French Dictionary *Plus* Grammar

French Dictionary *Plus* Grammar

HarperResource
An Imprint of HarperCollins*Publishers*

third edition 2004

HarperCollins Pu[illegible]
Westerhill Road, Bishopbrig[illegible]
Great Brit[illegible]

www.collinsdictionaries.com

Collins is an imprint of HarperCollins Publishers

ISBN 0-00-712629-8

HarperCollins Publishers, Inc.
10 East 53rd Street, New York, NY 10022

ISBN 0-06-057576-X

Library of Congress Cataloging-in-Publication Data
has been applied for

www.harpercollins.com

First HarperCollins edition published 1998

HarperCollins books may be purchased for educational, business, or sales promotional use. For information, please write to: Special Markets Department, HarperCollins Publishers Inc., 10 East 53rd Street, New York, NY 10022

A catalogue record for this book is available from the British Library

Dictionary text typeset by Morton Word Processing Ltd, Scarborough
Grammar text typeset by Ruth Noble, Peebles

Printed in Italy by Legoprint S.P.A.

TABLE DES MATIÈRES

Introduction	**vi**
Abréviations employées dans le texte	**viii**
Symboles phonétiques	**x**
Le verbe français	**xii**
Les nombres	**xiv**
L'heure et la date	**xvi**
FRANÇAIS-ANGLAIS	**1-453**
ANGLAIS-FRANÇAIS	**455-877**
Grammaire: mode d'emploi	
Table des matières	**4**
Grammaire	**6-255**

CONTENTS

Introduction	**vi**
Abbreviations used in the dictionary	**viii**
Phonetic symbols	**x**
French verb forms	**xii**
Numbers	**xiv**
Time and date	**xvi**
FRENCH-ENGLISH	**1-453**
ENGLISH-FRENCH	**455-877**
Using the Grammar	
Contents	**4**
Grammar	**6-255**

Pierre-Henri Cousin, Lorna Sinclair, Lesley A. Robertson
Jean-François Allain, Catherine E. Love

editorial team
Megan Thomson, Cécile Aubinière-Robb, Harry Campbell
Keith Foley, Janet Gough, Jean-Benoît Ormal-Grenon
Elspeth Anderson, Susan Dunsmore, Christine Penman
Val McNulty, Caitlin McMahon

series editor
Lorna Sinclair

editorial management
Vivian Marr

INTRODUCTION

You may be starting French for the first time, or you may wish to extend your knowledge of the language. Perhaps you want to read and study French books, newspapers and magazines, or perhaps simply have a conversation with French speakers. Whatever the reason, whether you're a student, a tourist or want to use French for business, this is the ideal book to help you understand and communicate. This modern, user-friendly dictionary gives priority to everyday vocabulary and the language of current affairs, business, computing and tourism, and, as in all Collins dictionaries, the emphasis is firmly placed on contemporary language and expressions.

HOW TO USE THE DICTIONARY

Below you will find an outline of how information is presented in your dictionary. Our aim is to give you the maximum amount of detail in the clearest and most helpful way.

Entries

A typical entry in your dictionary will be made up of the following elements:

Phonetic transcription

Phonetics appear in square brackets immediately after the headword. They are shown using the International Phonetic Alphabet (IPA), and a complete list of the symbols used in this system can be found on pages viii and ix.

Grammatical information

All words belong to one of the following parts of speech: noun, verb, adjective, adverb, pronoun, article, conjunction, preposition. Nouns can be singular or plural and, in French, masculine or feminine. Verbs can be transitive, intransitive, reflexive or impersonal. Parts of speech appear in *italics* immediately after the phonetic spelling of the headword. The gender of the translation also appears in *italics* immediately following the key element of the translation.

Often a word can have more than one part of speech. Just as the English word **chemical** can be an adjective or a noun, the French word **rose** can be an adjective ("pink") or a feminine noun ("rose"). In the same way the verb **to walk** is sometimes transitive, ie it takes an object ("to walk the dog") and sometimes intransitive, ie it doesn't take an object ("to walk to school"). To help you find the meaning you are looking for quickly and for clarity of presentation, the different part of speech categories are separated by a black lozenge ♦.

Meaning divisions

Most words have more than one meaning. Take, for example, **punch** which can be, amongst other things, a blow with the fist or an object used for making holes. Other words are translated differently depending on the context in which they are used. The transitive verb **to roll up**, for example, can be translated by "rouler" or "retrousser" depending on *what* it is you are rolling up. To help you select the most appropriate translation in every context, entries are divided according to meaning. Different meanings are introduced by an "indicator" in *italics* and in brackets. Thus, the examples given above will be shown as follows:

punch *n* (*blow*) coup *m* de poing; (*tool*) poinçon *m*

roll up *vt* (*carpet, cloth, map*) rouler; (*sleeves*) retrousser

Likewise, some words can have a different meaning when used to talk about a specific subject area or field. For example, **bishop**, which we generally use to mean a high-ranking clergyman, is also the name of a chess piece. To show English speakers which translation to use, we have added "subject field labels" in capitals and in brackets, in this case (*CHESS*):

bishop *n* évêque *m*; (*CHESS*) fou *m*

Field labels are often shortened to save space. You will find a complete list of abbreviations used in the dictionary on pages vi and vii.

Translations

Most English words have a direct translation in French and vice versa, as shown in the examples given above. Sometimes, however, no exact equivalent exists in the target language. In such cases we have given an approximate equivalent, indicated by the sign ≈. An example is **National Insurance**, the French equivalent of which is "Sécurité Sociale". There is no exact equivalent since the systems of the two countries are quite different:

National Insurance *n* (*BRIT*) ≈ Sécurité Sociale

On occasion it is impossible to find even an approximate equivalent. This may be the case, for example, with the names of types of food:

mince pie *n sorte de tarte aux fruits secs*

Here the translation (which doesn't exist) is replaced by an explanation. For increased clarity the explanation, or "gloss", is shown in *italics*.

It is often the case that a word, or a particular meaning of a word, cannot be translated in isolation. The translation of **Dutch**, for example, is "hollandais(e), néerlandais(e)". However, the phrase **to go Dutch** is rendered by "partager les frais". Even an expression as simple as **washing powder** needs a separate translation since it translates as "lessive (en poudre)", not "poudre à laver". This is where your dictionary will prove to be particularly informative and useful since it contains an abundance of compounds, phrases and idiomatic expressions.

Levels of formality and familiarity

In English you instinctively know when to say **I don't have any money** and when to say **I'm broke** or **I'm a bit short of cash**. When you are trying to understand someone who is speaking French, however, or when you yourself try to speak French, it is important to know what is polite and what is less so, and what you can say in a relaxed situation but not in a formal context. To help you with this, on the French-English side we have added the label (*fam*) to show that a French meaning or expression is colloquial, while those meanings or expressions which are vulgar are given an exclamation mark (*fam!*), warning you they can cause serious offence. Note also that on the English-French side, translations which are vulgar are followed by an exclamation mark in brackets.

Key words

Words labelled in the text as *KEYWORDS*, such as **be** and **do** or their French equivalents **être** and **faire**, have been given special treatment because they form the basic elements of the language. This extra help will ensure that you know how to use these complex words with confidence.

Cultural information

Entries which appear separated from the main text by a line above and below them explain aspects of culture in French and English-speaking countries. Subject areas covered include politics, education, media and national festivals, for example **Assemblée nationale**, **baccalauréat**, **BBC** and **Hallowe'en**.

ABRÉVIATIONS ABBREVIATIONS

abréviation	***ab(b)r***	abbreviation
adjectif, locution adjective	***adj***	adjective, adjectival phrase
administration	***ADMIN***	administration
adverbe, locution adverbiale	***adv***	adverb, adverbial phrase
agriculture	***AGR***	agriculture
anatomie	***ANAT***	anatomy
architecture	***ARCHIT***	architecture
article défini	***art déf***	definite article
article indéfini	***art indéf***	indefinite article
automobile	***AUT(O)***	the motor car and motoring
aviation, voyages aériens	***AVIAT***	flying, air travel
biologie	***BIO(L)***	biology
botanique	***BOT***	botany
anglais de Grande-Bretagne	***BRIT***	British English
chimie	***CHIMIE, CHEM***	chemistry
cinéma	***CINÉ, CINE***	cinema
langue familière (! emploi vulgaire)	***col(!)***	colloquial usage (! particularly offensive)
commerce, finance, banque	***COMM***	commerce, finance, banking
informatique	***COMPUT***	computing
conjonction	***conj***	conjunction
construction	***CONSTR***	building
nom utilisé comme adjectif, ne peut s'employer ni comme attribut, ni après le nom qualifié	***cpd***	compound element: noun used as an adjective and which cannot follow the noun it qualifies
cuisine, art culinaire	***CULIN***	cookery
article défini	***def art***	definite article
déterminant: adjectif démonstratif, indéfini etc	***dét***	determiner: demonstrative etc.
économie	***ECON***	economics
électricité, électronique	***ELEC***	electricity, electronics
exclamation, interjection	***excl***	exclamation, interjection
féminin	***f***	feminine
langue familière (! emploi vulgaire)	***fam (!)***	colloquial usage (! particularly offensive)
emploi figuré	***fig***	figurative use
(verbe anglais) dont la particule est inséparable du verbe	***fus***	(phrasal verb) where the particle cannot be separated from the main verb
dans la plupart des sens; généralement	***gén, gen***	in most or all senses; generally
géographie, géologie	***GEO***	geography, geology
géométrie	***GEOM***	geometry
histoire	***HIST***	history
article indéfini	***indef art***	indefinite article
informatique	***INFORM***	computing
invariable	***inv***	invariable
irrégulier	***irrég, irreg***	irregular
domaine juridique	***JUR***	law
grammaire, linguistique	***LING***	grammar, linguistics
masculin	***m***	masculine
mathématiques, algèbre	***MATH***	mathematics, calculus
médecine	***MÉD, MED***	medical term, medicine

ABRÉVIATIONS   ABBREVIATIONS

masculin ou féminin, suivant le sexe	***m/f***	either masculine or feminine depending on sex
domaine militaire, armée	***MIL***	military matters
musique	***MUS***	music
nom	***n***	noun
navigation, nautisme	***NAVIG, NAUT***	sailing, navigation
nom non comptable: ne peut s'utiliser au pluriel	***no pl***	collective (uncountable) noun: is not used in the plural
nom ou adjectif numéral	***num***	numeral adjective or noun
	o.s.	oneself
péjoratif	***péj, pej***	derogatory, pejorative
photographie	***PHOT(O)***	photography
physiologie	***PHYSIOL***	physiology
pluriel	***pl***	plural
politique	***POL***	politics
participe passé	***pp***	past participle
préposition	***prép, prep***	preposition
psychologie, psychiatrie	***PSYCH***	psychology, psychiatry
temps du passé	***pt***	past tense
quelque chose	***qch***	
quelqu'un	***qn***	
religions, domaine ecclésiastique	***REL***	religions, church service
	sb	somebody
enseignement, système scolaire et universitaire	***SCOL***	schooling, schools and universities
singulier	***sg***	singular
	sth	something
subjonctif	***sub***	subjunctive
sujet (grammatical)	***su(b)j***	(grammatical) subject
techniques, technologie	***TECH***	technical term, technology
télécommunications	***TEL***	telecommunications
théâtre	***THÉÂT, THEAT***	theatre
télévision	***TV***	television
typographie	***TYP(O)***	typography, printing
anglais des USA	***US***	American English
verbe	***vb***	verb
verbe ou groupe verbal à fonction intransitive	***vi***	verb or phrasal verb used intransitively
verbe ou groupe verbal à fonction transitive	***vt***	verb or phrasal verb used transitively
zoologie	***ZOOL***	zoology
marque déposée	®	registered trademark
indique une équivalence culturelle	≈	introduces a cultural equivalent
pas de liaison devant h aspiré	'	no liaison before aspirate h

TRANSCRIPTION PHONÉTIQUE

Consonnes		*Consonants*
NB. p, b, t, d, k, g sont suivis d'une aspiration en anglais.		NB. p, b, t, d, k, g are not aspirated in French.
poupée	p	puppy
bombe	b	baby
tente thermal	t	tent
dinde	d	daddy
coq qui képi	k	cork kiss chord
gag bague	g	gag guess
sale ce nation	s	so rice kiss
zéro rose	z	cousin buzz
tache chat	ʃ	sheep sugar
gilet juge	ʒ	pleasure beige
	tʃ	church
	dʒ	judge general
fer phare	f	farm raffle
valve	v	very rev
	θ	thin maths
	ð	that other
lent salle	l	little ball
rare rentrer	ʀ	
	r	rat rare
maman femme	m	mummy comb
non nonne	n	no ran
agneau vigne	ɲ	
	ŋ	singing bank
hop!	h	hat reheat
yeux paille pied	j	yet
nouer oui	w	wall bewail
huile lui	ɥ	
	x	loch

Divers		*Miscellaneous*
pour l'anglais: le r final se prononce en liaison devant une voyelle	*	
pour l'anglais: précède la syllabe accentuée	'	in French transcription: no liaison before aspirate h

En règle générale, la prononciation est donnée entre crochets après chaque entrée. Toutefois, du côté anglais-français et dans le cas des expressions composées de deux ou plusieurs mots non réunis par un trait d'union et faisant l'objet d'une entrée séparée, la prononciation doit être cherchée sous chacun des mots constitutifs de l'expression en question.

PHONETIC TRANSCRIPTION

Voyelles / Vowels

NB. La mise en équivalence de certains sons n'indique qu'une ressemblance approximative.

NB. The pairing of some vowel sounds only indicates approximate equivalence.

Voyelles		Vowels
ici vie lyre	i iː	heel bead
	ɪ	hit pity
jouer été	e	
lait jouet merci	ɛ	set tent
plat amour	a æ	bat apple
bas pâte	ɑ ɑː	after car calm
	ʌ	fun cousin
le premier	ə	over above
beurre peur	œ	
peu deux	ø əː	urn fern work
or homme	ɔ	wash pot
mot eau gauche	o ɔː	born cork
genou roue	u	full soot
	uː	boon lewd
rue urne	y	

Diphtongues / Diphthongs

Diphtongues		Diphthongs
	ɪə	beer tier
	ɛə	tear fair there
	eɪ	date plaice day
	aɪ	life buy cry
	au	owl foul now
	əu	low no
	ɔɪ	boil boy oily
	uə	poor tour

Nasales / Nasal Vowels

Nasales		Nasal Vowels
matin plein	ɛ̃	
brun	œ̃	
sang an dans	ɑ̃	
non pont	ɔ̃	

In general, we give the pronunciation of each entry in square brackets after the word in question. However, on the English-French side, where the entry is composed of two or more unhyphenated words, each of which is given elsewhere in this dictionary, you will find the pronunciation of each word in its alphabetical position.

FRENCH VERB FORMS

1 Participe présent ***2*** Participe passé ***3*** Présent ***4*** Imparfait ***5*** Futur ***6*** Conditionnel ***7*** Subjonctif présent

acquérir ***1*** acquérant ***2*** acquis ***3*** acquiers, acquérons, acquièrent ***4*** acquérais ***5*** acquerrai ***7*** acquière

ALLER ***1*** allant ***2*** allé ***3*** vais, vas, va, allons, allez, vont ***4*** allais ***5*** irai ***6*** irais ***7*** aille

asseoir ***1*** asseyant ***2*** assis ***3*** assieds, asseyons, asseyez, asseyent ***4*** asseyais ***5*** assiérai ***7*** asseye

atteindre ***1*** atteignant ***2*** atteint ***3*** atteins, atteignons ***4*** atteignais ***7*** atteigne

AVOIR ***1*** ayant ***2*** eu ***3*** ai, as, a, avons, avez, ont ***4*** avais ***5*** aurai ***6*** aurais ***7*** aie, aies, ait, ayons, ayez, aient

battre ***1*** battant ***2*** battu ***3*** bats, bat, battons ***4*** battais ***7*** batte

boire ***1*** buvant ***2*** bu ***3*** bois, buvons, boivent ***4*** buvais ***7*** boive

bouillir ***1*** bouillant ***2*** bouilli ***3*** bous, bouillons ***4*** bouillais ***7*** bouille

conclure ***1*** concluant ***2*** conclu ***3*** conclus, concluons ***4*** concluais ***7*** conclue

conduire ***1*** conduisant ***2*** conduit ***3*** conduis, conduisons ***4*** conduisais ***7*** conduise

connaître ***1*** connaissant ***2*** connu ***3*** connais, connaît, connaissons ***4*** connaissais ***7*** connaisse

coudre ***1*** cousant ***2*** cousu ***3*** couds, cousons, cousez, cousent ***4*** cousais ***7*** couse

courir ***1*** courant ***2*** couru ***3*** cours, courons ***4*** courais ***5*** courrai ***7*** coure

couvrir ***1*** couvrant ***2*** couvert ***3*** couvre, couvrons ***4*** couvrais ***7*** couvre

craindre ***1*** craignant ***2*** craint ***3*** crains, craignons ***4*** craignais ***7*** craigne

croire ***1*** croyant ***2*** cru ***3*** crois, croyons, croient ***4*** croyais ***7*** croie

croître ***1*** croissant ***2*** crû, crue, crus, crues ***3*** croîs, croissons ***4*** croissais ***7*** croisse

cueillir ***1*** cueillant ***2*** cueilli ***3*** cueille, cueillons ***4*** cueillais ***5*** cueillerai ***7*** cueille

devoir ***1*** devant ***2*** dû, due, dus, dues ***3*** dois, devons, doivent ***4*** devais ***5*** devrai ***7*** doive

dire ***1*** disant ***2*** dit ***3*** dis, disons, dites, disent ***4*** disais ***7*** dise

dormir ***1*** dormant ***2*** dormi ***3*** dors, dormons ***4*** dormais ***7*** dorme

écrire ***1*** écrivant ***2*** écrit ***3*** écris, écrivons ***4*** écrivais ***7*** écrive

ÊTRE ***1*** étant ***2*** été ***3*** suis, es, est, sommes, êtes, sont ***4*** étais ***5*** serai ***6*** serais ***7*** sois, sois, soit, soyons, soyez, soient

FAIRE ***1*** faisant ***2*** fait ***3*** fais, fais, fait, faisons, faites, font ***4*** faisais ***5*** ferai ***6*** ferais ***7*** fasse

falloir ***2*** fallu ***3*** faut ***4*** fallait ***5*** faudra ***7*** faille

FINIR ***1*** finissant ***2*** fini ***3*** finis, finis, finit, finissons, finissez, finissent ***4*** finissais ***5*** finirai ***6*** finirais ***7*** finisse

fuir ***1*** fuyant ***2*** fui ***3*** fuis, fuyons, fuient ***4*** fuyais ***7*** fuie

joindre ***1*** joignant ***2*** joint ***3*** joins, joignons ***4*** joignais ***7*** joigne

lire ***1*** lisant ***2*** lu ***3*** lis, lisons ***4*** lisais ***7*** lise

luire ***1*** luisant ***2*** lui ***3*** luis, luisons ***4*** luisais ***7*** luise

maudire ***1*** maudissant ***2*** maudit ***3*** maudis, maudissons ***4*** maudissait ***7*** maudisse

mentir ***1*** mentant ***2*** menti ***3*** mens, mentons ***4*** mentais ***7*** mente

mettre ***1*** mettant ***2*** mis ***3*** mets, mettons ***4*** mettais ***7*** mette

mourir ***1*** mourant ***2*** mort ***3*** meurs, mourons, meurent ***4*** mourais ***5*** mourrai ***7*** meure

naître ***1*** naissant ***2*** né ***3*** nais, naît, naissons ***4*** naissais ***7*** naisse

offrir ***1*** offrant ***2*** offert ***3*** offre, offrons ***4*** offrais ***7*** offre

PARLER ***1*** parlant ***2*** parlé ***3*** parle, parles, parle, parlons, parlez, parlent ***4*** parlais, parlais, parlait, parlions, parliez, parlaient ***5*** parlerai, parleras, parlera, parlerons, parlerez, parleront ***6*** parlerais, parlerais, parlerait, parlerions, parleriez, parleraient ***7***

1 **Participe présent *2* Participe passé *3* Présent *4* Imparfait *5* Futur *6* Conditionnel *7* Subjonctif présent**

parle, parles, parle, parlions, parliez, parlent *impératif* parle! parlez!

partir ***1*** partant ***2*** parti ***3*** pars, partons ***4*** partais ***7*** parte

plaire ***1*** plaisant ***2*** plu ***3*** plais, plaît, plaisons ***4*** plaisais ***7*** plaise

pleuvoir ***1*** pleuvant ***2*** plu ***3*** pleut, pleuvent ***4*** pleuvait ***5*** pleuvra ***7*** pleuve

pourvoir ***1*** pourvoyant ***2*** pourvu ***3*** pourvois, pourvoyons, pourvoient ***4*** pourvoyais ***7*** pourvoie

pouvoir ***1*** pouvant ***2*** pu ***3*** peux, peut, pouvons, peuvent ***4*** pouvais ***5*** pourrai ***7*** puisse

prendre ***1*** prenant ***2*** pris ***3*** prends, prenons, prennent ***4*** prenais ***7*** prenne

prévoir *like voir* ***5*** prévoirai

RECEVOIR ***1*** recevant ***2*** reçu ***3*** reçois, reçois, reçoit, recevons, recevez, reçoivent ***4*** recevais ***5*** recevrai ***6*** recevrais ***7*** reçoive

RENDRE ***1*** rendant ***2*** rendu ***3*** rends, rends, rend, rendons, rendez, rendent ***4*** rendais ***5*** rendrai ***6*** rendrais ***7*** rende

résoudre ***1*** résolvant ***2*** résolu ***3*** résous, résout, résolvons ***4*** résolvais ***7*** résolve

rire ***1*** riant ***2*** ri ***3*** ris, rions ***4*** riais ***7*** rie

savoir ***1*** sachant ***2*** su ***3*** sais, savons, savent ***4*** savais ***5*** saurai ***7*** sache *impératif* sache, sachons, sachez

servir ***1*** servant ***2*** servi ***3*** sers, servons ***4*** servais ***7*** serve

sortir ***1*** sortant ***2*** sorti ***3*** sors, sortons ***4*** sortais ***7*** sorte

souffrir ***1*** souffrant ***2*** souffert ***3*** souffre, souffrons ***4*** souffrais ***7*** souffre

suffire ***1*** suffisant ***2*** suffi ***3*** suffis, suffisons ***4*** suffisais ***7*** suffise

suivre ***1*** suivant ***2*** suivi ***3*** suis, suivons ***4*** suivais ***7*** suive

taire ***1*** taisant ***2*** tu ***3*** tais, taisons ***4*** taisais ***7*** taise

tenir ***1*** tenant ***2*** tenu ***3*** tiens, tenons, tiennent ***4*** tenais ***5*** tiendrai ***7*** tienne

vaincre ***1*** vainquant ***2*** vaincu ***3*** vaincs, vainc, vainquons ***4*** vainquais ***7*** vainque

valoir ***1*** valant ***2*** valu ***3*** vaux, vaut, valons ***4*** valais ***5*** vaudrai ***7*** vaille

venir ***1*** venant ***2*** venu ***3*** viens, venons, viennent ***4*** venais ***5*** viendrai ***7*** vienne

vivre ***1*** vivant ***2*** vécu ***3*** vis, vivons ***4*** vivais ***7*** vive

voir ***1*** voyant ***2*** vu ***3*** vois, voyons, voient ***4*** voyais ***5*** verrai ***7*** voie

vouloir ***1*** voulant ***2*** voulu ***3*** veux, veut, voulons, veulent ***4*** voulais ***5*** voudrai ***7*** veuille *impératif* veuillez

For additional information on French verb formation, see pp. 6-131 of Grammar section.

LES NOMBRES		*NUMBERS*
un (une)	**1**	one
deux	**2**	two
trois	**3**	three
quatre	**4**	four
cinq	**5**	five
six	**6**	six
sept	**7**	seven
huit	**8**	eight
neuf	**9**	nine
dix	**10**	ten
onze	**11**	eleven
douze	**12**	twelve
treize	**13**	thirteen
quatorze	**14**	fourteen
quinze	**15**	fifteen
seize	**16**	sixteen
dix-sept	**17**	seventeen
dix-huit	**18**	eighteen
dix-neuf	**19**	nineteen
vingt	**20**	twenty
vingt et un (une)	**21**	twenty-one
vingt-deux	**22**	twenty-two
trente	**30**	thirty
quarante	**40**	forty
cinquante	**50**	fifty
soixante	**60**	sixty
soixante-dix	**70**	seventy
soixante et onze	**71**	seventy-one
soixante-douze	**72**	seventy-two
quatre-vingts	**80**	eighty
quatre-vingt-un (-une)	**81**	eighty-one
quatre-vingt-dix	**90**	ninety
quatre-vingt-onze	**91**	ninety-one
cent	**100**	a hundred
cent un (une)	**101**	a hundred and one
trois cents	**300**	three hundred
trois cent un (une)	**301**	three hundred and one
mille	**1 000**	a thousand
un million	**1 000 000**	a million

LES NOMBRES	*NUMBERS*
premier (première), 1er	first, 1st
deuxième, 2e *or* 2ème	second, 2nd
troisième, 3e *or* 3ème	third, 3rd
quatrième	fourth, 4th
cinquième	fifth, 5th
sixième	sixth, 6th
septième	seventh
huitième	eighth
neuvième	ninth
dixième	tenth
onzième	eleventh
douzième	twelfth
treizième	thirteenth
quatorzième	fourteenth
quinzième	fifteenth
seizième	sixteenth
dix-septième	seventeenth
dix-huitième	eighteenth
dix-neuvième	nineteenth
vingtième	twentieth
vingt-et-unième	twenty-first
vingt-deuxième	twenty-second
trentième	thirtieth
centième	hundredth
cent-unième	hundred-and-first
millième	thousandth

## L'HEURE	## THE TIME
quelle heure est-il?	*what time is it?*
il est ...	*it's ...*
minuit	midnight
une heure (du matin)	one o'clock (in the morning) , one (am)
une heure cinq	five past one
une heure dix	ten past one
une heure et quart	a quarter past one, one fifteen
une heure vingt-cinq	twenty-five past one, one twenty-five
une heure et demie, une heure trente	half past one, one thirty
deux heures moins vingt-cinq, une heure trente-cinq	twenty-five to two, one thirty-five
deux heures moins vingt, une heure quarante	twenty to two, one forty
deux heures moins le quart, une heure quarante-cinq	a quarter to two, one forty-five
deux heures moins dix, une heure cinquante	ten to two, one fifty
midi	twelve o'clock, midday, noon
deux heures (de l'après-midi)	two o'clock (in the afternoon), two (pm)
sept heures (du soir)	seven o'clock (in the evening), seven (pm)
à quelle heure?	*at what time?*
à minuit	at midnight
à sept heures	at seven o'clock
à une heure	at one o'clock
dans vingt minutes	in twenty minutes
il y a dix minutes	ten minutes ago

## LA DATE	## THE DATE
aujourd'hui	today
demain	tomorrow
après-demain	the day after tomorrow
hier	yesterday
avant-hier	the day before yesterday
la veille	the day before, the previous day
le lendemain	the next *or* following day

le matin	morning
le soir	evening
ce matin	this morning
ce soir	this evening
cet après-midi	this afternoon
hier matin	yesterday morning
hier soir	yesterday evening
demain matin	tomorrow morning
demain soir	tomorrow evening
dans la nuit du samedi au dimanche	during Saturday night, during the night of Saturday to Sunday
il viendra samedi	he's coming on Saturday
le samedi	on Saturdays
tous les samedis	every Saturday
samedi passé *ou* dernier	last Saturday
samedi prochain	next Saturday
samedi en huit	a week on Saturday
samedi en quinze	a fortnight *or* two weeks on Saturday
du lundi au samedi	from Monday to Saturday
tous les jours	every day
une fois par semaine	once a week
une fois par mois	once a month
deux fois par semaine	twice a week
il y a une semaine *ou* huit jours	a week ago
il y a quinze jours	a fortnight *or* two weeks ago
l'année passée *ou* dernière	last year
dans deux jours	in two days
dans huit jours *ou* une semaine	in a week
dans quinze jours	in a fortnight *or* two weeks
le mois prochain	next month
l'année prochaine	next year

quel jour sommes-nous?	*what day is it?*
le 1er/24 octobre 1996	the 1st/24th of October 1996, October 1st/24th 1996
en 1996	in 1996
mille neuf cent quatre-vingt seize	nineteen ninety-six
44 av. J.-C.	44 BC
14 apr. J.-C.	14 AD
au XIXe (siècle)	in the nineteenth century
dans les années trente	in the thirties
il était une fois ...	once upon a time ...

A a

A, a [ɑ] *nm inv* A, a ♦ *abr* = **anticyclone, are**; (= *ampère*) amp; (= *autoroute*) ≈ M (*BRIT*); **A comme Anatole** A for Andrew (*BRIT*) *ou* Able (*US*); **de a à z** from a to z; **prouver qch par a + b** to prove sth conclusively.

a [a] *vb voir* **avoir.**

MOT-CLÉ

à [a] (*à + le* = **au,** *à + les* = **aux**) *prép* **1** (*endroit, situation*) at, in; **être ~ Paris/au Portugal** to be in Paris/Portugal; **être ~ la maison/~ l'école** to be at home/at school; **~ la campagne** in the country; **c'est ~ 10 km/~ 20 minutes (d'ici)** it's 10 km/20 minutes away

2 (*direction*) to; **aller ~ Paris/au Portugal** to go to Paris/Portugal; **aller ~ la maison/~ l'école** to go home/to school; **~ la campagne** to the country

3 (*temps*): **~ 3 heures/minuit** at 3 o'clock/midnight; **au printemps** in the spring; **au mois de juin** in June; **au départ** at the start, at the outset; **~ demain/la semaine prochaine!** see you tomorrow/next week!; **visites de 5 heures ~ 6 heures** visiting from 5 to *ou* till 6 o'clock

4 (*attribution, appartenance*) to; **le livre est ~ Paul/~ lui/~ nous** this book is Paul's/his/ours; **donner qch ~ qn** to give sth to sb; **un ami ~ moi** a friend of mine; **c'est ~ moi de le faire** it's up to me to do it

5 (*moyen*) with; **se chauffer au gaz** to have gas heating; **~ bicyclette** on a *ou* by bicycle; **~ la main/machine** by hand/machine; **~ la télévision/la radio** on television/the radio

6 (*provenance*) from; **boire ~ la bouteille** to drink from the bottle

7 (*caractérisation, manière*): **l'homme aux yeux bleus** the man with the blue eyes; **~ la russe** the Russian way; **glace ~ la framboise** raspberry ice cream

8 (*but, destination*): **tasse ~ café** coffee cup; **maison ~ vendre** house for sale; **problème ~ régler** problem to sort out

9 (*rapport, évaluation, distribution*): **100 km/unités ~ l'heure** 100 km/units per *ou* an hour; **payé ~ l'heure** paid by the hour; **cinq ~ six** five to six

10 (*conséquence, résultat*): **~ ce qu'il prétend** according to him; **~ leur grande surprise** much to their surprise; **~ nous trois nous n'avons pas su le faire** we couldn't do it even between the three of us; **ils sont arrivés ~ 4** 4 of them arrived (together).

Å *abr* (= *Angstrom*) Å *ou* A.

A2 *abr* (= *Antenne 2*) *French TV channel.*

AB *abr* = *assez bien.*

abaissement [abɛsmɑ̃] *nm* lowering; pulling down.

abaisser [abese] *vt* to lower, bring down; (*manette*) to pull down; (*fig*) to debase; to humiliate; **s'~** *vi* to go down; (*fig*) to demean o.s.; **s'~ à faire/à qch** to stoop *ou* descend to doing/to sth.

abandon [abɑ̃dɔ̃] *nm* abandoning; deserting; giving up; withdrawal; surrender, relinquishing; (*fig*) lack of constraint; relaxed pose *ou* mood; **être à l'~** to be in a state of neglect; **laisser à l'~** to abandon.

abandonné, e [abɑ̃dɔne] *adj* (*solitaire*) deserted; (*route, usine*) disused; (*jardin*) abandoned.

abandonner [abɑ̃dɔne] *vt* to leave, abandon, desert; (*projet, activité*) to abandon, give up; (*SPORT*) to retire *ou* withdraw from; (*céder*) to surrender, relinquish; **s'~** *vi* to let o.s. go; **s'~ à** (*paresse, plaisirs*) to give o.s. up to; **~ qch à qn** to give sth up to sb.

abasourdir [abazuʀdiʀ] *vt* to stun, stagger.

abat [aba] *etc vb voir* **abattre.**

abat-jour [abaʒuʀ] *nm inv* lampshade.

abats [aba] *vb voir* **abattre** ♦ *nmpl* (*de bœuf, porc*) offal *sg* (*BRIT*), entrails (*US*); (*de volaille*) giblets.

abattage [abataʒ] *nm* cutting down, felling.

abattant [abatɑ̃] *vb voir* **abattre** ♦ *nm* leaf, flap.

abattement [abatmɑ̃] *nm* (*physique*) enfeeblement; (*moral*) dejection, despondency; (*déduction*) reduction; **~ fiscal** ≈ tax allowance.

abattis [abati] *vb voir* **abattre** ♦ *nmpl* giblets.

abattoir [abatwaʀ] *nm* abattoir (*BRIT*), slaughterhouse.

abattre [abatʀ(ə)] *vt* (*arbre*) to cut down, fell; (*mur, maison*) to pull down; (*avion, personne*)

to shoot down; (*animal*) to shoot, kill; (*fig: physiquement*) to wear out, tire out; (*: moralement*) to demoralize; **s'~** *vi* to crash down; **s'~ sur** (*suj: pluie*) to beat down on; (*: coups, injures*) to rain down on; **~ ses cartes** (*aussi fig*) to lay one's cards on the table; **~ du travail** *ou* **de la besogne** to get through a lot of work.
abattu, e [abaty] *pp de* **abattre** ♦ *adj* (*déprimé*) downcast.
abbatiale [abasjal] *nf* abbey (*church*).
abbaye [abei] *nf* abbey.
abbé [abe] *nm* priest; (*d'une abbaye*) abbot; **M l'~** Father.
abbesse [abɛs] *nf* abbess.
abc, ABC [abese] *nm* alphabet primer; (*fig*) rudiments *pl*.
abcès [apsɛ] *nm* abscess.
abdication [abdikɑsjɔ̃] *nf* abdication.
abdiquer [abdike] *vi* to abdicate ♦ *vt* to renounce, give up.
abdomen [abdɔmɛn] *nm* abdomen.
abdominal, e, aux [abdɔminal, -o] *adj* abdominal ♦ *nmpl*: **faire des abdominaux** to do exercises for the stomach muscles.
abécédaire [abesedɛʀ] *nm* alphabet primer.
abeille [abɛj] *nf* bee.
aberrant, e [abɛʀɑ̃, -ɑ̃t] *adj* absurd.
aberration [abɛʀɑsjɔ̃] *nf* aberration.
abêtir [abetiʀ] *vt* to make morons (*ou* a moron) of.
abêtissant, e [abetisɑ̃, -ɑ̃t] *adj* stultifying.
abhorrer [abɔʀe] *vt* to abhor, loathe.
abîme [abim] *nm* abyss, gulf.
abîmer [abime] *vt* to spoil, damage; **s'~** *vi* to get spoilt *ou* damaged; (*fruits*) to spoil; (*tomber*) to sink, founder; **s'~ les yeux** to ruin one's eyes *ou* eyesight.
abject, e [abʒɛkt] *adj* abject, despicable.
abjurer [abʒyʀe] *vt* to abjure, renounce.
ablatif [ablatif] *nm* ablative.
ablation [ablɑsjɔ̃] *nf* removal.
ablutions [ablysjɔ̃] *nfpl*: **faire ses ~** to perform one's ablutions.
abnégation [abnegɑsjɔ̃] *nf* (self-)abnegation.
aboie [abwa] *etc vb voir* **aboyer**.
aboiement [abwamɑ̃] *nm* bark, barking *no pl*.
aboierai [abwajəʀe] *etc vb voir* **aboyer**.
abois [abwa] *nmpl*: **aux ~** at bay.
abolir [abɔliʀ] *vt* to abolish.
abolition [abɔlisjɔ̃] *nf* abolition.
abolitionniste [abɔlisjɔnist(ə)] *adj, nm/f* abolitionist.
abominable [abɔminabl(ə)] *adj* abominable.
abomination [abɔminɑsjɔ̃] *nf* abomination.
abondamment [abɔ̃damɑ̃] *adv* abundantly.
abondance [abɔ̃dɑ̃s] *nf* abundance; (*richesse*) affluence; **en ~** in abundance.
abondant, e [abɔ̃dɑ̃, -ɑ̃t] *adj* plentiful, abundant, copious.
abonder [abɔ̃de] *vi* to abound, be plentiful; **~ en** to be full of, abound in; **~ dans le sens de qn** to concur with sb.
abonné, e [abɔne] *nm/f* subscriber; season ticket holder ♦ *adj*: **être ~ à un journal** to subscribe to *ou* have a subscription to a periodical; **être ~ au téléphone** to be on the (tele)phone.
abonnement [abɔnmɑ̃] *nm* subscription; (*pour transports en commun, concerts*) season ticket.
abonner [abɔne] *vt*: **s'~ à** to subscribe to, take out a subscription to.
abord [abɔʀ] *nm*: **être d'un ~ facile** to be approachable; **être d'un ~ difficile** (*personne*) to be unapproachable; (*lieu*) to be hard to reach *ou* difficult to get to; **de prime ~, au premier ~** at first sight; **d'~** *adv* first; **tout d'~** first of all.
abordable [abɔʀdabl(ə)] *adj* (*personne*) approachable; (*marchandise*) reasonably priced; (*prix*) affordable, reasonable.
abordage [abɔʀdaʒ] *nm* boarding.
aborder [abɔʀde] *vi* to land ♦ *vt* (*sujet, difficulté*) to tackle; (*personne*) to approach; (*rivage etc*) to reach; (*NAVIG: attaquer*) to board; (*: heurter*) to collide with.
abords [abɔʀ] *nmpl* surroundings.
aborigène [abɔʀiʒɛn] *nm* aborigine, native.
Abou Dhabî, Abu Dhabî [abudabi] *nm* Abu Dhabi.
aboulique [abulik] *adj* totally lacking in willpower.
aboutir [abutiʀ] *vi* (*négociations etc*) to succeed; (*abcès*) to come to a head; **~ à/dans/sur** to end up at/in/on.
aboutissants [abutisɑ̃] *nmpl voir* **tenants.**
aboutissement [abutismɑ̃] *nm* success; (*de concept, projet*) successful realization; (*d'années de travail*) successful conclusion.
aboyer [abwaje] *vi* to bark.
abracadabrant, e [abʀakadabʀɑ̃, -ɑ̃t] *adj* incredible, preposterous.
abrasif, ive [abʀazif, -iv] *adj, nm* abrasive.
abrégé [abʀeʒe] *nm* summary; **en ~** in a shortened *ou* abbreviated form.
abréger [abʀeʒe] *vt* (*texte*) to shorten, abridge; (*mot*) to shorten, abbreviate; (*réunion, voyage*) to cut short, shorten.
abreuver [abʀœve] *vt* to water; (*fig*): **~ qn de** to shower *ou* swamp sb with; (*injures etc*) to shower sb with; **s'~** *vi* to drink.
abreuvoir [abʀœvwaʀ] *nm* watering place.
abréviation [abʀevjɑsjɔ̃] *nf* abbreviation.
abri [abʀi] *nm* shelter; **à l'~** under cover; **être/se mettre à l'~** to be/get under cover *ou* shelter; **à l'~ de** sheltered from; (*fig*) safe from.
Abribus [abʀibys] *nm* ® bus shelter.
abricot [abʀiko] *nm* apricot.
abricotier [abʀikɔtje] *nm* apricot tree.
abrité, e [abʀite] *adj* sheltered.
abriter [abʀite] *vt* to shelter; (*loger*) to accommodate; **s'~** to shelter, take cover.

abrogation [abʀɔgɑsjɔ̃] *nf* (*JUR*) repeal, abrogation.
abroger [abʀɔʒe] *vt* to repeal, abrogate.
abrupt, e [abʀypt] *adj* sheer, steep; (*ton*) abrupt.
abruti, e [abʀyti] *nm/f* (*fam*) idiot, moron.
abrutir [abʀytiʀ] *vt* to daze; (*fatiguer*) to exhaust; (*abêtir*) to stupefy.
abrutissant, e [abʀytisɑ̃, -ɑ̃t] *adj* (*bruit, travail*) stupefying.
abscisse [apsis] *nf* X axis, abscissa.
absence [apsɑ̃s] *nf* absence; (*MÉD*) blackout; (*distraction*) mental blank; **en l'~ de** in the absence of.
absent, e [apsɑ̃, -ɑ̃t] *adj* absent; (*chose*) missing, lacking; (*distrait: air*) vacant, faraway ♦ *nm/f* absentee.
absentéisme [apsɑ̃teism(ə)] *nm* absenteeism.
absenter [apsɑ̃te]: **s'~** *vi* to take time off work; (*sortir*) to leave, go out.
abside [apsid] *nf* (*ARCHIT*) apse.
absinthe [apsɛ̃t] *nf* (*boisson*) absinth(e); (*BOT*) wormwood, absinth(e).
absolu, e [apsɔly] *adj* absolute; (*caractère*) rigid, uncompromising ♦ *nm* (*PHILOSOPHIE*): **l'~** the Absolute; **dans l'~** in the absolute, in a vacuum.
absolument [apsɔlymɑ̃] *adv* absolutely.
absolution [apsɔlysjɔ̃] *nf* absolution; (*JUR*) dismissal (*of case*).
absolutisme [apsɔlytism(ə)] *nm* absolutism.
absolvais [apsɔlvɛ] *etc vb voir* **absoudre**.
absorbant, e [apsɔʀbɑ̃, -ɑ̃t] *adj* absorbent; (*tâche*) absorbing, engrossing.
absorbé, e [apsɔʀbe] *adj* absorbed, engrossed.
absorber [apsɔʀbe] *vt* to absorb; (*gén MÉD: manger, boire*) to take; (*ÉCON: firme*) to take over, absorb.
absorption [apsɔʀpsjɔ̃] *nf* absorption.
absoudre [apsudʀ(ə)] *vt* to absolve; (*JUR*) to dismiss.
absous, oute [apsu, -ut] *pp de* **absoudre**.
abstenir [apstəniʀ]: **s'~** *vi* (*POL*) to abstain; **s'~ de qch/de faire** to refrain from sth/from doing.
abstention [apstɑ̃sjɔ̃] *nf* abstention.
abstentionnisme [apstɑ̃sjɔnism(ə)] *nm* abstaining.
abstentionniste [apstɑ̃sjɔnist(ə)] *nm* abstentionist.
abstenu, e [apstəny] *pp de* **abstenir**.
abstiendrai [apstjɛ̃dʀe], **abstiens** [apstjɛ̃] *etc voir* **abstenir**.
abstinence [apstinɑ̃s] *nf* abstinence; **faire ~** to abstain (*from meat on Fridays*).
abstint [apstɛ̃] *etc vb voir* **abstenir**.
abstraction [apstʀaksjɔ̃] *nf* abstraction; **faire ~ de** to set *ou* leave aside; **~ faite de ...** leaving aside ....
abstraire [apstʀɛʀ] *vt* to abstract; **s'~** *vi*: **s'~ (de)** (*s'isoler*) to cut o.s. off (from).
abstrait, e [apstʀɛ, -ɛt] *pp de* **abstraire** ♦ *adj* abstract ♦ *nm*: **dans l'~** in the abstract.
abstraitement [apstʀɛtmɑ̃] *adv* abstractly.
abstrayais [apstʀɛjɛ] *etc vb voir* **abstraire**.
absurde [apsyʀd(ə)] *adj* absurd ♦ *nm* absurdity; (*PHILOSOPHIE*): **l'~** absurd; **par l'~** ad absurdio.
absurdité [apsyʀdite] *nf* absurdity.
abus [aby] *nm* (*excès*) abuse, misuse; (*injustice*) abuse; **~ de confiance** breach of trust; (*détournement de fonds*) embezzlement.
abuser [abyze] *vi* to go too far, overstep the mark ♦ *vt* to deceive, mislead; **s'~** *vi* (*se méprendre*) to be mistaken; **~ de** *vt* (*force, droit*) to misuse; (*alcool*) to take to excess; (*violer, duper*) to take advantage of.
abusif, ive [abyzif, -iv] *adj* exorbitant; (*punition*) excessive; (*pratique*) improper.
abusivement [abyzivmɑ̃] *adv* exorbitantly; excessively; improperly.
AC *sigle f* = **appellation contrôlée**.
acabit [akabi] *nm*: **du même ~** of the same type.
acacia [akasja] *nm* (*BOT*) acacia.
académicien, ne [akademisjɛ̃, -ɛn] *nm/f* academician.
académie [akademi] *nf* (*société*) learned society; (*école: d'art, de danse*) academy; (*ART: nu*) nude; (*SCOL: circonscription*) ≈ regional education authority; **l'A~ (française)** the French Academy; *see boxed note*.

ACADÉMIE FRANÇAISE

The **Académie française** *was founded by Cardinal Richelieu in 1635, during the reign of Louis XIII. It is made up of forty elected scholars and writers who are known as 'les Quarante' or 'les Immortels'. One of the* **Académie's** *functions is to keep an eye on the development of the French language and its recommendations are frequently the subject of lively public debate. It has produced several editions of its famous dictionary and also awards various literary prizes.*

académique [akademik] *adj* academic.
Acadie [akadi] *nf*: **l'~** the Maritime Provinces.
acadien, ne [akadjɛ̃, -ɛn] *adj* Acadian, of *ou* from the Maritime Provinces.
acajou [akaʒu] *nm* mahogany.
acariâtre [akaʀjɑtʀ(ə)] *adj* sour(-tempered) (*BRIT*), cantankerous.
accablant, e [akɑblɑ̃, -ɑ̃t] *adj* (*témoignage, preuve*) overwhelming.
accablement [akɑbləmɑ̃] *nm* deep despondency.
accabler [akɑble] *vt* to overwhelm, overcome; (*suj: témoignage*) to condemn, damn; **~ qn d'injures** to heap *ou* shower abuse on sb; **~ qn de travail** to overburden sb with work; **accablé de dettes/soucis** weighed down

with debts/cares.
accalmie [akalmi] *nf* lull.
accaparant, e [akaparɑ̃, -ɑ̃t] *adj* that takes up all one's time *ou* attention.
accaparer [akapaʀe] *vt* to monopolize; (*suj: travail etc*) to take up (all) the time *ou* attention of.
accéder [aksede]: ~ **à** *vt* (*lieu*) to reach; (*fig: pouvoir*) to accede to; (*: poste*) to attain; (*accorder: requête*) to grant, accede to.
accélérateur [akseleʀatœʀ] *nm* accelerator.
accélération [akseleʀɑsjɔ̃] *nf* speeding up; acceleration.
accéléré [akseleʀe] *nm*: **en** ~ (*CINÉ*) speeded up.
accélérer [akseleʀe] *vt* (*mouvement, travaux*) to speed up ♦ *vi* (*AUTO*) to accelerate.
accent [aksɑ̃] *nm* accent; (*inflexions expressives*) tone (of voice); (*PHONÉTIQUE, fig*) stress; **aux ~s de** (*musique*) to the strains of; **mettre l'~ sur** (*fig*) to stress; ~ **aigu/grave/circonflexe** acute/grave/ circumflex accent.
accentuation [aksɑ̃tɥɑsjɔ̃] *nf* accenting; stressing.
accentué, e [aksɑ̃tɥe] *adj* marked, pronounced.
accentuer [aksɑ̃tɥe] *vt* (*LING: orthographe*) to accent; (*: phonétique*) to stress, accent; (*fig*) to accentuate, emphasize; (*: effort, pression*) to increase; **s'~** *vi* to become more marked *ou* pronounced.
acceptable [aksɛptabl(ə)] *adj* satisfactory, acceptable.
acceptation [aksɛptɑsjɔ̃] *nf* acceptance.
accepter [aksɛpte] *vt* to accept; (*tolérer*): ~ **que qn fasse** to agree to sb doing; ~ **de faire** to agree to do.
acception [aksɛpsjɔ̃] *nf* meaning, sense; **dans toute l'~ du terme** in the full sense *ou* meaning of the word.
accès [aksɛ] *nm* (*à un lieu, INFORM*) access; (*MÉD*) attack; (*: de toux*) fit, bout ♦ *nmpl* (*routes etc*) means of access, approaches; **d'~ facile/malaisé** easily/not easily accessible; **donner ~ à** (*lieu*) to give access to; (*carrière*) to open the door to; **avoir ~ auprès de qn** to have access to sb; **l'~ aux quais est interdit aux personnes non munies d'un billet** ticket-holders only on platforms, no access to platforms without a ticket; ~ **de colère** fit of anger; ~ **de joie** burst of joy.
accessible [aksesibl(ə)] *adj* accessible; (*personne*) approachable; (*livre, sujet*): ~ **à qn** within the reach of sb; (*sensible*): ~ **à la pitié/l'amour** open to pity/love.
accession [aksɛsjɔ̃] *nf*: ~ **à** accession to; (*à un poste*) attainment of; ~ **à la propriété** home-ownership.
accessit [aksesit] *nm* (*SCOL*) ≈ certificate of merit.
accessoire [akseswaʀ] *adj* secondary, of secondary importance; (*frais*) incidental ♦ *nm* accessory; (*THÉÂT*) prop.
accessoirement [akseswaʀmɑ̃] *adv* secondarily; incidentally.
accessoiriste [akseswaʀist(ə)] *nm/f* (*TV, CINÉ*) property man/woman.
accident [aksidɑ̃] *nm* accident; **par** ~ by chance; ~ **de parcours** mishap; ~ **de la route** road accident; ~ **du travail** accident at work; industrial injury *ou* accident; **~s de terrain** unevenness of the ground.
accidenté, e [aksidɑ̃te] *adj* damaged *ou* injured (in an accident); (*relief, terrain*) uneven; hilly.
accidentel, le [aksidɑ̃tɛl] *adj* accidental.
accidentellement [aksidɑ̃tɛlmɑ̃] *adv* (*par hasard*) accidentally; (*mourir*) in an accident.
accise [ɑksiz] *nf*: **droit d'~(s)** excise duty.
acclamation [aklamɑsjɔ̃] *nf*: **par** ~ (*vote*) by acclamation; **~s** *nfpl* cheers, cheering *sg*.
acclamer [aklame] *vt* to cheer, acclaim.
acclimatation [aklimatɑsjɔ̃] *nf* acclimatization.
acclimater [aklimate] *vt* to acclimatize; **s'~** *vi* to become acclimatized.
accointances [akwɛ̃tɑ̃s] *nfpl*: **avoir des ~ avec** to have contacts with.
accolade [akɔlad] *nf* (*amicale*) embrace; (*signe*) brace; **donner l'~ à qn** to embrace sb.
accoler [akɔle] *vt* to place side by side.
accommodant, e [akɔmɔdɑ̃, -ɑ̃t] *adj* accommodating, easy-going.
accommodement [akɔmɔdmɑ̃] *nm* compromise.
accommoder [akɔmɔde] *vt* (*CULIN*) to prepare; (*points de vue*) to reconcile; ~ **qch à** (*adapter*) to adapt sth to; **s'~ de** to put up with; (*se contenter de*) to make do with; **s'~ à** (*s'adapter*) to adapt to.
accompagnateur, trice [akɔ̃paɲatœʀ, -tʀis] *nm/f* (*MUS*) accompanist; (*de voyage*) guide; (*de voyage organisé*) courier; (*d'enfants*) accompanying adult.
accompagnement [akɔ̃paɲmɑ̃] *nm* (*MUS*) accompaniment; (*MIL*) support.
accompagner [akɔ̃paɲe] *vt* to accompany, be *ou* go *ou* come with; (*MUS*) to accompany; **s'~ de** to bring, be accompanied by.
accompli, e [akɔ̃pli] *adj* accomplished.
accomplir [akɔ̃pliʀ] *vt* (*tâche, projet*) to carry out; (*souhait*) to fulfil; **s'~** *vi* to be fulfilled.
accomplissement [akɔ̃plismɑ̃] *nm* carrying out; fulfilment (*BRIT*), fulfillment (*US*).
accord [akɔʀ] *nm* (*entente, convention, LING*) agreement; (*entre des styles, tons etc*) harmony; (*consentement*) agreement, consent; (*MUS*) chord; **donner son** ~ to give one's agreement; **mettre 2 personnes d'~** to make 2 people come to an agreement, reconcile 2 people; **se mettre d'~** to come to an agreement (with each other); **être d'~** to agree; **être d'~ avec qn** to agree with sb; **d'~!** OK!,

right!; **d'un commun** ~ of one accord; ~ **parfait** (*MUS*) tonic chord.
accord-cadre, *pl* **accords-cadres** [akɔʀkɑdʀ(ə)] *nm* framework *ou* outline agreement.
accordéon [akɔʀdeɔ̃] *nm* (*MUS*) accordion.
accordéoniste [akɔʀdeɔnist(ə)] *nm/f* accordionist.
accorder [akɔʀde] *vt* (*faveur, délai*) to grant; (*attribuer*): ~ **de l'importance/de la valeur à qch** to attach importance/value to sth; (*harmoniser*) to match; (*MUS*) to tune; **s'**~ to get on together; (*être d'accord*) to agree; (*couleurs, caractères*) to go together, match; (*LING*) to agree; **je vous accorde que ...** I grant you that ....
accordeur [akɔʀdœʀ] *nm* (*MUS*) tuner.
accoster [akɔste] *vt* (*NAVIG*) to draw alongside; (*personne*) to accost ♦ *vi* (*NAVIG*) to berth.
accotement [akɔtmɑ̃] *nm* (*de route*) verge (*BRIT*), shoulder; ~ **stabilisé/non stabilisé** hard shoulder/soft verge *ou* shoulder.
accoter [akɔte] *vt*: ~ **qch contre/à** to lean *ou* rest sth against/on; **s'**~ **contre/à** to lean against/on.
accouchement [akuʃmɑ̃] *nm* delivery, (child)birth; (*travail*) labour (*BRIT*), labor (*US*); ~ **à terme** delivery at (full) term; ~ **sans douleur** natural childbirth.
accoucher [akuʃe] *vi* to give birth, have a baby; (*être en travail*) to be in labour (*BRIT*) *ou* labor (*US*) ♦ *vt* to deliver; ~ **d'un garçon** to give birth to a boy.
accoucheur [akuʃœʀ] *nm*: **(médecin)** ~ obstetrician.
accoucheuse [akuʃøz] *nf* midwife.
accouder [akude]: **s'**~ *vi*: **s'**~ **à/contre/sur** to rest one's elbows on/against/on; **accoudé à la fenêtre** leaning on the windowsill.
accoudoir [akudwaʀ] *nm* armrest.
accouplement [akupləmɑ̃] *nm* coupling; mating.
accoupler [akuple] *vt* to couple; (*pour la reproduction*) to mate; **s'**~ to mate.
accourir [akuʀiʀ] *vi* to rush *ou* run up.
accoutrement [akutʀəmɑ̃] *nm* (*péj*) getup (*BRIT*), outfit.
accoutrer [akutʀe] (*péj*) *vt* to do *ou* get up; **s'**~ to do *ou* get o.s. up.
accoutumance [akutymɑ̃s] *nf* (*gén*) adaptation; (*MÉD*) addiction.
accoutumé, e [akutyme] *adj* (*habituel*) customary, usual; **comme à l'**~**e** as is customary *ou* usual.
accoutumer [akutyme] *vt*: ~ **qn à qch/faire** to accustom sb to sth/to doing; **s'**~ **à** to get accustomed *ou* used to.
accréditer [akʀedite] *vt* (*nouvelle*) to substantiate; ~ **qn (auprès de)** to accredit sb (to).
accro [akʀo] *nm/f* (*fam*: = *accroché(e)*) addict.
accroc [akʀo] *nm* (*déchirure*) tear; (*fig*) hitch, snag; **sans** ~ without a hitch; **faire un** ~ **à** (*vêtement*) to make a tear in, tear; (*fig: règle etc*) to infringe.
accrochage [akʀɔʃaʒ] *nm* hanging (up); hitching (up); (*AUTO*) (minor) collision; (*MIL*) encounter, engagement; (*dispute*) clash, brush.
accroche-cœur [akʀɔʃkœʀ] *nm* kiss-curl.
accrocher [akʀɔʃe] *vt* (*suspendre*): ~ **qch à** to hang sth (up) on; (*attacher: remorque*): ~ **qch à** to hitch sth (up) to; (*heurter*) to catch; to hit; (*déchirer*): ~ **qch (à)** to catch sth (on); (*MIL*) to engage; (*fig*) to catch, attract ♦ *vi* to stick, get stuck; (*fig: pourparlers etc*) to hit a snag; (*plaire: disque etc*) to catch on; **s'**~ (*se disputer*) to have a clash *ou* brush; (*ne pas céder*) to hold one's own, hang on in (*fam*); **s'**~ **à** (*rester pris à*) to catch on; (*agripper, fig*) to hang on *ou* cling to.
accrocheur, euse [akʀɔʃœʀ, -øz] *adj* (*vendeur, concurrent*) tenacious; (*publicité*) eye-catching; (*titre*) catchy, eye-catching.
accroire [akʀwaʀ] *vt*: **faire** *ou* **laisser** ~ **à qn qch/que** to give sb to believe sth/that.
accroîs [akʀwa], **accroissais** [akʀwasɛ] *etc vb voir* **accroître**.
accroissement [akʀwasmɑ̃] *nm* increase.
accroître [akʀwatʀ(ə)] *vt*, **s'**~ *vi* to increase.
accroupi, e [akʀupi] *adj* squatting, crouching (down).
accroupir [akʀupiʀ]: **s'**~ *vi* to squat, crouch (down).
accru, e [akʀy] *pp de* **accroître**.
accu [aky] *nm* (*fam*: = *accumulateur*) accumulator, battery.
accueil [akœj] *nm* welcome; (*endroit*) reception (desk); (*: dans une gare*) information kiosk; **comité/centre d'**~ reception committee/centre.
accueillant, e [akœjɑ̃, -ɑ̃t] *adj* welcoming, friendly.
accueillir [akœjiʀ] *vt* to welcome; (*loger*) to accommodate.
acculer [akyle] *vt*: ~ **qn à** *ou* **contre** to drive sb back against; ~ **qn dans** to corner sb in; ~ **qn à** (*faillite*) to drive sb to the brink of.
accumulateur [akymylatœʀ] *nm* accumulator, battery.
accumulation [akymylɑsjɔ̃] *nf* accumulation; **chauffage/radiateur à** ~ (night-)storage heating/heater.
accumuler [akymyle] *vt* to accumulate, amass; **s'**~ *vi* to accumulate; to pile up.
accusateur, trice [akyzatœʀ, -tʀis] *nm/f* accuser ♦ *adj* accusing; (*document, preuve*) incriminating.
accusatif [akyzatif] *nm* (*LING*) accusative.
accusation [akyzɑsjɔ̃] *nf* (*gén*) accusation; (*JUR*) charge; (*partie*): **l'**~ the prosecution; **mettre en** ~ to indict; **acte d'**~ bill of indictment.
accusé, e [akyze] *nm/f* accused; (*prévenu(e)*)

defendant ♦ *nm*: ~ **de réception** acknowledgement of receipt.
accuser [akyze] *vt* to accuse; (*fig*) to emphasize, bring out; (*: montrer*) to show; **s'~** *vi* (*s'accentuer*) to become more marked; ~ **qn de** to accuse sb of; (*JUR*) to charge sb with; ~ **qn/qch de qch** (*rendre responsable*) to blame sb/sth for sth; **s'~ de qch/d'avoir fait qch** to admit sth/having done sth; to blame o.s. for sth/for having done sth; ~ **réception de** to acknowledge receipt of; ~ **le coup** (*aussi fig*) to be visibly affected.
acerbe [asɛʀb(ə)] *adj* caustic, acid.
acéré, e [aseʀe] *adj* sharp.
acétate [asetat] *nm* acetate.
acétique [asetik] *adj*: **acide** ~ acetic acid.
acétone [asetɔn] *nf* acetone.
acétylène [asetilɛn] *nm* acetylene.
ACF *sigle m* (= *Automobile Club de France*) ≈ AA (*BRIT*), ≈ AAA (*US*).
ach. *abr* = *achète*.
acharné, e [aʃaʀne] *adj* (*lutte, adversaire*) fierce, bitter; (*travail*) relentless, unremitting.
acharnement [aʃaʀnəmɑ̃] *nm* fierceness; relentlessness.
acharner [aʃaʀne]: **s'~** *vi*: **s'~ sur** to go at fiercely, hound; **s'~ contre** to set o.s. against; to dog, pursue; (*suj: malchance*) to hound; **s'~ à faire** to try doggedly to do; to persist in doing.
achat [aʃa] *nm* buying *no pl*; (*article acheté*) purchase; **faire l'~ de** to buy, purchase; **faire des ~s** to do some shopping, buy a few things.
acheminement [aʃminmɑ̃] *nm* conveyance.
acheminer [aʃmine] *vt* (*courrier*) to forward, dispatch; (*troupes*) to convey, transport; (*train*) to route; **s'~ vers** to head for.
acheter [aʃte] *vt* to buy, purchase; (*soudoyer*) to buy, bribe; ~ **qch à** (*marchand*) to buy *ou* purchase sth from; (*ami etc: offrir*) to buy sth for; ~ **à crédit** to buy on credit.
acheteur, euse [aʃtœʀ, -øz] *nm/f* buyer; shopper; (*COMM*) buyer; (*JUR*) vendee, purchaser.
achevé, e [aʃve] *adj*: **d'un ridicule** ~ thoroughly *ou* absolutely ridiculous; **d'un comique** ~ absolutely hilarious.
achèvement [aʃɛvmɑ̃] *nm* completion, finishing.
achever [aʃve] *vt* to complete, finish; (*blessé*) to finish off; **s'~** *vi* to end.
achoppement [aʃɔpmɑ̃] *nm*: **pierre d'~** stumbling block.
acide [asid] *adj* sour, sharp; (*ton*) acid, biting; (*CHIMIE*) acid(ic) ♦ *nm* acid.
acidifier [asidifje] *vt* to acidify.
acidité [asidite] *nf* sharpness; acidity.
acidulé, e [asidyle] *adj* slightly acid; **bonbons ~s** acid drops (*BRIT*), ≈ lemon drops (*US*).
acier [asje] *nm* steel; ~ **inoxydable** stainless steel.
aciérie [asjeʀi] *nf* steelworks *sg*.
acné [akne] *nf* acne.
acolyte [akɔlit] *nm* (*péj*) associate.
acompte [akɔ̃t] *nm* deposit; (*versement régulier*) instalment; (*sur somme due*) payment on account; (*sur salaire*) advance; **un ~ de 100 €** €100 on account.
acoquiner [akɔkine]: **s'~ avec** *vt* (*péj*) to team up with.
Açores [asɔʀ] *nfpl*: **les ~** the Azores.
à-côté [akote] *nm* side-issue; (*argent*) extra.
à-coup [aku] *nm* (*du moteur*) (hic)cough; (*fig*) jolt; **sans ~s** smoothly; **par ~s** by fits and starts.
acoustique [akustik] *nf* (*d'une salle*) acoustics *pl*; (*science*) acoustics *sg* ♦ *adj* acoustic.
acquéreur [akeʀœʀ] *nm* buyer, purchaser; **se porter/se rendre ~ de qch** to announce one's intention to purchase/to purchase sth.
acquérir [akeʀiʀ] *vt* to acquire; (*par achat*) to purchase, acquire; (*valeur*) to gain; (*résultats*) to achieve; **ce que ses efforts lui ont acquis** what his efforts have won *ou* gained (for) him.
acquiers [akjɛʀ] *etc vb voir* **acquérir**.
acquiescement [akjɛsmɑ̃] *nm* acquiescence, agreement.
acquiescer [akjese] *vi* (*opiner*) to agree; (*consentir*): ~ **(à qch)** to acquiesce *ou* assent (to sth).
acquis, e [aki, -iz] *pp de* **acquérir** ♦ *nm* (accumulated) experience; (*avantage*) gain ♦ *adj* (*voir acquérir*) acquired; gained; achieved; **être ~ à** (*plan, idée*) to be in full agreement with; **son aide nous est ~e** we can count on *ou* be sure of his help; **tenir qch pour ~** to take sth for granted.
acquisition [akizisjɔ̃] *nf* acquisition; (*achat*) purchase; **faire l'~ de** to acquire; to purchase.
acquit [aki] *vb voir* **acquérir** ♦ *nm* (*quittance*) receipt; **pour ~** received; **par ~ de conscience** to set one's mind at rest.
acquittement [akitmɑ̃] *nm* acquittal; payment, settlement.
acquitter [akite] *vt* (*JUR*) to acquit; (*facture*) to pay, settle; **s'~ de** to discharge; (*promesse, tâche*) to fulfil (*BRIT*), fulfill (*US*), carry out.
âcre [ɑkʀ(ə)] *adj* acrid, pungent.
âcreté [ɑkʀəte] *nf* acridness, pungency.
acrimonie [akʀimɔni] *nf* acrimony.
acrobate [akʀɔbat] *nm/f* acrobat.
acrobatie [akʀɔbasi] *nf* (*art*) acrobatics *sg* (*exercice*) acrobatic feat; ~ **aérienne** aerobatics *sg*.
acrobatique [akʀɔbatik] *adj* acrobatic.
acronyme [akʀɔnim] *nm* acronym.
Acropole [akʀɔpɔl] *nf*: **l'~** the Acropolis.
acrylique [akʀilik] *adj, nm* acrylic.
acte [akt(ə)] *nm* act, action; (*THÉÂT*) act; **~s** *nmpl* (*compte-rendu*) proceedings; **prendre ~**

de to note, take note of; **faire ~ de présence** to put in an appearance; **faire ~ de candidature** to submit an application; **~ d'accusation** charge (*BRIT*), bill of indictment; **~ de baptême** baptismal certificate; **~ de mariage/naissance** marriage/birth certificate; **~ de vente** bill of sale.

acteur [aktœʀ] *nm* actor.

actif, ive [aktif, -iv] *adj* active ♦ *nm* (*COMM*) assets *pl*; (*LING*) active (voice); (*fig*): **avoir à son ~** to have to one's credit; **~s** *nmpl* people in employment; **mettre à son ~** to add to one's list of achievements; **l'~ et le passif** assets and liabilities; **prendre une part active à qch** to take an active part in sth; **population active** working population.

action [aksjɔ̃] *nf* (*gén*) action; (*COMM*) share; **une bonne/mauvaise ~** a good/an unkind deed; **mettre en ~** to put into action; **passer à l'~** to take action; **sous l'~ de** under the effect of; **l'~ syndicale** (the) union action; **un film d'~** an action film *ou* movie; **~ en diffamation** libel action; **~ de grâce(s)** (*REL*) thanksgiving.

actionnaire [aksjɔnɛʀ] *nm/f* shareholder.

actionner [aksjɔne] *vt* to work; to activate; to operate.

active [aktiv] *adj f voir* **actif**.

activement [aktivmɑ̃] *adv* actively.

activer [aktive] *vt* to speed up; (*CHIMIE*) to activate; **s'~** *vi* (*s'affairer*) to bustle about; (*se hâter*) to hurry up.

activisme [aktivism(ə)] *nm* activism.

activiste [aktivist(ə)] *nm/f* activist.

activité [aktivite] *nf* activity; **en ~** (*volcan*) active; (*fonctionnaire*) in active life; (*militaire*) on active service.

actrice [aktʀis] *nf* actress.

actualiser [aktɥalize] *vt* to actualize; (*mettre à jour*) to bring up to date.

actualité [aktɥalite] *nf* (*d'un problème*) topicality; (*événements*): **l'~** current events; **les ~s** (*CINÉ, TV*) the news; **l'~ politique/sportive** the political/sports *ou* sporting news; **les ~s télévisées** the television news; **d'~** topical.

actuel, le [aktɥɛl] *adj* (*présent*) present; (*d'actualité*) topical; (*non virtuel*) actual; **à l'heure ~le** at this moment in time, at the moment.

actuellement [aktɥɛlmɑ̃] *adv* at present, at the present time.

acuité [akɥite] *nf* acuteness.

acuponcteur, acupuncteur [akypɔ̃ktœʀ] *nm* acupuncturist.

acuponcture, acupuncture [akypɔ̃ktyʀ] *nf* acupuncture.

adage [adaʒ] *nm* adage.

adagio [ada(d)ʒjo] *adv, nm* adagio.

adaptable [adaptabl(ə)] *adj* adaptable.

adaptateur, trice [adaptatœʀ, -tʀis] *nm/f* adapter.

adaptation [adaptɑsjɔ̃] *nf* adaptation.

adapter [adapte] *vt* to adapt; **s'~ (à)** (*suj: personne*) to adapt (to); (*: objet, prise etc*) to apply (to); **~ qch à** (*approprier*) to adapt sth to (fit); **~ qch sur/dans/à** (*fixer*) to fit sth on/into/to.

addenda [adɛ̃da] *nm inv* addenda.

Addis-Ababa [adisababa], **Addis-Abeba** [adisabəba] *n* Addis Ababa.

additif [aditif] *nm* additional clause; (*substance*) additive; **~ alimentaire** food additive.

addition [adisjɔ̃] *nf* addition; (*au café*) bill.

additionnel, le [adisjɔnɛl] *adj* additional.

additionner [adisjɔne] *vt* to add (up); **s'~** *vi* to add up; **~ un produit d'eau** to add water to a product.

adduction [adyksjɔ̃] *nf* (*de gaz, d'eau*) conveyance.

ADEP *sigle f* (*= Agence nationale pour le développement de l'éducation permanente*) *national body which promotes adult education.*

adepte [adɛpt(ə)] *nm/f* follower.

adéquat, e [adekwa, -at] *adj* appropriate, suitable.

adéquation [adekwɑsjɔ̃] *nf* appropriateness; (*LING*) adequacy.

adhérence [adeʀɑ̃s] *nf* adhesion.

adhérent, e [adeʀɑ̃, -ɑ̃t] *nm/f* (*de club*) member.

adhérer [adeʀe] *vi* (*coller*) to adhere, stick; **~ à** (*coller*) to adhere *ou* stick to; (*se rallier à: parti, club*) to join; to be a member of; (*: opinion, mouvement*) to support.

adhésif, ive [adezif, -iv] *adj* adhesive, sticky ♦ *nm* adhesive.

adhésion [adezjɔ̃] *nf* (*à un club*) joining; membership; (*à une opinion*) support.

ad hoc [adɔk] *adj* ad hoc.

adieu, x [adjø] *excl* goodbye ♦ *nm* farewell; **dire ~ à qn** to say goodbye *ou* farewell to sb; **dire ~ à qch** (*renoncer*) to say *ou* wave goodbye to sth.

adipeux, euse [adipø, -øz] *adj* bloated, fat; (*ANAT*) adipose.

adjacent, e [adʒasɑ̃, -ɑ̃t] *adj*: **~ (à)** adjacent (to).

adjectif [adʒɛktif] *nm* adjective; **~ attribut** adjectival complement; **~ épithète** attributive adjective.

adjectival, e, aux [adʒɛktival, -o] *adj* adjectival.

adjoignais [adʒwaɲɛ] *etc vb voir* **adjoindre**.

adjoindre [adʒwɛ̃dʀ(ə)] *vt*: **~ qch à** to attach sth to; (*ajouter*) to add sth to; **~ qn à** (*personne*) to appoint sb as an assistant to; (*comité*) to appoint sb to, attach sb to; **s'~** *vt* (*collaborateur etc*) to take on, appoint.

adjoint, e [adʒwɛ̃, -wɛ̃t] *pp de* **adjoindre** ♦ *nm/f* assistant; **directeur ~** assistant manager.

adjonction [adʒɔ̃ksjɔ̃] *nf* (*voir adjoindre*) attaching; addition; appointment.

adjudant [adʒydɑ̃] *nm* (*MIL*) warrant officer;

~-chef ≈ warrant officer 1st class (*BRIT*), ≈ chief warrant officer (*US*).
adjudicataire [adʒydikatɛʀ] *nm/f* successful bidder, purchaser; (*pour travaux*) successful tenderer (*BRIT*) *ou* bidder (*US*).
adjudicateur, trice [adʒydikatœʀ, -tʀis] *nm/f* (*aux enchères*) seller.
adjudication [adʒydikɑsjɔ̃] *nf* sale by auction; (*pour travaux*) invitation to tender (*BRIT*) *ou* bid (*US*).
adjuger [adʒyʒe] *vt* (*prix, récompense*) to award; (*lors d'une vente*) to auction (off); **s'~** *vt* to take for o.s; **adjugé!** (*vendu*) gone!, sold!
adjurer [adʒyʀe] *vt*: ~ **qn de faire** to implore *ou* beg sb to do.
adjuvant [adʒyvɑ̃] *nm* (*médicament*) adjuvant; (*additif*) additive; (*stimulant*) stimulant.
admettre [admɛtʀ(ə)] *vt* (*visiteur, nouveau-venu*) to admit, let in; (*candidat: SCOL*) to pass; (*TECH: gaz, eau, air*) to admit; (*tolérer*) to allow, accept; (*reconnaître*) to admit, acknowledge; (*supposer*) to suppose; **j'admets que ...** I admit that ...; **je n'admets pas que tu fasses cela** I won't allow you to do that; **admettons que ...** let's suppose that ...; **admettons** let's suppose so.
administrateur, trice [administʀatœʀ, -tʀis] *nm/f* (*COMM*) director; (*ADMIN*) administrator; ~ **délégué** managing director; ~ **judiciaire** receiver.
administratif, ive [administʀatif, -iv] *adj* administrative ♦ *nm* person in administration.
administration [administʀɑsjɔ̃] *nf* administration; **l'A~** ≈ the Civil Service.
administré, e [administʀe] *nm/f* ≈ citizen.
administrer [administʀe] *vt* (*firme*) to manage, run; (*biens, remède, sacrement etc*) to administer.
admirable [admiʀabl(ə)] *adj* admirable, wonderful.
admirablement [admiʀabləmɑ̃] *adv* admirably.
admirateur, trice [admiʀatœʀ, -tʀis] *nm/f* admirer.
admiratif, ive [admiʀatif, -iv] *adj* admiring.
admiration [admiʀɑsjɔ̃] *nf* admiration; **être en ~ devant** to be lost in admiration before.
admirativement [admiʀativmɑ̃] *adv* admiringly.
admirer [admiʀe] *vt* to admire.
admis, e [admi, -iz] *pp de* **admettre**.
admissibilité [admisibilite] *nf* eligibility; admissibility, acceptability.
admissible [admisibl(ə)] *adj* (*candidat*) eligible; (*comportement*) admissible, acceptable; (*JUR*) receivable.
admission [admisjɔ̃] *nf* admission; **tuyau d'~** intake pipe; **demande d'~** application for membership; **service des ~s** admissions.
admonester [admɔnɛste] *vt* to admonish.
ADN *sigle m* (= *acide désoxyribonucléique*) DNA.
ado [ado] *nm/f* (*fam*: = *adolescent(e)*) adolescent, teenager.
adolescence [adɔlesɑ̃s] *nf* adolescence.
adolescent, e [adɔlesɑ̃, -ɑ̃t] *nm/f* adolescent, teenager.
adonner [adɔne]: **s'~ à** *vt* (*sport*) to devote o.s. to; (*boisson*) to give o.s. over to.
adopter [adɔpte] *vt* to adopt; (*projet de loi etc*) to pass.
adoptif, ive [adɔptif, -iv] *adj* (*parents*) adoptive; (*fils, patrie*) adopted.
adoption [adɔpsjɔ̃] *nf* adoption; **son pays/sa ville d'~** his adopted country/town.
adorable [adɔʀabl(ə)] *adj* adorable.
adoration [adɔʀɑsjɔ̃] *nf* adoration; (*REL*) worship; **être en ~ devant** to be lost in adoration before.
adorer [adɔʀe] *vt* to adore; (*REL*) to worship.
adosser [adose] *vt*: ~ **qch à** *ou* **contre** to stand sth against; **s'~ à** *ou* **contre** to lean with one's back against; **être adossé à** *ou* **contre** to be leaning with one's back against.
adoucir [adusiʀ] *vt* (*goût, température*) to make milder; (*avec du sucre*) to sweeten; (*peau, voix, eau*) to soften; (*caractère, personne*) to mellow; (*peine*) to soothe, allay; **s'~** *vi* to become milder; to soften; to mellow.
adoucissement [adusismɑ̃] *nm* becoming milder; sweetening; softening; mellowing; soothing.
adoucisseur [adusisœʀ] *nm*: ~ **(d'eau)** water softener.
adr. *abr* = **adresse, adresser**.
adrénaline [adʀenalin] *nf* adrenaline.
adresse [adʀɛs] *nf* (*voir adroit*) skill, dexterity; (*domicile, INFORM*) address; **à l'~ de** (*pour*) for the benefit of.
adresser [adʀese] *vt* (*lettre: expédier*) to send; (*écrire l'adresse sur*) to address; (*injure, compliments*) to address; ~ **qn à un docteur/bureau** to refer *ou* send sb to a doctor/an office; ~ **la parole à qn** to speak to *ou* address sb; **s'~ à** (*parler à*) to speak to, address; (*s'informer auprès de*) to go and see, go and speak to; (*bureau*) to enquire at; (*suj: livre, conseil*) to be aimed at.
Adriatique [adʀijatik] *nf*: **l'~** the Adriatic.
adroit, e [adʀwa, -wat] *adj* (*joueur, mécanicien*) skilful (*BRIT*), skillful (*US*), dext(e)rous; (*politicien etc*) shrewd, skilled.
adroitement [adʀwatmɑ̃] *adv* skilfully (*BRIT*), skillfully (*US*), dext(e)rously; shrewdly.
AdS *sigle f* = *Académie des Sciences*.
aduler [adyle] *vt* to adulate.
adulte [adylt(ə)] *nm/f* adult, grown-up ♦ *adj* (*personne, attitude*) adult, grown-up; (*chien, arbre*) fully-grown, mature; **l'âge ~** adulthood; **formation/film pour ~s** adult training/film.
adultère [adyltɛʀ] *adj* adulterous ♦ *nm/f* adulterer/adulteress ♦ *nm* (*acte*) adultery.
adultérin, e [adylteʀɛ̃, -in] *adj* born of adul

tery.
advenir [advəniʀ] *vi* to happen; **qu'est-il advenu de?** what has become of?; **quoi qu'il advienne** whatever befalls *ou* happens.
adventiste [advɑ̃tist(ə)] *nm/f* (*REL*) Adventist.
adverbe [advɛʀb(ə)] *nm* adverb; ~ **de manière** adverb of manner.
adverbial, e, aux [advɛʀbjal, -o] *adj* adverbial.
adversaire [advɛʀsɛʀ] *nm/f* (*SPORT*, *gén*) opponent, adversary; (*MIL*) adversary, enemy.
adverse [advɛʀs(ə)] *adj* opposing.
adversité [advɛʀsite] *nf* adversity.
AE *sigle m* (= *adjoint d'enseignement*) *non-certificated teacher.*
AELE *sigle f* (= *Association européenne de libre-échange*) EFTA (= *European Free Trade Association*).
AEN *sigle f* (= *Agence pour l'énergie nucléaire*) ≈ AEA (= *Atomic Energy Authority*).
aérateur [aeʀatœʀ] *nm* ventilator.
aération [aeʀɑsjɔ̃] *nf* airing; (*circulation de l'air*) ventilation; **conduit d'~** ventilation shaft; **bouche d'~** air vent.
aéré, e [aeʀe] *adj* (*pièce, local*) airy, well-ventilated; (*tissu*) loose-woven; **centre ~** outdoor centre.
aérer [aeʀe] *vt* to air; (*fig*) to lighten; **s'~** *vi* to get some (fresh) air.
aérien, ne [aeʀjɛ̃, -ɛn] *adj* (*AVIAT*) air *cpd*, aerial; (*câble, métro*) overhead; (*fig*) light; **compagnie ~ne** airline (company); **ligne ~ne** airline.
aérobic [aeʀɔbik] *nf* aerobics *sg*.
aérobie [aeʀɔbi] *adj* aerobic.
aéro-club [aeʀɔklœb] *nm* flying club.
aérodrome [aeʀɔdʀom] *nm* airfield, aerodrome.
aérodynamique [aeʀɔdinamik] *adj* aerodynamic, streamlined ♦ *nf* aerodynamics *sg*.
aérofrein [aeʀofʀɛ̃] *nm* air brake.
aérogare [aeʀɔgaʀ] *nf* airport (buildings); (*en ville*) air terminal.
aéroglisseur [aeʀɔglisœʀ] *nm* hovercraft.
aérogramme [aeʀɔgʀam] *nm* air letter, aerogram(me).
aéromodélisme [aeʀɔmɔdelism(ə)] *nm* model aircraft making.
aéronaute [aeʀɔnot] *nm/f* aeronaut.
aéronautique [aeʀɔnotik] *adj* aeronautical ♦ *nf* aeronautics *sg*.
aéronaval, e [aeʀɔnaval] *adj* air and sea *cpd* ♦ *nf*: **l'A~e** ≈ the Fleet Air Arm (*BRIT*), ≈ the Naval Air Force (*US*).
aéronef [aeʀɔnɛf] *nm* aircraft.
aérophagie [aeʀɔfaʒi] *nf* aerophagy.
aéroport [aeʀɔpɔʀ] *nm* airport; ~ **d'embarquement** departure airport.
aéroporté, e [aeʀɔpɔʀte] *adj* airborne, airlifted.
aéroportuaire [aeʀɔpɔʀtɥɛʀ] *adj* of an *ou* the airport, airport *cpd*.
aéropostal, e, aux [aeʀɔpɔstal, -o] *adj* airmail *cpd*.
aérosol [aeʀɔsɔl] *nm* aerosol.
aérospatial, e, aux [aeʀɔspasjal, -o] *adj* aerospace ♦ *nf* the aerospace industry.
aérostat [aeʀɔsta] *nm* aerostat.
aérotrain [aeʀɔtʀɛ̃] *nm* hovertrain.
AF *sigle fpl* = **allocations familiales** ♦ *sigle f* (*Suisse*) = *Assemblée fédérale.*
AFAT [afat] *sigle m* (= *Auxiliaire féminin de l'armée de terre*) *member of the women's army.*
affabilité [afabilite] *nf* affability.
affable [afabl(ə)] *adj* affable.
affabulateur, trice [afabylatœʀ, -tʀis] *nm/f* storyteller.
affabulation [afabylɑsjɔ̃] *nf* invention, fantasy.
affabuler [afabyle] *vi* to make up stories.
affacturage [afaktyʀaʒ] *nm* factoring.
affadir [afadiʀ] *vt* to make insipid *ou* tasteless.
affaiblir [afebliʀ] *vt* to weaken; **s'~** *vi* to weaken, grow weaker; (*vue*) to grow dim.
affaiblissement [afeblismɑ̃] *nm* weakening.
affaire [afɛʀ] *nf* (*problème, question*) matter; (*criminelle, judiciaire*) case; (*scandaleuse etc*) affair; (*entreprise*) business; (*marché, transaction*) (business) deal, (piece of) business *no pl*; (*occasion intéressante*) good deal, bargain; **~s** *nfpl* affairs; (*activité commerciale*) business *sg*; (*effets personnels*) things, belongings; **tirer qn/se tirer d'~** to get sb/o.s. out of trouble; **ceci fera l'~** this will do (nicely); **avoir ~ à** (*comme adversaire*) to be faced with; (*en contact*) to be dealing with; **tu auras ~ à moi!** (*menace*) you'll have me to contend with!; **c'est une ~ de goût/d'argent** it's a question *ou* matter of taste/money; **c'est l'~ d'une minute/heure** it'll only take a minute/an hour; **ce sont mes ~s** (*cela me concerne*) that's my business; **toutes ~s cessantes** forthwith; **les ~s étrangères** (*POL*) foreign affairs.
affairé, e [afeʀe] *adj* busy.
affairer [afeʀe]: **s'~** *vi* to busy o.s., bustle about.
affairisme [afeʀism(ə)] *nm* (political) racketeering.
affaissement [afɛsmɑ̃] *nm* subsidence; collapse.
affaisser [afese]: **s'~** *vi* (*terrain, immeuble*) to subside, sink; (*personne*) to collapse.
affaler [afale]: **s'~** *vi*: **s'~ dans/sur** to collapse *ou* slump into/onto.
affamé, e [afame] *adj* starving, famished.
affamer [afame] *vt* to starve.
affectation [afɛktɑsjɔ̃] *nf* (*voir affecter*) allotment; appointment; posting; (*voir affecté*) affectedness.
affecté, e [afɛkte] *adj* affected.
affecter [afɛkte] *vt* (*émouvoir*) to affect, move; (*feindre*) to affect, feign; (*telle ou telle forme*

etc) to take on, assume; ~ **qch à** to allocate *ou* allot sth to; ~ **qn à** to appoint sb to; (*diplomate*) to post sb to; ~ **qch de** (*de coefficient*) to modify sth by.
affectif, ive [afɛktif, -iv] *adj* emotional, affective.
affection [afɛksjɔ̃] *nf* affection; (*mal*) ailment; **avoir de l'~ pour** to feel affection for; **prendre en ~** to become fond of.
affectionner [afɛksjɔne] *vt* to be fond of.
affectueusement [afɛktɥøzmɑ̃] *adv* affectionately.
affectueux, euse [afɛktɥø, -øz] *adj* affectionate.
afférent, e [afeʀɑ̃, -ɑ̃t] *adj*: ~ **à** pertaining *ou* relating to.
affermir [afɛʀmiʀ] *vt* to consolidate, strengthen.
aff. étr. *abr* (= *Affaires étrangères*) *voir* **affaire**.
affichage [afiʃaʒ] *nm* billposting, billsticking; (*électronique*) display; **"~ interdit"** "stick no bills", "billsticking prohibited"; ~ **à cristaux liquides** liquid crystal display, LCD; ~ **numérique** *ou* **digital** digital display.
affiche [afiʃ] *nf* poster; (*officielle*) (public) notice; (*THÉÂT*) bill; **être à l'~** (*THÉÂT*) to be on; **tenir l'~** to run.
afficher [afiʃe] *vt* (*affiche*) to put up, post up; (*réunion*) to put up a notice about; (*électroniquement*) to display; (*fig*) to exhibit, display; **s'~** (*péj*) to flaunt o.s.; **"défense d'~"** "stick no bills".
affichette [afiʃɛt] *nf* small poster *ou* notice.
affilé, e [afile] *adj* sharp.
affilée [afile]: **d'~** *adv* at a stretch.
affiler [afile] *vt* to sharpen.
affiliation [afiljɑsjɔ̃] *nf* affiliation.
affilié, e [afilje] *adj*: **être ~ à** to be affiliated to ♦ *nm/f* affiliated party *ou* member.
affilier [afilje] *vt*: **s'~ à** to become affiliated to.
affiner [afine] *vt* to refine; **s'~** *vi* to become (more) refined.
affinité [afinite] *nf* affinity.
affirmatif, ive [afiʀmatif, -iv] *adj* affirmative ♦ *nf*: **répondre par l'affirmative** to reply in the affirmative; **dans l'affirmative** (*si oui*) if (the answer is) yes ..., if he does (*ou* you do *etc*) ....
affirmation [afiʀmɑsjɔ̃] *nf* assertion.
affirmativement [afiʀmativmɑ̃] *adv* affirmatively, in the affirmative.
affirmer [afiʀme] *vt* (*prétendre*) to maintain, assert; (*autorité etc*) to assert; **s'~** to assert o.s.; to assert itself.
affleurer [aflœʀe] *vi* to show on the surface.
affliction [afliksjɔ̃] *nf* affliction.
affligé, e [afliʒe] *adj* distressed, grieved; ~ **de** (*maladie, tare*) afflicted with.
affligeant, e [afliʒɑ̃, -ɑ̃t] *adj* distressing.
affliger [afliʒe] *vt* (*peiner*) to distress, grieve.
affluence [aflyɑ̃s] *nf* crowds *pl*; **heures d'~** rush hour *sg*; **jours d'~** busiest days.
affluent [aflyɑ̃] *nm* tributary.
affluer [aflye] *vi* (*secours, biens*) to flood in, pour in; (*sang*) to rush, flow.
afflux [afly] *nm* flood, influx; rush.
affolant, e [afɔlɑ̃, -ɑ̃t] *adj* terrifying.
affolé, e [afɔle] *adj* panic-stricken, panicky.
affolement [afɔlmɑ̃] *nm* panic.
affoler [afɔle] *vt* to throw into a panic; **s'~** *vi* to panic.
affranchir [afʀɑ̃ʃiʀ] *vt* to put a stamp *ou* stamps on; (*à la machine*) to frank (*BRIT*), meter (*US*); (*esclave*) to enfranchise, emancipate; (*fig*) to free, liberate; **s'~ de** to free o.s. from; **machine à ~** franking machine, postage meter.
affranchissement [afʀɑ̃ʃismɑ̃] *nm* franking (*BRIT*), metering (*US*); freeing; (*POSTES: prix payé*) postage; **tarifs d'~** postage rates.
affres [afʀ(ə)] *nfpl*: **dans les ~ de** in the throes of.
affréter [afʀete] *vt* to charter.
affreusement [afʀøzmɑ̃] *adv* dreadfully, awfully.
affreux, euse [afʀø, -øz] *adj* dreadful, awful.
affriolant, e [afʀijɔlɑ̃, -ɑ̃t] *adj* tempting, enticing.
affront [afʀɔ̃] *nm* affront.
affrontement [afʀɔ̃tmɑ̃] *nm* (*MIL, POL*) clash, confrontation.
affronter [afʀɔ̃te] *vt* to confront, face; **s'~** to confront each other.
affubler [afyble] *vt* (*péj*): ~ **qn de** to rig *ou* deck sb out in; (*surnom*) to attach to sb.
affût [afy] *nm* (*de canon*) gun carriage; **à l'~ (de)** (*gibier*) lying in wait (for); (*fig*) on the look-out (for).
affûter [afyte] *vt* to sharpen, grind.
afghan, e [afgɑ̃, -an] *adj* Afghan.
Afghanistan [afganistɑ̃] *nm*: **l'~** Afghanistan.
afin [afɛ̃]: ~ **que** *conj* so that, in order that; ~ **de faire** in order to do, so as to do.
AFNOR [afnɔʀ] *sigle f* (= *Association française de normalisation*) *industrial standards authority*.
a fortiori [afɔʀsjɔʀi] *adv* all the more, a fortiori.
AFP *sigle f* = *Agence France-Presse*.
AFPA *sigle f* = *Association pour la formation professionnelle des adultes*.
africain, e [afʀikɛ̃, -ɛn] *adj* African ♦ *nm/f*: **A~, e** African.
afrikaans [afʀikɑ̃] *nm, adj inv* Afrikaans.
Afrikaner [afʀikanɛʀ] *nm/f* Afrikaner.
Afrique [afʀik] *nf*: **l'~** Africa; **l'~ australe/du Nord/du Sud** southern/North/South Africa.
afro [afʀo] *adj inv*: **coupe ~** afro hairstyle ♦ *nm/f*: **A~** Afro.
afro-américain, e [afʀoameʀikɛ̃, -ɛn] *adj* Afro-American.
afro-asiatique [afʀɔazjatik] *adj* Afro-Asian.
AG *sigle f* = *assemblée générale*.
ag. *abr* = **agence**.

agaçant, e [agasɑ̃, -ɑ̃t] *adj* irritating, aggravating.
agacement [agasmɑ̃] *nm* irritation, aggravation.
agacer [agase] *vt* to pester, tease; (*involontairement*) to irritate, aggravate; (*aguicher*) to excite, lead on.
agapes [agap] *nfpl* (*humoristique: festin*) feast.
agate [agat] *nf* agate.
AGE *sigle f* = *assemblée générale extraordinaire.*
âge [ɑʒ] *nm* age; **quel ~ as-tu?** how old are you?; **une femme d'un certain ~** a middle-aged woman, a woman who is getting on (in years); **bien porter son ~** to wear well; **prendre de l'~** to be getting on (in years), grow older; **limite d'~** age limit; **dispense d'~** special exemption from age limit; **troisième ~** (*période*) retirement; (*personnes âgées*) senior citizens; **l'~ ingrat** the awkward *ou* difficult age; **~ légal** legal age; **~ mental** mental age; **l'~ mûr** maturity, middle age; **~ de raison** age of reason.
âgé, e [ɑʒe] *adj* old, elderly; **~ de 10 ans** 10 years old.
agence [aʒɑ̃s] *nf* agency, office; (*succursale*) branch; **~ immobilière** estate agent's (office) (*BRIT*), real estate office (*US*); **~ matrimoniale** marriage bureau; **~ de placement** employment agency; **~ de publicité** advertising agency; **~ de voyages** travel agency.
agencé, e [aʒɑ̃se] *adj*: **bien/mal ~** well/badly put together; well/badly laid out *ou* arranged.
agencement [aʒɑ̃smɑ̃] *nm* putting together; arrangement, laying out.
agencer [aʒɑ̃se] *vt* to put together; (*local*) to arrange, lay out.
agenda [aʒɛ̃da] *nm* diary.
agenouiller [aʒnuje]: **s'~** *vi* to kneel (down).
agent [aʒɑ̃] *nm* (*aussi*: **~ de police**) policeman; (*ADMIN*) official, officer; (*fig: élément, facteur*) agent; **~ d'assurances** insurance broker; **~ de change** stockbroker; **~ commercial** sales representative; **~ immobilier** estate agent (*BRIT*), realtor (*US*); **~ (secret)** (secret) agent.
agglo [aglo] *nm* (*fam*) = **aggloméré.**
agglomérat [aglɔmeʀa] *nm* (*GÉO*) agglomerate.
agglomération [aglɔmeʀɑsjɔ̃] *nf* town; (*AUTO*) built-up area; **l'~ parisienne** the urban area of Paris.
aggloméré [aglɔmeʀe] *nm* (*bois*) chipboard; (*pierre*) conglomerate.
agglomérer [aglɔmeʀe] *vt* to pile up; (*TECH: bois, pierre*) to compress; **s'~** *vi* to pile up.
agglutiner [aglytine] *vt* to stick together; **s'~** *vi* to congregate.
aggravant, e [agʀavɑ̃, -ɑ̃t] *adj*: **circonstances ~es** aggravating circumstances.
aggravation [agʀavɑsjɔ̃] *nf* worsening, aggravation; increase.
aggraver [agʀave] *vt* to worsen, aggravate; (*JUR: peine*) to increase; **s'~** *vi* to worsen; **~ son cas** to make one's case worse.
agile [aʒil] *adj* agile, nimble.
agilement [aʒilmɑ̃] *adv* nimbly.
agilité [aʒilite] *nf* agility, nimbleness.
agio [aʒjo] *nm* (bank) charges *pl*.
agir [aʒiʀ] *vi* (*se comporter*) to behave, act; (*faire quelque chose*) to act, take action; (*avoir de l'effet*) to act; **il s'agit de** it's a matter *ou* question of; it is about; (*il importe que*): **il s'agit de faire** we (*ou* you *etc*) must do; **de quoi s'agit-il?** what is it about?
agissements [aʒismɑ̃] *nmpl* (*gén péj*) schemes, intrigues.
agitateur, trice [aʒitatœʀ, -tʀis] *nm/f* agitator.
agitation [aʒitɑsjɔ̃] *nf* (hustle and) bustle; (*trouble*) agitation, excitement; (*politique*) unrest, agitation.
agité, e [aʒite] *adj* (*remuant*) fidgety, restless; (*troublé*) agitated, perturbed; (*journée*) hectic; (*mer*) rough; (*sommeil*) disturbed, broken.
agiter [aʒite] *vt* (*bouteille, chiffon*) to shake; (*bras, mains*) to wave; (*préoccuper, exciter*) to trouble, perturb; **s'~** *vi* to bustle about; (*dormeur*) to toss and turn; (*enfant*) to fidget; (*POL*) to grow restless; **"~ avant l'emploi"** "shake before use".
agneau, x [aɲo] *nm* lamb; (*toison*) lambswool.
agnelet [aɲlɛ] *nm* little lamb.
agnostique [agnɔstik] *adj, nm/f* agnostic.
agonie [agɔni] *nf* mortal agony, death pangs *pl*; (*fig*) death throes *pl*.
agonir [agɔniʀ] *vt*: **~ qn d'injures** to hurl abuse at sb.
agoniser [agɔnize] *vi* to be dying; (*fig*) to be in its death throes.
agrafe [agʀaf] *nf* (*de vêtement*) hook, fastener; (*de bureau*) staple; (*MÉD*) clip.
agrafer [agʀafe] *vt* to fasten; to staple.
agrafeuse [agʀaføz] *nf* stapler.
agraire [agʀɛʀ] *adj* agrarian; (*mesure, surface*) land *cpd*.
agrandir [agʀɑ̃diʀ] *vt* (*magasin, domaine*) to extend, enlarge; (*trou*) to enlarge, make bigger; (*PHOTO*) to enlarge, blow up; **s'~** *vi* to be extended; to be enlarged.
agrandissement [agʀɑ̃dismɑ̃] *nm* extension; enlargement; (*photographie*) enlargement.
agrandisseur [agʀɑ̃disœʀ] *nm* (*PHOTO*) enlarger.
agréable [agʀeabl(ə)] *adj* pleasant, nice.
agréablement [agʀeabləmɑ̃] *adv* pleasantly.
agréé, e [agʀee] *adj*: **concessionnaire ~** registered dealer; **magasin ~** registered dealer('s).
agréer [agʀee] *vt* (*requête*) to accept; **~ à** *vt* to please, suit; **veuillez ~ ...** (*formule épistolaire*) yours faithfully.
agrég [agʀɛg] *nf* (*fam*) = **agrégation.**

agrégat [agʀega] *nm* aggregate.
agrégation [agʀegɑsjɔ̃] *nf highest teaching diploma in France*; *see boxed note*.

> **AGRÉGATION**
>
> *The* **agrégation**, *informally known as the* **'agrég'**, *is a prestigious competitive examination for the recruitment of secondary school teachers in France. The number of candidates always far exceeds the number of vacant posts. Most teachers of 'classes préparatoires' and most university lecturers have passed the* **agrégation**.

agrégé, e [agʀeʒe] *nm/f* holder of the *agrégation*.
agréger [agʀeʒe]: **s'**~ *vi* to aggregate.
agrément [agʀemɑ̃] *nm* (*accord*) consent, approval; (*attraits*) charm, attractiveness; (*plaisir*) pleasure; **voyage d'**~ pleasure trip.
agrémenter [agʀemɑ̃te] *vt*: ~ **(de)** to embellish (with), adorn (with).
agrès [agʀɛ] *nmpl* (gymnastics) apparatus *sg*.
agresser [agʀese] *vt* to attack.
agresseur [agʀɛsœʀ] *nm* aggressor.
agressif, ive [agʀɛsif, -iv] *adj* aggressive.
agression [agʀɛsjɔ̃] *nf* attack; (*POL, MIL, PSYCH*) aggression.
agressivement [agʀɛsivmɑ̃] *adv* aggressively.
agressivité [agʀɛsivite] *nf* aggressiveness.
agreste [agʀɛst(ə)] *adj* rustic.
agricole [agʀikɔl] *adj* agricultural, farm *cpd*.
agriculteur, trice [agʀikyltœʀ, -tʀis] *nm/f* farmer.
agriculture [agʀikyltyʀ] *nf* agriculture; farming.
agripper [agʀipe] *vt* to grab, clutch; (*pour arracher*) to snatch, grab; **s'**~ **à** to cling (on) to, clutch, grip.
agro-alimentaire [agʀɔalimɑ̃tɛʀ] *adj* farming *cpd* ♦ *nm*: **l'**~ agribusiness.
agronomie [agʀɔnɔmi] *nf* agronomy.
agrumes [agʀym] *nmpl* citrus fruit(s).
aguerrir [ageʀiʀ] *vt* to harden; **s'**~ **(contre)** to become hardened (to).
aguets [agɛ]: **aux** ~ *adv*: **être aux** ~ to be on the look-out.
aguichant, e [agiʃɑ̃, -ɑ̃t] *adj* enticing.
aguicher [agiʃe] *vt* to entice.
aguicheur, euse [agiʃœʀ, -øz] *adj* enticing.
ah [ɑ] *excl* ah!; ~ **bon?** really?, is that so?; ~ **mais** ... yes, but ...; ~ **non!** oh no!
ahuri, e [ayʀi] *adj* (*stupéfait*) flabbergasted; (*idiot*) dim-witted.
ahurir [ayʀiʀ] *vt* to stupefy, stagger.
ahurissant, e [ayʀisɑ̃, -ɑ̃t] *adj* stupefying, staggering, mind-boggling.
ai [e] *vb voir* **avoir**.
aide [ɛd] *nm/f* assistant ♦ *nf* assistance, help; (*secours financier*) aid; **à l'**~ **de** with the help *ou* aid of; **aller à l'**~ **de qn** to go to sb's aid, go to help sb; **venir en** ~ **à qn** to help sb, come to sb's assistance; **appeler (qn) à l'**~ to call for help (from sb); **à l'**~! help!; ~ **de camp** *nm* aide-de-camp; ~ **comptable** *nm* accountant's assistant; ~ **électricien** *nm* electrician's mate; ~ **familiale** *nf* mother's help, ≈ home help; ~ **judiciaire** *nf* legal aid; ~ **de laboratoire** *nm/f* laboratory assistant; ~ **ménagère** *nf* ≈ home help; ~ **sociale** *nf* (*assistance*) state aid; ~ **soignant, e** *nm/f* auxiliary nurse.
aide-éducateur, trice [ɛdedykatœʀ,tʀis] *nm/f* classroom assistant.
aide-mémoire [ɛdmemwaʀ] *nm inv* (key facts) handbook.
aider [ede] *vt* to help; ~ **à qch** to help (towards) sth; ~ **qn à faire qch** to help sb to do sth; **s'**~ **de** (*se servir de*) to use, make use of.
aie [ɛ] *etc vb voir* **avoir**.
aïe [aj] *excl* ouch!
AIEA *sigle f* (= *Agence internationale de l'énergie nucléaire*) IAEA (= *International Atomic Energy Agency*).
aïeul, e [ajœl] *nm/f* grandparent, grandfather, grandmother; (*ancêtre*) forebear.
aïeux [ajø] *nmpl* grandparents; forebears, forefathers.
aigle [ɛgl(ə)] *nm* eagle.
aiglefin [ɛgləfɛ̃] *nm* = **églefin**.
aigre [ɛgʀ(ə)] *adj* sour, sharp; (*fig*) sharp, cutting; **tourner à l'**~ to turn sour.
aigre-doux, -douce [ɛgʀədu, -dus] *adj* (*fruit*) bitter-sweet; (*sauce*) sweet and sour.
aigrefin [ɛgʀəfɛ̃] *nm* swindler.
aigrelet, te [ɛgʀəlɛ, -ɛt] *adj* (*taste*) sourish; (*voix, son*) sharpish.
aigrette [ɛgʀɛt] *nf* (*plume*) feather.
aigreur [ɛgʀœʀ] *nf* sourness; sharpness; ~**s d'estomac** heartburn *sg*.
aigri, e [egʀi] *adj* embittered.
aigrir [egʀiʀ] *vt* (*personne*) to embitter; (*caractère*) to sour; **s'**~ *vi* to become embittered; to sour; (*lait etc*) to turn sour.
aigu, ë [egy] *adj* (*objet, arête*) sharp, pointed; (*son, voix*) high-pitched, shrill; (*note*) high(-pitched); (*douleur, intelligence*) acute, sharp.
aigue-marine, *pl* **aigues-marines** [ɛgmaʀin] *nf* aquamarine.
aiguillage [egɥijaʒ] *nm* (*RAIL*) points *pl*.
aiguille [egɥij] *nf* needle; (*de montre*) hand; ~ **à tricoter** knitting needle.
aiguiller [egɥije] *vt* (*orienter*) to direct; (*RAIL*) to shunt.
aiguillette [egɥijɛt] *nf* (*CULIN*) aiguillette.
aiguilleur [egɥijœʀ] *nm* (*RAIL*) pointsman; ~ **du ciel** air traffic controller.
aiguillon [egɥijɔ̃] *nm* (*d'abeille*) sting; (*fig*) spur, stimulus.
aiguillonner [egɥijɔne] *vt* to spur *ou* goad on.
aiguiser [egize] *vt* to sharpen, grind; (*fig*) to stimulate; (*: esprit*) to sharpen; (*: sens*) to excite.

aiguisoir [egizwaʀ] *nm* sharpener.
aïkido [ajkido] *nm* aikido.
ail [aj] *nm* garlic.
aile [ɛl] *nf* wing; (*de voiture*) wing (*BRIT*), fender (*US*); **battre de l'~** (*fig*) to be in a sorry state; **voler de ses propres ~s** to stand on one's own two feet; **~ libre** hang-glider.
ailé, e [ele] *adj* winged.
aileron [ɛlʀɔ̃] *nm* (*de requin*) fin; (*d'avion*) aileron.
ailette [ɛlɛt] *nf* (*TECH*) fin; (*: de turbine*) blade.
ailier [elje] *nm* (*SPORT*) winger.
aille [aj] *etc vb voir* **aller**.
ailleurs [ajœʀ] *adv* elsewhere, somewhere else; **partout/nulle part ~** everywhere/nowhere else; **d'~** *adv* (*du reste*) moreover, besides; **par ~** *adv* (*d'autre part*) moreover, furthermore.
ailloli [ajɔli] *nm* garlic mayonnaise.
aimable [ɛmabl(ə)] *adj* kind, nice; **vous êtes bien ~** that's very nice *ou* kind of you, how kind (of you)!
aimablement [ɛmabləmɑ̃] *adv* kindly.
aimant [ɛmɑ̃] *nm* magnet.
aimant, e [ɛmɑ̃, -ɑ̃t] *adj* loving, affectionate.
aimanté, e [ɛmɑ̃te] *adj* magnetic.
aimanter [ɛmɑ̃te] *vt* to magnetize.
aimer [eme] *vt* to love; (*d'amitié, affection, par goût*) to like; (*souhait*): **j'aimerais ...** I would like ...; **s'~** to love each other; to like each other; **je n'aime pas beaucoup Paul** I don't like Paul much, I don't care much for Paul; **~ faire qch** to like doing sth, like to do sth; **aimeriez-vous que je vous accompagne?** would you like me to come with you?; **j'aimerais (bien) m'en aller** I should (really) like to go; **bien ~ qn/qch** to like sb/sth; **j'aime mieux Paul (que Pierre)** I prefer Paul (to Pierre); **j'aime mieux** *ou* **autant vous dire que** I may as well tell you that; **j'aimerais autant** *ou* **mieux y aller maintenant** I'd sooner *ou* rather go now; **j'aime assez aller au cinéma** I quite like going to the cinema.
aine [ɛn] *nf* groin.
aîné, e [ene] *adj* elder, older; (*le plus âgé*) eldest, oldest ♦ *nm/f* oldest child *ou* one, oldest boy *ou* son/girl *ou* daughter; **~s** *nmpl* (*fig: anciens*) elders; **il est mon ~ (de 2 ans)** he's (2 years) older than me, he's 2 years my senior.
aînesse [ɛnɛs] *nf*: **droit d'~** birthright.
ainsi [ɛ̃si] *adv* (*de cette façon*) like this, in this way, thus; (*ce faisant*) thus ♦ *conj* thus, so; **~ que** (*comme*) (just) as; (*et aussi*) as well as; **pour ~ dire** so to speak, as it were; **~ donc** and so; **~ soit-il** (*REL*) so be it; **et ~ de suite** and so on (and so forth).
aïoli [ajɔli] *nm* = **ailloli**.
air [ɛʀ] *nm* air; (*mélodie*) tune; (*expression*) look, air; (*atmosphère, ambiance*): **dans l'~** in the air (*fig*); **prendre de grands ~s (avec qn)** to give o.s. airs (with sb); **en l'~** (up) into the air; **tirer en l'~** to fire shots in the air; **paroles/menaces en l'~** idle words/threats; **prendre l'~** to get some (fresh) air; (*avion*) to take off; **avoir l'~ triste** to look *ou* seem sad; **avoir l'~ de qch** to look like sth; **avoir l'~ de faire** to look as though one is doing, appear to be doing; **courant d'~** draught (*BRIT*), draft (*US*); **le grand ~** the open air; **mal de l'~** air-sickness; **tête en l'~** scatterbrain; **~ comprimé** compressed air; **~ conditionné** air-conditioning.
airbag [ɛʀbag] *nm* air bag.
aire [ɛʀ] *nf* (*zone, fig, MATH*) area; (*nid*) eyrie (*BRIT*), aerie (*US*); **~ d'atterrissage** landing strip; landing patch; **~ de jeu** play area; **~ de lancement** launching site; **~ de stationnement** parking area.
airelle [ɛʀɛl] *nf* bilberry.
aisance [ɛzɑ̃s] *nf* ease; (*COUTURE*) easing, freedom of movement; (*richesse*) affluence; **être dans l'~** to be well-off *ou* affluent.
aise [ɛz] *nf* comfort ♦ *adj*: **être bien ~ de/que** to be delighted to/that; **~s** *nfpl*: **aimer ses ~s** to like one's (creature) comforts; **prendre ses ~s** to make o.s. comfortable; **frémir d'~** to shudder with pleasure; **être à l'~** *ou* **à son ~** to be comfortable; (*pas embarrassé*) to be at ease; (*financièrement*) to be comfortably off; **se mettre à l'~** to make o.s. comfortable; **être mal à l'~** *ou* **à son ~** to be uncomfortable; (*gêné*) to be ill at ease; **mettre qn à l'~** to put sb at his (*ou* her) ease; **mettre qn mal à l'~** to make sb feel ill at ease; **à votre ~** please yourself, just as you like; **en faire à son ~** to do as one likes; **en prendre à son ~ avec qch** to be free and easy with sth, do as one likes with sth.
aisé, e [eze] *adj* easy; (*assez riche*) well-to-do, well-off.
aisément [ezemɑ̃] *adv* easily.
aisselle [ɛsɛl] *nf* armpit.
ait [ɛ] *vb voir* **avoir**.
ajonc [aʒɔ̃] *nm* gorse *no pl*.
ajouré, e [aʒuʀe] *adj* openwork *cpd*.
ajournement [aʒuʀnəmɑ̃] *nm* adjournment; deferment, postponement.
ajourner [aʒuʀne] *vt* (*réunion*) to adjourn; (*décision*) to defer, postpone; (*candidat*) to refer; (*conscrit*) to defer.
ajout [aʒu] *nm* addition.
ajouter [aʒute] *vt* to add; (*INFORM*) to append; **~ à** *vt* (*accroître*) to add to; **s'~ à** to add to; **~ que** to add that; **~ foi à** to lend *ou* give credence to.
ajustage [aʒystaʒ] *nm* fitting.
ajusté, e [aʒyste] *adj*: **bien ~** (*robe etc*) close-fitting.
ajustement [aʒystəmɑ̃] *nm* adjustment.
ajuster [aʒyste] *vt* (*régler*) to adjust; (*vêtement*) to alter; (*arranger*): **~ sa cravate** to adjust one's tie; (*coup de fusil*) to aim; (*cible*) to aim at; (*adapter*): **~ qch à** to fit sth to.

ajusteur [aʒystœʀ] *nm* metal worker.
al *abr* = **année-lumière.**
alaise [alɛz] *nf* = **alèse.**
alambic [alɑ̃bik] *nm* still.
alambiqué, e [alɑ̃bike] *adj* convoluted, overcomplicated.
alangui, e [alɑ̃gi] *adj* languid.
alanguir [alɑ̃giʀ]: **s'~** *vi* to grow languid.
alarmant, e [alaʀmɑ̃, -ɑ̃t] *adj* alarming.
alarme [alaʀm(ə)] *nf* alarm; **donner l'~** to give *ou* raise the alarm; **jeter l'~** to cause alarm.
alarmer [alaʀme] *vt* to alarm; **s'~** *vi* to become alarmed.
alarmiste [alaʀmist(ə)] *adj* alarmist.
Alaska [alaska] *nm*: **l'~** Alaska.
albanais, e [albanɛ, -ɛz] *adj* Albanian ♦ *nm* (*LING*) Albanian ♦ *nm/f*: **A~, e** Albanian.
Albanie [albani] *nf*: **l'~** Albania.
albâtre [albɑtʀ(ə)] *nm* alabaster.
albatros [albatʀos] *nm* albatross.
albigeois, e [albiʒwa, -waz] *adj* of *ou* from Albi.
albinos [albinos] *nm/f* albino.
album [albɔm] *nm* album; **~ à colorier** colouring book; **~ de timbres** stamp album.
albumen [albymɛn] *nm* albumen.
albumine [albymin] *nf* albumin; **avoir** *ou* **faire de l'~** to suffer from albuminuria.
alcalin, e [alkalɛ̃, -in] *adj* alkaline.
alchimie [alʃimi] *nf* alchemy.
alchimiste [alʃimist(ə)] *nm* alchemist.
alcool [alkɔl] *nm*: **l'~** alcohol; **un ~** a spirit, a brandy; **~ à brûler** methylated spirits (*BRIT*), wood alcohol (*US*); **~ à 90°** surgical spirit; **~ camphré** camphorated alcohol; **~ de prune** *etc* plum *etc* brandy.
alcoolémie [alkɔlemi] *nf* blood alcohol level.
alcoolique [alkɔlik] *adj, nm/f* alcoholic.
alcoolisé, e [alkɔlize] *adj* alcoholic.
alcoolisme [alkɔlism(ə)] *nm* alcoholism.
alco(o)test [alkɔtɛst] *nm* ® (*objet*) Breathalyser ®; (*test*) breath-test; **faire subir l'~ à qn** to Breathalyze ® sb.
alcôve [alkov] *nf* alcove, recess.
aléas [alea] *nmpl* hazards.
aléatoire [aleatwaʀ] *adj* uncertain; (*INFORM, STATISTIQUE*) random.
alémanique [alemanik] *adj*: **la Suisse ~** German-speaking Switzerland.
ALENA [alena] *sigle m* (= *Accord de libre-échange nord-américain*) NAFTA (= *North American Free Trade Agreement*).
alentour [alɑ̃tuʀ] *adv* around (about); **~s** *nmpl* surroundings; **aux ~s de** in the vicinity *ou* neighbourhood of, around about; (*temps*) around about.
Aléoutiennes [aleusjɛn] *nfpl*: **les (îles) ~** the Aleutian Islands.
alerte [alɛʀt(ə)] *adj* agile, nimble; (*style*) brisk, lively ♦ *nf* alert; warning; **donner l'~** to give the alert; **à la première ~** at the first sign of trouble *ou* danger; **~ à la bombe** bomb scare.
alerter [alɛʀte] *vt* to alert.
alèse [alɛz] *nf* (*drap*) undersheet, drawsheet.
aléser [aleze] *vt* to ream.
alevin [alvɛ̃] *nm* alevin, young fish.
alevinage [alvinaʒ] *nm* fish farming.
Alexandrie [alɛksɑ̃dʀi] *n* Alexandria.
alexandrin [alɛksɑ̃dʀɛ̃] *nm* alexandrine.
alezan, e [alzɑ̃, -an] *adj* chestnut.
algarade [algaʀad] *nf* row, dispute.
algèbre [alʒɛbʀ(ə)] *nf* algebra.
algébrique [alʒebʀik] *adj* algebraic.
Alger [alʒe] *n* Algiers.
Algérie [alʒeʀi] *nf*: **l'~** Algeria.
algérien, ne [alʒeʀjɛ̃, -ɛn] *adj* Algerian ♦ *nm/f*: **A~, ne** Algerian.
algérois, e [alʒeʀwa, -waz] *adj* of *ou* from Algiers ♦ *nm*: **l'A~** (*région*) the Algiers region.
algorithme [algɔʀitm(ə)] *nm* algorithm.
algue [alg(ə)] *nf* (*gén*) seaweed *no pl*; (*BOT*) alga (*pl* -ae).
alias [aljas] *adv* alias.
alibi [alibi] *nm* alibi.
aliénation [aljenɑsjɔ̃] *nf* alienation.
aliéné, e [aljene] *nm/f* insane person, lunatic (*péj*).
aliéner [aljene] *vt* to alienate; (*bien, liberté*) to give up; **s'~** *vt* to alienate.
alignement [aliɲmɑ̃] *nm* alignment, lining up; **à l'~** in line.
aligner [aliɲe] *vt* to align, line up; (*idées, chiffres*) to string together; (*adapter*): **~ qch sur** to bring sth into alignment with; **s'~** (*soldats etc*) to line up; **s'~ sur** (*POL*) to align o.s. with.
aliment [alimɑ̃] *nm* food; **~ complet** whole food.
alimentaire [alimɑ̃tɛʀ] *adj* food *cpd*; (*péj: besogne*) done merely to earn a living; **produits ~s** foodstuffs, foods.
alimentation [alimɑ̃tɑsjɔ̃] *nf* feeding; supplying, supply; (*commerce*) food trade; (*produits*) groceries *pl*; (*régime*) diet; (*INFORM*) feed; **~ (générale)** (general) grocer's; **~ de base** staple diet; **~ en feuilles/en continu/en papier** form/stream/sheet feed.
alimenter [alimɑ̃te] *vt* to feed; (*TECH*): **~ (en)** to supply (with), feed (with); (*fig*) to sustain, keep going.
alinéa [alinea] *nm* paragraph; **"nouvel ~"** "new line".
aliter [alite]: **s'~** *vi* to take to one's bed; **infirme alité** bedridden person *ou* invalid.
alizé [alize] *adj, nm*: **(vent) ~** trade wind.
allaitement [alɛtmɑ̃] *nm* feeding; **~ maternel/au biberon** breast-/bottle-feeding; **~ mixte** mixed feeding.
allaiter [alete] *vt* (*suj: femme*) to (breast-)feed, nurse; (*suj: animal*) to suckle; **~ au biberon** to bottle-feed.

allant [alɑ̃] *nm* drive, go.
alléchant, e [aleʃɑ̃, -ɑ̃t] *adj* tempting, enticing.
allécher [aleʃe] *vt*: ~ **qn** to make sb's mouth water; to tempt sb, entice sb.
allée [ale] *nf* (*de jardin*) path; (*en ville*) avenue, drive; ~**s et venues** comings and goings.
allégation [alegɑsjɔ̃] *nf* allegation.
alléger [aleʒe] *vt* (*voiture*) to make lighter; (*chargement*) to lighten; (*souffrance*) to alleviate, soothe.
allégorie [alegɔʀi] *nf* allegory.
allégorique [alegɔʀik] *adj* allegorical.
allègre [alɛgʀ(ə)] *adj* lively, jaunty (*BRIT*); (*personne*) gay, cheerful.
allégresse [alegʀɛs] *nf* elation, gaiety.
allegretto [al(l)egʀɛt(t)o] *adv, nm* allegretto.
allegro [al(l)egʀo] *adv, nm* allegro.
alléguer [alege] *vt* to put forward (as proof *ou* an excuse).
Allemagne [alǝmaɲ] *nf*: **l'**~ Germany; **l'**~ **de l'Est/Ouest** East/West Germany; **l'**~ **fédérale (RFA)** the Federal Republic of Germany (FRG).
allemand, e [almɑ̃, -ɑ̃d] *adj* German ♦ *nm* (*LING*) German ♦ *nm/f*: **A**~, **e** German; **A**~ **de l'Est/l'Ouest** East/West German.
aller [ale] *nm* (*trajet*) outward journey; (*billet*): ~ **(simple)** single (*BRIT*) *ou* one-way ticket; ~ **(et) retour (AR)** (*trajet*) return trip *ou* journey (*BRIT*), round trip (*US*); (*billet*) return (*BRIT*) *ou* round-trip (*US*) ticket ♦ *vi* (*gén*) to go; ~ **à** (*convenir*) to suit; (*suj: forme, pointure etc*) to fit; **cela me va** (*couleur*) that suits me; (*vêtement*) that suits me; that fits me; (*projet, disposition*) that suits me, that's fine *ou* OK by me; ~ **à la chasse/pêche** to go hunting/fishing; ~ **avec** (*couleurs, style etc*) to go (well) with; **je vais le faire/me fâcher** I'm going to do it/to get angry; ~ **voir/chercher qn** to go and see/look for sb; **comment allez-vous?** how are you?; **comment ça va?** how are you?; (*affaires etc*) how are things?; **ça va? — oui (ça va)!** how are things? — fine!; **ça va (comme ça)** that's fine (as it is); **il va bien/mal** he's well/not well, he's fine/ill; **ça va bien/mal** (*affaires etc*) it's going well/not going well; **tout va bien** everything's fine; **ça ne va pas!** (*mauvaise humeur etc*) that's not on!, hey, come on!; **ça ne va pas sans difficultés** it's not without difficulties; ~ **mieux** to be better; **il y va de leur vie** their lives are at stake; **se laisser** ~ to let o.s. go; **s'en** ~ *vi* (*partir*) to be off, go, leave; (*disparaître*) to go away; ~ **jusqu'à** to go as far as; **ça va de soi, ça va sans dire** that goes without saying; **tu y vas un peu fort** you're going a bit (too) far; **allez!** go on!; come on!; **allons-y!** let's go!; **allez, au revoir** right *ou* OK then, bye-bye!
allergène [alɛʀʒɛn] *nm* allergen.
allergie [alɛʀʒi] *nf* allergy.
allergique [alɛʀʒik] *adj* allergic; ~ **à** allergic to.
allez [ale] *vb voir* **aller**.
alliage [aljaʒ] *nm* alloy.
alliance [aljɑ̃s] *nf* (*MIL, POL*) alliance; (*mariage*) marriage; (*bague*) wedding ring; **neveu par** ~ nephew by marriage.
allié, e [alje] *nm/f* ally; **parents et** ~**s** relatives and relatives by marriage.
allier [alje] *vt* (*métaux*) to alloy; (*POL, gén*) to ally; (*fig*) to combine; **s'**~ to become allies; (*éléments, caractéristiques*) to combine; **s'**~ **à** to become allied to *ou* with.
alligator [aligatɔʀ] *nm* alligator.
allitération [aliteʀɑsjɔ̃] *nf* alliteration.
allô [alo] *excl* hullo, hallo.
allocataire [alɔkatɛʀ] *nm/f* beneficiary.
allocation [alɔkɑsjɔ̃] *nf* allowance; ~ **(de) chômage** unemployment benefit; ~ **(de) logement** rent allowance; ~**s familiales** ≈ child benefit *no pl*; ~**s de maternité** maternity allowance.
allocution [alɔkysjɔ̃] *nf* short speech.
allongé, e [alɔ̃ʒe] *adj* (*étendu*): **être** ~ to be stretched out *ou* lying down; (*long*) long; (*étiré*) elongated; (*oblong*) oblong; **rester** ~ to be lying down; **mine** ~**e** long face.
allonger [alɔ̃ʒe] *vt* to lengthen, make longer; (*étendre: bras, jambe*) to stretch (out); (*sauce*) to spin out, make go further; **s'**~ *vi* to get longer; (*se coucher*) to lie down, stretch out; ~ **le pas** to hasten one's step(s).
allouer [alwe] *vt*: ~ **qch à** to allocate sth to, allot sth to.
allumage [alymaʒ] *nm* (*AUTO*) ignition.
allume-cigare [alymsigaʀ] *nm inv* cigar lighter.
allume-gaz [alymgɑz] *nm inv* gas lighter.
allumer [alyme] *vt* (*lampe, phare, radio*) to put *ou* switch on; (*pièce*) to put *ou* switch the light(s) on in; (*feu, bougie, cigare, pipe, gaz*) to light; (*chauffage*) to put on; **s'**~ *vi* (*lumière, lampe*) to come *ou* go on; ~ **(la lumière** *ou* **l'électricité)** to put on the light.
allumette [alymɛt] *nf* match; (*morceau de bois*) matchstick; (*CULIN*): ~ **au fromage** cheese straw; ~ **de sûreté** safety match.
allumeuse [alymøz] *nf* (*péj*) tease (*woman*).
allure [alyʀ] *nf* (*vitesse*) speed; (*: à pied*) pace; (*démarche*) walk; (*maintien*) bearing; (*aspect, air*) look; **avoir de l'**~ to have style *ou* a certain elegance; **à toute** ~ at top *ou* full speed.
allusion [alyzjɔ̃] *nf* allusion; (*sous-entendu*) hint; **faire** ~ **à** to allude *ou* refer to; to hint at.
alluvions [alyvjɔ̃] *nfpl* alluvial deposits, alluvium *sg*.
almanach [almana] *nm* almanac.
aloès [alɔɛs] *nm* (*BOT*) aloe.
aloi [alwa] *nm*: **de bon/mauvais** ~ of genuine/doubtful worth *ou* quality.

MOT-CLÉ

alors [alɔʀ] *adv* **1** (*à ce moment-là*) then, at that time; **il habitait ~ à Paris** he lived in Paris at that time; **jusqu'~** up till *ou* until then
2 (*par conséquent*) then; **tu as fini? ~ je m'en vais** have you finished? I'm going then
3 (*expressions*): **~? quoi de neuf?** well *ou* so? what's new?; **et ~?** so (what)?; **ça ~!** (well) really!
~ que *conj* **1** (*au moment où*) when, as; **il est arrivé alors que je partais** he arrived as I was leaving
2 (*pendant que*) while, when; **~ qu'il était à Paris, il a visité ...** while *ou* when he was in Paris, he visited ...
3 (*tandis que*) whereas, while; **~ que son frère travaillait dur, lui se reposait** while his brother was working hard, HE would rest.

alouette [alwɛt] *nf* (sky)lark.
alourdir [aluʀdiʀ] *vt* to weigh down, make heavy; **s'~** *vi* to grow heavy *ou* heavier.
aloyau [alwajo] *nm* sirloin.
alpaga [alpaga] *nm* (*tissu*) alpaca.
alpage [alpaʒ] *nm* high mountain pasture.
Alpes [alp(ə)] *nfpl*: **les ~** the Alps.
alpestre [alpɛstʀ(ə)] *adj* alpine.
alphabet [alfabɛ] *nm* alphabet; (*livre*) ABC (book), primer.
alphabétique [alfabetik] *adj* alphabetic(al); **par ordre ~** in alphabetical order.
alphabétisation [alfabetizɑsjɔ̃] *nf* literacy teaching.
alphabétiser [alfabetize] *vt* to teach to read and write; (*pays*) to eliminate illiteracy in.
alphanumérique [alfanymeʀik] *adj* alphanumeric.
alpin, e [alpɛ̃, -in] *adj* (*plante etc*) alpine; (*club*) climbing.
alpinisme [alpinism(ə)] *nm* mountaineering, climbing.
alpiniste [alpinist(ə)] *nm/f* mountaineer, climber.
Alsace [alzas] *nf*: **l'~** Alsace.
alsacien, ne [alzasjɛ̃, -ɛn] *adj* Alsatian.
altercation [altɛʀkɑsjɔ̃] *nf* altercation.
alter ego [altɛʀego] *nm* alter ego.
altérer [alteʀe] *vt* (*faits, vérité*) to falsify, distort; (*qualité*) to debase, impair; (*données*) to corrupt; (*donner soif à*) to make thirsty; **s'~** *vi* to deteriorate; to spoil.
alternance [altɛʀnɑ̃s] *nf* alternation; **en ~** alternately; **formation en ~** sandwich course.
alternateur [altɛʀnatœʀ] *nm* alternator.
alternatif, ive [altɛʀnatif, -iv] *adj* alternating ♦ *nf* alternative.
alternativement [altɛʀnativmɑ̃] *adv* alternately.
alterner [altɛʀne] *vt* to alternate ♦ *vi*: **~ (avec)** to alternate (with); **(faire) ~ qch avec qch** to alternate sth with sth.
Altesse [altɛs] *nf* Highness.
altier, ière [altje, -jɛʀ] *adj* haughty.
altimètre [altimɛtʀ(ə)] *nm* altimeter.
altiport [altipɔʀ] *nm* mountain airfield.
altiste [altist(ə)] *nm/f* viola player, violist.
altitude [altityd] *nf* altitude, height; **à 1 000 m d'~** at a height *ou* an altitude of 1000 m; **en ~** at high altitudes; **perdre/prendre de l'~** to lose/gain height; **voler à haute/basse ~** to fly at a high/low altitude.
alto [alto] *nm* (*instrument*) viola ♦ *nf* (contr)alto.
altruisme [altʀɥism(ə)] *nm* altruism.
altruiste [altʀɥist(ə)] *adj* altruistic.
aluminium [alyminjɔm] *nm* aluminium (*BRIT*), aluminum (*US*).
alun [alœ̃] *nm* alum.
alunir [alyniʀ] *vi* to land on the moon.
alunissage [alynisaʒ] *nm* (moon) landing.
alvéole [alveɔl] *nm ou f* (*de ruche*) alveolus.
alvéolé, e [alveɔle] *adj* honeycombed.
AM *sigle f* = **assurance maladie.**
amabilité [amabilite] *nf* kindness; **il a eu l'~ de** he was kind *ou* good enough to.
amadou [amadu] *nm* touchwood, amadou.
amadouer [amadwe] *vt* to coax, cajole; (*adoucir*) to mollify, soothe.
amaigrir [amegʀiʀ] *vt* to make thin *ou* thinner.
amaigrissant, e [amegʀisɑ̃, -ɑ̃t] *adj*: **régime ~** slimming (*BRIT*) *ou* weight-reduction (*US*) diet.
amalgame [amalgam] *nm* amalgam; (*fig: de gens, d'idées*) hotch-potch, mixture.
amalgamer [amalgame] *vt* to amalgamate.
amande [amɑ̃d] *nf* (*de l'amandier*) almond; (*de noyau de fruit*) kernel; **en ~** (*yeux*) almond *cpd*, almond-shaped.
amandier [amɑ̃dje] *nm* almond (tree).
amanite [amanit] *nf* (*BOT*) *mushroom of the genus Amanita*; **~ tue-mouches** fly agaric.
amant [amɑ̃] *nm* lover.
amarre [amaʀ] *nf* (*NAVIG*) (mooring) rope *ou* line; **~s** *nfpl* moorings.
amarrer [amaʀe] *vt* (*NAVIG*) to moor; (*gén*) to make fast.
amaryllis [amaʀilis] *nf* amaryllis.
amas [amɑ] *nm* heap, pile.
amasser [amɑse] *vt* to amass; **s'~** *vi* to pile up, accumulate; (*foule*) to gather.
amateur [amatœʀ] *nm* amateur; **en ~** (*péj*) amateurishly; **musicien/sportif ~** amateur musician/sportsman; **~ de musique/sport** *etc* music/sport *etc* lover.
amateurisme [amatœʀism(ə)] *nm* amateurism; (*péj*) amateurishness.
Amazone [amazɔn] *nf*: **l'~** the Amazon.
amazone [amazɔn] *nf* horsewoman; **en ~** sidesaddle.
Amazonie [amazɔni] *nf*: **l'~** Amazonia.
ambages [ɑ̃baʒ]: **sans ~** *adv* without beating about the bush, plainly.
ambassade [ɑ̃basad] *nf* embassy; (*mission*): **en**

~ on a mission.
ambassadeur, drice [ɑ̃basadœʀ, -dʀis] *nm/f* ambassador/ambassadress.
ambiance [ɑ̃bjɑ̃s] *nf* atmosphere; **il y a de l'~** everyone's having a good time.
ambiant, e [ɑ̃bjɑ̃, -ɑ̃t] *adj* (*air, milieu*) surrounding; (*température*) ambient.
ambidextre [ɑ̃bidɛkstʀ(ə)] *adj* ambidextrous.
ambigu, ë [ɑ̃bigy] *adj* ambiguous.
ambiguïté [ɑ̃bigɥite] *nf* ambiguousness *no pl*, ambiguity.
ambitieux, euse [ɑ̃bisjø, -øz] *adj* ambitious.
ambition [ɑ̃bisjɔ̃] *nf* ambition.
ambitionner [ɑ̃bisjɔne] *vt* to have as one's aim *ou* ambition.
ambivalent, e [ɑ̃bivalɑ̃, -ɑ̃t] *adj* ambivalent.
amble [ɑ̃bl(ə)] *nm*: **aller l'~** to amble.
ambre [ɑ̃bʀ(ə)] *nm*: **~ (jaune)** amber; **~ gris** ambergris.
ambré, e [ɑ̃bʀe] *adj* (*couleur*) amber; (*parfum*) ambergris-scented.
ambulance [ɑ̃bylɑ̃s] *nf* ambulance.
ambulancier, ière [ɑ̃bylɑ̃sje, -jɛʀ] *nm/f* ambulanceman/woman (*BRIT*), paramedic (*US*).
ambulant, e [ɑ̃bylɑ̃, -ɑ̃t] *adj* travelling, itinerant.
âme [ɑm] *nf* soul; **rendre l'~** to give up the ghost; **bonne ~** (*aussi ironique*) kind soul; **un joueur/tricheur dans l'~** a gambler/cheat through and through; **~ sœur** kindred spirit.
amélioration [ameljɔʀɑsjɔ̃] *nf* improvement.
améliorer [ameljɔʀe] *vt* to improve; **s'~** *vi* to improve, get better.
aménagement [amenaʒmɑ̃] *nm* fitting out; laying out; development; **~s** *nmpl* developments; **l'~ du territoire** ≈ town and country planning; **~s fiscaux** tax adjustments.
aménager [amenaʒe] *vt* (*agencer: espace, local*) to fit out; (*: terrain*) to lay out; (*: quartier, territoire*) to develop; (*installer*) to fix up, put in; **ferme aménagée** converted farmhouse.
amende [amɑ̃d] *nf* fine; **mettre à l'~** to penalize; **faire ~ honorable** to make amends.
amendement [amɑ̃dmɑ̃] *nm* (*JUR*) amendment.
amender [amɑ̃de] *vt* (*loi*) to amend; (*terre*) to enrich; **s'~** *vi* to mend one's ways.
amène [amɛn] *adj* affable; **peu ~** unkind.
amener [amne] *vt* to bring; (*causer*) to bring about; (*baisser: drapeau, voiles*) to strike; **s'~** *vi* (*fam*) to show up, turn up; **~ qn à qch/à faire** to lead sb to sth/to do.
amenuiser [amənɥize]: **s'~** *vi* to dwindle; (*chances*) to grow slimmer, lessen.
amer, amère [amɛʀ] *adj* bitter.
amèrement [amɛʀmɑ̃] *adv* bitterly.
américain, e [ameʀikɛ̃, -ɛn] *adj* American ♦ *nm* (*LING*) American (English) ♦ *nm/f*: **A~, e** American; **en vedette ~e** as a special guest (star).
américaniser [ameʀikanize] *vt* to Americanize.
américanisme [ameʀikanism(ə)] *nm* Americanism.
amérindien, ne [ameʀɛ̃djɛ̃, -ɛn] *adj* Amerindian, American Indian.
Amérique [ameʀik] *nf* America; **l'~ centrale** Central America; **l'~ latine** Latin America; **l'~ du Nord** North America; **l'~ du Sud** South America.
Amerloque [amɛʀlɔk] *nm/f* (*fam*) Yank, Yankee.
amerrir [ameʀiʀ] *vi* to land (on the sea); (*capsule spatiale*) to splash down.
amerrissage [ameʀisaʒ] *nm* landing (on the sea); splash-down.
amertume [amɛʀtym] *nf* bitterness.
améthyste [ametist(ə)] *nf* amethyst.
ameublement [amœbləmɑ̃] *nm* furnishing; (*meubles*) furniture; **articles d'~** furnishings; **tissus d'~** soft furnishings, furnishing fabrics.
ameuter [amøte] *vt* (*badauds*) to draw a crowd of; (*peuple*) to rouse, stir up.
ami, e [ami] *nm/f* friend; (*amant/maîtresse*) boyfriend/girlfriend ♦ *adj*: **pays/groupe ~** friendly country/group; **être (très) ~ avec qn** to be (very) friendly with sb; **être ~ de l'ordre** to be a lover of order; **un ~ des arts** a patron of the arts; **un ~ des chiens** a dog lover; **petit ~/petite ~e** (*fam*) boyfriend/girlfriend.
amiable [amjabl(ə)]: **à l'~** *adv* (*JUR*) out of court; (*gén*) amicably.
amiante [amjɑ̃t] *nm* asbestos.
amibe [amib] *nf* amoeba (*pl* -ae).
amical, e, aux [amikal, -o] *adj* friendly ♦ *nf* (*club*) association.
amicalement [amikalmɑ̃] *adv* in a friendly way; (*formule épistolaire*) regards.
amidon [amidɔ̃] *nm* starch.
amidonner [amidɔne] *vt* to starch.
amincir [amɛ̃siʀ] *vt* (*objet*) to thin (down); **s'~** *vi* to get thinner *ou* slimmer; **~ qn** to make sb thinner *ou* slimmer.
amincissant, e [amɛ̃sisɑ̃, -ɑ̃t] *adj* slimming.
aminé, e [amine] *adj*: **acide ~** amino acid.
amiral, aux [amiʀal, -o] *nm* admiral.
amirauté [amiʀote] *nf* admiralty.
amitié [amitje] *nf* friendship; **prendre en ~** to take a liking to; **faire *ou* présenter ses ~s à qn** to send sb one's best wishes; **~s** (*formule épistolaire*) (with) best wishes.
ammoniac [amɔnjak] *nm*: **(gaz) ~** ammonia.
ammoniaque [amɔnjak] *nf* ammonia (water).
amnésie [amnezi] *nf* amnesia.
amnésique [amnezik] *adj* amnesic.
Amnesty International [amnɛsti-] *n* Amnesty International.
amniocentèse [amnjosɛ̃tɛz] *nf* amniocentesis.
amnistie [amnisti] *nf* amnesty.
amnistier [amnistje] *vt* to amnesty.

amocher [amɔʃe] *vt* (*fam*) to mess up.
amoindrir [amwɛ̃dʀiʀ] *vt* to reduce.
amollir [amɔliʀ] *vt* to soften.
amonceler [amɔ̃sle] *vt*, **s'~** *vi* to pile *ou* heap up; (*fig*) to accumulate.
amoncellement [amɔ̃sɛlmɑ̃] *nm* piling *ou* heaping up; accumulation; (*tas*) pile, heap; accumulation.
amont [amɔ̃]: **en ~** *adv* upstream; (*sur une pente*) uphill; **en ~ de** *prép* upstream from; uphill from, above.
amoral, e, aux [amɔʀal, -o] *adj* amoral.
amorce [amɔʀs(ə)] *nf* (*sur un hameçon*) bait; (*explosif*) cap; (*tube*) primer; (*: contenu*) priming; (*fig: début*) beginning(s), start.
amorcer [amɔʀse] *vt* to bait; to prime; (*commencer*) to begin, start.
amorphe [amɔʀf(ə)] *adj* passive, lifeless.
amortir [amɔʀtiʀ] *vt* (*atténuer: choc*) to absorb, cushion; (*bruit, douleur*) to deaden; (*COMM: dette*) to pay off, amortize; (*: mise de fonds, matériel*) to write off; **~ un abonnement** to make a season ticket pay (for itself).
amortissable [amɔʀtisabl(ə)] *adj* (*COMM*) that can be paid off.
amortissement [amɔʀtismɑ̃] *nm* (*de matériel*) writing off; (*d'une dette*) paying off.
amortisseur [amɔʀtisœʀ] *nm* shock absorber.
amour [amuʀ] *nm* love; (*liaison*) love affair, love; (*statuette etc*) cupid; **un ~ de** a lovely little; **faire l'~** to make love.
amouracher [amuʀaʃe]: **s'~ de** *vt* (*péj*) to become infatuated with.
amourette [amuʀɛt] *nf* passing fancy.
amoureusement [amuʀøzmɑ̃] *adv* lovingly.
amoureux, euse [amuʀø, -øz] *adj* (*regard, tempérament*) amorous; (*vie, problèmes*) love *cpd*; (*personne*): **~ (de qn)** in love (with sb) ♦ *nm/f* lover ♦ *nmpl* courting couple(s); **tomber ~ de qn** to fall in love with sb; **être ~ de qch** to be passionately fond of sth; **un ~ de la nature** a nature lover.
amour-propre, *pl* **amours-propres** [amuʀpʀɔpʀ(ə)] *nm* self-esteem.
amovible [amɔvibl(ə)] *adj* removable, detachable.
ampère [ɑ̃pɛʀ] *nm* amp(ere).
ampèremètre [ɑ̃pɛʀmɛtʀ(ə)] *nm* ammeter.
amphétamine [ɑ̃fetamin] *nf* amphetamine.
amphi [ɑ̃fi] *nm* (*SCOL fam: = amphithéâtre*) lecture hall *ou* theatre.
amphibie [ɑ̃fibi] *adj* amphibious.
amphibien [ɑ̃fibjɛ̃] *nm* (*ZOOL*) amphibian.
amphithéâtre [ɑ̃fiteɑtʀ(ə)] *nm* amphitheatre; (*d'université*) lecture hall *ou* theatre.
amphore [ɑ̃fɔʀ] *nf* amphora.
ample [ɑ̃pl(ə)] *adj* (*vêtement*) roomy, ample; (*gestes, mouvement*) broad; (*ressources*) ample; **jusqu'à plus ~ informé** (*ADMIN*) until further details are available.
amplement [ɑ̃pləmɑ̃] *adv* amply; **~ suffisant** ample, more than enough.
ampleur [ɑ̃plœʀ] *nf* scale, size; extent, magnitude.
ampli [ɑ̃pli] *nm* (*fam: = amplificateur*) amplifier, amp.
amplificateur [ɑ̃plifikatœʀ] *nm* amplifier.
amplification [ɑ̃plifikɑsjɔ̃] *nf* amplification; expansion, increase.
amplifier [ɑ̃plifje] *vt* (*son, oscillation*) to amplify; (*fig*) to expand, increase.
amplitude [ɑ̃plityd] *nf* amplitude; (*des températures*) range.
ampoule [ɑ̃pul] *nf* (*électrique*) bulb; (*de médicament*) phial; (*aux mains, pieds*) blister.
ampoulé, e [ɑ̃pule] *adj* (*péj*) pompous, bombastic.
amputation [ɑ̃pytɑsjɔ̃] *nf* amputation.
amputer [ɑ̃pyte] *vt* (*MÉD*) to amputate; (*fig*) to cut *ou* reduce drastically; **~ qn d'un bras/pied** to amputate sb's arm/foot.
Amsterdam [amstɛʀdam] *n* Amsterdam.
amulette [amylɛt] *nf* amulet.
amusant, e [amyzɑ̃, -ɑ̃t] *adj* (*divertissant, spirituel*) entertaining, amusing; (*comique*) funny, amusing.
amusé, e [amyze] *adj* amused.
amuse-gueule [amyzgœl] *nm inv* appetizer, snack.
amusement [amyzmɑ̃] *nm* (*voir amusé*) amusement; (*voir amuser*) entertaining, amusing; (*jeu etc*) pastime, diversion.
amuser [amyze] *vt* (*divertir*) to entertain, amuse; (*égayer, faire rire*) to amuse; (*détourner l'attention de*) to distract; **s'~** *vi* (*jouer*) to amuse o.s., play; (*se divertir*) to enjoy o.s., have fun; (*fig*) to mess around; **s'~ de qch** (*trouver comique*) to find sth amusing; **s'~ avec** *ou* **de qn** (*duper*) to make a fool of sb.
amusette [amyzɛt] *nf* idle pleasure, trivial pastime.
amuseur [amyzœʀ] *nm* entertainer; (*péj*) clown.
amygdale [amidal] *nf* tonsil; **opérer qn des ~s** to take sb's tonsils out.
amygdalite [amidalit] *nf* tonsillitis.
AN *sigle f* = **Assemblée nationale**.
an [ɑ̃] *nm* year; **être âgé de** *ou* **avoir 3 ~s** to be 3 (years old); **en l'~ 1980** in the year 1980; **le jour de l'~, le premier de l'~, le nouvel ~** New Year's Day.
anabolisant [anabɔlizɑ̃] *nm* anabolic steroid.
anachronique [anakʀɔnik] *adj* anachronistic.
anachronisme [anakʀɔnism(ə)] *nm* anachronism.
anaconda [anakɔ̃da] *nm* (*ZOOL*) anaconda.
anaérobie [anaeʀɔbi] *adj* anaerobic.
anagramme [anagʀam] *nf* anagram.
ANAH *sigle f* = *Agence nationale pour l'amélioration de l'habitat*.
anal, e, aux [anal, -o] *adj* anal.
analgésique [analʒezik] *nm* analgesic.
anallergique [analɛʀʒik] *adj* hypoallergenic.
analogie [analɔʒi] *nf* analogy.

analogique [analɔʒik] *adj* (*LOGIQUE: raisonnement*) analogical; (*calculateur, montre etc*) analogue; (*INFORM*) analog.
analogue [analɔg] *adj*: ~ **(à)** analogous (to), similar (to).
analphabète [analfabɛt] *nm/f* illiterate.
analphabétisme [analfabetism(ə)] *nm* illiteracy.
analyse [analiz] *nf* analysis; (*MÉD*) test; **faire l'~ de** to analyse; **une ~ approfondie** an in-depth analysis; **en dernière ~** in the last analysis; **avoir l'esprit d'~** to have an analytical turn of mind; **~ grammaticale** grammatical analysis, parsing (*SCOL*).
analyser [analize] *vt* to analyse; (*MÉD*) to test.
analyste [analist(ə)] *nm/f* analyst; (*psychanalyste*) (psycho)analyst.
analyste-programmeur, euse, *pl* **analystes-programmeurs, euses** [analist-pʀɔgʀamœʀ, -øz] *nm/f* systems analyst.
analytique [analitik] *adj* analytical.
analytiquement [analitikmɑ̃] *adv* analytically.
ananas [anana] *nm* pineapple.
anarchie [anaʀʃi] *nf* anarchy.
anarchique [anaʀʃik] *adj* anarchic.
anarchisme [anaʀʃism(ə)] *nm* anarchism.
anarchiste [anaʀʃist(ə)] *adj* anarchistic ♦ *nm/f* anarchist.
anathème [anatɛm] *nm*: **jeter l'~ sur, lancer l'~ contre** to anathematize, curse.
anatomie [anatɔmi] *nf* anatomy.
anatomique [anatɔmik] *adj* anatomical.
ancestral, e, aux [ɑ̃sɛstʀal, -o] *adj* ancestral.
ancêtre [ɑ̃sɛtʀ(ə)] *nm/f* ancestor; (*fig*): **l'~ de** the forerunner of.
anche [ɑ̃ʃ] *nf* reed.
anchois [ɑ̃ʃwa] *nm* anchovy.
ancien, ne [ɑ̃sjɛ̃, -ɛn] *adj* old; (*de jadis, de l'antiquité*) ancient; (*précédent, ex-*) former, old ♦ *nm* (*mobilier ancien*): **l'~** antiques *pl* ♦ *nm/f* (*dans une tribu etc*) elder; **un ~ ministre** a former minister; **mon ~ne voiture** my previous car; **être plus ~ que qn dans une maison** to have been in a firm longer than sb; (*dans l'hiérarchie*) to be senior to sb in a firm; **~ combattant** ex-serviceman; **~ (élève)** (*SCOL*) ex-pupil (*BRIT*), alumnus (*US*).
anciennement [ɑ̃sjɛnmɑ̃] *adv* formerly.
ancienneté [ɑ̃sjɛnte] *nf* oldness; antiquity; (*ADMIN*) (length of) service; seniority.
ancrage [ɑ̃kʀaʒ] *nm* anchoring; (*NAVIG*) anchorage; (*CONSTR*) anchor.
ancre [ɑ̃kʀ(ə)] *nf* anchor; **jeter/lever l'~** to cast/weigh anchor; **à l'~** at anchor.
ancrer [ɑ̃kʀe] *vt* (*CONSTR*) to anchor; (*fig*) to fix firmly; **s'~** *vi* (*NAVIG*) to (cast) anchor.
andalou, ouse [ɑ̃dalu, -uz] *adj* Andalusian.
Andalousie [ɑ̃daluzi] *nf*: **l'~** Andalusia.
andante [ɑ̃dɑ̃t] *adv, nm* andante.
Andes [ɑ̃d] *nfpl*: **les ~** the Andes.
Andorre [ɑ̃dɔʀ] *nf* Andorra.
andouille [ɑ̃duj] *nf* (*CULIN*) *sausage made of chitterlings*; (*fam*) clot, nit.
andouillette [ɑ̃dujɛt] *nf small andouille*.
âne [ɑn] *nm* donkey, ass; (*péj*) dunce, fool.
anéantir [aneɑ̃tiʀ] *vt* to annihilate, wipe out; (*fig*) to obliterate, destroy; (*déprimer*) to overwhelm.
anecdote [anɛkdɔt] *nf* anecdote.
anecdotique [anɛkdɔtik] *adj* anecdotal.
anémie [anemi] *nf* anaemia.
anémié, e [anemje] *adj* anaemic; (*fig*) enfeebled.
anémique [anemik] *adj* anaemic.
anémone [anemɔn] *nf* anemone; **~ de mer** sea anemone.
ânerie [ɑnʀi] *nf* stupidity; (*parole etc*) stupid *ou* idiotic comment *etc*.
anéroïde [aneʀɔid] *adj voir* **baromètre**.
ânesse [ɑnɛs] *nf* she-ass.
anesthésie [anɛstezi] *nf* anaesthesia; **sous ~** under anaesthetic; **~ générale/locale** general/local anaesthetic; **faire une ~ locale à qn** to give sb a local anaesthetic.
anesthésier [anɛstezje] *vt* to anaesthetize.
anesthésique [anɛstezik] *adj* anaesthetic.
anesthésiste [anɛstezist(ə)] *nm/f* anaesthetist.
anfractuosité [ɑ̃fʀaktɥozite] *nf* crevice.
ange [ɑ̃ʒ] *nm* angel; **être aux ~s** to be over the moon; **~ gardien** guardian angel.
angélique [ɑ̃ʒelik] *adj* angelic(al) ♦ *nf* angelica.
angelot [ɑ̃ʒlo] *nm* cherub.
angélus [ɑ̃ʒelys] *nm* angelus; (*cloches*) evening bells *pl*.
angevin, e [ɑ̃ʒvɛ̃, -in] *adj* of *ou* from Anjou; of *ou* from Angers.
angine [ɑ̃ʒin] *nf* sore throat, throat infection; **~ de poitrine** angina (pectoris).
angiome [ɑ̃ʒjom] *nm* angioma.
anglais, e [ɑ̃glɛ, -ɛz] *adj* English ♦ *nm* (*LING*) English ♦ *nm/f*: **A~, e** Englishman/woman; **les A~** the English; **filer à l'~e** to take French leave; **à l'~e** (*CULIN*) boiled.
anglaises [ɑ̃glɛz] *nfpl* (*cheveux*) ringlets.
angle [ɑ̃gl(ə)] *nm* angle; (*coin*) corner; **~ droit/obtus/aigu/mort** right/obtuse/acute/dead angle.
Angleterre [ɑ̃glətɛʀ] *nf*: **l'~** England.
anglican, e [ɑ̃glikɑ̃, -an] *adj, nm/f* Anglican.
anglicanisme [ɑ̃glikanism(ə)] *nm* Anglicanism.
anglicisme [ɑ̃glisism(ə)] *nm* anglicism.
angliciste [ɑ̃glisist(ə)] *nm/f* English scholar; (*étudiant*) student of English.
anglo... [ɑ̃glɔ] *préfixe* Anglo-, anglo(-).
anglo-américain, e [ɑ̃glɔameʀikɛ̃, -ɛn] *adj* Anglo-American ♦ *nm* (*LING*) American English.
anglo-arabe [ɑ̃glɔaʀab] *adj* Anglo-Arab.
anglo-canadien, ne [ɑ̃glɔkanadjɛ̃, -ɛn] *adj* Anglo-Canadian ♦ *nm* (*LING*) Canadian English.
anglo-normand, e [ɑ̃glɔnɔʀmɑ̃, -ɑ̃d] *adj*

Anglo-Norman; **les îles ~es** the Channel Islands.
anglophile [ɑ̃glɔfil] *adj* anglophilic.
anglophobe [ɑ̃glɔfɔb] *adj* anglophobic.
anglophone [ɑ̃glɔfɔn] *adj* English-speaking.
anglo-saxon, ne [ɑ̃glɔsaksɔ̃, -ɔn] *adj* Anglo-Saxon.
angoissant, e [ɑ̃gwasɑ̃, -ɑ̃t] *adj* harrowing.
angoisse [ɑ̃gwas] *nf*: **l'~** anguish *no pl*.
angoissé, e [ɑ̃gwase] *adj* anguished; (*personne*) full of anxieties *ou* hang-ups (*fam*).
angoisser [ɑ̃gwase] *vt* to harrow, cause anguish to ♦ *vi* to worry, fret.
Angola [ɑ̃gɔla] *nm*: **l'~** Angola.
angolais, e [ɑ̃gɔlɛ, -ɛz] *adj* Angolan.
angora [ɑ̃gɔʀa] *adj, nm* angora.
anguille [ɑ̃gij] *nf* eel; **~ de mer** conger (eel); **il y a ~ sous roche** (*fig*) there's something going on, there's something beneath all this.
angulaire [ɑ̃gylɛʀ] *adj* angular.
anguleux, euse [ɑ̃gylø, -øz] *adj* angular.
anhydride [anidʀid] *nm* anhydride.
anicroche [anikʀɔʃ] *nf* hitch, snag.
animal, e, aux [animal, -o] *adj, nm* animal; **~ domestique/sauvage** domestic/wild animal.
animalier [animalje] *adj*: **peintre ~** animal painter.
animateur, trice [animatœʀ, -tʀis] *nm/f* (*de télévision*) host; (*de music-hall*) compère; (*de groupe*) leader, organizer; (*CINÉ: technicien*) animator.
animation [animɑsjɔ̃] *nf* (*voir animé*) busyness; liveliness; (*CINÉ: technique*) animation; (*activité*): **~s** *nfpl* activities; **centre d'~** ≈ community centre.
animé, e [anime] *adj* (*rue, lieu*) busy, lively; (*conversation, réunion*) lively, animated; (*opposé à inanimé, aussi LING*) animate.
animer [anime] *vt* (*ville, soirée*) to liven up, enliven; (*mettre en mouvement*) to drive; (*stimuler*) to drive, impel; **s'~** *vi* to liven up, come to life.
animosité [animozite] *nf* animosity.
anis [ani] *nm* (*CULIN*) aniseed; (*BOT*) anise.
anisette [anizɛt] *nf* anisette.
Ankara [ɑ̃kaʀa] *n* Ankara.
ankyloser [ɑ̃kiloze]: **s'~** *vi* to get stiff, ankylose.
annales [anal] *nfpl* annals.
anneau, x [ano] *nm* ring; (*de chaîne*) link; (*SPORT*): **exercices aux ~x** ring exercises.
année [ane] *nf* year; **souhaiter la bonne ~ à qn** to wish sb a Happy New Year; **tout au long de l'~** all year long; **d'une ~ à l'autre** from one year to the next; **d'~ en ~** from year to year; **l'~ scolaire/fiscale** the school/tax year.
année-lumière, *pl* **années-lumières** [anelymjɛʀ] *nf* light year.
annexe [anɛks(ə)] *adj* (*problème*) related; (*document*) appended; (*salle*) adjoining ♦ *nf* (*bâtiment*) annex(e); (*de document, ouvrage*) annex, appendix; (*jointe à une lettre, un dossier*) enclosure.
annexer [anɛkse] *vt* to annex; **s'~** (*pays*) to annex; **~ qch à** (*joindre*) to append sth to.
annexion [anɛksjɔ̃] *nf* annexation.
annihiler [aniile] *vt* to annihilate.
anniversaire [anivɛʀsɛʀ] *nm* birthday; (*d'un événement, bâtiment*) anniversary ♦ *adj*: **jour ~** anniversary.
annonce [anɔ̃s] *nf* announcement; (*signe, indice*) sign; (*aussi*: **~ publicitaire**) advertisement; (*CARTES*) declaration; **~ personnelle** personal message; **les petites ~s** the small *ou* classified ads.
annoncer [anɔ̃se] *vt* to announce; (*être le signe de*) to herald; (*CARTES*) to declare; **je vous annonce que ...** I wish to tell you that ...; **s'~ bien/difficile** to look promising/difficult; **~ la couleur** (*fig*) to lay one's cards on the table.
annonceur, euse [anɔ̃sœʀ, -øz] *nm/f* (*TV, RADIO: speaker*) announcer; (*publicitaire*) advertiser.
annonciateur, trice [anɔ̃sjatœʀ, -tʀis] *adj*: **~ d'un événement** presaging an event.
Annonciation [anɔ̃sjɑsjɔ̃] *nf*: **l'~** (*REL*) the Annunciation; (*jour*) Annunciation Day.
annotation [anɔtɑsjɔ̃] *nf* annotation.
annoter [anɔte] *vt* to annotate.
annuaire [anɥɛʀ] *nm* yearbook, annual; **~ téléphonique** (telephone) directory, phone book.
annuel, le [anɥɛl] *adj* annual, yearly.
annuellement [anɥɛlmɑ̃] *adv* annually, yearly.
annuité [anɥite] *nf* annual instalment.
annulaire [anylɛʀ] *nm* ring *ou* third finger.
annulation [anylɑsjɔ̃] *nf* cancellation; annulment; quashing, repeal.
annuler [anyle] *vt* (*rendez-vous, voyage*) to cancel, call off; (*mariage*) to annul; (*jugement*) to quash (*BRIT*), repeal (*US*); (*résultats*) to declare void; (*MATH, PHYSIQUE*) to cancel out; **s'~** to cancel each other out.
anoblir [anɔbliʀ] *vt* to ennoble.
anode [anɔd] *nf* anode.
anodin, e [anɔdɛ̃, -in] *adj* harmless; (*sans importance*) insignificant, trivial.
anomalie [anɔmali] *nf* anomaly.
ânon [ɑnɔ̃] *nm* baby donkey; (*petit âne*) little donkey.
ânonner [ɑnɔne] *vi, vt* to read in a drone; (*hésiter*) to read in a fumbling manner.
anonymat [anɔnima] *nm* anonymity; **garder l'~** to remain anonymous.
anonyme [anɔnim] *adj* anonymous; (*fig*) impersonal.
anonymement [anɔnimmɑ̃] *adv* anonymously.
anorak [anɔʀak] *nm* anorak.
anorexie [anɔʀɛksi] *nf* anorexia.
anorexique [anɔʀɛksik] *adj, nm/f* anorexic.

anormal, e, aux [anɔʀmal, -o] *adj* abnormal; (*insolite*) unusual, abnormal.
anormalement [anɔʀmalmɑ̃] *adv* abnormally; unusually.
ANPE *sigle f* (= *Agence nationale pour l'emploi*) *national employment agency (functions include job creation)*.
anse [ɑ̃s] *nf* handle; (*GÉO*) cove.
antagonisme [ɑ̃tagɔnism(ə)] *nm* antagonism.
antagoniste [ɑ̃tagɔnist(ə)] *adj* antagonistic ♦ *nm* antagonist.
antan [ɑ̃tɑ̃]: **d'~** *adj* of yesteryear, of long ago.
antarctique [ɑ̃taʀktik] *adj* Antarctic ♦ *nm*: **l'A~** the Antarctic; **le cercle A~** the Antarctic Circle; **l'océan A~** the Antarctic Ocean.
antécédent [ɑ̃tesedɑ̃] *nm* (*LING*) antecedent; **~s** *nmpl* (*MÉD etc*) past history *sg*; **~s professionnels** record, career to date.
antédiluvien, ne [ɑ̃tedilyvjɛ̃, -ɛn] *adj* (*fig*) ancient, antediluvian.
antenne [ɑ̃tɛn] *nf* (*de radio, télévision*) aerial; (*d'insecte*) antenna (*pl* -ae), feeler; (*poste avancé*) outpost; (*petite succursale*) subbranch; **sur l'~** on the air; **passer à/avoir l'~** to go/be on the air; **2 heures d'~** 2 hours' broadcasting time; **hors ~** off the air; **~ chirurgicale** (*MIL*) advance surgical unit.
antépénultième [ɑ̃tepenyltjɛm] *adj* antepenultimate.
antérieur, e [ɑ̃teʀjœʀ] *adj* (*d'avant*) previous, earlier; (*de devant*) front; **~ à** prior *ou* previous to; **passé/futur ~** (*LING*) past/future anterior.
antérieurement [ɑ̃teʀjœʀmɑ̃] *adv* earlier; (*précédemment*) previously; **~ à** prior *ou* previous to.
antériorité [ɑ̃teʀjɔʀite] *nf* precedence (*in time*).
anthologie [ɑ̃tɔlɔʒi] *nf* anthology.
anthracite [ɑ̃tʀasit] *nm* anthracite ♦ *adj*: **(gris)** ~ charcoal (grey).
anthropologie [ɑ̃tʀɔpɔlɔʒi] *nf* anthropology.
anthropologue [ɑ̃tʀɔpɔlɔg] *nm/f* anthropologist.
anthropomorphisme [ɑ̃tʀɔpɔmɔʀfism(ə)] *nm* anthropomorphism.
anthropophage [ɑ̃tʀɔpɔfaʒ] *adj* cannibalistic.
anthropophagie [ɑ̃tʀɔpɔfaʒi] *nf* cannibalism, anthropophagy.
anti... [ɑ̃ti] *préfixe* anti....
antiaérien, ne [ɑ̃tiaeʀjɛ̃, -ɛn] *adj* anti-aircraft; **abri ~** air-raid shelter.
antialcoolique [ɑ̃tialkɔlik] *adj* anti-alcohol; **ligue ~** temperance league.
antiatomique [ɑ̃tiatɔmik] *adj*: **abri ~** fallout shelter.
antibiotique [ɑ̃tibjɔtik] *nm* antibiotic.
antibrouillard [ɑ̃tibʀujaʀ] *adj*: **phare ~** fog lamp.
antibruit [ɑ̃tibʀɥi] *adj inv*: **mur ~** (*sur autoroute*) sound-muffling wall.
antibuée [ɑ̃tibɥe] *adj inv*: **dispositif ~** demister; **bombe ~** demister spray.

anticancéreux, euse [ɑ̃tikɑ̃seʀø, -øz] *adj* cancer *cpd*.
anticasseur(s) [ɑ̃tikɑsœʀ] *adj*: **loi/mesure ~** law/measure against damage done by demonstrators.
antichambre [ɑ̃tiʃɑ̃bʀ(ə)] *nf* antechamber, anteroom; **faire ~** to wait (for an audience).
antichar [ɑ̃tiʃaʀ] *adj* antitank.
antichoc [ɑ̃tiʃɔk] *adj* shockproof.
anticipation [ɑ̃tisipɑsjɔ̃] *nf* anticipation; (*COMM*) payment in advance; **par ~** in anticipation, in advance; **livre/film d'~** science fiction book/film.
anticipé, e [ɑ̃tisipe] *adj* (*règlement, paiement*) early, in advance; (*joie etc*) anticipated, early; **avec mes remerciements ~s** thanking you in advance *ou* anticipation.
anticiper [ɑ̃tisipe] *vt* to anticipate, foresee; (*paiement*) to pay *ou* make in advance ♦ *vi* to look *ou* think ahead; (*en racontant*) to jump ahead; (*prévoir*) to anticipate; **~ sur** to anticipate.
anticlérical, e, aux [ɑ̃tikleʀikal, -o] *adj* anticlerical.
anticoagulant, e [ɑ̃tikɔagylɑ̃, -ɑ̃t] *adj, nm* anticoagulant.
anticolonialisme [ɑ̃tikɔlɔnjalism(ə)] *nm* anticolonialism.
anticonceptionnel, le [ɑ̃tikɔ̃sɛpsjɔnɛl] *adj* contraceptive.
anticonformisme [ɑ̃tikɔ̃fɔʀmism(ə)] *nm* nonconformism.
anticonstitutionnel, le [ɑ̃tikɔ̃stitysjɔnɛl] *adj* unconstitutional.
anticorps [ɑ̃tikɔʀ] *nm* antibody.
anticyclone [ɑ̃tisiklon] *nm* anticyclone.
antidater [ɑ̃tidate] *vt* to backdate, predate.
antidémocratique [ɑ̃tidemɔkʀatik] *adj* antidemocratic; (*peu démocratique*) undemocratic.
antidépresseur [ɑ̃tidepʀɛsœʀ] *nm* antidepressant.
antidérapant, e [ɑ̃tideʀapɑ̃, -ɑ̃t] *adj* nonskid.
antidopage [ɑ̃tidɔpaʒ], **antidoping** [ɑ̃tidɔpiŋ] *adj* (*lutte*) antidoping; (*contrôle*) dope *cpd*.
antidote [ɑ̃tidɔt] *nm* antidote.
antienne [ɑ̃tjɛn] *nf* (*fig*) chant, refrain.
antigang [ɑ̃tigɑ̃g] *adj inv*: **brigade ~** commando unit.
antigel [ɑ̃tiʒɛl] *nm* antifreeze.
antigène [ɑ̃tiʒɛn] *nm* antigen.
antigouvernemental, e, aux [ɑ̃tiguvɛʀnəmɑ̃tal, -o] *adj* antigovernment.
Antigua et Barbude [ɑ̃tigaebaʀbyd] *nf* Antigua and Barbuda.
antihistaminique [ɑ̃tiistaminik] *nm* antihistamine.
anti-inflammatoire [ɑ̃tiɛ̃flamatwaʀ] *adj* anti-inflammatory.
anti-inflationniste [ɑ̃tiɛ̃flɑsjɔnist(ə)] *adj* anti-inflationary.
antillais, e [ɑ̃tijɛ, -ɛz] *adj* West Indian.
Antilles [ɑ̃tij] *nfpl*: **les ~** the West Indies; **les**

Grandes/Petites ~ the Greater/Lesser Antilles.
antilope [ɑ̃tilɔp] *nf* antelope.
antimilitarisme [ɑ̃timilitaʀism(ə)] *nm* antimilitarism.
antimilitariste [ɑ̃timilitaʀist(ə)] *adj* antimilitarist.
antimissile [ɑ̃timisil] *adj* antimissile.
antimite(s) [ɑ̃timit] *adj, nm*: **(produit)** ~ mothproofer, moth repellent.
antimondialisation [ɑ̃timɔ̃djalizasjɔ̃] *nf* antiglobalization.
antinucléaire [ɑ̃tinykleɛʀ] *adj* antinuclear.
antioxydant [ɑ̃tiɔksidɑ̃] *nm* antioxidant.
antiparasite [ɑ̃tipaʀazit] *adj* (*RADIO, TV*) anti-interference; **dispositif** ~ suppressor.
antipathie [ɑ̃tipati] *nf* antipathy.
antipathique [ɑ̃tipatik] *adj* unpleasant, disagreeable.
antipelliculaire [ɑ̃tipelikylɛʀ] *adj* antidandruff.
antiphrase [ɑ̃tifʀɑz] *nf*: **par** ~ ironically.
antipodes [ɑ̃tipɔd] *nmpl* (*GÉO*): **les** ~ the antipodes; (*fig*): **être aux** ~ **de** to be the opposite extreme of.
antipoison [ɑ̃tipwazɔ̃] *adj inv*: **centre** ~ poison centre.
antipoliomyélitique [ɑ̃tipɔljɔmjelitik] *adj* polio *cpd*.
antiprotectionniste [ɑ̃tipʀɔtɛksjɔnist(ə)] *adj* free-trade.
antiquaire [ɑ̃tikɛʀ] *nm/f* antique dealer.
antique [ɑ̃tik] *adj* antique; (*très vieux*) ancient, antiquated.
antiquité [ɑ̃tikite] *nf* (*objet*) antique; **l'A**~ Antiquity; **magasin/marchand d'**~**s** antique shop/dealer.
antirabique [ɑ̃tiʀabik] *adj* rabies *cpd*.
antiraciste [ɑ̃tiʀasist(ə)] *adj* antiracist, antiracialist.
antireflet [ɑ̃tiʀəflɛ] *adj inv* (*verres*) antireflective.
antirépublicain, e [ɑ̃tiʀepyblikɛ̃, -ɛn] *adj* antirepublican.
antirides [ɑ̃tiʀid] *adj* (*crème*) antiwrinkle.
antirouille [ɑ̃tiʀuj] *adj inv*: **peinture** ~ antirust paint; **traitement** ~ rustproofing.
antisémite [ɑ̃tisemit] *adj* anti-Semitic.
antisémitisme [ɑ̃tisemitism(ə)] *nm* anti-Semitism.
antiseptique [ɑ̃tisɛptik] *adj, nm* antiseptic.
antisocial, e, aux [ɑ̃tisɔsjal, -o] *adj* antisocial.
antispasmodique [ɑ̃tispasmɔdik] *adj, nm* antispasmodic.
antisportif, ive [ɑ̃tispɔʀtif, -iv] *adj* unsporting; (*hostile au sport*) antisport.
antitétanique [ɑ̃titetanik] *adj* tetanus *cpd*.
antithèse [ɑ̃titɛz] *nf* antithesis.
antitrust [ɑ̃titʀœst] *adj inv* (*loi, mesures*) antimonopoly.
antituberculeux, euse [ɑ̃titybɛʀkylø, -øz] *adj* tuberculosis *cpd*.
antitussif, ive [ɑ̃titysif, -iv] *adj* antitussive cough *cpd*.
antivariolique [ɑ̃tivaʀjɔlik] *adj* smallpox *cpd*.
antivol [ɑ̃tivɔl] *adj, nm*: **(dispositif)** ~ antitheft device; (*pour vélo*) padlock.
antonyme [ɑ̃tɔnim] *nm* antonym.
antre [ɑ̃tʀ(ə)] *nm* den, lair.
anus [anys] *nm* anus.
Anvers [ɑ̃vɛʀ] *n* Antwerp.
anxiété [ɑ̃ksjete] *nf* anxiety.
anxieusement [ɑ̃ksjøzmɑ̃] *adv* anxiously.
anxieux, euse [ɑ̃ksjø, -øz] *adj* anxious, worried; **être** ~ **de faire** to be anxious to do.
AOC *sigle f see boxed note.*

> **AOC**
>
> *AOC ('appellation d'origine contrôlée') is the highest French wine classification. It indicates that the wine meets strict requirements concerning vineyard of origin, type of grape, method of production and alcoholic strength.*

aorte [aɔʀt(ə)] *nf* aorta.
août [u] *nm* August; *voir aussi* **juillet**; **Assomption.**
aoûtien, ne [ausjɛ̃, -ɛn] *nm/f* August holiday-maker.
AP *sigle f* = **Assistance publique.**
apaisant, e [apɛzɑ̃, -ɑ̃t] *adj* soothing.
apaisement [apɛzmɑ̃] *nm* calming; soothing; (*aussi POL*) appeasement; ~**s** *nmpl* soothing reassurances; (*pour calmer*) pacifying words.
apaiser [apeze] *vt* (*colère*) to calm, quell, soothe; (*faim*) to appease, assuage; (*douleur*) to soothe; (*personne*) to calm (down), pacify; **s'**~ *vi* (*tempête, bruit*) to die down, subside.
apanage [apanaʒ] *nm*: **être l'**~ **de** to be the privilege *ou* prerogative of.
aparté [apaʀte] *nm* (*THÉÂT*) aside; (*entretien*) private conversation; **en** ~ *adv* in an aside (*BRIT*); (*entretien*) in private.
apartheid [apaʀtɛd] *nm* apartheid.
apathie [apati] *nf* apathy.
apathique [apatik] *adj* apathetic.
apatride [apatʀid] *nm/f* stateless person.
Apennins [apɔnɛ̃] *nmpl*: **les** ~ the Apennines.
apercevoir [apɛʀsəvwaʀ] *vt* to see; **s'**~ **de** *vt* to notice; **s'**~ **que** to notice that; **sans s'en** ~ without realizing *ou* noticing.
aperçu, e [apɛʀsy] *pp de* **apercevoir** ♦ *nm* (*vue d'ensemble*) general survey; (*intuition*) insight.
apéritif, ive [apeʀitif, -iv] *adj* which stimulates the appetite ♦ *nm* (*boisson*) aperitif; (*réunion*) (pre-lunch *ou* -dinner) drinks *pl*; **prendre l'**~ to have an aperitif.
apesanteur [apəzɑ̃tœʀ] *nf* weightlessness.
à-peu-près [apøpʀɛ] *nm inv* (*péj*) vague approximation.
apeuré, e [apœʀe] *adj* frightened, scared.

aphasie [afazi] *nm* aphasia.
aphone [afɔn] *adj* voiceless.
aphorisme [afɔʀism(ə)] *nm* aphorism.
aphrodisiaque [afʀɔdizjak] *adj, nm* aphrodisiac.
aphte [aft(ə)] *nm* mouth ulcer.
aphteuse [aftøz] *adj f*: **fièvre ~** foot-and-mouth disease.
à-pic [apik] *nm* cliff, drop.
apicole [apikɔl] *adj* beekeeping *cpd*.
apiculteur, trice [apikyltœʀ, -tʀis] *nm/f* beekeeper.
apiculture [apikyltyʀ] *nf* beekeeping, apiculture.
apitoiement [apitwamɑ̃] *nm* pity, compassion.
apitoyer [apitwaje] *vt* to move to pity; **~ qn sur qn/qch** to move sb to pity for sb/over sth; **s'~ (sur qn/qch)** to feel pity *ou* compassion (for sb/over sth).
ap. J.-C. *abr* (= *après Jésus-Christ*) AD.
APL *sigle f* (= *aide personnalisée au logement*) *type of loan for house purchase.*
aplanir [aplaniʀ] *vt* to level; (*fig*) to smooth away, iron out.
aplati, e [aplati] *adj* flat, flattened.
aplatir [aplatiʀ] *vt* to flatten; **s'~** *vi* to become flatter; (*écrasé*) to be flattened; (*fig*) to lie flat on the ground; (*: fam*) to fall flat on one's face; (*: péj*) to grovel.
aplomb [aplɔ̃] *nm* (*équilibre*) balance, equilibrium; (*fig*) self-assurance; (*: péj*) nerve; **d'~** *adv* steady; (*CONSTR*) plumb.
apocalypse [apɔkalips(ə)] *nf* apocalypse.
apocalyptique [apɔkaliptik] *adj* (*fig*) apocalyptic.
apocryphe [apɔkʀif] *adj* apocryphal.
apogée [apɔʒe] *nm* (*fig*) peak, apogee.
apolitique [apɔlitik] *adj* (*indifférent*) apolitical; (*indépendant*) unpolitical, non-political.
apologie [apɔlɔʒi] *nf* praise; (*JUR*) vindication.
apoplexie [apɔplɛksi] *nf* apoplexy.
a posteriori [apɔsteʀjɔʀi] *adv* after the event, with hindsight, a posteriori.
apostolat [apɔstɔla] *nm* (*REL*) apostolate, discipleship; (*gén*) evangelism.
apostolique [apɔstɔlik] *adj* apostolic.
apostrophe [apɔstʀɔf] *nf* (*signe*) apostrophe; (*appel*) interpellation.
apostropher [apɔstʀɔfe] *vt* (*interpeller*) to shout at, address sharply.
apothéose [apɔteoz] *nf* pinnacle (of achievement); (*MUS etc*) grand finale.
apothicaire [apɔtikɛʀ] *nm* apothecary.
apôtre [apotʀ(ə)] *nm* apostle, disciple.
Appalaches [apalaʃ] *nmpl*: **les ~** the Appalachian Mountains.
appalachien, ne [apalaʃjɛ̃, -ɛn] *adj* Appalachian.
apparaître [apaʀɛtʀ(ə)] *vi* to appear ♦ *vb avec attribut* to appear, seem.
apparat [apaʀa] *nm*: **tenue/dîner d'~** ceremonial dress/dinner.
appareil [apaʀɛj] *nm* (*outil, machine*) piece of apparatus, device; (*électrique etc*) appliance; (*politique, syndical*) machinery; (*avion*) (aero)plane (*BRIT*), (air)plane (*US*), aircraft *inv*; (*téléphonique*) telephone; (*dentier*) brace (*BRIT*), braces (*US*); **~ digestif/reproducteur** digestive/reproductive system *ou* apparatus; **l'~ productif** the means of production; **qui est à l'~?** who's speaking?; **dans le plus simple ~** in one's birthday suit; **~ (photographique)** camera; **~ 24 x 36** *ou* **petit format** 35 mm camera.
appareillage [apaʀɛjaʒ] *nm* (*appareils*) equipment; (*NAVIG*) casting off, getting under way.
appareiller [apaʀeje] *vi* (*NAVIG*) to cast off, get under way ♦ *vt* (*assortir*) to match up.
appareil-photo, *pl* **appareils-photos** [apaʀɛjfɔtɔ] *nm* camera.
apparemment [apaʀamɑ̃] *adv* apparently.
apparence [apaʀɑ̃s] *nf* appearance; **malgré les ~s** despite appearances; **en ~** apparently, seemingly.
apparent, e [apaʀɑ̃, -ɑ̃t] *adj* visible; (*évident*) obvious; (*superficiel*) apparent; **coutures ~es** topstitched seams; **poutres ~es** exposed beams.
apparenté, e [apaʀɑ̃te] *adj*: **~ à** related to; (*fig*) similar to.
apparenter [apaʀɑ̃te]: **s'~ à** *vt* to be similar to.
apparier [apaʀje] *vt* (*gants*) to pair, match.
appariteur [apaʀitœʀ] *nm* attendant, porter (*in French universities*).
apparition [apaʀisjɔ̃] *nf* appearance; (*surnaturelle*) apparition; **faire son ~** to appear.
appartement [apaʀtəmɑ̃] *nm* flat (*BRIT*), apartment (*US*).
appartenance [apaʀtənɑ̃s] *nf*: **~ à** belonging to, membership of.
appartenir [apaʀtəniʀ]: **~ à** *vt* to belong to; (*faire partie de*) to belong to, be a member of; **il lui appartient de** it is up to him to.
appartiendrai [apaʀtjɛ̃dʀe], **appartiens** [apaʀtjɛ̃] *etc voir* **appartenir**.
apparu, e [apaʀy] *pp de* **apparaître**.
appas [apɑ] *nmpl* (*d'une femme*) charms.
appât [apɑ] *nm* (*PÊCHE*) bait; (*fig*) lure, bait.
appâter [apɑte] *vt* (*hameçon*) to bait; (*poisson, fig*) to lure, entice.
appauvrir [apovʀiʀ] *vt* to impoverish; **s'~** *vi* to grow poorer, become impoverished.
appauvrissement [apovʀismɑ̃] *nm* impoverishment.
appel [apɛl] *nm* call; (*nominal*) roll call; (*: SCOL*) register; (*MIL: recrutement*) call-up; (*JUR*) appeal; **faire ~ à** (*invoquer*) to appeal to; (*avoir recours à*) to call on; (*nécessiter*) to call for, require; **faire** *ou* **interjeter ~** (*JUR*) to appeal, lodge an appeal; **faire l'~** to call the roll; to call the register; **indicatif d'~** call sign; **numéro d'~** (*TÉL*) number; **produit**

d'~ (*COMM*) loss leader; **sans ~** (*fig*) final, irrevocable; **~ d'air** in-draught; **~ d'offres** (*COMM*) invitation to tender; **faire un ~ de phares** to flash one's headlights; **~ (téléphonique)** (tele)phone call.
appelé [aple] *nm* (*MIL*) conscript.
appeler [aple] *vt* to call; (*TÉL*) to call, ring; (*faire venir: médecin etc*) to call, send for; (*fig: nécessiter*) to call for, demand; **~ au secours** to call for help; **~ qn à l'aide** *ou* **au secours** to call to sb to help; **~ qn à un poste/des fonctions** to appoint sb to a post/assign duties to sb; **être appelé à** (*fig*) to be destined to; **~ qn à comparaître** (*JUR*) to summon sb to appear; **en ~ à** to appeal to; **s'~**: **elle s'appelle Gabrielle** her name is Gabrielle, she's called Gabrielle; **comment ça s'appelle?** what is it *ou* that called?
appellation [apelɑsjɔ̃] *nf* designation, appellation; **vin d'~ contrôlée** "appellation contrôlée" wine, *wine guaranteed of a certain quality*.
appelle [apɛl] *etc vb voir* **appeler**.
appendice [apɛ̃dis] *nm* appendix.
appendicite [apɑ̃disit] *nf* appendicitis.
appentis [apɑ̃ti] *nm* lean-to.
appert [apɛʀ] *vb*: **il ~ que** it appears that, it is evident that.
appesantir [apzɑ̃tiʀ]: **s'~** *vi* to grow heavier; **s'~ sur** (*fig*) to dwell at length on.
appétissant, e [apetisɑ̃, -ɑ̃t] *adj* appetizing, mouth-watering.
appétit [apeti] *nm* appetite; **couper l'~ à qn** to take away sb's appetite; **bon ~!** enjoy your meal!
applaudimètre [aplodimɛtʀ(ə)] *nm* applause meter.
applaudir [aplodiʀ] *vt* to applaud ♦ *vi* to applaud, clap; **~ à** *vt* (*décision*) to applaud, commend.
applaudissements [aplodismɑ̃] *nmpl* applause *sg*, clapping *sg*.
applicable [aplikabl(ə)] *adj* applicable.
applicateur [aplikatœʀ] *nm* applicator.
application [aplikɑsjɔ̃] *nf* application; (*d'une loi*) enforcement; **mettre en ~** to implement.
applique [aplik] *nf* wall lamp.
appliqué, e [aplike] *adj* (*élève etc*) industrious, assiduous; (*science*) applied.
appliquer [aplike] *vt* to apply; (*loi*) to enforce; (*donner: gifle, châtiment*) to give; **s'~** *vi* (*élève etc*) to apply o.s.; **s'~ à** (*loi, remarque*) to apply to; **s'~ à faire qch** to apply o.s. to doing sth, take pains to do sth; **s'~ sur** (*coïncider avec*) to fit over.
appoint [apwɛ̃] *nm* (extra) contribution *ou* help; **avoir/faire l'~** (*en payant*) to have/give the right change *ou* money; **chauffage d'~** extra heating.
appointements [apwɛ̃tmɑ̃] *nmpl* salary *sg*, stipend (*surtout REL*).
appointer [apwɛ̃te] *vt*: **être appointé à l'année/au mois** to be paid yearly/monthly.
appontage [apɔ̃taʒ] *nm* landing (*on an aircraft carrier*).
appontement [apɔ̃tmɑ̃] *nm* landing stage, wharf.
apponter [apɔ̃te] *vi* (*avion, hélicoptère*) to land.
apport [apɔʀ] *nm* supply; (*argent, biens etc*) contribution.
apporter [apɔʀte] *vt* to bring; (*preuve*) to give, provide; (*modification*) to make; (*suj: remarque*) to contribute, add.
apposer [apoze] *vt* to append; (*sceau etc*) to affix.
apposition [apozisjɔ̃] *nf* appending; affixing; (*LING*): **en ~** in apposition.
appréciable [apʀesjabl(ə)] *adj* (*important*) appreciable, significant.
appréciation [apʀesjɑsjɔ̃] *nf* appreciation; estimation, assessment; **~s** *nfpl* (*avis*) assessment *sg*, appraisal *sg*.
apprécier [apʀesje] *vt* to appreciate; (*évaluer*) to estimate, assess; **j'apprécierais que tu ...** I should appreciate (it) if you ....
appréhender [apʀeɑ̃de] *vt* (*craindre*) to dread; (*arrêter*) to apprehend; **~ que** to fear that; **~ de faire** to dread doing.
appréhensif, ive [apʀeɑ̃sif, -iv] *adj* apprehensive.
appréhension [apʀeɑ̃sjɔ̃] *nf* apprehension.
apprendre [apʀɑ̃dʀ(ə)] *vt* to learn; (*événement, résultats*) to learn of, hear of; **~ qch à qn** (*informer*) to tell sb (of) sth; (*enseigner*) to teach sb sth; **tu me l'apprends!** that's news to me!; **~ à faire qch** to learn to do sth; **~ à qn à faire qch** to teach sb to do sth.
apprenti, e [apʀɑ̃ti] *nm/f* apprentice; (*fig*) novice, beginner.
apprentissage [apʀɑ̃tisaʒ] *nm* learning; (*COMM, SCOL: période*) apprenticeship; **école** *ou* **centre d'~** training school *ou* centre; **faire l'~ de qch** (*fig*) to be initiated into sth.
apprêt [apʀɛ] *nm* (*sur un cuir, une étoffe*) dressing; (*sur un mur*) size; (*sur un papier*) finish; **sans ~** (*fig*) without artifice, unaffectedly.
apprêté, e [apʀete] *adj* (*fig*) affected.
apprêter [apʀete] *vt* to dress, finish; **s'~** *vi*: **s'~ à qch/à faire qch** to prepare for sth/for doing sth.
appris, e [apʀi, -iz] *pp de* **apprendre**.
apprivoisé, e [apʀivwaze] *adj* tame, tamed.
apprivoiser [apʀivwaze] *vt* to tame.
approbateur, trice [apʀɔbatœʀ, -tʀis] *adj* approving.
approbatif, ive [apʀɔbatif, -iv] *adj* approving.
approbation [apʀɔbɑsjɔ̃] *nf* approval; **digne d'~** (*conduite, travail*) praiseworthy, commendable.
approchant, e [apʀɔʃɑ̃, -ɑ̃t] *adj* similar, close; **quelque chose d'~** something similar.
approche [apʀɔʃ] *nf* approaching; (*arrivée, attitude*) approach; **~s** *nfpl* (*abords*) surroundings; **à l'~ du bateau/de l'ennemi** as the

ship/enemy approached *ou* drew near; **l'~ d'un problème** the approach to a problem; **travaux d'~** (*fig*) manoeuvrings.
approché, e [apʀɔʃe] *adj* approximate.
approcher [apʀɔʃe] *vi* to approach, come near ♦ *vt* (*vedette, artiste*) to come close to, approach; (*rapprocher*): ~ **qch (de qch)** to bring *ou* put *ou* move sth near (to sth); ~ **de** *vt* to draw near to; (*quantité, moment*) to approach; **s'~ de** *vt* to approach, go *ou* come *ou* move near to; **approchez-vous** come *ou* go nearer.
approfondi, e [apʀɔfɔ̃di] *adj* thorough, detailed.
approfondir [apʀɔfɔ̃diʀ] *vt* to deepen; (*question*) to go further into; **sans ~** without going too deeply into it.
appropriation [apʀɔpʀijɑsjɔ̃] *nf* appropriation.
approprié, e [apʀɔpʀije] *adj*: ~ **(à)** appropriate (to), suited to.
approprier [apʀɔpʀije] *vt* (*adapter*) adapt; **s'~** *vt* to appropriate, take over.
approuver [apʀuve] *vt* to agree with; (*autoriser: loi, projet*) to approve, pass; (*trouver louable*) to approve of; **je vous approuve entièrement/ne vous approuve pas** I agree with you entirely/don't agree with you; **lu et approuvé** (read and) approved.
approvisionnement [apʀɔvizjɔnmɑ̃] *nm* supplying; (*provisions*) supply, stock.
approvisionner [apʀɔvizjɔne] *vt* to supply; (*compte bancaire*) to pay funds into; ~ **qn en** to supply sb with; **s'~** *vi*: **s'~ dans un certain magasin/au marché** to shop in a certain shop/at the market; **s'~ en** to stock up with.
approximatif, ive [apʀɔksimatif, -iv] *adj* approximate, rough; (*imprécis*) vague.
approximation [apʀɔksimɑsjɔ̃] *nf* approximation.
approximativement [apʀɔksimativmɑ̃] *adv* approximately, roughly; vaguely.
appt *abr* = **appartement**.
appui [apɥi] *nm* support; **prendre ~ sur** to lean on; (*objet*) to rest on; **point d'~** fulcrum; (*fig*) something to lean on; **à l'~ de** (*pour prouver*) in support of; **à l'~** *adv* to support one's argument; **l'~ de la fenêtre** the windowsill, the window ledge.
appuie [apɥi] *etc vb voir* **appuyer**.
appui-tête, appuie-tête [apɥitɛt] *nm inv* headrest.
appuyé, e [apɥije] *adj* (*regard*) meaningful; (: *insistant*) intent, insistent; (*excessif: politesse, compliment*) exaggerated, overdone.
appuyer [apɥije] *vt* (*poser*): ~ **qch sur/contre/à** to lean *ou* rest sth on/against/on; (*soutenir: personne, demande*) to support, back (up) ♦ *vi*: ~ **sur** (*bouton, frein*) to press, push; (*mot, détail*) to stress, emphasize; (*suj: chose: peser sur*) to rest (heavily) on, press against; **s'~ sur** *vt* to lean on; (*compter sur*) to rely on; **s'~ sur qn** to lean on sb; ~ **contre** (*toucher: mur, porte*) to lean *ou* rest against; ~ **à droite** *ou* **sur sa droite** to bear (to the) right; ~ **sur le champignon** to put one's foot down.
apr. *abr* = **après**.
âpre [ɑpʀ(ə)] *adj* acrid, pungent; (*fig*) harsh; (*lutte*) bitter; ~ **au gain** grasping, greedy.
après [apʀɛ] *prép* after ♦ *adv* afterwards; **2 heures ~** 2 hours later; ~ **qu'il est parti/avoir fait** after he left/having done; **courir ~ qn** to run after sb; **crier ~ qn** to shout at sb; **être toujours ~ qn** (*critiquer etc*) to be always on at sb; ~ **quoi** after which; **d'~** *prép* (*selon*) according to; **d'~ lui** according to him; **d'~ moi** in my opinion; ~ **coup** *adv* after the event, afterwards; ~ **tout** *adv* (*au fond*) after all; **et (puis) ~?** so what?
après-demain [apʀɛdmɛ̃] *adv* the day after tomorrow.
après-guerre [apʀɛgɛʀ] *nm* post-war years *pl*; **d'~** *adj* post-war.
après-midi [apʀɛmidi] *nm ou nf inv* afternoon.
après-rasage [apʀɛʀazaʒ] *nm inv*: **(lotion) ~** after-shave (lotion).
après-ski [apʀɛski] *nm inv* (*chaussure*) snow boot; (*moment*) après-ski.
après-vente [apʀɛvɑ̃t] *adj inv* after-sales *cpd*.
âpreté [ɑpʀəte] *nf* (*voir âpre*) pungency; harshness; bitterness.
à-propos [apʀɔpo] *nm* (*d'une remarque*) aptness; **faire preuve d'~** to show presence of mind, do the right thing; **avec ~** suitably, aptly.
apte [apt(ə)] *adj*: ~ **à qch/faire qch** capable of sth/doing sth; ~ **(au service)** (*MIL*) fit (for service).
aptitude [aptityd] *nf* ability, aptitude.
apurer [apyʀe] *vt* (*COMM*) to clear.
aquaculture [akwakyltyʀ] *nf* fish farming.
aquaplanage [akwaplanaʒ] *nm* (*AUTO*) aquaplaning.
aquaplane [akwaplan] *nm* (*planche*) aquaplane; (*sport*) aquaplaning.
aquaplaning [akwaplaniŋ] *nm* aquaplaning.
aquarelle [akwaʀɛl] *nf* (*tableau*) watercolour (*BRIT*), watercolor (*US*); (*genre*) watercolo(u)rs *pl*, aquarelle.
aquarelliste [akwaʀelist(ə)] *nm/f* painter in watercolo(u)rs.
aquarium [akwaʀjɔm] *nm* aquarium.
aquatique [akwatik] *adj* aquatic, water *cpd*.
aqueduc [akdyk] *nm* aqueduct.
aqueux, euse [akø, -øz] *adj* aqueous.
aquilin [akilɛ̃] *adj m*: **nez ~** aquiline nose.
AR *sigle m* (= *accusé de réception*): **lettre/paquet avec ~** ≈ recorded delivery letter/parcel; (*AVIAT, RAIL etc*) = **aller (et) retour** ♦ *abr* (*AUTO*) = **arrière**.
arabe [aʀab] *adj* Arabic; (*désert, cheval*) Arabian; (*nation, peuple*) Arab ♦ *nm* (*LING*) Arabic ♦ *nm/f*: **A~** Arab.
arabesque [aʀabɛsk(ə)] *nf* arabesque.

Arabie [aʀabi] *nf*: **l'~** Arabia; **l'~ Saoudite** *ou* **Séoudite** Saudi Arabia.
arable [aʀabl(ə)] *adj* arable.
arachide [aʀaʃid] *nf* groundnut (plant); (*graine*) peanut, groundnut.
araignée [aʀeɲe] *nf* spider; **~ de mer** spider crab.
araser [aʀɑze] *vt* to level; (*en rabotant*) to plane (down).
aratoire [aʀatwaʀ] *adj*: **instrument ~** plough-ing implement.
arbalète [aʀbalɛt] *nf* crossbow.
arbitrage [aʀbitʀaʒ] *nm* refereeing; umpiring; arbitration.
arbitraire [aʀbitʀɛʀ] *adj* arbitrary.
arbitre [aʀbitʀ(ə)] *nm* (*SPORT*) referee; (*: TENNIS, CRICKET*) umpire; (*fig*) arbiter, judge; (*JUR*) arbitrator.
arbitrer [aʀbitʀe] *vt* to referee; to umpire; to arbitrate.
arborer [aʀbɔʀe] *vt* to bear, display; (*avec ostentation*) to sport.
arborescence [aʀbɔʀesɑ̃s] *nf* tree structure.
arboricole [aʀbɔʀikɔl] *adj* (*animal*) arboreal; (*technique*) arboricultural.
arboriculture [aʀbɔʀikyltyʀ] *nf* arboriculture; **~ fruitière** fruit (tree) growing.
arbre [aʀbʀ(ə)] *nm* tree; (*TECH*) shaft; **~ à cames** (*AUTO*) camshaft; **~ fruitier** fruit tree; **~ généalogique** family tree; **~ de Noël** Christmas tree; **~ de transmission** (*AUTO*) driveshaft.
arbrisseau, x [aʀbʀiso] *nm* shrub.
arbuste [aʀbyst(ə)] *nm* small shrub, bush.
arc [aʀk] *nm* (*arme*) bow; (*GÉOM*) arc; (*ARCHIT*) arch; **~ de cercle** arc of a circle; **en ~ de cercle** *adj* semi-circular.
arcade [aʀkad] *nf* arch(way); **~s** *nfpl* arcade *sg*, arches; **~ sourcilière** arch of the eyebrows.
arcanes [aʀkan] *nmpl* mysteries.
arc-boutant, *pl* **arcs-boutants** [aʀkbutɑ̃] *nm* flying buttress.
arc-bouter [aʀkbute]: **s'~** *vi*: **s'~ contre** to lean *ou* press against.
arceau, x [aʀso] *nm* (*métallique etc*) hoop.
arc-en-ciel, *pl* **arcs-en-ciel** [aʀkɑ̃sjɛl] *nm* rainbow.
archaïque [aʀkaik] *adj* archaic.
archaïsme [aʀkaism(ə)] *nm* archaism.
archange [aʀkɑ̃ʒ] *nm* archangel.
arche [aʀʃ(ə)] *nf* arch; **~ de Noé** Noah's Ark.
archéologie [aʀkeɔlɔʒi] *nf* arch(a)eology.
archéologique [aʀkeɔlɔʒik] *adj* arch(a)eological.
archéologue [aʀkeɔlɔg] *nm/f* arch(a)eologist.
archer [aʀʃe] *nm* archer.
archet [aʀʃɛ] *nm* bow.
archevêché [aʀʃəveʃe] *nm* archbishopric; (*palais*) archbishop's palace.
archevêque [aʀʃəvɛk] *nm* archbishop.
archi... [aʀʃi] *préfixe* (*très*) dead, extra.
archibondé, e [aʀʃibɔ̃de] *adj* chock-a-block (*BRIT*), packed solid.
archiduc [aʀʃidyk] *nm* archduke.
archiduchesse [aʀʃidyʃɛs] *nf* archduchess.
archipel [aʀʃipɛl] *nm* archipelago.
architecte [aʀʃitɛkt(ə)] *nm* architect.
architectural, e, aux [aʀʃitɛktyʀal, -o] *adj* architectural.
architecture [aʀʃitɛktyʀ] *nf* architecture.
archive [aʀʃiv] *nf* file; **~s** *nfpl* archives.
archiver [aʀʃive] *vt* to file.
archiviste [aʀʃivist(ə)] *nm/f* archivist.
arçon [aʀsɔ̃] *nm* voir **cheval**.
arctique [aʀktik] *adj* Arctic ♦ *nm*: **l'A~** the Arctic; **le cercle A~** the Arctic Circle; **l'océan A~** the Arctic Ocean.
ardemment [aʀdamɑ̃] *adv* ardently, fervently.
ardent, e [aʀdɑ̃, -ɑ̃t] *adj* (*soleil*) blazing; (*fièvre*) raging; (*amour*) ardent, passionate; (*prière*) fervent.
ardeur [aʀdœʀ] *nf* blazing heat; (*fig*) fervour, ardour.
ardoise [aʀdwaz] *nf* slate.
ardu, e [aʀdy] *adj* arduous, difficult; (*pente*) steep, abrupt.
are [aʀ] *nm* are, 100 square metres.
arène [aʀɛn] *nf* arena; (*fig*): **l'~ politique** the political arena; **~s** *nfpl* bull-ring *sg*.
arête [aʀɛt] *nf* (*de poisson*) bone; (*d'une montagne*) ridge; (*GÉOM etc*) edge (*where two faces meet*).
arg. *abr* = **argus**.
argent [aʀʒɑ̃] *nm* (*métal*) silver; (*monnaie*) money; (*couleur*) silver; **en avoir pour son ~** to get value for money; **~ comptant** (hard) cash; **~ liquide** ready money, (ready) cash; **~ de poche** pocket money.
argenté, e [aʀʒɑ̃te] *adj* silver(y); (*métal*) silver-plated.
argenter [aʀʒɑ̃te] *vt* to silver(-plate).
argenterie [aʀʒɑ̃tʀi] *nf* silverware; (*en métal argenté*) silver plate.
argentin, e [aʀʒɑ̃tɛ̃, -in] *adj* Argentinian, Argentine ♦ *nm/f*: **A~, e** Argentinian, Argentine.
Argentine [aʀʒɑ̃tin] *nf*: **l'~** Argentina, the Argentine.
argile [aʀʒil] *nf* clay.
argileux, euse [aʀʒilø, -øz] *adj* clayey.
argot [aʀgo] *nm* slang; *see boxed note*.

ARGOT

***Argot** was the term originally used to describe the jargon of the criminal underworld, characterized by colourful images and distinctive intonation and designed to confuse the outsider. Some French authors write in **argot** and so have helped it spread and grow. More generally, the special vocabulary used by any social or professional group is also known as **argot**.*

argotique [aʀɡɔtik] *adj* slang *cpd*; (*très familier*) slangy.
arguer [aʀɡɥe]: ~ **de** *vt* to put forward as a reason; ~ **que** to argue that.
argument [aʀɡymɑ̃] *nm* argument.
argumentaire [aʀɡymɑ̃tɛʀ] *nm* list of sales points; (*brochure*) sales leaflet.
argumentation [aʀɡymɑ̃tɑsjɔ̃] *nf* (*fait d'argumenter*) arguing; (*ensemble des arguments*) argument.
argumenter [aʀɡymɑ̃te] *vi* to argue.
argus [aʀɡys] *nm guide to second-hand car etc prices.*
arguties [aʀɡysi] *nfpl* pettifoggery *sg* (*BRIT*), quibbles.
aride [aʀid] *adj* arid.
aridité [aʀidite] *nf* aridity.
arien, ne [aʀjɛ̃, -ɛn] *adj* Arian.
aristocrate [aʀistɔkʀat] *nm/f* aristocrat.
aristocratie [aʀistɔkʀasi] *nf* aristocracy.
aristocratique [aʀistɔkʀatik] *adj* aristocratic.
arithmétique [aʀitmetik] *adj* arithmetic(al) ♦ *nf* arithmetic.
armada [aʀmada] *nf* (*fig*) army.
armagnac [aʀmaɲak] *nm* armagnac.
armateur [aʀmatœʀ] *nm* shipowner.
armature [aʀmatyʀ] *nf* framework; (*de tente etc*) frame; (*de corset*) bone; (*de soutien-gorge*) wiring.
arme [aʀm(ə)] *nf* weapon; (*section de l'armée*) arm; ~**s** *nfpl* weapons, arms; (*blason*) (coat of) arms; **les ~s** (*profession*) soldiering *sg*; **à ~s égales** on equal terms; **en ~s** up in arms; **passer par les ~s** to execute (by firing squad); **prendre/présenter les ~s** to take up/present arms; **se battre à l'~ blanche** to fight with blades; ~ **à feu** firearm; ~**s de destruction massive** weapons of mass destruction.
armé, e [aʀme] *adj* armed; ~ **de** armed with.
armée [aʀme] *nf* army; ~ **de l'air** Air Force; **l'~ du Salut** the Salvation Army; ~ **de terre** Army.
armement [aʀməmɑ̃] *nm* (*matériel*) arms *pl*, weapons *pl*; (*: d'un pays*) arms *pl*, armament; (*action d'équiper: d'un navire*) fitting out; ~**s nucléaires** nuclear armaments; **course aux ~s** arms race.
Arménie [aʀmeni] *nf*: **l'~** Armenia.
arménien, ne [aʀmenjɛ̃, -ɛn] *adj* Armenian ♦ *nm* (*LING*) Armenian ♦ *nm/f*: **A~, ne** Armenian.
armer [aʀme] *vt* to arm; (*arme à feu*) to cock; (*appareil-photo*) to wind on; ~ **qch de** to fit sth with; (*renforcer*) to reinforce sth with; ~ **qn de** to arm *ou* equip sb with; **s'~ de** to arm o.s. with.
armistice [aʀmistis] *nm* armistice; **l'A~** ≈ Remembrance (*BRIT*) *ou* Veterans (*US*) Day.
armoire [aʀmwaʀ] *nf* (tall) cupboard; (*penderie*) wardrobe (*BRIT*), closet (*US*); ~ **à pharmacie** medicine chest.
armoiries [aʀmwaʀi] *nfpl* coat of arms *sg*.
armure [aʀmyʀ] *nf* armour *no pl*, suit of armour.
armurerie [aʀmyʀʀi] *nf* arms factory; (*magasin*) gunsmith's (shop).
armurier [aʀmyʀje] *nm* gunsmith; (*MIL, d'armes blanches*) armourer.
ARN *sigle m* (= *acide ribonucléique*) RNA.
arnaque [aʀnak] *nf*: **de l'~** daylight robbery.
arnaquer [aʀnake] *vt* to do (*fam*), swindle; **se faire ~** to be had (*fam*) *ou* done.
arnaqueur [aʀnakœʀ] *nm* swindler.
arnica [aʀnika] *nm*: **(teinture d')~** arnica.
aromates [aʀɔmat] *nmpl* seasoning *sg*, herbs (and spices).
aromathérapie [aʀɔmateʀapi] *nf* aromatherapy.
aromatique [aʀɔmatik] *adj* aromatic.
aromatiser [aʀɔmatize] *vt* to flavour.
arôme [aʀom] *nm* aroma; (*d'une fleur etc*) fragrance.
arpège [aʀpɛʒ] *nm* arpeggio.
arpentage [aʀpɑ̃taʒ] *nm* (land) surveying.
arpenter [aʀpɑ̃te] *vt* to pace up and down.
arpenteur [aʀpɑ̃tœʀ] *nm* land surveyor.
arqué, e [aʀke] *adj* arched; (*jambes*) bow *cpd*, bandy.
arr. *abr* = **arrondissement**.
arrachage [aʀaʃaʒ] *nm*: ~ **des mauvaises herbes** weeding.
arraché [aʀaʃe] *nm* (*SPORT*) snatch; **obtenir à l'~** (*fig*) to snatch.
arrache-pied [aʀaʃpje]: **d'~** *adv* relentlessly.
arracher [aʀaʃe] *vt* to pull out; (*page etc*) to tear off, tear out; (*déplanter: légume*) to lift; (*: herbe, souche*) to pull up; (*bras etc: par explosion*) to blow off; (*: par accident*) to tear off; **s'~** *vt* (*article très recherché*) to fight over; ~ **qch à qn** to snatch sth from sb; (*fig*) to wring sth out of sb, wrest sth from sb; ~ **qn à** (*solitude, rêverie*) to drag sb out of; (*famille etc*) to tear *ou* wrench sb away from; **se faire ~ une dent** to have a tooth out *ou* pulled (*US*); **s'~ de** (*lieu*) to tear o.s. away from; (*habitude*) to force o.s. out of.
arraisonner [aʀɛzɔne] *vt* to board and search.
arrangeant, e [aʀɑ̃ʒɑ̃, -ɑ̃t] *adj* accommodating, obliging.
arrangement [aʀɑ̃ʒmɑ̃] *nm* arrangement.
arranger [aʀɑ̃ʒe] *vt* to arrange; (*réparer*) to fix, put right; (*régler*) to settle, sort out; (*convenir à*) to suit, be convenient for; **s'~** (*se mettre d'accord*) to come to an agreement *ou* arrangement; (*s'améliorer: querelle, situation*) to be sorted out; (*se débrouiller*): **s'~ pour que** ... to arrange things so that ...; **je vais m'~** I'll manage; **ça va s'~** it'll sort itself out; **s'~ pour faire** to make sure that *ou* see to it that one can do.
arrangeur [aʀɑ̃ʒœʀ] *nm* (*MUS*) arranger.

arrestation [aʀɛstɑsjɔ̃] *nf* arrest.
arrêt [aʀɛ] *nm* stopping; (*de bus etc*) stop; (*JUR*) judgment, decision; (*FOOTBALL*) save; ~**s** *nmpl* (*MIL*) arrest *sg*; **être à l'~** to be stopped, have come to a halt; **rester** *ou* **tomber en ~ devant** to stop short in front of; **sans ~** without stopping, non-stop; (*fréquemment*) continually; ~ **d'autobus** bus stop; ~ **facultatif** request stop; ~ **de mort** capital sentence; ~ **de travail** stoppage (of work).
arrêté, e [aʀete] *adj* (*idées*) firm, fixed ♦ *nm* order, decree; ~ **municipal** ≈ bylaw, byelaw.
arrêter [aʀete] *vt* to stop; (*chauffage etc*) to turn off, switch off; (*COMM: compte*) to settle; (*COUTURE: point*) to fasten off; (*fixer: date etc*) to appoint, decide on; (*criminel, suspect*) to arrest; **s'~** *vi* to stop; (*s'interrompre*) to stop o.s.; ~ **de faire** to stop doing; **arrête de te plaindre** stop complaining; **ne pas ~ de faire** to keep on doing; **s'~ de faire** to stop doing; **s'~ sur** (*suj: choix, regard*) to fall on.
arrhes [aʀ] *nfpl* deposit *sg*.
arrière [aʀjɛʀ] *nm* back; (*SPORT*) fullback ♦ *adj inv*: **siège/roue ~** back *ou* rear seat/wheel; ~**s** *nmpl* (*fig*): **protéger ses ~s** to protect the rear; **à l'~** *adv* behind, at the back; **en ~** *adv* behind; (*regarder*) back, behind; (*tomber, aller*) backwards; **en ~ de** *prép* behind.
arriéré, e [aʀjeʀe] *adj* (*péj*) backward ♦ *nm* (*d'argent*) arrears *pl*.
arrière-boutique [aʀjɛʀbutik] *nf* back shop.
arrière-cour [aʀjɛʀkuʀ] *nf* backyard.
arrière-cuisine [aʀjɛʀkɥizin] *nf* scullery.
arrière-garde [aʀjɛʀgaʀd(ə)] *nf* rearguard.
arrière-goût [aʀjɛʀgu] *nm* aftertaste.
arrière-grand-mère, *pl* **arrière-grand-mères** [aʀjɛʀgʀɑ̃mɛʀ] *nf* great-grandmother.
arrière-grand-père, *pl* **arrière-grands-pères** [aʀjɛʀgʀɑ̃pɛʀ] *nm* great-grandfather.
arrière-grands-parents [aʀjɛʀgʀɑ̃paʀɑ̃] *nmpl* great-grandparents.
arrière-pays [aʀjɛʀpei] *nm inv* hinterland.
arrière-pensée [aʀjɛʀpɑ̃se] *nf* ulterior motive; (*doute*) mental reservation.
arrière-petite-fille, *pl* **arrière-petites-filles** [aʀjɛʀpətitfij] *nf* great-granddaughter.
arrière-petit-fils, *pl* **arrière-petits-fils** [aʀjɛʀpətifis] *nm* great-grandson.
arrière-petits-enfants [aʀjɛʀpətizɑ̃fɑ̃] *nmpl* great-grandchildren.
arrière-plan [aʀjɛʀplɑ̃] *nm* background; **d'~** *adj* (*INFORM*) background *cpd*.
arriérer [aʀjeʀe]: **s'~** *vi* (*COMM*) to fall into arrears.
arrière-saison [aʀjɛʀsɛzɔ̃] *nf* late autumn.
arrière-salle [aʀjɛʀsal] *nf* back room.
arrière-train [aʀjɛʀtʀɛ̃] *nm* hindquarters *pl*.
arrimer [aʀime] *vt* to stow; (*fixer*) to secure, fasten securely.
arrivage [aʀivaʒ] *nm* arrival.
arrivant, e [aʀivɑ̃, -ɑ̃t] *nm/f* newcomer.
arrivée [aʀive] *nf* arrival; (*ligne d'arrivée*) finish; ~ **d'air/de gaz** air/gas inlet; **courrier à l'~** incoming mail; **à mon ~** when I arrived.
arriver [aʀive] *vi* to arrive; (*survenir*) to happen, occur; **j'arrive!** (I'm) just coming!; **il arrive à Paris à 8 h** he gets to *ou* arrives in Paris at 8; ~ **à destination** to arrive at one's destination; ~ **à** (*atteindre*) to reach; ~ **à (faire) qch** (*réussir*) to manage (to do) sth; ~ **à échéance** to fall due; **en ~ à faire** to end up doing, get to the point of doing; **il arrive que** it happens that; **il lui arrive de faire** he sometimes does.
arrivisme [aʀivism(ə)] *nm* ambition, ambitiousness.
arriviste [aʀivist(ə)] *nm/f* go-getter.
arrobase [aʀɔbaz] *nf* (*INFORM*) @, 'at' sign.
arrogance [aʀɔgɑ̃s] *nf* arrogance.
arrogant, e [aʀɔgɑ̃, -ɑ̃t] *adj* arrogant.
arroger [aʀɔʒe]: **s'~** *vt* to assume (without right); **s'~ le droit de ...** to assume the right to ....
arrondi, e [aʀɔ̃di] *adj* round ♦ *nm* roundness.
arrondir [aʀɔ̃diʀ] *vt* (*forme, objet*) to round; (*somme*) to round off; **s'~** *vi* to become round(ed); ~ **ses fins de mois** to supplement one's pay.
arrondissement [aʀɔ̃dismɑ̃] *nm* (*ADMIN*) ≈ district.
arrosage [aʀozaʒ] *nm* watering; **tuyau d'~** hose(pipe).
arroser [aʀoze] *vt* to water; (*victoire etc*) to celebrate (over a drink); (*CULIN*) to baste.
arroseur [aʀozœʀ] *nm* (*tourniquet*) sprinkler.
arroseuse [aʀozøz] *nf* water cart.
arrosoir [aʀozwaʀ] *nm* watering can.
arrt *abr* = **arrondissement.**
arsenal, aux [aʀsənal, -o] *nm* (*NAVIG*) naval dockyard; (*MIL*) arsenal; (*fig*) gear, paraphernalia.
art [aʀ] *nm* art; **avoir l'~ de faire** (*fig: personne*) to have a talent for doing; **les ~s** the arts; **livre/critique d'~** art book/critic; **objet d'~** objet d'art; ~ **dramatique** dramatic art; ~**s martiaux** martial arts; ~**s et métiers** applied arts and crafts; ~**s ménagers** home economics *sg*; ~**s plastiques** plastic arts.
art. *abr* = **article.**
artère [aʀtɛʀ] *nf* (*ANAT*) artery; (*rue*) main road.
artériel, le [aʀteʀjɛl] *adj* arterial.
artériosclérose [aʀteʀjɔskleʀoz] *nf* arteriosclerosis.
arthrite [aʀtʀit] *nf* arthritis.
arthrose [aʀtʀoz] *nf* (degenerative) osteoarthritis.
artichaut [aʀtiʃo] *nm* artichoke.
article [aʀtikl(ə)] *nm* article; (*COMM*) item, article; (*INFORM*) record, item; **faire l'~** (*COMM*) to do one's sales spiel; **faire l'~ de** (*fig*) to sing the praises of; **à l'~ de la mort** at the point of death; ~ **défini/indéfini** definite/indefinite article; ~ **de fond**

(*PRESSE*) feature article; **~s de bureau** office equipment; **~s de voyage** travel goods *ou* items.

articulaire [aʀtikylɛʀ] *adj* of the joints, articular.

articulation [aʀtikylɑsjɔ̃] *nf* articulation; (*ANAT*) joint.

articulé, e [aʀtikyle] *adj* (*membre*) jointed; (*poupée*) with moving joints.

articuler [aʀtikyle] *vt* to articulate; **s'~ (sur)** (*ANAT, TECH*) to articulate (with); **s'~ autour de** (*fig*) to centre around *ou* on, turn on.

artifice [aʀtifis] *nm* device, trick.

artificiel, le [aʀtifisjɛl] *adj* artificial.

artificiellement [aʀtifisjɛlmɑ̃] *adv* artificially.

artificier [aʀtifisje] *nm* pyrotechnist.

artificieux, euse [aʀtifisjø, -øz] *adj* guileful, deceitful.

artillerie [aʀtijʀi] *nf* artillery, ordnance.

artilleur [aʀtijœʀ] *nm* artilleryman, gunner.

artisan [aʀtizɑ̃] *nm* artisan, (self-employed) craftsman; **l'~ de la victoire/du malheur** the architect of victory/of the disaster.

artisanal, e, aux [aʀtizanal, -o] *adj* of *ou* made by craftsmen; (*péj*) cottage industry *cpd*, unsophisticated.

artisanalement [aʀtizanalmɑ̃] *adv* by craftsmen.

artisanat [aʀtizana] *nm* arts and crafts *pl*.

artiste [aʀtist(ə)] *nm/f* artist; (*THÉÂT, MUS*) artist, performer; (*: de variétés*) entertainer.

artistique [aʀtistik] *adj* artistic.

artistiquement [aʀtistikmɑ̃] *adv* artistically.

aryen, ne [aʀjɛ̃, -ɛn] *adj* Aryan.

AS *sigle fpl* (*ADMIN*) = **assurances sociales** ♦ *sigle f* (*SPORT: = Association sportive*) ≈ FC (= *Football Club*).

as *vb* [a] *voir* **avoir** ♦ *nm* [ɑs] ace.

a/s *abr* (= *aux soins de*) c/o.

ASBL *sigle f* (= *association sans but lucratif*) non-profit-making organization.

asc. *abr* = **ascenseur**.

ascendance [asɑ̃dɑ̃s] *nf* (*origine*) ancestry; (*ASTROLOGIE*) ascendant.

ascendant, e [asɑ̃dɑ̃, -ɑ̃t] *adj* upward ♦ *nm* influence; **~s** *nmpl* ascendants.

ascenseur [asɑ̃sœʀ] *nm* lift (*BRIT*), elevator (*US*).

ascension [asɑ̃sjɔ̃] *nf* ascent; climb; **l'A~** (*REL*) the Ascension; (*: jour férié*) Ascension (Day); **(île de) l'A~** Ascension Island; *see boxed note*.

> **FÊTE DE L'ASCENSION**
>
> *The* **fête de l'Ascension** *is a public holiday in France. It always falls on a Thursday, usually in May. Many French people take Friday off work too and enjoy a long weekend.*

ascète [asɛt] *nm/f* ascetic.

ascétique [asetik] *adj* ascetic.

ascétisme [asetism(ə)] *nm* asceticism.

ascorbique [askɔʀbik] *adj*: **acide ~** ascorbic acid.

ASE *sigle f* (= *Agence spatiale européenne*) ESA (= *European Space Agency*).

asepsie [asɛpsi] *nf* asepsis.

aseptique [asɛptik] *adj* aseptic.

aseptiser [asɛptize] *vt* to sterilize; (*plaie*) to disinfect.

asexué, e [asɛksɥe] *adj* asexual.

asiatique [azjatik] *adj* Asian, Asiatic ♦ *nm/f*: **A~** Asian.

Asie [azi] *nf*: **l'~** Asia.

asile [azil] *nm* (*refuge*) refuge, sanctuary; (*POL*): **droit d'~** (political) asylum; (*pour malades, vieillards etc*) home; **accorder l'~ politique à qn** to grant *ou* give sb political asylum; **chercher/trouver ~ quelque part** to seek/find refuge somewhere.

asocial, e, aux [asɔsjal, -o] *adj* antisocial.

aspect [aspɛ] *nm* appearance, look; (*fig*) aspect, side; (*LING*) aspect; **à l'~ de** at the sight of.

asperge [aspɛʀʒ(ə)] *nf* asparagus *no pl*.

asperger [aspɛʀʒe] *vt* to spray, sprinkle.

aspérité [aspeʀite] *nf* excrescence, protruding bit (of rock *etc*).

aspersion [aspɛʀsjɔ̃] *nf* spraying, sprinkling.

asphalte [asfalt(ə)] *nm* asphalt.

asphyxiant, e [asfiksjɑ̃, -ɑ̃t] *adj* suffocating; **gaz ~** poison gas.

asphyxie [asfiksi] *nf* suffocation, asphyxia, asphyxiation.

asphyxier [asfiksje] *vt* to suffocate, asphyxiate; (*fig*) to stifle; **mourir asphyxié** to die of suffocation *ou* asphyxiation.

aspic [aspik] *nm* (*ZOOL*) asp; (*CULIN*) aspic.

aspirant, e [aspiʀɑ̃, -ɑ̃t] *adj*: **pompe ~e** suction pump ♦ *nm* (*NAVIG*) midshipman.

aspirateur [aspiʀatœʀ] *nm* vacuum cleaner, Hoover ®.

aspiration [aspiʀɑsjɔ̃] *nf* inhalation; sucking (up); drawing up; **~s** *nfpl* aspirations.

aspirer [aspiʀe] *vt* (*air*) to inhale; (*liquide*) to suck (up); (*suj: appareil*) to suck *ou* draw up; **~ à** *vt* to aspire to.

aspirine [aspiʀin] *nf* aspirin.

assagir [asaʒiʀ] *vt*, **s'~** *vi* to quieten down, sober down.

assaillant, e [asajɑ̃, -ɑ̃t] *nm/f* assailant, attacker.

assaillir [asajiʀ] *vt* to assail, attack; **~ qn de** (*questions*) to assail *ou* bombard sb with.

assainir [aseniʀ] *vt* to clean up; (*eau, air*) to purify.

assainissement [asenismɑ̃] *nm* cleaning up; purifying.

assaisonnement [asɛzɔnmɑ̃] *nm* seasoning.

assaisonner [asɛzɔne] *vt* to season; **bien assaisonné** highly seasoned.

assassin [asasɛ̃] *nm* murderer; assassin.

assassinat [asasina] *nm* murder; assassination.

assassiner [asasine] *vt* to murder; (*surtout POL*) to assassinate.
assaut [aso] *nm* assault, attack; **prendre d'~** to (take by) storm, assault; **donner l'~ (à)** to attack; **faire ~ de** (*rivaliser*) to vie with *ou* rival each other in.
assèchement [asɛʃmɑ̃] *nm* draining, drainage.
assécher [aseʃe] *vt* to drain.
ASSEDIC [asedik] *sigle f* (= *Association pour l'emploi dans l'industrie et le commerce*) *unemployment insurance scheme*.
assemblage [asɑ̃blaʒ] *nm* assembling; (*MENUISERIE*) joint; **un ~ de** (*fig*) a collection of; **langage d'~** (*INFORM*) assembly language.
assemblée [asɑ̃ble] *nf* (*réunion*) meeting; (*public, assistance*) gathering; assembled people; (*POL*) assembly; (*REL*): **l'~ des fidèles** the congregation; **l'A~ nationale (AN)** the (French) National Assembly; *see boxed note.*

> **ASSEMBLÉE NATIONALE**
>
> *The* **Assemblée nationale** *is the lower house of the French Parliament, the upper house being the 'Sénat'. It is housed in the Palais Bourbon in Paris. Its members, or '***députés***', are elected every five years.*

assembler [asɑ̃ble] *vt* (*joindre, monter*) to assemble, put together; (*amasser*) to gather (together), collect (together); **s'~** *vi* to gather, collect.
assembleur [asɑ̃blœʀ] *nm* assembler, fitter; (*INFORM*) assembler.
assener, asséner [asene] *vt*: **~ un coup à qn** to deal sb a blow.
assentiment [asɑ̃timɑ̃] *nm* assent, consent; (*approbation*) approval.
asseoir [aswaʀ] *vt* (*malade, bébé*) to sit up; (*personne debout*) to sit down; (*autorité, réputation*) to establish; **s'~** *vi* to sit (o.s.) up; to sit (o.s.) down; **faire ~ qn** to ask sb to sit down; **~ qch sur** to build sth on; (*appuyer*) to base sth on.
assermenté, e [asɛʀmɑ̃te] *adj* sworn, on oath.
assertion [asɛʀsjɔ̃] *nf* assertion.
asservir [asɛʀviʀ] *vt* to subjugate, enslave.
asservissement [asɛʀvismɑ̃] *nm* (*action*) enslavement; (*état*) slavery.
assesseur [asesœʀ] *nm* (*JUR*) assessor.
asseyais [asɛjɛ] *etc vb voir* **asseoir**.
assez [ase] *adv* (*suffisamment*) enough, sufficiently; (*passablement*) rather, quite, fairly; **~!** enough!, that'll do!; **~/pas ~ cuit** well enough done/underdone; **est-il ~ fort/rapide?** is he strong/fast enough?; **il est passé ~ vite** he went past rather *ou* quite *ou* fairly fast; **~ de pain/livres** enough *ou* sufficient bread/books; **vous en avez ~?** have you got enough?; **en avoir ~ de qch** (*en être fatigué*) to have had enough of sth; **travailler ~** to work (hard) enough.
assidu, e [asidy] *adj* assiduous, painstaking; (*régulier*) regular; **~ auprès de qn** attentive towards sb.
assiduité [asidɥite] *nf* assiduousness, painstaking; regularity; attentiveness; **~s** *nfpl* assiduous attentions.
assidûment [asidymɑ̃] *adv* assiduously, painstakingly; attentively.
assied [asje] *etc vb voir* **asseoir**.
assiégé, e [asjeʒe] *adj* under siege, besieged.
assiéger [asjeʒe] *vt* to besiege, lay siege to; (*suj: foule, touristes*) to mob, besiege.
assiérai [asjeʀe] *etc vb voir* **asseoir**.
assiette [asjɛt] *nf* plate; (*contenu*) plate(ful); (*équilibre*) seat; (*de colonne*) seating; (*de navire*) trim; **~ anglaise** assorted cold meats; **~ creuse** (soup) dish, soup plate; **~ à dessert** dessert *ou* side plate; **~ de l'impôt** basis of (tax) assessment; **~ plate** (dinner) plate.
assiettée [asjete] *nf* plateful.
assignation [asiɲɑsjɔ̃] *nf* assignation; (*JUR*) summons; (*: de témoin*) subpoena; **~ à résidence** compulsory order of residence.
assigner [asiɲe] *vt*: **~ qch à** to assign *ou* allot sth to; (*valeur, importance*) to attach sth to; (*somme*) to allocate sth to; (*limites*) to set *ou* fix sth to; (*cause, effet*) to ascribe *ou* attribute sth to; **~ qn à** (*affecter*) to assign sb to; **~ qn à résidence** (*JUR*) to give sb a compulsory order of residence.
assimilable [asimilabl(ə)] *adj* easily assimilated *ou* absorbed.
assimilation [asimilɑsjɔ̃] *nf* assimilation, absorption.
assimiler [asimile] *vt* to assimilate, absorb; (*comparer*): **~ qch/qn à** to liken *ou* compare sth/sb to; **s'~** *vi* (*s'intégrer*) to be assimilated *ou* absorbed; **ils sont assimilés aux infirmières** (*ADMIN*) they are classed as nurses.
assis, e [asi, -iz] *pp de* **asseoir** ♦ *adj* sitting (down), seated ♦ *nf* (*CONSTR*) course; (*GÉO*) stratum (*pl* -a); (*fig*) basis (*pl* bases), foundation; **~ en tailleur** sitting cross-legged.
assises [asiz] *nfpl* (*JUR*) assizes; (*congrès*) (annual) conference.
assistanat [asistana] *nm* assistantship; (*à l'université*) probationary lectureship.
assistance [asistɑ̃s] *nf* (*public*) audience; (*aide*) assistance; **porter** *ou* **prêter ~ à qn** to give sb assistance; **A~ publique (AP)** *public health service*; **enfant de l'A~ (publique)** (*formerly*) child in care.
assistant, e [asistɑ̃, -ɑ̃t] *nm/f* assistant; (*d'université*) probationary lecturer; **les ~s** *nmpl* (*auditeurs etc*) those present; **~e sociale** social worker.
assisté, e [asiste] *adj* (*AUTO*) power assisted ♦ *nm/f* person receiving aid from the State.
assister [asiste] *vt* to assist; **~ à** *vt* (*scène, événement*) to witness; (*conférence*) to attend,

be (present) at; (*spectacle, match*) to be at, see.

association [asɔsjasjɔ̃] *nf* association; (*COMM*) partnership; ~ **d'idées/images** association of ideas/images.

associé, e [asɔsje] *nm/f* associate; (*COMM*) partner.

associer [asɔsje] *vt* to associate; ~ **qn à** (*profits*) to give sb a share of; (*affaire*) to make sb a partner in; (*joie, triomphe*) to include sb in; ~ **qch à** (*joindre, allier*) to combine sth with; **s'~** *vi* to join together; (*COMM*) to form a partnership ♦ *vt* (*collaborateur*) to take on (as a partner); **s'~ à** to be combined with; (*opinions, joie de qn*) to share in; **s'~ à** *ou* **avec qn pour faire** to join (forces) *ou* join together with sb to do.

assoie [aswa] *etc vb voir* **asseoir**.

assoiffé, e [aswafe] *adj* thirsty; (*fig*): ~ **de** (*sang*) thirsting for; (*gloire*) thirsting after.

assoirai [asware], **assois** [aswa] *etc vb voir* **asseoir**.

assolement [asɔlmɑ̃] *nm* (systematic) rotation of crops.

assombrir [asɔ̃bʀiʀ] *vt* to darken; (*fig*) to fill with gloom; **s'~** *vi* to darken; (*devenir nuageux, fig: visage*) to cloud over; (*fig*) to become gloomy.

assommer [asɔme] *vt* (*étourdir, abrutir*) to knock out, stun; (*fam: ennuyer*) to bore stiff.

Assomption [asɔ̃psjɔ̃] *nf*: **l'~** the Assumption; *see boxed note.*

LE 15 AOÛT

The **fête de l'Assomption**, *more commonly known as 'le 15 août' is a national holiday in France. Traditionally, large numbers of holidaymakers leave home on 15th August, frequently causing chaos on the French roads.*

assorti, e [asɔʀti] *adj* matched, matching; **fromages/légumes ~s** assorted cheeses/vegetables; ~ **à** matching; ~ **de** accompanied with; (*conditions, conseils*) coupled with; **bien/mal ~** well/ill-matched.

assortiment [asɔʀtimɑ̃] *nm* (*choix*) assortment, selection; (*harmonie de couleurs, formes*) arrangement; (*COMM: lot, stock*) selection.

assortir [asɔʀtiʀ] *vt* to match; **s'~** to go well together, match; ~ **qch à** to match sth with; ~ **qch de** to accompany sth with; **s'~ de** to be accompanied by.

assoupi, e [asupi] *adj* dozing, sleeping; (*fig*) (be)numbed; (*sens*) dulled.

assoupir [asupiʀ]: **s'~** *vi* (*personne*) to doze off; (*sens*) to go numb.

assoupissement [asupismɑ̃] *nm* (*sommeil*) dozing; (*fig: somnolence*) drowsiness.

assouplir [asupliʀ] *vt* to make supple, soften; (*membres, corps*) to limber up, make supple; (*fig*) to relax; (*: caractère*) to soften, make more flexible; **s'~** *vi* to soften; to limber up; to relax; to become more flexible.

assouplissement [asuplismɑ̃] *nm* softening; limbering up; relaxation; **exercices d'~** limbering up exercises.

assourdir [asuʀdiʀ] *vt* (*bruit*) to deaden, muffle; (*suj: bruit*) to deafen.

assourdissant, e [asuʀdisɑ̃, -ɑ̃t] *adj* (*bruit*) deafening.

assouvir [asuviʀ] *vt* to satisfy, appease.

assoyais [aswajɛ] *etc vb voir* **asseoir**.

ASSU [asy] *sigle f* = *Association du sport scolaire et universitaire.*

assujetti, e [asyʒeti] *adj*: ~ **(à)** subject (to); (*ADMIN*): ~ **à l'impôt** subject to tax(ation).

assujettir [asyʒetiʀ] *vt* to subject, subjugate; (*fixer: planches, tableau*) to fix securely; ~ **qn à** (*règle, impôt*) to subject sb to.

assujettissement [asyʒetismɑ̃] *nm* subjection, subjugation.

assumer [asyme] *vt* (*fonction, emploi*) to assume, take on; (*accepter: conséquence, situation*) to accept.

assurance [asyʀɑ̃s] *nf* (*certitude*) assurance; (*confiance en soi*) (self-)confidence; (*contrat*) insurance (policy); (*secteur commercial*) insurance; **prendre une ~ contre** to take out insurance *ou* an insurance policy against; ~ **contre l'incendie** fire insurance; ~ **contre le vol** insurance against theft; **société d'~, compagnie d'~s** insurance company; ~ **maladie (AM)** health insurance; ~ **au tiers** third party insurance; ~ **tous risques** (*AUTO*) comprehensive insurance; **~s sociales (AS)** ≈ National Insurance (*BRIT*), ≈ Social Security (*US*).

assurance-vie, *pl* **assurances-vie** [asyʀɑ̃svi] *nf* life assurance *ou* insurance.

assurance-vol, *pl* **assurances-vol** [asyʀɑ̃svɔl] *nf* insurance against theft.

assuré, e [asyʀe] *adj* (*victoire etc*) certain, sure; (*démarche, voix*) assured, (self-)confident; (*certain*): ~ **de** confident of; (*ASSURANCES*) insured ♦ *nm/f* insured (person); ~ **social** ≈ member of the National Insurance (*BRIT*) *ou* Social Security (*US*) scheme.

assurément [asyʀemɑ̃] *adv* assuredly, most certainly.

assurer [asyʀe] *vt* (*COMM*) to insure; (*stabiliser*) to steady, stabilize; (*victoire etc*) to ensure, make certain; (*frontières, pouvoir*) to make secure; (*service, garde*) to provide, operate; ~ **qch à qn** (*garantir*) to secure *ou* guarantee sth for sb; (*certifier*) to assure sb of sth; ~ **à qn que** to assure sb that; **je vous assure que non/si** I assure you that that is not the case/is the case; ~ **qn de** to assure sb of; ~ **ses arrières** (*fig*) to be sure one has something to fall back on; **s'~ (contre)** (*COMM*) to insure o.s. (against); **s'~ de/que** (*vérifier*) to make sure of/that: **s'~ (de)** (*aide*

de qn) to secure; **s'~ sur la vie** to take out a life insurance; **s'~ le concours/la collaboration de qn** to secure sb's aid/collaboration.
assureur [asyʀœʀ] *nm* insurance agent; (*société*) insurers *pl*.
Assyrie [asiʀi] *nf*: **l'~** Assyria.
assyrien, ne [asiʀjɛ̃, -ɛn] *adj* Assyrian ♦ *nm/f*: **A~, ne** Assyrian.
astérisque [asteʀisk(ə)] *nm* asterisk.
astéroïde [asteʀɔid] *nm* asteroid.
asthmatique [asmatik] *adj* asthmatic.
asthme [asm(ə)] *nm* asthma.
asticot [astiko] *nm* maggot.
asticoter [astikɔte] *vt* (*fam*) to needle, get at.
astigmate [astigmat] *adj* (*MÉD*: *personne*) astigmatic, having an astigmatism.
astiquer [astike] *vt* to polish, shine.
astrakan [astʀakɑ̃] *nm* astrakhan.
astral, e, aux [astʀal, -o] *adj* astral.
astre [astʀ(ə)] *nm* star.
astreignant, e [astʀɛɲɑ̃, -ɑ̃t] *adj* demanding.
astreindre [astʀɛ̃dʀ(ə)] *vt*: **~ qn à qch** to force sth upon sb; **~ qn à faire** to compel *ou* force sb to do; **s'~ à** to compel *ou* force o.s. to.
astringent, e [astʀɛ̃ʒɑ̃, -ɑ̃t] *adj* astringent.
astrologie [astʀɔlɔʒi] *nf* astrology.
astrologique [astʀɔlɔʒik] *adj* astrological.
astrologue [astʀɔlɔg] *nm/f* astrologer.
astronaute [astʀɔnot] *nm/f* astronaut.
astronautique [astʀɔnotik] *nf* astronautics *sg*.
astronome [astʀɔnɔm] *nm/f* astronomer.
astronomie [astʀɔnɔmi] *nf* astronomy.
astronomique [astʀɔnɔmik] *adj* astronomic(al).
astrophysicien, ne [astʀɔfizisjɛ̃, -ɛn] *nm/f* astrophysicist.
astrophysique [astʀɔfizik] *nf* astrophysics *sg*.
astuce [astys] *nf* shrewdness, astuteness; (*truc*) trick, clever way; (*plaisanterie*) wisecrack.
astucieusement [astysjøzmɑ̃] *adv* shrewdly, cleverly, astutely.
astucieux, euse [astysjø, -øz] *adj* shrewd, clever, astute.
asymétrique [asimetʀik] *adj* asymmetric(al).
AT *sigle m* (= *Ancien Testament*) OT.
atavisme [atavism(ə)] *nm* atavism, heredity.
atelier [atəlje] *nm* workshop; (*de peintre*) studio.
atermoiements [atɛʀmwamɑ̃] *nmpl* procrastination *sg*.
atermoyer [atɛʀmwaje] *vi* to temporize, procrastinate.
athée [ate] *adj* atheistic ♦ *nm/f* atheist.
athéisme [ateism(ə)] *nm* atheism.
Athènes [atɛn] *n* Athens.
athénien, ne [atenjɛ̃, -ɛn] *adj* Athenian.
athlète [atlɛt] *nm/f* (*SPORT*) athlete; (*costaud*) muscleman.
athlétique [atletik] *adj* athletic.
athlétisme [atletism(ə)] *nm* athletics *sg*; **faire de l'~** to do athletics; **tournoi d'~** athletics meeting.
Atlantide [atlɑ̃tid] *nf*: **l'~** Atlantis.
atlantique [atlɑ̃tik] *adj* Atlantic ♦ *nm*: **l'(océan) A~** the Atlantic (Ocean).
atlantiste [atlɑ̃tist(ə)] *adj, nm/f* Atlanticist.
Atlas [atlɑs] *nm*: **l'~** the Atlas Mountains.
atlas [atlɑs] *nm* atlas.
atmosphère [atmɔsfɛʀ] *nf* atmosphere.
atmosphérique [atmɔsfeʀik] *adj* atmospheric.
atoll [atɔl] *nm* atoll.
atome [atom] *nm* atom.
atomique [atɔmik] *adj* atomic, nuclear; (*usine*) nuclear; (*nombre, masse*) atomic.
atomiseur [atɔmizœʀ] *nm* atomizer.
atomiste [atɔmist(ə)] *nm/f* (*aussi*: **savant, ingénieur** *etc* ~) atomic scientist.
atone [atɔn] *adj* lifeless; (*LING*) unstressed, unaccented.
atours [atuʀ] *nmpl* attire *sg*, finery *sg*.
atout [atu] *nm* trump; (*fig*) asset; (*: plus fort*) trump card; **"~ pique/trèfle"** "spades/clubs are trumps".
ATP *sigle f* (= *Association des tennismen professionnels*) ATP (= *Association of Tennis Professionals*) ♦ *sigle mpl* (= *arts et traditions populaires*): **musée des ~** ≈ folk museum.
âtre [ɑtʀ(ə)] *nm* hearth.
atroce [atʀɔs] *adj* atrocious, horrible.
atrocement [atʀɔsmɑ̃] *adv* atrociously, horribly.
atrocité [atʀɔsite] *nf* atrocity.
atrophie [atʀɔfi] *nf* atrophy.
atrophier [atʀɔfje]: **s'~** *vi* to atrophy.
atropine [atʀɔpin] *nf* (*CHIMIE*) atropine.
attabler [atable]: **s'~** *vi* to sit down at (the) table; **s'~ à la terrasse** to sit down (at a table) on the terrace.
attachant, e [ataʃɑ̃, -ɑ̃t] *adj* engaging, likeable.
attache [ataʃ] *nf* clip, fastener; (*fig*) tie; **~s** *nfpl* (*relations*) connections; **à l'~** (*chien*) tied up.
attaché, e [ataʃe] *adj*: **être ~ à** (*aimer*) to be attached to ♦ *nm* (*ADMIN*) attaché; **~ de presse/d'ambassade** press/embassy attaché; **~ commercial** commercial attaché.
attaché-case [ataʃekɛz] *nm inv* attaché case (*BRIT*), briefcase.
attachement [ataʃmɑ̃] *nm* attachment.
attacher [ataʃe] *vt* to tie up; (*étiquette*) to attach, tie on; (*souliers*) to do up ♦ *vi* (*poêle, riz*) to stick; **s'~** (*robe etc*) to do up; **s'~ à** (*par affection*) to become attached to; **s'~ à faire qch** to endeavour to do sth; **~ qch à** to tie *ou* fasten *ou* attach sth to; **~ qn à** (*fig: lier*) to attach sb to; **~ du prix/de l'importance à** to attach great value/attach importance to.
attaquant [atakɑ̃] *nm* (*MIL*) attacker; (*SPORT*) striker, forward.
attaque [atak] *nf* attack; (*cérébrale*) stroke; (*d'épilepsie*) fit; **être/se sentir d'~** to be/feel on form; **~ à main armée** armed attack.
attaquer [atake] *vt* to attack; (*en justice*) to

bring an action against, sue; (*travail*) to tackle, set about ♦ *vi* to attack; **s'~ à** to attack; (*épidémie, misère*) to tackle, attack.

attardé, e [ataʀde] *adj* (*passants*) late; (*enfant*) backward; (*conceptions*) old-fashioned.

attarder [ataʀde]: **s'~** *vi* (*sur qch, en chemin*) to linger; (*chez qn*) to stay on.

atteignais [ateɲɛ] *etc vb voir* **atteindre**.

atteindre [atɛ̃dʀ(ə)] *vt* to reach; (*blesser*) to hit; (*contacter*) to reach, contact, get in touch with; (*émouvoir*) to affect.

atteint, e [atɛ̃, -ɛ̃t] *pp de* **atteindre** ♦ *adj* (*MÉD*): **être ~ de** to be suffering from ♦ *nf* attack; **hors d'~e** out of reach; **porter ~e à** to strike a blow at, undermine.

attelage [atlaʒ] *nm* (*de remorque etc*) coupling (*BRIT*), (trailer) hitch (*US*); (*animaux*) team; (*harnachement*) harness; (*: de bœufs*) yoke.

atteler [atle] *vt* (*cheval, bœufs*) to hitch up; (*wagons*) to couple; **s'~ à** (*travail*) to buckle down to.

attelle [atɛl] *nf* splint.

attenant, e [atnɑ̃, -ɑ̃t] *adj*: **~ (à)** adjoining.

attendant [atɑ̃dɑ̃]: **en ~** *adv* (*dans l'intervalle*) meanwhile, in the meantime.

attendre [atɑ̃dʀ(ə)] *vt* to wait for; (*être destiné ou réservé à*) to await, be in store for ♦ *vi* to wait; **je n'attends plus rien (de la vie)** I expect nothing more (from life); **attendez que je réfléchisse** wait while I think; **s'~ à (ce que)** (*escompter*) to expect (that); **je ne m'y attendais pas** I didn't expect that; **ce n'est pas ce à quoi je m'attendais** that's not what I expected; **~ un enfant** to be expecting a baby; **~ de pied ferme** to wait determinedly; **~ de faire/d'être** to wait until one does/is; **~ que** to wait until; **~ qch de** to expect sth of; **faire ~ qn** to keep sb waiting; **se faire ~** to keep people (*ou* us *etc*) waiting; **en attendant** *adv voir* **attendant**.

attendri, e [atɑ̃dʀi] *adj* tender.

attendrir [atɑ̃dʀiʀ] *vt* to move (to pity); (*viande*) to tenderize; **s'~ (sur)** to be moved *ou* touched (by).

attendrissant, e [atɑ̃dʀisɑ̃, -ɑ̃t] *adj* moving, touching.

attendrissement [atɑ̃dʀismɑ̃] *nm* (*tendre*) emotion; (*apitoyé*) pity.

attendrisseur [atɑ̃dʀisœʀ] *nm* tenderizer.

attendu, e [atɑ̃dy] *pp de* **attendre** ♦ *adj* long-awaited; (*prévu*) expected ♦ *nm*: **~s** *reasons adduced for a judgment*; **~ que** *conj* considering that, since.

attentat [atɑ̃ta] *nm* (*contre une personne*) assassination attempt; (*contre un bâtiment*) attack; **~ à la bombe** bomb attack; **~ à la pudeur** (*exhibitionnisme*) indecent exposure *no pl*; (*agression*) indecent assault *no pl*.

attente [atɑ̃t] *nf* wait; (*espérance*) expectation; **contre toute ~** contrary to (all) expectations.

attenter [atɑ̃te]: **~ à** *vt* (*liberté*) to violate; **~ à la vie de qn** to make an attempt on sb's life; **~ à ses jours** to make an attempt on one's life.

attentif, ive [atɑ̃tif, -iv] *adj* (*auditeur*) attentive; (*soin*) scrupulous; (*travail*) careful; **~ à** paying attention to; (*devoir*) mindful of; **~ à faire** careful to do.

attention [atɑ̃sjɔ̃] *nf* attention; (*prévenance*) attention, thoughtfulness *no pl*; **mériter ~** to be worthy of attention; **à l'~ de** for the attention of; **porter qch à l'~ de qn** to bring sth to sb's attention; **attirer l'~ de qn sur qch** to draw sb's attention to sth; **faire ~ (à)** to be careful (of); **faire ~ (à ce) que** to be *ou* make sure that; **~!** careful!, watch!, watch *ou* mind (*BRIT*) out!; **~, si vous ouvrez cette lettre** (*sanction*) just watch out, if you open that letter; **~, respectez les consignes de sécurité** be sure to observe the safety instructions.

attentionné, e [atɑ̃sjɔne] *adj* thoughtful, considerate.

attentisme [atɑ̃tism(ə)] *nm* wait-and-see policy.

attentiste [atɑ̃tist(ə)] *adj* (*politique*) wait-and-see ♦ *nm/f* believer in a wait-and-see policy.

attentivement [atɑ̃tivmɑ̃] *adv* attentively.

atténuant, e [atenɥɑ̃, -ɑ̃t] *adj*: **circonstances ~es** extenuating circumstances.

atténuer [atenɥe] *vt* to alleviate, ease; (*diminuer*) to lessen; (*amoindrir*) to mitigate the effects of; **s'~** *vi* to ease; (*violence etc*) to abate.

atterrer [ateʀe] *vt* to dismay, appal.

atterrir [ateʀiʀ] *vi* to land.

atterrissage [ateʀisaʒ] *nm* landing; **~ sur le ventre/sans visibilité/forcé** belly/blind/forced landing.

attestation [atɛstɑsjɔ̃] *nf* certificate, testimonial; **~ médicale** doctor's certificate.

attester [atɛste] *vt* to testify to, vouch for; (*démontrer*) to attest, testify to; **~ que** to testify that.

attiédir [atjediʀ]: **s'~** *vi* to become lukewarm; (*fig*) to cool down.

attifé, e [atife] *adj* (*fam*) got up (*BRIT*), decked out.

attifer [atife] *vt* to get (*BRIT*) *ou* do up, deck out.

attique [atik] *nm*: **appartement en ~** penthouse (flat (*BRIT*) *ou* apartment (*US*)).

attirail [atiʀaj] *nm* gear; (*péj*) paraphernalia.

attirance [atiʀɑ̃s] *nf* attraction; (*séduction*) lure.

attirant, e [atiʀɑ̃, -ɑ̃t] *adj* attractive, appealing.

attirer [atiʀe] *vt* to attract; (*appâter*) to lure, entice; **~ qn dans un coin/vers soi** to draw sb into a corner/towards one; **~ l'attention de qn** to attract sb's attention; **~ l'attention de qn sur qch** to draw sb's attention to sth; **~ des ennuis à qn** to make trouble for sb;

s'~ des ennuis to bring trouble upon o.s., get into trouble.
attiser [atize] *vt* (*feu*) to poke (up), stir up; (*fig*) to fan the flame of, stir up.
attitré, e [atitʀe] *adj* qualified; (*agréé*) accredited, appointed.
attitude [atityd] *nf* attitude; (*position du corps*) bearing.
attouchements [atuʃmɑ̃] *nmpl* touching *sg*; (*sexuels*) fondling *sg*, stroking *sg*.
attractif, ive [atʀaktif, -iv] *adj* attractive.
attraction [atʀaksjɔ̃] *nf* attraction; (*de cabaret, cirque*) number.
attrait [atʀɛ] *nm* appeal, attraction; (*plus fort*) lure; **~s** *nmpl* attractions; **éprouver de l'~ pour** to be attracted to.
attrape [atʀap] *nf voir* **farce**.
attrape-nigaud [atʀapnigo] *nm* con.
attraper [atʀape] *vt* to catch; (*habitude, amende*) to get, pick up; (*fam: duper*) to take in (*BRIT*), con.
attrayant, e [atʀɛjɑ̃, -ɑ̃t] *adj* attractive.
attribuer [atʀibɥe] *vt* (*prix*) to award; (*rôle, tâche*) to allocate, assign; (*imputer*): **~ qch à** to attribute sth to, ascribe sth to, put sth down to; **s'~** *vt* (*s'approprier*) to claim for o.s.
attribut [atʀiby] *nm* attribute; (*LING*) complement.
attribution [atʀibysjɔ̃] *nf* (*voir attribuer*) awarding; allocation, assignment; attribution; **~s** *nfpl* (*compétence*) attributions; **complément d'~** (*LING*) indirect object.
attristant, e [atʀistɑ̃, -ɑ̃t] *adj* saddening.
attrister [atʀiste] *vt* to sadden; **s'~ de qch** to be saddened by sth.
attroupement [atʀupmɑ̃] *nm* crowd, mob.
attrouper [atʀupe]: **s'~** *vi* to gather.
au [o] *prép + dét voir* **à**.
aubade [obad] *nf* dawn serenade.
aubaine [obɛn] *nf* godsend; (*financière*) windfall; (*COMM*) bonanza.
aube [ob] *nf* dawn, daybreak; (*REL*) alb; **à l'~** at dawn *ou* daybreak; **à l'~ de** (*fig*) at the dawn of.
aubépine [obepin] *nf* hawthorn.
auberge [obɛʀʒ(ə)] *nf* inn; **~ de jeunesse** youth hostel.
aubergine [obɛʀʒin] *nf* aubergine (*BRIT*), eggplant (*US*).
aubergiste [obɛʀʒist(ə)] *nm/f* inn-keeper, hotel-keeper.
auburn [obœʀn] *adj inv* auburn.
aucun, e [okœ̃, -yn] *dét* no, *tournure négative* + any; (*positif*) any ♦ *pron* none, *tournure négative* + any; (*positif*) any(one); **il n'y a ~ livre** there isn't any book, there is no book; **je n'en vois ~ qui** I can't see any which, I (can) see none which; **~ homme** no man; **sans ~ doute** without any doubt; **sans ~e hésitation** without hesitation; **plus qu'~ autre** more than any other; **plus qu'~ de ceux qui ...** more than any of those who ...; **en ~e façon** in no way at all; **~ des deux** neither of the two; **~ d'entre eux** none of them; **d'~s** (*certains*) some.
aucunement [okynmɑ̃] *adv* in no way, not in the least.
audace [odas] *nf* daring, boldness; (*péj*) audacity; **il a eu l'~ de ...** he had the audacity to ...; **vous ne manquez pas d'~!** you're not lacking in nerve *ou* cheek!
audacieux, euse [odasjø, -øz] *adj* daring, bold.
au-dedans [odədɑ̃] *adv, prép* inside.
au-dehors [odəɔʀ] *adv, prép* outside.
au-delà [odla] *adv* beyond ♦ *nm*: **l'~** the hereafter; **~ de** *prép* beyond.
au-dessous [odsu] *adv* underneath; below; **~ de** *prép* under(neath), below; (*limite, somme etc*) below, under; (*dignité, condition*) below.
au-dessus [odsy] *adv* above; **~ de** *prép* above.
au-devant [odvɑ̃]: **~ de** *prép*: **aller ~ de** to go (out) and meet; (*souhaits de qn*) to anticipate.
audible [odibl(ə)] *adj* audible.
audience [odjɑ̃s] *nf* audience; (*JUR*: *séance*) hearing; **trouver ~ auprès de** to arouse much interest among, get the (interested) attention of.
audimat [odimat] *nm* (*taux d'écoute*) ratings *pl*.
audiogramme [odjɔgʀam] *nm* audiogramme.
audio-visuel, le [odjɔvizɥɛl] *adj* audio-visual ♦ *nm* (*équipement*) audio-visual aids *pl*; (*méthodes*) audio-visual methods *pl*; **l'~** radio and television.
auditeur, trice [oditœʀ, -tʀis] *nm/f* (*à la radio*) listener; (*à une conférence*) member of the audience, listener; **~ libre** unregistered student (*attending lectures*), auditor (*US*).
auditif, ive [oditif, -iv] (*mémoire*) auditory; **appareil ~** hearing aid.
audition [odisjɔ̃] *nf* (*ouïe, écoute*) hearing (*JUR*: *de témoins*) examination; (*MUS, THÉÂT épreuve*) audition.
auditionner [odisjɔne] *vt, vi* to audition.
auditoire [oditwaʀ] *nm* audience.
auditorium [oditɔʀjɔm] *nm* (public) studio.
auge [oʒ] *nf* trough.
augmentation [ɔgmɑ̃tɑsjɔ̃] *nf* (*action*) increasing; raising; (*résultat*) increase; **~ (de salaire)** rise (in salary) (*BRIT*), (pay) raise (*US*).
augmenter [ɔgmɑ̃te] *vt* to increase; (*salaire, prix*) to increase, raise, put up; (*employé*) to increase the salary of, give a (salary) rise (*BRIT*) *ou* (pay) raise (*US*) to ♦ *vi* to increase; **~ de poids/volume** to gain (in) weight/volume.
augure [ɔgyʀ] *nm* soothsayer, oracle; **de bon/mauvais ~** of good/ill omen.
augurer [ɔgyʀe] *vt*: **~ qch de** to foresee sth (coming) from *ou* out of; **~ bien de** to augur well for.
auguste [ɔgyst(ə)] *adj* august, noble, majestic.

aujourd'hui [oʒuʀdɥi] *adv* today; ~ **en huit/quinze** a week/two weeks today, a week/two weeks from now; **à dater** *ou* **partir d'**~ from today('s date).
aumône [ɔmon] *nf* alms *sg* (*pl inv*); **faire l'**~ **(à qn)** to give alms (to sb); **faire l'**~ **de qch à qn** (*fig*) to favour sb with sth.
aumônerie [ɔmonʀi] *nf* chaplaincy.
aumônier [ɔmonje] *nm* chaplain.
auparavant [opaʀavɑ̃] *adv* before(hand).
auprès [opʀɛ]: ~ **de** *prép* next to, close to; (*recourir, s'adresser*) to; (*en comparaison de*) compared with, next to; (*dans l'opinion de*) in the opinion of.
auquel [okɛl] *prép + pron voir* **lequel**.
aurai [ɔʀe] *etc vb voir* **avoir**.
auréole [ɔʀeɔl] *nf* halo; (*tache*) ring.
auréolé, e [ɔʀeɔle] *adj* (*fig*): ~ **de gloire** crowned with *ou* in glory.
auriculaire [ɔʀikylɛʀ] *nm* little finger.
aurore [ɔʀɔʀ] *nf* dawn, daybreak; ~ **boréale** northern lights *pl*.
ausculter [ɔskylte] *vt* to sound.
auspices [ɔspis] *nmpl*: **sous les** ~ **de** under the patronage *ou* auspices of; **sous de bons/mauvais** ~ under favourable/unfavourable auspices.
aussi [osi] *adv* (*également*) also, too; (*de comparaison*) as ♦ *conj* therefore, consequently; ~ **fort que** as strong as; **lui** ~ (*sujet*) he too; (*objet*) him too; ~ **bien que** (*de même que*) as well as.
aussitôt [osito] *adv* straight away, immediately; ~ **que** as soon as; ~ **envoyé** as soon as it is (*ou* was) sent; ~ **fait** no sooner done.
austère [ɔstɛʀ] *adj* austere; (*sévère*) stern.
austérité [ɔsteʀite] *nf* austerity; **plan/budget d'**~ austerity plan/budget.
austral, e [ɔstʀal] *adj* southern; **l'océan A**~ the Antarctic Ocean; **les Terres A~es** Antarctica.
Australie [ɔstʀali] *nf*: **l'**~ Australia.
australien, ne [ɔstʀaljɛ̃, -ɛn] *adj* Australian ♦ *nm/f*: **A~, ne** Australian.
autant [otɑ̃] *adv* so much; (*comparatif*): ~ **(que)** as much (as); (*nombre*) as many (as); ~ **(de)** so much (*ou* many); as much (*ou* many); **n'importe qui aurait pu en faire** ~ anyone could have done the same *ou* as much; ~ **partir** we (*ou* you *etc*) may as well leave; ~ **ne rien dire** best not say anything; ~ **dire que** ... one might as well say that ...; **fort** ~ **que courageux** as strong as he is brave; **il n'est pas découragé pour** ~ he isn't discouraged for all that; **pour** ~ **que** *conj* assuming, as long as; **d'**~ *adv* accordingly, in proportion; **d'**~ **plus/mieux (que)** all the more/the better (since).
autarcie [otaʀsi] *nf* autarky, self-sufficiency.
autel [ɔtɛl] *nm* altar.
auteur [otœʀ] *nm* author; **l'**~ **de cette remarque** the person who said that; **droit d'**~ copyright.
auteur-compositeur [otœʀkɔ̃pozitœʀ] *nm/f* composer-songwriter.
authenticité [ɔtɑ̃tisite] *nf* authenticity.
authentifier [ɔtɑ̃tifje] *vt* to authenticate.
authentique [ɔtɑ̃tik] *adj* authentic, genuine.
autiste [otist] *adj* autistic.
auto [ɔto] *nf* car; **~s tamponneuses** bumper cars, dodgems.
auto... [ɔto] *préfixe* auto..., self-.
autobiographie [ɔtɔbjɔgʀafi] *nf* autobiography.
autobiographique [ɔtɔbjɔgʀafik] *adj* autobiographical.
autobronzant [ɔtɔbʀɔ̃zɑ̃] *nm* self-tanning cream (*or* lotion *etc*).
autobus [ɔtɔbys] *nm* bus.
autocar [ɔtɔkaʀ] *nm* coach.
autochtone [ɔtɔktɔn] *nm/f* native.
autocollant, e [ɔtɔkɔlɑ̃, -ɑ̃t] *adj* self-adhesive; (*enveloppe*) self-seal ♦ *nm* sticker.
auto-couchettes [ɔtɔkuʃɛt] *adj inv*: **train** ~ car sleeper train, motorail ® train (*BRIT*).
autocratique [ɔtɔkʀatik] *adj* autocratic.
autocritique [ɔtɔkʀitik] *nf* self-criticism.
autocuiseur [ɔtɔkwizœʀ] *nm* (*CULIN*) pressure cooker.
autodéfense [ɔtɔdefɑ̃s] *nf* self-defence; **groupe d'**~ vigilante committee.
autodétermination [ɔtɔdetɛʀminɑsjɔ̃] *nf* self-determination.
autodidacte [ɔtɔdidakt(ə)] *nm/f* self-taught person.
autodiscipline [ɔtɔdisiplin] *nf* self-discipline.
autodrome [ɔtɔdʀom] *nm* motor-racing stadium.
auto-école [ɔtɔekɔl] *nf* driving school.
autofinancement [ɔtɔfinɑ̃smɑ̃] *nm* self-financing.
autogéré, e [ɔtɔʒeʀe] *adj* self-managed, managed internally.
autogestion [ɔtɔʒɛstjɔ̃] *nf* joint worker-management control.
autographe [ɔtɔgʀaf] *nm* autograph.
autoguidé, e [ɔtɔgide] *adj* self-guided.
auto-immun, e [ɔtɔimœ̃, -yn] *adj* autoimmune.
automate [ɔtɔmat] *nm* (*robot*) automaton; (*machine*) (automatic) machine.
automatique [ɔtɔmatik] *adj, nm* automatic; **l'**~ (*TÉL*) ≈ direct dialling.
automatiquement [ɔtɔmatikmɑ̃] *adv* automatically.
automatisation [ɔtɔmatizɑsjɔ̃] *nf* automation.
automatiser [ɔtɔmatize] *vt* to automate.
automédication [ɔtɔmedikɑsjɔ̃] *nf* self-medication.
automitrailleuse [ɔtɔmitʀɑjøz] *nf* armoured car.
automnal, e, aux [ɔtɔnal, -o] *adj* autumnal.
automne [ɔtɔn] *nm* autumn (*BRIT*), fall (*US*).
automobile [ɔtɔmɔbil] *adj* motor *cpd* ♦ *nf* (mo-

tor) car; **l'~** motoring; (*industrie*) the car *ou* automobile (*US*) industry.

automobiliste [ɔtɔmɔbilist(ə)] *nm/f* motorist.

autonettoyant, e [ɔtɔnɛtwajɑ̃, -ɑ̃t] *adj*: **four ~** self-cleaning oven.

autonome [ɔtɔnɔm] *adj* autonomous; (*INFORM*) stand-alone; **(en mode) ~** off line.

autonomie [ɔtɔnɔmi] *nf* autonomy; (*POL*) self-government, autonomy; **~ de vol** range.

autonomiste [ɔtɔnɔmist(ə)] *nm/f* separatist.

autoportrait [ɔtɔpɔʀtʀɛ] *nm* self-portrait.

autopsie [ɔtɔpsi] *nf* post-mortem (examination), autopsy.

autopsier [ɔtɔpsje] *vt* to carry out a post-mortem *ou* an autopsy on.

autoradio [ɔtɔʀadjo] *nf* car radio.

autorail [ɔtɔʀɑj] *nm* railcar.

autorisation [ɔtɔʀizɑsjɔ̃] *nf* permission, authorization; (*papiers*) permit; **donner à qn l'~ de** to give sb permission to, authorize sb to; **avoir l'~ de faire** to be allowed *ou* have permission to do, be authorized to do.

autorisé, e [ɔtɔʀize] *adj* (*opinion, sources*) authoritative; (*permis*): **~ à faire** authorized *ou* permitted to do; **dans les milieux ~s** in official circles.

autoriser [ɔtɔʀize] *vt* to give permission for, authorize; (*fig*) to allow (of), sanction; **~ qn à faire** to give permission to sb to do, authorize sb to do.

autoritaire [ɔtɔʀitɛʀ] *adj* authoritarian.

autoritarisme [ɔtɔʀitaʀism(ə)] *nm* authoritarianism.

autorité [ɔtɔʀite] *nf* authority; **faire ~** to be authoritative; **~s constituées** constitutional authorities.

autoroute [ɔtɔʀut] *nf* motorway (*BRIT*), expressway (*US*); **~ de l'information** information superhighway.

autoroutier, ière [ɔtɔʀutje, -jɛʀ] *adj* motorway *cpd* (*BRIT*), expressway *cpd* (*US*).

autosatisfaction [ɔtɔsatisfaksjɔ̃] *nf* self-satisfaction.

auto-stop [ɔtɔstɔp] *nm*: **l'~** hitch-hiking; **faire de l'~** to hitch-hike; **prendre qn en ~** to give sb a lift.

auto-stoppeur, euse [ɔtɔstɔpœʀ, -øz] *nm/f* hitch-hiker, hitcher (*BRIT*).

autosuffisant, e [ɔtɔsyfizɑ̃, -ɑ̃t] *adj* self-sufficient.

autosuggestion [ɔtɔsygʒɛstjɔ̃] *nf* autosuggestion.

autour [otuʀ] *adv* around; **~ de** *prép* around; (*environ*) around, about; **tout ~** *adv* all around.

MOT-CLÉ

autre [otʀ(ə)] *adj* **1** (*différent*) other, different; **je préférerais un ~ verre** I'd prefer another *ou* a different glass; **d'~s verres** different glasses; **se sentir ~** to feel different; **la difficulté est ~** the difficulty is *ou* lies elsewhere

2 (*supplémentaire*) other; **je voudrais un ~ verre d'eau** I'd like another glass of water

3: **~ chose** something else; **~ part** somewhere else; **d'~ part** on the other hand

♦ *pron* **1**: **un ~** another (one); **nous/vous ~s** us/you; **d'~s** others; **l'~** the other (one); **les ~s** the others; (*autrui*) others; **l'un et l'~** both of them; **ni l'un ni l'~** neither of them; **se détester l'un l'~/les uns les ~s** to hate each other *ou* one another; **d'une semaine/minute à l'~** from one week/minute *ou* moment to the next; (*incessamment*) any week/minute *ou* moment now; **de temps à ~** from time to time; **entre ~s** among other things

2 (*expressions*): **j'en ai vu d'~s** I've seen worse; **à d'~s!** pull the other one!

---

autrefois [otʀəfwa] *adv* in the past.

autrement [otʀəmɑ̃] *adv* differently; (*d'une manière différente*) in another way; (*sinon*) otherwise; **je n'ai pas pu faire ~** I couldn't do anything else, I couldn't do otherwise; **~ dit** in other words; (*c'est-à-dire*) that is to say.

Autriche [otʀiʃ] *nf*: **l'~** Austria.

autrichien, ne [otʀiʃjɛ̃, -ɛn] *adj* Austrian ♦ *nm/f*: **A~, ne** Austrian.

autruche [otʀyʃ] *nf* ostrich; **faire l'~** (*fig*) to bury one's head in the sand.

autrui [otʀɥi] *pron* others.

auvent [ovɑ̃] *nm* canopy.

auvergnat, e [ɔvɛʀɲa, -at] *adj* of *ou* from the Auvergne.

Auvergne [ɔvɛʀɲ(ə)] *nf*: **l'~** the Auvergne.

aux [o] *prép + dét voir* **à**.

auxiliaire [ɔksiljɛʀ] *adj, nm/f* auxiliary.

auxquels, auxquelles [okɛl] *prép + pron voir* **lequel**.

AV *sigle m* (*BANQUE*: = *avis de virement*) *advice of bank transfer* ♦ *abr* (*AUTO*) = **avant**.

av. *abr* (= *avenue*) Av(e).

avachi, e [avaʃi] *adj* limp, flabby; (*chaussure, vêtement*) out-of-shape; (*personne*): **~ sur qch** slumped on *ou* across sth.

avais [avɛ] *etc vb voir* **avoir**.

aval [aval] *nm* (*accord*) endorsement, backing; (*GÉO*): **en ~** downstream, downriver; (*sur une pente*) downhill; **en ~ de** downstream *ou* downriver from; downhill from.

avalanche [avalɑ̃ʃ] *nf* avalanche; **~ poudreuse** powder snow avalanche.

avaler [avale] *vt* to swallow.

avaliser [avalize] *vt* (*plan, entreprise*) to back support; (*COMM, JUR*) to guarantee.

avance [avɑ̃s] *nf* (*de troupes etc*) advance (*progrès*) progress; (*d'argent*) advance; (*opposé à retard*) lead; being ahead of schedule **~s** *nfpl* overtures; (*amoureuses*) advances **une ~ de 300 m/4 h** (*SPORT*) a 300 m/4 hour lead; **(être) en ~** (to be) early; (*sur un programme*) (to be) ahead of schedule; **on n'est**

pas en ~! we're kind of late!; **être en ~ sur qn** to be ahead of sb; **d'~, à l'~, par ~** in advance; **~ (du) papier** (*INFORM*) paper advance.

avancé, e [avɑ̃se] *adj* advanced; (*travail etc*) well on, well under way; (*fruit, fromage*) overripe ♦ *nf* projection; overhang; **il est ~ pour son âge** he is advanced for his age.

avancement [avɑ̃smɑ̃] *nm* (*professionnel*) promotion; (*de travaux*) progress.

avancer [avɑ̃se] *vi* to move forward, advance; (*projet, travail*) to make progress; (*être en saillie*) to overhang; to project; (*montre, réveil*) to be fast; (*: d'habitude*) to gain ♦ *vt* to move forward, advance; (*argent*) to advance; (*montre, pendule*) to put forward; (*faire progresser: travail etc*) to advance, move on; **s'~** *vi* to move forward, advance; (*fig*) to commit o.s.; (*faire saillie*) to overhang; to project; **j'avance (d'une heure)** I'm (an hour) fast.

avanies [avani] *nfpl* snubs (*BRIT*), insults.

avant [avɑ̃] *prép* before ♦ *adv*: **trop/plus ~** too far/further forward ♦ *adj inv*: **siège/roue ~** front seat/wheel ♦ *nm* front; (*SPORT: joueur*) forward; **~ qu'il parte/de partir** before he leaves/leaving; **~ qu'il (ne) pleuve** before it rains (*ou* rained); **~ tout** (*surtout*) above all; **à l'~** (*dans un véhicule*) in (the) front; **en ~** *adv* forward(s); **en ~ de** *prép* in front of; **aller de l'~** to steam ahead (*fig*), make good progress.

avantage [avɑ̃taʒ] *nm* advantage; (*TENNIS*): **~ service/dehors** advantage *ou* van (*BRIT*) *ou* ad (*US*) in/out; **tirer ~ de** to take advantage of; **vous auriez ~ à faire** you would be well-advised to do, it would be to your advantage to do; **à l'~ de qn** to sb's advantage; **être à son ~** to be at one's best; **~s en nature** benefits in kind; **~s sociaux** fringe benefits.

avantager [avɑ̃taʒe] *vt* (*favoriser*) to favour; (*embellir*) to flatter.

avantageux, euse [avɑ̃taʒø, -øz] *adj* attractive; (*intéressant*) attractively priced; (*portrait, coiffure*) flattering; **conditions avantageuses** favourable terms.

avant-bras [avɑ̃bʀa] *nm inv* forearm.

avant-centre [avɑ̃sɑ̃tʀ(ə)] *nm* centre-forward.

avant-coureur [avɑ̃kuʀœʀ] *adj inv* (*bruit etc*) precursory; **signe ~** advance indication *ou* sign.

avant-dernier, ière [avɑ̃dɛʀnje, -jɛʀ] *adj, nm/f* next to last, last but one.

avant-garde [avɑ̃gaʀd(ə)] *nf* (*MIL*) vanguard; (*fig*) avant-garde; **d'~** avant-garde.

avant-goût [avɑ̃gu] *nm* foretaste.

avant-hier [avɑ̃tjɛʀ] *adv* the day before yesterday.

avant-poste [avɑ̃pɔst(ə)] *nm* outpost.

avant-première [avɑ̃pʀəmjɛʀ] *nf* (*de film*) preview; **en ~** as a preview, in a preview showing.

avant-projet [avɑ̃pʀɔʒɛ] *nm* preliminary draft.

avant-propos [avɑ̃pʀɔpo] *nm* foreword.

avant-veille [avɑ̃vɛj] *nf*: **l'~** two days before.

avare [avaʀ] *adj* miserly, avaricious ♦ *nm/f* miser; **~ de compliments** stingy *ou* sparing with one's compliments.

avarice [avaʀis] *nf* avarice, miserliness.

avaricieux, euse [avaʀisjø, -øz] *adj* miserly, niggardly.

avarié, e [avaʀje] *adj* (*viande, fruits*) rotting, going off (*BRIT*); (*NAVIG: navire*) damaged.

avaries [avaʀi] *nfpl* (*NAVIG*) damage *sg*.

avatar [avataʀ] *nm* misadventure; (*transformation*) metamorphosis (*pl* -phoses).

avec [avɛk] *prép* with; (*à l'égard de*) to(wards), with ♦ *adv* (*fam*) with it (*ou* him *etc*); **~ habileté/lenteur** skilfully/slowly; **~ eux/ces maladies** with them/these diseases; **~ ça** (*malgré ça*) for all that; **et ~ ça?** (*dans un magasin*) anything *ou* something else?

avenant, e [avnɑ̃, -ɑ̃t] *adj* pleasant ♦ *nm* (*ASSURANCES*) additional clause; **à l'~** *adv* in keeping.

avènement [avɛnmɑ̃] *nm* (*d'un roi*) accession, succession; (*d'un changement*) advent; (*d'une politique, idée*) coming.

avenir [avniʀ] *nm*: **l'~** the future; **à l'~** in future; **sans ~** with no future, without a future; **carrière/politicien d'~** career/politician with prospects *ou* a future.

Avent [avɑ̃] *nm*: **l'~** Advent.

aventure [avɑ̃tyʀ] *nf*: **l'~** adventure; **une ~** an adventure; (*amoureuse*) an affair; **partir à l'~** to go off in search of adventure; (*au hasard*) to go where one's fancy takes one; **roman/film d'~** adventure story/film.

aventurer [avɑ̃tyʀe] *vt* (*somme, réputation, vie*) to stake; (*remarque, opinion*) to venture; **s'~** *vi* to venture; **s'~ à faire qch** to venture into sth.

aventureux, euse [avɑ̃tyʀø, -øz] *adj* adventurous, venturesome; (*projet*) risky, chancy.

aventurier, ière [avɑ̃tyʀje, -jɛʀ] *nm/f* adventurer ♦ *nf* (*péj*) adventuress.

avenu, e [avny] *adj*: **nul et non ~** null and void.

avenue [avny] *nf* avenue.

avéré, e [aveʀe] *adj* recognized, acknowledged.

avérer [aveʀe]: **s'~** *vb avec attribut*: **s'~ faux/coûteux** to prove (to be) wrong/expensive.

averse [avɛʀs(ə)] *nf* shower.

aversion [avɛʀsjɔ̃] *nf* aversion, loathing.

averti, e [avɛʀti] *adj* (well-)informed.

avertir [avɛʀtiʀ] *vt*: **~ qn (de qch/que)** to warn sb (of sth/that); (*renseigner*) to inform sb (of sth/that); **~ qn de ne pas faire qch** to warn sb not to do sth.

avertissement [avɛʀtismɑ̃] *nm* warning.

avertisseur [avɛʀtisœʀ] *nm* horn, siren; ~

(d'incendie) (fire) alarm.
aveu, x [avø] *nm* confession; **passer aux ~x** to make a confession; **de l'~ de** according to.
aveuglant, e [avœglɑ̃, -ɑ̃t] *adj* blinding.
aveugle [avœgl(ə)] *adj* blind ♦ *nm/f* blind person; **les ~s** the blind; **test en (double) ~** (double) blind test.
aveuglement [avœgləmɑ̃] *nm* blindness.
aveuglément [avœglemɑ̃] *adv* blindly.
aveugler [avœgle] *vt* to blind.
aveuglette [avœglɛt]: **à l'~** groping one's way along; (*fig*) in the dark, blindly.
avez [ave] *vb voir* **avoir.**
aviateur, trice [avjatœʀ, -tʀis] *nm/f* aviator, pilot.
aviation [avjɑsjɔ̃] *nf* (*secteur commercial*) aviation; (*sport, métier de pilote*) flying; (*MIL*) air force; **terrain d'~** airfield; **~ de chasse** fighter force.
aviculteur, trice [avikyltœʀ, -tʀis] *nm/f* poultry farmer; bird breeder.
aviculture [avikyltyʀ] *nf* (*de volailles*) poultry farming.
avide [avid] *adj* eager; (*péj*) greedy, grasping; **~ de** (*sang etc*) thirsting for; **~ d'honneurs/ d'argent** greedy for honours/money; **~ de connaître/d'apprendre** eager to know/learn.
avidité [avidite] *nf* eagerness; greed.
avilir [aviliʀ] *vt* to debase.
avilissant, e [avilisɑ̃, -ɑ̃t] *adj* degrading.
aviné, e [avine] *adj* drunken.
avion [avjɔ̃] *nm* (aero)plane (*BRIT*), (air)plane (*US*); **aller (quelque part) en ~** to go (somewhere) by plane, fly (somewhere); **par ~** by airmail; **~ de chasse** fighter; **~ de ligne** airliner; **~ à réaction** jet (plane).
avion-cargo [avjɔ̃kaʀgo] *nm* air freighter.
avion-citerne [avjɔ̃sitɛʀn(ə)] *nm* air tanker.
aviron [aviʀɔ̃] *nm* oar; (*sport*): **l'~** rowing.
avis [avi] *nm* opinion; (*notification*) notice; (*COMM*): **~ de crédit/débit** credit/debit advice; **à mon ~** in my opinion; **je suis de votre ~** I share your opinion, I am of your opinion; **être d'~ que** to be of the opinion that; **changer d'~** to change one's mind; **sauf ~ contraire** unless you hear to the contrary; **sans ~ préalable** without notice; **jusqu'à nouvel ~** until further notice; **~ de décès** death announcement.
avisé, e [avize] *adj* sensible, wise; **être bien/ mal ~ de faire** to be well-/ill-advised to do.
aviser [avize] *vt* (*voir*) to notice, catch sight of; (*informer*): **~ qn de/que** to advise *ou* inform *ou* notify sb of/that ♦ *vi* to think about things, assess the situation; **s'~ de qch/que** to become suddenly aware of sth/that; **s'~ de faire** to take it into one's head to do.
aviver [avive] *vt* (*douleur, chagrin*) to intensify; (*intérêt, désir*) to sharpen; (*colère, querelle*) to stir up; (*couleur*) to brighten up.
av. J.-C. *abr* (= *avant Jésus-Christ*) BC.
avocat, e [avɔka, -at] *nm/f* (*JUR*) ≈ barrister (*BRIT*), lawyer; (*fig*) advocate, champion ♦ *nm* (*CULIN*) avocado (pear); **se faire l'~ du diable** to be the devil's advocate; **l'~ de la défense/partie civile** the counsel for the defence/plaintiff; **~ d'affaires** business lawyer; **~ général** assistant public prosecutor.
avocat-conseil, *pl* **avocats-conseils** [avɔkakɔ̃sɛj] *nm* ≈ barrister (*BRIT*).
avocat-stagiaire, *pl* **avocats-stagiaires** [avɔkastaʒjɛʀ] *nm* ≈ barrister doing his articles (*BRIT*).
avoine [avwan] *nf* oats *pl.*

MOT-CLÉ

avoir [avwaʀ] *nm* assets *pl*, resources *pl*; (*COMM*) credit; **~ fiscal** tax credit
♦ *vt* **1** (*posséder*) to have; **elle a 2 enfants/une belle maison** she has (got) 2 children/a lovely house; **il a les yeux bleus** he has (got) blue eyes
2 (*éprouver*): **qu'est-ce que tu as?, qu'as-tu?** what's wrong?, what's the matter?; *voir aussi* **faim, peur** *etc*
3 (*âge, dimensions*) to be; **il a 3 ans** he is 3 (years old); **le mur a 3 mètres de haut** the wall is 3 metres high
4 (*fam: duper*) to do, have; **on vous a eu!** you've been done *ou* had!
5: en ~ contre qn to have a grudge against sb; **en ~ assez** to be fed up; **j'en ai pour une demi-heure** it'll take me half an hour; **n'~ que faire de qch** to have no use for sth
♦ *vb aux* **1** to have; **~ mangé/dormi** to have eaten/slept; **hier je n'ai pas mangé** I didn't eat yesterday
2 (*avoir +à +infinitif*): **~ à faire qch** to have to do sth; **vous n'avez qu'à lui demander** you only have to ask him; **tu n'as pas à me poser des questions** it's not for you to ask me questions
♦ *vb impers* **1: il y a** (*+ singulier*) there is; (*+ pluriel*) there are; **qu'y a-t-il?, qu'est-ce qu'il y a?** what's the matter?, what is it?; **il doit y avoir une explication** there must be an explanation; **il n'y a qu'à ...** we (*ou* you *etc*) will just have to ...; **il ne peut y en ~ qu'un** there can only be one
2 (*temporel*): **il y a 10 ans** 10 years ago; **il y a 10 ans/longtemps que je le connais** I've known him for 10 years/a long time; **il y a 10 ans qu'il est arrivé** it's 10 years since he arrived.

avoisinant, e [avwazinɑ̃, -ɑ̃t] *adj* neighbouring.
avoisiner [avwazine] *vt* to be near *ou* close to (*fig*) to border *ou* verge on.
avons [avɔ̃] *vb voir* **avoir.**
avortement [avɔʀtəmɑ̃] *nm* abortion.
avorter [avɔʀte] *vi* (*MÉD*) to have an abortion (*fig*) to fail; **faire ~** to abort; **se faire ~** to have an abortion.

avorton [avɔʀtɔ̃] *nm (péj)* little runt.
avouable [avwabl(ə)] *adj* respectable; **des pensées non ~s** unrepeatable thoughts.
avoué, e [avwe] *adj* avowed ♦ *nm (JUR)* ≈ solicitor *(BRIT)*, lawyer.
avouer [avwe] *vt (crime, défaut)* to confess (to) ♦ *vi (se confesser)* to confess; *(admettre)* to admit; ~ **avoir fait/que** to admit *ou* confess to having done/that; ~ **que oui/non** to admit that that is so/not so.
avril [avʀil] *nm* April; *voir aussi* **juillet**; *see boxed note.*

POISSON D'AVRIL

The traditional April Fools' Day prank in France involves attaching a cut-out paper fish, known as a 'poisson d'avril' to the back of one's victim, without being caught.

axe [aks(ə)] *nm* axis (*pl* axes); *(de roue etc)* axle; **dans l'~ de** directly in line with; *(fig)* main line; ~ **routier** trunk road, main road.
axer [akse] *vt:* ~ **qch sur** to centre sth on.
axial, e, aux [aksjal, -o] *adj* axial.
axiome [aksjom] *nm* axiom.
ayant [ɛjɑ̃] *vb voir* **avoir** ♦ *nm:* ~ **droit** assignee; ~ **droit à** *(pension etc)* person eligible for.
ayons [ɛjɔ̃] *etc vb voir* **avoir.**
azalée [azale] *nf* azalea.
Azerbaïdjan [azɛʀbaidʒɑ̃] *nm* Azerbaijan.
azerbaïdjanais, e [azɛʀbaidʒanɛ, -ɛz] *adj* Azerbaijani ♦ *nm (LING)* Azerbaijani ♦ *nm/f:* **A~, e** Azerbaijani.
azimut [azimyt] *nm* azimuth; **tous ~s** *adj (fig)* omnidirectional.
azote [azɔt] *nm* nitrogen.
azoté, e [azɔte] *adj* nitrogenous.
AZT *sigle m (= azidothymidine)* AZT.
aztèque [aztɛk] *adj* Aztec.
azur [azyʀ] *nm (couleur)* azure, sky blue; *(ciel)* sky, skies *pl.*
azyme [azim] *adj:* **pain ~** unleavened bread.

B b

B, b [be] *nm inv* B, b ♦ *abr* = *bien*; **B comme Bertha** B for Benjamin *(BRIT) ou* Baker *(US).*
BA *sigle f (= bonne action)* good deed.
baba [baba] *adj inv:* **en être ~** *(fam)* to be flabbergasted ♦ *nm:* ~ **au rhum** rum baba.
babil [babi] *nm* prattle.
babillage [babijaʒ] *nm* chatter.
babiller [babije] *vi* to prattle, chatter; *(bébé)* to babble.
babines [babin] *nfpl* chops.
babiole [babjɔl] *nf (bibelot)* trinket; *(vétille)* trifle.
bâbord [bɑbɔʀ] *nm:* **à** *ou* **par ~** to port, on the port side.
babouin [babwɛ̃] *nm* baboon.
baby-foot [babifut] *nm inv* table football.
babylonien, ne [babilɔnjɛ̃, -ɛn] *adj* Babylonian.
baby-sitter [babisitœʀ] *nm/f* baby-sitter.
baby-sitting [babisitiŋ] *nm* baby-sitting.
bac [bak] *nm (SCOL)* = **baccalauréat**; *(bateau)* ferry; *(récipient)* tub; *(: PHOTO etc)* tray; *(: INDUSTRIE)* tank; ~ **à glace** ice-tray; ~ **à légumes** vegetable compartment *ou* rack.
baccalauréat [bakalɔʀea] *nm* ≈ GCE A-levels *pl (BRIT)*, ≈ high school diploma *(US)*; *see boxed note.*

BACCALAURÉAT

The **baccalauréat** *or 'bac' is the school-leaving examination taken at a French 'lycée' at the age of 17 or 18; it marks the end of seven years of secondary education. Several subject combinations are available, although in all cases a broad range is studied. Successful candidates can go on to university, if they so wish.*

bâche [bɑʃ] *nf* tarpaulin, canvas sheet.
bachelier, ière [baʃəlje, -jɛʀ] *nm/f* holder of the baccalauréat.
bâcher [bɑʃe] *vt* to cover (with a canvas sheet *ou* a tarpaulin).
bachot [baʃo] *nm* = **baccalauréat.**
bachotage [baʃɔtaʒ] *nm (SCOL)* cramming.
bachoter [baʃɔte] *vi (SCOL)* to cram.
bacille [basil] *nm* bacillus (*pl* -i).
bâcler [bɑkle] *vt* to botch (up).
bacon [bekɔn] *nm* bacon.
bactéricide [bakteʀisid] *nm (MÉD)* bactericide.
bactérie [bakteʀi] *nf* bacterium (*pl* -ia).
bactérien, ne [bakteʀjɛ̃, -ɛn] *adj* bacterial.
bactériologie [bakteʀjɔlɔʒi] *nf* bacteriology.
bactériologique [bakteʀjɔlɔʒik] *adj* bacteriological.
bactériologiste [bakteʀjɔlɔʒist(ə)] *nm/f* bacteriologist.
badaud, e [bado, -od] *nm/f* idle onlooker.
baderne [badɛʀn(ə)] *nf (péj):* **(vieille) ~** old fossil.
badge [badʒ(ə)] *nm* badge.
badigeon [badiʒɔ̃] *nm* distemper; colourwash.
badigeonner [badiʒɔne] *vt* to distemper; to colourwash; *(péj: barbouiller)* to daub; *(MÉD)* to paint.
badin, e [badɛ̃, -in] *adj* light-hearted, playful.
badinage [badinaʒ] *nm* banter.
badine [badin] *nf* switch *(stick).*
badiner [badine] *vi:* ~ **avec qch** to treat sth lightly; **ne pas ~ avec qch** not to trifle with

sth.

badminton [badmintɔn] *nm* badminton.

BAFA [bafa] *sigle m* (= *Brevet d'aptitude aux fonctions d'animation*) *diploma for youth leaders and workers*.

baffe [baf] *nf* (*fam*) slap, clout.

Baffin [bafin] *nf*: **terre de** ~ Baffin Island.

baffle [bɑfl(ə)] *nm* baffle (board).

bafouer [bafwe] *vt* to deride, ridicule.

bafouillage [bafujaʒ] *nm* (*fam*: *propos incohérents*) jumble of words.

bafouiller [bafuje] *vi, vt* to stammer.

bâfrer [bɑfʀe] *vi, vt* (*fam*) to guzzle, gobble.

bagage [bagaʒ] *nm*: ~**s** luggage *sg*, baggage *sg*; ~ **littéraire** (stock of) literary knowledge; ~**s à main** hand-luggage.

bagarre [bagaʀ] *nf* fight, brawl; **il aime la** ~ he loves a fight, he likes fighting.

bagarrer [bagaʀe]: **se** ~ *vi* to (have a) fight.

bagarreur, euse [bagaʀœʀ, -øz] *adj* pugnacious ♦ *nm/f*: **il est** ~ he loves a fight.

bagatelle [bagatɛl] *nf* trifle, trifling sum (*ou* matter).

Bagdad, Baghdâd [bagdad] *n* Baghdad.

bagnard [baɲaʀ] *nm* convict.

bagne [baɲ] *nm* penal colony; **c'est le** ~ (*fig*) it's forced labour.

bagnole [baɲɔl] *nf* (*fam*) car, wheels *pl* (*BRIT*).

bagout [bagu] *nm* glibness; **avoir du** ~ to have the gift of the gab.

bague [bag] *nf* ring; ~ **de fiançailles** engagement ring; ~ **de serrage** clip.

baguenauder [bagnode]: **se** ~ *vi* to trail around, loaf around.

baguer [bage] *vt* to ring.

baguette [bagɛt] *nf* stick; (*cuisine chinoise*) chopstick; (*de chef d'orchestre*) baton; (*pain*) stick of (French) bread; (*CONSTR*: *moulure*) beading; **mener qn à la** ~ to rule sb with a rod of iron; ~ **magique** magic wand; ~ **de sourcier** divining rod; ~ **de tambour** drumstick.

Bahamas [baamas] *nfpl*: **les (îles)** ~ the Bahamas.

Bahrein [baʀɛn] *nm* Bahrain *ou* Bahrein.

bahut [bay] *nm* chest.

bai, e [bɛ] *adj* (*cheval*) bay.

baie [bɛ] *nf* (*GÉO*) bay; (*fruit*) berry; ~ **(vitrée)** picture window.

baignade [bɛɲad] *nf* (*action*) bathing; (*bain*) bathe; (*endroit*) bathing place.

baigné, e [beɲe] *adj*: ~ **de** bathed in; (*trempé*) soaked with; (*inondé*) flooded with.

baigner [beɲe] *vt* (*bébé*) to bath ♦ *vi*: ~ **dans son sang** to lie in a pool of blood; ~ **dans la brume** to be shrouded in mist; **se** ~ *vi* to go swimming *ou* bathing; (*dans une baignoire*) to have a bath; **ça baigne!** (*fam*) everything's great!

baigneur, euse [bɛɲœʀ, -øz] *nm/f* bather ♦ *nm* (*poupée*) baby doll.

baignoire [bɛɲwaʀ] *nf* bath(tub); (*THÉÂT*) ground-floor box.

bail, baux [baj, bo] *nm* lease; **donner *ou* prendre qch à** ~ to lease sth.

bâillement [bɑjmɑ̃] *nm* yawn.

bâiller [bɑje] *vi* to yawn; (*être ouvert*) to gape.

bailleur [bajœʀ] *nm*: ~ **de fonds** sponsor, backer; (*COMM*) sleeping *ou* silent partner.

bâillon [bɑjɔ̃] *nm* gag.

bâillonner [bɑjɔne] *vt* to gag.

bain [bɛ̃] *nm* (*dans une baignoire, PHOTO, TECH*) bath; (*dans la mer, une piscine*) swim; **costume de** ~ bathing costume (*BRIT*), swimsuit; **prendre un** ~ to have a bath; **se mettre dans le** ~ (*fig*) to get into (the way of) it *ou* things; ~ **de bouche** mouthwash; ~ **de foule** walkabout; ~ **de pieds** footbath; (*au bord de la mer*) paddle; ~ **de siège** hip bath; ~ **de soleil** sunbathing *no pl*; **prendre un** ~ **de soleil** to sunbathe; ~**s de mer** sea bathing *sg*; ~**s(-douches) municipaux** public baths.

bain-marie, *pl* **bains-marie** [bɛ̃maʀi] *nm* double boiler; **faire chauffer au** ~ (*boîte etc*) to immerse in boiling water.

baïonnette [bajɔnɛt] *nf* bayonet; (*ÉLEC*): **douille à** ~ bayonet socket; **ampoule à** ~ bulb with a bayonet fitting.

baisemain [bɛzmɛ̃] *nm* kissing a lady's hand.

baiser [beze] *nm* kiss ♦ *vt* (*main, front*) to kiss; (*fam!*) to screw (*!*).

baisse [bɛs] *nf* fall, drop; (*COMM*): "~ **sur la viande**" "meat prices down"; **en** ~ (*cours, action*) falling; **à la** ~ downwards.

baisser [bese] *vt* to lower; (*radio, chauffage*) to turn down; (*AUTO*: *phares*) to dip (*BRIT*), lower (*US*) ♦ *vi* to fall, drop, go down; **se** ~ *vi* to bend down.

bajoues [baʒu] *nfpl* chaps, chops.

bal [bal] *nm* dance; (*grande soirée*) ball; ~ **costumé/masqué** fancy-dress/masked ball; ~ **musette** dance (*with accordion accompaniment*).

balade [balad] *nf* walk, stroll; (*en voiture*) drive; **faire une** ~ to go for a walk *ou* stroll; to go for a drive.

balader [balade] *vt* (*traîner*) to trail around; **se** ~ *vi* to go for a walk *ou* stroll; to go for a drive.

baladeur [baladœʀ] *nm* personal stereo.

baladeuse [baladøz] *nf* inspection lamp.

baladin [baladɛ̃] *nm* wandering entertainer.

balafre [balafʀ(ə)] *nf* gash, slash; (*cicatrice*) scar.

balafrer [balafʀe] *vt* to gash, slash.

balai [balɛ] *nm* broom, brush; (*AUTO*: *d'essuie-glace*) blade; (*MUS*: *de batterie etc*) brush; **donner un coup de** ~ to give the floor a sweep; ~ **mécanique** carpet sweeper.

balai-brosse, *pl* **balais-brosses** [balɛbʀɔs] *nm* (long-handled) scrubbing brush.

balance [balɑ̃s] *nf* (*à plateaux*) scales *pl*; (*de précision*) balance; (*COMM, POL*): ~ **des comptes *ou* paiements** balance of pay

ments; (*signe*): **la B~** Libra, the Scales; **être de la B~** to be Libra; ~ **commerciale** balance of trade; ~ **des forces** balance of power; ~ **romaine** steelyard.
balancelle [balɑ̃sɛl] *nf* garden hammock-seat.
balancer [balɑ̃se] *vt* to swing; (*lancer*) to fling, chuck; (*renvoyer, jeter*) to chuck out ♦ *vi* to swing; **se** ~ *vi* to swing; (*bateau*) to rock; (*branche*) to sway; **se** ~ **de qch** (*fam*) not to give a toss about sth.
balancier [balɑ̃sje] *nm* (*de pendule*) pendulum; (*de montre*) balance wheel; (*perche*) (balancing) pole.
balançoire [balɑ̃swaʀ] *nf* swing; (*sur pivot*) seesaw.
balayage [balɛjaʒ] *nm* sweeping; scanning.
balayer [baleje] *vt* (*feuilles etc*) to sweep up, brush up; (*pièce, cour*) to sweep; (*chasser*) to sweep away *ou* aside; (*suj: radar*) to scan; (*: phares*) to sweep across.
balayette [balɛjɛt] *nf* small brush.
balayeur, euse [balɛjœʀ, -øz] *nm/f* roadsweeper ♦ *nf* (*engin*) roadsweeper.
balayures [balɛjyʀ] *nfpl* sweepings.
balbutiement [balbysimɑ̃] *nm* (*paroles*) stammering *no pl*; ~**s** *nmpl* (*fig: débuts*) first faltering steps.
balbutier [balbysje] *vi, vt* to stammer.
balcon [balkɔ̃] *nm* balcony; (*THÉÂT*) dress circle.
baldaquin [baldakɛ̃] *nm* canopy.
Bâle [bɑl] *n* Basle *ou* Basel.
Baléares [baleɑʀ] *nfpl*: **les** ~ the Balearic Islands.
baleine [balɛn] *nf* whale; (*de parapluie*) rib; (*de corset*) bone.
baleinier [balenje] *nm* (*NAVIG*) whaler.
baleinière [balenjɛʀ] *nf* whaleboat.
balisage [balizaʒ] *nm* (*signaux*) beacons *pl*; buoys *pl*; runway lights *pl*; signs *pl*, markers *pl*.
balise [baliz] *nf* (*NAVIG*) beacon, (marker) buoy; (*AVIAT*) runway light, beacon; (*AUTO, SKI*) sign, marker.
baliser [balize] *vt* to mark out (with beacons *ou* lights *etc*).
balistique [balistik] *adj* (*engin*) ballistic ♦ *nf* ballistics.
balivernes [balivɛʀn(ə)] *nfpl* twaddle *sg* (*BRIT*), nonsense *sg*.
balkanique [balkanik] *adj* Balkan.
Balkans [balkɑ̃] *nmpl*: **les** ~ the Balkans.
ballade [balad] *nf* ballad.
ballant, e [balɑ̃, -ɑ̃t] *adj* dangling.
ballast [balast] *nm* ballast.
balle [bal] *nf* (*de fusil*) bullet; (*de sport*) ball; (*du blé*) chaff; (*paquet*) bale; (*fam: franc*) franc; ~ **perdue** stray bullet.
ballerine [balʀin] *nf* ballet dancer; (*chaussure*) pump, ballerina.
ballet [balɛ] *nm* ballet; (*fig*): ~ **diplomatique** diplomatic to-ings and fro-ings.
ballon [balɔ̃] *nm* (*de sport*) ball; (*jouet, AVIAT, de bande dessinée*) balloon; (*de vin*) glass; ~ **d'essai** (*météorologique*) pilot balloon; (*fig*) feeler(s); ~ **de football** football; ~ **d'oxygène** oxygen bottle.
ballonner [balɔne] *vt*: **j'ai le ventre ballonné** I feel bloated.
ballon-sonde, *pl* **ballons-sondes** [balɔ̃sɔ̃d] *nm* sounding balloon.
ballot [balo] *nm* bundle; (*péj*) nitwit.
ballottage [balɔtaʒ] *nm* (*POL*) second ballot.
ballotter [balɔte] *vi* to roll around; (*bateau etc*) to toss ♦ *vt* to shake *ou* throw about; to toss; **être ballotté entre** (*fig*) to be shunted between; (*: indécis*) to be torn between.
ballottine [balɔtin] *nf* (*CULIN*): ~ **de volaille** *meat loaf made with poultry*.
ball-trap [baltʀap] *nm* (*appareil*) trap; (*tir*) clay pigeon shooting.
balluchon [balyʃɔ̃] *nm* bundle (of clothes).
balnéaire [balneɛʀ] *adj* seaside *cpd*.
balnéothérapie [balneɔteʀapi] *nf* spa bath therapy.
BALO *sigle m* (= *Bulletin des annonces légales obligatoires*) ≈ Public Notices (*in newspapers etc*).
balourd, e [baluʀ, -uʀd(ə)] *adj* clumsy ♦ *nm/f* clodhopper.
balourdise [baluʀdiz] *nf* clumsiness; (*gaffe*) blunder.
balte [balt] *adj* Baltic ♦ *nm/f*: **B~** native of the Baltic States.
baltique [baltik] *adj* Baltic ♦ *nf*: **la (mer) B~** the Baltic (Sea).
baluchon [balyʃɔ̃] *nm* = **balluchon**.
balustrade [balystʀad] *nf* railings *pl*, handrail.
bambin [bɑ̃bɛ̃] *nm* little child.
bambou [bɑ̃bu] *nm* bamboo.
ban [bɑ̃] *nm* round of applause, cheer; **être/mettre au** ~ **de** to be outlawed/to outlaw from; **le** ~ **et l'arrière-**~ **de sa famille** every last one of his relatives; ~**s (de mariage)** banns, bans.
banal, e [banal] *adj* banal, commonplace; (*péj*) trite; **four/moulin** ~ village oven/mill.
banalisé, e [banalize] *adj* (*voiture de police*) unmarked.
banalité [banalite] *nf* banality; (*remarque*) truism, trite remark.
banane [banan] *nf* banana.
bananeraie [bananʀɛ] *nf* banana plantation.
bananier [bananje] *nm* banana tree; (*bateau*) banana boat.
banc [bɑ̃] *nm* seat, bench; (*de poissons*) shoal; ~ **des accusés** dock; ~ **d'essai** (*fig*) testing ground; ~ **de sable** sandbank; ~ **des témoins** witness box; ~ **de touche** dugout.
bancaire [bɑ̃kɛʀ] *adj* banking, bank *cpd*.
bancal, e [bɑ̃kal] *adj* wobbly; (*personne*) bow-legged; (*fig: projet*) shaky.
bandage [bɑ̃daʒ] *nm* bandaging; (*pansement*) bandage; ~ **herniaire** truss.

bande [bɑ̃d] *nf* (*de tissu etc*) strip; (*MÉD*) bandage; (*motif, dessin*) stripe; (*CINÉ*) film; (*INFORM*) tape; (*RADIO, groupe*) band; (*péj*): **une ~ de** a bunch *ou* crowd of; **par la ~** in a roundabout way; **donner de la ~** to list; **faire ~ à part** to keep to o.s.; **~ dessinée (BD)** strip cartoon (*BRIT*), comic strip; **~ magnétique** magnetic tape; **~ perforée** punched tape; **~ de roulement** (*de pneu*) tread; **~ sonore** sound track; **~ de terre** strip of land; **~ Velpeau** ® (*MÉD*) crêpe bandage; *see boxed note*.

BANDE DESSINÉE

The **bande dessinée** *or 'BD' enjoys a huge following amongst adults as well as children in France, where the comic strip is accorded both literary and artistic status. Every year, an international exhibition takes place in Angoulême at the end of January. Astérix, Tintin, Lucky Luke and Gaston Lagaffe are some of the most famous cartoon characters.*

bandé, e [bɑ̃de] *adj* bandaged; **les yeux ~s** blindfold.
bande-annonce, *pl* **bandes-annonces** [bɑ̃danɔ̃s] *nf* (*CINÉ*) trailer.
bandeau, x [bɑ̃do] *nm* headband; (*sur les yeux*) blindfold; (*MÉD*) head bandage.
bandelette [bɑ̃dlɛt] *nf* strip of cloth, bandage.
bander [bɑ̃de] *vt* to bandage; (*muscle*) to tense; (*arc*) to bend ♦ *vi* (*fam!*) to have a hard on (*!*); **~ les yeux à qn** to blindfold sb.
banderole [bɑ̃dʀɔl] *nf* banderole; (*dans un défilé etc*) streamer.
bande-son, *pl* **bandes-son** [bɑ̃dsɔ̃] *nf* (*CINÉ*) soundtrack.
bande-vidéo, *pl* **bandes-vidéo** [bɑ̃dvideo] *nf* video tape.
bandit [bɑ̃di] *nm* bandit.
banditisme [bɑ̃ditism(ə)] *nm* violent crime, armed robberies *pl*.
bandoulière [bɑ̃duljɛʀ] *nf*: **en ~** (slung *ou* worn) across the shoulder.
Bangkok [bɑ̃ŋkɔk] *n* Bangkok.
Bangladesh [bɑ̃gladɛʃ] *nm*: **le ~** Bangladesh.
banjo [bɑ̃(d)ʒo] *nm* banjo.
banlieue [bɑ̃ljø] *nf* suburbs *pl*; **quartiers de ~** suburban areas; **trains de ~** commuter trains.
banlieusard, e [bɑ̃ljøzaʀ, -aʀd(ə)] *nm/f* suburbanite.
bannière [banjɛʀ] *nf* banner.
bannir [baniʀ] *vt* to banish.
banque [bɑ̃k] *nf* bank; (*activités*) banking; **~ des yeux/du sang** eye/blood bank; **~ d'affaires** merchant bank; **~ de dépôt** deposit bank; **~ de données** (*INFORM*) data bank; **~ d'émission** bank of issue.
banqueroute [bɑ̃kʀut] *nf* bankruptcy.
banquet [bɑ̃kɛ] *nm* (*de club*) dinner; (*de noces*) reception; (*d'apparat*) banquet.
banquette [bɑ̃kɛt] *nf* seat.
banquier [bɑ̃kje] *nm* banker.
banquise [bɑ̃kiz] *nf* ice field.
bantou, e [bɑ̃tu] *adj* Bantu.
baptême [batɛm] *nm* (*sacrement*) baptism; (*cérémonie*) christening, baptism; (*d'un navire*) launching; (*d'une cloche*) consecration, dedication; **~ de l'air** first flight.
baptiser [batize] *vt* to christen; to baptize; to launch; to consecrate, dedicate.
baptismal, e, aux [batismal, -o] *adj*: **eau ~e** baptismal water.
baptiste [batist(ə)] *adj, nm/f* Baptist.
baquet [bakɛ] *nm* tub, bucket.
bar [baʀ] *nm* bar; (*poisson*) bass.
baragouin [baʀagwɛ̃] *nm* gibberish.
baragouiner [baʀagwine] *vi* to gibber, jabber.
baraque [baʀak] *nf* shed; (*fam*) house; **~ foraine** fairground stand.
baraqué, e [baʀake] *adj* well-built, hefty.
baraquements [baʀakmɑ̃] *nmpl* huts (*for refugees, workers etc*).
baratin [baʀatɛ̃] *nm* (*fam*) smooth talk, patter.
baratiner [baʀatine] *vt* to chat up.
baratte [baʀat] *nf* churn.
Barbade [baʀbad] *nf*: **la ~** Barbados.
barbant, e [baʀbɑ̃, -ɑ̃t] *adj* (*fam*) deadly (boring).
barbare [baʀbaʀ] *adj* barbaric ♦ *nm/f* barbarian.
Barbarie [baʀbaʀi] *nf*: **la ~** the Barbary Coast.
barbarie [baʀbaʀi] *nf* barbarism; (*cruauté*) barbarity.
barbarisme [baʀbaʀism(ə)] *nm* (*LING*) barbarism.
barbe [baʀb(ə)] *nf* beard; **(au nez et) à la ~ de qn** (*fig*) under sb's very nose; **quelle ~!** (*fam*) what a drag *ou* bore!; **~ à papa** candy-floss (*BRIT*), cotton candy (*US*).
barbecue [baʀbəkju] *nm* barbecue.
barbelé [baʀbəle] *nm* barbed wire *no pl*.
barber [baʀbe] *vt* (*fam*) to bore stiff.
barbiche [baʀbiʃ] *nf* goatee.
barbichette [baʀbiʃɛt] *nf* small goatee.
barbiturique [baʀbityʀik] *nm* barbiturate.
barboter [baʀbɔte] *vi* to paddle, dabble ♦ *v* (*fam*) to filch.
barboteuse [baʀbɔtøz] *nf* rompers *pl*.
barbouiller [baʀbuje] *vt* to daub; (*péj*: *écrire dessiner*) to scribble; **avoir l'estomac bar bouillé** to feel queasy *ou* sick.
barbu, e [baʀby] *adj* bearded.
barbue [baʀby] *nf* (*poisson*) brill.
Barcelone [baʀsəlɔn] *n* Barcelona.
barda [baʀda] *nm* (*fam*) kit, gear.
barde [baʀd(ə)] *nf* (*CULIN*) piece of fat bacon ♦ *nm* (*poète*) bard.
bardé, e [baʀde] *adj*: **~ de médailles** *etc* be decked with medals *etc*.
bardeaux [baʀdo] *nmpl* shingle *no pl*.
barder [baʀde] *vt* (*CULIN*: *rôti, volaille*) to bar ♦ *vi* (*fam*): **ça va ~** sparks will fly.
barème [baʀɛm] *nm* scale; (*liste*) table; **~ de**

salaires salary scale.
barge [baʀʒ] *nf* barge.
barguigner [baʀgiɲe] *vi*: **sans** ~ without (any) humming and hawing *ou* shilly-shallying.
baril [baʀil] *nm* (*tonneau*) barrel; (*de poudre*) keg.
barillet [baʀijɛ] *nm* (*de revolver*) cylinder.
bariolé, e [baʀjɔle] *adj* many-coloured, rainbow-coloured.
barman [baʀman] *nm* barman.
baromètre [baʀɔmɛtʀ(ə)] *nm* barometer; ~ **anéroïde** aneroid barometer.
baron [baʀɔ̃] *nm* baron.
baronne [baʀɔn] *nf* baroness.
baroque [baʀɔk] *adj* (*ART*) baroque; (*fig*) weird.
baroud [baʀud] *nm*: ~ **d'honneur** gallant last stand.
baroudeur [baʀudœʀ] *nm* (*fam*) fighter.
barque [baʀk(ə)] *nf* small boat.
barquette [baʀkɛt] *nf* small boat-shaped tart; (*récipient: en aluminium*) tub; (*: en bois*) basket.
barracuda [baʀakyda] *nm* barracuda.
barrage [baʀaʒ] *nm* dam; (*sur route*) roadblock, barricade; ~ **de police** police roadblock.
barre [baʀ] *nf* (*de fer etc*) rod, bar; (*NAVIG*) helm; (*écrite*) line, stroke; (*DANSE*) barre; (*niveau*): **la livre a franchi la ~ des 1,70 €** the pound has broken the €1.70 barrier; (*JUR*): **comparaître à la** ~ to appear as a witness; **être à** *ou* **tenir la** ~ (*NAVIG*) to be at the helm; **coup de** ~ (*fig*): **c'est le coup de ~!** it's daylight robbery!; **j'ai le coup de ~!** I'm all in!; ~ **fixe** (*GYM*) horizontal bar; ~ **de mesure** (*MUS*) bar line; ~ **à mine** crowbar; **~s parallèles/asymétriques** (*GYM*) parallel/asymmetric bars.
barreau, x [baʀo] *nm* bar; (*JUR*): **le** ~ the Bar.
barrer [baʀe] *vt* (*route etc*) to block; (*mot*) to cross out; (*chèque*) to cross (*BRIT*); (*NAVIG*) to steer; **se** ~ *vi* (*fam*) to clear off.
barrette [baʀɛt] *nf* (*pour cheveux*) (hair) slide (*BRIT*) *ou* clip (*US*); (*REL: bonnet*) biretta; (*broche*) brooch.
barreur [baʀœʀ] *nm* helmsman; (*aviron*) coxswain.
barricade [baʀikad] *nf* barricade.
barricader [baʀikade] *vt* to barricade; **se** ~ **chez soi** (*fig*) to lock o.s. in.
barrière [baʀjɛʀ] *nf* fence; (*obstacle*) barrier; (*porte*) gate; **la Grande B~** the Great Barrier Reef; ~ **de dégel** (*ADMIN: on roadsigns*) no heavy vehicles - road liable to subsidence due to thaw; **~s douanières** trade barriers.
barrique [baʀik] *nf* barrel, cask.
barrir [baʀiʀ] *vi* to trumpet.
baryton [baʀitɔ̃] *nm* baritone.
BAS *sigle m* (= *bureau d'aide sociale*) ≈ social security office (*BRIT*), ≈ Welfare office (*US*).
bas, basse [bɑ, bɑs] *adj* low; (*action*) low, ignoble ♦ *nm* (*vêtement*) stocking; (*partie inférieure*): **le ~ de** the lower part *ou* foot *ou* bottom of ♦ *nf* (*MUS*) bass ♦ *adv* low; (*parler*) softly; **plus** ~ lower down; more softly; (*dans un texte*) further on, below; **la tête basse** with lowered head; (*fig*) with head hung low; **avoir la vue basse** to be shortsighted; **au ~ mot** at the lowest estimate; **enfant en ~ âge** infant, young child; **en** ~ down below; at (*ou* to) the bottom; (*dans une maison*) downstairs; **en ~ de** at the bottom of; **de ~ en haut** upwards; from the bottom to the top; **des hauts et des ~** ups and downs; **un ~ de laine** (*fam: économies*) money under the mattress (*fig*); **mettre** ~ *vi* to give birth; **à ~ la dictature!** down with dictatorship!; ~ **morceaux** (*viande*) cheap cuts.
basalte [bazalt(ə)] *nm* basalt.
basané, e [bazane] *adj* tanned, bronzed; (*immigré etc*) swarthy.
bas-côté [bakote] *nm* (*de route*) verge (*BRIT*), shoulder (*US*); (*d'église*) (side) aisle.
bascule [baskyl] *nf*: **(jeu de)** ~ seesaw; **(balance à)** ~ scales *pl*; **fauteuil à** ~ rocking chair; **système à** ~ tip-over device; rocker device.
basculer [baskyle] *vi* to fall over, topple (over); (*benne*) to tip up ♦ *vt* (*aussi*: **faire** ~) to topple over; to tip out, tip up.
base [bɑz] *nf* base; (*POL*): **la** ~ the rank and file, the grass roots; (*fondement, principe*) basis (*pl* bases); **jeter les ~s de** to lay the foundations of; **à la ~ de** (*fig*) at the root of; **sur la ~ de** (*fig*) on the basis of; **de** ~ basic; **à ~ de café** *etc* coffee *etc* -based; ~ **de données** (*INFORM*) database; ~ **de lancement** launching site.
base-ball [bɛzbol] *nm* baseball.
baser [bɑze] *vt*: ~ **qch sur** to base sth on; **se ~ sur** (*données, preuves*) to base one's argument on; **être basé à/dans** (*MIL*) to be based at/in.
bas-fond [bɑfɔ̃] *nm* (*NAVIG*) shallow; **~s** *nmpl* (*fig*) dregs.
BASIC [bazik] *nm* BASIC.
basilic [bazilik] *nm* (*CULIN*) basil.
basilique [bazilik] *nf* basilica.
basket(-ball) [baskɛt(bol)] *nm* basketball.
baskets [baskɛt] *nfpl* (*chaussures*) trainers (*BRIT*), sneakers (*US*).
basketteur, euse [baskɛtœʀ, -øz] *nm/f* basketball player.
basquaise [baskɛz] *adj f* Basque ♦ *nf*: **B~** Basque.
basque [bask(ə)] *adj, nm* (*LING*) Basque ♦ *nm/f*: **B~** Basque; **le Pays** ~ the Basque country.
basques [bask(ə)] *nfpl* skirts; **pendu aux ~ de qn** constantly pestering sb; (*mère etc*) hanging on sb's apron strings.
bas-relief [bɑʀəljɛf] *nm* bas-relief.
basse [bɑs] *adj f, nf voir* **bas**.

basse-cour, *pl* **basses-cours** [baskuʀ] *nf* farmyard; (*animaux*) farmyard animals.
bassement [basmɑ̃] *adv* basely.
bassesse [basɛs] *nf* baseness; (*acte*) base act.
basset [basɛ] *nm* (*ZOOL*) basset (hound).
bassin [basɛ̃] *nm* (*cuvette*) bowl; (*pièce d'eau*) pond, pool; (*de fontaine, GÉO*) basin; (*ANAT*) pelvis; (*portuaire*) dock; ~ **houiller** coalfield.
bassine [basin] *nf* basin; (*contenu*) bowl, bowlful.
bassiner [basine] *vt* (*plaie*) to bathe; (*lit*) to warm with a warming pan; (*fam: ennuyer*) to bore; (*: importuner*) to bug, pester.
bassiste [basist(ə)] *nm/f* (double) bass player.
basson [basɔ̃] *nm* bassoon.
bastide [bastid] *nf* (*maison*) country house (*in Provence*); (*ville*) walled town (*in SW France*).
bastingage [bastɛ̃gaʒ] *nm* (ship's) rail.
bastion [bastjɔ̃] *nm* (*aussi fig, POL*) bastion.
bas-ventre [bavɑ̃tʀ(ə)] *nm* (lower part of the) stomach.
bât [ba] *nm* packsaddle.
bataille [bataj] *nf* battle; **en** ~ (*en travers*) at an angle; (*en désordre*) awry; ~ **rangée** pitched battle.
bataillon [batajɔ̃] *nm* battalion.
bâtard, e [bataʀ, -aʀd(ə)] *adj* (*enfant*) illegitimate; (*fig*) hybrid ♦ *nm/f* illegitimate child, bastard (*péj*) ♦ *nm* (*BOULANGERIE*) ≈ Vienna loaf; **chien** ~ mongrel.
batavia [batavja] *nf* ≈ Webb lettuce.
bateau, x [bato] *nm* boat; (*grand*) ship ♦ *adj inv* (*banal, rebattu*) hackneyed; ~ **de pêche/à moteur** fishing/motor boat.
bateau-citerne [batositɛʀn(ə)] *nm* tanker.
bateau-mouche [batomuʃ] *nm* (passenger) pleasure boat (*on the Seine*).
bateau-pilote [batopilɔt] *nm* pilot ship.
bateleur, euse [batlœʀ, -øz] *nm/f* street performer.
batelier, ière [batəlje, -jɛʀ] *nm/f* ferryman/woman.
bat-flanc [baflɑ̃] *nm inv raised boards for sleeping, in cells, army huts etc.*
bâti, e [bati] *adj* (*terrain*) developed ♦ *nm* (*armature*) frame; (*COUTURE*) tacking; **bien** ~ (*personne*) well-built.
batifoler [batifɔle] *vi* to frolic *ou* lark about.
batik [batik] *nm* batik.
bâtiment [batimɑ̃] *nm* building; (*NAVIG*) ship, vessel; (*industrie*): **le** ~ the building trade.
bâtir [batiʀ] *vt* to build; (*COUTURE: jupe, ourlet*) to tack; **fil à** ~ (*COUTURE*) tacking thread.
bâtisse [batis] *nf* building.
bâtisseur, euse [batisœʀ, -øz] *nm/f* builder.
batiste [batist(ə)] *nf* (*COUTURE*) batiste, cambric.
bâton [batɔ̃] *nm* stick; **mettre des ~s dans les roues à qn** to put a spoke in sb's wheel; **à ~s rompus** informally; ~ **de rouge (à lèvres)** lipstick; ~ **de ski** ski stick.
bâtonnet [batɔnɛ] *nm* short stick *ou* rod.
bâtonnier [batɔnje] *nm* (*JUR*) ≈ President of the Bar.
batraciens [batʀasjɛ̃] *nmpl* amphibians.
battage [bataʒ] *nm* (*publicité*) (hard) plugging.
battant, e [batɑ̃, -ɑ̃t] *vb voir* **battre** ♦ *adj*: **pluie ~e** lashing rain ♦ *nm* (*de cloche*) clapper; (*de volets*) shutter, flap; (*de porte*) side; (*fig: personne*) fighter; **porte à double** ~ double door; **tambour** ~ briskly.
batte [bat] *nf* (*SPORT*) bat.
battement [batmɑ̃] *nm* (*de cœur*) beat; (*intervalle*) interval (*between classes, trains etc*); ~ **de paupières** blinking *no pl* (of eyelids); **un** ~ **de 10 minutes, 10 minutes de** ~ 10 minutes to spare.
batterie [batʀi] *nf* (*MIL, ÉLEC*) battery; (*MUS*) drums *pl*, drum kit; ~ **de cuisine** kitchen utensils *pl*; (*casseroles etc*) pots and pans *pl*; **une** ~ **de tests** a string of tests.
batteur [batœʀ] *nm* (*MUS*) drummer; (*appareil*) whisk.
batteuse [batøz] *nf* (*AGR*) threshing machine.
battoir [batwaʀ] *nm* (*à linge*) beetle (*for laundry*); (*à tapis*) (carpet) beater.
battre [batʀ(ə)] *vt* to beat; (*suj: pluie, vagues*) to beat *ou* lash against; (*œufs etc*) to beat up, whisk; (*blé*) to thresh; (*cartes*) to shuffle; (*passer au peigne fin*) to scour ♦ *vi* (*cœur*) to beat; (*volets etc*) to bang, rattle; **se** ~ *vi* to fight; ~ **la mesure** to beat time; ~ **en brèche** (*MIL: mur*) to batter; (*fig: théorie*) to demolish; (*: institution etc*) to attack; ~ **son plein** to be at its height, be going full swing; ~ **pavillon britannique** to fly the British flag; ~ **des mains** to clap one's hands; ~ **des ailes** to flap its wings; ~ **de l'aile** (*fig*) to be in a bad way *ou* in bad shape; ~ **la semelle** to stamp one's feet; ~ **en retraite** to beat a retreat.
battu, e [baty] *pp de* **battre** ♦ *nf* (*chasse*) beat; (*policière etc*) search, hunt.
baud [bo(d)] *nm* baud.
baudruche [bodʀyʃ] *nf*: **ballon en** ~ (toy) balloon; (*fig*) windbag.
baume [bom] *nm* balm.
bauxite [boksit] *nf* bauxite.
bavard, e [bavaʀ, -aʀd(ə)] *adj* (very) talkative; gossipy.
bavardage [bavaʀdaʒ] *nm* chatter *no pl*; gossip *no pl*.
bavarder [bavaʀde] *vi* to chatter; (*indiscrètement*) to gossip; (*: révéler un secret*) to blab.
bavarois, e [bavaʀwa, -waz] *adj* Bavarian ♦ *nm ou nf* (*CULIN*) bavarois.
bave [bav] *nf* dribble; (*de chien etc*) slobber, slaver (*BRIT*), drool (*US*); (*d'escargot*) slime.
baver [bave] *vi* to dribble; to slobber, slaver (*BRIT*), drool (*US*); (*encre, couleur*) to run; **en** ~ (*fam*) to have a hard time (of it).
bavette [bavɛt] *nf* bib.
baveux, euse [bavø, -øz] *adj* dribbling; (*omelette*) runny.

Bavière [bavjɛʀ] *nf*: **la** ~ Bavaria.
bavoir [bavwaʀ] *nm* (*de bébé*) bib.
bavure [bavyʀ] *nf* smudge; (*fig*) hitch; blunder.
bayer [baje] *vi*: ~ **aux corneilles** to stand gaping.
bazar [bazaʀ] *nm* general store; (*fam*) jumble.
bazarder [bazaʀde] *vt* (*fam*) to chuck out.
BCBG *sigle a* (= *bon chic bon genre*) ≈ preppy.
BCE *sigle f* (= *Banque centrale européenne*) ECB.
BCG *sigle m* (= *bacille Calmette-Guérin*) BCG.
bcp *abr* = **beaucoup**.
BD *sigle f* = **bande dessinée**; (= *base de données*) DB.
bd *abr* = **boulevard**.
b.d.c. *abr* (*TYPO*: = *bas de casse*) l.c.
béant, e [beɑ̃, -ɑ̃t] *adj* gaping.
béarnais, e [beaʀnɛ, -ɛz] *adj* of *ou* from the Béarn.
béat, e [bea, -at] *adj* showing open-eyed wonder; (*sourire etc*) blissful.
béatitude [beatityd] *nf* bliss.
beau (**bel**), **belle**, **beaux** [bo, bɛl] *adj* beautiful, lovely; (*homme*) handsome ♦ *nf* (*SPORT*) decider ♦ *adv*: **il fait** ~ the weather's fine ♦ *nm*: **avoir le sens du** ~ to have an aesthetic sense; **le temps est au** ~ the weather is set fair; **un** ~ **geste** (*fig*) a fine gesture; **un** ~ **salaire** a good salary; **un** ~ **gâchis/rhume** a fine mess/nasty cold; **en faire/dire de belles** to do/say (some) stupid things; **le** ~ **monde** high society; ~ **parleur** smooth talker; **un** ~ **jour** one (fine) day; **de plus belle** more than ever, even more; **bel et bien** well and truly; (*vraiment*) really (and truly); **le plus** ~ **c'est que ...** the best of it is that ...; **c'est du** ~! that's great, that is!; **on a** ~ **essayer** however hard *ou* no matter how hard we try; **il a** ~ **jeu de protester** it's easy for him to protest; **faire le** ~ (*chien*) to sit up and beg.
beauceron, ne [bosʀɔ̃, -ɔn] *adj* of *ou* from the Beauce.

MOT-CLÉ

beaucoup [boku] *adv* **1** a lot; **il boit** ~ he drinks a lot; **il ne boit pas** ~ he doesn't drink much *ou* a lot
2 (*suivi de plus, trop etc*) much, a lot, far; **il est** ~ **plus grand** he is much *ou* a lot *ou* far taller
3: ~ **de** (*nombre*) many, a lot of; (*quantité*) a lot of; **pas** ~ **de** (*nombre*) not many, not a lot of; (*quantité*) not much, not a lot of; ~ **d'étudiants/de touristes** a lot of *ou* many students/tourists; ~ **de courage** a lot of courage; **il n'a pas** ~ **d'argent** he hasn't got much *ou* a lot of money; **il n'y a pas** ~ **de touristes** there aren't many *ou* a lot of tourists
4: **de** ~ by far
♦ *pron*: ~ **le savent** lots of people know that.

beau-fils, *pl* **beaux-fils** [bofis] *nm* son-in-law; (*remariage*) stepson.
beau-frère, *pl* **beaux-frères** [bofʀɛʀ] *nm* brother-in-law.
beau-père, *pl* **beaux-pères** [bopɛʀ] *nm* father-in-law; (*remariage*) stepfather.
beauté [bote] *nf* beauty; **de toute** ~ beautiful; **en** ~ *adv* with a flourish, brilliantly.
beaux-arts [bozaʀ] *nmpl* fine arts.
beaux-parents [bopaʀɑ̃] *nmpl* wife's/husband's family *sg ou pl*, in-laws.
bébé [bebe] *nm* baby.
bébé-éprouvette, *pl* **bébés-éprouvette** [beepʀuvɛt] *nm* test-tube baby.
bec [bɛk] *nm* beak, bill; (*de plume*) nib; (*de cafetière etc*) spout; (*de casserole etc*) lip; (*d'une clarinette etc*) mouthpiece; (*fam*) mouth; **clouer le** ~ **à qn** (*fam*) to shut sb up; **ouvrir le** ~ (*fam*) to open one's mouth; ~ **de gaz** (street) gaslamp; ~ **verseur** pouring lip.
bécane [bekan] *nf* (*fam*) bike.
bécarre [bekaʀ] *nm* (*MUS*) natural.
bécasse [bekas] *nf* (*ZOOL*) woodcock; (*fam*) silly goose.
bec-de-cane, *pl* **becs-de-cane** [bɛkdəkan] *nm* (*poignée*) door handle.
bec-de-lièvre, *pl* **becs-de-lièvre** [bɛkdəljɛvʀ(ə)] *nm* harelip.
bêche [bɛʃ] *nf* spade.
bêcher [beʃe] *vt* (*terre*) to dig; (*personne: critiquer*) to slate; (*: snober*) to look down on.
bêcheur, euse [bɛʃœʀ, -øz] *adj* (*fam*) stuck-up ♦ *nm/f* fault-finder; (*snob*) stuck-up person.
bécoter [bekɔte]: **se** ~ *vi* to smooch.
becquée [beke] *nf*: **donner la** ~ **à** to feed.
becqueter [bɛkte] *vt* (*fam*) to eat.
bedaine [bədɛn] *nf* paunch.
bédé [bede] *nf* (*fam*) = **bande dessinée**.
bedeau, x [bədo] *nm* beadle.
bedonnant, e [bədɔnɑ̃, -ɑ̃t] *adj* paunchy, pot-bellied.
bée [be] *adj*: **bouche** ~ gaping.
beffroi [befʀwa] *nm* belfry.
bégaiement [begɛmɑ̃] *nm* stammering, stuttering.
bégayer [begeje] *vt, vi* to stammer.
bégonia [begɔnja] *nm* (*BOT*) begonia.
bègue [bɛg] *nm/f*: **être** ~ to have a stammer.
bégueule [begœl] *adj* prudish.
beige [bɛʒ] *adj* beige.
beignet [bɛɲɛ] *nm* fritter.
bel [bɛl] *adj m voir* **beau**.
bêler [bele] *vi* to bleat.
belette [bəlɛt] *nf* weasel.
belge [bɛlʒ(ə)] *adj* Belgian ♦ *nm/f*: **B**~ Belgian; *see boxed note*.

FÊTE NATIONALE BELGE

The **fête nationale belge** *on 21st July, marks the day in 1831 when Leopold of Saxe-Coburg Gotha was crowned King Leopold 1.*

Belgique [bɛlʒik] *nf*: **la** ~ Belgium.
Belgrade [bɛlgʀad] *n* Belgrade.
bélier [belje] *nm* ram; (*engin*) (battering) ram; (*signe*): **le B**~ Aries, the Ram; **être du B**~ to be Aries.
Bélize [beliz] *nm*: **le** ~ Belize.
bellâtre [bɛlɑtʀ(ə)] *nm* dandy.
belle [bɛl] *adj f, nf voir* **beau.**
belle-famille, *pl* **belles-familles** [bɛlfamij] *nf* (*fam*) in-laws *pl.*
belle-fille, *pl* **belles-filles** [bɛlfij] *nf* daughter-in-law; (*remariage*) stepdaughter.
belle-mère, *pl* **belles-mères** [bɛlmɛʀ] *nf* mother-in-law; (*remariage*) stepmother.
belle-sœur, *pl* **belles-sœurs** [bɛlsœʀ] *nf* sister-in-law.
belliciste [belisist(ə)] *adj* warmongering.
belligérance [beliʒeʀɑ̃s] *nf* belligerence.
belligérant, e [beliʒeʀɑ̃, -ɑ̃t] *adj* belligerent.
belliqueux, euse [belikø, -øz] *adj* aggressive, warlike.
belote [bəlɔt] *nf* belote (*card game*).
belvédère [bɛlvedɛʀ] *nm* panoramic viewpoint (*or small building there*).
bémol [bemɔl] *nm* (*MUS*) flat.
ben [bɛ̃] *excl* (*fam*) well.
bénédiction [benediksjɔ̃] *nf* blessing.
bénéfice [benefis] *nm* (*COMM*) profit; (*avantage*) benefit; **au** ~ **de** in aid of.
bénéficiaire [benefisjɛʀ] *nm/f* beneficiary.
bénéficier [benefisje] *vi*: ~ **de** to enjoy; (*profiter*) to benefit by *ou* from; (*obtenir*) to get, be given.
bénéfique [benefik] *adj* beneficial.
Benelux [benelyks] *nm*: **le** ~ Benelux, the Benelux countries.
benêt [bənɛ] *nm* simpleton.
bénévolat [benevɔla] *nm* voluntary service *ou* work.
bénévole [benevɔl] *adj* voluntary, unpaid.
bénévolement [benevɔlmɑ̃] *adv* voluntarily.
Bengale [bɛ̃gal] *nm*: **le** ~ Bengal; **le golfe du** ~ the Bay of Bengal.
bengali [bɛ̃gali] *adj* Bengali, Bengalese ♦ *nm* (*LING*) Bengali.
Bénin [benɛ̃] *nm*: **le** ~ Benin.
bénin, igne [benɛ̃, -iɲ] *adj* minor, mild; (*tumeur*) benign.
bénir [beniʀ] *vt* to bless.
bénit, e [beni, -it] *adj* consecrated; **eau** ~**e** holy water.
bénitier [benitje] *nm* stoup, font (*for holy water*).
benjamin, e [bɛ̃ʒamɛ̃, -in] *nm/f* youngest child; (*SPORT*) under-13.
benne [bɛn] *nf* skip; (*de téléphérique*) (cable) car; ~ **basculante** tipper (*BRIT*), dump *ou* dumper truck.
benzine [bɛ̃zin] *nf* benzine.
béotien, ne [beɔsjɛ̃, -ɛn] *nm/f* philistine.
BEP *sigle m* (= *Brevet d'études professionnelles*) *school-leaving diploma, taken at approx. 18 years.*
BEPA [bepa] *sigle m* (= *Brevet d'études professionnelles agricoles*) *school-leaving diploma in agriculture, taken at approx. 18 years.*
BEPC *sigle m* (= *Brevet d'études du premier cycle*) *former school certificate (taken at approx. 16 years).*
béquille [bekij] *nf* crutch; (*de bicyclette*) stand.
berbère [bɛʀbɛʀ] *adj* Berber ♦ *nm* (*LING*) Berber ♦ *nm/f*: **B**~ Berber.
bercail [bɛʀkaj] *nm* fold.
berceau, x [bɛʀso] *nm* cradle, crib.
bercer [bɛʀse] *vt* to rock, cradle; (*suj: musique etc*) to lull; ~ **qn de** (*promesses etc*) to delude sb with.
berceur, euse [bɛʀsœʀ, -øz] *adj* soothing ♦ *nf* (*chanson*) lullaby.
BERD [bɛʀd] *sigle f* (= *Banque européenne pour la reconstruction et le développement*) EBRD.
béret (**basque**) [beʀɛ(bask(ə))] *nm* beret.
bergamote [bɛʀgamɔt] *nf* (*BOT*) bergamot.
berge [bɛʀʒ(ə)] *nf* bank.
berger, ère [bɛʀʒe, -ɛʀ] *nm/f* shepherd/shepherdess; ~ **allemand** (*chien*) alsatian (dog) (*BRIT*), German shepherd (dog) (*US*).
bergerie [bɛʀʒəʀi] *nf* sheep pen.
bergeronnette [bɛʀʒəʀɔnɛt] *nf* wagtail.
béribéri [beʀibeʀi] *nm* beriberi.
Berlin [bɛʀlɛ̃] *n* Berlin; ~**-Est/-Ouest** East/West Berlin.
berline [bɛʀlin] *nf* (*AUTO*) saloon (car) (*BRIT*), sedan (*US*).
berlingot [bɛʀlɛ̃go] *nm* (*emballage*) carton (*pyramid shaped*); (*bonbon*) lozenge.
berlinois, e [bɛʀlinwa, -waz] *adj* of *ou* from Berlin ♦ *nm/f*: **B**~**, e** Berliner.
berlue [bɛʀly] *nf*: **j'ai la** ~ I must be seeing things.
bermuda [bɛʀmyda] *nm* (*short*) Bermuda shorts.
Bermudes [bɛʀmyd] *nfpl*: **les (îles)** ~ Bermuda.
Berne [bɛʀn(ə)] *n* Bern.
berne [bɛʀn(ə)] *nf*: **en** ~ at half-mast; **mettre en** ~ to fly at half-mast.
berner [bɛʀne] *vt* to fool.
bernois, e [bɛʀnwa, -waz] *adj* Bernese.
berrichon, ne [bɛʀiʃɔ̃, -ɔn] *adj* of *ou* from the Berry.
besace [bəzas] *nf* beggar's bag.
besogne [bəzɔɲ] *nf* work *no pl*, job.
besogneux, euse [bəzɔɲø, -øz] *adj* hard-working.
besoin [bəzwɛ̃] *nm* need; (*pauvreté*): **le** ~ need, want; **le** ~ **d'argent/de gloire** the need for money/glory; ~**s (naturels)** nature's needs; **faire ses** ~**s** to relieve o.s.; **avoir** ~ **de qch/faire qch** to need sth/to do sth; **il n'y a pas** ~ **de (faire)** there is no need to (do); **au** ~, **si** ~ **est** if need be; **pour les** ~**s de la cause** for the purpose in hand.

bestial, e, aux [bɛstjal, -o] *adj* bestial, brutish ♦ *nmpl* cattle.
bestiole [bɛstjɔl] *nf* (tiny) creature.
bétail [betaj] *nm* livestock, cattle *pl*.
bétaillère [betajɛʀ] *nf* livestock truck.
bête [bɛt] *nf* animal; (*bestiole*) insect, creature ♦ *adj* stupid, silly; **les ~s** (the) animals; **chercher la petite ~** to nit-pick; **~ noire** pet hate, bugbear (*BRIT*); **~ sauvage** wild beast; **~ de somme** beast of burden.
bêtement [bɛtmɑ̃] *adv* stupidly; **tout ~** quite simply.
Bethléem [bɛtleɛm] *n* Bethlehem.
bêtifier [betifje] *vi* to talk nonsense.
bêtise [betiz] *nf* stupidity; (*action, remarque*) stupid thing (to say *ou* do); (*bonbon*) *type of mint sweet* (*BRIT*) *ou candy* (*US*); **faire/dire une ~** to do/say something stupid.
béton [betɔ̃] *nm* concrete; **(en) ~** (*fig: alibi, argument*) cast iron; **~ armé** reinforced concrete; **~ précontraint** prestressed concrete.
bétonner [betɔne] *vt* to concrete (over).
bétonnière [betɔnjɛʀ] *nf* cement mixer.
bette [bɛt] *nf* (*BOT*) (Swiss) chard.
betterave [bɛtʀav] *nf* (*rouge*) beetroot (*BRIT*), beet (*US*); **~ sucrière** sugar beet.
beugler [bøgle] *vi* to low; (*péj: radio etc*) to blare ♦ *vt* (*péj: chanson etc*) to bawl out.
Beur [bœʀ] *adj, nm/f see boxed note.*

BEUR

Beur *is a term used to refer to a person born in France of North African immigrant parents. It is not racist and is often used by the media, anti-racist groups and second-generation North Africans themselves. The word itself comes from back slang, or 'verlan'.*

beurre [bœʀ] *nm* butter; **mettre du ~ dans les épinards** (*fig*) to add a little to the kitty; **~ de cacao** cocoa butter; **~ noir** brown butter (sauce).
beurrer [bœʀe] *vt* to butter.
beurrier [bœʀje] *nm* butter dish.
beuverie [bœvʀi] *nf* drinking session.
bévue [bevy] *nf* blunder.
Beyrouth [beʀut] *n* Beirut.
Bhoutan [butɑ̃] *nm*: **le ~** Bhutan.
bi... [bi] *préfixe* bi..., two-.
Biafra [bjafʀa] *nm*: **le ~** Biafra.
biafrais, e [bjafʀɛ, -ɛz] *adj* Biafran.
biais [bjɛ] *nm* (*moyen*) device, expedient; (*aspect*) angle; (*bande de tissu*) piece of cloth cut on the bias; **en ~, de ~** (*obliquement*) at an angle; (*fig*) indirectly.
biaiser [bjeze] *vi* (*fig*) to sidestep the issue.
biathlon [biatlɔ̃] *nm* biathlon.
bibelot [biblo] *nm* trinket, curio.
biberon [bibʀɔ̃] *nm* (feeding) bottle; **nourrir au ~** to bottle-feed.
bible [bibl(ə)] *nf* bible.
bibliobus [biblijɔbys] *nm* mobile library van.
bibliographie [biblijɔgʀafi] *nf* bibliography.
bibliophile [biblijɔfil] *nm/f* book-lover.
bibliothécaire [biblijɔtekɛʀ] *nm/f* librarian.
bibliothèque [biblijɔtɛk] *nf* library; (*meuble*) bookcase; **~ municipale** public library.
biblique [biblik] *adj* biblical.
bic ® [bik] *nm*: **(pointe) ~** ballpoint pen.
bicarbonate [bikaʀbɔnat] *nm*: **~ (de soude)** bicarbonate of soda.
bicentenaire [bisɑ̃tnɛʀ] *nm* bicentenary.
biceps [bisɛps] *nm* biceps.
biche [biʃ] *nf* doe.
bichonner [biʃɔne] *vt* to groom.
bicolore [bikɔlɔʀ] *adj* two-coloured (*BRIT*), two-colored (*US*).
bicoque [bikɔk] *nf* (*péj*) shack, dump.
bicorne [bikɔʀn(ə)] *nm* cocked hat.
bicyclette [bisiklɛt] *nf* bicycle.
bidasse [bidas] *nm* (*fam*) squaddie (*BRIT*).
bide [bid] *nm* (*fam: ventre*) belly; (*THÉÂT*) flop.
bidet [bidɛ] *nm* bidet.
bidirectionnel, le [bidiʀɛksjɔnɛl] *adj* bidirectional.
bidoche [bidɔʃ] *nf* (*fam*) meat.
bidon [bidɔ̃] *nm* can ♦ *adj inv* (*fam*) phoney.
bidonnant, e [bidɔnɑ̃, -ɑ̃t] *adj* (*fam*) hilarious.
bidonville [bidɔ̃vil] *nm* shanty town.
bidule [bidyl] *nm* (*fam*) thingamajig.
bielle [bjɛl] *nf* connecting rod; (*AUTO*) track rod.
biélorusse [bjelɔʀys] *adj* Belarussian ♦ *nm/f*: **B~** Belarussian.
Biélorussie [bjelɔʀysi] *nf* Belorussia.

MOT-CLÉ

bien [bjɛ̃] *nm* **1** (*avantage, profit*): **faire le ~** to do good; **faire du ~ à qn** to do sb good; **ça fait du ~ de faire** it does you good to do; **dire du ~ de** to speak well of; **c'est pour son ~** it's for his own good; **changer en ~** to change for the better; **le ~ public** the public good; **vouloir du ~ à qn** (*vouloir aider*) to have sb's (best) interests at heart; **je te veux du ~** (*pour mettre en confiance*) I don't wish you any harm

2 possession, property; **son ~ le plus précieux** his most treasured possession; **avoir du ~** to have property; **~s (de consommation** *etc***)** (consumer *etc*) goods; **~s durables** (consumer) durables

3 (*moral*): **le ~** good; **distinguer le ~ du mal** to tell good from evil

♦ *adv* **1** (*de façon satisfaisante*) well; **elle travaille/mange ~** she works/eats well; **aller** *or* **se porter ~** to be well; **croyant ~ faire, je/il ...** thinking I/he was doing the right thing, I/he ...

2 (*valeur intensive*) quite; **~ jeune** quite young; **~ assez** quite enough; **~ mieux** (very) much better; **~ du temps/des gens** quite a time/a number of people; **j'espère ~**

y aller I do hope to go; **je veux ~ le faire** (*concession*) I'm quite willing to do it; **il faut ~ le faire** it has to be done; **il y a ~ 2 ans** at least 2 years ago; **il semble ~ que** it really seems that; **peut-être ~** it could well be; **aimer ~** to like; **Paul est ~ venu, n'est-ce pas?** Paul HAS come, hasn't he?; **où peut-il ~ être passé?** where on earth can he have got to?
3 (*conséquence, résultat*): **si ~ que** with the result that; **on verra ~** we'll see; **faire ~ de ...** to be right to ...
♦ *excl* right!, OK!, fine!; **eh ~!** well!; **(c'est) ~ fait!** it serves you (*ou* him *etc*) right!; **~ sûr!, ~ entendu!** certainly!, of course!
♦ *adj inv* **1** (*en bonne forme, à l'aise*): **je me sens ~, je suis ~** I feel fine; **je ne me sens pas ~, je ne suis pas ~** I don't feel well; **on est ~ dans ce fauteuil** this chair is very comfortable
2 (*joli, beau*) good-looking; **tu es ~ dans cette robe** you look good in that dress
3 (*satisfaisant*) good; **elle est ~, cette maison/secrétaire** it's a good house/she's a good secretary; **c'est très ~ (comme ça)** it's fine (like that); **ce n'est pas si ~ que ça** it's not as good *ou* great as all that; **c'est ~?** is that all right?
4 (*moralement*) right; (: *personne*) good, nice; (*respectable*) respectable; **ce n'est pas ~ de ...** it's not right to ...; **elle est ~, cette femme** she's a nice woman, she's a good sort; **des gens ~** respectable people
5 (*en bons termes*): **être ~ avec qn** to be on good terms with sb.

bien-aimé, e [bjɛ̃neme] *adj, nm/f* beloved.
bien-être [bjɛ̃nɛtʀ(ə)] *nm* well-being.
bienfaisance [bjɛ̃fəzɑ̃s] *nf* charity.
bienfaisant, e [bjɛ̃fəzɑ̃, -ɑ̃t] *adj* (*chose*) beneficial.
bienfait [bjɛ̃fɛ] *nm* act of generosity, benefaction; (*de la science etc*) benefit.
bienfaiteur, trice [bjɛ̃fɛtœʀ, -tʀis] *nm/f* benefactor/benefactress.
bien-fondé [bjɛ̃fɔ̃de] *nm* soundness.
bien-fonds [bjɛ̃fɔ̃] *nm* property.
bienheureux, euse [bjɛ̃nœʀø, -øz] *adj* happy; (*REL*) blessed, blest.
biennal, e, aux [bjenal, -o] *adj* biennial.
bien-pensant, e [bjɛ̃pɑ̃sɑ̃, -ɑ̃t] *adj* right-thinking ♦ *nm/f*: **les ~s** right-minded people.
bien que [bjɛ̃k(ə)] *conj* although.
bienséance [bjɛ̃seɑ̃s] *nf* propriety, decorum *no pl*; **les ~s** (*convenances*) the proprieties.
bienséant, e [bjɛ̃seɑ̃, -ɑ̃t] *adj* proper, seemly.
bientôt [bjɛ̃to] *adv* soon; **à ~** see you soon.
bienveillance [bjɛ̃vɛjɑ̃s] *nf* kindness.
bienveillant, e [bjɛ̃vɛjɑ̃, -ɑ̃t] *adj* kindly.
bienvenu, e [bjɛ̃vny] *adj* welcome ♦ *nm/f*: **être le ~/la ~e** to be welcome ♦ *nf*: **souhaiter la ~e à** to welcome; **~e à** welcome to.
bière [bjɛʀ] *nf* (*boisson*) beer; (*cercueil*) bier; **~ blonde** lager; **~ brune** brown ale; **~ (à la) pression** draught beer.
biffer [bife] *vt* to cross out.
bifteck [biftɛk] *nm* steak.
bifurcation [bifyʀkɑsjɔ̃] *nf* fork (*in road*); (*fig*) new direction.
bifurquer [bifyʀke] *vi* (*route*) to fork; (*véhicule*) to turn off.
bigame [bigam] *adj* bigamous.
bigamie [bigami] *nf* bigamy.
bigarré, e [bigaʀe] *adj* multicoloured (*BRIT*), multicolored (*US*); (*disparate*) motley.
bigarreau, x [bigaʀo] *nm type of cherry.*
bigleux, euse [biglø, -øz] *adj* (*fam*: *qui louche*) cross-eyed; (: *qui voit mal*) short-sighted; **il est complètement ~** he's as blind as a bat.
bigorneau, x [bigɔʀno] *nm* winkle.
bigot, e [bigo, -ɔt] (*péj*) *adj* bigoted ♦ *nm/f* bigot.
bigoterie [bigɔtʀi] *nf* bigotry.
bigoudi [bigudi] *nm* curler.
bigrement [bigʀəmɑ̃] *adv* (*fam*) fantastically.
bijou, x [biʒu] *nm* jewel.
bijouterie [biʒutʀi] *nf* (*magasin*) jeweller's (shop) (*BRIT*), jewelry store (*US*); (*bijoux*) jewellery, jewelry.
bijoutier, ière [biʒutje, -jɛʀ] *nm/f* jeweller (*BRIT*), jeweler (*US*).
bikini [bikini] *nm* bikini.
bilan [bilɑ̃] *nm* (*COMM*) balance sheet(s); (*annuel*) end of year statement; (*fig*) (net) outcome; (: *de victimes*) toll; **faire le ~ de** to assess; to review; **déposer son ~** to file a bankruptcy statement; **~ de santé** (*MÉD*) check-up; **~ social** *statement of a firm's policies towards its employees.*
bilatéral, e, aux [bilateʀal, -o] *adj* bilateral.
bilboquet [bilbɔkɛ] *nm* (*jouet*) cup-and-ball game.
bile [bil] *nf* bile; **se faire de la ~** (*fam*) to worry o.s. sick.
biliaire [biljɛʀ] *adj* biliary.
bilieux, euse [biljø, -øz] *adj* bilious; (*fig: colérique*) testy.
bilingue [bilɛ̃g] *adj* bilingual.
bilinguisme [bilɛ̃gɥism(ə)] *nm* bilingualism.
billard [bijaʀ] *nm* billiards *sg*; (*table*) billiard table; **c'est du ~** (*fam*) it's a cinch; **passer sur le ~** (*fam*) to have an (*ou* one's) operation; **~ électrique** pinball.
bille [bij] *nf* ball; (*du jeu de billes*) marble; (*de bois*) log; **jouer aux ~s** to play marbles.
billet [bijɛ] *nm* (*aussi*: **~ de banque**) (bank)note; (*de cinéma, de bus etc*) ticket; (*courte lettre*) note; **~ à ordre** *ou* **de commerce** (*COMM*) promissory note, IOU; **~ d'avion/de train** plane/train ticket; **~ circulaire** round-trip ticket; **~ doux** love letter; **~ de faveur** complimentary ticket; **~ de loterie** lottery ticket; **~ de quai** platform ticket.
billetterie [bijɛtʀi] *nf* ticket office; (*distribu

teur) ticket dispenser; (*BANQUE*) cash dispenser.
billion [biljɔ̃] *nm* billion (*BRIT*), trillion (*US*).
billot [bijo] *nm* block.
BIMA *sigle m* = *Bulletin d'information du ministère de l'agriculture.*
bimbeloterie [bɛ̃blɔtʀi] *nf* (*objets*) fancy goods.
bimensuel, le [bimɑ̃sɥɛl] *adj* bimonthly, twice-monthly.
bimestriel, le [bimɛstʀijɛl] *adj* bimonthly, two-monthly.
bimoteur [bimɔtœʀ] *adj* twin-engined.
binaire [binɛʀ] *adj* binary.
biner [bine] *vt* to hoe.
binette [binɛt] *nf* (*outil*) hoe.
binoclard, e [binɔklaʀ, ɑʀd(ə)] (*fam*) *adj* specky ♦ *nm/f* four-eyes.
binocle [binɔkl(ə)] *nm* pince-nez.
binoculaire [binɔkylɛʀ] *adj* binocular.
binôme [binom] *nm* binomial.
bio... [bjɔ] *préfixe* bio....
biochimie [bjɔʃimi] *nf* biochemistry.
biochimique [bjɔʃimik] *adj* biochemical.
biochimiste [bjɔʃimist(ə)] *nm/f* biochemist.
biodégradable [bjɔdegʀadabl(ə)] *adj* biodegradable.
biodiversité [bjodivɛʀsite] *nf* biodiversity.
bioéthique [bjoetik] *nf* bioethics *sg*.
biographe [bjɔgʀaf] *nm/f* biographer.
biographie [bjɔgʀafi] *nf* biography.
biographique [bjɔgʀafik] *adj* biographical.
biologie [bjɔlɔʒi] *nf* biology.
biologique [bjɔlɔʒik] *adj* biological.
biologiste [bjɔlɔʒist(ə)] *nm/f* biologist.
biomasse [bjomas] *nf* biomass.
biopsie [bjɔpsi] *nf* (*MÉD*) biopsy.
biosphère [bjɔsfɛʀ] *nf* biosphere.
biotope [bjɔtɔp] *nm* biotope.
bipartisme [bipaʀtism(ə)] *nm* two-party system.
bipartite [bipaʀtit] *adj* (*POL*) two-party, bipartisan.
bipède [bipɛd] *nm* biped, two-footed creature.
biphasé, e [bifaze] *adj* (*ÉLEC*) two-phase.
biplace [biplas] *adj, nm* (*avion*) two-seater.
biplan [biplɑ̃] *nm* biplane.
bique [bik] *nf* nanny goat; (*péj*) old hag.
biquet, te [bikɛ, -ɛt] *nm/f*: **mon** ~ (*fam*) my lamb.
BIRD [biʀd] *sigle f* (= *Banque internationale pour la reconstruction et le développement*) IBRD.
biréacteur [biʀeaktœʀ] *nm* twin-engined jet.
birman, e [biʀmɑ̃, -an] *adj* Burmese.
Birmanie [biʀmani] *nf*: **la** ~ Burma.
bis, e [bi, biz] *adj* (*couleur*) greyish brown ♦ *adv* [bis]: **12** ~ 12a *ou* A ♦ *excl, nm* [bis] encore ♦ *nf* (*baiser*) kiss; (*vent*) North wind.
bisaïeul, e [bisajœl] *nm/f* great-grandfather/great-grandmother.
bisannuel, le [bizanɥɛl] *adj* biennial.
bisbille [bisbij] *nf*: **être en** ~ **avec qn** to be at loggerheads with sb.
Biscaye [biske] *nf*: **le golfe de** ~ the Bay of Biscay.
biscornu, e [biskɔʀny] *adj* crooked; (*bizarre*) weird(-looking).
biscotte [biskɔt] *nf* (breakfast) rusk.
biscuit [biskɥi] *nm* biscuit (*BRIT*), cookie (*US*); (*gateau*) sponge cake; ~ **à la cuiller** sponge finger.
biscuiterie [biskɥitʀi] *nf* biscuit manufacturing.
bise [biz] *adj f, nf voir* **bis**.
biseau, x [bizo] *nm* bevelled edge; **en** ~ bevelled.
biseauter [bizote] *vt* to bevel.
bisexué, e [bisɛksɥe] *adj* bisexual.
bisexuel, le [bisɛksɥɛl] *adj, nm/f* bisexual.
bismuth [bismyt] *nm* bismuth.
bison [bizɔ̃] *nm* bison.
bisou [bizu] *nm* (*fam*) kiss.
bisque [bisk(ə)] *nf*: ~ **d'écrevisses** shrimp bisque.
bissectrice [bisɛktʀis] *nf* bisector.
bisser [bise] *vt* (*faire rejouer: artiste, chanson*) to encore; (*rejouer: morceau*) to give an encore of.
bissextile [bisɛkstil] *adj*: **année** ~ leap year.
bistouri [bistuʀi] *nm* lancet.
bistre [bistʀ(ə)] *adj* (*couleur*) bistre; (*peau, teint*) tanned.
bistro(t) [bistʀo] *nm* bistro, café.
BIT *sigle m* (= *Bureau international du travail*) ILO.
bit [bit] *nm* (*INFORM*) bit.
biterrois, e [bitɛʀwa, -waz] *adj* of *ou* from Béziers.
bitte [bit] *nf*: ~ **d'amarrage** bollard (*NAUT*).
bitume [bitym] *nm* asphalt.
bitumer [bityme] *vt* to asphalt.
bivalent, e [bivalɑ̃, -ɑ̃t] *adj* bivalent.
bivouac [bivwak] *nm* bivouac.
bizarre [bizaʀ] *adj* strange, odd.
bizarrement [bizaʀmɑ̃] *adv* strangely, oddly.
bizarrerie [bizaʀʀi] *nf* strangeness, oddness.
blackbouler [blakbule] *vt* (*à une élection*) to blackball.
blafard, e [blafaʀ, -aʀd(ə)] *adj* wan.
blague [blag] *nf* (*propos*) joke; (*farce*) trick; **sans** ~! no kidding!; ~ **à tabac** tobacco pouch.
blaguer [blage] *vi* to joke ♦ *vt* to tease.
blagueur, euse [blagœʀ, -øz] *adj* teasing ♦ *nm/f* joker.
blair [blɛʀ] *nm* (*fam*) conk.
blaireau, x [blɛʀo] *nm* (*ZOOL*) badger; (*brosse*) shaving brush.
blairer [bleʀe] *vt*: **je ne peux pas le** ~ I can't bear *ou* stand him.
blâmable [blɑmabl(ə)] *adj* blameworthy.
blâme [blɑm] *nm* blame; (*sanction*) reprimand.
blâmer [blɑme] *vt* (*réprouver*) to blame; (*réprimander*) to reprimand.

blanc, blanche [blɑ̃, blɑ̃ʃ] *adj* white; (*non imprimé*) blank; (*innocent*) pure ♦ *nm/f* white, white man/woman ♦ *nm* (*couleur*) white; (*linge*): **le** ~ whites *pl*; (*espace non écrit*) blank; (*aussi*: ~ **d'œuf**) (egg-)white; (*aussi*: ~ **de poulet**) breast, white meat; (*aussi*: **vin** ~) white wine ♦ *nf* (*MUS*) minim (*BRIT*), half-note (*US*); (*fam: drogue*) smack; **d'une voix blanche** in a toneless voice; **aux cheveux ~s** white-haired; **le ~ de l'œil** the white of the eye; **laisser en** ~ to leave blank; **chèque en** ~ blank cheque; **à** ~ *adv* (*chauffer*) white-hot; (*tirer, charger*) with blanks; **saigner à** ~ to bleed white; ~ **cassé** off-white.
blanc-bec, *pl* **blancs-becs** [blɑ̃bɛk] *nm* greenhorn.
blanchâtre [blɑ̃ʃɑtʀ(ə)] *adj* (*teint, lumière*) whitish.
blancheur [blɑ̃ʃœʀ] *nf* whiteness.
blanchir [blɑ̃ʃiʀ] *vt* (*gén*) to whiten; (*linge, fig: argent*) to launder; (*CULIN*) to blanch; (*fig: disculper*) to clear ♦ *vi* to grow white; (*cheveux*) to go white; **blanchi à la chaux** whitewashed.
blanchissage [blɑ̃ʃisaʒ] *nm* (*du linge*) laundering.
blanchisserie [blɑ̃ʃisʀi] *nf* laundry.
blanchisseur, euse [blɑ̃ʃisœʀ, -øz] *nm/f* launderer.
blanc-seing, *pl* **blancs-seings** [blɑ̃sɛ̃] *nm* signed blank paper.
blanquette [blɑ̃kɛt] *nf* (*CULIN*): ~ **de veau** veal in a white sauce, blanquette de veau.
blasé, e [blaze] *adj* blasé.
blaser [blaze] *vt* to make blasé.
blason [blazɔ̃] *nm* coat of arms.
blasphémateur, trice [blasfematœʀ, -tʀis] *nm/f* blasphemer.
blasphématoire [blasfematwaʀ] *adj* blasphemous.
blasphème [blasfɛm] *nm* blasphemy.
blasphémer [blasfeme] *vi* to blaspheme ♦ *vt* to blaspheme against.
blatte [blat] *nf* cockroach.
blazer [blazɛʀ] *nm* blazer.
blé [ble] *nm* wheat; ~ **en herbe** wheat on the ear; ~ **noir** buckwheat.
bled [blɛd] *nm* (*péj*) hole; (*en Afrique du Nord*): **le** ~ the interior.
blême [blɛm] *adj* pale.
blêmir [blemiʀ] *vi* (*personne*) to (turn) pale; (*lueur*) to grow pale.
blennorragie [blenɔʀaʒi] *nf* blennorrhoea.
blessant, e [blɛsɑ̃, -ɑ̃t] *adj* hurtful.
blessé, e [blese] *adj* injured ♦ *nm/f* injured person, casualty; **un ~ grave, un grand** ~ a seriously injured *ou* wounded person.
blesser [blese] *vt* to injure; (*délibérément*: *MIL etc*) to wound; (*suj: souliers etc, offenser*) to hurt; **se** ~ to injure o.s.; **se ~ au pied** *etc* to injure one's foot *etc*.
blessure [blesyʀ] *nf* injury; wound.
blet, te [blɛ, blɛt] *adj* overripe.
blette [blɛt] *nf* = **bette**.
bleu, e [blø] *adj* blue; (*bifteck*) very rare ♦ *nm* (*couleur*) blue; (*novice*) greenhorn; (*contusion*) bruise; (*vêtement*: *aussi*: ~**s**) overalls *pl* (*BRIT*), coveralls *pl* (*US*); **avoir une peur ~e** to be scared stiff; **zone ~e** ≈ restricted parking area; **fromage** ~ blue cheese; **au** ~ (*CULIN*) au bleu; ~ **(de lessive)** ≈ blue bag; ~ **de methylène** (*MÉD*) methylene blue; ~ **marine/nuit/roi** navy/midnight/royal blue.
bleuâtre [bløɑtʀ(ə)] *adj* (*fumée etc*) bluish, blueish.
bleuet [bløɛ] *nm* cornflower.
bleuir [bløiʀ] *vt, vi* to turn blue.
bleuté, e [bløte] *adj* blue-shaded.
blindage [blɛ̃daʒ] *nm* armo(u)r-plating.
blindé, e [blɛ̃de] *adj* armoured (*BRIT*), armored (*US*); (*fig*) hardened ♦ *nm* armoured *ou* armored car; (*char*) tank.
blinder [blɛ̃de] *vt* to armour (*BRIT*), armor (*US*); (*fig*) to harden.
blizzard [blizaʀ] *nm* blizzard.
bloc [blɔk] *nm* (*de pierre etc, INFORM*) block; (*de papier à lettres*) pad; (*ensemble*) group, block; **serré à** ~ tightened right down; **en** ~ as a whole; wholesale; **faire** ~ to unite; ~ **opératoire** operating *ou* theatre block; ~ **sanitaire** toilet block; ~ **sténo** shorthand notebook.
blocage [blɔkaʒ] *nm* (*voir bloquer*) blocking; jamming; freezing; (*PSYCH*) hang-up.
bloc-cuisine, *pl* **blocs-cuisines** [blɔkkɥizin] *nm* kitchen unit.
bloc-cylindres, *pl* **blocs-cylindres** [blɔksilɛ̃dʀ(ə)] *nm* cylinder block.
bloc-évier, *pl* **blocs-éviers** [blɔkevje] *nm* sink unit.
bloc-moteur, *pl* **blocs-moteurs** [blɔkmɔtœʀ] *nm* engine block.
bloc-notes, *pl* **blocs-notes** [blɔknɔt] *nm* note pad.
blocus [blɔkys] *nm* blockade.
blond, e [blɔ̃, -ɔ̃d] *adj* fair; (*plus clair*) blond (*sable, blés*) golden ♦ *nm/f* fair-haired *ou* blond man/woman; ~ **cendré** ash blond.
blondeur [blɔ̃dœʀ] *nf* fairness; blondness.
blondin, e [blɔ̃dɛ̃, -in] *nm/f* fair-haired *ou* blond child *ou* young person.
blondinet, te [blɔ̃dinɛ, -ɛt] *nm/f* blondy.
blondir [blɔ̃diʀ] *vi* (*personne, cheveux*) to go fair *ou* blond.
bloquer [blɔke] *vt* (*passage*) to block; (*pièce mobile*) to jam; (*crédits, compte*) to freeze (*personne, négociations etc*) to hold up; (*regrouper*) to group; ~ **les freins** to jam on the brakes.
blottir [blɔtiʀ]: **se** ~ *vi* to huddle up.
blousant, e [bluzɑ̃, ɑ̃t] *adj* blousing out.
blouse [bluz] *nf* overall.
blouser [bluze] *vi* to blouse out.
blouson [bluzɔ̃] *nm* blouson (jacket); ~ **noir** (*fig*) ≈ rocker.

blue-jean(s) [bludʒin(s)] *nm* jeans.
blues [bluz] *nm* blues *pl.*
bluet [blyɛ] *nm* = **bleuet.**
bluff [blœf] *nm* bluff.
bluffer [blœfe] *vi, vt* to bluff.
BN *sigle f* = *Bibliothèque nationale.*
BNP *sigle f* = *Banque nationale de Paris.*
boa [bɔa] *nm* (*ZOOL*): ~ **(constricteur)** boa (constrictor); (*tour de cou*) (feather *ou* fur) boa.
bob [bɔb] *nm* (*SPORT*) bobsleigh.
bobard [bɔbaʀ] *nm* (*fam*) tall story.
bobèche [bɔbɛʃ] *nf* candle-ring.
bobine [bɔbin] *nf* (*de fil*) reel; (*de machine à coudre*) spool; (*de machine à écrire*) ribbon; (*ÉLEC*) coil; ~ **(d'allumage)** (*AUTO*) coil; ~ **de pellicule** (*PHOTO*) roll of film.
bobo [bobo] *nm* (*aussi fig*) sore spot.
bob(sleigh) [bɔb(slɛg)] *nm* bob(sleigh).
bocage [bɔkaʒ] *nm* (*GÉO*) bocage, *farmland criss-crossed by hedges and trees*; (*bois*) grove, copse (*BRIT*).
bocal, aux [bɔkal, -o] *nm* jar.
bock [bɔk] *nm* (beer) glass; (*contenu*) glass of beer.
bœuf [bœf, *pl* bø] *nm* ox (*pl* oxen), steer; (*CULIN*) beef; (*MUS: fam*) jam session.
bof [bɔf] *excl* (*fam: indifférence*) don't care!; (*: pas terrible*) nothing special.
bogue [bɔg] *nf* (*BOT*) husk ♦ *nm* (*ORDIN*) bug; ~ **de l'an 2000** millennium bug.
Bohème [bɔɛm] *nf*: **la** ~ Bohemia.
bohème [bɔɛm] *adj* happy-go-lucky, unconventional.
bohémien, ne [bɔemjɛ̃, -ɛn] *adj* Bohemian ♦ *nm/f* gipsy.
boire [bwaʀ] *vt* to drink; (*s'imprégner de*) to soak up; ~ **un coup** to have a drink.
bois [bwa] *vb voir* **boire** ♦ *nm* wood; (*ZOOL*) antler; (*MUS*): **les** ~ the woodwind; **de** ~, **en** ~ wooden; ~ **vert** green wood; ~ **mort** deadwood; ~ **de lit** bedstead.
boisé, e [bwaze] *adj* woody, wooded.
boiser [bwaze] *vt* (*galerie de mine*) to timber; (*chambre*) to panel; (*terrain*) to plant with trees.
boiseries [bwazʀi] *nfpl* panelling *sg.*
boisson [bwasɔ̃] *nf* drink; **pris de** ~ drunk, intoxicated; ~**s alcoolisées** alcoholic beverages *ou* drinks; ~**s non alcoolisées** soft drinks.
boit [bwa] *vb voir* **boire.**
boîte [bwat] *nf* box; (*fam: entreprise*) firm, company; **aliments en** ~ canned *ou* tinned (*BRIT*) foods; ~ **de sardines/petits pois** can *ou* tin (*BRIT*) of sardines/peas; **mettre qn en** ~ (*fam*) to have a laugh at sb's expense; ~ **d'allumettes** box of matches; (*vide*) matchbox; ~ **de conserves** can *ou* tin (*BRIT*) (of food); ~ **crânienne** cranium; ~ **à gants** glove compartment; ~ **aux lettres** letter box, mailbox (*US*); (*INFORM*) mailbox; ~ **à musique** musical box; ~ **noire** (*AVIAT*) black box; ~ **de nuit** night club; ~ **à ordures** dustbin (*BRIT*), trash can (*US*); ~ **postale (BP)** PO box; ~ **de vitesses** gear box; ~ **vocale** (*dispositif*) voice mail.
boiter [bwate] *vi* to limp; (*fig*) to wobble; (*raisonnement*) to be shaky.
boiteux, euse [bwatø, -øz] *adj* lame; wobbly; shaky.
boîtier [bwatje] *nm* case; (*d'appareil-photo*) body; ~ **de montre** watch case.
boitiller [bwatije] *vi* to limp slightly, have a slight limp.
boive [bwav] *etc vb voir* **boire.**
bol [bɔl] *nm* bowl; (*contenu*): **un** ~ **de café** *etc* a bowl of coffee *etc*; **un** ~ **d'air** a breath of fresh air; **en avoir ras le** ~ (*fam*) to have had a bellyful.
bolée [bɔle] *nf* bowlful.
boléro [bɔleʀo] *nm* bolero.
bolet [bɔlɛ] *nm* boletus (mushroom).
bolide [bɔlid] *nm* racing car; **comme un** ~ like a rocket.
Bolivie [bɔlivi] *nf*: **la** ~ Bolivia.
bolivien, ne [bɔlivjɛ̃, -ɛn] *adj* Bolivian ♦ *nm/f*: **B~, ne** Bolivian.
bolognais, e [bɔlɔɲɛ, -ɛz] *adj* Bolognese.
Bologne [bɔlɔɲ] *n* Bologna.
bombardement [bɔ̃baʀdəmɑ̃] *nm* bombing.
bombarder [bɔ̃baʀde] *vt* to bomb; ~ **qn de** (*cailloux, lettres*) to bombard sb with; ~ **qn directeur** to thrust sb into the director's seat.
bombardier [bɔ̃baʀdje] *nm* (*avion*) bomber; (*aviateur*) bombardier.
bombe [bɔ̃b] *nf* bomb; (*atomiseur*) (aerosol) spray; (*ÉQUITATION*) riding cap; **faire la** ~ (*fam*) to go on a binge; ~ **atomique** atomic bomb; ~ **à retardement** time bomb.
bombé, e [bɔ̃be] *adj* rounded; (*mur*) bulging; (*front*) domed; (*route*) steeply cambered.
bomber [bɔ̃be] *vi* to bulge; (*route*) to camber ♦ *vt*: ~ **le torse** to swell out one's chest.

MOT-CLÉ

bon, bonne [bɔ̃, bɔn] *adj* **1** (*agréable, satisfaisant*) good; **un** ~ **repas/restaurant** a good meal/restaurant; **être** ~ **en maths** to be good at maths

2 (*charitable*): **être** ~ **(envers)** to be good (to), to be kind (to); **vous êtes trop** ~ you're too kind

3 (*correct*) right; **le** ~ **numéro/moment** the right number/moment

4 (*souhaits*): ~ **anniversaire** happy birthday; ~ **voyage** have a good trip; **bonne chance** good luck; **bonne année** happy New Year; **bonne nuit** good night

5 (*approprié*): ~ **à/pour** fit to/for; ~ **à jeter** fit for the bin; **c'est** ~ **à savoir** that's useful to know; **à quoi** ~ **(...)?** what's the point *ou* use (of ...)?

6 (*intensif*): **ça m'a pris 2 bonnes heures** it

took me a good 2 hours; **un ~ nombre de** a good number of
7: ~ **enfant** *adj inv* accommodating, easy-going; **bonne femme** (*péj*) woman; **de bonne heure** early; ~ **marché** cheap; ~ **mot** witticism; **pour faire ~ poids ...** to make up for it ...; ~ **sens** common sense; ~ **vivant** jovial chap; **bonnes œuvres** charitable works, charities; **bonne sœur** nun
♦ *nm* **1** (*billet*) voucher; (*aussi*: ~ **cadeau**) gift voucher; ~ **de caisse** cash voucher; ~ **d'essence** petrol coupon; ~ **à tirer** pass for press; ~ **du Trésor** Treasury bond
2: **avoir du** ~ to have its good points; **il y a du ~ dans ce qu'il dit** there's some sense in what he says; **pour de** ~ for good
♦ *nm/f*: **un ~ à rien** a good-for-nothing
♦ *adv*: **il fait** ~ it's *ou* the weather is fine; **sentir** ~ to smell good; **tenir** ~ to stand firm; **juger ~ de faire ...** to think fit to do ...
♦ *excl* right!, good!; **ah ~?** really?; ~, **je reste** right, I'll stay; *voir aussi* **bonne.**

bonasse [bɔnas] *adj* soft, meek.
bonbon [bɔ̃bɔ̃] *nm* (boiled) sweet.
bonbonne [bɔ̃bɔn] *nf* demijohn; carboy.
bonbonnière [bɔ̃bɔnjɛʀ] *nf* sweet (*BRIT*) *ou* candy (*US*) box.
bond [bɔ̃] *nm* leap; (*d'une balle*) rebound, ricochet; **faire un** ~ to leap in the air; **d'un seul** ~ in one bound, with one leap; ~ **en avant** (*fig: progrès*) leap forward.
bonde [bɔ̃d] *nf* (*d'évier etc*) plug; (*: trou*) plughole; (*de tonneau*) bung; bunghole.
bondé, e [bɔ̃de] *adj* packed (full).
bondieuserie [bɔ̃djøzʀi] *nf* (*péj: objet*) religious knick-knack.
bondir [bɔ̃diʀ] *vi* to leap; ~ **de joie** (*fig*) to jump for joy; ~ **de colère** (*fig*) to be hopping mad.
bonheur [bɔnœʀ] *nm* happiness; **avoir le ~ de** to have the good fortune to; **porter ~ (à qn)** to bring (sb) luck; **au petit** ~ haphazardly; **par** ~ fortunately.
bonhomie [bɔnɔmi] *nf* goodnaturedness.
bonhomme [bɔnɔm], *pl* **bonshommes** [bɔ̃zɔm] *nm* fellow ♦ *adj* good-natured; **un vieux** ~ an old chap; **aller son ~ de chemin** to carry on in one's own sweet way; ~ **de neige** snowman.
boni [bɔni] *nm* profit.
bonification [bɔnifikɑsjɔ̃] *nf* bonus.
bonifier [bɔnifje] *vt*, **se** ~ *vi* to improve.
boniment [bɔnimɑ̃] *nm* patter *no pl*.
bonjour [bɔ̃ʒuʀ] *excl, nm* hello; (*selon l'heure*) good morning (*ou* afternoon); **donner** *ou* **souhaiter le ~ à qn** to bid sb good morning *ou* afternoon.
Bonn [bɔn] *n* Bonn.
bonne [bɔn] *adj f voir* **bon** ♦ *nf* (*domestique*) maid; ~ **à tout faire** general help; ~ **d'enfant** nanny.
bonne-maman, *pl* **bonnes-mamans** [bɔnmamɑ̃] granny, grandma, gran.
bonnement [bɔnmɑ̃] *adv*: **tout** ~ quite simply.
bonnet [bɔnɛ] *nm* bonnet, hat; (*de soutien-gorge*) cup; ~ **d'âne** dunce's cap; ~ **de bain** bathing cap; ~ **de nuit** nightcap.
bonneterie [bɔnɛtʀi] *nf* hosiery.
bon-papa, *pl* **bons-papas** [bɔ̃papa] *nm* grandpa, grandad.
bonsoir [bɔ̃swaʀ] *excl* good evening.
bonté [bɔ̃te] *nf* kindness *no pl*; **avoir la ~ de** to be kind *ou* good enough to.
bonus [bɔnys] *nm* (*assurances*) no-claims bonus.
bonze [bɔ̃z] *nm* (*REL*) bonze.
boomerang [bumʀɑ̃g] *nm* boomerang.
boots [buts] *nfpl* boots.
borborygme [bɔʀbɔʀigm(ə)] *nm* rumbling noise.
bord [bɔʀ] *nm* (*de table, verre, falaise*) edge; (*de rivière, lac*) bank; (*de route*) side; (*de vêtement*) edge, border; (*de chapeau*) brim; **(monter) à** ~ (to go) on board; **jeter par-dessus** ~ to throw overboard; **le commandant de ~/les hommes du** ~ the ship's master/crew; **du même** ~ (*fig*) of the same opinion; **au ~ de la mer/route** at the seaside/roadside; **être au ~ des larmes** to be on the verge of tears; **virer de** ~ (*NAVIG*) to tack; **sur les ~s** (*fig*) slightly; **de tous ~s** on all sides; ~ **du trottoir** kerb (*BRIT*), curb (*US*).
bordage [bɔʀdaʒ] *nm* (*NAVIG*) planking *no pl*; plating *no pl*.
bordeaux [bɔʀdo] *nm* Bordeaux ♦ *adj inv* maroon.
bordée [bɔʀde] *nf* broadside; **une ~ d'injures** a volley of abuse; **tirer une** ~ to go on the town.
bordel [bɔʀdɛl] *nm* brothel; (*fam!*) bloody (*BRIT*) *ou* goddamn (*US*) mess (*!*) ♦ *excl* hell!
bordelais, e [bɔʀdəlɛ, -ɛz] *adj* of *ou* from Bordeaux.
border [bɔʀde] *vt* (*être le long de*) to border, line; (*garnir*): ~ **qch de** to line sth with; to trim sth with; (*qn dans son lit*) to tuck up.
bordereau, x [bɔʀdəʀo] *nm* docket, slip.
bordure [bɔʀdyʀ] *nf* border; (*sur un vêtement*) trim(ming), border; **en ~ de** on the edge of.
boréal, e, aux [bɔʀeal, -o] *adj* boreal, northern.
borgne [bɔʀɲ(ə)] *adj* one-eyed; **hôtel** ~ shady hotel; **fenêtre** ~ obstructed window.
bornage [bɔʀnaʒ] *nm* (*d'un terrain*) demarcation.
borne [bɔʀn(ə)] *nf* boundary stone; (*aussi*: ~ **kilométrique**) kilometre-marker, ≈ milestone; **~s** *nfpl* (*fig*) limits; **dépasser les ~s** to go too far; **sans ~(s)** boundless.
borné, e [bɔʀne] *adj* narrow; (*obtus*) narrow-minded.
Bornéo [bɔʀneo] *nm*: **le** ~ Borneo.
borner [bɔʀne] *vt* (*délimiter*) to limit; (*limiter*

to confine; **se ~ à faire** to content o.s. with doing; to limit o.s. to doing.
bosniaque [bɔznjak] *adj* Bosnian ♦ *nm/f*: **B~** Bosnian.
Bosnie [bɔsni] *nf* Bosnia.
bosnien, ne [bɔznjɛ̃, -ɛn] *adj* Bosnian ♦ *nm/f*: **B~, ne** Bosnian.
Bosphore [bɔsfɔʀ] *nm*: **le ~** the Bosphorus.
bosquet [bɔskɛ] *nm* copse (*BRIT*), grove.
bosse [bɔs] *nf* (*de terrain etc*) bump; (*enflure*) lump; (*du bossu, du chameau*) hump; **avoir la ~ des maths** *etc* to have a gift for maths *etc*; **il a roulé sa ~** he's been around.
bosseler [bɔsle] *vt* (*ouvrer*) to emboss; (*abîmer*) to dent.
bosser [bɔse] *vi* (*fam*) to work; (*: dur*) to slog (hard) (*BRIT*), slave (away).
bosseur, euse [bɔsœʀ, -øz] *nm/f* (hard) worker, slogger (*BRIT*).
bossu, e [bɔsy] *nm/f* hunchback.
bot [bo] *adj m*: **pied ~** club foot.
botanique [bɔtanik] *nf* botany ♦ *adj* botanic(al).
botaniste [bɔtanist(ə)] *nm/f* botanist.
Botswana [bɔtswana] *nm*: **le ~** Botswana.
botte [bɔt] *nf* (*soulier*) (high) boot; (*ESCRIME*) thrust; (*gerbe*): **~ de paille** bundle of straw; **~ de radis/d'asperges** bunch of radishes/asparagus; **~s de caoutchouc** wellington boots.
botter [bɔte] *vt* to put boots on; (*donner un coup de pied à*) to kick; (*fam*): **ça me botte** I fancy that.
bottier [bɔtje] *nm* bootmaker.
bottillon [bɔtijɔ̃] *nm* bootee.
bottin [bɔtɛ̃] *nm* ® directory.
bottine [bɔtin] *nf* ankle boot.
botulisme [bɔtylism(ə)] *nm* botulism.
bouc [buk] *nm* goat; (*barbe*) goatee; **~ émissaire** scapegoat.
boucan [bukɑ̃] *nm* din, racket.
bouche [buʃ] *nf* mouth; **une ~ à nourrir** a mouth to feed; **les ~s inutiles** the non-productive members of the population; **faire du ~ à ~ à qn** to give sb the kiss of life (*BRIT*), give sb mouth-to-mouth resuscitation; **de ~ à oreille** confidentially; **pour la bonne ~** (*pour la fin*) till last; **faire venir l'eau à la ~** to make one's mouth water; **~ cousue!** mum's the word!; **~ d'aération** air vent; **~ de chaleur** hot air vent; **~ d'égout** manhole; **~ d'incendie** fire hydrant; **~ de métro** métro entrance.
bouché, e [buʃe] *adj* (*flacon etc*) stoppered; (*temps, ciel*) overcast; (*carrière*) blocked; (*péj: personne*) thick; (*trompette*) muted; **avoir le nez ~** to have a blocked(-up) nose.
bouchée [buʃe] *nf* mouthful; **ne faire qu'une ~ de** (*fig*) to make short work of; **pour une ~ de pain** (*fig*) for next to nothing; **~s à la reine** chicken vol-au-vents.
boucher [buʃe] *nm* butcher ♦ *vt* (*pour colmater*) to stop up; to fill up; (*obstruer*) to block (up); **se ~** (*tuyau etc*) to block up, get blocked up; **se ~ le nez** to hold one's nose.
bouchère [buʃɛʀ] *nf* butcher; (*femme du boucher*) butcher's wife.
boucherie [buʃʀi] *nf* butcher's (shop); (*métier*) butchery; (*fig*) slaughter, butchery.
bouche-trou [buʃtʀu] *nm* (*fig*) stop-gap.
bouchon [buʃɔ̃] *nm* (*en liège*) cork; (*autre matière*) stopper; (*fig: embouteillage*) holdup; (*PÊCHE*) float; **~ doseur** measuring cap.
bouchonner [buʃɔne] *vt* to rub down ♦ *vi* to form a traffic jam.
bouchot [buʃo] *nm* mussel bed.
bouclage [buklaʒ] *nm* sealing off.
boucle [bukl(ə)] *nf* (*forme, figure, aussi INFORM*) loop; (*objet*) buckle; **~ (de cheveux)** curl; **~ d'oreilles** earring.
bouclé, e [bukle] *adj* curly; (*tapis*) uncut.
boucler [bukle] *vt* (*fermer: ceinture etc*) to fasten; (*: magasin*) to shut; (*terminer*) to finish off; (*: circuit*) to complete; (*budget*) to balance; (*enfermer*) to shut away; (*: condamné*) to lock up; (*: quartier*) to seal off ♦ *vi* to curl; **faire ~** (*cheveux*) to curl; **~ la boucle** (*AVIAT*) to loop the loop.
bouclette [buklɛt] *nf* small curl.
bouclier [buklije] *nm* shield.
bouddha [buda] *nm* Buddha.
bouddhisme [budism(ə)] *nm* Buddhism.
bouddhiste [budist(ə)] *nm/f* Buddhist.
bouder [bude] *vi* to sulk ♦ *vt* (*chose*) to turn one's nose up at; (*personne*) to refuse to have anything to do with.
bouderie [budʀi] *nf* sulking *no pl*.
boudeur, euse [budœʀ, -øz] *adj* sullen, sulky.
boudin [budɛ̃] *nm* (*CULIN*) black pudding; (*TECH*) roll; **~ blanc** white pudding.
boudiné, e [budine] *adj* (*doigt*) podgy; (*serré*): **~ dans** (*vêtement*) bulging out of.
boudoir [budwaʀ] *nm* boudoir; (*biscuit*) sponge finger.
boue [bu] *nf* mud.
bouée [bwe] *nf* buoy; (*de baigneur*) rubber ring; **~ (de sauvetage)** lifebuoy; (*fig*) lifeline.
boueux, euse [bwø, -øz] *adj* muddy ♦ *nm* (*fam*) refuse (*BRIT*) *ou* garbage (*US*) collector.
bouffant, e [bufɑ̃, -ɑ̃t] *adj* puffed out.
bouffe [buf] *nf* (*fam*) grub, food.
bouffée [bufe] *nf* puff; **~ de chaleur** (*gén*) blast of hot air; (*MÉD*) hot flush (*BRIT*) *ou* flash (*US*); **~ de fièvre/de honte** flush of fever/shame; **~ d'orgueil** fit of pride.
bouffer [bufe] *vi* (*fam*) to eat; (*COUTURE*) to puff out ♦ *vt* (*fam*) to eat.
bouffi, e [bufi] *adj* swollen.
bouffon, ne [bufɔ̃, -ɔn] *adj* farcical, comical ♦ *nm* jester.
bouge [buʒ] *nm* (*bar louche*) (low) dive; (*taudis*) hovel.
bougeoir [buʒwaʀ] *nm* candlestick.

bougeotte [buʒɔt] *nf*: **avoir la ~** to have the fidgets.
bouger [buʒe] *vi* to move; (*dent etc*) to be loose; (*changer*) to alter; (*agir*) to stir ♦ *vt* to move; **se ~** (*fam*) to move (oneself).
bougie [buʒi] *nf* candle; (*AUTO*) spark(ing) plug.
bougon, ne [bugɔ̃, -ɔn] *adj* grumpy.
bougonner [bugɔne] *vi, vt* to grumble.
bougre [bugʀ(ə)] *nm* chap; (*fam*): **ce ~ de ...** that confounded ....
boui-boui [bwibwi] *nm* (*fam*) greasy spoon.
bouillabaisse [bujabɛs] *nf type of fish soup.*
bouillant, e [bujɑ̃, -ɑ̃t] *adj* (*qui bout*) boiling; (*très chaud*) boiling (hot); (*fig: ardent*) hotheaded; **~ de colère** *etc* seething with anger *etc.*
bouille [buj] *nf* (*fam*) mug.
bouilleur [bujœʀ] *nm*: **~ de cru** (home) distiller.
bouillie [buji] *nf* gruel; (*de bébé*) cereal; **en ~** (*fig*) crushed.
bouillir [bujiʀ] *vi* to boil ♦ *vt* (*aussi*: **faire ~**: *CULIN*) to boil; **~ de colère** *etc* to seethe with anger *etc.*
bouilloire [bujwaʀ] *nf* kettle.
bouillon [bujɔ̃] *nm* (*CULIN*) stock *no pl*; (*bulles, écume*) bubble; **~ de culture** culture medium.
bouillonnement [bujɔnmɑ̃] *nm* (*d'un liquide*) bubbling; (*des idées*) ferment.
bouillonner [bujɔne] *vi* to bubble; (*fig*) to bubble up; (*torrent*) to foam.
bouillotte [bujɔt] *nf* hot-water bottle.
boulanger, ère [bulɑ̃ʒe, -ɛʀ] *nm/f* baker ♦ *nf* (*femme du boulanger*) baker's wife.
boulangerie [bulɑ̃ʒʀi] *nf* bakery, baker's (shop); (*commerce*) bakery; **~ industrielle** bakery.
boulangerie-pâtisserie, *pl* **boulangeries-pâtisseries** [bulɑ̃ʒʀipɑtisʀi] *nf* baker's and confectioner's (shop).
boule [bul] *nf* (*gén*) ball; (*pour jouer*) bowl; (*de machine à écrire*) golf ball; **roulé en ~** curled up in a ball; **se mettre en ~** (*fig*) to fly off the handle, blow one's top; **perdre la ~** (*fig: fam*) to go off one's rocker; **~ de gomme** (*bonbon*) gum(drop), pastille; **~ de neige** snowball; **faire ~ de neige** (*fig*) to snowball.
bouleau, x [bulo] *nm* (silver) birch.
bouledogue [buldɔg] *nm* bulldog.
bouler [bule] *vi* (*fam*): **envoyer ~ qn** to send sb packing; **je me suis fait ~** (*à un examen*) they flunked me.
boulet [bulɛ] *nm* (*aussi*: **~ de canon**) cannonball; (*de bagnard*) ball and chain; (*charbon*) (coal) nut.
boulette [bulɛt] *nf* ball.
boulevard [bulvaʀ] *nm* boulevard.
bouleversant, e [bulvɛʀsɑ̃, -ɑ̃t] *adj* (*récit*) deeply distressing; (*nouvelle*) shattering.
bouleversé, e [bulvɛʀse] *adj* (*ému*) deeply distressed; shattered.
bouleversement [bulvɛʀsəmɑ̃] *nm* (*politique, social*) upheaval.
bouleverser [bulvɛʀse] *vt* (*émouvoir*) to overwhelm; (*causer du chagrin à*) to distress; (*pays, vie*) to disrupt; (*papiers, objets*) to turn upside down, upset.
boulier [bulje] *nm* abacus; (*de jeu*) scoring board.
boulimie [bulimi] *nf* bulimia; compulsive eating.
boulimique [bulimik] *adj* bulimic.
boulingrin [bulɛ̃gʀɛ̃] *nm* lawn.
bouliste [bulist(ə)] *nm/f* bowler.
boulocher [bulɔʃe] *vi* (*laine etc*) to develop little snarls.
boulodrome [bulɔdʀɔm] *nm* bowling pitch.
boulon [bulɔ̃] *nm* bolt.
boulonner [bulɔne] *vt* to bolt.
boulot [bulo] *nm* (*fam: travail*) work.
boulot, te [bulo, -ɔt] *adj* plump, tubby.
boum [bum] *nm* bang ♦ *nf* party.
bouquet [bukɛ] *nm* (*de fleurs*) bunch (of flowers), bouquet; (*de persil etc*) bunch; (*parfum*) bouquet; (*fig*) crowning piece; **c'est le ~!** that's the last straw!; **~ garni** (*CULIN*) bouquet garni.
bouquetin [buktɛ̃] *nm* ibex.
bouquin [bukɛ̃] *nm* (*fam*) book.
bouquiner [bukine] *vi* (*fam*) to read.
bouquiniste [bukinist(ə)] *nm/f* bookseller.
bourbeux, euse [buʀbø, -øz] *adj* muddy.
bourbier [buʀbje] *nm* (quag)mire.
bourde [buʀd(ə)] *nf* (*erreur*) howler; (*gaffe*) blunder.
bourdon [buʀdɔ̃] *nm* bumblebee.
bourdonnement [buʀdɔnmɑ̃] *nm* buzzing *no pl*, buzz; **avoir des ~s d'oreilles** to have a buzzing (noise) in one's ears.
bourdonner [buʀdɔne] *vi* to buzz; (*moteur*) to hum.
bourg [buʀ] *nm* small market town (*ou* village).
bourgade [buʀgad] *nf* township.
bourgeois, e [buʀʒwa, -waz] *adj* (*péj*) ≈ (upper) middle class; bourgeois; (*maison etc*) very comfortable ♦ *nm/f* (*autrefois*) burgher.
bourgeoisie [buʀʒwazi] *nf* ≈ upper middle classes *pl*; bourgeoisie; **petite ~** middle classes.
bourgeon [buʀʒɔ̃] *nm* bud.
bourgeonner [buʀʒɔne] *vi* to bud.
Bourgogne [buʀgɔɲ] *nf*: **la ~** Burgundy ♦ *nm*: **b~** burgundy (wine).
bourguignon, ne [buʀgiɲɔ̃, -ɔn] *adj* of *ou* from Burgundy, Burgundian; **bœuf ~** bœuf bourguignon.
bourlinguer [buʀlɛ̃ge] *vi* to knock about a lot, get around a lot.
bourrade [buʀad] *nf* shove, thump.
bourrage [buʀaʒ] *nm* (*papier*) jamming; **~ de**

crâne brainwashing; (*SCOL*) cramming.

bourrasque [buʀask(ə)] *nf* squall.

bourratif, ive [buʀatif, -iv] *adj* filling, stodgy.

bourre [buʀ] *nf* (*de coussin, matelas etc*) stuffing.

bourré, e [buʀe] *adj* (*rempli*): ~ **de** crammed full of; (*fam: ivre*) pickled, plastered.

bourreau, x [buʀo] *nm* executioner; (*fig*) torturer; ~ **de travail** workaholic, glutton for work.

bourrelé, e [buʀle] *adj*: **être** ~ **de remords** to be racked by remorse.

bourrelet [buʀlɛ] *nm* draught (*BRIT*) *ou* draft (*US*) excluder; (*de peau*) fold *ou* roll (of flesh).

bourrer [buʀe] *vt* (*pipe*) to fill; (*poêle*) to pack; (*valise*) to cram (full); ~ **de** to cram (full) with, stuff with; ~ **de coups** to hammer blows on, pummel; ~ **le crâne à qn** to pull the wool over sb's eyes; (*endoctriner*) to brainwash sb.

bourricot [buʀiko] *nm* small donkey.

bourrique [buʀik] *nf* (*âne*) ass.

bourru, e [buʀy] *adj* surly, gruff.

bourse [buʀs(ə)] *nf* (*subvention*) grant; (*porte-monnaie*) purse; **sans** ~ **délier** without spending a penny; **la B**~ the Stock Exchange; ~ **du travail** ≈ trades union council (regional headquarters).

boursicoter [buʀsikɔte] *vi* (*COMM*) to dabble on the Stock Market.

boursier, ière [buʀsje, -jɛʀ] *adj* (*COMM*) Stock Market *cpd* ♦ *nm/f* (*SCOL*) grant-holder.

boursouflé, e [buʀsufle] *adj* swollen, puffy; (*fig*) bombastic, turgid.

boursoufler [buʀsufle] *vt* to puff up, bloat; **se** ~ *vi* (*visage*) to swell *ou* puff up; (*peinture*) to blister.

boursouflure [buʀsuflyʀ] *nf* (*du visage*) swelling, puffiness; (*de la peinture*) blister; (*fig: du style*) pomposity.

bous [bu] *vb voir* **bouillir**.

bousculade [buskylad] *nf* (*hâte*) rush; (*poussée*) crush.

bousculer [buskyle] *vt* to knock over; to knock into; (*fig*) to push, rush.

bouse [buz] *nf*: ~ **(de vache)** (cow) dung *no pl* (*BRIT*), manure *no pl*.

bousiller [buzije] *vt* (*fam*) to wreck.

boussole [busɔl] *nf* compass.

bout [bu] *vb voir* **bouillir** ♦ *nm* bit; (*extrémité: d'un bâton etc*) tip; (*: d'une ficelle, table, rue, période*) end; **au** ~ **de** at the end of, after; **au** ~ **du compte** at the end of the day; **pousser qn à** ~ to push sb to the limit (of his patience); **venir à** ~ **de** to manage to finish (off) *ou* overcome; ~ **à** ~ end to end; **à tout** ~ **de champ** at every turn; **d'un** ~ **à l'autre, de** ~ **en** ~ from one end to the other; **à** ~ **portant** at point-blank range; **un** ~ **de chou** (*enfant*) a little tot; ~ **d'essai** (*CINÉ etc*) screen test; ~ **filtre** filter tip.

boutade [butad] *nf* quip, sally.

boute-en-train [butɑ̃tʀɛ̃] *nm inv* live wire (*fig*).

bouteille [butɛj] *nf* bottle; (*de gaz butane*) cylinder.

boutiquaire [butikɛʀ] *adj*: **niveau** ~ shopping level.

boutique [butik] *nf* shop (*BRIT*), store (*US*); (*de grand couturier, de mode*) boutique.

boutiquier, ière [butikje, -jɛʀ] *nm/f* shopkeeper (*BRIT*), storekeeper (*US*).

boutoir [butwaʀ] *nm*: **coup de** ~ (*choc*) thrust; (*fig: propos*) barb.

bouton [butɔ̃] *nm* (*de vêtement, électrique etc*) button; (*BOT*) bud; (*sur la peau*) spot; (*de porte*) knob; ~ **de manchette** cuff-link; ~ **d'or** buttercup.

boutonnage [butɔnaʒ] *nm* (*action*) buttoning(-up); **un manteau à double** ~ a coat with two rows of buttons.

boutonner [butɔne] *vt* to button up, do up; **se** ~ to button one's clothes up.

boutonneux, euse [butɔnø, -øz] *adj* spotty.

boutonnière [butɔnjɛʀ] *nf* buttonhole.

bouton-poussoir, *pl* **boutons-poussoirs** [butɔ̃puswaʀ] *nm* pushbutton.

bouton-pression, *pl* **boutons-pression** [butɔ̃pʀesjɔ̃] *nm* press stud, snap fastener.

bouture [butyʀ] *nf* cutting; **faire des** ~**s** to take cuttings.

bouvreuil [buvʀœj] *nm* bullfinch.

bovidé [bɔvide] *nm* bovine.

bovin, e [bɔvɛ̃, -in] *adj* bovine ♦ *nm*: ~**s** cattle.

bowling [bɔliŋ] *nm* (tenpin) bowling; (*salle*) bowling alley.

box [bɔks] *nm* lock-up (garage); (*de salle, dortoir*) cubicle; (*d'écurie*) loose-box; **le** ~ **des accusés** the dock.

box(-calf) [bɔks(kalf)] *nm inv* box calf.

boxe [bɔks(ə)] *nf* boxing.

boxer [bɔkse] *vi* to box ♦ *nm* [bɔksɛʀ] (*chien*) boxer.

boxeur [bɔksœʀ] *nm* boxer.

boyau, x [bwajo] *nm* (*corde de raquette etc*) (cat) gut; (*galerie*) passage(way); (narrow) gallery; (*pneu de bicyclette*) tubeless tyre ♦ *nmpl* (*viscères*) entrails, guts.

boycottage [bɔikɔtaʒ] *nm* (*d'un produit*) boycotting.

boycotter [bɔjkɔte] *vt* to boycott.

BP *sigle f* = **boîte postale**.

BPAL *sigle f* (= *base de plein air et de loisir*) open-air leisure centre.

BPF *sigle* (= *bon pour francs*) *printed on cheques before space for amount to be inserted.*

brabançon, ne [bʀabɑ̃sɔ̃, -ɔn] *adj* of *ou* from Brabant.

Brabant [bʀabɑ̃] *nm*: **le** ~ Brabant.

bracelet [bʀaslɛ] *nm* bracelet.

bracelet-montre [bʀaslɛmɔ̃tʀ(ə)] *nm* wristwatch.

braconnage [bʀakɔnaʒ] *nm* poaching.

braconner [bʀakɔne] *vi* to poach.
braconnier [bʀakɔnje] *nm* poacher.
brader [bʀade] *vt* to sell off, sell cheaply.
braderie [bʀadʀi] *nf* clearance sale; (*par des particuliers*) ≈ car boot sale (*BRIT*), ≈ garage sale (*US*); (*magasin*) discount store; (*sur marché*) cut-price (*BRIT*) *ou* cut-rate (*US*) stall.
braguette [bʀagɛt] *nf* fly, flies *pl* (*BRIT*), zipper (*US*).
braillard, e [bʀɑjaʀ, -aʀd] *adj* (*fam*) bawling, yelling.
braille [bʀɑj] *nm* Braille.
braillement [bʀɑjmɑ̃] *nm* (*cri*) bawling *no pl*, yelling *no pl*.
brailler [bʀɑje] *vi* to bawl, yell ♦ *vt* to bawl out, yell out.
braire [bʀɛʀ] *vi* to bray.
braise [bʀɛz] *nf* embers *pl*.
braiser [bʀeze] *vt* to braise; **bœuf braisé** braised steak.
bramer [bʀɑme] *vi* to bell; (*fig*) to wail.
brancard [bʀɑ̃kaʀ] *nm* (*civière*) stretcher; (*bras, perche*) shaft.
brancardier [bʀɑ̃kaʀdje] *nm* stretcher-bearer.
branchages [bʀɑ̃ʃaʒ] *nmpl* branches, boughs.
branche [bʀɑ̃ʃ] *nf* branch; (*de lunettes*) side(-piece).
branché, e [bʀɑ̃ʃe] *adj* (*fam*) switched-on, trendy ♦ *nm/f* (*fam*) trendy.
branchement [bʀɑ̃ʃmɑ̃] *nm* connection.
brancher [bʀɑ̃ʃe] *vt* to connect (up); (*en mettant la prise*) to plug in; ~ **qn/qch sur** (*fig*) to get sb/sth launched onto.
branchies [bʀɑ̃ʃi] *nfpl* gills.
brandade [bʀɑ̃dad] *nf* brandade (*cod dish*).
brandebourgeois, e [bʀɑ̃dəbuʀʒwa, -waz] *adj* of *ou* from Brandenburg.
brandir [bʀɑ̃diʀ] *vt* (*arme*) to brandish, wield; (*document*) to flourish, wave.
brandon [bʀɑ̃dɔ̃] *nm* firebrand.
branlant, e [bʀɑ̃lɑ̃, -ɑ̃t] *adj* (*mur, meuble*) shaky.
branle [bʀɑ̃l] *nm*: **mettre en** ~ to set swinging; **donner le** ~ **à** to set in motion.
branle-bas [bʀɑ̃lbɑ] *nm inv* commotion.
branler [bʀɑ̃le] *vi* to be shaky, be loose ♦ *vt*: ~ **la tête** to shake one's head.
braquage [bʀakaʒ] *nm* (*fam*) stick-up, hold-up; (*AUTO*): **rayon de** ~ turning circle.
braque [bʀak] *nm* (*ZOOL*) pointer.
braquer [bʀake] *vi* (*AUTO*) to turn (the wheel) ♦ *vt* (*revolver etc*): ~ **qch sur** to aim sth at, point sth at; (*mettre en colère*): ~ **qn** to antagonize sb, put sb's back up; ~ **son regard sur** to fix one's gaze on; **se** ~ *vi*: **se** ~ **(contre)** to take a stand (against).
bras [bʀa] *nm* arm; (*de fleuve*) branch ♦ *nmpl* (*fig: travailleurs*) labour *sg* (*BRIT*), labor *sg* (*US*), hands; ~ **dessus** ~ **dessous** arm in arm; **à** ~ **raccourcis** with fists flying; **à tour de** ~ with all one's might; **baisser les** ~ to give up; ~ **droit** (*fig*) right hand man; ~ **de fer** arm-wrestling; **une partie de** ~ **de fer** (*fig*) a trial of strength; ~ **de levier** lever arm; ~ **de mer** arm of the sea, sound.
brasero [bʀɑzeʀo] *nm* brazier.
brasier [bʀɑzje] *nm* blaze, (blazing) inferno; (*fig*) inferno.
Brasilia [bʀazilja] *n* Brasilia.
bras-le-corps [bʀalkɔʀ]: **à** ~ *adv* (a)round the waist.
brassage [bʀasaʒ] *nm* (*de la bière*) brewing; (*fig*) mixing.
brassard [bʀasaʀ] *nm* armband.
brasse [bʀas] *nf* (*nage*) breast-stroke; (*mesure*) fathom; ~ **papillon** butterfly(-stroke).
brassée [bʀase] *nf* armful; **une** ~ **de** (*fig*) a number of.
brasser [bʀase] *vt* (*bière*) to brew; (*remuer: salade*) to toss; (*: cartes*) to shuffle; (*fig*) to mix; ~ **l'argent/les affaires** to handle a lot of money/business.
brasserie [bʀasʀi] *nf* (*restaurant*) bar (*selling food*), brasserie; (*usine*) brewery.
brasseur [bʀasœʀ] *nm* (*de bière*) brewer; ~ **d'affaires** big businessman.
brassière [bʀasjɛʀ] *nf* (baby's) vest (*BRIT*) *ou* undershirt (*US*); (*de sauvetage*) life jacket.
bravache [bʀavaʃ] *nm* blusterer, braggart.
bravade [bʀavad] *nf*: **par** ~ out of bravado.
brave [bʀav] *adj* (*courageux*) brave; (*bon, gentil*) good, kind.
bravement [bʀavmɑ̃] *adv* bravely; (*résolument*) boldly.
braver [bʀave] *vt* to defy.
bravo [bʀavo] *excl* bravo! ♦ *nm* cheer.
bravoure [bʀavuʀ] *nf* bravery.
BRB *sigle f* (*POLICE*: = *Brigade de répression du banditisme*) ≈ serious crime squad.
break [bʀɛk] *nm* (*AUTO*) estate car (*BRIT*), station wagon (*US*).
brebis [bʀəbi] *nf* ewe; ~ **galeuse** black sheep.
brèche [bʀɛʃ] *nf* breach, gap; **être sur la** ~ (*fig*) to be on the go.
bredouille [bʀəduj] *adj* empty-handed.
bredouiller [bʀəduje] *vi, vt* to mumble, stammer.
bref, brève [bʀɛf, bʀɛv] *adj* short, brief ♦ *adv* in short ♦ *nf* (*voyelle*) short vowel; (*information*) brief news item; **d'un ton** ~ sharply, curtly; **en** ~ in short, in brief; **à** ~ **délai** shortly.
brelan [bʀəlɑ̃] *nm*: **un** ~ three of a kind; **un** ~ **d'as** three aces.
breloque [bʀəlɔk] *nf* charm.
brème [bʀɛm] *nf* bream.
Brésil [bʀezil] *nm*: **le** ~ Brazil.
brésilien, ne [bʀeziljɛ̃, -ɛn] *adj* Brazilian ♦ *nm/f*: **B~, ne** Brazilian.
bressan, e [bʀɛsɑ̃, -an] *adj* of *ou* from Bresse.
Bretagne [bʀətaɲ] *nf*: **la** ~ Brittany.
bretelle [bʀətɛl] *nf* (*de fusil etc*) sling; (*de vêtement*) strap; (*d'autoroute*) slip road

(*BRIT*), entrance *ou* exit ramp (*US*); ~**s** *nfpl* (*pour pantalon*) braces (*BRIT*), suspenders (*US*); ~ **de contournement** (*AUTO*) bypass; ~ **de raccordement** (*AUTO*) access road.

breton, ne [bʀətɔ̃, -ɔn] *adj* Breton ♦ *nm* (*LING*) Breton ♦ *nm/f*: **B~, ne** Breton.

breuvage [bʀœvaʒ] *nm* beverage, drink.

brève [bʀɛv] *adj f, nf voir* **bref**.

brevet [bʀəvɛ] *nm* diploma, certificate; ~ **(d'invention)** patent; ~ **d'apprentissage** certificate of apprenticeship; ~ **(des collèges)** *school certificate, taken at approx. 16 years.*

breveté, e [bʀəvte] *adj* patented; (*diplômé*) qualified.

breveter [bʀəvte] *vt* to patent.

bréviaire [bʀevjɛʀ] *nm* breviary.

BRGM *sigle m* = *Bureau de recherches géologiques et minières.*

briard, e [bʀijaʀ, -aʀd(ə)] *adj* of *ou* from Brie ♦ *nm* (*chien*) briard.

bribes [bʀib] *nfpl* bits, scraps; (*d'une conversation*) snatches; **par** ~ piecemeal.

bric [bʀik]: **de** ~ **et de broc** *adv* with any old thing.

bric-à-brac [bʀikabʀak] *nm inv* bric-a-brac, jumble.

bricolage [bʀikɔlaʒ] *nm*: **le** ~ do-it-yourself (jobs); (*péj*) patched-up job.

bricole [bʀikɔl] *nf* (*babiole, chose insignifiante*) trifle; (*petit travail*) small job.

bricoler [bʀikɔle] *vi* to do odd jobs; (*en amateur*) to do DIY jobs; (*passe-temps*) to potter about ♦ *vt* (*réparer*) to fix up; (*mal réparer*) to tinker with; (*trafiquer: voiture etc*) to doctor, fix.

bricoleur, euse [bʀikɔlœʀ, -øz] *nm/f* handyman/woman, DIY enthusiast.

bride [bʀid] *nf* bridle; (*d'un bonnet*) string, tie; **à** ~ **abattue** flat out, hell for leather; **tenir en** ~ to keep in check; **lâcher la** ~ **à, laisser la** ~ **sur le cou à** to give free rein to.

bridé, e [bʀide] *adj*: **yeux** ~**s** slit eyes.

brider [bʀide] *vt* (*réprimer*) to keep in check; (*cheval*) to bridle; (*CULIN: volaille*) to truss.

bridge [bʀidʒ(ə)] *nm* bridge.

brie [bʀi] *nm* Brie (*cheese*).

brièvement [bʀijɛvmɑ̃] *adv* briefly.

brièveté [bʀijɛvte] *nf* brevity.

brigade [bʀigad] *nf* squad; (*MIL*) brigade.

brigadier [bʀigadje] *nm* (*POLICE*) ≈ sergeant; (*MIL*) bombardier; corporal.

brigadier-chef, *pl* **brigadiers-chefs** [bʀigadjeʃɛf] *nm* ≈ lance-sergeant.

brigand [bʀigɑ̃] *nm* brigand.

brigandage [bʀigɑ̃daʒ] *nm* robbery.

briguer [bʀige] *vt* to aspire to; (*suffrages*) to canvass.

brillamment [bʀijamɑ̃] *adv* brilliantly.

brillant, e [bʀijɑ̃, -ɑ̃t] *adj* brilliant; bright; (*luisant*) shiny, shining ♦ *nm* (*diamant*) brilliant.

briller [bʀije] *vi* to shine.

brimade [bʀimad] *nf* vexation, harassment *no pl*; bullying *no pl*.

brimbaler [bʀɛ̃bale] *vb* = **bringuebaler**.

brimer [bʀime] *vt* to harass; to bully.

brin [bʀɛ̃] *nm* (*de laine, ficelle etc*) strand; (*fig*): **un** ~ **de** a bit of; **un** ~ **mystérieux** *etc* (*fam*) a weeny bit mysterious *etc*; ~ **d'herbe** blade of grass; ~ **de muguet** sprig of lily of the valley; ~ **de paille** wisp of straw.

brindille [bʀɛ̃dij] *nf* twig.

bringue [bʀɛ̃g] *nf* (*fam*): **faire la** ~ to go on a binge.

bringuebaler [bʀɛ̃gbale] *vi* to shake (about) ♦ *vt* to cart about.

brio [bʀijo] *nm* brilliance; (*MUS*) brio; **avec** ~ brilliantly, with panache.

brioche [bʀijɔʃ] *nf* brioche (bun); (*fam: ventre*) paunch.

brioché, e [bʀijɔʃe] *adj* brioche-style.

brique [bʀik] *nf* brick; (*fam*) 10,000 francs ♦ *adj inv* brick red.

briquer [bʀike] *vt* (*fam*) to polish up.

briquet [bʀikɛ] *nm* (cigarette) lighter.

briqueterie [bʀiktʀi] *nf* brickyard.

bris [bʀi] *nm*: ~ **de clôture** (*JUR*) breaking in; ~ **de glaces** (*AUTO*) breaking of windows.

brisant [bʀizɑ̃] *nm* reef; (*vague*) breaker.

brise [bʀiz] *nf* breeze.

brisé, e [bʀize] *adj* broken; ~ **(de fatigue)** exhausted; **d'une voix** ~**e** in a voice broken with emotion; **pâte** ~**e** shortcrust pastry.

brisées [bʀize] *nfpl*: **aller** *ou* **marcher sur les** ~ **de qn** to compete with sb in his own province.

brise-glace(s) [bʀizglas] *nm inv* (*navire*) icebreaker.

brise-jet [bʀizʒɛ] *nm inv* tap swirl.

brise-lames [bʀizlam] *nm inv* breakwater.

briser [bʀize] *vt* to break; **se** ~ *vi* to break.

brise-tout [bʀiztu] *nm inv* wrecker.

briseur, euse [bʀizœʀ, -øz] *nm/f*: ~ **de grève** strike-breaker.

brise-vent [bʀizvɑ̃] *nm inv* windbreak.

bristol [bʀistɔl] *nm* (*carte de visite*) visiting card.

britannique [bʀitanik] *adj* British ♦ *nm/f*: **B~** Briton, British person; **les B~s** the British.

broc [bʀo] *nm* pitcher.

brocante [bʀɔkɑ̃t] *nf* (*objets*) secondhand goods *pl*, junk; (*commerce*) secondhand trade; junk dealing.

brocanteur, euse [bʀɔkɑ̃tœʀ, -øz] *nm/f* junkshop owner; junk dealer.

brocart [bʀɔkaʀ] *nm* brocade.

broche [bʀɔʃ] *nf* brooch; (*CULIN*) spit; (*fiche*) spike, peg; (*MÉD*) pin; **à la** ~ spit-roasted, roasted on a spit.

broché, e [bʀɔʃe] *adj* (*livre*) paper-backed; (*tissu*) brocaded.

brochet [bʀɔʃɛ] *nm* pike *inv*.

brochette [bʀɔʃɛt] *nf* skewer; ~ **de décorations** row of medals.

brochure [bRɔʃyR] *nf* pamphlet, brochure, booklet.
brocoli [bRɔkɔli] *nm* broccoli.
brodequins [bRɔdkɛ̃] *nmpl* (*de marche*) (lace-up) boots.
broder [bRɔde] *vt* to embroider ♦ *vi*: ~ **(sur des faits** *ou* **une histoire)** to embroider the facts.
broderie [bRɔdRi] *nf* embroidery.
bromure [bRɔmyR] *nm* bromide.
broncher [bRɔ̃ʃe] *vi*: **sans** ~ without flinching, without turning a hair.
bronches [bRɔ̃ʃ] *nfpl* bronchial tubes.
bronchite [bRɔ̃ʃit] *nf* bronchitis.
broncho-pneumonie [bRɔ̃kɔpnømɔni] *nf* broncho-pneumonia *no pl*.
bronzage [bRɔ̃zaʒ] *nm* (*hâle*) (sun)tan.
bronze [bRɔ̃z] *nm* bronze.
bronzé, e [bRɔ̃ze] *adj* tanned.
bronzer [bRɔ̃ze] *vt* to tan ♦ *vi* to get a tan; **se** ~ to sunbathe.
brosse [bRɔs] *nf* brush; **donner un coup de** ~ **à qch** to give sth a brush; **coiffé en** ~ with a crewcut; ~ **à cheveux** hairbrush; ~ **à dents** toothbrush; ~ **à habits** clothesbrush.
brosser [bRɔse] *vt* (*nettoyer*) to brush; (*fig: tableau etc*) to paint; to draw; **se** ~ to brush one's clothes; **se** ~ **les dents** to brush one's teeth; **tu peux te** ~! (*fam*) you can sing for it!
brou [bRu] *nm*: ~ **de noix** (*pour bois*) walnut stain; (*liqueur*) walnut liqueur.
brouette [bRuɛt] *nf* wheelbarrow.
brouhaha [bRuaa] *nm* hubbub.
brouillage [bRujaʒ] *nm* (*d'une émission*) jamming.
brouillard [bRujaR] *nm* fog; **être dans le** ~ (*fig*) to be all at sea.
brouille [bRuj] *nf* quarrel.
brouillé, e [bRuje] *adj* (*fâché*): **il est** ~ **avec ses parents** he has fallen out with his parents; (*teint*) muddy.
brouiller [bRuje] *vt* to mix up; to confuse; (*RADIO*) to cause interference to; (*: délibérément*) to jam; (*rendre trouble*) to cloud; (*désunir: amis*) to set at odds; **se** ~ *vi* (*ciel, vue*) to cloud over; (*détails*) to become confused; **se** ~ **(avec)** to fall out (with); ~ **les pistes** to cover one's tracks; (*fig*) to confuse the issue.
brouillon, ne [bRujɔ̃, -ɔn] *adj* disorganized, unmethodical ♦ *nm* (first) draft; **cahier de** ~ rough (work) book.
broussailles [bRusɑj] *nfpl* undergrowth *sg*.
broussailleux, euse [bRusɑjø, -øz] *adj* bushy.
brousse [bRus] *nf*: **la** ~ the bush.
brouter [bRute] *vt* to graze on ♦ *vi* to graze; (*AUTO*) to judder.
broutille [bRutij] *nf* trifle.
broyer [bRwaje] *vt* to crush; ~ **du noir** to be down in the dumps.
bru [bRy] *nf* daughter-in-law.
brucelles [bRysɛl] *nfpl*: **(pinces)** ~ tweezers.
brugnon [bRyɲɔ̃] *nm* nectarine.
bruine [bRɥin] *nf* drizzle.
bruiner [bRɥine] *vb impers*: **il bruine** it's drizzling, there's a drizzle.
bruire [bRɥiR] *vi* (*eau*) to murmur; (*feuilles, étoffe*) to rustle.
bruissement [bRɥismɑ̃] *nm* murmuring; rustling.
bruit [bRɥi] *nm*: **un** ~ a noise, a sound; (*fig: rumeur*) a rumour (*BRIT*), a rumor (*US*); **le** ~ noise; **pas/trop de** ~ no/too much noise; **sans** ~ without a sound, noiselessly; **faire du** ~ to make a noise; ~ **de fond** background noise.
bruitage [bRɥitaʒ] *nm* sound effects *pl*.
bruiteur, euse [bRɥitœR, -øz] *nm/f* sound-effects engineer.
brûlant, e [bRylɑ̃, -ɑ̃t] *adj* burning (hot); (*liquide*) boiling (hot); (*regard*) fiery; (*sujet*) red-hot.
brûlé, e [bRyle] *adj* (*fig: démasqué*) blown; (*: homme politique etc*) discredited ♦ *nm*: **odeur de** ~ smell of burning.
brûle-pourpoint [bRylpuRpwɛ̃]: **à** ~ *adv* point-blank.
brûler [bRyle] *vt* to burn; (*suj: eau bouillante*) to scald; (*consommer: électricité, essence*) to use; (*feu rouge, signal*) to go through (without stopping) ♦ *vi* to burn; (*jeu*): **tu brûles** you're getting warm *ou* hot; **se** ~ to burn o.s.; to scald o.s.; **se** ~ **la cervelle** to blow one's brains out; ~ **les étapes** to make rapid progress; (*aller trop vite*) to cut corners; ~ **(d'impatience) de faire qch** to burn with impatience to do sth, be dying to do sth.
brûleur [bRylœR] *nm* burner.
brûlot [bRylo] *nm* (*CULIN*) flaming brandy; **un** ~ **de contestation** (*fig*) a hotbed of dissent.
brûlure [bRylyR] *nf* (*lésion*) burn; (*sensation*) burning *no pl*, burning sensation; ~**s d'estomac** heartburn *sg*.
brume [bRym] *nf* mist.
brumeux, euse [bRymø, -øz] *adj* misty; (*fig*) hazy.
brumisateur [bRymizatœR] *nm* atomizer.
brun, e [bRœ̃, -yn] *adj* brown; (*cheveux, personne*) dark ♦ *nm* (*couleur*) brown ♦ *nf* (*cigarette*) *cigarette made of dark tobacco*; (*bière*) ≈ brown ale, stout.
brunâtre [bRynɑtR(ə)] *adj* brownish.
brunch [bRœntʃ] *nm* brunch.
Brunei [bRynei] *nm*: **le** ~ Brunei.
brunir [bRyniR] *vi* (*aussi*: **se** ~) to get a tan ♦ *vt* to tan.
brushing [bRœʃiŋ] *nm* blow-dry.
brusque [bRysk(ə)] *adj* (*soudain*) abrupt, sudden; (*rude*) abrupt, brusque.
brusquement [bRyskəmɑ̃] *adv* (*soudainement*) abruptly, suddenly.
brusquer [bRyske] *vt* to rush.
brusquerie [bRyskəRi] *nf* abruptness, brusqueness.

brut, e [bʀyt] *adj* raw, crude, rough; (*diamant*) uncut; (*soie, minéral, INFORM: données*) raw; (*COMM*) gross ♦ *nf* brute; **(champagne)** ~ brut champagne; **(pétrole)** ~ crude (oil).
brutal, e, aux [bʀytal, -o] *adj* brutal.
brutalement [bʀytalmɑ̃] *adv* brutally.
brutaliser [bʀytalize] *vt* to handle roughly, manhandle.
brutalité [bʀytalite] *nf* brutality *no pl*.
brute [bʀyt] *adj f, nf voir* **brut**.
Bruxelles [bʀysɛl] *n* Brussels.
bruxellois, e [bʀysɛlwa, -waz] *adj* of *ou* from Brussels ♦ *nm/f*: **B~, e** inhabitant *ou* native of Brussels.
bruyamment [bʀɥijamɑ̃] *adv* noisily.
bruyant, e [bʀɥijɑ̃, -ɑ̃t] *adj* noisy.
bruyère [bʀyjɛʀ] *nf* heather.
BT *sigle m* (= *Brevet de technicien*) *vocational training certificate, taken at approx. 18 years.*
BTA *sigle m* (= *Brevet de technicien agricole*) *agricultural training certificate, taken at approx. 18 years.*
BTP *sigle mpl* (= *Bâtiments et travaux publics*) *public buildings and works sector.*
BTS *sigle m* (= *Brevet de technicien supérieur*) *vocational training certificate taken at end of 2-year higher education course.*
BU *sigle f* = *Bibliothèque universitaire.*
bu, e [by] *pp de* **boire**.
buanderie [bɥɑ̃dʀi] *nf* laundry.
Bucarest [bykaʀɛst] *n* Bucharest.
buccal, e, aux [bykal, -o] *adj*: **par voie ~e** orally.
bûche [byʃ] *nf* log; **prendre une** ~ (*fig*) to come a cropper (*BRIT*), fall flat on one's face; ~ **de Noël** Yule log.
bûcher [byʃe] *nm* pyre; bonfire ♦ *vi* (*fam: étudier*) to swot (*BRIT*), grind (*US*) ♦ *vt* to swot up (*BRIT*), cram.
bûcheron [byʃʀɔ̃] *nm* woodcutter.
bûchette [byʃɛt] *nf* (*de bois*) stick, twig; (*pour compter*) rod.
bûcheur, euse [byʃœʀ, -øz] *nm/f* (*fam: étudiant*) swot (*BRIT*), grind (*US*).
bucolique [bykɔlik] *adj* bucolic, pastoral.
Budapest [bydapɛst] *n* Budapest.
budget [bydʒɛ] *nm* budget.
budgétaire [bydʒetɛʀ] *adj* budgetary, budget *cpd*.
budgétiser [bydʒetize] *vt* to budget (for).
buée [bɥe] *nf* (*sur une vitre*) mist; (*de l'haleine*) steam.
Buenos Aires [bwenɔzɛʀ] *n* Buenos Aires.
buffet [byfɛ] *nm* (*meuble*) sideboard; (*de réception*) buffet; ~ **(de gare)** (station) buffet, snack bar.
buffle [byfl(ə)] *nm* buffalo.
buis [bɥi] *nm* box tree; (*bois*) box(wood).
buisson [bɥisɔ̃] *nm* bush.
buissonnière [bɥisɔnjɛʀ] *adj f*: **faire l'école** ~ to play truant (*BRIT*), skip school.
bulbe [bylb(ə)] *nm* (*BOT, ANAT*) bulb; (*coupole*) onion-shaped dome.
bulgare [bylgaʀ] *adj* Bulgarian ♦ *nm* (*LING*) Bulgarian ♦ *nm/f*: **B~** Bulgarian, Bulgar.
Bulgarie [bylgaʀi] *nf*: **la** ~ Bulgaria.
bulldozer [buldozœʀ] *nm* bulldozer.
bulle [byl] *adj, nm*: **(papier)** ~ manil(l)a paper ♦ *nf* bubble; (*de bande dessinée*) balloon; (*papale*) bull; ~ **de savon** soap bubble.
bulletin [byltɛ̃] *nm* (*communiqué, journal*) bulletin; (*papier*) form; (*: de bagages*) ticket; (*SCOL*) report; ~ **d'informations** news bulletin; ~ **météorologique** weather report; ~ **de naissance** birth certificate; ~ **de salaire** pay slip; ~ **de santé** medical bulletin; ~ **(de vote)** ballot paper.
buraliste [byʀalist(ə)] *nm/f* (*de bureau de tabac*) tobacconist; (*de poste*) clerk.
bure [byʀ] *nf* homespun; (*de moine*) frock.
bureau, x [byʀo] *nm* (*meuble*) desk; (*pièce, service*) office; ~ **de change** (foreign) exchange office *ou* bureau; ~ **d'embauche** ≈ job centre; ~ **d'études** design office; ~ **de location** box office; ~ **de placement** employment agency; ~ **de poste** post office; ~ **de tabac** tobacconist's (shop), smoke shop (*US*); ~ **de vote** polling station.
bureaucrate [byʀokʀat] *nm* bureaucrat.
bureaucratie [byʀokʀasi] *nf* bureaucracy.
bureaucratique [byʀokʀatik] *adj* bureaucratic.
bureautique [byʀɔtik] *nf* office automation.
burette [byʀɛt] *nf* (*de mécanicien*) oilcan; (*de chimiste*) burette.
burin [byʀɛ̃] *nm* cold chisel; (*ART*) burin.
buriné, e [byʀine] *adj* (*fig: visage*) craggy, seamed.
Burkina(-Faso) [byʀkina(faso)] *nm*: **le** ~ Burkina Faso.
burlesque [byʀlɛsk(ə)] *adj* ridiculous; (*LITTÉRATURE*) burlesque.
burnous [byʀnu(s)] *nm* burnous.
Burundi [buʀundi] *nm*: **le** ~ Burundi.
BUS *sigle m* = *Bureau universitaire de statistiques.*
bus *vb* [by] *voir* **boire** ♦ *nm* [bys] (*véhicule, aussi INFORM*) bus.
busard [byzaʀ] *nm* harrier.
buse [byz] *nf* buzzard.
busqué, e [byske] *adj*: **nez** ~ hook(ed) nose.
buste [byst(ə)] *nm* (*ANAT*) chest; (*: de femme*) bust; (*sculpture*) bust.
bustier [bystje] *nm* (*soutien-gorge*) long-line bra.
but [by] *vb voir* **boire** ♦ *nm* (*cible*) target; (*fig*) goal, aim; (*FOOTBALL etc*) goal; **de ~ en blanc** point-blank; **avoir pour ~ de faire** to aim to do; **dans le ~ de** with the intention of.
butane [bytan] *nm* butane; (*domestique*) calor gas ® (*BRIT*), butane.
buté, e [byte] *adj* stubborn, obstinate ♦ *nf* (*ARCHIT*) abutment; (*TECH*) stop.

buter [byte] *vi*: ~ **contre** *ou* **sur** to bump into; (*trébucher*) to stumble against ♦ *vt* to antagonize; **se** ~ *vi* to get obstinate, dig in one's heels.
buteur [bytœʀ] *nm* striker.
butin [bytɛ̃] *nm* booty, spoils *pl*; (*d'un vol*) loot.
butiner [bytine] *vi* to gather nectar.
butor [bytɔʀ] *nm* (*fig*) lout.
butte [byt] *nf* mound, hillock; **être en** ~ **à** to be exposed to.
buvable [byvabl(ə)] *adj* (*eau, vin*) drinkable; (*MÉD: ampoule etc*) to be taken orally; (*fig: roman etc*) reasonable.
buvais [byvɛ] *etc vb voir* **boire**.
buvard [byvaʀ] *nm* blotter.
buvette [byvɛt] *nf* refreshment room *ou* stall; (*comptoir*) bar.
buveur, euse [byvœʀ, -øz] *nm/f* drinker.
buvons [byvɔ̃] *etc vb voir* **boire**.
BVP *sigle m* (= *Bureau de vérification de la publicité*) *advertising standards authority*.
Byzance [bizɑ̃s] *n* Byzantium.
byzantin, e [bizɑ̃tɛ̃, -in] *adj* Byzantine.
BZH *abr* (= *Breizh*) Brittany.

C c

C, c [se] *nm inv* C, c ♦ *abr* (= *centime*) c; (= *Celsius*) C; **C comme Célestin** C for Charlie.
c' [s] *dét voir* **ce**.
CA *sigle m* = **chiffre d'affaires, conseil d'administration, corps d'armée** ♦ *sigle f* = **chambre d'agriculture**.
ca *abr* (= *centiare*) *1 m²*.
ça [sa] *pron* (*pour désigner*) this; (*: plus loin*) that; (*comme sujet indéfini*) it; ~ **m'étonne que** it surprises me that; ~ **va?** how are you?; how are things?; (*d'accord?*) OK?, all right?; ~ **alors!** (*désapprobation*) well!, really!; (*étonnement*) heavens!; **c'est** ~ that's right.
çà [sa] *adv*: ~ **et là** here and there.
cabale [kabal] *nf* (*THÉÂT, POL*) cabal, clique.
caban [kabɑ̃] *nm* reefer jacket, donkey jacket.
cabane [kaban] *nf* hut, cabin.
cabanon [kabanɔ̃] *nm* chalet; (country) cottage.
cabaret [kabaʀɛ] *nm* night club.
cabas [kabɑ] *nm* shopping bag.
cabestan [kabɛstɑ̃] *nm* capstan.
cabillaud [kabijo] *nm* cod *inv*.
cabine [kabin] *nf* (*de bateau*) cabin; (*de plage*) (beach) hut; (*de piscine etc*) cubicle; (*de camion, train*) cab; (*d'avion*) cockpit; ~ **(d'ascenseur)** lift cage; ~ **d'essayage** fitting room; ~ **de projection** projection room; ~ **spatiale** space capsule; ~ **(téléphonique)** call *ou* (tele)phone box, (tele)phone booth.
cabinet [kabinɛ] *nm* (*petite pièce*) closet; (*de médecin*) surgery (*BRIT*), office (*US*); (*de notaire etc*) office; (*: clientèle*) practice; (*POL*) cabinet; (*d'un ministre*) advisers *pl*; ~**s** *nmpl* (*w.-c.*) toilet *sg*, loo *sg* (*fam BRIT*); ~ **d'affaires** business consultants' (bureau), business partnership; ~ **de toilette** toilet; ~ **de travail** study.
câble [kɑbl(ə)] *nm* cable; **le** ~ (*TV*) cable television, cablevision (*US*).
câblé, e [kɑble] *adj* (*fam*) switched on; (*TECH*) linked to cable television.
câbler [kɑble] *vt* to cable; ~ **un quartier** (*TV*) to put cable television into an area.
câblogramme [kɑblɔgʀam] *nm* cablegram.
cabosser [kabɔse] *vt* to dent.
cabot [kabo] *nm* (*péj: chien*) mutt.
cabotage [kabɔtaʒ] *nm* coastal navigation.
caboteur [kabɔtœʀ] *nm* coaster.
cabotin, e [kabɔtɛ̃, -in] *nm/f* (*péj: personne maniérée*) poseur; (*: acteur*) ham ♦ *adj* dramatic, theatrical.
cabotinage [kabɔtinaʒ] *nm* playacting; third-rate acting, ham acting.
cabrer [kɑbʀe]: **se** ~ *vi* (*cheval*) to rear up; (*avion*) to nose up; (*fig*) to revolt, rebel; to jib.
cabri [kabʀi] *nm* kid.
cabriole [kabʀijɔl] *nf* caper; (*gymnastique etc*) somersault.
cabriolet [kabʀijɔlɛ] *nm* convertible.
CAC [kak] *sigle f* (= *Compagnie des agents de change*): **indice** ~ ≈ FT index (*BRIT*), ≈ Dow Jones average (*US*).
caca [kaka] *nm* (*langage enfantin*) pooh; (*couleur*): ~ **d'oie** greeny-yellow; **faire** ~ (*fam*) to do a pooh.
cacahuète [kakaɥɛt] *nf* peanut.
cacao [kakao] *nm* cocoa (powder); (*boisson*) cocoa.
cachalot [kaʃalo] *nm* sperm whale.
cache [kaʃ] *nm* mask, card (*for masking*) ♦ *nf* hiding place.
cache-cache [kaʃkaʃ] *nm*: **jouer à** ~ to play hide-and-seek.
cache-col [kaʃkɔl] *nm* scarf (*pl* scarves).
cachemire [kaʃmiʀ] *nm* cashmere ♦ *adj*: **dessin** ~ paisley pattern; **le C**~ Kashmir.
cache-nez [kaʃne] *nm inv* scarf (*pl* scarves), muffler.
cache-pot [kaʃpo] *nm inv* flower-pot holder.
cache-prise [kaʃpʀiz] *nm inv* socket cover.
cacher [kaʃe] *vt* to hide, conceal; ~ **qch à qn** to hide *ou* conceal sth from sb; **se** ~ to hide; to be hidden *ou* concealed; **il ne s'en cache pas** he makes no secret of it.
cache-sexe [kaʃsɛks] *nm inv* G-string.
cachet [kaʃɛ] *nm* (*comprimé*) tablet; (*sceau: du roi*) seal; (*: de la poste*) postmark; (*rétribution*)

fee; (*fig*) style, character.
cacheter [kaʃte] *vt* to seal; **vin cacheté** vintage wine.
cachette [kaʃɛt] *nf* hiding place; **en ~** on the sly, secretly.
cachot [kaʃo] *nm* dungeon.
cachotterie [kaʃɔtʀi] *nf* mystery; **faire des ~s** to be secretive.
cachottier, ière [kaʃɔtje, -jɛʀ] *adj* secretive.
cachou [kaʃu] *nm*: **pastille de ~** cachou (*sweet*).
cacophonie [kakɔfɔni] *nf* cacophony, din.
cacophonique [kakɔfɔnik] *adj* cacophonous.
cactus [kaktys] *nm* cactus.
c-à-d *abr* (= *c'est-à-dire*) i.e.
cadastre [kadastʀ(ə)] *nm* land register.
cadavéreux, euse [kadaveʀø, -øz] *adj* (*teint, visage*) deathly pale.
cadavérique [kadaveʀik] *adj* deathly (pale), deadly pale.
cadavre [kadavʀ(ə)] *nm* corpse, (dead) body.
Caddie [kadi] *nm* ® (supermarket) trolley.
cadeau, x [kado] *nm* present, gift; **faire un ~ à qn** to give sb a present *ou* gift; **faire ~ de qch à qn** to make a present of sth to sb, give sb sth as a present.
cadenas [kadna] *nm* padlock.
cadenasser [kadnase] *vt* to padlock.
cadence [kadɑ̃s] *nf* (*MUS*) cadence; (*: rythme*) rhythm; (*de travail etc*) rate; **~s** *nfpl* (*en usine*) production rate *sg*; **en ~** rhythmically; in time.
cadencé, e [kadɑ̃se] *adj* rhythmic(al); **au pas ~** (*MIL*) in quick time.
cadet, te [kadɛ, -ɛt] *adj* younger; (*le plus jeune*) youngest ♦ *nm/f* youngest child *ou* one, youngest boy *ou* son/girl *ou* daughter; **il est mon ~ de deux ans** he's 2 years younger than me, he's 2 years my junior; **les ~s** (*SPORT*) the minors (*15 - 17 years*); **le ~ de mes soucis** the least of my worries.
cadrage [kadʀaʒ] *nm* framing (*of shot*).
cadran [kadʀɑ̃] *nm* dial; **~ solaire** sundial.
cadre [kadʀ(ə)] *nm* frame; (*environnement*) surroundings *pl*; (*limites*) scope ♦ *nm/f* (*ADMIN*) managerial employee, executive ♦ *adj*: **loi ~** outline *ou* blueprint law; **~ moyen/supérieur** (*ADMIN*) middle/senior management employee, junior/senior executive; **rayer qn des ~s** to discharge sb; to dismiss sb; **dans le ~ de** (*fig*) within the framework *ou* context of.
cadrer [kadʀe] *vi*: **~ avec** to tally *ou* correspond with ♦ *vt* (*CINÉ, PHOTO*) to frame.
cadreur, euse [kadʀœʀ, -øz] *nm/f* (*CINÉ*) cameraman/woman.
caduc, uque [kadyk] *adj* obsolete; (*BOT*) deciduous.
CAF *sigle f* (= *Caisse d'allocations familiales*) *family allowance office*.
caf *abr* (= *coût, assurance, fret*) cif.
cafard [kafaʀ] *nm* cockroach; **avoir le ~** to be down in the dumps, be feeling low.
cafardeux, euse [kafaʀdø, -øz] *adj* (*personne, ambiance*) depressing, melancholy.
café [kafe] *nm* coffee; (*bistro*) café ♦ *adj inv* coffee *cpd*; **~ crème** coffee with cream; **~ au lait** white coffee; **~ noir** black coffee; **~ en grains** coffee beans; **~ en poudre** instant coffee; **~ tabac** *tobacconist's or newsagent's also serving coffee and spirits*; **~ liégeois** *coffee ice cream with whipped cream*.
café-concert, *pl* **cafés-concerts** [kafekɔ̃sɛʀ] *nm* (*aussi*: **caf'conc'**) *café with a cabaret*.
caféine [kafein] *nf* caffeine.
cafétéria [kafeteʀja] *nf* cafeteria.
café-théâtre, *pl* **cafés-théâtres** [kafeteatʀ(ə)] *nm café used as a venue by (experimental) theatre groups*.
cafetier, ière [kaftje, -jɛʀ] *nm/f* café-owner ♦ *nf* (*pot*) coffee-pot.
cafouillage [kafujaʒ] *nm* shambles *sg*.
cafouiller [kafuje] *vi* to get in a shambles; (*machine etc*) to work in fits and starts.
cage [kaʒ] *nf* cage; **~ (des buts)** goal; **en ~** in a cage, caged up *ou* in; **~ d'ascenseur** lift shaft; **~ d'escalier** (stair)well; **~ thoracique** rib cage.
cageot [kaʒo] *nm* crate.
cagibi [kaʒibi] *nm* shed.
cagneux, euse [kaɲø, -øz] *adj* knock-kneed.
cagnotte [kaɲɔt] *nf* kitty.
cagoule [kagul] *nf* cowl; hood; (*SKI etc*) cagoule.
cahier [kaje] *nm* notebook; (*TYPO*) signature; (*revue*): **~s** journal; **~ de revendications/doléances** list of claims/grievances; **~ de brouillons** roughbook, jotter; **~ des charges** specification; **~ d'exercices** exercise book.
cahin-caha [kaɛ̃kaa] *adv*: **aller ~** to jog along; (*fig*) to be so-so.
cahot [kao] *nm* jolt, bump.
cahoter [kaɔte] *vi* to bump along, jog along.
cahoteux, euse [kaɔtø, -øz] *adj* bumpy.
cahute [kayt] *nf* shack, hut.
caïd [kaid] *nm* big chief, boss.
caillasse [kajas] *nf* (*pierraille*) loose stones *pl*.
caille [kaj] *nf* quail.
caillé, e [kaje] *adj*: **lait ~** curdled milk, curds *pl*.
caillebotis [kajbɔti] *nm* duckboard.
cailler [kaje] *vi* (*lait*) to curdle; (*sang*) to clot; (*fam*) to be cold.
caillot [kajo] *nm* (blood) clot.
caillou, x [kaju] *nm* (little) stone.
caillouter [kajute] *vt* (*chemin*) to metal.
caillouteux, euse [kajutø, -øz] *adj* stony; pebbly.
cailloutis [kajuti] *nm* (*petits graviers*) gravel.
caïman [kaimɑ̃] *nm* cayman.
Caïmans [kaimɑ̃] *nfpl*: **les ~** the Cayman Islands.
Caire [kɛʀ] *nm*: **Le ~** Cairo.
caisse [kɛs] *nf* box; (*où l'on met la recette*) cash-

box; (*: machine*) till; (*où l'on paye*) cash desk (*BRIT*), checkout counter; (*: au supermarché*) checkout; (*de banque*) cashier's desk; (*TECH*) case, casing; **faire sa** ~ (*COMM*) to count the takings; ~ **claire** (*MUS*) side *ou* snare drum; ~ **éclair** express checkout; ~ **enregistreuse** cash register; ~ **d'épargne (CE)** savings bank; ~ **noire** slush fund; ~ **de retraite** pension fund; ~ **de sortie** checkout; *voir* **grosse**.

caissier, ière [kesje, -jɛʀ] *nm/f* cashier.

caisson [kɛsɔ̃] *nm* box, case.

cajoler [kaʒɔle] *vt* to wheedle, coax; to surround with love and care, make a fuss of.

cajoleries [kaʒɔlʀi] *nfpl* coaxing *sg*, flattery *sg*.

cajou [kaʒu] *nm* cashew nut.

cake [kɛk] *nm* fruit cake.

CAL *sigle m* (= *Comité d'action lycéen*) *pupils' action group seeking to reform school system.*

cal [kal] *nm* callus.

cal. *abr* = **calorie**.

calamar [kalamaʀ] *nm* = **calmar**.

calaminé, e [kalamine] *adj* (*AUTO*) coked up.

calamité [kalamite] *nf* calamity, disaster.

calandre [kalɑ̃dʀ(ə)] *nf* radiator grill; (*machine*) calender, mangle.

calanque [kalɑ̃k] *nf* rocky inlet.

calcaire [kalkɛʀ] *nm* limestone ♦ *adj* (*eau*) hard; (*GÉO*) limestone *cpd*.

calciné, e [kalsine] *adj* burnt to ashes.

calcium [kalsjɔm] *nm* calcium.

calcul [kalkyl] *nm* calculation; **le** ~ (*SCOL*) arithmetic; ~ **différentiel/intégral** differential/integral calculus; ~ **mental** mental arithmetic; ~ **(biliaire)** (gall)stone; ~ **(rénal)** (kidney) stone; **d'après mes ~s** by my reckoning.

calculateur [kalkylatœʀ] *nm*, **calculatrice** [kalkylatʀis] *nf* calculator.

calculé, e [kalkyle] *adj*: **risque** ~ calculated risk.

calculer [kalkyle] *vt* to calculate, work out, reckon; (*combiner*) to calculate; ~ **qch de tête** to work sth out in one's head.

calculette [kalkylɛt] *nf* (pocket) calculator.

cale [kal] *nf* (*de bateau*) hold; (*en bois*) wedge, chock; ~ **sèche** *ou* **de radoub** dry dock.

calé, e [kale] *adj* (*fam*) clever, bright.

calebasse [kalbɑs] *nf* calabash, gourd.

calèche [kalɛʃ] *nf* horse-drawn carriage.

caleçon [kalsɔ̃] *nm* pair of underpants, trunks *pl*; ~ **de bain** bathing trunks *pl*.

calembour [kalɑ̃buʀ] *nm* pun.

calendes [kalɑ̃d] *nfpl*: **renvoyer aux** ~ **grecques** to postpone indefinitely.

calendrier [kalɑ̃dʀije] *nm* calendar; (*fig*) timetable.

cale-pied [kalpje] *nm inv* toe clip.

calepin [kalpɛ̃] *nm* notebook.

caler [kale] *vt* to wedge, chock up; ~ **(son moteur/véhicule)** to stall (one's engine/vehicle); **se** ~ **dans un fauteuil** to make o.s. comfortable in an armchair.

calfater [kalfate] *vt* to caulk.

calfeutrage [kalføtʀaʒ] *nm* draughtproofing (*BRIT*), draftproofing (*US*).

calfeutrer [kalføtʀe] *vt* to (make) draughtproof (*BRIT*) *ou* draftproof (*US*); **se** ~ to make o.s. snug and comfortable.

calibre [kalibʀ(ə)] *nm* (*d'un fruit*) grade; (*d'une arme*) bore, calibre (*BRIT*), caliber (*US*); (*fig*) calibre, caliber.

calibrer [kalibʀe] *vt* to grade.

calice [kalis] *nm* (*REL*) chalice; (*BOT*) calyx.

calicot [kaliko] *nm* (*tissu*) calico.

calife [kalif] *nm* caliph.

Californie [kalifɔʀni] *nf*: **la** ~ California.

californien, ne [kalifɔʀnjɛ̃, -ɛn] *adj* Californian.

califourchon [kalifuʀʃɔ̃]: **à** ~ *adv* astride; **à** ~ **sur** astride, straddling.

câlin, e [kɑlɛ̃, -in] *adj* cuddly, cuddlesome; tender.

câliner [kɑline] *vt* to fondle, cuddle.

câlineries [kɑlinʀi] *nfpl* cuddles.

calisson [kalisɔ̃] *nm* *diamond-shaped sweet or candy made with ground almonds.*

calleux, euse [kalø, -øz] *adj* horny, callous.

calligraphie [kaligʀafi] *nf* calligraphy.

callosité [kalozite] *nf* callus.

calmant [kalmɑ̃] *nm* tranquillizer, sedative; (*contre la douleur*) painkiller.

calmar [kalmaʀ] *nm* squid.

calme [kalm(ə)] *adj* calm, quiet ♦ *nm* calm(ness), quietness; **sans perdre son** ~ without losing one's cool *ou* calmness; ~ **plat** (*NAVIG*) dead calm.

calmement [kalməmɑ̃] *adv* calmly, quietly.

calmer [kalme] *vt* to calm (down); (*douleur, inquiétude*) to ease, soothe; **se** ~ to calm down.

calomniateur, trice [kalɔmnjatœʀ, -tʀis] *nm/f* slanderer; libeller.

calomnie [kalɔmni] *nf* slander; (*écrite*) libel.

calomnier [kalɔmnje] *vt* to slander; to libel.

calomnieux, euse [kalɔmnjø, -øz] *adj* slanderous; libellous.

calorie [kalɔʀi] *nf* calorie.

calorifère [kalɔʀifɛʀ] *nm* stove.

calorifique [kalɔʀifik] *adj* calorific.

calorifuge [kalɔʀifyʒ] *adj* (heat-)insulating, heat-retaining.

calot [kalo] *nm* forage cap.

calotte [kalɔt] *nf* (*coiffure*) skullcap; (*gifle*) slap; **la** ~ (*péj: clergé*) the cloth, the clergy; ~ **glaciaire** icecap.

calque [kalk(ə)] *nm* (*aussi*: **papier** ~) tracing paper; (*dessin*) tracing; (*fig*) carbon copy.

calquer [kalke] *vt* to trace; (*fig*) to copy exactly.

calvados [kalvados] *nm* Calvados (*apple brandy*).

calvaire [kalvɛʀ] *nm* (*croix*) wayside cross, calvary; (*souffrances*) suffering, martyrdom.

calvitie [kalvisi] *nf* baldness.

camaïeu [kamajø] *nm*: **(motif en)** ~ monochrome motif.
camarade [kamaʀad] *nm/f* friend, pal; (*POL*) comrade.
camaraderie [kamaʀadʀi] *nf* friendship.
camarguais, e [kamaʀgɛ, -ɛz] *adj* of *ou* from the Camargue.
Camargue [kamaʀg] *nf*: **la** ~ the Camargue.
cambiste [kɑ̃bist(ə)] *nm* (*COMM*) foreign exchange dealer, exchange agent.
Cambodge [kɑ̃bɔdʒ] *nm*: **le** ~ Cambodia.
cambodgien, ne [kɑ̃bɔdʒjɛ̃, -ɛn] *adj* Cambodian ♦ *nm/f*: **C~, ne** Cambodian.
cambouis [kɑ̃bwi] *nm* dirty oil *ou* grease.
cambré, e [kɑ̃bʀe] *adj*: **avoir les reins ~s** to have an arched back; **avoir le pied très** ~ to have very high arches *ou* insteps.
cambrer [kɑ̃bʀe] *vt* to arch; **se** ~ to arch one's back; ~ **la taille** *ou* **les reins** to arch one's back.
cambriolage [kɑ̃bʀijɔlaʒ] *nm* burglary.
cambrioler [kɑ̃bʀijɔle] *vt* to burgle (*BRIT*), burglarize (*US*).
cambrioleur, euse [kɑ̃bʀijɔlœʀ, -øz] *nm/f* burglar.
cambrure [kɑ̃bʀyʀ] *nf* (*du pied*) arch; (*de la route*) camber; ~ **des reins** small of the back.
cambuse [kɑ̃byz] *nf* storeroom.
came [kam] *nf*: **arbre à ~s** camshaft; **arbre à ~s en tête** overhead camshaft.
camée [kame] *nm* cameo.
caméléon [kameleɔ̃] *nm* chameleon.
camélia [kamelja] *nm* camellia.
camelot [kamlo] *nm* street pedlar.
camelote [kamlɔt] *nf* rubbish, trash, junk.
camembert [kamɑ̃bɛʀ] *nm* Camembert (*cheese*).
caméra [kameʀa] *nf* (*CINÉ, TV*) camera; (*d'amateur*) cine-camera.
caméraman [kameʀaman] *nm* cameraman/woman.
Cameroun [kamʀun] *nm*: **le** ~ Cameroon.
camerounais, e [kamʀunɛ, -ɛz] *adj* Cameroonian.
caméscope [kameskɔp] ® *nm* camcorder ®.
camion [kamjɔ̃] *nm* lorry (*BRIT*), truck; (*plus petit, fermé*) van; (*charge*): ~ **de sable/cailloux** lorry-load (*BRIT*) *ou* truck-load of sand/stones; ~ **de dépannage** breakdown (*BRIT*) *ou* tow (*US*) truck.
camion-citerne, *pl* **camions-citernes** [kamjɔ̃sitɛʀn(ə)] *nm* tanker.
camionnage [kamjɔnaʒ] *nm* haulage (*BRIT*), trucking (*US*); **frais/entreprise de** ~ haulage costs/business.
camionnette [kamjɔnɛt] *nf* (small) van.
camionneur [kamjɔnœʀ] *nm* (*entrepreneur*) haulage contractor (*BRIT*), trucker (*US*); (*chauffeur*) lorry (*BRIT*) *ou* truck driver; van driver.
camisole [kamizɔl] *nf*: ~ **(de force)** strait-jacket.
camomille [kamɔmij] *nf* camomile; (*boisson*) camomile tea.
camouflage [kamuflaʒ] *nm* camouflage.
camoufler [kamufle] *vt* to camouflage; (*fig*) to conceal, cover up.
camouflet [kamuflɛ] *nm* (*fam*) snub.
camp [kɑ̃] *nm* camp; (*fig*) side; ~ **de nudistes/vacances** nudist/holiday camp; ~ **de concentration** concentration camp.
campagnard, e [kɑ̃paɲaʀ, -aʀd(ə)] *adj* country *cpd* ♦ *nm/f* countryman/woman.
campagne [kɑ̃paɲ] *nf* country, countryside; (*MIL, POL, COMM*) campaign; **en** ~ (*MIL*) in the field; **à la** ~ in/to the country; **faire** ~ **pour** to campaign for; ~ **électorale** election campaign; ~ **de publicité** advertising campaign.
campanile [kɑ̃panil] *nm* (*tour*) bell tower.
campé, e [kɑ̃pe] *adj*: **bien** ~ (*personnage, tableau*) well-drawn.
campement [kɑ̃pmɑ̃] *nm* camp, encampment.
camper [kɑ̃pe] *vi* to camp ♦ *vt* (*chapeau etc*) to pull *ou* put on firmly; (*dessin*) to sketch; **se** ~ **devant** to plant o.s. in front of.
campeur, euse [kɑ̃pœʀ, -øz] *nm/f* camper.
camphre [kɑ̃fʀ(ə)] *nm* camphor.
camphré, e [kɑ̃fʀe] *adj* camphorated.
camping [kɑ̃piŋ] *nm* camping; **(terrain de)** ~ campsite, camping site; **faire du** ~ to go camping; **faire du** ~ **sauvage** to camp rough.
camping-car [kɑ̃piŋkaʀ] *nm* caravanette, camper (*US*).
campus [kɑ̃pys] *nm* campus.
camus, e [kamy, -yz] *adj*: **nez** ~ pug nose.
Canada [kanada] *nm*: **le** ~ Canada.
canadair [kanadɛʀ] *nm* ® fire-fighting plane.
canadien, ne [kanadjɛ̃, -ɛn] *adj* Canadian ♦ *nm/f*: **C~, ne** Canadian ♦ *nf* (*veste*) fur-lined jacket.
canaille [kanɑj] *nf* (*péj*) scoundrel; (*populace*) riff-raff ♦ *adj* raffish, rakish.
canal, aux [kanal, -o] *nm* canal; (*naturel*) channel; (*ADMIN*): **par le** ~ **de** through (the medium of), via; ~ **de distribution/télévision** distribution/television channel; ~ **de Panama/Suez** Panama/Suez Canal.
canalisation [kanalizɑsjɔ̃] *nf* (*tuyau*) pipe.
canaliser [kanalize] *vt* to canalize; (*fig*) to channel.
canapé [kanape] *nm* settee, sofa; (*CULIN*) canapé, open sandwich.
canapé-lit, *pl* **canapés-lits** [kanapeli] *nm* sofa bed.
canaque [kanak] *adj* of *ou* from New Caledonia ♦ *nm/f*: **C~** native of New Caledonia.
canard [kanaʀ] *nm* duck.
canari [kanaʀi] *nm* canary.
Canaries [kanaʀi] *nfpl*: **les (îles)** ~ the Canary Islands, the Canaries.
cancaner [kɑ̃kane] *vi* to gossip (maliciously); (*canard*) to quack.
cancanier, ière [kɑ̃kanje, -jɛʀ] *adj* gossiping.

cancans [kɑ̃kɑ̃] *nmpl* (malicious) gossip *sg*.
cancer [kɑ̃sɛʀ] *nm* cancer; (*signe*): **le C~** Cancer, the Crab; **être du C~** to be Cancer; **il a un ~** he has cancer.
cancéreux, euse [kɑ̃seʀø, -øz] *adj* cancerous; (*personne*) suffering from cancer.
cancérigène [kɑ̃seʀiʒɛn] *adj* carcinogenic.
cancérologue [kɑ̃seʀɔlɔg] *nm/f* cancer specialist.
cancre [kɑ̃kʀ(ə)] *nm* dunce.
cancrelat [kɑ̃kʀəla] *nm* cockroach.
candélabre [kɑ̃delɑbʀ(ə)] *nm* candelabrum; (*lampadaire*) street lamp, lamppost.
candeur [kɑ̃dœʀ] *nf* ingenuousness.
candi [kɑ̃di] *adj inv*: **sucre ~** (sugar-)candy.
candidat, e [kɑ̃dida, -at] *nm/f* candidate; (*à un poste*) applicant, candidate.
candidature [kɑ̃didatyʀ] *nf* candidacy; application; **poser sa ~** to submit an application, apply.
candide [kɑ̃did] *adj* ingenuous, guileless, naïve.
cane [kan] *nf* (female) duck.
caneton [kantɔ̃] *nm* duckling.
canette [kanɛt] *nf* (*de bière*) (flip-top) bottle; (*de machine à coudre*) spool.
canevas [kanva] *nm* (*COUTURE*) canvas (for tapestry work); (*fig*) framework, structure.
caniche [kaniʃ] *nm* poodle.
caniculaire [kanikylɛʀ] *adj* (*chaleur, jour*) scorching.
canicule [kanikyl] *nf* scorching heat; midsummer heat, dog days *pl*.
canif [kanif] *nm* penknife, pocket knife.
canin, e [kanɛ̃, -in] *adj* canine ♦ *nf* canine (tooth), eye tooth; **exposition ~e** dog show.
caniveau, x [kanivo] *nm* gutter.
cannabis [kanabis] *nm* cannabis.
canne [kan] *nf* (walking) stick; **~ à pêche** fishing rod; **~ à sucre** sugar cane; **les ~s blanches** (*les aveugles*) the blind.
canné, e [kane] *adj* (*chaise*) cane *cpd*.
cannelé, e [kanle] *adj* fluted.
cannelle [kanɛl] *nf* cinnamon.
cannelure [kanlyʀ] *nf* fluting *no pl*.
canner [kane] *vt* (*chaise*) to make *ou* repair with cane.
cannibale [kanibal] *nm/f* cannibal.
cannibalisme [kanibalism(ə)] *nm* cannibalism.
canoë [kanɔe] *nm* canoe; (*sport*) canoeing; **~ (kayak)** kayak.
canon [kanɔ̃] *nm* (*arme*) gun; (*HIST*) cannon; (*d'une arme: tube*) barrel; (*fig*) model; (*MUS*) canon ♦ *adj*: **droit ~** canon law; **~ rayé** rifled barrel.
cañon [kaɲɔ̃] *nm* canyon.
canonique [kanɔnik] *adj*: **âge ~** respectable age.
canoniser [kanɔnize] *vt* to canonize.
canonnade [kanɔnad] *nf* cannonade.
canonnier [kanɔnje] *nm* gunner.
canonnière [kanɔnjɛʀ] *nf* gunboat.
canot [kano] *nm* boat, ding(h)y; **~ pneumatique** rubber *ou* inflatable ding(h)y; **~ de sauvetage** lifeboat.
canotage [kanɔtaʒ] *nm* rowing.
canoter [kanɔte] *vi* to go rowing.
canoteur, euse [kanɔtœʀ, -øz] *nm/f* rower.
canotier [kanɔtje] *nm* boater.
Cantal [kɑ̃tal] *nm*: **le ~** Cantal.
cantate [kɑ̃tat] *nf* cantata.
cantatrice [kɑ̃tatʀis] *nf* (opera) singer.
cantilène [kɑ̃tilɛn] *nf* (*MUS*) cantilena.
cantine [kɑ̃tin] *nf* canteen; (*réfectoire d'école*) dining hall.
cantique [kɑ̃tik] *nm* hymn.
canton [kɑ̃tɔ̃] *nm* district (*consisting of several communes*); (*en Suisse*) canton; *see boxed note*.

CANTON

A French **canton** *is an administrative division represented by a councillor in the 'Conseil général'. It comprises a number of 'communes' and is, in turn, a subdivision of an 'arrondissement'. In Switzerland the* **cantons** *are the 23 autonomous political divisions which make up the Swiss confederation.*

cantonade [kɑ̃tɔnad]: **à la ~** *adv* to everyone in general; (*crier*) from the rooftops.
cantonais, e [kɑ̃tɔnɛ, -ɛz] *adj* Cantonese ♦ *nm* (*LING*) Cantonese.
cantonal, e, aux [kɑ̃tɔnal, -o] *adj* cantonal, ≈ district.
cantonnement [kɑ̃tɔnmɑ̃] *nm* (*lieu*) billet; (*action*) billeting.
cantonner [kɑ̃tɔne] *vt* (*MIL*) to billet (*BRIT*), quarter; to station; **se ~ dans** to confine o.s. to.
cantonnier [kɑ̃tɔnje] *nm* roadmender.
canular [kanylaʀ] *nm* hoax.
CAO *sigle f* (= *conception assistée par ordinateur*) CAD.
caoutchouc [kautʃu] *nm* rubber; **~ mousse** foam rubber; **en ~** rubber *cpd*.
caoutchouté, e [kautʃute] *adj* rubberized.
caoutchouteux, euse [kautʃutø, -øz] *adj* rubbery.
CAP *sigle m* (= *Certificat d'aptitude professionnelle*) *vocational training certificate taken at secondary school*.
cap [kap] *nm* (*GÉO*) cape; headland; (*fig*) hurdle; watershed; (*NAVIG*): **changer de ~** to change course; **mettre le ~ sur** to head *ou* steer for; **doubler** *ou* **passer le ~** (*fig*) to get over the worst; **Le C~** Cape Town; **le ~ de Bonne Espérance** the Cape of Good Hope; **le ~ Horn** Cape Horn; **les îles du C~ Vert** (*aussi*: **le C~-Vert**) the Cape Verde Islands.
capable [kapabl(ə)] *adj* able, capable; **~ de qch/faire** capable of sth/doing; **il est ~ d'oublier** he could easily forget; **spectacle ~ d'intéresser** show likely to be of interest.

capacité [kapasite] *nf* (*compétence*) ability; (*JUR, INFORM, d'un récipient*) capacity; ~ **(en droit)** *basic legal qualification.*
caparaçonner [kaparasɔne] *vt* (*fig*) to clad.
cape [kap] *nf* cape, cloak; **rire sous** ~ to laugh up one's sleeve.
capeline [kaplin] *nf* wide-brimmed hat.
CAPES [kapɛs] *sigle m* (= *Certificat d'aptitude au professorat de l'enseignement du second degré*) *secondary teaching diploma*; see boxed note.

> **CAPES**
>
> *The French* **CAPES** *('certificat d'aptitude au professorat de l'enseignement du second degré') is a competitive examination sat by prospective secondary school teachers after the 'licence'. Successful candidates become fully qualified teachers 'professeurs certifiés'.*

capésien, ne [kapesjɛ̃, -ɛn] *nm/f person who holds the CAPES.*
CAPET [kapɛt] *sigle m* (= *Certificat d'aptitude au professorat de l'enseignement technique*) *technical teaching diploma.*
capharnaüm [kafarnaɔm] *nm* shambles *sg.*
capillaire [kapilɛr] *adj* (*soins, lotion*) hair *cpd*; (*vaisseau etc*) capillary; **artiste** ~ hair artist *ou* designer.
capillarité [kapilarite] *nf* capillary action.
capilliculteur [kapilikyltœr] *nm* hair-care specialist.
capilotade [kapilɔtad]: **en** ~ *adv* crushed to a pulp; smashed to pieces.
capitaine [kapitɛn] *nm* captain; ~ **des pompiers** fire chief (*BRIT*), fire marshal (*US*); ~ **au long cours** master mariner.
capitainerie [kapitɛnri] *nf* (*du port*) harbour (*BRIT*) *ou* harbor (*US*) master's (office).
capital, e, aux [kapital, -o] *adj* major; fundamental; (*JUR*) capital ♦ *nm* capital; (*fig*) stock; asset ♦ *nf* (*ville*) capital; (*lettre*) capital (letter) ♦*nmpl* (*fonds*) capital *sg*, money *sg*; **peine** ~**e** capital punishment; ~ **(social)** authorized capital; ~ **d'exploitation** working capital.
capitaliser [kapitalize] *vt* to amass, build up; (*COMM*) to capitalize ♦ *vi* to save.
capitalisme [kapitalism(ə)] *nm* capitalism.
capitaliste [kapitalist(ə)] *adj, nm/f* capitalist.
capiteux, euse [kapitø, -øz] *adj* (*vin, parfum*) heady; (*sensuel*) sensuous, alluring.
capitonnage [kapitɔnaʒ] *nm* padding.
capitonné, e [kapitɔne] *adj* padded.
capitonner [kapitɔne] *vt* to pad.
capitulation [kapitylɑsjɔ̃] *nf* capitulation.
capituler [kapityle] *vi* to capitulate.
caporal, aux [kapɔral, -o] *nm* lance corporal.
caporal-chef, *pl* **caporaux-chefs** [kapɔralʃɛf, kapɔro-] *nm* corporal.
capot [kapo] *nm* (*AUTO*) bonnet (*BRIT*), hood (*US*).
capote [kapɔt] *nf* (*de voiture*) hood (*BRIT*), top (*US*); (*de soldat*) greatcoat; ~ **(anglaise)** (*fam*) rubber, condom.
capoter [kapɔte] *vi* to overturn; (*négociations*) to founder.
câpre [kɑpr(ə)] *nf* caper.
caprice [kapris] *nm* whim, caprice; passing fancy; ~**s** *nmpl* (*de la mode etc*) vagaries; **faire un** ~ to throw a tantrum; **faire des** ~**s** to be temperamental.
capricieux, euse [kaprisjø, -øz] *adj* capricious; whimsical; temperamental.
Capricorne [kaprikɔrn] *nm*: **le** ~ Capricorn, the Goat; **être du** ~ to be Capricorn.
capsule [kapsyl] *nf* (*de bouteille*) cap; (*amorce*) primer; cap; (*BOT etc, spatiale*) capsule.
captage [kaptaʒ] *nm* (*d'une émission de radio*) picking-up; (*d'énergie, d'eau*) harnessing.
capter [kapte] *vt* (*ondes radio*) to pick up; (*eau*) to harness; (*fig*) to win, capture.
capteur [kaptœr] *nm*: ~ **solaire** solar collector.
captieux, euse [kapsjø, -øz] *adj* specious.
captif, ive [kaptif, -iv] *adj, nm/f* captive.
captivant, e [kaptivɑ̃, -ɑ̃t] *adj* captivating.
captiver [kaptive] *vt* to captivate.
captivité [kaptivite] *nf* captivity; **en** ~ in captivity.
capture [kaptyr] *nf* capture, catching *no pl*; catch.
capturer [kaptyre] *vt* to capture, catch.
capuche [kapyʃ] *nf* hood.
capuchon [kapyʃɔ̃] *nm* hood; (*de stylo*) cap, top.
capucin [kapysɛ̃] *nm* Capuchin monk.
capucine [kapysin] *nf* (*BOT*) nasturtium.
Cap-Vert [kabvɛr] *nm*: **le** ~ Cape Verde.
caquelon [kaklɔ̃] *nm* (*ustensile de cuisson*) fondue pot.
caquet [kakɛ] *nm*: **rabattre le** ~ **à qn** to bring sb down a peg or two.
caqueter [kakte] *vi* (*poule*) to cackle; (*fig*) to prattle.
car [kar] *nm* coach (*BRIT*), bus ♦ *conj* because, for; ~ **de police** police van; ~ **de reportage** broadcasting *ou* radio van.
carabine [karabin] *nf* carbine, rifle; ~ **à air comprimé** airgun.
carabiné, e [karabine] *adj* violent; (*cocktail, amende*) stiff.
Caracas [karakas] *n* Caracas.
caracoler [karakɔle] *vi* to caracole, prance.
caractère [karaktɛr] *nm* (*gén*) character; **en** ~**s gras** in bold type; **en petits** ~**s** in small print; **en** ~**s d'imprimerie** in block capitals; **avoir du** ~ to have character; **avoir bon/mauvais** ~ to be good-/ill-natured *ou* tempered; ~ **de remplacement** wild card (*INFORM*); ~**s/seconde (cps)** characters per second (cps).
caractériel, le [karakterjɛl] *adj* (*enfant*) (emotionally) disturbed ♦ *nm/f* problem child; **troubles** ~**s** emotional problems.

caractérisé, e [kaʀakteʀize] *adj*: **c'est une grippe/de l'insubordination ~e** it is a clear(-cut) case of flu/insubordination.
caractériser [kaʀakteʀize] *vt* to characterize; **se ~ par** to be characterized *ou* distinguished by.
caractéristique [kaʀakteʀistik] *adj, nf* characteristic.
carafe [kaʀaf] *nf* decanter; carafe.
carafon [kaʀafɔ̃] *nm* small carafe.
caraïbe [kaʀaib] *adj* Caribbean; **les C~s** *nfpl* the Caribbean (Islands); **la mer des C~s** the Caribbean Sea.
carambolage [kaʀɑ̃bɔlaʒ] *nm* multiple crash, pileup.
caramel [kaʀamɛl] *nm* (*bonbon*) caramel, toffee; (*substance*) caramel.
caraméliser [kaʀamelize] *vt* to caramelize.
carapace [kaʀapas] *nf* shell.
carapater [kaʀapate]: **se ~** *vi* to take to one's heels, scram.
carat [kaʀa] *nm* carat; **or à 18 ~s** 18-carat gold.
caravane [kaʀavan] *nf* caravan.
caravanier [kaʀavanje] *nm* caravanner.
caravaning [kaʀavaniŋ] *nm* caravanning; (*emplacement*) caravan site.
caravelle [kaʀavɛl] *nf* caravel.
carbonate [kaʀbɔnat] *nm* (*CHIMIE*): **~ de soude** sodium carbonate.
carbone [kaʀbɔn] *nm* carbon; (*feuille*) carbon, sheet of carbon paper; (*double*) carbon (copy).
carbonique [kaʀbɔnik] *adj*: **gaz ~** carbon dioxide; **neige ~** dry ice.
carbonisé, e [kaʀbɔnize] *adj* charred; **mourir ~** to be burned to death.
carboniser [kaʀbɔnize] *vt* to carbonize; (*brûler complètement*) to burn down, reduce to ashes.
carburant [kaʀbyʀɑ̃] *nm* (motor) fuel.
carburateur [kaʀbyʀatœʀ] *nm* carburettor.
carburation [kaʀbyʀɑsjɔ̃] *nf* carburation.
carburer [kaʀbyʀe] *vi* (*moteur*): **bien/mal ~** to be well/badly tuned.
carcan [kaʀkɑ̃] *nm* (*fig*) yoke, shackles *pl*.
carcasse [kaʀkas] *nf* carcass; (*de véhicule etc*) shell.
carcéral, e, aux [kaʀseʀal, -o] *adj* prison *cpd*.
carcinogène [kaʀsinɔʒɛn] *adj* carcinogenic.
cardan [kaʀdɑ̃] *nm* universal joint.
carder [kaʀde] *vt* to card.
cardiaque [kaʀdjak] *adj* cardiac, heart *cpd* ♦ *nm/f* heart patient; **être ~** to have a heart condition.
cardigan [kaʀdigɑ̃] *nm* cardigan.
cardinal, e, aux [kaʀdinal, -o] *adj* cardinal ♦ *nm* (*REL*) cardinal.
cardiologie [kaʀdjɔlɔʒi] *nf* cardiology.
cardiologue [kaʀdjɔlɔg] *nm/f* cardiologist, heart specialist.
cardio-vasculaire [kaʀdjɔvaskylɛʀ] *adj* cardiovascular.
cardon [kaʀdɔ̃] *nm* cardoon.
carême [kaʀɛm] *nm*: **le C~** Lent.
carence [kaʀɑ̃s] *nf* incompetence, inadequacy; (*manque*) deficiency; **~ vitaminique** vitamin deficiency.
carène [kaʀɛn] *nf* hull.
caréner [kaʀene] *vt* (*NAVIG*) to careen; (*carrosserie*) to streamline.
caressant, e [kaʀɛsɑ̃, -ɑ̃t] *adj* affectionate; caressing, tender.
caresse [kaʀɛs] *nf* caress.
caresser [kaʀese] *vt* to caress, stroke, fondle; (*fig: projet, espoir*) to toy with.
cargaison [kaʀgɛzɔ̃] *nf* cargo, freight.
cargo [kaʀgo] *nm* cargo boat, freighter; **~ mixte** cargo and passenger ship.
cari [kaʀi] *nm* = **curry**.
caricatural, e, aux [kaʀikatyʀal, -o] *adj* caricatural, caricature-like.
caricature [kaʀikatyʀ] *nf* caricature; (*politique etc*) (satirical) cartoon.
caricaturer [kaʀikatyʀe] *vt* (*personne*) to caricature; (*politique etc*) to satirize.
caricaturiste [kaʀikatyʀist(ə)] *nm/f* caricaturist; (satirical) cartoonist.
carie [kaʀi] *nf*: **la ~ (dentaire)** tooth decay; **une ~** a bad tooth.
carié, e [kaʀje] *adj*: **dent ~e** bad *ou* decayed tooth.
carillon [kaʀijɔ̃] *nm* (*d'église*) bells *pl*; (*de pendule*) chimes *pl*; (*de porte*): **~ (électrique)** (electric) door chime *ou* bell.
carillonner [kaʀijɔne] *vi* to ring, chime, peal.
caritatif, ive [kaʀitatif, -iv] *adj* charitable.
carlingue [kaʀlɛ̃g] *nf* cabin.
carmélite [kaʀmelit] *nf* Carmelite nun.
carmin [kaʀmɛ̃] *adj inv* crimson.
carnage [kaʀnaʒ] *nm* carnage, slaughter.
carnassier, ière [kaʀnasje, -jɛʀ] *adj* carnivorous ♦ *nm* carnivore.
carnation [kaʀnɑsjɔ̃] *nf* complexion; **~s** *nfpl* (*PEINTURE*) flesh tones.
carnaval [kaʀnaval] *nm* carnival.
carné, e [kaʀne] *adj* meat *cpd*, meat-based.
carnet [kaʀnɛ] *nm* (*calepin*) notebook; (*de tickets, timbres etc*) book; (*d'école*) school report; (*journal intime*) diary; **~ d'adresses** address book; **~ de chèques** cheque book (*BRIT*), checkbook (*US*); **~ de commandes** order book; **~ de notes** (*SCOL*) (school) report; **~ à souches** counterfoil book.
carnier [kaʀnje] *nm* gamebag.
carnivore [kaʀnivɔʀ] *adj* carnivorous ♦ *nm* carnivore.
Carolines [kaʀɔlin] *nfpl*: **les ~** the Caroline Islands.
carotide [kaʀɔtid] *nf* carotid (artery).
carotte [kaʀɔt] *nf* (*aussi fig*) carrot.
Carpates [kaʀpat] *nfpl*: **les ~** the Carpathians, the Carpathian Mountains.
carpe [kaʀp(ə)] *nf* carp.

carpette [karpɛt] *nf* rug.
carquois [karkwa] *nm* quiver.
carre [kar] *nf* (*de ski*) edge.
carré, e [kare] *adj* square; (*fig: franc*) straightforward ♦ *nm* (*de terrain, jardin*) patch, plot; (*NAVIG: salle*) wardroom; (*MATH*) square; (*CARTES*): ~ **d'as/de rois** four aces/kings; **élever un nombre au** ~ to square a number; **mètre/kilomètre** ~ square metre/kilometre; ~ **de soie** silk headsquare *ou* headscarf; ~ **d'agneau** loin of lamb.
carreau, x [karo] *nm* (*en faïence etc*) (floor) tile; (wall) tile; (*de fenêtre*) (window) pane; (*motif*) check, square; (*CARTES: couleur*) diamonds *pl*; (*: carte*) diamond; **tissu à ~x** checked fabric; **papier à ~x** squared paper.
carrefour [karfur] *nm* crossroads *sg*.
carrelage [karlaʒ] *nm* tiling; (tiled) floor.
carreler [karle] *vt* to tile.
carrelet [karlɛ] *nm* (*poisson*) plaice.
carreleur [karlœr] *nm* (floor) tiler.
carrément [karemɑ̃] *adv* (*franchement*) straight out, bluntly; (*sans détours, sans hésiter*) straight; (*nettement*) definitely; **il l'a ~ mis à la porte** he threw him straight out.
carrer [kare]: **se ~** *vi*: **se ~ dans un fauteuil** to settle o.s. comfortably *ou* ensconce o.s. in an armchair.
carrière [karjɛr] *nf* (*de roches*) quarry; (*métier*) career; **militaire de** ~ professional soldier; **faire ~ dans** to make one's career in.
carriériste [karjerist(ə)] *nm/f* careerist.
carriole [karjɔl] *nf* (*péj*) old cart.
carrossable [karɔsabl(ə)] *adj* suitable for (motor) vehicles.
carrosse [karɔs] *nm* (horse-drawn) coach.
carrosserie [karɔsri] *nf* body, bodywork *no pl* (*BRIT*); (*activité, commerce*) coachwork (*BRIT*), (car) body manufacturing; **atelier de ~** (*pour réparations*) body shop, panel beaters' (yard) (*BRIT*).
carrossier [karɔsje] *nm* coachbuilder (*BRIT*), (car) body repairer; (*dessinateur*) car designer.
carrousel [karuzɛl] *nm* (*ÉQUITATION*) carousel; (*fig*) merry-go-round.
carrure [karyr] *nf* build; (*fig*) stature.
cartable [kartabl(ə)] *nm* (*d'écolier*) satchel, (school)bag.
carte [kart(ə)] *nf* (*de géographie*) map; (*marine, du ciel*) chart; (*de fichier, d'abonnement etc, à jouer*) card; (*au restaurant*) menu; (*aussi:* ~ **postale**) (post)card; (*aussi:* ~ **de visite**) (visiting) card; **avoir/donner ~ blanche** to have/give carte blanche *ou* a free hand; **tirer les ~s à qn** to read sb's cards; **jouer aux ~s** to play cards; **jouer ~s sur table** (*fig*) to put one's cards on the table; **à la ~** (*au restaurant*) à la carte; ~ **bancaire** cash card; ~ **à circuit imprimé** printed circuit; ~ **à puce** smartcard; ~ **de crédit** credit card; ~ **d'état-major** ≈ Ordnance (*BRIT*) *ou* Geological (*US*) Survey map; ~ **de fidélité** loyalty card; **la ~ grise** (*AUTO*) ≈ the (car) registration document; ~ **d'identité** identity card; ~ **jeune** young person's railcard; ~ **perforée** punch(ed) card; ~ **de séjour** residence permit; ~ **routière** road map; **la ~ verte** (*AUTO*) the green card; **la ~ des vins** the wine list.
cartel [kartɛl] *nm* cartel.
carte-lettre, *pl* **cartes-lettres** [kartəlɛtr(ə)] *nf* letter-card.
carte-mère, *pl* **cartes-mères** [kartəmɛr] *nf* (*INFORM*) mother board.
carter [kartɛr] *nm* (*AUTO: d'huile*) sump (*BRIT*), oil pan (*US*); (*: de la boîte de vitesses*) casing; (*de bicyclette*) chain guard.
carte-réponse, *pl* **cartes-réponses** [kart(ə)repɔ̃s] *nf* reply card.
cartésien, ne [kartezjɛ̃, -ɛn] *adj* Cartesian.
Carthage [kartɑʒ] *n* Carthage.
carthaginois, e [kartaʒinwa, -waz] *adj* Carthaginian.
cartilage [kartilaʒ] *nm* (*ANAT*) cartilage.
cartilagineux, euse [kartilaʒinø, -øz] *adj* (*viande*) gristly.
cartographe [kartɔgraf] *nm/f* cartographer.
cartographie [kartɔgrafi] *nf* cartography, map-making.
cartomancie [kartɔmɑ̃si] *nf* fortune-telling, card-reading.
cartomancien, ne [kartɔmɑ̃sjɛ̃, -ɛn] *nm/f* fortune-teller (*with cards*).
carton [kartɔ̃] *nm* (*matériau*) cardboard; (*boîte*) (cardboard) box; (*d'invitation*) invitation card; (*ART*) sketch; cartoon; **en ~** cardboard *cpd*; **faire un ~** (*au tir*) to have a go at the rifle range; to score a hit; ~ **(à dessin)** portfolio.
cartonnage [kartɔnaʒ] *nm* cardboard (packing).
cartonné, e [kartɔne] *adj* (*livre*) hardback, cased.
carton-pâte [kartɔ̃pɑt] *nm* pasteboard; **de ~** (*fig*) cardboard *cpd*.
cartouche [kartuʃ] *nf* cartridge; (*de cigarettes*) carton.
cartouchière [kartuʃjɛr] *nf* cartridge belt.
cas [kɑ] *nm* case; **faire peu de ~/grand ~ de** to attach little/great importance to; **le ~ échéant** if need be; **en aucun ~** on no account, under no circumstances (whatsoever); **au ~ où** in case; **dans ce ~** in that case; **en ~ de** in case of, in the event of; **en ~ de besoin** if need be; **en ~ d'urgence** in an emergency; **en ce ~** in that case; **en tout ~** in any case, at any rate; ~ **de conscience** matter of conscience; ~ **de force majeure** case of absolute necessity; (*ASSURANCES*) act of God; ~ **limite** borderline case; ~ **social** social problem.
Casablanca [kazablɑ̃ka] *n* Casablanca.

casanier, ière [kazanje, -jɛʀ] *adj* stay-at-home.
casaque [kazak] *nf* (*de jockey*) blouse.
cascade [kaskad] *nf* waterfall, cascade; (*fig*) stream, torrent.
cascadeur, euse [kaskadœʀ, -øz] *nm/f* stuntman/girl.
case [kɑz] *nf* (*hutte*) hut; (*compartiment*) compartment; (*pour le courrier*) pigeonhole; (*de mots croisés, d'échiquier*) square; (*sur un formulaire*) box.
casemate [kazmat] *nf* blockhouse.
caser [kɑze] *vt* (*mettre*) to put; (*loger*) to put up; (*péj*) to find a job for; to marry off; **se** ~ (*personne*) to settle down.
caserne [kazɛʀn(ə)] *nf* barracks.
casernement [kazɛʀnəmɑ̃] *nm* barrack buildings *pl*.
cash [kaʃ] *adv*: **payer** ~ to pay cash down.
casier [kɑzje] *nm* (*à journaux etc*) rack; (*de bureau*) filing cabinet; (*: à cases*) set of pigeonholes; (*case*) compartment; pigeonhole; (*: à clef*) locker; (*PÊCHE*) lobster pot; ~ **à bouteilles** bottle rack; ~ **judiciaire** police record.
casino [kazino] *nm* casino.
casque [kask(ə)] *nm* helmet; (*chez le coiffeur*) (hair-)dryer; (*pour audition*) (head-)phones *pl*, headset; **les C~s bleus** the UN peacekeeping force.
casquer [kaske] *vi* (*fam*) to cough up, stump up (*BRIT*).
casquette [kaskɛt] *nf* cap.
cassable [kɑsabl(ə)] *adj* (*fragile*) breakable.
cassant, e [kɑsɑ̃, -ɑ̃t] *adj* brittle; (*fig*) brusque, abrupt.
cassate [kasat] *nf*: **(glace)** ~ cassata.
cassation [kɑsɑsjɔ̃] *nf*: **se pourvoir en** ~ to lodge an appeal; **recours en** ~ appeal to the Supreme Court.
casse [kas] *nf* (*pour voitures*): **mettre à la** ~ to scrap, send to the breakers (*BRIT*); (*dégâts*): **il y a eu de la** ~ there were a lot of breakages; (*TYPO*): **haut/bas de** ~ upper/lower case.
cassé, e [kɑse] *adj* (*voix*) cracked; (*vieillard*) bent.
casse-cou [kɑsku] *adj inv* daredevil, reckless; **crier** ~ **à qn** to warn sb (*against a risky undertaking*).
casse-croûte [kɑskʀut] *nm inv* snack.
casse-noisette(s) [kɑsnwazɛt], **casse-noix** [kɑsnwa] *nm inv* nutcrackers *pl*.
casse-pieds [kɑspje] *adj, nm/f inv* (*fam*): **il est** ~**, c'est un** ~ he's a pain (in the neck).
casser [kɑse] *vt* to break; (*ADMIN*: *gradé*) to demote; (*JUR*) to quash; (*COMM*): ~ **les prix** to slash prices; **se** ~ *vi* to break; (*fam*) to go, leave ♦ *vt*: **se** ~ **la jambe/une jambe** to break one's leg/a leg; **à tout** ~ fantastic, brilliant; **se** ~ **net** to break clean off.
casserole [kasʀɔl] *nf* saucepan; **à la** ~ (*CULIN*) braised.
casse-tête [kɑstɛt] *nm inv* (*fig*) brain teaser; (*difficultés*) headache (*fig*).
cassette [kasɛt] *nf* (*bande magnétique*) cassette; (*coffret*) casket; ~ **numérique** digital compact cassette.
casseur [kɑsœʀ] *nm* hooligan; rioter.
cassis [kasis] *nm* blackcurrant; (*de la route*) dip, bump.
cassonade [kasɔnad] *nf* brown sugar.
cassoulet [kasulɛ] *nm* *sausage and bean hotpot*.
cassure [kɑsyʀ] *nf* break, crack.
castagnettes [kastaɲɛt] *nfpl* castanets.
caste [kast(ə)] *nf* caste.
castillan, e [kastijɑ̃, -an] *adj* Castilian ♦ *nm* (*LING*) Castilian.
Castille [kastij] *nf*: **la** ~ Castile.
castor [kastɔʀ] *nm* beaver.
castrer [kastʀe] *vt* (*mâle*) to castrate; (*femelle*) to spay; (*cheval*) to geld; (*chat, chien*) to doctor (*BRIT*), fix (*US*).
cataclysme [kataklism(ə)] *nm* cataclysm.
catacombes [katakɔ̃b] *nfpl* catacombs.
catadioptre [katadjɔptʀ(ə)] *nm* = **cataphote**.
catafalque [katafalk(ə)] *nm* catafalque.
catalan, e [katalɑ̃, -an] *adj* Catalan, Catalonian ♦ *nm* (*LING*) Catalan.
Catalogne [katalɔɲ] *nf*: **la** ~ Catalonia.
catalogue [katalɔg] *nm* catalogue.
cataloguer [katalɔge] *vt* to catalogue, list; (*péj*) to put a label on.
catalyse [kataliz] *nf* catalysis.
catalyser [katalize] *vt* to catalyze.
catalyseur [katalizœʀ] *nm* catalyst.
catalytique [katalitik] *adj* catalytic.
catamaran [katamaʀɑ̃] *nm* (*voilier*) catamaran.
cataphote [katafɔt] *nm* reflector.
cataplasme [kataplasm(ə)] *nm* poultice.
catapulte [katapylt(ə)] *nf* catapult.
catapulter [katapylte] *vt* to catapult.
cataracte [kataʀakt(ə)] *nf* cataract; **opérer qn de la** ~ to operate on sb for a cataract.
catarrhe [kataʀ] *nm* catarrh.
catarrheux, euse [kataʀø, -øz] *adj* catarrhal.
catastrophe [katastʀɔf] *nf* catastrophe, disaster; **atterrir en** ~ to make an emergency landing; **partir en** ~ to rush away.
catastropher [katastʀɔfe] *vt* (*personne*) to shatter.
catastrophique [katastʀɔfik] *adj* catastrophic, disastrous.
catch [katʃ] *nm* (all-in) wrestling.
catcheur, euse [katʃœʀ, -øz] *nm/f* (all-in) wrestler.
catéchiser [kateʃize] *vt* to indoctrinate; to lecture.
catéchisme [kateʃism(ə)] *nm* catechism.
catéchumène [katekymɛn] *nm/f* catechumen, *person attending religious instruction prior to baptism*.
catégorie [kategɔʀi] *nf* category; (*BOUCHERIE*):

morceaux de première/deuxième ~ prime/ second cuts.
catégorique [kategɔʀik] *adj* categorical.
catégoriquement [kategɔʀikmɑ̃] *adv* categorically.
catégoriser [kategɔʀize] *vt* to categorize.
caténaire [katenɛʀ] *nf* (*RAIL*) catenary.
cathédrale [katedʀal] *nf* cathedral.
cathéter [katetɛʀ] *nm* (*MÉD*) catheter.
cathode [katɔd] *nf* cathode.
cathodique [katɔdik] *adj*: **rayons ~s** cathode rays; **tube/écran ~** cathode-ray tube/ screen.
catholicisme [katɔlisism(ə)] *nm* (Roman) Catholicism.
catholique [katɔlik] *adj, nm/f* (Roman) Catholic; **pas très ~** a bit shady *ou* fishy.
catimini [katimini]: **en ~** *adv* on the sly, on the quiet.
catogan [katɔgɑ̃] *nm* bow (*tying hair on neck*).
Caucase [kɔkɑz] *nm*: **le ~** the Caucasus (Mountains).
caucasien, ne [kɔkɑzjɛ̃, -ɛn] *adj* Caucasian.
cauchemar [kɔʃmaʀ] *nm* nightmare.
cauchemardesque [kɔʃmaʀdɛsk(ə)] *adj* nightmarish.
caudal, e, aux [kodal, -o] *adj* caudal, tail *cpd*.
causal, e [kozal] *adj* causal.
causalité [kozalite] *nf* causality.
causant, e [kozɑ̃, -ɑ̃t] *adj* chatty, talkative.
cause [koz] *nf* cause; (*JUR*) lawsuit, case; brief; **faire ~ commune avec qn** to take sides with sb; **être ~ de** to be the cause of; **à ~ de** because of, owing to; **pour ~ de** on account of; owing to; **(et) pour ~** and for (a very) good reason; **être en ~** (*intérêts*) to be at stake; (*personne*) to be involved; (*qualité*) to be in question; **mettre en ~** to implicate; to call into question; **remettre en ~** to challenge, call into question; **c'est hors de ~** it's out of the question; **en tout état de ~** in any case.
causer [koze] *vt* to cause ♦ *vi* to chat, talk.
causerie [kozʀi] *nf* talk.
causette [kozɛt] *nf*: **faire la** *ou* **un brin de ~** to have a chat.
caustique [kostik] *adj* caustic.
cauteleux, euse [kotlø, -øz] *adj* wily.
cautériser [kɔteʀize] *vt* to cauterize.
caution [kosjɔ̃] *nf* guarantee, security; deposit; (*JUR*) bail (bond); (*fig*) backing, support; **payer la ~ de qn** to stand bail for sb; **se porter ~ pour qn** to stand security for sb; **libéré sous ~** released on bail; **sujet à ~** unconfirmed.
cautionnement [kosjɔnmɑ̃] *nm* (*somme*) guarantee, security.
cautionner [kosjɔne] *vt* to guarantee; (*soutenir*) to support.
cavalcade [kavalkad] *nf* (*fig*) stampede.
cavale [kaval] *nf*: **en ~** on the run.
cavalerie [kavalʀi] *nf* cavalry.
cavalier, ière [kavalje, -jɛʀ] *adj* (*désinvolte*) offhand ♦ *nm/f* rider; (*au bal*) partner ♦ *nm* (*ÉCHECS*) knight; **faire ~ seul** to go it alone; **allée** *ou* **piste cavalière** riding path.
cavalièrement [kavaljɛʀmɑ̃] *adv* offhandedly.
cave [kav] *nf* cellar; (*cabaret*) (cellar) nightclub ♦ *adj*: **yeux ~s** sunken eyes; **joues ~s** hollow cheeks.
caveau, x [kavo] *nm* vault.
caverne [kavɛʀn(ə)] *nf* cave.
caverneux, euse [kavɛʀnø, -øz] *adj* cavernous.
caviar [kavjaʀ] *nm* caviar(e).
cavité [kavite] *nf* cavity.
Cayenne [kajɛn] *n* Cayenne.
CB [sibi] *sigle f* (= *citizens' band, canaux banalisés*) CB.
CC *sigle m* = **corps consulaire, compte courant.**
CCI *sigle f* = **Chambre de commerce et d'industrie.**
CCP *sigle m* = **compte chèque postal.**
CD *sigle m* (= *chemin départemental*) secondary road, ≈ B road (*BRIT*); (= *compact disc*) CD; (= *comité directeur*) steering committee; (*POL*) = **corps diplomatique.**
CDD *sigle m* (= *contrat à durée déterminée*) fixed-term contract.
CDF, CdF *sigle mpl* (= *Charbonnages de France*) *national coal board.*
CDI *sigle m* (= *Centre de documentation et d'information*) *school library*; (= *contrat à durée indéterminée*) permanent *ou* open-ended contract.
CD-I *sigle m* (= *compact disc interactif*) CD-I®.
CD-Rom [sedeʀɔm] *nm inv* (= *Compact Disc Read Only Memory*) CD-Rom.
CDS *sigle m* (= *Centre des démocrates sociaux*) *political party.*
CE *sigle f* (= *Communauté européenne*) EC; (*COMM*) = **caisse d'épargne** ♦ *sigle m* (*INDUSTRIE*) = **comité d'entreprise**; (*SCOL*) = **cours élémentaire.**

MOT-CLÉ

ce, cette [sə, sɛt] (*devant nm* **cet** + *voyelle ou h aspiré*; *pl* **ces**) *dét* (*proximité*) this; these *pl*; (*non-proximité*) that; those *pl*; **cette maison(-ci/là)** this/that house; **cette nuit** (*qui vient*) tonight; (*passée*) last night

♦ *pron* **1**: **c'est** it's, it is; **c'est petit/grand/un livre** it's *ou* it is small/big/a book; **c'est un peintre** he's *ou* he is a painter; **ce sont des peintres** they're *ou* they are painters; **c'est le facteur** *etc* (*à la porte*) it's the postman *etc*; **qui est-ce?** who is it?; (*en désignant*) who is he/she?; **qu'est-ce?** what is it?; **c'est toi qui lui as parlé** it was you who spoke to him

2: **c'est que**: **c'est qu'il est lent/qu'il n'a pas faim** the fact is, he's slow/he's not hungry

3 (*expressions*): **c'est ça** (*correct*) that's it, that's right; **c'est toi qui le dis!** that's what YOU say!; *voir aussi* **c'est-à-dire; -ci; est-ce**

que; n'est-ce pas.
4: ~ **qui**, ~ **que** what; (*chose qui*): **il est bête, ~ qui me chagrine** he's stupid, which saddens me; **tout ~ qui bouge** everything that *ou* which moves; **tout ~ que je sais** all I know; ~ **dont j'ai parlé** what I talked about; ~ **que c'est grand!** it's so big!

CEA *sigle m* (= *Commissariat à l'énergie atomique*) ≈ AEA (= *Atomic Energy Authority*) (*BRIT*), ≈ AEC (= *Atomic Energy Commission*) (*US*).
CECA [seka] *sigle f* (= *Communauté européenne du charbon et de l'acier*) ECSC (= *European Coal and Steel Community*).
ceci [səsi] *pron* this.
cécité [sesite] *nf* blindness.
céder [sede] *vt* to give up ♦ *vi* (*pont, barrage*) to give way; (*personne*) to give in; ~ **à** to yield to, give in to.
CEDEX [sedɛks] *sigle m* (= *courrier d'entreprise à distribution exceptionnelle*) *accelerated postal service for bulk users*.
cédille [sedij] *nf* cedilla.
cèdre [sɛdʀ(ə)] *nm* cedar.
CEE *sigle f* (= *Communauté économique européenne*) EEC.
CEG *sigle m* (= *Collège d'enseignement général*) ≈ junior secondary school (*BRIT*), ≈ junior high school (*US*).
CEI *sigle f* (= *Communauté des États indépendants*) CIS.
ceindre [sɛ̃dʀ(ə)] *vt* (*mettre*) to put on; (*entourer*): ~ **qch de qch** to put sth round sth.
ceinture [sɛ̃tyʀ] *nf* belt; (*taille*) waist; (*fig*) ring; belt; circle; ~ **de sauvetage** lifebelt (*BRIT*), life preserver (*US*); ~ **de sécurité** safety *ou* seat belt; ~ **(de sécurité) à enrouleur** inertia reel seat belt; ~ **verte** green belt.
ceinturer [sɛ̃tyʀe] *vt* (*saisir*) to grasp (round the waist); (*entourer*) to surround.
ceinturon [sɛ̃tyʀɔ̃] *nm* belt.
cela [səla] *pron* that; (*comme sujet indéfini*) it; ~ **m'étonne que** it surprises me that; **quand/où ~?** when/where (was that)?
célébrant [selebʀɑ̃] *nm* (*REL*) celebrant.
célébration [selebʀɑsjɔ̃] *nf* celebration.
célèbre [selɛbʀ(ə)] *adj* famous.
célébrer [selebʀe] *vt* to celebrate; (*louer*) to extol.
célébrité [selebʀite] *nf* fame; (*star*) celebrity.
céleri [sɛlʀi] *nm*: ~**(-rave)** celeriac; ~ **(en branche)** celery.
célérité [seleʀite] *nf* speed, swiftness.
céleste [selɛst(ə)] *adj* celestial; heavenly.
célibat [seliba] *nm* celibacy; bachelor/spinsterhood.
célibataire [selibatɛʀ] *adj* single, unmarried ♦ *nm/f* bachelor/unmarried *ou* single woman; **mère ~** single *ou* unmarried mother.
celle, celles [sɛl] *pron voir* **celui**.
cellier [selje] *nm* storeroom.
cellophane [selɔfan] *nf* ® cellophane.
cellulaire [selylɛʀ] *adj* (*BIO*) cell *cpd*, cellular; **voiture** *ou* **fourgon ~** prison *ou* police van; **régime ~** confinement.
cellule [selyl] *nf* (*gén*) cell; ~ **(photoélectrique)** electronic eye.
cellulite [selylit] *nf* cellulite.
celluloïd [selylɔid] *nm* ® Celluloid.
cellulose [selyloz] *nf* cellulose.
celte [sɛlt(ə)], **celtique** [sɛltik] *adj* Celt, Celtic.

MOT-CLÉ

celui, celle [səlɥi, sɛl] (*mpl* **ceux,** *fpl* **celles**) *pron*
1: ~**-ci/là, celle-ci/là** this one/that one; **ceux-ci, celles-ci** these (ones); **ceux-là, celles-là** those (ones); ~ **de mon frère** my brother's; ~ **du salon/du dessous** the one in (*ou* from) the lounge/below
2: ~ **qui bouge** the one which *ou* that moves; (*personne*) the one who moves; ~ **que je vois** the one (which *ou* that) I see; (*personne*) the one (whom) I see; ~ **dont je parle** the one I'm talking about
3 (*valeur indéfinie*): ~ **qui veut** whoever wants.

cénacle [senakl(ə)] *nm* (literary) coterie *ou* set.
cendre [sɑ̃dʀ(ə)] *nf* ash; ~**s** (*d'un foyer*) ash(es), cinders; (*volcaniques*) ash *sg*; (*d'un défunt*) ashes; **sous la ~** (*CULIN*) in (the) embers.
cendré, e [sɑ̃dʀe] *adj* (*couleur*) ashen; **(piste)** ~**e** cinder track.
cendreux, euse [sɑ̃dʀø, -øz] *adj* (*terrain, substance*) cindery; (*teint*) ashen.
cendrier [sɑ̃dʀije] *nm* ashtray.
cène [sɛn] *nf*: **la ~** (Holy) Communion; (*ART*) the Last Supper.
censé, e [sɑ̃se] *adj*: **être ~ faire** to be supposed to do.
censément [sɑ̃semɑ̃] *adv* supposedly.
censeur [sɑ̃sœʀ] *nm* (*SCOL*) deputy-head (*BRIT*), vice-principal (*US*); (*CINÉ, POL*) censor.
censure [sɑ̃syʀ] *nf* censorship.
censurer [sɑ̃syʀe] *vt* (*CINÉ, PRESSE*) to censor; (*POL*) to censure.
cent [sɑ̃] *num* a hundred, one hundred; **pour ~ (%)** per cent (%); **faire les ~ pas** to pace up and down ♦ *nm* (*US, Canada, partie de l'euro etc*) cent.
centaine [sɑ̃tɛn] *nf*: **une ~ (de)** about a hundred, a hundred or so; (*COMM*) a hundred; **plusieurs ~s (de)** several hundred; **des ~s (de)** hundreds (of).
centenaire [sɑ̃tnɛʀ] *adj* hundred-year-old ♦ *nm/f* centenarian ♦ *nm* (*anniversaire*) centenary.
centième [sɑ̃tjɛm] *num* hundredth.
centigrade [sɑ̃tigʀad] *nm* centigrade.

centigramme [sɑ̃tigʀam] *nm* centigramme.
centilitre [sɑ̃tilitʀ(ə)] *nm* centilitre (*BRIT*), centiliter (*US*).
centime [sɑ̃tim] *nm* centime.
centimètre [sɑ̃timɛtʀ(ə)] *nm* centimetre (*BRIT*), centimeter (*US*); (*ruban*) tape measure, measuring tape.
centrafricain, e [sɑ̃tʀafʀikɛ̃, -ɛn] *adj* of *ou* from the Central African Republic.
central, e, aux [sɑ̃tʀal, -o] *adj* central ♦ *nm*: ~ **(téléphonique)** (telephone) exchange ♦ *nf*: ~**e d'achat** (*COMM*) central buying service; ~**e électrique/nucléaire** electric/nuclear power station; ~**e syndicale** group of affiliated trade unions.
centralisation [sɑ̃tʀalizɑsjɔ̃] *nf* centralization.
centraliser [sɑ̃tʀalize] *vt* to centralize.
centralisme [sɑ̃tʀalism(ə)] *nm* centralism.
centraméricain, e [sɑ̃tʀameʀikɛ̃, -ɛn] *adj* Central American.
centre [sɑ̃tʀ(ə)] *nm* centre (*BRIT*), center (*US*); ~ **commercial/sportif/culturel** shopping/ sports/arts centre; ~ **aéré** outdoor centre; ~ **d'appels** call centre; ~ **d'apprentissage** training college; ~ **d'attraction** centre of attraction; ~ **de gravité** centre of gravity; ~ **de loisirs** leisure centre; ~ **d'enfouissement des déchets** landfill site; ~ **hospitalier** hospital complex; ~ **de tri** (*POSTES*) sorting office; ~**s nerveux** (*ANAT*) nerve centres.
centrer [sɑ̃tʀe] *vt* to centre (*BRIT*), center (*US*) ♦ *vi* (*FOOTBALL*) to centre the ball.
centre-ville, *pl* **centres-villes** [sɑ̃tʀəvil] *nm* town centre (*BRIT*) *ou* center (*US*), downtown (area) (*US*).
centrifuge [sɑ̃tʀifyʒ] *adj*: **force** ~ centrifugal force.
centrifuger [sɑ̃tʀifyʒe] *vt* to centrifuge.
centrifugeuse [sɑ̃tʀifyʒøz] *nf* (*pour fruits*) juice extractor.
centripète [sɑ̃tʀipɛt] *adj*: **force** ~ centripetal force.
centrisme [sɑ̃tʀism(ə)] *nm* centrism.
centriste [sɑ̃tʀist(ə)] *adj, nm/f* centrist.
centuple [sɑ̃typl(ə)] *nm*: **le** ~ **de qch** a hundred times sth; **au** ~ a hundredfold.
centupler [sɑ̃typle] *vi, vt* to increase a hundredfold.
CEP *sigle m* = **Certificat d'études (primaires)**.
cépage [sepaʒ] *nm* (type of) vine.
cèpe [sɛp] *nm* (edible) boletus.
cependant [səpɑ̃dɑ̃] *adv* however, nevertheless.
céramique [seʀamik] *adj* ceramic ♦ *nf* ceramic; (*art*) ceramics *sg*.
céramiste [seʀamist(ə)] *nm/f* ceramist.
cerbère [sɛʀbɛʀ] *nm* (*fig*: *péj*) bad-tempered doorkeeper.
cerceau, x [sɛʀso] *nm* (*d'enfant, de tonnelle*) hoop.
cercle [sɛʀkl(ə)] *nm* circle; (*objet*) band, hoop; **décrire un** ~ (*avion*) to circle; (*projectile*) to describe a circle; ~ **d'amis** circle of friends; ~ **de famille** family circle; ~ **vicieux** vicious circle.
cercler [sɛʀkle] *vt*: **lunettes cerclées d'or** gold-rimmed glasses.
cercueil [sɛʀkœj] *nm* coffin.
céréale [seʀeal] *nf* cereal.
céréalier, ière [seʀealje, -jɛʀ] *adj* (*production, cultures*) cereal *cpd*.
cérébral, e, aux [seʀebʀal, -o] *adj* (*ANAT*) cerebral, brain *cpd*; (*fig*) mental, cerebral.
cérémonial [seʀemɔnjal] *nm* ceremonial.
cérémonie [seʀemɔni] *nf* ceremony; ~**s** *nfpl* (*péj*) fuss *sg*, to-do *sg*.
cérémonieux, euse [seʀemɔnjø, -øz] *adj* ceremonious, formal.
CERES [seʀɛs] *sigle m* (= *Centre d'etudes, de recherches et d'éducation socialiste*) (*formerly*) *intellectual section of the French Socialist party*.
cerf [sɛʀ] *nm* stag.
cerfeuil [sɛʀfœj] *nm* chervil.
cerf-volant [sɛʀvɔlɑ̃] *nm* kite; **jouer au** ~ to fly a kite.
cerisaie [səʀizɛ] *nf* cherry orchard.
cerise [səʀiz] *nf* cherry.
cerisier [səʀizje] *nm* cherry (tree).
CERN [sɛʀn] *sigle m* (= *Centre européen de recherche nucléaire*) CERN.
cerné, e [sɛʀne] *adj*: **les yeux** ~**s** with dark rings *ou* shadows under the eyes.
cerner [sɛʀne] *vt* (*MIL etc*) to surround; (*fig: problème*) to delimit, define.
cernes [sɛʀn(ə)] *nfpl* (dark) rings, shadows (under the eyes).
certain, e [sɛʀtɛ̃, -ɛn] *adj* certain; (*sûr*): ~ **(de/ que)** certain *ou* sure (of/ that) ♦ *dét* certain; **d'un** ~ **âge** past one's prime, not so young; **un** ~ **temps** (quite) some time; **sûr et** ~ absolutely certain; ~**s** *pron* some.
certainement [sɛʀtɛnmɑ̃] *adv* (*probablement*) most probably *ou* likely; (*bien sûr*) certainly, of course.
certes [sɛʀt(ə)] *adv* admittedly; of course; indeed (yes).
certificat [sɛʀtifika] *nm* certificate; **C**~ **d'études (primaires) (CEP)** *former school leaving certificate* (*taken at the end of primary education*); **C**~ **de fin d'études secondaires (CFES)** school leaving certificate.
certifié, e [sɛʀtifje] *adj*: **professeur** ~ qualified teacher; (*ADMIN*): **copie** ~**e conforme (à l'original)** certified copy (of the original).
certifier [sɛʀtifje] *vt* to certify, guarantee; ~ **à qn que** to assure sb that, guarantee to sb that; ~ **qch à qn** to guarantee sth to sb.
certitude [sɛʀtityd] *nf* certainty.
cérumen [seʀymɛn] *nm* (ear)wax.
cerveau, x [sɛʀvo] *nm* brain; ~ **électronique** electronic brain.
cervelas [sɛʀvəla] *nm* saveloy.
cervelle [sɛʀvɛl] *nf* (*ANAT*) brain; (*CULIN*)

brain(s); **se creuser la** ~ to rack one's brains.
cervical, e, aux [sɛʀvikal, -o] *adj* cervical.
cervidés [sɛʀvide] *nmpl* cervidae.
CES *sigle m* (= *Collège d'enseignement secondaire*) ≈ (junior) secondary school (*BRIT*), ≈ junior high school (*US*).
ces [se] *dét voir* **ce.**
césarienne [sezaʀjɛn] *nf* caesarean (*BRIT*) *ou* cesarean (*US*) (section).
cessantes [sɛsɑ̃t] *adj fpl*: **toutes affaires** ~ forthwith.
cessation [sɛsɑsjɔ̃] *nf*: ~ **des hostilités** cessation of hostilities; ~ **de paiements/commerce** suspension of payments/trading.
cesse [sɛs]: **sans** ~ *adv* continually, constantly; continuously; **il n'avait de** ~ **que** he would not rest until.
cesser [sese] *vt* to stop ♦ *vi* to stop, cease; ~ **de faire** to stop doing; **faire** ~ (*bruit, scandale*) to put a stop to.
cessez-le-feu [seselfø] *nm inv* ceasefire.
cession [sɛsjɔ̃] *nf* transfer.
c'est [sɛ] *pron + vb voir* **ce.**
c'est-à-dire [sɛtadiʀ] *adv* that is (to say); (*demander de préciser*): ~? what does that mean?; ~ **que ...** (*en conséquence*) which means that ...; (*manière d'excuse*) well, in fact ....
CET *sigle m* (= *Collège d'enseignement technique*) (*formerly*) *technical school.*
cet [sɛt] *dét voir* **ce.**
cétacé [setase] *nm* cetacean.
cette [sɛt] *dét voir* **ce.**
ceux [sø] *pron voir* **celui.**
cévenol, e [sevnɔl] *adj* of *ou* from the Cévennes region.
cf. *abr* (= *confer*) cf, cp.
CFAO *sigle f* (= *conception de fabrication assistée par ordinateur*) CAM.
CFC *sigle mpl* (= *chlorofluorocarbures*) CFC.
CFDT *sigle f* (= *Confédération française démocratique du travail*) *trade union.*
CFES *sigle m* = **Certificat de fin d'études secondaires.**
CFF *sigle m* (= *Chemins de fer fédéraux*) *Swiss railways.*
CFL *sigle m* (= *Chemins de fer luxembourgeois*) *Luxembourg railways.*
CFP *sigle m* = *Centre de formation professionnelle* ♦ *sigle f* = *Compagnie française des pétroles.*
CFTC *sigle f* (= *Confédération française des travailleurs chrétiens*) *trade union.*
CGC *sigle f* (= *Confédération générale des cadres*) *management union.*
CGPME *sigle f* = *Confédération générale des petites et moyennes entreprises.*
CGT *sigle f* (= *Confédération générale du travail*) *trade union.*
CH *abr* (= *Confédération helvétique*) CH.
ch. *abr* = **charges, chauffage, cherche.**
chacal [ʃakal] *nm* jackal.
chacun, e [ʃakœ̃, -yn] *pron* each; (*indéfini*) everyone, everybody.
chagrin, e [ʃagʀɛ̃, -in] *adj* morose ♦ *nm* grief, sorrow; **avoir du** ~ to be grieved *ou* sorrowful.
chagriner [ʃagʀine] *vt* to grieve, distress; (*contrarier*) to bother, worry.
chahut [ʃay] *nm* uproar.
chahuter [ʃayte] *vt* to rag, bait ♦ *vi* to make an uproar.
chahuteur, euse [ʃaytœʀ, -øz] *nm/f* rowdy.
chai [ʃɛ] *nm* wine and spirit store(house).
chaîne [ʃɛn] *nf* chain; (*RADIO, TV*) channel; (*INFORM*) string; ~**s** *nfpl* (*liens, asservissement*) fetters, bonds; **travail à la** ~ production line work; **réactions en** ~ chain reactions; **faire la** ~ to form a (human) chain; ~ **alimentaire** food chain; ~ **compacte** music centre; ~ **d'entraide** mutual aid association; ~ **(haute-fidélité** *ou* **hi-fi)** hi-fi system; ~ **(de montage** *ou* **de fabrication)** production *ou* assembly line; ~ **(de montagnes)** (mountain) range; ~ **de solidarité** solidarity network; ~ **(stéréo** *ou* **audio)** stereo (system).
chaînette [ʃɛnɛt] *nf* (small) chain.
chaînon [ʃɛnɔ̃] *nm* link.
chair [ʃɛʀ] *nf* flesh ♦ *adj*: **(couleur)** ~ flesh-coloured; **avoir la** ~ **de poule** to have goosepimples *ou* gooseflesh; **bien en** ~ plump, well-padded; **en** ~ **et en os** in the flesh; ~ **à saucisses** sausage meat.
chaire [ʃɛʀ] *nf* (*d'église*) pulpit; (*d'université*) chair.
chaise [ʃɛz] *nf* chair; ~ **de bébé** high chair; ~ **électrique** electric chair; ~ **longue** deckchair.
chaland [ʃalɑ̃] *nm* (*bateau*) barge.
châle [ʃɑl] *nm* shawl.
chalet [ʃalɛ] *nm* chalet.
chaleur [ʃalœʀ] *nf* heat; (*fig*) warmth; fire, fervour (*BRIT*), fervor (*US*); heat; **en** ~ (*ZOOL*) on heat.
chaleureusement [ʃalœʀøzmɑ̃] *adv* warmly.
chaleureux, euse [ʃalœʀø, -øz] *adj* warm.
challenge [ʃalɑ̃ʒ] *nm* contest, tournament.
challenger [ʃalɑ̃ʒɛʀ] *nm* (*SPORT*) challenger.
chaloupe [ʃalup] *nf* launch; (*de sauvetage*) lifeboat.
chalumeau, x [ʃalymo] *nm* blowlamp (*BRIT*), blowtorch.
chalut [ʃaly] *nm* trawl (net); **pêcher au** ~ to trawl.
chalutier [ʃalytje] *nm* trawler; (*pêcheur*) trawlerman.
chamade [ʃamad] *nf*: **battre la** ~ to beat wildly.
chamailler [ʃamɑje]: **se** ~ *vi* to squabble, bicker.
chamarré, e [ʃamaʀe] *adj* richly brocaded.
chambard [ʃɑ̃baʀ] *nm* rumpus.
chambardement [ʃɑ̃baʀdəmɑ̃] *nm*: **c'est le grand** ~ everything has been (*ou* is being)

turned upside down.
chambarder [ʃɑ̃baʀde] *vt* to turn upside down.
chamboulement [ʃɑ̃bulmɑ̃] *nm* disruption.
chambouler [ʃɑ̃bule] *vt* to disrupt, turn upside down.
chambranle [ʃɑ̃bʀɑ̃l] *nm* (door) frame.
chambre [ʃɑ̃bʀ(ə)] *nf* bedroom; (*TECH*) chamber; (*POL*) chamber, house; (*JUR*) court; (*COMM*) chamber; federation; **faire ~ à part** to sleep in separate rooms; **stratège/alpiniste en ~** armchair strategist/mountaineer; **~ à un lit/deux lits** single/twin-bedded room; **~ pour une/deux personne(s)** single/double room; **~ d'accusation** court of criminal appeal; **~ d'agriculture** *body responsible for the agricultural interests of a département*; **~ à air** (*de pneu*) (inner) tube; **~ d'amis** spare *ou* guest room; **~ de combustion** combustion chamber; **~ de commerce et d'industrie (CCI)** chamber of commerce and industry; **~ à coucher** bedroom; **la C~ des députés** the Chamber of Deputies, ≈ the House (of Commons) (*BRIT*), ≈ the House of Rep- resentatives (*US*); **~ forte** strongroom; **~ froide** *ou* **frigorifique** cold room; **~ à gaz** gas chamber; **~ d'hôte** ≈ bed and breakfast (*in private home*); **~ des machines** engine-room; **~ des métiers (CM)** *chamber of commerce for trades*; **~ meublée** bedsit(ter) (*BRIT*), furnished room; **~ noire** (*PHOTO*) dark room.
chambrée [ʃɑ̃bʀe] *nf* room.
chambrer [ʃɑ̃bʀe] *vt* (*vin*) to bring to room temperature.
chameau, x [ʃamo] *nm* camel.
chamois [ʃamwa] *nm* chamois ♦ *adj*: **(couleur) ~** fawn, buff.
champ [ʃɑ̃] *nm* (*aussi INFORM*) field; (*PHOTO*): **dans le ~** in the picture; **prendre du ~** to draw back; **laisser le ~ libre à qn** to leave sb a clear field; **~ d'action** sphere of operation(s); **~ de bataille** battlefield; **~ de courses** racecourse; **~ d'honneur** field of honour; **~ de manœuvre** (*MIL*) parade ground; **~ de mines** minefield; **~ de tir** shooting *ou* rifle range; **~ visuel** field of vision.
Champagne [ʃɑ̃paɲ] *nf*: **la ~** Champagne, the Champagne region.
champagne [ʃɑ̃paɲ] *nm* champagne.
champenois, e [ʃɑ̃pənwa, -waz] *adj* of *ou* from Champagne; (*vin*): **méthode ~e** champagne-type.
champêtre [ʃɑ̃pɛtʀ(ə)] *adj* country *cpd*, rural.
champignon [ʃɑ̃piɲɔ̃] *nm* mushroom; (*terme générique*) fungus (*pl* -i); (*fam: accélérateur*) accelerator, gas pedal (*US*); **~ de couche** *ou* **de Paris** button mushroom; **~ vénéneux** toadstool, poisonous mushroom.
champion, ne [ʃɑ̃pjɔ̃, -ɔn] *adj, nm/f* champion.
championnat [ʃɑ̃pjɔna] *nm* championship.
chance [ʃɑ̃s] *nf*: **la ~** luck; **une ~** a stroke *ou* piece of luck *ou* good fortune; (*occasion*) a lucky break; **~s** *nfpl* (*probabilités*) chances; **avoir de la ~** to be lucky; **il a des ~s de gagner** he has a chance of winning; **il y a de fortes ~s pour que Paul soit malade** it's highly probable that Paul is ill; **bonne ~!** good luck!; **encore une ~ que tu viennes!** it's lucky you're coming; **je n'ai pas de ~** I'm out of luck; (*toujours*) I never have any luck; **donner sa ~ à qn** to give sb a chance.
chancelant, e [ʃɑ̃slɑ̃, -ɑ̃t] *adj* (*personne*) tottering; (*santé*) failing.
chanceler [ʃɑ̃sle] *vi* to totter.
chancelier [ʃɑ̃səlje] *nm* (*allemand*) chancellor; (*d'ambassade*) secretary.
chancellerie [ʃɑ̃sɛlʀi] *nf* (*en France*) ministry of justice; (*en Allemagne*) chancellery; (*d'ambassade*) chancery.
chanceux, euse [ʃɑ̃sø, -øz] *adj* lucky, fortunate.
chancre [ʃɑ̃kʀ(ə)] *nm* canker.
chandail [ʃɑ̃daj] *nm* (thick) jumper *ou* sweater.
Chandeleur [ʃɑ̃dlœʀ] *nf*: **la ~** Candlemas.
chandelier [ʃɑ̃dəlje] *nm* candlestick; (*à plusieurs branches*) candelabra.
chandelle [ʃɑ̃dɛl] *nf* (tallow) candle; (*TENNIS*): **faire une ~** to lob; (*AVIAT*): **monter en ~** to climb vertically; **tenir la ~** to play gooseberry; **dîner aux ~s** candlelight dinner.
change [ʃɑ̃ʒ] *nm* (*COMM*) exchange; **opérations de ~** (foreign) exchange transactions; **contrôle des ~s** exchange control; **gagner/perdre au ~** to be better/worse off (for it); **donner le ~ à qn** (*fig*) to lead sb up the garden path.
changeant, e [ʃɑ̃ʒɑ̃, -ɑ̃t] *adj* changeable, fickle.
changement [ʃɑ̃ʒmɑ̃] *nm* change; **~ de vitesse** (*dispositif*) gears *pl*; (*action*) gear change.
changer [ʃɑ̃ʒe] *vt* (*modifier*) to change, alter; (*remplacer, COMM, rhabiller*) to change ♦ *vi* to change, alter; **se ~** to change (o.s.); **~ de** (*remplacer: adresse, nom, voiture etc*) to change one's; (*échanger, alterner: côté, place, train etc*) to change + *npl*; **~ d'air** to get a change of air; **~ de couleur/direction** to change colour/direction; **~ d'idée** to change one's mind; **~ de place avec qn** to change places with sb; **~ de vitesse** (*AUTO*) to change gear; **~ qn/qch de place** to move sb/sth to another place; **~ (de train** *etc***)** to change (trains *etc*); **~ qch en** to change sth into.
changeur [ʃɑ̃ʒœʀ] *nm* (*personne*) moneychanger; **~ automatique** change machine; **~ de disques** record changer, autochange.
chanoine [ʃanwan] *nm* canon.
chanson [ʃɑ̃sɔ̃] *nf* song.
chansonnette [ʃɑ̃sɔnɛt] *nf* ditty.
chansonnier [ʃɑ̃sɔnje] *nm* cabaret artist (*spe-*

cializing in political satire); (*recueil*) song book.
chant [ʃɑ̃] *nm* song; (*art vocal*) singing; (*d'église*) hymn; (*de poème*) canto; (*TECH*): **posé de** *ou* **sur** ~ placed edgeways; ~ **de Noël** Christmas carol.
chantage [ʃɑ̃taʒ] *nm* blackmail; **faire du** ~ to use blackmail; **soumettre qn à un** ~ to blackmail sb.
chantant, e [ʃɑ̃tɑ̃, -ɑ̃t] *adj* (*accent, voix*) sing-song.
chanter [ʃɑ̃te] *vt, vi* to sing; ~ **juste/faux** to sing in tune/out of tune; **si cela lui chante** (*fam*) if he feels like it *ou* fancies it.
chanterelle [ʃɑ̃tʀɛl] *nf* chanterelle (*edible mushroom*).
chanteur, euse [ʃɑ̃tœʀ, -øz] *nm/f* singer; ~ **de charme** crooner.
chantier [ʃɑ̃tje] *nm* (building) site; (*sur une route*) roadworks *pl*; **mettre en** ~ to start work on; ~ **naval** shipyard.
chantilly [ʃɑ̃tiji] *nf voir* **crème**.
chantonner [ʃɑ̃tɔne] *vi, vt* to sing to oneself, hum.
chantre [ʃɑ̃tʀ(ə)] *nm* (*fig*) eulogist.
chanvre [ʃɑ̃vʀ(ə)] *nm* hemp.
chaos [kao] *nm* chaos.
chaotique [kaɔtik] *adj* chaotic.
chap. *abr* (= *chapitre*) ch.
chapardage [ʃapaʀdaʒ] *nm* pilfering.
chaparder [ʃapaʀde] *vt* to pinch.
chapeau, x [ʃapo] *nm* hat; (*PRESSE*) introductory paragraph; ~! well done!; ~ **melon** bowler hat; ~ **mou** trilby; ~**x de roues** hub caps.
chapeauter [ʃapote] *vt* (*ADMIN*) to head, oversee.
chapelain [ʃaplɛ̃] *nm* (*REL*) chaplain.
chapelet [ʃaplɛ] *nm* (*REL*) rosary; (*fig*): **un** ~ **de** a string of; **dire son** ~ to tell one's beads.
chapelier, ière [ʃapəlje, -jɛʀ] *nm/f* hatter; milliner.
chapelle [ʃapɛl] *nf* chapel; ~ **ardente** chapel of rest.
chapellerie [ʃapɛlʀi] *nf* (*magasin*) hat shop; (*commerce*) hat trade.
chapelure [ʃaplyʀ] *nf* (dried) breadcrumbs *pl*.
chaperon [ʃapʀɔ̃] *nm* chaperon.
chaperonner [ʃapʀɔne] *vt* to chaperon.
chapiteau, x [ʃapito] *nm* (*ARCHIT*) capital; (*de cirque*) marquee, big top.
chapitre [ʃapitʀ(ə)] *nm* chapter; (*fig*) subject, matter; **avoir voix au** ~ to have a say in the matter.
chapitrer [ʃapitʀe] *vt* to lecture, reprimand.
chapon [ʃapɔ̃] *nm* capon.
chaque [ʃak] *dét* each, every; (*indéfini*) every.
char [ʃaʀ] *nm* (*à foin etc*) cart, waggon; (*de carnaval*) float; ~ **(d'assaut)** tank.
charabia [ʃaʀabja] *nm* (*péj*) gibberish, gobbledygook (*BRIT*).
charade [ʃaʀad] *nf* riddle; (*mimée*) charade.
charbon [ʃaʀbɔ̃] *nm* coal; ~ **de bois** charcoal.
charbonnage [ʃaʀbɔnaʒ] *nm*: **les** ~**s de France** the (French) Coal Board *sg*.
charbonnier [ʃaʀbɔnje] *nm* coalman.
charcuterie [ʃaʀkytʀi] *nf* (*magasin*) pork butcher's shop and delicatessen; (*produits*) cooked pork meats *pl*.
charcutier, ière [ʃaʀkytje, -jɛʀ] *nm/f* pork butcher.
chardon [ʃaʀdɔ̃] *nm* thistle.
chardonneret [ʃaʀdɔnʀɛ] *nm* goldfinch.
charentais, e [ʃaʀɑ̃tɛ, -ɛz] *adj* of *ou* from Charente ♦ *nf* (*pantoufle*) slipper.
charge [ʃaʀʒ(ə)] *nf* (*fardeau*) load; (*explosif, ÉLEC, MIL, JUR*) charge; (*rôle, mission*) responsibility; ~**s** *nfpl* (*du loyer*) service charges; **à la** ~ **de** (*dépendant de*) dependent upon, supported by; (*aux frais de*) chargeable to, payable by; **j'accepte, à** ~ **de revanche** I accept, provided I can do the same for you (in return) one day; **prendre en** ~ to take charge of; (*suj: véhicule*) to take on; (*dépenses*) to take care of; ~ **utile** (*AUTO*) live load; (*COMM*) payload; ~**s sociales** social security contributions.
chargé [ʃaʀʒe] *adj* (*voiture, animal, personne*) laden; (*fusil, batterie, caméra*) loaded; (*occupé: emploi du temps, journée*) busy, full; (*estomac*) heavy, full; (*langue*) furred; (*décoration, style*) heavy, ornate ♦ *nm*: ~ **d'affaires** chargé d'affaires; ~ **de cours** ≈ lecturer; ~ **de** (*responsable de*) responsible for.
chargement [ʃaʀʒəmɑ̃] *nm* (*action*) loading; charging; (*objets*) load.
charger [ʃaʀʒe] *vt* (*voiture, fusil, caméra, INFORM*) to load; (*batterie*) to charge ♦ *vi* (*MIL etc*) to charge; **se** ~ **de** *vt* to see to, take care of; ~ **qn de qch/faire qch** to give sb the responsibility for sth/of doing sth; to put sb in charge of sth/doing sth; **se** ~ **de faire qch** to take it upon o.s. to do sth.
chargeur [ʃaʀʒœʀ] *nm* (*dispositif: d'arme à feu*) magazine; (*: PHOTO*) cartridge; ~ **de batterie** (*ÉLEC*) battery charger.
chariot [ʃaʀjo] *nm* trolley; (*charrette*) waggon; (*de machine à écrire*) carriage; ~ **élévateur** fork-lift truck.
charisme [kaʀism(ə)] *nm* charisma.
charitable [ʃaʀitabl(ə)] *adj* charitable; kind.
charité [ʃaʀite] *nf* charity; **faire la** ~ to give to charity; to do charitable works; **faire la** ~ **à** to give (something) to; **fête/vente de** ~ fête/sale in aid of charity.
charivari [ʃaʀivaʀi] *nm* hullabaloo.
charlatan [ʃaʀlatɑ̃] *nm* charlatan.
charlotte [ʃaʀlɔt] *nf* (*CULIN*) charlotte.
charmant, e [ʃaʀmɑ̃, -ɑ̃t] *adj* charming.
charme [ʃaʀm(ə)] *nm* charm; ~**s** *nmpl* (*appas*) charms; **c'est ce qui en fait le** ~ that is its attraction; **faire du** ~ to be charming, turn on the charm; **aller** *ou* **se porter comme un** ~ to be in the pink.
charmer [ʃaʀme] *vt* to charm; **je suis charmé**

de I'm delighted to.

charmeur, euse [ʃaʀmœʀ, -øz] *nm/f* charmer; ~ **de serpents** snake charmer.

charnel, le [ʃaʀnɛl] *adj* carnal.

charnier [ʃaʀnje] *nm* mass grave.

charnière [ʃaʀnjɛʀ] *nf* hinge; (*fig*) turning-point.

charnu, e [ʃaʀny] *adj* fleshy.

charogne [ʃaʀɔɲ] *nf* carrion *no pl*; (*fam!*) bastard (*!*).

charolais, e [ʃaʀɔlɛ, -ɛz] *adj* of *ou* from the Charolais.

charpente [ʃaʀpɑ̃t] *nf* frame(work); (*fig*) structure, framework; (*carrure*) build, frame.

charpenté, e [ʃaʀpɑ̃te] *adj*: **bien** *ou* **solidement** ~ (*personne*) well-built; (*texte*) well-constructed.

charpenterie [ʃaʀpɑ̃tʀi] *nf* carpentry.

charpentier [ʃaʀpɑ̃tje] *nm* carpenter.

charpie [ʃaʀpi] *nf*: **en** ~ (*fig*) in shreds *ou* ribbons.

charretier [ʃaʀtje] *nm* carter; **de** ~ (*péj*: *langage, manières*) uncouth.

charrette [ʃaʀɛt] *nf* cart.

charrier [ʃaʀje] *vt* to carry (along); to cart, carry ♦ *vi* (*fam*) to exaggerate.

charrue [ʃaʀy] *nf* plough (*BRIT*), plow (*US*).

charte [ʃaʀt(ə)] *nf* charter.

charter [tʃaʀtœʀ] *nm* (*vol*) charter flight; (*avion*) charter plane.

chasse [ʃas] *nf* hunting; (*au fusil*) shooting; (*poursuite*) chase; (*aussi*: ~ **d'eau**) flush; **la** ~ **est ouverte** the hunting season is open; **la** ~ **est fermée** it is the close (*BRIT*) *ou* closed (*US*) season; **aller à la** ~ to go hunting; **prendre en** ~, **donner la** ~ **à** to give chase to; **tirer la** ~ **(d'eau)** to flush the toilet, pull the chain; ~ **aérienne** aerial pursuit; ~ **à courre** hunting; ~ **à l'homme** manhunt; ~ **gardée** private hunting grounds *pl*; ~ **sous-marine** underwater fishing.

châsse [ʃɑs] *nf* reliquary, shrine.

chassé-croisé, *pl* **chassés-croisés** [ʃasekʀwaze] *nm* (*DANSE*) chassé-croisé; (*fig*) mix-up (*where people miss each other in turn*).

chasse-neige [ʃasnɛʒ] *nm inv* snowplough (*BRIT*), snowplow (*US*).

chasser [ʃase] *vt* to hunt; (*expulser*) to chase away *ou* out, drive away *ou* out; (*dissiper*) to chase *ou* sweep away; to dispel, drive away.

chasseur, euse [ʃasœʀ, -øz] *nm/f* hunter ♦ *nm* (*avion*) fighter; (*domestique*) page (boy), messenger (boy); ~ **d'images** roving photographer; ~ **de têtes** (*fig*) headhunter; ~**s alpins** mountain infantry.

chassieux, euse [ʃasjø, -øz] *adj* sticky, gummy.

châssis [ʃɑsi] *nm* (*AUTO*) chassis; (*cadre*) frame; (*de jardin*) cold frame.

chaste [ʃast(ə)] *adj* chaste.

chasteté [ʃastəte] *nf* chastity.

chasuble [ʃazybl(ə)] *nf* chasuble; **robe** ~ pinafore dress (*BRIT*), jumper (*US*).

chat [ʃa] *nm* cat; ~ **sauvage** wildcat.

châtaigne [ʃɑtɛɲ] *nf* chestnut.

châtaignier [ʃɑteɲe] *nm* chestnut (tree).

châtain [ʃɑtɛ̃] *adj inv* chestnut (brown); (*personne*) chestnut-haired.

château, x [ʃɑto] *nm* castle; ~ **d'eau** water tower; ~ **fort** stronghold, fortified castle; ~ **de sable** sandcastle.

châtelain, e [ʃɑtlɛ̃, -ɛn] *nm/f* lord/lady of the manor ♦ *nf* (*ceinture*) chatelaine.

châtier [ʃɑtje] *vt* to punish, castigate; (*fig: style*) to polish, refine.

chatière [ʃatjɛʀ] *nf* (*porte*) cat flap.

châtiment [ʃɑtimɑ̃] *nm* punishment, castigation; ~ **corporel** corporal punishment.

chatoiement [ʃatwamɑ̃] *nm* shimmer(ing).

chaton [ʃatɔ̃] *nm* (*ZOOL*) kitten; (*BOT*) catkin; (*de bague*) bezel; stone.

chatouillement [ʃatujmɑ̃] *nm* (*gén*) tickling; (*dans le nez, la gorge*) tickle.

chatouiller [ʃatuje] *vt* to tickle; (*l'odorat, le palais*) to titillate.

chatouilleux, euse [ʃatujø, -øz] *adj* ticklish; (*fig*) touchy, over-sensitive.

chatoyant, e [ʃatwajɑ̃, -ɑ̃t] *adj* (*reflet, étoffe*) shimmering; (*couleurs*) sparkling.

chatoyer [ʃatwaje] *vi* to shimmer.

châtrer [ʃɑtʀe] *vt* (*mâle*) to castrate; (*femelle*) to spay; (*cheval*) to geld; (*chat, chien*) to doctor (*BRIT*), fix (*US*); (*fig*) to mutilate.

chatte [ʃat] *nf* (she-)cat.

chatterton [ʃatɛʀtɔn] *nm* (*ruban isolant*: *ÉLEC*) (adhesive) insulating tape.

chaud, e [ʃo, -od] *adj* (*gén*) warm; (*très chaud*) hot; (*fig: félicitations*) hearty; (*discussion*) heated; **il fait** ~ it's warm; it's hot; **manger** ~ to have something hot to eat; **avoir** ~ to be warm; to be hot; **tenir** ~ to keep hot; **ça me tient** ~ it keeps me warm; **tenir au** ~ to keep in a warm place; **rester au** ~ to stay in the warm.

chaudement [ʃodmɑ̃] *adv* warmly; (*fig*) hotly.

chaudière [ʃodjɛʀ] *nf* boiler.

chaudron [ʃodʀɔ̃] *nm* cauldron.

chaudronnerie [ʃodʀɔnʀi] *nf* (*usine*) boilerworks; (*activité*) boilermaking; (*boutique*) coppersmith's workshop.

chauffage [ʃofaʒ] *nm* heating; ~ **au gaz/à l'électricité/au charbon** gas/electric/solid fuel heating; ~ **central** central heating; ~ **par le sol** underfloor heating.

chauffagiste [ʃofaʒist(ə)] *nm* (*installateur*) heating engineer.

chauffant, e [ʃofɑ̃, -ɑ̃t]: **couverture** ~**e** electric blanket; **plaque** ~**e** hotplate.

chauffard [ʃofaʀ] *nm* (*péj*) reckless driver; roadhog; (*après un accident*) hit-and-run driver.

chauffe-bain [ʃofbɛ̃] *nm* = **chauffe-eau**.

chauffe-biberon [ʃofbibʀɔ̃] *nm* (baby's) bottle

warmer.
chauffe-eau [ʃofo] *nm inv* water heater.
chauffe-plats [ʃofpla] *nm inv* dish warmer.
chauffer [ʃofe] *vt* to heat ♦ *vi* to heat up, warm up; (*trop chauffer: moteur*) to overheat; **se** ~ (*se mettre en train*) to warm up; (*au soleil*) to warm o.s.
chaufferie [ʃofʀi] *nf* boiler room.
chauffeur [ʃofœʀ] *nm* driver; (*privé*) chauffeur; **voiture avec/sans** ~ chauffeur-driven/self-drive car.
chauffeuse [ʃoføz] *nf* fireside chair.
chauler [ʃole] *vt* (*mur*) to whitewash.
chaume [ʃom] *nm* (*du toit*) thatch; (*tiges*) stubble.
chaumière [ʃomjɛʀ] *nf* (thatched) cottage.
chaussée [ʃose] *nf* road(way); (*digue*) causeway.
chausse-pied [ʃospje] *nm* shoe-horn.
chausser [ʃose] *vt* (*bottes, skis*) to put on; (*enfant*) to put shoes on; (*suj: soulier*) to fit; ~ **du 38/42** to take size 38/42; ~ **grand/bien** to be big-/well-fitting; **se** ~ to put one's shoes on.
chausse-trappe [ʃostʀap] *nf* trap.
chaussette [ʃosɛt] *nf* sock.
chausseur [ʃosœʀ] *nm* (*marchand*) footwear specialist, shoemaker.
chausson [ʃosɔ̃] *nm* slipper; (*de bébé*) bootee; ~ **(aux pommes)** (apple) turnover.
chaussure [ʃosyʀ] *nf* shoe; (*commerce*): **la** ~ the shoe industry *ou* trade; ~**s basses** flat shoes; ~**s montantes** ankle boots; ~**s de ski** ski boots.
chaut [ʃo] *vb*: **peu me** ~ it matters little to me.
chauve [ʃov] *adj* bald.
chauve-souris, *pl* **chauves-souris** [ʃovsuʀi] *nf* bat.
chauvin, e [ʃovɛ̃, -in] *adj* chauvinistic; jingoistic.
chauvinisme [ʃovinism(ə)] *nm* chauvinism; jingoism.
chaux [ʃo] *nf* lime; **blanchi à la** ~ whitewashed.
chavirer [ʃaviʀe] *vi* to capsize, overturn.
chef [ʃɛf] *nm* head, leader; (*patron*) boss; (*de cuisine*) chef; **au premier** ~ extremely, to the nth degree; **de son propre** ~ on his *ou* her own initiative; **général/commandant en** ~ general-/commander-in-chief; ~ **d'accusation** (*JUR*) charge, count (of indictment); ~ **d'atelier** (shop) foreman; ~ **de bureau** head clerk; ~ **de clinique** senior hospital lecturer; ~ **d'entreprise** company head; ~ **d'équipe** team leader; ~ **d'état** head of state; ~ **de famille** head of the family; ~ **de file** (*de parti etc*) leader; ~ **de gare** station master; ~ **d'orchestre** conductor (*BRIT*), leader (*US*); ~ **de rayon** department(al) supervisor; ~ **de service** departmental head.
chef-d'œuvre, *pl* **chefs-d'œuvre** [ʃɛdœvʀ(ə)] *nm* masterpiece.
chef-lieu, *pl* **chefs-lieux** [ʃɛfljø] *nm* county town.
cheftaine [ʃɛftɛn] *nf* (guide) captain.
cheik(h) [ʃɛk] *nm* sheik.
chemin [ʃəmɛ̃] *nm* path; (*itinéraire, direction, trajet*) way; **en** ~, ~ **faisant** on the way; ~ **de fer** railway (*BRIT*), railroad (*US*); **par** ~ **de fer** by rail; **les** ~**s de fer** the railways (*BRIT*), the railroad (*US*); ~ **de terre** dirt track.
cheminée [ʃəmine] *nf* chimney; (*à l'intérieur*) chimney piece, fireplace; (*de bateau*) funnel.
cheminement [ʃəminmɑ̃] *nm* progress; course.
cheminer [ʃəmine] *vi* to walk (along).
cheminot [ʃəmino] *nm* railwayman (*BRIT*), railroad worker (*US*).
chemise [ʃəmiz] *nf* shirt; (*dossier*) folder; ~ **de nuit** nightdress.
chemiserie [ʃəmizʀi] *nf* (gentlemen's) outfitters'.
chemisette [ʃəmizɛt] *nf* short-sleeved shirt.
chemisier [ʃəmizje] *nm* blouse.
chenal, aux [ʃənal, -o] *nm* channel.
chenapan [ʃənapɑ̃] *nm* (*garnement*) rascal; (*péj: vaurien*) rogue.
chêne [ʃɛn] *nm* oak (tree); (*bois*) oak.
chenet [ʃənɛ] *nm* fire-dog, andiron.
chenil [ʃənil] *nm* kennels *pl*.
chenille [ʃənij] *nf* (*ZOOL*) caterpillar; (*AUTO*) caterpillar track; **véhicule à** ~**s** tracked vehicle, caterpillar.
chenillette [ʃənijɛt] *nf* tracked vehicle.
cheptel [ʃɛptɛl] *nm* livestock.
chèque [ʃɛk] *nm* cheque (*BRIT*), check (*US*); **faire/toucher un** ~ to write/cash a cheque; **par** ~ by cheque; ~ **barré/sans provision** crossed (*BRIT*)/bad cheque; ~ **en blanc** blank cheque; ~ **au porteur** cheque to bearer; ~ **postal** post office cheque, ≈ giro cheque (*BRIT*); ~ **de voyage** traveller's cheque.
chèque-cadeau, *pl* **chèques-cadeaux** [ʃɛkkado] *nm* gift token.
chèque-repas, *pl* **chèques-repas** [ʃɛkʀəpɑ], **chèque-restaurant,** *pl* **chèques-restaurant** [ʃɛkʀɛstɔʀɑ̃] *nm* ≈ luncheon voucher.
chéquier [ʃekje] *nm* cheque book (*BRIT*), checkbook (*US*).
cher, ère [ʃɛʀ] *adj* (*aimé*) dear; (*coûteux*) expensive, dear ♦ *adv*: **coûter/payer** ~ to cost/pay a lot ♦ *nf*: **la bonne chère** good food; **cela coûte** ~ it's expensive, it costs a lot of money; **mon** ~, **ma chère** my dear.
chercher [ʃɛʀʃe] *vt* to look for; (*gloire etc*) to seek; (*INFORM*) to search; ~ **des ennuis/la bagarre** to be looking for trouble/a fight; **aller** ~ to go for, go and fetch; ~ **à faire** to try to do.
chercheur, euse [ʃɛʀʃœʀ, -øz] *nm/f* researcher, research worker; ~ **de** seeker of; hunter of; ~ **d'or** gold digger.
chère [ʃɛʀ] *adj f*, *nf voir* **cher**.

chèrement [ʃɛʀmɑ̃] *adv* dearly.
chéri, e [ʃeʀi] *adj* beloved, dear; **(mon)** ~ darling.
chérir [ʃeʀiʀ] *vt* to cherish.
cherté [ʃɛʀte] *nf*: **la ~ de la vie** the high cost of living.
chérubin [ʃeʀybɛ̃] *nm* cherub.
chétif, ive [ʃetif, -iv] *adj* puny, stunted.
cheval, aux [ʃəval, -o] *nm* horse; (*AUTO*): ~ **(vapeur) (CV)** horsepower *no pl*; **50 chevaux (au frein)** 50 brake horsepower, 50 b.h.p.; **10 chevaux (fiscaux)** 10 horsepower (*for tax purposes*); **faire du** ~ to ride; **à** ~ on horseback; **à ~ sur** astride, straddling; (*fig*) overlapping; ~ **d'arçons** vaulting horse; ~ **à bascule** rocking horse; ~ **de bataille** charger; (*fig*) hobby-horse; ~ **de course** race horse; **chevaux de bois** (*des manèges*) wooden (fairground) horses; (*manège*) merry-go-round.
chevaleresque [ʃəvalʀɛsk(ə)] *adj* chivalrous.
chevalerie [ʃəvalʀi] *nf* chivalry; knighthood.
chevalet [ʃəvalɛ] *nm* easel.
chevalier [ʃəvalje] *nm* knight; ~ **servant** escort.
chevalière [ʃəvaljɛʀ] *nf* signet ring.
chevalin, e [ʃəvalɛ̃, -in] *adj* of horses, equine; (*péj*) horsy; **boucherie ~e** horse-meat butcher's.
cheval-vapeur, *pl* **chevaux-vapeur** [ʃəvalvapœʀ, ʃəvo-] *nm voir* **cheval**.
chevauchée [ʃəvoʃe] *nf* ride; cavalcade.
chevauchement [ʃəvoʃmɑ̃] *nm* overlap.
chevaucher [ʃəvoʃe] *vi* (*aussi*: **se ~**) to overlap (each other) ♦ *vt* to be astride, straddle.
chevaux [ʃəvo] *nmpl voir* **cheval**.
chevelu, e [ʃəvly] *adj* with a good head of hair, hairy (*péj*).
chevelure [ʃəvlyʀ] *nf* hair *no pl*.
chevet [ʃəvɛ] *nm*: **au ~ de qn** at sb's bedside; **lampe de ~** bedside lamp.
cheveu, x [ʃəvø] *nm* hair ♦ *nmpl* (*chevelure*) hair *sg*; **avoir les ~x courts/en brosse** to have short hair/a crew cut; **se faire couper les ~x** to get *ou* have one's hair cut; **tiré par les ~x** (*histoire*) far-fetched.
cheville [ʃəvij] *nf* (*ANAT*) ankle; (*de bois*) peg; (*pour enfoncer une vis*) plug; **être en ~ avec qn** to be in cahoots with sb; ~ **ouvrière** (*fig*) kingpin.
chèvre [ʃɛvʀ(ə)] *nf* (she-)goat; **ménager la ~ et le chou** to try to please everyone.
chevreau, x [ʃəvʀo] *nm* kid.
chèvrefeuille [ʃɛvʀəfœj] *nm* honeysuckle.
chevreuil [ʃəvʀœj] *nm* roe deer *inv*; (*CULIN*) venison.
chevron [ʃəvʀɔ̃] *nm* (*poutre*) rafter; (*motif*) chevron, v(-shape); **à ~s** chevron-patterned; (*petits*) herringbone.
chevronné, e [ʃəvʀɔne] *adj* seasoned, experienced.
chevrotant, e [ʃəvʀɔtɑ̃, -ɑ̃t] *adj* quavering.
chevroter [ʃəvʀɔte] *vi* (*personne, voix*) to quaver.
chevrotine [ʃəvʀɔtin] *nf* buckshot *no pl*.
chewing-gum [ʃwiŋgɔm] *nm* chewing gum.

MOT-CLÉ

chez [ʃe] *prép* **1** (*à la demeure de*) at; (: *direction*) to; ~ **qn** at/to sb's house *ou* place; ~ **moi** at home; (*direction*) home
2 (*à l'entreprise de*): **il travaille ~ Renault** he works for Renault, he works at Renault('s)
3 (*+profession*) at; (: *direction*) to; ~ **le boulanger/dentiste** at *ou* to the baker's/dentist's
4 (*dans le caractère, l'œuvre de*) in; ~ **les renards/Racine** in foxes/Racine; ~ **les Français** among the French; ~ **lui, c'est un devoir** for him, it's a duty
♦ *nm inv*: **mon ~ moi/ton ~ toi** *etc* my/your *etc* home *ou* place.

chez-soi [ʃeswa] *nm inv* home.
Chf. cent. *abr* (= *chauffage central*) c.h.
chiadé, e [ʃjade] *adj* (*fam*: *fignolé, soigné*) wicked.
chialer [ʃjale] *vi* (*fam*) to blubber; **arrête de ~!** stop blubbering!
chiant, e [ʃjɑ̃, -ɑ̃t] *adj* (*fam!*) bloody annoying (*BRIT!*), damn annoying; **qu'est-ce qu'il est ~!** he's such a bloody pain! (*!*).
chic [ʃik] *adj inv* chic, smart; (*généreux*) nice, decent ♦ *nm* stylishness; **avoir le ~ de** *ou* **pour** to have the knack of *ou* for; **de ~** *adv* off the cuff; ~! great!, terrific!
chicane [ʃikan] *nf* (*obstacle*) zigzag; (*querelle*) squabble.
chicaner [ʃikane] *vi* (*ergoter*): ~ **sur** to quibble about.
chiche [ʃiʃ] *adj* (*mesquin*) niggardly, mean; (*pauvre*) meagre (*BRIT*), meager (*US*) ♦ *excl* (*en réponse à un défi*) you're on!; **tu n'es pas ~ de lui parler!** you wouldn't (dare) speak to her!
chichement [ʃiʃmɑ̃] *adv* (*pauvrement*) meagrely (*BRIT*), meagerly (*US*); (*mesquinement*) meanly.
chichi [ʃiʃi] *nm* (*fam*) fuss; **faire des ~s** to make a fuss.
chicorée [ʃikɔʀe] *nf* (*café*) chicory; (*salade*) endive; ~ **frisée** curly endive.
chicot [ʃiko] *nm* stump.
chien [ʃjɛ̃] *nm* dog; (*de pistolet*) hammer; **temps de ~** rotten weather; **vie de ~** dog's life; **couché en ~ de fusil** curled up; ~ **d'aveugle** guide dog; ~ **de chasse** gun dog; ~ **de garde** guard dog; ~ **policier** police dog; ~ **de race** pedigree dog; ~ **de traîneau** husky.
chiendent [ʃjɛ̃dɑ̃] *nm* couch grass.
chien-loup, *pl* **chiens-loups** [ʃjɛ̃lu] *nm* wolfhound.
chienne [ʃjɛn] *nf* (she-)dog, bitch.
chier [ʃje] *vi* (*fam!*) to crap (*!*), shit (*!*); **faire ~**

qn (*importuner*) to bug sb; (*causer des ennuis à*) to piss sb around (*!*); **se faire ~** (*s'ennuyer*) to be bored rigid.

chiffe [ʃif] *nf*: **il est mou comme une ~, c'est une ~ molle** he's spineless *ou* wet.

chiffon [ʃifɔ̃] *nm* (piece of) rag.

chiffonné, e [ʃifɔne] *adj* (*fatigué: visage*) worn-looking.

chiffonner [ʃifɔne] *vt* to crumple, crease; (*tracasser*) to concern.

chiffonnier [ʃifɔnje] *nm* ragman, rag-and-bone man; (*meuble*) chiffonier.

chiffrable [ʃifʀabl(ə)] *adj* numerable.

chiffre [ʃifʀ(ə)] *nm* (*représentant un nombre*) figure; numeral; (*montant, total*) total, sum; (*d'un code*) code, cipher; **~s romains/arabes** roman/arabic figures *ou* numerals; **en ~s ronds** in round figures; **écrire un nombre en ~s** to write a number in figures; **~ d'affaires (CA)** turnover; **~ de ventes** sales figures.

chiffrer [ʃifʀe] *vt* (*dépense*) to put a figure to, assess; (*message*) to (en)code, cipher ♦ *vi*: **~ à, se ~ à** to add up to.

chignole [ʃiɲɔl] *nf* drill.

chignon [ʃiɲɔ̃] *nm* chignon, bun.

chiite [ʃiit] *adj* Shiite ♦ nm/f: **C~** Shiite.

Chili [ʃili] *nm*: **le ~** Chile.

chilien, ne [ʃiljɛ̃, -ɛn] *adj* Chilean ♦ *nm/f*: **C~, ne** Chilean.

chimère [ʃimɛʀ] *nf* (wild) dream; pipe dream, idle fancy.

chimérique [ʃimeʀik] *adj* (*utopique*) fanciful.

chimie [ʃimi] *nf* chemistry.

chimio [ʃimjɔ], **chimiothérapie** [ʃimjɔteʀapi] *nf* chemotherapy.

chimique [ʃimik] *adj* chemical; **produits ~s** chemicals.

chimiste [ʃimist(ə)] *nm/f* chemist.

chimpanzé [ʃɛ̃pɑ̃ze] *nm* chimpanzee.

chinchilla [ʃɛ̃ʃila] *nm* chinchilla.

Chine [ʃin] *nf*: **la ~** China; **la ~ libre, la république de ~** the Republic of China, Nationalist China (*Taiwan*).

chine [ʃin] *nm* rice paper; (*porcelaine*) china (vase).

chiné, e [ʃine] *adj* flecked.

chinois, e [ʃinwa, -waz] *adj* Chinese; (*fig: péj*) pernickety, fussy ♦ *nm* (*LING*) Chinese ♦ *nm/f*: **C~, e** Chinese.

chinoiserie(s) [ʃinwazʀi] *nf(pl)* (*péj*) red tape, fuss.

chiot [ʃjo] *nm* pup(py).

chiper [ʃipe] *vt* (*fam*) to pinch.

chipie [ʃipi] *nf* shrew.

chipolata [ʃipɔlata] *nf* chipolata.

chipoter [ʃipɔte] *vi* (*manger*) to nibble; (*ergoter*) to quibble, haggle.

chips [ʃips] *nfpl* (*aussi*: **pommes ~**) crisps (*BRIT*), (potato) chips (*US*).

chique [ʃik] *nf* quid, chew.

chiquenaude [ʃiknod] *nf* flick, flip.

chiquer [ʃike] *vi* to chew tobacco.

chiromancie [kiʀɔmɑ̃si] *nf* palmistry.

chiromancien, ne [kiʀɔmɑ̃sjɛ̃, -ɛn] *nm/f* palmist.

chiropracteur [kiʀɔpʀaktœʀ] *nm*, **chiropraticien, ne** [kiʀɔpʀatisjɛ̃, -ɛn] *nm/f* chiropractor.

chirurgical, e, aux [ʃiʀyʀʒikal, -o] *adj* surgical.

chirurgie [ʃiʀyʀʒi] *nf* surgery; **~ esthétique** cosmetic *ou* plastic surgery.

chirurgien [ʃiʀyʀʒjɛ̃] *nm* surgeon; **~ dentiste** dental surgeon.

chiure [ʃjyʀ] *nf*: **~s de mouche** fly specks.

ch.-l. *abr* = **chef-lieu.**

chlore [klɔʀ] *nm* chlorine.

chloroforme [klɔʀɔfɔʀm(ə)] *nm* chloroform.

chlorophylle [klɔʀɔfil] *nf* chlorophyll.

chlorure [klɔʀyʀ] *nm* chloride.

choc [ʃɔk] *nm* impact; shock; crash; (*moral*) shock; (*affrontement*) clash ♦ *adj*: **prix ~** amazing *ou* incredible price/prices; **de ~** (*troupe, traitement*) shock *cpd*; (*patron etc*) high-powered; **~ opératoire/nerveux** post-operative/nervous shock; **~ en retour** return shock; (*fig*) backlash.

chocolat [ʃɔkɔla] *nm* chocolate; (*boisson*) (hot) chocolate; **~ à cuire** cooking chocolate; **~ au lait** milk chocolate; **~ en poudre** drinking chocolate.

chocolaté, e [ʃɔkɔlate] *adj* chocolate *cpd*, chocolate-flavoured.

chocolaterie [ʃɔkɔlatʀi] *nf* (*fabrique*) chocolate factory.

chocolatier, ière [ʃɔkɔlatje, -jɛʀ] *nm/f* chocolate maker.

chœur [kœʀ] *nm* (*chorale*) choir; (*OPÉRA, THÉÂT*) chorus; (*ARCHIT*) choir, chancel; **en ~** in chorus.

choir [ʃwaʀ] *vi* to fall.

choisi, e [ʃwazi] *adj* (*de premier choix*) carefully chosen; select; **textes ~s** selected writings.

choisir [ʃwaziʀ] *vt* to choose; (*entre plusiers*) to choose, select; **~ de faire qch** to choose *ou* opt to do sth.

choix [ʃwa] *nm* choice; selection; **avoir le ~** to have the choice; **je n'avais pas le ~** I had no choice; **de premier ~** (*COMM*) class *ou* grade one; **de ~** choice *cpd*, selected; **au ~** as you wish *ou* prefer; **de mon/son ~** of my/his *ou* her choosing.

choléra [kɔleʀa] *nm* cholera.

cholestérol [kɔlɛsteʀɔl] *nm* cholesterol.

chômage [ʃomaʒ] *nm* unemployment; **mettre au ~** to make redundant, put out of work; **être au ~** to be unemployed *ou* out of work; **~ partiel** short-time working; **~ structurel** structural unemployment; **~ technique** lay-offs *pl*.

chômer [ʃome] *vi* to be unemployed, be idle; **jour chômé** public holiday.

chômeur, euse [ʃomœʀ, -øz] *nm/f* unemployed person, person out of work.

chope [ʃɔp] *nf* tankard.
choquant, e [ʃɔkɑ̃, -ɑ̃t] *adj* shocking.
choquer [ʃɔke] *vt* (*offenser*) to shock; (*commotionner*) to shake (up).
choral, e [kɔʀal] *adj* choral ♦ *nf* choral society, choir.
chorégraphe [kɔʀegʀaf] *nm/f* choreographer.
chorégraphie [kɔʀegʀafi] *nf* choreography.
choriste [kɔʀist(ə)] *nm/f* choir member; (*OPÉRA*) chorus member.
chorus [kɔʀys] *nm*: **faire ~ (avec)** to voice one's agreement (with).
chose [ʃoz] *nf* thing ♦ *nm* (*fam*: *machin*) thingamajig ♦ *adj inv*: **être/se sentir tout ~** (*bizarre*) to be/feel a bit odd; (*malade*) to be/feel out of sorts; **dire bien des ~s à qn** to give sb's regards to sb; **parler de ~(s) et d'autre(s)** to talk about one thing and another; **c'est peu de ~** it's nothing much.
chou, x [ʃu] *nm* cabbage ♦ *adj inv* cute; **mon petit ~** (my) sweetheart; **faire ~ blanc** to draw a blank; **feuille de ~** (*fig: journal*) rag; **~ à la crème** cream bun (*made of choux pastry*); **~ de Bruxelles** Brussels sprout.
choucas [ʃuka] *nm* jackdaw.
chouchou, te [ʃuʃu, -ut] *nm/f* (*SCOL*) teacher's pet.
chouchouter [ʃuʃute] *vt* to pet.
choucroute [ʃukʀut] *nf* sauerkraut; **~ garnie** sauerkraut with cooked meats and potatoes.
chouette [ʃwɛt] *nf* owl ♦ *adj* (*fam*) great, smashing.
chou-fleur, *pl* **choux-fleurs** [ʃuflœʀ] *nm* cauliflower.
chou-rave, *pl* **choux-raves** [ʃuʀav] *nm* kohlrabi.
choyer [ʃwaje] *vt* to cherish; to pamper.
CHR *sigle m* = *Centre hospitalier régional*.
chrétien, ne [kʀetjɛ̃, -ɛn] *adj, nm/f* Christian.
chrétiennement [kʀetjɛnmɑ̃] *adv* in a Christian way *ou* spirit.
chrétienté [kʀetjɛ̃te] *nf* Christendom.
Christ [kʀist] *nm*: **le ~** Christ; **c~** (*crucifix etc*) figure of Christ; **Jésus ~** Jesus Christ.
christianiser [kʀistjanize] *vt* to convert to Christianity.
christianisme [kʀistjanism(ə)] *nm* Christianity.
Christmas [kʀistmas] *nf*: **(l'île) ~** Christmas Island.
chromatique [kʀɔmatik] *adj* chromatic.
chrome [kʀom] *nm* chromium; (*revêtement*) chrome, chromium.
chromé, e [kʀome] *adj* chrome-plated, chromium-plated.
chromosome [kʀɔmozom] *nm* chromosome.
chronique [kʀɔnik] *adj* chronic ♦ *nf* (*de journal*) column, page; (*historique*) chronicle; (*RADIO, TV*): **la ~ sportive/théâtrale** the sports/theatre review; **la ~ locale** local news and gossip.
chroniqueur [kʀɔnikœʀ] *nm* columnist; chronicler.
chrono [kʀɔno] *nm* (*fam*) = **chronomètre**.
chronologie [kʀɔnɔlɔʒi] *nf* chronology.
chronologique [kʀɔnɔlɔʒik] *adj* chronological.
chronologiquement [kʀɔnɔlɔʒikmɑ̃] *adv* chronologically.
chronomètre [kʀɔnɔmɛtʀ(ə)] *nm* stopwatch.
chronométrer [kʀɔnɔmetʀe] *vt* to time.
chronométreur [kʀɔnɔmetʀœʀ] *nm* timekeeper.
chrysalide [kʀizalid] *nf* chrysalis.
chrysanthème [kʀizɑ̃tɛm] *nm* chrysanthemum.
CHU *sigle m* (= *Centre hospitalo-universitaire*) ≈ (teaching) hospital.
chu, e [ʃy] *pp de* **choir**.
chuchotement [ʃyʃɔtmɑ̃] *nm* whisper.
chuchoter [ʃyʃɔte] *vt, vi* to whisper.
chuintement [ʃɥɛ̃tmɑ̃] *nm* hiss.
chuinter [ʃɥɛ̃te] *vi* to hiss.
chut *excl* [ʃyt] sh! ♦ *vb* [ʃy] *voir* **choir**.
chute [ʃyt] *nf* fall; (*de bois, papier: déchet*) scrap; **la ~ des cheveux** hair loss; **faire une ~ (de 10 m)** to fall (10 m); **~s de pluie/neige** rain/snowfalls; **~ (d'eau)** waterfall; **~ du jour** nightfall; **~ libre** free fall; **~ des reins** small of the back.
Chypre [ʃipʀ] *nm*: **le ~** Cyprus.
chypriote [ʃipʀiɔt] *adj, nm/f* = **cypriote**.
-ci, ci- [si] *adv voir* **par, ci-contre, ci-joint** *etc* ♦ *dét*: **ce garçon-ci/-là** this/that boy; **ces femmes-ci/-là** these/those women.
CIA *sigle f* CIA.
cial *abr* = **commercial**.
ciao [tʃao] *excl* (*fam*) (bye-)bye.
ci-après [siapʀɛ] *adv* hereafter.
cibiste [sibist(ə)] *nm* CB enthusiast.
cible [sibl(ə)] *nf* target.
cibler [sible] *vt* to target.
ciboire [sibwaʀ] *nm* ciborium (*vessel*).
ciboule [sibul] *nf* (large) chive.
ciboulette [sibulɛt] *nf* (small) chive.
ciboulot [sibulo] *nm* (*fam*) head, nut; **il n'a rien dans le ~** he's got nothing between his ears.
cicatrice [sikatʀis] *nf* scar.
cicatriser [sikatʀize] *vt* to heal; **se ~** to heal (up), form a scar.
ci-contre [sikɔ̃tʀ(ə)] *adv* opposite.
CICR *sigle m* (= *Comité international de la Croix-Rouge*) ICRC.
ci-dessous [sidəsu] *adv* below.
ci-dessus [sidəsy] *adv* above.
ci-devant [sidəvɑ̃] *nm/f inv aristocrat who lost his/her title in the French Revolution.*
CIDEX *sigle m* (= *Courrier individuel à distribution exceptionnelle*) *system which groups letter boxes in country areas, rather than each house having its letter box at its front door.*
CIDJ *sigle m* (= *Centre d'information et de documentation de la jeunesse*) *careers advisory*

service.
cidre [sidʀ(ə)] *nm* cider.
cidrerie [sidʀəʀi] *nf* cider factory.
CIDUNATI [sidynati] *sigle m* (= *Comité interprofessionnel de défense de l'union nationale des artisans et travailleurs indépendants*) *union of self-employed craftsmen.*
Cie *abr* (= *compagnie*) Co.
ciel [sjɛl] *nm* sky; (*REL*) heaven; **~s** *nmpl* (*PEINTURE etc*) skies; **cieux** *nmpl* sky *sg*, skies; (*REL*) heaven *sg*; **à ~ ouvert** open-air; (*mine*) opencast; **tomber du ~** (*arriver à l'improviste*) to appear out of the blue; (*être stupéfait*) to be unable to believe one's eyes; **C~!** good heavens!; **~ de lit** canopy.
cierge [sjɛʀʒ(ə)] *nm* candle; **~ pascal** Easter candle.
cieux [sjø] *nmpl voir* **ciel**.
cigale [sigal] *nf* cicada.
cigare [sigaʀ] *nm* cigar.
cigarette [sigaʀɛt] *nf* cigarette; **~ (à) bout filtre** filter cigarette.
ci-gît [siʒi] *adv* here lies.
cigogne [sigɔɲ] *nf* stork.
ciguë [sigy] *nf* hemlock.
ci-inclus, e [siɛ̃kly, -yz] *adj, adv* enclosed.
ci-joint, e [siʒwɛ̃, -ɛ̃t] *adj, adv* enclosed; **veuillez trouver ~** please find enclosed.
cil [sil] *nm* (eye)lash.
ciller [sije] *vi* to blink.
cimaise [simɛz] *nf* picture rail.
cime [sim] *nf* top; (*montagne*) peak.
ciment [simɑ̃] *nm* cement; **~ armé** reinforced concrete.
cimenter [simɑ̃te] *vt* to cement.
cimenterie [simɑ̃tʀi] *nf* cement works *sg*.
cimetière [simtjɛʀ] *nm* cemetery; (*d'église*) churchyard; **~ de voitures** scrapyard.
cinéaste [sineast(ə)] *nm/f* film-maker.
ciné-club [sineklœb] *nm* film club; film society.
cinéma [sinema] *nm* cinema; **aller au ~** to go to the cinema *ou* pictures *ou* movies; **~ d'animation** cartoon (film).
cinémascope [sinemaskɔp] *nm* ® Cinemascope ®.
cinémathèque [sinematɛk] *nf* film archives *pl ou* library.
cinématographie [sinematɔgʀafi] *nf* cinematography.
cinématographique [sinematɔgʀafik] *adj* film *cpd*, cinema *cpd*.
cinéphile [sinefil] *nm/f* film buff.
cinérama [sineʀama] *nm* ®: **en ~** in Cinerama ®.
cinétique [sinetik] *adj* kinetic.
cing(h)alais, e [sɛ̃galɛ, -ɛz] *adj* Sin(g)halese.
cinglant, e [sɛ̃glɑ̃, -ɑ̃t] *adj* (*propos, ironie*) scathing, biting; (*échec*) crushing.
cinglé, e [sɛ̃gle] *adj* (*fam*) crazy.
cingler [sɛ̃gle] *vt* to lash; (*fig*) to sting ♦ *vi* (*NAVIG*): **~ vers** to make *ou* head for.
cinq [sɛ̃k] *num* five.
cinquantaine [sɛ̃kɑ̃tɛn] *nf*: **une ~ (de)** about fifty; **avoir la ~** (*âge*) to be around fifty.
cinquante [sɛ̃kɑ̃t] *num* fifty.
cinquantenaire [sɛ̃kɑ̃tnɛʀ] *adj, nm/f* fifty-year-old.
cinquantième [sɛ̃kɑ̃tjɛm] *num* fiftieth.
cinquième [sɛ̃kjɛm] *num* fifth.
cinquièmement [sɛ̃kjɛmmɑ̃] *adv* fifthly.
cintre [sɛ̃tʀ(ə)] *nm* coat-hanger; (*ARCHIT*) arch; **plein ~** semicircular arch.
cintré, e [sɛ̃tʀe] *adj* curved; (*chemise*) fitted, slim-fitting.
CIO *sigle m* (= *Comité international olympique*) IOC (= *International Olympic Committee*).
cirage [siʀaʒ] *nm* (shoe) polish.
circoncis, e [siʀkɔ̃si, -iz] *adj* circumcized.
circoncision [siʀkɔ̃sizjɔ̃] *nf* circumcision.
circonférence [siʀkɔ̃feʀɑ̃s] *nf* circumference.
circonflexe [siʀkɔ̃flɛks(ə)] *adj*: **accent ~** circumflex accent.
circonlocution [siʀkɔ̃lɔkysjɔ̃] *nf* circumlocution.
circonscription [siʀkɔ̃skʀipsjɔ̃] *nf* district; **~ électorale** (*d'un député*) constituency; **~ militaire** military area.
circonscrire [siʀkɔ̃skʀiʀ] *vt* to define, delimit; (*incendie*) to contain; (*propriété*) to mark out; (*sujet*) to define.
circonspect, e [siʀkɔ̃spɛkt] *adj* circumspect, cautious.
circonspection [siʀkɔ̃spɛksjɔ̃] *nf* circumspection, caution.
circonstance [siʀkɔ̃stɑ̃s] *nf* circumstance; (*occasion*) occasion; **œuvre de ~** occasional work; **air de ~** fitting air; **tête de ~** appropriate demeanour (*BRIT*) *ou* demeanor (*US*); **~s atténuantes** mitigating circumstances.
circonstancié, e [siʀkɔ̃stɑ̃sje] *adj* detailed.
circonstanciel, le [siʀkɔ̃stɑ̃sjɛl] *adj* **complément/proposition ~(le)** adverbial phrase/clause.
circonvenir [siʀkɔ̃vniʀ] *vt* to circumvent.
circonvolutions [siʀkɔ̃vɔlysjɔ̃] *nfpl* twists convolutions.
circuit [siʀkɥi] *nm* (*trajet*) tour, (round) trip (*ÉLEC, TECH*) circuit; **~ automobile** motor circuit; **~ de distribution** distribution network; **~ fermé** closed circuit; **~ intégré** integrated circuit.
circulaire [siʀkylɛʀ] *adj, nf* circular.
circulation [siʀkylasjɔ̃] *nf* circulation; (*AUTO*) **la ~** (the) traffic; **bonne/mauvaise ~** good bad circulation; **mettre en ~** to put into circulation.
circulatoire [siʀkylatwaʀ] *adj*: **avoir des troubles ~s** to have problems with one's circulation.
circuler [siʀkyle] *vi* to drive (along); to walk along; (*train etc*) to run; (*sang, devises*) to circulate; **faire ~** (*nouvelle*) to spread (about)

circulate; (*badauds*) to move on.
cire [siʀ] *nf* wax; ~ **à cacheter** sealing wax.
ciré [siʀe] *nm* oilskin.
cirer [siʀe] *vt* to wax, polish.
cireur [siʀœʀ] *nm* shoeshine-boy.
cireuse [siʀøz] *nf* floor polisher.
cireux, euse [siʀø, -øz] *adj* (*fig: teint*) sallow, waxen.
cirque [siʀk(ə)] *nm* circus; (*arène*) amphitheatre (*BRIT*), amphitheater (*US*); (*GÉO*) cirque; (*fig: désordre*) chaos, bedlam; (*: chichis*) carry-on.
cirrhose [siʀoz] *nf*: ~ **du foie** cirrhosis of the liver.
cisailler [sizɑje] *vt* to clip.
cisaille(s) [sizɑj] *nf(pl)* (gardening) shears *pl*.
ciseau, x [sizo] *nm*: ~ **(à bois)** chisel ♦ *nmpl* (pair of) scissors; **sauter en ~x** to do a scissors jump; ~ **à froid** cold chisel.
ciseler [sizle] *vt* to chisel, carve.
ciselure [sizlyʀ] *nf* engraving; (*bois*) carving.
Cisjordanie [sisʒɔʀdani] *nf*: **la** ~ the West Bank (of Jordan).
citadelle [sitadɛl] *nf* citadel.
citadin, e [sitadɛ̃, -in] *nm/f* city dweller ♦ *adj* town *cpd*, city *cpd*, urban.
citation [sitɑsjɔ̃] *nf* (*d'auteur*) quotation; (*JUR*) summons *sg*; (*MIL: récompense*) mention.
cité [site] *nf* town; (*plus grande*) city; ~ **ouvrière** (workers') housing estate; ~ **universitaire** students' residences *pl*.
cité-dortoir, *pl* **cités-dortoirs** [sitedɔʀtwaʀ] *nf* dormitory town.
cité-jardin, *pl* **cités-jardins** [siteʒaʀdɛ̃] *nf* garden city.
citer [site] *vt* (*un auteur*) to quote (from); (*nommer*) to name; (*JUR*) to summon; ~ **(en exemple)** (*personne*) to hold up (as an example); **je ne veux** ~ **personne** I don't want to name names.
citerne [sitɛʀn(ə)] *nf* tank.
cithare [sitaʀ] *nf* zither.
citoyen, ne [sitwajɛ̃, -ɛn] *nm/f* citizen.
citoyenneté [sitwajɛnte] *nf* citizenship.
citrique [sitʀik] *adj*: **acide** ~ citric acid.
citron [sitʀɔ̃] *nm* lemon; ~ **pressé** (fresh) lemon juice; ~ **vert** lime.
citronnade [sitʀɔnad] *nf* lemonade.
citronné, e [sitʀɔne] *adj* (*boisson*) lemon-flavoured (*BRIT*) *ou* -flavored (*US*); (*eau de toilette*) lemon-scented.
citronnelle [sitʀɔnɛl] *nf* citronella.
citronnier [sitʀɔnje] *nm* lemon tree.
citrouille [sitʀuj] *nf* pumpkin.
cive(s) [siv] *nf(pl)* (*BOT*) chive(s); (*CULIN*) chives.
civet [sivɛ] *nm* stew; ~ **de lièvre** jugged hare.
civette [sivɛt] *nf* (*BOT*) chives *pl*; (*ZOOL*) civet (cat).
civière [sivjɛʀ] *nf* stretcher.
civil, e [sivil] *adj* (*JUR, ADMIN, poli*) civil; (*non militaire*) civilian ♦ *nm* civilian; **en** ~ in civilian clothes; **dans le** ~ in civilian life.
civilement [sivilmɑ̃] *adv* (*poliment*) civilly; **se marier** ~ to have a civil wedding.
civilisation [sivilizɑsjɔ̃] *nf* civilization.
civilisé, e [sivilize] *adj* civilized.
civiliser [sivilize] *vt* to civilize.
civilité [sivilite] *nf* civility; **présenter ses ~s** to present one's compliments.
civique [sivik] *adj* civic; **instruction** ~ (*SCOL*) civics *sg*.
civisme [sivism(ə)] *nm* public-spiritedness.
cl. *abr* (= *centilitre*) cl.
clafoutis [klafuti] *nm* batter pudding (*containing fruit*).
claie [klɛ] *nf* grid, riddle.
clair, e [klɛʀ] *adj* light; (*chambre*) light, bright; (*eau, son, fig*) clear ♦ *adv*: **voir** ~ to see clearly ♦ *nm*: **mettre au** ~ (*notes etc*) to tidy up; **tirer qch au** ~ to clear sth up, clarify sth; **bleu** ~ light blue; **pour être** ~ so as to make it plain; **y voir** ~ (*comprendre*) to understand, see; **le plus** ~ **de son temps/argent** the better part of his time/money; **en** ~ (*non codé*) in clear; ~ **de lune** moonlight.
claire [klɛʀ] *nf*: **(huître de)** ~ fattened oyster.
clairement [klɛʀmɑ̃] *adv* clearly.
claire-voie [klɛʀvwa]: **à** ~ *adj* letting the light through; openwork *cpd*.
clairière [klɛʀjɛʀ] *nf* clearing.
clair-obscur, *pl* **clairs-obscurs** [klɛʀɔpskyʀ] *nm* half-light; (*fig*) uncertainty.
clairon [klɛʀɔ̃] *nm* bugle.
claironner [klɛʀɔne] *vt* (*fig*) to trumpet, shout from the rooftops.
clairsemé, e [klɛʀsəme] *adj* sparse.
clairvoyance [klɛʀvwajɑ̃s] *nf* clear-sightedness.
clairvoyant, e [klɛʀvwajɑ̃, -ɑ̃t] *adj* perceptive, clear-sighted.
clam [klam] *nm* (*ZOOL*) clam.
clamer [klame] *vt* to proclaim.
clameur [klamœʀ] *nf* clamour (*BRIT*), clamor (*US*).
clan [klɑ̃] *nm* clan.
clandestin, e [klɑ̃dɛstɛ̃, -in] *adj* clandestine, covert; (*POL*) underground, clandestine; **passager** ~ stowaway.
clandestinement [klɑ̃dɛstinmɑ̃] *adv* secretly; **s'embarquer** ~ to stow away.
clandestinité [klɑ̃dɛstinite] *nf*: **dans la** ~ (*en secret*) under cover; (*en se cachant: vivre*) underground; **entrer dans la** ~ to go underground.
clapet [klapɛ] *nm* (*TECH*) valve.
clapier [klapje] *nm* (rabbit) hutch.
clapotement [klapɔtmɑ̃] *nm* lap(ping).
clapoter [klapɔte] *vi* to lap.
clapotis [klapɔti] *nm* lap(ping).
claquage [klakaʒ] *nm* pulled *ou* strained muscle.
claque [klak] *nf* (*gifle*) slap; (*THÉÂT*) claque ♦ *nm* (*chapeau*) opera hat.

claquement [klakmɑ̃] *nm* (*de porte: bruit répété*) banging; (*: bruit isolé*) slam.
claquemurer [klakmyʀe]: **se ~** *vi* to shut o.s. away, closet o.s.
claquer [klake] *vi* (*drapeau*) to flap; (*porte*) to bang, slam; (*coup de feu*) to ring out ♦ *vt* (*porte*) to slam, bang; (*doigts*) to snap; **elle claquait des dents** her teeth were chattering; **se ~ un muscle** to pull *ou* strain a muscle.
claquettes [klakɛt] *nfpl* tap-dancing *sg*.
clarification [klaʀifikɑsjɔ̃] *nf* (*fig*) clarification.
clarifier [klaʀifje] *vt* (*fig*) to clarify.
clarinette [klaʀinɛt] *nf* clarinet.
clarinettiste [klaʀinetist(ə)] *nm/f* clarinettist.
clarté [klaʀte] *nf* lightness; brightness; (*d'un son, de l'eau*) clearness; (*d'une explication*) clarity.
classe [klɑs] *nf* class; (*SCOL: local*) class(room); (*: leçon*) class; (*: élèves*) class, form; **1ère/2ème ~** 1st/2nd class; **un (soldat de) deuxième ~** (*MIL: armée de terre*) ≈ private (soldier); (*: armée de l'air*) ≈ aircraftman (*BRIT*), ≈ airman basic (*US*); **de ~** luxury *cpd*; **faire ses ~s** (*MIL*) to do one's (recruit's) training; **faire la ~** (*SCOL*) to be a *ou* the teacher; to teach; **aller en ~ verte/de neige/de mer** to go to the countryside/skiing/to the seaside with the school; **~ préparatoire** *class which prepares students for the Grandes Écoles entry exams*; **~ sociale** social class; **~ touriste** economy class; *see boxed note*.

CLASSES PRÉPARATOIRES

Classes préparatoires *are the two years of intensive study which coach students for the competitive entry examinations to the 'grandes écoles'. These extremely demanding courses follow the 'baccalauréat', and are usually done at a 'lycée'. Schools which provide such classes are more highly regarded than those which do not.*

classement [klɑsmɑ̃] *nm* classifying; filing; grading; closing; (*rang: SCOL*) place; (*: SPORT*) placing; (*liste: SCOL*) class list (in order of merit); (*: SPORT*) placings *pl*; **premier au ~ général** (*SPORT*) first overall.
classer [klɑse] *vt* (*idées, livres*) to classify; (*papiers*) to file; (*candidat, concurrent*) to grade; (*personne: juger: péj*) to rate; (*JUR: affaire*) to close; **se ~ premier/dernier** to come first/last; (*SPORT*) to finish first/last.
classeur [klɑsœʀ] *nm* file; (*meuble*) filing cabinet; **~ à feuillets mobiles** ring binder.
classification [klasifikɑsjɔ̃] *nf* classification.
classifier [klasifje] *vt* to classify.
classique [klasik] *adj* classical; (*habituel*) standard, classic ♦ *nm* classic; classical author; **études ~s** classical studies, classics.
claudication [klodikɑsjɔ̃] *nf* limp.
clause [kloz] *nf* clause.
claustrer [klostʀe] *vt* to confine.
claustrophobie [klostʀɔfɔbi] *nf* claustrophobia.
clavecin [klavsɛ̃] *nm* harpsichord.
claveciniste [klavsinist(ə)] *nm/f* harpsichordist.
clavicule [klavikyl] *nf* clavicle, collarbone.
clavier [klavje] *nm* keyboard.
clé *ou* **clef** [kle] *nf* key; (*MUS*) clef; (*de mécanicien*) spanner (*BRIT*), wrench (*US*) ♦ *adj*: **problème/position ~** key problem/position; **mettre sous ~** to place under lock and key; **prendre la ~ des champs** to run away, make off; **prix ~s en main** (*d'une voiture*) on-the-road price; (*d'un appartement*) price with immediate entry; **~ de sol/de fa/d'ut** treble/bass/alto clef; **livre/film** *etc* **à ~** *book/film etc in which real people are depicted under fictitious names*; **à la ~** (*à la fin*) at the end of it all; **~ anglaise = ~ à molette**; **~ de contact** ignition key; **~ à molette** adjustable spanner (*BRIT*) *ou* wrench, monkey wrench; **~ de voûte** keystone.
clématite [klematit] *nf* clematis.
clémence [klemɑ̃s] *nf* mildness; leniency.
clément, e [klemɑ̃, -ɑ̃t] *adj* (*temps*) mild; (*indulgent*) lenient.
clémentine [klemɑ̃tin] *nf* (*BOT*) clementine.
clenche [klɑ̃ʃ] *nf* latch.
cleptomane [klɛptɔman] *nm/f* = **kleptomane**.
clerc [klɛʀ] *nm*: **~ de notaire** *ou* **d'avoué** lawyer's clerk.
clergé [klɛʀʒe] *nm* clergy.
clérical, e, aux [kleʀikal, -o] *adj* clerical.
cliché [kliʃe] *nm* (*PHOTO*) negative; print; (*TYPO*) (printing) plate; (*LING*) cliché.
client, e [klijɑ̃, -ɑ̃t] *nm/f* (*acheteur*) customer, client; (*d'hôtel*) guest, patron; (*du docteur*) patient; (*de l'avocat*) client.
clientèle [klijɑ̃tɛl] *nf* (*du magasin*) customers *pl*, clientèle; (*du docteur, de l'avocat*) practice; **accorder sa ~ à** to give one's custom to; **retirer sa ~ à** to take one's business away from.
cligner [kliɲe] *vi*: **~ des yeux** to blink (one's eyes); **~ de l'œil** to wink.
clignotant [kliɲɔtɑ̃] *nm* (*AUTO*) indicator.
clignoter [kliɲɔte] *vi* (*étoiles etc*) to twinkle; (*lumière: à intervalles réguliers*) to flash; (*: vaciller*) to flicker; (*yeux*) to blink.
climat [klima] *nm* climate.
climatique [klimatik] *adj* climatic.
climatisation [klimatizɑsjɔ̃] *nf* air conditioning.
climatisé, e [klimatize] *adj* air-conditioned.
climatiseur [klimatizœʀ] *nm* air conditioner.
clin d'œil [klɛ̃dœj] *nm* wink; **en un ~** in a flash.
clinique [klinik] *adj* clinical ♦ *nf* nursing home (private) clinic.

clinquant, e [klɛ̃kɑ̃, -ɑ̃t] *adj* flashy.
clip [klip] *nm* (*pince*) clip; (*vidéo*) pop (*ou* promotional) video.
clique [klik] *nf* (*péj*: *bande*) clique, set; **prendre ses ~s et ses claques** to pack one's bags.
cliquer [klike] *vi* (*INFORM*) to click; ~ **deux fois** to double-click.
cliqueter [klikte] *vi* to clash; (*ferraille, clefs, monnaie*) to jangle, jingle; (*verres*) to chink.
cliquetis [klikti] *nm* jangle, jingle; chink.
clitoris [klitɔʀis] *nm* clitoris.
clivage [klivaʒ] *nm* cleavage; (*fig*) rift, split.
cloaque [klɔak] *nm* (*fig*) cesspit.
clochard, e [klɔʃaʀ, -aʀd(ə)] *nm/f* tramp.
cloche [klɔʃ] *nf* (*d'église*) bell; (*fam*) clot; (*chapeau*) cloche (hat); ~ **à fromage** cheese-cover.
cloche-pied [klɔʃpje]: **à** ~ *adv* on one leg, hopping (along).
clocher [klɔʃe] *nm* church tower; (*en pointe*) steeple ♦ *vi* (*fam*) to be *ou* go wrong; **de** ~ (*péj*) parochial.
clocheton [klɔʃtɔ̃] *nm* pinnacle.
clochette [klɔʃɛt] *nf* bell.
clodo [klɔdo] *nm* (*fam*: = *clochard*) tramp.
cloison [klwazɔ̃] *nf* partition (wall); ~ **étanche** (*fig*) impenetrable barrier, brick wall (*fig*).
cloisonner [klwazɔne] *vt* to partition (off); to divide up; (*fig*) to compartmentalize.
cloître [klwatʀ(ə)] *nm* cloister.
cloîtrer [klwatʀe] *vt*: **se** ~ to shut o.s. away; (*REL*) to enter a convent *ou* monastery.
clone [klɔn] *nm* clone.
clope [klɔp] *nm ou f* (*fam*) fag (*BRIT*), cigarette.
clopin-clopant [klɔpɛ̃klɔpɑ̃] *adv* hobbling along; (*fig*) so-so.
clopiner [klɔpine] *vi* to hobble along.
cloporte [klɔpɔʀt(ə)] *nm* woodlouse (*pl* -lice).
cloque [klɔk] *nf* blister.
cloqué, e [klɔke] *adj*: **étoffe ~e** seersucker.
cloquer [klɔke] *vi* (*peau, peinture*) to blister.
clore [klɔʀ] *vt* to close; ~ **une session** (*INFORM*) to log out.
clos, e [klo, -oz] *pp de* **clore** ♦ *adj voir* **maison, huis, vase** ♦ *nm* (enclosed) field.
clôt [klo] *vb voir* **clore**.
clôture [klotyʀ] *nf* closure, closing; (*barrière*) enclosure, fence.
clôturer [klotyʀe] *vt* (*terrain*) to enclose, close off; (*festival, débats*) to close.
clou [klu] *nm* nail; (*MÉD*) boil; **~s** *nmpl* = **passage clouté; pneus à ~s** studded tyres; **le ~ du spectacle** the highlight of the show; ~ **de girofle** clove.
clouer [klue] *vt* to nail down (*ou* up); (*fig*): ~ **sur/contre** to pin to/against.
clouté, e [klute] *adj* studded.
clown [klun] *nm* clown; **faire le** ~ (*fig*) to clown (about), play the fool.
clownerie [klunʀi] *nf* clowning *no pl*; **faire des ~s** to clown around.
CLT *sigle f* = *Compagnie Luxembourgeoise de Télévision.*
club [klœb] *nm* club.
CM *sigle f* = **chambre des métiers** ♦ *sigle m* = **conseil municipal**; (*SCOL*) = **cours moyen**.
cm. *abr* (= *centimètre*) cm.
CMU *sigle f* (= *couverture maladie universelle*) *system of free health care for those on low incomes.*
CNAT *sigle f* (= *Commission nationale d'aménagement du territoire*) *national development agency.*
CNC *sigle m* (= *Conseil national de la consommation*) *national consumers' council.*
CNCL *sigle f* (= *Commission nationale de la communication et des libertés*) *independent broadcasting authority.*
CNDP *sigle m* = *Centre national de documentation pédagogique.*
CNE *sigle f* (= *Caisse nationale d'épargne*) *national savings bank.*
CNED *sigle m* (= *Centre national d'enseignement à distance*) ≈ Open University.
CNIL *sigle f* (= *Commission nationale de l'informatique et des libertés*) *board which enforces law on data protection.*
CNIT *sigle m* (= *Centre national des industries et des techniques*) *exhibition centre in Paris.*
CNJA *sigle m* (= *Centre national des jeunes agriculteurs*) *farmers' union.*
CNL *sigle f* (= *Confédération nationale du logement*) *consumer group for housing.*
CNP *sigle f* (= *Caisse nationale de prévoyance*) *savings bank.*
CNPF *sigle m* (= *Conseil national du patronat français*) *national council of employers.*
CNRS *sigle m* = *Centre national de la recherche scientifique.*
c/o *abr* (= *care of*) c/o.
coagulant [kɔagylɑ̃] *nm* (*MÉD*) coagulant.
coaguler [kɔagyle] *vi, vt*, **se** ~ *vi* to coagulate.
coaliser [kɔalize]: **se** ~ *vi* to unite, join forces.
coalition [kɔalisjɔ̃] *nf* coalition.
coasser [kɔase] *vi* to croak.
coauteur [kootœʀ] *nm* co-author.
coaxial, e, aux [koaksjal, -o] *adj* coaxial.
cobaye [kɔbaj] *nm* guinea-pig.
COBOL, Cobol [kɔbɔl] *nm* COBOL, Cobol.
cobra [kɔbʀa] *nm* cobra.
coca [kɔka] *nm* ® Coke ®.
cocagne [kɔkaɲ] *nf*: **pays de** ~ land of plenty; **mât de** ~ greasy pole (*fig*).
cocaïne [kɔkain] *nf* cocaine.
cocarde [kɔkaʀd(ə)] *nf* rosette.
cocardier, ière [kɔkaʀdje, -jɛʀ] *adj* jingoistic, chauvinistic; militaristic.
cocasse [kɔkas] *adj* comical, funny.
coccinelle [kɔksinɛl] *nf* ladybird (*BRIT*), ladybug (*US*).
coccyx [kɔksis] *nm* coccyx.
cocher [kɔʃe] *nm* coachman ♦ *vt* to tick off; (*entailler*) to notch.
cochère [kɔʃɛʀ]

cochon, ne [kɔʃɔ̃, -ɔn] *nm* pig ♦ *nm/f* (*péj: sale*) (filthy) pig; (*: méchant*) swine ♦ *adj* (*fam*) dirty, smutty; ~ **d'Inde** guinea-pig; ~ **de lait** (*CULIN*) sucking pig.
cochonnaille [kɔʃɔnaj] *nf* (*péj: charcuterie*) (cold) pork.
cochonnerie [kɔʃɔnʀi] *nf* (*fam: saleté*) filth; (*: marchandises*) rubbish, trash.
cochonnet [kɔʃɔnɛ] *nm* (*BOULES*) jack.
cocker [kɔkɛʀ] *nm* cocker spaniel.
cocktail [kɔktɛl] *nm* cocktail; (*réception*) cocktail party.
coco [koko] *nm voir* **noix**; (*fam*) bloke (*BRIT*), dude (*US*).
cocon [kɔkɔ̃] *nm* cocoon.
cocorico [kɔkɔʀiko] *excl, nm* cock-a-doodle-do.
cocotier [kɔkɔtje] *nm* coconut palm.
cocotte [kɔkɔt] *nf* (*en fonte*) casserole; **ma** ~ (*fam*) sweetie (pie); ~ **(minute)** ® pressure cooker; ~ **en papier** paper shape.
cocu [kɔky] *nm* cuckold.
code [kɔd] *nm* code; **se mettre en** ~**(s)** to dip (*BRIT*) *ou* dim (*US*) one's (head)lights; ~ **à barres** bar code; ~ **de caractère** (*INFORM*) character code; ~ **civil** Common Law; ~ **machine** machine code; ~ **pénal** penal code; ~ **postal** (*numéro*) postcode (*BRIT*), zip code (*US*); ~ **de la route** highway code; ~ **secret** cipher.
codéine [kɔdein] *nf* codeine.
coder [kɔde] *vt* to (en)code.
codétenu, e [kɔdɛtny] *nm/f* fellow prisoner *ou* inmate.
codicille [kɔdisil] *nm* codicil.
codifier [kɔdifje] *vt* to codify.
codirecteur, trice [kɔdiʀɛktœʀ, -tʀis] *nm/f* co-director.
coéditeur, trice [kɔeditœʀ, -tʀis] *nm/f* co-publisher; (*rédacteur*) co-editor.
coefficient [kɔefisjɑ̃] *nm* coefficient; ~ **d'erreur** margin of error.
coéquipier, ière [kɔekipje, -jɛʀ] *nm/f* team-mate, partner.
coercition [kɔɛʀsisjɔ̃] *nf* coercion.
cœur [kœʀ] *nm* heart; (*CARTES: couleur*) hearts *pl*; (*: carte*) heart; (*CULIN*): ~ **de laitue/d'artichaut** lettuce/artichoke heart; (*fig*): ~ **du débat** heart of the debate; ~ **de l'été** height of summer; ~ **de la forêt** depths *pl* of the forest; **affaire de** ~ love affair; **avoir bon** ~ to be kind-hearted; **avoir mal au** ~ to feel sick; **contre** *ou* **sur son** ~ to one's breast; **opérer qn à** ~ **ouvert** to perform open-heart surgery on sb; **recevoir qn à** ~ **ouvert** to welcome sb with open arms; **parler à** ~ **ouvert** to open one's heart; **de tout son** ~ with all one's heart; **avoir le** ~ **gros** *ou* **serré** to have a heavy heart; **en avoir le** ~ **net** to be clear in one's own mind (about it); **par** ~ by heart; **de bon** ~ willingly; **avoir à** ~ **de faire** to be very keen to do; **cela lui tient à** ~ that's (very) close to his heart; **prendre les choses à** ~ to take things to heart; **à** ~ **joie** to one's heart's content; **être de tout** ~ **avec qn** to be (completely) in accord with sb.
coexistence [kɔɛgzistɑ̃s] *nf* coexistence.
coexister [kɔegziste] *vi* to coexist.
coffrage [kɔfʀaʒ] *nm* (*CONSTR: dispositif*) form(work).
coffre [kɔfʀ(ə)] *nm* (*meuble*) chest; (*coffre-fort*) safe; (*d'auto*) boot (*BRIT*), trunk (*US*); **avoir du** ~ (*fam*) to have a lot of puff.
coffre-fort, *pl* **coffres-forts** [kɔfʀəfɔʀ] *nm* safe.
coffrer [kɔfʀe] *vt* (*fam*) to put inside, lock up.
coffret [kɔfʀɛ] *nm* casket; ~ **à bijoux** jewel box.
cogérant, e [kɔʒeʀɑ̃, -ɑ̃t] *nm/f* joint manager/manageress.
cogestion [kɔʒestjɔ̃] *nf* joint management.
cogiter [kɔʒite] *vi* to cogitate.
cognac [kɔɲak] *nm* brandy, cognac.
cognement [kɔɲmɑ̃] *nm* knocking.
cogner [kɔɲe] *vi* to knock, bang; **se** ~ to bump o.s.
cohabitation [kɔabitɑsjɔ̃] *nf* living together; (*POL, JUR*) cohabitation.
cohabiter [kɔabite] *vi* to live together.
cohérence [kɔeʀɑ̃s] *nf* coherence.
cohérent, e [kɔeʀɑ̃, -ɑ̃t] *adj* coherent.
cohésion [kɔezjɔ̃] *nf* cohesion.
cohorte [kɔɔʀt(ə)] *nf* troop.
cohue [kɔy] *nf* crowd.
coi, coite [kwa, kwat] *adj*: **rester** ~ to remain silent.
coiffe [kwaf] *nf* headdress.
coiffé, e [kwafe] *adj*: **bien/mal** ~ with tidy/untidy hair; ~ **d'un béret** wearing a beret; ~ **en arrière** with one's hair brushed *ou* combed back; ~ **en brosse** with a crew cut.
coiffer [kwafe] *vt* (*fig*) to cover, top; ~ **qn** to do sb's hair; ~ **qn d'un béret** to put a beret on sb; **se** ~ to do one's hair; to put on a *ou* one's hat.
coiffeur, euse [kwafœʀ, -øz] *nm/f* hairdresser ♦ *nf* (*table*) dressing table.
coiffure [kwafyʀ] *nf* (*cheveux*) hairstyle, hair-do; (*chapeau*) hat, headgear *no pl*; (*art*): **la** ~ hairdressing.
coin [kwɛ̃] *nm* corner; (*pour graver*) die; (*pour coincer*) wedge; (*poinçon*) hallmark; **l'épicerie du** ~ the local grocer; **dans le** ~ (*aux alentours*) in the area, around about; locally; **au** ~ **du feu** by the fireside; **du** ~ **de l'œil** out of the corner of one's eye; **regard en** ~ side(ways) glance; **sourire en** ~ half-smile.
coincé, e [kwɛ̃se] *adj* stuck, jammed; (*fig: inhibé*) inhibited, with hang-ups.
coincer [kwɛ̃se] *vt* to jam; (*fam*) to catch (out), to nab; **se** ~ to get stuck *ou* jammed.
coïncidence [kɔɛ̃sidɑ̃s] *nf* coincidence.
coïncider [kɔɛ̃side] *vi*: ~ **(avec)** to coincide (with); (*correspondre: témoignage etc*) to correspond *ou* tally (with).

coin-coin [kwɛ̃kwɛ̃] *nm inv* quack.
coing [kwɛ̃] *nm* quince.
coït [kɔit] *nm* coitus.
coite [kwat] *adj f voir* **coi.**
coke [kɔk] *nm* coke.
col [kɔl] *nm* (*de chemise*) collar; (*encolure, cou*) neck; (*de montagne*) pass; ~ **roulé** polo-neck; ~ **de l'utérus** cervix.
coléoptère [kɔleɔptɛʀ] *nm* beetle.
colère [kɔlɛʀ] *nf* anger; **une** ~ a fit of anger; **être en** ~ **(contre qn)** to be angry (with sb); **mettre qn en** ~ to make sb angry; **se mettre en** ~ to get angry.
coléreux, euse [kɔleʀø, -øz] *adj*, **colérique** [kɔleʀik] *adj* quick-tempered, irascible.
colibacille [kɔlibasil] *nm* colon bacillus.
colibacillose [kɔlibasiloz] *nf* colibacillosis.
colifichet [kɔlifiʃɛ] *nm* trinket.
colimaçon [kɔlimasɔ̃] *nm*: **escalier en** ~ spiral staircase.
colin [kɔlɛ̃] *nm* hake.
colin-maillard [kɔlɛ̃majaʀ] *nm* (*jeu*) blind man's buff.
colique [kɔlik] *nf* diarrhoea (*BRIT*), diarrhea (*US*); (*douleurs*) colic (pains *pl*); (*fam: personne ou chose ennuyeuse*) pain.
colis [kɔli] *nm* parcel; **par** ~ **postal** by parcel post.
colistier, ière [kɔlistje, -jɛʀ] *nm/f* fellow candidate.
colite [kɔlit] *nf* colitis.
coll. *abr* = **collection**; (= *collaborateurs*): **et** ~ et al.
collaborateur, trice [kɔlabɔʀatœʀ, -tʀis] *nm/f* (*aussi POL*) collaborator; (*d'une revue*) contributor.
collaboration [kɔlabɔʀɑsjɔ̃] *nf* collaboration.
collaborer [kɔlabɔʀe] *vi* to collaborate; ~ **à** to collaborate on; (*revue*) to contribute to.
collage [kɔlaʒ] *nm* (*ART*) collage.
collagène [kɔlaʒɛn] *nm* collagen.
collant, e [kɔlɑ̃, -ɑ̃t] *adj* sticky; (*robe etc*) clinging, skintight; (*péj*) clinging ♦ *nm* (*bas*) tights *pl*.
collatéral, e, aux [kɔlateʀal, -o] *nm/f* collateral.
collation [kɔlɑsjɔ̃] *nf* light meal.
colle [kɔl] *nf* glue; (*à papiers peints*) (wallpaper) paste; (*devinette*) teaser, riddle; (*SCOL fam*) detention; ~ **forte** superglue ®.
collecte [kɔlɛkt(ə)] *nf* collection; **faire une** ~ to take up a collection.
collecter [kɔlɛkte] *vt* to collect.
collecteur [kɔlɛktœʀ] *nm* (*égout*) main sewer.
collectif, ive [kɔlɛktif, -iv] *adj* collective; (*visite, billet etc*) group *cpd* ♦ *nm*: ~ **budgétaire** mini-budget (*BRIT*), mid-term budget; **immeuble** ~ block of flats.
collection [kɔlɛksjɔ̃] *nf* collection; (*ÉDITION*) series; **pièce de** ~ collector's item; **faire (la)** ~ **de** to collect; **(toute) une** ~ **de ...** (*fig*) a (complete) set of ....
collectionner [kɔlɛksjɔne] *vt* (*tableaux, timbres*) to collect.
collectionneur, euse [kɔlɛksjɔnœʀ, -øz] *nm/f* collector.
collectivement [kɔlɛktivmɑ̃] *adv* collectively.
collectiviser [kɔlɛktivize] *vt* to collectivize.
collectivisme [kɔlɛktivism(ə)] *nm* collectivism.
collectiviste [kɔlɛktivist(ə)] *adj* collectivist.
collectivité [kɔlɛktivite] *nf* group; **la** ~ the community, the collectivity; **les ~s locales** local authorities.
collège [kɔlɛʒ] *nm* (*école*) (secondary) school; (*assemblée*) body; ~ **d'enseignement secondaire (CES)** ≈ junior secondary school (*BRIT*), ≈ junior high school (*US*); *see boxed note*.

COLLÈGE

A **collège** *is a state secondary school for children between 11 and 15 years of age. Pupils follow a national curriculum which prescribes a common core along with several options. Schools are free to arrange their own timetable and choose their own teaching methods. Before leaving this phase of their education, students are assessed by examination and course work for their 'brevet des collèges'.*

collégial, e, aux [kɔleʒjal, -o] *adj* collegiate.
collégien, ne [kɔleʒjɛ̃, -ɛn] *nm/f* secondary school pupil (*BRIT*), high school student (*US*).
collègue [kɔlɛg] *nm/f* colleague.
coller [kɔle] *vt* (*papier, timbre*) to stick (on); (*affiche*) to stick up; (*appuyer, placer contre*): ~ **son front à la vitre** to press one's face to the window; (*enveloppe*) to stick down; (*morceaux*) to stick *ou* glue together; (*fam: mettre, fourrer*) to stick, shove; (*SCOL fam*) to keep in, give detention to ♦ *vi* (*être collant*) to be sticky; (*adhérer*) to stick; ~ **qch sur** to stick (*ou* paste *ou* glue) sth on(to); ~ **à** to stick to; (*fig*) to cling to.
collerette [kɔlʀɛt] *nf* ruff; (*TECH*) flange.
collet [kɔlɛ] *nm* (*piège*) snare, noose; (*cou*): **prendre qn au** ~ to grab sb by the throat; ~ **monté** *adj inv* straight-laced.
colleter [kɔlte] *vt* (*adversaire*) to collar, grab by the throat; **se** ~ **avec** to wrestle with.
colleur [kɔlœʀ] *nm*: ~ **d'affiches** bill-poster.
collier [kɔlje] *nm* (*bijou*) necklace; (*de chien, TECH*) collar; ~ **(de barbe), barbe en** ~ narrow beard along the line of the jaw; ~ **de serrage** choke collar.
collimateur [kɔlimatœʀ] *nm*: **être dans le** ~ (*fig*) to be in the firing line; **avoir qn/qch dans le** ~ (*fig*) to have sb/sth in one's sights.
colline [kɔlin] *nf* hill.
collision [kɔlizjɔ̃] *nf* collision, crash; **entrer en** ~ **(avec)** to collide (with).
colloque [kɔlɔk] *nm* colloquium, symposium.

collusion [kɔlyzjɔ̃] *nf* collusion.
collutoire [kɔlytwaʀ] *nm* (*MÉD*) oral medication; (*en bombe*) throat spray.
collyre [kɔliʀ] *nm* (*MÉD*) eye lotion.
colmater [kɔlmate] *vt* (*fuite*) to seal off; (*brèche*) to plug, fill in.
Cologne [kɔlɔɲ] *n* Cologne.
colombage [kɔlɔ̃baʒ] *nm* half-timbering; **une maison à ~s** a half-timbered house.
colombe [kɔlɔ̃b] *nf* dove.
Colombie [kɔlɔ̃bi] *nf*: **la ~** Colombia.
colombien, ne [kɔlɔ̃bjɛ̃, -ɛn] *adj* Colombian ♦ *nm/f*: **C~, ne** Colombian.
colon [kɔlɔ̃] *nm* settler; (*enfant*) boarder (*in children's holiday camp*).
côlon [kolɔ̃] *nm* colon (*MÉD*).
colonel [kɔlɔnɛl] *nm* colonel; (*armée de l'air*) group captain.
colonial, e, aux [kɔlɔnjal, -o] *adj* colonial.
colonialisme [kɔlɔnjalism(ə)] *nm* colonialism.
colonialiste [kɔlɔnjalist(ə)] *adj, nm/f* colonialist.
colonie [kɔlɔni] *nf* colony; ~ **(de vacances)** holiday camp (*for children*).
colonisation [kɔlɔnizɑsjɔ̃] *nf* colonization.
coloniser [kɔlɔnize] *vt* to colonize.
colonnade [kɔlɔnad] *nf* colonnade.
colonne [kɔlɔn] *nf* column; **se mettre en ~ par deux/quatre** to get into twos/fours; **en ~ par deux** in double file; ~ **de secours** rescue party; ~ **(vertébrale)** spine, spinal column.
colonnette [kɔlɔnɛt] *nf* small column.
colophane [kɔlɔfan] *nf* rosin.
colorant [kɔlɔʀɑ̃] *nm* colo(u)ring.
coloration [kɔlɔʀɑsjɔ̃] *nf* colour(ing) (*BRIT*), color(ing) (*US*); **se faire faire une ~** (*chez le coiffeur*) to have one's hair dyed.
coloré, e [kɔlɔʀe] *adj* (*fig*) colo(u)rful.
colorer [kɔlɔʀe] *vt* to colour (*BRIT*), color (*US*); **se ~** *vi* to turn red; to blush.
coloriage [kɔlɔʀjaʒ] *nm* colo(u)ring.
colorier [kɔlɔʀje] *vt* to colo(u)r (in); **album à ~** colouring book.
coloris [kɔlɔʀi] *nm* colo(u)r, shade.
coloriste [kɔlɔʀist(ə)] *nm/f* colo(u)rist.
colossal, e, aux [kɔlɔsal, -o] *adj* colossal, huge.
colosse [kɔlɔs] *nm* giant.
colostrum [kɔlɔstʀɔm] *nm* colostrum.
colporter [kɔlpɔʀte] *vt* to peddle.
colporteur, euse [kɔlpɔʀtœʀ, -øz] *nm/f* pedlar.
colt [kɔlt] *nm* revolver, Colt ®.
coltiner [kɔltine] *vt* to lug about.
colza [kɔlza] *nm* rape(seed).
coma [kɔma] *nm* coma.
comateux, euse [kɔmatø, -øz] *adj* comatose.
combat [kɔ̃ba] *vb voir* **combattre** ♦ *nm* fight; fighting *no pl*; ~ **de boxe** boxing match; ~ **de rues** street fighting *no pl*; ~ **singulier** single combat.
combatif, ive [kɔ̃batif, -iv] *adj* with a lot of fight.
combativité [kɔ̃bativite] *nf* fighting spirit.
combattant [kɔ̃batɑ̃] *vb voir* **combattre** ♦ *nm* combatant; (*d'une rixe*) brawler; **ancien ~** war veteran.
combattre [kɔ̃batʀ(ə)] *vi* to fight ♦ *vt* to fight; (*épidémie, ignorance*) to combat.
combien [kɔ̃bjɛ̃] *adv* (*quantité*) how much; (*nombre*) how many; (*exclamatif*) how; ~ **de** how much; how many; ~ **de temps** how long, how much time; ~ **coûte/pèse ceci?** how much does this cost/weigh?; **vous mesurez ~?** what size are you?; **ça fait ~ en largeur?** how wide is that?
combinaison [kɔ̃binɛzɔ̃] *nf* combination; (*astuce*) device, scheme; (*de femme*) slip; (*d'aviateur*) flying suit; (*d'homme-grenouille*) wetsuit; (*bleu de travail*) boilersuit (*BRIT*), coveralls *pl* (*US*).
combine [kɔ̃bin] *nf* trick; (*péj*) scheme, fiddle (*BRIT*).
combiné [kɔ̃bine] *nm* (*aussi*: ~ **téléphonique**) receiver; (*SKI*) combination (event); (*vêtement de femme*) corselet.
combiner [kɔ̃bine] *vt* to combine; (*plan, horaire*) to work out, devise.
comble [kɔ̃bl(ə)] *adj* (*salle*) packed (full) ♦ *nm* (*du bonheur, plaisir*) height; **~s** *nmpl* (*CONSTR*) attic *sg*, loft *sg*; **de fond en ~** from top to bottom; **pour ~ de malchance** to cap it all; **c'est le ~!** that beats everything!, that takes the biscuit! (*BRIT*); **sous les ~s** in the attic.
combler [kɔ̃ble] *vt* (*trou*) to fill in; (*besoin, lacune*) to fill; (*déficit*) to make good; (*satisfaire*) to gratify, fulfil (*BRIT*), fulfill (*US*); ~ **qn de joie** to fill sb with joy; ~ **qn d'honneurs** to shower sb with honours.
combustible [kɔ̃bystibl(ə)] *adj* combustible ♦ *nm* fuel.
combustion [kɔ̃bystjɔ̃] *nf* combustion.
COMECON [kɔmekɔn] *sigle m* Comecon.
comédie [kɔmedi] *nf* comedy; (*fig*) playacting *no pl*; **jouer la ~** (*fig*) to put on an act; ~ **musicale** musical; *see boxed note*.

> **COMÉDIE FRANÇAISE**
>
> **Founded in 1680 by Louis XIV, the Comédie française** *is the French national theatre. The company is subsidized by the state and mainly performs in the Palais-Royal in Paris, tending to concentrate on classical French drama.*

comédien, ne [kɔmedjɛ̃, -ɛn] *nm/f* actor/actress; (*comique*) comedy actor/actress, comedian/comedienne; (*fig*) sham.
COMES [kɔmɛs] *sigle m* = *Commissariat à l'énergie solaire.*
comestible [kɔmɛstibl(ə)] *adj* edible; **~s** *nmpl* foods.
comète [kɔmɛt] *nf* comet.
comice [kɔmis] *nm*: ~ **agricole** agricultural show.

comique [kɔmik] *adj* (*drôle*) comical; (*THÉÂT*) comic ♦ *nm* (*artiste*) comic, comedian; **le ~ de qch** the funny *ou* comical side of sth.

comité [kɔmite] *nm* committee; **petit ~** select group; **~ directeur** management committee; **~ d'entreprise (CE)** works council; **~ des fêtes** festival committee.

commandant [kɔmɑ̃dɑ̃] *nm* (*gén*) commander, commandant; (*MIL*: *grade*) major; (*: armée de l'air*) squadron leader; (*NAVIG*) captain; **~ (de bord)** (*AVIAT*) captain.

commande [kɔmɑ̃d] *nf* (*COMM*) order; (*INFORM*) command; **~s** *nfpl* (*AVIAT etc*) controls; **passer une ~ (de)** to put in an or- der (for); **sur ~** to order; **~ à distance** remote control; **véhicule à double ~** vehicle with dual controls.

commandement [kɔmɑ̃dmɑ̃] *nm* command; (*ordre*) command, order; (*REL*) commandment.

commander [kɔmɑ̃de] *vt* (*COMM*) to order; (*diriger, ordonner*) to command; **~ à** (*MIL*) to command; (*contrôler, maîtriser*) to have control over; **~ à qn de faire** to command *ou* order sb to do.

commanditaire [kɔmɑ̃ditɛʀ] *nm* sleeping (*BRIT*) *ou* silent (*US*) partner.

commandite [kɔmɑ̃dit] *nf*: **(société en) ~** limited partnership.

commanditer [kɔmɑ̃dite] *vt* (*COMM*) to finance, back; to commission.

commando [kɔmɑ̃do] *nm* commando (squad).

MOT-CLÉ

comme [kɔm] *prép* **1** (*comparaison*) like; **tout ~ son père** just like his father; **fort ~ un bœuf** as strong as an ox; **joli ~ tout** ever so pretty

2 (*manière*) like; **faites-le ~ ça** do it like this, do it this way; **~ ça** *ou* **cela on n'aura pas d'ennuis** that way we won't have any problems; **~ ci, ~ ça** so-so, middling; **comment ça va? — ~ ça** how are things? — OK; **~ on dit** as they say

3 (*en tant que*) as a; **donner ~ prix** to give as a prize; **travailler ~ secrétaire** to work as a secretary

4: **~ quoi** (*d'où il s'ensuit que*) which shows that; **il a écrit une lettre ~ quoi il** ... he's written a letter saying that ...

5: **~ il faut** *phr adv* properly; *phr adj* (*correct*) proper, correct

♦ *conj* **1** (*ainsi que*) as; **elle écrit ~ elle parle** she writes as she talks; **~ si** as if

2 (*au moment où, alors que*) as; **il est parti ~ j'arrivais** he left as I arrived

3 (*parce que, puisque*) as, since; **~ il était en retard, il** ... as he was late, he ...

♦ *adv*: **~ il est fort/c'est bon!** he's so strong/ it's so good!; **il est malin ~ c'est pas permis** he's as smart as anything.

commémoratif, ive [kɔmemɔʀatif, -iv] *adj* commemorative; **un monument ~** a memorial.

commémoration [kɔmemɔʀɑsjɔ̃] *nf* commemoration.

commémorer [kɔmemɔʀe] *vt* to commemorate.

commencement [kɔmɑ̃smɑ̃] *nm* beginning, start, commencement; **~s** *nmpl* (*débuts*) beginnings.

commencer [kɔmɑ̃se] *vt* to begin, start, commence ♦ *vi* to begin, start, commence; **~ à** *ou* **de faire** to begin *ou* start doing; **~ par qch** to begin with sth; **~ par faire qch** to begin by doing sth.

commensal, e, aux [kɔmɑ̃sal, -o] *nm/f* companion at table.

comment [kɔmɑ̃] *adv* how; **~?** (*que dites-vous*) (I beg your) pardon?; **~!** what! ♦ *nm*: **le ~ et le pourquoi** the whys and wherefores; **et ~!** and how!; **~ donc!** of course!; **~ faire?** how will we do it?; **~ se fait-il que?** how is it that?

commentaire [kɔmɑ̃tɛʀ] *nm* comment; remark; **~ (de texte)** (*SCOL*) commentary; **~ sur image** voice-over.

commentateur, trice [kɔmɑ̃tatœʀ, -tʀis] *nm/f* commentator.

commenter [kɔmɑ̃te] *vt* (*jugement, événement*) to comment (up)on; (*RADIO, TV*: *match, manifestation*) to cover, give a commentary on.

commérages [kɔmeʀaʒ] *nmpl* gossip *sg*.

commerçant, e [kɔmɛʀsɑ̃, -ɑ̃t] *adj* commercial; trading; (*rue*) shopping *cpd*; (*personne*) commercially shrewd ♦ *nm/f* shopkeeper, trader.

commerce [kɔmɛʀs(ə)] *nm* (*activité*) trade, commerce; (*boutique*) business; **le petit ~** small shopowners *pl*, small traders *pl*; **faire ~ de** to trade in; (*fig*: *péj*) to trade on; **chambre de ~** Chamber of Commerce; **livres de ~** (account) books; **vendu dans le ~** sold in the shops; **vendu hors-~** sold directly to the public; **~ en** *ou* **de gros/détail** wholesale/retail trade; **~ intérieur/ extérieur** home/foreign trade; **~ électronique** e-commerce; **~ équitable** fair trade.

commercer [kɔmɛʀse] *vi*: **~ avec** to trade with.

commercial, e, aux [kɔmɛʀsjal, -o] *adj* commercial, trading; (*péj*) commercial ♦ *nm*: **les commerciaux** the commercial people.

commercialisable [kɔmɛʀsjalizabl(ə)] *adj* marketable.

commercialisation [kɔmɛʀsjalizɑsjɔ̃] *nf* marketing.

commercialiser [kɔmɛʀsjalize] *vt* to market.

commère [kɔmɛʀ] *nf* gossip.

commettant [kɔmetɑ̃] *vb voir* **commettre** ♦ *nm* (*JUR*) principal.

commettre [kɔmɛtʀ(ə)] *vt* to commit; **se ~** to compromise one's good name.

commis [kɔmi] *vb voir* **commettre** ♦ *nm* (*de magasin*) (shop) assistant (*BRIT*), sales clerk (*US*); (*de banque*) clerk; ~ **voyageur** commercial traveller (*BRIT*) *ou* traveler (*US*).
commis, e [kɔmi, -iz] *pp de* **commettre**.
commisération [kɔmizeʀɑsjɔ̃] *nf* commiseration.
commissaire [kɔmisɛʀ] *nm* (*de police*) ≈ (police) superintendent (*BRIT*), ≈ (police) captain (*US*); (*de rencontre sportive etc*) steward; ~ **du bord** (*NAVIG*) purser; ~ **aux comptes** (*ADMIN*) auditor.
commissaire-priseur, *pl* **commissaires-priseurs** [kɔmisɛʀpʀizœʀ] *nm* (official) auctioneer.
commissariat [kɔmisaʀja] *nm* police station; (*ADMIN*) commissionership.
commission [kɔmisjɔ̃] *nf* (*comité, pourcentage*) commission; (*message*) message; (*course*) errand; ~**s** *nfpl* (*achats*) shopping *sg*; ~ **d'examen** examining board.
commissionnaire [kɔmisjɔnɛʀ] *nm* delivery boy (*ou* man); messenger; (*TRANSPORTS*) (forwarding) agent.
commissure [kɔmisyʀ] *nf*: **les ~s des lèvres** the corners of the mouth.
commode [kɔmɔd] *adj* (*pratique*) convenient, handy; (*facile*) easy; (*air, personne*) easy-going; (*personne*): **pas** ~ awkward (to deal with) ♦ *nf* chest of drawers.
commodité [kɔmɔdite] *nf* convenience.
commotion [kɔmosjɔ̃] *nf*: ~ **(cérébrale)** concussion.
commotionné, e [kɔmosjɔne] *adj* shocked, shaken.
commuer [kɔmɥe] *vt* to commute.
commun, e [kɔmœ̃, -yn] *adj* common; (*pièce*) communal, shared; (*réunion, effort*) joint ♦ *nf* (*ADMIN*) commune, ≈ district; (*: urbaine*) ≈ borough; ~**s** *nmpl* (*bâtiments*) outbuildings; **cela sort du** ~ it's out of the ordinary; **le ~ des mortels** the common run of people; **sans ~e mesure** incomparable; **être ~ à** (*suj: chose*) to be shared by; **en** ~ (*faire*) jointly; **mettre en** ~ to pool, share; **peu** ~ unusual; **d'un ~ accord** of one accord; with one accord.
communal, e, aux [kɔmynal, -o] *adj* (*ADMIN*) of the commune, ≈ (district *ou* borough) council *cpd*.
communard, e [kɔmynaʀ, -aʀd(ə)] *nm/f* (*HIST*) Communard; (*péj: communiste*) commie.
communautaire [kɔmynotɛʀ] *adj* community *cpd*.
communauté [kɔmynote] *nf* community; (*JUR*): **régime de la** ~ communal estate settlement.
commune [kɔmyn] *adj f, nf voir* **commun**.
communément [kɔmynemɑ̃] *adv* commonly.
Communes [kɔmyn] *nfpl* (*BRIT: parlement*) Commons.
communiant, e [kɔmynjɑ̃, -ɑ̃t] *nm/f* communicant; **premier** ~ child taking his first communion.
communicant, e [kɔmynikɑ̃, -ɑ̃t] *adj* communicating.
communicatif, ive [kɔmynikatif, -iv] *adj* (*personne*) communicative; (*rire*) infectious.
communication [kɔmynikɑsjɔ̃] *nf* communication; ~ **(téléphonique)** (telephone) call; **avoir la ~ (avec)** to get *ou* be through (to); **vous avez la** ~ you're through; **donnez-moi la ~ avec** put me through to; **mettre qn en ~ avec qn** (*en contact*) to put sb in touch with sb; (*au téléphone*) to connect sb with sb; ~ **interurbaine** long-distance call; ~ **en PCV** reverse charge (*BRIT*) *ou* collect (*US*) call; ~ **avec préavis** personal call.
communier [kɔmynje] *vi* (*REL*) to receive communion; (*fig*) to be united.
communion [kɔmynjɔ̃] *nf* communion.
communiqué [kɔmynike] *nm* communiqué; ~ **de presse** press release.
communiquer [kɔmynike] *vt* (*nouvelle, dossier*) to pass on, convey; (*maladie*) to pass on; (*peur etc*) to communicate; (*chaleur, mouvement*) to transmit ♦ *vi* to communicate; ~ **avec** (*suj: salle*) to communicate with; **se ~ à** (*se propager*) to spread to.
communisant, e [kɔmynizɑ̃, -ɑ̃t] *adj* communistic ♦ *nm/f* communist sympathizer.
communisme [kɔmynism(ə)] *nm* communism.
communiste [kɔmynist(ə)] *adj, nm/f* communist.
commutateur [kɔmytatœʀ] *nm* (*ÉLEC*) (change-over) switch, commutator.
commutation [kɔmytɑsjɔ̃] *nf* (*INFORM*): ~ **de messages** message switching; ~ **de paquets** packet switching.
Comores [kɔmɔʀ] *nfpl*: **les (îles)** ~ the Comoros (Islands).
comorien, ne [kɔmɔʀjɛ̃, -ɛn] *adj* of *ou* from the Comoros.
compact, e [kɔ̃pakt] *adj* dense; compact.
compagne [kɔ̃paɲ] *nf* companion.
compagnie [kɔ̃paɲi] *nf* (*firme, MIL*) company; (*groupe*) gathering; (*présence*): **la ~ de qn** sb's company; **homme/femme de** ~ escort; **tenir ~ à qn** to keep sb company; **fausser ~ à qn** to give sb the slip, slip *ou* sneak away from sb; **en ~ de** in the company of; **Dupont et ~, Dupont et Cie** Dupont and Company, Dupont and Co; ~ **aérienne** airline (company).
compagnon [kɔ̃paɲɔ̃] *nm* companion; (*autrefois: ouvrier*) craftsman; journeyman.
comparable [kɔ̃paʀabl(ə)] *adj*: ~ **(à)** comparable (to).
comparaison [kɔ̃paʀɛzɔ̃] *nf* comparison; (*métaphore*) simile; **en ~ (de)** in comparison (with); **par ~ (à)** by comparison (with).
comparaître [kɔ̃paʀɛtʀ(ə)] *vi*: ~ **(devant)** to appear (before).
comparatif, ive [kɔ̃paʀatif, -iv] *adj, nm* com-

parative.
comparativement [kɔ̃paʀativmɑ̃] *adv* comparatively; ~ **à** by comparison with.
comparé, e [kɔ̃paʀe] *adj*: **littérature** *etc* **~e** comparative literature *etc.*
comparer [kɔ̃paʀe] *vt* to compare; ~ **qch/qn à** *ou* **et** (*pour choisir*) to compare sth/sb with *ou* and; (*pour établir une similitude*) to compare sth/sb to *ou* and.
comparse [kɔ̃paʀs(ə)] *nm/f* (*péj*) associate, stooge.
compartiment [kɔ̃paʀtimɑ̃] *nm* compartment.
compartimenté, e [kɔ̃paʀtimɑ̃te] *adj* partitioned; (*fig*) compartmentalized.
comparu, e [kɔ̃paʀy] *pp de* **comparaître.**
comparution [kɔ̃paʀysjɔ̃] *nf* appearance.
compas [kɔ̃pa] *nm* (*GÉOM*) (pair of) compasses *pl*; (*NAVIG*) compass.
compassé, e [kɔ̃pɑse] *adj* starchy, formal.
compassion [kɔ̃pɑsjɔ̃] *nf* compassion.
compatibilité [kɔ̃patibilite] *nf* compatibility.
compatible [kɔ̃patibl(ə)] *adj*: ~ **(avec)** compatible (with).
compatir [kɔ̃patiʀ] *vi*: ~ **(à)** to sympathize (with).
compatissant, e [kɔ̃patisɑ̃, -ɑ̃t] *adj* sympathetic.
compatriote [kɔ̃patʀijɔt] *nm/f* compatriot, fellow countryman/woman.
compensateur, trice [kɔ̃pɑ̃satœʀ, -tʀis] *adj* compensatory.
compensation [kɔ̃pɑ̃sɑsjɔ̃] *nf* compensation; (*BANQUE*) clearing; **en** ~ in *ou* as compensation.
compensé, e [kɔ̃pɑ̃se] *adj*: **semelle ~e** platform sole.
compenser [kɔ̃pɑ̃se] *vt* to compensate for, make up for.
compère [kɔ̃pɛʀ] *nm* accomplice; fellow musician *ou* comedian *etc.*
compétence [kɔ̃petɑ̃s] *nf* competence.
compétent, e [kɔ̃petɑ̃, -ɑ̃t] *adj* (*apte*) competent, capable; (*JUR*) competent.
compétitif, ive [kɔ̃petitif, -iv] *adj* competitive.
compétition [kɔ̃petisjɔ̃] *nf* (*gén*) competition; (*SPORT*: *épreuve*) event; **la** ~ competitive sport; **être en** ~ **avec** to be competing with; **la** ~ **automobile** motor racing.
compétitivité [kɔ̃petitivite] *nf* competitiveness.
compilateur [kɔ̃pilatœʀ] *nm* (*INFORM*) compiler.
compiler [kɔ̃pile] *vt* to compile.
complainte [kɔ̃plɛ̃t] *nf* lament.
complaire [kɔ̃plɛʀ]: **se** ~ *vi*: **se** ~ **dans/parmi** to take pleasure in/in being among.
complaisais [kɔ̃plɛzɛ] *etc vb voir* **complaire.**
complaisamment [kɔ̃plɛzamɑ̃] *adv* kindly; complacently.
complaisance [kɔ̃plɛzɑ̃s] *nf* kindness; (*péj*) indulgence; (*: fatuité*) complacency; **attestation de** ~ *certificate produced to oblige a patient etc*; **pavillon de** ~ flag of convenience.
complaisant, e [kɔ̃plɛzɑ̃, -ɑ̃t] *vb voir* **complaire** ♦ *adj* (*aimable*) kind; obliging; (*péj*) accommodating; (*: fat*) complacent.
complaît [kɔ̃plɛ] *vb voir* **complaire.**
complément [kɔ̃plemɑ̃] *nm* complement; (*reste*) remainder; (*LING*) complement; ~ **d'information** (*ADMIN*) supplementary *ou* further information; ~ **d'agent** agent; ~ **(d'objet) direct/indirect** direct/indirect object; ~ **(circonstanciel) de lieu/temps** adverbial phrase of place/time; ~ **de nom** possessive phrase.
complémentaire [kɔ̃plemɑ̃tɛʀ] *adj* complementary; (*additionnel*) supplementary.
complet, ète [kɔ̃plɛ, -ɛt] *adj* complete; (*plein: hôtel etc*) full ♦ *nm* (*aussi*: **~-veston**) suit; **au (grand)** ~ all together.
complètement [kɔ̃plɛtmɑ̃] *adv* (*en entier*) completely; (*absolument: fou, faux etc*) absolutely; (*à fond: étudier etc*) fully, in depth.
compléter [kɔ̃plete] *vt* (*porter à la quantité voulue*) to complete; (*augmenter*) to complement, supplement; to add to; **se** ~ (*personnes*) to complement one another; (*collection etc*) to become complete.
complexe [kɔ̃plɛks(ə)] *adj* complex ♦ *nm* (*PSYCH*) complex, hang-up; (*bâtiments*): ~ **hospitalier/industriel** hospital/industrial complex.
complexé, e [kɔ̃plɛkse] *adj* mixed-up, hung-up.
complexité [kɔ̃plɛksite] *nf* complexity.
complication [kɔ̃plikɑsjɔ̃] *nf* complexity, intricacy; (*difficulté, ennui*) complication; **~s** *nfpl* (*MÉD*) complications.
complice [kɔ̃plis] *nm* accomplice.
complicité [kɔ̃plisite] *nf* complicity.
compliment [kɔ̃plimɑ̃] *nm* (*louange*) compliment; **~s** *nmpl* (*félicitations*) congratulations.
complimenter [kɔ̃plimɑ̃te] *vt*: ~ **qn (sur** *ou* **de)** to congratulate *ou* compliment sb (on).
compliqué, e [kɔ̃plike] *adj* complicated, complex, intricate; (*personne*) complicated.
compliquer [kɔ̃plike] *vt* to complicate; **se** ~ *vi* (*situation*) to become complicated; **se** ~ **la vie** to make life difficult *ou* complicated for o.s.
complot [kɔ̃plo] *nm* plot.
comploter [kɔ̃plɔte] *vi, vt* to plot.
complu, e [kɔ̃ply] *pp de* **complaire.**
comportement [kɔ̃pɔʀtəmɑ̃] *nm* behaviour (*BRIT*), behavior (*US*); (*TECH*: *d'une pièce, d'un véhicule*) behavio(u)r, performance.
comporter [kɔ̃pɔʀte] *vt* to be composed of, consist of, comprise; (*être équipé de*) to have; (*impliquer*) to entail, involve; **se** ~ *vi* to behave; (*TECH*) to behave, perform.
composant [kɔ̃pozɑ̃] *nm* component, constituent.
composante [kɔ̃pozɑ̃t] *nf* component.

composé, e [kɔ̃poze] *adj* (*visage, air*) studied; (*BIO, CHIMIE, LING*) compound ♦ *nm* (*CHIMIE, LING*) compound; ~ **de** made up of.
composer [kɔ̃poze] *vt* (*musique, texte*) to compose; (*mélange, équipe*) to make up; (*faire partie de*) to make up, form; (*TYPO*) to (type)set ♦ *vi* (*SCOL*) to sit *ou* do a test; (*transiger*) to come to terms; **se** ~ **de** to be composed of, be made up of; ~ **un numéro** (*au téléphone*) to dial a number.
composite [kɔ̃pozit] *adj* heterogeneous.
compositeur, trice [kɔ̃pozitœʀ, -tʀis] *nm/f* (*MUS*) composer; (*TYPO*) compositor, typesetter.
composition [kɔ̃pozisjɔ̃] *nf* composition; (*SCOL*) test; (*TYPO*) (type)setting, composition; **de bonne** ~ (*accommodant*) easy to deal with; **amener qn à** ~ to get sb to come to terms; ~ **française** (*SCOL*) French essay.
compost [kɔ̃pɔst] *nm* compost.
composter [kɔ̃pɔste] *vt* to date-stamp; to punch.
composteur [kɔ̃pɔstœʀ] *nm* date stamp; punch; (*TYPO*) composing stick.
compote [kɔ̃pɔt] *nf* stewed fruit *no pl*; ~ **de pommes** stewed apples.
compotier [kɔ̃pɔtje] *nm* fruit dish *ou* bowl.
compréhensible [kɔ̃pʀeɑ̃sibl(ə)] *adj* comprehensible; (*attitude*) understandable.
compréhensif, ive [kɔ̃pʀeɑ̃sif, -iv] *adj* understanding.
compréhension [kɔ̃pʀeɑ̃sjɔ̃] *nf* understanding; comprehension.
comprendre [kɔ̃pʀɑ̃dʀ(ə)] *vt* to understand; (*se composer de*) to comprise, consist of; (*inclure*) to include; **se faire** ~ to make o.s. understood; to get one's ideas across; **mal** ~ to misunderstand.
compresse [kɔ̃pʀɛs] *nf* compress.
compresser [kɔ̃pʀese] *vt* to squash in, crush together.
compresseur [kɔ̃pʀɛsœʀ] *adj m voir* **rouleau**.
compressible [kɔ̃pʀesibl(ə)] *adj* (*PHYSIQUE*) compressible; (*dépenses*) reducible.
compression [kɔ̃pʀɛsjɔ̃] *nf* compression; (*d'un crédit etc*) reduction.
comprimé, e [kɔ̃pʀime] *adj*: **air** ~ compressed air ♦ *nm* tablet.
comprimer [kɔ̃pʀime] *vt* to compress; (*fig: crédit etc*) to reduce, cut down.
compris, e [kɔ̃pʀi, -iz] *pp de* **comprendre** ♦ *adj* (*inclus*) included; ~**?** understood?, is that clear?; ~ **entre** (*situé*) contained between; **la maison** ~**e/non** ~**e, y/non** ~ **la maison** including/excluding the house; **service** ~ service (charge) included; **100 € tout** ~ €100 all inclusive *ou* all-in.
compromettant, e [kɔ̃pʀɔmetɑ̃, -ɑ̃t] *adj* compromising.
compromettre [kɔ̃pʀɔmɛtʀ(ə)] *vt* to compromise.
compromis [kɔ̃pʀɔmi] *vb voir* **compromettre** ♦ *nm* compromise.
compromission [kɔ̃pʀɔmisjɔ̃] *nf* compromise, deal.
comptabiliser [kɔ̃tabilize] *vt* (*valeur*) to post; (*fig*) to evaluate.
comptabilité [kɔ̃tabilite] *nf* (*activité, technique*) accounting, accountancy; (*d'une société: comptes*) accounts *pl*, books *pl*; (*: service*) accounts office *ou* department; ~ **à partie double** double-entry book-keeping.
comptable [kɔ̃tabl(ə)] *nm/f* accountant ♦ *adj* accounts *cpd*, accounting.
comptant [kɔ̃tɑ̃] *adv*: **payer** ~ to pay cash; **acheter** ~ to buy for cash.
compte [kɔ̃t] *nm* count, counting; (*total, montant*) count, (right) number; (*bancaire, facture*) account; ~**s** *nmpl* accounts, books; (*fig*) explanation *sg*; **ouvrir un** ~ to open an account; **rendre des** ~**s à qn** (*fig*) to be answerable to sb; **faire le** ~ **de** to count up, make a count of; **tout** ~ **fait** on the whole; **à ce** ~**-là** (*dans ce cas*) in that case; (*à ce train-là*) at that rate; **en fin de** ~ (*fig*) all things considered, weighing it all up; **au bout du** ~ in the final analysis; **à bon** ~ at a favourable price; (*fig*) lightly; **avoir son** ~ (*fig: fam*) to have had it; **pour le** ~ **de** on behalf of; **pour son propre** ~ for one's own benefit; **sur le** ~ **de qn** (*à son sujet*) about sb; **travailler à son** ~ to work for oneself; **mettre qch sur le** ~ **de qn** (*le rendre responsable*) to attribute sth to sb; **prendre qch à son** ~ to take responsibility for sth; **trouver son** ~ **à qch** to do well out of sth; **régler un** ~ (*s'acquitter de qch*) to settle an account; (*se venger*) to get one's own back; **rendre** ~ **(à qn) de qch** to give (sb) an account of sth; **tenir** ~ **de qch** to take sth into account; ~ **tenu de** taking into account; ~ **chèque(s)** current account; ~ **chèque postal (CCP)** Post Office account; ~ **client** (*sur bilan*) accounts receivable; ~ **courant (CC)** current account; ~ **de dépôt** deposit account; ~ **d'exploitation** operating ac- count; ~ **fournisseur** (*sur bilan*) accounts payable; ~ **à rebours** countdown; ~ **rendu** account, report; (*de film, livre*) review; *voir aussi* **rendre**.
compte-gouttes [kɔ̃tgut] *nm inv* dropper.
compter [kɔ̃te] *vt* to count; (*facturer*) to charge for; (*avoir à son actif, comporter*) to have; (*prévoir*) to allow, reckon; (*tenir compte de, inclure*) to include; (*penser, espérer*): ~ **réussir/revenir** to expect to succeed/return ♦ *vi* to count; (*être économe*) to economize; (*être non négligeable*) to count, matter; (*valoir*): ~ **pour** to count for; (*figurer*): ~ **parmi** to be *ou* rank among; ~ **sur** to count (up)on; ~ **avec qch/qn** to reckon with *ou* take account of sth/sb; ~ **sans qch/qn** to reckon without sth/sb; **sans** ~ **que** besides which; ~ **du 10 janvier** (*COMM*) (as) from 10th January.

compte-tours [kɔ̃ttuʀ] *nm inv* rev(olution) counter.

compteur [kɔ̃tœʀ] *nm* meter; ~ **de vitesse** speedometer.

comptine [kɔ̃tin] *nf* nursery rhyme.

comptoir [kɔ̃twaʀ] *nm* (*de magasin*) counter; (*de café*) counter, bar; (*colonial*) trading post.

compulser [kɔ̃pylse] *vt* to consult.

comte, comtesse [kɔ̃t, kɔ̃tɛs] *nm/f* count/ countess.

con, ne [kɔ̃, kɔn] *adj* (*fam!*) bloody (*BRIT*) *ou* damned stupid (*!*).

concasser [kɔ̃kɑse] *vt* (*pierre, sucre*) to crush; (*poivre*) to grind.

concave [kɔ̃kav] *adj* concave.

concéder [kɔ̃sede] *vt* to grant; (*défaite, point*) to concede; ~ **que** to concede that.

concentration [kɔ̃sɑ̃tʀɑsjɔ̃] *nf* concentration.

concentrationnaire [kɔ̃sɑ̃tʀɑsjɔnɛʀ] *adj* of *ou* in concentration camps.

concentré [kɔ̃sɑ̃tʀe] *nm* concentrate; ~ **de tomates** tomato purée.

concentrer [kɔ̃sɑ̃tʀe] *vt* to concentrate; **se** ~ to concentrate.

concentrique [kɔ̃sɑ̃tʀik] *adj* concentric.

concept [kɔ̃sɛpt] *nm* concept.

concepteur, trice [kɔ̃sɛptœʀ, -tʀis] *nm/f* designer.

conception [kɔ̃sɛpsjɔ̃] *nf* conception; (*d'une machine etc*) design.

concernant [kɔ̃sɛʀnɑ̃] *prép* (*se rapportant à*) concerning; (*en ce qui concerne*) as regards.

concerner [kɔ̃sɛʀne] *vt* to concern; **en ce qui me concerne** as far as I am concerned; **en ce qui concerne ceci** as far as this is concerned, with regard to this.

concert [kɔ̃sɛʀ] *nm* concert; **de** ~ *adv* in unison; together.

concertation [kɔ̃sɛʀtɑsjɔ̃] *nf* (*échange de vues*) dialogue; (*rencontre*) meeting.

concerter [kɔ̃sɛʀte] *vt* to devise; **se** ~ *vi* (*collaborateurs etc*) to put our (*ou* their *etc*) heads together, consult (each other).

concertiste [kɔ̃sɛʀtist(ə)] *nm/f* concert artist.

concerto [kɔ̃sɛʀto] *nm* concerto.

concession [kɔ̃sesjɔ̃] *nf* concession.

concessionnaire [kɔ̃sesjɔnɛʀ] *nm/f* agent, dealer.

concevable [kɔ̃svabl(ə)] *adj* conceivable.

concevoir [kɔ̃svwaʀ] *vt* (*idée, projet*) to conceive (of); (*méthode, plan d'appartement, décoration etc*) to plan, design; (*enfant*) to conceive; **maison bien/mal conçue** well-/badly-designed *ou* -planned house.

concierge [kɔ̃sjɛʀʒ(ə)] *nm/f* caretaker; (*d'hôtel*) head porter.

conciergerie [kɔ̃sjɛʀʒəʀi] *nf* caretaker's lodge.

concile [kɔ̃sil] *nm* council, synod.

conciliable [kɔ̃siljabl(ə)] *adj* (*opinions etc*) reconcilable.

conciliabules [kɔ̃siljabyl] *nmpl* (private) discussions, confabulations (*BRIT*).

conciliant, e [kɔ̃siljɑ̃, -ɑ̃t] *adj* conciliatory.

conciliateur, trice [kɔ̃siljatœʀ, -tʀis] *nm/f* mediator, go-between.

conciliation [kɔ̃siljɑsjɔ̃] *nf* conciliation.

concilier [kɔ̃silje] *vt* to reconcile; **se** ~ **qn/ l'appui de qn** to win sb over/sb's support.

concis, e [kɔ̃si, -iz] *adj* concise.

concision [kɔ̃sizjɔ̃] *nf* concision, conciseness.

concitoyen, ne [kɔ̃sitwajɛ̃, -ɛn] *nm/f* fellow citizen.

conclave [kɔ̃klav] *nm* conclave.

concluant, e [kɔ̃klyɑ̃, -ɑ̃t] *vb voir* **conclure** ♦ *adj* conclusive.

conclure [kɔ̃klyʀ] *vt* to conclude; (*signer: accord, pacte*) to enter into; (*déduire*): ~ **qch de qch** to deduce sth from sth; ~ **à l'acquittement** to decide in favour of an acquittal; ~ **au suicide** to come to the conclusion (*ou* (*JUR*) to pronounce) that it is a case of suicide; ~ **un marché** to clinch a deal; **j'en conclus que** from that I conclude that.

conclusion [kɔ̃klyzjɔ̃] *nf* conclusion; ~**s** *nfpl* (*JUR*) submissions; findings; **en** ~ in conclusion.

concocter [kɔ̃kɔkte] *vt* to concoct.

conçois [kɔ̃swa], **conçoive** [kɔ̃swav] *etc vb voir* **concevoir**.

concombre [kɔ̃kɔ̃bʀ(ə)] *nm* cucumber.

concomitant, e [kɔ̃kɔmitɑ̃, -ɑ̃t] *adj* concomitant.

concordance [kɔ̃kɔʀdɑ̃s] *nf* concordance; **la** ~ **des temps** (*LING*) the sequence of tenses.

concordant, e [kɔ̃kɔʀdɑ̃, -ɑ̃t] *adj* (*témoignages, versions*) corroborating.

concorde [kɔ̃kɔʀd(ə)] *nf* concord.

concorder [kɔ̃kɔʀde] *vi* to tally, agree.

concourir [kɔ̃kuʀiʀ] *vi* (*SPORT*) to compete; ~ **à** *vt* (*effet etc*) to work towards.

concours [kɔ̃kuʀ] *vb voir* **concourir** ♦ *nm* competition; (*SCOL*) competitive examination; (*assistance*) aid, help; **recrutement par voie de** ~ recruitment by (competitive) examination; **apporter son** ~ **à** to give one's support to; ~ **de circonstances** combination of circumstances; ~ **hippique** horse show; *voir* **hors**.

concret, ète [kɔ̃kʀɛ, -ɛt] *adj* concrete.

concrètement [kɔ̃kʀɛtmɑ̃] *adv* in concrete terms.

concrétisation [kɔ̃kʀetizɑsjɔ̃] *nf* realization.

concrétiser [kɔ̃kʀetize] *vt* to realize; **se** ~ *vi* to materialize.

conçu, e [kɔ̃sy] *pp de* **concevoir**.

concubin, e [kɔ̃kybɛ̃, -in] *nm/f* (*JUR*) cohabitant.

concubinage [kɔ̃kybinaʒ] *nm* (*JUR*) cohabitation.

concupiscence [kɔ̃kypisɑ̃s] *nf* concupiscence.

concurremment [kɔ̃kyʀamɑ̃] *adv* concurrently; jointly.

concurrence [kɔ̃kyʀɑ̃s] *nf* competition; **jusqu'à ~ de** up to; **~ déloyale** unfair competition.
concurrencer [kɔ̃kyʀɑ̃se] *vt* to compete with; **ils nous concurrencent dangereusement** they are a serious threat to us.
concurrent, e [kɔ̃kyʀɑ̃, -ɑ̃t] *adj* competing ♦ *nm/f* (*SPORT, ÉCON etc*) competitor; (*SCOL*) candidate.
concurrentiel, le [kɔ̃kyʀɑ̃sjɛl] *adj* competitive.
conçus [kɔ̃sy] *vb voir* **concevoir**.
condamnable [kɔ̃dɑnabl(ə)] *adj* (*action, opinion*) reprehensible.
condamnation [kɔ̃dɑnɑsjɔ̃] *nf* (*action*) condemnation; sentencing; (*peine*) sentence; conviction; **~ à mort** death sentence.
condamné, e [kɔ̃dɑne] *nm/f* (*JUR*) convict.
condamner [kɔ̃dɑne] *vt* (*blâmer*) to condemn; (*JUR*) to sentence; (*porte, ouverture*) to fill in, block up; (*malade*) to give up (hope for); (*obliger*): **~ qn à qch/à faire** to condemn sb to sth/to do; **~ qn à 2 ans de prison** to sentence sb to 2 years' imprisonment; **~ qn à une amende** to impose a fine on sb.
condensateur [kɔ̃dɑ̃satœʀ] *nm* condenser.
condensation [kɔ̃dɑ̃sɑsjɔ̃] *nf* condensation.
condensé [kɔ̃dɑ̃se] *nm* digest.
condenser [kɔ̃dɑ̃se] *vt*, **se ~** *vi* to condense.
condescendance [kɔ̃desɑ̃dɑ̃s] *nf* condescension.
condescendant, e [kɔ̃desɑ̃dɑ̃, -ɑ̃t] *adj* (*personne, attitude*) condescending.
condescendre [kɔ̃desɑ̃dʀ(ə)] *vi*: **~ à** to condescend to.
condiment [kɔ̃dimɑ̃] *nm* condiment.
condisciple [kɔ̃disipl(ə)] *nm/f* school fellow, fellow student.
condition [kɔ̃disjɔ̃] *nf* condition; **~s** *nfpl* (*tarif, prix*) terms; (*circonstances*) conditions; **sans ~** *adj* unconditional ♦ *adv* unconditionally; **sous ~ que** on condition that; **à ~ de** *ou* **que** provided that; **en bonne ~** in good condition; **mettre en ~** (*SPORT etc*) to get fit; (*PSYCH*) to condition (mentally); **~s de vie** living conditions.
conditionnel, le [kɔ̃disjɔnɛl] *adj* conditional ♦ *nm* conditional (tense).
conditionnement [kɔ̃disjɔnmɑ̃] *nm* (*emballage*) packaging; (*fig*) conditioning.
conditionner [kɔ̃disjɔne] *vt* (*déterminer*) to determine; (*COMM: produit*) to package; (*fig: personne*) to condition; **air conditionné** air conditioning; **réflexe conditionné** conditioned reflex.
condoléances [kɔ̃dɔleɑ̃s] *nfpl* condolences.
conducteur, trice [kɔ̃dyktœʀ, -tʀis] *adj* (*ÉLEC*) conducting ♦ *nm/f* (*AUTO etc*) driver; (*machine*) operator ♦ *nm* (*ÉLEC etc*) conductor.
conduire [kɔ̃dɥiʀ] *vt* (*véhicule, passager*) to drive; (*délégation, troupeau*) to lead; **se ~** *vi* to behave; **~ vers/à** to lead towards/to; **~ qn quelque part** to take sb somewhere; to drive sb somewhere.
conduit, e [kɔ̃dɥi, -it] *pp de* **conduire** ♦ *nm* (*TECH*) conduit, pipe; (*ANAT*) duct, canal.
conduite [kɔ̃dɥit] *nf* (*en auto*) driving; (*comportement*) behaviour (*BRIT*), behavior (*US*); (*d'eau, de gaz*) pipe; **sous la ~ de** led by; **~ forcée** pressure pipe; **~ à gauche** left-hand drive; **~ intérieure** saloon (car).
cône [kon] *nm* cone; **en forme de ~** cone-shaped.
conf. *abr* (= *confort*): **tt ~** all mod cons (*BRIT*).
confection [kɔ̃fɛksjɔ̃] *nf* (*fabrication*) making; (*COUTURE*): **la ~** the clothing industry, the rag trade (*fam*); **vêtement de ~** ready-to-wear *ou* off-the-peg garment.
confectionner [kɔ̃fɛksjɔne] *vt* to make.
confédération [kɔ̃fedeʀɑsjɔ̃] *nf* confederation.
conférence [kɔ̃feʀɑ̃s] *nf* (*exposé*) lecture; (*pourparlers*) conference; **~ de presse** press conference; **~ au sommet** summit (conference).
conférencier, ière [kɔ̃feʀɑ̃sje, -jɛʀ] *nm/f* lecturer.
conférer [kɔ̃feʀe] *vt*: **~ à qn** (*titre, grade*) to confer on sb; **~ à qch/qn** (*aspect etc*) to endow sth/sb with, give (to) sth/sb.
confesser [kɔ̃fese] *vt* to confess; **se ~** *vi* (*REL*) to go to confession.
confesseur [kɔ̃fesœʀ] *nm* confessor.
confession [kɔ̃fɛsjɔ̃] *nf* confession; (*culte: catholique etc*) denomination.
confessionnal, aux [kɔ̃fesjɔnal, -o] *nm* confessional.
confessionnel, le [kɔ̃fesjɔnɛl] *adj* denominational.
confetti [kɔ̃feti] *nm* confetti *no pl*.
confiance [kɔ̃fjɑ̃s] *nf* confidence, trust; faith; **avoir ~ en** to have confidence *ou* faith in, trust; **faire ~ à** to trust; **en toute ~** with complete confidence; **de ~** trustworthy, reliable; **mettre qn en ~** to win sb's trust; **vote de ~** (*POL*) vote of confidence; **inspirer ~ à** to inspire confidence in; **~ en soi** self-confidence; *voir* **question**.
confiant, e [kɔ̃fjɑ̃, -ɑ̃t] *adj* confident; trusting.
confidence [kɔ̃fidɑ̃s] *nf* confidence.
confident, e [kɔ̃fidɑ̃, -ɑ̃t] *nm/f* confidant, confidante.
confidentiel, le [kɔ̃fidɑ̃sjɛl] *adj* confidential.
confidentiellement [kɔ̃fidɑ̃sjɛlmɑ̃] *adv* in confidence, confidentially.
confier [kɔ̃fje] *vt*: **~ à qn** (*objet en dépôt, travail etc*) to entrust to sb; (*secret, pensée*) to confide to sb; **se ~ à qn** to confide in sb.
configuration [kɔ̃figyʀɑsjɔ̃] *nf* configuration, layout; (*INFORM*) configuration.
configurer [kɔ̃figyʀe] *vt* to configure.
confiné, e [kɔ̃fine] *adj* enclosed; (*air*) stale.
confiner [kɔ̃fine] *vt*: **~ à** to confine to

(*toucher*) to border on; **se** ~ **dans** *ou* **à** to confine o.s. to.
confins [kɔ̃fɛ̃] *nmpl*: **aux** ~ **de** on the borders of.
confirmation [kɔ̃fiʀmɑsjɔ̃] *nf* confirmation.
confirmer [kɔ̃fiʀme] *vt* to confirm; ~ **qn dans une croyance/ses fonctions** to strengthen sb in a belief/his duties.
confiscation [kɔ̃fiskɑsjɔ̃] *nf* confiscation.
confiserie [kɔ̃fizʀi] *nf* (*magasin*) confectioner's *ou* sweet shop (*BRIT*), candy store (*US*); ~**s** *nfpl* (*bonbons*) confectionery *sg*, sweets, candy *no pl*.
confiseur, euse [kɔ̃fizœʀ, -øz] *nm/f* confectioner.
confisquer [kɔ̃fiske] *vt* to confiscate.
confit, e [kɔ̃fi, -it] *adj*: **fruits** ~**s** crystallized fruits ♦ *nm*: ~ **d'oie** potted goose.
confiture [kɔ̃fityʀ] *nf* jam; ~ **d'oranges** (orange) marmalade.
conflagration [kɔ̃flagʀɑsjɔ̃] *nf* cataclysm.
conflictuel, le [kɔ̃fliktɥɛl] *adj* full of clashes *ou* conflicts.
conflit [kɔ̃fli] *nm* conflict.
confluent [kɔ̃flyɑ̃] *nm* confluence.
confondre [kɔ̃fɔ̃dʀ(ə)] *vt* (*jumeaux, faits*) to confuse, mix up; (*témoin, menteur*) to confound; **se** ~ *vi* to merge; **se** ~ **en excuses** to offer profuse apologies, apologize profusely; ~ **qch/qn avec qch/qn d'autre** to mistake sth/sb for sth/sb else.
confondu, e [kɔ̃fɔ̃dy] *pp de* **confondre** ♦ *adj* (*stupéfait*) speechless, overcome; **toutes catégories** ~**es** taking all categories together.
conformation [kɔ̃fɔʀmɑsjɔ̃] *nf* conformation.
conforme [kɔ̃fɔʀm(ə)] *adj*: ~ **à** (*en accord avec*) in accordance with, in keeping with; (*identique à*) true to; **copie certifiée** ~ (*ADMIN*) certified copy; ~ **à la commande** as per order.
conformé, e [kɔ̃fɔʀme] *adj*: **bien** ~ well-formed.
conformément [kɔ̃fɔʀmemɑ̃] *adv*: ~ **à** in accordance with.
conformer [kɔ̃fɔʀme] *vt*: ~ **qch à** to model sth on; **se** ~ **à** to conform to.
conformisme [kɔ̃fɔʀmism(ə)] *nm* conformity.
conformiste [kɔ̃fɔʀmist(ə)] *adj, nm/f* conformist.
conformité [kɔ̃fɔʀmite] *nf* conformity; agreement; **en** ~ **avec** in accordance with.
confort [kɔ̃fɔʀ] *nm* comfort; **tout** ~ (*COMM*) with all mod cons (*BRIT*) *ou* modern conveniences.
confortable [kɔ̃fɔʀtabl(ə)] *adj* comfortable.
confortablement [kɔ̃fɔʀtabləmɑ̃] *adv* comfortably.
conforter [kɔ̃fɔʀte] *vt* to reinforce, strengthen.
confrère [kɔ̃fʀɛʀ] *nm* colleague; fellow member.
confrérie [kɔ̃fʀeʀi] *nf* brotherhood.
confrontation [kɔ̃fʀɔ̃tɑsjɔ̃] *nf* confrontation.
confronté, e [kɔ̃fʀɔ̃te] *adj*: ~ **à** confronted by, facing.
confronter [kɔ̃fʀɔ̃te] *vt* to confront; (*textes*) to compare, collate.
confus, e [kɔ̃fy, -yz] *adj* (*vague*) confused; (*embarrassé*) embarrassed.
confusément [kɔ̃fyzemɑ̃] *adv* (*distinguer, ressentir*) vaguely; (*parler*) confusedly.
confusion [kɔ̃fyzjɔ̃] *nf* (*voir confus*) confusion; embarrassment; (*voir confondre*) confusion; mixing up; (*erreur*) confusion; ~ **des peines** (*JUR*) concurrency of sentences.
congé [kɔ̃ʒe] *nm* (*vacances*) holiday; (*arrêt de travail*) time off *no pl*; leave *no pl*; (*MIL*) leave *no pl*; (*avis de départ*) notice; **en** ~ on holiday; off (work); on leave; **semaine/jour de** ~ week/day off; **prendre** ~ **de qn** to take one's leave of sb; **donner son** ~ **à** to hand *ou* give in one's notice to; ~ **de maladie** sick leave; ~ **de maternité** maternity leave; ~**s payés** paid holiday *ou* leave.
congédier [kɔ̃ʒedje] *vt* to dismiss.
congélateur [kɔ̃ʒelatœʀ] *nm* freezer, deep freeze.
congélation [kɔ̃ʒelɑsjɔ̃] *nf* freezing; (*de l'huile*) congealing.
congeler [kɔ̃ʒle] *vt*, **se** ~ *vi* to freeze.
congénère [kɔ̃ʒenɛʀ] *nm/f* fellow (bear *ou* lion *etc*), fellow creature.
congénital, e, aux [kɔ̃ʒenital, -o] *adj* congenital.
congère [kɔ̃ʒɛʀ] *nf* snowdrift.
congestion [kɔ̃ʒɛstjɔ̃] *nf* congestion; ~ **cérébrale** stroke; ~ **pulmonaire** congestion of the lungs.
congestionner [kɔ̃ʒɛstjɔne] *vt* to congest; (*MÉD*) to flush.
conglomérat [kɔ̃glɔmeʀa] *nm* conglomerate.
Congo [kɔ̃go] *nm*: **le** ~ (*pays, fleuve*) the Congo.
congolais, e [kɔ̃gɔlɛ, -ɛz] *adj* Congolese ♦ *nm/f*: **C~, e** Congolese.
congratuler [kɔ̃gʀatyle] *vt* to congratulate.
congre [kɔ̃gʀ(ə)] *nm* conger (eel).
congrégation [kɔ̃gʀegɑsjɔ̃] *nf* (*REL*) congregation; (*gén*) assembly; gathering.
congrès [kɔ̃gʀɛ] *nm* congress.
congressiste [kɔ̃gʀesist(ə)] *nm/f* delegate, participant (at a congress).
congru, e [kɔ̃gʀy] *adj*: **la portion** ~**e** the smallest *ou* meanest share.
conifère [kɔnifɛʀ] *nm* conifer.
conique [kɔnik] *adj* conical.
conjecture [kɔ̃ʒɛktyʀ] *nf* conjecture, speculation *no pl*.
conjecturer [kɔ̃ʒɛktyʀe] *vt, vi* to conjecture.
conjoint, e [kɔ̃ʒwɛ̃, -wɛ̃t] *adj* joint ♦ *nm/f* spouse.
conjointement [kɔ̃ʒwɛ̃tmɑ̃] *adv* jointly.
conjonctif, ive [kɔ̃ʒɔ̃ktif, -iv] *adj*: **tissu** ~ connective tissue.
conjonction [kɔ̃ʒɔ̃ksjɔ̃] *nf* (*LING*) conjunction.

conjonctivite [kɔ̃ʒɔ̃ktivit] *nf* conjunctivitis.
conjoncture [kɔ̃ʒɔ̃ktyʀ] *nf* circumstances *pl*; **la ~ (économique)** the economic climate *ou* situation.
conjoncturel, le [kɔ̃ʒɔ̃ktyʀɛl] *adj*: **variations/ tendances ~les** economic fluctuations/ trends.
conjugaison [kɔ̃ʒygɛzɔ̃] *nf* (*LING*) conjugation.
conjugal, e, aux [kɔ̃ʒygal, -o] *adj* conjugal; married.
conjugué, e [kɔ̃ʒyge] *adj* combined.
conjuguer [kɔ̃ʒyge] *vt* (*LING*) to conjugate; (*efforts etc*) to combine.
conjuration [kɔ̃ʒyʀɑsjɔ̃] *nf* conspiracy.
conjuré, e [kɔ̃ʒyʀe] *nm/f* conspirator.
conjurer [kɔ̃ʒyʀe] *vt* (*sort, maladie*) to avert; (*implorer*): **~ qn de faire qch** to beseech *ou* entreat sb to do sth.
connais [kɔnɛ], **connaissais** [kɔnɛsɛ] *etc vb voir* **connaître**.
connaissance [kɔnɛsɑ̃s] *nf* (*savoir*) knowledge *no pl*; (*personne connue*) acquaintance; (*conscience, perception*) consciousness; **~s** *nfpl* knowledge *no pl*; **être sans ~** to be unconscious; **perdre/reprendre ~** to lose/regain consciousness; **à ma/sa ~** to (the best of) my/his knowledge; **faire ~ avec qn** *ou* **la ~ de qn** (*rencontrer*) to meet sb; (*apprendre à connaître*) to get to know sb; **avoir ~ de** to be aware of; **prendre ~ de** (*document etc*) to peruse; **en ~ de cause** with full knowledge of the facts; **de ~** (*personne, visage*) familiar.
connaissant [kɔnɛsɑ̃] *etc vb voir* **connaître**.
connaissement [kɔnɛsmɑ̃] *nm* bill of lading.
connaisseur, euse [kɔnɛsœʀ, -øz] *nm/f* connoisseur ♦ *adj* expert.
connaître [kɔnɛtʀ(ə)] *vt* to know; (*éprouver*) to experience; (*avoir*) to have; to enjoy; **~ de nom/vue** to know by name/sight; **se ~** to know each other; (*soi-même*) to know o.s.; **ils se sont connus à Genève** they (first) met in Geneva; **s'y ~ en qch** to know about sth.
connasse [kɔnas] *nf* (*fam!*) stupid bitch (*!*) *ou* cow (*!*).
connecté, e [kɔnɛkte] *adj* (*INFORM*) on line.
connecter [kɔnɛkte] *vt* to connect.
connerie [kɔnʀi] *nf* (*fam*) (bloody) stupid (*BRIT*) *ou* damn-fool (*US*) thing to do *ou* say.
connexe [kɔnɛks(ə)] *adj* closely related.
connexion [kɔnɛksjɔ̃] *nf* connection.
connivence [kɔnivɑ̃s] *nf* connivance.
connotation [kɔnɔtɑsjɔ̃] *nf* connotation.
connu, e [kɔny] *pp de* **connaître** ♦ *adj* (*célèbre*) well-known.
conque [kɔ̃k] *nf* (*coquille*) conch (shell).
conquérant, e [kɔ̃keʀɑ̃, -ɑ̃t] *nm/f* conqueror.
conquérir [kɔ̃keʀiʀ] *vt* to conquer, win.
conquerrai [kɔ̃kɛʀʀe] *etc vb voir* **conquérir**.
conquête [kɔ̃kɛt] *nf* conquest.
conquière, conquiers [kɔ̃kjɛʀ] *etc vb voir* **conquérir**.
conquis, e [kɔ̃ki, -iz] *pp de* **conquérir**.
consacrer [kɔ̃sakʀe] *vt* (*REL*): **~ qch (à)** to consecrate sth (to); (*fig: usage etc*) to sanction, establish; (*employer*): **~ qch à** to devote *ou* dedicate sth to; **se ~ à qch/faire** to dedicate *ou* devote o.s. to sth/to doing.
consanguin, e [kɔ̃sɑ̃gɛ̃, -in] *adj* between blood relations; **frère ~** half-brother (*on father's side*); **mariage ~** intermarriage.
consciemment [kɔ̃sjamɑ̃] *adv* consciously.
conscience [kɔ̃sjɑ̃s] *nf* conscience; (*perception*) consciousness; **avoir/prendre ~ de** to be/become aware of; **perdre/reprendre ~** to lose/regain consciousness; **avoir bonne/ mauvaise ~** to have a clear/guilty conscience; **en (toute) ~** in all conscience; **~ professionnelle** professional conscience.
consciencieux, euse [kɔ̃sjɑ̃sjø, -øz] *adj* conscientious.
conscient, e [kɔ̃sjɑ̃, -ɑ̃t] *adj* conscious; **~ de** aware *ou* conscious of.
conscription [kɔ̃skʀipsjɔ̃] *nf* conscription.
conscrit [kɔ̃skʀi] *nm* conscript.
consécration [kɔ̃sekʀɑsjɔ̃] *nf* consecration.
consécutif, ive [kɔ̃sekytif, -iv] *adj* consecutive; **~ à** following upon.
consécutivement [kɔ̃sekytivmɑ̃] *adv* consecutively; **~ à** following on.
conseil [kɔ̃sɛj] *nm* (*avis*) piece of advice, advice *no pl*; (*assemblée*) council; (*expert*): **~ en recrutement** recruitment consultant ♦ *adj*: **ingénieur-~** engineering consultant; **tenir ~** to hold a meeting; to deliberate; **donner un ~** *ou* **des ~s à qn** to give sb (a piece of) advice; **demander ~ à qn** to ask sb's advice; **prendre ~ (auprès de qn)** to take advice (from sb); **~ d'administration (CA)** board (of directors); **~ de classe** (*SCOL*) *meeting of teachers, parents and class representatives to discuss pupils' progress*; **~ de discipline** disciplinary committee; **~ général** regional council; **~ de guerre** court-martial; **le ~ des ministres** ≈ the Cabinet; **~ municipal (CM)** town council; **~ régional** *regional board of elected representatives*; **~ de révision** recruitment *ou* draft (*US*) board; *see boxed note*.

> **CONSEIL GÉNÉRAL**
>
> *Each 'département' of France, is run by a* **'Conseil général'** *whose remit covers personnel, transport infrastructure, housing, school grants and economic development. The council is made up of 'conseillers généraux' each of whom represents a 'canton' and is elected for a six-year term. Half of the council's members are elected every three years.*

conseiller[1] [kɔ̃seje] *vt* (*personne*) to advise; (*méthode, action*) to recommend, advise; **~ qch à qn** to recommend sth to sb; **~ à qn de faire qch** to advise sb to do sth.

conseiller[2], ère [kɔ̃seje, -ɛʀ] *nm/f* adviser; ~ **général** regional councillor; ~ **matrimonial** marriage guidance counsellor; ~ **municipal** town councillor.
consensuel, le [kɔ̃sɑ̃sɥɛl] *adj* consensual.
consensus [kɔ̃sɛ̃sys] *nm* consensus.
consentement [kɔ̃sɑ̃tmɑ̃] *nm* consent.
consentir [kɔ̃sɑ̃tiʀ] *vt*: ~ **(à qch/faire)** to agree *ou* consent (to sth/to doing); ~ **qch à qn** to grant sb sth.
conséquence [kɔ̃sekɑ̃s] *nf* consequence, outcome; ~**s** *nfpl* consequences, repercussions; **en** ~ (*donc*) consequently; (*de façon appropriée*) accordingly; **ne pas tirer à** ~ to be unlikely to have any repercussions; **sans** ~ unimportant; **de** ~ important.
conséquent, e [kɔ̃sekɑ̃, -ɑ̃t] *adj* logical, rational; (*fam: important*) substantial; **par** ~ consequently.
conservateur, trice [kɔ̃sɛʀvatœʀ, -tʀis] *adj* conservative ♦ *nm/f* (*POL*) conservative; (*de musée*) curator.
conservation [kɔ̃sɛʀvɑsjɔ̃] *nf* retention; keeping; preserving; preservation.
conservatisme [kɔ̃sɛʀvatism(ə)] *nm* conservatism.
conservatoire [kɔ̃sɛʀvatwaʀ] *nm* academy; (*ÉCOLOGIE*) conservation area.
conserve [kɔ̃sɛʀv(ə)] *nf* (*gén pl*) canned *ou* tinned (*BRIT*) food; ~**s de poisson** canned *ou* tinned (*BRIT*) fish; **en** ~ canned, tinned (*BRIT*); **de** ~ (*ensemble*) in concert; (*naviguer*) in convoy.
conservé, e [kɔ̃sɛʀve] *adj*: **bien** ~ (*personne*) well-preserved.
conserver [kɔ̃sɛʀve] *vt* (*faculté*) to retain, keep; (*habitude*) to keep up; (*amis, livres*) to keep; (*préserver, aussi CULIN*) to preserve; **se** ~ *vi* (*aliments*) to keep; **"~ au frais"** "store in a cool place".
conserverie [kɔ̃sɛʀvəʀi] *nf* canning factory.
considérable [kɔ̃sideʀabl(ə)] *adj* considerable, significant, extensive.
considération [kɔ̃sideʀɑsjɔ̃] *nf* consideration; (*estime*) esteem, respect; ~**s** *nfpl* (*remarques*) reflections; **prendre en** ~ to take into consideration *ou* account; **ceci mérite** ~ this is worth considering; **en** ~ **de** given, because of.
considéré, e [kɔ̃sideʀe] *adj* respected; **tout bien** ~ all things considered.
considérer [kɔ̃sideʀe] *vt* to consider; (*regarder*) to consider, study; ~ **qch comme** to regard sth as.
consigne [kɔ̃siɲ] *nf* (*COMM*) deposit; (*de gare*) left luggage (office) (*BRIT*), checkroom (*US*); (*punition: SCOL*) detention; (*: MIL*) confinement to barracks; (*ordre, instruction*) instructions *pl*; ~ **automatique** left-luggage locker; ~**s de sécurité** safety instructions.
consigné, e [kɔ̃siɲe] *adj* (*COMM: bouteille, emballage*) returnable; **non** ~ non-returnable.
consigner [kɔ̃siɲe] *vt* (*note, pensée*) to record; (*marchandises*) to deposit; (*punir: MIL*) to confine to barracks; (*: élève*) to put in detention; (*COMM*) to put a deposit on.
consistance [kɔ̃sistɑ̃s] *nf* consistency.
consistant, e [kɔ̃sistɑ̃, -ɑ̃t] *adj* thick; solid.
consister [kɔ̃siste] *vi*: ~ **en/dans/à faire** to consist of/in/in doing.
consœur [kɔ̃sœʀ] *nf* (lady) colleague; fellow member.
consolation [kɔ̃sɔlɑsjɔ̃] *nf* consolation *no pl*, comfort *no pl*.
console [kɔ̃sɔl] *nf* console; ~ **graphique** *ou* **de visualisation** (*INFORM*) visual display unit, VDU; ~ **de jeux vidéo** games console.
consoler [kɔ̃sɔle] *vt* to console; **se** ~ **(de qch)** to console o.s. (for sth).
consolider [kɔ̃sɔlide] *vt* to strengthen, reinforce; (*fig*) to consolidate; **bilan consolidé** consolidated balance sheet.
consommateur, trice [kɔ̃sɔmatœʀ, -tʀis] *nm/f* (*ÉCON*) consumer; (*dans un café*) customer.
consommation [kɔ̃sɔmɑsjɔ̃] *nf* consumption; (*JUR*) consummation; (*boisson*) drink; ~ **aux 100 km** (*AUTO*) (fuel) consumption per 100 km, ≈ miles per gallon (mpg), ≈ gas mileage (*US*); **de** ~ (*biens, société*) consumer *cpd*.
consommé, e [kɔ̃sɔme] *adj* consummate ♦ *nm* consommé.
consommer [kɔ̃sɔme] *vt* (*suj: personne*) to eat *ou* drink, consume; (*suj: voiture, usine, poêle*) to use, consume; (*JUR*) to consummate ♦ *vi* (*dans un café*) to (have a) drink.
consonance [kɔ̃sɔnɑ̃s] *nf* consonance; **nom à** ~ **étrangère** foreign-sounding name.
consonne [kɔ̃sɔn] *nf* consonant.
consortium [kɔ̃sɔʀsjɔm] *nm* consortium.
consorts [kɔ̃sɔʀ] *nmpl*: **et** ~ (*péj*) and company, and his bunch *ou* like.
conspirateur, trice [kɔ̃spiʀatœʀ, -tʀis] *nm/f* conspirator, plotter.
conspiration [kɔ̃spiʀɑsjɔ̃] *nf* conspiracy.
conspirer [kɔ̃spiʀe] *vi* to conspire, plot; ~ **à** (*tendre à*) to conspire to.
conspuer [kɔ̃spɥe] *vt* to boo, shout down.
constamment [kɔ̃stamɑ̃] *adv* constantly.
constance [kɔ̃stɑ̃s] *nf* permanence, constancy; (*d'une amitié*) steadfastness; **travailler avec** ~ to work steadily; **il faut de la** ~ **pour la supporter** (*fam*) you need a lot of patience to put up with her.
constant, e [kɔ̃stɑ̃, -ɑ̃t] *adj* constant; (*personne*) steadfast ♦ *nf* constant.
Constantinople [kɔ̃stɑ̃tinɔpl(ə)] *n* Constantinople.
constat [kɔ̃sta] *nm* (*d'huissier*) certified report (*by bailiff*); (*de police*) report; (*observation*) (observed) fact, observation; (*affirmation*) statement; ~ **(à l'amiable)** (*jointly agreed*) *statement for insurance purposes*.
constatation [kɔ̃statɑsjɔ̃] *nf* noticing; certifying; (*remarque*) observation.

constater [kɔ̃state] *vt* (*remarquer*) to note, notice; (*ADMIN, JUR: attester*) to certify; (*dégâts*) to note; ~ **que** (*dire*) to state that.
constellation [kɔ̃stelɑsjɔ̃] *nf* constellation.
constellé, e [kɔ̃stele] *adj*: ~ **de** (*étoiles*) studded *ou* spangled with; (*taches*) spotted with.
consternant, e [kɔ̃stɛʀnɑ̃ -ɑ̃t] *adj* (*nouvelle*) dismaying; (*attristant, étonnant: bêtise*) appalling.
consternation [kɔ̃stɛʀnɑsjɔ̃] *nf* consternation, dismay.
consterner [kɔ̃stɛʀne] *vt* to dismay.
constipation [kɔ̃stipɑsjɔ̃] *nf* constipation.
constipé, e [kɔ̃stipe] *adj* constipated; (*fig*) stiff.
constituant, e [kɔ̃stitɥɑ̃, -ɑ̃t] *adj* (*élément*) constituent; **assemblée** ~**e** (*POL*) constituent assembly.
constitué, e [kɔ̃stitɥe] *adj*: ~ **de** made up *ou* composed of; **bien** ~ of sound constitution; well-formed.
constituer [kɔ̃stitɥe] *vt* (*comité, équipe*) to set up, form; (*dossier, collection*) to put together, build up; (*suj: éléments, parties: composer*) to make up, constitute; (*représenter, être*) to constitute; **se** ~ **prisonnier** to give o.s. up; **se** ~ **partie civile** *to bring an independent action for damages*.
constitution [kɔ̃stitysjɔ̃] *nf* setting up; building up; (*composition*) composition, make-up; (*santé, POL*) constitution.
constitutionnel, le [kɔ̃stitysjɔnɛl] *adj* constitutional.
constructeur [kɔ̃stʀyktœʀ] *nm* manufacturer, builder.
constructif, ive [kɔ̃stʀyktif, -iv] *adj* (*positif*) constructive.
construction [kɔ̃stʀyksjɔ̃] *nf* construction, building.
construire [kɔ̃stʀɥiʀ] *vt* to build, construct; **se** ~: **l'immeuble s'est construit très vite** the building went up *ou* was built very quickly.
consul [kɔ̃syl] *nm* consul.
consulaire [kɔ̃sylɛʀ] *adj* consular.
consulat [kɔ̃syla] *nm* consulate.
consultant, e [kɔ̃syltɑ̃, -ɑ̃t] *adj* consultant.
consultatif, ive [kɔ̃syltatif, -iv] *adj* advisory.
consultation [kɔ̃syltɑsjɔ̃] *nf* consultation; ~**s** *nfpl* (*POL*) talks; **être en** ~ (*délibération*) to be in consultation; (*médecin*) to be consulting; **aller à la** ~ (*MÉD*) to go to the surgery (*BRIT*) *ou* doctor's office (*US*); **heures de** ~ (*MÉD*) surgery (*BRIT*) *ou* office (*US*) hours.
consulter [kɔ̃sylte] *vt* to consult ♦ *vi* (*médecin*) to hold surgery (*BRIT*), be in (the office) (*US*); **se** ~ to confer.
consumer [kɔ̃syme] *vt* to consume; **se** ~ *vi* to burn; **se** ~ **de chagrin/douleur** to be consumed with sorrow/grief.
consumérisme [kɔ̃symeʀism(ə)] *nm* consumerism.
contact [kɔ̃takt] *nm* contact; **au** ~ **de** (*air, peau*) on contact with; (*gens*) through contact with; **mettre/couper le** ~ (*AUTO*) to switch on/off the ignition; **entrer en** ~ (*fils, objets*) to come into contact, make contact; **se mettre en** ~ **avec** (*RADIO*) to make contact with; **prendre** ~ **avec** (*relation d'affaires, connaissance*) to get in touch *ou* contact with.
contacter [kɔ̃takte] *vt* to contact, get in touch with.
contagieux, euse [kɔ̃taʒjø, -øz] *adj* contagious; infectious.
contagion [kɔ̃taʒjɔ̃] *nf* contagion.
container [kɔ̃tɛnɛʀ] *nm* container.
contamination [kɔ̃taminɑsjɔ̃] *nf* infection; contamination.
contaminer [kɔ̃tamine] *vt* (*par un virus*) to infect; (*par des radiations*) to contaminate.
conte [kɔ̃t] *nm* tale; ~ **de fées** fairy tale.
contemplatif, ive [kɔ̃tɑ̃platif, -iv] *adj* contemplative.
contemplation [kɔ̃tɑ̃plɑsjɔ̃] *nf* contemplation; (*REL, PHILOSOPHIE*) meditation.
contempler [kɔ̃tɑ̃ple] *vt* to contemplate, gaze at.
contemporain, e [kɔ̃tɑ̃pɔʀɛ̃, -ɛn] *adj, nm/f* contemporary.
contenance [kɔ̃tnɑ̃s] *nf* (*d'un récipient*) capacity; (*attitude*) bearing, attitude; **perdre** ~ to lose one's composure; **se donner une** ~ to give the impression of composure; **faire bonne** ~ **(devant)** to put on a bold front (in the face of).
conteneur [kɔ̃tnœʀ] *nm* container; ~ **(de bouteilles)** bottle bank.
conteneurisation [kɔ̃tnœʀizɑsjɔ̃] *nf* containerization.
contenir [kɔ̃tniʀ] *vt* to contain; (*avoir une capacité de*) to hold; **se** ~ (*se retenir*) to control o.s. *ou* one's emotions, contain o.s.
content, e [kɔ̃tɑ̃, -ɑ̃t] *adj* pleased, glad; ~ **de** pleased with; **je serais** ~ **que tu ...** I would be pleased if you ....
contentement [kɔ̃tɑ̃tmɑ̃] *nm* contentment, satisfaction.
contenter [kɔ̃tɑ̃te] *vt* to satisfy, please; (*envie*) to satisfy; **se** ~ **de** to content o.s. with.
contentieux [kɔ̃tɑ̃sjø] *nm* (*COMM*) litigation; (*service*) litigation department; (*POL etc*) contentious issues *pl*.
contenu, e [kɔ̃tny] *pp de* **contenir** ♦ *nm* (*d'un bol*) contents *pl*; (*d'un texte*) content.
conter [kɔ̃te] *vt* to recount, relate; **en** ~ **de belles à qn** to tell tall stories to sb.
contestable [kɔ̃tɛstabl(ə)] *adj* questionable.
contestataire [kɔ̃tɛstatɛʀ] *adj* (*journal, étudiant*) anti-establishment ♦ *nm/f* (anti-establishment) protester.
contestation [kɔ̃tɛstɑsjɔ̃] *nf* questioning, contesting; (*POL*): **la** ~ anti-establishment activity, protest.
conteste [kɔ̃tɛst(ə)]: **sans** ~ *adv* unquestion-

ably, indisputably.
contesté, e [kɔ̃tɛste] *adj (roman, écrivain)* controversial.
contester [kɔ̃tɛste] *vt* to question, contest ♦ *vi (POL, gén)* to protest, rebel (against established authority).
conteur, euse [kɔ̃tœʀ, -øz] *nm/f* story-teller.
contexte [kɔ̃tɛkst(ə)] *nm* context.
contiendrai [kɔ̃tjɛ̃dʀe], **contiens** [kɔ̃tjɛ̃] *etc vb voir* **contenir**.
contigu, ë [kɔ̃tigy] *adj*: ~ **(à)** adjacent (to).
continent [kɔ̃tinɑ̃] *nm* continent.
continental, e, aux [kɔ̃tinɑ̃tal, -o] *adj* continental.
contingences [kɔ̃tɛ̃ʒɑ̃s] *nfpl* contingencies.
contingent [kɔ̃tɛ̃ʒɑ̃] *nm (MIL)* contingent; *(COMM)* quota.
contingenter [kɔ̃tɛ̃ʒɑ̃te] *vt (COMM)* to fix a quota on.
contins [kɔ̃tɛ̃] *etc vb voir* **contenir**.
continu, e [kɔ̃tiny] *adj* continuous; **(courant)** ~ direct current, DC.
continuation [kɔ̃tinɥɑsjɔ̃] *nf* continuation.
continuel, le [kɔ̃tinɥɛl] *adj (qui se répète)* constant, continual; *(continu)* continuous.
continuellement [kɔ̃tinɥɛlmɑ̃] *adv* continually; continuously.
continuer [kɔ̃tinɥe] *vt (travail, voyage etc)* to continue (with), carry on (with), go on with; *(prolonger: alignement, rue)* to continue ♦ *vi (pluie, vie, bruit)* to continue, go on; *(voyageur)* to go on; **se** ~ *vi* to carry on; ~ **à** *ou* **de faire** to go on *ou* continue doing.
continuité [kɔ̃tinɥite] *nf* continuity; continuation.
contondant, e [kɔ̃tɔ̃dɑ̃, -ɑ̃t] *adj*: **arme** ~**e** blunt instrument.
contorsion [kɔ̃tɔʀsjɔ̃] *nf* contortion.
contorsionner [kɔ̃tɔʀsjɔne]: **se** ~ *vi* to contort o.s., writhe about.
contorsionniste [kɔ̃tɔʀsjɔnist(ə)] *nm/f* contortionist.
contour [kɔ̃tuʀ] *nm* outline, contour; ~**s** *nmpl (d'une rivière etc)* windings.
contourner [kɔ̃tuʀne] *vt* to bypass, walk *(ou* drive) round.
contraceptif, ive [kɔ̃tʀasɛptif, -iv] *adj, nm* contraceptive.
contraception [kɔ̃tʀasɛpsjɔ̃] *nf* contraception.
contracté, e [kɔ̃tʀakte] *adj (muscle)* tense, contracted; *(personne: tendu)* tense, tensed up; **article** ~ *(LING)* contracted article.
contracter [kɔ̃tʀakte] *vt (muscle etc)* to tense, contract; *(maladie, dette, obligation)* to contract; *(assurance)* to take out; **se** ~ *vi (métal, muscles)* to contract.
contraction [kɔ̃tʀaksjɔ̃] *nf* contraction.
contractuel, le [kɔ̃tʀaktɥɛl] *adj* contractual ♦ *nm/f (agent)* traffic warden; *(employé)* contract employee.
contradiction [kɔ̃tʀadiksjɔ̃] *nf* contradiction.
contradictoire [kɔ̃tʀadiktwaʀ] *adj* contradictory, conflicting; **débat** ~ (open) debate.
contraignant, e [kɔ̃tʀɛɲɑ̃, -ɑ̃t] *vb voir* **contraindre** ♦ *adj* restricting.
contraindre [kɔ̃tʀɛ̃dʀ(ə)] *vt*: ~ **qn à faire** to force *ou* compel sb to do.
contraint, e [kɔ̃tʀɛ̃, -ɛ̃t] *pp de* **contraindre** ♦ *adj (mine, air)* constrained, forced ♦ *nf* constraint; **sans** ~**e** unrestrainedly, unconstrainedly.
contraire [kɔ̃tʀɛʀ] *adj, nm* opposite; ~ **à** contrary to; **au** ~ *adv* on the contrary.
contrairement [kɔ̃tʀɛʀmɑ̃] *adv*: ~ **à** contrary to, unlike.
contralto [kɔ̃tʀalto] *nm* contralto.
contrariant, e [kɔ̃tʀaʀjɑ̃, -ɑ̃t] *adj (personne)* contrary, perverse; *(incident)* annoying.
contrarier [kɔ̃tʀaʀje] *vt (personne)* to annoy, bother; *(fig)* to impede; to thwart, frustrate.
contrariété [kɔ̃tʀaʀjete] *nf* annoyance.
contraste [kɔ̃tʀast(ə)] *nm* contrast.
contraster [kɔ̃tʀaste] *vt, vi* to contrast.
contrat [kɔ̃tʀa] *nm* contract; *(fig: accord, pacte)* agreement; ~ **de travail** employment contract.
contravention [kɔ̃tʀavɑ̃sjɔ̃] *nf (infraction)*: ~ **à** contravention of; *(amende)* fine; *(PV pour stationnement interdit)* parking ticket; **dresser** ~ **à** *(automobiliste)* to book; to write out a parking ticket for.
contre [kɔ̃tʀ(ə)] *prép* against; *(en échange)* (in exchange) for; **par** ~ on the other hand.
contre-amiral, aux [kɔ̃tʀamiʀal, -o] *nm* rear admiral.
contre-attaque [kɔ̃tʀatak] *nf* counterattack.
contre-attaquer [kɔ̃tʀatake] *vi* to counterattack.
contre-balancer [kɔ̃tʀəbalɑ̃se] *vt* to counterbalance; *(fig)* to offset.
contrebande [kɔ̃tʀəbɑ̃d] *nf (trafic)* contraband, smuggling; *(marchandise)* contraband, smuggled goods *pl*; **faire la** ~ **de** to smuggle.
contrebandier, ière [kɔ̃tʀəbɑ̃dje, -jɛʀ] *nm/f* smuggler.
contrebas [kɔ̃tʀəbɑ]: **en** ~ *adv* (down) below.
contrebasse [kɔ̃tʀəbɑs] *nf* (double) bass.
contrebassiste [kɔ̃tʀəbɑsist(ə)] *nm/f* (double) bass player.
contre-braquer [kɔ̃tʀəbʀake] *vi* to steer into a skid.
contrecarrer [kɔ̃tʀəkaʀe] *vt* to thwart.
contrechamp [kɔ̃tʀəʃɑ̃] *nm (CINÉ)* reverse shot.
contrecœur [kɔ̃tʀəkœʀ]: **à** ~ *adv* (be)grudgingly, reluctantly.
contrecoup [kɔ̃tʀəku] *nm* repercussions *pl*; **par** ~ as an indirect consequence.
contre-courant [kɔ̃tʀəkuʀɑ̃]: **à** ~ *adv* against the current.
contredire [kɔ̃tʀədiʀ] *vt (personne)* to contradict; *(témoignage, assertion, faits)* to refute; **se** ~ to contradict o.s.
contredit, e [kɔ̃tʀədi, -it] *pp de* **contredire**

♦ *nm*: **sans ~** without question.
contrée [kɔ̃tʀe] *nf* region; land.
contre-écrou [kɔ̃tʀekʀu] *nm* lock nut.
contre-enquête [kɔ̃tʀɑ̃kɛt] *nf* counter-inquiry.
contre-espionnage [kɔ̃tʀɛspjɔnaʒ] *nm* counter-espionage.
contre-exemple [kɔ̃tʀɛgzɑ̃pl(ə)] *nf* counter-example.
contre-expertise [kɔ̃tʀɛkspɛʀtiz] *nf* second (expert) assessment.
contrefaçon [kɔ̃tʀəfasɔ̃] *nf* forgery; **~ de brevet** patent infringement.
contrefaire [kɔ̃tʀəfɛʀ] *vt* (*document, signature*) to forge, counterfeit; (*personne, démarche*) to mimic; (*dénaturer: sa voix etc*) to disguise.
contrefait, e [kɔ̃tʀəfɛ, -ɛt] *pp de* **contrefaire** ♦ *adj* misshapen, deformed.
contrefasse [kɔ̃tʀəfas], **contreferai** [kɔ̃tʀəfʀe] *etc vb voir* **contrefaire**.
contre-filet [kɔ̃tʀəfilɛ] *nm* (*CULIN*) sirloin.
contreforts [kɔ̃tʀəfɔʀ] *nmpl* foothills.
contre-haut [kɔ̃tʀəo]: **en ~** *adv* (up) above.
contre-indication [kɔ̃tʀɛ̃dikɑsjɔ̃] *nf* contra-indication.
contre-indiqué, e [kɔ̃tʀɛ̃dike] *adj* (*MÉD*) contraindicated.
contre-interrogatoire [kɔ̃tʀɛ̃tɛʀɔgatwaʀ] *nm*: **faire subir un ~ à qn** to cross-examine sb.
contre-jour [kɔ̃tʀəʒuʀ]: **à ~** *adv* against the light.
contremaître [kɔ̃tʀəmɛtʀ(ə)] *nm* foreman.
contre-manifestant, e [kɔ̃tʀəmanifɛstɑ̃, -ɑ̃t] *nm/f* counter-demonstrator.
contre-manifestation [kɔ̃tʀəmanifɛstɑsjɔ̃] *nf* counter-demonstration.
contremarque [kɔ̃tʀəmaʀk(ə)] *nf* (*ticket*) pass-out ticket.
contre-offensive [kɔ̃tʀɔfɑ̃siv] *nf* counter-offensive.
contre-ordre [kɔ̃tʀɔʀdʀ(ə)] *nm* = **controrde**.
contrepartie [kɔ̃tʀəpaʀti] *nf* compensation; **en ~** in compensation; in return.
contre-performance [kɔ̃tʀəpɛʀfɔʀmɑ̃s] *nf* below-average performance.
contrepèterie [kɔ̃tʀəpetʀi] *nf* spoonerism.
contre-pied [kɔ̃tʀəpje] *nm* (*inverse, opposé*): **le ~ de** ... the exact opposite of ...; **prendre le ~ de** to take the opposing view of; to take the opposite course to; **prendre qn à ~** (*SPORT*) to wrong-foot sb.
contre-plaqué [kɔ̃tʀəplake] *nm* plywood.
contre-plongée [kɔ̃tʀəplɔ̃ʒe] *nf* low-angle shot.
contrepoids [kɔ̃tʀəpwa] *nm* counterweight, counterbalance; **faire ~** to act as a counter-balance.
contrepoil [kɔ̃tʀəpwal]: **à ~** *adv* the wrong way.
contrepoint [kɔ̃tʀəpwɛ̃] *nm* counterpoint.
contrepoison [kɔ̃tʀəpwazɔ̃] *nm* antidote.
contrer [kɔ̃tʀe] *vt* to counter.
contre-révolution [kɔ̃tʀəʀevɔlysjɔ̃] *nf* counter-revolution.
contre-révolutionnaire [kɔ̃tʀəʀevɔlysjɔnɛʀ] *nm/f* counter-revolutionary.
contresens [kɔ̃tʀəsɑ̃s] *nm* misinterpretation; (*mauvaise traduction*) mistranslation; (*absurdité*) nonsense *no pl*; **à ~** *adv* the wrong way.
contresigner [kɔ̃tʀəsiɲe] *vt* to countersign.
contretemps [kɔ̃tʀətɑ̃] *nm* hitch, contretemps; **à ~** *adv* (*MUS*) out of time; (*fig*) at an inopportune moment.
contre-terrorisme [kɔ̃tʀətɛʀɔʀism(ə)] *nm* counter-terrorism.
contre-terroriste [kɔ̃tʀətɛʀɔʀist(ə)] *nm/f* counter-terrorist.
contre-torpilleur [kɔ̃tʀətɔʀpijœʀ] *nm* destroyer.
contrevenant, e [kɔ̃tʀəvnɑ̃, -ɑ̃t] *vb voir* **contrevenir** ♦ *nm/f* offender.
contrevenir [kɔ̃tʀəvniʀ]: **~ à** *vt* to contravene.
contre-voie [kɔ̃tʀəvwa]: **à ~** *adv* (*en sens inverse*) on the wrong track; (*du mauvais côté*) on the wrong side.
contribuable [kɔ̃tʀibɥabl(ə)] *nm/f* taxpayer.
contribuer [kɔ̃tʀibɥe]: **~ à** *vt* to contribute towards.
contribution [kɔ̃tʀibysjɔ̃] *nf* contribution; **les ~s** (*bureaux*) the tax office; **mettre à ~** to call upon; **~s directes/indirectes** direct/indirect taxation.
contrit, e [kɔ̃tʀi, -it] *adj* contrite.
contrôlable [kɔ̃tʀolabl(ə)] *adj* (*maîtrisable: situation, débit*) controllable; (*alibi, déclarations*) verifiable.
contrôle [kɔ̃tʀol] *nm* checking *no pl*, check; supervision; monitoring; (*test*) test, examination; **perdre le ~ de son véhicule** to lose control of one's vehicle; **~ des changes** (*COMM*) exchange controls; **~ continu** (*SCOL*) continuous assessment; **~ d'identité** identity check; **~ des naissances** birth control; **~ des prix** price control.
contrôler [kɔ̃tʀole] *vt* (*vérifier*) to check; (*surveiller*) to supervise; to monitor, control; (*maîtriser, COMM: firme*) to control; **se ~** to control o.s.
contrôleur, euse [kɔ̃tʀolœʀ, -øz] *nm/f* (*de train*) (ticket) inspector; (*de bus*) (bus) conductor/tress; **~ de la navigation aérienne, ~ aérien** air traffic controller; **~ financier** financial controller.
contrordre [kɔ̃tʀɔʀdʀ(ə)] *nm* counter-order, countermand; **sauf ~** unless otherwise directed.
controverse [kɔ̃tʀɔvɛʀs(ə)] *nf* controversy.
controversé, e [kɔ̃tʀɔvɛʀse] *adj* (*personnage, question*) controversial.
contumace [kɔ̃tymas]: **par ~** *adv* in absentia.
contusion [kɔ̃tyzjɔ̃] *nf* bruise, contusion.
contusionné, e [kɔ̃tyzjɔne] *adj* bruised.
conurbation [kɔnyʀbɑsjɔ̃] *nf* conurbation.
convaincant, e [kɔ̃vɛ̃kɑ̃, -ɑ̃t] *vb voir* **convaincre**

♦ *adj* convincing.

convaincre [kɔ̃vɛ̃kʀ(ə)] *vt*: ~ **qn (de qch)** to convince sb (of sth); ~ **qn (de faire)** to persuade sb (to do); ~ **qn de** (*JUR*: *délit*) to convict sb of.

convaincu, e [kɔ̃vɛ̃ky] *pp de* **convaincre** ♦ *adj*: **d'un ton** ~ with conviction.

convainquais [kɔ̃vɛ̃kɛ] *etc vb voir* **convaincre**.

convalescence [kɔ̃valesɑ̃s] *nf* convalescence; **maison de** ~ convalescent home.

convalescent, e [kɔ̃valesɑ̃, -ɑ̃t] *adj, nm/f* convalescent.

convenable [kɔ̃vnabl(ə)] *adj* suitable; (*décent*) acceptable, proper; (*assez bon*) decent, acceptable; adequate, passable.

convenablement [kɔ̃vnabləmɑ̃] *adv* (*placé, choisi*) suitably; (*s'habiller, s'exprimer*) properly; (*payé, logé*) decently.

convenance [kɔ̃vnɑ̃s] *nf*: **à ma/votre** ~ to my/your liking; ~**s** *nfpl* proprieties.

convenir [kɔ̃vniʀ] *vt* to be suitable; ~ **à** to suit; **il convient de** it is advisable to; (*bienséant*) it is right *ou* proper to; ~ **de** (*bienfondé de qch*) to admit (to), acknowledge; (*date, somme etc*) to agree upon; ~ **que** (*admettre*) to admit that, acknowledge the fact that; ~ **de faire qch** to agree to do sth; **il a été convenu que** it has been agreed that; **comme convenu** as agreed.

convention [kɔ̃vɑ̃sjɔ̃] *nf* convention; ~**s** *nfpl* (*convenances*) convention *sg*, social conventions; **de** ~ conventional; ~ **collective** (*ÉCON*) collective agreement.

conventionnalisme [kɔ̃vɑ̃sjɔnalism(ə)] *nm* (*des idées*) conventionality.

conventionné, e [kɔ̃vɑ̃sjɔne] *adj* (*ADMIN*) *applying charges laid down by the state*.

conventionnel, le [kɔ̃vɑ̃sjɔnɛl] *adj* conventional.

conventionnellement [kɔ̃vɑ̃sjɔnɛlmɑ̃] *adv* conventionally.

conventuel, le [kɔ̃vɑ̃tɥɛl] *adj* monastic; monastery *cpd*; conventual, convent *cpd*.

convenu, e [kɔ̃vnu] *pp de* **convenir** ♦ *adj* agreed.

convergent, e [kɔ̃vɛʀʒɑ̃, -ɑ̃t] *adj* convergent.

converger [kɔ̃vɛʀʒe] *vi* to converge; ~ **vers** *ou* **sur** to converge on.

conversation [kɔ̃vɛʀsɑsjɔ̃] *nf* conversation; **avoir de la** ~ to be a good conversationalist.

converser [kɔ̃vɛʀse] *vi* to converse.

conversion [kɔ̃vɛʀsjɔ̃] *nf* conversion; (*SKI*) kick turn.

convertible [kɔ̃vɛʀtibl(ə)] *adj* (*ÉCON*) convertible; **(canapé)** ~ sofa bed.

convertir [kɔ̃vɛʀtiʀ] *vt*: ~ **qn (à)** to convert sb (to); ~ **qch en** to convert sth into; **se** ~ **(à)** to be converted (to).

convertisseur [kɔ̃vɛʀtisœʀ] *nm* (*ÉLEC*) converter.

convexe [kɔ̃vɛks(ə)] *adj* convex.

conviction [kɔ̃viksjɔ̃] *nf* conviction.

conviendrai [kɔ̃vjɛ̃dʀe], **conviens** [kɔ̃vjɛ̃] *etc vb voir* **convenir**.

convier [kɔ̃vje] *vt*: ~ **qn à** (*dîner etc*) to (cordially) invite sb to; ~ **qn à faire** to urge sb to do.

convint [kɔ̃vɛ̃] *etc vb voir* **convenir**.

convive [kɔ̃viv] *nm/f* guest (*at table*).

convivial, e [kɔ̃vivjal] *adj* (*INFORM*) user-friendly.

convocation [kɔ̃vɔkɑsjɔ̃] *nf* (*voir convoquer*) convening, convoking; summoning; invitation; (*document*) notification to attend; summons *sg*.

convoi [kɔ̃vwa] *nm* (*de voitures, prisonniers*) convoy; (*train*) train; ~ **(funèbre)** funeral procession.

convoiter [kɔ̃vwate] *vt* to covet.

convoitise [kɔ̃vwatiz] *nf* covetousness; (*sexuelle*) lust, desire.

convoler [kɔ̃vɔle] *vi*: ~ **(en justes noces)** to be wed.

convoquer [kɔ̃vɔke] *vt* (*assemblée*) to convene, convoke; (*subordonné, témoin*) to summon; (*candidat*) to ask to attend; ~ **qn (à)** (*réunion*) to invite sb (to attend).

convoyer [kɔ̃vwaje] *vt* to escort.

convoyeur [kɔ̃vwajœʀ] *nm* (*NAVIG*) escort ship; ~ **de fonds** security guard.

convulsé, e [kɔ̃vylse] *adj* (*visage*) distorted.

convulsif, ive [kɔ̃vylsif, -iv] *adj* convulsive.

convulsions [kɔ̃vylsjɔ̃] *nfpl* convulsions.

coopérant [kɔɔpeʀɑ̃] *nm* ≈ person doing Voluntary Service Overseas (*BRIT*), ≈ member of the Peace Corps (*US*).

coopératif, ive [kɔɔpeʀatif, -iv] *adj, nf* co-operative.

coopération [kɔɔpeʀɑsjɔ̃] *nf* co-operation; (*ADMIN*): **la C**~ ≈ Voluntary Service Overseas (*BRIT*) *ou* the Peace Corps (*US*) (*done as alternative to military service*).

coopérer [kɔɔpeʀe] *vi*: ~ **(à)** to co-operate (in).

coordination [kɔɔʀdinɑsjɔ̃] *nf* coordination.

coordonnateur, trice [kɔɔʀdɔnatœʀ, -tʀis] *adj* coordinating ♦ *nm/f* coordinator.

coordonné, e [kɔɔʀdɔne] *adj* coordinated ♦ *nf* (*LING*) coordinate clause; ~**s** *nmpl* (*vêtements*) coordinates; ~**es** *nfpl* (*MATH*) coordinates; (*détails personnels*) address, phone number, schedule *etc*; whereabouts.

coordonner [kɔɔʀdɔne] *vt* to coordinate.

copain, copine [kɔpɛ̃, kɔpin] *nm/f* mate (*BRIT*), pal ♦ *adj*: **être** ~ **avec** to be pally with.

copeau, x [kɔpo] *nm* shaving; (*de métal*) turning.

Copenhague [kɔpənag] *n* Copenhagen.

copie [kɔpi] *nf* copy; (*SCOL*) script, paper; exercise; ~ **certifiée conforme** certified copy; ~ **papier** (*INFORM*) hard copy.

copier [kɔpje] *vt, vi* to copy; ~ **sur** to copy from.

copieur [kɔpjœʀ] *nm* (photo)copier.

copieusement [kɔpjøzmɑ̃] *adv* copiously.

copieux, euse [kɔpjø, -øz] *adj* copious, hearty.
copilote [kɔpilɔt] *nm* (*AVIAT*) co-pilot; (*AUTO*) co-driver, navigator.
copinage [kɔpinaʒ] *nm*: **obtenir qch par ~** to get sth through contacts.
copine [kɔpin] *nf voir* **copain**.
copiste [kɔpist(ə)] *nm/f* copyist, transcriber.
coproduction [kɔpʀɔdyksjɔ̃] *nf* coproduction, joint production.
copropriétaire [kɔpʀɔpʀijetɛʀ] *nm/f* co-owner.
copropriété [kɔpʀɔpʀijete] *nf* co-ownership, joint ownership; **acheter en ~** to buy on a co-ownership basis.
copulation [kɔpylɑsjɔ̃] *nf* copulation.
copyright [kɔpiʀajt] *nm* copyright.
coq [kɔk] *nm* cock, rooster ♦ *adj inv* (*BOXE*): **poids ~** bantamweight; **~ de bruyère** grouse; **~ du village** (*fig*: *péj*) ladykiller.
coq-à-l'âne [kɔkalɑn] *nm inv* abrupt change of subject.
coque [kɔk] *nf* (*de noix, mollusque*) shell; (*de bateau*) hull; **à la ~** (*CULIN*) (soft-)boiled.
coquelet [kɔklɛ] *nm* (*CULIN*) cockerel.
coquelicot [kɔkliko] *nm* poppy.
coqueluche [kɔklyʃ] *nf* whooping-cough; (*fig*): **être la ~ de qn** to be sb's flavour of the month.
coquet, te [kɔkɛ, -ɛt] *adj* appearance-conscious; (*joli*) pretty.
coquetier [kɔktje] *nm* egg-cup.
coquettement [kɔkɛtmɑ̃] *adv* (*s'habiller*) attractively; (*meubler*) prettily.
coquetterie [kɔkɛtʀi] *nf* appearance-consciousness.
coquillage [kɔkijaʒ] *nm* (*mollusque*) shellfish *inv*; (*coquille*) shell.
coquille [kɔkij] *nf* shell; (*TYPO*) misprint; **~ de beurre** shell of butter; **~ d'œuf** *adj* (*couleur*) eggshell; **~ de noix** nutshell; **~ St Jacques** scallop.
coquillettes [kɔkijɛt] *nfpl* pasta shells.
coquin, e [kɔkɛ̃, -in] *adj* mischievous, roguish; (*polisson*) naughty ♦ *nm/f* (*péj*) rascal.
cor [kɔʀ] *nm* (*MUS*) horn; (*MÉD*): **~ (au pied)** corn; **réclamer à ~ et à cri** to clamour for; **~ anglais** cor anglais; **~ de chasse** hunting horn.
corail, aux [kɔʀaj, -o] *nm* coral *no pl*.
Coran [kɔʀɑ̃] *nm*: **le ~** the Koran.
coraux [kɔʀo] *pl de* **corail**.
corbeau, x [kɔʀbo] *nm* crow.
corbeille [kɔʀbɛj] *nf* basket; (*BOURSE*): **la ~** ≈ the floor (of the Stock Exchange); **~ de mariage** (*fig*) wedding presents *pl*; **~ à ouvrage** work-basket; **~ à pain** breadbasket; **~ à papier** waste paper basket *ou* bin.
corbillard [kɔʀbijaʀ] *nm* hearse.
cordage [kɔʀdaʒ] *nm* rope; **~s** *nmpl* (*de voilure*) rigging *sg*.
corde [kɔʀd(ə)] *nf* rope; (*de violon, raquette, d'arc*) string; (*trame*): **la ~** the thread; (*ATHLÉTISME, AUTO*): **la ~** the rails *pl*; **les ~s** (*BOXE*) the ropes; **les (instruments à) ~s** (*MUS*) the strings, the stringed instruments; **semelles de ~** rope soles; **tenir la ~** (*ATHLÉTISME, AUTO*) to be in the inside lane; **tomber des ~s** to rain cats and dogs; **tirer sur la ~** to go too far; **la ~ sensible** the right chord; **usé jusqu'à la ~** threadbare; **~ à linge** washing *ou* clothes line; **~ lisse** (climbing) rope; **~ à nœuds** knotted climbing rope; **~ raide** tightrope; **~ à sauter** skipping rope; **~s vocales** vocal cords.
cordeau, x [kɔʀdo] *nm* string, line; **tracé au ~** as straight as a die.
cordée [kɔʀde] *nf* (*d'alpinistes*) rope, roped party.
cordelière [kɔʀdəljɛʀ] *nf* cord (belt).
cordial, e, aux [kɔʀdjal, -o] *adj* warm, cordial ♦ *nm* cordial, pick-me-up.
cordialement [kɔʀdjalmɑ̃] *adv* cordially, heartily; (*formule épistolaire*) (kind) regards.
cordialité [kɔʀdjalite] *nf* warmth, cordiality.
cordillère [kɔʀdijɛʀ] *nf*: **la ~ des Andes** the Andes cordillera *ou* range.
cordon [kɔʀdɔ̃] *nm* cord, string; **~ sanitaire/de police** sanitary/police cordon; **~ littoral** sandbank, sandbar; **~ ombilical** umbilical cord.
cordon-bleu [kɔʀdɔ̃blø] *adj, nm/f* cordon bleu.
cordonnerie [kɔʀdɔnʀi] *nf* shoe repairer's *ou* mender's (shop).
cordonnier [kɔʀdɔnje] *nm* shoe repairer *ou* mender, cobbler.
cordouan, e [kɔʀduɑ̃, -an] *adj* Cordovan.
Cordoue [kɔʀdu] *n* Cordoba.
Corée [kɔʀe] *nf*: **la ~** Korea; **la ~ du Sud/du Nord** South/North Korea; **la République (démocratique populaire) de ~** the (Democratic People's) Republic of Korea.
coréen, ne [kɔʀeɛ̃, -ɛn] *adj* Korean ♦ *nm* (*LING*) Korean ♦ *nm/f*: **C~, ne** Korean.
coreligionnaire [kɔʀəliʒjɔnɛʀ] *nm/f* fellow Christian/Muslim/Jew *etc*.
Corfou [kɔʀfu] *n* Corfu.
coriace [kɔʀjas] *adj* tough.
coriandre [kɔʀjɑ̃dʀ(ə)] *nf* coriander.
Corinthe [kɔʀɛ̃t] *n* Corinth.
cormoran [kɔʀmɔʀɑ̃] *nm* cormorant.
cornac [kɔʀnak] *nm* elephant driver.
corne [kɔʀn(ə)] *nf* horn; (*de cerf*) antler; (*de la peau*) callus; **~ d'abondance** horn of plenty; **~ de brume** (*NAVIG*) foghorn.
cornée [kɔʀne] *nf* cornea.
corneille [kɔʀnɛj] *nf* crow.
cornélien, ne [kɔʀneljɛ̃, -ɛn] *adj* (*débat etc*) where love and duty conflict.
cornemuse [kɔʀnəmyz] *nf* bagpipes *pl*; **joueur de ~** piper.
corner *nm* [kɔʀnɛʀ] (*FOOTBALL*) corner (kick) ♦ *vb* [kɔʀne] *vt* (*pages*) to make dog-eared ♦ *vi* (*klaxonner*) to blare out.
cornet [kɔʀnɛ] *nm* (paper) cone; (*de glace*) cor-

net, cone; ~ **à pistons** cornet.
cornette [kɔʀnɛt] *nf* cornet (*headgear*).
corniaud [kɔʀnjo] *nm* (*chien*) mongrel; (*péj*) twit, clot.
corniche [kɔʀniʃ] *nf* (*de meuble, neigeuse*) cornice; (*route*) coast road.
cornichon [kɔʀniʃɔ̃] *nm* gherkin.
Cornouailles [kɔʀnwaj] *nf(pl)* Cornwall.
cornue [kɔʀny] *nf* retort.
corollaire [kɔʀɔlɛʀ] *nm* corollary.
corolle [kɔʀɔl] *nf* corolla.
coron [kɔʀɔ̃] *nm* mining cottage; mining village.
coronaire [kɔʀɔnɛʀ] *adj* coronary.
corporation [kɔʀpɔʀɑsjɔ̃] *nf* corporate body; (*au Moyen-Âge*) guild.
corporel, le [kɔʀpɔʀɛl] *adj* bodily; (*punition*) corporal; **soins** ~**s** care *sg* of the body.
corps [kɔʀ] *nm* (*gén*) body; (*cadavre*) (dead) body; **à son ~ défendant** against one's will; **à ~ perdu** headlong; **perdu ~ et biens** lost with all hands; **prendre** ~ to take shape; **faire ~ avec** to be joined to; to form one body with; ~ **d'armée (CA)** army corps; ~ **de ballet** corps de ballet; ~ **constitués** (*POL*) constitutional bodies; **le ~ consulaire (CC)** the consular corps; ~ **à** ~ *adv* hand-to-hand ♦ *nm* clinch; **le ~ du délit** (*JUR*) corpus delicti; **le ~ diplomatique (CD)** the diplomatic corps; **le ~ électoral** the electorate; **le ~ enseignant** the teaching profession; ~ **étranger** (*MÉD*) foreign body; ~ **expéditionnaire** task force; ~ **de garde** guardroom; ~ **législatif** legislative body; **le ~ médical** the medical profession.
corpulence [kɔʀpylɑ̃s] *nf* build, (*embonpoint*) stoutness (*BRIT*), corpulence; **de forte** ~ of large build.
corpulent, e [kɔʀpylɑ̃, -ɑ̃t] *adj* stout (*BRIT*), corpulent.
corpus [kɔʀpys] *nm* (*LING*) corpus.
correct, e [kɔʀɛkt] *adj* (*exact*) accurate, correct; (*bienséant, honnête*) correct; (*passable*) adequate.
correctement [kɔʀɛktəmɑ̃] *adv* accurately; correctly; adequately.
correcteur, trice [kɔʀɛktœʀ, -tʀis] *nm/f* (*SCOL*) examiner, marker; (*TYPO*) proofreader.
correctif, ive [kɔʀɛktif, -iv] *adj* corrective ♦ *nm* (*mise au point*) rider, qualification.
correction [kɔʀɛksjɔ̃] *nf* (*voir corriger*) correction; marking; (*voir correct*) correctness; (*rature, surcharge*) correction, emendation; (*coups*) thrashing; ~ **sur écran** (*INFORM*) screen editing; ~ **(des épreuves)** proofreading.
correctionnel, le [kɔʀɛksjɔnɛl] *adj* (*JUR*): **tribunal** ~ ≈ criminal court.
corrélation [kɔʀelɑsjɔ̃] *nf* correlation.
correspondance [kɔʀɛspɔ̃dɑ̃s] *nf* correspondence; (*de train, d'avion*) connection; **ce train assure la ~ avec l'avion de 10 heures** this train connects with the 10 o'clock plane; **cours par** ~ correspondence course; **vente par** ~ mail-order business.
correspondancier, ière [kɔʀɛspɔ̃dɑ̃sje, -jɛʀ] *nm/f* correspondence clerk.
correspondant, e [kɔʀɛspɔ̃dɑ̃, -ɑ̃t] *nm/f* correspondent; (*TÉL*) person phoning (*ou* being phoned).
correspondre [kɔʀɛspɔ̃dʀ(ə)] *vi* (*données, témoignages*) to correspond, tally; (*chambres*) to communicate; ~ **à** to correspond to; ~ **avec qn** to correspond with sb.
Corrèze [kɔʀɛz] *nf*: **la** ~ the Corrèze.
corrézien, ne [kɔʀezjɛ̃, -ɛn] *adj* of *ou* from the Corrèze.
corrida [kɔʀida] *nf* bullfight.
corridor [kɔʀidɔʀ] *nm* corridor, passage.
corrigé [kɔʀiʒe] *nm* (*SCOL*) correct version; fair copy.
corriger [kɔʀiʒe] *vt* (*devoir*) to correct, mark; (*texte*) to correct, emend; (*erreur, défaut*) to correct, put right; (*punir*) to thrash; ~ **qn de** (*défaut*) to cure sb of; **se ~ de** to cure o.s. of.
corroborer [kɔʀɔbɔʀe] *vt* to corroborate.
corroder [kɔʀɔde] *vt* to corrode.
corrompre [kɔʀɔ̃pʀ(ə)] *vt* (*dépraver*) to corrupt; (*acheter: témoin etc*) to bribe.
corrompu, e [kɔʀɔ̃py] *adj* corrupt.
corrosif, ive [kɔʀozif, -iv] *adj* corrosive.
corrosion [kɔʀozjɔ̃] *nf* corrosion.
corruption [kɔʀypsjɔ̃] *nf* corruption; bribery.
corsage [kɔʀsaʒ] *nm* (*d'une robe*) bodice; (*chemisier*) blouse.
corsaire [kɔʀsɛʀ] *nm* pirate, corsair; privateer.
corse [kɔʀs(ə)] *adj* Corsican ♦ *nm/f*: **C~** Corsican ♦ *nf*: **la C~** Corsica.
corsé, e [kɔʀse] *adj* vigorous; (*café etc*) full-flavoured (*BRIT*) *ou* -flavored (*US*); (*goût*) full; (*fig*) spicy; tricky.
corselet [kɔʀsəlɛ] *nm* corselet.
corser [kɔʀse] *vt* (*difficulté*) to aggravate; (*intrigue*) to liven up; (*sauce*) to add spice to.
corset [kɔʀsɛ] *nm* corset; (*d'une robe*) bodice; ~ **orthopédique** surgical corset.
corso [kɔʀso] *nm*: ~ **fleuri** procession of floral floats.
cortège [kɔʀtɛʒ] *nm* procession.
cortisone [kɔʀtizɔn] *nf* (*MÉD*) cortisone.
corvée [kɔʀve] *nf* chore, drudgery *no pl*; (*MIL*) fatigue (duty).
cosaque [kɔzak] *nm* cossack.
cosignataire [kosiɲatɛʀ] *adj, nm/f* co-signatory.
cosinus [kosinys] *nm* (*MATH*) cosine.
cosmétique [kɔsmetik] *nm* (*pour les cheveux*) hair-oil; (*produit de beauté*) beauty care product.
cosmétologie [kɔsmetɔlɔʒi] *nf* beauty care.
cosmique [kɔsmik] *adj* cosmic.
cosmonaute [kɔsmɔnot] *nm/f* cosmonaut, astronaut.

cosmopolite [kɔsmɔpɔlit] *adj* cosmopolitan.
cosmos [kɔsmɔs] *nm* outer space; cosmos.
cosse [kɔs] *nf* (*BOT*) pod, hull.
cossu, e [kɔsy] *adj* opulent-looking, well-to-do.
Costa Rica [kɔstaʀika] *nm*: **le ~** Costa Rica.
costaricien, ne [kɔstaʀisjɛ̃, -ɛn] *adj* Costa Rican ♦ *nm/f*: **C~, ne** Costa Rican.
costaud, e [kɔsto, -od] *adj* strong, sturdy.
costume [kɔstym] *nm* (*d'homme*) suit; (*de théâtre*) costume.
costumé, e [kɔstyme] *adj* dressed up.
costumier, ière [kɔstymje, -jɛʀ] *nm/f* (*fabricant, loueur*) costumier; (*THÉÂT*) wardrobe master/mistress.
cotangente [kɔtɑ̃ʒɑ̃t] *nf* (*MATH*) cotangent.
cotation [kɔtɑsjɔ̃] *nf* quoted value.
cote [kɔt] *nf* (*en Bourse etc*) quotation; quoted value; (*d'un cheval*): **la ~ de** the odds *pl* on; (*d'un candidat etc*) rating; (*mesure: sur une carte*) spot height; (*: sur un croquis*) dimension; (*de classement*) (classification) mark; reference number; **avoir la ~** to be very popular; **inscrit à la ~** quoted on the Stock Exchange; **~ d'alerte** danger *ou* flood level; **~ mal taillée** (*fig*) compromise; **~ de popularité** popularity rating.
coté, e [kɔte] *adj*: **être ~** to be listed *ou* quoted; **être ~ en Bourse** to be quoted on the Stock Exchange; **être bien/mal ~** to be highly/poorly rated.
côte [kot] *nf* (*rivage*) coast(line); (*pente*) slope; (*: sur une route*) hill; (*ANAT*) rib; (*d'un tricot, tissu*) rib, ribbing *no pl*; **~ à ~** *adv* side by side; **la C~ (d'Azur)** the (French) Riviera; **la C~ d'Ivoire** the Ivory Coast.
côté [kote] *nm* (*gén*) side; (*direction*) way, direction; **de chaque ~ (de)** on each side of; **de tous les ~s** from all directions; **de quel ~ est-il parti?** which way *ou* in which direction did he go?; **de ce/de l'autre ~** this/the other way; **d'un ~ ... de l'autre ~** (*alternative*) on (the) one hand ... on the other (hand); **du ~ de** (*provenance*) from; (*direction*) towards; **du ~ de Lyon** (*proximité*) near Lyons; **du ~ gauche** on the left-hand side; **de ~** *adv* sideways; on one side; to one side; aside; **laisser de ~** to leave on one side; **mettre de ~** to put on one side, put aside; **de mon ~** (*quant à moi*) for my part; **à ~** *adv* (right) nearby; beside; next door; (*d'autre part*) besides; **à ~ de** beside; next to; (*fig*) in comparison to; **à ~ (de la cible)** off target, wide (of the mark); **être aux ~s de** to be by the side of.
coteau, x [kɔto] *nm* hill.
côtelé, e [kotle] *adj* ribbed; **pantalon en velours ~** corduroy trousers *pl*.
côtelette [kotlɛt] *nf* chop.
coter [kɔte] *vt* (*BOURSE*) to quote.
coterie [kɔtʀi] *nf* set.
côtier, ière [kotje, -jɛʀ] *adj* coastal.
cotisation [kɔtizɑsjɔ̃] *nf* subscription, dues *pl*; (*pour une pension*) contributions *pl*.
cotiser [kɔtize] *vi*: **~ (à)** to pay contributions (to); (*à une association*) to subscribe (to); **se ~** to club together.
coton [kɔtɔ̃] *nm* cotton; **~ hydrophile** cotton wool (*BRIT*), absorbent cotton (*US*).
cotonnade [kɔtɔnad] *nf* cotton (fabric).
Coton-Tige [kɔtɔ̃tiʒ] *nm* ® cotton bud ®.
côtoyer [kotwaje] *vt* to be close to; (*rencontrer*) to rub shoulders with; (*longer*) to run alongside; (*fig: friser*) to be bordering *ou* verging on.
cotte [kɔt] *nf*: **~ de mailles** coat of mail.
cou [ku] *nm* neck.
couac [kwak] *nm* (*fam*) bum note.
couard, e [kwaʀ, -aʀd(ə)] *adj* cowardly.
couchage [kuʃaʒ] *nm voir* **sac**.
couchant [kuʃɑ̃] *adj*: **soleil ~** setting sun.
couche [kuʃ] *nf* (*strate: gén, GÉO*) layer, stratum (*pl* -a); (*de peinture, vernis*) coat; (*de poussière, crème*) layer; (*de bébé*) nappy (*BRIT*), diaper (*US*); **~ d'ozone** ozone layer; **~s** *nfpl* (*MÉD*) confinement *sg*; **~s sociales** social levels *ou* strata.
couché, e [kuʃe] *adj* (*étendu*) lying down; (*au lit*) in bed.
couche-culotte, *pl* **couches-culottes** [kuʃkylɔt] *nf* (plastic-coated) disposable nappy (*BRIT*) *ou* diaper (*US*).
coucher [kuʃe] *nm* (*du soleil*) setting ♦ *vt* (*personne*) to put to bed; (*: loger*) to put up; (*objet*) to lay on its side; (*écrire*) to inscribe, couch ♦ *vi* (*dormir*) to sleep, spend the night; **~ avec qn** to sleep with sb, go to bed with sb; **se ~** *vi* (*pour dormir*) to go to bed; (*pour se reposer*) to lie down; (*soleil*) to set, go down; **à prendre avant le ~** (*MÉD*) take at night *ou* before going to bed; **~ de soleil** sunset.
couchette [kuʃɛt] *nf* couchette; (*de marin*) bunk.
coucheur [kuʃœʀ] *nm*: **mauvais ~** awkward customer.
couci-couça [kusikusa] *adv* (*fam*) so-so.
coucou [kuku] *nm* cuckoo ♦ *excl* peek-a-boo.
coude [kud] *nm* (*ANAT*) elbow; (*de tuyau, de la route*) bend; **~ à ~** *adv* shoulder to shoulder, side by side.
coudée [kude] *nf*: **avoir ses ~s franches** (*fig*) to have a free rein.
cou-de-pied, *pl* **cous-de-pied** [kudpje] *nm* instep.
coudoyer [kudwaje] *vt* to brush past *ou* against; (*fig*) to rub shoulders with.
coudre [kudʀ(ə)] *vt* (*bouton*) to sew on; (*robe*) to sew (up) ♦ *vi* to sew.
couenne [kwan] *nf* (*de lard*) rind.
couette [kwɛt] *nf* duvet, (continental) quilt; **~s** *nfpl* (*cheveux*) bunches.
couffin [kufɛ̃] *nm* Moses basket; (straw) basket.
couilles [kuj] *nfpl* (*fam!*) balls (*!*).
couiner [kwine] *vi* to squeal.

coulage [kulaʒ] *nm* (*COMM*) loss of stock (*due to theft or negligence*).
coulant, e [kulɑ̃, -ɑ̃t] *adj* (*indulgent*) easy-going; (*fromage etc*) runny.
coulée [kule] *nf* (*de lave, métal en fusion*) flow; ~ **de neige** snowslide.
couler [kule] *vi* to flow, run; (*fuir: stylo, récipient*) to leak; (*sombrer: bateau*) to sink ♦ *vt* (*cloche, sculpture*) to cast; (*bateau*) to sink; (*fig*) to ruin, bring down; (*: passer*): ~ **une vie heureuse** to enjoy a happy life; **se** ~ **dans** (*interstice etc*) to slip into; **faire** ~ (*eau*) to run; **faire** ~ **un bain** to run a bath; **il a coulé une bielle** (*AUTO*) his big end went; ~ **de source** to follow on naturally; ~ **à pic** to sink *ou* go straight to the bottom.
couleur [kulœʀ] *nf* colour (*BRIT*), color (*US*); (*CARTES*) suit; ~**s** *nfpl* (*du teint*) colo(u)r *sg*; **les** ~**s** (*MIL*) the colo(u)rs; **en** ~**s** (*film*) in colo(u)r; **télévision en** ~**s** colo(u)r television; **de** ~ (*homme, femme*) colo(u)red; **sous** ~ **de** on the pretext of.
couleuvre [kulœvʀ(ə)] *nf* grass snake.
coulisse [kulis] *nf* (*TECH*) runner; ~**s** *nfpl* (*THÉÂT*) wings; (*fig*): **dans les** ~**s** behind the scenes; **porte à** ~ sliding door.
coulisser [kulise] *vi* to slide, run.
couloir [kulwaʀ] *nm* corridor, passage; (*d'avion*) aisle; (*de bus*) gangway; (*: sur la route*) bus lane; (*SPORT: de piste*) lane; (*GÉO*) gully; ~ **aérien** air corridor *ou* lane; ~ **de navigation** shipping lane.
coulpe [kulp(ə)] *nf*: **battre sa** ~ to repent openly.
coup [ku] *nm* (*heurt, choc*) knock; (*affectif*) blow, shock; (*agressif*) blow; (*avec arme à feu*) shot; (*de l'horloge*) chime; stroke; (*SPORT*) stroke; shot; blow; (*fam: fois*) time; (*ÉCHECS*) move; ~ **de coude/genou** nudge (with the elbow)/with the knee; **à** ~**s de hache/marteau** (hitting) with an axe/a hammer; ~ **de tonnerre** clap of thunder; ~ **de sonnette** ring of the bell; ~ **de crayon/pinceau** stroke of the pencil/brush; **donner un** ~ **de balai** to sweep up, give the floor a sweep; **donner un** ~ **de chiffon** to go round with the duster; **avoir le** ~ (*fig*) to have the knack; **être dans le/hors du** ~ to be/not to be in on it; **boire un** ~ to have a drink; **d'un seul** ~ (*subitement*) suddenly; (*à la fois*) at one go; in one blow; **du** ~ so (you see); **du premier** ~ first time *ou* go, at the first attempt; **du même** ~ at the same time; **à** ~ **sûr** definitely, without fail; **après** ~ afterwards; ~ **sur** ~ in quick succession; **être sur un** ~ to be on to something; **sur le** ~ outright; **sous le** ~ **de** (*surprise etc*) under the influence of; **tomber sous le** ~ **de la loi** to constitute a statutory offence; **à tous les** ~**s** every time; **il a raté son** ~ he missed his turn; **pour le** ~ for once; ~ **bas** (*fig*): **donner un** ~ **bas à qn** to hit sb below the belt; ~ **de chance** stroke of luck; ~ **de chapeau** (*fig*) pat on the back; ~ **de couteau** stab (of a knife); ~ **dur** hard blow; ~ **d'éclat** (great) feat; ~ **d'envoi** kick-off; ~ **d'essai** first attempt; ~ **d'état** coup d'état; ~ **de feu** shot; ~ **de filet** (*POLICE*) haul; ~ **de foudre** (*fig*) love at first sight; ~ **fourré** stab in the back; ~ **franc** free kick; ~ **de frein** (sharp) braking *no pl*; ~ **de fusil** rifle shot; ~ **de grâce** coup de grâce; ~ **du lapin** (*AUTO*) whiplash; ~ **de main: donner un** ~ **de main à qn** to give sb a (helping) hand; ~ **de maître** master stroke; ~ **d'œil** glance; ~ **de pied** kick; ~ **de poing** punch; ~ **de soleil** sunburn *no pl*; ~ **de téléphone** phone call; ~ **de tête** (*fig*) (sudden) impulse; ~ **de théâtre** (*fig*) dramatic turn of events; ~ **de vent** gust of wind; **en** ~ **de vent** (*rapidement*) in a tearing hurry.
coupable [kupabl(ə)] *adj* guilty; (*pensée*) guilty, culpable ♦ *nm/f* (*gén*) culprit; (*JUR*) guilty party; ~ **de** guilty of.
coupant, e [kupɑ̃, -ɑ̃t] *adj* (*lame*) sharp; (*fig: voix, ton*) cutting.
coupe [kup] *nf* (*verre*) goblet; (*à fruits*) dish; (*SPORT*) cup; (*de cheveux, de vêtement*) cut; (*graphique, plan*) (cross) section; **être sous la** ~ **de** to be under the control of; **faire des** ~**s sombres dans** to make drastic cuts in.
coupé, e [kupe] *adj* (*communications, route*) cut, blocked; (*vêtement*): **bien/mal** ~ well/badly cut ♦ *nm* (*AUTO*) coupé.
coupe-circuit [kupsiʀkɥi] *nm inv* cutout, circuit breaker.
coupée [kupe] *nf* (*NAVIG*) gangway.
coupe-feu [kupfø] *nm inv* firebreak.
coupe-gorge [kupgɔʀʒ(ə)] *nm inv* cut-throats' den.
coupe-ongles [kupɔ̃gl(ə)] *nm inv* (*pince*) nail clippers; (*ciseaux*) nail scissors.
coupe-papier [kuppapje] *nm inv* paper knife.
couper [kupe] *vt* to cut; (*retrancher*) to cut (out), take out; (*route, courant*) to cut off; (*appétit*) to take away; (*fièvre*) to take down, reduce; (*vin, cidre*) to blend; (*: à table*) to dilute (with water) ♦ *vi* to cut; (*prendre un raccourci*) to take a short-cut; (*CARTES: diviser le paquet*) to cut; (*: avec l'atout*) to trump; **se** ~ (*se blesser*) to cut o.s.; (*en témoignant etc*) to give o.s. away; ~ **l'appétit à qn** to spoil sb's appetite; ~ **la parole à qn** to cut sb short; ~ **les vivres à qn** to cut off sb's vital supplies; ~ **le contact** *ou* **l'allumage** (*AUTO*) to turn off the ignition; ~ **les ponts avec qn** to break with sb; **se faire** ~ **les cheveux** to have *ou* get one's hair cut.
couperet [kupʀɛ] *nm* cleaver, chopper.
couperosé, e [kupʀoze] *adj* blotchy.
couple [kupl(ə)] *nm* couple; ~ **de torsion** torque.
coupler [kuple] *vt* to couple (together).
couplet [kuplɛ] *nm* verse.
coupleur [kuplœʀ] *nm*: ~ **acoustique** acoustic

coupler.
coupole [kupɔl] *nf* dome; cupola.
coupon [kupɔ̃] *nm* (*ticket*) coupon; (*de tissu*) remnant; roll.
coupon-réponse, *pl* **coupons-réponses** [kupɔ̃ʀepɔ̃s] *nm* reply coupon.
coupure [kupyʀ] *nf* cut; (*billet de banque*) note; (*de journal*) cutting; ~ **de courant** power cut.
cour [kuʀ] *nf* (*de ferme, jardin*) (court)yard; (*d'immeuble*) back yard; (*JUR, royale*) court; **faire la ~ à qn** to court sb; ~ **d'appel** appeal court (*BRIT*), appellate court (*US*); ~ **d'assises** court of assizes, ≈ Crown Court (*BRIT*); ~ **de cassation** final court of appeal; ~ **des comptes** (*ADMIN*) revenue court; ~ **martiale** court-martial; ~ **de récréation** (*SCOL*) schoolyard, playground.
courage [kuʀaʒ] *nm* courage, bravery.
courageusement [kuʀaʒøzmɑ̃] *adv* bravely, courageously.
courageux, euse [kuʀaʒø, -øz] *adj* brave, courageous.
couramment [kuʀamɑ̃] *adv* commonly; (*parler*) fluently.
courant, e [kuʀɑ̃, -ɑ̃t] *adj* (*fréquent*) common; (*COMM, gén: normal*) standard; (*en cours*) current ♦ *nm* current; (*fig*) movement; trend; **être au ~ (de)** (*fait, nouvelle*) to know (about); **mettre qn au ~ (de)** (*fait, nouvelle*) to tell sb (about); (*nouveau travail etc*) to teach sb the basics (of), brief sb (about); **se tenir au ~ (de)** (*techniques etc*) to keep o.s. up-to-date (on); **dans le ~ de** (*pendant*) in the course of; ~ **octobre** *etc* in the course of October *etc*; **le 10 ~** (*COMM*) the 10th inst; ~ **d'air** draught (*BRIT*), draft (*US*); ~ **électrique** (electric) current, power.
courbature [kuʀbatyʀ] *nf* ache.
courbaturé, e [kuʀbatyʀe] *adj* aching.
courbe [kuʀb(ə)] *adj* curved ♦ *nf* curve; ~ **de niveau** contour line.
courber [kuʀbe] *vt* to bend; ~ **la tête** to bow one's head; **se ~** *vi* (*branche etc*) to bend, curve; (*personne*) to bend (down).
courbette [kuʀbɛt] *nf* low bow.
coure [kuʀ] *etc vb voir* **courir**.
coureur, euse [kuʀœʀ, -øz] *nm/f* (*SPORT*) runner (*ou* driver); (*péj*) womanizer/manhunter; ~ **cycliste/automobile** racing cyclist/driver.
courge [kuʀʒ(ə)] *nf* (*BOT*) gourd; (*CULIN*) marrow.
courgette [kuʀʒɛt] *nf* courgette (*BRIT*), zucchini (*US*).
courir [kuʀiʀ] *vi* (*gén*) to run; (*se dépêcher*) to rush; (*fig: rumeurs*) to go round; (*COMM: intérêt*) to accrue ♦ *vt* (*SPORT: épreuve*) to compete in; (*risque*) to run; (*danger*) to face; ~ **les cafés/bals** to do the rounds of the cafés/dances; **le bruit court que** the rumour is going round that; **par les temps qui courent** at the present time; ~ **après qn** to run after sb, chase (after) sb; **laisser ~** to let things alone; **faire ~ qn** to make sb run around (all over the place); **tu peux (toujours) ~!** you've got a hope!
couronne [kuʀɔn] *nf* crown; (*de fleurs*) wreath, circlet; ~ **(mortuaire)** (funeral) wreath.
couronnement [kuʀɔnmɑ̃] *nm* coronation, crowning; (*fig*) crowning achievement.
couronner [kuʀɔne] *vt* to crown.
courons [kuʀɔ̃], **courrai** [kuʀe] *etc vb voir* **courir**.
courre [kuʀ] *vb voir* **chasse**.
courriel [kuʀjɛl] *nm* e-mail; **envoyer qch par ~** to e-mail sth.
courrier [kuʀje] *nm* mail, post; (*lettres à écrire*) letters *pl*; (*rubrique*) column; **qualité ~** letter quality; **long/moyen ~** *adj* (*AVIAT*) long-/medium-haul; ~ **du cœur** problem page; ~ **électronique** electronic mail, E-mail.
courroie [kuʀwɑ] *nf* strap; (*TECH*) belt; ~ **de transmission/ventilateur** driving/fan belt.
courrons [kuʀɔ̃] *etc vb voir* **courir**.
courroucé, e [kuʀuse] *adj* wrathful.
cours [kuʀ] *vb voir* **courir** ♦ *nm* (*leçon*) lesson; class; (*série de leçons*) course; (*cheminement*) course; (*écoulement*) flow; (*avenue*) walk; (*COMM*) rate; price; (*BOURSE*) quotation; **donner libre ~ à** to give free expression to; **avoir ~** (*monnaie*) to be legal tender; (*fig*) to be current; (*SCOL*) to have a class *ou* lecture; **en ~** (*année*) current; (*travaux*) in progress; **en ~ de route** on the way; **au ~ de** in the course of, during; **le ~ du change** the exchange rate; ~ **d'eau** waterway; ~ **élémentaire (CE)** *2nd and 3rd years of primary school*; ~ **moyen (CM)** *4th and 5th years of primary school*; ~ **préparatoire** ≈ infants' class (*BRIT*), ≈ 1st grade (*US*); ~ **du soir** night school.
course [kuʀs(ə)] *nf* running; (*SPORT: épreuve*) race; (*trajet: du soleil*) course; (*: d'un projectile*) flight; (*: d'une pièce mécanique*) travel; (*excursion*) outing; climb; (*d'un taxi, autocar*) journey, trip; (*petite mission*) errand; **~s** *nfpl* (*achats*) shopping *sg*; (*HIPPISME*) races; **faire les** *ou* **ses ~s** to go shopping; **jouer aux ~s** to bet on the races; **à bout de ~** (*épuisé*) exhausted; ~ **automobile** car race; ~ **de côte** (*AUTO*) hill climb; ~ **par étapes** *ou* **d'étapes** race in stages; ~ **d'obstacles** obstacle race; ~ **à pied** walking race; ~ **de vitesse** sprint; **~s de chevaux** horse racing.
coursier, ière [kuʀsje, -jɛʀ] *nm/f* courier.
court, e [kuʀ, kuʀt(ə)] *adj* short ♦ *adv* short ♦ *nm*: ~ **(de tennis)** (tennis) court; **tourner ~** to come to a sudden end; **couper ~ à** to cut short; **à ~ de** short of; **prendre qn de ~** to catch sb unawares; **pour faire ~** briefly, to cut a long story short; **ça fait ~** that's not very long; **tirer à la ~e paille** to draw lots; **faire la ~e échelle à qn** to give sb a leg up; ~ **métrage** (*CINÉ*) short (film).

court-bouillon, *pl* **courts-bouillons** [kuRbujɔ̃] *nm* court-bouillon.
court-circuit, *pl* **courts-circuits** [kuRsiRkɥi] *nm* short-circuit.
court-circuiter [kuRsiRkɥite] *vt* (*fig*) to bypass.
courtier, ière [kuRtje, -jɛR] *nm/f* broker.
courtisan [kuRtizɑ̃] *nm* courtier.
courtisane [kuRtizan] *nf* courtesan.
courtiser [kuRtize] *vt* to court, woo.
courtois, e [kuRtwa, -waz] *adj* courteous.
courtoisement [kuRtwazmɑ̃] *adv* courteously.
courtoisie [kuRtwazi] *nf* courtesy.
couru, e [kuRy] *pp de* **courir** ♦ *adj* (*spectacle etc*) popular; **c'est ~ (d'avance)!** (*fam*) it's a safe bet!
cousais [kuzɛ] *etc vb voir* **coudre.**
couscous [kuskus] *nm* couscous.
cousin, e [kuzɛ̃, -in] *nm/f* cousin ♦ *nm* (*ZOOL*) mosquito; **~ germain** first cousin.
cousons [kuzɔ̃] *etc vb voir* **coudre.**
coussin [kusɛ̃] *nm* cushion; **~ d'air** (*TECH*) air cushion.
cousu, e [kuzy] *pp de* **coudre** ♦ *adj*: **~ d'or** rolling in riches.
coût [ku] *nm* cost; **le ~ de la vie** the cost of living.
coûtant [kutɑ̃] *adj m*: **au prix ~** at cost price.
couteau, x [kuto] *nm* knife; **~ à cran d'arrêt** flick-knife; **~ de cuisine** kitchen knife; **~ à pain** bread knife; **~ de poche** pocket knife.
couteau-scie, *pl* **couteaux-scies** [kutosi] *nm* serrated(-edged) knife.
coutelier, ière [kutəlje, -jɛR] *adj*: **l'industrie ~ière** the cutlery industry ♦ *nm/f* cutler.
coutellerie [kutɛlRi] *nf* cutlery shop; cutlery.
coûter [kute] *vt* to cost ♦ *vi*: **~ à qn** to cost sb a lot; **~ cher** to be expensive; **~ cher à qn** (*fig*) to cost sb dear *ou* dearly; **combien ça coûte?** how much is it?, what does it cost?; **coûte que coûte** at all costs.
coûteux, euse [kutø, -øz] *adj* costly, expensive.
coutume [kutym] *nf* custom; **de ~** usual, customary.
coutumier, ière [kutymje, -jɛR] *adj* customary: **elle est coutumière du fait** that's her usual trick.
couture [kutyR] *nf* sewing; dress-making; (*points*) seam.
couturier [kutyRje] *nm* fashion designer, couturier.
couturière [kutyRjɛR] *nf* dressmaker.
couvée [kuve] *nf* brood, clutch.
couvent [kuvɑ̃] *nm* (*de sœurs*) convent; (*de frères*) monastery; (*établissement scolaire*) convent (school).
couver [kuve] *vt* to hatch; (*maladie*) to be sickening for ♦ *vi* (*feu*) to smoulder (*BRIT*), smolder (*US*); (*révolte*) to be brewing; **~ qn/qch des yeux** to look lovingly at sb/sth; (*convoiter*) to look longingly at sb/sth.
couvercle [kuvɛRkl(ə)] *nm* lid; (*de bombe aérosol etc, qui se visse*) cap, top.
couvert, e [kuvɛR, -ɛRt(ə)] *pp de* **couvrir** ♦ *adj* (*ciel*) overcast; (*coiffé d'un chapeau*) wearing a hat ♦ *nm* place setting; (*place à table*) place; (*au restaurant*) cover charge; **~s** *nmpl* place settings; cutlery *sg*; **~ de** covered with *ou* in; **bien ~** (*habillé*) well wrapped up; **mettre le ~** to lay the table; **à ~** under cover; **sous le ~ de** under the shelter of; (*fig*) under cover of.
couverture [kuvɛRtyR] *nf* (*de lit*) blanket; (*de bâtiment*) roofing; (*de livre, fig: d'un espion etc, ASSURANCES*) cover; (*PRESSE*) coverage; **de ~** (*lettre etc*) covering; **~ chauffante** electric blanket.
couveuse [kuvøz] *nf* (*à poules*) sitter, brooder; (*de maternité*) incubator.
couvre [kuvR(ə)] *etc vb voir* **couvrir.**
couvre-chef [kuvRəʃɛf] *nm* hat.
couvre-feu, x [kuvRəfø] *nm* curfew.
couvre-lit [kuvRəli] *nm* bedspread.
couvre-pieds [kuvRəpje] *nm inv* quilt.
couvreur [kuvRœR] *nm* roofer.
couvrir [kuvRiR] *vt* to cover; (*dominer, étouffer: voix, pas*) to drown out; (*erreur*) to cover up; (*ZOOL: s'accoupler à*) to cover; **se ~** (*ciel*) to cloud over; (*s'habiller*) to cover up, wrap up; (*se coiffer*) to put on one's hat; (*par une assurance*) to cover o.s.; **se ~ de** (*fleurs, boutons*) to become covered in.
cover-girl [kɔvœRgœRl] *nf* model.
cow-boy [kobɔj] *nm* cowboy.
coyote [kɔjɔt] *nm* coyote.
CP *sigle m* = **cours préparatoire.**
CPAM *sigle f* (= *Caisse primaire d'assurances maladie*) *health insurance office.*
cps *abr* (= *caractères par seconde*) cps.
cpt *abr* = **comptant.**
CQFD *abr* (= *ce qu'il fallait démontrer*) QED (= *quod erat demonstrandum*).
CR *sigle m* = **compte rendu.**
crabe [kRɑb] *nm* crab.
crachat [kRaʃa] *nm* spittle *no pl*, spit *no pl*.
craché, e [kRaʃe] *adj*: **son père tout ~** the spitting image of his (*ou* her) father.
cracher [kRaʃe] *vi* to spit ♦ *vt* to spit out; (*fig: lave etc*) to belch (out); **~ du sang** to spit blood.
crachin [kRaʃɛ̃] *nm* drizzle.
crachiner [kRaʃine] *vi* to drizzle.
crachoir [kRaʃwaR] *nm* spittoon; (*de dentiste*) bowl.
crachotement [kRaʃɔtmɑ̃] *nm* crackling *no pl*.
crachoter [kRaʃɔte] *vi* (*haut-parleur, radio*) to crackle.
crack [kRak] *nm* (*intellectuel*) whizzkid; (*sportif*) ace; (*poulain*) hot favourite (*BRIT*) *ou* favorite (*US*).
Cracovie [kRakɔvi] *n* Cracow.
cradingue [kRadɛ̃g] *adj* (*fam*) disgustingly dirty, filthy-dirty.
craie [kRɛ] *nf* chalk.

craignais [kʀɛɲɛ] *etc vb voir* **craindre**.
craindre [kʀɛ̃dʀ(ə)] *vt* to fear, be afraid of; (*être sensible à: chaleur, froid*) to be easily damaged by; ~ **de/que** to be afraid of/that; **je crains qu'il (ne) vienne** I am afraid he may come.
crainte [kʀɛ̃t] *nf* fear; **de** ~ **de/que** for fear of/that.
craintif, ive [kʀɛ̃tif, -iv] *adj* timid.
craintivement [kʀɛ̃tivmɑ̃] *adv* timidly.
cramer [kʀame] *vi* (*fam*) to burn.
cramoisi, e [kʀamwazi] *adj* crimson.
crampe [kʀɑ̃p] *nf* cramp; ~ **d'estomac** stomach cramp.
crampon [kʀɑ̃pɔ̃] *nm* (*de semelle*) stud; (*ALPINISME*) crampon.
cramponner [kʀɑ̃pɔne]: **se** ~ *vi*: **se** ~ **(à)** to hang *ou* cling on (to).
cran [kʀɑ̃] *nm* (*entaille*) notch; (*de courroie*) hole; (*courage*) guts *pl*; ~ **d'arrêt/de sûreté** safety catch; ~ **de mire** bead.
crâne [kʀɑn] *nm* skull.
crâner [kʀɑne] *vi* (*fam*) to swank, show off.
crânien, ne [kʀɑnjɛ̃, -ɛn] *adj* cranial, skull *cpd*, brain *cpd*.
crapaud [kʀapo] *nm* toad.
crapule [kʀapyl] *nf* villain.
crapuleux, euse [kʀapylø, -øz] *adj*: **crime** ~ villainous crime.
craquelure [kʀaklyʀ] *nf* crack; crackle *no pl*.
craquement [kʀakmɑ̃] *nm* crack, snap; (*du plancher*) creak, creaking *no pl*.
craquer [kʀake] *vi* (*bois, plancher*) to creak; (*fil, branche*) to snap; (*couture*) to come apart, burst; (*fig*) to break down, fall apart; (*: être enthousiasmé*) to go wild ♦ *vt*: ~ **une allumette** to strike a match.
crasse [kʀas] *nf* grime, filth ♦ *adj* (*fig: ignorance*) crass.
crasseux, euse [kʀasø, øz] *adj* filthy.
crassier [kʀasje] *nm* slag heap.
cratère [kʀatɛʀ] *nm* crater.
cravache [kʀavaʃ] *nf* (riding) crop.
cravacher [kʀavaʃe] *vt* to use the crop on.
cravate [kʀavat] *nf* tie.
cravater [kʀavate] *vt* to put a tie on; (*fig*) to grab round the neck.
crawl [kʀol] *nm* crawl.
crawlé, e [kʀole] *adj*: **dos** ~ backstroke.
crayeux, euse [kʀɛjø, -øz] *adj* chalky.
crayon [kʀɛjɔ̃] *nm* pencil; (*de rouge à lèvres etc*) stick, pencil; **écrire au** ~ to write in pencil; ~ **à bille** ball-point pen; ~ **de couleur** crayon; ~ **optique** light pen.
crayon-feutre, *pl* **crayons-feutres** [kʀɛjɔ̃føtʀ(ə)] *nm* felt(-tip) pen.
crayonner [kʀɛjɔne] *vt* to scribble, sketch.
CRDP *sigle m* (= *Centre régional de documentation pédagogique*) *teachers' resource centre*.
créance [kʀeɑ̃s] *nf* (*COMM*) (financial) claim, (recoverable) debt; **donner** ~ **à qch** to lend credence to sth.
créancier, ière [kʀeɑ̃sje, -jɛʀ] *nm/f* creditor.
créateur, trice [kʀeatœʀ, -tʀis] *adj* creative ♦ *nm/f* creator; **le C**~ (*REL*) the Creator.
créatif, ive [kʀeatif, -iv] *adj* creative.
création [kʀeɑsjɔ̃] *nf* creation.
créativité [kʀeativite] *nf* creativity.
créature [kʀeatyʀ] *nf* creature.
crécelle [kʀesɛl] *nf* rattle.
crèche [kʀɛʃ] *nf* (*de Noël*) crib; (*garderie*) crèche, day nursery; *see boxed note*.

CRÈCHE

*In France the Christmas crib (***crèche***) usually contains figurines representing a miller, a wood-cutter and other villagers as well as the Holy Family and the traditional cow, donkey and shepherds. The Three Wise Men are added to the nativity scene at Epiphany (6 January, Twelfth Night).*

crédence [kʀedɑ̃s] *nf* (small) sideboard.
crédibilité [kʀedibilite] *nf* credibility.
crédible [kʀedibl(ə)] *adj* credible.
CREDIF [kʀedif] *sigle m* (= *Centre de recherche et d'étude pour la diffusion du français*) *official body promoting use of the French language*.
crédit [kʀedi] *nm* (*gén*) credit; ~**s** *nmpl* funds; **acheter à** ~ to buy on credit *ou* on easy terms; **faire** ~ **à qn** to give sb credit; ~ **municipal** pawnshop; ~ **relais** bridging loan.
crédit-bail, *pl* **crédits-bails** [kʀedibɑj] *nm* (*ÉCON*) leasing.
créditer [kʀedite] *vt*: ~ **un compte (de)** to credit an account (with).
créditeur, trice [kʀeditœʀ, -tʀis] *adj* in credit, credit *cpd* ♦ *nm/f* customer in credit.
credo [kʀedo] *nm* credo, creed.
crédule [kʀedyl] *adj* credulous, gullible.
crédulité [kʀedylite] *nf* credulity, gullibility.
créer [kʀee] *vt* to create; (*THÉÂT: pièce*) to produce (for the first time); (*: rôle*) to create.
crémaillère [kʀemajɛʀ] *nf* (*RAIL*) rack; (*tige crantée*) trammel; **direction à** ~ (*AUTO*) rack and pinion steering; **pendre la** ~ to have a house-warming party.
crémation [kʀemɑsjɔ̃] *nf* cremation.
crématoire [kʀematwaʀ] *adj*: **four** ~ crematorium.
crématorium [kʀematɔʀjɔm] *nm* crematorium.
crème [kʀɛm] *nf* cream; (*entremets*) cream dessert ♦ *adj inv* cream; **un (café)** ~ ≈ a white coffee; ~ **chantilly** whipped cream, crème Chantilly; ~ **fouettée** whipped cream; ~ **glacée** ice cream; ~ **à raser** shaving cream.
crémerie [kʀɛmʀi] *nf* dairy; (*tearoom*) teashop.
crémeux, euse [kʀemø, -øz] *adj* creamy.
crémier, ière [kʀemje, -jɛʀ] *nm/f* dairyman/woman.
créneau, x [kʀeno] *nm* (*de fortification*) cren-

el(le); (*fig, aussi COMM*) gap, slot; (*AUTO*): **faire un** ~ to reverse into a parking space (*between cars alongside the kerb*).
créole [kReɔl] *adj, nm/f* Creole.
créosote [kReozɔt] *nf* creosote.
crêpe [kRɛp] *nf* (*galette*) pancake ♦ *nm* (*tissu*) crêpe; (*de deuil*) black mourning crêpe; (*ruban*) black armband (*ou* hatband *ou* ribbon); **semelle (de)** ~ crêpe sole; ~ **de Chine** crêpe de Chine.
crêpé, e [kRepe] *adj* (*cheveux*) backcombed.
crêperie [kRɛpRi] *nf* pancake shop *ou* restaurant.
crépi [kRepi] *nm* roughcast.
crépir [kRepiR] *vt* to roughcast.
crépitement [kRepitmɑ̃] *nm* (*du feu*) crackling *no pl*; (*d'une arme automatique*) rattle *no pl*.
crépiter [kRepite] *vi* to sputter, splutter, crackle.
crépon [kRepɔ̃] *nm* seersucker.
CREPS [kRɛps] *sigle m* (= *Centre régional d'éducation physique et sportive*) ≈ sports *ou* leisure centre.
crépu, e [kRepy] *adj* frizzy, fuzzy.
crépuscule [kRepyskyl] *nm* twilight, dusk.
crescendo [kReʃɛndo] *nm, adv* (*MUS*) crescendo; **aller** ~ (*fig*) to rise higher and higher, grow ever greater.
cresson [kResɔ̃] *nm* watercress.
Crète [kRɛt] *nf*: **la** ~ Crete.
crête [kRɛt] *nf* (*de coq*) comb; (*de vague, montagne*) crest.
crétin, e [kRetɛ̃, -in] *nm/f* cretin.
crétois, e [kRetwa, -waz] *adj* Cretan.
cretonne [kRətɔn] *nf* cretonne.
creuser [kRøze] *vt* (*trou, tunnel*) to dig; (*sol*) to dig a hole in; (*bois*) to hollow out; (*fig*) to go (deeply) into; **ça creuse** that gives you a real appetite; **se** ~ **(la cervelle)** to rack one's brains.
creuset [kRøzɛ] *nm* crucible; (*fig*) melting pot; (severe) test.
creux, euse [kRø, -øz] *adj* hollow ♦ *nm* hollow; (*fig: sur graphique etc*) trough; **heures creuses** slack periods; off-peak periods; **le** ~ **de l'estomac** the pit of the stomach.
crevaison [kRəvɛzɔ̃] *nf* puncture, flat.
crevant, e [kRəvɑ, -ɑ̃t] *adj* (*fam: fatigant*) knackering; (: *très drôle*) priceless.
crevasse [kRəvas] *nf* (*dans le sol*) crack, fissure; (*de glacier*) crevasse; (*de la peau*) crack.
crevé, e [kRəve] *adj* (*fam: fatigué*) worn out, dead beat.
crève-cœur [kRɛvkœR] *nm inv* heartbreak.
crever [kRəve] *vt* (*papier*) to tear, break; (*tambour, ballon*) to burst ♦ *vi* (*pneu*) to burst; (*automobiliste*) to have a puncture (*BRIT*) *ou* a flat (tire) (*US*); (*abcès, outre, nuage*) to burst (open); (*fam*) to die; **cela lui a crevé un œil** it blinded him in one eye; ~ **l'écran** to have real screen presence.
crevette [kRəvɛt] *nf*: ~ **(rose)** prawn; ~ **grise** shrimp.
CRF *sigle f* (= *Croix-Rouge française*) French Red Cross.
cri [kRi] *nm* cry, shout; (*d'animal: spécifique*) cry, call; **à grands** ~**s** at the top of one's voice; **c'est le dernier** ~ (*fig*) it's the latest fashion.
criant, e [kRijɑ̃, -ɑ̃t] *adj* (*injustice*) glaring.
criard, e [kRijaR, -aRd(ə)] *adj* (*couleur*) garish, loud; (*voix*) yelling.
crible [kRibl(ə)] *nm* riddle; (*mécanique*) screen, jig; **passer qch au** ~ to put sth through a riddle; (*fig*) to go over sth with a fine-tooth comb.
criblé, e [kRible] *adj*: ~ **de** riddled with.
cric [kRik] *nm* (*AUTO*) jack.
cricket [kRikɛt] *nm* cricket.
criée [kRije] *nf*: **(vente à la)** ~ (sale by) auction.
crier [kRije] *vi* (*pour appeler*) to shout, cry (out); (*de peur, de douleur etc*) to scream, yell; (*fig: grincer*) to squeal, screech ♦ *vt* (*ordre, injure*) to shout (out), yell (out); **sans** ~ **gare** without warning; ~ **grâce** to cry for mercy; ~ **au secours** to shout for help.
crieur, euse [kRijœR, -øz] *nm/f*: ~ **de journaux** newspaper seller.
crime [kRim] *nm* crime; (*meurtre*) murder.
Crimée [kRime] *nf*: **la** ~ the Crimea.
criminaliste [kRiminalist(ə)] *nm/f* specialist in criminal law.
criminalité [kRiminalite] *nf* criminality, crime.
criminel, le [kRiminɛl] *adj* criminal ♦ *nm/f* criminal; murderer; ~ **de guerre** war criminal.
criminologie [kRiminɔlɔʒi] *nf* criminology.
criminologiste [kRiminɔlɔʒist(ə)] *nm/f* criminologist.
criminologue [kRiminɔlɔg] *nm/f* criminologist.
crin [kRɛ̃] *nm* hair *no pl*; (*fibre*) horsehair; **à tous** ~**s, à tout** ~ diehard, out-and-out.
crinière [kRinjɛR] *nf* mane.
crique [kRik] *nf* creek, inlet.
criquet [kRikɛ] *nm* grasshopper.
crise [kRiz] *nf* crisis (*pl* crises); (*MÉD*) attack; fit; ~ **cardiaque** heart attack; ~ **de foi** crisis of belief; ~ **de foie** bilious attack; ~ **de nerfs** attack of nerves.
crispant, e [kRispɑ̃, -ɑ̃t] *adj* annoying, irritating.
crispation [kRispɑsjɔ̃] *nf* (*spasme*) twitch; (*contraction*) contraction; tenseness.
crispé, e [kRispe] *adj* tense, nervous.
crisper [kRispe] *vt* to tense; (*poings*) to clench; **se** ~ to tense; to clench; (*personne*) to get tense.
crissement [kRismɑ̃] *nm* crunch; rustle; screech.
crisser [kRise] *vi* (*neige*) to crunch; (*tissu*) to rustle; (*pneu*) to screech.
cristal, aux [kRistal, -o] *nm* crystal ♦ *nmpl* (*objets*) crystal(ware) *sg*; ~ **de plomb** (lead)

crystal; ~ **de roche** rock-crystal; **cristaux de soude** washing soda *sg*.
cristallin, e [kʀistalɛ̃, -in] *adj* crystal-clear ♦ *nm* (*ANAT*) crystalline lens.
cristalliser [kʀistalize] *vi, vt*, **se** ~ *vi* to crystallize.
critère [kʀitɛʀ] *nm* criterion (*pl* -ia).
critiquable [kʀitikabl(ə)] *adj* open to criticism.
critique [kʀitik] *adj* critical ♦ *nm/f* (*de théâtre, musique*) critic ♦ *nf* criticism; (*THÉÂT etc: article*) review; **la** ~ (*activité*) criticism; (*personnes*) the critics *pl*.
critiquer [kʀitike] *vt* (*dénigrer*) to criticize; (*évaluer, juger*) to assess, examine (critically).
croasser [kʀɔase] *vi* to caw.
croate [kʀɔat] *adj* Croatian ♦ *nm* (*LING*) Croat, Croatian.
Croatie [kʀɔasi] *nf*: **la** ~ Croatia.
croc [kʀo] *nm* (*dent*) fang; (*de boucher*) hook.
croc-en-jambe, *pl* **crocs-en-jambe** [kʀɔkɑ̃ʒɑ̃b] *nm*: **faire un** ~ **à qn** to trip sb up.
croche [kʀɔʃ] *nf* (*MUS*) quaver (*BRIT*), eighth note (*US*); **double** ~ semiquaver (*BRIT*), sixteenth note (*US*).
croche-pied [kʀɔʃpje] *nm* = **croc-en-jambe**.
crochet [kʀɔʃɛ] *nm* hook; (*clef*) picklock; (*détour*) detour; (*BOXE*): ~ **du gauche** left hook; (*TRICOT: aiguille*) crochet hook; (*: technique*) crochet; ~**s** *nmpl* (*TYPO*) square brackets; **vivre aux** ~**s de qn** to live *ou* sponge off sb.
crocheter [kʀɔʃte] *vt* (*serrure*) to pick.
crochu, e [kʀɔʃy] *adj* hooked; claw-like.
crocodile [kʀɔkɔdil] *nm* crocodile.
crocus [kʀɔkys] *nm* crocus.
croire [kʀwaʀ] *vt* to believe; ~ **qn honnête** to believe sb (to be) honest; **se** ~ **fort** to think one is strong; ~ **que** to believe *ou* think that; **vous croyez?** do you think so?; ~ **être/faire** to think one is/does; ~ **à**, ~ **en** to believe in.
croîs [kʀwa] *etc vb voir* **croître**.
croisade [kʀwazad] *nf* crusade.
croisé, e [kʀwaze] *adj* (*veston*) double-breasted ♦ *nm* (*guerrier*) crusader ♦ *nf* (*fenêtre*) window, casement; ~**e d'ogives** intersecting ribs; **à la** ~**e des chemins** at the crossroads.
croisement [kʀwazmɑ̃] *nm* (*carrefour*) crossroads *sg*; (*BIO*) crossing; crossbreed.
croiser [kʀwaze] *vt* (*personne, voiture*) to pass; (*route*) to cross, cut across; (*BIO*) to cross ♦ *vi* (*NAVIG*) to cruise; ~ **les jambes/bras** to cross one's legs/fold one's arms; **se** ~ (*personnes, véhicules*) to pass each other; (*routes*) to cross, intersect; (*lettres*) to cross (in the post); (*regards*) to meet; **se** ~ **les bras** (*fig*) to twiddle one's thumbs.
croiseur [kʀwazœʀ] *nm* cruiser (*warship*).
croisière [kʀwazjɛʀ] *nf* cruise; **vitesse de** ~ (*AUTO etc*) cruising speed.
croisillon [kʀwazijɔ̃] *nm*: **motif/fenêtre à** ~**s** lattice pattern/window.
croissais [kʀwasɛ] *etc vb voir* **croître**.
croissance [kʀwasɑ̃s] *nf* growing, growth; **troubles de la** ~ growing pains; **maladie de** ~ growth disease; ~ **économique** economic growth.
croissant, e [kʀwasɑ̃, -ɑ̃t] *vb voir* **croître** ♦ *adj* growing; rising ♦ *nm* (*à manger*) croissant; (*motif*) crescent; ~ **de lune** crescent moon.
croître [kʀwatʀ(ə)] *vi* to grow; (*lune*) to wax.
croix [kʀwa] *nf* cross; **en** ~ *adj, adv* in the form of a cross; **la C**~ **Rouge** the Red Cross.
croquant, e [kʀɔkɑ̃, -ɑ̃t] *adj* crisp, crunchy ♦ *nm/f* (*péj*) yokel, (country) bumpkin.
croque-madame [kʀɔkmadam] *nm inv toasted cheese sandwich with a fried egg on top.*
croque-mitaine [kʀɔkmitɛn] *nm* bog(e)y-man (*pl* -men).
croque-monsieur [kʀɔkməsjø] *nm inv toasted ham and cheese sandwich.*
croque-mort [kʀɔkmɔʀ] *nm* (*péj*) pallbearer.
croquer [kʀɔke] *vt* (*manger*) to crunch; to munch; (*dessiner*) to sketch ♦ *vi* to be crisp *ou* crunchy; **chocolat à** ~ plain dessert chocolate.
croquet [kʀɔkɛ] *nm* croquet.
croquette [kʀɔkɛt] *nf* croquette.
croquis [kʀɔki] *nm* sketch.
cross(-country), *pl* **cross(-countries)** [kʀɔs(kuntʀi)] *nm* cross-country race *ou* run; cross-country racing *ou* running.
crosse [kʀɔs] *nf* (*de fusil*) butt; (*de revolver*) grip; (*d'évêque*) crook, crosier; (*de hockey*) hockey stick.
crotale [kʀɔtal] *nm* rattlesnake.
crotte [kʀɔt] *nf* droppings *pl*; ~**!** (*fam*) damn!
crotté, e [kʀɔte] *adj* muddy, mucky.
crottin [kʀɔtɛ̃] *nm*: ~ **(de cheval)** (horse) dung *ou* manure.
croulant, e [kʀulɑ̃, -ɑ̃t] *nm/f* (*fam*) old fogey.
crouler [kʀule] *vi* (*s'effondrer*) to collapse; (*être délabré*) to be crumbling.
croupe [kʀup] *nf* croup, rump; **en** ~ pillion.
croupier [kʀupje] *nm* croupier.
croupion [kʀupjɔ̃] *nm* (*d'un oiseau*) rump; (*CULIN*) parson's nose.
croupir [kʀupiʀ] *vi* to stagnate.
CROUS [kʀus] *sigle m* (= *Centre régional des œuvres universitaires et scolaires*) *students' representative body.*
croustade [kʀustad] *nf* (*CULIN*) croustade.
croustillant, e [kʀustijɑ̃, -ɑ̃t] *adj* crisp; (*fig*) spicy.
croustiller [kʀustije] *vi* to be crisp *ou* crusty.
croûte [kʀut] *nf* crust; (*du fromage*) rind; (*de vol-au-vent*) case; (*MÉD*) scab; **en** ~ (*CULIN*) in pastry, in a pie; ~ **aux champignons** mushrooms on toast; ~ **au fromage** cheese on toast *no pl*; ~ **de pain** (*morceau*) crust (of bread); ~ **terrestre** earth's crust.
croûton [kʀutɔ̃] *nm* (*CULIN*) crouton; (*bout du pain*) crust, heel.

croyable [kʀwajabl(ə)] *adj* believable, credible.

croyais [kʀwajɛ] *etc vb voir* **croire.**

croyance [kʀwajɑ̃s] *nf* belief.

croyant, e [kʀwajɑ̃, -ɑ̃t] *vb voir* **croire** ♦ *adj*: **être/ne pas être** ~ to be/not to be a believer ♦ *nm/f* believer.

Crozet [kʀɔzɛ] *n*: **les îles** ~ the Crozet Islands.

CRS *sigle fpl* (= *Compagnies républicaines de sécurité*) *state security police force* ♦ *sigle m member of the CRS.*

cru, e [kʀy] *pp de* **croire** ♦ *adj* (*non cuit*) raw; (*lumière, couleur*) harsh; (*description*) crude; (*paroles, langage: franc*) blunt; (*: grossier*) crude ♦ *nm* (*vignoble*) vineyard; (*vin*) wine ♦ *nf* (*d'un cours d'eau*) swelling, rising; **de son (propre)** ~ (*fig*) of his own devising; **monter à** ~ to ride bareback; **du** ~ local; **en** ~**e** in spate.

crû [kʀy] *pp de* **croître.**

cruauté [kʀyote] *nf* cruelty.

cruche [kʀyʃ] *nf* pitcher, (earthenware) jug.

crucial, e, aux [kʀysjal, -o] *adj* crucial.

crucifier [kʀysifje] *vt* to crucify.

crucifix [kʀysifi] *nm* crucifix.

crucifixion [kʀysifiksjɔ̃] *nf* crucifixion.

cruciforme [kʀysifɔʀm(ə)] *adj* cruciform, cross-shaped.

cruciverbiste [kʀysivɛʀbist(ə)] *nm/f* crossword puzzle enthusiast.

crudité [kʀydite] *nf* crudeness *no pl*; harshness *no pl*; ~**s** *nfpl* (*CULIN*) mixed salads (*as hors d'œuvre*).

crue [kʀy] *nf voir* **cru.**

cruel, le [kʀyɛl] *adj* cruel.

cruellement [kʀyɛlmɑ̃] *adv* cruelly.

crûment [kʀymɑ̃] *adv* (*voir cru*) harshly; bluntly; crudely.

crus, crûs [kʀy] *etc vb voir* **croire; croître.**

crustacés [kʀystase] *nmpl* shellfish.

crypte [kʀipt(ə)] *nf* crypt.

CSA *sigle f* (= *Conseil supérieur de l'audiovisuel*) *French broadcasting regulatory body*, ≈ IBA (*BRIT*), ≈ FCC (*US*).

CSCE *sigle f* (= *Conférence sur la sécurité et la coopération en Europe*) CSCE.

cse *abr* = **cause.**

CSEN *sigle f* (= *Confédération des syndicats de l'éducation nationale*) *group of teachers' unions.*

CSG *sigle f* (= *contribution sociale généralisée*) *supplementary social security contribution in aid of the underprivileged.*

Cte *abr* = **Comtesse.**

CU *sigle f* = *communauté urbaine.*

Cuba [kyba] *nm*: **le** ~ Cuba.

cubage [kybaʒ] *nm* cubage, cubic content.

cubain, e [kybɛ̃, -ɛn] *adj* Cuban ♦ *nm/f*: **C~, e** Cuban.

cube [kyb] *nm* cube; (*jouet*) brick, building block; **gros** ~ powerful motorbike; **mètre** ~ cubic metre; **2 au** ~ **= 8** 2 cubed is 8; **élever au** ~ to cube.

cubique [kybik] *adj* cubic.

cubisme [kybism(ə)] *nm* cubism.

cubiste [kybist(ə)] *adj, nm/f* cubist.

cubitus [kybitys] *nm* ulna.

cueillette [kœjɛt] *nf* picking, gathering; harvest *ou* crop (of fruit).

cueillir [kœjiʀ] *vt* (*fruits, fleurs*) to pick, gather; (*fig*) to catch.

cuiller *ou* **cuillère** [kɥijɛʀ] *nf* spoon; ~ **à café** coffee spoon; (*CULIN*) ≈ teaspoonful; ~ **à soupe** soup spoon; (*CULIN*) ≈ tablespoonful.

cuillerée [kɥijʀe] *nf* spoonful; (*CULIN*): ~ **à soupe/café** tablespoonful/teaspoonful.

cuir [kɥiʀ] *nm* leather; (*avant tannage*) hide; ~ **chevelu** scalp.

cuirasse [kɥiʀas] *nf* breastplate.

cuirassé [kɥiʀase] *nm* (*NAVIG*) battleship.

cuire [kɥiʀ] *vt* (*aliments*) to cook; (*au four*) to bake; (*poterie*) to fire ♦ *vi* to cook; (*picoter*) to smart, sting, burn; **bien cuit** (*viande*) well done; **trop cuit** overdone; **pas assez cuit** underdone; **cuit à point** medium done; done to a turn.

cuisant, e [kɥizɑ̃, -ɑ̃t] *vb voir* **cuire** ♦ *adj* (*douleur*) smarting, burning; (*fig: souvenir, échec*) bitter.

cuisine [kɥizin] *nf* (*pièce*) kitchen; (*art culinaire*) cookery, cooking; (*nourriture*) cooking, food; **faire la** ~ to cook.

cuisiné, e [kɥizine] *adj*: **plat** ~ ready-made meal *ou* dish.

cuisiner [kɥizine] *vt* to cook; (*fam*) to grill ♦ *vi* to cook.

cuisinette [kɥizinɛt] *nf* kitchenette.

cuisinier, ière [kɥizinje, -jɛʀ] *nm/f* cook ♦ *nf* (*poêle*) cooker.

cuisis [kɥizi] *etc vb voir* **cuire.**

cuissardes [kɥisaʀd] *nfpl* (*de pêcheur*) waders; (*de femme*) thigh boots.

cuisse [kɥis] *nf* (*ANAT*) thigh; (*CULIN*) leg.

cuisson [kɥisɔ̃] *nf* cooking; (*de poterie*) firing.

cuissot [kɥiso] *nm* haunch.

cuistre [kɥistʀ(ə)] *nm* prig.

cuit, e [kɥi, -it] *pp de* **cuire** ♦ *nf* (*fam*): **prendre une** ~**e** to get plastered *ou* smashed.

cuivre [kɥivʀ(ə)] *nm* copper; **les** ~**s** (*MUS*) the brass; ~ **rouge** copper; ~ **jaune** brass.

cuivré, e [kɥivʀe] *adj* coppery; (*peau*) bronzed.

cul [ky] *nm* (*fam!*) arse (*BRIT !*), ass (*US !*), bum (*BRIT*); ~ **de bouteille** bottom of a bottle.

culasse [kylas] *nf* (*AUTO*) cylinder-head; (*de fusil*) breech.

culbute [kylbyt] *nf* somersault; (*accidentelle*) tumble, fall.

culbuter [kylbyte] *vi* to (take a) tumble, fall (head over heels).

culbuteur [kylbytœʀ] *nm* (*AUTO*) rocker arm.

cul-de-jatte, *pl* **culs-de-jatte** [kydʒat] *nm/f* legless cripple.

cul-de-sac, *pl* **culs-de-sac** [kydsak] *nm* cul-de-sac.

culinaire [kylinɛʀ] *adj* culinary.
culminant, e [kylminɑ̃, -ɑ̃t] *adj*: **point ~** highest point; (*fig*) height, climax.
culminer [kylmine] *vi* to reach its highest point; to tower.
culot [kylo] *nm* (*d'ampoule*) cap; (*effronterie*) cheek, nerve.
culotte [kylɔt] *nf* (*de femme*) panties *pl*, knickers *pl* (*BRIT*); (*d'homme*) underpants *pl*; (*pantalon*) trousers *pl* (*BRIT*), pants *pl* (*US*); **~ de cheval** riding breeches *pl*.
culotté, e [kylɔte] *adj* (*pipe*) seasoned; (*cuir*) mellowed; (*effronté*) cheeky.
culpabiliser [kylpabilize] *vt*: **~ qn** to make sb feel guilty.
culpabilité [kylpabilite] *nf* guilt.
culte [kylt(ə)] *adj*: **livre/film ~** cult film/book ♦ *nm* (*religion*) religion; (*hommage, vénération*) worship; (*protestant*) service.
cultivable [kyltivabl(ə)] *adj* cultivable.
cultivateur, trice [kyltivatœʀ, -tʀis] *nm/f* farmer.
cultivé, e [kyltive] *adj* (*personne*) cultured, cultivated.
cultiver [kyltive] *vt* to cultivate; (*légumes*) to grow, cultivate.
culture [kyltyʀ] *nf* cultivation; growing; (*connaissances etc*) culture; **(champs de) ~s** land(s) under cultivation; **~ physique** physical training.
culturel, le [kyltyʀɛl] *adj* cultural.
culturisme [kyltyʀism(ə)] *nm* body-building.
culturiste [kyltyʀist(ə)] *nm/f* body-builder.
cumin [kymɛ̃] *nm* (*CULIN*) caraway seeds *pl*; cumin.
cumul [kymyl] *nm* (*voir cumuler*) holding (*ou* drawing) concurrently; **~ de peines** sentences to run consecutively.
cumulable [kymylabl(ə)] *adj* (*fonctions*) which may be held concurrently.
cumuler [kymyle] *vt* (*emplois, honneurs*) to hold concurrently; (*salaires*) to draw concurrently; (*JUR*: *droits*) to accumulate.
cupide [kypid] *adj* greedy, grasping.
cupidité [kypidite] *nf* greed.
curable [kyʀabl(ə)] *adj* curable.
Curaçao [kyʀaso] *n* Curaçao ♦ *nm*: **c~** curaçao.
curare [kyʀaʀ] *nm* curare.
curatif, ive [kyʀatif, -iv] *adj* curative.
cure [kyʀ] *nf* (*MÉD*) course of treatment; (*REL*) cure, ≈ living; presbytery, ≈ vicarage; **faire une ~ de fruits** to go on a fruit cure *ou* diet; **faire une ~ thermale** to take the waters; **n'avoir ~ de** to pay no attention to; **~ d'amaigrissement** slimming course; **~ de repos** rest cure; **~ de sommeil** sleep therapy.
curé [kyʀe] *nm* parish priest; **M le ~** ≈ Vicar.
cure-dent [kyʀdɑ̃] *nm* toothpick.
curée [kyʀe] *nf* (*fig*) scramble for the pickings.
cure-ongles [kyʀɔ̃gl(ə)] *nm inv* nail cleaner.
cure-pipe [kyʀpip] *nm* pipe cleaner.
curer [kyʀe] *vt* to clean out; **se ~ les dents** to pick one's teeth.
curetage [kyʀtaʒ] *nm* (*MÉD*) curettage.
curieusement [kyʀjøzmɑ̃] *adv* oddly.
curieux, euse [kyʀjø, -øz] *adj* (*étrange*) strange, curious; (*indiscret*) curious, inquisitive; (*intéressé*) inquiring, curious ♦ *nmpl* (*badauds*) onlookers, bystanders.
curiosité [kyʀjozite] *nf* curiosity, inquisitiveness; (*objet*) curio(sity); (*site*) unusual feature *ou* sight.
curiste [kyʀist(ə)] *nm/f* *person taking the waters at a spa.*
curriculum vitae (CV) [kyʀikylɔmvite] *nm inv* curriculum vitae (CV).
curry [kyʀi] *nm* curry; **poulet au ~** curried chicken, chicken curry.
curseur [kyʀsœʀ] *nm* (*INFORM*) cursor; (*de règle*) slide; (*de fermeture-éclair*) slider.
cursif, ive [kyʀsif, -iv] *adj*: **écriture cursive** cursive script.
cursus [kyʀsys] *nm* degree course.
cutané, e [kytane] *adj* cutaneous, skin *cpd*.
cuti-réaction [kytiʀeaksjɔ̃] *nf* (*MÉD*) skin-test.
cuve [kyv] *nf* vat; (*à mazout etc*) tank.
cuvée [kyve] *nf* vintage.
cuvette [kyvɛt] *nf* (*récipient*) bowl, basin; (*du lavabo*) (wash)basin; (*des w.-c.*) pan; (*GÉO*) basin.
CV *sigle m* (*AUTO*) = **cheval vapeur**; (*ADMIN*) = **curriculum vitae**.
CVS *sigle adj* (= *corrigées des variations saisonnières*) seasonally adjusted.
cx *abr* (= *coefficient de pénétration dans l'air*) drag coefficient.
cyanure [sjanyʀ] *nm* cyanide.
cybercafé [sibɛʀkafe] *nm* cybercafé.
cyberculture [sibɛʀkyltyr] *nf* cyberculture.
cybernétique [sibɛʀnetik] *nf* cybernetics *sg*.
cyclable [siklabl(ə)] *adj*: **piste ~** cycle track.
cyclamen [siklamɛn] *nm* cyclamen.
cycle [sikl(ə)] *nm* cycle; (*SCOL*): **premier/second ~** ≈ middle/upper school (*BRIT*), ≈ junior/senior high school (*US*).
cyclique [siklik] *adj* cyclic(al).
cyclisme [siklism(ə)] *nm* cycling.
cycliste [siklist(ə)] *nm/f* cyclist ♦ *adj* cycle *cpd*; **coureur ~** racing cyclist.
cyclo-cross [siklɔkʀɔs] *nm* (*SPORT*) cyclo-cross; (*épreuve*) cyclo-cross race.
cyclomoteur [siklɔmɔtœʀ] *nm* moped.
cyclomotoriste [siklɔmɔtɔʀist(ə)] *nm/f* moped rider.
cyclone [siklon] *nm* hurricane.
cyclotourisme [siklɔtuʀism(ə)] *nm* (bi)cycle touring.
cygne [siɲ] *nm* swan.
cylindre [silɛ̃dʀ(ə)] *nm* cylinder; **moteur à 4 ~s en ligne** straight-4 engine.
cylindrée [silɛ̃dʀe] *nf* (*AUTO*) (cubic) capacity; **une (voiture de) grosse ~** a big-engined car.
cylindrique [silɛ̃dʀik] *adj* cylindrical.

cymbale [sɛ̃bal] *nf* cymbal.
cynique [sinik] *adj* cynical.
cyniquement [sinikmɑ̃] *adv* cynically.
cynisme [sinism(ə)] *nm* cynicism.
cyprès [sipʀɛ] *nm* cypress.
cypriote [sipʀijɔt] *adj* Cypriot ♦ *nm/f*: **C~** Cypriot.
cyrillique [siʀilik] *adj* Cyrillic.
cystite [sistit] *nf* cystitis.
cytise [sitiz] *nm* laburnum.
cytologie [sitɔlɔʒi] *nf* cytology.

D d

D, d [de] *nm inv* D, d ♦ *abr*: **D** (*MÉTÉO*: = *dépression*) low, depression; **D comme Désiré** D for David (*BRIT*) *ou* Dog (*US*); *voir* **système**.
d' *prép, dét voir* **de**.
Dacca [daka] *n* Dacca.
dactylo [daktilo] *nf* (*aussi*: ~**graphe**) typist; (*aussi*: ~**graphie**) typing, typewriting.
dactylographier [daktilɔgʀafje] *vt* to type (out).
dada [dada] *nm* hobby-horse.
dadais [dadɛ] *nm* ninny, lump.
dague [dag] *nf* dagger.
dahlia [dalja] *nm* dahlia.
dahoméen, ne [daɔmeɛ̃, -ɛn] *adj* Dahomean.
Dahomey [daɔmɛ] *nm*: **le** ~ Dahomey.
daigner [deɲe] *vt* to deign.
daim [dɛ̃] *nm* (fallow) deer *inv*; (*peau*) buckskin; (*imitation*) suede.
dais [dɛ] *nm* (*tenture*) canopy.
Dakar [dakaʀ] *n* Dakar.
dal. *abr* (= *décalitre*) dal.
dallage [dalaʒ] *nm* paving.
dalle [dal] *nf* slab; (*au sol*) paving stone, flag(stone); **que** ~ nothing at all, damn all (*BRIT*).
daller [dale] *vt* to pave.
dalmate [dalmat] *adj* Dalmatian.
Dalmatie [dalmasi] *nf*: **la** ~ Dalmatia.
dalmatien, ne [dalmasjɛ̃, -ɛn] *nm/f* (*chien*) Dalmatian.
daltonien, ne [daltɔnjɛ̃, -ɛn] *adj* colour-blind (*BRIT*), color-blind (*US*).
daltonisme [daltɔnism(ə)] *nm* colour (*BRIT*) *ou* color (*US*) blindness.
dam [dam] *nm*: **au grand** ~ **de** much to the detriment (*ou* annoyance) of.
Damas [dama] *n* Damascus.
damas [dama] *nm* (*étoffe*) damask.
damassé, e [damase] *adj* damask *cpd*.
dame [dam] *nf* lady; (*CARTES, ÉCHECS*) queen; ~**s** *nfpl* (*jeu*) draughts *sg* (*BRIT*), checkers *sg* (*US*); **les (toilettes des)** ~**s** the ladies' (toilets); ~ **de charité** benefactress; ~ **de compagnie** lady's companion.
dame-jeanne, *pl* **dames-jeannes** [damʒɑn] *nf* demijohn.
damer [dame] *vt* to ram *ou* pack down; ~ **le pion à** (*fig*) to get the better of.
damier [damje] *nm* draughtboard (*BRIT*), checkerboard (*US*); (*dessin*) check (pattern); **en** ~ check.
damner [dɑne] *vt* to damn.
dancing [dɑ̃siŋ] *nm* dance hall.
dandiner [dɑ̃dine]: **se** ~ *vi* to sway about; (*en marchant*) to waddle along.
Danemark [danmaʀk] *nm*: **le** ~ Denmark.
danger [dɑ̃ʒe] *nm* danger; **mettre en** ~ to endanger, put in danger; **être en** ~ **de mort** to be in peril of one's life; **être hors de** ~ to be out of danger.
dangereusement [dɑ̃ʒʀøzmɑ̃] *adv* dangerously.
dangereux, euse [dɑ̃ʒʀø, -øz] *adj* dangerous.
danois, e [danwa, -waz] *adj* Danish ♦ *nm* (*LING*) Danish ♦ *nm/f*: **D~, e** Dane.

MOT-CLÉ

dans [dɑ̃] *prép* **1** (*position*) in; (*à l'intérieur de*) inside; **c'est** ~ **le tiroir/le salon** it's in the drawer/lounge; ~ **la boîte** in *ou* inside the box; **marcher** ~ **la ville/la rue** to walk about the town/along the street; **je l'ai lu** ~ **le journal** I read it in the newspaper; **être** ~ **les meilleurs** to be among *ou* one of the best
2 (*direction*) into; **elle a couru** ~ **le salon** she ran into the lounge
3 (*provenance*) out of, from; **je l'ai pris** ~ **le tiroir/salon** I took it out of *ou* from the drawer/lounge; **boire** ~ **un verre** to drink out of *ou* from a glass
4 (*temps*) in; ~ **2 mois** in 2 months, in 2 months' time
5 (*approximation*) about; ~ **les 20 €** about €20.

dansant, e [dɑ̃sɑ̃, -ɑ̃t] *adj*: **soirée** ~**e** evening of dancing; (*bal*) dinner dance.
danse [dɑ̃s] *nf*: **la** ~ dancing; (*classique*) (ballet) dancing; **une** ~ a dance; ~ **du ventre** belly dancing.
danser [dɑ̃se] *vi, vt* to dance.
danseur, euse [dɑ̃sœʀ, -øz] *nm/f* ballet dancer; (*au bal etc*) dancer; (*: cavalier*) partner; ~ **de claquettes** tap-dancer; **en danseuse** (*à vélo*) standing on the pedals.
Danube [danyb] *nm*: **le** ~ the Danube.
DAO *sigle m* (= *dessin assisté par ordinateur*) CAD.
dard [daʀ] *nm* sting (*organ*).
Dardanelles [daʀdanɛl] *nfpl*: **les** ~ the Dardanelles.
darder [daʀde] *vt* to shoot, send forth.
dare-dare [daʀdaʀ] *adv* in double quick time.

Dar-es-Salaam, Dar-es-Salam [daʀɛsalam] *n* Dar-es-Salaam.
darne [daʀn] *nf* steak (*of fish*).
darse [daʀs(ə)] *nf* sheltered dock (*in a Mediterranean port*).
dartre [daʀtʀ(ə)] *nf* (*MÉD*) sore.
datation [datɑsjɔ̃] *nf* dating.
date [dat] *nf* date; **faire ~** to mark a milestone; **de longue ~** *adj* longstanding; **~ de naissance** date of birth; **~ limite** deadline; (*d'un aliment*: *aussi*: **~ limite de vente**) sell-by date.
dater [date] *vt, vi* to date; **~ de** to date from, go back to; **à ~ de** (as) from.
dateur [datœʀ] *nm* (*de montre*) date indicator; **timbre ~** date stamp.
datif [datif] *nm* dative.
datte [dat] *nf* date.
dattier [datje] *nm* date palm.
daube [dob] *nf*: **bœuf en ~** beef casserole.
dauphin [dofɛ̃] *nm* (*ZOOL*) dolphin; (*du roi*) dauphin; (*fig*) heir apparent.
Dauphiné [dofine] *nm*: **le ~** the Dauphiné.
dauphinois, e [dofinwa, -waz] *adj* of *ou* from the Dauphiné.
daurade [dɔʀad] *nf* sea bream.
davantage [davɑ̃taʒ] *adv* more; (*plus longtemps*) longer; **~ de** more; **~ que** more than.
DB *sigle f* (*MIL*) = *division blindée.*
DCA *sigle f* (= *défense contre avions*) anti-aircraft defence.
DCC *sigle f* ® (= *digital compact cassette*) DCC ®.
DCT *sigle m* (= *diphtérie coqueluche tétanos*) DPT.
DDASS [dɑs] *sigle f* (= *Direction départementale d'action sanitaire et sociale*) ≈ DHSS (= *Department of Health and Social Security*) (*BRIT*), ≈ SSA (= *Social Security Administration*) (*US*).
DDT *sigle m* (= *dichloro-diphénol-trichloréthane*) DDT.

MOT-CLÉ

de (d') (*de +le* = **du,** *de +les* = **des**) *prép* **1** (*appartenance*) of; **le toit ~ la maison** the roof of the house; **la voiture d'Elisabeth/~ mes parents** Elizabeth's/my parents' car
2 (*provenance*) from; **il vient ~ Londres** he comes from London; **~ Londres à Paris** from London to Paris; **elle est sortie du cinéma** she came out of the cinema
3 (*moyen*) with; **je l'ai fait ~ mes propres mains** I did it with my own two hands
4 (*caractérisation, mesure*): **un mur ~ brique/bureau d'acajou** a brick wall/mahogany desk; **un billet ~ 50 €** a €50 note; **une pièce ~ 2 m ~ large** *ou* **large ~ 2 m** a room 2 m wide, a 2m-wide room; **un bébé ~ 10 mois** a 10-month-old baby; **12 mois ~ crédit/travail** 12 months' credit/work; **elle est payée 8 € ~ l'heure** she's paid €8 an hour *ou* per hour; **augmenter ~ 10 €** to increase by €10; **3 jours ~ libres** 3 free days, 3 days free; **un verre d'eau** a glass of water; **il mange ~ tout** he'll eat anything
5 (*rapport*) from; **~ 4 à 6** from 4 to 6
6 (*de la part de*): **estimé ~ ses collègues** respected by his colleagues
7 (*cause*): **mourir ~ faim** to die of hunger; **rouge ~ colère** red with fury
8 (*vb +de +infin*) to; **il m'a dit ~ rester** he told me to stay
9 (*en apposition*): **cet imbécile ~ Paul** that idiot Paul; **le terme ~ franglais** the term "franglais"
♦ *dét* **1** (*phrases affirmatives*) some (*souvent omis*); **du vin, ~ l'eau, des pommes** (some) wine, (some) water, (some) apples; **des enfants sont venus** some children came; **pendant des mois** for months
2 (*phrases interrogatives et négatives*) any; **a-t-il du vin?** has he got any wine?; **il n'a pas ~ pommes/d'enfants** he hasn't (got) any apples/children, he has no apples/children.

dé [de] *nm* (*à jouer*) die *ou* dice (*pl* dice); (*aussi*: **~ à coudre**) thimble; **~s** *nmpl* (*jeu*) (game of) dice; **un coup de ~s** a throw of the dice; **couper en ~s** (*CULIN*) to dice.
DEA *sigle m* (= *Diplôme d'études approfondies*) *post-graduate diploma.*
dealer [dilœʀ] *nm* (*fam*) (drug) pusher.
déambulateur [deɑ̃bylatœʀ] *nm* zimmer ®.
déambuler [deɑ̃byle] *vi* to stroll about.
déb. *abr* = **débutant**; (*COMM*) = *à débattre.*
débâcle [debɑkl(ə)] *nf* rout.
déballage [debalaʒ] *nm* (*de marchandises*) display (*of loose goods*); (*fig: fam*) outpourings *pl.*
déballer [debale] *vt* to unpack.
débandade [debɑ̃dad] *nf* scattering; (*déroute*) rout.
débander [debɑ̃de] *vt* to unbandage.
débaptiser [debatize] *vt* (*rue*) to rename.
débarbouiller [debaʀbuje] *vt* to wash; **se ~** to wash (one's face).
débarcadère [debaʀkadɛʀ] *nm* landing stage (*BRIT*), wharf.
débardeur [debaʀdœʀ] *nm* docker, stevedore; (*maillot*) slipover, tank top.
débarquement [debaʀkəmɑ̃] *nm* unloading, landing; disembarcation; (*MIL*) landing; **le D~** the Normandy landings.
débarquer [debaʀke] *vt* to unload, land ♦ *vi* to disembark; (*fig*) to turn up.
débarras [debaʀa] *nm* lumber room; (*placard*) junk cupboard; (*remise*) outhouse; **bon ~!** good riddance!
débarrasser [debaʀase] *vt* to clear ♦ *vi* (*enlever le couvert*) to clear away; **~ qn de** (*vêtements, paquets*) to relieve sb of; (*habitude, ennemi*) to rid sb of; **~ qch de** (*fouillis etc*) to clear sth of; **se ~ de** *vt* to get rid of; to rid o.s. of.
débat [deba] *vb voir* **débattre** ♦ *nm* discussion

debate; ~**s** *nmpl* (*POL*) proceedings, debates.
débattre [debatʀ(ə)] *vt* to discuss, debate; **se ~** *vi* to struggle.
débauchage [deboʃaʒ] *nm* (*licenciement*) laying off (of staff); (*par un concurrent*) poaching.
débauche [deboʃ] *nf* debauchery; **une ~ de** (*fig*) a profusion of; (*: de couleurs*) a riot of.
débauché, e [deboʃe] *adj* debauched ♦ *nm/f* profligate.
débaucher [deboʃe] *vt* (*licencier*) to lay off, dismiss; (*salarié d'une autre entreprise*) to poach; (*entraîner*) to lead astray, debauch; (*inciter à la grève*) to incite.
débile [debil] *adj* weak, feeble; (*fam: idiot*) dim-witted ♦ *nm/f*: ~ **mental, e** mental defective.
débilitant, e [debilitɑ̃, -ɑ̃t] *adj* debilitating.
débilité [debilite] *nf* debility; (*fam: idiotie*) stupidity; ~ **mentale** mental debility.
débiner [debine]: **se ~** *vi* to do a bunk (*BRIT*), clear out.
débit [debi] *nm* (*d'un liquide, fleuve*) (rate of) flow; (*d'un magasin*) turnover (of goods); (*élocution*) delivery; (*bancaire*) debit; **avoir un ~ de 10 €** to be €10 in debit; ~ **de boissons** drinking establishment; ~ **de tabac** tobacconist's (shop) (*BRIT*), tobacco *ou* smoke shop (*US*).
débiter [debite] *vt* (*compte*) to debit; (*liquide, gaz*) to yield, produce, give out; (*couper: bois, viande*) to cut up; (*vendre*) to retail; (*péj: paroles etc*) to come out with, churn out.
débiteur, trice [debitœʀ, -tʀis] *nm/f* debtor ♦ *adj* in debit; (*compte*) debit *cpd*.
déblai [deblɛ] *nm* (*nettoyage*) clearing; ~**s** *nmpl* (*terre*) earth; (*décombres*) rubble.
déblaiement [deblɛmɑ̃] *nm* clearing; **travaux de ~** earth moving *sg*.
déblatérer [deblateʀe] *vi*: ~ **contre** to go on about.
déblayer [debleje] *vt* to clear; ~ **le terrain** (*fig*) to clear the ground.
déblocage [deblɔkaʒ] *nm* (*des prix, cours*) unfreezing.
débloquer [deblɔke] *vt* (*frein, fonds*) to release; (*prix*) to unfreeze ♦ *vi* (*fam*) to talk rubbish.
débobiner [debɔbine] *vt* to unwind.
déboires [debwaʀ] *nmpl* setbacks.
déboisement [debwazmɑ̃] *nm* deforestation.
déboiser [debwaze] *vt* to clear of trees; (*région*) to deforest; **se ~** *vi* (*colline, montagne*) to become bare of trees.
déboîter [debwate] *vt* (*AUTO*) to pull out; **se ~ le genou** *etc* to dislocate one's knee *etc*.
débonnaire [debɔnɛʀ] *adj* easy-going, good-natured.
débordant, e [debɔʀdɑ̃, -ɑ̃t] *adj* (*joie*) unbounded; (*activité*) exuberant.
débordé, e [debɔʀde] *adj*: **être ~ de** (*travail, demandes*) to be snowed under with.
débordement [debɔʀdəmɑ̃] *nm* overflowing.
déborder [debɔʀde] *vi* to overflow; (*lait etc*) to boil over ♦ *vt* (*MIL, SPORT*) to outflank; ~ **(de) qch** (*dépasser*) to extend beyond sth; ~ **de** (*joie, zèle*) to be brimming over with *ou* bursting with.
débouché [debuʃe] *nm* (*pour vendre*) outlet; (*perspective d'emploi*) opening; (*sortie*): **au ~ de la vallée** where the valley opens out (onto the plain).
déboucher [debuʃe] *vt* (*évier, tuyau etc*) to unblock; (*bouteille*) to uncork, open ♦ *vi*: ~ **de** to emerge from, come out of; ~ **sur** to come out onto; to open out onto; (*fig*) to arrive at, lead up to.
débouler [debule] *vi* to go (*ou* come) tumbling down; (*sans tomber*) to come careering down ♦ *vt*: ~ **l'escalier** to belt down the stairs.
déboulonner [debulɔne] *vt* to dismantle; (*fig: renvoyer*) to dismiss; (*: détruire le prestige de*) to discredit.
débours [debuʀ] *nmpl* outlay.
débourser [debuʀse] *vt* to pay out, lay out.
déboussoler [debusɔle] *vt* to disorientate, disorient.
debout [dəbu] *adv*: **être ~** (*personne*) to be standing, stand; (*: levé, éveillé*) to be up (and about); (*chose*) to be upright; **être encore ~** (*fig: en état*) to be still going; to be still standing; to be still up; **mettre qn ~** to get sb to his feet; **mettre qch ~** to stand sth up; **se mettre ~** to get up (on one's feet); **se tenir ~** to stand; **~!** get up!; **cette histoire ne tient pas ~** this story doesn't hold water.
débouter [debute] *vt* (*JUR*) to dismiss; ~ **qn de sa demande** to dismiss sb's petition.
déboutonner [debutɔne] *vt* to undo, unbutton; **se ~** *vi* to come undone *ou* unbuttoned.
débraillé, e [debʀɑje] *adj* slovenly, untidy.
débrancher [debʀɑ̃ʃe] *vt* (*appareil électrique*) to unplug; (*télephone, courant électrique*) to disconnect, cut off.
débrayage [debʀɛjaʒ] *nm* (*AUTO*) clutch; (*: action*) disengaging the clutch; (*grève*) stoppage; **faire un double ~** to double-declutch.
débrayer [debʀeje] *vi* (*AUTO*) to declutch, disengage the clutch; (*cesser le travail*) to stop work.
débridé, e [debʀide] *adj* unbridled, unrestrained.
débrider [debʀide] *vt* (*cheval*) to unbridle; (*CULIN: volaille*) to untruss.
débris [debʀi] *nm* (*fragment*) fragment ♦ *nmpl* (*déchets*) pieces, debris *sg*; rubbish *sg* (*BRIT*), garbage *sg* (*US*).
débrouillard, e [debʀujaʀ, -aʀd(ə)] *adj* smart, resourceful.
débrouillardise [debʀujaʀdiz] *nf* smartness, resourcefulness.
débrouiller [debʀuje] *vt* to disentangle, untangle; (*fig*) to sort out, unravel; **se ~** *vi* to man-

age.

débroussailler [debʀusɑje] *vt* to clear (of brushwood).

débusquer [debyske] *vt* to drive out (from cover).

début [deby] *nm* beginning, start; **~s** *nmpl* beginnings; (*de carrière*) début *sg*; **faire ses ~s** to start out; **au ~** in *ou* at the beginning, at first; **au ~ de** at the beginning *ou* start of; **dès le ~** from the start.

débutant, e [debytɑ̃, -ɑ̃t] *nm/f* beginner, novice.

débuter [debyte] *vi* to begin, start; (*faire ses débuts*) to start out.

deçà [dəsa]: **en ~ de** *prép* this side of; **en ~** *adv* on this side.

décacheter [dekaʃte] *vt* to unseal, open.

décade [dekad] *nf* (*10 jours*) (period of) ten days; (*10 ans*) decade.

décadence [dekadɑ̃s] *nf* decadence; decline.

décadent, e [dekadɑ̃, -ɑ̃t] *adj* decadent.

décaféiné, e [dekafeine] *adj* decaffeinated, caffeine-free.

décalage [dekalaʒ] *nm* move forward *ou* back; shift forward *ou* back; (*écart*) gap; (*désaccord*) discrepancy; **~ horaire** time difference (between time zones), time-lag.

décalaminer [dekalamine] *vt* to decoke.

décalcification [dekalsifikɑsjɔ̃] *nf* decalcification.

décalcifier [dekalsifje]: **se ~** *vr* to decalcify.

décalcomanie [dekalkɔmani] *nf* transfer.

décaler [dekale] *vt* (*dans le temps: avancer*) to bring forward; (*: retarder*) to put back; (*changer de position*) to shift forward *ou* back; **~ de 10 cm** to move forward *ou* back by 10 cm; **~ de 2 h** to bring *ou* move forward 2 hours; to put back 2 hours.

décalitre [dekalitʀ(ə)] *nm* decalitre (*BRIT*), decaliter (*US*).

décalogue [dekalɔg] *nm* Decalogue.

décalquer [dekalke] *vt* to trace; (*par pression*) to transfer.

décamètre [dekamɛtʀ(ə)] *nm* decametre (*BRIT*), decameter (*US*).

décamper [dekɑ̃pe] *vi* to clear out *ou* off.

décan [dekɑ̃] *nm* (*ASTROLOGIE*) decan.

décanter [dekɑ̃te] *vt* to (allow to) settle (and decant); **se ~** *vi* to settle.

décapage [dekapaʒ] *nm* stripping; scouring; sanding.

décapant [dekapɑ̃] *nm* acid solution; scouring agent; paint stripper.

décaper [dekape] *vt* to strip; (*avec abrasif*) to scour; (*avec papier de verre*) to sand.

décapiter [dekapite] *vt* to behead; (*par accident*) to decapitate; (*fig*) to cut the top off; (*: organisation*) to remove the top people from.

décapotable [dekapɔtabl(ə)] *adj* convertible.

décapoter [dekapɔte] *vt* to put down the top of.

décapsuler [dekapsyle] *vt* to take the cap *ou* top off.

décapsuleur [dekapsylœʀ] *nm* bottle-opener.

décarcasser [dekaʀkase] *vt*: **se ~ pour qn/pour faire qch** (*fam*) to slog one's guts out for sb/to do sth.

décathlon [dekatlɔ̃] *nm* decathlon.

décati, e [dekati] *adj* faded, aged.

décédé, e [desede] *adj* deceased.

décéder [desede] *vi* to die.

décelable [des(ə)labl(ə)] *adj* discernible.

déceler [desle] *vt* to discover, detect; (*révéler*) to indicate, reveal.

décélération [deseleʀɑsjɔ̃] *nf* deceleration.

décélérer [deseleʀe] *vi* to decelerate, slow down.

décembre [desɑ̃bʀ(ə)] *nm* December; *voir aussi* **juillet**.

décemment [desamɑ̃] *adv* decently.

décence [desɑ̃s] *nf* decency.

décennal, e, aux [desenal, -o] *adj* (*qui dure dix ans*) having a term of ten years, ten-year; (*qui revient tous les dix ans*) ten-yearly.

décennie [desni] *nf* decade.

décent, e [desɑ̃, -ɑ̃t] *adj* decent.

décentralisation [desɑ̃tʀalizɑsjɔ̃] *nf* decentralization.

décentraliser [desɑ̃tʀalize] *vt* to decentralize.

décentrer [desɑ̃tʀe] *vt* to decentre; **se ~** to move off-centre.

déception [desɛpsjɔ̃] *nf* disappointment.

décerner [desɛʀne] *vt* to award.

décès [desɛ] *nm* death, decease; **acte de ~** death certificate.

décevant, e [dɛsvɑ̃, -ɑ̃t] *adj* disappointing.

décevoir [dɛsvwaʀ] *vt* to disappoint.

déchaîné, e [deʃene] *adj* unbridled, raging.

déchaînement [deʃɛnmɑ̃] *nm* (*de haine, violence*) outbreak, outburst.

déchaîner [deʃene] *vt* (*passions, colère*) to unleash; (*rires etc*) to give rise to, arouse; **se ~** *vi* to be unleashed; (*rires*) to burst out; (*se mettre en colère*) to fly into a rage; **se ~ contre qn** to unleash one's fury on sb.

déchanter [deʃɑ̃te] *vi* to become disillusioned.

décharge [deʃaʀʒ(ə)] *nf* (*dépôt d'ordures*) rubbish tip *ou* dump; (*électrique*) electrical discharge; (*salve*) volley of shots; **à la ~ de** in defence of.

déchargement [deʃaʀʒəmɑ̃] *nm* unloading.

décharger [deʃaʀʒe] *vt* (*marchandise, véhicule*) to unload; (*ÉLEC*) to discharge; (*arme: neutraliser*) to unload; (*: faire feu*) to discharge, fire; **~ qn de** (*responsabilité*) to relieve sb of, release sb from; **~ sa colère (sur)** to vent one's anger (on); **~ sa conscience** to unburden one's conscience; **se ~ dans** (*se déverser*) to flow into; **se ~ d'une affaire sur qn** to hand a matter over to sb.

décharné, e [deʃaʀne] *adj* bony, emaciated, fleshless.

déchaussé, e [deʃose] *adj* (*dent*) loose.

déchausser [deʃose] *vt* (*personne*) to take the shoes off; (*skis*) to take off; **se ~** to take off one's shoes; (*dent*) to come *ou* work loose.
dèche [dɛʃ] *nf* (*fam*): **être dans la ~** to be flat broke.
déchéance [deʃeɑ̃s] *nf* (*déclin*) degeneration, decay, decline; (*chute*) fall.
déchet [deʃɛ] *nm* (*de bois, tissu etc*) scrap; (*perte: gén COMM*) wastage, waste; **~s** *nmpl* (*ordures*) refuse *sg*, rubbish *sg* (*BRIT*), garbage *sg* (*US*); **~s radioactifs** radioactive waste.
déchiffrage [deʃifʀaʒ] *nm* sight-reading.
déchiffrer [deʃifʀe] *vt* to decipher.
déchiqueté, e [deʃikte] *adj* jagged(-edged), ragged.
déchiqueter [deʃikte] *vt* to tear *ou* pull to pieces.
déchirant, e [deʃiʀɑ̃, -ɑ̃t] *adj* heart-breaking, heart-rending.
déchiré, e [deʃiʀe] *adj* torn; (*fig*) heart-broken.
déchirement [deʃiʀmɑ̃] *nm* (*chagrin*) wrench, heartbreak; (*gén pl: conflit*) rift, split.
déchirer [deʃiʀe] *vt* to tear, rip; (*mettre en morceaux*) to tear up; (*pour ouvrir*) to tear off; (*arracher*) to tear out; (*fig*) to tear apart; **se ~** *vi* to tear, rip; **se ~ un muscle/tendon** to tear a muscle/tendon.
déchirure [deʃiʀyʀ] *nf* (*accroc*) tear, rip; **~ musculaire** torn muscle.
déchoir [deʃwaʀ] *vi* (*personne*) to lower o.s., demean o.s; **~ de** to fall from.
déchu, e [deʃy] *pp de* **déchoir** ♦ *adj* fallen; (*roi*) deposed.
décibel [desibɛl] *nm* decibel.
décidé, e [deside] *adj* (*personne, air*) determined; **c'est ~** it's decided; **être ~ à faire** to be determined to do.
décidément [desidemɑ̃] *adv* undoubtedly; really.
décider [deside] *vt*: **~ qch** to decide on sth; **~ de faire/que** to decide to do/that; **~ qn (à faire qch)** to persuade *ou* induce sb (to do sth); **~ de qch** to decide upon sth; (*suj: chose*) to determine sth; **se ~** *vi* (*personne*) to decide, make up one's mind; (*problème, affaire*) to be resolved; **se ~ à qch** to decide on sth; **se ~ à faire** to decide *ou* make up one's mind to do; **se ~ pour qch** to decide on *ou* in favour of sth.
décideur [desidœʀ] *nm* decision-maker.
décilitre [desilitʀ(ə)] *nm* decilitre (*BRIT*), deciliter (*US*).
décimal, e, aux [desimal, -o] *adj, nf* decimal.
décimalisation [desimalizɑsjɔ̃] *nf* decimalization.
décimaliser [desimalize] *vt* to decimalize.
décimer [desime] *vt* to decimate.
décimètre [desimɛtʀ(ə)] *nm* decimetre (*BRIT*), decimeter (*US*); **double ~** (20 cm) ruler.
décisif, ive [desizif, -iv] *adj* decisive; (*qui l'emporte*): **le facteur/l'argument ~** the deciding factor/argument.
décision [desizjɔ̃] *nf* decision; (*fermeté*) decisiveness, decision; **prendre une ~** to make a decision; **prendre la ~ de faire** to take the decision to do; **emporter** *ou* **faire la ~** to be decisive.
déclamation [deklamɑsjɔ̃] *nf* declamation; (*péj*) ranting, spouting.
déclamatoire [deklamatwaʀ] *adj* declamatory.
déclamer [deklame] *vt* to declaim; (*péj*) to spout ♦ *vi*: **~ contre** to rail against.
déclarable [deklaʀabl(ə)] *adj* (*marchandise*) dutiable; (*revenus*) declarable.
déclaration [deklaʀɑsjɔ̃] *nf* declaration; registration; (*discours: POL etc*) statement; (*compte rendu*) report; **fausse ~** misrepresentation; **~ (d'amour)** declaration; **~ de décès** registration of death; **~ de guerre** declaration of war; **~ (d'impôts)** statement of income, tax declaration, ≈ tax return; **~ (de sinistre)** (insurance) claim; **~ de revenus** statement of income.
déclaré, e [deklaʀe] *adj* (*juré*) avowed.
déclarer [deklaʀe] *vt* to declare, announce; (*revenus, employés, marchandises*) to declare; (*décès, naissance*) to register; (*vol etc: à la police*) to report; **se ~** *vi* (*feu, maladie*) to break out; **~ la guerre** to declare war.
déclassé, e [deklɑse] *adj* relegated, downgraded; (*matériel*) (to be) sold off.
déclassement [deklɑsmɑ̃] *nm* relegation, downgrading; (*RAIL etc*) change of class.
déclasser [deklɑse] *vt* to relegate, downgrade; (*déranger: fiches, livres*) to get out of order.
déclenchement [deklɑ̃ʃmɑ̃] *nm* release; setting off.
déclencher [deklɑ̃ʃe] *vt* (*mécanisme etc*) to release; (*sonnerie*) to set off, activate; (*attaque, grève*) to launch; (*provoquer*) to trigger off; **se ~** *vi* to release itself; to go off.
déclencheur [deklɑ̃ʃœʀ] *nm* release mechanism.
déclic [deklik] *nm* trigger mechanism; (*bruit*) click.
déclin [deklɛ̃] *nm* decline.
déclinaison [deklinɛzɔ̃] *nf* declension.
décliner [dekline] *vi* to decline ♦ *vt* (*invitation*) to decline, refuse; (*responsabilité*) to refuse to accept; (*nom, adresse*) to state; (*LING*) to decline; **se ~** (*LING*) to decline.
déclivité [deklivite] *nf* slope, incline; **en ~** sloping, on the incline.
décloisonner [deklwazɔne] *vt* to decompartmentalize.
déclouer [deklue] *vt* to unnail.
décocher [dekɔʃe] *vt* to hurl; (*flèche, regard*) to shoot.
décoction [dekɔksjɔ̃] *nf* decoction.
décodage [dekɔdaʒ] *nm* deciphering, decoding.
décoder [dekɔde] *vt* to decipher, decode.
décodeur [dekɔdœʀ] *nm* decoder.

décoiffé, e [dekwafe] *adj*: **elle est toute ~e** her hair is in a mess.
décoiffer [dekwafe] *vt*: **~ qn** to disarrange *ou* mess up sb's hair; to take sb's hat off; **se ~** to take off one's hat.
décoincer [dekwɛ̃se] *vt* to unjam, loosen.
déçois [deswa] *etc*, **déçoive** [deswav] *etc vb voir* **décevoir**.
décolérer [dekɔleʀe] *vi*: **il ne décolère pas** he's still angry, he hasn't calmed down.
décollage [dekɔlaʒ] *nm* (*AVIAT*, *ÉCON*) takeoff.
décollé, e [dekɔle] *adj*: **oreilles ~es** sticking-out ears.
décollement [dekɔlmɑ̃] *nm* (*MÉD*): **~ de la rétine** retinal detachment.
décoller [dekɔle] *vt* to unstick ♦ *vi* to take off; (*projet, entreprise*) to take off, get off the ground; **se ~** *vi* to come unstuck.
décolleté, e [dekɔlte] *adj* low-necked, low-cut; (*femme*) wearing a low-cut dress ♦ *nm* low neck(line); (*épaules*) (bare) neck and shoulders; (*plongeant*) cleavage.
décolleter [dekɔlte] *vt* (*vêtement*) to give a low neckline to; (*TECH*) to cut.
décolonisation [dekɔlɔnizɑsjɔ̃] *nf* decolonization.
décoloniser [dekɔlɔnize] *vt* to decolonize.
décolorant [dekɔlɔʀɑ̃] *nm* decolorant, bleaching agent.
décoloration [dekɔlɔʀɑsjɔ̃] *nf*: **se faire faire une ~** (*chez le coiffeur*) to have one's hair bleached *ou* lightened.
décoloré, e [dekɔlɔʀe] *adj* (*vêtement*) faded; (*cheveux*) bleached.
décolorer [dekɔlɔʀe] *vt* (*tissu*) to fade; (*cheveux*) to bleach, lighten; **se ~** *vi* to fade.
décombres [dekɔ̃bʀ(ə)] *nmpl* rubble *sg*, debris *sg*.
décommander [dekɔmɑ̃de] *vt* to cancel; (*invités*) to put off; **se ~** to cancel, cry off.
décomposé, e [dekɔ̃poze] *adj* (*pourri*) decomposed; (*visage*) haggard, distorted.
décomposer [dekɔ̃poze] *vt* to break up; (*CHIMIE*) to decompose; (*MATH*) to factorize; **se ~** *vi* to decompose.
décomposition [dekɔ̃pozisjɔ̃] *nf* breaking up; decomposition; factorization; **en ~** (*organisme*) in a state of decay, decomposing.
décompresser [dekɔ̃pʀese] *vi* (*fam: se détendre*) to unwind.
décompresseur [dekɔ̃pʀesœʀ] *nm* decompressor.
décompression [dekɔ̃pʀesjɔ̃] *nf* decompression.
décomprimer [dekɔ̃pʀime] *vt* to decompress.
décompte [dekɔ̃t] *nm* deduction; (*facture*) breakdown (of an account), detailed account.
décompter [dekɔ̃te] *vt* to deduct.
déconcentration [dekɔ̃sɑ̃tʀɑsjɔ̃] *nf* (*des industries etc*) dispersal; **~ des pouvoirs** devolution.
déconcentré, e [dekɔ̃sɑ̃tʀe] *adj* (*sportif etc*) who has lost (his/her) concentration.
déconcentrer [dekɔ̃sɑ̃tʀe] *vt* (*ADMIN*) to disperse; **se ~** *vi* to lose (one's) concentration.
déconcertant, e [dekɔ̃sɛʀtɑ̃, -ɑ̃t] *adj* disconcerting.
déconcerter [dekɔ̃sɛʀte] *vt* to disconcert, confound.
déconditionner [dekɔ̃disjɔne] *vt*: **~ l'opinion américaine** to change the way the Americans have been forced to think.
déconfit, e [dekɔ̃fi, -it] *adj* crestfallen, downcast.
déconfiture [dekɔ̃fityʀ] *nf* collapse, ruin; (*morale*) defeat.
décongélation [dekɔ̃ʒelɑsjɔ̃] *nf* defrosting, thawing.
décongeler [dekɔ̃ʒle] *vt* to thaw (out).
décongestionner [dekɔ̃ʒɛstjɔne] *vt* (*MÉD*) to decongest; (*rues*) to relieve congestion in.
déconnecter [dekɔnɛkte] *vt* to disconnect.
déconner [dekɔne] *vi* (*fam!*: *en parlant*) to talk (a load of) rubbish (*BRIT*) *ou* garbage (*US*); (*: faire des bêtises*) to muck about; **sans ~** no kidding.
déconseiller [dekɔ̃seje] *vt*: **~ qch (à qn)** to advise (sb) against sth; **~ à qn de faire** to advise sb against doing; **c'est déconseillé** it's not advised *ou* advisable.
déconsidérer [dekɔ̃sideʀe] *vt* to discredit.
décontamination [dekɔ̃taminɑsjɔ̃] *nf* decontamination.
décontaminer [dekɔ̃tamine] *vt* to decontaminate.
décontenancer [dekɔ̃tnɑ̃se] *vt* to disconcert, discountenance.
décontracté, e [dekɔ̃tʀakte] *adj* relaxed.
décontracter [dekɔ̃tʀakte] *vt*, **se ~** *vi* to relax.
décontraction [dekɔ̃tʀaksjɔ̃] *nf* relaxation.
déconvenue [dekɔ̃vny] *nf* disappointment.
décor [dekɔʀ] *nm* décor; (*paysage*) scenery; **~s** *nmpl* (*THÉÂT*) scenery *sg*, decor *sg*; (*CINÉ*) set *sg*; **changement de ~** (*fig*) change of scene; **entrer dans le ~** (*fig*) to run off the road; **en ~ naturel** (*CINÉ*) on location.
décorateur, trice [dekɔʀatœʀ, -tʀis] *nm/f* (interior) decorator; (*CINÉ*) set designer.
décoratif, ive [dekɔʀatif, -iv] *adj* decorative.
décoration [dekɔʀɑsjɔ̃] *nf* decoration.
décorer [dekɔʀe] *vt* to decorate.
décortiqué, e [dekɔʀtike] *adj* shelled; hulled.
décortiquer [dekɔʀtike] *vt* to shell; (*riz*) to hull; (*fig*) to dissect.
décorum [dekɔʀɔm] *nm* decorum; etiquette.
décote [dekɔt] *nf* tax relief.
découcher [dekuʃe] *vi* to spend the night away.
découdre [dekudʀ(ə)] *vt* (*vêtement, couture*) to unpick, take the stitching out of; (*bouton*) to take off; **se ~** *vi* to come unstitched; (*bouton*) to come off; **en ~** (*fig*) to fight, do battle.

découler [dekule] *vi*: ~ **de** to ensue *ou* follow from.
découpage [dekupaʒ] *nm* cutting up; carving; (*image*) cut-out (figure); ~ **électoral** division into constituencies.
découper [dekupe] *vt* (*papier, tissu etc*) to cut up; (*volaille, viande*) to carve; (*détacher: manche, article*) to cut out; **se** ~ **sur** (*ciel, fond*) to stand out against.
découplé, e [dekuple] *adj*: **bien** ~ well-built, well-proportioned.
découpure [dekupyʀ] *nf*: ~**s** (*morceaux*) cut-out bits; (*d'une côte, arête*) indentations, jagged outline *sg*.
décourageant, e [dekuʀaʒɑ̃, ɑ̃t] *adj* discouraging; (*personne, attitude*) discouraging, negative.
découragement [dekuʀaʒmɑ̃] *nm* discouragement, despondency.
décourager [dekuʀaʒe] *vt* to discourage, dishearten; (*dissuader*) to discourage, put off; **se** ~ *vi* to lose heart, become discouraged; ~ **qn de faire/de qch** to discourage sb from doing/from sth, put sb off doing/sth.
décousu, e [dekuzy] *pp de* **découdre** ♦ *adj* unstitched; (*fig*) disjointed, disconnected.
découvert, e [dekuvɛʀ, -ɛʀt(ə)] *pp de* **découvrir** ♦ *adj* (*tête*) bare, uncovered; (*lieu*) open, exposed ♦ *nm* (*bancaire*) overdraft ♦ *nf* discovery; **à** ~ *adv* (*MIL*) exposed, without cover; (*fig*) openly ♦ *adj* (*COMM*) overdrawn; **à visage** ~ openly; **aller à la** ~**e de** to go in search of.
découvrir [dekuvʀiʀ] *vt* to discover; (*apercevoir*) to see; (*enlever ce qui couvre ou protège*) to uncover; (*montrer, dévoiler*) to reveal; **se** ~ to take off one's hat; (*se déshabiller*) to take something off; (*au lit*) to uncover o.s.; (*ciel*) to clear; **se** ~ **des talents** to find hidden talents in o.s.
décrasser [dekʀase] *vt* to clean.
décrêper [dekʀepe] *vt* (*cheveux*) to straighten.
décrépi, e [dekʀepi] *adj* peeling; with roughcast rendering removed.
décrépit, e [dekʀepi, -it] *adj* decrepit.
décrépitude [dekʀepityd] *nf* decrepitude; decay.
decrescendo [dekʀeʃɛndo] *nm* (*MUS*) decrescendo; **aller** ~ (*fig*) to decline, be on the wane.
décret [dekʀɛ] *nm* decree.
décréter [dekʀete] *vt* to decree; (*ordonner*) to order.
décret-loi [dekʀɛlwa] *nm* statutory order.
décrié, e [dekʀije] *adj* disparaged.
décrire [dekʀiʀ] *vt* to describe; (*courbe, cercle*) to follow, describe.
décrisper [dekʀispe] *vt* to defuse.
décrit, e [dekʀi, -it] *pp de* **décrire**.
décrivais [dekʀivɛ] *etc vb voir* **décrire**.
décrochement [dekʀɔʃmɑ̃] *nm* (*d'un mur etc*) recess.
décrocher [dekʀɔʃe] *vt* (*dépendre*) to take down; (*téléphone*) to take off the hook; (*: pour répondre*): ~ **(le téléphone)** to pick up *ou* lift the receiver; (*fig: contrat etc*) to get, land ♦ *vi* to drop out; to switch off; **se** ~ *vi* (*tableau, rideau*) to fall down.
décroîs [dekʀwa] *etc vb voir* **décroître**.
décroiser [dekʀwaze] *vt* (*bras*) to unfold; (*jambes*) to uncross.
décroissant, e [dekʀwasɑ̃, -ɑ̃t] *vb voir* **décroître** ♦ *adj* decreasing, declining, diminishing; **par ordre** ~ in descending order.
décroître [dekʀwatʀ(ə)] *vi* to decrease, decline, diminish.
décrotter [dekʀɔte] *vt* (*chaussures*) to clean the mud from; **se** ~ **le nez** to pick one's nose.
décru, e [dekʀy] *pp de* **décroître**.
décrue [dekʀy] *nf* drop in level (of the waters).
décrypter [dekʀipte] *vt* to decipher.
déçu, e [desy] *pp de* **décevoir** ♦ *adj* disappointed.
déculotter [dekylɔte] *vt*: ~ **qn** to take off *ou* down sb's trousers; **se** ~ to take off *ou* down one's trousers.
déculpabiliser [dekylpabilize] *vt* (*personne*) to relieve of guilt; (*chose*) to decriminalize.
décuple [dekypl(ə)] *nm*: **le** ~ **de** ten times; **au** ~ tenfold.
décupler [dekyple] *vt, vi* to increase tenfold.
déçut [desy] *etc vb voir* **décevoir**.
dédaignable [dedɛɲabl(ə)] *adj*: **pas** ~ not to be despised.
dédaigner [dedeɲe] *vt* to despise, scorn; (*négliger*) to disregard, spurn; ~ **de faire** to consider it beneath one to do, not deign to do.
dédaigneusement [dedɛɲøzmɑ̃] *adv* scornfully, disdainfully.
dédaigneux, euse [dedɛɲø, -øz] *adj* scornful, disdainful.
dédain [dedɛ̃] *nm* scorn, disdain.
dédale [dedal] *nm* maze.
dedans [dədɑ̃] *adv* inside; (*pas en plein air*) indoors, inside ♦ *nm* inside; **au** ~ on the inside; inside; **en** ~ (*vers l'intérieur*) inwards; *voir aussi* **là**.
dédicace [dedikas] *nf* (*imprimée*) dedication; (*manuscrite, sur une photo etc*) inscription.
dédicacer [dedikase] *vt*: ~ **(à qn)** to sign (for sb), autograph (for sb), inscribe (to sb).
dédié, e [dedje] *adj*: **ordinateur** ~ dedicated computer.
dédier [dedje] *vt* to dedicate.
dédire [dediʀ]: **se** ~ *vi* to go back on one's word; (*se rétracter*) to retract, recant.
dédit, e [dedi, -it] *pp de* **dédire** ♦ *nm* (*COMM*) forfeit, penalty.
dédommagement [dedɔmaʒmɑ̃] *nm* compensation.
dédommager [dedɔmaʒe] *vt*: ~ **qn (de)** to compensate sb (for); (*fig*) to repay sb (for).

dédouaner [dedwane] *vt* to clear through customs.
dédoublement [dedubləmɑ̃] *nm* splitting; (*PSYCH*): ~ **de la personnalité** split *ou* dual personality.
dédoubler [deduble] *vt* (*classe, effectifs*) to split (into two); (*couverture etc*) to unfold; (*manteau*) to remove the lining of; ~ **un train/les trains** to run a relief train/additional trains; **se** ~ *vi* (*PSYCH*) to have a split personality.
dédramatiser [dedʀamatize] *vt* (*situation*) to defuse; (*événement*) to play down.
déductible [dedyktibl(ə)] *adj* deductible.
déduction [dedyksjɔ̃] *nf* (*d'argent*) deduction; (*raisonnement*) deduction, inference.
déduire [dedɥiʀ] *vt*: ~ **qch (de)** (*ôter*) to deduct sth (from); (*conclure*) to deduce *ou* infer sth (from).
déesse [deɛs] *nf* goddess.
DEFA *sigle m* (= *Diplôme d'État relatif aux fonctions d'animation*) *diploma for senior youth leaders.*
défaillance [defajɑ̃s] *nf* (*syncope*) blackout; (*fatigue*) (sudden) weakness *no pl*; (*technique*) fault, failure; (*morale etc*) weakness; ~ **cardiaque** heart failure.
défaillant, e [defajɑ̃, -ɑ̃t] *adj* defective; (*JUR*: *témoin*) defaulting.
défaillir [defajiʀ] *vi* to faint; to feel faint; (*mémoire etc*) to fail.
défaire [defɛʀ] *vt* (*installation, échafaudage*) to take down, dismantle; (*paquet etc, nœud, vêtement*) to undo; (*bagages*) to unpack; (*ouvrage*) to undo, unpick; (*cheveux*) to take out; **se** ~ *vi* to come undone; **se** ~ **de** *vt* (*se débarrasser de*) to get rid of; (*se séparer de*) to part with; ~ **le lit** (*pour changer les draps*) to strip the bed; (*pour se coucher*) to turn back the bedclothes.
défait, e [defɛ, -ɛt] *pp de* **défaire** ♦ *adj* (*visage*) haggard, ravaged ♦ *nf* defeat.
défaites [defɛt] *vb voir* **défaire**.
défaitisme [defetism(ə)] *nm* defeatism.
défaitiste [defetist(ə)] *adj, nm/f* defeatist.
défalcation [defalkɑsjɔ̃] *nf* deduction.
défalquer [defalke] *vt* to deduct.
défasse [defas] *etc vb voir* **défaire**.
défausser [defose] *vt* to get rid of; **se** ~ *vi* (*CARTES*) to discard.
défaut [defo] *nm* (*moral*) fault, failing, defect; (*d'étoffe, métal*) fault, flaw, defect; (*manque, carence*): ~ **de** lack of; shortage of; (*INFORM*) bug; ~ **de la cuirasse** (*fig*) chink in the armour (*BRIT*) *ou* armor (*US*); **en** ~ at fault; in the wrong; **faire** ~ (*manquer*) to be lacking; **à** ~ *adv* failing that; **à** ~ **de** for lack *ou* want of; **par** ~ (*JUR*) in his (*ou* her *etc*) absence.
défaveur [defavœʀ] *nf* disfavour (*BRIT*), disfavor (*US*).
défavorable [defavɔʀabl(ə)] *adj* unfavourable (*BRIT*), unfavorable (*US*).
défavoriser [defavɔʀize] *vt* to put at a disadvantage.
défectif, ive [defɛktif, -iv] *adj*: **verbe** ~ defective verb.
défection [defɛksjɔ̃] *nf* defection, failure to give support *ou* assistance; failure to appear; **faire** ~ (*d'un parti etc*) to withdraw one's support, leave.
défectueux, euse [defɛktɥø, -øz] *adj* faulty, defective.
défectuosité [defɛkɥozite] *nf* defectiveness *no pl*; (*défaut*) defect, fault.
défendable [defɑ̃dabl(ə)] *adj* defensible.
défendeur, eresse [defɑ̃dœʀ, -dʀɛs] *nm/f* (*JUR*) defendant.
défendre [defɑ̃dʀ(ə)] *vt* to defend; (*interdire*) to forbid; ~ **à qn qch/de faire** to forbid sb sth/to do; **il est défendu de cracher** spitting (is) prohibited *ou* is not allowed; **c'est défendu** it is forbidden; **se** ~ to defend o.s.; **il se défend** (*fig*) he can hold his own; **ça se défend** (*fig*) it holds together; **se** ~ **de/contre** (*se protéger*) to protect o.s. from/against; **se** ~ **de** (*se garder de*) to refrain from; (*nier*): **se** ~ **de vouloir** to deny wanting.
défenestrer [defənɛstʀe] *vt* to throw out of the window.
défense [defɑ̃s] *nf* defence (*BRIT*), defense (*US*); (*d'éléphant etc*) tusk; **ministre de la** ~ Minister of Defence (*BRIT*), Defence Secretary; **la** ~ **nationale** defence, the defence of the realm (*BRIT*); **la** ~ **contre avions** anti-aircraft defence; **"**~ **de fumer/cracher"** "no smoking/spitting", "smoking/spitting prohibited"; **prendre la** ~ **de qn** to stand up for sb; ~ **des consommateurs** consumerism.
défenseur [defɑ̃sœʀ] *nm* defender; (*JUR*) counsel for the defence.
défensif, ive [defɑ̃sif, -iv] *adj, nf* defensive; **être sur la défensive** to be on the defensive.
déféquer [defeke] *vi* to defecate.
déferai [defʀe] *etc vb voir* **défaire**.
déférence [defeʀɑ̃s] *nf* deference.
déférent, e [defeʀɑ̃, -ɑ̃t] *adj* (*poli*) deferential, deferent.
déférer [defeʀe] *vt* (*JUR*) to refer; ~ **à** *vt* (*requête, décision*) to defer to; ~ **qn à la justice** to hand sb over to justice.
déferlant, e [defɛʀlɑ̃, -ɑ̃t] *adj*: **vague** ~**e** breaker.
déferlement [defɛʀləmɑ̃] *nm* breaking; surge.
déferler [defɛʀle] *vi* (*vagues*) to break; (*fig*) to surge.
défi [defi] *nm* (*provocation*) challenge; (*bravade*) defiance; **mettre qn au** ~ **de faire qch** to challenge sb to do sth; **relever un** ~ to take up *ou* accept a challenge.
défiance [defjɑ̃s] *nf* mistrust, distrust.
déficeler [defisle] *vt* (*paquet*) to undo, untie.
déficience [defisjɑ̃s] *nf* deficiency.
déficient, e [defisjɑ̃, -ɑ̃t] *adj* deficient.
déficit [defisit] *nm* (*COMM*) deficit; (*PSYCH etc*:

manque) defect; ~ **budgétaire** budget deficit; **être en** ~ to be in deficit.
déficitaire [defisitɛʀ] *adj* (*année, récolte*) bad; **entreprise/budget** ~ business/budget in deficit.
défier [defje] *vt* (*provoquer*) to challenge; (*fig*) to defy, brave; **se** ~ **de** (*se méfier de*) to distrust, mistrust; ~ **qn de faire** to challenge *ou* defy sb to do; ~ **qn à** to challenge sb to; ~ **toute comparaison/concurrence** to be incomparable/unbeatable.
défigurer [defigyʀe] *vt* to disfigure; (*suj: boutons etc*) to mar *ou* spoil (the looks of); (*fig: œuvre*) to mutilate, deface.
défilé [defile] *nm* (*GÉO*) (narrow) gorge *ou* pass; (*soldats*) parade; (*manifestants*) procession, march; **un** ~ **de** (*voitures, visiteurs etc*) a stream of.
défiler [defile] *vi* (*troupes*) to march past; (*sportifs*) to parade; (*manifestants*) to march; (*visiteurs*) to pour, stream; **se** ~ *vi* (*se dérober*) to slip away, sneak off; **faire** ~ (*bande, film*) to put on; (*INFORM*) to scroll.
défini, e [defini] *adj* definite.
définir [definiʀ] *vt* to define.
définissable [definisabl(ə)] *adj* definable.
définitif, ive [definitif, -iv] *adj* (*final*) final, definitive; (*pour longtemps*) permanent, definitive; (*sans appel*) final, definite ♦ *nf*: **en définitive** eventually; (*somme toute*) when all is said and done.
définition [definisjɔ̃] *nf* definition; (*de mots croisés*) clue; (*TV*) (picture) resolution.
définitivement [definitivmɑ̃] *adv* definitively; permanently; definitely.
défit [defi] *etc vb voir* **défaire.**
déflagration [deflagʀɑsjɔ̃] *nf* explosion.
déflation [deflɑsjɔ̃] *nf* deflation.
déflationniste [deflɑsjɔnist(ə)] *adj* deflationist, deflationary.
déflecteur [deflɛktœʀ] *nm* (*AUTO*) quarterlight (*BRIT*), deflector (*US*).
déflorer [deflɔʀe] *vt* (*jeune fille*) to deflower; (*fig*) to spoil the charm of.
défoncé, e [defɔ̃se] *adj* smashed in; broken down; (*route*) full of potholes ♦ *nm/f* addict.
défoncer [defɔ̃se] *vt* (*caisse*) to stave in; (*porte*) to smash in *ou* down; (*lit, fauteuil*) to burst (the springs of); (*terrain, route*) to rip *ou* plough up; **se** ~ *vi* (*se donner à fond*) to give it all one's got.
défont [defɔ̃] *vb voir* **défaire.**
déformant, e [defɔʀmɑ̃, -ɑ̃t] *adj*: **glace** ~**e** *ou* **miroir** ~ distorting mirror.
déformation [defɔʀmɑsjɔ̃] *nf* loss of shape; deformation; distortion; ~ **professionnelle** conditioning by one's job.
déformer [defɔʀme] *vt* to put out of shape; (*corps*) to deform; (*pensée, fait*) to distort; **se** ~ *vi* to lose its shape.
défoulement [defulmɑ̃] *nm* release of tension; unwinding.
défouler [defule]: **se** ~ *vi* (*PSYCH*) to work off one's tensions, release one's pent-up feelings; (*gén*) to unwind, let off steam.
défraîchi, e [defʀeʃi] *adj* faded; (*article à vendre*) shop-soiled.
défraîchir [defʀeʃiʀ]: **se** ~ *vi* to fade; to become shop-soiled.
défrayer [defʀeje] *vt*: ~ **qn** to pay sb's expenses; ~ **la chronique** to be in the news; ~ **la conversation** to be the main topic of conversation.
défrichement [defʀiʃmɑ̃] *nm* clearance.
défricher [defʀiʃe] *vt* to clear (for cultivation).
défriser [defʀize] *vt* (*cheveux*) to straighten; (*fig*) to annoy.
défroisser [defʀwase] *vt* to smooth out.
défroque [defʀɔk] *nf* cast-off.
défroqué [defʀɔke] *nm* former monk (*ou* priest).
défroquer [defʀɔke] *vi* (*aussi*: **se** ~) to give up the cloth, renounce one's vows.
défunt, e [defœ̃, -œ̃t] *adj*: **son** ~ **père** his late father ♦ *nm/f* deceased.
dégagé, e [degaʒe] *adj* clear; (*ton, air*) casual, jaunty.
dégagement [degaʒmɑ̃] *nm* emission; freeing; clearing; (*espace libre*) clearing; passage; clearance; (*FOOTBALL*) clearance; **voie de** ~ slip road; **itinéraire de** ~ alternative route (*to relieve traffic congestion*).
dégager [degaʒe] *vt* (*exhaler*) to give off, emit; (*délivrer*) to free, extricate; (*MIL: troupes*) to relieve; (*désencombrer*) to clear; (*isoler, mettre en valeur*) to bring out; (*crédits*) to release; **se** ~ *vi* (*odeur*) to emanate, be given off; (*passage, ciel*) to clear; ~ **qn de** (*engagement, parole etc*) to release *ou* free sb from; **se** ~ **de** (*fig: engagement etc*) to get out of; (*: promesse*) to go back on.
dégaine [degɛn] *nf* awkward way of walking.
dégainer [degene] *vt* to draw.
dégarni, e [degaʀni] *adj* bald.
dégarnir [degaʀniʀ] *vt* (*vider*) to empty, clear; **se** ~ *vi* to empty; to be cleaned out *ou* cleared; (*tempes, crâne*) to go bald.
dégâts [degɑ] *nmpl* damage *sg*; **faire des** ~ to damage.
dégauchir [degoʃiʀ] *vt* (*TECH*) to surface.
dégazer [degɑze] *vi* (*pétrolier*) to clean its tanks.
dégel [deʒɛl] *nm* thaw; (*fig: des prix etc*) unfreezing.
dégeler [deʒle] *vt* to thaw (out); (*fig*) to unfreeze ♦ *vi* to thaw (out); **se** ~ *vi* (*fig*) to thaw out.
dégénéré, e [deʒeneʀe] *adj, nm/f* degenerate.
dégénérer [deʒeneʀe] *vi* to degenerate; (*empirer*) to go from bad to worse; (*devenir*): ~ **en** to degenerate into.
dégénérescence [deʒeneʀesɑ̃s] *nf* degeneration.

dégingandé, e [deʒɛ̃gɑ̃de] *adj* gangling, lanky.
dégivrage [deʒivʀaʒ] *nm* defrosting; de-icing.
dégivrer [deʒivʀe] *vt* (*frigo*) to defrost; (*vitres*) to de-ice.
dégivreur [deʒivʀœʀ] *nm* defroster; de-icer.
déglinguer [deglɛ̃ge] *vt* to bust.
déglutir [deglytiʀ] *vt, vi* to swallow.
déglutition [deglytisjɔ̃] *nf* swallowing.
dégonflé, e [degɔ̃fle] *adj* (*pneu*) flat; (*fam*) chicken ♦ *nm/f* (*fam*) chicken.
dégonfler [degɔ̃fle] *vt* (*pneu, ballon*) to let down, deflate ♦ *vi* (*désenfler*) to go down; **se** ~ *vi* (*fam*) to chicken out.
dégorger [degɔʀʒe] *vi* (*CULIN*): **faire** ~ to leave to sweat; (*aussi*: **se** ~: *rivière*): ~ **dans** to flow into ♦ *vt* to disgorge.
dégoter [degɔte] *vt* (*fam*) to dig up, find.
dégouliner [deguline] *vi* to trickle, drip; ~ **de** to be dripping with.
dégoupiller [degupije] *vt* (*grenade*) to take the pin out of.
dégourdi, e [deguʀdi] *adj* smart, resourceful.
dégourdir [deguʀdiʀ] *vt* to warm (up); **se** ~ **(les jambes)** to stretch one's legs.
dégoût [degu] *nm* disgust, distaste.
dégoûtant, e [degutɑ̃, -ɑ̃t] *adj* disgusting.
dégoûté, e [degute] *adj* disgusted; ~ **de** sick of.
dégoûter [degute] *vt* to disgust; **cela me dégoûte** I find this disgusting *ou* revolting; ~ **qn de qch** to put sb off sth; **se** ~ **de** to get *ou* become sick of.
dégoutter [degute] *vi* to drip; ~ **de** to be dripping with.
dégradant, e [degʀadɑ̃, -ɑ̃t] *adj* degrading.
dégradation [degʀadɑsjɔ̃] *nf* reduction in rank; defacement; degradation, debasement; deterioration; (*aussi*: ~**s**: *dégâts*) damage *no pl*.
dégradé, e [degʀade] *adj* (*couleur*) shaded off; (*teintes*) faded; (*cheveux*) layered ♦ *nm* (*PEINTURE*) gradation.
dégrader [degʀade] *vt* (*MIL*: *officier*) to degrade; (*abîmer*) to damage, deface; (*avilir*) to degrade, debase; **se** ~ *vi* (*relations, situation*) to deteriorate.
dégrafer [degʀafe] *vt* to unclip, unhook, unfasten.
dégraissage [degʀɛsaʒ] *nm* (*ÉCON*) cutbacks *pl*; ~ **et nettoyage à sec** dry cleaning.
dégraissant [degʀɛsɑ̃] *nm* spot remover.
dégraisser [degʀese] *vt* (*soupe*) to skim; (*vêtement*) to take the grease marks out of; (*ÉCON*) to cut back; (*: entreprise*) to slim down.
degré [dəgʀe] *nm* degree; (*d'escalier*) step; **brûlure au 1er/2ème** ~ 1st/2nd degree burn; **équation du 1er/2ème** ~ linear/quadratic equation; **le premier** ~ (*SCOL*) primary level; **alcool à 90** ~**s** surgical spirit; **vin de 10** ~**s** 10° wine (*on Gay-Lussac scale*); **par** ~**(s)** *adv* by degrees, gradually.
dégressif, ive [degʀesif, -iv] *adj* on a decreasing scale, degressive; **tarif** ~ decreasing rate of charge.
dégrèvement [degʀɛvmɑ̃] *nm* tax relief.
dégrever [degʀəve] *vt* to grant tax relief to; to reduce the tax burden on.
dégriffé, e [degʀife] *adj* (*vêtement*) sold without the designer's label.
dégringolade [degʀɛ̃gɔlad] *nf* tumble; (*fig*) collapse.
dégringoler [degʀɛ̃gɔle] *vi* to tumble (down); (*fig: prix, monnaie etc*) to collapse.
dégriser [degʀize] *vt* to sober up.
dégrossir [degʀosiʀ] *vt* (*bois*) to trim; (*fig*) to work out roughly; (*: personne*) to knock the rough edges off.
déguenillé, e [degnije] *adj* ragged, tattered.
déguerpir [degɛʀpiʀ] *vi* to clear off.
dégueulasse [degœlas] *adj* (*fam*) disgusting.
dégueuler [degœle] *vi* (*fam*) to puke, throw up.
déguisé, e [degize] *adj* disguised; dressed up; ~ **en** disguised (*ou* dressed up) as.
déguisement [degizmɑ̃] *nm* disguise; (*habits: pour s'amuser*) dressing-up clothes; (*: pour tromper*) disguise.
déguiser [degize] *vt* to disguise; **se** ~ **(en)** (*se costumer*) to dress up (as); (*pour tromper*) to disguise o.s. (as).
dégustation [degystɑsjɔ̃] *nf* tasting; sampling; savouring (*BRIT*), savoring (*US*); (*séance*): ~ **de vin(s)** wine-tasting.
déguster [degyste] *vt* (*vins*) to taste; (*fromages etc*) to sample; (*savourer*) to enjoy, savour (*BRIT*), savor (*US*).
déhancher [deɑ̃ʃe]: **se** ~ *vi* to sway one's hips; to lean (one's weight) on one hip.
dehors [dəɔʀ] *adv* outside; (*en plein air*) outdoors, outside ♦ *nm* outside ♦ *nmpl* (*apparences*) appearances, exterior *sg*; **mettre** *ou* **jeter** ~ to throw out; **au** ~ outside; (*en apparence*) outwardly; **au** ~ **de** outside; **de** ~ from outside; **en** ~ outside; outwards; **en** ~ **de** apart from.
déifier [deifje] *vt* to deify.
déjà [deʒa] *adv* already; (*auparavant*) before, already; **as-tu** ~ **été en France?** have you been to France before?; **c'est** ~ **pas mal** that's not too bad (at all); **c'est** ~ **quelque chose** (at least) it's better than nothing; **quel nom,** ~**?** what was the name again?
déjanter [deʒɑ̃te]: **se** ~ *vi* (*pneu*) to come off the rim.
déjà-vu [deʒavy] *nm*: **c'est du** ~ there's nothing new in that.
déjeté, e [dɛʒte] *adj* lop-sided, crooked.
déjeuner [deʒœne] *vi* to (have) lunch; (*le matin*) to have breakfast ♦ *nm* lunch; (*petit déjeuner*) breakfast; ~ **d'affaires** business lunch.
déjouer [deʒwe] *vt* to elude; to foil, thwart.

déjuger [deʒyʒe]: **se ~** *vi* to go back on one's opinion.

delà [dəla] *adv*: **par ~, en ~ (de), au ~ (de)** beyond.

délabré, e [delɑbʀe] *adj* dilapidated, broken-down.

délabrement [delɑbʀəmɑ̃] *nm* decay, dilapidation.

délabrer [delɑbʀe]: **se ~** *vi* to fall into decay, become dilapidated.

délacer [delase] *vt* to unlace, undo.

délai [delɛ] *nm* (*attente*) waiting period; (*sursis*) extension (of time); (*temps accordé*: *aussi*: **~s**) time limit; **sans ~** without delay; **à bref ~** shortly, very soon; at short notice; **dans les ~s** within the time limit; **un ~ de 30 jours** a period of 30 days; **comptez un ~ de livraison de 10 jours** allow 10 days for delivery.

délaissé, e [delese] *adj* abandoned, deserted; neglected.

délaisser [delese] *vt* (*abandonner*) to abandon, desert; (*négliger*) to neglect.

délassant, e [delɑsɑ̃, -ɑ̃t] *adj* relaxing.

délassement [delɑsmɑ̃] *nm* relaxation.

délasser [delɑse] *vt* (*reposer*) to relax; (*divertir*) to divert, entertain; **se ~** *vi* to relax.

délateur, trice [delatœʀ, -tʀis] *nm/f* informer.

délation [delɑsjɔ̃] *nf* denouncement, informing.

délavé, e [delave] *adj* faded.

délayage [delɛjaʒ] *nm* mixing; thinning down.

délayer [deleje] *vt* (*CULIN*) to mix (with water *etc*); (*peinture*) to thin down; (*fig*) to pad out, spin out.

delco [dɛlko] *nm* ® (*AUTO*) distributor; **tête de ~** distributor cap.

délectation [delɛktɑsjɔ̃] *nf* delight.

délecter [delɛkte]: **se ~** *vi*: **se ~ de** to revel *ou* delight in.

délégation [delegɑsjɔ̃] *nf* delegation; **~ de pouvoir** delegation of power.

délégué, e [delege] *adj* delegated ♦ *nm/f* delegate; representative; **ministre ~ à** minister with special responsibility for.

déléguer [delege] *vt* to delegate.

délestage [delɛstaʒ] *nm*: **itinéraire de ~** alternative route (*to relieve traffic congestion*).

délester [delɛste] *vt* (*navire*) to unballast; **~ une route** to relieve traffic congestion on a road by diverting traffic.

Delhi [dɛli] *n* Delhi.

délibérant, e [delibeʀɑ̃, -ɑ̃t] *adj*: **assemblée ~e** deliberative assembly.

délibératif, ive [delibeʀatif, -iv] *adj*: **avoir voix délibérative** to have voting rights.

délibération [delibeʀɑsjɔ̃] *nf* deliberation.

délibéré, e [delibeʀe] *adj* (*conscient*) deliberate; (*déterminé*) determined, resolute; **de propos ~** (*à dessein, exprès*) intentionally.

délibérément [delibeʀemɑ̃] *adv* deliberately; (*résolument*) resolutely.

délibérer [delibeʀe] *vi* to deliberate.

délicat, e [delika, -at] *adj* delicate; (*plein de tact*) tactful; (*attentionné*) thoughtful; (*exigeant*) fussy, particular; **procédés peu ~s** unscrupulous methods.

délicatement [delikatmɑ̃] *adv* delicately; (*avec douceur*) gently.

délicatesse [delikatɛs] *nf* delicacy; tactfulness; thoughtfulness; **~s** *nfpl* attentions, consideration *sg*.

délice [delis] *nm* delight.

délicieusement [delisjøzmɑ̃] *adv* deliciously; delightfully.

délicieux, euse [delisjø, -øz] *adj* (*au goût*) delicious; (*sensation, impression*) delightful.

délictueux, euse [deliktɥø, -øz] *adj* criminal.

délié, e [delje] *adj* nimble, agile; (*mince*) slender, fine ♦ *nm*: **les ~s** the upstrokes (*in handwriting*).

délier [delje] *vt* to untie; **~ qn de** (*serment etc*) to free *ou* release sb from.

délimitation [delimitɑsjɔ̃] *nf* delimitation.

délimiter [delimite] *vt* to delimit.

délinquance [delɛ̃kɑ̃s] *nf* criminality; **~ juvénile** juvenile delinquency.

délinquant, e [delɛ̃kɑ̃, -ɑ̃t] *adj, nm/f* delinquent.

déliquescence [delikesɑ̃s] *nf*: **en ~** in a state of decay.

déliquescent, e [delikesɑ̃, -ɑ̃t] *adj* decaying.

délirant, e [deliʀɑ̃, -ɑ̃t] *adj* (*MÉD*: *fièvre*) delirious; (*imagination*) frenzied; (*fam*: *déraisonnable*) crazy.

délire [deliʀ] *nm* (*fièvre*) delirium; (*fig*) frenzy; (*: folie*) lunacy.

délirer [deliʀe] *vi* to be delirious; (*fig*) to be raving.

délit [deli] *nm* (criminal) offence; **~ de droit commun** violation of common law; **~ de fuite** failure to stop after an accident; **~ d'initiés** insider dealing *ou* trading; **~ de presse** violation of the press laws.

délivrance [delivʀɑ̃s] *nf* freeing, release; (*sentiment*) relief.

délivrer [delivʀe] *vt* (*prisonnier*) to (set) free, release; (*passeport, certificat*) to issue; **~ qn de** (*ennemis*) to set sb free from, deliver *ou* free sb from; (*fig*) to rid sb of.

déloger [delɔʒe] *vt* (*locataire*) to turn out; (*objet coincé, ennemi*) to dislodge.

déloyal, e, aux [delwajal, -o] *adj* (*personne, conduite*) disloyal; (*procédé*) unfair.

Delphes [dɛlf] *n* Delphi.

delta [dɛlta] *nm* (*GÉO*) delta.

deltaplane [dɛltaplan] *nm* ® hang-glider.

déluge [delyʒ] *nm* (*biblique*) Flood, Deluge; (*grosse pluie*) downpour, deluge; (*grand nombre*): **~ de** flood of.

déluré, e [delyʀe] *adj* smart, resourceful; (*péj*) forward, pert.

démagnétiser [demaɲetize] *vt* to demagnetize.

démagogie [demagɔʒi] *nf* demagogy.
démagogique [demagɔʒik] *adj* demagogic, popularity-seeking; (*POL*) vote-catching.
démagogue [demagɔg] *adj* demagogic ♦ *nm* demagogue.
démaillé, e [demɑje] *adj* (*bas*) laddered (*BRIT*), with a run (*ou* runs).
demain [dəmɛ̃] *adv* tomorrow; ~ **matin/soir** tomorrow morning/evening; ~ **midi** tomorrow at midday; **à** ~! see you tomorrow!
demande [dəmɑ̃d] *nf* (*requête*) request; (*revendication*) demand; (*ADMIN, formulaire*) application; (*ÉCON*): **la** ~ demand; **"~s d'emploi"** "situations wanted"; **à la** ~ **générale** by popular request; ~ **en mariage** (marriage) proposal; **faire sa** ~ **(en mariage)** to propose (marriage); ~ **de naturalisation** application for naturalization; ~ **de poste** job application.
demandé, e [dəmɑ̃de] *adj* (*article etc*): **très** ~ (very) much in demand.
demander [dəmɑ̃de] *vt* to ask for; (*question: date, heure, chemin*) to ask; (*requérir, nécessiter*) to require, demand; ~ **qch à qn** to ask sb for sth, ask sb sth; **ils demandent 2 secrétaires et un ingénieur** they're looking for 2 secretaries and an engineer; ~ **la main de qn** to ask for sb's hand (in marriage); ~ **pardon à qn** to apologize to sb; ~ **à** *ou* **de voir/faire** to ask to see/ask if one can do; ~ **à qn de faire** to ask sb to do; ~ **que/pourquoi** to ask that/why; **se** ~ **si/pourquoi** *etc* to wonder if/why *etc*; (*sens purement réfléchi*) to ask o.s. if/why *etc*; **on vous demande au téléphone** you're wanted on the phone, there's someone for you on the phone; **il ne demande que ça** that's all he wants; **je ne demande pas mieux** I'm asking nothing more; **il ne demande qu'à faire** all he wants is to do.
demandeur, euse [dəmɑ̃dœʀ, -øz] *nm/f*: ~ **d'emploi** job-seeker.
démangeaison [demɑ̃ʒɛzɔ̃] *nf* itching.
démanger [demɑ̃ʒe] *vi* to itch; **la main me démange** my hand is itching; **l'envie** *ou* **ça me démange de faire** I'm itching to do.
démantèlement [demɑ̃tɛlmɑ̃] *nm* breaking up.
démanteler [demɑ̃tle] *vt* to break up; to demolish.
démaquillant [demakijɑ̃] *nm* make-up remover.
démaquiller [demakije] *vt*: **se** ~ to remove one's make-up.
démarcage [demaʀkaʒ] *nm* = **démarquage**.
démarcation [demaʀkɑsjɔ̃] *nf* demarcation.
démarchage [demaʀʃaʒ] *nm* (*COMM*) door-to-door selling.
démarche [demaʀʃ(ə)] *nf* (*allure*) gait, walk; (*intervention*) step; approach; (*fig: intellectuelle*) thought processes *pl*; approach; **faire** *ou* **entreprendre des** ~**s** to take action; **faire des** ~**s auprès de qn** to approach sb.
démarcheur, euse [demaʀʃœʀ, -øz] *nm/f* (*COMM*) door-to-door salesman/woman; (*POL etc*) canvasser.
démarquage [demaʀkaʒ] *nm* marking down.
démarque [demaʀk(ə)] *nf* (*COMM: d'un article*) mark-down.
démarqué, e [demaʀke] *adj* (*FOOTBALL*) unmarked; (*COMM*) reduced; **prix** ~**s** marked-down prices.
démarquer [demaʀke] *vt* (*prix*) to mark down; (*joueur*) to stop marking; **se** ~ *vi* (*SPORT*) to shake off one's marker.
démarrage [demaʀaʒ] *nm* starting *no pl*, start; ~ **en côte** hill start.
démarrer [demaʀe] *vt* to start up ♦ *vi* (*conducteur*) to start (up); (*véhicule*) to move off; (*travaux, affaire*) to get moving; (*coureur: accélérer*) to pull away.
démarreur [demaʀœʀ] *nm* (*AUTO*) starter.
démasquer [demaske] *vt* to unmask; **se** ~ to unmask; (*fig*) to drop one's mask.
démâter [demɑte] *vt* to dismast ♦ *vi* to be dismasted.
démêlant, e [demelɑ̃, -ɑ̃t] *adj*: **baume** ~, **crème** ~**e** (hair) conditioner.
démêler [demele] *vt* to untangle, disentangle.
démêlés [demele] *nmpl* problems.
démembrement [demɑ̃bʀəmɑ̃] *nm* dismemberment.
démembrer [demɑ̃bʀe] *vt* to dismember.
déménagement [demenaʒmɑ̃] *nm* (*du point de vue du locataire etc*) move; (*: du déménageur*) removal (*BRIT*), moving (*US*); **entreprise/camion de** ~ removal (*BRIT*) *ou* moving (*US*) firm/van.
déménager [demenaʒe] *vt* (*meubles*) to (re)move ♦ *vi* to move (house).
déménageur [demenaʒœʀ] *nm* removal man (*BRIT*), (furniture) mover (*US*); (*entrepreneur*) furniture remover.
démence [demɑ̃s] *nf* madness, insanity; (*MÉD*) dementia.
démener [demne]: **se** ~ *vi* to thrash about; (*fig*) to exert o.s.
dément, e [demɑ̃, -ɑ̃t] *vb voir* **démentir** ♦ *adj* (*fou*) mad (*BRIT*), crazy; (*fam*) brilliant, fantastic.
démenti [demɑ̃ti] *nm* refutation.
démentiel, le [demɑ̃sjɛl] *adj* insane.
démentir [demɑ̃tiʀ] *vt* (*nouvelle, témoin*) to refute; (*suj: faits etc*) to belie, refute; ~ **que** to deny that; **ne pas se** ~ not to fail, keep up.
démerder [demɛʀde]: **se** ~ *vi* (*fam!*) to bloody well manage for o.s.
démériter [demeʀite] *vi*: ~ **auprès de qn** to come down in sb's esteem.
démesure [deməzyʀ] *nf* immoderation, immoderateness.
démesuré, e [deməzyʀe] *adj* immoderate, disproportionate.
démesurément [deməzyʀemɑ̃] *adv* dispropor-

tionately.
démettre [demɛtʀ(ə)] *vt:* ~ **qn de** (*fonction, poste*) to dismiss sb from; **se** ~ **(de ses fonctions)** to resign (from) one's duties; **se** ~ **l'épaule** *etc* to dislocate one's shoulder *etc*.
demeurant [dəmœʀɑ̃]: **au** ~ *adv* for all that.
demeure [dəmœʀ] *nf* residence; **dernière** ~ (*fig*) last resting place; **mettre qn en** ~ **de faire** to enjoin *ou* order sb to do; **à** ~ *adv* permanently.
demeuré, e [dəmœʀe] *adj* backward ♦ *nm/f* backward person.
demeurer [dəmœʀe] *vi* (*habiter*) to live; (*séjourner*) to stay; (*rester*) to remain; **en** ~ **là** (*suj: personne*) to leave it at that; (*: choses*) to be left at that.
demi, e [dəmi] *adj:* **et** ~: **trois heures/bouteilles et** ~**e** three and a half hours/bottles, three hours/bottles and a half ♦ *nm* (*bière: = 0.25 litre*) ≈ half-pint; (*FOOTBALL*) half-back; **il est 2 heures et** ~**e** it's half past 2; **il est midi et** ~ it's half past 12; ~ **de mêlée/d'ouverture** (*RUGBY*) scrum/fly half; **à** ~ *adv* half-; **ouvrir à** ~ to half-open; **faire les choses à** ~ to do things by halves; **à la** ~**e** (*heure*) on the half-hour.
demi... [dəmi] *préfixe* half-, semi..., demi-.
demi-bas [dəmibɑ] *nm inv* (*chaussette*) knee-sock.
demi-bouteille [dəmibutɛj] *nf* half-bottle.
demi-cercle [dəmisɛʀkl(ə)] *nm* semicircle; **en** ~ *adj* semicircular ♦ *adv* in a semicircle.
demi-douzaine [dəmiduzɛn] *nf* half-dozen, half a dozen.
demi-finale [dəmifinal] *nf* semifinal.
demi-finaliste [dəmifinalist(ə)] *nm/f* semifinalist.
demi-fond [dəmifɔ̃] *nm* (*SPORT*) medium-distance running.
demi-frère [dəmifʀɛʀ] *nm* half-brother.
demi-gros [dəmigʀo] *nm inv* wholesale trade.
demi-heure [dəmijœʀ] *nf:* **une** ~ a half-hour, half an hour.
demi-jour [dəmiʒuʀ] *nm* half-light.
demi-journée [dəmiʒuʀne] *nf* half-day, half a day.
démilitariser [demilitaʀize] *vt* to demilitarize.
demi-litre [dəmilitʀ(ə)] *nm* half-litre (*BRIT*), half-liter (*US*), half a litre *ou* liter.
demi-livre [dəmilivʀ(ə)] *nf* half-pound, half a pound.
demi-longueur [dəmilɔ̃gœʀ] *nf* (*SPORT*) half-length, half a length.
demi-lune [dəmilyn]: **en** ~ *adj inv* semicircular.
demi-mal [dəmimal] *nm:* **il n'y a que** ~ there's not much harm done.
demi-mesure [dəmimzyʀ] *nf* half-measure.
demi-mot [dəmimo]: **à** ~ *adv* without having to spell things out.
déminer [demine] *vt* to clear of mines.
démineur [deminœʀ] *nm* bomb disposal expert.
demi-pension [dəmipɑ̃sjɔ̃] *nf* half-board; **être en** ~ (*SCOL*) to take school meals.
demi-pensionnaire [dəmipɑ̃sjɔnɛʀ] *nm/f* (*SCOL*) half-boarder.
demi-place [dəmiplas] *nf* half-price; (*TRANSPORTS*) half-fare.
démis, e [demi, -iz] *pp de* **démettre** ♦ *adj* (*épaule etc*) dislocated.
demi-saison [dəmisɛzɔ̃] *nf:* **vêtements de** ~ spring *ou* autumn clothing.
demi-sel [dəmisɛl] *adj inv* slightly salted.
demi-sœur [dəmisœʀ] *nf* half-sister.
demi-sommeil [dəmisɔmɛj] *nm* doze.
demi-soupir [dəmisupiʀ] *nm* (*MUS*) quaver (*BRIT*) *ou* eighth note (*US*) rest.
démission [demisjɔ̃] *nf* resignation; **donner sa** ~ to give *ou* hand in one's notice, hand in one's resignation.
démissionnaire [demisjɔnɛʀ] *adj* outgoing ♦ *nm/f* person resigning.
démissionner [demisjɔne] *vi* (*de son poste*) to resign, give *ou* hand in one's notice.
demi-tarif [dəmitaʀif] *nm* half-price; (*TRANSPORTS*) half-fare.
demi-ton [dəmitɔ̃] *nm* (*MUS*) semitone.
demi-tour [dəmituʀ] *nm* about-turn; **faire un** ~ (*MIL etc*) to make an about-turn; **faire** ~ to turn (and go) back; (*AUTO*) to do a U-turn.
démobilisation [demɔbilizɑsjɔ̃] *nf* demobilization; (*fig*) demotivation, demoralization.
démobiliser [demɔbilize] *vt* to demobilize; (*fig*) to demotivate, demoralize.
démocrate [demɔkʀat] *adj* democratic ♦ *nm/f* democrat.
démocrate-chrétien, ne [demɔkʀatkʀetjɛ̃, -ɛn] *nm/f* Christian Democrat.
démocratie [demɔkʀasi] *nf* democracy; ~ **populaire/libérale** people's/liberal democracy.
démocratique [demɔkʀatik] *adj* democratic.
démocratiquement [demɔkʀatikmɑ̃] *adv* democratically.
démocratisation [demɔkʀatizɑsjɔ̃] *nf* democratization.
démocratiser [demɔkʀatize] *vt* to democratize.
démodé, e [demɔde] *adj* old-fashioned.
démoder [demɔde]: **se** ~ *vi* to go out of fashion.
démographe [demɔgʀaf] *nm/f* demographer.
démographie [demɔgʀafi] *nf* demography.
démographique [demɔgʀafik] *adj* demographic; **poussée** ~ increase in population.
demoiselle [dəmwazɛl] *nf* (*jeune fille*) young lady; (*célibataire*) single lady, maiden lady; ~ **d'honneur** bridesmaid.
démolir [demɔliʀ] *vt* to demolish; (*fig: personne*) to do for.
démolisseur [demɔlisœʀ] *nm* demolition worker.
démolition [demɔlisjɔ̃] *nf* demolition.

démon [demɔ̃] *nm* demon, fiend; evil spirit; (*enfant turbulent*) devil, demon; **le ~ du jeu/des femmes** a mania for gambling/women; **le D~** the Devil.
démonétiser [demɔnetize] *vt* to demonetize.
démoniaque [demɔnjak] *adj* fiendish.
démonstrateur, trice [demɔ̃stʀatœʀ, -tʀis] *nm/f* demonstrator.
démonstratif, ive [demɔ̃stʀatif, -iv] *adj, nm* (*aussi* LING) demonstrative.
démonstration [demɔ̃stʀɑsjɔ̃] *nf* demonstration; (*aérienne, navale*) display.
démontable [demɔ̃tabl(ə)] *adj* folding.
démontage [demɔ̃taʒ] *nm* dismantling.
démonté, e [demɔ̃te] *adj* (*fig*) raging, wild.
démonte-pneu [demɔ̃təpnø] *nm* tyre lever (*BRIT*), tire iron (*US*).
démonter [demɔ̃te] *vt* (*machine etc*) to take down, dismantle; (*pneu, porte*) to take off; (*cavalier*) to throw, unseat; (*fig: personne*) to disconcert; **se ~** *vi* (*personne*) to lose countenance.
démontrable [demɔ̃tʀabl(ə)] *adj* demonstrable.
démontrer [demɔ̃tʀe] *vt* to demonstrate, show.
démoralisant, e [demɔʀalizɑ̃, -ɑ̃t] *adj* demoralizing.
démoralisateur, trice [demɔʀalizatœʀ, -tʀis] *adj* demoralizing.
démoraliser [demɔʀalize] *vt* to demoralize.
démordre [demɔʀdʀ(ə)] *vi*: **ne pas ~ de** to refuse to give up, stick to.
démouler [demule] *vt* (*gâteau*) to turn out.
démoustiquer [demustike] *vt* to clear of mosquitoes.
démultiplication [demyltiplikɑsjɔ̃] *nf* reduction; reduction ratio.
démuni, e [demyni] *adj* (*sans argent*) impoverished; **~ de** without, lacking in.
démunir [demyniʀ] *vt*: **~ qn de** to deprive sb of; **se ~ de** to part with, give up.
démuseler [demyzle] *vt* to unmuzzle.
démystifier [demistifje] *vt* to demystify.
démythifier [demitifje] *vt* to demythologize.
dénatalité [denatalite] *nf* fall in the birth rate.
dénationalisation [denasjɔnalizɑsjɔ̃] *nf* denationalization.
dénationaliser [denasjɔnalize] *vt* to denationalize.
dénaturé, e [denatyʀe] *adj* (*alcool*) denaturized; (*goûts*) unnatural.
dénaturer [denatyʀe] *vt* (*goût*) to alter (completely); (*pensée, fait*) to distort, misrepresent.
dénégations [denegɑsjɔ̃] *nfpl* denials.
déneigement [denɛʒmɑ̃] *nm* snow clearance.
déneiger [deneʒe] *vt* to clear snow from.
déni [deni] *nm*: **~ (de justice)** denial of justice.
déniaiser [denjeze] *vt*: **~ qn** to teach sb about life.
dénicher [deniʃe] *vt* to unearth.
dénicotinisé, e [denikɔtinize] *adj* nicotine-free.
denier [dənje] *nm* (*monnaie*) *formerly, a coin of small value*; (*de bas*) denier; **~ du culte** contribution to parish upkeep; **~s publics** public money; **de ses (propres) ~s** out of one's own pocket.
dénier [denje] *vt* to deny; **~ qch à qn** to deny sb sth.
dénigrement [denigʀəmɑ̃] *nm* denigration; **campagne de ~** smear campaign.
dénigrer [denigʀe] *vt* to denigrate, run down.
dénivelé, e [denivle] *adj* (*chaussée*) on a lower level ♦ *nm* difference in height.
déniveler [denivle] *vt* to make uneven; to put on a lower level.
dénivellation [denivɛlɑsjɔ̃] *nf*, **dénivellement** [denivɛlmɑ̃] *nm* difference in level; (*pente*) ramp; (*creux*) dip.
dénombrer [denɔ̃bʀe] *vt* (*compter*) to count; (*énumérer*) to enumerate, list.
dénominateur [denɔminatœʀ] *nm* denominator; **~ commun** common denominator.
dénomination [denɔminɑsjɔ̃] *nf* designation, appellation.
dénommé, e [denɔme] *adj*: **le ~ Dupont** the man by the name of Dupont.
dénommer [denɔme] *vt* to name.
dénoncer [denɔ̃se] *vt* to denounce; **se ~** to give o.s. up, come forward.
dénonciation [denɔ̃sjɑsjɔ̃] *nf* denunciation.
dénoter [denɔte] *vt* to denote.
dénouement [denumɑ̃] *nm* outcome, conclusion; (*THÉÂT*) dénouement.
dénouer [denwe] *vt* to unknot, undo.
dénoyauter [denwajote] *vt* to stone; **appareil à ~** stoner.
dénoyauteur [denwajotœʀ] *nm* stoner.
denrée [dɑ̃ʀe] *nf* commodity; (*aussi*: **~ alimentaire**) food(stuff).
dense [dɑ̃s] *adj* dense.
densité [dɑ̃site] *nf* denseness; (*PHYSIQUE*) density.
dent [dɑ̃] *nf* tooth (*pl* teeth); **avoir/garder une ~ contre qn** to have/hold a grudge against sb; **se mettre qch sous la ~** to eat sth; **être sur les ~s** to be on one's last legs; **faire ses ~s** to teethe, cut (one's) teeth; **en ~s de scie** serrated; (*irrégulier*) jagged; **avoir les ~s longues** (*fig*) to be ruthlessly ambitious; **~ de lait/sagesse** milk/wisdom tooth.
dentaire [dɑ̃tɛʀ] *adj* dental; **cabinet ~** dental surgery; **école ~** dental school.
denté, e [dɑ̃te] *adj*: **roue ~e** cog wheel.
dentelé, e [dɑ̃tle] *adj* jagged, indented.
dentelle [dɑ̃tɛl] *nf* lace *no pl*.
dentelure [dɑ̃tlyʀ] *nf* (*aussi*: **~s**) jagged outline.
dentier [dɑ̃tje] *nm* denture.
dentifrice [dɑ̃tifʀis] *adj, nm*: **(pâte) ~** toothpaste; **eau ~** mouthwash.
dentiste [dɑ̃tist(ə)] *nm/f* dentist.

dentition [dɑ̃tisjɔ̃] *nf* teeth *pl*, dentition.
dénucléariser [denykleaʀize] *vt* to make nuclear-free.
dénudé, e [denyde] *adj* bare.
dénuder [denyde] *vt* to bare; **se** ~ (*personne*) to strip.
dénué, e [denɥe] *adj*: ~ **de** lacking in; (*intérêt*) devoid of.
dénuement [denymɑ̃] *nm* destitution.
dénutrition [denytʀisjɔ̃] *nf* undernourishment.
déodorant [deɔdɔʀɑ̃] *nm* deodorant.
déodoriser [deɔdɔʀize] *vt* to deodorize.
déontologie [deɔ̃tɔlɔʒi] *nf* code of ethics; (professional) code of practice.
dép. *abr* (*ADMIN*: = *département*) dept; (= *départ*) dep.
dépannage [depanaʒ] *nm*: **service/camion de** ~ (*AUTO*) breakdown service/truck.
dépanner [depane] *vt* (*voiture, télévision*) to fix, repair; (*fig*) to bail out, help out.
dépanneur [depanœʀ] *nm* (*AUTO*) breakdown mechanic; (*TV*) television engineer.
dépanneuse [depanøz] *nf* breakdown lorry (*BRIT*), tow truck (*US*).
dépareillé, e [depaʀeje] *adj* (*collection, service*) incomplete; (*gant, volume, objet*) odd.
déparer [depaʀe] *vt* to spoil, mar.
départ [depaʀ] *nm* leaving *no pl*, departure; (*SPORT*) start; (*sur un horaire*) departure; **à son** ~ when he left; **au** ~ (*au début*) initially, at the start; **courrier au** ~ outgoing mail.
départager [depaʀtaʒe] *vt* to decide between.
département [depaʀtəmɑ̃] *nm* department; *see boxed note*.

DÉPARTEMENT

France is divided into 96 administrative units called **départements**. *These local government divisions are headed by a state-appointed 'préfet', and administered by an elected 'Conseil général'.* **Départements** *are usually named after prominent geographical features such as rivers or mountain ranges.*

départemental, e, aux [depaʀtəmɑ̃tal, -o] *adj* departmental.
départementaliser [depaʀtəmɑ̃talize] *vt* to devolve authority to.
départir [depaʀtiʀ]: **se** ~ **de** *vt* to abandon, depart from.
dépassé, e [depɑse] *adj* superseded, outmoded; (*fig*) out of one's depth.
dépassement [depɑsmɑ̃] *nm* (*AUTO*) overtaking *no pl*.
dépasser [depɑse] *vt* (*véhicule, concurrent*) to overtake; (*endroit*) to pass, go past; (*somme, limite*) to exceed; (*fig: en beauté etc*) to surpass, outshine; (*être en saillie sur*) to jut out above (*ou* in front of); (*dérouter*): **cela me dépasse** it's beyond me ♦ *vi* (*AUTO*) to overtake; (*jupon*) to show; **se** ~ to excel o.s.
dépassionner [depasjɔne] *vt* (*débat etc*) to take the heat out of.
dépaver [depave] *vt* to remove the cobblestones from.
dépaysé, e [depeize] *adj* disorientated.
dépaysement [depeizmɑ̃] *nm* disorientation; change of scenery.
dépayser [depeize] *vt* (*désorienter*) to disorientate; (*changer agréablement*) to provide with a change of scenery.
dépecer [depəse] *vt* (*suj: boucher*) to joint, cut up; (*suj: animal*) to dismember.
dépêche [depɛʃ] *nf* dispatch; ~ **(télégraphique)** telegram, wire.
dépêcher [depeʃe] *vt* to dispatch; **se** ~ *vi* to hurry; **se** ~ **de faire qch** to hasten to do sth, hurry (in order) to do sth.
dépeindre [depɛ̃dʀ(ə)] *vt* to depict.
dépénalisation [depenalizɑsjɔ̃] *nf* decriminalization.
dépendance [depɑ̃dɑ̃s] *nf* (*interdépendance*) dependence *no pl*, dependency; (*bâtiment*) outbuilding.
dépendant, e [depɑ̃dɑ̃, -ɑ̃t] *vb voir* **dépendre** ♦ *adj* (*financièrement*) dependent.
dépendre [depɑ̃dʀ(ə)] *vt* (*tableau*) to take down; ~ **de** *vt* to depend on; to be dependent on; (*appartenir*) to belong to.
dépens [depɑ̃] *nmpl*: **aux** ~ **de** at the expense of.
dépense [depɑ̃s] *nf* spending *no pl*, expense, expenditure *no pl*; (*fig*) consumption; (*: de temps, de forces*) expenditure; **pousser qn à la** ~ to make sb incur an expense; ~ **physique** (physical) exertion; ~**s de fonctionnement** revenue expenditure; ~**s d'investissement** capital expenditure; ~**s publiques** public expenditure.
dépenser [depɑ̃se] *vt* to spend; (*gaz, eau*) to use; (*fig*) to expend, use up; **se** ~ (*se fatiguer*) to exert o.s.
dépensier, ière [depɑ̃sje, -jɛʀ] *adj*: **il est** ~ he's a spendthrift.
déperdition [depɛʀdisjɔ̃] *nf* loss.
dépérir [depeʀiʀ] *vi* (*personne*) to waste away; (*plante*) to wither.
dépersonnaliser [depɛʀsɔnalize] *vt* to depersonalize.
dépêtrer [depetʀe] *vt*: **se** ~ **de** (*situation*) to extricate o.s. from.
dépeuplé, e [depœple] *adj* depopulated.
dépeuplement [depœpləmɑ̃] *nm* depopulation.
dépeupler [depœple] *vt* to depopulate; **se** ~ to be depopulated.
déphasage [defɑzaʒ] *nm* (*fig*) being out of touch.
déphasé, e [defɑze] *adj* (*ÉLEC*) out of phase; (*fig*) out of touch.
déphaser [defɑze] *vt* (*fig*) to put out of touch.
dépilation [depilɑsjɔ̃] *nf* hair loss; hair re-

moval.
dépilatoire [depilatwaʀ] *adj* depilatory, hair-removing.
dépiler [depile] *vt* (*épiler*) to depilate, remove hair from.
dépistage [depistaʒ] *nm* (*MÉD*) screening.
dépister [depiste] *vt* to detect; (*MÉD*) to screen; (*voleur*) to track down; (*poursuivants*) to throw off the scent.
dépit [depi] *nm* vexation, frustration; **en ~ de** *prép* in spite of; **en ~ du bon sens** contrary to all good sense.
dépité, e [depite] *adj* vexed, frustrated.
dépiter [depite] *vt* to vex, frustrate.
déplacé, e [deplase] *adj* (*propos*) out of place, uncalled-for; **personne ~e** displaced person.
déplacement [deplasmɑ̃] *nm* moving; shifting; transfer; (*voyage*) trip, travelling *no pl* (*BRIT*), traveling *no pl* (*US*); **en ~** away (on a trip); **~ d'air** displacement of air; **~ de vertèbre** slipped disc.
déplacer [deplase] *vt* (*table, voiture*) to move, shift; (*employé*) to transfer, move; **se ~** *vi* (*objet*) to move; (*organe*) to become displaced; (*personne: bouger*) to move, walk; (*: voyager*) to travel ♦ *vt* (*vertèbre etc*) to displace.
déplaire [deplɛʀ] *vi*: **ceci me déplaît** I don't like this, I dislike this; **il cherche à nous ~** he's trying to displease us *ou* be disagreeable to us; **se ~ quelque part** to dislike it *ou* be unhappy somewhere.
déplaisant, e [deplɛzɑ̃, -ɑ̃t] *vb voir* **déplaire** ♦ *adj* disagreeable, unpleasant.
déplaisir [deplezir] *nm* displeasure, annoyance.
déplaît [deplɛ] *vb voir* **déplaire**.
dépliant [deplijɑ̃] *nm* leaflet.
déplier [deplije] *vt* to unfold; **se ~** (*parachute*) to open.
déplisser [deplise] *vt* to smooth out.
déploiement [deplwamɑ̃] *nm* (*voir déployer*) deployment; display.
déplomber [deplɔ̃be] *vt* (*caisse, compteur*) to break (open) the seal of.
déplorable [deplɔʀabl(ə)] *adj* deplorable; lamentable.
déplorer [deplɔʀe] *vt* (*regretter*) to deplore; (*pleurer sur*) to lament.
déployer [deplwaje] *vt* to open out, spread; (*MIL*) to deploy; (*montrer*) to display, exhibit.
déplu [deply] *pp de* **déplaire**.
dépointer [depwɛ̃te] *vi* to clock out.
dépoli, e [depɔli] *adj*: **verre ~** frosted glass.
dépolitiser [depɔlitize] *vt* to depoliticize.
dépopulation [depɔpylasjɔ̃] *nf* depopulation.
déportation [depɔʀtɑsjɔ̃] *nf* deportation.
déporté, e [depɔʀte] *nm/f* deportee; (*1939-45*) concentration camp prisoner.
déporter [depɔʀte] *vt* (*POL*) to deport; (*dévier*) to carry off course; **se ~** *vi* (*voiture*) to swerve.
déposant, e [depozɑ̃, -ɑ̃t] *nm/f* (*épargnant*) depositor.
dépose [depoz] *nf* taking out; taking down.
déposé, e [depoze] *adj* registered; *voir aussi* **marque**.
déposer [depoze] *vt* (*gén: mettre, poser*) to lay down, put down, set down; (*à la banque, à la consigne*) to deposit; (*caution*) to put down; (*passager*) to drop (off), set down; (*démonter: serrure, moteur*) to take out; (*: rideau*) to take down; (*roi*) to depose; (*ADMIN: faire enregistrer*) to file; to register ♦ *vi* to form a sediment *ou* deposit; (*JUR*): **~ (contre)** to testify *ou* give evidence (against); **se ~** *vi* to settle; **~ son bilan** (*COMM*) to go into (voluntary) liquidation.
dépositaire [depozitɛʀ] *nm/f* (*JUR*) depository; (*COMM*) agent; **~ agréé** authorized agent.
déposition [depozisjɔ̃] *nf* (*JUR*) deposition.
déposséder [depɔsede] *vt* to dispossess.
dépôt [depo] *nm* (*à la banque, sédiment*) deposit; (*entrepôt, réserve*) warehouse, store; (*gare*) depot; (*prison*) cells *pl*; **~ d'ordures** rubbish (*BRIT*) *ou* garbage (*US*) dump, tip (*BRIT*); **~ de bilan** (voluntary) liquidation; **~ légal** registration of copyright.
dépoter [depɔte] *vt* (*plante*) to take from the pot, transplant.
dépotoir [depɔtwaʀ] *nm* dumping ground, rubbish (*BRIT*) *ou* garbage (*US*) dump; **~ nucléaire** nuclear (waste) dump.
dépouille [depuj] *nf* (*d'animal*) skin, hide; (*humaine*): **~ (mortelle)** mortal remains *pl*.
dépouillé, e [depuje] *adj* (*fig*) bare, bald; **~ de** stripped of; lacking in.
dépouillement [depujmɑ̃] *nm* (*de scrutin*) count, counting *no pl*.
dépouiller [depuje] *vt* (*animal*) to skin; (*spolier*) to deprive of one's possessions; (*documents*) to go through, peruse; **~ qn/qch de** to strip sb/sth of; **~ le scrutin** to count the votes.
dépourvu, e [depuʀvy] *adj*: **~ de** lacking in, without; **au ~** *adv*: **prendre qn au ~** to catch sb unawares.
dépoussiérer [depusjeʀe] *vt* to remove dust from.
dépravation [depʀavɑsjɔ̃] *nf* depravity.
dépravé, e [depʀave] *adj* depraved.
dépraver [depʀave] *vt* to deprave.
dépréciation [depʀesjɑsjɔ̃] *nf* depreciation.
déprécier [depʀesje] *vt*, **se ~** *vi* to depreciate.
déprédations [depʀedɑsjɔ̃] *nfpl* damage *sg*.
dépressif, ive [depʀesif, -iv] *adj* depressive.
dépression [depʀɛsjɔ̃] *nf* depression; **~ (nerveuse)** (nervous) breakdown.
déprimant, e [depʀimɑ̃, -ɑ̃t] *adj* depressing.
déprime [depʀim] *nf* (*fam*): **la ~** depression.
déprimé, e [depʀime] *adj* (*découragé*) depressed.
déprimer [depʀime] *vt* to depress.

déprogrammer [depʀɔgʀame] *vt* (*supprimer*) to cancel.
DEPS *sigle* (= *dernier entré premier sorti*) LIFO (= *last in first out*).
dépt *abr* (= *département*) dept.
dépuceler [depysle] *vt* (*fam*) to take the virginity of.

MOT-CLÉ

depuis [dəpɥi] *prép* **1** (*point de départ dans le temps*) since; **il habite Paris ~ 1983/l'an dernier** he has been living in Paris since 1983/last year; **~ quand?** since when? **~ quand le connaissez-vous?** how long have you known him?; **~ lors** since then
2 (*temps écoulé*) for; **il habite Paris ~ 5 ans** he has been living in Paris for 5 years; **je le connais ~ 3 ans** I've known him for 3 years; **~ combien de temps êtes-vous ici?** how long have you been here?
3 (*lieu*): **il a plu ~ Metz** it's been raining since Metz; **elle a téléphoné ~ Valence** she rang from Valence
4 (*quantité, rang*) from; **~ les plus petits jusqu'aux plus grands** from the youngest to the oldest
♦ *adv* (*temps*) since (then); **je ne lui ai pas parlé ~** I haven't spoken to him since (then); **~ que** *conj* (ever) since; **~ qu'il m'a dit ça** (ever) since he said that to me

dépuratif, ive [depyʀatif, -iv] *adj* depurative, purgative.
députation [depytɑsjɔ̃] *nf* deputation; (*fonction*) position of deputy, ≈ parliamentary seat (*BRIT*), ≈ seat in Congress (*US*).
député, e [depyte] *nm/f* (*POL*) deputy, ≈ Member of Parliament (*BRIT*), ≈ Congressman/woman (*US*).
députer [depyte] *vt* to delegate; **~ qn auprès de** to send sb (as a representative) to.
déracinement [deʀasinmɑ̃] *nm* (*gén*) uprooting; (*d'un préjugé*) eradication.
déraciner [deʀasine] *vt* to uproot.
déraillement [deʀɑjmɑ̃] *nm* derailment.
dérailler [deʀɑje] *vi* (*train*) to be derailed, go off *ou* jump the rails; (*fam*) to be completely off the track; **faire ~** to derail.
dérailleur [deʀɑjœʀ] *nm* (*de vélo*) dérailleur gears *pl*.
déraison [deʀɛzɔ̃] *nf* unreasonableness.
déraisonnable [deʀɛzɔnabl(ə)] *adj* unreasonable.
déraisonner [deʀɛzɔne] *vi* to talk nonsense, rave.
dérangement [deʀɑ̃ʒmɑ̃] *nm* (*gêne, déplacement*) trouble; (*gastrique etc*) disorder; (*mécanique*) breakdown; **en ~** (*téléphone*) out of order.
déranger [deʀɑ̃ʒe] *vt* (*personne*) to trouble, bother, disturb; (*projets*) to disrupt, upset; (*objets, vêtements*) to disarrange; **se ~** to put o.s. out; (*se déplacer*) to (take the trouble to) come (*ou* go) out; **est-ce que cela vous dérange si ...?** do you mind if ...?; **ça te dérangerait de faire ...?** would you mind doing ...?; **ne vous dérangez pas** don't go to any trouble; don't disturb yourself.
dérapage [deʀapaʒ] *nm* skid, skidding *no pl*; going out of control.
déraper [deʀape] *vi* (*voiture*) to skid; (*personne, semelles, couteau*) to slip; (*fig: économie etc*) to go out of control.
dératé, e [deʀate] *nm/f*: **courir comme un ~** to run like the clappers.
dératiser [deʀatize] *vt* to rid of rats.
déréglé, e [deʀegle] *adj* (*mœurs*) dissolute.
dérèglement [deʀɛgləmɑ̃] *nm* upsetting *no pl*, upset.
déréglementation [deʀɛgləmɑ̃tɑsjɔ̃] *nf* deregulation.
dérégler [deʀegle] *vt* (*mécanisme*) to put out of order, cause to break down; (*estomac*) to upset; **se ~** *vi* to break down, go wrong.
dérider [deʀide] *vt*, **se ~** *vi* to brighten *ou* cheer up.
dérision [deʀizjɔ̃] *nf* derision; **tourner en ~** to deride; **par ~** in mockery.
dérisoire [deʀizwaʀ] *adj* derisory.
dérivatif [deʀivatif] *nm* distraction.
dérivation [deʀivɑsjɔ̃] *nf* derivation; diversion.
dérive [deʀiv] *nf* (*de dériveur*) centre-board; **aller à la ~** (*NAVIG, fig*) to drift; **~ des continents** (*GÉO*) continental drift.
dérivé, e [deʀive] *adj* derived ♦ *nm* (*LING*) derivative; (*TECH*) by-product ♦ *nf* (*MATH*) derivative.
dériver [deʀive] *vt* (*MATH*) to derive; (*cours d'eau etc*) to divert ♦ *vi* (*bateau*) to drift; **~ de** to derive from.
dériveur [deʀivœʀ] *nm* sailing dinghy.
dermatite [dɛʀmatit] *nf* dermatitis.
dermato [dɛʀmato] *nm/f* (*fam*: = *dermatologue*) dermatologist.
dermatologie [dɛʀmatɔlɔʒi] *nf* dermatology.
dermatologue [dɛʀmatɔlɔg] *nm/f* dermatologist.
dermatose [dɛʀmatoz] *nf* dermatosis.
dermite [dɛʀmit] *nf* = **dermatite**.
dernier, ière [dɛʀnje, -jɛʀ] *adj* (*dans le temps, l'espace*) last; (*le plus récent: gén avant n*) latest, last; (*final, ultime: effort*) final; (*échelon, grade*) top, highest ♦ *nm* (*étage*) top floor; **lundi/le mois ~** last Monday/month; **du ~ chic** extremely smart; **le ~ cri** the last word (in fashion); **les ~s honneurs** the last tribute; **le ~ soupir**: **rendre le ~ soupir** to breathe one's last; **en ~** *adv* last; **ce ~, cette dernière** the latter.
dernièrement [dɛʀnjɛʀmɑ̃] *adv* recently.
dernier-né, dernière-née [dɛʀnjene, dɛʀnjɛʀne] *nm/f* (*enfant*) last-born.
dérobade [deʀɔbad] *nf* side-stepping *no pl*.

dérobé, e [deRɔbe] *adj (porte)* secret, hidden; **à la ~e** surreptitiously.
dérober [deRɔbe] *vt* to steal; *(cacher)*: **~ qch à (la vue de) qn** to conceal *ou* hide sth from sb('s view); **se ~** *vi (s'esquiver)* to slip away; *(fig)* to shy away; **se ~ sous** *(s'effondrer)* to give way beneath; **se ~ à** *(justice, regards)* to hide from; *(obligation)* to shirk.
dérogation [deRɔgɑsjɔ̃] *nf* (special) dispensation.
déroger [deRɔʒe]: **~ à** *vt* to go against, depart from.
dérouiller [deRuje] *vt*: **se ~ les jambes** to stretch one's legs.
déroulement [deRulmɑ̃] *nm (d'une opération etc)* progress.
dérouler [deRule] *vt (ficelle)* to unwind; *(papier)* to unroll; **se ~** *vi* to unwind; to unroll, come unrolled; *(avoir lieu)* to take place; *(se passer)* to go.
déroutant, e [deRutɑ̃, -ɑ̃t] *adj* disconcerting.
déroute [deRut] *nf (MIL)* rout; *(fig)* total collapse; **mettre en ~** to rout; **en ~** routed.
dérouter [deRute] *vt (avion, train)* to reroute, divert; *(étonner)* to disconcert, throw (out).
derrick [deRik] *nm* derrick *(over oil well)*.
derrière [dɛRjɛR] *adv, prép* behind ♦ *nm (d'une maison)* back; *(postérieur)* behind, bottom; **les pattes de ~** the back legs, the hind legs; **par ~** from behind; *(fig)* in an underhand way, behind one's back.
derviche [dɛRviʃ] *nm* dervish.
DES *sigle m (= diplôme d'études supérieures) university post-graduate degree.*
des [de] *dét, prép + dét voir* **de**.
dès [dɛ] *prép* from; **~ que** *conj* as soon as; **~ à présent** here and now; **~ son retour** as soon as he was *(ou* is) back; **~ réception** upon receipt; **~ lors** *adv* from then on; **~ lors que** *conj* from the moment (that).
désabusé, e [dezabyze] *adj* disillusioned.
désaccord [dezakɔR] *nm* disagreement.
désaccordé, e [dezakɔRde] *adj (MUS)* out of tune.
désacraliser [desakRalize] *vt* to deconsecrate; *(fig: profession, institution)* to take the mystique out of.
désaffecté, e [dezafɛkte] *adj* disused.
désaffection [dezafɛksjɔ̃] *nf*: **~ pour** estrangement from.
désagréable [dezagReable(ə)] *adj* unpleasant, disagreeable.
désagréablement [dezagReabləmɑ̃] *adv* disagreeably, unpleasantly.
désagrégation [dezagRegɑsjɔ̃] *nf* disintegration.
désagréger [dezagReʒe]: **se ~** *vi* to disintegrate, break up.
désagrément [dezagRemɑ̃] *nm* annoyance, trouble *no pl*.
désaltérant, e [dezalteRɑ̃, -ɑ̃t] *adj* thirst-quenching.
désaltérer [dezalteRe] *vt*: **se ~** to quench one's thirst; **ça désaltère** it's thirst-quenching, it quenches your thirst.
désamorcer [dezamɔRse] *vt* to remove the primer from; *(fig)* to defuse; *(: prévenir)* to forestall.
désappointé, e [dezapwɛ̃te] *adj* disappointed.
désapprobateur, trice [dezapRɔbatœR, -tRis] *adj* disapproving.
désapprobation [dezapRɔbɑsjɔ̃] *nf* disapproval.
désapprouver [dezapRuve] *vt* to disapprove of.
désarçonner [dezaRsɔne] *vt* to unseat, throw; *(fig)* to throw, nonplus *(BRIT)*, disconcert.
désargenté, e [dezaRʒɑ̃te] *adj* impoverished.
désarmant, e [dezaRmɑ̃, -ɑ̃t] *adj* disarming.
désarmé, e [dezaRme] *adj (fig)* disarmed.
désarmement [dezaRməmɑ̃] *nm* disarmament.
désarmer [dezaRme] *vt (MIL, aussi fig)* to disarm; *(NAVIG)* to lay up; *(fusil)* to unload; *(: mettre le cran de sûreté)* to put the safety catch on ♦ *vi (pays)* to disarm; *(haine)* to wane; *(personne)* to give up.
désarrimer [dezaRime] *vt* to shift.
désarroi [dezaRwa] *nm* helplessness, disarray.
désarticulé, e [dezaRtikyle] *adj (pantin, corps)* dislocated.
désarticuler [dezaRtikyle] *vt*: **se ~** to contort (o.s.).
désassorti, e [dezasɔRti] *adj* unmatching, unmatched; *(magasin, marchand)* sold out.
désastre [dezastR(ə)] *nm* disaster.
désastreux, euse [dezastRø, -øz] *adj* disastrous.
désavantage [dezavɑ̃taʒ] *nm* disadvantage; *(inconvénient)* drawback, disadvantage.
désavantager [dezavɑ̃taʒe] *vt* to put at a disadvantage.
désavantageux, euse [dezavɑ̃taʒø, -øz] *adj* unfavourable, disadvantageous.
désaveu [dezavø] *nm* repudiation; *(déni)* disclaimer.
désavouer [dezavwe] *vt* to disown, repudiate, disclaim.
désaxé, e [dezakse] *adj (fig)* unbalanced.
désaxer [dezakse] *vt (roue)* to put out of true; *(personne)* to throw off balance.
desceller [desele] *vt (pierre)* to pull free.
descendance [desɑ̃dɑ̃s] *nf (famille)* descendants *pl*, issue; *(origine)* descent.
descendant, e [desɑ̃dɑ̃, -ɑ̃t] *vb voir* **descendre** ♦ *nm/f* descendant.
descendeur, euse [desɑ̃dœR, -øz] *nm/f (SPORT)* downhiller.
descendre [desɑ̃dR(ə)] *vt (escalier, montagne)* to go *(ou* come) down; *(valise, paquet)* to take *ou* get down; *(étagère etc)* to lower; *(fam: abattre)* to shoot down; *(: boire)* to knock back ♦ *vi* to go *(ou* come) down; *(passager: s'arrêter)* to get out, alight; *(niveau, tempéra-*

ture) to go *ou* come down, fall, drop; (*marée*) to go out; ~ **à pied/en voiture** to walk/drive down, go down on foot/by car; ~ **de** (*famille*) to be descended from; ~ **du train** to get out of *ou* off the train; ~ **d'un arbre** to climb down from a tree; ~ **de cheval** to dismount, get off one's horse; ~ **à l'hôtel** to stay at a hotel; ~ **dans la rue** (*manifester*) to take to the streets; ~ **en ville** to go into town, go down town.

descente [desɑ̃t] *nf* descent, going down; (*chemin*) way down; (*SKI*) downhill (race); **au milieu de la** ~ halfway down; **freinez dans les** ~**s** use the brakes going downhill; ~ **de lit** bedside rug; ~ **(de police)** (police) raid.

descriptif, ive [dɛskʀiptif, -iv] *adj* descriptive ♦ *nm* explanatory leaflet.

description [dɛskʀipsjɔ̃] *nf* description.

désembourber [dezɑ̃buʀbe] *vt* to pull out of the mud.

désembourgeoiser [dezɑ̃buʀʒwaze] *vt*: ~ **qn** to get sb out of his (*ou* her) middle-class attitudes.

désembuer [dezɑ̃bɥe] *vt* to demist.

désemparé, e [dezɑ̃paʀe] *adj* bewildered, distraught; (*bateau, avion*) crippled.

désemparer [dezɑ̃paʀe] *vi*: **sans** ~ without stopping.

désemplir [dezɑ̃pliʀ] *vi*: **ne pas** ~ to be always full.

désenchanté, e [dezɑ̃ʃɑ̃te] *adj* disenchanted, disillusioned.

désenchantement [dezɑ̃ʃɑ̃tmɑ̃] *nm* disenchantment, disillusion.

désenclaver [dezɑ̃klave] *vt* to open up.

désencombrer [dezɑ̃kɔ̃bʀe] *vt* to clear.

désenfler [dezɑ̃fle] *vi* to become less swollen.

désengagement [dezɑ̃gaʒmɑ̃] *nm* (*POL*) disengagement.

désensabler [dezɑ̃sable] *vt* to pull out of the sand.

désensibiliser [desɑ̃sibilize] *vt* (*MÉD*) to desensitize.

désenvenimer [dezɑ̃vnime] *vt* (*plaie*) to remove the poison from; (*fig*) to take the sting out of.

désépaissir [dezepesiʀ] *vt* to thin (out).

déséquilibre [dezekilibʀ(ə)] *nm* (*position*): **être en** ~ to be unsteady; (*fig: des forces, du budget*) imbalance; (*PSYCH*) unbalance.

déséquilibré, e [dezekilibʀe] *nm/f* (*PSYCH*) unbalanced person.

déséquilibrer [dezekilibʀe] *vt* to throw off balance.

désert, e [dezɛʀ, -ɛʀt(ə)] *adj* deserted ♦ *nm* desert.

déserter [dezɛʀte] *vi, vt* to desert.

déserteur [dezɛʀtœʀ] *nm* deserter.

désertion [dezɛʀsjɔ̃] *nf* desertion.

désertique [dezɛʀtik] *adj* desert *cpd*; (*inculte*) barren, empty.

désescalade [dezɛskalad] *nf* (*MIL*) de-escalation.

désespérant, e [dezɛspeʀɑ̃, -ɑ̃t] *adj* hopeless, despairing.

désespéré, e [dezɛspeʀe] *adj* desperate; (*regard*) despairing; **état** ~ (*MÉD*) hopeless condition.

désespérément [dezɛspeʀemɑ̃] *adv* desperately.

désespérer [dezɛspeʀe] *vt* to drive to despair ♦ *vi*, **se** ~ *vi* to despair; ~ **de** to despair of.

désespoir [dezɛspwaʀ] *nm* despair; **être *ou* faire le** ~ **de qn** to be the despair of sb; **en** ~ **de cause** in desperation.

déshabillé, e [dezabije] *adj* undressed ♦ *nm* négligée.

déshabiller [dezabije] *vt* to undress; **se** ~ to undress (o.s.).

déshabituer [dezabitɥe] *vt*: **se** ~ **de** to get out of the habit of.

désherbant [dezɛʀbɑ̃] *nm* weed-killer.

désherber [dezɛʀbe] *vt* to weed.

déshérité, e [dezeʀite] *adj* disinherited ♦ *nm/f*: **les** ~**s** (*pauvres*) the underprivileged, the deprived.

déshériter [dezeʀite] *vt* to disinherit.

déshonneur [dezɔnœʀ] *nm* dishonour (*BRIT*), dishonor (*US*), disgrace.

déshonorer [dezɔnɔʀe] *vt* to dishonour (*BRIT*), dishonor (*US*), bring disgrace upon; **se** ~ to bring dishono(u)r on o.s.

déshumaniser [dezymanize] *vt* to dehumanize.

déshydratation [dezidʀatasjɔ̃] *nf* dehydration.

déshydraté, e [dezidʀate] *adj* dehydrated.

déshydrater [dezidʀate] *vt* to dehydrate.

desiderata [dezideʀata] *nmpl* requirements.

design [dizajn] *adj* (*mobilier*) designer *cpd* ♦ *nm* (industrial) design.

désignation [deziɲasjɔ̃] *nf* naming, appointment; (*signe, mot*) name, designation.

designer [dizajnɛʀ] *nm* designer.

désigner [deziɲe] *vt* (*montrer*) to point out, indicate; (*dénommer*) to denote, refer to; (*nommer: candidat etc*) to name, appoint.

désillusion [dezilyzjɔ̃] *nf* disillusion(ment).

désillusionner [dezilyzjɔne] *vt* to disillusion.

désincarné, e [dezɛ̃kaʀne] *adj* disembodied.

désinence [dezinɑ̃s] *nf* ending, inflexion.

désinfectant, e [dezɛ̃fɛktɑ̃, -ɑ̃t] *adj, nm* disinfectant.

désinfecter [dezɛ̃fɛkte] *vt* to disinfect.

désinfection [dezɛ̃fɛksjɔ̃] *nf* disinfection.

désinformation [dezɛ̃fɔʀmasjɔ̃] *nf* disinformation.

désintégration [dezɛ̃tegʀasjɔ̃] *nf* disintegration.

désintégrer [dezɛ̃tegʀe] *vt*, **se** ~ *vi* to disintegrate.

désintéressé, e [dezɛ̃teʀese] *adj* (*généreux, bénévole*) disinterested, unselfish.

désintéressement [dezɛ̃teʀɛsmɑ̃] *nm* (*géné-*

rosité) disinterestedness.
désintéresser [dezɛ̃teʀese] *vt*: **se ~ (de)** to lose interest (in).
désintérêt [dezɛ̃teʀɛ] *nm* (*indifférence*) disinterest.
désintoxication [dezɛ̃tɔksikɑsjɔ̃] *nf* treatment for alcoholism (*ou* drug addiction); **faire une cure de ~** to have *ou* undergo treatment for alcoholism (*ou* drug addiction).
désintoxiquer [dezɛ̃tɔksike] *vt* to treat for alcoholism (*ou* drug addiction).
désinvolte [dezɛ̃vɔlt(ə)] *adj* casual, off-hand.
désinvolture [dezɛ̃vɔltyʀ] *nf* casualness.
désir [deziʀ] *nm* wish; (*fort, sensuel*) desire.
désirable [deziʀabl(ə)] *adj* desirable.
désirer [deziʀe] *vt* to want, wish for; (*sexuellement*) to desire; **je désire ...** (*formule de politesse*) I would like ...; **il désire que tu l'aides** he would like *ou* he wants you to help him; **~ faire** to want *ou* wish to do; **ça laisse à ~** it leaves something to be desired.
désireux, euse [deziʀø, -øz] *adj*: **~ de faire** anxious to do.
désistement [dezistəmɑ̃] *nm* withdrawal.
désister [deziste]: **se ~** *vi* to stand down, withdraw.
désobéir [dezɔbeiʀ] *vi*: **~ (à qn/qch)** to disobey (sb/sth).
désobéissance [dezɔbeisɑ̃s] *nf* disobedience.
désobéissant, e [dezɔbeisɑ̃, -ɑ̃t] *adj* disobedient.
désobligeant, e [dezɔbliʒɑ̃, -ɑ̃t] *adj* disagreeable, unpleasant.
désobliger [dezɔbliʒe] *vt* to offend.
désodorisant [dezɔdɔʀizɑ̃] *nm* air freshener, deodorizer.
désodoriser [dezɔdɔʀize] *vt* to deodorize.
désœuvré, e [dezœvʀe] *adj* idle.
désœuvrement [dezœvʀəmɑ̃] *nm* idleness.
désolant, e [dezɔlɑ̃, -ɑ̃t] *adj* distressing.
désolation [dezɔlɑsjɔ̃] *nf* (*affliction*) distress, grief; (*d'un paysage etc*) desolation, devastation.
désolé, e [dezɔle] *adj* (*paysage*) desolate; **je suis ~** I'm sorry.
désoler [dezɔle] *vt* to distress, grieve; **se ~** to be upset.
désolidariser [desɔlidaʀize] *vt*: **se ~ de** *ou* **d'avec** to dissociate o.s. from.
désopilant, e [dezɔpilɑ̃, -ɑ̃t] *adj* screamingly funny, hilarious.
désordonné, e [dezɔʀdɔne] *adj* untidy, disorderly.
désordre [dezɔʀdʀ(ə)] *nm* disorder(liness), untidiness; (*anarchie*) disorder; **~s** *nmpl* (*POL*) disturbances, disorder *sg*; **en ~** in a mess, untidy.
désorganiser [dezɔʀganize] *vt* to disorganize.
désorienté, e [dezɔʀjɑ̃te] *adj* disorientated; (*fig*) bewildered.
désorienter [dezɔʀjɑ̃te] *vt* (*fig*) to confuse.
désormais [dezɔʀmɛ] *adv* in future, from now on.
désosser [dezɔse] *vt* to bone.
despote [dɛspɔt] *nm* despot; (*fig*) tyrant.
despotique [dɛspɔtik] *adj* despotic.
despotisme [dɛspɔtism(ə)] *nm* despotism.
desquamer [dɛskwame]: **se ~** *vi* to flake off.
desquels, desquelles [dekɛl] *prép + pron voir* **lequel.**
DESS *sigle m* (= *Diplôme d'études supérieures spécialisées*) *post-graduate diploma.*
dessaisir [deseziʀ] *vt*: **~ un tribunal d'une affaire** to remove a case from a court; **se ~ de** *vt* to give up, part with.
dessaler [desale] *vt* (*eau de mer*) to desalinate; (*CULIN*: *morue etc*) to soak; (*fig fam*: *délurer*): **~ qn** to teach sb a thing or two ♦ *vi* (*voilier*) to capsize.
Desse *abr* = **duchesse.**
desséché, e [deseʃe] *adj* dried up.
dessèchement [desɛʃmɑ̃] *nm* drying out; dryness; hardness.
dessécher [deseʃe] *vt* (*terre, plante*) to dry out, parch; (*peau*) to dry out; (*volontairement: aliments etc*) to dry, dehydrate; (*fig: cœur*) to harden; **se ~** *vi* to dry out; (*peau, lèvres*) to go dry.
dessein [desɛ̃] *nm* design; **dans le ~ de** with the intention of; **à ~** intentionally, deliberately.
desseller [desele] *vt* to unsaddle.
desserrer [deseʀe] *vt* to loosen; (*frein*) to release; (*poing, dents*) to unclench; (*objets alignés*) to space out; **ne pas ~ les dents** not to open one's mouth.
dessert [desɛʀ] *vb voir* **desservir** ♦ *nm* dessert, pudding.
desserte [desɛʀt(ə)] *nf* (*table*) side table; (*transport*): **la ~ du village est assurée par autocar** there is a coach service to the village; **chemin** *ou* **voie de ~** service road.
desservir [desɛʀviʀ] *vt* (*ville, quartier*) to serve; (*: suj: voie de communication*) to lead into; (*suj: vicaire: paroisse*) to serve; (*nuire à: personne*) to do a disservice to; (*débarrasser*): **~ (la table)** to clear the table.
dessiller [desije] *vt* (*fig*): **~ les yeux à qn** to open sb's eyes.
dessin [desɛ̃] *nm* (*œuvre, art*) drawing; (*motif*) pattern, design; (*contour*) (out)line; **le ~ industriel** draughtsmanship (*BRIT*), draftsmanship (*US*); **~ animé** cartoon (film); **~ humoristique** cartoon.
dessinateur, trice [desinatœʀ, -tʀis] *nm/f* drawer; (*de bandes dessinées*) cartoonist; (*industriel*) draughtsman (*BRIT*), draftsman (*US*); **dessinatrice de mode** fashion designer.
dessiner [desine] *vt* to draw; (*concevoir: carrosserie, maison*) to design; (*suj: robe: taille*) to show off; **se ~** *vi* (*forme*) to be outlined; (*fig: solution*) to emerge.
dessoûler [desule] *vt, vi* to sober up.

dessous [dəsu] *adv* underneath, beneath ♦ *nm* underside; (*étage inférieur*): **les voisins du ~** the downstairs neighbours ♦ *nmpl* (*sous-vêtements*) underwear *sg*; (*fig*) hidden aspects; **en ~** underneath; below; (*fig: en catimini*) slyly, on the sly; **par ~** underneath; below; **de ~ le lit** from under the bed; **au-~** *adv* below; **au-~ de** *prép* below; (*peu digne de*) beneath; **au-~ de tout** the (absolute) limit; **avoir le ~** to get the worst of it.
dessous-de-bouteille [dəsudbutɛj] *nm* bottle mat.
dessous-de-plat [dəsudpla] *nm inv* tablemat.
dessous-de-table [dəsudtabl(ə)] *nm* (*fig*) bribe, under-the-counter payment.
dessus [dəsy] *adv* on top; (*collé, écrit*) on it ♦ *nm* top; (*étage supérieur*): **les voisins/l'appartement du ~** the upstairs neighbours/flat; **en ~** above; **par ~** *adv* over it ♦ *prép* over; **au-~** above; **au-~ de** above; **avoir/prendre le ~** to have/get the upper hand; **reprendre le ~** to get over it; **bras ~ bras dessous** arm in arm; **sens ~ dessous** upside down; *voir* **ci-; là-**.
dessus-de-lit [dəsydli] *nm inv* bedspread.
déstabiliser [destabilize] *vt* (*POL*) to destabilize.
destin [dɛstɛ̃] *nm* fate; (*avenir*) destiny.
destinataire [dɛstinatɛʀ] *nm/f* (*POSTES*) addressee; (*d'un colis*) consignee; (*d'un mandat*) payee; **aux risques et périls du ~** at owner's risk.
destination [dɛstinɑsjɔ̃] *nf* (*lieu*) destination; (*usage*) purpose; **à ~ de** (*avion etc*) bound for; (*voyageur*) bound for, travelling to.
destinée [dɛstine] *nf* fate; (*existence, avenir*) destiny.
destiner [dɛstine] *vt*: **~ qn à** (*poste, sort*) to destine sb for, intend sb to *+ verbe*; **~ qn/qch à** (*prédestiner*) to mark sb/sth out for, destine sb/sth to *+ verbe*; **~ qch à** (*envisager d'affecter*) to intend to use sth for; **~ qch à qn** (*envisager de donner*) to intend to give sth to sb, intend sb to have sth; (*adresser*) to intend sth for sb; **se ~ à l'enseignement** to intend to become a teacher; **être destiné à** (*sort*) to be destined to *+ verbe*; (*usage*) to be intended *ou* meant for; (*suj: sort*) to be in store for.
destituer [dɛstitɥe] *vt* to depose; **~ qn de ses fonctions** to relieve sb of his duties.
destitution [dɛstitysjɔ̃] *nf* deposition.
destructeur, trice [dɛstʀyktœʀ, -tʀis] *adj* destructive.
destructif, ive [dɛstʀyktif, -iv] *adj* destructive.
destruction [dɛstʀyksjɔ̃] *nf* destruction.
déstructuré, e [destʀyktyʀe] *adj*: **vêtements ~s** casual clothes.
déstructurer [destʀyktyʀe] *vt* to break down, take to pieces.
désuet, ète [desɥɛ, -ɛt] *adj* outdated, outmoded.
désuétude [desɥetyd] *nf*: **tomber en ~** to fall into disuse, become obsolete.
désuni, e [dezyni] *adj* divided, disunited.
désunion [dezynjɔ̃] *nf* disunity.
désunir [dezyniʀ] *vt* to disunite; **se ~** *vi* (*athlète*) to get out of one's stride.
détachable [detaʃabl(ə)] *adj* (*coupon etc*) tear-off *cpd*; (*capuche etc*) detachable.
détachant [detaʃɑ̃] *nm* stain remover.
détaché, e [detaʃe] *adj* (*fig*) detached ♦ *nm/f* (*représentant*) person on secondment (*BRIT*) *ou* a posting.
détachement [detaʃmɑ̃] *nm* detachment; (*fonctionnaire, employé*): **être en ~** to be on secondment (*BRIT*) *ou* a posting.
détacher [detaʃe] *vt* (*enlever*) to detach, remove; (*délier*) to untie; (*ADMIN*): **~ qn (auprès de** *ou* **à)** to send sb on secondment (to) (*BRIT*), post sb (to); (*MIL*) to detail; (*vêtement: nettoyer*) to remove the stains from; **se ~** *vi* (*tomber*) to come off; to come out; (*se défaire*) to come undone; (*SPORT*) to pull *ou* break away; (*se délier: chien, prisonnier*) to break loose; **se ~ sur** to stand out against; **se ~ de** (*se désintéresser*) to grow away from.
détail [detaj] *nm* detail; (*COMM*): **le ~** retail; **prix de ~** retail price; **au ~** *adv* (*COMM*) retail; (*: individuellement*) separately; **donner le ~ de** to give a detailed account of; (*compte*) to give a breakdown of; **en ~** in detail.
détaillant, e [detajɑ̃, -ɑ̃t] *nm/f* retailer.
détaillé, e [detaje] *adj* (*recit*) detailed.
détailler [detaje] *vt* (*COMM*) to sell retail; to sell separately; (*expliquer*) to explain in detail; to detail; (*examiner*) to look over, examine.
détaler [detale] *vi* (*lapin*) to scamper off; (*fam: personne*) to make off, scarper (*fam*).
détartrant [detaʀtʀɑ̃] *nm* descaling agent (*BRIT*), scale remover.
détartrer [detaʀtʀe] *vt* to descale; (*dents*) to scale.
détaxe [detaks(ə)] *nf* (*réduction*) reduction in tax; (*suppression*) removal of tax; (*remboursement*) tax refund.
détaxer [detakse] *vt* (*réduire*) to reduce the tax on; (*ôter*) to remove the tax on.
détecter [detɛkte] *vt* to detect.
détecteur [detɛktœʀ] *nm* detector, sensor; **~ de mensonges** lie detector; **~ (de mines)** mine detector.
détection [detɛksjɔ̃] *nf* detection.
détective [detɛktiv] *nm* (*BRIT: policier*) detective; **~ (privé)** private detective *ou* investigator.
déteindre [detɛ̃dʀ(ə)] *vi* to fade; (*fig*): **~ sur** to rub off on.
déteint, e [detɛ̃, -ɛ̃t] *pp de* **déteindre**.
dételer [dɛtle] *vt* to unharness; (*voiture, wagon*) to unhitch ♦ *vi* (*fig: s'arrêter*) to leave off

(working).

détendeur [detɑ̃dœʀ] *nm* (*de bouteille à gaz*) regulator.

détendre [detɑ̃dʀ(ə)] *vt* (*fil*) to slacken, loosen; (*personne, atmosphère*) to relax; (*: situation*) to relieve; **se** ~ to lose its tension; to relax.

détendu, e [detɑ̃dy] *adj* relaxed.

détenir [detniʀ] *vt* (*fortune, objet, secret*) to be in possession of; (*prisonnier*) to detain; (*record*) to hold; ~ **le pouvoir** to be in power.

détente [detɑ̃t] *nf* relaxation; (*POL*) détente; (*d'une arme*) trigger; (*d'un athlète qui saute*) spring.

détenteur, trice [detɑ̃tœʀ, -tʀis] *nm/f* holder.

détention [detɑ̃sjɔ̃] *nf* (*voir détenir*) possession; detention; holding; ~ **préventive** (pretrial) custody.

détenu, e [detny] *pp de* **détenir** ♦ *nm/f* prisoner.

détergent [detɛʀʒɑ̃] *nm* detergent.

détérioration [deteʀjɔʀɑsjɔ̃] *nf* damaging; deterioration.

détériorer [deteʀjɔʀe] *vt* to damage; **se** ~ *vi* to deteriorate.

déterminant, e [detɛʀminɑ̃, -ɑ̃t] *adj*: **un facteur** ~ a determining factor ♦ *nm* (*LING*) determiner.

détermination [detɛʀminɑsjɔ̃] *nf* determining; (*résolution*) decision; (*fermeté*) determination.

déterminé, e [detɛʀmine] *adj* (*résolu*) determined; (*précis*) specific, definite.

déterminer [detɛʀmine] *vt* (*fixer*) to determine; (*décider*): ~ **qn à faire** to decide sb to do; **se** ~ **à faire** to make up one's mind to do.

déterminisme [detɛʀminism(ə)] *nm* determinism.

déterré, e [deteʀe] *nm/f*: **avoir une mine de** ~ to look like death warmed up (*BRIT*) *ou* warmed over (*US*).

déterrer [deteʀe] *vt* to dig up.

détersif, ive [detɛʀsif, -iv] *adj, nm* detergent.

détestable [detɛstabl(ə)] *adj* foul, detestable.

détester [detɛste] *vt* to hate, detest.

détiendrai [detjɛ̃dʀe], **détiens** [detjɛ̃] *etc vb voir* **détenir**.

détonant, e [detɔnɑ̃, -ɑ̃t] *adj*: **mélange** ~ explosive mixture.

détonateur [detɔnatœʀ] *nm* detonator.

détonation [detɔnɑsjɔ̃] *nf* detonation, bang, report (of a gun).

détoner [detɔne] *vi* to detonate, explode.

détonner [detɔne] *vi* (*MUS*) to go out of tune; (*fig*) to clash.

détordre [detɔʀdʀ(ə)] *vt* to untwist, unwind.

détour [detuʀ] *nm* detour; (*tournant*) bend, curve; (*fig: subterfuge*) roundabout means; **sans** ~ (*fig*) plainly.

détourné, e [detuʀne] *adj* (*sentier, chemin, moyen*) roundabout.

détournement [detuʀnəmɑ̃] *nm* diversion, rerouting; ~ **d'avion** hijacking; ~ **(de fonds)** embezzlement *ou* misappropriation (of funds); ~ **de mineur** corruption of a minor.

détourner [detuʀne] *vt* to divert; (*avion*) to divert, reroute; (*: par la force*) to hijack; (*yeux, tête*) to turn away; (*de l'argent*) to embezzle, misappropriate; **se** ~ to turn away; ~ **la conversation** to change the subject; ~ **qn de son devoir** to divert sb from his duty; ~ **l'attention (de qn)** to distract *ou* divert (sb's) attention.

détracteur, trice [detʀaktœʀ, -tʀis] *nm/f* disparager, critic.

détraqué, e [detʀake] *adj* (*machine, santé*) broken-down ♦ *nm/f* (*fam*): **c'est un** ~ he's unhinged.

détraquer [detʀake] *vt* to put out of order; (*estomac*) to upset; **se** ~ *vi* to go wrong.

détrempe [detʀɑ̃p] *nf* (*ART*) tempera.

détrempé, e [detʀɑ̃pe] *adj* (*sol*) sodden, waterlogged.

détremper [detʀɑ̃pe] *vt* (*peinture*) to water down.

détresse [detʀɛs] *nf* distress; **en** ~ (*avion etc*) in distress; **appel/signal de** ~ distress call/signal.

détriment [detʀimɑ̃] *nm*: **au** ~ **de** to the detriment of.

détritus [detʀitys] *nmpl* rubbish *sg*, refuse *sg*, garbage *sg* (*US*).

détroit [detʀwa] *nm* strait; **le** ~ **de Bering** *ou* **Behring** the Bering Strait; **le** ~ **de Gibraltar** the Straits of Gibraltar; **le** ~ **du Bosphore** the Bosphorus; **le** ~ **de Magellan** the Strait of Magellan, the Magellan Strait.

détromper [detʀɔ̃pe] *vt* to disabuse; **se** ~: **détrompez-vous** don't believe it.

détrôner [detʀone] *vt* to dethrone, depose; (*fig*) to oust, dethrone.

détrousser [detʀuse] *vt* to rob.

détruire [detʀɥiʀ] *vt* to destroy; (*fig: santé, réputation*) to ruin; (*documents*) to shred.

détruit, e [detʀɥi, -it] *pp de* **détruire**.

dette [dɛt] *nf* debt; ~ **publique** *ou* **de l'État** national debt.

DEUG [døg] *sigle m* = *Diplôme d'études universitaires générales*; *see boxed note*.

DEUG

French students sit their **DEUG** *('diplôme d'études universitaires générales') after two years at university. The can then choose to leave university altogether, or go on to study for their 'licence'. The certificate specifies the student's major subject and may be awarded with distinction.*

deuil [dœj] *nm* (*perte*) bereavement; (*période*) mourning; (*chagrin*) grief; **porter le** ~ to wear mourning; **prendre le/être en** ~ to go into/be in mourning.

DEUST [dœst] *sigle m* = *Diplôme d'études universitaires scientifiques et techniques.*

deux [dø] *num* two; **les ~** both; **ses ~ mains** both his hands, his two hands; **à ~ pas** a short distance away; **tous les ~ mois** every two months, every other month; **~ points** colon *sg*.
deuxième [døzjɛm] *num* second.
deuxièmement [døzjɛmmɑ̃] *adv* secondly, in the second place.
deux-pièces [døpjɛs] *nm inv* (*tailleur*) two-piece (suit); (*de bain*) two-piece (swimsuit); (*appartement*) two-roomed flat (*BRIT*) *ou* apartment (*US*).
deux-roues [døʀu] *nm* two-wheeled vehicle.
deux-temps [døtɑ̃] *adj* two-stroke.
devais [dəvɛ] *etc vb voir* **devoir**.
dévaler [devale] *vt* to hurtle down.
dévaliser [devalize] *vt* to rob, burgle.
dévalorisant, e [devalɔʀizɑ̃, -ɑ̃t] *adj* depreciatory.
dévalorisation [devalɔʀizɑsjɔ̃] *nf* depreciation.
dévaloriser [devalɔʀize] *vt*, **se ~** *vi* to depreciate.
dévaluation [devalɥɑsjɔ̃] *nf* depreciation; (*ÉCON*: *mesure*) devaluation.
dévaluer [devalɥe] *vt*, **se ~** *vi* to devalue.
devancer [dəvɑ̃se] *vt* to be ahead of; (*distancer*) to get ahead of; (*arriver avant*) to arrive before; (*prévenir*) to anticipate; **~ l'appel** (*MIL*) to enlist before call-up.
devancier, ière [dəvɑ̃sje, -jɛʀ] *nm/f* precursor.
devant [dəvɑ̃] *vb voir* **devoir** ♦ *adv* in front; (*à distance: en avant*) ahead ♦ *prép* in front of; ahead of; (*avec mouvement: passer*) past; (*fig*) before, in front of; (*: face à*) faced with, in the face of; (*: vu*) in view of ♦ *nm* front; **prendre les ~s** to make the first move; **de ~** (*roue, porte*) front; **les pattes de ~** the front legs, the forelegs; **par ~** (*boutonner*) at the front; (*entrer*) the front way; **par-~ notaire** in the presence of a notary; **aller au-~ de qn** to go out to meet sb; **aller au-~ de** (*désirs de qn*) to anticipate; **aller au-~ des ennuis** *ou* **difficultés** to be asking for trouble.
devanture [dəvɑ̃tyʀ] *nf* (*façade*) (shop) front; (*étalage*) display; (shop) window.
dévastateur, trice [devastatœʀ, -tʀis] *adj* devastating.
dévastation [devastɑsjɔ̃] *nf* devastation.
dévaster [devaste] *vt* to devastate.
déveine [devɛn] *nf* rotten luck *no pl*.
développement [devlɔpmɑ̃] *nm* development.
développer [devlɔpe] *vt*, **se ~** *vi* to develop.
devenir [dəvniʀ] *vb avec attribut* to become; **~ instituteur** to become a teacher; **que sont-ils devenus?** what has become of them?
devenu, e [dəvny] *pp de* **devenir**.
dévergondé, e [devɛʀgɔ̃de] *adj* wild, shameless.
dévergonder [devɛʀgɔ̃de] *vt*, **se ~** *vi* to get into bad ways.
déverrouiller [devɛʀuje] *vt* to unbolt.
devers [dəvɛʀ] *adv*: **par ~ soi** to oneself.
déverser [devɛʀse] *vt* (*liquide*) to pour (out); (*ordures*) to tip (out); **se ~ dans** (*fleuve, mer*) to flow into.
déversoir [devɛʀswaʀ] *nm* overflow.
dévêtir [devetiʀ] *vt*, **se ~** *vi* to undress.
devez [dəve] *vb voir* **devoir**.
déviation [devjɑsjɔ̃] *nf* deviation; (*AUTO*) diversion (*BRIT*), detour (*US*); **~ de la colonne (vertébrale)** curvature of the spine.
dévider [devide] *vt* to unwind.
dévidoir [devidwaʀ] *nm* reel.
deviendrai [dəvjɛ̃dʀe], **deviens** [dəvjɛ̃] *etc vb voir* **devenir**.
dévier [devje] *vt* (*fleuve, circulation*) to divert; (*coup*) to deflect ♦ *vi* to veer (off course); **(faire) ~** (*projectile*) to deflect; (*véhicule*) to push off course.
devin [dəvɛ̃] *nm* soothsayer, seer.
deviner [dəvine] *vt* to guess; (*prévoir*) to foretell, foresee; (*apercevoir*) to distinguish.
devinette [dəvinɛt] *nf* riddle.
devint [dəvɛ̃] *etc vb voir* **devenir**.
devis [dəvi] *nm* estimate, quotation; **~ descriptif/estimatif** detailed/preliminary estimate.
dévisager [devizaʒe] *vt* to stare at.
devise [dəviz] *nf* (*formule*) motto, watchword; (*ÉCON*: *monnaie*) currency; **~s** *nfpl* (*argent*) currency *sg*.
deviser [dəvize] *vi* to converse.
dévisser [devise] *vt* to unscrew, undo; **se ~** *vi* to come unscrewed.
de visu [devizy] *adv*: **se rendre compte de qch ~** to see sth for o.s.
dévitaliser [devitalize] *vt* (*dent*) to remove the nerve from.
dévoiler [devwale] *vt* to unveil.
devoir [dəvwaʀ] *nm* duty; (*SCOL*) piece of homework, homework *no pl*; (*: en classe*) exercise ♦ *vt* (*argent, respect*): **~ qch (à qn)** to owe (sb) sth; (*suivi de l'infinitif: obligation*): **il doit le faire** he has to do it, he must do it; (*: fatalité*): **cela devait arriver un jour** it was bound to happen; (*: intention*): **il doit partir demain** he is (due) to leave tomorrow; (*: probabilité*): **il doit être tard** it must be late; **se faire un ~ de faire qch** to make it one's duty to do sth; **~s de vacances** homework set for the holidays; **se ~ de faire qch** to be duty bound to do sth; **je devrais faire** I ought to *ou* should do; **tu n'aurais pas dû** you ought not to have *ou* shouldn't have; **comme il se doit** (*comme il faut*) as is right and proper.
dévolu, e [devɔly] *adj*: **~ à** allotted to ♦ *nm*: **jeter son ~ sur** to fix one's choice on.
devons [dəvɔ̃] *vb voir* **devoir**.
dévorant, e [devɔʀɑ̃, -ɑ̃t] *adj* (*faim, passion*) raging.
dévorer [devɔʀe] *vt* to devour; (*suj: feu, soucis*) to consume; **~ qn/qch des yeux** *ou* **du re-**

gard (*fig*) to eye sb/sth intently; (: *convoitise*) to eye sb/sth greedily.
dévot, e [devo, -ɔt] *adj* devout, pious ♦ *nm/f* devout person; **un faux** ~ a falsely pious person.
dévotion [devosjɔ̃] *nf* devoutness; **être à la** ~ **de qn** to be totally devoted to sb; **avoir une** ~ **pour qn** to worship sb.
dévoué, e [devwe] *adj* devoted.
dévouement [devumɑ̃] *nm* devotion, dedication.
dévouer [devwe]: **se** ~ *vi* (*se sacrifier*): **se** ~ **(pour)** to sacrifice o.s. (for); (*se consacrer*): **se** ~ **à** to devote *ou* dedicate o.s. to.
dévoyé, e [devwaje] *adj* delinquent.
dévoyer [devwaje] *vt* to lead astray; **se** ~ *vi* to go off the rails; ~ **l'opinion publique** to influence public opinion.
devrai [dəvʀe] *etc vb voir* **devoir**.
dextérité [dɛksteʀite] *nf* skill, dexterity.
dfc *abr* (= *désire faire connaissance*) *in personal column of newspaper*.
DG *sigle m* = **directeur général**.
dg. *abr* (= *décigramme*) dg.
DGE *sigle f* (= *Dotation globale d'équipement*) *state contribution to local government budget*.
DGSE *sigle f* (= *Direction générale des services extérieurs*) ≈ MI6 (*BRIT*), ≈ CIA (*US*).
DI *sigle f* (*MIL*) = *division d'infanterie*.
dia [dja] *abr* = **diapositive**.
diabète [djabɛt] *nm* diabetes *sg*.
diabétique [djabetik] *nm/f* diabetic.
diable [djɑbl(ə)] *nm* devil; **une musique du** ~ an unholy racket; **il fait une chaleur du** ~ it's fiendishly hot; **avoir le** ~ **au corps** to be the very devil.
diablement [djɑbləmɑ̃] *adv* fiendishly.
diableries [djɑbləʀi] *nfpl* (*d'enfant*) devilment *sg*, mischief *sg*.
diablesse [djɑblɛs] *nf* (*petite fille*) little devil.
diablotin [djɑblɔtɛ̃] *nm* imp; (*pétard*) cracker.
diabolique [djɑbɔlik] *adj* diabolical.
diabolo [djabɔlo] *nm* (*jeu*) diabolo; (*boisson*) lemonade and fruit cordial; ~**(-menthe)** lemonade and mint cordial.
diacre [djakʀ(ə)] *nm* deacon.
diadème [djadɛm] *nm* diadem.
diagnostic [djagnɔstik] *nm* diagnosis *sg*.
diagnostiquer [djagnɔstike] *vt* to diagnose.
diagonal, e, aux [djagɔnal, -o] *adj*, *nf* diagonal; **en** ~**e** diagonally; **lire en** ~**e** (*fig*) to skim through.
diagramme [djagʀam] *nm* chart, graph.
dialecte [djalɛkt(ə)] *nm* dialect.
dialectique [djalɛktik] *adj* dialectic(al).
dialogue [djalɔg] *nm* dialogue; ~ **de sourds** dialogue of the deaf.
dialoguer [djalɔge] *vi* to converse; (*POL*) to have a dialogue.
dialoguiste [djalɔgist(ə)] *nm/f* dialogue writer.
dialyse [djaliz] *nf* dialysis.
diamant [djamɑ̃] *nm* diamond.
diamantaire [djamɑ̃tɛʀ] *nm* diamond dealer.
diamétralement [djametʀalmɑ̃] *adv* diametrically; ~ **opposés** (*opinions*) diametrically opposed.
diamètre [djamɛtʀ(ə)] *nm* diameter.
diapason [djapazɔ̃] *nm* tuning fork; (*fig*): **être/se mettre au** ~ **(de)** to be/get in tune (with).
diaphane [djafan] *adj* diaphanous.
diaphragme [djafʀagm(ə)] *nm* (*ANAT, PHOTO*) diaphragm; (*contraceptif*) diaphragm, cap; **ouverture du** ~ (*PHOTO*) aperture.
diapo [djapo], **diapositive** [djapozitiv] *nf* transparency, slide.
diaporama [djapɔʀama] *nm* slide show.
diapré, e [djapʀe] *adj* many-coloured (*BRIT*), many-colored (*US*).
diarrhée [djaʀe] *nf* diarrhoea (*BRIT*), diarrhea (*US*).
diatribe [djatʀib] *nf* diatribe.
dichotomie [dikɔtɔmi] *nf* dichotomy.
dictaphone [diktafɔn] *nm* Dictaphone ®.
dictateur [diktatœʀ] *nm* dictator.
dictatorial, e, aux [diktatɔʀjal, -o] *adj* dictatorial.
dictature [diktatyʀ] *nf* dictatorship.
dictée [dikte] *nf* dictation; **prendre sous** ~ to take down (*sth dictated*).
dicter [dikte] *vt* to dictate.
diction [diksjɔ̃] *nf* diction, delivery; **cours de** ~ speech production lesson(s).
dictionnaire [diksjɔnɛʀ] *nm* dictionary; ~ **géographique** gazetteer.
dicton [diktɔ̃] *nm* saying, dictum.
didacticiel [didaktisjɛl] *nm* educational software.
didactique [didaktik] *adj* didactic.
dièse [djɛz] *nm* (*MUS*) sharp.
diesel [djezɛl] *nm*, *adj inv* diesel.
diète [djɛt] *nf* diet; **être à la** ~ to be on a diet.
diététicien, ne [djetetisjɛ̃, -ɛn] *nm/f* dietician.
diététique [djetetik] *nf* dietetics *sg* ♦ *adj*: **magasin** ~ health food shop (*BRIT*) *ou* store (*US*).
dieu, x [djø] *nm* god; **D**~ God; **le bon D**~ the good Lord; **mon D**~! good heavens!
diffamant, e [difamɑ̃, -ɑ̃t] *adj* slanderous, defamatory; libellous.
diffamation [difamɑsjɔ̃] *nf* slander; (*écrite*) libel; **attaquer qn en** ~ to sue sb for slander (*ou* libel).
diffamatoire [difamatwaʀ] *adj* slanderous, defamatory; libellous.
diffamer [difame] *vt* to slander, defame; to libel.
différé [difeʀe] *adj* (*INFORM*): **traitement** ~ batch processing; **crédit** ~ deferred credit ♦ *nm* (*TV*): **en** ~ (pre-)recorded.
différemment [difeʀamɑ̃] *adv* differently.
différence [difeʀɑ̃s] *nf* difference; **à la** ~ **de** unlike.

différenciation [difeʀɑ̃sjɑsjɔ̃] *nf* differentiation.
différencier [difeʀɑ̃sje] *vt* to differentiate; **se** ~ *vi* (*organisme*) to become differentiated; **se** ~ **de** to differentiate o.s. from; (*être différent*) to differ from.
différend [difeʀɑ̃] *nm* difference (of opinion), disagreement.
différent, e [difeʀɑ̃, -ɑ̃t] *adj*: ~ **(de)** different (from); ~**s objets** different *ou* various objects; **à** ~**es reprises** on various occasions.
différentiel, le [difeʀɑ̃sjɛl] *adj, nm* differential.
différer [difeʀe] *vt* to postpone, put off ♦ *vi*: ~ **(de)** to differ (from); ~ **de faire** (*tarder*) to delay doing.
difficile [difisil] *adj* difficult; (*exigeant*) hard to please, difficult (to please); **faire le** *ou* **la** ~ to be hard to please, be difficult.
difficilement [difisilmɑ̃] *adv* (*marcher, s'expliquer etc*) with difficulty; ~ **lisible/compréhensible** difficult *ou* hard to read/understand.
difficulté [difikylte] *nf* difficulty; **en** ~ (*bateau, alpiniste*) in trouble *ou* difficulties; **avoir de la** ~ **à faire** to have difficulty (in) doing.
difforme [difɔʀm(ə)] *adj* deformed, misshapen.
difformité [difɔʀmite] *nf* deformity.
diffracter [difʀakte] *vt* to diffract.
diffus, e [dify, -yz] *adj* diffuse.
diffuser [difyze] *vt* (*chaleur, bruit, lumière*) to diffuse; (*émission, musique*) to broadcast; (*nouvelle, idée*) to circulate; (*COMM: livres, journaux*) to distribute.
diffuseur [difyzœʀ] *nm* diffuser; distributor.
diffusion [difyzjɔ̃] *nf* diffusion; broadcast(ing); circulation; distribution.
digérer [diʒeʀe] *vt* (*suj: personne*) to digest; (*: machine*) to process; (*fig: accepter*) to stomach, put up with.
digeste [diʒɛst(ə)] *adj* easily digestible.
digestible [diʒɛstibl(ə)] *adj* digestible.
digestif, ive [diʒɛstif, -iv] *adj* digestive ♦ *nm* (after-dinner) liqueur.
digestion [diʒɛstjɔ̃] *nf* digestion.
digit [didʒit] *nm*: ~ **binaire** binary digit.
digital, e, aux [diʒital, -o] *adj* digital.
digitale [diʒital] *nf* digitalis, foxglove.
digne [diɲ] *adj* dignified; ~ **de** worthy of; ~ **de foi** trustworthy.
dignitaire [diɲitɛʀ] *nm* dignitary.
dignité [diɲite] *nf* dignity.
digression [digʀesjɔ̃] *nf* digression.
digue [dig] *nf* dike, dyke; (*pour protéger la côte*) sea wall.
dijonnais, e [diʒɔnɛ, -ɛz] *adj* of *ou* from Dijon ♦ *nm/f*: **D**~**, e** inhabitant *ou* native of Dijon.
diktat [diktat] *nm* diktat.
dilapidation [dilapidɑsjɔ̃] *nf* (*voir vb*) squandering; embezzlement, misappropriation.
dilapider [dilapide] *vt* to squander, waste; (*détourner: biens, fonds publics*) to embezzle, misappropriate.
dilater [dilate] *vt* to dilate; (*gaz, métal*) to cause to expand; (*ballon*) to distend; **se** ~ *vi* to expand.
dilemme [dilɛm] *nm* dilemma.
dilettante [diletɑ̃t] *nm/f* dilettante; **en** ~ in a dilettantish way.
dilettantisme [diletɑ̃tism(ə)] *nm* dilettant(e)ism.
diligence [diliʒɑ̃s] *nf* stagecoach, diligence; (*empressement*) despatch; **faire** ~ to make haste.
diligent, e [diliʒɑ̃, -ɑ̃t] *adj* prompt and efficient; diligent.
diluant [dilɥɑ̃] *nm* thinner(s).
diluer [dilɥe] *vt* to dilute.
dilution [dilysjɔ̃] *nf* dilution.
diluvien, ne [dilyvjɛ̃, -ɛn] *adj*: **pluie** ~**ne** torrential rain.
dimanche [dimɑ̃ʃ] *nm* Sunday; **le** ~ **des Rameaux/de Pâques** Palm/Easter Sunday; *voir aussi* **lundi**.
dîme [dim] *nf* tithe.
dimension [dimɑ̃sjɔ̃] *nf* (*grandeur*) size; (*gén pl: cotes, MATH: de l'espace*) dimension.
diminué, e [diminɥe] *adj* (*personne: physiquement*) run-down; (*: mentalement*) less alert.
diminuer [diminɥe] *vt* to reduce, decrease; (*ardeur etc*) to lessen; (*personne: physiquement*) to undermine; (*dénigrer*) to belittle ♦ *vi* to decrease, diminish.
diminutif [diminytif] *nm* (*LING*) diminutive; (*surnom*) pet name.
diminution [diminysjɔ̃] *nf* decreasing, diminishing.
dînatoire [dinatwaʀ] *adj*: **goûter** ~ ≈ high tea (*BRIT*); **apéritif** ~ ≈ evening buffet.
dinde [dɛ̃d] *nf* turkey; (*femme stupide*) goose.
dindon [dɛ̃dɔ̃] *nm* turkey.
dindonneau, x [dɛ̃dɔno] *nm* turkey poult.
dîner [dine] *nm* dinner ♦ *vi* to have dinner; ~ **d'affaires/de famille** business/family dinner.
dînette [dinɛt] *nf* (*jeu*): **jouer à la** ~ to play at tea parties.
dingue [dɛ̃g] *adj* (*fam*) crazy.
dinosaure [dinozɔʀ] *nm* dinosaur.
diocèse [djɔsɛz] *nm* diocese.
diode [djɔd] *nf* diode.
diphasé, e [difɑze] *adj* (*ÉLEC*) two-phase.
diphtérie [difteʀi] *nf* diphtheria.
diphtongue [diftɔ̃g] *nf* diphthong.
diplomate [diplɔmat] *adj* diplomatic ♦ *nm* diplomat; (*fig: personne habile*) diplomatist; (*CULIN: gâteau*) *dessert made of sponge cake, candied fruit and custard*, ≈ trifle (*BRIT*).
diplomatie [diplɔmasi] *nf* diplomacy.
diplomatique [diplɔmatik] *adj* diplomatic.
diplôme [diplom] *nm* diploma certificate; (*examen*) (diploma) examination.
diplômé, e [diplome] *adj* qualified.

dire [diʀ] *nm*: **au ~ de** according to; **leurs ~s** what they say ⧫ *vt* to say; (*secret, mensonge*) to tell; ~ **l'heure/la vérité** to tell the time/the truth; **dis pardon/merci** say sorry/thank you; ~ **qch à qn** to tell sb sth; ~ **à qn qu'il fasse** *ou* **de faire** to tell sb to do; ~ **que** to say that; **on dit que** they say that; **comme on dit** as they say; **on dirait que** it looks (*ou* sounds *etc*) as though; **on dirait du vin** you'd *ou* one would think it was wine; **que dites-vous de** (*penser*) what do you think of; **si cela lui dit** if he feels like it, if he fancies it; **cela ne me dit rien** that doesn't appeal to me; **à vrai** ~ truth to tell; **pour ainsi** ~ so to speak; **cela va sans** ~ that goes without saying; **dis donc!, dites donc!** (*pour attirer l'attention*) hey!; (*au fait*) by the way; **et ~ que ...** and to think that ...; **ceci** *ou* **cela dit** that being said; (*à ces mots*) whereupon; **c'est dit, voilà qui est dit** so that's settled; **il n'y a pas à** ~ there's no getting away from it; **c'est ~ si ...** that just shows that ...; **c'est beaucoup/peu** ~ that's saying a lot/not saying much; **se** ~ (*à soi-même*) to say to oneself; (*se prétendre*): **se ~ malade** *etc* to say (that) one is ill *etc*; **ça se dit ... en anglais** that is ... in English; **cela ne se dit pas comme ça** you don't say it like that; **se ~ au revoir** to say goodbye (to each other).

direct, e [diʀɛkt] *adj* direct ⧫ *nm* (*train*) through train; **en** ~ (*émission*) live; **train/bus** ~ express train/bus.

directement [diʀɛktəmɑ̃] *adv* directly.

directeur, trice [diʀɛktœʀ, -tʀis] *nm/f* (*d'entreprise*) director; (*de service*) manager/eress; (*d'école*) head(teacher) (*BRIT*), principal (*US*); **comité** ~ management *ou* steering committee; ~ **général** general manager; ~ **de thèse** ≈ PhD supervisor.

direction [diʀɛksjɔ̃] *nf* management; conducting; supervision; (*AUTO*) steering; (*sens*) direction; **sous la ~ de** (*MUS*) conducted by; **en ~ de** (*avion, train, bateau*) for; **"toutes ~s"** (*AUTO*) "all routes".

directive [diʀɛktiv] *nf* directive, instruction.

directorial, e, aux [diʀɛktɔʀjal, -o] *adj* (*bureau*) director's; manager's; head teacher's.

directrice [diʀɛktʀis] *adj f, nf voir* **directeur**.

dirent [diʀ] *vb voir* **dire**.

dirigeable [diʀiʒabl(ə)] *adj, nm*: **(ballon)** ~ dirigible.

dirigeant, e [diʀiʒɑ̃, -ɑ̃t] *adj* managerial; (*classes*) ruling ⧫ *nm/f* (*d'un parti etc*) leader; (*d'entreprise*) manager, member of the management.

diriger [diʀiʒe] *vt* (*entreprise*) to manage, run; (*véhicule*) to steer; (*orchestre*) to conduct; (*recherches, travaux*) to supervise, be in charge of; (*braquer: regard, arme*): ~ **sur** to point *ou* level *ou* aim at; (*fig: critiques*): ~ **contre** to aim at; **se** ~ (*s'orienter*) to find one's way; **se ~ vers** *ou* **sur** to make *ou* head for.

dirigisme [diʀiʒism(ə)] *nm* (*ÉCON*) state intervention, interventionism.

dirigiste [diʀiʒist(ə)] *adj* interventionist.

dis [di], **disais** [dizɛ] *etc vb voir* **dire**.

discal, e, aux [diskal, -o] *adj* (*MÉD*): **hernie ~e** slipped disc.

discernement [disɛʀnəmɑ̃] *nm* discernment, judgment.

discerner [disɛʀne] *vt* to discern, make out.

disciple [disipl(ə)] *nm/f* disciple.

disciplinaire [disiplinɛʀ] *adj* disciplinary.

discipline [disiplin] *nf* discipline.

discipliné, e [disipline] *adj* (well-)disciplined.

discipliner [disipline] *vt* to discipline; (*cheveux*) to control.

discobole [diskɔbɔl] *nm/f* discus thrower.

discographie [diskɔgʀafi] *nf* discography.

discontinu, e [diskɔ̃tiny] *adj* intermittent; (*bande: sur la route*) broken.

discontinuer [diskɔ̃tinɥe] *vi*: **sans** ~ without stopping, without a break.

disconvenir [diskɔ̃vniʀ] *vi*: **ne pas ~ de qch/que** not to deny sth/that.

discophile [diskɔfil] *nm/f* record enthusiast.

discordance [diskɔʀdɑ̃s] *nf* discordance; conflict.

discordant, e [diskɔʀdɑ̃, -ɑ̃t] *adj* discordant; conflicting.

discorde [diskɔʀd(ə)] *nf* discord, dissension.

discothèque [diskɔtɛk] *nf* (*disques*) record collection; (*: dans une bibliothèque*): ~ **(de prêt)** record library; (*boîte de nuit*) disco(thèque).

discourais [diskuʀɛ] *etc vb voir* **discourir**.

discourir [diskuʀiʀ] *vi* to discourse, hold forth.

discours [diskuʀ] *vb voir* **discourir** ⧫ *nm* speech; ~ **direct/indirect** (*LING*) direct/indirect *ou* reported speech.

discourtois, e [diskuʀtwa, waz] *adj* discourteous.

discrédit [diskʀedi] *nm*: **jeter le ~ sur** to discredit.

discréditer [diskʀedite] *vt* to discredit.

discret, ète [diskʀɛ, -ɛt] *adj* discreet; (*fig: musique, style*) unobtrusive; (*: endroit*) quiet.

discrètement [diskʀɛtmɑ̃] *adv* discreetly.

discrétion [diskʀesjɔ̃] *nf* discretion; **à la ~ de qn** at sb's discretion; in sb's hands; **à** ~ (*boisson etc*) unlimited, as much as one wants.

discrétionnaire [diskʀesjɔnɛʀ] *adj* discretionary.

discrimination [diskʀiminɑsjɔ̃] *nf* discrimination; **sans** ~ indiscriminately.

discriminatoire [diskʀiminatwaʀ] *adj* discriminatory.

disculper [diskylpe] *vt* to exonerate.

discussion [diskysjɔ̃] *nf* discussion.

discutable [diskytabl(ə)] *adj* (*contestable*) doubtful; (*à débattre*) debatable.

discuté, e [diskyte] *adj* controversial.

discuter [diskyte] *vt* (*contester*) to question, dispute; (*débattre: prix*) to discuss ♦ *vi* to talk; (*ergoter*) to argue; ~ **de** to discuss.
dise [diz] *etc vb voir* **dire**.
disert, e [dizɛʀ, -ɛʀt(ə)] *adj* loquacious.
disette [dizɛt] *nf* food shortage.
diseuse [dizøz] *nf*: ~ **de bonne aventure** fortuneteller.
disgrâce [disgʀɑs] *nf* disgrace; **être en** ~ to be in disgrace.
disgracié, e [disgʀasje] *adj* (*en disgrâce*) disgraced.
disgracieux, euse [disgʀasjø, -øz] *adj* ungainly, awkward.
disjoindre [disʒwɛ̃dʀ(ə)] *vt* to take apart; **se** ~ *vi* to come apart.
disjoint, e [disʒwɛ̃, -wɛ̃t] *pp de* **disjoindre** ♦ *adj* loose.
disjoncteur [disʒɔ̃ktœʀ] *nm* (*ÉLEC*) circuit breaker.
dislocation [dislɔkɑsjɔ̃] *nf* dislocation.
disloquer [dislɔke] *vt* (*membre*) to dislocate; (*chaise*) to dismantle; (*troupe*) to disperse; **se** ~ *vi* (*parti, empire*) to break up; **se** ~ **l'épaule** to dislocate one's shoulder.
disons [dizɔ̃] *etc vb voir* **dire**.
disparaître [dispaʀɛtʀ(ə)] *vi* to disappear; (*à la vue*) to vanish, disappear; to be hidden *ou* concealed; (*être manquant*) to go missing, disappear; (*se perdre: traditions etc*) to die out; (*personne: mourir*) to die; **faire** ~ (*objet, tache, trace*) to remove; (*personne*) to get rid of.
disparate [dispaʀat] *adj* disparate; (*couleurs*) ill-assorted.
disparité [dispaʀite] *nf* disparity.
disparition [dispaʀisjɔ̃] *nf* disappearance.
disparu, e [dispaʀy] *pp de* **disparaître** ♦ *nm/f* missing person; (*défunt*) departed; **être porté** ~ to be reported missing.
dispendieux, euse [dispɑ̃djø, -øz] *adj* extravagant, expensive.
dispensaire [dispɑ̃sɛʀ] *nm* community clinic.
dispense [dispɑ̃s] *nf* exemption; (*permission*) special permission; ~ **d'âge** special exemption from age limit.
dispenser [dispɑ̃se] *vt* (*donner*) to lavish, bestow; (*exempter*): ~ **qn de** to exempt sb from; **se** ~ **de** *vt* to avoid, get out of.
disperser [dispɛʀse] *vt* to scatter; (*fig: son attention*) to dissipate; **se** ~ *vi* to scatter; (*fig*) to dissipate one's efforts.
dispersion [dispɛʀsjɔ̃] *nf* scattering; (*des efforts*) dissipation.
disponibilité [dispɔnibilite] *nf* availability; (*ADMIN*): **être en** ~ to be on leave of absence; ~**s** *nfpl* (*COMM*) liquid assets.
disponible [dispɔnibl(ə)] *adj* available.
dispos [dispo] *adj m*: **(frais et)** ~ fresh (as a daisy).
disposé, e [dispoze] *adj* (*d'une certaine manière*) arranged, laid-out; **bien/mal** ~ (*humeur*) in a good/bad mood; **bien/mal** ~ **pour** *ou* **envers qn** well/badly disposed towards sb; ~ **à** (*prêt à*) willing *ou* prepared to.
disposer [dispoze] *vt* (*arranger, placer*) to arrange; (*inciter*): ~ **qn à qch/faire qch** to dispose *ou* incline sb towards sth/to do sth ♦ *vi*: **vous pouvez** ~ you may leave; ~ **de** *vt* to have (at one's disposal); **se** ~ **à faire** to prepare to do, be about to do.
dispositif [dispozitif] *nm* device; (*fig*) system, plan of action; set-up; (*d'un texte de loi*) operative part; ~ **de sûreté** safety device.
disposition [dispozisjɔ̃] *nf* (*arrangement*) arrangement, layout; (*humeur*) mood; (*tendance*) tendency; ~**s** *nfpl* (*mesures*) steps, measures; (*préparatifs*) arrangements; (*de loi, testament*) provisions; (*aptitudes*) bent *sg*, aptitude *sg*; **à la** ~ **de qn** at sb's disposal.
disproportion [dispʀɔpɔʀsjɔ̃] *nf* disproportion.
disproportionné, e [dispʀɔpɔʀsjɔne] *adj* disproportionate, out of all proportion.
dispute [dispyt] *nf* quarrel, argument.
disputer [dispyte] *vt* (*match*) to play; (*combat*) to fight; (*course*) to run; **se** ~ *vi* to quarrel, have a quarrel; (*match, combat, course*) to take place; ~ **qch à qn** to fight with sb for *ou* over sth.
disquaire [diskɛʀ] *nm/f* record dealer.
disqualification [diskalifikɑsjɔ̃] *nf* disqualification.
disqualifier [diskalifje] *vt* to disqualify; **se** ~ *vi* to bring discredit on o.s.
disque [disk(ə)] *nm* (*MUS*) record; (*INFORM*) disk, disc; (*forme, pièce*) disc; (*SPORT*) discus; ~ **compact** compact disc; ~ **compact interactif** CD-I ®; ~ **dur** hard disk; ~ **d'embrayage** (*AUTO*) clutch plate; ~ **laser** compact disc; ~ **de stationnement** parking disc; ~ **système** system disk.
disquette [diskɛt] *nf* diskette, floppy (disk); ~ **(à) simple/double densité** single/double density disk; ~ **une face/double face** single-/double-sided disk.
dissection [disɛksjɔ̃] *nf* dissection.
dissemblable [disɑ̃blabl(ə)] *adj* dissimilar.
dissemblance [disɑ̃blɑ̃s] *nf* dissimilarity, difference.
dissémination [diseminɑsjɔ̃] *nf* (*voir vb*) scattering; dispersal; (*des armes*) proliferation.
disséminer [disemine] *vt* to scatter; (*troupes: sur un territoire*) to disperse.
dissension [disɑ̃sjɔ̃] *nf* dissension; ~**s** *nfpl* dissension.
disséquer [diseke] *vt* to dissect.
dissertation [disɛʀtɑsjɔ̃] *nf* (*SCOL*) essay.
disserter [disɛʀte] *vi*: ~ **sur** to discourse upon.
dissidence [disidɑ̃s] *nf* (*concept*) dissidence; **rejoindre la** ~ to join the dissidents.
dissident, e [disidɑ̃, -ɑ̃t] *adj, nm/f* dissident.
dissimilitude [disimilityd] *nf* dissimilarity.
dissimulateur, trice [disimyltœʀ, -tʀis] *adj*

dissembling ♦ *nm/f* dissembler.
dissimulation [disimylɑsjɔ̃] *nf* concealing; (*duplicité*) dissimulation; ~ **de bénéfices/de revenus** concealment of profits/income.
dissimulé, e [disimyle] (*personne: secret*) secretive; (*: fourbe, hypocrite*) deceitful.
dissimuler [disimyle] *vt* to conceal; **se** ~ to conceal o.s.; to be concealed.
dissipation [disipɑsjɔ̃] *nf* squandering; unruliness; (*débauche*) dissipation.
dissipé, e [disipe] *adj* (*indiscipliné*) unruly.
dissiper [disipe] *vt* to dissipate; (*fortune*) to squander, fritter away; **se** ~ *vi* (*brouillard*) to clear, disperse; (*doutes*) to disappear, melt away; (*élève*) to become undisciplined *ou* unruly.
dissociable [disɔsjabl(ə)] *adj* separable.
dissocier [disɔsje] *vt* to dissociate; **se** ~ *vi* (*éléments, groupe*) to break up, split up; **se** ~ **de** (*groupe, point de vue*) to dissociate o.s. from.
dissolu, e [disɔly] *adj* dissolute.
dissoluble [disɔlybl(ə)] *adj* (*POL: assemblée*) dissolvable.
dissolution [disɔlysjɔ̃] *nf* dissolving; (*POL, JUR*) dissolution.
dissolvant, e [disɔlvɑ̃, -ɑ̃t] *vb voir* **dissoudre** ♦ *nm* (*CHIMIE*) solvent; ~ **(gras)** nail polish remover.
dissonant, e [disɔnɑ̃, -ɑ̃t] *adj* discordant.
dissoudre [disudʀ(ə)] *vt*, **se** ~ *vi* to dissolve.
dissous, oute [disu, -ut] *pp de* **dissoudre.**
dissuader [disɥade] *vt*: ~ **qn de faire/de qch** to dissuade sb from doing/from sth.
dissuasif, ive [disɥazif, iv] *adj* dissuasive.
dissuasion [disɥɑzjɔ̃] *nf* dissuasion; **force de** ~ deterrent power.
distance [distɑ̃s] *nf* distance; (*fig: écart*) gap; **à** ~ at *ou* from a distance; (*mettre en marche, commander*) by remote control; **(situé) à** ~ (*INFORM*) remote; **tenir qn à** ~ to keep sb at a distance; **se tenir à** ~ to keep one's distance; **à une** ~ **de 10 km, à 10 km de** ~ 10 km away, at a distance of 10 km; **à 2 ans de** ~ with a gap of 2 years; **prendre ses** ~**s** to space out; **garder ses** ~**s** to keep one's distance; **tenir la** ~ (*SPORT*) to cover the distance, last the course; ~ **focale** (*PHOTO*) focal length.
distancer [distɑ̃se] *vt* to outdistance, leave behind.
distancier [distɑ̃sje]: **se** ~ *vi* to distance o.s.
distant, e [distɑ̃, -ɑ̃t] *adj* (*réservé*) distant, aloof; (*éloigné*) distant, far away; ~ **de** (*lieu*) far away *ou* a long way from; ~ **de 5 km (d'un lieu)** 5 km away (from a place).
distendre [distɑ̃dʀ(ə)] *vt*, **se** ~ *vi* to distend.
distillation [distilɑsjɔ̃] *nf* distillation, distilling.
distillé, e [distile] *adj*: **eau** ~**e** distilled water.
distiller [distile] *vt* to distil; (*fig*) to exude; to elaborate.
distillerie [distilʀi] *nf* distillery.
distinct, e [distɛ̃(kt), distɛ̃kt(ə)] *adj* distinct.
distinctement [distɛ̃ktəmɑ̃] *adv* distinctly.
distinctif, ive [distɛ̃ktif, -iv] *adj* distinctive.
distinction [distɛ̃ksjɔ̃] *nf* distinction.
distingué, e [distɛ̃ge] *adj* distinguished.
distinguer [distɛ̃ge] *vt* to distinguish; **se** ~ *vi* (*s'illustrer*) to distinguish o.s.; (*différer*): **se** ~ **(de)** to distinguish o.s. *ou* be distinguished (from).
distinguo [distɛ̃go] *nm* distinction.
distorsion [distɔʀsjɔ̃] *nf* (*gén*) distorsion; (*fig: déséquilibre*) disparity, imbalance.
distraction [distʀaksjɔ̃] *nf* (*manque d'attention*) absent-mindedness; (*oubli*) lapse (in concentration *ou* attention); (*détente*) diversion, recreation; (*passe-temps*) distraction, entertainment.
distraire [distʀɛʀ] *vt* (*déranger*) to distract; (*divertir*) to entertain, divert; (*détourner: somme d'argent*) to divert, misappropriate; **se** ~ to amuse *ou* enjoy o.s.
distrait, e [distʀɛ, -ɛt] *pp de* **distraire** ♦ *adj* absent-minded.
distraitement [distʀɛtmɑ̃] *adv* absent-mindedly.
distrayant, e [distʀɛjɑ̃, -ɑ̃t] *vb voir* **distraire** ♦ *adj* entertaining.
distribanque [distʀibɑ̃k] *nm* cash dispenser.
distribuer [distʀibɥe] *vt* to distribute; to hand out; (*CARTES*) to deal (out); (*courrier*) to deliver.
distributeur [distʀibytœʀ] *nm* (*AUTO, COMM*) distributor; (*automatique*) (vending) machine; ~ **de billets** (*RAIL*) ticket machine; (*BANQUE*) cash dispenser.
distribution [distʀibysjɔ̃] *nf* distribution; (*postale*) delivery; (*choix d'acteurs*) casting; **circuits de** ~ (*COMM*) distribution network; ~ **des prix** (*SCOL*) prize giving.
district [distʀik(t)] *nm* district.
dit, e [di, dit] *pp de* **dire** ♦ *adj* (*fixé*): **le jour** ~ the arranged day; (*surnommé*): **X,** ~ **Pierrot** X, known as *ou* called Pierrot.
dites [dit] *vb voir* **dire.**
dithyrambique [ditiʀɑ̃bik] *adj* eulogistic.
DIU *sigle m* (*= dispositif intra-utérin*) IUD.
diurétique [djyʀetik] *adj, nm* diuretic.
diurne [djyʀn(ə)] *adj* diurnal, daytime *cpd*.
divagations [divagɑsjɔ̃] *nfpl* ramblings; ravings.
divaguer [divage] *vi* to ramble; (*malade*) to rave.
divan [divɑ̃] *nm* divan.
divan-lit [divɑ̃li] *nm* divan (bed).
divergence [divɛʀʒɑ̃s] *nf* divergence; **des** ~**s d'opinion au sein de ...** differences of opinion within ....
divergent, e [divɛʀʒɑ̃, -ɑ̃t] *adj* divergent.
diverger [divɛʀʒe] *vi* to diverge.
divers, e [divɛʀ, -ɛʀs(ə)] *adj* (*varié*) diverse, varied; (*différent*) different, various ♦ *dét* (*plusieurs*) various, several; **(frais)** ~ (*COMM*)

sundries, miscellaneous (expenses); "~" (*rubrique*) "miscellaneous".
diversement [divɛʀsəmɑ̃] *adv* in various *ou* diverse ways.
diversification [divɛʀsifikɑsjɔ̃] *nf* diversification.
diversifier [divɛʀsifje] *vt*, **se ~** *vi* to diversify.
diversion [divɛʀsjɔ̃] *nf* diversion; **faire ~** to create a diversion.
diversité [divɛʀsite] *nf* diversity, variety.
divertir [divɛʀtiʀ] *vt* to amuse, entertain; **se ~** to amuse *ou* enjoy o.s.
divertissant, e [divɛʀtisɑ̃, -ɑ̃t] *adj* entertaining.
divertissement [divɛʀtismɑ̃] *nm* entertainment; (*MUS*) divertimento, divertissement.
dividende [dividɑ̃d] *nm* (*MATH, COMM*) dividend.
divin, e [divɛ̃, -in] *adj* divine; (*fig: excellent*) heavenly, divine.
divinateur, trice [divinatœʀ, -tʀis] *adj* perspicacious.
divinatoire [divinatwaʀ] *adj* (*art, science*) divinatory; **baguette ~** divining rod.
diviniser [divinize] *vt* to deify.
divinité [divinite] *nf* divinity.
divisé, e [divize] *adj* divided.
diviser [divize] *vt* (*gén, MATH*) to divide; (*morceler, subdiviser*) to divide (up), split (up); **se ~ en** to divide into; **~ par** to divide by.
diviseur [divizœʀ] *nm* (*MATH*) divisor.
divisible [divizibl(ə)] *adj* divisible.
division [divizjɔ̃] *nf* (*gén*) division; **~ du travail** (*ÉCON*) division of labour.
divisionnaire [divisjɔnɛʀ] *adj*: **commissaire ~** ≈ chief superintendent (*BRIT*), ≈ police chief (*US*).
divorce [divɔʀs(ə)] *nm* divorce.
divorcé, e [divɔʀse] *nm/f* divorcee.
divorcer [divɔʀse] *vi* to get a divorce, get divorced; **~ de** *ou* **d'avec qn** to divorce sb.
divulgation [divylgɑsjɔ̃] *nf* disclosure.
divulguer [divylge] *vt* to divulge, disclose.
dix [di, dis, diz] *num* ten.
dix-huit [dizɥit] *num* eighteen.
dix-huitième [dizɥitjɛm] *num* eighteenth.
dixième [dizjɛm] *num* tenth.
dix-neuf [diznœf] *num* nineteen.
dix-neuvième [diznœvjɛm] *num* nineteenth.
dix-sept [disɛt] *num* seventeen.
dix-septième [disɛtjɛm] *num* seventeenth.
dizaine [dizɛn] *nf* (*10*) ten; (*environ 10*): **une ~ (de)** about ten, ten or so.
Djakarta [dʒakaʀta] *n* Djakarta.
Djibouti [dʒibuti] *n* Djibouti.
dl *abr* (= *décilitre*) dl.
DM *abr* (= *Deutschmark*) DM.
dm. *abr* (= *décimètre*) dm.
do [do] *nm* (*note*) C; (*en chantant la gamme*) do(h).
docile [dɔsil] *adj* docile.
docilement [dɔsilmɑ̃] *adv* docilely.
docilité [dɔsilite] *nf* docility.
dock [dɔk] *nm* dock; (*hangar, bâtiment*) warehouse.
docker [dɔkɛʀ] *nm* docker.
docte [dɔkt(ə)] *adj* (*péj*) learned.
docteur, e [dɔktœʀ] *nm/f* doctor; **~ en médecine** doctor of medicine.
doctoral, e, aux [dɔktɔʀal, -o] *adj* pompous, bombastic.
doctorat [dɔktɔʀa] *nm*: **~ (d'Université)** ≈ doctorate; **~ d'État** ≈ PhD; **~ de troisième cycle** ≈ doctorate.
doctoresse [dɔktɔʀɛs] *nf* lady doctor.
doctrinaire [dɔktʀinɛʀ] *adj* doctrinaire; (*sententieux*) pompous, sententious.
doctrinal, e, aux [dɔktʀinal, o] *adj* doctrinal.
doctrine [dɔktʀin] *nf* doctrine.
document [dɔkymɑ̃] *nm* document.
documentaire [dɔkymɑ̃tɛʀ] *adj, nm* documentary.
documentaliste [dɔkymɑ̃talist(ə)] *nm/f* archivist; (*PRESSE, TV*) researcher.
documentation [dɔkymɑ̃tɑsjɔ̃] *nf* documentation, literature; (*PRESSE, TV: service*) research.
documenté, e [dɔkymɑ̃te] *adj* well-informed, well-documented; well-researched.
documenter [dɔkymɑ̃te] *vt*: **se ~ (sur)** to gather information *ou* material (on *ou* about).
Dodécanèse [dɔdekanɛz] *nm* Dodecanese (Islands).
dodeliner [dɔdline] *vi*: **~ de la tête** to nod one's head gently.
dodo [dɔdo] *nm*: **aller faire ~** to go to beddy-byes.
dodu, e [dɔdy] *adj* plump.
dogmatique [dɔgmatik] *adj* dogmatic.
dogmatisme [dɔgmatism(ə)] *nm* dogmatism.
dogme [dɔgm(ə)] *nm* dogma.
dogue [dɔg] *nm* mastiff.
doigt [dwa] *nm* finger; **à deux ~s de** within an ace (*BRIT*) *ou* an inch of; **un ~ de lait/whisky** a drop of milk/whisky; **désigner** *ou* **montrer du ~** to point at; **au ~ et à l'œil** to the letter; **connaître qch sur le bout du ~** to know sth backwards; **mettre le ~ sur la plaie** (*fig*) to find the sensitive spot; **~ de pied** toe.
doigté [dwate] *nm* (*MUS*) fingering; (*fig: habileté*) diplomacy, tact.
doigtier [dwatje] *nm* fingerstall.
dois [dwa] *etc vb voir* **devoir**.
doive [dwav] *etc vb voir* **devoir**.
doléances [dɔleɑ̃s] *nfpl* complaints; (*réclamations*) grievances.
dolent, e [dɔlɑ̃, -ɑ̃t] *adj* doleful, mournful.
dollar [dɔlaʀ] *nm* dollar.
dolmen [dɔlmɛn] *nm* dolmen.
DOM [deoɛm, dɔm] *sigle m ou mpl* = *Département(s) d'outre-mer*; *see boxed note*.

DOM

France has four overseas 'départements d'outre-mer', or **DOMs***: French Guiana, Guadeloupe, Martinique and Réunion. Since 1982 each of these places has also had regional status. France also has five overseas 'territoires d'outre-mer', or 'TOMs': French and Southern Antarctic Territories, French Polynesia, Mayotte, New Caledonia and Wallis and Futuna. Citizens of both DOMs and TOMs have French nationality.*

domaine [dɔmɛn] *nm* estate, property; (*fig*) domain, field; **tomber dans le ~ public** (*livre etc*) to be out of copyright; **dans tous les ~s** in all areas.

domanial, e, aux [dɔmanjal, -o] *adj* national, state *cpd*.

dôme [dom] *nm* dome.

domestication [dɔmɛstikɑsjɔ̃] *nf* (*voir domestiquer*) domestication; harnessing.

domesticité [dɔmɛstisite] *nf* (domestic) staff.

domestique [dɔmɛstik] *adj* domestic ♦ *nm/f* servant, domestic.

domestiquer [dɔmɛstike] *vt* to domesticate; (*vent, marées*) to harness.

domicile [dɔmisil] *nm* home, place of residence; **à ~** at home; **élire ~ à** to take up residence in; **sans ~ fixe** of no fixed abode; **~ conjugal** marital home; **~ légal** domicile.

domicilié, e [dɔmisilje] *adj*: **être ~ à** to have one's home in *ou* at.

dominant, e [dɔminɑ̃, -ɑ̃t] *adj* dominant; (*plus important*) predominant ♦ *nf* (*caractéristique*) dominant characteristic; (*couleur*) dominant colour.

dominateur, trice [dɔminatœʀ, -tʀis] *adj* dominating; (*qui aime à dominer*) domineering.

domination [dɔminɑsjɔ̃] *nf* domination.

dominer [dɔmine] *vt* to dominate; (*passions etc*) to control, master; (*surpasser*) to outclass, surpass; (*surplomber*) to tower above, dominate ♦ *vi* to be in the dominant position; **se ~** to control o.s.

dominicain, e [dɔminikɛ̃, -ɛn] *adj* Dominican.

dominical, e, aux [dɔminikal, -o] *adj* Sunday *cpd*, dominical.

Dominique [dɔminik] *nf*: **la ~** Dominica.

domino [dɔmino] *nm* domino; **~s** *nmpl* (*jeu*) dominoes *sg*.

dommage [dɔmaʒ] *nm* (*préjudice*) harm, injury; (*dégâts, pertes*) damage *no pl*; **c'est ~ de faire/que** it's a shame *ou* pity to do/that; **~s corporels** physical injury.

dommages-intérêts [dɔmaʒ(əz)ɛ̃teʀɛ] *nmpl* damages.

dompter [dɔ̃te] *vt* to tame.

dompteur, euse [dɔ̃tœʀ, -øz] *nm/f* trainer; (*de lion*) liontamer.

DOM-TOM [dɔmtɔm] *sigle m ou mpl* = *Département(s) d'outre-mer/Territoire(s) d'outre-mer.*

don [dɔ̃] *nm* (*cadeau*) gift; (*charité*) donation; (*aptitude*) gift, talent; **avoir des ~s pour** to have a gift *ou* talent for; **faire ~ de** to make a gift of; **~ en argent** cash donation.

donateur, trice [dɔnatœʀ, -tʀis] *nm/f* donor.

donation [dɔnɑsjɔ̃] *nf* donation.

donc [dɔ̃k] *conj* therefore, so; (*après une digression*) so, then; (*intensif*): **voilà ~ la solution** so there's the solution; **je disais ~ que ...** as I was saying, ...; **venez ~ dîner à la maison** do come for dinner; **allons ~!** come now!; **faites ~** go ahead.

donjon [dɔ̃ʒɔ̃] *nm* keep.

don Juan [dɔ̃ʒɥɑ̃] *nm* Don Juan.

donnant, e [dɔnɑ̃, -ɑ̃t] *adj*: **~, ~** fair's fair.

donne [dɔn] *nf* (*CARTES*): **il y a mauvaise** *ou* **fausse ~** there's been a misdeal.

donné, e [dɔne] *adj* (*convenu*) given; (*pas cher*) very cheap ♦ *nf* (*MATH, INFORM*) datum (*pl* data); **c'est ~** it's a gift; **étant ~ ...** given ....

donner [dɔne] *vt* to give; (*vieux habits etc*) to give away; (*spectacle*) to put on; (*film*) to show; **~ qch à qn** to give sb sth, give sth to sb; **~ sur** (*suj: fenêtre, chambre*) to look (out) onto; **~ dans** (*piège etc*) to fall into; **faire ~ l'infanterie** (*MIL*) to send in the infantry; **~ l'heure à qn** to tell sb the time; **~ le ton** (*fig*) to set the tone; **~ à penser/entendre que ...** to make one think/give one to understand that ...; **se ~ à fond (à son travail)** to give one's all (to one's work); **se ~ du mal** *ou* **de la peine (pour faire qch)** to go to a lot of trouble (to do sth); **s'en ~ à cœur joie** (*fam*) to have a great time (of it).

donneur, euse [dɔnœʀ, -øz] *nm/f* (*MÉD*) donor; (*CARTES*) dealer; **~ de sang** blood donor.

MOT-CLÉ

dont [dɔ̃] *pron relatif* **1** (*appartenance: objets*) whose, of which; (*: êtres animés*) whose; **la maison ~ le toit est rouge** the house whose roof is red; **l'homme ~ je connais la sœur** the man whose sister I know

2 (*parmi lesquel(le)s*): **2 livres, ~ l'un est ...** 2 books, one of which is ...; **il y avait plusieurs personnes, ~ Gabrielle** there were several people, among them Gabrielle; **10 blessés, ~ 2 grièvement** 10 injured, 2 of them seriously

3 (*complément d'adjectif, de verbe*): **le fils ~ il est si fier** the son he's so proud of; **ce ~ je parle** what I'm talking about; **la façon ~ il l'a fait** the way (in which) he did it.

donzelle [dɔ̃zɛl] *nf* (*péj*) young madam.

dopage [dɔpaʒ] *nm* doping.

dopant [dɔpɑ̃] *nm* dope.

doper [dɔpe] *vt* to dope; **se ~** to take dope.

doping [dɔpiŋ] *nm* doping; (*excitant*) dope.

dorade [dɔʀad] *nf* = **daurade**.

doré, e [dɔʀe] *adj* golden; (*avec dorure*) gilt,

gilded.
dorénavant [dɔrenavɑ̃] *adv* from now on, henceforth.
dorer [dɔre] *vt* (*cadre*) to gild; **(faire)** ~ (*CULIN*) to brown; (*: gâteau*) to glaze; **se ~ au soleil** to sunbathe; ~ **la pilule à qn** to sugar the pill for sb.
dorloter [dɔrlɔte] *vt* to pamper, cosset (*BRIT*); **se faire** ~ to be pampered *ou* cosseted.
dormant, e [dɔrmɑ̃, -ɑ̃t] *adj*: **eau ~e** still water.
dorme [dɔrm(ə)] *etc vb voir* **dormir**.
dormeur, euse [dɔrmœr, -øz] *nm/f* sleeper.
dormir [dɔrmir] *vi* to sleep; (*être endormi*) to be asleep; ~ **à poings fermés** to sleep very soundly.
dorsal, e, aux [dɔrsal, -o] *adj* dorsal; *voir* **rouleau**.
dortoir [dɔrtwar] *nm* dormitory.
dorure [dɔryr] *nf* gilding.
doryphore [dɔrifɔr] *nm* Colorado beetle.
dos [do] *nm* back; (*de livre*) spine; **"voir au ~"** "see over"; **robe décolletée dans le** ~ low-backed dress; **de** ~ from the back, from behind; ~ **à** ~ back to back; **sur le** ~ on one's back; **à ~ de chameau** riding on a camel; **avoir bon** ~ to be a good excuse; **se mettre qn à** ~ to turn sb against one.
dosage [dozaʒ] *nm* mixture.
dos-d'âne [dodɑn] *nm* humpback; **pont en** ~ humpbacked bridge.
dose [doz] *nf* (*MÉD*) dose; **forcer la** ~ (*fig*) to overstep the mark.
doser [doze] *vt* to measure out; (*mélanger*) to mix in the correct proportions; (*fig*) to expend in the right amounts *ou* proportions; to strike a balance between.
doseur [dozœr] *nm* measure; **bouchon** ~ measuring cap.
dossard [dosar] *nm* number (*worn by competitor*).
dossier [dosje] *nm* (*renseignements, fichier*) file; (*enveloppe*) folder, file; (*de chaise*) back; (*PRESSE*) feature; **le ~ social/monétaire** (*fig*) the social/financial question; ~ **suspendu** suspension file.
dot [dɔt] *nf* dowry.
dotation [dɔtɑsjɔ̃] *nf* grant; endowment.
doté, e [dɔte] *adj*: ~ **de** equipped with.
doter [dɔte] *vt*: ~ **qn/qch de** to equip sb/sth with.
douairière [dwɛrjɛr] *nf* dowager.
douane [dwan] *nf* (*poste, bureau*) customs *pl*; (*taxes*) (customs) duty; **passer la** ~ to go through customs; **en** ~ (*marchandises, entrepôt*) bonded.
douanier, ière [dwanje, -jɛr] *adj* customs *cpd* ♦ *nm* customs officer.
doublage [dublaʒ] *nm* (*CINÉ*) dubbing.
double [dubl(ə)] *adj, adv* double ♦ *nm* (*2 fois plus*): **le ~ (de)** twice as much (*ou* many) (as), double the amount (*ou* number) (of); (*autre exemplaire*) duplicate, copy; (*sosie*) double; (*TENNIS*) doubles *sg*; **voir** ~ to see double; **en ~ (exemplaire)** in duplicate; **faire ~ emploi** to be redundant; **à ~ sens** with a double meaning; **à ~ tranchant** two-edged; ~ **carburateur** twin carburettor; **à ~s commandes** dual-control; ~ **messieurs/mixte** men's/mixed doubles *sg*; ~ **toit** (*de tente*) fly sheet; ~ **vue** second sight.
doublé, e [duble] *adj* (*vêtement*): ~ **(de)** lined (with).
double-cliquer [dubl(ə)klike] *vi* (*INFORM*) to double-click.
doublement [dubləmɑ̃] *nm* doubling; twofold increase ♦ *adv* doubly; (*pour deux raisons*) in two ways, on two counts.
doubler [duble] *vt* (*multiplier par 2*) to double; (*vêtement*) to line; (*dépasser*) to overtake, pass; (*film*) to dub; (*acteur*) to stand in for ♦ *vi* to double, increase twofold; **se ~ de** to be coupled with; ~ **(la classe)** (*SCOL*) to repeat a year; ~ **un cap** (*NAVIG*) to round a cape; (*fig*) to get over a hurdle.
doublure [dublyr] *nf* lining; (*CINÉ*) stand-in.
douce [dus] *adj f voir* **doux**.
douceâtre [dusɑtr(ə)] *adj* sickly sweet.
doucement [dusmɑ̃] *adv* gently; (*à voix basse*) softly; (*lentement*) slowly.
doucereux, euse [dusrø, -øz] *adj* (*péj*) sugary.
douceur [dusœr] *nf* softness; sweetness; mildness; gentleness; ~**s** *nfpl* (*friandises*) sweets (*BRIT*), candy *sg* (*US*); **en** ~ gently.
douche [duʃ] *nf* shower; ~**s** *nfpl* shower room *sg*; **prendre une** ~ to have *ou* take a shower; ~ **écossaise** (*fig*), ~ **froide** (*fig*) let-down.
doucher [duʃe] *vt*: ~ **qn** to give sb a shower; (*mouiller*) to drench sb; (*fig*) to give sb a telling-off; **se** ~ to have *ou* take a shower.
doudoune [dudun] *nf* padded jacket; (*fam*) boob.
doué, e [dwe] *adj* gifted, talented; ~ **de** endowed with; **être ~ pour** to have a gift for.
douille [duj] *nf* (*ÉLEC*) socket; (*de projectile*) case.
douillet, te [dujɛ, -ɛt] *adj* cosy; (*péj*) soft.
douleur [dulœr] *nf* pain; (*chagrin*) grief, distress; **ressentir des ~s** to feel pain; **il a eu la ~ de perdre son père** he suffered the grief of losing his father.
douloureux, euse [dulurø, -øz] *adj* painful.
doute [dut] *nm* doubt; **sans** ~ *adv* no doubt; (*probablement*) probably; **sans nul** *ou* **aucun** ~ without (a) doubt; **hors de** ~ beyond doubt; **nul ~ que** there's no doubt that; **mettre en** ~ to call into question; **mettre en ~ que** to question whether.
douter [dute] *vt* to doubt; ~ **de** *vt* (*allié*) to doubt, have (one's) doubts about; (*résultat*) to be doubtful of; ~ **que** to doubt whether *ou* if; **j'en doute** I have my doubts; **se ~ de qch/que** to suspect sth/that; **je m'en doutais** I suspected as much; **il ne se doutait de rien**

he didn't suspect a thing.

douteux, euse [dutø, -øz] *adj* (*incertain*) doubtful; (*discutable*) dubious, questionable; (*péj*) dubious-looking.

douve [duv] *nf* (*de château*) moat; (*de tonneau*) stave.

Douvres [duvʀ(ə)] *n* Dover.

doux, douce [du, dus] *adj* (*lisse, moelleux, pas vif: couleur, non calcaire: eau*) soft; (*sucré, agréable*) sweet; (*peu fort: moutarde etc, clément: climat*) mild; (*pas brusque*) gentle; **en douce** (*partir etc*) on the quiet.

douzaine [duzɛn] *nf* (*12*) dozen; (*environ 12*): **une ~ (de)** a dozen or so, twelve or so.

douze [duz] *num* twelve; **les D~** (*membres de la CEE*) the Twelve.

douzième [duzjɛm] *num* twelfth.

doyen, ne [dwajɛ̃, -ɛn] *nm/f* (*en âge, ancienneté*) most senior member; (*de faculté*) dean.

DPLG *sigle* (= *diplômé par le gouvernement*) *extra certificate for architects, engineers etc.*

Dr *abr* (= *docteur*) Dr.

dr. *abr* (= *droit(e)*) R, r.

draconien, ne [dʀakɔnjɛ̃, -ɛn] *adj* draconian, stringent.

dragage [dʀagaʒ] *nm* dredging.

dragée [dʀaʒe] *nf* sugared almond; (*MÉD*) (sugar-coated) pill.

dragéifié, e [dʀaʒeifje] *adj* (*MÉD*) sugar-coated.

dragon [dʀagɔ̃] *nm* dragon.

drague [dʀag] *nf* (*filet*) dragnet; (*bateau*) dredger.

draguer [dʀage] *vt* (*rivière: pour nettoyer*) to dredge; (*: pour trouver qch*) to drag; (*fam*) to try and pick up, chat up (*BRIT*) ♦ *vi* (*fam*) to try and pick sb up, chat sb up (*BRIT*).

dragueur [dʀagœʀ] *nm* (*aussi*: **~ de mines**) minesweeper; (*fam*): **quel ~!** he's a great one for picking up girls!

drain [dʀɛ̃] *nm* (*MÉD*) drain.

drainage [dʀɛnaʒ] *nm* drainage.

drainer [dʀene] *vt* to drain; (*fig: visiteurs, région*) to drain off.

dramatique [dʀamatik] *adj* dramatic; (*tragique*) tragic ♦ *nf* (*TV*) (television) drama.

dramatisation [dʀamatizɑsjɔ̃] *nf* dramatization.

dramatiser [dʀamatize] *vt* to dramatize.

dramaturge [dʀamatyʀʒ(ə)] *nm* dramatist, playwright.

drame [dʀam] *nm* (*THÉÂT*) drama; (*catastrophe*) drama, tragedy; **~ familial** family drama.

drap [dʀa] *nm* (*de lit*) sheet; (*tissu*) woollen fabric; **~ de plage** beach towel.

drapé [dʀape] *nm* (*d'un vêtement*) hang.

drapeau, x [dʀapo] *nm* flag; **sous les ~x** with the colours (*BRIT*) *ou* colors (*US*), in the army.

draper [dʀape] *vt* to drape; (*robe, jupe*) to arrange.

draperies [dʀapʀi] *nfpl* hangings.

drap-housse, *pl* **draps-housses** [dʀaus] *nm* fitted sheet.

drapier [dʀapje] *nm* (woollen) cloth manufacturer; (*marchand*) clothier.

drastique [dʀastik] *adj* drastic.

dressage [dʀɛsaʒ] *nm* training.

dresser [dʀese] *vt* (*mettre vertical, monter: tente*) to put up, erect; (*fig: liste, bilan, contrat*) to draw up; (*animal*) to train; **se ~** *vi* (*falaise, obstacle*) to stand; (*avec grandeur, menace*) to tower (up); (*personne*) to draw o.s. up; **~ l'oreille** to prick up one's ears; **~ la table** to set *ou* lay the table; **~ qn contre qn d'autre** to set sb against sb else; **~ un procès-verbal** *ou* **une contravention à qn** to book sb.

dresseur, euse [dʀɛsœʀ, -øz] *nm/f* trainer.

dressoir [dʀɛswaʀ] *nm* dresser.

dribbler [dʀible] *vt, vi* (*SPORT*) to dribble.

drille [dʀij] *nm*: **joyeux ~** cheerful sort.

drogue [dʀɔg] *nf* drug; **la ~** drugs *pl*; **~ dure/douce** hard/soft drugs *pl*.

drogué, e [dʀɔge] *nm/f* drug addict.

droguer [dʀɔge] *vt* (*victime*) to drug; (*malade*) to give drugs to; **se ~** (*aux stupéfiants*) to take drugs; (*péj: de médicaments*) to dose o.s. up.

droguerie [dʀɔgʀi] *nf* ≈ hardware shop (*BRIT*) *ou* store (*US*).

droguiste [dʀɔgist(ə)] *nm* ≈ keeper (*ou* owner) of a hardware shop *ou* store.

droit, e [dʀwa, dʀwat] *adj* (*non courbe*) straight; (*vertical*) upright, straight; (*fig: loyal, franc*) upright, straight(forward); (*opposé à gauche*) right, right-hand ♦ *adv* straight ♦ *nm* (*prérogative, BOXE*) right; (*taxe*) duty, tax; (*: d'inscription*) fee; (*lois, branche*): **le ~** law ♦ *nf* (*POL*) right (wing); (*ligne*) straight line; **~ au but** *ou* **au fait/cœur** straight to the point/heart; **avoir le ~ de** to be allowed to; **avoir ~ à** to be entitled to; **être en ~ de** to have a *ou* the right to; **faire ~ à** to grant, accede to; **être dans son ~** to be within one's rights; **à bon ~** (*justement*) with good reason; **de quel ~?** by what right?; **à qui de ~** to whom it may concern; **à ~e** on the right; (*direction*) (to the) right; **à ~e de** to the right of; **de ~e** (*POL*) right-wing; **~ d'auteur** copyright; **avoir ~ de cité (dans)** (*fig*) to belong (to); **~ coutumier** common law; **~ de regard** right of access *ou* inspection; **~ de réponse** right to reply; **~ de visite** (right of) access; **~ de vote** (right to) vote; **~s d'auteur** royalties; **~s de douane** customs duties; **~s de l'homme** human rights; **~s d'inscription** enrolment *ou* registration fees.

droitement [dʀwatmɑ̃] *adv* (*agir*) uprightly.

droitier, ière [dʀwatje, -jɛʀ] *nm/f* right-handed person.

droiture [dʀwatyʀ] *nf* uprightness, straightness.

drôle [dRol] *adj* (*amusant*) funny, amusing; (*bizarre*) funny, peculiar; **un ~ de ...** (*bizarre*) a strange *ou* funny ...; (*intensif*) an incredible ..., a terrific ....
drôlement [dRolmɑ̃] *adv* funnily; peculiarly; (*très*) terribly, awfully; **il fait ~ froid** it's awfully cold.
drôlerie [dRolRi] *nf* funniness; funny thing.
dromadaire [dRɔmadɛR] *nm* dromedary.
dru, e [dRy] *adj* (*cheveux*) thick, bushy; (*pluie*) heavy ♦ *adv* (*pousser*) thickly; (*tomber*) heavily.
drugstore [dRœgstɔR] *nm* drugstore.
druide [dRɥid] *nm* Druid.
ds *abr* = **dans.**
DST *sigle f* (= *Direction de la surveillance du territoire*) *internal security service*, ≈ MI5 (*BRIT*).
DT *sigle m* (= *diphtérie tétanos*) *vaccine.*
DTCP *sigle m* (= *diphtérie tétanos coqueluche polio*) *vaccine.*
DTP *sigle m* (= *diphtérie tétanos polio*) *vaccine.*
DTTAB *sigle m* (= *diphtérie tétanos typhoïde A et B*) *vaccine.*
du [dy] *prép + dét, dét voir* **de.**
dû, due [dy] *pp de* **devoir** ♦ *adj* (*somme*) owing, owed; (*: venant à échéance*) due; (*causé par*): **~ à** due to ♦ *nm* due; (*somme*) dues *pl*.
dualisme [dɥalism(ə)] *nm* dualism.
Dubaï, Dubay [dybaj] *n* Dubai.
dubitatif, ive [dybitatif, -iv] *adj* doubtful, dubious.
Dublin [dyblɛ̃] *n* Dublin.
duc [dyk] *nm* duke.
duché [dyʃe] *nm* dukedom, duchy.
duchesse [dyʃɛs] *nf* duchess.
DUEL [dyɛl] *sigle m* = *Diplôme universitaire d'études littéraires.*
duel [dɥɛl] *nm* duel.
DUES [dyɛs] *sigle m* = *Diplôme universitaire d'études scientifiques.*
duettiste [dɥetist(ə)] *nm/f* duettist.
duffel-coat [dœfœlkot] *nm* duffelcoat.
dûment [dymɑ̃] *adv* duly.
dumping [dœmpiŋ] *nm* dumping.
dune [dyn] *nf* dune.
Dunkerque [dœ̃kɛRk] *n* Dunkirk.
duo [dɥo] *nm* (*MUS*) duet; (*fig: couple*) duo, pair.
dupe [dyp] *nf* dupe ♦ *adj*: **(ne pas) être ~ de** (not) to be taken in by.
duper [dype] *vt* to dupe, deceive.
duperie [dypRi] *nf* deception, dupery.
duplex [dyplɛks] *nm* (*appartement*) split-level apartment, duplex; (*TV*): **émission en ~** link-up.
duplicata [dyplikata] *nm* duplicate.
duplicateur [dyplikatœR] *nm* duplicator; **~ à alcool** spirit duplicator.
duplicité [dyplisite] *nf* duplicity.
duquel [dykɛl] *prép + pron voir* **lequel.**
dur, e [dyR] *adj* (*pierre, siège, travail, problème*) hard; (*lumière, voix, climat*) harsh; (*sévère*) hard, harsh; (*cruel*) hard(-hearted); (*porte, col*) stiff; (*viande*) tough ♦ *adv* hard ♦ *nf*: **à la ~e** rough; **mener la vie ~e à qn** to give sb a hard time; **~ d'oreille** hard of hearing.
durabilité [dyRabilite] *nf* durability.
durable [dyRabl(ə)] *adj* lasting.
durablement [dyRabləmɑ̃] *adv* for the long term.
durant [dyRɑ̃] *prép* (*au cours de*) during; (*pendant*) for; **~ des mois, des mois ~** for months.
durcir [dyRsiR] *vt, vi*, **se ~** *vi* to harden.
durcissement [dyRsismɑ̃] *nm* hardening.
durée [dyRe] *nf* length; (*d'une pile etc*) life; (*déroulement: des opérations etc*) duration; **pour une ~ illimitée** for an unlimited length of time; **de courte ~** (*séjour, répit*) brief, short-term; **de longue ~** (*effet*) long-term; **pile de longue ~** long-life battery.
durement [dyRmɑ̃] *adv* harshly.
durent [dyR] *vb voir* **devoir.**
durer [dyRe] *vi* to last.
dureté [dyRte] *nf* (*voir dur*) hardness; harshness; stiffness; toughness.
durillon [dyRijɔ̃] *nm* callus.
durit [dyRit] *nf* ® (car radiator) hose.
DUT *sigle m* = *Diplôme universitaire de technologie.*
dut [dy] *etc vb voir* **devoir.**
duvet [dyvɛ] *nm* down; **(sac de couchage en) ~** down-filled sleeping bag.
duveteux, euse [dyvtø, -øz] *adj* downy.
DVD *sigle m* (= *digital versatile disc*) DVD.
dynamique [dinamik] *adj* dynamic.
dynamiser [dinamize] *vt* to pep up, enliven; (*équipe, service*) to inject some dynamism into.
dynamisme [dinamism(ə)] *nm* dynamism.
dynamite [dinamit] *nf* dynamite.
dynamiter [dinamite] *vt* to (blow up with) dynamite.
dynamo [dinamo] *nf* dynamo.
dynastie [dinasti] *nf* dynasty.
dysenterie [disɑ̃tRi] *nf* dysentery.
dyslexie [dislɛksi] *nf* dyslexia, word blindness.
dyslexique [dislɛksik] *adj* dyslexic.
dyspepsie [dispɛpsi] *nf* dyspepsia.

E e

E, e [ə] *nm inv* E, e ♦ *abr* (= *Est*) E; **E comme Eugène** E for Edward (*BRIT*) *ou* Easy (*US*).
EAO *sigle m* (= *enseignement assisté par ordinateur*) CAL (= *computer-aided learning*).
EAU *sigle mpl* (= *Émirats arabes unis*) UAE (= *United Arab Emirates*).
eau, x [o] *nf* water ♦ *nfpl* waters; **prendre l'~** (*chaussure etc*) to leak, let in water; **prendre les ~x** to take the waters; **faire ~** to leak; **tomber à l'~** (*fig*) to fall through; **à l'~ de rose** slushy, sentimental; **~ bénite** holy water; **~ de Cologne** eau de Cologne; **~ courante** running water; **~ distillée** distilled water; **~ douce** fresh water; **~ de Javel** bleach; **~ lourde** heavy water; **~ minérale** mineral water; **~ oxygénée** hydrogen peroxide; **~ plate** still water; **~ de pluie** rainwater; **~ salée** salt water; **~ de toilette** toilet water; **~x ménagères** dirty water (*from washing up etc*); **~x territoriales** territorial waters; **~x usées** liquid waste.
eau-de-vie, *pl* **eaux-de-vie** [odvi] *nf* brandy.
eau-forte, *pl* **eaux-fortes** [ofɔʀt(ə)] *nf* etching.
ébahi, e [ebai] *adj* dumbfounded, flabbergasted.
ébahir [ebaiʀ] *vt* to astonish, astound.
ébats [eba] *vb voir* **ébattre** ♦ *nmpl* frolics, gambols.
ébattre [ebatʀ(ə)]: **s'~** *vi* to frolic.
ébauche [eboʃ] *nf* (rough) outline, sketch.
ébaucher [eboʃe] *vt* to sketch out, outline; (*fig*): **~ un sourire/geste** to give a hint of a smile/make a slight gesture; **s'~** *vi* to take shape.
ébène [ebɛn] *nf* ebony.
ébéniste [ebenist(ə)] *nm* cabinetmaker.
ébénisterie [ebenistʀi] *nf* cabinetmaking; (*bâti*) cabinetwork.
éberlué, e [ebɛʀlɥe] *adj* astounded, flabbergasted.
éblouir [ebluiʀ] *vt* to dazzle.
éblouissant, e [ebluisɑ̃, -ɑ̃t] *adj* dazzling.
éblouissement [ebluismɑ̃] *nm* dazzle; (*faiblesse*) dizzy turn.
ébonite [ebɔnit] *nf* vulcanite.
éborgner [ebɔʀɲe] *vt*: **~ qn** to blind sb in one eye.
éboueur [ebwœʀ] *nm* dustman (*BRIT*), garbageman (*US*).
ébouillanter [ebujɑ̃te] *vt* to scald; (*CULIN*) to blanch; **s'~** to scald o.s.
éboulement [ebulmɑ̃] *nm* falling rocks *pl*, rock fall; (*amas*) heap of boulders *etc*.
ébouler [ebule]: **s'~** *vi* to crumble, collapse.
éboulis [ebuli] *nmpl* fallen rocks.
ébouriffé, e [ebuʀife] *adj* tousled, ruffled.
ébouriffer [ebuʀife] *vt* to tousle, ruffle.
ébranlement [ebʀɑ̃lmɑ̃] *nm* shaking.
ébranler [ebʀɑ̃le] *vt* to shake; (*rendre instable: mur, santé*) to weaken; **s'~** *vi* (*partir*) to move off.
ébrécher [ebʀeʃe] *vt* to chip.
ébriété [ebʀijete] *nf*: **en état d'~** in a state of intoxication.
ébrouer [ebʀue]: **s'~** *vi* (*souffler*) to snort; (*s'agiter*) to shake o.s.
ébruiter [ebʀɥite] *vt*, **s'~** *vi* to spread.
ébullition [ebylisjɔ̃] *nf* boiling point; **en ~** boiling; (*fig*) in an uproar.
écaille [ekɑj] *nf* (*de poisson*) scale; (*de coquillage*) shell; (*matière*) tortoiseshell; (*de roc etc*) flake.
écaillé, e [ekɑje] *adj* (*peinture*) flaking.
écailler [ekɑje] *vt* (*poisson*) to scale; (*huître*) to open; **s'~** *vi* to flake *ou* peel (off).
écarlate [ekaʀlat] *adj* scarlet.
écarquiller [ekaʀkije] *vt*: **~ les yeux** to stare wide-eyed.
écart [ekaʀ] *nm* gap; (*embardée*) swerve; (*saut*) sideways leap; (*fig*) departure, deviation; **à l'~** *adv* out of the way; **à l'~ de** *prép* away from; (*fig*) out of; **faire le grand ~** (*DANSE, GYMNASTIQUE*) to do the splits; **~ de conduite** misdemeanour.
écarté, e [ekaʀte] *adj* (*lieu*) out-of-the-way, remote; (*ouvert*): **les jambes ~es** legs apart; **les bras ~s** arms outstretched.
écarteler [ekaʀtəle] *vt* to quarter; (*fig*) to tear.
écartement [ekaʀtəmɑ̃] *nm* space, gap; (*RAIL*) gauge.
écarter [ekaʀte] *vt* (*séparer*) to move apart, separate; (*éloigner*) to push back, move away; (*ouvrir: bras, jambes*) to spread, open; (*: rideau*) to draw (back); (*éliminer: candidat, possibilité*) to dismiss; (*CARTES*) to discard; **s'~** *vi* to part; (*personne*) to move away; **s'~ de** to wander from.
ecchymose [ekimoz] *nf* bruise.
ecclésiastique [eklezjastik] *adj* ecclesiastical ♦ *nm* ecclesiastic.
écervelé, e [esɛʀvəle] *adj* scatterbrained, featherbrained.
ECG *sigle m* (= *électrocardiogramme*) ECG.
échafaud [eʃafo] *nm* scaffold.
échafaudage [eʃafodaʒ] *nm* scaffolding; (*fig*) heap, pile.
échafauder [eʃafode] *vt* (*plan*) to construct.
échalas [eʃala] *nm* stake, pole; (*personne*) beanpole.
échalote [eʃalɔt] *nf* shallot.
échancré, e [eʃɑ̃kʀe] *adj* (*robe, corsage*) low-necked; (*côte*) indented.
échancrure [eʃɑ̃kʀyʀ] *nf* (*de robe*) scoop neck-

line; (*de côte, arête rocheuse*) indentation.
échange [eʃɑ̃ʒ] *nm* exchange; **en ~** in exchange; **en ~ de** in exchange *ou* return for; **libre ~** free trade; **~ de lettres/politesses/vues** exchange of letters/civilities/views; **~s commerciaux** trade; **~s culturels** cultural exchanges.
échangeable [eʃɑ̃ʒabl(ə)] *adj* exchangeable.
échanger [eʃɑ̃ʒe] *vt*: **~ qch (contre)** to exchange sth (for).
échangeur [eʃɑ̃ʒœʀ] *nm* (*AUTO*) interchange.
échantillon [eʃɑ̃tijɔ̃] *nm* sample.
échantillonnage [eʃɑ̃tijɔnaʒ] *nm* selection of samples.
échappatoire [eʃapatwaʀ] *nf* way out.
échappée [eʃape] *nf* (*vue*) vista; (*CYCLISME*) breakaway.
échappement [eʃapmɑ̃] *nm* (*AUTO*) exhaust; **~ libre** cutout.
échapper [eʃape]: **~ à** *vt* (*gardien*) to escape (from); (*punition, péril*) to escape; **~ à qn** (*détail, sens*) to escape sb; (*objet qu'on tient: aussi*: **~ des mains de qn**) to slip out of sb's hands; **laisser ~** to let fall; (*cri etc*) to let out; **s'~** *vi* to escape; **l'~ belle** to have a narrow escape.
écharde [eʃaʀd(ə)] *nf* splinter (of wood).
écharpe [eʃaʀp(ə)] *nf* scarf (*pl* scarves); (*de maire*) sash; (*MÉD*) sling; **prendre en ~** (*dans une collision*) to hit sideways on.
écharper [eʃaʀpe] *vt* to tear to pieces.
échasse [eʃɑs] *nf* stilt.
échassier [eʃɑsje] *nm* wader.
échauder [eʃode] *vt*: **se faire ~** (*fig*) to get one's fingers burnt.
échauffement [eʃofmɑ̃] *nm* overheating; (*SPORT*) warm-up.
échauffer [eʃofe] *vt* (*métal, moteur*) to overheat; (*fig: exciter*) to fire, excite; **s'~** *vi* (*SPORT*) to warm up; (*discussion*) to become heated.
échauffourée [eʃofuʀe] *nf* clash, brawl; (*MIL*) skirmish.
échéance [eʃeɑ̃s] *nf* (*d'un paiement: date*) settlement date; (*: somme due*) financial commitment(s); (*fig*) deadline; **à brève/longue ~** *adj* short-/long-term ♦ *adv* in the short/long term.
échéancier [eʃeɑ̃sje] *nm* schedule.
échéant [eʃeɑ̃]: **le cas ~** *adv* if the case arises.
échec [eʃɛk] *nm* failure; (*ÉCHECS*): **~ et mat/au roi** checkmate/check; **~s** *nmpl* (*jeu*) chess *sg*; **mettre en ~** to put in check; **tenir en ~** to hold in check; **faire ~ à** to foil, thwart.
échelle [eʃɛl] *nf* ladder; (*fig, d'une carte*) scale; **à l'~ de** on the scale of; **sur une grande/petite ~** on a large/small scale; **faire la courte ~ à qn** to give sb a leg up; **~ de corde** rope ladder.
échelon [eʃlɔ̃] *nm* (*d'échelle*) rung; (*ADMIN*) grade.
échelonner [eʃlɔne] *vt* to space out, spread out; **(versement) échelonné** (payment) by instalments.
écheveau, x [ɛʃvo] *nm* skein, hank.
échevelé, e [eʃəvle] *adj* tousled, dishevelled; (*fig*) wild, frenzied.
échine [eʃin] *nf* backbone, spine.
échiner [eʃine]: **s'~** *vi* (*se fatiguer*) to work o.s. to the bone.
échiquier [eʃikje] *nm* chessboard.
écho [eko] *nm* echo; **~s** *nmpl* (*potins*) gossip *sg*, rumours; (*PRESSE: rubrique*) "news in brief"; **rester sans ~** (*suggestion etc*) to come to nothing; **se faire l'~ de** to repeat, spread about.
échographie [ekɔgʀafi] *nf* ultrasound (scan).
échoir [eʃwaʀ] *vi* (*dette*) to fall due; (*délais*) to expire; **~ à** *vt* to fall to.
échoppe [eʃɔp] *nf* stall, booth.
échouer [eʃwe] *vi* to fail; (*débris etc : sur la plage*) to be washed up; (*aboutir: personne dans un café etc*) to arrive ♦ *vt* (*bateau*) to ground; **s'~** *vi* to run aground.
échu, e [eʃy] *pp de* **échoir** ♦ *adj* due, mature.
échut [eʃy] *etc vb voir* **échoir**.
éclabousser [eklabuse] *vt* to splash; (*fig*) to tarnish.
éclaboussure [eklabusyʀ] *nf* splash; (*fig*) stain.
éclair [eklɛʀ] *nm* (*d'orage*) flash of lightning, lightning *no pl*; (*PHOTO: de flash*) flash; (*fig*) flash, spark; (*gâteau*) éclair.
éclairage [eklɛʀaʒ] *nm* lighting.
éclairagiste [eklɛʀaʒist(ə)] *nm/f* lighting engineer.
éclaircie [eklɛʀsi] *nf* bright *ou* sunny interval.
éclaircir [eklɛʀsiʀ] *vt* to lighten; (*fig*) to clear up, clarify; (*CULIN*) to thin (down); **s'~** *vi* (*ciel*) to brighten up, clear; (*cheveux*) to go thin; (*situation etc*) to become clearer; **s'~ la voix** to clear one's throat.
éclaircissement [eklɛʀsismɑ̃] *nm* clearing up, clarification.
éclairer [ekleʀe] *vt* (*lieu*) to light (up); (*personne: avec une lampe de poche etc*) to light the way for; (*fig: instruire*) to enlighten; (*: rendre comprehensible*) to shed light on ♦ *vi*: **~ mal/bien** to give a poor/good light; **s'~** *vi* (*phare, rue*) to light up; (*situation etc*) to become clearer; **s'~ à la bougie/l'électricité** to use candlelight/have electric lighting.
éclaireur, euse [eklɛʀœʀ, -øz] *nm/f* (*scout*) (boy) scout/(girl) guide ♦ *nm* (*MIL*) scout; **partir en ~** to go off to reconnoitre.
éclat [ekla] *nm* (*de bombe, de verre*) fragment; (*du soleil, d'une couleur etc*) brightness, brilliance; (*d'une cérémonie*) splendour; (*scandale*): **faire un ~** to cause a commotion; **action d'~** outstanding action; **voler en ~s** to shatter; **des ~s de verre** broken glass; flying glass; **~ de rire** burst *ou* roar of laughter; **~ de voix** shout.
éclatant, e [eklatɑ̃, -ɑ̃t] *adj* brilliant, bright;

(*succès*) resounding; (*revanche*) devastating.

éclater [eklate] *vi* (*pneu*) to burst; (*bombe*) to explode; (*guerre, épidémie*) to break out; (*groupe, parti*) to break up; ~ **de rire/en sanglots** to burst out laughing/sobbing.

éclectique [eklɛktik] *adj* eclectic.

éclipse [eklips(ə)] *nf* eclipse.

éclipser [eklipse] *vt* to eclipse; **s'~** *vi* to slip away.

éclopé, e [eklɔpe] *adj* lame.

éclore [eklɔʀ] *vi* (*œuf*) to hatch; (*fleur*) to open (out).

éclosion [eklozjɔ̃] *nf* blossoming.

écluse [eklyz] *nf* lock.

éclusier [eklyzje] *nm* lock keeper.

éco- [eko] *préfixe* eco-.

écœurant, e [ekœʀɑ̃, -ɑ̃t] *adj* sickening; (*gâteau etc*) sickly.

écœurement [ekœʀmɑ̃] *nm* disgust.

écœurer [ekœʀe] *vt*: ~ **qn** to make sb feel sick; (*fig: démoraliser*) to disgust sb.

école [ekɔl] *nf* school; **aller à l'~** to go to school; **faire ~** to collect a following; **les grandes ~s** *prestige university-level colleges with competitive entrance examinations*; ~ **maternelle** nursery school; ~ **primaire** primary (*BRIT*) *ou* grade (*US*) school; ~ **secondaire** secondary (*BRIT*) *ou* high (*US*) school; ~ **privée/publique/élementaire** private/state/elementary school; ~ **de dessin** art school; ~ **hôtelière** catering college; ~ **normale (d'instituteurs) (ENI)** *primary school teachers' training college*; ~ **normale supérieure (ENS)** *grande école for training secondary school teachers*; ~ **de secrétariat** secretarial college; *see boxed note*.

> **ÉCOLE MATERNELLE**
>
> *Nursery school (kindergarten)* **(école maternelle)** *is publicly funded in France and, though not compulsory, is attended by most children between the ages of two and six. Statutory education begins with primary school (grade school)* **(école primaire)** *at the age of six and lasts until 10 or 11.*

écolier, ière [ekɔlje, -jɛʀ] *nm/f* schoolboy/girl.

écolo [ekɔlo] *nm/f* (*fam*) ecologist ♦ *adj* ecological.

écologie [ekɔlɔʒi] *nf* ecology; (*sujet scolaire*) environmental studies *pl*.

écologique [ekɔlɔʒik] *adj* ecological; environmental.

écologiste [ekɔlɔʒist(ə)] *nm/f* ecologist; environmentalist.

éconduire [ekɔ̃dɥiʀ] *vt* to dismiss.

économat [ekɔnɔma] *nm* (*fonction*) bursarship (*BRIT*), treasurership (*US*); (*bureau*) bursar's office (*BRIT*), treasury (*US*).

économe [ekɔnɔm] *adj* thrifty ♦ *nm/f* (*de lycée etc*) bursar (*BRIT*), treasurer (*US*).

économie [ekɔnɔmi] *nf* (*vertu*) economy, thrift; (*gain: d'argent, de temps etc*) saving; (*science*) economics *sg*; (*situation économique*) economy; ~**s** *nfpl* (*pécule*) savings; **une ~ de temps/d'argent** a saving in time/of money; ~ **dirigée** planned economy; ~ **de marché** market economy.

économique [ekɔnɔmik] *adj* (*avantageux*) economical; (*ÉCON*) economic.

économiquement [ekɔnɔmikmɑ̃] *adv* economically; **les ~ faibles** (*ADMIN*) the low-paid, people on low incomes.

économiser [ekɔnɔmize] *vt, vi* to save.

économiseur [ekɔnɔmizœʀ] *nm* (*INFORM*): ~ **d'écran** screen saver.

économiste [ekɔnɔmist(ə)] *nm/f* economist.

écoper [ekɔpe] *vi* to bale out; (*fig*) to cop it; ~ **(de)** *vt* to get.

écorce [ekɔʀs(ə)] *nf* bark; (*de fruit*) peel.

écorché, e [ekɔʀʃe] *adj*: ~ **vif** flayed alive ♦ *nm* cut-away drawing.

écorcher [ekɔʀʃe] *vt* (*animal*) to skin; (*égratigner*) to graze; ~ **une langue** to speak a language brokenly; **s'~ le genou** *etc* to scrape *ou* graze one's knee *etc*.

écorchure [ekɔʀʃyʀ] *nf* graze.

écorner [ekɔʀne] *vt* (*taureau*) to dehorn; (*livre*) to make dog-eared.

écossais, e [ekɔsɛ, -ɛz] *adj* Scottish, Scots; (*whisky, confiture*) Scotch; (*écharpe, tissu*) tartan ♦ *nm* (*LING*) Scots; (*: gaélique*) Gaelic; (*tissu*) tartan (cloth) ♦ *nm/f*: **É~, e** Scot, Scotsman/woman; **les É~** the Scots.

Écosse [ekɔs] *nf* Scotland.

écosser [ekɔse] *vt* to shell.

écosystème [ekɔsistɛm] *nm* ecosystem.

écot [eko] *nm*: **payer son ~** to pay one's share.

écoulement [ekulmɑ̃] *nm* (*de faux billets*) circulation; (*de stock*) selling.

écouler [ekule] *vt* to dispose of; **s'~** *vi* (*eau*) to flow (out); (*foule*) to drift away; (*jours, temps*) to pass (by).

écourter [ekuʀte] *vt* to curtail, cut short.

écoute [ekut] *nf* (*NAVIG: cordage*) sheet; (*RADIO, TV*): **temps d'~** (listening *ou* viewing) time; **heure de grande ~** peak listening *ou* viewing time; **prendre l'~** to tune in; **rester à l'~ (de)** to stay tuned in (to); **~s téléphoniques** phone tapping *sg*.

écouter [ekute] *vt* to listen to.

écouteur [ekutœʀ] *nm* (*TÉL*) (additional) earpiece; **~s** *nmpl* (*RADIO*) headphones, headset *sg*.

écoutille [ekutij] *nf* hatch.

écrabouiller [ekʀabuje] *vt* to squash, crush.

écran [ekʀɑ̃] *nm* screen; (*INFORM*) VDU screen; ~ **de fumée/d'eau** curtain of smoke/water; **porter à l'~** (*CINÉ*) to adapt for the screen; **le petit ~** television, the small screen.

écrasant, e [ekʀazɑ̃, -ɑ̃t] *adj* overwhelming.

écraser [ekʀaze] *vt* to crush; (*piéton*) to run

over; (*INFORM*) to overwrite; **se faire** ~ to be run over; **écrase(-toi)!** shut up!; **s'~ (au sol)** to crash; **s'~ contre** to crash into.
écrémer [ekʀeme] *vt* to skim.
écrevisse [ekʀəvis] *nf* crayfish *inv*.
écrier [ekʀije]: **s'~** *vi* to exclaim.
écrin [ekʀɛ̃] *nm* case, box.
écrire [ekʀiʀ] *vt*, *vi* to write ♦ *vi*: **ça s'écrit comment?** how is it spelt?; ~ **à qn que** to write and tell sb that; **s'~** to write to one another.
écrit, e [ekʀi, -it] *pp de* **écrire** ♦ *adj*: **bien/mal** ~ well/badly written ♦ *nm* document; (*examen*) written paper; **par** ~ in writing.
écriteau, x [ekʀito] *nm* notice, sign.
écritoire [ekʀitwaʀ] *nf* writing case.
écriture [ekʀityʀ] *nf* writing; (*COMM*) entry; **~s** *nfpl* (*COMM*) accounts, books; **l'É~ (sainte), les É~s** the Scriptures.
écrivain [ekʀivɛ̃] *nm* writer.
écrivais [ekʀivɛ] *etc vb voir* **écrire**.
écrou [ekʀu] *nm* nut.
écrouer [ekʀue] *vt* to imprison; (*provisoirement*) to remand in custody.
écroulé, e [ekʀule] *adj* (*de fatigue*) exhausted; (*par un malheur*) overwhelmed; ~ **(de rire)** in stitches.
écroulement [ekʀulmɑ̃] *nm* collapse.
écrouler [ekʀule]: **s'~** *vi* to collapse.
écru, e [ekʀy] *adj* (*toile*) raw, unbleached; (*couleur*) off-white, écru.
écu [eky] *nm* (*bouclier*) shield; (*monnaie: ancienne*) crown; (*: de la CEE*) ecu.
écueil [ekœj] *nm* reef; (*fig*) pitfall; stumbling block.
écuelle [ekɥɛl] *nf* bowl.
éculé, e [ekyle] *adj* (*chaussure*) down-at-heel; (*fig: péj*) hackneyed.
écume [ekym] *nf* foam; (*CULIN*) scum; ~ **de mer** meerschaum.
écumer [ekyme] *vt* (*CULIN*) to skim; (*fig*) to plunder ♦ *vi* (*mer*) to foam; (*fig*) to boil with rage.
écumoire [ekymwaʀ] *nf* skimmer.
écureuil [ekyʀœj] *nm* squirrel.
écurie [ekyʀi] *nf* stable.
écusson [ekysɔ̃] *nm* badge.
écuyer, ère [ekɥije, -ɛʀ] *nm/f* rider.
eczéma [ɛgzema] *nm* eczema.
éd. *abr* = **édition**.
édam [edam] *nm* (*fromage*) edam.
edelweiss [edɛlvajs] *nm inv* edelweiss.
éden [edɛn] *nm* Eden.
édenté, e [edɑ̃te] *adj* toothless.
EDF *sigle f* (= *Électricité de France*) *national electricity company*.
édifiant, e [edifjɑ̃, -ɑ̃t] *adj* edifying.
édification [edifikɑsjɔ̃] (*d'un bâtiment*) building, erection.
édifice [edifis] *nm* building, edifice.
édifier [edifje] *vt* to build, erect; (*fig*) to edify.
édiles [edil] *nmpl* city fathers.
Édimbourg [edɛ̃buʀ] *n* Edinburgh.
édit [edi] *nm* edict.
édit. *abr* = **éditeur**.
éditer [edite] *vt* (*publier*) to publish; (*: disque*) to produce; (*préparer: texte, INFORM*) to edit.
éditeur, trice [editœʀ, -tʀis] *nm/f* publisher; editor.
édition [edisjɔ̃] *nf* editing *no pl*; (*série d'exemplaires*) edition; (*industrie du livre*): **l'~** publishing; ~ **sur écran** (*INFORM*) screen editing.
édito [edito] *nm* (*fam: éditorial*) editorial, leader.
éditorial, aux [editɔʀjal, -o] *nm* editorial, leader.
éditorialiste [editɔʀjalist(ə)] *nm/f* editorial *ou* leader writer.
édredon [edʀədɔ̃] *nm* eiderdown, comforter (*US*).
éducateur, trice [edykatœʀ, -tʀis] *nm/f* teacher; ~ **spécialisé** specialist teacher.
éducatif, ive [edykatif, -iv] *adj* educational.
éducation [edykɑsjɔ̃] *nf* education; (*familiale*) upbringing; (*manières*) (good) manners *pl*; **bonne/mauvaise** ~ good/bad upbringing; **sans** ~ bad-mannered, ill-bred; **l'É~ (nationale)** ≈ the Department for Education; ~ **permanente** continuing education; ~ **physique** physical education.
édulcorer [edylkɔʀe] *vt* to sweeten; (*fig*) to tone down.
éduquer [edyke] *vt* to educate; (*élever*) to bring up; (*faculté*) to train; **bien/mal éduqué** well/badly brought up.
EEG *sigle m* (= *électroencéphalogramme*) EEG.
effacé, e [efase] *adj* (*fig*) retiring, unassuming.
effacer [efase] *vt* to erase, rub out; (*bande magnétique*) to erase; (*INFORM: fichier, fiche*) to delete, erase; **s'~** *vi* (*inscription etc*) to wear off; (*pour laisser passer*) to step aside; ~ **le ventre** to pull one's stomach in.
effarant, e [efaʀɑ̃, -ɑ̃t] *adj* alarming.
effaré, e [efaʀe] *adj* alarmed.
effarement [efaʀmɑ̃] *nm* alarm.
effarer [efaʀe] *vt* to alarm.
effarouchement [efaʀuʃmɑ̃] *nm* alarm.
effaroucher [efaʀuʃe] *vt* to frighten *ou* scare away; (*personne*) to alarm.
effectif, ive [efɛktif, -iv] *adj* real; effective ♦ *nm* (*MIL*) strength; (*SCOL*) total number of pupils, size; **~s** numbers, strength *sg*; (*COMM*) manpower *sg*; **réduire l'~ de** to downsize.
effectivement [efɛktivmɑ̃] *adv* effectively; (*réellement*) actually, really; (*en effet*) indeed.
effectuer [efɛktɥe] *vt* (*opération, mission*) to carry out; (*déplacement, trajet*) to make, complete; (*mouvement*) to execute, make; **s'~** to be carried out.
efféminé, e [efemine] *adj* effeminate.
effervescence [efɛʀvesɑ̃s] *nf* (*fig*): **en** ~ in a turmoil.

effervescent, e [efɛʀvesɑ̃, -ɑ̃t] *adj* (*cachet, boisson*) effervescent; (*fig*) agitated, in a turmoil.
effet [efɛ] *nm* (*résultat, artifice*) effect; (*impression*) impression; (*COMM*) bill; (*JUR*: *d'une loi, d'un jugement*): **avec ~ rétroactif** applied retrospectively; **~s** *nmpl* (*vêtements etc*) things; **~ de style/couleur/lumière** stylistic/colour/lighting effect; **~s de voix** dramatic effects with one's voice; **faire de l'~** (*médicament, menace*) to have an effect, be effective; **sous l'~ de** under the effect of; **donner de l'~ à une balle** (*TENNIS*) to put some spin on a ball; **à cet ~** to that end; **en ~** *adv* indeed; **~ (de commerce)** bill of exchange; **~ de serre** greenhouse effect; **~s spéciaux** (*CINÉ*) special effects.
effeuiller [efœje] *vt* to remove the leaves (*ou* petals) from.
efficace [efikas] *adj* (*personne*) efficient; (*action, médicament*) effective.
efficacité [efikasite] *nf* efficiency; effectiveness.
effigie [efiʒi] *nf* effigy; **brûler qn en ~** to burn an effigy of sb.
effilé, e [efile] *adj* slender; (*pointe*) sharp; (*carrosserie*) streamlined.
effiler [efile] *vt* (*cheveux*) to thin (out); (*tissu*) to fray.
effilocher [efilɔʃe]: **s'~** *vi* to fray.
efflanqué, e [eflɑ̃ke] *adj* emaciated.
effleurement [eflœʀmɑ̃] *nm*: **touche à ~** touch-sensitive control *ou* key.
effleurer [eflœʀe] *vt* to brush (against); (*sujet*) to touch upon; (*suj*: *idée, pensée*): **~ qn** to cross sb's mind.
effluves [eflyv] *nmpl* exhalation(s).
effondré, e [efɔ̃dʀe] *adj* (*abattu: par un malheur, échec*) overwhelmed.
effondrement [efɔ̃dʀəmɑ̃] *nm* collapse.
effondrer [efɔ̃dʀe]: **s'~** *vi* to collapse.
efforcer [efɔʀse]: **s'~ de** *vt*: **s'~ de faire** to try hard to do.
effort [efɔʀ] *nm* effort; **faire un ~** to make an effort; **faire tous ses ~s** to try one's hardest; **faire l'~ de ...** to make the effort to ...; **sans ~** *adj* effortless ♦ *adv* effortlessly; **~ de mémoire** attempt to remember; **~ de volonté** effort of will.
effraction [efʀaksjɔ̃] *nf* breaking-in; **s'introduire par ~ dans** to break into.
effrangé, e [efʀɑ̃ʒe] *adj* fringed; (*effiloché*) frayed.
effrayant, e [efʀɛjɑ̃, -ɑ̃t] *adj* frightening, fearsome; (*sens affaibli*) dreadful.
effrayer [efʀeje] *vt* to frighten, scare; (*rebuter*) to put off; **s'~ (de)** to be frightened *ou* scared (by).
effréné, e [efʀene] *adj* wild.
effritement [efʀitmɑ̃] *nm* crumbling; erosion; slackening off.
effriter [efʀite]: **s'~** *vi* to crumble; (*monnaie*) to be eroded; (*valeurs*) to slacken off.
effroi [efʀwɑ] *nm* terror, dread *no pl*.
effronté, e [efʀɔ̃te] *adj* insolent.
effrontément [efʀɔ̃temɑ̃] *adv* insolently.
effronterie [efʀɔ̃tʀi] *nf* insolence.
effroyable [efʀwajabl(ə)] *adj* horrifying, appalling.
effusion [efyzjɔ̃] *nf* effusion; **sans ~ de sang** without bloodshed.
égailler [egaje]: **s'~** *vi* to scatter, disperse.
égal, e, aux [egal, -o] *adj* (*identique, ayant les mêmes droits*) equal; (*plan: surface*) even, level; (*constant: vitesse*) steady; (*équitable*) even ♦ *nm/f* equal; **être ~ à** (*prix, nombre*) to be equal to; **ça lui est ~** it's all the same to him, it doesn't matter to him, he doesn't mind; **c'est ~, ...** all the same, ...; **sans ~** matchless, unequalled; **à l'~ de** (*comme*) just like; **d'~ à ~** as equals.
également [egalmɑ̃] *adv* equally; evenly; steadily; (*aussi*) too, as well.
égaler [egale] *vt* to equal.
égalisateur, trice [egalizatœʀ, -tʀis] *adj* (*SPORT*): **but ~** equalizing goal, equalizer.
égalisation [egalizɑsjɔ̃] *nf* (*SPORT*) equalization.
égaliser [egalize] *vt* (*sol, salaires*) to level (out); (*chances*) to equalize ♦ *vi* (*SPORT*) to equalize.
égalitaire [egalitɛʀ] *adj* egalitarian.
égalitarisme [egalitaʀism(ə)] *nm* egalitarianism.
égalité [egalite] *nf* equality; evenness; steadiness; (*MATH*) identity; **être à ~ (de points)** to be level; **~ de droits** equality of rights; **~ d'humeur** evenness of temper.
égard [egaʀ] *nm*: **~s** *nmpl* consideration *sg*; **à cet ~** in this respect; **à certains ~s/tous ~s** in certain respects/all respects; **eu ~ à** in view of; **par ~ pour** out of consideration for; **sans ~ pour** without regard for; **à l'~ de** *prép* towards; (*en ce qui concerne*) concerning, as regards.
égaré, e [egaʀe] *adj* lost.
égarement [egaʀmɑ̃] *nm* distraction; aberration.
égarer [egaʀe] *vt* (*objet*) to mislay; (*moralement*) to lead astray; **s'~** *vi* to get lost, lose one's way; (*objet*) to go astray; (*fig: dans une discussion*) to wander.
égayer [egeje] *vt* (*personne*) to amuse; (*: remonter*) to cheer up; (*récit, endroit*) to brighten up, liven up.
Égée [eʒe] *adj*: **la mer ~** the Aegean (Sea).
égéen, ne [eʒeɛ̃, -ɛn] *adj* Aegean.
égérie [eʒeʀi] *nf*: **l'~ de qn/qch** the brains behind sb/sth.
égide [eʒid] *nf*: **sous l'~ de** under the aegis of.
églantier [eglɑ̃tje] *nm* wild *ou* dog rose(-bush).
églantine [eglɑ̃tin] *nf* wild *ou* dog rose.
églefin [egləfɛ̃] *nm* haddock.

église [egliz] *nf* church.
égocentrique [egɔsɑ̃tʀik] *adj* egocentric, self-centred.
égocentrisme [egɔsɑ̃tʀism(ə)] *nm* egocentricity.
égoïne [egɔin] *nf* handsaw.
égoïsme [egɔism(ə)] *nm* selfishness, egoism.
égoïste [egɔist(ə)] *adj* selfish, egoistic ♦ *nm/f* egoist.
égoïstement [egɔistəmɑ̃] *adv* selfishly.
égorger [egɔʀʒe] *vt* to cut the throat of.
égosiller [egozije]: **s'~** *vi* to shout o.s. hoarse.
égotisme [egɔtism(ə)] *nm* egotism, egoism.
égout [egu] *nm* sewer; **eaux d'~** sewage.
égoutier [egutje] *nm* sewer worker.
égoutter [egute] *vt* (*linge*) to wring out; (*vaisselle, fromage*) to drain ♦ *vi*, **s'~** *vi* to drip.
égouttoir [egutwaʀ] *nm* draining board; (*mobile*) draining rack.
égratigner [egʀatiɲe] *vt* to scratch; **s'~** to scratch o.s.
égratignure [egʀatiɲyʀ] *nf* scratch.
égrener [egʀəne] *vt*: **~ une grappe**, **~ des raisins** to pick grapes off a bunch; **s'~** *vi* (*fig: heures etc*) to pass by; (*: notes*) to chime out.
égrillard, e [egʀijaʀ, -aʀd(ə)] *adj* ribald, bawdy.
Égypte [eʒipt] *nf*: **l'~** Egypt.
égyptien, ne [eʒipsjɛ̃, -ɛn] *adj* Egyptian ♦ *nm/f*: **É~, ne** Egyptian.
égyptologue [eʒiptɔlɔg] *nm/f* Egyptologist.
eh [e] *excl* hey!; **~ bien** well.
éhonté, e [eɔ̃te] *adj* shameless, brazen (*BRIT*).
éjaculation [eʒakylɑsjɔ̃] *nf* ejaculation.
éjaculer [eʒakyle] *vi* to ejaculate.
éjectable [eʒɛktabl(ə)] *adj*: **siège ~** ejector seat.
éjecter [eʒɛkte] *vt* (*TECH*) to eject; (*fam*) to kick *ou* chuck out.
éjection [eʒɛksjɔ̃] *nf* ejection.
élaboration [elabɔʀɑsjɔ̃] *nf* elaboration.
élaboré, e [elabɔʀe] *adj* (*complexe*) elaborate.
élaborer [elabɔʀe] *vt* to elaborate; (*projet, stratégie*) to work out; (*rapport*) to draft.
élagage [elagaʒ] *nm* pruning.
élaguer [elage] *vt* to prune.
élan [elɑ̃] *nm* (*ZOOL*) elk, moose; (*SPORT: avant le saut*) run up; (*de véhicule etc*) momentum; (*fig: de tendresse etc*) surge; **prendre son ~/de l'~** to take a run up/gather speed; **perdre son ~** to lose one's momentum.
élancé, e [elɑ̃se] *adj* slender.
élancement [elɑ̃smɑ̃] *nm* shooting pain.
élancer [elɑ̃se]: **s'~** *vi* to dash, hurl o.s.; (*fig: arbre, clocher*) to soar (upwards).
élargir [elaʀʒiʀ] *vt* to widen; (*vêtement*) to let out; (*JUR*) to release; **s'~** *vi* to widen; (*vêtement*) to stretch.
élargissement [elaʀʒismɑ̃] *nm* widening; letting out.
élasticité [elastisite] *nf* (*aussi ÉCON*) elasticity; **~ de l'offre/de la demande** flexibility of supply/demand.
élastique [elastik] *adj* elastic ♦ *nm* (*de bureau*) rubber band; (*pour la couture*) elastic *no pl*.
élastomère [elastɔmɛʀ] *nm* elastomer.
Elbe [ɛlb] *nf*: **l'île d'~** (the Island of) Elba; (*fleuve*): **l'~** the Elbe.
eldorado [ɛldɔʀado] *nm* Eldorado.
électeur, trice [elɛktœʀ, -tʀis] *nm/f* elector, voter.
électif, ive [elɛktif, -iv] *adj* elective.
élection [elɛksjɔ̃] *nf* election; **~s** *nfpl* (*POL*) election(s); **sa terre/patrie d'~** the land/country of one's choice; **~ partielle** ≈ by-election; **~s législatives/présidentielles** general/presidential election *sg*; *see boxed note*.

ÉLECTIONS LÉGISLATIVES

Élections législatives are held in France every five years to elect 'députés' to the 'Assemblée Nationale'. The president is chosen in the 'élection presidentielle' which comes round every seven years. Voting is by direct universal suffrage and is divided into two rounds. The ballots always take place on a Sunday.

électoral, e, aux [elɛktɔʀal, -o] *adj* electoral, election *cpd*.
électoralisme [elɛktɔʀalism(ə)] *nm* electioneering.
électorat [elɛktɔʀa] *nm* electorate.
électricien, ne [elɛktʀisjɛ̃, -ɛn] *nm/f* electrician.
électricité [elɛktʀisite] *nf* electricity; **allumer/éteindre l'~** to put on/off the light; **~ statique** static electricity.
électrification [elɛktʀifikɑsjɔ̃] *nf* (*RAIL*) electrification; (*d'un village etc*) laying on of electricity.
électrifier [elɛktʀifje] *vt* (*RAIL*) to electrify.
électrique [elɛktʀik] *adj* electric(al).
électriser [elɛktʀize] *vt* to electrify.
électro... [elɛktʀɔ] *préfixe* electro....
électro-aimant [elɛktʀɔɛmɑ̃] *nm* electromagnet.
électrocardiogramme [elɛktʀɔkaʀdjɔgʀam] *nm* electrocardiogram.
électrocardiographe [elɛktʀɔkaʀdjɔgʀaf] *nm* electrocardiograph.
électrochoc [elɛktʀɔʃɔk] *nm* electric shock treatment.
électrocuter [elɛktʀɔkyte] *vt* to electrocute.
électrocution [elɛktʀɔkysjɔ̃] *nf* electrocution.
électrode [elɛktʀɔd] *nf* electrode.
électro-encéphalogramme [elɛktʀɔɑ̃sefalɔgʀam] *nm* electroencephalogram.
électrogène [elɛktʀɔʒɛn] *adj*: **groupe ~** generating set.
électrolyse [elɛktʀɔliz] *nf* electrolysis *sg*.
électromagnétique [elɛktʀɔmaɲetik] *adj* electromagnetic.
électroménager [elɛktʀɔmenaʒe] *adj*: **appa-**

reils ~s domestic (electrical) appliances ♦ *nm*: **l'~** household appliances.
électron [elɛktʀɔ̃] *nm* electron.
électronicien, ne [elɛktʀɔnisjɛ̃, -ɛn] *nm/f* electronics (*BRIT*) *ou* electrical (*US*) engineer.
électronique [elɛktʀɔnik] *adj* electronic ♦ *nf* (*science*) electronics *sg*.
électronucléaire [elɛktʀɔnykleɛʀ] *adj* nuclear power *cpd* ♦ *nm*: **l'~** nuclear power.
électrophone [elɛktʀɔfɔn] *nm* record player.
électrostatique [elɛktʀɔstatik] *adj* electrostatic ♦ *nf* electrostatics *sg*.
élégamment [elegamɑ̃] *adv* elegantly.
élégance [elegɑ̃s] *nf* elegance.
élégant, e [elegɑ̃, -ɑ̃t] *adj* elegant; (*solution*) neat, elegant; (*attitude, procédé*) courteous, civilized.
élément [elemɑ̃] *nm* element; (*pièce*) component, part; **~s** *nmpl* elements.
élémentaire [elemɑ̃tɛʀ] *adj* elementary; (*CHIMIE*) elemental.
éléphant [elefɑ̃] *nm* elephant; **~ de mer** elephant seal.
éléphanteau, x [elefɑ̃to] *nm* baby elephant.
éléphantesque [elefɑ̃tɛsk(ə)] *adj* elephantine.
élevage [ɛlvaʒ] *nm* breeding; (*de bovins*) cattle breeding *ou* rearing; (*ferme*) cattle farm.
élévateur [elevatœʀ] *nm* elevator.
élévation [elevɑsjɔ̃] *nf* (*gén*) elevation; (*voir élever*) raising; (*voir s'élever*) rise.
élevé, e [ɛlve] *adj* (*prix, sommet*) high; (*fig: noble*) elevated; **bien/mal ~** well-/ill-mannered.
élève [elɛv] *nm/f* pupil; **~ infirmière** student nurse.
élever [ɛlve] *vt* (*enfant*) to bring up, raise; (*bétail, volaille*) to breed; (*abeilles*) to keep; (*hausser: taux, niveau*) to raise; (*fig: âme, esprit*) to elevate; (*monument*) to put up, erect; **s'~** *vi* (*avion, alpiniste*) to go up; (*niveau, température, aussi: cri etc*) to rise; (*difficultés*) to arise; **s'~ à** (*suj: frais, dégâts*) to amount to, add up to; **s'~ contre** to rise up against; **~ une protestation/critique** to raise a protest/make a criticism; **~qn au rang de** to raise *ou* elevate sb to the rank of; **~ un nombre au carré/au cube** to square/cube a number.
éleveur, euse [ɛlvœʀ, -øz] *nm/f* stock breeder.
elfe [ɛlf(ə)] *nm* elf.
élidé, e [elide] *adj* elided.
éligibilité [eliʒibilite] *nf* eligibility.
éligible [eliʒibl(ə)] *adj* eligible.
élimé, e [elime] *adj* worn (thin), threadbare.
élimination [eliminɑsjɔ̃] *nf* elimination.
éliminatoire [eliminatwaʀ] *adj* eliminatory; (*SPORT*) disqualifying ♦ *nf* (*SPORT*) heat.
éliminer [elimine] *vt* to eliminate.
élire [eliʀ] *vt* to elect; **~ domicile à** to take up residence in *ou* at.
élite [elit] *nf* elite; **tireur d'~** crack rifleman; **chercheur d'~** top-notch researcher.
élitisme [elitism(ə)] *nm* elitism.
élitiste [elitist(ə)] *adj* elitist.
élixir [eliksiʀ] *nm* elixir.
elle [ɛl] *pron* (*sujet*) she; (*: chose*) it; (*complément*) her; it; **~s** (*sujet*) they; (*complément*) them; **~-même** herself; itself; **~s-mêmes** themselves; *voir* **il**.
ellipse [elips(ə)] *nf* ellipse; (*LING*) ellipsis *sg*.
elliptique [eliptik] *adj* elliptical.
élocution [elɔkysjɔ̃] *nf* delivery; **défaut d'~** speech impediment.
éloge [elɔʒ] *nm* praise (*gén no pl*); **faire l'~ de** to praise.
élogieusement [elɔʒjøzmɑ̃] *adv* very favourably.
élogieux, euse [elɔʒjø, -øz] *adj* laudatory, full of praise.
éloigné, e [elwaɲe] *adj* distant, far-off.
éloignement [elwaɲmɑ̃] *nm* removal; putting off; estrangement; (*fig: distance*) distance.
éloigner [elwaɲe] *vt* (*objet*): **~ qch (de)** to move *ou* take sth away (from); (*personne*): **~ qn (de)** to take sb away *ou* remove sb (from); (*échéance*) to put off, postpone; (*soupçons, danger*) to ward off; **s'~ (de)** (*personne*) to go away (from); (*véhicule*) to move away (from); (*affectivement*) to become estranged (from).
élongation [elɔ̃gɑsjɔ̃] *nf* strained muscle.
éloquence [elɔkɑ̃s] *nf* eloquence.
éloquent, e [elɔkɑ̃, -ɑ̃t] *adj* eloquent.
élu, e [ely] *pp de* **élire** ♦ *nm/f* (*POL*) elected representative.
élucider [elyside] *vt* to elucidate.
élucubrations [elykybʀɑsjɔ̃] *nfpl* wild imaginings.
éluder [elyde] *vt* to evade.
élus [ely] *etc vb voir* **élire**.
élusif, ive [elyzif, -iv] *adj* elusive.
Élysée [elize] *nm*: **(le palais de) l'~** the Élysée palace; **les Champs ~s** the Champs Élysées; *see boxed note*.

PALAIS DE L'ÉLYSÉE

The **palais de l'Élysée**, *situated in the heart of Paris just off the Champs Élysées, is the official residence of the French President. Built in the eighteenth century, it has performed its present function since 1876. A shortened form of its name,* **l'Élysée** *is frequently used to mean the presidency itself.*

émacié, e [emasje] *adj* emaciated.
émail, aux [emaj, -o] *nm* enamel.
e-mail [imɛl] *nm* e-mail; **envoyer qch par ~** to e-mail sth.
émaillé, e [emaje] *adj* enamelled; (*fig*): **~ de** dotted with.
émailler [emaje] *vt* to enamel.
émanation [emanɑsjɔ̃] *nf* emanation.
émancipation [emɑ̃sipɑsjɔ̃] *nf* emancipation.
émancipé, e [emɑ̃sipe] *adj* emancipated.

émanciper [emɑ̃sipe] *vt* to emancipate; **s'~** (*fig*) to become emancipated *ou* liberated.
émaner [emane]: **~ de** *vt* to emanate from; (*ADMIN*) to proceed from.
émarger [emaʀʒe] *vt* to sign; **~ de 1 000 € à un budget** to receive €1000 out of a budget.
émasculer [emaskyle] *vt* to emasculate.
emballage [ɑ̃balaʒ] *nm* wrapping; packing; (*papier*) wrapping; (*carton*) packaging.
emballer [ɑ̃bale] *vt* to wrap (up); (*dans un carton*) to pack (up); (*fig: fam*) to thrill (to bits); **s'~** *vi* (*moteur*) to race; (*cheval*) to bolt; (*fig: personne*) to get carried away.
emballeur, euse [ɑ̃balœʀ, -øz] *nm/f* packer.
embarcadère [ɑ̃baʀkadɛʀ] *nm* landing stage (*BRIT*), pier.
embarcation [ɑ̃baʀkɑsjɔ̃] *nf* (small) boat, (small) craft *inv*.
embardée [ɑ̃baʀde] *nf* swerve; **faire une ~** to swerve.
embargo [ɑ̃baʀgo] *nm* embargo; **mettre l'~ sur** to put an embargo on, embargo.
embarquement [ɑ̃baʀkəmɑ̃] *nm* embarkation; loading; boarding.
embarquer [ɑ̃baʀke] *vt* (*personne*) to embark; (*marchandise*) to load; (*fam*) to cart off; (*: arrêter*) to nick ♦ *vi* (*passager*) to board; (*NAVIG*) to ship water; **s'~** *vi* to board; **s'~ dans** (*affaire, aventure*) to embark upon.
embarras [ɑ̃baʀa] *nm* (*obstacle*) hindrance; (*confusion*) embarrassment; (*ennuis*): **être dans l'~** to be in a predicament *ou* an awkward position; (*gêne financière*) to be in difficulties; **~ gastrique** stomach upset.
embarrassant, e [ɑ̃baʀasɑ̃, -ɑ̃t] *adj* cumbersome; embarrassing; awkward.
embarrassé, e [ɑ̃baʀase] *adj* (*encombré*) encumbered; (*gêné*) embarrassed; (*explications etc*) awkward.
embarrasser [ɑ̃baʀase] *vt* (*encombrer*) to clutter (up); (*gêner*) to hinder, hamper; (*fig*) to cause embarrassment to; to put in an awkward position; **s'~ de** to burden o.s. with.
embauche [ɑ̃boʃ] *nf* hiring; **bureau d'~** labour office.
embaucher [ɑ̃boʃe] *vt* to take on, hire; **s'~ comme** to get (o.s.) a job as.
embauchoir [ɑ̃boʃwaʀ] *nm* shoetree.
embaumer [ɑ̃bome] *vt* to embalm; (*parfumer*) to fill with its fragrance; **~ la lavande** to be fragrant with (the scent of) lavender.
embellie [ɑ̃beli] *nf* bright spell, brighter period.
embellir [ɑ̃beliʀ] *vt* to make more attractive; (*une histoire*) to embellish ♦ *vi* to grow lovelier *ou* more attractive.
embellissement [ɑ̃belismɑ̃] *nm* embellishment.
embêtant, e [ɑ̃bɛtɑ̃, -ɑ̃t] *adj* annoying.
embêtement [ɑ̃bɛtmɑ̃] *nm* problem, difficulty; **~s** *nmpl* trouble *sg*.
embêter [ɑ̃bete] *vt* to bother; **s'~** *vi* (*s'ennuyer*) to be bored; **il ne s'embête pas!** (*ironique*) he does all right for himself!
emblée [ɑ̃ble]: **d'~** *adv* straightaway.
emblème [ɑ̃blɛm] *nm* emblem.
embobiner [ɑ̃bɔbine] *vt* (*enjôler*): **~ qn** to get round sb.
emboîtable [ɑ̃bwatabl(ə)] *adj* interlocking.
emboîter [ɑ̃bwate] *vt* to fit together; **s'~ dans** to fit into; **s'~ (l'un dans l'autre)** to fit together; **~ le pas à qn** to follow in sb's footsteps.
embolie [ɑ̃bɔli] *nf* embolism.
embonpoint [ɑ̃bɔ̃pwɛ̃] *nm* stoutness (*BRIT*), corpulence; **prendre de l'~** to grow stout (*BRIT*) *ou* corpulent.
embouché, e [ɑ̃buʃe] *adj*: **mal ~** foul-mouthed.
embouchure [ɑ̃buʃyʀ] *nf* (*GÉO*) mouth; (*MUS*) mouthpiece.
embourber [ɑ̃buʀbe]: **s'~** *vi* to get stuck in the mud; (*fig*): **s'~ dans** to sink into.
embourgeoiser [ɑ̃buʀʒwaze]: **s'~** *vi* to adopt a middle-class outlook.
embout [ɑ̃bu] *nm* (*de canne*) tip; (*de tuyau*) nozzle.
embouteillage [ɑ̃butɛjaʒ] *nm* traffic jam, (traffic) holdup (*BRIT*).
embouteiller [ɑ̃buteje] *vt* (*suj: véhicules etc*) to block.
emboutir [ɑ̃butiʀ] *vt* (*TECH*) to stamp; (*heurter*) to crash into, ram.
embranchement [ɑ̃bʀɑ̃ʃmɑ̃] *nm* (*routier*) junction; (*classification*) branch.
embrancher [ɑ̃bʀɑ̃ʃe] *vt* (*tuyaux*) to join; **~ qch sur** to join sth to.
embraser [ɑ̃bʀɑze]: **s'~** *vi* to flare up.
embrassade [ɑ̃bʀasad] *nf* (*gén pl*) hugging and kissing *no pl*.
embrasse [ɑ̃bʀas] *nf* (*de rideau*) tie-back, loop.
embrasser [ɑ̃bʀase] *vt* to kiss; (*sujet, période*) to embrace, encompass; (*carrière*) to embark on; (*métier*) to go in for, take up; **~ du regard** to take in (*with eyes*); **s'~** to kiss (each other).
embrasure [ɑ̃bʀɑzyʀ] *nf*: **dans l'~ de la porte** in the door(way).
embrayage [ɑ̃bʀɛjaʒ] *nm* clutch.
embrayer [ɑ̃bʀeje] *vi* (*AUTO*) to let in the clutch ♦ *vt* (*fig: affaire*) to set in motion; **~ sur qch** to begin on sth.
embrigader [ɑ̃bʀigade] *vt* to recruit.
embrocher [ɑ̃bʀɔʃe] *vt* to (put on a) spit (*ou* skewer).
embrouillamini [ɑ̃bʀujamini] *nm* (*fam*) muddle.
embrouillé, e [ɑ̃bʀuje] *adj* (*affaire*) confused, muddled.
embrouiller [ɑ̃bʀuje] *vt* (*fils*) to tangle (up); (*fiches, idées, personne*) to muddle up; **s'~** *vi* to get in a muddle.
embroussaillé, e [ɑ̃bʀusɑje] *adj* overgrown, scrubby; (*cheveux*) bushy, shaggy.

embruns [ɑ̃bʀœ̃] *nmpl* sea spray *sg*.
embryologie [ɑ̃bʀijɔlɔʒi] *nf* embryology.
embryon [ɑ̃bʀijɔ̃] *nm* embryo.
embryonnaire [ɑ̃bʀijɔnɛʀ] *adj* embryonic.
embûches [ɑ̃byʃ] *nfpl* pitfalls, traps.
embué, e [ɑ̃bɥe] *adj* misted up; **yeux ~s de larmes** eyes misty with tears.
embuscade [ɑ̃byskad] *nf* ambush; **tendre une ~ à** to lay an ambush for.
embusqué, e [ɑ̃byske] *adj* in ambush ♦ *nm* (*péj*) shirker, skiver (*BRIT*).
embusquer [ɑ̃byske] **s'~** *vi* to take up position (for an ambush).
éméché, e [emeʃe] *adj* tipsy, merry.
émeraude [ɛmʀod] *nf* emerald ♦ *adj inv* emerald-green.
émergence [emɛʀʒɑ̃s] *nf* (*fig*) emergence.
émerger [emɛʀʒe] *vi* to emerge; (*faire saillie, aussi fig*) to stand out.
émeri [ɛmʀi] *nm*: **toile** *ou* **papier ~** emery paper.
émérite [emeʀit] *adj* highly skilled.
émerveillement [emɛʀvɛjmɑ̃] *nm* wonderment.
émerveiller [emɛʀveje] *vt* to fill with wonder; **s'~ de** to marvel at.
émet [emɛ] *etc vb voir* **émettre**.
émétique [emetik] *nm* emetic.
émetteur, trice [emɛtœʀ, -tʀis] *adj* transmitting; **(poste) ~** transmitter.
émetteur-récepteur, *pl* **émetteurs-récepteurs** [emetœʀʀesɛptœʀ] *nm* transceiver.
émettre [emɛtʀ(ə)] *vt* (*son, lumière*) to give out, emit; (*message etc: RADIO*) to transmit; (*billet, timbre, emprunt, chèque*) to issue; (*hypothèse, avis*) to voice, put forward; (*vœu*) to express ♦ *vi*: **~ sur ondes courtes** to broadcast on short wave.
émeus [emø] *etc vb voir* **émouvoir**.
émeute [emøt] *nf* riot.
émeutier, ière [emøtje, -jɛʀ] *nm/f* rioter.
émeuve [emœv] *etc vb voir* **émouvoir**.
émietter [emjete] *vt* (*pain, terre*) to crumble; (*fig*) to split up, disperse; **s'~** *vi* (*pain, terre*) to crumble.
émigrant, e [emigʀɑ̃, -ɑ̃t] *nm/f* emigrant.
émigration [emigʀɑsjɔ̃] *nf* emigration.
émigré, e [emigʀe] *nm/f* expatriate.
émigrer [emigʀe] *vi* to emigrate.
émincer [emɛ̃se] *vt* (*CULIN*) to slice thinly.
éminemment [eminamɑ̃] *adv* eminently.
éminence [eminɑ̃s] *nf* distinction; (*colline*) knoll, hill; **Son É~** His Eminence; **~ grise** éminence grise.
éminent, e [eminɑ̃, -ɑ̃t] *adj* distinguished.
émir [emiʀ] *nm* emir.
émirat [emiʀa] *nm* emirate; **les É~s arabes unis (EAU)** the United Arab Emirates (UAE).
émis, e [emi, -iz] *pp de* **émettre**.
émissaire [emisɛʀ] *nm* emissary.
émission [emisjɔ̃] *nf* (*voir émettre*) emission; transmission; issue; (*RADIO, TV*) programme, broadcast.
émit [emi] *etc vb voir* **émettre**.
emmagasinage [ɑ̃magazinaʒ] *nm* storage; storing away.
emmagasiner [ɑ̃magazine] *vt* to (put into) store; (*fig*) to store up.
emmailloter [ɑ̃majɔte] *vt* to wrap up.
emmanchure [ɑ̃mɑ̃ʃyʀ] *nf* armhole.
emmêlement [ɑ̃mɛlmɑ̃] *nm* (*état*) tangle.
emmêler [ɑ̃mele] *vt* to tangle (up); (*fig*) to muddle up; **s'~** to get into a tangle.
emménagement [ɑ̃menaʒmɑ̃] *nm* settling in.
emménager [ɑ̃menaʒe] *vi* to move in; **~ dans** to move into.
emmener [ɑ̃mne] *vt* to take (with one); (*comme otage, capture*) to take away; **~ qn au concert** to take sb to a concert.
emment(h)al [emɛ̃tal] *nm* (*fromage*) Emmenthal.
emmerder [ɑ̃mɛʀde] (*fam!*) *vt* to bug, bother; **s'~** *vi* (*s'ennuyer*) to be bored stiff; **je t'emmerde!** to hell with you!
emmitoufler [ɑ̃mitufle] *vt* to wrap up (warmly); **s'~** to wrap (o.s.) up (warmly).
emmurer [ɑ̃myʀe] *vt* to wall up, immure.
émoi [emwa] *nm* (*agitation, effervescence*) commotion; (*trouble*) agitation; **en ~** (*sens*) excited, stirred.
émollient, e [emɔljɑ̃, -ɑ̃t] *adj* (*MÉD*) emollient.
émoluments [emɔlymɑ̃] *nmpl* remuneration *sg*, fee *sg*.
émonder [emɔ̃de] *vt* (*arbre etc*) to prune; (*amande etc*) to blanch.
émotif, ive [emɔtif, -iv] *adj* emotional.
émotion [emosjɔ̃] *nf* emotion; **avoir des ~s** (*fig*) to get a fright; **donner des ~s à** to give a fright to; **sans ~** without emotion, coldly.
émotionnant, e [emosjɔnɑ̃, -ɑ̃t] *adj* upsetting.
émotionnel, le [emosjɔnɛl] *adj* emotional.
émotionner [emosjɔne] *vt* to upset.
émoulu, e [emuly] *adj*: **frais ~ de** fresh from, just out of.
émoussé, e [emuse] *adj* blunt.
émousser [emuse] *vt* to blunt; (*fig*) to dull.
émoustiller [emustije] *vt* to titillate, arouse.
émouvant, e [emuvɑ̃, -ɑ̃t] *adj* moving.
émouvoir [emuvwaʀ] *vt* (*troubler*) to stir, affect; (*toucher, attendrir*) to move; (*indigner*) to rouse; (*effrayer*) to disturb, worry; **s'~** *vi* to be affected; to be moved; to be roused; to be disturbed *ou* worried.
empailler [ɑ̃paje] *vt* to stuff.
empailleur, euse [ɑ̃pajœʀ, -øz] *nm/f* (*d'animaux*) taxidermist.
empaler [ɑ̃pale] *vt* to impale.
empaquetage [ɑ̃paktaʒ] *nm* packing, packaging.
empaqueter [ɑ̃pakte] *vt* to pack up.
emparer [ɑ̃paʀe]: **s'~ de** *vt* (*objet*) to seize, grab; (*comme otage, MIL*) to seize; (*suj: peur*

etc) to take hold of.
empâter [ɑ̃pɑte]: **s'~** *vi* to thicken out.
empattement [ɑ̃patmɑ̃] *nm* (*AUTO*) wheelbase; (*TYPO*) serif.
empêché, e [ɑ̃peʃe] *adj* detained.
empêchement [ɑ̃pɛʃmɑ̃] *nm* (unexpected) obstacle, hitch.
empêcher [ɑ̃peʃe] *vt* to prevent; ~ **qn de faire** to prevent *ou* stop sb (from) doing; ~ **que qch (n')arrive/qn (ne) fasse** to prevent sth from happening/sb from doing; **il n'empêche que** nevertheless, be that as it may; **il n'a pas pu s'~ de rire** he couldn't help laughing.
empêcheur [ɑ̃pɛʃœʀ] *nm*: ~ **de danser en rond** spoilsport, killjoy (*BRIT*).
empeigne [ɑ̃pɛɲ] *nf* upper (*of shoe*).
empennage [ɑ̃penaʒ] *nm* (*AVIAT*) tailplane.
empereur [ɑ̃pʀœʀ] *nm* emperor.
empesé, e [ɑ̃pəze] *adj* (*fig*) stiff, starchy.
empeser [ɑ̃pəze] *vt* to starch.
empester [ɑ̃pɛste] *vt* (*lieu*) to stink out ♦ *vi* to stink, reek; ~ **le tabac/le vin** to stink *ou* reek of tobacco/wine.
empêtrer [ɑ̃petʀe] *vt*: **s'~ dans** (*fils etc, aussi fig*) to get tangled up in.
emphase [ɑ̃fɑz] *nf* pomposity, bombast; **avec ~** pompously.
emphatique [ɑ̃fatik] *adj* emphatic.
empiècement [ɑ̃pjɛsmɑ̃] *nm* (*COUTURE*) yoke.
empierrer [ɑ̃pjeʀe] *vt* (*route*) to metal.
empiéter [ɑ̃pjete]: ~ **sur** *vt* to encroach upon.
empiffrer [ɑ̃pifʀe]: **s'~** *vi* (*péj*) to stuff o.s.
empiler [ɑ̃pile] *vt* to pile (up), stack (up); **s'~** *vi* to pile up.
empire [ɑ̃piʀ] *nm* empire; (*fig*) influence; **style E~** Empire style; **sous l'~ de** in the grip of.
empirer [ɑ̃piʀe] *vi* to worsen, deteriorate.
empirique [ɑ̃piʀik] *adj* empirical.
empirisme [ɑ̃piʀism(ə)] *nm* empiricism.
emplacement [ɑ̃plasmɑ̃] *nm* site; **sur l'~ de** on the site of.
emplâtre [ɑ̃plɑtʀ(ə)] *nm* plaster; (*fam*) twit.
emplette [ɑ̃plɛt] *nf*: **faire l'~ de** to purchase; **~s** shopping *sg*; **faire des ~s** to go shopping.
emplir [ɑ̃pliʀ] *vt* to fill; **s'~ (de)** to fill (with).
emploi [ɑ̃plwa] *nm* use; (*COMM, ÉCON*): **l'~** employment; (*poste*) job, situation; **d'~ facile** easy to use; **le plein ~** full employment; **~ du temps** timetable, schedule.
emploie [ɑ̃plwa] *etc vb voir* **employer**.
employé, e [ɑ̃plwaje] *nm/f* employee; ~ **de bureau/banque** office/bank employee *ou* clerk; ~ **de maison** domestic (servant).
employer [ɑ̃plwaje] *vt* (*outil, moyen, méthode, mot*) to use; (*ouvrier, main-d'œuvre*) to employ; **s'~ à qch/à faire** to apply *ou* devote o.s. to sth/to doing.
employeur, euse [ɑ̃plwajœʀ, -øz] *nm/f* employer.
empocher [ɑ̃pɔʃe] *vt* to pocket.
empoignade [ɑ̃pwaɲad] *nf* row, set-to.
empoigne [ɑ̃pwaɲ] *nf*: **foire d'~** free-for-all.
empoigner [ɑ̃pwaɲe] *vt* to grab; **s'~** (*fig*) to have a row *ou* set-to.
empois [ɑ̃pwa] *nm* starch.
empoisonnement [ɑ̃pwazɔnmɑ̃] *nm* poisoning; (*fam: ennui*) annoyance, irritation.
empoisonner [ɑ̃pwazɔne] *vt* to poison; (*empester: air, pièce*) to stink out; (*fam*): ~ **qn** to drive sb mad; **s'~** to poison o.s.; ~ **l'atmosphère** (*aussi fig*) to poison the atmosphere; **il nous empoisonne l'existence** he's the bane of our life.
empoissonner [ɑ̃pwasɔne] *vt* (*étang, rivière*) to stock with fish.
emporté, e [ɑ̃pɔʀte] *adj* (*personne, caractère*) fiery.
emportement [ɑ̃pɔʀtəmɑ̃] *nm* fit of rage, anger *no pl*.
emporte-pièce [ɑ̃pɔʀtəpjɛs] *nm inv* (*TECH*) punch; **à l'~** *adj* (*fig*) incisive.
emporter [ɑ̃pɔʀte] *vt* to take (with one); (*en dérobant ou enlevant, emmener: blessés, voyageurs*) to take away; (*entraîner*) to carry away *ou* along; (*arracher*) to tear off; (*suj: rivière, vent*) to carry away; (*MIL: position*) to take; (*avantage, approbation*) to win; **s'~** *vi* (*de colère*) to fly into a rage, lose one's temper; **la maladie qui l'a emporté** the illness which caused his death; **l'~** to gain victory; **l'~ (sur)** to get the upper hand (of); (*méthode etc*) to prevail (over); **boissons à ~** take-away drinks.
empoté, e [ɑ̃pɔte] *adj* (*maladroit*) clumsy.
empourpré, e [ɑ̃puʀpʀe] *adj* crimson.
empreint, e [ɑ̃pʀɛ̃, -ɛ̃t] *adj*: ~ **de** marked with; tinged with ♦ *nf* (*de pied, main*) print; (*fig*) stamp, mark; **~e (digitale)** fingerprint.
empressé, e [ɑ̃pʀese] *adj* attentive; (*péj*) overanxious to please, overattentive.
empressement [ɑ̃pʀɛsmɑ̃] *nm* eagerness.
empresser [ɑ̃pʀese]: **s'~** *vi*: **s'~ auprès de qn** to surround sb with attentions; **s'~ de faire** to hasten to do.
emprise [ɑ̃pʀiz] *nf* hold, ascendancy; **sous l'~ de** under the influence of.
emprisonnement [ɑ̃pʀizɔnmɑ̃] *nm* imprisonment.
emprisonner [ɑ̃pʀizɔne] *vt* to imprison, jail.
emprunt [ɑ̃pʀœ̃] *nm* borrowing *no pl*, loan (*from debtor's point of view*); (*LING etc*) borrowing; **nom d'~** assumed name; ~ **d'État** government *ou* state loan; ~ **public à 5%** 5% public loan.
emprunté, e [ɑ̃pʀœ̃te] *adj* (*fig*) ill-at-ease, awkward.
emprunter [ɑ̃pʀœ̃te] *vt* to borrow; (*itinéraire*) to take, follow; (*style, manière*) to adopt, assume.
emprunteur, euse [ɑ̃pʀœ̃tœʀ, -øz] *nm/f* borrower.
empuantir [ɑ̃pɥɑ̃tiʀ] *vt* to stink out.
EMT *sigle f* (= *éducation manuelle et technique*)

handwork as a school subject.
ému, e [emy] *pp de* **émouvoir** ♦ *adj* excited; touched; moved.
émulation [emylɑsjɔ̃] *nf* emulation.
émule [emyl] *nm/f* imitator.
émulsion [emylsjɔ̃] *nf* emulsion; (*cosmétique*) (water-based) lotion.
émut [emy] *etc vb voir* **émouvoir**.
EN *sigle f* (= *Éducation nationale*) *voir* **éducation**.

MOT-CLÉ

en [ɑ̃] *prép* **1** (*endroit, pays*) in; (*direction*) to; **habiter ~ France/ville** to live in France/town; **aller ~ France/ville** to go to France/town
2 (*moment, temps*) in; **~ été/juin** in summer/June; **~ 3 jours/20 ans** in 3 days/20 years
3 (*moyen*) by; **~ avion/taxi** by plane/taxi
4 (*composition*) made of; **c'est ~ verre** it's (made of) glass; **un collier ~ argent** a silver necklace; **~ 2 volumes/une pièce** in 2 volumes/one piece
5 (*description, état*): **une femme (habillée) ~ rouge** a woman (dressed) in red; **peindre qch ~ rouge** to paint sth red; **~ T/étoile** T-/star-shaped; **~ chemise/chaussettes** in one's shirt sleeves/socks: **~ soldat** as a soldier; **~ civil** in civilian clothes; **cassé ~ plusieurs morceaux** broken into several pieces; **~ réparation** being repaired, under repair; **~ vacances** on holiday; **~ bonne santé** healthy, in good health; **~ deuil** in mourning; **le même ~ plus grand** the same but *ou* only bigger
6 (*avec gérondif*) while; on; **~ dormant** while sleeping, as one sleeps; **~ sortant** on going out, as he *etc* went out; **sortir ~ courant** to run out; **~ apprenant la nouvelle, il s'est évanoui** he fainted at the news *ou* when he heard the news
7 (*matière*): **fort ~ math** good at maths; **expert ~** expert in
8 (*conformité*): **~ tant que** as; **~ bon politicien, il ...** good politician that he is, he ..., like a good *ou* true politician, he ...; **je te parle ~ ami** I'm talking to you as a friend
♦ *pron* **1** (*indéfini*): **j'~ ai/veux** I have/want some; **~ as-tu?** have you got any?; **je n'~ veux pas** I don't want any; **j'~ ai 2** I've got 2; **combien y ~ a-t-il?** how many (of them) are there?; **j'~ ai assez** I've got enough (of it *ou* them); (*j'en ai marre*) I've had enough; **où ~ étais-je?** where was I?
2 (*provenance*) from there; **j'~ viens** I've come from there
3 (*cause*): **il ~ est malade/perd le sommeil** he is ill/can't sleep because of it
4 (*de la part de*): **elle ~ est aimée** she is loved by him (*ou* them *etc*)
5 (*complément de nom, d'adjectif, de verbe*): **j'~ connais les dangers** I know its *ou* the dangers; **j'~ suis fier/ai besoin** I am proud of it/need it; **il ~ est ainsi** *ou* **de même pour moi** it's the same for me, same here.

ENA [ena] *sigle f* (= *École nationale d'administration*) *grande école for training civil servants.*
énarque [enaʀk(ə)] *nm/f* former ENA student.
encablure [ɑ̃kablyʀ] *nf* (*NAVIG*) cable's length.
encadrement [ɑ̃kɑdʀəmɑ̃] *nm* framing; training; (*de porte*) frame; **~ du crédit** credit restrictions.
encadrer [ɑ̃kɑdʀe] *vt* (*tableau, image*) to frame; (*fig: entourer*) to surround; (*personnel, soldats etc*) to train; (*COMM: crédit*) to restrict.
encadreur [ɑ̃kɑdʀœʀ] *nm* (picture) framer.
encaisse [ɑ̃kɛs] *nf* cash in hand; **~ or/métallique** gold/gold and silver reserves.
encaissé, e [ɑ̃kese] *adj* (*vallée*) steep-sided; (*rivière*) with steep banks.
encaisser [ɑ̃kese] *vt* (*chèque*) to cash; (*argent*) to collect; (*fig: coup, défaite*) to take.
encaisseur [ɑ̃kɛsœʀ] *nm* collector (*of debts etc*).
encan [ɑ̃kɑ̃]: **à l'~** *adv* by auction.
encanailler [ɑ̃kanɑje]: **s'~** *vi* to become vulgar *ou* common; to mix with the riffraff.
encart [ɑ̃kaʀ] *nm* insert; **~ publicitaire** publicity insert.
encarter [ɑ̃kaʀte] *vt* to insert.
en-cas [ɑ̃kɑ] *nm inv* snack.
encastrable [ɑ̃kastʀabl(ə)] *adj* (*four, élément*) that can be built in.
encastré, e [ɑ̃kastʀe] *adj* (*four, baignoire*) built-in.
encastrer [ɑ̃kastʀe] *vt*: **~ qch dans** (*mur*) to embed sth in(to); (*boîtier*) to fit sth into; **s'~ dans** to fit into; (*heurter*) to crash into.
encaustiquage [ɑ̃kɔstikaʒ] *nm* polishing, waxing.
encaustique [ɑ̃kɔstik] *nf* polish, wax.
encaustiquer [ɑ̃kɔstike] *vt* to polish, wax.
enceinte [ɑ̃sɛ̃t] *adj f*: **~ (de 6 mois)** (6 months) pregnant ♦ *nf* (*mur*) wall; (*espace*) enclosure; **~ (acoustique)** speaker.
encens [ɑ̃sɑ̃] *nm* incense.
encenser [ɑ̃sɑ̃se] *vt* to (in)cense; (*fig*) to praise to the skies.
encensoir [ɑ̃sɑ̃swaʀ] *nm* thurible (*BRIT*), censer.
encéphalogramme [ɑ̃sefalɔgʀam] *nm* encephalogram.
encercler [ɑ̃sɛʀkle] *vt* to surround.
enchaîné [ɑ̃ʃene] *nm* (*CINÉ*) link shot.
enchaînement [ɑ̃ʃɛnmɑ̃] *nm* (*fig*) linking.
enchaîner [ɑ̃ʃene] *vt* to chain up; (*mouvements, séquences*) to link (together) ♦ *vi* to carry on.
enchanté, e [ɑ̃ʃɑ̃te] *adj* (*ravi*) delighted; (*ensorcelé*) enchanted; **~ (de faire votre connaissance)** pleased to meet you, how do you do?

enchantement [ɑ̃ʃɑ̃tmɑ̃] *nm* delight; (*magie*) enchantment; **comme par** ~ as if by magic.
enchanter [ɑ̃ʃɑ̃te] *vt* to delight.
enchanteur, teresse [ɑ̃ʃɑ̃tœʀ, -tʀɛs] *adj* enchanting.
enchâsser [ɑ̃ʃɑse] *vt*: ~ **qch (dans)** to set sth (in).
enchère [ɑ̃ʃɛʀ] *nf* bid; **faire une** ~ to (make a) bid; **mettre/vendre aux** ~**s** to put up for (sale by)/sell by auction; **les** ~**s montent** the bids are rising; **faire monter les** ~**s** (*fig*) to raise the bidding.
enchérir [ɑ̃ʃeʀiʀ] *vi*: ~ **sur qn** (*aux enchères, aussi fig*) to outbid sb.
enchérisseur, euse [ɑ̃ʃeʀisœʀ, -øz] *nm/f* bidder.
enchevêtrement [ɑ̃ʃvɛtʀəmɑ̃] *nm* tangle.
enchevêtrer [ɑ̃ʃvetʀe] *vt* to tangle (up).
enclave [ɑ̃klav] *nf* enclave.
enclaver [ɑ̃klave] *vt* to enclose, hem in.
enclencher [ɑ̃klɑ̃ʃe] *vt* (*mécanisme*) to engage; (*fig: affaire*) to set in motion; **s'**~ *vi* to engage.
enclin, e [ɑ̃klɛ̃, -in] *adj*: ~ **à qch/à faire** inclined *ou* prone to sth/to do.
enclore [ɑ̃klɔʀ] *vt* to enclose.
enclos [ɑ̃klo] *nm* enclosure; (*clôture*) fence.
enclume [ɑ̃klym] *nf* anvil.
encoche [ɑ̃kɔʃ] *nf* notch.
encoder [ɑ̃kɔde] *vt* to encode.
encodeur [ɑ̃kɔdœʀ] *nm* encoder.
encoignure [ɑ̃kɔɲyʀ] *nf* corner.
encoller [ɑ̃kɔle] *vt* to paste.
encolure [ɑ̃kɔlyʀ] *nf* (*tour de cou*) collar size; (*col, cou*) neck.
encombrant, e [ɑ̃kɔ̃bʀɑ̃, -ɑ̃t] *adj* cumbersome, bulky.
encombre [ɑ̃kɔ̃bʀ(ə)]: **sans** ~ *adv* without mishap *ou* incident.
encombré, e [ɑ̃kɔ̃bʀe] *adj* (*pièce, passage*) cluttered; (*lignes téléphoniques*) engaged; (*marché*) saturated.
encombrement [ɑ̃kɔ̃bʀəmɑ̃] *nm* (*d'un lieu*) cluttering (up); (*d'un objet: dimensions*) bulk.
encombrer [ɑ̃kɔ̃bʀe] *vt* to clutter (up); (*gêner*) to hamper; **s'**~ **de** (*bagages etc*) to load *ou* burden o.s. with; ~ **le passage** to block *ou* obstruct the way.
encontre [ɑ̃kɔ̃tʀ(ə)]: **à l'**~ **de** *prép* against, counter to.
encorbellement [ɑ̃kɔʀbɛlmɑ̃] *nm*: **fenêtre en** ~ oriel window.
encorder [ɑ̃kɔʀde] *vt*: **s'**~ (*ALPINISME*) to rope up.

MOT-CLÉ

encore [ɑ̃kɔʀ] *adv* **1** (*continuation*) still; **il y travaille** ~ he's still working on it; **pas** ~ not yet
2 (*de nouveau*) again; **j'irai** ~ **demain** I'll go again tomorrow; ~ **une fois** (once) again; ~ **un effort** one last effort; ~ **deux jours** two more days
3 (*intensif*) even, still; ~ **plus fort/mieux** even louder/better, louder/better still; **hier** ~ even yesterday; **non seulement ..., mais** ~ ... not only ..., but also ...; ~**!** (*insatisfaction*) not again!; **quoi** ~**?** what now?
4 (*restriction*) even so *ou* then, only; ~ **pourrais-je le faire si ...** even so, I might be able to do it if ...; **si** ~ if only
encore que *conj* although.

encourageant, e [ɑ̃kuʀaʒɑ̃, -ɑ̃t] *adj* encouraging.
encouragement [ɑ̃kuʀaʒmɑ̃] *nm* encouragement; (*récompense*) incentive.
encourager [ɑ̃kuʀaʒe] *vt* to encourage; ~ **qn à faire qch** to encourage sb to do sth.
encourir [ɑ̃kuʀiʀ] *vt* to incur.
encrasser [ɑ̃kʀase] *vt* to foul up; (*AUTO etc*) to soot up.
encre [ɑ̃kʀ(ə)] *nf* ink; ~ **de Chine** Indian ink; ~ **indélébile** indelible ink; ~ **sympathique** invisible ink.
encrer [ɑ̃kʀe] *vt* to ink.
encreur [ɑ̃kʀœʀ] *adj m*: **rouleau** ~ inking roller.
encrier [ɑ̃kʀije] *nm* inkwell.
encroûter [ɑ̃kʀute]: **s'**~ *vi* (*fig*) to get into a rut, get set in one's ways.
encyclique [ɑ̃siklik] *nf* encyclical.
encyclopédie [ɑ̃siklɔpedi] *nf* encyclopaedia (*BRIT*), encyclopedia (*US*).
encyclopédique [ɑ̃siklɔpedik] *adj* encyclopaedic (*BRIT*), encyclopedic (*US*).
endémique [ɑ̃demik] *adj* endemic.
endetté, e [ɑ̃dete] *adj* in debt; (*fig*): **très** ~ **envers qn** deeply indebted to sb.
endettement [ɑ̃dɛtmɑ̃] *nm* debts *pl*.
endetter [ɑ̃dete] *vt*, **s'**~ *vi* to get into debt.
endeuiller [ɑ̃dœje] *vt* to plunge into mourning; **manifestation endeuillée par** event over which a tragic shadow was cast by.
endiablé, e [ɑ̃djɑble] *adj* furious; (*enfant*) boisterous.
endiguer [ɑ̃dige] *vt* to dyke (up); (*fig*) to check, hold back.
endimancher [ɑ̃dimɑ̃ʃe] *vt*: **s'**~ to put on one's Sunday best; **avoir l'air endimanché** to be all done up to the nines (*fam*).
endive [ɑ̃div] *nf* chicory *no pl*.
endocrine [ɑ̃dɔkʀin] *adj f*: **glande** ~ endocrine (gland).
endoctrinement [ɑ̃dɔktʀinmɑ̃] *nm* indoctrination.
endoctriner [ɑ̃dɔktʀine] *vt* to indoctrinate.
endolori, e [ɑ̃dɔlɔʀi] *adj* painful.
endommager [ɑ̃dɔmaʒe] *vt* to damage.
endormant, e [ɑ̃dɔʀmɑ̃, -ɑ̃t] *adj* dull, boring.
endormi, e [ɑ̃dɔʀmi] *pp de* **endormir** ♦ *adj* (*personne*) asleep; (*fig: indolent, lent*) sluggish; (*engourdi: main, pied*) numb.
endormir [ɑ̃dɔʀmiʀ] *vt* to put to sleep; (*suj: chaleur etc*) to send to sleep; (*MÉD: dent, nerf*)

to anaesthetize; (*fig: soupçons*) to allay; **s'~** *vi* to fall asleep, go to sleep.
endoscope [ɑ̃dɔskɔp] *nm* (*MÉD*) endoscope.
endoscopie [ɑ̃dɔskɔpi] *nf* endoscopy.
endosser [ɑ̃dose] *vt* (*responsabilité*) to take, shoulder; (*chèque*) to endorse; (*uniforme, tenue*) to put on, don.
endroit [ɑ̃dʀwa] *nm* place; (*localité*): **les gens de l'~** the local people; (*opposé à l'envers*) right side; **à cet ~** in this place; **à l'~** right side out; the right way up; (*vêtement*) the right way out; **à l'~ de** *prép* regarding, with regard to; **par ~s** in places.
enduire [ɑ̃dɥiʀ] *vt* to coat; **~ qch de** to coat sth with.
enduit, e [ɑ̃dɥi, -it] *pp de* **enduire** ♦ *nm* coating.
endurance [ɑ̃dyʀɑ̃s] *nf* endurance.
endurant, e [ɑ̃dyʀɑ̃, -ɑ̃t] *adj* tough, hardy.
endurcir [ɑ̃dyʀsiʀ] *vt* (*physiquement*) to toughen; (*moralement*) to harden; **s'~** *vi* to become tougher; to become hardened.
endurer [ɑ̃dyʀe] *vt* to endure, bear.
énergétique [enɛʀʒetik] *adj* (*ressources etc*) energy *cpd*; (*aliment*) energizing.
énergie [enɛʀʒi] *nf* (*PHYSIQUE*) energy; (*TECH*) power; (*fig: physique*) energy; (*: morale*) vigour, spirit; **~ éolienne/solaire** wind/solar power.
énergique [enɛʀʒik] *adj* energetic; vigorous; (*mesures*) drastic, stringent.
énergiquement [enɛʀʒikmɑ̃] *adv* energetically; drastically.
énergisant, e [enɛʀʒizɑ̃, -ɑ̃t] *adj* energizing.
énergumène [enɛʀgymɛn] *nm* rowdy character *ou* customer.
énervant, e [enɛʀvɑ̃, -ɑ̃t] *adj* irritating.
énervé, e [enɛʀve] *adj* nervy, on edge; (*agacé*) irritated.
énervement [enɛʀvəmɑ̃] *nm* nerviness; irritation.
énerver [enɛʀve] *vt* to irritate, annoy; **s'~** *vi* to get excited, get worked up.
enfance [ɑ̃fɑ̃s] *nf* (*âge*) childhood; (*fig*) infancy; (*enfants*) children *pl*; **c'est l'~ de l'art** it's child's play; **petite ~** infancy; **souvenir/ami d'~** childhood memory/friend; **retomber en ~** to lapse into one's second childhood.
enfant [ɑ̃fɑ̃] *nm/f* child (*pl* children); **~ adoptif/naturel** adopted/natural child; **bon ~** *adj* good-natured, easy-going; **~ de chœur** *nm* (*REL*) altar boy; **~ prodige** child prodigy; **~ unique** only child.
enfanter [ɑ̃fɑ̃te] *vi* to give birth ♦ *vt* to give birth to.
enfantillage [ɑ̃fɑ̃tijaʒ] *nm* (*péj*) childish behaviour *no pl*.
enfantin, e [ɑ̃fɑ̃tɛ̃, -in] *adj* childlike; (*péj*) childish; (*langage*) child *cpd*.
enfer [ɑ̃fɛʀ] *nm* hell; **allure/bruit d'~** horrendous speed/noise.
enfermer [ɑ̃fɛʀme] *vt* to shut up; (*à clef, interner*) to lock up; **s'~** to shut o.s. away; **s'~ à clé** to lock o.s. in; **s'~ dans la solitude/le mutisme** to retreat into solitude/silence.
enferrer [ɑ̃feʀe]: **s'~** *vi*: **s'~ dans** to tangle o.s. up in.
enfiévré, e [ɑ̃fjevʀe] *adj* (*fig*) feverish.
enfilade [ɑ̃filad] *nf*: **une ~ de** a series *ou* line of; **prendre des rues en ~** to cross directly from one street into the next.
enfiler [ɑ̃file] *vt* (*vêtement*): **~ qch** to slip sth on, slip into sth; (*insérer*): **~ qch dans** to stick sth into; (*rue, couloir*) to take; (*perles*) to string; (*aiguille*) to thread; **s'~ dans** to disappear into.
enfin [ɑ̃fɛ̃] *adv* at last; (*en énumérant*) lastly; (*de restriction, résignation*) still; (*eh bien*) well; (*pour conclure*) in a word.
enflammé, e [ɑ̃flame] *adj* (*torche, allumette*) burning; (*MÉD: plaie*) inflamed; (*fig: nature, discours, déclaration*) fiery.
enflammer [ɑ̃flame] *vt* to set fire to; (*MÉD*) to inflame; **s'~** *vi* to catch fire; to become inflamed.
enflé, e [ɑ̃fle] *adj* swollen; (*péj: style*) bombastic, turgid.
enfler [ɑ̃fle] *vi* to swell (up); **s'~** *vi* to swell.
enflure [ɑ̃flyʀ] *nf* swelling.
enfoncé, e [ɑ̃fɔ̃se] *adj* staved-in, smashed-in; (*yeux*) deep-set.
enfoncement [ɑ̃fɔ̃smɑ̃] *nm* (*recoin*) nook.
enfoncer [ɑ̃fɔ̃se] *vt* (*clou*) to drive in; (*faire pénétrer*): **~ qch dans** to push (*ou* drive) sth into; (*forcer: porte*) to break open; (*: plancher*) to cause to cave in; (*défoncer: côtes etc*) to smash; (*fam: surpasser*) to lick, beat (hollow) ♦ *vi* (*dans la vase etc*) to sink in; (*sol, surface porteuse*) to give way; **s'~** *vi* to sink; **s'~ dans** to sink into; (*forêt, ville*) to disappear into; **~ un chapeau sur la tête** to cram *ou* jam a hat on one's head; **~ qn dans la dette** to drag sb into debt.
enfouir [ɑ̃fwiʀ] *vt* (*dans le sol*) to bury; (*dans un tiroir etc*) to tuck away; **s'~ dans/sous** to bury o.s. in/under.
enfourcher [ɑ̃fuʀʃe] *vt* to mount; **~ son dada** (*fig*) to get on one's hobby-horse.
enfourner [ɑ̃fuʀne] *vt* to put in the oven; (*poterie*) to put in the kiln; **~ qch dans** to shove *ou* stuff sth into; **s'~ dans** (*suj: personne*) to dive into.
enfreignais [ɑ̃fʀeɲɛ] *etc vb voir* **enfreindre**.
enfreindre [ɑ̃fʀɛ̃dʀ(ə)] *vt* to infringe, break.
enfuir [ɑ̃fɥiʀ]: **s'~** *vi* to run away *ou* off.
enfumer [ɑ̃fyme] *vt* to smoke out.
enfuyais [ɑ̃fɥijɛ] *etc vb voir* **enfuir**.
engagé, e [ɑ̃gaʒe] *adj* (*littérature etc*) engagé, committed.
engageant, e [ɑ̃gaʒɑ̃, -ɑ̃t] *adj* attractive, appealing.
engagement [ɑ̃gaʒmɑ̃] *nm* taking on, engaging; starting; investing; (*promesse*) commitment; (*MIL: combat*) engagement; (*: recrute-*

ment) enlistment; (*SPORT*) entry; **prendre l'~ de faire** to undertake to do; **sans ~** (*COMM*) without obligation.
engager [ɑ̃gaʒe] *vt* (*embaucher*) to take on, engage; (*commencer*) to start; (*lier*) to bind, commit; (*impliquer, entraîner*) to involve; (*investir*) to invest, lay out; (*faire intervenir*) to engage; (*SPORT: concurrents, chevaux*) to enter; (*inciter*): **~ qn à faire** to urge sb to do; (*faire pénétrer*): **~ qch dans** to insert sth into; **~ qn à qch** to urge sth on sb; **s'~** to get taken on; (*MIL*) to enlist; (*promettre, politiquement*) to commit o.s.; (*débuter*) to start (up); **s'~ à faire** to undertake to do; **s'~ dans** (*rue, passage*) to enter, turn into; (*s'emboîter*) to engage *ou* fit into; (*fig: affaire, discussion*) to enter into, embark on.
engazonner [ɑ̃gɑzɔne] *vt* to turf.
engeance [ɑ̃ʒɑ̃s] *nf* mob.
engelure [ɑ̃ʒlyʀ] *nf* chilblain.
engendrer [ɑ̃ʒɑ̃dʀe] *vt* to father; (*fig*) to create, breed.
engin [ɑ̃ʒɛ̃] *nm* machine; instrument; vehicle; (*péj*) gadget; (*AVIAT: avion*) aircraft *inv*; (*: missile*) missile; **~ blindé** armoured vehicle; **~ (explosif)** (explosive) device; **~s (spéciaux)** missiles.
englober [ɑ̃glɔbe] *vt* to include.
engloutir [ɑ̃glutiʀ] *vt* to swallow up; (*fig: dépenses*) to devour; **s'~** to be engulfed.
englué, e [ɑ̃glye] sticky.
engoncé, e [ɑ̃gɔ̃se] *adj*: **~ dans** cramped in.
engorgement [ɑ̃gɔʀʒəmɑ̃] *nm* blocking; (*MÉD*) engorgement.
engorger [ɑ̃gɔʀʒe] *vt* to obstruct, block; **s'~** *vi* to become blocked.
engouement [ɑ̃gumɑ̃] *nm* (sudden) passion.
engouffrer [ɑ̃gufʀe] *vt* to swallow up, devour; **s'~ dans** to rush into.
engourdi, e [ɑ̃guʀdi] *adj* numb.
engourdir [ɑ̃guʀdiʀ] *vt* to numb; (*fig*) to dull, blunt; **s'~** *vi* to go numb.
engrais [ɑ̃gʀɛ] *nm* manure; **~ (chimique)** (chemical) fertilizer; **~ organique/inorganique** organic/inorganic fertilizer.
engraisser [ɑ̃gʀese] *vt* to fatten (up); (*terre: fertiliser*) to fertilize ♦ *vi* (*péj*) to get fat(ter).
engranger [ɑ̃gʀɑ̃ʒe] *vt* (*foin*) to bring in; (*fig*) to store away.
engrenage [ɑ̃gʀənaʒ] *nm* gears *pl*, gearing; (*fig*) chain.
engueuler [ɑ̃gœle] *vt* (*fam*) to bawl at *ou* out.
enguirlander [ɑ̃giʀlɑ̃de] *vt* (*fam*) to give sb a bawling out, bawl at.
enhardir [ɑ̃aʀdiʀ]: **s'~** *vi* to grow bolder.
ENI [eni] *sigle f* = **école normale (d'instituteurs)**.
énième [enjɛm] *adj* = **nième**.
énigmatique [enigmatik] *adj* enigmatic.
énigmatiquement [enigmatikmɑ̃] *adv* enigmatically.
énigme [enigm(ə)] *nf* riddle.
enivrant, e [ɑ̃nivʀɑ̃, -ɑ̃t] *adj* intoxicating.
enivrer [ɑ̃nivʀe] *vt*: **s'~** to get drunk; **s'~ de** (*fig*) to become intoxicated with.
enjambée [ɑ̃ʒɑ̃be] *nf* stride; **d'une ~** with one stride.
enjamber [ɑ̃ʒɑ̃be] *vt* to stride over; (*suj: pont etc*) to span, straddle.
enjeu, x [ɑ̃ʒø] *nm* stakes *pl*.
enjoindre [ɑ̃ʒwɛ̃dʀ(ə)] *vt*: **~ à qn de faire** to enjoin *ou* order sb to do.
enjôler [ɑ̃ʒole] *vt* to coax, wheedle.
enjôleur, euse [ɑ̃ʒolœʀ, -øz] *adj* (*sourire, paroles*) winning.
enjolivement [ɑ̃ʒɔlivmɑ̃] *nm* embellishment.
enjoliver [ɑ̃ʒɔlive] *vt* to embellish.
enjoliveur [ɑ̃ʒɔlivœʀ] *nm* (*AUTO*) hub cap.
enjoué, e [ɑ̃ʒwe] *adj* playful.
enlacer [ɑ̃lɑse] *vt* (*étreindre*) to embrace, hug; (*suj: lianes*) to wind round, entwine.
enlaidir [ɑ̃lediʀ] *vt* to make ugly ♦ *vi* to become ugly.
enlevé, e [ɑ̃lve] *adj* (*morceau de musique*) played brightly.
enlèvement [ɑ̃lɛvmɑ̃] *nm* removal; (*rapt*) abduction, kidnapping; **l'~ des ordures ménagères** refuse collection.
enlever [ɑ̃lve] *vt* (*ôter: gén*) to remove; (*: vêtement, lunettes*) to take off; (*: MÉD: organe*) to remove; (*emporter: ordures etc*) to collect, take away; (*kidnapper*) to abduct, kidnap; (*obtenir: prix, contrat*) to win; (*MIL: position*) to take; (*morceau de piano etc*) to execute with spirit *ou* brio; (*prendre*): **~ qch à qn** to take sth (away) from sb; **s'~** *vi* (*tache*) to come out *ou* off; **la maladie qui nous l'a enlevé** (*euphémisme*) the illness which took him from us.
enliser [ɑ̃lize]: **s'~** *vi* to sink, get stuck; (*dialogue etc*) to get bogged down.
enluminure [ɑ̃lyminyʀ] *nf* illumination.
ENM *sigle f* (= *École nationale de la magistrature*) *grande école for law students*.
enneigé, e [ɑ̃neʒe] *adj* snowy; (*col*) snowed-up; (*maison*) snowed-in.
enneigement [ɑ̃nɛʒmɑ̃] *nm* depth of snow, snowfall; **bulletin d'~** snow report.
ennemi, e [ɛnmi] *adj* hostile; (*MIL*) enemy *cpd* ♦ *nm/f* enemy; **être ~ de** to be strongly averse *ou* opposed to.
ennième [ɛnjɛm] *adj* = **nième**.
ennoblir [ɑ̃nɔbliʀ] *vt* to ennoble.
ennui [ɑ̃nɥi] *nm* (*lassitude*) boredom; (*difficulté*) trouble *no pl*; **avoir des ~s** to have problems; **s'attirer des ~s** to cause problems for o.s.
ennuie [ɑ̃nɥi] *etc vb voir* **ennuyer**.
ennuyé, e [ɑ̃nɥije] *adj* (*air, personne*) preoccupied, worried.
ennuyer [ɑ̃nɥije] *vt* to bother; (*lasser*) to bore; **s'~** *vi* to be bored; **s'~ de** (*regretter*) to miss; **si cela ne vous ennuie pas** if it's no trouble to you.
ennuyeux, euse [ɑ̃nɥijø, -øz] *adj* boring, tedious; (*agaçant*) annoying.

énoncé [enɔ̃se] *nm* terms *pl*; wording; (*LING*) utterance.
énoncer [enɔ̃se] *vt* to say, express; (*conditions*) to set out, lay down, state.
énonciation [enɔ̃sjɑsjɔ̃] *nf* statement.
enorgueillir [ɑ̃nɔʀgœjiʀ]: **s'~ de** *vt* to pride o.s. on; to boast.
énorme [enɔʀm(ə)] *adj* enormous, huge.
énormément [enɔʀmemɑ̃] *adv* enormously, tremendously; **~ de neige/gens** an enormous amount of snow/number of people.
énormité [enɔʀmite] *nf* enormity, hugeness; (*propos*) outrageous remark.
en part. *abr* (= *en particulier*) esp.
enquérir [ɑ̃keʀiʀ]: **s'~ de** *vt* to inquire about.
enquête [ɑ̃kɛt] *nf* (*de journaliste, de police*) investigation; (*judiciaire, administrative*) inquiry; (*sondage d'opinion*) survey.
enquêter [ɑ̃kete] *vi* to investigate; to hold an inquiry; (*faire un sondage*): **~ (sur)** to do a survey (on), carry out an opinion poll (on).
enquêteur, euse *ou* **trice** [ɑ̃kɛtœʀ, -øz, -tʀis] *nm/f* officer in charge of an investigation; person conducting a survey; pollster.
enquiers, enquière [ɑ̃kjɛʀ] *etc vb voir* **enquérir**.
enquiquiner [ɑ̃kikine] *vt* to rile, irritate.
enquis, e [ɑ̃ki, -iz] *pp de* **enquérir**.
enraciné, e [ɑ̃ʀasine] *adj* deep-rooted.
enragé, e [ɑ̃ʀaʒe] *adj* (*MÉD*) rabid, with rabies; (*furieux*) furiously angry; (*fig*) fanatical; **~ de** wild about.
enrageant, e [ɑ̃ʀaʒɑ̃, -ɑ̃t] *adj* infuriating.
enrager [ɑ̃ʀaʒe] *vi* to be furious, be in a rage; **faire ~ qn** to make sb wild with anger.
enrayer [ɑ̃ʀeje] *vt* to check, stop; **s'~** *vi* (*arme à feu*) to jam.
enrégimenter [ɑ̃ʀeʒimɑ̃te] *vt* (*péj*) to enlist.
enregistrement [ɑ̃ʀʒistʀəmɑ̃] *nm* recording; (*ADMIN*) registration; **~ des bagages** (*à l'aéroport*) baggage check-in; **~ magnétique** tape-recording.
enregistrer [ɑ̃ʀʒistʀe] *vt* (*MUS, INFORM etc*) to record; (*remarquer, noter*) to note, record; (*COMM: commande*) to note, enter; (*fig: mémoriser*) to make a mental note of; (*ADMIN*) to register; (*aussi:* **faire ~**: *bagages: par train*) to register; (*: à l'aéroport*) to check in.
enregistreur, euse [ɑ̃ʀʒistʀœʀ, -øz] *adj* (*machine*) recording *cpd* ♦ *nm* (*appareil*): **~ de vol** (*AVIAT*) flight recorder.
enrhumé, e [ɑ̃ʀyme] *adj*: **il est ~** he has a cold.
enrhumer [ɑ̃ʀyme]: **s'~** *vi* to catch a cold.
enrichir [ɑ̃ʀiʃiʀ] *vt* to make rich(er); (*fig*) to enrich; **s'~** to get rich(er).
enrichissant, e [ɑ̃ʀiʃisɑ̃, -ɑ̃t] *adj* instructive.
enrichissement [ɑ̃ʀiʃismɑ̃] *nm* enrichment.
enrober [ɑ̃ʀɔbe] *vt*: **~ qch de** to coat sth with; (*fig*) to wrap sth up in.
enrôlement [ɑ̃ʀolmɑ̃] *nm* enlistment.
enrôler [ɑ̃ʀole] *vt* to enlist; **s'~ (dans)** to enlist (in).
enroué, e [ɑ̃ʀwe] *adj* hoarse.
enrouer [ɑ̃ʀwe]: **s'~** *vi* to go hoarse.
enrouler [ɑ̃ʀule] *vt* (*fil, corde*) to wind (up); **s'~** to coil up; **~ qch autour de** to wind sth (a)round.
enrouleur, euse [ɑ̃ʀulœʀ, -øz] *adj* (*TECH*) winding ♦ *nm voir* **ceinture**.
enrubanné, e [ɑ̃ʀybane] *adj* trimmed with ribbon.
ENS *sigle f* = **école normale supérieure**.
ensabler [ɑ̃sɑble] *vt* (*port, canal*) to silt up, sand up; (*embarcation*) to strand (on a sandbank); **s'~** *vi* to silt up; to get stranded.
ensacher [ɑ̃saʃe] *vt* to pack into bags.
ENSAM *sigle f* (= *École nationale supérieure des arts et métiers*) *grande école for engineering students*.
ensanglanté, e [ɑ̃sɑ̃glɑ̃te] *adj* covered with blood.
enseignant, e [ɑ̃sɛɲɑ̃, -ɑ̃t] *adj* teaching ♦ *nm/f* teacher.
enseigne [ɑ̃sɛɲ] *nf* sign ♦ *nm*: **~ de vaisseau** lieutenant; **à telle ~ que** so much so that; **être logés à la même ~** (*fig*) to be in the same boat; **~ lumineuse** neon sign.
enseignement [ɑ̃sɛɲmɑ̃] *nm* teaching; **~ ménager** home economics; **~ primaire** primary (*BRIT*) *ou* grade school (*US*) education; **~ secondaire** secondary (*BRIT*) *ou* high school (*US*) education.
enseigner [ɑ̃seɲe] *vt, vi* to teach; **~ qch à qn/à qn que** to teach sb sth/sb that.
ensemble [ɑ̃sɑ̃bl(ə)] *adv* together ♦ *nm* (*assemblage, MATH*) set; (*totalité*): **l'~ du/de la** the whole *ou* entire; (*vêtement féminin*) ensemble, suit; (*unité, harmonie*) unity; (*résidentiel*) housing development; **aller ~** to go together; **impression/idée d'~** overall *ou* general impression/idea; **dans l'~** (*en gros*) on the whole; **dans son ~** overall, in general; **~ vocal/musical** vocal/musical ensemble.
ensemblier [ɑ̃sɑ̃blije] *nm* interior designer.
ensemencer [ɑ̃smɑ̃se] *vt* to sow.
enserrer [ɑ̃seʀe] *vt* to hug (tightly).
ENSET [ɛnsɛt] *sigle f* (= *École normale supérieure de l'enseignement technique*) *grande école for training technical teachers*.
ensevelir [ɑ̃səvliʀ] *vt* to bury.
ensilage [ɑ̃silaʒ] *nm* (*aliment*) silage.
ensoleillé, e [ɑ̃sɔleje] *adj* sunny.
ensoleillement [ɑ̃sɔlɛjmɑ̃] *nm* period *ou* hours *pl* of sunshine.
ensommeillé, e [ɑ̃sɔmeje] *adj* sleepy, drowsy.
ensorceler [ɑ̃sɔʀsəle] *vt* to enchant, bewitch.
ensuite [ɑ̃sɥit] *adv* then, next; (*plus tard*) afterwards, later; **~ de quoi** after which.
ensuivre [ɑ̃sɥivʀ(ə)]: **s'~** *vi* to follow, ensue; **il s'ensuit que** ... it follows that ...; **et tout ce qui s'ensuit** and all that goes with it.
entaché, e [ɑ̃taʃe] *adj*: **~ de** marred by; **~ de nullité** null and void.

entacher [ɑ̃taʃe] *vt* to soil.
entaille [ɑ̃taj] *nf* (*encoche*) notch; (*blessure*) cut; **se faire une** ~ to cut o.s.
entailler [ɑ̃taje] *vt* to notch; to cut; **s'~ le doigt** to cut one's finger.
entamer [ɑ̃tame] *vt* to start; (*hostilités, pourparlers*) to open; (*fig: altérer*) to make a dent in; to damage.
entartrer [ɑ̃taʀtʀe]: **s'~** *vi* to fur up; (*dents*) to become covered with plaque.
entassement [ɑ̃tɑsmɑ̃] *nm* (*tas*) pile, heap.
entasser [ɑ̃tɑse] *vt* (*empiler*) to pile up, heap up; (*tenir à l'étroit*) to cram together; **s'~** *vi* to pile up; to cram; **s'~ dans** to cram into.
entendement [ɑ̃tɑ̃dmɑ̃] *nm* understanding.
entendre [ɑ̃tɑ̃dʀ(ə)] *vt* to hear; (*comprendre*) to understand; (*vouloir dire*) to mean; (*vouloir*): ~ **être obéi/que** to intend *ou* mean to be obeyed/that; **j'ai entendu dire que** I've heard (it said) that; **je suis heureux de vous l'~ dire** I'm pleased to hear you say it; ~ **parler de** to hear of; **laisser** ~ **que, donner à** ~ **que** to let it be understood that; ~ **raison** to see sense, listen to reason; **qu'est- ce qu'il ne faut pas** ~! whatever next!; **j'ai mal entendu** I didn't catch what was said; **je vous entends très mal** I can hardly hear you; **s'~** *vi* (*sympathiser*) to get on; (*se mettre d'accord*) to agree; **s'~ à qch/à faire** (*être compétent*) to be good at sth/doing; **ça s'entend** (*est audible*) it's audible; **je m'entends** I mean; **entendons-nous!** let's be clear what we mean.
entendu, e [ɑ̃tɑ̃dy] *pp de* **entendre** ♦ *adj* (*réglé*) agreed; (*au courant: air*) knowing; **étant ~ que** since (it's understood *ou* agreed that); **(c'est)** ~ all right, agreed; **c'est** ~ (*concession*) all right, granted; **bien** ~ of course.
entente [ɑ̃tɑ̃t] *nf* (*entre amis, pays*) understanding, harmony; (*accord, traité*) agreement, understanding; **à double** ~ (*sens*) with a double meaning.
entériner [ɑ̃teʀine] *vt* to ratify, confirm.
entérite [ɑ̃teʀit] *nf* enteritis *no pl*.
enterrement [ɑ̃tɛʀmɑ̃] *nm* burying; (*cérémonie*) funeral, burial; (*cortège funèbre*) funeral procession.
enterrer [ɑ̃teʀe] *vt* to bury.
entêtant, e [ɑ̃tɛtɑ̃, -ɑ̃t] *adj* heady.
entêté, e [ɑ̃tete] *adj* stubborn.
en-tête [ɑ̃tɛt] *nm* heading; (*de papier à lettres*) letterhead; **papier à** ~ headed notepaper.
entêtement [ɑ̃tɛtmɑ̃] *nm* stubbornness.
entêter [ɑ̃tete]: **s'~** *vi*: **s'~ (à faire)** to persist (in doing).
enthousiasmant, e [ɑ̃tuzjasmɑ̃, -ɑ̃t] *adj* exciting.
enthousiasme [ɑ̃tuzjasm(ə)] *nm* enthusiasm; **avec** ~ enthusiastically.
enthousiasmé, e [ɑ̃tuzjasme] *adj* filled with enthusiasm.
enthousiasmer [ɑ̃tuzjasme] *vt* to fill with enthusiasm; **s'~ (pour qch)** to get enthusiastic (about sth).
enthousiaste [ɑ̃tuzjast(ə)] *adj* enthusiastic.
enticher [ɑ̃tiʃe]: **s'~ de** *vt* to become infatuated with.
entier, ière [ɑ̃tje, -jɛʀ] *adj* (*non entamé, en totalité*) whole; (*total, complet*) complete; (*fig: caractère*) unbending, averse to compromise ♦ *nm* (*MATH*) whole; **en** ~ totally; in its entirety; **se donner tout ~ à qch** to devote o.s. completely to sth; **lait** ~ full-cream milk; **pain** ~ wholemeal bread; **nombre** ~ whole number.
entièrement [ɑ̃tjɛʀmɑ̃] *adv* entirely, completely, wholly.
entité [ɑ̃tite] *nf* entity.
entomologie [ɑ̃tɔmɔlɔʒi] *nf* entomology.
entonner [ɑ̃tɔne] *vt* (*chanson*) to strike up.
entonnoir [ɑ̃tɔnwaʀ] *nm* (*ustensile*) funnel; (*trou*) shell-hole, crater.
entorse [ɑ̃tɔʀs(ə)] *nf* (*MÉD*) sprain; (*fig*): ~ **à la loi/au règlement** infringement of the law/rule; **se faire une ~ à la cheville/au poignet** to sprain one's ankle/wrist.
entortiller [ɑ̃tɔʀtije] *vt* (*envelopper*): ~ **qch dans/avec** to wrap sth in/with; (*enrouler*): ~ **qch autour de** to twist *ou* wind sth (a)round; (*fam*): ~ **qn** to get (a)round sb; (*: duper*) to hoodwink sb (*BRIT*), trick sb; **s'~ dans** (*draps*) to roll o.s. up in; (*fig: réponses*) to get tangled up in.
entourage [ɑ̃tuʀaʒ] *nm* circle; family (circle); (*d'une vedette etc*) entourage; (*ce qui enclôt*) surround.
entouré, e [ɑ̃tuʀe] *adj* (*recherché, admiré*) popular; ~ **de** surrounded by.
entourer [ɑ̃tuʀe] *vt* to surround; (*apporter son soutien à*) to rally round; ~ **de** to surround with; (*trait*) to encircle with; **s'~ de** to surround o.s. with; **s'~ de précautions** to take all possible precautions.
entourloupette [ɑ̃tuʀlupɛt] *nf* mean trick.
entournures [ɑ̃tuʀnyʀ] *nfpl*: **gêné aux** ~ in financial difficulties; (*fig*) a bit awkward.
entracte [ɑ̃tʀakt(ə)] *nm* interval.
entraide [ɑ̃tʀɛd] *nf* mutual aid *ou* assistance.
entraider [ɑ̃tʀede]: **s'~** *vi* to help each other.
entrailles [ɑ̃tʀɑj] *nfpl* entrails; (*humaines*) bowels.
entrain [ɑ̃tʀɛ̃] *nm* spirit; **avec** ~ (*répondre, travailler*) energetically; **faire qch sans** ~ to do sth half-heartedly *ou* without enthusiasm.
entraînant, e [ɑ̃tʀɛnɑ̃, -ɑ̃t] *adj* (*musique*) stirring, rousing.
entraînement [ɑ̃tʀɛnmɑ̃] *nm* training; (*TECH*): ~ **à chaîne/galet** chain/wheel drive; **manquer d'~** to be unfit; ~ **par ergots/friction** (*INFORM*) tractor/friction feed.
entraîner [ɑ̃tʀene] *vt* (*tirer: wagons*) to pull; (*charrier*) to carry *ou* drag along; (*TECH*) to drive; (*emmener: personne*) to take (off); (*mener à l'assaut, influencer*) to lead; (*SPORT*)

to train; (*impliquer*) to entail; (*causer*) to lead to, bring about; ~ **qn à faire** (*inciter*) to lead sb to do; **s'**~ (*SPORT*) to train; **s'**~ **à qch/à faire** to train o.s. for sth/to do.
entraîneur [ɑ̃tʀɛnœʀ] *nm* (*SPORT*) coach, trainer; (*HIPPISME*) trainer.
entraîneuse [ɑ̃tʀɛnøz] *nf* (*de bar*) hostess.
entrapercevoir [ɑ̃tʀapɛʀsəvwaʀ] *vt* to catch a glimpse of.
entrave [ɑ̃tʀav] *nf* hindrance.
entraver [ɑ̃tʀave] *vt* (*circulation*) to hold up; (*action, progrès*) to hinder, hamper.
entre [ɑ̃tʀ(ə)] *prép* between; (*parmi*) among(st); **l'un d'**~ **eux/nous** one of them/us; **le meilleur d'**~ **eux/nous** the best of them/us; **ils préfèrent rester** ~ **eux** they prefer to keep to themselves; ~ **autres (choses)** among other things; ~ **nous, ...** between ourselves ..., between you and me ...; **ils se battent** ~ **eux** they are fighting among(st) themselves.
entrebâillé, e [ɑ̃tʀəbɑje] *adj* half-open, ajar.
entrebâillement [ɑ̃tʀəbɑjmɑ̃] *nm*: **dans l'**~ **(de la porte)** in the half-open door.
entrebâiller [ɑ̃tʀəbɑje] *vt* to half open.
entrechat [ɑ̃tʀəʃa] *nm* leap.
entrechoquer [ɑ̃tʀəʃɔke]: **s'**~ *vi* to knock *ou* bang together.
entrecôte [ɑ̃tʀəkot] *nf* entrecôte *ou* rib steak.
entrecoupé, e [ɑ̃tʀəkupe] *adj* (*paroles, voix*) broken.
entrecouper [ɑ̃tʀəkupe] *vt*: ~ **qch de** to intersperse sth with; ~ **un récit/voyage de** to interrupt a story/journey with; **s'**~ (*traits, lignes*) to cut across each other.
entrecroiser [ɑ̃tʀəkʀwaze] *vt*, **s'**~ *vi* to intertwine.
entrée [ɑ̃tʀe] *nf* entrance; (*accès: au cinéma etc*) admission; (*billet*) (admission) ticket; (*CULIN*) first course; (*COMM: de marchandises*) entry; (*INFORM*) entry, input; ~**s** *nfpl*: **avoir ses** ~**s chez** *ou* **auprès de** to be a welcome visitor to; **d'**~ *adv* from the outset; **erreur d'**~ input error; **"**~ **interdite"** "no admittance *ou* entry"; ~ **des artistes** stage door; ~ **en matière** introduction; ~ **en scène** entrance; ~ **de service** service entrance.
entrefaites [ɑ̃tʀəfɛt]: **sur ces** ~ *adv* at this juncture.
entrefilet [ɑ̃tʀəfilɛ] *nm* (*article*) paragraph, short report.
entregent [ɑ̃tʀəʒɑ̃] *nm*: **avoir de l'**~ to have an easy manner.
entre-jambes [ɑ̃tʀəʒɑ̃b] *nm inv* crotch.
entrelacement [ɑ̃tʀəlasmɑ̃] *nm*: **un** ~ **de ...** a network of ....
entrelacer [ɑ̃tʀəlase] *vt*, **s'**~ *vi* to intertwine.
entrelarder [ɑ̃tʀəlaʀde] *vt* to lard; (*fig*): **entrelardé de** interspersed with.
entremêler [ɑ̃tʀəmele] *vt*: ~ **qch de** to (inter)mingle sth with.
entremets [ɑ̃tʀəmɛ] *nm* (cream) dessert.
entremetteur, euse [ɑ̃tʀəmɛtœʀ, -øz] *nm/f* go-between.
entremettre [ɑ̃tʀəmɛtʀ(ə)]: **s'**~ *vi* to intervene.
entremise [ɑ̃tʀəmiz] *nf* intervention; **par l'**~ **de** through.
entrepont [ɑ̃tʀəpɔ̃] *nm* steerage; **dans l'**~ in steerage.
entreposer [ɑ̃tʀəpoze] *vt* to store, put into storage.
entrepôt [ɑ̃tʀəpo] *nm* warehouse.
entreprenant, e [ɑ̃tʀəpʀənɑ̃, -ɑ̃t] *vb voir* **entreprendre** ♦ *adj* (*actif*) enterprising; (*trop galant*) forward.
entreprendre [ɑ̃tʀəpʀɑ̃dʀ(ə)] *vt* (*se lancer dans*) to undertake; (*commencer*) to begin *ou* start (upon); (*personne*) to buttonhole; ~ **qn sur un sujet** to tackle sb on a subject; ~ **de faire** to undertake to do.
entrepreneur [ɑ̃tʀəpʀənœʀ] *nm*: ~ **(en bâtiment)** (building) contractor; ~ **de pompes funèbres** funeral director, undertaker.
entreprenne [ɑ̃tʀəpʀɛn] *etc vb voir* **entreprendre**.
entrepris, e [ɑ̃tʀəpʀi, -iz] *pp de* **entreprendre** ♦ *nf* (*société*) firm, business; (*action*) undertaking, venture.
entrer [ɑ̃tʀe] *vi* to go (*ou* come) in, enter ♦ *vt* (*INFORM*) to input, enter; **(faire)** ~ **qch dans** to get sth into; ~ **dans** (*gén*) to enter; (*pièce*) to go (*ou* come) into, enter; (*club*) to join; (*heurter*) to run into; (*partager: vues, craintes de qn*) to share; (*être une composante de*) to go into; (*faire partie de*) to form part of; ~ **au couvent** to enter a convent; ~ **à l'hôpital** to go into hospital; ~ **dans le système** (*INFORM*) to log in; ~ **en fureur** to become angry; ~ **en ébullition** to start to boil; ~ **en scène** to come on stage; **laisser** ~ **qn/qch** to let sb/sth in; **faire** ~ (*visiteur*) to show in.
entresol [ɑ̃tʀəsɔl] *nm* entresol, mezzanine.
entre-temps [ɑ̃tʀətɑ̃] *adv* meanwhile, (in the) meantime.
entretenir [ɑ̃tʀətniʀ] *vt* to maintain; (*amitié*) to keep alive; (*famille, maîtresse*) to support, keep; ~ **qn (de)** to speak to sb (about); **s'**~ **(de)** to converse (about); ~ **qn dans l'erreur** to let sb remain in ignorance.
entretenu, e [ɑ̃tʀətny] *pp de* **entretenir** ♦ *adj* (*femme*) kept; **bien/mal** ~ (*maison, jardin*) well/badly kept.
entretien [ɑ̃tʀətjɛ̃] *nm* maintenance; (*discussion*) discussion, talk; (*audience*) interview; **frais d'**~ maintenance charges.
entretiendrai [ɑ̃tʀətjɛ̃dʀe], **entretiens** [ɑ̃tʀətjɛ̃] *etc vb voir* **entretenir**.
entretuer [ɑ̃tʀətɥe]: **s'**~ *vi* to kill one another.
entreverrai [ɑ̃tʀəvɛʀe], **entrevit** [ɑ̃tʀəvi] *etc vb voir* **entrevoir**.
entrevoir [ɑ̃tʀəvwaʀ] *vt* (*à peine*) to make out; (*brièvement*) to catch a glimpse of.

entrevu, e [ɑ̃tʀəvy] *pp de* **entrevoir** ♦ *nf* meeting; (*audience*) interview.
entrouvert, e [ɑ̃tʀuvɛʀ, -ɛʀt(ə)] *pp de* **entrouvrir** ♦ *adj* half-open.
entrouvrir [ɑ̃tʀuvʀiʀ] *vt*, **s'~** *vi* to half open.
énumération [enymeʀɑsjɔ̃] *nf* enumeration.
énumérer [enymeʀe] *vt* to list, enumerate.
envahir [ɑ̃vaiʀ] *vt* to invade; (*suj: inquiétude, peur*) to come over.
envahissant, e [ɑ̃vaisɑ̃, -ɑ̃t] *adj* (*péj: personne*) interfering, intrusive.
envahissement [ɑ̃vaismɑ̃] *nm* invasion.
envahisseur [ɑ̃vaisœʀ] *nm* (*MIL*) invader.
envasement [ɑ̃nvɑzmɑ̃] *nm* silting up.
envaser [ɑ̃vɑze]: **s'~** *vi* to get bogged down (in the mud).
enveloppe [ɑ̃vlɔp] *nf* (*de lettre*) envelope; (*TECH*) casing; outer layer; **mettre sous ~** to put in an envelope; **~ autocollante** self-seal envelope; **~ budgétaire** budget; **~ à fenêtre** window envelope.
envelopper [ɑ̃vlɔpe] *vt* to wrap; (*fig*) to envelop, shroud; **s'~ dans un châle/une couverture** to wrap o.s. in a shawl/blanket.
envenimer [ɑ̃vnime] *vt* to aggravate; **s'~** *vi* (*plaie*) to fester; (*situation, relations*) to worsen.
envergure [ɑ̃vɛʀgyʀ] *nf* (*d'un oiseau, avion*) wingspan; (*fig: étendue*) scope; (*: valeur*) calibre.
enverrai [ɑ̃veʀe] *etc vb voir* **envoyer**.
envers [ɑ̃vɛʀ] *prép* towards, to ♦ *nm* other side; (*d'une étoffe*) wrong side; **à l'~** upside down; back to front; (*vêtement*) inside out; **~ et contre tous** *ou* **tout** against all opposition.
enviable [ɑ̃vjabl(ə)] *adj* enviable; **peu ~** unenviable.
envie [ɑ̃vi] *nf* (*sentiment*) envy; (*souhait*) desire, wish; (*tache sur la peau*) birthmark; (*filet de peau*) hangnail; **avoir ~ de** to feel like; (*désir plus fort*) to want; **avoir ~ de faire** to feel like doing; to want to do; **avoir ~ que** to wish that; **donner à qn l'~ de faire** to make sb want to do; **ça lui fait ~** he would like that.
envier [ɑ̃vje] *vt* to envy; **~ qch à qn** to envy sb sth; **n'avoir rien à ~ à** to have no cause to be envious of.
envieux, euse [ɑ̃vjø, -øz] *adj* envious.
environ [ɑ̃viʀɔ̃] *adv*: **~ 3 h/2 km, 3 h/2 km ~** (around) about 3 o'clock/2 km, 3 o'clock/2 km or so.
environnant, e [ɑ̃viʀɔnɑ̃, -ɑ̃t] *adj* surrounding.
environnement [ɑ̃viʀɔnmɑ̃] *nm* environment.
environnementaliste [ɑ̃viʀɔnmɑ̃talist(ə)] *nm/f* environmentalist.
environner [ɑ̃viʀɔne] *vt* to surround.
environs [ɑ̃viʀɔ̃] *nmpl* surroundings; **aux ~ de** around.
envisageable [ɑ̃vizaʒabl(ə)] *adj* conceivable.
envisager [ɑ̃vizaʒe] *vt* (*examiner, considérer*) to view, contemplate; (*avoir en vue*) to envisage; **~ de faire** to consider doing.
envoi [ɑ̃vwa] *nm* sending; (*paquet*) parcel, consignment; **~ contre remboursement** (*COMM*) cash on delivery.
envoie [ɑ̃vwa] *etc vb voir* **envoyer**.
envol [ɑ̃vɔl] *nm* takeoff.
envolée [ɑ̃vɔle] *nf* (*fig*) flight.
envoler [ɑ̃vɔle]: **s'~** *vi* (*oiseau*) to fly away *ou* off; (*avion*) to take off; (*papier, feuille*) to blow away; (*fig*) to vanish (into thin air).
envoûtant, e [ɑ̃vutɑ̃, -ɑ̃t] *adj* enchanting.
envoûtement [ɑ̃vutmɑ̃] *nm* bewitchment.
envoûter [ɑ̃vute] *vt* to bewitch.
envoyé, e [ɑ̃vwaje] *nm/f* (*POL*) envoy; (*PRESSE*) correspondent ♦ *adj*: **bien ~** (*remarque, réponse*) well-aimed.
envoyer [ɑ̃vwaje] *vt* to send; (*lancer*) to hurl, throw; **~ une gifle/un sourire à qn** to aim a blow/flash a smile at sb; **~ les couleurs** to run up the colours; **~ chercher** to send for; **~ par le fond** (*bateau*) to send to the bottom.
envoyeur, euse [ɑ̃vwajœʀ, -øz] *nm/f* sender.
enzyme [ɑ̃zim] *nf ou m* enzyme.
ÉOLE [eɔl] *sigle m* (*= est-ouest-liaison-express*) *Paris high-speed, east-west subway service.*
éolien, ne [eɔljɛ̃, -ɛn] *adj* wind *cpd*.
EOR *sigle m* (*= élève officier de réserve*) ≈ military cadet.
éosine [eɔzin] *nf* eosin (*antiseptic used in France to treat skin ailments*).
épagneul, e [epaɲœl] *nm/f* spaniel.
épais, se [epɛ, -ɛs] *adj* thick.
épaisseur [epɛsœʀ] *nf* thickness.
épaissir [epesiʀ] *vt*, **s'~** *vi* to thicken.
épaississement [epesismɑ̃] *nm* thickening.
épanchement [epɑ̃ʃmɑ̃] *nm*: **un ~ de sinovie** water on the knee; **~s** *nmpl* (*fig*) (sentimental) outpourings.
épancher [epɑ̃ʃe] *vt* to give vent to; **s'~** *vi* to open one's heart; (*liquide*) to pour out.
épandage [epɑ̃daʒ] *nm* manure spreading.
épanoui, e [epanwi] *adj* (*éclos, ouvert, développé*) blooming; (*radieux*) radiant.
épanouir [epanwiʀ]: **s'~** *vi* (*fleur*) to bloom, open out; (*visage*) to light up; (*fig: se développer*) to blossom (out); (*: mentalement*) to open up.
épanouissement [epanwismɑ̃] *nm* blossoming; opening up.
épargnant, e [epaʀɲɑ̃, -ɑ̃t] *nm/f* saver, investor.
épargne [epaʀɲ(ə)] *nf* saving; **l'~-logement** property investment.
épargner [epaʀɲe] *vt* to save; (*ne pas tuer ou endommager*) to spare ♦ *vi* to save; **~ qch à qn** to spare sb sth.
éparpillement [epaʀpijmɑ̃] *nm* (*de papier*) scattering; (*des efforts*) dissipation.
éparpiller [epaʀpije] *vt* to scatter; (*pour répartir*) to disperse; (*fig: efforts*) to dissipate; **s'~**

vi to scatter; (*fig*) to dissipate one's efforts.
épars, e [epaʀ, -aʀs(ə)] *adj* (*maisons*) scattered; (*cheveux*) sparse.
épatant, e [epatɑ̃, -ɑ̃t] *adj* (*fam*) super, splendid.
épaté, e [epate] *adj*: **nez** ~ flat nose (with wide nostrils).
épater [epate] *vt* to amaze; (*impressionner*) to impress.
épaule [epol] *nf* shoulder.
épaulé-jeté, *pl* **épaulés-jetés** [epoleʒəte] *nm* (*SPORT*) clean-and-jerk.
épaulement [epolmɑ̃] *nm* escarpment; (*mur*) retaining wall.
épauler [epole] *vt* (*aider*) to back up, support; (*arme*) to raise (to one's shoulder) ♦ *vi* to (take) aim.
épaulette [epolɛt] *nf* (*MIL, d'un veston*) epaulette; (*de combinaison*) shoulder strap.
épave [epav] *nf* wreck.
épée [epe] *nf* sword.
épeler [eple] *vt* to spell.
éperdu, e [epɛʀdy] *adj* (*personne*) overcome; (*sentiment*) passionate; (*fuite*) frantic.
éperdument [epɛʀdymɑ̃] *adv* (*aimer*) wildly; (*espérer*) fervently.
éperlan [epɛʀlɑ̃] *nm* (*ZOOL*) smelt.
éperon [epʀɔ̃] *nm* spur.
éperonner [epʀɔne] *vt* to spur (on); (*navire*) to ram.
épervier [epɛʀvje] *nm* (*ZOOL*) sparrowhawk; (*PÊCHE*) casting net.
éphèbe [efɛb] *nm* beautiful young man.
éphémère [efemɛʀ] *adj* ephemeral, fleeting.
éphéméride [efemeʀid] *nf* block *ou* tear-off calendar.
épi [epi] *nm* (*de blé, d'orge*) ear; ~ **de cheveux** tuft of hair; **stationnement/se garer en** ~ parking/to park at an angle to the kerb.
épice [epis] *nf* spice.
épicé, e [epise] *adj* highly spiced, spicy; (*fig*) spicy.
épicéa [episea] *nm* spruce.
épicentre [episɑ̃tʀ(ə)] *nm* epicentre.
épicer [epise] *vt* to spice; (*fig*) to add spice to.
épicerie [episʀi] *nf* (*magasin*) grocer's shop; (*denrées*) groceries *pl*; ~ **fine** delicatessen (shop).
épicier, ière [episje, -jɛʀ] *nm/f* grocer.
épicurien, ne [epikyʀjɛ̃, -ɛn] *adj* epicurean.
épidémie [epidemi] *nf* epidemic.
épidémique [epidemik] *adj* epidemic.
épiderme [epidɛʀm(ə)] *nm* skin, epidermis.
épidermique [epidɛʀmik] *adj* skin *cpd*, epidermic.
épier [epje] *vt* to spy on, watch closely; (*occasion*) to look out for.
épieu, x [epjø] *nm* (hunting-)spear.
épigramme [epigʀam] *nf* epigram.
épigraphe [epigʀaf] *nf* epigraph.
épilation [epilɑsjɔ̃] *nf* removal of unwanted hair.
épilatoire [epilatwaʀ] *adj* depilatory, hair-removing.
épilepsie [epilɛpsi] *nf* epilepsy.
épileptique [epilɛptik] *adj, nm/f* epileptic.
épiler [epile] *vt* (*jambes*) to remove the hair from; (*sourcils*) to pluck; **s'~ les jambes** to remove the hair from one's legs; **s'~ les sourcils** to pluck one's eyebrows; **se faire** ~ to get unwanted hair removed; **crème à** ~ hair-removing *ou* depilatory cream; **pince à** ~ eyebrow tweezers.
épilogue [epilɔg] *nm* (*fig*) conclusion, dénouement.
épiloguer [epilɔge] *vi*: ~ **sur** to hold forth on.
épinard [epinaʀ] *nm* (*aussi*: ~**s**) spinach *sg*.
épine [epin] *nf* thorn, prickle; (*d'oursin etc*) spine, prickle; ~ **dorsale** backbone.
épineux, euse [epinø, -øz] *adj* thorny, prickly.
épinglage [epɛ̃glaʒ] *nm* pinning.
épingle [epɛ̃gl(ə)] *nf* pin; **tirer son** ~ **du jeu** to play one's game well; **tiré à quatre ~s** well turned-out; **monter qch en** ~ to build sth up, make a thing of sth (*fam*); ~ **à chapeau** hatpin; ~ **à cheveux** hairpin; **virage en** ~ **à cheveux** hairpin bend; ~ **de cravate** tie pin; ~ **de nourrice** *ou* **de sûreté** *ou* **double** safety pin, nappy (*BRIT*) *ou* diaper (*US*) pin.
épingler [epɛ̃gle] *vt* (*badge, décoration*): ~ **qch sur** to pin sth on(to); (*COUTURE: tissu, robe*) to pin together; (*fam*) to catch, nick.
épinière [epinjɛʀ] *adj f voir* **moelle**.
Epiphanie [epifani] *nf* Epiphany.
épique [epik] *adj* epic.
épiscopal, e, aux [episkɔpal, -o] *adj* episcopal.
épiscopat [episkɔpa] *nm* bishopric, episcopate.
épisiotomie [epizjɔtomi] *nf* (*MÉD*) episiotomy.
épisode [epizɔd] *nm* episode; **film/roman à ~s** serialized film/novel, serial.
épisodique [epizɔdik] *adj* occasional.
episodiquement [epizɔdikmɑ̃] *adv* occasionally.
épissure [episyʀ] *nf* splice.
épistémologie [epistemɔlɔʒi] *nf* epistemology.
épistolaire [epistɔlɛʀ] *adj* epistolary; **être en relations ~s avec qn** to correspond with sb.
épitaphe [epitaf] *nf* epitaph.
épithète [epitɛt] *nf* (*nom, surnom*) epithet; **adjectif** ~ attributive adjective.
épître [epitʀ(ə)] *nf* epistle.
éploré, e [eplɔʀe] *adj* in tears, tearful.
épluchage [eplyʃaʒ] *nm* peeling; (*de dossier etc*) careful reading *ou* analysis.
épluche-légumes [eplyʃlegym] *nm inv* potato peeler.
éplucher [eplyʃe] *vt* (*fruit, légumes*) to peel; (*comptes, dossier*) to go over with a fine-tooth comb.
éplucheur [eplyʃœʀ] *nm* (automatic) peeler.
épluchures [eplyʃyʀ] *nfpl* peelings.

épointer [epwɛ̃te] *vt* to blunt.
éponge [epɔ̃ʒ] *nf* sponge; **passer l'~ (sur)** (*fig*) to let bygones be bygones (with regard to); **jeter l'~** (*fig*) to throw in the towel; **~ métallique** scourer.
éponger [epɔ̃ʒe] *vt* (*liquide*) to mop *ou* sponge up; (*surface*) to sponge; (*fig: déficit*) to soak up, absorb; **s'~ le front** to mop one's brow.
épopée [epɔpe] *nf* epic.
époque [epɔk] *nf* (*de l'histoire*) age, era; (*de l'année, la vie*) time; **d'~** *adj* (*meuble*) period *cpd*; **à cette ~** at this (*ou* that) time *ou* period; **faire ~** to make history.
épouiller [epuje] *vt* to pick lice off; (*avec un produit*) to delouse.
époumoner [epumɔne]: **s'~** *vi* to shout (*ou* sing) o.s. hoarse.
épouse [epuz] *nf* wife (*pl* wives).
épouser [epuze] *vt* to marry; (*fig: idées*) to espouse; (*: forme*) to fit.
époussetage [epustaʒ] *nm* dusting.
épousseter [epuste] *vt* to dust.
époustouflant, e [epustuflɑ̃, -ɑ̃t] *adj* staggering, mind-boggling.
époustoufler [epustufle] *vt* to flabbergast, astound.
épouvantable [epuvɑ̃tabl(ə)] *adj* appalling, dreadful.
épouvantablement [epuvɑ̃tabləmɑ̃] *adj* terribly, dreadfully.
épouvantail [epuvɑ̃taj] *nm* (*à moineaux*) scarecrow; (*fig*) bog(e)y; bugbear.
épouvante [epuvɑ̃t] *nf* terror; **film d'~** horror film.
épouvanter [epuvɑ̃te] *vt* to terrify.
époux [epu] *nm* husband ♦ *nmpl*: **les ~** the (married) couple, the husband and wife.
éprendre [epʀɑ̃dʀ(ə)]: **s'~ de** *vt* to fall in love with.
épreuve [epʀœv] *nf* (*d'examen*) test; (*malheur, difficulté*) trial, ordeal; (*PHOTO*) print; (*TYPO*) proof; (*SPORT*) event; **à l'~ des balles/du feu** (*vêtement*) bulletproof/fireproof; **à toute ~** unfailing; **mettre à l'~** to put to the test; **~ de force** trial of strength; (*fig*) showdown; **~ de résistance** test of resistance; **~ de sélection** (*SPORT*) heat.
épris, e [epʀi, -iz] *vb voir* **éprendre** ♦ *adj*: **~ de** in love with.
éprouvant, e [epʀuvɑ̃, -ɑ̃t] *adj* trying.
éprouvé, e [epʀuve] *adj* tested, proven.
éprouver [epʀuve] *vt* (*tester*) to test; (*mettre à l'épreuve*) to put to the test; (*marquer, faire souffrir*) to afflict, distress; (*ressentir*) to experience.
éprouvette [epʀuvɛt] *nf* test tube.
EPS *sigle f* (= *Éducation physique et sportive*) ≈ PE.
épuisant, e [epɥizɑ̃, -ɑ̃t] *adj* exhausting.
épuisé, e [epɥize] *adj* exhausted; (*livre*) out of print.
épuisement [epɥizmɑ̃] *nm* exhaustion; **jusqu'à ~ des stocks** while stocks last.
épuiser [epɥize] *vt* (*fatiguer*) to exhaust, wear *ou* tire out; (*stock, sujet*) to exhaust; **s'~** *vi* to wear *ou* tire o.s. out, exhaust o.s.; (*stock*) to run out.
épuisette [epɥizɛt] *nf* landing net; shrimping net.
épuration [epyʀɑsjɔ̃] *nf* purification; purging; refinement.
épure [epyʀ] *nf* working drawing.
épurer [epyʀe] *vt* (*liquide*) to purify; (*parti, administration*) to purge; (*langue, texte*) to refine.
équarrir [ekaʀiʀ] *vt* (*pierre, arbre*) to square (off); (*animal*) to quarter.
équateur [ekwatœʀ] *nm* equator; **(la république de) l'É~** Ecuador.
équation [ekwɑsjɔ̃] *nf* equation; **mettre en ~** to equate; **~ du premier/second degré** simple/quadratic equation.
équatorial, e, aux [ekwatɔʀjal, -o] *adj* equatorial.
équatorien, ne [ekwatɔʀjɛ̃, -ɛn] *adj* Ecuadorian ♦ *nm/f*: **É~, ne** Ecuadorian.
équerre [ekɛʀ] *nf* (*à dessin*) (set) square; (*pour fixer*) brace; **en ~** at right angles; **à l'~, d'~** straight; **double ~** T-square.
équestre [ekɛstʀ(ə)] *adj* equestrian.
équeuter [ekøte] *vt* (*CULIN*) to remove the stalk(s) from.
équidé [ekide] *nm* (*ZOOL*) member of the horse family.
équidistance [ekɥidistɑ̃s] *nf*: **à ~ (de)** equidistant (from).
équidistant, e [ekɥidistɑ̃, -ɑ̃t] *adj*: **~ (de)** equidistant (from).
équilatéral, e, aux [ekɥilateʀal, -o] *adj* equilateral.
équilibrage [ekilibʀaʒ] *nm* (*AUTO*): **~ des roues** wheel balancing.
équilibre [ekilibʀ(ə)] *nm* balance; (*d'une balance*) equilibrium; **~ budgétaire** balanced budget; **garder/perdre l'~** to keep/lose one's balance; **être en ~** to be balanced; **mettre en ~** to make steady; **avoir le sens de l'~** to be well-balanced.
équilibré, e [ekilibʀe] *adj* (*fig*) well-balanced, stable.
équilibrer [ekilibʀe] *vt* to balance; **s'~** (*poids*) to balance; (*fig: défauts etc*) to balance each other out.
équilibriste [ekilibʀist(ə)] *nm/f* tightrope walker.
équinoxe [ekinɔks] *nm* equinox.
équipage [ekipaʒ] *nm* crew; **en grand ~** in great array.
équipe [ekip] *nf* team; (*bande: parfois péj*) bunch; **travailler par ~s** to work in shifts; **travailler en ~** to work as a team; **faire ~ avec** to team up with; **~ de chercheurs** research team; **~ de secours** *ou* **de sauvetage** rescue team.

équipé, e [ekipe] *adj* (*cuisine etc*) equipped, fitted(-out) ♦ *nf* escapade.
équipement [ekipmɑ̃] *nm* equipment; ~**s** *nmpl* amenities, facilities; installations; **biens/dépenses d'**~ capital goods/expenditure; **ministère de l'É**~ department of public works; ~**s sportifs/collectifs** sports/community facilities *ou* resources.
équiper [ekipe] *vt* to equip; (*voiture, cuisine*) to equip, fit out; ~ **qn/qch de** to equip sb/sth with; **s'**~ (*sportif*) to equip o.s., kit o.s. out.
équipier, ière [ekipje, -jɛʀ] *nm/f* team member.
équitable [ekitabl(ə)] *adj* fair.
équitablement [ekitabləmɑ̃] *adv* fairly, equitably.
équitation [ekitɑsjɔ̃] *nf* (horse-)riding; **faire de l'**~ to go (horse-)riding.
équité [ekite] *nf* equity.
équivaille [ekivaj] *etc vb voir* **équivaloir**.
équivalence [ekivalɑ̃s] *nf* equivalence.
équivalent, e [ekivalɑ̃, -ɑ̃t] *adj, nm* equivalent.
équivaloir [ekivalwaʀ]: ~ **à** *vt* to be equivalent to; (*représenter*) to amount to.
équivaut [ekivo] *etc vb voir* **équivaloir**.
équivoque [ekivɔk] *adj* equivocal, ambiguous; (*louche*) dubious ♦ *nf* ambiguity.
érable [eʀabl(ə)] *nm* maple.
éradication [eʀadikɑsjɔ̃] *nf* eradication.
éradiquer [eʀadike] *vt* to eradicate.
érafler [eʀɑfle] *vt* to scratch; **s'**~ **la main/les jambes** to scrape *ou* scratch one's hand/legs.
éraflure [eʀɑflyʀ] *nf* scratch.
éraillé, e [eʀɑje] *adj* (*voix*) rasping, hoarse.
ère [ɛʀ] *nf* era; **en l'an 1050 de notre** ~ in the year 1050 A.D.
érection [eʀɛksjɔ̃] *nf* erection.
éreintant, e [eʀɛ̃tɑ̃, -ɑ̃t] *adj* exhausting.
éreinté, e [eʀɛ̃te] *adj* exhausted.
éreintement [eʀɛ̃tmɑ̃] *nm* exhaustion.
éreinter [eʀɛ̃te] *vt* to exhaust, wear out; (*fig: critiquer*) to slate; **s'**~ **(à faire qch/à qch)** to wear o.s. out (doing sth/with sth).
ergonomie [ɛʀgɔnɔmi] *nf* ergonomics *sg*.
ergonomique [ɛʀgɔnɔmik] *adj* ergonomic.
ergot [ɛʀgo] *nm* (*de coq*) spur; (*TECH*) lug.
ergoter [ɛʀgɔte] *vi* to split hairs, argue over details.
ergoteur, euse [ɛʀgɔtœʀ, -øz] *nm/f* hair-splitter.
ériger [eʀiʒe] *vt* (*monument*) to erect; ~ **qch en principe/loi** to make sth a principle/law; **s'**~ **en critique (de)** to set o.s. up as a critic (of).
ermitage [ɛʀmitaʒ] *nm* retreat.
ermite [ɛʀmit] *nm* hermit.
éroder [eʀɔde] *vt* to erode.
érogène [eʀɔʒɛn] *adj* erogenous.
érosion [eʀozjɔ̃] *nf* erosion.
érotique [eʀɔtik] *adj* erotic.
érotiquement [eʀɔtikmɑ̃] *adv* erotically.
érotisme [eʀɔtism(ə)] *nm* eroticism.
errance [ɛʀɑ̃s] *nf* wandering.
errant, e [ɛʀɑ̃, -ɑ̃t] *adj*: **un chien** ~ a stray dog.
erratum, a [ɛʀatɔm, -a] *nm* erratum (*pl* -a).
errements [ɛʀmɑ̃] *nmpl* misguided ways.
errer [ɛʀe] *vi* to wander.
erreur [ɛʀœʀ] *nf* mistake, error; (*INFORM: de programme*) bug; (*morale*): ~**s** *nfpl* errors; **être dans l'**~ to be wrong; **induire qn en** ~ to mislead sb; **par** ~ by mistake; **sauf** ~ unless I'm mistaken; **faire** ~ to be mistaken; ~ **de date** mistake in the date; ~ **de fait** error of fact; ~ **d'impression** (*TYPO*) misprint; ~ **judiciaire** miscarriage of justice; ~ **de jugement** error of judgment; ~ **matérielle** *ou* **d'écriture** clerical error; ~ **tactique** tactical error.
erroné, e [ɛʀɔne] *adj* wrong, erroneous.
ersatz [ɛʀzats] *nm* substitute, ersatz; ~ **de café** coffee substitute.
éructer [eʀykte] *vi* to belch.
érudit, e [eʀydi, -it] *adj* erudite, learned ♦ *nm/f* scholar.
érudition [eʀydisjɔ̃] *nf* erudition, scholarship.
éruptif, ive [eʀyptif, -iv] *adj* eruptive.
éruption [eʀypsjɔ̃] *nf* eruption; (*cutanée*) outbreak; (*: boutons*) rash; (*fig: de joie, colère, folie*) outburst.
es [ɛ] *vb voir* **être**.
ès [ɛs] *prép*: **licencié** ~ **lettres/sciences** ≈ Bachelor of Arts/Science; **docteur** ~ **lettres** ≈ doctor of philosophy, PhD.
E/S *abr* (= *entrée/sortie*) I/O (= *in/out*).
esbroufe [ɛsbʀuf] *nf*: **faire de l'**~ to have people on.
escabeau, x [ɛskabo] *nm* (*tabouret*) stool; (*échelle*) stepladder.
escadre [ɛskadʀ(ə)] *nf* (*NAVIG*) squadron; (*AVIAT*) wing.
escadrille [ɛskadʀij] *nf* (*AVIAT*) flight.
escadron [ɛskadʀɔ̃] *nm* squadron.
escalade [ɛskalad] *nf* climbing *no pl*; (*POL etc*) escalation.
escalader [ɛskalade] *vt* to climb, scale.
escalator [ɛskalatɔʀ] *nm* escalator.
escale [ɛskal] *nf* (*NAVIG*) call; (*: port*) port of call; (*AVIAT*) stop(over); **faire** ~ **à** to put in at, call in at; to stop over at; ~ **technique** (*AVIAT*) refuelling stop.
escalier [ɛskalje] *nm* stairs *pl*; **dans l'**~ *ou* **les** ~**s** on the stairs; **descendre l'**~ *ou* **les** ~**s** to go downstairs; ~ **mécanique** *ou* **roulant** escalator; ~ **de secours** fire escape; ~ **de service** backstairs; ~ **à vis** *ou* **en colimaçon** spiral staircase.
escalope [ɛskalɔp] *nf* escalope.
escamotable [ɛskamɔtabl(ə)] *adj* (*train d'atterrissage, antenne*) retractable; (*table, lit*) fold-away.
escamoter [ɛskamɔte] *vt* (*esquiver*) to get round, evade; (*faire disparaître*) to conjure away; (*dérober: portefeuille etc*) to snatch; (*train d'atterrissage*) to retract; (*mots*) to miss

out.

escapade [ɛskapad] *nf*: **faire une ~** to go on a jaunt; (*s'enfuir*) to run away *ou* off.

escarbille [ɛskaʀbij] *nf* bit of grit.

escarcelle [ɛskaʀsɛl] *nf*: **faire tomber dans l'~** (*argent*) to bring in.

escargot [ɛskaʀgo] *nm* snail.

escarmouche [ɛskaʀmuʃ] *nf* (*MIL*) skirmish; (*fig: propos hostiles*) angry exchange.

escarpé, e [ɛskaʀpe] *adj* steep.

escarpement [ɛskaʀpəmɑ̃] *nm* steep slope.

escarpin [ɛskaʀpɛ̃] *nm* flat(-heeled) shoe.

escarre [ɛskaʀ] *nf* bedsore.

Escaut [ɛsko] *nm*: **l'~** the Scheldt.

escient [esjɑ̃] *nm*: **à bon ~** advisedly.

esclaffer [ɛsklafe]: **s'~** *vi* to guffaw.

esclandre [ɛsklɑ̃dʀ(ə)] *nm* scene, fracas.

esclavage [ɛsklavaʒ] *nm* slavery.

esclavagiste [ɛsklavaʒist(ə)] *adj* pro-slavery ♦ *nm/f* supporter of slavery.

esclave [ɛsklav] *nm/f* slave; **être ~ de** (*fig*) to be a slave of.

escogriffe [ɛskɔgʀif] *nm* (*péj*) beanpole.

escompte [ɛskɔ̃t] *nm* discount.

escompter [ɛskɔ̃te] *vt* (*COMM*) to discount; (*espérer*) to expect, reckon upon; **~ que** to reckon *ou* expect that.

escorte [ɛskɔʀt(ə)] *nf* escort; **faire ~ à** to escort.

escorter [ɛskɔʀte] *vt* to escort.

escorteur [ɛskɔʀtœʀ] *nm* (*NAVIG*) escort (ship).

escouade [ɛskwad] *nf* squad; (*fig: groupe de personnes*) group.

escrime [ɛskʀim] *nf* fencing; **faire de l'~** to fence.

escrimer [ɛskʀime]: **s'~** *vi*: **s'~ à faire** to wear o.s. out doing.

escrimeur, euse [ɛskʀimœʀ, -øz] *nm/f* fencer.

escroc [ɛskʀo] *nm* swindler, con-man.

escroquer [ɛskʀɔke] *vt*: **~ qn (de qch)/qch à qn** to swindle sb (out of sth)/sth out of sb.

escroquerie [ɛskʀɔkʀi] *nf* swindle.

ésotérique [ezɔteʀik] *adj* esoteric.

espace [ɛspas] *nm* space; **~ publicitaire** advertising space; **~ vital** living space.

espacé, e [ɛspase] *adj* spaced out.

espacement [ɛspasmɑ̃] *nm*: **~ proportionnel** proportional spacing (*on printer*).

espacer [ɛspase] *vt* to space out; **s'~** *vi* (*visites etc*) to become less frequent.

espadon [ɛspadɔ̃] *nm* swordfish *inv*.

espadrille [ɛspadʀij] *nf* rope-soled sandal.

Espagne [ɛspaɲ(ə)] *nf*: **l'~** Spain.

espagnol, e [ɛspaɲɔl] *adj* Spanish ♦ *nm* (*LING*) Spanish ♦ *nm/f*: **E~, e** Spaniard.

espagnolette [ɛspaɲɔlɛt] *nf* (window) catch; **fermé à l'~** resting on the catch.

espalier [ɛspalje] *nm* (*arbre fruitier*) espalier.

espèce [ɛspɛs] *nf* (*BIO, BOT, ZOOL*) species *inv*; (*gén: sorte*) sort, kind, type; (*péj*): **~ de maladroit/de brute!** you clumsy oaf/you brute!; **~s** *nfpl* (*COMM*) cash *sg*; (*REL*) species; **de toute ~** of all kinds *ou* sorts; **en l'~** *adv* in the case in point; **payer en ~s** to pay (in) cash; **cas d'~** individual case; **l'~ humaine** humankind.

espérance [ɛspeʀɑ̃s] *nf* hope; **~ de vie** life expectancy.

espéranto [ɛspeʀɑ̃to] *nm* esperanto.

espérer [ɛspeʀe] *vt* to hope for; **j'espère (bien)** I hope so; **~ que/faire** to hope that/to do; **~ en** to trust in.

espiègle [ɛspjɛgl(ə)] *adj* mischievous.

espièglerie [ɛspjɛgləʀi] *nf* mischievousness; (*tour, farce*) piece of mischief, prank.

espion, ne [ɛspjɔ̃, -ɔn] *nm/f* spy; **avion ~** spy plane.

espionnage [ɛspjɔnaʒ] *nm* espionage, spying; **film/roman d'~** spy film/novel.

espionner [ɛspjɔne] *vt* to spy (up)on.

espionnite [ɛspjɔnit] *nf* spy mania.

esplanade [ɛsplanad] *nf* esplanade.

espoir [ɛspwaʀ] *nm* hope; **l'~ de qch/de faire qch** the hope of sth/of doing sth; **avoir bon ~ que ...** to have high hopes that ...; **garder l'~ que ...** to remain hopeful that ...; **un ~ de la boxe/du ski** one of boxing's/skiing's hopefuls, one of the hopes of boxing/skiing; **sans ~** *adj* hopeless.

esprit [ɛspʀi] *nm* (*pensée, intellect*) mind; (*humour, ironie*) wit; (*mentalité, d'une loi etc, fantôme etc*) spirit; **l'~ d'équipe/de compétition** team/competitive spirit; **faire de l'~** to try to be witty; **reprendre ses ~s** to come to; **perdre l'~** to lose one's mind; **avoir bon/mauvais ~** to be of a good/bad disposition; **avoir l'~ à faire qch** to have a mind to do sth; **avoir l'~ critique** to be critical; **~ de contradiction** contrariness; **~ de corps** esprit de corps; **~ de famille** family loyalty; **l'~ malin** (*le diable*) the Evil One; **~s chagrins** faultfinders.

esquif [ɛskif] *nm* skiff.

esquimau, de, x [ɛskimo, -od] *adj* Eskimo ♦ *nm* (*LING*) Eskimo; (*glace*): **E~** ® ice lolly (*BRIT*), popsicle (*US*) ♦ *nm/f*: **E~, de** Eskimo; **chien ~** husky.

esquinter [ɛskɛ̃te] *vt* (*fam*) to mess up; **s'~** *vi*: **s'~ à faire qch** to knock o.s. out doing sth.

esquisse [ɛskis] *nf* sketch; **l'~ d'un sourire/changement** a hint of a smile/of change.

esquisser [ɛskise] *vt* to sketch; **s'~** *vi* (*amélioration*) to begin to be detectable; **~ un sourire** to give a hint of a smile.

esquive [ɛskiv] *nf* (*BOXE*) dodging; (*fig*) sidestepping.

esquiver [ɛskive] *vt* to dodge; **s'~** *vi* to slip away.

essai [esɛ] *nm* trying; (*tentative*) attempt, try; (*RUGBY*) try; (*LITTÉRATURE*) essay; **~s** *nmpl* (*AUTO*) trials; **à l'~** on a trial basis; **~ gratuit** (*COMM*) free trial.

essaim [esɛ̃] *nm* swarm.

essaimer [eseme] *vi* to swarm; (*fig*) to spread, expand.
essayage [esɛjaʒ] *nm* (*d'un vêtement*) trying on, fitting; **salon d'~** fitting room; **cabine d'~** fitting room (*cubicle*).
essayer [eseje] *vt* (*gén*) to try; (*vêtement, chaussures*) to try (on); (*restaurant, méthode, voiture*) to try (out) ♦ *vi* to try; ~ **de faire** to try *ou* attempt to do; **s'~ à faire** to try one's hand at doing; **essayez un peu!** (*menace*) just you try!
essayeur, euse [esɛjœʀ, -øz] *nm/f* (*chez un tailleur etc*) fitter.
essayiste [esejist(ə)] *nm/f* essayist.
ESSEC [ɛsɛk] *sigle f* (= *École supérieure des sciences économiques et sociales*) *grande école for management and business studies.*
essence [esɑ̃s] *nf* (*de voiture*) petrol (*BRIT*), gas(oline) (*US*); (*extrait de plante, PHILOSOPHIE*) essence; (*espèce: d'arbre*) species *inv*; **prendre de l'~** to get (some) petrol *ou* gas; **par ~** (*essentiellement*) essentially; ~ **de citron/rose** lemon/rose oil; ~ **de térébenthine** turpentine.
essentiel, le [esɑ̃sjɛl] *adj* essential ♦ *nm*: **l'~ d'un discours/d'une œuvre** the essence of a speech/work of art; **emporter l'~** to take the essentials; **c'est l'~** (*ce qui importe*) that's the main thing; **l'~ de** (*la majeure partie*) the main part of.
essentiellement [esɑ̃sjɛlmɑ̃] *adv* essentially.
esseulé, e [esœle] *adj* forlorn.
essieu, x [esjø] *nm* axle.
essor [esɔʀ] *nm* (*de l'économie etc*) rapid expansion; **prendre son ~** (*oiseau*) to fly off.
essorage [esɔʀaʒ] *nm* wringing out; spin-drying; spinning; shaking.
essorer [esɔʀe] *vt* (*en tordant*) to wring (out); (*par la force centrifuge*) to spin-dry; (*salade*) to spin; (*: en secouant*) to shake dry.
essoreuse [esɔʀøz] *nf* mangle, wringer; (*à tambour*) spin-dryer.
essouffler [esufle] *vt* to make breathless; **s'~** *vi* to get out of breath; (*fig: économie*) to run out of steam.
essuie [esɥi] *etc vb voir* **essuyer**.
essuie-glace [esɥiglas] *nm* windscreen (*BRIT*) *ou* windshield (*US*) wiper.
essuie-mains [esɥimɛ̃] *nm inv* hand towel.
essuierai [esɥiʀe] *etc vb voir* **essuyer**.
essuie-tout [esɥitu] *nm inv* kitchen paper.
essuyer [esɥije] *vt* to wipe; (*fig: subir*) to suffer; **s'~** (*après le bain*) to dry o.s.; ~ **la vaisselle** to dry up, dry the dishes.
est [ɛ] *vb voir* **être** ♦ *nm* [ɛst]: **l'~** the east ♦ *adj inv* east; (*région*) east(ern); **à l'~** in the east; (*direction*) to the east, east(wards); **à l'~ de** (to the) east of; **les pays de l'E~** the eastern countries.
estafette [ɛstafɛt] *nf* (*MIL*) dispatch rider.
estafilade [ɛstafilad] *nf* gash, slash.
est-allemand, e [ɛstalmɑ̃, -ɑ̃d] *adj* East German.
estaminet [ɛstaminɛ] *nm* tavern.
estampe [ɛstɑ̃p] *nf* print, engraving.
estamper [ɛstɑ̃pe] *vt* (*monnaies etc*) to stamp; (*fam: escroquer*) to swindle.
estampille [ɛstɑ̃pij] *nf* stamp.
est-ce que [ɛskə] *adv*: ~ **c'est cher/c'était bon?** is it expensive/was it good?; **quand est-ce qu'il part?** when does he leave?, when is he leaving?; **où est-ce qu'il va?** where's he going?; **qui est-ce qui le connaît/a fait ça?** who knows him/did that?; *voir aussi* **que**.
este [ɛst(ə)] *adj* Estonian ♦ *nm/f*: **E~** Estonian.
esthète [ɛstɛt] *nm/f* aesthete.
esthéticienne [ɛstetisjɛn] *nf* beautician.
esthétique [ɛstetik] *adj* (*sens, jugement*) aesthetic; (*beau*) attractive, aesthetically pleasing ♦ *nf* aesthetics *sg*; **l'~ industrielle** industrial design.
esthétiquement [ɛstetikmɑ̃] *adv* aesthetically.
estimable [ɛstimabl(ə)] *adj* respected.
estimatif, ive [ɛstimatif, -iv] *adj* estimated.
estimation [ɛstimɑsjɔ̃] *nf* valuation; assessment; **d'après mes ~s** according to my calculations.
estime [ɛstim] *nf* esteem, regard; **avoir de l'~ pour qn** to think highly of sb.
estimer [ɛstime] *vt* (*respecter*) to esteem, hold in high regard; (*expertiser*) to value; (*évaluer*) to assess, estimate; (*penser*): ~ **que/être** to consider that/o.s. to be; **s'~ satisfait/heureux** to feel satisfied/happy; **j'estime la distance à 10 km** I reckon the distance to be 10 km.
estival, e, aux [ɛstival, -o] *adj* summer *cpd*; **station ~e** (summer) holiday resort.
estivant, e [ɛstivɑ̃, -ɑ̃t] *nm/f* (summer) holiday-maker.
estoc [ɛstɔk] *nm*: **frapper d'~ et de taille** to cut and thrust.
estocade [ɛstɔkad] *nf* death-blow.
estomac [ɛstɔma] *nm* stomach; **avoir mal à l'~** to have stomach ache; **avoir l'~ creux** to have an empty stomach.
estomaqué, e [ɛstɔmake] *adj* flabbergasted.
estompe [ɛstɔ̃p] *nf* stump; (*dessin*) stump drawing.
estompé, e [ɛstɔ̃pe] *adj* blurred.
estomper [ɛstɔ̃mpe] *vt* (*ART*) to shade off; (*fig*) to blur, dim; **s'~** *vi* (*sentiments*) to soften; (*contour*) to become blurred.
Estonie [ɛstɔni] *nf*: **l'~** Estonia.
estonien, ne [ɛstɔnjɛ̃, -ɛn] *adj* Estonian ♦ *nm* (*LING*) Estonian ♦ *nm/f*: **E~, ne** Estonian.
estrade [ɛstʀad] *nf* platform, rostrum.
estragon [ɛstʀagɔ̃] *nm* tarragon.
estropié, e [ɛstʀɔpje] *nm/f* cripple.
estropier [ɛstʀɔpje] *vt* to cripple, maim; (*fig*) to twist, distort.
estuaire [ɛstɥɛʀ] *nm* estuary.
estudiantin, e [ɛstydjɑ̃tɛ̃, -in] *adj* student *cpd*.

esturgeon [ɛstyʀʒɔ̃] *nm* sturgeon.
et [e] *conj* and; ~ **lui?** what about him?; ~ **alors?**, ~ **(puis) après?** so what?; (*ensuite*) and then?
ét. *abr* = **étage.**
ETA [eta] *sigle m* (*POL*) ETA.
étable [etabl(ə)] *nf* cowshed.
établi, e [etabli] *adj* established ♦ *nm* (work)bench.
établir [etabliʀ] *vt* (*papiers d'identité, facture*) to make out; (*liste, programme*) to draw up; (*gouvernement, artisan etc: aider à s'installer*) to set up, establish; (*entreprise, atelier, camp*) to set up; (*réputation, usage, fait, culpabilité, relations*) to establish; (*SPORT: record*) to set; **s'~** *vi* (*se faire: entente etc*) to be established; **s'~ (à son compte)** to set up in business; **s'~ à/près de** to settle in/near.
établissement [etablismɑ̃] *nm* making out; drawing up; setting up, establishing; (*entreprise, institution*) establishment; ~ **de crédit** credit institution; ~ **hospitalier** hospital complex; ~ **industriel** industrial plant, factory; ~ **scolaire** school, educational establishment.
étage [etaʒ] *nm* (*d'immeuble*) storey (*BRIT*), story (*US*), floor; (*de fusée*) stage; (*GÉO: de culture, végétation*) level; **au 2ème ~** on the 2nd (*BRIT*) *ou* 3rd (*US*) floor; **à l'~** upstairs; **maison à deux ~s** two-storey *ou* -story house; **de bas ~** *adj* low-born; (*médiocre*) inferior.
étager [etaʒe] *vt* (*cultures*) to lay out in tiers; **s'~** *vi* (*prix*) to range; (*zones, cultures*) to lie on different levels.
étagère [etaʒɛʀ] *nf* (*rayon*) shelf; (*meuble*) shelves *pl*, set of shelves.
étai [etɛ] *nm* stay, prop.
étain [etɛ̃] *nm* tin; (*ORFÈVRERIE*) pewter *no pl*.
étais [etɛ] *etc vb voir* **être.**
étal [etal] *nm* stall.
étalage [etalaʒ] *nm* display; (*vitrine*) display window; **faire ~ de** to show off, parade.
étalagiste [etalaʒist(ə)] *nm/f* window-dresser.
étale [etal] *adj* (*mer*) slack.
étalement [etalmɑ̃] *nm* spreading; (*échelonnement*) staggering.
étaler [etale] *vt* (*carte, nappe*) to spread (out); (*peinture, liquide*) to spread; (*échelonner: paiements, dates, vacances*) to spread, stagger; (*exposer: marchandises*) to display; (*richesses, connaissances*) to parade; **s'~** *vi* (*liquide*) to spread out; (*fam*) to come a cropper (*BRIT*), fall flat on one's face; **s'~ sur** (*suj: paiements etc*) to be spread over.
étalon [etalɔ̃] *nm* (*mesure*) standard; (*cheval*) stallion; **l'~-or** the gold standard.
étalonner [etalɔne] *vt* to calibrate.
étamer [etame] *vt* (*casserole*) to tin(plate); (*glace*) to silver.
étamine [etamin] *nf* (*BOT*) stamen; (*tissu*) butter muslin.
étanche [etɑ̃ʃ] *adj* (*récipient; aussi fig*) watertight; (*montre, vêtement*) waterproof; ~ **à l'air** airtight.
étanchéité [etɑ̃ʃeite] *nf* watertightness; airtightness.
étancher [etɑ̃ʃe] *vt* (*liquide*) to stop (flowing); ~ **sa soif** to quench *ou* slake one's thirst.
étançon [etɑ̃sɔ̃] *nm* (*TECH*) prop.
étançonner [etɑ̃sɔne] *vt* to prop up.
étang [etɑ̃] *nm* pond.
étant [etɑ̃] *vb voir* **être, donné.**
étape [etap] *nf* stage; (*lieu d'arrivée*) stopping place; (*: CYCLISME*) staging point; **faire ~ à** to stop off at; **brûler les ~s** (*fig*) to cut corners.
état [eta] *nm* (*POL, condition*) state; (*d'un article d'occasion etc*) condition, state; (*liste*) inventory, statement; (*condition: professionnelle*) profession, trade; (*: sociale*) status; **en mauvais ~** in poor condition; **en ~ (de marche)** in (working) order; **remettre en ~** to repair; **hors d'~** out of order; **être en ~/hors d'~ de faire** to be in a state/in no fit state to do; **en tout ~ de cause** in any event; **être dans tous ses ~s** to be in a state; **faire ~ de** (*alléguer*) to put forward; **en ~ d'arrestation** under arrest; ~ **de grâce** (*REL*) state of grace; (*fig*) honeymoon period; **en ~ de grâce** (*fig*) inspired; **en ~ d'ivresse** under the influence of drink; ~ **de choses** (*situation*) state of affairs; ~ **civil** civil status; (*bureau*) registry office (*BRIT*); ~ **d'esprit** frame of mind; ~ **des lieux** inventory of fixtures; ~ **de santé** state of health; ~ **de siège/d'urgence** state of siege/emergency, ~ **de veille** (*PSYCH*) waking state; **~s d'âme** moods; **les É~s barbaresques** the Barbary States; **les É~s du Golfe** the Gulf States; **~s de service** service record *sg*.
étatique [etatik] *adj* state *cpd*, State *cpd*.
étatisation [etatizɑsjɔ̃] *nf* nationalization.
étatiser [etatize] *vt* to bring under state control.
étatisme [etatism(ə)] *nm* state control.
étatiste [etatist(ə)] *adj* (*doctrine etc*) of state control ♦ *nm/f* partisan of state control.
état-major, *pl* **états-majors** [etamaʒɔʀ] *nm* (*MIL*) staff; (*d'un parti etc*) top advisers *pl*; (*d'une entreprise*) top management.
État-providence [etapʀɔvidɑ̃s] *nm* welfare state.
États-Unis [etazyni] *nmpl*: **les ~ (d'Amérique)** the United States (of America).
étau, x [eto] *nm* vice (*BRIT*), vise (*US*).
étayer [eteje] *vt* to prop *ou* shore up; (*fig*) to back up.
et c(a)etera [ɛtseteʀa], **etc.** *adv* et cetera, and so on, etc.
été [ete] *pp de* **être** ♦ *nm* summer; **en ~** in summer.
éteignais [etɛɲɛ] *etc vb voir* **éteindre.**
éteignoir [etɛɲwaʀ] *nm* (candle) snuffer; (*péj*) killjoy, wet blanket.

éteindre [etɛ̃dʀ(ə)] *vt* (*lampe, lumière, radio, chauffage*) to turn *ou* switch off; (*cigarette, incendie, bougie*) to put out, extinguish; (*JUR*: *dette*) to extinguish; **s'~** *vi* to go off; to go out; (*mourir*) to pass away.

éteint, e [etɛ̃, -ɛ̃t] *pp de* **éteindre** ♦ *adj* (*fig*) lacklustre, dull; (*volcan*) extinct; **tous feux ~s** (*AUTO*: *rouler*) without lights.

étendard [etɑ̃daʀ] *nm* standard.

étendre [etɑ̃dʀ(ə)] *vt* (*appliquer: pâte, liquide*) to spread; (*déployer: carte etc*) to spread out; (*sur un fil: lessive, linge*) to hang up *ou* out; (*bras, jambes, par terre: blessé*) to stretch out; (*diluer*) to dilute, thin; (*fig: agrandir*) to extend; (*fam*: *adversaire*) to floor; **s'~** *vi* (*augmenter, se propager*) to spread; (*terrain, forêt etc*): **s'~ jusqu'à/de ... à** to stretch as far as/from ... to; **s'~ (sur)** (*s'allonger*) to stretch out (upon); (*se coucher*) to lie down (on); (*fig: expliquer*) to elaborate *ou* enlarge (upon).

étendu, e [etɑ̃dy] *adj* extensive ♦ *nf* (*d'eau, de sable*) stretch, expanse; (*importance*) extent.

éternel, le [etɛʀnɛl] *adj* eternal; **les neiges ~les** perpetual snow.

éternellement [etɛʀnɛlmɑ̃] *adv* eternally.

éterniser [etɛʀnize]: **s'~** *vi* to last for ages; (*personne*) to stay for ages.

éternité [etɛʀnite] *nf* eternity; **il y a** *ou* **ça fait une ~ que** it's ages since; **de toute ~** from time immemorial.

éternuement [etɛʀnymɑ̃] *nm* sneeze.

éternuer [etɛʀnɥe] *vi* to sneeze.

êtes [ɛt] *vb voir* **être**.

étêter [etete] *vt* (*arbre*) to poll(ard); (*clou, poisson*) to cut the head off.

éther [etɛʀ] *nm* ether.

éthéré, e [eteʀe] *adj* ethereal.

Éthiopie [etjɔpi] *nf*: **l'~** Ethiopia.

éthiopien, ne [etjɔpjɛ̃, -ɛn] *adj* Ethiopian.

éthique [etik] *adj* ethical ♦ *nf* ethics *sg*.

ethnie [ɛtni] *nf* ethnic group.

ethnique [ɛtnik] *adj* ethnic.

ethnographe [ɛtnɔgʀaf] *nm/f* ethnographer.

ethnographie [ɛtnɔgʀafi] *nf* ethnography.

ethnographique [ɛtnɔgʀafik] *adj* ethnographic(al).

ethnologie [ɛtnɔlɔʒi] *nf* ethnology.

ethnologique [ɛtnɔlɔʒik] *adj* ethnological.

ethnologue [ɛtnɔlɔg] *nm/f* ethnologist.

éthylique [etilik] *adj* alcoholic.

éthylisme [etilism(ə)] *nm* alcoholism.

étiage [etjaʒ] *nm* low water.

étiez [etje] *vb voir* **être**.

étincelant, e [etɛ̃slɑ̃, -ɑ̃t] *adj* sparkling.

étinceler [etɛ̃sle] *vi* to sparkle.

étincelle [etɛ̃sɛl] *nf* spark.

étioler [etjɔle]: **s'~** *vi* to wilt.

étions [etjɔ̃] *vb voir* **être**.

étique [etik] *adj* skinny, bony.

étiquetage [etiktaʒ] *nm* labelling.

étiqueter [etikte] *vt* to label.

étiquette [etikɛt] *vb voir* **étiqueter** ♦ *nf* label; (*protocole*): **l'~** etiquette.

étirer [etiʀe] *vt* to stretch; (*ressort*) to stretch out; **s'~** *vi* (*personne*) to stretch; (*convoi, route*): **s'~ sur** to stretch out over.

étoffe [etɔf] *nf* material, fabric; **avoir l'~ d'un chef** *etc* to be cut out to be a leader *etc*; **avoir de l'~** to be a forceful personality.

étoffer [etɔfe] *vt*, **s'~** *vi* to fill out.

étoile [etwal] *nf* star ♦ *adj*: **danseuse** *ou* **danseur ~** leading dancer; **la bonne/mauvaise ~ de qn** sb's lucky/unlucky star; **à la belle ~** (out) in the open; **~ filante** shooting star; **~ de mer** starfish; **~ polaire** pole star.

étoilé, e [etwale] *adj* starry.

étole [etɔl] *nf* stole.

étonnamment [etɔnamɑ̃] *adv* amazingly.

étonnant, e [etɔnɑ̃, -ɑ̃t] *adj* surprising.

étonné, e [etɔne] *adj* surprised.

étonnement [etɔnmɑ̃] *nm* surprise; **à mon grand ~ ...** to my great surprise *ou* amazement....

étonner [etɔne] *vt* to surprise; **s'~ que/de** to be surprised that/at; **cela m'étonnerait (que)** (*j'en doute*) I'd be (very) surprised (if).

étouffant, e [etufɑ̃, -ɑ̃t] *adj* stifling.

étouffé, e [etufe] *adj* (*asphyxié*) suffocated; (*assourdi: cris, rires*) smothered ♦ *nf*: **à l'~e** (*CULIN*: *poisson, légumes*) steamed; (*: viande*) braised.

étouffement [etufmɑ̃] *nm* suffocation.

étouffer [etufe] *vt* to suffocate; (*bruit*) to muffle; (*scandale*) to hush up ♦ *vi* to suffocate; (*avoir trop chaud; aussi fig*) to feel stifled; **s'~** *vi* (*en mangeant etc*) to choke.

étouffoir [etufwaʀ] *nm* (*MUS*) damper.

étourderie [etuʀdəʀi] *nf* heedlessness *no pl*; thoughtless blunder; **faute d'~** careless mistake.

étourdi, e [etuʀdi] *adj* (*distrait*) scatterbrained, heedless.

étourdiment [etuʀdimɑ̃] *adv* rashly.

étourdir [etuʀdiʀ] *vt* (*assommer*) to stun, daze; (*griser*) to make dizzy *ou* giddy.

étourdissant, e [etuʀdisɑ̃, -ɑ̃t] *adj* staggering.

étourdissement [etuʀdismɑ̃] *nm* dizzy spell.

étourneau, x [etuʀno] *nm* starling.

étrange [etʀɑ̃ʒ] *adj* strange.

étrangement [etʀɑ̃ʒmɑ̃] *adv* strangely.

étranger, ère [etʀɑ̃ʒe, -ɛʀ] *adj* foreign; (*pas de la famille, non familier*) strange ♦ *nm/f* foreigner; stranger ♦ *nm*: **l'~** foreign countries; **à l'~** abroad; **de l'~** from abroad; **~ à** (*mal connu*) unfamiliar to; (*sans rapport*) irrelevant to.

étrangeté [etʀɑ̃ʒte] *nf* strangeness.

étranglé, e [etʀɑ̃gle] *adj*: **d'une voix ~e** in a strangled voice.

étranglement [etʀɑ̃gləmɑ̃] *nm* (*d'une vallée etc*) constriction, narrow passage.

étrangler [etʀɑ̃gle] *vt* to strangle; (*fig: presse, libertés*) to stifle; **s'~** *vi* (*en mangeant etc*) to choke; (*se resserrer*) to make a bottleneck.

étrave [etʀav] *nf* stem.

MOT-CLÉ

être [ɛtʀ(ə)] *nm* being; ~ **humain** human being
♦ *vb +attrib* **1** (*état, description*) to be; **il est instituteur** he is *ou* he's a teacher; **vous êtes grand/intelligent/fatigué** you are *ou* you're tall/clever/tired
2 (*+à*: *appartenir*) to be; **le livre est à Paul** the book is Paul's *ou* belongs to Paul; **c'est à moi/eux** it is *ou* it's mine/theirs
3 (*+de*: *provenance*): **il est de Paris** he is from Paris; (: *appartenance*): **il est des nôtres** he is one of us
4 (*date*): **nous sommes le 10 janvier** it's the 10th of January (today)
♦ *vi* to be; **je ne serai pas ici demain** I won't be here tomorrow
♦ *vb aux* **1** to have; to be; ~ **arrivé/allé** to have arrived/gone; **il est parti** he has left, he has gone
2 (*forme passive*) to be; ~ **fait par** to be made by; **il a été promu** he has been promoted
3 (*+à +inf*: *obligation, but*): **c'est à réparer** it needs repairing; **c'est à essayer** it should be tried; **il est à espérer que ...** it is *ou* it's to be hoped that ...
♦ *vb impers* **1**: **il est** *+adjectif* it is *+adjective*; **il est impossible de le faire** it's impossible to do it
2 (*heure, date*): **il est 10 heures** it is *ou* it's 10 o'clock
3 (*emphatique*): **c'est moi** it's me; **c'est à lui de le faire** it's up to him to do it; *voir aussi* **est-ce que, n'est-ce pas, c'est-à-dire, ce.**

étreindre [etʀɛ̃dʀ(ə)] *vt* to clutch, grip; (*amoureusement, amicalement*) to embrace; **s'**~ to embrace.

étreinte [etʀɛ̃t] *nf* clutch, grip; embrace; **resserrer son** ~ **autour de** (*fig*) to tighten one's grip on *ou* around.

étrenner [etʀene] *vt* to use (*ou* wear) for the first time.

étrennes [etʀɛn] *nfpl* (*cadeaux*) New Year's present; (*gratifications*) ≈ Christmas box *sg*, ≈ Christmas bonus.

étrier [etʀije] *nm* stirrup.

étriller [etʀije] *vt* (*cheval*) to curry; (*fam: battre*) to slaughter (*fig*).

étriper [etʀipe] *vt* to gut; (*fam*): ~ **qn** to tear sb's guts out.

étriqué, e [etʀike] *adj* skimpy.

étroit, e [etʀwa, -wat] *adj* narrow; (*vêtement*) tight; (*fig: serré*) close, tight; **à l'**~ cramped; ~ **d'esprit** narrow-minded.

étroitement [etʀwatmɑ̃] *adv* closely.

étroitesse [etʀwatɛs] *nf* narrowness; ~ **d'esprit** narrow-mindedness.

Étrurie [etʀyʀi] *nf*: **l'**~ Etruria.

étrusque [etʀysk(ə)] *adj* Etruscan.

étude [etyd] *nf* studying; (*ouvrage, rapport, MUS*) study; (*de notaire: bureau*) office; (*: charge*) practice; (*SCOL: salle de travail*) study room; ~**s** *nfpl* (*SCOL*) studies; **être à l'**~ (*projet etc*) to be under consideration; **faire des** ~**s (de droit/médecine)** to study (law/medicine); ~**s secondaires/supérieures** secondary/higher education; ~ **de cas** case study; ~ **de faisabilité** feasibility study; ~ **de marché** (*ÉCON*) market research.

étudiant, e [etydjɑ̃, -ɑ̃t] *adj, nm/f* student.

étudié, e [etydje] *adj* (*démarche*) studied; (*système*) carefully designed; (*prix*) keen.

étudier [etydje] *vt, vi* to study.

étui [etɥi] *nm* case.

étuve [etyv] *nf* steamroom; (*appareil*) sterilizer.

étuvée [etyve]: **à l'**~ *adv* braised.

étymologie [etimɔlɔʒi] *nf* etymology.

étymologique [etimɔlɔʒik] *adj* etymological.

eu, eue [y] *pp de* **avoir**.

EU(A) *sigle mpl* (= *États-Unis (d'Amérique)*) US(A).

eucalyptus [økaliptys] *nm* eucalyptus.

Eucharistie [økaʀisti] *nf*: **l'**~ the Eucharist, the Lord's Supper.

eucharistique [økaʀistik] *adj* eucharistic.

euclidien, ne [øklidjɛ̃, -ɛn] *adj* Euclidian.

eugénique [øʒenik] *adj* eugenic ♦ *nf* eugenics *sg*.

eugénisme [øʒenism(ə)] *nm* eugenics *sg*.

euh [ø] *excl* er.

eunuque [ønyk] *nm* eunuch.

euphémique [øfemik] *adj* euphemistic.

euphémisme [øfemism(ə)] *nm* euphemism.

euphonie [øfɔni] *nf* euphony.

euphorbe [øfɔʀb(ə)] *nf* (*BOT*) spurge.

euphorie [øfɔʀi] *nf* euphoria.

euphorique [øfɔʀik] *adj* euphoric.

euphorisant, e [øfɔʀizɑ̃, -ɑ̃t] *adj* exhilarating.

Euphrate [øfʀat] *nm*: **l'**~ the Euphrates *sg*.

eurafricain, e [øʀafʀikɛ̃, -ɛn] *adj* Eurafrican.

eurasiatique [øʀazjatik] *adj* Eurasiatic.

Eurasie [øʀazi] *nf*: **l'**~ Eurasia.

eurasien, ne [øʀazjɛ̃, -ɛn] *adj* Eurasian.

EURATOM [øʀatɔm] *sigle f* Euratom.

eurent [yʀ(ə)] *vb voir* **avoir**.

euro [øʀo] *nm* (*monnaie*) euro.

euro- [øʀo] *préfixe* Euro-.

eurocrate [øʀɔkʀat] *nm/f* (*péj*) Eurocrat.

eurodevise [øʀɔdəviz] *nf* Eurocurrency.

eurodollar [øʀodɔlaʀ] *nm* Eurodollar.

Euroland [øʀolɑ̃d] *nm* Euroland.

Europe [øʀɔp] *nf*: **l'**~ Europe; **l'**~ **centrale** Central Europe; **l'**~ **verte** European agriculture.

européanisation [øʀɔpeanizɑsjɔ̃] *nf* Europeanization.

européaniser [øʀɔpeanize] *vt* to Europeanize.

européen, ne [øʀɔpeɛ̃, -ɛn] *adj* European ♦ *nm/f*: **E**~**, ne** European.

eurosceptique [øʀosɛptik] *nm/f* Eurosceptic.

Eurovision [øʀovizjɔ̃] *nf* Eurovision.

eus [y] *etc vb voir* **avoir**.
euthanasie [øtanazi] *nf* euthanasia.
eux [ø] *pron* (*sujet*) they; (*objet*) them; **~, ils ont fait** ... THEY did ....
EV *abr (= en ville) used on mail to be delivered by hand, courier etc within the same town.*
évacuation [evakɥɑsjɔ̃] *nf* evacuation.
évacué, e [evakɥe] *nm/f* evacuee.
évacuer [evakɥe] *vt* (*salle, région*) to evacuate, clear; (*occupants, population*) to evacuate; (*toxine etc*) to evacuate, discharge.
évadé, e [evade] *adj* escaped ♦ *nm/f* escapee.
évader [evade]: **s'~** *vi* to escape.
évaluation [evalɥɑsjɔ̃] *nf* assessment, evaluation.
évaluer [evalɥe] *vt* to assess, evaluate.
évanescent, e [evanesɑ̃, -ɑ̃t] *adj* evanescent.
évangélique [evɑ̃ʒelik] *adj* evangelical.
évangélisation [evɑ̃gelizɑsjɔ̃] *nf* evangelization.
évangéliser [evɑ̃ʒelize] *vt* to evangelize.
évangéliste [evɑ̃ʒelist(ə)] *nm* evangelist.
évangile [evɑ̃ʒil] *nm* gospel; (*texte de la Bible*): **É~** Gospel; **ce n'est pas l'É~** (*fig*) it's not gospel.
évanoui, e [evanwi] *adj* in a faint; **tomber ~** to faint.
évanouir [evanwiʀ]: **s'~** *vi* to faint, pass out; (*disparaître*) to vanish, disappear.
évanouissement [evanwismɑ̃] *nm* (*syncope*) fainting fit; (*MÉD*) loss of consciousness.
évaporation [evapɔʀɑsjɔ̃] *nf* evaporation.
évaporé, e [evapɔʀe] *adj* giddy, scatterbrained.
évaporer [evapɔʀe]: **s'~** *vi* to evaporate.
évasé, e [evɑze] *adj* (*jupe etc*) flared.
évaser [evɑze] *vt* (*tuyau*) to widen, open out; (*jupe, pantalon*) to flare; **s'~** *vi* to widen, open out.
évasif, ive [evazif, -iv] *adj* evasive.
évasion [evazjɔ̃] *nf* escape; **littérature d'~** escapist literature; **~ des capitaux** (*ÉCON*) flight of capital; **~ fiscale** tax avoidance.
évasivement [evazivmɑ̃] *adv* evasively.
évêché [eveʃe] *nm* (*fonction*) bishopric; (*palais*) bishop's palace.
éveil [evɛj] *nm* awakening; **être en ~** to be alert; **mettre qn en ~, donner l'~ à qn** to arouse sb's suspicions; **activités d'~** early-learning activities.
éveillé, e [eveje] *adj* awake; (*vif*) alert, sharp.
éveiller [eveje] *vt* to (a)waken; **s'~** *vi* to (a)waken; (*fig*) to be aroused.
événement [evɛnmɑ̃] *nm* event.
éventail [evɑ̃taj] *nm* fan; (*choix*) range; **en ~** fanned out; fan-shaped.
éventaire [evɑ̃tɛʀ] *nm* stall, stand.
éventé, e [evɑ̃te] *adj* (*parfum, vin*) stale.
éventer [evɑ̃te] *vt* (*secret, complot*) to uncover; (*avec un éventail*) to fan; **s'~** *vi* (*parfum, vin*) to go stale.
éventrer [evɑ̃tʀe] *vt* to disembowel; (*fig*) to tear *ou* rip open.
éventualité [evɑ̃tɥalite] *nf* eventuality; possibility; **dans l'~ de** in the event of; **parer à toute ~** to guard against all eventualities.
éventuel, le [evɑ̃tɥɛl] *adj* possible.
éventuellement [evɑ̃tɥɛlmɑ̃] *adv* possibly.
évêque [evɛk] *nm* bishop.
Everest [ɛvʀɛst] *nm*: **(mont) ~** (Mount) Everest.
évertuer [evɛʀtɥe]: **s'~** *vi*: **s'~ à faire** to try very hard to do.
éviction [eviksjɔ̃] *nf* ousting, supplanting; (*de locataire*) eviction.
évidemment [evidamɑ̃] *adv* obviously.
évidence [evidɑ̃s] *nf* obviousness; (*fait*) obvious fact; **se rendre à l'~** to bow before the evidence; **nier l'~** to deny the evidence; **à l'~** evidently; **de toute ~** quite obviously *ou* evidently; **en ~** conspicuous; **mettre en ~** to bring to the fore.
évident, e [evidɑ̃, -ɑ̃t] *adj* obvious, evident; **ce n'est pas ~** (*cela pose des problèmes*) it's not (all that) straightforward, it's not as simple as all that.
évider [evide] *vt* to scoop out.
évier [evje] *nm* (kitchen) sink.
évincement [evɛ̃smɑ̃] *nm* ousting.
évincer [evɛ̃se] *vt* to oust, supplant.
évitable [evitabl(ə)] *adj* avoidable.
évitement [evitmɑ̃] *nm*: **place d'~** (*AUTO*) passing place.
éviter [evite] *vt* to avoid; **~ de faire/que qch ne se passe** to avoid doing/sth happening; **~ qch à qn** to spare sb sth.
évocateur, trice [evɔkatœʀ, -tʀis] *adj* evocative, suggestive.
évocation [evɔkɑsjɔ̃] *nf* evocation.
évolué, e [evɔlɥe] *adj* advanced; (*personne*) broad-minded.
évoluer [evɔlɥe] *vi* (*enfant, maladie*) to develop; (*situation, moralement*) to evolve, develop; (*aller et venir: danseur etc*) to move about, circle.
évolutif, ive [evɔlytif, -iv] *adj* evolving.
évolution [evɔlysjɔ̃] *nf* development; evolution; **~s** *nfpl* movements.
évolutionnisme [evɔlysjɔnism(ə)] *nm* evolutionism.
évoquer [evɔke] *vt* to call to mind, evoke; (*mentionner*) to mention.
ex. *abr* (*= exemple*) ex.
ex- [ɛks] *préfixe* ex-.
exacerbé, e [ɛgzasɛʀbe] *adj* (*orgueil, sensibilité*) exaggerated.
exacerber [ɛgzasɛʀbe] *vt* to exacerbate.
exact, e [ɛgzakt] *adj* (*précis*) exact, accurate, precise; (*correct*) correct; (*ponctuel*) punctual; **l'heure ~e** the right *ou* exact time.
exactement [ɛgzaktəmɑ̃] *adv* exactly, accurately, precisely; correctly; (*c'est cela même*) exactly.
exaction [ɛgzaksjɔ̃] *nf* (*d'argent*) exaction; (*gén*

pl: actes de violence) abuse(s).
exactitude [ɛgzaktityd] *nf* exactitude, accurateness, precision.
ex aequo [ɛgzeko] *adj* equally placed; **classé 1er** ~ placed equal first.
exagération [ɛgzaʒeʀɑsjɔ̃] *nf* exaggeration.
exagéré, e [ɛgzaʒeʀe] *adj* (*prix etc*) excessive.
exagérément [ɛgzaʒeʀemɑ̃] *adv* excessively.
exagérer [ɛgzaʒeʀe] *vt* to exaggerate ♦ *vi* (*abuser*) to go too far; (*dépasser les bornes*) to overstep the mark; (*déformer les faits*) to exaggerate; **s'**~ **qch** to exaggerate sth.
exaltant, e [ɛgzaltɑ̃, -ɑ̃t] *adj* exhilarating.
exaltation [ɛgzaltɑsjɔ̃] *nf* exaltation.
exalté, e [ɛgzalte] *adj* (over)excited ♦ *nm/f* (*péj*) fanatic.
exalter [ɛgzalte] *vt* (*enthousiasmer*) to excite, elate; (*glorifier*) to exalt.
examen [ɛgzamɛ̃] *nm* examination; (*SCOL*) exam, examination; **à l'**~ (*dossier, projet*) under consideration; (*COMM*) on approval; ~ **blanc** mock exam(ination); ~ **de la vue** sight test.
examinateur, trice [ɛgzaminatœʀ, -tʀis] *nm/f* examiner.
examiner [ɛgzamine] *vt* to examine.
exaspérant, e [ɛgzaspeʀɑ̃, -ɑ̃t] *adj* exasperating.
exaspération [ɛgzaspeʀɑsjɔ̃] *nf* exasperation.
exaspéré, e [ɛgzaspeʀe] *adj* exasperated.
exaspérer [ɛgzaspeʀe] *vt* to exasperate; (*aggraver*) to exacerbate.
exaucer [ɛgzose] *vt* (*vœu*) to grant, fulfil; ~ **qn** to grant sb's wishes.
ex cathedra [ɛkskatedʀa] *adj, adv* ex cathedra.
excavateur [ɛkskavatœʀ] *nm* excavator, mechanical digger.
excavation [ɛkskavɑsjɔ̃] *nf* excavation.
excavatrice [ɛkskavatʀis] *nf* = **excavateur**.
excédent [ɛksedɑ̃] *nm* surplus; **en** ~ surplus; **payer 60 € d'**~ (*de bagages*) to pay €60 excess luggage; ~ **de bagages** excess luggage; ~ **commercial** trade surplus.
excédentaire [ɛksedɑ̃tɛʀ] *adj* surplus, excess.
excéder [ɛksede] *vt* (*dépasser*) to exceed; (*agacer*) to exasperate; **excédé de fatigue** exhausted; **excédé de travail** worn out with work.
excellence [ɛkselɑ̃s] *nf* excellence; (*titre*) Excellency; **par** ~ par excellence.
excellent, e [ɛkselɑ̃, -ɑ̃t] *adj* excellent.
exceller [ɛksele] *vi*: ~ **(dans)** to excel (in).
excentricité [ɛksɑ̃tʀisite] *nf* eccentricity.
excentrique [ɛksɑ̃tʀik] *adj* eccentric; (*quartier*) outlying ♦ *nm/f* eccentric.
excentriquement [ɛksɑ̃tʀikmɑ̃] *adv* eccentrically.
excepté, e [ɛksɛpte] *adj, prép*: **les élèves ~s**, ~ **les élèves** except for *ou* apart from the pupils; ~ **si/quand** except if/when; ~ **que** except that.
excepter [ɛksɛpte] *vt* to except.
exception [ɛksɛpsjɔ̃] *nf* exception; **faire** ~ to be an exception; **faire une** ~ to make an exception; **sans** ~ without exception; **à l'**~ **de** except for, with the exception of; **d'**~ (*mesure, loi*) special, exceptional.
exceptionnel, le [ɛksɛpsjɔnɛl] *adj* exceptional; (*prix*) special.
exceptionnellement [ɛksɛpsjɔnɛlmɑ̃] *adv* exceptionally; (*par exception*) by way of an exception, on this occasion.
excès [ɛksɛ] *nm* surplus ♦ *nmpl* excesses; **à l'**~ (*méticuleux, généreux*) to excess; **avec** ~ to excess; **sans** ~ in moderation; **tomber dans l'**~ **inverse** to go to the opposite extreme; ~ **de langage** immoderate language; ~ **de pouvoir** abuse of power; ~ **de vitesse** speeding *no pl*, exceeding the speed limit; ~ **de zèle** overzealousness *no pl*.
excessif, ive [ɛksesif, -iv] *adj* excessive.
excessivement [ɛksesivmɑ̃] *adv* (*trop: cher*) excessively, inordinately; (*très: riche, laid*) extremely, incredibly; **manger/boire** ~ to eat/drink to excess.
exciper [ɛksipe]: ~ **de** *vt* to plead.
excipient [ɛksipjɑ̃] *nm* (*MÉD*) inert base, excipient.
exciser [ɛksize] *vt* (*MÉD*) to excise.
excision [ɛksizjɔ̃] *nf* (*MÉD*) excision; (*rituelle*) circumcision.
excitant, e [ɛksitɑ̃, -ɑ̃t] *adj* exciting ♦ *nm* stimulant.
excitation [ɛksitɑsjɔ̃] *nf* (*état*) excitement.
excité, e [ɛksite] *adj* excited.
exciter [ɛksite] *vt* to excite; (*suj: café etc*) to stimulate; **s'**~ *vi* to get excited; ~ **qn à** (*révolte etc*) to incite sb to.
exclamation [ɛksklamɑsjɔ̃] *nf* exclamation.
exclamer [ɛksklame]: **s'**~ *vi* to exclaim.
exclu, e [ɛkskly] *pp de* **exclure** ♦ *adj*: **il est/n'est pas** ~ **que ...** it's out of the question/not impossible that ...; **ce n'est pas exclu** it's not impossible, I don't rule that out.
exclure [ɛksklyʀ] *vt* (*faire sortir*) to expel; (*ne pas compter*) to exclude, leave out; (*rendre impossible*) to exclude, rule out.
exclusif, ive [ɛksklyzif, -iv] *adj* exclusive; **avec la mission exclusive/dans le but** ~ **de ...** with the sole mission/aim of ...; **agent** ~ sole agent.
exclusion [ɛksklyzjɔ̃] *nf* expulsion; **à l'**~ **de** with the exclusion *ou* exception of.
exclusivement [ɛksklyzivmɑ̃] *adv* exclusively.
exclusivité [ɛksklyzivite] *nf* exclusiveness; (*COMM*) exclusive rights *pl*; **passer en** ~ (*film*) to go on general release.
excommunier [ɛkskɔmynje] *vt* to excommunicate.
excréments [ɛkskʀemɑ̃] *nmpl* excrement *sg*, faeces.
excréter [ɛkskʀete] *vt* to excrete.
excroissance [ɛkskʀwasɑ̃s] *nf* excrescence, outgrowth.

excursion [ɛkskyʀsjɔ̃] *nf* (*en autocar*) excursion, trip; (*à pied*) walk, hike; **faire une** ~ to go on an excursion *ou* a trip; to go on a walk *ou* hike.
excursionniste [ɛkskyʀsjɔnist(ə)] *nm/f* tripper; hiker.
excusable [ɛkskyzabl(ə)] *adj* excusable.
excuse [ɛkskyz] *nf* excuse; ~**s** *nfpl* apology *sg*, apologies; **faire des** ~**s** to apologize; **faire ses** ~**s** to offer one's apologies; **mot d'**~ (*SCOL*) note from one's parent(s) (*to explain absence etc*); **lettre d'**~**s** letter of apology.
excuser [ɛkskyze] *vt* to excuse; ~ **qn de qch** (*dispenser*) to excuse sb from sth; **s'**~ **(de)** to apologize (for); **"excusez-moi"** "I'm sorry"; (*pour attirer l'attention*) "excuse me"; **se faire** ~ to ask to be excused.
exécrable [ɛgzekʀabl(ə)] *adj* atrocious.
exécrer [ɛgzekʀe] *vt* to loathe, abhor.
exécutant, e [ɛgzekytɑ̃, -ɑ̃t] *nm/f* performer.
exécuter [ɛgzekyte] *vt* (*prisonnier*) to execute; (*tâche etc*) to execute, carry out; (*MUS: jouer*) to perform, execute; (*INFORM*) to run; **s'**~ *vi* to comply.
exécuteur, trice [ɛgzekytœʀ, -tʀis] *nm/f* (*testamentaire*) executor ♦ *nm* (*bourreau*) executioner.
exécutif, ive [ɛgzekytif, -iv] *adj*, *nm* (*POL*) executive.
exécution [ɛgzekysjɔ̃] *nf* execution; carrying out; **mettre à** ~ to carry out.
exécutoire [ɛgzekytwaʀ] *adj* (*JUR*) (legally) binding.
exégèse [ɛgzeʒɛz] *nf* exegesis.
exégète [ɛgzeʒɛt] *nm* exegete.
exemplaire [ɛgzɑ̃plɛʀ] *adj* exemplary ♦ *nm* copy.
exemple [ɛgzɑ̃pl(ə)] *nm* example; **par** ~ for instance, for example; (*valeur intensive*) really!; **sans** ~ (*bêtise, gourmandise etc*) unparalleled; **donner l'**~ to set an example; **prendre** ~ **sur** to take as a model; **à l'**~ **de** just like; **pour l'**~ (*punir*) as an example.
exempt, e [ɛgzɑ̃, -ɑ̃t] *adj*: ~ **de** (*dispensé de*) exempt from; (*sans*) free from; ~ **de taxes** tax-free.
exempter [ɛgzɑ̃te] *vt*: ~ **de** to exempt from.
exercé, e [ɛgzɛʀse] *adj* trained.
exercer [ɛgzɛʀse] *vt* (*pratiquer*) to exercise, practise; (*faire usage de: prérogative*) to exercise; (*effectuer: influence, contrôle, pression*) to exert; (*former*) to exercise, train ♦ *vi* (*médecin*) to be in practice; **s'**~ (*sportif, musicien*) to practise; (*se faire sentir: pression etc*): **s'**~ **(sur** *ou* **contre)** to be exerted (on); **s'**~ **à faire qch** to train o.s. to do sth.
exercice [ɛgzɛʀsis] *nm* practice; exercising; (*tâche, travail*) exercise; (*COMM, ADMIN: période*) accounting period; **l'**~ (*sportive etc*) exercise; (*MIL*) drill; **en** ~ (*juge*) in office; (*médecin*) practising; **dans l'**~ **de ses fonctions** in the discharge of his duties; ~**s d'assouplissement** limbering-up (exercises).
exergue [ɛgzɛʀg(ə)] *nm*: **mettre en** ~ (*inscription*) to inscribe; **porter en** ~ to be inscribed with.
exhalaison [ɛgzalɛzɔ̃] *nf* exhalation.
exhaler [ɛgzale] *vt* (*parfum*) to exhale; (*souffle, son, soupir*) to utter, breathe; **s'**~ *vi* to rise (up).
exhausser [ɛgzose] *vt* to raise (up).
exhausteur [ɛgzostœʀ] *nm* extractor fan.
exhaustif, ive [ɛgzostif, -iv] *adj* exhaustive.
exhiber [ɛgzibe] *vt* (*montrer: papiers, certificat*) to present, produce; (*péj*) to display, flaunt; **s'**~ (*personne*) to parade; (*suj: exhibitionniste*) to expose o.s.
exhibitionnisme [ɛgzibisjɔnism(ə)] *nm* exhibitionism.
exhibitionniste [ɛgzibisjɔnist(ə)] *nm/f* exhibitionist.
exhortation [ɛgzɔʀtɑsjɔ̃] *nf* exhortation.
exhorter [ɛgzɔʀte] *vt*: ~ **qn à faire** to urge sb to do.
exhumer [ɛgzyme] *vt* to exhume.
exigeant, e [ɛgziʒɑ̃, -ɑ̃t] *adj* demanding; (*péj*) hard to please.
exigence [ɛgziʒɑ̃s] *nf* demand, requirement.
exiger [ɛgziʒe] *vt* to demand, require.
exigible [ɛgziʒibl(ə)] *adj* (*COMM, JUR*) payable.
exigu, ë [ɛgzigy] *adj* cramped, tiny.
exiguïté [ɛgzigɥite] *nf* (*d'un lieu*) cramped nature.
exil [ɛgzil] *nm* exile; **en** ~ in exile.
exilé, e [ɛgzile] *nm/f* exile.
exiler [ɛgzile] *vt* to exile; **s'**~ to go into exile.
existant, e [ɛgzistɑ̃, -ɑ̃t] *adj* (*actuel, présent*) existing.
existence [ɛgzistɑ̃s] *nf* existence; **dans l'**~ in life.
existentialisme [ɛgzistɑ̃sjalism(ə)] *nm* existentialism.
existentiel, le [ɛgzistɑ̃sjɛl] *adj* existential.
exister [ɛgziste] *vi* to exist; **il existe un/des** there is a/are (some).
exode [ɛgzɔd] *nm* exodus.
exonération [ɛgzɔneʀɑsjɔ̃] *nf* exemption.
exonéré, e [ɛgzɔneʀe] *adj*: ~ **de TVA** zero-rated (for VAT).
exonérer [ɛgzɔneʀe] *vt*: ~ **de** to exempt from.
exorbitant, e [ɛgzɔʀbitɑ̃, -ɑ̃t] *adj* exorbitant.
exorbité, e [ɛgzɔʀbite] *adj*: **yeux** ~**s** bulging eyes.
exorciser [ɛgzɔʀsize] *vt* to exorcize.
exorde [ɛgzɔʀd(ə)] *nm* introduction.
exotique [ɛgzɔtik] *adj* exotic.
exotisme [ɛgzɔtism(ə)] *nm* exoticism.
expansif, ive [ɛkspɑ̃sif, -iv] *adj* expansive, communicative.
expansion [ɛkspɑ̃sjɔ̃] *nf* expansion.
expansionniste [ɛkspɑ̃sjɔnist(ə)] *adj* expansionist.
expansivité [ɛkspɑ̃sivite] *nf* expansiveness.

expatrié, e [ɛkspatʀije] *nm/f* expatriate.
expatrier [ɛkspatʀije] *vt* (*argent*) to take *ou* send out of the country; **s'~** to leave one's country.
expectative [ɛkspɛktativ] *nf*: **être dans l'~** to be waiting to see.
expectorant, e [ɛkspɛktɔʀɑ̃, -ɑ̃t] *adj*: **sirop ~** expectorant (syrup).
expectorer [ɛkspɛktɔʀe] *vi* to expectorate.
expédient [ɛkspedjɑ̃] *nm* (*parfois péj*) expedient; **vivre d'~s** to live by one's wits.
expédier [ɛkspedje] *vt* (*lettre, paquet*) to send; (*troupes, renfort*) to dispatch; (*péj*: *travail etc*) to dispose of, dispatch.
expéditeur, trice [ɛkspeditœʀ, -tʀis] *nm/f* (*POSTES*) sender.
expéditif, ive [ɛkspeditif, -iv] *adj* quick, expeditious.
expédition [ɛkspedisjɔ̃] *nf* sending; (*scientifique, sportive, MIL*) expedition; **~ punitive** punitive raid.
expéditionnaire [ɛkspedisjɔnɛʀ] *adj*: **corps ~** (*MIL*) task force.
expérience [ɛkspeʀjɑ̃s] *nf* (*de la vie, des choses*) experience; (*scientifique*) experiment; **avoir de l'~** to have experience, be experienced; **avoir l'~ de** to have experience of; **faire l'~ de qch** to experience sth; **~ de chimie/d'électricité** chemical/electrical experiment.
expérimental, e, aux [ɛkspeʀimɑ̃tal, -o] *adj* experimental.
expérimentalement [ɛkspeʀimɑ̃talmɑ̃] *adv* experimentally.
expérimenté, e [ɛkspeʀimɑ̃te] *adj* experienced.
expérimenter [ɛkspeʀimɑ̃te] *vt* (*machine, technique*) to test out, experiment with.
expert, e [ɛkspɛʀ, -ɛʀt(ə)] *adj*: **~ en** expert in ♦ *nm* (*spécialiste*) expert; **~ en assurances** insurance valuer.
expert-comptable, *pl* **experts-comptables** [ɛkspɛʀkɔ̃tabl(ə)] *nm* ≈ chartered (*BRIT*) *ou* certified public (*US*) accountant.
expertise [ɛkspɛʀtiz] *nf* valuation; assessment; valuer's (*ou* assessor's) report; (*JUR*) (forensic) examination.
expertiser [ɛkspɛʀtize] *vt* (*objet de valeur*) to value; (*voiture accidentée etc*) to assess damage to.
expier [ɛkspje] *vt* to expiate, atone for.
expiration [ɛkspiʀɑsjɔ̃] *nf* expiry (*BRIT*), expiration; breathing out *no pl*.
expirer [ɛkspiʀe] *vi* (*prendre fin, littéraire*: *mourir*) to expire; (*respirer*) to breathe out.
explétif, ive [ɛkspletif, -iv] *adj* (*LING*) expletive.
explicable [ɛksplikabl(ə)] *adj*: **pas ~** inexplicable.
explicatif, ive [ɛksplikatif, -iv] *adj* (*mot, texte, note*) explanatory.
explication [ɛksplikɑsjɔ̃] *nf* explanation; (*discussion*) discussion; **~ de texte** (*SCOL*) critical analysis (of a text).
explicite [ɛksplisit] *adj* explicit.
explicitement [ɛksplisitmɑ̃] *adv* explicitly.
expliciter [ɛksplisite] *vt* to make explicit.
expliquer [ɛksplike] *vt* to explain; **~ (à qn) comment/que** to point out *ou* explain (to sb) how/that; **s'~** (*se faire comprendre: personne*) to explain o.s.; (*discuter*) to discuss things; (*se disputer*) to have it out; (*comprendre*): **je m'explique son retard/absence** I understand his lateness/absence; **son erreur s'explique** one can understand his mistake.
exploit [ɛksplwa] *nm* exploit, feat.
exploitable [ɛskplwatabl(ə)] *adj* (*gisement etc*) that can be exploited; **~ par une machine** machine-readable.
exploitant [ɛksplwatɑ̃] *nm* farmer.
exploitation [ɛksplwatɑsjɔ̃] *nf* exploitation; running; (*entreprise*): **~ agricole** farming concern.
exploiter [ɛksplwate] *vt* to exploit; (*entreprise, ferme*) to run, operate.
exploiteur, euse [ɛksplwatœʀ, -øz] *nm/f* (*péj*) exploiter.
explorateur, trice [ɛksplɔʀatœʀ, -tʀis] *nm/f* explorer.
exploration [ɛksplɔʀɑsjɔ̃] *nf* exploration.
explorer [ɛksplɔʀe] *vt* to explore.
exploser [ɛksploze] *vi* to explode, blow up; (*engin explosif*) to go off; (*fig: joie, colère*) to burst out, explode; (*: personne: de colère*) to explode, flare up; **faire ~** (*bombe*) to explode, detonate; (*bâtiment, véhicule*) to blow up.
explosif, ive [ɛksplozif, -iv] *adj, nm* explosive.
explosion [ɛksplozjɔ̃] *nf* explosion; **~ de joie/colère** outburst of joy/rage; **~ démographique** population explosion.
exponentiel, le [ɛkspɔnɑ̃sjɛl] *adj* exponential.
exportateur, trice [ɛkspɔʀtatœʀ, -tʀis] *adj* exporting ♦ *nm* exporter.
exportation [ɛkspɔʀtɑsjɔ̃] *nf* export.
exporter [ɛkspɔʀte] *vt* to export.
exposant [ɛkspozɑ̃] *nm* exhibitor; (*MATH*) exponent.
exposé, e [ɛkspoze] *nm* (*écrit*) exposé; (*oral*) talk ♦ *adj*: **~ au sud** facing south, with a southern aspect; **bien ~** well situated; **très ~** very exposed.
exposer [ɛkspoze] *vt* (*montrer: marchandise*) to display; (*: peinture*) to exhibit, show; (*parler de: problème, situation*) to explain, expose, set out; (*mettre en danger, orienter: maison etc*) to expose; **~ qn/qch à** to expose sb/sth to; **~ sa vie** to risk one's life; **s'~ à** (*soleil, danger*) to expose o.s. to; (*critiques, punition*) to lay o.s. open to.
exposition [ɛkspozisjɔ̃] *nf* (*voir exposer*) displaying; exhibiting; explanation, exposition; exposure; (*voir exposé*) aspect, situation; (*manifestation*) exhibition; (*PHOTO*) exposure;

(*introduction*) exposition.
exprès [ɛkspʀɛ] *adv* (*délibérément*) on purpose; (*spécialement*) specially; **faire ~ de faire qch** to do sth on purpose.
exprès, esse [ɛkspʀɛs] *adj* (*ordre, défense*) express, formal ♦ *adj inv, adv* (*POSTES*) express; **envoyer qch en ~** to send sth express.
express [ɛkspʀɛs] *adj, nm*: **(café) ~** espresso; **(train) ~** fast train.
expressément [ɛkspʀesemɑ̃] *adv* expressly, specifically.
expressif, ive [ɛkspʀesif, -iv] *adj* expressive.
expression [ɛkspʀɛsjɔ̃] *nf* expression; **réduit à sa plus simple ~** reduced to its simplest terms; **liberté/moyens d'~** freedom/means of expression; **~ toute faite** set phrase.
expressionnisme [ɛkspʀɛsjɔnism(ə)] *nm* expressionism.
expressivité [ɛkspʀesivite] *nf* expressiveness.
exprimer [ɛkspʀime] *vt* (*sentiment, idée*) to express; (*faire sortir: jus, liquide*) to press out; **s'~** *vi* (*personne*) to express o.s.
expropriation [ɛkspʀɔpʀijɑsjɔ̃] *nf* expropriation; **frapper d'~** to put a compulsory purchase order on.
exproprier [ɛkspʀɔpʀije] *vt* to buy up (*ou* buy the property of) by compulsory purchase, expropriate.
expulser [ɛkspylse] *vt* (*d'une salle, d'un groupe*) to expel; (*locataire*) to evict; (*FOOTBALL*) to send off.
expulsion [ɛkspylsjɔ̃] *nf* expulsion; eviction; sending off.
expurger [ɛkspyʀʒe] *vt* to expurgate, bowdlerize.
exquis, e [ɛkski, -iz] *adj* (*gâteau, parfum, élégance*) exquisite; (*personne, temps*) delightful.
exsangue [ɛksɑ̃g] *adj* bloodless, drained of blood.
exsuder [ɛksyde] *vt* to exude.
extase [ɛkstɑz] *nf* ecstasy; **être en ~** to be in raptures.
extasier [ɛkstɑzje]: **s'~** *vi*: **s'~ sur** to go into raptures over.
extatique [ɛkstatik] *adj* ecstatic.
extenseur [ɛkstɑ̃sœʀ] *nm* (*SPORT*) chest expander.
extensible [ɛkstɑ̃sibl(ə)] *adj* extensible.
extensif, ive [ɛkstɑ̃sif, -iv] *adj* extensive.
extension [ɛkstɑ̃sjɔ̃] *nf* (*d'un muscle, ressort*) stretching; (*MÉD*): **à l'~** in traction; (*fig*) extension; expansion.
exténuant [ɛkstenɥɑ̃, -ɑ̃t] *adj* exhausting.
exténuer [ɛkstenɥe] *vt* to exhaust.
extérieur, e [ɛksteʀjœʀ] *adj* (*de dehors: porte, mur etc*) outer, outside; (*: commerce, politique*) foreign; (*: influences, pressions*) external; (*au dehors: escalier, w.-c.*) outside; (*apparent: calme, gaieté etc*) outer ♦ *nm* (*d'une maison, d'un récipient etc*) outside, exterior; (*d'une personne: apparence*) exterior; (*d'un pays, d'un groupe social*): **l'~** the outside world; **à l'~** (*dehors*) outside; (*fig: à l'étranger*) abroad.
extérieurement [ɛksteʀjœʀmɑ̃] *adv* (*de dehors*) on the outside; (*en apparence*) on the surface.
extérioriser [ɛksteʀjɔʀize] *vt* to exteriorize.
extermination [ɛkstɛʀminɑsjɔ̃] *nf* extermination, wiping out.
exterminer [ɛkstɛʀmine] *vt* to exterminate, wipe out.
externat [ɛkstɛʀna] *nm* day school.
externe [ɛkstɛʀn(ə)] *adj* external, outer ♦ *nm/f* (*MÉD*) non-resident medical student, extern (*US*); (*SCOL*) day pupil.
extincteur [ɛkstɛ̃ktœʀ] *nm* (fire) extinguisher.
extinction [ɛkstɛ̃ksjɔ̃] *nf* extinction; (*JUR: d'une dette*) extinguishment; **~ de voix** (*MÉD*) loss of voice.
extirper [ɛkstiʀpe] *vt* (*tumeur*) to extirpate; (*plante*) to root out, pull up; (*préjugés*) to eradicate.
extorquer [ɛkstɔʀke] *vt* (*de l'argent, un renseignement*): **~ qch à qn** to extort sth from sb.
extorsion [ɛkstɔʀsjɔ̃] *nf*: **~ de fonds** extortion of money.
extra [ɛkstʀa] *adj inv* first-rate; (*marchandises*) top-quality ♦ *nm inv* extra help ♦ *préfixe* extra(-).
extraction [ɛkstʀaksjɔ̃] *nf* extraction.
extrader [ɛkstʀade] *vt* to extradite.
extradition [ɛkstʀadisjɔ̃] *nf* extradition.
extra-fin, e [ɛkstʀafɛ̃, -in] *adj* extra-fine.
extra-fort, e [ɛkstʀafɔʀ] *adj* extra strong.
extraire [ɛkstʀɛʀ] *vt* to extract.
extrait, e [ɛkstʀɛ, -ɛt] *pp de* **extraire** ♦ *nm* (*de plante*) extract; (*de film, livre*) extract, excerpt; **~ de naissance** birth certificate.
extra-lucide [ɛkstʀalysid] *adj*: **voyante ~** clairvoyant.
extraordinaire [ɛkstʀaɔʀdinɛʀ] *adj* extraordinary; (*POL, ADMIN*) special; **ambassadeur ~** ambassador extraordinary; **assemblée ~** extraordinary meeting; **par ~** by some unlikely chance.
extraordinairement [ɛksʀaɔʀdinɛʀmɑ̃] *adv* extraordinarily.
extrapoler [ɛksʀapɔle] *vt, vi* to extrapolate.
extra-sensoriel, le [ɛkstʀasɑ̃sɔʀjɛl] *adj* extrasensory.
extra-terrestre [ɛkstʀatɛʀɛstʀ(ə)] *nm/f* extraterrestrial.
extra-utérin, e [ɛkstʀayteʀɛ̃, -in] *adj* extrauterine.
extravagance [ɛkstʀavagɑ̃s] *nf* extravagance *no pl*; extravagant behaviour *no pl*.
extravagant, e [ɛkstʀavagɑ̃, -ɑ̃t] *adj* (*personne, attitude*) extravagant; (*idée*) wild.
extraverti, e [ɛkstʀavɛʀti] *adj* extrovert.
extrayais [ɛkstʀɛjɛ] *etc vb voir* **extraire**.
extrême [ɛkstʀɛm] *adj, nm* extreme; (*intensif*): **d'une ~ simplicité/brutalité** extremely

simple/brutal; **d'un ~ à l'autre** from one extreme to another; **à l'~** in the extreme; **à l'~ rigueur** in the absolute extreme.

extrêmement [ɛkstʀɛmmɑ̃] *adv* extremely.

extrême-onction, *pl* **extrêmes-onctions** [ɛkstʀɛmɔ̃ksjɔ̃] *nf* (*REL*) last rites *pl*, Extreme Unction.

Extrême-Orient [ɛkstʀɛmɔʀjɑ̃] *nm*: **l'~** the Far East.

extrême-oriental, e, aux [ɛkstʀɛmɔʀjɑ̃tal, -o] *adj* Far Eastern.

extrémisme [ɛkstʀemism(ə)] *nm* extremism.

extrémiste [ɛkstʀemist(ə)] *adj, nm/f* extremist.

extrémité [ɛkstʀemite] *nf* (*bout*) end; (*situation*) straits *pl*, plight; (*geste désespéré*) extreme action; **~s** *nfpl* (*pieds et mains*) extremities; **à la dernière ~** (*à l'agonie*) on the point of death.

extroverti, e [ɛkstʀɔvɛʀti] *adj* = **extraverti**.

exubérance [ɛgzybeʀɑ̃s] *nf* exuberance.

exubérant, e [ɛgzybeʀɑ̃, -ɑ̃t] *adj* exuberant.

exulter [ɛgzylte] *vi* to exult.

exutoire [ɛgzytwaʀ] *nm* outlet, release.

ex-voto [ɛksvɔto] *nm inv* ex-voto.

eye-liner [ajlajnœʀ] *nm* eyeliner.

F f

F, f [ɛf] *nm inv* F, f ♦ *abr* = **féminin**; (= *franc*) fr.; (= *Fahrenheit*) F; (= *frère*) Br(o).; (= *femme*) W; (*appartement*): **un F2/F3** a 2-/3-roomed flat (*BRIT*) *ou* apartment (*US*); **F comme François** F for Frederick (*BRIT*) *ou* Fox (*US*).

fa [fɑ] *nm inv* (*MUS*) F; (*en chantant la gamme*) fa.

fable [fɑbl(ə)] *nf* fable; (*mensonge*) story, tale.

fabricant [fabʀikɑ̃] *nm* manufacturer, maker.

fabrication [fabʀikɑsjɔ̃] *nf* manufacture, making.

fabrique [fabʀik] *nf* factory.

fabriquer [fabʀike] *vt* to make; (*industriellement*) to manufacture, make; (*construire: voiture*) to manufacture, build; (*: maison*) to build; (*fig: inventer: histoire, alibi*) to make up; (*fam*): **qu'est-ce qu'il fabrique?** what is he up to?; **~ en série** to mass-produce.

fabulateur, trice [fabylatœʀ, -tʀis] *nm/f*: **c'est un ~** he fantasizes, he makes up stories.

fabulation [fabylɑsjɔ̃] *nf* (*PSYCH*) fantasizing.

fabuleusement [fabyløzmɑ̃] *adv* fabulously, fantastically.

fabuleux, euse [fabylø, -øz] *adj* fabulous, fantastic.

fac [fak] *abr f* (*fam*: = *faculté*) Uni (*BRIT fam*), ≈ college (*US*).

façade [fasad] *nf* front, façade; (*fig*) façade.

face [fas] *nf* face; (*fig: aspect*) side ♦ *adj*: **le côté ~** heads; **perdre/sauver la ~** to lose/save face; **regarder qn en ~** to look sb in the face; **la maison/le trottoir d'en ~** the house/pavement opposite; **en ~ de** *prép* opposite; (*fig*) in front of; **de ~** *adv* from the front; face on; **~ à** *prép* facing; (*fig*) faced with, in the face of; **faire ~ à** to face; **faire ~ à la demande** (*COMM*) to meet the demand; **~ à ~** *adv* facing each other ♦ *nm inv* encounter.

face-à-main, *pl* **faces-à-main** [fasamɛ̃] *nm* lorgnette.

facéties [fasesi] *nfpl* jokes, pranks.

facétieux, euse [fasesjø, -øz] *adj* mischievous.

facette [fasɛt] *nf* facet.

fâché, e [fɑʃe] *adj* angry; (*désolé*) sorry.

fâcher [fɑʃe] *vt* to anger; **se ~** *vi* to get angry; **se ~ avec** (*se brouiller*) to fall out with.

fâcherie [fɑʃʀi] *nf* quarrel.

fâcheusement [fɑʃøzmɑ̃] *adv* unpleasantly; (*impressionné etc*) badly; **avoir ~ tendance à** to have an irritating tendency to.

fâcheux, euse [fɑʃø, -øz] *adj* unfortunate, regrettable.

facho [faʃo] *adj, nm/f* (*fam*: = *fasciste*) fascist.

facial, e, aux [fasjal, -o] *adj* facial.

faciès [fasjɛs] *nm* (*visage*) features *pl*.

facile [fasil] *adj* easy; (*accommodant*) easy-going; **~ d'emploi** (*INFORM*) user-friendly.

facilement [fasilmɑ̃] *adv* easily.

facilité [fasilite] *nf* easiness; (*disposition, don*) aptitude; (*moyen, occasion, possibilité*): **il a la ~ de rencontrer les gens** he has every opportunity to meet people; **~s** *nfpl* facilities; (*COMM*) terms; **~s de crédit** credit terms; **~s de paiement** easy terms.

faciliter [fasilite] *vt* to make easier.

façon [fasɔ̃] *nf* (*manière*) way; (*d'une robe etc*) making-up; cut; (*: main-d'œuvre*) labour (*BRIT*), labor (*US*); (*imitation*): **châle ~ cachemire** cashmere-style shawl; **~s** *nfpl* (*péj*) fuss *sg*; **faire des ~s** (*péj: être affecté*) to be affected; (*: faire des histoires*) to make a fuss; **de quelle ~?** (in) what way?; **sans ~** *adv* without fuss ♦ *adj* unaffected; **d'une autre ~** in another way; **en aucune ~** in no way; **de ~ à** so as to; **de ~ à ce que, de (telle) ~ que** so that; **de toute ~** anyway, in any case; **(c'est une) ~ de parler** it's a way of putting it; **travail à ~** tailoring.

façonner [fasɔne] *vt* (*fabriquer*) to manufacture; (*travailler: matière*) to shape, fashion; (*fig*) to mould, shape.

fac-similé [faksimile] *nm* facsimile.

facteur, trice [faktœʀ, -tʀis] *nm/f* postman/woman (*BRIT*), mailman/woman (*US*) ♦ *nm* (*MATH, gén*) factor; **~ d'orgues** organ builder; **~ de pianos** piano maker; **~ rhésus** rhesus factor.

factice [faktis] *adj* artificial.

faction [faksjɔ̃] *nf* (*groupe*) faction; (*MIL*) guard *ou* sentry (duty); watch; **en ~** on guard; standing watch.
factionnaire [faksjɔnɛʀ] *nm* guard, sentry.
factoriel, le [faktɔʀjɛl] *adj, nf* factorial.
factotum [faktɔtɔm] *nm* odd-job man, dogsbody (*BRIT*).
factuel, le [faktɥɛl] *adj* factual.
facturation [faktyʀɑsjɔ̃] *nf* invoicing; (*bureau*) invoicing (office).
facture [faktyʀ] *nf* (*à payer: gén*) bill; (*: COMM*) invoice; (*d'un artisan, artiste*) technique, workmanship.
facturer [faktyʀe] *vt* to invoice.
facturier, ière [faktyʀje, -jɛʀ] *nm/f* invoice clerk.
facultatif, ive [fakyltatif, -iv] *adj* optional; (*arrêt de bus*) request *cpd*.
faculté [fakylte] *nf* (*intellectuelle, d'université*) faculty; (*pouvoir, possibilité*) power.
fadaises [fadɛz] *nfpl* twaddle *sg*.
fade [fad] *adj* insipid.
fading [fadiŋ] *nm* (*RADIO*) fading.
fagot [fago] *nm* (*de bois*) bundle of sticks.
fagoté, e [fagɔte] *adj* (*fam*): **drôlement ~** oddly dressed.
faible [fɛbl(ə)] *adj* weak; (*voix, lumière, vent*) faint; (*élève, copie*) poor; (*rendement, intensité, revenu etc*) low ♦ *nm* weak point; (*pour quelqu'un*) weakness, soft spot; **~ d'esprit** feeble-minded.
faiblement [fɛbləmɑ̃] *adv* weakly; (*peu: éclairer etc*) faintly.
faiblesse [fɛblɛs] *nf* weakness.
faiblir [febliʀ] *vi* to weaken; (*lumière*) to dim; (*vent*) to drop.
faïence [fajɑ̃s] *nf* earthenware *no pl*; (*objet*) piece of earthenware.
faignant, e [fɛɲɑ̃, -ɑ̃t] *nm/f* = **fainéant, e**.
faille [faj] *vb voir* **falloir** ♦ *nf* (*GÉO*) fault; (*fig*) flaw, weakness.
failli, e [faji] *adj, nm/f* bankrupt.
faillible [fajibl(ə)] *adj* fallible.
faillir [fajiʀ] *vi*: **j'ai failli tomber/lui dire** I almost *ou* nearly fell/told him; **~ à une promesse/un engagement** to break a promise/an agreement.
faillite [fajit] *nf* bankruptcy; (*échec: d'une politique etc*) collapse; **être en ~** to be bankrupt; **faire ~** to go bankrupt.
faim [fɛ̃] *nf* hunger; (*fig*): **~ d'amour/de richesse** hunger *ou* yearning for love/wealth; **avoir ~** to be hungry; **rester sur sa ~** (*aussi fig*) to be left wanting more.
fainéant, e [fɛneɑ̃, -ɑ̃t] *nm/f* idler, loafer.
fainéantise [feneɑ̃tiz] *nf* idleness, laziness.

MOT-CLÉ

faire [fɛʀ] *vt* **1** (*fabriquer, être l'auteur de*) to make; (*produire*) to produce; (*construire: maison, bateau*) to build; **~ du vin/une offre/un film** to make wine/an offer/a film; **~ du bruit** to make a noise
2 (*effectuer: travail, opération*) to do; **que faites-vous?** (*quel métier etc*) what do you do?; (*quelle activité: au moment de la question*) what are you doing?; **que ~?** what are we going to do?, what can be done (about it)?; **~ la lessive/le ménage** to do the washing/the housework
3 (*études*) to do; (*sport, musique*) to play; **~ du droit/du français** to do law/French; **~ du rugby/piano** to play rugby/the piano; **~ du cheval/du ski** to go riding/skiing
4 (*visiter*): **~ les magasins** to go shopping; **~ l'Europe** to tour *ou* do Europe
5 (*simuler*): **~ le malade/l'ignorant** to act the invalid/the fool
6 (*transformer, avoir un effet sur*): **~ de qn un frustré/avocat** to make sb frustrated/a lawyer; **ça ne me fait rien** (*m'est égal*) I don't care *ou* mind; (*me laisse froid*) it has no effect on me; **ça ne fait rien** it doesn't matter; **~ que** (*impliquer*) to mean that
7 (*calculs, prix, mesures*): **2 et 2 font 4** 2 and 2 are *ou* make 4; **ça fait 10 m/15 F** it's 10 m/15 F; **je vous le fais 10 F** I'll let you have it for 10 F
8 (*vb +de*): **qu'a-t-il fait de sa valise/de sa sœur?** what has he done with his case/his sister?
9: **ne ~ que: il ne fait que critiquer** (*sans cesse*) all he (ever) does is criticize; (*seulement*) he's only criticizing
10 (*dire*) to say; **vraiment? fit-il** really? he said
11 (*maladie*) to have; **~ du diabète/de la tension** to have diabetes *sg*/high blood pressure
♦ *vi* **1** (*agir, s'y prendre*) to act, do; **il faut ~ vite** we (*ou* you *etc*) must act quickly; **comment a-t-il fait pour?** how did he manage to?; **faites comme chez vous** make yourself at home; **je n'ai pas pu ~ autrement** there was nothing else I could do
2 (*paraître*) to look; **~ vieux/démodé** to look old/old-fashioned; **ça fait bien** it looks good; **tu fais jeune dans cette robe** that dress makes you look young(er)
♦ *vb substitut* to do; **ne le casse pas comme je l'ai fait** don't break it as I did; **je peux le voir? — faites!** can I see it? — please do; **remets-le en place — je viens de le ~** put it back in its place — I just have (done)
♦ *vb impers* **1**: **il fait beau** *etc* the weather is fine *etc*; *voir aussi* **jour; froid** *etc*
2 (*temps écoulé, durée*): **ça fait 2 ans qu'il est parti** it's 2 years since he left; **ça fait 2 ans qu'il y est** he's been there for 2 years
♦ *vb semi-aux* **1**: **~ +***infinitif* (*action directe*) to make; **~ tomber/bouger qch** to make sth fall/move; **~ démarrer un moteur/chauffer de l'eau** to start up an engine/heat some water; **cela fait dormir** it makes you sleep; ~

travailler les enfants to make the children work *ou* get the children to work; **il m'a fait traverser la rue** he helped me to cross the road
2 (*indirectement, par un intermédiaire*): ~ **réparer qch** to get *ou* have sth repaired; ~ **punir les enfants** to have the children punished; **il m'a fait ouvrir la porte** he got me to open the door
se ~ *vi* **1** (*vin, fromage*) to mature
2: **cela se fait beaucoup/ne se fait pas** it's done a lot/not done
3 (*+nom ou pron*): **se** ~ **une jupe** to make o.s. a skirt; **se** ~ **des amis** to make friends; **se** ~ **du souci** to worry; **se** ~ **des illusions** to delude o.s.; **se** ~ **beaucoup d'argent** to make a lot of money; **il ne s'en fait pas** he doesn't worry
4 (*+adj*) (*devenir*): **se** ~ **vieux** to be getting old; (*délibérément*): **se** ~ **beau** to do o.s. up
5: **se** ~ **à** (*s'habituer*) to get used to; **je n'arrive pas à me** ~ **à la nourriture/au climat** I can't get used to the food/climate
6 (*+infinitif*): **se** ~ **examiner la vue/opérer** to have one's eyes tested/have an operation; **se** ~ **couper les cheveux** to get one's hair cut; **il va se** ~ **tuer/punir** he's going to get himself killed/get (himself) punished; **il s'est fait aider** he got somebody to help him; **il s'est fait aider par Simon** he got Simon to help him; **se** ~ ~ **un vêtement** to get a garment made for o.s.
7 (*impersonnel*): **comment se fait-il/faisait-il que?** how is it/was it that?; **il peut se** ~ **que nous utilisions ...** it's possible that we could use ...

aire-part [fɛʀpaʀ] *nm inv* announcement (*of birth, marriage etc*).
air-play [fɛʀplɛ] *adj inv* fair.
ais [fɛ] *vb voir* **faire.**
aisabilité [fəzabilite] *nf* feasibility.
aisable [fəzabl(ə)] *adj* feasible.
aisais [fəzɛ] *etc vb voir* **faire.**
aisan, e [fəzɑ̃, -an] *nm/f* pheasant.
aisandé, e [fəzɑ̃de] *adj* high (*bad*); (*fig péj*) corrupt, decadent.
aisceau, x [fɛso] *nm* (*de lumière etc*) beam; (*de branches etc*) bundle.
aiseur, euse [fəzœʀ, -øz] *nm/f* (*gén: péj*): ~ **de** maker of ♦ *nm* (bespoke) tailor; ~ **d'embarras** fusspot; ~ **de projets** schemer.
aisons [fəzɔ̃] *etc vb voir* **faire.**
aisselle [fɛsɛl] *nf* cheese strainer.
ait [fɛ] *vb voir* **faire** ♦ *nm* (*événement*) event, occurrence; (*réalité, donnée*) fact; **le** ~ **que/de manger** the fact that/of eating; **être le** ~ **de** (*causé par*) to be the work of; **être au** ~ **(de)** to be informed (of); **mettre qn au** ~ to inform sb, put sb in the picture; **au** ~ (*à propos*) by the way; **en venir au** ~ to get to the point; **de** ~ *adj* (*opposé à: de droit*) de facto ♦ *adv* in fact; **du** ~ **de ceci/qu'il a menti** because of *ou* on account of this/his having lied; **de ce** ~ therefore, for this reason; **en** ~ in fact; **en** ~ **de repas** by way of a meal; **prendre** ~ **et cause pour qn** to support sb, side with sb; **prendre qn sur le** ~ to catch sb in the act; **dire à qn son** ~ to give sb a piece of one's mind; **hauts ~s** (*exploits*) exploits; ~ **d'armes** feat of arms; ~ **divers** (short) news item; **les ~s et gestes de qn** sb's actions *ou* doings.
fait, e [fɛ, fɛt] *pp de* **faire** ♦ *adj* (*mûr: fromage, melon*) ripe; (*maquillé: yeux*) made-up; (*vernis: ongles*) painted, polished; **un homme** ~ a grown man; **tout(e)** ~**(e)** (*préparé à l'avance*) ready-made; **c'en est** ~ **de notre tranquillité** that's the end of our peace; **c'est bien** ~ **(pour lui** *ou* **eux** *etc***)** it serves him (*ou* them *etc*) right.
faîte [fɛt] *nm* top; (*fig*) pinnacle, height.
faites [fɛt] *vb voir* **faire.**
faîtière [fɛtjɛʀ] *nf* (*de tente*) ridge pole.
fait-tout *nm inv*, **faitout** *nm* [fɛtu] stewpot.
fakir [fakiʀ] *nm* (*THÉÂT*) wizard.
falaise [falɛz] *nf* cliff.
falbalas [falbala] *nmpl* fripperies, frills.
fallacieux, euse [falasjø, -øz] *adj* (*raisonnement*) fallacious; (*apparences*) deceptive; (*espoir*) illusory.
falloir [falwaʀ] *vb impers*: **il faut faire les lits** we (*ou* you *etc*) have to *ou* must make the beds; **il faut que je fasse les lits** I have to *ou* must make the beds; **il a fallu qu'il parte** he had to leave; **il faudrait qu'elle rentre** she ought to go home; **il va** ~ **100 €** we'll (*ou* I'll *etc*) need €100; **il doit** ~ **du temps** that must take time; **il vous faut tourner à gauche après l'église** you have to turn left past the church; **nous avons ce qu'il (nous) faut** we have what we need; **il faut qu'il ait oublié** he must have forgotten; **il a fallu qu'il l'apprenne** he would have to hear about it; **il ne fallait pas** (*pour remercier*) you shouldn't have (done); **faut le faire!** (it) takes some doing! ♦ *vi*: **s'en** ~: **il s'en est fallu de 10 €/5 minutes** we (*ou* they *etc*) were €10 short/5 minutes late (*ou* early); **il s'en faut de beaucoup qu'il soit ...** he is far from being ...; **il s'en est fallu de peu que cela n'arrive** it very nearly happened; **ou peu s'en faut** or just about, or as good as; **comme il faut** *adj* proper ♦ *adv* properly.
fallu [faly] *pp de* **falloir.**
falot, e [falo, -ɔt] *adj* dreary, colourless (*BRIT*), colorless (*US*) ♦ *nm* lantern.
falsification [falsifikɑsjɔ̃] *nf* falsification.
falsifier [falsifje] *vt* to falsify.
famé, e [fame] *adj*: **mal** ~ disreputable, of ill repute.
famélique [famelik] *adj* half-starved.
fameux, euse [famø, -øz] *adj* (*illustre: parfois péj*) famous; (*bon: repas, plat etc*) first-rate,

first-class; (*intensif*): **un ~ problème** *etc* a real problem *etc*; **pas ~** not great, not much good.
familial, e, aux [familjal, -o] *adj* family *cpd* ♦ *nf* (*AUTO*) family estate car (*BRIT*), station wagon (*US*).
familiariser [familjaʀize] *vt*: **~ qn avec** to familiarize sb with; **se ~ avec** to familiarize o.s. with.
familiarité [familjaʀite] *nf* familiarity; informality; **~s** *nfpl* familiarities; **~ avec** (*sujet, science*) familiarity with.
familier, ière [familje, -jɛʀ] *adj* (*connu, impertinent*) familiar; (*dénotant une certaine intimité*) informal, friendly; (*LING*) informal, colloquial ♦ *nm* regular (visitor).
familièrement [familjɛʀmɑ̃] *adv* (*sans façon: s'entretenir*) informally; (*cavalièrement*) familiarly.
famille [famij] *nf* family; **il a de la ~ à Paris** he has relatives in Paris.
famine [famin] *nf* famine.
fan [fan] *nm/f* fan.
fana [fana] *adj, nm/f* (*fam*) = **fanatique**.
fanal, aux [fanal, -o] *nm* beacon; lantern.
fanatique [fanatik] *adj*: **~ (de)** fanatical (about) ♦ *nm/f* fanatic.
fanatisme [fanatism(ə)] *nm* fanaticism.
fane [fan] *nf* top.
fané, e [fane] *adj* faded.
faner [fane]: **se ~** *vi* to fade.
faneur, euse [fanœʀ, -øz] *nm/f* haymaker ♦ *nf* (*TECH*) tedder.
fanfare [fɑ̃faʀ] *nf* (*orchestre*) brass band; (*musique*) fanfare; **en ~** (*avec bruit*) noisily.
fanfaron, ne [fɑ̃faʀɔ̃, -ɔn] *nm/f* braggart.
fanfaronnades [fɑ̃faʀɔnad] *nfpl* bragging *no pl*.
fanfreluches [fɑ̃fʀəlyʃ] *nfpl* trimming *no pl*.
fange [fɑ̃ʒ] *nf* mire.
fanion [fanjɔ̃] *nm* pennant.
fanon [fanɔ̃] *nm* (*de baleine*) plate of baleen; (*repli de peau*) dewlap, wattle.
fantaisie [fɑ̃tezi] *nf* (*spontanéité*) fancy, imagination; (*caprice*) whim; extravagance; (*MUS*) fantasia ♦ *adj*: **bijou (de) ~** (piece of) costume jewellery (*BRIT*) *ou* jewelry (*US*); **pain (de) ~** fancy bread.
fantaisiste [fɑ̃tezist(ə)] *adj* (*péj*) unorthodox, eccentric ♦ *nm/f* (*de music-hall*) variety artist *ou* entertainer.
fantasmagorique [fɑ̃tasmagɔʀik] *adj* phantasmagorical.
fantasme [fɑ̃tasm(ə)] *nm* fantasy.
fantasmer [fɑ̃tasme] *vi* to fantasize.
fantasque [fɑ̃task(ə)] *adj* whimsical, capricious; fantastic.
fantassin [fɑ̃tasɛ̃] *nm* infantryman.
fantastique [fɑ̃tastik] *adj* fantastic.
fantoche [fɑ̃tɔʃ] *nm* (*péj*) puppet.
fantomatique [fɑ̃tɔmatik] *adj* ghostly.
fantôme [fɑ̃tom] *nm* ghost, phantom.
FAO *sigle f* (= *Food and Agricultural Organization*) FAO.
faon [fɑ̃] *nm* fawn (*deer*).
faramineux, euse [faʀaminø, -øz] *adj* (*fam*) fantastic.
farandole [faʀɑ̃dɔl] *nf* farandole.
farce [faʀs(ə)] *nf* (*viande*) stuffing; (*blague*) (practical) joke; (*THÉÂT*) farce; **faire une ~ à qn** to play a (practical) joke on sb; **~s et attrapes** jokes and novelties.
farceur, euse [faʀsœʀ, -øz] *nm/f* practical joker; (*fumiste*) clown.
farci, e [faʀsi] *adj* (*CULIN*) stuffed.
farcir [faʀsiʀ] *vt* (*viande*) to stuff; (*fig*): **~ qch de** to stuff sth with; **se ~** (*fam*): **je me suis farci la vaisselle** I've got stuck *ou* landed with the washing-up.
fard [faʀ] *nm* make-up; **~ à joues** blusher.
fardeau, x [faʀdo] *nm* burden.
farder [faʀde] *vt* to make up; (*vérité*) to disguise; **se ~** to make o.s. up.
farfelu, e [faʀfəly] *adj* wacky (*fam*), harebrained.
farfouiller [faʀfuje] *vi* (*péj*) to rummage around.
fariboles [faʀibɔl] *nfpl* nonsense *no pl*.
farine [faʀin] *nf* flour; **~ de blé** wheatflour; **~ de maïs** cornflour (*BRIT*), cornstarch (*US*); **~ lactée** (*pour bouillie*) gruel.
fariner [faʀine] *vt* to flour.
farineux, euse [faʀinø, -øz] *adj* (*sauce, pomme*) floury ♦ *nmpl* (*aliments*) starchy foods.
farniente [faʀnjɛnte] *nm* idleness.
farouche [faʀuʃ] *adj* shy, timid; (*sauvage*) savage, wild; (*violent*) fierce.
farouchement [faʀuʃmɑ̃] *adv* fiercely.
fart [faʀ(t)] *nm* (ski) wax.
farter [faʀte] *vt* to wax.
fascicule [fasikyl] *nm* volume.
fascinant, e [fasinɑ̃, -ɑ̃t] *adj* fascinating.
fascination [fasinɑsjɔ̃] *nf* fascination.
fasciner [fasine] *vt* to fascinate.
fascisant, e [faʃizɑ̃, -ɑ̃t] *adj* fascistic.
fascisme [faʃism(ə)] *nm* fascism.
fasciste [faʃist(ə)] *adj, nm/f* fascist.
fasse [fas] *etc vb voir* **faire**.
faste [fast(ə)] *nm* splendour (*BRIT*), splendor (*US*) ♦ *adj*: **c'est un jour ~** it's his (*ou* our *etc*) lucky day.
fastidieux, euse [fastidjø, -øz] *adj* tedious, tiresome.
fastueux, euse [fastɥø, -øz] *adj* sumptuous, luxurious.
fat [fa] *adj m* conceited, smug.
fatal, e [fatal] *adj* fatal; (*inévitable*) inevitable.
fatalement [fatalmɑ̃] *adv* inevitably.
fatalisme [fatalism(ə)] *nm* fatalism.
fataliste [fatalist(ə)] *adj* fatalistic.
fatalité [fatalite] *nf* (*destin*) fate; (*coïncidence*) fateful coincidence; (*caractère inévitable*) inevitability.
fatidique [fatidik] *adj* fateful.

fatigant, e [fatigɑ̃, -ɑ̃t] *adj* tiring; (*agaçant*) tiresome.
fatigue [fatig] *nf* tiredness, fatigue; (*détérioration*) fatigue; **les ~s du voyage** the wear and tear of the journey.
fatigué, e [fatige] *adj* tired.
fatiguer [fatige] *vt* to tire, make tired; (*TECH*) to put a strain on, strain; (*fig: importuner*) to wear out ♦ *vi* (*moteur*) to labour (*BRIT*), labor (*US*), strain; **se ~** *vi* to get tired; to tire o.s. (out); **se ~ à faire qch** to tire o.s. out doing sth.
fatras [fatʀa] *nm* jumble, hotchpotch.
fatuité [fatɥite] *nf* conceitedness, smugness.
faubourg [fobuʀ] *nm* suburb.
faubourien, ne [foburjɛ̃, -ɛn] *adj* (*accent*) working-class.
fauché, e [foʃe] *adj* (*fam*) broke.
faucher [foʃe] *vt* (*herbe*) to cut; (*champs, blés*) to reap; (*fig*) to cut down; to mow down; (*fam: voler*) to pinch, nick.
faucheur, euse [foʃœʀ, -øz] *nm/f* reaper, mower.
faucille [fosij] *nf* sickle.
faucon [fokɔ̃] *nm* falcon, hawk.
faudra [fodʀa] *etc vb voir* **falloir.**
faufil [fofil] *nm* (*COUTURE*) tacking thread.
faufilage [fofilaʒ] *nm* (*COUTURE*) tacking.
faufiler [fofile] *vt* to tack, baste; **se ~** *vi*: **se ~ dans** to edge one's way into; **se ~ parmi/entre** to thread one's way among/between.
faune [fon] *nf* (*ZOOL*) wildlife, fauna; (*fig péj*) set, crowd ♦ *nm* faun; **~ marine** marine (animal) life.
faussaire [fosɛʀ] *nm/f* forger.
fausse [fos] *adj f voir* **faux.**
faussement [fosmɑ̃] *adv* (*accuser*) wrongly, wrongfully; (*croire*) falsely, erroneously.
fausser [fose] *vt* (*objet*) to bend, buckle; (*fig*) to distort; **~ compagnie à qn** to give sb the slip.
fausset [fosɛ] *nm*: **voix de ~** falsetto voice.
fausseté [foste] *nf* wrongness; falseness.
faut [fo] *vb voir* **falloir.**
faute [fot] *nf* (*erreur*) mistake, error; (*péché, manquement*) misdemeanour; (*FOOTBALL etc*) offence; (*TENNIS*) fault; (*responsabilité*): **par la ~ de** through the fault of, because of; **c'est de sa/ma ~** it's his/my fault; **être en ~** to be in the wrong; **prendre qn en ~** to catch sb out; **~ de** (*temps, argent*) for *ou* through lack of; **~ de mieux** for want of anything *ou* something better; **sans ~** *adv* without fail; **~ de frappe** typing error; **~ d'inattention** careless mistake; **~ d'orthographe** spelling mistake; **~ professionnelle** professional misconduct *no pl.*
fauteuil [fotœj] *nm* armchair; **~ à bascule** rocking chair; **~ club** (big) easy chair; **~ d'orchestre** seat in the front stalls (*BRIT*) *ou* the orchestra (*US*); **~ roulant** wheelchair.
fauteur [fotœʀ] *nm*: **~ de troubles** trouble-maker.
fautif, ive [fotif, -iv] *adj* (*incorrect*) incorrect, inaccurate; (*responsable*) at fault, in the wrong; (*coupable*) guilty ♦ *nm/f* culprit.
fauve [fov] *nm* wildcat; (*peintre*) Fauve ♦ *adj* (*couleur*) fawn.
fauvette [fovɛt] *nf* warbler.
fauvisme [fovism(ə)] *nm* (*ART*) Fauvism.
faux[1] [fo] *nf* scythe.
faux[2], fausse [fo, fos] *adj* (*inexact*) wrong; (*piano, voix*) out of tune; (*falsifié*) fake, forged; (*sournois, postiche*) false ♦ *adv* (*MUS*) out of tune ♦ *nm* (*copie*) fake, forgery; (*opposé au vrai*): **le ~** falsehood; **le ~ numéro/la fausse clé** the wrong number/key; **faire fausse route** to go the wrong way; **faire ~ bond à qn** to let sb down; **~ ami** (*LING*) faux ami; **~ col** detachable collar; **~ départ** (*SPORT, fig*) false start; **~ frais** *nmpl* extras, incidental expenses; **~ frère** (*fig péj*) false friend; **~ mouvement** awkward movement; **~ nez** false nose; **~ nom** assumed name; **~ pas** tripping *no pl*; (*fig*) faux pas; **~ témoignage** (*délit*) perjury; **fausse alerte** false alarm; **fausse clé** skeleton key; **fausse couche** (*MÉD*) miscarriage; **fausse joie** vain joy; **fausse note** wrong note.
faux-filet [fofilɛ] *nm* sirloin.
faux-fuyant [fofɥijɑ̃] *nm* equivocation.
faux-monnayeur [fomɔnɛjœʀ] *nm* counterfeiter, forger.
faux-semblant [fosɑ̃blɑ̃] *nm* pretence (*BRIT*), pretense (*US*).
faux-sens [fosɑ̃s] *nm* mistranslation.
faveur [favœʀ] *nf* favour (*BRIT*), favor (*US*); **traitement de ~** preferential treatment; **à la ~ de** under cover of; (*grâce à*) thanks to; **en ~ de** in favo(u)r of.
favorable [favɔʀabl(ə)] *adj* favo(u)rable.
favori, te [favɔʀi, -it] *adj, nm/f* favo(u)rite.
favoris [favɔʀi] *nmpl* (*barbe*) sideboards (*BRIT*), sideburns.
favoriser [favɔʀize] *vt* to favour (*BRIT*), favor (*US*).
favoritisme [favɔʀitism(ə)] *nm* (*péj*) favo(u)ritism.
fayot [fajo] *nm* (*fam*) crawler.
FB *abr* (= *franc belge*) BF, FB.
FBI *sigle m* FBI.
FC *sigle m* (= *Football Club*) FC.
fébrile [febʀil] *adj* feverish, febrile; **capitaux ~s** (*ÉCON*) hot money.
fébrilement [febʀilmɑ̃] *adv* feverishly.
fécal, e, aux [fekal, -o] *adj voir* **matière.**
FECOM [fekɔm] *sigle m* (= *Fonds européen de coopération militaire*) EMCF.
fécond, e [fekɔ̃, -ɔ̃d] *adj* fertile.
fécondation [fekɔ̃dasjɔ̃] *nf* fertilization.
féconder [fekɔ̃de] *vt* to fertilize.
fécondité [fekɔ̃dite] *nf* fertility.
fécule [fekyl] *nf* potato flour.
féculent [fekylɑ̃] *nm* starchy food.

fédéral, e, aux [fedeʀal, -o] *adj* federal.
fédéralisme [fedeʀalism(ə)] *nm* federalism.
fédéraliste [fedeʀalist(ə)] *adj* federalist.
fédération [fedeʀɑsjɔ̃] *nf* federation; **la F~ française de football** the French football association.
fée [fe] *nf* fairy.
féerie [feʀi] *nf* enchantment.
féerique [feʀik] *adj* magical, fairytale *cpd*.
feignant, e [fɛɲɑ̃, -ɑ̃t] *nm/f* = **fainéant, e**.
feindre [fɛ̃dʀ(ə)] *vt* to feign ♦ *vi* to dissemble; ~ **de faire** to pretend to do.
feint, e [fɛ̃, fɛ̃t] *pp de* **feindre** ♦ *adj* feigned ♦ *nf* (*SPORT: escrime*) feint; (*: football, rugby*) dummy (*BRIT*), fake (*US*): (*fam: ruse*) sham.
feinter [fɛ̃te] *vi* (*SPORT: escrime*) to feint; (*: football, rugby*) to dummy (*BRIT*), fake (*US*) ♦ *vt* (*fam: tromper*) to fool.
fêlé, e [fele] *adj* (*aussi fig*) cracked.
fêler [fele] *vt* to crack.
félicitations [felisitɑsjɔ̃] *nfpl* congratulations.
félicité [felisite] *nf* bliss.
féliciter [felisite] *vt*: ~ **qn (de)** to congratulate sb (on).
félin, e [felɛ̃, -in] *adj* feline ♦ *nm* (big) cat.
félon, ne [felɔ̃, -ɔn] *adj* perfidious, treacherous.
félonie [felɔni] *nf* treachery.
fêlure [felyʀ] *nf* crack.
femelle [fəmɛl] *adj* (*aussi ÉLEC, TECH*) female ♦ *nf* female.
féminin, e [feminɛ̃, -in] *adj* feminine; (*sexe*) female; (*équipe, vêtements etc*) women's; (*parfois péj: homme*) effeminate ♦ *nm* (*LING*) feminine.
féminiser [feminize] *vt* to feminize; (*rendre efféminé*) to make effeminate; **se** ~ *vi*: **cette profession se féminise** this profession is attracting more women.
féminisme [feminism(ə)] *nm* feminism.
féministe [feminist(ə)] *adj, nf* feminist.
féminité [feminite] *nf* femininity.
femme [fam] *nf* woman; (*épouse*) wife (*pl* wives); **être très** ~ to be very much a woman; **devenir** ~ to attain womanhood; ~ **d'affaires** businesswoman; ~ **de chambre** chambermaid; ~ **fatale** femme fatale; ~ **au foyer** housewife; ~ **d'intérieur** (real) homemaker; ~ **de ménage** domestic help, cleaning lady; ~ **du monde** society woman; ~**-objet** sex object; ~ **de tête** determined, intellectual woman.
fémoral, e, aux [femɔʀal, -o] *adj* femoral.
fémur [femyʀ] *nm* femur, thighbone.
FEN [fɛn] *sigle f* (= *Fédération de l'Éducation nationale*) *teachers' trade union*.
fenaison [fənɛzɔ̃] *nf* haymaking.
fendillé, e [fɑ̃dije] *adj* (*terre etc*) crazed.
fendre [fɑ̃dʀ(ə)] *vt* (*couper en deux*) to split; (*fissurer*) to crack; (*fig: traverser*) to cut through; to push one's way through; **se** ~ *vi* to crack.
fendu, e [fɑ̃dy] *adj* (*mur*) cracked; (*jupe*) slit.

fenêtre [fənɛtʀ(ə)] *nf* window; ~ **à guillotin** sash window.
fennec [fenɛk] *nm* fennec.
fenouil [fənuj] *nm* fennel.
fente [fɑ̃t] *nf* slit; (*fissure*) crack.
féodal, e, aux [feɔdal, -o] *adj* feudal.
féodalisme [feɔdalism(ə)] *nm* feudalism.
feodalité [feɔdalite] *nf* feudalism.
fer [fɛʀ] *nm* iron; (*de cheval*) shoe; ~**s** *pl* (*MÉD* forceps; **mettre aux ~s** (*enchaîner*) to put i chains; **au ~ rouge** with a red-hot iron; **santé/main de** ~ iron constitution/hand; ~ **cheval** horseshoe; **en ~ à cheval** (*fig* horseshoe-shaped; ~ **forgé** wrought iron; ~ **à friser** curling tongs; ~ **de lance** spearhead ~ **(à repasser)** iron; ~ **à souder** solderin iron.
ferai [fəʀe] *etc vb voir* **faire**.
fer-blanc [fɛʀblɑ̃] *nm* tin(plate).
ferblanterie [fɛʀblɑ̃tʀi] *nf* tinplate makin (*produit*) tinware.
ferblantier [fɛʀblɑ̃tje] *nm* tinsmith.
férié, e [feʀje] *adj*: **jour** ~ public holiday.
férir [feʀiʀ]: **sans coup** ~ *adv* without meetin any opposition.
fermage [fɛʀmaʒ] *nm* tenant farming.
ferme [fɛʀm(ə)] *adj* firm ♦ *adv* (*travailler et* hard; (*discuter*) ardently ♦ *nf* (*exploitatio* farm; (*maison*) farmhouse; **tenir** ~ to stan firm.
fermé, e [fɛʀme] *adj* closed, shut; (*gaz, eau et* off; (*fig: personne*) uncommunicative; (*: m lieu*) exclusive.
fermement [fɛʀməmɑ̃] *adv* firmly.
ferment [fɛʀmɑ̃] *nm* ferment.
fermentation [fɛʀmɑ̃tɑsjɔ̃] *nf* fermentation.
fermenter [fɛʀmɑ̃te] *vi* to ferment.
fermer [fɛʀme] *vt* to close, shut; (*cess l'exploitation de*) to close down, shut dow (*eau, lumière, électricité, robinet*) to put of turn off; (*aéroport, route*) to close ♦ *vi* close, shut; to close down, shut down; **se** *vi* (*yeux*) to close, shut; (*fleur, blessure*) close up; ~ **à clef** to lock; ~ **au verrou** bolt; ~ **les yeux (sur qch)** (*fig*) to close one eyes (to sth); **se ~ à** (*pitié, amour*) to clo one's heart *ou* mind to.
fermeté [fɛʀməte] *nf* firmness.
fermette [fɛʀmɛt] *nf* farmhouse.
fermeture [fɛʀmətyʀ] *nf* (*voir fermer*) closin shutting; closing *ou* shutting down; putti *ou* turning off; (*dispositif*) catch; fastenin fastener; **heure de** ~ (*COMM*) closing tim **jour de** ~ (*COMM*) day on which the sh (*etc*) is closed; ~ **éclair** ® *ou* **à glissière** z (fastener) (*BRIT*), zipper.
fermier, ière [fɛʀmje, -jɛʀ] *nm/f* farmer ♦ (*femme de fermier*) farmer's wife ♦ *a* **beurre/cidre** ~ farm butter/cider.
fermoir [fɛʀmwaʀ] *nm* clasp.
féroce [feʀɔs] *adj* ferocious, fierce.
férocement [feʀɔsmɑ̃] *adv* ferociously.

férocité [ferɔsite] *nf* ferocity, ferociousness.
ferons [fəʀɔ̃] *etc vb voir* **faire.**
ferraille [fɛʀɑj] *nf* scrap iron; **mettre à la ~** to scrap; **bruit de ~** clanking.
ferrailler [fɛʀɑje] *vi* to clank.
ferrailleur [fɛʀɑjœʀ] *nm* scrap merchant.
ferrant [fɛʀɑ̃] *adj m voir* **maréchal-ferrant.**
ferré, e [fɛʀe] *adj* (*chaussure*) hobnailed; (*canne*) steel-tipped; **~ sur** (*fam: savant*) well up on.
ferrer [fɛʀe] *vt* (*cheval*) to shoe; (*chaussure*) to nail; (*canne*) to tip; (*poisson*) to strike.
ferreux, euse [fɛʀø, -øz] *adj* ferrous.
ferronnerie [fɛʀɔnʀi] *nf* ironwork; **~ d'art** wrought iron work.
ferronnier [fɛʀɔnje] *nm* craftsman in wrought iron; (*marchand*) ironware merchant.
ferroviaire [fɛʀɔvjɛʀ] *adj* rail *cpd*, railway *cpd* (*BRIT*), railroad *cpd* (*US*).
ferrugineux, euse [feʀyʒinø, -øz] *adj* ferruginous.
ferrure [fɛʀyʀ] *nf* (ornamental) hinge.
ferry(-boat) [fɛʀe(bot)] *nm* ferry.
fertile [fɛʀtil] *adj* fertile; **~ en incidents** eventful, packed with incidents.
fertilisant [fɛʀtilizɑ̃] *nm* fertilizer.
fertilisation [fɛʀtilizɑsjɔ̃] *nf* fertilization.
fertiliser [fɛʀtilize] *vt* to fertilize.
fertilité [fɛʀtilite] *nf* fertility.
féru, e [feʀy] *adj*: **~ de** with a keen interest in.
férule [feʀyl] *nf*: **être sous la ~ de qn** to be under sb's (iron) rule.
fervent, e [fɛʀvɑ̃, -ɑ̃t] *adj* fervent.
ferveur [fɛʀvœʀ] *nf* fervour (*BRIT*), fervor (*US*).
fesse [fɛs] *nf* buttock; **les ~s** the bottom *sg*, the buttocks.
fessée [fese] *nf* spanking.
fessier [fesje] *nm* (*fam*) behind.
festin [fɛstɛ̃] *nm* feast.
festival [fɛstival] *nm* festival.
festivalier [fɛstivalje] *nm* festival-goer.
festivités [fɛstivite] *nfpl* festivities, merry-making *sg*.
feston [fɛstɔ̃] *nm* (*ARCHIT*) festoon; (*COUTURE*) scallop.
festoyer [fɛstwaje] *vi* to feast.
fêtard [fɛtaʀ] *nm* (*péj*) high liver, merry-maker.
fête [fɛt] *nf* (*religieuse*) feast; (*publique*) holiday; (*en famille etc*) celebration; (*kermesse*) fête, fair, festival; (*du nom*) feast day, name day; **faire la ~** to live it up; **faire ~ à qn** to give sb a warm welcome; **se faire une ~ de** to look forward to; to enjoy; **ça va être sa ~!** (*fam*) he's going to get it!; **jour de ~** holiday; **les ~s (de fin d'année)** the festive season; **la salle des ~s** the village hall; **la ~ des Mères/Pères** Mother's/Father's Day; **~ de charité** charity fair *ou* fête; **~ foraine** (fun)fair; **~mobile** movable feast (day); **la F~ Nationale** the national holiday; *see boxed note.*

FÊTE DE LA MUSIQUE

The **fête de la Musique** *is a music festival which has taken place every year since 1981. On 21 June throughout France local musicians perform free of charge in parks, streets and squares.*

Fête-Dieu [fɛtdjø] *nf*: **la ~** Corpus Christi.
fêter [fete] *vt* to celebrate; (*personne*) to have a celebration for.
fétiche [fetiʃ] *nm* fetish; **animal ~, objet ~** mascot.
fétichisme [fetiʃism(ə)] *nm* fetishism.
fétichiste [fetiʃist(ə)] *adj* fetishist.
fétide [fetid] *adj* fetid.
fétu [fety] *nm*: **~ de paille** wisp of straw.
feu[1] [fø] *adj inv*: **~ son père** his late father.
feu[2], x [fø] *nm* (*gén*) fire; (*signal lumineux*) light; (*de cuisinière*) ring; (*sensation de brûlure*) burning (sensation); **~x** *nmpl* fire *sg*; (*AUTO*) (traffic) lights; **tous ~x éteints** (*NAVIG, AUTO*) without lights; **au ~!** (*incendie*) fire!; **à ~ doux/vif** over a slow/brisk heat; **à petit ~** (*CULIN*) over a gentle heat; (*fig*) slowly; **faire ~** to fire; **ne pas faire long ~** (*fig*) not to last long; **commander le ~** (*MIL*) to give the order to (open) fire; **tué au ~** (*MIL*) killed in action; **mettre à ~** (*fusée*) to fire off; **pris entre deux ~x** caught in the crossfire; **en ~** on fire; **être tout ~ tout flamme (pour)** (*passion*) to be aflame with passion (for); (*enthousiasme*) to be fired with enthusiasm (for); **prendre ~** to catch fire; **mettre le ~ à** to set fire to, set on fire; **faire du ~** to make a fire; **avez-vous du ~?** (*pour cigarette*) have you (got) a light?; **~ rouge/vert/orange** (*AUTO*) red/green/amber (*BRIT*) *ou* yellow (*US*) light; **donner le ~ vert à qch/qn** (*fig*) to give sth/sb the go-ahead *ou* green light; **~ arrière** (*AUTO*) rear light; **~ d'artifice** firework; (*spectacle*) fireworks *pl*; **~ de camp** campfire; **~ de cheminée** chimney fire; **~ de joie** bonfire; **~ de paille** (*fig*) flash in the pan; **~x de brouillard** (*AUTO*) fog lights *ou* lamps; **~x de croisement** (*AUTO*) dipped (*BRIT*) *ou* dimmed (*US*) headlights; **~x de position** (*AUTO*) sidelights; **~x de route** (*AUTO*) headlights (on full (*BRIT*) *ou* high (*US*) beam); **~x de stationnement** parking lights.
feuillage [fœjaʒ] *nm* foliage, leaves *pl*.
feuille [fœj] *nf* (*d'arbre*) leaf (*pl* leaves); **~ (de papier)** sheet (of paper); **rendre ~ blanche** (*SCOL*) to give in a blank paper; **~ d'or/de métal** gold/metal leaf; **~ de chou** (*péj: journal*) rag; **~ d'impôts** tax form; **~ de maladie** medical expenses claim form; **~ morte** dead leaf; **~ de paye** pay slip; **~ de présence** attendance sheet; **~ de température** temperature chart; **~ de vigne** (*BOT*) vine leaf; (*sur statue*) fig leaf; **~ volante** loose sheet.

feuillet [fœjɛ] *nm* leaf (*pl* leaves), page.
feuilletage [fœjtaʒ] *nm* (*aspect feuilleté*) flakiness.
feuilleté, e [fœjte] *adj* (*CULIN*) flaky; (*verre*) laminated.
feuilleter [fœjte] *vt* (*livre*) to leaf through.
feuilleton [fœjtɔ̃] *nm* serial.
feuillette [fœjɛt] *etc vb voir* **feuilleter**.
feuillu, e [fœjy] *adj* leafy ♦ *nm* broad-leaved tree.
feulement [følmɑ̃] *nm* growl.
feutre [føtʀ(ə)] *nm* felt; (*chapeau*) felt hat; (*stylo*) felt-tip(ped pen).
feutré, e [føtʀe] *adj* feltlike; (*pas, voix*) muffled.
feutrer [føtʀe] *vt* to felt; (*fig: bruits*) to muffle ♦ *vi*, **se** ~ *vi* (*tissu*) to felt.
feutrine [føtʀin] *nf* (lightweight) felt.
fève [fɛv] *nf* broad bean; (*dans la galette des Rois*) charm (*hidden in cake eaten on Twelfth Night*).
février [fevʀije] *nm* February; *voir aussi* **juillet**.
fez [fɛz] *nm* fez.
FF *abr* (*HIST = franc français*) FF.
FFA *sigle fpl* (*HIST = Forces françaises en Allemagne*) *French forces in Germany*.
FFF *abr* = **Fédération française de football.**
FFI *sigle fpl* = *Forces françaises de l'intérieur* (*1942-45*) ♦ *sigle m member of the FFI*.
FFL *sigle fpl* (= *Forces françaises libres*) Free French Army.
Fg *abr* = **faubourg**.
FGA *sigle m* (= *Fonds de garantie automobile*) *fund financed through insurance premiums, to compensate victims of uninsured losses*.
FGEN *sigle f* (= *Fédération générale de l'éducation nationale*) *teachers' trade union*.
fi [fi] *excl*: **faire** ~ **de** to snap one's fingers at.
fiabilité [fjabilite] *nf* reliability.
fiable [fjabl(ə)] *adj* reliable.
fiacre [fjakʀ(ə)] *nm* (hackney) cab.
fiançailles [fjɑ̃sɑj] *nfpl* engagement *sg*.
fiancé, e [fjɑ̃se] *nm/f* fiancé/fiancée ♦ *adj*: **être** ~ **(à)** to be engaged (to).
fiancer [fjɑ̃se]: **se** ~ *vi*: **se** ~ **(avec)** to become engaged (to).
fiasco [fjasko] *nm* fiasco.
fibranne [fibʀan] *nf* bonded fibre *ou* fiber (*US*).
fibre [fibʀ(ə)] *nf* fibre, fiber (*US*); **avoir la** ~ **paternelle/militaire** to be a born father/soldier; ~ **optique** optical fibre *ou* fiber; ~ **de verre** fibreglass (*BRIT*), fiberglass (*US*), glass fibre *ou* fiber.
fibreux, euse [fibʀø, -øz] *adj* fibrous; (*viande*) stringy.
fibrome [fibʀom] *nm* (*MÉD*) fibroma.
ficelage [fislaʒ] *nm* tying (up).
ficelé, e [fisle] *adj* (*fam*): **être mal** ~ (*habillé*) to be badly got up; **bien/mal** ~ (*conçu*: *roman, projet*) well/badly put together.
ficeler [fisle] *vt* to tie up.
ficelle [fisɛl] *nf* string *no pl*; (*morceau*) piece *ou* length of string; (*pain*) stick of French bread; ~**s** *pl* (*fig*) strings; **tirer sur la** ~ (*fig*) to go too far.
fiche [fiʃ] *nf* (*carte*) (index) card; (*INFORM*) record; (*formulaire*) form; (*ÉLEC*) plug; ~ **de paye** pay slip; ~ **signalétique** (*POLICE*) identification card; ~ **technique** data sheet, specification *ou* spec sheet.
ficher [fiʃe] *vt* (*dans un fichier*) to file; (*: POLICE*) to put on file; (*fam*) to do; (*: donner*) to give; (*: mettre*) to stick *ou* shove; (*planter*): ~ **qch dans** to stick *ou* drive sth into; ~ **qn à la porte** (*fam*) to chuck sb out; **fiche(-moi) le camp** (*fam*) clear off; **fiche-moi la paix** (*fam*) leave me alone; **se** ~ **dans** (*s'enfoncer*) to get stuck in, embed itself in; **se** ~ **de** (*fam*) to make fun of; not to care about.
fichier [fiʃje] *nm* (*gén, INFORM*) file; (*à cartes*) card index; ~ **actif** *ou* **en cours d'utilisation** (*INFORM*) active file; ~ **d'adresses** mailing list; ~ **d'archives** (*INFORM*) archive file.
fichu, e [fiʃy] *pp de* **ficher** (*fam*) ♦ *adj* (*fam: fini, inutilisable*) bust, done for; (*: intensif*) wretched, darned ♦ *nm* (*foulard*) (head)scarf (*pl* -scarves); **être** ~ **de** to be capable of; **mal** ~ feeling lousy; useless; **bien** ~ great.
fictif, ive [fiktif, -iv] *adj* fictitious.
fiction [fiksjɔ̃] *nf* fiction; (*fait imaginé*) invention.
fictivement [fiktivmɑ̃] *adv* fictitiously.
fidèle [fidɛl] *adj*: ~ **(à)** faithful (to) ♦ *nm/f* (*REL*): **les** ~**s** the faithful; (*à l'église*) the congregation.
fidèlement [fidɛlmɑ̃] *adv* faithfully.
fidélité [fidelite] *nf* faithfulness.
Fidji [fidʒi] *nfpl*: **(les îles)** ~ Fiji.
fiduciaire [fidysjɛʀ] *adj* fiduciary; **héritier** ~ heir, trustee; **monnaie** ~ flat money.
fief [fjɛf] *nm* fief; (*fig*) preserve; stronghold.
fieffé, e [fjefe] *adj* (*ivrogne, menteur*) arrant, out-and-out.
fiel [fjɛl] *nm* gall.
fiente [fjɑ̃t] *nf* (bird) droppings *pl*.
fier[1] [fje]: **se** ~ **à** *vt* to trust.
fier[2], **fière** [fjɛʀ] *adj* proud; ~ **de** proud of; **avoir fière allure** to cut a fine figure.
fièrement [fjɛʀmɑ̃] *adv* proudly.
fierté [fjɛʀte] *nf* pride.
fièvre [fjɛvʀ(ə)] *nf* fever; **avoir de la** ~**/39 de** ~ to have a high temperature/a temperature of 39°C; ~ **typhoïde** typhoid fever.
fiévreusement [fjevʀøzmɑ̃] *adv* (*fig*) feverishly.
fiévreux, euse [fjevʀø, -øz] *adj* feverish.
FIFA [fifa] *sigle f* (= *Fédération internationale de Football association*) FIFA.
fifre [fifʀ(ə)] *nm* fife; (*personne*) fife-player.
fig *abr* (= *figure*) fig.
figer [fiʒe] *vt* to congeal; (*fig: personne*) to freeze, root to the spot; **se** ~ *vi* to congeal; to freeze; (*institutions etc*) to become set, stop evolving.

fignoler [fiɲɔle] *vt* to put the finishing touches to.
figue [fig] *nf* fig.
figuier [figje] *nm* fig tree.
figurant, e [figyʀɑ̃, -ɑ̃t] *nm/f* (*THÉÂT*) walk-on; (*CINÉ*) extra.
figuratif, ive [figyʀatif, -iv] *adj* representational, figurative.
figuration [figyʀɑsjɔ̃] *nf* walk-on parts *pl*; extras *pl*.
figure [figyʀ] *nf* (*visage*) face; (*image, tracé, forme, personnage*) figure; (*illustration*) picture, diagram; **faire ~ de** to look like; **faire bonne ~** to put up a good show; **faire triste ~** to be a sorry sight; **~ de rhétorique** figure of speech.
figuré, e [figyʀe] *adj* (*sens*) figurative.
figurer [figyʀe] *vi* to appear ♦ *vt* to represent; **se ~ que** to imagine that; **figurez-vous que** ... would you believe that ...?
figurine [figyʀin] *nf* figurine.
fil [fil] *nm* (*brin, fig: d'une histoire*) thread; (*du téléphone*) cable, wire; (*textile de lin*) linen; (*d'un couteau: tranchant*) edge; **au ~ des années** with the passing of the years; **au ~ de l'eau** with the stream *ou* current; **de ~ en aiguille** one thing leading to another; **ne tenir qu'à un ~** (*vie, réussite etc*) to hang by a thread; **donner du ~ à retordre à qn** to make life difficult for sb; **donner/recevoir un coup de ~** to make/get a phone call; **~ à coudre** (sewing) thread *ou* yarn; **~ dentaire** dental floss; **~ électrique** electric wire; **~ de fer** wire; **~ de fer barbelé** barbed wire; **~ à pêche** fishing line; **~ à plomb** plumbline; **~ à souder** soldering wire.
filament [filamɑ̃] *nm* (*ÉLEC*) filament; (*de liquide*) trickle, thread.
filandreux, euse [filɑ̃dʀø, -øz] *adj* stringy.
filant, e [filɑ̃, -ɑ̃t] *adj*: **étoile ~e** shooting star.
filasse [filas] *adj inv* white blond.
filature [filatyʀ] *nf* (*fabrique*) mill; (*policière*) shadowing *no pl*, tailing *no pl*; **prendre qn en ~** to shadow *ou* tail sb.
fil-de-fériste [fildəfeʀist(ə)] *nm/f* high-wire artist.
file [fil] *nf* line; **~ (d'attente)** queue (*BRIT*), line (*US*); **prendre la ~** to join the (end of the) queue *ou* line; **prendre la ~ de droite** (*AUTO*) to move into the right-hand lane; **se mettre en ~** to form a line; (*AUTO*) to get into lane; **stationner en double ~** (*AUTO*) to double-park; **à la ~** *adv* (*d'affilée*) in succession; (*à la suite*) one after another; **à la** *ou* **en ~ indienne** in single file.
filer [file] *vt* (*tissu, toile, verre*) to spin; (*dérouler: câble etc*) to pay *ou* let out; (*prendre en filature*) to shadow, tail; (*fam: donner*): **~ qch à qn** to slip sb sth ♦ *vi* (*bas, maille, liquide, pâte*) to run; (*aller vite*) to fly past *ou* by; (*fam: partir*) to make off; **~ à l'anglaise** to take French leave; **~ doux** to behave o.s., toe the line; **~ un mauvais coton** to be in a bad way.
filet [filɛ] *nm* net; (*CULIN*) fillet; (*d'eau, de sang*) trickle; **tendre un ~** (*suj: police*) to set a trap; **~ (à bagages)** (*RAIL*) luggage rack; **~ (à provisions)** string bag.
filetage [filtaʒ] *nm* threading; thread.
fileter [filte] *vt* to thread.
filial, e, aux [filjal, -o] *adj* filial ♦ *nf* (*COMM*) subsidiary; affiliate.
filiation [filjɑsjɔ̃] *nf* filiation.
filière [filjɛʀ] *nf*: **passer par la ~** to go through the (administrative) channels; **suivre la ~** to work one's way up (through the hierarchy).
filiforme [filifɔʀm(ə)] *adj* spindly; threadlike.
filigrane [filigʀan] *nm* (*d'un billet, timbre*) watermark; **en ~** (*fig*) showing just beneath the surface.
filin [filɛ̃] *nm* (*NAVIG*) rope.
fille [fij] *nf* girl; (*opposé à fils*) daughter; **vieille ~** old maid; **~ de joie** prostitute; **~ de salle** waitress.
fille-mère, *pl* **filles-mères** [fijmɛʀ] *nf* unmarried mother.
fillette [fijɛt] *nf* (little) girl.
filleul, e [fijœl] *nm/f* godchild, godson/daughter.
film [film] *nm* (*pour photo*) (roll of) film; (*œuvre*) film, picture, movie; (*couche*) film; **~ muet/parlant** silent/talking picture *ou* movie; **~ alimentaire** clingfilm; **~ d'animation** animated film; **~ policier** thriller.
filmer [filme] *vt* to film.
filon [filɔ̃] *nm* vein, lode; (*fig*) lucrative line, moneyspinner.
filou [filu] *nm* (*escroc*) swindler.
fils [fis] *nm* son; **~ de famille** moneyed young man; **~ à papa** (*péj*) daddy's boy.
filtrage [filtʀaʒ] *nm* filtering.
filtrant, e [filtʀɑ̃, -ɑ̃t] *adj* (*huile solaire etc*) filtering.
filtre [filtʀ(ə)] *nm* filter; **"~ ou sans ~?"** (*cigarettes*) "tipped or plain?"; **~ à air** air filter.
filtrer [filtʀe] *vt* to filter; (*fig: candidats, visiteurs*) to screen ♦ *vi* to filter (through).
fin[1] [fɛ̃] *nf* end; **~s** *nfpl* (*but*) ends; **à (la) ~ mai, ~ mai** at the end of May; **en ~ de semaine** at the end of the week; **prendre ~** to come to an end; **toucher à sa ~** to be drawing to a close; **mettre ~ à** to put an end to; **mener à bonne ~** to bring to a successful conclusion; **à cette ~** to this end; **à toutes ~s utiles** for your information; **à la ~** in the end, eventually; **sans ~** *adj* endless ♦ *adv* endlessly; **~ de non-recevoir** (*JUR, ADMIN*) objection; **~ de section** (*de ligne d'autobus*) (fare) stage.
fin[2], **e** [fɛ̃, fin] *adj* (*papier, couche, fil*) thin; (*cheveux, poudre, pointe, visage*) fine; (*taille*) neat, slim; (*esprit, remarque*) subtle; shrewd ♦ *adv* (*moudre, couper*) finely ♦ *nm*: **vouloir jouer au plus ~ (avec qn)** to try to outsmart sb ♦ *nf*

(*alcool*) liqueur brandy; **c'est ~!** (*ironique*) how clever!; ~ **prêt/soûl** quite ready/drunk; **un ~ gourmet** a gourmet; **un ~ tireur** a crack shot; **avoir la vue/l'ouïe ~e** to have sharp eyes/ears, have keen eyesight/ hearing; **or/linge/vin ~** fine gold/linen/wine; **le ~ fond de** the very depths of; **le ~ mot de** the real story behind; **la ~e fleur de** the flower of; **une ~e mouche** (*fig*) a sharp customer; **~es herbes** mixed herbs.
final, e [final] *adj, nf* final ♦ *nm* (*MUS*) finale; **quarts de ~e** quarter finals; **8èmes/16èmes de ~e** 2nd/1st round (*in 5 round knock-out competition*).
finalement [finalmɑ̃] *adv* finally, in the end; (*après tout*) after all.
finaliste [finalist(ə)] *nm/f* finalist.
finalité [finalite] *nf* (*but*) aim, goal; (*fonction*) purpose.
finance [finɑ̃s] *nf* finance; **~s** *nfpl* (*situation financière*) finances; (*activités financières*) finance *sg*; **moyennant ~** for a fee *ou* consideration.
financement [finɑ̃smɑ̃] *nm* financing.
financer [finɑ̃se] *vt* to finance.
financier, ière [finɑ̃sje, -jɛʀ] *adj* financial ♦ *nm* financier.
financièrement [finɑ̃sjɛʀmɑ̃] *adv* financially.
finasser [finase] *vi* (*péj*) to wheel and deal.
finaud, e [fino, -od] *adj* wily.
fine [fin] *adj f, nf voir* **fin, e**.
finement [finmɑ̃] *adv* thinly; finely; neatly, slimly; subtly; shrewdly.
finesse [finɛs] *nf* thinness; fineness; neatness, slimness; subtlety; shrewdness; **~s** *nfpl* (*subtilités*) niceties; finer points.
fini, e [fini] *adj* finished; (*MATH*) finite; (*intensif*): **un menteur ~** a liar through and through ♦ *nm* (*d'un objet manufacturé*) finish.
finir [finiʀ] *vt* to finish ♦ *vi* to finish, end; **~ quelque part** to end *ou* finish up somewhere; **~ de faire** to finish doing; (*cesser*) to stop doing; **~ par faire** to end *ou* finish up doing; **il finit par m'agacer** he's beginning to get on my nerves; **~ en pointe/tragédie** to end in a point/in tragedy; **en ~ avec** to be *ou* have done with; **à n'en plus ~** (*route, discussions*) never-ending; **il va mal ~** he will come to a bad end; **c'est bientôt fini?** (*reproche*) have you quite finished?
finish [finiʃ] *nm* (*SPORT*) finish.
finissage [finisaʒ] *nm* finishing.
finisseur, euse [finisœʀ, -øz] *nm/f* (*SPORT*) strong finisher.
finition [finisjɔ̃] *nf* finishing; finish.
finlandais, e [fɛ̃lɑ̃dɛ, -ɛz] *adj* Finnish ♦ *nm/f*: **F~, e** Finn.
Finlande [fɛ̃lɑ̃d] *nf*: **la ~** Finland.
finnois, e [finwa, -waz] *adj* Finnish ♦ *nm* (*LING*) Finnish.
fiole [fjɔl] *nf* phial.
fiord [fjɔʀ(d)] *nm* = **fjord**.
fioriture [fjɔʀityʀ] *nf* embellishment, flourish.
fioul [fjul] *nm* fuel oil.
firent [fiʀ] *vb voir* **faire**.
firmament [fiʀmamɑ̃] *nm* firmament, skies *pl*.
firme [fiʀm(ə)] *nf* firm.
fis [fi] *vb voir* **faire**.
fisc [fisk] *nm* tax authorities *pl*, ≈ Inland Revenue (*BRIT*), ≈ Internal Revenue Service (*US*).
fiscal, e, aux [fiskal, -o] *adj* tax *cpd*, fiscal.
fiscaliser [fiskalize] *vt* to subject to tax.
fiscaliste [fiskalist(ə)] *nm/f* tax specialist.
fiscalité [fiskalite] *nf* tax system; (*charges*) taxation.
fissible [fisibl(ə)] *adj* fissile.
fission [fisjɔ̃] *nf* fission.
fissure [fisyʀ] *nf* crack.
fissurer [fisyʀe] *vt*, **se ~** *vi* to crack.
fiston [fistɔ̃] *nm* (*fam*) son, lad.
fit [fi] *vb voir* **faire**.
FIV *sigle f* (= *fécondation in vitro*) IVF.
fixage [fiksaʒ] *nm* (*PHOTO*) fixing.
fixateur [fiksatœʀ] *nm* (*PHOTO*) fixer; (*pour cheveux*) hair cream.
fixatif [fiksatif] *nm* fixative.
fixation [fiksɑsjɔ̃] *nf* fixing; fastening; setting; (*de ski*) binding; (*PSYCH*) fixation.
fixe [fiks(ə)] *adj* fixed; (*emploi*) steady, regular ♦ *nm* (*salaire*) basic salary; **à heure ~** at a set time; **menu à prix ~** set menu.
fixé, e [fikse] *adj* (*heure, jour*) appointed; **être ~ (sur)** to have made up one's mind (about); to know for certain (about).
fixement [fiksəmɑ̃] *adv* fixedly, steadily.
fixer [fikse] *vt* (*attacher*): **~ qch (à/sur)** to fix *ou* fasten sth (to/onto); (*déterminer*) to fix, set; (*CHIMIE, PHOTO*) to fix; (*poser son regard sur*) to look hard at, stare at; **se ~** (*s'établir*) to settle down; **~ son choix sur qch** to decide on sth; **se ~ sur** (*suj: attention*) to focus on.
fixité [fiksite] *nf* fixedness.
fjord [fjɔʀ(d)] *nm* fjord, fiord.
fl. *abr* (= *fleuve*) r, R; (= *florin*) fl.
flacon [flakɔ̃] *nm* bottle.
flagada [flagada] *adj inv* (*fam: fatigué*) shattered.
flagellation [flaʒɛlɑsjɔ̃] *nf* flogging.
flageller [flaʒele] *vt* to flog, scourge.
flageoler [flaʒɔle] *vi* to have knees like jelly.
flageolet [flaʒɔlɛ] *nm* (*MUS*) flageolet; (*CULIN*) dwarf kidney bean.
flagornerie [flagɔʀnəʀi] *nf* toadying, fawning.
flagorneur, euse [flagɔʀnœʀ, -øz] *nm/f* toady, fawner.
flagrant, e [flagʀɑ̃, -ɑ̃t] *adj* flagrant, blatant; **en ~ délit** in the act, in flagrante delicto.
flair [flɛʀ] *nm* sense of smell; (*fig*) intuition.
flairer [fleʀe] *vt* (*humer*) to sniff (at); (*détecter*) to scent.
flamand, e [flamɑ̃, -ɑ̃d] *adj* Flemish ♦ *nm* (*LING*) Flemish ♦ *nm/f*: **F~, e** Fleming; **les F~s** the Flemish.

flamant [flamɑ̃] *nm* flamingo.
flambant [flɑ̃bɑ̃] *adv*: ~ **neuf** brand new.
flambé, e [flɑ̃be] *adj* (*CULIN*) flambé ♦ *nf* blaze; (*fig*) flaring-up, explosion.
flambeau, x [flɑ̃bo] *nm* (flaming) torch; **se passer le** ~ (*fig*) to hand down the (*ou* a) tradition.
flambée [flɑ̃be] *nf* (*feu*) blaze; (*COMM*): ~ **des prix** (sudden) shooting up of prices.
flamber [flɑ̃be] *vi* to blaze (up) ♦ *vt* (*poulet*) to singe; (*aiguille*) to sterilize.
flambeur, euse [flɑ̃bœʀ, -øz] *nm/f* big-time gambler.
flamboyant, e [flɑ̃bwajɑ̃, -ɑ̃t] *adj* blazing; flaming.
flamboyer [flɑ̃bwaje] *vi* to blaze (up); (*fig*) to flame.
flamenco [flamɛnko] *nm* flamenco.
flamingant, e [flamɛ̃gɑ̃, -ɑ̃t] *adj* Flemish-speaking ♦ *nm/f*: **F~, e** Flemish speaker; (*POL*) Flemish nationalist.
flamme [flam] *nf* flame; (*fig*) fire, fervour; **en** ~**s** on fire, ablaze.
flammèche [flamɛʃ] *nf* (flying) spark.
flammerole [flamʀɔl] *nf* will-o'-the-wisp.
flan [flɑ̃] *nm* (*CULIN*) custard tart *ou* pie.
flanc [flɑ̃] *nm* side; (*MIL*) flank; **à** ~ **de colline** on the hillside; **prêter le** ~ **à** (*fig*) to lay o.s. open to.
flancher [flɑ̃ʃe] *vi* (*cesser de fonctionner*) to fail, pack up; (*armée*) to quit.
Flandre [flɑ̃dʀ(ə)] *nf*: **la** ~ (*aussi*: **les** ~**s**) Flanders.
flanelle [flanɛl] *nf* flannel.
flâner [flɑne] *vi* to stroll.
flânerie [flɑnʀi] *nf* stroll.
flâneur, euse [flɑnœʀ, -øz] *adj* idle ♦ *nm/f* stroller.
flanquer [flɑ̃ke] *vt* to flank; (*fam*: *jeter*): ~ **par terre/à la porte** to fling to the ground/chuck out; (*: donner*): ~ **la frousse à qn** to put the wind up sb, give sb an awful fright.
flapi, e [flapi] *adj* dog-tired.
flaque [flak] *nf* (*d'eau*) puddle; (*d'huile, de sang etc*) pool.
flash, *pl* **flashes** [flaʃ] *nm* (*PHOTO*) flash; ~ **(d'information)** newsflash.
flasque [flask(ə)] *adj* flabby ♦ *nf* (*flacon*) flask.
flatter [flate] *vt* to flatter; (*caresser*) to stroke; **se** ~ **de qch** to pride o.s. on sth.
flatterie [flatʀi] *nf* flattery.
flatteur, euse [flatœʀ, -øz] *adj* flattering ♦ *nm/f* flatterer.
flatulence [flatylɑ̃s], **flatuosité** [flatɥozite] *nf* (*MÉD*) flatulence, wind.
FLB *abr* (= *franco long du bord*) FAS ♦ *sigle m* (*POL*) = *Front de libération de la Bretagne*.
FLC *sigle m* = *Front de libération de la Corse*.
fléau, x [fleo] *nm* scourge, curse; (*de balance*) beam; (*pour le blé*) flail.
fléchage [fleʃaʒ] *nm* (*d'un itinéraire*) signposting.
flèche [flɛʃ] *nf* arrow; (*de clocher*) spire; (*de grue*) jib; (*trait d'esprit, critique*) shaft; **monter en** ~ (*fig*) to soar, rocket; **partir en** ~ (*fig*) to be off like a shot; **à** ~ **variable** (*avion*) swing-wing *cpd*.
flécher [fleʃe] *vt* to arrow, mark with arrows.
fléchette [fleʃɛt] *nf* dart; ~**s** *nfpl* (*jeu*) darts *sg*.
fléchir [fleʃiʀ] *vt* (*corps, genou*) to bend; (*fig*) to sway, weaken ♦ *vi* (*poutre*) to sag, bend; (*fig*) to weaken, flag; (*: baisser: prix*) to fall off.
fléchissement [fleʃismɑ̃] *nm* bending; sagging; flagging; (*de l'économie*) dullness.
flegmatique [flɛgmatik] *adj* phlegmatic.
flegme [flɛgm(ə)] *nm* composure.
flemmard, e [flemaʀ, -aʀd(ə)] *nm/f* lazybones *sg*, loafer.
flemme [flɛm] *nf* (*fam*): **j'ai la** ~ **de faire** I can't be bothered to do.
flétan [fletɑ̃] *nm* (*ZOOL*) halibut.
flétrir [fletʀiʀ] *vt* to wither; (*stigmatiser*) to condemn (in the most severe terms); **se** ~ *vi* to wither.
fleur [flœʀ] *nf* flower; (*d'un arbre*) blossom; **être en** ~ (*arbre*) to be in blossom; **tissu à** ~**s** flowered *ou* flowery fabric; **la (fine)** ~ **de** (*fig*) the flower of; **être** ~ **bleue** to be soppy *ou* sentimental; **à** ~ **de terre** just above the ground; **faire une** ~ **à qn** to do sb a favour (*BRIT*) *ou* favor (*US*); ~ **de lis** fleur-de-lis.
fleurer [flœʀe] *vt*: ~ **la lavande** to have the scent of lavender.
fleuret [flœʀɛ] *nm* (*arme*) foil; (*sport*) fencing.
fleurette [flœʀɛt] *nf*: **conter** ~ **à qn** to whisper sweet nothings to sb.
fleuri, e [flœʀi] *adj* in flower *ou* bloom; surrounded by flowers; (*fig*: *style*) flowery; (*: teint*) glowing.
fleurir [flœʀiʀ] *vi* (*rose*) to flower; (*arbre*) to blossom; (*fig*) to flourish ♦ *vt* (*tombe*) to put flowers on; (*chambre*) to decorate with flowers.
fleuriste [flœʀist(ə)] *nm/f* florist.
fleuron [flœʀɔ̃] *nm* jewel (*fig*).
fleuve [flœv] *nm* river; **roman-**~ saga; **discours-**~ interminable speech.
flexibilité [flɛksibilite] *nf* flexibility.
flexible [flɛksibl(ə)] *adj* flexible.
flexion [flɛksjɔ̃] *nf* flexing, bending; (*LING*) inflection.
flibustier [flibystje] *nm* buccaneer.
flic [flik] *nm* (*fam*: *péj*) cop.
flingue [flɛ̃g] *nm* (*fam*) shooter.
flipper *nm* [flipœʀ] pinball (machine) ♦ *vi* [flipe] (*fam*: *être déprimé*) to feel down, be on a downer; (*: être exalté*) to freak out.
flirt [flœʀt] *nm* flirting; (*personne*) boyfriend, girlfriend.
flirter [flœʀte] *vi* to flirt.
FLN *sigle m* = *Front de libération nationale (during the Algerian war)*.
FLNKS *sigle m* (= *Front de libération nationale kanak et socialiste*) *political movement in New*

Caledonia.

flocon [flɔkɔ̃] *nm* flake; (*de laine etc: boulette*) flock; **~s d'avoine** oatflakes, porridge oats.

floconneux, euse [flɔkɔnø, -øz] *adj* fluffy, fleecy.

flonflons [flɔ̃flɔ̃] *nmpl* blare *sg*.

flopée [flɔpe] *nf*: **une ~ de** loads of.

floraison [flɔʀɛzɔ̃] *nf* (*voir fleurir*) flowering; blossoming; flourishing.

floral, e, aux [flɔʀal, -o] *adj* floral, flower *cpd*.

floralies [flɔʀali] *nfpl* flower show *sg*.

flore [flɔʀ] *nf* flora.

Florence [flɔʀɑ̃s] *n* (*ville*) Florence.

florentin, e [flɔʀɑ̃tɛ̃, -in] *adj* Florentine.

floriculture [flɔʀikyltyʀ] *nf* flower-growing.

florissant, e [flɔʀisɑ̃, -ɑ̃t] *vb voir* **fleurir** ♦ *adj* flourishing; (*santé, teint, mine*) blooming.

flot [flo] *nm* flood, stream; (*marée*) flood tide; **~s** *nmpl* (*de la mer*) waves; **être à ~** (*NAVIG*) to be afloat; (*fig*) to be on an even keel; **à ~s** (*couler*) in torrents; **entrer à ~s** to stream *ou* pour in.

flottage [flɔtaʒ] *nm* (*du bois*) floating.

flottaison [flɔtɛzɔ̃] *nf*: **ligne de ~** waterline.

flottant, e [flɔtɑ̃, -ɑ̃t] *adj* (*vêtement*) loose(-fitting); (*cours, barême*) floating.

flotte [flɔt] *nf* (*NAVIG*) fleet; (*fam*) water; rain.

flottement [flɔtmɑ̃] *nm* (*fig*) wavering, hesitation; (*ÉCON*) floating.

flotter [flɔte] *vi* to float; (*nuage, odeur*) to drift; (*drapeau*) to fly; (*vêtements*) to hang loose ♦ *vb impers* (*fam: pleuvoir*): **il flotte** it's raining ♦ *vt* to float; **faire ~** to float.

flotteur [flɔtœʀ] *nm* float.

flottille [flɔtij] *nf* flotilla.

flou, e [flu] *adj* fuzzy, blurred; (*fig*) woolly (*BRIT*), vague; (*non ajusté: robe*) loose(-fitting).

flouer [flue] *vt* to swindle.

FLQ *abr* (= *franco long du quai*) FAQ.

fluctuant, e [flyktɥɑ̃, -ɑ̃t] *adj* (*prix, cours*) fluctuating; (*opinions*) changing.

fluctuation [flyktɥasjɔ̃] *nf* fluctuation.

fluctuer [flyktɥe] *vi* to fluctuate.

fluet, te [flyɛ, -ɛt] *adj* thin, slight; (*voix*) thin.

fluide [flyid] *adj* fluid; (*circulation etc*) flowing freely ♦ *nm* fluid; (*force*) (mysterious) power.

fluidifier [flyidifje] *vt* to make fluid.

fluidité [flyidite] *nf* fluidity; free flow.

fluor [flyɔʀ] *nm* fluorine.

fluoré, e [flyɔʀe] *adj* fluoridated.

fluorescent, e [flyɔʀesɑ̃, -ɑ̃t] *adj* fluorescent.

flûte [flyt] *nf* (*aussi*: **~ traversière**) flute; (*verre*) flute glass; (*pain*) long loaf (*pl* loaves); **petite ~** piccolo (*pl* -s); **~!** drat it!; **~ (à bec)** recorder; **~ de Pan** panpipes *pl*.

flûtiste [flytist(ə)] *nm/f* flautist, flute player.

fluvial, e, aux [flyvjal, -o] *adj* river *cpd*, fluvial.

flux [fly] *nm* incoming tide; (*écoulement*) flow; **le ~ et le reflux** the ebb and flow.

fluxion [flyksjɔ̃] *nf*: **~ de poitrine** pneumonia.

FM *sigle f* (= *frequency modulation*) FM.

Fme *abr* (= *femme*) W.

FMI *sigle m* (= *Fonds monétaire international*) IMF.

FN *sigle m* (= *Front national*) ≈ NF (= *National Front*).

FNAC [fnak] *sigle f* (= *Fédération nationale des achats des cadres*) *chain of discount shops* (*hi-fi, photo etc*).

FNAH *sigle m* = *Fonds national d'amélioration de l'habitat.*

FNEF [fnɛf] *sigle f* (= *Fédération nationale des étudiants de France*) *student union.*

FNSEA *sigle f* (= *Fédération nationale des syndicats d'exploitants agricoles*) *farmers' union.*

FO *sigle f* (= *Force ouvrière*) *trades union.*

foc [fɔk] *nm* jib.

focal, e, aux [fɔkal, -o] *adj* focal ♦ *nf* focal length.

focaliser [fɔkalize] *vt* to focus.

foehn [føn] *nm* foehn, föhn.

fœtal, e, aux [fetal, -o] *adj* fetal, foetal (*BRIT*).

fœtus [fetys] *nm* fetus, foetus (*BRIT*).

foi [fwa] *nf* faith; **sous la ~ du serment** under *ou* on oath; **ajouter ~ à** to lend credence to; **faire ~** (*prouver*) to be evidence; **digne de ~** reliable; **sur la ~ de** on the word *ou* strength of; **être de bonne/mauvaise ~** to be in good faith/not to be in good faith; **ma ~!** well!

foie [fwa] *nm* liver; **~ gras** foie gras.

foin [fwɛ̃] *nm* hay; **faire les ~s** to make hay; **faire du ~** (*fam*) to kick up a row.

foire [fwaʀ] *nf* fair; (*fête foraine*) (fun) fair; (*fig: désordre, confusion*) bear garden; **faire la ~** to whoop it up; **~ (exposition)** trade fair.

fois [fwa] *nf* time; **une/deux ~** once/twice; **trois/vingt ~** three/twenty times; **2 ~ 2** 2 times 2; **deux/quatre ~ plus grand (que)** twice/four times as big (as); **une ~** (*passé*) once; (*futur*) sometime; **une (bonne) ~ pour toutes** once and for all; **encore une ~** again, once more; **il était une ~** once upon a time; **une ~ que c'est fait** once it's done; **une ~ parti** once he (*ou* I *etc*) had left; **des ~** (*parfois*) sometimes; **si des ~ ...** (*fam*) if ever ...; **non mais des ~!** (*fam*) (now) look here!; **à la ~** (*ensemble*) (all) at once; **à la ~ grand et beau** both tall and handsome.

foison [fwazɔ̃] *nf*: **une ~ de** an abundance of; **à ~** *adv* in plenty.

foisonnant, e [fwazɔnɑ̃, -ɑ̃t] *adj* teeming.

foisonnement [fwazɔnmɑ̃] *nm* profusion, abundance.

foisonner [fwazɔne] *vi* to abound; **~ en** *ou* **de** to abound in.

fol [fɔl] *adj m voir* **fou**.

folâtre [fɔlɑtʀ(ə)] *adj* playful.

folâtrer [fɔlɑtʀe] *vi* to frolic (about).

folichon, ne [fɔliʃɔ̃, -ɔn] *adj*: **ça n'a rien de ~** it's not a lot of fun.

folie [fɔli] *nf* (*d'une décision, d'un acte*) madness, folly; (*état*) madness, insanity; (*acte*) folly; **la ~ des grandeurs** delusions of grandeur; **faire des ~s** (*en dépenses*) to be extravagant.
folklore [fɔlklɔʀ] *nm* folklore.
folklorique [fɔlklɔʀik] *adj* folk *cpd*; (*fam*) weird.
folle [fɔl] *adj f, nf voir* **fou**.
follement [fɔlmɑ̃] *adv* (*très*) madly, wildly.
follet [fɔlɛ] *adj m*: **feu ~** will-o'-the-wisp.
fomentateur, trice [fɔmɑ̃tatœʀ, -tʀis] *nm/f* agitator.
fomenter [fɔmɑ̃te] *vt* to stir up, foment.
foncé, e [fɔ̃se] *adj* dark; **bleu ~** dark blue.
foncer [fɔ̃se] *vt* to make darker; (*CULIN: moule etc*) to line ♦ *vi* to go darker; (*fam: aller vite*) to tear *ou* belt along; **~ sur** to charge at.
fonceur, euse [fɔ̃sœʀ, -øz] *nm/f* whizz kid.
foncier, ière [fɔ̃sje, -jɛʀ] *adj* (*honnêteté etc*) basic, fundamental; (*malhonnêteté*) deep-rooted; (*COMM*) real estate *cpd*.
foncièrement [fɔ̃sjɛʀmɑ̃] *adv* basically; (*absolument*) thoroughly.
fonction [fɔ̃ksjɔ̃] *nf* (*rôle, MATH, LING*) function; (*emploi, poste*) post, position; **~s** (*professionnelles*) duties; **entrer en ~s** to take up one's post *ou* duties; to take up office; **voiture de ~** company car; **être ~ de** (*dépendre de*) to depend on; **en ~ de** (*par rapport à*) according to; **faire ~ de** to serve as; **la ~ publique** the state *ou* civil (*BRIT*) service.
fonctionnaire [fɔ̃ksjɔnɛʀ] *nm/f* state employee *ou* official; (*dans l'administration*) ≈ civil servant (*BRIT*).
fonctionnariser [fɔ̃ksjɔnaʀize] *vt* (*ADMIN: personne*) to give the status of a state employee to.
fonctionnel, le [fɔ̃ksjɔnɛl] *adj* functional.
fonctionnellement [fɔ̃ksjɔnɛlmɑ̃] *adv* functionally.
fonctionnement [fɔ̃ksjɔnmɑ̃] *nm* working; functioning; operation.
fonctionner [fɔ̃ksjɔne] *vi* to work, function; (*entreprise*) to operate, function; **faire ~** to work, operate.
fond [fɔ̃] *nm voir aussi* **fonds**; (*d'un récipient, trou*) bottom; (*d'une salle, scène*) back; (*d'un tableau, décor*) background; (*opposé à la forme*) content; (*petite quantité*): **un ~ de verre** a drop; (*SPORT*): **le ~** long distance (running); **course/épreuve de ~** long-distance race/trial; **au ~ de** at the bottom of; at the back of; **aller au ~ des choses** to get to the root of things; **le ~ de sa pensée** his (*ou* her) true thoughts *ou* feelings; **sans ~** *adj* bottomless; **envoyer par le ~** (*NAVIG: couler*) to sink, scuttle; **à ~** *adv* (*connaître, soutenir*) thoroughly; (*appuyer, visser*) right down *ou* home; **à ~ (de train)** *adv* (*fam*) full tilt; **dans le ~, au ~** *adv* (*en somme*) basically, really; **de ~ en comble** *adv* from top to bottom; **~ sonore** background noise; background music; **~ de teint** (make-up) foundation.
fondamental, e, aux [fɔ̃damɑ̃tal, -o] *adj* fundamental.
fondamentalement [fɔ̃damɑ̃talmɑ̃] *adv* fundamentally.
fondamentalisme [fɔ̃damɑ̃talism(ə)] *nm* fundamentalism.
fondamentaliste [fɔ̃damɑ̃talist(ə)] *adj, nm/f* fundamentalist.
fondant, e [fɔ̃dɑ̃, -ɑ̃t] *adj* (*neige*) melting; (*poire*) that melts in the mouth; (*chocolat*) fondant.
fondateur, trice [fɔ̃datœʀ, -tʀis] *nm/f* founder; **membre ~** founder (*BRIT*) *ou* founding (*US*) member.
fondation [fɔ̃dasjɔ̃] *nf* founding; (*établissement*) foundation; **~s** *nfpl* (*d'une maison*) foundations; **travail de ~** foundation works *pl*.
fondé, e [fɔ̃de] *adj* (*accusation etc*) well-founded ♦ *nm*: **~ de pouvoir** authorized representative; **mal ~** unfounded; **être ~ à croire** to have grounds for believing *ou* good reason to believe.
fondement [fɔ̃dmɑ̃] *nm* (*derrière*) behind; **~s** *nmpl* foundations; **sans ~** *adj* (*rumeur etc*) groundless, unfounded.
fonder [fɔ̃de] *vt* to found; (*fig*): **~ qch sur** to base sth on; **se ~ sur** (*suj: personne*) to base o.s. on; **~ un foyer** (*se marier*) to set up home.
fonderie [fɔ̃dʀi] *nf* smelting works *sg*.
fondeur, euse [fɔ̃dœʀ, øz] *nm/f* (*skieur*) long-distance skier ♦ *nm*: **(ouvrier) ~** caster.
fondre [fɔ̃dʀ(ə)] *vt* to melt; (*dans l'eau: sucre, sel*) to dissolve; (*fig: mélanger*) to merge, blend ♦ *vi* to melt; to dissolve; (*fig*) to melt away; (*se précipiter*): **~ sur** to swoop down on; **se ~** *vi* (*se combiner, se confondre*) to merge into each other; to dissolve; **~ en larmes** to dissolve into tears.
fondrière [fɔ̃dʀijɛʀ] *nf* rut.
fonds [fɔ̃] *nm* (*de bibliothèque*) collection; (*COMM*): **~ (de commerce)** business; (*fig*): **~ de probité** *etc* fund of integrity *etc* ♦ *nmpl* (*argent*) funds; **à ~ perdus** *adv* with little or no hope of getting the money back; **être en ~** to be in funds; **mise de ~** investment, (capital) outlay; **F~ monétaire international (FMI)** International Monetary Fund (IMF); **~ de roulement** *nm* float.
fondu, e [fɔ̃dy] *adj* (*beurre, neige*) melted; (*métal*) molten ♦ *nm* (*CINÉ*): **~ (enchaîné)** dissolve ♦ *nf* (*CULIN*) fondue.
fongicide [fɔ̃ʒisid] *nm* fungicide.
font [fɔ̃] *vb voir* **faire**.
fontaine [fɔ̃tɛn] *nf* fountain; (*source*) spring.
fontanelle [fɔ̃tanɛl] *nf* fontanelle.
fonte [fɔ̃t] *nf* melting; (*métal*) cast iron; **la ~ des neiges** the (spring) thaw.
fonts baptismaux [fɔ̃batismo] *nmpl* (baptis-

mal) font *sg*.
foot(ball) [fut(bol)] *nm* football, soccer.
footballeur, euse [futbolœʀ, -øz] *nm/f* footballer (*BRIT*), football *ou* soccer player.
footing [futiŋ] *nm* jogging; **faire du** ~ to go jogging.
for [fɔʀ] *nm*: **dans** *ou* **en son** ~ **intérieur** in one's heart of hearts.
forage [fɔʀaʒ] *nm* drilling, boring.
forain, e [fɔʀɛ̃, -ɛn] *adj* fairground *cpd* ♦ *nm* (*marchand*) stallholder; (*acteur etc*) fairground entertainer.
forban [fɔʀbɑ̃] *nm* (*pirate*) pirate; (*escroc*) crook.
forçat [fɔʀsa] *nm* convict.
force [fɔʀs(ə)] *nf* strength; (*puissance: surnaturelle etc*) power; (*PHYSIQUE, MÉCANIQUE*) force; ~**s** *nfpl* (*physiques*) strength *sg*; (*MIL*) forces; (*effectifs*): **d'importantes ~s de police** large contingents of police; **avoir de la** ~ to be strong; **être à bout de** ~ to have no strength left; **à la** ~ **du poignet** (*fig*) by the sweat of one's brow; **à** ~ **de faire** by dint of doing; **arriver en** ~ (*nombreux*) to arrive in force; **cas de** ~ **majeure** case of absolute necessity; (*ASSURANCES*) act of God; ~ **de la nature** natural force; **de** ~ *adv* forcibly, by force; **de toutes mes/ses** ~**s** with all my/his strength; **par la** ~ using force; **par la** ~ **des choses/d'habitude** by force of circumstances/habit; **à toute** ~ (*absolument*) at all costs; **faire** ~ **de rames/voiles** to ply the oars/cram on sail; **être de** ~ **à faire** to be up to doing; **de première** ~ first class; **la** ~ **armée** (*les troupes*) the army; ~ **d'âme** fortitude; ~ **de frappe** strike force; ~ **d'inertie** force of inertia; **la** ~ **publique** the authorities responsible for public order; ~**s d'intervention** (*MIL, POLICE*) peace-keeping force *sg*; **les** ~**s de l'ordre** the police.
forcé, e [fɔʀse] *adj* forced; (*bain*) unintended; (*inevitable*): **c'est** ~! it's inevitable!, it HAS to be!
forcément [fɔʀsemɑ̃] *adv* necessarily; inevitably; (*bien sûr*) of course.
forcené, e [fɔʀsəne] *adj* frenzied ♦ *nm/f* maniac.
forceps [fɔʀsɛps] *nm* forceps *pl*.
forcer [fɔʀse] *vt* (*contraindre*): ~ **qn à faire** to force sb to do; (*porte, serrure, plante*) to force; (*moteur, voix*) to strain ♦ *vi* (*SPORT*) to overtax o.s.; **se** ~ **à faire qch** to force o.s. to do sth; ~ **la dose/l'allure** to overdo it/ increase the pace; ~ **l'attention/le respect** to command attention/respect; ~ **la consigne** to bypass orders.
forcing [fɔʀsiŋ] *nm* (*SPORT*): **faire le** ~ to pile on the pressure.
forcir [fɔʀsiʀ] *vi* (*grossir*) to broaden out; (*vent*) to freshen.
forclore [fɔʀklɔʀ] *vt* (*JUR: personne*) to debar.
forclusion [fɔʀklyzjɔ̃] *nf* (*JUR*) debarment.
forer [fɔʀe] *vt* to drill, bore.
forestier, ière [fɔʀɛstje, -jɛʀ] *adj* forest *cpd*.
foret [fɔʀɛ] *nm* drill.
forêt [fɔʀɛ] *nf* forest; **Office National des F~s** (*ADMIN*) ≈ Forestry Commission (*BRIT*), ≈ National Forest Service (*US*); **la F~ Noire** the Black Forest.
foreuse [fɔʀøz] *nf* (electric) drill.
forfait [fɔʀfɛ] *nm* (*COMM*) fixed *ou* set price; all-in deal *ou* price; (*crime*) infamy; **déclarer** ~ to withdraw; **gagner par** ~ to win by a walkover; **travailler à** ~ to work for a lump sum.
forfaitaire [fɔʀfɛtɛʀ] *adj* set; inclusive.
forfait-vacances, *pl* **forfaits-vacances** [fɔʀfɛvakɑ̃s] *nm* package holiday.
forfanterie [fɔʀfɑ̃tʀi] *nf* boastfulness *no pl*.
forge [fɔʀʒ(ə)] *nf* forge, smithy.
forgé, e [fɔʀʒe] *adj*: ~ **de toutes pièces** (*histoire*) completely fabricated.
forger [fɔʀʒe] *vt* to forge; (*fig: personnalité*) to form; (*: prétexte*) to contrive, make up.
forgeron [fɔʀʒəʀɔ̃] *nm* (black)smith.
formaliser [fɔʀmalize]: **se** ~ *vi*: **se** ~ **(de)** to take offence (at).
formalisme [fɔʀmalism(ə)] *nm* formality.
formalité [fɔʀmalite] *nf* formality.
format [fɔʀma] *nm* size; **petit** ~ small size (*PHOTO*) 35 mm (film).
formater [fɔʀmate] *vt* (*disque*) to format; **non formaté** unformatted.
formateur, trice [fɔʀmatœʀ, -tʀis] *adj* formative.
formation [fɔʀmɑsjɔ̃] *nf* forming; (*éducation*) training; (*MUS*) group; (*MIL, AVIAT, GÉO*) formation; **la** ~ **permanente** *ou* **continue** continuing education; **la** ~ **professionnelle** vocational training.
forme [fɔʀm(ə)] *nf* (*gén*) form; (*d'un objet*) shape, form; ~**s** *nfpl* (*bonnes manières*) proprieties; (*d'une femme*) figure *sg*; **en** ~ **de poire** pear-shaped, in the shape of a pear; **sous** ~ **de** in the form of; in the guise of; **sous** ~ **de cachets** in the form of tablets; **être en (bonne** *ou* **pleine)** ~, **avoir la** ~ (*SPORT etc*) to be on form; **en bonne et due** ~ in due form; **pour la** ~ for the sake of form; **sans autre** ~ **de procès** (*fig*) without further ado; **prendre** ~ to take shape.
formel, le [fɔʀmɛl] *adj* (*preuve, décision*) definite, positive; (*logique*) formal.
formellement [fɔʀmɛlmɑ̃] *adv* (*interdit*) strictly.
former [fɔʀme] *vt* (*gén*) to form; (*éduquer: soldat, ingénieur etc*) to train; **se** ~ to form; to train.
formidable [fɔʀmidabl(ə)] *adj* tremendous.
formidablement [fɔʀmidabləmɑ̃] *adv* tremendously.
formol [fɔʀmɔl] *nm* formalin, formol.
formosan, e [fɔʀmozɑ̃, -an] *adj* Formosan.
Formose [fɔʀmoz] *nm* Formosa.

formulaire [fɔʀmylɛʀ] *nm* form.
formulation [fɔʀmylɑsjɔ̃] *nf* (*voir vb*) formulation; expression.
formule [fɔʀmyl] *nf* (*gén*) formula; (*formulaire*) form; **selon la ~ consacrée** as one says; **~ de politesse** polite phrase; (*en fin de lettre*) letter ending.
formuler [fɔʀmyle] *vt* (*émettre: réponse, vœux*) to formulate; (*expliciter: sa pensée*) to express.
forniquer [fɔʀnike] *vi* to fornicate.
FORPRONU [fɔʀpʀɔny] *sigle f* (= *Force de protection des Nations unies*) UNPROFOR.
fort, e [fɔʀ, fɔʀt(ə)] *adj* strong; (*intensité, rendement*) high, great; (*corpulent*) large; (*doué*): **être ~ (en)** to be good (at) ♦ *adv* (*serrer, frapper*) hard; (*sonner*) loud(ly); (*beaucoup*) greatly, very much; (*très*) very ♦ *nm* (*édifice*) fort; (*point fort*) strong point, forte; (*gén pl: personne, pays*): **le ~, les ~s** the strong; **c'est un peu ~!** it's a bit much!; **à plus ~e raison** even more so, all the more reason; **avoir ~ à faire avec qn** to have a hard job with sb; **se faire ~ de faire** to claim one can do; **~ bien/peu** very well/few; **au plus ~ de** (*au milieu de*) in the thick of, at the height of; **~e tête** rebel.
fortement [fɔʀtəmɑ̃] *adv* strongly; (*s'intéresser*) deeply.
forteresse [fɔʀtəʀɛs] *nf* fortress.
fortifiant [fɔʀtifjɑ̃] *nm* tonic.
fortifications [fɔʀtifikɑsjɔ̃] *nfpl* fortifications.
fortifier [fɔʀtifje] *vt* to strengthen, fortify; (*MIL*) to fortify; **se ~** *vi* (*personne, santé*) to grow stronger.
fortin [fɔʀtɛ̃] *nm* (small) fort.
fortiori [fɔʀtjɔʀi]: **à ~** *adv* all the more so.
FORTRAN [fɔʀtʀɑ̃] *nm* FORTRAN.
fortuit, e [fɔʀtɥi, -it] *adj* fortuitous, chance *cpd*.
fortuitement [fɔʀtɥitmɑ̃] *adv* fortuitously.
fortune [fɔʀtyn] *nf* fortune; **faire ~** to make one's fortune; **de ~** *adj* makeshift; (*compagnon*) chance *cpd*.
fortuné, e [fɔʀtyne] *adj* wealthy, well-off.
forum [fɔʀɔm] *nm* forum.
fosse [fos] *nf* (*grand trou*) pit; (*tombe*) grave; **la ~ aux lions/ours** the lions' den/bear pit; **~ commune** common *ou* communal grave; **~ (d'orchestre)** (orchestra) pit; **~ à purin** cesspit; **~ septique** septic tank; **~s nasales** nasal fossae.
fossé [fose] *nm* ditch; (*fig*) gulf, gap.
fossette [fosɛt] *nf* dimple.
fossile [fosil] *nm* fossil ♦ *adj* fossilized, fossil *cpd*.
fossilisé, e [fosilize] *adj* fossilized.
fossoyeur [foswajœʀ] *nm* gravedigger.
fou (fol), folle [fu, fɔl] *adj* mad, crazy; (*déréglé etc*) wild, erratic; (*mèche*) stray; (*herbe*) wild; (*fam: extrême, très grand*) terrific, tremendous ♦ *nm/f* madman/woman ♦ *nm* (*du roi*) jester, fool; (*ÉCHECS*) bishop; **~ à lier, ~ furieux (folle furieuse)** raving mad; **être ~ de** to be mad *ou* crazy about; (*chagrin, joie, colère*) to be wild with; **faire le ~** to play *ou* act the fool; **avoir le ~ rire** to have the giggles.
foucade [fukad] *nf* caprice.
foudre [fudʀ(ə)] *nf* lightning; **~s** *nfpl* (*fig: colère*) wrath *sg*.
foudroyant, e [fudʀwajɑ̃, -ɑ̃t] *adj* devastating; (*maladie, poison*) violent.
foudroyer [fudʀwaje] *vt* to strike down; **~ qn du regard** to look daggers at sb; **il a été foudroyé** he was struck by lightning.
fouet [fwɛ] *nm* whip; (*CULIN*) whisk; **de plein ~** *adv* head on.
fouettement [fwɛtmɑ̃] *nm* lashing *no pl*.
fouetter [fwete] *vt* to whip; to whisk.
fougasse [fugas] *nf* *type of flat pastry*.
fougère [fuʒɛʀ] *nf* fern.
fougue [fug] *nf* ardour (*BRIT*), ardor (*US*), spirit.
fougueusement [fugøzmɑ̃] *adv* ardently.
fougueux, euse [fugø, -øz] *adj* fiery, ardent.
fouille [fuj] *nf* search; **~s** *nfpl* (*archéologiques*) excavations; **passer à la ~** to be searched.
fouillé, e [fuje] *adj* detailed.
fouiller [fuje] *vt* to search; (*creuser*) to dig; (*: suj: archéologue*) to excavate; (*approfondir: étude etc*) to go into ♦ *vi* (*archéologue*) to excavate; **~ dans/parmi** to rummage in/among.
fouillis [fuji] *nm* jumble, muddle.
fouine [fwin] *nf* stone marten.
fouiner [fwine] *vi* (*péj*): **~ dans** to nose around *ou* about in.
fouineur, euse [fwinœʀ, -øz] *adj* nosey ♦ *nm/f* nosey parker, snooper.
fouir [fwiʀ] *vt* to dig.
fouisseur, euse [fwisœʀ, -øz] *adj* burrowing.
foulage [fulaʒ] *nm* pressing.
foulante [fulɑ̃t] *adj f*: **pompe ~** force pump.
foulard [fulaʀ] *nm* scarf (*pl* scarves).
foule [ful] *nf* crowd; **une ~ de** masses of; **venir en ~** to come in droves.
foulée [fule] *nf* stride; **dans la ~ de** on the heels of.
fouler [fule] *vt* to press; (*sol*) to tread upon; **se ~** *vi* (*fam*) to overexert o.s.; **se ~ la cheville** to sprain one's ankle; **~ aux pieds** to trample underfoot.
foulure [fulyʀ] *nf* sprain.
four [fuʀ] *nm* oven; (*de potier*) kiln; (*THÉÂT: échec*) flop; **allant au ~** ovenproof.
fourbe [fuʀb(ə)] *adj* deceitful.
fourberie [fuʀbəʀi] *nf* deceit.
fourbi [fuʀbi] *nm* (*fam*) gear, junk.
fourbir [fuʀbiʀ] *vt*: **~ ses armes** (*fig*) to get ready for the fray.
fourbu, e [fuʀby] *adj* exhausted.
fourche [fuʀʃ(ə)] *nf* pitchfork; (*de bicyclette*) fork.
fourcher [fuʀʃe] *vi*: **ma langue a fourché** it

was a slip of the tongue.
fourchette [furʃɛt] *nf* fork; (*STATISTIQUE*) bracket, margin.
fourchu, e [furʃy] *adj* split; (*arbre etc*) forked.
fourgon [furgɔ̃] *nm* van; (*RAIL*) wag(g)on; ~ **mortuaire** hearse.
fourgonnette [furgɔnɛt] *nf* (delivery) van.
fourmi [furmi] *nf* ant; **avoir des ~s** (*fig*) to have pins and needles.
fourmilière [furmiljɛr] *nf* ant-hill; (*fig*) hive of activity.
fourmillement [furmijmɑ̃] *nm* (*démangeaison*) pins and needles *pl*; (*grouillement*) swarming *no pl*.
fourmiller [furmije] *vi* to swarm; ~ **de** to be teeming with, be swarming with.
fournaise [furnɛz] *nf* blaze; (*fig*) furnace, oven.
fourneau, x [furno] *nm* stove.
fournée [furne] *nf* batch.
fourni, e [furni] *adj* (*barbe, cheveux*) thick; (*magasin*): **bien ~ (en)** well stocked (with).
fournil [furni] *nm* bakehouse.
fournir [furnir] *vt* to supply; (*preuve, exemple*) to provide, supply; (*effort*) to put in; ~ **qch à qn** to supply sth to sb, supply *ou* provide sb with sth; ~ **qn en** (*COMM*) to supply sb with; **se ~ chez** to shop at.
fournisseur, euse [furnisœr, -øz] *nm/f* supplier; (*INTERNET*): ~ **d'accès à Internet** (Internet) service provider.
fourniture [furnityr] *nf* supply(ing); **~s** *nfpl* supplies; **~s de bureau** office supplies, stationery; **~s scolaires** school stationery.
fourrage [furaʒ] *nm* fodder.
fourrager [furaʒe] *vi*: ~ **dans/parmi** to rummage through/among.
fourrager, ère [furaʒe, -ɛr] *adj* fodder *cpd* ♦ *nf* (*MIL*) fourragère.
fourré, e [fure] *adj* (*bonbon, chocolat*) filled; (*manteau, botte*) fur-lined ♦ *nm* thicket.
fourreau, x [furo] *nm* sheath; (*de parapluie*) cover; **robe ~** figure-hugging dress.
fourrer [fure] *vt* (*fam*): ~ **qch dans** to stick *ou* shove sth into; **se ~ dans/sous** to get into/under; **se ~ dans** (*une mauvaise situation*) to land o.s. in.
fourre-tout [furtu] *nm inv* (*sac*) holdall; (*péj*) junk room (*ou* cupboard); (*fig*) rag-bag.
fourreur [furœr] *nm* furrier.
fourrière [furjɛr] *nf* pound.
fourrure [furyr] *nf* fur; (*sur l'animal*) coat; **manteau/col de ~** fur coat/collar.
fourvoyer [furvwaje]: **se ~** *vi* to go astray, stray; **se ~ dans** to stray into.
foutre [futr(ə)] *vt* (*fam!*) = **ficher** (*fam*).
foutu, e [futy] *adj* (*fam!*) = **fichu.**
foyer [fwaje] *nm* (*de cheminée*) hearth; (*fig*) seat, centre; (*famille*) family; (*domicile*) home; (*local de réunion*) (social) club; (*résidence*) hostel; (*salon*) foyer; (*OPTIQUE, PHOTO*) focus; **lunettes à double ~** bi-focal glasses.
FP *sigle f* (= *franchise postale*) *exemption from postage*.
FPA *sigle f* (= *Formation professionnelle pour adultes*) adult education.
FPLP *sigle m* (= *Front populaire de la libération de la Palestine*) PFLP (= *Popular Front for the Liberation of Palestine*).
FR3 [ɛfɛrtrwa] *sigle f* (= *France Régions 3*) *TV channel*.
fracas [fraka] *nm* din; crash.
fracassant, e [frakasɑ̃, -ɑ̃t] *adj* sensational, staggering.
fracasser [frakase] *vt* to smash; **se ~ contre** *ou* **sur** to crash against.
fraction [fraksjɔ̃] *nf* fraction.
fractionnement [fraksjɔnmɑ̃] *nm* division.
fractionner [fraksjɔne] *vt* to divide (up), split (up).
fracture [fraktyr] *nf* fracture; ~ **du crâne** fractured skull; ~ **de la jambe** broken leg.
fracturer [fraktyre] *vt* (*coffre, serrure*) to break open; (*os, membre*) to fracture.
fragile [fraʒil] *adj* fragile, delicate; (*fig*) frail.
fragiliser [fraʒilize] *vt* to weaken, make fragile.
fragilité [fraʒilite] *nf* fragility.
fragment [fragmɑ̃] *nm* (*d'un objet*) fragment, piece; (*d'un texte*) passage, extract.
fragmentaire [fragmɑ̃tɛr] *adj* sketchy.
fragmenter [fragmɑ̃te] *vt* to split up.
frai [frɛ] *nm* spawn; (*ponte*) spawning.
fraîche [frɛʃ] *adj f voir* **frais.**
fraîchement [frɛʃmɑ̃] *adv* (*sans enthousiasme*) coolly; (*récemment*) freshly, newly.
fraîcheur [frɛʃœr] *nf* (*voir frais*) coolness; freshness.
fraîchir [frɛʃir] *vi* to get cooler; (*vent*) to freshen.
frais, fraîche [frɛ, frɛʃ] *adj* (*air, eau, accueil*) cool; (*petit pois, œufs, nouvelles, couleur, troupes*) fresh; **le voilà ~!** he's in a (right) mess! ♦ *adv* (*récemment*) newly, fresh(ly); **il fait ~** it's cool; **servir ~** chill before serving, serve chilled ♦ *nm*: **mettre au ~** to put in a cool place; **prendre le ~** to take a breath of cool air ♦ *nmpl* (*débours*) expenses; (*COMM*) costs; charges; **faire des ~** to spend; to go to a lot of expense; **faire les ~ de** to bear the brunt of; **faire les ~ de la conversation** (*parler*) to do most of the talking; (*en être le sujet*) to be the topic of conversation; **il en a été pour ses ~** he could have spared himself the trouble; **rentrer dans ses ~** to recover one's expenses; ~ **de déplacement** travel(ling) expenses; ~ **d'entretien** upkeep; ~ **généraux** overheads; ~ **de scolarité** school fees, tuition (*US*).
fraise [frɛz] *nf* strawberry; (*TECH*) countersink (bit); (*de dentiste*) drill; ~ **des bois** wild strawberry.
fraiser [freze] *vt* to countersink; (*CULIN*: *pâte*)

to knead.
fraiseuse [fʀɛzøz] *nf* (*TECH*) milling machine.
fraisier [fʀezje] *nm* strawberry plant.
framboise [fʀɑ̃bwaz] *nf* raspberry.
framboisier [fʀɑ̃bwazje] *nm* raspberry bush.
franc, franche [fʀɑ̃, fʀɑ̃ʃ] *adj* (*personne*) frank, straightforward; (*visage*) open; (*net: refus, couleur*) clear; (*: coupure*) clean; (*intensif*) downright; (*exempt*): ~ **de port** post free, postage paid; (*zone, port*) free; (*boutique*) duty-free ♦ *adv*: **parler** ~ to be frank *ou* candid ♦ *nm* franc.
français, e [fʀɑ̃sɛ, -ɛz] *adj* French ♦ *nm* (*LING*) French ♦ *nm/f*: **F~, e** Frenchman/woman; **les F~** the French.
franc-comtois, e, *mpl* **francs-comtois** [fʀɑ̃kɔ̃twa, -waz] *adj* of *ou* from (the) Franche-Comté.
France [fʀɑ̃s] *nf*: **la** ~ France; **en** ~ in France.
Francfort [fʀɑ̃kfɔʀ] *n* Frankfurt.
franche [fʀɑ̃ʃ] *adj f voir* **franc**.
Franche-Comté [fʀɑ̃ʃkɔ̃te] *nf* Franche-Comté.
franchement [fʀɑ̃ʃmɑ̃] *adv* (*voir* **franc**) frankly; clearly; (*tout à fait*) downright ♦ *excl* well, really!
franchir [fʀɑ̃ʃiʀ] *vt* (*obstacle*) to clear, get over; (*seuil, ligne, rivière*) to cross; (*distance*) to cover.
franchisage [fʀɑ̃ʃizaʒ] *nm* (*COMM*) franchising.
franchise [fʀɑ̃ʃiz] *nf* frankness; (*douanière, d'impôt*) exemption; (*ASSURANCES*) excess; (*COMM*) franchise; ~ **de bagages** baggage allowance.
franchissable [fʀɑ̃ʃisabl(ə)] *adj* (*obstacle*) surmountable.
francilien, ne [fʀɑ̃siljɛ̃, -ɛn] *adj* of *ou* from the Île-de-France region ♦ *nm/f*: **F~, ne** person from the Île-de-France region.
franciscain, e [fʀɑ̃siskɛ̃, -ɛn] *adj* Franciscan.
franciser [fʀɑ̃size] *vt* to gallicize, Frenchify.
franc-jeu [fʀɑ̃ʒø] *nm*: **jouer** ~ to play fair.
franc-maçon, *pl* **francs-maçons** [fʀɑ̃masɔ̃] *nm* Freemason.
franc-maçonnerie [fʀɑ̃masɔnʀi] *nf* Freemasonry.
franco [fʀɑ̃ko] *adv* (*COMM*): ~ **(de port)** postage paid.
franco... [fʀɑ̃ko] *préfixe* franco-.
franco-canadien [fʀɑ̃kɔkanadjɛ̃] *nm* (*LING*) Canadian French.
francophile [fʀɑ̃kɔfil] *adj* Francophile.
francophobe [fʀɑ̃kɔfɔb] *adj* Francophobe.
francophone [fʀɑ̃kɔfɔn] *adj* French-speaking ♦ *nm/f* French speaker.
francophonie [fʀɑ̃kɔfɔni] *nf* French-speaking communities *pl*.
franco-québécois [fʀɑ̃kɔkebekwa] *nm* (*LING*) Quebec French.
franc-parler [fʀɑ̃paʀle] *nm inv* outspokenness.
franc-tireur [fʀɑ̃tiʀœʀ] *nm* (*MIL*) irregular; (*fig*) freelance.
frange [fʀɑ̃ʒ] *nf* fringe; (*cheveux*) fringe (*BRIT*), bangs (*US*).
frangé, e [fʀɑ̃ʒe] *adj* (*tapis, nappe*): ~ **de** trimmed with.
frangin [fʀɑ̃ʒɛ̃] *nm* (*fam*) brother.
frangine [fʀɑ̃ʒin] *nf* (*fam*) sis, sister.
frangipane [fʀɑ̃ʒipan] *nf* almond paste.
franglais [fʀɑ̃glɛ] *nm* Franglais.
franquette [fʀɑ̃kɛt]: **à la bonne** ~ *adv* without any fuss.
frappant, e [fʀapɑ̃, -ɑ̃t] *adj* striking.
frappe [fʀap] *nf* (*d'une dactylo, pianiste, machine à écrire*) touch; (*BOXE*) punch; (*péj*) hood, thug.
frappé, e [fʀape] *adj* (*CULIN*) iced; ~ **de panique** panic-stricken; ~ **de stupeur** thunderstruck, dumbfounded.
frapper [fʀape] *vt* to hit, strike; (*étonner*) to strike; (*monnaie*) to strike, stamp; **se** ~ *vi* (*s'inquiéter*) to get worked up; ~ **à la porte** to knock at the door; ~ **dans ses mains** to clap one's hands; ~ **du poing sur** to bang one's fist on; ~ **un grand coup** (*fig*) to strike a blow.
frasques [fʀask(ə)] *nfpl* escapades; **faire des ~s** to get up to mischief.
fraternel, le [fʀatɛʀnɛl] *adj* brotherly, fraternal.
fraternellement [fʀatɛʀnɛlmɑ̃] *adv* in a brotherly way.
fraterniser [fʀatɛʀnize] *vi* to fraternize.
fraternité [fʀatɛʀnite] *nf* brotherhood.
fratricide [fʀatʀisid] *adj* fratricidal.
fraude [fʀod] *nf* fraud; (*SCOL*) cheating; **passer qch en** ~ to smuggle sth in (*ou* out); ~ **fiscale** tax evasion.
frauder [fʀode] *vi, vt* to cheat; ~ **le fisc** to evade paying tax(es).
fraudeur, euse [fʀodœʀ, -øz] *nm/f* person guilty of fraud; (*candidat*) candidate who cheats; (*au fisc*) tax evader.
frauduleux, euse [fʀodylø, -øz] *adj* fraudulent.
frauduleusement [fʀodyløzmɑ̃] *adv* fraudulently.
frayer [fʀeje] *vt* to open up, clear ♦ *vi* to spawn; (*fréquenter*): ~ **avec** to mix *ou* associate with; **se** ~ **un passage dans** to clear o.s. a path through, force one's way through.
frayeur [fʀɛjœʀ] *nf* fright.
fredaines [fʀədɛn] *nfpl* mischief *sg*, escapades.
fredonner [fʀədɔne] *vt* to hum.
freezer [fʀizœʀ] *nm* freezing compartment.
frégate [fʀegat] *nf* frigate.
frein [fʀɛ̃] *nm* brake; **mettre un** ~ **à** (*fig*) to put a brake on, check; **sans** ~ (*sans limites*) unchecked; ~ **à main** handbrake; ~ **moteur** engine braking; **~s à disques** disc brakes; **~s à tambour** drum brakes.
freinage [fʀɛnaʒ] *nm* braking; **distance de** ~ braking distance; **traces de** ~ tyre (*BRIT*) *ou* tire (*US*) marks.

freiner [fʀene] *vi* to brake ♦ *vt* (*progrès etc*) to check.
frelaté, e [fʀəlate] *adj* adulterated; (*fig*) tainted.
frêle [fʀɛl] *adj* frail, fragile.
frelon [fʀəlɔ̃] *nm* hornet.
freluquet [fʀəlykɛ] *nm* (*péj*) whippersnapper.
frémir [fʀemiʀ] *vi* (*de froid, de peur*) to tremble, shiver; (*de joie*) to quiver; (*eau*) to (begin to) bubble.
frémissement [fʀemismɑ̃] *nm* shiver; quiver; bubbling *no pl.*
frêne [fʀɛn] *nm* ash (tree).
frénésie [fʀenezi] *nf* frenzy.
frénétique [fʀenetik] *adj* frenzied, frenetic.
frénétiquement [fʀenetikmɑ̃] *adv* frenetically.
fréon [fʀeɔ̃] *nm* ® Freon ®.
fréquemment [fʀekamɑ̃] *adv* frequently.
fréquence [fʀekɑ̃s] *nf* frequency.
fréquent, e [fʀekɑ̃, -ɑ̃t] *adj* frequent.
fréquentable [fʀekɑ̃tabl(ə)] *adj*: **il est peu** ~ he's not the type one can associate oneself with.
fréquentation [fʀekɑ̃tɑsjɔ̃] *nf* frequenting; seeing; ~**s** *nfpl* company *sg.*
fréquenté, e [fʀekɑ̃te] *adj*: **très** ~ (very) busy; **mal** ~ patronized by disreputable elements.
fréquenter [fʀekɑ̃te] *vt* (*lieu*) to frequent; (*personne*) to see; **se** ~ to see a lot of each other.
frère [fʀɛʀ] *nm* brother ♦ *adj*: **partis/pays** ~**s** sister parties/countries.
fresque [fʀɛsk(ə)] *nf* (*ART*) fresco.
fret [fʀɛ] *nm* freight.
fréter [fʀete] *vt* to charter.
frétiller [fʀetije] *vi* to wriggle; to quiver; ~ **de la queue** to wag its tail.
fretin [fʀətɛ̃] *nm*: **le menu** ~ the small fry.
freudien, ne [fʀødjɛ̃, -ɛn] *adj* Freudian.
freux [fʀø] *nm* (*ZOOL*) rook.
friable [fʀijabl(ə)] *adj* crumbly.
friand, e [fʀijɑ̃, -ɑ̃d] *adj*: ~ **de** very fond of ♦ *nm* (*CULIN*) small minced-meat (*BRIT*) *ou* ground-meat (*US*) pie; (*: sucré*) small almond cake.
friandise [fʀijɑ̃diz] *nf* sweet.
fric [fʀik] *nm* (*fam*) cash, bread.
fricassée [fʀikase] *nf* fricassee.
fric-frac [fʀikfʀak] *nm* break-in.
friche [fʀiʃ]: **en** ~ *adj*, *adv* (lying) fallow.
friction [fʀiksjɔ̃] *nf* (*massage*) rub, rub-down; (*chez le coiffeur*) scalp massage; (*TECH, fig*) friction.
frictionner [fʀiksjɔne] *vt* to rub (down); to massage.
frigidaire [fʀiʒidɛʀ] *nm* ® refrigerator.
frigide [fʀiʒid] *adj* frigid.
frigidité [fʀiʒidite] *nf* frigidity.
frigo [fʀigo] *nm* (*= frigidaire*) fridge.
frigorifier [fʀigɔʀifje] *vt* to refrigerate; (*fig: personne*) to freeze.
frigorifique [fʀigɔʀifik] *adj* refrigerating.
frileusement [fʀiløzmɑ̃] *adv* with a shiver.
frileux, euse [fʀilø, -øz] *adj* sensitive to (the) cold; (*fig*) overcautious.
frimas [fʀimɑ] *nmpl* wintry weather *sg.*
frime [fʀim] *nf* (*fam*): **c'est de la** ~ it's all put on; **pour la** ~ just for show.
frimer [fʀime] *vi* to put on an act.
frimeur, euse [fʀimœʀ, -øz] *nm/f* poser.
frimousse [fʀimus] *nf* (sweet) little face.
fringale [fʀɛ̃gal] *nf*: **avoir la** ~ to be ravenous.
fringant, e [fʀɛ̃gɑ̃, -ɑ̃t] *adj* dashing.
fringues [fʀɛ̃g] *nfpl* (*fam*) clothes, gear *no pl.*
fripé, e [fʀipe] *adj* crumpled.
friperie [fʀipʀi] *nf* (*commerce*) secondhand clothes shop; (*vêtements*) secondhand clothes.
fripes [fʀip] *nfpl* secondhand clothes.
fripier, ière [fʀipje, -jɛʀ] *nm/f* secondhand clothes dealer.
fripon, ne [fʀipɔ̃, -ɔn] *adj* roguish, mischievous ♦ *nm/f* rascal, rogue.
fripouille [fʀipuj] *nf* scoundrel.
frire [fʀiʀ] *vt* (*aussi*: **faire** ~), *vi* to fry.
Frisbee [fʀizbi] *nm* ® Frisbee ®.
frise [fʀiz] *nf* frieze.
frisé, e [fʀize] *adj* curly, curly-haired ♦ *nf*: **(chicorée)** ~**e** curly endive.
friser [fʀize] *vt* to curl; (*fig: surface*) to skim graze; (*: mort*) to come within a hair's breadth of; (*: hérésie*) to verge on ♦ *vi* (*cheveux*) to curl; (*personne*) to have curly hair **se faire** ~ to have one's hair curled.
frisette [fʀizɛt] *nf* little curl.
frisotter [fʀizɔte] *vi* (*cheveux*) to curl tightly.
frisquet [fʀiskɛ] *adj* chilly.
frisson [fʀisɔ̃], **frissonnement** [fʀisɔnmɑ̃] *nm* shudder, shiver; quiver.
frissonner [fʀisɔne] *vi* (*personne*) to shudder shiver; (*feuilles*) to quiver.
frit, e [fʀi, fʀit] *pp de* **frire** ♦ *adj* fried ♦ *nf*: **(pommes)** ~**es** chips (*BRIT*), French fries.
friterie [fʀitʀi] *nf* ≈ chip shop (*BRIT*), ≈ hamburger stand (*US*).
friteuse [fʀitøz] *nf* chip pan (*BRIT*), deep (fat fryer.
friture [fʀityʀ] *nf* (*huile*) (deep) fat; (*plat*): ~ **(de poissons)** fried fish; (*RADIO*) crackle crackling *no pl*; ~**s** *nfpl* (*aliments frits*) fried food *sg.*
frivole [fʀivɔl] *adj* frivolous.
frivolité [fʀivɔlite] *nf* frivolity.
froc [fʀɔk] *nm* (*REL*) habit; (*fam: pantalon*) trousers *pl*, pants *pl.*
froid, e [fʀwa, fʀwad] *adj* cold ♦ *nm* cold; (*absence de sympathie*) coolness *no pl*; **il fait** ~ it's cold; **avoir** ~ to be cold; **prendre** ~ to catch a chill *ou* cold; **à** ~ *adv* (*démarrer*) (from) cold; **(pendant) les grands** ~**s** (in) the depths of winter, (during) the cold season **jeter un** ~ (*fig*) to cast a chill; **être en** ~ **avec** to be on bad terms with; **battre** ~ **à qn** to give sb the cold shoulder.

froidement [fʀwadmɑ̃] *adv (accueillir)* coldly; *(décider)* coolly.
froideur [fʀwadœʀ] *nf* coolness *no pl*.
froisser [fʀwase] *vt* to crumple (up), crease; *(fig)* to hurt, offend; **se ~** *vi* to crumple, crease; to take offence *(BRIT) ou* offense *(US)*; **se ~ un muscle** to strain a muscle.
frôlement [fʀolmɑ̃] *nm (contact)* light touch.
frôler [fʀole] *vt* to brush against; *(suj: projectile)* to skim past; *(fig)* to come within a hair's breadth of, come very close to.
fromage [fʀɔmaʒ] *nm* cheese; **~ blanc** soft white cheese; **~ de tête** pork brawn.
fromager, ère [fʀɔmaʒe, -ɛʀ] *nm/f* cheese merchant ♦ *adj (industrie)* cheese *cpd*.
fromagerie [fʀɔmaʒʀi] *nf* cheese dairy.
froment [fʀɔmɑ̃] *nm* wheat.
fronce [fʀɔ̃s] *nf (de tissu)* gather.
froncement [fʀɔ̃smɑ̃] *nm*: **~ de sourcils** frown.
froncer [fʀɔ̃se] *vt* to gather; **~ les sourcils** to frown.
frondaison [fʀɔ̃dɛzɔ̃] *nf* foliage.
fronde [fʀɔ̃d] *nf* sling; *(fig)* rebellion, rebelliousness.
frondeur, euse [fʀɔ̃dœʀ, -øz] *adj* rebellious.
front [fʀɔ̃] *nm* forehead, brow; *(MIL, MÉTÉOROLOGIE, POL)* front; **avoir le ~ de faire** to have the effrontery *ou* front to do; **de ~** *adv (se heurter)* head-on; *(rouler)* together *(i.e. 2 or 3 abreast)*; *(simultanément)* at once; **faire ~ à** to face up to; **~ de mer** (sea) front.
frontal, e, aux [fʀɔ̃tal, -o] *adj* frontal.
frontalier, ière [fʀɔ̃talje, -jɛʀ] *adj* border *cpd*, frontier *cpd* ♦ *nm/f*: **(travailleurs) ~s** workers who cross the border to go to work, commuters from across the border.
frontière [fʀɔ̃tjɛʀ] *nf (GÉO, POL)* frontier, border; *(fig)* frontier, boundary.
frontispice [fʀɔ̃tispis] *nm* frontispiece.
fronton [fʀɔ̃tɔ̃] *nm* pediment; *(de pelote basque)* (front) wall.
frottement [fʀɔtmɑ̃] *nm* rubbing, scraping; **~s** *nmpl (fig: difficultés)* friction *sg*.
frotter [fʀɔte] *vi* to rub, scrape ♦ *vt* to rub; *(pour nettoyer)* to rub (up); *(: avec une brosse)* to scrub; **~ une allumette** to strike a match; **se ~ à qn** to cross swords with sb; **se ~ à qch** to come up against sth; **se ~ les mains** *(fig)* to rub one's hands (gleefully).
frottis [fʀɔti] *nm (MÉD)* smear.
frottoir [fʀɔtwaʀ] *nm (d'allumettes)* friction strip; *(pour encaustiquer)* (long-handled) brush.
frou-frou, *pl* **frous-frous** [fʀufʀu] *nm* rustle.
frousse [fʀus] *nf (fam: peur)*: **avoir la ~** to be in a blue funk.
fructifier [fʀyktifje] *vi* to yield a profit; **faire ~** to turn to good account.
fructueux, euse [fʀyktɥø, -øz] *adj* fruitful; profitable.
frugal, e, aux [fʀygal, -o] *adj* frugal.
frugalement [fʀygalmɑ̃] *adv* frugally.
frugalité [fʀygalite] *nf* frugality.
fruit [fʀɥi] *nm* fruit *gén no pl*; **~s de mer** *(CULIN)* seafood(s); **~s secs** dried fruit *sg*.
fruité, e [fʀɥite] *adj (vin)* fruity.
fruiterie [fʀɥitʀi] *nf (boutique)* greengrocer's *(BRIT)*, fruit (and vegetable) store *(US)*.
fruitier, ière [fʀɥitje, -jɛʀ] *adj*: **arbre ~** fruit tree ♦ *nm/f* fruiterer *(BRIT)*, fruit merchant *(US)*.
fruste [fʀyst(ə)] *adj* unpolished, uncultivated.
frustrant, e [fʀystʀɑ̃, -ɑ̃t] *adj* frustrating.
frustration [fʀystʀɑsjɔ̃] *nf* frustration.
frustré, e [fʀystʀe] *adj* frustrated.
frustrer [fʀystʀe] *vt* to frustrate; *(priver)*: **~ qn de qch** to deprive sb of sth.
FS *abr (= franc suisse)* FS, SF.
FSE *sigle m (= foyer socio-éducatif)* community home.
FTP *sigle mpl (= Francs-tireurs et partisans) Communist Resistance in 1940-45.*
fuchsia [fyʃja] *nm* fuchsia.
fuel(-oil) [fjul(ɔjl)] *nm* fuel oil; *(pour chauffer)* heating oil.
fugace [fygas] *adj* fleeting.
fugitif, ive [fyʒitif, -iv] *adj (lueur, amour)* fleeting; *(prisonnier etc)* runaway ♦ *nm/f* fugitive, runaway.
fugue [fyg] *nf (d'un enfant)* running away *no pl*; *(MUS)* fugue; **faire une ~** to run away, abscond.
fuir [fɥiʀ] *vt* to flee from; *(éviter)* to shun ♦ *vi* to run away; *(gaz, robinet)* to leak.
fuite [fɥit] *nf* flight; *(écoulement)* leak, leakage; *(divulgation)* leak; **être en ~** to be on the run; **mettre en ~** to put to flight; **prendre la ~** to take flight.
fulgurant, e [fylgyʀɑ̃, -ɑ̃t] *adj* lightning *cpd*, dazzling.
fulminant, e [fylminɑ̃, -ɑ̃t] *adj (lettre, regard)* furious; **~ de colère** raging with anger.
fulminer [fylmine] *vi*: **~ (contre)** to thunder forth (against).
fumant, e [fymɑ̃, -ɑ̃t] *adj* smoking; *(liquide)* steaming; **un coup ~** *(fam)* a master stroke.
fumé, e [fyme] *adj (CULIN)* smoked; *(verre)* tinted ♦ *nf* smoke; **partir en ~e** to go up in smoke.
fume-cigarette [fymsigaʀɛt] *nm inv* cigarette holder.
fumer [fyme] *vi* to smoke; *(liquide)* to steam ♦ *vt* to smoke; *(terre, champ)* to manure.
fumerie [fymʀi] *nf*: **~ d'opium** opium den.
fumerolles [fymʀɔl] *nfpl* gas and smoke *(from volcano)*.
fûmes [fym] *vb voir* **être**.
fumet [fymɛ] *nm* aroma.
fumeur, euse [fymœʀ, -øz] *nm/f* smoker; **(compartiment) ~s** smoking compartment.
fumeux, euse [fymø, -øz] *adj (péj)* woolly *(BRIT)*, hazy.
fumier [fymje] *nm* manure.
fumigation [fymigɑsjɔ̃] *nf* fumigation.

fumigène [fymiʒɛn] *adj* smoke *cpd.*
fumiste [fymist(ə)] *nm* (*ramoneur*) chimney sweep ♦ *nm/f* (*péj: paresseux*) shirker; (*charlatan*) phoney.
fumisterie [fymistəʀi] *nf* (*péj*) fraud, con.
fumoir [fymwaʀ] *nm* smoking room.
funambule [fynɑ̃byl] *nm* tightrope walker.
funèbre [fynɛbʀ(ə)] *adj* funeral *cpd*; (*fig*) doleful; funereal.
funérailles [fyneʀɑj] *nfpl* funeral *sg.*
funéraire [fyneʀɛʀ] *adj* funeral *cpd*, funerary.
funeste [fynɛst(ə)] *adj* disastrous; deathly.
funiculaire [fynikylɛʀ] *nm* funicular (railway).
FUNU [fyny] *sigle f* (= *Force d'urgence des Nations unies*) UNEF (= *United Nations Emergency Forces*).
fur [fyʀ]: **au ~ et à mesure** *adv* as one goes along; **au ~ et à mesure que** as; **au ~ et à mesure de leur progression** as they advance (*ou* advanced).
furax [fyʀaks] *adj inv* (*fam*) livid.
furent [fyʀ] *vb voir* **être.**
furet [fyʀɛ] *nm* ferret.
fureter [fyʀte] *vi* (*péj*) to nose about.
fureur [fyʀœʀ] *nf* fury; (*passion*): **~ de** passion for; **faire ~** to be all the rage.
furibard, e [fyʀibaʀ, -aʀd(ə)] *adj* (*fam*) livid, absolutely furious.
furibond, e [fyʀibɔ̃, -ɔ̃d] *adj* livid, absolutely furious.
furie [fyʀi] *nf* fury; (*femme*) shrew, vixen; **en ~** (*mer*) raging.
furieusement [fyʀjøzmɑ̃] *adv* furiously.
furieux, euse [fyʀjø, -øz] *adj* furious.
furoncle [fyʀɔ̃kl(ə)] *nm* boil.
furtif, ive [fyʀtif, -iv] *adj* furtive.
furtivement [fyʀtivmɑ̃] *adv* furtively.
fus [fy] *vb voir* **être.**
fusain [fyzɛ̃] *nm* (*BOT*) spindle-tree; (*ART*) charcoal.
fuseau, x [fyzo] *nm* (*pantalon*) (ski-)pants *pl*; (*pour filer*) spindle; **en ~** (*jambes*) tapering; (*colonne*) bulging; **~ horaire** time zone.
fusée [fyze] *nf* rocket; **~ éclairante** flare.
fuselage [fyzlaʒ] *nm* fuselage.
fuselé, e [fyzle] *adj* slender; (*galbé*) tapering.
fuser [fyze] *vi* (*rires etc*) to burst forth.
fusible [fyzibl(ə)] *nm* (*ÉLEC: fil*) fuse wire; (*: fiche*) fuse.
fusil [fyzi] *nm* (*de guerre, à canon rayé*) rifle, gun; (*de chasse, à canon lisse*) shotgun, gun; **~ à deux coups** double-barrelled rifle *ou* shotgun; **~ sous-marin** spear-gun.
fusilier [fyzilje] *nm* (*MIL*) rifleman.
fusillade [fyzijad] *nf* gunfire *no pl*, shooting *no pl*; (*combat*) gun battle.
fusiller [fyzije] *vt* to shoot; **~ qn du regard** to look daggers at sb.
fusil-mitrailleur, *pl* **fusils-mitrailleurs** [fyzimitʀɑjœʀ] *nm* machine gun.
fusion [fyzjɔ̃] *nf* fusion, melting; (*fig*) merging; (*COMM*) merger; **en ~** (*métal, roches*) molten.
fusionnement [fyzjɔnmɑ̃] *nm* merger.
fusionner [fyzjɔne] *vi* to merge.
fustiger [fystiʒe] *vt* to denounce.
fut [fy] *vb voir* **être.**
fût [fy] *vb voir* **être** ♦ *nm* (*tonneau*) barrel, cask; (*de canon*) stock; (*d'arbre*) bole, trunk; (*de colonne*) shaft.
futaie [fytɛ] *nf* forest, plantation.
futé, e [fyte] *adj* crafty.
fûtes [fyt] *vb voir* **être.**
futile [fytil] *adj* (*inutile*) futile; (*frivole*) frivolous.
futilement [fytilmɑ̃] *adv* frivolously.
futilité [fytilite] *nf* futility; frivolousness; (*chose futile*) futile pursuit (*ou* thing *etc*).
futon [fytɔ̃] *nm* futon.
futur, e [fytyʀ] *adj, nm* future; **son ~ époux** her husband-to-be; **au ~** (*LING*) in the future.
futuriste [fytyʀist(ə)] *adj* futuristic.
futurologie [fytyʀɔlɔʒi] *nf* futurology.
fuyant, e [fɥijɑ̃, -ɑ̃t] *vb voir* **fuir** ♦ *adj* (*regard etc*) evasive; (*lignes etc*) receding; (*perspective*) vanishing.
fuyard, e [fɥijaʀ, -aʀd(ə)] *nm/f* runaway.
fuyons [fɥijɔ̃] *etc vb voir* **fuir.**

G g

G, g [ʒe] *nm inv* G, g ♦ *abr* (= *gramme*) g; (= *gauche*) L, l; **G comme Gaston** G for George; **le G7** (*POL*) the G7 nations, the Group of Seven.
gabardine [gabaʀdin] *nf* gabardine.
gabarit [gabaʀi] *nm* (*fig: dimension, taille*) size; (*: valeur*) calibre; (*TECH*) template; **du même ~** (*fig*) of the same type, of that ilk.
gabegie [gabʒi] *nf* (*péj*) chaos.
Gabon [gabɔ̃] *nm*: **le ~** Gabon.
gabonais, e [gabɔnɛ, -ɛz] *adj* Gabonese.
gâcher [gɑʃe] *vt* (*gâter*) to spoil, ruin; (*gaspiller*) to waste; (*plâtre*) to temper; (*mortier*) to mix.
gâchette [gɑʃɛt] *nf* trigger.
gâchis [gɑʃi] *nm* (*désordre*) mess; (*gaspillage*) waste *no pl.*
gadget [gadʒɛt] *nm* thingumajig; (*nouveauté*) gimmick.
gadin [gadɛ̃] *nm* (*fam*): **prendre un ~** to come a cropper (*BRIT*).
gadoue [gadu] *nf* sludge.
gaélique [gaelik] *adj* Gaelic ♦ *nm* (*LING*) Gaelic.
gaffe [gaf] *nf* (*instrument*) boat hook; (*fam: e*

reur) blunder; **faire ~** (*fam*) to watch out.
gaffer [gafe] *vi* to blunder.
gaffeur, euse [gafœʀ, -øz] *nm/f* blunderer.
gag [gag] *nm* gag.
gaga [gaga] *adj* (*fam*) gaga.
gage [gaʒ] *nm* (*dans un jeu*) forfeit; (*fig: de fidélité*) token; **~s** *nmpl* (*salaire*) wages; (*garantie*) guarantee *sg*; **mettre en ~** to pawn; **laisser en ~** to leave as security.
gager [gaʒe] *vt*: **~ que** to bet *ou* wager that.
gageure [gaʒyʀ] *nf*: **c'est une ~** it's attempting the impossible.
gagnant, e [gaɲɑ̃, -ɑ̃t] *adj*: **billet/numéro ~** winning ticket/number ♦ *adv*: **jouer ~** (*aux courses*) to be bound to win ♦ *nm/f* winner.
gagne-pain [gaɲpɛ̃] *nm inv* job.
gagne-petit [gaɲpəti] *nm inv* low wage earner.
gagner [gaɲe] *vt* (*concours, procès, pari*) to win; (*somme d'argent, revenu*) to earn; (*aller vers, atteindre*) to reach; (*s'emparer de*) to overcome; (*envahir*) to spread to; (*se concilier*): **~ qn** to win sb over ♦ *vi* to win; (*fig*) to gain; **~ du temps/de la place** to gain time/save space; **~ sa vie** to earn one's living; **~ du terrain** (*aussi fig*) to gain ground; **~ qn de vitesse** (*aussi fig*) to outstrip sb; **~ à faire** (*s'en trouver bien*) to be better off doing; **il y gagne** it's in his interest, it's to his advantage.
gagneur [gaɲœʀ] *nm* winner.
gai, e [ge] *adj* cheerful; (*livre, pièce de théâtre*) light-hearted; (*un peu ivre*) merry.
gaiement [gemɑ̃] *adv* cheerfully.
gaieté [gete] *nf* cheerfulness; **~s** *nfpl* (*souvent ironique*) delights; **de ~ de cœur** with a light heart.
gaillard, e [gajaʀ, -aʀd(ə)] *adj* (*robuste*) sprightly; (*grivois*) bawdy, ribald ♦ *nm/f* (strapping) fellow/wench.
gaillardement [gajaʀdəmɑ̃] *adv* cheerfully.
gain [gɛ̃] *nm* (*revenu*) earnings *pl*; (*bénéfice: gén pl*) profits *pl*; (*au jeu: gén pl*) winnings *pl*; (*fig: de temps, place*) saving; (*: avantage*) benefit; (*: lucre*) gain; **avoir ~ de cause** to win the case; (*fig*) to be proved right; **obtenir ~ de cause** (*fig*) to win out.
gaine [gɛn] *nf* (*corset*) girdle; (*fourreau*) sheath; (*de fil électrique etc*) outer covering.
gaine-culotte, *pl* **gaines-culottes** [gɛnkylɔt] *nf* pantie girdle.
gainer [gene] *vt* to cover.
gala [gala] *nm* official reception; **soirée de ~** gala evening.
galamment [galamɑ̃] *adv* courteously.
galant, e [galɑ̃, -ɑ̃t] *adj* (*courtois*) courteous, gentlemanly; (*entreprenant*) flirtatious, gallant; (*aventure, poésie*) amorous; **en ~e compagnie** (*homme*) with a lady friend; (*femme*) with a gentleman friend.
galanterie [galɑ̃tʀi] *nf* gallantry.
galantine [galɑ̃tin] *nf* galantine.
Galapagos [galapagɔs] *nfpl*: **les (îles) ~** the Galapagos Islands.
galaxie [galaksi] *nf* galaxy.
galbe [galb(ə)] *nm* curve(s); shapeliness.
galbé, e [galbe] *adj* (*jambes*) (well-)rounded; **bien ~** shapely.
gale [gal] *nf* (*MÉD*) scabies *sg*; (*de chien*) mange.
galéjade [galeʒad] *nf* tall story.
galère [galɛʀ] *nf* galley.
galérer [galeʀe] *vi* (*fam*) to work hard, slave (away).
galerie [galʀi] *nf* gallery; (*THÉÂT*) circle; (*de voiture*) roof rack; (*fig: spectateurs*) audience; **~ marchande** shopping mall; **~ de peinture** (private) art gallery.
galérien [galeʀjɛ̃] *nm* galley slave.
galet [galɛ] *nm* pebble; (*TECH*) wheel; **~s** *nmpl* pebbles, shingle *sg*.
galette [galɛt] *nf* (*gâteau*) flat pastry cake; (*crêpe*) savoury pancake; **la ~ des Rois** *cake traditionally eaten on Twelfth Night*.
galeux, euse [galø, -øz] *adj*: **un chien ~** a mangy dog.
Galice [galis] *nf*: **la ~** Galicia (*in Spain*).
Galicie [galisi] *nf*: **la ~** Galicia (*in Central Europe*).
galiléen, ne [galileɛ̃, -ɛn] *adj* Galilean.
galimatias [galimatja] *nm* (*péj*) gibberish.
galipette [galipɛt] *nf*: **faire des ~s** to turn somersaults.
Galles [gal] *nfpl*: **le pays de ~** Wales.
gallicisme [galisism(ə)] *nm* French idiom; (*tournure fautive*) gallicism.
gallois, e [galwa, -waz] *adj* Welsh ♦ *nm* (*LING*) Welsh ♦ *nm/f*: **G~, e** Welshman/woman.
gallo-romain, e [galoʀɔmɛ̃, -ɛn] *adj* Gallo-Roman.
galoche [galɔʃ] *nf* clog.
galon [galɔ̃] *nm* (*MIL*) stripe; (*décoratif*) piece of braid; **prendre du ~** to be promoted.
galop [galo] *nm* gallop; **au ~** at a gallop; **~ d'essai** (*fig*) trial run.
galopade [galɔpad] *nf* stampede.
galopant, e [galɔpɑ̃, -ɑ̃t] *adj*: **inflation ~e** galloping inflation; **démographie ~e** exploding population.
galoper [galɔpe] *vi* to gallop.
galopin [galɔpɛ̃] *nm* urchin, ragamuffin.
galvaniser [galvanize] *vt* to galvanize.
galvaudé, e [galvode] *adj* (*expression*) hackneyed; (*mot*) clichéd.
galvauder [galvode] *vt* to debase.
gambade [gɑ̃bad] *nf*: **faire des ~s** to skip *ou* frisk about.
gambader [gɑ̃bade] *vi* to skip *ou* frisk about.
gamberger [gɑ̃bɛʀʒe] (*fam*) *vi* to (have a) think ♦ *vt* to dream up.
Gambie [gɑ̃bi] *nf*: **la ~** (*pays*) Gambia; (*fleuve*) the Gambia.
gamelle [gamɛl] *nf* mess tin; billy can; (*fam*): **ramasser une ~** to fall flat on one's face.
gamin, e [gamɛ̃, -in] *nm/f* kid ♦ *adj* mischie-

vous, playful.
gaminerie [gaminʀi] *nf* mischievousness, playfulness.
gamme [gam] *nf* (*MUS*) scale; (*fig*) range.
gammé, e [game] *adj*: **croix ~e** swastika.
Gand [gɑ̃] *n* Ghent.
gang [gɑ̃g] *nm* gang.
Gange [gɑ̃ʒ] *nm*: **le** ~ the Ganges.
ganglion [gɑ̃glijɔ̃] *nm* ganglion; (*lymphatique*) gland; **avoir des ~s** to have swollen glands.
gangrène [gɑ̃gʀɛn] *nf* gangrene; (*fig*) corruption; corrupting influence.
gangster [gɑ̃gstɛʀ] *nm* gangster.
gangstérisme [gɑ̃gsteʀism(ə)] *nm* gangsterism.
gangue [gɑ̃g] *nf* coating.
ganse [gɑ̃s] *nf* braid.
gant [gɑ̃] *nm* glove; **prendre des ~s** (*fig*) to handle the situation with kid gloves; **relever le** ~ (*fig*) to take up the gauntlet; ~ **de crin** massage glove; ~ **de toilette** (face) flannel (*BRIT*), face cloth; **~s de boxe** boxing gloves; **~s de caoutchouc** rubber gloves.
ganté, e [gɑ̃te] *adj*: ~ **de blanc** wearing white gloves.
ganterie [gɑ̃tʀi] *nf* glove trade; (*magasin*) glove shop.
garage [gaʀaʒ] *nm* garage; ~ **à vélos** bicycle shed.
garagiste [gaʀaʒist(ə)] *nm/f* (*propriétaire*) garage owner; (*mécanicien*) garage mechanic.
garant, e [gaʀɑ̃, -ɑ̃t] *nm/f* guarantor ♦ *nm* guarantee; **se porter** ~ **de** to vouch for; to be answerable for.
garantie [gaʀɑ̃ti] *nf* guarantee, warranty; (*gage*) security, surety; **(bon de)** ~ guarantee *ou* warranty slip; ~ **de bonne exécution** performance bond.
garantir [gaʀɑ̃tiʀ] *vt* to guarantee; (*protéger*): ~ **de** to protect from; **je vous garantis que** I can assure you that; **garanti pure laine/2 ans** guaranteed pure wool/for 2 years.
garce [gaʀs(ə)] *nf* (*péj*) bitch.
garçon [gaʀsɔ̃] *nm* boy; (*célibataire*) bachelor; (*jeune homme*) boy, lad; (*aussi*: ~ **de café**) waiter; ~ **boucher/coiffeur** butcher's/hairdresser's assistant; ~ **de courses** messenger; ~ **d'écurie** stable lad; ~ **manqué** tomboy.
garçonnet [gaʀsɔnɛ] *nm* small boy.
garçonnière [gaʀsɔnjɛʀ] *nf* bachelor flat.
garde [gaʀd(ə)] *nm* (*de prisonnier*) guard; (*de domaine etc*) warden; (*soldat, sentinelle*) guardsman ♦ *nf* guarding; looking after; (*soldats, BOXE, ESCRIME*) guard; (*faction*) watch; (*d'une arme*) hilt; (*TYPO*: *aussi*: **page** *ou* **feuille de** ~) flyleaf; (*: collée*) endpaper; **de** ~ *adj, adv* on duty; **monter la** ~ to stand guard; **être sur ses ~s** to be on one's guard; **mettre en** ~ to warn; **mise en** ~ warning; **prendre** ~ **(à)** to be careful (of); **avoir la** ~ **des enfants** (*après divorce*) to have custody of the children; ~ **champêtre** *nm* rural policeman; ~ **du corps** *nm* bodyguard; ~ **d'enfants** *nf* child minder; ~ **forestier** *nm* forest warden; ~ **mobile** *nm, nf* mobile guard; ~ **des Sceaux** *nm* ≈ Lord Chancellor (*BRIT*), ≈ Attorney General (*US*); ~ **à vue** *nf* (*JUR*) ≈ police custody.
garde-à-vous [gaʀdavu] *nm inv*: **être/se mettre au** ~ to be at/stand to attention; ~ **(fixe)!** (*MIL*) attention!
garde-barrière, *pl* **gardes-barrière(s)** [gaʀdəbaʀjɛʀ] *nm/f* level-crossing keeper.
garde-boue [gaʀdəbu] *nm inv* mudguard.
garde-chasse, *pl* **gardes-chasse(s)** [gaʀdəʃas] *nm* gamekeeper.
garde-côte [gaʀdəkot] *nm* (*vaisseau*) coastguard boat.
garde-feu [gaʀdəfø] *nm inv* fender.
garde-fou [gaʀdəfu] *nm* railing, parapet.
garde-malade, *pl* **gardes-malade(s)** [gaʀdəmalad] *nf* home nurse.
garde-manger [gaʀdmɑ̃ʒe] *nm inv* (*boîte*) meat safe; (*placard*) pantry, larder.
garde-meuble [gaʀdəmœbl(ə)] *nm* furniture depository.
garde-pêche [gaʀdəpɛʃ] *nm inv* (*personne*) water bailiff; (*navire*) fisheries protection ship.
garder [gaʀde] *vt* (*conserver*) to keep; (*: sur soi vêtement, chapeau*) to keep on; (*surveiller: enfants*) to look after; (*: immeuble, lieu, prisonnier*) to guard; **se** ~ *vi* (*aliment: se conserver*) to keep; **se** ~ **de faire** to be careful not to do; ~ **le lit/la chambre** to stay in bed/indoors; ~ **le silence** to keep silent *ou* quiet; ~ **la ligne** to keep one's figure; ~ **à vue** to keep in custody; **pêche/chasse gardée** private fishing/hunting (ground).
garderie [gaʀdəʀi] *nf* day nursery, crèche.
garde-robe [gaʀdəʀɔb] *nf* wardrobe.
gardeur, euse [gaʀdœʀ, -øz] *nm/f* (*de vaches*) cowherd; (*de chèvres*) goatherd.
gardian [gaʀdjɑ̃] *nm* cowboy (*in the Camargue*).
gardien, ne [gaʀdjɛ̃, -ɛn] *nm/f* (*garde*) guard; (*de prison*) warder; (*de domaine, réserve*) warden; (*de musée etc*) attendant; (*de phare, cimetière*) keeper; (*d'immeuble*) caretaker; (*fig*) guardian; ~ **de but** goalkeeper; ~ **de nuit** night watchman; ~ **de la paix** policeman.
gardiennage [gaʀdjɛnaʒ] *nm* (*emploi*) caretaking; **société de** ~ security firm.
gardon [gaʀdɔ̃] *nm* roach.
gare [gaʀ] *nf* (railway) station, train station (*US*) ♦ *excl*: ~ **à** ... mind ...!, watch out for ...! ~ **à ne pas** ... mind you don't ...; ~ **à toi** watch out!; **sans crier** ~ without warning; ~ **maritime** harbour station; ~ **routière** coach (*BRIT*) *ou* bus station; (*camions*) haulage (*BRIT*) *ou* trucking (*US*) depot; ~ **de triage** marshalling yard.
garenne [gaʀɛn] *nf voir* **lapin**.
garer [gaʀe] *vt* to park; **se** ~ to park; (*pour lais*

ser passer) to draw into the side.
gargantuesque [gaʀgɑ̃tɥɛsk(ə)] *adj* gargantuan.
gargariser [gaʀgaʀize]: **se** ~ *vi* to gargle; **se** ~ **de** (*fig*) to revel in.
gargarisme [gaʀgaʀism(ə)] *nm* gargling *no pl*; (*produit*) gargle.
gargote [gaʀgɔt] *nf* cheap restaurant, greasy spoon (*fam*).
gargouille [gaʀguj] *nf* gargoyle.
gargouillement [gaʀgujmɑ̃] *nm* = **gargouillis**.
gargouiller [gaʀguje] *vi* (*estomac*) to rumble; (*eau*) to gurgle.
gargouillis [gaʀguji] *nm* (*gén pl: voir vb*) rumbling; gurgling.
garnement [gaʀnəmɑ̃] *nm* rascal, scallywag.
garni, e [gaʀni] *adj* (*plat*) served with vegetables (*and chips or pasta or rice*) ♦ *nm* (*appartement*) furnished accommodation *no pl* (*BRIT*) *ou* accommodations *pl* (*US*).
garnir [gaʀniʀ] *vt* to decorate; (*remplir*) to fill; (*recouvrir*) to cover; **se** ~ *vi* (*pièce, salle*) to fill up; ~ **qch de** (*orner*) to decorate sth with; to trim sth with; (*approvisionner*) to fill *ou* stock sth with; (*protéger*) to fit sth with; (*CULIN*) to garnish sth with.
garnison [gaʀnizɔ̃] *nf* garrison.
garniture [gaʀnityʀ] *nf* (*CULIN: légumes*) vegetables *pl*; (*: persil etc*) garnish; (*: farce*) filling; (*décoration*) trimming; (*protection*) fittings *pl*; ~ **de cheminée** mantelpiece ornaments *pl*; ~ **de frein** (*AUTO*) brake lining; ~ **intérieure** (*AUTO*) interior trim; ~ **périodique** sanitary towel (*BRIT*) *ou* napkin (*US*).
garrigue [gaʀig] *nf* scrubland.
garrot [gaʀo] *nm* (*MÉD*) tourniquet; (*torture*) garrotte.
garrotter [gaʀɔte] *vt* to tie up; (*fig*) to muzzle.
gars [gɑ] *nm* lad; (*type*) guy.
Gascogne [gaskɔɲ] *nf*: **la** ~ Gascony.
gascon, ne [gaskɔ̃, -ɔn] *adj* Gascon ♦ *nm*: **G**~ (*hâbleur*) braggart.
gas-oil [gɑzɔjl] *nm* diesel oil.
gaspillage [gaspijaʒ] *nm* waste.
gaspiller [gaspije] *vt* to waste.
gaspilleur, euse [gaspijœʀ, -øz] *adj* wasteful.
gastrique [gastʀik] *adj* gastric, stomach *cpd*.
gastro-entérite [gastʀoɑ̃teʀit] *nf* (*MÉD*) gastro-enteritis.
gastro-intestinal, e, aux [gastʀoɛ̃tɛstinal, -o] *adj* gastrointestinal.
gastronome [gastʀɔnɔm] *nm/f* gourmet.
gastronomie [gastʀɔnɔmi] *nf* gastronomy.
gastronomique [gastʀɔnɔmik] *adj*: **menu** ~ gourmet menu.
gâteau, x [gɑto] *nm* cake ♦ *adj inv* (*fam: trop indulgent*): **papa-/maman-**~ doting father/mother; ~ **d'anniversaire** birthday cake; ~ **de riz** ≈ rice pudding; ~ **sec** biscuit.
gâter [gɑte] *vt* to spoil; **se** ~ *vi* (*dent, fruit*) to go bad; (*temps, situation*) to change for the worse.
gâterie [gɑtʀi] *nf* little treat.
gâteux, euse [gɑtø, -øz] *adj* senile.
gâtisme [gɑtism(ə)] *nm* senility.
GATT [gat] *sigle m* (= *General Agreement on Tariffs and Trade*) GATT.
gauche [goʃ] *adj* left, left-hand; (*maladroit*) awkward, clumsy ♦ *nf* (*POL*) left (wing); (*BOXE*) left; **à** ~ on the left; (*direction*) (to the) left; **à** ~ **de** (on *ou* to the) left of; **à la** ~ **de** to the left of; **de** ~ (*POL*) left-wing.
gauchement [goʃmɑ̃] *adv* awkwardly, clumsily.
gaucher, ère [goʃe, -ɛʀ] *adj* left-handed.
gaucherie [goʃʀi] *nf* awkwardness, clumsiness.
gauchir [goʃiʀ] *vt* (*planche, objet*) to warp; (*fig: fait, idée*) to distort.
gauchisant, e [goʃizɑ̃, -ɑ̃t] *adj* with left-wing tendencies.
gauchisme [goʃism(ə)] *nm* leftism.
gauchiste [goʃist(ə)] *adj, nm/f* leftist.
gaufre [gofʀ(ə)] *nf* (*pâtisserie*) waffle; (*de cire*) honeycomb.
gaufrer [gofʀe] *vt* (*papier*) to emboss; (*tissu*) to goffer.
gaufrette [gofʀɛt] *nf* wafer.
gaufrier [gofʀije] *nm* (*moule*) waffle iron.
Gaule [gol] *nf*: **la** ~ Gaul.
gaule [gol] *nf* (*perche*) (long) pole; (*canne à pêche*) fishing rod.
gauler [gole] *vt* (*arbre*) to beat (*using a long pole to bring down fruit etc*); (*fruits*) to beat down (*with a pole*).
gaullisme [golism(ə)] *nm* Gaullism.
gaulliste [golist(ə)] *adj, nm/f* Gaullist.
gaulois, e [golwa, -waz] *adj* Gallic; (*grivois*) bawdy ♦ *nm/f*: **G**~, **e** Gaul.
gauloiserie [golwazʀi] *nf* bawdiness.
gausser [gose]: **se** ~ **de** *vt* to deride.
gaver [gave] *vt* to force-feed; (*fig*): ~ **de** to cram with, fill up with; (*personne*): **se** ~ **de** to stuff o.s. with.
gay [gɛ] *adj, nm* (*fam*) gay.
gaz [gɑz] *nm inv* gas; **mettre les** ~ (*AUTO*) to put one's foot down; **chambre/masque à** ~ gas chamber/mask; ~ **en bouteille** bottled gas; ~ **butane** Calor gas ® (*BRIT*), butane gas; ~ **carbonique** carbon dioxide; ~ **hilarant** laughing gas; ~ **lacrymogène** tear gas; ~ **naturel** natural gas; ~ **de ville** town gas (*BRIT*), manufactured domestic gas.
gaze [gɑz] *nf* gauze.
gazéifié, e [gazeifje] *adj* carbonated, aerated.
gazelle [gazɛl] *nf* gazelle.
gazer [gɑze] *vt* to gas ♦ *vi* (*fam*) to be going *ou* working well.
gazette [gazɛt] *nf* news sheet.
gazeux, euse [gɑzø, -øz] *adj* gaseous; (*eau*) sparkling; (*boisson*) fizzy.
gazoduc [gɑzɔdyk] *nm* gas pipeline.
gazole [gɑzɔl] *nm* = **gas-oil**.
gazomètre [gɑzɔmɛtʀ(ə)] *nm* gasometer.

gazon [gɑzɔ̃] *nm* (*herbe*) turf, grass; (*pelouse*) lawn.
gazonner [gɑzɔne] *vt* (*terrain*) to grass over.
gazouillement [gazujmɑ̃] *nm* (*voir vb*) chirping; babbling.
gazouiller [gazuje] *vi* (*oiseau*) to chirp; (*enfant*) to babble.
gazouillis [gazuji] *nmpl* chirp *sg*.
GB *sigle f* (= *Grande Bretagne*) GB.
gd *abr* (= *grand*) L.
GDF *sigle m* (= *Gaz de France*) *national gas company*.
geai [ʒɛ] *nm* jay.
géant, e [ʒeɑ̃, -ɑ̃t] *adj* gigantic, giant; (*COMM*) giant-size ♦ *nm/f* giant.
geignement [ʒɛɲmɑ̃] *nm* groaning, moaning.
geindre [ʒɛ̃dʀ(ə)] *vi* to groan, moan.
gel [ʒɛl] *nm* frost; (*de l'eau*) freezing; (*fig: des salaires, prix*) freeze; freezing; (*produit de beauté*) gel.
gélatine [ʒelatin] *nf* gelatine.
gélatineux, euse [ʒelatinø, -øz] *adj* jelly-like, gelatinous.
gelé, e [ʒəle] *adj* frozen ♦ *nf* jelly; (*gel*) frost; ~ **blanche** hoarfrost, white frost.
geler [ʒəle] *vt, vi* to freeze; **il gèle** it's freezing.
gélule [ʒelyl] *nf* capsule.
gelures [ʒəlyʀ] *nfpl* frostbite *sg*.
Gémeaux [ʒemo] *nmpl*: **les** ~ Gemini, the Twins; **être des** ~ to be Gemini.
gémir [ʒemiʀ] *vi* to groan, moan.
gémissement [ʒemismɑ̃] *nm* groan, moan.
gemme [ʒɛm] *nf* gem(stone).
gémonies [ʒemɔni] *nfpl*: **vouer qn aux** ~ to subject sb to public scorn.
gén. *abr* (= *généralement*) gen.
gênant, e [ʒɛnɑ̃, -ɑ̃t] *adj* (*objet*) awkward, in the way; (*histoire, personne*) embarrassing.
gencive [ʒɑ̃siv] *nf* gum.
gendarme [ʒɑ̃daʀm(ə)] *nm* gendarme.
gendarmer [ʒɑ̃daʀme]: **se** ~ *vi* to kick up a fuss.
gendarmerie [ʒɑ̃daʀməʀi] *nf military police force in countryside and small towns; their police station or barracks*.
gendre [ʒɑ̃dʀ(ə)] *nm* son-in-law.
gène [ʒɛn] *nm* (*BIO*) gene.
gêne [ʒɛn] *nf* (*à respirer, bouger*) discomfort, difficulty; (*dérangement*) bother, trouble; (*manque d'argent*) financial difficulties *pl ou* straits *pl*; (*confusion*) embarrassment; **sans** ~ *adj* inconsiderate.
gêné, e [ʒene] *adj* embarrassed; (*dépourvu d'argent*) short (of money).
généalogie [ʒenealɔʒi] *nf* genealogy.
généalogique [ʒenealɔʒik] *adj* genealogical.
gêner [ʒene] *vt* (*incommoder*) to bother; (*encombrer*) to hamper; (*bloquer le passage*) to be in the way of; (*déranger*) to bother; (*embarrasser*): ~ **qn** to make sb feel ill-at-ease; **se** ~ to put o.s. out; **ne vous gênez pas!** (*ironique*) go right ahead!, don't mind me!; **je vais me** ~**!** (*ironique*) why should I care?
général, e, aux [ʒeneʀal, -o] *adj, nm* general ♦ *nf*: **(répétition)** ~**e** final dress rehearsal; **en** ~ usually, in general; **à la satisfaction** ~**e** to everyone's satisfaction.
généralement [ʒeneʀalmɑ̃] *adv* generally.
généralisable [ʒeneʀalizabl(ə)] *adj* generally applicable.
généralisation [ʒeneʀalizɑsjɔ̃] *nf* generalization.
généraliser [ʒeneʀalize] *vt, vi* to generalize; **se** ~ *vi* to become widespread.
généraliste [ʒeneʀalist(ə)] *nm/f* (*MÉD*) general practitioner, GP.
généralité [ʒeneʀalite] *nf*: **la** ~ **des ...** the majority of ...; ~**s** *nfpl* generalities; (*introduction*) general points.
générateur, trice [ʒeneʀatœʀ, -tʀis] *adj*: ~ **de** which causes *ou* brings about ♦ *nf* (*ÉLEC*) generator.
génération [ʒeneʀɑsjɔ̃] *nf* (*aussi INFORM*) generation.
généreusement [ʒeneʀøzmɑ̃] *adv* generously.
généreux, euse [ʒeneʀø, -øz] *adj* generous.
générique [ʒeneʀik] *adj* generic ♦ *nm* (*CINÉ, TV*) credits *pl*, credit titles *pl*.
générosité [ʒeneʀozite] *nf* generosity.
Gênes [ʒɛn] *n* Genoa.
genèse [ʒənɛz] *nf* genesis.
genêt [ʒənɛ] *nm* (*BOT*) broom *no pl*.
généticien, ne [ʒenetisjɛ̃, -ɛn] *nm/f* geneticist.
génétique [ʒenetik] *adj* genetic ♦ *nf* genetics *sg*.
génétiquement [ʒenetikmɑ̃] *adv* genetically.
gêneur, euse [ʒɛnœʀ, -øz] *nm/f* (*personne qui gêne*) obstacle; (*importun*) intruder.
Genève [ʒənɛv] Geneva.
genevois, e [ʒənəvwa, -waz] *adj* Genevan.
genévrier [ʒənevʀije] *nm* juniper.
génial, e, aux [ʒenjal, -o] *adj* of genius; (*fam*) fantastic, brilliant.
génie [ʒeni] *nm* genius; (*MIL*): **le** ~ ≈ the Engineers *pl*; **avoir du** ~ to have genius; ~ **civil** civil engineering; ~ **génétique** genetic engineering.
genièvre [ʒənjɛvʀ(ə)] *nm* (*BOT*) juniper (tree); (*boisson*) geneva; **grain de** ~ juniper berry.
génisse [ʒenis] *nf* heifer; **foie de** ~ ox liver.
génital, e, aux [ʒenital, -o] *adj* genital.
génitif [ʒenitif] *nm* genitive.
génocide [ʒenɔsid] *nm* genocide.
génois, e [ʒenwa, -waz] *adj* Genoese ♦ *nf* (*gâteau*) ≈ sponge cake.
genou, x [ʒnu] *nm* knee; **à** ~**x** on one's knees; **se mettre à** ~**x** to kneel down.
genouillère [ʒənujɛʀ] *nf* (*SPORT*) kneepad.
genre [ʒɑ̃ʀ] *nm* (*espèce, sorte*) kind, type, sort; (*allure*) manner; (*LING*) gender; (*ART*) genre; (*ZOOL etc*) genus; **se donner du** ~ to give o.s. airs; **avoir bon** ~ to have style; **avoir mauvais** ~ to be ill-mannered.
gens [ʒɑ̃] *nmpl* (*f in some phrases*) people *pl*; **les**

~ **d'Église** the clergy; **les ~ du monde** society people; ~ **de maison** domestics.
gentiane [ʒɑ̃sjan] *nf* gentian.
gentil, le [ʒɑ̃ti, -ij] *adj* kind; (*enfant: sage*) good; (*sympa: endroit etc*) nice; **c'est très ~ à vous** it's very kind *ou* good *ou* nice of you.
gentilhommière [ʒɑ̃tijɔmjɛʀ] *nf* (small) manor house *ou* country seat.
gentillesse [ʒɑ̃tijɛs] *nf* kindness.
gentillet, te [ʒɑ̃tijɛ, -ɛt] *adj* nice little.
gentiment [ʒɑ̃timɑ̃] *adv* kindly.
génuflexion [ʒenyflɛksjɔ̃] *nf* genuflexion.
géodésique [ʒeɔdezik] *adj* geodesic.
géographe [ʒeɔgʀaf] *nm/f* geographer.
géographie [ʒeɔgʀafi] *nf* geography.
géographique [ʒeɔgʀafik] *adj* geographical.
geôlier [ʒolje] *nm* jailer.
géologie [ʒeɔlɔʒi] *nf* geology.
géologique [ʒeɔlɔʒik] *adj* geological.
géologiquement [ʒeɔlɔʒikmɑ̃] *adv* geologically.
géologue [ʒeɔlɔg] *nm/f* geologist.
géomètre [ʒeɔmɛtʀ(ə)] *nm*: **(arpenteur-)~** (land) surveyor.
géométrie [ʒeɔmetʀi] *nf* geometry; **à ~ variable** (*AVIAT*) swing-wing.
géométrique [ʒeɔmetʀik] *adj* geometric.
géophysique [ʒeɔfizik] *nf* geophysics *sg*.
géopolitique [ʒeɔpɔlitik] *nf* geopolitics *sg*.
Géorgie [ʒeɔʀʒi] *nf*: **la ~** (*URSS, USA*) Georgia; **la ~ du Sud** South Georgia.
géorgien, ne [ʒeɔʀʒjɛ̃, -ɛn] *adj* Georgian.
géostationnaire [ʒeɔstasjɔnɛʀ] *adj* geostationary.
géothermique [ʒeɔtɛʀmik] *adj*: **énergie ~** geothermal energy.
gérance [ʒeʀɑ̃s] *nf* management; **mettre en ~** to appoint a manager for; **prendre en ~** to take over (the management of).
géranium [ʒeʀanjɔm] *nm* geranium.
gérant, e [ʒeʀɑ̃, -ɑ̃t] *nm/f* manager/manageress; ~ **d'immeuble** managing agent.
gerbe [ʒɛʀb(ə)] *nf* (*de fleurs, d'eau*) spray; (*de blé*) sheaf (*pl* sheaves); (*fig*) shower, burst.
gercé, e [ʒɛʀse] *adj* chapped.
gercer [ʒɛʀse] *vi*, **se ~** *vi* to chap.
gerçure [ʒɛʀsyʀ] *nf* crack.
gérer [ʒeʀe] *vt* to manage.
gériatrie [ʒeʀjatʀi] *nf* geriatrics *sg*.
gériatrique [ʒeʀjatʀik] *adj* geriatric.
germain, e [ʒɛʀmɛ̃, -ɛn] *adj*: **cousin ~** first cousin.
germanique [ʒɛʀmanik] *adj* Germanic.
germaniste [ʒɛʀmanist(ə)] *nm/f* German scholar.
germe [ʒɛʀm(ə)] *nm* germ.
germer [ʒɛʀme] *vi* to sprout; (*semence, aussi fig*) to germinate.
gérondif [ʒeʀɔ̃dif] *nm* gerund; (*en latin*) gerundive.
gérontologie [ʒɛʀɔ̃tɔlɔʒi] *nf* gerontology.
gérontologue [ʒeʀɔ̃tɔlɔg] *nm/f* gerontologist.
gésier [ʒezje] *nm* gizzard.
gésir [ʒeziʀ] *vi* to be lying (down); *voir aussi* **ci-gît**.
gestation [ʒɛstɑsjɔ̃] *nf* gestation.
geste [ʒɛst(ə)] *nm* gesture; move; motion; **il fit un ~ de la main pour m'appeler** he signed to me to come over, he waved me over; **ne faites pas un ~** (*ne bougez pas*) don't move.
gesticuler [ʒɛstikyle] *vi* to gesticulate.
gestion [ʒɛstjɔ̃] *nf* management; ~ **des disques** (*INFORM*) housekeeping; ~ **de fichier(s)** (*INFORM*) file management.
gestionnaire [ʒɛstjɔnɛʀ] *nm/f* administrator; ~ **de fichier** (*INFORM*) file manager.
geyser [ʒezɛʀ] *nm* geyser.
Ghana [gana] *nm*: **le ~** Ghana.
ghanéen, ne [ganeɛ̃, -ɛn] *adj* Ghanaian.
ghetto [gɛto] *nm* ghetto.
gibecière [ʒibsjɛʀ] *nf* (*de chasseur*) gamebag; (*sac en bandoulière*) shoulder bag.
gibelotte [ʒiblɔt] *nf rabbit fricassee in white wine.*
gibet [ʒibɛ] *nm* gallows *pl*.
gibier [ʒibje] *nm* (*animaux*) game; (*fig*) prey.
giboulée [ʒibule] *nf* sudden shower.
giboyeux, euse [ʒibwajø, -øz] *adj* well-stocked with game.
Gibraltar [ʒibʀaltaʀ] *nm* Gibraltar.
gibus [ʒibys] *nm* opera hat.
giclée [ʒikle] *nf* spurt, squirt.
gicler [ʒikle] *vi* to spurt, squirt.
gicleur [ʒiklœʀ] *nm* (*AUTO*) jet.
GIE *sigle m* = **groupement d'intérêt économique.**
gifle [ʒifl(ə)] *nf* slap (in the face).
gifler [ʒifle] *vt* to slap (in the face).
gigantesque [ʒigɑ̃tɛsk(ə)] *adj* gigantic.
gigantisme [ʒigɑ̃tism(ə)] *nm* (*MÉD*) gigantism; (*des mégalopoles*) vastness.
gigaoctet [ʒigaɔktɛ] *nm* gigabyte.
GIGN *sigle m* (= *Groupe d'intervention de la gendarmerie nationale*) *special crack force of the gendarmerie*, ≈ SAS (*BRIT*).
gigogne [ʒigɔɲ] *adj*: **lits ~s** truckle (*BRIT*) *ou* trundle (*US*) beds; **tables/poupées ~s** nest of tables/dolls.
gigolo [ʒigɔlo] *nm* gigolo.
gigot [ʒigo] *nm* leg (of mutton *ou* lamb).
gigoter [ʒigɔte] *vi* to wriggle (about).
gilet [ʒilɛ] *nm* waistcoat; (*pull*) cardigan; (*de corps*) vest; ~ **pare-balles** bulletproof jacket; ~ **de sauvetage** life jacket.
gin [dʒin] *nm* gin.
gingembre [ʒɛ̃ʒɑ̃bʀ(ə)] *nm* ginger.
gingivite [ʒɛ̃ʒivit] *nf* inflammation of the gums, gingivitis.
ginseng [ʒinsɛŋ] *nm* ginseng.
girafe [ʒiʀaf] *nf* giraffe.
giratoire [ʒiʀatwaʀ] *adj*: **sens ~** roundabout.
girofle [ʒiʀɔfl(ə)] *nm*: **clou de ~** clove.
giroflée [ʒiʀɔfle] *nf* wallflower.

girolle [ʒiʀɔl] *nf* chanterelle.
giron [ʒiʀɔ̃] *nm* (*genoux*) lap; (*fig: sein*) bosom.
Gironde [ʒiʀɔ̃d] *nf*: **la** ~ the Gironde.
girophare [ʒiʀɔfaʀ] *nm* revolving (flashing) light.
girouette [ʒiʀwɛt] *nf* weather vane *ou* cock.
gis [ʒi], **gisais** [ʒizɛ] *etc vb voir* **gésir**.
gisement [ʒizmɑ̃] *nm* deposit.
gît [ʒi] *vb voir* **gésir**.
gitan, e [ʒitɑ̃, -an] *nm/f* gipsy.
gîte [ʒit] *nm* home; shelter; (*du lièvre*) form; ~ **(rural)** (country) holiday cottage *ou* apartment.
gîter [ʒite] *vi* (*NAVIG*) to list.
givrage [ʒivʀaʒ] *nm* icing.
givrant, e [ʒivʀɑ̃, -ɑ̃t] *adj*: **brouillard** ~ freezing fog.
givre [ʒivʀ(ə)] *nm* (hoar)frost.
givré, e [ʒivʀe] *adj*: **citron ~/orange ~e** lemon/orange sorbet (*served in fruit skin*).
glabre [glɑbʀ(ə)] *adj* hairless; (*menton*) clean-shaven.
glaçage [glasaʒ] *nm* (*au sucre*) icing; (*au blanc d'œuf, de la viande*) glazing.
glace [glas] *nf* ice; (*crème glacée*) ice cream; (*verre*) sheet of glass; (*miroir*) mirror; (*de voiture*) window; **~s** *nfpl* (*GÉO*) ice sheets, ice *sg*; **de** ~ (*fig: accueil, visage*) frosty, icy; **rester de** ~ to remain unmoved.
glacé, e [glase] *adj* icy; (*boisson*) iced.
glacer [glase] *vt* to freeze; (*boisson*) to chill, ice; (*gâteau*) to ice (*BRIT*), frost (*US*); (*papier, tissu*) to glaze; (*fig*): ~ **qn** to chill sb; (*fig*) to make sb's blood run cold.
glaciaire [glasjɛʀ] *adj* (*période*) ice *cpd*; (*relief*) glacial.
glacial, e [glasjal] *adj* icy.
glacier [glasje] *nm* (*GÉO*) glacier; (*marchand*) ice-cream maker.
glacière [glasjɛʀ] *nf* icebox.
glaçon [glasɔ̃] *nm* icicle; (*pour boisson*) ice cube.
gladiateur [gladjatœʀ] *nm* gladiator.
glaïeul [glajœl] *nm* gladiola.
glaire [glɛʀ] *nf* (*MÉD*) phlegm *no pl*.
glaise [glɛz] *nf* clay.
glaive [glɛv] *nm* two-edged sword.
gland [glɑ̃] *nm* (*de chêne*) acorn; (*décoration*) tassel; (*ANAT*) glans.
glande [glɑ̃d] *nf* gland.
glander [glɑ̃de] *vi* (*fam*) to fart around (*BRIT !*), screw around (*US !*).
glaner [glane] *vt, vi* to glean.
glapir [glapiʀ] *vi* to yelp.
glapissement [glapismɑ̃] *nm* yelping.
glas [glɑ] *nm* knell, toll.
glauque [glok] *adj* dull blue-green.
glissade [glisad] *nf* (*par jeu*) slide; (*chute*) slip; (*dérapage*) skid; **faire des ~s** to slide.
glissant, e [glisɑ̃, -ɑ̃t] *adj* slippery.
glisse [glis] *nf*: **sports de** ~ *sports involving sliding or gliding* (*eg skiing, surfing, windsurfing*).
glissement [glismɑ̃] *nm* sliding; (*fig*) shift; ~ **de terrain** landslide.
glisser [glise] *vi* (*avancer*) to glide *ou* slide along; (*coulisser, tomber*) to slide; (*déraper*) to slip; (*être glissant*) to be slippery ♦ *vt*: ~ **qch sous/dans/à** to slip sth under/into/to; ~ **sur** (*fig: détail etc*) to skate over; **se** ~ **dans/entre** to slip into/between.
glissière [glisjɛʀ] *nf* slide channel; **à** ~ (*porte, fenêtre*) sliding; ~ **de sécurité** (*AUTO*) crash barrier.
glissoire [gliswaʀ] *nf* slide.
global, e, aux [glɔbal, -o] *adj* overall.
globalement [glɔbalmɑ̃] *adv* taken as a whole.
globe [glɔb] *nm* globe; **sous** ~ under glass; ~ **oculaire** eyeball; **le** ~ **terrestre** the globe.
globe-trotter [glɔbtʀɔtœʀ] *nm* globe-trotter.
globule [glɔbyl] *nm* (*du sang*): ~ **blanc/rouge** white/red corpuscle.
globuleux, euse [glɔbylø, -øz] *adj*: **yeux** ~ protruding eyes.
gloire [glwaʀ] *nf* glory; (*mérite*) distinction, credit; (*personne*) celebrity.
glorieux, euse [glɔʀjø, -øz] *adj* glorious.
glorifier [glɔʀifje] *vt* to glorify, extol; **se** ~ **de** to glory in.
gloriole [glɔʀjɔl] *nf* vainglory.
glose [gloz] *nf* gloss.
glossaire [glɔsɛʀ] *nm* glossary.
glotte [glɔt] *nf* (*ANAT*) glottis.
glouglouter [gluglute] *vi* to gurgle.
gloussement [glusmɑ̃] *nm* (*de poule*) cluck; (*rire*) chuckle.
glousser [gluse] *vi* to cluck; (*rire*) to chuckle.
glouton, ne [glutɔ̃, -ɔn] *adj* gluttonous, greedy.
gloutonnerie [glutɔnʀi] *nf* gluttony.
glu [gly] *nf* birdlime.
gluant, e [glyɑ̃, -ɑ̃t] *adj* sticky, gummy.
glucide [glysid] *nm* carbohydrate.
glucose [glykoz] *nm* glucose.
gluten [glytɛn] *nm* gluten.
glycérine [gliseʀin] *nf* glycerine.
glycine [glisin] *nf* wisteria.
GMT *sigle adj* (= *Greenwich Mean Time*) GMT.
gnangnan [ɲɑ̃ɲɑ̃] *adj inv* (*fam: livre, film*) soppy.
GNL *sigle m* (= *gaz naturel liquéfié*) LNG (= *liquefied natural gas*).
gnôle [njol] *nf* (*fam*) booze *no pl*; **un petit verre de** ~ a drop of the hard stuff.
gnome [gnom] *nm* gnome.
gnon [ɲɔ̃] *nm* (*fam: coup de poing*) bash; (*: marque*) dent.
GO *sigle fpl* (= *grandes ondes*) LW ♦ *sigle m* (= *gentil organisateur*) *title given to leaders on Club Méditerranée holidays; extended to refer to easy-going leader of any group*.
go [go]: **tout de** ~ *adv* straight out.
goal [gol] *nm* goalkeeper.
gobelet [gɔblɛ] *nm* (*en métal*) tumbler; (*en

plastique) beaker; (*à dés*) cup.
gober [gɔbe] *vt* to swallow.
goberger [gɔbɛʀʒe]: **se** ~ *vi* to cosset o.s.
Gobi [gɔbi] *n*: **désert de** ~ Gobi Desert.
godasse [gɔdas] *nf* (*fam*) shoe.
godet [gɔdɛ] *nm* pot; (*COUTURE*) unpressed pleat.
godiller [gɔdije] *vi* (*NAVIG*) to scull; (*SKI*) to wedeln.
goéland [gɔelɑ̃] *nm* (sea)gull.
goélette [gɔelɛt] *nf* schooner.
goémon [gɔemɔ̃] *nm* wrack.
gogo [gɔgo] *nm* (*péj*) mug, sucker; **à** ~ *adv* galore.
goguenard, e [gɔgnaʀ, -aʀd(ə)] *adj* mocking.
goguette [gɔgɛt] *nf*: **en** ~ on the binge.
goinfre [gwɛ̃fʀ(ə)] *nm* glutton.
goinfrer [gwɛ̃fʀe]: **se** ~ *vi* to make a pig of o.s.; **se** ~ **de** to guzzle.
goitre [gwatʀ(ə)] *nm* goitre.
golf [gɔlf] *nm* (*jeu*) golf; (*terrain*) golf course; ~ **miniature** crazy *ou* miniature golf.
golfe [gɔlf(ə)] *nm* gulf; bay; **le** ~ **d'Aden** the Gulf of Aden; **le** ~ **de Gascogne** the Bay of Biscay; **le** ~ **du Lion** the Gulf of Lions; **le** ~ **Persique** the Persian Gulf.
golfeur, euse [gɔlfœʀ, -øz] *nm/f* golfer.
gominé, e [gɔmine] *adj* slicked down.
gomme [gɔm] *nf* (*à effacer*) rubber (*BRIT*), eraser; (*résine*) gum; **boule** *ou* **pastille de** ~ throat pastille.
gommé, e [gɔme] *adj*: **papier** ~ gummed paper.
gommer [gɔme] *vt* (*effacer*) to rub out (*BRIT*), erase; (*enduire de gomme*) to gum.
gond [gɔ̃] *nm* hinge; **sortir de ses ~s** (*fig*) to fly off the handle.
gondole [gɔ̃dɔl] *nf* gondola; (*pour l'étalage*) shelves *pl*, gondola.
gondoler [gɔ̃dɔle]: **se** ~ *vi* to warp, buckle; (*fam: rire*) to hoot with laughter; to be in stitches.
gondolier [gɔ̃dɔlje] *nm* gondolier.
gonflable [gɔ̃flabl(ə)] *adj* inflatable.
gonflage [gɔ̃flaʒ] *nm* inflating, blowing up.
gonflé, e [gɔ̃fle] *adj* swollen; (*ventre*) bloated; (*fam: culotté*): **être** ~ to have a nerve.
gonflement [gɔ̃fləmɑ̃] *nm* inflation; (*MÉD*) swelling.
gonfler [gɔ̃fle] *vt* (*pneu, ballon*) to inflate, blow up; (*nombre, importance*) to inflate ♦ *vi* (*pied etc*) to swell (up); (*CULIN: pâte*) to rise.
gonfleur [gɔ̃flœʀ] *nm* air pump.
gong [gɔ̃g] *nm* gong.
gonzesse [gɔ̃zɛs] *nf* (*fam*) chick, bird (*BRIT*).
goret [gɔʀɛ] *nm* piglet.
gorge [gɔʀʒ(ə)] *nf* (*ANAT*) throat; (*poitrine*) breast; (*GÉO*) gorge; (*rainure*) groove; **avoir mal à la** ~ to have a sore throat; **avoir la** ~ **serrée** to have a lump in one's throat.
gorgé, e [gɔʀʒe] *adj*: ~ **de** filled with; (*eau*) saturated with ♦ *nf* mouthful; sip; gulp; **boire à petites/grandes ~es** to take little sips/big gulps.
gorille [gɔʀij] *nm* gorilla; (*fam*) bodyguard.
gosier [gozje] *nm* throat.
gosse [gɔs] *nm/f* kid.
gothique [gɔtik] *adj* gothic.
gouache [gwaʃ] *nf* gouache.
gouaille [gwaj] *nf* street wit, cocky humour (*BRIT*) *ou* humor (*US*).
goudron [gudʀɔ̃] *nm* (*asphalte*) tar(mac) (*BRIT*), asphalt; (*du tabac*) tar.
goudronner [gudʀɔne] *vt* to tar(mac) (*BRIT*), asphalt.
gouffre [gufʀ(ə)] *nm* abyss, gulf.
goujat [guʒa] *nm* boor.
goujon [guʒɔ̃] *nm* gudgeon.
goulée [gule] *nf* gulp.
goulet [gulɛ] *nm* bottleneck.
goulot [gulo] *nm* neck; **boire au** ~ to drink from the bottle.
goulu, e [guly] *adj* greedy.
goulûment [gulymɑ̃] *adv* greedily.
goupille [gupij] *nf* (metal) pin.
goupiller [gupije] *vt* to pin (together).
goupillon [gupijɔ̃] *nm* (*REL*) sprinkler; (*brosse*) bottle brush; **le** ~ (*fig*) the cloth, the clergy.
gourd, e [guʀ, guʀd(ə)] *adj* numb (with cold); (*fam*) oafish.
gourde [guʀd(ə)] *nf* (*récipient*) flask; (*fam*) (clumsy) clot *ou* oaf.
gourdin [guʀdɛ̃] *nm* club, bludgeon.
gourmand, e [guʀmɑ̃, -ɑ̃d] *adj* greedy.
gourmandise [guʀmɑ̃diz] *nf* greed; (*bonbon*) sweet (*BRIT*), piece of candy (*US*).
gourmet [guʀmɛ] *nm* epicure.
gourmette [guʀmɛt] *nf* chain bracelet.
gourou [guʀu] *nm* guru.
gousse [gus] *nf* (*de vanille etc*) pod; ~ **d'ail** clove of garlic.
gousset [gusɛ] *nm* (*de gilet*) fob.
goût [gu] *nm* taste; (*fig: appréciation*) taste, liking; **le (bon)** ~ good taste; **de bon** ~ in good taste, tasteful; **de mauvais** ~ in bad taste, tasteless; **avoir bon/mauvais** ~ (*aliment*) to taste nice/nasty; (*personne*) to have good/bad taste; **avoir du/manquer de** ~ to have/lack taste; **avoir du** ~ **pour** to have a liking for; **prendre** ~ **à** to develop a taste *ou* a liking for.
goûter [gute] *vt* (*essayer*) to taste; (*apprécier*) to enjoy ♦ *vi* to have (afternoon) tea ♦ *nm* (afternoon) tea; ~ **à** to taste, sample; ~ **de** to have a taste of; ~ **d'enfants/ d'anniversaire** children's tea/birthday party.
goutte [gut] *nf* drop; (*MÉD*) gout; (*alcool*) nip (*BRIT*), tot (*BRIT*), drop (*US*); **~s** *nfpl* (*MÉD*) drops; ~ **à** ~ *adv* a drop at a time; **tomber** ~ **à** ~ to drip.
goutte-à-goutte [gutagut] *nm inv* (*MÉD*) drip; **alimenter au** ~ to drip-feed.
gouttelette [gutlɛt] *nf* droplet.
goutter [gute] *vi* to drip.

gouttière [gutjɛʀ] *nf* gutter.
gouvernail [guvɛʀnaj] *nm* rudder; (*barre*) helm, tiller.
gouvernant, e [guvɛʀnɑ̃, -ɑ̃t] *adj* ruling *cpd* ♦ *nf* housekeeper; (*d'un enfant*) governess.
gouverne [guvɛʀn(ə)] *nf*: **pour sa ~** for his guidance.
gouvernement [guvɛʀnəmɑ̃] *nm* government.
gouvernemental, e, aux [guvɛʀnəmɑ̃tal, -o] *adj* (*politique*) government *cpd*; (*journal, parti*) pro-government.
gouverner [guvɛʀne] *vt* to govern; (*diriger*) to steer; (*fig*) to control.
gouverneur [guvɛʀnœʀ] *nm* governor; (*MIL*) commanding officer.
goyave [gɔjav] *nf* guava.
GPL *sigle m* (= *gaz de pétrole liquéfié*) LPG (= *liquefied petroleum gas*).
GQG *sigle m* (= *grand quartier général*) GHQ.
grabataire [gʀabatɛʀ] *adj* bedridden ♦ *nm/f* bedridden invalid.
grâce [gʀɑs] *nf* grace; (*faveur*) favour; (*JUR*) pardon; **~s** *nfpl* (*REL*) grace *sg*; **de bonne/mauvaise ~** with (a) good/bad grace; **dans les bonnes ~s de qn** in favour with sb; **faire ~ à qn de qch** to spare sb sth; **rendre ~(s) à** to give thanks to; **demander ~** to beg for mercy; **droit de ~** right of reprieve; **recours en ~** plea for pardon; **~ à** *prép* thanks to.
gracier [gʀasje] *vt* to pardon.
gracieusement [gʀasjøzmɑ̃] *adv* graciously, kindly; (*gratuitement*) freely; (*avec grâce*) gracefully.
gracieux, euse [gʀasjø, -øz] *adj* (*charmant, élégant*) graceful; (*aimable*) gracious, kind; **à titre ~** free of charge.
gracile [gʀasil] *adj* slender.
gradation [gʀadɑsjɔ̃] *nf* gradation.
grade [gʀad] *nm* (*MIL*) rank; (*SCOL*) degree; **monter en ~** to be promoted.
gradé [gʀade] *nm* (*MIL*) officer.
gradin [gʀadɛ̃] *nm* (*dans un théâtre*) tier; (*de stade*) step; **~s** *nmpl* (*de stade*) terracing *no pl* (*BRIT*), standing area; **en ~s** terraced.
graduation [gʀadɥɑsjɔ̃] *nf* graduation.
gradué, e [gʀadɥe] *adj* (*exercices*) graded (for difficulty); (*thermomètre, verre*) graduated.
graduel, le [gʀadɥɛl] *adj* gradual; progressive.
graduer [gʀadɥe] *vt* (*effort etc*) to increase gradually; (*règle, verre*) to graduate.
graffiti [gʀafiti] *nmpl* graffiti.
grain [gʀɛ̃] *nm* (*gén*) grain; (*de chapelet*) bead; (*NAVIG*) squall; (*averse*) heavy shower; (*fig: petite quantité*): **un ~ de** a touch of; **~ de beauté** beauty spot; **~ de café** coffee bean; **~ de poivre** peppercorn; **~ de poussière** speck of dust; **~ de raisin** grape.
graine [gʀɛn] *nf* seed; **mauvaise ~** bad lot; **une ~ de voyou** a hooligan in the making.
graineterie [gʀɛntʀi] *nf* seed merchant's (shop).
grainetier, -ière [gʀɛntje, -jɛʀ] *nm/f* seed merchant.
graissage [gʀɛsaʒ] *nm* lubrication, greasing.
graisse [gʀɛs] *nf* fat; (*lubrifiant*) grease; **~ saturée** saturated fat.
graisser [gʀese] *vt* to lubricate, grease; (*tacher*) to make greasy.
graisseux, euse [gʀɛsø, -øz] *adj* greasy; (*ANAT*) fatty.
grammaire [gʀamɛʀ] *nf* grammar.
grammatical, e, aux [gʀamatikal, -o] *adj* grammatical.
gramme [gʀam] *nm* gramme.
grand, e [gʀɑ̃, gʀɑ̃d] *adj* (*haut*) tall; (*gros, vaste, large*) big, large; (*long*) long; (*sens abstraits*) great ♦ *adv*: **~ ouvert** wide open; **un ~ buveur** a heavy drinker; **un ~ homme** a great man; **son ~ frère** his big *ou* older brother; **avoir ~ besoin de** to be in dire *ou* desperate need of; **il est ~ temps de** it's high time to; **il est assez ~ pour** he's big *ou* old enough to; **voir ~** to think big; **en ~** on a large scale; **au ~ air** in the open (air); **les ~s blessés/brûlés** the severely injured/burned; **de ~ matin** at the crack of dawn; **~ écart** splits *pl*; **~ ensemble** housing scheme; **~ jour** broad daylight; **~ livre** (*COMM*) ledger; **~ magasin** department store; **~ malade** very sick person; **~ public** general public; **~e personne** grown-up; **~e surface** hypermarket, superstore; **~es écoles** *prestige university-level colleges with competitive entrance examinations*; **~es lignes** (*RAIL*) main lines; **~es vacances** summer holidays; *see boxed note*.

> **GRANDES ÉCOLES**
>
> *The* **grandes écoles** *are highly respected institutes of higher education which train students for specific careers. Students who have spent two years after the 'baccalauréat' in the 'classes préparatoires' are recruited by competitive entry examination. The prestigious* **grandes écoles** *have a strong corporate identity and tend to furnish France with its intellectual, administrative and political élite.*

grand-angle, *pl* **grands-angles** [gʀɑ̃tɑ̃gl(ə)] *nm* (*PHOTO*) wide-angle lens.
grand-angulaire, *pl* **grands-angulaires** [gʀɑ̃tɑ̃gylɛʀ] *nm* (*PHOTO*) wide-angle lens.
grand-chose [gʀɑ̃ʃoz] *nm/f inv*: **pas ~** not much.
Grande-Bretagne [gʀɑ̃dbʀətaɲ] *nf*: **la ~** (Great) Britain; **en ~** in (Great) Britain.
grandement [gʀɑ̃dmɑ̃] *adv* (*tout à fait*) greatly; (*largement*) easily; (*généreusement*) lavishly.
grandeur [gʀɑ̃dœʀ] *nf* (*dimension*) size; (*fig: ampleur, importance*) magnitude; (*: gloire, puissance*) greatness; **~ nature** *adj* life-size.
grand-guignolesque [gʀɑ̃giɲɔlɛsk(ə)] *adj* gruesome.

grandiloquent, e [gʀɑ̃dilɔkɑ̃, -ɑ̃t] *adj* bombastic, grandiloquent.
grandiose [gʀɑ̃djoz] *adj* (*paysage, spectacle*) imposing.
grandir [gʀɑ̃diʀ] *vi* (*enfant, arbre*) to grow; (*bruit, hostilité*) to increase, grow ♦ *vt*: ~ **qn** (*suj: vêtement, chaussure*) to make sb look taller; (*fig*) to make sb grow in stature.
grandissant, e [gʀɑ̃disɑ̃, -ɑ̃t] growing.
grand-mère, *pl* **grand(s)-mères** [gʀɑ̃mɛʀ] *nf* grandmother.
grand-messe [gʀɑ̃mɛs] *nf* high mass.
grand-oncle, *pl* **grands-oncles** [gʀɑ̃tɔ̃kl(ə), gʀɑ̃zɔ̃kl(ə)] *nm* great-uncle.
grand-peine [gʀɑ̃pɛn]: **à** ~ *adv* with (great) difficulty.
grand-père, *pl* **grands-pères** [gʀɑ̃pɛʀ] *nm* grandfather.
grand-route [gʀɑ̃ʀut] *nf* main road.
grand-rue [gʀɑ̃ʀy] *nf* high street.
grands-parents [gʀɑ̃paʀɑ̃] *nmpl* grandparents.
grand-tante, *pl* **grand(s)-tantes** [gʀɑ̃tɑ̃t] *nf* great-aunt.
grand-voile [gʀɑ̃vwal] *nf* mainsail.
grange [gʀɑ̃ʒ] *nf* barn.
granit(e) [gʀanit] *nm* granite.
granitique [gʀanitik] *adj* granite; (*terrain*) granitic.
granule [gʀanyl] *nm* small pill.
granulé [gʀanyle] *nm* granule.
granuleux, euse [gʀanylø, -øz] *adj* granular.
graphe [gʀaf] *nm* graph.
graphie [gʀafi] *nf* written form.
graphique [gʀafik] *adj* graphic ♦ *nm* graph.
graphisme [gʀafism(ə)] *nm* graphic arts *pl*; graphics *sg*; (*écriture*) handwriting.
graphiste [gʀafist(ə)] *nm/f* graphic designer.
graphologie [gʀafɔlɔʒi] *nf* graphology.
graphologue [gʀafɔlɔg] *nm/f* graphologist.
grappe [gʀap] *nf* cluster; ~ **de raisin** bunch of grapes.
grappiller [gʀapije] *vt* to glean.
grappin [gʀapɛ̃] *nm* grapnel; **mettre le** ~ **sur** (*fig*) to get one's claws on.
gras, se [gʀɑ, gʀɑs] *adj* (*viande, soupe*) fatty; (*personne*) fat; (*surface, main, cheveux*) greasy; (*terre*) sticky; (*toux*) loose, phlegmy; (*rire*) throaty; (*plaisanterie*) coarse; (*crayon*) soft-lead; (*TYPO*) bold ♦ *nm* (*CULIN*) fat; **faire la** ~**se matinée** to have a lie-in (*BRIT*), sleep late; **matière** ~**se** fat (content).
gras-double [gʀɑdubl(ə)] *nm* (*CULIN*) tripe.
grassement [gʀɑsmɑ̃] *adv* (*généreusement*): ~ **payé** handsomely paid; (*grossièrement: rire*) coarsely.
grassouillet, te [gʀasujɛ, -ɛt] *adj* podgy, plump.
gratifiant, e [gʀatifjɑ̃, -ɑ̃t] *adj* gratifying, rewarding.
gratification [gʀatifikɑsjɔ̃] *nf* bonus.
gratifier [gʀatifje] *vt*: ~ **qn de** to favour (*BRIT*) *ou* favor (*US*) sb with; to reward sb with; (*sourire etc*) to favo(u)r sb with.
gratin [gʀatɛ̃] *nm* (*CULIN*) cheese- (*ou* crumb-) topped dish; (*: croûte*) topping; **au** ~ au gratin; **tout le** ~ **parisien** all the best people of Paris.
gratiné, e [gʀatine] *adj* (*CULIN*) au gratin; (*fam*) hellish ♦ *nf* (*soupe*) onion soup au gratin.
gratis [gʀatis] *adv, adj* free.
gratitude [gʀatityd] *nf* gratitude.
gratte-ciel [gʀatsjɛl] *nm inv* skyscraper.
grattement [gʀatmɑ̃] *nm* (*bruit*) scratching (noise).
gratte-papier [gʀatpapje] *nm inv* (*péj*) penpusher.
gratter [gʀate] *vt* (*frotter*) to scrape; (*enlever*) to scrape off; (*bras, bouton*) to scratch; **se** ~ to scratch o.s.
grattoir [gʀatwaʀ] *nm* scraper.
gratuit, e [gʀatɥi, -ɥit] *adj* (*entrée*) free; (*billet*) free, complimentary; (*fig*) gratuitous.
gratuité [gʀatɥite] *nf* being free (of charge); gratuitousness.
gratuitement [gʀatɥitmɑ̃] *adv* (*sans payer*) free; (*sans preuve, motif*) gratuitously.
gravats [gʀavɑ] *nmpl* rubble *sg*.
grave [gʀav] *adj* (*dangereux: maladie, accident*) serious, bad; (*sérieux: sujet, problème*) serious, grave; (*personne, air*) grave, solemn; (*voix, son*) deep, low-pitched ♦ *nm* (*MUS*) low register; **ce n'est pas** ~**!** it's all right, don't worry; **blessé** ~ seriously injured person.
graveleux, euse [gʀavlø, -øz] *adj* (*terre*) gravelly; (*fruit*) gritty; (*contes, propos*) smutty.
gravement [gʀavmɑ̃] *adv* seriously; badly; gravely.
graver [gʀave] *vt* (*plaque, nom*) to engrave; (*fig*): ~ **qch dans son esprit/sa mémoire** to etch sth in one's mind/memory.
graveur [gʀavœʀ] *nm* engraver.
gravier [gʀavje] *nm* (loose) gravel *no pl*.
gravillons [gʀavijɔ̃] *nmpl* gravel *sg*, loose chippings *ou* gravel.
gravir [gʀaviʀ] *vt* to climb (up).
gravitation [gʀavitɑsjɔ̃] *nf* gravitation.
gravité [gʀavite] *nf* (*voir grave*) seriousness; gravity; (*PHYSIQUE*) gravity.
graviter [gʀavite] *vi*: ~ **autour de** to revolve around.
gravure [gʀavyʀ] *nf* engraving; (*reproduction*) print; plate.
GRE *sigle f* (= *garantie contre les risques à l'exportation*) ≈ service provided by ECGD (= *Export Credit Guarantees Department*).
gré [gʀe] *nm*: **à son** ~ *adj* to his liking ♦ *adv* as he pleases; **au** ~ **de** according to, following; **contre le** ~ **de qn** against sb's will; **de son (plein)** ~ of one's own free will; **de** ~ **ou de force** whether one likes it or not; **de bon** ~ willingly; **bon** ~ **mal** ~ like it or not; willy-nilly; **de** ~ **à** ~ (*COMM*) by mutual agree-

ment; **savoir (bien) ~ à qn de qch** to be (most) grateful to sb for sth.

grec, grecque [gʀɛk] *adj* Greek; (*classique: vase etc*) Grecian ♦ *nm* (*LING*) Greek ♦ *nm/f*: **G~, Grecque** Greek.

Grèce [gʀɛs] *nf*: **la ~** Greece.

gredin, e [gʀədɛ̃, -in] *nm/f* rogue, rascal.

gréement [gʀemɑ̃] *nm* rigging.

greffe [gʀɛf] *nf* graft; transplant ♦ *nm* (*JUR*) office.

greffer [gʀefe] *vt* (*BOT, MÉD: tissu*) to graft; (*MÉD: organe*) to transplant.

greffier [gʀefje] *nm* clerk of the court.

grégaire [gʀegɛʀ] *adj* gregarious.

grège [gʀɛʒ] *adj*: **soie ~** raw silk.

grêle [gʀɛl] *adj* (very) thin ♦ *nf* hail.

grêlé, e [gʀele] *adj* pockmarked.

grêler [gʀele] *vb impers*: **il grêle** it's hailing ♦ *vt*: **la région a été grêlée** the region was damaged by hail.

grêlon [gʀɛlɔ̃] *nm* hailstone.

grelot [gʀəlo] *nm* little bell.

grelottant, e [gʀəlɔtɑ̃, -ɑ̃t] *adj* shivering, shivery.

grelotter [gʀəlɔte] *vi* (*trembler*) to shiver.

Grenade [gʀənad] *n* Granada ♦ *nf* (*île*) Grenada.

grenade [gʀənad] *nf* (*explosive*) grenade; (*BOT*) pomegranate; **~ lacrymogène** teargas grenade.

grenadier [gʀənadje] *nm* (*MIL*) grenadier; (*BOT*) pomegranate tree.

grenadine [gʀənadin] *nf* grenadine.

grenat [gʀəna] *adj inv* dark red.

grenier [gʀənje] *nm* (*de maison*) attic; (*de ferme*) loft.

grenouille [gʀənuj] *nf* frog.

grenouillère [gʀənujɛʀ] *nf* (*de bébé*) leggings; (*: combinaison*) sleepsuit.

grenu, e [gʀəny] *adj* grainy, grained.

grès [gʀɛ] *nm* (*roche*) sandstone; (*poterie*) stoneware.

grésil [gʀezi] *nm* (fine) hail.

grésillement [gʀezijmɑ̃] *nm* sizzling; crackling.

grésiller [gʀezije] *vi* to sizzle; (*RADIO*) to crackle.

grève [gʀɛv] *nf* (*d'ouvriers*) strike; (*plage*) shore; **se mettre en/faire ~** to go on/be on strike; **~ bouchon** partial strike (*in key areas of a company*); **~ de la faim** hunger strike; **~ perlée** go-slow (*BRIT*), slowdown (*US*); **~ sauvage** wildcat strike; **~ de solidarité** sympathy strike; **~ surprise** lightning strike; **~ sur le tas** sit down strike; **~ tournante** strike by rota; **~ du zèle** work-to-rule (*BRIT*), slowdown (*US*).

grever [gʀəve] *vt* (*budget, économie*) to put a strain on; **grevé d'impôts** crippled by taxes; **grevé d'hypothèques** heavily mortgaged.

gréviste [gʀevist(ə)] *nm/f* striker.

gribouillage [gʀibujaʒ] *nm* scribble, scrawl.

gribouiller [gʀibuje] *vt* to scribble, scrawl ♦ *vi* to doodle.

gribouillis [gʀibuji] *nm* (*dessin*) doodle; (*action*) doodling *no pl*; (*écriture*) scribble.

grief [gʀijɛf] *nm* grievance; **faire ~ à qn de** to reproach sb for.

grièvement [gʀijɛvmɑ̃] *adv* seriously.

griffe [gʀif] *nf* claw; (*fig*) signature; (*: d'un couturier, parfumeur*) label, signature.

griffé, e [gʀife] *adj* designer(-label) *cpd*.

griffer [gʀife] *vt* to scratch.

griffon [gʀifɔ̃] *nm* (*chien*) griffon.

griffonnage [gʀifɔnaʒ] *nm* scribble.

griffonner [gʀifɔne] *vt* to scribble.

griffure [gʀifyʀ] *nf* scratch.

grignoter [gʀiɲɔte] *vt, vi* to nibble.

gril [gʀil] *nm* steak *ou* grill pan.

grillade [gʀijad] *nf* grill.

grillage [gʀijaʒ] *nm* (*treillis*) wire netting; (*clôture*) wire fencing.

grillager [gʀijaʒe] *vt* (*objet*) to put wire netting on; (*périmètre, jardin*) to put wire fencing around.

grille [gʀij] *nf* (*portail*) (metal) gate; (*clôture*) railings *pl*; (*d'égout*) (metal) grate; (*fig*) grid.

grille-pain [gʀijpɛ̃] *nm inv* toaster.

griller [gʀije] *vt* (*aussi*: **faire ~**: *pain*) to toast; (*: viande*) to grill (*BRIT*), broil (*US*); (*: café*) to roast; (*fig: ampoule etc*) to burn out, blow; **~ un feu rouge** to jump the lights (*BRIT*), run a stoplight (*US*) ♦ *vi* (*brûler*) to be roasting.

grillon [gʀijɔ̃] *nm* (*ZOOL*) cricket.

grimace [gʀimas] *nf* grimace; (*pour faire rire*): **faire des ~s** to pull *ou* make faces.

grimacer [gʀimase] *vi* to grimace.

grimacier, ière [gʀimasje, -jɛʀ] *adj*: **c'est un enfant ~** that child is always pulling faces.

grimer [gʀime] *vt* to make up.

grimoire [gʀimwaʀ] *nm* (*illisible*) unreadable scribble; (*livre de magie*) book of magic spells.

grimpant, e [gʀɛ̃pɑ̃, -ɑ̃t] *adj*: **plante ~e** climbing plant, climber.

grimper [gʀɛ̃pe] *vi, vt* to climb ♦ *nm*: **le ~** (*SPORT*) rope-climbing; **~ à/sur** to climb (up)/climb onto.

grimpeur, euse [gʀɛ̃pœʀ, -øz] *nm/f* climber.

grinçant, e [gʀɛ̃sɑ̃, -ɑ̃t] *adj* grating.

grincement [gʀɛ̃smɑ̃] *nm* grating (noise); creaking (noise).

grincer [gʀɛ̃se] *vi* (*porte, roue*) to grate; (*plancher*) to creak; **~ des dents** to grind one's teeth.

grincheux, euse [gʀɛ̃ʃø, -øz] *adj* grumpy.

gringalet [gʀɛ̃galɛ] *adj m* puny ♦ *nm* weakling.

griotte [gʀijɔt] *nf* Morello cherry.

grippal, e, aux [gʀipal, -o] *adj* (*état*) flu-like.

grippe [gʀip] *nf* flu, influenza; **avoir la ~** to have (the) flu; **prendre qn/qch en ~** (*fig*) to take a sudden dislike to sb/sth.

grippé, e [gʀipe] *adj*: **être ~** to have (the) flu; (*moteur*) to have seized up (*BRIT*) *ou*

jammed.
gripper [gʀipe] *vt, vi* to jam.
grippe-sou [gʀipsu] *nm/f* penny pincher.
gris, e [gʀi, gʀiz] *adj* grey (*BRIT*), gray (*US*); (*ivre*) tipsy ♦ *nm* (*couleur*) grey (*BRIT*), gray (*US*); **il fait ~** it's a dull *ou* grey day; **faire ~e mine** to look miserable *ou* morose; **faire ~e mine à qn** to give sb a cool reception.
grisaille [gʀizɑj] *nf* greyness (*BRIT*), grayness (*US*), dullness.
grisant, e [gʀizɑ̃, -ɑ̃t] *adj* intoxicating, exhilarating.
grisâtre [gʀizɑtʀ(ə)] *adj* greyish (*BRIT*), grayish (*US*).
griser [gʀize] *vt* to intoxicate; **se ~ de** (*fig*) to become intoxicated with.
griserie [gʀizʀi] *nf* intoxication.
grisonnant, e [gʀizɔnɑ̃, -ɑ̃t] *adj* greying (*BRIT*), graying (*US*).
grisonner [gʀizɔne] *vi* to be going grey (*BRIT*) *ou* gray (*US*).
Grisons [gʀizɔ̃] *nmpl*: **les ~** Graubünden.
grisou [gʀizu] *nm* firedamp.
gris-vert [gʀivɛʀ] *adj* grey-green.
grive [gʀiv] *nf* (*ZOOL*) thrush.
grivois, e [gʀivwa, -waz] *adj* saucy.
grivoiserie [gʀivwazʀi] *nf* sauciness.
Groenland [gʀɔɛnlɑ̃d] *nm*: **le ~** Greenland.
groenlandais, e [gʀɔɛnlɑ̃dɛ, -ɛz] *adj* of *ou* from Greenland ♦ *nm/f*: **G~, e** Greenlander.
grog [gʀɔg] *nm* grog.
groggy [gʀɔgi] *adj inv* dazed.
grogne [gʀɔɲ] *nf* grumble.
grognement [gʀɔɲmɑ̃] *nm* grunt; growl.
grogner [gʀɔɲe] *vi* to growl; (*fig*) to grumble.
grognon, ne [gʀɔ̃ɲɔ̃, -ɔn] *adj* grumpy, grouchy.
groin [gʀwɛ̃] *nm* snout.
grommeler [gʀɔmle] *vi* to mutter to o.s.
grondement [gʀɔ̃dmɑ̃] *nm* rumble; growl.
gronder [gʀɔ̃de] *vi* (*canon, moteur, tonnerre*) to rumble; (*animal*) to growl; (*fig: révolte*) to be brewing ♦ *vt* to scold.
groom [gʀum] *nm* page, bellhop (*US*).
gros, se [gʀo, gʀos] *adj* big, large; (*obèse*) fat; (*problème, quantité*) great; (*travaux, dégâts*) extensive; (*large: trait, fil*) thick, heavy ♦ *adv*: **risquer/gagner ~** to risk/win a lot ♦ *nm* (*COMM*): **le ~** the wholesale business; **écrire ~** to write in big letters; **prix de ~** wholesale price; **par ~ temps/~se mer** in rough weather/heavy seas; **le ~ de** the main body of; (*du travail etc*) the bulk of; **en avoir ~ sur le cœur** to be upset; **en ~** roughly; (*COMM*) wholesale; **~ intestin** large intestine; **~ lot** jackpot; **~ mot** coarse word, vulgarity; **~ œuvre** shell (of building); **~ plan** (*PHOTO*) close-up; **~ porteur** wide-bodied aircraft, jumbo (jet); **~ sel** cooking salt; **~ titre** headline; **~se caisse** big drum.
groseille [gʀozɛj] *nf*: **~ (rouge)/(blanche)** red/white currant; **~ à maquereau** gooseberry.
groseillier [gʀozeje] *nm* red *ou* white currant bush; gooseberry bush.
grosse [gʀos] *adj f voir* **gros** ♦ *nf* (*COMM*) gross.
grossesse [gʀosɛs] *nf* pregnancy; **~ nerveuse** phantom pregnancy.
grosseur [gʀosœʀ] *nf* size; fatness; (*tumeur*) lump.
grossier, ière [gʀosje, -jɛʀ] *adj* coarse; (*travail*) rough; crude; (*évident: erreur*) gross.
grossièrement [gʀosjɛʀmɑ̃] *adv* coarsely; roughly; crudely; (*en gros*) roughly.
grossièreté [gʀosjɛʀte] *nf* coarseness; rudeness.
grossir [gʀosiʀ] *vi* (*personne*) to put on weight; (*fig*) to grow, get bigger; (*rivière*) to swell ♦ *vt* to increase; (*exagérer*) to exaggerate; (*au microscope*) to magnify, enlarge; (*suj: vêtement*): **~ qn** to make sb look fatter.
grossissant, e [gʀosisɑ̃, -ɑ̃t] *adj* magnifying, enlarging.
grossissement [gʀosismɑ̃] *nm* (*optique*) magnification.
grossiste [gʀosist(ə)] *nm/f* wholesaler.
grosso modo [gʀosomɔdo] *adv* roughly.
grotesque [gʀɔtɛsk(ə)] *adj* grotesque.
grotte [gʀɔt] *nf* cave.
grouiller [gʀuje] *vi* (*foule*) to mill about; (*fourmis*) to swarm about; **~ de** to be swarming with.
groupe [gʀup] *nm* group; **cabinet de ~** group practice; **médecine de ~** group practice; **~ électrogène** generator; **~ de parole** support group; **~ de pression** pressure group; **~ sanguin** blood group; **~ scolaire** school complex.
groupement [gʀupmɑ̃] *nm* grouping; (*groupe*) group; **~ d'intérêt économique (GIE)** ≈ trade association.
grouper [gʀupe] *vt* to group; (*ressources, moyens*) to pool; **se ~** to get together.
groupuscule [gʀupyskyl] *nm* clique.
gruau [gʀyo] *nm*: **pain de ~** wheaten bread.
grue [gʀy] *nf* crane; **faire le pied de ~** (*fam*) to hang around (waiting), kick one's heels (*BRIT*).
gruger [gʀyʒe] *vt* to cheat, dupe.
grumeaux [gʀymo] *nmpl* (*CULIN*) lumps.
grumeleux, euse [gʀymlø, -øz] *adj* (*sauce etc*) lumpy; (*peau etc*) bumpy.
grutier [gʀytje] *nm* crane driver.
gruyère [gʀyjɛʀ] *nm* gruyère (*BRIT*) *ou* Swiss cheese.
Guadeloupe [gwadlup] *nf*: **la ~** Guadeloupe.
guadeloupéen, ne [gwadlupeɛ̃, -ɛn] *adj* Guadelupian.
Guatémala [gwatemala] *nm*: **le ~** Guatemala.
guatémalien, ne [gwatemaljɛ̃, -ɛn] *adj* Guatemalan.
guatémaltèque [gwatemaltɛk] *adj* Guatemalan.
GUD [gyd] *sigle m* (= *Groupe Union Défense*) *student union*.
gué [ge] *nm* ford; **passer à ~** to ford.

guenilles [gənij] *nfpl* rags.
guenon [gənɔ̃] *nf* female monkey.
guépard [gepaʀ] *nm* cheetah.
guêpe [gɛp] *nf* wasp.
guêpier [gepje] *nm* (*fig*) trap.
guère [gɛʀ] *adv* (*avec adjectif, adverbe*): **ne ... ~** hardly; (*avec verbe*): **ne ... ~** *tournure négative* + much; hardly ever; *tournure négative* + (very) long; **il n'y a ~ que/de** there's hardly anybody (*ou* anything) but/hardly any.
guéridon [geʀidɔ̃] *nm* pedestal table.
guérilla [geʀija] *nf* guerrilla warfare.
guérillero [geʀijeʀo] *nm* guerrilla.
guérir [geʀiʀ] *vt* (*personne, maladie*) to cure; (*membre, plaie*) to heal ♦ *vi* (*personne*) to recover, be cured; (*plaie, chagrin*) to heal; **~ de** to be cured of, recover from; **~ qn de** to cure sb of.
guérison [geʀizɔ̃] *nf* curing; healing; recovery.
guérissable [geʀisabl(ə)] *adj* curable.
guérisseur, euse [geʀisœʀ, -øz] *nm/f* healer.
guérite [geʀit] *nf* (*MIL*) sentry box; (*sur un chantier*) (workman's) hut.
Guernesey [gɛʀnəzɛ] *nf* Guernsey.
guernesiais, e [gɛʀnəzjɛ, -ɛz] *adj* of *ou* from Guernsey.
guerre [gɛʀ] *nf* war; (*méthode*): **~ atomique/de tranchées** atomic/trench warfare *no pl*; **en ~** at war; **faire la ~ à** to wage war against; **de ~ lasse** (*fig*) tired of fighting *ou* resisting; **de bonne ~** fair and square; **~ civile/mondiale** civil/world war; **~ froide/sainte** cold/holy war; **~ d'usure** war of attrition.
guerrier, ière [gɛʀje, -jɛʀ] *adj* warlike ♦ *nm/f* warrior.
guerroyer [gɛʀwaje] *vi* to wage war.
guet [gɛ] *nm*: **faire le ~** to be on the watch *ou* look-out.
guet-apens, *pl* **guets-apens** [gɛtapɑ̃] *nm* ambush.
guêtre [gɛtʀ(ə)] *nf* gaiter.
guetter [gete] *vt* (*épier*) to watch (intently); (*attendre*) to watch (out) for; (*: pour surprendre*) to be lying in wait for.
guetteur [gɛtœʀ] *nm* look-out.
gueule [gœl] *nf* mouth; (*fam: visage*) mug; (*: bouche*) gob (*!*), mouth; **ta ~!** (*fam*) shut up!; **~ de bois** (*fam*) hangover.
gueule-de-loup, *pl* **gueules-de-loup** [gœldəlu] *nf* snapdragon.
gueuler [gœle] *vi* (*fam*) to bawl.
gueuleton [gœltɔ̃] *nm* (*fam*) blowout (*BRIT*), big meal.
gueux [gø] *nm* beggar; (*coquin*) rogue.
gui [gi] *nm* mistletoe.
guibole [gibɔl] *nf* (*fam*) leg.
guichet [giʃɛ] *nm* (*de bureau, banque*) counter, window; (*d'une porte*) wicket, hatch; **les ~s** (*à la gare, au théâtre*) the ticket office; **jouer à ~s fermés** to play to a full house.
guichetier, ière [giʃtje, -jɛʀ] *nm/f* counter clerk.
guide [gid] *nm* guide; (*livre*) guide(book) ♦ *nf* (*fille scout*) (girl) guide (*BRIT*), girl scout (*US*); **~s** *nfpl* (*d'un cheval*) reins.
guider [gide] *vt* to guide.
guidon [gidɔ̃] *nm* handlebars *pl*.
guigne [giɲ] *nf* (*fam*): **avoir la ~** to be jinxed.
guignol [giɲɔl] *nm* ≈ Punch and Judy show; (*fig*) clown.
guillemets [gijmɛ] *nmpl*: **entre ~** in inverted commas *ou* quotation marks; **~ de répétition** ditto marks.
guilleret, te [gijʀɛ, -ɛt] *adj* perky, bright.
guillotine [gijɔtin] *nf* guillotine.
guillotiner [gijɔtine] *vt* to guillotine.
guimauve [gimov] *nf* (*BOT*) marshmallow; (*fig*) sentimentality, sloppiness.
guimbarde [gɛ̃baʀd(ə)] *nf* old banger (*BRIT*), jalopy.
guindé, e [gɛ̃de] *adj* stiff, starchy.
Guinée [gine] *nf*: **la (République de) ~** (the Republic of) Guinea; **la ~ équatoriale** Equatorial Guinea.
Guinée-Bissau [ginebiso] *nf*: **la ~** Guinea-Bissau.
guinéen, ne [gineɛ̃, -ɛn] *adj* Guinean.
guingois [gɛ̃gwa]: **de ~** *adv* askew.
guinguette [gɛ̃gɛt] *nf open-air café or dance hall.*
guirlande [giʀlɑ̃d] *nf* garland; (*de papier*) paper chain; **~ lumineuse** (fairy (*BRIT*)) lights *pl*; **~ de Noël** tinsel *no pl*.
guise [giz] *nf*: **à votre ~** as you wish *ou* please; **en ~ de** by way of.
guitare [gitaʀ] *nf* guitar.
guitariste [gitaʀist(ə)] *nm/f* guitarist, guitar player.
gustatif, ive [gystatif, -iv] *adj* gustatory; *voir* **papille**.
guttural, e, aux [gytyʀal, -o] *adj* guttural.
guyanais, e [gɥijanɛ, -ɛz] *adj* Guyanese, Guyanan; (*français*) Guianese, Guianan.
Guyane [gɥijan] *nf*: **la ~** Guyana; **la ~ (française)** (French) Guiana.
gvt *abr* (= *gouvernement*) govt.
gymkhana [ʒimkana] *nm* rally; **~ motocycliste** (motorbike) scramble (*BRIT*), motocross.
gymnase [ʒimnɑz] *nm* gym(nasium).
gymnaste [ʒimnast(ə)] *nm/f* gymnast.
gymnastique [ʒimnastik] *nf* gymnastics *sg*; (*au réveil etc*) keep-fit exercises *pl*; **~ corrective** remedial gymnastics.
gynécologie [ʒinekɔlɔʒi] *nf* gynaecology (*BRIT*), gynecology (*US*).
gynécologique [ʒinekɔlɔʒik] *adj* gynaecological (*BRIT*), gynecological (*US*).
gynécologue [ʒinekɔlɔg] *nm/f* gynaecologist (*BRIT*), gynecologist (*US*).
gypse [ʒips(ə)] *nm* gypsum.
gyrophare [ʒiʀɔfaʀ] *nm* (*sur une voiture*) revolving (flashing) light.

H h

H, h [aʃ] *nm inv* H, h ♦ *abr* (= *homme*) M; (= *hydrogène*) H; (= *heure*): **à l'heure** ~ at zero hour; **bombe** ~ H bomb; **H comme Henri** H for Harry (*BRIT*) *ou* How (*US*).
ha. *abr* (= *hectare*) ha.
hab. *abr* = **habitant.**
habile [abil] *adj* skilful; (*malin*) clever.
habilement [abilmɑ̃] *adv* skilfully; cleverly.
habileté [abilte] *nf* skill, skilfulness; cleverness.
habilité, e [abilite] *adj*: ~ **à faire** entitled to do, empowered to do.
habiliter [abilite] *vt* empower, entitle.
habillage [abijaʒ] *nm* dressing.
habillé, e [abije] *adj* dressed; (*chic*) dressy; (*TECH*): ~ **de** covered with; encased in.
habillement [abijmɑ̃] *nm* clothes *pl*; (*profession*) clothing industry.
habiller [abije] *vt* to dress; (*fournir en vêtements*) to clothe; **s'**~ to dress (o.s.); (*se déguiser, mettre des vêtements chic*) to dress up; **s'**~ **de/en** to dress in/dress up as; **s'**~ **chez/à** to buy one's clothes from/at.
habilleuse [abijøz] *nf* (*CINÉ, THÉÂT*) dresser.
habit [abi] *nm* outfit; ~**s** *nmpl* (*vêtements*) clothes; ~ **(de soirée)** tails *pl*; evening dress; **prendre l'**~ (*REL: entrer en religion*) to enter (holy) orders.
habitable [abitabl(ə)] *adj* (in)habitable.
habitacle [abitakl(ə)] *nm* cockpit; (*AUTO*) passenger cell.
habitant, e [abitɑ̃, -ɑ̃t] *nm/f* inhabitant; (*d'une maison*) occupant, occupier; **loger chez l'**~ to stay with the locals.
habitat [abita] *nm* housing conditions *pl*; (*BOT, ZOOL*) habitat.
habitation [abitɑsjɔ̃] *nf* living; (*demeure*) residence, home; (*maison*) house; ~**s à loyer modéré (HLM)** *low-rent, state-owned housing*, ≈ council housing *sg* (*BRIT*), ≈ public housing units (*US*).
habité, e [abite] *adj* inhabited; lived in.
habiter [abite] *vt* to live in; (*suj: sentiment*) to dwell in ♦ *vi*: ~ **à/dans** to live in *ou* at/in; ~ **chez** *ou* **avec qn** to live with sb; ~ **16 rue Montmartre** to live at number 16 rue Montmartre; ~ **rue Montmartre** to live in rue Montmartre.
habitude [abityd] *nf* habit; **avoir l'**~ **de faire** to be in the habit of doing; **avoir l'**~ **des enfants** to be used to children; **prendre l'**~ **de faire qch** to get into the habit of doing sth; **perdre une** ~ to get out of a habit; **d'**~ usually; **comme d'**~ as usual; **par** ~ out of habit.
habitué, e [abitɥe] *adj*: **être** ~ **à** to be used *ou* accustomed to ♦ *nm/f* regular visitor; (*client*) regular (customer).
habituel, le [abitɥɛl] *adj* usual.
habituellement [abitɥɛlmɑ̃] *adv* usually.
habituer [abitɥe] *vt*: ~ **qn à** to get sb used to; **s'**~ **à** to get used to.
'hâbleur, euse ['ɑblœʀ, -øz] *adj* boastful.
'hache ['aʃ] *nf* axe.
'haché, e ['aʃe] *adj* minced (*BRIT*), ground (*US*); (*persil*) chopped; (*fig*) jerky.
'hache-légumes ['aʃlegym] *nm inv* vegetable chopper.
'hacher ['aʃe] *vt* (*viande*) to mince (*BRIT*), grind (*US*); (*persil*) to chop; ~ **menu** to mince *ou* grind finely; to chop finely.
'hachette ['aʃɛt] *nf* hatchet.
'hache-viande ['aʃvjɑ̃d] *nm inv* (meat) mincer (*BRIT*) *ou* grinder (*US*); (*couteau*) (meat) cleaver.
'hachis ['aʃi] *nm* mince *no pl* (*BRIT*), hamburger meat (*US*); ~ **de viande** minced (*BRIT*) *ou* ground (*US*) meat.
'hachisch ['aʃiʃ] *nm* hashish.
'hachoir ['aʃwaʀ] *nm* chopper; (meat) mincer (*BRIT*) *ou* grinder (*US*); (*planche*) chopping board.
'hachurer ['aʃyʀe] *vt* to hatch.
'hachures ['aʃyʀ] *nfpl* hatching *sg*.
'hagard, e ['agaʀ, -aʀd(ə)] *adj* wild, distraught.
'haie ['ɛ] *nf* hedge; (*SPORT*) hurdle; (*fig: rang*) line, row; **200 m** ~**s** 200 m hurdles; ~ **d'honneur** guard of honour.
'haillons ['ɑjɔ̃] *nmpl* rags.
'haine ['ɛn] *nf* hatred.
'haineux, euse ['ɛnø, -øz] *adj* full of hatred.
'haïr ['aiʀ] *vt* to detest, hate; **se** ~ to hate each other.
'hais ['ɛ], **'haïs** ['ai] *etc vb voir* **haïr.**
'haïssable ['aisabl(ə)] *adj* detestable.
Haïti [aiti] *n* Haiti.
haïtien, ne [aisjɛ̃, -ɛn] *adj* Haitian.
'halage ['alaʒ] *nm*: **chemin de** ~ towpath.
'hâle ['ɑl] *nm* (sun)tan.
'hâlé, e ['ɑle] *adj* (sun)tanned, sunburnt.
haleine [alɛn] *nf* breath; **perdre** ~ to get out of breath; **à perdre** ~ until one is gasping for breath; **avoir mauvaise** ~ to have bad breath; **reprendre** ~ to get one's breath back; **hors d'**~ out of breath; **tenir en** ~ to hold spellbound; (*en attente*) to keep in suspense; **de longue** ~ *adj* long-term.
'haler ['ale] *vt* to haul in; (*remorquer*) to tow.
'haleter ['alte] *vi* to pant.
'hall ['ɔl] *nm* hall.
hallali [alali] *nm* kill.
'halle ['al] *nf* (covered) market; ~**s** *nfpl* central food market *sg*.
'hallebarde ['albaʀd] *nf* halberd; **il pleut des**

~**s** (*fam*) it's bucketing down.
hallucinant, e [alysinɑ̃, -ɑ̃t] *adj* staggering.
hallucination [alysinɑsjɔ̃] *nf* hallucination.
hallucinatoire [alysinatwaʀ] *adj* hallucinatory.
halluciné, e [alysine] *nm/f* person suffering from hallucinations; (*fou*) (raving) lunatic.
hallucinogène [a(l)lysinɔʒɛn] *adj* hallucinogenic ♦ *nm* hallucinogen.
'halo ['alo] *nm* halo.
halogène [alɔʒɛn] *nm*: **lampe (à)** ~ halogen lamp.
'halte ['alt(ə)] *nf* stop, break; (*escale*) stopping place; (*RAIL*) halt ♦ *excl* stop!; **faire** ~ to stop.
'halte-garderie, *pl* **'haltes-garderies** ['altgaʀdəʀi] *nf* crèche.
haltère [altɛʀ] *nm* (*à boules, disques*) dumbbell, barbell; **(poids et)** ~**s** weightlifting.
haltérophile [alteʀɔfil] *nm/f* weightlifter.
haltérophilie [alteʀɔfili] *nf* weightlifting.
'hamac ['amak] *nm* hammock.
'Hambourg ['ɑ̃buʀ] *n* Hamburg.
'hamburger ['ɑ̃buʀgœʀ] *nm* hamburger.
'hameau, x ['amo] *nm* hamlet.
hameçon [amsɔ̃] *nm* (fish) hook.
'hampe ['ɑ̃p] *nf* (*de drapeau etc*) pole; (*de lance*) shaft.
'hamster ['amstɛʀ] *nm* hamster.
'hanche ['ɑ̃ʃ] *nf* hip.
'hand-ball ['ɑ̃dbal] *nm* handball.
'handballeur, euse ['ɑ̃dbalœʀ, -øz] *nm/f* handball player.
'handicap ['ɑ̃dikap] *nm* handicap.
'handicapé, e ['ɑ̃dikape] *adj* handicapped ♦ *nm/f* physically (*ou* mentally) handicapped person; ~ **moteur** spastic.
'handicaper ['ɑ̃dikape] *vt* to handicap.
'hangar ['ɑ̃gaʀ] *nm* shed; (*AVIAT*) hangar.
'hanneton ['antɔ̃] *nm* cockchafer.
'Hanovre ['anɔvʀ(ə)] *n* Hanover.
'hanovrien, ne ['anɔvʀjɛ̃, -ɛn] *adj* Hanoverian.
'hanter ['ɑ̃te] *vt* to haunt.
'hantise ['ɑ̃tiz] *nf* obsessive fear.
'happer ['ape] *vt* to snatch; (*suj: train etc*) to hit.
'harangue ['aʀɑ̃g] *nf* harangue.
'haranguer ['aʀɑ̃ge] *vt* to harangue.
'haras ['aʀɑ] *nm* stud farm.
'harassant, e ['aʀasɑ̃, -ɑ̃t] *adj* exhausting.
'harcèlement ['aʀsɛlmɑ̃] *nm* harassment; ~ **sexuel** sexual harassment.
'harceler ['aʀsəle] *vt* (*MIL, CHASSE*) to harass, harry; (*importuner*) to plague.
'hardes ['aʀd(ə)] *nfpl* rags.
'hardi, e ['aʀdi] *adj* bold, daring.
'hardiesse ['aʀdjɛs] *nf* audacity; **avoir la** ~ **de** to have the audacity *ou* effrontery to.
'harem ['aʀɛm] *nm* harem.
'hareng ['aʀɑ̃] *nm* herring.
'hargne ['aʀɲ(ə)] *nf* aggressivity, aggressiveness.
'hargneusement ['aʀɲøzmɑ̃] *adv* belligerently, aggressively.
'hargneux, -euse ['aʀɲø, -øz] *adj* (*propos, personne*) belligerent, aggressive; (*chien*) fierce.
'haricot ['aʀiko] *nm* bean; ~ **blanc/rouge** haricot/kidney bean; ~ **vert** French (*BRIT*) *ou* green bean.
harmonica [aʀmɔnika] *nm* mouth organ.
harmonie [aʀmɔni] *nf* harmony.
harmonieux, euse [aʀmɔnjø, -øz] *adj* harmonious.
harmonique [aʀmɔnik] *adj, nm ou nf* harmonic.
harmoniser [aʀmɔnize] *vt* to harmonize; **s'**~ (*couleurs, teintes*) to go well together.
harmonium [aʀmɔnjɔm] *nm* harmonium.
'harnaché, e ['aʀnaʃe] *adj* (*fig*) rigged out.
'harnachement ['aʀnaʃmɑ̃] *nm* (*habillement*) rig-out; (*équipement*) harness, equipment.
'harnacher ['aʀnaʃe] *vt* to harness.
'harnais ['aʀnɛ] *nm* harness.
'haro ['aʀo] *nm*: **crier** ~ **sur qn/qch** to inveigh against sb/sth.
'harpe ['aʀp(ə)] *nf* harp.
'harpie ['aʀpi] *nf* harpy.
'harpiste ['aʀpist(ə)] *nm/f* harpist.
'harpon ['aʀpɔ̃] *nm* harpoon.
'harponner ['aʀpɔne] *vt* to harpoon; (*fam*) to collar.
'hasard ['azaʀ] *nm*: **le** ~ chance, fate; **un** ~ a coincidence; (*aubaine, chance*) a stroke of luck; **au** ~ (*sans but*) aimlessly; (*à l'aveuglette*) at random, haphazardly; **par** ~ by chance; **comme par** ~ as if by chance; **à tout** ~ on the off chance; (*en cas de besoin*) just in case.
'hasarder ['azaʀde] *vt* (*mot*) to venture; (*fortune*) to risk; **se** ~ **à faire** to risk doing, venture to do.
'hasardeux, euse ['azaʀdø, -øz] *adj* hazardous, risky; (*hypothèse*) rash.
'haschisch ['aʃiʃ] *nm* hashish.
'hâte ['ɑt] *nf* haste; **à la** ~ hurriedly, hastily; **en** ~ posthaste, with all possible speed; **avoir** ~ **de** to be eager *ou* anxious to.
'hâter ['ɑte] *vt* to hasten; **se** ~ to hurry; **se** ~ **de** to hurry *ou* hasten to.
'hâtif, ive ['ɑtif, -iv] *adj* (*travail*) hurried; (*décision*) hasty; (*légume*) early.
'hâtivement ['ɑtivmɑ̃] *adv* hurriedly; hastily.
'hauban ['obɑ̃] *nm* (*NAVIG*) shroud.
'hausse ['os] *nf* rise, increase; (*de fusil*) backsight adjuster; **à la** ~ upwards; **en** ~ rising.
'hausser ['ose] *vt* to raise; ~ **les épaules** to shrug (one's shoulders); **se** ~ **sur la pointe des pieds** to stand (up) on tiptoe *ou* tippytoe (*US*).
'haut, e ['o, 'ot] *adj* high; (*grand*) tall; (*son, voix*) high(-pitched) ♦ *adv* high ♦ *nm* top (part); **de 3 m de** ~, ~ **de 3 m** 3 m high, 3 m in height; **en** ~**e montagne** high up in the mountains; **en** ~ **lieu** in high places; **à** ~**e**

voix, (tout) ~ aloud, out loud; **des ~s et des bas** ups and downs; **du ~ de** from the top of; **tomber de** ~ to fall from a height; (*fig*) to have one's hopes dashed; **dire qch bien** ~ to say sth plainly; **prendre qch de (très)** ~ to react haughtily to sth; **traiter qn de** ~ to treat sb with disdain; **de ~ en bas** from top to bottom; downwards; ~ **en couleur** (*chose*) highly coloured; (*personne*): **un personnage ~ en couleur** a colourful character; **plus** ~ higher up, further up; (*dans un texte*) above; (*parler*) louder; **en** ~ up above; at (*ou* to) the top; (*dans une maison*) upstairs; **en ~ de** at the top of; ~ **les mains!** hands up!, stick 'em up!; **la ~e couture/coiffure** haute couture/ coiffure; **~e fidélité** hi-fi, high fidelity; **la ~e finance** high finance; **~e trahison** high treason.

'hautain, e ['otɛ̃, -ɛn] *adj* (*personne, regard*) haughty.

'hautbois ['obwɑ] *nm* oboe.

'hautboïste ['obɔist(ə)] *nm/f* oboist.

'haut-de-forme, *pl* **'hauts-de-forme** ['odfɔʀm(ə)] *nm* top hat.

'haute-contre, *pl* **'hautes-contre** ['otkɔ̃tʀ(ə)] *nf* counter-tenor.

'hautement ['otmɑ̃] *adv* (*ouvertement*) openly; (*supérieurement*): ~ **qualifié** highly qualified.

'hauteur ['otœʀ] *nf* height; (*GÉO*) height, hill; (*fig*) loftiness; haughtiness; **à ~ de** up to (the level of); **à ~ des yeux** at eye level; **à la ~ de** (*sur la même ligne*) level with; by; (*fig*) equal to; **à la** ~ (*fig*) up to it, equal to the task.

'Haute-Volta ['otvɔlta] *nf*: **la** ~ Upper Volta.

'haut-fond, *pl* **'hauts-fonds** ['ofɔ̃] *nm* shallow.

'haut-fourneau, *pl* **'hauts-fourneaux** ['ofuʀno] *nm* blast *ou* smelting furnace.

'haut-le-cœur ['olkœʀ] *nm inv* retch, heave.

'haut-le-corps ['olkɔʀ] *nm inv* start, jump.

'haut-parleur, *pl* **'haut-parleurs** ['opaʀlœʀ] *nm* (loud)speaker.

'hauturier, ière ['otyʀje, -jɛʀ] *adj* (*NAVIG*) deep-sea.

'havanais, e ['avanɛ, -ɛz] *adj* of *ou* from Havana.

'Havane ['avan] *nf*: **la** ~ Havana ♦ *nm*: **'h~** (*cigare*) Havana.

'hâve ['ɑv] *adj* gaunt.

'havrais, e ['ɑvʀɛ, -ɛz] *adj* of *ou* from Le Havre.

'havre ['ɑvʀ(ə)] *nm* haven.

'havresac ['ɑvʀəsak] *nm* haversack.

Hawaï [awai] *n* Hawaii; **les îles** ~ the Hawaiian Islands.

hawaïen, ne [awajɛ̃, -ɛn] *adj* Hawaiian ♦ *nm* (*LING*) Hawaiian.

'Haye ['ɛ] *n*: **la** ~ the Hague.

'hayon ['ɛjɔ̃] *nm* tailgate.

HCR *sigle m* (= *Haut-Commissariat des Nations unies pour les réfugiés*) UNHCR.

hdb. *abr* (= *heures de bureau*) o.h. (= *office hours*).

'hé ['e] *excl* hey!

hebdo [ɛbdo] *nm* (*fam*) weekly.

hebdomadaire [ɛbdɔmadɛʀ] *adj, nm* weekly.

hébergement [ebɛʀʒəmɑ̃] *nm* accommodation, lodging; taking in.

héberger [ebɛʀʒe] *vt* to accommodate, lodge; (*réfugiés*) to take in.

hébergeur [ebɛʀʒœʀ] *nm* (*COMPUT*) host.

hébété, e [ebete] *adj* dazed.

hébétude [ebetyd] *nf* stupor.

hébraïque [ebʀaik] *adj* Hebrew, Hebraic.

hébreu, x [ebʀø] *adj m, nm* Hebrew.

Hébrides [ebʀid] *nf*: **les** ~ the Hebrides.

HEC *sigle fpl* (= *École des hautes études commerciales*) *grande école for management and business studies.*

hécatombe [ekatɔ̃b] *nf* slaughter.

hectare [ɛktaʀ] *nm* hectare, 10,000 square metres.

hecto... [ɛkto] *préfixe* hecto....

hectolitre [ɛktɔlitʀ(ə)] *nm* hectolitre.

hédoniste [edɔnist(ə)] *adj* hedonistic.

hégémonie [eʒemɔni] *nf* hegemony.

'hein ['ɛ̃] *excl* eh?; (*sollicitant l'approbation*): **tu m'approuves,** ~? so I did the right thing then?; **Paul est venu,** ~? Paul came, did he?; **que fais-tu,** ~? hey! what are you doing?

'hélas ['elɑs] *excl* alas! ♦ *adv* unfortunately.

'héler ['ele] *vt* to hail.

hélice [elis] *nf* propeller.

hélicoïdal, e, aux [elikɔidal, -o] *adj* helical; helicoid.

hélicoptère [elikɔptɛʀ] *nm* helicopter.

hélio(gravure) [eljɔgʀavyʀ] *nf* heliogravure.

héliomarin, e [eljɔmaʀɛ̃, -in] *adj*: **centre** ~ *centre offering sea and sun therapy.*

héliotrope [eljɔtʀɔp] *nm* (*BOT*) heliotrope.

héliport [elipɔʀ] *nm* heliport.

héliporté, e [elipɔʀte] *adj* transported by helicopter.

hélium [eljɔm] *nm* helium.

hellénique [elenik] *adj* Hellenic.

hellénisant, e [elenizɑ̃, -ɑ̃t], **helléniste** [elenist(ə)] *nm/f* hellenist.

Helsinki [ɛlzinki] *n* Helsinki.

helvète [ɛlvɛt] *adj* Helvetian ♦ *nm/f*: **H~** Helvetian.

Helvétie [ɛlvesi] *nf*: **la** ~ Helvetia.

helvétique [ɛlvetik] *adj* Swiss.

hématologie [ematɔlɔʒi] *nf* haematology.

hématome [ematom] *nm* haematoma.

hémicycle [emisikl(ə)] *nm* semicircle; (*POL*): **l'~** *the benches (in French parliament).*

hémiplégie [emipleʒi] *nf* paralysis of one side, hemiplegia.

hémisphère [emisfɛʀ] *nf*: ~ **nord/sud** northern/southern hemisphere.

hémisphérique [emisfeʀik] *adj* hemispherical.

hémoglobine [emɔglɔbin] *nf* haemoglobin

(*BRIT*), hemoglobin (*US*).
hémophile [emɔfil] *adj* haemophiliac (*BRIT*), hemophiliac (*US*).
hémophilie [emɔfili] *nf* haemophilia (*BRIT*), hemophilia (*US*).
hémorragie [emɔʀaʒi] *nf* bleeding *no pl*, haemorrhage (*BRIT*), hemorrhage (*US*); ~ **cérébrale** cerebral haemorrhage; ~ **interne** internal bleeding *ou* haemorrhage.
hémorroïdes [emɔʀɔid] *nfpl* piles, haemorrhoids (*BRIT*), hemorrhoids (*US*).
hémostatique [emɔstatik] *adj* haemostatic (*BRIT*), hemostatic (*US*).
'henné ['ene] *nm* henna.
'hennir ['eniʀ] *vi* to neigh, whinny.
'hennissement ['enismɑ̃] *nm* neighing, whinnying.
'hep ['ɛp] *excl* hey!
hépatite [epatit] *nf* hepatitis, liver infection.
héraldique [eʀaldik] *adj* heraldry.
herbacé, e [ɛʀbase] *adj* herbaceous.
herbage [ɛʀbaʒ] *nm* pasture.
herbe [ɛʀb(ə)] *nf* grass; (*CULIN, MÉD*) herb; **en** ~ unripe; (*fig*) budding; **touffe/brin d'**~ clump/blade of grass.
herbeux, euse [ɛʀbø, -øz] *adj* grassy.
herbicide [ɛʀbisid] *nm* weed-killer.
herbier [ɛʀbje] *nm* herbarium.
herbivore [ɛʀbivɔʀ] *nm* herbivore.
herboriser [ɛʀbɔʀize] *vi* to collect plants.
herboriste [ɛʀbɔʀist(ə)] *nm/f* herbalist.
herboristerie [ɛʀbɔʀistʀi] *nf* (*magasin*) herbalist's shop; (*commerce*) herb trade.
herculéen, ne [ɛʀkyleɛ̃, -ɛn] *adj* (*fig*) herculean.
'hère ['ɛʀ] *nm*: **pauvre** ~ poor wretch.
héréditaire [eʀeditɛʀ] *adj* hereditary.
hérédité [eʀedite] *nf* heredity.
hérésie [eʀezi] *nf* heresy.
hérétique [eʀetik] *nm/f* heretic.
'hérissé, e ['eʀise] *adj* bristling; ~ **de** spiked with; (*fig*) bristling with.
'hérisser ['eʀise] *vt*: ~ **qn** (*fig*) to ruffle sb; **se** ~ *vi* to bristle, bristle up.
'hérisson ['eʀisɔ̃] *nm* hedgehog.
héritage [eʀitaʒ] *nm* inheritance; (*fig*) heritage; (*: legs*) legacy; **faire un (petit)** ~ to come into (a little) money.
hériter [eʀite] *vi*: ~ **de qch (de qn)** to inherit sth (from sb); ~ **de qn** to inherit sb's property.
héritier, ière [eʀitje, -jɛʀ] *nm/f* heir/heiress.
hermaphrodite [ɛʀmafʀɔdit] *adj* (*BOT, ZOOL*) hermaphrodite.
hermétique [ɛʀmetik] *adj* (*à l'air*) airtight; (*à l'eau*) watertight; (*fig: écrivain, style*) abstruse; (*: visage*) impenetrable.
hermétiquement [ɛʀmetikmɑ̃] *adv* hermetically.
hermine [ɛʀmin] *nf* ermine.
'hernie ['ɛʀni] *nf* hernia.
héroïne [eʀɔin] *nf* heroine; (*drogue*) heroin.
héroïnomane [eʀɔinɔman] *nm/f* heroin addict.
héroïque [eʀɔik] *adj* heroic.
héroïquement [eʀɔikmɑ̃] *adv* heroically.
héroïsme [eʀɔism(ə)] *nm* heroism.
'héron ['eʀɔ̃] *nm* heron.
'héros ['eʀo] *nm* hero.
herpès [ɛʀpɛs] *nm* herpes.
'herse ['ɛʀs(ə)] *nf* harrow; (*de château*) portcullis.
hertz [ɛʀts] *nm* (*ÉLEC*) hertz.
hertzien, ne [ɛʀtsjɛ̃, -ɛn] *adj* (*ÉLEC*) Hertzian.
hésitant, e [ezitɑ̃, -ɑ̃t] *adj* hesitant.
hésitation [ezitɑsjɔ̃] *nf* hesitation.
hésiter [ezite] *vi*: ~ **(à faire)** to hesitate (to do); ~ **sur qch** to hesitate over sth.
hétéro [eteʀo] *adj inv* (= *hétérosexuel(le)*) hetero.
hétéroclite [eteʀɔklit] *adj* heterogeneous; (*objets*) sundry.
hétérogène [eteʀɔʒɛn] *adj* heterogeneous.
hétérosexuel, le [eteʀɔsɛksɥɛl] *adj* heterosexual.
'hêtre ['ɛtʀ(ə)] *nm* beech.
heure [œʀ] *nf* hour; (*SCOL*) period; (*moment, moment fixé*) time; **c'est l'**~ it's time; **pourriez-vous me donner l'**~**, s'il vous plaît?** could you tell me the time, please?; **quelle** ~ **est-il?** what time is it?; **2** ~**s (du matin)** 2 o'clock (in the morning); **à la bonne** ~**!** (*parfois ironique*) splendid!; **être à l'**~ to be on time; (*montre*) to be right; **le bus passe à l'**~ the bus runs on the hour; **mettre à l'**~ to set right; **100 km à l'**~ ≈ 60 miles an *ou* per hour; **à toute** ~ at any time; **24** ~**s sur 24** round the clock, 24 hours a day; **à l'**~ **qu'il est** at this time (of day); (*fig*) now; **à l'**~ **actuelle** at the present time; **sur l'**~ at once; **pour l'**~ for the time being; **d'**~ **en** ~ from one hour to the next; (*régulièrement*) hourly; **d'une** ~ **à l'autre** from hour to hour; **de bonne** ~ early; **2** ~**s de marche/travail** 2 hours' walking/work; **une** ~ **d'arrêt** an hour's break *ou* stop; ~ **d'été** summer time (*BRIT*), daylight saving time (*US*); ~ **de pointe** rush hour; ~**s de bureau** office hours; ~**s supplémentaires** overtime *sg*.
heureusement [œʀøzmɑ̃] *adv* (*par bonheur*) fortunately, luckily; ~ **que** ... it's a good job that ..., fortunately ....
heureux, euse [œʀø, -øz] *adj* happy; (*chanceux*) lucky, fortunate; (*judicieux*) felicitous, fortunate; **être** ~ **de qch** to be pleased *ou* happy about sth; **être** ~ **de faire/que** to be pleased *ou* happy to do/that; **s'estimer** ~ **de qch/que** to consider o.s. fortunate with/that; **encore** ~ **que** ... just as well that ....
'heurt ['œʀ] *nm* (*choc*) collision; ~**s** *nmpl* (*fig*) clashes.
'heurté, e ['œʀte] *adj* (*fig*) jerky, uneven; (*: couleurs*) clashing.
'heurter ['œʀte] *vt* (*mur*) to strike, hit; (*personne*) to collide with; (*fig*) to go against, up-

set; **se ~** (*couleurs, tons*) to clash; **se ~ à** to collide with; (*fig*) to come up against; **~ qn de front** to clash head-on with sb.

'heurtoir ['œʀtwaʀ] *nm* door knocker.

hévéa [evea] *nm* rubber tree.

hexagonal, e, aux [ɛgzagɔnal, -o] *adj* hexagonal; (*français*) French (*see note at hexagone*).

hexagone [ɛgzagɔn] *nm* hexagon; (*la France*) France (*because of its roughly hexagonal shape*).

HF *sigle f* (= *haute fréquence*) HF.

hiatus [jatys] *nm* hiatus.

hibernation [ibɛʀnɑsjɔ̃] *nf* hibernation.

hiberner [ibɛʀne] *vi* to hibernate.

hibiscus [ibiskys] *nm* hibiscus.

'hibou, x ['ibu] *nm* owl.

'hic ['ik] *nm* (*fam*) snag.

'hideusement ['idøzmɑ̃] *adv* hideously.

'hideux, euse ['idø, -øz] *adj* hideous.

hier [jɛʀ] *adv* yesterday; **~ matin/soir/midi** yesterday morning/evening/at midday; **toute la journée d'~** all day yesterday; **toute la matinée d'~** all yesterday morning.

'hiérarchie ['jeʀaʀʃi] *nf* hierarchy.

'hiérarchique ['jeʀaʀʃik] *adj* hierarchic.

'hiérarchiquement ['jeʀaʀʃikmɑ̃] *adv* hierarchically.

'hiérarchiser ['jeʀaʀʃize] *vt* to organize into a hierarchy.

'hiéroglyphe ['jeʀɔglif] *nm* hieroglyphic.

'hiéroglyphique ['jeʀɔglifik] *adj* hieroglyphic.

'hi-fi ['ifi] *nf inv* hi-fi.

hilarant, e [ilaʀɑ̃, -ɑ̃t] *adj* hilarious.

hilare [ilaʀ] *adj* mirthful.

hilarité [ilaʀite] *nf* hilarity, mirth.

Himalaya [imalaja] *nm*: **l'~** the Himalayas *pl*.

himalayen, ne [imalajɛ̃, -ɛn] *adj* Himalayan.

hindou, e [ɛ̃du] *adj, nm/f* Hindu; (*Indien*) Indian.

hindouisme [ɛ̃duism(ə)] *nm* Hinduism.

Hindoustan [ɛ̃dustɑ̃] *nm*: **l'~** Hindustan.

'hippie ['ipi] *nm/f* hippy.

hippique [ipik] *adj* equestrian, horse *cpd*.

hippisme [ipism(ə)] *nm* (horse-)riding.

hippocampe [ipɔkɑ̃p] *nm* sea horse.

hippodrome [ipɔdʀom] *nm* racecourse.

hippophagique [ipɔfaʒik] *adj*: **boucherie ~** horse butcher's.

hippopotame [ipɔpɔtam] *nm* hippopotamus.

hirondelle [iʀɔ̃dɛl] *nf* swallow.

hirsute [iʀsyt] *adj* (*personne*) hairy; (*barbe*) shaggy; (*tête*) tousled.

hispanique [ispanik] *adj* Hispanic.

hispanisant, e [ispanizɑ̃, -ɑ̃t], **hispaniste** [ispanist(ə)] *nm/f* Hispanist.

hispano-américain, e [ispanoameʀikɛ̃, -ɛn] *adj* Spanish-American.

hispano-arabe [ispanoaʀab] *adj* Hispano-Moresque.

'hisser ['ise] *vt* to hoist, haul up; **se ~ sur** to haul o.s. up onto.

histoire [istwaʀ] *nf* (*science, événements*) history; (*anecdote, récit, mensonge*) story; (*affaire*) business *no pl*; (*chichis: gén pl*) fuss *no pl*; **~s** *nfpl* (*ennuis*) trouble *sg*; **l'~ de France** French history, the history of France; **l'~ sainte** biblical history; **une ~ de** (*fig*) a question of.

histologie [istɔlɔʒi] *nf* histology.

historien, ne [istɔʀjɛ̃, -ɛn] *nm/f* historian.

historique [istɔʀik] *adj* historical; (*important*) historic ♦ *nm* (*exposé, récit*): **faire l'~ de** to give the background to.

historiquement [istɔʀikmɑ̃] *adv* historically.

'hit-parade ['itpaʀad] *nm*: **le ~** the charts.

HIV *sigle m* (= *human immunodeficiency virus*) HIV.

hiver [ivɛʀ] *nm* winter; **en ~** in winter.

hivernal, e, aux [ivɛʀnal, -o] *adj* (*de l'hiver*) winter *cpd*; (*comme en hiver*) wintry.

hivernant, e [ivɛʀnɑ̃, -ɑ̃t] *n* winter holiday-maker.

hiverner [ivɛʀne] *vi* to winter.

HLM *sigle m ou f* (= *habitations à loyer modéré*) *low-rent, state-owned housing*; **un(e) ~** ≈ a council flat (*ou* house) (*BRIT*), ≈ a public housing unit (*US*).

Hme *abr* (= *homme*) M.

HO *abr* (= *hors œuvre*) labour not included (*on invoices*).

'hobby ['ɔbi] *nm* hobby.

'hochement ['ɔʃmɑ̃] *nm*: **~ de tête** nod; shake of the head.

'hocher ['ɔʃe] *vt*: **~ la tête** to nod; (*signe négatif ou dubitatif*) to shake one's head.

'hochet ['ɔʃɛ] *nm* rattle.

'hockey ['ɔkɛ] *nm*: **~ (sur glace/gazon)** (ice/field) hockey.

'hockeyeur, euse ['ɔkɛjœʀ, -øz] *nm/f* hockey player.

'holà ['ɔla] *nm*: **mettre le ~ à qch** to put a stop to sth.

'holding ['ɔldiŋ] *nm* holding company.

'hold-up ['ɔldœp] *nm inv* hold-up.

'hollandais, e ['ɔlɑ̃dɛ, -ɛz] *adj* Dutch ♦ *nm* (*LING*) Dutch ♦ *nm/f*: **H~, e** Dutchman/woman; **les H~** the Dutch.

'Hollande ['ɔlɑ̃d] *nf*: **la ~** Holland ♦ *nm*: **h~** (*fromage*) Dutch cheese.

holocauste [ɔlɔkost(ə)] *nm* holocaust.

hologramme [ɔlɔgʀam] *nm* hologram.

'homard ['ɔmaʀ] *nm* lobster.

homéopathe [ɔmeɔpat] *n* homoeopath.

homéopathie [ɔmeɔpati] *nf* homoeopathy.

homéopathique [ɔmeɔpatik] *adj* homoeopathic.

homérique [ɔmeʀik] *adj* Homeric.

homicide [ɔmisid] *nm* murder ♦ *nm/f* murderer/eress; **~ involontaire** manslaughter.

hommage [ɔmaʒ] *nm* tribute; **~s** *nmpl*: **présenter ses ~s** to pay one's respects; **rendre ~ à** to pay tribute *ou* homage to; **en ~ de** as a token of; **faire ~ de qch à qn** to present sb with sth.

homme [ɔm] *nm* man; (*espèce humaine*): **l'~** man, mankind; **~ d'affaires** businessman; **~ des cavernes** caveman; **~ d'Église** churchman, clergyman; **~ d'État** statesman; **~ de loi** lawyer; **~ de main** hired man; **~ de paille** stooge; **l'~ de la rue** the man in the street; **~ à tout faire** odd-job man.

homme-grenouille, *pl* **hommes-grenouilles** [ɔmgʀənuj] *nm* frogman.

homme-orchestre, *pl* **hommes-orchestres** [ɔmɔʀkɛstʀ(ə)] *nm* one-man band.

homme-sandwich, *pl* **hommes-sandwichs** [ɔmsɑ̃dwitʃ] *nm* sandwich (board) man.

homo [ɔmo] *adj, nm/f* = **homosexuel.**

homogène [ɔmɔʒɛn] *adj* homogeneous.

homogénéisé, e [ɔmɔʒeneize] *adj*: **lait ~** homogenized milk.

homogénéité [ɔmɔʒeneite] *nf* homogeneity.

homologation [ɔmɔlɔgɑsjɔ̃] *nf* ratification; official recognition.

homologue [ɔmɔlɔg] *nm/f* counterpart, opposite number.

homologué, e [ɔmɔlɔge] *adj* (*SPORT*) officially recognized, ratified; (*tarif*) authorized.

homologuer [ɔmɔlɔge] *vt* (*JUR*) to ratify; (*SPORT*) to recognize officially, ratify.

homonyme [ɔmɔnim] *nm* (*LING*) homonym; (*d'une personne*) namesake.

homosexualité [ɔmɔsɛksɥalite] *nf* homosexuality.

homosexuel, le [ɔmɔsɛksɥɛl] *adj* homosexual.

'Honduras ['ɔ̃dyʀas] *nm*: **le ~** Honduras.

'hondurien, ne ['ɔ̃dyʀjɛ̃, -ɛn] *adj* Honduran.

'Hong-Kong ['ɔ̃gkɔ̃g] *n* Hong Kong.

'hongre ['ɔ̃gʀ(ə)] *adj* (*cheval*) gelded ♦ *nm* gelding.

'Hongrie ['ɔ̃gʀi] *nf*: **la ~** Hungary.

'hongrois, e ['ɔ̃gʀwa, -waz] *adj* Hungarian ♦ *nm* (*LING*) Hungarian ♦ *nm/f*: **'H~, e** Hungarian.

honnête [ɔnɛt] *adj* (*intègre*) honest; (*juste, satisfaisant*) fair.

honnêtement [ɔnɛtmɑ̃] *adv* honestly.

honnêteté [ɔnɛtte] *nf* honesty.

honneur [ɔnœʀ] *nm* honour; (*mérite*): **l'~ lui revient** the credit is his; **à qui ai-je l'~?** to whom have I the pleasure of speaking?; **"j'ai l'~ de ..."** "I have the honour of ..."; **en l'~ de** (*personne*) in honour of; (*événement*) on the occasion of; **faire ~ à** (*engagements*) to honour; (*famille, professeur*) to be a credit to; (*fig: repas etc*) to do justice to; **être à l'~** to be in the place of honour; **être en ~** to be in favour; **membre d'~** honorary member; **table d'~** top table.

Honolulu [ɔnɔlyly] *n* Honolulu.

honorable [ɔnɔʀabl(ə)] *adj* worthy, honourable; (*suffisant*) decent.

honorablement [ɔnɔʀabləmɑ̃] *adv* honourably; decently.

honoraire [ɔnɔʀɛʀ] *adj* honorary; **~s** *nmpl* fees; **professeur ~** professor emeritus.

honorer [ɔnɔʀe] *vt* to honour; (*estimer*) to hold in high regard; (*faire honneur à*) to do credit to; **~ qn de** to honour sb with; **s'~ de** to pride o.s. upon.

honorifique [ɔnɔʀifik] *adj* honorary.

'honte ['ɔ̃t] *nf* shame; **avoir ~ de** to be ashamed of; **faire ~ à qn** to make sb (feel) ashamed.

'honteusement ['ɔ̃tøzmɑ̃] *adv* ashamedly; shamefully.

'honteux, euse ['ɔ̃tø, -øz] *adj* ashamed; (*conduite, acte*) shameful, disgraceful.

hôpital, aux [ɔpital, -o] *nm* hospital.

'hoquet ['ɔkɛ] *nm* hiccough; **avoir le ~** to have (the) hiccoughs.

'hoqueter ['ɔkte] *vi* to hiccough.

horaire [ɔʀɛʀ] *adj* hourly ♦ *nm* timetable, schedule; **~s** *nmpl* (*heures de travail*) hours; **~ flexible** *ou* **mobile** *ou* **à la carte** *ou* **souple** flex(i)time.

'horde ['ɔʀd(ə)] *nf* horde.

'horions ['ɔʀjɔ̃] *nmpl* blows.

horizon [ɔʀizɔ̃] *nm* horizon; (*paysage*) landscape, view; **sur l'~** on the skyline *ou* horizon.

horizontal, e, aux [ɔʀizɔ̃tal, -o] *adj* horizontal ♦ *nf*: **à l'~e** on the horizontal.

horizontalement [ɔʀizɔ̃talmɑ̃] *adv* horizontally.

horloge [ɔʀlɔʒ] *nf* clock; **l'~ parlante** the speaking clock; **~ normande** grandfather clock; **~ physiologique** biological clock.

horloger, ère [ɔʀlɔʒe, -ɛʀ] *nm/f* watchmaker; clockmaker.

horlogerie [ɔʀlɔʒʀi] *nf* watchmaking; watchmaker's (shop); clockmaker's (shop); **pièces d'~** watch parts *ou* components.

'hormis ['ɔʀmi] *prép* save.

hormonal, e, aux [ɔʀmɔnal, -o] *adj* hormonal.

hormone [ɔʀmɔn] *nf* hormone.

horodaté, e [ɔʀɔdate] *adj* (*ticket*) time- and date-stamped; (*stationnement*) pay and display.

horodateur, trice [ɔʀɔdatœʀ, -tʀis] *adj* (*appareil*) for stamping the time and date ♦ *nm/f* (parking) ticket machine.

horoscope [ɔʀɔskɔp] *nm* horoscope.

horreur [ɔʀœʀ] *nf* horror; **avoir ~ de** to loathe, detest; **quelle ~!** how awful!; **cela me fait ~** I find that awful.

horrible [ɔʀibl(ə)] *adj* horrible.

horriblement [ɔʀibləmɑ̃] *adv* horribly.

horrifiant, e [ɔʀifjɑ̃, -ɑ̃t] *adj* horrifying.

horrifier [ɔʀifje] *vt* to horrify.

horrifique [ɔʀifik] *adj* horrific.

horripilant, e [ɔʀipilɑ̃, -ɑ̃t] *adj* exasperating.

horripiler [ɔʀipile] *vt* to exasperate.

'hors ['ɔʀ] *prép* except (for); **~ de** out of; **~ ligne, ~ pair** outstanding; **~ de propos** inopportune; **~ série** (*sur mesure*) made-to-order; (*exceptionnel*) exceptional; **~ service (HS), ~**

d'usage out of service; **être ~ de soi** to be beside o.s.
'hors-bord ['ɔRbɔR] *nm inv* outboard motor; (*canot*) speedboat (with outboard motor).
'hors-concours ['ɔRkɔ̃kuR] *adj inv* ineligible to compete; (*fig*) in a class of one's own.
'hors-d'œuvre ['ɔRdœvR(ə)] *nm inv* hors d'œuvre.
'hors-jeu ['ɔRʒø] *nm inv* being offside *no pl.*
'hors-la-loi ['ɔRlalwa] *nm inv* outlaw.
'hors-piste(s) ['ɔRpist] *nm inv* (*SKI*) cross-country.
hors-taxe [ɔRtaks] *adj* (*sur une facture, prix*) excluding VAT; (*boutique, marchandises*) duty-free.
'hors-texte ['ɔRtɛkst(ə)] *nm inv* plate.
hortensia [ɔRtɑ̃sja] *nm* hydrangea.
horticole [ɔRtikɔl] *adj* horticultural.
horticulteur, trice [ɔRtikyltœR, -tRis] *nm/f* horticulturalist (*BRIT*), horticulturist (*US*).
horticulture [ɔRtikyltyR] *nf* horticulture.
hospice [ɔspis] *nm* (*de vieillards*) home; (*asile*) hospice.
hospitalier, ière [ɔspitalje, -jɛR] *adj* (*accueillant*) hospitable; (*MÉD: service, centre*) hospital *cpd.*
hospitalisation [ɔspitalizɑsjɔ̃] *nf* hospitalization.
hospitaliser [ɔspitalize] *vt* to take (*ou* send) to hospital, hospitalize.
hospitalité [ɔspitalite] *nf* hospitality.
hospitalo-universitaire [ɔspitalɔynivɛRsitɛR] *adj*: **centre ~ (CHU)** ≈ (teaching) hospital.
hostie [ɔsti] *nf* host (*REL*).
hostile [ɔstil] *adj* hostile.
hostilité [ɔstilite] *nf* hostility; **~s** *nfpl* hostilities.
hôte [ot] *nm* (*maître de maison*) host; (*client*) patron; (*fig*) inhabitant, occupant ♦ *nm/f* (*invité*) guest; **~ payant** paying guest.
hôtel [otɛl] *nm* hotel; **aller à l'~** to stay in a hotel; **~ (particulier)** (private) mansion; **~ de ville** town hall.
hôtelier, ière [otəlje, -jɛR] *adj* hotel *cpd* ♦ *nm/f* hotelier, hotel-keeper.
hôtellerie [otɛlRi] *nf* (*profession*) hotel business; (*auberge*) inn.
hôtesse [otɛs] *nf* hostess; **~ de l'air** air hostess (*BRIT*) *ou* stewardess; **~ (d'accueil)** receptionist.
'hotte ['ɔt] *nf* (*panier*) basket (*carried on the back*); (*de cheminée*) hood; **~ aspirante** cooker hood.
'houblon ['ublɔ̃] *nm* (*BOT*) hop; (*pour la bière*) hops *pl.*
'houe ['u] *nf* hoe.
'houille ['uj] *nf* coal; **~ blanche** hydroelectric power.
'houiller, ère ['uje, -ɛR] *adj* coal *cpd*; (*terrain*) coal-bearing ♦ *nf* coal mine.
'houle ['ul] *nf* swell.
'houlette ['ulɛt] *nf*: **sous la ~ de** under the guidance of.
'houleux, euse ['ulø, -øz] *adj* heavy, swelling; (*fig*) stormy, turbulent.
'houppe ['up] *nf*, **'houppette** ['upɛt] *nf* powder puff; (*cheveux*) tuft.
'hourra ['uRa] *nm* cheer ♦ *excl* hurrah!
'houspiller ['uspije] *vt* to scold.
'housse ['us] *nf* cover; (*pour protéger provisoirement*) dust cover; (*pour recouvrir à neuf*) loose *ou* stretch cover; **~ (penderie)** hanging wardrobe.
'houx ['u] *nm* holly.
HS *abr* = **hors service.**
HT *abr* = **hors taxe.**
'hublot ['yblo] *nm* porthole.
'huche ['yʃ] *nf*: **~ à pain** bread bin.
'huées ['ɥe] *nfpl* boos.
'huer ['ɥe] *vt* to boo; (*hibou, chouette*) to hoot.
huile [ɥil] *nf* oil; (*ART*) oil painting; (*fam*) bigwig; **mer d'~** (*très calme*) glassy sea, sea of glass; **faire tache d'~** (*fig*) to spread; **~ d'arachide** groundnut oil; **~ essentielle** essential oil; **~ de foie de morue** cod-liver oil; **~ de ricin** castor oil; **~ solaire** suntan oil; **~ de table** salad oil.
huiler [ɥile] *vt* to oil.
huilerie [ɥilRi] *nf* (*usine*) oil-works.
huileux, euse [ɥilø, -øz] *adj* oily.
huilier [ɥilje] *nm* (oil and vinegar) cruet.
huis [ɥi] *nm*: **à ~ clos** in camera.
huissier [ɥisje] *nm* usher; (*JUR*) ≈ bailiff.
'huit ['ɥi(t)] *num* eight; **samedi en ~** a week on Saturday; **dans ~ jours** in a week('s time).
'huitaine ['ɥitɛn] *nf*: **une ~ de** about eight, eight or so; **une ~ de jours** a week or so.
'huitante ['ɥitɑ̃t] *num* (*Suisse*) eighty.
'huitième ['ɥitjɛm] *num* eighth.
huître [ɥitR(ə)] *nf* oyster.
'hululement ['ylylmɑ̃] *nm* hooting.
'hululer ['ylyle] *vi* to hoot.
humain, e [ymɛ̃, -ɛn] *adj* human; (*compatissant*) humane ♦ *nm* human (being).
humainement [ymɛnmɑ̃] *adv* humanly; humanely.
humanisation [ymanizɑsjɑ̃] *nf* humanization.
humaniser [ymanize] *vt* to humanize.
humaniste [ymanist(ə)] *nm/f* (*LING*) classicist; humanist.
humanitaire [ymanitɛR] *adj* humanitarian.
humanitarisme [ymanitaRism(ə)] *nm* humanitarianism.
humanité [ymanite] *nf* humanity.
humanoïde [ymanɔid] *nm/f* humanoid.
humble [œ̃bl(ə)] *adj* humble.
humblement [œ̃bləmɑ̃] *adv* humbly.
humecter [ymɛkte] *vt* to dampen; **s'~ les lèvres** to moisten one's lips.
'humer ['yme] *vt* to inhale; (*pour sentir*) to smell.
humérus [ymeRys] *nm* (*ANAT*) humerus.
humeur [ymœR] *nf* mood; (*tempérament*) temper; (*irritation*) bad temper; **de bonne/**

mauvaise ~ in a good/bad mood; **être d'~ à faire qch** to be in the mood for doing sth.
humide [ymid] *adj* (*linge*) damp; (*main, yeux*) moist; (*climat, chaleur*) humid; (*saison, route*) wet.
humidificateur [ymidifikatœʀ] *nm* humidifier.
humidifier [ymidifje] *vt* to humidify.
humidité [ymidite] *nf* humidity; dampness; **traces d'~** traces of moisture *ou* damp.
humiliant, e [ymiljɑ̃, -ɑ̃t] *adj* humiliating.
humiliation [ymiljɑsjɔ̃] *nf* humiliation.
humilier [ymilje] *vt* to humiliate; **s'~ devant qn** to humble o.s. before sb.
humilité [ymilite] *nf* humility.
humoriste [ymɔʀist(ə)] *nm/f* humorist.
humoristique [ymɔʀistik] *adj* humorous; humoristic.
humour [ymuʀ] *nm* humour; **avoir de l'~** to have a sense of humour; **~ noir** sick humour.
humus [ymys] *nm* humus.
'huppé, e ['ype] *adj* crested; (*fam*) posh.
'hurlement ['yʀləmɑ̃] *nm* howling *no pl*, howl; yelling *no pl*, yell.
'hurler ['yʀle] *vi* to howl, yell; (*fig: vent*) to howl; (*: couleurs etc*) to clash; **~ à la mort** (*suj: chien*) to bay at the moon.
hurluberlu [yʀlybɛʀly] *nm* (*péj*) crank ♦ *adj* cranky.
'hutte ['yt] *nf* hut.
hybride [ibʀid] *adj* hybrid.
hydratant, e [idʀatɑ̃, -ɑ̃t] *adj* (*crème*) moisturizing.
hydrate [idʀat] *nm*: **~s de carbone** carbohydrates.
hydrater [idʀate] *vt* to hydrate.
hydraulique [idʀolik] *adj* hydraulic.
hydravion [idʀavjɔ̃] *nm* seaplane, hydroplane.
hydro... [idʀɔ] *préfixe* hydro....
hydrocarbure [idʀɔkaʀbyʀ] *nm* hydrocarbon.
hydrocution [idʀɔkysjɔ̃] *nf* immersion syncope.
hydro-électrique [idʀɔelɛktʀik] *adj* hydroelectric.
hydrogène [idʀɔʒɛn] *nm* hydrogen.
hydroglisseur [idʀɔglisœʀ] *nm* hydroplane.
hydrographie [idʀɔgʀafi] *nf* (*fleuves*) hydrography.
hydrophile [idʀɔfil] *adj voir* **coton**.
hyène [jɛn] *nf* hyena.
hygiène [iʒjɛn] *nf* hygiene; **~ intime** personal hygiene.
hygiénique [iʒenik] *adj* hygienic.
hymne [imn(ə)] *nm* hymn; **~ national** national anthem.
hyper... [ipɛʀ] *préfixe* hyper....
hypermarché [ipɛʀmaʀʃe] *nm* hypermarket.
hypermétrope [ipɛʀmetʀɔp] *adj* long-sighted.
hypernerveux, euse [ipɛʀnɛʀvø, -øz] *adj* highly-strung.
hypersensible [ipɛʀsɑ̃sibl(ə)] *adj* hypersensitive.
hypertendu, e [ipɛʀtɑ̃dy] *adj* having high blood pressure, hypertensive.
hypertension [ipɛʀtɑ̃sjɔ̃] *nf* high blood pressure, hypertension.
hypertexte [ipɛʀtɛkst] *nm* (*INFORM*) hypertext.
hypnose [ipnoz] *nf* hypnosis.
hypnotique [ipnɔtik] *adj* hypnotic.
hypnotiser [ipnɔtize] *vt* to hypnotize.
hypnotiseur [ipnɔtizœʀ] *nm* hypnotist.
hypnotisme [ipnɔtism(ə)] *nm* hypnotism.
hypocondriaque [ipɔkɔ̃dʀijak] *adj* hypochondriac.
hypocrisie [ipɔkʀizi] *nf* hypocrisy.
hypocrite [ipɔkʀit] *adj* hypocritical ♦ *nm/f* hypocrite.
hypocritement [ipɔkʀitmɑ̃] *adv* hypocritically.
hypotendu, e [ipɔtɑ̃dy] *adj* having low blood pressure, hypotensive.
hypotension [ipɔtɑ̃sjɔ̃] *nf* low blood pressure, hypotension.
hypoténuse [ipɔtenyz] *nf* hypotenuse.
hypothécaire [ipɔtekɛʀ] *adj* hypothecary; **garantie/prêt ~** mortgage security/loan.
hypothèque [ipɔtɛk] *nf* mortgage.
hypothéquer [ipɔteke] *vt* to mortgage.
hypothermie [ipɔtɛʀmi] *nf* hypothermia.
hypothèse [ipɔtɛz] *nf* hypothesis; **dans l'~ où** assuming that.
hypothétique [ipɔtetik] *adj* hypothetical.
hypothétiquement [ipɔtetikmɑ̃] *adv* hypothetically.
hystérectomie [isteʀɛktɔmi] *nf* hysterectomy.
hystérie [isteʀi] *nf* hysteria; **~ collective** mass hysteria.
hystérique [isteʀik] *adj* hysterical.
Hz *abr* (= *Hertz*) Hz.

I i

I, i [i] *nm inv* I, i; **I comme Irma** I for Isaac (*BRIT*) *ou* Item (*US*).
IAC *sigle f* (= *insémination artificielle entre conjoints*) AIH.
IAD *sigle f* (= *insémination artificielle par donneur extérieur*) AID.
ibère [ibɛʀ] *adj* Iberian ♦ *nm/f*: **I~** Iberian.
ibérique [ibeʀik] *adj*: **la péninsule ~** the Iberian peninsula.
ibid. [ibid] *abr* (= *ibidem*) ibid., ib.
iceberg [isbɛʀg] *nm* iceberg.
ici [isi] *adv* here; **jusqu'~** as far as this; (*temporel*) until now; **d'~ là** by then; (*en atten-*

dant) in the meantime; **d'~ peu** before long.
icône [ikon] *nf* (*aussi INFORM*) icon.
iconoclaste [ikɔnɔklast(ə)] *nm/f* iconoclast.
iconographie [ikɔnɔgʀafi] *nf* iconography; (*illustrations*) (collection of) illustrations.
id. [id] *abr* (= *idem*) id.
idéal, e, aux [ideal, -o] *adj* ideal ♦ *nm* ideal; (*système de valeurs*) ideals *pl*.
idéalement [idealmɑ̃] *adv* ideally.
idéalisation [idealizɑsjɔ̃] *nf* idealization.
idéaliser [idealize] *vt* to idealize.
idéalisme [idealism(ə)] *nm* idealism.
idéaliste [idealist(ə)] *adj* idealistic ♦ *nm/f* idealist.
idée [ide] *nf* idea; (*illusion*): **se faire des ~s** to imagine things, get ideas into one's head; **avoir dans l'~ que** to have an idea that; **mon ~, c'est que** ... I suggest that ..., I think that ...; **à l'~ de/que** at the idea of/that, at the thought of/that; **je n'ai pas la moindre ~** I haven't the faintest idea; **avoir ~ que** to have an idea that; **avoir des ~s larges/étroites** to be broad-/narrow-minded; **venir à l'~ de qn** to occur to sb; **en voilà des ~s!** the very idea!; **~ fixe** idée fixe, obsession; **~s noires** black *ou* dark thoughts; **~s reçues** accepted ideas *ou* wisdom.
identifiable [idɑ̃tifjabl(ə)] *adj* identifiable.
identification [idɑ̃tifikɑsjɔ̃] *nf* identification.
identifier [idɑ̃tifje] *vt* to identify; **~ qch/qn à** to identify sth/sb with; **s'~ avec** *ou* **à qn/qch** (*héros etc*) to identify with sb/sth.
identique [idɑ̃tik] *adj*: **~ (à)** identical (to).
identité [idɑ̃tite] *nf* identity; **~ judiciaire** (*POLICE*) ≈ Criminal Records Office.
idéogramme [ideɔgʀam] *nm* ideogram.
idéologie [ideɔlɔʒi] *nf* ideology.
idéologique [ideɔlɔʒik] *adj* ideological.
idiomatique [idjɔmatik] *adj*: **expression ~** idiom, idiomatic expression.
idiome [idjom] *nm* (*LING*) idiom.
idiot, e [idjo, idjɔt] *adj* idiotic ♦ *nm/f* idiot.
idiotie [idjɔsi] *nf* idiocy; (*propos*) idiotic remark *etc*.
idiotisme [idjɔtism(ə)] *nm* idiom, idiomatic phrase.
idoine [idwan] *adj* fitting.
idolâtrer [idɔlɑtʀe] *vt* to idolize.
idolâtrie [idɔlɑtʀi] *nf* idolatry.
idole [idɔl] *nf* idol.
IDS *sigle f* (= *Initiative de défense stratégique*) SDI.
idylle [idil] *nf* idyll.
idyllique [idilik] *adj* idyllic.
if [if] *nm* yew.
IFOP [ifɔp] *sigle m* (= *Institut français d'opinion publique*) *French market research institute*.
IGF *sigle m* (= *impôt sur les grandes fortunes*) *wealth tax*.
IGH *sigle m* = *immeuble de grande hauteur*.
igloo [iglu] *nm* igloo.
IGN *sigle m* = *Institut géographique national*.
ignare [iɲaʀ] *adj* ignorant.
ignifuge [ignifyʒ] *adj* fireproofing ♦ *nm* fireproofing (substance).
ignifuger [ignifyʒe] *vt* to fireproof.
ignoble [iɲɔbl(ə)] *adj* vile.
ignominie [iɲɔmini] *nf* ignominy; (*acte*) ignominious *ou* base act.
ignominieux, euse [iɲɔminjø, øz] *adj* ignominious.
ignorance [iɲɔʀɑ̃s] *nf* ignorance; **dans l'~ de** in ignorance of, ignorant of.
ignorant, e [iɲɔʀɑ̃, -ɑ̃t] *adj* ignorant ♦ *nm/f*: **faire l'~** to pretend one doesn't know; **~ de** ignorant of, not aware of; **~ en** ignorant of, knowing nothing of.
ignoré, e [iɲɔʀe] *adj* unknown.
ignorer [iɲɔʀe] *vt* (*ne pas connaître*) not to know, be unaware *ou* ignorant of; (*être sans expérience de: plaisir, guerre etc*) not to know about, have no experience of; (*bouder: personne*) to ignore; **j'ignore comment/si** I do not know how/if; **~ que** to be unaware that, not to know that; **je n'ignore pas que** ... I'm not forgetting that ..., I'm not unaware that ...; **je l'ignore** I don't know.
IGPN *sigle f* (= *Inspection générale de la police nationale*) *police disciplinary body*.
IGS *sigle f* (= *Inspection générale des services*) *police disciplinary body for Paris*.
iguane [igwan] *nm* iguana.
il [il] *pron* he; (*animal, chose, en tournure impersonnelle*) it; *NB: en anglais les navires et les pays sont en général assimilés aux femelles, et les bébés aux choses, si le sexe n'est pas spécifié*; **~s** they; **~ neige** it's snowing; *voir aussi* **avoir**.
île [il] *nf* island; **les Î~s** the West Indies; **l'~ de Beauté** Corsica; **l'~ Maurice** Mauritius; **les ~s anglo- normandes** the Channel Islands; **les ~s Britanniques** the British Isles; **les ~s Cocos** *ou* **Keeling** the Cocos *ou* Keeling Islands; **les ~s Cook** the Cook Islands; **les ~s Scilly** the Scilly Isles, the Scillies; **les ~s Shetland** the Shetland Islands, Shetland; **les ~s Sorlingues = les ~s Scilly**; **les ~s Vierges** the Virgin Islands.
iliaque [iljak] *adj* (*ANAT*): **os/artère ~** iliac bone/artery.
illégal, e, aux [ilegal, -o] *adj* illegal, unlawful (*ADMIN*).
illégalement [ilegalmɑ̃] *adv* illegally.
illégalité [ilegalite] *nf* illegality; unlawfulness; **être dans l'~** to be outside the law.
illégitime [ileʒitim] *adj* illegitimate; (*optimisme, sévérité*) unjustified, unwarranted.
illégitimement [ileʒitimmɑ̃] *adv* illegitimately.
illégitimité [ileʒitimite] *nf* illegitimacy; **gouverner dans l'~** to rule illegally.
illettré, e [iletʀe] *adj, nm/f* illiterate.
illicite [ilisit] *adj* illicit.
illicitement [ilisitmɑ̃] *adv* illicitly.

illico [iliko] *adv* (*fam*) pronto.
illimité, e [ilimite] *adj* (*immense*) boundless, unlimited; (*congé, durée*) indefinite, unlimited.
illisible [ilizibl(ə)] *adj* illegible; (*roman*) unreadable.
illisiblement [ilizibləmɑ̃] *adv* illegibly.
illogique [ilɔʒik] *adj* illogical.
illogisme [ilɔʒism(ə)] *nm* illogicality.
illumination [ilyminɑsjɔ̃] *nf* illumination, floodlighting; (*inspiration*) flash of inspiration; **~s** *nfpl* illuminations, lights.
illuminé, e [ilymine] *adj* lit up; illuminated, floodlit ♦ *nm/f* (*fig: péj*) crank.
illuminer [ilymine] *vt* to light up; (*monument, rue: pour une fête*) to illuminate, floodlight; **s'~** *vi* to light up.
illusion [ilyzjɔ̃] *nf* illusion; **se faire des ~s** to delude o.s.; **faire ~** to delude *ou* fool people; **~ d'optique** optical illusion.
illusionner [ilyzjɔne] *vt* to delude; **s'~ (sur qn/qch)** to delude o.s. (about sb/sth).
illusionnisme [ilyzjɔnism(ə)] *nm* conjuring.
illusionniste [ilyzjɔnist(ə)] *nm/f* conjuror.
illusoire [ilyzwaʀ] *adj* illusory, illusive.
illustrateur [ilystʀatœʀ] *nm* illustrator.
illustratif, ive [ilystʀatif, -iv] *adj* illustrative.
illustration [ilystʀɑsjɔ̃] *nf* illustration; (*d'un ouvrage: photos*) illustrations *pl*.
illustre [ilystʀ(ə)] *adj* illustrious, renowned.
illustré, e [ilystʀe] *adj* illustrated ♦ *nm* illustrated magazine; (*pour enfants*) comic.
illustrer [ilystʀe] *vt* to illustrate; **s'~** to become famous, win fame.
îlot [ilo] *nm* small island, islet; (*de maisons*) block; (*petite zone*): **un ~ de verdure** an island of greenery, a patch of green.
ils [il] *pron voir* **il**.
image [imaʒ] *nf* (*gén*) picture; (*comparaison, ressemblance,* OPTIQUE) image; **~ de** picture *ou* image of; **~ d'Épinal** (social) stereotype; **~ de marque** brand image; (*d'une personne*) (public) image; (*d'une entreprise*) corporate image; **~ pieuse** holy picture.
imagé, e [imaʒe] *adj* full of imagery.
imaginable [imaʒinabl(ə)] *adj* imaginable; **difficilement ~** hard to imagine.
imaginaire [imaʒinɛʀ] *adj* imaginary.
imaginatif, ive [imaʒinatif, -iv] *adj* imaginative.
imagination [imaʒinɑsjɔ̃] *nf* imagination; (*chimère*) fancy, imagining; **avoir de l'~** to be imaginative, have a good imagination.
imaginer [imaʒine] *vt* to imagine; (*croire*): **qu'allez-vous ~ là?** what on earth are you thinking of?; (*inventer: expédient, mesure*) to devise, think up; **s'~** *vt* (*se figurer: scène etc*) to imagine, picture; **s'~ à 60 ans** to picture *ou* imagine o.s. at 60; **s'~ que** to imagine that; **s'~ pouvoir faire qch** to think one can do sth; **j'imagine qu'il a voulu plaisanter** I suppose he was joking; **~ de faire** (*se mettre dans l'idée de*) to dream up the idea of doing.
imbattable [ɛ̃batabl(ə)] *adj* unbeatable.
imbécile [ɛ̃besil] *adj* idiotic ♦ *nm/f* idiot; (*MÉD*) imbecile.
imbécillité [ɛ̃besilite] *nf* idiocy; imbecility; idiotic action (*ou* remark *etc*).
imberbe [ɛ̃bɛʀb(ə)] *adj* beardless.
imbiber [ɛ̃bibe] *vt*: **~ qch de** to moisten *ou* wet sth with; **s'~ de** to become saturated with; **imbibé(e) d'eau** (*chaussures, étoffe*) saturated; (*terre*) waterlogged.
imbriqué, e [ɛ̃bʀike] *adj* overlapping.
imbriquer [ɛ̃bʀike]: **s'~** *vi* to overlap (each other); (*fig*) to become interlinked *ou* interwoven.
imbroglio [ɛ̃bʀɔljo] *nm* imbroglio.
imbu, e [ɛ̃by] *adj*: **~ de** full of; **~ de soi-même/sa supériorité** full of oneself/one's superiority.
imbuvable [ɛ̃byvabl(ə)] *adj* undrinkable.
imitable [imitabl(ə)] *adj* imitable; **facilement ~** easily imitated.
imitateur, trice [imitatœʀ, -tʀis] *nm/f* (*gén*) imitator; (*MUSIC-HALL: d'une personnalité*) impersonator.
imitation [imitɑsjɔ̃] *nf* imitation; impersonation; **sac ~ cuir** bag in imitation *ou* simulated leather; **à l'~ de** in imitation of.
imiter [imite] *vt* to imitate; (*personne*) to imitate, impersonate; (*contrefaire: signature, document*) to forge, copy; (*ressembler à*) to look like; **il se leva et je l'imitai** he got up and I did likewise.
imm. *abr* = **immeuble**.
immaculé, e [imakyle] *adj* spotless, immaculate; **l'I~e Conception** (*REL*) the Immaculate Conception.
immanent, e [imanɑ̃, -ɑ̃t] *adj* immanent.
immangeable [ɛ̃mɑ̃ʒabl(ə)] *adj* inedible, uneatable.
immanquable [ɛ̃mɑ̃kabl(ə)] *adj* (*cible*) impossible to miss; (*fatal, inévitable*) bound to happen, inevitable.
immanquablement [ɛ̃mɑ̃kabləmɑ̃] *adv* inevitably.
immatériel, le [imateʀjɛl] *adj* ethereal; (*PHILOSOPHIE*) immaterial.
immatriculation [imatʀikylɑsjɔ̃] *nf* registration.
immatriculer [imatʀikyle] *vt* to register; **faire/se faire ~** to register; **voiture immatriculée dans la Seine** car with a Seine registration (number).
immature [imatyʀ] *adj* immature.
immaturité [imatyʀite] *nf* immaturity.
immédiat, e [imedja, -at] *adj* immediate ♦ *nm*: **dans l'~** for the time being; **dans le voisinage ~ de** in the immediate vicinity of.
immédiatement [imedjatmɑ̃] *adv* immediately.
immémorial, e, aux [imemɔʀjal, -o] *adj* ancient, age-old.

immense [imɑ̃s] *adj* immense.
immensément [imɑ̃semɑ̃] *adv* immensely.
immensité [imɑ̃site] *nf* immensity.
immerger [imɛʀʒe] *vt* to immerse, submerge; (*câble etc*) to lay under water; (*déchets*) to dump at sea; **s'~** *vi* (*sous-marin*) to dive, submerge.
immérité, e [imeʀite] *adj* undeserved.
immersion [imɛʀsjɔ̃] *nf* immersion.
immettable [ɛ̃mɛtabl(ə)] *adj* unwearable.
immeuble [imœbl(ə)] *nm* building ♦ *adj* (*JUR*) immovable, real; ~ **locatif** block of rented flats (*BRIT*), rental building (*US*); ~ **de rapport** investment property.
immigrant, e [imigʀɑ̃, -ɑ̃t] *nm/f* immigrant.
immigration [imigʀɑsjɔ̃] *nf* immigration.
immigré, e [imigʀe] *nm/f* immigrant.
immigrer [imigʀe] *vi* to immigrate.
imminence [iminɑ̃s] *nf* imminence.
imminent, e [iminɑ̃, -ɑ̃t] *adj* imminent, impending.
immiscer [imise]: **s'~** *vi*: **s'~ dans** to interfere in *ou* with.
immixtion [imiksjɔ̃] *nf* interference.
immobile [imɔbil] *adj* still, motionless; (*pièce de machine*) fixed; (*fig*) unchanging; **rester/se tenir** ~ to stay/keep still.
immobilier, ière [imɔbilje, -jɛʀ] *adj* property *cpd*, in real property ♦ *nm*: **l'~** the property *ou* the real estate business.
immobilisation [imɔbilizɑsjɔ̃] *nf* immobilization; **~s** *nfpl* (*JUR*) fixed assets.
immobiliser [imɔbilize] *vt* (*gén*) to immobilize; (*circulation, véhicule, affaires*) to bring to a standstill; **s'~** (*personne*) to stand still; (*machine, véhicule*) to come to a halt *ou* a standstill.
immobilisme [imɔbilism(ə)] *nm* strong resistance *ou* opposition to change.
immobilité [imɔbilite] *nf* immobility.
immodéré, e [imɔdeʀe] *adj* immoderate, inordinate.
immodérément [imɔdeʀemɑ̃] *adv* immoderately.
immoler [imɔle] *vt* to sacrifice.
immonde [imɔ̃d] *adj* foul; (*sale: ruelle, taudis*) squalid.
immondices [imɔ̃dis] *nfpl* (*ordures*) refuse *sg*; (*saletés*) filth *sg*.
immoral, e, aux [imɔʀal, -o] *adj* immoral.
immoralisme [imɔʀalism(ə)] *nm* immoralism.
immoralité [imɔʀalite] *nf* immorality.
immortaliser [imɔʀtalize] *vt* to immortalize.
immortel, le [imɔʀtɛl] *adj* immortal ♦ *nf* (*BOT*) everlasting (flower).
immuable [imɥabl(ə)] *adj* (*inébranlable*) immutable; (*qui ne change pas*) unchanging; (*personne*): ~ **dans ses convictions** immoveable (in one's convictions).
immunisation [imynizɑsjɔ̃] *nf* immunization.
immuniser [imynize] *vt* (*MÉD*) to immunize; ~ **qn contre** to immunize sb against; (*fig*) to make sb immune to.
immunitaire [imynitɛʀ] *adj* immune.
immunité [imynite] *nf* immunity; ~ **diplomatique** diplomatic immunity; ~ **parlementaire** parliamentary privilege.
immunologie [imynɔlɔʒi] *nf* immunology.
immutabilité [imytabilite] *nf* immutability.
impact [ɛ̃pakt] *nm* impact; **point d'~** point of impact.
impair, e [ɛ̃pɛʀ] *adj* odd ♦ *nm* faux pas, blunder; **numéros ~s** odd numbers.
impalpable [ɛ̃palpabl(ə)] *adj* impalpable.
impaludation [ɛ̃palydɑsjɔ̃] *nf* inoculation against malaria.
imparable [ɛ̃paʀabl(ə)] *adj* unstoppable.
impardonnable [ɛ̃paʀdɔnabl(ə)] *adj* unpardonable, unforgivable; **vous êtes ~ d'avoir fait cela** it's unforgivable of you to have done that.
imparfait, e [ɛ̃paʀfɛ, -ɛt] *adj* imperfect ♦ *nm* (*LING*) imperfect (tense).
imparfaitement [ɛ̃paʀfɛtmɑ̃] *adv* imperfectly.
impartial, e, aux [ɛ̃paʀsjal, -o] *adj* impartial, unbiased.
impartialité [ɛ̃paʀsjalite] *nf* impartiality.
impartir [ɛ̃paʀtiʀ] *vt*: ~ **qch à qn** to assign sth to sb; (*dons*) to bestow sth upon sb; **dans les délais impartis** in the time allowed.
impasse [ɛ̃pɑs] *nf* dead-end, cul-de-sac; (*fig*) deadlock; **être dans l'~** (*négociations*) to have reached deadlock; ~ **budgétaire** budget deficit.
impassibilité [ɛ̃pasibilite] *nf* impassiveness.
impassible [ɛ̃pasibl(ə)] *adj* impassive.
impassiblement [ɛ̃pasibləmɑ̃] *adv* impassively.
impatiemment [ɛ̃pasjamɑ̃] *adv* impatiently.
impatience [ɛ̃pasjɑ̃s] *nf* impatience.
impatient, e [ɛ̃pasjɑ̃, -ɑ̃t] *adj* impatient; ~ **de faire qch** keen *ou* impatient to do sth.
impatienter [ɛ̃pasjɑ̃te] *vt* to irritate, annoy; **s'~** *vi* to get impatient; **s'~ de/contre** to lose patience at/with, grow impatient at/with.
impayable [ɛ̃pɛjabl(ə)] *adj* (*drôle*) priceless.
impayé, e [ɛ̃peje] *adj* unpaid, outstanding.
impeccable [ɛ̃pekabl(ə)] *adj* faultless, impeccable; (*propre*) spotlessly clean; (*chic*) impeccably dressed; (*fam*) smashing.
impeccablement [ɛ̃pekabləmɑ̃] *adv* impeccably.
impénétrable [ɛ̃penetʀabl(ə)] *adj* impenetrable.
impénitent, e [ɛ̃penitɑ̃, -ɑ̃t] *adj* unrepentant.
impensable [ɛ̃pɑ̃sabl(ə)] *adj* unthinkable, unbelievable.
imper [ɛ̃pɛʀ] *nm* (= *imperméable*) mac.
impératif, ive [ɛ̃peʀatif, -iv] *adj* imperative; (*JUR*) mandatory ♦ *nm* (*LING*) imperative; **~s** *nmpl* requirements; demands.
impérativement [ɛ̃peʀativmɑ̃] *adv* imperatively.
impératrice [ɛ̃peʀatʀis] *nf* empress.

imperceptible [ɛ̃pɛʀsɛptibl(ə)] *adj* imperceptible.
imperceptiblement [ɛ̃pɛʀsɛptibləmɑ̃] *adv* imperceptibly.
imperdable [ɛ̃pɛʀdabl(ə)] *adj* that cannot be lost.
imperfectible [ɛ̃pɛʀfɛktibl(ə)] *adj* which cannot be perfected.
imperfection [ɛ̃pɛʀfɛksjɔ̃] *nf* imperfection.
impérial, e, aux [ɛ̃peʀjal, -o] *adj* imperial ♦ *nf* upper deck; **autobus à ~e** double-decker bus.
impérialisme [ɛ̃peʀjalism(ə)] *nm* imperialism.
impérialiste [ɛ̃peʀjalist(ə)] *adj* imperialist.
impérieusement [ɛ̃peʀjøzmɑ̃] *adv*: **avoir ~ besoin de qch** to have urgent need of sth.
impérieux, euse [ɛ̃peʀjø, -øz] *adj* (*caractère, ton*) imperious; (*obligation, besoin*) pressing, urgent.
impérissable [ɛ̃peʀisabl(ə)] *adj* undying, imperishable.
imperméabilisation [ɛ̃pɛʀmeabilizɑsjɔ̃] *nf* waterproofing.
imperméabiliser [ɛ̃pɛʀmeabilize] *vt* to waterproof.
imperméable [ɛ̃pɛʀmeabl(ə)] *adj* waterproof; (*GÉO*) impermeable; (*fig*): **~ à** impervious to ♦ *nm* raincoat; **~ à l'air** airtight.
impersonnel, le [ɛ̃pɛʀsɔnɛl] *adj* impersonal.
impertinemment [ɛ̃pɛʀtinamɑ̃] *adv* impertinently.
impertinence [ɛ̃pɛʀtinɑ̃s] *nf* impertinence.
impertinent, e [ɛ̃pɛʀtinɑ̃, -ɑ̃t] *adj* impertinent.
imperturbable [ɛ̃pɛʀtyʀbabl(ə)] *adj* (*personne*) imperturbable; (*sang-froid*) unshakeable; **rester ~** to remain unruffled.
imperturbablement [ɛ̃pɛʀtyʀbabləmɑ̃] *adv* imperturbably; unshakeably.
impétrant, e [ɛ̃petʀɑ̃, -ɑ̃t] *nm/f* (*JUR*) applicant.
impétueux, euse [ɛ̃petɥø, -øz] *adj* fiery.
impétuosité [ɛ̃petɥozite] *nf* fieriness.
impie [ɛ̃pi] *adj* impious, ungodly.
impiété [ɛ̃pjete] *nf* impiety.
impitoyable [ɛ̃pitwajabl(ə)] *adj* pitiless, merciless.
impitoyablement [ɛ̃pitwajabləmɑ̃] *adv* mercilessly.
implacable [ɛ̃plakabl(ə)] *adj* implacable.
implacablement [ɛ̃plakabləmɑ̃] *adv* implacably.
implant [ɛ̃plɑ̃] *nm* (*MÉD*) implant.
implantation [ɛ̃plɑ̃tɑsjɔ̃] *nf* establishment; settling; implantation.
implanter [ɛ̃plɑ̃te] *vt* (*usine, industrie, usage*) to establish; (*colons etc*) to settle; (*idée, préjugé*) to implant; **s'~ dans** to be established in; to settle in; to become implanted in.
implémenter [ɛ̃plemɑ̃te] *vt* to implement.
implication [ɛ̃plikɑsjɔ̃] *nf* implication.
implicite [ɛ̃plisit] *adj* implicit.
implicitement [ɛ̃plisitmɑ̃] *adv* implicitly.
impliquer [ɛ̃plike] *vt* to imply; **~ qn (dans)** to implicate sb (in).
implorant, e [ɛ̃plɔʀɑ̃, -ɑ̃t] *adj* imploring.
implorer [ɛ̃plɔʀe] *vt* to implore.
imploser [ɛ̃ploze] *vi* to implode.
implosion [ɛ̃plozjɔ̃] *nf* implosion.
impoli, e [ɛ̃pɔli] *adj* impolite, rude.
impoliment [ɛ̃pɔlimɑ̃] *adv* impolitely.
impolitesse [ɛ̃pɔlitɛs] *nf* impoliteness, rudeness; (*propos*) impolite *ou* rude remark.
impondérable [ɛ̃pɔ̃deʀabl(ə)] *nm* imponderable.
impopulaire [ɛ̃pɔpylɛʀ] *adj* unpopular.
impopularité [ɛ̃pɔpylaʀite] *nf* unpopularity.
importable [ɛ̃pɔʀtabl(ə)] *adj* (*COMM: marchandise*) importable; (*vêtement: immettable*) unwearable.
importance [ɛ̃pɔʀtɑ̃s] *nf* importance; **avoir de l'~** to be important; **sans ~** unimportant; **d'~** important, considerable; **quelle ~?** what does it matter?
important, e [ɛ̃pɔʀtɑ̃, -ɑ̃t] *adj* important; (*en quantité*) considerable, sizeable; (*: gamme, dégâts*) extensive; (*péj: airs, ton*) self-important ♦ *nm*: **l'~** the important thing.
importateur, trice [ɛ̃pɔʀtatœʀ, -tʀis] *adj* importing ♦ *nm/f* importer; **pays ~ de blé** wheat-importing country.
importation [ɛ̃pɔʀtɑsjɔ̃] *nf* import; introduction; (*produit*) import.
importer [ɛ̃pɔʀte] *vt* (*COMM*) to import; (*maladies, plantes*) to introduce ♦ *vi* (*être important*) to matter; **~ à qn** to matter to sb; **il importe de** it is important to; **il importe qu'il fasse** he must do, it is important that he should do; **peu m'importe** I don't mind, I don't care; **peu importe** it doesn't matter; **peu importe (que)** it doesn't matter (if); **peu importe le prix** never mind the price; *voir aussi* **n'importe**.
import-export [ɛ̃pɔʀɛkspɔʀ] *nm* import-export business.
importun, e [ɛ̃pɔʀtœ̃, -yn] *adj* irksome, importunate; (*arrivée, visite*) inopportune, ill-timed ♦ *nm* intruder.
importuner [ɛ̃pɔʀtyne] *vt* to bother.
imposable [ɛ̃pozabl(ə)] *adj* taxable.
imposant, e [ɛ̃pozɑ̃, -ɑ̃t] *adj* imposing.
imposé, e [ɛ̃poze] *adj* (*soumis à l'impôt*) taxed; (*GYM etc: figures*) set.
imposer [ɛ̃poze] *vt* (*taxer*) to tax; (*REL*): **~ les mains** to lay on hands; **~ qch à qn** to impose sth on sb; **s'~** (*être nécessaire*) to be imperative; (*montrer sa proéminence*) to stand out, emerge; (*artiste: se faire connaître*) to win recognition, come to the fore; **en ~** to be imposing; **en ~ à** to impress; **ça s'impose** it's essential, it's vital.
imposition [ɛ̃pozisjɔ̃] *nf* (*ADMIN*) taxation.
impossibilité [ɛ̃pɔsibilite] *nf* impossibility; **être dans l'~ de faire** to be unable to do, find it impossible to do.

impossible [ɛ̃pɔsibl(ə)] *adj* impossible ♦ *nm*: **l'~** the impossible; **~ à faire** impossible to do; **il m'est ~ de le faire** it is impossible for me to do it, I can't possibly do it; **faire l'~ (pour que)** to do one's utmost (so that); **si, par ~** ... if, by some miracle ....

imposteur [ɛ̃pɔstœʀ] *nm* impostor.

imposture [ɛ̃pɔstyʀ] *nf* imposture, deception.

impôt [ɛ̃po] *nm* tax; (*taxes*) taxation, taxes *pl*; **~s** *nmpl* (*contributions*) (income) tax *sg*; **payer 100 € d'~s** to pay €100 in tax; **~ direct/indirect** direct/indirect tax; **~ sur le chiffre d'affaires** tax on turnover; **~ foncier** land tax; **~ sur la fortune** wealth tax; **~ sur les plus-values** capital gains tax; **~ sur le revenu** income tax; **~ sur le RPP** personal income tax; **~ sur les sociétés** tax on companies; **~s locaux** rates, local taxes (*US*), ≈ council tax (*BRIT*).

impotence [ɛ̃pɔtɑ̃s] *nf* disability.

impotent, e [ɛ̃pɔtɑ̃, -ɑ̃t] *adj* disabled.

impraticable [ɛ̃pʀatikabl(ə)] *adj* (*projet*) impracticable, unworkable; (*piste*) impassable.

imprécation [ɛ̃pʀekɑsjɔ̃] *nf* imprecation.

imprécis, e [ɛ̃pʀesi, -iz] *adj* (*contours, souvenir*) imprecise, vague; (*tir*) inaccurate, imprecise.

imprécision [ɛ̃pʀesizjɔ̃] *nf* imprecision.

imprégner [ɛ̃pʀeɲe] *vt* (*tissu, tampon*): **~ (de)** to soak *ou* impregnate (with); (*lieu, air*): **~ (de)** to fill (with); (*suj: amertume, ironie*) to pervade; **s'~ de** to become impregnated with; to be filled with; (*fig*) to absorb.

imprenable [ɛ̃pʀənabl(ə)] *adj* (*forteresse*) impregnable; **vue ~** unimpeded outlook.

impresario [ɛ̃pʀesaʀjo] *nm* manager, impresario.

impression [ɛ̃pʀesjɔ̃] *nf* impression; (*d'un ouvrage, tissu*) printing; (*PHOTO*) exposure; **faire bonne ~** to make a good impression; **donner une ~ de/l'~ que** to give the impression of/that; **avoir l'~ de/que** to have the impression of/that; **faire ~** to make an impression; **~s de voyage** impressions of one's journey.

impressionnable [ɛ̃pʀesjɔnabl(ə)] *adj* impressionable.

impressionnant, e [ɛ̃pʀesjɔnɑ̃, -ɑ̃t] *adj* impressive; upsetting.

impressionner [ɛ̃pʀesjɔne] *vt* (*frapper*) to impress; (*troubler*) to upset; (*PHOTO*) to expose.

impressionnisme [ɛ̃pʀesjɔnism(ə)] *nm* impressionism.

impressionniste [ɛ̃pʀesjɔnist(ə)] *adj, nm/f* impressionist.

imprévisible [ɛ̃pʀevizibl(ə)] *adj* unforeseeable; (*réaction, personne*) unpredictable.

imprévoyance [ɛ̃pʀevwajɑ̃s] *nf* lack of foresight.

imprévoyant, e [ɛ̃pʀevwajɑ̃, -ɑ̃t] *adj* lacking in foresight; (*en matière d'argent*) improvident.

imprévu, e [ɛ̃pʀevy] *adj* unforeseen, unexpected ♦ *nm* unexpected incident; **l'~** the unexpected; **en cas d'~** if anything unexpected happens; **sauf ~** barring anything unexpected.

imprimante [ɛ̃pʀimɑ̃t] *nf* (*INFORM*) printer; **~ à bulle d'encre** bubblejet printer; **~ à jet d'encre** ink-jet printer; **~ à laser** laser printer; **~ (ligne par) ligne** line printer; **~ à marguerite** daisy-wheel printer; **~ matricielle** dot-matrix printer; **~ thermique** thermal printer.

imprimé [ɛ̃pʀime] *nm* (*formulaire*) printed form; (*POSTES*) printed matter *no pl*; (*tissu*) printed fabric; **un ~ à fleurs/pois** (*tissu*) a floral/polka-dot print.

imprimer [ɛ̃pʀime] *vt* to print; (*INFORM*) to print (out); (*apposer: visa, cachet*) to stamp; (*empreinte etc*) to imprint; (*publier*) to publish; (*communiquer: mouvement, impulsion*) to impart, transmit.

imprimerie [ɛ̃pʀimʀi] *nf* printing; (*établissement*) printing works *sg*; (*atelier*) printing house, printery.

imprimeur [ɛ̃pʀimœʀ] *nm* printer; **imprimeur-éditeur/-libraire** printer and publisher/bookseller.

improbable [ɛ̃pʀɔbabl(ə)] *adj* unlikely, improbable.

improductif, ive [ɛ̃pʀɔdyktif, -iv] *adj* unproductive.

impromptu, e [ɛ̃pʀɔ̃pty] *adj* impromptu; (*départ*) sudden.

imprononçable [ɛ̃pʀɔnɔ̃sabl(ə)] *adj* unpronounceable.

impropre [ɛ̃pʀɔpʀ(ə)] *adj* inappropriate; **~ à** unsuitable for.

improprement [ɛ̃pʀɔpʀəmɑ̃] *adv* improperly.

impropriété [ɛ̃pʀɔpʀijete] *nf*: **~ (de langage)** incorrect usage *no pl*.

improvisation [ɛ̃pʀɔvizɑsjɔ̃] *nf* improvization.

improvisé, e [ɛ̃pʀɔvize] *adj* makeshift, improvized; (*jeu etc*) scratch, improvized; **avec des moyens ~s** using whatever comes to hand.

improviser [ɛ̃pʀɔvize] *vt, vi* to improvize; **s'~** (*secours, réunion*) to be improvized; **s'~ cuisinier** to (decide to) act as cook; **~ qn cuisinier** to get sb to act as cook.

improviste [ɛ̃pʀɔvist(ə)]: **à l'~** *adv* unexpectedly, without warning.

imprudemment [ɛ̃pʀydamɑ̃] *adv* carelessly; unwisely, imprudently.

imprudence [ɛ̃pʀydɑ̃s] *nf* carelessness *no pl*; imprudence *no pl*; act of carelessness; foolish *ou* unwise action.

imprudent, e [ɛ̃pʀydɑ̃, -ɑ̃t] *adj* (*conducteur, geste, action*) careless; (*remarque*) unwise, imprudent; (*projet*) foolhardy.

impubère [ɛ̃pybɛʀ] *adj* below the age of puberty.

impubliable [ɛ̃pyblijabl(ə)] *adj* unpublishable.

impudemment [ɛ̃pydamɑ̃] *adv* impudently.
impudence [ɛ̃pydɑ̃s] *nf* impudence.
impudent, e [ɛ̃pydɑ̃, -ɑ̃t] *adj* impudent.
impudeur [ɛ̃pydœʀ] *nf* shamelessness.
impudique [ɛ̃pydik] *adj* shameless.
impuissance [ɛ̃pɥisɑ̃s] *nf* helplessness; ineffectualness; impotence.
impuissant, e [ɛ̃pɥisɑ̃, -ɑ̃t] *adj* helpless; (*sans effet*) ineffectual; (*sexuellement*) impotent ♦ *nm* impotent man; ~ **à faire qch** powerless to do sth.
impulsif, ive [ɛ̃pylsif, -iv] *adj* impulsive.
impulsion [ɛ̃pylsjɔ̃] *nf* (*ÉLEC, instinct*) impulse; (*élan, influence*) impetus.
impulsivement [ɛ̃pylsivmɑ̃] *adv* impulsively.
impulsivité [ɛ̃pylsivite] *nf* impulsiveness.
impunément [ɛ̃pynemɑ̃] *adv* with impunity.
impuni, e [ɛ̃pyni] *adj* unpunished.
impunité [ɛ̃pynite] *nf* impunity.
impur, e [ɛ̃pyʀ] *adj* impure.
impureté [ɛ̃pyʀte] *nf* impurity.
imputable [ɛ̃pytabl(ə)] *adj* (*attribuable*): ~ **à** imputable to, ascribable to; (*COMM: somme*): ~ **sur** chargeable to.
imputation [ɛ̃pytɑsjɔ̃] *nf* imputation, charge.
imputer [ɛ̃pyte] *vt* (*attribuer*): ~ **qch à** to ascribe *ou* impute sth to; (*COMM*): ~ **qch à** *ou* **sur** to charge sth to.
imputrescible [ɛ̃pytʀesibl(ə)] *adj* rotproof.
in [in] *adj inv* in, trendy.
INA [ina] *sigle m* (= *Institut national de l'audiovisuel*) *library of television archives*.
inabordable [inabɔʀdabl(ə)] *adj* (*lieu*) inaccessible; (*cher*) prohibitive.
inaccentué, e [inaksɑ̃tɥe] *adj* (*LING*) unstressed.
inacceptable [inaksɛptabl(ə)] *adj* unacceptable.
inaccessible [inaksesibl(ə)] *adj* inaccessible; (*objectif*) unattainable; (*insensible*): ~ **à** impervious to.
inaccoutumé, e [inakutyme] *adj* unaccustomed.
inachevé, e [inaʃve] *adj* unfinished.
inactif, ive [inaktif, -iv] *adj* inactive, idle.
inaction [inaksjɔ̃] *nf* inactivity.
inactivité [inaktivite] *nf* (*ADMIN*): **en** ~ out of active service.
inadaptation [inadaptɑsjɔ̃] *nf* (*PSYCH*) maladjustment.
inadapté, e [inadapte] *adj* (*PSYCH: adulte, enfant*) maladjusted ♦ *nm/f* (*péj: adulte: asocial*) misfit; ~ **à** not adapted to, unsuited to.
inadéquat, e [inadekwa, wat] *adj* inadequate.
inadéquation [inadekwɑsjɔ̃] *nf* inadequacy.
inadmissible [inadmisibl(ə)] *adj* inadmissible.
inadvertance [inadvɛʀtɑ̃s]: **par** ~ *adv* inadvertently.
inaliénable [inaljenabl(ə)] *adj* inalienable.
inaltérable [inalteʀabl(ə)] *adj* (*matière*) stable; (*fig*) unchanging; ~ **à** unaffected by; **couleur ~ (au lavage/à la lumière)** fast colour/fade-resistant colour.
inamovible [inamɔvibl(ə)] *adj* fixed; (*JUR*) irremovable.
inanimé, e [inanime] *adj* (*matière*) inanimate; (*évanoui*) unconscious; (*sans vie*) lifeless.
inanité [inanite] *nf* futility.
inanition [inanisjɔ̃] *nf*: **tomber d'~** to faint with hunger (and exhaustion).
inaperçu, e [inapɛʀsy] *adj*: **passer** ~ to go unnoticed.
inappétence [inapetɑ̃s] *nf* lack of appetite.
inapplicable [inaplikabl(ə)] *adj* inapplicable.
inapplication [inaplikɑsjɔ̃] *nf* lack of application.
inappliqué, e [inaplike] *adj* lacking in application.
inappréciable [inapʀesjabl(ə)] *adj* (*service*) invaluable; (*différence, nuance*) inappreciable.
inapte [inapt(ə)] *adj*: ~ **à** incapable of; (*MIL*) unfit for.
inaptitude [inaptityd] *nf* inaptitude; unfitness.
inarticulé, e [inaʀtikyle] *adj* inarticulate.
inassimilable [inasimilabl(ə)] *adj* that cannot be assimilated.
inassouvi, e [inasuvi] *adj* unsatisfied, unfulfilled.
inattaquable [inatakabl(ə)] *adj* (*MIL*) unassailable; (*texte, preuve*) irrefutable.
inattendu, e [inatɑ̃dy] *adj* unexpected ♦ *nm*: **l'~** the unexpected.
inattentif, ive [inatɑ̃tif, -iv] *adj* inattentive; ~ **à** (*dangers, détails*) heedless of.
inattention [inatɑ̃sjɔ̃] *nf* inattention; (*inadvertance*): **une minute d'~** a minute of inattention, a minute's carelessness; **par** ~ inadvertently; **faute d'~** careless mistake.
inaudible [inodibl(ə)] *adj* inaudible.
inaugural, e, aux [inɔgyʀal, -o] *adj* (*cérémonie*) inaugural, opening; (*vol, voyage*) maiden.
inauguration [inɔgyʀɑsjɔ̃] *nf* unveiling; opening; **discours/cérémonie d'~** inaugural speech/ceremony.
inaugurer [inɔgyʀe] *vt* (*monument*) to unveil; (*exposition, usine*) to open; (*fig*) to inaugurate.
inauthenticité [inɔtɑ̃tisite] *nf* inauthenticity.
inavouable [inavwabl(ə)] *adj* undisclosable; (*honteux*) shameful.
inavoué, e [inavwe] *adj* unavowed.
INC *sigle m* (= *Institut national de la consommation*) *consumer research organization*.
inca [ɛ̃ka] *adj inv* Inca ♦ *nm/f*: **I~** Inca.
incalculable [ɛ̃kalkylabl(ə)] *adj* incalculable; **un nombre ~ de** countless numbers of.
incandescence [ɛ̃kɑ̃desɑ̃s] *nf* incandescence; **en** ~ incandescent, white-hot; **porter à** ~ to heat white-hot; **lampe/manchon à** ~ incandescent lamp/(gas) mantle.
incandescent, e [ɛ̃kɑ̃desɑ̃, -ɑ̃t] *adj* incandescent, white-hot.
incantation [ɛ̃kɑ̃tɑsjɔ̃] *nf* incantation.

incantatoire [ɛ̃kɑ̃tatwaʀ] *adj*: **formule ~** incantation.
incapable [ɛ̃kapabl(ə)] *adj* incapable; **~ de faire** incapable of doing; (*empêché*) unable to do.
incapacitant, e [ɛ̃kapasitɑ̃, -ɑ̃t] *adj* (*MIL*) incapacitating.
incapacité [ɛ̃kapasite] *nf* incapability; (*JUR*) incapacity; **être dans l'~ de faire** to be unable to do; **~ permanente/de travail** permanent/industrial disablement; **~ électorale** ineligibility to vote.
incarcération [ɛ̃kaʀseʀɑsjɔ̃] *nf* incarceration.
incarcérer [ɛ̃kaʀseʀe] *vt* to incarcerate.
incarnat, e [ɛ̃kaʀna, -at] *adj* (rosy) pink.
incarnation [ɛ̃kaʀnɑsjɔ̃] *nf* incarnation.
incarné, e [ɛ̃kaʀne] *adj* incarnate; (*ongle*) ingrown.
incarner [ɛ̃kaʀne] *vt* to embody, personify; (*THÉÂT*) to play; (*REL*) to incarnate; **s'~ dans** (*REL*) to be incarnate in.
incartade [ɛ̃kaʀtad] *nf* prank, escapade.
incassable [ɛ̃kɑsabl(ə)] *adj* unbreakable.
incendiaire [ɛ̃sɑ̃djɛʀ] *adj* incendiary; (*fig: discours*) inflammatory ♦ *nm/f* fire-raiser, arsonist.
incendie [ɛ̃sɑ̃di] *nm* fire; **~ criminel** arson *no pl*; **~ de forêt** forest fire.
incendier [ɛ̃sɑ̃dje] *vt* (*mettre le feu à*) to set fire to, set alight; (*brûler complètement*) to burn down.
incertain, e [ɛ̃sɛʀtɛ̃, -ɛn] *adj* uncertain; (*temps*) uncertain, unsettled; (*imprécis: contours*) indistinct, blurred.
incertitude [ɛ̃sɛʀtityd] *nf* uncertainty.
incessamment [ɛ̃sɛsamɑ̃] *adv* very shortly.
incessant, e [ɛ̃sɛsɑ̃, -ɑ̃t] *adj* incessant, unceasing.
incessible [ɛ̃sesibl(ə)] *adj* (*JUR*) non-transferable.
inceste [ɛ̃sɛst(ə)] *nm* incest.
incestueux, euse [ɛ̃sɛstɥø, -øz] *adj* incestuous.
inchangé, e [ɛ̃ʃɑ̃ʒe] *adj* unchanged, unaltered.
inchantable [ɛ̃ʃɑ̃tabl(ə)] *adj* unsingable.
inchauffable [ɛ̃ʃofabl(ə)] *adj* impossible to heat.
incidemment [ɛ̃sidamɑ̃] *adv* in passing.
incidence [ɛ̃sidɑ̃s] *nf* (*effet, influence*) effect; (*PHYSIQUE*) incidence.
incident [ɛ̃sidɑ̃] *nm* incident; **~ de frontière** border incident; **~ de parcours** minor hitch *ou* setback; **~ technique** technical difficulties *pl*, technical hitch.
incinérateur [ɛ̃sineʀatœʀ] *nm* incinerator.
incinération [ɛ̃sineʀɑsjɔ̃] *nf* (*d'ordures*) incineration; (*crémation*) cremation.
incinérer [ɛ̃sineʀe] *vt* (*ordures*) to incinerate; (*mort*) to cremate.
incise [ɛ̃siz] *nf* (*LING*) interpolated clause.
inciser [ɛ̃size] *vt* to make an incision in; (*abcès*) to lance.
incisif, ive [ɛ̃sizif, -iv] *adj* incisive, cutting ♦ *nf* incisor.
incision [ɛ̃sizjɔ̃] *nf* incision; (*d'un abcès*) lancing.
incitation [ɛ̃sitɑsjɔ̃] *nf* (*encouragement*) incentive; (*provocation*) incitement.
inciter [ɛ̃site] *vt*: **~ qn à (faire) qch** to prompt *ou* encourage sb to do sth; (*à la révolte etc*) to incite sb to do sth.
incivil, e [ɛ̃sivil] *adj* uncivil.
incivilité [ɛ̃sivilite] *nf* incivility.
inclinable [ɛ̃klinabl(ə)] *adj* (*dossier etc*) tilting; **siège à dossier ~** reclining seat.
inclinaison [ɛ̃klinɛzɔ̃] *nf* (*déclivité: d'une route etc*) incline; (*: d'un toit*) slope; (*état penché: d'un mur*) lean; (*: de la tête*) tilt; (*: d'un navire*) list.
inclination [ɛ̃klinɑsjɔ̃] *nf* (*penchant*) inclination, tendency; **montrer de l'~ pour les sciences** *etc* to show an inclination for the sciences *etc*; **~s égoïstes/altruistes** egoistic/altruistic tendencies; **~ de (la) tête** nod (of the head); **~ (de buste)** bow.
incliner [ɛ̃kline] *vt* (*bouteille*) to tilt; (*tête*) to incline; (*inciter*): **~ qn à qch/à faire** to encourage sb towards sth/to do ♦ *vi*: **~ à qch/à faire** (*tendre à, pencher pour*) to incline towards sth/doing, tend towards sth/to do; **s'~** (*route*) to slope; (*toit*) to be sloping; **s'~ (devant)** to bow (before).
inclure [ɛ̃klyʀ] *vt* to include; (*joindre à un envoi*) to enclose; **jusqu'au 10 mars inclus** until 10th March inclusive.
inclus, e [ɛ̃kly, -yz] *pp de* **inclure** ♦ *adj* (*joint à un envoi*) enclosed; (*compris: frais, dépense*) included; (*MATH: ensemble*): **~ dans** included in; **jusqu'au troisième chapitre ~** up to and including the third chapter.
inclusion [ɛ̃klyzjɔ̃] *nf* (*voir inclure*) inclusion; enclosing.
inclusivement [ɛ̃klyzivmɑ̃] *adv* inclusively.
inclut [ɛ̃kly] *vb voir* **inclure**.
incoercible [ɛ̃kɔɛʀsibl(ə)] *adj* uncontrollable.
incognito [ɛ̃kɔɲito] *adv* incognito ♦ *nm*: **garder l'~** to remain incognito.
incohérence [ɛ̃kɔeʀɑ̃s] *nf* inconsistency; incoherence.
incohérent, e [ɛ̃kɔeʀɑ̃, -ɑ̃t] *adj* inconsistent; incoherent.
incollable [ɛ̃kɔlabl(ə)] *adj* (*riz*) that does not stick; (*fam: personne*): **il est ~** he's got all the answers.
incolore [ɛ̃kɔlɔʀ] *adj* colourless.
incomber [ɛ̃kɔ̃be]: **~ à** *vt* (*suj: devoirs, responsabilité*) to rest *ou* be incumbent upon; (*: frais, travail*) to be the responsibility of.
incombustible [ɛ̃kɔ̃bystibl(ə)] *adj* incombustible.
incommensurable [ɛ̃kɔmɑ̃syʀabl(ə)] *adj* immeasurable.
incommodant, e [ɛ̃kɔmɔdɑ̃, -ɑ̃t] *adj* (*bruit*) an-

noying; (*chaleur*) uncomfortable.
incommode [ɛ̃kɔmɔd] *adj* inconvenient; (*posture, siège*) uncomfortable.
incommodément [ɛ̃kɔmɔdemɑ̃] *adv* (*installé, assis*) uncomfortably; (*logé, situé*) inconveniently.
incommoder [ɛ̃kɔmɔde] *vt*: ~ **qn** to bother *ou* inconvenience sb; (*embarrasser*) to make sb feel uncomfortable *ou* ill at ease.
incommodité [ɛ̃kɔmɔdite] *nf* inconvenience.
incommunicable [ɛ̃kɔmynikabl(ə)] *adj* (*JUR*: *droits, privilèges*) non-transferable; (*pensée*) incommunicable.
incomparable [ɛ̃kɔ̃paʀabl(ə)] *adj* not comparable; (*inégalable*) incomparable, matchless.
incomparablement [ɛ̃kɔ̃paʀabləmɑ̃] *adv* incomparably.
incompatibilité [ɛ̃kɔ̃patibilite] *nf* incompatibility; ~ **d'humeur** (mutual) incompatibility.
incompatible [ɛ̃kɔ̃patibl(ə)] *adj* incompatible.
incompétence [ɛ̃kɔ̃petɑ̃s] *nf* lack of expertise; incompetence.
incompétent, e [ɛ̃kɔ̃petɑ̃, -ɑ̃t] *adj* (*ignorant*) inexpert; (*incapable*) incompetent, not competent.
incomplet, ète [ɛ̃kɔ̃plɛ, -ɛt] *adj* incomplete.
incomplètement [ɛ̃kɔ̃plɛtmɑ̃] *adv* not completely, incompletely.
incompréhensible [ɛ̃kɔ̃pʀeɑ̃sibl(ə)] *adj* incomprehensible.
incompréhensif, ive [ɛ̃kɔ̃pʀeɑ̃sif, -iv] *adj* lacking in understanding, unsympathetic.
incompréhension [ɛ̃kɔ̃pʀeɑ̃sjɔ̃] *nf* lack of understanding.
incompressible [ɛ̃kɔ̃pʀesibl(ə)] *adj* (*PHYSIQUE*) incompressible; (*fig: dépenses*) that cannot be reduced; (*JUR*: *peine*) irreducible.
incompris, e [ɛ̃kɔ̃pʀi, -iz] *adj* misunderstood.
inconcevable [ɛ̃kɔ̃svabl(ə)] *adj* (*conduite etc*) inconceivable; (*mystère*) incredible.
inconciliable [ɛ̃kɔ̃siljabl(ə)] *adj* irreconcilable.
inconditionnel, le [ɛ̃kɔ̃disjɔnɛl] *adj* unconditional; (*partisan*) unquestioning ♦ *nm/f* (*partisan*) unquestioning supporter.
inconditionnellement [ɛ̃kɔ̃disjɔnɛlmɑ̃] *adv* unconditionally.
inconduite [ɛ̃kɔ̃dɥit] *nf* bad *ou* unsuitable behaviour *no pl*.
inconfort [ɛ̃kɔ̃fɔʀ] *nm* lack of comfort, discomfort.
inconfortable [ɛ̃kɔ̃fɔʀtabl(ə)] *adj* uncomfortable.
inconfortablement [ɛ̃kɔ̃fɔʀtabləmɑ̃] *adv* uncomfortably.
incongru, e [ɛ̃kɔ̃gʀy] *adj* unseemly; (*remarque*) ill-chosen, incongruous.
incongruité [ɛ̃kɔ̃gʀyite] *nf* unseemliness; incongruity; (*parole incongrue*) ill-chosen remark.
inconnu, e [ɛ̃kɔny] *adj* unknown; (*sentiment, plaisir*) new, strange ♦ *nm/f* stranger; unknown person (*ou* artist *etc*) ♦ *nm*: **l'**~ the unknown ♦ *nf* (*MATH*) unknown; (*fig*) unknown factor.
inconsciemment [ɛ̃kɔ̃sjamɑ̃] *adv* unconsciously.
inconscience [ɛ̃kɔ̃sjɑ̃s] *nf* unconsciousness; recklessness.
inconscient, e [ɛ̃kɔ̃sjɑ̃, -ɑ̃t] *adj* unconscious; (*irréfléchi*) reckless ♦ *nm* (*PSYCH*): **l'**~ the subconscious, the unconscious; ~ **de** unaware of.
inconséquence [ɛ̃kɔ̃sekɑ̃s] *nf* inconsistency; thoughtlessness; (*action, parole*) thoughtless thing to do (*ou* say).
inconséquent, e [ɛ̃kɔ̃sekɑ̃, -ɑ̃t] *adj* (*illogique*) inconsistent; (*irréfléchi*) thoughtless.
inconsidéré, e [ɛ̃kɔ̃sideʀe] *adj* ill-considered.
inconsidérément [ɛ̃kɔ̃sideʀemɑ̃] *adv* thoughtlessly.
inconsistant, e [ɛ̃kɔ̃sistɑ̃, -ɑ̃t] *adj* flimsy, weak; (*crème etc*) runny.
inconsolable [ɛ̃kɔ̃sɔlabl(ə)] *adj* inconsolable.
inconstance [ɛ̃kɔ̃stɑ̃s] *nf* inconstancy, fickleness.
inconstant, e [ɛ̃kɔ̃stɑ̃, -ɑ̃t] *adj* inconstant, fickle.
inconstitutionnel, le [ɛ̃kɔ̃stitysjɔnɛl] *adj* unconstitutional.
incontestable [ɛ̃kɔ̃tɛstabl(ə)] *adj* unquestionable, indisputable.
incontestablement [ɛ̃kɔ̃tɛstabləmɑ̃] *adv* unquestionably, indisputably.
incontesté, e [ɛ̃kɔ̃tɛste] *adj* undisputed.
incontinence [ɛ̃kɔ̃tinɑ̃s] *nf* (*MÉD*) incontinence.
incontinent, e [ɛ̃kɔ̃tinɑ̃, -ɑ̃t] *adj* (*MÉD*) incontinent ♦ *adv* (*tout de suite*) forthwith.
incontournable [ɛ̃kɔ̃tuʀnabl(ə)] *adj* unavoidable.
incontrôlable [ɛ̃kɔ̃tʀolabl(ə)] *adj* unverifiable.
incontrôlé, e [ɛ̃kɔ̃tʀole] *adj* uncontrolled.
inconvenance [ɛ̃kɔ̃vnɑ̃s] *nf* (*parole, action*) impropriety.
inconvenant, e [ɛ̃kɔ̃vnɑ̃, -ɑ̃t] *adj* unseemly, improper.
inconvénient [ɛ̃kɔ̃venjɑ̃] *nm* (*d'une situation, d'un projet*) disadvantage, drawback; (*d'un remède, changement etc*) risk, inconvenience; **si vous n'y voyez pas d'**~ if you have no objections; **y a-t-il un ~ à ...?** (*risque*) isn't there a risk in ...?; (*objection*) is there any objection to ...?
inconvertible [ɛ̃kɔ̃vɛʀtibl(ə)] *adj* inconvertible.
incorporation [ɛ̃kɔʀpɔʀɑsjɔ̃] *nf* (*MIL*) call-up.
incorporé, e [ɛ̃kɔʀpɔʀe] *adj* (*micro etc*) built-in.
incorporel, le [ɛ̃kɔʀpɔʀɛl] *adj* (*JUR*): **biens ~s** intangible property.
incorporer [ɛ̃kɔʀpɔʀe] *vt*: ~ **(à)** to mix in (with); (*paragraphe etc*): ~ **(dans)** to incorporate (in); (*territoire, immigrants*): ~ **(dans)**

to incorporate (into); (*MIL: appeler*) to recruit, call up; (*: affecter*): ~ **qn dans** to enlist sb into.
incorrect, e [ɛ̃kɔʀɛkt] *adj* (*impropre, inconvenant*) improper; (*défectueux*) faulty; (*inexact*) incorrect; (*impoli*) impolite; (*déloyal*) underhand.
incorrectement [ɛ̃kɔʀɛktəmɑ̃] *adv* improperly; faultily; incorrectly; impolitely; in an underhand way.
incorrection [ɛ̃kɔʀɛksjɔ̃] *nf* impropriety; incorrectness; underhand nature; (*terme impropre*) impropriety; (*action, remarque*) improper behaviour (*ou* remark).
incorrigible [ɛ̃kɔʀiʒibl(ə)] *adj* incorrigible.
incorruptible [ɛ̃kɔʀyptibl(ə)] *adj* incorruptible.
incrédibilité [ɛ̃kʀedibilite] *nf* incredibility.
incrédule [ɛ̃kʀedyl] *adj* incredulous; (*REL*) unbelieving.
incrédulité [ɛ̃kʀedylite] *nf* incredulity; **avec** ~ incredulously.
increvable [ɛ̃kʀəvabl(ə)] *adj* (*pneu*) puncture-proof; (*fam*) tireless.
incriminer [ɛ̃kʀimine] *vt* (*personne*) to incriminate; (*action, conduite*) to bring under attack; (*bonne foi, honnêteté*) to call into question; **livre/article incriminé** offending book/article.
incrochetable [ɛ̃kʀɔʃtabl(ə)] *adj* (*serrure*) that can't be picked, burglarproof.
incroyable [ɛ̃kʀwajabl(ə)] *adj* incredible, unbelievable.
incroyablement [ɛ̃kʀwajabləmɑ̃] *adv* incredibly, unbelievably.
incroyant, e [ɛ̃kʀwajɑ̃, -ɑ̃t] *nm/f* non-believer.
incrustation [ɛ̃kʀystɑsjɔ̃] *nf* inlaying *no pl*; inlay; (*dans une chaudière etc*) fur *no pl*, scale *no pl*.
incruster [ɛ̃kʀyste] *vt* (*ART*): ~ **qch dans/qch de** to inlay sth into/sth with; (*radiateur etc*) to coat with scale *ou* fur; **s'**~ *vi* (*invité*) to take root; (*radiateur etc*) to become coated with fur *ou* scale; **s'**~ **dans** (*suj: corps étranger, caillou*) to become embedded in.
incubateur [ɛ̃kybatœʀ] *nm* incubator.
incubation [ɛ̃kybɑsjɔ̃] *nf* incubation.
inculpation [ɛ̃kylpɑsjɔ̃] *nf* charging *no pl*; charge; **sous l'**~ **de** on a charge of.
inculpé, e [ɛ̃kylpe] *nm/f* accused.
inculper [ɛ̃kylpe] *vt*: ~ **(de)** to charge (with).
inculquer [ɛ̃kylke] *vt*: ~ **qch à** to inculcate sth in, instil sth into.
inculte [ɛ̃kylt(ə)] *adj* uncultivated; (*esprit, peuple*) uncultured; (*barbe*) unkempt.
incultivable [ɛ̃kyltivabl(ə)] *adj* (*terrain*) unworkable.
inculture [ɛ̃kyltyʀ] *nf* lack of education.
incurable [ɛ̃kyʀabl(ə)] *adj* incurable.
incurie [ɛ̃kyʀi] *nf* carelessness.
incursion [ɛ̃kyʀsjɔ̃] *nf* incursion, foray.
incurvé, e [ɛ̃kyʀve] *adj* curved.
incurver [ɛ̃kyʀve] *vt* (*barre de fer*) to bend into a curve; **s'**~ *vi* (*planche, route*) to bend.
Inde [ɛ̃d] *nf*: **l'**~ India.
indécemment [ɛ̃desamɑ̃] *adv* indecently.
indécence [ɛ̃desɑ̃s] *nf* indecency; (*propos, acte*) indecent remark (*ou* act *etc*).
indécent, e [ɛ̃desɑ̃, -ɑ̃t] *adj* indecent.
indéchiffrable [ɛ̃deʃifʀabl(ə)] *adj* indecipherable.
indéchirable [ɛ̃deʃiʀabl(ə)] *adj* tearproof.
indécis, e [ɛ̃desi, -iz] *adj* indecisive; (*perplexe*) undecided.
indécision [ɛ̃desizjɔ̃] *nf* indecision, indecisiveness.
indéclinable [ɛ̃deklinabl(ə)] *adj* (*LING: mot*) indeclinable.
indécomposable [ɛ̃dekɔ̃pozabl(ə)] *adj* that cannot be broken down.
indécrottable [ɛ̃dekʀɔtabl(ə)] *adj* (*fam*) hopeless.
indéfectible [ɛ̃defɛktibl(ə)] *adj* (*attachement*) indestructible.
indéfendable [ɛ̃defɑ̃dabl(ə)] *adj* indefensible.
indéfini, e [ɛ̃defini] *adj* (*imprécis, incertain*) undefined; (*illimité, LING*) indefinite.
indéfiniment [ɛ̃definimɑ̃] *adv* indefinitely.
indéfinissable [ɛ̃definisabl(ə)] *adj* indefinable.
indéformable [ɛ̃defɔʀmabl(ə)] *adj* that keeps its shape.
indélébile [ɛ̃delebil] *adj* indelible.
indélicat, e [ɛ̃delika, -at] *adj* tactless; (*malhonnête*) dishonest.
indélicatesse [ɛ̃delikatɛs] *nf* tactlessness; dishonesty.
indémaillable [ɛ̃demɑjabl(ə)] *adj* run-resist.
indemne [ɛ̃dɛmn(ə)] *adj* unharmed.
indemnisable [ɛ̃dɛmnizabl(ə)] *adj* entitled to compensation.
indemnisation [ɛ̃dɛmnizɑsjɔ̃] *nf* (*somme*) indemnity, compensation.
indemniser [ɛ̃dɛmnize] *vt*: ~ **qn (de)** to compensate sb (for); **se faire** ~ to get compensation.
indemnité [ɛ̃dɛmnite] *nf* (*dédommagement*) compensation *no pl*; (*allocation*) allowance; ~ **de licenciement** redundancy payment; ~ **de logement** housing allowance; ~ **parlementaire** ≈ M.P.'s (*BRIT*) *ou* Congressman's (*US*) salary.
indémontable [ɛ̃demɔ̃tabl(ə)] *adj* (*meuble etc*) that cannot be dismantled, in one piece.
indéniable [ɛ̃denjabl(ə)] *adj* undeniable, indisputable.
indéniablement [ɛ̃denjabləmɑ̃] *adv* undeniably.
indépendamment [ɛ̃depɑ̃damɑ̃] *adv* independently; ~ **de** independently of; (*abstraction faite de*) irrespective of; (*en plus de*) over and above.
indépendance [ɛ̃depɑ̃dɑ̃s] *nf* independence; ~ **matérielle** financial independence.
indépendant, e [ɛ̃depɑ̃dɑ̃, -ɑ̃t] *adj* independ-

ent; ~ **de** independent of; **chambre** ~**e** room with private entrance; **travailleur** ~ self-employed worker.
indépendantiste [ɛ̃depɑ̃dɑ̃tist(ə)] *adj, nm/f* separatist.
indéracinable [ɛ̃deʀasinabl(ə)] *adj* (*fig: croyance etc*) ineradicable.
indéréglable [ɛ̃deʀeglabl(ə)] *adj* which will not break down.
indescriptible [ɛ̃dɛskʀiptibl(ə)] *adj* indescribable.
indésirable [ɛ̃deziʀabl(ə)] *adj* undesirable.
indestructible [ɛ̃dɛstʀyktibl(ə)] *adj* indestructible; (*marque, impression*) indelible.
indéterminable [ɛ̃detɛʀminabl(ə)] *adj* indeterminable.
indétermination [ɛ̃detɛʀminɑsjɔ̃] *nf* indecision, indecisiveness.
indéterminé, e [ɛ̃detɛʀmine] *adj* unspecified; indeterminate; indeterminable.
index [ɛ̃dɛks] *nm* (*doigt*) index finger; (*d'un livre etc*) index; **mettre à l'**~ to blacklist.
indexation [ɛ̃dɛksɑsjɔ̃] *nf* indexing.
indexé, e [ɛ̃dɛkse] *adj* (*ÉCON*): ~ **(sur)** index-linked (to).
indexer [ɛ̃dɛkse] *vt* (*salaire, emprunt*): ~ **(sur)** to index (on).
indicateur [ɛ̃dikatœʀ] *nm* (*POLICE*) informer; (*livre*) guide; (*: liste*) directory; (*TECH*) gauge; indicator; (*ÉCON*) indicator ♦ *adj*: **poteau** ~ signpost; **tableau** ~ indicator (board); ~ **des chemins de fer** railway timetable; ~ **de direction** (*AUTO*) indicator; ~ **immobilier** property gazette; ~ **de niveau** level, gauge; ~ **de pression** pressure gauge; ~ **de rues** street directory; ~ **de vitesse** speedometer.
indicatif, ive [ɛ̃dikatif, -iv] *adj*: **à titre** ~ for (your) information ♦ *nm* (*LING*) indicative; (*d'une émission*) theme *ou* signature tune; (*TÉL*) dialling code; ~ **d'appel** (*RADIO*) call sign.
indication [ɛ̃dikɑsjɔ̃] *nf* indication; (*renseignement*) information *no pl*; ~**s** *nfpl* (*directives*) instructions; ~ **d'origine** (*COMM*) place of origin.
indice [ɛ̃dis] *nm* (*marque, signe*) indication, sign; (*POLICE: lors d'une enquête*) clue; (*JUR: présomption*) piece of evidence; (*SCIENCE, ÉCON, TECH*) index; (*ADMIN*) grading; rating; ~ **du coût de la vie** cost-of-living index; ~ **inférieur** subscript; ~ **d'octane** octane rating; ~ **des prix** price index; ~ **de traitement** salary grading.
indicible [ɛ̃disibl(ə)] *adj* inexpressible.
indien, ne [ɛ̃djɛ̃, -ɛn] *adj* Indian ♦ *nm/f*: **I**~, **ne** (*d'Amérique*) (American *ou* Red) Indian; (*d'Inde*) Indian.
indifféremment [ɛ̃difeʀamɑ̃] *adv* (*sans distinction*) equally; indiscriminately.
indifférence [ɛ̃difeʀɑ̃s] *nf* indifference.
indifférencié, e [ɛ̃difeʀɑ̃sje] *adj* undifferentiated.
indifférent, e [ɛ̃difeʀɑ̃, -ɑ̃t] *adj* (*peu intéressé*) indifferent; ~ **à** (*insensible à*) indifferent to, unconcerned about; (*peu intéressant pour*) indifferent to; immaterial to; **ça m'est** ~ **(que ...)** it doesn't matter to me (whether ...).
indifférer [ɛ̃difeʀe] *vt*: **cela m'indiffère** I'm indifferent about it.
indigence [ɛ̃diʒɑ̃s] *nf* poverty; **être dans l'**~ to be destitute.
indigène [ɛ̃diʒɛn] *adj* native, indigenous; (*de la région*) local ♦ *nm/f* native.
indigent, e [ɛ̃diʒɑ̃, -ɑ̃t] *adj* destitute, poverty-stricken; (*fig*) poor.
indigeste [ɛ̃diʒɛst(ə)] *adj* indigestible.
indigestion [ɛ̃diʒɛstjɔ̃] *nf* indigestion *no pl*; **avoir une** ~ to have indigestion.
indignation [ɛ̃diɲɑsjɔ̃] *nf* indignation; **avec** ~ indignantly.
indigne [ɛ̃diɲ] *adj*: ~ **(de)** unworthy (of).
indigné, e [ɛ̃diɲe] *adj* indignant.
indignement [ɛ̃diɲmɑ̃] *adv* shamefully.
indigner [ɛ̃diɲe] *vt* to make indignant; **s'**~ **(de/contre)** to be (*ou* become) indignant (at).
indignité [ɛ̃diɲite] *nf* unworthiness *no pl*; (*acte*) shameful act.
indigo [ɛ̃digo] *nm* indigo.
indiqué, e [ɛ̃dike] *adj* (*date, lieu*) given, appointed; (*adéquat*) appropriate, suitable; (*conseillé*) advisable; (*remède, traitement*) appropriate.
indiquer [ɛ̃dike] *vt* (*désigner*): ~ **qch/qn à qn** to point sth/sb out to sb; (*suj: pendule, aiguille*) to show; (*suj: étiquette, plan*) to show, indicate; (*faire connaître: médecin, restaurant*): ~ **qch/qn à qn** to tell sb of sth/sb; (*renseigner sur*) to point out, tell; (*déterminer: date, lieu*) to give, state; (*dénoter*) to indicate, point to; ~ **du doigt** to point out; ~ **de la main** to indicate with one's hand; ~ **du regard** to glance towards *ou* in the direction of; **pourriez-vous m'**~ **les toilettes/l'heure?** could you direct me to the toilets/tell me the time?
indirect, e [ɛ̃diʀɛkt] *adj* indirect.
indirectement [ɛ̃diʀɛktəmɑ̃] *adv* indirectly (*apprendre*) in a roundabout way.
indiscernable [ɛ̃disɛʀnabl(ə)] *adj* indiscernible.
indiscipline [ɛ̃disiplin] *nf* lack of discipline.
indiscipliné, e [ɛ̃disipline] *adj* undisciplined (*fig*) unmanageable.
indiscret, ète [ɛ̃diskʀɛ, -ɛt] *adj* indiscreet.
indiscrétion [ɛ̃diskʀesjɔ̃] *nf* indiscretion; **sans** ~, ... without wishing to be indiscreet, ...
indiscutable [ɛ̃diskytabl(ə)] *adj* indisputable.
indiscutablement [ɛ̃diskytabləmɑ̃] *adv* indisputably.
indiscuté, e [ɛ̃dispyte] *adj* (*incontesté: droit chef*) undisputed.
indispensable [ɛ̃dispɑ̃sabl(ə)] *adj* indispensable, essential; ~ **à qn/pour faire qch** essen

tial for sb/to do sth.
indisponibilité [ɛ̃dispɔnibilite] *nf* unavailability.
indisponible [ɛ̃dispɔnibl(ə)] *adj* unavailable.
indisposé, e [ɛ̃dispoze] *adj* indisposed, unwell.
indisposer [ɛ̃dispoze] *vt* (*incommoder*) to upset; (*déplaire à*) to antagonize.
indisposition [ɛ̃dispozisjɔ̃] *nf* (slight) illness, indisposition.
indissociable [ɛ̃disɔsjabl(ə)] *adj* indissociable.
indissoluble [ɛ̃disɔlybl(ə)] *adj* indissoluble.
indissolublement [ɛ̃disɔlybləmɑ̃] *adv* indissolubly.
indistinct, e [ɛ̃distɛ̃, -ɛ̃kt(ə)] *adj* indistinct.
indistinctement [ɛ̃distɛ̃ktəmɑ̃] *adv* (*voir, prononcer*) indistinctly, (*sans distinction*) without distinction, indiscriminately.
individu [ɛ̃dividy] *nm* individual.
individualiser [ɛ̃dividɥalize] *vt* to individualize; (*personnaliser*) to tailor to individual requirements; **s'~** to develop one's own identity.
individualisme [ɛ̃dividɥalism(ə)] *nm* individualism.
individualiste [ɛ̃dividɥalist(ə)] *nm/f* individualist.
individualité [ɛ̃dividɥalite] *nf* individuality.
individuel, le [ɛ̃dividɥɛl] *adj* (*gén*) individual; (*opinion, livret, contrôle, avantages*) personal; **chambre ~le** single room; **maison ~le** detached house; **propriété ~le** personal *ou* private property.
individuellement [ɛ̃dividɥɛlmɑ̃] *adv* individually.
indivis, e [ɛ̃divi, -iz] *adj* (*JUR: bien, propriété, succession*) indivisible; (*: cohéritiers, propriétaires*) joint.
indivisible [ɛ̃divizibl(ə)] *adj* indivisible.
Indochine [ɛ̃dɔʃin] *nf*: **l'~** Indochina.
indochinois, e [ɛ̃dɔʃinwa, -waz] *adj* Indochinese.
indocile [ɛ̃dɔsil] *adj* unruly.
indo-européen, ne [ɛ̃dɔøʀɔpeɛ̃, -ɛn] *adj* Indo-European ♦ *nm* (*LING*) Indo-European.
indolence [ɛ̃dɔlɑ̃s] *nf* indolence.
indolent, e [ɛ̃dɔlɑ̃, -ɑ̃t] *adj* indolent.
indolore [ɛ̃dɔlɔʀ] *adj* painless.
indomptable [ɛ̃dɔ̃tabl(ə)] *adj* untameable; (*fig*) invincible, indomitable.
indompté, e [ɛ̃dɔ̃te] *adj* (*cheval*) unbroken.
Indonésie [ɛ̃donezi] *nf*: **l'~** Indonesia.
indonésien, ne [ɛ̃dɔnezjɛ̃, -ɛn] *adj* Indonesian ♦ *nm/f*: **I~, ne** Indonesian.
indu, e [ɛ̃dy] *adj*: **à des heures ~es** at an ungodly hour.
indubitable [ɛ̃dybitabl(ə)] *adj* indubitable.
indubitablement [ɛ̃dybitabləmɑ̃] *adv* indubitably.
induction [ɛ̃dyksjɔ̃] *nf* induction.
induire [ɛ̃dɥiʀ] *vt*: **~ qch de** to induce sth from; **~ qn en erreur** to lead sb astray, mislead sb.
indulgence [ɛ̃dylʒɑ̃s] *nf* indulgence; leniency; **avec ~** indulgently; leniently.
indulgent, e [ɛ̃dylʒɑ̃, -ɑ̃t] *adj* (*parent, regard*) indulgent; (*juge, examinateur*) lenient.
indûment [ɛ̃dymɑ̃] *adv* without due cause; (*illégitimement*) wrongfully.
industrialisation [ɛ̃dystʀijalizɑsjɔ̃] *nf* industrialization.
industrialiser [ɛ̃dystʀijalize] *vt* to industrialize; **s'~** to become industrialized.
industrie [ɛ̃dystʀi] *nf* industry; **~ automobile/textile** car/textile industry; **~ du spectacle** entertainment business.
industriel, le [ɛ̃dystʀijɛl] *adj* industrial; (*produit industriellement: pain etc*) mass-produced, factory-produced ♦ *nm* industrialist; (*fabricant*) manufacturer.
industriellement [ɛ̃dystʀijɛlmɑ̃] *adv* industrially.
industrieux, euse [ɛ̃dystʀijø, -øz] *adj* industrious.
inébranlable [inebʀɑ̃labl(ə)] *adj* (*masse, colonne*) solid; (*personne, certitude, foi*) steadfast, unwavering.
inédit, e [inedi, -it] *adj* (*correspondance etc*) (hitherto) unpublished; (*spectacle, moyen*) novel, original.
ineffable [inefabl(ə)] *adj* inexpressible, ineffable.
ineffaçable [inefasabl(ə)] *adj* indelible.
inefficace [inefikas] *adj* (*remède, moyen*) ineffective; (*machine, employé*) inefficient.
inefficacité [inefikasite] *nf* ineffectiveness; inefficiency.
inégal, e, aux [inegal, -o] *adj* unequal; (*irrégulier*) uneven.
inégalable [inegalabl(e)] *adj* matchless.
inégalé, e [inegale] *adj* unmatched, unequalled.
inégalement [inegalmɑ̃] *adv* unequally.
inégalité [inegalite] *nf* inequality; unevenness *no pl*; **~ de 2 hauteurs** difference *ou* disparity between 2 heights; **~s de terrain** uneven ground.
inélégance [inelegɑ̃s] *nf* inelegance.
inélégant, e [inelegɑ̃, -ɑ̃t] *adj* inelegant; (*indélicat*) discourteous.
inéligible [ineliʒibl(ə)] *adj* ineligible.
inéluctable [inelyktabl(ə)] *adj* inescapable.
inéluctablement [inelyktabləmɑ̃] *adv* inescapably.
inemployable [inɑ̃plwajabl(ə)] *adj* unusable.
inemployé, e [inɑ̃plwaje] *adj* unused.
inénarrable [inenaʀabl(ə)] *adj* hilarious.
inepte [inɛpt(ə)] *adj* inept.
ineptie [inɛpsi] *nf* ineptitude; (*propos*) nonsense *no pl*.
inépuisable [inepɥizabl(ə)] *adj* inexhaustible.
inéquitable [inekitabl(ə)] *adj* inequitable.
inerte [inɛʀt(ə)] *adj* lifeless; (*apathique*) passive, inert; (*PHYSIQUE, CHIMIE*) inert.

inertie [inɛʀsi] *nf* inertia.
inescompté, e [inɛskɔ̃te] *adj* unexpected, unhoped-for.
inespéré, e [inɛspeʀe] *adj* unhoped-for, unexpected.
inesthétique [inɛstetik] *adj* unsightly.
inestimable [inɛstimabl(e)] *adj* priceless; (*fig: bienfait*) invaluable.
inévitable [inevitabl(ə)] *adj* unavoidable; (*fatal, habituel*) inevitable.
inévitablement [inevitabləmɑ̃] *adv* inevitably.
inexact, e [inɛgzakt] *adj* inaccurate, inexact; (*non ponctuel*) unpunctual.
inexactement [inɛgzaktəmɑ̃] *adv* inaccurately.
inexactitude [inɛgzaktityd] *nf* inaccuracy.
inexcusable [inɛkskyzabl(ə)] *adj* inexcusable, unforgivable.
inexécutable [inɛgzekytabl(ə)] *adj* impracticable, unworkable; (*MUS*) unplayable.
inexistant, e [inɛgzistɑ̃, -ɑ̃t] *adj* non-existent.
inexorable [inɛgzɔʀabl(ə)] *adj* inexorable; (*personne: dur*): ~ **(à)** unmoved (by).
inexorablement [inɛgzɔʀabləmɑ̃] *adv* inexorably.
inexpérience [inɛkspeʀjɑ̃s] *nf* inexperience, lack of experience.
inexpérimenté, e [inɛkspeʀimɑ̃te] *adj* inexperienced; (*arme, procédé*) untested.
inexplicable [inɛksplikabl(ə)] *adj* inexplicable.
inexplicablement [inɛksplikabləmɑ̃] *adv* inexplicably.
inexpliqué, e [inɛksplike] *adj* unexplained.
inexploitable [inɛksplwatabl(ə)] *adj* (*gisement, richesse*) unexploitable; (*données, renseignements*) unusable.
inexploité, e [inɛksplwate] *adj* unexploited, untapped.
inexploré, e [inɛksplɔʀe] *adj* unexplored.
inexpressif, ive [inɛkspʀesif, -iv] *adj* inexpressive; (*regard etc*) expressionless.
inexpressivité [inɛkspʀesivite] *nf* expressionlessness.
inexprimable [inɛkspʀimabl(ə)] *adj* inexpressible.
inexprimé, e [inɛkspʀime] *adj* unspoken, unexpressed.
inexpugnable [inɛkspygnabl(ə)] *adj* impregnable.
inextensible [inɛkstɑ̃sibl(ə)] *adj* (*tissu*) non-stretch.
in extenso [inɛkstɛ̃so] *adv* in full.
inextinguible [inɛkstɛ̃gibl(ə)] *adj* (*soif*) unquenchable; (*rire*) uncontrollable.
in extremis [inɛkstʀemis] *adv* at the last minute ♦ *adj* last-minute; (*testament*) death bed *cpd*.
inextricable [inɛkstʀikabl(ə)] *adj* inextricable.
inextricablement [inɛkstʀikabləmɑ̃] *adv* inextricably.
infaillibilité [ɛ̃fajibilite] *nf* infallibility.
infaillible [ɛ̃fajibl(ə)] *adj* infallible; (*instinct*) infallible, unerring.
infailliblement [ɛ̃fajibləmɑ̃] *adv* (*certainement*) without fail.
infaisable [ɛ̃fəzabl(ə)] *adj* (*travail etc*) impossible, impractical.
infamant, e [ɛ̃famɑ̃, -ɑ̃t] *adj* libellous, defamatory.
infâme [ɛ̃fɑm] *adj* vile.
infamie [ɛ̃fami] *nf* infamy.
infanterie [ɛ̃fɑ̃tʀi] *nf* infantry.
infanticide [ɛ̃fɑ̃tisid] *nm/f* child-murderer/eress ♦ *nm* (*meurtre*) infanticide.
infantile [ɛ̃fɑ̃til] *adj* (*MÉD*) infantile, child *cpd*; (*péj: ton, réaction*) infantile, childish.
infantilisme [ɛ̃fɑ̃tilism(ə)] *nm* infantilism.
infarctus [ɛ̃faʀktys] *nm*: ~ **(du myocarde)** coronary (thrombosis).
infatigable [ɛ̃fatigabl(ə)] *adj* tireless, indefatigable.
infatigablement [ɛ̃fatigabləmɑ̃] *adv* tirelessly, indefatigably.
infatué, e [ɛ̃fatɥe] *adj* conceited; ~ **de** full of.
infécond, e [ɛ̃fekɔ̃, -ɔ̃d] *adj* infertile, barren.
infect, e [ɛ̃fɛkt] *adj* vile, foul; (*repas, vin*) revolting, foul.
infecter [ɛ̃fɛkte] *vt* (*atmosphère, eau*) to contaminate; (*MÉD*) to infect; **s'~** to become infected *ou* septic.
infectieux, euse [ɛ̃fɛksjø, -øz] *adj* infectious.
infection [ɛ̃fɛksjɔ̃] *nf* infection.
inféoder [ɛ̃feɔde] *vt*: **s'~ à** to pledge allegiance to.
inférer [ɛ̃feʀe] *vt*: ~ **qch de** to infer sth from.
inférieur, e [ɛ̃feʀjœʀ] *adj* lower; (*en qualité, intelligence*) inferior ♦ *nm/f* inferior; ~ **à** (*somme, quantité*) less *ou* smaller than; (*moins bon que*) inferior to; (*tâche: pas à la hauteur de*) unequal to.
infériorité [ɛ̃feʀjɔʀite] *nf* inferiority; ~ **en nombre** inferiority in numbers.
infernal, e, aux [ɛ̃fɛʀnal, -o] *adj* (*chaleur rythme*) infernal; (*méchanceté, complot*) diabolical.
infester [ɛ̃fɛste] *vt* to infest; **infesté de moustiques** infested with mosquitoes, mosquito-ridden.
infidèle [ɛ̃fidɛl] *adj* unfaithful; (*REL*) infidel.
infidélité [ɛ̃fidelite] *nf* unfaithfulness *no pl*.
infiltration [ɛ̃filtʀɑsjɔ̃] *nf* infiltration.
infiltrer [ɛ̃filtʀe]: **s'~** *vi*: **s'~ dans** to penetrate into; (*liquide*) to seep into; (*fig: noyauter*) to infiltrate.
infime [ɛ̃fim] *adj* minute, tiny; (*inférieur*) lowly.
infini, e [ɛ̃fini] *adj* infinite ♦ *nm* infinity; **à l'~** (*MATH*) to infinity; (*discourir*) ad infinitum endlessly; (*agrandir, varier*) infinitely; (*à perte de vue*) endlessly (into the distance).
infiniment [ɛ̃finimɑ̃] *adv* infinitely; ~ **grand, petit** (*MATH*) infinitely great/infinitessimal.
infinité [ɛ̃finite] *nf*: **une ~ de** an infinite number of.

infinitésimal, e, aux [ɛ̃finitezimal, -o] *adj* infinitessimal.
infinitif, ive [ɛ̃finitif, -iv] *adj, nm* infinitive.
infirme [ɛ̃fiʀm(ə)] *adj* disabled ♦ *nm/f* disabled person; ~ **mental** mentally-handicapped person; ~ **moteur** spastic; ~ **de guerre** war cripple; ~ **du travail** industrially disabled person.
infirmer [ɛ̃fiʀme] *vt* to invalidate.
infirmerie [ɛ̃fiʀməʀi] *nf* sick bay.
infirmier, ière [ɛ̃fiʀmje, -jɛʀ] *nm/f* nurse ♦ *adj*: **élève** ~ student nurse; **infirmière chef** sister; **infirmière diplômée** registered nurse; **infirmière visiteuse** visiting nurse, ≈ district nurse (*BRIT*).
infirmité [ɛ̃fiʀmite] *nf* disability.
inflammable [ɛ̃flamabl(ə)] *adj* (in)flammable.
inflammation [ɛ̃flamɑsjɔ̃] *nf* inflammation.
inflammatoire [ɛ̃flamatwaʀ] *adj* (*MÉD*) inflammatory.
inflation [ɛ̃flɑsjɔ̃] *nf* inflation.
inflationniste [ɛ̃flɑsjɔnist(ə)] *adj* inflationist.
infléchir [ɛ̃fleʃiʀ] *vt* (*fig: politique*) to reorientate, redirect; **s'**~ *vi* (*poutre, tringle*) to bend, sag.
inflexibilité [ɛ̃flɛksibilite] *nf* inflexibility.
inflexible [ɛ̃flɛksibl(ə)] *adj* inflexible.
inflexion [ɛ̃flɛksjɔ̃] *nf* inflexion; ~ **de la tête** slight nod (of the head).
infliger [ɛ̃fliʒe] *vt*: ~ **qch (à qn)** to inflict sth (on sb); (*amende, sanction*) to impose sth (on sb).
influençable [ɛ̃flyɑ̃sabl(ə)] *adj* easily influenced.
influence [ɛ̃flyɑ̃s] *nf* influence; (*d'un médicament*) effect.
influencer [ɛ̃flyɑ̃se] *vt* to influence.
influent, e [ɛ̃flyɑ̃, -ɑ̃t] *adj* influential.
influer [ɛ̃flye]: ~ **sur** *vt* to have an influence upon.
influx [ɛ̃fly] *nm*: ~ **nerveux** (nervous) impulse.
infobulle [ɛ̃fobyl] *nf* (*COMPUT*) tooltip.
infographie [ɛ̃fɔgʀafi] *nf* computer graphics *sg*.
informateur, trice [ɛ̃fɔʀmatœʀ, -tʀis] *nm/f* informant.
informaticien, ne [ɛ̃fɔʀmatisjɛ̃, -ɛn] *nm/f* computer scientist.
informatif, ive [ɛ̃fɔʀmatif, -iv] *adj* informative.
information [ɛ̃fɔʀmɑsjɔ̃] *nf* (*renseignement*) piece of information; (*PRESSE, TV: nouvelle*) item of news; (*diffusion de renseignements, INFORM*) information; (*JUR*) inquiry, investigation; ~**s** *nfpl* (*TV*) news *sg*; **voyage d'**~ fact-finding trip; **agence d'**~ news agency; **journal d'**~ quality (*BRIT*) *ou* serious newspaper.
informatique [ɛ̃fɔʀmatik] *nf* (*technique*) data processing; (*science*) computer science ♦ *adj* computer *cpd*.
informatisation [ɛ̃fɔʀmatizɑsjɔ̃] *nf* computerization.
informatiser [ɛ̃fɔʀmatize] *vt* to computerize.
informe [ɛ̃fɔʀm(ə)] *adj* shapeless.
informé, e [ɛ̃fɔʀme] *adj*: **jusqu'à plus ample** ~ until further information is available.
informel, le [ɛ̃fɔʀmɛl] *adj* informal.
informer [ɛ̃fɔʀme] *vt*: ~ **qn (de)** to inform sb (of) ♦ *vi* (*JUR*): ~ **contre qn/sur qch** to initiate inquiries about sb/sth; **s'**~ **(sur)** to inform o.s. (about); **s'**~ **(de qch/si)** to inquire *ou* find out (about sth/whether *ou* if).
informulé, e [ɛ̃fɔʀmyle] *adj* unformulated.
infortune [ɛ̃fɔʀtyn] *nf* misfortune.
infos [ɛ̃fo] *nfpl* (= *informations*) news.
infraction [ɛ̃fʀaksjɔ̃] *nf* offence; ~ **à** violation *ou* breach of; **être en** ~ to be in breach of the law.
infranchissable [ɛ̃fʀɑ̃ʃisabl(ə)] *adj* impassable; (*fig*) insuperable.
infrarouge [ɛ̃fʀaʀuʒ] *adj, nm* infrared.
infrason [ɛ̃fʀasɔ̃] *nm* infrasonic vibration.
infrastructure [ɛ̃fʀastʀyktyʀ] *nf* (*d'une route etc*) substructure; (*AVIAT, MIL*) ground installations *pl*; (*touristique etc*) facilities.
infréquentable [ɛ̃fʀekɑ̃tabl(ə)] *adj* not to be associated with.
infroissable [ɛ̃fʀwasabl(ə)] *adj* crease-resistant.
infructueux, euse [ɛ̃fʀyktɥø, -øz] *adj* fruitless, unfruitful.
infus, e [ɛ̃fy, -yz] *adj*: **avoir la science** ~**e** to have innate knowledge.
infuser [ɛ̃fyze] *vt* (*aussi*: **faire** ~: *thé*) to brew; (*: tisane*) to infuse ♦ *vi* to brew; to infuse; **laisser** ~ (to leave) to brew.
infusion [ɛ̃fyzjɔ̃] *nf* (*tisane*) infusion, herb tea.
ingambe [ɛ̃gɑ̃b] *adj* spry, nimble.
ingénier [ɛ̃ʒenje]: **s'**~ *vi*: **s'**~ **à faire** to strive to do.
ingénierie [ɛ̃ʒeniʀi] *nf* engineering.
ingénieur [ɛ̃ʒenjœʀ] *nm* engineer; ~ **agronome/chimiste** agricultural/chemical engineer; ~ **conseil** consulting engineer; ~ **du son** sound engineer.
ingénieusement [ɛ̃ʒenjøzmɑ̃] *adv* ingeniously.
ingénieux, euse [ɛ̃ʒenjø, -øz] *adj* ingenious, clever.
ingéniosité [ɛ̃ʒenjozite] *nf* ingenuity.
ingénu, e [ɛ̃ʒeny] *adj* ingenuous, artless ♦ *nf* (*THÉÂT*) ingénue.
ingénuité [ɛ̃ʒenɥite] *nf* ingenuousness.
ingénument [ɛ̃ʒenymɑ̃] *adv* ingenuously.
ingérence [ɛ̃ʒeʀɑ̃s] *nf* interference.
ingérer [ɛ̃ʒeʀe]: **s'**~ *vi*: **s'**~ **dans** to interfere in.
ingouvernable [ɛ̃guvɛʀnabl(ə)] *adj* ungovernable.
ingrat, e [ɛ̃gʀa, -at] *adj* (*personne*) ungrateful; (*sol*) poor; (*travail, sujet*) arid, thankless; (*visage*) unprepossessing.
ingratitude [ɛ̃gʀatityd] *nf* ingratitude.

ingrédient [ɛ̃gʀedjɑ̃] *nm* ingredient.
inguérissable [ɛ̃geʀisabl(ə)] *adj* incurable.
ingurgiter [ɛ̃gyʀʒite] *vt* to swallow; **faire ~ qch à qn** to make sb swallow sth; (*fig: connaissances*) to force sth into sb.
inhabile [inabil] *adj* clumsy; (*fig*) inept.
inhabitable [inabitabl(ə)] *adj* uninhabitable.
inhabité, e [inabite] *adj* (*régions*) uninhabited; (*maison*) unoccupied.
inhabituel, le [inabitɥɛl] *adj* unusual.
inhalateur [inalatœʀ] *nm* inhaler; **~ d'oxygène** oxygen mask.
inhalation [inalɑsjɔ̃] *nf* (*MÉD*) inhalation; **faire des ~s** to use an inhalation bath.
inhaler [inale] *vt* to inhale.
inhérent, e [ineʀɑ̃, -ɑ̃t] *adj*: **~ à** inherent in.
inhiber [inibe] *vt* to inhibit.
inhibition [inibisjɔ̃] *nf* inhibition.
inhospitalier, ière [inɔspitalje, -jɛʀ] *adj* inhospitable.
inhumain, e [inymɛ̃, -ɛn] *adj* inhuman.
inhumation [inymɑsjɔ̃] *nf* interment, burial.
inhumer [inyme] *vt* to inter, bury.
inimaginable [inimaʒinabl(ə)] *adj* unimaginable.
inimitable [inimitabl(ə)] *adj* inimitable.
inimitié [inimitje] *nf* enmity.
ininflammable [inɛ̃flamabl(ə)] *adj* nonflammable.
inintelligent, e [inɛ̃teliʒɑ̃, -ɑ̃t] *adj* unintelligent.
inintelligible [inɛ̃teliʒibl(ə)] *adj* unintelligible.
inintelligiblement [inɛ̃teliʒibləmɑ̃] *adv* unintelligibly.
inintéressant, e [inɛ̃teʀɛsɑ̃, -ɑ̃t] *adj* uninteresting.
ininterrompu, e [inɛ̃tɛʀɔ̃py] *adj* (*file, série*) unbroken; (*flot, vacarme*) uninterrupted, nonstop; (*effort*) unremitting, continuous.
iniquité [inikite] *nf* iniquity.
initial, e, aux [inisjal, -o] *adj, nf* initial; **~es** *nfpl* initials.
initialement [inisjalmɑ̃] *adv* initially.
initialiser [inisjalize] *vt* to initialize.
initiateur, trice [inisjatœʀ, -tʀis] *nm/f* initiator; (*d'une mode, technique*) innovator, pioneer.
initiation [inisjɑsjɔ̃] *nf* initiation.
initiatique [inisjatik] *adj* (*rites, épreuves*) initiatory.
initiative [inisjativ] *nf* initiative; **prendre l'~ de qch/de faire** to take the initiative for sth/of doing; **avoir de l'~** to have initiative, show enterprise; **esprit/qualités d'~** spirit/qualities of initiative; **à** *ou* **sur l'~ de qn** on sb's initiative; **de sa propre ~** on one's own initiative.
initié, e [inisje] *adj* initiated ♦ *nm/f* initiate.
initier [inisje] *vt* to initiate; **~ qn à** to initiate sb into; (*faire découvrir: art, jeu*) to introduce sb to; **s'~ à** (*métier, profession, technique*) to become initiated into.
injectable [ɛ̃ʒɛktabl(ə)] *adj* injectable.
injecté, e [ɛ̃ʒɛkte] *adj*: **yeux ~s de sang** bloodshot eyes.
injecter [ɛ̃ʒɛkte] *vt* to inject.
injection [ɛ̃ʒɛksjɔ̃] *nf* injection; **à ~** (*AUTO*) fuel injection *cpd*.
injonction [ɛ̃ʒɔ̃ksjɔ̃] *nf* injunction, order; **~ de payer** (*JUR*) order to pay.
injouable [ɛ̃jwabl(ə)] *adj* unplayable.
injure [ɛ̃ʒyʀ] *nf* insult, abuse *no pl*.
injurier [ɛ̃ʒyʀje] *vt* to insult, abuse.
injurieux, euse [ɛ̃ʒyʀjø, -øz] *adj* abusive, insulting.
injuste [ɛ̃ʒyst(ə)] *adj* unjust, unfair.
injustement [ɛ̃jystəmɑ̃] *adv* unjustly, unfairly.
injustice [ɛ̃ʒystis] *nf* injustice.
injustifiable [ɛ̃jystifjabl(ə)] *adj* unjustifiable.
injustifié, e [ɛ̃jystifje] *adj* unjustified, unwarranted.
inlassable [ɛ̃lɑsabl(ə)] *adj* tireless, indefatigable.
inlassablement [ɛ̃lasabləmɑ̃] *adv* tirelessly.
inné, e [ine] *adj* innate, inborn.
innocemment [inɔsamɑ̃] *adv* innocently.
innocence [inɔsɑ̃s] *nf* innocence.
innocent, e [inɔsɑ̃, -ɑ̃t] *adj* innocent ♦ *nm/f* innocent person; **faire l'~** to play *ou* come the innocent.
innocenter [inɔsɑ̃te] *vt* to clear, prove innocent.
innocuité [inɔkɥite] *nf* innocuousness.
innombrable [inɔ̃bʀabl(ə)] *adj* innumerable.
innommable [inɔmabl(ə)] *adj* unspeakable.
innovateur, trice [inɔvatœʀ, -tʀis] *adj* innovatory.
innovation [inɔvɑsjɔ̃] *nf* innovation.
innover [inɔve] *vi*: **~ en matière d'art** to break new ground in the field of art.
inobservance [inɔpsɛʀvɑ̃s] *nf* nonobservance.
inobservation [inɔpsɛʀvɑsjɔ̃] *nf* nonobservation, inobservance.
inoccupé, e [inɔkype] *adj* unoccupied.
inoculer [inɔkyle] *vt*: **~ qch à qn** (*volontairement*) to inoculate sb with sth; (*accidentellement*) to infect sb with sth; **~ qn contre** to inoculate sb against.
inodore [inɔdɔʀ] *adj* (*gaz*) odourless; (*fleur*) scentless.
inoffensif, ive [inɔfɑ̃sif, -iv] *adj* harmless, innocuous.
inondable [inɔ̃dabl(ə)] *adj* (*zone etc*) liable to flooding.
inondation [inɔ̃dɑsjɔ̃] *nf* flooding *no pl*; (*torrent, eau*) flood.
inonder [inɔ̃de] *vt* to flood; (*fig*) to inundate, overrun; **~ de** (*fig*) to flood *ou* swamp with.
inopérable [inɔpeʀabl(ə)] *adj* inoperable.
inopérant, e [inɔpeʀɑ̃, -ɑ̃t] *adj* inoperative, ineffective.
inopiné, e [inɔpine] *adj* unexpected, sudden.
inopinément [inɔpinemɑ̃] *adv* unexpectedly.

inopportun, e [inɔpɔʀtœ̃, -yn] *adj* ill-timed, untimely; inappropriate; (*moment*) inopportune.
inorganisation [inɔʀganizɑsjɔ̃] *nf* lack of organization.
inorganisé, e [inɔʀganize] *adj* (*travailleurs*) non-organized.
inoubliable [inublijabl(ə)] *adj* unforgettable.
inouï, e [inwi] *adj* unheard-of, extraordinary.
inox [inɔks] *adj, nm* (= *inoxydable*) stainless (steel).
inoxydable [inɔksidabl(ə)] *adj* stainless; (*couverts*) stainless steel *cpd*.
inqualifiable [ɛ̃kalifjabl(ə)] *adj* unspeakable.
inquiet, ète [ɛ̃kjɛ, -ɛt] *adj* (*par nature*) anxious; (*momentanément*) worried; ~ **de qch/au sujet de qn** worried about sth/sb.
inquiétant, e [ɛ̃kjetɑ̃, -ɑ̃t] *adj* worrying, disturbing.
inquiéter [ɛ̃kjete] *vt* to worry, disturb; (*harceler*) to harass; **s'~** to worry, become anxious; **s'~ de** to worry about; (*s'enquérir de*) to inquire about.
inquiétude [ɛ̃kjetyd] *nf* anxiety; **donner de l'~** *ou* **des ~s à** to worry; **avoir de l'~** *ou* **des ~s au sujet de** to feel anxious *ou* worried about.
inquisiteur, trice [ɛ̃kizitœʀ, -tʀis] *adj* (*regards, questions*) inquisitive, prying.
inquisition [ɛ̃kizisjɔ̃] *nf* inquisition.
INR *sigle m* = *Institut national (belge) de radiodiffusion.*
INRA [inʀa] *sigle m* = *Institut national de la recherche agronomique.*
inracontable [ɛ̃ʀakɔ̃tabl(ə)] *adj* (*trop osé*) unrepeatable; (*trop compliqué*): **l'histoire est ~** the story is too complicated to relate.
insaisissable [ɛ̃sezisabl(ə)] *adj* elusive.
insalubre [ɛ̃salybʀ(ə)] *adj* unhealthy, insalubrious.
insalubrité [ɛ̃salybʀite] *nf* unhealthiness, insalubrity.
insanité [ɛ̃sanite] *nf* madness *no pl*, insanity *no pl*.
insatiable [ɛ̃sasjabl(ə)] *adj* insatiable.
insatisfaction [ɛ̃satisfaksjɔ̃] *nf* dissatisfaction.
insatisfait, e [ɛ̃satisfɛ, -ɛt] *adj* (*non comblé*) unsatisfied; (*: passion, envie*) unfulfilled; (*mécontent*) dissatisfied.
inscription [ɛ̃skʀipsjɔ̃] *nf* (*sur un mur, écriteau etc*) inscription; (*à une institution: voir s'inscrire*) enrolment; registration.
inscrire [ɛ̃skʀiʀ] *vt* (*marquer: sur son calepin etc*) to note *ou* write down; (*: sur un mur, une affiche etc*) to write; (*: dans la pierre, le métal*) to inscribe; (*mettre: sur une liste, un budget etc*) to put down; (*enrôler: soldat*) to enlist; **~ qn à** (*club, école etc*) to enrol sb at; **s'~** (*pour une excursion etc*) to put one's name down; **s'~ (à)** (*club, parti*) to join; (*université*) to register *ou* enrol (at); (*examen, concours*) to register *ou* enter (for); **s'~ dans** (*se situer: négociations etc*) to come within the scope of; **s'~ en faux contre** to deny (strongly); (*JUR*) to challenge.
inscrit, e [ɛ̃skʀi, it] *pp de* **inscrire** ♦ *adj* (*étudiant, électeur etc*) registered.
insécable [ɛ̃sekabl(ə)] *adj* (*INFORM*) indivisible.
insecte [ɛ̃sɛkt(ə)] *nm* insect.
insecticide [ɛ̃sɛktisid] *nm* insecticide.
insécurité [ɛ̃sekyʀite] *nf* insecurity, lack of security.
INSEE [inse] *sigle m* (= *Institut national de la statistique et des études économiques*) *national institute of statistical and economic information.*
insémination [ɛ̃seminɑsjɔ̃] *nf* insemination.
insensé, e [ɛ̃sɑ̃se] *adj* insane, mad.
insensibiliser [ɛ̃sɑ̃sibilize] *vt* to anaesthetize; (*à une allergie*) to desensitize; **~ à qch** (*fig*) to cause to become insensitive to sth.
insensibilité [ɛ̃sɑ̃sibilite] *nf* insensitivity.
insensible [ɛ̃sɑ̃sibl(ə)] *adj* (*nerf, membre*) numb; (*dur, indifférent*) insensitive; (*imperceptible*) imperceptible.
insensiblement [ɛ̃sɑ̃sibləmɑ̃] *adv* (*doucement, peu à peu*) imperceptibly.
inséparable [ɛ̃sepaʀabl(ə)] *adj*: **~ (de)** inseparable (from) ♦ *nmpl*: **~s** (*oiseaux*) lovebirds.
insérer [ɛ̃seʀe] *vt* to insert; **s'~ dans** to fit into; (*fig*) to come within.
INSERM [ɛ̃sɛʀm] *sigle m* (= *Institut national de la santé et de la recherche médicale*) *national institute for medical research.*
insert [ɛ̃sɛʀ] *nm enclosed fireplace burning solid fuel.*
insertion [ɛ̃sɛʀsjɔ̃] *nf* (*d'une personne*) integration.
insidieusement [ɛ̃sidjøzmɑ̃] *adv* insidiously.
insidieux, euse [ɛ̃sidjø, -øz] *adj* insidious.
insigne [ɛ̃siɲ] *nm* (*d'un parti, club*) badge ♦ *adj* distinguished; **~s** *nmpl* (*d'une fonction*) insignia *pl*.
insignifiant, e [ɛ̃siɲifjɑ̃, -ɑ̃t] *adj* insignificant; (*somme, affaire, détail*) trivial, insignificant.
insinuant, e [ɛ̃sinɥɑ̃, -ɑ̃t] *adj* ingratiating.
insinuation [ɛ̃sinɥɑsjɔ̃] *nf* innuendo, insinuation.
insinuer [ɛ̃sinɥe] *vt* to insinuate, imply; **s'~ dans** to seep into; (*fig*) to worm one's way into, creep into.
insipide [ɛ̃sipid] *adj* insipid.
insistance [ɛ̃sistɑ̃s] *nf* insistence; **avec ~** insistently.
insistant, e [ɛ̃sistɑ̃, -ɑ̃t] *adj* insistent.
insister [ɛ̃siste] *vi* to insist; (*s'obstiner*) to keep on; **~ sur** (*détail, note*) to stress; **~ pour qch/pour faire qch** to be insistent about sth/about doing sth.
insociable [ɛ̃sɔsjabl(ə)] *adj* unsociable.
insolation [ɛ̃sɔlɑsjɔ̃] *nf* (*MÉD*) sunstroke *no pl*; (*ensoleillement*) period of sunshine.
insolence [ɛ̃sɔlɑ̃s] *nf* insolence *no pl*; **avec ~** in-

solently.
insolent, e [ɛ̃sɔlɑ̃, -ɑ̃t] *adj* insolent.
insolite [ɛ̃sɔlit] *adj* strange, unusual.
insoluble [ɛ̃sɔlybl(ə)] *adj* insoluble.
insolvable [ɛ̃sɔlvabl(ə)] *adj* insolvent.
insomniaque [ɛ̃sɔmnjak] *adj, nm/f* insomniac.
insomnie [ɛ̃sɔmni] *nf* insomnia *no pl*, sleeplessness *no pl*; **avoir des ~s** to suffer from insomnia.
insondable [ɛ̃sɔ̃dabl(ə)] *adj* unfathomable.
insonore [ɛ̃sɔnɔʀ] *adj* soundproof.
insonorisation [ɛ̃sɔnɔʀizɑsjɔ̃] *nf* soundproofing.
insonoriser [ɛ̃sɔnɔʀize] *vt* to soundproof.
insouciance [ɛ̃susjɑ̃s] *nf* carefree attitude; heedless attitude.
insouciant, e [ɛ̃susjɑ̃, -ɑ̃t] *adj* carefree; (*imprévoyant*) heedless.
insoumis, e [ɛ̃sumi, -iz] *adj* (*caractère, enfant*) rebellious, refractory; (*contrée, tribu*) unsubdued; (*MIL: soldat*) absent without leave ♦ *nm* (*MIL: soldat*) absentee.
insoumission [ɛ̃sumisjɔ̃] *nf* rebelliousness; (*MIL*) absence without leave.
insoupçonnable [ɛ̃supsɔnabl(ə)] *adj* above suspicion.
insoupçonné, e [ɛ̃supsɔne] *adj* unsuspected.
insoutenable [ɛ̃sutnabl(ə)] *adj* (*argument*) untenable; (*chaleur*) unbearable.
inspecter [ɛ̃spɛkte] *vt* to inspect.
inspecteur, trice [ɛ̃spɛktœʀ, -tʀis] *nm/f* inspector; (*des assurances*) assessor; **~ d'Académie** (regional) director of education; **~ (de l'enseignement) primaire** primary school inspector; **~ des finances** ≈ tax inspector (*BRIT*), ≈ Internal Revenue Service agent (*US*); **~ (de police)** (police) inspector.
inspection [ɛ̃spɛksjɔ̃] *nf* inspection.
inspirateur, trice [ɛ̃spiʀatœʀ, -tʀis] *nm/f* (*instigateur*) instigator; (*animateur*) inspirer.
inspiration [ɛ̃spiʀɑsjɔ̃] *nf* inspiration; breathing in *no pl*; (*idée*) flash of inspiration, brainwave; **sous l'~ de** prompted by.
inspiré, e [ɛ̃spiʀe] *adj*: **être bien/mal ~ de faire qch** to be well-advised/ill-advised to do sth.
inspirer [ɛ̃spiʀe] *vt* (*gén*) to inspire ♦ *vi* (*aspirer*) to breathe in; **s'~ de** (*suj: artiste*) to draw one's inspiration from; (*suj: tableau*) to be inspired by; **~ qch à qn** (*œuvre, project, action*) to inspire sb with sth; (*dégoût, crainte, horreur*) to fill sb with sth; **ça ne m'inspire pas** I'm not keen on the idea.
instabilité [ɛ̃stabilite] *nf* instability.
instable [ɛ̃stabl(ə)] *adj* (*meuble, équilibre*) unsteady; (*population, temps*) unsettled; (*paix, régime, caractère*) unstable.
installateur [ɛ̃stalatœʀ] *nm* fitter.
installation [ɛ̃stalɑsjɔ̃] *nf* installation; putting in *ou* up; fitting out; settling in; (*appareils etc*) fittings *pl*, installations *pl*; **~s** *nfpl* installations; (*industrielles*) plant *sg*; (*de loisirs*) facilities.
installé, e [ɛ̃stale] *adj*: **bien/mal ~** well/poorly equipped; (*personne*) well/not very well set up *ou* organized.
installer [ɛ̃stale] *vt* (*loger*): **~ qn** to get sb settled, install sb; (*asseoir, coucher*) to settle (down); (*placer*) to put, place; (*meuble*) to put in; (*rideau, étagère, tente*) to put up; (*gaz, électricité etc*) to put in, install; (*appartement*) to fit out; (*aménager*): **~ une salle de bains dans une pièce** to fit out a room with a bathroom suite; **s'~** (*s'établir: artisan, dentiste etc*) to set o.s. up; (*se loger*): **s'~ à l'hôtel/chez qn** to move into a hotel/in with sb; (*emménager*) to settle in; (*sur un siège, à un emplacement*) to settle (down); (*fig: maladie, grève*) to take a firm hold *ou* grip.
instamment [ɛ̃stamɑ̃] *adv* urgently.
instance [ɛ̃stɑ̃s] *nf* (*JUR: procédure*) (legal) proceedings *pl*; (*ADMIN: autorité*) authority; **~s** *nfpl* (*prières*) entreaties; **affaire en ~** matter pending; **courrier en ~** mail ready for posting; **être en ~ de divorce** to be awaiting a divorce; **train en ~ de départ** train on the point of departure; **tribunal de première ~** court of first instance; **en seconde ~** on appeal.
instant [ɛ̃stɑ̃] *nm* moment, instant; **dans un ~** in a moment; **à l'~** this instant; **je l'ai vu à l'~** I've just this minute seen him, I saw him a moment ago; **à l'~ (même) où** at the (very) moment that *ou* when, (just) as; **à chaque ~, à tout ~** at any moment; constantly; **pour l'~** for the moment, for the time being; **par ~s** at times; **de tous les ~s** perpetual; **dès l'~ où** *ou* **que** ... from the moment when ..., since that moment when ....
instantané, e [ɛ̃stɑ̃tane] *adj* (*lait, café*) instant; (*explosion, mort*) instantaneous ♦ *nm* snapshot.
instantanément [ɛ̃stɑ̃tanemɑ̃] *adv* instantaneously.
instar [ɛ̃staʀ]: **à l'~ de** *prép* following the example of, like.
instaurer [ɛ̃stɔʀe] *vt* to institute; **s'~** *vi* to set o.s. up; (*collaboration etc*) to be established.
instigateur, trice [ɛ̃stigatœʀ, -tʀis] *nm/f* instigator.
instigation [ɛ̃stigɑsjɔ̃] *nf*: **à l'~ de qn** at sb's instigation.
instiller [ɛ̃stile] *vt* to instil, apply.
instinct [ɛ̃stɛ̃] *nm* instinct; **d'~** (*spontanément*) instinctively; **~ grégaire** herd instinct; **~ de conservation** instinct of self-preservation.
instinctif, ive [ɛ̃stɛ̃ktif, -iv] *adj* instinctive.
instinctivement [ɛ̃stɛ̃ktivmɑ̃] *adv* instinctively.
instituer [ɛ̃stitɥe] *vt* to institute, set up; **s'~ défenseur d'une cause** to set o.s up as defender of a cause.
institut [ɛ̃stity] *nm* institute; **~ de beauté** beauty salon; **~ médico-légal** mortuary; **l~**

universitaire de technologie (IUT) technical college.

instituteur, trice [ɛ̃stitytœʀ, -tʀis] *nm/f* (primary (*BRIT*) *ou* grade (*US*) school) teacher.

institution [ɛ̃stitysjɔ̃] *nf* institution; (*collège*) private school.

institutionnaliser [ɛ̃stitysjɔnalize] *vt* to institutionalize.

instructeur, trice [ɛ̃stʀyktœʀ, -tʀis] *adj* (*MIL*): **sergent** ~ drill sergeant; (*JUR*): **juge** ~ examining (*BRIT*) *ou* committing (*US*) magistrate ♦ *nm/f* instructor.

instructif, ive [ɛ̃stʀyktif, -iv] *adj* instructive.

instruction [ɛ̃stʀyksjɔ̃] *nf* (*enseignement, savoir*) education; (*JUR*) (preliminary) investigation and hearing; (*directive*) instruction; (*ADMIN: document*) directive; **~s** *nfpl* instructions; (*mode d'emploi*) directions, instructions; ~ **civique** civics *sg*; ~ **primaire/publique** primary/public education; ~ **religieuse** religious instruction; ~ **professionnelle** vocational training.

instruire [ɛ̃stʀɥiʀ] *vt* (*élèves*) to teach; (*recrues*) to train; (*JUR: affaire*) to conduct the investigation for; **s'~** to educate o.s.; **s'~ auprès de qn de qch** (*s'informer*) to find sth out from sb; ~ **qn de qch** (*informer*) to inform *ou* advise sb of sth; ~ **contre qn** (*JUR*) to investigate sb.

instruit, e [ɛ̃stʀɥi, -it] *pp de* **instruire** ♦ *adj* educated.

instrument [ɛ̃stʀymɑ̃] *nm* instrument; ~ **à cordes/vent** stringed/wind instrument; ~ **de mesure** measuring instrument; ~ **de musique** musical instrument; ~ **de travail** (working) tool.

instrumental, e, aux [ɛ̃stʀymɑ̃tal, -o] *adj* instrumental.

instrumentation [ɛ̃stʀymɑ̃tɑsjɔ̃] *nf* instrumentation.

instrumentiste [ɛ̃stʀymɑ̃tist(ə)] *nm/f* instrumentalist.

insu [ɛ̃sy] *nm*: **à l'~ de qn** without sb knowing.

insubmersible [ɛ̃sybmɛʀsibl(ə)] *adj* unsinkable.

insubordination [ɛ̃sybɔʀdinɑsjɔ̃] *nf* rebelliousness; (*MIL*) insubordination.

insubordonné, e [ɛ̃sybɔʀdɔne] *adj* insubordinate.

insuccès [ɛ̃syksɛ] *nm* failure.

insuffisamment [ɛ̃syfizamɑ̃] *adv* insufficiently.

insuffisance [ɛ̃syfizɑ̃s] *nf* insufficiency; inadequacy; **~s** *nfpl* (*lacunes*) inadequacies; ~ **cardiaque** cardiac insufficiency *no pl*; ~ **hépatique** liver deficiency.

insuffisant, e [ɛ̃syfizɑ̃, -ɑ̃t] *adj* insufficient; (*élève, travail*) inadequate.

insuffler [ɛ̃syfle] *vt*: ~ **qch dans** to blow sth into; ~ **qch à qn** to inspire sb with sth.

insulaire [ɛ̃sylɛʀ] *adj* island *cpd*; (*attitude*) insular.

insularité [ɛ̃sylaʀite] *nf* insularity.

insuline [ɛ̃sylin] *nf* insulin.

insultant, e [ɛ̃syltɑ̃, -ɑ̃t] *adj* insulting.

insulte [ɛ̃sylt(ə)] *nf* insult.

insulter [ɛ̃sylte] *vt* to insult.

insupportable [ɛ̃sypɔʀtabl(ə)] *adj* unbearable.

insurgé, e [ɛ̃syʀʒe] *adj, nm/f* insurgent, rebel.

insurger [ɛ̃syʀʒe]: **s'~** *vi*: **s'~ (contre)** to rise up *ou* rebel (against).

insurmontable [ɛ̃syʀmɔ̃tabl(ə)] *adj* (*difficulté*) insuperable; (*aversion*) unconquerable.

insurpassable [ɛ̃syʀpɑsabl(ə)] *adj* unsurpassable, unsurpassed.

insurrection [ɛ̃syʀɛksjɔ̃] *nf* insurrection, revolt.

insurrectionnel, le [ɛ̃syʀɛksjɔnɛl] *adj* insurrectionary.

intact, e [ɛ̃takt] *adj* intact.

intangible [ɛ̃tɑ̃ʒibl(ə)] *adj* intangible; (*principe*) inviolable.

intarissable [ɛ̃taʀisabl(ə)] *adj* inexhaustible.

intégral, e, aux [ɛ̃tegʀal, -o] *adj* complete ♦ *nf* (*MATH*) integral; (*œuvres complètes*) complete works.

intégralement [ɛ̃tegʀalmɑ̃] *adv* in full, fully.

intégralité [ɛ̃tegʀalite] *nf* (*d'une somme, d'un revenu*) whole (*ou* full) amount; **dans son ~** in its entirety.

intégrant, e [ɛ̃tegʀɑ̃, -ɑ̃t] *adj*: **faire partie ~e de** to be an integral part of, be part and parcel of.

intégration [ɛ̃tegʀɑsjɔ̃] *nf* integration.

intégrationniste [ɛ̃tegʀɑsjɔnist(ə)] *adj, nm/f* integrationist.

intègre [ɛ̃tɛgʀ(ə)] *adj* perfectly honest, upright.

intégré, e [ɛ̃tegʀe] *adj*: **circuit ~** integrated circuit.

intégrer [ɛ̃tegʀe] *vt*: ~ **qch à** *ou* **dans** to integrate sth into; **s'~ à** *ou* **dans** to become integrated into.

intégrisme [ɛ̃tegʀism(ə)] *nm* fundamentalism.

intégriste [ɛ̃tegʀist(ə)] *adj, nm/f* fundamentalist.

intégrité [ɛ̃tegʀite] *nf* integrity.

intellect [ɛ̃telɛkt] *nm* intellect.

intellectualisme [ɛ̃telɛktɥalism(ə)] *nm* intellectualism.

intellectuel, le [ɛ̃telɛktɥɛl] *adj, nm/f* intellectual; (*péj*) highbrow.

intellectuellement [ɛ̃telɛktɥɛlmɑ̃] *adv* intellectually.

intelligemment [ɛ̃teliʒamɑ̃] *adv* intelligently.

intelligence [ɛ̃teliʒɑ̃s] *nf* intelligence; (*compréhension*): **l'~ de** the understanding of; (*complicité*): **regard d'~** glance of complicity, meaningful *ou* knowing look; (*accord*): **vivre en bonne ~ avec qn** to be on good terms with sb; **~s** *nfpl* (*MIL, fig*) secret contacts; **être d'~** to have an understanding; ~ **artificielle** artificial intelligence (A.I.).

intelligent, e [ɛ̃teliʒɑ̃, -ɑ̃t] *adj* intelligent; (*ca-*

pable): ~ **en affaires** competent in business.
intelligentsia [ɛ̃telidʒɛnsja] *nf* intelligentsia.
intelligible [ɛ̃teliʒibl(ə)] *adj* intelligible.
intello [ɛ̃telo] *adj, nm/f* (*fam*) highbrow.
intempérance [ɛ̃tɑ̃peʀɑ̃s] *nf* overindulgence *no pl*; intemperance *no pl*.
intempérant, e [ɛ̃tɑ̃peʀɑ̃, -ɑ̃t] *adj* overindulgent; (*moralement*) intemperate.
intempéries [ɛ̃tɑ̃peʀi] *nfpl* bad weather *sg*.
intempestif, ive [ɛ̃tɑ̃pɛstif, -iv] *adj* untimely.
intenable [ɛ̃tnabl(ə)] *adj* unbearable.
intendance [ɛ̃tɑ̃dɑ̃s] *nf* (*MIL*) supply corps; (*: bureau*) supplies office; (*SCOL*) bursar's office.
intendant, e [ɛ̃tɑ̃dɑ̃, -ɑ̃t] *nm/f* (*MIL*) quartermaster; (*SCOL*) bursar; (*d'une propriété*) steward.
intense [ɛ̃tɑ̃s] *adj* intense.
intensément [ɛ̃tɑsemɑ̃] *adv* intensely.
intensif, ive [ɛ̃tɑ̃sif, -iv] *adj* intensive; **cours** ~ crash course; ~ **en main-d'œuvre** labour-intensive; ~ **en capital** capital-intensive.
intensification [ɛ̃tɑ̃sifikɑsjɔ̃] *nf* intensification.
intensifier [ɛ̃tɑ̃sifje] *vt*, **s'**~ *vi* to intensify.
intensité [ɛ̃tɑ̃site] *nf* intensity.
intensivement [ɛ̃tɑ̃sivmɑ̃] *adv* intensively.
intenter [ɛ̃tɑ̃te] *vt*: ~ **un procès contre** *ou* **à qn** to start proceedings against sb.
intention [ɛ̃tɑ̃sjɔ̃] *nf* intention; (*JUR*) intent; **avoir l'**~ **de faire** to intend to do, have the intention of doing; **dans l'**~ **de faire qch** with a view to doing sth; **à l'**~ **de** *prép* for; (*renseignement*) for the benefit *ou* information of; (*film, ouvrage*) aimed at; **à cette** ~ with this aim in view; **sans** ~ unintentionally; **faire qch sans mauvaise** ~ to do sth without ill intent; **agir dans une bonne** ~ to act with good intentions.
intentionné, e [ɛ̃tɑ̃sjɔne] *adj*: **bien** ~ well-meaning *ou* -intentioned; **mal** ~ ill-intentioned.
intentionnel, le [ɛ̃tɑ̃sjɔnɛl] *adj* intentional, deliberate.
intentionnellement [ɛ̃tɑ̃sjɔnɛlmɑ̃] *adv* intentionally, deliberately.
inter [ɛ̃tɛʀ] *nm* (*TÉL*: = *interurbain*) long-distance call service; (*SPORT*): ~ **gauche/droit** inside-left/-right.
interactif, ive [ɛ̃tɛʀaktif, -iv] *adj* (*aussi INFORM*) interactive.
interaction [ɛ̃tɛʀaksjɔ̃] *nf* interaction.
interarmées [ɛ̃tɛʀaʀme] *adj inv* inter-army, combined.
interbancaire [ɛ̃tɛʀbɑ̃kɛʀ] *adj* interbank.
intercalaire [ɛ̃tɛʀkalɛʀ] *adj, nm*: **(feuillet)** ~ insert; **(fiche)** ~ divider.
intercaler [ɛ̃tɛʀkale] *vt* to insert; **s'**~ **entre** to come in between; to slip in between.
intercéder [ɛ̃tɛʀsede] *vi*: ~ **(pour qn)** to intercede (on behalf of sb).
intercepter [ɛ̃tɛʀsɛpte] *vt* to intercept; (*lumière, chaleur*) to cut off.
intercepteur [ɛ̃tɛʀsɛptœʀ] *nm* (*AVIAT*) interceptor.
interception [ɛ̃tɛʀsɛpsjɔ̃] *nf* interception; **avion d'**~ interceptor.
intercession [ɛ̃tɛʀsesjɔ̃] *nf* intercession.
interchangeable [ɛ̃tɛʀʃɑ̃ʒabl(ə)] *adj* interchangeable.
interclasse [ɛ̃tɛʀklɑs] *nm* (*SCOL*) break (between classes).
interclubs [ɛ̃tɛʀklœb] *adj inv* interclub.
intercommunal, e, aux [ɛ̃tɛʀkɔmynal, -o] *adj* intervillage, intercommunity.
intercommunautaire [ɛ̃tɛʀkɔmynotɛʀ] *adj* intercommunity.
interconnexion [ɛ̃tɛʀkɔnɛksjɔ̃] *nf* (*INFORM*) networking.
intercontinental, e, aux [ɛ̃tɛʀkɔ̃tinɑ̃tal, -o] *adj* intercontinental.
intercostal, e, aux [ɛ̃tɛʀkɔstal, -o] *adj* intercostal, between the ribs.
interdépartemental, e, aux [ɛ̃tɛʀdepaʀtəmɑ̃tal, -o] *adj* interdepartmental.
interdépendance [ɛ̃tɛʀdepɑ̃dɑ̃s] *nf* interdependence.
interdépendant, e [ɛ̃tɛʀdepɑ̃dɑ̃, -ɑ̃t] *adj* interdependent.
interdiction [ɛ̃tɛʀdiksjɔ̃] *nf* ban; ~ **de faire qch** ban on doing sth; ~ **de séjour** (*JUR*) *order banning ex-prisoner from frequenting specified places*.
interdire [ɛ̃tɛʀdiʀ] *vt* to forbid; (*ADMIN: stationnement, meeting, passage*) to ban, prohibit; (*: journal, livre*) to ban; ~ **qch à qn** to forbid sb sth; ~ **à qn de faire** to forbid sb to do, prohibit sb from doing; (*suj: empêchement*) to prevent *ou* preclude sb from doing; **s'**~ **qch** (*éviter*) to refrain *ou* abstain from sth; (*se refuser*): **il s'interdit d'y penser** he doesn't allow himself to think about it.
interdisciplinaire [ɛ̃tɛʀdisiplinɛʀ] *adj* interdisciplinary.
interdit, e [ɛ̃tɛʀdi, -it] *pp de* **interdire** ♦ *adj* (*stupéfait*) taken aback; (*défendu*) forbidden, prohibited ♦ *nm* interdict, prohibition; **film** ~ **aux moins de 18/13 ans** ≈ 18-/PG-rated film; **sens** ~ one way; **stationnement** ~ no parking; ~ **de chéquier** having cheque book facilities suspended; ~ **de séjour** subject to an *interdiction de séjour*.
intéressant, e [ɛ̃teʀɛsɑ̃, -ɑ̃t] *adj* interesting; **faire l'**~ to draw attention to o.s.
intéressé, e [ɛ̃teʀese] *adj* (*parties*) involved, concerned; (*amitié, motifs*) self-interested ♦ *nm*: **l'**~ the interested party; **les** ~**s** those concerned *ou* involved.
intéressement [ɛ̃teʀɛsmɑ̃] *nm* (*COMM*) profit-sharing.
intéresser [ɛ̃teʀese] *vt* to interest; (*toucher*) to be of interest *ou* concern to; (*ADMIN: concerner*) to affect, concern; (*COMM: travailleur*) to give a share in the profits to; (*: partenaire*) to

interest (in the business); **s'~ à** to take an interest in, be interested in; **~ qn à qch** to get sb interested in sth.

intérêt [ɛ̃teʀɛ] *nm* (*aussi COMM*) interest; (*égoïsme*) self-interest; **porter de l'~ à qn** to take an interest in sb; **agir par ~** to act out of self-interest; **avoir des ~s dans** (*COMM*) to have a financial interest *ou* a stake in; **avoir ~ à faire** to do well to do; **il y a ~ à ...** it would be a good thing to ...; **~ composé** compound interest.

interface [ɛ̃tɛʀfas] *nf* (*INFORM*) interface.

interférence [ɛ̃tɛʀfeʀɑ̃s] *nf* interference.

interférer [ɛ̃tɛʀfeʀe] *vi*: **~ (avec)** to interfere (with).

intergouvernemental, e, aux [ɛ̃tɛʀguvɛʀnəmɑ̃tal, -o] *adj* intergovernmental.

intérieur, e [ɛ̃teʀjœʀ] *adj* (*mur, escalier, poche*) inside; (*commerce, politique*) domestic; (*cour, calme, vie*) inner; (*navigation*) inland ♦ *nm* (*d'une maison, d'un récipient etc*) inside; (*d'un pays, aussi: décor, mobilier*) interior; (*POL*): **l'I~** (the Department of) the Interior, ≈ the Home Office (*BRIT*); **à l'~ (de)** inside; (*fig*) within; **de l'~** (*fig*) from the inside; **en ~** (*CINÉ*) in the studio; **vêtement d'~** indoor garment.

intérieurement [ɛ̃teʀjœʀmɑ̃] *adv* inwardly.

intérim [ɛ̃teʀim] *nm* interim period; **assurer l'~ (de)** to deputize (for); **par ~** *adj* interim ♦ *adv* in a temporary capacity.

intérimaire [ɛ̃teʀimɛʀ] *adj* temporary, interim ♦ *nm/f* (*secrétaire etc*) temporary, temp (*BRIT*); (*suppléant*) deputy.

intérioriser [ɛ̃teʀjɔʀize] *vt* to internalize.

interjection [ɛ̃tɛʀʒɛksjɔ̃] *nf* interjection.

interjeter [ɛ̃tɛʀʒəte] *vt* (*JUR*): **~ appel** to lodge an appeal.

interligne [ɛ̃tɛʀliɲ] *nm* inter-line space ♦ *nf* (*TYPO*) lead, leading; **simple/double ~** single/double spacing.

interlocuteur, trice [ɛ̃tɛʀlɔkytœʀ, -tʀis] *nm/f* speaker; (*POL*): **~ valable** valid representative; **son ~** the person he *ou* she was speaking to.

interlope [ɛ̃tɛʀlɔp] *adj* illicit; (*milieu, bar*) shady.

interloquer [ɛ̃tɛʀlɔke] *vt* to take aback.

interlude [ɛ̃tɛʀlyd] *nm* interlude.

intermède [ɛ̃tɛʀmɛd] *nm* interlude.

intermédiaire [ɛ̃tɛʀmedjɛʀ] *adj* intermediate; middle; half-way ♦ *nm/f* intermediary; (*COMM*) middleman; **sans ~** directly; **par l'~ de** through.

interminable [ɛ̃tɛʀminabl(ə)] *adj* never-ending.

interminablement [ɛ̃tɛʀminabləmɑ̃] *adv* interminably.

interministériel, le [ɛ̃tɛʀministeʀjɛl] *adj*: **comité ~** interdepartmental committee.

intermittence [ɛ̃tɛʀmitɑ̃s] *nf*: **par ~** intermittently, sporadically.

intermittent, e [ɛ̃tɛʀmitɑ̃, -ɑ̃t] *adj* intermittent, sporadic.

internat [ɛ̃tɛʀna] *nm* (*SCOL*) boarding school.

international, e, aux [ɛ̃tɛʀnasjɔnal, -o] *adj, nm/f* international.

internationalisation [ɛ̃tɛʀnasjɔnalizɑsjɔ̃] *nf* internationalization.

internationaliser [ɛ̃tɛʀnasjɔnalize] *vt* to internationalize.

internationalisme [ɛ̃tɛʀnasjɔnalism(ə)] *nm* internationalism.

internaute [ɛ̃tɛʀnot] *nm/f* Internet user.

interne [ɛ̃tɛʀn(ə)] *adj* internal ♦ *nm/f* (*SCOL*) boarder; (*MÉD*) houseman (*BRIT*), intern (*US*).

internement [ɛ̃tɛʀnəmɑ̃] *nm* (*POL*) internment; (*MÉD*) confinement.

interner [ɛ̃tɛʀne] *vt* (*POL*) to intern; (*MÉD*) to confine to a mental institution.

Internet [ɛ̃tɛʀnɛt] *nm*: **l'~** the Internet; **sur ~** on (the) Internet.

interparlementaire [ɛ̃tɛʀpaʀləmɑ̃tɛʀ] *adj* interparliamentary.

interpellation [ɛ̃tɛʀpelɑsjɔ̃] *nf* interpellation; (*POL*) question.

interpeller [ɛ̃tɛʀpele] *vt* (*appeler*) to call out to; (*apostropher*) to shout at; (*POLICE*) to take in for questioning; (*POL*) to question; **s'~** to exchange insults.

interphone [ɛ̃tɛʀfɔn] *nm* intercom.

interplanétaire [ɛ̃tɛʀplanetɛʀ] *adj* interplanetary.

interposer [ɛ̃tɛʀpoze] *vt* to interpose; **s'~** *vi* to intervene; **par personnes interposées** through a third party.

interprétariat [ɛ̃tɛʀpʀetaʀja] *nm* interpreting.

interprétation [ɛ̃tɛʀpʀetɑsjɔ̃] *nf* interpretation.

interprète [ɛ̃tɛʀpʀɛt] *nm/f* interpreter; (*porte-parole*) spokesman.

interpréter [ɛ̃tɛʀpʀete] *vt* to interpret.

interprofessionnel, le [ɛ̃tɛʀpʀɔfesjɔnɛl] *adj* interprofessional.

interrogateur, trice [ɛ̃teʀɔgatœʀ, -tʀis] *adj* questioning, inquiring ♦ *nm/f* (*SCOL*) (oral) examiner.

interrogatif, ive [ɛ̃teʀɔgatif, -iv] *adj* (*LING*) interrogative.

interrogation [ɛ̃teʀɔgɑsjɔ̃] *nf* question; (*SCOL*) (written *ou* oral) test.

interrogatoire [ɛ̃teʀɔgatwaʀ] *nm* (*POLICE*) questioning *no pl*; (*JUR*) cross-examination, interrogation.

interroger [ɛ̃teʀɔʒe] *vt* to question; (*INFORM*) to interrogate; (*SCOL*: *candidat*) to test; **~ qn (sur qch)** to question sb (about sth); **~ qn du regard** to look questioningly at sb, give sb a questioning look; **s'~ sur qch** to ask o.s. about sth, ponder (about) sth.

interrompre [ɛ̃teʀɔ̃pʀ(ə)] *vt* (*gén*) to interrupt; (*travail, voyage*) to break off, interrupt; **s'~** to break off.

interrupteur [ɛ̃teʀyptœʀ] *nm* switch; **~ à bas-**

cule (*INFORM*) toggle switch.
interruption [ɛ̃terypsjɔ̃] *nf* interruption; **sans** ~ without a break; ~ **de grossesse** termination of pregnancy; ~ **volontaire de grossesse** voluntary termination of pregnancy, abortion.
interscolaire [ɛ̃tɛrskɔlɛr] *adj* interschool(s).
intersection [ɛ̃tɛrsɛksjɔ̃] *nf* intersection.
intersidéral, e, aux [ɛ̃tɛrsideral, -o] *adj* intersidereal, interstellar.
interstice [ɛ̃tɛrstis] *nm* crack, slit.
intersyndical, e, aux [ɛ̃tɛrsɛ̃dikal, -o] *adj* interunion.
interurbain [ɛ̃tɛryrbɛ̃] (*TÉL*) *nm* long-distance call service ♦ *adj* long-distance.
intervalle [ɛ̃tɛrval] *nm* (*espace*) space; (*de temps*) interval; **dans l'**~ in the meantime; **à 2 mois d'**~ after a space of 2 months; **à** ~**s rapprochés** at close intervals; **par** ~**s** at intervals.
intervenant, e [ɛ̃tɛrvənɑ̃, -ɑ̃t] *vb voir* **intervenir** ♦ *nm/f* speaker (*at conference*).
intervenir [ɛ̃tɛrvənir] *vi* (*gén*) to intervene; (*survenir*) to take place; (*faire une conférence*) to give a talk *ou* lecture; ~ **auprès de/en faveur de qn** to intervene with/on behalf of sb; **la police a dû** ~ police had to step in *ou* intervene; **les médecins ont dû** ~ the doctors had to operate.
intervention [ɛ̃tɛrvɑ̃sjɔ̃] *nf* intervention; (*conférence*) talk, paper; ~ **(chirurgicale)** operation.
interventionnisme [ɛ̃tɛrvɑ̃sjɔnism(ə)] *nm* interventionism.
interventionniste [ɛ̃tɛrvɑ̃sjɔnist(ə)] *adj* interventionist.
intervenu, e [ɛ̃tɛrv(ə)ny] *pp de* **intervenir.**
intervertible [ɛ̃tɛrvɛrtibl(ə)] *adj* interchangeable.
intervertir [ɛ̃tɛrvɛrtir] *vt* to invert (the order of), reverse.
interviendrai [ɛ̃tɛrvjɛ̃dre], **interviens** [ɛ̃tɛrvjɛ̃] *etc vb voir* **intervenir.**
interview [ɛ̃tɛrvju] *nf* interview.
interviewer [ɛ̃tɛrvjuve] *vt* to interview ♦ *nm* [ɛ̃tɛrvjuvœr] (*journaliste*) interviewer.
intervins [ɛ̃tɛrvɛ̃] *etc vb voir* **intervenir.**
intestat [ɛ̃tɛsta] *adj* (*JUR*): **décéder** ~ to die intestate.
intestin, e [ɛ̃tɛstɛ̃, -in] *adj* internal ♦ *nm* intestine; ~ **grêle** small intestine.
intestinal, e, aux [ɛ̃tɛstinal, -o] *adj* intestinal.
intime [ɛ̃tim] *adj* intimate; (*vie, journal*) private; (*convictions*) inmost; (*dîner, cérémonie*) held among friends, quiet ♦ *nm/f* close friend.
intimement [ɛ̃timmɑ̃] *adv* (*profondément*) deeply, firmly; (*étroitement*) intimately.
intimer [ɛ̃time] *vt* (*JUR*) to notify; ~ **à qn l'ordre de faire** to order sb to do.
intimidant, e [ɛ̃timidɑ̃, -ɑ̃t] *adj* intimidating.
intimidation [ɛ̃timidɑsjɔ̃] intimidation; **manœuvres d'**~ (*action*) acts of intimidation; (*stratégie*) intimidatory tactics.
intimider [ɛ̃timide] *vt* to intimidate.
intimité [ɛ̃timite] *nf* intimacy; (*vie privée*) privacy; private life; **dans l'**~ in private; (*sans formalités*) with only a few friends, quietly.
intitulé [ɛ̃tityle] *nm* title.
intituler [ɛ̃tityle] *vt*: **comment a-t-il intitulé son livre?** what title did he give his book?; **s'**~ to be entitled; (*personne*) to call o.s.
intolérable [ɛ̃tɔlerabl(ə)] *adj* intolerable.
intolérance [ɛ̃tɔlerɑ̃s] *nf* intolerance; ~ **aux antibiotiques** intolerance to antibiotics.
intolérant, e [ɛ̃tɔlerɑ̃, -ɑ̃t] *adj* intolerant.
intonation [ɛ̃tɔnɑsjɔ̃] *nf* intonation.
intouchable [ɛ̃tuʃabl(ə)] *adj* (*fig*) above the law, sacrosanct; (*REL*) untouchable.
intoxication [ɛ̃tɔksikɑsjɔ̃] *nf* poisoning *no pl*; (*toxicomanie*) drug addiction; (*fig*) brainwashing; ~ **alimentaire** food poisoning.
intoxiqué, e [ɛ̃tɔksike] *nm/f* addict.
intoxiquer [ɛ̃tɔksike] *vt* to poison; (*fig*) to brainwash; **s'**~ to poison o.s.
intradermique [ɛ̃tradɛrmik] *adj, nf*: **(injection)** ~ intradermal *ou* intracutaneous injection.
intraduisible [ɛ̃tradɥizibl(ə)] *adj* untranslatable; (*fig*) inexpressible.
intraitable [ɛ̃trɛtabl(ə)] *adj* inflexible, uncompromising.
intramusculaire [ɛ̃tramyskylɛr] *adj, nf*: **(injection)** ~ intramuscular injection.
intranet [ɛ̃tranɛt] *nm* intranet.
intransigeance [ɛ̃trɑ̃ziʒɑ̃s] *nf* intransigence.
intransigeant, e [ɛ̃trɑ̃ziʒɑ̃, -ɑ̃t] *adj* intransigent; (*morale, passion*) uncompromising.
intransitif, ive [ɛ̃trɑ̃zitif, -iv] *adj* (*LING*) intransitive.
intransportable [ɛ̃trɑ̃spɔrtabl(ə)] *adj* (*blessé*) unable to travel.
intraveineux, euse [ɛ̃travɛnø, -øz] *adj* intravenous.
intrépide [ɛ̃trepid] *adj* dauntless, intrepid.
intrépidité [ɛ̃trepidite] *nf* dauntlessness.
intrigant, e [ɛ̃trigɑ̃, -ɑ̃t] *nm/f* schemer.
intrigue [ɛ̃trig] *nf* intrigue; (*scénario*) plot.
intriguer [ɛ̃trige] *vi* to scheme ♦ *vt* to puzzle intrigue.
intrinsèque [ɛ̃trɛ̃sɛk] *adj* intrinsic.
introductif, ive [ɛ̃trɔdyktif, -iv] *adj* introductory.
introduction [ɛ̃trɔdyksjɔ̃] *nf* introduction **paroles/chapitre d'**~ introductory words chapter; **lettre d'**~ letter of introduction.
introduire [ɛ̃trɔdɥir] *vt* to introduce; (*visiteur*) to show in; (*aiguille, clef*): ~ **qch dans** to insert *ou* introduce sth into; (*personne*): ~ **à qch** to introduce to sth; (*: présenter*): ~ **qn à qn/dans un club** to introduce sb to sb/to a club; (*INFORM*) to input, enter; **s'**~ (*techniques, usages*) to be introduced; **s'**~ **dans** to gain entry into; to get o.s. accepted into (*eau, fumée*) to get into; ~ **au clavier** to key

in.
introduit, e [ɛ̃tʀɔdɥi, -it] *pp de* **introduire** ♦ *adj*: **bien ~** (*personne*) well-received.
introniser [ɛ̃tʀɔnize] *vt* to enthrone.
introspection [ɛ̃tʀɔspɛksjɔ̃] *nf* introspection.
introuvable [ɛ̃tʀuvabl(ə)] *adj* which cannot be found; (*COMM*) unobtainable.
introverti, e [ɛ̃tʀɔvɛʀti] *nm/f* introvert.
intrus, e [ɛ̃tʀy, -yz] *nm/f* intruder.
intrusion [ɛ̃tʀyzjɔ̃] *nf* intrusion; (*ingérence*) interference.
intuitif, ive [ɛ̃tɥitif, -iv] *adj* intuitive.
intuition [ɛ̃tɥisjɔ̃] *nf* intuition; **avoir une ~** to have a feeling; **avoir l'~ de qch** to have an intuition of sth; **avoir de l'~** to have intuition.
intuitivement [ɛ̃tɥitivmɑ̃] *adv* intuitively.
inusable [inyzabl(ə)] *adj* hard-wearing.
inusité, e [inyzite] *adj* rarely used.
inutile [inytil] *adj* useless; (*superflu*) unnecessary.
inutilement [inytilmɑ̃] *adv* needlessly.
inutilisable [inytilizabl(ə)] *adj* unusable.
inutilisé, e [inytilize] *adj* unused.
inutilité [inytilite] *nf* uselessness.
invaincu, e [ɛ̃vɛ̃ky] *adj* unbeaten; (*armée, peuple*) unconquered.
invalide [ɛ̃valid] *adj* disabled ♦ *nm/f*: **~ de guerre** disabled ex-serviceman; **~ du travail** industrially disabled person.
invalider [ɛ̃valide] *vt* to invalidate.
invalidité [ɛ̃validite] *nf* disability.
invariable [ɛ̃vaʀjabl(ə)] *adj* invariable.
invariablement [ɛ̃vaʀjabləmɑ̃] *adv* invariably.
invasion [ɛ̃vɑzjɔ̃] *nf* invasion.
invective [ɛ̃vɛktiv] *nf* invective.
invectiver [ɛ̃vɛktive] *vt* to hurl abuse at ♦ *vi*: **~ contre** to rail against.
invendable [ɛ̃vɑ̃dabl(ə)] *adj* unsaleable, unmarketable.
invendu, e [ɛ̃vɑ̃dy] *adj* unsold ♦ *nm* return; **~s** *nmpl* unsold goods.
inventaire [ɛ̃vɑ̃tɛʀ] *nm* inventory; (*COMM: liste*) stocklist; (*: opération*) stocktaking *no pl*; (*fig*) survey; **faire un ~** to make an inventory; (*COMM*) to take stock; **faire** *ou* **procéder à l'~** to take stock.
inventer [ɛ̃vɑ̃te] *vt* to invent; (*subterfuge*) to devise, invent; (*histoire, excuse*) to make up, invent; **~ de faire** to hit on the idea of doing.
inventeur, trice [ɛ̃vɑ̃tœʀ, -tʀis] *nm/f* inventor.
inventif, ive [ɛ̃vɑ̃tif, -iv] *adj* inventive.
invention [ɛ̃vɑ̃sjɔ̃] *nf* invention; (*imagination, inspiration*) inventiveness.
inventivité [ɛ̃vɑ̃tivite] *nf* inventiveness.
inventorier [ɛ̃vɑ̃tɔʀje] *vt* to make an inventory of.
invérifiable [ɛ̃veʀifjabl(ə)] *adj* unverifiable.
inverse [ɛ̃vɛʀs(ə)] *adj* (*ordre*) reverse; (*sens*) opposite; (*rapport*) inverse ♦ *nm* reverse; inverse; **en proportion ~** in inverse proportion; **dans le sens ~ des aiguilles d'une montre** anti-clockwise; **en sens ~** in (*ou* from) the opposite direction; **à l'~** conversely.
inversement [ɛ̃vɛʀsəmɑ̃] *adv* conversely.
inverser [ɛ̃vɛʀse] *vt* to reverse, invert; (*ÉLEC*) to reverse.
inversion [ɛ̃vɛʀsjɔ̃] *nf* reversal; inversion.
invertébré, e [ɛ̃vɛʀtebʀe] *adj, nm* invertebrate.
inverti, e [ɛ̃vɛʀti] *nm/f* homosexual.
investigation [ɛ̃vɛstigɑsjɔ̃] *nf* investigation, inquiry.
investir [ɛ̃vɛstiʀ] *vt* to invest; **s'~** *vi* (*PSYCH*) to involve o.s.; **~ qn de** to vest *ou* invest sb with.
investissement [ɛ̃vɛstismɑ̃] *nm* investment; (*PSYCH*) involvement.
investisseur [ɛ̃vɛstisœʀ] *nm* investor.
investiture [ɛ̃vɛstityʀ] *nf* investiture; (*à une élection*) nomination.
invétéré, e [ɛ̃veteʀe] *adj* (*habitude*) ingrained; (*bavard, buveur*) inveterate.
invincible [ɛ̃vɛ̃sibl(ə)] *adj* invincible, unconquerable.
invinciblement [ɛ̃vɛ̃sibləmɑ̃] *adv* (*fig*) invincibly.
inviolabilité [ɛ̃vjɔlabilite] *nf*: **~ parlementaire** parliamentary immunity.
inviolable [ɛ̃vjɔlabl(ə)] *adj* inviolable.
invisible [ɛ̃vizibl(ə)] *adj* invisible; (*fig: personne*) not available.
invitation [ɛ̃vitɑsjɔ̃] *nf* invitation; **à/sur l'~ de qn** at/on sb's invitation; **carte/lettre d'~** invitation card/letter.
invite [ɛ̃vit] *nf* invitation.
invité, e [ɛ̃vite] *nm/f* guest.
inviter [ɛ̃vite] *vt* to invite; **~ qn à faire qch** to invite sb to do sth; (*suj: chose*) to induce *ou* tempt sb to do sth.
invivable [ɛ̃vivabl(ə)] *adj* unbearable, impossible.
involontaire [ɛ̃vɔlɔ̃tɛʀ] *adj* (*mouvement*) involuntary; (*insulte*) unintentional; (*complice*) unwitting.
involontairement [ɛ̃vɔlɔ̃tɛʀmɑ̃] *adv* involuntarily.
invoquer [ɛ̃vɔke] *vt* (*Dieu, muse*) to call upon, invoke; (*prétexte*) to put forward (as an excuse); (*témoignage*) to call upon; (*loi, texte*) to refer to; **~ la clémence de qn** to beg sb *ou* appeal to sb for clemency.
invraisemblable [ɛ̃vʀɛsɑ̃blabl(ə)] *adj* unlikely, improbable; (*bizarre*) incredible.
invraisemblance [ɛ̃vʀɛsɑ̃blɑ̃s] *nf* unlikelihood *no pl*, improbability.
invulnérable [ɛ̃vylneʀabl(ə)] *adj* invulnerable.
iode [jɔd] *nm* iodine.
iodé, e [jɔde] *adj* iodized.
ion [jɔ̃] *nm* ion.
ionique [jɔnik] *adj* (*ARCHIT*) Ionic; (*SCIENCE*) ionic.
ioniseur [jɔnizœʀ] *nm* ionizer.
iota [jɔta] *nm*: **sans changer un ~** without

changing one iota *ou* the tiniest bit.
IPC *sigle m* (= *Indice des prix à la consommation*) CPI.
IR. *abr* = **infrarouge.**
IRA *sigle f* (= *Irish Republican Army*) IRA.
irai [iʀe] *etc vb voir* **aller.**
Irak [iʀɑk] *nm*: **l'~** Iraq *ou* Irak.
irakien, ne [iʀakjɛ̃, -ɛn] *adj* Iraqi ♦ *nm/f*: **I~, ne** Iraqi.
Iran [iʀɑ̃] *nm*: **l'~** Iran.
iranien, ne [iʀanjɛ̃, -ɛn] *adj* Iranian ♦ *nm* (*LING*) Iranian ♦ *nm/f*: **I~, ne** Iranian.
Iraq [iʀɑk] = **Irak.**
iraquien, ne [iʀakjɛ̃, -ɛn] = **irakien, ne.**
irascible [iʀasibl(ə)] *adj* short-tempered, irascible.
irions [iʀjɔ̃] *etc vb voir* **aller.**
iris [iʀis] *nm* iris.
irisé, e [iʀize] *adj* iridescent.
irlandais, e [iʀlɑ̃dɛ, -ɛz] *adj, nm* (*LING*) Irish ♦ *nm/f*: **I~, e** Irishman/woman; **les I~** the Irish.
Irlande [iʀlɑ̃d] *nf*: **l'~** (*pays*) Ireland; (*état*) the Irish Republic, the Republic of Ireland, Eire; **~ du Nord** Northern Ireland, Ulster; **~ du Sud** Southern Ireland, Irish Republic, Eire; **la mer d'~** the Irish Sea.
ironie [iʀɔni] *nf* irony.
ironique [iʀɔnik] *adj* ironical.
ironiquement [iʀɔnikmɑ̃] *adv* ironically.
ironiser [iʀɔnize] *vi* to be ironical.
irons [iʀɔ̃] *etc vb voir* **aller.**
IRPP *sigle m* (= *impôt sur le revenu des personnes physiques*) income tax.
irradiation [iʀadjɑsjɔ̃] *nf* irradiation.
irradier [iʀadje] *vi* to radiate ♦ *vt* to irradiate.
irraisonné, e [iʀɛzɔne] *adj* irrational, unreasoned.
irrationnel, le [iʀasjɔnɛl] *adj* irrational.
irrattrapable [iʀatʀapabl(ə)] *adj* (*retard*) that cannot be made up; (*bévue*) that cannot be made good.
irréalisable [iʀealizabl(ə)] *adj* unrealizable; (*projet*) impracticable.
irréalisme [iʀealism(ə)] *nm* lack of realism.
irréaliste [iʀealist(ə)] *adj* unrealistic.
irréalité [iʀealite] *nf* unreality.
irrecevable [iʀsəvabl(ə)] *adj* unacceptable.
irréconciliable [iʀekɔ̃siljabl(ə)] *adj* irreconcilable.
irrécouvrable [iʀekuvʀabl(ə)] *adj* irrecoverable.
irrécupérable [iʀekypeʀabl(ə)] *adj* unreclaimable, beyond repair; (*personne*) beyond redemption *ou* recall.
irrécusable [iʀekyzabl(ə)] *adj* (*témoignage*) unimpeachable; (*preuve*) incontestable, indisputable.
irréductible [iʀedyktibl(ə)] *adj* indomitable, implacable; (*MATH*: *fraction, équation*) irreducible.
irréductiblement [iʀedyktibləmɑ̃] *adv* implacably.
irréel, le [iʀeɛl] *adj* unreal.
irréfléchi, e [iʀefleʃi] *adj* thoughtless.
irréfutable [iʀefytabl(ə)] *adj* irrefutable.
irréfutablement [iʀefytabləmɑ̃] *adv* irrefutably.
irrégularité [iʀegylaʀite] *nf* irregularity; unevenness *no pl.*
irrégulier, ière [iʀegylje, -jɛʀ] *adj* irregular; (*surface, rythme, écriture*) uneven, irregular; (*élève, athlète*) erratic.
irrégulièrement [iʀegyljɛʀmɑ̃] *adv* irregularly.
irrémédiable [iʀemedjabl(ə)] *adj* irreparable.
irrémédiablement [iʀemedjabləmɑ̃] *adv* irreparably.
irremplaçable [iʀɑ̃plasabl(ə)] *adj* irreplaceable.
irréparable [iʀepaʀabl(ə)] *adj* beyond repair, irreparable; (*fig*) irreparable.
irrépréhensible [iʀepʀeɑ̃sibl(ə)] *adj* irreprehensible.
irrépressible [iʀepʀesibl(ə)] *adj* irrepressible.
irréprochable [iʀepʀɔʃabl(ə)] *adj* irreproachable, beyond reproach; (*tenue, toilette*) impeccable.
irrésistible [iʀezistibl(ə)] *adj* irresistible; (*preuve, logique*) compelling.
irrésistiblement [iʀezistibləmɑ̃] *adv* irresistibly.
irrésolu, e [iʀezɔly] *adj* irresolute.
irrésolution [iʀezɔlysjɔ̃] *nf* irresoluteness.
irrespectueux, euse [iʀɛspɛktɥø, -øz] *adj* disrespectful.
irrespirable [iʀɛspiʀabl(ə)] *adj* unbreathable; (*fig*) oppressive, stifling.
irresponsabilité [iʀɛspɔ̃sabilite] *nf* irresponsibility.
irresponsable [iʀɛspɔ̃sabl(ə)] *adj* irresponsible.
irrévérencieux, euse [iʀeveʀɑ̃sjø, -øz] *adj* irreverent.
irréversible [iʀevɛʀsibl(ə)] *adj* irreversible.
irréversiblement [iʀevɛʀsibləmɑ̃] *adv* irreversibly.
irrévocable [iʀevɔkabl(ə)] *adj* irrevocable.
irrévocablement [iʀevɔkabləmɑ̃] *adv* irrevocably.
irrigation [iʀigɑsjɔ̃] *nf* irrigation.
irriguer [iʀige] *vt* to irrigate.
irritabilité [iʀitabilite] *nf* irritability.
irritable [iʀitabl(ə)] *adj* irritable.
irritant, e [iʀitɑ̃, -ɑ̃t] *adj* irritating; (*MÉD*) irritant.
irritation [iʀitɑsjɔ̃] *nf* irritation.
irrité, e [iʀite] *adj* irritated.
irriter [iʀite] *vt* (*agacer*) to irritate, annoy (*MÉD*: *enflammer*) to irritate; **s'~ contre qn, de qch** to get annoyed *ou* irritated with sb at sth.
irruption [iʀypsjɔ̃] *nf* irruption *no pl*; **faire ~ dans** to burst into.
ISBN *sigle m* (= *International Standard Boo*

Number) ISBN.
Islam [islam] *nm* Islam.
islamique [islamik] *adj* Islamic.
islamiste [islamist(ə)] *adj, nm/f* Islamic.
islandais, e [islɑ̃dɛ, -ɛz] *adj* Icelandic ♦ *nm* (*LING*) Icelandic ♦ *nm/f*: **I~, e** Icelander.
Islande [islɑ̃d] *nf*: **l'~** Iceland.
ISMH *sigle m* (= *Inventaire supplémentaire des monuments historiques*): **monument inscrit à l'~** ≈ listed building.
isocèle [izɔsɛl] *adj* isosceles.
isolant, e [izɔlɑ̃, -ɑ̃t] *adj* insulating; (*insonorisant*) soundproofing ♦ *nm* insulator.
isolateur [izɔlatœʀ] *nm* (*ÉLEC*) insulator.
isolation [izɔlasjɔ̃] *nf* insulation; **~ acoustique/thermique** sound/thermal insulation.
isolationnisme [izɔlasjɔnism(ə)] *nm* isolationism.
isolé, e [izɔle] *adj* isolated; (*ÉLEC*) insulated.
isolement [izɔlmɑ̃] *nm* isolation; solitary confinement.
isolément [izɔlemɑ̃] *adv* in isolation.
isoler [izɔle] *vt* to isolate; (*prisonnier*) to put in solitary confinement; (*ville*) to cut off, isolate; (*ÉLEC*) to insulate.
isoloir [izɔlwaʀ] *nm* polling booth.
isorel [izɔʀɛl] *nm* ® hardboard.
isotherme [izɔtɛʀm(ə)] *adj* (*camion*) refrigerated.
Israël [isʀaɛl] *nm*: **l'~** Israel.
israélien, ne [isʀaeljɛ̃, -ɛn] *adj* Israeli ♦ *nm/f*: **I~, ne** Israeli.
israélite [isʀaelit] *adj* Jewish; (*dans l'Ancien Testament*) Israelite ♦ *nm/f*: **I~** Jew/Jewess; Israelite.
issu, e [isy] *adj*: **~ de** descended from; (*fig*) stemming from ♦ *nf* (*ouverture, sortie*) exit; (*solution*) way out, solution; (*dénouement*) outcome; **à l'~e de** at the conclusion *ou* close of; **rue sans ~e** dead end, no through road (*BRIT*), no outlet (*US*); **~e de secours** emergency exit.
Istamboul *ou* **Istanbul** [istɑ̃bul] *n* Istanbul.
isthme [ism(ə)] *nm* isthmus.
Italie [itali] *nf*: **l'~** Italy.
italien, ne [italjɛ̃, -ɛn] *adj* Italian ♦ *nm* (*LING*) Italian ♦ *nm/f*: **I~, ne** Italian.
italique [italik] *nm*: **en ~(s)** in italics.
item [itɛm] *nm* item; (*question*) question, test.
itinéraire [itineʀɛʀ] *nm* itinerary, route.
itinérant, e [itineʀɑ̃, -ɑ̃t] *adj* itinerant, travelling.
ITP *sigle m* (= *ingénieur des travaux publics*) civil engineer.
IUT *sigle m* = **Institut universitaire de technologie.**
IVG *sigle f* (= *interruption volontaire de grossesse*) abortion.
ivoire [ivwaʀ] *nm* ivory.
ivoirien, ne [ivwaʀjɛ̃, -ɛn] *adj* of *ou* from the Ivory Coast.
ivraie [ivʀɛ] *nf*: **séparer le bon grain de l'~** (*fig*) to separate the wheat from the chaff.
ivre [ivʀ(ə)] *adj* drunk; **~ de** (*colère*) wild with; (*bonheur*) drunk *ou* intoxicated with; **~ mort** dead drunk.
ivresse [ivʀɛs] *nf* drunkenness; (*euphorie*) intoxication.
ivrogne [ivʀɔɲ] *nm/f* drunkard.

J j

J, j [ʒi] *nm inv* J, j ♦ *abr* (= *jour*): **jour ~** D-day; (= *Joule*) J; **J comme Joseph** J for Jack (*BRIT*) *ou* Jig (*US*).
j' [ʒ] *pron voir* **je.**
jabot [ʒabo] *nm* (*ZOOL*) crop; (*de vêtement*) jabot.
JAC [ʒak] *sigle f* (= *Jeunesse agricole catholique*) *youth organization.*
jacasser [ʒakase] *vi* to chatter.
jachère [ʒaʃɛʀ] *nf*: **(être) en ~** (to lie) fallow.
jacinthe [ʒasɛ̃t] *nf* hyacinth; **~ des bois** bluebell.
jack [dʒak] *nm* jack plug.
jacquard [ʒakaʀ] *adj inv* Fair Isle.
jacquerie [ʒakʀi] *nf* riot.
jade [ʒad] *nm* jade.
jadis [ʒadis] *adv* in times past, formerly.
jaguar [ʒagwaʀ] *nm* (*ZOOL*) jaguar.
jaillir [ʒajiʀ] *vi* (*liquide*) to spurt out, gush out; (*lumière*) to flood out; (*fig*) to rear up; to burst out.
jaillissement [ʒajismɑ̃] *nm* spurt, gush.
jais [ʒɛ] *nm* jet; **(d'un noir) de ~** jet-black.
jalon [ʒalɔ̃] *nm* range pole; (*fig*) milestone; **poser des ~s** (*fig*) to pave the way.
jalonner [ʒalɔne] *vt* to mark out; (*fig*) to mark, punctuate.
jalousement [ʒaluzmɑ̃] *adv* jealously.
jalouser [ʒaluze] *vt* to be jealous of.
jalousie [ʒaluzi] *nf* jealousy; (*store*) (venetian) blind.
jaloux, ouse [ʒalu, -uz] *adj* jealous; **être ~ de qn/qch** to be jealous of sb/sth.
jamaïquain, e [ʒamaikɛ̃, -ɛn] *adj* Jamaican.
Jamaïque [ʒamaik] *nf*: **la ~** Jamaica.
jamais [ʒamɛ] *adv* never; (*sans négation*) ever; **ne ... ~** never; **~ de la vie!** never!; **si ~ ...** if ever ...; **à (tout) ~, pour ~** for ever, for ever and ever.
jambage [ʒɑ̃baʒ] *nm* (*de lettre*) downstroke; (*de porte*) jamb.
jambe [ʒɑ̃b] *nf* leg; **à toutes ~s** as fast as one's legs can carry one.
jambières [ʒɑ̃bjɛʀ] *nfpl* legwarmers; (*SPORT*)

shin pads.
jambon [ʒɑ̃bɔ̃] *nm* ham.
jambonneau, x [ʒɑ̃bɔno] *nm* knuckle of ham.
jante [ʒɑ̃t] *nf* (wheel) rim.
janvier [ʒɑ̃vje] *nm* January; *voir aussi* **juillet**.
Japon [ʒapɔ̃] *nm*: **le** ~ Japan.
japonais, e [ʒapɔnɛ, -ɛz] *adj* Japanese ♦ *nm* (*LING*) Japanese ♦ *nm/f*: **J~, e** Japanese.
japonaiserie [ʒapɔnɛzʀi] *nf* (*bibelot*) Japanese curio.
jappement [ʒapmɑ̃] *nm* yap, yelp.
japper [ʒape] *vi* to yap, yelp.
jaquette [ʒakɛt] *nf* (*de cérémonie*) morning coat; (*de femme*) jacket; (*de livre*) dust cover, (dust) jacket.
jardin [ʒaʀdɛ̃] *nm* garden; ~ **d'acclimatation** zoological gardens *pl*; ~ **botanique** botanical gardens *pl*; ~ **d'enfants** nursery school; ~ **potager** vegetable garden; ~ **public** (public) park, public gardens *pl*; ~**s suspendus** hanging gardens.
jardinage [ʒaʀdinaʒ] *nm* gardening.
jardiner [ʒaʀdine] *vi* to garden, do some gardening.
jardinet [ʒaʀdinɛ] *nm* little garden.
jardinier, ière [ʒaʀdinje, -jɛʀ] *nm/f* gardener ♦ *nf* (*de fenêtre*) window box; **jardinière d'enfants** nursery school teacher; **jardinière (de légumes)** (*CULIN*) mixed vegetables.
jargon [ʒaʀgɔ̃] *nm* (*charabia*) gibberish; (*publicitaire, scientifique etc*) jargon.
jarre [ʒaʀ] *nf* (earthenware) jar.
jarret [ʒaʀɛ] *nm* back of knee; (*CULIN*) knuckle, shin.
jarretelle [ʒaʀtɛl] *nf* suspender (*BRIT*), garter (*US*).
jarretière [ʒaʀtjɛʀ] *nf* garter.
jars [ʒaʀ] *nm* (*ZOOL*) gander.
jaser [ʒɑze] *vi* to chatter, prattle; (*indiscrètement*) to gossip.
jasmin [ʒasmɛ̃] *nm* jasmin.
jaspe [ʒasp(ə)] *nm* jasper.
jaspé, e [ʒaspe] *adj* marbled, mottled.
jatte [ʒat] *nf* basin, bowl.
jauge [ʒoʒ] *nf* (*capacité*) capacity, tonnage; (*instrument*) gauge; ~ **(de niveau) d'huile** dipstick.
jauger [ʒoʒe] *vt* to gauge the capacity of; (*fig*) to size up; ~ **3 000 tonneaux** to measure 3,000 tons.
jaunâtre [ʒonɑtʀ(ə)] *adj* (*couleur, teint*) yellowish.
jaune [ʒon] *adj, nm* yellow ♦ *nm/f* (*péj*) Asiatic; (*briseur de grève*) blackleg ♦ *adv* (*fam*): **rire** ~ to laugh on the other side of one's face; ~ **d'œuf** (egg) yolk.
jaunir [ʒoniʀ] *vi, vt* to turn yellow.
jaunisse [ʒonis] *nf* jaundice.
Java [ʒava] *nf* Java.
java [ʒava] *nf* (*fam*): **faire la** ~ to live it up, have a real party.
javanais, e [ʒavanɛ, -ɛz] *adj* Javanese.
Javel [ʒavɛl] *nf voir* **eau**.
javelliser [ʒavelise] *vt* (*eau*) to chlorinate.
javelot [ʒavlo] *nm* javelin; (*SPORT*): **faire du** ~ to throw the javelin.
jazz [dʒaz] *nm* jazz.
J.-C. *abr* = **Jésus-Christ**.
JCR *sigle f* (= *Jeunesse communiste révolutionnaire*) *communist youth movement.*
je, j' [ʒ(ə)] *pron* I.
jean [dʒin] *nm* jeans *pl*.
jeannette [ʒanɛt] *nf* (*planchette*) sleeveboard; (*petite fille scout*) Brownie.
JEC [ʒɛk] *sigle f* (= *Jeunesse étudiante chrétienne*) *youth organization.*
jeep [(d)ʒip] *nf* ® (*AUTO*) jeep ®.
jérémiades [ʒeʀemjad] *nfpl* moaning *sg*.
jerrycan [ʒeʀikan] *nm* jerrycan.
Jersey [ʒɛʀzɛ] *nf* Jersey.
jersey [ʒɛʀzɛ] *nm* jersey; (*TRICOT*): **pointe de** ~ stocking stitch.
jersiais, e [ʒɛʀzjɛ, -ɛz] *adj* Jersey *cpd*, of or from Jersey.
Jérusalem [ʒeʀyzalɛm] *n* Jerusalem.
jésuite [ʒezɥit] *nm* Jesuit.
Jésus-Christ [ʒezykʀi(st)] *n* Jesus Christ; **600 avant/après** ~ *ou* **J.-C.** 600 B.C./A.D.
jet[1] [ʒɛ] *nm* (*lancer*) throwing *no pl*, throw; (*jaillissement*) jet; spurt; (*de tuyau*) nozzle; (*fig*): **premier** ~ (*ébauche*) rough outline; **arroser au** ~ to hose; **d'un (seul)** ~ (*d'un seul coup*) at (*ou* in) one go; **du premier** ~ at the first attempt *ou* shot; ~ **d'eau** spray; (*fontaine*) fountain.
jet[2] [dʒɛt] *nm* (*avion*) jet.
jetable [ʒətabl(ə)] *adj* disposable.
jeté [ʒəte] *nm* (*TRICOT*): **un** ~ make one; ~ **de table** (table) runner; ~ **de lit** bedspread.
jetée [ʒəte] *nf* jetty; pier.
jeter [ʒəte] *vt* (*gén*) to throw; (*se défaire de*) to throw away *ou* out; (*son, lueur etc*) to give out; ~ **qch à qn** to throw sth to sb; (*de façon agressive*) to throw sth at sb; (*NAVIG*): ~ **l'ancre** to cast anchor; ~ **un coup d'œil (à)** to take a look (at); ~ **les bras en avant/la tête en arrière** to throw one's arms forward/ one's head back(ward); ~ **l'effroi parmi** to spread fear among; ~ **un sort à qn** to cast a spell on sb; ~ **qn dans la misère** to reduce sb to poverty; ~ **qn dehors/en prison** to throw sb out/into prison; ~ **l'éponge** (*fig*) to throw in the towel; ~ **des fleurs à qn** (*fig*) to say lovely things to sb; ~ **la pierre à qn** (*accuser, blâmer*) to accuse sb; **se** ~ **sur** to throw o.s. onto; **se** ~ **dans** (*suj: fleuve*) to flow into; **se** ~ **par la fenêtre** to throw o.s. out of the window; **se** ~ **à l'eau** (*fig*) to take the plunge.
jeton [ʒətɔ̃] *nm* (*au jeu*) counter; (*de téléphone*) token; ~**s de présence** (director's) fees.
jette [ʒɛt] *etc vb voir* **jeter**.
jeu, x [ʒø] *nm* (*divertissement, TECH: d'une pièce*) play; (*défini par des règles, TENNIS: partie*

FOOTBALL etc: façon de jouer) game; (*THÉÂT etc*) acting; (*fonctionnement*) working, interplay; (*série d'objets, jouet*) set; (*CARTES*) hand; (*au casino*): **le** ~ gambling; **cacher son** ~ (*fig*) to keep one's cards hidden, conceal one's hand; **c'est un** ~ **d'enfant!** (*fig*) it's child's play!; **en** ~ at stake; at work; (*FOOTBALL*) in play; **remettre en** ~ to throw in; **entrer/mettre en** ~ to come/bring into play; **par** ~ (*pour s'amuser*) for fun; **d'entrée de** ~ (*tout de suite, dès le début*) from the outset; **entrer dans le** ~**/le** ~ **de qn** (*fig*) to play the game/sb's game; **jouer gros** ~ to play for high stakes; **se piquer/se prendre au** ~ to get excited over/get caught up in the game; ~ **de boules** game of bowls; (*endroit*) bowling pitch; (*boules*) set of bowls; ~ **de cartes** card game; (*paquet*) pack of cards; ~ **de construction** building set; ~ **d'échecs** chess set; ~ **d'écritures** (*COMM*) paper transaction; ~ **de hasard** game of chance; ~ **de mots** pun; **le** ~ **de l'oie** snakes and ladders *sg*; ~ **d'orgue(s)** organ stop; ~ **de patience** puzzle; ~ **de physionomie** facial expressions *pl*; ~ **de société** parlour game; ~ **vidéo** computer game; ~**x de lumière** lighting effects; **J**~**x olympiques (JO)** Olympic Games.

jeu-concours, *pl* **jeux-concours** [jøkɔ̃kuʀ] *nm* competition.

jeudi [ʒødi] *nm* Thursday; ~ **saint** Maundy Thursday; *voir aussi* **lundi**.

jeun [ʒœ̃]: **à** ~ *adv* on an empty stomach.

jeune [ʒœn] *adj* young ♦ *adv*: **faire/s'habiller** ~ to look/dress young; **les** ~**s** young people, the young; ~ **fille** *nf* girl; ~ **homme** *nm* young man; ~ **loup** *nm* (*POL, ÉCON*) young go-getter; ~ **premier** leading man; ~**s gens** *nmpl* young people; ~**s mariés** *nmpl* newly weds.

jeûne [ʒøn] *nm* fast.

jeûner [ʒøne] *vt* to fast, go without food.

jeunesse [ʒœnɛs] *nf* youth; (*aspect*) youthfulness; (*jeunes*) young people *pl*, youth.

JF *sigle f* = **jeune fille**.

JH *sigle m* = **jeune homme**.

JI *sigle m* = **juge d'instruction**.

jiu-jitsu [ʒyʒitsy] *nm inv* (*SPORT*) jujitsu.

JMF *sigle f* (= *Jeunesses musicales de France*) *association to promote music among the young*.

JO *sigle m* = **Journal officiel** ♦ *sigle mpl* = **Jeux olympiques**.

joaillerie [ʒɔɑjʀi] *nf* jewel trade; jewellery (*BRIT*), jewelry (*US*).

joaillier, ière [ʒɔɑje, -jɛʀ] *nm/f* jeweller (*BRIT*), jeweler (*US*).

job [dʒɔb] *nm* job.

jobard [ʒɔbaʀ] *nm* (*péj*) sucker, mug.

JOC [ʒɔk] *sigle f* (= *Jeunesse ouvrière chrétienne*) *youth organization*.

jockey [ʒɔkɛ] *nm* jockey.

jodler [ʒɔdle] *vi* to yodel.

jogging [dʒɔgiŋ] *nm* tracksuit (*BRIT*), sweatsuit (*US*); **faire du** ~ to jog, go jogging.

joie [ʒwa] *nf* joy.

joignais [ʒwaɲɛ] *etc vb voir* **joindre**.

joindre [ʒwɛ̃dʀ(ə)] *vt* to join; (*à une lettre*): ~ **qch à** to enclose sth with; (*contacter*) to contact, get in touch with; ~ **les mains/talons** to put one's hands/heels together; ~ **les deux bouts** (*fig: du mois*) to make ends meet; **se** ~ (*mains etc*) to come together; **se** ~ **à qn** to join sb; **se** ~ **à qch** to join in sth.

joint, e [ʒwɛ̃, -ɛ̃t] *pp de* **joindre** ♦ *adj*: ~ **(à)** (*lettre, paquet*) attached (to), enclosed (with); **pièce** ~**e** enclosure ♦ *nm* joint; (*ligne*) join; (*de ciment etc*) pointing *no pl*; **chercher/trouver le** ~ (*fig*) to look for/come up with the answer; ~ **de cardan** cardan joint; ~ **de culasse** cylinder head gasket; ~ **de robinet** washer; ~ **universel** universal joint.

jointure [ʒwɛ̃tyʀ] *nf* (*ANAT: articulation*) joint; (*TECH: assemblage*) joint; (*: ligne*) join.

joker [ʒɔkɛʀ] *nm* (*CARTES*) joker; (*INFORM*): **(caractère** *m*) ~ wildcard.

joli, e [ʒɔli] *adj* pretty, attractive; **une** ~**e somme/situation** a nice little sum/situation; **un** ~ **gâchis** *etc* a nice mess *etc*; **c'est du** ~**!** that's very nice!; **tout ça, c'est bien** ~ **mais** ... that's all very well but ....

joliment [ʒɔlimɑ̃] *adv* prettily, attractively; (*fam: très*) pretty.

jonc [ʒɔ̃] *nm* (bul)rush; (*bague, bracelet*) band.

joncher [ʒɔ̃ʃe] *vt* (*suj: choses*) to be strewed on; **jonché de** strewn with.

jonction [ʒɔ̃ksjɔ̃] *nf* joining; **(point de)** ~ (*de routes*) junction; (*de fleuves*) confluence; **opérer une** ~ (*MIL etc*) to rendez-vous.

jongler [ʒɔ̃gle] *vi* to juggle; (*fig*): ~ **avec** to juggle with, play with.

jongleur, euse [ʒɔ̃glœʀ, -øz] *nm/f* juggler.

jonquille [ʒɔ̃kij] *nf* daffodil.

Jordanie [ʒɔʀdani] *nf*: **la** ~ Jordan.

jordanien, ne [ʒɔʀdanjɛ̃, -ɛn] *adj* Jordanian ♦ *nm/f*: **J**~**, ne** Jordanian.

jouable [ʒwabl(ə)] *adj* playable.

joue [ʒu] *nf* cheek; **mettre en** ~ to take aim at.

jouer [ʒwe] *vt* (*partie, carte, coup, MUS: morceau*) to play; (*somme d'argent, réputation*) to stake, wager; (*pièce, rôle*) to perform; (*film*) to show; (*simuler: sentiment*) to affect, feign ♦ *vi* to play; (*THÉÂT, CINÉ*) to act, perform; (*bois, porte: se voiler*) to warp; (*clef, pièce: avoir du jeu*) to be loose; (*entrer ou être en jeu*) to come into play, come into it; ~ **sur** (*miser*) to gamble on; ~ **de** (*MUS*) to play; ~ **du couteau/des coudes** to use knives/one's elbows; ~ **à** (*jeu, sport, roulette*) to play; ~ **au héros** to act *ou* play the hero; ~ **avec** (*risquer*) to gamble with; **se** ~ **de** (*difficultés*) to make light of; **se** ~ **de qn** to deceive *ou* dupe sb; ~ **un tour à qn** to play a trick on sb; ~ **la comédie** (*fig*) to put on an act, put it on; ~ **aux courses** to back horses, bet on horses; ~ **à la baisse/hausse** (*BOURSE*) to

play for a fall/rise; ~ **serré** to play a close game; ~ **de malchance** to be dogged with ill-luck; ~ **sur les mots** to play with words; **à toi/nous de** ~ it's your/our go *ou* turn.
jouet [ʒwɛ] *nm* toy; **être le** ~ **de** (*illusion etc*) to be the victim of.
joueur, euse [ʒwœʀ, -øz] *nm/f* player ♦ *adj* (*enfant, chat*) playful; **être beau/mauvais** ~ to be a good/bad loser.
joufflu, e [ʒufly] *adj* chubby(-cheeked).
joug [ʒu] *nm* yoke.
jouir [ʒwiʀ]: ~ **de** *vt* to enjoy.
jouissance [ʒwisɑ̃s] *nf* pleasure; (*JUR*) use.
jouisseur, euse [ʒwisœʀ, -øz] *nm/f* sensualist.
joujou [ʒuʒu] *nm* (*fam*) toy.
jour [ʒuʀ] *nm* day; (*opposé à la nuit*) day, daytime; (*clarté*) daylight; (*fig: aspect*): **sous un** ~ **favourable/nouveau** in a favourable/new light; (*ouverture*) opening; (*COUTURE*) openwork *no pl*; **au** ~ **le** ~ from day to day; **de nos** ~**s** these days, nowadays; **tous les** ~**s** every day; **de** ~ **en** ~ day by day; **d'un** ~ **à l'autre** from one day to the next; **du** ~ **au lendemain** overnight; **il fait** ~ it's daylight; **en plein** ~ in broad daylight; **au** ~ in daylight; **au petit** ~ at daybreak; **au grand** ~ (*fig*) in the open; **mettre au** ~ to uncover, disclose; **être à** ~ to be up to date; **mettre à** ~ to bring up to date, update; **mise à** ~ updating; **donner le** ~ **à** to give birth to; **voir le** ~ to be born; **se faire** ~ (*fig*) to become clear; ~ **férié** public holiday; **le** ~ **J** D-day.
Jourdain [ʒuʀdɛ̃] *nm*: **le** ~ the (River) Jordan.
journal, aux [ʒuʀnal, -o] *nm* (news)paper; (*personnel*) journal, diary; ~ **de bord** log; ~ **de mode** fashion magazine; **le J~ officiel (de la République française) (JO)** *bulletin giving details of laws and official announcements*; ~ **parlé/télévisé** radio/television news *sg*.
journalier, ière [ʒuʀnalje, -jɛʀ] *adj* daily; (*banal*) everyday ♦ *nm* day labourer.
journalisme [ʒuʀnalism(ə)] *nm* journalism.
journaliste [ʒuʀnalist(ə)] *nm/f* journalist.
journalistique [ʒuʀnalistik] *adj* journalistic.
journée [ʒuʀne] *nf* day; **la** ~ **continue** the 9 to 5 working day (*with short lunch break*).
journellement [ʒuʀnɛlmɑ̃] *adv* (*tous les jours*) daily; (*souvent*) every day.
joute [ʒut] *nf* (*tournoi*) duel; (*verbale*) duel, battle of words.
jouvence [ʒuvɑ̃s] *nf*: **bain de** ~ rejuvenating experience.
jouxter [ʒukste] *vt* to adjoin.
jovial [ʒɔvjal] *adj* jovial, jolly.
jovialité [ʒɔvjalite] *nf* joviality.
joyau, x [ʒwajo] *nm* gem, jewel.
joyeusement [ʒwajøzmɑ̃] *adv* joyfully, gladly.
joyeux, euse [ʒwajø, -øz] *adj* joyful, merry; ~ **Noël!** merry *ou* happy Christmas!; ~ **anniversaire!** many happy returns!
JT *sigle m* = **journal télévisé.**
jubilation [ʒybilɑsjɔ̃] *nf* jubilation.
jubilé [ʒybile] *nm* jubilee.
jubiler [ʒybile] *vi* to be jubilant, exult.
jucher [ʒyʃe] *vt*: ~ **qch sur** to perch sth (up)on ♦ *vi* (*oiseau*): ~ **sur** to perch (up)on; **se** ~ **sur** to perch o.s. (up)on.
judaïque [ʒydaik] *adj* (*loi*) Judaic; (*religion*) Jewish.
judaïsme [ʒydaism(ə)] *nm* Judaism.
judas [ʒyda] *nm* (*trou*) spy-hole.
Judée [ʒyde] *nf*: **la** ~ Jud(a)ea.
judéo- [ʒydeɔ] *préfixe* Judeo-.
judéo-allemand, e [ʒydeɔalmɑ̃, -ɑ̃d] *adj, nm* Yiddish.
judéo-chrétien, ne [ʒydeɔkʀetjɛ̃, -ɛn] *adj* Judeo-Christian.
judiciaire [ʒydisjɛʀ] *adj* judicial.
judicieusement [ʒydisjøzmɑ̃] *adv* judiciously.
judicieux, euse [ʒydisjø, -øz] *adj* judicious.
judo [ʒydo] *nm* judo.
judoka [ʒydɔka] *nm/f* judoka.
juge [ʒyʒ] *nm* judge; ~ **d'instruction** examining (*BRIT*) *ou* committing (*US*) magistrate; ~ **de paix** justice of the peace; ~ **de touche** linesman.
jugé [ʒyʒe]: **au** ~ *adv* by guesswork.
jugement [ʒyʒmɑ̃] *nm* judgment; (*JUR: au pénal*) sentence; (*: au civil*) decision; ~ **de valeur** value judgment.
jugeote [ʒyʒɔt] *nf* (*fam*) gumption.
juger [ʒyʒe] *vt* to judge ♦ *nm*: **au** ~ by guesswork; ~ **qn/qch satisfaisant** to consider sb/sth (to be) satisfactory; ~ **que** to think *ou* consider that; ~ **bon de faire** to consider it a good idea to do, see fit to do; ~ **de** *vt* to judge; **jugez de ma surprise** imagine my surprise.
jugulaire [ʒygylɛʀ] *adj* jugular ♦ *nf* (*MIL*) chinstrap.
juguler [ʒygyle] *vt* (*maladie*) to halt; (*révolte*) to suppress; (*inflation etc*) to control, curb.
juif, ive [ʒɥif, -iv] *adj* Jewish ♦ *nm/f*: **J~, ive** Jew/Jewess *ou* Jewish woman.
juillet [ʒɥijɛ] *nm* July; **le premier** ~ the first of July (*BRIT*), July first (*US*); **le deux/onze** ~ the second/eleventh of July, July second/eleventh; **il est venu le 5** ~ he came on 5th July *ou* July 5th; **en** ~ in July; **début/fin** ~ at the beginning/end of July; *see boxed note*.

14 JUILLET

Le 14 juillet *is a national holiday in France and commemorates the storming of the Bastille during the French Revolution. Throughout the country there are celebrations, which feature parades, music, dancing and firework displays. In Paris, a military parade along the Champs-Élysées is attended by the President.*

juin [ʒɥɛ̃] *nm* June; *voir aussi* **juillet**.
juive [ʒwiv] *voir* **juif.**

jumeau, elle, x [ʒymo, -ɛl] *adj, nm/f* twin; **maisons jumelles** semidetached houses.
jumelage [ʒymlaʒ] *nm* twinning.
jumeler [ʒymle] *vt* to twin; **roues jumelées** double wheels; **billets jumelés** (*Loterie*) double series tickets; **pari jumelé** double bet.
jumelle [ʒymɛl] *adj f, nf voir* **jumeau** ♦ *vb voir* **jumeler**.
jumelles [ʒymɛl] *nfpl* binoculars.
jument [ʒymɑ̃] *nf* mare.
jungle [ʒɔ̃gl(ə)] *nf* jungle.
junior [ʒynjɔʀ] *adj* junior.
junte [ʒœ̃t] *nf* junta.
jupe [ʒyp] *nf* skirt.
jupe-culotte, *pl* **jupes-culottes** [ʒypkylɔt] *nf* divided skirt, culotte(s).
jupette [ʒypɛt] *nf* short skirt.
jupon [ʒypɔ̃] *nm* waist slip *ou* petticoat.
Jura [ʒyʀa] *nm*: **le** ~ the Jura (Mountains).
jurassien, ne [ʒyʀasjɛ̃, -ɛn] *adj* of *ou* from the Jura Mountains.
juré, e [ʒyʀe] *nm/f* juror ♦ *adj*: **ennemi** ~ sworn *ou* avowed enemy.
jurer [ʒyʀe] *vt* (*obéissance etc*) to swear, vow ♦ *vi* (*dire des jurons*) to swear, curse; (*dissoner*): ~ **(avec)** to clash (with); (*s'engager*): ~ **de faire/que** to swear *ou* vow to do/that; (*affirmer*): ~ **que** to swear *ou* vouch that; ~ **de qch** (*s'en porter garant*) to swear to sth; **ils ne jurent que par lui** they swear by him; **je vous jure!** honestly!
juridiction [ʒyʀidiksjɔ̃] *nf* jurisdiction; (*tribunal, tribunaux*) court(s) of law.
juridique [ʒyʀidik] *adj* legal.
juridiquement [ʒyʀidikmɑ̃] *adv* (*devant la justice*) juridically; (*du point de vue du droit*) legally.
jurisconsulte [ʒyʀikɔ̃sylt(ə)] *nm* jurisconsult.
jurisprudence [ʒyʀispʀydɑ̃s] *nf* (*JUR*: *décisions*) (legal) precedents; (*principes juridiques*) jurisprudence; **faire** ~ (*faire autorité*) to set a precedent.
juriste [ʒyʀist(ə)] *nm/f* jurist; lawyer.
juron [ʒyʀɔ̃] *nm* curse, swearword.
jury [ʒyʀi] *nm* (*JUR*) jury; (*SCOL*) board (of examiners), jury.
jus [ʒy] *nm* juice; (*de viande*) gravy, (meat) juice; ~ **de fruits** fruit juice; ~ **de raisin/tomates** grape/tomato juice.
jusant [ʒyzɑ̃] *nm* ebb (tide).
jusqu'au-boutiste [ʒyskobutist(ə)] *nm/f* extremist, hardliner.
jusque [ʒysk(ə)]: **jusqu'à** *prép* (*endroit*) as far as, (up) to; (*moment*) until, till; (*limite*) up to; ~ **sur/dans** up to, as far as; (*y compris*) even on/in; **jusque vers** until about; **jusqu'à ce que** *conj* until; **jusque-là** (*temps*) until then; (*espace*) up to there; **jusqu'ici** (*temps*) until now; (*espace*) up to here; **jusqu'à présent** until now, so far.
justaucorps [ʒystokɔʀ] *nm inv* (*DANSE, SPORT*) leotard.
juste [ʒyst(ə)] *adj* (*équitable*) just, fair; (*légitime*) just, justified; (*exact, vrai*) right; (*étroit, insuffisant*) tight ♦ *adv* right; tight; (*chanter*) in tune; (*seulement*) just; ~ **assez/au-dessus** just enough/above; **pouvoir tout ~ faire** to be only just able to do; **au** ~ exactly, actually; **comme de** ~ of course, naturally; **le ~ milieu** the happy medium; **à ~ titre** rightfully.
justement [ʒystəmɑ̃] *adv* rightly; justly; (*précisément*): **c'est ~ ce qu'il fallait faire** that's just *ou* precisely what needed doing.
justesse [ʒystɛs] *nf* (*précision*) accuracy; (*d'une remarque*) aptness; (*d'une opinion*) soundness; **de** ~ just, by a narrow margin.
justice [ʒystis] *nf* (*équité*) fairness, justice; (*ADMIN*) justice; **rendre la** ~ to dispense justice; **traduire en** ~ to bring before the courts; **obtenir** ~ to obtain justice; **rendre ~ à qn** to do sb justice; **se faire** ~ to take the law into one's own hands; (*se suicider*) to take one's life.
justiciable [ʒystisjabl(ə)] *adj*: ~ **de** (*JUR*) answerable to.
justicier, ière [ʒystisje, -jɛʀ] *nm/f* judge, righter of wrongs.
justifiable [ʒystifjabl(ə)] *adj* justifiable.
justificatif, ive [ʒystifikatif, -iv] *adj* (*document etc*) supporting ♦ *nm* supporting proof.
justification [ʒystifikɑsjɔ̃] *nf* justification.
justifier [ʒystifje] *vt* to justify; ~ **de** *vt* to prove; **non justifié** unjustified; **justifié à droite/gauche** ranged right/left.
jute [ʒyt] *nm* jute.
juteux, euse [ʒytø, -øz] *adj* juicy.
juvénile [ʒyvenil] *adj* young, youthful.
juxtaposer [ʒykstapoze] *vt* to juxtapose.
juxtaposition [ʒykstapozisjɔ̃] *nf* juxtaposition.

K k

K, k [kɑ] *nm inv* K, k ♦ *abr* (= *kilo*) kg; (= *kilooctet*) K; **K comme Kléber** K for King.
K7 [kasɛt] *abr* = **cassette**.
Kaboul, Kabul [kabul] *n* Kabul.
kabyle [kabil] *adj* Kabyle ♦ *nm* (*LING*) Kabyle ♦ *nm/f*: **K~** Kabyle.
Kabylie [kabili] *nf*: **la** ~ Kabylia.
kafkaïen, ne [kafkajɛ̃, -ɛn] *adj* Kafkaesque.
kaki [kaki] *adj inv* khaki.
Kalahari [kalaaʀi] *n*: **désert de** ~ Kalahari Desert.
kaléidoscope [kaleidɔskɔp] *nm* kaleidoscope.
Kampala [kɑ̃pala] *n* Kampala.
Kampuchéa [kɑ̃putʃea] *nm*: **le ~ (démocrati-**

que) (the People's Republic of) Kampuchea.
kangourou [kɑ̃guʀu] *nm* kangaroo.
kaolin [kaɔlɛ̃] *nm* kaolin.
kapok [kapɔk] *nm* kapok.
karaoke [kaʀaoke] *nm* karaoke.
karaté [kaʀate] *nm* karate.
kart [kaʀt] *nm* go-cart.
karting [kaʀtiŋ] *nm* go-carting, karting.
kascher [kaʃɛʀ] *adj inv* kosher.
kayac, kayak [kajak] *nm* kayak.
Kazakhstan [kaʒakstɑ̃] *nm* Kazakhstan.
Kenya [kenja] *nm*: **le** ~ Kenya.
kenyan, e [kenjɑ̃, -an] *adj* Kenyan ♦ *nm/f*: **K~, ne** Kenyan.
képi [kepi] *nm* kepi.
Kerguelen [kɛʀgelɛn]: **les (îles)** ~ Kerguelen.
kermesse [kɛʀmɛs] *nf* bazaar, (charity) fête; village fair.
kérosène [keʀozɛn] *nm* jet fuel; rocket fuel.
kg *abr* (= *kilogramme*) kg.
KGB *sigle m* KGB.
khmer, ère [kmɛʀ] *adj* Khmer ♦ *nm* (*LING*) Khmer.
khôl [kol] *nm* khol.
kibboutz [kibuts] *nm* kibbutz.
kidnapper [kidnape] *vt* to kidnap.
kidnappeur, euse [kidnapœʀ, -øz] *nm/f* kidnapper.
kidnapping [kidnapiŋ] *nm* kidnapping.
Kilimandjaro [kilimɑ̃dʒaʀo] *nm*: **le** ~ Mount Kilimanjaro.
kilo [kilo] *nm* kilo.
kilogramme [kilɔgʀam] *nm* kilogramme (*BRIT*), kilogram (*US*).
kilométrage [kilɔmetʀaʒ] *nm* number of kilometres travelled, ≈ mileage.
kilomètre [kilɔmɛtʀ(ə)] *nm* kilometre (*BRIT*), kilometer (*US*); **~s-heure** kilometres per hour.
kilométrique [kilɔmetʀik] *adj* (*distance*) in kilometres; **compteur** ~ ≈ mileage indicator.
kilooctet [kilɔɔktɛ] *nm* kilobyte.
kilowatt [kilɔwat] *nm* kilowatt.
kinésithérapeute [kineziteʀapøt] *nm/f* physiotherapist.
kinésithérapie [kineziteʀapi] *nf* physiotherapy.
kiosque [kjɔsk(ə)] *nm* kiosk, stall; (*TÉL etc*) *telephone and/or videotext information service.*
Kirghizistan [kiʀgizistɑ̃] *nm* Kirghizia.
kirsch [kiʀʃ] *nm* kirsch.
kitchenette [kitʃ(ə)nɛt] *nf* kitchenette.
kiwi [kiwi] *nm* (*ZOOL*) kiwi; (*BOT*) kiwi (fruit).
klaxon [klaksɔn] *nm* horn.
klaxonner [klaksɔne] *vi, vt* to hoot (*BRIT*), honk (one's horn) (*US*).
kleptomane [klɛptɔman] *nm/f* kleptomaniac.
km *abr* (= *kilomètre*) km.
knock-out [nɔkawt] *nm* knock-out.
Ko *abr* (*INFORM*: = *kilooctet*) K.
K.-O. [kao] *adj inv* (knocked) out, out for the count.
koala [kɔala] *nm* koala (bear).
kolkhoze [kɔlkoz] *nm* kolkhoz.
Kosovo [kɔsɔvo] *nm* Kosovo.
Koweit *ou* **Kuweit** [kɔwɛt] *nm*: **le** ~ Kuwait, Koweit.
koweitien, ne [kɔwɛtjɛ̃, -ɛn] *adj* Kuwaiti ♦ *nm/f*: **K~, ne** Kuwaiti.
krach [kʀak] *nm* (*ÉCON*) crash.
kraft [kʀaft] *nm* brown *ou* kraft paper.
Kremlin [kʀɛmlɛ̃] *nm*: **le** ~ the Kremlin.
Kuala Lumpur [kwalalympuʀ] *n* Kuala Lumpur.
kurde [kyʀd(ə)] *adj* Kurdish ♦ *nm* (*LING*) Kurdish ♦ *nm/f*: **K~** Kurd.
Kurdistan [kyʀdistɑ̃] *nm*: **le** ~ Kurdistan.
Kuweit [kɔwɛt] = **Koweit**.
kW *abr* (= *kilowatt*) kW.
kW/h *abr* (= *kilowatt/heure*) kW/h.
kyrielle [kiʀjɛl] *nf*: **une ~ de** a stream of.
kyste [kist(ə)] *nm* cyst.

L l

L, l [ɛl] *nm inv* L, l ♦ *abr* (= *litre*) l; (*SCOL*): **L ès L = Licence ès Lettres; L en D = Licence en Droit; L comme Louis** L for Lucy (*BRIT*) *ou* Love (*US*).
l' [l] *art déf voir* **le**.
la [la] *art déf, pron voir* **le** ♦ *nm* (*MUS*) A; (*en chantant la gamme*) la.
là [la] *adv* (*voir aussi* **-ci, celui**) there; (*ici*) here; (*dans le temps*) then; **est-ce que Catherine est ~?** is Catherine there (*ou* here)?; **c'est ~ que** this is where; ~ **où** where; **de** ~ (*fig*) hence; **par** ~ (*fig*) by that; **tout est** ~ (*fig*) that's what it's all about.
là-bas [labɑ] *adv* there.
label [labɛl] *nm* stamp, seal.
labeur [labœʀ] *nm* toil *no pl*, toiling *no pl*.
labo [labo] *nm* (= *laboratoire*) lab.
laborantin, e [labɔʀɑ̃tɛ̃, -in] *nm/f* laboratory assistant.
laboratoire [labɔʀatwaʀ] *nm* laboratory; ~ **de langues/d'analyses** language/(medical) analysis laboratory.
laborieux, euse [labɔʀjø, -øz] *adj* (*tâche*) laborious; **classes ~euses** working classes.
laborieusement [labɔʀjøzmɑ̃] *adv* laboriously.
labour [labuʀ] *nm* ploughing *no pl* (*BRIT*), plowing *no pl* (*US*); **~s** *nmpl* (*champs*) ploughed fields; **cheval de** ~ plough- *ou* cart-horse; **bœuf de** ~ ox (*pl* oxen).
labourage [labuʀaʒ] *nm* ploughing (*BRIT*)

plowing (*US*).
labourer [labuʀe] *vt* to plough (*BRIT*), plow (*US*); (*fig*) to make deep gashes *ou* furrows in.
laboureur [labuʀœʀ] *nm* ploughman (*BRIT*), plowman (*US*).
labrador [labʀadɔʀ] *nm* (*chien*) labrador; (*GÉO*): **le L~** Labrador.
labyrinthe [labiʀɛ̃t] *nm* labyrinth, maze.
lac [lak] *nm* lake; **le ~ Léman** Lake Geneva; **les Grands L~s** the Great Lakes; *voir aussi* **lacs**.
lacer [lase] *vt* to lace *ou* do up.
lacérer [laseʀe] *vt* to tear to shreds.
lacet [lasɛ] *nm* (*de chaussure*) lace; (*de route*) sharp bend; (*piège*) snare; **chaussures à ~s** lace-up *ou* lacing shoes.
lâche [lɑʃ] *adj* (*poltron*) cowardly; (*desserré*) loose, slack; (*morale, mœurs*) lax ♦ *nm/f* coward.
lâchement [lɑʃmɑ̃] *adv* (*par peur*) like a coward; (*par bassesse*) despicably.
lâcher [lɑʃe] *nm* (*de ballons, oiseaux*) release ♦ *vt* to let go of; (*ce qui tombe, abandonner*) to drop; (*oiseau, animal: libérer*) to release, set free; (*fig: mot, remarque*) to let slip, come out with; (*SPORT: distancer*) to leave behind ♦ *vi* (*fil, amarres*) to break, give way; (*freins*) to fail; ~ **les amarres** (*NAVIG*) to cast off (the moorings); ~ **prise** to let go.
lâcheté [lɑʃte] *nf* cowardice; (*bassesse*) lowness.
lacis [lasi] *nm* (*de ruelles*) maze.
laconique [lakɔnik] *adj* laconic.
laconiquement [lakɔnikmɑ̃] *adv* laconically.
lacrymal, e, aux [lakʀimal, -o] *adj* (*canal, glande*) tear *cpd*.
lacrymogène [lakʀimɔʒɛn] *adj*: **grenade/gaz ~** tear gas grenade/tear gas.
lacs [lɑ] *nm* (*piège*) snare.
lactation [laktɑsjɔ̃] *nf* lactation.
lacté, e [lakte] *adj* milk *cpd*.
lactique [laktik] *adj*: **acide/ferment ~** lactic acid/ferment.
lactose [laktoz] *nm* lactose, milk sugar.
lacune [lakyn] *nf* gap.
lacustre [lakystʀ(ə)] *adj* lake *cpd*, lakeside *cpd*.
lad [lad] *nm* stable-lad.
là-dedans [ladədɑ̃] *adv* inside (there), in it; (*fig*) in that.
là-dehors [ladəɔʀ] *adv* out there.
là-derrière [ladɛʀjɛʀ] *adv* behind there; (*fig*) behind that.
là-dessous [ladsu] *adv* underneath, under there; (*fig*) behind that.
là-dessus [ladsy] *adv* on there; (*fig*) at that point; (*: à ce sujet*) about that.
là-devant [ladvɑ̃] *adv* there (in front).
ladite [ladit] *dét voir* **ledit**.
ladre [lɑdʀ(ə)] *adj* miserly.
lagon [lagɔ̃] *nm* lagoon.
Lagos [lagɔs] *n* Lagos.
lagune [lagyn] *nf* lagoon.
là-haut [lao] *adv* up there.
laïc [laik] *adj, nm/f* = **laïque**.
laïciser [laisize] *vt* to secularize.
laïcité [laisite] *nf* secularity, secularism.
laid, e [lɛ, lɛd] *adj* ugly; (*fig: acte*) mean, cheap.
laideron [lɛdʀɔ̃] *nm* ugly girl.
laideur [lɛdœʀ] *nf* ugliness *no pl*; meanness *no pl*.
laie [lɛ] *nf* wild sow.
lainage [lɛnaʒ] *nm* woollen garment; (*étoffe*) woollen material.
laine [lɛn] *nf* wool; ~ **peignée** worsted (wool); ~ **à tricoter** knitting wool; ~ **de verre** glass wool; ~ **vierge** new wool.
laineux, euse [lɛnø, -øz] *adj* woolly.
lainier, ière [lenje, -jɛʀ] *adj* (*industrie etc*) woollen.
laïque [laik] *adj* lay, civil; (*SCOL*) state *cpd* (*as opposed to private and Roman Catholic*) ♦ *nm/f* layman/woman.
laisse [lɛs] *nf* (*de chien*) lead, leash; **tenir en ~** to keep on a lead *ou* leash.
laissé-pour-compte, laissée-, laissés- [lesepuʀkɔ̃t] *adj* (*COMM*) unsold; (*: refusé*) returned ♦ *nm/f* (*fig*) reject; **les laissés-pour-compte de la reprise économique** those who are left out of the economic upturn.
laisser [lese] *vt* to leave ♦ *vb aux*: ~ **qn faire** to let sb do; **se ~ exploiter** to let o.s. be exploited; **se ~ aller** to let o.s. go; ~ **qn tranquille** to let *ou* leave sb alone; **laisse-toi faire** let me (*ou* him) do it; **rien ne laisse penser que ...** there is no reason to think that ...; **cela ne laisse pas de surprendre** nonetheless it is surprising.
laisser-aller [leseale] *nm* carelessness, slovenliness.
laisser-faire [lesefɛʀ] *nm* laissez-faire.
laissez-passer [lesepɑse] *nm inv* pass.
lait [lɛ] *nm* milk; **frère/sœur de ~** foster brother/sister; ~ **écrémé/concentré/condensé** skimmed/condensed/evaporated milk; ~ **en poudre** powdered milk, milk powder; ~ **de chèvre/vache** goat's/cow's milk; ~ **maternel** mother's milk; ~ **démaquillant/de beauté** cleansing/beauty lotion.
laitage [lɛtaʒ] *nm* milk product.
laiterie [lɛtʀi] *nf* dairy.
laiteux, euse [lɛtø, -øz] *adj* milky.
laitier, ière [letje, -jɛʀ] *adj* dairy ♦ *nm/f* milkman/dairywoman.
laiton [lɛtɔ̃] *nm* brass.
laitue [lety] *nf* lettuce.
laïus [lajys] *nm* (*péj*) spiel.
lama [lama] *nm* llama.
lambeau, x [lɑ̃bo] *nm* scrap; **en ~x** in tatters, tattered.
lambin, e [lɑ̃bɛ̃, -in] *adj* (*péj*) slow.
lambiner [lɑ̃bine] *vi* (*péj*) to dawdle.
lambris [lɑ̃bʀi] *nm* panelling *no pl*.
lambrissé, e [lɑ̃bʀise] *adj* panelled.

lame [lam] *nf* blade; (*vague*) wave; (*lamelle*) strip; ~ **de fond** ground swell *no pl*; ~ **de rasoir** razor blade.

lamé [lame] *nm* lamé.

lamelle [lamɛl] *nf* (*lame*) small blade; (*morceau*) sliver; (*de champignon*) gill; **couper en ~s** to slice thinly.

lamentable [lamɑ̃tabl(ə)] *adj* (*déplorable*) appalling; (*pitoyable*) pitiful.

lamentablement [lamɑ̃tabləmɑ̃] *adv* (*échouer*) miserably; (*se conduire*) appallingly.

lamentation [lamɑ̃tɑsjɔ̃] *nf* wailing *no pl*, lamentation; moaning *no pl*.

lamenter [lamɑ̃te]: **se ~** *vi*: **se ~ (sur)** to moan (over).

laminage [laminaʒ] *nm* lamination.

laminer [lamine] *vt* to laminate; (*fig: écraser*) to wipe out.

laminoir [laminwaʀ] *nm* rolling mill; **passer au ~** (*fig*) to go (*ou* put) through the mill.

lampadaire [lɑ̃padɛʀ] *nm* (*de salon*) standard lamp; (*dans la rue*) street lamp.

lampe [lɑ̃p(ə)] *nf* lamp; (*TECH*) valve; ~ **à alcool** spirit lamp; ~ **à bronzer** sunlamp; ~ **de poche** torch (*BRIT*), flashlight (*US*); ~ **à souder** blowlamp; ~ **témoin** warning light.

lampée [lɑ̃pe] *nf* gulp, swig.

lampe-tempête, *pl* **lampes-tempête** [lɑ̃ptɑ̃pɛt] *nf* storm lantern.

lampion [lɑ̃pjɔ̃] *nm* Chinese lantern.

lampiste [lɑ̃pist(ə)] *nm* light (maintenance) man; (*fig*) underling.

lamproie [lɑ̃pʀwa] *nf* lamprey.

lance [lɑ̃s] *nf* spear; ~ **d'arrosage** garden hose; ~ **à eau** water hose; ~ **d'incendie** fire hose.

lancée [lɑ̃se] *nf*: **être/continuer sur sa ~** to be under way/keep going.

lance-flammes [lɑ̃sflam] *nm inv* flamethrower.

lance-fusées [lɑ̃sfyze] *nm inv* rocket launcher.

lance-grenades [lɑ̃sgʀənad] *nm inv* grenade launcher.

lancement [lɑ̃smɑ̃] *nm* launching *no pl*, launch; **offre de ~** introductory offer.

lance-missiles [lɑ̃smisil] *nm inv* missile launcher.

lance-pierres [lɑ̃spjɛʀ] *nm inv* catapult.

lancer [lɑ̃se] *nm* (*SPORT*) throwing *no pl*, throw; (*PÊCHE*) rod and reel fishing ♦ *vt* to throw; (*émettre, projeter*) to throw out, send out; (*produit, fusée, bateau, artiste*) to launch; (*injure*) to hurl, fling; (*proclamation, mandat d'arrêt*) to issue; (*emprunt*) to float; (*moteur*) to send roaring away; ~ **qch à qn** to throw sth to sb; (*de façon agressive*) to throw sth at sb; ~ **un cri** *ou* **un appel** to shout *ou* call out; **se ~** *vi* (*prendre de l'élan*) to build up speed; (*se précipiter*): **se ~ sur** *ou* **contre** to rush at; **se ~ dans** (*discussion*) to launch into; (*aventure*) to embark on; (*les affaires, la politique*) to go into; ~ **du poids** *nm* putting the shot.

lance-roquettes [lɑ̃sʀɔkɛt] *nm inv* rocket launcher.

lance-torpilles [lɑ̃stɔʀpij] *nm inv* torpedo tube.

lanceur, euse [lɑ̃sœʀ, -øz] *nm/f* bowler; (*BASEBALL*) pitcher ♦ *nm* (*ESPACE*) launcher.

lancinant, e [lɑ̃sinɑ̃, -ɑ̃t] *adj* (*regrets etc*) haunting; (*douleur*) shooting.

lanciner [lɑ̃sine] *vi* to throb; (*fig*) to nag.

landais, e [lɑ̃dɛ, -ɛz] *adj* of *ou* from the Landes.

landau [lɑ̃do] *nm* pram (*BRIT*), baby carriage (*US*).

lande [lɑ̃d] *nf* moor.

Landes [lɑ̃d] *nfpl*: **les ~** the Landes.

langage [lɑ̃gaʒ] *nm* language; ~ **d'assemblage** (*INFORM*) assembly language; ~ **du corps** body language; ~ **évolué/machine** (*INFORM*) high-level/machine language; ~ **de programmation** (*INFORM*) programming language.

lange [lɑ̃ʒ] *nm* flannel blanket; **~s** *nmpl* swaddling clothes.

langer [lɑ̃ʒe] *vt* to change (the nappy (*BRIT*) *ou* diaper (*US*) of); **table à ~** changing table.

langoureux, euse [lɑ̃guʀø, -øz] *adj* languorous.

langoureusement [lɑ̃guʀøzmɑ̃] *adv* languorously.

langouste [lɑ̃gust(ə)] *nf* crayfish *inv*.

langoustine [lɑ̃gustin] *nf* Dublin Bay prawn.

langue [lɑ̃g] *nf* (*ANAT, CULIN*) tongue; (*LING*) language; (*bande*): ~ **de terre** spit of land; **tirer la ~ (à)** to stick out one's tongue (at); **donner sa ~ au chat** to give up, give in; **de ~ française** French-speaking; ~ **de bois** officialese; ~ **maternelle** native language, mother tongue; ~ **verte** slang; ~ **vivante** modern language.

langue-de-chat [lɑ̃gdəʃa] *nf* finger biscuit.

languedocien, ne [lɑ̃gdɔsjɛ̃, -ɛn] *adj* of *ou* from the Languedoc.

languette [lɑ̃gɛt] *nf* tongue.

langueur [lɑ̃gœʀ] *nf* languidness.

languir [lɑ̃giʀ] *vi* to languish; (*conversation*) to flag; **se ~** *vi* to be languishing; **faire ~ qn** to keep sb waiting.

languissant, e [lɑ̃gisɑ̃, -ɑ̃t] *adj* languid.

lanière [lanjɛʀ] *nf* (*de fouet*) lash; (*de valise, bretelle*) strap.

lanoline [lanɔlin] *nf* lanolin.

lanterne [lɑ̃tɛʀn(ə)] *nf* (*portable*) lantern; (*électrique*) light, lamp; (*de voiture*) (side)light; ~ **rouge** (*fig*) tail-ender; ~ **vénitienne** Chinese lantern.

lanterneau, x [lɑ̃tɛʀno] *nm* skylight.

lanterner [lɑ̃tɛʀne] *vi*: **faire ~ qn** to keep sb hanging around.

Laos [laɔs] *nm*: **le ~** Laos.

laotien, ne [laɔsjɛ̃, -ɛn] *adj* Laotian.

lapalissade [lapalisad] *nf* statement of the obvious.

La Paz [lapaz] *n* La Paz.

laper [lape] *vt* to lap up.

lapereau, x [lapʀo] *nm* young rabbit.
lapidaire [lapidɛʀ] *adj* stone *cpd*; (*fig*) terse.
lapider [lapide] *vt* to stone.
lapin [lapɛ̃] *nm* rabbit; (*fourrure*) cony; **coup du ~** rabbit punch; **poser un ~ à qn** to stand sb up; **~ de garenne** wild rabbit.
lapis(-lazuli) [lapis(lazyli)] *nm inv* lapis lazuli.
lapon, e [lapɔ̃, -ɔn] *adj* Lapp, Lappish ♦ *nm* (*LING*) Lapp, Lappish ♦ *nm/f*: **L~, e** Lapp, Laplander.
Laponie [lapɔni] *nf*: **la ~** Lapland.
laps [laps] *nm*: **~ de temps** space of time, time *no pl*.
lapsus [lapsys] *nm* slip.
laquais [lakɛ] *nm* lackey.
laque [lak] *nf* lacquer; (*brute*) shellac; (*pour cheveux*) hair spray ♦ *nm* lacquer; piece of lacquer ware.
laqué, e [lake] *adj* lacquered.
laquelle [lakɛl] *pron voir* **lequel**.
larbin [laʀbɛ̃] *nm* (*péj*) flunkey.
larcin [laʀsɛ̃] *nm* theft.
lard [laʀ] *nm* (*graisse*) fat; (*bacon*) (streaky) bacon.
larder [laʀde] *vt* (*CULIN*) to lard.
lardon [laʀdɔ̃] *nm* (*CULIN*) piece of chopped bacon; (*fam: enfant*) kid.
large [laʀʒ(ə)] *adj* wide; broad; (*fig*) generous ♦ *adv*: **calculer/voir ~** to allow extra/think big ♦ *nm* (*largeur*): **5 m de ~** 5 m wide *ou* in width; (*mer*): **le ~** the open sea; **en ~** *adv* sideways; **au ~ de** off; **~ d'esprit** broad-minded; **ne pas en mener ~** to have one's heart in one's boots.
largement [laʀʒəmɑ̃] *adv* widely; (*de loin*) greatly; (*amplement, au minimum*) easily; (*sans compter: donner etc*) generously.
largesse [laʀʒɛs] *nf* generosity; **~s** *nfpl* liberalities.
largeur [laʀʒœʀ] *nf* (*qu'on mesure*) width; (*impression visuelle*) wideness, width; breadth; broadness.
larguer [laʀge] *vt* to drop; (*fam: se débarrasser de*) to get rid of; **~ les amarres** to cast off (the moorings).
larme [laʀm(ə)] *nf* tear; (*fig*): **une ~ de** a drop of; **en ~s** in tears; **pleurer à chaudes ~s** to cry one's eyes out, cry bitterly.
larmoyant, e [laʀmwajɑ̃, -ɑ̃t] *adj* tearful.
larmoyer [laʀmwaje] *vi* (*yeux*) to water; (*se plaindre*) to whimper.
larron [laʀɔ̃] *nm* thief (*pl* thieves).
larve [laʀv(ə)] *nf* (*ZOOL*) larva (*pl* -ae); (*fig*) worm.
larvé, e [laʀve] *adj* (*fig*) latent.
laryngite [laʀɛ̃ʒit] *nf* laryngitis.
laryngologiste [laʀɛ̃gɔlɔʒist(ə)] *nm/f* throat specialist.
larynx [laʀɛ̃ks] *nm* larynx.
las, lasse [lɑ, lɑs] *adj* weary.
lasagne [lazaɲ] *nf* lasagne.
lascar [laskaʀ] *nm* character; (*malin*) rogue.
lascif, ive [lasif, -iv] *adj* lascivious.
laser [lazɛʀ] *nm*: **(rayon) ~** laser (beam); **chaîne** *ou* **platine ~** compact disc (player); **disque ~** compact disc.
lassant, e [lɑsɑ̃, -ɑ̃t] *adj* tiresome, wearisome.
lasse [lɑs] *adj f voir* **las**.
lasser [lɑse] *vt* to weary, tire; **se ~ de** to grow weary *ou* tired of.
lassitude [lɑsityd] *nf* lassitude, weariness.
lasso [laso] *nm* lasso; **prendre au ~** to lasso.
latent, e [latɑ̃, -ɑ̃t] *adj* latent.
latéral, e, aux [lateʀal, -o] *adj* side *cpd*, lateral.
latéralement [lateʀalmɑ̃] *adv* edgeways; (*arriver, souffler*) from the side.
latex [latɛks] *nm inv* latex.
latin, e [latɛ̃, -in] *adj* Latin ♦ *nm* (*LING*) Latin ♦ *nm/f*: **L~, e** Latin; **j'y perds mon ~** it's all Greek to me.
latiniste [latinist(ə)] *nm/f* Latin scholar (*ou* student).
latino-américain, e [latinɔameʀikɛ̃, -ɛn] *adj* Latin-American.
latitude [latityd] *nf* latitude; (*fig*): **avoir la ~ de faire** to be left free *ou* be at liberty to do; **à 48° de ~ Nord** at latitude 48° North; **sous toutes les ~s** (*fig*) world-wide, throughout the world.
latrines [latʀin] *nfpl* latrines.
latte [lat] *nf* lath, slat; (*de plancher*) board.
lattis [lati] *nm* lathwork.
laudanum [lodanɔm] *nm* laudanum.
laudatif, ive [lodatif, -iv] *adj* laudatory.
lauréat, e [lɔʀea, -at] *nm/f* winner.
laurier [lɔʀje] *nm* (*BOT*) laurel; (*CULIN*) bay leaves *pl*; **~s** *nmpl* (*fig*) laurels.
laurier-rose, *pl* **lauriers-roses** [lɔʀjeʀoz] *nm* oleander.
laurier-tin, *pl* **lauriers-tins** [lɔʀjetɛ̃] *nm* laurustinus.
lavable [lavabl(ə)] *adj* washable.
lavabo [lavabo] *nm* washbasin; **~s** *nmpl* toilet *sg*.
lavage [lavaʒ] *nm* washing *no pl*, wash; **~ d'estomac/d'intestin** stomach/intestinal wash; **~ de cerveau** brainwashing *no pl*.
lavande [lavɑ̃d] *nf* lavender.
lavandière [lavɑ̃djɛʀ] *nf* washerwoman.
lave [lav] *nf* lava *no pl*.
lave-glace [lavglas] *nm* (*AUTO*) windscreen (*BRIT*) *ou* windshield (*US*) washer.
lave-linge [lavlɛ̃ʒ] *nm inv* washing machine.
lavement [lavmɑ̃] *nm* (*MÉD*) enema.
laver [lave] *vt* to wash; (*tache*) to wash off; (*fig: affront*) to avenge; **se ~** to have a wash, wash; **se ~ les mains/dents** to wash one's hands/clean one's teeth; **~ la vaisselle/le linge** to wash the dishes/clothes; **~ qn de** (*accusation*) to clear sb of.
laverie [lavʀi] *nf*: **~ (automatique)** launderette.
lavette [lavɛt] *nf* (*chiffon*) dish cloth; (*brosse*) dish mop; (*fam: homme*) wimp, drip.

laveur, euse [lavœʀ, -øz] *nm/f* cleaner.
lave-vaisselle [lavvɛsɛl] *nm inv* dishwasher.
lavis [lavi] *nm* (*technique*) washing; (*dessin*) wash drawing.
lavoir [lavwaʀ] *nm* wash house; (*bac*) washtub.
laxatif, ive [laksatif, -iv] *adj, nm* laxative.
laxisme [laksism(ə)] *nm* laxity.
laxiste [laksist(ə)] *adj* lax.
layette [lɛjɛt] *nf* layette.
layon [lɛjɔ̃] *nm* trail.
lazaret [lazaʀɛ] *nm* quarantine area.
lazzi [ladzi] *nm* gibe.
LCR *sigle f* (= *Ligue communiste révolutionnaire*) *political party.*

MOT-CLÉ

le (l'), la [l(ə)] (*pl* **les**) *art déf* **1** the; ~ **livre/la pomme/l'arbre** the book/the apple/the tree; **les étudiants** the students
2 (*noms abstraits*): ~ **courage/l'amour/la jeunesse** courage/love/youth
3 (*indiquant la possession*): **se casser la jambe** *etc* to break one's leg *etc*; **levez la main** put your hand up; **avoir les yeux gris/~ nez rouge** to have grey eyes/a red nose
4 (*temps*): **le matin/soir** in the morning/evening; mornings/evenings; ~ **jeudi** *etc* (*d'habitude*) on Thursdays *etc*; (*ce jeudi-là etc*) on (the) Thursday; **nous venons ~ 3 décembre** (*parlé*) we're coming on the 3rd of December *ou* on December the 3rd; (*écrit*) we're coming (on) 3rd *ou* 3 December
5 (*distribution, évaluation*) a, an; **2 € ~ mètre/kilo** €2 a *ou* per metre/kilo; ~ **tiers/quart de** a third/quarter of
♦ *pron* **1** (*personne: mâle*) him; (: *femelle*) her; (: *pluriel*) them; **je ~/la/les vois** I can see him/her/them
2 (*animal, chose: singulier*) it; (: *pluriel*) them; **je ~ (ou la) vois** I can see it; **je les vois** I can see them
3 (*remplaçant une phrase*): **je ne ~ savais pas** I didn't know (about it); **il était riche et ne l'est plus** he was once rich but no longer is.

lé [le] *nm* (*de tissu*) width; (*de papier peint*) strip, length.
leader [lidœʀ] *nm* leader.
leadership [lidœʀʃip] *nm* (*POL*) leadership.
leasing [liziŋ] *nm* leasing.
lèche-bottes [lɛʃbɔt] *nm inv* bootlicker.
lèchefrite [lɛʃfʀit] *nf* dripping pan *ou* tray.
lécher [leʃe] *vt* to lick; (*laper: lait, eau*) to lick *ou* lap up; (*finir, polir*) to over-refine; ~ **les vitrines** to go window-shopping; **se ~ les doigts/lèvres** to lick one's fingers/lips.
lèche-vitrines [lɛʃvitʀin] *nm inv*: **faire du ~** to go window-shopping.
leçon [ləsɔ̃] *nf* lesson; **faire la ~** to teach; **faire la ~ à** (*fig*) to give a lecture to; **~s de conduite** driving lessons; **~s particulières** private lessons *ou* tuition *sg* (*BRIT*).
lecteur, trice [lɛktœʀ, -tʀis] *nm/f* reader; (*d'université*) (foreign language) assistant (*BRIT*), (foreign) teaching assistant (*US*) ♦ *nm* (*TECH*): ~ **de cassettes** cassette player; (*INFORM*): ~ **de disquette(s)** *ou* **de disque** disk drive; ~ **compact-disc** *ou* **CD** CD (player).
lectorat [lɛktɔʀa] *nm* (foreign language *ou* teaching) assistantship.
lecture [lɛktyʀ] *nf* reading.
LED [lɛd] *sigle f* (= *light emitting diode*) LED.
ledit [lədi], **ladite** [ladit], *mpl* **lesdits** [ledi], *fpl* **lesdites** [ledit] *dét* the aforesaid.
légal, e, aux [legal, -o] *adj* legal.
légalement [legalmɑ̃] *adv* legally.
légalisation [legalizɑsjɔ̃] *nf* legalization.
légaliser [legalize] *vt* to legalize.
légalité [legalite] *nf* legality, lawfulness; **être dans/sortir de la ~** to be within/step outside the law.
légat [lega] *nm* (*REL*) legate.
légataire [legatɛʀ] *nm* legatee.
légendaire [leʒɑ̃dɛʀ] *adj* legendary.
légende [leʒɑ̃d] *nf* (*mythe*) legend; (*de carte, plan*) key, legend; (*de dessin*) caption.
léger, ère [leʒe, -ɛʀ] *adj* light; (*bruit, retard*) slight; (*boisson, parfum*) weak; (*couche, étoffe*) thin; (*superficiel*) thoughtless; (*volage*) free and easy; flighty; (*peu sérieux*) lightweight; **blessé ~** slightly injured person; **à la légère** *adv* (*parler, agir*) rashly, thoughtlessly.
légèrement [leʒɛʀmɑ̃] *adv* lightly; thoughtlessly, rashly; ~ **plus grand** slightly bigger.
légèreté [leʒɛʀte] *nf* lightness; thoughtlessness.
légiférer [leʒifeʀe] *vi* to legislate.
légion [leʒjɔ̃] *nf* legion; **la L~ étrangère** the Foreign Legion; **la L~ d'honneur** the Legion of Honour; *see boxed note.*

LÉGION D'HONNEUR

Created by Napoleon in 1802 to reward services to the French nation, the **Légion d'honneur** *is a prestigious group of men and women headed by the President of the Republic, the 'Grand Maître'. Members receive a nominal tax-free payment each year.*

légionnaire [leʒjɔnɛʀ] *nm* (*MIL*) legionnaire (*de la Légion d'honneur*) holder of the Legion of Honour.
législateur [leʒislatœʀ] *nm* legislator, lawmaker.
législatif, ive [leʒislatif, -iv] *adj* legislative; **législatives** *nfpl* general election *sg*.
législation [leʒislasjɔ̃] *nf* legislation.
législature [leʒislatyʀ] *nf* legislature; (*période*) term (of office).
légiste [leʒist(ə)] *nm* jurist ♦ *adj*: **médecin ~** forensic scientist (*BRIT*), medical examiner (*US*).

légitime [leʒitim] *adj* (*JUR*) lawful, legitimate; (*enfant*) legitimate; (*fig*) rightful, legitimate; **en état de ~ défense** in self-defence.
légitimement [leʒitimmɑ̃] *adv* lawfully; legitimately; rightfully.
légitimer [leʒitime] *vt* (*enfant*) to legitimize; (*justifier: conduite etc*) to justify.
légitimité [leʒitimite] *nf* (*JUR*) legitimacy.
legs [lɛg] *nm* legacy.
léguer [lege] *vt*: **~ qch à qn** (*JUR*) to bequeath sth to sb; (*fig*) to hand sth down *ou* pass sth on to sb.
légume [legym] *nm* vegetable; **~s verts** green vegetables; **~s secs** pulses.
légumier [legymje] *nm* vegetable dish.
leitmotiv [lejtmɔtiv] *nm* leitmotiv, leitmotif.
Léman [lemɑ̃] *nm voir* **lac**.
lendemain [lɑ̃dmɛ̃] *nm*: **le ~** the next *ou* following day; **le ~ matin/soir** the next *ou* following morning/evening; **le ~ de** the day after; **au ~ de** in the days following; in the wake of; **penser au ~** to think of the future; **sans ~** short-lived; **de beaux ~s** bright prospects; **des ~s qui chantent** a rosy future.
lénifiant, e [lenifjɑ̃, -ɑ̃t] *adj* soothing.
léniniste [leninist(ə)] *adj, nm/f* Leninist.
lent, e [lɑ̃, lɑ̃t] *adj* slow.
lente [lɑ̃t] *nf* nit.
lentement [lɑ̃tmɑ̃] *adv* slowly.
lenteur [lɑ̃tœʀ] *nf* slowness *no pl*; **~s** *nfpl* (*actions, décisions lentes*) slowness *sg*.
lentille [lɑ̃tij] *nf* (*OPTIQUE*) lens *sg*; (*BOT*) lentil; **~ d'eau** duckweed; **~s de contact** contact lenses.
léonin, e [leɔnɛ̃, -in] *adj* (*fig: contrat etc*) one-sided.
léopard [leɔpaʀ] *nm* leopard.
LEP [lɛp] *sigle m* (= *lycée d'enseignement professionnel*) *secondary school for vocational training, pre-1986*.
lèpre [lɛpʀ(ə)] *nf* leprosy.
lépreux, euse [lepʀø, -øz] *nm/f* leper ♦ *adj* (*fig*) flaking, peeling.

MOT-CLÉ

lequel, laquelle [ləkɛl, lakɛl] (*mpl* **lesquels,** *fpl* **lesquelles;** *à + lequel* = **auquel,** *de + lequel* = **duquel**) *pron* **1** (*interrogatif*) which, which one
2 (*relatif: personne: sujet*) who; (*: objet, après préposition*) whom; (*sujet: possessif*) whose; (*: chose*) which; **je l'ai proposé au directeur, ~ est d'accord** I suggested it to the director, who agrees; **la femme à laquelle j'ai acheté mon chien** the woman from whom I bought my dog; **le pont sur ~ nous sommes passés** the bridge (over) which we crossed; **un homme sur la compétence duquel on peut compter** a man whose competence one can count on
♦ *adj*: **auquel cas** in which case.

les [le] *voir* **le**.
lesbienne [lɛsbjɛn] *nf* lesbian.
lesdits [ledi], **lesdites** [ledit] *dét voir* **ledit**.
lèse-majesté [lɛzmaʒɛste] *nf inv*: **crime de ~** crime of lese-majesty.
léser [leze] *vt* to wrong; (*MÉD*) to injure.
lésiner [lezine] *vt*: **~ (sur)** to skimp (on).
lésion [lezjɔ̃] *nf* lesion, damage *no pl*; **~s cérébrales** brain damage.
Lesotho [lezɔto] *nm*: **le ~** Lesotho.
lesquels, lesquelles [lekɛl] *pron voir* **lequel**.
lessivable [lesivabl(ə)] *adj* washable.
lessive [lesiv] *nf* (*poudre*) washing powder; (*linge*) washing *no pl*, wash; (*opération*) washing *no pl*; **faire la ~** to do the washing.
lessivé, e [lesive] *adj* (*fam*) washed out.
lessiver [lesive] *vt* to wash.
lessiveuse [lesivøz] *nf* (*récipient*) washtub.
lessiviel [lesivjɛl] *adj* detergent.
lest [lɛst] *nm* ballast; **jeter** *ou* **lâcher du ~** (*fig*) to make concessions.
leste [lɛst(ə)] *adj* (*personne, mouvement*) sprightly, nimble; (*désinvolte: manières*) offhand; (*osé: plaisanterie*) risqué.
lestement [lɛstəmɑ̃] *adv* nimbly.
lester [lɛste] *vt* to ballast.
letchi [lɛtʃi] *nm* = **litchi**.
léthargie [letaʀʒi] *nf* lethargy.
léthargique [letaʀʒik] *adj* lethargic.
letton, ne [lɛtɔ̃, -ɔn] *adj* Latvian, Lett.
Lettonie [lɛtɔni] *nf*: **la ~** Latvia.
lettre [lɛtʀ(ə)] *nf* letter; **~s** *nfpl* (*étude, culture*) literature *sg*; (*SCOL*) arts (subjects); **à la ~** (*au sens propre*) literally; (*ponctuellement*) to the letter; **en ~s majuscules** *ou* **capitales** in capital letters, in capitals; **en toutes ~s** in words, in full; **~ de change** bill of exchange; **~ piégée** letter bomb; **~ de voiture (aérienne)** (air) waybill, (air) bill of lading; **~s de noblesse** pedigree.
lettré, e [letʀe] *adj* well-read, scholarly.
lettre-transfert, *pl* **lettres-transferts** [lɛtʀətʀɑ̃sfɛʀ] *nf* (pressure) transfer.
leu [lø] *voir* **queue**.
leucémie [løsemi] *nf* leukaemia.

MOT-CLÉ

leur [lœʀ] *adj possessif* their; **~ maison** their house; **~s amis** their friends; **à ~ approche** as they came near; **à ~ vue** at the sight of them
♦ *pron* **1** (*objet indirect*) (to) them; **je ~ ai dit la vérité** I told them the truth; **je le ~ ai donné** I gave it to them, I gave them it
2 (*possessif*): **le(la) ~, les ~s** theirs.

leurre [lœʀ] *nm* (*appât*) lure; (*fig*) delusion; (*: piège*) snare.
leurrer [lœʀe] *vt* to delude, deceive.
levain [ləvɛ̃] *nm* leaven; **sans ~** unleavened.
levant, e [ləvɑ̃, -ɑ̃t] *adj*: **soleil ~** rising sun ♦*nm*: **le L~** the Levant; **au soleil ~** at sunrise.
levantin, e [ləvɑ̃tɛ̃, -in] *adj* Levantine ♦ *nm/f*:

L~, e Levantine.
levé, e [ləve] *adj*: **être** ~ to be up ♦ *nm*: ~ **de terrain** land survey; **à mains ~es** (*vote*) by a show of hands; **au pied** ~ at a moment's notice.
levée [ləve] *nf* (*POSTES*) collection; (*CARTES*) trick; ~ **de boucliers** general outcry; ~ **du corps** *collection of the body from house of the deceased, before funeral*; ~ **d'écrou** release from custody; ~ **de terre** levee; ~ **de troupes** levy.
lever [ləve] *vt* (*vitre, bras etc*) to raise; (*soulever de terre, supprimer: interdiction, siège*) to lift; (*: difficulté*) to remove; (*séance*) to close; (*impôts, armée*) to levy; (*CHASSE: lièvre*) to start; (*: perdrix*) to flush; (*fam: fille*) to pick up ♦ *vi* (*CULIN*) to rise ♦ *nm*: **au** ~ on getting up; **se** ~ *vi* to get up; (*soleil*) to rise; (*jour*) to break; (*brouillard*) to lift; **ça va se** ~ the weather will clear; ~ **du jour** daybreak; ~ **du rideau** (*THÉÂT*) curtain; ~ **de rideau** (*pièce*) curtain raiser; ~ **de soleil** sunrise.
lève-tard [lɛvtaʀ] *nm/f inv* late riser.
lève-tôt [lɛvto] *nm/f inv* early riser, early bird.
levier [ləvje] *nm* lever; **faire** ~ **sur** to lever up (*ou* off); ~ **de changement de vitesse** gear lever.
lévitation [levitɑsjɔ̃] *nf* levitation.
levraut [ləvʀo] *nm* (*ZOOL*) leveret.
lèvre [lɛvʀ(ə)] *nf* lip; **~s** *nfpl* (*d'une plaie*) edges; **petites/grandes ~s** labia minora/majora; **du bout des ~s** half-heartedly.
lévrier [levʀije] *nm* greyhound.
levure [ləvyʀ] *nf* yeast; ~ **chimique** baking powder.
lexical, e, aux [lɛksikal, -o] *adj* lexical.
lexicographe [lɛksikɔgʀaf] *nm/f* lexicographer.
lexicographie [lɛksikɔgʀafi] *nf* lexicography, dictionary writing.
lexicologie [lɛksikɔlɔʒi] *nf* lexicology.
lexique [lɛksik] *nm* vocabulary, lexicon; (*glossaire*) vocabulary.
lézard [lezaʀ] *nm* lizard; (*peau*) lizardskin.
lézarde [lezaʀd(ə)] *nf* crack.
lézarder [lezaʀde]: **se** ~ *vi* to crack.
liaison [ljɛzɔ̃] *nf* (*rapport*) connection, link; (*RAIL, AVIAT etc*) link; (*relation: d'amitié*) friendship; (*: d'affaires*) relationship; (*: amoureuse*) affair; (*CULIN, PHONÉTIQUE*) liaison; **entrer/être en** ~ **avec** to get/be in contact with; ~ **radio** radio contact; ~ **(de transmission de données)** (*INFORM*) data link.
liane [ljan] *nf* creeper.
liant, e [ljɑ̃, -ɑ̃t] *adj* sociable.
liasse [ljas] *nf* wad, bundle.
Liban [libɑ̃] *nm*: **le** ~ (the) Lebanon.
libanais [libanɛ, -ɛz] *adj* Lebanese ♦ *nm/f*: **L~, e** Lebanese.
libations [libɑsjɔ̃] *nfpl* libations.
libelle [libɛl] *nm* lampoon.
libellé [libele] *nm* wording.
libeller [libele] *vt* (*chèque, mandat*): ~ **(au nom de)** to make out (to); (*lettre*) to word.
libellule [libelyl] *nf* dragonfly.
libéral, e, aux [libeʀal, -o] *adj, nm/f* liberal; **les professions ~es** the professions.
libéralement [libɛʀalmɑ̃] *adv* liberally.
libéralisation [libeʀalizɑsjɔ̃] *nf* liberalization; ~ **du commerce** easing of trade restrictions.
libéraliser [libeʀalize] *vt* to liberalize.
libéralisme [libeʀalism(ə)] *nm* liberalism.
libéralité [libeʀalite] *nf* liberality *no pl*, generosity *no pl*.
libérateur, trice [libeʀatœʀ, -tʀis] *adj* liberating ♦ *nm/f* liberator.
libération [libeʀɑsjɔ̃] *nf* liberation, freeing; release; discharge; ~ **conditionnelle** release on parole.
libéré, e [libeʀe] *adj* liberated; ~ **de** freed from; **être** ~ **sous caution/sur parole** to be released on bail/on parole.
libérer [libeʀe] *vt* (*délivrer*) to free, liberate; (*: moralement, PSYCH*) to liberate; (*relâcher: prisonnier*) to release; (*: soldat*) to discharge; (*dégager: gaz, cran d'arrêt*) to release; (*ÉCON: échanges commerciaux*) to ease restrictions on; **se** ~ (*de rendez-vous*) to try and be free, get out of previous engagements; ~ **qn de** (*liens, dette*) to free sb from; (*promesse*) to release sb from.
Libéria [libeʀja] *nm*: **le** ~ Liberia.
libérien, ne [libeʀjɛ̃, -ɛn] *adj* Liberian ♦ *nm/f*: **L~, ne** Liberian.
libéro [libeʀo] *nm* (*FOOTBALL*) sweeper.
libertaire [libɛʀtɛʀ] *adj* libertarian.
liberté [libɛʀte] *nf* freedom; (*loisir*) free time; **~s** *nfpl* (*privautés*) liberties; **mettre/être en** ~ to set/be free; **en** ~ **provisoire/surveillée/conditionnelle** on bail/probation/parole; ~ **d'association** right of association; ~ **de conscience** freedom of conscience; ~ **du culte** freedom of worship; ~ **d'esprit** independence of mind; ~ **d'opinion** freedom of thought; ~ **de la presse** freedom of the press; ~ **de réunion** right to hold meetings; ~ **syndicale** union rights *pl*; **~s individuelles** personal freedom *sg*; **~s publiques** civil rights.
libertin, e [libɛʀtɛ̃, -in] *adj* libertine, licentious.
libertinage [libɛʀtinaʒ] *nm* licentiousness.
libidineux, euse [libidinø, -øz] *adj* libidinous, lustful.
libido [libido] *nf* libido.
libraire [libʀɛʀ] *nm/f* bookseller.
libraire-éditeur, *pl* **libraires-éditeurs** [libʀɛʀeditœʀ] *nm* publisher and bookseller.
librairie [libʀeʀi] *nf* bookshop.
librairie-papeterie, *pl* **librairies-papeteries** [libʀeʀipapetʀi] bookseller's and stationer's.
libre [libʀ(ə)] *adj* free; (*route*) clear; (*place etc*) vacant, free; (*fig: propos, manières*) open;

(*SCOL*) private and Roman Catholic (*as opposed to "laïque"*); **de** ~ (*place*) free; ~ **de qch/de faire** free from sth/to do; **vente** ~ (*COMM*) unrestricted sale; ~ **arbitre** free will; ~ **concurrence** free-market economy; ~ **entreprise** free enterprise.
libre-échange [libʀeʃɑ̃ʒ] *nm* free trade.
librement [libʀəmɑ̃] *adv* freely.
libre-penseur, euse [libʀəpɑ̃sœʀ, -øz] *nm/f* free thinker.
libre-service [libʀəsɛʀvis] *nm inv* (*magasin*) self-service store; (*restaurant*) self-service restaurant.
librettiste [libʀetist(ə)] *nm/f* librettist.
Libye [libi] *nf*: **la** ~ Libya.
libyen, ne [libjɛ̃, -ɛn] *adj* Libyan ♦ *nm/f*: **L~, ne** Libyan.
lice [lis] *nf*: **entrer en** ~ (*fig*) to enter the lists.
licence [lisɑ̃s] *nf* (*permis*) permit; (*diplôme*) (first) degree; (*liberté*) liberty; (*poétique, orthographique*) licence (*BRIT*), license (*US*); (*des mœurs*) licentiousness; ~ **ès lettres/en droit** arts/law degree; *see boxed note*.

LICENCE

After the 'DEUG', French university students undertake a third year of study to complete their **licence**. *This is roughly equivalent to a Bachelor's degree in Britain.*

licencié, e [lisɑ̃sje] *nm/f* (*SCOL*): ~ **ès lettres/en droit** ≈ Bachelor of Arts/Law, arts/law graduate; (*SPORT*) permit-holder.
licenciement [lisɑ̃simɑ̃] *nm* dismissal; redundancy; laying off *no pl*.
licencier [lisɑ̃sje] *vt* (*renvoyer*) to dismiss; (*débaucher*) to make redundant; to lay off.
licencieux, euse [lisɑ̃sjø, -øz] *adj* licentious.
lichen [likɛn] *nm* lichen.
licite [lisit] *adj* lawful.
licorne [likɔʀn(ə)] *nf* unicorn.
licou [liku] *nm* halter.
lie [li] *nf* dregs *pl*, sediment.
lié, e [lje] *adj*: **très** ~ **avec** (*fig*) very friendly with *ou* close to; ~ **par** (*serment, promesse*) bound by; **avoir partie ~e (avec qn)** to be involved (with sb).
Liechtenstein [liʃtɛnʃtajn] *nm*: **le** ~ Liechtenstein.
lie-de-vin [lidvɛ̃] *adj inv* wine(-coloured).
liège [ljɛʒ] *nm* cork.
liégeois, e [ljeʒwa, -waz] *adj* of *ou* from Liège ♦ *nm/f*: **L~, e** inhabitant *ou* native of Liège; **café/chocolat** ~ *coffee/chocolate ice cream topped with whipped cream*.
lien [ljɛ̃] *nm* (*corde, fig: affectif, culturel*) bond; (*rapport*) link, connection; (*analogie*) link; ~ **de parenté** family tie.
lier [lje] *vt* (*attacher*) to tie up; (*joindre*) to link up; (*fig: unir, engager*) to bind; (*CULIN*) to thicken; ~ **qch à** (*attacher*) to tie sth to; (*associer*) to link sth to; ~ **conversation (avec)** to strike up a conversation (with); **se** ~ **avec** to make friends with.
lierre [ljɛʀ] *nm* ivy.
liesse [ljɛs] *nf*: **être en** ~ to be jubilant.
lieu, x [ljø] *nm* place; **~x** *nmpl* (*locaux*) premises; (*endroit: d'un accident etc*) scene *sg*; **en** ~ **sûr** in a safe place; **en haut** ~ in high places; **vider** *ou* **quitter les ~x** to leave the premises; **arriver/être sur les ~x** to arrive/be on the scene; **en premier** ~ in the first place; **en dernier** ~ lastly; **avoir** ~ to take place; **avoir** ~ **de faire** to have grounds *ou* good reason for doing; **tenir** ~ **de** to take the place of; (*servir de*) to serve as; **donner** ~ **à** to give rise to, give cause for; **au** ~ **de** instead of; **au** ~ **qu'il y aille** instead of him going; ~ **commun** commonplace; ~ **géométrique** locus; ~ **de naissance** place of birth.
lieu-dit, *pl* **lieux-dits** [ljødi] *nm* locality.
lieue [ljø] *nf* league.
lieutenant [ljøtnɑ̃] *nm* lieutenant; ~ **de vaisseau** (*NAVIG*) lieutenant.
lieutenant-colonel, *pl* **lieutenants-colonels** [ljøtnɑ̃kɔlɔnɛl] *nm* (*armée de terre*) lieutenant colonel; (*armée de l'air*) wing commander (*BRIT*), lieutenant colonel (*US*).
lièvre [ljɛvʀ(ə)] *nm* hare; (*coureur*) pacemaker; **lever un** ~ (*fig*) to bring up a prickly subject.
liftier, ière [liftje, -jɛʀ] lift (*BRIT*) *ou* elevator (*US*) attendant.
lifting [liftiŋ] *nm* face lift.
ligament [ligamɑ̃] *nm* ligament.
ligature [ligatyʀ] *nf* ligature.
lige [liʒ] *adj*: **homme** ~ (*péj*) henchman.
ligne [liɲ] *nf* (*gén*) line; (*TRANSPORTS: liaison*) service; (*: trajet*) route; (*silhouette*): **garder la** ~ to keep one's figure; **en** ~ (*INFORM*) on line; **en** ~ **droite** as the crow flies; **"à la ~"** "new paragraph"; **entrer en** ~ **de compte** to be taken into account; to come into it; ~ **de but/médiane** goal/halfway line; ~ **d'arrivée/de départ** finishing/starting line; ~ **de conduite** course of action; ~ **directrice** guiding line; ~ **fixe** (*TEL*) fixed line (phone); ~ **d'horizon** skyline; ~ **de mire** line of sight; ~ **de touche** touchline.
ligné, e [liɲe] *adj*: **papier** ~ ruled paper ♦ *nf* (*race, famille*) line, lineage; (*postérité*) descendants *pl*.
ligneux, euse [liɲø, -øz] *adj* ligneous, woody.
lignite [liɲit] *nm* lignite.
ligoter [ligɔte] *vt* to tie up.
ligue [lig] *nf* league.
liguer [lige]: **se** ~ *vi* to form a league; **se** ~ **contre** (*fig*) to combine against.
lilas [lila] *nm* lilac.
lillois, e [lilwa, -waz] *adj* of *ou* from Lille.
limace [limas] *nf* slug.
limaille [limaj] *nf*: ~ **de fer** iron filings *pl*.
limande [limɑ̃d] *nf* dab.

limande-sole [limɑ̃dsol] *nf* lemon sole.
limbes [lɛ̃b] *nmpl* limbo *sg*; **être dans les ~** (*fig: projet etc*) to be up in the air.
lime [lim] *nf* (*TECH*) file; (*BOT*) lime; **~ à ongles** nail file.
limer [lime] *vt* (*bois, métal*) to file (down); (*ongles*) to file; (*fig: prix*) to pare down.
limier [limje] *nm* (*ZOOL*) bloodhound; (*détective*) sleuth.
liminaire [liminɛʀ] *adj* (*propos*) introductory.
limitatif, ive [limitatif, -iv] *adj* restrictive.
limitation [limitɑsjɔ̃] *nf* limitation, restriction; **sans ~ de temps** with no time limit; **~ des naissances** birth control; **~ de vitesse** speed limit.
limite [limit] *nf* (*de terrain*) boundary; (*partie ou point extrême*) limit; **dans la ~ de** within the limits of; **à la ~** (*au pire*) if the worst comes (*ou* came) to the worst; **sans ~s** (*bêtise, richesse, pouvoir*) limitless, boundless; **vitesse/charge ~** maximum speed/load; **cas ~** borderline case; **date ~** deadline; **date ~ de vente/consommation** sell-by/best-before date; **prix ~** upper price limit; **~ d'âge** maximum age, age limit.
limiter [limite] *vt* (*restreindre*) to limit, restrict; (*délimiter*) to border, form the boundary of; **se ~ (à qch/à faire)** (*personne*) to limit *ou* confine o.s. (to sth/to doing sth); **se ~ à** (*chose*) to be limited to.
limitrophe [limitʀɔf] *adj* border *cpd*; **~ de** bordering on.
limogeage [limɔʒaʒ] *nm* dismissal.
limoger [limɔʒe] *vt* to dismiss.
limon [limɔ̃] *nm* silt.
limonade [limɔnad] *nf* lemonade (*BRIT*), (lemon) soda (*US*).
limonadier, ière [limɔnadje, -jɛʀ] *nm/f* (*commerçant*) café owner; (*fabricant de limonade*) soft drinks manufacturer.
limoneux, euse [limɔnø, -øz] *adj* muddy.
limousin, e [limuzɛ̃, -in] *adj* of *ou* from Limousin ♦ *nm* (*région*): **le L~** the Limousin ♦ *nf* limousine.
limpide [lɛ̃pid] *adj* limpid.
lin [lɛ̃] *nm* (*BOT*) flax; (*tissu, toile*) linen.
linceul [lɛ̃sœl] *nm* shroud.
linéaire [lineɛʀ] *adj* linear ♦ *nm*: **~ (de vente)** shelves *pl*.
linéament [lineamɑ̃] *nm* outline.
linge [lɛ̃ʒ] *nm* (*serviettes etc*) linen; (*pièce de tissu*) cloth; (*aussi*: **~ de corps**) underwear; (*aussi*: **~ de toilette**) towel; (*lessive*) washing; **~ sale** dirty linen.
lingère [lɛ̃ʒɛʀ] *nf* linen maid.
lingerie [lɛ̃ʒʀi] *nf* lingerie, underwear.
lingot [lɛ̃go] *nm* ingot.
linguiste [lɛ̃gɥist(ə)] *nm/f* linguist.
linguistique [lɛ̃gɥistik] *adj* linguistic ♦ *nf* linguistics *sg*.
lino(léum) [linɔ(leɔm)] *nm* lino(leum).
linotte [linɔt] *nf*: **tête de ~** bird brain.
linteau, x [lɛ̃to] *nm* lintel.
lion, ne [ljɔ̃, ljɔn] *nm/f* lion/lioness; (*signe*): **le L~** Leo, the Lion; **être du L~** to be Leo; **~ de mer** sealion.
lionceau, x [ljɔ̃so] *nm* lion cub.
liposuccion [liposyksjɔ̃] *nf* liposuction.
lippu, e [lipy] *adj* thick-lipped.
liquéfier [likefje] *vt* to liquefy; **se ~** *vi* (*gaz etc*) to liquefy; (*fig: personne*) to succumb.
liqueur [likœʀ] *nf* liqueur.
liquidateur, trice [likidatœʀ, -tʀis] *nm/f* (*JUR*) receiver; **~ judiciaire** official liquidator.
liquidation [likidɑsjɔ̃] *nf* liquidation; (*COMM*) clearance (sale); **~ judiciaire** compulsory liquidation.
liquide [likid] *adj* liquid ♦ *nm* liquid; (*COMM*): **en ~** in ready money *ou* cash.
liquider [likide] *vt* (*société, biens, témoin gênant*) to liquidate; (*compte, problème*) to settle; (*COMM: articles*) to clear, sell off.
liquidités [likidite] *nfpl* (*COMM*) liquid assets.
liquoreux, euse [likɔʀø, -øz] *adj* syrupy.
lire [liʀ] *nf* (*monnaie*) lira ♦ *vt, vi* to read; **~ qch à qn** to read sth (out) to sb.
lis *vb* [li] *voir* **lire** ♦ *nm* [lis] = **lys**.
lisais [lizɛ] *etc vb voir* **lire**.
Lisbonne [lizbɔn] *n* Lisbon.
lise [liz] *etc vb voir* **lire**.
liseré [lizʀe] *nm* border, edging.
liseron [lizʀɔ̃] *nm* bindweed.
liseuse [lizøz] *nf* book-cover; (*veste*) bedjacket.
lisible [lizibl(ə)] *adj* legible; (*digne d'être lu*) readable.
lisiblement [liziblәmɑ̃] *adv* legibly.
lisière [lizjɛʀ] *nf* (*de forêt*) edge; (*de tissu*) selvage.
lisons [lizɔ̃] *vb voir* **lire**.
lisse [lis] *adj* smooth.
lisser [lise] *vt* to smooth.
listage [listaʒ] *nm* (*INFORM*) listing.
liste [list(ə)] *nf* list; (*INFORM*) listing; **faire la ~ de** to list, make out a list of; **~ d'attente** waiting list; **~ civile** civil list; **~ électorale** electoral roll; **~ de mariage** wedding (present) list; **~ noire** hit list.
lister [liste] *vt* (*aussi INFORM*) to list; **~ la mémoire** to dump.
listéria [listeʀja] *nf* listeria.
listing [listiŋ] *nm* (*INFORM*) listing; **qualité ~** draft quality.
lit [li] *nm* (*gén*) bed; **faire son ~** to make one's bed; **aller/se mettre au ~** to go to/get into bed; **prendre le ~** to take to one's bed; **d'un premier ~** (*JUR*) of a first marriage; **~ de camp** campbed (*BRIT*), cot (*US*); **~ d'enfant** cot (*BRIT*), crib (*US*).
litanie [litani] *nf* litany.
lit-cage, *pl* **lits-cages** [likaʒ] *nm* folding bed.
litchi [litʃi] *nm* lychee.
literie [litʀi] *nf* bedding; (*linge*) bedding, bedclothes *pl*.
litho [lito], **lithographie** [litɔgʀafi] *nf*

litho(graphy); (*épreuve*) litho(graph).
litière [litjɛʀ] *nf* litter.
litige [litiʒ] *nm* dispute; **en** ~ in contention.
litigieux, euse [litiʒjø, -øz] *adj* litigious, contentious.
litote [litɔt] *nf* understatement.
litre [litʀ(ə)] *nm* litre; (*récipient*) litre measure.
littéraire [liteʀɛʀ] *adj* literary.
littéral, e, aux [liteʀal, -o] *adj* literal.
littéralement [liteʀalmɑ̃] *adv* literally.
littérature [liteʀatyʀ] *nf* literature.
littoral, e, aux [litɔʀal, -o] *adj* coastal ♦ *nm* coast.
Lituanie [litɥani] *nf*: **la** ~ Lithuania.
lituanien, ne [litɥanjɛ̃, -ɛn] *adj* Lithuanian ♦ *nm* (*LING*) Lithuanian ♦ *nm/f*: **L~, ne** Lithuanian.
liturgie [lityʀʒi] *nf* liturgy.
liturgique [lityʀʒik] *adj* liturgical.
livide [livid] *adj* livid, pallid.
living(-room) [liviŋ(ʀum)] *nm* living room.
livrable [livʀabl(ə)] *adj* (*COMM*) that can be delivered.
livraison [livʀɛzɔ̃] *nf* delivery; ~ **à domicile** home delivery (service).
livre [livʀ(ə)] *nm* book; (*imprimerie etc*): **le** ~ the book industry ♦ *nf* (*poids, monnaie*) pound; **traduire qch à** ~ **ouvert** to translate sth off the cuff *ou* at sight; ~ **blanc** official report (*prepared by independent body, following war, natural disaster etc*); ~ **de bord** (*NAVIG*) logbook; ~ **de comptes** account(s) book; ~ **de cuisine** cookery book (*BRIT*), cookbook; ~ **de messe** mass *ou* prayer book; ~ **d'or** visitors' book; ~ **de poche** paperback (*cheap and pocket size*); ~ **verte** green pound.
livré, e [livʀe] *nf* livery ♦ *adj*: ~ **à** (*l'anarchie etc*) given over to; ~ **à soi-même** left to oneself *ou* one's own devices.
livrer [livʀe] *vt* (*COMM*) to deliver; (*otage, coupable*) to hand over; (*secret, information*) to give away; **se** ~ **à** (*se confier*) to confide in; (*se rendre*) to give o.s. up to; (*s'abandonner à: débauche etc*) to give o.s. up *ou* over to; (*faire: pratiques, actes*) to indulge in; (*travail*) to be engaged in, engage in; (*: sport*) to practise; (*: enquête*) to carry out; ~ **bataille** to give battle.
livresque [livʀɛsk(ə)] *adj* (*péj*) bookish.
livret [livʀɛ] *nm* booklet; (*d'opéra*) libretto (*pl* -s); ~ **de caisse d'épargne** (savings) bankbook; ~ **de famille** (official) family record book; ~ **scolaire** (school) report book.
livreur, euse [livʀœʀ, -øz] *nm/f* delivery boy *ou* man/girl *ou* woman.
LO *sigle f* (= *Lutte ouvrière*) *political party*.
lob [lɔb] *nm* lob.
lobe [lɔb] *nm*: ~ **de l'oreille** ear lobe.
lobé, e [lɔbe] *adj* (*ARCHIT*) foiled.
lober [lɔbe] *vt* to lob.
local, e, aux [lɔkal, -o] *adj* local ♦ *nm* (*salle*) premises *pl* ♦ *nmpl* premises.
localement [lɔkalmɑ̃] *adv* locally.
localisé, e [lɔkalize] *adj* localized.
localiser [lɔkalize] *vt* (*repérer*) to locate, place; (*limiter*) to localize, confine.
localité [lɔkalite] *nf* locality.
locataire [lɔkatɛʀ] *nm/f* tenant; (*de chambre*) lodger.
locatif, ive [lɔkatif, -iv] *adj* (*charges, réparations*) incumbent upon the tenant; (*valeur*) rental; (*immeuble*) with rented flats, used as a letting *ou* rental (*US*) concern.
location [lɔkɑsjɔ̃] *nf* (*par le locataire*) renting; (*par l'usager: de voiture etc*) hiring (*BRIT*), renting (*US*); (*par le propriétaire*) renting out, letting; hiring out (*BRIT*); (*de billets, places*) booking; (*bureau*) booking office; **"~ de voitures"** "car hire (*BRIT*) *ou* rental (*US*)".
location-vente [lɔkɑsjɔ̃vɑ̃t] *nf form of hire purchase* (*BRIT*) *ou instalment plan* (*US*).
lock-out [lɔkawt] *nm inv* lockout.
locomoteur, trice [lɔkɔmɔtœʀ, -tʀis] *adj, nf* locomotive.
locomotion [lɔkɔmosjɔ̃] *nf* locomotion.
locomotive [lɔkɔmɔtiv] *nf* locomotive, engine; (*fig*) pacesetter, pacemaker.
locuteur, trice [lɔkytœʀ, -tʀis] *nm/f* (*LING*) speaker.
locution [lɔkysjɔ̃] *nf* phrase.
loden [lɔdɛn] *nm* loden.
lofer [lɔfe] *vi* (*NAVIG*) to luff.
logarithme [lɔgaʀitm(ə)] *nm* logarithm.
loge [lɔʒ] *nf* (*THÉÂT: d'artiste*) dressing room; (*: de spectateurs*) box; (*de concierge, franc-maçon*) lodge.
logeable [lɔʒabl(ə)] *adj* habitable; (*spacieux*) roomy.
logement [lɔʒmɑ̃] *nm* flat (*BRIT*), apartment (*US*); accommodation *no pl* (*BRIT*), accommodations *pl* (*US*); **le** ~ housing; **chercher un** ~ to look for a flat *ou* apartment, look for accommodation(s); **construire des** ~**s bon marché** to build cheap housing *sg*; **crise du** ~ housing shortage; ~ **de fonction** (*ADMIN*) company flat *ou* apartment, accommodation(s) provided with one's job.
loger [lɔʒe] *vt* to accommodate ♦ *vi* to live; **se** ~: **trouver à se** ~ to find accommodation; **se** ~ **dans** (*suj: balle, flèche*) to lodge itself in.
logeur, euse [lɔʒœʀ, -øz] *nm/f* landlord/landlady.
loggia [lɔdʒja] *nf* loggia.
logiciel [lɔʒisjɛl] *nm* software.
logicien, ne [lɔʒisjɛ̃, -ɛn] *nm/f* logician.
logique [lɔʒik] *adj* logical ♦ *nf* logic; **c'est** ~ it stands to reason.
logiquement [lɔʒikmɑ̃] *adv* logically.
logis [lɔʒi] *nm* home; abode, dwelling.
logisticien, ne [lɔʒistisjɛ̃, -ɛn] *nm/f* logistician.
logistique [lɔʒistik] *nf* logistics *sg* ♦ *adj* logistic.
logo [lɔgo], **logotype** [lɔgɔtip] *nm* logo.
loi [lwa] *nf* law; **faire la** ~ to lay down the law;

les ~s de la mode (*fig*) the dictates of fashion; **proposition de** ~ (private member's) bill; **projet de** ~ (government) bill.

loi-cadre, *pl* **lois-cadres** [lwakadʀ(ə)] *nf* (*POL*) blueprint law.

loin [lwɛ̃] *adv* far; (*dans le temps: futur*) a long way off; (*: passé*) a long time ago; **plus** ~ further; **moins** ~ **(que)** not as far (as); ~ **de** far from; **pas** ~ **de 100 €** not far off €100; **au** ~ far off; **de** ~ *adv* from a distance; (*fig: de beaucoup*) by far; **il vient de** ~ he's come a long way; he comes from a long way away; **de** ~ **en** ~ here and there; (*de temps en temps*) (every) now and then; ~ **de là** (*au contraire*) far from it.

lointain, e [lwɛ̃tɛ̃, -ɛn] *adj* faraway, distant; (*dans le futur, passé*) distant, far-off; (*cause, parent*) remote, distant ♦ *nm*: **dans le** ~ in the distance.

loi-programme, *pl* **lois-programmes** [lwapʀɔgʀam] *nf* (*POL*) *act providing framework for government programme.*

loir [lwaʀ] *nm* dormouse (*pl* -mice).

Loire [lwaʀ] *nf*: **la** ~ the Loire.

loisible [lwazibl(ə)] *adj*: **il vous est** ~ **de ...** you are free to ....

loisir [lwaziʀ] *nm*: **heures de** ~ spare time; ~**s** *nmpl* leisure *sg*; (*activités*) leisure activities; **avoir le** ~ **de faire** to have the time *ou* opportunity to do; **(tout) à** ~ (*en prenant son temps*) at leisure; (*autant qu'on le désire*) at one's pleasure.

lombaire [lɔ̃bɛʀ] *adj* lumbar.

lombalgie [lɔ̃balʒi] *nf* back pain.

lombard, e [lɔ̃baʀ, -aʀd(ə)] *adj* Lombard.

Lombardie [lɔ̃baʀdi] *nf*: **la** ~ Lombardy.

londonien, ne [lɔ̃dɔnjɛ̃, -ɛn] *adj* London *cpd*, of London ♦ *nm/f*: **L~, ne** Londoner.

Londres [lɔ̃dʀ(ə)] *n* London.

long, longue [lɔ̃, lɔ̃g] *adj* long ♦ *adv*: **en savoir** ~ to know a great deal ♦ *nm*: **de 3 m de** ~ 3 m long, 3 m in length ♦ *nf*: **à la longue** in the end; **faire** ~ **feu** to fizzle out; **ne pas faire** ~ **feu** not to last long; **au** ~ **cours** (*NAVIG*) ocean *cpd*, ocean-going; **de longue date** *adj* long-standing; **longue durée** *adj* long-term; **de longue haleine** *adj* long-term; **être** ~ **à faire** to take a long time to do; **en** ~ *adv* lengthwise, lengthways; **(tout) le** ~ **de** (all) along; **tout au** ~ **de** (*année, vie*) throughout; **de** ~ **en large** (*marcher*) to and fro, up and down; **en** ~ **et en large** (*fig*) in every detail.

longanimité [lɔ̃ganimite] *nf* forbearance.

long-courrier [lɔ̃kuʀje] *nm* (*AVIAT*) long-haul aircraft.

longe [lɔ̃ʒ] *nf* (*corde: pour attacher*) tether; (*pour mener*) lead; (*CULIN*) loin.

longer [lɔ̃ʒe] *vt* to go (*ou* walk *ou* drive) along(side); (*suj: mur, route*) to border.

longévité [lɔ̃ʒevite] *nf* longevity.

longiligne [lɔ̃ʒiliɲ] *adj* long-limbed.

longitude [lɔ̃ʒityd] *nf* longitude; **à 45° de** ~ **ouest** at 45° longitude west.

longitudinal, e, aux [lɔ̃ʒitydinal, -o] *adj* longitudinal, lengthways; (*entaille, vallée*) running lengthways.

longtemps [lɔ̃tɑ̃] *adv* (for) a long time, (for) long; **ça ne va pas durer** ~ it won't last long; **avant** ~ before long; **pour/pendant** ~ for a long time; **je n'en ai pas pour** ~ I shan't be long; **mettre** ~ **à faire** to take a long time to do; **il en a pour** ~ he'll be a long time; **il y a** ~ **que je travaille** I have been working (for) a long time; **il n'y a pas** ~ **que je l'ai rencontré** it's not long since I met him.

longue [lɔ̃g] *adj f voir* **long**.

longuement [lɔ̃gmɑ̃] *adv* (*longtemps: parler, regarder*) for a long time; (*en détail: expliquer, raconter*) at length.

longueur [lɔ̃gœʀ] *nf* length; ~**s** *nfpl* (*fig: d'un film etc*) tedious parts; **sur une** ~ **de 10 km** for *ou* over 10 km; **en** ~ *adv* lengthwise, lengthways; **tirer en** ~ to drag on; **à** ~ **de journée** all day long; **d'une** ~ (*gagner*) by a length; ~ **d'onde** wavelength.

longue-vue [lɔ̃gvy] *nf* telescope.

looping [lupiŋ] *nm* (*AVIAT*): **faire des** ~**s** to loop the loop.

lopin [lɔpɛ̃] *nm*: ~ **de terre** patch of land.

loquace [lɔkas] *adj* talkative, loquacious.

loque [lɔk] *nf* (*personne*) wreck; ~**s** *nfpl* (*habits*) rags; **être** *ou* **tomber en** ~**s** to be in rags.

loquet [lɔkɛ] *nm* latch.

lorgner [lɔʀɲe] *vt* to eye; (*convoiter*) to have one's eye on.

lorgnette [lɔʀɲɛt] *nf* opera glasses *pl*.

lorgnon [lɔʀɲɔ̃] *nm* (*face-à-main*) lorgnette; (*pince-nez*) pince-nez.

loriot [lɔʀjo] *nm* (golden) oriole.

lorrain, e [lɔʀɛ̃, -ɛn] *adj* of *ou* from Lorraine; **quiche** ~**e** quiche lorraine.

lors [lɔʀ]: ~ **de** *prép* (*au moment de*) at the time of; (*pendant*) during; ~ **même que** even though.

lorsque [lɔʀsk(ə)] *conj* when, as.

losange [lɔzɑ̃ʒ] *nm* diamond; (*GÉOM*) lozenge; **en** ~ diamond-shaped.

lot [lo] *nm* (*part*) share; (*de loterie*) prize; (*fig: destin*) fate, lot; (*COMM, INFORM*) batch; ~ **de consolation** consolation prize.

loterie [lɔtʀi] *nf* lottery; (*tombola*) raffle; **L~ nationale** (*formerly*) *French national lottery.*

loti, e [lɔti] *adj*: **bien/mal** ~ well-/badly off, lucky/unlucky.

lotion [losjɔ̃] *nf* lotion; ~ **après rasage** aftershave (lotion); ~ **capillaire** hair lotion.

lotir [lɔtiʀ] *vt* (*terrain: diviser*) to divide into plots; (*: vendre*) to sell by lots.

lotissement [lɔtismɑ̃] *nm* (*groupe de maisons, d'immeubles*) housing development; (*parcelle*) (building) plot, lot.

loto [lɔto] *nm* lotto; *see boxed note.*

LE LOTO

Le Loto *is a state-run national lottery with large cash prizes. Participants select seven numbers out of a possible 49. There is a sliding scale of winnings: if you have all seven numbers correct you win top prize, if you have six right you win a smaller sum and so on. The draw is shown on television twice weekly.*

lotte [lɔt] *nf* (*ZOOL: de rivière*) burbot; (*: de mer*) monkfish.

louable [lwabl(ə)] *adj* (*appartement, garage*) rentable; (*action, personne*) praiseworthy, commendable.

louage [lwaʒ] *nm*: **voiture de ~** hired (*BRIT*) *ou* rented (*US*) car; (*à louer*) hire (*BRIT*) *ou* rental (*US*) car.

louange [lwɑ̃ʒ] *nf*: **à la ~ de** in praise of; **~s** *nfpl* praise *sg*.

loubar(d) [lubaʀ] *nm* (*fam*) lout.

louche [luʃ] *adj* shady, dubious ♦ *nf* ladle.

loucher [luʃe] *vi* to squint; (*fig*): **~ sur** to have one's (beady) eye on.

louer [lwe] *vt* (*maison: suj: propriétaire*) to let, rent (out); (*: locataire*) to rent; (*voiture etc*) to hire out (*BRIT*), rent (out); to hire (*BRIT*), rent, (*réserver*) to book; (*faire l'éloge de*) to praise; **"à ~"** "to let" (*BRIT*), "for rent" (*US*); **~ qn de** to praise sb for; **se ~ de** to congratulate o.s. on.

loufoque [lufɔk] *adj* (*fam*) crazy, zany.

loukoum [lukum] *nm* Turkish delight.

loulou [lulu] *nm* (*chien*) spitz; **~ de Poméranie** Pomeranian (dog).

loup [lu] *nm* wolf (*pl* wolves); (*poisson*) bass; (*masque*) (eye) mask; **jeune ~** young go-getter; **~ de mer** (*marin*) old seadog.

loupe [lup] *nf* magnifying glass; **~ de noyer** burr walnut; **à la ~** (*fig*) in minute detail.

louper [lupe] *vt* (*fam: manquer*) to miss; (*: gâcher*) to mess up, bungle.

lourd, e [luʀ, luʀd(ə)] *adj* heavy; (*chaleur, temps*) sultry; (*fig: personne, style*) heavy-handed ♦ *adv*: **peser ~** to be heavy; **~ de** (*menaces*) charged with; (*conséquences*) fraught with; **artillerie/industrie ~e** heavy artillery/industry.

lourdaud, e [luʀdo, -od] *adj* oafish.

lourdement [luʀdəmɑ̃] *adv* heavily; **se tromper ~** to make a big mistake.

lourdeur [luʀdœʀ] *nf* heaviness; **~ d'estomac** indigestion *no pl*.

loustic [lustik] *nm* (*fam péj*) joker.

loutre [lutʀ(ə)] *nf* otter; (*fourrure*) otter skin.

louve [luv] *nf* she-wolf.

louveteau, x [luvto] *nm* (*ZOOL*) wolf-cub; (*scout*) cub (scout).

louvoyer [luvwaje] *vi* (*NAVIG*) to tack; (*fig*) to hedge, evade the issue.

lover [lɔve]: **se ~** *vi* to coil up.

loyal, e, aux [lwajal, -o] *adj* (*fidèle*) loyal, faithful; (*fair-play*) fair.

loyalement [lwajalmɑ̃] *adv* loyally, faithfully; fairly.

loyalisme [lwajalism(ə)] *nm* loyalty.

loyauté [lwajote] *nf* loyalty, faithfulness; fairness.

loyer [lwaje] *nm* rent; **~ de l'argent** interest rate.

LP *sigle m* (= *lycée professionnel*) *secondary school for vocational training.*

LPO *sigle f* (= *Ligue pour la protection des oiseaux*) *bird protection society.*

LSD *sigle m* (= *Lyserg Säure Diäthylamid*) LSD.

lu, e [ly] *pp de* **lire**.

lubie [lybi] *nf* whim, craze.

lubricité [lybʀisite] *nf* lust.

lubrifiant [lybʀifjɑ̃] *nm* lubricant.

lubrifier [lybʀifje] *vt* to lubricate.

lubrique [lybʀik] *adj* lecherous.

lucarne [lykaʀn(ə)] *nf* skylight.

lucide [lysid] *adj* (*conscient*) lucid, conscious; (*perspicace*) clear-headed.

lucidité [lysidite] *nf* lucidity.

luciole [lysjɔl] *nf* firefly.

lucratif, ive [lykʀatif, -iv] *adj* lucrative; profitable; **à but non ~** non profit-making.

ludique [lydik] *adj* play *cpd*, playing.

ludothèque [lydɔtɛk] *nf* toy library.

luette [lɥɛt] *nf* uvula.

lueur [lɥœʀ] *nf* (*chatoyante*) glimmer *no pl*; (*métallique, mouillée*) gleam *no pl*; (*rougeoyante*) glow *no pl*; (*pâle*) (faint) light; (*fig*) spark; (*: d'espérance*) glimmer, gleam.

luge [lyʒ] *nf* sledge (*BRIT*), sled (*US*); **faire de la ~** to sledge (*BRIT*), sled (*US*), toboggan.

lugubre [lygybʀ(ə)] *adj* gloomy; dismal.

MOT-CLÉ

lui [lɥi] *pp de* **luire**

♦ *pron* **1** (*objet indirect: mâle*) (to) him; (*: femelle*) (to) her; (*: chose, animal*) (to) it; **je ~ ai parlé** I have spoken to him (*ou* to her); **il ~ a offert un cadeau** he gave him (*ou* her) a present; **je le ~ ai donné** I gave it to him (*ou* her)

2 (*après préposition, comparatif: personne*) him; (*: chose, animal*) it; **elle est contente de ~** she is pleased with him; **je la connais mieux que ~** I know her better than he does; **cette voiture est à ~** this car belongs to him, this is HIS car

3 (*sujet, forme emphatique*) he; **~, il est à Paris** HE is in Paris; **c'est ~ qui l'a fait** HE did it.

lui-même [lɥimɛm] *pron* (*personne*) himself; (*chose*) itself.

luire [lɥiʀ] *vi* (*gén*) to shine, gleam; (*surface mouillée*) to glisten; (*reflets chauds, cuivrés*) to glow.

luisant, e [lɥizɑ̃, -ɑ̃t] *vb voir* **luire** ♦ *adj* shining,

gleaming.
lumbago [lɔ̃bago] *nm* lumbago.
lumière [lymjɛʀ] *nf* light; ~**s** *nfpl* (*d'une personne*) knowledge *sg*, wisdom *sg*; **à la ~ de** by the light of; (*fig: événements*) in the light of; **fais de la ~** let's have some light, give us some light; **faire (toute) la ~ sur** (*fig*) to clarify (completely); **mettre en ~** (*fig*) to highlight; **~ du jour/soleil** day/sunlight.
luminaire [lyminɛʀ] *nm* lamp, light.
lumineux, euse [lyminø, -øz] *adj* (*émettant de la lumière*) luminous; (*éclairé*) illuminated; (*ciel, journée, couleur*) bright; (*relatif à la lumière: rayon etc*) of light, light *cpd*; (*fig: regard*) radiant.
luminosité [lyminɔzite] *nf* (*TECH*) luminosity.
lump [lœ̃p] *nm*: **œufs de ~** lump-fish roe.
lunaire [lynɛʀ] *adj* lunar, moon *cpd*.
lunatique [lynatik] *adj* whimsical, temperamental.
lunch [lœntʃ] *nm* (*réception*) buffet lunch.
lundi [lœ̃di] *nm* Monday; **on est ~** it's Monday; **le ~ 20 août** Monday 20th August; **il est venu ~** he came on Monday; **le(s) ~(s)** on Mondays; **à ~!** see you (on) Monday!; **~ de Pâques** Easter Monday; **~ de Pentecôte** Whit Monday (*BRIT*).
lune [lyn] *nf* moon; **pleine/nouvelle ~** full/new moon; **être dans la ~** (*distrait*) to have one's head in the clouds; **~ de miel** honeymoon.
luné, e [lyne] *adj*: **bien/mal ~** in a good/bad mood.
lunette [lynɛt] *nf*: ~**s** *nfpl* glasses, spectacles; (*protectrices*) goggles; **~ d'approche** telescope; **~ arrière** (*AUTO*) rear window; **~s noires** dark glasses; **~s de soleil** sunglasses.
lurent [lyʀ] *vb voir* **lire**.
lurette [lyʀɛt] *nf*: **il y a belle ~** ages ago.
luron, ne [lyʀɔ̃, -ɔn] *nm/f* lad/lass; **joyeux** *ou* **gai ~** gay dog.
lus [ly] *etc vb voir* **lire**.
lustre [lystʀ(ə)] *nm* (*de plafond*) chandelier; (*fig: éclat*) lustre.
lustrer [lystʀe] *vt*: **~ qch** (*faire briller*) to make sth shine; (*user*) to make sth shiny.
lut [ly] *vb voir* **lire**.
luth [lyt] *nm* lute.
luthier [lytje] *nm* (stringed-)instrument maker.
lutin [lytɛ̃] *nm* imp, goblin.
lutrin [lytʀɛ̃] *nm* lectern.
lutte [lyt] *nf* (*conflit*) struggle; (*SPORT*): **la ~** wrestling; **de haute ~** after a hard-fought struggle; **~ des classes** class struggle; **~ libre** (*SPORT*) all-in wrestling.
lutter [lyte] *vi* to fight, struggle; (*SPORT*) to wrestle.
lutteur, euse [lytœʀ, -øz] *nm/f* (*SPORT*) wrestler; (*fig*) battler, fighter.
luxation [lyksɑsjɔ̃] *nf* dislocation.
luxe [lyks(ə)] *nm* luxury; **un ~ de** (*détails, précautions*) a wealth of; **de ~** *adj* luxury *cpd*.
Luxembourg [lyksɑ̃buʀ] *nm*: **le ~** Luxembourg.
luxembourgeois, e [lyksɑ̃buʀʒwa, -waz] *adj* of *ou* from Luxembourg ♦ *nm/f*: **L~, e** inhabitant *ou* native of Luxembourg.
luxer [lykse] *vt*: **se ~ l'épaule** to dislocate one's shoulder.
luxueusement [lyksɥøzmɑ̃] *adv* luxuriously.
luxueux, euse [lyksɥø, -øz] *adj* luxurious.
luxure [lyksyʀ] *nf* lust.
luxuriant, e [lyksyʀjɑ̃, -ɑ̃t] *adj* luxuriant, lush.
luzerne [lyzɛʀn(ə)] *nf* lucerne, alfalfa.
lycée [lise] *nm* (state) secondary (*BRIT*) *ou* high (*US*) school; **~ technique** technical secondary *ou* high school; *see boxed note*.

LYCÉE

French pupils spend the last three years of their secondary education at a **lycée**, *where they sit their 'baccalauréat' before leaving school or going on to higher education. There are various types of* **lycée**, *including the 'lycées d'enseignement technologique', providing technical courses, and the 'lycées d'enseignement professionnel' providing vocational courses. Some* **lycées**, *particularly those with a wide catchment area or those which run specialist courses, have boarding facilities.*

lycéen, ne [liseɛ̃, -ɛn] *nm/f* secondary school pupil.
Lycra [likʀa] *nm* ® Lycra ®.
lymphatique [lɛ̃fatik] *adj* (*fig*) lethargic, sluggish.
lymphe [lɛ̃f] *nf* lymph.
lyncher [lɛ̃ʃe] *vt* to lynch.
lynx [lɛ̃ks] *nm* lynx.
Lyon [ljɔ̃] *n* Lyons.
lyonnais, e [ljɔnɛ, -ɛz] *adj* of *ou* from Lyons; (*CULIN*) Lyonnaise.
lyophilisé, e [ljɔfilize] *adj* freeze-dried.
lyre [liʀ] *nf* lyre.
lyrique [liʀik] *adj* lyrical; (*OPÉRA*) lyric; **artiste ~** opera singer; **comédie ~** comic opera; **théâtre ~** opera house (*for light opera*).
lyrisme [liʀism(ə)] *nm* lyricism.
lys [lis] *nm* lily.

M m

M, m [ɛm] *nm inv* M, m ♦ *abr* = **majeur, masculin, mètre, Monsieur**; (= *million*) M; **M comme Marcel** M for Mike.
m' [m] *pron voir* **me**.
MA *sigle m* = **maître auxiliaire**.
ma [ma] *adj possessif voir* **mon**.
maboul, e [mabul] *adj* (*fam*) loony.
macabre [makɑbʀ(ə)] *adj* macabre, gruesome.
macadam [makadam] *nm* tarmac (*BRIT*), asphalt.
Macao [makao] *nf* Macao.
macaron [makaʀɔ̃] *nm* (*gâteau*) macaroon; (*insigne*) (round) badge.
macaroni(s) [makaʀɔni] *nm(pl)* macaroni *sg*; ~ **au fromage** *ou* **au gratin** macaroni cheese (*BRIT*), macaroni and cheese (*US*).
Macédoine [masedwan] *nf* Macedonia.
macédoine [masedwan] *nf*: ~ **de fruits** fruit salad; ~ **de légumes** mixed vegetables *pl*.
macédonien, ne [masedɔnjɛ̃, -ɛn] *adj* Macedonian ♦ *nm/f*: **M~, ne** Macedonian.
macérer [maseʀe] *vi, vt* to macerate; (*dans du vinaigre*) to pickle.
mâchefer [mɑʃfɛʀ] *nm* clinker, cinders *pl*.
mâcher [mɑʃe] *vt* to chew; **ne pas ~ ses mots** not to mince one's words; ~ **le travail à qn** (*fig*) to spoonfeed sb, do half sb's work for him.
machiavélique [makjavelik] *adj* Machiavellian.
machin [maʃɛ̃] *nm* (*fam*) thingamajig, thing; (*personne*): **M~** what's-his(*ou*-her)-name.
machinal, e, aux [maʃinal, -o] *adj* mechanical, automatic.
machination [maʃinɑsjɔ̃] *nf* scheming, frame-up.
machine [maʃin] *nf* machine; (*locomotive; de navire etc*) engine; (*fig: rouages*) machinery; (*fam: personne*): **M~** what's-her-name; **faire ~ arrière** (*NAVIG*) to go astern; (*fig*) to backpedal; ~ **à laver/coudre/tricoter** washing/sewing/knitting machine; ~ **à écrire** typewriter; ~ **à sous** fruit machine; ~ **à vapeur** steam engine.
machine-outil, *pl* **machines-outils** [maʃinuti] *nf* machine tool.
machinerie [maʃinʀi] *nf* machinery, plant; (*d'un navire*) engine room.
machinisme [maʃinism(ə)] *nm* mechanization.
machiniste [maʃinist(ə)] *nm* (*THÉÂT*) scene shifter; (*de bus, métro*) driver.
mâchoire [mɑʃwaʀ] *nf* jaw; ~ **de frein** brake shoe.
mâchonner [mɑʃɔne] *vt* to chew (at).
mâcon [mɑkɔ̃] *nm* Mâcon wine.
maçon [masɔ̃] *nm* bricklayer; (*constructeur*) builder.
maçonner [masɔne] *vt* (*revêtir*) to face, render (with cement); (*boucher*) to brick up.
maçonnerie [masɔnʀi] *nf* (*murs: de brique*) brickwork; (*: de pierre*) masonry, stonework; (*activité*) bricklaying; building; ~ **de béton** concrete.
maçonnique [masɔnik] *adj* masonic.
macramé [makʀame] *nm* macramé.
macrobiotique [makʀɔbjɔtik] *adj* macrobiotic.
macrocosme [makʀɔkɔsm(ə)] *nm* macrocosm.
macro-économie [makʀɔekɔnɔmi] *nf* macroeconomics *sg*.
macrophotographie [makʀofɔtɔgʀafi] *nf* macrophotography.
maculer [makyle] *vt* to stain; (*TYPO*) to mackle.
Madagascar [madagaskaʀ] *nf* Madagascar.
Madame [madam], *pl* **Mesdames** [medam] *nf*: ~ **X** Mrs X ['mɪsɪz]; **occupez-vous de ~/Monsieur/Mademoiselle** please serve this lady/gentleman/(young) lady; **bonjour ~/Monsieur/Mademoiselle** good morning; (*ton déférent*) good morning Madam/Sir/Madam; (*le nom est connu*) good morning Mrs X/Mr X/Miss X; **~/Monsieur/Mademoiselle!** (*pour appeler*) excuse me!; (*ton déférent*) Madam/Sir/Miss!; **~/Monsieur/Mademoiselle** (*sur lettre*) Dear Madam/Sir/Madam; **chère ~/cher Monsieur/chère Mademoiselle** Dear Mrs X/Mr X/Miss X; ~ **la Directrice** the director; the manageress; the headteacher; **Mesdames** Ladies.
Madeleine [madlɛn]: **îles de la ~** *nfpl* Magdalen Islands.
madeleine [madlɛn] *nf* madeleine, ≈ sponge finger cake.
Madelinot, e [madlino, -ɔt] *nm/f* inhabitant *ou* native of the Magdalen Islands.
Mademoiselle [madmwazɛl], *pl* **Mesdemoiselles** [medmwazɛl] *nf* Miss; *voir aussi* **Madame**.
Madère [madɛʀ] *nf* Madeira ♦ *nm*: **m~** Madeira (wine).
madone [madɔn] *nf* madonna.
madré, e [madʀe] *adj* crafty, wily.
Madrid [madʀid] *n* Madrid.
madrier [madʀije] *nm* beam.
madrigal, aux [madʀigal, -o] *nm* madrigal.
madrilène [madʀilɛn] *adj* of *ou* from Madrid.
maestria [maɛstʀija] *nf* (masterly) skill.
maestro [maɛstʀo] *nm* maestro.
maf(f)ia [mafja] *nf* Maf(f)ia.
magasin [magazɛ̃] *nm* (*boutique*) shop; (*entrepôt*) warehouse; (*d'arme, appareil-photo*) magazine; **en ~** (*COMM*) in stock; **faire les ~s** to go (a)round the shops, do the shops; ~

d'alimentation grocer's shop (*BRIT*), grocery store (*US*).
magasinier [magazinje] *nm* warehouseman.
magazine [magazin] *nm* magazine.
mage [maʒ] *nm*: **les Rois M~s** the Magi, the (Three) Wise Men.
Maghreb [magʀɛb] *nm*: **le ~** the Maghreb, North(-West) Africa.
maghrébin, e [magʀebɛ̃, -in] *adj* of *ou* from the Maghreb ♦ *nm/f*: **M~, e** North African, Maghrebi.
magicien, ne [maʒisjɛ̃, -ɛn] *nm/f* magician.
magie [maʒi] *nf* magic; **~ noire** black magic.
magique [maʒik] *adj* (*occulte*) magic; (*fig*) magical.
magistral, e, aux [maʒistʀal, -o] *adj* (*œuvre, adresse*) masterly; (*ton*) authoritative; (*gifle etc*) sound, resounding; (*ex cathedra*): **enseignement ~** lecturing, lectures *pl*; **cours ~** lecture.
magistrat [maʒistʀa] *nm* magistrate.
magistrature [maʒistʀatyʀ] *nf* magistracy, magistrature; **~ assise** judges *pl*, bench; **~ debout** state prosecutors *pl*.
magma [magma] *nm* (*GÉO*) magma; (*fig*) jumble.
magnanerie [maɲanʀi] *nf* silk farm.
magnanime [maɲanim] *adj* magnanimous.
magnanimité [maɲanimite] *nf* magnanimity.
magnat [magna] *nm* tycoon, magnate.
magner [maɲe]: **se ~** *vi* (*fam*) to get a move on.
magnésie [maɲezi] *nf* magnesia.
magnésium [maɲezjɔm] *nm* magnesium.
magnétique [maɲetik] *adj* magnetic.
magnétiser [maɲetize] *vt* to magnetize; (*fig*) to mesmerize, hypnotize.
magnétiseur, euse [maɲetizœʀ, -øz] *nm/f* hypnotist.
magnétisme [maɲetism(ə)] *nm* magnetism.
magnéto [maɲeto] *nm* (= *magnétocassette*) cassette deck; (= *magnétophone*) tape recorder.
magnétocassette [maɲetɔkasɛt] *nm* cassette deck.
magnétophone [maɲetɔfɔn] *nm* tape recorder; **~ à cassettes** cassette recorder.
magnétoscope [maɲetɔskɔp] *nm*: **~ (à cassette)** video (recorder).
magnificence [maɲifisɑ̃s] *nf* (*faste*) magnificence, splendour (*BRIT*), splendor (*US*); (*générosité*) munificence, lavishness.
magnifier [maɲifje] *vt* (*glorifier*) to glorify; (*idéaliser*) to idealize.
magnifique [maɲifik] *adj* magnificent.
magnifiquement [maɲifikmɑ̃] *adv* magnificently.
magnolia [maɲɔlja] *nm* magnolia.
magnum [magnɔm] *nm* magnum.
magot [mago] *nm* (*argent*) pile (of money); (*économies*) nest egg.
magouille [maguj] *nf* (*fam*) scheming.
mahométan, e [maɔmetɑ̃, -an] *adj* Mohammedan, Mahometan.
mai [mɛ] *nm* May; *voir aussi* **juillet**; *see boxed note*.

LE PREMIER MAI

Le premier mai *is a public holiday in France and commemorates the trades union demonstrations in the United States in 1886 when workers demanded the right to an eight-hour working day. Sprigs of lily of the valley are traditionally exchanged.* **Le 8 mai** *is also a public holiday and commemorates the surrender of the German army to Eisenhower on 7 May, 1945. It is marked by parades of ex-servicemen and ex-servicewomen in most towns. The social upheavals of May and June 1968, with their student demonstrations, workers' strikes and general rioting, are usually referred to as 'les événements de mai 68'. De Gaulle's Government survived, but reforms in education and a move towards decentralization ensued.*

maigre [mɛgʀ(ə)] *adj* (very) thin, skinny; (*viande*) lean; (*fromage*) low-fat; (*végétation*) thin, sparse; (*fig*) poor, meagre, skimpy ♦ *adv*: **faire ~** not to eat meat; **jours ~s** days of abstinence, fish days.
maigrelet, te [mɛgʀəlɛ, -ɛt] *adj* skinny, scrawny.
maigreur [mɛgʀœʀ] *nf* thinness.
maigrichon, ne [megʀiʃɔ̃, -ɔn] *adj* = **maigrelet, te**.
maigrir [megʀiʀ] *vi* to get thinner, lose weight ♦ *vt*: **~ qn** (*suj: vêtement*) to make sb look slim(mer).
mailing [mɛliŋ] *nm* direct mail *no pl*; **un ~** a mailshot.
maille [mɑj] *nf* (*boucle*) stitch; (*ouverture*) hole (in the mesh); **avoir ~ à partir avec qn** to have a brush with sb; **~ à l'endroit/à l'envers** knit one/purl one; (*boucle*) plain/purl stitch.
maillechort [majʃɔʀ] *nm* nickel silver.
maillet [majɛ] *nm* mallet.
maillon [mɑjɔ̃] *nm* link.
maillot [majo] *nm* (*aussi*: **~ de corps**) vest; (*de danseur*) leotard; (*de sportif*) jersey; **~ de bain** bathing costume (*BRIT*), swimsuit; (*d'homme*) bathing trunks *pl*; **~ deux pièces** two-piece swimsuit, bikini.
main [mɛ̃] *nf* hand; **la ~ dans la ~** hand in hand; **à deux ~s** with both hands; **à une ~** with one hand; **à la ~** (*tenir, avoir*) in one's hand; (*faire, tricoter etc*) by hand; **se donner la ~** to hold hands; **donner** *ou* **tendre la ~ à qn** to hold out one's hand to sb; **se serrer la ~** to shake hands; **serrer la ~ à qn** to shake hands with sb; **sous la ~** to *ou* at hand; **haut les ~s!** hands up!; **à ~ levée** (*ART*) freehand;

à ~s levées (*voter*) with a show of hands; **attaque à ~ armée** armed attack; **à ~ droite/gauche** to the right/left; **à remettre en ~s propres** to be delivered personally; **de première ~** (*renseignement*) first-hand; (*COMM*: *voiture etc*) with only one previous owner; **faire ~ basse sur** to help o.s. to; **mettre la dernière ~ à** to put the finishing touches to; **mettre la ~ à la pâte** (*fig*) to lend a hand; **avoir/passer la ~** (*CARTES*) to lead/hand over the lead; **s'en laver les ~s** (*fig*) to wash one's hands of it; **se faire/perdre la ~** to get one's hand in/lose one's touch; **avoir qch bien en ~** to have got the hang of sth; **en un tour de ~** (*fig*) in the twinkling of an eye; **~ courante** handrail.

mainate [mɛnat] *nm* myna(h) bird.

main-d'œuvre [mɛ̃dœvʀ(ə)] *nf* manpower, labour (*BRIT*), labor (*US*).

main-forte [mɛ̃fɔʀt(ə)] *nf*: **prêter ~ à qn** to come to sb's assistance.

mainmise [mɛ̃miz] *nf* seizure; (*fig*): **avoir la ~ sur** to have a grip *ou* a stranglehold on.

maint, e [mɛ̃, mɛ̃t] *adj* many a; **~s** many; **à ~es reprises** time and (time) again.

maintenance [mɛ̃tnɑ̃s] *nf* maintenance, servicing.

maintenant [mɛ̃tnɑ̃] *adv* now; (*actuellement*) nowadays.

maintenir [mɛ̃tniʀ] *vt* (*retenir, soutenir*) to support; (*contenir: foule etc*) to keep in check; (*conserver*) to maintain, preserve, uphold; (*affirmer*) to maintain; **se ~** *vi* (*paix, temps*) to hold; (*préjugé*) to persist; (*malade*) to remain stable.

maintien [mɛ̃tjɛ̃] *nm* maintaining, upholding; (*attitude*) bearing; **~ de l'ordre** maintenance of law and order.

maintiendrai [mɛ̃tjɛ̃dʀe], **maintiens** [mɛ̃tjɛ̃] *etc vb voir* **maintenir**.

maire [mɛʀ] *nm* mayor.

mairie [meʀi] *nf* (*endroit*) town hall; (*administration*) town council.

mais [mɛ] *conj* but; **~ non!** of course not!; **~ enfin** but after all; (*indignation*) look here!; **~ encore?** is that all?

maïs [mais] *nm* maize (*BRIT*), Indian corn (*BRIT*), corn (*US*).

maison [mɛzɔ̃] *nf* (*bâtiment*) house; (*chez-soi*) home; (*COMM*) firm; (*famille*): **ami de la ~** friend of the family ♦ *adj inv* (*CULIN*) home-made; (*: au restaurant*) made by the chef; (*COMM*) in-house, own; (*fam*) first-rate; **à la ~** at home; (*direction*) home; **~ d'arrêt** (short-stay) prison; **~ centrale** prison; **~ close** brothel; **~ de correction** ≈ remand home (*BRIT*), ≈ reformatory (*US*); **~ de la culture** ≈ arts centre; **~ des jeunes** ≈ youth club; **~ mère** parent company; **~ de passe** = **~ close**; **~ de repos** convalescent home; **~ de retraite** old people's home; **~ de santé** mental home; *see boxed note*.

MAISONS DES JEUNES

Maisons des jeunes et de la culture *are centres for young people which combine the functions of youth club and community arts centre. They organize a wide range of sporting and cultural activities (theatre, music, exhibitions), and their members also help out in the community. The centres receive some of their funding from the state.*

Maison-Blanche [mɛzɔ̃blɑ̃ʃ] *nf*: **la ~** the White House.

maisonnée [mɛzɔne] *nf* household, family.

maisonnette [mɛzɔnɛt] *nf* small house.

maître, esse [mɛtʀ(ə), mɛtʀɛs] *nm/f* master/mistress; (*SCOL*) teacher, schoolmaster/mistress ♦ *nm* (*peintre etc*) master; (*titre*): **M~ (Me)** Maître, *term of address for lawyers etc* ♦ *nf* (*amante*) mistress ♦ *adj* (*principal, essentiel*) main; **maison de ~** family seat; **être ~ de** (*soi-même, situation*) to be in control of; **se rendre ~ de** (*pays, ville*) to gain control of; (*situation, incendie*) to bring under control; **être passé ~ dans l'art de** to be a (past) master in the art of; **une maîtresse femme** a forceful woman; **~ d'armes** fencing master; **~ auxiliaire (MA)** (*SCOL*) temporary teacher; **~ chanteur** blackmailer; **~ de chapelle** choirmaster; **~ de conférences** ≈ senior lecturer (*BRIT*), ≈ assistant professor (*US*); **~ d'hôtel** (*domestique*) butler; (*d'hôtel*) head waiter; **~ de maison** host; **~ nageur** lifeguard; **~ d'œuvre** (*CONSTR*) project manager; **~ d'ouvrage** (*CONSTR*) client; **~ queux** chef; **maîtresse de maison** hostess; (*ménagère*) housewife (*pl* -wives).

maître-assistant, e, *pl* **maîtres-assistants, es** [mɛtʀasistɑ̃, -ɑ̃t] *nm/f* ≈ lecturer.

maître-autel, *pl* **maîtres-autels** [mɛtʀotɛl] *nm* high altar.

maîtrise [metʀiz] *nf* (*aussi*: **~ de soi**) self-control; (*habileté*) skill, mastery; (*suprématie*) mastery, command; (*diplôme*) ≈ master's degree; (*chefs d'équipe*) supervisory staff; *see boxed note*.

MAÎTRISE

The **maîtrise** *is a French degree which is awarded to university students if they successfully complete two more years' study after the 'DEUG'. Students wishing to go on to do research or to take the 'agrégation' must hold a* **maîtrise**.

maîtriser [metʀize] *vt* (*cheval, incendie*) to (bring under) control; (*sujet*) to master; (*émotion*) to control; **se ~** to control o.s.

majesté [maʒɛste] *nf* majesty.

majestueux, euse [maʒɛstɥø, -øz] *adj* majestic.

majeur, e [maʒœʀ] *adj* (*important*) major; (*JUR*) of age; (*fig*) adult ♦ *nm/f* (*JUR*) person who has come of age *ou* attained his (*ou* her) majority ♦ *nm* (*doigt*) middle finger; **en ~e partie** for the most part; **la ~e partie de** the major part of.

major [maʒɔʀ] *nm* adjutant; (*SCOL*): **~ de la promotion** first in one's year.

majoration [maʒɔʀɑsjɔ̃] *nf* increase.

majordome [maʒɔʀdɔm] *nm* major-domo.

majorer [maʒɔʀe] *vt* to increase.

majorette [maʒɔʀɛt] *nf* majorette.

majoritaire [maʒɔʀitɛʀ] *adj* majority *cpd*; **système/scrutin ~** majority system/ballot.

majorité [maʒɔʀite] *nf* (*gén*) majority; (*parti*) party in power; **en ~** (*composé etc*) mainly.

Majorque [maʒɔʀk(ə)] *nf* Majorca.

majorquin, e [maʒɔʀkɛ̃, -in] *adj* Majorcan ♦ *nm/f*: **M~, e** Majorcan.

majuscule [maʒyskyl] *adj, nf*: **(lettre) ~** capital (letter).

MAL [mal] *sigle f* (= *Maison d'animation et des loisirs*) *cultural centre*.

mal, maux [mal, mo] *nm* (*opposé au bien*) evil; (*tort, dommage*) harm; (*douleur physique*) pain, ache; (*maladie*) illness, sickness *no pl*; (*difficulté, peine*) trouble; (*souffrance morale*) pain ♦ *adv* badly ♦ *adj*: **c'est ~ (de faire)** it's bad *ou* wrong (to do); **être ~** to be uncomfortable; **être ~ avec qn** to be on bad terms with sb; **être au plus ~** (*malade*) to be very bad; (*brouillé*) to be at daggers drawn; **il comprend ~** he has difficulty in understanding; **il a ~ compris** he misunderstood; **~ tourner** to go wrong; **dire/penser du ~ de** to speak/think ill of; **ne vouloir de ~ à personne** to wish nobody any ill; **il n'a rien fait de ~** he has done nothing wrong; **avoir du ~ à faire qch** to have trouble doing sth; **se donner du ~ pour faire qch** to go to a lot of trouble to do sth; **ne voir aucun ~ à** to see no harm in; **craignant ~ faire** fearing he *etc* was doing the wrong thing; **sans penser** *ou* **songer à ~** without meaning any harm; **faire du ~ à qn** to hurt sb; to harm sb; **se faire ~** to hurt o.s.; **se faire ~ au pied** to hurt one's foot; **ça fait ~** it hurts; **j'ai ~ (ici)** it hurts (here); **j'ai ~ au dos** my back aches, I've got a pain in my back; **avoir ~ à la tête/à la gorge/aux dents** to have a headache/a sore throat/toothache; **avoir le ~ de l'air** to be airsick; **avoir le ~ du pays** to be homesick; **~ de mer** seasickness; **~ de la route** carsickness; **~ en point** *adj inv* in a bad state; **maux de ventre** stomach ache *sg*; *voir* **cœur**.

Malabar [malabaʀ] *nm*: **le ~, la côte de ~** the Malabar (Coast).

malabar [malabaʀ] *nm* (*fam*) muscle man.

malade [malad] *adj* ill, sick; (*poitrine, jambe*) bad; (*plante*) diseased; (*fig: entreprise, monde*) ailing ♦ *nm/f* invalid, sick person; (*à l'hôpital etc*) patient; **tomber ~** to fall ill; **être ~ du cœur** to have heart trouble *ou* a bad heart; **grand ~** seriously ill person; **~ mental** mentally sick *ou* ill person.

maladie [maladi] *nf* (*spécifique*) disease, illness; (*mauvaise santé*) illness, sickness; (*fig: manie*) mania; **être rongé par la ~** to be wasting away; **~ d'Alzheimer** Alzheimer's disease; **~ de peau** skin disease.

maladif, ive [maladif, -iv] *adj* sickly; (*curiosité, besoin*) pathological.

maladresse [maladʀɛs] *nf* clumsiness *no pl*; (*gaffe*) blunder.

maladroit, e [maladʀwa, -wat] *adj* clumsy.

maladroitement [maladʀwatmɑ̃] *adv* clumsily.

mal-aimé, e [maleme] *nm/f* unpopular person; (*de la scène politique, de la société*) persona non grata.

malais, e [malɛ, -ɛz] *adj* Malay, Malayan ♦ *nm* (*LING*) Malay ♦ *nm/f*: **M~, e** Malay, Malayan.

malaise [malɛz] *nm* (*MÉD*) feeling of faintness; feeling of discomfort; (*fig*) uneasiness, malaise; **avoir un ~** to feel faint *ou* dizzy.

malaisé, e [maleze] *adj* difficult.

Malaisie [malɛzi] *nf*: **la ~** Malaya, West Malaysia; **la péninsule de ~** the Malay Peninsula.

malappris, e [malapʀi, -iz] *nm/f* ill-mannered *ou* boorish person.

malaria [malaʀja] *nf* malaria.

malavisé, e [malavize] *adj* ill-advised, unwise.

Malawi [malawi] *nm*: **le ~** Malawi.

malaxer [malakse] *vt* (*pétrir*) to knead; (*mêler*) to mix.

Malaysia [malɛzja] *nf*: **la ~** Malaysia.

malbouffe [malbuf] *nf* (*fam*): **la ~** junk food.

malchance [malʃɑ̃s] *nf* misfortune; **par ~** unfortunately; **quelle ~!** what bad luck!

malchanceux, euse [malʃɑ̃sø, -øz] *adj* unlucky.

malcommode [malkɔmɔd] *adj* impractical, inconvenient.

Maldives [maldiv] *nfpl*: **les ~** the Maldive Islands.

maldonne [maldɔn] *nf* (*CARTES*) misdeal; **il y a ~** (*fig*) there's been a misunderstanding.

mâle [mɑl] *adj* (*aussi ÉLEC, TECH*) male; (*viril: voix, traits*) manly ♦ *nm* male.

malédiction [malediksjɔ̃] *nf* curse.

maléfice [malefis] *nm* evil spell.

maléfique [malefik] *adj* evil, baleful.

malencontreusement [malɑ̃kɔ̃tʀøzmɑ̃] *adv* (*arriver*) at the wrong moment; (*rappeler, mentionner*) inopportunely.

malencontreux, euse [malɑ̃kɔ̃tʀø, -øz] *adj* unfortunate, untoward.

malentendant, e [malɑ̃tɑ̃dɑ̃, -ɑ̃t] *nm/f*: **les ~s** the hard of hearing.

malentendu [malɑ̃tɑ̃dy] *nm* misunderstanding.

malfaçon [malfasɔ̃] *nf* fault.

malfaisant, e [malfəzɑ̃, -ɑ̃t] *adj* evil, harmful.
malfaiteur [malfɛtœʀ] *nm* lawbreaker, criminal; (*voleur*) thief (*pl* thieves).
malfamé, e [malfame] *adj* disreputable, of ill repute.
malfrat [malfʀɑ] *nm* villain, crook.
malgache [malgaʃ] *adj* Malagasy, Madagascan ♦ *nm* (*LING*) Malagasy ♦ *nm/f*: **M~** Malagasy, Madagascan.
malgré [malgʀe] *prép* in spite of, despite; **~ tout** *adv* in spite of everything.
malhabile [malabil] *adj* clumsy.
malheur [malœʀ] *nm* (*situation*) adversity, misfortune; (*événement*) misfortune; (*: plus fort*) disaster, tragedy; **par ~** unfortunately; **quel ~!** what a shame *ou* pity!; **faire un ~** (*fam: un éclat*) to do something desperate; (*: avoir du succès*) to be a smash hit.
malheureusement [malœʀøzmɑ̃] *adv* unfortunately.
malheureux, euse [malœʀø, -øz] *adj* (*triste*) unhappy, miserable; (*infortuné, regrettable*) unfortunate; (*malchanceux*) unlucky; (*insignifiant*) wretched ♦ *nm/f* (*infortuné, misérable*) poor soul; (*indigent, miséreux*) unfortunate creature; **les ~** the destitute; **avoir la main malheureuse** (*au jeu*) to be unlucky; (*tout casser*) to be ham-fisted.
malhonnête [malɔnɛt] *adj* dishonest; (*impoli*) rude.
malhonnêtement [malɔnɛtmɑ̃] *adv* dishonestly.
malhonnêteté [malɔnɛtte] *nf* dishonesty; rudeness *no pl*.
Mali [mali] *nm*: **le ~** Mali.
malice [malis] *nf* mischievousness; (*méchanceté*): **par ~** out of malice *ou* spite; **sans ~** guileless.
malicieusement [malisjøzmɑ̃] *adv* mischievously.
malicieux, euse [malisjø, -øz] *adj* mischievous.
malien, ne [maljɛ̃, -ɛn] *adj* Malian.
malignité [maliɲite] *nf* (*d'une tumeur, d'un mal*) malignancy.
malin, igne [malɛ̃, -iɲ] *adj* (*futé: f gén:* **maline**) smart, shrewd; (*: sourire*) knowing; (*MÉD, influence*) malignant; **faire le ~** to show off; **éprouver un ~ plaisir à** to take malicious pleasure in.
malingre [malɛ̃gʀ(ə)] *adj* puny.
malintentionné, e [malɛ̃tɑ̃sjɔne] *adj* ill-intentioned, malicious.
malle [mal] *nf* trunk; (*AUTO*): **~ (arrière)** boot (*BRIT*), trunk (*US*).
malléable [maleabl(ə)] *adj* malleable.
malle-poste, *pl* **malles-poste** [malpɔst(ə)] *nf* mail coach.
mallette [malɛt] *nf* (*valise*) (small) suitcase; (*aussi*: **~ de voyage**) overnight case; (*pour documents*) attaché case.
malmener [malməne] *vt* to manhandle; (*fig*) to give a rough ride to.
malnutrition [malnytʀisjɔ̃] *nf* malnutrition.
malodorant, e [malɔdɔʀɑ̃, -ɑ̃t] *adj* foul-smelling.
malotru [malɔtʀy] *nm* lout, boor.
malouin, e [malwɛ̃, -in] *adj* of *ou* from Saint Malo.
Malouines [malwin] *nfpl*: **les ~** the Falklands, the Falkland Islands.
malpoli, e [malpɔli] *nm/f* rude individual.
malpropre [malpʀɔpʀ(ə)] *adj* (*personne, vêtement*) dirty; (*travail*) slovenly; (*histoire, plaisanterie*) unsavoury (*BRIT*), unsavory (*US*), smutty; (*malhonnête*) dishonest.
malpropreté [malpʀɔpʀəte] *nf* dirtiness.
malsain, e [malsɛ̃, -ɛn] *adj* unhealthy.
malséant, e [malseɑ̃, -ɑ̃t] *adj* unseemly, unbecoming.
malsonnant, e [malsɔnɑ̃, -ɑ̃t] *adj* offensive.
malt [malt] *nm* malt; **pur ~** (*whisky*) malt (whisky).
maltais, e [maltɛ, -ɛz] *adj* Maltese.
Malte [malt(ə)] *nf* Malta.
malté, e [malte] *adj* (*lait etc*) malted.
maltraiter [maltʀete] *vt* (*brutaliser*) to manhandle, ill-treat; (*critiquer, éreinter*) to slate (*BRIT*), roast.
malus [malys] *nm* (*ASSURANCES*) car insurance weighting, penalty.
malveillance [malvɛjɑ̃s] *nf* (*animosité*) ill will; (*intention de nuire*) malevolence; (*JUR*) malicious intent *no pl*.
malveillant, e [malvɛjɑ̃, -ɑ̃t] *adj* malevolent, malicious.
malvenu, e [malvəny] *adj*: **être ~ de** *ou* **à faire qch** not to be in a position to do sth.
malversation [malvɛʀsɑsjɔ̃] *nf* embezzlement, misappropriation (of funds).
mal-vivre [malvivʀ] *nm inv* malaise.
maman [mamɑ̃] *nf* mum(my) (*BRIT*), mom (*US*).
mamelle [mamɛl] *nf* teat.
mamelon [mamlɔ̃] *nm* (*ANAT*) nipple; (*colline*) knoll, hillock.
mamie [mami] *nf* (*fam*) granny.
mammifère [mamifɛʀ] *nm* mammal.
mammouth [mamut] *nm* mammoth.
manager [manadʒɛʀ] *nm* (*SPORT*) manager; (*COMM*): **~ commercial** commercial director.
manceau, elle, x [mɑ̃so, -ɛl] *adj* of *ou* from Le Mans.
manche [mɑ̃ʃ] *nf* (*de vêtement*) sleeve; (*d'un jeu, tournoi*) round; (*GÉO*): **la M~** the (English) Channel ♦ *nm* (*d'outil, casserole*) handle; (*de pelle, pioche etc*) shaft; (*de violon, guitare*) neck; (*fam*) clumsy oaf; **faire la ~** to pass the hat; **~ à air** *nf* (*AVIAT*) wind-sock; **~ à balai** *nm* broomstick; (*AVIAT, INFORM*) joystick.
manchette [mɑ̃ʃɛt] *nf* (*de chemise*) cuff; (*coup*) forearm blow; (*titre*) headline.
manchon [mɑ̃ʃɔ̃] *nm* (*de fourrure*) muff; **~ à incandescence** incandescent (gas) mantle.

manchot [mɑ̃ʃo] *nm* one-armed man; armless man; (*ZOOL*) penguin.
mandarine [mɑ̃daʀin] *nf* mandarin (orange), tangerine.
mandat [mɑ̃da] *nm* (*postal*) postal *ou* money order; (*d'un député etc*) mandate; (*procuration*) power of attorney, proxy; (*POLICE*) warrant; ~ **d'amener** summons *sg*; ~ **d'arrêt** warrant for arrest; ~ **de dépôt** committal order; ~ **de perquisition** (*POLICE*) search warrant.
mandataire [mɑ̃datɛʀ] *nm/f* (*représentant, délégué*) representative; (*JUR*) proxy.
mandat-carte, *pl* **mandats-cartes** [mɑ̃dakaʀt(ə)] *nm* money order (*in postcard form*).
mandater [mɑ̃date] *vt* (*personne*) to appoint; (*POL: député*) to elect.
mandat-lettre, *pl* **mandats-lettres** [mɑ̃dalɛtʀ(ə)] *nm* money order (*with space for correspondence*).
mandchou, e [mɑ̃tʃu] *adj* Manchu, Manchurian ♦ *nm* (*LING*) Manchu ♦ *nm/f*: **M~, e** Manchu.
Mandchourie [mɑ̃tʃuʀi] *nf*: **la** ~ Manchuria.
mander [mɑ̃de] *vt* to summon.
mandibule [mɑ̃dibyl] *nf* mandible.
mandoline [mɑ̃dɔlin] *nf* mandolin(e).
manège [manɛʒ] *nm* riding school; (*à la foire*) roundabout (*BRIT*), merry-go-round; (*fig*) game, ploy; **faire un tour de** ~ to go for a ride on a *ou* the roundabout *etc*; ~ **(de chevaux de bois)** roundabout (*BRIT*), merry-go-round.
manette [manɛt] *nf* lever, tap; ~ **de jeu** (*INFORM*) joystick.
manganèse [mɑ̃ganɛz] *nm* manganese.
mangeable [mɑ̃ʒabl(ə)] *adj* edible, eatable.
mangeaille [mɑ̃ʒɑj] *nf* (*péj*) grub.
mangeoire [mɑ̃ʒwaʀ] *nf* trough, manger.
manger [mɑ̃ʒe] *vt* to eat; (*ronger: suj: rouille etc*) to eat into *ou* away; (*utiliser, consommer*) to eat up ♦ *vi* to eat.
mange-tout [mɑ̃ʒtu] *nm inv* mange-tout.
mangeur, euse [mɑ̃ʒœʀ, -øz] *nm/f* eater.
mangouste [mɑ̃gust(ə)] *nf* mongoose.
mangue [mɑ̃g] *nf* mango.
maniabilité [manjabilite] *nf* (*d'un outil*) handiness; (*d'un véhicule, voilier*) manoeuvrability.
maniable [manjabl(ə)] *adj* (*outil*) handy; (*voiture, voilier*) easy to handle, manoeuvrable (*BRIT*), maneuverable (*US*); (*fig: personne*) easily influenced, manipulable.
maniaque [manjak] *adj* (*pointilleux, méticuleux*) finicky, fussy; (*atteint de manie*) suffering from a mania ♦ *nm/f* maniac.
manie [mani] *nf* mania; (*tic*) odd habit.
maniement [manimɑ̃] *nm* handling; ~ **d'armes** arms drill.
manier [manje] *vt* to handle; **se** ~ *vi* (*fam*) to get a move on.
manière [manjɛʀ] *nf* (*façon*) way, manner; (*genre, style*) style; ~**s** *nfpl* (*attitude*) manners; (*chichis*) fuss *sg*; **de** ~ **à** so as to; **de telle** ~ **que** in such a way that; **de cette** ~ in this way *ou* manner; **d'une** ~ **générale** generally speaking, as a general rule; **de toute** ~ in any case; **d'une certaine** ~ in a (certain) way; **faire des** ~**s** to put on airs; **employer la** ~ **forte** to use strong-arm tactics; **adverbe de** ~ adverb of manner.
maniéré, e [manjeʀe] *adj* affected.
manif [manif] *nf* (= *manifestation*) demo (*pl* -s).
manifestant, e [manifɛstɑ̃, -ɑ̃t] *nm/f* demonstrator.
manifestation [manifɛstɑsjɔ̃] *nf* (*de joie, mécontentement*) expression, demonstration; (*symptôme*) outward sign; (*fête etc*) event; (*POL*) demonstration.
manifeste [manifɛst(ə)] *adj* obvious, evident ♦ *nm* manifesto (*pl* -s).
manifestement [manifɛstəmɑ̃] *adv* obviously.
manifester [manifɛste] *vt* (*volonté, intentions*) to show, indicate; (*joie, peur*) to express, show ♦ *vi* (*POL*) to demonstrate; **se** ~ *vi* (*émotion*) to show *ou* express itself; (*difficultés*) to arise; (*symptômes*) to appear; (*témoin etc*) to come forward.
manigance [manigɑ̃s] *nf* scheme.
manigancer [manigɑ̃se] *vt* to plot, devise.
Manille [manij] *n* Manila.
manioc [manjɔk] *nm* cassava, manioc.
manipulateur, trice [manipylatœʀ, -tʀis] *adj* (*technicien*) technician, operator; (*prestidigitateur*) conjurer; (*péj*) manipulator.
manipulation [manipylɑsjɔ̃] *nf* handling; manipulation.
manipuler [manipyle] *vt* to handle; (*fig*) to manipulate.
manivelle [manivɛl] *nf* crank.
manne [man] *nf* (*REL*) manna; (*fig*) godsend.
mannequin [mankɛ̃] *nm* (*COUTURE*) dummy; (*MODE*) model.
manœuvrable [manœvʀabl(ə)] *adj* (*bateau, véhicule*) manoeuvrable (*BRIT*), maneuverable (*US*).
manœuvre [manœvʀ(ə)] *nf* (*gén*) manoeuvre (*BRIT*), maneuver (*US*) ♦ *nm* (*ouvrier*) labourer (*BRIT*), laborer (*US*).
manœuvrer [manœvʀe] *vt* to manoeuvre (*BRIT*), maneuver (*US*); (*levier, machine*) to operate; (*personne*) to manipulate ♦ *vi* to manoeuvre *ou* maneuver.
manoir [manwaʀ] *nm* manor *ou* country house.
manomètre [manɔmɛtʀ(ə)] *nm* gauge, manometer.
manquant, e [mɑ̃kɑ̃, -ɑ̃t] *adj* missing.
manque [mɑ̃k] *nm* (*insuffisance*): ~ **de** lack of; (*vide*) emptiness, gap; (*MÉD*) withdrawal; ~**s** *nmpl* (*lacunes*) faults, defects; **par** ~ **de** for want of; ~ **à gagner** loss of profit *ou* earnings.

manqué, e [mɑ̃ke] *adj* failed; **garçon ~** tomboy.
manquement [mɑ̃kmɑ̃] *nm*: **~ à** (*discipline, règle*) breach of.
manquer [mɑ̃ke] *vi* (*faire défaut*) to be lacking; (*être absent*) to be missing; (*échouer*) to fail ♦ *vt* to miss ♦ *vb impers*: **il (nous) manque encore 10 €** we are still €10 short; **il manque des pages (au livre)** there are some pages missing *ou* some pages are missing (from the book); **l'argent qui leur manque** the money they need *ou* are short of; **le pied/la voix lui manqua** he missed his footing/his voice failed him; **~ à qn** (*absent etc*): **il/cela me manque** I miss him/that; **~ à** *vt* (*règles etc*) to be in breach of, fail to observe; **~ de** *vt* to lack; (*COMM*) to be out of (stock of); **ne pas ~ de faire**: **il n'a pas manqué de le dire** he certainly said it; **~ (de) faire**: **il a manqué (de) se tuer** he very nearly got killed; **il ne manquerait plus qu'il fasse** all we need now is for him to do; **je n'y manquerai pas** leave it to me, I'll definitely do it.
mansarde [mɑ̃saʀd(ə)] *nf* attic.
mansardé, e [mɑ̃saʀde] *adj* attic *cpd*.
mansuétude [mɑ̃sɥetyd] *nf* leniency.
mante [mɑ̃t] *nf*: **~ religieuse** praying mantis.
manteau, x [mɑ̃to] *nm* coat; **~ de cheminée** mantelpiece; **sous le ~** (*fig*) under cover.
mantille [mɑ̃tij] *nf* mantilla.
Mantoue [mɑ̃tu] *n* Mantua.
manucure [manykyʀ] *nf* manicurist.
manuel, le [manɥɛl] *adj* manual ♦ *nm/f* manually gifted pupil *etc* (*as opposed to intellectually gifted*) ♦ *nm* (*ouvrage*) manual, handbook.
manuellement [manɥɛlmɑ̃] *adv* manually.
manufacture [manyfaktyʀ] *nf* (*établissement*) factory; (*fabrication*) manufacture.
manufacturé, e [manyfaktyʀe] *adj* manufactured.
manufacturier, ière [manyfaktyʀje, -jɛʀ] *nm/f* factory owner.
manuscrit, e [manyskʀi, -it] *adj* handwritten ♦ *nm* manuscript.
manutention [manytɑ̃sjɔ̃] *nf* (*COMM*) handling; (*local*) storehouse.
manutentionnaire [manytɑ̃sjɔnɛʀ] *nm/f* warehouseman/woman, packer.
manutentionner [manytɑ̃sjɔne] *vt* to handle.
MAP *sigle f* (*PHOTO*: *= mise au point*) focusing.
mappemonde [mapmɔ̃d] *nf* (*plane*) map of the world; (*sphère*) globe.
maquereau, x [makʀo] *nm* mackerel *inv*; (*fam*: *proxénète*) pimp.
maquerelle [makʀɛl] *nf* (*fam*) madam.
maquette [makɛt] *nf* (*d'un décor, bâtiment, véhicule*) (scale) model; (*TYPO*) mockup; (*: d'une page illustrée, affiche*) paste-up; (*: prêt à la réproduction*) artwork.
maquignon [makiɲɔ̃] *nm* horse-dealer.
maquillage [makijaʒ] *nm* making up; faking; (*produits*) make-up.
maquiller [makije] *vt* (*personne, visage*) to make up; (*truquer: passeport, statistique*) to fake; (*: voiture volée*) to do over (*respray etc*); **se ~** to make o.s. up.
maquilleur, euse [makijœʀ, -øz] *nm/f* make-up artist.
maquis [maki] *nm* (*GÉO*) scrub; (*fig*) tangle; (*MIL*) maquis, underground fighting *no pl*.
maquisard, e [makizaʀ, -aʀd(ə)] *nm/f* maquis, member of the Resistance.
marabout [maʀabu] *nm* (*ZOOL*) marabou(t).
maraîcher, ère [maʀeʃe, maʀɛʃɛʀ] *adj*: **cultures maraîchères** market gardening *sg* ♦ *nm/f* market gardener.
marais [maʀɛ] *nm* marsh, swamp; **~ salant** saltworks.
marasme [maʀasm(ə)] *nm* (*POL, ÉCON*) stagnation, sluggishness; (*accablement*) dejection, depression.
marathon [maʀatɔ̃] *nm* marathon.
marâtre [maʀɑtʀ(ə)] *nf* cruel mother.
maraude [maʀod] *nf* pilfering, thieving (*of poultry, crops*); (*dans un verger*) scrumping; (*vagabondage*) prowling; **en ~** on the prowl; (*taxi*) cruising.
maraudeur, euse [maʀodœʀ, -øz] *nm/f* marauder; prowler.
marbre [maʀbʀ(ə)] *nm* (*pierre, statue*) marble; (*d'une table, commode*) marble top; (*TYPO*) stone, bed; **rester de ~** to remain stonily indifferent.
marbrer [maʀbʀe] *vt* to mottle, blotch; (*TECH: papier*) to marble.
marbrerie [maʀbʀəʀi] *nf* (*atelier*) marble mason's workshop; (*industrie*) marble industry.
marbrier [maʀbʀije] *nm* monumental mason.
marbrière [maʀbʀijɛʀ] *nf* marble quarry.
marbrures [maʀbʀyʀ] *nfpl* blotches *pl*; (*TECH*) marbling *sg*.
marc [maʀ] *nm* (*de raisin, pommes*) marc; **~ de café** coffee grounds *pl ou* dregs *pl*.
marcassin [maʀkasɛ̃] *nm* young wild boar.
marchand, e [maʀʃɑ̃, -ɑ̃d] *nm/f* shopkeeper, tradesman/woman; (*au marché*) stallholder; (*spécifique*): **~ de cycles/tapis** bicycle/carpet dealer; **~ de charbon/vins** coal/wine merchant ♦ *adj*: **prix/valeur ~(e)** market price/value; **qualité ~e** standard quality; **~ en gros/au détail** wholesaler/retailer; **~ de biens** real estate agent; **~ de canons** (*péj*) arms dealer; **~ de couleurs** ironmonger (*BRIT*), hardware dealer (*US*); **~/e de fruits** fruiterer (*BRIT*), fruit seller (*US*); **~/e de journaux** newsagent (*BRIT*), newsdealer (*US*); **~/e de légumes** greengrocer (*BRIT*), produce dealer (*US*); **~/e de poisson** fishmonger (*BRIT*), fish seller (*US*); **~/e de(s) quatre-saisons** costermonger (*BRIT*), street vendor (selling fresh fruit and vegetables); **~ de sable** (*fig*) sandman; **~ de tableaux** art dealer.

marchandage [maRʃɑ̃daʒ] *nm* bargaining; (*péj: électoral*) bargaining, manoeuvring.

marchander [maRʃɑ̃de] *vt* (*article*) to bargain *ou* haggle over; (*éloges*) to be sparing with ♦ *vi* to bargain, haggle.

marchandisage [maRʃɑ̃dizaʒ] *nm* merchandizing.

marchandise [maRʃɑ̃diz] *nf* goods *pl*, merchandise *no pl*.

marche [maRʃ(ə)] *nf* (*d'escalier*) step; (*activité*) walking; (*promenade, trajet, allure*) walk; (*démarche*) walk, gait; (*MIL etc, MUS*) march; (*fonctionnement*) running; (*progression*) progress; course; **à une heure de** ~ an hour's walk (away); **ouvrir/fermer la** ~ to lead the way/bring up the rear; **dans le sens de la** ~ (*RAIL*) facing the engine; **en** ~ (*monter etc*) while the vehicle is moving *ou* in motion; **mettre en** ~ to start; **remettre qch en** ~ to set *ou* start sth going again; **se mettre en** ~ (*personne*) to get moving; (*machine*) to start; ~ **arrière** (*AUTO*) reverse (gear); **faire** ~ **arrière** (*AUTO*) to reverse; (*fig*) to backtrack, back-pedal; ~ **à suivre** (correct) procedure; (*sur notice*) (step by step) instructions *pl*.

marché [maRʃe] *nm* (*lieu, COMM, ÉCON*) market; (*ville*) trading centre; (*transaction*) bargain, deal; **par-dessus le** ~ into the bargain; **faire son** ~ to do one's shopping; **mettre le** ~ **en main à qn** to tell sb to take it or leave it; ~ **au comptant** (*BOURSE*) spot market; **M**~ **commun** Common Market; ~ **aux fleurs** flower market; ~ **noir** black market; **faire du** ~ **noir** to buy and sell on the black market; ~ **aux puces** flea market; ~ **à terme** (*BOURSE*) forward market; ~ **du travail** labour market.

marchepied [maRʃəpje] *nm* (*RAIL*) step; (*AUTO*) running board; (*fig*) stepping stone.

marcher [maRʃe] *vi* to walk; (*MIL*) to march; (*aller: voiture, train, affaires*) to go; (*prospérer*) to go well; (*fonctionner*) to work, run; (*fam*) to go along, agree; (*: croire naïvement*) to be taken in; ~ **sur** to walk on; (*mettre le pied sur*) to step on *ou* in; (*MIL*) to march upon; ~ **dans** (*herbe etc*) to walk in *ou* on; (*flaque*) to step in; **faire** ~ **qn** (*pour rire*) to pull sb's leg; (*pour tromper*) to lead sb up the garden path.

marcheur, euse [maRʃœR, -øz] *nm/f* walker.

marcotter [maRkɔte] *vt* to layer.

mardi [maRdi] *nm* Tuesday; **M**~ **gras** Shrove Tuesday; *voir aussi* **lundi**.

mare [maR] *nf* pond; ~ **de sang** pool of blood.

marécage [maRekaʒ] *nm* marsh, swamp.

marécageux, euse [maRekaʒø, -øz] *adj* marshy, swampy.

maréchal, aux [maReʃal, -o] *nm* marshal; ~ **des logis** (*MIL*) sergeant.

maréchal-ferrant, *pl* **maréchaux-ferrants** [maReʃalfeRɑ̃, maReʃo-] *nm* blacksmith, farrier (*BRIT*).

maréchaussée [maReʃose] *nf* (*humoristique: gendarmes*) constabulary (*BRIT*), police.

marée [maRe] *nf* tide; (*poissons*) fresh (sea) fish; ~ **haute/basse** high/low tide; ~ **montante/descendante** rising/ebb tide; ~ **noire** oil slick.

marelle [maRɛl] *nf*: **(jouer à) la** ~ (to play) hopscotch.

marémotrice [maRemɔtRis] *adj f* tidal.

mareyeur, euse [maRɛjœR, -øz] *nm/f* wholesale (sea) fish merchant.

margarine [maRgaRin] *nf* margarine.

marge [maRʒ(ə)] *nf* margin; **en** ~ in the margin; **en** ~ **de** (*fig*) on the fringe of; (*en dehors de*) cut off from; (*qui se rapporte à*) connected with; ~ **bénéficiaire** profit margin, mark-up; ~ **de sécurité** safety margin.

margelle [maRʒɛl] *nf* coping.

margeur [maRʒœR] *nm* margin stop.

marginal, e, aux [maRʒinal, -o] *adj* marginal ♦ *nm/f* dropout.

marguerite [maRgəRit] *nf* marguerite, (oxeye) daisy; (*INFORM*) daisy wheel.

marguillier [maRgije] *nm* churchwarden.

mari [maRi] *nm* husband.

mariage [maRjaʒ] *nm* (*union, état, fig*) marriage; (*noce*) wedding; ~ **civil/religieux** registry office (*BRIT*) *ou* civil/church wedding; **un** ~ **de raison/d'amour** a marriage of convenience/a love match; ~ **blanc** unconsummated marriage; ~ **en blanc** white wedding.

marié, e [maRje] *adj* married ♦ *nm/f* (bride)groom/bride; **les** ~**s** the bride and groom; **les (jeunes)** ~**s** the newly-weds.

marier [maRje] *vt* to marry; (*fig*) to blend; **se** ~ **(avec)** to marry, get married (to); (*fig*) to blend (with).

marijuana [maRiʒwana] *nf* marijuana.

marin, e [maRɛ̃, -in] *adj* sea *cpd*, marine ♦ *nm* sailor ♦ *nf* navy; (*ART*) seascape; (*couleur*) navy (blue); **avoir le pied** ~ to be a good sailor; (*garder son équilibre*) to have one's sea legs; ~**e de guerre** navy; ~**e marchande** merchant navy; ~**e à voiles** sailing ships *pl*.

marina [maRina] *nf* marina.

marinade [maRinad] *nf* marinade.

marine [maRin] *adj f, nf voir* **marin** ♦ *adj inv* navy (blue) ♦ *nm* (*MIL*) marine.

mariner [maRine] *vi, vt* to marinate, marinade.

marinier [maRinje] *nm* bargee.

marinière [maRinjɛR] *nf* (*blouse*) smock ♦ *adj inv*: **moules** ~ (*CULIN*) mussels in white wine.

marionnette [maRjɔnɛt] *nf* puppet.

marital, e, aux [maRital, -o] *adj*: **autorisation** ~**e** husband's permission.

maritalement [maRitalmɑ̃] *adv*: **vivre** ~ to live together (as husband and wife).

maritime [maRitim] *adj* sea *cpd*, maritime; (*ville*) coastal, seaside; (*droit*) shipping, maritime.

marjolaine [maRʒɔlɛn] *nf* marjoram.

mark [maʀk] *nm* (*monnaie*) mark.
marketing [maʀkətiŋ] *nm* (*COMM*) marketing.
marmaille [maʀmɑj] *nf* (*péj*) (gang of) brats *pl*.
marmelade [maʀməlad] *nf* (*compote*) stewed fruit, compote; ~ **d'oranges** (orange) marmalade; **en** ~ (*fig*) crushed (to a pulp).
marmite [maʀmit] *nf* (cooking-)pot.
marmiton [maʀmitɔ̃] *nm* kitchen boy.
marmonner [maʀmɔne] *vt, vi* to mumble, mutter.
marmot [maʀmo] *nm* (*fam*) brat.
marmotte [maʀmɔt] *nf* marmot.
marmotter [maʀmɔte] *vt* (*prière*) to mumble, mutter.
marne [maʀn(ə)] *nf* (*GÉO*) marl.
Maroc [maʀɔk] *nm*: **le** ~ Morocco.
marocain, e [maʀɔkɛ̃, -ɛn] *adj* Moroccan ♦ *nm/f*: **M~, e** Moroccan.
maroquin [maʀɔkɛ̃] *nm* (*peau*) morocco (leather); (*fig*) (minister's) portfolio.
maroquinerie [maʀɔkinʀi] *nf* (*industrie*) leather craft; (*commerce*) leather shop; (*articles*) fine leather goods *pl*.
maroquinier [maʀɔkinje] *nm* (*fabricant*) leather craftsman; (*marchand*) leather dealer.
marotte [maʀɔt] *nf* fad.
marquant, e [maʀkɑ̃, -ɑ̃t] *adj* outstanding.
marque [maʀk(ə)] *nf* mark; (*SPORT, JEU*) score; (*COMM*: *de produits*) brand, make; (*: de disques*) label; (*insigne: d'une fonction*) badge; (*fig*): ~ **d'affection** token of affection; ~ **de joie** sign of joy; **à vos ~s!** (*SPORT*) on your marks!; **de** ~ *adj* (*COMM*) brand-name *cpd*; proprietary; (*fig*) high-class; (*: personnage, hôte*) distinguished; **produit de** ~ (*COMM*) quality product; ~ **déposée** registered trademark; ~ **de fabrique** trademark.
marqué, e [maʀke] *adj* marked.
marquer [maʀke] *vt* to mark; (*inscrire*) to write down; (*bétail*) to brand; (*SPORT*: *but etc*) to score; (*: joueur*) to mark; (*accentuer: taille etc*) to emphasize; (*manifester: refus, intérêt*) to show ♦ *vi* (*événement, personnalité*) to stand out, be outstanding; (*SPORT*) to score; ~ **qn de son influence/empreinte** to have an influence/leave its impression on sb; ~ **un temps d'arrêt** to pause momentarily; ~ **le pas** (*fig*) to mark time; **il a marqué ce jour-là d'une pierre blanche** that was a red-letter day for him; ~ **les points** (*tenir la marque*) to keep the score.
marqueté, e [maʀkəte] *adj* inlaid.
marqueterie [maʀkətʀi] *nf* inlaid work, marquetry.
marqueur, euse [maʀkœʀ, -øz] *nm/f* (*SPORT*: *de but*) scorer ♦ *nm* (*crayon feutre*) marker pen.
marquis, e [maʀki, -iz] *nm/f* marquis *ou* marquess/marchioness ♦ *nf* (*auvent*) glass canopy *ou* awning.
Marquises [maʀkiz] *nfpl*: **les (îles)** ~ the Marquesas Islands.
marraine [maʀɛn] *nf* godmother; (*d'un navire, d'une rose etc*) namer.
Marrakech [maʀakɛʃ] *n* Marrakech *ou* Marrakesh.
marrant, e [maʀɑ̃, -ɑ̃t] *adj* (*fam*) funny.
marre [maʀ] *adv* (*fam*): **en avoir** ~ **de** to be fed up with.
marrer [maʀe]: **se** ~ *vi* (*fam*) to have a (good) laugh.
marron, ne [maʀɔ̃, -ɔn] *nm* (*fruit*) chestnut ♦ *adj inv* brown ♦ *adj* (*péj*) crooked; (*: faux*) bogus; **~s glacés** marrons glacés.
marronnier [maʀɔnje] *nm* chestnut (tree).
Mars [maʀs] *nm ou f* Mars.
mars [maʀs] *nm* March; *voir aussi* **juillet**.
marseillais, e [maʀsɛjɛ, -ɛz] *adj* of *ou* from Marseilles ♦ *nf*: **la M~e** *the French national anthem*; *see boxed note*.

> **MARSEILLAISE**
>
> *The* **Marseillaise** *has been France's national anthem since 1879. The words of the 'Chant de guerre de l'armée du Rhin', as the song was originally called, were written to an anonymous tune by an army captain called Rouget de Lisle in 1792. Adopted as a marching song by the Marseille battalion, it was finally popularized as the* **Marseillaise**.

marsouin [maʀswɛ̃] *nm* porpoise.
marsupiaux [maʀsypjo] *nmpl* marsupials.
marteau, x [maʀto] *nm* hammer; (*de porte*) knocker; ~ **pneumatique** pneumatic drill.
marteau-pilon, *pl* **marteaux-pilons** [maʀtopilɔ̃] *nm* power hammer.
marteau-piqueur, *pl* **marteaux-piqueurs** [maʀtopikœʀ] *nm* pneumatic drill.
martel [maʀtɛl] *nm*: **se mettre** ~ **en tête** to worry o.s.
martèlement [maʀtɛlmɑ̃] *nm* hammering.
marteler [maʀtəle] *vt* to hammer; (*mots, phrases*) to rap out.
martial, e, aux [maʀsjal, -o] *adj* martial; **cour ~e** court-martial.
martien, ne [maʀsjɛ̃, -ɛn] *adj* Martian, of *ou* from Mars.
martinet [maʀtinɛ] *nm* (*fouet*) small whip; (*ZOOL*) swift.
martingale [maʀtɛ̃gal] *nf* (*COUTURE*) half-belt; (*JEU*) winning formula.
martiniquais, e [maʀtinikɛ, -ɛz] *adj* of *ou* from Martinique.
Martinique [maʀtinik] *nf*: **la** ~ Martinique.
martin-pêcheur, *pl* **martins-pêcheurs** [maʀtɛ̃pɛʃœʀ] *nm* kingfisher.
martre [maʀtʀ(ə)] *nf* marten; ~ **zibeline** sable.
martyr, e [maʀtiʀ] *nm/f* martyr ♦ *adj* martyred; **enfants ~s** battered children.
martyre [maʀtiʀ] *nm* martyrdom; (*fig: sens af-*

faibli) agony, torture; **souffrir le ~** to suffer agonies.

martyriser [maʀtiʀize] *vt* (*REL*) to martyr; (*fig*) to bully; (*: enfant*) to batter.

marxisme [maʀksism(ə)] *nm* Marxism.

marxiste [maʀksist(ə)] *adj, nm/f* Marxist.

mas [mɑ(s)] *nm traditional house or farm in Provence.*

mascara [maskaʀa] *nm* mascara.

mascarade [maskaʀad] *nf* masquerade.

mascotte [maskɔt] *nf* mascot.

masculin, e [maskylɛ̃, -in] *adj* masculine; (*sexe, population*) male; (*équipe, vêtements*) men's; (*viril*) manly ♦ *nm* masculine.

masochisme [mazɔʃism(ə)] *nm* masochism.

masochiste [mazɔʃist(ə)] *adj* masochistic ♦ *nm/f* masochist.

masque [mask(ə)] *nm* mask; **~ de beauté** face pack; **~ à gaz** gas mask; **~ de plongée** diving mask.

masqué, e [maske] *adj* masked.

masquer [maske] *vt* (*cacher: porte, goût*) to hide, conceal; (*dissimuler: vérité, projet*) to mask, obscure.

massacrant, e [masakʀɑ̃, -ɑ̃t] *adj*: **humeur ~e** foul temper.

massacre [masakʀ(ə)] *nm* massacre, slaughter; **jeu de ~** (*fig*) wholesale slaughter.

massacrer [masakʀe] *vt* to massacre, slaughter; (*fig: adversaire*) to slaughter; (*: texte etc*) to murder.

massage [masaʒ] *nm* massage.

masse [mas] *nf* mass; (*péj*): **la ~** the masses *pl*; (*ÉLEC*) earth; (*maillet*) sledgehammer; **~s** *nfpl* masses; **une ~ de, des ~s de** (*fam*) masses *ou* loads of; **en ~** *adv* (*en bloc*) in bulk; (*en foule*) en masse ♦ *adj* (*exécutions, production*) mass *cpd*; **~ monétaire** (*ÉCON*) money supply; **~ salariale** (*COMM*) wage(s) bill.

massepain [maspɛ̃] *nm* marzipan.

masser [mase] *vt* (*assembler*) to gather; (*pétrir*) to massage; **se ~** *vi* to gather.

masseur, euse [masœʀ, -øz] *nm/f* (*personne*) masseur/masseuse ♦ *nm* (*appareil*) massager.

massicot [masiko] *nm* (*TYPO*) guillotine.

massif, ive [masif, -iv] *adj* (*porte*) solid, massive; (*visage*) heavy, large; (*bois, or*) solid; (*dose*) massive; (*déportations etc*) mass *cpd* ♦ *nm* (*montagneux*) massif; (*de fleurs*) clump, bank.

massivement [masivmɑ̃] *adv* (*répondre*) en masse; (*administrer, injecter*) in massive doses.

mass media [masmedja] *nmpl* mass media.

massue [masy] *nf* club, bludgeon ♦ *adj inv*: **argument ~** sledgehammer argument.

mastectomie [mastɛktɔmi] *nf* mastectomy.

mastic [mastik] *nm* (*pour vitres*) putty; (*pour fentes*) filler.

masticage [mastikaʒ] *nm* (*d'une fente*) filling; (*d'une vitre*) puttying.

mastication [mastikɑsjɔ̃] *nf* chewing, mastication.

mastiquer [mastike] *vt* (*aliment*) to chew, masticate; (*fente*) to fill; (*vitre*) to putty.

mastoc [mastɔk] *adj inv* hefty.

mastodonte [mastɔdɔ̃t] *nm* monster (*fig*).

masturbation [mastyʀbɑsjɔ̃] *nf* masturbation.

masturber [mastyʀbe] *vt*: **se ~** to masturbate.

m'as-tu-vu [matyvy] *nm/f inv* show-off.

masure [mazyʀ] *nf* tumbledown cottage.

mat, e [mat] *adj* (*couleur, métal*) mat(t); (*bruit, son*) dull ♦ *adj inv* (*ÉCHECS*): **être ~** to be checkmate.

mât [mɑ] *nm* (*NAVIG*) mast; (*poteau*) pole, post.

matamore [matamɔʀ] *nm* braggart, blusterer.

match [matʃ] *nm* match; **~ nul** draw, tie (*US*); **faire ~ nul** to draw (*BRIT*), tie (*US*); **~ aller** first leg; **~ retour** second leg, return match.

matelas [matla] *nm* mattress; **~ pneumatique** air bed *ou* mattress; **~ à ressorts** spring *ou* interior-sprung mattress.

matelasser [matlase] *vt* to pad.

matelot [matlo] *nm* sailor, seaman.

mater [mate] *vt* (*personne*) to bring to heel, subdue; (*révolte*) to put down; (*fam*) to watch, look at.

matérialisation [mateʀjalizɑsjɔ̃] *nf* materialization.

matérialiser [mateʀjalize]: **se ~** *vi* to materialize.

matérialisme [mateʀjalism(ə)] *nm* materialism.

matérialiste [mateʀjalist(ə)] *adj* materialistic ♦ *nm/f* materialist.

matériau, x [mateʀjo] *nm* material; **~x** *nmpl* material(s); **~x de construction** building materials.

matériel, le [mateʀjɛl] *adj* material; (*organisation, aide, obstacle*) practical; (*fig: péj: personne*) materialistic ♦ *nm* equipment *no pl*; (*de camping etc*) gear *no pl*; **il n'a pas le temps ~ de le faire** he doesn't have the time (needed) to do it; **~ d'exploitation** (*COMM*) plant; **~ roulant** rolling stock.

matériellement [mateʀjɛlmɑ̃] *adv* (*financièrement*) materially; **~ à l'aise** comfortably off; **je n'en ai ~ pas le temps** I simply do not have the time.

maternel, le [matɛʀnɛl] *adj* (*amour, geste*) motherly, maternal; (*grand-père, oncle*) maternal ♦ *nf* (*aussi*: **école ~le**) (state) nursery school.

materner [matɛʀne] *vt* (*personne*) to mother.

maternisé, e [matɛʀnize] *adj*: **lait ~** (infant) formula.

maternité [matɛʀnite] *nf* (*établissement*) maternity hospital; (*état de mère*) motherhood, maternity; (*grossesse*) pregnancy.

math [mat] *nfpl* maths (*BRIT*), math (*US*).

mathématicien, ne [matematisjɛ̃, -ɛn] *nm/f* mathematician.

mathématique [matematik] *adj* mathematical.

mathématiques [matematik] *nfpl* mathematics *sg.*
matheux, euse [matø, -øz] *nm/f* (*fam*) maths (*BRIT*) *ou* math (*US*) student; (*fort en math*) mathematical genius.
maths [mat] *nfpl* maths (*BRIT*), math (*US*).
matière [matjɛʀ] *nf* (*PHYSIQUE*) matter; (*COMM, TECH*) material; (*fig: d'un livre etc*) subject matter; (*SCOL*) subject; **en ~ de** as regards; **donner ~ à** to give cause to; **~ plastique** plastic; **~s fécales** faeces; **~s grasses** fat (content) *sg*; **~s premières** raw materials.
MATIF [matif] *sigle m* (= *Marché à terme des instruments financiers*) *body which regulates the activities of the French Stock Exchange*; *see boxed note.*

> **HÔTEL MATIGNON**
>
> *The* **hôtel Matignon** *is the Paris office and residence of the French Prime Minister. By extension, the term 'Matignon' is often used to refer to the Prime Minister and his or her staff.*

matin [matɛ̃] *nm, adv* morning; **le ~** (*pendant le ~*) in the morning; **demain ~** tomorrow morning; **le lendemain ~** (the) next morning; **du ~ au soir** from morning till night; **une heure du ~** one o'clock in the morning; **de grand** *ou* **bon ~** early in the morning.
matinal, e, aux [matinal, -o] *adj* (*toilette, gymnastique*) morning *cpd*; (*de bonne heure*) early; **être ~** (*personne*) to be up early; (*: habituellement*) to be an early riser.
mâtiné, e [mɑtine] *adj* crossbred, mixed race *cpd*.
matinée [matine] *nf* morning; (*spectacle*) matinée, afternoon performance.
matois, e [matwa, -waz] *adj* wily.
matou [matu] *nm* tom(cat).
matraquage [matʀakaʒ] *nm* beating up; **~ publicitaire** plug, plugging.
matraque [matʀak] *nf* (*de malfaiteur*) cosh (*BRIT*), club; (*de policier*) truncheon (*BRIT*), billy (*US*).
matraquer [matʀake] *vt* to beat up (with a truncheon *ou* billy); to cosh (*BRIT*), club; (*fig: touristes etc*) to rip off; (*: disque*) to plug.
matriarcal, e, aux [matʀijaʀkal, -o] *adj* matriarchal.
matrice [matʀis] *nf* (*ANAT*) womb; (*TECH*) mould; (*MATH etc*) matrix.
matricule [matʀikyl] *nf* (*aussi*: **registre ~**) roll, register ♦ *nm* (*aussi*: **numéro ~**: *MIL*) regimental number; (*: ADMIN*) reference number.
matrimonial, e, aux [matʀimɔnjal, -o] *adj* marital, marriage *cpd*.
matrone [matʀɔn] *nf* matron.
mâture [mɑtyʀ] *nf* masts *pl*.
maturité [matyʀite] *nf* maturity; (*d'un fruit*) ripeness, maturity.
maudire [modiʀ] *vt* to curse.
maudit, e [modi, -it] *adj* (*fam: satané*) blasted, confounded.
maugréer [mogʀee] *vi* to grumble.
mauresque [mɔʀɛsk(ə)] *adj* Moorish.
Maurice [mɔʀis] *nf*: **(l'île) ~** Mauritius.
mauricien, ne [mɔʀisjɛ̃, -ɛn] *adj* Mauritian.
Mauritanie [mɔʀitani] *nf*: **la ~** Mauritania.
mauritanien, ne [mɔʀitanjɛ̃, -ɛn] *adj* Mauritanian.
mausolée [mozɔle] *nm* mausoleum.
maussade [mosad] *adj* (*air, personne*) sullen; (*ciel, temps*) dismal.
mauvais, e [mɔvɛ, -ɛz] *adj* bad; (*faux*): **le ~ numéro** the wrong number; (*méchant, malveillant*) malicious, spiteful ♦ *nm*: **le ~** the bad side ♦ *adv*: **il fait ~** the weather is bad; **sentir ~** to have a nasty smell, smell nasty; **la mer est ~e** the sea is rough; **~ coucheur** awkward customer; **~ coup** (*fig*) criminal venture; **~ garçon** tough; **~ pas** tight spot; **~ plaisant** hoaxer; **~ traitements** ill treatment *sg*; **~e herbe** weed; **~e langue** gossip, scandalmonger (*BRIT*); **~e passe** difficult situation; (*période*) bad patch; **~e tête** rebellious *ou* headstrong customer.
mauve [mov] *adj* (*couleur*) mauve ♦ *nf* (*BOT*) mallow.
mauviette [movjɛt] *nf* (*péj*) weakling.
maux [mo] *nmpl voir* **mal**.
max. *abr* (= *maximum*) max.
maximal, e, aux [maksimal, -o] *adj* maximal.
maxime [maksim] *nf* maxim.
maximum [maksimɔm] *adj, nm* maximum; **atteindre un/son ~** to reach a/his peak; **au ~** *adv* (*le plus possible*) to the full; as much as one can; (*tout au plus*) at the (very) most *ou* maximum.
Mayence [majɑ̃s] *n* Mainz.
mayonnaise [majɔnɛz] *nf* mayonnaise.
Mayotte [majɔt] *nf* Mayotte.
mazout [mazut] *nm* (fuel) oil; **chaudière/poêle à ~** oil-fired boiler/stove.
mazouté, e [mazute] *adj* oil-polluted.
MDM *sigle mpl* (= *Médecins du Monde*) *medical association for aid to Third World countries.*
M^{e} *abr* = **Maître**.
me, m' [m(ə)] *pron* me; (*réfléchi*) myself.
méandres [meɑ̃dʀ(ə)] *nmpl* meanderings.
mec [mɛk] *nm* (*fam*) guy, bloke (*BRIT*).
mécanicien, ne [mekanisjɛ̃, -ɛn] *nm/f* mechanic; (*RAIL*) (train *ou* engine) driver; **~ navigant** *ou* **de bord** (*AVIAT*) flight engineer.
mécanicien-dentiste [mekanisjɛ̃dɑ̃tist(ə)], **mécanicienne-dentiste** [mekanisjɛn-] (*pl* **~s-~s**) *nm/f* dental technician.
mécanique [mekanik] *adj* mechanical ♦ *nf* (*science*) mechanics *sg*; (*technologie*) mechanical engineering; (*mécanisme*) mechanism; engineering; works *pl*; **ennui ~** engine trouble *no pl*; **s'y connaître en ~** to be me-

chanically minded; ~ **hydraulique** hydraulics *sg*; ~ **ondulataire** wave mechanics *sg*.
mécaniquement [mekanikmɑ̃] *adv* mechanically.
mécanisation [mekanizɑsjɔ̃] *nf* mechanization.
mécaniser [mekanize] *vt* to mechanize.
mécanisme [mekanism(ə)] *nm* mechanism; ~ **du taux de change** exchange rate mechanism.
mécano [mekano] *nm* (*fam*) mechanic.
mécanographie [mekanɔɡʀafi] *nf* (mechanical) data processing.
mécène [mesɛn] *nm* patron.
méchamment [meʃamɑ̃] *adv* nastily, maliciously, spitefully; viciously.
méchanceté [meʃɑ̃ste] *nf* (*d'une personne, d'une parole*) nastiness, maliciousness, spitefulness; (*parole, action*) nasty *ou* spiteful *ou* malicious remark (*ou* action).
méchant, e [meʃɑ̃, -ɑ̃t] *adj* nasty, malicious, spiteful; (*enfant: pas sage*) naughty; (*animal*) vicious; (*avant le nom: valeur péjorative*) nasty; miserable; (*: intensive*) terrific.
mèche [mɛʃ] *nf* (*de lampe, bougie*) wick; (*d'un explosif*) fuse; (*MÉD*) pack, dressing; (*de vilebrequin, perceuse*) bit; (*de dentiste*) drill; (*de fouet*) lash; (*de cheveux*) lock; **se faire faire des** ~**s** (*chez le coiffeur*) to have one's hair streaked, have highlights put in one's hair; **vendre la** ~ to give the game away; **de** ~ **avec** in league with.
méchoui [meʃwi] *nm* *whole sheep barbecue*.
mécompte [mekɔ̃t] *nm* (*erreur*) miscalculation; (*déception*) disappointment.
méconnais [mekɔnɛ] *etc vb voir* **méconnaître**.
méconnaissable [mekɔnɛsabl(ə)] *adj* unrecognizable.
méconnaissais [mekɔnɛsɛ] *etc vb voir* **méconnaître**.
méconnaissance [mekɔnɛsɑ̃s] *nf* ignorance.
méconnaître [mekɔnɛtʀ(ə)] *vt* (*ignorer*) to be unaware of; (*mésestimer*) to misjudge.
méconnu, e [mekɔny] *pp de* **méconnaître** ♦ *adj* (*génie etc*) unrecognized.
mécontent, e [mekɔ̃tɑ̃, -ɑ̃t] *adj*: ~ **(de)** (*insatisfait*) discontented *ou* dissatisfied *ou* displeased (with); (*contrarié*) annoyed (at) ♦ *nm/f* malcontent, dissatisfied person.
mécontentement [mekɔ̃tɑ̃tmɑ̃] *nm* dissatisfaction, discontent, displeasure; annoyance.
mécontenter [mekɔ̃tɑ̃te] *vt* to displease.
Mecque [mɛk] *nf*: **la** ~ Mecca.
mécréant, e [mekʀeɑ̃, -ɑ̃t] *adj* (*peuple*) infidel; (*personne*) atheistic.
méd. *abr* = **médecin**.
médaille [medaj] *nf* medal.
médaillé, e [medaje] *nm/f* (*SPORT*) medalholder.
médaillon [medajɔ̃] *nm* (*portrait*) medallion; (*bijou*) locket; (*CULIN*) médaillon; **en** ~ *adj* (*carte etc*) inset.
médecin [medsɛ̃] *nm* doctor; ~ **du bord** (*NAVIG*) ship's doctor; ~ **généraliste** general practitioner, GP; ~ **légiste** forensic scientist (*BRIT*), medical examiner (*US*); ~ **traitant** family doctor, GP.
médecine [medsin] *nf* medicine; ~ **générale** general medicine; ~ **infantile** paediatrics *sg* (*BRIT*), pediatrics *sg* (*US*); ~ **légale** forensic medicine; ~ **préventive** preventive medicine; ~ **du travail** occupational *ou* industrial medicine; ~**s parallèles** *ou* **douces** alternative medicine.
médian, e [medjɑ̃, -an] *adj* median.
médias [medja] *nmpl*: **les** ~ the media.
médiateur, trice [medjatœʀ, -tʀis] *nm/f* (*voir médiation*) mediator; arbitrator.
médiathèque [medjatɛk] *nf* media library.
médiation [medjɑsjɔ̃] *nf* mediation; (*dans conflit social etc*) arbitration.
médiatique [medjatik] *adj* media *cpd*.
médiatisé, e [medjatize] *adj* reported in the media; **ce procès a été très** ~ (*péj*) this trial was turned into a media event.
médiator [medjatɔʀ] *nm* plectrum.
médical, e, aux [medikal, -o] *adj* medical; **visiteur** *ou* **délégué** ~ medical rep *ou* representative.
médicalement [medikalmɑ̃] *adv* medically.
médicament [medikamɑ̃] *nm* medicine, drug.
médicamenteux, euse [medikamɑ̃tø, -øz] *adj* medicinal.
médication [medikɑsjɔ̃] *nf* medication.
médicinal, e, aux [medisinal, -o] *adj* medicinal.
médico-légal, e, aux [medikɔlegal, -o] *adj* forensic.
médico-social, e, aux [medikɔsɔsjal, -o] *adj*: **assistance** ~**e** medical and social assistance.
médiéval, e, aux [medjeval, -o] *adj* medieval.
médiocre [medjɔkʀ(ə)] *adj* mediocre, poor.
médiocrité [medjɔkʀite] *nf* mediocrity.
médire [mediʀ] *vi*: ~ **de** to speak ill of.
médisance [medizɑ̃s] *nf* scandalmongering *no pl* (*BRIT*), mud-slinging *no pl*; (*propos*) piece of scandal *ou* malicious gossip.
médisant, e [medizɑ̃, -ɑ̃t] *vb voir* **médire** ♦ *adj* slanderous, malicious.
médit, e [medi, -it] *pp de* **médire**.
méditatif, ive [meditatif, -iv] *adj* thoughtful.
méditation [meditɑsjɔ̃] *nf* meditation.
méditer [medite] *vt* (*approfondir*) to meditate on, ponder (over); (*combiner*) to meditate ♦ *vi* to meditate; ~ **de faire** to contemplate doing, plan to do.
Méditerranée [mediteʀane] *nf*: **la (mer)** ~ the Mediterranean (Sea).
méditerranéen, ne [mediteʀaneɛ̃, -ɛn] *adj* Mediterranean ♦ *nm/f*: **M**~, **ne** Mediterranean.
médium [medjɔm] *nm* medium (*spiritualist*).
médius [medjys] *nm* middle finger.

méduse [medyz] *nf* jellyfish.
méduser [medyze] *vt* to dumbfound.
meeting [mitiŋ] *nm* (*POL, SPORT*) rally, meeting; ~ **d'aviation** air show.
méfait [mefɛ] *nm* (*faute*) misdemeanour, wrongdoing; ~**s** *nmpl* (*ravages*) ravages.
méfiance [mefjɑ̃s] *nf* mistrust, distrust.
méfiant, e [mefjɑ̃, -ɑ̃t] *adj* mistrustful, distrustful.
méfier [mefje]: **se** ~ *vi* to be wary; (*faire attention*) to be careful; **se** ~ **de** *vt* to mistrust, distrust, be wary of; to be careful about.
mégalomane [megalɔman] *adj* megalomaniac.
mégalomanie [megalɔmani] *nf* megalomania.
mégalopole [megalɔpɔl] *nf* megalopolis.
méga-octet [megaɔktɛ] *nm* megabyte.
mégarde [megaʀd(ə)] *nf*: **par** ~ accidentally; (*par erreur*) by mistake.
mégatonne [megatɔn] *nf* megaton.
mégère [meʒɛʀ] *nf* (*péj*: *femme*) shrew.
mégot [mego] *nm* cigarette end *ou* butt.
mégoter [megɔte] *vi* to nitpick.
meilleur, e [mɛjœʀ] *adj*, *adv* better; (*valeur superlative*) best ♦ *nm*: **le** ~ (*celui qui ...*) the best (one); (*ce qui ...*) the best ♦ *nf*: **la** ~**e** the best (one); **le** ~ **des deux** the better of the two; **de** ~**e heure** earlier; ~ **marché** cheaper.
méjuger [meʒyʒe] *vt* to misjudge.
mél [mɛl] *nm* e mail.
mélancolie [melɑ̃kɔli] *nf* melancholy, gloom.
mélancolique [melɑ̃kɔlik] *adj* melancholy, gloomy.
Mélanésie [melanezi] *nf*: **la** ~ Melanesia.
mélange [melɑ̃ʒ] *nm* (*opération*) mixing; blending; (*résultat*) mixture; blend; **sans** ~ unadulterated.
mélanger [melɑ̃ʒe] *vt* (*substances*) to mix; (*vins, couleurs*) to blend; (*mettre en désordre, confondre*) to mix up, muddle (up); **se** ~ (*liquides, couleurs*) to blend, mix.
mélanine [melanin] *nf* melanin.
mélasse [melas] *nf* treacle, molasses *sg*.
mêlée [mele] *nf* (*bataille, cohue*) mêlée, scramble; (*lutte, conflit*) tussle, scuffle; (*RUGBY*) scrum(mage).
mêler [mele] *vt* (*substances, odeurs, races*) to mix; (*embrouiller*) to muddle (up), mix up; **se** ~ to mix; (*se joindre, s'allier*) to mingle; **se** ~ **à** (*suj: personne*) to join; to mix with; (*: odeurs etc*) to mingle with; **se** ~ **de** (*suj: personne*) to meddle with, interfere in; **mêle-toi de tes affaires!** mind your own business!; ~ **à** *ou* **avec** *ou* **de** to mix with; to mingle with; ~ **qn à** (*affaire*) to get sb mixed up *ou* involved in.
mélo [melo] *nm, adj* = **mélodrame, mélodramatique**.
mélodie [melɔdi] *nf* melody.
mélodieux, euse [melɔdjø, -øz] *adj* melodious, tuneful.
mélodique [melɔdik] *adj* melodic.
mélodramatique [melɔdʀamatik] *adj* melodramatic.
mélodrame [melɔdʀam] *nm* melodrama.
mélomane [melɔman] *nm/f* music lover.
melon [məlɔ̃] *nm* (*BOT*) (honeydew) melon; (*aussi*: **chapeau** ~) bowler (hat); ~ **d'eau** watermelon.
mélopée [melɔpe] *nf* monotonous chant.
membrane [mɑ̃bʀan] *nf* membrane.
membre [mɑ̃bʀ(ə)] *nm* (*ANAT*) limb; (*personne, pays, élément*) member ♦ *adj* member; **être** ~ **de** to be a member of; ~ **(viril)** (male) organ.
mémé [meme] *nf* (*fam*) granny; (*: vieille femme*) old dear.

MOT-CLÉ

même [mɛm] *adj* **1** (*avant le nom*) same; **en** ~ **temps** at the same time; **ils ont les** ~**s goûts** they have the same *ou* similar tastes
2 (*après le nom*: *renforcement*): **il est la loyauté** ~ he is loyalty itself; **ce sont ses paroles/celles-là** ~ they are his very words/ the very ones
♦ *pron*: **le(la)** ~ the same one
♦ *adv* **1** (*renforcement*): **il n'a** ~ **pas pleuré** he didn't even cry; ~ **lui l'a dit** even *HE* said it; **ici** ~ at this very place; ~ **si** even if
2: **à** ~: **à** ~ **la bouteille** straight from the bottle; **à** ~ **la peau** next to the skin; **être à** ~ **de faire** to be in a position to do, be able to do; **mettre qn à** ~ **de faire** to enable sb to do
3: **de** ~ likewise; **faire de** ~ to do likewise *ou* the same; **lui de** ~ so does (*ou* did *ou* is) he; **de** ~ **que** just as; **il en va de** ~ **pour** the same goes for.

mémento [memɛ̃to] *nm* (*agenda*) appointments diary; (*ouvrage*) summary.
mémoire [memwaʀ] *nf* memory ♦ *nm* (*ADMIN, JUR*) memorandum (*pl* -a); (*SCOL*) dissertation, paper; **avoir la** ~ **des visages/chiffres** to have a (good) memory for faces/figures; **n'avoir aucune** ~ to have a terrible memory; **avoir de la** ~ to have a good memory; **à la** ~ **de** to the *ou* in memory of; **pour** ~ *adv* for the record; **de** ~ *adv* from memory; **de** ~ **d'homme** in living memory; **mettre en** ~ (*INFORM*) to store; ~ **morte** ROM; ~ **rémanente** *ou* **non volatile** non-volatile memory; ~ **vive** RAM.
mémoires [memwaʀ] *nmpl* memoirs.
mémorable [memɔʀabl(ə)] *adj* memorable.
mémorandum [memɔʀɑ̃dɔm] *nm* memorandum (*pl* -a); (*carnet*) notebook.
mémorial, aux [memɔʀjal, -o] *nm* memorial.
mémoriser [memɔʀize] *vt* to memorize; (*INFORM*) to store.
menaçant, e [mənasɑ̃, -ɑ̃t] *adj* threatening, menacing.
menace [mənas] *nf* threat; ~ **en l'air** empty threat.
menacer [mənase] *vt* to threaten; ~ **qn de qch/de faire qch** to threaten sb with sth/to

do sth.

ménage [menaʒ] *nm* (*travail*) housekeeping, housework; (*couple*) (married) couple; (*famille, ADMIN*) household; **faire le ~** to do the housework; **faire des ~s** to work as a cleaner (*in people's homes*); **monter son ~** to set up house; **se mettre en ~ (avec)** to set up house (with); **heureux en ~** happily married; **faire bon ~ avec** to get on well with; **~ de poupée** doll's kitchen set; **~ à trois** love triangle.

ménagement [menaʒmɑ̃] *nm* care and attention; **~s** *nmpl* (*égards*) consideration *sg*, attention *sg*.

ménager [menaʒe] *vt* (*traiter avec mesure*) to handle with tact; to treat considerately; (*utiliser*) to use with care; (*: avec économie*) to use sparingly; (*prendre soin de*) to take (great) care of, look after; (*organiser*) to arrange; (*installer*) to put in; to make; **se ~** to look after o.s.; **~ qch à qn** (*réserver*) to have sth in store for sb.

ménager, ère [menaʒe, -ɛʀ] *adj* household *cpd*, domestic ♦ *nf* (*femme*) housewife (*pl* -wives); (*couverts*) canteen (of cutlery).

ménagerie [menaʒʀi] *nf* menagerie.

mendiant, e [mɑ̃djɑ̃, -ɑ̃t] *nm/f* beggar.

mendicité [mɑ̃disite] *nf* begging.

mendier [mɑ̃dje] *vi* to beg ♦ *vt* to beg (for); (*fig: éloges, compliments*) to fish for.

menées [məne] *nfpl* intrigues, manœuvres (*BRIT*), maneuvers (*US*); (*COMM*) activities.

mener [məne] *vt* to lead; (*enquête*) to conduct; (*affaires*) to manage, conduct, run ♦ *vi*: **~ (à la marque)** to lead, be in the lead; **~ à/dans** (*emmener*) to take to/into; **~ qch à bonne fin** *ou* **à terme** *ou* **à bien** to see sth through (to a successful conclusion), complete sth successfully.

meneur, euse [mənœʀ, -øz] *nm/f* leader; (*péj: agitateur*) ringleader; **~ d'hommes** born leader; **~ de jeu** host, quizmaster (*BRIT*).

menhir [meniʀ] *nm* standing stone.

méningite [menɛ̃ʒit] *nf* meningitis *no pl*.

ménisque [menisk] *nm* (*ANAT*) meniscus.

ménopause [menɔpoz] *nf* menopause.

menotte [mənɔt] *nf* (*langage enfantin*) handie; **~s** *nfpl* handcuffs; **passer les ~s à** to handcuff.

mens [mɑ̃] *vb voir* **mentir**.

mensonge [mɑ̃sɔ̃ʒ] *nm*: **le ~** lying *no pl*; **un ~** a lie.

mensonger, ère [mɑ̃sɔ̃ʒe, -ɛʀ] *adj* false.

menstruation [mɑ̃stʀyɑsjɔ̃] *nf* menstruation.

menstruel, le [mɑ̃stʀyɛl] *adj* menstrual.

mensualiser [mɑ̃sɥalize] *vt* to pay monthly.

mensualité [mɑ̃sɥalite] *nf* (*somme payée*) monthly payment; (*somme perçue*) monthly salary.

mensuel, le [mɑ̃sɥɛl] *adj* monthly ♦ *nm/f* (*employé*) employee paid monthly ♦ *nm* (*PRESSE*) monthly.

mensuellement [mɑ̃sɥɛlmɑ̃] *adv* monthly.

mensurations [mɑ̃syʀɑsjɔ̃] *nfpl* measurements.

mentais [mɑ̃tɛ] *etc vb voir* **mentir**.

mental, e, aux [mɑ̃tal, -o] *adj* mental.

mentalement [mɑ̃talmɑ̃] *adv* in one's head, mentally.

mentalité [mɑ̃talite] *nf* mentality.

menteur, euse [mɑ̃tœʀ, -øz] *nm/f* liar.

menthe [mɑ̃t] *nf* mint; **~ (à l'eau)** peppermint cordial.

mentholé, e [mɑ̃tɔle] *adj* menthol *cpd*, mentholated.

mention [mɑ̃sjɔ̃] *nf* (*note*) note, comment; (*SCOL*): **~ (très) bien/passable** *(very) good/satisfactory pass*; **faire ~ de** to mention; **"rayer la ~ inutile"** "delete as appropriate".

mentionner [mɑ̃sjɔne] *vt* to mention.

mentir [mɑ̃tiʀ] *vi* to lie.

menton [mɑ̃tɔ̃] *nm* chin.

mentonnière [mɑ̃tɔnjɛʀ] *nf* chin strap.

menu, e [məny] *adj* (*mince*) thin; (*petit*) tiny; (*frais, difficulté*) minor ♦ *adv* (*couper, hacher*) very fine ♦ *nm* menu; **par le ~** (*raconter*) in minute detail; **~ touristique** popular *ou* tourist menu; **~e monnaie** small change.

menuet [mənɥɛ] *nm* minuet.

menuiserie [mənɥizʀi] *nf* (*travail*) joinery, carpentry; (*d'amateur*) woodwork; (*local*) joiner's workshop; (*ouvrages*) woodwork *no pl*.

menuisier [mənɥizje] *nm* joiner, carpenter.

méprendre [mepʀɑ̃dʀ(ə)]: **se ~** *vi*: **se ~ sur** to be mistaken about.

mépris, e [mepʀi, -iz] *pp de* **méprendre** ♦ *nm* (*dédain*) contempt, scorn; (*indifférence*): **le ~ de** contempt *ou* disregard for; **au ~ de** regardless of, in defiance of.

méprisable [mepʀizabl(ə)] *adj* contemptible, despicable.

méprisant, e [mepʀizɑ̃, -ɑ̃t] *adj* contemptuous, scornful.

méprise [mepʀiz] *nf* mistake, error; (*malentendu*) misunderstanding.

mépriser [mepʀize] *vt* to scorn, despise; (*gloire, danger*) to scorn, spurn.

mer [mɛʀ] *nf* sea; (*marée*) tide; **~ fermée** inland sea; **en ~** at sea; **prendre la ~** to put out to sea; **en haute** *ou* **pleine ~** off shore, on the open sea; **la ~ Adriatique** the Adriatic (Sea); **la ~ des Antilles** *ou* **des Caraïbes** the Caribbean (Sea); **la ~ Baltique** the Baltic (Sea); **la ~ Caspienne** the Caspian Sea; **la ~ de Corail** the Coral Sea; **la ~ Égée** the Aegean (Sea); **la ~ Ionienne** the Ionian Sea; **la ~ Morte** the Dead Sea; **la ~ Noire** the Black Sea; **la ~ du Nord** the North Sea; **la ~ Rouge** the Red Sea; **la ~ des Sargasses** the Sargasso Sea, the Sargasso Sea; **les ~s du Sud** the South Seas; **la ~ Tyrrhénienne** the Tyrrhenian Sea.

mercantile [mɛʀkɑ̃til] *adj* (*péj*) mercenary.

mercantilisme [mɛʀkɑ̃tilism(ə)] *nm* (*esprit*

mercantile) mercenary attitude.
mercenaire [mɛʀsənɛʀ] *nm* mercenary.
mercerie [mɛʀsəʀi] *nf* (*COUTURE*) haberdashery (*BRIT*), notions *pl* (*US*); (*boutique*) haberdasher's shop (*BRIT*), notions store (*US*).
merci [mɛʀsi] *excl* thank you ♦ *nf*: **à la ~ de qn/qch** at sb's mercy/the mercy of sth; ~ **beaucoup** thank you very much; ~ **de** *ou* **pour** thank you for; **sans ~** *adj* merciless ♦ *adv* mercilessly.
mercier, ière [mɛʀsje, -jɛʀ] *nm/f* haberdasher.
mercredi [mɛʀkʀədi] *nm* Wednesday; ~ **des Cendres** Ash Wednesday; *voir aussi* **lundi**.
mercure [mɛʀkyʀ] *nm* mercury.
merde [mɛʀd(ə)] (*fam!*) *nf* shit (*!*) ♦ *excl* (bloody) hell (*!*).
merdeux, euse [mɛʀdø, -øz] *nm/f* (*fam!*) little bugger (*BRIT !*), little devil.
mère [mɛʀ] *nf* mother ♦ *adj inv* mother *cpd*; ~ **célibataire** single parent, unmarried mother.
merguez [mɛʀgɛz] *nf* *spicy North African sausage.*
méridien [meʀidjɛ̃] *nm* meridian.
méridional, e, aux [meʀidjɔnal, -o] *adj* southern; (*du midi de la France*) Southern (French) ♦ *nm/f* Southerner.
meringue [məʀɛ̃g] *nf* meringue.
mérinos [meʀinos] *nm* merino.
merisier [məʀizje] *nm* wild cherry (tree).
méritant, e [meʀitɑ̃, -ɑ̃t] *adj* deserving.
mérite [meʀit] *nm* merit; **le ~ (de ceci) lui revient** the credit (for this) is his.
mériter [meʀite] *vt* to deserve; ~ **de réussir** to deserve to succeed; **il mérite qu'on fasse ...** he deserves people to do ....
méritocratie [meʀitɔkʀasi] *nf* meritocracy.
méritoire [meʀitwaʀ] *adj* praiseworthy, commendable.
merlan [mɛʀlɑ̃] *nm* whiting.
merle [mɛʀl(ə)] *nm* blackbird.
mérou [meʀu] *nm* grouper (*fish*).
merveille [mɛʀvɛj] *nf* marvel, wonder; **faire ~** *ou* **des ~s** to work wonders; **à ~** perfectly, wonderfully.
merveilleux, euse [mɛʀvɛjø, -øz] *adj* marvellous, wonderful.
mes [me] *adj possessif voir* **mon**.
mésalliance [mezaljɑ̃s] *nf* misalliance, mismatch.
mésallier [mezalje]: **se ~** *vi* to marry beneath (*ou* above) o.s.
mésange [mezɑ̃ʒ] *nf* tit(mouse) (*pl* -mice); ~ **bleue** bluetit.
mésaventure [mezavɑ̃tyʀ] *nf* misadventure, misfortune.
Mesdames [medam] *nfpl voir* **Madame**.
Mesdemoiselles [medmwazɛl] *nfpl voir* **Mademoiselle**.
mésentente [mezɑ̃tɑ̃t] *nf* dissension, disagreement.
mésestimer [mezɛstime] *vt* to underestimate, underrate.
Mésopotamie [mezɔpɔtami] *nf*: **la ~** Mesopotamia.
mésopotamien, ne [mezɔpɔtamjɛ̃, -ɛn] *adj* Mesopotamian.
mesquin, e [mɛskɛ̃, -in] *adj* mean, petty.
mesquinerie [mɛskinʀi] *nf* meanness *no pl*, pettiness *no pl*.
mess [mɛs] *nm* mess.
message [mesaʒ] *nm* message; ~ **d'erreur** (*INFORM*) error message; ~ **(de guidage)** (*INFORM*) prompt; ~ **publicitaire** ad, advertisement; ~ **téléphoné** telegram dictated by telephone.
messager, ère [mesaʒe, -ɛʀ] *nm/f* messenger.
messagerie [mesaʒʀi] *nf*: ~ **(électronique)** (electronic) bulletin board; ~ **rose** *lonely hearts and contact service on videotext*; ~ **vocale** (*service*) voice mail; **~s aériennes/maritimes** air freight/shipping service *sg*; **~s de presse** press distribution service.
messe [mɛs] *nf* mass; **aller à la ~** to go to mass; ~ **de minuit** midnight mass; **faire des ~s basses** (*fig, péj*) to mutter.
messie [mesi] *nm*: **le M~** the Messiah.
Messieurs [mesjø] *nmpl voir* **Monsieur**.
mesure [məzyʀ] *nf* (*évaluation, dimension*) measurement; (*étalon, récipient, contenu*) measure; (*MUS*: *cadence*) time, tempo; (*: division*) bar; (*retenue*) moderation; (*disposition*) measure, step; **unité/système de ~** unit/system of measurement; **sur ~** (*costume*) made-to-measure; (*fig*) personally adapted; **à la ~ de** (*fig: personne*) worthy of; (*chambre etc*) on the same scale as; **dans la ~ où** insofar as, inasmuch as; **dans une certaine ~** to some *ou* a certain extent; **à ~ que** as; **en ~** (*MUS*) in time *ou* tempo; **être en ~ de** to be in a position to; **dépasser la ~** (*fig*) to overstep the mark.
mesuré, e [məzyʀe] *adj* (*ton, effort*) measured; (*personne*) restrained.
mesurer [məzyʀe] *vt* to measure; (*juger*) to weigh up, assess; (*limiter*) to limit, ration; (*modérer*) to moderate; (*proportionner*): ~ **qch à** to match sth to, gear sth to; **se ~ avec** to have a confrontation with; to tackle; **il mesure 1 m 80** he's 1 m 80 tall.
met [mɛ] *vb voir* **mettre**.
métabolisme [metabɔlism(ə)] *nm* metabolism.
métairie [meteʀi] *nf* smallholding.
métal, aux [metal, -o] *nm* metal.
métalangage [metalɑ̃gaʒ] *nm* metalanguage.
métallique [metalik] *adj* metallic.
métallisé, e [metalize] *adj* metallic.
métallurgie [metalyʀʒi] *nf* metallurgy.
métallurgique [metalyʀʒik] *adj* steel *cpd*, metal *cpd*.
métallurgiste [metalyʀʒist(ə)] *nm/f* (*ouvrier*) steel *ou* metal worker; (*industriel*) metallurgist.
métamorphose [metamɔʀfoz] *nf* metamor-

phosis (*pl* -oses).
métamorphoser [metamɔRfoze] *vt* to transform.
métaphore [metafɔR] *nf* metaphor.
métaphorique [metafɔRik] *adj* metaphorical, figurative.
métaphoriquement [metafɔRikmɑ̃] *adv* metaphorically.
métaphysique [metafizik] *nf* metaphysics *sg* ♦ *adj* metaphysical.
métapsychique [metapsiʃik] *adj* psychic, parapsychological.
métayer, ère [meteje, metɛjɛR] *nm/f* (tenant) farmer.
météo [meteo] *nf* (*bulletin*) (weather) forecast; (*service*) ≈ Met Office (*BRIT*), ≈ National Weather Service (*US*).
météore [meteɔR] *nm* meteor.
météorite [meteɔRit] *nm ou f* meteorite.
météorologie [meteɔRɔlɔʒi] *nf* (*étude*) meteorology; (*service*) ≈ Meteorological Office (*BRIT*), ≈ National Weather Service (*US*).
météorologique [meteɔRɔlɔʒik] *adj* meteorological, weather *cpd*.
météorologue [meteɔRɔlɔg] *nm/f*, **météorologiste** [meteɔRɔlɔʒist(ə)] *nm/f* meteorologist, weather forecaster.
métèque [metɛk] *nm* (*péj*) wop (*!*).
méthane [metan] *nm* methane.
méthanier [metanje] *nm* (*bateau*) (liquefied) gas carrier *ou* tanker.
méthode [metɔd] *nf* method; (*livre, ouvrage*) manual, tutor.
méthodique [metɔdik] *adj* methodical.
méthodiquement [metɔdikmɑ̃] *adv* methodically.
méthodiste [metɔdist(ə)] *adj, nm/f* (*REL*) Methodist.
méthylène [metilɛn] *nm*: **bleu de** ~ *nm* methylene blue.
méticuleux, euse [metikylø, -øz] *adj* meticulous.
métier [metje] *nm* (*profession: gén*) job; (*: manuel*) trade; (*: artisanal*) craft; (*technique, expérience*) (acquired) skill *ou* technique; (*aussi*: ~ **à tisser**) (weaving) loom; **être du** ~ to be in the trade *ou* profession.
métis, se [metis] *adj, nm/f* half-caste, half-breed.
métisser [metise] *vt* to cross(breed).
métrage [metRaʒ] *nm* (*de tissu*) length; (*CINÉ*) footage, length; **long/moyen/court** ~ feature *ou* full-length/medium-length/short film.
mètre [mɛtR(ə)] *nm* metre (*BRIT*), meter (*US*); (*règle*) (metre *ou* meter) rule; (*ruban*) tape measure; ~ **carré/cube** square/cubic metre *ou* meter.
métrer [metRe] *vt* (*TECH*) to measure (in metres *ou* meters); (*CONSTR*) to survey.
métreur, euse [metRœR, -øz] *nm/f*: ~ **(vérificateur), métreuse (vérificatrice)** (quantity) surveyor.
métrique [metRik] *adj* metric ♦ *nf* metrics *sg*.
métro [metRo] *nm* underground (*BRIT*), subway (*US*).
métronome [metRɔnɔm] *nm* metronome.
métropole [metRɔpɔl] *nf* (*capitale*) metropolis; (*pays*) home country.
métropolitain, e [metRɔpɔlitɛ̃, -ɛn] *adj* metropolitan.
mets [mɛ] *nm* dish ♦ *vb voir* **mettre**.
mettable [mɛtabl(ə)] *adj* fit to be worn, decent.
metteur [mɛtœR] *nm*: ~ **en scène** (*THÉÂT*) producer; (*CINÉ*) director; ~ **en ondes** (*RADIO*) producer.

MOT-CLÉ

mettre [mɛtR(ə)] *vt* **1** (*placer*) to put; ~ **en bouteille/en sac** to bottle/put in bags *ou* sacks; ~ **qch à la poste** to post sth (*BRIT*), mail sth; ~ **en examen (pour)** to charge (with) (*BRIT*), indict (for) (*US*); ~ **une note gaie/amusante** to inject a cheerful/an amusing note; ~ **qn debout/assis** to help sb up *ou* to their feet/help sb to sit down
2 (*vêtements: revêtir*) to put on; (*: porter*) to wear; **mets ton gilet** put your cardigan on; **je ne mets plus mon manteau** I no longer wear my coat
3 (*faire fonctionner: chauffage, électricité*) to put on; (*: reveil, minuteur*) to set; (*installer: gaz, eau*) to put in, lay on; ~ **en marche** to start up
4 (*consacrer*): ~ **du temps/2 heures à faire qch** to take time/2 hours to do sth *ou* over sth; **y** ~ **du sien** to pull one's weight
5 (*noter, écrire*) to say, put (down); **qu'est-ce qu'il a mis sur la carte?** what did he say *ou* write on the card?; **mettez au pluriel** ... put ... into the plural
6 (*supposer*): **mettons que** ... let's suppose *ou* say that ...
7 (*faire +vb*): **faire** ~ **le gaz/l'électricité** to have gas/electricity put in *ou* installed
se ~ *vi* **1** (*se placer*): **vous pouvez vous** ~ **là** you can sit (*ou* stand) there; **où ça se met?** where does it go?; **se** ~ **au lit** to get into bed; **se** ~ **au piano** to sit down at the piano; **se** ~ **à l'eau** to get into the water; **se** ~ **de l'encre sur les doigts** to get ink on one's fingers
2 (*s'habiller*): **se** ~ **en maillot de bain** to get into *ou* put on a swimsuit; **n'avoir rien à se** ~ to have nothing to wear
3 (*dans rapports*): **se** ~ **bien/mal avec qn** to get on the right/wrong side of sb; **se** ~ **qn à dos** to get on sb's bad side; **se** ~ **avec qn** (*prendre parti*) to side with sb; (*faire équipe*) to team up with sb; (*en ménage*) to move in with sb
4: **se** ~ **à** to begin, start; **se** ~ **à faire** to begin *ou* start doing *ou* to do; **se** ~ **au piano** to

start learning the piano; **se ~ au régime** to go on a diet; **se ~ au travail/à l'étude** to get down to work/one's studies; **il est temps de s'y ~** it's time we got down to it *ou* got on with it.

meublant, e [mœblɑ̃, -ɑ̃t] *adj* (*tissus etc*) effective (in the room).
meuble [mœbl(ə)] *nm* (*objet*) piece of furniture; (*ameublement*) furniture *no pl* ♦ *adj* (*terre*) loose, friable; (*JUR*): **biens ~s** movables.
meublé [mœble] *nm* (*pièce*) furnished room; (*appartement*) furnished flat (*BRIT*) *ou* apartment (*US*).
meubler [mœble] *vt* to furnish; (*fig*): **~ qch (de)** to fill sth (with); **se ~** to furnish one's house.
meugler [møgle] *vi* to low, moo.
meule [møl] *nf* (*à broyer*) millstone; (*à aiguiser*) grindstone; (*à polir*) buffwheel; (*de foin, blé*) stack; (*de fromage*) round.
meunerie [mønʀi] *nf* (*industrie*) flour trade; (*métier*) milling.
meunier, ière [mønje, -jɛʀ] *nm* miller ♦ *nf* miller's wife ♦ *adj f* (*CULIN*) meunière.
meurs [mœʀ] *etc vb voir* **mourir**.
meurtre [mœʀtʀ(ə)] *nm* murder.
meurtrier, ière [mœʀtʀije, -jɛʀ] *adj* (*arme, épidémie, combat*) deadly; (*accident*) fatal; (*carrefour, route*) lethal; (*fureur, instincts*) murderous ♦ *nm/f* murderer/murderess ♦ *nf* (*ouverture*) loophole.
meurtrir [mœʀtʀiʀ] *vt* to bruise; (*fig*) to wound.
meurtrissure [mœʀtʀisyʀ] *nf* bruise; (*fig*) scar.
meus [mœ] *etc vb voir* **mouvoir**.
Meuse [mœz] *nf*: **la ~** the Meuse.
meute [møt] *nf* pack.
meuve [mœv] *etc vb voir* **mouvoir**.
mévente [mevɑ̃t] *nf* slump (in sales).
mexicain, e [mɛksikɛ̃, -ɛn] *adj* Mexican ♦ *nm/f*: **M~, e** Mexican.
Mexico [mɛksiko] *n* Mexico City.
Mexique [mɛksik] *nm*: **le ~** Mexico.
mezzanine [mɛdzanin] *nf* mezzanine (floor).
MF *sigle mpl = millions de francs* ♦ *sigle f* (*RADIO*: = *modulation de fréquence*) FM.
Mgr *abr* = **Monseigneur**.
mi [mi] *nm* (*MUS*) E; (*en chantant la gamme*) mi.
mi... [mi] *préfixe* half(-); mid-; **à la ~-janvier** in mid-January; **~-bureau, ~-chambre** half office, half bedroom; **à ~-jambes/-corps** (up *ou* down) to the knees/waist; **à ~-hauteur/-pente** halfway up (*ou* down)/up (*ou* down) the hill.
miaou [mjau] *nm* miaow.
miaulement [mjolmɑ̃] *nm* (*cri*) miaow; (*continu*) miaowing *no pl*.
miauler [mjole] *vi* to miaow.
mi-bas [mibɑ] *nm inv* knee-length sock.
mica [mika] *nm* mica.
mi-carême [mikaʀɛm] *nf*: **la ~** the third Thursday in Lent.
miche [miʃ] *nf* round *ou* cob loaf.
mi-chemin [miʃmɛ̃]: **à ~** *adv* halfway, midway.
mi-clos, e [miklo, -kloz] *adj* half-closed.
micmac [mikmak] *nm* (*péj*) carry-on.
mi-côte [mikot]: **à ~** *adv* halfway up (*ou* down) the hill.
mi-course [mikuʀs]: **à ~** *adv* halfway through the race.
micro [mikʀo] *nm* mike, microphone; (*INFORM*) micro; **~ cravate** lapel mike.
microbe [mikʀɔb] *nm* germ, microbe.
microbiologie [mikʀɔbjɔlɔʒi] *nf* microbiology.
microchirurgie [mikʀɔʃiʀyʀʒi] *nf* microsurgery.
microclimat [mikʀoklima] *nm* microclimate.
microcosme [mikʀɔkɔsm(ə)] *nm* microcosm.
micro-édition [mikʀɔedisjɔ̃] *nf* desk-top publishing.
micro-électronique [mikʀɔelɛktʀɔnik] *nf* microelectronics *sg*.
microfiche [mikʀɔfiʃ] *nf* microfiche.
microfilm [mikʀɔfilm] *nm* microfilm.
micro-onde [mikʀɔɔ̃d] *nf*: **four à ~s** microwave oven.
micro-ordinateur [mikʀɔɔʀdinatœʀ] *nm* microcomputer.
micro-organisme [mikʀɔɔʀganism(ə)] *nm* micro-organism.
microphone [mikʀɔfɔn] *nm* microphone.
microplaquette [mikʀɔplakɛt] *nf* microchip.
microprocesseur [mikʀɔpʀɔsɛsœʀ] *nm* microprocessor.
microscope [mikʀɔskɔp] *nm* microscope; **au ~** under *ou* through the microscope.
microscopique [mikʀɔskɔpik] *adj* microscopic.
microsillon [mikʀɔsijɔ̃] *nm* long-playing record.
MIDEM [midɛm] *sigle m* (= *Marché international du disque et de l'édition musicale*) *music industry trade fair*.
midi [midi] *nm* (*milieu du jour*) midday, noon; (*moment du déjeuner*) lunchtime; (*sud*) south; (*: de la France*): **le M~** the South (of France), the Midi; **à ~** at 12 (o'clock) *ou* midday *ou* noon; **tous les ~s** every lunchtime; **le repas de ~** lunch; **en plein ~** (right) in the middle of the day; (*sud*) facing south.
midinette [midinɛt] *nf* silly young townie.
mie [mi] *nf* inside (of the loaf).
miel [mjɛl] *nm* honey; **être tout ~** (*fig*) to be all sweetness and light.
mielleux, euse [mjɛlø, -øz] *adj* (*péj*) sugary, honeyed.
mien, ne [mjɛ̃, mjɛn] *adj, pron*: **le (la) ~(ne), les ~s** mine; **les ~s** (*ma famille*) my family.
miette [mjɛt] *nf* (*de pain, gâteau*) crumb; (*fig: de la conversation etc*) scrap; **en ~s** (*fig*) in

pieces *ou* bits.

MOT-CLÉ

mieux [mjø] *adv* **1** (*d'une meilleure façon*): ~ **(que)** better (than); **elle travaille/mange** ~ she works/eats better; **aimer** ~ to prefer; **j'attendais** ~ **de vous** I expected better of you; **elle va** ~ she is better; **de** ~ **en** ~ better and better

2 (*de la meilleure façon*) best; **ce que je sais le** ~ what I know best; **les livres les** ~ **faits** the best made books

3 (*intensif*): **vous feriez** ~ **de faire ...** you would be better to do ...; **crier à qui** ~ ~ to try to shout each other down

♦ *adj* **1** (*plus à l'aise, en meilleure forme*) better; **se sentir** ~ to feel better

2 (*plus satisfaisant*) better; **c'est** ~ **ainsi** it's better like this; **c'est le** ~ **des deux** it's the better of the two; **le(la)** ~, **les** ~ the best; **demandez-lui, c'est le** ~ ask him, it's the best thing

3 (*plus joli*) better-looking; (*plus gentil*) nicer; **il est** ~ **que son frère** (*plus beau*) he's better-looking than his brother; (*plus gentil*) he's nicer than his brother; **il est** ~ **sans moustache** he looks better without a moustache

4: **au** ~ at best; **au** ~ **avec** on the best of terms with; **pour le** ~ for the best; **qui** ~ **est** even better, better still

♦ *nm* **1** (*progrès*) improvement

2: **de mon/ton** ~ as best I/you can (*ou* could); **faire de son** ~ to do one's best; **du** ~ **qu'il peut** the best he can; **faute de** ~ for want of anything better, failing anything better.

mieux-être [mjøzɛtʀ(ə)] *nm* greater well-being; (*financier*) improved standard of living.
mièvre [mjɛvʀ(ə)] *adj* sickly sentimental.
mignon, ne [miɲɔ̃, -ɔn] *adj* sweet, cute.
migraine [migʀɛn] *nf* headache; migraine.
migrant, e [migʀɑ̃, -ɑ̃t] *adj, nm/f* migrant.
migrateur, trice [migʀatœʀ, -tʀis] *adj* migratory.
migration [migʀɑsjɔ̃] *nf* migration.
mijaurée [miʒɔʀe] *nf* pretentious (young) madam.
mijoter [miʒɔte] *vt* to simmer; (*préparer avec soin*) to cook lovingly; (*affaire, projet*) to plot, cook up ♦ *vi* to simmer.
mil [mil] *num* = **mille**.
Milan [milɑ̃] *n* Milan.
milanais, e [milanɛ, -ɛz] *adj* Milanese.
mildiou [mildju] *nm* mildew.
milice [milis] *nf* militia.
milicien, ne [milisjɛ̃, -ɛn] *nm/f* militiaman/woman.
milieu, x [miljø] *nm* (*centre*) middle; (*fig*) middle course *ou* way; (*aussi*: **juste** ~) happy medium; (*BIO, GÉO*) environment; (*entourage social*) milieu; (*familial*) background; circle; (*pègre*): **le** ~ the underworld; **au** ~ **de** in the middle of; **au beau** *ou* **en plein** ~ **(de)** right in the middle (of); ~ **de terrain** (*FOOTBALL*: *joueur*) midfield player; (*: joueurs*) midfield.
militaire [militɛʀ] *adj* military ♦ *nm* serviceman; **service** ~ military service.
militant, e [militɑ̃, -ɑ̃t] *adj, nm/f* militant.
militantisme [militɑ̃tism(ə)] *nm* militancy.
militariser [militaʀize] *vt* to militarize.
militarisme [militaʀism(ə)] *nm* (*péj*) militarism.
militer [milite] *vi* to be a militant; ~ **pour/contre** to militate in favour of/against.
milk-shake [milkʃɛk] *nm* milk shake.
mille [mil] *num* a *ou* one thousand ♦ *nm* (*mesure*): ~ **(marin)** nautical mile; **mettre dans le** ~ to hit the bull's-eye; (*fig*) to be bang on (target).
millefeuille [milfœj] *nm* cream *ou* vanilla slice.
millénaire [milenɛʀ] *nm* millennium ♦ *adj* thousand-year-old; (*fig*) ancient.
mille-pattes [milpat] *nm inv* centipede.
millésime [milezim] *nm* year.
millésimé, e [milezime] *adj* vintage *cpd*.
millet [mijɛ] *nm* millet.
milliard [miljaʀ] *nm* milliard, thousand million (*BRIT*), billion (*US*).
milliardaire [miljaʀdɛʀ] *nm/f* multimillionaire (*BRIT*), billionaire (*US*).
millième [miljɛm] *num* thousandth.
millier [milje] *nm* thousand; **un** ~ **(de)** a thousand or so, about a thousand; **par** ~**s** in (their) thousands, by the thousand.
milligramme [miligʀam] *nm* milligramme (*BRIT*), milligram (*US*).
millimètre [milimɛtʀ(ə)] *nm* millimetre (*BRIT*), millimeter (*US*).
millimétré, e [milimetʀe] *adj*: **papier** ~ graph paper.
million [miljɔ̃] *nm* million; **deux** ~**s de** two million; **riche à** ~**s** worth millions.
millionième [miljɔnjɛm] *num* millionth.
millionnaire [miljɔnɛʀ] *nm/f* millionaire.
mi-lourd [miluʀ] *adj m, nm* light heavyweight.
mime [mim] *nm/f* (*acteur*) mime(r); (*imitateur*) mimic ♦ *nm* (*art*) mime, miming.
mimer [mime] *vt* to mime; (*singer*) to mimic, take off.
mimétisme [mimetism(ə)] *nm* (*BIO*) mimicry.
mimique [mimik] *nf* (funny) face; (*signes*) gesticulations *pl*, sign language *no pl*.
mimosa [mimoza] *nm* mimosa.
mi-moyen [mimwajɛ̃] *adj m, nm* welterweight.
MIN *sigle m* (= *Marché d'intérêt national*) *wholesale market for fruit, vegetables and agricultural produce.*
min. *abr* (= *minimum*) min.
minable [minabl(ə)] *adj* (*personne*) shabby(-looking); (*travail*) pathetic.

minaret [minaʀɛ] *nm* minaret.
minauder [minode] *vi* to mince, simper.
minauderies [minodʀi] *nfpl* simperings.
mince [mɛ̃s] *adj* thin; (*personne, taille*) slim; (*fig: profit, connaissances*) slight, small; (*: prétexte*) weak ♦ *excl*: ~ **(alors)**! darn it!
minceur [mɛ̃sœʀ] *nf* thinness; slimness, slenderness.
mincir [mɛ̃siʀ] *vi* to get slimmer *ou* thinner.
mine [min] *nf* (*physionomie*) expression, look; (*extérieur*) exterior, appearance; (*de crayon*) lead; (*gisement, exploitation, explosif*) mine; ~**s** *nfpl* (*péj*) simpering airs; **les M~s** (*ADMIN*) *the national mining and geological service; the government vehicle testing department*; **avoir bonne** ~ (*personne*) to look well; (*ironique*) to look an utter idiot; **avoir mauvaise** ~ to look unwell; **faire** ~ **de faire** to make a pretence of doing; **ne pas payer de** ~ to be not much to look at; ~ **de rien** *adv* with a casual air; although you wouldn't think so; ~ **de charbon** coalmine; ~ **à ciel ouvert** opencast (*BRIT*) *ou* open-air (*US*) mine.
miner [mine] *vt* (*saper*) to undermine, erode; (*MIL*) to mine.
minerai [minʀɛ] *nm* ore.
minéral, e, aux [mineʀal, -o] *adj* mineral; (*CHIMIE*) inorganic ♦ *nm* mineral.
minéralier [mineʀalje] *nm* (*bateau*) ore tanker.
minéralisé, e [mineʀalize] *adj* mineralized.
minéralogie [mineʀalɔʒi] *nf* mineralogy.
minéralogique [mineʀalɔʒik] *adj* mineralogical; **plaque** ~ number (*BRIT*) *ou* license (*US*) plate; **numéro** ~ registration (*BRIT*) *ou* license (*US*) number.
minet, te [minɛ, -ɛt] *nm/f* (*chat*) pussy-cat; (*péj*) young trendy.
mineur, e [minœʀ] *adj* minor ♦ *nm/f* (*JUR*) minor ♦ *nm* (*travailleur*) miner; (*MIL*) sapper; ~ **de fond** face worker.
miniature [minjatyʀ] *adj, nf* miniature.
miniaturisation [minjatyʀizɑsjɔ̃] *nf* miniaturization.
miniaturiser [minjatyʀize] *vt* to miniaturize.
minibus [minibys] *nm* minibus.
mini-cassette [minikasɛt] *nf* cassette (recorder).
minichaîne [miniʃɛn] *nf* mini system.
minier, ière [minje, -jɛʀ] *adj* mining.
mini-jupe [miniʒyp] *nf* mini-skirt.
minimal, e, aux [minimal, -o] *adj* minimum.
minimaliste [minimalist(ə)] *adj* (*ART*) minimalist.
minime [minim] *adj* minor, minimal ♦ *nm/f* (*SPORT*) junior.
minimessage [minimesaʒ] *nm* text message.
minimiser [minimize] *vt* to minimize; (*fig*) to play down.
minimum [minimɔm] *adj, nm* minimum; **au** ~ at the very least; ~ **vital** (*salaire*) living wage; (*niveau de vie*) subsistance level.
mini-ordinateur [miniɔʀdinatœʀ] *nm* minicomputer.
ministère [ministɛʀ] *nm* (*cabinet*) government; (*département*) ministry (*BRIT*), department; (*REL*) ministry; ~ **public** (*JUR*) Prosecution, State Prosecutor.
ministériel, le [ministeʀjɛl] *adj* government *cpd*; ministerial, departmental; (*partisan*) pro-government.
ministrable [ministʀabl(ə)] *adj* (*POL*): **il est** ~ he's a potential minister.
ministre [ministʀ(ə)] *nm* minister (*BRIT*), secretary; (*REL*) minister; ~ **d'État** senior minister *ou* secretary.
Minitel [minitɛl] *nm* ® *videotext terminal and service*; *see boxed note*.

> **MINITEL**
>
> **Minitel** *is a computer system provided by France-Télécom to telephone subscribers. The terminal is supplied free of charge. The system serves as a computerized telephone directory as well as providing a wide variety of services, including train timetables, stock market and situations vacant. Services are accessed by dialling the relevant number on the telephone, and charges are added to the subscriber's telephone bill.*

minium [minjɔm] *nm* red lead paint.
minois [minwa] *nm* little face.
minorer [minɔʀe] *vt* to cut, reduce.
minoritaire [minɔʀitɛʀ] *adj* minority *cpd*.
minorité [minɔʀite] *nf* minority; **être en** ~ to be in the *ou* a minority; **mettre en** ~ (*POL*) to defeat.
Minorque [minɔʀk] *nf* Minorca.
minorquin, e [minɔʀkɛ̃, -in] *adj* Minorcan.
minoterie [minɔtʀi] *nf* flour-mill.
minuit [minɥi] *nm* midnight.
minuscule [minyskyl] *adj* minute, tiny ♦ *nf*: **(lettre)** ~ small letter.
minutage [minytaʒ] *nm* timing.
minute [minyt] *nf* minute; (*JUR: original*) minute, draft ♦ *excl* just a minute!, hang on!; **à la** ~ (*présent*) (just) this instant; (*passé*) there and then; **entrecôte** ~ minute steak.
minuter [minyte] *vt* to time.
minuterie [minytʀi] *nf* time switch.
minuteur [minytœʀ] *nm* timer.
minutie [minysi] *nf* meticulousness; minute detail; **avec** ~ meticulously; in minute detail.
minutieusement [minysjøzmɑ̃] *adv* (*organiser, travailler*) meticulously; (*examiner*) minutely.
minutieux, euse [minysjø, -øz] *adj* (*personne*) meticulous; (*inspection*) minutely detailed; (*travail*) requiring painstaking attention to detail.
mioche [mjɔʃ] *nm* (*fam*) nipper, brat.
mirabelle [miʀabɛl] *nf* (*fruit*) (cherry) plum; (*eau-de-vie*) plum brandy.

miracle [miʀɑkl(ə)] *nm* miracle.
miraculé, e [miʀakyle] *adj* who has been miraculously cured (*ou* rescued).
miraculeux, euse [miʀakylø, -øz] *adj* miraculous.
mirador [miʀadɔʀ] *nm* (*MIL*) watchtower.
mirage [miʀaʒ] *nm* mirage.
mire [miʀ] *nf* (*d'un fusil*) sight; (*TV*) test card; **point de** ~ target; (*fig*) focal point; **ligne de** ~ line of sight.
mirent [miʀ] *vb voir* **mettre**.
mirer [miʀe] *vt* (*œufs*) to candle; **se** ~ *vi*: **se** ~ **dans** (*suj: personne*) to gaze at one's reflection in; (*: chose*) to be mirrored in.
mirifique [miʀifik] *adj* wonderful.
mirobolant, e [miʀɔbɔlɑ̃, -ɑ̃t] *adj* fantastic.
miroir [miʀwaʀ] *nm* mirror.
miroiter [miʀwate] *vi* to sparkle, shimmer; **faire** ~ **qch à qn** to paint sth in glowing colours for sb, dangle sth in front of sb's eyes.
miroiterie [miʀwatʀi] *nf* (*usine*) mirror factory; (*magasin*) mirror dealer's (shop).
Mis *abr* = **marquis**.
mis, e [mi, miz] *pp de* **mettre** ♦ *adj* (*couvert, table*) set, laid; (*personne*): **bien** ~ well dressed ♦ *nf* (*argent: au jeu*) stake; (*tenue*) clothing; attire; **être de** ~**e** to be acceptable *ou* in season; ~**e en bouteilles** bottling; ~**e en examen** charging, indictment; ~**e à feu** blast-off; ~**e de fonds** capital outlay; ~**e à jour** updating; ~**e à mort** kill; ~**e à pied** (*d'un employé*) suspension; lay-off; ~**e sur pied** (*d'une affaire, entreprise*) setting up; ~**e en plis** set; ~**e au point** (*PHOTO*) focusing; (*fig*) clarification; ~**e à prix** reserve (*BRIT*) *ou* upset price; ~**e en scène** production.
misaine [mizɛn] *nf*: **mât de** ~ foremast.
misanthrope [mizɑ̃tʀɔp] *nm/f* misanthropist.
Mise *abr* = **marquise**.
mise [miz] *adj f, nf voir* **mis**.
miser [mize] *vt* (*enjeu*) to stake, bet; ~ **sur** *vt* (*cheval, numéro*) to bet on; (*fig*) to bank *ou* count on.
misérable [mizeʀabl(ə)] *adj* (*lamentable, malheureux*) pitiful, wretched; (*pauvre*) poverty-stricken; (*insignifiant, mesquin*) miserable ♦ *nm/f* wretch; (*miséreux*) poor wretch.
misère [mizɛʀ] *nf* (*pauvreté*) (extreme) poverty, destitution; ~**s** *nfpl* (*malheurs*) woes, miseries; (*ennuis*) little troubles; **être dans la** ~ to be destitute *ou* poverty-stricken; **salaire de** ~ starvation wage; **faire des** ~**s à qn** to torment sb; ~ **noire** utter destitution, abject poverty.
miséreux, euse [mizeʀø, -øz] *adj* poverty-stricken ♦ *nm/f* down-and-out.
miséricorde [mizeʀikɔʀd(ə)] *nf* mercy, forgiveness.
miséricordieux, euse [mizeʀikɔʀdjø, -øz] *adj* merciful, forgiving.
misogyne [mizɔʒin] *adj* misogynous ♦ *nm/f* misogynist.
missel [misɛl] *nm* missal.
missile [misil] *nm* missile.
mission [misjɔ̃] *nf* mission; **partir en** ~ (*ADMIN, POL*) to go on an assignment.
missionnaire [misjɔnɛʀ] *nm/f* missionary.
missive [misiv] *nf* missive.
mistral [mistʀal] *nm* mistral (wind).
mit [mi] *vb voir* **mettre**.
mitaine [mitɛn] *nf* mitt(en).
mite [mit] *nf* clothes moth.
mité, e [mite] *adj* moth-eaten.
mi-temps [mitɑ̃] *nf inv* (*SPORT: période*) half (*pl* halves); (*: pause*) half-time; **à** ~ *adj, adv* part-time.
miteux, euse [mitø, -øz] *adj* seedy, shabby.
mitigé, e [mitiʒe] *adj* (*conviction, ardeur*) lukewarm; (*sentiments*) mixed.
mitonner [mitɔne] *vt* (*préparer*) to cook with loving care; (*fig*) to cook up quietly.
mitoyen, ne [mitwajɛ̃, -ɛn] *adj* common, party *cpd*; **maisons** ~**nes** semi-detached houses; (*plus de deux*) terraced (*BRIT*) *ou* row (*US*) houses.
mitraille [mitʀɑj] *nf* (*balles de fonte*) grapeshot; (*décharge d'obus*) shellfire.
mitrailler [mitʀɑje] *vt* to machine-gun; (*fig: photographier*) to snap away at; ~ **qn de** to pelt *ou* bombard sb with.
mitraillette [mitʀɑjɛt] *nf* submachine gun.
mitrailleur [mitʀɑjœʀ] *nm* machine gunner ♦ *adj m*: **fusil** ~ machine gun.
mitrailleuse [mitʀɑjøz] *nf* machine gun.
mitre [mitʀ(ə)] *nf* mitre.
mitron [mitʀɔ̃] *nm* baker's boy.
mi-voix [mivwa]: **à** ~ *adv* in a low *ou* hushed voice.
mixage [miksaʒ] *nm* (*CINÉ*) (sound) mixing.
mixer, mixeur [miksœʀ] *nm* (*CULIN*) (food) mixer.
mixité [miksite] *nf* (*SCOL*) coeducation.
mixte [mikst(ə)] *adj* (*gén*) mixed; (*SCOL*) mixed, coeducational; **à usage** ~ dual purpose; **cuisinière** ~ combined gas and electric cooker; **équipe** ~ combined team.
mixture [mikstyʀ] *nf* mixture; (*fig*) concoction.
MJC *sigle f* (= *maison des jeunes et de la culture*) *community arts centre and youth club.*
ml *abr* (= *millilitre*) ml.
MLF *sigle m* (= *Mouvement de libération de la femme*) Women's Movement.
Mlle, *pl* **Mlles** *abr* = **Mademoiselle**.
MM *abr* = **Messieurs**; *voir* **Monsieur**.
Mme, *pl* **Mmes** *abr* = **Madame**.
mn. *abr* (= *minute*) min.
mnémotechnique [mnemɔtɛknik] *adj* mnemonic.
MNS *sigle m* (= *maître nageur sauveteur*) ≈ lifeguard.
MO *sigle f* (= *main-d'œuvre*) *labour costs (on in*

voices).

Mo *abr* = **méga-octet, métro**.

mobile [mɔbil] *adj* mobile; (*amovible*) loose, removable; (*pièce de machine*) moving; (*élément de meuble etc*) movable ♦ *nm* (*motif*) motive; (*œuvre d'art*) mobile; (*PHYSIQUE*) moving object *ou* body.

mobilier, ière [mɔbilje, -jɛʀ] *adj* (*JUR*) personal ♦ *nm* (*meubles*) furniture; **valeurs mobilières** transferable securities; **vente mobilière** sale of personal property *ou* chattels.

mobilisation [mɔbilizɑsjɔ̃] *nf* mobilization.

mobiliser [mɔbilize] *vt* (*MIL, gén*) to mobilize.

mobilité [mɔbilite] *nf* mobility.

mobylette [mɔbilɛt] *nf* ® moped.

mocassin [mɔkasɛ̃] *nm* moccasin.

moche [mɔʃ] *adj* (*fam: laid*) ugly; (*: mauvais, méprisable*) rotten.

modalité [mɔdalite] *nf* form, mode; **~s** *nfpl* (*d'un accord etc*) clauses, terms; **~s de paiement** methods of payment.

mode [mɔd] *nf* fashion; (*commerce*) fashion trade *ou* industry ♦ *nm* (*manière*) form, mode, method; (*LING*) mood; (*INFORM, MUS*) mode; **travailler dans la ~** to be in the fashion business; **à la ~** fashionable, in fashion; **~ dialogué** (*INFORM*) interactive *ou* conversational mode; **~ d'emploi** directions *pl* (for use); **~ de vie** way of life.

modelage [mɔdlaʒ] *nm* modelling.

modelé [mɔdle] *nm* (*GÉO*) relief; (*du corps etc*) contours *pl*.

modèle [mɔdɛl] *adj* model ♦ *nm* model; (*qui pose: de peintre*) sitter; (*type*) type; (*gabarit, patron*) pattern; **~ courant** *ou* **de série** (*COMM*) production model; **~ déposé** registered design; **~ réduit** small-scale model.

modeler [mɔdle] *vt* (*ART*) to model, mould; (*suj: vêtement, érosion*) to mould, shape; **~ qch sur/d'après** to model sth on.

modélisation [mɔdelizɑsjɔ̃] *nf* (*MATH*) modelling.

modéliste [mɔdelist(ə)] *nm/f* (*COUTURE*) designer; (*de modèles réduits*) model maker.

modem [mɔdɛm] *nm* modem.

Modène [mɔdɛn] *n* Modena.

modérateur, trice [mɔdeʀatœʀ, -tʀis] *adj* moderating ♦ *nm/f* moderator.

modération [mɔdeʀɑsjɔ̃] *nf* moderation; **~ de peine** reduction of sentence.

modéré, e [mɔdeʀe] *adj, nm/f* moderate.

modérément [mɔdeʀemɑ̃] *adv* moderately, in moderation.

modérer [mɔdeʀe] *vt* to moderate; **se ~** *vi* to restrain o.s.

moderne [mɔdɛʀn(ə)] *adj* modern ♦ *nm* (*ART*) modern style; (*ameublement*) modern furniture.

modernisation [mɔdɛʀnizɑsjɔ̃] *nf* modernization.

moderniser [mɔdɛʀnize] *vt* to modernize.

modernisme [mɔdɛʀnism(ə)] *nm* modernism.

modernité [mɔdɛʀnite] *nf* modernity.

modeste [mɔdɛst(ə)] *adj* modest; (*origine*) humble, lowly.

modestement [mɔdɛstəmɑ̃] *adv* modestly.

modestie [mɔdɛsti] *nf* modesty; **fausse ~** false modesty.

modicité [mɔdisite] *nf*: **la ~ des prix** *etc* the low prices *etc*.

modificatif, ive [mɔdifikatif, -iv] *adj* modifying.

modification [mɔdifikɑsjɔ̃] *nf* modification.

modifier [mɔdifje] *vt* to modify, alter; (*LING*) to modify; **se ~** *vi* to alter.

modique [mɔdik] *adj* (*salaire, somme*) modest.

modiste [mɔdist(ə)] *nf* milliner.

modulaire [mɔdylɛʀ] *adj* modular.

modulation [mɔdylɑsjɔ̃] *nf* modulation; **~ de fréquence (FM** *ou* **MF)** frequency modulation (FM).

module [mɔdyl] *nm* module.

moduler [mɔdyle] *vt* to modulate; (*air*) to warble.

moelle [mwal] *nf* marrow; (*fig*) pith, core; **~ épinière** spinal chord.

moelleux, euse [mwalø, -øz] *adj* soft; (*au goût, à l'ouïe*) mellow; (*gracieux, souple*) smooth.

moellon [mwalɔ̃] *nm* rubble stone.

mœurs [mœʀ] *nfpl* (*conduite*) morals; (*manières*) manners; (*pratiques sociales*) habits; (*mode de vie*) life style *sg*; (*d'une espèce animale*) behaviour *sg* (*BRIT*), behavior *sg* (*US*); **femme de mauvaises ~** loose woman; **passer dans les ~** to become the custom; **contraire aux bonnes ~** contrary to proprieties.

mohair [mɔɛʀ] *nm* mohair.

moi [mwa] *pron* me; (*emphatique*): **~, je ...** for my part, I ..., I myself ... ♦ *nm inv* (*PSYCH*) ego, self; **à ~!** (*à l'aide*) help (me)!

moignon [mwaɲɔ̃] *nm* stump.

moi-même [mwamɛm] *pron* myself; (*emphatique*) I myself.

moindre [mwɛ̃dʀ(ə)] *adj* lesser; lower; **le(la) ~, les ~s** the least; the slightest; **le(la) ~ de** the least of; **c'est la ~ des choses** it's nothing at all.

moindrement [mwɛ̃dʀəmɑ̃] *adv*: **pas le ~** not in the least.

moine [mwan] *nm* monk, friar.

moineau, x [mwano] *nm* sparrow.

MOT-CLÉ

moins [mwɛ̃] *adv* **1** (*comparatif*): **~ (que)** less (than); **~ grand que** less tall than, not as tall as; **il a 3 ans de ~ que moi** he's 3 years younger than me; **il est ~ intelligent que moi** he's not as clever as me, he's less clever than me; **~ je travaille, mieux je me porte** the less I work, the better I feel

2 (*superlatif*): **le ~** (the) least; **c'est ce que j'aime le ~** it's what I like (the) least; **le(la) ~ doué(e)** the least gifted; **au ~, du ~** at least; **pour le ~** at the very least

3: ~ **de** (*quantité*) less (than); (*nombre*) fewer (than); ~ **de sable/d'eau** less sand/water; ~ **de livres/gens** fewer books/people; ~ **de 2 ans** less than 2 years; ~ **de midi** not yet midday
4: **de** ~, **en** ~: **10 €/3 jours de** ~ €10/3 days less; **3 livres en** ~ 3 books fewer; 3 books too few; **de l'argent en** ~ less money; **le soleil en** ~ but for the sun, minus the sun; **de** ~ **en** ~ less and less; **en** ~ **de deux** in a flash *ou* a trice
5: **à** ~ **de, à** ~ **que** unless; **à** ~ **de faire** unless we do (*ou* he does *etc*); **à** ~ **que tu ne fasses** unless you do; **à** ~ **d'un accident** barring any accident
♦ *prép*: **4** ~ **2** 4 minus 2; **10 heures** ~ **5** 5 to 10; **il fait** ~ **5** it's 5 (degrees) below (freezing), it's minus 5; **il est** ~ **5** it's 5 to
♦ *nm* (*signe*) minus sign.

moins-value [mwɛ̃valy] *nf* (*ÉCON, COMM*) depreciation.
moire [mwaʀ] *nf* moiré.
moiré, e [mwaʀe] *adj* (*tissu, papier*) moiré, watered; (*reflets*) shimmering.
mois [mwa] *nm* month; (*salaire, somme dû*) (monthly) pay *ou* salary; **treizième** ~, **double** ~ extra month's salary.
moïse [mɔiz] *nm* Moses basket.
moisi, e [mwazi] *adj* mouldy (*BRIT*), moldy (*US*), mildewed ♦ *nm* mould, mold, mildew; **odeur de** ~ musty smell.
moisir [mwaziʀ] *vi* to go mouldy (*BRIT*) *ou* moldy (*US*); (*fig*) to rot; (*personne*) to hang about ♦ *vt* to make mouldy *ou* moldy.
moisissure [mwazisyʀ] *nf* mould *no pl* (*BRIT*), mold *no pl* (*US*).
moisson [mwasɔ̃] *nf* harvest; (*époque*) harvest (time); (*fig*): **faire une** ~ **de** to gather a wealth of.
moissonner [mwasɔne] *vt* to harvest, reap; (*fig*) to collect.
moissonneur, euse [mwasɔnœʀ, -øz] *nm/f* harvester, reaper ♦ *nf* (*machine*) harvester.
moissonneuse-batteuse, *pl* **moissonneuses-batteuses** [mwasɔnøzbatøz] *nf* combine harvester.
moite [mwat] *adj* (*peau, mains*) sweaty, sticky; (*atmosphère*) muggy.
moitié [mwatje] *nf* half (*pl* halves); (*épouse*): **sa** ~ his better half; **la** ~ half; **la** ~ **de** half (of), half the amount (*ou* number) of; **la** ~ **du temps/des gens** half the time/the people; **à la** ~ **de** halfway through; ~ **moins grand** half as tall; ~ **plus long** half as long again, longer by half; **à** ~ half (*avant le verbe*), half- (*avant l'adjectif*); **à** ~ **prix** (at) half price, half-price; **de** ~ by half; ~ ~ half-and-half.
moka [mɔka] *nm* (*café*) mocha coffee; (*gâteau*) mocha cake.
mol [mɔl] *adj m voir* **mou**.
molaire [mɔlɛʀ] *nf* molar.
moldave [mɔldav] *adj* Moldavian.
Moldavie [mɔldavi] *nf*: **la** ~ Moldavia.
môle [mol] *nm* jetty.
moléculaire [mɔlekylɛʀ] *adj* molecular.
molécule [mɔlekyl] *nf* molecule.
moleskine [mɔlɛskin] *nf* imitation leather.
molester [mɔlɛste] *vt* to manhandle, mau (about).
molette [mɔlɛt] *nf* toothed *ou* cutting wheel.
mollasse [mɔlas] *adj* (*péj: sans énergie*) slug gish; (*: flasque*) flabby.
molle [mɔl] *adj f voir* **mou**.
mollement [mɔlmɑ̃] *adv* softly; (*péj*) slug gishly; (*protester*) feebly.
mollesse [mɔlɛs] *nf* (*voir mou*) softness; flab biness; limpness; sluggishness; feebleness.
mollet [mɔlɛ] *nm* calf (*pl* calves) ♦ *adj m*: **œuf** ~ soft-boiled egg.
molletière [mɔltjɛʀ] *adj f*: **bande** ~ puttee.
molleton [mɔltɔ̃] *nm* (*TEXTILES*) felt.
molletonné, e [mɔltɔne] *adj* (*gants etc*) fleece lined.
mollir [mɔliʀ] *vi* (*jambes*) to give way; (*NAVIG vent*) to drop, die down; (*fig: personne*) to re lent; (*: courage*) to fail, flag.
mollusque [mɔlysk(ə)] *nm* (*ZOOL*) mollusc (*fig: personne*) lazy lump.
molosse [mɔlɔs] *nm* big ferocious dog.
môme [mom] *nm/f* (*fam: enfant*) brat; (*: fille*) bird (*BRIT*), chick.
moment [mɔmɑ̃] *nm* moment; (*occasion*): **profiter du** ~ to take (advantage of) the op portunity; **ce n'est pas le** ~ this is not th right time; **à un certain** ~ at some point; **un** ~ **donné** at a certain point; **à quel** ~ when exactly?; **au même** ~ at the sam time; (*instant*) at the same moment; **pour u bon** ~ for a good while; **pour le** ~ for th moment, for the time being; **au** ~ **de** at th time of; **au** ~ **où** as; at a time when; **à tou** ~ at any time *ou* moment; (*continuellemen*) constantly, continually; **en ce** ~ at the mo ment; (*aujourd'hui*) at present; **sur le** ~ a the time; **par** ~**s** now and then, at times; **d'un** ~ **à l'autre** any time (now); **du** ~ **où** *o* **que** seeing that, since; **n'avoir pas un** ~ **à soi** not to have a minute to oneself.
momentané, e [mɔmɑ̃tane] *adj* temporary momentary.
momentanément [mɔmɑ̃tanemɑ̃] *adv* for moment, for a while.
momie [mɔmi] *nf* mummy.
mon [mɔ̃], **ma** [ma], *pl* **mes** [me] *adj possess* my.
monacal, e, aux [mɔnakal, -o] *adj* monastic.
Monaco [mɔnako] *nm*: **le** ~ Monaco.
monarchie [mɔnaʀʃi] *nf* monarchy.
monarchiste [mɔnaʀʃist(ə)] *adj, nm/f* mona chist.
monarque [mɔnaʀk(ə)] *nm* monarch.
monastère [mɔnastɛʀ] *nm* monastery.
monastique [mɔnastik] *adj* monastic.

monceau, x [mɔ̃so] *nm* heap.
mondain, e [mɔ̃dɛ̃, -ɛn] *adj* (*soirée, vie*) society *cpd*; (*obligations*) social; (*peintre, écrivain*) fashionable; (*personne*) society *cpd* ♦ *nm/f* society man/woman, socialite ♦ *nf*: **la M~e, la police ~e** ≈ the vice squad.
mondanités [mɔ̃danite] *nfpl* (*vie mondaine*) society life *sg*; (*paroles*) (society) small talk *sg*; (*PRESSE*) (society) gossip column *sg*.
monde [mɔ̃d] *nm* world; (*personnes mondaines*): **le ~** (high) society; (*milieu*): **être du même ~** to move in the same circles; (*gens*): **il y a du ~** (*beaucoup de gens*) there are a lot of people; (*quelques personnes*) there are some people; **y a-t-il du ~ dans le salon?** is there anybody in the lounge?; **beaucoup/peu de ~** many/few people; **le meilleur** *etc* **du ~** the best *etc* in the world *ou* on earth; **mettre au ~** to bring into the world; **pas le moins du ~** not in the least; **se faire un ~ de qch** to make a great deal of fuss about sth; **tour du ~** round-the-world trip; **homme/femme du ~** society man/woman.
mondial, e, aux [mɔ̃djal, -o] *adj* (*population*) world *cpd*; (*influence*) world-wide.
mondialement [mɔ̃djalmɑ̃] *adv* throughout the world.
mondialisation [mɔ̃djalizɑsjɔ̃] *nf* (*d'une technique*) global application; (*d'un conflit*) global spread.
mondovision [mɔ̃dɔvizjɔ̃] *nf* (world coverage by) satellite television.
monégasque [mɔnegask(ə)] *adj* Monegasque, of *ou* from Monaco ♦ *nm/f*: **M~** Monegasque.
monétaire [mɔnetɛʀ] *adj* monetary.
monétarisme [mɔnetaʀism(ə)] *nm* monetarism.
monétique [mɔnetik] *nf* electronic money.
mongol, e [mɔ̃gɔl] *adj* Mongol, Mongolian ♦ *nm* (*LING*) Mongolian ♦ *nm/f*: **M~, e** (*de la Mongolie*) Mongolian.
Mongolie [mɔ̃gɔli] *nf*: **la ~** Mongolia.
mongolien, ne [mɔ̃gɔljɛ̃, -ɛn] *adj, nm/f* mongol.
mongolisme [mɔ̃gɔlism(ə)] *nm* mongolism, Down's syndrome.
moniteur, trice [mɔnitœʀ, -tʀis] *nm/f* (*SPORT*) instructor/instructress; (*de colonie de vacances*) supervisor ♦ *nm* (*écran*) monitor; **~ cardiaque** cardiac monitor; **~ d'auto-école** driving instructor.
monitorage [mɔnitɔʀaʒ] *nm* monitoring.
monitorat [mɔnitɔʀa] *nm* (*formation*) instructor's training (course); (*fonction*) instructorship.
monnaie [mɔnɛ] *nf* (*pièce*) coin; (*ÉCON, gén: moyen d'échange*) currency; (*petites pièces*): **avoir de la ~** to have (some) change; **faire de la ~** to get (some) change; **avoir/faire la ~ de 5 €** to have change of/get change for €5; **faire** *ou* **donner à qn la ~ de 5 €** to give sb change for €5, change €5 for sb; **rendre à qn la ~ (sur 5 €)** to give sb the change (from *ou* out of €5); **servir de ~ d'échange** (*fig*) to be used as a bargaining counter *ou* as bargaining counters; **payer en ~ de singe** to fob (sb) off with empty promises; **c'est ~ courante** it's a common occurrence; **~ légale** legal tender.
monnayable [mɔnɛjabl(ə)] *adj* (*vendable*) convertible into cash; **mes services sont ~s** my services are worth money.
monnayer [mɔneje] *vt* to convert into cash; (*talent*) to capitalize on.
monnayeur [mɔnɛjœʀ] *nm voir* **faux.**
mono [mɔno] *nf* (= *monophonie*) mono ♦ *nm* (= *monoski*) monoski.
monochrome [mɔnɔkʀom] *adj* monochrome.
monocle [mɔnɔkl(ə)] *nm* monocle, eyeglass.
monocoque [mɔnɔkɔk] *adj* (*voiture*) monocoque ♦ *nm* (*voilier*) monohull.
monocorde [mɔnɔkɔʀd(ə)] *adj* monotonous.
monoculture [mɔnɔkyltyʀ] *nf* single-crop farming, monoculture.
monogamie [mɔnɔgami] *nf* monogamy.
monogramme [mɔnɔgʀam] *nm* monogram.
monokini [mɔnɔkini] *nm* one-piece bikini, bikini pants *pl*.
monolingue [mɔnɔlɛ̃g] *adj* monolingual.
monolithique [mɔnɔlitik] *adj* (*lit, fig*) monolithic.
monologue [mɔnɔlɔg] *nm* monologue, soliloquy; **~ intérieur** stream of consciousness.
monologuer [mɔnɔlɔge] *vi* to soliloquize.
monôme [mɔnom] *nm* (*MATH*) monomial; (*d'étudiants*) students' rag procession.
monoparental, e, aux [mɔnɔpaʀɑ̃tal, -o] *adj*: **famille ~e** single-parent *ou* one-parent family.
monophasé, e [mɔnɔfɑze] *adj* single-phase *cpd*.
monophonie [mɔnɔfɔni] *nf* monophony.
monoplace [mɔnɔplas] *adj, nm, nf* single-seater, one-seater.
monoplan [mɔnɔplɑ̃] *nm* monoplane.
monopole [mɔnɔpɔl] *nm* monopoly.
monopolisation [mɔnɔpɔlizɑsjɔ̃] *nf* monopolization.
monopoliser [mɔnɔpɔlize] *vt* to monopolize.
monorail [mɔnɔʀɑj] *nm* monorail; monorail train.
monoski [mɔnɔski] *nm* monoski.
monosyllabe [mɔnɔsilab] *nm* monosyllable, word of one syllable.
monosyllabique [mɔnosilabik] *adj* monosyllabic.
monotone [mɔnɔtɔn] *adj* monotonous.
monotonie [mɔnɔtɔni] *nf* monotony.
monseigneur [mɔ̃sɛɲœʀ] *nm* (*archevêque, évêque*) Your (*ou* His) Grace; (*cardinal*) Your (*ou* His) Eminence; **Mgr Thomas** Bishop Thomas; Cardinal Thomas.
Monsieur [məsjø], *pl* **Messieurs** [mesjø] *titre* Mr ['mɪstə*] ♦ *nm* (*homme quelconque*): **un/le**

m~ a/the gentleman; *voir aussi* **Madame**.
monstre [mɔ̃stʀ(ə)] *nm* monster ♦ *adj* (*fam: effet, publicité*) massive; **un travail** ~ a fantastic amount of work; an enormous job; ~ **sacré** superstar.
monstrueux, euse [mɔ̃stʀyø, -øz] *adj* monstrous.
monstruosité [mɔ̃stʀyozite] *nf* monstrosity.
mont [mɔ̃] *nm*: **par ~s et par vaux** up hill and down dale; **le M~ Blanc** Mont Blanc; ~ **de Vénus** mons veneris.
montage [mɔ̃taʒ] *nm* putting up; (*d'un bijou*) mounting, setting; (*d'une machine etc*) assembly; (*PHOTO*) photomontage; (*CINÉ*) editing; ~ **sonore** sound editing.
montagnard, e [mɔ̃taɲaʀ, -aʀd(ə)] *adj* mountain *cpd* ♦ *nm/f* mountain-dweller.
montagne [mɔ̃taɲ] *nf* (*cime*) mountain; (*région*): **la** ~ the mountains *pl*; **la haute** ~ the high mountains; **les ~s Rocheuses** the Rocky Mountains, the Rockies; **~s russes** big dipper *sg*, switchback *sg*.
montagneux, euse [mɔ̃taɲø, -øz] *adj* mountainous; hilly.
montant, e [mɔ̃tɑ̃, -ɑ̃t] *adj* (*mouvement, marée*) rising; (*chemin*) uphill; (*robe, corsage*) high-necked ♦ *nm* (*somme, total*) (sum) total, (total) amount; (*de fenêtre*) upright; (*de lit*) post.
mont-de-piété, *pl* **monts-de-piété** [mɔ̃dpjete] *nm* pawnshop.
monte [mɔ̃t] *nf* (*accouplement*): **la** ~ stud; (*d'un jockey*) seat.
monté, e [mɔ̃te] *adj*: **être** ~ **contre qn** to be angry with sb; (*fourni, équipé*): ~ **en** equipped with.
monte-charge [mɔ̃tʃaʀʒ(ə)] *nm inv* goods lift, hoist.
montée [mɔ̃te] *nf* rising, rise; (*escalade*) ascent, climb; (*chemin*) way up; (*côte*) hill; **au milieu de la** ~ halfway up; **le moteur chauffe dans les ~s** the engine overheats going uphill.
monte-plats [mɔ̃tpla] *nm inv* service lift.
monter [mɔ̃te] *vt* (*escalier, côte*) to go (*ou* come) up; (*valise, paquet*) to take (*ou* bring) up; (*cheval*) to mount; (*femelle*) to cover, serve; (*tente, échafaudage*) to put up; (*machine*) to assemble; (*bijou*) to mount, set; (*COUTURE*) to sew on; (*: manche*) to set in; (*CINÉ*) to edit; (*THÉÂT*) to put on, stage; (*société, coup etc*) to set up; (*fournir, équiper*) to equip ♦ *vi* to go (*ou* come) up; (*avion, voiture*) to climb, go up; (*chemin, niveau, température, voix, prix*) to go up, rise; (*brouillard, bruit*) to rise, come up; (*passager*) to get on; (*à cheval*): ~ **bien/mal** to ride well/badly; ~ **à cheval/bicyclette** to get on *ou* mount a horse/bicycle; (*faire du cheval etc*) to ride (a horse); to (ride a) bicycle; ~ **à pied/en voiture** to walk/drive up, go up on foot/by car; ~ **dans le train/l'avion** to get into the train/plane, board the train/plane; ~ **sur** to climb up onto; ~ **sur** *ou* **à un arbre/une échelle** to climb (up) a tree/ladder; ~ **à bord** to (get on) board; ~ **à la tête de qn** to go to sb's head; ~ **sur les planches** to go on the stage; ~ **en grade** to be promoted; **se** ~ (*s'équiper*) to equip o.s., get kitted out (*BRIT*); **se** ~ **à** (*frais etc*) to add up to, come to; ~ **qn contre qn** to set sb against sb; ~ **la tête à qn** to give sb ideas.
monteur, euse [mɔ̃tœʀ, -øz] *nm/f* (*TECH*) fitter; (*CINÉ*) (film) editor.
monticule [mɔ̃tikyl] *nm* mound.
montmartrois, e [mɔ̃maʀtʀwa, -waz] *adj* of *ou* from Montmartre.
montre [mɔ̃tʀ(ə)] *nf* watch; (*ostentation*): **pour la** ~ for show; ~ **en main** exactly, to the minute; **faire** ~ **de** to show, display; **contre la** ~ (*SPORT*) against the clock; ~ **de plongée** diver's watch.
Montréal [mɔ̃ʀeal] *n* Montreal.
montréalais, e [mɔ̃ʀealɛ, -ɛz] *adj* of *ou* from Montreal ♦ *nm/f*: **M~, e** Montrealer.
montre-bracelet, *pl* **montres-bracelets** [mɔ̃tʀəbʀaslɛ] *nf* wrist watch.
montrer [mɔ̃tʀe] *vt* to show; **se** ~ to appear; ~ **qch à qn** to show sb sth; ~ **qch du doigt** to point to sth, point one's finger at sth; **se** ~ **intelligent** to prove (to be) intelligent.
montreur, euse [mɔ̃tʀœʀ, -øz] *nm/f*: ~ **de marionnettes** puppeteer.
monture [mɔ̃tyʀ] *nf* (*bête*) mount; (*d'une bague*) setting; (*de lunettes*) frame.
monument [mɔnymɑ̃] *nm* monument; ~ **aux morts** war memorial.
monumental, e, aux [mɔnymɑ̃tal, -o] *adj* monumental.
moquer [mɔke]: **se** ~ **de** *vt* to make fun of, laugh at; (*fam: se désintéresser de*) not to care about; (*tromper*): **se** ~ **de qn** to take sb for a ride.
moquerie [mɔkʀi] *nf* mockery *no pl*.
moquette [mɔkɛt] *nf* fitted carpet, wall-to-wall carpeting *no pl*.
moquetter [mɔkete] *vt* to carpet.
moqueur, euse [mɔkœʀ, -øz] *adj* mocking.
moral, e, aux [mɔʀal, -o] *adj* moral ♦ *nm* morale ♦ *nf* (*conduite*) morals *pl*; (*règles*) moral code, ethic; (*valeurs*) moral standards *pl*, morality; (*science*) ethics *sg*, moral philosophy; (*conclusion: d'une fable etc*) moral; **au** ~, **sur le plan** ~ morally; **avoir le** ~ **à zéro** to be really down; **faire la ~e à** to lecture, preach at.
moralement [mɔʀalmɑ̃] *adv* morally.
moralisateur, trice [mɔʀalizatœʀ, -tʀis] *adj* moralizing, sanctimonious ♦ *nm/f* moralizer.
moraliser [mɔʀalize] *vt* (*sermonner*) to lecture, preach at.
moraliste [mɔʀalist(ə)] *nm/f* moralist ♦ *adj* moralistic.
moralité [mɔʀalite] *nf* (*d'une action, attitude*) morality; (*conduite*) morals *pl*; (*conclusion,*

enseignement) moral.
moratoire [mɔratwar] *adj m*: **intérêts ~s** (*ÉCON*) interest on arrears.
morave [mɔrav] *adj* Moravian.
Moravie [mɔravi] *nf*: **la ~** Moravia.
morbide [mɔrbid] *adj* morbid.
morceau, x [mɔrso] *nm* piece, bit; (*d'une œuvre*) passage, extract; (*MUS*) piece; (*CULIN*: *de viande*) cut; **mettre en ~x** to pull to pieces *ou* bits.
morceler [mɔrsəle] *vt* to break up, divide up.
morcellement [mɔrsɛlmɑ̃] *nm* breaking up.
mordant, e [mɔrdɑ̃, -ɑ̃t] *adj* scathing, cutting; (*froid*) biting ♦ *nm* (*dynamisme, énergie*) spirit; (*fougue*) bite, punch.
mordicus [mɔrdikys] *adv* (*fam*) obstinately, stubbornly.
mordiller [mɔrdije] *vt* to nibble at, chew at.
mordoré, e [mɔrdɔre] *adj* lustrous bronze.
mordre [mɔrdr(ə)] *vt* to bite; (*suj: lime, vis*) to bite into ♦ *vi* (*poisson*) to bite; **~ dans** to bite into; **~ sur** (*fig*) to go over into, overlap into; **~ à qch** (*comprendre, aimer*) to take to; **~ à l'hameçon** to bite, rise to the bait.
mordu, e [mɔrdy] *pp de* **mordre** ♦ *adj* (*amoureux*) smitten ♦ *nm/f*: **un ~ de jazz/de voile** a jazz/sailing fanatic *ou* buff.
morfondre [mɔrfɔ̃dr(ə)]: **se ~** *vi* to mope.
morgue [mɔrg(ə)] *nf* (*arrogance*) haughtiness; (*lieu: de la police*) morgue; (*: à l'hôpital*) mortuary.
moribond, e [mɔribɔ̃, -ɔ̃d] *adj* dying, moribund.
morille [mɔrij] *nf* morel (*mushroom*).
mormon, e [mɔrmɔ̃, -ɔn] *adj, nm/f* Mormon.
morne [mɔrn(ə)] *adj* (*personne, visage*) glum, gloomy; (*temps, vie*) dismal, dreary.
morose [mɔroz] *adj* sullen, morose; (*marché*) sluggish.
morphine [mɔrfin] *nf* morphine.
morphinomane [mɔrfinɔman] *nm/f* morphine addict.
morphologie [mɔrfɔlɔʒi] *nf* morphology.
morphologique [mɔrfɔlɔʒik] *adj* morphological.
mors [mɔr] *nm* bit.
morse [mɔrs(ə)] *nm* (*ZOOL*) walrus; (*TÉL*) Morse (code).
morsure [mɔrsyr] *nf* bite.
mort[1] [mɔr] *nf* death; **se donner la ~** to take one's own life; **de ~** (*silence, pâleur*) deathly; **blessé à ~** fatally wounded *ou* injured; **à la vie, à la ~** for better, for worse; **~ clinique** brain death; **~ subite du nourrisson, ~ au berceau** cot death.
mort[2], e [mɔr, mɔrt(ə)] *pp de* **mourir** ♦ *adj* dead ♦ *nm/f* (*défunt*) dead man/woman; (*victime*): **il y a eu plusieurs ~s** several people were killed, there were several killed ♦ *nm* (*CARTES*) dummy; **~ ou vif** dead or alive; **~ de peur/fatigue** frightened to death/dead tired; **~s et blessés** casualties; **faire le ~** to play dead; (*fig*) to lie low.
mortadelle [mɔrtadɛl] *nf* mortadella (*type of luncheon meat*).
mortalité [mɔrtalite] *nf* mortality, death rate.
mort-aux-rats [mɔrtɔra] *nf inv* rat poison.
mortel, le [mɔrtɛl] *adj* (*poison etc*) deadly, lethal; (*accident, blessure*) fatal; (*REL, danger, frayeur*) mortal; (*fig: froid*) deathly; (*: ennui, soirée*) deadly (boring) ♦ *nm/f* mortal.
mortellement [mɔrtɛlmɑ̃] *adv* (*blessé etc*) fatally, mortally; (*pâle etc*) deathly; (*fig: ennuyeux etc*) deadly.
morte-saison, *pl* **mortes-saisons** [mɔrtəsɛzɔ̃] *nf* slack *ou* off season.
mortier [mɔrtje] *nm* (*gén*) mortar.
mortifier [mɔrtifje] *vt* to mortify.
mort-né, e [mɔrne] *adj* (*enfant*) stillborn; (*fig*) abortive.
mortuaire [mɔrtɥɛr] *adj* funeral *cpd*; **avis ~s** death announcements, intimations; **chapelle ~** mortuary chapel; **couronne ~** (funeral) wreath; **domicile ~** house of the deceased; **drap ~** pall.
morue [mɔry] *nf* (*ZOOL*) cod *inv*; (*CULIN*: *salée*) salt-cod.
morutier [mɔrytje] *nm* (*pêcheur*) cod fisherman; (*bateau*) cod fishing boat.
morvandeau, elle, x [mɔrvɑ̃do, -ɛl] *adj* of *ou* from the Morvan region.
morveux, euse [mɔrvø, -øz] *adj* (*fam*) snotty-nosed.
mosaïque [mɔzaik] *nf* (*ART*) mosaic; (*fig*) patchwork.
Moscou [mɔsku] *n* Moscow.
moscovite [mɔskɔvit] *adj* of *ou* from Moscow, Moscow *cpd* ♦ *nm/f*: **M~** Muscovite.
mosquée [mɔske] *nf* mosque.
mot [mo] *nm* word; (*message*) line, note; (*bon mot etc*) saying; **le ~ de la fin** the last word; **~ à ~** *adj, adv* word for word; **~ pour ~** word for word, verbatim; **sur** *ou* **à ces ~s** with these words; **en un ~** in a word; **à ~s couverts** in veiled terms; **prendre qn au ~** to take sb at his word; **se donner le ~** to send the word round; **avoir son ~ à dire** to have a say; **~ d'ordre** watchword; **~ de passe** password; **~s croisés** crossword (puzzle) *sg*.
motard [mɔtar] *nm* biker; (*policier*) motorcycle cop.
motel [mɔtɛl] *nm* motel.
moteur, trice [mɔtœr, -tris] *adj* (*ANAT, PHYSIOL*) motor; (*TECH*) driving; (*AUTO*): **à 4 roues motrices** 4-wheel drive ♦ *nm* engine, motor; (*fig*) mover, mainspring; **à ~** power-driven, motor *cpd*; **~ à deux temps** two-stroke engine; **~ à explosion** internal combustion engine; **~ à réaction** jet engine; **~ thermique** heat engine.
motif [mɔtif] *nm* (*cause*) motive; (*décoratif*) design, pattern, motif; (*d'un tableau*) subject, motif; (*MUS*) figure, motif; **~s** *nmpl* (*JUR*) grounds *pl*; **sans ~** *adj* groundless.

motion [mosjɔ̃] *nf* motion; ~ **de censure** motion of censure, vote of no confidence.
motivation [mɔtivɑsjɔ̃] *nf* motivation.
motivé, e [mɔtive] *adj* (*acte*) justified; (*personne*) motivated.
motiver [mɔtive] *vt* (*justifier*) to justify, account for; (*ADMIN, JUR, PSYCH*) to motivate.
moto [mɔto] *nf* (motor)bike; ~ **verte** *ou* **de trial** trail (*BRIT*) *ou* dirt (*US*) bike.
moto-cross [mɔtɔkʀɔs] *nm* motocross.
motoculteur [mɔtɔkyltœʀ] *nm* (motorized) cultivator.
motocyclette [mɔtɔsiklɛt] *nf* motorbike, motorcycle.
motocyclisme [mɔtɔsiklism(ə)] *nm* motorcycle racing.
motocycliste [mɔtɔsiklist(ə)] *nm/f* motorcyclist.
motoneige [mɔtɔnɛʒ] *nf* snow bike.
motorisé, e [mɔtɔʀize] *adj* (*troupe*) motorized; (*personne*) having one's own transport.
motrice [mɔtʀis] *adj f voir* **moteur**.
motte [mɔt] *nf*: ~ **de terre** lump of earth, clod (of earth); ~ **de gazon** turf, sod; ~ **de beurre** lump of butter.
motus [mɔtys] *excl*: ~ **(et bouche cousue)!** mum's the word!
mou (mol), molle [mu, mɔl] *adj* soft; (*péj: visage, traits*) flabby; (*: geste*) limp; (*: personne*) sluggish; (*: résistance, protestations*) feeble ♦ *nm* (*homme mou*) wimp; (*abats*) lights *pl*, lungs *pl*; (*de la corde*): **avoir du** ~ to be slack; **donner du** ~ to slacken, loosen; **avoir les jambes molles** to be weak at the knees.
mouchard, e [muʃaʀ, -aʀd(ə)] *nm/f* (*péj: SCOL*) sneak; (*: POLICE*) stool pigeon, grass (*BRIT*) ♦ *nm* (*appareil*) control device; (*: de camion*) tachograph.
mouche [muʃ] *nf* fly; (*ESCRIME*) button; (*de taffetas*) patch; **prendre la** ~ to go into a huff; **faire** ~ to score a bull's-eye.
moucher [muʃe] *vt* (*enfant*) to blow the nose of; (*chandelle*) to snuff (out); **se** ~ to blow one's nose.
moucheron [muʃʀɔ̃] *nm* midge.
moucheté, e [muʃte] *adj* (*cheval*) dappled; (*laine*) flecked; (*ESCRIME*) buttoned.
mouchoir [muʃwaʀ] *nm* handkerchief, hanky; ~ **en papier** tissue, paper hanky.
moudre [mudʀ(ə)] *vt* to grind.
moue [mu] *nf* pout; **faire la** ~ to pout; (*fig*) to pull a face.
mouette [mwɛt] *nf* (sea)gull.
mouf(f)ette [mufɛt] *nf* skunk.
moufle [mufl(ə)] *nf* (*gant*) mitt(en); (*TECH*) pulley block.
mouflon [muflɔ̃] *nm* mouf(f)lon.
mouillage [mujaʒ] *nm* (*NAVIG: lieu*) anchorage, moorings *pl*.
mouillé, e [muje] *adj* wet.
mouiller [muje] *vt* (*humecter*) to wet, moisten; (*tremper*): ~ **qn/qch** to make sb/sth wet; (*CULIN: ragoût*) to add stock *ou* wine to; (*couper, diluer*) to water down; (*mine etc*) to lay ♦ *vi* (*NAVIG*) to lie *ou* be at anchor; **se** ~ to get wet; (*fam*) to commit o.s.; to get (o.s.) involved; ~ **l'ancre** to drop *ou* cast anchor.
mouillette [mujɛt] *nf* (bread) finger.
mouillure [mujyʀ] *nf* wet *no pl*; (*tache*) wet patch.
moulage [mulaʒ] *nm* moulding (*BRIT*), molding (*US*); casting; (*objet*) cast.
moulais [mulɛ] *etc vb voir* **moudre**.
moulant, e [mulɑ̃, -ɑ̃t] *adj* figure-hugging.
moule [mul] *vb voir* **moudre** ♦ *nf* (*mollusque*) mussel ♦ *nm* (*creux, CULIN*) mould (*BRIT*), mold (*US*); (*modèle plein*) cast; ~ **à gâteau** *nm* cake tin (*BRIT*) *ou* pan (*US*); ~ **à gaufre** *nm* waffle iron; ~ **à tarte** *nm* pie *ou* flan dish.
moulent [mul] *vb voir* **moudre, mouler**.
mouler [mule] *vt* (*brique*) to mould (*BRIT*), mold (*US*); (*statue*) to cast; (*visage, bas-relief*) to make a cast of; (*lettre*) to shape with care; (*suj: vêtement*) to hug, fit closely round; ~ **qch sur** (*fig*) to model sth on.
moulin [mulɛ̃] *nm* mill; (*fam*) engine; ~ **à café** coffee mill; ~ **à eau** watermill; ~ **à légumes** (vegetable) shredder; ~ **à paroles** (*fig*) chatterbox; ~ **à poivre** pepper mill; ~ **à prières** prayer wheel; ~ **à vent** windmill.
mouliner [muline] *vt* to shred.
moulinet [mulinɛ] *nm* (*de treuil*) winch; (*de canne à pêche*) reel; (*mouvement*): **faire des** ~**s avec qch** to whirl sth around.
moulinette [mulinɛt] *nf* ® (vegetable) shredder.
moulons [mulɔ̃] *etc vb voir* **moudre**.
moulu, e [muly] *pp de* **moudre** ♦ *adj* (*café*) ground.
moulure [mulyʀ] *nf* (*ornement*) moulding (*BRIT*), molding (*US*).
mourant, e [muʀɑ̃, -ɑ̃t] *vb voir* **mourir** ♦ *adj* dying ♦ *nm/f* dying man/woman.
mourir [muʀiʀ] *vi* to die; (*civilisation*) to die out; ~ **assassiné** to be murdered; ~ **de froid/faim/vieillesse** to die of exposure/hunger/old age; ~ **de faim/d'ennui** (*fig*) to be starving/be bored to death; ~ **d'envie de faire** to be dying to do; **s'ennuyer à** ~ to be bored to death.
mousquetaire [muskətɛʀ] *nm* musketeer.
mousqueton [muskətɔ̃] *nm* (*fusil*) carbine; (*anneau*) snap-link, karabiner.
moussant, e [musɑ̃, -ɑ̃t] *adj* foaming; **bain** ~ foam *ou* bubble bath, bath foam.
mousse [mus] *nf* (*BOT*) moss; (*écume: sur eau, bière*) froth, foam; (*: shampooing*) lather; (*de champagne*) bubbles *pl*; (*CULIN*) mousse; (*en caoutchouc etc*) foam ♦ *nm* (*NAVIG*) ship's boy; **bain de** ~ bubble bath; **bas** ~ stretch stockings; **balle** ~ rubber ball; ~ **carbonique** (fire-fighting) foam; ~ **de nylon** nylon foam; (*tissu*) stretch nylon; ~ **à raser** shaving foam.

mousseline [muslin] *nf* (*TEXTILES*) muslin; chiffon; **pommes** ~ (*CULIN*) creamed potatoes.
mousser [muse] *vi* to foam; to lather.
mousseux, euse [musø, -øz] *adj* (*chocolat*) frothy; (*eau*) foamy, frothy; (*vin*) sparkling ♦ *nm*: **(vin)** ~ sparkling wine.
mousson [musɔ̃] *nf* monsoon.
moussu, e [musy] *adj* mossy.
moustache [mustaʃ] *nf* moustache; **~s** *nfpl* (*d'animal*) whiskers *pl*.
moustachu, e [mustaʃy] *adj* wearing a moustache.
moustiquaire [mustikɛʀ] *nf* (*rideau*) mosquito net; (*chassis*) mosquito screen.
moustique [mustik] *nm* mosquito.
moutarde [mutaʀd(ə)] *nf* mustard ♦ *adj inv* mustard(-coloured).
moutardier [mutaʀdje] *nm* mustard jar.
mouton [mutɔ̃] *nm* (*ZOOL, péj*) sheep *inv*; (*peau*) sheepskin; (*CULIN*) mutton.
mouture [mutyʀ] *nf* grinding; (*péj*) rehash.
mouvant, e [muvɑ̃, -ɑ̃t] *adj* unsettled; changing; shifting.
mouvement [muvmɑ̃] *nm* (*gén, aussi: mécanisme*) movement; (*ligne courbe*) contours *pl*; (*fig: tumulte, agitation*) activity, bustle; (*: impulsion*) impulse; reaction; (*geste*) gesture; (*MUS: rythme*) tempo (*pl* -s *ou* tempi); **en** ~ in motion; on the move; **mettre qch en** ~ to set sth in motion, set sth going; ~ **d'humeur** fit *ou* burst of temper; ~ **d'opinion** trend of (public) opinion; **le** ~ **perpétuel** perpetual motion.
mouvementé, e [muvmɑ̃te] *adj* (*vie, poursuite*) eventful; (*réunion*) turbulent.
mouvoir [muvwaʀ] *vt* (*levier, membre*) to move; (*machine*) to drive; **se** ~ to move.
moyen, ne [mwajɛ̃, -ɛn] *adj* average; (*tailles, prix*) medium; (*de grandeur moyenne*) medium-sized ♦ *nm* (*façon*) means *sg*, way ♦ *nf* average; (*STATISTIQUE*) mean; (*SCOL: à l'examen*) pass mark; (*AUTO*) average speed; **~s** *nmpl* (*capacités*) means; **au** ~ **de** by means of; **y a-t-il** ~ **de ...?** is it possible to ...?, can one ...?; **par quel ~?** how?, which way?, by which means?; **par tous les ~s** by every possible means, every possible way; **avec les ~s du bord** (*fig*) with what's available *ou* what comes to hand; **employer les grands ~s** to resort to drastic measures; **par ses propres ~s** all by oneself; **en ~ne** on (an) average; **faire la ~ne** to work out the average; ~ **de locomotion/d'expression** means of transport/expression; ~ **âge** Middle Ages; ~ **de transport** means of transport; **~ne d'âge** average age; **~ne entreprise** (*COMM*) medium-sized firm.
moyenâgeux, euse [mwajɛnaʒø, -øz] *adj* medieval.
moyen-courrier [mwajɛ̃kuʀje] *nm* (*AVIAT*) medium-haul aircraft.
moyennant [mwajɛnɑ̃] *prép* (*somme*) for; (*service, conditions*) in return for; (*travail, effort*) with.
moyennement [mwajɛnmɑ̃] *adv* fairly, moderately; (*faire qch*) fairly *ou* moderately well.
Moyen-Orient [mwajɛnɔʀjɑ̃] *nm*: **le** ~ the Middle East.
moyeu, x [mwajø] *nm* hub.
mozambicain, e [mɔzɑ̃bikɛ̃, -ɛn] *adj* Mozambican.
Mozambique [mɔzɑ̃bik] *nm*: **le** ~ Mozambique.
MRAP *sigle m* = *Mouvement contre le racisme, l'antisémitisme et pour la paix.*
MRP *sigle m* (= *Mouvement républicain populaire*) *political party.*
ms *abr* (= *manuscrit*) MS., ms.
MST *sigle f* (= *maladie sexuellement transmissible*) STD (= *sexually transmitted disease*).
MTC *sigle m* (= *mécanisme du taux de change*) ERM.
mû, mue [my] *pp de* **mouvoir**.
mucosité [mykozite] *nf* mucus *no pl*.
mucus [mykys] *nm* mucus *no pl*.
mue [my] *pp de* **mouvoir** ♦ *nf* moulting (*BRIT*), molting (*US*); sloughing; breaking of the voice.
muer [mɥe] *vi* (*oiseau, mammifère*) to moult (*BRIT*), molt (*US*); (*serpent*) to slough; (*jeune garçon*): **il mue** his voice is breaking; **se** ~ **en** to transform into.
muet, te [mɥɛ, -ɛt] *adj* dumb; (*fig*): ~ **d'admiration** *etc* speechless with admiration *etc*; (*joie, douleur, CINÉ*) silent; (*LING: lettre*) silent, mute; (*carte*) blank ♦ *nm/f* mute ♦ *nm*: **le** ~ (*CINÉ*) the silent cinema *ou* movies (*esp US*).
mufle [myfl(ə)] *nm* muzzle; (*goujat*) boor ♦ *adj* boorish.
mugir [myʒiʀ] *vi* (*bœuf*) to bellow; (*vache*) to low, moo; (*fig*) to howl.
mugissement [myʒismɑ̃] *nm* (*voir mugir*) bellowing; lowing, mooing; howling.
muguet [mygɛ] *nm* (*BOT*) lily of the valley; (*MÉD*) thrush.
mulâtre, tresse [mylɑtʀ(ə), -tʀɛs] *nm/f* mulatto.
mule [myl] *nf* (*ZOOL*) (she-)mule.
mules [myl] *nfpl* (*pantoufles*) mules.
mulet [mylɛ] *nm* (*ZOOL*) (he-)mule; (*poisson*) mullet.
muletier, ière [myltje, -jɛʀ] *adj*: **sentier** *ou* **chemin** ~ mule track.
mulot [mylo] *nm* fieldmouse (*pl* -mice).
multicolore [myltikɔlɔʀ] *adj* multicoloured (*BRIT*), multicolored (*US*).
multicoque [myltikɔk] *nm* multihull.
multidisciplinaire [myltidisiplinɛʀ] *adj* multidisciplinary.
multiforme [myltifɔʀm(ə)] *adj* many-sided.
multilatéral, e, aux [myltilateʀal, -o] *adj*

multilateral.
multimilliardaire [myltimiljardɛʀ], **multimillionnaire** [myltimiljɔnɛʀ] *adj, nm/f* multimillionaire.
multinational, e, aux [myltinasjɔnal, -o] *adj, nf* multinational.
multiple [myltipl(ə)] *adj* multiple, numerous; (*varié*) many, manifold ♦ *nm* (*MATH*) multiple.
multiplex [myltiplɛks] *nm* (*RADIO*) live link-up.
multiplicateur [myltiplikatœʀ] *nm* multiplier.
multiplication [myltiplikɑsjɔ̃] *nf* multiplication.
multiplicité [myltiplisite] *nf* multiplicity.
multiplier [myltiplije] *vt* to multiply; **se** ~ *vi* to multiply; (*fig: personne*) to be everywhere at once.
multiprogrammation [myltipʀɔgʀamɑsjɔ̃] *nf* (*INFORM*) multiprogramming.
multipropriété [myltipʀɔpʀijete] *nf* timesharing *no pl*.
multirisque [myltiʀisk] *adj*: **assurance** ~ multiple-risk insurance.
multisalles [myltisal] *adj*: **(cinéma)** ~ multiplex (cinema).
multitraitement [myltitʀɛtmɑ̃] *nm* (*INFORM*) multiprocessing.
multitude [myltityd] *nf* multitude; mass; **une** ~ **de** a vast number of, a multitude of.
Munich [mynik] *n* Munich.
munichois, e [mynikwa, -waz] *adj* of *ou* from Munich.
municipal, e, aux [mynisipal, -o] *adj* municipal; town *cpd*.
municipalité [mynisipalite] *nf* (*corps municipal*) town council, corporation; (*commune*) town, municipality.
munificence [mynifisɑ̃s] *nf* munificence.
munir [myniʀ] *vt*: ~ **qn/qch de** to equip sb/sth with; **se** ~ **de** to provide o.s. with.
munitions [mynisjɔ̃] *nfpl* ammunition *sg*.
muqueuse [mykøz] *nf* mucous membrane.
mur [myʀ] *nm* wall; (*fig*) stone *ou* brick wall; **faire le** ~ (*interne, soldat*) to jump the wall; ~ **du son** sound barrier.
mûr, e [myʀ] *adj* ripe; (*personne*) mature ♦ *nf* (*de la ronce*) blackberry; (*du mûrier*) mulberry.
muraille [myʀɑj] *nf* (high) wall.
mural, e, aux [myʀal, -o] *adj* wall *cpd* ♦ *nm* (*ART*) mural.
mûre [myʀ] *nf voir* **mûr**.
mûrement [myʀmɑ̃] *adv*: **ayant** ~ **réfléchi** having given the matter much thought.
murène [myʀɛn] *nf* moray (eel).
murer [myʀe] *vt* (*enclos*) to wall (in); (*porte, issue*) to wall up; (*personne*) to wall up *ou* in.
muret [myʀɛ] *nm* low wall.
mûrier [myʀje] *nm* mulberry tree; (*ronce*) blackberry bush.
mûrir [myʀiʀ] *vi* (*fruit, blé*) to ripen; (*abcès, furoncle*) to come to a head; (*fig: idée, personne*) to mature; (*projet*) to develop ♦ *vt* (*fruit, blé*) to ripen; (*personne*) to (make) mature; (*pensée, projet*) to nurture.
murmure [myʀmyʀ] *nm* murmur; ~**s** *nmpl* (*plaintes*) murmurings, mutterings.
murmurer [myʀmyʀe] *vi* to murmur; (*se plaindre*) to mutter, grumble.
mus [my] *etc vb voir* **mouvoir**.
musaraigne [myzaʀɛɲ] *nf* shrew.
musarder [myzaʀde] *vi* to idle (about); (*en marchant*) to dawdle (along).
musc [mysk] *nm* musk.
muscade [myskad] *nf* (*aussi*: **noix** ~) nutmeg.
muscat [myska] *nm* (*raisin*) muscat grape; (*vin*) muscatel (wine).
muscle [myskl(ə)] *nm* muscle.
musclé, e [myskle] *adj* (*personne, corps*) muscular; (*fig: politique, régime etc*) strong-arm *cpd*.
muscler [myskle] *vt* to develop the muscles of.
musculaire [myskylɛʀ] *adj* muscular.
musculation [myskylɑsjɔ̃] *nf*: **exercices de** ~ muscle-developing exercises.
musculature [myskylatyʀ] *nf* muscle structure, muscles *pl*, musculature.
muse [myz] *nf* muse.
museau, x [myzo] *nm* muzzle.
musée [myze] *nm* museum; (*de peinture*) art gallery.
museler [myzle] *vt* to muzzle.
muselière [myzəljɛʀ] *nf* muzzle.
musette [myzɛt] *nf* (*sac*) lunchbag ♦ *adj inv* (*orchestre etc*) accordion *cpd*.
muséum [myzeɔm] *nm* museum.
musical, e, aux [myzikal, -o] *adj* musical.
music-hall [myzikol] *nm* variety theatre; (*genre*) variety.
musicien, ne [myzisjɛ̃, -ɛn] *adj* musical ♦ *nm/f* musician.
musique [myzik] *nf* music; (*fanfare*) band; **faire de la** ~ to make music; (*jouer d'un instrument*) to play an instrument; ~ **de chambre** chamber music; ~ **de fond** background music.
musqué, e [myske] *adj* musky.
must [mœst] *nm* must.
musulman, e [myzylmɑ̃, -an] *adj, nm/f* Moslem, Muslim.
mutant, e [mytɑ̃, -ɑ̃t] *nm/f* mutant.
mutation [mytɑsjɔ̃] *nf* (*ADMIN*) transfer; (*BIO*) mutation.
muter [myte] *vt* (*ADMIN*) to transfer.
mutilation [mytilɑsjɔ̃] *nf* mutilation.
mutilé, e [mytile] *nm/f* disabled person (*through loss of limbs*); ~ **de guerre** disabled ex-serviceman; **grand** ~ severely disabled person.
mutiler [mytile] *vt* to mutilate, maim; (*fig*) to mutilate, deface.
mutin, e [mytɛ̃, -in] *adj* (*enfant, air, ton*) mischievous, impish ♦ *nm/f* (*MIL, NAVIG*) muti

neer.
mutiner [mytine]: **se** ~ *vi* to mutiny.
mutinerie [mytinʀi] *nf* mutiny.
mutisme [mytism(ə)] *nm* silence.
mutualiste [mytɥalist(ə)] *adj*: **société** ~ mutual benefit society, ≈ Friendly Society.
mutualité [mytɥalite] *nf* (*assurance*) mutual (benefit) insurance scheme.
mutuel, le [mytɥɛl] *adj* mutual ♦ *nf* mutual benefit society.
mutuellement [mytɥɛlmɑ̃] *adv* each other, one another.
Myanmar [mjanmaʀ] *nm* Myanmar.
myocarde [mjɔkaʀd(ə)] *nm voir* **infarctus.**
myope [mjɔp] *adj* short-sighted.
myopie [mjɔpi] *nf* short-sightedness, myopia.
myosotis [mjozɔtis] *nm* forget-me-not.
myriade [miʀjad] *nf* myriad.
myrtille [miʀtij] *nf* bilberry (*BRIT*), blueberry (*US*), whortleberry.
mystère [mistɛʀ] *nm* mystery.
mystérieusement [misteʀjøzmɑ̃] *adv* mysteriously.
mystérieux, euse [misteʀjø, -øz] *adj* mysterious.
mysticisme [mistisism(ə)] *nm* mysticism.
mystificateur, trice [mistifikatœʀ, -tʀis] *nm/f* hoaxer, practical joker.
mystification [mistifikɑsjɔ̃] *nf* (*tromperie, mensonge*) hoax; (*mythe*) mystification.
mystifier [mistifje] *vt* to fool, take in; (*tromper*) to mystify.
mystique [mistik] *adj* mystic, mystical ♦ *nm/f* mystic.
mythe [mit] *nm* myth.
mythifier [mitifje] *vt* to turn into a myth, mythologize.
mythique [mitik] *adj* mythical.
mythologie [mitɔlɔʒi] *nf* mythology.
mythologique [mitɔlɔʒik] *adj* mythological.
mythomane [mitɔman] *adj, nm/f* mythomaniac.

N n

N, n [ɛn] *nm inv* N, n ♦ *abr* (= *nord*) N; **N comme Nicolas** N for Nelly (*BRIT*) *ou* Nan (*US*).
n' [n] *adv voir* **ne.**
nabot [nabo] *nm* dwarf.
nacelle [nasɛl] *nf* (*de ballon*) basket.
nacre [nakʀ(ə)] *nf* mother-of-pearl.
nacré, e [nakʀe] *adj* pearly.
nage [naʒ] *nf* swimming; (*manière*) style of swimming, stroke; **traverser/s'éloigner à la** ~ to swim across/away; **en** ~ bathed in perspiration; ~ **indienne** sidestroke; ~ **libre** freestyle; ~ **papillon** butterfly.
nageoire [naʒwaʀ] *nf* fin.
nager [naʒe] *vi* to swim; (*fig: ne rien comprendre*) to be all at sea; ~ **dans** to be swimming in; (*vêtements*) to be lost in; ~ **dans le bonheur** to be overjoyed.
nageur, euse [naʒœʀ, -øz] *nm/f* swimmer.
naguère [nagɛʀ] *adv* (*il y a peu de temps*) not long ago; (*autrefois*) formerly.
naïf, ïve [naif, naiv] *adj* naïve.
nain, e [nɛ̃, nɛn] *adj, nm/f* dwarf.
Nairobi [naiʀɔbi] *n* Nairobi.
nais [nɛ], **naissais** [nɛsɛ] *etc vb voir* **naître.**
naissance [nɛsɑ̃s] *nf* birth; **donner** ~ **à** to give birth to; (*fig*) to give rise to; **prendre** ~ to originate; **aveugle de** ~ born blind; **Français de** ~ French by birth; **à la** ~ **des cheveux** at the roots of the hair; **lieu de** ~ place of birth.
naissant, e [nɛsɑ̃, -ɑ̃t] *vb voir* **naître** ♦ *adj* budding, incipient; (*jour*) dawning.
naît [nɛ] *vb voir* **naître.**
naître [nɛtʀ(ə)] *vi* to be born; (*conflit, complications*): ~ **de** to arise from, be born out of; ~ **à** (*amour, poésie*) to awaken to; **il est né en 1960** he was born in 1960; **il naît plus de filles que de garçons** there are more girls born than boys; **faire** ~ (*fig*) to give rise to, arouse.
naïvement [naivmɑ̃] *adv* naïvely.
naïveté [naivte] *nf* naïvety.
Namibie [namibi] *nf*: **la** ~ Namibia.
nana [nana] *nf* (*fam: fille*) bird (*BRIT*), chick.
nancéien, ne [nɑ̃sejɛ̃, -ɛn] *adj* of *ou* from Nancy.
nantais, e [nɑ̃tɛ, -ɛz] *adj* of *ou* from Nantes.
nantir [nɑ̃tiʀ] *vt*: ~ **qn de** to provide sb with; **les nantis** (*péj*) the well-to-do.
NAP *sigle a* (= *Neuilly Auteuil Passy*) ≈ preppy, ≈ Sloane Ranger *cpd* (*BRIT*).
napalm [napalm] *nm* napalm.
naphtaline [naftalin] *nf*: **boules de** ~ mothballs.
Naples [napl(ə)] *n* Naples.
napolitain, e [napɔlitɛ̃, -ɛn] *adj* Neapolitan; **tranche** ~**e** Neapolitan ice cream.
nappe [nap] *nf* tablecloth; (*fig*) sheet; layer; ~ **de mazout** oil slick; ~ **(phréatique)** water table.
napper [nape] *vt*: ~ **qch de** to coat sth with.
napperon [napʀɔ̃] *nm* table-mat; ~ **individuel** place mat.
naquis [naki] *etc vb voir* **naître.**
narcisse [naʀsis] *nm* narcissus.
narcissique [naʀsisik] *adj* narcissistic.
narcissisme [naʀsisism(ə)] *nm* narcissism.
narcodollars [naʀkodɔlaʀ] *nmpl* drug money *no pl.*
narcotique [naʀkɔtik] *adj, nm* narcotic.
narguer [naʀge] *vt* to taunt.
narine [naʀin] *nf* nostril.

narquois, e [narkwa, -waz] *adj* derisive, mocking.
narrateur, trice [naratœr, -tris] *nm/f* narrator.
narration [narɑsjɔ̃] *nf* narration, narrative; (*SCOL*) essay.
narrer [nare] *vt* to tell the story of, recount.
NASA [nasa] *sigle f* (= *National Aeronautics and Space Administration*) NASA.
nasal, e, aux [nazal, -o] *adj* nasal.
naseau, x [nazo] *nm* nostril.
nasillard, e [nazijar, -ard(ə)] *adj* nasal.
nasiller [nazije] *vi* to speak with a (nasal) twang.
Nassau [naso] *n* Nassau.
nasse [nas] *nf* fish-trap.
natal, e [natal] *adj* native.
nataliste [natalist(ə)] *adj* supporting a rising birth rate.
natalité [natalite] *nf* birth rate.
natation [natɑsjɔ̃] *nf* swimming; **faire de la ~** to go swimming (*regularly*); **~ synchronisée** synchronized swimming.
natif, ive [natif, -iv] *adj* native.
nation [nɑsjɔ̃] *nf* nation; **les N~s unies (NU)** the United Nations (UN).
national, e, aux [nasjɔnal, -o] *adj* national ♦ *nf*: **(route) ~e** ≈ A road (*BRIT*), ≈ state highway (*US*); **obsèques ~es** state funeral.
nationalisation [nasjɔnalizɑsjɔ̃] *nf* nationalization.
nationaliser [nasjɔnalize] *vt* to nationalize.
nationalisme [nasjɔnalism(ə)] *nm* nationalism.
nationaliste [nasjɔnalist(ə)] *adj, nm/f* nationalist.
nationalité [nasjɔnalite] *nf* nationality; **de ~ française** of French nationality.
natte [nat] *nf* (*tapis*) mat; (*cheveux*) plait.
natter [nate] *vt* (*cheveux*) to plait.
naturalisation [natyralizɑsjɔ̃] *nf* naturalization.
naturaliser [natyralize] *vt* to naturalize; (*empailler*) to stuff.
naturaliste [natyralist(ə)] *nm/f* naturalist; (*empailleur*) taxidermist.
nature [natyr] *nf* nature ♦ *adj, adv* (*CULIN*) plain, without seasoning or sweetening; (*café, thé: sans lait*) black; (*: sans sucre*) without sugar; **payer en ~** to pay in kind; **peint d'après ~** painted from life; **être de ~ à faire qch** (*propre à*) to be the sort of thing (*ou* person) to do sth; **~ morte** still-life.
naturel, le [natyrɛl] *adj* (*gén, aussi: enfant*) natural ♦ *nm* naturalness; (*caractère*) disposition, nature; (*autochtone*) native; **au ~** (*CULIN*) in water; in its own juices.
naturellement [natyrɛlmɑ̃] *adv* naturally; (*bien sûr*) of course.
naturisme [natyrism(ə)] *nm* naturism.
naturiste [natyrist(ə)] *nm/f* naturist.
naufrage [nofraʒ] *nm* (ship)wreck; (*fig*) wreck; **faire ~** to be shipwrecked.
naufragé, e [nofraʒe] *nm/f* shipwreck victim, castaway.
Nauru [nɔry] *nm* Nauru.
nauséabond, e [nozeabɔ̃, -ɔ̃d] *adj* foul, nauseous.
nausée [noze] *nf* nausea; **avoir la ~** to feel sick; **avoir des ~s** to have waves of nausea, feel nauseous *ou* sick.
nautique [notik] *adj* nautical, water *cpd*; **sports ~s** water sports.
nautisme [notism(ə)] *nm* water sports *pl*.
naval, e [naval] *adj* naval.
navarrais, e [navarɛ, -ɛz] *adj* Navarrian.
navet [navɛ] *nm* turnip; (*péj*) third-rate film.
navette [navɛt] *nf* shuttle; (*en car etc*) shuttle (service); **faire la ~ (entre)** to go to and fro (between), shuttle (between); **~ spatiale** space shuttle.
navigabilité [navigabilite] *nf* (*d'un navire*) seaworthiness; (*d'un avion*) airworthiness.
navigable [navigabl(ə)] *adj* navigable.
navigant, e [navigɑ̃, -ɑ̃t] *adj* (*AVIAT: personnel*) flying ♦ *nm/f*: **les ~s** the flying staff *ou* personnel.
navigateur [navigatœr] *nm* (*NAVIG*) seafarer, sailor; (*AVIAT*) navigator; (*INFORM*) browser.
navigation [navigɑsjɔ̃] *nf* navigation, sailing; (*COMM*) shipping; **compagnie de ~** shipping company; **~ spatiale** space navigation.
naviguer [navige] *vi* to navigate, sail.
navire [navir] *nm* ship; **~ de guerre** warship; **~ marchand** merchantman.
navire-citerne, *pl* **navires-citernes** [navirsitɛrn(ə)] *nm* tanker.
navire-hôpital, *pl* **navires-hôpitaux** [navirɔpital, -to] *nm* hospital ship.
navrant, e [navrɑ̃, -ɑ̃t] *adj* (*affligeant*) upsetting; (*consternant*) annoying.
navrer [navre] *vt* to upset, distress; **je suis navré (de/de faire/que)** I'm so sorry (for/for doing/that).
nazaréen, ne [nazareɛ̃, -ɛn] *adj* Nazarene.
Nazareth [nazarɛt] *n* Nazareth.
NB *abr* (= *nota bene*) NB.
nbr. *abr* = **nombreux.**
nbses *abr* = **nombreuses.**
n.c. *abr* = *non communiqué, non coté.*
ND *sigle f* = *Notre Dame.*
n.d. *abr* = *non daté, non disponible.*
NDA *sigle f* = *note de l'auteur.*
NDE *sigle f* = *note de l'éditeur.*
NDLR *sigle f* = *note de la rédaction.*
ne, n' [n(ə)] *adv voir* **pas, plus, jamais** *etc*; (*explétif*) *non traduit.*
né, e [ne] *pp de* **naître**; **~ en 1960** born in 1960; **~e Scott** née Scott; **~(e) de ... et de ...** son/daughter of ... and of ...; **~ d'une mère française** having a French mother; **~ pour commander** born to lead ♦ *adj*: **un comédien ~** a born comedian.
néanmoins [neɑ̃mwɛ̃] *adv* nevertheless, yet.
néant [neɑ̃] *nm* nothingness; **réduire à ~** to bring to nought; (*espoir*) to dash.

nébuleux, euse [nebylø, -øz] *adj* (*ciel*) cloudy; (*fig*) nebulous ♦ *nf* (*ASTRONOMIE*) nebula.
nébuliser [nebylize] *vt* (*liquide*) to spray.
nébulosité [nebylozite] *nf* cloud cover; ~ **variable** cloudy in places.
nécessaire [nesesɛʀ] *adj* necessary ♦ *nm* necessary; (*sac*) kit; **faire le** ~ to do the necessary; **n'emporter que le strict** ~ to take only what is strictly necessary; ~ **de couture** sewing kit; ~ **de toilette** toilet bag; ~ **de voyage** overnight bag.
nécessairement [nesesɛʀmɑ̃] *adv* necessarily.
nécessité [nesesite] *nf* necessity; **se trouver dans la** ~ **de faire qch** to find it necessary to do sth; **par** ~ out of necessity.
nécessiter [nesesite] *vt* to require.
nécessiteux, euse [nesesitø, -øz] *adj* needy.
nec plus ultra [nekplysyltʀa] *nm*: **le** ~ **de** the last word in.
nécrologie [nekʀɔlɔʒi] *nf* obituary.
nécrologique [nekʀɔlɔʒik] *adj*: **article** ~ obituary; **rubrique** ~ obituary column.
nécromancie [nekʀɔmɑ̃si] *nf* necromancy.
nécromancien, ne [nekʀɔmɑ̃sjɛ̃, -ɛn] *nm/f* necromancer.
nécrose [nekʀoz] *nf* necrosis.
nectar [nɛktaʀ] *nm* nectar.
nectarine [nɛktaʀin] *nf* nectarine.
néerlandais, e [neɛʀlɑ̃dɛ, -ɛz] *adj* Dutch, of the Netherlands ♦ *nm* (*LING*) Dutch ♦ *nm/f*: **N~, e** Dutchman/woman; **les N~** the Dutch.
nef [nɛf] *nf* (*d'église*) nave.
néfaste [nefast(ə)] *adj* baneful; ill-fated.
négatif, ive [negatif, iv] *adj* negative ♦ *nm* (*PHOTO*) negative.
négation [negɑsjɔ̃] *nf* denial; (*LING*) negation.
négativement [negativmɑ̃] *adv*: **répondre** ~ to give a negative response.
négligé, e [negliʒe] *adj* (*en désordre*) slovenly ♦ *nm* (*tenue*) negligee.
négligeable [negliʒabl(ə)] *adj* insignificant, negligible.
négligemment [negliʒamɑ̃] *adv* carelessly.
négligence [negliʒɑ̃s] *nf* carelessness *no pl*; (*faute*) careless omission.
négligent, e [negliʒɑ̃, -ɑ̃t] *adj* careless; (*JUR etc*) negligent.
négliger [negliʒe] *vt* (*épouse, jardin*) to neglect; (*tenue*) to be careless about; (*avis, précautions*) to disregard, overlook; ~ **de faire** to fail to do, not bother to do; **se** ~ to neglect o.s.
négoce [negɔs] *nm* trade.
négociable [negɔsjabl(ə)] *adj* negotiable.
négociant [negɔsjɑ̃] *nm* merchant.
négociateur [negɔsjatœʀ] *nm* negotiator.
négociation [negɔsjɑsjɔ̃] *nf* negotiation; **~s collectives** collective bargaining *sg*.
négocier [negɔsje] *vi, vt* to negotiate.
nègre [nɛgʀ(ə)] *nm* (*péj*) Negro; (*péj*: *écrivain*) ghost writer ♦ *adj* Negro.
négresse [negʀɛs] *nf* (*péj*) Negress.
négrier [negʀije] *nm* (*fig*) slave driver.
neige [nɛʒ] *nf* snow; **battre les œufs en** ~ (*CULIN*) to whip *ou* beat the egg whites until stiff; ~ **carbonique** dry ice; ~ **fondue** (*par terre*) slush; (*qui tombe*) sleet.
neiger [neʒe] *vi* to snow.
neigeux, euse [nɛʒø, -øz] *adj* snowy, snow-covered.
nénuphar [nenyfaʀ] *nm* water-lily.
néo-calédonien, ne [neɔkaledɔnjɛ̃, -ɛn] *adj* New Caledonian ♦ *nm/f*: **N~, ne** native of New Caledonia.
néocapitalisme [neokapitalism(ə)] *nm* neo-capitalism.
néo-colonialisme [neokɔlɔnjalism(ə)] *nm* neo-colonialism.
néologisme [neɔlɔʒism(ə)] *nm* neologism.
néon [neɔ̃] *nm* neon.
néo-natal, e [neɔnatal] *adj* neonatal.
néophyte [neɔfit] *nm/f* novice.
néo-zélandais, e [neɔzelɑ̃dɛ, -ɛz] *adj* New Zealand *cpd* ♦ *nm/f*: **N~, e** New Zealander.
Népal [nepal] *nm*: **le** ~ Nepal.
népalais, e [nepalɛ, -ɛz] *adj* Nepalese, Nepali ♦ *nm* (*LING*) Nepalese, Nepali ♦ *nm/f*: **N~, e** Nepalese, Nepali.
néphrétique [nefʀetik] *adj* (*MÉD*: *colique*) nephritic.
néphrite [nefʀit] *nf* (*MÉD*) nephritis.
népotisme [nepɔtism(ə)] *nm* nepotism.
nerf [nɛʀ] *nm* nerve; (*fig*) spirit; (*: forces*) stamina; **~s** *nmpl* nerves; **être** *ou* **vivre sur les ~s** to live on one's nerves; **être à bout de ~s** to be at the end of one's tether; **passer ses ~s sur qn** to take it out on sb.
nerveusement [nɛʀvøzmɑ̃] *adv* nervously.
nerveux, euse [nɛʀvø, -øz] *adj* nervous; (*cheval*) highly-strung; (*voiture*) nippy, responsive; (*tendineux*) sinewy.
nervosité [nɛʀvozite] *nf* nervousness; (*émotivité*) excitability.
nervure [nɛʀvyʀ] *nf* (*de feuille*) vein; (*ARCHIT, TECH*) rib.
n'est-ce pas [nɛspɑ] *adv* isn't it?, won't you? *etc, selon le verbe qui précède*; **c'est bon, ~?** it's good, isn't it?; **il a peur, ~?** he's afraid, isn't he?; ~ **que c'est bon?** don't you think it's good?; **lui, ~, il peut se le permettre** he, of course, can afford to do that, can't he?
Net [nɛt] *nm* (*Internet*): **le** ~ the Net; **surfer le** ~ to surf the Net.
net, nette [nɛt] *adj* (*sans équivoque, distinct*) clear; (*photo*) sharp; (*évident*) definite; (*propre*) neat, clean; (*COMM*: *prix, salaire, poids*) net ♦ *adv* (*refuser*) flatly ♦ *nm*: **mettre au** ~ to copy out; **s'arrêter** ~ to stop dead; **la lame a cassé** ~ the blade snapped clean through; **faire place nette** to make a clean sweep; ~ **d'impôt** tax free.
nettement [nɛtmɑ̃] *adv* (*distinctement*) clearly; (*évidemment*) definitely; (*avec comparatif, superlatif*): ~ **mieux** definitely *ou* clearly bet-

ter.

netteté [nɛtte] *nf* clearness.

nettoie [nɛtwa] *etc vb voir* **nettoyer.**

nettoiement [nɛtwamɑ̃] *nm* (*ADMIN*) cleaning; **service du** ~ refuse collection.

nettoierai [nɛtwaʀe] *etc vb voir* **nettoyer.**

nettoyage [nɛtwajaʒ] *nm* cleaning; ~ **à sec** dry cleaning.

nettoyant [nɛtwajɑ̃] *nm* (*produit*) cleaning agent.

nettoyer [nɛtwaje] *vt* to clean; (*fig*) to clean out.

neuf [nœf] *num* nine.

neuf, neuve [nœf, nœv] *adj* new ♦ *nm*: **repeindre à** ~ to redecorate; **remettre à** ~ to do up (as good as new), refurbish; **n'acheter que du** ~ to buy everything new; **quoi de** ~? what's new?

neurasthénique [nøʀastenik] *adj* neurasthenic.

neurochirurgie [nøʀoʃiʀyʀʒi] *nf* neurosurgery.

neurochirurgien [nøʀoʃiʀyʀʒjɛ̃] *nm* neurosurgeon.

neuroleptique [nøʀɔlɛptik] *adj* neuroleptic.

neurologie [nøʀɔlɔʒi] *nf* neurology.

neurologique [nøʀɔlɔʒik] *adj* neurological.

neurologue [nøʀɔlɔg] *nm/f* neurologist.

neurone [nøʀɔn] *nm* neuron(e).

neuropsychiatre [nøʀopsikjatʀ(ə)] *nm/f* neuropsychiatrist.

neutralisation [nøtʀalizɑsjɔ̃] *nf* neutralization.

neutraliser [nøtʀalize] *vt* to neutralize.

neutralisme [nøtʀalism(ə)] *nm* neutralism.

neutraliste [nøtʀalist(ə)] *adj* neutralist.

neutralité [nøtʀalite] *nf* neutrality.

neutre [nøtʀ(ə)] *adj, nm* (*aussi LING*) neutral.

neutron [nøtʀɔ̃] *nm* neutron.

neuve [nœv] *adj f voir* **neuf.**

neuvième [nœvjɛm] *num* ninth.

névé [neve] *nm* permanent snowpatch.

neveu, x [nəvø] *nm* nephew.

névralgie [nevʀalʒi] *nf* neuralgia.

névralgique [nevʀalʒik] *adj* (*fig: sensible*) sensitive; **centre** ~ nerve centre.

névrite [nevʀit] *nf* neuritis.

névrose [nevʀoz] *nf* neurosis.

névrosé, e [nevʀoze] *adj, nm/f* neurotic.

névrotique [nevʀɔtik] *adj* neurotic.

New York [njujɔʀk] *n* New York.

new-yorkais, e [njujɔʀkɛ, -ɛz] *adj* of *ou* from New York, New York *cpd* ♦ *nm/f*: **New-Yorkais, e** New Yorker.

nez [ne] *nm* nose; **rire au** ~ **de qn** to laugh in sb's face; **avoir du** ~ to have flair; **avoir le** ~ **fin** to have foresight; ~ **à** ~ **avec** face to face with; **à vue de** ~ roughly.

NF *sigle mpl = nouveaux francs* ♦ *sigle f (INDUSTRIE: = norme française) industrial standard.*

ni [ni] *conj*: ~ **l'un** ~ **l'autre ne sont** *ou* **n'est** neither one nor the other is; **il n'a rien dit** ~ **fait** he hasn't said or done anything.

Niagara [njagaʀa] *nm*: **les chutes du** ~ the Niagara Falls.

niais, e [njɛ, -ɛz] *adj* silly, thick.

niaiserie [njɛzʀi] *nf* gullibility; (*action, propos, futilité*) silliness.

Nicaragua [nikɑʀagwa] *nm*: **le** ~ Nicaragua.

nicaraguayen, ne [nikɑʀagwajɛ̃, -ɛn] *adj* Nicaraguan ♦ *nm/f*: **N~, ne** Nicaraguan.

Nice [nis] *n* Nice.

niche [niʃ] *nf* (*du chien*) kennel; (*de mur*) recess, niche; (*farce*) trick.

nichée [niʃe] *nf* brood, nest.

nicher [niʃe] *vi* to nest; **se** ~ **dans** (*personne: se blottir*) to snuggle into; (*: se cacher*) to hide in; (*objet*) to lodge itself in.

nichon [niʃɔ̃] *nm* (*fam*) boob, tit.

nickel [nikɛl] *nm* nickel.

niçois, e [niswa, -waz] *adj* of *ou* from Nice; (*CULIN*) Nicoise.

Nicosie [nikɔsi] *n* Nicosia.

nicotine [nikɔtin] *nf* nicotine.

nid [ni] *nm* nest; (*fig: repaire etc*) den, lair; ~ **d'abeilles** (*COUTURE, TEXTILE*) honeycomb stitch; ~ **de poule** pothole.

nièce [njɛs] *nf* niece.

nième [ɛnjɛm] *adj*: **la** ~ **fois** the nth *ou* umpteenth time.

nier [nje] *vt* to deny.

nigaud, e [nigo, -od] *nm/f* booby, fool.

Niger [niʒɛʀ] *nm*: **le** ~ Niger; (*fleuve*) the Niger.

Nigéria [niʒeʀja] *nm ou nf* Nigeria.

nigérian, e [niʒeʀjɑ̃, -an] *adj* Nigerian ♦ *nm/f*: **N~, e** Nigerian.

nigérien, ne [niʒeʀjɛ̃, -ɛn] *adj* of *ou* from Niger.

night-club [najtklœb] *nm* nightclub.

nihilisme [niilism(ə)] *nm* nihilism.

nihiliste [niilist(ə)] *adj* nihilist, nihilistic.

Nil [nil] *nm*: **le** ~ the Nile.

n'importe [nɛ̃pɔʀt(ə)] *adv*: ~! no matter!; ~ **qui/quoi/où** anybody/anything/anywhere; ~ **quoi!** (*fam: désapprobation*) what rubbish!; ~ **quand** any time; ~ **quel/quelle** any; ~ **lequel/laquelle** any (one); ~ **comment** (*sans soin*) carelessly; ~ **comment, il part ce soir** he's leaving tonight in any case.

nippes [nip] *nfpl* (*fam*) togs.

nippon, e *ou* **ne** [nipɔ̃, -ɔn] *adj* Japanese.

nique [nik] *nf*: **faire la** ~ **à** to thumb one's nose at (*fig*).

nitouche [nituʃ] *nf* (*péj*): **c'est une sainte** ~ she looks as if butter wouldn't melt in her mouth.

nitrate [nitʀat] *nm* nitrate.

nitrique [nitʀik] *adj*: **acide** ~ nitric acid.

nitroglycérine [nitʀɔgliseʀin] *nf* nitroglycerin(e).

niveau, x [nivo] *nm* level; (*des élèves, études*) standard; **au** ~ **de** at the level of; (*personne*) on a level with; **de** ~ **(avec)** level (with); **le**

~ **de la mer** sea level; ~ **(à bulle)** spirit level; ~ **(d'eau)** water level; ~ **de vie** standard of living.
niveler [nivle] *vt* to level.
niveleuse [nivløz] *nf* (*TECH*) grader.
nivellement [nivɛlmɑ̃] *nm* levelling.
nivernais, e [nivɛʀnɛ, -ɛz] *adj* of *ou* from Nevers (and region) ♦ *nm/f*: **N~, e** inhabitant *ou* native of Nevers (and region).
NL *sigle f* = *nouvelle lune*.
NN *abr* (= *nouvelle norme*) *revised standard of hotel classification.*
n° *abr* (= *numéro*) no.
nobiliaire [nɔbiljɛʀ] *adj f voir* **particule**.
noble [nɔbl(ə)] *adj* noble; (*de qualité: métal etc*) precious ♦ *nm/f* noble(man/woman).
noblesse [nɔblɛs] *nf* (*classe sociale*) nobility; (*d'une action etc*) nobleness.
noce [nɔs] *nf* wedding; (*gens*) wedding party (*ou* guests *pl*); **il l'a épousée en secondes ~s** she was his second wife; **faire la ~** (*fam*) to go on a binge; **~s d'or/d'argent/de diamant** golden/silver/diamond wedding.
noceur [nɔsœʀ] *nm* (*fam*): **c'est un sacré ~** he's a real party animal.
nocif, ive [nɔsif, -iv] *adj* harmful, noxious.
noctambule [nɔktɑ̃byl] *nm* night-bird.
nocturne [nɔktyʀn(ə)] *adj* nocturnal ♦ *nf* (*SPORT*) floodlit fixture; (*d'un magasin*) late opening.
Noël [nɔɛl] *nm* Christmas; **la (fête de) ~** Christmas time.
nœud [nø] *nm* (*de corde, du bois, NAVIG*) knot; (*ruban*) bow; (*fig: liens*) bond, tie; (: *d'une question*) crux; (*THÉÂT etc*): **le ~ de l'action** the web of events; ~ **coulant** noose; ~ **gordien** Gordian knot; ~ **papillon** bow tie.
noie [nwa] *etc vb voir* **noyer**.
noir, e [nwaʀ] *adj* black; (*obscur, sombre*) dark ♦ *nm/f* black man/woman ♦ *nm*: **dans le ~** in the dark ♦ *nf* (*MUS*) crotchet (*BRIT*), quarter note (*US*); **il fait ~** it is dark; **au ~** *adv* (*acheter, vendre*) on the black market; **travail au ~** moonlighting.
noirâtre [nwaʀɑtʀ(ə)] *adj* (*teinte*) blackish.
noirceur [nwaʀsœʀ] *nf* blackness; darkness.
noircir [nwaʀsiʀ] *vt, vi* to blacken.
noise [nwaz] *nf*: **chercher ~ à** to try and pick a quarrel with.
noisetier [nwaztje] *nm* hazel (tree).
noisette [nwazɛt] *nf* hazelnut; (*morceau: de beurre etc*) small knob ♦ *adj* (*yeux*) hazel.
noix [nwa] *nf* walnut; (*fam*) twit; (*CULIN*): **une ~ de beurre** a knob of butter; **à la ~** (*fam*) worthless; ~ **de cajou** cashew nut; ~ **de coco** coconut; ~ **muscade** nutmeg; ~ **de veau** (*CULIN*) round fillet of veal.
nom [nɔ̃] *nm* name; (*LING*) noun; **connaître qn de ~** to know sb by name; **au ~ de** in the name of; ~ **d'une pipe** *ou* **d'un chien!** (*fam*) for goodness' sake!; ~ **de Dieu!** (*fam!*) bloody hell! (*BRIT*), my God!; ~ **commun/propre** common/proper noun; ~ **composé** (*LING*) compound noun; ~ **déposé** trade name; ~ **d'emprunt** assumed name; ~ **de famille** surname; ~ **de fichier** file name; ~ **de jeune fille** maiden name.
nomade [nɔmad] *adj* nomadic ♦ *nm/f* nomad.
nombre [nɔ̃bʀ(ə)] *nm* number; **venir en ~** to come in large numbers; **depuis ~ d'années** for many years; **ils sont au ~ de 3** there are 3 of them; **au ~ de mes amis** among my friends; **sans ~** countless; **(bon) ~ de** (*beaucoup, plusieurs*) a (large) number of; ~ **premier/entier** prime/whole number.
nombreux, euse [nɔ̃bʀø, -øz] *adj* many, numerous; (*avec nom sg: foule etc*) large; **peu ~** few; small; **de ~ cas** many cases.
nombril [nɔ̃bʀi] *nm* navel.
nomenclature [nɔmɑ̃klatyʀ] *nf* wordlist; list of items.
nominal, e, aux [nɔminal, -o] *adj* nominal; (*appel, liste*) of names.
nominatif, ive [nɔminatif, -iv] *nm* (*LING*) nominative ♦ *adj*: **liste ~ive** list of names; **carte ~ive** calling card; **titre ~** registered name.
nomination [nɔminɑsjɔ̃] *nf* nomination.
nommément [nɔmemɑ̃] *adv* (*désigner*) by name.
nommer [nɔme] *vt* (*baptiser*) to name, give a name to; (*qualifier*) to call; (*mentionner*) to name, give the name of; (*élire*) to appoint, nominate; **se ~**: **il se nomme Pascal** his name's Pascal, he's called Pascal.
non [nɔ̃] *adv* (*réponse*) no; (*suivi d'un adjectif, adverbe*) not; **Paul est venu, ~?** Paul came, didn't he?; **répondre** *ou* **dire que ~** to say no; ~ **pas que** not that; ~ **plus: moi ~ plus** neither do I, I don't either; **je préférerais que ~** I would prefer not; **il se trouve que ~** perhaps not; **je pense que ~** I don't think so; ~ **mais!** well really!; ~ **mais des fois!** you must be joking!; ~ **alcoolisé** non-alcoholic; ~ **loin/seulement** not far/only.
nonagénaire [nɔnaʒenɛʀ] *nm/f* nonagenarian.
non-agression [nɔnagʀesjɔ̃] *nf*: **pacte de ~** non-aggression pact.
non aligné, e [nɔnaliɲe] *adj* (*POL*) non-aligned.
nonante [nɔnɑ̃t] *num* (*Belgique, Suisse*) ninety.
non-assistance [nɔnasistɑ̃s] *nf* (*JUR*): ~ **à personne en danger** *failure to render assistance to a person in danger.*
nonce [nɔ̃s] *nm* (*REL*) nuncio.
nonchalamment [nɔ̃ʃalamɑ̃] *adv* nonchalantly.
nonchalance [nɔ̃ʃalɑ̃s] *nf* nonchalance, casualness.
nonchalant, e [nɔ̃ʃalɑ̃, -ɑ̃t] *adj* nonchalant, casual.
non-conformisme [nɔ̃kɔ̃fɔʀmism(ə)] *nm* nonconformism.
non-conformiste [nɔ̃kɔ̃fɔʀmist(ə)] *adj, nm/f* non-conformist.
non-conformité [nɔ̃kɔ̃fɔʀmite] *nf* noncon-

formity.
non-croyant, e [nɔ̃kʀwajɑ̃, -ɑ̃t] *nm/f* (*REL*) non-believer.
non(-)engagé, e [nɔnɑ̃gaʒe] *adj* non-aligned.
non-fumeur [nɔ̃fymœʀ] *nm* non-smoker.
non-ingérence [nɔnɛ̃ʒeʀɑ̃s] *nf* non-interference.
non-initié, e [nɔ̃ninisje] *nm/f* lay person; **les ~s** the uninitiated.
non-inscrit, e [nɔnɛ̃skʀi, -it] *nm/f* (*POL*: *député*) independent.
non-intervention [nɔnɛ̃tɛʀvɑ̃sjɔ̃] *nf* non-intervention.
non-lieu [nɔ̃ljø] *nm*: **il y a eu ~** the case was dismissed.
nonne [nɔn] *nf* nun.
nonobstant [nɔnɔpstɑ̃] *prép* notwithstanding.
non-paiement [nɔ̃pɛmɑ̃] *nm* non-payment.
non-prolifération [nɔ̃pʀɔlifeʀɑsjɔ̃] *nf* non-proliferation.
non-résident [nɔ̃ʀesidɑ̃] *nm* (*ÉCON*) non-resident.
non-retour [nɔ̃ʀətuʀ] *nm*: **point de ~** point of no return.
non-sens [nɔ̃sɑ̃s] *nm* absurdity.
non-spécialiste [nɔ̃spesjalist(ə)] *nm/f* non-specialist.
non-stop [nɔnstɔp] *adj inv* nonstop.
non-syndiqué, e [nɔ̃sɛ̃dike] *nm/f* non-union member.
non-violence [nɔ̃vjɔlɑ̃s] *nf* nonviolence.
non-violent, e [nɔ̃vjɔlɑ̃, -ɑ̃t] *adj* non-violent.
nord [nɔʀ] *nm* North ♦ *adj* northern; north; **au ~** (*situation*) in the north; (*direction*) to the north; **au ~ de** north of, to the north of; **perdre le ~** to lose the place (*fig*).
nord-africain, e [nɔʀafʀikɛ̃, -ɛn] *adj* North-African ♦ *nm/f*: **Nord-Africain, e** North African.
nord-américain, e [nɔʀameʀikɛ̃, -ɛn] *adj* North American ♦ *nm/f*: **Nord-Américain, e** North American.
nord-coréen, ne [nɔʀkɔʀeɛ̃, -ɛn] *adj* North Korean ♦ *nm/f*: **Nord-Coréen, ne** North Korean.
nord-est [nɔʀɛst] *nm* North-East.
nordique [nɔʀdik] *adj* (*pays, race*) Nordic; (*langues*) Scandinavian, Nordic ♦ *nm/f*: **N~** Scandinavian.
nord-ouest [nɔʀwɛst] *nm* North-West.
nord-vietnamien, ne [nɔʀvjɛtnamjɛ̃, -ɛn] *adj* North Vietnamese ♦ *nm/f*: **Nord-Vietnamien, ne** North Vietnamese.
normal, e, aux [nɔʀmal, -o] *adj* normal ♦ *nf*: **la ~e** the norm, the average.
normalement [nɔʀmalmɑ̃] *adv* (*en général*) normally; (*comme prévu*): **~, il le fera demain** he should be doing it tomorrow, he's supposed to do it tomorrow.
normalien, ne [nɔʀmaljɛ̃, -ɛn] *nm/f student of École normale supérieure.*
normalisation [nɔʀmalizɑsjɔ̃] *nf* standardization; normalization.
normaliser [nɔʀmalize] *vt* (*COMM, TECH*) to standardize; (*POL*) to normalize.
normand, e [nɔʀmɑ̃, -ɑ̃d] *adj* (*de Normandie*) Norman ♦ *nm/f*: **N~, e** (*de Normandie*) Norman.
Normandie [nɔʀmɑ̃di] *nf*: **la ~** Normandy.
norme [nɔʀm(ə)] *nf* norm; (*TECH*) standard.
Norvège [nɔʀvɛʒ] *nf*: **la ~** Norway.
norvégien, ne [nɔʀveʒjɛ̃, -ɛn] *adj* Norwegian ♦ *nm* (*LING*) Norwegian ♦ *nm/f*: **N~, ne** Norwegian.
nos [no] *adj possessif voir* **notre**.
nostalgie [nɔstalʒi] *nf* nostalgia.
nostalgique [nɔstalʒik] *adj* nostalgic.
notabilité [nɔtabilite] *nf* notability.
notable [nɔtabl(ə)] *adj* notable, noteworthy; (*marqué*) noticeable, marked ♦ *nm* prominent citizen.
notablement [nɔtabləmɑ̃] *adv* notably; (*sensiblement*) noticeably.
notaire [nɔtɛʀ] *nm* notary; solicitor.
notamment [nɔtamɑ̃] *adv* in particular, among others.
notariat [nɔtaʀja] *nm* profession of notary (*ou* solicitor).
notarié, e [nɔtaʀje] *adj*: **acte ~** deed drawn up by a notary (*ou* solicitor).
notation [nɔtɑsjɔ̃] *nf* notation.
note [nɔt] *nf* (*écrite, MUS*) note; (*SCOL*) mark (*BRIT*), grade; (*facture*) bill; **prendre des ~s** to take notes; **prendre ~ de** to note; (*par écrit*) to note, write down; **dans la ~** exactly right; **forcer la ~** to exaggerate; **une ~ de tristesse/de gaieté** a sad/happy note; **~ de service** memorandum.
noté, e [nɔte] *adj*: **être bien/mal ~** (*employé etc*) to have a good/bad record.
noter [nɔte] *vt* (*écrire*) to write down, note; (*remarquer*) to note, notice; (*SCOL, ADMIN*: *donner une appréciation*) to mark, give a grade to; **notez bien que ...** (please) note that ....
notice [nɔtis] *nf* summary, short article (*brochure*): **~ explicative** explanatory leaflet instruction booklet.
notification [nɔtifikɑsjɔ̃] *nf* notification.
notifier [nɔtifje] *vt*: **~ qch à qn** to notify sb of sth, notify sth to sb.
notion [nosjɔ̃] *nf* notion, idea; **~s** *nfpl* (*rudiments*) rudiments.
notoire [nɔtwaʀ] *adj* widely known; (*en mal*) notorious; **le fait est ~** the fact is common knowledge.
notoriété [nɔtɔʀjete] *nf*: **c'est de ~ publique** it's common knowledge.
notre, nos [nɔtʀ(ə), no] *adj possessif* our.
nôtre [notʀ(ə)] *adj* ours ♦ *pron*: **le/la ~** ours; **les ~s** ours; (*alliés etc*) our own people; **soyez des ~s** join us.
nouba [nuba] *nf* (*fam*): **faire la ~** to live it up.
nouer [nwe] *vt* to tie, knot; (*fig: alliance etc*) to strike up; **~ la conversation** to start a con

versation; **se** ~ *vi*: **c'est là où l'intrigue se noue** it's at that point that the strands of the plot come together; **ma gorge se noua** a lump came to my throat.
noueux, euse [nwø, -øz] *adj* gnarled.
nougat [nuga] *nm* nougat.
nougatine [nugatin] *nf kind of nougat.*
nouille [nuj] *nf (pâtes)*: ~**s** noodles; pasta *sg*; *(fam)* noodle *(BRIT)*, fathead.
nounou [nunu] *nf* nanny.
nounours [nunuʀs] *nm* teddy (bear).
nourri, e [nuʀi] *adj (feu etc)* sustained.
nourrice [nuʀis] *nf* ≈ baby-minder; *(autrefois)* wet-nurse.
nourrir [nuʀiʀ] *vt* to feed; *(fig: espoir)* to harbour, nurse; **logé nourri** with board and lodging; ~ **au sein** to breast-feed; **se** ~ **de légumes** to live on vegetables.
nourrissant, e [nuʀisɑ̃, -ɑ̃t] *adj* nourishing, nutritious.
nourrisson [nuʀisɔ̃] *nm* (unweaned) infant.
nourriture [nuʀityʀ] *nf* food.
nous [nu] *pron (sujet)* we; *(objet)* us.
nous-mêmes [numɛm] *pron* ourselves.
nouveau (nouvel), elle, x [nuvo, -ɛl] *adj* new; *(original)* novel ♦ *nm/f* new pupil *(ou* employee) ♦ *nm*: **il y a du** ~ there's something new ♦ *nf* (piece of) news *sg*; *(LITTÉRATURE)* short story; **nouvelles** *nfpl (PRESSE, TV)* news; **de** ~, **à** ~ again; **je suis sans nouvelles de lui** I haven't heard from him; **Nouvel An** New Year; ~ **venu, nouvelle venue** newcomer; ~**x mariés** newly-weds.
nouveau-né, e [nuvone] *nm/f* newborn (baby).
nouveauté [nuvote] *nf* novelty; *(chose nouvelle)* innovation, something new; *(COMM)* new film *(ou* book *ou* creation *etc)*.
nouvel *adj m*, **nouvelle** *adj f, nf* [nuvɛl] *voir* **nouveau.**
Nouvelle-Angleterre [nuvɛlɑ̃glətɛʀ] *nf*: **la** ~ New England.
Nouvelle-Calédonie [nuvɛlkaledɔni] *nf*: **la** ~ New Caledonia.
Nouvelle-Écosse [nuvɛlekɔs] *nf*: **la** ~ Nova Scotia.
Nouvelle-Galles du Sud [nuvɛlgaldysyd] *nf*: **la** ~ New South Wales.
Nouvelle-Guinée [nuvɛlgine] *nf*: **la** ~ New Guinea.
nouvellement [nuvɛlmɑ̃] *adv (arrivé etc)* recently, newly.
Nouvelle-Orléans [nuvɛlɔʀleɑ̃] *nf*: **la** ~ New Orleans.
Nouvelles-Hébrides [nuvɛlsebʀid] *nfpl*: **les** ~ the New Hebrides.
Nouvelle-Zélande [nuvɛlzelɑ̃d] *nf*: **la** ~ New Zealand.
nouvelliste [nuvelist(ə)] *nm/f* editor *ou* writer of short stories.
novateur, trice [nɔvatœʀ, -tʀis] *adj* innovative ♦ *nm/f* innovator.
novembre [nɔvɑ̃bʀ(ə)] *nm* November; *voir aussi* **juillet**; *see boxed note.*

LE 11 NOVEMBRE

Le 11 novembre *is a public holiday in France and commemorates the signing of the armistice, near Compiègne, at the end of the First World War.*

novice [nɔvis] *adj* inexperienced ♦ *nm/f* novice.
noviciat [nɔvisja] *nm (REL)* noviciate.
noyade [nwajad] *nf* drowning *no pl.*
noyau, x [nwajo] *nm (de fruit)* stone; *(BIO, PHYSIQUE)* nucleus; *(ÉLEC, GÉO, fig: centre)* core; *(fig: d'artistes etc)* group; *(: de résistants etc)* cell.
noyautage [nwajotaʒ] *nm (POL)* infiltration.
noyauter [nwajote] *vt (POL)* to infiltrate.
noyé, e [nwaje] *nm/f* drowning *(ou* drowned) man/woman ♦ *adj (fig: dépassé)* out of one's depth.
noyer [nwaje] *nm* walnut (tree); *(bois)* walnut ♦ *vt* to drown; *(fig)* to flood; to submerge; *(AUTO: moteur)* to flood; **se** ~ to be drowned, drown; *(suicide)* to drown o.s; ~ **son chagrin** to drown one's sorrows; ~ **le poisson** to duck the issue.
NSP *sigle m (REL) = Notre Saint Père*; *(dans les sondages: = ne sais pas)* don't know.
NT *sigle m (= Nouveau Testament)* NT.
NU *sigle fpl (= Nations unies)* UN.
nu, e [ny] *adj* naked; *(membres)* naked, bare; *(chambre, fil, plaine)* bare ♦ *nm (ART)* nude; **le** ~ **intégral** total nudity; **se mettre** ~ to strip; **mettre à** ~ to bare.
nuage [nɥaʒ] *nm* cloud; **être dans les** ~**s** *(distrait)* to have one's head in the clouds; ~ **de lait** drop of milk.
nuageux, euse [nɥaʒø, -øz] *adj* cloudy.
nuance [nɥɑ̃s] *nf (de couleur, sens)* shade; **il y a une** ~ **(entre)** there's a slight difference (between); **une** ~ **de tristesse** a tinge of sadness.
nuancé, e [nɥɑ̃se] *adj (opinion)* finely-shaded, subtly differing; **être** ~ **dans ses opinions** to have finely-shaded opinions.
nuancer [nɥɑ̃se] *vt (pensée, opinion)* to qualify.
nubile [nybil] *adj* nubile.
nucléaire [nykleɛʀ] *adj* nuclear ♦ *nm* nuclear power.
nudisme [nydism(ə)] *nm* nudism.
nudiste [nydist(ə)] *adj, nm/f* nudist.
nudité [nydite] *nf (voir nu)* nudity, nakedness; bareness.
nuée [nɥe] *nf*: **une** ~ **de** a cloud *ou* host *ou* swarm of.
nues [ny] *nfpl*: **tomber des** ~ to be taken aback; **porter qn aux** ~ to praise sb to the skies.
nui [nɥi] *pp de* **nuire.**
nuire [nɥiʀ] *vi* to be harmful; ~ **à** to harm, do damage to.

nuisance [nɥizɑ̃s] *nf* nuisance; **~s** *nfpl* pollution *sg*.

nuisible [nɥizibl(ə)] *adj* harmful; **(animal)** ~ pest.

nuisis [nɥizi] *etc vb voir* **nuire**.

nuit [nɥi] *nf* night; **payer sa** ~ to pay for one's overnight accommodation; **il fait** ~ it's dark; **cette** ~ (*hier*) last night; (*aujourd'hui*) tonight; **de** ~ (*vol, service*) night *cpd*; ~ **blanche** sleepless night; ~ **de noces** wedding night; ~ **de Noël** Christmas Eve.

nuitamment [nɥitamɑ̃] *adv* by night.

nuitées [nɥite] *nfpl* overnight stays, beds occupied (*in statistics*).

nul, nulle [nyl] *adj* (*aucun*) no; (*minime*) nil, non-existent; (*non valable*) null; (*péj*) useless, hopeless ♦ *pron* none, no one; **résultat** ~, **match** ~ draw; **nulle part** *adv* nowhere.

nullement [nylmɑ̃] *adv* by no means.

nullité [nylite] *nf* nullity; (*péj*) hopelessness; (*: personne*) hopeless individual, nonentity.

numéraire [nymeʀɛʀ] *nm* cash; metal currency.

numéral, e, aux [nymeʀal, -o] *adj* numeral.

numérateur [nymeʀatœʀ] *nm* numerator.

numération [nymeʀɑsjɔ̃] *nf*: ~ **décimale/binaire** decimal/binary notation; ~ **globulaire** blood count.

numérique [nymeʀik] *adj* numerical; (*INFORM*) digital.

numériquement [nymeʀikmɑ̃] *adv* numerically.

numériser [nymeʀize] *vt* (*INFORM*) to digitize.

numéro [nymeʀo] *nm* number; (*spectacle*) act, turn; **faire** *ou* **composer un** ~ to dial a number; ~ **d'identification personnel** personal identification number (PIN); ~ **d'immatriculation** *ou* **minéralogique** *ou* **de police** registration (*BRIT*) *ou* license (*US*) number; ~ **de téléphone** (tele)phone number; ~ **vert** ≈ Freefone ® number (*BRIT*), ≈ toll-free number (*US*).

numérotage [nymeʀɔtaʒ] *nm* numbering.

numérotation [nymeʀɔtɑsjɔ̃] *nf* numeration.

numéroter [nymeʀɔte] *vt* to number.

numerus clausus [nymeʀysklozys] *nm inv* restriction *ou* limitation of numbers.

numismate [nymismat] *nm/f* numismatist, coin collector.

nu-pieds [nypje] *nm inv* sandal ♦ *adj inv* barefoot.

nuptial, e, aux [nypsjal, -o] *adj* nuptial; wedding *cpd*.

nuptialité [nypsjalite] *nf*: **taux de** ~ marriage rate.

nuque [nyk] *nf* nape of the neck.

nu-tête [nytɛt] *adj inv* bareheaded.

nutritif, ive [nytʀitif, -iv] *adj* nutritional; (*aliment*) nutritious, nourishing.

nutrition [nytʀisjɔ̃] *nf* nutrition.

nutritionnel, le [nytʀisjɔnɛl] *adj* nutritional.

nutritionniste [nytʀisjɔnist(ə)] *nm/f* nutritionist.

nylon [nilɔ̃] *nm* nylon.

nymphomane [nɛ̃fɔman] *adj, nf* nymphomaniac.

O o

O, o [o] *nm inv* O, o ♦ *abr* (= *ouest*) W; **O comme Oscar** ≈ O for Oliver (*BRIT*) *ou* Oboe (*US*).

OAS *sigle f* (= *Organisation de l'armée secrète*) *organization opposed to Algerian independence (1961-63)*.

oasis [ɔazis] *nf ou m* oasis (*pl* oases).

obédience [ɔbedjɑ̃s] *nf* allegiance.

obéir [ɔbeiʀ] *vi* to obey; ~ **à** to obey; (*suj: moteur, véhicule*) to respond to.

obéissance [ɔbeisɑ̃s] *nf* obedience.

obéissant, e [ɔbeisɑ̃, -ɑ̃t] *adj* obedient.

obélisque [ɔbelisk(ə)] *nm* obelisk.

obèse [ɔbɛz] *adj* obese.

obésité [ɔbezite] *nf* obesity.

objecter [ɔbʒɛkte] *vt* (*prétexter*) to plead, put forward as an excuse; ~ **qch à** (*argument*) to put forward sth against; ~ **(à qn) que** to object (to sb) that.

objecteur [ɔbʒɛktœʀ] *nm*: ~ **de conscience** conscientious objector.

objectif, ive [ɔbʒɛktif, -iv] *adj* objective ♦ *nm* (*OPTIQUE, PHOTO*) lens *sg*; (*MIL, fig*) objective; ~ **grand angulaire/à focale variable** wide-angle/zoom lens.

objection [ɔbʒɛksjɔ̃] *nf* objection; ~ **de conscience** conscientious objection.

objectivement [ɔbʒɛktivmɑ̃] *adv* objectively.

objectivité [ɔbʒɛktivite] *nf* objectivity.

objet [ɔbʒɛ] *nm* (*chose*) object; (*d'une discussion, recherche*) subject; **être** *ou* **faire l'~ de** (*discussion*) to be the subject of; (*soins*) to be given *ou* shown; **sans** ~ *adj* purposeless, (*sans fondement*) groundless; ~ **d'art** objet d'art; **~s personnels** personal items; **~s de toilette** toiletries; **~s trouvés** lost property *sg* (*BRIT*), lost-and-found *sg* (*US*).

objurgations [ɔbʒyʀgɑsjɔ̃] *nfpl* objurgations (*prières*) entreaties.

obligataire [ɔbligatɛʀ] *adj* bond *cpd* ♦ *nm/f* bondholder, debenture holder.

obligation [ɔbligɑsjɔ̃] *nf* obligation; (*gén p devoir*) duty; (*COMM*) bond, debenture; **sans ~ d'achat** with no obligation (to buy); **être dans l'~ de faire** to be obliged to do; **avoir l'~ de faire** to be under an obligation to do; **~s familiales** family obligations *ou* responsibilities; **~s militaires** military obligations *ou* duties.

obligatoire [ɔbligatwaʀ] *adj* compulsory, obligatory.
obligatoirement [ɔbligatwaʀmɑ̃] *adv* compulsorily; (*fatalement*) necessarily.
obligé, e [ɔbliʒe] *adj* (*redevable*): **être très ~ à qn** to be most obliged to sb; (*contraint*): **je suis (bien) ~ (de le faire)** I have to (do it); (*nécessaire: conséquence*) necessary; **c'est ~!** it's inevitable!
obligeamment [ɔbliʒamɑ̃] *adv* obligingly.
obligeance [ɔbliʒɑ̃s] *nf*: **avoir l'~ de** to be kind *ou* good enough to.
obligeant, e [ɔbliʒɑ̃, -ɑ̃t] *adj* obliging; kind.
obliger [ɔbliʒe] *vt* (*contraindre*): **~ qn à faire** to force *ou* oblige sb to do; (*JUR: engager*) to bind; (*rendre service à*) to oblige.
oblique [ɔblik] *adj* oblique; **regard ~** sidelong glance; **en ~** *adv* diagonally.
obliquer [ɔblike] *vi*: **~ vers** to turn off towards.
oblitération [ɔbliteʀɑsjɔ̃] *nf* cancelling *no pl*, cancellation; obstruction.
oblitérer [ɔbliteʀe] *vt* (*timbre-poste*) to cancel; (*MÉD: canal, vaisseau*) to obstruct.
oblong, oblongue [ɔblɔ̃, ɔblɔ̃g] *adj* oblong.
obnubiler [ɔbnybile] *vt* to obsess.
obole [ɔbɔl] *nf* offering.
obscène [ɔpsɛn] *adj* obscene.
obscénité [ɔpsenite] *nf* obscenity.
obscur, e [ɔpskyʀ] *adj* (*sombre*) dark; (*fig: raisons*) obscure; (*: sentiment, malaise*) vague; (*: personne, vie*) humble, lowly.
obscurcir [ɔpskyʀsiʀ] *vt* to darken; (*fig*) to obscure; **s'~** *vi* to grow dark.
obscurité [ɔpskyʀite] *nf* darkness; **dans l'~** in the dark, in darkness; (*anonymat, médiocrité*) in obscurity.
obsédant, e [ɔpsedɑ̃, -ɑ̃t] *adj* obsessive.
obsédé, e [ɔpsede] *nm/f* fanatic; **~(e) sexuel(le)** sex maniac.
obséder [ɔpsede] *vt* to obsess, haunt.
obsèques [ɔpsɛk] *nfpl* funeral *sg*.
obséquieux, euse [ɔpsekjø, -øz] *adj* obsequious.
observance [ɔpsɛʀvɑ̃s] *nf* observance.
observateur, trice [ɔpsɛʀvatœʀ, -tʀis] *adj* observant, perceptive ♦ *nm/f* observer.
observation [ɔpsɛʀvɑsjɔ̃] *nf* observation; (*d'un règlement etc*) observance; (*commentaire*) observation, remark; (*reproche*) reproof; **en ~** (*MÉD*) under observation.
observatoire [ɔpsɛʀvatwaʀ] *nm* observatory; (*lieu élevé*) observation post, vantage point.
observer [ɔpsɛʀve] *vt* (*regarder*) to observe, watch; (*examiner*) to examine; (*scientifiquement, aussi: règlement, jeûne etc*) to observe; (*surveiller*) to watch; (*remarquer*) to observe, notice; **faire ~ qch à qn** (*dire*) to point out sth to sb; **s'~** (*se surveiller*) to keep a check on o.s.
obsession [ɔpsesjɔ̃] *nf* obsession; **avoir l'~ de** to have an obsession with.
obsessionnel, le [ɔpsesjɔnɛl] *adj* obsessive.
obsolescent, e [ɔpsɔlesɑ̃, -ɑ̃t] *adj* obsolescent.
obstacle [ɔpstakl(ə)] *nm* obstacle; (*ÉQUITATION*) jump, hurdle; **faire ~ à** (*lumière*) to block out; (*projet*) to hinder, put obstacles in the path of; **~s antichars** tank defences.
obstétricien, ne [ɔpstetʀisjɛ̃, -ɛn] *nm/f* obstetrician.
obstétrique [ɔpstetʀik] *nf* obstetrics *sg*.
obstination [ɔpstinɑsjɔ̃] *nf* obstinacy.
obstiné, e [ɔpstine] *adj* obstinate.
obstinément [ɔpstinemɑ̃] *adv* obstinately.
obstiner [ɔpstine]: **s'~** *vi* to insist, dig one's heels in; **s'~ à faire** to persist (obstinately) in doing; **s'~ sur qch** to keep working at sth, labour away at sth.
obstruction [ɔpstʀyksjɔ̃] *nf* obstruction, blockage; (*SPORT*) obstruction; **faire de l'~** (*fig*) to be obstructive.
obstruer [ɔpstʀye] *vt* to block, obstruct; **s'~** *vi* to become blocked.
obtempérer [ɔptɑ̃peʀe] *vi* to obey; **~ à** to obey, comply with.
obtenir [ɔptəniʀ] *vt* to obtain, get; (*total*) to arrive at, reach; (*résultat*) to achieve, obtain; **~ de pouvoir faire** to obtain permission to do; **~ qch à qn** to obtain sth for sb; **~ de qn qu'il fasse** to get sb to agree to do(ing).
obtention [ɔptɑ̃sjɔ̃] *nf* obtaining.
obtenu, e [ɔpt(ə)ny] *pp de* **obtenir**.
obtiendrai [ɔptjɛ̃dʀe], **obtiens** [ɔptjɛ̃], **obtint** [ɔptɛ̃] *etc vb voir* **obtenir**.
obturateur [ɔptyʀatœʀ] *nm* (*PHOTO*) shutter; **~ à rideau** focal plane shutter.
obturation [ɔptyʀɑsjɔ̃] *nf* closing (up); **~ (dentaire)** filling; **vitesse d'~** (*PHOTO*) shutter speed.
obturer [ɔptyʀe] *vt* to close (up); (*dent*) to fill.
obtus, e [ɔpty, -yz] *adj* obtuse.
obus [ɔby] *nm* shell; **~ explosif** high-explosive shell; **~ incendiaire** incendiary device, fire bomb.
obvier [ɔbvje]: **~ à** *vt* to obviate.
OC *sigle fpl* (= *ondes courtes*) SW.
occasion [ɔkɑzjɔ̃] *nf* (*aubaine, possibilité*) opportunity; (*circonstance*) occasion; (*COMM: article non neuf*) secondhand buy; (*: acquisition avantageuse*) bargain; **à plusieurs ~s** on several occasions; **à la première ~** at the first *ou* earliest opportunity; **avoir l'~ de faire** to have the opportunity to do; **être l'~ de** to occasion, give rise to; **à l'~** *adv* sometimes, on occasions; (*un jour*) some time; **à l'~ de** on the occasion of; **d'~** *adj, adv* secondhand.
occasionnel, le [ɔkazjɔnɛl] *adj* (*fortuit*) chance *cpd*; (*non régulier*) occasional; (*: travail*) casual.
occasionner [ɔkazjɔne] *vt* to cause, bring about; **~ qch à qn** to cause sb sth.
occident [ɔksidɑ̃] *nm*: **l'O~** the West.
occidental, e, aux [ɔksidɑ̃tal, -o] *adj* western;

(*POL*) Western ♦ *nm/f* Westerner.
occidentaliser [ɔksidɑ̃talize] *vt* (*coutumes, mœurs*) to westernize.
occiput [ɔksipyt] *nm* back of the head, occiput.
occire [ɔksiʀ] *vt* to slay.
occitan, e [ɔksitɑ̃, -an] *adj* of the langue d'oc, of Provençal French.
occlusion [ɔklyzjɔ̃] *nf*: ~ **intestinale** obstruction of the bowel.
occulte [ɔkylt(ə)] *adj* occult, supernatural.
occulter [ɔkylte] *vt* (*fig*) to overshadow.
occupant, e [ɔkypɑ̃, -ɑ̃t] *adj* occupying ♦ *nm/f* (*d'un appartement*) occupier, occupant; (*d'un véhicule*) occupant ♦ *nm* (*MIL*) occupying forces *pl*; (*POL: d'usine etc*) occupier.
occupation [ɔkypɑsjɔ̃] *nf* occupation; **l'O**~ the Occupation (of France).
occupationnel, le [ɔkypɑsjɔnɛl] *adj*: **thérapie ~le** occupational therapy.
occupé, e [ɔkype] *adj* (*MIL, POL*) occupied; (*personne: affairé, pris*) busy; (*esprit: absorbé*) occupied; (*place, sièges*) taken; (*toilettes, ligne*) engaged.
occuper [ɔkype] *vt* to occupy; (*poste, fonction*) to hold; (*main-d'œuvre*) to employ; **s'~ (à qch)** to occupy o.s. *ou* keep o.s. busy (with sth); **s'~ de** (*être responsable de*) to be in charge of; (*se charger de: affaire*) to take charge of, deal with; (*: clients etc*) to attend to; (*s'intéresser à, pratiquer: politique etc*) to be involved in; **ça occupe trop de place** it takes up too much room.
occurrence [ɔkyʀɑ̃s] *nf*: **en l'~** in this case.
OCDE *sigle f* (= *Organisation de coopération et de développement économique*) OECD.
océan [ɔseɑ̃] *nm* ocean; **l'~ Indien** the Indian Ocean.
Océanie [ɔseani] *nf*: **l'~** Oceania, South Sea Islands.
océanique [ɔseanik] *adj* oceanic.
océanographe [ɔseanɔgʀaf] *nm/f* oceanographer.
océanographie [ɔseanɔgʀafi] *nf* oceanography.
océanologie [ɔseanɔlɔʒi] *nf* oceanology.
ocelot [ɔslo] *nm* (*ZOOL*) ocelot; (*fourrure*) ocelot fur.
ocre [ɔkʀ(ə)] *adj inv* ochre.
octane [ɔktan] *nm* octane.
octante [ɔktɑ̃t] *num* (*Belgique, Suisse*) eighty.
octave [ɔktav] *nf* octave.
octet [ɔktɛ] *nm* byte.
octobre [ɔktɔbʀ(ə)] *nm* October; *voir aussi* **juillet**.
octogénaire [ɔktɔʒenɛʀ] *adj, nm/f* octogenarian.
octogonal, e, aux [ɔktɔgɔnal, -o] *adj* octagonal.
octogone [ɔktɔgɔn] *nm* octagon.
octroi [ɔktʀwa] *nm* granting.
octroyer [ɔktʀwaje] *vt*: ~ **qch à qn** to grant sth to sb, grant sb sth.
oculaire [ɔkylɛʀ] *adj* ocular, eye *cpd* ♦ *nm* (*de microscope*) eyepiece.
oculiste [ɔkylist(ə)] *nm/f* eye specialist, oculist.
ode [ɔd] *nf* ode.
odeur [ɔdœʀ] *nf* smell.
odieusement [ɔdjøzmɑ̃] *adv* odiously.
odieux, euse [ɔdjø, -øz] *adj* odious, hateful.
odontologie [ɔdɔ̃tɔlɔʒi] *nf* odontology.
odorant, e [ɔdɔʀɑ̃, -ɑ̃t] *adj* sweet-smelling, fragrant.
odorat [ɔdɔʀa] *nm* (sense of) smell; **avoir l'~ fin** to have a keen sense of smell.
odoriférant, e [ɔdɔʀifeʀɑ̃, -ɑ̃t] *adj* sweet-smelling, fragrant.
odyssée [ɔdise] *nf* odyssey.
OEA *sigle f* (= *Organisation des États américains*) OAS.
œcuménique [ekymenik] *adj* ecumenical.
œdème [edɛm] *nm* oedema (*BRIT*), edema (*US*).
œil [œj], *pl* **yeux** [jø] *nm* eye; **avoir un ~ poché** *ou* **au beurre noir** to have a black eye; **à l'~** (*fam*) for free; **à l'~ nu** with the naked eye; **tenir qn à l'~** to keep an eye *ou* a watch on sb; **avoir l'~ à** to keep an eye on; **faire de l'~ à qn** to make eyes at sb; **voir qch d'un bon/mauvais ~** to view sth in a favourable/an unfavourable light; **à l'~ vif** with a lively expression; **à mes/ses yeux** in my/his eyes; **de ses propres yeux** with his own eyes; **fermer les yeux (sur)** (*fig*) to turn a blind eye (to); **les yeux fermés** (*aussi fig*) with one's eyes shut; **fermer l'~** to get a moment's sleep; **~ pour ~, dent pour dent** an eye for an eye, a tooth for a tooth; **pour les beaux yeux de qn** (*fig*) for love of sb; **~ de verre** glass eye.
œil-de-bœuf, *pl* **œils-de-bœuf** [œjdəbœf] *nm* bull's-eye (window).
œillade [œjad] *nf*: **lancer une ~ à qn** to wink at sb, give sb a wink; **faire des ~s à** to make eyes at.
œillères [œjɛʀ] *nfpl* blinkers (*BRIT*), blinders (*US*); **avoir des ~** (*fig*) to be blinkered, wear blinders.
œillet [œjɛ] *nm* (*BOT*) carnation; (*trou*) eyelet.
œnologue [enɔlɔg] *nm/f* wine expert.
œsophage [ezɔfaʒ] *nm* oesophagus (*BRIT*), esophagus (*US*).
œstrogène [ɛstʀɔʒɛn] *adj* oestrogen (*BRIT*) estrogen (*US*).
œuf [œf, *pl* ø] *nm* egg; **étouffer dans l'~** to nip in the bud; **~ à la coque/dur/mollet** boiled hard-boiled/soft-boiled egg; **~ au plat/poché** fried/poached egg; **~s brouillés** scrambled eggs; **~ de Pâques** Easter egg; **~ à repriser** darning egg.
œuvre [œvʀ(ə)] *nf* (*tâche*) task, undertaking (*ouvrage achevé, livre, tableau etc*) work; (*ensemble de la production artistique*) works *pl*

(*organisation charitable*) charity ♦ *nm* (*d'un artiste*) works *pl*; (*CONSTR*): **le gros** ~ the shell; ~**s** *nfpl* (*actes*) deeds, works; **être/se mettre à l'**~ to be at/get (down) to work; **mettre en** ~ (*moyens*) to make use of; (*plan, loi, projet etc*) to implement; ~ **d'art** work of art; **bonnes** ~**s** good works *ou* deeds; ~**s de bienfaisance** charitable works.

OFCE *sigle m* (= *Observatoire français des conjonctures économiques*) *economic research institute*.

offensant, e [ɔfɑ̃sɑ̃, -ɑ̃t] *adj* offensive, insulting.

offense [ɔfɑ̃s] *nf* (*affront*) insult; (*REL*: *péché*) transgression, trespass.

offenser [ɔfɑ̃se] *vt* to offend, hurt; (*principes, Dieu*) to offend against; **s'**~ **de** to take offence (*BRIT*) *ou* offense (*US*) at.

offensif, ive [ɔfɑ̃sif, -iv] *adj* (*armes, guerre*) offensive ♦ *nf* offensive; (*fig*: *du froid, de l'hiver*) onslaught; **passer à l'offensive** to go into the attack *ou* offensive.

offert, e [ɔfɛʀ, -ɛʀt(ə)] *pp de* **offrir**.

offertoire [ɔfɛʀtwaʀ] *nm* offertory.

office [ɔfis] *nm* (*charge*) office; (*agence*) bureau, agency; (*REL*) service ♦ *nm ou nf* (*pièce*) pantry; **faire** ~ **de** to act as; to do duty as; **d'**~ *adv* automatically; **bons** ~**s** (*POL*) good offices; ~ **du tourisme** tourist bureau.

officialiser [ɔfisjalize] *vt* to make official.

officiel, le [ɔfisjɛl] *adj, nm/f* official.

officiellement [ɔfisjɛlmɑ̃] *adv* officially.

officier [ɔfisje] *nm* officer ♦ *vi* (*REL*) to officiate; ~ **de l'état civil** registrar; ~ **ministériel** member of the legal profession; ~ **de police** ≈ police officer.

officieusement [ɔfisjøzmɑ̃] *adv* unofficially.

officieux, euse [ɔfisjø, -øz] *adj* unofficial.

officinal, e, aux [ɔfisinal, -o] *adj*: **plantes** ~**es** medicinal plants.

officine [ɔfisin] *nf* (*de pharmacie*) dispensary; (*ADMIN*: *pharmacie*) pharmacy; (*gén péj*: *bureau*) agency, office.

offrais [ɔfʀɛ] *etc vb voir* **offrir**.

offrande [ɔfʀɑ̃d] *nf* offering.

offrant [ɔfʀɑ̃] *nm*: **au plus** ~ to the highest bidder.

offre [ɔfʀ(ə)] *vb voir* **offrir** ♦ *nf* offer; (*aux enchères*) bid; (*ADMIN*: *soumission*) tender; (*ÉCON*): **l'**~ supply; ~ **d'emploi** job advertised; **"**~**s d'emploi"** "situations vacant"; ~ **publique d'achat (OPA)** takeover bid; ~**s de service** offer of service.

offrir [ɔfʀiʀ] *vt*: ~ **(à qn)** to offer (to sb); (*faire cadeau*) to give to (sb); **s'**~ *vi* (*se présenter*: *occasion, paysage*) to present itself ♦ *vt* (*se payer*: *vacances, voiture*) to treat o.s. to; ~ **(à qn) de faire qch** to offer to do sth (for sb); ~ **à boire à qn** to offer sb a drink; **s'**~ **à faire qch** to offer *ou* volunteer to do sth; **s'**~ **comme guide/en otage** to offer one's services as (a) guide/offer o.s. as (a) hostage; **s'**~ **aux regards** (*suj*: *personne*) to expose o.s. to the public gaze.

offset [ɔfsɛt] *nm* offset (printing).

offusquer [ɔfyske] *vt* to offend; **s'**~ **de** to take offence (*BRIT*) *ou* offense (*US*) at, be offended by.

ogive [ɔʒiv] *nf* (*ARCHIT*) diagonal rib; (*d'obus, de missile*) nose cone; **voûte en** ~ rib vault; **arc en** ~ lancet arch; ~ **nucléaire** nuclear warhead.

OGM *sigle m* (= *organisme génétiquement modifié*) GM organism.

ogre [ɔgʀ(ə)] *nm* ogre.

oh [o] *excl* oh!; ~ **la la!** oh (dear)!; **pousser des** ~**! et des ah!** to gasp with admiration.

oie [wa] *nf* (*ZOOL*) goose (*pl* **geese**); ~ **blanche** (*fig*) young innocent.

oignon [ɔɲɔ̃] *nm* (*CULIN*) onion; (*de tulipe etc*: *bulbe*) bulb; (*MÉD*) bunion; **ce ne sont pas tes** ~**s** (*fam*) that's none of your business.

oindre [wɛ̃dʀ(ə)] *vt* to anoint.

oiseau, x [wazo] *nm* bird; ~ **de proie** bird of prey.

oiseau-mouche, *pl* **oiseaux-mouches** [wazomuʃ] *nm* hummingbird.

oiseleur [wazlœʀ] *nm* bird-catcher.

oiselier, ière [wazəlje, -jɛʀ] *nm/f* bird-seller.

oisellerie [wazɛlʀi] *nf* bird shop.

oiseux, euse [wazø, -øz] *adj* pointless, idle; (*sans valeur, importance*) trivial.

oisif, ive [wazif, -iv] *adj* idle ♦ *nm/f* (*péj*) man/lady of leisure.

oisillon [wazijɔ̃] *nm* little *ou* baby bird.

oisiveté [wazivte] *nf* idleness.

OIT *sigle f* (= *Organisation internationale du travail*) ILO.

OK [okɛ] *excl* OK!, all right!

OL *sigle fpl* (= *ondes longues*) LW.

oléagineux, euse [ɔleaʒinø, -øz] *adj* oleaginous, oil-producing.

oléiculture [ɔleikyltyʀ] *nm* olive growing.

oléoduc [ɔleɔdyk] *nm* (oil) pipeline.

olfactif, ive [ɔlfaktif, -iv] *adj* olfactory.

olibrius [ɔlibʀijys] *nm* oddball.

oligarchie [ɔligaʀʃi] *nf* oligarchy.

oligo-élément [ɔligɔelemɑ̃] *nm* trace element.

oligopole [ɔligɔpɔl] *nm* oligopoly.

olivâtre [ɔlivɑtʀ(ə)] *adj* olive-greenish; (*teint*) sallow.

olive [ɔliv] *nf* (*BOT*) olive ♦ *adj inv* olive(-green).

oliveraie [ɔlivʀɛ] *nf* olive grove.

olivier [ɔlivje] *nm* olive (tree); (*bois*) olive (wood).

olographe [ɔlɔgʀaf] *adj*: **testament** ~ *will written, dated and signed by the testator*.

OLP *sigle f* (= *Organisation de libération de la Palestine*) PLO.

olympiade [ɔlɛ̃pjad] *nf* (*période*) Olympiad; **les** ~**s** (*jeux*) the Olympiad *sg*.

olympique [ɔlɛ̃pik] *adj* Olympic.

OM *sigle fpl* (= *ondes moyennes*) MW.

Oman [ɔman] *nm*: **l'~, le sultanat d'~** (the Sultanate of) Oman.
ombilical, e, aux [ɔ̃bilikal, -o] *adj* umbilical.
ombrage [ɔ̃bʀaʒ] *nm* (*ombre*) (leafy) shade; (*fig*): **prendre ~ de** to take umbrage at; **faire** *ou* **porter ~ à qn** to offend sb.
ombragé, e [ɔ̃bʀaʒe] *adj* shaded, shady.
ombrageux, euse [ɔ̃bʀaʒø, -øz] *adj* (*cheval*) skittish, nervous; (*personne*) touchy, easily offended.
ombre [ɔ̃bʀ(ə)] *nf* (*espace non ensoleillé*) shade; (*ombre portée, tache*) shadow; **à l'~** in the shade; (*fam: en prison*) behind bars; **à l'~ de** in the shade of; (*tout près de, fig*) in the shadow of; **tu me fais de l'~** you're in my light; **ça nous donne de l'~** it gives us (some) shade; **il n'y a pas l'~ d'un doute** there's not the shadow of a doubt; **dans l'~** in the shade; **vivre dans l'~** (*fig*) to live in obscurity; **laisser dans l'~** (*fig*) to leave in the dark; **~ à paupières** eyeshadow; **~ portée** shadow; **~s chinoises** (*spectacle*) shadow show *sg*.
ombrelle [ɔ̃bʀɛl] *nf* parasol, sunshade.
ombrer [ɔ̃bʀe] *vt* to shade.
omelette [ɔmlɛt] *nf* omelette; **~ baveuse** runny omelette; **~ au fromage/au jambon** cheese/ham omelette; **~ aux herbes** omelette with herbs; **~ norvégienne** baked Alaska.
omettre [ɔmɛtʀ(ə)] *vt* to omit, leave out; **~ de faire** to fail *ou* omit to do.
omis, e [ɔmi, -iz] *pp de* **omettre**.
omission [ɔmisjɔ̃] *nf* omission.
omnibus [ɔmnibys] *nm* slow *ou* stopping train.
omnipotent, e [ɔmnipɔtɑ̃, -ɑ̃t] *adj* omnipotent.
omnipraticien, ne [ɔmnipʀatisjɛ̃, -ɛn] *nm/f* (*MÉD*) general practitioner.
omniprésent, e [ɔmnipʀezɑ̃, -ɑ̃t] *adj* omnipresent.
omniscient, e [ɔmnisjɑ̃, -ɑ̃t] *adj* omniscient.
omnisports [ɔmnispɔʀ] *adj inv* (*club*) general sports *cpd*; (*salle*) multi-purpose *cpd*; (*terrain*) all-purpose *cpd*.
omnium [ɔmnjɔm] *nm* (*COMM*) corporation; (*CYCLISME*) omnium; (*COURSES*) open handicap.
omnivore [ɔmnivɔʀ] *adj* omnivorous.
omoplate [ɔmɔplat] *nf* shoulder blade.
OMS *sigle f* (= *Organisation mondiale de la santé*) WHO.

MOT-CLÉ

on [ɔ̃] *pron* **1** (*indéterminé*) you, one; **~ peut le faire ainsi** you *ou* one can do it like this, it can be done like this; **~ dit que** ... they say that ..., it is said that ...
2 (*quelqu'un*): **~ les a attaqués** they were attacked; **~ vous demande au téléphone** there's a phone call for you, you're wanted on the phone; **~ frappe à la porte** someone's knocking at the door
3 (*nous*) we; **~ va y aller demain** we're going tomorrow
4 (*les gens*) they; **autrefois, ~ croyait** ... they used to believe ...
5: **~ ne peut plus** *adv*: **~ ne peut plus stupide** as stupid as can be.

once [ɔ̃s] *nf*: **une ~ de** an ounce of.
oncle [ɔ̃kl(ə)] *nm* uncle.
onction [ɔ̃ksjɔ̃] *nf voir* **extrême-onction**.
onctueux, euse [ɔ̃ktɥø, -øz] *adj* creamy, smooth; (*fig*) smooth, unctuous.
onde [ɔ̃d] *nf* (*PHYSIQUE*) wave; **sur l'~** on the waters; **sur les ~s** on the radio; **mettre en ~s** to produce for the radio; **~ de choc** shock wave; **~s courtes (OC)** short wave *sg*; **petites ~s (PO)**, **~s moyennes (OM)** medium wave *sg*; **grandes ~s (GO)**, **~s longues (OL)** long wave *sg*; **~s sonores** sound waves.
ondée [ɔ̃de] *nf* shower.
on-dit [ɔ̃di] *nm inv* rumour.
ondoyer [ɔ̃dwaje] *vi* to ripple, wave ♦ *vt* (*REL*) to baptize (*in an emergency*).
ondulant, e [ɔ̃dylɑ̃, -ɑ̃t] *adj* (*démarche*) swaying; (*ligne*) undulating.
ondulation [ɔ̃dylɑsjɔ̃] *nf* undulation; wave.
ondulé, e [ɔ̃dyle] *adj* undulating; wavy.
onduler [ɔ̃dyle] *vi* to undulate; (*cheveux*) to wave.
onéreux, euse [ɔneʀø, -øz] *adj* costly; **à titre ~** in return for payment.
ONF *sigle m* (= *Office national des forêts*) ≈ Forestry Commission (*BRIT*), ≈ National Forest Service (*US*).
ongle [ɔ̃gl(ə)] *nm* (*ANAT*) nail; **manger** *ou* **ronger ses ~s** to bite one's nails; **se faire les ~s** to do one's nails.
onglet [ɔ̃glɛ] *nm* (*rainure*) (thumbnail) groove; (*bande de papier*) tab.
onguent [ɔ̃gɑ̃] *nm* ointment.
onirique [ɔniʀik] *adj* dreamlike, dream *cpd*.
onirisme [ɔniʀism(ə)] *nm* dreams *pl*.
onomatopée [ɔnɔmatɔpe] *nf* onomatopoeia.
ont [ɔ̃] *vb voir* **avoir**.
ontarien, ne [ɔ̃taʀjɛ̃, -ɛn] *adj* Ontarian.
ONU [ɔny] *sigle f* (= *Organisation des Nations unies*) UN(O).
onusien, ne [ɔnyzjɛ̃, -ɛn] *adj* of the UN(O), of the United Nations (Organization).
onyx [ɔniks] *nm* onyx.
onze [ɔ̃z] *num* eleven.
onzième [ɔ̃zjɛm] *num* eleventh.
op [ɔp] *nf* (= *opération*): **salle d'~** (operating) theatre.
OPA *sigle f* = **offre publique d'achat**.
opacité [ɔpasite] *nf* opaqueness.
opale [ɔpal] *nf* opal.
opalescent, e [ɔpalesɑ̃, -ɑ̃t] *adj* opalescent.
opalin, e [ɔpalɛ̃, -in] *adj, nf* opaline.
opaque [ɔpak] *adj* (*vitre, verre*) opaque; (*brouillard, nuit*) impenetrable.
OPE *sigle f* (= *offre publique d'échange*) take-

over bid where bidder offers shares in his company in exchange for shares in target company.

OPEP [ɔpɛp] *sigle f* (= *Organisation des pays exportateurs de pétrole*) OPEC.

opéra [ɔpeʀa] *nm* opera; (*édifice*) opera house.

opérable [ɔpeʀabl(ə)] *adj* operable.

opéra-comique, *pl* **opéras-comiques** [ɔpeʀakɔmik] *nm* light opera, opéra comique.

opérant, e [ɔpeʀɑ̃, -ɑ̃t] *adj* (*mesure*) effective.

opérateur, trice [ɔpeʀatœʀ, -tʀis] *nm/f* operator; ~ **(de prise de vues)** cameraman.

opération [ɔpeʀɑsjɔ̃] *nf* operation; (*COMM*) dealing; **salle/table d'~** operating theatre/table; ~ **de sauvetage** rescue operation; ~ **à cœur ouvert** open-heart surgery *no pl*.

opérationnel, le [ɔpeʀasjɔnel] *adj* operational.

opératoire [ɔpeʀatwaʀ] *adj* (*manœuvre, méthode*) operating; (*choc etc*) post-operative.

opéré, e [ɔpeʀe] *nm/f* post-operative patient.

opérer [ɔpeʀe] *vt* (*MÉD*) to operate on; (*faire, exécuter*) to carry out, make ♦ *vi* (*remède: faire effet*) to act, work; (*procéder*) to proceed; (*MÉD*) to operate; **s'~** *vi* (*avoir lieu*) to occur, take place; **se faire ~** to have an operation; **se faire ~ des amygdales/du cœur** to have one's tonsils out/have a heart operation.

opérette [ɔpeʀɛt] *nf* operetta, light opera.

ophtalmique [ɔftalmik] *adj* ophthalmic.

ophtalmologie [ɔftalmɔlɔʒi] *nf* ophthalmology.

ophtalmologue [ɔftalmɔlɔg] *nm/f* ophthalmologist.

opiacé, e [ɔpjase] *adj* opiate.

opiner [ɔpine] *vi*: ~ **de la tête** to nod assent ♦ *vt*: ~ **à** to consent to.

opiniâtre [ɔpinjɑtʀ(ə)] *adj* stubborn.

opiniâtreté [ɔpinjɑtʀəte] *nf* stubbornness.

opinion [ɔpinjɔ̃] *nf* opinion; **l'~ (publique)** public opinion; **avoir bonne/mauvaise ~ de** to have a high/low opinion of.

opiomane [ɔpjɔman] *nm/f* opium addict.

opium [ɔpjɔm] *nm* opium.

OPJ *sigle m* (= *officier de police judiciaire*) ≈ DC (= *Detective Constable*).

opportun, e [ɔpɔʀtœ̃, -yn] *adj* timely, opportune; **en temps ~** at the appropriate time.

opportunément [ɔpɔʀtynemɑ̃] *adv* opportunely.

opportunisme [ɔpɔʀtynism(ə)] *nm* opportunism.

opportuniste [ɔpɔʀtynist(ə)] *adj, nm/f* opportunist.

opportunité [ɔpɔʀtynite] *nf* timeliness, opportuneness.

opposant, e [ɔpozɑ̃, -ɑ̃t] *adj* opposing ♦ *nm/f* opponent.

opposé, e [ɔpoze] *adj* (*direction, rive*) opposite; (*faction*) opposing; (*couleurs*) contrasting; (*opinions, intérêts*) conflicting; (*contre*): ~ **à** opposed to, against ♦ *nm*: **l'~** the other *ou* opposite side (*ou* direction); (*contraire*) the opposite; **être ~ à** to be opposed to; **à l'~** (*fig*) on the other hand; **à l'~ de** on the other *ou* opposite side from; (*fig*) contrary to, unlike.

opposer [ɔpoze] *vt* (*meubles, objets*) to place opposite each other; (*personnes, armées, équipes*) to oppose; (*couleurs, termes, tons*) to contrast; (*comparer: livres, avantages*) to contrast; ~ **qch à** (*comme obstacle, défense*) to set sth against; (*comme objection*) to put sth forward against; (*en contraste*) to set sth opposite; to match sth with; **s'~** (*sens réciproque*) to conflict; to clash; to face each other; to contrast; **s'~ à** (*interdire, empêcher*) to oppose; (*tenir tête à*) to rebel against; **sa religion s'y oppose** it's against his religion; **s'~ à ce que qn fasse** to be opposed to sb's doing.

opposition [ɔpozisjɔ̃] *nf* opposition; **par ~** in contrast; **par ~ à** as opposed to, in contrast with; **entrer en ~ avec** to come into conflict with; **être en ~ avec** (*idées, conduite*) to be at variance with; **faire ~ à un chèque** to stop a cheque.

oppressant, e [ɔpʀesɑ̃, ɑ̃t] *adj* oppressive.

oppresser [ɔpʀese] *vt* to oppress; **se sentir oppressé** to feel breathless.

oppresseur [ɔpʀesœʀ] *nm* oppressor.

oppressif, ive [ɔpʀesif, -iv] *adj* oppressive.

oppression [ɔpʀesjɔ̃] *nf* oppression; (*malaise*) feeling of suffocation.

opprimer [ɔpʀime] *vt* (*asservir: peuple, faibles*) to oppress; (*étouffer: liberté, opinion*) to suppress, stifle; (*suj: chaleur etc*) to suffocate, oppress.

opprobre [ɔpʀɔbʀ(ə)] *nm* disgrace.

opter [ɔpte] *vi*: ~ **pour** to opt for; ~ **entre** to choose between.

opticien, ne [ɔptisjɛ̃, -ɛn] *nm/f* optician.

optimal, e, aux [ɔptimal, -o] *adj* optimal.

optimisation [ɔptimizɑsjɔ̃] *nf* optimization.

optimiser [ɔptimize] *vt* to optimize.

optimisme [ɔptimism(ə)] *nm* optimism.

optimiste [ɔptimist(ə)] *adj* optimistic ♦ *nm/f* optimist.

optimum [ɔptimɔm] *adj, nm* optimum.

option [ɔpsjɔ̃] *nf* option; (*AUTO: supplément*) optional extra; **matière à ~** (*SCOL*) optional subject (*BRIT*), elective (*US*); **prendre une ~ sur** to take (out) an option on; ~ **par défaut** (*INFORM*) default (option).

optionnel, le [ɔpsjɔnɛl] *adj* optional.

optique [ɔptik] *adj* (*nerf*) optic; (*verres*) optical ♦ *nf* (*PHOTO: lentilles etc*) optics *pl*; (*science, industrie*) optics *sg*; (*fig: manière de voir*) perspective.

opulence [ɔpylɑ̃s] *nf* wealth, opulence.

opulent, e [ɔpylɑ̃, -ɑ̃t] *adj* wealthy, opulent; (*formes, poitrine*) ample, generous.

OPV *sigle f* (= *offre publique de vente*) public offer of sale.
or [ɔʀ] *nm* gold ♦ *conj* now, but; **d'~** (*fig*) golden; **en ~** gold *cpd*; (*occasion*) golden; **un mari/enfant en ~** a treasure; **une affaire en ~** (*achat*) a real bargain; (*commerce*) a gold mine; **plaqué ~** gold-plated; **~ noir** black gold.
oracle [ɔʀɑkl(ə)] *nm* oracle.
orage [ɔʀaʒ] *nm* (thunder)storm.
orageux, euse [ɔʀaʒø, -øz] *adj* stormy.
oraison [ɔʀɛzɔ̃] *nf* orison, prayer; **~ funèbre** funeral oration.
oral, e, aux [ɔʀal, -o] *adj* (*déposition, promesse*) oral, verbal; (*MÉD*): **par voie ~e** by mouth, orally ♦ *nm* (*SCOL*) oral.
oralement [ɔʀalmɑ̃] *adv* orally.
orange [ɔʀɑ̃ʒ] *adj inv*, *nf* orange; **~ sanguine** blood orange; **~ pressée** freshly-squeezed orange juice.
orangé, e [ɔʀɑ̃ʒe] *adj* orangey, orange-coloured.
orangeade [ɔʀɑ̃ʒad] *nf* orangeade.
oranger [ɔʀɑ̃ʒe] *nm* orange tree.
orangeraie [ɔʀɑ̃ʒʀɛ] *nf* orange grove.
orangerie [ɔʀɑ̃ʒʀi] *nf* orangery.
orang-outan(g) [ɔʀɑ̃utɑ̃] *nm* orangutan.
orateur [ɔʀatœʀ] *nm* speaker; orator.
oratoire [ɔʀatwaʀ] *nm* (*lieu, chapelle*) oratory; (*au bord du chemin*) wayside shrine ♦ *adj* oratorical.
oratorio [ɔʀatɔʀjo] *nm* oratorio.
orbital, e, aux [ɔʀbital, -o] *adj* orbital; **station ~e** space station.
orbite [ɔʀbit] *nf* (*ANAT*) (eye-)socket; (*PHYSIQUE*) orbit; **mettre sur ~** to put into orbit; (*fig*) to launch; **dans l'~ de** (*fig*) within the sphere of influence of.
Orcades [ɔʀkad] *nfpl*: **les ~** the Orkneys, the Orkney Islands.
orchestral, e, aux [ɔʀkɛstʀal, -o] *adj* orchestral.
orchestrateur, trice [ɔʀkɛstʀatœʀ, -tʀis] *nm/f* orchestrator.
orchestration [ɔʀkɛstʀɑsjɔ̃] *nf* orchestration.
orchestre [ɔʀkɛstʀ(ə)] *nm* orchestra; (*de jazz, danse*) band; (*places*) stalls *pl* (*BRIT*), orchestra (*US*).
orchestrer [ɔʀkɛstʀe] *vt* (*MUS*) to orchestrate; (*fig*) to mount, stage-manage.
orchidée [ɔʀkide] *nf* orchid.
ordinaire [ɔʀdinɛʀ] *adj* ordinary; (*coutumier: maladresse etc*) usual; (*de tous les jours*) everyday; (*modèle, qualité*) standard ♦ *nm* ordinary; (*menus*) everyday fare ♦ *nf* (*essence*) ≈ two-star (petrol) (*BRIT*), ≈ regular (gas) (*US*); **d'~** usually, normally; **à l'~** usually, ordinarily.
ordinairement [ɔʀdinɛʀmɑ̃] *adv* ordinarily, usually.
ordinal, e, aux [ɔʀdinal, -o] *adj* ordinal.
ordinateur [ɔʀdinatœʀ] *nm* computer; **mettre sur ~** to computerize, put on computer; **~ de bureau** desktop computer; **~ domestique** home computer; **~ individuel** *ou* **personnel** personal computer; **~ portatif** laptop (computer).
ordination [ɔʀdinɑsjɔ̃] *nf* ordination.
ordonnance [ɔʀdɔnɑ̃s] *nf* organization; (*groupement, disposition*) layout; (*MÉD*) prescription; (*JUR*) order; (*MIL*) orderly, batman (*BRIT*); **d'~** (*MIL*) regulation *cpd*; **officier d'~** aide-de-camp.
ordonnateur, trice [ɔʀdɔnatœʀ, -tʀis] *nm/f* (*d'une cérémonie, fête*) organizer; **~ des pompes funèbres** funeral director.
ordonné, e [ɔʀdɔne] *adj* tidy, orderly; (*MATH*) ordered ♦ *nf* (*MATH*) Y-axis, ordinate.
ordonner [ɔʀdɔne] *vt* (*agencer*) to organize, arrange; (*: meubles, appartement*) to lay out, arrange; (*donner un ordre*): **~ à qn de faire** to order sb to do; (*MATH*) to (arrange in) order; (*REL*) to ordain; (*MÉD*) to prescribe; (*JUR*) to order; **s'~** (*faits*) to organize themselves.
ordre [ɔʀdʀ(ə)] *nm* (*gén*) order; (*propreté et soin*) orderliness, tidiness; (*association professionnelle, honorifique*) association; (*COMM*): **à l'~ de** payable to; (*nature*): **d'~ pratique** of a practical nature; **~s** *nmpl* (*REL*) holy orders; **avoir de l'~** to be tidy *ou* orderly; **mettre en ~** to tidy (up), put in order; **mettre bon ~ à** to put to rights, sort out; **procéder par ~** to take things one at a time; **être aux ~s de qn/sous les ~s de qn** to be at sb's disposal/under sb's command; **rappeler qn à l'~** to call sb to order; **jusqu'à nouvel ~** until further notice; **dans le même ~ d'idées** in this connection; **par ~ d'entrée en scène** in order of appearance; **un ~ de grandeur** some idea of the size (*ou* amount); **de premier ~** first-rate; **~ de grève** strike call; **~ du jour** (*d'une réunion*) agenda; (*MIL*) order of the day; **à l'~ du jour** on the agenda; (*fig*) topical; (*MIL: citer*) in dispatches; **~ de mission** (*MIL*) orders *pl*; **~ public** law and order; **~ de route** marching orders *pl*.
ordure [ɔʀdyʀ] *nf* filth *no pl*; (*propos, écrit*) obscenity, (piece of) filth; **~s** *nfpl* (*balayures, déchets*) rubbish *sg*, refuse *sg*; **~s ménagères** household refuse.
ordurier, ière [ɔʀdyʀje, -jɛʀ] *adj* lewd, filthy.
oreille [ɔʀɛj] *nf* (*ANAT*) ear; (*de marmite, tasse*) handle; (*TECH: d'un écrou*) wing; **avoir de l'~** to have a good ear (for music); **avoir l'~ fine** to have good *ou* sharp ears; **l'~ basse** crestfallen, dejected; **se faire tirer l'~** to take a lot of persuading; **dire qch à l'~ de qn** to have a word in sb's ear (about sth).
oreiller [ɔʀeje] *nm* pillow.
oreillette [ɔʀɛjɛt] *nf* (*ANAT*) auricle.
oreillons [ɔʀɛjɔ̃] *nmpl* mumps *sg*.
ores [ɔʀ]: **d'~ et déjà** *adv* already.
orfèvre [ɔʀfɛvʀ(ə)] *nm* goldsmith; silversmith.
orfèvrerie [ɔʀfɛvʀəʀi] *nf* (*art, métier*) gold-

smith's (*ou* silversmith's) trade; (*ouvrage*) (silver *ou* gold) plate.
orfraie [ɔʀfʀɛ] *nm* white-tailed eagle; **pousser des cris d'~** to yell at the top of one's voice.
organe [ɔʀgan] *nm* organ; (*véhicule, instrument*) instrument; (*voix*) voice; (*porte-parole*) representative, mouthpiece; **~s de commande** (*TECH*) controls; **~s de transmission** (*TECH*) transmission system *sg*.
organigramme [ɔʀganigʀam] *nm* (*hiérarchique, structurel*) organization chart; (*des opérations*) flow chart.
organique [ɔʀganik] *adj* organic.
organisateur, trice [ɔʀganizatœʀ, -tʀis] *nm/f* organizer.
organisation [ɔʀganizɑsjɔ̃] *nf* organization; **O~ des Nations unies (ONU)** United Nations (Organization) (UN, UNO); **O~ mondiale de la santé (OMS)** World Health Organization (WHO); **O~ du traité de l'Atlantique Nord (OTAN)** North Atlantic Treaty Organization (NATO).
organisationnel, le [ɔʀganizasjɔnɛl] *adj* organizational.
organiser [ɔʀganize] *vt* to organize; (*mettre sur pied: service etc*) to set up; **s'~** to get organized.
organisme [ɔʀganism(ə)] *nm* (*BIO*) organism; (*corps humain*) body; (*ADMIN, POL etc*) body, organism.
organiste [ɔʀganist(ə)] *nm/f* organist.
orgasme [ɔʀgasm(ə)] *nm* orgasm, climax.
orge [ɔʀʒ(ə)] *nf* barley.
orgeat [ɔʀʒa] *nm*: **sirop d'~** barley water.
orgelet [ɔʀʒəlɛ] *nm* sty(e).
orgie [ɔʀʒi] *nf* orgy.
orgue [ɔʀg(ə)] *nm* organ; **~s** *nfpl* organ *sg*; **~ de Barbarie** barrel *ou* street organ.
orgueil [ɔʀgœj] *nm* pride.
orgueilleux, euse [ɔʀgœjø, -øz] *adj* proud.
Orient [ɔʀjɑ̃] *nm*: **l'~** the East, the Orient.
orientable [ɔʀjɑ̃tabl(ə)] *adj* (*phare, lampe etc*) adjustable.
oriental, e, aux [ɔʀjɑ̃tal, -o] *adj* oriental, eastern; (*frontière*) eastern ♦ *nm/f*: **O~, e** Oriental.
orientation [ɔʀjɑ̃tɑsjɔ̃] *nf* positioning; adjustment; orientation; direction; (*d'une maison etc*) aspect; (*d'un journal*) leanings *pl*; **avoir le sens de l'~** to have a (good) sense of direction; **course d'~** orienteering exercise; **~ professionnelle** careers advice *ou* guidance; (*service*) careers advisory service.
orienté, e [ɔʀjɑ̃te] *adj* (*fig: article, journal*) slanted; **bien/mal ~** (*appartement*) well/badly positioned; **~ au sud** facing south, with a southern aspect.
orienter [ɔʀjɑ̃te] *vt* (*situer*) to position; (*placer, disposer: pièce mobile*) to adjust, position; (*tourner*) to direct, turn; (*voyageur, touriste, recherches*) to direct; (*fig: élève*) to orientate; **s'~** (*se repérer*) to find one's bearings; **s'~ vers** (*fig*) to turn towards.
orienteur, euse [ɔʀjɑ̃tœʀ, -øz] *nm/f* (*SCOL*) careers adviser.
orifice [ɔʀifis] *nm* opening, orifice.
oriflamme [ɔʀiflam] *nf* banner, standard.
origan [ɔʀigɑ̃] *nm* oregano.
originaire [ɔʀiʒinɛʀ] *adj* original; **être ~ de** (*pays, lieu*) to be a native of; (*provenir de*) to originate from; to be native to.
original, e, aux [ɔʀiʒinal, -o] *adj* original; (*bizarre*) eccentric ♦ *nm/f* (*fam: excentrique*) eccentric; (*: fantaisiste*) joker ♦ *nm* (*document etc, ART*) original; (*dactylographie*) top copy.
originalité [ɔʀiʒinalite] *nf* (*d'un nouveau modèle*) originality *no pl*; (*excentricité, bizarrerie*) eccentricity.
origine [ɔʀiʒin] *nf* origin; (*d'un message, appel téléphonique*) source; (*d'une révolution, réussite*) root; **~s** *nfpl* (*d'une personne*) origins; **d'~** of origin; (*pneus etc*) original; (*bureau postal*) dispatching; **d'~ française** of French origin; **dès l'~** at *ou* from the outset; **à l'~** originally; **avoir son ~ dans** to have its origins in, originate in.
originel, le [ɔʀiʒinɛl] *adj* original.
originellement [ɔʀiʒinɛlmɑ̃] *adv* (*à l'origine*) originally; (*dès l'origine*) from the beginning.
oripeaux [ɔʀipo] *nmpl* rags.
ORL *sigle f* (= *oto-rhino-laryngologie*) ENT ♦ *sigle m/f* (= *oto-rhino-laryngologiste*) ENT specialist; **être en ~** (*malade*) to be in the ENT hospital *ou* department.
orme [ɔʀm(ə)] *nm* elm.
orné, e [ɔʀne] *adj* ornate; **~ de** adorned *ou* decorated with.
ornement [ɔʀnəmɑ̃] *nm* ornament; (*fig*) embellishment, adornment; **~s sacerdotaux** vestments.
ornemental, e, aux [ɔʀnəmɑ̃tal, -o] *adj* ornamental.
ornementer [ɔʀnəmɑ̃te] *vt* to ornament.
orner [ɔʀne] *vt* to decorate, adorn; **~ qch de** to decorate sth with.
ornière [ɔʀnjɛʀ] *nf* rut; (*fig*): **sortir de l'~** (*routine*) to get out of the rut; (*impasse*) to get out of a spot.
ornithologie [ɔʀnitɔlɔʒi] *nf* ornithology.
ornithologue [ɔʀnitɔlɔg] *nm/f* ornithologist; **~ amateur** birdwatcher.
orphelin, e [ɔʀfəlɛ̃, -in] *adj* orphan(ed) ♦ *nm/f* orphan; **~ de père/mère** fatherless/motherless.
orphelinat [ɔʀfəlina] *nm* orphanage.
ORSEC [ɔʀsɛk] *sigle f* (= *Organisation des secours*): **le plan ~** *disaster contingency plan.*
ORSECRAD [ɔʀsɛkʀad] *sigle m* = *ORSEC en cas d'accident nucléaire.*
orteil [ɔʀtɛj] *nm* toe; **gros ~** big toe.
ORTF *sigle m* (= *Office de radio-diffusion télévision française*) *(former) French broadcasting corporation.*
orthodontiste [ɔʀtɔdɔ̃tist(ə)] *nm/f* orthodon-

tist.
orthodoxe [ɔʀtɔdɔks(ə)] *adj* orthodox.
orthodoxie [ɔʀtɔdɔksi] *nf* orthodoxy.
orthogénie [ɔʀtɔʒeni] *nf* family planning.
orthographe [ɔʀtɔgʀaf] *nf* spelling.
orthographier [ɔʀtɔgʀafje] *vt* to spell; **mal orthographié** misspelt.
orthopédie [ɔʀtɔpedi] *nf* orthopaedics *sg* (*BRIT*), orthopedics *sg* (*US*).
orthopédique [ɔʀtɔpedik] *adj* orthopaedic (*BRIT*), orthopedic (*US*).
orthopédiste [ɔʀtɔpedist(ə)] *nm/f* orthopaedic (*BRIT*) *ou* orthopedic (*US*) specialist.
orthophonie [ɔʀtɔfɔni] *nf* (*MÉD*) speech therapy; (*LING*) correct pronunciation.
orthophoniste [ɔʀtɔfɔnist(ə)] *nm/f* speech therapist.
ortie [ɔʀti] *nf* (stinging) nettle; ~ **blanche** white dead-nettle.
OS *sigle m* = **ouvrier spécialisé**.
os [ɔs, *pl* o] *nm* bone; **sans** ~ (*BOUCHERIE*) off the bone, boned; ~ **à moelle** marrowbone.
oscillation [ɔsilɑsjɔ̃] *nf* oscillation; ~**s** *nfpl* (*fig*) fluctuations.
osciller [ɔsile] *vi* (*pendule*) to swing; (*au vent etc*) to rock; (*TECH*) to oscillate; (*fig*): ~ **entre** to waver *ou* fluctuate between.
osé, e [oze] *adj* daring, bold.
oseille [ozɛj] *nf* sorrel.
oser [oze] *vi, vt* to dare; ~ **faire** to dare (to) do.
osier [ozje] *nm* (*BOT*) willow; **d'**~, **en** ~ wicker(work) *cpd*.
Oslo [ɔslo] *n* Oslo.
osmose [ɔsmoz] *nf* osmosis.
ossature [ɔsatyʀ] *nf* (*ANAT*: *squelette*) frame, skeletal structure; (*: du visage*) bone structure; (*fig*) framework.
osselet [ɔslɛ] *nm* (*ANAT*) ossicle; **jouer aux** ~**s** to play jacks.
ossements [ɔsmɑ̃] *nmpl* bones.
osseux, euse [ɔsø, -øz] *adj* bony; (*tissu, maladie, greffe*) bone *cpd*.
ossifier [ɔsifje]: **s'**~ *vi* to ossify.
ossuaire [ɔsɥɛʀ] *nm* ossuary.
Ostende [ɔstɑ̃d] *n* Ostend.
ostensible [ɔstɑ̃sibl(ə)] *adj* conspicuous.
ostensiblement [ɔstɑ̃sibləmɑ̃] *adv* conspicuously.
ostensoir [ɔstɑ̃swaʀ] *nm* monstrance.
ostentation [ɔstɑ̃tɑsjɔ̃] *nf* ostentation; **faire** ~ **de** to parade, make a display of.
ostentatoir [ɔstɑ̃tatwaʀ] *adj* ostentatious.
ostracisme [ɔstʀasism(ə)] *nm* ostracism; **frapper d'**~ to ostracize.
ostréicole [ɔstʀeikɔl] *adj* oyster *cpd*.
ostréiculture [ɔstʀeikyltyʀ] *nf* oyster-farming.
otage [ɔtaʒ] *nm* hostage; **prendre qn comme** ~ to take sb hostage.
OTAN [ɔtɑ̃] *sigle f* (= *Organisation du traité de l'Atlantique Nord*) NATO.
otarie [ɔtaʀi] *nf* sea-lion.
OTASE [ɔtaz] *sigle f* (= *Organisation du traité de l'Asie du Sud-Est*) SEATO (= *Southeast Asia Treaty Organization*).
ôter [ote] *vt* to remove; (*soustraire*) to take away; ~ **qch à qn** to take sth (away) from sb; ~ **qch de** to remove sth from; **6 ôté de 10 égale 4** 6 from 10 equals *ou* is 4.
otite [ɔtit] *nf* ear infection.
oto-rhino(-laryngologiste) [ɔtɔʀinɔ(-laʀɛ̃gɔlɔʒist(ə))] *nm/f* ear, nose and throat specialist.
ottomane [ɔtɔman] *nf* ottoman.
ou [u] *conj* or; ~ ... ~ either ... or; ~ **bien** or (else).

MOT-CLÉ

où [u] *pron relatif* **1** (*position, situation*) where, that (*souvent omis*); **la chambre** ~ **il était** the room (that) he was in, the room where he was; **la ville** ~ **je l'ai rencontré** the town where I met him; **la pièce d'**~ **il est sorti** the room he came out of; **le village d'**~ **je viens** the village I come from; **les villes par** ~ **il est passé** the towns he went through
2 (*temps, état*) that (*souvent omis*); **le jour** ~ **il est parti** the day (that) he left; **au prix** ~ **c'est** at the price it is
♦ *adv* **1** (*interrogation*) where; ~ **est-il/va-t-il?** where is he/is he going?; **par** ~**?** which way?; **d'**~ **vient que ...?** how come ...?
2 (*position*) where; **je sais** ~ **il est** I know where he is; ~ **que l'on aille** wherever you go.

OUA *sigle f* (= *Organisation de l'unité africaine*) OAU (= *Organization of African Unity*).
ouais [wɛ] *excl* yeah.
ouate [wat] *nf* cotton wool (*BRIT*), cotton (*US*); (*bourre*) padding, wadding; ~ **(hydrophile)** cotton wool (*BRIT*), (absorbent) cotton (*US*).
ouaté, e [wate] *adj* cotton-wool; (*doublé*) padded; (*fig: atmosphère*) cocoon-like; (*: pas, bruit*) muffled.
oubli [ubli] *nm* (*acte*): **l'**~ **de** forgetting; (*étourderie*) forgetfulness *no pl*; (*négligence*) omission, oversight; (*absence de souvenirs*) oblivion; ~ **de soi** self-effacement, self-negation.
oublier [ublije] *vt* (*gén*) to forget; (*ne pas voir: erreurs etc*) to miss; (*ne pas mettre: virgule, nom*) to leave out, forget; (*laisser quelque part: chapeau etc*) to leave behind; **s'**~ to forget o.s; (*enfant, animal*) to have an accident (*euphemism*); ~ **l'heure** to forget (about) the time.
oubliettes [ublijɛt] *nfpl* dungeon *sg*; **(jeter) aux** ~ (*fig*) (to put) completely out of mind.
oublieux, euse [ublijø, -øz] *adj* forgetful.
oued [wɛd] *nm* wadi.
ouest [wɛst] *nm* west ♦ *adj inv* west; (*région*) western; **à l'**~ in the west; (to the) west, westwards; **à l'**~ **de** (to the) west of; **vent d'**~ westerly wind.

ouest-allemand, e [wɛstalmɑ̃, -ɑ̃d] *adj* West German.
ouf [uf] *excl* phew!
Ouganda [ugɑ̃da] *nm*: **l'~** Uganda.
ougandais, e [ugɑ̃dɛ, -ɛz] *adj* Ugandan.
oui [wi] *adv* yes; **répondre (par)** ~ to answer yes; **mais ~, bien sûr** yes, of course; **je pense que** ~ I think so; **pour un** ~ **ou pour un non** for no apparent reason.
ouï-dire [widiʀ]: **par** ~ *adv* by hearsay.
ouïe [wi] *nf* hearing; **~s** *nfpl* (*de poisson*) gills; (*de violon*) sound-hole *sg*.
ouïr [wiʀ] *vt* to hear; **avoir ouï dire que** to have heard it said that.
ouistiti [wistiti] *nm* marmoset.
ouragan [uʀagɑ̃] *nm* hurricane; (*fig*) storm.
Oural [uʀal] *nm*: **l'~** (*fleuve*) the Ural; (*aussi*: **les monts** ~) the Urals, the Ural Mountains.
ouralo-altaïque [uʀalɔaltaik] *adj, nm* Ural-Altaic.
ourdir [uʀdiʀ] *vt* (*complot*) to hatch.
ourdou [uʀdu] *adj inv* Urdu ♦ *nm* (*LING*) Urdu.
ourlé, e [uʀle] *adj* hemmed; (*fig*) rimmed.
ourler [uʀle] *vt* to hem.
ourlet [uʀlɛ] *nm* hem; (*de l'oreille*) rim; **faire un** ~ **à** to hem.
ours [uʀs] *nm* bear; ~ **brun/blanc** brown/polar bear; ~ **marin** fur seal; ~ **mal léché** uncouth fellow; ~ **(en peluche)** teddy (bear).
ourse [uʀs(ə)] *nf* (*ZOOL*) she-bear; **la Grande/Petite O~** the Great/Little Bear, Ursa Major/Minor.
oursin [uʀsɛ̃] *nm* sea urchin.
ourson [uʀsɔ̃] *nm* (bear-)cub.
ouste [ust(ə)] *excl* hop it!
outil [uti] *nm* tool.
outillage [utijaʒ] *nm* set of tools; (*d'atelier*) equipment *no pl*.
outiller [utije] *vt* (*ouvrier, usine*) to equip.
outrage [utʀaʒ] *nm* insult; **faire subir les derniers ~s à** (*femme*) to ravish; ~ **aux bonnes mœurs** (*JUR*) outrage to public decency; ~ **à magistrat** (*JUR*) contempt of court; ~ **à la pudeur** (*JUR*) indecent behaviour *no pl*.
outragé, e [utʀaʒe] *adj* offended; outraged.
outrageant, e [utʀaʒɑ̃, -ɑ̃t] *adj* offensive.
outrager [utʀaʒe] *vt* to offend gravely; (*fig: contrevenir à*) to outrage, insult.
outrageusement [utʀaʒøzmɑ̃] *adv* outrageously.
outrance [utʀɑ̃s] *nf* excessiveness *no pl*, excess; **à** ~ *adv* excessively, to excess.
outrancier, ière [utʀɑ̃sje, -jɛʀ] *adj* extreme.
outre [utʀ(ə)] *nf* goatskin, water skin ♦ *prép* besides ♦ *adv*: **passer** ~ to carry on regardless; **passer** ~ **à** to disregard, take no notice of; **en** ~ besides, moreover; ~ **que** apart from the fact that; ~ **mesure** immoderately; unduly.
outré, e [utʀe] *adj* (*flatterie, éloge*) excessive, exaggerated; (*indigné, scandalisé*) outraged.
outre-Atlantique [utʀatlɑ̃tik] *adv* across the Atlantic.
outrecuidance [utʀəkɥidɑ̃s] *nf* presumptuousness *no pl*.
outre-Manche [utʀəmɑ̃ʃ] *adv* across the Channel.
outremer [utʀəmɛʀ] *adj inv* ultramarine.
outre-mer [utʀəmɛʀ] *adv* overseas; **d'~** overseas.
outrepasser [utʀəpɑse] *vt* to go beyond, exceed.
outrer [utʀe] *vt* (*pensée, attitude*) to exaggerate; (*indigner: personne*) to outrage.
outre-Rhin [utʀəʀɛ̃] *adv* across the Rhine, in Germany.
outsider [awtsajdœʀ] *nm* outsider.
ouvert, e [uvɛʀ, -ɛʀt(ə)] *pp de* **ouvrir** ♦ *adj* open; (*robinet, gaz etc*) on; **à bras ~s** with open arms.
ouvertement [uvɛʀtəmɑ̃] *adv* openly.
ouverture [uvɛʀtyʀ] *nf* opening; (*MUS*) overture; (*POL*): **l'~** the widening of the political spectrum; (*PHOTO*): ~ **(du diaphragme)** aperture; **~s** *nfpl* (*propositions*) overtures; ~ **d'esprit** open-mindedness; **heures d'~** (*COMM*) opening hours; **jours d'~** (*COMM*) days of opening.
ouvrable [uvʀabl(ə)] *adj*: **jour** ~ working day, weekday; **heures ~s** business hours.
ouvrage [uvʀaʒ] *nm* (*tâche, de tricot etc, MIL*) work *no pl*; (*objet*: *COUTURE, ART*) (piece of) work; (*texte, livre*) work; **panier** *ou* **corbeille à** ~ work basket; ~ **d'art** (*GÉNIE CIVIL*) *bridge or tunnel etc*.
ouvragé, e [uvʀaʒe] *adj* finely embroidered (*ou* worked *ou* carved).
ouvrant, e [uvʀɑ̃, -ɑ̃t] *vb voir* **ouvrir** ♦ *adj*: **toit** ~ sunroof.
ouvré, e [uvʀe] *adj* finely-worked; **jour** ~ working day.
ouvre-boîte(s) [uvʀəbwat] *nm inv* tin (*BRIT*) *ou* can opener.
ouvre-bouteille(s) [uvʀəbutɛj] *nm inv* bottle-opener.
ouvreuse [uvʀøz] *nf* usherette.
ouvrier, ière [uvʀije, -jɛʀ] *nm/f* worker ♦ *nf* (*ZOOL*) worker (bee) ♦ *adj* working-class; (*problèmes, conflit*) industrial, labour *cpd* (*BRIT*), labor *cpd* (*US*); (*revendications*) workers'; **classe ouvrière** working class; ~ **agricole** farmworker; ~ **qualifié** skilled worker; ~ **spécialisé (OS)** semiskilled worker; ~ **d'usine** factory worker.
ouvrir [uvʀiʀ] *vt* (*gén*) to open; (*brèche, passage*) to open up; (*commencer l'exploitation de, créer*) to open (up); (*eau, électricité, chauffage, robinet*) to turn on; (*MÉD*: *abcès*) to open up, cut open ♦ *vi* to open; to open up; (*CARTES*): ~ **à trèfle** to open in clubs; **s'~** *vi* to open; **s'~ à** (*art etc*) to open one's mind to; **s'~ à qn (de qch)** to open one's heart to sb (about sth); **s'~ les veines** to slash *ou* cut one's wrists; ~ **sur** to open onto; ~ **l'appétit**

à qn to whet sb's appetite; ~ **des horizons** to open up new horizons; ~ **l'esprit** to broaden one's horizons; ~ **une session** (*INFORM*) to log in.
ouvroir [uvʀwaʀ] *nm* workroom, sewing room.
ovaire [ɔvɛʀ] *nm* ovary.
ovale [ɔval] *adj* oval.
ovation [ɔvɑsjɔ̃] *nf* ovation.
ovationner [ɔvɑsjɔne] *vt*: ~ **qn** to give sb an ovation.
ovin, e [ɔvɛ̃, -in] *adj* ovine.
OVNI [ɔvni] *sigle m* (= *objet volant non identifié*) UFO.
ovoïde [ɔvɔid] *adj* egg-shaped.
ovulation [ɔvylɑsjɔ̃] *nf* (*PHYSIOL*) ovulation.
ovule [ɔvyl] *nm* (*PHYSIOL*) ovum (*pl* ova); (*MÉD*) pessary.
oxfordien, ne [ɔksfɔʀdjɛ̃, -ɛn] *adj* Oxonian ♦ *nm/f*: **O~, ne** Oxonian.
oxydable [ɔksidabl(ə)] *adj* liable to rust.
oxyde [ɔksid] *nm* oxide; ~ **de carbone** carbon monoxide.
oxyder [ɔkside]: **s'~** *vi* to become oxidized.
oxygène [ɔksiʒɛn] *nm* oxygen; (*fig*): **cure d'~** fresh air cure.
oxygéné, e [ɔksiʒene] *adj*: **eau ~e** hydrogen peroxide; **cheveux ~s** bleached hair.
ozone [ozɔn] *nm* ozone; **trou dans la couche d'~** ozone hole.

P p

P, p [pe] *nm inv* P, p ♦ *abr* (= *Père*) Fr; (= *page*) p; **P comme Pierre** P for Peter.
PA *sigle fpl* = **petites annonces**.
PAC *sigle f* (= *Politique agricole commune*) CAP.
pacage [pakaʒ] *nm* grazing, pasture.
pace-maker [pɛsmɛkœʀ] *nm* pacemaker.
pachyderme [paʃidɛʀm(ə)] *nm* pachyderm; elephant.
pacificateur, trice [pasifikatœʀ, -tʀis] *adj* pacificatory.
pacification [pasifikɑsjɔ̃] *nf* pacification.
pacifier [pasifje] *vt* to pacify.
pacifique [pasifik] *adj* (*personne*) peaceable; (*intentions, coexistence*) peaceful ♦ *nm*: **le P~, l'océan P~** the Pacific (Ocean).
pacifiquement [pasifikmɑ̃] *adv* peaceably; peacefully.
pacifisme [pasifism(ə)] *nm* pacifism.
pacifiste [pasifist(ə)] *nm/f* pacifist.
pack [pak] *nm* pack.
pacotille [pakɔtij] *nf* (*péj*) cheap goods *pl*; **de ~** cheap.
pacte [pakt(ə)] *nm* pact, treaty.
pactiser [paktize] *vi*: ~ **avec** to come to terms with.
pactole [paktɔl] *nm* gold mine (*fig*).
paddock [padɔk] *nm* paddock.
Padoue [padu] *n* Padua.
PAF *sigle f* (= *Police de l'air et des frontières*) *police authority responsible for civil aviation, border control etc* ♦ *sigle m* (= *paysage audiovisuel français*) *French broadcasting scene*.
pagaie [pagɛ] *nf* paddle.
pagaille [pagaj] *nf* mess, shambles *sg*; **il y en a en ~** there are loads *ou* heaps of them.
paganisme [paganism(ə)] *nm* paganism.
pagayer [pageje] *vi* to paddle.
page [paʒ] *nf* page; (*passage: d'un roman*) passage ♦ *nm* page (boy); **mise en ~** layout; **à la ~** (*fig*) up-to-date; ~ **d'accueil** (*INFORM*) home page; ~ **blanche** blank page; ~ **de garde** endpaper.
page-écran, *pl* **pages-écrans** [paʒekʀɑ̃] *nf* (*INFORM*) screen page.
pagination [paʒinɑsjɔ̃] *nf* pagination.
paginer [paʒine] *vt* to paginate.
pagne [paɲ] *nm* loincloth.
pagode [pagɔd] *nf* pagoda.
paie [pɛ] *nf* = **paye**.
paiement [pɛmɑ̃] *nm* = **payement**.
païen, ne [pajɛ̃, -ɛn] *adj, nm/f* pagan, heathen.
paillard, e [pajaʀ, -aʀd(ə)] *adj* bawdy.
paillasse [pajas] *nf* (*matelas*) straw mattress; (*d'un évier*) draining board.
paillasson [pɑjasɔ̃] *nm* doormat.
paille [pɑj] *nf* straw; (*défaut*) flaw; **être sur la ~** to be ruined; ~ **de fer** steel wool.
paillé, e [pɑje] *adj* with a straw seat.
pailleté, e [pajte] *adj* sequined.
paillette [pajɛt] *nf* speck, flake; **~s** *nfpl* (*décoratives*) sequins, spangles; **lessive en ~s** soapflakes *pl*.
pain [pɛ̃] *nm* (*substance*) bread; (*unité*) loaf (*pl* loaves) (of bread); (*morceau*): ~ **de cire** *etc* bar of wax *etc*; (*CULIN*): ~ **de poisson/légumes** fish/vegetable loaf; **petit ~** (bread) roll; ~ **bis/complet** brown/wholemeal (*BRIT*) *ou* wholewheat (*US*) bread; ~ **de campagne** farmhouse bread; ~ **d'épice** ≈ gingerbread; ~ **grillé** toast; ~ **de mie** sandwich loaf; ~ **perdu** French toast; ~ **de seigle** rye bread; ~ **de sucre** sugar loaf.
pair, e [pɛʀ] *adj* (*nombre*) even ♦ *nm* peer; **aller de ~ (avec)** to go hand in hand *ou* together (with); **au ~** (*FINANCE*) at par; **valeur au ~** par value; **jeune fille au ~** au pair.
paire [pɛʀ] *nf* pair; **une ~ de lunettes/tenailles** a pair of glasses/pincers; **faire la ~: les deux font la ~** they are two of a kind.
pais [pɛ] *vb voir* **paître**.
paisible [pezibl(ə)] *adj* peaceful, quiet.
paisiblement [peziblәmɑ̃] *adv* peacefully, quietly.
paître [pɛtʀ(ə)] *vi* to graze.

paix [pɛ] *nf* peace; (*fig*) peacefulness, peace; **faire la ~ avec** to make peace with; **avoir la ~** to have peace (and quiet).
Pakistan [pakistɑ̃] *nm*: **le ~** Pakistan.
pakistanais, e [pakistanɛ, -ɛz] *adj* Pakistani.
PAL *sigle m* (= *Phase Alternation Line*) PAL.
palabrer [palabʀe] *vi* to argue endlessly.
palabres [palabʀ(ə)] *nfpl ou mpl* endless discussions.
palace [palas] *nm* luxury hotel.
palais [palɛ] *nm* palace; (*ANAT*) palate; **le P~ Bourbon** *the seat of the French National Assembly*; **le P~ de l'Élysée** the Élysée Palace; **~ des expositions** exhibition centre; **le P~ de Justice** the Law Courts *pl*.
palan [palɑ̃] *nm* hoist.
Palatin [palatɛ̃]: **le (mont) ~** the Palatine (Hill).
pale [pal] *nf* (*d'hélice, de rame*) blade; (*de roue*) paddle.
pâle [pɑl] *adj* pale; (*fig*): **une ~ imitation** a pale imitation; **bleu ~** pale blue; **~ de colère** white *ou* pale with anger.
palefrenier [palfʀənje] *nm* groom (*for horses*).
paléontologie [paleɔ̃tɔlɔʒi] *nf* paleontology.
paléontologiste [paleɔ̃tɔlɔʒist(ə)], **paléontologue** [paleɔ̃tɔlɔg] *nm/f* paleontologist.
Palerme [palɛʀm(ə)] *n* Palermo.
Palestine [palɛstin] *nf*: **la ~** Palestine.
palestinien, ne [palɛstinjɛ̃, -ɛn] *adj* Palestinian ♦ *nm/f*: **P~, ne** Palestinian.
palet [palɛ] *nm* disc; (*HOCKEY*) puck.
paletot [palto] *nm* (short) coat.
palette [palɛt] *nf* palette; (*produits*) range.
palétuvier [paletyvje] *nm* mangrove.
pâleur [pɑlœʀ] *nf* paleness.
palier [palje] *nm* (*d'escalier*) landing; (*fig*) level, plateau; (*: phase stable*) levelling (*BRIT*) *ou* leveling (*US*) off, new level; (*TECH*) bearing; **nos voisins de ~** our neighbo(u)rs across the landing (*BRIT*) *ou* the hall (*US*); **en ~** *adv* level; **par ~s** in stages.
palière [paljɛʀ] *adj f* landing *cpd*.
pâlir [pɑliʀ] *vi* to turn *ou* go pale; (*couleur*) to fade; **faire ~ qn** (*de jalousie*) to make sb green (with envy).
palissade [palisad] *nf* fence.
palissandre [palisɑ̃dʀ(ə)] *nm* rosewood.
palliatif [paljatif] *nm* palliative; (*expédient*) stopgap measure.
pallier [palje] *vt*, **~ à** *vt* to offset, make up for.
palmarès [palmaʀɛs] *nm* record (of achievements); (*SCOL*) prize list; (*SPORT*) list of winners.
palme [palm(ə)] *nf* (*BOT*) palm leaf (*pl* leaves); (*symbole*) palm; (*de plongeur*) flipper; **~s (académiques)** *decoration for services to education*.
palmé, e [palme] *adj* (*pattes*) webbed.
palmeraie [palməʀɛ] *nf* palm grove.
palmier [palmje] *nm* palm tree.
palmipède [palmipɛd] *nm* palmiped, web-footed bird.
palois, e [palwa, -waz] *adj* of *ou* from Pau ♦ *nm/f*: **P~, e** inhabitant *ou* native of Pau.
palombe [palɔ̃b] *nf* woodpigeon, ringdove.
pâlot, te [pɑlo, -ɔt] *adj* pale, peaky.
palourde [paluʀd(ə)] *nf* clam.
palpable [palpabl(ə)] *adj* tangible, palpable.
palper [palpe] *vt* to feel, finger.
palpitant, e [palpitɑ̃, -ɑ̃t] *adj* thrilling, gripping.
palpitation [palpitɑsjɔ̃] *nf* palpitation.
palpiter [palpite] *vi* (*cœur, pouls*) to beat; (*: plus fort*) to pound, throb; (*narines, chair*) to quiver.
paludisme [palydism(ə)] *nm* malaria.
palustre [palystʀ(ə)] *adj* (*coquillage etc*) marsh *cpd*; (*fièvre*) malarial.
pâmer [pɑme]: **se ~** *vi* to swoon; (*fig*): **se ~ devant** to go into raptures over.
pâmoison [pɑmwazɔ̃] *nf*: **tomber en ~** to swoon.
pampa [pɑ̃pa] *nf* pampas *pl*.
pamphlet [pɑ̃flɛ] *nm* lampoon, satirical tract.
pamphlétaire [pɑ̃fletɛʀ] *nm/f* lampoonist.
pamplemousse [pɑ̃pləmus] *nm* grapefruit.
pan [pɑ̃] *nm* section, piece; (*côté: d'un prisme, d'une tour*) side, face ♦ *excl* bang!; **~ de chemise** shirt tail; **~ de mur** section of wall.
panacée [panase] *nf* panacea.
panachage [panaʃaʒ] *nm* blend, mix; (*POL*) *voting for candidates from different parties instead of for the set list of one party*.
panache [panaʃ] *nm* plume; (*fig*) spirit, panache.
panaché, e [panaʃe] *adj*: **œillet ~** variegated carnation; **glace ~e** mixed ice cream; **salade ~e** mixed salad; **bière ~e** shandy.
panais [panɛ] *nm* parsnip.
Panama [panama] *nm*: **le ~** Panama.
panaméen, ne [panameɛ̃, -ɛn] *adj* Panamanian ♦ *nm/f*: **P~, ne** Panamanian.
panaris [panaʀi] *nm* whitlow.
pancarte [pɑ̃kaʀt(ə)] *nf* sign, notice; (*dans un défilé*) placard.
pancréas [pɑ̃kʀeɑs] *nm* pancreas.
panda [pɑ̃da] *nm* panda.
pané, e [pane] *adj* fried in breadcrumbs.
panégyrique [paneʒiʀik] *nm*: **faire le ~ de qn** to extol sb's merits *ou* virtues.
panier [panje] *nm* basket; (*à diapositives*) magazine; **mettre au ~** to chuck away; **~ de crabes**: **c'est un ~ de crabes** (*fig*) they're constantly at one another's throats; **~ percé** (*fig*) spendthrift; **~ à provisions** shopping basket; **~ à salade** (*CULIN*) salad shaker; (*POLICE*) paddy wagon, police van.
panier-repas, *pl* **paniers-repas** [panjeʀ(ə)pɑ] *nm* packed lunch.
panification [panifikɑsjɔ̃] *nf* bread-making.
panique [panik] *adj* panicky ♦ *nf* panic.
paniquer [panike] *vi* to panic.
panne [pan] *nf* (*d'un mécanisme, moteur*)

breakdown; **être/tomber en** ~ to have broken down/break down; **être en** ~ **d'essence** *ou* **en** ~ **sèche** to have run out of petrol (*BRIT*) *ou* gas (*US*); **mettre en** ~ (*NAVIG*) to bring to; ~ **d'électricité** *ou* **de courant** power *ou* electrical failure.

panneau, x [pano] *nm* (*écriteau*) sign, notice; (*de boiserie, de tapisserie etc*) panel; **tomber dans le** ~ (*fig*) to walk into the trap; ~ **d'affichage** notice (*BRIT*) *ou* bulletin (*US*) board; ~ **électoral** board for election poster; ~ **indicateur** signpost; ~ **publicitaire** hoarding (*BRIT*), billboard (*US*); ~ **de signalisation** roadsign; ~ **solaire** solar panel.

panneau-réclame, *pl* **panneaux-réclame** [panoʀeklam] *nm* hoarding (*BRIT*), billboard (*US*).

panonceau, x [panɔ̃so] *nm* (*de magasin etc*) sign; (*de médecin etc*) plaque.

panoplie [panɔpli] *nf* (*jouet*) outfit; (*d'armes*) display; (*fig*) array.

panorama [panɔʀama] *nm* (*vue*) all-round view, panorama; (*peinture*) panorama; (*fig: étude complète*) complete overview.

panoramique [panɔʀamik] *adj* panoramic; (*carrosserie*) with panoramic windows ♦ *nm* (*CINÉ, TV*) panoramic shot.

panse [pɑ̃s] *nf* paunch.

pansement [pɑ̃smɑ̃] *nm* dressing, bandage; ~ **adhésif** sticking plaster (*BRIT*), bandaid ® (*US*).

panser [pɑ̃se] *vt* (*plaie*) to dress, bandage; (*bras*) to put a dressing on, bandage; (*cheval*) to groom.

pantalon [pɑ̃talɔ̃] *nm* (*aussi*: ~**s, paire de** ~**s**) trousers *pl* (*BRIT*), pants *pl* (*US*), pair of trousers *ou* pants; ~ **de ski** ski pants *pl*.

pantalonnade [pɑ̃talɔnad] *nf* slapstick (comedy).

pantelant, e [pɑ̃tlɑ̃, -ɑ̃t] *adj* gasping for breath, panting.

panthère [pɑ̃tɛʀ] *nf* panther.

pantin [pɑ̃tɛ̃] *nm* (*jouet*) jumping jack; (*péj: personne*) puppet.

pantois [pɑ̃twa] *adj m*: **rester** ~ to be flabbergasted.

pantomime [pɑ̃tɔmim] *nf* mime; (*pièce*) mime show; (*péj*) fuss, carry-on.

pantouflard, e [pɑ̃tuflaʀ, -aʀd(ə)] *adj* (*péj*) stay-at-home.

pantoufle [pɑ̃tufl(ə)] *nf* slipper.

panure [panyʀ] *nf* breadcrumbs *pl*.

PAO *sigle f* (= *publication assistée par ordinateur*) desk-top publishing.

paon [pɑ̃] *nm* peacock.

papa [papa] *nm* dad(dy).

papauté [papote] *nf* papacy.

papaye [papaj] *nf* pawpaw.

pape [pap] *nm* pope.

paperasse [papʀas] *nf* (*péj*) bumf *no pl*, papers *pl*; forms *pl*.

paperasserie [papʀasʀi] *nf* (*péj*) red tape *no pl*; paperwork *no pl*.

papeterie [papetʀi] *nf* (*fabrication du papier*) paper-making (industry); (*usine*) paper mill; (*magasin*) stationer's (shop (*BRIT*)); (*articles*) stationery.

papetier, ière [paptje, -jɛʀ] *nm/f* paper-maker; stationer.

papetier-libraire, *pl* **papetiers-libraires** [paptjelibʀɛʀ] *nm* bookseller and stationer.

papier [papje] *nm* paper; (*feuille*) sheet *ou* piece of paper; (*article*) article; (*écrit officiel*) document; ~**s** *nmpl* (*aussi*: ~**s d'identité**) (identity) papers; **sur le** ~ (*théoriquement*) on paper; **noircir du** ~ to write page after page; ~ **couché/glacé** art/glazed paper; ~ **(d')aluminium** aluminium (*BRIT*) *ou* aluminum (*US*) foil, tinfoil; ~ **d'Arménie** incense paper; ~ **bible** India *ou* bible paper; ~ **de brouillon** rough *ou* scrap paper; ~ **bulle** manil(l)a paper; ~ **buvard** blotting paper; ~ **calque** tracing paper; ~ **carbone** carbon paper; ~ **collant** Sellotape ® (*BRIT*), Scotch ® (*US*) *ou* sticky tape; ~ **en continu** continuous stationery; ~ **à dessin** drawing paper; ~ **d'emballage** wrapping paper; ~ **gommé** gummed paper; ~ **hygiénique** toilet paper; ~ **journal** newsprint; (*pour emballer*) newspaper; ~ **à lettres** writing paper, notepaper; ~ **mâché** papier-mâché; ~ **machine** typing paper; ~ **peint** wallpaper; ~ **pelure** India paper; ~ **à pliage accordéon** fanfold paper; ~ **de soie** tissue paper; ~ **thermique** thermal paper; ~ **de tournesol** litmus paper; ~ **de verre** sandpaper.

papier-filtre, *pl* **papiers-filtres** [papjefiltʀ(ə)] *nm* filter paper.

papier-monnaie, *pl* **papiers-monnaies** [papjemɔnɛ] *nm* paper money.

papille [papij] *nf*: ~**s gustatives** taste buds.

papillon [papijɔ̃] *nm* butterfly; (*fam: contravention*) (parking) ticket; (*TECH: écrou*) wing *ou* butterfly nut; ~ **de nuit** moth.

papillonner [papijɔne] *vi* to flit from one thing (*ou* person) to another.

papillote [papijɔt] *nf* (*pour cheveux*) curlpaper; (*de gigot*) (paper) frill.

papilloter [papijɔte] *vi* (*yeux*) to blink; (*paupières*) to flutter; (*lumière*) to flicker.

papotage [papɔtaʒ] *nm* chitchat.

papoter [papɔte] *vi* to chatter.

papou, e [papu] *adj* Papuan.

Papouasie-Nouvelle-Guinée [papwazinuvɛlgine] *nf*: **la** ~ Papua-New-Guinea.

paprika [papʀika] *nm* paprika.

papyrus [papiʀys] *nm* papyrus.

pâque [pɑk] *nf*: **la** ~ Passover; *voir aussi* **Pâques.**

paquebot [pakbo] *nm* liner.

pâquerette [pɑkʀɛt] *nf* daisy.

Pâques [pɑk] *nm, nfpl* Easter; **faire ses** ~ to do one's Easter duties; **l'île de** ~ Easter Island.

paquet [pakɛ] *nm* packet; (*colis*) parcel; (*bal-

lot) bundle; (*dans négociations*) package (deal); (*fig: tas*): ~ **de** pile *ou* heap of; ~**s** *nmpl* (*bagages*) bags; **mettre le** ~ (*fam*) to give one's all; ~ **de mer** big wave.

paquetage [paktaʒ] *nm* (*MIL*) kit, pack.

paquet-cadeau, *pl* **paquets-cadeaux** [pakɛkado] *nm* gift-wrapped parcel.

par [paʀ] *prép* by; **finir** *etc* ~ to end *etc* with; ~ **amour** out of love; **passer** ~ **Lyon/la côte** to go via *ou* through Lyons/along by the coast; ~ **la fenêtre** (*jeter, regarder*) out of the window; **3** ~ **jour/personne** 3 a *ou* per day/head; **deux** ~ **deux** two at a time; (*marcher etc*) in twos; ~ **où?** which way?; ~ **ici** this way; (*dans le coin*) round here; ~**-ci,** ~**-là** here and there.

para [paʀa] *nm* (= *parachutiste*) para.

parabole [paʀabɔl] *nf* (*REL*) parable; (*GÉOM*) parabola.

parabolique [paʀabɔlik] *adj* parabolic; **antenne** ~ satellite dish.

parachever [paʀaʃve] *vt* to perfect.

parachutage [paʀaʃytaʒ] *nm* (*de soldats, vivres*) parachuting-in; **nous sommes contre le** ~ **d'un candidat parisien dans notre circonscription** (*POL, fig*) we are against a Parisian candidate being landed on us.

parachute [paʀaʃyt] *nm* parachute.

parachuter [paʀaʃyte] *vt* (*soldat etc*) to parachute, (*fig*) to pitchfork; **il a été parachuté à la tête de l'entreprise** he was brought in from outside as head of the company.

parachutisme [paʀaʃytism(ə)] *nm* parachuting.

parachutiste [paʀaʃytist(ə)] *nm/f* parachutist; (*MIL*) paratrooper.

parade [paʀad] *nf* (*spectacle, défilé*) parade; (*ESCRIME, BOXE*) parry; (*ostentation*): **faire** ~ **de** to display, show off; (*défense, riposte*): **trouver la** ~ **à une attaque** to find the answer to an attack; **de** ~ *adj* ceremonial; (*superficiel*) superficial, outward.

parader [paʀade] *vi* to swagger (around), show off.

paradis [paʀadi] *nm* heaven, paradise; **P**~ **terrestre** (*REL*) Garden of Eden; (*fig*) heaven on earth.

paradisiaque [paʀadizjak] *adj* heavenly, divine.

paradoxal, e, aux [paʀadɔksal, -o] *adj* paradoxical.

paradoxalement [paʀadɔksalmɑ̃] *adv* paradoxically.

paradoxe [paʀadɔks(ə)] *nm* paradox.

parafe [paʀaf] *nm*, **parafer** [paʀafe] *vt* = **paraphe, parapher**.

paraffine [paʀafin] *nf* paraffin; paraffin wax.

paraffiné, e [paʀafine] *adj*: **papier** ~ wax(ed) paper.

parafoudre [paʀafudʀ(ə)] *nm* (*ÉLEC*) lightning conductor.

parages [paʀaʒ] *nmpl* (*NAVIG*) waters; **dans les** ~ **(de)** in the area *ou* vicinity (of).

paragraphe [paʀagʀaf] *nm* paragraph.

Paraguay [paʀagwɛ] *nm*: **le** ~ Paraguay.

paraguayen, ne [paʀagwajɛ̃, -ɛn] *adj* Paraguayan ♦ *nm/f*: **P**~**, ne** Paraguayan.

paraître [paʀɛtʀ(ə)] *vb avec attribut* to seem, look, appear ♦ *vi* to appear; (*être visible*) to show; (*PRESSE, ÉDITION*) to be published, come out, appear; (*briller*) to show off; **laisser** ~ **qch** to let (sth) show ♦ *vb impers*: **il paraît que** it seems *ou* appears that; **il me paraît que** it seems to me that; **il paraît absurde de** it seems absurd to; **il ne paraît pas son âge** he doesn't look his age; ~ **en justice** to appear before the court(s); ~ **en scène/en public/à l'écran** to appear on stage/in public/on the screen.

parallèle [paʀalɛl] *adj* parallel; (*police, marché*) unofficial; (*société, énergie*) alternative ♦ *nm* (*comparaison*): **faire un** ~ **entre** to draw a parallel between; (*GÉO*) parallel ♦ *nf* parallel (line); **en** ~ in parallel; **mettre en** ~ (*choses opposées*) to compare; (*choses semblables*) to parallel.

parallèlement [paʀalɛlmɑ̃] *adv* in parallel; (*fig: en même temps*) at the same time.

parallélépipède [paʀalelepipɛd] *nm* parallelepiped.

parallélisme [paʀalelism(ə)] *nm* parallelism; (*AUTO*) wheel alignment.

parallélogramme [paʀalelɔgʀam] *nm* parallelogram.

paralyser [paʀalize] *vt* to paralyze.

paralysie [paʀalizi] *nf* paralysis.

paralytique [paʀalitik] *adj, nm/f* paralytic.

paramédical, e, aux [paʀamedikal, -o] *adj* paramedical.

paramètre [paʀamɛtʀ(ə)] *nm* parameter.

paramilitaire [paʀamilitɛʀ] *adj* paramilitary.

paranoïa [paʀanɔja] *nf* paranoia.

paranoïaque [paʀanɔjak] *nm/f* paranoiac.

paranormal, e, aux [paʀanɔʀmal, -o] *adj* paranormal.

parapet [paʀapɛ] *nm* parapet.

paraphe [paʀaf] *nm* (*trait*) flourish; (*signature*) initials *pl*; signature.

parapher [paʀafe] *vt* to initial; to sign.

paraphrase [paʀafʀɑz] *nf* paraphrase.

paraphraser [paʀafʀɑze] *vt* to paraphrase.

paraplégie [paʀapleʒi] *nf* paraplegia.

paraplégique [paʀapleʒik] *adj, nm/f* paraplegic.

parapluie [paʀaplɥi] *nm* umbrella; ~ **atomique** *ou* **nucléaire** nuclear umbrella; ~ **pliant** telescopic umbrella.

parapsychique [paʀapsiʃik] *adj* parapsychological.

parapsychologie [paʀapsikɔlɔʒi] *nf* parapsychology.

parapublic, ique [paʀapyblik] *adj partly state-controlled.*

parascolaire [paʀaskɔlɛʀ] *adj* extracurricular.

parasitaire [paʀazitɛʀ] *adj* parasitic(al).
parasite [paʀazit] *nm* parasite ⧫ *adj* (*BOT, BIO*) parasitic(al); ~**s** *nmpl* (*TÉL*) interference *sg*.
parasitisme [paʀasitism(ə)] *nm* parasitism.
parasol [paʀasɔl] *nm* parasol, sunshade.
paratonnerre [paʀatɔnɛʀ] *nm* lightning conductor.
paravent [paʀavɑ̃] *nm* folding screen; (*fig*) screen.
parc [paʀk] *nm* (public) park, gardens *pl*; (*de château etc*) grounds *pl*; (*pour le bétail*) pen, enclosure; (*d'enfant*) playpen; (*MIL: entrepôt*) depot; (*ensemble d'unités*) stock; (*de voitures etc*) fleet; ~ **d'attractions** amusement park; ~ **automobile** (*d'un pays*) number of cars on the roads; ~ **à huîtres** oyster bed; ~ **à thème** theme park; ~ **national** national park; ~ **naturel** nature reserve; ~ **de stationnement** car park; ~ **zoologique** zoological gardens *pl*.
parcelle [paʀsɛl] *nf* fragment, scrap; (*de terrain*) plot, parcel.
parcelliser [paʀselize] *vt* to divide *ou* split up.
parce que [paʀsk(ə)] *conj* because.
parchemin [paʀʃəmɛ̃] *nm* parchment.
parcheminé, e [paʀʃəmine] *adj* wrinkled; (*papier*) with a parchment finish.
parcimonie [paʀsimɔni] *nf* parsimony, parsimoniousness.
parcimonieux, euse [paʀsimɔnjø, -øz] *adj* parsimonious, miserly.
parc(o)mètre [paʀk(ɔ)mɛtʀ(ə)] *nm* parking meter.
parcotrain [paʀkɔtʀɛ̃] *nm* station car park (*BRIT*) *ou* parking lot (*US*), park-and-ride car park (*BRIT*).
parcourir [paʀkuʀiʀ] *vt* (*trajet, distance*) to cover; (*article, livre*) to skim *ou* glance through; (*lieu*) to go all over, travel up and down; (*suj: frisson, vibration*) to run through; ~ **des yeux** to run one's eye over.
parcours [paʀkuʀ] *vb voir* **parcourir** ⧫ *nm* (*trajet*) journey; (*itinéraire*) route; (*SPORT: terrain*) course; (*: tour*) round; run; lap; ~ **du combattant** assault course.
parcouru, e [paʀkuʀy] *pp de* **parcourir**.
par-delà [paʀdəla] *prép* beyond.
par-dessous [paʀdəsu] *prép, adv* under(neath).
pardessus [paʀdəsy] *nm* overcoat.
par-dessus [paʀdəsy] *prép* over (the top of) ⧫ *adv* over (the top); ~ **le marché** on top of it all.
par-devant [paʀdəvɑ̃] *prép* in the presence of, before ⧫ *adv* at the front; round the front.
pardon [paʀdɔ̃] *nm* forgiveness *no pl* ⧫ *excl* (*excuses*) (I'm) sorry; (*pour interpeller etc*) excuse me; (*demander de répéter*) (I beg your) pardon? (*BRIT*), pardon me? (*US*).
pardonnable [paʀdɔnabl(ə)] *adj* forgivable, excusable.
pardonner [paʀdɔne] *vt* to forgive; ~ **qch à qn** to forgive sb for sth; **qui ne pardonne pas** (*maladie, erreur*) fatal.
paré, e [paʀe] *adj* ready, prepared.
pare-balles [paʀbal] *adj inv* bulletproof.
pare-boue [paʀbu] *nm inv* mudflap.
pare-brise [paʀbʀiz] *nm inv* windscreen (*BRIT*), windshield (*US*).
pare-chocs [paʀʃɔk] *nm inv* bumper (*BRIT*), fender (*US*).
pare-étincelles [paʀetɛ̃sɛl] *nm inv* fireguard.
pare-feu [paʀfø] *nm inv* firebreak ⧫ *adj inv*: **portes** ~ fire (resistant) doors.
pareil, le [paʀɛj] *adj* (*identique*) the same, alike; (*similaire*) similar; (*tel*): **un courage/livre** ~ such courage/a book, courage/a book like this; **de** ~**s livres** such books ⧫ *adv*: **habillés** ~ dressed the same (way), dressed alike; **faire** ~ to do the same (thing); **j'en veux un** ~ I'd like one just like it; **rien de** ~ no (*ou* any) such thing, nothing (*ou* anything) like it; **ses** ~**s** one's fellow men; one's peers; **ne pas avoir son (sa)** ~**(le)** to be second to none; ~ **à** the same as; similar to; **sans** ~ unparalleled, unequalled; **c'est du** ~ **au même** it comes to the same thing, it's six (of one) and half-a-dozen (of the other); **en** ~ **cas** in such a case; **rendre la** ~**le à qn** to pay sb back in his own coin.
pareillement [paʀɛjmɑ̃] *adv* the same, alike; in such a way; (*également*) likewise.
parement [paʀmɑ̃] *nm* (*CONSTR, revers d'un col, d'une manche*) facing; (*REL*): ~ **d'autel** antependium.
parent, e [paʀɑ̃, -ɑ̃t] *nm/f*: **un/une** ~**/e** a relative *ou* relation ⧫ *adj*: **être** ~ **de** to be related to; ~**s** *nmpl* (*père et mère*) parents; (*famille, proches*) relatives, relations; ~ **unique** lone parent; ~**s par alliance** relatives *ou* relations by marriage; ~**s en ligne directe** blood relations.
parental, e, aux [paʀɑ̃tal, -o] *adj* parental.
parenté [paʀɑ̃te] *nf* (*lien*) relationship; (*personnes*) relatives *pl*, relations *pl*.
parenthèse [paʀɑ̃tɛz] *nf* (*ponctuation*) bracket, parenthesis; (*MATH*) bracket; (*digression*) parenthesis, digression; **ouvrir/fermer la** ~ to open/close the brackets; **entre** ~**s** in brackets; (*fig*) incidentally.
parer [paʀe] *vt* to adorn; (*CULIN*) to dress, trim; (*éviter*) to ward off; ~ **à** (*danger*) to ward off; (*inconvénient*) to deal with; **se** ~ **de** (*fig: qualité, titre*) to assume; ~ **à toute éventualité** to be ready for every eventuality; ~ **au plus pressé** to attend to what's most urgent.
pare-soleil [paʀsɔlɛj] *nm inv* sun visor.
paresse [paʀɛs] *nf* laziness.
paresser [paʀese] *vi* to laze around.
paresseusement [paʀɛsøzmɑ̃] *adv* lazily; sluggishly.
paresseux, euse [paʀɛsø, -øz] *adj* lazy; (*fig*) slow, sluggish ⧫ *nm* (*ZOOL*) sloth.
parfaire [paʀfɛʀ] *vt* to perfect, complete.

parfait, e [parfɛ, -ɛt] *pp de* **parfaire** ♦ *adj* perfect ♦ *nm* (*LING*) perfect (tense); (*CULIN*) parfait ♦ *excl* fine, excellent.
parfaitement [parfɛtmɑ̃] *adv* perfectly ♦ *excl* (most) certainly.
parfaites [parfɛt], **parfasse** [parfas], **parferai** [parfre] *etc vb voir* **parfaire.**
parfois [parfwa] *adv* sometimes.
parfum [parfœ̃] *nm* (*produit*) perfume, scent; (*odeur: de fleur*) scent, fragrance; (*: de tabac, vin*) aroma; (*goût: de glace, milk-shake*) flavour (*BRIT*), flavor (*US*).
parfumé, e [parfyme] *adj* (*fleur, fruit*) fragrant; (*papier à lettres etc*) scented; (*femme*) wearing perfume *ou* scent, perfumed; (*aromatisé*): ~ **au café** coffee-flavoured (*BRIT*) *ou* -flavored (*US*).
parfumer [parfyme] *vt* (*suj: odeur, bouquet*) to perfume; (*mouchoir*) to put scent *ou* perfume on; (*crème, gâteau*) to flavour (*BRIT*), flavor (*US*); **se** ~ to put on (some) perfume *ou* scent; (*d'habitude*) to use perfume *ou* scent.
parfumerie [parfymri] *nf* (*commerce*) perfumery; (*produits*) perfumes *pl*; (*boutique*) perfume shop (*BRIT*) *ou* store (*US*).
pari [pari] *nm* bet, wager; (*SPORT*) bet; ~ **mutuel urbain (PMU)** *system of betting on horses.*
paria [parja] *nm* outcast.
parier [parje] *vt* to bet; **j'aurais parié que si/non** I'd have said he (*ou* you *etc*) would/wouldn't.
parieur [parjœr] *nm* (*turfiste etc*) punter.
Paris [pari] *n* Paris.
parisien, ne [parizjɛ̃, -ɛn] *adj* Parisian; (*GÉO, ADMIN*) Paris *cpd* ♦ *nm/f*: **P~, ne** Parisian.
paritaire [paritɛr] *adj*: **commission** ~ joint commission.
parité [parite] *nf* parity; ~ **de change** (*ÉCON*) exchange parity.
parjure [parʒyr] *nm* (*faux serment*) false oath, perjury; (*violation de serment*) breach of oath, perjury ♦ *nm/f* perjurer.
parjurer [parʒyre]: **se** ~ *vi* to perjure o.s.
parka [parka] *nf* parka.
parking [parkiŋ] *nm* (*lieu*) car park (*BRIT*), parking lot (*US*).
parlant, e [parlɑ̃, -ɑ̃t] *adj* (*fig*) graphic, vivid; (*: comparaison, preuve*) eloquent; (*CINÉ*) talking ♦ *adv*: **généralement** ~ generally speaking.
parlé, e [parle] *adj*: **langue** ~**e** spoken language.
parlement [parləmɑ̃] *nm* parliament; **le P~ européen** the European Parliament.
parlementaire [parləmɑ̃tɛr] *adj* parliamentary ♦ *nm/f* (*député*) ≈ Member of Parliament (*BRIT*) *ou* Congress (*US*); parliamentarian; (*négociateur*) negotiator, mediator.
parlementarisme [parləmɑ̃tarism(ə)] *nm* parliamentary government.
parlementer [parləmɑ̃te] *vi* (*ennemis*) to negotiate, parley; (*s'entretenir, discuter*) to argue at length, have lengthy talks.
parler [parle] *nm* speech; dialect ♦ *vi* to speak, talk; (*avouer*) to talk; ~ **(à qn) de** to talk *ou* speak (to sb) about; ~ **pour qn** (*intercéder*) to speak for sb; ~ **en l'air** to say the first thing that comes into one's head; ~ **le/en français** to speak French/in French; ~ **affaires** to talk business; ~ **en dormant/du nez** to talk in one's sleep/through one's nose; **sans** ~ **de** (*fig*) not to mention, to say nothing of; **tu parles!** you must be joking!; **n'en parlons plus!** let's forget it!
parleur [parlœr] *nm*: **beau** ~ fine talker.
parloir [parlwar] *nm* (*d'une prison, d'un hôpital*) visiting room; (*REL*) parlour (*BRIT*), parlor (*US*).
parlote [parlɔt] *nf* chitchat.
Parme [parm(ə)] *n* Parma.
parme [parm(ə)] *adj* violet (blue).
parmesan [parməzɑ̃] *nm* Parmesan (cheese).
parmi [parmi] *prép* among(st).
parodie [parɔdi] *nf* parody.
parodier [parɔdje] *vt* (*œuvre, auteur*) to parody.
paroi [parwa] *nf* wall; (*cloison*) partition; ~ **rocheuse** rock face.
paroisse [parwas] *nf* parish.
paroissial, e, aux [parwasjal, -o] *adj* parish *cpd.*
paroissien, ne [parwasjɛ̃, -ɛn] *nm/f* parishioner ♦ *nm* prayer book.
parole [parɔl] *nf* (*faculté*): **la** ~ speech; (*mot, promesse*) word; (*REL*): **la bonne** ~ the word of God; ~**s** *nfpl* (*MUS*) words, lyrics; **tenir** ~ to keep one's word; **avoir la** ~ to have the floor; **n'avoir qu'une** ~ to be true to one's word; **donner la** ~ **à qn** to hand over to sb; **prendre la** ~ to speak; **demander la** ~ to ask for permission to speak; **perdre la** ~ to lose the power of speech; (*fig*) to lose one's tongue; **je le crois sur** ~ I'll take his word for it, I'll take him at his word; **temps de** ~ (*TV, RADIO etc*) discussion time; **ma** ~! my word!, good heavens!; ~ **d'honneur** word of honour (*BRIT*) *ou* honor (*US*).
parolier, ière [parɔlje, -jɛr] *nm/f* lyricist; (*OPÉRA*) librettist.
paroxysme [parɔksism(ə)] *nm* height, paroxysm.
parpaing [parpɛ̃] *nm* bond-stone, parpen.
parquer [parke] *vt* (*voiture, matériel*) to park; (*bestiaux*) to pen (in *ou* up); (*prisonniers*) to pack in.
parquet [parkɛ] *nm* (parquet) floor; (*JUR: bureau*) public prosecutor's office; **le** ~ **(général)** (*magistrats*) ≈ the Bench.
parqueter [parkəte] *vt* to lay a parquet floor in.
parrain [parɛ̃] *nm* godfather; (*d'un navire*) namer; (*d'un nouvel adhérent*) sponsor, pro-

poser.
parrainage [paʀɛnaʒ] *nm* sponsorship.
parrainer [paʀene] *vt* (*nouvel adhérent*) to sponsor, propose; (*entreprise*) to promote, sponsor.
parricide [paʀisid] *nm, nf* parricide.
pars [paʀ] *vb voir* **partir**.
parsemer [paʀsəme] *vt* (*suj: feuilles, papiers*) to be scattered over; ~ **qch de** to scatter sth with.
parsi, e [paʀsi] *adj* Parsee.
part [paʀ] *vb voir* **partir** ♦ *nf* (*qui revient à qn*) share; (*fraction, partie*) part; (*de gâteau, fromage*) portion; (*FINANCE*) (non-voting) share; **prendre ~ à** (*débat etc*) to take part in; (*soucis, douleur de qn*) to share in; **faire ~ de qch à qn** to announce sth to sb, inform sb of sth; **pour ma ~** as for me, as far as I'm concerned; **à ~ entière** *adj* full; **de la ~ de** (*au nom de*) on behalf of; (*donné par*) from; **c'est de la ~ de qui?** (*au téléphone*) who's calling *ou* speaking (please)?; **de toute(s) ~(s)** from all sides *ou* quarters; **de ~ et d'autre** on both sides, on either side; **de ~ en ~** right through; **d'une ~ ... d'autre ~** on the one hand ... on the other hand; **nulle/autre/quelque ~** nowhere/elsewhere/somewhere; **à ~** *adv* separately; (*de côté*) aside ♦ *prép* apart from, except for ♦ *adj* exceptional, special; **pour une large** *ou* **bonne ~** to a great extent; **prendre qch en bonne/mauvaise ~** to take sth well/badly; **faire la ~ des choses** to make allowances; **faire la ~ du feu** (*fig*) to cut one's losses; **faire la ~ (trop) belle à qn** to give sb more than his (*ou* her) share.
part. *abr* = **particulier**.
partage [paʀtaʒ] *nm* (*voir partager*) sharing (out) *no pl*, share-out; sharing; dividing up; (*POL: de suffrages*) share; **recevoir qch en ~** to receive sth as one's share (*ou* lot); **sans ~** undivided.
partagé, e [paʀtaʒe] *adj* (*opinions etc*) divided; (*amour*) shared; **temps ~** (*INFORM*) time sharing; **être ~ entre** to be shared between; **être ~ sur** to be divided about.
partager [paʀtaʒe] *vt* to share; (*distribuer, répartir*) to share (out); (*morceler, diviser*) to divide (up); **se ~** *vt* (*héritage etc*) to share between themselves (*ou* ourselves *etc*).
partance [paʀtɑ̃s]: **en ~** *adv* outbound, due to leave; **en ~ pour** (bound) for.
partant, e [paʀtɑ̃, -ɑ̃t] *vb voir* **partir** ♦ *adj*: **être ~ pour qch** (*d'accord pour*) to be quite ready for sth ♦ *nm* (*SPORT*) starter; (*HIPPISME*) runner.
partenaire [paʀtənɛʀ] *nm/f* partner; **~s sociaux** management and workforce.
parterre [paʀtɛʀ] *nm* (*de fleurs*) (flower) bed, border; (*THÉÂT*) stalls *pl*.
parti [paʀti] *nm* (*POL*) party; (*décision*) course of action; (*personne à marier*) match; **tirer ~ de** to take advantage of, turn to good account; **prendre le ~ de faire** to make up one's mind to do, resolve to do; **prendre le ~ de qn** to stand up for sb, side with sb; **prendre ~ (pour/contre)** to take sides *ou* a stand (for/against); **prendre son ~ de** to come to terms with; **~ pris** bias.
partial, e, aux [paʀsjal, -o] *adj* biased, partial.
partialement [paʀsjalmɑ̃] *adv* in a biased way.
partialité [paʀsjalite] *nf* bias, partiality.
participant, e [paʀtisipɑ̃, -ɑ̃t] *nm/f* participant; (*à un concours*) entrant; (*d'une société*) member.
participation [paʀtisipɑsjɔ̃] *nf* participation; sharing; (*COMM*) interest; **la ~ aux bénéfices** profit-sharing; **la ~ ouvrière** worker participation; **"avec la ~ de ..."** "featuring ...".
participe [paʀtisip] *nm* participle; **~ passé/présent** past/present participle.
participer [paʀtisipe]: **~ à** *vt* (*course, réunion*) to take part in; (*profits etc*) to share in; (*frais etc*) to contribute to; (*entreprise: financièrement*) to cooperate in; (*chagrin, succès de qn*) to share (in); **~ de** *vt* to partake of.
particulariser [paʀtikylaʀize] *vt*: **se ~** to mark o.s. (*ou* itself) out.
particularisme [paʀtikylaʀism(ə)] *nm* sense of identity.
particularité [paʀtikylaʀite] *nf* particularity; (*distinctive*) characteristic, feature.
particule [paʀtikyl] *nf* particle; **~ (nobiliaire)** nobiliary particle.
particulier, ière [paʀtikylje, -jɛʀ] *adj* (*personnel, privé*) private; (*spécial*) special, particular; (*caractéristique*) characteristic, distinctive; (*spécifique*) particular ♦ *nm* (*individu: ADMIN*) private individual; **"~ vend ..."** (*COMM*) "for sale privately ...", "for sale by owner ..." (*US*); **~ à** peculiar to; **en ~** *adv* (*surtout*) in particular, particularly; (*à part*) separately; (*en privé*) in private.
particulièrement [paʀtikyljɛʀmɑ̃] *adv* particularly.
partie [paʀti] *nf* (*gén*) part; (*profession, spécialité*) field, subject; (*JUR etc: protagonistes*) party; (*de cartes, tennis etc*) game; (*fig: lutte, combat*) struggle, fight; **une ~ de campagne/de pêche** an outing in the country/a fishing party *ou* trip; **en ~** *adv* partly, in part; **faire ~ de** to belong to; (*suj: chose*) to be part of; **prendre qn à ~** to take sb to task; (*malmener*) to set on sb; **en grande ~** largely, in the main; **ce n'est que ~ remise** it will be for another time *ou* the next time; **avoir ~ liée avec qn** to be in league with sb; **~ civile** (*JUR*) *party claiming damages in a criminal case*.
partiel, le [paʀsjɛl] *adj* partial ♦ *nm* (*SCOL*) class exam.
partiellement [paʀsjɛlmɑ̃] *adv* partially, partly.
partir [paʀtiʀ] *vi* (*gén*) to go; (*quitter*) to go,

leave; (*s'éloigner*) to go (*ou* drive *etc*) away *ou* off; (*moteur*) to start; (*pétard*) to go off; (*bouchon*) to come out; (*bouton*) to come off; ~ **de** (*lieu: quitter*) to leave; (*: commencer à*) to start from; (*date*) to run *ou* start from; ~ **pour/à** (*lieu, pays etc*) to leave for/go off to; **à ~ de** from.

partisan, e [partizɑ̃, -an] *nm/f* partisan; (*d'un parti, régime etc*) supporter ♦ *adj* (*lutte, querelle*) partisan, one-sided; **être ~ de qch/faire** to be in favour (*BRIT*) *ou* favor (*US*) of sth/doing.

partitif, ive [partitif, -iv] *adj*: **article ~** partitive article.

partition [partisjɔ̃] *nf* (*MUS*) score; (*POL*) partition.

partout [partu] *adv* everywhere; ~ **où il allait** everywhere *ou* wherever he went; **trente ~** (*TENNIS*) thirty all.

paru [pary] *pp de* **paraître**.

parure [paryr] *nf* (*bijoux etc*) finery *no pl*; jewellery *no pl* (*BRIT*), jewelry *no pl* (*US*); (*assortiment*) set.

parus [pary] *etc vb voir* **paraître**.

parution [parysjɔ̃] *nf* publication, appearance.

parvenir [parvənir]: ~ **à** *vt* (*atteindre*) to reach; (*obtenir, arriver à*) to attain; (*réussir*): ~ **à faire** to manage to do, succeed in doing; **faire ~ qch à qn** to have sth sent to sb.

parvenu, e [parvəny] *pp de* **parvenir** ♦ *nm/f* (*péj*) parvenu, upstart.

parviendrai [parvjɛ̃dre], **parviens** [parvjɛ̃] *etc voir* **parvenir**.

parvis [parvi] *nm* square (*in front of a church*).

MOT-CLÉ

pas[1] [pɑ] *adv* **1** (*en corrélation avec ne, non etc*) not; **il ne pleure ~** (*habituellement*) he does not *ou* doesn't cry; (*maintenant*) he's not *ou* isn't crying; **je ne mange ~ de viande** I don't *ou* do not eat meat; **il n'a ~ pleuré/ne pleurera ~** he did not *ou* didn't/will not *ou* won't cry; **ils n'ont ~ de voiture/d'enfants** they haven't got a car/any children, they have no car/children; **il m'a dit de ne ~ le faire** he told me not to do it; **non ~ que ...** not that ...

2 (*employé sans ne etc*): ~ **moi** not me, not I, I don't (*ou* can't *etc*); **elle travaille, (mais) lui ~** *ou* ~ **lui** she works but he doesn't *ou* does not; **une pomme ~ mûre** an apple which isn't ripe; ~ **plus tard qu'hier** only yesterday; ~ **du tout** not at all; ~ **de sucre, merci** no sugar, thanks; **ceci est à vous ou ~?** is this yours or not?, is this yours or isn't it?

3: ~ **mal** (*joli: personne, maison*) not bad; ~ **mal fait** not badly done *ou* made; **comment ça va? — ~ mal** how are things? — not bad; ~ **mal de** quite a lot of.

pas[2] [pɑ] *nm* (*allure, mesure*) pace; (*démarche*) tread; (*enjambée, DANSE, fig: étape*) step; (*bruit*) (foot)step; (*trace*) footprint; (*allure*) pace; (*d'un cheval*) walk; (*mesure*) pace; (*TECH: de vis, d'écrou*) thread; ~ **à ~** step by step; **au ~** at walking pace; **de ce ~** (*à l'instant même*) straightaway, at once; **marcher à grands ~** to stride along; **mettre qn au ~** to bring sb to heel; **au ~ de gymnastique/de course** at a jog trot/at a run; **à ~ de loup** stealthily; **faire les cent ~** to pace up and down; **faire les premiers ~** to make the first move; **retourner** *ou* **revenir sur ses ~** to retrace one's steps; **se tirer d'un mauvais ~** to get o.s. out of a tight spot; **sur le ~ de la porte** on the doorstep; **le ~ de Calais** (*détroit*) the Straits *pl* of Dover; ~ **de porte** (*fig*) key money.

pascal, e, aux [paskal, -o] *adj* Easter *cpd*.

passable [pɑsabl(ə)] *adj* passable, tolerable.

passablement [pɑsabləmɑ̃] *adv* (*pas trop mal*) reasonably well; (*beaucoup*) quite a lot.

passade [pɑsad] *nf* passing fancy, whim.

passage [pɑsaʒ] *nm* (*fait de passer*) *voir* **passer**; (*lieu, prix de la traversée, extrait de livre etc*) passage; (*chemin*) way; (*itinéraire*): **sur le ~ du cortège** along the route of the procession; **"laissez/n'obstruez pas le ~"** "keep clear/do not obstruct"; **au ~** (*en passant*) as I (*ou* he *etc*) went by; **de ~** (*touristes*) passing through; (*amants etc*) casual; ~ **clouté** pedestrian crossing; **"~ interdit"** "no entry"; ~ **à niveau** level (*BRIT*) *ou* grade (*US*) crossing; **"~ protégé"** *right of way over secondary road(s) on your right*; ~ **souterrain** subway (*BRIT*), underpass; ~ **à tabac** beating-up; ~ **à vide** (*fig*) bad patch.

passager, ère [pɑsaʒe, -ɛr] *adj* passing; (*hôte*) short-stay *cpd*; (*oiseau*) migratory ♦ *nm/f* passenger; ~ **clandestin** stowaway.

passagèrement [pɑsaʒɛrmɑ̃] *adv* temporarily, for a short time.

passant, e [pɑsɑ̃, -ɑ̃t] *adj* (*rue, endroit*) busy ♦ *nm/f* passer-by ♦ *nm* (*pour ceinture etc*) loop; **en ~**: **remarquer qch en ~** to notice sth in passing.

passation [pɑsɑsjɔ̃] *nf* (*JUR: d'un acte*) signing; ~ **des pouvoirs** transfer *ou* handover of power.

passe [pɑs] *nf* (*SPORT, magnétique*) pass; (*NAVIG*) channel ♦ *nm* (*passe-partout*) master *ou* skeleton key; **être en ~ de faire** to be on the way to doing; **être dans une bonne/mauvaise ~** (*fig*) to be going through a good/bad patch; ~ **d'armes** (*fig*) heated exchange.

passé, e [pɑse] *adj* (*événement, temps*) past; (*couleur, tapisserie*) faded; (*précédent*): **dimanche ~** last Sunday ♦ *prép* after ♦ *nm* past; (*LING*) past (tense); **il est ~ midi** *ou* **midi ~** it's gone (*BRIT*) *ou* past twelve; ~ **de mode** out of fashion; ~ **composé** perfect (tense); ~ **simple** past historic.

passe-droit [pɑsdʀwa] *nm* special privilege.
passéiste [pɑseist(ə)] *adj* backward-looking.
passementerie [pɑsmɑ̃tʀi] *nf* trimmings *pl*.
passe-montagne [pɑsmɔ̃taɲ] *nm* balaclava.
passe-partout [pɑspaʀtu] *nm inv* master *ou* skeleton key ♦ *adj inv* all-purpose.
passe-passe [pɑspɑs] *nm*: **tour de ~** trick, sleight of hand *no pl*.
passe-plat [pɑspla] *nm* serving hatch.
passeport [pɑspɔʀ] *nm* passport.
passer [pɑse] *vi* (*se rendre, aller*) to go; (*voiture, piétons: défiler*) to pass (by), go by; (*faire une halte rapide: facteur, laitier etc*) to come, call; (*: pour rendre visite*) to call *ou* drop in; (*courant, air, lumière, franchir un obstacle etc*) to get through; (*accusé, projet de loi*): **~ devant** to come before; (*film, émission*) to be on; (*temps, jours*) to pass, go by; (*liquide, café*) to go through; (*être digéré, avalé*) to go down; (*couleur, papier*) to fade; (*mode*) to die out; (*douleur*) to pass, go away; (*CARTES*) to pass; (*SCOL*) to go up (to the next class); (*devenir*): **~ président** to be appointed *ou* become president ♦ *vt* (*frontière, rivière etc*) to cross; (*douane*) to go through; (*examen*) to sit, take; (*visite médicale etc*) to have; (*journée, temps*) to spend; (*donner*): **~ qch à qn** to pass sth to sb; to give sb sth; (*transmettre*): **~ qch à qn** to pass sth on to sb; (*enfiler: vêtement*) to slip on; (*faire entrer, mettre*): **(faire) ~ qch dans/par** to get sth into/through; (*café*) to pour the water on; (*thé, soupe*) to strain; (*film, pièce*) to show, put on; (*disque*) to play, put on; (*marché, accord*) to agree on; (*tolérer*): **~ qch à qn** to let sb get away with sth; **se ~** *vi* (*avoir lieu: scène, action*) to take place; (*se dérouler: entretien etc*) to go; (*arriver*): **que s'est-il passé?** what happened?; (*s'écouler: semaine etc*) to pass, go by; **se ~ de** *vt* to go *ou* do without; **se ~ les mains sous l'eau/de l'eau sur le visage** to put one's hands under the tap/run water over one's face; **en passant** in passing; **~ par** to go through; **passez devant/par ici** go in front/this way; **~ sur** *vt* (*faute, détail inutile*) to pass over; **~ dans les mœurs/l'usage** to become the custom/normal usage; **~ avant qch/qn** (*fig*) to come before sth/sb; **laisser ~** (*air, lumière, personne*) to let through; (*occasion*) to let slip, miss; (*erreur*) to overlook; **faire ~** (*message*) to get over *ou* across; **faire ~ à qn le goût de qch** to cure sb of his (*ou* her) taste for sth; **~ à la radio/ fouille** to be X-rayed/searched; **~ à la radio/télévision** to be on the radio/on television; **~ à table** to sit down to eat; **~ au salon** to go into the sitting room; **~ à l'opposition** to go over to the opposition; **~ aux aveux** to confess, make a confession; **~ à l'action** to go into action; **~ pour riche** to be taken for a rich man; **il passait pour avoir** he was said to have; **faire ~ qn/qch pour** to make sb/sth out to be; **passe encore de le penser, mais de le dire!** it's one thing to think it, but to say it!; **passons!** let's say no more (about it); **et j'en passe!** and that's not all!; **~ en seconde, ~ la seconde** (*AUTO*) to change into second; **~ qch en fraude** to smuggle sth in (*ou* out); **~ la main par la portière** to stick one's hand out of the door; **~ le balai/l'aspirateur** to sweep up/hoover; **~ commande/la parole à qn** to hand over to sb; **je vous passe M X** (*je vous mets en communication avec lui*) I'm putting you through to Mr X; (*je lui passe l'appareil*) here is Mr X, I'll hand you over to Mr X; **~ prendre** to (come and) collect.
passereau, x [pɑsʀo] *nm* sparrow.
passerelle [pɑsʀɛl] *nf* footbridge; (*de navire, avion*) gangway; (*NAVIG*): **~ (de commandement)** bridge.
passe-temps [pɑstɑ̃] *nm inv* pastime.
passette [pɑsɛt] *nf* (tea-)strainer.
passeur, euse [pɑsœʀ, -øz] *nm/f* smuggler.
passible [pasibl(ə)] *adj*: **~ de** liable to.
passif, ive [pasif, -iv] *adj* passive ♦ *nm* (*LING*) passive; (*COMM*) liabilities *pl*.
passion [pɑsjɔ̃] *nf* passion; **avoir la ~ de** to have a passion for; **fruit de la ~** passion fruit.
passionnant, e [pɑsjɔnɑ̃, -ɑ̃t] *adj* fascinating.
passionné, e [pɑsjɔne] *adj* (*personne, tempérament*) passionate; (*description*) impassioned ♦ *nm/f*: **c'est un ~ d'échecs** he's a chess fanatic; **être ~ de** *ou* **pour qch** to have a passion for sth.
passionnel, le [pɑsjɔnɛl] *adj* of passion.
passionnément [pɑsjɔnemɑ̃] *adv* passionately.
passionner [pɑsjɔne] *vt* (*personne*) to fascinate, grip; (*débat, discussion*) to inflame; **se ~ pour** to take an avid interest in; to have a passion for.
passivement [pasivmɑ̃] *adv* passively.
passivité [pasivite] *nf* passivity, passiveness.
passoire [pɑswaʀ] *nf* sieve; (*à légumes*) colander; (*à thé*) strainer.
pastel [pastɛl] *nm, adj inv* (*ART*) pastel.
pastèque [pastɛk] *nf* watermelon.
pasteur [pastœʀ] *nm* (*protestant*) minister, pastor.
pasteurisation [pastœʀizɑsjɔ̃] *nf* pasteurization.
pasteuriser [pastœʀize] *vt* to pasteurize.
pastiche [pastiʃ] *nm* pastiche.
pastille [pastij] *nf* (*à sucer*) lozenge, pastille; (*de papier etc*) (small) disc; **~s pour la toux** cough drops *ou* lozenges.
pastis [pastis] *nm anise-flavoured alcoholic drink*.
pastoral, e, aux [pastɔʀal, -o] *adj* pastoral.
patagon, ne [patagɔ̃, -ɔn] *adj* Patagonian.
Patagonie [patagɔni] *nf*: **la ~** Patagonia.
patate [patat] *nf* spud; **~ douce** sweet potato.
pataud, e [pato, -od] *adj* lumbering.

patauger [patoʒe] *vi* (*pour s'amuser*) to splash about; (*avec effort*) to wade about; (*fig*) to flounder; ~ **dans** (*en marchant*) to wade through.
patch [patʃ] *nm* nicotine patch.
patchouli [patʃuli] *nm* patchouli.
patchwork [patʃwœʀk] *nm* patchwork.
pâte [pɑt] *nf* (*à tarte*) pastry; (*à pain*) dough; (*à frire*) batter; (*substance molle*) paste; cream; ~**s** *nfpl* (*macaroni etc*) pasta *sg*; **fromage à ~ dure/molle** hard/soft cheese; ~ **d'amandes** almond paste; ~ **brisée** shortcrust (*BRIT*) *ou* pie crust (*US*) pastry; ~ **à choux/feuilletée** choux/puff *ou* flaky (*BRIT*) pastry; ~ **de fruits** crystallized fruit *no pl*; ~ **à modeler** modelling clay, Plasticine ® (*BRIT*); ~ **à papier** paper pulp.
pâté [pɑte] *nm* (*charcuterie: terrine*) pâté; (*tache*) ink blot; (*de sable*) sandpie; ~ **(en croûte)** ≈ meat pie; ~ **de foie** liver pâté; ~ **de maisons** block (of houses).
pâtée [pɑte] *nf* mash, feed.
patelin [patlɛ̃] *nm* little place.
patente [patɑ̃t] *nf* (*COMM*) trading licence (*BRIT*) *ou* license (*US*).
patenté, e [patɑ̃te] *adj* (*COMM*) licensed; (*fig: attitré*) registered, (officially) recognized.
patère [patɛʀ] *nf* (coat-)peg.
paternalisme [patɛʀnalism(ə)] *nm* paternalism.
paternaliste [patɛʀnalist(ə)] *adj* paternalistic.
paternel, le [patɛʀnɛl] *adj* (*amour, soins*) fatherly; (*ligne, autorité*) paternal.
paternité [patɛʀnite] *nf* paternity, fatherhood.
pâteux, euse [pɑtø, -øz] *adj* thick; pasty; **avoir la bouche** *ou* **langue pâteuse** to have a furred (*BRIT*) *ou* coated tongue.
pathétique [patetik] *adj* pathetic, moving.
pathologie [patɔlɔʒi] *nf* pathology.
pathologique [patɔlɔʒik] *adj* pathological.
patibulaire [patibylɛʀ] *adj* sinister.
patiemment [pasjamɑ̃] *adv* patiently.
patience [pasjɑ̃s] *nf* patience; **être à bout de ~** to have run out of patience; **perdre/prendre ~** to lose (one's)/have patience.
patient, e [pasjɑ̃, -ɑ̃t] *adj, nm/f* patient.
patienter [pasjɑ̃te] *vi* to wait.
patin [patɛ̃] *nm* skate; (*sport*) skating; (*de traîneau, luge*) runner; (*pièce de tissu*) cloth pad (*used as slippers to protect polished floor*); ~ **(de frein)** brake block; ~**s (à glace)** (ice) skates; ~**s à roulettes** roller skates.
patinage [patinaʒ] *nm* skating; ~ **artistique/de vitesse** figure/speed skating.
patine [patin] *nf* sheen.
patiner [patine] *vi* to skate; (*embrayage*) to slip; (*roue, voiture*) to spin; **se ~** *vi* (*meuble, cuir*) to acquire a sheen, become polished.
patineur, euse [patinœʀ, -øz] *nm/f* skater.
patinoire [patinwaʀ] *nf* skating rink, (ice) rink.
patio [patjo] *nm* patio.
pâtir [pɑtiʀ]: ~ **de** *vt* to suffer because of.
pâtisserie [pɑtisʀi] *nf* (*boutique*) cake shop; (*métier*) confectionery; (*à la maison*) pastry- *ou* cake-making, baking; ~**s** *nfpl* (*gâteaux*) pastries, cakes.
pâtissier, ière [pɑtisje, -jɛʀ] *nm/f* pastrycook; confectioner.
patois [patwa] *nm* dialect, patois.
patriarche [patʀijaʀʃ(ə)] *nm* patriarch.
patrie [patʀi] *nf* homeland.
patrimoine [patʀimwan] *nm* inheritance, patrimony; (*culture*) heritage; ~ **génétique** *ou* **héréditaire** genetic inheritance.
patriote [patʀijɔt] *adj* patriotic ♦ *nm/f* patriot.
patriotique [patʀijɔtik] *adj* patriotic.
patriotisme [patʀijɔtism(ə)] *nm* patriotism.
patron, ne [patʀɔ̃, -ɔn] *nm/f* (*chef*) boss, manager/eress; (*propriétaire*) owner, proprietor/tress; (*employeur*) employer; (*MÉD*) ≈ senior consultant; (*REL*) patron saint ♦ *nm* (*COUTURE*) pattern; ~ **de thèse** supervisor (of postgraduate thesis).
patronage [patʀɔnaʒ] *nm* patronage; (*organisation, club*) (parish) youth club; (parish) children's club.
patronal, e, aux [patʀɔnal, -o] *adj* (*syndicat, intérêts*) employers'.
patronat [patʀɔna] *nm* employers *pl*.
patronner [patʀɔne] *vt* to sponsor, support.
patronnesse [patʀɔnɛs] *adj f*: **dame ~** patroness.
patronyme [patʀɔnim] *nm* name.
patronymique [patʀɔnimik] *adj*: **nom ~** patronymic (name).
patrouille [patʀuj] *nf* patrol.
patrouiller [patʀuje] *vi* to patrol, be on patrol.
patrouilleur [patʀujœʀ] *nm* (*AVIAT*) scout (plane); (*NAVIG*) patrol boat.
patte [pat] *nf* (*jambe*) leg; (*pied: de chien, chat*) paw; (*: d'oiseau*) foot; (*languette*) strap; (*: de poche*) flap; (*favoris*): ~**s (de lapin)** (short) sideburns; **à ~s d'éléphant** *adj* (*pantalon*) flared; ~**s de mouche** (*fig*) spidery scrawl *sg*; ~**s d'oie** (*fig*) crow's feet.
pattemouille [patmuj] *nf* damp cloth (*for ironing*).
pâturage [pɑtyʀaʒ] *nm* pasture.
pâture [pɑtyʀ] *nf* food.
paume [pom] *nf* palm.
paumé, e [pome] *nm/f* (*fam*) drop-out.
paumer [pome] *vt* (*fam*) to lose.
paupérisation [popeʀizɑsjɔ̃] *nf* pauperization.
paupérisme [popeʀism(ə)] *nm* pauperism.
paupière [popjɛʀ] *nf* eyelid.
paupiette [popjɛt] *nf*: ~**s de veau** veal olives.
pause [poz] *nf* (*arrêt*) break; (*en parlant, MUS*) pause.
pause-café, *pl* **pauses-café** [pozkafe] *nf* coffee-break.
pauvre [povʀ(ə)] *adj* poor ♦ *nm/f* poor man/woman; **les ~s** the poor; ~ **en calcium** low in calcium.

pauvrement [povʀəmɑ̃] *adv* poorly.
pauvreté [povʀəte] *nf* (*état*) poverty.
pavage [pavaʒ] *nm* paving; cobbles *pl*.
pavaner [pavane]: **se** ~ *vi* to strut about.
pavé, e [pave] *adj* (*cour*) paved; (*rue*) cobbled ♦ *nm* (*bloc*) paving stone; cobblestone; (*pavage*) paving; (*bifteck*) slab of steak; (*fam: livre*) hefty tome; **être sur le** ~ (*sans domicile*) to be on the streets; (*sans emploi*) to be out of a job; ~ **numérique** (*INFORM*) keypad.
pavillon [pavijɔ̃] *nm* (*de banlieue*) small (detached) house; (*kiosque*) lodge; pavilion; (*d'hôpital*) ward; (*MUS: de cor etc*) bell; (*ANAT: de l'oreille*) pavilion, pinna; (*NAVIG*) flag; ~ **de complaisance** flag of convenience.
pavoiser [pavwaze] *vt* to deck with flags ♦ *vi* to put out flags; (*fig*) to rejoice, exult.
pavot [pavo] *nm* poppy.
payable [pɛjabl(ə)] *adj* payable.
payant, e [pɛjɑ̃, -ɑ̃t] *adj* (*spectateurs etc*) paying; (*billet*) that you pay for, to be paid for; (*fig: entreprise*) profitable; **c'est** ~ you have to pay, there is a charge.
paye [pɛj] *nf* pay, wages *pl*.
payement [pɛjmɑ̃] *nm* payment.
payer [peje] *vt* (*créancier, employé, loyer*) to pay; (*achat, réparations, fig: faute*) to pay for ♦ *vi* to pay; (*métier*) to pay, be well-paid; (*effort, tactique etc*) to pay off; **il me l'a fait** ~ **10 €** he charged me €10 for it; ~ **qn de** (*ses efforts, peines*) to reward sb for; ~ **qch à qn** to buy sth for sb, buy sb sth; **ils nous ont payé le voyage** they paid for our trip; ~ **de sa personne** to give of oneself; ~ **d'audace** to act with great daring; ~ **cher qch** to pay dear(ly) for sth; **cela ne paie pas de mine** it doesn't look much; **se** ~ **qch** to buy o.s. sth; **se** ~ **de mots** to shoot one's mouth off; **se** ~ **la tête de qn** to take the mickey out of sb (*BRIT*), make a fool of sb; (*duper*) to take sb for a ride.
payeur, euse [pɛjœʀ, -øz] *adj* (*organisme, bureau*) payments *cpd* ♦ *nm/f* payer.
pays [pei] *nm* (*territoire, habitants*) country, land; (*région*) region; (*village*) village; **du** ~ *adj* local; **le** ~ **de Galles** Wales.
paysage [peizaʒ] *nm* landscape.
paysager, ère [peizaʒe, -ɛʀ] *adj* (*jardin, parc*) landscaped.
paysagiste [peizaʒist(ə)] *nm/f* (*de jardin*) landscape gardener; (*ART*) landscapist, landscape painter.
paysan, ne [peizɑ̃, -an] *nm/f* countryman/woman; farmer; (*péj*) peasant ♦ *adj* country *cpd*, farming; farmers'.
paysannat [peizana] *nm* peasantry.
Pays-Bas [peiba] *nmpl*: **les** ~ the Netherlands.
PC *sigle m* (*POL*) = *parti communiste*; (*INFORM: = personal computer*) PC; (= *prêt conventionné*) *type of loan for house purchase*; (*CONSTR*) = **permis de construire**; (*MIL*) = **poste de commandement**.
pcc *abr* (= *pour copie conforme*) c.c.
Pce *abr* = **prince**.
Pcesse *abr* = **princesse**.
PCV *abr* (= *percevoir*) *voir* **communication**.
p de p *abr* = **pas de porte**.
PDG *sigle m* = **président directeur général**.
p.ê. *abr* = **peut-être**.
PEA *sigle m* (= *plan d'épargne en actions*) *building society savings plan*.
péage [peaʒ] *nm* toll; (*endroit*) tollgate; **pont à** ~ toll bridge.
peau, x [po] *nf* skin; (*cuir*): **gants de** ~ leather gloves; **être bien/mal dans sa** ~ to be at ease/odds with oneself; **se mettre dans la** ~ **de qn** to put o.s. in sb's place *ou* shoes; **faire** ~ **neuve** (*se renouveler*) to change one's image; ~ **de chamois** (*chiffon*) chamois leather, shammy; ~ **d'orange** orange peel.
peaufiner [pofine] *vt* to polish (up).
Peau-Rouge [poʀuʒ] *nm/f* Red Indian, red skin.
peccadille [pekadij] *nf* trifle, peccadillo.
péché [peʃe] *nm* sin; ~ **mignon** weakness.
pêche [pɛʃ] *nf* (*sport, activité*) fishing; (*poissons pêchés*) catch; (*fruit*) peach; **aller à la** ~ to go fishing; **avoir la** ~ (*fam*) to be on (top) form; ~ **à la ligne** (*en rivière*) angling; ~ **sous-marine** deep-sea fishing.
pêche-abricot, *pl* **pêches-abricots** [pɛʃabʀiko] *nf* yellow peach.
pécher [peʃe] *vi* (*REL*) to sin; (*fig: personne*) to err; (*: chose*) to be flawed; ~ **contre la bienséance** to break the rules of good behaviour.
pêcher [peʃe] *nm* peach tree ♦ *vi* to go fishing; (*en rivière*) to go angling ♦ *vt* (*attraper*) to catch, land; (*chercher*) to fish for; ~ **au chalut** to trawl.
pécheur, eresse [peʃœʀ, peʃʀɛs] *nm/f* sinner.
pêcheur [pɛʃœʀ] *nm* (*voir pêcher*) fisherman; angler; ~ **de perles** pearl diver.
pectine [pɛktin] *nf* pectin.
pectoral, e, aux [pɛktɔʀal, -o] *adj* (*ANAT*) pectoral; (*sirop*) throat *cpd*, cough *cpd* ♦ *nmpl* pectoral muscles.
pécule [pekyl] *nm* savings *pl*, nest egg; (*d'un détenu*) earnings *pl* (*paid on release*).
pécuniaire [pekynjɛʀ] *adj* financial.
pédagogie [pedagɔʒi] *nf* educational methods *pl*, pedagogy.
pédagogique [pedagɔʒik] *adj* educational; **formation** ~ teacher training.
pédagogue [pedagɔg] *nm/f* teacher; education(al)ist.
pédale [pedal] *nf* pedal; **mettre la** ~ **douce** to soft-pedal.
pédaler [pedale] *vi* to pedal.
pédalier [pedalje] *nm* pedal and gear mechanism.
pédalo [pedalo] *nm* pedalo, pedal-boat.
pédant, e [pedɑ̃, -ɑ̃t] *adj* (*péj*) pedantic ♦ *nm/f* pedant.

pédantisme [pedɑ̃tism(ə)] *nm* pedantry.

pédéraste [pederast(ə)] *nm* homosexual, pederast.

pédérastie [pederasti] *nf* homosexuality, pederasty.

pédestre [pedɛstr(ə)] *adj*: **tourisme** ~ hiking; **randonnée** ~ (*activité*) rambling; (*excursion*) ramble.

pédiatre [pedjatr(ə)] *nm/f* paediatrician (*BRIT*), pediatrician *ou* pediatrist (*US*), child specialist.

pédiatrie [pedjatri] *nf* paediatrics *sg* (*BRIT*), pediatrics *sg* (*US*).

pédicure [pedikyr] *nm/f* chiropodist.

pedigree [pedigre] *nm* pedigree.

peeling [piliŋ] *nm* exfoliation treatment.

PEEP *sigle f* = *Fédération des parents d'élèves de l'enseignement public.*

pègre [pɛgr(ə)] *nf* underworld.

peignais [pɛɲɛ] *etc vb voir* **peindre**.

peigne [pɛɲ] *vb voir* **peindre, peigner** ♦ *nm* comb.

peigné, e [peɲe] *adj*: **laine** ~**e** wool worsted; combed wool.

peigner [peɲe] *vt* to comb (the hair of); **se** ~ to comb one's hair.

peignez [pɛɲe] *etc vb voir* **peindre**.

peignoir [pɛɲwar] *nm* dressing gown; ~ **de bain** bathrobe; ~ **de plage** beach robe.

peignons [pɛɲɔ̃] *vb voir* **peindre**.

peinard, e [pɛnar, -ard(ə)] *adj* (*emploi*) cushy (*BRIT*), easy; (*personne*): **on est** ~ **ici** we're left in peace here.

peindre [pɛ̃dr(ə)] *vt* to paint; (*fig*) to portray, depict.

peine [pɛn] *nf* (*affliction*) sorrow, sadness *no pl*; (*mal, effort*) trouble *no pl*, effort; (*difficulté*) difficulty; (*punition, châtiment*) punishment; (*JUR*) sentence; **faire de la** ~ **à qn** to distress *ou* upset sb; **prendre la** ~ **de faire** to go to the trouble of doing; **se donner de la** ~ to make an effort; **ce n'est pas la** ~ **de faire** there's no point in doing, it's not worth doing; **ce n'est pas la** ~ **que vous fassiez** there's no point (in) you doing; **avoir de la** ~ **à faire** to have difficulty doing; **donnez-vous** *ou* **veuillez-vous donner la** ~ **d'entrer** please do come in; **c'est** ~ **perdue** it's a waste of time (and effort); **à** ~ *adv* scarcely, hardly, barely; **à** ~ ... **que** hardly ... than; **c'est à** ~ **si** ... it's (*ou* it was) a job to ...; **sous** ~: **sous** ~ **d'être puni** for fear of being punished; **défense d'afficher sous** ~ **d'amende** billposters will be fined; ~ **capitale** capital punishment; ~ **de mort** death sentence *ou* penalty.

peiner [pene] *vi* to work hard; to struggle; (*moteur, voiture*) to labour (*BRIT*), labor (*US*) ♦ *vt* to grieve, sadden.

peint, e [pɛ̃, pɛ̃t] *pp de* **peindre**.

peintre [pɛ̃tr(ə)] *nm* painter; ~ **en bâtiment** house painter, painter and decorator; ~ **d'enseignes** signwriter.

peinture [pɛ̃tyr] *nf* painting; (*couche de couleur, couleur*) paint; (*surfaces peintes: aussi*: ~**s**) paintwork; **je ne peux pas le voir en** ~ I can't stand the sight of him; ~ **mate/brillante** matt/gloss paint; "~ **fraîche**" "wet paint".

péjoratif, ive [peʒɔratif, -iv] *adj* pejorative, derogatory.

Pékin [pekɛ̃] *n* Peking.

pékinois, e [pekinwa, -waz] *adj* Pekin(g)ese ♦ *nm* (*chien*) peke, pekin(g)ese; (*LING*) Mandarin, Pekin(g)ese ♦ *nm/f*: **P**~**, e** Pekin(g)ese.

PEL *sigle m* (= *plan d'épargne logement*) *savings scheme providing lower-interest mortgages.*

pelade [pəlad] *nf* alopecia.

pelage [pəlaʒ] *nm* coat, fur.

pelé, e [pəle] *adj* (*chien*) hairless; (*vêtement*) threadbare; (*terrain*) bare.

pêle-mêle [pɛlmɛl] *adv* higgledy-piggledy.

peler [pəle] *vt, vi* to peel.

pèlerin [pɛlrɛ̃] *nm* pilgrim.

pèlerinage [pɛlrinaʒ] *nm* (*voyage*) pilgrimage; (*lieu*) place of pilgrimage, shrine.

pèlerine [pɛlrin] *nf* cape.

pélican [pelikɑ̃] *nm* pelican.

pelisse [pəlis] *nf* fur-lined cloak.

pelle [pɛl] *nf* shovel; (*d'enfant, de terrassier*) spade; ~ **à gâteau** cake slice; ~ **mécanique** mechanical digger.

pelletée [pɛlte] *nf* shovelful; spadeful.

pelleter [pɛlte] *vt* to shovel (up).

pelleteuse [pɛltøz] *nf* mechanical digger, excavator.

pelletier [pɛltje] *nm* furrier.

pellicule [pelikyl] *nf* film; ~**s** *nfpl* (*MÉD*) dandruff *sg*.

Péloponnèse [pelɔpɔnɛz] *nm*: **le** ~ the Peloponnese.

pelote [pəlɔt] *nf* (*de fil, laine*) ball; (*d'épingles*) pin cushion; ~ **basque** pelota.

peloter [pəlɔte] *vt* (*fam*) to feel (up); **se** ~ to pet.

peloton [pəlɔtɔ̃] *nm* (*groupe: personnes*) group; (*: pompiers, gendarmes*) squad; (*: SPORT*) pack; (*de laine*) ball; ~ **d'exécution** firing squad.

pelotonner [pəlɔtɔne]: **se** ~ *vi* to curl (o.s.) up.

pelouse [pəluz] *nf* lawn; (*HIPPISME*) *spectating area inside racetrack.*

peluche [pəlyʃ] *nf* (bit of) fluff; **animal en** ~ soft toy, fluffy animal.

pelucher [p(ə)lyʃe] *vi* to become fluffy, fluff up.

pelucheux, euse [p(ə)lyʃø, -øz] *adj* fluffy.

pelure [pəlyr] *nf* peeling, peel *no pl*; ~ **d'oignon** onion skin.

pénal, e, aux [penal, -o] *adj* penal.

pénalisation [penalizɑsjɔ̃] *nf* (*SPORT*) sanction, penalty.

pénaliser [penalize] *vt* to penalize.

pénalité [penalite] *nf* penalty.

penalty, ies [penalti, -z] *nm* (*SPORT*) penalty (kick).
pénard, e [penaʀ, -aʀd(ə)] *adj* = **peinard.**
pénates [penat] *nmpl*: **regagner ses** ~ to return to the bosom of one's family.
penaud, e [pəno, -od] *adj* sheepish, contrite.
penchant [pɑ̃ʃɑ̃] *nm*: **un** ~ **à faire/à qch** a tendency to do/to sth; **un** ~ **pour qch** a liking *ou* fondness for sth.
penché, e [pɑ̃ʃe] *adj* slanting.
pencher [pɑ̃ʃe] *vi* to tilt, lean over ♦ *vt* to tilt; **se** ~ *vi* to lean over; (*se baisser*) to bend down; **se** ~ **sur** to bend over; (*fig: problème*) to look into; **se** ~ **au dehors** to lean out; ~ **pour** to be inclined to favour (*BRIT*) *ou* favor (*US*).
pendable [pɑ̃dabl(ə)] *adj*: **tour** ~ rotten trick; **c'est un cas** ~! he (*ou* she) deserves to be shot!
pendaison [pɑ̃dɛzɔ̃] *nf* hanging.
pendant, e [pɑ̃dɑ̃, -ɑ̃t] *adj* hanging (out); (*ADMIN, JUR*) pending ♦ *nm* counterpart; matching piece ♦ *prép* during; **faire** ~ **à** to match; to be the counterpart of; ~ **que** while; ~**s d'oreilles** drop *ou* pendant earrings.
pendeloque [pɑ̃dlɔk] *nf* pendant.
pendentif [pɑ̃dɑ̃tif] *nm* pendant.
penderie [pɑ̃dʀi] *nf* wardrobe; (*placard*) walk-in cupboard.
pendiller [pɑ̃dije] *vi* to flap (about).
pendre [pɑ̃dʀ(ə)] *vt, vi* to hang; **se** ~ **(à)** (*se suicider*) to hang o.s. (on); **se** ~ **à** (*se suspendre*) to hang from; ~ **à** to hang (down) from; ~ **qch à** (*mur*) to hang sth (up) on; (*plafond*) to hang sth (up) from.
pendu, e [pɑ̃dy] *pp de* **pendre** ♦ *nm/f* hanged man (*ou* woman).
pendulaire [pɑ̃dylɛʀ] *adj* pendular, of a pendulum.
pendule [pɑ̃dyl] *nf* clock ♦ *nm* pendulum.
pendulette [pɑ̃dylɛt] *nf* small clock.
pêne [pɛn] *nm* bolt.
pénétrant, e [penetʀɑ̃, -ɑ̃t] *adj* (*air, froid*) biting; (*pluie*) that soaks right through you; (*fig: odeur*) noticeable; (*œil, regard*) piercing; (*clairvoyant, perspicace*) perceptive ♦ *nf* (*route*) expressway.
pénétration [penetʀasjɔ̃] *nf* (*fig: d'idées etc*) penetration; (*perspicacité*) perception.
pénétré, e [penetʀe] *adj* (*air, ton*) earnest; **être** ~ **de soi-même/son importance** to be full of oneself/one's own importance.
pénétrer [penetʀe] *vi* to come *ou* get in ♦ *vt* to penetrate; ~ **dans** to enter; (*suj: froid, projectile*) to penetrate; (*: air, eau*) to come into, get into; (*mystère, secret*) to fathom; **se** ~ **de qch** to get sth firmly set in one's mind.
pénible [penibl(ə)] *adj* (*astreignant*) hard; (*affligeant*) painful; (*personne, caractère*) tiresome; **il m'est** ~ **de** ... I'm sorry to ....
péniblement [penibləmɑ̃] *adv* with difficulty.
péniche [peniʃ] *nf* barge; ~ **de débarquement** landing craft *inv*.
pénicilline [penisilin] *nf* penicillin.
péninsulaire [penɛ̃sylɛʀ] *adj* peninsular.
péninsule [penɛ̃syl] *nf* peninsula.
pénis [penis] *nm* penis.
pénitence [penitɑ̃s] *nf* (*repentir*) penitence; (*peine*) penance; (*punition, châtiment*) punishment; **mettre un enfant en** ~ ≈ to make a child stand in the corner; **faire** ~ to do a penance.
pénitencier [penitɑ̃sje] *nm* prison, penitentiary (*US*).
pénitent, e [penitɑ̃, -ɑ̃t] *adj* penitent.
pénitentiaire [penitɑ̃sjɛʀ] *adj* prison *cpd*, penitentiary (*US*).
pénombre [penɔ̃bʀ(ə)] *nf* half-light.
pensable [pɑ̃sabl(ə)] *adj*: **ce n'est pas** ~ it's unthinkable.
pensant, e [pɑ̃sɑ̃, -ɑ̃t] *adj*: **bien** ~ right-thinking.
pense-bête [pɑ̃sbɛt] *nm* aide-mémoire, mnemonic device.
pensée [pɑ̃se] *nf* thought; (*démarche, doctrine*) thinking *no pl*; (*BOT*) pansy; **se représenter qch par la** ~ to conjure up a mental picture of sth; **en** ~ in one's mind.
penser [pɑ̃se] *vi* to think ♦ *vt* to think; (*concevoir: problème, machine*) to think out; ~ **à** to think of; (*songer à: ami, vacances*) to think of *ou* about; (*réfléchir à: problème, offre*): ~ **à qch** to think about sth, think sth over; ~ **à faire qch** to think of doing sth; ~ **faire qch** to be thinking of doing sth, intend to do sth; **faire** ~ **à** to remind one of; **n'y pensons plus** let's forget it; **vous n'y pensez pas!** don't let it bother you!; **sans** ~ **à mal** without meaning any harm; **je le pense aussi** I think so too; **je pense que oui/non** I think so/don't think so.
penseur [pɑ̃sœʀ] *nm* thinker; **libre** ~ free-thinker.
pensif, ive [pɑ̃sif, -iv] *adj* pensive, thoughtful.
pension [pɑ̃sjɔ̃] *nf* (*allocation*) pension; (*prix du logement*) board and lodging, bed and board; (*maison particulière*) boarding house; (*hôtel*) guesthouse, hotel; (*école*) boarding school; **prendre** ~ **chez** to take board and lodging at; **prendre qn en** ~ to take sb (in) as a lodger; **mettre en** ~ to send to boarding school; ~ **alimentaire** (*d'étudiant*) living allowance; (*de divorcée*) maintenance allowance; alimony; ~ **complète** full board; ~ **de famille** boarding house, guesthouse; ~ **de guerre/d'invalidité** war/disablement pension.
pensionnaire [pɑ̃sjɔnɛʀ] *nm/f* boarder; guest.
pensionnat [pɑ̃sjɔna] *nm* boarding school.
pensionné, e [pɑ̃sjɔne] *nm/f* pensioner.
pensivement [pɑ̃sivmɑ̃] *adv* pensively, thoughtfully.
pensum [pɛ̃sɔm] *nm* (*SCOL*) punishment exercise; (*fig*) chore.
pentagone [pɛ̃tagɔn] *nm* pentagon; **le P**~ the

Pentagon.

pentathlon [pɛ̃tatlɔ̃] *nm* pentathlon.

pente [pɑ̃t] *nf* slope; **en ~** *adj* sloping.

Pentecôte [pɑ̃tkot] *nf*: **la ~** Whitsun (*BRIT*), Pentecost; (*dimanche*) Whitsunday (*BRIT*); **lundi de ~** Whit Monday (*BRIT*).

pénurie [penyʀi] *nf* shortage; **~ de main-d'œuvre** undermanning.

PEP [pɛp] *sigle m* (= *plan d'épargne populaire*) *individual savings plan*.

pépé [pepe] *nm* (*fam*) grandad.

pépère [pepɛʀ] *adj* (*fam*) cushy (*fam*), quiet ♦ *nm* (*fam*) grandad.

pépier [pepje] *vi* to chirp, tweet.

pépin [pepɛ̃] *nm* (*BOT*: *graine*) pip; (*fam*: *ennui*) snag, hitch; (*: parapluie*) brolly (*BRIT*), umbrella.

pépinière [pepinjɛʀ] *nf* nursery; (*fig*) nest, breeding-ground.

pépiniériste [pepinjeʀist(ə)] *nm* nurseryman.

pépite [pepit] *nf* nugget.

PEPS *abr* (= *premier entré premier sorti*) first in first out.

PER [pɛʀ] *sigle m* (= *plan d'épargne retraite*) *type of personal pension plan*.

perçant, e [pɛʀsɑ̃, -ɑ̃t] *adj* (*vue, regard, yeux*) sharp, keen; (*cri, voix*) piercing, shrill.

percée [pɛʀse] *nf* (*trouée*) opening; (*MIL, COMM, fig*) breakthrough; (*SPORT*) break.

perce-neige [pɛʀsənɛʒ] *nm ou f inv* snowdrop.

perce-oreille [pɛʀsɔʀɛj] *nm* earwig.

percepteur [pɛʀsɛptœʀ] *nm* tax collector.

perceptible [pɛʀsɛptibl(ə)] *adj* (*son, différence*) perceptible; (*impôt*) payable, collectable.

perception [pɛʀsɛpsjɔ̃] *nf* perception; (*d'impôts etc*) collection; (*bureau*) tax (collector's) office.

percer [pɛʀse] *vt* to pierce; (*ouverture etc*) to make; (*mystère, énigme*) to penetrate ♦ *vi* to come through; (*réussir*) to break through; **~ une dent** to cut a tooth.

perceuse [pɛʀsøz] *nf* drill; **~ à percussion** hammer drill.

percevable [pɛʀsəvabl(ə)] *adj* collectable, payable.

percevoir [pɛʀsəvwaʀ] *vt* (*distinguer*) to perceive, detect; (*taxe, impôt*) to collect; (*revenu, indemnité*) to receive.

perche [pɛʀʃ(ə)] *nf* (*ZOOL*) perch; (*bâton*) pole; **~ à son** (sound) boom.

percher [pɛʀʃe] *vt*: **~ qch sur** to perch sth on ♦ *vi*, **se ~** *vi* (*oiseau*) to perch.

perchiste [pɛʀʃist(ə)] *nm/f* (*SPORT*) pole vaulter; (*TV etc*) boom operator.

perchoir [pɛʀʃwaʀ] *nm* perch; (*fig*) *presidency of the French National Assembly*.

perclus, e [pɛʀkly, -yz] *adj*: **~ de** (*rhumatismes*) crippled with.

perçois [pɛʀswa] *etc vb voir* **percevoir**.

percolateur [pɛʀkɔlatœʀ] *nm* percolator.

perçu, e [pɛʀsy] *pp de* **percevoir**.

percussion [pɛʀkysjɔ̃] *nf* percussion.

percussionniste [pɛʀkysjɔnist(ə)] *nm/f* percussionist.

percutant, e [pɛʀkytɑ̃, -ɑ̃t] *adj* (*article etc*) resounding, forceful.

percuter [pɛʀkyte] *vt* to strike; (*suj: véhicule*) to crash into ♦ *vi*: **~ contre** to crash into.

percuteur [pɛʀkytœʀ] *nm* firing pin, hammer.

perdant, e [pɛʀdɑ̃, -ɑ̃t] *nm/f* loser ♦ *adj* losing.

perdition [pɛʀdisjɔ̃] *nf* (*morale*) ruin; **en ~** (*NAVIG*) in distress; **lieu de ~** den of vice.

perdre [pɛʀdʀ(ə)] *vt* to lose; (*gaspiller: temps, argent*) to waste; (*: occasion*) to waste, miss; (*personne: moralement etc*) to ruin ♦ *vi* to lose; (*sur une vente etc*) to lose out; (*récipient*) to leak; **se ~** *vi* (*s'égarer*) to get lost, lose one's way; (*fig: se gâter*) to go to waste; (*disparaître*) to disappear, vanish; **il ne perd rien pour attendre** it can wait, it'll keep.

perdreau, x [pɛʀdʀo] *nm* (young) partridge.

perdrix [pɛʀdʀi] *nf* partridge.

perdu, e [pɛʀdy] *pp de* **perdre** ♦ *adj* (*enfant, cause, objet*) lost; (*isolé*) out-of-the-way; (*COMM: emballage*) non-returnable; (*récolte etc*) ruined; (*malade*): **il est ~** there's no hope left for him; **à vos moments ~s** in your spare time.

père [pɛʀ] *nm* father; **~s** *nmpl* (*ancêtres*) forefathers; **de ~ en fils** from father to son; **~ de famille** father; family man; **mon ~** (*REL*) Father; **le ~ Noël** Father Christmas.

pérégrinations [peʀegʀinɑsjɔ̃] *nfpl* travels.

péremption [peʀɑ̃psjɔ̃] *nf*: **date de ~** expiry date.

péremptoire [peʀɑ̃ptwaʀ] *adj* peremptory.

pérennité [peʀenite] *nf* durability, lasting quality.

péréquation [peʀekwɑsjɔ̃] *nf* (*des salaires*) realignment; (*des prix, impôts*) equalization.

perfectible [pɛʀfɛktibl(ə)] *adj* perfectible.

perfection [pɛʀfɛksjɔ̃] *nf* perfection; **à la ~** *adv* to perfection.

perfectionné, e [pɛʀfɛksjɔne] *adj* sophisticated.

perfectionnement [pɛʀfɛksjɔnmɑ̃] *nm* improvement.

perfectionner [pɛʀfɛksjɔne] *vt* to improve, perfect; **se ~ en anglais** to improve one's English.

perfectionniste [pɛʀfɛksjɔnist(ə)] *nm/f* perfectionist.

perfide [pɛʀfid] *adj* perfidious, treacherous.

perfidie [pɛʀfidi] *nf* treachery.

perforant, e [pɛʀfɔʀɑ̃, -ɑ̃t] *adj* (*balle*) armour-piercing (*BRIT*), armor-piercing (*US*).

perforateur, trice [pɛʀfɔʀatœʀ, -tʀis] *nm/f* punch-card operator ♦ *nm* (*perceuse*) borer; drill ♦ *nf* (*perceuse*) borer; drill; (*pour cartes*) card-punch; (*de bureau*) punch.

perforation [pɛʀfɔʀɑsjɔ̃] *nf* perforation; punching; (*trou*) hole.

perforatrice [pɛʀfɔʀatʀis] *nf voir* **perforateur**.

perforé, e [pɛʀfɔʀe] *adj*: **bande ~** punched

tape; **carte ~** punch card.
perforer [pɛʀfɔʀe] *vt* to perforate, punch a hole (*ou* holes) in; (*ticket, bande, carte*) to punch.
perforeuse [pɛʀfɔʀøz] *nf* (*machine*) (card) punch; (*personne*) card punch operator.
performance [pɛʀfɔʀmɑ̃s] *nf* performance.
performant, e [pɛʀfɔʀmɑ̃, -ɑ̃t] *adj* (*ÉCON: produit, entreprise*) high-return *cpd*; (*TECH: appareil, machine*) high-performance *cpd*.
perfusion [pɛʀfyzjɔ̃] *nf* perfusion; **faire une ~ à qn** to put sb on a drip.
péricliter [peʀiklite] *vi* to go downhill.
péridurale [peʀidyʀal] *nf* epidural.
périgourdin, e [peʀiguʀdɛ̃, -in] *adj* of *ou* from the Perigord.
péril [peʀil] *nm* peril; **au ~ de sa vie** at the risk of his life; **à ses risques et ~s** at his (*ou* her) own risk.
périlleux, euse [peʀijø, -øz] *adj* perilous.
périmé, e [peʀime] *adj* (out)dated; (*ADMIN*) out-of-date, expired.
périmètre [peʀimɛtʀ(ə)] *nm* perimeter.
périnatal, e [peʀinatal] *adj* perinatal.
période [peʀjɔd] *nf* period.
périodique [peʀjɔdik] *adj* (*phases*) periodic; (*publication*) periodical; (*MATH: fraction*) recurring ♦ *nm* periodical; **garniture** *ou* **serviette ~** sanitary towel (*BRIT*) *ou* napkin (*US*).
périodiquement [peʀjɔdikmɑ̃] *adv* periodically.
péripéties [peʀipesi] *nfpl* events, episodes.
périphérie [peʀifeʀi] *nf* periphery; (*d'une ville*) outskirts *pl*.
périphérique [peʀifeʀik] *adj* (*quartiers*) outlying; (*ANAT, TECH*) peripheral; (*station de radio*) operating from a neighbouring country ♦ *nm* (*INFORM*) peripheral; (*AUTO*): **(boulevard) ~** ring road (*BRIT*), circular route (*US*).
périphrase [peʀifʀɑz] *nf* circumlocution.
périple [peʀipl(ə)] *nm* journey.
périr [peʀiʀ] *vi* to die, perish.
périscolaire [peʀiskɔlɛʀ] *adj* extracurricular.
périscope [peʀiskɔp] *nm* periscope.
périssable [peʀisabl(ə)] *adj* perishable.
péristyle [peʀistil] *nm* peristyle.
péritonite [peʀitɔnit] *nf* peritonitis.
perle [pɛʀl(ə)] *nf* pearl; (*de plastique, métal, sueur*) bead; (*personne, chose*) gem, treasure; (*erreur*) gem, howler.
perlé, e [pɛʀle] *adj* (*rire*) rippling, tinkling; (*travail*) exquisite; (*orge*) pearl *cpd*; **grève ~e** go-slow, selective strike (action).
perler [pɛʀle] *vi* to form in droplets.
perlier, ière [pɛʀlje, -jɛʀ] *adj* pearl *cpd*.
permanence [pɛʀmanɑ̃s] *nf* permanence; (*local*) (duty) office; strike headquarters; (*service des urgences*) emergency service; (*SCOL*) study room; **assurer une ~** (*service public, bureaux*) to operate *ou* maintain a basic service; **être de ~** to be on call *ou* duty; **en ~** *adv* (*toujours*) permanently; (*continûment*) continuously.
permanent, e [pɛʀmanɑ̃, -ɑ̃t] *adj* permanent; (*spectacle*) continuous; (*armée, comité*) standing ♦ *nf* perm ♦ *nm/f* (*d'un syndicat, parti*) paid official.
perméable [pɛʀmeabl(ə)] *adj* (*terrain*) permeable; **~ à** (*fig*) receptive *ou* open to.
permettre [pɛʀmɛtʀ(ə)] *vt* to allow, permit; **~ à qn de faire/qch** to allow sb to do/sth; **se ~ de faire qch** to take the liberty of doing sth; **permettez!** excuse me!
permis, e [pɛʀmi, -iz] *pp de* **permettre** ♦ *nm* permit, licence (*BRIT*), license (*US*); **~ de chasse** hunting permit; **~ (de conduire)** (driving) licence (*BRIT*), (driver's) license (*US*); **~ de construire** planning permission (*BRIT*), building permit (*US*); **~ d'inhumer** burial certificate; **~ poids lourds** ≈ HGV (driving) licence (*BRIT*), ≈ class E (driver's) license (*US*); **~ de séjour** residence permit; **~ de travail** work permit.
permissif, ive [pɛʀmisif, -iv] *adj* permissive.
permission [pɛʀmisjɔ̃] *nf* permission; (*MIL*) leave; (*: papier*) pass; **en ~** on leave; **avoir la ~ de faire** to have permission to do, be allowed to do.
permissionnaire [pɛʀmisjɔnɛʀ] *nm* soldier on leave.
permutable [pɛʀmytabl(ə)] *adj* which can be changed *ou* switched around.
permuter [pɛʀmyte] *vt* to change around, permutate ♦ *vi* to change, swap.
pernicieux, euse [pɛʀnisjø, -øz] *adj* pernicious.
péroné [peʀɔne] *nm* fibula.
pérorer [peʀɔʀe] *vi* to hold forth.
Pérou [peʀu] *nm*: **le ~** Peru.
perpendiculaire [pɛʀpɑ̃dikylɛʀ] *adj, nf* perpendicular.
perpendiculairement [pɛʀpɑ̃dikylɛʀmɑ̃] *adv* perpendicularly.
perpète [pɛʀpɛt] *nf*: **à ~** (*fam: loin*) miles away; (*: longtemps*) forever.
perpétrer [pɛʀpetʀe] *vt* to perpetrate.
perpétuel, le [pɛʀpetɥɛl] *adj* perpetual; (*ADMIN etc*) permanent; for life.
perpétuellement [pɛʀpetɥɛlmɑ̃] *adv* perpetually, constantly.
perpétuer [pɛʀpetɥe] *vt* to perpetuate; **se ~** (*usage, injustice*) to be perpetuated; (*espèces*) to survive.
perpétuité [pɛʀpetɥite] *nf*: **à ~** *adj, adv* for life; **être condamné à ~** to be sentenced to life imprisonment, receive a life sentence.
perplexe [pɛʀplɛks(ə)] *adj* perplexed, puzzled.
perplexité [pɛʀplɛksite] *nf* perplexity.
perquisition [pɛʀkizisjɔ̃] *nf* (police) search.
perquisitionner [pɛʀkizisjɔne] *vi* to carry out a search.
perron [pɛʀɔ̃] *nm* steps *pl* (*in front of mansion etc*).

perroquet [pɛʀɔkɛ] *nm* parrot.
perruche [peʀyʃ] *nf* budgerigar (*BRIT*), budgie (*BRIT*), parakeet (*US*).
perruque [peʀyk] *nf* wig.
persan, e [pɛʀsɑ̃, -an] *adj* Persian ♦ *nm* (*LING*) Persian.
perse [pɛʀs(ə)] *adj* Persian ♦ *nm* (*LING*) Persian ♦ *nm/f*: **P~** Persian ♦ *nf*: **la P~** Persia.
persécuter [pɛʀsekyte] *vt* to persecute.
persécution [pɛʀsekysjɔ̃] *nf* persecution.
persévérance [pɛʀseveʀɑ̃s] *nf* perseverance.
persévérant, e [pɛʀseveʀɑ̃, -ɑ̃t] *adj* persevering.
persévérer [pɛʀseveʀe] *vi* to persevere; **~ à croire que** to continue to believe that.
persiennes [pɛʀsjɛn] *nfpl* (slatted) shutters.
persiflage [pɛʀsiflaʒ] *nm* mockery *no pl*.
persifleur, euse [pɛʀsiflœʀ, -øz] *adj* mocking.
persil [pɛʀsi] *nm* parsley.
persillé, e [pɛʀsije] *adj* (sprinkled) with parsley; (*fromage*) veined; (*viande*) marbled, with fat running through.
Persique [pɛʀsik] *adj*: **le golfe ~** the (Persian) Gulf.
persistance [pɛʀsistɑ̃s] *nf* persistence.
persistant, e [pɛʀsistɑ̃, -ɑ̃t] *adj* persistent; (*feuilles*) evergreen; **à feuillage ~** evergreen.
persister [pɛʀsiste] *vi* to persist; **~ à faire qch** to persist in doing sth.
personnage [pɛʀsɔnaʒ] *nm* (*notable*) personality; figure; (*individu*) character, individual; (*THÉÂT*) character; (*PEINTURE*) figure.
personnaliser [pɛʀsɔnalize] *vt* to personalize; (*appartement*) to give a personal touch to.
personnalité [pɛʀsɔnalite] *nf* personality; (*personnage*) prominent figure.
personne [pɛʀsɔn] *nf* person ♦ *pron* nobody, no one; (*quelqu'un*) anybody, anyone; **~s** *nfpl* people *pl*; **il n'y a ~** there's nobody in *ou* there, there isn't anybody in *ou* there; **10 € par ~** €10 per person *ou* a head; **en ~** personally, in person; **~ âgée** elderly person; **~ à charge** (*JUR*) dependent; **~ morale** *ou* **civile** (*JUR*) legal entity.
personnel, le [pɛʀsɔnɛl] *adj* personal; (*égoïste: personne*) selfish, self-centred; (*idée, opinion*): **j'ai des idées ~les à ce sujet** I have my own ideas about that ♦ *nm* personnel, staff; **service du ~** personnel department.
personnellement [pɛʀsɔnɛlmɑ̃] *adv* personally.
personnification [pɛʀsɔnifikɑsjɔ̃] *nf* personification; **c'est la ~ de la cruauté** he's cruelty personified.
personnifier [pɛʀsɔnifje] *vt* to personify; to typify; **c'est l'honnêteté personnifiée** he (*ou* she *etc*) is honesty personified.
perspective [pɛʀspɛktiv] *nf* (*ART*) perspective; (*vue, coup d'œil*) view; (*point de vue*) viewpoint, angle; (*chose escomptée, envisagée*) prospect; **en ~** in prospect.
perspicace [pɛʀspikas] *adj* clear-sighted, gifted with (*ou* showing) insight.
perspicacité [pɛʀspikasite] *nf* insight, perspicacity.
persuader [pɛʀsɥade] *vt*: **~ qn (de/de faire)** to persuade sb (of/to do); **j'en suis persuadé** I'm quite sure *ou* convinced (of it).
persuasif, ive [pɛʀsɥazif, -iv] *adj* persuasive.
persuasion [pɛʀsɥɑzjɔ̃] *nf* persuasion.
perte [pɛʀt(ə)] *nf* loss; (*de temps*) waste; (*fig: morale*) ruin; **~s** *nfpl* losses; **à ~** (*COMM*) at a loss; **à ~ de vue** as far as the eye can (*ou* could) see; (*fig*) interminably; **en pure ~** for absolutely nothing; **courir à sa ~** to be on the road to ruin; **être en ~ de vitesse** (*fig*) to be losing momentum; **avec ~ et fracas** forcibly; **~ de chaleur** heat loss; **~ sèche** dead loss; **~s blanches** (vaginal) discharge *sg*.
pertinemment [pɛʀtinamɑ̃] *adv* to the point; (*savoir*) perfectly well, full well.
pertinence [pɛʀtinɑ̃s] *nf* pertinence, relevance; discernment.
pertinent, e [pɛʀtinɑ̃, -ɑ̃t] *adj* (*remarque*) apt, pertinent, relevant; (*analyse*) discerning, judicious.
perturbateur, trice [pɛʀtyʀbatœʀ, -tʀis] *adj* disruptive.
perturbation [pɛʀtyʀbɑsjɔ̃] *nf* (*dans un service public*) disruption; (*agitation, trouble*) perturbation; **~ (atmosphérique)** atmospheric disturbance.
perturber [pɛʀtyʀbe] *vt* to disrupt; (*PSYCH*) to perturb, disturb.
péruvien, ne [peʀyvjɛ̃, -ɛn] *adj* Peruvian ♦ *nm/f*: **P~, ne** Peruvian.
pervenche [pɛʀvɑ̃ʃ] *nf* periwinkle; (*fam*) traffic warden (*BRIT*), meter maid (*US*).
pervers, e [pɛʀvɛʀ, -ɛʀs(ə)] *adj* perverted, depraved; (*malfaisant*) perverse.
perversion [pɛʀvɛʀsjɔ̃] *nf* perversion.
perversité [pɛʀvɛʀsite] *nf* depravity; perversity.
perverti, e [pɛʀvɛʀti] *nm/f* pervert.
pervertir [pɛʀvɛʀtiʀ] *vt* to pervert.
pesage [pəzaʒ] *nm* weighing; (*HIPPISME: action*) weigh-in; (*: salle*) weighing room; (*: enceinte*) enclosure.
pesamment [pəzamɑ̃] *adv* heavily.
pesant, e [pəzɑ̃, -ɑ̃t] *adj* heavy; (*fig*) burdensome ♦ *nm*: **valoir son ~ de** to be worth one's weight in.
pesanteur [pəzɑ̃tœʀ] *nf* gravity.
pèse-bébé [pɛzbebe] *nm* (baby) scales *pl*.
pesée [pəze] *nf* weighing; (*BOXE*) weigh-in; (*pression*) pressure.
pèse-lettre [pɛzlɛtʀ(ə)] *nm* letter scales *pl*.
pèse-personne [pɛzpɛʀsɔn] *nm* (bathroom) scales *pl*.
peser [pəze] *vt, vb avec attribut* to weigh; (*considérer, comparer*) to weigh up ♦ *vi* to be heavy; (*fig*) to carry weight; **~ sur** (*levier, bouton*) to press, push; (*fig: accabler*) to lie heavy on;

(: *influencer*) to influence; ~ **à qn** to weigh heavy on sb.
pessaire [pesɛʀ] *nm* pessary.
pessimisme [pesimism(ə)] *nm* pessimism.
pessimiste [pesimist(ə)] *adj* pessimistic ♦ *nm/f* pessimist.
peste [pɛst(ə)] *nf* plague; (*fig*) pest, nuisance.
pester [pɛste] *vi*: ~ **contre** to curse.
pesticide [pɛstisid] *nm* pesticide.
pestiféré, e [pɛstifeʀe] *nm/f* plague victim.
pestilentiel, le [pɛstilɑ̃sjɛl] *adj* foul.
pet [pɛ] *nm* (*fam!*) fart (*!*).
pétale [petal] *nm* petal.
pétanque [petɑ̃k] *nf type of bowls*; *see boxed note*.

PÉTANQUE

Pétanque *is a version of the game of 'boules', played on a variety of hard surfaces. Standing with their feet together, players throw steel bowls at a wooden jack.* **Pétanque** *originated in the South of France and is still very much associated with that area.*

pétarade [petaʀad] *nf* backfiring *no pl*.
pétarader [petaʀade] *vi* to backfire.
pétard [petaʀ] *nm* (*feu d'artifice*) banger (*BRIT*), firecracker; (*de cotillon*) cracker; (*RAIL*) detonator.
pet-de-nonne, *pl* **pets-de-nonne** [pɛdnɔn] *nm* ≈ choux bun.
péter [pete] *vi* (*fam: casser, sauter*) to burst; to bust; (*fam!*) to fart (*!*).
pète-sec [pɛtsɛk] *adj inv* abrupt, sharp(-tongued).
pétillant, e [petijɑ̃, -ɑ̃t] *adj* sparkling.
pétiller [petije] *vi* (*flamme, bois*) to crackle; (*mousse, champagne*) to bubble; (*pierre, métal*) to glisten; (*yeux*) to sparkle; (*fig*): ~ **d'esprit** to sparkle with wit.
petit, e [pəti, -it] *adj* (*gén*) small; (*main, objet, colline, en âge: enfant*) small, little; (*mince, fin: personne, taille, pluie*) slight; (*voyage*) short, little; (*bruit etc*) faint, slight; (*mesquin*) mean; (*peu important*) minor ♦ *nm/f* (*petit enfant*) little one, child ♦ *nmpl* (*d'un animal*) young *pl*; **faire des ~s** to have kittens (*ou* puppies *etc*); **en** ~ in miniature; **mon** ~ son; little one; **ma ~e** dear; little one; **pauvre** ~ poor little thing; **la classe des ~s** the infant class; **pour ~s et grands** for children and adults; **les tout-~s** the little ones, the tiny tots; ~ **à** ~ bit by bit, gradually; **~(e) ami/e** boyfriend/girlfriend; **les ~es annonces** the small ads; ~ **déjeuner** breakfast; ~ **doigt** little finger; **le ~ écran** the small screen; ~ **four** petit four; ~ **pain** (bread) roll; **~e monnaie** small change; **~e vérole** smallpox; **~s pois** petit pois *pl*, garden peas; **~es gens** people of modest means.
petit-beurre, *pl* **petits-beurre** [pətibœʀ] *nm* *sweet butter biscuit* (*BRIT*) *ou cookie* (*US*).
petit(e)-bourgeois(e), *pl* **petit(e)s-bourgeois(es)** [pəti(t)buʀʒwa(z)] *adj* (*péj*) petit-bourgeois, middle-class.
petite-fille, *pl* **petites-filles** [pətitfij] *nf* granddaughter.
petitement [pətitmɑ̃] *adv* poorly; meanly; **être logé** ~ to be in cramped accommodation.
petitesse [pətitɛs] *nf* smallness; (*d'un salaire, de revenus*) modestness; (*mesquinerie*) meanness.
petit-fils, *pl* **petits-fils** [pətifis] *nm* grandson.
pétition [petisjɔ̃] *nf* petition.
pétitionnaire [petisjɔnɛʀ] *nm/f* petitioner.
pétitionner [petisjɔne] *vi* to petition.
petit-lait, *pl* **petits-laits** [pətilɛ] *nm* whey *no pl*.
petit-nègre [pətinɛgʀ(ə)] *nm* (*péj*) pidgin French.
petits-enfants [pətizɑ̃fɑ̃] *nmpl* grandchildren.
petit-suisse, *pl* **petits-suisses** [pətisɥis] *nm* *small individual pot of cream cheese*.
pétoche [petɔʃ] *nf* (*fam*): **avoir la** ~ to be scared out of one's wits.
pétri, e [petʀi] *adj*: ~ **d'orgueil** filled with pride.
pétrifier [petʀifje] *vt* to petrify; (*fig*) to paralyze, transfix.
pétrin [petʀɛ̃] *nm* kneading-trough; (*fig*): **dans le** ~ in a jam *ou* fix.
pétrir [petʀiʀ] *vt* to knead.
pétrochimie [petʀɔʃimi] *nf* petrochemistry.
pétrochimique [petʀɔʃimik] *adj* petrochemical.
pétrodollar [petʀodɔlaʀ] *nm* petrodollar.
pétrole [petʀɔl] *nm* oil; (*aussi*: ~ **lampant**) paraffin (*BRIT*), kerosene (*US*).
pétrolier, ière [petʀɔlje, -jɛʀ] *adj* oil *cpd*; (*pays*) oil-producing ♦ *nm* (*navire*) oil tanker; (*financier*) oilman; (*technicien*) petroleum engineer.
pétrolifère [petʀɔlifɛʀ] *adj* oil(-bearing).
P et T *sigle fpl = postes et télécommunications.*
pétulant, e [petylɑ̃, -ɑ̃t] *adj* exuberant.

MOT-CLÉ

peu [pø] *adv* **1** (*modifiant verbe, adjectif, adverbe*): **il boit** ~ he doesn't drink (very) much; **il est ~ bavard** he's not very talkative; ~ **avant/après** shortly before/afterwards; **pour ~ qu'il fasse** if he should do, if by any chance he does
2 (*modifiant nom*): ~ **de**: ~ **de gens/d'arbres** few *ou* not (very) many people/trees; **il a ~ d'espoir** he hasn't (got) much hope, he has little hope; **pour ~ de temps** for (only) a short while; **à ~ de frais** for very little cost
3: ~ **à** ~ little by little; **à ~ près** just about, more or less; **à ~ près 10 kg/10 €** approximately 10 kg/€10
♦ *nm* **1**: **le ~ de gens qui** the few people who; **le ~ de sable qui** what little sand, the little sand which
2: **un** ~ a little; **un petit** ~ a little bit; **un** ~

d'espoir a little hope; **elle est un ~ bavarde** she's rather talkative; **un ~ plus/moins de** slightly more/less (*ou* fewer) than; **pour un ~ il ..., un ~ plus et il ...** he very nearly *ou* all but ...; **essayez un ~!** have a go!, just try it!
♦ *pron*: **~ le savent** few know (it); **avant** *ou* **sous ~** shortly, before long; **depuis ~** for a short *ou* little while; (*au passé*) a short *ou* little while ago; **de ~** (only) just; **c'est ~ de chose** it's nothing; **il est de ~ mon cadet** he's just a little *ou* bit younger than me.

peuplade [pœplad] *nf* (*horde, tribu*) tribe, people.
peuple [pœpl(ə)] *nm* people; (*masse indifférenciée*): **un ~ de vacanciers** a crowd of holiday-makers; **il y a du ~** there are a lot of people.
peuplé, e [pœple] *adj*: **très/peu ~** densely/sparsely populated.
peupler [pœple] *vt* (*pays, région*) to populate; (*étang*) to stock; (*suj: hommes, poissons*) to inhabit; (*fig: imagination, rêves*) to fill; **se ~** *vi* (*ville, région*) to become populated; (*fig: s'animer*) to fill (up), be filled.
peuplier [pøplije] *nm* poplar (tree).
peur [pœʀ] *nf* fear; **avoir ~ (de/de faire/que)** to be frightened *ou* afraid (of/of doing/that); **prendre ~** to take fright; **faire ~ à** to frighten; **de ~ de/que** for fear of/that; **j'ai ~ qu'il ne soit trop tard** I'm afraid it might be too late; **j'ai ~ qu'il (ne) vienne (pas)** I'm afraid he may (not) come.
peureux, euse [pœʀø, -øz] *adj* fearful, timorous.
peut [pø] *vb voir* **pouvoir**.
peut-être [pøtɛtʀ(ə)] *adv* perhaps, maybe; **~ que** perhaps, maybe; **~ bien qu'il fera/est** he may well do/be.
peuvent [pœv], **peux** [pø] *etc vb voir* **pouvoir**.
p. ex. *abr* (= *par exemple*) e.g.
phalange [falɑ̃ʒ] *nf* (*ANAT*) phalanx (*pl* phalanges); (*MIL, fig*) phalanx (*pl* -es).
phallique [falik] *adj* phallic.
phallocrate [falɔkʀat] *nm* male chauvinist.
phallocratie [falɔkʀasi] *nf* male chauvinism.
phallus [falys] *nm* phallus.
pharaon [faʀaɔ̃] *nm* Pharaoh.
phare [faʀ] *nm* (*en mer*) lighthouse; (*d'aéroport*) beacon; (*de véhicule*) headlight, headlamp (*BRIT*) ♦ *adj*: **produit ~** leading product; **se mettre en ~s, mettre ses ~s** to put on one's headlights; **~s de recul** reversing (*BRIT*) *ou* back-up (*US*) lights.
pharmaceutique [faʀmasøtik] *adj* pharmaceutic(al).
pharmacie [faʀmasi] *nf* (*science*) pharmacology; (*magasin*) chemist's (*BRIT*), pharmacy; (*officine*) dispensary; (*produits*) pharmaceuticals *pl*; (*armoire*) medicine chest *ou* cupboard, first-aid cupboard.
pharmacien, ne [faʀmasjɛ̃, -ɛn] *nm/f* pharmacist, chemist (*BRIT*).
pharmacologie [faʀmakɔlɔʒi] *nf* pharmacology.
pharyngite [faʀɛ̃ʒit] *nf* pharyngitis *no pl*.
pharynx [faʀɛ̃ks] *nm* pharynx.
phase [fɑz] *nf* phase.
phénoménal, e, aux [fenɔmenal, -o] phenomenal.
phénomène [fenɔmɛn] *nm* phenomenon (*pl* -a); (*monstre*) freak.
philanthrope [filɑ̃tʀɔp] *nm/f* philanthropist.
philanthropie [filɑ̃tʀɔpi] *nf* philanthropy.
philanthropique [filɑ̃tʀɔpik] *adj* philanthropic.
philatélie [filateli] *nf* philately, stamp collecting.
philatélique [filatelik] *adj* philatelic.
philatéliste [filatelist(ə)] *nm/f* philatelist, stamp collector.
philharmonique [filaʀmɔnik] *adj* philharmonic.
philippin, e [filipɛ̃, -in] *adj* Filipino.
Philippines [filipin] *nfpl*: **les ~** the Philippines.
philistin [filistɛ̃] *nm* philistine.
philo [filo] *nf* (*fam*: = *philosophie*) philosophy.
philosophe [filɔzɔf] *nm/f* philosopher ♦ *adj* philosophical.
philosopher [filɔzɔfe] *vi* to philosophize.
philosophie [filɔzɔfi] *nf* philosophy.
philosophique [filɔzɔfik] *adj* philosophical.
philosophiquement [filɔzɔfikmɑ̃] *adv* philosophically.
philtre [filtʀ(ə)] *nm* philtre, love potion.
phlébite [flebit] *nf* phlebitis.
phlébologue [flebɔlɔg] *nm/f* vein specialist.
phobie [fɔbi] *nf* phobia.
phonétique [fɔnetik] *adj* phonetic ♦ *nf* phonetics *sg*.
phonétiquement [fɔnetikmɑ̃] *adv* phonetically.
phonographe [fɔnɔgʀaf] *nm* (wind-up) gramophone.
phoque [fɔk] *nm* seal; (*fourrure*) sealskin.
phosphate [fɔsfat] *nm* phosphate.
phosphaté, e [fɔsfate] *adj* phosphate-enriched.
phosphore [fɔsfɔʀ] *nm* phosphorus.
phosphoré, e [fɔsfɔʀe] *adj* phosphorous.
phosphorescent, e [fɔsfɔʀesɑ̃, -ɑ̃t] *adj* luminous.
phosphorique [fɔsfɔʀik] *adj*: **acide ~** phosphoric acid.
photo [fɔto] *nf* (= *photographie*) photo ♦ *adj*: **appareil/pellicule ~** camera/film; **en ~** in *ou* on a photo; **prendre en ~** to take a photo of; **aimer la/faire de la ~** to like taking/take photos; **~ en couleurs** colour photo; **~ d'identité** passport photo.
photo... [fɔtɔ] *préfixe* photo....
photocopie [fɔtɔkɔpi] *nf* (*procédé*) photocopying; (*document*) photocopy.

photocopier [fɔtɔkɔpje] *vt* to photocopy.
photocopieur [fɔtɔkɔpjœʀ] *nm*, **photocopieuse** [fɔtɔkɔpjøz] *nf* (photo)copier.
photo-électrique [fɔtɔelɛktʀik] *adj* photoelectric.
photo-finish, *pl* **photos-finish** [fɔtofiniʃ] *nf* (*appareil*) photo finish camera; (*photo*) photo finish picture; **il y a eu ~ pour la troisième place** there was a photo finish for third place.
photogénique [fɔtɔʒenik] *adj* photogenic.
photographe [fɔtɔgʀaf] *nm/f* photographer.
photographie [fɔtɔgʀafi] *nf* (*procédé, technique*) photography; (*cliché*) photograph; **faire de la ~** to have photography as a hobby; (*comme métier*) to be a photographer.
photographier [fɔtɔgʀafje] *vt* to photograph, take.
photographique [fɔtɔgʀafik] *adj* photographic.
photogravure [fɔtɔgʀavyʀ] *nf* photoengraving.
photomaton [fɔtɔmatɔ̃] *nm* photo-booth, photomat.
photomontage [fɔtɔmɔ̃taʒ] *nm* photomontage.
photo-robot [fɔtɔʀɔbo] *nf* Identikit ® (picture).
photosensible [fɔtɔsɑ̃sibl(ə)] *adj* photosensitive.
photostat [fɔtɔsta] *nm* photostat.
phrase [fʀɑz] *nf* (*LING*) sentence; (*propos, MUS*) phrase; **~s** *nfpl* (*péj*) flowery language *sg*.
phraséologie [fʀazeɔlɔʒi] *nf* phraseology; (*rhétorique*) flowery language.
phraseur, euse [fʀazœʀ, -øz] *nm/f*: **c'est un ~** he uses such flowery language.
phrygien, ne [fʀiʒjɛ̃, -ɛn] *adj*: **bonnet ~** Phrygian cap.
phtisie [ftizi] *nf* consumption.
phylloxéra [filɔkseʀa] *nm* phylloxera.
physicien, ne [fizisjɛ̃, -ɛn] *nm/f* physicist.
physiologie [fizjɔlɔʒi] *nf* physiology.
physiologique [fizjɔlɔʒik] *adj* physiological.
physiologiquement [fizjɔlɔʒikmɑ̃] *adv* physiologically.
physionomie [fizjɔnɔmi] *nf* face; (*d'un paysage etc*) physiognomy.
physionomiste [fizjɔnɔmist(ə)] *nm/f* good judge of faces; person who has a good memory for faces.
physiothérapie [fizjɔteʀapi] *nf* natural medicine, alternative medicine.
physique [fizik] *adj* physical ♦ *nm* physique ♦ *nf* physics *sg*; **au ~** physically.
physiquement [fizikmɑ̃] *adv* physically.
phytothérapie [fitɔteʀapi] *nf* herbal medicine.
p.i. *abr* = **par intérim**; *voir* **intérim**.
piaffer [pjafe] *vi* to stamp.
piaillement [pjɑjmɑ̃] *nm* squawking *no pl*.
piailler [pjɑje] *vi* to squawk.
pianiste [pjanist(ə)] *nm/f* pianist.
piano [pjano] *nm* piano; **~ à queue** grand piano.
pianoter [pjanɔte] *vi* to tinkle away (at the piano); (*tapoter*): **~ sur** to drum one's fingers on.
piaule [pjol] *nf* (*fam*) pad.
piauler [pjole] *vi* (*enfant*) to whimper; (*oiseau*) to cheep.
PIB *sigle m* (= *produit intérieur brut*) GDP.
pic [pik] *nm* (*instrument*) pick(axe); (*montagne*) peak; (*ZOOL*) woodpecker; **à ~** *adv* vertically; (*fig*) just at the right time; **couler à ~** (*bateau*) to go straight down; **~ à glace** ice pick.
picard, e [pikaʀ, -aʀd(ə)] *adj* of *ou* from Picardy.
Picardie [pikaʀdi] *nf*: **la ~** Picardy.
picaresque [pikaʀɛsk(ə)] *adj* picaresque.
piccolo [pikɔlo] *nm* piccolo.
pichenette [piʃnɛt] *nf* flick.
pichet [piʃɛ] *nm* jug.
pickpocket [pikpɔkɛt] *nm* pickpocket.
pick-up [pikœp] *nm inv* record player.
picorer [pikɔʀe] *vt* to peck.
picot [piko] *nm* sprocket; **entraînement par roue à ~s** sprocket feed.
picotement [pikɔtmɑ̃] *nm* smarting *no pl*, prickling *no pl*.
picoter [pikɔte] *vt* (*suj: oiseau*) to peck ♦ *vi* (*irriter*) to smart, prickle.
pictural, e, aux [piktyʀal, -o] *adj* pictorial.
pie [pi] *nf* magpie; (*fig*) chatterbox ♦ *adj inv*: **cheval ~** piebald; **vache ~** black and white cow.
pièce [pjɛs] *nf* (*d'un logement*) room; (*THÉÂT*) play; (*de mécanisme, machine*) part; (*de monnaie*) coin; (*COUTURE*) patch; (*document*) document; (*de drap, fragment, d'une collection*) piece; (*de bétail*) head; **mettre en ~s** to smash to pieces; **deux euros ~** two euros each; **vendre à la ~** to sell separately *ou* individually; **travailler/payer à la ~** to do piecework/pay piece rate; **de toutes ~s**: **c'est inventé de toutes ~s** it's a complete fabrication; **un maillot une ~** a one-piece swimsuit; **un deux-~s cuisine** a two-room(ed) flat (*BRIT*) *ou* apartment (*US*) with kitchen; **tout d'une ~** (*personne: franc*) blunt; (*: sans souplesse*) inflexible; **~ à conviction** exhibit; **~ d'eau** ornamental lake *ou* pond; **~ d'identité**: **avez-vous une ~ d'identité?** have you got any (means of) identification?; **~ montée** tiered cake; **~ de rechange** spare (part); **~ de résistance** pièce de résistance; (*plat*) main dish; **~s détachées** spares, (spare) parts; **en ~s détachées** (*à monter*) in kit form; **~s justificatives** supporting documents.
pied [pje] *nm* foot (*pl* feet); (*de verre*) stem; (*de table*) leg; (*de lampe*) base; (*plante*) plant; **~s**

nus barefoot; **à** ~ on foot; **à** ~ **sec** without getting one's feet wet; **à** ~ **d'œuvre** ready to start (work); **au** ~ **de la lettre** literally; **au** ~ **levé** at a moment's notice; **de** ~ **en cap** from head to foot; **en** ~ (*portrait*) full-length; **avoir** ~ to be able to touch the bottom, not to be out of one's depth; **avoir le** ~ **marin** to be a good sailor; **perdre** ~ to lose one's footing; (*fig*) to get out of one's depth; **sur** ~ (*AGR*) on the stalk, uncut; (*debout, rétabli*) up and about; **mettre sur** ~ (*entreprise*) to set up; **mettre à** ~ to suspend; to lay off; **mettre qn au** ~ **du mur** to get sb with his (*ou* her) back to the wall; **sur le** ~ **de guerre** ready for action; **sur un** ~ **d'égalité** on an equal footing; **sur** ~ **d'intervention** on stand-by; **faire du** ~ **à qn** (*prévenir*) to give sb a (warning) kick; (*galamment*) to play footsie with sb; **mettre les** ~**s quelque part** to set foot somewhere; **faire des** ~**s et des mains** (*fig*) to move heaven and earth, pull out all the stops; **c'est le** ~! (*fam*) it's terrific!; **se lever du bon** ~**/du** ~ **gauche** to get out of bed on the right/wrong side; ~ **de lit** footboard; ~ **de nez: faire un** ~ **de nez à** to thumb one's nose at; ~ **de vigne** vine.

pied-à-terre [pjetatɛʀ] *nm inv* pied-à-terre.

pied-bot, *pl* **pieds-bots** [pjebo] *nm* person with a club foot.

pied-de-biche, *pl* **pieds-de-biche** [pjedbiʃ] *nm* claw; (*COUTURE*) presser foot.

pied-de-poule [pjedpul] *adj inv* hound's-tooth.

piédestal, aux [pjedɛstal, -o] *nm* pedestal.

pied-noir, *pl* **pieds-noirs** [pjenwaʀ] *nm* Algerian-born Frenchman.

piège [pjɛʒ] *nm* trap; **prendre au** ~ to trap.

piéger [pjeʒe] *vt* (*animal, fig*) to trap; (*avec une bombe*) to booby-trap; **lettre/voiture piégée** letter-/car-bomb.

pierraille [pjɛʀɑj] *nf* loose stones *pl*.

pierre [pjɛʀ] *nf* stone; **première** ~ (*d'un édifice*) foundation stone; **mur de** ~**s sèches** drystone wall; **faire d'une** ~ **deux coups** to kill two birds with one stone; ~ **à briquet** flint; ~ **fine** semiprecious stone; ~ **ponce** pumice stone; ~ **de taille** freestone *no pl*; ~ **tombale** tombstone, gravestone; ~ **de touche** touchstone.

pierreries [pjɛʀʀi] *nfpl* gems, precious stones.

pierreux, euse [pjɛʀø, -øz] *adj* stony.

piété [pjete] *nf* piety.

piétinement [pjetinmɑ̃] *nm* stamping *no pl*.

piétiner [pjetine] *vi* (*trépigner*) to stamp (one's foot); (*marquer le pas*) to stand about; (*fig*) to be at a standstill ♦ *vt* to trample on.

piéton, ne [pjetɔ̃, -ɔn] *nm/f* pedestrian ♦ *adj* pedestrian *cpd*.

piétonnier, ière [pjetɔnje, -jɛʀ] *adj* pedestrian *cpd*.

piètre [pjɛtʀ(ə)] *adj* poor, mediocre.

pieu, x [pjø] *nm* (*piquet*) post; (*pointu*) stake; (*fam: lit*) bed.

pieusement [pjøzmɑ̃] *adv* piously.

pieuvre [pjœvʀ(ə)] *nf* octopus.

pieux, euse [pjø, -øz] *adj* pious.

pif [pif] *nm* (*fam*) conk (*BRIT*), beak; **au** ~ = **au pifomètre**.

piffer [pife] *vt* (*fam*): **je ne peux pas le** ~ I can't stand him.

pifomètre [pifɔmɛtʀ(ə)] *nm* (*fam*): **choisir** *etc* **au** ~ to follow one's nose when choosing *etc*.

pige [piʒ] *nf* piecework rate.

pigeon [piʒɔ̃] *nm* pigeon; ~ **voyageur** homing pigeon.

pigeonnant, e [piʒɔnɑ̃, -ɑ̃t] *adj* full, well-developed.

pigeonneau, x [piʒɔno] *nm* young pigeon.

pigeonnier [piʒɔnje] *nm* pigeon loft, dovecot(e).

piger [piʒe] *vi* (*fam*) to get it ♦ *vt* (*fam*) to get, understand.

pigiste [piʒist(ə)] *nm/f* (*typographe*) typesetter on piecework; (*journaliste*) freelance journalist (*paid by the line*).

pigment [pigmɑ̃] *nm* pigment.

pignon [piɲɔ̃] *nm* (*de mur*) gable; (*d'engrenage*) cog(wheel), gearwheel; (*graine*) pine kernel; **avoir** ~ **sur rue** (*fig*) to have a prosperous business.

pile [pil] *nf* (*tas, pilier*) pile; (*ÉLEC*) battery ♦ *adj*: **le côté** ~ tails ♦ *adv* (*net, brusquement*) dead; (*à temps, à point nommé*) just at the right time; **à deux heures** ~ at two on the dot; **jouer à** ~ **ou face** to toss up (for it); ~ **ou face?** heads or tails?

piler [pile] *vt* to crush, pound.

pileux, euse [pilø, -øz] *adj*: **système** ~ (body) hair.

pilier [pilje] *nm* (*colonne, support*) pillar; (*personne*) mainstay; (*RUGBY*) prop (forward).

pillage [pijaʒ] *nm* pillaging, plundering, looting.

pillard, e [pijaʀ, -aʀd(ə)] *nm/f* looter; plunderer.

piller [pije] *vt* to pillage, plunder, loot.

pilleur, euse [pijœʀ, -øz] *nm/f* looter.

pilon [pilɔ̃] *nm* (*instrument*) pestle; (*de volaille*) drumstick; **mettre un livre au** ~ to pulp a book.

pilonner [pilɔne] *vt* to pound.

pilori [pilɔʀi] *nm*: **mettre** *ou* **clouer au** ~ to pillory.

pilotage [pilɔtaʒ] *nm* piloting; flying; ~ **automatique** automatic piloting; ~ **sans visibilité** blind flying.

pilote [pilɔt] *nm* pilot; (*de char, voiture*) driver ♦ *adj* pilot *cpd*; **usine/ferme** ~ experimental factory/farm; ~ **de chasse/d'essai/de ligne** fighter/test/airline pilot; ~ **de course** racing driver.

piloter [pilɔte] *vt* (*navire*) to pilot; (*avion*) to fly; (*automobile*) to drive; (*fig*): ~ **qn** to guide sb round; **piloté par menu** (*INFORM*) menu-driven.

pilotis [pilɔti] *nm* pile; stilt.

pilule [pilyl] *nf* pill; **prendre la** ~ to be on the pill; ~ **du lendemain** morning-after pill.

pimbêche [pɛ̃bɛʃ] *nf* (*péj*) stuck-up girl.

piment [pimɑ̃] *nm* (*BOT*) pepper, capsicum; (*fig*) spice, piquancy; ~ **rouge** (*CULIN*) chilli.

pimenté, e [pimɑ̃te] *adj* hot and spicy.

pimenter [pimɑ̃te] *vt* (*plat*) to season (with peppers *ou* chillis); (*fig*) to add *ou* give spice to.

pimpant, e [pɛ̃pɑ̃, -ɑ̃t] *adj* spruce.

pin [pɛ̃] *nm* pine (tree); (*bois*) pine(wood).

pinacle [pinakl(ə)] *nm*: **porter qn au** ~ (*fig*) to praise sb to the skies.

pinard [pinaʀ] *nm* (*fam*) (cheap) wine, plonk (*BRIT*).

pince [pɛ̃s] *nf* (*outil*) pliers *pl*; (*de homard, crabe*) pincer, claw; (*COUTURE*: *pli*) dart; ~ **à sucre/glace** sugar/ice tongs *pl*; ~ **à épiler** tweezers *pl*; ~ **à linge** clothes peg (*BRIT*) *ou* pin (*US*); ~ **universelle** (universal) pliers *pl*; ~**s de cycliste** bicycle clips.

pincé, e [pɛ̃se] *adj* (*air*) stiff; (*mince: bouche*) pinched ♦ *nf*: **une** ~**e de** a pinch of.

pinceau, x [pɛ̃so] *nm* (paint)brush.

pincement [pɛ̃smɑ̃] *nm*: ~ **au cœur** twinge of regret.

pince-monseigneur, *pl* **pinces-monseigneur** [pɛ̃smɔ̃sɛɲœʀ] *nf* crowbar.

pince-nez [pɛ̃sne] *nm inv* pince-nez.

pincer [pɛ̃se] *vt* to pinch; (*MUS*: *cordes*) to pluck; (*COUTURE*) to dart, put darts in; (*fam*) to nab; **se** ~ **le doigt** to squeeze *ou* nip one's finger; **se** ~ **le nez** to hold one's nose.

pince-sans-rire [pɛ̃ssɑ̃ʀiʀ] *adj inv* deadpan.

pincettes [pɛ̃sɛt] *nfpl* tweezers; (*pour le feu*) (fire) tongs.

pinçon [pɛ̃sɔ̃] *nm* pinch mark.

pinède [pinɛd] *nf* pinewood, pine forest.

pingouin [pɛ̃gwɛ̃] *nm* penguin.

ping-pong [piŋpɔ̃ŋ] *nm* table tennis.

pingre [pɛ̃gʀ(ə)] *adj* niggardly.

pinson [pɛ̃sɔ̃] *nm* chaffinch.

pintade [pɛ̃tad] *nf* guinea-fowl.

pin up [pinœp] *nf inv* pin-up (girl).

pioche [pjɔʃ] *nf* pickaxe.

piocher [pjɔʃe] *vt* to dig up (with a pickaxe); (*fam*) to swot (*BRIT*) *ou* grind (*US*) at; ~ **dans** to dig into.

piolet [pjɔlɛ] *nm* ice axe.

pion, ne [pjɔ̃, pjɔn] *nm/f* (*SCOL*: *péj*) *student paid to supervise schoolchildren* ♦ *nm* (*ÉCHECS*) pawn; (*DAMES*) piece, draught (*BRIT*), checker (*US*).

pionnier [pjɔnje] *nm* pioneer.

pipe [pip] *nf* pipe; **fumer la** *ou* **une** ~ to smoke a pipe; ~ **de bruyère** briar pipe.

pipeau, x [pipo] *nm* (reed-)pipe.

pipe-line [piplin] *nm* pipeline.

piper [pipe] *vt* (*dé*) to load; (*carte*) to mark; **sans** ~ **mot** (*fam*) without a squeak; **les dés sont pipés** (*fig*) the dice are loaded.

pipette [pipɛt] *nf* pipette.

pipi [pipi] *nm* (*fam*): **faire** ~ to have a wee.

piquant, e [pikɑ̃, -ɑ̃t] *adj* (*barbe, rosier etc*) prickly; (*saveur, sauce*) hot, pungent; (*fig: description, style*) racy; (*: mordant, caustique*) biting ♦ *nm* (*épine*) thorn, prickle; (*de hérisson*) quill, spine; (*fig*) spiciness, spice.

pique [pik] *nf* (*arme*) pike; (*fig*): **envoyer** *ou* **lancer des** ~**s à qn** to make cutting remarks to sb ♦ *nm* (*CARTES*: *couleur*) spades *pl*; (*: carte*) spade.

piqué, e [pike] *adj* (*COUTURE*) (machine-) stitched; quilted; (*livre, glace*) mildewed; (*vin*) sour; (*MUS*: *note*) staccato; (*fam*: *personne*) nuts ♦ *nm* (*AVIAT*) dive; (*TEXTILE*) piqué.

pique-assiette [pikasjɛt] *nm/f inv* (*péj*) scrounger, sponger.

pique-fleurs [pikflœʀ] *nm inv* flower holder.

pique-nique [piknik] *nm* picnic.

pique-niquer [piknike] *vi* to (have a) picnic.

pique-niqueur, euse [piknikœʀ, -øz] *nm/f* picnicker.

piquer [pike] *vt* (*percer*) to prick; (*planter*): ~ **qch dans** to stick sth into; (*fixer*): ~ **qch à** *ou* **sur** to pin sth onto; (*MÉD*) to give an injection to; (*: animal blessé etc*) to put to sleep; (*suj: insecte, fumée, ortie*) to sting; (*: poivre*) to burn; (*: froid*) to bite; (*COUTURE*) to machine (stitch); (*intérêt etc*) to arouse; (*fam*: *prendre*) to pick up; (*: voler*) to pinch; (*: arrêter*) to nab ♦ *vi* (*oiseau, avion*) to go into a dive; (*saveur*) to be pungent; to be sour; **se** ~ (*avec une aiguille*) to prick o.s.; (*se faire une piqûre*) to inject o.s.; (*se vexer*) to get annoyed; **se** ~ **de faire** to pride o.s. on doing; ~ **sur** to swoop down on; to head straight for; ~ **du nez** (*avion*) to go into a nose-dive; ~ **une tête** (*plonger*) to dive headfirst; ~ **un galop/un cent mètres** to break into a gallop/put on a sprint; ~ **une crise** to throw a fit; ~ **au vif** (*fig*) to sting.

piquet [pikɛ] *nm* (*pieu*) post, stake; (*de tente*) peg; **mettre un élève au** ~ to make a pupil stand in the corner; ~ **de grève** (strike) picket; ~ **d'incendie** fire-fighting squad.

piqueté, e [pikte] *adj*: ~ **de** dotted with.

piquette [pikɛt] *nf* (*fam*) cheap wine, plonk (*BRIT*).

piqûre [pikyʀ] *nf* (*d'épingle*) prick; (*d'ortie*) sting; (*de moustique*) bite; (*MÉD*) injection, shot (*US*); (*COUTURE*) (straight) stitch; straight stitching; (*de ver*) hole; (*tache*) (spot of) mildew; **faire une** ~ **à qn** to give sb an injection.

piranha [piʀana] *nm* piranha.

piratage [piʀataʒ] *nm* piracy.

pirate [piʀat] *adj* pirate *cpd* ♦ *nm* pirate; (*fig: escroc*) crook, shark; ~ **de l'air** hijacker.

pirater [piʀate] *vt* to pirate.

piraterie [piʀatʀi] *nf* (act of) piracy; ~

aérienne hijacking.
pire [piR] *adj* (*comparatif*) worse; (*superlatif*): **le (la) ~** ... the worst ... ♦ *nm*: **le ~ (de)** the worst (of).
Pirée [piRe] *n* Piraeus.
pirogue [piRɔg] *nf* dugout (canoe).
pirouette [piRwɛt] *nf* pirouette; (*fig: volte-face*) about-turn.
pis [pi] *nm* (*de vache*) udder; (*pire*): **le ~** the worst ♦ *adj, adv* worse; **qui ~ est** what is worse; **au ~ aller** if the worst comes to the worst, at worst.
pis-aller [pizale] *nm inv* stopgap.
pisciculture [pisikyltyR] *nf* fish farming.
piscine [pisin] *nf* (swimming) pool; **~ couverte** indoor (swimming) pool.
Pise [piz] *n* Pisa.
pissenlit [pisɑ̃li] *nm* dandelion.
pisser [pise] *vi* (*fam!*) to pee.
pissotière [pisɔtjɛR] *nf* (*fam*) public urinal.
pistache [pistaʃ] *nf* pistachio (nut).
pistard [pistaR] *nm* (*CYCLISME*) track cyclist.
piste [pist(ə)] *nf* (*d'un animal, sentier*) track, trail; (*indice*) lead; (*de stade, de magnétophone, INFORM*) track; (*de cirque*) ring; (*de danse*) floor; (*de patinage*) rink; (*de ski*) run; (*AVIAT*) runway; **~ cavalière** bridle path; **~ cyclable** cycle track, bikeway (*US*); **~ sonore** sound track.
pister [piste] *vt* to track, trail.
pisteur [pistœR] *nm* (*SKI*) member of the ski patrol.
pistil [pistil] *nm* pistil.
pistolet [pistɔlɛ] *nm* (*arme*) pistol, gun; (*à peinture*) spray gun; **~ à bouchon/air comprimé** popgun/airgun; **~ à eau** water pistol.
pistolet-mitrailleur, *pl* **pistolets-mitrailleurs** [pistɔlɛmitRajœR] *nm* submachine gun.
piston [pistɔ̃] *nm* (*TECH*) piston; (*MUS*) valve; (*fig: appui*) string-pulling.
pistonner [pistɔne] *vt* (*candidat*) to pull strings for.
pitance [pitɑ̃s] *nf* (*péj*) (means of) sustenance.
piteusement [pitøzmɑ̃] *adv* (*échouer*) miserably.
piteux, euse [pitø, -øz] *adj* pitiful, sorry (*avant le nom*); **en ~ état** in a sorry state.
pitié [pitje] *nf* pity; **sans ~** *adj* pitiless, merciless; **faire ~** to inspire pity; **il me fait ~** I pity him, I feel sorry for him; **avoir ~ de** (*compassion*) to pity, feel sorry for; (*merci*) to have pity *ou* mercy on; **par ~!** for pity's sake!
piton [pitɔ̃] *nm* (*clou*) peg, bolt; **~ rocheux** rocky outcrop.
pitoyable [pitwajabl(ə)] *adj* pitiful.
pitre [pitR(ə)] *nm* clown.
pitrerie [pitRəRi] *nf* tomfoolery *no pl*.
pittoresque [pitɔRɛsk(ə)] *adj* picturesque; (*expression, détail*) colourful (*BRIT*), colorful (*US*).
pivert [pivɛR] *nm* green woodpecker.
pivoine [pivwan] *nf* peony.
pivot [pivo] *nm* pivot; (*d'une dent*) post.
pivoter [pivɔte] *vi* (*fauteuil*) to swivel; (*porte*) to revolve; **~ sur ses talons** to swing round.
pixel [piksɛl] *nm* pixel.
pizza [pidza] *nf* pizza.
PJ *sigle f* = **police judiciaire** ♦ *sigle fpl* (= *pièces jointes*) encl.
PL *sigle m* (*AUTO*) = **poids lourd**.
Pl. *abr* = **place**.
placage [plakaʒ] *nm* (*bois*) veneer.
placard [plakaR] *nm* (*armoire*) cupboard; (*affiche*) poster, notice; (*TYPO*) galley; **~ publicitaire** display advertisement.
placarder [plakaRde] *vt* (*affiche*) to put up; (*mur*) to stick posters on.
place [plas] *nf* (*emplacement, situation, classement*) place; (*de ville, village*) square; (*ÉCON*): **~ financière/boursière** money/stock market; (*espace libre*) room, space; (*de parking*) space; (*siège: de train, cinéma, voiture*) seat; (*prix: au cinéma etc*) price; (*: dans un bus, taxi*) fare; (*emploi*) job; **en ~** (*mettre*) in its place; **de ~ en ~, par ~s** here and there, in places; **sur ~** on the spot; **faire ~ à** to give way to; **faire de la ~ à** to make room for; **ça prend de la ~** it takes up a lot of room *ou* space; **prendre ~** to take one's place; **remettre qn à sa ~** to put sb in his (*ou* her) place; **ne pas rester** *ou* **tenir en ~** to be always on the go; **à la ~ de** in place of, instead of; **une quatre ~s** (*AUTO*) a four-seater; **il y a 20 ~s assises/debout** there are 20 seats/there is standing room for 20; **~ forte** fortified town; **~ d'honneur** place (*ou* seat) of honour (*BRIT*) *ou* honor (*US*).
placé, e [plase] *adj* (*HIPPISME*) placed; **haut ~** (*fig*) high-ranking; **être bien/mal ~** to be well/badly placed; (*spectateur*) to have a good/bad seat; **être bien/mal ~ pour faire** to be in/not to be in a position to do.
placebo [plasebo] *nm* placebo.
placement [plasmɑ̃] *nm* placing; (*FINANCE*) investment; **agence** *ou* **bureau de ~** employment agency.
placenta [plasɑ̃ta] *nm* placenta.
placer [plase] *vt* to place, put; (*convive, spectateur*) to seat; (*capital, argent*) to place, invest; (*dans la conversation*) to put *ou* get in; **~ qn chez** to get sb a job at (*ou* with); **se ~ au premier rang** to go and stand (*ou* sit) in the first row.
placide [plasid] *adj* placid.
placidité [plasidite] *nf* placidity.
placier, ière [plasje, -jɛR] *nm/f* commercial rep(resentative), salesman/woman.
Placoplâtre [plakoplatR] *nm* ® plasterboard.
plafond [plafɔ̃] *nm* ceiling.
plafonner [plafɔne] *vt* (*pièce*) to put a ceiling (up) in ♦ *vi* to reach one's (*ou* a) ceiling.
plafonnier [plafɔnje] *nm* ceiling light; (*AUTO*)

interior light.
plage [plaʒ] *nf* beach; (*station*) (seaside) resort; (*fig*) band, bracket; (*de disque*) track, band; ~ **arrière** (*AUTO*) parcel *ou* back shelf.
plagiaire [plaʒjɛʀ] *nm/f* plagiarist.
plagiat [plaʒja] *nm* plagiarism.
plagier [plaʒje] *vt* to plagiarize.
plagiste [plaʒist(ə)] *nm/f* beach attendant.
plaid [plɛd] *nm* (tartan) car rug, lap robe (*US*).
plaidant, e [plɛdɑ̃, -ɑ̃t] *adj* litigant.
plaider [plede] *vi* (*avocat*) to plead; (*plaignant*) to go to court, litigate ♦ *vt* to plead; ~ **pour** (*fig*) to speak for.
plaideur, euse [plɛdœʀ, -øz] *nm/f* litigant.
plaidoirie [plɛdwaʀi] *nf* (*JUR*) speech for the defence (*BRIT*) *ou* defense (*US*).
plaidoyer [plɛdwaje] *nm* (*JUR*) speech for the defence (*BRIT*) *ou* defense (*US*); (*fig*) plea.
plaie [plɛ] *nf* wound.
plaignant, e [plɛɲɑ̃, -ɑ̃t] *vb voir* **plaindre** ♦ *nm/f* plaintiff.
plaindre [plɛ̃dʀ(ə)] *vt* to pity, feel sorry for; **se** ~ *vi* (*gémir*) to moan; (*protester, rouspéter*): **se** ~ **(à qn) (de)** to complain (to sb) (about); (*souffrir*): **se** ~ **de** to complain of.
plaine [plɛn] *nf* plain.
plain-pied [plɛ̃pje]: **de** ~ *adv* at street-level; (*fig*) straight; **de** ~ **(avec)** on the same level (as).
plaint, e [plɛ̃, -ɛ̃t] *pp de* **plaindre** ♦ *nf* (*gémissement*) moan, groan; (*doléance*) complaint; **porter** ~**e** to lodge a complaint.
plaintif, ive [plɛ̃tif, -iv] *adj* plaintive.
plaire [plɛʀ] *vi* to be a success, be successful; to please; ~ **à**: **cela me plaît** I like it; **essayer de** ~ **à qn** (*en étant serviable etc*) to try and please sb; **elle plaît aux hommes** she's a success with men, men like her; **se** ~ **quelque part** to like being somewhere, like it somewhere; **se** ~ **à faire** to take pleasure in doing; **ce qu'il vous plaira** what(ever) you like *ou* wish; **s'il vous plaît** please.
plaisamment [plɛzamɑ̃] *adv* pleasantly.
plaisance [plɛzɑ̃s] *nf* (*aussi*: **navigation de** ~) (pleasure) sailing, yachting.
plaisancier [plɛzɑ̃sje] *nm* amateur sailor, yachting enthusiast.
plaisant, e [plɛzɑ̃, -ɑ̃t] *adj* pleasant; (*histoire, anecdote*) amusing.
plaisanter [plɛzɑ̃te] *vi* to joke ♦ *vt* (*personne*) to tease, make fun of; **pour** ~ for a joke; **on ne plaisante pas avec cela** that's no joking matter; **tu plaisantes!** you're joking *ou* kidding!
plaisanterie [plɛzɑ̃tʀi] *nf* joke; joking *no pl*.
plaisantin [plɛzɑ̃tɛ̃] *nm* joker; (*fumiste*) fly-by-night.
plaise [plɛz] *etc vb voir* **plaire**.
plaisir [pleziʀ] *nm* pleasure; **faire** ~ **à qn** (*délibérément*) to be nice to sb, please sb; (*suj: cadeau, nouvelle etc*): **ceci me fait** ~ I'm delighted *ou* very pleased with this; **prendre** ~ **à/à faire** to take pleasure in/in doing; **j'ai le** ~ **de** ... it is with great pleasure that I ...; **M. et Mme X ont le** ~ **de vous faire part de** ... M. and Mme X are pleased to announce ...; **se faire un** ~ **de faire qch** to be (only too) pleased to do sth; **faites-moi le** ~ **de** ... would you mind ..., would you be kind enough to ...; **à** ~ freely; for the sake of it; **au** ~ **(de vous revoir)** (I hope to) see you again; **pour le** *ou* **pour son** *ou* **par** ~ for pleasure.
plaît [plɛ] *vb voir* **plaire**.
plan, e [plɑ̃, -an] *adj* flat ♦ *nm* plan; (*GÉOM*) plane; (*fig*) level, plane; (*CINÉ*) shot; **au premier/second** ~ in the foreground/middle distance; **à l'arrière** ~ in the background; **mettre qch au premier** ~ (*fig*) to consider sth to be of primary importance; **sur le** ~ **sexuel** sexually, as far as sex is concerned; **laisser/rester en** ~ to abandon/be abandoned; ~ **d'action** plan of action; ~ **directeur** (*ÉCON*) master plan; ~ **d'eau** lake; pond; ~ **de travail** work-top, work surface; ~ **de vol** (*AVIAT*) flight plan.
planche [plɑ̃ʃ] *nf* (*pièce de bois*) plank, (wooden) board; (*illustration*) plate; (*de salades, radis, poireaux*) bed; (*d'un plongeoir*) (diving) board; **les** ~**s** (*THÉÂT*) the boards; **en** ~**s** *adj* wooden; **faire la** ~ (*dans l'eau*) to float on one's back; **avoir du pain sur la** ~ to have one's work cut out; ~ **à découper** chopping board; ~ **à dessin** drawing board; ~ **à pain** breadboard; ~ **à repasser** ironing board; ~ **(à roulettes)** (*planche*) skateboard; (*sport*) skateboarding; ~ **de salut** (*fig*) sheet anchor; ~ **à voile** (*planche*) windsurfer, sailboard; (*sport*) windsurfing.
plancher [plɑ̃ʃe] *nm* floor; (*planches*) floorboards *pl*; (*fig*) minimum level ♦ *vi* to work hard.
planchiste [plɑ̃ʃist(ə)] *nm/f* windsurfer.
plancton [plɑ̃ktɔ̃] *nm* plankton.
planer [plane] *vi* (*oiseau, avion*) to glide; (*fumée, vapeur*) to float, hover; (*drogué*) to be (on a) high; ~ **sur** (*fig*) to hang over; to hover above.
planétaire [planetɛʀ] *adj* planetary.
planétarium [planetaʀjɔm] *nm* planetarium.
planète [planɛt] *nf* planet.
planeur [planœʀ] *nm* glider.
planification [planifikɑsjɔ̃] *nf* (economic) planning.
planifier [planifje] *vt* to plan.
planisphère [planisfɛʀ] *nm* planisphere.
planning [planiŋ] *nm* programme (*BRIT*), program (*US*), schedule; ~ **familial** family planning.
planque [plɑ̃k] *nf* (*fam: combine, filon*) cushy (*BRIT*) *ou* easy number; (*: cachette*) hideout.
planquer [plɑ̃ke] *vt* (*fam*) to hide (away), stash away; **se** ~ to hide.
plant [plɑ̃] *nm* seedling, young plant.
plantaire [plɑ̃tɛʀ] *adj voir* **voûte**.

plantation [plɑ̃tɑsjɔ̃] *nf* planting; (*de fleurs, légumes*) bed; (*exploitation*) plantation.
plante [plɑ̃t] *nf* plant; ~ **d'appartement** house *ou* pot plant; ~ **du pied** sole (of the foot); ~ **verte** house plant.
planter [plɑ̃te] *vt* (*plante*) to plant; (*enfoncer*) to hammer *ou* drive in; (*tente*) to put up, pitch; (*drapeau, échelle, décors*) to put up; (*fam: mettre*) to dump; (*: abandonner*): ~ **là** to ditch; **se** ~ *vi* (*fam: se tromper*) to get it wrong; ~ **qch dans** to hammer *ou* drive sth into; to stick sth into; **se** ~ **dans** to sink into; to get stuck in; **se** ~ **devant** to plant o.s. in front of.
planteur [plɑ̃tœʀ] *nm* planter.
planton [plɑ̃tɔ̃] *nm* orderly.
plantureux, euse [plɑ̃tyʀø, -øz] *adj* (*repas*) copious, lavish; (*femme*) buxom.
plaquage [plakaʒ] *nm* (*RUGBY*) tackle.
plaque [plak] *nf* plate; (*de verre*) sheet; (*de verglas, d'eczéma*) patch; (*dentaire*) plaque; (*avec inscription*) plaque; ~ **(minéralogique** *ou* **de police** *ou* **d'immatriculation)** number (*BRIT*) *ou* license (*US*) plate; ~ **de beurre** slab of butter; ~ **chauffante** hotplate; ~ **de chocolat** bar of chocolate; ~ **de cuisson** hob; ~ **d'identité** identity disc; ~ **tournante** (*fig*) centre (*BRIT*), center (*US*).
plaqué, e [plake] *adj*: ~ **or/argent** gold-/silver-plated ♦ *nm*: ~ **or/argent** gold/silver plate; ~ **acajou** with a mahogany veneer.
plaquer [plake] *vt* (*bijou*) to plate; (*bois*) to veneer; (*aplatir*): ~ **qch sur/contre** to make sth stick *ou* cling to, (*RUGBY*) to bring down; (*fam: laisser tomber*) to drop, ditch; **se** ~ **contre** to flatten o.s. against; ~ **qn contre** to pin sb to.
plaquette [plakɛt] *nf* tablet; (*de chocolat*) bar; (*de beurre*) slab, packet; (*livre*) small volume; (*MÉD: de pilules, gélules*) pack, packet; (*INFORM*) circuit board; ~ **de frein** (*AUTO*) brake pad.
plasma [plasma] *nm* plasma.
plastic [plastik] *nm* plastic explosive.
plastifié, e [plastifje] *adj* plastic-coated.
plastifier [plastifje] *vt* (*document, photo*) to laminate.
plastiquage [plastikaʒ] *nm* bombing, bomb attack.
plastique [plastik] *adj* plastic ♦ *nm* plastic ♦ *nf* plastic arts *pl*; (*d'une statue*) modelling.
plastiquer [plastike] *vt* to blow up.
plastiqueur [plastikœʀ] *nm* terrorist (*planting a plastic bomb*).
plastron [plastʀɔ̃] *nm* shirt front.
plastronner [plastʀɔne] *vi* to swagger.
plat, e [pla, -at] *adj* flat; (*fade: vin*) flat-tasting, insipid; (*personne, livre*) dull ♦ *nm* (*récipient, CULIN*) dish; (*d'un repas*): **le premier** ~ the first course; (*partie plate*): **le** ~ **de la main** the flat of the hand; (*: d'une route*) flat (part); **à** ~ **ventre** *adv* face down; (*tomber*) flat on one's face; **à** ~ *adj* (*pneu, batterie*) flat; (*fam: fatigué*) dead beat, tired out; ~ **cuisiné** pre-cooked meal (*ou* dish); ~ **du jour** dish of the day; ~ **de résistance** main course; ~**s préparés** convenience food(s).
platane [platan] *nm* plane tree.
plateau, x [plato] *nm* (*support*) tray; (*d'une table*) top; (*d'une balance*) pan; (*GÉO*) plateau; (*de tourne-disques*) turntable; (*CINÉ*) set; (*TV*): **nous avons 2 journalistes sur le** ~ **ce soir** we have 2 journalists with us tonight; ~ **à fromages** cheeseboard.
plateau-repas, *pl* **plateaux-repas** [platoʀəpɑ] *nm* tray meal, TV dinner (*US*).
plate-bande, *pl* **plates-bandes** [platbɑ̃d] *nf* flower bed.
platée [plate] *nf* dish(ful).
plate-forme, *pl* **plates-formes** [platfɔʀm(ə)] *nf* platform; ~ **de forage/pétrolière** drilling/oil rig.
platine [platin] *nm* platinum ♦ *nf* (*d'un tourne-disque*) turntable; ~ **disque/cassette** record/cassette deck; ~ **laser** *ou* **compact-disc** compact disc (player).
platitude [platityd] *nf* platitude.
platonique [platɔnik] *adj* platonic.
plâtras [plɑtʀa] *nm* rubble *no pl*.
plâtre [plɑtʀ(ə)] *nm* (*matériau*) plaster; (*statue*) plaster statue; (*MÉD*) (plaster) cast; ~**s** *nmpl* plasterwork *sg*; **avoir un bras dans le** ~ to have an arm in plaster.
plâtrer [plɑtʀe] *vt* to plaster; (*MÉD*) to set *ou* put in a (plaster) cast.
plâtrier [plɑtʀije] *nm* plasterer.
plausible [plozibl(ə)] *adj* plausible.
play-back [plɛbak] *nm* miming.
play-boy [plɛbɔj] *nm* playboy.
plébiscite [plebisit] *nm* plebiscite.
plébisciter [plebisite] *vt* (*approuver*) to give overwhelming support to; (*élire*) to elect by an overwhelming majority.
plectre [plɛktʀ(ə)] *nm* plectrum.
plein, e [plɛ̃, -ɛn] *adj* full; (*porte, roue*) solid; (*chienne, jument*) big (with young) ♦ *nm*: **faire le** ~ **(d'essence)** to fill up (with petrol (*BRIT*) *ou* gas (*US*)) ♦ *prép*: **avoir de l'argent** ~ **les poches** to have loads of money; ~ **de** full of; **avoir les mains** ~**es** to have one's hands full; **à** ~**es mains** (*ramasser*) in handfuls; (*empoigner*) firmly; **à** ~ **régime** at maximum revs; (*fig*) at full speed; **à** ~ **temps** full-time; **en** ~ **air** in the open air; **jeux en** ~ **air** outdoor games; **en** ~**e mer** on the open sea; **en** ~ **soleil** in direct sunlight; **en** ~**e nuit/rue** in the middle of the night/street; **en** ~ **milieu** right in the middle; **en** ~ **jour** in broad daylight; **les** ~**s** the downstrokes (*in handwriting*); **faire le** ~ **des voix** to get the maximum number of votes possible; **en** ~ **sur** right on; **en avoir** ~ **le dos** (*fam*) to have had it up to here.
pleinement [plɛnmɑ̃] *adv* fully; to the full.

plein-emploi [plɛnɑ̃plwa] *nm* full employment.
plénière [plenjɛʀ] *adj f*: **assemblée** ~ plenary assembly.
plénipotentiaire [plenipɔtɑ̃sjɛʀ] *nm* plenipotentiary.
plénitude [plenityd] *nf* fullness.
pléthore [pletɔʀ] *nf*: ~ **de** overabundance *ou* plethora of.
pléthorique [pletɔʀik] *adj* (*classes*) overcrowded; (*documentation*) excessive.
pleurer [plœʀe] *vi* to cry; (*yeux*) to water ♦ *vt* to mourn (for); ~ **sur** *vt* to lament (over), bemoan; ~ **de rire** to laugh till one cries.
pleurésie [plœʀezi] *nf* pleurisy.
pleureuse [plœʀøz] *nf* professional mourner.
pleurnicher [plœʀniʃe] *vi* to snivel, whine.
pleurs [plœʀ] *nmpl*: **en** ~ in tears.
pleut [plø] *vb voir* **pleuvoir.**
pleutre [pløtʀ(ə)] *adj* cowardly.
pleuvait [pløvɛ] *etc vb voir* **pleuvoir.**
pleuviner [pløvine] *vb impers* to drizzle.
pleuvoir [pløvwaʀ] *vb impers* to rain ♦ *vi* (*fig*): ~ **(sur)** to shower down (upon), be showered upon; **il pleut** it's raining; **il pleut des cordes** *ou* **à verse** *ou* **à torrents** it's pouring (down), it's raining cats and dogs.
pleuvra [pløvʀa] *etc vb voir* **pleuvoir.**
Plexiglas [plɛksiglɑs] *nm* ® Plexiglas ® (*US*).
pli [pli] *nm* fold; (*de jupe*) pleat; (*de pantalon*) crease; (*aussi*: **faux** ~) crease; (*enveloppe*) envelope; (*lettre*) letter; (*CARTES*) trick; **prendre le** ~ **de faire** to get into the habit of doing; **ça ne fait pas un** ~**!** don't you worry!; ~ **d'aisance** inverted pleat.
pliable [plijabl(ə)] *adj* pliable, flexible.
pliage [plijaʒ] *nm* folding; (*ART*) origami.
pliant, e [plijɑ̃, -ɑ̃t] *adj* folding ♦ *nm* folding stool, campstool.
plier [plije] *vt* to fold; (*pour ranger*) to fold up; (*table pliante*) to fold down; (*genou, bras*) to bend ♦ *vi* to bend; (*fig*) to yield; **se** ~ **à** to submit to; ~ **bagages** (*fig*) to pack up (and go).
plinthe [plɛ̃t] *nf* skirting board.
plissé, e [plise] *adj* (*jupe, robe*) pleated; (*peau*) wrinkled; (*GÉO*) folded ♦ *nm* (*COUTURE*) pleats *pl*.
plissement [plismɑ̃] *nm* (*GÉO*) fold.
plisser [plise] *vt* (*chiffonner: papier, étoffe*) to crease; (*rider: front*) to furrow, wrinkle; (*: bouche*) to pucker; (*jupe*) to put pleats in; **se** ~ *vi* (*vêtement, étoffe*) to crease.
pliure [plijyʀ] *nf* (*du bras, genou*) bend; (*d'un ourlet*) fold.
plomb [plɔ̃] *nm* (*métal*) lead; (*d'une cartouche*) (lead) shot; (*PÊCHE*) sinker; (*sceau*) (lead) seal; (*ÉLEC*) fuse; **de** ~ (*soleil*) blazing; **sans** ~ (*essence*) unleaded; **sommeil de** ~ heavy *ou* very deep sleep; **mettre à** ~ to plumb.
plombage [plɔ̃baʒ] *nm* (*de dent*) filling.
plomber [plɔ̃be] *vt* (*canne, ligne*) to weight (with lead); (*colis, wagon*) to put a lead seal on; (*TECH: mur*) to plumb; (*dent*) to fill (*BRIT*), stop (*US*); (*INFORM*) to protect.
plomberie [plɔ̃bʀi] *nf* plumbing.
plombier [plɔ̃bje] *nm* plumber.
plonge [plɔ̃ʒ] *nf*: **faire la** ~ to be a washer-up (*BRIT*) *ou* dishwasher (*person*).
plongeant, e [plɔ̃ʒɑ̃, -ɑ̃t] *adj* (*vue*) from above; (*tir, décolleté*) plunging.
plongée [plɔ̃ʒe] *nf* (*SPORT*) diving *no pl*; (*: sans scaphandre*) skin diving; (*de sous-marin*) submersion, dive; **en** ~ (*sous-marin*) submerged; (*prise de vue*) high angle.
plongeoir [plɔ̃ʒwaʀ] *nm* diving board.
plongeon [plɔ̃ʒɔ̃] *nm* dive.
plonger [plɔ̃ʒe] *vi* to dive ♦ *vt*: ~ **qch dans** to plunge sth into; ~ **dans un sommeil profond** to sink straight into a deep sleep; ~ **qn dans l'embarras** to throw sb into a state of confusion.
plongeur, euse [plɔ̃ʒœʀ, -øz] *nm/f* diver; (*de café*) washer-up (*BRIT*), dishwasher (*person*).
plot [plo] *nm* (*ÉLEC*) contact.
ploutocratie [plutɔkʀasi] *nf* plutocracy.
ploutocratique [plutɔkʀatik] *adj* plutocratic.
ployer [plwaje] *vt* to bend ♦ *vi* to bend; (*plancher*) to sag.
plu [ply] *pp de* **plaire, pleuvoir.**
pluie [plɥi] *nf* rain; (*averse, ondée*): **une** ~ **brève** a shower; (*fig*): ~ **de** shower of; **une** ~ **fine** fine rain; **retomber en** ~ to shower down; **sous la** ~ in the rain.
plumage [plymaʒ] *nm* plumage *no pl*, feathers *pl*.
plume [plym] *nf* feather; (*pour écrire*) (pen) nib; (*fig*) pen; **dessin à la** ~ pen and ink drawing.
plumeau, x [plymo] *nm* feather duster.
plumer [plyme] *vt* to pluck.
plumet [plymɛ] *nm* plume.
plumier [plymje] *nm* pencil box.
plupart [plypaʀ]: **la** ~ *pron* the majority, most (of them); **la** ~ **des** most, the majority of; **la** ~ **du temps/d'entre nous** most of the time/of us; **pour la** ~ *adv* for the most part, mostly.
pluralisme [plyʀalism(ə)] *nm* pluralism.
pluralité [plyʀalite] *nf* plurality.
pluridisciplinaire [plyʀidisiplinɛʀ] *adj* multidisciplinary.
pluriel [plyʀjɛl] *nm* plural; **au** ~ in the plural.
plus¹ [ply] *vb voir* **plaire.**

MOT-CLÉ

plus² [ply] *adv* **1** (*forme négative*): **ne ...** ~ no more, no longer; **je n'ai** ~ **d'argent** I've got no more money *ou* no money left; **il ne travaille** ~ he's no longer working, he doesn't work any more
2 [ply, plyz *+voyelle*] (*comparatif*) more, ...+er; (*superlatif*): **le** ~ the most, the ...+est; ~ **grand/intelligent (que)** bigger/more intelli-

gent (than); **le ~ grand/intelligent** the biggest/most intelligent; **tout au ~** at the very most
3 [plys] (*davantage*) more; **il travaille ~ (que)** he works more (than); **~ il travaille, ~ il est heureux** the more he works, the happier he is; **~ de pain** more bread; **~ de 10 personnes/3 heures/4 kilos** more than *ou* over 10 people/3 hours/4 kilos; **3 heures de ~ que** 3 hours more than; **~ de minuit** after *ou* past midnight; **de ~** what's more, moreover; **il a 3 ans de ~ que moi** he's 3 years older than me; **3 kilos en ~** 3 kilos more; **en ~ de** in addition to; **de ~ en ~** more and more; **en ~ de cela** ... what is more ...; **~ ou moins** more or less; **ni ~ ni moins** no more, no less; **sans ~** (but) no more than that, (but) that's all; **qui ~ est** what is more
♦ *prép* [plys]: **4 ~ 2** 4 plus 2.

plusieurs [plyzjœʀ] *dét, pron* several; **ils sont ~** there are several of them.
plus-que-parfait [plyskəpaʀfɛ] *nm* pluperfect, past perfect.
plus-value [plyvaly] *nf* (*d'un bien*) appreciation; (*bénéfice*) capital gain; (*budgétaire*) surplus.
plut [ply] *vb voir* **plaire, pleuvoir**.
plutonium [plytɔnjɔm] *nm* plutonium.
plutôt [plyto] *adv* rather; **je ferais ~ ceci** I'd rather *ou* sooner do this; **fais ~ comme ça** try this way instead; **~ que (de) faire** rather than *ou* instead of doing.
pluvial, e, aux [plyvjal, -o] *adj* (*eaux*) rain *cpd*.
pluvieux, euse [plyvjø, -øz] *adj* rainy, wet.
pluviosité [plyvjɔzite] *nf* rainfall.
PM *sigle f* = *Police militaire*.
p.m. *abr* (= *pour mémoire*) for the record.
PME *sigle fpl* = *petites et moyennes entreprises*.
PMI *sigle fpl* = *petites et moyennes industries* ♦ *sigle f* = **protection maternelle et infantile**.
PMU *sigle m* = *pari mutuel urbain*; (*café*) betting agency; *see boxed note*.

PMU

The **PMU** *('pari mutuel urbain') is a Government-regulated network of betting counters run from bars displaying the PMU sign. Punters buy fixed-price tickets predicting winners or finishing positions in horse races. The traditional bet is the 'tiercé', a triple bet, although other multiple bets ('quarté' and so on) are becoming increasingly popular.*

PNB *sigle m* (= *produit national brut*) GNP.
pneu [pnø] *nm* (*de roue*) tyre (*BRIT*), tire (*US*); (*message*) letter sent by pneumatic tube.
pneumatique [pnømatik] *adj* pneumatic; (*gonflable*) inflatable ♦ *nm* tyre (*BRIT*), tire (*US*).
pneumonie [pnømɔni] *nf* pneumonia.
PO *sigle fpl* (= *petites ondes*) MW.
po [po] *abr voir* **science**.
Pô [po] *nm*: **le ~** the Po.
p.o. *abr* (= *par ordre*) p.p. (*on letters etc*).
poche [pɔʃ] *nf* pocket; (*déformation*): **faire une/des ~(s)** to bag; (*sous les yeux*) bag, pouch; (*ZOOL*) pouch ♦ *nm* (= *livre de ~*) (pocket-size) paperback; **de ~** pocket *cpd*; **en être de sa ~** to be out of pocket; **c'est dans la ~** it's in the bag.
poché, e [pɔʃe] *adj*: **œuf ~** poached egg; **œil ~** black eye.
pocher [pɔʃe] *vt* (*CULIN*) to poach; (*ART*) to sketch ♦ *vi* (*vêtement*) to bag.
poche-revolver, *pl* **poches-revolver** [pɔʃʀəvɔlvɛʀ] *nf* hip pocket.
pochette [pɔʃɛt] *nf* (*de timbres*) wallet, envelope; (*d'aiguilles etc*) case; (*sac: de femme*) clutch bag, purse; (*: d'homme*) bag; (*sur veston*) breast pocket; (*mouchoir*) breast pocket handkerchief; **~ d'allumettes** book of matches; **~ de disque** record sleeve; **~ surprise** lucky bag.
pochoir [pɔʃwaʀ] *nm* (*ART: cache*) stencil; (*: tampon*) transfer.
podium [pɔdjɔm] *nm* podium (*pl* -ia).
poêle [pwal] *nm* stove ♦ *nf*: **~ (à frire)** frying pan.
poêlon [pwalɔ̃] *nm* casserole.
poème [pɔɛm] *nm* poem.
poésie [pɔezi] *nf* (*poème*) poem; (*art*): **la ~** poetry.
poète [pɔɛt] *nm* poet, (*fig*) dreamer ♦ *adj* poetic.
poétique [pɔetik] *adj* poetic.
pognon [pɔɲɔ̃] *nm* (*fam: argent*) dough.
poids [pwa] *nm* weight; (*SPORT*) shot; **vendre au ~** to sell by weight; **de ~** *adj* (*argument etc*) weighty; **prendre du ~** to put on weight; **faire le ~** (*fig*) to measure up; **~ plume/ mouche/coq/moyen** (*BOXE*) feather/fly/ bantam/ middleweight; **~ et haltères** *nmpl* weight lifting *sg*; **~ lourd** (*BOXE*) heavyweight; (*camion: aussi*: **PL**) (big) lorry (*BRIT*), truck (*US*); (*: ADMIN*) large goods vehicle (*BRIT*), truck (*US*); **~ mort** dead weight; **~ utile** net weight.
poignant, e [pwaɲɑ̃, -ɑ̃t] *adj* poignant, harrowing.
poignard [pwaɲaʀ] *nm* dagger.
poignarder [pwaɲaʀde] *vt* to stab, knife.
poigne [pwaɲ] *nf* grip; (*fig*) firm-handedness; **à ~** firm-handed.
poignée [pwaɲe] *nf* (*de sel etc, fig*) handful; (*de couvercle, porte*) handle; **~ de main** handshake.
poignet [pwaɲɛ] *nm* (*ANAT*) wrist; (*de chemise*) cuff.
poil [pwal] *nm* (*ANAT*) hair; (*de pinceau, brosse*) bristle; (*de tapis, tissu*) strand; (*pelage*) coat; (*ensemble des poils*): **avoir du ~ sur la**

poitrine to have hair(s) on one's chest, have a hairy chest; **à** ~ *adj* (*fam*) starkers; **au** ~ *adj* (*fam*) hunky-dory; **de tout** ~ of all kinds; **être de bon/mauvais** ~ to be in a good/bad mood; ~ **à gratter** itching powder.

poilu, e [pwaly] *adj* hairy.

poinçon [pwɛ̃sɔ̃] *nm* awl; bodkin; (*marque*) hallmark.

poinçonner [pwɛ̃sɔne] *vt* (*marchandise*) to stamp; (*bijou etc*) to hallmark; (*billet, ticket*) to clip, punch.

poinçonneuse [pwɛ̃sɔnøz] *nf* (*outil*) punch.

poindre [pwɛ̃dʀ(ə)] *vi* (*fleur*) to come up; (*aube*) to break; (*jour*) to dawn.

poing [pwɛ̃] *nm* fist; **dormir à ~s fermés** to sleep soundly.

point [pwɛ̃] *vb voir* **poindre** ♦ *nm* (*marque, signe*) dot; (*: de ponctuation*) full stop, period (*US*); (*moment, de score etc, fig: question*) point; (*endroit*) spot; (*COUTURE, TRICOT*) stitch ♦ *adv* = **pas**; **ne** ... ~ not (at all); **faire le** ~ (*NAVIG*) to take a bearing; (*fig*) to take stock (of the situation); **faire le** ~ **sur** to review; **en tout** ~ in every respect; **sur le** ~ **de faire** (just) about to do; **au** ~ **que, à tel** ~ **que** so much so that; **mettre au** ~ (*mécanisme, procédé*) to develop; (*appareil-photo*) to focus; (*affaire*) to settle; **à** ~ (*CULIN*) just right; (*: viande*) medium; **à** ~ **(nommé)** just at the right time; ~ **de croix/tige/chaînette** (*COUTURE*) cross/stem/chain stitch; ~ **mousse/jersey** (*TRICOT*) garter/stocking stitch; ~ **de départ/d'arrivée/d'arrêt** departure/arrival/stopping point; ~ **chaud** (*MIL, POL*) hot spot; ~ **de chute** landing place; (*fig*) stopping-off point; ~ **(de côté)** stitch (*pain*); ~ **culminant** summit; (*fig*) height, climax; ~ **d'eau** spring; water point; ~ **d'exclamation** exclamation mark; ~ **faible** weak spot; ~ **final** full stop, period (*US*); ~ **d'interrogation** question mark; ~ **mort** (*FINANCE*) break-even point; **au** ~ **mort** (*AUTO*) in neutral; (*affaire, entreprise*) at a standstill; ~ **noir** (*sur le visage*) blackhead; (*AUTO*) accident black spot; ~ **de non-retour** point of no return; ~ **de repère** landmark; (*dans le temps*) point of reference; ~ **de vente** retail outlet; ~ **de vue** viewpoint; (*fig: opinion*) point of view; **du** ~ **de vue de** from the point of view of; **~s cardinaux** points of the compass, cardinal points; **~s de suspension** suspension points.

pointage [pwɛ̃taʒ] *nm* ticking off; checking in.

pointe [pwɛ̃t] *nf* point; (*de la côte*) headland; (*allusion*) dig; sally; (*fig*): **une** ~ **d'ail/d'accent** a touch *ou* hint of garlic/of an accent; **~s** *nfpl* (*DANSE*) points, point shoes; **être à la** ~ **de** (*fig*) to be in the forefront of; **faire** *ou* **pousser une** ~ **jusqu'à** ... to press on as far as ...; **sur la** ~ **des pieds** on tiptoe; **en** ~ *adv* (*tailler*) into a point ♦ *adj* pointed, tapered; **de** ~ *adj* (*technique etc*) leading; (*vitesse*) maximum, top; **heures/jours de** ~ peak hours/days; **faire du 180 en** ~ (*AUTO*) to have a top *ou* maximum speed of 180; **faire des ~s** (*DANSE*) to dance on points; ~ **d'asperge** asparagus tip; ~ **de courant** surge (of current); ~ **de tension** (*INFORM*) spike; ~ **de vitesse** burst of speed.

pointer [pwɛ̃te] *vt* (*cocher*) to tick off; (*employés etc*) to check in; (*diriger: canon, longue-vue, doigt*): ~ **vers qch** to point at sth; (*MUS: note*) to dot ♦ *vi* (*employé*) to clock in; (*pousses*) to come through; (*jour*) to break; ~ **les oreilles** (*chien*) to prick up its ears.

pointeur, euse [pwɛ̃tœʀ, -øz] *nm/f* timekeeper ♦ *nf* timeclock.

pointillé [pwɛ̃tije] *nm* (*trait*) dotted line; (*ART*) stippling *no pl*.

pointilleux, euse [pwɛ̃tijø, -øz] *adj* particular, pernickety.

pointu, e [pwɛ̃ty] *adj* pointed; (*clou*) sharp; (*voix*) shrill; (*analyse*) precise.

pointure [pwɛ̃tyʀ] *nf* size.

point-virgule, *pl* **points-virgules** [pwɛ̃viʀgyl] *nm* semi-colon.

poire [pwaʀ] *nf* pear; (*fam: péj*) mug; ~ **électrique** (*pear-shaped*) switch; ~ **à injections** syringe.

poireau, x [pwaʀo] *nm* leek.

poireauter [pwaʀote] *vi* (*fam*) to hang about (waiting).

poirier [pwaʀje] *nm* pear tree; (*GYMNASTIQUE*): **faire le** ~ to do a headstand.

pois [pwa] *nm* (*BOT*) pea; (*sur une étoffe*) dot, spot; **à** ~ (*cravate etc*) spotted, polka-dot *cpd*; ~ **chiche** chickpea; ~ **de senteur** sweet pea; ~ **cassés** split peas.

poison [pwazɔ̃] *nm* poison.

poisse [pwas] *nf* rotten luck.

poisser [pwase] *vt* to make sticky.

poisseux, euse [pwasø, -øz] *adj* sticky.

poisson [pwasɔ̃] *nm* fish *gén inv*; **les P~s** (*ASTROL: signe*) Pisces, the Fish; **être des P~s** to be Pisces; **pêcher** *ou* **prendre du** ~ *ou* **des ~s** to fish; ~ **d'avril** April fool; (*blague*) April fool's day trick; ~ **rouge** goldfish.

poisson-chat, *pl* **poissons-chats** [pwasɔ̃ʃa] *nm* catfish.

poissonnerie [pwasɔnʀi] *nf* fishmonger's (*BRIT*), fish store (*US*).

poissonneux, euse [pwasɔnø, -øz] *adj* abounding in fish.

poissonnier, ière [pwasɔnje, -jɛʀ] *nm/f* fishmonger (*BRIT*), fish merchant (*US*) ♦ *nf* (*ustensile*) fish kettle.

poisson-scie, *pl* **poissons-scies** [pwasɔ̃si] *nm* sawfish.

poitevin, e [pwatvɛ̃, -in] *adj* (*région*) of *ou* from Poitou; (*ville*) of *ou* from Poitiers.

poitrail [pwatʀaj] *nm* (*d'un cheval etc*) breast.
poitrine [pwatʀin] *nf* (*ANAT*) chest; (*seins*) bust, bosom; (*CULIN*) breast; ~ **de bœuf** brisket.
poivre [pwavʀ(ə)] *nm* pepper; ~ **en grains/moulu** whole/ground pepper; ~ **de cayenne** cayenne (pepper); ~ **et sel** *adj* (*cheveux*) pepper-and-salt.
poivré, e [pwavʀe] *adj* peppery.
poivrer [pwavʀe] *vt* to pepper.
poivrier [pwavʀije] *nm* (*BOT*) pepper plant.
poivrière [pwavʀijɛʀ] *nf* pepperpot, pepper shaker (*US*).
poivron [pwavʀɔ̃] *nm* pepper, capsicum; ~ **vert/rouge** green/red pepper.
poix [pwa] *nf* pitch (*tar*).
poker [pɔkɛʀ] *nm*: **le** ~ poker; **partie de** ~ (*fig*) gamble; ~ **d'as** four aces.
polaire [pɔlɛʀ] *adj* polar.
polarisation [pɔlaʀizɑsjɔ̃] *nf* (*PHYSIQUE, ÉLEC*) polarization; (*fig*) focusing.
polariser [pɔlaʀize] *vt* to polarize; (*fig: attirer*) to attract; (*: réunir, concentrer*) to focus; **être polarisé sur** (*personne*) to be completely bound up with *ou* absorbed by.
pôle [pol] *nm* (*GÉO, ÉLEC*) pole; **le** ~ **Nord/Sud** the North/South Pole; ~ **d'attraction** (*fig*) centre of attraction.
polémique [pɔlemik] *adj* controversial, polemic(al) ♦ *nf* controversy.
polémiquer [pɔlemike] *vi* to be involved in controversy.
polémiste [pɔlemist(ə)] *nm/f* polemist, polemicist.
poli, e [pɔli] *adj* polite; (*lisse*) smooth; polished.
police [pɔlis] *nf* police; (*discipline*): **assurer la** ~ **de** *ou* **dans** to keep order in; **peine de simple** ~ *sentence given by a magistrates' or police court*; ~ **(d'assurance)** (insurance) policy; ~ **(de caractères)** (*TYPO, INFORM*) typeface; ~ **judiciaire (PJ)** ≈ Criminal Investigation Department (CID) (*BRIT*), ≈ Federal Bureau of Investigation (FBI) (*US*); ~ **des mœurs** ≈ vice squad; ~ **secours** ≈ emergency services *pl*.
polichinelle [pɔliʃinɛl] *nm* Punch; (*péj*) buffoon; **secret de** ~ open secret.
policier, ière [pɔlisje, -jɛʀ] *adj* police *cpd* ♦ *nm* policeman; (*aussi*: **roman** ~) detective novel.
policlinique [pɔliklinik] *nf* ≈ outpatients *sg* (clinic).
poliment [pɔlimɑ̃] *adv* politely.
polio(myélite) [pɔljɔ(mjelit)] *nf* polio(-myelitis).
polio(myélitique) [pɔljɔ(mjelitik)] *nm/f* polio patient *ou* case.
polir [pɔliʀ] *vt* to polish.
polisson, ne [pɔlisɔ̃, -ɔn] *adj* naughty.
politesse [pɔlitɛs] *nf* politeness; ~**s** *nfpl* (exchange of) courtesies; **rendre une** ~ **à qn** to return sb's favour (*BRIT*) *ou* favor (*US*).
politicard [pɔlitikaʀ] *nm* (*péj*) politico, political schemer.
politicien, ne [pɔlitisjɛ̃, -ɛn] *adj* political ♦ *nm/f* politician.
politique [pɔlitik] *adj* political ♦ *nf* (*science, activité*) politics *sg*; (*principes, tactique*) policy, policies *pl* ♦ *nm* (*politicien*) politician; ~ **étrangère/intérieure** foreign/domestic policy.
politique-fiction [pɔlitikfiksjɔ̃] *nf* political fiction.
politiquement [pɔlitikmɑ̃] *adv* politically.
politisation [pɔlitizɑsjɔ̃] *nf* politicization.
politiser [pɔlitize] *vt* to politicize; ~ **qn** to make sb politically aware.
pollen [pɔlɛn] *nm* pollen.
polluant, e [pɔlɥɑ̃, -ɑ̃t] *adj* polluting ♦ *nm* polluting agent, pollutant.
polluer [pɔlɥe] *vt* to pollute.
pollueur, euse [pɔlɥœʀ, -øz] *nm/f* polluter.
pollution [pɔlysjɔ̃] *nf* pollution.
polo [pɔlo] *nm* (*sport*) polo; (*tricot*) polo shirt.
Pologne [pɔlɔɲ] *nf*: **la** ~ Poland.
polonais, e [pɔlɔnɛ, -ɛz] *adj* Polish ♦ *nm* (*LING*) Polish ♦ *nm/f*: **P**~, **e** Pole.
poltron, ne [pɔltʀɔ̃, -ɔn] *adj* cowardly.
poly... [pɔli] *préfixe* poly....
polyamide [pɔliamid] *nf* polyamide.
polychrome [pɔlikʀom] *adj* polychrome, polychromatic.
polyclinique [pɔliklinik] *nf* (private) clinic (*treating different illnesses*).
polycopie [pɔlikɔpi] *nf* (*procédé*) duplicating; (*reproduction*) duplicated copy.
polycopié, e [pɔlikɔpje] *adj* duplicated ♦ *nm* handout, duplicated notes *pl*.
polycopier [pɔlikɔpje] *vt* to duplicate.
polyculture [pɔlikyltyʀ] *nf* mixed farming.
polyester [pɔliɛstɛʀ] *nm* polyester.
polyéthylène [pɔlietilɛn] *nm* polyethylene.
polygame [pɔligam] *adj* polygamous.
polygamie [pɔligami] *nf* polygamy.
polyglotte [pɔliglɔt] *adj* polyglot.
polygone [pɔligɔn] *nm* polygon.
Polynésie [pɔlinezi] *nf*: **la** ~ Polynesia; **la** ~ **française** French Polynesia.
polynésien, ne [pɔlinezjɛ̃, -ɛn] *adj* Polynesian.
polynôme [pɔlinom] *nm* polynomial.
polype [pɔlip] *nm* polyp.
polystyrène [pɔlistiʀɛn] *nm* polystyrene.
polytechnicien, ne [pɔlitɛknisjɛ̃, -ɛn] *nm/f student or former student of the École polytechnique.*
Polytechnique [pɔlitɛknik] *nf*: **(École) p**~ *prestigious military academy producing high-ranking officers and engineers.*
polyvalent, e [pɔlivalɑ̃, -ɑ̃t] *adj* (*vaccin*) polyvalent; (*personne*) versatile; (*salle*) multipurpose ♦ *nm* ≈ tax inspector.
pomélo [pɔmelo] *nm* pomelo, grapefruit.
Poméranie [pɔmeʀani] *nf*: **la** ~ Pomerania.

pommade [pɔmad] *nf* ointment, cream.
pomme [pɔm] *nf* (*BOT*) apple; (*boule décorative*) knob; (*pomme de terre*): **steak ~s (frites)** steak and chips (*BRIT*) *ou* (French) fries (*US*); **tomber dans les ~s** (*fam*) to pass out; ~ **d'Adam** Adam's apple; **~s allumettes** French fries (*thin-cut*); ~ **d'arrosoir** (sprinkler) rose; ~ **de pin** pine *ou* fir cone; ~ **de terre** potato; **~s vapeur** boiled potatoes.
pommé, e [pɔme] *adj* (*chou etc*) firm.
pommeau, x [pɔmo] *nm* (*boule*) knob; (*de selle*) pommel.
pommelé, e [pɔmle] *adj*: **gris ~** dapple grey.
pommette [pɔmɛt] *nf* cheekbone.
pommier [pɔmje] *nm* apple tree.
pompe [pɔ̃p] *nf* pump; (*faste*) pomp (and ceremony); ~ **à eau/essence** water/petrol pump; ~ **à huile** oil pump; ~ **à incendie** fire engine (*apparatus*); **~s funèbres** undertaker's *sg*, funeral parlour *sg* (*BRIT*), mortician's *sg* (*US*).
Pompéi [pɔ̃pei] *n* Pompeii.
pompéien, ne [pɔ̃pejɛ̃, -ɛn] *adj* Pompeiian.
pomper [pɔ̃pe] *vt* to pump; (*évacuer*) to pump out; (*aspirer*) to pump up; (*absorber*) to soak up ♦ *vi* to pump.
pompeusement [pɔ̃pøzmɑ̃] *adv* pompously.
pompeux, euse [pɔ̃pø, -øz] *adj* pompous.
pompier [pɔ̃pje] *nm* fireman ♦ *adj m* (*style*) pretentious, pompous.
pompiste [pɔ̃pist(ə)] *nm/f* petrol (*BRIT*) *ou* gas (*US*) pump attendant.
pompon [pɔ̃pɔ̃] *nm* pompom, bobble.
pomponner [pɔ̃pɔne] *vt* to titivate (*BRIT*), dress up.
ponce [pɔ̃s] *nf*: **pierre ~** pumice stone.
poncer [pɔ̃se] *vt* to sand (down).
ponceuse [pɔ̃søz] *nf* sander.
poncif [pɔ̃sif] *nm* cliché.
ponction [pɔ̃ksjɔ̃] *nf* (*d'argent etc*) withdrawal; ~ **lombaire** lumbar puncture.
ponctualité [pɔ̃ktɥalite] *nf* punctuality.
ponctuation [pɔ̃ktɥɑsjɔ̃] *nf* punctuation.
ponctuel, le [pɔ̃ktɥɛl] *adj* (*à l'heure, aussi TECH*) punctual; (*fig: opération etc*) one-off, single; (*scrupuleux*) punctilious, meticulous.
ponctuellement [pɔ̃ktɥɛlmɑ̃] *adv* punctually; punctiliously, meticulously.
ponctuer [pɔ̃ktɥe] *vt* to punctuate; (*MUS*) to phrase.
pondéré, e [pɔ̃deʀe] *adj* level-headed, composed.
pondérer [pɔ̃deʀe] *vt* to balance.
pondeuse [pɔ̃døz] *nf* layer, laying hen.
pondre [pɔ̃dʀ(ə)] *vt* to lay; (*fig*) to produce ♦ *vi* to lay.
poney [pɔnɛ] *nm* pony.
pongiste [pɔ̃ʒist(ə)] *nm/f* table tennis player.
pont [pɔ̃] *nm* bridge; (*AUTO*): ~ **arrière/avant** rear/front axle; (*NAVIG*) deck; **faire le ~** to take the extra day off; **faire un ~ d'or à qn** to offer sb a fortune to take a job; ~ **aérien** airlift; ~ **basculant** bascule bridge; ~ **d'envol** flight deck; ~ **élévateur** hydraulic ramp; ~ **de graissage** ramp (*in garage*); ~ **à péage** tollbridge; ~ **roulant** travelling crane; ~ **suspendu** suspension bridge; ~ **tournant** swing bridge; **P~s et Chaussées** highways department; *see boxed note*.

> **FAIRE LE PONT**
>
> *The expression 'faire le pont' refers to the practice of taking a Monday or Friday off to make a long weekend if a public holiday falls on a Tuesday or Thursday. The French commonly take an extra day off work to give four consecutive days' holiday at 'l'Ascension', 'le 14 juillet' and 'le 15 août'.*

ponte [pɔ̃t] *nf* laying; (*œufs pondus*) clutch ♦ *nm* (*fam*) big shot.
pontife [pɔ̃tif] *nm* pontiff.
pontifier [pɔ̃tifje] *vi* to pontificate.
pont-levis, *pl* **ponts-levis** [pɔ̃lvi] *nm* drawbridge.
ponton [pɔ̃tɔ̃] *nm* pontoon (*on water*).
pop [pɔp] *adj inv* pop ♦ *nm*: **le ~** pop (music).
pop-corn [pɔpkɔʀn] *nm* popcorn.
popeline [pɔplin] *nf* poplin.
populace [pɔpylas] *nf* (*péj*) rabble.
populaire [pɔpylɛʀ] *adj* popular; (*manifestation*) mass *cpd*, of the people; (*milieux, clientèle*) working-class; (*LING: mot etc*) used by the lower classes (of society).
populariser [pɔpylaʀize] *vt* to popularize.
popularité [pɔpylaʀite] *nf* popularity.
population [pɔpylɑsjɔ̃] *nf* population; ~ **active/agricole** working/farming population.
populeux, euse [pɔpylø, -øz] *adj* densely populated.
porc [pɔʀ] *nm* (*ZOOL*) pig; (*CULIN*) pork; (*peau*) pigskin.
porcelaine [pɔʀsəlɛn] *nf* (*substance*) porcelain, china; (*objet*) piece of china(ware).
porcelet [pɔʀsəlɛ] *nm* piglet.
porc-épic, *pl* **porcs-épics** [pɔʀkepik] *nm* porcupine.
porche [pɔʀʃ(ə)] *nm* porch.
porcher, ère [pɔʀʃe, -ɛʀ] *nm/f* pig-keeper.
porcherie [pɔʀʃəʀi] *nf* pigsty.
porcin, e [pɔʀsɛ̃, -in] *adj* (*race*) porcine; (*élevage*) pig *cpd*; (*fig*) piglike.
pore [pɔʀ] *nm* pore.
poreux, euse [pɔʀø, -øz] *adj* porous.
porno [pɔʀno] *adj* porno ♦ *nm* porn.
pornographie [pɔʀnɔgʀafi] *nf* pornography.
pornographique [pɔʀnɔgʀafik] *adj* pornographic.
port [pɔʀ] *nm* (*NAVIG*) harbour (*BRIT*), harbor (*US*), port; (*ville, aussi INFORM*) port; (*de l'uniforme etc*) wearing; (*pour lettre*) postage; (*pour colis, aussi: posture*) carriage; ~ **de commerce/de pêche** commercial/fishing port; **arriver à bon ~** to arrive safe and

sound; ~ **d'arme** (*JUR*) carrying of a firearm; ~ **d'attache** (*NAVIG*) port of registry; (*fig*) home base; ~ **d'escale** port of call; ~ **franc** free port.

portable [pɔʀtabl(ə)] *adj* (*vêtement*) wearable; (*portatif*) transportable; (*téléphone*) mobile ♦ *nm* (*ordinateur*) laptop; (*téléphone*) mobile (*fam*).

portail [pɔʀtaj] *nm* gate; (*de cathédrale*) portal.

portant, e [pɔʀtɑ̃, -ɑ̃t] *adj* (*murs*) structural, supporting; (*roues*) running; **bien/mal** ~ in good/poor health.

portatif, ive [pɔʀtatif, -iv] *adj* portable.

porte [pɔʀt(ə)] *nf* door; (*de ville, forteresse, SKI*) gate; **mettre à la** ~ to throw out; **prendre la** ~ to leave, go away; **à ma/sa** ~ (*tout près*) on my/his (*ou* her) doorstep; ~ **(d'embarquement)** (*AVIAT*) (departure) gate; ~ **d'entrée** front door; ~ **à** ~ *nm* door-to-door selling; ~ **de secours** emergency exit; ~ **de service** service entrance.

porté, e [pɔʀte] *adj*: **être** ~ **à faire qch** to be apt to do sth, tend to do sth; **être** ~ **sur qch** to be partial to sth.

porte-à-faux [pɔʀtafo] *nm*: **en** ~ cantilevered; (*fig*) in an awkward position.

porte-aiguilles [pɔʀtegɥij] *nm inv* needle case.

porte-avions [pɔʀtavjɔ̃] *nm inv* aircraft carrier.

porte-bagages [pɔʀtbagaʒ] *nm inv* luggage rack (*ou* basket *etc*).

porte-bébé [pɔʀtbebe] *nm* baby sling *ou* carrier.

porte-bonheur [pɔʀtbɔnœʀ] *nm inv* lucky charm.

porte-bouteilles [pɔʀtbutɛj] *nm inv* bottle carrier; (*à casiers*) wine rack.

porte-cartes [pɔʀtəkaʀt(ə)] *nm inv* (*de cartes d'identité*) card holder; (*de cartes géographiques*) map wallet.

porte-cigarettes [pɔʀtsigaʀɛt] *nm inv* cigarette case.

porte-clefs [pɔʀtəkle] *nm inv* key ring.

porte-conteneurs [pɔʀtəkɔ̃tnœʀ] *nm inv* container ship.

porte-couteau, x [pɔʀtkuto] *nm* knife rest.

porte-crayon [pɔʀtkʀɛjɔ̃] *nm* pencil holder.

porte-documents [pɔʀtdɔkymɑ̃] *nm inv* attaché *ou* document case.

porte-drapeau, x [pɔʀtdʀapo] *nm* standard bearer.

portée [pɔʀte] *nf* (*d'une arme*) range; (*fig: importance*) impact, import; (*: capacités*) scope, capability; (*de chatte etc*) litter; (*MUS*) stave, staff (*pl* staves); **à/hors de** ~ **(de)** within/out of reach (of); **à** ~ **de (la) main** within (arm's) reach; **à** ~ **de voix** within earshot; **à la** ~ **de qn** (*fig*) at sb's level, within sb's capabilities; **à la** ~ **de toutes les bourses** to suit every pocket, within everyone's means.

portefaix [pɔʀtəfɛ] *nm inv* porter.

porte-fenêtre, *pl* **portes-fenêtres** [pɔʀtfənɛtʀ(ə)] *nf* French window.

portefeuille [pɔʀtəfœj] *nm* wallet; (*POL, BOURSE*) portfolio; **faire un lit en** ~ to make an apple-pie bed.

porte-jarretelles [pɔʀtʒaʀtɛl] *nm inv* suspender belt (*BRIT*), garter belt (*US*).

porte-jupe [pɔʀtəʒyp] *nm* skirt hanger.

portemanteau, x [pɔʀtmɑ̃to] *nm* coat rack.

porte-mine [pɔʀtəmin] *nm* propelling (*BRIT*) *ou* mechanical (*US*) pencil.

porte-monnaie [pɔʀtmɔnɛ] *nm inv* purse.

porte-parapluies [pɔʀtpaʀaplɥi] *nm inv* umbrella stand.

porte-parole [pɔʀtpaʀɔl] *nm inv* spokesperson.

porte-plume [pɔʀtəplym] *nm inv* penholder.

porter [pɔʀte] *vt* (*charge ou sac etc, aussi: fœtus*) to carry; (*sur soi: vêtement, barbe, bague*) to wear; (*fig: responsabilité etc*) to bear, carry; (*inscription, marque, titre, patronyme, suj: arbre: fruits, fleurs*) to bear; (*jugement*) to pass; (*apporter*): ~ **qch quelque part/à qn** to take sth somewhere/to sb; (*inscrire*): ~ **qch sur** to put sth down on; to enter sth in ♦ *vi* (*voix, regard, canon*) to carry; (*coup, argument*) to hit home; **se** ~ *vi* (*se sentir*): **se** ~ **bien/mal** to be well/unwell; (*aller*): **se** ~ **vers** to go towards; ~ **sur** (*peser*) to rest on; (*accent*) to fall on; (*conférence etc*) to concern; (*heurter*) to strike; **être porté à faire** to be apt *ou* inclined to do; **elle portait le nom de Rosalie** she was called Rosalie; ~ **qn au pouvoir** to bring sb to power; ~ **bonheur à qn** to bring sb luck; ~ **qn à croire** to lead sb to believe; ~ **son âge** to look one's age; ~ **un toast** to drink a toast; ~ **de l'argent au crédit d'un compte** to credit an account with some money; **se** ~ **partie civile** *to associate in a court action with the public prosecutor*; **se** ~ **garant de qch** to guarantee sth, vouch for sth; **se** ~ **candidat à la députation** ≈ to stand for Parliament (*BRIT*), ≈ run for Congress (*US*); **se faire** ~ **malade** to report sick; ~ **la main à son chapeau** to raise one's hand to one's hat; ~ **son effort sur** to direct one's efforts towards; ~ **un fait à la connaissance de qn** to bring a fact to sb's attention.

porte-savon [pɔʀtsavɔ̃] *nm* soap dish.

porte-serviettes [pɔʀtsɛʀvjɛt] *nm inv* towel rail.

portes-ouvertes [pɔʀtuvɛʀt(ə)] *adj inv*: **journée** ~ open day.

porteur, euse [pɔʀtœʀ, -øz] *adj* (*COMM*) strong, promising; (*nouvelle, chèque etc*): **être** ~ **de** to be the bearer of ♦ *nm/f* (*de messages*) bearer ♦ *nm* (*de bagages*) porter; (*COMM: de chèque*) bearer; (*: d'actions*) holder; **(avion) gros** ~ wide-bodied aircraft, jumbo (jet).

porte-voix [pɔʀtəvwa] *nm inv* megaphone, loudhailer (*BRIT*).

portier [pɔʀtje] *nm* doorman, commissionaire (*BRIT*).

portière [pɔʀtjɛʀ] *nf* door.
portillon [pɔʀtijɔ̃] *nm* gate.
portion [pɔʀsjɔ̃] *nf* (*part*) portion, share; (*partie*) portion, section.
portique [pɔʀtik] *nm* (*GYMNASTIQUE*) crossbar; (*ARCHIT*) portico; (*RAIL*) gantry.
porto [pɔʀto] *nm* port (wine).
portoricain, e [pɔʀtɔʀikɛ̃, -ɛn] *adj* Puerto Rican.
Porto Rico [pɔʀtɔʀiko] *nf* Puerto Rico.
portrait [pɔʀtʀɛ] *nm* portrait; (*photographie*) photograph; (*fig*): **elle est le ~ de sa mère** she's the image of her mother.
portraitiste [pɔʀtʀetist(ə)] *nm/f* portrait painter.
portrait-robot [pɔʀtʀeʀɔbo] *nm* Identikit ® *ou* Photo-fit ® (*BRIT*) picture.
portuaire [pɔʀtɥɛʀ] *adj* port *cpd*, harbour *cpd* (*BRIT*), harbor *cpd* (*US*).
portugais, e [pɔʀtygɛ, -ɛz] *adj* Portuguese ♦ *nm* (*LING*) Portuguese ♦ *nm/f*: **P~, e** Portuguese.
Portugal [pɔʀtygal] *nm*: **le ~** Portugal.
POS *sigle m* (= *plan d'occupation des sols*) zoning ordinances *ou* regulations.
pose [poz] *nf* (*de moquette*) laying; (*de rideaux, papier peint*) hanging; (*attitude, d'un modèle*) pose; (*PHOTO*) exposure.
posé, e [poze] *adj* calm, unruffled.
posément [pozemɑ̃] *adv* calmly.
posemètre [pozmɛtʀ(ə)] *nm* exposure meter.
poser [poze] *vt* (*déposer*): **~ qch (sur)/qn à** to put sth down (on)/drop sb at; (*placer*): **~ qch sur/quelque part** to put sth on/somewhere; (*installer: moquette, carrelage*) to lay; (*rideaux, papier peint*) to hang; (*MATH*: *chiffre*) to put (down); (*question*) to ask; (*principe, conditions*) to lay *ou* set down; (*problème*) to formulate; (*difficulté*) to pose; (*personne: mettre en valeur*) to give standing to ♦ *vi* (*modèle*) to pose; to sit; **se ~** (*oiseau, avion*) to land; (*question*) to arise; **se ~ en** to pass o.s. off as, pose as; **~ son** *ou* **un regard sur qn/qch** to turn one's gaze on sb/sth; **~ sa candidature** to apply; (*POL*) to put o.s. up for election.
poseur, euse [pozœʀ, -øz] *nm/f* (*péj*) show-off, poseur; **~ de parquets/carrelages** floor/tile layer.
positif, ive [pozitif, -iv] *adj* positive.
position [pozisjɔ̃] *nf* position; **prendre ~** (*fig*) to take a stand.
positionner [pozisjɔne] *vt* to position; (*compte en banque*) to calculate the balance of.
positivement [pozitivmɑ̃] *adv* positively.
posologie [pɔsɔlɔʒi] *nf* directions *pl* for use, dosage.
possédant, e [pɔsedɑ̃, -ɑ̃t] *adj* (*classe*) wealthy ♦ *nm/f*: **les ~s** the haves, the wealthy.
possédé, e [pɔsede] *nm/f* person possessed.
posséder [pɔsede] *vt* to own, possess; (*qualité, talent*) to have, possess; (*bien connaître: métier, langue*) to have mastered, have a thorough knowledge of; (*sexuellement, aussi: suj: colère etc*) to possess; (*fam: duper*) to take in.
possesseur [pɔsesœʀ] *nm* owner.
possessif, ive [pɔsesif, -iv] *adj, nm* (*aussi LING*) possessive.
possession [pɔsesjɔ̃] *nf* ownership *no pl*; possession; **être/entrer en ~ de qch** to be in/take possession of sth.
possibilité [pɔsibilite] *nf* possibility; **~s** *nfpl* (*moyens*) means; (*potentiel*) potential *sg*; **avoir la ~ de faire** to be in a position to do; to have the opportunity to do.
possible [pɔsibl(ə)] *adj* possible; (*projet, entreprise*) feasible ♦ *nm*: **faire son ~** to do all one can, do one's utmost; **(ce n'est) pas ~!** impossible!; **le plus/moins de livres ~** as many/few books as possible; **dès que ~** as soon as possible; **gentil** *etc* **au ~** as nice *etc* as it is possible to be.
postal, e, aux [pɔstal, -o] *adj* postal, post office *cpd*; **sac ~** mailbag, postbag.
postdater [pɔstdate] *vt* to postdate.
poste [pɔst(ə)] *nf* (*service*) post, postal service; (*administration, bureau*) post office ♦ *nm* (*fonction, MIL*) post; (*TÉL*) extension; (*de radio etc*) set; (*de budget*) item; **~s** *nfpl* post office *sg*; **P~s télécommunications et télédiffusion (PTT)** *postal and telecommunications service*; **agent** *ou* **employé des ~s** post office worker; **mettre à la ~** to post; **~ de commandement (PC)** *nm* (*MIL etc*) headquarters; **~ de contrôle** *nm* checkpoint; **~ de douane** *nm* customs post; **~ émetteur** *nm* transmitting set; **~ d'essence** *nm* filling station; **~ d'incendie** *nm* fire point; **~ de péage** *nm* tollgate; **~ de pilotage** *nm* cockpit; **~ (de police)** *nm* police station; **~ de radio** *nm* radio set; **~ restante (PR)** *nf* poste restante (*BRIT*), general delivery (*US*); **~ de secours** *nm* first-aid post; **~ de télévision** *nm* television set; **~ de travail** *nm* work station.
poster *vt* [pɔste] to post ♦ *nm* [pɔstɛʀ] poster; **se ~** to position o.s.
postérieur, e [pɔsteʀjœʀ] *adj* (*date*) later; (*partie*) back ♦ *nm* (*fam*) behind.
postérieurement [pɔsteʀjœʀmɑ̃] *adv* later, subsequently; **~ à** after.
posteriori [pɔsteʀjɔʀi]: **a ~** *adv* with hindsight, a posteriori.
postérité [pɔsteʀite] *nf* posterity.
postface [pɔstfas] *nf* appendix.
posthume [pɔstym] *adj* posthumous.
postiche [pɔstiʃ] *adj* false ♦ *nm* hairpiece.
postier, ière [pɔstje, -jɛʀ] *nm/f* post office worker.
postillon [pɔstijɔ̃] *nm*: **envoyer des ~s** to splutter.
postillonner [pɔstijɔne] *vi* to splutter.
post-natal, e [pɔstnatal] *adj* postnatal.
postopératoire [pɔstɔpeʀatwaʀ] *adj* postoperative.

postscolaire [pɔstskɔlɛʀ] *adj* further, continuing.
post-scriptum [pɔstskʀiptɔm] *nm inv* postscript.
postsynchronisation [pɔstsɛ̃kʀɔnizɑsjɔ̃] *nf* dubbing.
postsynchroniser [pɔstsɛ̃kʀɔnize] *vt* to dub.
postulant, e [pɔstylɑ̃, -ɑ̃t] *nm/f* (*candidat*) applicant; (*REL*) postulant.
postulat [pɔstyla] *nm* postulate.
postuler [pɔstyle] *vt* (*emploi*) to apply for, put in for.
posture [pɔstyʀ] *nf* posture, position; (*fig*) position.
pot [po] *nm* jar, pot; (*en plastique, carton*) carton; (*en métal*) tin; (*fam*): **avoir du** ~ to be lucky; **boire** *ou* **prendre un** ~ (*fam*) to have a drink; **découvrir le** ~ **aux roses** to find out what's been going on; ~ **catalytique** catalytic converter; ~ **(de chambre)** (chamber)pot; ~ **d'échappement** exhaust pipe; ~ **de fleurs** plant pot, flowerpot; (*plante*) pot plant; ~ **à tabac** tobacco jar.
potable [pɔtabl(ə)] *adj* (*fig: boisson*) drinkable; (*: travail, devoir*) decent; **eau (non)** ~ (not) drinking water.
potache [pɔtaʃ] *nm* schoolboy.
potage [pɔtaʒ] *nm* soup.
potager, ère [pɔtaʒe, -ɛʀ] *adj* (*plante*) edible, vegetable *cpd*; **(jardin)** ~ kitchen *ou* vegetable garden.
potasse [pɔtas] *nf* potassium hydroxide; (*engrais*) potash.
potasser [pɔtase] *vt* (*fam*) to swot up (*BRIT*), cram.
potassium [pɔtasjɔm] *nm* potassium.
pot-au-feu [pɔtofø] *nm inv* (beef) stew; (*viande*) stewing beef ♦ *adj* (*fam: personne*) stay-at-home.
pot-de-vin, *pl* **pots-de-vin** [podvɛ̃] *nm* bribe.
pote [pɔt] *nm* (*fam*) mate (*BRIT*), pal.
poteau, x [pɔto] *nm* post; ~ **de départ/arrivée** starting/finishing post; ~ **(d'exécution)** execution post, stake; ~ **indicateur** signpost; ~ **télégraphique** telegraph pole; ~**x (de but)** goal-posts.
potée [pɔte] *nf* hotpot (*of pork and cabbage*).
potelé, e [pɔtle] *adj* plump, chubby.
potence [pɔtɑ̃s] *nf* gallows *sg*; **en** ~ T-shaped.
potentat [pɔtɑ̃ta] *nm* potentate; (*fig: péj*) despot.
potentiel, le [pɔtɑ̃sjɛl] *adj, nm* potential.
potentiellement [pɔtɑ̃sjɛlmɑ̃] *adv* potentially.
poterie [pɔtʀi] *nf* (*fabrication*) pottery; (*objet*) piece of pottery.
potiche [pɔtiʃ] *nf* large vase.
potier [pɔtje] *nm* potter.
potins [pɔtɛ̃] *nmpl* gossip *sg*.
potion [posjɔ̃] *nf* potion.
potiron [pɔtiʀɔ̃] *nm* pumpkin.
pot-pourri, *pl* **pots-pourris** [popuʀi] *nm* (*MUS*) potpourri, medley.
pou, x [pu] *nm* louse (*pl* lice).
pouah [pwa] *excl* ugh!, yuk!
poubelle [pubɛl] *nf* (dust)bin.
pouce [pus] *nm* thumb; **se tourner** *ou* **se rouler les** ~**s** (*fig*) to twiddle one's thumbs; **manger sur le** ~ to eat on the run, snatch something to eat.
poudre [pudʀ(ə)] *nf* powder; (*fard*) (face) powder; (*explosif*) gunpowder; **en** ~: **café en** ~ instant coffee; **savon en** ~ soap powder; **lait en** ~ dried *ou* powdered milk; ~ **à canon** gunpowder; ~ **à éternuer** sneezing powder; ~ **à récurer** scouring powder; ~ **de riz** face powder.
poudrer [pudʀe] *vt* to powder.
poudrerie [pudʀəʀi] *nf* gunpowder factory.
poudreux, euse [pudʀø, -øz] *adj* dusty; (*neige*) powdery, powder *cpd*.
poudrier [pudʀije] *nm* (powder) compact.
poudrière [pudʀijɛʀ] *nf* powder magazine; (*fig*) powder keg.
poudroyer [pudʀwaje] *vi* to rise in clouds *ou* a flurry.
pouf [puf] *nm* pouffe.
pouffer [pufe] *vi*: ~ **(de rire)** to snigger; to giggle.
pouffiasse [pufjas] *nf* (*fam*) fat cow; (*prostituée*) tart.
pouilleux, euse [pujø, -øz] *adj* flea-ridden; (*fig*) seedy.
poulailler [pulɑje] *nm* henhouse; (*THÉÂT*): **le** ~ the gods *sg*.
poulain [pulɛ̃] *nm* foal; (*fig*) protégé.
poularde [pulaʀd(ə)] *nf* fatted chicken.
poule [pul] *nf* (*ZOOL*) hen; (*CULIN*) (boiling) fowl; (*SPORT*) (round-robin) tournament; (*RUGBY*) group; (*fam*) bird (*BRIT*), chick, broad (*US*); (*prostituée*) tart; ~ **d'eau** moorhen; ~ **mouillée** coward; ~ **pondeuse** laying hen, layer; ~ **au riz** chicken and rice.
poulet [pulɛ] *nm* chicken; (*fam*) cop.
poulette [pulɛt] *nf* (*jeune poule*) pullet.
pouliche [puliʃ] *nf* filly.
poulie [puli] *nf* pulley.
poulpe [pulp(ə)] *nm* octopus.
pouls [pu] *nm* pulse (*ANAT*); **prendre le** ~ **de qn** to feel sb's pulse.
poumon [pumɔ̃] *nm* lung; ~ **d'acier** *ou* **artificiel** iron *ou* artificial lung.
poupe [pup] *nf* stern; **en** ~ astern.
poupée [pupe] *nf* doll; **jouer à la** ~ to play with one's doll (*ou* dolls); **de** ~ (*très petit*): **jardin de** ~ doll's garden, pocket-handkerchief-sized garden.
poupin, e [pupɛ̃, -in] *adj* chubby.
poupon [pupɔ̃] *nm* babe-in-arms.
pouponner [pupɔne] *vi* to fuss (around).
pouponnière [pupɔnjɛʀ] *nf* crèche, day nursery.
pour [puʀ] *prép* for ♦ *nm*: **le** ~ **et le contre** the pros and cons; ~ **faire** (so as) to do, in order to do; ~ **avoir fait** for having done; ~ **que** so

that, in order that; ~ **moi** (*à mon avis, pour ma part*) for my part, personally; ~ **riche qu'il soit** rich though he may be; ~ **30 euros d'essence** 30 euros' worth of petrol; ~ **cent** per cent; ~ **ce qui est de** as for; **y être** ~ **quelque chose** to have something to do with it.

pourboire [puRbwaR] *nm* tip.

pourcentage [puRsɑ̃taʒ] *nm* percentage; **travailler au** ~ to work on commission.

pourchasser [puRʃase] *vt* to pursue.

pourfendeur [puRfɑ̃dœR] *nm* sworn opponent.

pourfendre [puRfɑ̃dR(ə)] *vt* to assail.

pourlécher [puRleʃe]: **se** ~ *vi* to lick one's lips.

pourparlers [puRparle] *nmpl* talks, negotiations; **être en** ~ **avec** to be having talks with.

pourpre [puRpR(ə)] *adj* crimson.

pourquoi [puRkwa] *adv, conj* why ♦ *nm inv*: **le** ~ **(de)** the reason (for).

pourrai [puRe] *etc vb voir* **pouvoir**.

pourri, e [puRi] *adj* rotten; (*roche, pierre*) crumbling; (*temps, climat*) filthy, foul ♦ *nm*: **sentir le** ~ to smell rotten.

pourrir [puRiR] *vi* to rot; (*fruit*) to go rotten *ou* bad; (*fig: situation*) to deteriorate ♦ *vt* to rot; (*fig: corrompre: personne*) to corrupt; (*: gâter: enfant*) to spoil thoroughly.

pourrissement [puRismɑ̃] *nm* deterioration.

pourriture [puRityR] *nf* rot.

pourrons [puRɔ̃] *etc vb voir* **pouvoir**.

poursuis [puRsɥi] *etc vb voir* **poursuivre**.

poursuite [puRsɥit] *nf* pursuit, chase; ~**s** *nfpl* (*JUR*) legal proceedings; **(course)** ~ track race; (*fig*) chase.

poursuivant, e [puRsɥivɑ̃, -ɑ̃t] *vb voir* **poursuivre** ♦ *nm/f* pursuer; (*JUR*) plaintiff.

poursuivre [puRsɥivR(ə)] *vt* to pursue, chase (after); (*relancer*) to hound, harry; (*obséder*) to haunt; (*JUR*) to bring proceedings against, prosecute; (*: au civil*) to sue; (*but*) to strive towards; (*voyage, études*) to carry on with, continue ♦ *vi* to carry on, go on; **se** ~ *vi* to go on, continue.

pourtant [puRtɑ̃] *adv* yet; **mais** ~ but nevertheless, but even so; **c'est** ~ **facile** (and) yet it's easy.

pourtour [puRtuR] *nm* perimeter.

pourvoi [puRvwa] *nm* appeal.

pourvoir [puRvwaR] *nm* (*COMM*) supply ♦ *vt*: ~ **qch/qn de** to equip sth/sb with ♦ *vi*: ~ **à** to provide for; (*emploi*) to fill; **se** ~ (*JUR*): **se** ~ **en cassation** to take one's case to the Court of Appeal.

pourvoyeur, euse [puRvwajœR, -øz] *nm/f* supplier.

pourvu, e [puRvy] *pp de* **pourvoir** ♦ *adj*: ~ **de** equipped with; ~ **que** *conj* (*si*) provided that, so long as; (*espérons que*) let's hope (that).

pousse [pus] *nf* growth; (*bourgeon*) shoot.

poussé, e [puse] *adj* sophisticated, advanced; (*moteur*) souped-up.

pousse-café [puskafe] *nm inv* (after-dinner) liqueur.

poussée [puse] *nf* thrust; (*coup*) push; (*MÉD*) eruption; (*fig*) upsurge.

pousse-pousse [puspus] *nm inv* rickshaw.

pousser [puse] *vt* to push; (*inciter*): ~ **qn à** to urge *ou* press sb to + *infinitif*; (*acculer*): ~ **qn à** to drive sb to; (*moteur, voiture*) to drive hard; (*émettre: cri etc*) to give; (*stimuler*) to urge on; to drive hard; (*poursuivre*) to carry on ♦ *vi* to push; (*croître*) to grow; (*aller*): ~ **plus loin** to push on a bit further; **se** ~ *vi* to move over; **faire** ~ (*plante*) to grow; ~ **le dévouement** *etc* **jusqu'à** ... to take devotion *etc* as far as ....

poussette [pusɛt] *nf* (*voiture d'enfant*) pushchair (*BRIT*), stroller (*US*).

poussette-canne, *pl* **poussettes-cannes** [pusɛtkan] *nf* baby buggy (*BRIT*), (folding) stroller (*US*).

poussier [pusje] *nm* coaldust.

poussière [pusjɛR] *nf* dust; (*grain*) speck of dust; **et des** ~**s** (*fig*) and a bit; ~ **de charbon** coaldust.

poussiéreux, euse [pusjeRø, -øz] *adj* dusty.

poussif, ive [pusif, -iv] *adj* wheezy, wheezing.

poussin [pusɛ̃] *nm* chick.

poussoir [puswaR] *nm* button.

poutre [putR(ə)] *nf* beam; (*en fer, ciment armé*) girder; ~**s apparentes** exposed beams.

poutrelle [putRɛl] *nf* (*petite poutre*) small beam; (*barre d'acier*) girder.

MOT-CLÉ

pouvoir [puvwaR] *nm* power; (*POL: dirigeants*): **le** ~ those in power; **les** ~**s publics** the authorities; **avoir** ~ **de faire** (*autorisation*) to have (the) authority to do; (*droit*) to have the right to do; ~ **absolu** absolute power; ~ **absorbant** absorbency; ~ **d'achat** purchasing power; ~ **calorifique** calorific value

♦ *vb semi-aux* **1** (*être en état de*) can, be able to; **je ne peux pas le réparer** I can't *ou* I am not able to repair it; **déçu de ne pas** ~ **le faire** disappointed not to be able to do it

2 (*avoir la permission*) can, may, be allowed to; **vous pouvez aller au cinéma** you can *or* may go to the pictures

3 (*probabilité, hypothèse*) may, might, could; **il a pu avoir un accident** he may *ou* might *or* could have had an accident; **il aurait pu le dire!** he might *ou* could have said (so)!

4 (*expressions*): **tu ne peux pas savoir!** you have no idea!; **tu peux le dire!** you can say that again!

♦ *vb impers* may, might, could; **il peut arriver que** it may *ou* might *ou* could happen that; **il pourrait pleuvoir** it might rain

♦ *vt* **1** can, be able to; **j'ai fait tout ce que j'ai pu** I did all I could; **je n'en peux plus** (*épuisé*) I'm exhausted; (*à bout*) I can't take

any more
2 (*vb +adj ou adv comparatif*): **je me porte on ne peut mieux** I'm absolutely fine, I couldn't be better; **elle est on ne peut plus gentille** she couldn't be nicer, she's as nice as can be
se ~ *vi*: **il se peut que** it may *ou* might be that; **cela se pourrait** that's quite possible.

PP *sigle f* (= *préventive de la pellagre: vitamine*) niacin ♦ *abr* (= *pages*) pp.
p.p. *abr* (= *par procuration*) p.p.
p.p.c.m. *sigle m* (*MATH*: = *plus petit commun multiple*) LCM (= *lowest common multiple*).
PQ *sigle f* (*Canada*: = *province de Québec*) PQ.
PR *sigle m* = *parti républicain* ♦ *sigle f* = **poste restante**.
pr *abr* = **pour**.
pragmatique [pʀagmatik] *adj* pragmatic.
pragmatisme [pʀagmatism(ə)] *nm* pragmatism.
Prague [pʀag] *n* Prague.
prairie [pʀeʀi] *nf* meadow.
praline [pʀalin] *nf* (*bonbon*) sugared almond; (*au chocolat*) praline.
praliné, e [pʀaline] *adj* (*amande*) sugared; (*chocolat, glace*) praline *cpd*.
praticable [pʀatikabl(ə)] *adj* (*route etc*) passable, practicable; (*projet*) practicable.
praticien, ne [pʀatisjɛ̃, -ɛn] *nm/f* practitioner.
pratiquant, e [pʀatikɑ̃, -ɑ̃t] *adj* practising (*BRIT*), practicing (*US*).
pratique [pʀatik] *nf* practice ♦ *adj* practical; (*commode: horaire etc*) convenient; (*: outil*) handy, useful; **dans la ~** in (actual) practice; **mettre en ~** to put into practice.
pratiquement [pʀatikmɑ̃] *adv* (*dans la pratique*) in practice; (*pour ainsi dire*) practically, virtually.
pratiquer [pʀatike] *vt* to practise (*BRIT*), practice (*US*); (*SPORT etc*) to go in for, play; (*appliquer: méthode, théorie*) to apply; (*intervention, opération*) to carry out; (*ouverture, abri*) to make ♦ *vi* (*REL*) to be a churchgoer.
pré [pʀe] *nm* meadow.
préados [pʀeado] *nmpl* preteens.
préalable [pʀealabl(ə)] *adj* preliminary; **condition ~ (de)** precondition (for), prerequisite (for); **sans avis ~** without prior *ou* previous notice; **au ~** first, beforehand.
préalablement [pʀealabləmɑ̃] *adv* first, beforehand.
Préalpes [pʀealp(ə)] *nfpl*: **les ~** the Pre-Alps.
préalpin, e [pʀealpɛ̃, -in] *adj* of the Pre-Alps.
préambule [pʀeɑ̃byl] *nm* preamble; (*fig*) prelude; **sans ~** straight away.
préau, x [pʀeo] *nm* (*d'une cour d'école*) covered playground; (*d'un monastère, d'une prison*) inner courtyard.
préavis [pʀeavi] *nm* notice; **~ de congé** notice; **communication avec ~** (*TÉL*) personal *ou* person-to-person call.
prébende [pʀebɑ̃d] *nf* (*péj*) remuneration.
précaire [pʀekɛʀ] *adj* precarious.
précaution [pʀekosjɔ̃] *nf* precaution; **avec ~** cautiously; **prendre des** *ou* **ses ~s** to take precautions; **par ~** as a precaution; **pour plus de ~** to be on the safe side; **~s oratoires** carefully phrased remarks.
précautionneux, euse [pʀekosjɔnø, -øz] *adj* cautious, careful.
précédemment [pʀesedamɑ̃] *adv* before, previously.
précédent, e [pʀesedɑ̃, -ɑ̃t] *adj* previous ♦ *nm* precedent; **sans ~** unprecedented; **le jour ~** the day before, the previous day.
précéder [pʀesede] *vt* to precede; (*marcher ou rouler devant*) to be in front of; (*arriver avant*) to get ahead of.
précepte [pʀesɛpt(ə)] *nm* precept.
précepteur, trice [pʀesɛptœʀ, -tʀis] *nm/f* (private) tutor.
préchauffer [pʀeʃofe] *vt* to preheat.
prêcher [pʀeʃe] *vt, vi* to preach.
prêcheur, euse [pʀɛʃœʀ, -øz] *adj* moralizing ♦ *nm/f* (*REL*) preacher; (*fig*) moralizer.
précieusement [pʀesjøzmɑ̃] *adv* (*avec soin*) carefully; (*avec préciosité*) preciously.
précieux, euse [pʀesjø, -øz] *adj* precious; (*collaborateur, conseils*) invaluable; (*style, écrivain*) précieux, precious.
préciosité [pʀesjozite] *nf* preciosity, preciousness.
précipice [pʀesipis] *nm* drop, chasm; (*fig*) abyss; **au bord du ~** at the edge of the precipice.
précipitamment [pʀesipitamɑ̃] *adv* hurriedly, hastily.
précipitation [pʀesipitɑsjɔ̃] *nf* (*hâte*) haste; **~s (atmosphériques)** *nfpl* precipitation *sg*.
précipité, e [pʀesipite] *adj* (*respiration*) fast; (*pas*) hurried; (*départ*) hasty.
précipiter [pʀesipite] *vt* (*faire tomber*): **~ qn/qch du haut de** to throw *ou* hurl sb/sth off *ou* from; (*hâter: marche*) to quicken; (*: départ*) to hasten; **se ~** *vi* (*événements*) to move faster; (*respiration*) to speed up; **se ~ sur/vers** to rush at/towards; **se ~ au-devant de qn** to throw o.s. before sb.
précis, e [pʀesi, -iz] *adj* precise; (*tir, mesures*) accurate, precise ♦ *nm* handbook.
précisément [pʀesizemɑ̃] *adv* precisely; **ma vie n'est pas ~ distrayante** my life is not exactly entertaining.
préciser [pʀesize] *vt* (*expliquer*) to be more specific about, clarify; (*spécifier*) to state, specify; **se ~** *vi* to become clear(er).
précision [pʀesizjɔ̃] *nf* precision; accuracy; (*détail*) point *ou* detail (*made clear or to be clarified*); **~s** *nfpl* further details.
précoce [pʀekɔs] *adj* early; (*enfant*) precocious; (*calvitie*) premature.
précocité [pʀekɔsite] *nf* earliness; precociousness.
préconçu, e [pʀekɔ̃sy] *adj* preconceived.

préconiser [prekɔnize] *vt* to advocate.
précontraint, e [prekɔ̃trɛ̃, -ɛ̃t] *adj*: **béton ~** prestressed concrete.
précuit, e [prekɥi, -it] *adj* precooked.
précurseur [prekyrsœr] *adj m* precursory ♦ *nm* forerunner, precursor.
prédateur [predatœr] *nm* predator.
prédécesseur [predesesœr] *nm* predecessor.
prédécoupé, e [predekupe] *adj* pre-cut.
prédestiner [predɛstine] *vt*: **~ qn à qch/à faire** to predestine sb for sth/to do.
prédicateur [predikatœr] *nm* preacher.
prédiction [prediksjɔ̃] *nf* prediction.
prédilection [predilɛksjɔ̃] *nf*: **avoir une ~ pour** to be partial to; **de ~** favourite (*BRIT*), favorite (*US*).
prédire [predir] *vt* to predict.
prédisposer [predispoze] *vt*: **~ qn à qch/à faire** to predispose sb to sth/to do.
prédisposition [predispozisjɔ̃] *nf* predisposition.
prédit, e [predi, -it] *pp de* **prédire**.
prédominance [predɔminɑ̃s] *nf* predominance.
prédominant, e [predɔminɑ̃, -ɑ̃t] *adj* predominant; prevailing.
prédominer [predɔmine] *vi* to predominate; (*avis*) to prevail.
pré-électoral, e, aux [preelɛktɔral, -o] *adj* pre-election *cpd*.
pré-emballé, e [preɑ̃bale] *adj* pre-packed.
prééminent, e [preeminɑ̃, -ɑ̃t] *adj* preeminent.
préemption [preɑ̃psjɔ̃] *nf*: **droit de ~** (*JUR*) pre-emptive right.
pré-encollé, e [preɑ̃kɔle] *adj* pre-pasted.
préétabli, e [preetabli] *adj* pre-established.
préexistant, e [preɛgzistɑ̃, -ɑ̃t] *adj* preexisting.
préfabriqué, e [prefabrike] *adj* prefabricated; (*péj*: *sourire*) artificial ♦ *nm* prefabricated material.
préface [prefas] *nf* preface.
préfacer [prefase] *vt* to write a preface for.
préfectoral, e, aux [prefɛktɔral, -o] *adj* prefectorial.
préfecture [prefɛktyr] *nf* prefecture; **~ de police** police headquarters *pl*; *see boxed note*.

> **PRÉFECTURE**
>
> *The* **préfecture** *is the administrative headquarters of the 'département'. The 'préfet', a senior civil servant appointed by the Government, is responsible for putting government policy into practice. France's 22 regions, each comprising a number of 'départements', also have a 'préfet de région'.*

préférable [preferabl(ə)] *adj* preferable.
préféré, e [prefere] *adj, nm/f* favourite (*BRIT*), favorite (*US*).
préférence [preferɑ̃s] *nf* preference; **de ~** preferably; **de** *ou* **par ~ à** in preference to, rather than; **donner la ~ à qn** to give preference to sb; **par ordre de ~** in order of preference; **obtenir la ~ sur** to have preference over.
préférentiel, le [preferɑ̃sjɛl] *adj* preferential.
préférer [prefere] *vt*: **~ qn/qch (à)** to prefer sb/sth (to), like sb/sth better (than); **~ faire** to prefer to do; **je préférerais du thé** I would rather have tea, I'd prefer tea.
préfet [prefɛ] *nm* prefect; **~ de police** ≈ Chief Constable (*BRIT*), ≈ Police Commissioner (*US*).
préfigurer [prefigyre] *vt* to prefigure.
préfixe [prefiks(ə)] *nm* prefix.
préhistoire [preistwar] *nf* prehistory.
préhistorique [preistɔrik] *adj* prehistoric.
préjudice [preʒydis] *nm* (*matériel*) loss; (*moral*) harm *no pl*; **porter ~ à** to harm, be detrimental to; **au ~ de** at the expense of.
préjudiciable [preʒydisjabl(ə)] *adj*: **~ à** prejudicial *ou* harmful to.
préjugé [preʒyʒe] *nm* prejudice; **avoir un ~ contre** to be prejudiced against; **bénéficier d'un ~ favorable** to be viewed favourably.
préjuger [preʒyʒe]: **~ de** *vt* to prejudge.
prélasser [prelɑse]: **se ~** *vi* to lounge.
prélat [prela] *nm* prelate.
prélavage [prelavaʒ] *nm* pre-wash.
prélèvement [prelɛvmɑ̃] *nm* deduction; withdrawal; **faire un ~ de sang** to take a blood sample.
prélever [prelve] *vt* (*échantillon*) to take; (*argent*): **~ (sur)** to deduct (from); (*: sur son compte*): **~ (sur)** to withdraw (from).
préliminaire [preliminɛr] *adj* preliminary; **~s** *nmpl* preliminaries; (*négociations*) preliminary talks.
prélude [prelyd] *nm* prelude; (*avant le concert*) warm-up.
prématuré, e [prematyre] *adj* premature; (*retraite*) early ♦ *nm* premature baby.
prématurément [prematyremɑ̃] *adv* prematurely.
préméditation [premeditɑsjɔ̃] *nf*: **avec ~** *adj* premeditated ♦ *adv* with intent.
préméditer [premedite] *vt* to premeditate, plan.
prémices [premis] *nfpl* beginnings.
premier, ière [prəmje, -jɛr] *adj* first; (*branche, marche, grade*) bottom; (*fig: fondamental*) basic; prime; (*en importance*) first, foremost ♦ *nm* (*~ étage*) first (*BRIT*) *ou* second (*US*) floor ♦ *nf* (*AUTO*) first (gear); (*RAIL, AVIAT etc*) first class; (*SCOL: classe*) *penultimate school year (age 16-17)*; (*THÉÂT*) first night; (*CINÉ*) première; (*exploit*) first; **au ~ abord** at first sight; **au** *ou* **du ~ coup** at the first attempt *ou* go; **de ~ ordre** first-class, first-rate; **de première qualité, de ~ choix** best *ou* top quality; **de première importance** of the highest importance; **de première nécessité** abso-

lutely essential; **le ~ venu** the first person to come along; **jeune ~** leading man; **le ~ de l'an** New Year's Day; **enfant du ~ lit** child of a first marriage; **en ~ lieu** in the first place; **~ âge** (*d'un enfant*) the first 3 months (of life); **P~ Ministre** Prime Minister.
premièrement [pʀəmjɛʀmɑ̃] *adv* firstly.
première-née, *pl* **premières-nées** [pʀəmjɛʀne] *nf* first-born.
premier-né, *pl* **premiers-nés** [pʀəmjene] *nm* first-born.
prémisse [pʀemis] *nf* premise.
prémolaire [pʀemɔlɛʀ] *nf* premolar.
prémonition [pʀemɔnisjɔ̃] *nf* premonition.
prémonitoire [pʀemɔnitwaʀ] *adj* premonitory.
prémunir [pʀemyniʀ]: **se ~** *vi*: **se ~ contre** to protect o.s. from, guard against.
prenant, e [pʀənɑ̃, -ɑ̃t] *vb voir* **prendre** ♦ *adj* absorbing, engrossing.
prénatal, e [pʀenatal] *adj* (*MÉD*) antenatal; (*allocation*) maternity *cpd*.
prendre [pʀɑ̃dʀ(ə)] *vt* to take; (*ôter*): **~ qch à** to take sth from; (*aller chercher*) to get, fetch; (*se procurer*) to get; (*réserver: place*) to book; (*acquérir: du poids, de la valeur*) to put on, gain; (*malfaiteur, poisson*) to catch; (*passager*) to pick up; (*personnel, aussi: couleur, goût*) to take on; (*locataire*) to take in; (*traiter: enfant, problème*) to handle; (*voix, ton*) to put on; (*prélever: pourcentage, argent*) to take off; (*coincer*): **se ~ les doigts dans** to get one's fingers caught in ♦ *vi* (*liquide, ciment*) to set; (*greffe, vaccin*) to take; (*mensonge*) to be successful; (*feu: foyer*) to go; (*: incendie*) to start; (*allumette*) to light; (*se diriger*): **~ à gauche** to turn (to the) left; **~ son origine** *ou* **sa source** (*mot, rivière*) to have its source; **~ qn pour** to take sb for; **se ~ pour** to think one is; **~ sur soi de faire qch** to take it upon o.s. to do sth; **~ qn en sympathie/horreur** to get to like/loathe sb; **à tout ~** all things considered; **s'en ~ à** (*agresser*) to set about; (*passer sa colère sur*) to take it out on; (*critiquer*) to attack; (*remettre en question*) to challenge; **se ~ d'amitié/d'affection pour** to befriend/become fond of; **s'y ~** (*procéder*) to set about it; **s'y ~ à l'avance** to see to it in advance; **s'y ~ à deux fois** to try twice, make two attempts.
preneur [pʀənœʀ] *nm*: **être ~** to be willing to buy; **trouver ~** to find a buyer.
prénom [pʀenɔ̃] *nm* first name.
prénommer [pʀenɔme] *vt*: **elle se prénomme Claude** her (first) name is Claude.
prénuptial, e, aux [pʀenypsjal, -o] *adj* premarital.
préoccupant, e [pʀeɔkypɑ̃, -ɑ̃t] *adj* worrying.
préoccupation [pʀeɔkypɑsjɔ̃] *nf* (*souci*) concern; (*idée fixe*) preoccupation.
préoccupé, e [pʀeɔkype] *adj* concerned; preoccupied.
préoccuper [pʀeɔkype] *vt* (*tourmenter, tracasser*) to concern; (*absorber, obséder*) to preoccupy; **se ~ de qch** to be concerned about sth; to show concern about sth.
préparateur, trice [pʀepaʀatœʀ, -tʀis] *nm/f* assistant.
préparatifs [pʀepaʀatif] *nmpl* preparations.
préparation [pʀepaʀɑsjɔ̃] *nf* preparation; (*SCOL*) piece of homework.
préparatoire [pʀepaʀatwaʀ] *adj* preparatory.
préparer [pʀepaʀe] *vt* to prepare; (*café, repas*) to make; (*examen*) to prepare for; (*voyage, entreprise*) to plan; **se ~** *vi* (*orage, tragédie*) to brew, be in the air; **se ~ (à qch/à faire)** to prepare (o.s.) *ou* get ready (for sth/to do); **~ qch à qn** (*surprise etc*) to have sth in store for sb; **~ qn à qch** (*nouvelle etc*) to prepare sb for sth.
prépondérance [pʀepɔ̃deʀɑ̃s] *nf*: **~ (sur)** predominance (over).
prépondérant, e [pʀepɔ̃deʀɑ̃, -ɑ̃t] *adj* major, dominating; **voix ~e** casting vote.
préposé, e [pʀepoze] *adj*: **~ à** in charge of ♦ *nm/f* (*gén: employé*) employee; (*ADMIN: facteur*) postman/woman (*BRIT*), mailman/woman (*US*); (*de la douane etc*) official; (*de vestiaire*) attendant.
préposer [pʀepoze] *vt*: **~ qn à qch** to appoint sb to sth.
préposition [pʀepozisjɔ̃] *nf* preposition.
prérentrée [pʀeʀɑ̃tʀe] *nf in-service training period before start of school term.*
préretraite [pʀeʀətʀɛt] *nf* early retirement.
prérogative [pʀeʀɔgativ] *nf* prerogative.
près [pʀɛ] *adv* near, close; **~ de** *prép* near (to), close to; (*environ*) nearly, almost; **de ~** *adv* closely; **à 5 kg ~** to within about 5 kg; **à cela ~ que** apart from the fact that; **je ne suis pas ~ de lui pardonner** I'm nowhere near ready to forgive him; **on n'est pas à un jour ~** one day (either way) won't make any difference, we're not going to quibble over the odd day.
présage [pʀezaʒ] *nm* omen.
présager [pʀezaʒe] *vt* (*prévoir*) to foresee; (*annoncer*) to portend.
pré-salé, *pl* **prés-salés** [pʀesale] *nm* (*CULIN*) salt-meadow lamb.
presbyte [pʀɛsbit] *adj* long-sighted (*BRIT*), far-sighted (*US*).
presbytère [pʀɛsbitɛʀ] *nm* presbytery.
presbytérien, ne [pʀɛsbiteʀjɛ̃, -ɛn] *adj, nm/f* Presbyterian.
presbytie [pʀɛsbisi] *nf* long-sightedness (*BRIT*), far-sightedness (*US*).
prescience [pʀesjɑ̃s] *nf* prescience, foresight.
préscolaire [pʀeskɔlɛʀ] *adj* preschool *cpd*.
prescription [pʀɛskʀipsjɔ̃] *nf* (*instruction*) order, instruction; (*MÉD, JUR*) prescription.
prescrire [pʀɛskʀiʀ] *vt* to prescribe; **se ~** *vi* (*JUR*) to lapse.
prescrit, e [pʀɛskʀi, -it] *pp de* **prescrire** ♦ *adj* (*date etc*) stipulated.

préséance [preseɑ̃s] *nf* precedence *no pl.*
présélection [preselɛksjɔ̃] *nf* (*de candidats*) short-listing; **effectuer une ~** to draw up a shortlist.
présélectionner [preselɛksjɔne] *vt* to preselect; (*dispositif*) to preset; (*candidats*) to make an initial selection from among, short-list (*BRIT*).
présence [prezɑ̃s] *nf* presence; (*au bureau etc*) attendance; **en ~** face to face; **en ~ de** in (the) presence of; (*fig*) in the face of; **faire acte de ~** to put in a token appearance; **~ d'esprit** presence of mind.
présent, e [prezɑ̃, -ɑ̃t] *adj, nm* present; (*ADMIN, COMM*): **la ~e lettre/loi** this letter/law ♦ *nm/f*: **les ~s** (*personnes*) those present ♦ *nf* (*COMM: lettre*): **la ~e** this letter; **à ~** now, at present; **dès à ~** here and now; **jusqu'à ~** up till now, until now; **à ~ que** now that.
présentable [prezɑ̃tabl(ə)] *adj* presentable.
présentateur, trice [prezɑ̃tatœr, -tris] *nm/f* presenter.
présentation [prezɑ̃tasjɔ̃] *nf* presentation; introduction; (*allure*) appearance.
présenter [prezɑ̃te] *vt* to present; (*invité, candidat*) to introduce; (*félicitations, condoléances*) to offer; (*montrer: billet, pièce d'identité*) to show, produce; (*faire inscrire: candidat*) to put forward; (*soumettre*) to submit ♦ *vi*: **~ mal/bien** to have an unattractive/a pleasing appearance; **se ~** *vi* (*sur convocation*) to report, come; (*se faire connaître*) to come forward; (*à une élection*) to stand; (*occasion*) to arise; **se ~ à un examen** to sit an exam; **se ~ bien/mal** to look good/not too good.
présentoir [prezɑ̃twar] *nm* (*étagère*) display shelf (*pl* shelves); (*vitrine*) showcase; (*étal*) display stand.
préservatif [prezɛrvatif] *nm* condom, sheath.
préservation [prezɛrvasjɔ̃] *nf* protection, preservation.
préserver [prezɛrve] *vt*: **~ de** (*protéger*) to protect from; (*sauver*) to save from.
présidence [prezidɑ̃s] *nf* presidency; chairmanship.
président [prezidɑ̃] *nm* (*POL*) president; (*d'une assemblée, COMM*) chairman; **~ directeur général (PDG)** chairman and managing director (*BRIT*), chairman and president (*US*); **~ du jury** (*JUR*) foreman of the jury; (*d'examen*) chief examiner.
présidente [prezidɑ̃t] *nf* president; (*femme du président*) president's wife; (*d'une réunion*) chairwoman.
présidentiable [prezidɑ̃sjabl(ə)] *adj, nm/f* potential president.
présidentiel, le [prezidɑ̃sjɛl] *adj* presidential; **~les** *nfpl* presidential election(s).
présider [prezide] *vt* to preside over; (*dîner*) to be the guest of honour (*BRIT*) *ou* honor (*US*) at; **~ à** *vt* to direct; to govern.
présomption [prezɔ̃psjɔ̃] *nf* presumption.
présomptueux, euse [prezɔ̃ptɥø, -øz] *adj* presumptuous.
presque [prɛsk(ə)] *adv* almost, nearly; **~ rien** hardly anything; **~ pas** hardly (at all); **~ pas de** hardly any; **personne, ou ~** next to nobody, hardly anyone; **la ~ totalité (de)** almost *ou* nearly all.
presqu'île [prɛskil] *nf* peninsula.
pressant, e [prɛsɑ̃, -ɑ̃t] *adj* urgent; (*personne*) insistent; **se faire ~** to become insistent.
presse [prɛs] *nf* press; (*affluence*): **heures de ~** busy times; **sous ~** gone to press; **mettre sous ~** to send to press; **avoir une bonne/mauvaise ~** to have a good/bad press; **~ féminine** women's magazines *pl*; **~ d'information** quality newspapers *pl*.
pressé, e [prese] *adj* in a hurry; (*air*) hurried; (*besogne*) urgent ♦ *nm*: **aller au plus ~** to see to first things first; **être ~ de faire qch** to be in a hurry to do sth; **orange ~e** freshly squeezed orange juice.
presse-citron [prɛssitrɔ̃] *nm inv* lemon squeezer.
presse-fruits [prɛsfrɥi] *nm inv* lemon squeezer.
pressentiment [presɑ̃timɑ̃] *nm* foreboding, premonition.
pressentir [presɑ̃tir] *vt* to sense; (*prendre contact avec*) to approach.
presse-papiers [prɛspapje] *nm inv* paperweight.
presse-purée [prɛspyre] *nm inv* potato masher.
presser [prese] *vt* (*fruit, éponge*) to squeeze; (*interrupteur, bouton*) to press, push; (*allure, affaire*) to speed up; (*débiteur etc*) to press; (*inciter*): **~ qn de faire** to urge *ou* press sb to do ♦ *vi* to be urgent; **se ~** (*se hâter*) to hurry (up); (*se grouper*) to crowd; **rien ne presse** there's no hurry; **se ~ contre qn** to squeeze up against sb; **~ le pas** to quicken one's step; **~ qn entre ses bras** to squeeze sb tight.
pressing [presiŋ] *nm* (*repassage*) steam-pressing; (*magasin*) dry-cleaner's.
pression [prɛsjɔ̃] *nf* pressure; (*bouton*) press stud (*BRIT*), snap fastener; **faire ~ sur** to put pressure on; **sous ~** pressurized, under pressure; (*fig*) keyed up; **~ artérielle** blood pressure.
pressoir [prɛswar] *nm* (wine *ou* oil *etc*) press.
pressurer [presyre] *vt* (*fig*) to squeeze.
pressurisé, e [presyrize] *adj* pressurized.
prestance [prɛstɑ̃s] *nf* presence, imposing bearing.
prestataire [prɛstatɛr] *nm/f* person receiving benefits; (*COMM*): **~ de services** provider of services.
prestation [prɛstasjɔ̃] *nf* (*allocation*) benefit; (*d'une assurance*) cover *no pl*; (*d'une entreprise*) service provided; (*d'un joueur, artiste*)

performance; ~ **de serment** taking the oath; ~ **de service** provision of a service; ~**s familiales** ≈ child benefit.

preste [pʀɛst(ə)] *adj* nimble.

prestement [pʀɛstəmɑ̃] *adv* nimbly.

prestidigitateur, trice [pʀɛstidiʒitatœʀ, -tʀis] *nm/f* conjurer.

prestidigitation [pʀɛstidiʒitɑsjɔ̃] *nf* conjuring.

prestige [pʀɛstiʒ] *nm* prestige.

prestigieux, euse [pʀɛstiʒjø, -øz] *adj* prestigious.

présumer [pʀezyme] *vt*: ~ **que** to presume *ou* assume that; ~ **de** to overrate; ~ **qn coupable** to presume sb guilty.

présupposé [pʀesypoze] *nm* presupposition.

présupposer [pʀesypoze] *vt* to presuppose.

présupposition [pʀesypozisjɔ̃] *nf* presupposition.

présure [pʀezyʀ] *nf* rennet.

prêt, e [pʀɛ, pʀɛt] *adj* ready ♦ *nm* lending *no pl*; (*somme prêtée*) loan; ~ **à faire** ready to do; ~ **à tout** ready for anything; ~ **sur gages** pawnbroking *no pl*.

prêt-à-porter, *pl* **prêts-à-porter** [pʀɛtapɔʀte] *nm* ready-to-wear *ou* off-the-peg (*BRIT*) clothes *pl*.

prétendant [pʀetɑ̃dɑ̃] *nm* pretender; (*d'une femme*) suitor.

prétendre [pʀetɑ̃dʀ(ə)] *vt* (*affirmer*): ~ **que** to claim that; (*avoir l'intention de*): ~ **faire qch** to mean *ou* intend to do sth; ~ **à** *vt* (*droit, titre*) to lay claim to.

prétendu, e [pʀetɑ̃dy] *adj* (*supposé*) so-called.

prétendument [pʀetɑ̃dymɑ̃] *adv* allegedly.

prête-nom [pʀɛtnɔ̃] *nm* (*péj*) figurehead; (*COMM etc*) dummy.

prétentieux, euse [pʀetɑ̃sjø, -øz] *adj* pretentious.

prétention [pʀetɑ̃sjɔ̃] *nf* pretentiousness; (*exigence, ambition*) claim; **sans** ~ unpretentious.

prêter [pʀete] *vt* (*livres, argent*): ~ **qch (à)** to lend sth (to); (*supposer*): ~ **à qn** (*caractère, propos*) to attribute to sb ♦ *vi* (*aussi*: **se** ~: *tissu, cuir*) to give; ~ **à** (*commentaires etc*) to be open to, give rise to; **se** ~ **à** to lend o.s. (*ou* itself) to; (*manigances etc*) to go along with; ~ **assistance à** to give help to; ~ **attention** to pay attention; ~ **serment** to take the oath; ~ **l'oreille** to listen.

prêteur, euse [pʀɛtœʀ, -øz] *nm/f* moneylender; ~ **sur gages** pawnbroker.

prétexte [pʀetɛkst(ə)] *nm* pretext, excuse; **sous aucun** ~ on no account; **sous (le)** ~ **que/de** on the pretext that/of.

prétexter [pʀetɛkste] *vt* to give as a pretext *ou* an excuse.

prêtre [pʀɛtʀ(ə)] *nm* priest.

prêtre-ouvrier, *pl* **prêtres-ouvriers** [pʀɛtʀuvʀije] *nm* worker-priest.

prêtrise [pʀɛtʀiz] *nf* priesthood.

preuve [pʀœv] *nf* proof; (*indice*) proof, evidence *no pl*; **jusqu'à** ~ **du contraire** until proved otherwise; **faire** ~ **de** to show; **faire ses** ~**s** to prove o.s. (*ou* itself); ~ **matérielle** material evidence.

prévaloir [pʀevalwaʀ] *vi* to prevail; **se** ~ **de** *vt* to take advantage of; (*tirer vanité de*) to pride o.s. on.

prévarication [pʀevaʀikɑsjɔ̃] *nf* maladministration.

prévaut [pʀevo] *etc vb voir* **prévaloir**.

prévenances [pʀɛvnɑ̃s] *nfpl* thoughtfulness *sg*, kindness *sg*.

prévenant, e [pʀɛvnɑ̃, -ɑ̃t] *adj* thoughtful, kind.

prévenir [pʀɛvniʀ] *vt* (*avertir*): ~ **qn (de)** to warn sb (about); (*informer*): ~ **qn (de)** to tell *ou* inform sb (about); (*éviter*) to avoid, prevent; (*anticiper*) to anticipate; (*influencer*): ~ **qn contre** to prejudice sb against.

préventif, ive [pʀevɑ̃tif, -iv] *adj* preventive.

prévention [pʀevɑ̃sjɔ̃] *nf* prevention; (*préjugé*) prejudice; (*JUR*) custody, detention; ~ **routière** road safety.

prévenu, e [pʀɛvny] *nm/f* (*JUR*) defendant, accused.

prévisible [pʀevizibl(ə)] *adj* foreseeable.

prévision [pʀevizjɔ̃] *nf*: ~**s** predictions; (*météorologiques, économiques*) forecast *sg*; **en** ~ **de** in anticipation of; ~**s météorologiques** *ou* **du temps** weather forecast *sg*.

prévisionnel, le [pʀevizjɔnɛl] *adj* concerned with future requirements.

prévit [pʀevi] *etc vb voir* **prévoir**.

prévoir [pʀevwaʀ] *vt* (*deviner*) to foresee; (*s'attendre à*) to expect, reckon on; (*prévenir*) to anticipate; (*organiser*) to plan; (*préparer, réserver*) to allow; **prévu pour 4 personnes** designed for 4 people; **prévu pour 10 h** scheduled for 10 o'clock.

prévoyance [pʀevwajɑ̃s] *nf* foresight; **société/caisse de** ~ provident society/contingency fund.

prévoyant, e [pʀevwajɑ̃, -ɑ̃t] *vb voir* **prévoir** ♦ *adj* gifted with (*ou* showing) foresight, far-sighted.

prévu, e [pʀevy] *pp de* **prévoir**.

prier [pʀije] *vi* to pray ♦ *vt* (*Dieu*) to pray to; (*implorer*) to beg; (*demander*): ~ **qn de faire** to ask sb to do; (*inviter*): ~ **qn à dîner** to invite sb to dinner; **se faire** ~ to need coaxing *ou* persuading; **je vous en prie** (*allez-y*) please do; (*de rien*) don't mention it; **je vous prie de faire** please (would you) do.

prière [pʀijɛʀ] *nf* prayer; (*demande instante*) plea, entreaty; "~ **de faire** ..." "please do ...".

primaire [pʀimɛʀ] *adj* primary; (*péj*: *personne*) simple-minded; (: *idées*) simplistic ♦ *nm* (*SCOL*) primary education.

primauté [pʀimote] *nf* (*fig*) primacy.

prime [pʀim] *nf* (*bonification*) bonus; (*subside*) allowance; (*COMM*: *cadeau*) free gift; (*ASSU-*

RANCES, BOURSE) premium ♦ *adj*: **de ~ abord** at first glance; ~ **de risque** danger money *no pl*; ~ **de transport** travel allowance.
primer [pʀime] *vt* (*l'emporter sur*) to prevail over; (*récompenser*) to award a prize to ♦ *vi* to dominate, prevail.
primesautier, ière [pʀimsotje, -jɛʀ] *adj* impulsive.
primeur [pʀimœʀ] *nf*: **avoir la ~ de** to be the first to hear (*ou* see *etc*); **~s** *nfpl* (*fruits, légumes*) early fruits and vegetables; **marchand de ~** greengrocer (*BRIT*), produce dealer (*US*).
primevère [pʀimvɛʀ] *nf* primrose.
primitif, ive [pʀimitif, -iv] *adj* primitive; (*originel*) original ♦ *nm/f* primitive.
primo [pʀimo] *adv* first (of all), firstly.
primordial, e, aux [pʀimɔʀdjal, -o] *adj* essential, primordial.
prince [pʀɛ̃s] *nm* prince; ~ **charmant** Prince Charming; ~ **de Galles** *nm inv* (*tissu*) check cloth; ~ **héritier** crown prince.
princesse [pʀɛ̃sɛs] *nf* princess.
princier, ière [pʀɛ̃sje, -jɛʀ] *adj* princely.
principal, e, aux [pʀɛ̃sipal, -o] *adj* principal, main ♦ *nm* (*SCOL*) head(teacher) (*BRIT*), principal (*US*); (*essentiel*) main thing ♦ *nf* (*LING*): **(proposition) ~e** main clause.
principalement [pʀɛ̃sipalmɑ̃] *adv* principally, mainly.
principauté [pʀɛ̃sipote] *nf* principality.
principe [pʀɛ̃sip] *nm* principle; **partir du ~ que** to work on the principle *ou* assumption that; **pour le ~** on principle, for the sake of it; **de ~** *adj* (*hostilité*) automatic; (*accord*) in principle; **par ~** on principle; **en ~** (*habituellement*) as a rule; (*théoriquement*) in principle.
printanier, ière [pʀɛ̃tanje, -jɛʀ] *adj* spring *cpd*; spring-like.
printemps [pʀɛ̃tɑ̃] *nm* spring; **au ~** in spring.
priori [pʀijɔʀi]: **a ~** *adv* at first glance; initially; a priori.
prioritaire [pʀijɔʀitɛʀ] *adj* having priority; (*AUTO*) having right of way; (*INFORM*) foreground.
priorité [pʀijɔʀite] *nf* (*AUTO*): **avoir la ~ (sur)** to have right of way (over); ~ **à droite** right of way to vehicles coming from the right; **en ~** as a (matter of) priority.
pris, e [pʀi, pʀiz] *pp de* **prendre** ♦ *adj* (*place*) taken; (*billets*) sold; (*journée, mains*) full; (*personne*) busy; (*crème, ciment*) set; (*MÉD*: *enflammé*): **avoir le nez/la gorge ~(e)** to have a stuffy nose/a bad throat; (*saisi*): **être ~ de peur/de fatigue** to be stricken with fear/ overcome with fatigue.
prise [pʀiz] *nf* (*d'une ville*) capture; (*PÊCHE, CHASSE*) catch; (*de judo ou catch, point d'appui ou pour empoigner*) hold; (*ÉLEC*: *fiche*) plug; (*: femelle*) socket; (*: au mur*) point; **en ~** (*AUTO*) in gear; **être aux ~s avec** to be grappling with; to be battling with; **lâcher ~** to let go; **donner ~ à** (*fig*) to give rise to; **avoir ~ sur qn** to have a hold over sb; ~ **en charge** (*taxe*) pick-up charge; (*par la sécurité sociale*) *undertaking to reimburse costs*; ~ **de contact** initial meeting, first contact; ~ **de courant** power point; ~ **d'eau** water (supply) point; tap; ~ **multiple** adaptor; ~ **d'otages** hostage-taking; ~ **à partie** (*JUR*) *action against a judge*; ~ **péritel** SCART socket; ~ **de sang** blood test; ~ **de son** sound recording; ~ **de tabac** pinch of snuff; ~ **de terre** earth; ~ **de vue** (*photo*) shot; (*action*): ~ **de vue(s)** filming, shooting.
priser [pʀize] *vt* (*tabac, héroïne*) to take; (*estimer*) to prize, value ♦ *vi* to take snuff.
prisme [pʀism(ə)] *nm* prism.
prison [pʀizɔ̃] *nf* prison; **aller/être en ~** to go to/be in prison *ou* jail; **faire de la ~** to serve time; **être condamné à 5 ans de ~** to be sentenced to 5 years' imprisonment *ou* 5 years in prison.
prisonnier, ière [pʀizɔnje, -jɛʀ] *nm/f* prisoner ♦ *adj* captive; **faire qn ~** to take sb prisoner.
prit [pʀi] *vb voir* **prendre**.
privatif, ive [pʀivatif, -iv] *adj* (*jardin etc*) private; (*peine*) which deprives one of one's liberties.
privations [pʀivɑsjɔ̃] *nfpl* privations, hardships.
privatisation [pʀivatizɑsjɔ̃] *nf* privatization.
privatiser [pʀivatize] *vt* to privatize.
privautés [pʀivote] *nfpl* liberties.
privé, e [pʀive] *adj* private; (*dépourvu*): ~ **de** without, lacking; **en ~**, **dans le ~** in private.
priver [pʀive] *vt*: ~ **qn de** to deprive sb of; **se ~ de** to go *ou* do without; **ne pas se ~ de faire** not to refrain from doing.
privilège [pʀivilɛʒ] *nm* privilege.
privilégié, e [pʀivileʒje] *adj* privileged.
privilégier [pʀivileʒje] *vt* to favour (*BRIT*), favor (*US*).
prix [pʀi] *nm* (*valeur*) price; (*récompense, SCOL*) prize; **mettre à ~** to set a reserve (*BRIT*) *ou* an upset (*US*) price on; **au ~ fort** at a very high price; **acheter qch à ~ d'or** to pay a (small) fortune for sth; **hors de ~** exorbitantly priced; **à aucun ~** not at any price; **à tout ~** at all costs; **grand ~** (*SPORT*) Grand Prix; ~ **d'achat/de vente/de revient** purchasing/selling/cost price; ~ **conseillé** manufacturer's recommended price (MRP).
pro [pʀo] *nm* (= *professionnel*) pro.
probabilité [pʀɔbabilite] *nf* probability; **selon toute ~** in all probability.
probable [pʀɔbabl(ə)] *adj* likely, probable.
probablement [pʀɔbabləmɑ̃] *adv* probably.
probant, e [pʀɔbɑ̃, -ɑ̃t] *adj* convincing.
probatoire [pʀɔbatwaʀ] *adj* (*examen, test*) preliminary; (*stage*) probationary, trial *cpd*.
probité [pʀɔbite] *nf* integrity, probity.
problématique [pʀɔblematik] *adj* problemat-

ic(al) ♦ *nf* problematics *sg*; (*problème*) problem.

problème [pʀɔblɛm] *nm* problem.

procédé [pʀɔsede] *nm* (*méthode*) process; (*comportement*) behaviour *no pl* (*BRIT*), behavior *no pl* (*US*).

procéder [pʀɔsede] *vi* to proceed; to behave; ~ **à** *vt* to carry out.

procédure [pʀɔsedyʀ] *nf* (*ADMIN, JUR*) procedure.

procès [pʀɔsɛ] *nm* (*JUR*) trial; (*: poursuites*) proceedings *pl*; **être en ~ avec** to be involved in a lawsuit with; **faire le ~ de qn/qch** (*fig*) to put sb/sth on trial; **sans autre forme de ~** without further ado.

processeur [pʀɔsesœʀ] *nm* processor.

procession [pʀɔsesjɔ̃] *nf* procession.

processus [pʀɔsesys] *nm* process.

procès-verbal, aux [pʀɔsɛvɛʀbal, -o] *nm* (*constat*) statement; (*aussi*: **PV**): **avoir un ~** to get a parking ticket; to be booked; (*de réunion*) minutes *pl*.

prochain, e [pʀɔʃɛ̃, -ɛn] *adj* next; (*proche*) impending; near ♦ *nm* fellow man; **la ~e fois/semaine ~e** next time/week; **à la ~e!** (*fam*), **à la ~e fois** see you!, till the next time!; **un ~ jour** (some day) soon.

prochainement [pʀɔʃɛnmɑ̃] *adv* soon, shortly.

proche [pʀɔʃ] *adj* nearby; (*dans le temps*) imminent; close at hand; (*parent, ami*) close; **~s** *nmpl* (*parents*) close relatives, next of kin; (*amis*): **l'un de ses ~s** one of those close to him (*ou* her); **être ~ (de)** to be near, be close (to); **de ~ en ~** gradually.

Proche-Orient [pʀɔʃɔʀjɑ̃] *nm*: **le ~** the Near East.

proclamation [pʀɔklamɑsjɔ̃] *nf* proclamation.

proclamer [pʀɔklame] *vt* to proclaim; (*résultat d'un examen*) to announce.

procréer [pʀɔkʀee] *vt* to procreate.

procuration [pʀɔkyʀɑsjɔ̃] *nf* proxy; power of attorney; **voter par ~** to vote by proxy.

procurer [pʀɔkyʀe] *vt* (*fournir*): **~ qch à qn** to get *ou* obtain sth for sb; (*causer: plaisir etc*): **~ qch à qn** to bring *ou* give sb sth; **se ~** *vt* to get.

procureur [pʀɔkyʀœʀ] *nm* public prosecutor; **~ général** public prosecutor (*in appeal court*).

prodigalité [pʀɔdigalite] *nf* (*générosité*) generosity; (*extravagance*) extravagance, wastefulness.

prodige [pʀɔdiʒ] *nm* (*miracle, merveille*) marvel, wonder; (*personne*) prodigy.

prodigieusement [pʀɔdiʒjøzmɑ̃] *adv* tremendously.

prodigieux, euse [pʀɔdiʒjø, -øz] *adj* prodigious; phenomenal.

prodigue [pʀɔdig] *adj* (*généreux*) generous; (*dépensier*) extravagant, wasteful; **fils ~** prodigal son.

prodiguer [pʀɔdige] *vt* (*argent, biens*) to be lavish with; (*soins, attentions*): **~ qch à qn** to lavish sth on sb.

producteur, trice [pʀɔdyktœʀ, -tʀis] *adj*: **~ de blé** wheat-producing; (*CINÉ*): **société productrice** film *ou* movie company ♦ *nm/f* producer.

productif, ive [pʀɔdyktif, -iv] *adj* productive.

production [pʀɔdyksjɔ̃] *nf* (*gén*) production; (*rendement*) output; (*produits*) products *pl*, goods *pl*; (*œuvres*): **la ~ dramatique du XVIIe siècle** the plays of the 17th century.

productivité [pʀɔdyktivite] *nf* productivity.

produire [pʀɔdɥiʀ] *vt, vi* to produce; **se ~** *vi* (*acteur*) to perform, appear; (*événement*) to happen, occur.

produit, e [pʀɔdɥi, -it] *pp de* **produire** ♦ *nm* (*gén*) product; **~ d'entretien** cleaning product; **~ national brut (PNB)** gross national product (GNP); **~ net** net profit; **~ pour la vaisselle** washing-up (*BRIT*) *ou* dish-washing (*US*) liquid; **~ des ventes** income from sales; **~s agricoles** farm produce *sg*; **~s alimentaires** foodstuffs; **~s de beauté** beauty products, cosmetics.

proéminent, e [pʀɔeminɑ̃, -ɑ̃t] *adj* prominent.

prof [pʀɔf] *nm* (*fam: = professeur*) teacher; professor; lecturer.

prof. [pʀɔf] *abr* = **professeur, professionnel**.

profane [pʀɔfan] *adj* (*REL*) secular; (*ignorant, non initié*) uninitiated ♦ *nm/f* layman.

profaner [pʀɔfane] *vt* to desecrate; (*fig: sentiment*) to defile; (*: talent*) to debase.

proférer [pʀɔfeʀe] *vt* to utter.

professer [pʀɔfese] *vt* to profess.

professeur, e [pʀɔfɛsœʀ] *nm/f* teacher; (*titulaire d'une chaire*) professor; **~ (de faculté)** (university) lecturer.

profession [pʀɔfɛsjɔ̃] *nf* (*libérale*) profession; (*gén*) occupation; **faire ~ de** (*opinion, religion*) to profess; **de ~** by profession; **"sans ~"** "unemployed"; (*femme mariée*) "housewife".

professionnel, le [pʀɔfesjɔnɛl] *adj* professional ♦ *nm/f* professional; (*ouvrier qualifié*) skilled worker.

professoral, e, aux [pʀɔfɛsɔʀal, -o] *adj* professorial; **le corps ~** the teaching profession.

professorat [pʀɔfɛsɔʀa] *nm*: **le ~** the teaching profession.

profil [pʀɔfil] *nm* profile; (*d'une voiture*) line, contour; **de ~** in profile.

profilé, e [pʀɔfile] *adj* shaped; (*aile etc*) streamlined.

profiler [pʀɔfile] *vt* to streamline; **se ~** *vi* (*arbre, tour*) to stand out, be silhouetted.

profit [pʀɔfi] *nm* (*avantage*) benefit, advantage; (*COMM, FINANCE*) profit; **au ~ de** in aid of; **tirer** *ou* **retirer ~ de** to profit from; **mettre à ~** to take advantage of; to turn to good account; **~s et pertes** (*COMM*) profit and loss(es).

profitable [pʀɔfitabl(ə)] *adj* beneficial; profitable.
profiter [pʀɔfite] *vi*: ~ **de** to take advantage of; to make the most of; ~ **de ce que** ... to take advantage of the fact that ...; ~ **à** to be of benefit to, benefit; to be profitable to.
profiteur, euse [pʀɔfitœʀ, -øz] *nm/f* (*péj*) profiteer.
profond, e [pʀɔfɔ̃, -ɔ̃d] *adj* deep; (*méditation, mépris*) profound; **au plus** ~ **de** in the depths of, at the (very) bottom of; **la France** ~**e** the heartlands of France.
profondément [pʀɔfɔ̃demɑ̃] *adv* deeply; profoundly.
profondeur [pʀɔfɔ̃dœʀ] *nf* depth.
profusément [pʀɔfyzemɑ̃] *adv* profusely.
profusion [pʀɔfyzjɔ̃] *nf* profusion; **à** ~ in plenty.
progéniture [pʀɔʒenityʀ] *nf* offspring *inv*.
progiciel [pʀɔʒisjɛl] *nm* (*INFORM*) (software) package; ~ **d'application** applications package, applications software *no pl*.
progouvernemental, e, aux [pʀɔguvɛʀnəmɑ̃tal, -o] *adj* pro-government *cpd*.
programmable [pʀɔgʀamabl(ə)] *adj* programmable.
programmateur, trice [pʀɔgʀamatœʀ, -tʀis] *nm/f* (*CINÉ, TV*) programme (*BRIT*) *ou* program (*US*) planner ♦ *nm* (*de machine à laver etc*) timer.
programmation [pʀɔgʀamɑsjɔ̃] *nf* programming.
programme [pʀɔgʀam] *nm* programme (*BRIT*), program (*US*); (*TV, RADIO*) program(me)s *pl*; (*SCOL*) syllabus, curriculum; (*INFORM*) program; **au** ~ **de ce soir** (*TV*) among tonight's program(me)s.
programmé, e [pʀɔgʀame] *adj*: **enseignement** ~ programmed learning.
programmer [pʀɔgʀame] *vt* (*TV, RADIO*) to put on, show; (*organiser, prévoir*) to schedule; (*INFORM*) to program.
programmeur, euse [pʀɔgʀamœʀ, -øz] *nm/f* (computer) programmer.
progrès [pʀɔgʀɛ] *nm* progress *no pl*; **faire des/être en** ~ to make/be making progress.
progresser [pʀɔgʀese] *vi* to progress; (*troupes etc*) to make headway *ou* progress.
progressif, ive [pʀɔgʀesif, -iv] *adj* progressive.
progression [pʀɔgʀesjɔ̃] *nf* progression; (*d'une troupe etc*) advance, progress.
progressiste [pʀɔgʀesist(ə)] *adj* progressive.
progressivement [pʀɔgʀesivmɑ̃] *adv* progressively.
prohiber [pʀɔibe] *vt* to prohibit, ban.
prohibitif, ive [pʀɔibitif, -iv] *adj* prohibitive.
prohibition [pʀɔibisjɔ̃] *nf* ban, prohibition; (*HIST*) Prohibition.
proie [pʀwa] *nf* prey *no pl*; **être la** ~ **de** to fall prey to; **être en** ~ **à** (*doutes, sentiment*) to be prey to; (*douleur, mal*) to be suffering.
projecteur [pʀɔʒɛktœʀ] *nm* projector; (*de théâtre, cirque*) spotlight.
projectile [pʀɔʒɛktil] *nm* missile; (*d'arme*) projectile, bullet (*ou* shell *etc*).
projection [pʀɔʒɛksjɔ̃] *nf* projection; showing; **conférence avec** ~**s** lecture with slides (*ou* a film).
projectionniste [pʀɔʒɛksjɔnist(ə)] *nm/f* (*CINÉ*) projectionist.
projet [pʀɔʒɛ] *nm* plan; (*ébauche*) draft; **faire des** ~**s** to make plans; ~ **de loi** bill.
projeter [pʀɔʒte] *vt* (*envisager*) to plan; (*film, photos*) to project; (*passer*) to show; (*ombre, lueur*) to throw, cast, project; (*jeter*) to throw up (*ou* off *ou* out); ~ **de faire qch** to plan to do sth.
prolétaire [pʀɔletɛʀ] *adj, nm/f* proletarian.
prolétariat [pʀɔletaʀja] *nm* proletariat.
prolétarien, -ne [pʀɔletaʀjɛ̃, -ɛn] *adj* proletarian.
prolifération [pʀɔlifeʀɑsjɔ̃] *nf* proliferation.
proliférer [pʀɔlifeʀe] *vi* to proliferate.
prolifique [pʀɔlifik] *adj* prolific.
prolixe [pʀɔliks(ə)] *adj* verbose.
prolo [pʀɔlo] *nm/f* (*fam*: = *prolétaire*) prole (*péj*).
prologue [pʀɔlɔg] *nm* prologue.
prolongateur [pʀɔlɔ̃gatœʀ] *nm* (*ÉLEC*) extension cable.
prolongation [pʀɔlɔ̃gɑsjɔ̃] *nf* prolongation; extension; ~**s** *nfpl* (*FOOTBALL*) extra time *sg*.
prolongement [pʀɔlɔ̃ʒmɑ̃] *nm* extension; ~**s** *nmpl* (*fig*) repercussions, effects; **dans le** ~ **de** running on from.
prolonger [pʀɔlɔ̃ʒe] *vt* (*débat, séjour*) to prolong; (*délai, billet, rue*) to extend; (*suj: chose*) to be a continuation *ou* an extension of; **se** ~ *vi* to go on.
promenade [pʀɔmnad] *nf* walk (*ou* drive *ou* ride); **faire une** ~ to go for a walk; **une** ~ **(à pied)/en voiture/à vélo** a walk/drive/(bicycle) ride.
promener [pʀɔmne] *vt* (*personne, chien*) to take out for a walk; (*fig*) to carry around; to trail round; (*doigts, regard*): ~ **qch sur** to run sth over; **se** ~ *vi* (*à pied*) to go for (*ou* be out for) a walk; (*en voiture*) to go for (*ou* be out for) a drive; (*fig*): **se** ~ **sur** to wander over.
promeneur, euse [pʀɔmnœʀ, -øz] *nm/f* walker, stroller.
promenoir [pʀɔmənwaʀ] *nm* gallery, (covered) walkway.
promesse [pʀɔmɛs] *nf* promise; ~ **d'achat** commitment to buy.
prometteur, euse [pʀɔmɛtœʀ, -øz] *adj* promising.
promettre [pʀɔmɛtʀ(ə)] *vt* to promise ♦ *vi* (*récolte, arbre*) to look promising; (*enfant, musicien*) to be promising; **se** ~ **de faire** to resolve *ou* mean to do; ~ **à qn de faire** to promise sb that one will do.
promeus [pʀɔmø] *etc vb voir* **promouvoir**.

promis, e [pʀɔmi, -iz] *pp de* **promettre** ♦ *adj*: **être ~ à qch** (*destiné*) to be destined for sth.
promiscuité [pʀɔmiskɥite] *nf* crowding; lack of privacy.
promit [pʀɔmi] *vb voir* **promettre**.
promontoire [pʀɔmɔ̃twaʀ] *nm* headland.
promoteur, trice [pʀɔmɔtœʀ, -tʀis] *nm/f* (*instigateur*) instigator, promoter; **~ (immobilier)** property developer (*BRIT*), real estate promoter (*US*).
promotion [pʀɔmɔsjɔ̃] *nf* (*avancement*) promotion; (*SCOL*) year (*BRIT*), class; **en ~** (*COMM*) on promotion, on (special) offer.
promotionnel, le [pʀɔmɔsjɔnɛl] *adj* (*article*) on promotion, on (special) offer; (*vente*) promotional.
promouvoir [pʀɔmuvwaʀ] *vt* to promote.
prompt, e [pʀɔ̃, pʀɔ̃t] *adj* swift, rapid; (*intervention, changement*) sudden; **~ à faire qch** quick to do sth.
promptement [pʀɔ̃ptəmɑ̃] *adv* swiftly.
prompteur [pʀɔ̃tœʀ] *nm* ® Autocue ® (*BRIT*), Teleprompter ® (*US*).
promptitude [pʀɔ̃tityd] *nf* swiftness, rapidity.
promu, e [pʀɔmy] *pp de* **promouvoir**.
promulguer [pʀɔmylge] *vt* to promulgate.
prôner [pʀone] *vt* (*louer*) to laud, extol; (*préconiser*) to advocate, commend.
pronom [pʀɔnɔ̃] *nm* pronoun.
pronominal, e, aux [pʀɔnɔminal, -o] *adj* pronominal; (*verbe*) reflexive, pronominal.
prononcé, e [pʀɔnɔ̃se] *adj* pronounced, marked.
prononcer [pʀɔnɔ̃se] *vt* (*son, mot, jugement*) to pronounce; (*dire*) to utter; (*allocution*) to deliver ♦ *vi* (*JUR*) to deliver *ou* give a verdict; **~ bien/mal** to have a good/poor pronunciation; **se ~** *vi* to reach a decision, give a verdict; **se ~ sur** to give an opinion on; **se ~ contre** to come down against; **ça se prononce comment?** how do you pronounce this?
prononciation [pʀɔnɔ̃sjɑsjɔ̃] *nf* pronunciation.
pronostic [pʀɔnɔstik] *nm* (*MÉD*) prognosis (*pl* -oses); (*fig: aussi*: **~s**) forecast.
pronostiquer [pʀɔnɔstike] *vt* (*MÉD*) to prognosticate; (*annoncer, prévoir*) to forecast, foretell.
pronostiqueur, euse [pʀɔnɔstikœʀ, -øz] *nm/f* forecaster.
propagande [pʀɔpagɑ̃d] *nf* propaganda; **faire de la ~ pour qch** to plug *ou* push sth.
propagandiste [pʀɔpagɑ̃dist(ə)] *nm/f* propagandist.
propagation [pʀɔpagɑsjɔ̃] *nf* propagation.
propager [pʀɔpaʒe] *vt* to spread; **se ~** *vi* to spread; (*PHYSIQUE*) to be propagated.
propane [pʀɔpan] *nm* propane.
propension [pʀɔpɑ̃sjɔ̃] *nf*: **~ à (faire) qch** propensity to (do) sth.
prophète [pʀɔfɛt], **prophétesse** [pʀɔfetɛs] *nm/f* prophet(ess).
prophétie [pʀɔfesi] *nf* prophecy.
prophétique [pʀɔfetik] *adj* prophetic.
prophétiser [pʀɔfetize] *vt* to prophesy.
prophylactique [pʀɔfilaktik] *adj* prophylactic.
propice [pʀɔpis] *adj* favourable (*BRIT*), favorable (*US*).
proportion [pʀɔpɔʀsjɔ̃] *nf* proportion; **il n'y a aucune ~ entre le prix demandé et le prix réel** the asking price bears no relation to the real price; **à ~ de** proportionally to, in proportion to; **en ~ (de)** in proportion (to); **hors de ~** out of proportion; **toute(s) ~(s) gardée(s)** making due allowance(s).
proportionné, e [pʀɔpɔʀsjɔne] *adj*: **bien ~** well-proportioned; **~ à** proportionate to.
proportionnel, le [pʀɔpɔʀsjɔnɛl] *adj* proportional; **~ à** proportional to ♦ *nf* proportional representation.
proportionnellement [pʀɔpɔʀsjɔnɛlmɑ̃] *adv* proportionally, proportionately.
proportionner [pʀɔpɔʀsjɔne] *vt*: **~ qch à** to proportion *ou* adjust sth to.
propos [pʀɔpo] *nm* (*paroles*) talk *no pl*, remark; (*intention, but*) intention, aim; (*sujet*): **à quel ~?** what about?; **à ~ de** about, regarding; **à tout ~** for no reason at all; **à ce ~** on that subject, in this connection; **à ~** *adv* by the way; (*opportunément*) (just) at the right moment; **hors de ~, mal à ~** *adv* at the wrong moment.
proposer [pʀɔpoze] *vt* (*suggérer*): **~ qch (à qn)/de faire** to suggest sth (to sb)/doing, propose sth (to sb)/to do; (*offrir*): **~ qch à qn/de faire** to offer sb sth/to do; (*candidat*) to nominate, put forward; (*loi, motion*) to propose; **se ~ (pour faire)** to offer one's services (to do); **se ~ de faire** to intend *ou* propose to do.
proposition [pʀɔpozisjɔ̃] *nf* suggestion; proposal; offer; (*LING*) clause; **sur la ~ de** at the suggestion of; **~ de loi** private bill.
propre [pʀɔpʀ(ə)] *adj* clean; (*net*) neat, tidy; (*qui ne salit pas: chien, chat*) house-trained; (*: enfant*) toilet-trained; (*fig: honnête*) honest; (*possessif*) own; (*sens*) literal; (*particulier*): **~ à** peculiar to, characteristic of; (*approprié*): **~ à** suitable *ou* appropriate for; (*de nature à*): **~ à faire** likely to do, that will do ♦ *nm*: **recopier au ~** to make a fair copy of; (*particularité*): **le ~ de** the peculiarity of, the distinctive feature of; **au ~** (*LING*) literally; **appartenir à qn en ~** to belong to sb (exclusively); **~ à rien** *nm/f* (*péj*) good-for-nothing.
proprement [pʀɔpʀəmɑ̃] *adv* cleanly; neatly, tidily; **à ~ parler** strictly speaking; **le village ~ dit** the actual village, the village itself.
propret, te [pʀɔpʀɛ, -ɛt] *adj* neat and tidy, spick-and-span.
propreté [pʀɔpʀəte] *nf* cleanliness, cleanness; neatness, tidiness.

propriétaire [pʀɔpʀijetɛʀ] *nm/f* owner; (*d'hôtel etc*) proprietor/tress, owner; (*pour le locataire*) landlord/lady; ~ **(immobilier)** house-owner; householder; ~ **récoltant** grower; ~ **(terrien)** landowner.
propriété [pʀɔpʀijete] *nf* (*droit*) ownership; (*objet, immeuble etc*) property *gén no pl*; (*villa*) residence, property; (*terres*) property *gén no pl*, land *gén no pl*; (*qualité, CHIMIE, MATH*) property; (*correction*) appropriateness, suitability; ~ **artistique et littéraire** artistic and literary copyright; ~ **industrielle** patent rights *pl*.
propulser [pʀɔpylse] *vt* (*missile*) to propel; (*projeter*) to hurl, fling.
propulsion [pʀɔpylsjɔ̃] *nf* propulsion.
prorata [pʀɔʀata] *nm inv*: **au** ~ **de** in proportion to, on the basis of.
prorogation [pʀɔʀɔgɑsjɔ̃] *nf* deferment; extension; adjournment.
proroger [pʀɔʀɔʒe] *vt* to put back, defer; (*prolonger*) to extend; (*assemblée*) to adjourn, prorogue.
prosaïque [pʀozaik] *adj* mundane, prosaic.
proscription [pʀɔskʀipsjɔ̃] *nf* banishment; (*interdiction*) banning; prohibition.
proscrire [pʀɔskʀiʀ] *vt* (*bannir*) to banish; (*interdire*) to ban, prohibit.
prose [pʀoz] *nf* prose (*style*).
prosélyte [pʀɔzelit] *nm/f* proselyte, convert.
prospecter [pʀɔspɛkte] *vt* to prospect; (*COMM*) to canvass.
prospecteur-placier, *pl* **prospecteurs-placiers** [pʀɔspɛktœʀplasje] *nm* placement officer.
prospectif, ive [pʀɔspɛktif, -iv] *adj* prospective.
prospectus [pʀɔspɛktys] *nm* (*feuille*) leaflet; (*dépliant*) brochure, leaflet.
prospère [pʀɔspɛʀ] *adj* prosperous; (*santé, entreprise*) thriving, flourishing.
prospérer [pʀɔspeʀe] *vi* to thrive.
prospérité [pʀɔspeʀite] *nf* prosperity.
prostate [pʀɔstat] *nf* prostate (gland).
prosterner [pʀɔstɛʀne]: **se** ~ *vi* to bow low, prostrate o.s.
prostituée [pʀɔstitɥe] *nf* prostitute.
prostitution [pʀɔstitysjɔ̃] *nf* prostitution.
prostré, e [pʀɔstʀe] *adj* prostrate.
protagoniste [pʀɔtagɔnist(ə)] *nm* protagonist.
protecteur, trice [pʀɔtɛktœʀ, -tʀis] *adj* protective; (*air, ton: péj*) patronizing ♦ *nm/f* (*défenseur*) protector; (*des arts*) patron.
protection [pʀɔtɛksjɔ̃] *nf* protection; (*d'un personnage influent: aide*) patronage; **écran de** ~ protective screen; ~ **civile** *state-financed civilian rescue service*; ~ **maternelle et infantile (PMI)** *social service concerned with child welfare*.
protectionnisme [pʀɔtɛksjɔnism(ə)] *nm* protectionism.
protectionniste [pʀɔtɛksjɔnist(ə)] *adj* protectionist.
protégé, e [pʀɔteʒe] *nm/f* protégé/e.
protège-cahier [pʀɔtɛʒkaje] *nm* exercise book cover.
protéger [pʀɔteʒe] *vt* to protect; (*aider, patronner: personne, arts*) to be a patron of; (*: carrière*) to further; **se** ~ **de/contre** to protect o.s. from.
protéine [pʀɔtein] *nf* protein.
protestant, e [pʀɔtɛstɑ̃, -ɑ̃t] *adj, nm/f* Protestant.
protestantisme [pʀɔtɛstɑ̃tism(ə)] *nm* Protestantism.
protestataire [pʀɔtɛstatɛʀ] *nm/f* protestor.
protestation [pʀɔtɛstɑsjɔ̃] *nf* (*plainte*) protest; (*déclaration*) protestation, profession.
protester [pʀɔtɛste] *vi*: ~ **(contre)** to protest (against *ou* about); ~ **de** (*son innocence, sa loyauté*) to protest.
prothèse [pʀɔtɛz] *nf* artificial limb, prosthesis (*pl* -ses); ~ **dentaire** (*appareil*) denture; (*science*) dental engineering.
protocolaire [pʀɔtɔkɔlɛʀ] *adj* formal; (*questions, règles*) of protocol.
protocole [pʀɔtɔkɔl] *nm* protocol; (*fig*) etiquette; ~ **d'accord** draft treaty; ~ **opératoire** (*MÉD*) operating procedure.
prototype [pʀɔtɔtip] *nm* prototype.
protubérance [pʀɔtybeʀɑ̃s] *nf* bulge, protuberance.
protubérant, e [pʀɔtybeʀɑ̃, -ɑ̃t] *adj* protruding, bulging, protuberant.
proue [pʀu] *nf* bow(s *pl*), prow.
prouesse [pʀuɛs] *nf* feat.
prouver [pʀuve] *vt* to prove.
provenance [pʀɔvnɑ̃s] *nf* origin; (*de mot, coutume*) source; **avion en** ~ **de** plane (arriving) from.
provençal, e, aux [pʀɔvɑ̃sal, -o] *adj* Provençal ♦ *nm* (*LING*) Provençal.
Provence [pʀɔvɑ̃s] *nf*: **la** ~ Provence.
provenir [pʀɔvniʀ]: ~ **de** *vt* to come from; (*résulter de*) to be due to, be the result of.
proverbe [pʀɔvɛʀb(ə)] *nm* proverb.
proverbial, e, aux [pʀɔvɛʀbjal, -o] *adj* proverbial.
providence [pʀɔvidɑ̃s] *nf*: **la** ~ providence.
providentiel, le [pʀɔvidɑ̃sjɛl] *adj* providential.
province [pʀɔvɛ̃s] *nf* province.
provincial, e, aux [pʀɔvɛ̃sjal, -o] *adj, nm/f* provincial.
proviseur [pʀɔvizœʀ] *nm* ≈ head(teacher) (*BRIT*), ≈ principal (*US*).
provision [pʀɔvizjɔ̃] *nf* (*réserve*) stock, supply; (*avance: à un avocat, avoué*) retainer, retaining fee; (*COMM*) funds *pl* (in account); reserve; ~**s** *nfpl* (*vivres*) provisions, food *no pl*; **faire** ~ **de** to stock up with; **placard** *ou* **armoire à** ~**s** food cupboard.
provisoire [pʀɔvizwaʀ] *adj* temporary; (*JUR*) provisional; **mise en liberté** ~ release on bail.

provisoirement [pʀɔvizwaʀmɑ̃] *adv* temporarily, for the time being.
provocant, e [pʀɔvɔkɑ̃, -ɑ̃t] *adj* provocative.
provocateur, trice [pʀɔvɔkatœʀ, -tʀis] *adj* provocative ♦ *nm* (*meneur*) agitator.
provocation [pʀɔvɔkɑsjɔ̃] *nf* provocation.
provoquer [pʀɔvɔke] *vt* (*défier*) to provoke; (*causer*) to cause, bring about; (*: curiosité*) to arouse, give rise to; (*: aveux*) to prompt, elicit; (*inciter*): ~ **qn à** to incite sb to.
prox. *abr* = **proximité**.
proxénète [pʀɔksenɛt] *nm* procurer.
proxénétisme [pʀɔksenetism(ə)] *nm* procuring.
proximité [pʀɔksimite] *nf* nearness, closeness, proximity; (*dans le temps*) imminence, closeness; **à** ~ near *ou* close by; **à** ~ **de** near (to), close to.
prude [pʀyd] *adj* prudish.
prudemment [pʀydamɑ̃] *adv* (*voir prudent*) carefully; cautiously; prudently; wisely, sensibly.
prudence [pʀydɑ̃s] *nf* carefulness; caution; prudence; **avec** ~ carefully; cautiously; wisely; **par (mesure de)** ~ as a precaution.
prudent, e [pʀydɑ̃, -ɑ̃t] *adj* (*pas téméraire*) careful, cautious, prudent; (*: en général*) safety-conscious; (*sage, conseillé*) wise, sensible; (*réservé*) cautious; **ce n'est pas** ~ it's risky; it's not sensible, **soyez** ~ take care, be careful.
prune [pʀyn] *nf* plum.
pruneau, x [pʀyno] *nm* prune.
prunelle [pʀynɛl] *nf* pupil; (*œil*) eye; (*BOT*) sloe; (*eau de vie*) sloe gin.
prunier [pʀynje] *nm* plum tree.
Prusse [pʀys] *nf*: **la** ~ Prussia.
PS *sigle m* = *parti socialiste*; (= *post-scriptum*) PS.
psalmodier [psalmɔdje] *vt* to chant; (*fig*) to drone out.
psaume [psom] *nm* psalm.
pseudonyme [psødɔnim] *nm* (*gén*) fictitious name; (*d'écrivain*) pseudonym, pen name; (*de comédien*) stage name.
PSIG *sigle m* (= *Peloton de surveillance et d'intervention de gendarmerie*) *type of police commando squad.*
PSU *sigle m* = *parti socialiste unifié.*
psy [psi] *nm/f* (*fam, péj*: = *psychiatre, psychologue*) shrink.
psychanalyse [psikanaliz] *nf* psychoanalysis.
psychanalyser [psikanalize] *vt* to psychoanalyze; **se faire** ~ to undergo (psycho-) analysis.
psychanalyste [psikanalist(ə)] *nm/f* psychoanalyst.
psychanalytique [psikanalitik] *adj* psychoanalytical.
psychédélique [psikedelik] *adj* psychedelic.
psychiatre [psikjatʀ(ə)] *nm/f* psychiatrist.
psychiatrie [psikjatʀi] *nf* psychiatry.
psychiatrique [psikjatʀik] *adj* psychiatric; (*hôpital*) mental, psychiatric.
psychique [psiʃik] *adj* psychological.
psychisme [psiʃism(ə)] *nm* psyche.
psychologie [psikɔlɔʒi] *nf* psychology.
psychologique [psikɔlɔʒik] *adj* psychological.
psychologiquement [psikɔlɔʒikmɑ̃] *adv* psychologically.
psychologue [psikɔlɔg] *nm/f* psychologist; **être** ~ (*fig*) to be a good psychologist.
psychomoteur, trice [psikɔmɔtœʀ, -tʀis] *adj* psychomotor.
psychopathe [psikɔpat] *nm/f* psychopath.
psychopédagogie [psikɔpedagɔʒi] *nf* educational psychology.
psychose [psikoz] *nf* (*MÉD*) psychosis (*pl* -ses); (*obsession, idée fixe*) obsessive fear.
psychosomatique [psikɔsɔmatik] *adj* psychosomatic.
psychothérapie [psikɔteʀapi] *nf* psychotherapy.
psychotique [psikɔtik] *adj* psychotic.
PTCA *sigle m* = *poids total en charge autorisé.*
Pte *abr* = **Porte**.
pte *abr* (= *pointe*) pt.
PTMA *sigle m* (= *poids total maximum autorisé*) maximum loaded weight.
PTT *sigle fpl voir* **poste**.
pu [py] *pp de* **pouvoir**.
puanteur [pɥɑ̃tœʀ] *nf* stink, stench.
pub [pyb] *nf* (*fam*: = *publicité*): **la** ~ advertising.
pubère [pybɛʀ] *adj* pubescent.
puberté [pybɛʀte] *nf* puberty.
pubis [pybis] *nm* (*bas-ventre*) pubes *pl*; (*os*) pubis.
public, ique [pyblik] *adj* public; (*école, instruction*) state *cpd*; (*scrutin*) open ♦ *nm* public; (*assistance*) audience; **en** ~ in public; **le grand** ~ the general public.
publication [pyblikɑsjɔ̃] *nf* publication.
publiciste [pyblisist(ə)] *nm/f* adman.
publicitaire [pyblisitɛʀ] *adj* advertising *cpd*; (*film, voiture*) publicity *cpd*; (*vente*) promotional ♦ *nm* adman; **rédacteur** ~ copywriter.
publicité [pyblisite] *nf* (*méthode, profession*) advertising; (*annonce*) advertisement; (*révélations*) publicity.
publier [pyblije] *vt* to publish; (*nouvelle*) to publicize, make public.
publipostage [pyblipɔstaʒ] *nm* mailshot, (mass) mailing.
publique [pyblik] *adj f voir* **public**.
publiquement [pyblikmɑ̃] *adv* publicly.
puce [pys] *nf* flea; (*INFORM*) chip; **(marché aux)** ~**s** flea market *sg*; **mettre la** ~ **à l'oreille de qn** to give sb something to think about.
puceau, x [pyso] *adj m*: **être** ~ to be a virgin.
pucelle [pysɛl] *adj f*: **être** ~ to be a virgin.
puceron [pysʀɔ̃] *nm* aphid.
pudeur [pydœʀ] *nf* modesty.
pudibond, e [pydibɔ̃, -ɔ̃d] *adj* prudish.
pudique [pydik] *adj* (*chaste*) modest; (*discret*)

discreet.
pudiquement [pydikmɑ̃] *adv* modestly.
puer [pɥe] *(péj) vi* to stink ♦ *vt* to stink of, reek of.
puéricultrice [pɥeʀikyltʀis] *nf* ≈ nursery nurse.
puériculture [pɥeʀikyltyʀ] *nf* infant care.
puéril, e [pɥeʀil] *adj* childish.
puérilement [pɥeʀilmɑ̃] *adv* childishly.
puérilité [pɥeʀilite] *nf* childishness; *(acte, idée)* childish thing.
pugilat [pyʒila] *nm* (fist) fight.
puis [pɥi] *vb voir* **pouvoir** ♦ *adv (ensuite)* then; *(dans une énumération)* next; *(en outre)*: **et ~** and (then); **et ~ (après *ou* quoi)?** so (what)?
puisard [pɥizaʀ] *nm (égout)* cesspool.
puiser [pɥize] *vt*: **~ (dans)** to draw (from); **~ dans qch** to dip into sth.
puisque [pɥisk(ə)] *conj* since; *(valeur intensive)*: **~ je te le dis!** I'm telling you!
puissamment [pɥisamɑ̃] *adv* powerfully.
puissance [pɥisɑ̃s] *nf* power; **en ~** *adj* potential; **2 (à la) ~ 5** 2 to the power (of) 5.
puissant, e [pɥisɑ̃, -ɑ̃t] *adj* powerful.
puisse [pɥis] *etc vb voir* **pouvoir**.
puits [pɥi] *nm* well; **~ artésien** artesian well; **~ de mine** mine shaft; **~ de science** fount of knowledge.
pull(-over) [pyl(ɔvœʀ)] *nm* sweater, jumper *(BRIT)*.
pulluler [pylyle] *vi* to swarm; *(fig: erreurs)* to abound, proliferate.
pulmonaire [pylmɔnɛʀ] *adj* lung *cpd*; *(artère)* pulmonary.
pulpe [pylp(ə)] *nf* pulp.
pulsation [pylsɑsjɔ̃] *nf (MÉD)* beat.
pulsé [pylse] *adj m*: **chauffage à air ~** warm air heating.
pulsion [pylsjɔ̃] *nf (PSYCH)* drive, urge.
pulvérisateur [pylveʀizatœʀ] *nm* spray.
pulvérisation [pylveʀizɑsjɔ̃] *nf* spraying.
pulvériser [pylveʀize] *vt (solide)* to pulverize; *(liquide)* to spray; *(fig: anéantir: adversaire)* to pulverize; *(: record)* to smash, shatter; *(: argument)* to demolish.
puma [pyma] *nm* puma, cougar.
punaise [pynɛz] *nf (ZOOL)* bug; *(clou)* drawing pin *(BRIT)*, thumb tack *(US)*.
punch [pɔ̃ʃ] *nm (boisson)* punch; [pœnʃ] *(BOXE)* punching ability; *(fig)* punch.
punching-ball [pœnʃiŋbol] *nm* punchball.
punir [pyniʀ] *vt* to punish; **~ qn de qch** to punish sb for sth.
punitif, ive [pynitif, -iv] *adj* punitive.
punition [pynisjɔ̃] *nf* punishment.
pupille [pypij] *nf (ANAT)* pupil ♦ *nm/f (enfant)* ward; **~ de l'État** child in care; **~ de la Nation** war orphan.
pupitre [pypitʀ(ə)] *nm (SCOL)* desk; *(REL)* lectern; *(de chef d'orchestre)* rostrum; *(INFORM)* console; **~ de commande** control panel.
pupitreur, euse [pypitʀœʀ, -øz] *nm/f (INFORM)* (computer) operator, keyboarder.
pur, e [pyʀ] *adj* pure; *(vin)* undiluted; *(whisky)* neat; *(intentions)* honourable *(BRIT)*, honorable *(US)* ♦ *nm (personne)* hard-liner; **en ~e perte** fruitlessly, to no avail.
purée [pyʀe] *nf*: **~ (de pommes de terre)** ≈ mashed potatoes *pl*; **~ de marrons** chestnut purée; **~ de pois** *(fig)* peasoup(er).
purement [pyʀmɑ̃] *adv* purely.
pureté [pyʀte] *nf* purity.
purgatif [pyʀgatif] *nm* purgative, purge.
purgatoire [pyʀgatwaʀ] *nm* purgatory.
purge [pyʀʒ(ə)] *nf (POL)* purge; *(MÉD)* purging *no pl*; purge.
purger [pyʀʒe] *vt (radiateur)* to flush (out), drain; *(circuit hydraulique)* to bleed; *(MÉD, POL)* to purge; *(JUR: peine)* to serve.
purification [pyʀifikɑsjɔ̃] *nf (de l'eau)* purification; **~ ethnique** ethnic cleansing.
purifier [pyʀifje] *vt* to purify; *(TECH: métal)* to refine.
purin [pyʀɛ̃] *nm* liquid manure.
puriste [pyʀist(ə)] *nm/f* purist.
puritain, e [pyʀitɛ̃, -ɛn] *adj, nm/f* Puritan.
puritanisme [pyʀitanism(ə)] *nm* Puritanism.
pur-sang [pyʀsɑ̃] *nm inv* thoroughbred, purebred.
purulent, e [pyʀylɑ̃, -ɑ̃t] *adj* purulent.
pus [py] *vb voir* **pouvoir** ♦ *nm* pus.
pusillanime [pyzilanim] *adj* fainthearted.
pustule [pystyl] *nf* pustule.
putain [pytɛ̃] *nf (fam!)* whore *(!)*; **ce/cette ~ de** ... this bloody *(BRIT) ou* goddamn *(US)* ... *(!)*.
putois [pytwa] *nm* polecat; **crier comme un ~** to yell one's head off.
putréfaction [pytʀefaksjɔ̃] *nf* putrefaction.
putréfier [pytʀefje] *vt*, **se ~** *vi* to putrefy, rot.
putride [pytʀid] *adj* putrid.
putsch [putʃ] *nm (POL)* putsch.
puzzle [pœzl(ə)] *nm* jigsaw (puzzle).
PV *sigle m* = **procès-verbal**.
PVC *sigle f (= polychlorure de vinyle)* PVC.
PVD *sigle mpl (= pays en voie de développement)* developing countries.
Px *abr* = **prix**.
pygmée [pigme] *nm* pygmy.
pyjama [piʒama] *nm* pyjamas *pl*, pair of pyjamas.
pylône [pilon] *nm* pylon.
pyramide [piʀamid] *nf* pyramid.
pyrénéen, ne [piʀeneɛ̃, -ɛn] *adj* Pyrenean.
Pyrénées [piʀene] *nfpl*: **les ~** the Pyrenees.
pyrex [piʀɛks] *nm* ® Pyrex ®.
pyrogravure [piʀɔgʀavyʀ] *nf* poker-work.
pyromane [piʀɔman] *nm/f* arsonist.
python [pitɔ̃] *nm* python.

Q q

Q, q [ky] *nm inv* Q, q ♦ *abr* (= *quintal*) q; **Q comme Quintal** Q for Queen.
Qatar [kataʀ] *nm*: **le ~** Qatar.
qcm *sigle m* (= *questionnaire à choix multiple*) multiple choice question paper.
QG *sigle m* (= *quartier général*) HQ.
QHS *sigle m* (= *quartier de haute sécurité*) high-security wing *ou* prison.
QI *sigle m* (= *quotient intellectuel*) IQ.
qqch. *abr* (= *quelque chose*) sth.
qqe(s) *abr* = **quelque(s)**.
qqn *abr* (= *quelqu'un*) sb, s.o.
quadra [k(w)adʀa] *nm/f* (*fam*) (= *quadragénaire*) person in his (*ou* her) forties; **les ~s** forty somethings (*fam*).
quadragénaire [kadʀaʒenɛʀ] *nm/f* (*de quarante ans*) forty-year-old; (*de quarante à cinquante ans*) man/woman in his/her forties.
quadrangulaire [kwadʀɑ̃gylɛʀ] *adj* quadrangular.
quadrature [kwadʀatyʀ] *nf*: **c'est la ~ du cercle** it's like trying to square the circle.
quadrichromie [kwadʀikʀɔmi] *nf* four-colour (*BRIT*) *ou* -color (*US*) printing.
quadrilatère [k(w)adʀilatɛʀ] *nm* (*GÉOM, MIL*) quadrilateral; (*terrain*) four-sided area.
quadrillage [kadʀijaʒ] *nm* (*lignes etc*) square pattern, criss-cross pattern.
quadrillé, e [kadʀije] *adj* (*papier*) squared.
quadriller [kadʀije] *vt* (*papier*) to mark out in squares; (*POLICE*: *ville, région etc*) to keep under tight control, be positioned throughout.
quadrimoteur [k(w)adʀimɔtœʀ] *nm* four-engined plane.
quadripartite [kwadʀipaʀtit] *adj* (*entre pays*) four-power; (*entre partis*) four-party.
quadriphonie [kadʀifɔni] *nf* quadraphony.
quadriréacteur [k(w)adʀiʀeaktœʀ] *nm* four-engined jet.
quadrupède [k(w)adʀypɛd] *nm* quadruped.
quadruple [k(w)adʀypl(ə)] *nm*: **le ~ de** four times as much as.
quadrupler [k(w)adʀyple] *vt, vi* to quadruple, increase fourfold.
quadruplés, ées [k(w)adʀyple] *nm/fpl* quadruplets, quads.
quai [ke] *nm* (*de port*) quay; (*de gare*) platform; (*de cours d'eau, canal*) embankment; **être à ~** (*navire*) to be alongside; (*train*) to be in the station; **le Q~ d'Orsay** *offices of the French Ministry for Foreign Affairs*; **le Q~ des Orfèvres** *central police headquarters*.
qualifiable [kalifjabl(ə)] *adj*: **ce n'est pas ~** it defies description.
qualificatif, ive [kalifikatif, -iv] *adj* (*LING*) qualifying ♦ *nm* (*terme*) term; (*LING*) qualifier.
qualification [kalifikɑsjɔ̃] *nf* qualification.
qualifier [kalifje] *vt* to qualify; (*appeler*): **~ qch/qn de** to describe sth/sb as; **se ~** *vi* (*SPORT*) to qualify; **être qualifié pour** to be qualified for.
qualitatif, ive [kalitatif, -iv] *adj* qualitative.
qualité [kalite] *nf* quality; (*titre, fonction*) position; **en ~ de** in one's capacity as; **ès ~s** in an official capacity; **avoir ~ pour** to have authority to; **de ~** *adj* quality *cpd*; **rapport ~-prix** value (for money).
quand [kɑ̃] *conj, adv* when; **~ je serai riche** when I'm rich; **~ même** (*cependant, pourtant*) nevertheless; (*tout de même*) all the same; really; **~ bien même** even though.
quant [kɑ̃]: **~ à** *prép* (*pour ce qui est de*) as for, as to; (*au sujet de*) regarding.
quant-à-soi [kɑ̃taswa] *nm*: **rester sur son ~** to remain aloof.
quantième [kɑ̃tjɛm] *nm* date, day (of month).
quantifiable [kɑ̃tifjabl(ə)] *adj* quantifiable.
quantifier [kɑ̃tifje] *vt* to quantify.
quantitatif, ive [kɑ̃titatif, -iv] *adj* quantitative.
quantitativement [kɑ̃titativmɑ̃] *adv* quantitatively.
quantité [kɑ̃tite] *nf* quantity, amount; (*SCIENCE*) quantity; (*grand nombre*): **une** *ou* **des ~(s) de** a great deal of; a lot of; **en grande ~** in large quantities; **en ~s industrielles** in vast amounts; **du travail en ~** a great deal of work; **~ de** many.
quarantaine [kaʀɑ̃tɛn] *nf* (*isolement*) quarantine; (*âge*): **avoir la ~** to be around forty; (*nombre*): **une ~ (de)** forty or so, about forty; **mettre en ~** to put into quarantine; (*fig*) to send to Coventry (*BRIT*), ostracize.
quarante [kaʀɑ̃t] *num* forty.
quarantième [kaʀɑ̃tjɛm] *num* fortieth.
quark [kwaʀk] *nm* quark.
quart [kaʀ] *nm* (*fraction*) quarter; (*surveillance*) watch; (*partie*): **un ~ de poulet/fromage** a chicken quarter/a quarter of a cheese; **un ~ de beurre** a quarter kilo of butter, ≈ a half pound of butter; **un ~ de vin** a quarter litre of wine; **une livre un ~** *ou* **et ~** one and a quarter pounds; **le ~ de** a quarter of; **~ d'heure** quarter of an hour; **2 h et** *ou* **un ~** (a) quarter past 2 *ou* after 2 (*US*); **il est le ~** it's (a) quarter past *ou* after (*US*); **une heure moins le ~** (a) quarter to one *ou* of one (*US*); **il est moins le ~** it's (a) quarter to; **être de/prendre le ~** to keep/take the watch; **~ de tour** quarter turn; **au ~ de tour** (*fig*) straight off; **~s de finale** (*SPORT*) quarter finals.
quarté [kaʀte] *nm* (*COURSES*) *system of forecast betting giving first four horses*.
quarteron [kaʀtəʀɔ̃] *nm* (*péj*) small bunch.

quartette [kwaʀtɛt] *nm* quartet(te).
quartier [kaʀtje] *nm* (*de ville*) district, area; (*de bœuf, de la lune*) quarter; (*de fruit, fromage*) piece; **~s** *nmpl* (*MIL, BLASON*) quarters; **cinéma/salle de ~** local cinema/hall; **avoir ~ libre** to be free; (*MIL*) to have leave from barracks; **ne pas faire de ~** to spare no one, give no quarter; **~ commerçant/résidentiel** shopping/residential area; **~ général (QG)** headquarters (HQ).
quartier-maître [kaʀtjemɛtʀ(ə)] *nm* ≈ leading seaman.
quasi [kazi] *adv* almost, nearly ♦ *préfixe*: **~-certitude** near certainty.
quasiment [kazimɑ̃] *adv* almost, very nearly.
quaternaire [kwatɛʀnɛʀ] *adj* (*GÉO*) Quaternary.
quatorze [katɔʀz(ə)] *num* fourteen.
quatorzième [katɔʀzjɛm] *num* fourteenth.
quatrain [katʀɛ̃] *nm* quatrain.
quatre [katʀ(ə)] *num* four; **à ~ pattes** on all fours; **tiré à ~ épingles** dressed up to the nines; **faire les ~ cent coups** to be a bit wild; **se mettre en ~ pour qn** to go out of one's way for sb; **~ à ~** (*monter, descendre*) four at a time; **à ~ mains** (*jouer*) four-handed.
quatre-vingt-dix [katʀəvɛ̃dis] *num* ninety.
quatre-vingts [katʀəvɛ̃] *num* eighty.
quatrième [katʀijɛm] *num* fourth.
quatuor [kwatɥɔʀ] *nm* quartet(te).

MOT-CLÉ

que [kə] *conj* **1** (*introduisant complétive*) that; **il sait ~ tu es là** he knows (that) you're here; **je veux ~ tu acceptes** I want you to accept; **il a dit ~ oui** he said he would (*ou* it was *etc*)
2 (*reprise d'autres conjonctions*): **quand il rentrera et qu'il aura mangé** when he gets back and (when) he has eaten; **si vous y allez ou ~ vous ...** if you go there or if you ...
3 (*en tête de phrase*: *hypothèse, souhait etc*): **qu'il le veuille ou non** whether he likes it or not; **qu'il fasse ce qu'il voudra**! let him do as he pleases!
4 (*but*): **tenez-le qu'il ne tombe pas** hold it so (that) it doesn't fall
5 (*après comparatif*) than; as; *voir aussi* **plus; aussi; autant** *etc*
6 (*seulement*): **ne ... ~** only; **il ne boit ~ de l'eau** he only drinks water
7 (*temps*): **elle venait à peine de sortir qu'il se mit à pleuvoir** she had just gone out when it started to rain, no sooner had she gone out than it started to rain; **il y a 4 ans qu'il est parti** it is 4 years since he left, he left 4 years ago
♦ *adv* (*exclamation*): **qu'il** *ou* **qu'est-ce qu'il est bête/court vite!** he's so silly!/he runs so fast!; **~ de livres!** what a lot of books!
♦ *pron* **1** (*relatif*: *personne*) whom; (: *chose*) that, which; **l'homme ~ je vois** the man (whom) I see; **le livre ~ tu vois** the book (that *ou* which) you see; **un jour ~ j'étais ...** a day when I was ...
2 (*interrogatif*) what; **~ fais-tu?, qu'est-ce ~ tu fais?** what are you doing?; **qu'est-ce ~ c'est?** what is it?, what's that?; **~ faire?** what can one do?; **~ préfères-tu, celui-ci ou celui-là?** which (one) do you prefer, this one or that one?

Québec [kebɛk] *n* (*ville*) Quebec ♦ *nm*: **le ~** Quebec (Province).
québécois, e [kebekwa, -waz] *adj* Quebec *cpd* ♦ *nm* (*LING*) Quebec French ♦ *nm/f*: **Q~, e** Quebecois, Quebec(k)er.

MOT-CLÉ

quel, quelle [kɛl] *adj* **1** (*interrogatif*: *personne*) who; (: *chose*) what; which; **~ est cet homme?** who is this man?; **~ est ce livre?** what is this book?; **~ livre/homme?** what book/man?; (*parmi un certain choix*) which book/man?; **~s acteurs préférez-vous?** which actors do you prefer?; **dans ~s pays êtes-vous allé?** which *ou* what countries did you go to?
2 (*exclamatif*): **quelle surprise/coïncidence!** what a surprise/coincidence!
3: **~ que soit le coupable** whoever is guilty; **~ que soit votre avis** whatever your opinion (may be).

quelconque [kɛlkɔ̃k] *adj* (*médiocre*) indifferent, poor; (*sans attrait*) ordinary, plain; (*indéfini*): **un ami/prétexte ~** some friend/pretext or other; **un livre ~ suffira** any book will do; **pour une raison ~** for some reason (or other).

MOT-CLÉ

quelque [kɛlkə] *adj* **1** some; a few; (*tournure interrogative*) any; **~ espoir** some hope; **il a ~s amis** he has a few *ou* some friends; **a-t-il ~s amis?** has he any friends?; **les ~s livres qui** the few books which; **20 kg et ~(s)** a bit over 20 kg; **il habite à ~ distance d'ici** he lives some distance *ou* way (away) from here
2: **~ ... que** whatever, whichever; **~ livre qu'il choisisse** whatever (*ou* whichever) book he chooses; **par ~ temps qu'il fasse** whatever the weather
3: **~ chose** something; (*tournure interrogative*) anything; **~ chose d'autre** something else; anything else; **y être pour ~ chose** to have something to do with it; **faire ~ chose à qn** to have an effect on sb, do something to sb; **~ part** somewhere; anywhere; **en ~ sorte** as it were
♦ *adv* **1** (*environ*): **~ 100 mètres** some 100 metres
2: **~ peu** rather, somewhat.

quelquefois [kɛlkəfwa] *adv* sometimes.

quelques-uns, -unes [kɛlkəzœ̃, -yn] *pron* some, a few; ~ **des lecteurs** some of the readers.

quelqu'un [kɛlkœ̃] *pron* someone, somebody, *tournure interrogative ou négative* + anyone *ou* anybody; ~ **d'autre** someone *ou* somebody else; anybody else.

quémander [kemɑ̃de] *vt* to beg for.

qu'en dira-t-on [kɑ̃diʀatɔ̃] *nm inv*: **le** ~ gossip, what people say.

quenelle [kənɛl] *nf* quenelle.

quenouille [kənuj] *nf* distaff.

querelle [kəʀɛl] *nf* quarrel; **chercher** ~ **à qn** to pick a quarrel with sb.

quereller [kəʀele]: **se** ~ *vi* to quarrel.

querelleur, euse [kəʀɛlœʀ, -øz] *adj* quarrelsome.

qu'est-ce que (*ou* qui) [kɛskə(ki)] *voir* **que, qui**.

question [kɛstjɔ̃] *nf* (*gén*) question; (*fig*) matter; issue; **il a été** ~ **de** we (*ou* they) spoke about; **il est** ~ **de les emprisonner** there's talk of them being jailed; **c'est une** ~ **de temps** it's a matter *ou* question of time; **de quoi est-il** ~**?** what is it about?; **il n'en est pas** ~ there's no question of it; **en** ~ in question; **hors de** ~ out of the question; **je ne me suis jamais posé la** ~ I've never thought about it; **(re)mettre en** ~ (*autorité, science*) to question; **poser la** ~ **de confiance** (*POL*) to ask for a vote of confidence; ~ **piège** (*d'apparence facile*) trick question; (*pour nuire*) loaded question; ~ **subsidiaire** tiebreaker.

questionnaire [kɛstjɔnɛʀ] *nm* questionnaire.

questionner [kɛstjɔne] *vt* to question.

quête [kɛt] *nf* (*collecte*) collection; (*recherche*) quest, search; **faire la** ~ (*à l'église*) to take the collection; (*artiste*) to pass the hat round; **se mettre en** ~ **de qch** to go in search of sth.

quêter [kete] *vi* (*à l'église*) to take the collection; (*dans la rue*) to collect money (for charity) ♦ *vt* to seek.

quetsche [kwɛtʃ(ə)] *nf* damson.

queue [kø] *nf* tail; (*fig: du classement*) bottom; (*: de poêle*) handle; (*: de fruit, feuille*) stalk; (*: de train, colonne, file*) rear; (*file: de personnes*) queue (*BRIT*), line (*US*); **en** ~ **(de train)** at the rear (of the train); **faire la** ~ to queue (up) (*BRIT*), line up (*US*); **se mettre à la** ~ to join the queue *ou* line; **histoire sans** ~ **ni tête** cock and bull story; **à la** ~ **leu leu** in single file; (*fig*) one after the other; ~ **de cheval** ponytail; **faire une** ~ **de poisson à qn** (*AUTO*) to cut in front of sb; **finir en** ~ **de poisson** (*film*) to come to an abrupt end.

queue-de-pie, *pl* **queues-de-pie** [kødpi] *nf* (*habit*) tails *pl*, tail coat.

queux [kø] *adj m voir* **maître.**

qui [ki] *pron* (*personne*) who, *prép* + whom; (*chose, animal*) which, that; (*interrogatif indirect: sujet*): **je me demande** ~ **est là?** I wonder who is there?; (*: objet*): **elle ne sait à** ~ **se plaindre** she doesn't know who to complain to *ou* to whom to complain; **qu'est-ce** ~ **est sur la table?** what is on the table?; **à** ~ **est ce sac?** whose bag is this?; **à** ~ **parlais-tu?** who were you talking to?, to whom were you talking?; **chez** ~ **allez-vous?** whose house are you going to?; **amenez** ~ **vous voulez** bring who(ever) you like; ~ **est-ce** ~...**?** who?; ~ **est-ce que** ...**?** who?; whom?; ~ **que ce soit** whoever it may be.

quiche [kiʃ] *nf* quiche; ~ **lorraine** quiche Lorraine.

quiconque [kikɔ̃k] *pron* (*celui qui*) whoever, anyone who; (*n'importe qui, personne*) anyone, anybody.

quidam [kɥidam] *nm* (*hum*) fellow.

quiétude [kjetyd] *nf* (*d'un lieu*) quiet, tranquillity; (*d'une personne*) peace (of mind), serenity; **en toute** ~ in complete peace; (*mentale*) with complete peace of mind.

quignon [kiɲɔ̃] *nm*: ~ **de pain** (*croûton*) crust of bread; (*morceau*) hunk of bread.

quille [kij] *nf* ninepin, skittle (*BRIT*); (*NAVIG: d'un bateau*) keel; **(jeu de)** ~**s** ninepins *sg*, skittles *sg* (*BRIT*).

quincaillerie [kɛ̃kɑjʀi] *nf* (*outils, métier*) hardware, ironmongery (*BRIT*); (*magasin*) hardware shop *ou* store (*US*), ironmonger's (*BRIT*).

quincaillier, ière [kɛ̃kɑje, -jɛʀ] *nm/f* hardware dealer, ironmonger (*BRIT*).

quinconce [kɛ̃kɔ̃s] *nm*: **en** ~ in staggered rows.

quinine [kinin] *nf* quinine.

quinqua [kɛ̃ka] *nm/f* (*fam*) (= *quinquagénaire*) person in his (*ou* her) fifties; **les** ~**s** fifty somethings (*fam*).

quinquagénaire [kɛ̃kaʒenɛʀ] *nm/f* (*de cinquante ans*) fifty-year old; (*de cinquante à soixante ans*) man/woman in his/her fifties.

quinquennal, e, aux [kɛ̃kenal, -o] *adj* five-year, quinquennial.

quintal, aux [kɛ̃tal, -o] *nm* quintal (*100 kg*).

quinte [kɛ̃t] *nf*: ~ **(de toux)** coughing fit.

quintessence [kɛ̃tesɑ̃s] *nf* quintessence, very essence.

quintette [kɛ̃tɛt] *nm* quintet(te).

quintuple [kɛ̃typl(ə)] *nm*: **le** ~ **de** five times as much as.

quintupler [kɛ̃typle] *vt, vi* to increase fivefold.

quintuplés, ées [kɛ̃typle] *nm/fpl* quintuplets.

quinzaine [kɛ̃zɛn] *nf*: **une** ~ **(de)** about fifteen, fifteen or so; **une** ~ **(de jours)** (*deux semaines*) a fortnight (*BRIT*), two weeks; ~ **publicitaire** *ou* **commerciale** (two-week) sale.

quinze [kɛ̃z] *num* fifteen; **demain en** ~ a fortnight (*BRIT*) *ou* two weeks tomorrow; **dans** ~ **jours** in a fortnight('s time) (*BRIT*), in two weeks(' time).

quinzième [kɛ̃zjɛm] *num* fifteenth.

quiproquo [kipʀɔko] *nm* (*méprise sur une personne*) mistake; (*malentendu sur un sujet*) misunderstanding; (*THÉÂT*) (case of) mistaken identity.
Quito [kito] *n* Quito.
quittance [kitɑ̃s] *nf* (*reçu*) receipt; (*facture*) bill.
quitte [kit] *adj*: **être ~ envers qn** to be no longer in sb's debt; (*fig*) to be quits with sb; **être ~ de** (*obligation*) to be clear of; **en être ~ à bon compte** to have got off lightly; **~ à faire** even if it means doing; **~ ou double** (*jeu*) double or quits; (*fig*): **c'est du ~ ou double** it's a big risk.
quitter [kite] *vt* to leave; (*espoir, illusion*) to give up; (*vêtement*) to take off; **se ~** (*couples, interlocuteurs*) to part; **ne quittez pas** (*au téléphone*) hold the line; **ne pas ~ qn d'une semelle** to stick to sb like glue.
quitus [kitys] *nm* final discharge; **donner ~ à** to discharge.
qui-vive [kiviv] *nm inv*: **être sur le ~** to be on the alert.
quoi [kwa] *pron* (*interrogatif*) what; **~ de neuf** *ou* **de nouveau?** what's new *ou* the news?; **as-tu de ~ écrire?** have you anything to write with?; **il n'a pas de ~ se l'acheter** he can't afford it, he hasn't got the money to buy it; **il y a de ~ être fier** that's something to be proud of; **"il n'y a pas de ~"** "(please) don't mention it", "not at all"; **~ qu'il arrive** whatever happens; **~ qu'il en soit** be that as it may; **~ que ce soit** anything at all; **en ~ puis-je vous aider?** how can I help you?; **à ~ bon?** what's the use *ou* point?; **et puis ~ encore!** what(ever) next!; **~ faire?** what's to be done?; **sans ~** (*ou sinon*) otherwise.
quoique [kwak(ə)] *conj* (al)though.
quolibet [kɔlibɛ] *nm* gibe, jeer.
quorum [kɔʀɔm] *nm* quorum.
quota [kwɔta] *nm* quota.
quote-part [kɔtpaʀ] *nf* share.
quotidien, ne [kɔtidjɛ̃, -ɛn] *adj* (*journalier*) daily; (*banal*) ordinary, everyday ♦ *nm* (*journal*) daily (paper); (*vie quotidienne*) daily life, day-to-day existence; **les grands ~s** the big (national) dailies.
quotidiennement [kɔtidjɛnmɑ̃] *adv* daily, every day.
quotient [kɔsjɑ̃] *nm* (*MATH*) quotient; **~ intellectuel (QI)** intelligence quotient (IQ).
quotité [kɔtite] *nf* (*FINANCE*) quota.

R r

R, r [ɛʀ] *nm inv* R, r ♦ *abr* = **route, rue; R comme Raoul** R for Robert (*BRIT*) *ou* Roger (*US*).
rab [ʀab] (*fam*), **rabiot** [ʀabjo] *nm* extra, more.
rabâcher [ʀabɑʃe] *vi* to harp on ♦ *vt* keep on repeating.
rabais [ʀabɛ] *nm* reduction, discount; **au ~** at a reduction *ou* discount.
rabaisser [ʀabese] *vt* (*rabattre*) to reduce; (*dénigrer*) to belittle.
rabane [ʀaban] *nf* raffia (matting).
Rabat [ʀaba(t)] *n* Rabat.
rabat [ʀaba] *vb voir* **rabattre** ♦ *nm* flap.
rabat-joie [ʀabaʒwa] *nm/f inv* killjoy (*BRIT*), spoilsport.
rabatteur, euse [ʀabatœʀ, -øz] *nm/f* (*de gibier*) beater; (*péj*) tout.
rabattre [ʀabatʀ(ə)] *vt* (*couvercle, siège*) to pull down; (*col*) to turn down; (*couture*) to stitch down; (*gibier*) to drive; (*somme d'un prix*) to deduct, take off; (*orgueil, prétentions*) to humble; (*TRICOT*) to decrease; **se ~** *vi* (*bords, couvercle*) to fall shut; (*véhicule, coureur*) to cut in; **se ~ sur** (*accepter*) to fall back on.
rabattu, e [ʀabaty] *pp de* **rabattre** ♦ *adj* turned down.
rabbin [ʀabɛ̃] *nm* rabbi.
rabique [ʀabik] *adj* rabies *cpd*.
râble [ʀɑbl(ə)] *nm* back; (*CULIN*) saddle.
râblé, e [ʀɑble] *adj* broad-backed, stocky.
rabot [ʀabo] *nm* plane.
raboter [ʀabɔte] *vt* to plane (down).
raboteux, euse [ʀabɔtø, -øz] *adj* uneven, rough.
rabougri, e [ʀabugʀi] *adj* stunted.
rabrouer [ʀabʀue] *vt* to snub, rebuff.
racaille [ʀakɑj] *nf* (*péj*) rabble, riffraff.
raccommodage [ʀakɔmɔdaʒ] *nm* mending *no pl*, repairing *no pl*; darning *no pl*.
raccommoder [ʀakɔmɔde] *vt* to mend, repair; (*chaussette etc*) to darn; (*fam*: *réconcilier: amis, ménage*) to bring together again; **se ~ (avec)** (*fam*) to patch it up (with).
raccompagner [ʀakɔ̃paɲe] *vt* to take *ou* see back.
raccord [ʀakɔʀ] *nm* link; **~ de maçonnerie** pointing *no pl*; **~ de peinture** join; touch-up.
raccordement [ʀakɔʀdəmɑ̃] *nm* joining up; connection.
raccorder [ʀakɔʀde] *vt* to join (up), link up; (*suj: pont etc*) to connect, link; **se ~ à** to join up with; (*fig: se rattacher à*) to tie in with; **~ au réseau du téléphone** to connect to the

telephone service.
raccourci [RakuRsi] *nm* short cut; **en** ~ in brief.
raccourcir [RakuRsiR] *vt* to shorten ♦ *vi* (*vêtement*) to shrink.
raccroc [RakRo]: **par** ~ *adv* by chance.
raccrocher [RakRɔʃe] *vt* (*tableau, vêtement*) to hang back up; (*récepteur*) to put down; (*fig: affaire*) to save ♦ *vi* (*TÉL*) to hang up, ring off; **se** ~ **à** *vt* to cling to, hang on to; **ne raccrochez pas** (*TÉL*) hold on, don't hang up.
race [Ras] *nf* race; (*d'animaux, fig: espèce*) breed; (*ascendance, origine*) stock, race; **de** ~ *adj* purebred, pedigree.
racé, e [Rase] *adj* thoroughbred.
rachat [Raʃa] *nm* buying; buying back; redemption; atonement.
racheter [Raʃte] *vt* (*article perdu*) to buy another; (*davantage*): ~ **du lait/3 œufs** to buy more milk/another 3 eggs *ou* 3 more eggs; (*après avoir vendu*) to buy back; (*d'occasion*) to buy; (*COMM: part, firme*) to buy up; (*: pension, rente*) to redeem; (*REL: pécheur*) to redeem; (*: péché*) to atone for, expiate; (*mauvaise conduite, oubli, défaut*) to make up for; **se** ~ (*REL*) to redeem o.s.; (*gén*) to make amends, make up for it.
rachidien, ne [Raʃidjɛ̃, -ɛn] *adj* rachidian, of the spine.
rachitique [Raʃitik] *adj* suffering from rickets; (*fig*) scraggy, scrawny.
rachitisme [Raʃitism(ə)] *nm* rickets *sg*.
racial, e, aux [Rasjal, -o] *adj* racial.
racine [Rasin] *nf* root; (*fig: attache*) roots *pl*; ~ **carrée/cubique** square/cube root; **prendre** ~ (*fig*) to take root; to put down roots.
racisme [Rasism(ə)] *nm* racism, racialism.
raciste [Rasist(ə)] *adj, nm/f* racist, racialist.
racket [Rakɛt] *nm* racketeering *no pl*.
racketteur [RakɛtœR] *nm* racketeer.
raclée [Rɑkle] *nf* (*fam*) hiding, thrashing.
raclement [Rɑkləmɑ̃] *nm* (*bruit*) scraping (noise).
racler [Rɑkle] *vt* (*os, plat*) to scrape; (*tache, boue*) to scrape off; (*fig: instrument*) to scrape on; (*suj: chose: frotter contre*) to scrape (against).
raclette [Rɑklɛt] *nf* (*CULIN*) raclette (*Swiss cheese dish*).
racloir [RɑklwaR] *nm* (*outil*) scraper.
racolage [Rakɔlaʒ] *nm* soliciting; touting.
racoler [Rakɔle] *vt* (*attirer: suj: prostituée*) to solicit; (*: parti, marchand*) to tout for; (*attraper*) to pick up.
racoleur, euse [RakɔlœR, -øz] *adj* (*péj: publicité*) cheap and alluring ♦ *nm* (*péj: de clients etc*) tout ♦ *nf* streetwalker.
racontars [Rakɔ̃taR] *nmpl* stories, gossip *sg*.
raconter [Rakɔ̃te] *vt*: ~ **(à qn)** (*décrire*) to relate (to sb), tell (sb) about; (*dire*) to tell (sb).
racorni, e [RakɔRni] *adj* hard(ened).
racornir [RakɔRniR] *vt* to harden.
radar [RadaR] *nm* radar; **système** ~ radar system; **écran** ~ radar screen.
rade [Rad] *nf* (natural) harbour; **en** ~ **de Toulon** in Toulon harbour; **rester en** ~ (*fig*) to be left stranded.
radeau, x [Rado] *nm* raft; ~ **de sauvetage** life raft.
radial, e, aux [Radjal, -o] *adj* radial; **pneu à carcasse** ~**e** radial tyre.
radiant, e [Radjɑ̃, -ɑ̃t] *adj* radiant.
radiateur [RadjatœR] *nm* radiator, heater; (*AUTO*) radiator; ~ **électrique/à gaz** electric/gas heater *ou* fire.
radiation [Radjɑsjɔ̃] *nf* (*d'un nom etc*) striking off *no pl*; (*PHYSIQUE*) radiation.
radical, e, aux [Radikal, -o] *adj* radical ♦ *nm* (*LING*) stem; (*MATH*) root sign; (*POL*) radical.
radicalement [Radikalmɑ̃] *adv* radically, completely.
radicaliser [Radikalize] *vt* (*durcir: opinions etc*) to harden; **se** ~ *vi* (*mouvement etc*) to become more radical.
radicalisme [Radikalism(ə)] *nm* (*POL*) radicalism.
radier [Radje] *vt* to strike off.
radiesthésie [Radjɛstezi] *nf* divination (by radiation).
radiesthésiste [Radjɛstezist(ə)] *nm/f* diviner.
radieux, euse [Radjø, -øz] *adj* (*visage, personne*) radiant; (*journée, soleil*) brilliant, glorious.
radin, e [Radɛ̃, -in] *adj* (*fam*) stingy.
radio [Radjo] *nf* radio; (*MÉD*) X-ray ♦ *nm* (*personne*) radio operator; **à la** ~ on the radio, **avoir la** ~ to have a radio; **passer à la** ~ to be on the radio; **se faire faire une** ~**/une** ~ **des poumons** to have an X-ray/a chest X-ray.
radio... [Radjɔ] *préfixe* radio....
radioactif, ive [Radjɔaktif, -iv] *adj* radioactive.
radioactivité [Radjɔaktivite] *nf* radioactivity.
radioamateur [RadjɔamatœR] *nm* (radio) ham.
radiobalise [Radjɔbaliz] *nf* radio beacon.
radiocassette [Radjɔkasɛt] *nf* cassette radio.
radiodiffuser [Radjɔdifyze] *vt* to broadcast.
radiodiffusion [Radjɔdifyzjɔ̃] *nf* (radio) broadcasting.
radioélectrique [RadjɔelɛktRik] *adj* radio *cpd*.
radiogoniomètre [RadjɔgɔnjɔmɛtR(ə)] *nm* direction finder, radiogoniometer.
radiographie [RadjɔgRafi] *nf* radiography; (*photo*) X-ray photograph, radiograph.
radiographier [RadjɔgRafje] *vt* to X-ray; **se faire** ~ to have an X-ray.
radioguidage [Radjɔgidaʒ] *nm* (*NAVIG, AVIAT*) radio control; (*AUTO*) (broadcast of) traffic information.
radioguider [Radjɔgide] *vt* (*NAVIG, AVIAT*) to guide by radio, control by radio.
radiologie [Radjɔlɔʒi] *nf* radiology.
radiologique [Radjɔlɔʒik] *adj* radiological.
radiologue [Radjɔlɔg] *nm/f* radiologist.

radionavigant [ʀadjɔnavigɑ̃] *nm* radio officer.
radiophare [ʀadjɔfaʀ] *nm* radio beacon.
radiophonique [ʀadjɔfɔnik] *adj*: **programme/émission/jeu** ~ radio programme/broadcast/game.
radioreportage [ʀadjɔʀəpɔʀtaʒ] *nm* radio report.
radio(-)réveil [ʀadjɔʀevɛj] *nm* clock radio.
radioscopie [ʀadjɔskɔpi] *nf* radioscopy.
radio-taxi [ʀadjɔtaksi] *nm* radiotaxi.
radiotélégraphie [ʀadjɔtelegʀafi] *nf* radiotelegraphy.
radiotéléphone [ʀadjɔtelefɔn] *nm* radiotelephone.
radiotélescope [ʀadjɔtelɛskɔp] *nm* radiotelescope.
radiotélévisé, e [ʀadjɔtelevize] *adj* broadcast on radio and television.
radiothérapie [ʀadjɔteʀapi] *nf* radiotherapy.
radis [ʀadi] *nm* radish; ~ **noir** horseradish *no pl*.
radium [ʀadjɔm] *nm* radium.
radoter [ʀadɔte] *vi* to ramble on.
radoub [ʀadu] *nm*: **bassin** *ou* **cale de** ~ dry dock.
radouber [ʀadube] *vt* to repair, refit.
radoucir [ʀadusiʀ]: **se** ~ *vi* (*se réchauffer*) to become milder; (*se calmer*) to calm down; to soften.
radoucissement [ʀadusismɑ̃] *nm* milder period, better weather.
rafale [ʀafal] *nf* (*vent*) gust (of wind); (*de balles, d'applaudissements*) burst; ~ **de mitrailleuse** burst of machine-gun fire.
raffermir [ʀafɛʀmiʀ] *vt*, **se** ~ *vi* (*tissus, muscle*) to firm up; (*fig*) to strengthen.
raffermissement [ʀafɛʀmismɑ̃] *nm* (*fig*) strengthening.
raffinage [ʀafinaʒ] *nm* refining.
raffiné, e [ʀafine] *adj* refined.
raffinement [ʀafinmɑ̃] *nm* refinement.
raffiner [ʀafine] *vt* to refine.
raffinerie [ʀafinʀi] *nf* refinery.
raffoler [ʀafɔle]: ~ **de** *vt* to be very keen on.
raffut [ʀafy] *nm* (*fam*) row, racket.
rafiot [ʀafjo] *nm* tub.
rafistoler [ʀafistɔle] *vt* (*fam*) to patch up.
rafle [ʀɑfl(ə)] *nf* (*de police*) roundup, raid.
rafler [ʀɑfle] *vt* (*fam*) to swipe, nick.
rafraîchir [ʀafʀeʃiʀ] *vt* (*atmosphère, température*) to cool (down); (*aussi*: **mettre à** ~) to chill; (*suj: air, eau*) to freshen up; (*: boisson*) to refresh; (*fig: rénover*) to brighten up ♦ *vi*: **mettre du vin/une boisson à** ~ to chill wine/a drink; **se** ~ to grow cooler; to freshen up; (*personne: en buvant etc*) to refresh o.s; ~ **la mémoire** *ou* **les idées à qn** to refresh sb's memory.
rafraîchissant, e [ʀafʀeʃisɑ̃, -ɑ̃t] *adj* refreshing.
rafraîchissement [ʀafʀeʃismɑ̃] *nm* cooling; (*boisson*) cool drink; ~**s** *nmpl* (*boissons, fruits etc*) refreshments.
ragaillardir [ʀagajaʀdiʀ] *vt* (*fam*) to perk *ou* buck up.
rage [ʀaʒ] *nf* (*MÉD*): **la** ~ rabies; (*fureur*) rage, fury; **faire** ~ to rage; ~ **de dents** (raging) toothache.
rager [ʀaʒe] *vi* to fume (with rage); **faire** ~ **qn** to enrage sb, get sb mad.
rageur, euse [ʀaʒœʀ, -øz] *adj* snarling; ill-tempered.
raglan [ʀaglɑ̃] *adj inv* raglan.
ragot [ʀago] *nm* (*fam*) malicious gossip *no pl*.
ragoût [ʀagu] *nm* (*plat*) stew.
ragoûtant, e [ʀagutɑ̃, -ɑ̃t] *adj*: **peu** ~ unpalatable.
rai [ʀɛ] *nm*: **un** ~ **de soleil/lumière** a shaft of sunshine/light.
raid [ʀɛd] *nm* (*MIL*) raid; (*attaque aérienne*) air raid; (*SPORT*) long-distance trek.
raide [ʀɛd] *adj* (*tendu*) taut, tight; (*escarpé*) steep; (*droit: cheveux*) straight; (*ankylosé, dur, guindé*) stiff; (*fam: cher*) steep, stiff; (*: sans argent*) flat broke; (*osé, licencieux*) daring ♦ *adv* (*en pente*) steeply; ~ **mort** stone dead.
raideur [ʀɛdœʀ] *nf* steepness; stiffness.
raidir [ʀediʀ] *vt* (*muscles*) to stiffen; (*câble*) to pull taut, tighten; **se** ~ *vi* to stiffen; to become taut; (*personne: se crisper*) to tense up; (*: devenir intransigeant*) to harden.
raidissement [ʀedismɑ̃] *nm* stiffening; tightening; hardening.
raie [ʀɛ] *nf* (*ZOOL*) skate, ray; (*rayure*) stripe; (*des cheveux*) parting.
raifort [ʀɛfɔʀ] *nm* horseradish.
rail [ʀɑj] *nm* (*barre d'acier*) rail; (*chemins de fer*) railways *pl* (*BRIT*), railroads *pl* (*US*); **les** ~**s** (*la voie ferrée*) the rails, the track *sg*; **par** ~ by rail; ~ **conducteur** live *ou* conductor rail.
railler [ʀɑje] *vt* to scoff at, jeer at.
raillerie [ʀɑjʀi] *nf* mockery.
railleur, euse [ʀɑjœʀ, -øz] *adj* mocking.
rail-route [ʀɑjʀut] *nm* road-rail.
rainurage [ʀenyʀaʒ] *nm* (*AUTO*) uneven road surface.
rainure [ʀenyʀ] *nf* groove; slot.
rais [ʀɛ] *nm inv* = **rai**.
raisin [ʀɛzɛ̃] *nm* (*aussi*: ~**s**) grapes *pl*; (*variété*): ~ **blanc/noir** white (*ou* green)/black grape; ~ **muscat** muscat grape; ~**s secs** raisins.
raison [ʀɛzɔ̃] *nf* reason; **avoir** ~ to be right; **donner** ~ **à qn** (*personne*) to agree with sb; (*fait*) to prove sb right; **avoir** ~ **de qn/qch** to get the better of sb/sth; **se faire une** ~ to learn to live with it; **perdre la** ~ to become insane; (*fig*) to take leave of one's senses; **recouvrer la** ~ to come to one's senses; **ramener qn à la** ~ to make sb see sense; **demander** ~ **à qn de** (*affront etc*) to demand satisfaction from sb for; **entendre** ~ to listen to reason, see reason; **plus que de** ~ too much, more than is reasonable; ~ **de plus** all the more reason; **à plus forte** ~ all the

more so; **en ~ de** (*à cause de*) because of; (*à proportion de*) in proportion to; **à ~ de** at the rate of; **~ d'État** reason of state; **~ d'être** raison d'être; **~ sociale** corporate name.

raisonnable [rɛzɔnabl(ə)] *adj* reasonable, sensible.

raisonnablement [rɛzɔnabləmɑ̃] *adv* reasonably.

raisonné, e [rɛzɔne] *adj* reasoned.

raisonnement [rɛzɔnmɑ̃] *nm* reasoning; arguing; argument.

raisonner [rɛzɔne] *vi* (*penser*) to reason; (*argumenter, discuter*) to argue ♦ *vt* (*personne*) to reason with; (*attitude: justifier*) to reason out; **se ~** to reason with oneself.

raisonneur, euse [rɛzɔnœr, -øz] *adj* (*péj*) quibbling.

rajeunir [raʒœniʀ] *vt* (*suj: coiffure, robe*): **~ qn** to make sb look younger; (*suj: cure etc*) to rejuvenate; (*fig: rafraîchir*) to brighten up; (*: moderniser*) to give a new look to; (*: en recrutant*) to inject new blood into ♦ *vi* (*personne*) to become (*ou* look) younger; (*entreprise, quartier*) to be modernized.

rajout [raʒu] *nm* addition.

rajouter [raʒute] *vt* (*commentaire*) to add; **~ du sel/un œuf** to add some more salt/another egg; **~ que** to add that; **en ~** to lay it on thick.

rajustement [raʒystəmɑ̃] *nm* adjustment.

rajuster [raʒyste] *vt* (*vêtement*) to straighten, tidy; (*salaires*) to adjust; (*machine*) to readjust; **se ~** to tidy *ou* straighten o.s. up.

râle [rɑl] *nm* groan; **~ d'agonie** death rattle.

ralenti [ralɑ̃ti] *nm*: **au ~** (*CINÉ*) in slow motion; (*fig*) at a slower pace; **tourner au ~** (*AUTO*) to tick over, idle.

ralentir [ralɑ̃tiʀ] *vt, vi,* **se ~** *vi* to slow down.

ralentissement [ralɑ̃tismɑ̃] *nm* slowing down.

râler [rɑle] *vi* to groan; (*fam*) to grouse, moan (and groan).

ralliement [ralimɑ̃] *nm* (*rassemblement*) rallying; (*adhésion: à une cause, une opinion*) winning over; **point/signe de ~** rallying point/sign.

rallier [ralje] *vt* (*rassembler*) to rally; (*rejoindre*) to rejoin; (*gagner à sa cause*) to win over; **se ~ à** (*avis*) to come over *ou* round to.

rallonge [ralɔ̃ʒ] *nf* (*de table*) (extra) leaf (*pl* leaves); (*argent etc*) extra *no pl*; (*ÉLEC*) extension (cable *ou* flex); (*fig: de crédit etc*) extension.

rallonger [ralɔ̃ʒe] *vt* to lengthen.

rallumer [ralyme] *vt* to light up again, relight; (*fig*) to revive; **se ~** *vi* (*lumière*) to come on again.

rallye [rali] *nm* rally; (*POL*) march.

ramages [ramaʒ] *nmpl* (*dessin*) leaf pattern *sg*; (*chants*) songs.

ramassage [ramɑsaʒ] *nm*: **~ scolaire** school bus service.

ramassé, e [ramɑse] *adj* (*trapu*) squat, stocky; (*concis: expression etc*) compact.

ramasse-miettes [ramɑsmjɛt] *nm inv* table-tidy.

ramasse-monnaie [ramɑsmɔnɛ] *nm inv* change-tray.

ramasser [ramɑse] *vt* (*objet tombé ou par terre, fam*) to pick up; (*recueillir*) to collect; (*récolter*) to gather; (*: pommes de terre*) to lift; **se ~** *vi* (*sur soi-même*) to huddle up; to crouch.

ramasseur, euse [ramɑsœr, -øz] *nm/f*: **~ de balles** ballboy/girl.

ramassis [ramɑsi] *nm* (*péj: de gens*) bunch; (*: de choses*) jumble.

rambarde [rɑ̃bard(ə)] *nf* guardrail.

rame [ram] *nf* (*aviron*) oar; (*de métro*) train; (*de papier*) ream; **~ de haricots** bean support; **faire force de ~s** to row hard.

rameau, x [ramo] *nm* (small) branch; (*fig*) branch; **les R~x** (*REL*) Palm Sunday *sg*.

ramener [ramne] *vt* to bring back; (*reconduire*) to take back; (*rabattre: couverture, visière*): **~ qch sur** to pull sth back over; **~ qch à** (*réduire à, aussi MATH*) to reduce sth to; **~ qn à la vie/raison** to bring sb back to life/bring sb to his (*ou* her) senses; **se ~** *vi* (*fam*) to roll *ou* turn up; **se ~ à** (*se réduire à*) to come *ou* boil down to.

ramequin [ramkɛ̃] *nm* ramekin.

ramer [rame] *vi* to row.

rameur, euse [ramœr, -øz] *nm/f* rower.

rameuter [ramøte] *vt* to gather together.

ramier [ramje] *nm*: **(pigeon) ~** woodpigeon.

ramification [ramifikɑsjɔ̃] *nf* ramification.

ramifier [ramifje]: **se ~** *vi* (*tige, secte, réseau*): **se ~ (en)** to branch out (into); (*veines, nerfs*) to ramify.

ramolli, e [ramɔli] *adj* soft.

ramollir [ramɔliʀ] *vt* to soften; **se ~** *vi* (*os, tissus*) to get (*ou* go) soft; (*beurre, asphalte*) to soften.

ramonage [ramɔnaʒ] *nm* (chimney-) sweeping.

ramoner [ramɔne] *vt* (*cheminée*) to sweep; (*pipe*) to clean.

ramoneur [ramɔnœr] *nm* (chimney) sweep.

rampe [rɑ̃p] *nf* (*d'escalier*) banister(s *pl*); (*dans un garage, d'un terrain*) ramp; (*THÉÂT*): **la ~** the footlights *pl*; (*lampes: lumineuse, de balisage*) floodlights *pl*; **passer la ~** (*toucher le public*) to get across to the audience; **~ de lancement** launching pad.

ramper [rɑ̃pe] *vi* (*reptile, animal*) to crawl; (*plante*) to creep.

rancard [rɑ̃kar] *nm* (*fam*) date; tip.

rancart [rɑ̃kar] *nm*: **mettre au ~** (*article, projet*) to scrap; (*personne*) to put on the scrapheap.

rance [rɑ̃s] *adj* rancid.

rancir [rɑ̃siʀ] *vi* to go off, go rancid.

rancœur [rɑ̃kœr] *nf* rancour (*BRIT*), rancor (*US*), resentment.

rançon [rɑ̃sɔ̃] *nf* ransom; (*fig*): **la ~ du succès**

etc the price of success *etc*.
rançonner [Rɑ̃sɔne] *vt* to hold to ransom.
rancune [Rɑ̃kyn] *nf* grudge, rancour (*BRIT*), rancor (*US*); **garder ~ à qn (de qch)** to bear sb a grudge (for sth); **sans ~!** no hard feelings!
rancunier, ière [Rɑ̃kynje, -jɛR] *adj* vindictive, spiteful.
randonnée [Rɑ̃dɔne] *nf* ride; (*à pied*) walk, ramble; hike, hiking *no pl*.
randonneur, euse [Rɑ̃dɔnœR, -øz] *nm/f* hiker.
rang [Rɑ̃] *nm* (*rangée*) row; (*de perles*) row, string, rope; (*grade, condition sociale, classement*) rank; **~s** *nmpl* (*MIL*) ranks; **se mettre en ~s/sur un ~** to get into *ou* form rows/a line; **sur 3 ~s** (lined up) 3 deep; **se mettre en ~s par 4** to form fours *ou* rows of 4; **se mettre sur les ~s** (*fig*) to get into the running; **au premier ~** in the first row; (*fig*) ranking first; **rentrer dans le ~** to get into line; **au ~ de** (*au nombre de*) among (the ranks of); **avoir ~ de** to hold the rank of.
rangé, e [Rɑ̃ʒe] *adj* (*sérieux*) orderly, steady.
rangée [Rɑ̃ʒe] *nf* row.
rangement [Rɑ̃ʒmɑ̃] *nm* tidying-up, putting-away; **faire des ~s** to tidy up.
ranger [Rɑ̃ʒe] *vt* (*classer, grouper*) to order, arrange; (*mettre à sa place*) to put away; (*voiture dans la rue*) to park; (*mettre de l'ordre dans*) to tidy up; (*arranger, disposer: en cercle etc*) to arrange; (*fig: classer*): **~ qn/qch parmi** to rank sb/sth among; **se ~** *vi* (*se placer, se disposer: autour d'une table etc*) to take one's place, sit round; (*véhicule, conducteur: s'écarter*) to pull over; (*: s'arrêter*) to pull in; (*piéton*) to step aside; (*s'assagir*) to settle down; **se ~ à** (*avis*) to come round to, fall in with.
ranimer [Ranime] *vt* (*personne évanouie*) to bring round; (*revigorer: forces, courage*) to restore; (*réconforter: troupes etc*) to kindle new life in; (*douleur, souvenir*) to revive; (*feu*) to rekindle.
rapace [Rapas] *nm* bird of prey ♦ *adj* (*péj*) rapacious, grasping; **~ diurne/nocturne** diurnal/nocturnal bird of prey.
rapatrié, e [RapatRije] *nm/f* repatriate (*esp French North African settler*).
rapatriement [RapatRimɑ̃] *nm* repatriation.
rapatrier [RapatRije] *vt* to repatriate; (*capitaux*) to bring (back) into the country.
râpe [Rɑp] *nf* (*CULIN*) grater; (*à bois*) rasp.
râpé, e [Rɑpe] *adj* (*tissu*) threadbare; (*CULIN*) grated.
râper [Rɑpe] *vt* (*CULIN*) to grate; (*gratter, râcler*) to rasp.
rapetasser [Raptase] *vt* (*fam*) to patch up.
rapetisser [Raptise] *vt*: **~ qch** to shorten sth; to make sth look smaller ♦ *vi*, **se ~** *vi* to shrink.
râpeux, euse [Rɑpø, -øz] *adj* rough.
raphia [Rafja] *nm* raffia.
rapide [Rapid] *adj* fast; (*prompt*) quick; (*intelligence*) quick ♦ *nm* express (train); (*de cours d'eau*) rapid.
rapidement [Rapidmɑ̃] *adv* fast; quickly.
rapidité [Rapidite] *nf* speed; quickness.
rapiécer [Rapjese] *vt* to patch.
rappel [Rapɛl] *nm* (*d'un ambassadeur, MIL*) recall; (*THÉÂT*) curtain call; (*MÉD: vaccination*) booster; (*ADMIN: de salaire*) back pay *no pl*; (*d'une aventure, d'un nom*) reminder; (*de limitation de vitesse: sur écriteau*) speed limit sign (*reminder*); (*TECH*) return; (*NAVIG*) sitting out; (*ALPINISME: aussi: ~ de corde*) abseiling *no pl*, roping down *no pl*; abseil; **~ à l'ordre** call to order.
rappeler [Raple] *vt* (*pour faire revenir, retéléphoner*) to call back; (*ambassadeur, MIL, INFORM*) to recall; (*acteur*) to call back (onto the stage); (*faire se souvenir*): **~ qch à qn** to remind sb of sth; **se ~** *vt* (*se souvenir de*) to remember, recall; **~ qn à la vie** to bring sb back to life; **~ qn à la décence** to recall sb to a sense of decency; **ça rappelle la Provence** it's reminiscent of Provence, it reminds you of Provence; **se ~ que...** to remember that....
rappelle [Rapɛl] *etc vb voir* **rappeler**.
rappliquer [Raplike] *vi* (*fam*) to turn up.
rapport [RapɔR] *nm* (*compte rendu*) report; (*profit*) yield, return; revenue; (*lien, analogie*) relationship; (*corrélation*) connection; (*proportion: MATH, TECH*) ratio (*pl* -s); **~s** *nmpl* (*entre personnes, pays*) relations; **avoir ~ à** to have something to do with, concern; **être en ~ avec** (*idée de corrélation*) to be related to; **être/se mettre en ~ avec qn** to be/get in touch with sb; **par ~ à** (*comparé à*) in relation to; (*à propos de*) with regard to; **sous le ~ de** from the point of view of; **sous tous (les) ~s** in all respects; **~s (sexuels)** (sexual) intercourse *sg*; **~ qualité-prix** value (for money).
rapporté, e [RapɔRte] *adj*: **pièce ~e** (*COUTURE*) patch.
rapporter [RapɔRte] *vt* (*rendre, ramener*) to bring back; (*apporter davantage*) to bring more; (*COUTURE*) to sew on; (*suj: investissement*) to yield; (*: activité*) to bring in; (*relater*) to report; (*JUR: annuler*) to revoke ♦ *vi* (*investissement*) to give a good return *ou* yield; (*activité*) to be very profitable; (*péj: moucharder*) to tell; **~ qch à** (*fig: rattacher*) to relate sth to; **se ~ à** (*correspondre à*) to relate to; **s'en ~ à** to rely on.
rapporteur, euse [RapɔRtœR, -øz] *nm/f* (*de procès, commission*) reporter; (*péj*) telltale ♦ *nm* (*GÉOM*) protractor.
rapproché, e [RapRɔʃe] *adj* (*proche*) near, close at hand; **~s** (*l'un de l'autre*) at close intervals.
rapprochement [RapRɔʃmɑ̃] *nm* (*réconciliation: de nations, familles*) reconciliation; (*analogie,*

rapport) parallel.

rapprocher [RapRɔʃe] *vt* (*chaise d'une table*): ~ **qch (de)** to bring sth closer (to); (*deux objets*) to bring closer together; (*réunir*) to bring together; (*comparer*) to establish a parallel between; **se** ~ *vi* to draw closer *ou* nearer; (*fig: familles, pays*) to come together; to come closer together; **se** ~ **de** to come closer to; (*présenter une analogie avec*) to be close to.

rapt [Rapt] *nm* abduction.

raquette [Rakɛt] *nf* (*de tennis*) racket; (*de ping-pong*) bat; (*à neige*) snowshoe.

rare [RaR] *adj* rare; (*main-d'œuvre, denrées*) scarce; (*cheveux, herbe*) sparse; **il est** ~ **que** it's rare that, it's unusual that; **se faire** ~ to become scarce; (*fig: personne*) to make oneself scarce.

raréfaction [RaRefaksjɔ̃] *nf* scarcity; (*de l'air*) rarefaction.

raréfier [RaRefje]: **se** ~ *vi* to grow scarce; (*air*) to rarefy.

rarement [RaRmɑ̃] *adv* rarely, seldom.

rareté [RaRte] *nf* (*voir rare*) rarity; scarcity.

rarissime [RaRisim] *adj* extremely rare.

RAS *abr* = *rien à signaler.*

ras, e [Rɑ, Rɑz] *adj* (*tête, cheveux*) close-cropped; (*poil, herbe*) short; (*mesure, cuillère*) level ♦ *adv* short; **faire table ~e** to make a clean sweep; **en ~e campagne** in open country; **à** ~ **bords** to the brim; **au** ~ **de** level with; **en avoir** ~ **le bol** (*fam*) to be fed up; ~ **du cou** *adj* (*pull, robe*) crew-neck.

rasade [Rɑzad] *nf* glassful.

rasant, e [Razɑ̃, ɑ̃t] *adj* (*MIL: balle, tir*) grazing; (*fam*) boring.

rascasse [Raskas] *nf* (*ZOOL*) scorpion fish.

rasé, e [Rɑze] *adj*: ~ **de frais** freshly shaven; ~ **de près** close-shaven.

rase-mottes [Rɑzmɔt] *nm inv*: **faire du** ~ to hedgehop; **vol en** ~ hedgehopping.

raser [Rɑze] *vt* (*barbe, cheveux*) to shave off; (*menton, personne*) to shave; (*fam: ennuyer*) to bore; (*démolir*) to raze (to the ground); (*frôler*) to graze, skim; **se** ~ to shave; (*fam*) to be bored (to tears).

rasoir [RɑzwaR] *nm* razor; ~ **électrique** electric shaver *ou* razor; ~ **mécanique** *ou* **de sûreté** safety razor.

rassasier [Rasazje] *vt* to satisfy; **être rassasié** (*dégoûté*) to be sated; to have had more than enough.

rassemblement [Rasɑ̃bləmɑ̃] *nm* (*groupe*) gathering; (*POL*) union; association; (*MIL*): **le** ~ parade.

rassembler [Rasɑ̃ble] *vt* (*réunir*) to assemble, gather; (*regrouper, amasser*) to gather together, collect; **se** ~ *vi* to gather; ~ **ses idées/ses esprits/son courage** to collect one's thoughts/gather one's wits/screw up one's courage.

rasseoir [RaswaR]: **se** ~ *vi* to sit down again.

rasséréner [RaseRene] *vt*: **se** ~ *vi* to recover one's serenity.

rassir [RasiR] *vi* to go stale.

rassis, e [Rasi, -iz] *adj* (*pain*) stale.

rassurant, e [RasyRɑ̃, -ɑ̃t] *adj* (*nouvelles etc*) reassuring.

rassuré, e [RasyRe] *adj*: **ne pas être très** ~ to be rather ill at ease.

rassurer [RasyRe] *vt* to reassure; **se** ~ to be reassured; **rassure-toi** don't worry.

rat [Ra] *nm* rat; ~ **d'hôtel** hotel thief (*pl* thieves); ~ **musqué** muskrat.

ratatiné, e [Ratatine] *adj* shrivelled (up), wrinkled.

ratatiner [Ratatine] *vt* to shrivel; (*peau*) to wrinkle; **se** ~ *vi* to shrivel; to become wrinkled.

ratatouille [Ratatuj] *nf* (*CULIN*) ratatouille.

rate [Rat] *nf* female rat; (*ANAT*) spleen.

raté, e [Rate] *adj* (*tentative*) unsuccessful, failed ♦ *nm/f* failure ♦ *nm* misfiring *no pl.*

râteau, x [Rɑto] *nm* rake.

râtelier [Rɑtəlje] *nm* rack; (*fam*) false teeth *pl.*

rater [Rate] *vi* (*ne pas partir: coup de feu*) to fail to go off; (*affaire, projet etc*) to go wrong, fail ♦ *vt* (*cible, train, occasion*) to miss; (*démonstration, plat*) to spoil; (*examen*) to fail; ~ **son coup** to fail, not to bring it off.

raticide [Ratisid] *nm* rat poison.

ratification [Ratifikɑsjɔ̃] *nf* ratification.

ratifier [Ratifje] *vt* to ratify.

ratio [Rasjo] *nm* ratio (*pl* -s).

ration [Rɑsjɔ̃] *nf* ration; (*fig*) share; ~ **alimentaire** food intake.

rationalisation [Rasjɔnalizɑsjɔ̃] *nf* rationalization.

rationaliser [Rasjɔnalize] *vt* to rationalize.

rationnel, le [Rasjɔnɛl] *adj* rational.

rationnellement [Rasjɔnɛlmɑ̃] *adv* rationally.

rationnement [Rasjɔnmɑ̃] *nm* rationing; **ticket de** ~ ration coupon.

rationner [Rasjɔne] *vt* to ration; (*personne*) to put on rations; **se** ~ to ration o.s.

ratisser [Ratise] *vt* (*allée*) to rake; (*feuilles*) to rake up; (*suj: armée, police*) to comb; ~ **large** to cast one's nets wide.

raton [Ratɔ̃] *nm*: ~ **laveur** raccoon.

RATP *sigle f* (= *Régie autonome des transports parisiens*) *Paris transport authority.*

rattacher [Rataʃe] *vt* (*animal, cheveux*) to tie up again; (*incorporer: ADMIN etc*): ~ **qch à** to join sth to, unite sth with; (*fig: relier*): ~ **qch à** to link sth with, relate sth to; (*: lier*): ~ **qn à** to bind *ou* tie sb to; **se** ~ **à** (*fig: avoir un lien avec*) to be linked (*ou* connected) with.

rattrapage [RatRapaʒ] *nm* (*SCOL*) remedial classes *pl*; (*ÉCON*) catching up.

rattraper [RatRape] *vt* (*fugitif*) to recapture; (*retenir, empêcher de tomber*) to catch (hold of); (*atteindre, rejoindre*) to catch up with; (*réparer: imprudence, erreur*) to make up for; **se** ~ *vi* (*regagner: du temps*) to make up for lost

time; (*: de l'argent etc*) to make good one's losses; (*réparer une gaffe etc*) to make up for it; **se ~ (à)** (*se raccrocher*) to stop o.s. falling (by catching hold of); **~ son retard/le temps perdu** to make up (for) lost time.
rature [RatyR] *nf* deletion, erasure.
raturer [RatyRe] *vt* to cross out, delete, erase.
rauque [Rok] *adj* raucous; hoarse.
ravagé, e [Ravaʒe] *adj* (*visage*) harrowed.
ravager [Ravaʒe] *vt* to devastate, ravage.
ravages [Ravaʒ] *nmpl* ravages; **faire des ~** to wreak havoc; (*fig: séducteur*) to break hearts.
ravalement [Ravalmɑ̃] *nm* restoration.
ravaler [Ravale] *vt* (*mur, façade*) to restore; (*déprécier*) to lower; (*avaler de nouveau*) to swallow again; **~ sa colère/son dégoût** to stifle one's anger/distaste.
ravaudage [Ravodaʒ] *nm* repairing, mending.
ravauder [Ravode] *vt* to repair, mend.
rave [Rav] *nf* (*BOT*) rape.
R avec AR *abr* (*= recommandé avec accusé de réception*) recorded delivery.
ravi, e [Ravi] *adj* delighted; **être ~ de/que** to be delighted with/that.
ravier [Ravje] *nm* hors d'œuvre dish.
ravigote [Ravigɔt] *adj*: **sauce ~** *oil and vinegar dressing with shallots*.
ravigoter [Ravigɔte] *vt* (*fam*) to buck up.
ravin [Ravɛ̃] *nm* gully, ravine.
raviner [Ravine] *vt* to furrow, gully.
ravioli [Ravjɔli] *nmpl* ravioli *sg*.
ravir [RaviR] *vt* (*enchanter*) to delight; (*enlever*): **~ qch à qn** to rob sb of sth; **à ~** *adv* delightfully, beautifully; **être beau à ~** to be ravishingly beautiful.
raviser [Ravize]: **se ~** *vi* to change one's mind.
ravissant, e [Ravisɑ̃, -ɑ̃t] *adj* delightful.
ravissement [Ravismɑ̃] *nm* (*enchantement, délice*) rapture.
ravisseur, euse [RavisœR, -øz] *nm/f* abductor, kidnapper.
ravitaillement [Ravitɑjmɑ̃] *nm* resupplying; refuelling; (*provisions*) supplies *pl*; **aller au ~** to go for fresh supplies; **~ en vol** (*AVIAT*) in-flight refuelling.
ravitailler [Ravitɑje] *vt* to resupply; (*véhicule*) to refuel; **se ~** *vi* to get fresh supplies.
raviver [Ravive] *vt* (*feu, douleur*) to revive; (*couleurs*) to brighten up.
ravoir [RavwaR] *vt* to get back.
rayé, e [Reje] *adj* (*à rayures*) striped; (*éraflé*) scratched.
rayer [Reje] *vt* (*érafler*) to scratch; (*barrer*) to cross *ou* score out; (*d'une liste: radier*) to cross *ou* strike off.
rayon [Rɛjɔ̃] *nm* (*de soleil etc*) ray; (*GÉOM*) radius; (*de roue*) spoke; (*étagère*) shelf (*pl* shelves); (*de grand magasin*) department; (*fig: domaine*) responsibility, concern; (*de ruche*) (honey)comb; **dans un ~ de** within a radius of; **~s** *nmpl* (*radiothérapie*) radiation; **~ d'action** range; **~ de braquage** (*AUTO*) turning circle; **~ laser** laser beam; **~ de soleil** sunbeam, ray of sunshine; **~s X** X-rays.
rayonnage [Rɛjɔnaʒ] *nm* set of shelves.
rayonnant, e [Rɛjɔnɑ̃, -ɑ̃t] *adj* radiant.
rayonne [Rɛjɔn] *nf* rayon.
rayonnement [Rɛjɔnmɑ̃] *nm* radiation; (*fig: éclat*) radiance; (*: influence*) influence.
rayonner [Rɛjɔne] *vi* (*chaleur, énergie*) to radiate; (*fig: émotion*) to shine forth; (*: visage*) to be radiant; (*avenues, axes etc*) to radiate; (*touriste*) to go touring (*from one base*).
rayure [RejyR] *nf* (*motif*) stripe; (*éraflure*) scratch; (*rainure, d'un fusil*) groove; **à ~s** striped.
raz-de-marée [RɑdmaRe] *nm inv* tidal wave.
razzia [Razja] *nf* raid, foray.
RBE *sigle m* (*= revenu brut d'exploitation*) gross profit (*of a farm*).
R-D *sigle f* (*= Recherche-Développement*) R & D.
RDA *sigle f* (*= République démocratique allemande*) GDR.
RDB *sigle m* (*STATISTIQUES: = revenu disponible brut*) *total income (of a family etc)*.
rdc *abr* = **rez-de-chaussée**.
ré [Re] *nm* (*MUS*) D; (*en chantant la gamme*) re.
réabonnement [Reabɔnmɑ̃] *nm* renewal of subscription.
réabonner [Reabɔne] *vt*: **~ qn à** to renew sb's subscription to; **se ~ (à)** to renew one's subscription (to).
réac [Reak] *adj, nm/f* (*fam: = réactionnaire*) reactionary.
réacteur [ReaktœR] *nm* jet engine; **~ nucléaire** nuclear reactor.
réactif [Reaktif] *nm* reagent.
réaction [Reaksjɔ̃] *nf* reaction; **par ~** jet-propelled; **avion/moteur à ~** jet (plane)/jet engine; **~ en chaîne** chain reaction.
réactionnaire [ReaksjɔnɛR] *adj, nm/f* reactionary.
réactualiser [Reaktɥalize] *vt* to update, bring up to date.
réadaptation [Readaptɑsjɔ̃] *nf* readjustment; rehabilitation.
réadapter [Readapte] *vt* to readjust; (*MÉD*) to rehabilitate; **se ~ (à)** to readjust (to).
réaffirmer [ReafiRme] *vt* to reaffirm, reassert.
réagir [ReaʒiR] *vi* to react.
réajuster [Reaʒyste] *vt* = **rajuster**.
réalisable [Realizabl(ə)] *adj* (*projet, plan*) feasible; (*COMM: valeur*) realizable.
réalisateur, trice [RealizatœR, -tRis] *nm/f* (*TV, CINÉ*) director.
réalisation [Realizɑsjɔ̃] *nf* carrying out; realization; fulfilment; achievement; production; (*œuvre*) production, work; (*création*) creation.
réaliser [Realize] *vt* (*projet, opération*) to carry out, realize; (*rêve, souhait*) to realize, fulfil; (*exploit*) to achieve; (*achat, vente*) to make; (*film*) to produce; (*se rendre compte de,*

COMM: *bien, capital*) to realize; **se** ~ *vi* to be realized.
réalisme [ʀealism(ə)] *nm* realism.
réaliste [ʀealist(ə)] *adj* realistic; (*peintre, roman*) realist ♦ *nm/f* realist.
réalité [ʀealite] *nf* reality; **en** ~ in (actual) fact; **dans la** ~ in reality; ~ **virtuelle** virtual reality.
réanimation [ʀeanimɑsjɔ̃] *nf* resuscitation; **service de** ~ intensive care unit.
réanimer [ʀeanime] *vt* (*MÉD*) to resuscitate.
réapparaître [ʀeapaʀɛtʀ(ə)] *vi* to reappear.
réapparition [ʀeapaʀisjɔ̃] *nf* reappearance.
réapprovisionner [ʀeapʀɔvizjɔne] *vt* (*magasin*) to restock; **se** ~ **(en)** to restock (with).
réarmement [ʀeaʀməmɑ̃] *nm* rearmament.
réarmer [ʀeaʀme] *vt* (*arme*) to reload ♦ *vi* (*état*) to rearm.
réassortiment [ʀeasɔʀtimɑ̃] *nm* (*COMM*) restocking.
réassortir [ʀeasɔʀtiʀ] *vt* to match up.
réassurance [ʀeasyʀɑ̃s] *nf* reinsurance.
réassurer [ʀeasyʀe] *vt* to reinsure.
réassureur [ʀeasyʀe] *nm* reinsurer.
rebaptiser [ʀəbatize] *vt* (*rue*) to rename.
rébarbatif, ive [ʀebaʀbatif, -iv] *adj* forbidding; (*style*) off-putting (*BRIT*), crabbed.
rebattre [ʀəbatʀ(ə)] *vt*: ~ **les oreilles à qn de qch** to keep harping on to sb about sth.
rebattu, e [ʀəbaty] *pp de* **rebattre** ♦ *adj* hackneyed.
rebelle [ʀəbɛl] *nm/f* rebel ♦ *adj* (*troupes*) rebel; (*enfant*) rebellious; (*mèche etc*) unruly; ~ **à qch** unamenable to sth; ~ **à faire** unwilling to do.
rebeller [ʀəbele]: **se** ~ *vi* to rebel.
rébellion [ʀebeljɔ̃] *nf* rebellion; (*rebelles*) rebel forces *pl*.
rebiffer [ʀəbife]: **se** ~ *vr* to fight back.
reboisement [ʀəbwazmɑ̃] *nm* reafforestation.
reboiser [ʀəbwaze] *vt* to replant with trees, reafforest.
rebond [ʀəbɔ̃] *nm* (*voir rebondir*) bounce; rebound.
rebondi, e [ʀəbɔ̃di] *adj* (*ventre*) rounded; (*joues*) chubby, well-rounded.
rebondir [ʀəbɔ̃diʀ] *vi* (*ballon: au sol*) to bounce; (*: contre un mur*) to rebound; (*fig: procès, action, conversation*) to get moving again, be suddenly revived.
rebondissement [ʀəbɔ̃dismɑ̃] *nm* new development.
rebord [ʀəbɔʀ] *nm* edge.
reboucher [ʀəbuʃe] *vt* (*flacon*) to put the stopper (*ou* top) back on, recork; (*trou*) to stop up.
rebours [ʀəbuʀ]: **à** ~ *adv* the wrong way.
rebouteux, euse [ʀəbutø, -øz] *nm/f* (*péj*) bonesetter.
reboutonner [ʀəbutɔne] *vt* (*vêtement*) to button up (again).
rebrousse-poil [ʀəbʀuspwal]: **à** ~ *adv* the wrong way.
rebrousser [ʀəbʀuse] *vt* (*cheveux, poils*) to brush back, brush up; ~ **chemin** to turn back.
rebuffade [ʀəbyfad] *nf* rebuff.
rébus [ʀebys] *nm inv* (*jeu d'esprit*) rebus; (*fig*) puzzle.
rebut [ʀəby] *nm*: **mettre au** ~ to scrap, discard.
rebutant, e [ʀəbytɑ̃, -ɑ̃t] *adj* (*travail, démarche*) off-putting, disagreeable.
rebuter [ʀəbyte] *vt* to put off.
récalcitrant, e [ʀekalsitʀɑ̃, -ɑ̃t] *adj* refractory, recalcitrant.
recaler [ʀəkale] *vt* (*SCOL*) to fail.
récapitulatif, ive [ʀekapitylatif, -iv] *adj* (*liste, tableau*) summary *cpd*, that sums up.
récapituler [ʀekapityle] *vt* to recapitulate; (*résumer*) to sum up.
recel [ʀəsɛl] *nm* receiving (stolen goods).
receler [ʀəsəle] *vt* (*produit d'un vol*) to receive; (*malfaiteur*) to harbour; (*fig*) to conceal.
receleur, euse [ʀəsəlœʀ, -øz] *nm/f* receiver.
récemment [ʀesamɑ̃] *adv* recently.
recensement [ʀəsɑ̃smɑ̃] *nm* census; inventory.
recenser [ʀəsɑ̃se] *vt* (*population*) to take a census of; (*inventorier*) to make an inventory of; (*dénombrer*) to list.
récent, e [ʀesɑ̃, -ɑ̃t] *adj* recent.
recentrer [ʀəsɑ̃tʀe] *vt* (*POL*) to move towards the centre.
récépissé [ʀesepise] *nm* receipt.
réceptacle [ʀesɛptakl(ə)] *nm* (*où les choses aboutissent*) recipient; (*où les choses sont stockées*) repository; (*BOT*) receptacle.
récepteur, trice [ʀesɛptœʀ, -tʀis] *adj* receiving ♦ *nm* receiver; ~ **(de papier)** (*INFORM*) stacker; ~ **(de radio)** radio set *ou* receiver.
réceptif, ive [ʀesɛptif, -iv] *adj*: ~ **(à)** receptive (to).
réception [ʀesɛpsjɔ̃] *nf* receiving *no pl*; (*d'une marchandise, commande*) receipt; (*accueil*) reception, welcome; (*bureau*) reception (desk); (*réunion mondaine*) reception, party; (*pièces*) reception rooms *pl*; (*SPORT*: *après un saut*) landing; (*du ballon*) catching *no pl*; **jour/heures de** ~ day/hours for receiving visitors (*ou* students *etc*).
réceptionnaire [ʀesɛpsjɔnɛʀ] *nm/f* receiving clerk.
réceptionner [ʀesɛpsjɔne] *vt* (*COMM*) to take delivery of; (*SPORT*: *ballon*) to catch (and control).
réceptionniste [ʀesɛpsjɔnist(ə)] *nm/f* receptionist.
réceptivité [ʀesɛptivite] *nf* (*à une influence*) receptiveness; (*à une maladie*) susceptibility.
récessif, ive [ʀesesif, -iv] *adj* (*BIOL*) recessive.
récession [ʀesesjɔ̃] *nf* recession.
recette [ʀəsɛt] *nf* (*CULIN*) recipe; (*fig*) formula, recipe; (*COMM*) takings *pl*; (*ADMIN*: *bureau*)

tax *ou* revenue office; ~**s** *nfpl* (*COMM*: *rentrées*) receipts; **faire** ~ (*spectacle, exposition*) to be a winner.

receveur, euse [RəsvœR, -øz] *nm/f* (*des contributions*) tax collector; (*des postes*) postmaster/mistress; (*d'autobus*) conductor/conductress; (*MÉD*: *de sang, organe*) recipient.

recevoir [RəsvwaR] *vt* to receive; (*lettre, prime*) to receive, get; (*client, patient, représentant*) to see; (*jour, soleil: suj: pièce*) to get; (*SCOL*: *candidat*) to pass ♦ *vi* to receive visitors; to give parties; to see patients *etc*; **se** ~ *vi* (*athlète*) to land; ~ **qn à diner** to invite sb to dinner; **il reçoit de 8 à 10** he's at home from 8 to 10, he will see visitors from 8 to 10; (*docteur, dentiste etc*) he sees patients from 8 to 10; **être reçu** (*à un examen*) to pass; **être bien/mal reçu** to be well/badly received.

rechange [Rəʃɑ̃ʒ]: **de** ~ *adj* (*pièces, roue*) spare; (*fig: solution*) alternative; **des vêtements de** ~ a change of clothes.

rechaper [Rəʃape] *vt* to remould (*BRIT*), remold (*US*), retread.

réchapper [Reʃape]: ~ **de** *ou* **à** *vt* (*accident, maladie*) to come through; **va-t-il en** ~**?** is he going to get over it?, is he going to come through (it)?

recharge [RəʃaRʒ(ə)] *nf* refill.

rechargeable [RəʃaRʒabl(ə)] *adj* refillable; rechargeable.

recharger [RəʃaRʒe] *vt* (*camion, fusil, appareil-photo*) to reload; (*briquet, stylo*) to refill; (*batterie*) to recharge.

réchaud [Reʃo] *nm* (portable) stove; platewarmer.

réchauffé [Reʃofe] *nm* (*nourriture*) reheated food; (*fig*) stale news (*ou* joke *etc*).

réchauffement [Reʃofmɑ̃] *nm* warming (up); **le** ~ **de la planète** global warming.

réchauffer [Reʃofe] *vt* (*plat*) to reheat; (*mains, personne*) to warm; **se** ~ *vi* to get warmer; **se** ~ **les doigts** to warm (up) one's fingers.

rêche [Rɛʃ] *adj* rough.

recherche [RəʃɛRʃ(ə)] *nf* (*action*): **la** ~ **de** the search for; (*raffinement*) affectedness, studied elegance; (*scientifique etc*): **la** ~ research; ~**s** *nfpl* (*de la police*) investigations; (*scientifiques*) research *sg*; **être/se mettre à la** ~ **de** to be/go in search of.

recherché, e [RəʃɛRʃe] *adj* (*rare, demandé*) much sought-after; (*entouré: acteur, femme*) in demand; (*raffiné*) studied, affected.

rechercher [RəʃɛRʃe] *vt* (*objet égaré, personne*) to look for, search for; (*témoins, coupable, main-d'œuvre*) to look for; (*causes d'un phénomène, nouveau procédé*) to try to find; (*bonheur etc, l'amitié de qn*) to seek; **"~ et remplacer"** (*INFORM*) "search and replace".

rechigner [Rəʃiɲe] *vi*: ~ **(à)** to balk (at).

rechute [Rəʃyt] *nf* (*MÉD*) relapse; (*dans le péché, le vice*) lapse; **faire une** ~ to have a relapse.

rechuter [Rəʃyte] *vi* (*MÉD*) to relapse.

récidive [Residiv] *nf* (*JUR*) second (*ou* subsequent) offence; (*fig*) repetition; (*MÉD*) recurrence.

récidiver [Residive] *vi* to commit a second (*ou* subsequent) offence; (*fig*) to do it again.

récidiviste [Residivist(ə)] *nm/f* second (*ou* habitual) offender, recidivist.

récif [Resif] *nm* reef.

récipiendaire [Resipjɑ̃dɛR] *nm* recipient (*of diploma etc*); (*d'une societé*) newly elected member.

récipient [Resipjɑ̃] *nm* container.

réciproque [ResipRɔk] *adj* reciprocal ♦ *nf*: **la** ~ (*l'inverse*) the converse.

réciproquement [ResipRɔkmɑ̃] *adv* reciprocally; **et** ~ and vice versa.

récit [Resi] *nm* (*action de narrer*) telling; (*conte, histoire*) story.

récital [Resital] *nm* recital.

récitant, e [Resitɑ̃, -ɑ̃t] *nm/f* narrator.

récitation [Resitɑsjɔ̃] *nf* recitation.

réciter [Resite] *vt* to recite.

réclamation [Reklamɑsjɔ̃] *nf* complaint; ~**s** *nfpl* (*bureau*) complaints department *sg*.

réclame [Reklam] *nf*: **la** ~ advertising; **une** ~ an ad(vertisement), an advert (*BRIT*); **faire de la** ~ **(pour qch/qn)** to advertise (sth/sb); **article en** ~ special offer.

réclamer [Reklame] *vt* (*aide, nourriture etc*) to ask for; (*revendiquer: dû, part, indemnité*) to claim, demand; (*nécessiter*) to demand, require ♦ *vi* to complain; **se** ~ **de** to give as one's authority; to claim filiation with.

reclassement [Rəklɑsmɑ̃] *nm* reclassifying; regrading; rehabilitation.

reclasser [Rəklɑse] *vt* (*fiches, dossiers*) to reclassify; (*fig: fonctionnaire etc*) to regrade; (*: ouvrier licencié*) to place, rehabilitate.

reclus, e [Rəkly, -yz] *nm/f* recluse.

réclusion [Reklyzjɔ̃] *nf* imprisonment; ~ **à perpétuité** life imprisonment.

recoiffer [Rəkwafe] *vt*: ~ **un enfant** to do a child's hair again; **se** ~ to do one's hair again.

recoin [Rəkwɛ̃] *nm* nook, corner; (*fig*) hidden recess.

reçois [Rəswa] *etc vb voir* **recevoir**.

reçoive [Rəswav] *etc vb voir* **recevoir**.

recoller [Rəkɔle] *vt* (*enveloppe*) to stick back down.

récolte [Rekɔlt(ə)] *nf* harvesting, gathering; (*produits*) harvest, crop; (*fig*) crop, collection; (*: d'observations*) findings.

récolter [Rekɔlte] *vt* to harvest, gather (in); (*fig*) to get.

recommandable [Rəkɔmɑ̃dabl(ə)] *adj* commendable; **peu** ~ not very commendable.

recommandation [Rəkɔmɑ̃dɑsjɔ̃] *nf* recommendation.

recommandé [Rəkɔmɑ̃de] *nm* (*méthode etc*)

recommended; (*POSTES*): **en** ~ by registered mail.

recommander [Rəkɔmɑ̃de] *vt* to recommend; (*suj: qualités etc*) to commend; (*POSTES*) to register; ~ **qch à qn** to recommend sth to sb; ~ **à qn de faire** to recommend sb to do; ~ **qn auprès de qn** *ou* **à qn** to recommend sb to sb; **il est recommandé de faire ...** it is recommended that one does ...; **se ~ à qn** to commend o.s. to sb; **se ~ de qn** to give sb's name as a reference.

recommencer [Rəkɔmɑ̃se] *vt* (*reprendre: lutte, séance*) to resume, start again; (*refaire: travail, explications*) to start afresh, start (over) again; (*récidiver: erreur*) to make again ♦ *vi* to start again; (*récidiver*) to do it again; ~ **à faire** to start doing again; **ne recommence pas!** don't do that again!

récompense [Rekɔ̃pɑ̃s] *nf* reward; (*prix*) award; **recevoir qch en ~** to get sth as a reward, be rewarded with sth.

récompenser [Rekɔ̃pɑ̃se] *vt*: ~ **qn (de** *ou* **pour)** to reward sb (for).

réconciliation [Rekɔ̃siljɑsjɔ̃] *nf* reconciliation.

réconcilier [Rekɔ̃silje] *vt* to reconcile; ~ **qn avec qn** to reconcile sb with sb; ~ **qn avec qch** to reconcile sb to sth; **se ~ (avec)** to be reconciled (with).

reconductible [Rəkɔ̃dyktibl(ə)] *adj* (*JUR: contrat, bail*) renewable.

reconduction [Rəkɔ̃dyksjɔ̃] *nf* renewal; (*POL: d'une politique*) continuation.

reconduire [Rəkɔ̃dɥiR] *vt* (*raccompagner*) to take *ou* see back; (*: à la porte*) to show out; (*: à son domicile*) to see home, take home; (*JUR, POL: renouveler*) to renew.

réconfort [Rekɔ̃fɔR] *nm* comfort.

réconfortant, e [Rekɔ̃fɔRtɑ̃, -ɑ̃t] *adj* (*idée, paroles*) comforting; (*boisson*) fortifying.

réconforter [Rekɔ̃fɔRte] *vt* (*consoler*) to comfort; (*revigorer*) to fortify.

reconnais [R(ə)kɔnɛ] *etc vb voir* **reconnaître**.

reconnaissable [Rəkɔnɛsabl(ə)] *adj* recognizable.

reconnaissais [R(ə)kɔnɛsɛ] *etc vb voir* **reconnaître**.

reconnaissance [Rəkɔnɛsɑ̃s] *nf* recognition; acknowledgement; (*gratitude*) gratitude, gratefulness; (*MIL*) reconnaissance, recce; **en ~** (*MIL*) on reconnaissance; ~ **de dette** acknowledgement of a debt, IOU.

reconnaissant, e [Rəkɔnɛsɑ̃, -ɑ̃t] *vb voir* **reconnaître** ♦ *adj* grateful; **je vous serais ~ de bien vouloir** I should be most grateful if you would (kindly).

reconnaître [Rəkɔnɛtr(ə)] *vt* to recognize; (*MIL: lieu*) to reconnoitre; (*JUR: enfant, dette, droit*) to acknowledge; ~ **que** to admit *ou* acknowledge that; ~ **qn/qch à** (*l'identifier grâce à*) to recognize sb/sth by; ~ **à qn: je lui reconnais certaines qualités** I recognize certain qualities in him; **se ~ quelque part** (*s'y retrouver*) to find one's way around (a place).

reconnu, e [R(ə)kɔny] *pp de* **reconnaître** ♦ *adj* (*indiscuté, connu*) recognized.

reconquérir [Rəkɔ̃keRiR] *vt* (*aussi fig*) to reconquer, recapture; (*sa dignité etc*) to recover.

reconquête [Rəkɔ̃kɛt] *nf* recapture; recovery.

reconsidérer [Rəkɔ̃sideRe] *vt* to reconsider.

reconstituant, e [Rəkɔ̃stitɥɑ̃, -ɑ̃t] *adj* (*régime*) strength-building ♦ *nm* tonic, pick-me-up.

reconstituer [Rəkɔ̃stitɥe] *vt* (*monument ancien*) to recreate, build a replica of; (*fresque, vase brisé*) to piece together, reconstitute; (*événement, accident*) to reconstruct; (*fortune, patrimoine*) to rebuild; (*BIO: tissus etc*) to regenerate.

reconstitution [Rəkɔ̃stitysjɔ̃] *nf* (*d'un accident etc*) reconstruction.

reconstruction [Rəkɔ̃stRyksjɔ̃] *nf* rebuilding, reconstruction.

reconstruire [Rəkɔ̃stRɥiR] *vt* to rebuild, reconstruct.

reconversion [Rəkɔ̃vɛRsjɔ̃] *nf* (*du personnel*) redeployment.

reconvertir [Rəkɔ̃vɛRtiR] *vt* (*usine*) to reconvert; (*personnel, troupes etc*) to redeploy; **se ~ dans** (*un métier, une branche*) to move into, be redeployed into.

recopier [Rəkɔpje] *vt* (*transcrire*) to copy out again, write out again; (*mettre au propre: devoir*) to make a clean *ou* fair copy of.

record [Rəkɔr] *nm, adj* record; ~ **du monde** world record.

recoucher [Rəkuʃe] *vt* (*enfant*) to put back to bed.

recoudre [RəkudR(ə)] *vt* (*bouton*) to sew back on; (*plaie, incision*) to sew (back) up, stitch up.

recoupement [Rəkupmɑ̃] *nm*: **faire un ~** *ou* **des ~s** to cross-check; **par ~** by cross-checking.

recouper [Rəkupe] *vt* (*tranche*) to cut again; (*vêtement*) to recut ♦ *vi* (*CARTES*) to cut again; **se ~** *vi* (*témoignages*) to tie *ou* match up.

recourais [RəkuRɛ] *etc vb voir* **recourir**.

recourbé, e [RəkuRbe] *adj* curved; hooked; bent.

recourber [RəkuRbe] *vt* (*branche, tige de métal*) to bend.

recourir [RəkuRiR] *vi* (*courir de nouveau*) to run again; (*refaire une course*) to race again; ~ **à** *vt* (*ami, agence*) to turn *ou* appeal to; (*force, ruse, emprunt*) to resort to, have recourse to.

recours [RəkuR] *vb voir* **recourir** ♦ *nm* (*JUR*) appeal; **avoir ~ à = recourir à; en dernier ~** as a last resort; **sans ~** final; with no way out; ~ **en grâce** plea for clemency (*ou* pardon).

recouru, e [RəkuRy] *pp de* **recourir**.

recousu, e [Rəkuzy] *pp de* **recoudre**.

recouvert, e [RəkuvɛR, -ɛRt(ə)] *pp de* **recouvrir**.

recouvrable [RəkuvRabl(ə)] *adj* (*somme*) recoverable.

recouvrais [RəkuvRɛ] *etc vb voir* **recouvrer, recouvrir.**
recouvrement [RəkuvRəmɑ̃] *nm* recovery.
recouvrer [RəkuvRe] *vt* (*vue, santé etc*) to recover, regain; (*impôts*) to collect; (*créance*) to recover.
recouvrir [RəkuvRiR] *vt* (*couvrir à nouveau*) to re-cover; (*couvrir entièrement, aussi fig*) to cover; (*cacher, masquer*) to conceal, hide; **se** ~ (*se superposer*) to overlap.
recracher [RəkRaʃe] *vt* to spit out.
récréatif, ive [RekReatif, -iv] *adj* of entertainment; recreational.
récréation [RekReɑsjɔ̃] *nf* recreation, entertainment; (*SCOL*) break.
recréer [RəkRee] *vt* to recreate.
récrier [RekRije]: **se** ~ *vi* to exclaim.
récriminations [RekRiminɑsjɔ̃] *nfpl* remonstrations, complaints.
récriminer [RekRimine] *vi*: ~ **contre qn/qch** to remonstrate against sb/sth.
recroqueviller [RəkRɔkvije]: **se** ~ *vi* (*feuilles*) to curl *ou* shrivel up; (*personne*) to huddle up.
recru, e [RəkRy] *adj*: ~ **de fatigue** exhausted ♦ *nf* recruit.
recrudescence [RəkRydesɑ̃s] *nf* fresh outbreak.
recrutement [RəkRytmɑ̃] *nm* recruiting, recruitment.
recruter [RəkRyte] *vt* to recruit.
rectal, e, aux [Rɛktal, -o] *adj*: **par voie ~e** rectally.
rectangle [Rɛktɑ̃gl(ə)] *nm* rectangle; ~ **blanc** (*TV*) "adults only" symbol.
rectangulaire [Rɛktɑ̃gylɛR] *adj* rectangular.
recteur [RɛktœR] *nm* ≈ (regional) director of education (*BRIT*), ≈ state superintendent of education (*US*).
rectificatif, ive [Rɛktifikatif, -iv] *adj* corrected ♦ *nm* correction.
rectification [Rɛktifikɑsjɔ̃] *nf* correction.
rectifier [Rɛktifje] *vt* (*tracé, virage*) to straighten; (*calcul, adresse*) to correct; (*erreur, faute*) to rectify, put right.
rectiligne [Rɛktiliɲ] *adj* straight; (*GÉOM*) rectilinear.
rectitude [Rɛktityd] *nf* rectitude, uprightness.
recto [Rɛkto] *nm* front (*of a sheet of paper*).
rectorat [RɛktɔRa] *nm* (*fonction*) *position of recteur*; (*bureau*) *recteur's office*; *see also* **recteur**.
rectum [Rɛktɔm] *nm* rectum.
reçu, e [Rəsy] *pp de* **recevoir** ♦ *adj* (*admis, consacré*) accepted ♦ *nm* (*COMM*) receipt.
recueil [Rəkœj] *nm* collection.
recueillement [Rəkœjmɑ̃] *nm* meditation, contemplation.
recueilli, e [Rəkœji] *adj* contemplative.
recueillir [RəkœjiR] *vt* to collect; (*voix, suffrages*) to win; (*accueillir: réfugiés, chat*) to take in; **se** ~ *vi* to gather one's thoughts; to meditate.
recuire [RəkɥiR] *vi*: **faire** ~ to recook.
recul [Rəkyl] *nm* retreat; recession; decline; (*d'arme à feu*) recoil, kick; **avoir un mouvement de** ~ to recoil, start back; **prendre du** ~ to stand back; **avec le** ~ with the passing of time, in retrospect.
reculade [Rəkylad] *nf* (*péj*) climb-down.
reculé, e [Rəkyle] *adj* remote.
reculer [Rəkyle] *vi* to move back, back away; (*AUTO*) to reverse, back (up); (*fig: civilisation, épidémie*) to (be on the) decline; (*: se dérober*) to shrink back ♦ *vt* to move back; to reverse, back (up); (*fig: possibilités, limites*) to extend; (*: date, décision*) to postpone; ~ **devant** (*danger, difficulté*) to shrink from; ~ **pour mieux sauter** (*fig*) to postpone the evil day.
reculons [Rəkylɔ̃]: **à** ~ *adv* backwards.
récupérable [RekypeRabl(ə)] *adj* (*créance*) recoverable; (*heures*) which can be made up; (*ferraille*) salvageable.
récupération [RekypeRɑsjɔ̃] *nf* (*de vieux métaux etc*) salvage, reprocessing; (*POL*) bringing into line.
récupérer [RekypeRe] *vt* (*rentrer en possession de*) to recover, get back; (*: forces*) to recover; (*déchets etc*) to salvage (for reprocessing); (*remplacer: journée, heures de travail*) to make up; (*délinquant etc*) to rehabilitate; (*POL*) to bring into line ♦ *vi* to recover.
récurer [RekyRe] *vt* to scour; **poudre à** ~ scouring powder.
reçus [Rəsy] *etc vb voir* **recevoir**.
récusable [Rekyzabl(ə)] *adj* (*témoin*) challengeable; (*témoignage*) impugnable.
récuser [Rekyze] *vt* to challenge; **se** ~ to decline to give an opinion.
recyclage [Rəsiklaʒ] *nm* reorientation; retraining; recycling; **cours de** ~ retraining course.
recycler [Rəsikle] *vt* (*SCOL*) to reorientate; (*employés*) to retrain; (*matériau*) to recycle; **se** ~ to retrain; to go on a retraining course.
rédacteur, trice [RedaktœR, -tRis] *nm/f* (*journaliste*) writer; subeditor; (*d'ouvrage de référence*) editor, compiler; ~ **en chef** chief editor; ~ **publicitaire** copywriter.
rédaction [Redaksjɔ̃] *nf* writing; (*rédacteurs*) editorial staff; (*bureau*) editorial office(s); (*SCOL: devoir*) essay, composition.
reddition [Redisjɔ̃] *nf* surrender.
redéfinir [RədefiniR] *vt* to redefine.
redemander [Rədmɑ̃de] *vt* (*renseignement*) to ask again for; (*nourriture*): ~ **de** to ask for more (*ou* another); (*objet prêté*): ~ **qch** to ask for sth back.
redémarrer [RədemaRe] *vi* (*véhicule*) to start again, get going again; (*fig: industrie etc*) to get going again.
rédemption [Redɑ̃psjɔ̃] *nf* redemption.

redéploiement [ʀədeplwamɑ̃] *nm* redeployment.
redescendre [ʀədesɑ̃dʀ(ə)] *vi* (*à nouveau*) to go back down; (*après la montée*) to go down (again) ♦ *vt* (*pente etc*) to go down.
redevable [ʀədvabl(ə)] *adj*: **être ~ de qch à qn** (*somme*) to owe sb sth; (*fig*) to be indebted to sb for sth.
redevance [ʀədvɑ̃s] *nf* (*TÉL*) rental charge; (*TV*) licence (*BRIT*) *ou* license (*US*) fee.
redevenir [ʀədvəniʀ] *vi* to become again.
rédhibitoire [ʀedibitwaʀ] *adj*: **vice ~** (*JUR*) *latent defect in merchandise that renders the sales contract void*; (*fig: défaut*) crippling.
rediffuser [ʀədifyze] *vt* (*RADIO, TV*) to repeat, broadcast again.
rediffusion [ʀədifyzjɔ̃] *nf* repeat (programme).
rédiger [ʀediʒe] *vt* to write; (*contrat*) to draw up.
redire [ʀədiʀ] *vt* to repeat; **trouver à ~ à** to find fault with.
redistribuer [ʀədistʀibɥe] *vt* (*cartes etc*) to deal again; (*richesses, tâches, revenus*) to redistribute.
redite [ʀədit] *nf* (needless) repetition.
redondance [ʀədɔ̃dɑ̃s] *nf* redundancy.
redonner [ʀədɔne] *vt* (*restituer*) to give back, return; (*du courage, des forces*) to restore.
redoublé, e [ʀəduble] *adj*: **à coups ~s** even harder, twice as hard.
redoubler [ʀəduble] *vi* (*tempête, violence*) to intensify, get even stronger *ou* fiercer *etc*; (*SCOL*) to repeat a year ♦ *vt* (*SCOL: classe*) to repeat; (*LING: lettre*) to double; **~ de** *vt* to be twice as + *adjectif*; **le vent redouble de violence** the wind is blowing twice as hard.
redoutable [ʀədutabl(ə)] *adj* formidable, fearsome.
redouter [ʀədute] *vt* to fear; (*appréhender*) to dread; **~ de faire** to dread doing.
redoux [ʀədu] *nm* milder spell.
redressement [ʀədʀɛsmɑ̃] *nm* (*de l'économie etc*) putting right; **maison de ~** reformatory; **~ fiscal** repayment of back taxes.
redresser [ʀədʀese] *vt* (*arbre, mât*) to set upright, right; (*pièce tordue*) to straighten out; (*AVIAT, AUTO*) to straighten up; (*situation, économie*) to put right; **se ~** *vi* (*objet penché*) to right itself; to straighten up; (*personne*) to sit (*ou* stand) up; to sit (*ou* stand) up straight; (*fig: pays, situation*) to recover; **~ (les roues)** (*AUTO*) to straighten up.
redresseur [ʀədʀɛsœʀ] *nm*: **~ de torts** righter of wrongs.
réducteur, trice [ʀedyktœʀ, -tʀis] *adj* simplistic.
réduction [ʀedyksjɔ̃] *nf* reduction; **en ~** *adv* in miniature, scaled-down.
réduire [ʀedɥiʀ] *vt* (*gén, aussi CULIN, MATH*) to reduce; (*prix, dépenses*) to cut, reduce; (*carte*) to scale down, reduce; (*MÉD: fracture*) to set; **~ qn/qch à** to reduce sb/sth to; **se ~ à** (*revenir à*) to boil down to; **se ~ en** (*se transformer en*) to be reduced to; **en être réduit à** to be reduced to.
réduit, e [ʀedɥi, -it] *pp de* **réduire** ♦ *adj* (*prix, tarif, échelle*) reduced; (*mécanisme*) scaled-down; (*vitesse*) reduced ♦ *nm* tiny room; recess.
rééchelonner [ʀeeʃlɔne] *vt* to reschedule.
rééditer [ʀeedite] *vt* to republish.
réédition [ʀeedisjɔ̃] *nf* new edition.
rééducation [ʀeedykɑsjɔ̃] *nf* (*d'un membre*) re-education; (*de délinquants, d'un blessé*) rehabilitation; **~ de la parole** speech therapy; **centre de ~** physiotherapy *ou* physical therapy (*US*) centre.
rééduquer [ʀeedyke] *vt* to reeducate; to rehabilitate.
réel, le [ʀeɛl] *adj* real ♦ *nm*: **le ~** reality.
réélection [ʀeelɛksjɔ̃] *nf* re-election.
rééligible [ʀeeliʒibl(ə)] *adj* re-eligible.
réélire [ʀeeliʀ] *vt* to re-elect.
réellement [ʀeɛlmɑ̃] *adv* really.
réembaucher [ʀeɑ̃boʃe] *vt* to take on again.
réemploi [ʀeɑ̃plwa] *nm* = **remploi**.
réemployer [ʀeɑ̃plwaje] *vt* (*méthode, produit*) to re-use; (*argent*) to reinvest; (*personnel, employé*) to re-employ.
rééquilibrer [ʀeekilibʀe] *vt* (*budget*) to balance (again).
réescompte [ʀeɛskɔ̃t] *nm* rediscount.
réessayer [ʀeɛseje] *vt* to try on again.
réévaluation [ʀeevalɥɑsjɔ̃] *nf* revaluation.
réévaluer [ʀeevalɥe] *vt* to revalue.
réexaminer [ʀeɛgzamine] *vt* to re-examine.
réexpédier [ʀeɛkspedje] *vt* (*à l'envoyeur*) to return, send back; (*au destinataire*) to send on, forward.
réexporter [ʀeɛkspɔʀte] *vt* to re-export.
réf. *abr* (= *référence(s)*): **V/~** Your ref.
refaire [ʀəfɛʀ] *vt* (*faire de nouveau, recommencer*) to do again; (*réparer, restaurer*) to do up; **se ~** *vi* (*en argent*) to make up one's losses; **se ~ une santé** to recuperate; **se ~ à qch** (*se réhabituer à*) to get used to sth again.
refasse [ʀəfas] *etc vb voir* **refaire**.
réfection [ʀefɛksjɔ̃] *nf* repair; **en ~** under repair.
réfectoire [ʀefɛktwaʀ] *nm* refectory.
referai [ʀ(ə)fʀe] *etc vb voir* **refaire**.
référé [ʀefeʀe] *nm* (*JUR*) *emergency interim proceedings ou ruling*.
référence [ʀefeʀɑ̃s] *nf* reference; **~s** *nfpl* (*recommandations*) reference *sg*; **faire ~ à** to refer to; **ouvrage de ~** reference work; **ce n'est pas une ~** (*fig*) that's no recommendation.
référendum [ʀefeʀɑ̃dɔm] *nm* referendum.
référer [ʀefeʀe]: **se ~ à** *vt* to refer to; **en ~ à qn** to refer the matter to sb.
refermer [ʀəfɛʀme] *vt* to close again, shut again.

refiler [ʀəfile] *vt* (*fam*): ~ **qch à qn** to palm (*BRIT*) *ou* fob sth off on sb; to pass sth on to sb.
refit [ʀəfi] *etc vb voir* **refaire.**
réfléchi, e [ʀefleʃi] *adj* (*caractère*) thoughtful; (*action*) well-thought-out; (*LING*) reflexive.
réfléchir [ʀefleʃiʀ] *vt* to reflect ♦ *vi* to think; ~ **à** *ou* **sur** to think about; **c'est tout réfléchi** my mind's made up.
réflecteur [ʀeflɛktœʀ] *nm* (*AUTO*) reflector.
reflet [ʀəflɛ] *nm* reflection; (*sur l'eau etc*) sheen *no pl*, glint; **~s** *nmpl* gleam *sg*.
refléter [ʀəflete] *vt* to reflect; **se** ~ *vi* to be reflected.
réflex [ʀeflɛks] *adj inv* (*PHOTO*) reflex.
réflexe [ʀeflɛks(ə)] *adj, nm* reflex; ~ **conditionné** conditioned reflex.
réflexion [ʀeflɛksjɔ̃] *nf* (*de la lumière etc, pensée*) reflection; (*fait de penser*) thought; (*remarque*) remark; **~s** *nfpl* (*méditations*) thought *sg*, reflection *sg*; **sans** ~ without thinking; ~ **faite, à la** ~**, après** ~ on reflection; **délai de** ~ cooling-off period; **groupe de** ~ think tank.
refluer [ʀəflye] *vi* to flow back; (*foule*) to surge back.
reflux [ʀəfly] *nm* (*de la mer*) ebb; (*fig*) backward surge.
refondre [ʀəfɔ̃dʀ(ə)] *vt* (*texte*) to recast.
refont [ʀ(ə)fɔ̃] *vb voir* **refaire.**
reformater [ʀəfɔʀmate] *vt* to reformat.
réformateur, trice [ʀefɔʀmatœʀ, -tʀis] *nm/f* reformer ♦ *adj* (*mesures*) reforming.
Réformation [ʀefɔʀmɑsjɔ̃] *nf*: **la** ~ the Reformation.
réforme [ʀefɔʀm(ə)] *nf* reform; (*MIL*) declaration of unfitness for service; discharge (*on health grounds*); (*REL*): **la R**~ the Reformation.
réformé, e [ʀefɔʀme] *adj, nm/f* (*REL*) Protestant.
reformer [ʀəfɔʀme] *vt*, **se** ~ *vi* to reform; ~ **les rangs** (*MIL*) to fall in again.
réformer [ʀefɔʀme] *vt* to reform; (*MIL*: *recrue*) to declare unfit for service; (*: soldat*) to discharge, invalid out; (*matériel*) to scrap.
réformisme [ʀefɔʀmism(ə)] *nm* reformism, policy of reform.
réformiste [ʀefɔʀmist(ə)] *adj, nm/f* (*POL*) reformist.
refoulé, e [ʀəfule] *adj* (*PSYCH*) repressed.
refoulement [ʀəfulmɑ̃] *nm* (*d'une armée*) driving back; (*PSYCH*) repression.
refouler [ʀəfule] *vt* (*envahisseurs*) to drive back, repulse; (*liquide*) to force back; (*fig*) to suppress; (*PSYCH*) to repress.
réfractaire [ʀefʀaktɛʀ] *adj* (*minerai*) refractory; (*brique*) fire *cpd*; (*maladie*) which is resistant to treatment; (*prêtre*) non-juring; **soldat** ~ draft evader; **être** ~ **à** to resist.
réfracter [ʀefʀakte] *vt* to refract.
réfraction [ʀefʀaksjɔ̃] *nf* refraction.
refrain [ʀəfʀɛ̃] *nm* (*MUS*) refrain, chorus; (*air, fig*) tune.
refréner, réfréner [ʀəfʀene, ʀefʀene] *vt* to curb, check.
réfrigérant, e [ʀefʀiʒeʀɑ̃, -ɑ̃t] *adj* refrigerant, cooling.
réfrigérateur [ʀefʀiʒeʀatœʀ] *nm* refrigerator; **~-congélateur** fridge-freezer.
réfrigération [ʀefʀiʒeʀɑsjɔ̃] *nf* refrigeration.
réfrigéré, e [ʀefʀiʒeʀe] *adj* (*camion, wagon*) refrigerated.
réfrigérer [ʀefʀiʒeʀe] *vt* to refrigerate; (*fam*: *glacer, aussi fig*) to cool.
refroidir [ʀəfʀwadiʀ] *vt* to cool; (*fig*) to have a cooling effect on ♦ *vi* to cool (down); **se** ~ *vi* (*prendre froid*) to catch a chill; (*temps*) to get cooler *ou* colder; (*fig*) to cool (off).
refroidissement [ʀəfʀwadismɑ̃] *nm* cooling; (*grippe etc*) chill.
refuge [ʀəfyʒ] *nm* refuge; (*pour piétons*) (traffic) island; **demander** ~ **à qn** to ask sb for refuge.
réfugié, e [ʀefyʒje] *adj, nm/f* refugee.
réfugier [ʀefyʒje]: **se** ~ *vi* to take refuge.
refus [ʀəfy] *nm* refusal; **ce n'est pas de** ~ I won't say no, it's very welcome.
refuser [ʀəfyze] *vt* to refuse; (*SCOL*: *candidat*) to fail ♦ *vi* to refuse; ~ **qch à qn/de faire** to refuse sb sth/to do; ~ **du monde** to have to turn people away; **se** ~ **à qch** *ou* **à faire qch** to refuse to do sth; **il ne se refuse rien** he doesn't stint himself; **se** ~ **à qn** to refuse sb.
réfutable [ʀefytabl(ə)] *adj* refutable.
réfuter [ʀefyte] *vt* to refute.
regagner [ʀəgaɲe] *vt* (*argent, faveur*) to win back; (*lieu*) to get back to; ~ **le temps perdu** to make up (for) lost time; ~ **du terrain** to regain ground.
regain [ʀəgɛ̃] *nm* (*herbe*) second crop of hay; (*renouveau*): **un** ~ **de** renewed + *nom*.
régal [ʀegal] *nm* treat; **un** ~ **pour les yeux** a pleasure *ou* delight to look at.
régalade [ʀegalad] *adv*: **à la** ~ from the bottle (held away from the lips).
régaler [ʀegale] *vt*: ~ **qn** to treat sb to a delicious meal; ~ **qn de** to treat sb to; **se** ~ *vi* to have a delicious meal; (*fig*) to enjoy o.s.
regard [ʀəgaʀ] *nm* (*coup d'œil*) look, glance; (*expression*) look (in one's eye); **parcourir/menacer du** ~ to cast an eye over/look threateningly at; **au** ~ **de** (*loi, morale*) from the point of view of; **en** ~ (*vis à vis*) opposite; **en** ~ **de** in comparison with.
regardant, e [ʀəgaʀdɑ̃, -ɑ̃t] *adj*: **très/peu** ~ **(sur)** quite fussy/very free (about); (*économe*) very tight-fisted/quite generous (with).
regarder [ʀəgaʀde] *vt* (*examiner, observer, lire*) to look at; (*film, télévision, match*) to watch; (*envisager: situation, avenir*) to view; (*considérer: son intérêt etc*) to be concerned with; (*être orienté vers*): ~ **(vers)** to face; (*concer-*

ner) to concern ♦ *vi* to look; ~ **à** *vt* (*dépense, qualité, détails*) to be fussy with *ou* over; ~ **à faire** to hesitate to do; **dépenser sans** ~ to spend freely; ~ **qn/qch comme** to regard sb/sth as; ~ **(qch) dans le dictionnaire/ l'annuaire** to look (sth up) in the dictionary/ directory; ~ **par la fenêtre** to look out of the window; **cela me regarde** it concerns me, it's my business.

régate(s) [Regat] *nf(pl)* regatta.

régénérer [Reʒenere] *vt* to regenerate; (*fig*) to revive.

régent [Reʒɑ̃] *nm* regent.

régenter [Reʒɑ̃te] *vt* to rule over; to dictate to.

régie [Reʒi] *nf* (*COMM, INDUSTRIE*) state-owned company; (*THÉÂT, CINÉ*) production; (*RADIO, TV*) control room; **la** ~ **de l'État** state control.

regimber [Rəʒɛ̃be] *vi* to balk, jib.

régime [Reʒim] *nm* (*POL, GÉO*) régime; (*ADMIN: carcéral, fiscal etc*) system; (*MÉD*) diet; (*TECH*) (engine) speed; (*fig*) rate, pace; (*de bananes, dattes*) bunch; **se mettre au/suivre un** ~ to go on/be on a diet; ~ **sans sel** salt-free diet; **à bas/haut** ~ (*AUTO*) at low/high revs; **à plein** ~ flat out, at full speed; ~ **matrimonial** marriage settlement.

régiment [Reʒimɑ̃] *nm* (*MIL: unité*) regiment; (*fig: fam*): **un** ~ **de** an army of; **un copain de** ~ a pal from military service *ou* (one's) army days.

région [Reʒjɔ̃] *nf* region; **la** ~ **parisienne** the Paris area.

régional, e, aux [Reʒjɔnal, -o] *adj* regional.

régionalisation [Reʒjɔnalizɑsjɔ̃] *nf* regionalization.

régionalisme [Reʒjɔnalism(ə)] *nm* regionalism.

régir [ReʒiR] *vt* to govern.

régisseur [ReʒisœR] *nm* (*d'un domaine*) steward; (*CINÉ, TV*) assistant director; (*THÉÂT*) stage manager.

registre [RəʒistR(ə)] *nm* (*livre*) register; logbook; ledger; (*MUS, LING*) register; (*d'orgue*) stop; ~ **de comptabilité** ledger; ~ **de l'état civil** register of births, marriages and deaths.

réglable [Reglabl(ə)] *adj* (*siège, flamme etc*) adjustable; (*achat*) payable.

réglage [Reglaʒ] *nm* (*d'une machine*) adjustment; (*d'un moteur*) tuning.

règle [Rɛgl(ə)] *nf* (*instrument*) ruler; (*loi, prescription*) rule; ~**s** *nfpl* (*PHYSIOL*) period *sg*; **avoir pour** ~ **de** to make it a rule that *ou* to; **en** ~ (*papiers d'identité*) in order; **être/se mettre en** ~ to be/put o.s. straight with the authorities; **en** ~ **générale** as a (general) rule; **être la** ~ to be the rule; **être de** ~ to be usual; ~ **à calcul** slide rule; ~ **de trois** (*MATH*) rule of three.

réglé, e [Regle] *adj* well-ordered; stable, steady; (*papier*) ruled; (*arrangé*) settled; (*femme*): **bien** ~**e** whose periods are regular.

règlement [Rɛgləmɑ̃] *nm* settling; (*paiement*) settlement; (*arrêté*) regulation; (*règles, statuts*) regulations *pl*, rules *pl*; ~ **à la commande** cash with order; ~ **de compte(s)** settling of scores; ~ **en espèces/par chèque** payment in cash/by cheque; ~ **intérieur** (*SCOL*) school rules *pl*; (*ADMIN*) by-laws *pl*; ~ **judiciaire** compulsory liquidation.

réglementaire [Rɛgləmɑ̃tɛR] *adj* conforming to the regulations; (*tenue, uniforme*) regulation *cpd*.

réglementation [Rɛgləmɑ̃tɑsjɔ̃] *nf* regulation, control; (*règlements*) regulations *pl*.

réglementer [Rɛgləmɑ̃te] *vt* to regulate, control.

régler [Regle] *vt* (*mécanisme, machine*) to regulate, adjust; (*moteur*) to tune; (*thermostat etc*) to set, adjust; (*emploi du temps etc*) to organize, plan; (*question, conflit, facture, dette*) to settle; (*fournisseur*) to settle up with, pay; (*papier*) to rule; ~ **qch sur** to model sth on; ~ **son compte à qn** to sort sb out, settle sb; ~ **un compte avec qn** to settle a score with sb.

réglisse [Reglis] *nf ou m* liquorice; **bâton de** ~ liquorice stick.

règne [Rɛɲ] *nm* (*d'un roi etc, fig*) reign; (*BIO*): **le** ~ **végétal/animal** the vegetable/animal kingdom.

régner [Reɲe] *vi* (*roi*) to rule, reign; (*fig*) to reign.

regonfler [R(ə)gɔ̃fle] *vt* (*ballon, pneu*) to reinflate, blow up again.

regorger [RəgɔRʒe] *vi* to overflow; ~ **de** to overflow with, be bursting with.

régresser [RegRese] *vi* (*phénomène*) to decline; (*enfant, malade*) to regress.

régressif, ive [RegResif, -iv] *adj* regressive.

régression [RegResjɔ̃] *nf* decline; regression; **être en** ~ to be on the decline.

regret [RəgRɛ] *nm* regret; **à** ~ with regret; **avec** ~ regretfully; **être au** ~ **de devoir/ne pas pouvoir faire** to regret to have to/that one is unable to do; **j'ai le** ~ **de vous informer que** ... I regret to inform you that ....

regrettable [RəgRɛtabl(ə)] *adj* regrettable.

regretter [RəgRete] *vt* to regret; (*personne*) to miss; ~ **d'avoir fait** to regret doing; ~ **que** to regret that, be sorry that; **non, je regrette** no, I'm sorry.

regroupement [R(ə)gRupmɑ̃] *nm* grouping together; (*groupe*) group.

regrouper [RəgRupe] *vt* (*grouper*) to group together; (*contenir*) to include, comprise; **se** ~ *vi* to gather (together).

régularisation [Regylarizɑsjɔ̃] *nf* (*de papiers, passeport*) putting in order; (*de sa situation: par le mariage*) regularization; (*d'un mécanisme*) regulation.

régulariser [RegylaRize] *vt* (*fonctionnement, trafic*) to regulate; (*passeport, papiers*) to put in order; (*sa situation*) to straighten out,

regularize.
régularité [ʀegylaʀite] *nf* regularity.
régulateur, trice [ʀegylatœʀ, -tʀis] *adj* regulating ♦ *nm* (*TECH*): ~ **de vitesse/de température** speed/temperature regulator.
régulation [ʀegylɑsjɔ̃] *nf* (*du trafic*) regulation; ~ **des naissances** birth control.
régulier, ière [ʀegylje, -jɛʀ] *adj* (*gén*) regular; (*vitesse, qualité*) steady; (*répartition, pression, paysage*) even; (*TRANSPORTS: ligne, service*) scheduled, regular; (*légal, réglementaire*) lawful, in order; (*fam: correct*) straight, on the level.
régulièrement [ʀegyljɛʀmɑ̃] *adv* regularly; steadily; evenly; normally.
régurgiter [ʀegyʀʒite] *vt* to regurgitate.
réhabiliter [ʀeabilite] *vt* to rehabilitate; (*fig*) to restore to favour (*BRIT*) *ou* favor (*US*).
réhabituer [ʀeabitɥe] *vt*: **se ~ à qch/à faire qch** to get used to sth again/to doing sth again.
rehausser [ʀəose] *vt* to heighten, raise; (*fig*) to set off, enhance.
réimporter [ʀeɛ̃pɔʀte] *vt* to reimport.
réimposer [ʀeɛ̃poze] *vt* (*FINANCE*) to reimpose; to tax again.
réimpression [ʀeɛ̃pʀɛsjɔ̃] *nf* reprinting; (*ouvrage*) reprint.
réimprimer [ʀeɛ̃pʀime] *vt* to reprint.
Reims [ʀɛ̃s] *n* Rheims.
rein [ʀɛ̃] *nm* kidney; **~s** *nmpl* (*dos*) back *sg*; **avoir mal aux ~s** to have backache; **~ artificiel** kidney machine.
réincarnation [ʀeɛ̃kaʀnɑsjɔ̃] *nf* reincarnation.
réincarner [ʀeɛ̃kaʀne]: **se ~** *vr* to be reincarnated.
reine [ʀɛn] *nf* queen.
reine-claude [ʀɛnklod] *nf* greengage.
reinette [ʀɛnɛt] *nf* rennet, pippin.
réinitialisation [ʀeinisjalizɑsjɔ̃] *nf* (*INFORM*) reset.
réinsérer [ʀeɛ̃seʀe] *vt* (*délinquant, handicapé etc*) to rehabilitate.
réinsertion [ʀeɛ̃sɛʀsjɔ̃] *nf* rehabilitation.
réintégrer [ʀeɛ̃tegʀe] *vt* (*lieu*) to return to; (*fonctionnaire*) to reinstate.
réitérer [ʀeiteʀe] *vt* to repeat, reiterate.
rejaillir [ʀəʒajiʀ] *vi* to splash up; **~ sur** to splash up onto; (*fig*) to rebound on; to fall upon.
rejet [ʀəʒɛ] *nm* (*action, aussi MÉD*) rejection; (*POÉSIE*) enjambement, rejet; (*BOT*) shoot.
rejeter [ʀəʒte] *vt* (*relancer*) to throw back; (*vomir*) to bring *ou* throw up; (*écarter*) to reject; (*déverser*) to throw out, discharge; (*reporter*): **~ un mot à la fin d'une phrase** to transpose a word to the end of a sentence; **se ~ sur qch** (*accepter faute de mieux*) to fall back on sth; **~ la tête/les épaules en arrière** to throw one's head/pull one's shoulders back; **~ la responsabilité de qch sur qn** to lay the responsibility for sth at sb's door.
rejeton [ʀəʒtɔ̃] *nm* offspring.
rejette [ʀ(ə)ʒɛt] *etc vb voir* **rejeter**.
rejoignais [ʀ(ə)ʒwaɲɛ] *etc vb voir* **rejoindre**.
rejoindre [ʀəʒwɛ̃dʀ(ə)] *vt* (*famille, régiment*) to rejoin, return to; (*lieu*) to get (back) to; (*suj: route etc*) to meet, join; (*rattraper*) to catch up (with); **se ~** *vi* to meet; **je te rejoins au café** I'll see *ou* meet you at the café.
réjoui, e [ʀeʒwi] *adj* joyous.
réjouir [ʀeʒwiʀ] *vt* to delight; **se ~** *vi* to be delighted; **se ~ de qch/de faire** to be delighted about sth/to do; **se ~ que** to be delighted that.
réjouissances [ʀeʒwisɑ̃s] *nfpl* (*joie*) rejoicing *sg*; (*fête*) festivities, merry-making *sg*.
réjouissant, e [ʀeʒwisɑ̃, -ɑ̃t] *adj* heartening, delightful.
relâche [ʀəlɑʃ]: **faire ~** *vi* (*navire*) to put into port; (*CINÉ*) to be closed; **c'est le jour de ~** (*CINÉ*) it's closed today; **sans ~** *adv* without respite *ou* a break.
relâché, e [ʀəlɑʃe] *adj* loose, lax.
relâchement [ʀəlɑʃmɑ̃] *nm* (*d'un prisonnier*) release; (*de la discipline, musculaire*) relaxation.
relâcher [ʀəlɑʃe] *vt* (*ressort, prisonnier*) to release; (*étreinte, cordes*) to loosen; (*discipline*) to relax ♦ *vi* (*NAVIG*) to put into port; **se ~** *vi* to loosen; (*discipline*) to become slack *ou* lax; (*élève etc*) to slacken off.
relais [ʀəlɛ] *nm* (*SPORT*): **(course de) ~** relay (race); (*RADIO, TV*) relay; (*intermédiaire*) go-between; **équipe de ~** shift team; (*SPORT*) relay team; **prendre le ~ (de)** to take over (from); **~ de poste** post house, coaching inn; **~ routier** ≈ transport café (*BRIT*), ≈ truck stop (*US*).
relance [ʀəlɑ̃s] *nf* boosting, revival; (*ÉCON*) reflation.
relancer [ʀəlɑ̃se] *vt* (*balle*) to throw back (again); (*moteur*) to restart; (*fig*) to boost, revive; (*personne*): **~ qn** to pester sb; to get on to sb again.
relater [ʀəlate] *vt* to relate, recount.
relatif, ive [ʀəlatif, -iv] *adj* relative.
relation [ʀəlɑsjɔ̃] *nf* (*récit*) account, report; (*rapport*) relation(ship); **~s** *nfpl* (*rapports*) relations; relationship; (*connaissances*) connections; **être/entrer en ~(s) avec** to be in contact *ou* be dealing/get in contact with; **mettre qn en ~(s) avec** to put sb in touch with; **~s internationales** international relations; **~s publiques (RP)** public relations (PR); **~s (sexuelles)** sexual relations, (sexual) intercourse *sg*.
relativement [ʀəlativmɑ̃] *adv* relatively; **~ à** in relation to.
relativiser [ʀəlativize] *vt* to see in relation to; to put into context.
relativité [ʀəlativite] *nf* relativity.
relax [ʀəlaks] *adj inv*, **relaxe** [ʀəlaks(ə)] *adj* relaxed, informal, casual; easy-going;

(fauteuil-)~ *nm* reclining chair.
relaxant, e [Rəlaksɑ̃, -ɑ̃t] *adj* (*cure, médicament*) relaxant; (*ambiance*) relaxing.
relaxation [R(ə)laksɑsjɔ̃] *nf* relaxation.
relaxer [Rəlakse] *vt* to relax; (*JUR*) to discharge; **se** ~ *vi* to relax.
relayer [Rəleje] *vt* (*collaborateur, coureur etc*) to relieve, take over from; (*RADIO, TV*) to relay; **se** ~ (*dans une activité*) to take it in turns.
relecture [R(ə)lɛktyR] *nf* rereading.
relégation [Rəlegɑsjɔ̃] *nf* (*SPORT*) relegation.
reléguer [Rəlege] *vt* to relegate; ~ **au second plan** to push into the background.
relent(s) [Rəlɑ̃] *nm(pl)* stench *sg*.
relevé, e [Rəlve] *adj* (*bord de chapeau*) turned-up; (*manches*) rolled-up; (*fig: style*) elevated; (*: sauce*) highly-seasoned ♦ *nm* (*lecture*) reading; (*de cotes*) plotting; (*liste*) statement; list; (*facture*) account; ~ **de compte** bank statement; ~ **d'identité bancaire (RIB)** (bank) account number.
relève [Rəlɛv] *nf* relief; (*équipe*) relief team (*ou* troops *pl*); **prendre la** ~ to take over.
relèvement [Rəlɛvmɑ̃] *nm* (*d'un taux, niveau*) raising.
relever [Rəlve] *vt* (*statue, meuble*) to stand up again; (*personne tombée*) to help up; (*vitre, plafond, niveau de vie*) to raise; (*pays, économie, entreprise*) to put back on its feet; (*col*) to turn up; (*style, conversation*) to elevate; (*plat, sauce*) to season; (*sentinelle, équipe*) to relieve; (*souligner: fautes, points*) to pick out; (*constater: traces etc*) to find, pick up; (*répliquer à: remarque*) to react to, reply to; (*: défi*) to accept, take up; (*noter: adresse etc*) to take down, note; (*: plan*) to sketch; (*: cotes etc*) to plot; (*compteur*) to read; (*ramasser: cahiers, copies*) to collect, take in ♦ *vi* (*jupe, bord*) to ride up; ~ **de** *vt* (*maladie*) to be recovering from; (*être du ressort de*) to be a matter for; (*ADMIN: dépendre de*) to come under; (*fig*) to pertain to; **se** ~ *vi* (*se remettre debout*) to get up; (*fig*): **se** ~ **(de)** to recover (from); ~ **qn de** (*vœux*) to release sb from; (*fonctions*) to relieve sb of; ~ **la tête** to look up; to hold up one's head.
relief [Rəljɛf] *nm* relief; (*de pneu*) tread pattern; ~**s** *nmpl* (*restes*) remains; **en** ~ in relief; (*photographie*) three-dimensional; **mettre en** ~ (*fig*) to bring out, highlight.
relier [Rəlje] *vt* to link up; (*livre*) to bind; ~ **qch à** to link sth to; **livre relié cuir** leather-bound book.
relieur, euse [RəljœR, -øz] *nm/f* (book)binder.
religieusement [R(ə)liʒjøzmɑ̃] *adv* religiously; (*enterré, mariés*) in church; **vivre** ~ to lead a religious life.
religieux, euse [Rəliʒjø, -øz] *adj* religious ♦ *nm* monk ♦ *nf* nun; (*gâteau*) cream bun.
religion [Rəliʒjɔ̃] *nf* religion; (*piété, dévotion*) faith; **entrer en** ~ to take one's vows.
reliquaire [RəlikɛR] *nm* reliquary.
reliquat [Rəlika] *nm* (*d'une somme*) balance; (*JUR: de succession*) residue.
relique [Rəlik] *nf* relic.
relire [RəliR] *vt* (*à nouveau*) to reread, read again; (*vérifier*) to read over; **se** ~ to read through what one has written.
reliure [RəljyR] *nf* binding; (*art, métier*): **la** ~ book-binding.
reloger [R(ə)lɔʒe] *vt* (*locataires, sinistrés*) to re-house.
relu, e [Rəly] *pp de* **relire**.
reluire [RəlɥiR] *vi* to gleam.
reluisant, e [Rəlɥizɑ̃, -ɑ̃t] *vb voir* **reluire** ♦ *adj* gleaming; **peu** ~ (*fig*) unattractive; unsavoury (*BRIT*), unsavory (*US*).
reluquer [R(ə)lyke] *vt* (*fam*) to eye (up), ogle.
remâcher [Rəmɑʃe] *vt* to chew *ou* ruminate over.
remailler [Rəmɑje] *vt* (*tricot*) to darn; (*filet*) to mend.
remaniement [Rəmanimɑ̃] *nm*: ~ **ministériel** Cabinet reshuffle.
remanier [Rəmanje] *vt* to reshape, recast; (*POL*) to reshuffle.
remarier [R(ə)maRje]: **se** ~ *vi* to remarry, get married again.
remarquable [RəmaRkabl(ə)] *adj* remarkable.
remarquablement [R(ə)maRkabləmɑ̃] *adv* remarkably.
remarque [RəmaRk(ə)] *nf* remark; (*écrite*) note.
remarquer [RəmaRke] *vt* (*voir*) to notice; (*dire*): ~ **que** to remark that; **se** ~ to be noticeable; **se faire** ~ to draw attention to o.s.; **faire** ~ **(à qn) que** to point out (to sb) that; **faire** ~ **qch (à qn)** to point sth out (to sb); **remarquez, ...** mark you, ..., mind you, ...
remballer [Rɑ̃bale] *vt* to wrap up (again); (*dans un carton*) to pack up (again).
rembarrer [Rɑ̃baRe] *vt*: ~ **qn** (*repousser*) to rebuff sb; (*remettre à sa place*) to put sb in his (*ou* her) place.
remblai [Rɑ̃blɛ] *nm* embankment.
remblayer [Rɑ̃bleje] *vt* to bank up; (*fossé*) to fill in.
rembobiner [Rɑ̃bɔbine] *vt* to rewind.
rembourrage [Rɑ̃buRaʒ] *nm* stuffing; padding.
rembourré, e [Rɑ̃buRe] *adj* padded.
rembourrer [Rɑ̃buRe] *vt* to stuff; (*dossier, vêtement, souliers*) to pad.
remboursable [Rɑ̃buRsabl(ə)] *adj* repayable.
remboursement [Rɑ̃buRsəmɑ̃] *nm* repayment; **envoi contre** ~ cash on delivery.
rembourser [Rɑ̃buRse] *vt* to pay back, repay.
rembrunir [Rɑ̃bRyniR]: **se** ~ *vi* to grow sombre (*BRIT*) *ou* somber (*US*).
remède [Rəmɛd] *nm* (*médicament*) medicine; (*traitement, fig*) remedy, cure; **trouver un** ~ **à** (*MÉD, fig*) to find a cure for.
remédier [Rəmedje]: ~ **à** *vt* to remedy.
remembrement [Rəmɑ̃bRəmɑ̃] *nm* (*AGR*) regrouping of lands.
remémorer [RəmemɔRe]: **se** ~ *vt* to recall,

recollect.

remerciements [ʀəmɛʀsimɑ̃] *nmpl* thanks; **(avec) tous mes ~** (with) grateful *ou* many thanks.

remercier [ʀəmɛʀsje] *vt* to thank; (*congédier*) to dismiss; **~ qn de/d'avoir fait** to thank sb for/for having done; **non, je vous remercie** no thank you.

remettre [ʀəmɛtʀ(ə)] *vt* (*vêtement*): **~ qch** to put sth back on, put sth on again; (*replacer*): **~ qch quelque part** to put sth back somewhere; (*ajouter*): **~ du sel/un sucre** to add more salt/another lump of sugar; (*rétablir: personne*): **~ qn** to set sb back on his (*ou* her) feet; (*rendre, restituer*): **~ qch à qn** to give sth back to sb, return sth to sb; (*donner, confier: paquet, argent*): **~ qch à qn** to hand sth over to sb, deliver sth to sb; (*prix, décoration*): **~ qch à qn** to present sb with sth; (*ajourner*): **~ qch (à)** to postpone sth *ou* put sth off (until); **se ~** *vi* to get better, recover; **se ~ de** to recover from, get over; **s'en ~ à** to leave it (up) to; **se ~ à faire/qch** to start doing/sth again; **~ une pendule à l'heure** to put a clock right; **~ un moteur/une machine en marche** to get an engine/a machine going again; **~ en état/en ordre** to repair/sort out; **~ en cause/question** to challenge/question again; **~ sa démission** to hand in one's notice; **~ qch à neuf** to make sth as good as new; **~ qn à sa place** (*fig*) to put sb in his (*ou* her) place.

réminiscence [ʀeminisɑ̃s] *nf* reminiscence.

remis, e [ʀəmi, -iz] *pp de* **remettre** ♦ *nf* delivery; presentation; (*rabais*) discount; (*local*) shed; **~ en marche/en ordre** starting up again/sorting out; **~ en cause/question** calling into question/challenging; **~ de fonds** remittance; **~ en jeu** (*FOOTBALL*) throw-in; **~ à neuf** restoration; **~ de peine** remission of sentence.

remiser [ʀəmize] *vt* to put away.

rémission [ʀemisjɔ̃]: **sans ~** *adj* irremediable ♦ *adv* unremittingly.

remodeler [ʀəmɔdle] *vt* to remodel; (*fig: restructurer*) to restructure.

rémois, e [ʀemwa, -waz] *adj* of *ou* from Rheims ♦ *nm/f*: **R~, e** inhabitant *ou* native of Rheims.

remontant [ʀəmɔ̃tɑ̃] *nm* tonic, pick-me-up.

remontée [ʀəmɔ̃te] *nf* rising; ascent; **~s mécaniques** (*SKI*) ski lifts, ski tows.

remonte-pente [ʀəmɔ̃tpɑ̃t] *nm* ski lift, (ski) tow.

remonter [ʀəmɔ̃te] *vi* (*à nouveau*) to go back up; (*sur un cheval*) to remount; (*après une descente*) to go up (again); (*dans une voiture*) to get back in; (*jupe*) to ride up ♦ *vt* (*pente*) to go up; (*fleuve*) to sail (*ou* swim *etc*) up; (*manches, pantalon*) to roll up; (*col*) to turn up; (*niveau, limite*) to raise; (*fig: personne*) to buck up; (*moteur, meuble*) to put back together, reassemble; (*garde-robe etc*) to renew, replenish; (*montre, mécanisme*) to wind up; **~ le moral à qn** to raise sb's spirits; **~ à** (*dater de*) to date *ou* go back to; **~ en voiture** to get back into the car.

remontoir [ʀəmɔ̃twaʀ] *nm* winding mechanism, winder.

remontrance [ʀəmɔ̃tʀɑ̃s] *nf* reproof, reprimand.

remontrer [ʀəmɔ̃tʀe] *vt* (*montrer de nouveau*): **~ qch (à qn)** to show sth again (to sb); (*fig*): **en ~ à** to prove one's superiority over.

remords [ʀəmɔʀ] *nm* remorse *no pl*; **avoir des ~** to feel remorse, be conscience-stricken.

remorque [ʀəmɔʀk(ə)] *nf* trailer; **prendre/être en ~** to tow/be on tow; **être à la ~** (*fig*) to tag along (behind).

remorquer [ʀəmɔʀke] *vt* to tow.

remorqueur [ʀəmɔʀkœʀ] *nm* tug(boat).

rémoulade [ʀemulad] *nf dressing with mustard and herbs*.

rémouleur [ʀemulœʀ] *nm* (knife- *ou* scissor-) grinder.

remous [ʀəmu] *nm* (*d'un navire*) (back)wash *no pl*; (*de rivière*) swirl, eddy ♦ *nmpl* (*fig*) stir *sg*.

rempailler [ʀɑ̃pɑje] *vt* to reseat (*with straw*).

rempart [ʀɑ̃paʀ] *nm* rampart; **faire à qn un ~ de son corps** to shield sb with one's (own) body.

rempiler [ʀɑ̃pile] *vt* (*dossiers, livres etc*) to pile up again ♦ *vi* (*MIL: fam*) to join up again.

remplaçant, e [ʀɑ̃plasɑ̃, -ɑ̃t] *nm/f* replacement, substitute, stand-in; (*THÉÂT*) understudy; (*SCOL*) supply (*BRIT*) *ou* substitute (*US*) teacher.

remplacement [ʀɑ̃plasmɑ̃] *nm* replacement; (*job*) replacement work *no pl*; (*suppléance: SCOL*) supply (*BRIT*) *ou* substitute (*US*) teacher; **assurer le ~ de qn** (*suj: remplaçant*) to stand in *ou* substitute for sb; **faire des ~s** (*professeur*) to do supply *ou* substitute teaching; (*médecin*) to do locum work.

remplacer [ʀɑ̃plase] *vt* to replace; (*prendre temporairement la place de*) to stand in for; (*tenir lieu de*) to take the place of, act as a substitute for; **~ qch/qn par** to replace sth/sb with.

rempli, e [ʀɑ̃pli] *adj* (*emploi du temps*) full, busy; **~ de** full of, filled with.

remplir [ʀɑ̃pliʀ] *vt* to fill (up); (*questionnaire*) to fill out *ou* up; (*obligations, fonction, condition*) to fulfil; **se ~** *vi* to fill up; **~ qch de** to fill sth with.

remplissage [ʀɑ̃plisaʒ] *nm* (*fig: péj*) padding.

remploi [ʀɑ̃plwa] *nm* re-use.

rempocher [ʀɑ̃pɔʃe] *vt* to put back into one's pocket.

remporter [ʀɑ̃pɔʀte] *vt* (*marchandise*) to take away; (*fig*) to win, achieve.

rempoter [ʀɑ̃pɔte] *vt* to repot.

remuant, e [ʀəmɥɑ̃, -ɑ̃t] *adj* restless.

remue-ménage [ʀəmymenaʒ] *nm inv* commotion.

remuer [Rəmɥe] *vt* to move; (*café, sauce*) to stir ♦ *vi* to move; (*fig: opposants*) to show signs of unrest; **se** ~ *vi* to move; (*se démener*) to stir o.s.; (*fam*) to get a move on.

rémunérateur, trice [RemyneRatœR, -tRis] *adj* remunerative, lucrative.

rémunération [RemyneRɑsjɔ̃] *nf* remuneration.

rémunérer [RemyneRe] *vt* to remunerate, pay.

renâcler [Rənɑkle] *vi* to snort; (*fig*) to grumble, balk.

renaissance [Rənɛsɑ̃s] *nf* rebirth, revival; **la R~** the Renaissance.

renaître [RənɛtR(ə)] *vi* to be revived; ~ **à la vie** to take on a new lease of life; ~ **à l'espoir** to find fresh hope.

rénal, e, aux [Renal, -o] *adj* renal, kidney *cpd*.

renard [RənaR] *nm* fox.

renardeau [RənaRdo] *nm* fox cub.

rencard [Rɑ̃kaR] *nm* = **rancard.**

rencart [Rɑ̃kaR] *nm* = **rancart.**

renchérir [Rɑ̃ʃeRiR] *vi* to become more expensive; (*fig*): ~ **(sur)** to add something (to).

renchérissement [Rɑ̃ʃeRismɑ̃] *nm* increase (in the cost *ou* price of).

rencontre [Rɑ̃kɔ̃tR(ə)] *nf* (*de cours d'eau*) confluence; (*véhicules*) collision; (*entrevue, congrès, match etc*) meeting; (*imprévue*) encounter; **faire la** ~ **de qn** to meet sb; **aller à la** ~ **de qn** to go and meet sb; **amours de** ~ casual love affairs.

rencontrer [Rɑ̃kɔ̃tRe] *vt* to meet; (*mot, expression*) to come across; (*difficultés*) to meet with; **se** ~ to meet; (*véhicules*) to collide.

rendement [Rɑ̃dmɑ̃] *nm* (*d'un travailleur, d'une machine*) output; (*d'une culture*) yield; (*d'un investissement*) return; **à plein** ~ at full capacity.

rendez-vous [Rɑ̃devu] *nm* (*rencontre*) appointment; (*: d'amoureux*) date; (*lieu*) meeting place; **donner** ~ **à qn** to arrange to meet sb; **recevoir sur** ~ to have an appointment system; **fixer un** ~ **à qn** to give sb an appointment; **avoir/prendre** ~ **(avec)** to have/make an appointment (with); **prendre** ~ **chez le médecin** to make an appointment with the doctor; ~ **spatial** *ou* **orbital** docking (in space).

rendormir [Rɑ̃dɔRmiR]: **se** ~ *vr* to go back to sleep.

rendre [Rɑ̃dR(ə)] *vt* (*livre, argent etc*) to give back, return; (*otages, politesse, JUR: verdict*) to return; (*honneurs*) to pay; (*sang, aliments*) to bring up; (*sons: suj: instrument*) to produce, make; (*exprimer, traduire*) to render; (*jugement*) to pronounce, render; (*faire devenir*): ~ **qn célèbre/qch possible** to make sb famous/sth possible; **se** ~ *vi* (*capituler*) to surrender, give o.s. up; (*aller*): **se** ~ **quelque part** to go somewhere; **se** ~ **à** (*arguments etc*) to bow to; (*ordres*) to comply with; **se** ~ **compte de qch** to realize sth; ~ **la vue/la santé à qn** to restore sb's sight/health; ~ **la liberté à qn** to set sb free; ~ **la monnaie** to give change; **se** ~ **insupportable/malade** to become unbearable/make o.s. ill.

rendu, e [Rɑ̃dy] *pp de* **rendre** ♦ *adj* (*fatigué*) exhausted.

renégat, e [Rənega, -at] *nm/f* renegade.

renégocier [Rənegɔsje] *vt* to renegociate.

rênes [Rɛn] *nfpl* reins.

renfermé, e [Rɑ̃fɛRme] *adj* (*fig*) withdrawn ♦ *nm*: **sentir le** ~ to smell stuffy.

renfermer [Rɑ̃fɛRme] *vt* to contain; **se** ~ **(sur soi-même)** to withdraw into o.s.

renfiler [Rɑ̃file] *vt* (*collier*) to rethread; (*pull*) to slip on.

renflé, e [Rɑ̃fle] *adj* bulging, bulbous.

renflement [Rɑ̃fləmɑ̃] *nm* bulge.

renflouer [Rɑ̃flue] *vt* to refloat; (*fig*) to set back on its (*ou* his/her *etc*) feet (again).

renfoncement [Rɑ̃fɔ̃smɑ̃] *nm* recess.

renforcer [Rɑ̃fɔRse] *vt* to reinforce; ~ **qn dans ses opinions** to confirm sb's opinion.

renfort [Rɑ̃fɔR]: ~**s** *nmpl* reinforcements; **en** ~ as a back-up; **à grand** ~ **de** with a great deal of.

renfrogné, e [Rɑ̃fRɔɲe] *adj* sullen, scowling.

renfrogner [Rɑ̃fRɔɲe]: **se** ~ *vi* to scowl.

rengager [Rɑ̃gaʒe] *vt* (*personnel*) to take on again; **se** ~ (*MIL*) to re-enlist.

rengaine [Rɑ̃gɛn] *nf* (*péj*) old tune.

rengainer [Rɑ̃gene] *vt* (*revolver*) to put back in its holster; (*épée*) to sheathe; (*fam: compliment, discours*) to save, withhold.

rengorger [Rɑ̃gɔRʒe]: **se** ~ *vi* (*fig*) to puff o.s. up.

renier [Rənje] *vt* (*parents*) to disown, repudiate; (*engagements*) to go back on; (*foi*) to renounce.

renifler [Rənifle] *vi* to sniff ♦ *vt* (*tabac*) to sniff up; (*odeur*) to sniff.

rennais, e [Rɛnɛ, -ɛz] *adj* of *ou* from Rennes ♦ *nm/f*: **R~, e** inhabitant *ou* native of Rennes.

renne [Rɛn] *nm* reindeer *inv*.

renom [Rənɔ̃] *nm* reputation; (*célébrité*) renown; **vin de grand** ~ celebrated *ou* highly renowned wine.

renommé, e [R(ə)nɔme] *adj* celebrated, renowned ♦ *nf* fame.

renoncement [Rənɔ̃smɑ̃] *nm* abnegation, renunciation.

renoncer [Rənɔ̃se] *vi*: ~ **à** *vt* to give up; ~ **à faire** to give up the idea of doing; **j'y renonce!** I give up!

renouer [Rənwe] *vt* (*cravate etc*) to retie; (*fig: conversation, liaison*) to renew, resume; ~ **avec** (*tradition*) to revive; (*habitude*) to take up again; ~ **avec qn** to take up with sb again.

renouveau, x [Rənuvo] *nm* revival; ~ **de succès** renewed success.

renouvelable [R(ə)nuvlabl(ə)] *adj* (*contrat, bail*)

renewable; (*expérience*) which can be renewed.

renouveler [ʀənuvle] *vt* to renew; (*exploit, méfait*) to repeat; **se ~** *vi* (*incident*) to recur, happen again, be repeated; (*cellules etc*) to be renewed *ou* replaced; (*artiste, écrivain*) to try something new.

renouvellement [ʀ(ə)nuvɛlmɑ̃] *nm* renewal; recurrence.

rénovation [ʀenɔvɑsjɔ̃] *nf* renovation; restoration; reform(ing); redevelopment.

rénover [ʀenɔve] *vt* (*immeuble*) to renovate, do up; (*meuble*) to restore; (*enseignement*) to reform; (*quartier*) to redevelop.

renseignement [ʀɑ̃sɛɲmɑ̃] *nm* information *no pl*, piece of information; (*MIL*) intelligence *no pl*; **prendre des ~s sur** to make inquiries about, ask for information about; **(guichet des) ~s** information desk; **(service des) ~s** (*TÉL*) directory inquiries (*BRIT*), information (*US*); **service de ~s** (*MIL*) intelligence service; **les ~s généraux** ≈ the secret police.

renseigner [ʀɑ̃seɲe] *vt*: **~ qn (sur)** to give information to sb (about); **se ~** *vi* to ask for information, make inquiries.

rentabiliser [ʀɑ̃tabilize] *vt* (*capitaux, production*) to make profitable.

rentabilité [ʀɑ̃tabilite] *nf* profitability; cost-effectiveness; (*d'un investissement*) return; **seuil de ~** break-even point.

rentable [ʀɑ̃tabl(ə)] *adj* profitable; cost-effective.

rente [ʀɑ̃t] *nf* income; (*pension*) pension; (*titre*) government stock *ou* bond; **~ viagère** life annuity.

rentier, ière [ʀɑ̃tje, -jɛʀ] *nm/f* person of private *ou* independent means.

rentrée [ʀɑ̃tʀe] *nf*: **~ (d'argent)** cash *no pl* coming in; **la ~ (des classes)** the start of the new school year; **la ~ (parlementaire)** the reopening *ou* reassembly of parliament; **faire sa ~** (*artiste, acteur*) to make a comeback; *see boxed note*.

> **RENTRÉE**
>
> *The* **rentrée (des classes)** *in September has wider connotations than just the start of the new school year. It is also the time when political and social life pick up again after the long summer break, and so marks an important point in the French calendar.*

rentrer [ʀɑ̃tʀe] *vi* (*entrer de nouveau*) to go (*ou* come) back in; (*entrer*) to go (*ou* come) in; (*revenir chez soi*) to go (*ou* come) (back) home; (*air, clou: pénétrer*) to go in; (*revenu, argent*) to come in ♦ *vt* (*foins*) to bring in; (*véhicule*) to put away; (*chemise dans pantalon etc*) to tuck in; (*griffes*) to draw in; (*train d'atterrissage*) to raise; (*fig: larmes, colère etc*) to hold back; **~ le ventre** to pull in one's stomach; **~ dans** to go (*ou* come) back into; to go (*ou* come) into; (*famille, patrie*) to go back *ou* return to; (*heurter*) to crash into; (*appartenir à*) to be included in; (*: catégorie etc*) to fall into; **~ dans l'ordre** to get back to normal; **~ dans ses frais** to recover one's expenses (*ou* initial outlay).

renverrai [ʀɑ̃vɛʀe] *etc vb voir* **renvoyer**.

renversant, e [ʀɑ̃vɛʀsɑ̃, -ɑ̃t] *adj* amazing, astounding.

renverse [ʀɑ̃vɛʀs(ə)]: **à la ~** *adv* backwards.

renversé, e [ʀɑ̃vɛʀse] *adj* (*écriture*) backhand; (*image*) reversed; (*stupéfait*) staggered.

renversement [ʀɑ̃vɛʀsəmɑ̃] *nm* (*d'un régime, des traditions*) overthrow; **~ de la situation** reversal of the situation.

renverser [ʀɑ̃vɛʀse] *vt* (*faire tomber: chaise, verre*) to knock over, overturn; (*piéton*) to knock down; (*liquide, contenu*) to spill, upset; (*retourner: verre, image*) to turn upside down, invert; (*: ordre des mots etc*) to reverse; (*fig: gouvernement etc*) to overthrow; (*stupéfier*) to bowl over, stagger; **se ~** *vi* to fall over; to overturn; to spill; **se ~ (en arrière)** to lean back; **~ la tête/le corps (en arrière)** to tip one's head back/throw oneself back; **~ la vapeur** (*fig*) to change course.

renvoi [ʀɑ̃vwa] *nm* dismissal; return; reflection; postponement; (*référence*) cross-reference; (*éructation*) belch.

renvoyer [ʀɑ̃vwaje] *vt* to send back; (*congédier*) to dismiss; (*TENNIS*) to return; (*lumière*) to reflect; (*son*) to echo; (*ajourner*): **~ qch (à)** to postpone sth (until); **~ qch à qn** (*rendre*) to return sth to sb; **~ qn à** (*fig*) to refer sb to.

réorganisation [ʀeɔʀganizɑsjɔ̃] *nf* reorganization.

réorganiser [ʀeɔʀganize] *vt* to reorganize.

réorienter [ʀeɔʀjɑ̃te] *vt* to reorient(ate), redirect.

réouverture [ʀeuvɛʀtyʀ] *nf* reopening.

repaire [ʀəpɛʀ] *nm* den.

repaître [ʀəpɛtʀ(ə)] *vt* to feast; to feed; **se ~ de** *vt* (*animal*) to feed on; (*fig*) to wallow *ou* revel in.

répandre [ʀepɑ̃dʀ(ə)] *vt* (*renverser*) to spill; (*étaler, diffuser*) to spread; (*lumière*) to shed; (*chaleur, odeur*) to give off; **se ~** *vi* to spill; to spread; **se ~ en** (*injures etc*) to pour out.

répandu, e [ʀepɑ̃dy] *pp de* **répandre** ♦ *adj* (*opinion, usage*) widespread.

réparable [ʀepaʀabl(ə)] *adj* (*montre etc*) repairable; (*perte etc*) which can be made up for.

reparaître [ʀəpaʀɛtʀ(ə)] *vi* to reappear.

réparateur, trice [ʀepaʀatœʀ, -tʀis] *nm/f* repairer.

réparation [ʀepaʀɑsjɔ̃] *nf* repairing *no pl*, repair; **en ~** (*machine etc*) under repair; **demander à qn ~ de** (*offense etc*) to ask sb to make amends for.

réparer [ʀepaʀe] *vt* to repair; (*fig: offense*) to make up for, atone for; (*: oubli, erreur*) to put right.

reparler [rəparle] *vi*: ~ **de qn/qch** to talk about sb/sth again; ~ **à qn** to speak to sb again.
repars [rəpar] *etc vb voir* **repartir**.
repartie [rəparti] *nf* retort; **avoir de la** ~ to be quick at repartee.
repartir [rəpartir] *vi* to set off again; to leave again; (*fig*) to get going again, pick up again; ~ **à zéro** to start from scratch (again).
répartir [repartir] *vt* (*pour attribuer*) to share out; (*pour disperser, disposer*) to divide up; (*poids, chaleur*) to distribute; (*étaler: dans le temps*): ~ **sur** to spread over; (*classer, diviser*): ~ **en** to divide into, split up into; **se** ~ *vt* (*travail, rôles*) to share out between themselves.
répartition [repartisjɔ̃] *nf* sharing out; dividing up; distribution.
repas [rəpɑ] *nm* meal; **à l'heure des** ~ at mealtimes.
repassage [rəpɑsaʒ] *nm* ironing.
repasser [rəpɑse] *vi* to come (*ou* go) back ♦ *vt* (*vêtement, tissu*) to iron; (*examen*) to retake, resit; (*film*) to show again; (*lame*) to sharpen; (*leçon, rôle: revoir*) to go over (again); (*plat, pain*): ~ **qch à qn** to pass sth back to sb.
repasseuse [rəpɑsøz] *nf* (*machine*) ironing machine.
repayer [rəpeje] *vt* to pay again.
repêchage [rəpɛʃaʒ] *nm* (*SCOL*): **question de** ~ question to give candidates a second chance.
repêcher [rəpeʃe] *vt* (*noyé*) to recover the body of, fish out; (*fam: candidat*) to pass (*by inflating marks*); to give a second chance to.
repeindre [rəpɛ̃dr(ə)] *vt* to repaint.
repentir [rəpɑ̃tir] *nm* repentance; **se** ~ *vi*: **se** ~ **(de)** to repent (of).
répercussions [repɛrkysjɔ̃] *nfpl* repercussions.
répercuter [repɛrkyte] *vt* (*réfléchir, renvoyer: son, voix*) to reflect; (*faire transmettre: consignes, charges etc*) to pass on; **se** ~ *vi* (*bruit*) to reverberate; (*fig*): **se** ~ **sur** to have repercussions on.
repère [rəpɛr] *nm* mark; (*monument etc*) landmark; **(point de)** ~ point of reference.
repérer [rəpere] *vt* (*erreur, connaissance*) to spot; (*abri, ennemi*) to locate; **se** ~ *vi* to get one's bearings; **se faire** ~ to be spotted.
répertoire [repɛrtwar] *nm* (*liste*) (alphabetical) list; (*carnet*) index notebook; (*INFORM*) directory; (*de carnet*) thumb index; (*indicateur*) directory, index; (*d'un théâtre, artiste*) repertoire.
répertorier [repɛrtɔrje] *vt* to itemize, list.
répéter [repete] *vt* to repeat; (*préparer: leçon: aussi vi*) to learn, go over; (*THÉÂT*) to rehearse; **se** ~ (*redire*) to repeat o.s.; (*se reproduire*) to be repeated, recur.
répéteur [repetœr] *nm* (*TÉL*) repeater.
répétitif, ive [repetitif, -iv] *adj* repetitive.
répétition [repetisjɔ̃] *nf* repetition; (*THÉÂT*) rehearsal; ~**s** *nfpl* (*leçons*) private coaching *sg*; **armes à** ~ repeater weapons; ~ **générale** final dress rehearsal.
repeupler [rəpœple] *vt* to repopulate; (*forêt, rivière*) to restock.
repiquage [rəpikaʒ] *nm* pricking out, planting out; re-recording.
repiquer [rəpike] *vt* (*plants*) to prick out, plant out; (*enregistrement*) to re-record.
répit [repi] *nm* respite; **sans** ~ without letting up.
replacer [rəplase] *vt* to replace, put back.
replanter [rəplɑ̃te] *vt* to replant.
replat [rəpla] *nm* ledge.
replâtrer [rəplɑtre] *vt* (*mur*) to replaster; (*fig*) to patch up.
replet, ète [rəplɛ, -ɛt] *adj* chubby, fat.
repli [rəpli] *nm* (*d'une étoffe*) fold; (*MIL, fig*) withdrawal.
replier [rəplije] *vt* (*rabattre*) to fold down *ou* over; **se** ~ *vi* (*troupes, armée*) to withdraw, fall back; **se** ~ **sur soi-même** to withdraw into oneself.
réplique [replik] *nf* (*repartie, fig*) reply; (*objection*) retort; (*THÉÂT*) line; (*copie*) replica; **donner la** ~ **à** to play opposite; **sans** ~ *adj* no-nonsense; irrefutable.
répliquer [replike] *vi* to reply; (*avec impertinence*) to answer back; (*riposter*) to retaliate.
replonger [rəplɔ̃ʒe] *vt*: ~ **qch dans** to plunge sth back into; **se** ~ **dans** (*journal etc*) to immerse o.s. in again.
répondant, e [repɔ̃dɑ̃, -ɑ̃t] *nm/f* (*garant*) guarantor, surety.
répondeur [repɔ̃dœr] *nm*: ~ **(automatique)** (*TÉL*) (telephone) answering machine.
répondre [repɔ̃dr(ə)] *vi* to answer, reply; (*freins, mécanisme*) to respond; ~ **à** *vt* to reply to, answer; (*avec impertinence*): ~ **à qn** to answer sb back; (*invitation, convocation*) to reply to; (*affection, salut*) to return; (*provocation, suj: mécanisme etc*) to respond to; (*correspondre à: besoin*) to answer; (*: conditions*) to meet; (*: description*) to match; ~ **que** to answer *ou* reply that; ~ **de** to answer for.
réponse [repɔ̃s] *nf* answer, reply; **avec** ~ **payée** (*POSTES*) reply-paid, post-paid (*US*); **avoir** ~ **à tout** to have an answer for everything; **en** ~ **à** in reply to; **carte-/bulletin-**~ reply card/slip.
report [rəpɔr] *nm* postponement; transfer; ~ **d'incorporation** (*MIL*) deferment.
reportage [rəpɔrtaʒ] *nm* (*bref*) report; (*écrit: documentaire*) story; article; (*en direct*) commentary; (*genre, activité*): **le** ~ reporting.
reporter *nm* [rəpɔrtɛr] reporter ♦ *vt* [rəpɔrte] (*total*): ~ **qch sur** to carry sth forward *ou* over to; (*ajourner*): ~ **qch (à)** to postpone sth (until); (*transférer*): ~ **qch sur** to transfer sth

to; **se ~ à** (*époque*) to think back to; (*document*) to refer to.
repos [Rəpo] *nm* rest; (*fig*) peace (and quiet); (*mental*) peace of mind; (*MIL*): ~! (stand) at ease!; **en ~** at rest; **au ~** at rest; (*soldat*) at ease; **de tout ~** safe.
reposant, e [R(ə)pozɑ̃, -ɑ̃t] *adj* restful; (*sommeil*) refreshing.
repose [Rəpoz] *nf* refitting.
reposé, e [Rəpoze] *adj* fresh, rested; **à tête ~e** in a leisurely way, taking time to think.
repose-pied [Rəpozpje] *nm inv* footrest.
reposer [Rəpoze] *vt* (*verre, livre*) to put down; (*rideaux, carreaux*) to put back; (*délasser*) to rest; (*problème*) to reformulate ♦ *vi* (*liquide, pâte*) to settle, rest; (*personne*): **ici repose ...** here lies ...; ~ **sur** to be built on; (*fig*) to rest on; **se ~** *vi* to rest; **se ~ sur qn** to rely on sb.
repoussant, e [Rəpusɑ̃, -ɑ̃t] *adj* repulsive.
repoussé, e [Rəpuse] *adj* (*cuir*) embossed (by hand).
repousser [Rəpuse] *vi* to grow again ♦ *vt* to repel, repulse; (*offre*) to turn down, reject; (*tiroir, personne*) to push back; (*différer*) to put back.
répréhensible [RepReɑ̃sibl(ə)] *adj* reprehensible.
reprendre [RəpRɑ̃dR(ə)] *vt* (*prisonnier, ville*) to recapture; (*objet prêté, donné*) to take back; (*chercher*): **je viendrai te ~ à 4 h** I'll come and fetch you *ou* I'll come back for you at 4; (*se resservir de*): ~ **du pain/un œuf** to take (*ou* eat) more bread/another egg; (*COMM*: *article usagé*) to take back; to take in part exchange; (*firme, entreprise*) to take over; (*travail, promenade*) to resume; (*emprunter: argument, idée*) to take up, use; (*refaire: article etc*) to go over again; (*jupe etc*) to alter; (*émission, pièce*) to put on again; (*réprimander*) to tell off; (*corriger*) to correct ♦ *vi* (*classes, pluie*) to start (up) again; (*activités, travaux, combats*) to resume, start (up) again; (*affaires, industrie*) to pick up; (*dire*): **reprit-il** he went on; **se ~** (*se ressaisir*) to recover, pull o.s. together; **s'y ~** to make another attempt; ~ **des forces** to recover one's strength; ~ **courage** to take new heart; ~ **ses habitudes/sa liberté** to get back into one's old habits/regain one's freedom; ~ **la route** to resume one's journey, set off again; ~ **connaissance** to come to, regain consciousness; ~ **haleine** *ou* **son souffle** to get one's breath back; ~ **la parole** to speak again.
repreneur [RəpRənœR] *nm* company fixer *ou* doctor.
reprenne [RəpRɛn] *etc vb voir* **reprendre**.
représailles [RəpRezɑj] *nfpl* reprisals, retaliation *sg*.
représentant, e [RəpRezɑ̃tɑ̃, -ɑ̃t] *nm/f* representative.
représentatif, ive [RəpRezɑ̃tatif, -iv] *adj* representative.
représentation [RəpRezɑ̃tɑsjɔ̃] *nf* representation; performing; (*symbole, image*) representation; (*spectacle*) performance; (*COMM*): **la ~** commercial travelling; sales representation; **frais de ~** (*d'un diplomate*) entertainment allowance.
représenter [RəpRezɑ̃te] *vt* to represent; (*donner: pièce, opéra*) to perform; **se ~** *vt* (*se figurer*) to imagine; to visualize ♦ *vi*: **se ~ à** (*POL*) to stand *ou* run again at; (*SCOL*) to resit.
répressif, ive [RepResif, -iv] *adj* repressive.
répression [RepResjɔ̃] *nf* (*voir réprimer*) suppression; repression; (*POL*): **la ~** repression; **mesures de ~** repressive measures.
réprimande [RepRimɑ̃d] *nf* reprimand, rebuke.
réprimander [RepRimɑ̃de] *vt* to reprimand, rebuke.
réprimer [RepRime] *vt* (*émotions*) to suppress; (*peuple etc*) repress.
repris, e [RəpRi, -iz] *pp de* **reprendre** ♦ *nm*: ~ **de justice** ex-prisoner, ex-convict.
reprise [RəpRiz] *nf* (*recommencement*) resumption; (*économique*) recovery; (*TV*) repeat; (*CINÉ*) rerun; (*BOXE etc*) round; (*AUTO*) acceleration *no pl*; (*COMM*) trade-in, part exchange; (*de location*) *sum asked for any extras or improvements made to the property*; (*raccommodage*) darn; mend; **la ~ des hostilités** the resumption of hostilities; **à plusieurs ~s** on several occasions, several times.
repriser [RəpRize] *vt* to darn; to mend; **aiguille/coton à ~** darning needle/thread.
réprobateur, trice [RepRɔbatœR, -tRis] *adj* reproving.
réprobation [RepRɔbɑsjɔ̃] *nf* reprobation.
reproche [RəpRɔʃ] *nm* (*remontrance*) reproach; **ton/air de ~** reproachful tone/look; **faire des ~s à qn** to reproach sb; **faire ~ à qn de qch** to reproach sb for sth; **sans ~(s)** beyond *ou* above reproach.
reprocher [RəpRɔʃe] *vt*: ~ **qch à qn** to reproach *ou* blame sb for sth; ~ **qch à** (*machine, théorie*) to have sth against; **se ~ qch/d'avoir fait qch** to blame o.s. for sth/for doing sth.
reproducteur, trice [RəpRɔdyktœR, -tRis] *adj* reproductive.
reproduction [RəpRɔdyksjɔ̃] *nf* reproduction; ~ **interdite** all rights (of reproduction) reserved.
reproduire [RəpRɔdɥiR] *vt* to reproduce; **se ~** *vi* (*BIO*) to reproduce; (*recommencer*) to recur, re-occur.
reprographie [RəpRɔgRafi] *nf* (photo)copying.
réprouvé, e [RepRuve] *nm/f* reprobate.
réprouver [RepRuve] *vt* to reprove.
reptation [Rɛptɑsjɔ̃] *nf* crawling.
reptile [Rɛptil] *nm* reptile.
repu, e [Rəpy] *pp de* **repaître** ♦ *adj* satisfied,

sated.
républicain, e [Repyblikɛ̃, -ɛn] *adj, nm/f* republican.
république [Repyblik] *nf* republic; **R~ arabe du Yémen** Yemen Arab Republic; **R~ Centrafricaine** Central African Republic; **R~ de Corée** South Korea; **R~ démocratique allemande (RDA)** German Democratic Republic (GDR); **R~ dominicaine** Dominican Republic; **R~ fédérale d'Allemagne (RFA)** Federal Republic of Germany (FRG); **R~ d'Irlande** Irish Republic, Eire; **R~ populaire de Chine** People's Republic of China; **R~ populaire démocratique de Corée** Democratic People's Republic of Korea; **R~ populaire du Yémen** People's Democratic Republic of Yemen.
répudier [Repydje] *vt* (*femme*) to repudiate; (*doctrine*) to renounce.
répugnance [Repyɲɑ̃s] *nf* repugnance, loathing; **avoir** *ou* **éprouver de la ~ pour** (*médicament, comportement, travail etc*) to have an aversion to; **avoir** *ou* **éprouver de la ~ à faire qch** to be reluctant to do sth.
répugnant, e [Repyɲɑ̃, -ɑ̃t] *adj* repulsive, loathsome.
répugner [Repyɲe]: **~ à** *vt*: **~ à qn** to repel *ou* disgust sb; **~ à faire** to be loath *ou* reluctant to do.
répulsion [Repylsjɔ̃] *nf* repulsion.
réputation [Repytɑsjɔ̃] *nf* reputation; **avoir la ~ d'être ...** to have a reputation for being ...; **connaître qn/qch de ~** to know sb/sth by repute; **de ~ mondiale** world-renowned.
réputé, e [Repyte] *adj* renowned; **être ~ pour** to have a reputation for, be renowned for.
requérir [Rəkerir] *vt* (*nécessiter*) to require, call for; (*au nom de la loi*) to call upon; (*JUR*: *peine*) to call for, demand.
requête [Rəkɛt] *nf* request, petition; (*JUR*) petition.
requiem [Rekɥijɛm] *nm* requiem.
requiers [RəkjɛR] *etc vb voir* **requérir**.
requin [Rəkɛ̃] *nm* shark.
requinquer [Rəkɛ̃ke] *vt* to set up, pep up.
requis, e [Rəki, -iz] *pp de* **requérir** ♦ *adj* required.
réquisition [Rekizisjɔ̃] *nf* requisition.
réquisitionner [Rekizisjɔne] *vt* to requisition.
réquisitoire [RekizitwaR] *nm* (*JUR*) closing speech for the prosecution; (*fig*): **~ contre** indictment of.
RER *sigle m* (*= Réseau express régional*) *Greater Paris high speed train service.*
rescapé, e [Rɛskape] *nm/f* survivor.
rescousse [Rɛskus] *nf*: **aller à la ~ de qn** to go to sb's aid *ou* rescue; **appeler qn à la ~** to call on sb for help.
réseau, x [Rezo] *nm* network.
réséda [Rezeda] *nm* (*BOT*) reseda, mignonette.
réservation [RezɛRvɑsjɔ̃] *nf* reservation; booking.
réserve [RezɛRv(ə)] *nf* (*retenue*) reserve; (*entrepôt*) storeroom; (*restriction, aussi: d'Indiens*) reservation; (*de pêche, chasse*) preserve; (*restrictions*): **faire des ~s** to have reservations; **officier de ~** reserve officer; **sous toutes ~s** with all reserve; (*dire*) with reservations; **sous ~ de** subject to; **sans ~** *adv* unreservedly; **en ~** in reserve; **de ~** (*provisions etc*) in reserve.
réservé, e [RezɛRve] *adj* (*discret*) reserved; (*chasse, pêche*) private; **~ à** *ou* **pour** reserved for.
réserver [RezɛRve] *vt* (*gén*) to reserve; (*chambre, billet etc*) to book, reserve; (*mettre de côté, garder*): **~ qch pour** *ou* **à** to keep *ou* save sth for; **~ qch à qn** to reserve (*ou* book) sth for sb; (*fig: destiner*) to have sth in store for sb; **se ~ le droit de faire** to reserve the right to do.
réserviste [RezɛRvist(ə)] *nm* reservist.
réservoir [RezɛRvwaR] *nm* tank.
résidence [Rezidɑ̃s] *nf* residence; **~ principale/secondaire** main/second home; **~ universitaire** hall of residence; **(en) ~ surveillée** (under) house arrest.
résident, e [Rezidɑ̃, -ɑ̃t] *nm/f* (*ressortissant*) foreign resident; (*d'un immeuble*) resident ♦ *adj* (*INFORM*) resident.
résidentiel, le [Rezidɑ̃sjɛl] *adj* residential.
résider [Rezide] *vi*: **~ à** *ou* **dans** *ou* **en** to reside in; **~ dans** (*fig*) to lie in.
résidu [Rezidy] *nm* residue *no pl*.
résiduel, le [Rezidɥɛl] *adj* residual.
résignation [Reziɲɑsjɔ̃] *nf* resignation.
résigné, e [Reziɲe] *adj* resigned.
résigner [Reziɲe] *vt* to relinquish, resign; **se ~** *vi*: **se ~ (à qch/à faire)** to resign o.s. (to sth/to doing).
résiliable [Reziljabl(ə)] *adj* which can be terminated.
résilier [Rezilje] *vt* to terminate.
résille [Rezij] *nf* (hair)net.
résine [Rezin] *nf* resin.
résiné, e [Rezine] *adj*: **vin ~** retsina.
résineux, euse [Rezinø, -øz] *adj* resinous ♦ *nm* coniferous tree.
résistance [Rezistɑ̃s] *nf* resistance; (*de réchaud, bouilloire: fil*) element.
résistant, e [Rezistɑ̃, -ɑ̃t] *adj* (*personne*) robust, tough; (*matériau*) strong, hard-wearing ♦ *nm/f* (*patriote*) Resistance worker *ou* fighter.
résister [Reziste] *vi* to resist; **~ à** *vt* (*assaut, tentation*) to resist; (*effort, souffrance*) to withstand; (*suj: matériau, plante*) to stand up to, withstand; (*personne: désobéir à*) to stand up to, oppose.
résolu, e [Rezɔly] *pp de* **résoudre** ♦ *adj* (*ferme*) resolute; **être ~ à qch/faire** to be set upon sth/doing.
résolument [Rezɔlymɑ̃] *adv* resolutely, steadfastly; **~ contre qch** firmly against sth.

résolution [Rezɔlysjɔ̃] *nf* solving; (*fermeté, décision, INFORM*) resolution; **prendre la ~ de** to make a resolution to.
résolvais [Rezɔlvɛ] *etc vb voir* **résoudre**.
résonance [Rezɔnɑ̃s] *nf* resonance.
résonner [Rezɔne] *vi* (*cloche, pas*) to reverberate, resound; (*salle*) to be resonant; **~ de** to resound with.
résorber [RezɔRbe]: **se ~** *vi* (*MÉD*) to be resorbed; (*fig*) to be absorbed.
résoudre [RezudR(ə)] *vt* to solve; **~ qn à faire qch** to get sb to make up his (*ou* her) mind to do sth; **~ de faire** to resolve to do; **se ~ à faire** to bring o.s. to do.
respect [Rɛspɛ] *nm* respect; **tenir en ~** to keep at bay.
respectabilité [Rɛspɛktabilite] *nf* respectability.
respectable [Rɛspɛktabl(ə)] *adj* respectable.
respecter [Rɛspɛkte] *vt* to respect; **faire ~** to enforce; **le lexicographe qui se respecte** (*fig*) any self-respecting lexicographer.
respectif, ive [Rɛspɛktif, -iv] *adj* respective.
respectivement [Rɛspɛktivmɑ̃] *adv* respectively.
respectueusement [Rɛspɛktɥøzmɑ̃] *adv* respectfully.
respectueux, euse [Rɛspɛktɥø, -øz] *adj* respectful; **~ de** respectful of.
respirable [RɛspiRabl(ə)] *adj*: **peu ~** unbreathable.
respiration [RɛspiRɑsjɔ̃] *nf* breathing *no pl*; **faire une ~ complète** to breathe in and out; **retenir sa ~** to hold one's breath; **~ artificielle** artificial respiration.
respiratoire [RɛspiRatwaR] *adj* respiratory.
respirer [RɛspiRe] *vi* to breathe; (*fig: se reposer*) to get one's breath, have a break; (*: être soulagé*) to breathe again ♦ *vt* to breathe (in), inhale; (*manifester: santé, calme etc*) to exude.
resplendir [Rɛsplɑ̃diR] *vi* to shine; (*fig*): **~ (de)** to be radiant (with).
resplendissant, e [Rɛsplɑ̃disɑ̃, -ɑ̃t] *adj* radiant.
responsabilité [Rɛspɔ̃sabilite] *nf* responsibility; (*légale*) liability; **refuser la ~ de** to deny responsibility (*ou* liability) for; **prendre ses ~s** to assume responsibility for one's actions; **~ civile** civil liability; **~ pénale/morale/collective** criminal/moral/collective responsibility.
responsable [Rɛspɔ̃sabl(ə)] *adj* responsible ♦ *nm/f* (*du ravitaillement etc*) person in charge; (*de parti, syndicat*) official; **~ de** responsible for; (*légalement: de dégâts etc*) liable for; (*chargé de*) in charge of, responsible for.
resquiller [Rɛskije] *vi* (*au cinéma, au stade*) to get in on the sly; (*dans le train*) to fiddle a free ride.
resquilleur, euse [RɛskijœR, -øz] *nm/f* (*qui n'est pas invité*) gatecrasher; (*qui ne paie pas*) fare dodger.
ressac [Rəsak] *nm* backwash.
ressaisir [RəseziR]: **se ~** *vi* to regain one's self-control; (*équipe sportive*) to rally.
ressasser [Rəsase] *vt* (*remâcher*) to keep turning over; (*redire*) to keep trotting out.
ressemblance [Rəsɑ̃blɑ̃s] *nf* (*visuelle*) resemblance, similarity, likeness; (*: ART*) likeness; (*analogie, trait commun*) similarity.
ressemblant, e [Rəsɑ̃blɑ̃, -ɑ̃t] *adj* (*portrait*) lifelike, true to life.
ressembler [Rəsɑ̃ble]: **~ à** *vt* to be like, resemble; (*visuellement*) to look like; **se ~** to be (*ou* look) alike.
ressemeler [Rəsəmle] *vt* to (re)sole.
ressens [R(ə)sɑ̃] *etc vb voir* **ressentir**.
ressentiment [Rəsɑ̃timɑ̃] *nm* resentment.
ressentir [Rəsɑ̃tiR] *vt* to feel; **se ~ de** to feel (*ou* show) the effects of.
resserre [RəsɛR] *nf* shed.
resserrement [R(ə)sɛRmɑ̃] *nm* narrowing; strengthening; (*goulet*) narrow part.
resserrer [RəseRe] *vt* (*pores*) to close; (*nœud, boulon*) to tighten (up); (*fig: liens*) to strengthen; **se ~** *vi* (*route, vallée*) to narrow; (*liens*) to strengthen; **se ~ (autour de)** to draw closer (around); to close in (on).
ressers [R(ə)sɛR] *etc vb voir* **resservir**.
resservir [RəsɛRviR] *vi* to do *ou* serve again ♦*vt*: **~ qch (à qn)** to serve sth up again (to sb); **~ de qch (à qn)** to give (sb) a second helping of sth; **~ qn (d'un plat)** to give sb a second helping (of a dish); **se ~ de** (*plat*) to take a second helping of; (*outil etc*) to use again.
ressort [RəsɔR] *vb voir* **ressortir** ♦ *nm* (*pièce*) spring; (*force morale*) spirit; (*recours*): **en dernier ~** as a last resort; (*compétence*): **être du ~ de** to fall within the competence of.
ressortir [RəsɔRtiR] *vi* to go (*ou* come) out (again); (*contraster*) to stand out; **~ de** (*résulter de*): **il ressort de ceci que** it emerges from this that; **~ à** (*JUR*) to come under the jurisdiction of; (*ADMIN*) to be the concern of; **faire ~** (*fig: souligner*) to bring out.
ressortissant, e [RəsɔRtisɑ̃, -ɑ̃t] *nm/f* national.
ressouder [Rəsude] *vt* to solder together again.
ressource [RəsuRs(ə)] *nf*: **avoir la ~ de** to have the possibility of; **~s** *nfpl* resources; (*fig*) possibilities; **leur seule ~ était de** the only course open to them was to; **~s d'énergie** energy resources.
ressusciter [Resysite] *vt* to resuscitate, restore to life; (*fig*) to revive, bring back ♦ *vi* to rise (from the dead); (*fig: pays*) to come back to life.
restant, e [Rɛstɑ̃, -ɑ̃t] *adj* remaining ♦ *nm*: **le ~ (de)** the remainder (of); **un ~ de** (*de trop*) some leftover; (*fig: vestige*) a remnant *ou* last trace of.
restaurant [RɛstɔRɑ̃] *nm* restaurant; **manger au ~** to eat out; **~ d'entreprise** staff canteen

ou cafeteria (*US*); ~ **universitaire (RU)** university refectory *ou* cafeteria (*US*).
restaurateur, trice [RɛstɔRatœR, -tRis] *nm/f* restaurant owner, restaurateur; (*de tableaux*) restorer.
restauration [RɛstɔRɑsjɔ̃] *nf* restoration; (*hôtellerie*) catering; ~ **rapide** fast food.
restaurer [RɛstɔRe] *vt* to restore; **se** ~ *vi* to have something to eat.
restauroute [RɛstɔRut] *nm* = **restoroute.**
reste [Rɛst(ə)] *nm* (*restant*): **le** ~ **(de)** the rest (of); (*de trop*): **un** ~ **(de)** some leftover; (*vestige*): **un** ~ **de** a remnant *ou* last trace of; (*MATH*) remainder; ~**s** *nmpl* leftovers; (*d'une cité etc, dépouille mortelle*) remains; **avoir du temps de** ~ to have time to spare; **ne voulant pas être en** ~ not wishing to be outdone; **partir sans attendre** *ou* **demander son** ~ (*fig*) to leave without waiting to hear more; **du** ~, **au** ~ *adv* besides, moreover; **pour le reste, quant au** ~ *adv* as for the rest.
rester [Rɛste] *vi* (*dans un lieu, un état, une position*) to stay, remain; (*subsister*) to remain, be left; (*durer*) to last, live on ♦ *vb impers*: **il reste du pain/2 œufs** there's some bread/there are 2 eggs left (over); **il reste du temps/10 minutes** there's some time/there are 10 minutes left; **il me reste assez de temps** I have enough time left; **voilà tout ce qui (me) reste** that's all I've got left; **ce qui reste à faire** what remains to be done; **ce qui me reste à faire** what remains for me to do; **(il) reste à savoir/établir si ...** it remains to be seen/established if *ou* whether ...; **il n'en reste pas moins que ...** the fact remains that ..., it's nevertheless a fact that ...; **en** ~ **à** (*stade, menaces*) to go no further than, only go as far as; **restons-en là** let's leave it at that; ~ **sur une impression** to retain an impression; **y** ~: **il a failli y** ~ he nearly met his end.
restituer [Rɛstitɥe] *vt* (*objet, somme*): ~ **qch (à qn)** to return *ou* restore sth (to sb); (*énergie*) to release; (*son*) to reproduce.
restitution [Rɛstitysjɔ̃] *nf* restoration.
restoroute [RɛstɔRut] *nm* motorway (*BRIT*) *ou* highway (*US*) restaurant.
restreindre [RɛstRɛ̃dR(ə)] *vt* to restrict, limit; **se** ~ (*dans ses dépenses etc*) to cut down; (*champ de recherches*) to narrow.
restreint, e [RɛstRɛ̃, -ɛ̃t] *pp de* **restreindre** ♦ *adj* restricted, limited.
restrictif, ive [RɛstRiktif, -iv] *adj* restrictive, limiting.
restriction [RɛstRiksjɔ̃] *nf* restriction; (*condition*) qualification; ~**s** *nfpl* (*mentales*) reservations; **sans** ~ *adv* unreservedly.
restructuration [RəstRyktyRɑsjɔ̃] *nf* restructuring.
restructurer [RəstRyktyRe] *vt* to restructure.
résultante [Rezyltɑ̃t] *nf* (*conséquence*) result, consequence.
résultat [Rezylta] *nm* result; (*conséquence*) outcome *no pl*, result; (*d'élection etc*) results *pl*; ~**s** *nmpl* (*d'une enquête*) findings; ~**s sportifs** sports results.
résulter [Rezylte]: ~ **de** *vt* to result from, be the result of; **il résulte de ceci que ...** the result of this is that ....
résumé [Rezyme] *nm* summary, résumé; **faire le** ~ **de** to summarize; **en** ~ *adv* in brief; (*pour conclure*) to sum up.
résumer [Rezyme] *vt* (*texte*) to summarize; (*récapituler*) to sum up; (*fig*) to epitomize, typify; **se** ~ *vi* (*personne*) to sum up (one's ideas); **se** ~ **à** to come down to.
resurgir [RəsyRʒiR] *vi* to reappear, re-emerge.
résurrection [RezyRɛksjɔ̃] *nf* resurrection; (*fig*) revival.
rétablir [RetabliR] *vt* to restore, re-establish; (*personne: suj: traitement*): ~ **qn** to restore sb to health, help sb recover; (*ADMIN*): ~ **qn dans son emploi/ses droits** to reinstate sb in his post/restore sb's rights; **se** ~ *vi* (*guérir*) to recover; (*silence, calme*) to return, be restored; (*GYM etc*): **se** ~ **(sur)** to pull o.s. up (onto).
rétablissement [Retablismɑ̃] *nm* restoring; recovery; pull-up.
rétamer [Retame] *vt* to re-coat, re-tin.
rétameur [RetamœR] *nm* tinker.
retaper [Rətape] *vt* (*maison, voiture etc*) to do up; (*fam: revigorer*) to buck up; (*redactylographier*) to retype.
retard [RətaR] *nm* (*d'une personne attendue*) lateness *no pl*; (*sur l'horaire, un programme, une échéance*) delay; (*fig: scolaire, mental etc*) backwardness; **être en** ~ (*pays*) to be backward; (*dans paiement, travail*) to be behind; **en** ~ **(de 2 heures)** (2 hours) late; **avoir un** ~ **de 2 km** (*SPORT*) to be 2 km behind; **rattraper son** ~ to catch up; **avoir du** ~ to be late; (*sur un programme*) to be behind (schedule); **prendre du** ~ (*train, avion*) to be delayed; (*montre*) to lose (time); **sans** ~ *adv* without delay; ~ **à l'allumage** (*AUTO*) retarded spark; ~ **scolaire** backwardness at school.
retardataire [RətaRdatɛR] *adj* late; (*enfant, idées*) backward ♦ *nm/f* latecomer; backward child.
retardé, e [RətaRde] *adj* backward.
retardement [RətaRdəmɑ̃]: **à** ~ *adj* delayed action *cpd*; **bombe à** ~ time bomb.
retarder [RətaRde] *vt* (*sur un horaire*): ~ **qn (d'une heure)** to delay sb (an hour); (*sur un programme*): ~ **qn (de 3 mois)** to set sb back *ou* delay sb (3 months); (*départ, date*): ~ **qch (de 2 jours)** to put sth back (2 days), delay sth (for *ou* by 2 days); (*horloge*) to put back ♦ *vi* (*montre*) to be slow; (*: habituellement*) to lose (time); **je retarde (d'une heure)** I'm (an hour) slow.
retendre [Rətɑ̃dR(ə)] *vt* (*câble etc*) to stretch again; (*MUS: cordes*) to retighten.

retenir [Rətnir] *vt* (*garder, retarder*) to keep, detain; (*maintenir: objet qui glisse, fig: colère, larmes, rire*) to hold back; (*: objet suspendu*) to hold; (*: chaleur, odeur*) to retain; (*fig: empêcher d'agir*): ~ **qn (de faire)** to hold sb back (from doing); (*se rappeler*) to retain; (*réserver*) to reserve; (*accepter*) to accept; (*prélever*): ~ **qch (sur)** to deduct sth (from); **se** ~ (*euphémisme*) to hold on; (*se raccrocher*): **se** ~ **à** to hold onto; (*se contenir*): **se** ~ **de faire** to restrain o.s. from doing; ~ **son souffle** *ou* **haleine** to hold one's breath; ~ **qn à dîner** to ask sb to stay for dinner; **je pose 3 et je retiens 2** put down 3 and carry 2.

rétention [Retɑ̃sjɔ̃] *nf*: ~ **d'urine** urine retention.

retentir [Rətɑ̃tiR] *vi* to ring out; (*salle*): ~ **de** to ring *ou* resound with; ~ **sur** *vt* (*fig*) to have an effect upon.

retentissant, e [Rətɑ̃tisɑ̃, -ɑ̃t] *adj* resounding; (*fig*) impact-making.

retentissement [Rətɑ̃tismɑ̃] *nm* (*retombées*) repercussions *pl*; effect, impact.

retenu, e [Rətny] *pp de* **retenir** ♦ *adj* (*place*) reserved; (*personne: empêché*) held up; (*propos: contenu, discret*) restrained ♦ *nf* (*prélèvement*) deduction; (*MATH*) number to carry over; (*SCOL*) detention; (*modération*) (self-)restraint; (*réserve*) reserve, reticence; (*AUTO*) tailback.

réticence [Retisɑ̃s] *nf* reticence *no pl*, reluctance *no pl*; **sans** ~ without hesitation.

réticent, e [Retisɑ̃, -ɑ̃t] *adj* reticent, reluctant.

retiendrai [Rətjɛ̃dRe], **retiens** [Rətjɛ̃] *etc vb voir* **retenir**.

rétif, ive [Retif, -iv] *adj* restive.

rétine [Retin] *nf* retina.

retint [Rətɛ̃] *etc vb voir* **retenir**.

retiré, e [RətiRe] *adj* (*solitaire*) secluded; (*éloigné*) remote.

retirer [RətiRe] *vt* to withdraw; (*vêtement, lunettes*) to take off, remove; (*enlever*): ~ **qch à qn** to take sth from sb; (*extraire*): ~ **qn/qch de** to take sb away from/sth out of, remove sb/sth from; (*reprendre: bagages, billets*) to collect, pick up; ~ **des avantages de** to derive advantages from; **se** ~ *vi* (*partir, reculer*) to withdraw; (*prendre sa retraite*) to retire; **se** ~ **de** to withdraw from; to retire from.

retombées [Rətɔ̃be] *nfpl* (*radioactives*) fallout *sg*; (*fig*) fallout; spin-offs.

retomber [Rətɔ̃be] *vi* (*à nouveau*) to fall again; (*rechuter*): ~ **malade/dans l'erreur** to fall ill again/fall back into error; (*atterrir: après un saut etc*) to land; (*tomber, redescendre*) to fall back; (*pendre*) to fall, hang (down); (*échoir*): ~ **sur qn** to fall on sb.

retordre [RətɔRdR(ə)] *vt*: **donner du fil à** ~ **à qn** to make life difficult for sb.

rétorquer [RetɔRke] *vt*: ~ **(à qn) que** to retort (to sb) that.

retors, e [Rətɔr, -ɔRs(ə)] *adj* wily.

rétorsion [RetɔRsjɔ̃] *nf*: **mesures de** ~ reprisals.

retouche [Rətuʃ] *nf* touching up *no pl*; alteration; **faire une** ~ *ou* **des** ~**s à** to touch up.

retoucher [Rətuʃe] *vt* (*photographie, tableau*) to touch up; (*texte, vêtement*) to alter.

retour [RətuR] *nm* return; **au** ~ (*en arrivant*) when we (*ou* they *etc*) get (*ou* got) back; (*en route*) on the way back; **pendant le** ~ on the way *ou* journey back; **à mon/ton** ~ on my/your return; **au** ~ **de** on the return of; **être de** ~ **(de)** to be back (from); **de** ~ **à .../chez moi** back at .../back home; **en** ~ *adv* in return; **par** ~ **du courrier** by return of post; **par un juste** ~ **des choses** by a favourable twist of fate; **match** ~ return match; ~ **en arrière** (*CINÉ*) flashback; (*mesure*) backward step; ~ **de bâton** kickback; ~ **de chariot** carriage return; ~ **à l'envoyeur** (*POSTES*) return to sender; ~ **de flamme** backfire; ~ **(automatique) à la ligne** (*INFORM*) wordwrap; ~ **de manivelle** (*fig*) backfire; ~ **offensif** renewed attack; ~ **aux sources** (*fig*) return to basics.

retournement [RətuRnəmɑ̃] *nm* (*d'une personne: revirement*) turning (round); ~ **de la situation** reversal of the situation.

retourner [RətuRne] *vt* (*dans l'autre sens: matelas, crêpe*) to turn (over); (*: caisse*) to turn upside down; (*: sac, vêtement*) to turn inside out; (*fig: argument*) to turn back; (*en remuant: terre, sol, foin*) to turn over; (*émouvoir: personne*) to shake; (*renvoyer, restituer*): ~ **qch à qn** to return sth to sb ♦ *vi* (*aller, revenir*): ~ **quelque part/à** to go back *ou* return somewhere/to; ~ **à** (*état, activité*) to return to, go back to; **se** ~ *vi* to turn over; (*tourner la tête*) to turn round; **s'en** ~ to go back; **se** ~ **contre** (*fig*) to turn against; **savoir de quoi il retourne** to know what it is all about; ~ **sa veste** (*fig*) to turn one's coat; ~ **en arrière** *ou* **sur ses pas** to turn back, retrace one's steps; ~ **aux sources** to go back to basics.

retracer [RətRase] *vt* to relate, recount.

rétracter [RetRakte] *vt*, **se** ~ *vi* to retract.

retraduire [RətRadɥiR] *vt* to translate again; (*dans la langue de départ*) to translate back.

retrait [RətRɛ] *nm* (*voir retirer*) withdrawal; collection; (*voir se retirer*) withdrawal; (*rétrécissement*) shrinkage; **en** ~ *adj* set back; **écrire en** ~ to indent; ~ **du permis (de conduire)** disqualification from driving (*BRIT*), revocation of driver's license (*US*).

retraite [RətRɛt] *nf* (*d'une armée, REL, refuge*) retreat; (*d'un employé*) retirement; (*revenu*) (retirement) pension; **être/mettre à la** ~ to be retired/pension off *ou* retire; **prendre sa** ~ to retire; ~ **anticipée** early retirement; ~ **aux flambeaux** torchlight tattoo.

retraité, e [RətRete] *adj* retired ♦ *nm/f* (old age) pensioner.

retraitement [RətRɛtmɑ̃] *nm* reprocessing.

retraiter [Rətʀete] *vt* to reprocess.

retranchement [Rətʀɑ̃ʃmɑ̃] *nm* entrenchment; **poursuivre qn dans ses derniers ~s** to drive sb into a corner.

retrancher [Rətʀɑ̃ʃe] *vt* (*passage, détails*) to take out, remove; (*nombre, somme*): **~ qch de** to take *ou* deduct sth from; (*couper*) to cut off; **se ~ derrière/dans** to entrench o.s. behind/in; (*fig*) to take refuge behind/in.

retranscrire [Rətʀɑ̃skʀiʀ] *vt* to retranscribe.

retransmettre [Rətʀɑ̃smɛtʀ(ə)] *vt* (*RADIO*) to broadcast, relay; (*TV*) to show.

retransmission [Rətʀɑ̃smisjɔ̃] *nf* broadcast; showing.

retravailler [Rətʀavaje] *vi* to start work again ♦ *vt* to work on again.

retraverser [Rətʀavɛʀse] *vt* (*dans l'autre sens*) to cross back over.

rétréci, e [ʀetʀesi] *adj* (*idées, esprit*) narrow.

rétrécir [ʀetʀesiʀ] *vt* (*vêtement*) to take in ♦ *vi* to shrink; **se ~** *vi* to narrow.

rétrécissement [ʀetʀesismɑ̃] *nm* narrowing.

retremper [Rətʀɑ̃pe] *vt*: **se ~ dans** (*fig*) to reimmerse o.s. in.

rétribuer [ʀetʀibɥe] *vt* (*travail*) to pay for; (*personne*) to pay.

rétribution [ʀetʀibysjɔ̃] *nf* payment.

rétro [ʀetʀo] *adj inv* old-style ♦ *nm* (= *rétroviseur*) (rear-view) mirror; **la mode ~** the nostalgia vogue.

rétroactif, ive [ʀetʀɔaktif, -iv] *adj* retroactive.

rétrocéder [ʀetʀɔsede] *vt* to retrocede.

rétrocession [ʀetʀɔsesjɔ̃] *nf* retrocession.

rétrofusée [ʀetʀɔfyze] *nf* retrorocket.

rétrograde [ʀetʀɔgʀad] *adj* reactionary, backward-looking.

rétrograder [ʀetʀɔgʀade] *vi* (*élève*) to fall back; (*économie*) to regress; (*AUTO*) to change down.

rétroprojecteur [ʀetʀɔpʀɔʒɛktœʀ] *nm* overhead projector.

rétrospectif, ive [ʀetʀɔspɛktif, -iv] *adj, nf* retrospective.

rétrospectivement [ʀetʀɔspɛktivmɑ̃] *adv* in retrospect.

retroussé, e [Rətʀuse] *adj*: **nez ~** turned-up nose.

retrousser [Rətʀuse] *vt* to roll up; (*fig: nez*) to wrinkle; (*: lèvres*) to curl up.

retrouvailles [Rətʀuvɑj] *nfpl* reunion *sg*.

retrouver [Rətʀuve] *vt* (*fugitif, objet perdu*) to find; (*occasion*) to find again; (*calme, santé*) to regain; (*reconnaître: expression, style*) to recognize; (*revoir*) to see again; (*rejoindre*) to meet (again), join; **se ~** *vi* to meet; (*s'orienter*) to find one's way; **se ~ quelque part** to find o.s. somewhere; to end up somewhere; **se ~ seul/sans argent** to find o.s. alone/with no money; **se ~ dans** (*calculs, dossiers, désordre*) to make sense of; **s'y ~** (*rentrer dans ses frais*) to break even.

rétroviseur [ʀetʀɔvizœʀ] *nm* (rear-view) mirror.

réunifier [ʀeynifje] *vt* to reunify.

Réunion [ʀeynjɔ̃] *nf*: **la ~, l'île de la ~** Réunion.

réunion [ʀeynjɔ̃] *nf* bringing together; joining; (*séance*) meeting.

réunionnais, e [ʀeynjɔnɛ, -ɛz] *adj* of *ou* from Réunion.

réunir [ʀeyniʀ] *vt* (*convoquer*) to call together; (*rassembler*) to gather together; (*cumuler*) to combine; (*rapprocher*) to bring together (again), reunite; (*rattacher*) to join (together); **se ~** *vi* (*se rencontrer*) to meet; (*s'allier*) to unite.

réussi, e [ʀeysi] *adj* successful.

réussir [ʀeysiʀ] *vi* to succeed, be successful; (*à un examen*) to pass; (*plante, culture*) to thrive, do well ♦ *vt* to make a success of; to bring off; **~ à faire** to succeed in doing; **~ à qn** to go right for sb; (*aliment*) to agree with sb; **le travail/le mariage lui réussit** work/married life agrees with him.

réussite [ʀeysit] *nf* success; (*CARTES*) patience.

réutiliser [ʀeytilize] *vt* to re-use.

revaloir [Rəvalwaʀ] *vt*: **je vous revaudrai cela** I'll repay you some day; (*en mal*) I'll pay you back for this.

revalorisation [Rəvalɔʀizɑsjɔ̃] *nf* revaluation; raising.

revaloriser [Rəvalɔʀize] *vt* (*monnaie*) to revalue; (*salaires, pensions*) to raise the level of; (*institution, tradition*) to reassert the value of.

revanche [Rəvɑ̃ʃ] *nf* revenge; **prendre sa ~ (sur)** to take one's revenge (on); **en ~** (*par contre*) on the other hand; (*en compensation*) in return.

rêvasser [ʀɛvase] *vi* to daydream.

rêve [ʀɛv] *nm* dream; (*activité psychique*): **le ~** dreaming; **paysage/silence de ~** dreamlike landscape/silence; **~ éveillé** daydreaming *no pl*, daydream.

rêvé, e [ʀeve] *adj* (*endroit, mari etc*) ideal.

revêche [Rəvɛʃ] *adj* surly, sour-tempered.

réveil [ʀevɛj] *nm* (*d'un dormeur*) waking up *no pl*; (*fig*) awakening; (*pendule*) alarm (clock); **au ~** when I (*ou* you *etc*) wake (*ou* woke) up, on waking (up); **sonner le ~** (*MIL*) to sound the reveille.

réveille-matin [ʀevɛjmatɛ̃] *nm inv* alarm clock.

réveiller [ʀeveje] *vt* (*personne*) to wake up; (*fig*) to awaken, revive; **se ~** *vi* to wake up; (*fig*) to be revived, reawaken.

réveillon [ʀevɛjɔ̃] *nm* Christmas Eve; (*de la Saint-Sylvestre*) New Year's Eve; Christmas Eve (*ou* New Year's Eve) party *ou* dinner.

réveillonner [ʀevɛjɔne] *vi* to celebrate Christmas Eve (*ou* New Year's Eve).

révélateur, trice [ʀevelatœʀ, -tʀis] *adj*: **~ (de qch)** revealing (sth) ♦ *nm* (*PHOTO*) developer.

révélation [ʀevelɑsjɔ̃] *nf* revelation.

révéler [revele] *vt* (*gén*) to reveal; (*divulguer*) to disclose, reveal; (*dénoter*) to reveal, show; (*faire connaître au public*): ~ **qn/qch** to make sb/sth widely known, bring sb/sth to the public's notice; **se** ~ *vi* to be revealed, reveal itself ♦ *vb avec attribut*: **se** ~ **facile/faux** to prove (to be) easy/false; **se** ~ **cruel/un allié sûr** to show o.s. to be cruel/a trustworthy ally.

revenant, e [rəvnɑ̃, -ɑ̃t] *nm/f* ghost.

revendeur, euse [rəvɑ̃dœr, -øz] *nm/f* (*détaillant*) retailer; (*d'occasions*) secondhand dealer.

revendicatif, ive [rəvɑ̃dikatif, -iv] *adj* (*mouvement*) of protest.

revendication [rəvɑ̃dikɑsjɔ̃] *nf* claim, demand; **journée de** ~ day of action (in support of one's claims).

revendiquer [rəvɑ̃dike] *vt* to claim, demand; (*responsabilité*) to claim ♦ *vi* to agitate in favour of one's claims.

revendre [rəvɑ̃dr(ə)] *vt* (*d'occasion*) to resell; (*détailler*) to sell; (*vendre davantage de*): ~ **du sucre/un foulard/deux bagues** to sell more sugar/another scarf/another two rings; **à** ~ *adv* (*en abondance*) to spare.

revenir [rəvnir] *vi* to come back; (*CULIN*): **faire** ~ to brown; (*coûter*): ~ **cher/à 10 € (à qn)** to cost (sb) a lot/€10; ~ **à** (*études, projet*) to return to, go back to; (*équivaloir à*) to amount to; ~ **à qn** (*rumeur, nouvelle*) to get back to sb, reach sb's ears; (*part, honneur*) to go to sb, be sb's; (*souvenir, nom*) to come back to sb; ~ **de** (*fig: maladie, étonnement*) to recover from; ~ **sur** (*question, sujet*) to go back over; (*engagement*) to go back on; ~ **à la charge** to return to the attack; ~ **à soi** to come round; **n'en pas** ~: **je n'en reviens pas** I can't get over it; ~ **sur ses pas** to retrace one's steps; **cela revient à dire que/au même** it amounts to saying that/to the same thing; ~ **de loin** (*fig*) to have been at death's door.

revente [rəvɑ̃t] *nf* resale.

revenu, e [rəvny] *pp de* **revenir** ♦ *nm* income; (*de l'État*) revenue; (*d'un capital*) yield; ~**s** *nmpl* income *sg*; ~ **national brut** gross national income.

rêver [reve] *vi*, *vt* to dream; (*rêvasser*) to (day)dream; ~ **de** (*voir en rêve*) to dream of *ou* about; ~ **de qch/de faire** to dream of sth/of doing; ~ **à** to dream of.

réverbération [reverberɑsjɔ̃] *nf* reflection.

réverbère [reverbɛr] *nm* street lamp *ou* light.

réverbérer [reverbere] *vt* to reflect.

reverdir [rəverdir] *vi* (*arbre etc*) to turn green again.

révérence [reverɑ̃s] *nf* (*vénération*) reverence; (*salut: d'homme*) bow; (*: de femme*) curtsey.

révérencieux, euse [reverɑ̃sjø, -øz] *adj* reverent.

révérend, e [reverɑ̃, -ɑ̃d] *adj*: **le** ~ **père Pascal** the Reverend Father Pascal.

révérer [revere] *vt* to revere.

rêverie [rɛvri] *nf* daydreaming *no pl*, daydream.

reverrai [rəvɛre] *etc vb voir* **revoir**.

revers [rəvɛr] *nm* (*de feuille, main*) back; (*d'étoffe*) wrong side; (*de pièce, médaille*) back, reverse; (*TENNIS, PING-PONG*) backhand; (*de veston*) lapel; (*de pantalon*) turn-up; (*fig: échec*) setback; ~ **de fortune** reverse of fortune; **d'un** ~ **de main** with the back of one's hand; **le** ~ **de la médaille** (*fig*) the other side of the coin; **prendre à** ~ (*MIL*) to take from the rear.

reverser [rəvɛrse] *vt* (*reporter: somme etc*): ~ **sur** to put back into; (*liquide*): ~ **(dans)** to pour some more (into).

réversible [revɛrsibl(ə)] *adj* reversible.

revêtement [rəvɛtmɑ̃] *nm* (*de paroi*) facing; (*des sols*) flooring; (*de chaussée*) surface; (*de tuyau etc: enduit*) coating.

revêtir [rəvetir] *vt* (*habit*) to don, put on; (*fig*) to take on; ~ **qn de** to dress sb in; (*fig*) to endow *ou* invest sb with; ~ **qch de** to cover sth with; (*fig*) to cloak sth in; ~ **d'un visa** to append a visa to.

rêveur, euse [rɛvœr, -øz] *adj* dreamy ♦ *nm/f* dreamer.

reviendrai [rəvjɛ̃dre] *etc vb voir* **revenir**.

revienne [rəvjɛn] *etc vb voir* **revenir**.

revient [rəvjɛ̃] *vb voir* **revenir** ♦ *nm*: **prix de** ~ cost price.

revigorer [rəvigɔre] *vt* to invigorate, revive, buck up.

revint [rəvɛ̃] *etc vb voir* **revenir**.

revirement [rəvirmɑ̃] *nm* change of mind; (*d'une situation*) reversal.

revis [rəvi] *etc vb voir* **revoir**.

révisable [revizabl(ə)] *adj* (*procès, taux etc*) reviewable, subject to review.

réviser [revize] *vt* (*texte, SCOL: matière*) to revise; (*comptes*) to audit; (*machine, installation, moteur*) to overhaul, service; (*JUR: procès*) to review.

révision [revizjɔ̃] *nf* revision; auditing *no pl*; overhaul, servicing *no pl*; review; **conseil de** ~ (*MIL*) recruiting board; **faire ses** ~**s** (*SCOL*) to do one's revision (*BRIT*), revise (*BRIT*), review (*US*); **la** ~ **des 10 000 km** (*AUTO*) the 10,000 km service.

révisionnisme [revizjɔnism(ə)] *nm* revisionism.

revisser [rəvise] *vt* to screw back again.

revit [rəvi] *vb voir* **revoir**.

revitaliser [rəvitalize] *vt* to revitalize.

revivifier [rəvivifje] *vt* to revitalize.

revivre [rəvivr(ə)] *vi* (*reprendre des forces*) to come alive again; (*traditions*) to be revived ♦ *vt* (*épreuve, moment*) to relive; **faire** ~ (*mode, institution, usage*) to bring back to life.

révocable [revɔkabl(ə)] *adj* (*délégué*) dismissible; (*contrat*) revocable.

révocation [revɔkɑsjɔ̃] *nf* dismissal; revocation.

revoir [ʀəvwaʀ] *vt* to see again; (*réviser*) to revise (*BRIT*), review (*US*) ♦ *nm*: **au ~** goodbye; **dire au ~ à qn** to say goodbye to sb; **se ~** (*amis*) to meet (again), see each other again.

révoltant, e [ʀevɔltɑ̃, -ɑ̃t] *adj* revolting.

révolte [ʀevɔlt(ə)] *nf* rebellion, revolt.

révolter [ʀevɔlte] *vt* to revolt, outrage; **se ~** *vi*: **se ~ (contre)** to rebel (against); **se ~ (à)** to be outraged (by).

révolu, e [ʀevɔly] *adj* past; (*ADMIN*): **âgé de 18 ans ~s** over 18 years of age; **après 3 ans ~s** when 3 full years have passed.

révolution [ʀevɔlysjɔ̃] *nf* revolution; **être en ~** (*pays etc*) to be in revolt; **la ~ industrielle** the industrial revolution.

révolutionnaire [ʀevɔlysjɔnɛʀ] *adj, nm/f* revolutionary.

révolutionner [ʀevɔlysjɔne] *vt* to revolutionize; (*fig*) to stir up.

revolver [ʀevɔlvɛʀ] *nm* gun; (*à barillet*) revolver.

révoquer [ʀevɔke] *vt* (*fonctionnaire*) to dismiss, remove from office; (*arrêt, contrat*) to revoke.

revoyais [ʀəvwajɛ] *etc vb voir* **revoir**.

revu, e [ʀəvy] *pp de* **revoir** ♦ *nf* (*inventaire, examen*) review; (*MIL: défilé*) review, march past; (*: inspection*) inspection, review; (*périodique*) review, magazine; (*pièce satirique*) revue; (*de music-hall*) variety show; **passer en ~** to review, inspect; (*fig*) to review; **~ de (la) presse** press review.

révulsé, e [ʀevylse] *adj* (*yeux*) rolled upwards; (*visage*) contorted.

Reykjavik [ʀɛkjavik] *n* Reykjavik.

rez-de-chaussée [ʀedʃose] *nm inv* ground floor.

rez-de-jardin [ʀedʒaʀdɛ̃] *nm inv* garden level.

RF *sigle f* = *République française*.

RFA *sigle f* (= *République fédérale d'Allemagne*) FRG.

RFO *sigle f* (= *Radio-Télévision Française d'Outre-mer*) *French overseas broadcasting service*.

RG *sigle mpl* (= *renseignements généraux*) *security section of the police force*.

rhabiller [ʀabije] *vt*: **se ~** to get dressed again, put one's clothes on again.

rhapsodie [ʀapsɔdi] *nf* rhapsody.

rhénan, e [ʀenɑ̃, -an] *adj* Rhine *cpd*, of the Rhine.

Rhénanie [ʀenani] *nf*: **la ~** the Rhineland.

rhéostat [ʀeɔsta] *nm* rheostat.

rhésus [ʀezys] *adj, nm* rhesus; **~ positif/ négatif** rhesus positive/negative.

rhétorique [ʀetɔʀik] *nf* rhetoric ♦ *adj* rhetorical.

rhéto-roman, e [ʀetɔʀɔmɑ̃, -an] *adj* Rhaeto-Romanic.

Rhin [ʀɛ̃] *nm*: **le ~** the Rhine.

rhinite [ʀinit] *nf* rhinitis.

rhinocéros [ʀinɔseʀɔs] *nm* rhinoceros.

rhinopharyngite [ʀinɔfaʀɛ̃ʒit] *nf* throat infection.

rhodanien, ne [ʀɔdanjɛ̃, -ɛn] *adj* Rhône *cpd*, of the Rhône.

Rhodes [ʀɔd] *n*: **(l'île de) ~** (the island of) Rhodes.

Rhodésie [ʀɔdezi] *nf*: **la ~** Rhodesia.

rhodésien, ne [ʀɔdezjɛ̃, -ɛn] *adj* Rhodesian.

rhododendron [ʀɔdɔdɛ̃dʀɔ̃] *nm* rhododendron.

Rhône [ʀon] *nm*: **le ~** the Rhone.

rhubarbe [ʀybaʀb(ə)] *nf* rhubarb.

rhum [ʀɔm] *nm* rum.

rhumatisant, e [ʀymatizɑ̃, -ɑ̃t] *adj, nm/f* rheumatic.

rhumatismal, e, aux [ʀymatismal, -o] *adj* rheumatic.

rhumatisme [ʀymatism(ə)] *nm* rheumatism *no pl*.

rhumatologie [ʀymatɔlɔʒi] *nf* rheumatology.

rhumatologue [ʀymatɔlɔg] *nm/f* rheumatologist.

rhume [ʀym] *nm* cold; **~ de cerveau** head cold; **le ~ des foins** hay fever.

rhumerie [ʀɔmʀi] *nf* (*distillerie*) rum distillery.

RI *sigle m* (*MIL*) = *régiment d'infanterie* ♦ *sigle mpl* (= *Républicains indépendants*) *political party*.

ri [ʀi] *pp de* **rire**.

riant, e [ʀjɑ̃, -ɑ̃t] *vb voir* **rire** ♦ *adj* smiling, cheerful; (*campagne, paysage*) pleasant.

RIB *sigle m* = **relevé d'identité bancaire**.

ribambelle [ʀibɑ̃bɛl] *nf*: **une ~ de** a herd *ou* swarm of.

ricain, e [ʀikɛ̃, -ɛn] *adj* (*fam*) Yank, Yankee.

ricanement [ʀikanmɑ̃] *nm* snigger; giggle.

ricaner [ʀikane] *vi* (*avec méchanceté*) to snigger; (*bêtement, avec gêne*) to giggle.

riche [ʀiʃ] *adj* (*gén*) rich; (*personne, pays*) rich, wealthy; **~ en** rich in; **~ de** full of; rich in.

richement [ʀiʃmɑ̃] *adv* richly.

richesse [ʀiʃɛs] *nf* wealth; (*fig*) richness; **~s** *nfpl* wealth *sg*; treasures; **~ en vitamines** high vitamin content.

richissime [ʀiʃisim] *adj* extremely rich *ou* wealthy.

ricin [ʀisɛ̃] *nm*: **huile de ~** castor oil.

ricocher [ʀikɔʃe] *vi*: **~ (sur)** to rebound (off); (*sur l'eau*) to bounce (on *ou* off); **faire ~** (*galet*) to skim.

ricochet [ʀikɔʃɛ] *nm* rebound; bounce; **faire ~** to rebound, bounce; (*fig*) to rebound; **faire des ~s** to skip stones; **par ~** *adv* on the rebound; (*fig*) as an indirect result.

rictus [ʀiktys] *nm* grin; (snarling) grimace.

ride [ʀid] *nf* wrinkle; (*fig*) ripple.

ridé, e [ʀide] *adj* wrinkled.

rideau, x [ʀido] *nm* curtain; **tirer/ouvrir les ~x** to draw/open the curtains; **~ de fer** metal shutter; (*POL*): **le ~ de fer** the Iron Curtain.

ridelle [ʀidɛl] *nf* slatted side (*of truck*).

rider [ʀide] *vt* to wrinkle; (*fig*) to ripple, ruffle

the surface of; **se** ~ *vi* to become wrinkled.
ridicule [ʀidikyl] *adj* ridiculous ♦ *nm* ridiculousness *no pl*; **le** ~ ridicule; (*travers: gén pl*) absurdities *pl*; **tourner en** ~ to ridicule.
ridiculement [ʀidikylmɑ̃] *adv* ridiculously.
ridiculiser [ʀidikylize] *vt* to ridicule; **se** ~ to make a fool of o.s.
ridule [ʀidyl] *nf* (*euph: ride*) little wrinkle.
rie [ʀi] *etc vb voir* **rire**.

MOT-CLÉ

rien [ʀjɛ̃] *pron* **1**: **(ne) ...** ~ nothing; *tournure negative* + anything; **qu'est-ce que vous avez? -** ~ what have you got? — nothing; **il n'a** ~ **dit/fait** he said/did nothing; he hasn't said/done anything; **il n'a** ~ (*n'est pas blessé*) he's all right; **ça ne fait** ~ it doesn't matter; **il n'y est pour** ~ he's got nothing to do with it
2 (*quelque chose*): **a-t-il jamais** ~ **fait pour nous?** has he ever done anything for us?
3: ~ **de**: ~ **d'intéressant** nothing interesting; ~ **d'autre** nothing else; ~ **du tout** nothing at all; **il n'a** ~ **d'un champion** he's no champion, there's nothing of the champion about him
4: ~ **que** just, only; nothing but; ~ **que pour lui faire plaisir** only *ou* just to please him; ~ **que la vérité** nothing but the truth; ~ **que cela** that alone
♦ *excl*: **de** ~! not at all!, don't mention it!; **il n'en est** ~! nothing of the sort!; ~ **à faire!** it's no good!, it's no use!
♦ *nm*: **un petit** ~ (*cadeau*) a little something; **des** ~**s** trivia *pl*; **un** ~ **de** a hint of; **en un** ~ **de temps** in no time at all; **avoir peur d'un** ~ to be frightened of the slightest thing.

rieur, euse [ʀjœʀ, -øz] *adj* cheerful.
rigide [ʀiʒid] *adj* stiff; (*fig*) rigid; (*moralement*) strict.
rigidité [ʀiʒidite] *nf* stiffness; **la** ~ **cadavérique** rigor mortis.
rigolade [ʀigɔlad] *nf*: **la** ~ fun; (*fig*): **c'est de la** ~ it's a big farce; (*c'est facile*) it's a cinch.
rigole [ʀigɔl] *nf* (*conduit*) channel; (*filet d'eau*) rivulet.
rigoler [ʀigɔle] *vi* (*rire*) to laugh; (*s'amuser*) to have (some) fun; (*plaisanter*) to be joking *ou* kidding.
rigolo, ote [ʀigɔlo, -ɔt] *adj* (*fam*) funny ♦ *nm/f* comic; (*péj*) fraud, phoney.
rigorisme [ʀigɔʀism(ə)] *nm* (moral) rigorism.
rigoriste [ʀigɔʀist(ə)] *adj* rigorist.
rigoureusement [ʀiguʀøzmɑ̃] *adv* rigorously; ~ **vrai/interdit** strictly true/forbidden.
rigoureux, euse [ʀiguʀø, -øz] *adj* (*morale*) rigorous, strict; (*personne*) stern, strict; (*climat, châtiment*) rigorous, harsh, severe; (*interdiction, neutralité*) strict; (*preuves, analyse, méthode*) rigorous.
rigueur [ʀigœʀ] *nf* rigour (*BRIT*), rigor (*US*); strictness; harshness; **"tenue de soirée de** ~**"** "evening dress (to be worn)"; **être de** ~ to be the usual thing, be the rule; **à la** ~ at a pinch; possibly; **tenir** ~ **à qn de qch** to hold sth against sb.
riions [ʀijɔ̃] *etc vb voir* **rire**.
rillettes [ʀijɛt] *nfpl* ≈ potted meat *sg*.
rime [ʀim] *nf* rhyme; **n'avoir ni** ~ **ni raison** to have neither rhyme nor reason.
rimer [ʀime] *vi*: ~ **(avec)** to rhyme (with); **ne** ~ **à rien** not to make sense.
Rimmel [ʀimɛl] *nm* ® mascara.
rinçage [ʀɛ̃saʒ] *nm* rinsing (out); (*opération*) rinse.
rince-doigts [ʀɛ̃sdwa] *nm inv* finger-bowl.
rincer [ʀɛ̃se] *vt* to rinse; (*récipient*) to rinse out; **se** ~ **la bouche** to rinse out one's mouth.
ring [ʀiŋ] *nm* (boxing) ring; **monter sur le** ~ (*aussi fig*) to enter the ring; (*: faire carrière de boxeur*) to take up boxing.
ringard, e [ʀɛ̃gaʀ, -aʀd(ə)] *adj* (*péj*) old-fashioned.
Rio de Janeiro [ʀiodʒanɛʀ(o)] *n* Rio de Janeiro.
rions [ʀiɔ̃] *vb voir* **rire**.
ripaille [ʀipɑj] *nf*: **faire** ~ to feast.
riper [ʀipe] *vi* to slip, slide.
ripoliné, e [ʀipɔline] *adj* enamel-painted.
riposte [ʀipɔst(ə)] *nf* retort, riposte; (*fig*) counter-attack, reprisal.
riposter [ʀipɔste] *vi* to retaliate ♦ *vt*: ~ **que** to retort that; ~ **à** *vt* to counter; to reply to.
rire [ʀiʀ] *vi* to laugh; (*se divertir*) to have fun; (*plaisanter*) to joke ♦ *nm* laugh; **le** ~ laughter; ~ **de** *vt* to laugh at; **se** ~ **de** to make light of; **tu veux** ~! you must be joking!; ~ **aux éclats/aux larmes** to roar with laughter/laugh until one cries; ~ **jaune** to force oneself to laugh; ~ **sous cape** to laugh up one's sleeve; ~ **au nez de qn** to laugh in sb's face; **pour** ~ (*pas sérieusement*) for a joke *ou* a laugh.
ris [ʀi] *vb voir* **rire** ♦ *nm*: ~ **de veau** (calf) sweetbread.
risée [ʀize] *nf*: **être la** ~ **de** to be the laughing stock of.
risette [ʀizɛt] *nf*: **faire** ~ **(à)** to give a nice little smile (to).
risible [ʀizibl(ə)] *adj* laughable, ridiculous.
risque [ʀisk(ə)] *nm* risk; **l'attrait du** ~ the lure of danger; **prendre des** ~**s** to take risks; **à ses** ~**s et périls** at his own risk; **au** ~ **de** at the risk of; ~ **d'incendie** fire risk; ~ **calculé** calculated risk.
risqué, e [ʀiske] *adj* risky; (*plaisanterie*) risqué, daring.
risquer [ʀiske] *vt* to risk; (*allusion, question*) to venture, hazard; **tu risques qu'on te renvoie** you risk being dismissed; **ça ne risque rien** it's quite safe; ~ **de**: **il risque de se tuer** he could get *ou* risks getting himself killed; **il a risqué de se tuer** he almost got himself

killed; **ce qui risque de se produire** what might *ou* could well happen; **il ne risque pas de recommencer** there's no chance of him doing that again; **se ~ dans** (*s'aventurer*) to venture into; **se ~ à faire** (*tenter*) to dare to do; **~ le tout pour le tout** to risk the lot.

risque-tout [riskətu] *nm/f inv* daredevil.

rissoler [risɔle] *vi, vt*: **(faire) ~** to brown.

ristourne [ristuʀn(ə)] *nf* rebate; discount.

rit [ri] *etc vb voir* **rire**.

rite [rit] *nm* rite; (*fig*) ritual.

ritournelle [rituʀnɛl] *nf* (*fig*) tune; **c'est toujours la même ~** (*fam*) it's always the same old story.

rituel, le [ritɥɛl] *adj, nm* ritual.

rituellement [ritɥɛlmɑ̃] *adv* religiously.

riv. *abr* (= *rivière*) R.

rivage [rivaʒ] *nm* shore.

rival, e, aux [rival, -o] *adj, nm/f* rival; **sans ~** *adj* unrivalled.

rivaliser [rivalize] *vi*: **~ avec** to rival, vie with; (*être comparable*) to hold its own against, compare with; **~ avec qn de** (*élégance etc*) to vie with *ou* rival sb in.

rivalité [rivalite] *nf* rivalry.

rive [riv] *nf* shore; (*de fleuve*) bank.

river [rive] *vt* (*clou, pointe*) to clinch; (*plaques*) to rivet together.

riverain, e [rivʀɛ̃, -ɛn] *adj* riverside *cpd*; lakeside *cpd*; roadside *cpd* ♦ *nm/f* riverside (*ou* lakeside) resident; local *ou* roadside resident.

rivet [rivɛ] *nm* rivet.

riveter [rivte] *vt* to rivet (together).

Riviera [rivjɛʀa] *nf*: **la ~ (italienne)** the Italian Riviera.

rivière [rivjɛʀ] *nf* river; **~ de diamants** diamond rivière.

rixe [riks(ə)] *nf* brawl, scuffle.

riz [ri] *nm* rice; **~ au lait** ≈ rice pudding.

rizière [rizjɛʀ] *nf* paddy field.

RMI *sigle m* (= *revenu minimum d'insertion*) ≈ income support (*BRIT*), ≈ welfare (*US*).

RN *sigle f* = **route nationale**.

RNIS *sigle m* (= *Réseau numérique à intégration de service*) ISDN.

robe [ʀɔb] *nf* dress; (*de juge, d'ecclésiastique*) robe; (*de professeur*) gown; (*pelage*) coat; **~ de soirée/de mariée** evening/wedding dress; **~ de baptême** christening robe; **~ de chambre** dressing gown; **~ de grossesse** maternity dress.

robinet [ʀɔbinɛ] *nm* tap, faucet (*US*); **~ du gaz** gas tap; **~ mélangeur** mixer tap.

robinetterie [ʀɔbinɛtʀi] *nf* taps *pl*, plumbing.

roboratif, ive [ʀɔbɔʀatif, -iv] *adj* bracing, invigorating.

robot [ʀɔbo] *nm* robot; **~ de cuisine** food processor.

robotique [ʀɔbɔtik] *nf* robotics *sg*.

robotiser [ʀɔbɔtize] *vt* (*personne, travailleur*) to turn into a robot; (*monde, vie*) to automate.

robuste [ʀɔbyst(ə)] *adj* robust, sturdy.

robustesse [ʀɔbystɛs] *nf* robustness, sturdiness.

roc [ʀɔk] *nm* rock.

rocade [ʀɔkad] *nf* (*AUTO*) bypass.

rocaille [ʀɔkɑj] *nf* (*pierres*) loose stones *pl*; (*terrain*) rocky *ou* stony ground; (*jardin*) rockery, rock garden ♦ *adj* (*style*) rocaille.

rocailleux, euse [ʀɔkɑjø, -øz] *adj* rocky, stony; (*voix*) harsh.

rocambolesque [ʀɔkɑ̃bɔlɛsk(ə)] *adj* fantastic, incredible.

roche [ʀɔʃ] *nf* rock.

rocher [ʀɔʃe] *nm* rock; (*ANAT*) petrosal bone.

rochet [ʀɔʃɛ] *nm*: **roue à ~** ratchet wheel.

rocheux, euse [ʀɔʃø, -øz] *adj* rocky; **les (montagnes) Rocheuses** the Rockies, the Rocky Mountains.

rock (and roll) [ʀɔk(ɛnʀɔl)] *nm* (*musique*) rock(-'n'-roll); (*danse*) rock.

rocker [ʀɔkœʀ] *nm* (*chanteur*) rock musician; (*adepte*) rock fan.

rocking-chair [ʀɔkiŋ(t)ʃɛʀ] *nm* rocking chair.

rodage [ʀɔdaʒ] *nm* running in (*BRIT*), breaking in (*US*); **en ~** (*AUTO*) running *ou* breaking in.

rodé, e [ʀɔde] *adj* run in (*BRIT*), broken in (*US*); (*personne*): **~ à qch** having got the hang of sth.

rodéo [ʀɔdeo] *nm* rodeo (*pl* -s).

roder [ʀɔde] *vt* (*moteur, voiture*) to run in (*BRIT*), break in (*US*); **~ un spectacle** to iron out the initial problems of a show.

rôder [ʀode] *vi* to roam *ou* wander about; (*de façon suspecte*) to lurk (about *ou* around).

rôdeur, euse [ʀodœʀ, -øz] *nm/f* prowler.

rodomontades [ʀɔdɔmɔ̃tad] *nfpl* bragging *sg*; sabre rattling *sg*.

rogatoire [ʀɔgatwaʀ] *adj*: **commission ~** letters rogatory.

rogne [ʀɔɲ] *nf*: **être en ~** to be mad *ou* in a temper; **se mettre en ~** to get mad *ou* in a temper.

rogner [ʀɔɲe] *vt* to trim; (*fig*) to whittle down; **~ sur** (*fig*) to cut down *ou* back on.

rognons [ʀɔɲɔ̃] *nmpl* kidneys.

rognures [ʀɔɲyʀ] *nfpl* trimmings.

rogue [ʀɔg] *adj* arrogant.

roi [ʀwa] *nm* king; **les R~s mages** the Three Wise Men, the Magi; **le jour** *ou* **la fête des R~s, les R~s** Twelfth Night; *see boxed note*.

FÊTE DES ROIS

The **fête des Rois** *is celebrated on 6 January, or Twelfth Night. Figurines representing the Three Wise Men are traditionally added to the Christmas crib ('crèche') and people eat 'galette des Rois', a flat cake with an almond filling in which a porcelain charm ('la fève') is hidden. Whoever finds the charm is king or queen for the day and can choose a partner.*

roitelet [ʀwatlɛ] *nm* wren; (*péj*) kinglet.
rôle [ʀol] *nm* role; (*contribution*) part.
rollmops [ʀɔlmɔps] *nm* rollmop.
romain, e [ʀɔmɛ̃, -ɛn] *adj* Roman ♦ *nm/f*: **R~, e** Roman ♦ *nf* (*CULIN*) cos (lettuce).
roman, e [ʀɔmɑ̃, -an] *adj* (*ARCHIT*) Romanesque; (*LING*) Romance *cpd*, Romanic ♦ *nm* novel; **~ policier** detective novel; **~ d'espionnage** spy novel *ou* story; **~ noir** thriller.
romance [ʀɔmɑ̃s] *nf* ballad.
romancer [ʀɔmɑ̃se] *vt* to romanticize.
romanche [ʀɔmɑ̃ʃ] *adj, nm* Romansh.
romancier, ière [ʀɔmɑ̃sje, -jɛʀ] *nm/f* novelist.
romand, e [ʀɔmɑ̃, -ɑ̃d] *adj* of *ou* from French-speaking Switzerland ♦ *nm/f*: **R~, e** French-speaking Swiss.
romanesque [ʀɔmanɛsk(ə)] *adj* (*fantastique*) fantastic; storybook *cpd*; (*sentimental*) romantic; (*LITTÉRATURE*) novelistic.
roman-feuilleton, *pl* **romans-feuilletons** [ʀɔmɑ̃fœjtɔ̃] *nm* serialized novel.
roman-fleuve, *pl* **romans-fleuves** [ʀɔmɑ̃flœv] *nm* saga, roman-fleuve.
romanichel, le [ʀɔmaniʃɛl] *nm/f* gipsy.
roman-photo, *pl* **romans-photos** [ʀɔmɑ̃fɔto] *nm* (romantic) picture story.
romantique [ʀɔmɑ̃tik] *adj* romantic.
romantisme [ʀɔmɑ̃tism(ə)] *nm* romanticism.
romarin [ʀɔmaʀɛ̃] *nm* rosemary.
rombière [ʀɔ̃bjɛʀ] *nf* (*péj*) old bag.
Rome [ʀɔm] *n* Rome.
rompre [ʀɔ̃pʀ(ə)] *vt* to break; (*entretien, fiançailles*) to break off ♦ *vi* (*fiancés*) to break it off; **se ~** *vi* to break; (*MÉD*) to burst, rupture; **se ~ les os** *ou* **le cou** to break one's neck; **~ avec** to break with; **à tout ~** *adv* wildly; **applaudir à tout ~** to bring down the house, applaud wildly; **~ la glace** (*fig*) to break the ice; **rompez (les rangs)!** (*MIL*) dismiss!, fall out!
rompu, e [ʀɔ̃py] *pp de* **rompre** ♦ *adj* (*fourbu*) exhausted, worn out; **~ à** with wide experience of; inured to.
romsteck [ʀɔ̃mstɛk] *nm* rump steak *no pl*.
ronce [ʀɔ̃s] *nf* (*BOT*) bramble branch; (*MENUISERIE*): **~ de noyer** burr walnut; **~s** *nfpl* brambles, thorns.
ronchonner [ʀɔ̃ʃɔne] *vi* (*fam*) to grouse, grouch.
rond, e [ʀɔ̃, ʀɔ̃d] *adj* round; (*joues, mollets*) well-rounded; (*fam: ivre*) tight; (*sincère, décidé*): **être ~ en affaires** to be on the level in business, do an honest deal ♦ *nm* (*cercle*) ring; (*fam: sou*): **je n'ai plus un ~** I haven't a penny left ♦ *nf* (*gén: de surveillance*) rounds *pl*, patrol; (*danse*) round (dance); (*MUS*) semibreve (*BRIT*), whole note (*US*) ♦ *adv*: **tourner ~** (*moteur*) to run smoothly; **ça ne tourne pas ~** (*fig*) there's something not quite right about it; **pour faire un compte ~** to make (it) a round figure, to round (it) off; **avoir le dos ~** to be round-shouldered; **en ~** (*s'asseoir, danser*) in a ring; **à la ~e** (*alentour*): **à 10 km à la ~e** for 10 km round; (*à chacun son tour*): **passer qch à la ~e** to pass sth (a)round; **faire des ~s de jambe** to bow and scrape; **~ de serviette** napkin ring.
rond-de-cuir, *pl* **ronds-de-cuir** [ʀɔ̃dkɥiʀ] *nm* (*péj*) penpusher.
rondelet, te [ʀɔ̃dlɛ, -ɛt] *adj* plump; (*fig: somme*) tidy; (*: bourse*) well-lined, fat.
rondelle [ʀɔ̃dɛl] *nf* (*TECH*) washer; (*tranche*) slice, round.
rondement [ʀɔ̃dmɑ̃] *adv* (*avec décision*) briskly; (*loyalement*) frankly.
rondeur [ʀɔ̃dœʀ] *nf* (*d'un bras, des formes*) plumpness; (*bonhomie*) friendly straightforwardness; **~s** *nfpl* (*d'une femme*) curves.
rondin [ʀɔ̃dɛ̃] *nm* log.
rond-point, *pl* **ronds-points** [ʀɔ̃pwɛ̃] *nm* roundabout (*BRIT*), traffic circle (*US*).
ronéotyper [ʀɔneɔtipe] *vt* to duplicate, roneo.
ronflant, e [ʀɔ̃flɑ̃, -ɑ̃t] *adj* (*péj*) high-flown, grand.
ronflement [ʀɔ̃fləmɑ̃] *nm* snore, snoring *no pl*.
ronfler [ʀɔ̃fle] *vi* to snore; (*moteur, poêle*) to hum; (*: plus fort*) to roar.
ronger [ʀɔ̃ʒe] *vt* to gnaw (at); (*suj: vers, rouille*) to eat into; **~ son frein** to champ (at) the bit (*fig*); **se ~ de souci, se ~ les sangs** to worry o.s. sick, fret; **se ~ les ongles** to bite one's nails.
rongeur, euse [ʀɔ̃ʒœʀ, -øz] *nm/f* rodent.
ronronnement [ʀɔ̃ʀɔnmɑ̃] *nm* purring; (*bruit*) purr.
ronronner [ʀɔ̃ʀɔne] *vi* to purr.
roque [ʀɔk] *nm* (*ÉCHECS*) castling.
roquefort [ʀɔkfɔʀ] *nm* Roquefort.
roquer [ʀɔke] *vi* to castle.
roquet [ʀɔkɛ] *nm* nasty little lap-dog.
roquette [ʀɔkɛt] *nf* rocket; **~ antichar** anti-tank rocket.
rosace [ʀozas] *nf* (*vitrail*) rose window, rosace; (*motif: de plafond etc*) rose.
rosaire [ʀozɛʀ] *nm* rosary.
rosbif [ʀɔsbif] *nm*: **du ~** roasting beef; (*cuit*) roast beef; **un ~** a joint of (roasting) beef.
rose [ʀoz] *nf* rose; (*vitrail*) rose window ♦ *adj* pink; **~ bonbon** *adj inv* candy pink; **~ des vents** compass card.
rosé, e [ʀoze] *adj* pinkish; **(vin) ~** rosé (wine).
roseau, x [ʀozo] *nm* reed.
rosée [ʀoze] *adj f voir* **rosé** ♦ *nf*: **goutte de ~** dewdrop.
roseraie [ʀozʀɛ] *nf* rose garden; (*plantation*) rose nursery.
rosette [ʀozɛt] *nf* rosette (*gen of the Légion d'honneur*).
rosier [ʀozje] *nm* rosebush, rose tree.
rosir [ʀoziʀ] *vi* to go pink.
rosse [ʀɔs] *nf* (*péj: cheval*) nag ♦ *adj* nasty, vicious.

rosser [Rɔse] *vt* (*fam*) to thrash.
rossignol [Rɔsiɲɔl] *nm* (*ZOOL*) nightingale; (*crochet*) picklock.
rot [Ro] *nm* belch; (*de bébé*) burp.
rotatif, ive [Rɔtatif, -iv] *adj* rotary ♦ *nf* rotary press.
rotation [Rɔtɑsjɔ̃] *nf* rotation; (*fig*) rotation, swap-around; (*renouvellement*) turnover; **par** ~ on a rota (*BRIT*) *ou* rotation (*US*) basis; ~ **des cultures** rotation of crops; ~ **des stocks** stock turnover.
rotatoire [Rɔtatwar] *adj*: **mouvement** ~ rotary movement.
roter [Rɔte] *vi* (*fam*) to burp, belch.
rôti [Roti] *nm*: **du** ~ roasting meat; (*cuit*) roast meat; **un** ~ **de bœuf/porc** a joint of (roasting) beef/pork.
rotin [Rɔtɛ̃] *nm* rattan (cane); **fauteuil en** ~ cane (arm)chair.
rôtir [RotiR] *vt* (*aussi*: **faire** ~) to roast ♦ *vi* to roast; **se** ~ **au soleil** to bask in the sun.
rôtisserie [RotisRi] *nf* (*restaurant*) steakhouse; (*comptoir, magasin*) roast meat counter (*ou* shop).
rôtissoire [Rotiswar] *nf* (roasting) spit.
rotonde [Rɔtɔ̃d] *nf* (*ARCHIT*) rotunda; (*RAIL*) engine shed.
rotondité [Rɔtɔ̃dite] *nf* roundness.
rotor [RɔtɔR] *nm* rotor.
Rotterdam [RɔtɛRdam] *n* Rotterdam.
rotule [Rɔtyl] *nf* kneecap, patella.
roturier, ière [RɔtyRje, -jɛR] *nm/f* commoner.
rouage [Rwaʒ] *nm* cog(wheel), gearwheel; (*de montre*) part; (*fig*) cog; ~**s** *nmpl* (*fig*) internal structure *sg*.
Rouanda [Rwɑ̃da] *nm*: **le** ~ Rwanda.
roubaisien, ne [Rubezjɛ̃, -ɛn] *adj* of *ou* from Roubaix.
roublard, e [Rublar, -aRd(ə)] *adj* (*péj*) crafty, wily.
rouble [Rubl(ə)] *nm* rouble.
roucoulement [Rukulmɑ̃] *nm* (*de pigeons, fig*) coo, cooing.
roucouler [Rukule] *vi* to coo; (*fig*: *péj*) to warble; (*: amoureux*) to bill and coo.
roue [Ru] *nf* wheel; **faire la** ~ (*paon*) to spread *ou* fan its tail; (*GYM*) to do a cartwheel; **descendre en** ~ **libre** to freewheel *ou* coast down; **pousser à la** ~ to put one's shoulder to the wheel; **grande** ~ (*à la foire*) big wheel; ~ **à aubes** paddle wheel; ~ **dentée** cogwheel; ~ **de secours** spare wheel.
roué, e [Rwe] *adj* wily.
rouennais, e [Rwanɛ, -ɛz] *adj* of *ou* from Rouen.
rouer [Rwe] *vt*: ~ **qn de coups** to give sb a thrashing.
rouet [Rwɛ] *nm* spinning wheel.
rouge [Ruʒ] *adj, nm/f* red ♦ *nm* red; (*fard*) rouge; **(vin)** ~ red wine; **passer au** ~ (*signal*) to go red; (*automobiliste*) to go through a red light; **porter au** ~ (*métal*) to bring to red heat; **sur la liste** ~ (*TÉL*) ex-directory (*BRIT*), unlisted (*US*); ~ **de honte/colère** red with shame/anger; **se fâcher tout/voir** ~ to blow one's top/see red; ~ **(à lèvres)** lipstick.
rougeâtre [RuʒɑtR(ə)] *adj* reddish.
rougeaud, e [Ruʒo, -od] *adj* (*teint*) red; (*personne*) red-faced.
rouge-gorge [Ruʒgɔrʒ(ə)] *nm* robin (redbreast).
rougeoiement [Ruʒwamɑ̃] *nm* reddish glow.
rougeole [Ruʒɔl] *nf* measles *sg*.
rougeoyant, e [Ruʒwajɑ̃, -ɑ̃t] *adj* (*ciel, braises*) glowing; (*aube, reflets*) glowing red.
rougeoyer [Ruʒwaje] *vi* to glow red.
rouget [Ruʒɛ] *nm* mullet.
rougeur [Ruʒœr] *nf* redness; (*du visage*) red face; ~**s** *nfpl* (*MÉD*) red blotches.
rougir [RuʒiR] *vi* (*de honte, timidité*) to blush, flush; (*de plaisir, colère*) to flush; (*fraise, tomate*) to go *ou* turn red; (*ciel*) to redden.
rouille [Ruj] *adj inv* rust-coloured, rusty ♦ *nf* rust; (*CULIN*) *spicy (Provençal) sauce served with fish dishes*.
rouillé, e [Ruje] *adj* rusty.
rouiller [Ruje] *vt* to rust ♦ *vi* to rust, go rusty; **se** ~ *vi* to rust; (*fig: mentalement*) to become rusty; (*: physiquement*) to grow stiff.
roulade [Rulad] *nf* (*GYM*) roll; (*CULIN*) rolled meat *no pl*; (*MUS*) roulade, run.
roulage [Rulaʒ] *nm* (*transport*) haulage.
roulant, e [Rulɑ̃, -ɑ̃t] *adj* (*meuble*) on wheels; (*surface, trottoir*) moving; **matériel** ~ (*RAIL*) rolling stock; **personnel** ~ (*RAIL*) train crews *pl*.
roulé, e [Rule] *adj*: **bien** ~**e** (*fam*: *femme*) shapely, curvy.
rouleau, x [Rulo] *nm* (*de papier, tissu, pièces de monnaie, SPORT*) roll; (*de machine à écrire*) roller, platen; (*à mise en plis, à peinture, vague*) roller; **être au bout du** ~ (*fig*) to be at the end of the line; ~ **compresseur** steamroller; ~ **à pâtisserie** rolling pin; ~ **de pellicule** roll of film.
roulé-boulé, *pl* **roulés-boulés** [Rulebule] (*SPORT*) roll.
roulement [Rulmɑ̃] *nm* (*bruit*) rumbling *no pl*, rumble; (*rotation*) rotation; turnover; (*: de capitaux*) circulation; **par** ~ on a rota (*BRIT*) *ou* rotation (*US*) basis; ~ **(à billes)** ball bearings *pl*; ~ **de tambour** drum roll; ~ **d'yeux** roll(ing) of the eyes.
rouler [Rule] *vt* to roll; (*papier, tapis*) to roll up; (*CULIN*: *pâte*) to roll out; (*fam*) to do, con ♦ *vi* (*bille, boule*) to roll; (*voiture, train*) to go, run; (*automobiliste*) to drive; (*cycliste*) to ride; (*bateau*) to roll; (*tonnerre*) to rumble, roll; (*dégringoler*): ~ **en bas de** to roll down; ~ **sur** (*suj: conversation*) to turn on; **se** ~ **dans** (*boue*) to roll in; (*couverture*) to roll o.s. (up) in; ~ **dans la farine** (*fam*) to con; ~ **les épaules/hanches** to sway one's shoulders/wiggle one's hips; ~ **les "r"** to roll one's r's;

~ **sur l'or** to be rolling in money, be rolling in it; ~ **(sa bosse)** to go places.
roulette [Rulɛt] *nf (de table, fauteuil)* castor; *(de pâtissier)* pastry wheel; *(jeu)*: **la** ~ roulette; **à** ~**s** on castors; **la** ~ **russe** Russian roulette.
roulis [Ruli] *nm* roll(ing).
roulotte [Rulɔt] *nf* caravan.
roumain, e [Rumɛ̃, -ɛn] *adj* Rumanian, Romanian ♦ *nm (LING)* Rumanian, Romanian ♦ *nm/f*: **R~, e** Rumanian, Romanian.
Roumanie [Rumani] *nf*: **la** ~ Rumania, Romania.
roupiller [Rupije] *vi (fam)* to sleep.
rouquin, e [Rukɛ̃, -in] *nm/f (péj)* redhead.
rouspéter [Ruspete] *vi (fam)* to moan, grouse.
rousse [Rus] *adj f voir* **roux**.
rousseur [RusœR] *nf*: **tache de** ~ freckle.
roussi [Rusi] *nm*: **ça sent le** ~ there's a smell of burning; *(fig)* I can smell trouble.
roussir [RusiR] *vt* to scorch ♦ *vi (feuilles)* to go *ou* turn brown; *(CULIN)*: **faire** ~ to brown.
routage [Rutaʒ] *nm* (collective) mailing.
routard, e [RutaR, -aRd(ə)] *nm/f* traveller.
route [Rut] *nf* road; *(fig: chemin)* way; *(itinéraire, parcours)* route; *(fig: voie)* road, path; **par (la)** ~ by road; **il y a 3 heures de** ~ it's a 3-hour ride *ou* journey; **en** ~ *adv* on the way; **en** ~! let's go!; **en cours de** ~ en route; **mettre en** ~ to start up; **se mettre en** ~ to set off; **faire** ~ **vers** to head towards; **faire fausse** ~ *(fig)* to be on the wrong track; ~ **nationale (RN)** ≈ A-road *(BRIT)*, ≈ state highway *(US)*.
routier, ière [Rutje, -jɛR] *adj* road *cpd* ♦ *nm (camionneur)* (long-distance) lorry *(BRIT) ou* truck driver; *(restaurant)* ≈ transport café *(BRIT)*, ≈ truck stop *(US)*; *(scout)* ≈ rover; *(cycliste)* road racer ♦ *nf (voiture)* touring car; **vieux** ~ old stager; **carte routière** road map.
routine [Rutin] *nf* routine; **visite/contrôle de** ~ routine visit/check.
routinier, ière [Rutinje, -jɛR] *adj (péj: travail)* humdrum, routine; *(: personne)* addicted to routine.
rouvert, e [RuvɛR, -ɛRt(ə)] *pp de* **rouvrir**.
rouvrir [RuvRiR] *vt, vi* to reopen, open again; **se** ~ *vi (blessure)* to open up again.
roux, rousse [Ru, Rus] *adj* red; *(personne)* red-haired ♦ *nm/f* redhead ♦ *nm (CULIN)* roux.
royal, e, aux [Rwajal, -o] *adj* royal; *(fig)* fit for a king, princely; blissful; thorough.
royalement [Rwajalmɑ̃] *adv* royally.
royaliste [Rwajalist(ə)] *adj, nm/f* royalist.
royaume [Rwajom] *nm* kingdom; *(fig)* realm; **le** ~ **des cieux** the kingdom of heaven.
Royaume-Uni [Rwajomyni] *nm*: **le** ~ the United Kingdom.
royauté [Rwajote] *nf (dignité)* kingship; *(régime)* monarchy.
RP *sigle f (= recette principale)* ≈ main post office; = *région parisienne* ♦ *sigle fpl (= relations publiques)* PR.
RPR *sigle m (= Rassemblement pour la République) political party.*
R.S.V.P. *abr (= répondez s'il vous plaît)* R.S.V.P.
RTB *sigle f = Radio-Télévision belge.*
Rte *abr* = **route**.
RTL *sigle f = Radio-Télévision Luxembourg.*
RTVE *sigle f = Radio-Télévision espagnole.*
RU [Ry] *sigle m* = **restaurant universitaire**.
ruade [Ryad] *nf* kick.
Ruanda [Rwɑ̃da] *nm*: **le** ~ Rwanda.
ruban [Rybɑ̃] *nm (gén)* ribbon; *(pour ourlet, couture)* binding; *(de téléscripteur etc)* tape; *(d'acier)* strip; ~ **adhésif** adhesive tape; ~ **carbone** carbon ribbon.
rubéole [Rybeɔl] *nf* German measles *sg*, rubella.
rubicond, e [Rybikɔ̃, -ɔ̃d] *adj* rubicund, ruddy.
rubis [Rybi] *nm* ruby; *(HORLOGERIE)* jewel; **payer** ~ **sur l'ongle** to pay cash on the nail.
rubrique [RybRik] *nf (titre, catégorie)* heading, rubric; *(PRESSE: article)* column.
ruche [Ryʃ] *nf* hive.
rucher [Ryʃe] *nm* apiary.
rude [Ryd] *adj (barbe, toile)* rough; *(métier, tâche)* hard, tough; *(climat)* severe, harsh; *(bourru)* harsh, rough; *(fruste)* rugged, tough; *(fam)* jolly good; **être mis à** ~ **épreuve** to be put through the mill.
rudement [Rydmɑ̃] *adv (tomber, frapper)* hard; *(traiter, reprocher)* harshly; *(fam: très)* terribly; *(: beaucoup)* terribly hard.
rudesse [Rydɛs] *nf* roughness; toughness; severity; harshness.
rudimentaire [Rydimɑ̃tɛR] *adj* rudimentary, basic.
rudiments [Rydimɑ̃] *nmpl* rudiments; basic knowledge *sg*; basic principles.
rudoyer [Rydwaje] *vt* to treat harshly.
rue [Ry] *nf* street; **être/jeter qn à la** ~ to be on the streets/throw sb out onto the street.
ruée [Rɥe] *nf* rush; **la** ~ **vers l'or** the gold rush.
ruelle [Rɥɛl] *nf* alley(way).
ruer [Rɥe] *vi (cheval)* to kick out; **se** ~ *vi*: **se** ~ **sur** to pounce on; **se** ~ **vers/dans/hors de** to rush *ou* dash towards/into/out of; ~ **dans les brancards** to become rebellious.
rugby [Rygbi] *nm* rugby (football); ~ **à treize/quinze** rugby league/union.
rugir [RyʒiR] *vi* to roar.
rugissement [Ryʒismɑ̃] *nm* roar, roaring *no pl*.
rugosité [Rygozite] *nf* roughness; *(aspérité)* rough patch.
rugueux, euse [Rygø, -øz] *adj* rough.
ruine [Rɥin] *nf* ruin; ~**s** *nfpl* ruins; **tomber en** ~ to fall into ruin(s).
ruiner [Rɥine] *vt* to ruin.
ruineux, euse [Rɥinø, -øz] *adj* terribly expensive to buy *(ou* run), ruinous; extravagant.
ruisseau, x [Rɥiso] *nm* stream, brook; *(caniveau)* gutter; *(fig)*: ~**x de larmes/sang** floods of tears/streams of blood.

ruisselant, e [ʀɥislɑ̃, -ɑ̃t] *adj* streaming.
ruisseler [ʀɥisle] *vi* to stream; ~ **(d'eau)** to be streaming (with water); ~ **de lumière** to stream with light.
ruissellement [ʀɥisɛlmɑ̃] *nm* streaming; ~ **de lumière** stream of light.
rumeur [ʀymœʀ] *nf* (*bruit confus*) rumbling; hubbub *no pl*; (*protestation*) murmur(ing); (*nouvelle*) rumour (*BRIT*), rumor (*US*).
ruminer [ʀymine] *vt* (*herbe*) to ruminate; (*fig*) to ruminate on *ou* over, chew over ♦ *vi* (*vache*) to chew the cud, ruminate.
rumsteck [ʀɔ̃mstɛk] *nm* = **romsteck**.
rupestre [ʀypɛstʀ(ə)] *adj* (*plante*) rock *cpd*; (*art*) wall *cpd*.
rupture [ʀyptyʀ] *nf* (*de câble, digue*) breaking; (*de tendon*) rupture, tearing; (*de négociations etc*) breakdown; (*de contrat*) breach; (*séparation, désunion*) break-up, split; **en** ~ **de ban** at odds with authority; **en** ~ **de stock** (*COMM*) out of stock.
rural, e, aux [ʀyʀal, -o] *adj* rural, country *cpd* ♦ *nmpl*: **les ruraux** country people.
ruse [ʀyz] *nf*: **la** ~ cunning, craftiness; trickery; **une** ~ a trick, a ruse; **par** ~ by trickery.
rusé, e [ʀyze] *adj* cunning, crafty.
russe [ʀys] *adj* Russian ♦ *nm* (*LING*) Russian ♦ *nm/f*: **R**~ Russian.
Russie [ʀysi] *nf*: **la** ~ Russia; **la** ~ **blanche** White Russia; **la** ~ **soviétique** Soviet Russia.
rustine [ʀystin] *nf* repair patch (*for bicycle inner tube*).
rustique [ʀystik] *adj* rustic; (*plante*) hardy.
rustre [ʀystʀ(ə)] *nm* boor.
rut [ʀyt] *nm*: **être en** ~ (*animal domestique*) to be in *ou* on heat; (*animal sauvage*) to be rutting.
rutabaga [ʀytabaga] *nm* swede.
rutilant, e [ʀytilɑ̃, -ɑ̃t] *adj* gleaming.
RV *sigle m* = **rendez-vous**.
Rwanda [ʀwɑ̃da] *nm*: **le** ~ Rwanda.
rythme [ʀitm(ə)] *nm* rhythm; (*vitesse*) rate; (*: de la vie*) pace, tempo; **au** ~ **de 10 par jour** at the rate of 10 a day.
rythmé, e [ʀitme] *adj* rhythmic(al).
rythmer [ʀitme] *vt* to give rhythm to.
rythmique [ʀitmik] *adj* rhythmic(al) ♦ *nf* rhythmics *sg*.

S s

S, s [ɛs] *nm inv* S, s ♦ *abr* (= *sud*) S; (= *seconde*) sec; (= *siècle*) c., century; **S comme Suzanne** S for Sugar.
s' [s] *pron voir* **se**.
s/ *abr* = **sur**.
SA *sigle f* = **société anonyme**; (= *Son Altesse*) HH.
sa [sa] *adj possessif voir* **son**.
sabbatique [sabatik] *adj*: **année** ~ sabbatical year.
sable [sɑbl(ə)] *nm* sand; ~**s mouvants** quicksand(s).
sablé [sɑble] *adj* (*allée*) sandy ♦ *nm* shortbread biscuit; **pâte** ~**e** (*CULIN*) shortbread dough.
sabler [sɑble] *vt* to sand; (*contre le verglas*) to grit; ~ **le champagne** to drink champagne.
sableux, euse [sɑblø, -øz] *adj* sandy.
sablier [sɑblije] *nm* hourglass; (*de cuisine*) egg timer.
sablière [sɑblijɛʀ] *nf* sand quarry.
sablonneux, euse [sɑblɔnø, -øz] *adj* sandy.
saborder [sabɔʀde] *vt* (*navire*) to scuttle; (*fig*) to wind up, shut down.
sabot [sabo] *nm* clog; (*de cheval, bœuf*) hoof; ~ **(de Denver)** (wheel) clamp; ~ **de frein** brake shoe.
sabotage [sabɔtaʒ] *nm* sabotage.
saboter [sabɔte] *vt* (*travail, morceau de musique*) to botch, make a mess of; (*machine, installation, négociation etc*) to sabotage.
saboteur, euse [sabɔtœʀ, -øz] *nm/f* saboteur.
sabre [sɑbʀ(ə)] *nm* sabre; **le** ~ (*fig*) the sword, the army.
sabrer [sɑbʀe] *vt* to cut down.
SAC [sak] *sigle m* (= *Service d'action civique*) *former Gaullist parapolice*.
sac [sak] *nm* bag; (*à charbon etc*) sack; (*pillage*) sack(ing); **mettre à** ~ to sack; ~ **à provisions/de voyage** shopping/travelling bag; ~ **de couchage** sleeping bag; ~ **à dos** rucksack; ~ **à main** handbag; ~ **de plage** beach bag.
saccade [sakad] *nf* jerk; **par** ~**s** jerkily; haltingly.
saccadé, e [sakade] *adj* jerky.
saccage [sakaʒ] *nm* havoc.
saccager [sakaʒe] *vt* (*piller*) to sack, lay waste; (*dévaster*) to create havoc in, wreck.
saccharine [sakaʀin] *nf* saccharin(e).
saccharose [sakaʀoz] *nm* sucrose.
SACEM [sasɛm] *sigle f* (= *Société des auteurs, compositeurs et éditeurs de musique*) *body re-*

sponsible for collecting and distributing royalties.

sacerdoce [sasɛʀdɔs] *nm* priesthood; (*fig*) calling, vocation.

sacerdotal, e, aux [sasɛʀdɔtal, -o] *adj* priestly, sacerdotal.

sachant [saʃɑ̃] *etc vb voir* **savoir**.

sache [saʃ] *etc vb voir* **savoir**.

sachet [saʃɛ] *nm* (small) bag; (*de lavande, poudre, shampooing*) sachet; **thé en ~s** tea bags; **~ de thé** tea bag.

sacoche [sakɔʃ] *nf* (*gén*) bag; (*de bicyclette*) saddlebag; (*du facteur*) (post-)bag; (*d'outils*) toolbag.

sacquer [sake] *vt* (*fam: candidat, employé*) to sack; (*: réprimander, mal noter*) to plough.

sacraliser [sakʀalize] *vt* to make sacred.

sacre [sakʀ(ə)] *nm* coronation; consecration.

sacré, e [sakʀe] *adj* sacred; (*fam: satané*) blasted; (*: fameux*): **un ~ ...** a heck of a ...; (*ANAT*) sacral.

sacrement [sakʀəmɑ̃] *nm* sacrament; **les derniers ~s** the last rites.

sacrer [sakʀe] *vt* (*roi*) to crown; (*évêque*) to consecrate ♦ *vi* to curse, swear.

sacrifice [sakʀifis] *nm* sacrifice; **faire le ~ de** to sacrifice.

sacrificiel, le [sakʀifisjɛl] *adj* sacrificial.

sacrifier [sakʀifje] *vt* to sacrifice; **~ à** *vt* to conform to; **se ~** to sacrifice o.s.; **articles sacrifiés** (*COMM*) items sold at rock-bottom *ou* give-away prices.

sacrilège [sakʀilɛʒ] *nm* sacrilege ♦ *adj* sacrilegious.

sacristain [sakʀistɛ̃] *nm* sexton; sacristan.

sacristie [sakʀisti] *nf* sacristy; (*culte protestant*) vestry.

sacro-saint, e [sakʀosɛ̃, -ɛ̃t] *adj* sacrosanct.

sadique [sadik] *adj* sadistic ♦ *nm/f* sadist.

sadisme [sadism(ə)] *nm* sadism.

sadomasochisme [sadɔmazoʃism(ə)] *nm* sadomasochism.

sadomasochiste [sadɔmazɔʃist(ə)] *nm/f* sadomasochist.

safari [safaʀi] *nm* safari; **faire un ~** to go on safari.

safari-photo [safaʀifɔto] *nm* photographic safari.

SAFER [safɛʀ] *sigle f* (*= Société d'aménagement foncier et d'établissement rural*) *organization with the right to buy land in order to retain it for agricultural use.*

safran [safʀɑ̃] *nm* saffron.

saga [saga] *nf* saga.

sagace [sagas] *adj* sagacious, shrewd.

sagacité [sagasite] *nf* sagacity, shrewdness.

sagaie [sagɛ] *nf* assegai.

sage [saʒ] *adj* wise; (*enfant*) good ♦ *nm* wise man; sage.

sage-femme [saʒfam] *nf* midwife (*pl* -wives).

sagement [saʒmɑ̃] *adv* (*raisonnablement*) wisely, sensibly; (*tranquillement*) quietly.

sagesse [saʒɛs] *nf* wisdom.

Sagittaire [saʒitɛʀ] *nm*: **le ~** Sagittarius, the Archer; **être du ~** to be Sagittarius.

Sahara [saaʀa] *nm*: **le ~** the Sahara (Desert); **le ~ occidental** (*pays*) Western Sahara.

saharien, ne [saaʀjɛ̃, -ɛn] *adj* Saharan ♦ *nf* safari jacket.

Sahel [saɛl] *nm*: **le ~** the Sahel.

sahélien, ne [saeljɛ̃, -ɛn] *adj* Sahelian.

saignant, e [sɛɲɑ̃, -ɑ̃t] *adj* (*viande*) rare; (*blessure, plaie*) bleeding.

saignée [seɲe] *nf* (*MÉD*) bleeding *no pl*, bloodletting *no pl*; (*ANAT*): **la ~ du bras** the bend of the arm; (*fig: MIL*) heavy losses *pl*; (*: prélèvement*) savage cut.

saignement [sɛɲmɑ̃] *nm* bleeding; **~ de nez** nosebleed.

saigner [seɲe] *vi* to bleed ♦ *vt* to bleed; (*animal*) to bleed to death; **~ qn à blanc** (*fig*) to bleed sb white; **~ du nez** to have a nosebleed.

Saigon [sajgɔ̃] *n* Saigon.

saillant, e [sajɑ̃, -ɑ̃t] *adj* (*pommettes, menton*) prominent; (*corniche etc*) projecting; (*fig*) salient, outstanding.

saillie [saji] *nf* (*sur un mur etc*) projection; (*trait d'esprit*) witticism; (*accouplement*) covering, serving; **faire ~** to project, stick out; **en ~, formant ~** projecting, overhanging.

saillir [sajiʀ] *vi* to project, stick out; (*veine, muscle*) to bulge ♦ *vt* (*ÉLEVAGE*) to cover, serve.

sain, e [sɛ̃, sɛn] *adj* healthy; (*dents, constitution*) healthy, sound; (*lectures*) wholesome; **~ et sauf** safe and sound, unharmed; **~ d'esprit** sound in mind, sane.

saindoux [sɛ̃du] *nm* lard.

sainement [sɛnmɑ̃] *adv* (*vivre*) healthily; (*raisonner*) soundly.

saint, e [sɛ̃, sɛ̃t] *adj* holy; (*fig*) saintly ♦ *nm/f* saint; **la S~e Vierge** the Blessed Virgin.

saint-bernard [sɛ̃bɛʀnaʀ] *nm inv* (*chien*) St Bernard.

Sainte-Hélène [sɛ̃telɛn] *nf* St Helena.

Sainte-Lucie [sɛ̃tlysi] *nf* Saint Lucia.

Saint-Esprit [sɛ̃tɛspʀi] *nm*: **le ~** the Holy Spirit *ou* Ghost.

sainteté [sɛ̃tte] *nf* holiness; saintliness.

Saint-Laurent [sɛ̃lɔʀɑ̃] *nm*: **le ~** the St Lawrence.

Saint-Marin [sɛ̃maʀɛ̃] *nm*: **le ~** San Marino.

Saint-Père [sɛ̃pɛʀ] *nm*: **le ~** the Holy Father, the Pontiff.

Saint-Pierre [sɛ̃pjɛʀ] *nm* Saint Peter; (*église*) Saint Peter's.

Saint-Pierre-et-Miquelon [sɛ̃pjɛʀemiklɔ̃] *nm* Saint Pierre and Miquelon.

Saint-Siège [sɛ̃sjɛʒ] *nm*: **le ~** the Holy See.

Saint-Sylvestre [sɛ̃silvɛstʀ(ə)] *nf*: **la ~** New Year's Eve.

Saint-Thomas [sɛ̃tɔmɑ] *nf* Saint Thomas.

Saint-Vincent et les Grenadines

[sɛ̃vɛ̃sɑ̃elegʀənadin] *nm* St Vincent and the Grenadines.

sais [sɛ] *etc vb voir* **savoir**.

saisie [sezi] *nf* seizure; **à la ~** (*texte*) being keyed; **~ (de données)** (data) capture.

saisine [sezin] *nf* (*JUR*) *submission of a case to the court*.

saisir [seziʀ] *vt* to take hold of, grab; (*fig: occasion*) to seize; (*comprendre*) to grasp; (*entendre*) to get, catch; (*suj: émotions*) to take hold of, come over; (*INFORM*) to capture, keyboard; (*CULIN*) to fry quickly; (*JUR: biens, publication*) to seize; (*: juridiction*): **~ un tribunal d'une affaire** to submit *ou* refer a case to a court; **se ~ de** *vt* to seize; **être saisi** (*frappé de*) to be overcome.

saisissant, e [sezisɑ̃, -ɑ̃t] *adj* startling, striking; (*froid*) biting.

saisissement [sezismɑ̃] *nm*: **muet/figé de ~** speechless/frozen with emotion.

saison [sɛzɔ̃] *nf* season; **la belle/mauvaise ~** the summer/winter months; **être de ~** to be in season; **en/hors ~** in/out of season; **haute/basse/morte ~** high/low/slack season; **la ~ des pluies/des amours** the rainy/mating season.

saisonnier, ière [sɛzɔnje, -jɛʀ] *adj* seasonal ♦ *nm* (*travailleur*) seasonal worker; (*vacancior*) seasonal holidaymaker.

sait [sɛ] *vb voir* **savoir**.

salace [salas] *adj* salacious.

salade [salad] *nf* (*BOT*) lettuce *etc* (*generic term*); (*CULIN*) (green) salad; (*fam*) tangle, muddle; **~s** *nfpl* (*fam*): **raconter des ~s** to tell tales (*fam*); **haricots en ~** bean salad; **~ de concombres** cucumber salad; **~ de fruits** fruit salad; **~ niçoise** salade niçoise; **~ russe** Russian salad.

saladier [saladje] *nm* (salad) bowl.

salaire [salɛʀ] *nm* (*annuel, mensuel*) salary; (*hebdomadaire, journalier*) pay, wages *pl*; (*fig*) reward; **~ de base** basic salary (*ou* wage); **~ de misère** starvation wage; **~ minimum interprofessionnel de croissance (SMIC)** *index-linked guaranteed minimum wage*.

salaison [salɛzɔ̃] *nf* salting; **~s** *nfpl* salt meat *sg*.

salamandre [salamɑ̃dʀ(ə)] *nf* salamander.

salami [salami] *nm* salami *no pl*, salami sausage.

salant [salɑ̃] *adj m*: **marais ~** salt pan.

salarial, e, aux [salaʀjal, -o] *adj* salary *cpd*, wage(s) *cpd*.

salariat [salaʀja] *nm* salaried staff.

salarié, e [salaʀje] *adj* salaried; wage-earning ♦ *nm/f* salaried employee; wage-earner.

salaud [salo] *nm* (*fam!*) sod (*!*), bastard (*!*).

sale [sal] *adj* dirty; (*fig: avant le nom*) nasty.

salé, e [sale] *adj* (*liquide, saveur*) salty; (*CULIN*) salted, salt *cpd*; (*fig*) spicy, juicy; (*: note, facture*) steep, stiff ♦ *nm* (*porc salé*) salt pork; **petit ~** ≈ boiling bacon.

salement [salmɑ̃] *adv* (*manger etc*) dirtily, messily.

saler [sale] *vt* to salt.

saleté [salte] *nf* (*état*) dirtiness; (*crasse*) dirt, filth; (*tache etc*) dirt *no pl*, something dirty, dirty mark; (*fig: tour*) filthy trick; (*: chose sans valeur*) rubbish *no pl*; (*: obscénité*) filth *no pl*; (*: microbe etc*) bug; **vivre dans la ~** to live in squalor.

salière [saljɛʀ] *nf* saltcellar.

saligaud [saligo] *nm* (*fam!*) bastard (*!*), sod (*!*).

salin, e [salɛ̃, -in] *adj* saline ♦ *nf* saltworks *sg*.

salinité [salinite] *nf* salinity, salt-content.

salir [saliʀ] *vt* to (make) dirty; (*fig*) to soil the reputation of; **se ~** to get dirty.

salissant, e [salisɑ̃, -ɑ̃t] *adj* (*tissu*) which shows the dirt; (*métier*) dirty, messy.

salissure [salisyʀ] *nf* dirt *no pl*; (*tache*) dirty mark.

salive [saliv] *nf* saliva.

saliver [salive] *vi* to salivate.

salle [sal] *nf* room; (*d'hôpital*) ward; (*de restaurant*) dining room; (*d'un cinéma*) auditorium; (*: public*) audience; **faire ~ comble** to have a full house; **~ d'armes** (*pour l'escrime*) arms room; **~ d'attente** waiting room; **~ de bain(s)** bathroom; **~ de bal** ballroom; **~ de cinéma** cinema; **~ de classe** classroom; **~ commune** (*d'hôpital*) ward; **~ de concert** concert hall; **~ de consultation** consulting room (*BRIT*), office (*US*); **~ de danse** dance hall; **~ de douches** shower-room; **~ d'eau** shower-room; **~ d'embarquement** (*à l'aéroport*) departure lounge; **~ d'exposition** showroom; **~ de jeux** games room; playroom; **~ des machines** engine room; **~ à manger** dining room; (*mobilier*) dining room suite; **~ obscure** cinema (*BRIT*), movie theater (*US*); **~ d'opération** (*d'hôpital*) operating theatre; **~ de projection** film theatre; **~ de séjour** living room; **~ de spectacle** theatre; cinema; **~ des ventes** saleroom.

salmonellose [salmɔneloz] *nf* (*MÉD*) salmonella poisoning.

Salomon [salɔmɔ̃]: **les îles ~** the Solomon Islands.

salon [salɔ̃] *nm* lounge, sitting room; (*mobilier*) lounge suite; (*exposition*) exhibition, show; (*mondain, littéraire*) salon; **~ de coiffure** hairdressing salon; **~ de thé** tearoom.

salopard [salɔpaʀ] *nm* (*fam!*) bastard (*!*).

salope [salɔp] *nf* (*fam!*) bitch (*!*).

saloper [salɔpe] *vt* (*fam!*) to muck up, mess up.

saloperie [salɔpʀi] *nf* (*fam!*) filth *no pl*; dirty trick; rubbish *no pl*.

salopette [salɔpɛt] *nf* dungarees *pl*; (*d'ouvrier*) overall(s).

salpêtre [salpɛtʀ(ə)] *nm* saltpetre.

salsifis [salsifi] *nm* salsify, oyster plant.

SALT [salt] *sigle* (= *Strategic Arms Limitation Talks ou Treaty*) SALT.

saltimbanque [saltɛ̃bɑ̃k] *nm/f* (travelling) acrobat.
salubre [salybʀ(ə)] *adj* healthy, salubrious.
salubrité [salybʀite] *nf* healthiness, salubrity; ~ **publique** public health.
saluer [salɥe] *vt* (*pour dire bonjour, fig*) to greet; (*pour dire au revoir*) to take one's leave; (*MIL*) to salute.
salut [saly] *nm* (*sauvegarde*) safety; (*REL*) salvation; (*geste*) wave; (*parole*) greeting; (*MIL*) salute ♦ *excl* (*fam: pour dire bonjour*) hi (there); (*: pour dire au revoir*) see you!, bye!; (*style relevé*) (all) hail.
salutaire [salytɛʀ] *adj* (*remède*) beneficial; (*conseils*) salutary.
salutations [salytɑsjɔ̃] *nfpl* greetings; **recevez mes ~ distinguées** *ou* **respectueuses** yours faithfully.
salutiste [salytist(ə)] *nm/f* Salvationist.
Salvador [salvadɔʀ] *nm*: **le** ~ El Salvador.
salve [salv(ə)] *nf* salvo; volley of shots; ~ **d'applaudissements** burst of applause.
Samarie [samaʀi] *nf*: **la** ~ Samaria.
samaritain [samaʀitɛ̃] *nm*: **le bon S~** the Good Samaritan.
samedi [samdi] *nm* Saturday; *voir aussi* **lundi**.
Samoa [samɔa] *nfpl*: **les (îles)** ~ Samoa, the Samoa Islands.
SAMU [samy] *sigle m* (= *service d'assistance médicale d'urgence*) ≈ ambulance (service) (*BRIT*), ≈ paramedics (*US*).
sanatorium [sanatɔʀjɔm] *nm* sanatorium (*pl* -a).
sanctifier [sɑ̃ktifje] *vt* to sanctify.
sanction [sɑ̃ksjɔ̃] *nf* sanction; (*fig*) penalty; **prendre des ~s contre** to impose sanctions on.
sanctionner [sɑ̃ksjɔne] *vt* (*loi, usage*) to sanction; (*punir*) to punish.
sanctuaire [sɑ̃ktɥɛʀ] *nm* sanctuary.
sandale [sɑ̃dal] *nf* sandal; **~s à lanières** strappy sandals.
sandalette [sɑ̃dalɛt] *nf* sandal.
sandow [sɑ̃do] *nm* ® luggage elastic.
sandwich [sɑ̃dwitʃ] *nm* sandwich; **pris en ~** sandwiched.
sang [sɑ̃] *nm* blood; **en ~** covered in blood; **jusqu'au ~** (*mordre, pincer*) till the blood comes; **se faire du mauvais ~** to fret, get in a state.
sang-froid [sɑ̃fʀwa] *nm* calm, sangfroid; **garder/perdre/reprendre son ~** to keep/lose/regain one's cool; **de ~** in cold blood.
sanglant, e [sɑ̃glɑ̃, -ɑ̃t] *adj* bloody, covered in blood; (*combat*) bloody; (*fig: reproche, affront*) cruel.
sangle [sɑ̃gl(ə)] *nf* strap; **~s** *nfpl* (*pour lit etc*) webbing *sg*.
sangler [sɑ̃gle] *vt* to strap up; (*animal*) to girth.
sanglier [sɑ̃glije] *nm* (wild) boar.
sanglot [sɑ̃glo] *nm* sob.
sangloter [sɑ̃glɔte] *vi* to sob.
sangsue [sɑ̃sy] *nf* leech.
sanguin, e [sɑ̃gɛ̃, -in] *adj* blood *cpd*; (*fig*) fiery ♦ *nf* blood orange; (*ART*) red pencil drawing.
sanguinaire [sɑ̃ginɛʀ] *adj* (*animal, personne*) bloodthirsty; (*lutte*) bloody.
sanguinolent, e [sɑ̃ginɔlɑ̃, -ɑ̃t] *adj* streaked with blood.
Sanisette [sanizɛt] *nf* ® coin-operated public lavatory.
sanitaire [sanitɛʀ] *adj* health *cpd*; **~s** *nmpl* (*salle de bain et w.-c.*) bathroom *sg*; **installation/appareil ~** bathroom plumbing/appliance.
sans [sɑ̃] *prép* without; **~ qu'il s'en aperçoive** without him *ou* his noticing; **~ scrupules** unscrupulous; **~ manches** sleeveless.
sans-abri [sɑ̃zabʀi] *nmpl* homeless.
sans-emploi [sɑ̃zɑ̃plwa] *nmpl* jobless.
sans-façon [sɑ̃fasɔ̃] *adj inv* fuss-free; free and easy.
sans-gêne [sɑ̃ʒɛn] *adj inv* inconsiderate ♦ *nm inv* (*attitude*) lack of consideration.
sans-logis [sɑ̃lɔʒi] *nmpl* homeless.
sans-souci [sɑ̃susi] *adj inv* carefree.
sans-travail [sɑ̃tʀavaj] *nmpl* unemployed, jobless.
santal [sɑ̃tal] *nm* sandal(wood).
santé [sɑ̃te] *nf* health; **avoir une ~ de fer** to be bursting with health; **être en bonne ~** to be in good health, be healthy; **boire à la ~ de qn** to drink (to) sb's health; **"à la ~ de"** "here's to"; **à ta** *ou* **votre ~!** cheers!; **service de ~** (*dans un port etc*) quarantine service; **la ~ publique** public health.
Santiago (du Chili) [sɑ̃tjago(dyʃili)] *n* Santiago (de Chile).
santon [sɑ̃tɔ̃] *nm* *ornamental figure at a Christmas crib*.
saoudien, ne [saudjɛ̃, -ɛn] *adj* Saudi (Arabian) ♦ *nm/f*: **S~, ne** Saudi (Arabian).
saoul, e [su, sul] *adj* = **soûl, e**.
sape [sap] *nf*: **travail de ~** (*MIL*) sap; (*fig*) insidious undermining process *ou* work; **~s** *nfpl* (*fam*) gear *sg*, togs.
saper [sape] *vt* to undermine, sap; **se ~** *vi* (*fam*) to dress.
sapeur [sapœʀ] *nm* sapper.
sapeur-pompier [sapœʀpɔ̃pje] *nm* fireman.
saphir [safiʀ] *nm* sapphire; (*d'électrophone*) needle, sapphire.
sapin [sapɛ̃] *nm* fir (tree); (*bois*) fir; **~ de Noël** Christmas tree.
sapinière [sapinjɛʀ] *nf* fir plantation *ou* forest.
SAR *sigle f* (= *Son Altesse Royale*) HRH.
sarabande [saʀabɑ̃d] *nf* saraband; (*fig*) hullabaloo; whirl.
sarbacane [saʀbakan] *nf* blowpipe, blowgun; (*jouet*) peashooter.
sarcasme [saʀkasm(ə)] *nm* sarcasm *no pl*; (*propos*) piece of sarcasm.
sarcastique [saʀkastik] *adj* sarcastic.
sarcastiquement [saʀkastikmɑ̃] *adv* sarcastically.

sarclage [saʀklaʒ] *nm* weeding.
sarcler [saʀkle] *vt* to weed.
sarcloir [saʀklwaʀ] *nm* (weeding) hoe, spud.
sarcophage [saʀkɔfaʒ] *nm* sarcophagus (*pl* -i).
Sardaigne [saʀdɛɲ] *nf*: **la** ~ Sardinia.
sarde [saʀd(ə)] *adj* Sardinian.
sardine [saʀdin] *nf* sardine; ~**s à l'huile** sardines in oil.
sardinerie [saʀdinʀi] *nf* sardine cannery.
sardinier, ière [saʀdinje, -jɛʀ] *adj* (*pêche, industrie*) sardine *cpd* ♦ *nm* (*bateau*) sardine boat.
sardonique [saʀdɔnik] *adj* sardonic.
sari [saʀi] *nm* sari.
SARL [saʀl] *sigle f* = **société à responsabilité limitée.**
sarment [saʀmɑ̃] *nm*: ~ **(de vigne)** vine shoot.
sarrasin [saʀazɛ̃] *nm* buckwheat.
sarrau [saʀo] *nm* smock.
Sarre [saʀ] *nf*: **la** ~ the Saar.
sarriette [saʀjɛt] *nf* savory.
sarrois, e [saʀwa, -waz] *adj* Saar *cpd* ♦ *nm/f*: **S**~, **e** inhabitant *ou* native of the Saar.
sas [sas] *nm* (*de sous-marin, d'engin spatial*) airlock; (*d'écluse*) lock.
satané, e [satane] *adj* (*fam*) confounded.
satanique [satanik] *adj* satanic, fiendish.
satelliser [satelize] *vt* (*fusée*) to put into orbit; (*fig: pays*) to make into a satellite.
satellite [satelit] *nm* satellite; **pays** ~ satellite country.
satellite-espion, *pl* **satellites-espions** [satelitɛspjɔ̃] *nm* spy satellite.
satellite-observatoire, *pl* **satellites-observatoires** [satelitɔpsɛʀvatwaʀ] *nm* observation satellite.
satellite-relais, *pl* **satellites-relais** [satelitʀəlɛ] *nm* (*TV*) relay satellite.
satiété [sasjete]: **à** ~ *adv* to satiety *ou* satiation; (*répéter*) ad nauseam.
satin [satɛ̃] *nm* satin.
satiné, e [satine] *adj* satiny; (*peau*) satin-smooth.
satinette [satinɛt] *nf* satinet, sateen.
satire [satiʀ] *nf* satire; **faire la** ~ to satirize.
satirique [satiʀik] *adj* satirical.
satiriser [satiʀize] *vt* to satirize.
satiriste [satiʀist(ə)] *nm/f* satirist.
satisfaction [satisfaksjɔ̃] *nf* satisfaction; **à ma grande** ~ to my great satisfaction; **obtenir** ~ to obtain *ou* get satisfaction; **donner** ~ **(à)** to give satisfaction (to).
satisfaire [satisfɛʀ] *vt* to satisfy; **se** ~ **de** to be satisfied *ou* content with; ~ **à** *vt* (*engagement*) to fulfil; (*revendications, conditions*) to satisfy, meet.
satisfaisant, e [satisfəzɑ̃, -ɑ̃t] *vb voir* **satisfaire** ♦ *adj* satisfactory; (*qui fait plaisir*) satisfying.
satisfait, e [satisfɛ, -ɛt] *pp de* **satisfaire** ♦ *adj* satisfied; ~ **de** happy *ou* satisfied with.
satisfasse [satisfas], **satisferai** [satisfʀe] *etc vb voir* **satisfaire.**
saturation [satyʀɑsjɔ̃] *nf* saturation; **arriver à** ~ to reach saturation point.
saturer [satyʀe] *vt* to saturate; ~ **qn/qch de** to saturate sb/sth with.
saturnisme [satyʀnism(ə)] *nm* (*MÉD*) lead poisoning.
satyre [satiʀ] *nm* satyr; (*péj*) lecher.
sauce [sos] *nf* sauce; (*avec un rôti*) gravy; **en** ~ in a sauce; ~ **blanche** white sauce; ~ **chasseur** sauce chasseur; ~ **tomate** tomato sauce.
saucer [sose] *vt* (*assiette*) to soak up the sauce from.
saucière [sosjɛʀ] *nf* sauceboat; gravy boat.
saucisse [sosis] *nf* sausage.
saucisson [sosisɔ̃] *nm* (slicing) sausage; ~ **à l'ail** garlic sausage.
saucissonner [sosisɔne] *vt* to cut up, slice ♦ *vi* to picnic.
sauf [sof] *prép* except; ~ **si** (*à moins que*) unless; ~ **avis contraire** unless you hear to the contrary; ~ **empêchement** barring (any) problems; ~ **erreur** if I'm not mistaken; ~ **imprévu** unless anything unforeseen arises, barring accidents.
sauf, sauve [sof, sov] *adj* unharmed, unhurt; (*fig: honneur*) intact, saved; **laisser la vie sauve à qn** to spare sb's life.
sauf-conduit [sofkɔ̃dɥi] *nm* safe-conduct.
sauge [soʒ] *nf* sage.
saugrenu, e [sogʀəny] *adj* preposterous, ludicrous.
saule [sol] *nm* willow (tree); ~ **pleureur** weeping willow.
saumâtre [somɑtʀ(ə)] *adj* briny; (*désagréable: plaisanterie*) unsavoury (*BRIT*), unsavory (*US*).
saumon [somɔ̃] *nm* salmon *inv* ♦ *adj inv* salmon (pink).
saumoné, e [somɔne] *adj*: **truite** ~**e** salmon trout.
saumure [somyʀ] *nf* brine.
sauna [sona] *nm* sauna.
saupoudrer [sopudʀe] *vt*: ~ **qch de** to sprinkle sth with.
saupoudreuse [sopudʀøz] *nf* dredger.
saur [sɔʀ] *adj m*: **hareng** ~ smoked *ou* red herring, kipper.
saurai [sɔʀe] *etc vb voir* **savoir.**
saut [so] *nm* jump; (*discipline sportive*) jumping; **faire un** ~ to (make a) jump *ou* leap; **faire un** ~ **chez qn** to pop over to sb's (place); **au** ~ **du lit** on getting out of bed; ~ **en hauteur/longueur** high/long jump; ~ **à la corde** skipping; ~ **de page** (*INFORM*) page break; ~ **en parachute** parachuting *no pl*; ~ **à la perche** pole vaulting; ~ **à l'élastique** bungee jumping; ~ **périlleux** somersault.
saute [sot] *nf*: ~ **de vent/température** sudden change of wind direction/in the temperature; **avoir des** ~**s d'humeur** to have sudden changes of mood.
sauté, e [sote] *adj* (*CULIN*) sauté ♦ *nm*: ~ **de**

veau sauté of veal.
saute-mouton [sotmutɔ̃] *nm*: **jouer à ~** to play leapfrog.
sauter [sote] *vi* to jump, leap; (*exploser*) to blow up, explode; (*: fusibles*) to blow; (*se rompre*) to snap, burst; (*se détacher*) to pop out (*ou* off) ♦ *vt* to jump (over), leap (over); (*fig: omettre*) to skip, miss (out); **faire ~** to blow up; to burst open; (*CULIN*) to sauté; **~ à pieds joints/à cloche-pied** to make a standing jump/to hop; **~ en parachute** to make a parachute jump; **~ à la corde** to skip; **~ de joie** to jump for joy; **~ de colère** to be hopping with rage *ou* hopping mad; **~ au cou de qn** to fly into sb's arms; **~ aux yeux** to be quite obvious; **~ au plafond** (*fig*) to hit the roof.
sauterelle [sotʀɛl] *nf* grasshopper.
sauterie [sotʀi] *nf* party, hop.
sauteur, euse [sotœʀ, -øz] *nm/f* (*athlète*) jumper ♦ *nf* (*casserole*) shallow pan, frying pan; **~ à la perche** pole vaulter; **~ à skis** skijumper.
sautillement [sotijmɑ̃] *nm* hopping; skipping.
sautiller [sotije] *vi* to hop; to skip.
sautoir [sotwaʀ] *nm* chain; (*SPORT: emplacement*) jumping pit; **~ (de perles)** string of pearls.
sauvage [sovaʒ] *adj* (*gén*) wild; (*peuplade*) savage; (*farouche*) unsociable; (*barbare*) wild, savage; (*non officiel*) unauthorized, unofficial ♦ *nm/f* savage; (*timide*) unsociable type, recluse.
sauvagement [sovaʒmɑ̃] *adv* savagely.
sauvageon, ne [sovaʒɔ̃, -ɔn] *nm/f* little savage.
sauvagerie [sovaʒʀi] *nf* wildness; savagery; unsociability.
sauve [sov] *adj f voir* **sauf**.
sauvegarde [sovgaʀd(ə)] *nf* safeguard; **sous la ~ de** under the protection of; **disquette/fichier de ~** (*INFORM*) backup disk/file.
sauvegarder [sovgaʀde] *vt* to safeguard; (*INFORM: enregistrer*) to save; (*: copier*) to back up.
sauve-qui-peut [sovkipø] *nm inv* stampede, mad rush ♦ *excl* run for your life!
sauver [sove] *vt* to save; (*porter secours à*) to rescue; (*récupérer*) to salvage, rescue; **se ~** *vi* (*s'enfuir*) to run away; (*fam: partir*) to be off; **~ qn de** to save sb from; **~ la vie à qn** to save sb's life; **~ les apparences** to keep up appearances.
sauvetage [sovtaʒ] *nm* rescue; **~ en montagne** mountain rescue; **ceinture de ~** lifebelt (*BRIT*), life preserver (*US*); **brassière** *ou* **gilet de ~** lifejacket (*BRIT*), life preserver (*US*).
sauveteur [sovtœʀ] *nm* rescuer.
sauvette [sovɛt]: **à la ~** *adv* (*vendre*) without authorization; (*se marier etc*) hastily, hurriedly; **vente à la ~** (unauthorized) street trading, (street) peddling.
sauveur [sovœʀ] *nm* saviour (*BRIT*), savior (*US*).
SAV *sigle m* = **service après-vente**.
savais [save] *etc vb voir* **savoir**.
savamment [savamɑ̃] *adv* (*avec érudition*) learnedly; (*habilement*) skilfully, cleverly.
savane [savan] *nf* savannah.
savant, e [savɑ̃, -ɑ̃t] *adj* scholarly, learned; (*calé*) clever ♦ *nm* scientist; **animal ~** performing animal.
savate [savat] *nf* worn-out shoe; (*SPORT*) French boxing.
saveur [savœʀ] *nf* flavour (*BRIT*), flavor (*US*); (*fig*) savour (*BRIT*), savor (*US*).
Savoie [savwa] *nf*: **la ~** Savoy.
savoir [savwaʀ] *vt* to know; (*être capable de*): **il sait nager** he knows how to swim, he can swim ♦ *nm* knowledge; **se ~** (*être connu*) to be known; **se ~ malade/incurable** to know that one is ill/incurably ill; **il est petit: tu ne peux pas ~!** you won't believe how small he is!; **vous n'êtes pas sans ~ que** you are not *ou* will not be unaware of the fact that; **je crois ~ que ...** I believe that ..., I think I know that ...; **je n'en sais rien** I (really) don't know; **à ~ (que)** that is, namely; **faire ~ qch à qn** to inform sb about sth, let sb know sth; **pas que je sache** not as far as I know; **sans le ~** *adv* unknowingly, unwittingly; **en ~ long** to know a lot.
savoir-faire [savwaʀfɛʀ] *nm inv* savoir-faire, know-how.
savoir-vivre [savwaʀvivʀ(ə)] *nm inv*: **le ~** savoir-faire, good manners *pl*.
savon [savɔ̃] *nm* (*produit*) soap; (*morceau*) bar *ou* tablet of soap; (*fam*): **passer un ~ à qn** to give sb a good dressing-down.
savonner [savɔne] *vt* to soap.
savonnerie [savɔnʀi] *nf* soap factory.
savonnette [savɔnɛt] *nf* bar *ou* tablet of soap.
savonneux, euse [savɔnø, -øz] *adj* soapy.
savons [savɔ̃] *vb voir* **savoir**.
savourer [savuʀe] *vt* to savour (*BRIT*), savor (*US*).
savoureux, euse [savuʀø, -øz] *adj* tasty; (*fig*) spicy, juicy.
savoyard, e [savwajaʀ, -aʀd(ə)] *adj* Savoyard.
Saxe [saks(ə)] *nf*: **la ~** Saxony.
saxo(phone) [saksɔ(fɔn)] *nm* sax(ophone).
saxophoniste [saksɔfɔnist(ə)] *nm/f* saxophonist, sax(ophone) player.
saynète [sɛnɛt] *nf* playlet.
SBB *sigle f* (= *Schweizerische Bundesbahn*) *Swiss federal railways*.
sbire [sbiʀ] *nm* (*péj*) henchman.
sc. *abr* = **scène**.
s/c *abr* (= *sous couvert de*) ≈ c/o.
scabreux, euse [skabʀø, -øz] *adj* risky; (*indécent*) improper, shocking.
scalpel [skalpɛl] *nm* scalpel.
scalper [skalpe] *vt* to scalp.

scampi [skɑ̃pi] *nmpl* scampi.
scandale [skɑ̃dal] *nm* scandal; (*tapage*): **faire du ~** to make a scene, create a disturbance; **faire ~** to scandalize people; **au grand ~ de** ... to the great indignation of ....
scandaleusement [skɑ̃daløzmɑ̃] *adv* scandalously, outrageously.
scandaleux, euse [skɑ̃dalø, -øz] *adj* scandalous, outrageous.
scandaliser [skɑ̃dalize] *vt* to scandalize; **se ~ (de)** to be scandalized (by).
scander [skɑ̃de] *vt* (*vers*) to scan; (*mots, syllabes*) to stress separately; (*slogans*) to chant.
scandinave [skɑ̃dinav] *adj* Scandinavian ♦ *nm/f*: **S~** Scandinavian.
Scandinavie [skɑ̃dinavi] *nf*: **la ~** Scandinavia.
scanner [skanɛʀ] *nm* (*MÉD*) scanner.
scanographie [skanɔgʀafi] *nf* (*MÉD*) scanning; (*image*) scan.
scaphandre [skafɑ̃dʀ(ə)] *nm* (*de plongeur*) diving suit; (*de cosmonaute*) space-suit; **~ autonome** aqualung.
scaphandrier [skafɑ̃dʀije] *nm* diver.
scarabée [skaʀabe] *nm* beetle.
scarlatine [skaʀlatin] *nf* scarlet fever.
scarole [skaʀɔl] *nf* endive.
scatologique [skatɔlɔʒik] *adj* scatological, lavatorial.
sceau, x [so] *nm* seal; (*fig*) stamp, mark; **sous le ~ du secret** under the seal of secrecy.
scélérat, e [seleʀa, -at] *nm/f* villain, blackguard ♦ *adj* villainous, blackguardly.
sceller [sele] *vt* to seal.
scellés [sele] *nmpl* seals.
scénario [senaʀjo] *nm* (*CINÉ*) screenplay, script; (*: idée, plan*) scenario; (*fig*) pattern; scenario.
scénariste [senaʀist(ə)] *nm/f* scriptwriter.
scène [sɛn] *nf* (*gén*) scene; (*estrade, fig: théâtre*) stage; **entrer en ~** to come on stage; **mettre en ~** (*THÉÂT*) to stage; (*CINÉ*) to direct; (*fig*) to present, introduce; **sur le devant de la ~** (*en pleine actualité*) in the forefront; **porter à la ~** to adapt for the stage; **faire une ~ (à qn)** to make a scene (with sb); **~ de ménage** domestic fight *ou* scene.
scénique [senik] *adj* (*effets*) theatrical; (*art*) scenic.
scepticisme [sɛptisism(ə)] *nm* scepticism.
sceptique [sɛptik] *adj* sceptical ♦ *nm/f* sceptic.
sceptre [sɛptʀ(ə)] *nm* sceptre.
schéma [ʃema] *nm* (*diagramme*) diagram, sketch; (*fig*) outline.
schématique [ʃematik] *adj* diagrammatic(al), schematic; (*fig*) oversimplified.
schématiquement [ʃematikmɑ̃] *adv* schematically, diagrammatically.
schématisation [ʃematizɑsjɔ̃] *nf* schematization; oversimplification.
schématiser [ʃematize] *vt* to schematize; to (over)simplify.
schismatique [ʃismatik] *adj* schismatic.
schisme [ʃism(ə)] *nm* schism; rift, split.
schiste [ʃist(ə)] *nm* schist.
schizophrène [skizɔfʀɛn] *nm/f* schizophrenic.
schizophrénie [skizɔfʀeni] *nf* schizophrenia.
sciatique [sjatik] *adj*: **nerf ~** sciatic nerve ♦ *nf* sciatica.
scie [si] *nf* saw; (*fam: rengaine*) catch-tune; (*: personne*) bore; **~ à bois** wood saw; **~ circulaire** circular saw; **~ à découper** fretsaw; **~ à métaux** hacksaw; **~ sauteuse** jigsaw.
sciemment [sjamɑ̃] *adv* knowingly, wittingly.
science [sjɑ̃s] *nf* science; (*savoir*) knowledge; (*savoir-faire*) art, skill; **~s humaines/sociales** social sciences; **~s naturelles** natural science *sg*, biology *sg*; **~s po** political studies.
science-fiction [sjɑ̃sfiksjɔ̃] *nf* science fiction.
scientifique [sjɑ̃tifik] *adj* scientific ♦ *nm/f* (*savant*) scientist; (*étudiant*) science student.
scientifiquement [sjɑ̃tifikmɑ̃] *adv* scientifically.
scier [sje] *vt* to saw; (*retrancher*) to saw off.
scierie [siʀi] *nf* sawmill.
scieur [sjœʀ] *nm*: **~ de long** pit sawyer.
Scilly [sili]: **les îles ~** the Scilly Isles, the Scillies, the Isles of Scilly.
scinder [sɛ̃de] *vt*, **se ~** *vi* to split (up).
scintillant, e [sɛ̃tijɑ̃, -ɑ̃t] *adj* sparkling.
scintillement [sɛ̃tijmɑ̃] *nm* sparkling *no pl*.
scintiller [sɛ̃tije] *vi* to sparkle.
scission [sisjɔ̃] *nf* split.
sciure [sjyʀ] *nf*: **~ (de bois)** sawdust.
sclérose [skleʀoz] *nf* sclerosis; (*fig*) ossification; **~ en plaques (SEP)** multiple sclerosis (MS).
sclérosé, e [skleʀoze] *adj* sclerosed, sclerotic; ossified.
scléroser [skleʀoze]: **se ~** *vi* to become sclerosed; (*fig*) to become ossified.
scolaire [skɔlɛʀ] *adj* school *cpd*; (*péj*) schoolish; **l'année ~** the school year; (*à l'université*) the academic year; **en âge ~** of school age.
scolarisation [skɔlaʀizɑsjɔ̃] *nf* (*d'un enfant*) schooling; **la ~ d'une région** the provision of schooling in a region; **le taux de ~** the proportion of children in full-time education.
scolariser [skɔlaʀize] *vt* to provide with schooling (*ou* schools).
scolarité [skɔlaʀite] *nf* schooling; **frais de ~** school fees (*BRIT*), tuition (*US*).
scolastique [skɔlastik] *adj* (*péj*) scholastic.
scoliose [skɔljoz] *nf* curvature of the spine, scoliosis.
scoop [skup] *nm* (*PRESSE*) scoop, exclusive.
scooter [skutœʀ] *nm* (motor) scooter.
scorbut [skɔʀbyt] *nm* scurvy.
score [skɔʀ] *nm* score; (*électoral etc*) result.
scories [skɔʀi] *nfpl* scoria *pl*.
scorpion [skɔʀpjɔ̃] *nm* (*signe*): **le S~** Scorpio, the Scorpion; **être du S~** to be Scorpio.
scotch [skɔtʃ] *nm* (*whisky*) scotch, whisky; (*ad-*

hésif) Sellotape ® (*BRIT*), Scotch tape ® (*US*).
scotcher [skɔtʃe] *vt* to sellotape ® (*BRIT*), scotchtape ® (*US*).
scout, e [skut] *adj, nm* scout.
scoutisme [skutism(ə)] *nm* (boy) scout movement; (*activités*) scouting.
scribe [skʀib] *nm* scribe; (*péj*) penpusher.
scribouillard [skʀibujaʀ] *nm* penpusher.
script [skʀipt(ə)] *nm* printing; (*CINÉ*) (shooting) script.
scripte [skʀipt(ə)] *nf* continuity girl.
script-girl [skʀiptgœʀl] *nf* continuity girl.
scriptural, e, aux [skʀiptyʀal, -o] *adj*: **monnaie ~e** bank money.
scrupule [skʀypyl] *nm* scruple; **être sans ~s** to be unscrupulous; **se faire un ~ de qch** to have scruples *ou* qualms about doing sth.
scrupuleusement [skʀypyløzmɑ̃] *adv* scrupulously.
scrupuleux, euse [skʀypylø, -øz] *adj* scrupulous.
scrutateur, trice [skʀytatœʀ, -tʀis] *adj* searching ♦ *nm/f* scrutineer.
scruter [skʀyte] *vt* to search, scrutinize; (*l'obscurité*) to peer into; (*motifs, comportement*) to examine, scrutinize.
scrutin [skʀytɛ̃] *nm* (*vote*) ballot; (*ensemble des opérations*) poll; **~ proportionnel/majoritaire** election on a proportional/majority basis; **~ à deux tours** poll with two ballots *ou* rounds; **~ de liste** list system.
sculpter [skylte] *vt* to sculpt; (*suj: érosion*) to carve.
sculpteur [skyltœʀ] *nm* sculptor.
sculptural, e, aux [skyltyʀal, -o] *adj* sculptural; (*fig*) statuesque.
sculpture [skyltyʀ] *nf* sculpture; **~ sur bois** wood carving.
sdb. *abr* = **salle de bain.**
S.D.F. *sigle m* (= *sans domicile fixe*) homeless person; **les ~** the homeless.
SDN *sigle f* (= *Société des Nations*) League of Nations.
SE *sigle f* (= *Son Excellence*) HE.

MOT-CLÉ

se (s') [s(ə)] *pron* **1** (*emploi réfléchi*) oneself; (: *masc*) himself; (: *fém*) herself; (: *sujet non humain*) itself; (: *pl*) themselves; **se voir comme l'on est** to see o.s. as one is
2 (*réciproque*) one another, each other; **ils s'aiment** they love one another *ou* each other
3 (*passif*): **cela se répare facilement** it is easily repaired
4 (*possessif*): **se casser la jambe/laver les mains** to break one's leg/wash one's hands.

séance [seɑ̃s] *nf* (*d'assemblée, récréative*) meeting, session; (*de tribunal*) sitting, session; (*musicale, CINÉ, THÉÂT*) performance; **ouvrir/lever la ~** to open/close the meeting; **~ tenante** forthwith.
séant, e [seɑ̃, -ɑ̃t] *adj* seemly, fitting ♦ *nm* posterior.
seau, x [so] *nm* bucket, pail; **~ à glace** ice bucket.
sébum [sebɔm] *nm* sebum.
sec, sèche [sɛk, sɛʃ] *adj* dry; (*raisins, figues*) dried; (*cœur, personne: insensible*) hard, cold; (*maigre, décharné*) spare, lean; (*réponse, ton*) sharp, curt; (*démarrage*) sharp, sudden ♦ *nm*: **tenir au ~** to keep in a dry place ♦ *adv* hard; (*démarrer*) sharply; **boire ~** to be a heavy drinker; **je le bois ~** I drink it straight *ou* neat; **à pied ~** without getting one's feet wet; **à ~** *adj* dried up; (*à court d'argent*) broke.
SECAM [sekam] *sigle m* (= *procédé séquentiel à mémoire*) SECAM.
sécante [sekɑ̃t] *nf* secant.
sécateur [sekatœʀ] *nm* secateurs *pl* (*BRIT*), shears *pl*, pair of secateurs *ou* shears.
sécession [sesesjɔ̃] *nf*: **faire ~** to secede; **la guerre de S~** the American Civil War.
séchage [seʃaʒ] *nm* drying; (*de bois*) seasoning.
sèche [sɛʃ] *adj f voir* **sec** ♦ *nf* (*fam*) cigarette, fag (*BRIT*).
sèche-cheveux [sɛʃʃəvø] *nm inv* hair-drier.
sèche-linge [sɛʃlɛ̃ʒ] *nm inv* drying cabinet.
sèche-mains [sɛʃmɛ̃] *nm inv* hand drier.
sèchement [sɛʃmɑ̃] *adv* (*frapper etc*) sharply; (*répliquer etc*) drily, sharply.
sécher [seʃe] *vt* to dry; (*dessécher: peau, blé*) to dry (out); (: *étang*) to dry up; (*bois*) to season; (*fam: classe, cours*) to skip, miss ♦ *vi* to dry; to dry out; to dry up; (*fam: candidat*) to be stumped; **se ~** (*après le bain*) to dry o.s.
sécheresse [sɛʃʀɛs] *nf* dryness; (*absence de pluie*) drought.
séchoir [seʃwaʀ] *nm* drier.
second, e [səgɔ̃, -ɔ̃d] *adj* second ♦ *nm* (*assistant*) second in command; (*étage*) second floor (*BRIT*), third floor (*US*); (*NAVIG*) first mate ♦ *nf* second; (*SCOL*) ≈ fifth form (*BRIT*), ≈ tenth grade (*US*); **en ~** (*en second rang*) in second place; **voyager en ~e** to travel second-class; **doué de ~e vue** having (the gift of) second sight; **trouver son ~ souffle** (*SPORT, fig*) to get one's second wind; **être dans un état ~** to be in a daze (*ou* trance); **de ~e main** second-hand.
secondaire [səgɔ̃dɛʀ] *adj* secondary.
seconder [səgɔ̃de] *vt* to assist; (*favoriser*) to back.
secouer [səkwe] *vt* to shake; (*passagers*) to rock; (*traumatiser*) to shake (up); **se ~** (*chien*) to shake itself; (*fam: se démener*) to shake o.s. up; **~ la poussière d'un tapis** to shake the dust off a carpet; **~ la tête** to shake one's head.
secourable [səkuʀabl(ə)] *adj* helpful.
secourir [səkuʀiʀ] *vt* (*aller sauver*) to (go and)

rescue; (*prodiguer des soins à*) to help, assist; (*venir en aide à*) to assist, aid.
secourisme [səkuʀism(ə)] *nm* (*premiers soins*) first aid; (*sauvetage*) life saving.
secouriste [səkuʀist(ə)] *nm/f* first-aid worker.
secourons [səkuʀɔ̃] *etc vb voir* **secourir.**
secours [səkuʀ] *vb voir* **secourir** ♦ *nm* help, aid, assistance ♦ *nmpl* aid *sg*; **cela lui a été d'un grand** ~ this was a great help to him; **au** ~! help!; **appeler au** ~ to shout *ou* call for help; **appeler qn à son** ~ to call sb to one's assistance; **porter** ~ **à qn** to give sb assistance, help sb; **les premiers** ~ first aid *sg*; **le** ~ **en montagne** mountain rescue.
secouru, e [səkuʀy] *pp de* **secourir.**
secousse [səkus] *nf* jolt, bump; (*électrique*) shock; (*fig: psychologique*) jolt, shock; ~ **sismique** *ou* **tellurique** earth tremor.
secret, ète [səkʀɛ, -ɛt] *adj* secret; (*fig: renfermé*) reticent, reserved ♦ *nm* secret; (*discrétion absolue*): **le** ~ secrecy; **en** ~ in secret, secretly; **au** ~ in solitary confinement; ~ **de fabrication** trade secret; ~ **professionnel** professional secrecy.
secrétaire [səkʀetɛʀ] *nm/f* secretary ♦ *nm* (*meuble*) writing desk, secretaire; ~ **d'ambassade** embassy secretary; ~ **de direction** private *ou* personal secretary; ~ **d'État** ≈ junior minister; ~ **général (SG)** Secretary-General, (*COMM*) company secretary; ~ **de mairie** town clerk; ~ **médicale** medical secretary; ~ **de rédaction** sub-editor.
secrétariat [s(ə)kʀetaʀja] *nm* (*profession*) secretarial work; (*bureau: d'entreprise, d'école*) (secretary's) office; (*: d'organisation internationale*) secretariat; (*POL etc: fonction*) secretaryship, office of Secretary.
secrètement [səkʀɛtmɑ̃] *adv* secretly.
sécréter [sekʀete] *vt* to secrete.
sécrétion [sekʀesjɔ̃] *nf* secretion.
sectaire [sɛktɛʀ] *adj* sectarian, bigoted.
sectarisme [sɛktaʀism(ə)] *nm* sectarianism.
secte [sɛkt(ə)] *nf* sect.
secteur [sɛktœʀ] *nm* sector; (*ADMIN*) district; (*ÉLEC*): **branché sur le** ~ plugged into the mains (supply); **fonctionne sur pile et** ~ battery or mains operated; **le** ~ **privé/public** (*ÉCON*) the private/public sector; **le** ~ **primaire/tertiaire** the primary/tertiary sector.
section [sɛksjɔ̃] *nf* section; (*de parcours d'autobus*) fare stage; (*MIL: unité*) platoon; ~ **rythmique** rhythm section.
sectionner [sɛksjɔne] *vt* to sever; **se** ~ *vi* to be severed.
sectionneur [sɛksjɔnœʀ] *nm* (*ÉLEC*) isolation switch.
sectoriel, le [sɛktɔʀjɛl] *adj* sector-based.
sectorisation [sɛktɔʀizɑsjɔ̃] *nf* division into sectors.
sectoriser [sɛktɔʀize] *vt* to divide into sectors.
sécu [seky] *nf* (*fam: = sécurité sociale*) ≈ dole (*BRIT*), ≈ Welfare (*US*).
séculaire [sekylɛʀ] *adj* secular; (*très vieux*) age-old.
séculariser [sekylaʀize] *vt* to secularize.
séculier, ière [sekylje, -jɛʀ] *adj* secular.
sécurisant, e [sekyʀizɑ̃, -ɑ̃t] *adj* secure, giving a sense of security.
sécuriser [sekyʀize] *vt* to give a sense of security to.
sécurité [sekyʀite] *nf* security; (*absence de danger*) safety; **impression de** ~ sense of security; **la** ~ **internationale** international security; **système de** ~ security (*ou* safety) system; **être en** ~ to be safe; **la** ~ **de l'emploi** job security; **la** ~ **routière** road safety; **la** ~ **sociale** ≈ (the) Social Security (*BRIT*), ≈ (the) Welfare (*US*).
sédatif, ive [sedatif, -iv] *adj, nm* sedative.
sédentaire [sedɑ̃tɛʀ] *adj* sedentary.
sédiment [sedimɑ̃] *nm* sediment; ~**s** *nmpl* (*alluvions*) sediment *sg*.
sédimentaire [sedimɑ̃tɛʀ] *adj* sedimentary.
sédimentation [sedimɑ̃tɑsjɔ̃] *nf* sedimentation.
séditieux, euse [sedisjø, -øz] *adj* insurgent; seditious.
sédition [sedisjɔ̃] *nf* insurrection; sedition.
séducteur, trice [sedyktœʀ, -tʀis] *adj* seductive ♦ *nm/f* seducer/seductress.
séduction [sedyksjɔ̃] *nf* seduction; (*charme, attrait*) appeal, charm.
séduire [sedɥiʀ] *vt* to charm; (*femme: abuser de*) to seduce; (*suj: chose*) to appeal to.
séduisant, e [sedɥizɑ̃, -ɑ̃t] *vb voir* **séduire** ♦ *adj* (*femme*) seductive; (*homme, offre*) very attractive.
séduit, e [sedɥi, -it] *pp de* **séduire.**
segment [sɛgmɑ̃] *nm* segment; (*AUTO*): ~ **(de piston)** piston ring; ~ **de frein** brake shoe.
segmenter [sɛgmɑ̃te] *vt*, **se** ~ *vi* to segment.
ségrégation [segʀegɑsjɔ̃] *nf* segregation.
ségrégationnisme [segʀegɑsjɔnism(ə)] *nm* segregationism.
ségrégationniste [segʀegɑsjɔnist(ə)] *adj* segregationist.
seiche [sɛʃ] *nf* cuttlefish.
séide [seid] *nm* (*péj*) henchman.
seigle [sɛgl(ə)] *nm* rye.
seigneur [sɛɲœʀ] *nm* lord; **le S**~ the Lord.
seigneurial, e, aux [sɛɲœʀjal, -o] *adj* lordly, stately.
sein [sɛ̃] *nm* breast; (*entrailles*) womb; **au** ~ **de** *prép* (*équipe, institution*) within; (*flots, bonheur*) in the midst of; **donner le** ~ **à** (*bébé*) to feed (at the breast); to breast-feed; **nourrir au** ~ to breast-feed.
Seine [sɛn] *nf*: **la** ~ the Seine.
séisme [seism(ə)] *nm* earthquake.
séismique *etc* [seismik] *voir* **sismique** *etc.*
SEITA [seita] *sigle f* = *Société d'exploitation indus-*

trielle des tabacs et allumettes.

seize [sɛz] *num* sixteen.

seizième [sɛzjɛm] *num* sixteenth.

séjour [seʒuʀ] *nm* stay; (*pièce*) living room.

séjourner [seʒuʀne] *vi* to stay.

sel [sɛl] *nm* salt; (*fig*) wit; spice; ~ **de cuisine/de table** cooking/table salt; ~ **gemme** rock salt; ~**s de bain** bathsalts.

sélect, e [selɛkt] *adj* select.

sélectif, ive [selɛktif, -iv] *adj* selective.

sélection [selɛksjɔ̃] *nf* selection; **faire/opérer une** ~ **parmi** to make a selection from among; **épreuve de** ~ (*SPORT*) trial (for selection); ~ **naturelle** natural selection.

sélectionné, e [selɛksjɔne] *adj* (*joueur*) selected; (*produit*) specially selected.

sélectionner [selɛksjɔne] *vt* to select.

sélectionneur, euse [selɛksjɔnœʀ, -øz] *nm/f* selector.

sélectivement [selɛktivmɑ̃] *adv* selectively.

sélectivité [selɛktivite] *nf* selectivity.

self [sɛlf] *nm* (*fam*) self-service.

self-service [sɛlfsɛʀvis] *adj* self-service ♦ *nm* self-service (restaurant); (*magasin*) self-service shop.

selle [sɛl] *nf* saddle; ~**s** *nfpl* (*MÉD*) stools; **aller à la** ~ (*MÉD*) to have a bowel movement; **se mettre en** ~ to mount, get into the saddle.

seller [sele] *vt* to saddle.

sellette [sɛlɛt] *nf*: **être sur la** ~ to be on the carpet (*fig*).

sellier [selje] *nm* saddler.

selon [səlɔ̃] *prép* according to; (*en se conformant à*) in accordance with; ~ **moi** as I see it; ~ **que** according to, depending on whether.

SEm *sigle f* (= *Son Éminence*) HE.

semailles [səmɑj] *nfpl* sowing *sg*.

semaine [səmɛn] *nf* week; (*salaire*) week's wages *ou* pay, weekly wages *ou* pay; **en** ~ during the week, on weekdays; **à la petite** ~ from day to day; **la** ~ **sainte** Holy Week.

semainier [səmenje] *nm* (*bracelet*) bracelet made up of seven bands; (*calendrier*) desk diary; (*meuble*) chest of (seven) drawers.

sémantique [semɑ̃tik] *adj* semantic ♦ *nf* semantics *sg*.

sémaphore [semafɔʀ] *nm* (*RAIL*) semaphore signal.

semblable [sɑ̃blabl(ə)] *adj* similar; (*de ce genre*): **de** ~**s mésaventures** such mishaps ♦ *nm* fellow creature *ou* man; ~ **à** similar to, like.

semblant [sɑ̃blɑ̃] *nm*: **un** ~ **de vérité** a semblance of truth; **faire** ~ **(de faire)** to pretend (to do).

sembler [sɑ̃ble] *vb avec attribut* to seem ♦ *vb impers*: **il semble (bien) que/inutile de** it (really) seems *ou* appears that/useless to; **il me semble (bien) que** it (really) seems to me that, I (really) think (that); **il me semble le connaître** I think *ou* I've a feeling I know him; ~ **être** to seem to be; **comme bon lui semble** as he sees fit; **me semble-t-il, à ce qu'il me semble** it seems to me, to my mind.

semelle [səmɛl] *nf* sole; (*intérieure*) insole, inner sole; **battre la** ~ to stamp one's feet (to keep them warm); (*fig*) to hang around (waiting); ~**s compensées** platform soles.

semence [səmɑ̃s] *nf* (*graine*) seed; (*clou*) tack.

semer [səme] *vt* to sow; (*fig: éparpiller*) to scatter; (*confusion*) to spread; (*: poursuivants*) to shake off; ~ **la discorde parmi** to sow discord among; **semé de** (*difficultés*) riddled with.

semestre [səmɛstʀ(ə)] *nm* half-year; (*SCOL*) semester.

semestriel, le [səmɛstʀijɛl] *adj* half-yearly; semestral.

semeur, euse [səmœʀ, -øz] *nm/f* sower.

semi-automatique [səmiɔtɔmatik] *adj* semi-automatic.

semiconducteur [səmikɔ̃dyktœʀ] *nm* (*INFORM*) semiconductor.

semi-conserve [səmikɔ̃sɛʀv(ə)] *nf* semi-perishable foodstuff.

semi-fini [səmifini] *adj m* (*produit*) semi-finished.

semi-liberté [səmilibɛʀte] *nf* (*JUR*) partial release from prison (*in order to follow a profession or undergo medical treatment*).

sémillant, e [semijɑ̃, -ɑ̃t] *adj* vivacious; dashing.

séminaire [seminɛʀ] *nm* seminar; (*REL*) seminary.

séminariste [seminaʀist(ə)] *nm* seminarist.

sémiologie [semjɔlɔʒi] *nf* semiology.

semi-public, ique [səmipyblik] *adj* (*JUR*) semi-public.

semi-remorque [səmiʀəmɔʀk(ə)] *nf* trailer ♦ *nm* articulated lorry (*BRIT*), semi(trailer) (*US*).

semis [səmi] *nm* (*terrain*) seedbed, seed plot; (*plante*) seedling.

sémite [semit] *adj* Semitic.

sémitique [semitik] *adj* Semitic.

semoir [səmwaʀ] *nm* seed-bag; seeder.

semonce [səmɔ̃s] *nf*: **un coup de** ~ a shot across the bows.

semoule [səmul] *nf* semolina; ~ **de riz** ground rice.

sempiternel, le [sɛ̃pitɛʀnɛl] *adj* eternal, never-ending.

sénat [sena] *nm* senate; *see boxed note*.

SÉNAT

The **Sénat** *is the upper house of the French Parliament and is housed in the Palais du Luxembourg in Paris. One-third of its members, 'sénateurs', are elected for a nine-year term every three years by an electoral college consisting of 'députés', and other elected representatives. The Sénat has a wide range of powers but can be overidden by the lower house, the "***Assemblée nationale***" in case of dispute.*

sénateur [senatœʀ] *nm* senator.
sénatorial, e, aux [senatɔʀjal, -o] *adj* senatorial, Senate *cpd*.
Sénégal [senegal] *nm*: **le** ~ Senegal.
sénégalais, e [senegalɛ, -ɛz] *adj* Senegalese.
sénevé [sɛnve] *nm* (*BOT*) mustard; (*graine*) mustard seed.
sénile [senil] *adj* senile.
sénilité [senilite] *nf* senility.
senior [senjɔʀ] *nm/f* (*SPORT*) senior.
sens [sɑ̃] *vb voir* **sentir** ♦ *nm* [sɑ̃s] (*PHYSIOL, instinct*) sense; (*signification*) meaning, sense; (*direction*) direction, way ♦ *nmpl* (*sensualité*) senses; **reprendre ses** ~ to regain consciousness; **avoir le** ~ **des affaires/de la mesure** to have business sense/a sense of moderation; **ça n'a pas de** ~ that doesn't make (any) sense; **en dépit du bon** ~ contrary to all good sense; **tomber sous le** ~ to stand to reason, be perfectly obvious; **en un** ~, **dans un** ~ in a way; **en ce** ~ **que** in the sense that; **à mon** ~ to my mind; **dans le** ~ **des aiguilles d'une montre** clockwise; **dans le** ~ **de la longeur/largeur** lengthways/widthways; **dans le mauvais** ~ the wrong way; in the wrong direction; **bon** ~ good sense; ~ **commun** common sense; ~ **dessus dessous** upside down; ~ **interdit**, ~ **unique** one-way street.
sensass [sɑ̃sas] *adj* (*fam*) fantastic.
sensation [sɑ̃sɑsjɔ̃] *nf* sensation; **faire** ~ to cause a sensation, create a stir; **à** ~ (*péj*) sensational.
sensationnel, le [sɑ̃sɑsjɔnɛl] *adj* sensational.
sensé, e [sɑ̃se] *adj* sensible.
sensibilisation [sɑ̃sibilizɑsjɔ̃] *nf* consciousness-raising: **une campagne de** ~ **de l'opinion** a campaign to raise public awareness.
sensibiliser [sɑ̃sibilize] *vt* to sensitize; ~ **qn (à)** to make sb sensitive (to).
sensibilité [sɑ̃sibilite] *nf* sensitivity; (*affectivité, émotivité*) sensitivity, sensibility.
sensible [sɑ̃sibl(ə)] *adj* sensitive; (*aux sens*) perceptible; (*appréciable: différence, progrès*) appreciable, noticeable; ~ **à** sensitive to.
sensiblement [sɑ̃sibləmɑ̃] *adv* (*notablement*) appreciably, noticeably; (*à peu près*): **ils ont** ~ **le même poids** they weigh approximately the same.
sensiblerie [sɑ̃sibləʀi] *nf* sentimentality; squeamishness.
sensitif, ive [sɑ̃sitif, -iv] *adj* (*nerf*) sensory; (*personne*) oversensitive.
sensoriel, le [sɑ̃sɔʀjɛl] *adj* sensory, sensorial.
sensualité [sɑ̃sɥalite] *nf* sensuality, sensuousness.
sensuel, le [sɑ̃sɥɛl] *adj* (*gén*) sensual; (*langage, style*) sensuous.
sent [sɑ̃] *vb voir* **sentir**.
sente [sɑ̃t] *nf* path.
sentence [sɑ̃tɑ̃s] *nf* (*jugement*) sentence; (*adage*) maxim.
sentencieusement [sɑ̃tɑ̃sjøzmɑ̃] *adv* sententiously.
sentencieux, euse [sɑ̃tɑ̃sjø, -øz] *adj* sententious.
senteur [sɑ̃tœʀ] *nf* scent, perfume.
senti, e [sɑ̃ti] *adj*: **bien** ~ (*mots etc*) well-chosen.
sentier [sɑ̃tje] *nm* path.
sentiment [sɑ̃timɑ̃] *nm* feeling; (*conscience, impression*): **avoir le** ~ **de/que** to be aware of/have the feeling that; **recevez mes** ~**s respectueux** yours faithfully; **faire du** ~ (*péj*) to be sentimental; **si vous me prenez par les** ~**s** if you appeal to my feelings.
sentimental, e, aux [sɑ̃timɑ̃tal, -o] *adj* sentimental; (*vie, aventure*) love *cpd*.
sentimentalisme [sɑ̃timɑ̃talism(ə)] *nm* sentimentalism.
sentimentalité [sɑ̃timɑ̃talite] *nf* sentimentality.
sentinelle [sɑ̃tinɛl] *nf* sentry, sentinel; **en** ~ standing guard; (*soldat: en faction*) on sentry duty.
sentir [sɑ̃tiʀ] *vt* (*par l'odorat*) to smell; (*par le goût*) to taste; (*au toucher, fig*) to feel; (*répandre une odeur de*) to smell of; (*: ressemblance*) to smell like; (*avoir la saveur de*) to taste of; to taste like; (*fig: dénoter, annoncer*) to be indicative of; to smack of; to foreshadow ♦ *vi* to smell; ~ **mauvais** to smell bad; **se** ~ **bien** to feel good; **se** ~ **mal** (*être indisposé*) to feel unwell *ou* ill; **se** ~ **le courage/la force de faire** to feel brave/strong enough to do; **ne plus se** ~ **de joie** to be beside o.s. with joy; **il ne peut pas le** ~ (*fam*) he can't stand him.
seoir [swaʀ]: ~ **à** *vt* to become, befit; **comme il (leur) sied** as it is fitting (to them).
Seoul [seul] *n* Seoul.
SEP *sigle f* (= *sclérose en plaques*) MS.
séparation [sepaʀɑsjɔ̃] *nf* separation; (*cloison*) division, partition; ~ **de biens** division of property (*in marriage settlement*); ~ **de corps** legal separation.
séparatisme [sepaʀatism(ə)] *nm* (*POL, REL*) separatism.
séparatiste [sepaʀatist(ə)] *adj, nm/f* (*POL*) separatist.
séparé, e [sepaʀe] *adj* (*appartements, pouvoirs*) separate; (*époux*) separated; ~ **de** separate from; separated from.
séparément [sepaʀemɑ̃] *adv* separately.
séparer [sepaʀe] *vt* (*gén*) to separate; (*suj: divergences etc*) to divide; to drive apart; (*: différences, obstacles*) to stand between; (*détacher*): ~ **qch de** to pull sth (off) from; (*dissocier*) to distinguish between; (*diviser*): ~ **qch par** to divide sth (up) with; ~ **une pièce en deux** to divide a room into two; **se** ~ (*époux*) to separate, part; (*prendre congé: amis etc*) to part, leave each other; (*adversaires*) to separate; (*se diviser: route, tige etc*)

to divide; (*se détacher*): **se ~ (de)** to split off (from); to come off; **se ~ de** (*époux*) to separate *ou* part from; (*employé, objet personnel*) to part with.
sépia [sepja] *nf* sepia.
sept [sɛt] *num* seven.
septante [sɛptɑ̃t] *num* (*Belgique, Suisse*) seventy.
septembre [sɛptɑ̃bʀ(ə)] *nm* September; *voir aussi* **juillet**.
septennal, e, aux [sɛptenal, -o] *adj* seven-year; (*festival*) seven-year, septennial.
septennat [sɛptena] *nm* seven-year term (of office); seven-year reign.
septentrional, e, aux [sɛptɑ̃tʀijɔnal, -o] *adj* northern.
septicémie [sɛptisemi] *nf* blood poisoning, septicaemia.
septième [sɛtjɛm] *num* seventh; **être au ~ ciel** to be on cloud nine.
septique [sɛptik] *adj*: **fosse ~** septic tank.
septuagénaire [sɛptɥaʒenɛʀ] *adj, nm/f* septuagenarian.
sépulcral, e, aux [sepylkʀal, -o] *adj* (*voix*) sepulchral.
sépulcre [sepylkʀ(ə)] *nm* sepulchre.
sépulture [sepyltyʀ] *nf* burial; (*tombeau*) burial place, grave.
séquelles [sekɛl] *nfpl* after-effects; (*fig*) aftermath *sg*; consequences.
séquence [sekɑ̃s] *nf* sequence.
séquentiel, le [sekɑ̃sjɛl] *adj* sequential.
séquestration [sekɛstʀɑsjɔ̃] *nf* illegal confinement; impounding.
séquestre [sekɛstʀ(ə)] *nm* impoundment; **mettre sous ~** to impound.
séquestrer [sekɛstʀe] *vt* (*personne*) to confine illegally; (*biens*) to impound.
serai [səʀe] *etc vb voir* **être**.
sérail [seʀaj] *nm* seraglio; harem; **rentrer au ~** to return to the fold.
serbe [sɛʀb(ə)] *adj* Serbian ♦ *nm* (*LING*) Serbian ♦ *nm/f*: **S~** Serb.
Serbie [sɛʀbi] *nf*: **la ~** Serbia.
serbo-croate [sɛʀbɔkʀɔat] *adj* Serbo-Croat, Serbo-Croatian ♦ *nm* (*LING*) Serbo-Croat.
serein, e [səʀɛ̃, -ɛn] *adj* serene; (*jugement*) dispassionate.
sereinement [səʀɛnmɑ̃] *adv* serenely.
sérénade [seʀenad] *nf* serenade; (*fam*) hullabaloo.
sérénité [seʀenite] *nf* serenity.
serez [səʀe] *vb voir* **être**.
serf, serve [sɛʀ, sɛʀv(ə)] *nm/f* serf.
serfouette [sɛʀfwɛt] *nf* weeding hoe.
serge [sɛʀʒ(ə)] *nf* serge.
sergent [sɛʀʒɑ̃] *nm* sergeant.
sergent-chef [sɛʀʒɑ̃ʃɛf] *nm* staff sergeant.
sergent-major [sɛʀʒɑ̃maʒɔʀ] *nm* ≈ quartermaster sergeant.
sériciculture [seʀisikyltyʀ] *nf* silkworm breeding, sericulture.
série [seʀi] *nf* (*de questions, d'accidents, TV*) series *inv*; (*de clés, casseroles, outils*) set; (*catégorie*: *SPORT*) rank; class; **en ~** in quick succession; (*COMM*) mass *cpd*; **de ~** *adj* standard; **hors ~** (*COMM*) custom-built; (*fig*) outstanding; **imprimante ~** (*INFORM*) serial printer; **soldes de fin de ~s** end of line special offers; **~ noire** *nm* (crime) thriller ♦ *nf* (*suite de malheurs*) run of bad luck.
sérier [seʀje] *vt* to classify, sort out.
sérieusement [seʀjøzmɑ̃] *adv* seriously; reliably; responsibly; **il parle ~** he's serious, he means it; **~?** are you serious?, do you mean it?
sérieux, euse [seʀjø, -øz] *adj* serious; (*élève, employé*) reliable, responsible; (*client, maison*) reliable, dependable; (*offre, proposition*) genuine, serious; (*grave, sévère*) serious, solemn; (*maladie, situation*) serious, grave; (*important*) considerable ♦ *nm* seriousness; reliability; **ce n'est pas ~** (*raisonnable*) that's not on; **garder son ~** to keep a straight face; **manquer de ~** not to be very responsible (*ou* reliable); **prendre qch/qn au ~** to take sth/sb seriously.
sérigraphie [seʀigʀafi] *nf* silk screen printing.
serin [səʀɛ̃] *nm* canary.
seriner [səʀine] *vt*: **~ qch à qn** to drum sth into sb.
seringue [səʀɛ̃g] *nf* syringe.
serions [səʀjɔ̃] *etc vb voir* **être**.
serment [sɛʀmɑ̃] *nm* (*juré*) oath; (*promesse*) pledge, vow; **prêter ~** to take the *ou* an oath; **faire le ~ de** to take a vow to, swear to; **sous ~** on *ou* under oath.
sermon [sɛʀmɔ̃] *nm* sermon; (*péj*) sermon, lecture.
sermonner [sɛʀmɔne] *vt* to lecture.
SERNAM [sɛʀnam] *sigle m* (= *Service national de messageries*) *rail delivery service*.
sérologie [seʀɔlɔʒi] *nf* serology.
séronégatif, ive [seʀonegatif, -iv] *adj* HIV negative.
séropositif, ive [seʀopozitif, -iv] *adj* HIV positive.
serpe [sɛʀp(ə)] *nf* billhook.
serpent [sɛʀpɑ̃] *nm* snake; **~ à sonnettes** rattlesnake; **~ monétaire (européen)** (European) monetary snake.
serpenter [sɛʀpɑ̃te] *vi* to wind.
serpentin [sɛʀpɑ̃tɛ̃] *nm* (*tube*) coil; (*ruban*) streamer.
serpillière [sɛʀpijɛʀ] *nf* floorcloth.
serrage [sɛʀaʒ] *nm* tightening; **collier de ~** clamp.
serre [sɛʀ] *nf* (*AGR*) greenhouse; **~ chaude** hothouse; **~ froide** unheated greenhouse.
serré, e [seʀe] *adj* (*tissu*) closely woven; (*réseau*) dense; (*écriture*) close; (*habits*) tight; (*fig: lutte, match*) tight, close-fought; (*passagers etc*) (tightly) packed; (*café*) strong ♦ *adv*: **jouer ~** to play it close, play a close game;

écrire ~ to write a cramped hand; **avoir la gorge ~e** to have a lump in one's throat.

serre-livres [sɛrlivr(ə)] *nm inv* book ends *pl*.

serrement [sɛrmɑ̃] *nm*: ~ **de main** handshake; ~ **de cœur** pang of anguish.

serrer [sere] *vt* (*tenir*) to grip *ou* hold tight; (*comprimer, coincer*) to squeeze; (*poings, mâchoires*) to clench; (*suj: vêtement*) to be too tight for; to fit tightly; (*rapprocher*) to close up, move closer together; (*ceinture, nœud, frein, vis*) to tighten ♦ *vi*: ~ **à droite** to keep to the right; to move into the right-hand lane; **se** ~ (*se rapprocher*) to squeeze up; **se** ~ **contre qn** to huddle up to sb; **se** ~ **les coudes** to stick together, back one another up; **se** ~ **la ceinture** to tighten one's belt; ~ **la main à qn** to shake sb's hand; ~ **qn dans ses bras** to hug sb, clasp sb in one's arms; ~ **la gorge à qn** (*suj: chagrin*) to bring a lump to sb's throat; ~ **les dents** to clench *ou* grit one's teeth; ~ **qn de près** to follow close behind sb; ~ **le trottoir** to hug the kerb; ~ **sa droite** to keep well to the right; ~ **la vis à qn** to crack down harder on sb; ~ **les rangs** to close ranks.

serres [sɛr] *nfpl* (*griffes*) claws, talons.

serre-tête [sɛrtɛt] *nm inv* (*bandeau*) headband; (*bonnet*) skullcap.

serrure [seryr] *nf* lock.

serrurerie [seryrri] *nf* (*métier*) locksmith's trade; (*ferronnerie*) ironwork; ~ **d'art** ornamental ironwork.

serrurier [seryrje] *nm* locksmith.

sers, sert [sɛr] *vb voir* **servir**.

sertir [sɛrtir] *vt* (*pierre*) to set; (*pièces métalliques*) to crimp.

sérum [serɔm] *nm* serum; ~ **antivenimeux** snakebite serum; ~ **sanguin** (blood) serum; ~ **de vérité** truth drug.

servage [sɛrvaʒ] *nm* serfdom.

servant [sɛrvɑ̃] *nm* server.

servante [sɛrvɑ̃t] *nf* (maid)servant.

serve [sɛrv] *nf voir* **serf** ♦ *vb voir* **servir**.

serveur, euse [sɛrvœr, -øz] *nm/f* waiter/ waitress ♦ *adj*: **centre** ~ (*INFORM*) service centre.

servi, e [sɛrvi] *adj*: **être bien** ~ to get a large helping (*ou* helpings); **vous êtes ~?** are you being served?

serviable [sɛrvjabl(ə)] *adj* obliging, willing to help.

service [sɛrvis] *nm* (*gén*) service; (*série de repas*): **premier** ~ first sitting; (*pourboire*) service (charge); (*assortiment de vaisselle*) set, service; (*linge de table*) set; (*bureau: de la vente etc*) department, section; (*travail*): **pendant le** ~ on duty; **~s** *nmpl* (*travail, ÉCON*) services, inclusive/exclusive of service; **faire le** ~ to serve; **être en** ~ **chez qn** (*domestique*) to be in sb's service; **être au** ~ **de** (*patron, patrie*) to be in the service of; **être au** ~ **de qn** (*collaborateur, voiture*) to be at sb's service; **porte de** ~ tradesman's entrance; **rendre** ~ **à** to help; **il aime rendre** ~ he likes to help; **rendre un** ~ **à qn** to do sb a favour; **heures de** ~ hours of duty; **être de** ~ to be on duty; **reprendre du** ~ to get back into action; **avoir 25 ans de** ~ to have completed 25 years' service; **être/mettre en** ~ to be in/put into service *ou* operation; **hors** ~ not in use; out of order; ~ **à thé/café** tea/ coffee set *ou* service; ~ **après-vente (SAV)** after-sales service; **en** ~ **commandé** on an official assignment; ~ **funèbre** funeral service; ~ **militaire** military service; ~ **d'ordre** police (*ou* stewards) in charge of maintaining order; **~s publics** public services, (public) utilities; **~s secrets** secret service *sg*; **~s sociaux** social services; *see boxed note*.

SERVICE MILITAIRE

French men over 18 years of age are required to do ten months' **service militaire** *if they pass their physical examination. Call-up can be delayed, however, if the conscript is a full-time student in higher education. Conscientious objectors are required to do two years' community service. Since 1970, women have been able to do military service, though few do.*

serviette [sɛrvjɛt] *nf* (*de table*) (table) napkin, serviette; (*de toilette*) towel; (*porte-documents*) briefcase; ~ **éponge** terry towel; ~ **hygiénique** sanitary towel.

servile [sɛrvil] *adj* servile.

servir [sɛrvir] *vt* (*gén*) to serve; (*dîneur: au restaurant*) to wait on; (*client: au magasin*) to serve, attend to; (*fig: aider*): ~ **qn** to aid sb; to serve sb's interests; to stand sb in good stead; (*COMM: rente*) to pay ♦ *vi* (*TENNIS*) to serve; (*CARTES*) to deal; (*être militaire*) to serve; ~ **qch à qn** to serve sb with sth, help sb to sth; **qu'est-ce que je vous sers?** what can I get you?; **se** ~ (*prendre d'un plat*) to help o.s.; (*s'approvisionner*): **se** ~ **chez** to shop at; **se** ~ **de** (*plat*) to help o.s. to; (*voiture, outil, relations*) to use; ~ **à qn** (*diplôme, livre*) to be of use to sb; **ça m'a servi pour faire** it was useful to me when I did; I used it to do; ~ **à qch/à faire** (*outil etc*) to be used for sth/for doing; **ça peut** ~ it may come in handy; **à quoi cela sert-il (de faire)?** what's the use (of doing)?; **cela ne sert à rien** it's no use; ~ **(à qn) de ...** to serve as ... (for sb); ~ **à dîner (à qn)** to serve dinner (to sb).

serviteur [sɛrvitœr] *nm* servant.

servitude [sɛrvityd] *nf* servitude; (*fig*) constraint; (*JUR*) easement.

servofrein [sɛrvɔfrɛ̃] *nm* servo(-assisted) brake.

servomécanisme [sɛrvɔmekanism(ə)] *nm* servo system.

ses [se] *adj possessif voir* **son**.

sésame [sezam] *nm* (*BOT*) sesame; (*graine*) sesame seed.
session [sesjɔ̃] *nf* session.
set [sɛt] *nm* set; (*napperon*) placemat; ~ **de table** set of placemats.
seuil [sœj] *nm* doorstep; (*fig*) threshold; **sur le ~ de sa maison** in the doorway of his house, on his doorstep; **au ~ de** (*fig*) on the threshold *ou* brink *ou* edge of; ~ **de rentabilité** (*COMM*) breakeven point.
seul, e [sœl] *adj* (*sans compagnie*) alone; (*avec nuance affective: isolé*) lonely; (*unique*): **un ~ livre** only one book, a single book; **le ~ livre** the only book; ~ **ce livre, ce livre ~** this book alone, only this book; **d'un ~ coup** (*soudainement*) all at once; (*à la fois*) at one blow ♦ *adv* (*vivre*) alone, on one's own; **parler tout ~** to talk to oneself; **faire qch (tout) ~** to do sth (all) on one's own *ou* (all) by oneself ♦ *nm, nf*: **il en reste un(e) ~(e)** there's only one left; **pas un(e) ~(e)** not a single; **à lui (tout) ~** single-handed, on his own; ~ **à ~** in private.
seulement [sœlmɑ̃] *adv* (*pas davantage*): ~ **5, 5 ~** only 5; (*exclusivement*): ~ **eux** only them, them alone; (*pas avant*): ~ **hier/à 10h** only yesterday/at 10 o'clock; (*mais, toutefois*): **il consent, ~ il demande des garanties** he agrees, only he wants guarantees; **non ~ ... mais aussi** *ou* **encore** not only ... but also.
sève [sɛv] *nf* sap.
sévère [sevɛʀ] *adj* severe.
sévèrement [sevɛʀmɑ̃] *adv* severely.
sévérité [seveʀite] *nf* severity.
sévices [sevis] *nmpl* (physical) cruelty *sg*, ill treatment *sg*.
Séville [sevil] *n* Seville.
sévir [seviʀ] *vi* (*punir*) to use harsh measures, crack down; (*suj: fléau*) to rage, be rampant; ~ **contre** (*abus*) to deal ruthlessly with, crack down on.
sevrage [səvʀaʒ] *nm* weaning; deprivation; (*d'un toxicomane*) withdrawal.
sevrer [səvʀe] *vt* to wean; (*fig*): ~ **qn de** to deprive sb of.
sexagénaire [sɛgzaʒenɛʀ] *adj, nm/f* sexagenarian.
SExc *sigle f* (= *Son Excellence*) HE.
sexe [sɛks(ə)] *nm* sex; (*organe mâle*) member.
sexisme [sɛksism(ə)] *nm* sexism.
sexiste [sɛksist(ə)] *adj, nm* sexist.
sexologie [sɛksɔlɔʒi] *nf* sexology.
sexologue [sɛksɔlɔg] *nm/f* sexologist, sex specialist.
sextant [sɛkstɑ̃] *nm* sextant.
sexualité [sɛksɥalite] *nf* sexuality.
sexué, e [sɛksɥe] *adj* sexual.
sexuel, le [sɛksɥɛl] *adj* sexual; **acte ~** sex act.
sexuellement [sɛksɥɛlmɑ̃] *adv* sexually.
seyait [sejɛ] *vb voir* **seoir**.
seyant, e [sɛjɑ̃, -ɑ̃t] *vb voir* **seoir** ♦ *adj* becoming.
Seychelles [seʃɛl] *nfpl*: **les ~** the Seychelles.
SFIO *sigle f* (= *Section française de l'internationale ouvrière*) *former name of French Socialist Party*.
SG *sigle m* = **secrétaire général**.
SGEN *sigle m* (= *Syndicat général de l'éducation nationale*) *trades union*.
shaker [ʃɛkœʀ] *nm* (cocktail) shaker.
shampooiner [ʃɑ̃pwine] *vt* to shampoo.
shampooineur, euse [ʃɑ̃pwinœʀ, -øz] *nm/f* (*personne*) junior (*who does the shampooing*).
shampooing [ʃɑ̃pwɛ̃] *nm* shampoo; **se faire un ~** to shampoo one's hair; ~ **colorant** (colour) rinse; ~ **traitant** medicated shampoo.
Shetland [ʃɛtlɑ̃d] *n*: **les îles ~** the Shetland Islands, Shetland.
shoot [ʃut] *nm* (*FOOTBALL*) shot.
shooter [ʃute] *vi* (*FOOTBALL*) to shoot; **se ~** (*drogué*) to mainline.
shopping [ʃɔpiŋ] *nm*: **faire du ~** to go shopping.
short [ʃɔʀt] *nm* (pair of) shorts *pl*.
SI *sigle m* = **syndicat d'initiative**.

MOT-CLÉ

si [si] *nm* (*MUS*) B; (*en chantant la gamme*) ti
♦ *adv* **1** (*oui*) yes; **"Paul n'est pas venu" — "~!"** "Paul hasn't come" — "Yes he has!"; **je vous assure que ~** I assure you he did/she is *etc*
2 (*tellement*) so; ~ **gentil/rapidement** so kind/fast; **(tant et) ~ bien que** so much so that; ~ **rapide qu'il soit** however fast he may be
♦ *conj* if; ~ **tu veux** if you want; **je me demande ~** I wonder if *ou* whether; ~ **j'étais toi** if I were you; ~ **seulement** if only; ~ **ce n'est que** apart from; **une des plus belles, ~ ce n'est la plus belle** one of the most beautiful, if not THE most beautiful; **s'il est aimable, eux par contre ...** while *ou* whereas he's nice, they (on the other hand) ...

siamois, e [sjamwa, -waz] *adj* Siamese; **frères/sœurs ~(es)** Siamese twins.
Sibérie [sibeʀi] *nf*: **la ~** Siberia.
sibérien, ne [sibeʀjɛ̃, -ɛn] *adj* Siberian ♦ *nm/f*: **S~, ne** Siberian.
sibyllin, e [sibilɛ̃, -in] *adj* sibylline.
SICAV [sikav] *sigle f* (= *société d'investissement à capital variable*) *open-ended investment trust; share in such a trust*.
Sicile [sisil] *nf*: **la ~** Sicily.
sicilien, ne [sisiljɛ̃, -ɛn] *adj* Sicilian.
SIDA, sida [sida] *nm* (= *syndrome immuno-déficitaire acquis*) AIDS *sg*.
sidéral, e, aux [sideʀal, -o] *adj* sideral.
sidérant, e [sideʀɑ̃, -ɑ̃t] *adj* staggering.
sidéré, e [sideʀe] *adj* staggered.
sidérurgie [sideʀyʀʒi] *nf* steel industry.
sidérurgique [sideʀyʀʒik] *adj* steel *cpd*.
sidérurgiste [sideʀyʀʒist(ə)] *nm/f* steel work-

er.

siècle [sjɛkl(ə)] *nm* century; (*époque*): **le ~ des lumières/de l'atome** the age of enlightenment/atomic age; (*REL*): **le ~** the world.

sied [sje] *vb voir* **seoir**.

siège [sjɛʒ] *nm* seat; (*d'entreprise*) head office; (*d'organisation*) headquarters *pl*; (*MIL*) siege; **lever le ~** to raise the siege; **mettre le ~ devant** to besiege; **présentation par le ~** (*MÉD*) breech presentation; **~ avant/arrière** (*AUTO*) front/back seat; **~ baquet** bucket seat; **~ social** registered office.

siéger [sjeʒe] *vi* (*assemblée, tribunal*) to sit; (*résider, se trouver*) to lie, be located.

sien, ne [sjɛ̃, sjɛn] *pron*: **le(la) ~(ne), les ~s(~nes)** *m* his; *f* hers; *non humain* its; **y mettre du ~** to pull one's weight; **faire des ~nes** (*fam*) to be up to one's (usual) tricks; **les ~s** (*sa famille*) one's family.

siérait [sjeʀɛ] *etc vb voir* **seoir**.

Sierra Leone [sjɛʀaleɔne] *nf*: **la ~** Sierra Leone.

sieste [sjɛst(ə)] *nf* (afternoon) snooze *ou* nap, siesta; **faire la ~** to have a snooze *ou* nap.

sieur [sjœʀ] *nm*: **le ~ Thomas** Mr Thomas; (*en plaisantant*) Master Thomas.

sifflant, e [siflɑ̃, -ɑ̃t] *adj* (*bruit*) whistling; (*toux*) wheezing; **(consonne) ~e** sibilant.

sifflement [sifləmɑ̃] *nm* whistle, whistling *no pl*; wheezing *no pl*; hissing *no pl*.

siffler [sifle] *vi* (*gén*) to whistle; (*avec un sifflet*) to blow (on) one's whistle; (*en respirant*) to wheeze; (*serpent, vapeur*) to hiss ♦ *vt* (*chanson*) to whistle; (*chien etc*) to whistle for; (*fille*) to whistle at; (*pièce, orateur*) to hiss, boo; (*faute*) to blow one's whistle at; (*fin du match, départ*) to blow one's whistle for; (*fam: verre, bouteille*) to guzzle, knock back (*BRIT*).

sifflet [siflɛ] *nm* whistle; **~s** *nmpl* (*de mécontentement*) whistles, boos; **coup de ~** whistle.

siffloter [siflɔte] *vi, vt* to whistle.

sigle [sigl(ə)] *nm* acronym, (set of) initials *pl*.

signal, aux [siɲal, -o] *nm* (*signe convenu, appareil*) signal; (*indice, écriteau*) sign; **donner le ~ de** to give the signal for; **~ d'alarme** alarm signal; **~ d'alerte/de détresse** warning/distress signal; **~ horaire** time signal; **~ optique/sonore** warning light/sound; visual/acoustic signal; **signaux (lumineux)** (*AUTO*) traffic signals; **signaux routiers** road signs; (*lumineux*) traffic lights.

signalement [siɲalmɑ̃] *nm* description, particulars *pl*.

signaler [siɲale] *vt* to indicate; to announce; to report; (*être l'indice de*) to indicate; (*faire remarquer*): **~ qch à qn/à qn que** to point out sth to sb/to sb that; (*appeler l'attention sur*): **~ qn à la police** to bring sb to the notice of the police; **se ~ par** to distinguish o.s. by; **se ~ à l'attention de qn** to attract sb's attention.

signalétique [siɲaletik] *adj*: **fiche ~** identification sheet.

signalisation [siɲalizɑsjɔ̃] *nf* signalling, signposting; signals *pl*; roadsigns *pl*; **panneau de ~** roadsign.

signaliser [siɲalize] *vt* to put up roadsigns on; to put signals on.

signataire [siɲatɛʀ] *nm/f* signatory.

signature [siɲatyʀ] *nf* signature; (*action*) signing.

signe [siɲ] *nm* sign; (*TYPO*) mark; **ne pas donner ~ de vie** to give no sign of life; **c'est bon ~** it's a good sign; **c'est ~ que** it's a sign that; **faire un ~ de la main/tête** to give a sign with one's hand/shake one's head; **faire ~ à qn** (*fig*) to get in touch with sb; **faire ~ à qn d'entrer** to motion (to) sb to come in; **en ~ de** as a sign *ou* mark of; **le ~ de la croix** the sign of the Cross; **~ de ponctuation** punctuation mark; **~ du zodiaque** sign of the zodiac; **~s particuliers** distinguishing marks.

signer [siɲe] *vt* to sign; **se ~** *vi* to cross o.s.

signet [siɲɛ] *nm* bookmark.

significatif, ive [siɲifikatif, -iv] *adj* significant.

signification [siɲifikɑsjɔ̃] *nf* meaning.

signifier [siɲifje] *vt* (*vouloir dire*) to mean, signify; (*faire connaître*): **~ qch (à qn)** to make sth known (to sb); (*JUR*): **~ qch à qn** to serve notice of sth on sb.

silence [silɑ̃s] *nm* silence; (*MUS*) rest; **garder le ~ (sur qch)** to keep silent (about sth), say nothing (about sth); **passer sous ~** to pass over (in silence); **réduire au ~** to silence.

silencieusement [silɑ̃sjøzmɑ̃] *adv* silently.

silencieux, euse [silɑ̃sjø, -øz] *adj* quiet, silent ♦ *nm* silencer (*BRIT*), muffler (*US*).

silex [silɛks] *nm* flint.

silhouette [silwɛt] *nf* outline, silhouette; (*lignes, contour*) outline; (*figure*) figure.

silice [silis] *nf* silica.

siliceux, euse [silisø, -øz] *adj* (*terrain*) chalky.

silicium [silisjɔm] *nm* silicon; **plaquette de ~** silicon chip.

silicone [silikon] *nf* silicone.

silicose [silikoz] *nf* silicosis, dust disease.

sillage [sijaʒ] *nm* wake; (*fig*) trail; **dans le ~ de** (*fig*) in the wake of.

sillon [sijɔ̃] *nm* (*d'un champ*) furrow; (*de disque*) groove.

sillonner [sijɔne] *vt* (*creuser*) to furrow; (*traverser*) to cross, criss-cross.

silo [silo] *nm* silo.

simagrées [simagʀe] *nfpl* fuss *sg*; airs and graces.

simiesque [simjɛsk(ə)] *adj* monkey-like, ape-like.

similaire [similɛʀ] *adj* similar.

similarité [similaʀite] *nf* similarity.

simili [simili] *nm* imitation; (*TYPO*) half-tone ♦ *nf* half-tone engraving.

simili... [simili] *préfixe* imitation *cpd*, artificial.

similicuir [similikɥiʀ] *nm* imitation leather.

similigravure [similigʀavyʀ] *nf* half-tone engraving.
similitude [similityd] *nf* similarity.
simple [sɛ̃pl(ə)] *adj* (*gén*) simple; (*non multiple*) single; **~s** *nmpl* (*MÉD*) medicinal plants; **~ messieurs** *nm* (*TENNIS*) men's singles *sg*; **un ~ particulier** an ordinary citizen; **une ~ formalité** a mere formality; **cela varie du ~ au double** it can double, it can double the price *etc*; **dans le plus ~ appareil** in one's birthday suit; **~ course** *adj* single; **~ d'esprit** *nm/f* simpleton; **~ soldat** private.
simplement [sɛ̃pləmɑ̃] *adv* simply.
simplet, te [sɛ̃plɛ, -ɛt] *adj* (*personne*) simple-minded.
simplicité [sɛ̃plisite] *nf* simplicity; **en toute ~** quite simply.
simplification [sɛ̃plifikɑsjɔ̃] *nf* simplification.
simplifier [sɛ̃plifje] *vt* to simplify.
simpliste [sɛ̃plist(ə)] *adj* simplistic.
simulacre [simylakʀ(ə)] *nm* enactment; (*péj*): **un ~ de** a pretence of, a sham.
simulateur, trice [simylatœʀ, -tʀis] *nm/f* shammer, pretender; (*qui se prétend malade*) malingerer ♦ *nm*: **~ de vol** flight simulator.
simulation [simylɑsjɔ̃] *nf* shamming, simulation; malingering.
simuler [simyle] *vt* to sham, simulate.
simultané, e [simyltane] *adj* simultaneous.
simultanéité [simyltaneite] *nf* simultaneity.
simultanément [simyltanemɑ̃] *adv* simultaneously.
Sinaï [sinai] *nm*: **le ~** Sinai.
sinapisme [sinapism(ə)] *nm* (*MÉD*) mustard poultice.
sincère [sɛ̃sɛʀ] *adj* sincere; genuine; heartfelt; **mes ~s condoléances** my deepest sympathy.
sincèrement [sɛ̃sɛʀmɑ̃] *adv* sincerely; genuinely.
sincérité [sɛ̃seʀite] *nf* sincerity; **en toute ~** in all sincerity.
sinécure [sinekyʀ] *nf* sinecure.
sine die [sinedje] *adv* sine die, indefinitely.
sine qua non [sinekwanɔn] *adj*: **condition ~** indispensable condition.
Singapour [sɛ̃gapuʀ] *nm*: **le ~** Singapore.
singe [sɛ̃ʒ] *nm* monkey; (*de grande taille*) ape.
singer [sɛ̃ʒe] *vt* to ape, mimic.
singeries [sɛ̃ʒʀi] *nfpl* antics; (*simagrées*) airs and graces.
singulariser [sɛ̃gylaʀize] *vt* to mark out; **se ~** to call attention to o.s.
singularité [sɛ̃gylaʀite] *nf* peculiarity.
singulier, ière [sɛ̃gylje, -jɛʀ] *adj* remarkable, singular; (*LING*) singular ♦ *nm* singular.
singulièrement [sɛ̃gyljɛʀmɑ̃] *adv* singularly, remarkably.
sinistre [sinistʀ(ə)] *adj* sinister; (*intensif*): **un ~ imbécile** an incredible idiot ♦ *nm* (*incendie*) blaze; (*catastrophe*) disaster; (*ASSURANCES*) damage (*giving rise to a claim*).
sinistré, e [sinistʀe] *adj* disaster-stricken ♦ *nm/f* disaster victim.
sinistrose [sinistʀoz] *nf* pessimism.
sino... [sino] *préfixe*: **~-indien** Sino-Indian, Chinese-Indian.
sinon [sinɔ̃] *conj* (*autrement, sans quoi*) otherwise, or else; (*sauf*) except, other than; (*si ce n'est*) if not.
sinueux, euse [sinɥø, -øz] *adj* winding; (*fig*) tortuous.
sinuosités [sinɥozite] *nfpl* winding *sg*, curves.
sinus [sinys] *nm* (*ANAT*) sinus; (*GÉOM*) sine.
sinusite [sinyzit] *nf* sinusitis, sinus infection.
sinusoïdal, e, aux [sinyzɔidal, -o] *adj* sinusoidal.
sinusoïde [sinyzɔid] *nf* sinusoid.
sionisme [sjɔnism(ə)] *nm* Zionism.
sioniste [sjɔnist(ə)] *adj, nm/f* Zionist.
siphon [sifɔ̃] *nm* (*tube, d'eau gazeuse*) siphon; (*d'évier etc*) U-bend.
siphonner [sifɔne] *vt* to siphon.
sire [siʀ] *nm* (*titre*): **S~** Sire; **un triste ~** an unsavoury individual.
sirène [siʀɛn] *nf* siren; **~ d'alarme** fire alarm; (*pendant la guerre*) air-raid siren.
sirop [siʀo] *nm* (*à diluer: de fruit etc*) syrup, cordial (*BRIT*); (*boisson*) fruit drink; (*pharmaceutique*) syrup, mixture; **~ de menthe** mint syrup *ou* cordial; **~ contre la toux** cough syrup *ou* mixture.
siroter [siʀɔte] *vt* to sip.
sirupeux, euse [siʀypø, -øz] *adj* syrupy.
sis, e [si, siz] *adj*: **~ rue de la Paix** located in the rue de la Paix.
sisal [sizal] *nm* (*BOT*) sisal.
sismique [sismik] *adj* seismic.
sismographe [sismɔgʀaf] *nm* seismograph.
sismologie [sismɔlɔʒi] *nf* seismology.
site [sit] *nm* (*paysage, environnement*) setting; (*d'une ville etc: emplacement*) site; **~ (pittoresque)** beauty spot; **~ Web** (*INFORM*) website; **~s touristiques** places of interest; **~s naturels/historiques** natural/historic sites.
sitôt [sito] *adv*: **~ parti** as soon as he *etc* had left; **~ après** straight after; **pas de ~** not for a long time; **~ (après) que** as soon as.
situation [sitɥɑsjɔ̃] *nf* (*gén*) situation; (*d'un édifice, d'une ville*) situation, position; (*emplacement*) location; **être en ~ de faire qch** to be in a position to do sth; **~ de famille** marital status.
situé, e [sitɥe] *adj*: **bien ~** well situated, in a good location; **~ à/près de** situated at/near.
situer [sitɥe] *vt* to site, situate; (*en pensée*) to set, place; **se ~** *vi*: **se ~ à/près de** to be situated at/near.
SIVOM [sivɔm] *sigle m* (*= Syndicat intercommunal à vocation multiple*) *association of "communes"*.
six [sis] *num* six.
sixième [sizjɛm] *num* sixth.
skaï [skaj] *nm* ® ≈ Leatherette ®.

skate(-board) [sket(bɔʀd)] *nm* (*sport*) skateboarding; (*planche*) skateboard.
sketch [skɛtʃ] *nm* (variety) sketch.
ski [ski] *nm* (*objet*) ski; (*sport*) skiing; **faire du ~** to ski; **~ alpin** Alpine skiing; **~ court** short ski; **~ évolutif** short ski method; **~ de fond** cross-country skiing; **~ nautique** water-skiing; **~ de piste** downhill skiing; **~ de randonnée** cross-country skiing.
ski-bob [skibɔb] *nm* skibob.
skier [skje] *vi* to ski.
skieur, euse [skjœʀ, -øz] *nm/f* skier.
skif(f) [skif] *nm* skiff.
slalom [slalɔm] *nm* slalom; **faire du ~ entre** to slalom between.
slalomer [slalɔme] *vi* (*entre des obstacles*) to weave in and out; (*SKI*) to slalom.
slalomeur, euse [slalɔmœʀ, -øz] *nm/f* (*SKI*) slalom skier.
slave [slav] *adj* Slav(onic), Slavic ♦ *nm* (*LING*) Slavonic ♦ *nm/f*: **S~** Slav.
slip [slip] *nm* (*sous-vêtement*) underpants *pl*, pants *pl* (*BRIT*), briefs *pl*; (*de bain: d'homme*) (bathing *ou* swimming) trunks *pl*; (*: du bikini*) (bikini) briefs *pl ou* bottoms *pl*.
slogan [slɔgɑ̃] *nm* slogan.
slovaque [slɔvak] *adj* Slovak ♦ *nm* (*LING*) Slovak ♦ *nm/f*: **S~** Slovak.
Slovaquie [slɔvaki] *nf*: **la ~** Slovakia.
slovène [slɔvɛn] *adj* Slovene ♦ *nm* (*LING*) Slovene ♦ *nm/f*: **S~** Slovene.
Slovénie [slɔveni] *nf*: **la ~** Slovenia.
slow [slo] *nm* (*danse*) slow number.
SM *sigle f* (= *Sa Majesté*) HM.
SMAG [smag] *sigle m* = *salaire minimum agricole garanti*.
smasher [smaʃe] *vi* to smash the ball ♦ *vt* (*balle*) to smash.
SME *sigle m* (= *Système monétaire européen*) EMS.
SMIC [smik] *sigle m* = **salaire minimum interprofessionnel de croissance**; *see boxed note*.

> **SMIC**
>
> *In France, the* **SMIC** *('salaire minimum interprofessionnel de croissance') is the minimum hourly rate which workers over the age of 18 must legally be paid. It is index-linked and is raised each time the cost of living rises by 2 per cent.*

smicard, e [smikaʀ, -aʀd(ə)] *nm/f* minimum wage earner.
smocks [smɔk] *nmpl* (*COUTURE*) smocking *no pl*.
smoking [smɔkiŋ] *nm* dinner *ou* evening suit.
SMUR [smyʀ] *sigle m* (= *service médical d'urgence et de réanimation*) *specialist mobile emergency unit*.
snack [snak] *nm* snack bar.
SNC *abr* = *service non compris*.
SNCB *sigle f* (= *Société nationale des chemins de fer belges*) *Belgian railways*.
SNCF *sigle f* (= *Société nationale des chemins de fer français*) *French railways*.
SNES [snɛs] *sigle m* (= *Syndicat national de l'enseignement secondaire*) *secondary teachers' union*.
SNE-sup [ɛsɛnəsyp] *sigle m* (= *Syndicat national de l'enseignement supérieur*) *university teachers' union*.
SNI *sigle m* (= *Syndicat national des instituteurs*) *primary teachers' union*.
SNJ *sigle m* (= *Syndicat national des journalistes*) *journalists' union*.
snob [snɔb] *adj* snobbish ♦ *nm/f* snob.
snober [snɔbe] *vt*: **~ qn** to give sb the cold shoulder, treat sb with disdain.
snobinard, e [snɔbinaʀ, -aʀd(ə)] *nm/f* snooty *ou* stuck-up person.
snobisme [snɔbism(ə)] *nm* snobbery.
SNSM *sigle f* (= *Société nationale de sauvetage en mer*) *national sea-rescue association*.
s.o. *abr* (= *sans objet*) no longer applicable.
sobre [sɔbʀ(ə)] *adj* temperate, abstemious; (*élégance, style*) restrained, sober; **~ de** (*gestes, compliments*) sparing of.
sobrement [sɔbʀəmɑ̃] *adv* in moderation, abstemiously; soberly.
sobriété [sɔbʀijete] *nf* temperance, abstemiousness; sobriety.
sobriquet [sɔbʀikɛ] *nm* nickname.
soc [sɔk] *nm* ploughshare.
sociabilité [sɔsjabilite] *nf* sociability.
sociable [sɔsjabl(ə)] *adj* sociable.
social, e, aux [sɔsjal, -o] *adj* social.
socialisant, e [sɔsjalizɑ̃, -ɑ̃t] *adj* with socialist tendencies.
socialisation [sɔsjalizɑsjɔ̃] *nf* socialisation.
socialiser [sɔsjalize] *vt* to socialize.
socialisme [sɔsjalism(ə)] *nm* socialism.
socialiste [sɔsjalist(ə)] *adj, nm/f* socialist.
sociétaire [sɔsjetɛʀ] *nm/f* member.
société [sɔsjete] *nf* society; (*d'abeilles, de fourmis*) colony; (*sportive*) club; (*COMM*) company; **la bonne ~** polite society; **se plaire dans la ~ de** to enjoy the society of; **l'archipel de la S~** the Society Islands; **la ~ d'abondance/de consommation** the affluent/consumer society; **~ par actions** joint stock company; **~ anonyme (SA)** ≈ limited company (Ltd) (*BRIT*), ≈ incorporated company (Inc.) (*US*); **~ d'investissement à capital variable (SICAV)** ≈ investment trust (*BRIT*), ≈ mutual fund (*US*); **~ à responsabilité limitée (SARL)** *type of limited liability company (with non-negotiable shares)*; **~ savante** learned society; **~ de services** service company.
socioculturel, le [sɔsjokyltyʀɛl] *adj* sociocultural.
socio-économique [sɔsjoekɔnɔmik] *adj* socioeconomic.
socio-éducatif, -ive [sɔsjoedykatif, -iv] *adj* so-

cioeducational.
sociolinguistique [sɔsjolɛ̃gɥistik] *adj* sociolinguistic.
sociologie [sɔsjɔlɔʒi] *nf* sociology.
sociologique [sɔsjɔlɔʒik] *adj* sociological.
sociologue [sɔsjɔlɔg] *nm/f* sociologist.
socio-professionnel, le [sɔsjopʀɔfɛsjɔnɛl] *adj* socioprofessional.
socle [sɔkl(ə)] *nm* (*de colonne, statue*) plinth, pedestal; (*de lampe*) base.
socquette [sɔkɛt] *nf* ankle sock.
soda [sɔda] *nm* (*boisson*) fizzy drink, soda (*US*).
sodium [sɔdjɔm] *nm* sodium.
sodomie [sɔdɔmi] *nf* sodomy; buggery.
sodomiser [sɔdɔmize] *vt* to sodomize; to bugger.
sœur [sœʀ] *nf* sister; (*religieuse*) nun, sister; ~ **Élisabeth** (*REL*) Sister Elizabeth; ~ **de lait** foster sister.
sofa [sɔfa] *nm* sofa.
Sofia [sɔfja] *n* Sofia.
SOFRES [sɔfʀɛs] *sigle f* (= *Société française d'enquête par sondage*) *company which conducts opinion polls*.
soi [swa] *pron* oneself; **cela va de** ~ that *ou* it goes without saying, it stands to reason.
soi-disant [swadizɑ̃] *adj inv* so-called ♦ *adv* supposedly.
soie [swa] *nf* silk; (*de porc, sanglier: poil*) bristle.
soient [swa] *vb voir* **être**.
soierie [swaʀi] *nf* (*industrie*) silk trade; (*tissu*) silk.
soif [swaf] *nf* thirst; (*fig*): ~ **de** thirst *ou* craving for; **avoir** ~ to be thirsty; **donner** ~ **à qn** to make sb thirsty.
soigné, e [swaɲe] *adj* (*tenue*) well-groomed, neat; (*travail*) careful, meticulous; (*fam*) whopping; stiff.
soigner [swaɲe] *vt* (*malade, maladie: suj: docteur*) to treat; (*: suj: infirmière, mère*) to nurse, look after; (*blessé*) to tend; (*travail, détails*) to take care over; (*jardin, chevelure, invités*) to look after.
soigneur [swaɲœʀ] *nm* (*CYCLISME, FOOTBALL*) trainer; (*BOXE*) second.
soigneusement [swaɲøzmɑ̃] *adv* carefully.
soigneux, euse [swaɲø, -øz] *adj* (*propre*) tidy, neat; (*méticuleux*) painstaking, careful; ~ **de** careful with.
soi-même [swamɛm] *pron* oneself.
soin [swɛ̃] *nm* (*application*) care; (*propreté, ordre*) tidiness, neatness; (*responsabilité*): **le** ~ **de qch** the care of sth; ~**s** *nmpl* (*à un malade, blessé*) treatment *sg*, medical attention *sg*; (*attentions, prévenance*) care and attention *sg*; (*hygiène*) care *sg*; ~**s de la chevelure/de beauté** hair/beauty care; ~**s du corps/ménage** care of one's body/the home; **avoir** *ou* **prendre** ~ **de** to take care of, look after; **avoir** *ou* **prendre** ~ **de faire** to take care to do; **sans** ~ *adj* careless; untidy; **les premiers** ~**s** first aid *sg*; **aux bons** ~**s de** c/o, care of; **être aux petits** ~**s pour qn** to wait on sb hand and foot, see to sb's every need; **confier qn aux** ~**s de qn** to hand sb over to sb's care.
soir [swaʀ] *nm, adv* evening; **le** ~ in the evening(s); **ce** ~ this evening, tonight; **à ce** ~! see you this evening (*ou* tonight)!; **la veille au** ~ the previous evening; **sept/dix heures du** ~ seven in the evening/ten at night; **le repas/journal du** ~ the evening meal/newspaper: **dimanche** ~ Sunday evening; **hier** ~ yesterday evening; **demain** ~ tomorrow evening, tomorrow night.
soirée [swaʀe] *nf* evening; (*réception*) party; **donner en** ~ (*film, pièce*) to give an evening performance of.
soit [swa] *vb voir* **être** ♦ *conj* (*à savoir*) namely, to wit; (*ou*): ~ ... ~ either ... or ♦ *adv* so be it, very well; ~ **un triangle ABC** let ABC be a triangle; ~ **que** ... ~ **que** *ou* **ou que** whether ... or whether.
soixantaine [swasɑ̃tɛn] *nf*: **une** ~ **(de)** sixty or so, about sixty; **avoir la** ~ to be around sixty.
soixante [swasɑ̃t] *num* sixty.
soixante-dix [swasɑ̃tdis] *num* seventy.
soixante-dixième [swasɑ̃tdizjɛm] *num* seventieth.
soixante-huitard, e [swazɑ̃tɥitaʀ, -aʀd(ə)] *adj* relating to the demonstrations of May 1968 ♦ *nm/f* participant in the demonstrations of May 1968.
soixantième [swasɑ̃tjɛm] *num* sixtieth.
soja [sɔʒa] *nm* soya; (*graines*) soya beans *pl*; **germes de** ~ beansprouts.
sol [sɔl] *nm* ground; (*de logement*) floor; (*revêtement*) flooring *no pl*; (*territoire, AGR, GÉO*) soil; (*MUS*) G; (*: en chantant la gamme*) so(h).
solaire [sɔlɛʀ] *adj* solar, sun *cpd*.
solarium [sɔlaʀjɔm] *nm* solarium.
soldat [sɔlda] *nm* soldier; **S**~ **inconnu** Unknown Warrior *ou* Soldier; ~ **de plomb** tin *ou* toy soldier.
solde [sɔld(ə)] *nf* pay ♦ *nm* (*COMM*) balance; ~**s** *nmpl ou nfpl* (*COMM*) sales; (*articles*) sale goods; **à la** ~ **de qn** (*péj*) in sb's pay; ~ **créditeur/débiteur** credit/debit balance; ~ **à payer** balance outstanding; **en** ~ at sale price; **aux** ~**s** at the sales.
solder [sɔlde] *vt* (*compte*) to settle; (*marchandise*) to sell at sale price, sell off; **se** ~ **par** (*fig*) to end in; **article soldé (à) 2 €** item reduced to €2.
soldeur, euse [sɔldœʀ, -øz] *nm/f* (*COMM*) discounter.
sole [sɔl] *nf* sole *inv* (*fish*).
soleil [sɔlɛj] *nm* sun; (*lumière*) sun(light); (*temps ensoleillé*) sun(shine); (*feu d'artifice*) Catherine wheel; (*ACROBATIE*) grand circle; (*BOT*) sunflower; **il y a** *ou* **il fait du** ~ it's sun-

ny; **au** ~ in the sun; **en plein** ~ in full sun; **le** ~ **levant/couchant** the rising/setting sun; **le** ~ **de minuit** the midnight sun.
solennel, le [sɔlanɛl] *adj* solemn; ceremonial.
solennellement [sɔlanɛlmɑ̃] *adv* solemnly.
solenniser [sɔlanize] *vt* to solemnize.
solennité [sɔlanite] *nf* (*d'une fête*) solemnity; ~**s** *nfpl* (*formalités*) formalities.
solénoïde [sɔlenɔid] *nm* (*ÉLEC*) solenoid.
solfège [sɔlfɛʒ] *nm* rudiments *pl* of music; (*exercices*) ear training *no pl*.
solfier [sɔlfje] *vt*: ~ **un morceau** to sing a piece using the sol-fa.
soli [sɔli] *pl de* **solo**.
solidaire [solidɛʀ] *adj* (*personnes*) who stand together, who show solidarity; (*pièces mécaniques*) interdependent; (*JUR*: *engagement*) binding on all parties; (*: débiteurs*) jointly liable; **être** ~ **de** (*collègues*) to stand by; (*mécanisme*) to be bound up with, be dependent on.
solidairement [sɔlidɛʀmɑ̃] *adv* jointly.
solidariser [sɔlidaʀize]: **se** ~ **avec** *vt* to show solidarity with.
solidarité [sɔlidaʀite] *nf* (*entre personnes*) solidarity; (*de mécanisme, phénomènes*) interdependence; **par** ~ **(avec)** (*cesser le travail etc*) in sympathy (with).
solide [sɔlid] *adj* solid; (*mur, maison, meuble*) solid, sturdy; (*connaissances, argument*) sound; (*personne*) robust, sturdy; (*estomac*) strong ♦ *nm* solid; **avoir les reins** ~**s** (*fig*) to be in a good financial position; to have sound financial backing.
solidement [sɔlidmɑ̃] *adv* solidly; (*fermement*) firmly.
solidifier [sɔlidifje] *vt*, **se** ~ *vi* to solidify.
solidité [sɔlidite] *nf* solidity; sturdiness.
soliloque [sɔlilɔk] *nm* soliloquy.
soliste [sɔlist(ə)] *nm/f* soloist.
solitaire [sɔlitɛʀ] *adj* (*sans compagnie*) solitary, lonely; (*isolé*) solitary, isolated, lone; (*lieu*) lonely ♦ *nm/f* recluse; loner ♦ *nm* (*diamant, jeu*) solitaire.
solitude [sɔlityd] *nf* loneliness; (*paix*) solitude.
solive [sɔliv] *nf* joist.
sollicitations [sɔlisitɑsjɔ̃] *nfpl* (*requêtes*) entreaties, appeals; (*attractions*) enticements; (*TECH*) stress *sg*.
solliciter [sɔlisite] *vt* (*personne*) to appeal to; (*emploi, faveur*) to seek; (*moteur*) to prompt; (*suj: occupations, attractions etc*): ~ **qn** to appeal to sb's curiosity *etc*; to entice sb; to make demands on sb's time; ~ **qn de faire** to appeal to sb *ou* request sb to do.
sollicitude [sɔlisityd] *nf* concern.
solo [solo] *nm*, *pl* **soli** [sɔli] (*MUS*) solo (*pl* -s *ou* soli).
sol-sol [sɔlsɔl] *adj inv* surface-to-surface.
solstice [sɔlstis] *nm* solstice; ~ **d'hiver/d'été** winter/summer solstice.
solubilisé, e [sɔlybilize] *adj* soluble.
solubilité [sɔlybilite] *nf* solubility.
soluble [sɔlybl(ə)] *adj* (*sucre, cachet*) soluble; (*problème etc*) soluble, solvable.
soluté [sɔlyte] *nm* solution.
solution [sɔlysjɔ̃] *nf* solution; ~ **de continuité** gap, break; ~ **de facilité** easy way out.
solutionner [sɔlysjɔne] *vt* to solve, find a solution for.
solvabilité [sɔlvabilite] *nf* solvency.
solvable [sɔlvabl(ə)] *adj* solvent.
solvant [sɔlvɑ̃] *nm* solvent.
Somalie [sɔmali] *nf*: **la** ~ Somalia.
somalien, ne [sɔmaljɛ̃, -ɛn] *adj* Somalian.
Somaliland [sɔmalilɑ̃d] *nm* Somaliland.
somatique [sɔmatik] *adj* somatic.
sombre [sɔ̃bʀ(ə)] *adj* dark; (*fig*) sombre, gloomy; (*sinistre*) awful, dreadful.
sombrer [sɔ̃bʀe] *vi* (*bateau*) to sink, go down; ~ **corps et biens** to go down with all hands; ~ **dans** (*misère, désespoir*) to sink into.
sommaire [sɔmɛʀ] *adj* (*simple*) basic; (*expéditif*) summary ♦ *nm* summary; **faire le** ~ **de** to make a summary of, summarize; **exécution** ~ summary execution.
sommairement [sɔmɛʀmɑ̃] *adv* basically; summarily.
sommation [sɔmɑsjɔ̃] *nf* (*JUR*) summons *sg*; (*avant de faire feu*) warning.
somme [sɔm] *nf* (*MATH*) sum; (*fig*) amount; (*argent*) sum, amount ♦ *nm*: **faire un** ~ to have a (short) nap; **faire la** ~ **de** to add up; **en** ~, ~ **toute** *adv* all in all.
sommeil [sɔmɛj] *nm* sleep; **avoir** ~ to be sleepy; **avoir le** ~ **léger** to be a light sleeper; **en** ~ (*fig*) dormant.
sommeiller [sɔmeje] *vi* to doze; (*fig*) to lie dormant.
sommelier [sɔməlje] *nm* wine waiter.
sommer [sɔme] *vt*: ~ **qn de faire** to command *ou* order sb to do; (*JUR*) to summon sb to do.
sommes [sɔm] *vb voir* **être**; *voir aussi* **somme**.
sommet [sɔmɛ] *nm* top; (*d'une montagne*) summit, top; (*fig: de la perfection, gloire*) height; (*GÉOM*: *d'angle*) vertex (*pl* vertices); (*conférence*) summit (conference).
sommier [sɔmje] *nm* bed base, bedspring (*US*); (*ADMIN*: *registre*) register; ~ **à ressorts** (interior sprung) divan base (*BRIT*), box spring (*US*); ~ **à lattes** slatted bed base.
sommité [sɔmite] *nf* prominent person, leading light.
somnambule [sɔmnɑ̃byl] *nm/f* sleepwalker.
somnambulisme [sɔmnɑ̃bylism(ə)] *nm* sleepwalking.
somnifère [sɔmnifɛʀ] *nm* sleeping drug; (*comprimé*) sleeping pill *ou* tablet.
somnolence [sɔmnɔlɑ̃s] *nf* drowsiness.
somnolent, e [sɔmnɔlɑ̃, -ɑ̃t] *adj* sleepy, drowsy.
somnoler [sɔmnɔle] *vi* to doze.
somptuaire [sɔ̃ptɥɛʀ] *adj*: **lois** ~**s** sumptuary laws; **dépenses** ~**s** extravagant expenditure

sg.

somptueusement [sɔ̃ptɥøzmɑ̃] *adv* sumptuously.

somptueux, euse [sɔ̃ptɥø, -øz] *adj* sumptuous; (*cadeau*) lavish.

somptuosité [sɔ̃ptɥozite] *nf* sumptuousness; (*d'un cadeau*) lavishness.

son [sɔ̃], **sa** [sa], *pl* **ses** [se] *adj possessif* (*antécédent humain mâle*) his; (*: femelle*) her; (*: valeur indéfinie*) one's, his/her; (*: non humain*) its; *voir note sous* **il**.

son [sɔ̃] *nm* sound; (*de blé etc*) bran; ~ **et lumière** *adj inv* son et lumière.

sonar [sɔnaʀ] *nm* (*NAVIG*) sonar.

sonate [sɔnat] *nf* sonata.

sondage [sɔ̃daʒ] *nm* (*de terrain*) boring, drilling; (*mer, atmosphère*) sounding; probe; (*enquête*) survey, sounding out of opinion; ~ **(d'opinion)** (opinion) poll.

sonde [sɔ̃d] *nf* (*NAVIG*) lead *ou* sounding line; (*MÉTÉOROLOGIE*) sonde; (*MÉD*) probe; catheter; (*d'alimentation*) feeding tube; (*TECH*) borer, driller; (*de forage, sondage*) drill; (*pour fouiller etc*) probe; ~ **à avalanche** pole (*for probing snow and locating victims*); ~ **spatiale** probe.

sonder [sɔ̃de] *vt* (*NAVIG*) to sound; (*atmosphère, plaie, bagages etc*) to probe; (*TECH*) to bore, drill; (*fig: personne*) to sound out; (*: opinion*) to probe; ~ **le terrain** (*fig*) to see how the land lies.

songe [sɔ̃ʒ] *nm* dream.

songer [sɔ̃ʒe] *vi* to dream; ~ **à** (*rêver à*) to muse over, think over; (*penser à*) to think of; (*envisager*) to contemplate, think of, consider; ~ **que** to consider that; to think that.

songerie [sɔ̃ʒʀi] *nf* reverie.

songeur, euse [sɔ̃ʒœʀ, -øz] *adj* pensive; **ça me laisse** ~ that makes me wonder.

sonnailles [sɔnɑj] *nfpl* jingle of bells.

sonnant, e [sɔnɑ̃, -ɑ̃t] *adj*: **en espèces** ~**es et trébuchantes** in coin of the realm; **à 8 heures** ~**es** on the stroke of 8.

sonné, e [sɔne] *adj* (*fam*) cracked; (*passé*): **il est midi** ~ it's gone twelve; **il a quarante ans bien** ~**s** he's well into his forties.

sonner [sɔne] *vi* (*retentir*) to ring; (*donner une impression*) to sound ♦ *vt* (*cloche*) to ring; (*glas, tocsin*) to sound; (*portier, infirmière*) to ring for; (*messe*) to ring the bell for; (*fam: suj: choc, coup*) to knock out; ~ **du clairon** to sound the bugle; ~ **bien/mal/creux** to sound good/bad/hollow; ~ **faux** (*instrument*) to sound out of tune; (*rire*) to ring false; ~ **les heures** to strike the hours; **minuit vient de** ~ midnight has just struck; ~ **chez qn** to ring sb's doorbell, ring at sb's door.

sonnerie [sɔnʀi] *nf* (*son*) ringing; (*sonnette*) bell; (*mécanisme d'horloge*) striking mechanism; ~ **d'alarme** alarm bell; ~ **de clairon** bugle call.

sonnet [sɔnɛ] *nm* sonnet.

sonnette [sɔnɛt] *nf* bell; ~ **d'alarme** alarm bell; ~ **de nuit** night-bell.

sono [sɔno] *nf* (= *sonorisation*) PA (system); (*d'une discothèque*) sound system.

sonore [sɔnɔʀ] *adj* (*voix*) sonorous, ringing; (*salle, métal*) resonant; (*ondes, film, signal*) sound *cpd*; (*LING*) voiced; **effets** ~**s** sound effects.

sonorisation [sɔnɔʀizɑsjɔ̃] *nf* (*installations*) public address system; (*d'une discothèque*) sound system.

sonoriser [sɔnɔʀize] *vt* (*film, spectacle*) to add the sound track to; (*salle*) to fit with a public address system.

sonorité [sɔnɔʀite] *nf* (*de piano, violon*) tone; (*de voix, mot*) sonority; (*d'une salle*) resonance; acoustics *pl*.

sonothèque [sɔnɔtɛk] *nf* sound library.

sont [sɔ̃] *vb voir* **être**.

sophisme [sɔfism(ə)] *nm* sophism.

sophiste [sɔfist(ə)] *nm/f* sophist.

sophistication [sɔfistikɑsjɔ̃] *nf* sophistication.

sophistiqué, e [sɔfistike] *adj* sophisticated.

soporifique [sɔpɔʀifik] *adj* soporific.

soprano [sɔpʀano] *nm/f* soprano (*pl* -s).

sorbet [sɔʀbɛ] *nm* water ice, sorbet.

sorbetière [sɔʀbətjɛʀ] *nf* ice-cream maker.

sorbier [sɔʀbje] *nm* service tree.

sorcellerie [sɔʀsɛlʀi] *nf* witchcraft *no pl*, sorcery *no pl*.

sorcier, ière [sɔʀsje, -jɛʀ] *nm/f* sorcerer/witch *ou* sorceress ♦ *adj*: **ce n'est pas** ~ (*fam*) it's as easy as pie.

sordide [sɔʀdid] *adj* sordid; squalid.

Sorlingues [sɔʀlɛ̃g] *nfpl*: **les (îles)** ~ the Scilly Isles, the Isles of Scilly, the Scillies.

sornettes [sɔʀnɛt] *nfpl* twaddle *sg*.

sort [sɔʀ] *vb voir* **sortir** ♦ *nm* (*fortune, destinée*) fate; (*condition, situation*) lot; (*magique*): **jeter un** ~ to cast a spell; **un coup du** ~ a blow dealt by fate; **le** ~ **en est jeté** the die is cast; **tirer au** ~ to draw lots; **tirer qch au** ~ to draw lots for sth.

sortable [sɔʀtabl(ə)] *adj*: **il n'est pas** ~ you can't take him anywhere.

sortant, e [sɔʀtɑ̃, -ɑ̃t] *vb voir* **sortir** ♦ *adj* (*numéro*) which comes up (*in a draw etc*); (*député, président*) outgoing.

sorte [sɔʀt(ə)] *vb voir* **sortir** ♦ *nf* sort, kind; **de la** ~ *adv* in that way; **en quelque** ~ in a way; **de** ~ **à** so as to, in order to; **de (telle)** ~ **que, en** ~ **que** (*de manière que*) so that; (*si bien que*) so much so that; **faire en** ~ **que** to see to it that.

sortie [sɔʀti] *nf* (*issue*) way out, exit; (*MIL*) sortie; (*fig: verbale*) outburst; sally; (*: parole incongrue*) odd remark; (*d'un gaz, de l'eau*) outlet; (*promenade*) outing; (*le soir: au restaurant etc*) night out; (*de produits*) export; (*de capitaux*) outflow; (*COMM: somme*): ~**s** items of expenditure; outgoings *sans sg*; (*INFORM*) output; (*d'imprimante*) printout; **à sa** ~ as he went out *ou* left; **à la ~ de l'école/l'usine** (*moment*) after school/work; when school/ the factory comes out; (*lieu*) at the school/ factory gates; **à la ~ de ce nouveau modèle** when this new model comes (*ou* came) out, when they bring (*ou* brought) out this new model; **~ de bain** (*vêtement*) bathrobe; **"~ de camions"** "vehicle exit"; **~ papier** hard copy; **~ de secours** emergency exit.

sortilège [sɔʀtilɛʒ] *nm* (magic) spell.

sortir [sɔʀtiʀ] *vi* (*gén*) to come out; (*partir, se promener, aller au spectacle etc*) to go out; (*bourgeon, plante, numéro gagnant*) to come up ♦ *vt* (*gén*) to take out; (*produit, ouvrage, modèle*) to bring out; (*boniments, incongruités*) to come out with; (*INFORM*) to output; (*: sur papier*) to print out; (*fam: expulser*) to throw out ♦ *nm*: **au ~ de l'hiver/l'enfance** as winter/childhood nears its end; **~ qch de** to take sth out of; **~ qn d'embarras** to get sb out of trouble; **~ de** (*gén*) to leave; (*endroit*) to go (*ou* come) out of, leave; (*rainure etc*) to come out of; (*maladie*) to get over; (*époque*) to get through; (*cadre, compétence*) to be outside; (*provenir de: famille etc*) to come from; **~ de table** to leave the table; **~ du système** (*INFORM*) to log out; **~ de ses gonds** (*fig*) to fly off the handle; **se ~ de** (*affaire, situation*) to get out of; **s'en ~** (*malade*) to pull through; (*d'une difficulté etc*) to come through all right; to get through, be able to manage.

SOS *sigle m* mayday, SOS.

sosie [sɔzi] *nm* double.

sot, sotte [so, sɔt] *adj* silly, foolish ♦ *nm/f* fool.

sottement [sɔtmɑ̃] *adv* foolishly.

sottise [sɔtiz] *nf* silliness *no pl*, foolishness *no pl*; (*propos, acte*) silly *ou* foolish thing (to do *ou* say).

sou [su] *nm*: **près de ses ~s** tight-fisted; **sans le ~** penniless; **~ à ~** penny by penny; **pas un ~ de bon sens** not a scrap *ou* an ounce of good sense; **de quatre ~s** worthless.

souahéli, e [swaeli] *adj* Swahili ♦ *nm* (*LING*) Swahili.

soubassement [subɑsmɑ̃] *nm* base.

soubresaut [subʀəso] *nm* (*de peur etc*) start; (*cahot: d'un véhicule*) jolt.

soubrette [subʀɛt] *nf* soubrette, maidservant.

souche [suʃ] *nf* (*d'arbre*) stump; (*de carnet*) counterfoil (*BRIT*), stub; **dormir comme une ~** to sleep like a log; **de vieille ~** of old stock.

souci [susi] *nm* (*inquiétude*) worry; (*préoccupation*) concern; (*BOT*) marigold; **se faire du ~** to worry; **avoir (le) ~ de** to have concern for; **par ~ de** for the sake of, out of concern for.

soucier [susje]: **se ~ de** *vt* to care about.

soucieux, euse [susjø, -øz] *adj* concerned, worried; **~ de** concerned about; **peu ~ de/ que** caring little about/whether.

soucoupe [sukup] *nf* saucer; **~ volante** flying saucer.

soudain, e [sudɛ̃, -ɛn] *adj* (*douleur, mort*) sudden ♦ *adv* suddenly, all of a sudden.

soudainement [sudɛnmɑ̃] *adv* suddenly.

soudaineté [sudɛnte] *nf* suddenness.

Soudan [sudɑ̃] *nm*: **le ~** the Sudan.

soudanais, e [sudanɛ, -ɛz] *adj* Sudanese.

soude [sud] *nf* soda.

soudé, e [sude] *adj* (*fig: pétales, organes*) joined (together).

souder [sude] *vt* (*avec fil à souder*) to solder; (*par soudure autogène*) to weld; (*fig*) to bind *ou* knit together; to fuse (together); **se ~** *vi* (*os*) to knit (together).

soudeur, euse [sudœʀ, -øz] *nm/f* (*ouvrier*) welder.

soudoyer [sudwaje] *vt* (*péj*) to bribe, buy over.

soudure [sudyʀ] *nf* soldering; welding; (*joint*) soldered joint; weld; **faire la ~** (*COMM*) to fill a gap; (*fig: assurer une transition*) to bridge the gap.

souffert, e [sufɛʀ, -ɛʀt(ə)] *pp de* **souffrir**.

soufflage [suflaʒ] *nm* (*du verre*) glass-blowing.

souffle [sufl(ə)] *nm* (*en expirant*) breath; (*en soufflant*) puff, blow; (*respiration*) breathing; (*d'explosion, de ventilateur*) blast; (*du vent*) blowing; (*fig*) inspiration; **retenir son ~** to hold one's breath; **avoir du/manquer de ~** to have a lot of puff/be short of breath; **être à bout de ~** to be out of breath; **avoir le ~ court** to be short-winded; **un ~ d'air** *ou* **de vent** a breath of air, a puff of wind; **~ au cœur** (*MÉD*) heart murmur.

soufflé, e [sufle] *adj* (*CULIN*) soufflé; (*fam: ahuri, stupéfié*) staggered ♦ *nm* (*CULIN*) soufflé.

souffler [sufle] *vi* (*gén*) to blow; (*haleter*) to puff (and blow) ♦ *vt* (*feu, bougie*) to blow out; (*chasser: poussière etc*) to blow away; (*TECH: verre*) to blow; (*suj: explosion*) to destroy (with its blast); (*dire*): **~ qch à qn** to whisper sth to sb; (*fam: voler*): **~ qch à qn** to pinch sth from sb; **~ son rôle à qn** to prompt sb; **ne pas ~ mot** not to breathe a word; **laisser ~ qn** (*fig*) to give sb a breather.

soufflet [suflɛ] *nm* (*instrument*) bellows *pl*; (*entre wagons*) vestibule; (*COUTURE*) gusset; (*gifle*) slap (in the face).

souffleur, euse [suflœʀ, -øz] *nm/f* (*THÉÂT*) prompter; (*TECH*) glass-blower.

souffrance [sufʀɑ̃s] *nf* suffering; **en ~** (*marchandise*) awaiting delivery; (*affaire*) pending.

souffrant, e [sufʀɑ̃, -ɑ̃t] *adj* unwell.

souffre-douleur [sufʀədulœʀ] *nm inv* whipping boy (*BRIT*), butt, underdog.

souffreteux, euse [sufʀətø, -øz] *adj* sickly.

souffrir [sufʀiʀ] *vi* to suffer; (*éprouver des douleurs*) to be in pain ♦ *vt* to suffer, endure; (*supporter*) to bear, stand; (*admettre: excep-*

tion etc) to allow *ou* admit of; ~ **de** (*maladie, froid*) to suffer from; ~ **des dents** to have trouble with one's teeth; **ne pas pouvoir** ~ **qch/que** ... not to be able to endure *ou* bear sth/that ...; **faire** ~ **qn** (*suj: personne*) to make sb suffer; (*: dents, blessure etc*) to hurt sb.

soufre [sufʀ(ə)] *nm* sulphur (*BRIT*), sulfur (*US*).

soufrer [sufʀe] *vt* (*vignes*) to treat with sulphur *ou* sulfur.

souhait [swɛ] *nm* wish; **tous nos ~s de** good wishes *ou* our best wishes for; **riche** *etc* **à** ~ as rich *etc* as one could wish; **à vos ~s!** bless you!

souhaitable [swɛtabl(ə)] *adj* desirable.

souhaiter [swete] *vt* to wish for; ~ **le bonjour à qn** to bid sb good day; ~ **la bonne année à qn** to wish sb a happy New Year; **il est à** ~ **que** it is to be hoped that.

souiller [suje] *vt* to dirty, soil; (*fig*) to sully, tarnish.

souillure [sujyʀ] *nf* stain.

soûl, e [su, sul] *adj* drunk; (*fig*): ~ **de musique/plaisirs** drunk with music/pleasure ♦ *nm*: **tout son** ~ to one's heart's content.

soulagement [sulaʒmɑ̃] *nm* relief.

soulager [sulaʒe] *vt* to relieve; ~ **qn de** to relieve sb of.

soûler [sule] *vt*: ~ **qn** to get sb drunk; (*suj: boisson*) to make sb drunk; (*fig*) to make sb's head spin *ou* reel; **se** ~ to get drunk; **se** ~ **de** (*fig*) to intoxicate o.s. with.

soûlerie [sulʀi] *nf* (*péj*) drunken binge.

soulèvement [sulɛvmɑ̃] *nm* uprising; (*GÉO*) upthrust.

soulever [sulve] *vt* to lift; (*vagues, poussière*) to send up; (*peuple*) to stir up (to revolt); (*enthousiasme*) to arouse; (*question, débat, protestations, difficultés*) to raise; **se** ~ *vi* (*peuple*) to rise up; (*personne couchée*) to lift o.s. up; (*couvercle etc*) to lift; **cela me soulève le cœur** it makes me feel sick.

soulier [sulje] *nm* shoe; **~s bas** low-heeled shoes; **~s plats/à talons** flat/heeled shoes.

souligner [suliɲe] *vt* to underline; (*fig*) to emphasize, stress.

soumettre [sumɛtʀ(ə)] *vt* (*pays*) to subject, subjugate; (*rebelles*) to put down, subdue; ~ **qn/qch à** to subject sb/sth to; ~ **qch à qn** (*projet etc*) to submit sth to sb; **se** ~ **(à)** (*se rendre, obéir*) to submit (to); **se** ~ **à** (*formalités etc*) to submit to; (*régime etc*) to submit o.s. to.

soumis, e [sumi, -iz] *pp de* **soumettre** ♦ *adj* submissive; **revenus** ~ **à l'impôt** taxable income.

soumission [sumisjɔ̃] *nf* (*voir se soumettre*) submission; (*docilité*) submissiveness; (*COMM*) tender.

soumissionner [sumisjɔne] *vt* (*COMM: travaux*) to bid for, tender for.

soupape [supap] *nf* valve; ~ **de sûreté** safety valve.

soupçon [supsɔ̃] *nm* suspicion; (*petite quantité*): **un** ~ **de** a hint *ou* touch of; **avoir** ~ **de** to suspect; **au dessus de tout** ~ above (all) suspicion.

soupçonner [supsɔne] *vt* to suspect; ~ **qn de qch/d'être** to suspect sb of sth/of being.

soupçonneux, euse [supsɔnø, -øz] *adj* suspicious.

soupe [sup] *nf* soup; ~ **au lait** *adj inv* quick-tempered; ~ **à l'oignon/de poisson** onion/fish soup; ~ **populaire** soup kitchen.

soupente [supɑ̃t] *nf* (*mansarde*) attic; (*placard*) cupboard (*BRIT*) *ou* closet (*US*) under the stairs.

souper [supe] *vi* to have supper ♦ *nm* supper; **avoir soupé de** (*fam*) to be sick and tired of.

soupeser [supəze] *vt* to weigh in one's hand(s), feel the weight of; (*fig*) to weigh up.

soupière [supjɛʀ] *nf* (soup) tureen.

soupir [supiʀ] *nm* sigh; (*MUS*) crotchet rest (*BRIT*), quarter note rest (*US*); **rendre le dernier** ~ to breathe one's last.

soupirail, aux [supiʀaj, -o] *nm* (small) basement window.

soupirant [supiʀɑ̃] *nm* (*péj*) suitor, wooer.

soupirer [supiʀe] *vi* to sigh; ~ **après qch** to yearn for sth.

souple [supl(ə)] *adj* supple; (*col*) soft; (*fig: règlement, caractère*) flexible; (*: démarche, taille*) lithe, supple; **disque(tte)** ~ (*INFORM*) floppy disk, diskette.

souplesse [suplɛs] *nf* suppleness; flexibility.

source [suʀs(ə)] *nf* (*point d'eau*) spring; (*d'un cours d'eau, fig*) source; **prendre sa** ~ **à/dans** (*suj: cours d'eau*) to have its source at/in; **tenir qch de bonne ~/de ~ sûre** to have sth on good authority/from a reliable source; ~ **thermale/d'eau minérale** hot *ou* thermal/mineral spring.

sourcier, ière [suʀsje, -jɛʀ] *nm* water diviner.

sourcil [suʀsij] *nm* (eye)brow.

sourcilière [suʀsiljɛʀ] *adj f voir* **arcade**.

sourciller [suʀsije] *vi*: **sans** ~ without turning a hair *ou* batting an eyelid.

sourcilleux, euse [suʀsijø, -øz] *adj* (*hautain, sévère*) haughty, supercilious; (*pointilleux*) finicky, pernickety.

sourd, e [suʀ, suʀd(ə)] *adj* deaf; (*bruit, voix*) muffled; (*couleur*) muted; (*douleur*) dull; (*lutte*) silent, hidden; (*LING*) voiceless ♦ *nm/f* deaf person; **être** ~ **à** to be deaf to.

sourdement [suʀdəmɑ̃] *adv* (*avec un bruit sourd*) dully; (*secrètement*) silently.

sourdine [suʀdin] *nf* (*MUS*) mute; **en** ~ *adv* softly, quietly; **mettre une** ~ **à** (*fig*) to tone down.

sourd-muet, sourde-muette [suʀmyɛ, suʀdmyɛt] *adj* deaf-and-dumb ♦ *nm/f* deaf-mute.

sourdre [suʀdʀ(ə)] *vi* (*eau*) to spring up; (*fig*) to rise.

souriant, e [suʀjɑ̃, -ɑ̃t] *vb voir* **sourire** ♦ *adj* cheerful.
souricière [suʀisjɛʀ] *nf* mousetrap; (*fig*) trap.
sourie [suʀi] *etc vb voir* **sourire**.
sourire [suʀiʀ] *nm* smile ♦ *vi* to smile; ~ **à qn** to smile at sb; (*fig*) to appeal to sb; (*: chance*) to smile on sb; **faire un** ~ **à qn** to give sb a smile; **garder le** ~ to keep smiling.
souris [suʀi] *nf* mouse (*pl* mice); (*INFORM*) mouse.
sournois, e [suʀnwa, -waz] *adj* deceitful, underhand.
sournoisement [suʀnwazmɑ̃] *adv* deceitfully.
sournoiserie [suʀnwazʀi] *nf* deceitfulness, underhandedness.
sous [su] *prép* (*gén*) under; ~ **la pluie/le soleil** in the rain/sunshine; ~ **mes yeux** before my eyes; ~ **terre** *adj, adv* underground; ~ **vide** *adj, adv* vacuum-packed; ~ **l'influence/l'action de** under the influence of/by the action of; ~ **antibiotiques/perfusion** on antibiotics/a drip; ~ **cet angle/ce rapport** from this angle/in this respect; ~ **peu** *adv* shortly, before long.
sous... [su, suz + *vowel*] *préfixe* sub-; under....
sous-alimentation [suzalimɑ̃tɑsjɔ̃] *nf* undernourishment.
sous-alimenté, e [suzalimɑ̃te] *adj* undernourished.
sous-bois [subwa] *nm inv* undergrowth.
sous-catégorie [sukategɔʀi] *nf* subcategory.
sous-chef [suʃɛf] *nm* deputy chief, second in command; ~ **de bureau** deputy head clerk.
sous-comité [sukɔmite] *nm* subcommittee.
sous-commission [sukɔmisjɔ̃] *nf* subcommittee.
sous-continent [sukɔ̃tinɑ̃] *nm* subcontinent.
sous-couche [sukuʃ] *nf* (*de peinture*) undercoat.
souscripteur, trice [suskʀiptœʀ, -tʀis] *nm/f* subscriber.
souscription [suskʀipsjɔ̃] *nf* subscription; **offert en** ~ available on subscription.
souscrire [suskʀiʀ]: ~ **à** *vt* to subscribe to.
sous-cutané, e [sukytane] *adj* subcutaneous.
sous-développé, e [sudevlɔpe] *adj* underdeveloped.
sous-développement [sudevlɔpmɑ̃] *nm* underdevelopment.
sous-directeur, trice [sudiʀɛktœʀ, -tʀis] *nm/f* assistant manager/manageress, submanager/manageress.
sous-emploi [suzɑ̃plwa] *nm* underemployment.
sous-employé, e [suzɑ̃plwaje] *adj* underemployed.
sous-ensemble [suzɑ̃sɑ̃bl(ə)] *nm* subset.
sous-entendre [suzɑ̃tɑ̃dʀ(ə)] *vt* to imply, infer.
sous-entendu, e [suzɑ̃tɑ̃dy] *adj* implied; (*LING*) understood ♦ *nm* innuendo, insinuation.
sous-équipé, e [suzekipe] *adj* underequipped; ~ **en infrastructures industrielles** (*ÉCON: pays, région*) with an insufficient industrial infrastructure.
sous-estimer [suzɛstime] *vt* to underestimate.
sous-exploiter [suzɛksplwate] *vt* to underexploit.
sous-exposer [suzɛkspoze] *vt* to underexpose.
sous-fifre [sufifʀ(ə)] *nm* (*péj*) underling.
sous-groupe [sugʀup] *nm* subgroup.
sous-homme [suzɔm] *nm* sub-human.
sous-jacent, e [suʒasɑ̃, -ɑ̃t] *adj* underlying.
sous-lieutenant [suljøtnɑ̃] *nm* sub-lieutenant.
sous-locataire [sulɔkatɛʀ] *nm/f* subtenant.
sous-location [sulɔkɑsjɔ̃] *nf* subletting.
sous-louer [sulwe] *vt* to sublet.
sous-main [sumɛ̃] *nm inv* desk blotter; **en** ~ *adv* secretly.
sous-marin, e [sumaʀɛ̃, -in] *adj* (*flore, volcan*) submarine; (*navigation, pêche, explosif*) underwater ♦ *nm* submarine.
sous-médicalisé, e [sumedikalize] *adj* lacking adequate medical care.
sous-nappe [sunap] *nf* undercloth.
sous-officier [suzɔfisje] *nm* ≈ non-commissioned officer (NCO).
sous-ordre [suzɔʀdʀ(ə)] *nm* subordinate; **créancier en** ~ creditor's creditor.
sous-payé, e [supeje] *adj* underpaid.
sous-préfecture [supʀefɛktyʀ] *nf* subprefecture.
sous-préfet [supʀefɛ] *nm* sub-prefect.
sous-production [supʀɔdyksjɔ̃] *nf* underproduction.
sous-produit [supʀɔdɥi] *nm* by-product; (*fig: péj*) pale imitation.
sous-programme [supʀɔgʀam] *nm* (*INFORM*) subroutine.
sous-pull [supul] *nm* thin poloneck sweater.
sous-secrétaire [susəkʀetɛʀ] *nm*: ~ **d'État** Under-Secretary of State.
soussigné, e [susiɲe] *adj*: **je** ~ I the undersigned.
sous-sol [susɔl] *nm* basement; (*GÉO*) subsoil.
sous-tasse [sutas] *nf* saucer.
sous-tendre [sutɑ̃dʀ(ə)] *vt* to underlie.
sous-titre [sutitʀ(ə)] *nm* subtitle.
sous-titré, e [sutitʀe] *adj* with subtitles.
soustraction [sustʀaksjɔ̃] *nf* subtraction.
soustraire [sustʀɛʀ] *vt* to subtract, take away; (*dérober*): ~ **qch à qn** to remove sth from sb; ~ **qn à** (*danger*) to shield sb from; **se** ~ **à** (*autorité, obligation, devoir*) to elude, escape from.
sous-traitance [sutʀɛtɑ̃s(ə)] *nf* subcontracting.
sous-traitant [sutʀɛtɑ̃] *nm* subcontractor.
sous-traiter [sutʀete] *vt, vi* to subcontract.
soustrayais [sustʀɛjɛ] *etc vb voir* **soustraire**.
sous-verre [suvɛʀ] *nm inv* glass mount.

sous-vêtement [suvɛtmɑ̃] *nm* undergarment, item of underwear; ~**s** *nmpl* underwear *sg.*
soutane [sutan] *nf* cassock, soutane.
soute [sut] *nf* hold; ~ **à bagages** baggage hold.
soutenable [sutnabl(ə)] *adj* (*opinion*) tenable, defensible.
soutenance [sutnɑ̃s] *nf*: ~ **de thèse** ≈ viva (voce).
soutènement [sutɛnmɑ̃] *nm*: **mur de** ~ retaining wall.
souteneur [sutnœʀ] *nm* procurer.
soutenir [sutniʀ] *vt* to support; (*assaut, choc, regard*) to stand up to, withstand; (*intérêt, effort*) to keep up; (*assurer*): ~ **que** to maintain that; **se** ~ (*dans l'eau etc*) to hold o.s. up; (*être soutenable: point de vue*) to be tenable; (*s'aider mutuellement*) to stand by each other; ~ **la comparaison avec** to bear *ou* stand comparison with; ~ **le regard de qn** to be able to look sb in the face.
soutenu, e [sutny] *pp de* **soutenir** ♦ *adj* (*efforts*) sustained, unflagging; (*style*) elevated; (*couleur*) strong.
souterrain, e [sutɛʀɛ̃, -ɛn] *adj* underground; (*fig*) subterranean ♦ *nm* underground passage.
soutien [sutjɛ̃] *nm* support; **apporter son** ~ **à** to lend one's support to; ~ **de famille** breadwinner.
soutiendrai [sutjɛ̃dʀe] *etc vb voir* **soutenir**.
soutien-gorge, *pl* **soutiens-gorge** [sutjɛ̃gɔʀʒ(ə)] *nm* bra; (*de maillot de bain*) top.
soutiens [sutjɛ̃], **soutint** [sutɛ̃] *etc vb voir* **soutenir**.
soutirer [sutiʀe] *vt*: ~ **qch à qn** to squeeze *ou* get sth out of sb.
souvenance [suvnɑ̃s] *nf*: **avoir** ~ **de** to recollect.
souvenir [suvniʀ] *nm* (*réminiscence*) memory; (*cadeau*) souvenir, keepsake; (*de voyage*) souvenir ♦ *vb*: **se** ~ **de** *vt* to remember; **se** ~ **que** to remember that; **garder le** ~ **de** to retain the memory of; **en** ~ **de** in memory *ou* remembrance of; **avec mes affectueux/meilleurs** ~**s,** ... with love from, .../ regards, ...
souvent [suvɑ̃] *adv* often; **peu** ~ seldom, infrequently; **le plus** ~ more often than not, most often.
souvenu, e [suvəny] *pp de* **se souvenir**.
souverain, e [suvʀɛ̃, -ɛn] *adj* sovereign; (*fig: mépris*) supreme ♦ *nm/f* sovereign, monarch.
souverainement [suvʀɛnmɑ̃] *adv* (*sans appel*) with sovereign power; (*extrêmement*) supremely, intensely.
souveraineté [suvʀɛnte] *nf* sovereignty.
souviendrai [suvjɛ̃dʀe], **souviens** [suvjɛ̃], **souvint** [suvɛ̃] *etc vb voir* **se souvenir**.
soviétique [sɔvjetik] *adj* Soviet ♦ *nm/f*: **S**~ Soviet citizen.
soviétiser [sɔvjetize] *vt* to sovietize.
soviétologue [sɔvjetɔlɔg] *nm/f* Kremlinologist.
soyeux, euse [swajø, -øz] *adj* silky.
soyez [swaje] *etc vb voir* **être**.
SPA *sigle f* (= *Société protectrice des animaux*) ≈ RSPCA (*BRIT*), ≈ SPCA (*US*).
spacieux, euse [spasjø, -øz] *adj* spacious; roomy.
spaciosité [spasjɔzite] *nf* spaciousness.
spaghettis [spageti] *nmpl* spaghetti *sg.*
sparadrap [spaʀadʀa] *nm* adhesive *ou* sticking (*BRIT*) plaster, bandaid ® (*US*).
Sparte [spaʀt(ə)] *nf* Sparta.
spartiate [spaʀsjat] *adj* Spartan; ~**s** *nfpl* (*sandales*) Roman sandals.
spasme [spazm(ə)] *nm* spasm.
spasmodique [spazmɔdik] *adj* spasmodic.
spatial, e, aux [spasjal, -o] *adj* (*AVIAT*) space *cpd*; (*PSYCH*) spatial.
spatule [spatyl] *nf* (*ustensile*) slice; spatula; (*bout*) tip.
speaker, ine [spikœʀ, -kʀin] *nm/f* announcer.
spécial, e, aux [spesjal, -o] *adj* special; (*bizarre*) peculiar.
spécialement [spesjalmɑ̃] *adv* especially, particularly; (*tout exprès*) specially; **pas** ~ not particularly.
spécialisation [spesjalizɑsjɔ̃] *nf* specialization.
spécialisé, e [spesjalize] *adj* specialised; **ordinateur** ~ dedicated computer.
spécialiser [spesjalize]: **se** ~ *vi* to specialize.
spécialiste [spesjalist(ə)] *nm/f* specialist.
spécialité [spesjalite] *nf* speciality; (*SCOL*) special field; ~ **pharmaceutique** patent medicine.
spécieux, euse [spesjø, -øz] *adj* specious.
spécification [spesifikɑsjɔ̃] *nf* specification.
spécificité [spesifisite] *nf* specificity.
spécifier [spesifje] *vt* to specify, state.
spécifique [spesifik] *adj* specific.
spécifiquement [spesifikmɑ̃] *adv* (*typiquement*) typically; (*tout exprès*) specifically.
spécimen [spesimɛn] *nm* specimen; (*revue etc*) specimen *ou* sample copy.
spectacle [spɛktakl(ə)] *nm* (*tableau, scène*) sight; (*représentation*) show; (*industrie*) show business, entertainment; **se donner en** ~ (*péj*) to make a spectacle *ou* an exhibition of o.s; **pièce/revue à grand** ~ spectacular (play/revue); **au** ~ **de** ... at the sight of ....
spectaculaire [spɛktakylɛʀ] *adj* spectacular.
spectateur, trice [spɛktatœʀ, -tʀis] *nm/f* (*CINÉ etc*) member of the audience; (*SPORT*) spectator; (*d'un événement*) onlooker, witness.
spectre [spɛktʀ(ə)] *nm* (*fantôme, fig*) spectre; (*PHYSIQUE*) spectrum (*pl* -a); ~ **solaire** solar spectrum.
spéculateur, trice [spekylatœʀ, -tʀis] *nm/f* speculator.
spéculatif, ive [spekylatif, -iv] *adj* speculative.

spéculation [spekylɑsjɔ̃] *nf* speculation.
spéculer [spekyle] *vi* to speculate; ~ **sur** (*COMM*) to speculate in; (*réfléchir*) to speculate on; (*tabler sur*) to bank *ou* rely on.
spéléologie [speleɔlɔʒi] *nf* (*étude*) speleology; (*activité*) potholing.
spéléologue [speleɔlɔg] *nm/f* speleologist; potholer.
spermatozoïde [spɛʀmatozɔid] *nm* sperm, spermatozoon (*pl* -zoa).
sperme [spɛʀm(ə)] *nm* semen, sperm.
spermicide [spɛʀmisid] *adj, nm* spermicide.
sphère [sfɛʀ] *nf* sphere.
sphérique [sfeʀik] *adj* spherical.
sphincter [sfɛ̃ktɛʀ] *nm* sphincter.
sphinx [sfɛ̃ks] *nm inv* sphinx; (*ZOOL*) hawkmoth.
spiral, aux [spiʀal, -o] *nm* hairspring.
spirale [spiʀal] *nf* spiral; **en** ~ in a spiral.
spire [spiʀ] *nf* (*d'une spirale*) turn; (*d'une coquille*) whorl.
spiritisme [spiʀitism(ə)] *nm* spiritualism, spiritism.
spirituel, le [spiʀitɥɛl] *adj* spiritual; (*fin, piquant*) witty; **musique ~le** sacred music; **concert** ~ concert of sacred music.
spirituellement [spiʀitɥɛlmɑ̃] *adv* spiritually; wittily.
spiritueux [spiʀitɥø] *nm* spirit.
splendeur [splɑ̃dœʀ] *nf* splendour (*BRIT*), splendor (*US*).
splendide [splɑ̃did] *adj* splendid, magnificent.
spolier [spɔlje] *vt*: ~ **qn (de)** to despoil sb (of).
spongieux, euse [spɔ̃ʒjø, -øz] *adj* spongy.
sponsor [spɔ̃sɔʀ] *nm* sponsor.
sponsoriser [spɔ̃sɔʀize] *vt* to sponsor.
spontané, e [spɔ̃tane] *adj* spontaneous.
spontanéité [spɔ̃taneite] *nf* spontaneity.
spontanément [spɔ̃tanemɑ̃] *adv* spontaneously.
sporadique [spɔʀadik] *adj* sporadic.
sporadiquement [spɔʀadikmɑ̃] *adv* sporadically.
sport [spɔʀ] *nm* sport ♦ *adj inv* (*vêtement*) casual; (*fair-play*) sporting; **faire du** ~ to do sport; ~ **individuel/d'équipe** individual/team sport; ~ **de combat** combative sport; **~s d'hiver** winter sports.
sportif, ive [spɔʀtif, -iv] *adj* (*journal, association, épreuve*) sports *cpd*; (*allure, démarche*) athletic; (*attitude, esprit*) sporting; **les résultats ~s** the sports results.
sportivement [spɔʀtivmɑ̃] *adv* sportingly.
sportivité [spɔʀtivite] *nf* sportsmanship.
spot [spɔt] *nm* (*lampe*) spot(light); (*annonce*): ~ **(publicitaire)** commercial (break).
spray [spʀɛ] *nm* spray, aerosol.
sprint [spʀint] *nm* sprint; **piquer un** ~ to put on a (final) spurt.
sprinter *nm* [spʀintœʀ] sprinter ♦ *vi* [spʀinte] to sprint.
squale [skwal] *nm* (*type of*) shark.
square [skwaʀ] *nm* public garden(s).
squash [skwaʃ] *nm* squash.
squat [skwat] *nm* (*lieu*) squat.
squatter *nm* [skwatœʀ] squatter ♦ *vt* [skwate] to squat.
squelette [skəlɛt] *nm* skeleton.
squelettique [skəletik] *adj* scrawny; (*fig*) skimpy.
Sri Lanka [sʀilɑ̃ka] *nm* Sri Lanka.
sri-lankais, e [sʀilɑ̃kɛ, -ɛz] *adj* Sri-Lankan.
SS *sigle f* = **sécurité sociale**; (= *Sa Sainteté*) HH.
ss *abr* = **sous.**
S/S *sigle m* (= *steamship*) SS.
SSR *sigle f* (= *Société suisse romande*) *the Swiss French-language broadcasting company*.
stabilisateur, trice [stabilizatœʀ, -tʀis] *adj* stabilizing ♦ *nm* stabilizer; (*véhicule*) anti-roll device; (*avion*) tailplane.
stabiliser [stabilize] *vt* to stabilize; (*terrain*) to consolidate.
stabilité [stabilite] *nf* stability.
stable [stabl(ə)] *adj* stable, steady.
stade [stad] *nm* (*SPORT*) stadium; (*phase, niveau*) stage.
stadier [stadje] *nm* steward (*working in a stadium*).
stage [staʒ] *nm* training period; training course; (*d'avocat stagiaire*) articles *pl*.
stagiaire [staʒjɛʀ] *nm/f, adj* trainee (*cpd*).
stagnant, e [stagnɑ̃, -ɑ̃t] *adj* stagnant.
stagnation [stagnɑsjɔ̃] *nf* stagnation.
stagner [stagne] *vi* to stagnate.
stalactite [stalaktit] *nf* stalactite.
stalagmite [stalagmit] *nf* stalagmite.
stalle [stal] *nf* stall, box.
stand [stɑ̃d] *nm* (*d'exposition*) stand; (*de foire*) stall; ~ **de tir** (*à la foire, SPORT*) shooting range; ~ **de ravitaillement** pit.
standard [stɑ̃daʀ] *adj inv* standard ♦ *nm* (*type, norme*) standard; (*TÉL*) switchboard.
standardisation [stɑ̃daʀdizɑsjɔ̃] *nf* standardization.
standardiser [stɑ̃daʀdize] *vt* to standardize.
standardiste [stɑ̃daʀdist(ə)] *nm/f* switchboard operator.
standing [stɑ̃diŋ] *nm* standing; **immeuble de grand** ~ block of luxury flats (*BRIT*), condo(minium) (*US*).
star [staʀ] *nf* star.
starlette [staʀlɛt] *nf* starlet.
starter [staʀtɛʀ] *nm* (*AUTO*) choke; (*SPORT*: *personne*) starter; **mettre le** ~ to pull out the choke.
station [stɑsjɔ̃] *nf* station; (*de bus*) stop; (*de villégiature*) resort; (*posture*): **la** ~ **debout** standing, an upright posture; ~ **balnéaire** seaside resort; ~ **de graissage** lubrication bay; ~ **de lavage** carwash; ~ **de ski** ski resort; ~ **de sports d'hiver** winter sports resort; ~ **de taxis** taxi rank (*BRIT*) *ou* stand (*US*); ~ **thermale** thermal spa; ~ **de travail** workstation.
stationnaire [stasjɔnɛʀ] *adj* stationary.

stationnement [stasjɔnmɑ̃] *nm* parking; **zone de ~ interdit** no parking area; **~ alterné** parking on alternate sides.
stationner [stasjɔne] *vi* to park.
station-service [stasjɔ̃sɛʀvis] *nf* service station.
statique [statik] *adj* static.
statisticien, ne [statistisjɛ̃, -ɛn] *nm/f* statistician.
statistique [statistik] *nf (science)* statistics *sg*; *(rapport, étude)* statistic ♦ *adj* statistical; **~s** *nfpl (données)* statistics *pl*.
statistiquement [statistikmɑ̃] *adv* statistically.
statue [staty] *nf* statue.
statuer [statɥe] *vi*: **~ sur** to rule on, give a ruling on.
statuette [statɥɛt] *nf* statuette.
statu quo [statykwo] *nm* status quo.
stature [statyʀ] *nf* stature; **de haute ~** of great stature.
statut [staty] *nm* status; **~s** *nmpl (JUR, ADMIN)* statutes.
statutaire [statytɛʀ] *adj* statutory.
St(e) *abr (= Saint(e))* St.
Sté *abr (= société)* soc.
steak [stɛk] *nm* steak.
stèle [stɛl] *nf* stela, stele.
stellaire [stelɛʀ] *adj* stellar.
stencil [stɛnsil] *nm* stencil.
sténodactylo [stenɔdaktilo] *nm/f* shorthand typist *(BRIT)*, stenographer *(US)*.
sténodactylographie [stenɔdaktilɔgʀafi] *nf* shorthand typing *(BRIT)*, stenography *(US)*.
sténo(graphe) [stenɔ(gʀaf)] *nm/f* shorthand typist *(BRIT)*, stenographer *(US)*.
sténo(graphie) [stenɔ(gʀafi)] *nf* shorthand; **prendre en ~** to take down in shorthand.
sténographier [stenɔgʀafje] *vt* to take down in shorthand.
sténographique [stenɔgʀafik] *adj* shorthand *cpd*.
stentor [stɑ̃tɔʀ] *nm*: **voix de ~** stentorian voice.
step [stɛp] *nm* ® step aerobics *sg* ®, step Reebok ®.
stéphanois, e [stefanwa, -waz] *adj* of *ou* from Saint-Étienne.
steppe [stɛp] *nf* steppe.
stère [stɛʀ] *nm* stere.
stéréo(phonie) [steʀeɔ(fɔni)] *nf* stereo(phony); **émission en ~** stereo broadcast.
stéréo(phonique) [steʀeɔ(fɔnik)] *adj* stereo(phonic).
stéréoscope [steʀeɔskɔp] *nm* stereoscope.
stéréoscopique [steʀeɔskɔpik] *adj* stereoscopic.
stéréotype [steʀeɔtip] *nm* stereotype.
stéréotypé, e [steʀeɔtipe] *adj* stereotyped.
stérile [steʀil] *adj* sterile; *(terre)* barren; *(fig)* fruitless, futile.
stérilement [steʀilmɑ̃] *adv* fruitlessly.
stérilet [steʀilɛ] *nm* coil, loop.
stérilisateur [steʀilizatœʀ] *nm* sterilizer.
stérilisation [steʀilizɑsjɔ̃] *nf* sterilization.
stériliser [steʀilize] *vt* to sterilize.
stérilité [steʀilite] *nf* sterility.
sternum [stɛʀnɔm] *nm* breastbone, sternum.
stéthoscope [stetɔskɔp] *nm* stethoscope.
stick [stik] *nm* stick.
stigmates [stigmat] *nmpl* scars, marks; *(REL)* stigmata *pl*.
stigmatiser [stigmatize] *vt* to denounce, stigmatize.
stimulant, e [stimylɑ̃, -ɑ̃t] *adj* stimulating ♦ *nm (MÉD)* stimulant; *(fig)* stimulus *(pl* -i), incentive.
stimulateur [stimylatœʀ] *nm*: **~ cardiaque** pacemaker.
stimulation [stimylɑsjɔ̃] *nf* stimulation.
stimuler [stimyle] *vt* to stimulate.
stimulus, i [stimylys, -i] *nm* stimulus *(pl* -i).
stipulation [stipylɑsjɔ̃] *nf* stipulation.
stipuler [stipyle] *vt* to stipulate, specify.
stock [stɔk] *nm* stock; **en ~** in stock.
stockage [stɔkaʒ] *nm* stocking; storage.
stocker [stɔke] *vt* to stock; *(déchets)* to store.
Stockholm [stɔkɔlm] *n* Stockholm.
stockiste [stɔkist(ə)] *nm* stockist.
stoïcisme [stɔisism(ə)] *nm* stoicism.
stoïque [stɔik] *adj* stoic, stoical.
stoïquement [stɔikmɑ̃] *adv* stoically.
stomacal, e, aux [stɔmakal, -o] *adj* gastric, stomach *cpd*.
stomatologie [stɔmatɔlɔʒi] *nf* stomatology.
stomatologue [stɔmatɔlɔg] *nm/f* stomatologist.
stop [stɔp] *nm (AUTO: écriteau)* stop sign; *(: signal)* brake-light; *(dans un télégramme)* stop ♦ *excl* stop!
stoppage [stɔpaʒ] *nm* invisible mending.
stopper [stɔpe] *vt* to stop, halt; *(COUTURE)* to mend ♦ *vi* to stop, halt.
store [stɔʀ] *nm* blind; *(de magasin)* shade, awning.
strabisme [stʀabism(ə)] *nm* squint(ing).
strangulation [stʀɑ̃gylɑsjɔ̃] *nf* strangulation.
strapontin [stʀapɔ̃tɛ̃] *nm* jump *ou* foldaway seat.
Strasbourg [stʀazbuʀ] *n* Strasbourg.
strass [stʀas] *nm* paste, strass.
stratagème [stʀataʒɛm] *nm* stratagem.
strate [stʀat] *nf (GÉO)* stratum, layer.
stratège [stʀatɛʒ] *nm* strategist.
stratégie [stʀateʒi] *nf* strategy.
stratégique [stʀateʒik] *adj* strategic.
stratégiquement [stʀateʒikmɑ̃] *adv* strategically.
stratifié, e [stʀatifje] *adj (GÉO)* stratified; *(TECH)* laminated.
stratosphère [stʀatɔsfɛʀ] *nf* stratosphere.
stress [stʀɛs] *nm inv* stress.
stressant, e [stʀɛsɑ̃, -ɑ̃t] *adj* stressful.

stresser [stʀɛse] *vt* to stress, cause stress in.
strict, e [stʀikt(ə)] *adj* strict; (*tenue, décor*) severe, plain; **son droit le plus** ~ his most basic right; **dans la plus** ~**e intimité** strictly in private; **le** ~ **nécessaire/minimum** the bare essentials/minimum.
strictement [stʀiktəmɑ̃] *adv* strictly; plainly.
strident, e [stʀidɑ̃, -ɑ̃t] *adj* shrill, strident.
stridulations [stʀidylɑsjɔ̃] *nfpl* stridulations, chirrings.
strie [stʀi] *nf* streak; (*ANAT, GÉO*) stria (*pl* -ae).
strier [stʀije] *vt* to streak; to striate.
strip-tease [stʀiptiz] *nm* striptease.
strip-teaseuse [stʀiptizøz] *nf* stripper, striptease artist.
striures [stʀijyʀ] *nfpl* streaking *sg*.
stroboscope [stʀɔbɔskɔp] *nm* strobe (light).
strophe [stʀɔf] *nf* verse, stanza.
structure [stʀyktyʀ] *nf* structure; ~**s d'accueil/touristiques** reception/tourist facilities.
structurer [stʀyktyʀe] *vt* to structure.
strychnine [stʀiknin] *nf* strychnine.
stuc [styk] *nm* stucco.
studieusement [stydjøzmɑ̃] *adv* studiously.
studieux, euse [stydjø, -øz] *adj* (*élève*) studious; (*vacances*) study *cpd*.
studio [stydjo] *nm* (*logement*) studio flat (*BRIT*) *ou* apartment (*US*); (*d'artiste, TV etc*) studio (*pl* -s).
stupéfaction [stypefaksjɔ̃] *nf* stupefaction, astonishment.
stupéfait, e [stypefɛ, -ɛt] *adj* astonished.
stupéfiant, e [stypefjɑ̃, -ɑ̃t] *adj* stunning, astonishing ♦ *nm* (*MÉD*) drug, narcotic.
stupéfier [stypefje] *vt* to stupefy; (*étonner*) to stun, astonish.
stupeur [stypœʀ] *nf* (*inertie, insensibilité*) stupor; (*étonnement*) astonishment, amazement.
stupide [stypid] *adj* stupid; (*hébété*) stunned.
stupidement [stypidmɑ̃] *adv* stupidly.
stupidité [stypidite] *nf* stupidity *no pl*; (*propos, action*) stupid thing (to say *ou* do).
stups [styp] *nmpl* (= *stupéfiants*): **brigade des** ~ narcotics bureau *ou* squad.
style [stil] *nm* style; **meuble/robe de** ~ piece of period furniture/period dress; ~ **de vie** lifestyle.
stylé, e [stile] *adj* well-trained.
stylet [stilɛ] *nm* (*poignard*) stiletto; (*CHIRURGIE*) stylet.
stylisé, e [stilize] *adj* stylized.
styliste [stilist(ə)] *nm/f* designer; stylist.
stylistique [stilistik] *nf* stylistics *sg* ♦ *adj* stylistic.
stylo [stilo] *nm*: ~ **(à encre)** (fountain) pen; ~ **(à) bille** ballpoint pen.
stylo-feutre [stilɔføtʀ(ə)] *nm* felt-tip pen.
su, e [sy] *pp de* **savoir** ♦ *nm*: **au** ~ **de** with the knowledge of.
suaire [sɥɛʀ] *nm* shroud.
suant, e [sɥɑ̃, -ɑ̃t] *adj* sweaty.
suave [sɥav] *adj* (*odeur*) sweet; (*voix*) suave, smooth; (*coloris*) soft, mellow.
subalterne [sybaltɛʀn(ə)] *adj* (*employé, officier*) junior; (*rôle*) subordinate, subsidiary ♦ *nm/f* subordinate, inferior.
subconscient [sypkɔ̃sjɑ̃] *nm* subconscious.
subdiviser [sybdivize] *vt* to subdivide.
subdivision [sybdivizjɔ̃] *nf* subdivision.
subir [sybiʀ] *vt* (*affront, dégâts, mauvais traitements*) to suffer; (*influence, charme*) to be under, be subjected to; (*traitement, opération, châtiment*) to undergo; (*personne*) to suffer, be subjected to.
subit, e [sybi, -it] *adj* sudden.
subitement [sybitmɑ̃] *adv* suddenly, all of a sudden.
subjectif, ive [sybʒɛktif, -iv] *adj* subjective.
subjectivement [sybʒɛktivmɑ̃] *adv* subjectively.
subjectivité [sybʒɛktivite] *nf* subjectivity.
subjonctif [sybʒɔ̃ktif] *nm* subjunctive.
subjuguer [sybʒyge] *vt* to subjugate.
sublime [syblim] *adj* sublime.
sublimer [syblime] *vt* to sublimate.
submergé, e [sybmɛʀʒe] *adj* submerged; (*fig*): ~ **de** snowed under with; overwhelmed with.
submerger [sybmɛʀʒe] *vt* to submerge; (*suj: foule*) to engulf; (*fig*) to overwhelm.
submersible [sybmɛʀsibl(ə)] *nm* submarine.
subordination [sybɔʀdinɑsjɔ̃] *nf* subordination.
subordonné, e [sybɔʀdɔne] *adj, nm/f* subordinate; ~ **à** (*personne*) subordinate to; (*résultats etc*) subject to, depending on.
subordonner [sybɔʀdɔne] *vt*: ~ **qn/qch à** to subordinate sb/sth to.
subornation [sybɔʀnɑsjɔ̃] *nf* bribing.
suborner [sybɔʀne] *vt* to bribe.
subrepticement [sybʀɛptismɑ̃] *adv* surreptitiously.
subroger [sybʀɔʒe] *vt* (*JUR*) to subrogate.
subside [sypsid] *nm* grant.
subsidiaire [sypsidjɛʀ] *adj* subsidiary; **question** ~ deciding question.
subsistance [sybzistɑ̃s] *nf* subsistence; **pourvoir à la** ~ **de qn** to keep sb, provide for sb's subsistence *ou* keep.
subsister [sybziste] *vi* (*rester*) to remain, subsist; (*vivre*) to live; (*survivre*) to live on.
subsonique [sybsɔnik] *adj* subsonic.
substance [sypstɑ̃s] *nf* substance; **en** ~ in substance.
substantiel, le [sypstɑ̃sjɛl] *adj* substantial.
substantif [sypstɑ̃tif] *nm* noun, substantive.
substantiver [sypstɑ̃tive] *vt* to nominalize.
substituer [sypstitɥe] *vt*: ~ **qn/qch à** to substitute sb/sth for; **se** ~ **à qn** (*représenter*) to substitute for sb; (*évincer*) to substitute o.s. for sb.
substitut [sypstity] *nm* (*JUR*) deputy public

prosecutor; (*succédané*) substitute.
substitution [sypstitysjɔ̃] *nf* substitution.
subterfuge [syptɛʀfyʒ] *nm* subterfuge.
subtil, e [syptil] *adj* subtle.
subtilement [syptilmɑ̃] *adv* subtly.
subtiliser [syptilize] *vt*: ~ **qch (à qn)** to spirit sth away (from sb).
subtilité [syptilite] *nf* subtlety.
subtropical, e, aux [sybtʀɔpikal, -o] *adj* subtropical.
suburbain, e [sybyʀbɛ̃, -ɛn] *adj* suburban.
subvenir [sybvəniʀ]: ~ **à** *vt* to meet.
subvention [sybvɑ̃sjɔ̃] *nf* subsidy, grant.
subventionner [sybvɑ̃sjɔne] *vt* to subsidize.
subversif, ive [sybvɛʀsif, -iv] *adj* subversive.
subversion [sybvɛʀsjɔ̃] *nf* subversion.
suc [syk] *nm* (*BOT*) sap; (*de viande, fruit*) juice; ~**s gastriques** gastric juices.
succédané [syksedane] *nm* substitute.
succéder [syksede]: ~ **à** *vt* (*directeur, roi etc*) to succeed; (*venir après: dans une série*) to follow, succeed; **se** ~ *vi* (*accidents, années*) to follow one another.
succès [syksɛ] *nm* success; **avec** ~ successfully; **sans** ~ unsuccessfully; **avoir du** ~ to be a success, be successful; **à** ~ successful; **livre à** ~ bestseller; ~ **de librairie** bestseller; ~ **(féminins)** conquests.
successeur [syksesœʀ] *nm* successor.
successif, ive [syksesif, -iv] *adj* successive.
succession [syksesjɔ̃] *nf* (*série, POL*) succession; (*JUR: patrimoine*) estate, inheritance; **prendre la** ~ **de** (*directeur*) to succeed, take over from; (*entreprise*) to take over.
successivement [syksesivmɑ̃] *adv* successively.
succinct, e [syksɛ̃, -ɛ̃t] *adj* succinct.
succinctement [syksɛ̃tmɑ̃] *adv* succinctly.
succion [syksjɔ̃] *nf*: **bruit de** ~ sucking noise.
succomber [sykɔ̃be] *vi* to die, succumb; (*fig*): ~ **à** to give way to, succumb to.
succulent, e [sykylɑ̃, -ɑ̃t] *adj* succulent.
succursale [sykyʀsal] *nf* branch; **magasin à** ~**s multiples** chain *ou* multiple store.
sucer [syse] *vt* to suck.
sucette [sysɛt] *nf* (*bonbon*) lollipop; (*de bébé*) dummy (*BRIT*), comforter, pacifier (*US*).
suçoter [sysɔte] *vt* to suck.
sucre [sykʀ(ə)] *nm* (*substance*) sugar; (*morceau*) lump of sugar, sugar lump *ou* cube; ~ **de canne/betterave** cane/beet sugar; ~ **en morceaux/cristallisé/en poudre** lump *ou* cube/granulated/caster sugar; ~ **glace** icing sugar; ~ **d'orge** barley sugar.
sucré, e [sykʀe] *adj* (*produit alimentaire*) sweetened; (*au goût*) sweet; (*péj*) sugary, honeyed.
sucrer [sykʀe] *vt* (*thé, café*) to sweeten, put sugar in; ~ **qn** to put sugar in sb's tea (*ou* coffee *etc*); **se** ~ to help o.s. to sugar, have some sugar; (*fam*) to line one's pocket(s).
sucrerie [sykʀəʀi] *nf* (*usine*) sugar refinery; ~**s** *nfpl* (*bonbons*) sweets, sweet things.
sucrier, ière [sykʀije, -jɛʀ] *adj* (*industrie*) sugar *cpd*; (*région*) sugar-producing ♦ *nm* (*fabricant*) sugar producer; (*récipient*) sugar bowl *ou* basin.
sud [syd] *nm*: **le** ~ the south ♦ *adj inv* south; (*côte*) south, southern; **au** ~ (*situation*) in the south; (*direction*) to the south; **au** ~ **de** (to the) south of.
sud-africain, e [sydafʀikɛ̃, -ɛn] *adj* South African ♦ *nm/f*: **Sud-Africain, e** South African.
sud-américain, e [sydameʀikɛ̃, -ɛn] *adj* South American ♦ *nm/f*: **Sud-Américain, e** South American.
sudation [sydɑsjɔ̃] *nf* sweating, sudation.
sud-coréen, ne [sydkɔʀeɛ̃, -ɛn] *adj* South Korean ♦ *nm/f*: **Sud-Coréen, ne** South Korean.
sud-est [sydɛst] *nm, adj inv* south-east.
sud-ouest [sydwɛst] *nm, adj inv* south-west.
sud-vietnamien, ne [sydvjɛtnamjɛ̃, -ɛn] *adj* South Vietnamese ♦ *nm/f*: **Sud-Vietnamien, ne** South Vietnamese.
Suède [sɥɛd] *nf*: **la** ~ Sweden.
suédois, e [sɥedwa, -waz] *adj* Swedish ♦ *nm* (*LING*) Swedish ♦ *nm/f*: **S~, e** Swede.
suer [sɥe] *vi* to sweat; (*suinter*) to ooze ♦ *vt* (*fig*) to exude; ~ **à grosses gouttes** to sweat profusely.
sueur [sɥœʀ] *nf* sweat; **en** ~ sweating, in a sweat; **avoir des** ~**s froides** to be in a cold sweat.
suffire [syfiʀ] *vi* (*être assez*): ~ **(à qn/pour qch/pour faire)** to be enough *ou* sufficient (for sb/for sth/to do); (*satisfaire*): **cela lui suffit** he's content with this, this is enough for him; **se** ~ *vi* to be self-sufficient; **cela suffit pour les irriter/qu'ils se fâchent** it's enough to annoy them/for them to get angry; **il suffit d'une négligence/qu'on oublie pour que ...** it only takes one act of carelessness/one only needs to forget for ...; **ça suffit!** that's enough!, that'll do!
suffisamment [syfizamɑ̃] *adv* sufficiently, enough; ~ **de** sufficient, enough.
suffisance [syfizɑ̃s] *nf* (*vanité*) self-importance, bumptiousness; (*quantité*): **en** ~ in plenty.
suffisant, e [syfizɑ̃, -ɑ̃t] *adj* (*temps, ressources*) sufficient; (*résultats*) satisfactory; (*vaniteux*) self-important, bumptious.
suffisons [syfizɔ̃] *etc vb voir* **suffire**.
suffixe [syfiks(ə)] *nm* suffix.
suffocant, e [syfɔkɑ̃, -ɑ̃t] *adj* (*étouffant*) suffocating; (*stupéfiant*) staggering.
suffocation [syfɔkɑsjɔ̃] *nf* suffocation.
suffoquer [syfɔke] *vt* to choke, suffocate; (*stupéfier*) to stagger, astound ♦ *vi* to choke, suffocate; ~ **de colère/d'indignation** to choke with anger/indignation.
suffrage [syfʀaʒ] *nm* (*POL: voix*) vote; (*: méthode*): ~ **universel/direct/indirect** universal/direct/indirect suffrage; (*du public etc*) approval *no pl*; ~**s exprimés** valid

votes.
suggérer [sygʒeʀe] *vt* to suggest; ~ **que/de faire** to suggest that/doing.
suggestif, ive [sygʒɛstif, -iv] *adj* suggestive.
suggestion [sygʒɛstjɔ̃] *nf* suggestion.
suggestivité [sygʒɛstivite] *nf* suggestiveness, suggestive nature.
suicidaire [sɥisidɛʀ] *adj* suicidal.
suicide [sɥisid] *nm* suicide ♦ *adj*: **opération** ~ suicide mission.
suicidé, e [sɥiside] *nm/f* suicide.
suicider [sɥiside]: **se** ~ *vi* to commit suicide.
suie [sɥi] *nf* soot.
suif [sɥif] *nm* tallow.
suinter [sɥɛ̃te] *vi* to ooze.
suis [sɥi] *vb voir* **être, suivre.**
suisse [sɥis] *adj* Swiss ♦ *nm* (*bedeau*) ≈ verger ♦ *nm/f*: **S**~ Swiss *pl inv* ♦ *nf*: **la S**~ Switzerland; **la S~ romande/allemande** French-speaking/German-speaking Switzerland; ~ **romand** Swiss French.
suisse-allemand, e [sɥisalmɑ̃, -ɑ̃d] *adj, nm/f* Swiss German.
Suissesse [sɥisɛs] *nf* Swiss (woman *ou* girl).
suit [sɥi] *vb voir* **suivre.**
suite [sɥit] *nf* (*continuation: d'énumération etc*) rest, remainder; (*: de feuilleton*) continuation; (*: second film etc sur le même thème*) sequel; (*série: de maisons, succès*): **une** ~ **de** a series *ou* succession of; (*MATH*) series *sg*; (*conséquence*) result; (*ordre, liaison logique*) coherence; (*appartement, MUS*) suite; (*escorte*) retinue, suite; ~**s** *nfpl* (*d'une maladie etc*) effects; **prendre la** ~ **de** (*directeur etc*) to succeed, take over from; **donner** ~ **à** (*requête, projet*) to follow up; **faire** ~ **à** to follow; **(faisant)** ~ **à votre lettre du** further to your letter of the; **sans** ~ *adj* incoherent, disjointed ♦ *adv* incoherently, disjointedly; **de** ~ *adv* (*d'affilée*) in succession; (*immédiatement*) at once; **par la** ~ afterwards, subsequently; **à la** ~ *adv* one after the other; **à la** ~ **de** (*derrière*) behind; (*en conséquence de*) following; **par** ~ **de** owing to, as a result of; **avoir de la** ~ **dans les idées** to show great singleness of purpose; **attendre la** ~ **des événements** to (wait and see) what happens.
suivant, e [sɥivɑ̃, -ɑ̃t] *vb voir* **suivre** ♦ *adj* next, following; (*ci-après*): **l'exercice** ~ the following exercise ♦ *prép* (*selon*) according to; ~ **que** according to whether; **au** ~! next!
suive [sɥiv] *etc vb voir* **suivre.**
suiveur [sɥivœʀ] *nm* (*CYCLISME*) (official) follower; (*péj*) (camp) follower.
suivi, e [sɥivi] *pp de* **suivre** ♦ *adj* (*régulier*) regular; (*COMM: article*) in general production; (*cohérent*) consistent; coherent ♦ *nm* follow-up; **très/peu** ~ (*cours*) well-/poorly-attended; (*mode*) widely/not widely adopted; (*feuilleton etc*) widely/not widely followed.
suivre [sɥivʀ(ə)] *vt* (*gén*) to follow; (*SCOL: cours*) to attend; (*: leçon*) to follow, attend to; (*: programme*) to keep up with; (*COMM: article*) to continue to stock ♦ *vi* to follow; (*élève: écouter*) to attend, pay attention; (*: assimiler le programme*) to keep up, follow; **se** ~ (*accidents, personnes, voitures etc*) to follow one after the other; (*raisonnement*) to be coherent; ~ **des yeux** to follow with one's eyes; **faire** ~ (*lettre*) to forward; ~ **son cours** (*suj: enquête etc*) to run *ou* take its course; **"à ~"** "to be continued".
sujet, te [syʒɛ, -ɛt] *adj*: **être** ~ **à** (*accidents*) to be prone to; (*vertige etc*) to be liable *ou* subject to ♦ *nm/f* (*d'un souverain*) subject ♦ *nm* subject; **un ~ de dispute/discorde/mécontentement** a cause for argument/dissension/dissatisfaction; **c'est à quel** ~? what is it about?; **avoir** ~ **de se plaindre** to have cause for complaint; **au** ~ **de** *prép* about; ~ **à caution** *adj* questionable; ~ **de conversation** topic *ou* subject of conversation; ~ **d'examen** (*SCOL*) examination question; examination paper; ~ **d'expérience** (*BIO etc*) experimental subject.
sujétion [syʒesjɔ̃] *nf* subjection; (*fig*) constraint.
sulfater [sylfate] *vt* to spray with copper sulphate.
sulfureux, euse [sylfyʀø, -øz] *adj* sulphurous (*BRIT*), sulfurous (*US*).
sulfurique [sylfyʀik] *adj*: **acide** ~ sulphuric (*BRIT*) *ou* sulfuric (*US*) acid.
sulfurisé, e [sylfyʀize] *adj*: **papier** ~ greaseproof (*BRIT*) *ou* wax (*US*) paper.
Sumatra [symatʀa] *nf* Sumatra.
summum [sɔmɔm] *nm*: **le** ~ **de** the height of.
sumo [symo] *nm inv* sumo (wrestling).
super [sypɛʀ] *adj inv* great, fantastic ♦ *nm* (= *supercarburant*) ≈ 4-star (*BRIT*), ≈ premium (*US*).
superbe [sypɛʀb(ə)] *adj* magnificent, superb ♦ *nf* arrogance.
superbement [sypɛʀbəmɑ̃] *adv* superbly.
supercarburant [sypɛʀkaʀbyʀɑ̃] *nm* ≈ 4-star petrol (*BRIT*), ≈ premium gas (*US*).
supercherie [sypɛʀʃəʀi] *nf* trick, trickery *no pl*; (*fraude*) fraud.
supérette [sypeʀɛt] *nf* minimarket.
superfétatoire [sypɛʀfetatwaʀ] *adj* superfluous.
superficie [sypɛʀfisi] *nf* (surface) area; (*fig*) surface.
superficiel, le [sypɛʀfisjɛl] *adj* superficial.
superficiellement [sypɛʀfisjɛlmɑ̃] *adv* superficially.
superflu, e [sypɛʀfly] *adj* superfluous ♦ *nm*: **le** ~ the superfluous.
superforme [sypɛʀfɔʀm(ə)] *nf* (*fam*) top form, excellent shape.
super-grand [sypɛʀgʀɑ̃] *nm* superpower.
super-huit [sypɛʀɥit] *adj*: **camera/film** ~ super-eight camera/film.

supérieur, e [sypeʀjœʀ] *adj* (*lèvre, étages, classes*) upper; (*plus élevé: température, niveau*): ~ **(à)** higher (than); (*meilleur: qualité, produit*): ~ **(à)** superior (to); (*excellent, hautain*) superior ♦ *nm/f* superior; **Mère ~e** Mother Superior; **à l'étage ~** on the next floor up; **~ en nombre** superior in number.
supérieurement [sypeʀjœʀmɑ̃] *adv* exceptionally well, exceptionally *+ adj.*
supériorité [sypeʀjɔʀite] *nf* superiority.
superlatif [sypɛʀlatif] *nm* superlative.
supermarché [sypɛʀmaʀʃe] *nm* supermarket.
supernova [sypɛʀnɔva] *nf* supernova.
superposable [sypɛʀpozabl(ə)] *adj* (*figures*) that may be superimposed; (*lits*) stackable.
superposer [sypɛʀpoze] *vt* to superpose; (*meubles, caisses*) to stack; (*faire chevaucher*) to superimpose; **se ~** (*images, souvenirs*) to be superimposed; **lits superposés** bunk beds.
superposition [sypɛʀpozisjɔ̃] *nf* superposition; superimposition.
superpréfet [sypɛʀpʀefɛ] *nm* *prefect in charge of a region.*
superproduction [sypɛʀpʀɔdyksjɔ̃] *nf* (*film*) spectacular.
superpuissance [sypɛʀpɥisɑ̃s] *nf* superpower.
supersonique [sypɛʀsɔnik] *adj* supersonic.
superstitieux, euse [sypɛʀstisjø, -øz] *adj* superstitious.
superstition [sypɛʀstisjɔ̃] *nf* superstition.
superstructure [sypɛʀstʀyktyʀ] *nf* superstructure.
supertanker [sypɛʀtɑ̃kœʀ] *nm* supertanker.
superviser [sypɛʀvize] *vt* to supervise.
supervision [sypɛʀvizjɔ̃] *nf* supervision.
suppl. *abr* = **supplément.**
supplanter [syplɑ̃te] *vt* to supplant.
suppléance [sypleɑ̃s] *nf* (*poste*) supply post (*BRIT*), substitute teacher's post (*US*).
suppléant, e [sypleɑ̃, -ɑ̃t] *adj* (*juge, fonctionnaire*) deputy *cpd*; (*professeur*) supply *cpd* (*BRIT*), substitute *cpd* (*US*) ♦ *nm/f* deputy; supply *ou* substitute teacher; **médecin ~** locum.
suppléer [syplee] *vt* (*ajouter: mot manquant etc*) to supply, provide; (*compenser: lacune*) to fill in; (*: défaut*) to make up for; (*remplacer: professeur*) to stand in for; (*: juge*) to deputize for; **~ à** *vt* to make up for; to substitute for.
supplément [syplemɑ̃] *nm* supplement; **un ~ de travail** extra *ou* additional work; **un ~ de frites** *etc* an extra portion of chips *etc*; **un ~ de 10 €** a supplement of €10, an extra *ou* additional €10; **ceci est en ~** (*au menu etc*) this is extra, there is an extra charge for this; **~ d'information** additional information.
supplémentaire [syplemɑ̃tɛʀ] *adj* additional, further; (*train, bus*) relief *cpd*, extra.
supplétif, ive [sypletif, -iv] *adj* (*MIL*) auxiliary.
suppliant, e [syplijɑ̃, -ɑ̃t] *adj* imploring.
supplication [syplikɑsjɔ̃] *nf* (*REL*) supplication; **~s** *nfpl* (*adjurations*) pleas, entreaties.
supplice [syplis] *nm* (*peine corporelle*) torture *no pl*; form of torture; (*douleur physique, morale*) torture, agony; **être au ~** to be in agony.
supplier [syplije] *vt* to implore, beseech.
supplique [syplik] *nf* petition.
support [sypɔʀ] *nm* support; (*pour livre, outils*) stand; **~ audio-visuel** audio-visual aid; **~ publicitaire** advertising medium.
supportable [sypɔʀtabl(ə)] *adj* (*douleur, température*) bearable; (*procédé, conduite*) tolerable.
supporter *nm* [sypɔʀtɛʀ] supporter, fan ♦ *vt* [sypɔʀte] (*poids, poussée, SPORT: concurrent, équipe*) to support; (*conséquences, épreuve*) to bear, endure; (*défauts, personne*) to tolerate, put up with; (*suj: chose: chaleur etc*) to withstand; (*suj: personne: chaleur, vin*) to take.
supposé, e [sypoze] *adj* (*nombre*) estimated; (*auteur*) supposed.
supposer [sypoze] *vt* to suppose; (*impliquer*) to presuppose; **en supposant** *ou* **à ~ que** supposing (that).
supposition [sypozisjɔ̃] *nf* supposition.
suppositoire [sypozitwaʀ] *nm* suppository.
suppôt [sypo] *nm* (*péj*) henchman.
suppression [sypʀesjɔ̃] *nf* (*voir supprimer*) removal; deletion; cancellation; suppression.
supprimer [sypʀime] *vt* (*cloison, cause, anxiété*) to remove; (*clause, mot*) to delete; (*congés, service d'autobus etc*) to cancel; (*publication, article*) to suppress; (*emplois, privilèges, témoin gênant*) to do away with; **~ qch à qn** to deprive sb of sth.
suppurer [sypyʀe] *vi* to suppurate.
supputations [sypytɑsjɔ̃] *nfpl* calculations, reckonings.
supputer [sypyte] *vt* to calculate, reckon.
supranational, e, aux [sypʀanasjɔnal, -o] *adj* supranational.
suprématie [sypʀemasi] *nf* supremacy.
suprême [sypʀɛm] *adj* supreme.
suprêmement [sypʀɛmmɑ̃] *adv* supremely.

MOT-CLÉ

sur [syʀ] *prép* **1** (*position*) on; (*pardessus*) over; (*au-dessus*) above; **pose-le ~ la table** put it on the table; **je n'ai pas d'argent ~ moi** I haven't any money on me

2 (*direction*) towards; **en allant ~ Paris** going towards Paris; **~ votre droite** on *ou* to your right

3 (*à propos de*) on, about; **un livre/une conférence ~ Balzac** a book/lecture on *ou* about Balzac

4 (*proportion, mesures*) out of; by; **un ~ 10** one in 10; (*SCOL*) one out of 10; **~ 20, 2 sont venus** out of 20, 2 came; **4 m ~ 2** 4 m by 2; **avoir accident ~ accident** to have one accident after another

5 (*cause*): ~ **sa recommandation** on *ou* at his recommendation; ~ **son invitation** at his invitation
sur ce *adv* whereupon; ~ **ce, il faut que je vous quitte** and now I must leave you.

sur, e [syʀ] *adj* sour.
sûr, e [syʀ] *adj* sure, certain; (*digne de confiance*) reliable; (*sans danger*) safe; **peu** ~ unreliable; ~ **de qch** sure *ou* certain of sth; **être** ~ **de qn** to be sure of sb; ~ **et certain** absolutely certain; ~ **de soi** self-assured, self-confident; **le plus** ~ **est de** the safest thing is to.
surabondance [syʀabɔ̃dɑ̃s] *nf* overabundance.
surabondant, e [syʀabɔ̃dɑ̃, -ɑ̃t] *adj* overabundant.
surabonder [syʀabɔ̃de] *vi* to be overabundant; ~ **de** to abound with, have an overabundance of.
suractivité [syʀaktivite] *nf* hyperactivity.
suraigu, ë [syʀegy] *adj* very shrill.
surajouter [syʀaʒute] *vt*: ~ **qch à** to add sth to.
suralimentation [syʀalimɑ̃tɑsjɔ̃] *nf* overfeeding; (*TECH*: *d'un moteur*) supercharging.
suralimenté, e [syʀalimɑ̃te] *adj* (*personne*) overfed; (*moteur*) supercharged.
suranné, e [syʀane] *adj* outdated, outmoded.
surarmement [syʀaʀməmɑ̃] *nm* (excess) stockpiling of arms (*ou* weapons).
surbaissé, e [syʀbese] *adj* lowered, low.
surcapacité [syʀkapasite] *nf* overcapacity.
surcharge [syʀʃaʀʒ(ə)] *nf* (*de passagers, marchandises*) excess load; (*de détails, d'ornements*) overabundance, excess; (*correction*) alteration; (*POSTES*) surcharge; **prendre des passagers en** ~ to take on excess *ou* extra passengers; ~ **de bagages** excess luggage; ~ **de travail** extra work.
surchargé, e [syʀʃaʀʒe] *adj* (*décoration, style*) over-elaborate, overfussy; (*voiture, emploi du temps*) overloaded.
surcharger [syʀʃaʀʒe] *vt* to overload; (*timbre-poste*) to surcharge; (*décoration*) to overdo.
surchauffe [syʀʃof] *nf* overheating.
surchauffé, e [syʀʃofe] *adj* overheated; (*fig: imagination*) overactive.
surchoix [syʀʃwa] *adj inv* top-quality.
surclasser [syʀklɑse] *vt* to outclass.
surconsommation [syʀkɔ̃sɔmɑsjɔ̃] *nf* (*ÉCON*) overconsumption.
surcoté, e [syʀkɔte] *adj* overpriced.
surcouper [syʀkupe] *vt* to overtrump.
surcroît [syʀkʀwa] *nm*: **un** ~ **de** additional + *nom*; **par** *ou* **de** ~ moreover; **en** ~ in addition.
surdi-mutité [syʀdimytite] *nf*: **atteint de** ~ deaf and dumb.
surdité [syʀdite] *nf* deafness; **atteint de** ~ **totale** profoundly deaf.
surdoué, e [syʀdwe] *adj* gifted.
sureau, x [syʀo] *nm* elder (tree).
sureffectif [syʀefɛktif] *nm* overmanning.
surélever [syʀɛlve] *vt* to raise, heighten.
sûrement [syʀmɑ̃] *adv* reliably; safely, securely; (*certainement*) certainly; ~ **pas** certainly not.
suremploi [syʀɑ̃plwa] *nm* (*ÉCON*) overemployment.
surenchère [syʀɑ̃ʃɛʀ] *nf* (*aux enchères*) higher bid; (*sur prix fixe*) overbid; (*fig*) overstatement; outbidding tactics *pl*; ~ **de violence** build-up of violence; ~ **électorale** political (*ou* electoral) one-upmanship.
surenchérir [syʀɑ̃ʃeʀiʀ] *vi* to bid higher; to raise one's bid; (*fig*) to try and outbid each other.
surendettement [syʀɑ̃dɛtmɑ̃] *nm* excessive debt.
surent [syʀ] *vb voir* **savoir**.
surentraîné, e [syʀɑ̃tʀene] *adj* overtrained.
suréquipé, e [syʀekipe] *adj* overequipped.
surestimer [syʀɛstime] *vt* (*tableau*) to overvalue; (*possibilité, personne*) to overestimate.
sûreté [syʀte] *nf* (*voir sûr*) reliability; safety; (*JUR*) guaranty; surety; **mettre en** ~ to put in a safe place; **pour plus de** ~ as an extra precaution; to be on the safe side; **la** ~ **de l'État** State security; **la S**~ **(nationale)** *division of the Ministère de l'Intérieur heading all police forces except the gendarmerie and the Paris préfecture de police.*
surexcité, e [syʀɛksite] *adj* overexcited.
surexciter [syʀɛksite] *vt* (*personne*) to overexcite; **cela surexcite ma curiosité** it really rouses my curiosity.
surexploiter [syʀɛksplwate] *vt* to overexploit.
surexposer [syʀɛkspoze] *vt* to overexpose.
surf [sœʀf] *nm* surfing; **faire du** ~ to go surfing.
surface [syʀfas] *nf* surface; (*superficie*) surface area; **faire** ~ to surface; **en** ~ *adv* near the surface; (*fig*) superficially; **la pièce fait 100 m² de** ~ the room has a surface area of 100m²; ~ **de réparation** (*SPORT*) penalty area; ~ **porteuse** *ou* **de sustentation** (*AVIAT*) aerofoil.
surfait, e [syʀfɛ, -ɛt] *adj* overrated.
surfeur, euse [sœʀfœʀ, -øz] *nm/f* surfer.
surfiler [syʀfile] *vt* (*COUTURE*) to oversew.
surfin, e [syʀfɛ̃, -in] *adj* superfine.
surgélateur [syʀʒelatœʀ] *nm* deep freeze.
surgélation [syʀʒelɑsjɔ̃] *nf* deep-freezing.
surgelé, e [syʀʒəle] *adj* (deep-)frozen.
surgeler [syʀʒəle] *vt* to (deep-)freeze.
surgir [syʀʒiʀ] *vi* (*personne, véhicule*) to appear suddenly; (*jaillir*) to shoot up; (*montagne etc*) to rise up, loom up; (*fig: problème, conflit*) to arise.
surhomme [syʀɔm] *nm* superman.
surhumain, e [syʀymɛ̃, -ɛn] *adj* superhuman.
surimposer [syʀɛ̃poze] *vt* to overtax.

surimpression [syʀɛ̃pʀesjɔ̃] *nf* (*PHOTO*) double exposure; **en ~** superimposed.
surimprimer [syʀɛ̃pʀime] *vt* to overstrike, overprint.
Surinam [syʀinam] *nm*: **le ~** Surinam.
surinfection [syʀɛ̃fɛksjɔ̃] *nf* (*MÉD*) secondary infection.
surjet [syʀʒɛ] *nm* (*COUTURE*) overcast seam.
sur-le-champ [syʀləʃɑ̃] *adv* immediately.
surlendemain [syʀlɑ̃dmɛ̃] *nm*: **le ~ (soir)** two days later (in the evening); **le ~ de** two days after.
surligneur [syʀliɲœʀ] *nm* (*feutre*) highlighter (pen).
surmenage [syʀmənaʒ] *nm* overwork; **le ~ intellectuel** mental fatigue.
surmené, e [syʀməne] *adj* overworked.
surmener [syʀməne] *vt*, **se ~** *vi* to overwork.
surmonter [syʀmɔ̃te] *vt* (*suj: coupole etc*) to surmount, top; (*vaincre*) to overcome, surmount.
surmultiplié, e [syʀmyltiplije] *adj*, *nf*: **(vitesse) ~e** overdrive.
surnager [syʀnaʒe] *vi* to float.
surnaturel, le [syʀnatyʀɛl] *adj*, *nm* supernatural.
surnom [syʀnɔ̃] *nm* nickname.
surnombre [syʀnɔ̃bʀ(ə)] *nm*: **être en ~** to be too many (*ou* one too many).
surnommer [syʀnɔme] *vt* to nickname.
surnuméraire [syʀnymeʀɛʀ] *nm/f* supernumerary.
suroît [syʀwa] *nm* sou'wester.
surpasser [syʀpɑse] *vt* to surpass; **se ~** to surpass o.s., excel o.s.
surpayer [syʀpeje] *vt* (*personne*) to overpay; (*article etc*) to pay too much for.
surpeuplé, e [syʀpœple] *adj* overpopulated.
surpeuplement [syʀpœpləmɑ̃] *nm* overpopulation.
surpiquer [syʀpike] *vt* (*COUTURE*) to overstitch.
surpiqûre [syʀpikyʀ] *nf* (*COUTURE*) overstitching.
surplace [syʀplas] *nm*: **faire du ~** to mark time.
surplis [syʀpli] *nm* surplice.
surplomb [syʀplɔ̃] *nm* overhang; **en ~** overhanging.
surplomber [syʀplɔ̃be] *vi* to be overhanging ♦ *vt* to overhang; (*dominer*) to tower above.
surplus [syʀply] *nm* (*COMM*) surplus; (*reste*): **~ de bois** wood left over; **au ~** moreover; **~ américains** American army surplus *sg*.
surpopulation [syʀpɔpylɑsjɔ̃] *nf* overpopulation.
surprenant, e [syʀpʀənɑ̃, -ɑ̃t] *vb voir* **surprendre** ♦ *adj* amazing.
surprendre [syʀpʀɑ̃dʀ(ə)] *vt* (*étonner, prendre à l'improviste*) to amaze, surprise; (*secret*) to discover; (*tomber sur: intrus etc*) to catch; (*fig*) to detect; to chance *ou* happen upon; (*clin d'œil*) to intercept; (*conversation*) to overhear; (*suj: orage, nuit etc*) to catch out, take by surprise; **~ la vigilance/bonne foi de qn** to catch sb out/betray sb's good faith; **se ~ à faire** to catch *ou* find o.s. doing.
surprime [syʀpʀim] *nf* additional premium.
surpris, e [syʀpʀi, -iz] *pp de* **surprendre** ♦ *adj*: **~ (de/que)** amazed *ou* surprised (at/that).
surprise [syʀpʀiz] *nf* surprise; **faire une ~ à qn** to give sb a surprise; **voyage sans ~s** uneventful journey; **par ~** *adv* by surprise.
surprise-partie [syʀpʀizpaʀti] *nf* party.
surprit [syʀpʀi] *vb voir* **surprendre**.
surproduction [syʀpʀɔdyksjɔ̃] *nf* overproduction.
surréaliste [syʀʀealist(ə)] *adj*, *nm/f* surrealist.
sursaut [syʀso] *nm* start, jump; **~ de** (*énergie, indignation*) sudden fit *ou* burst of; **en ~** *adv* with a start.
sursauter [syʀsote] *vi* to (give a) start, jump.
surseoir [syʀswaʀ]: **~ à** *vt* to defer; (*JUR*) to stay.
sursis [syʀsi] *nm* (*JUR*: *gén*) suspended sentence; (*à l'exécution capitale, aussi fig*) reprieve; (*MIL*): **~ (d'appel *ou* d'incorporation)** deferment; **condamné à 5 mois (de prison) avec ~** given a 5-month suspended (prison) sentence.
sursitaire [syʀsitɛʀ] *nm* (*MIL*) deferred conscript.
sursois [syʀswa], **sursoyais** [syʀswaje] *etc vb voir* **surseoir**.
surtaxe [syʀtaks(ə)] *nf* surcharge.
surtension [syʀtɑ̃sjɔ̃] *nf* (*ÉLEC*) overvoltage.
surtout [syʀtu] *adv* (*avant tout, d'abord*) above all; (*spécialement, particulièrement*) especially; **il aime le sport, ~ le football** he likes sport, especially football; **cet été, il a ~ fait de la pêche** this summer he went fishing more than anything (else); **~ pas d'histoires!** no fuss now!; **~, ne dites rien!** whatever you do - don't say anything!; **~ pas!** certainly *ou* definitely not!; **~ que ...** especially as ....
survécu, e [syʀveky] *pp de* **survivre**.
surveillance [syʀvɛjɑ̃s] *nf* watch; (*POLICE, MIL*) surveillance; **sous ~ médicale** under medical supervision; **la ~ du territoire** internal security; *voir aussi* **DST**.
surveillant, e [syʀvɛjɑ̃, -ɑ̃t] *nm/f* (*de prison*) warder; (*SCOL*) monitor; (*de travaux*) supervisor, overseer.
surveiller [syʀveje] *vt* (*enfant, élèves, bagages*) to watch, keep an eye on; (*malade*) to watch over; (*prisonnier, suspect*) to keep (a) watch on; (*territoire, bâtiment*) to (keep) watch over; (*travaux, cuisson*) to supervise; (*SCOL: examen*) to invigilate; **se ~** to keep a check *ou* watch on o.s.; **~ son langage/sa ligne** to watch one's language/figure.
survenir [syʀvəniʀ] *vi* (*incident, retards*) to occur, arise; (*événement*) to take place; (*per-*

sonne) to appear, arrive.
survenu, e [syʀv(ə)ny] *pp de* **survenir**.
survêt(ement) [syʀvɛt(mɑ̃)] *nm* tracksuit (*BRIT*), sweat suit (*US*).
survie [syʀvi] *nf* survival; (*REL*) afterlife; **équipement de ~** survival equipment; **une ~ de quelques mois** a few more months of life.
surviens [syʀvjɛ̃], **survint** [syʀvɛ̃] *etc vb voir* **survenir**.
survit [suʀvi] *etc vb voir* **survivre**.
survitrage [syʀvitʀaʒ] *nm* double-glazing.
survivance [syʀvivɑ̃s] *nf* relic.
survivant, e [syʀvivɑ̃, -ɑ̃t] *vb voir* **survivre** ♦ *nm/f* survivor.
survivre [syʀvivʀ(ə)] *vi* to survive; **~ à** *vt* (*accident etc*) to survive; (*personne*) to outlive; **la victime a peu de chance de ~** the victim has little hope of survival.
survol [syʀvɔl] *nm* flying over.
survoler [syʀvɔle] *vt* to fly over; (*fig: livre*) to skim through; (*: question, problèmes*) to skim over.
survolté, e [syʀvɔlte] *adj* (*ÉLEC*) stepped up, boosted; (*fig*) worked up.
sus [sy(s)]: **en ~ de** *prép* in addition to, over and above; **en ~** *adv* in addition; **~ à** *excl*: **~ au tyran!** at the tyrant! ♦ *vb* [sy] *voir* **savoir**.
susceptibilité [sysɛptibilite] *nf* sensitivity *no pl*.
susceptible [sysɛptibl(ə)] *adj* touchy, sensitive; **~ d'amélioration** *ou* **d'être amélioré** that can be improved, open to improvement; **~ de faire** (*capacité*) able to do; (*probabilité*) liable to do.
susciter [sysite] *vt* (*admiration*) to arouse; (*obstacles, ennuis*): **~ (à qn)** to create (for sb).
susdit, e [sysdi, -dit] *adj* foresaid.
susmentionné, e [sysmɑ̃sjɔne] *adj* above-mentioned.
susnommé, e [sysnɔme] *adj* above-named.
suspect, e [syspɛ(kt), -ɛkt(ə)] *adj* suspicious; (*témoignage, opinions, vin etc*) suspect ♦ *nm/f* suspect; **peu ~ de** most unlikely to be suspected of.
suspecter [syspɛkte] *vt* to suspect; (*honnêteté de qn*) to question, have one's suspicions about; **~ qn d'être/d'avoir fait qch** to suspect sb of being/having done sth.
suspendre [syspɑ̃dʀ(ə)] *vt* (*accrocher: vêtement*): **~ qch (à)** to hang sth up (on); (*fixer: lustre etc*): **~ qch à** to hang sth from; (*interrompre, démettre*) to suspend; (*remettre*) to defer; **se ~ à** to hang from.
suspendu, e [syspɑ̃dy] *pp de* **suspendre** ♦ *adj* (*accroché*): **~ à** hanging on (*ou* from); (*perché*): **~ au-dessus de** suspended over; (*AUTO*): **bien/mal ~** with good/poor suspension; **être ~ aux lèvres de qn** to hang upon sb's every word.
suspens [syspɑ̃]: **en ~** *adv* (*affaire*) in abeyance; **tenir en ~** to keep in suspense.
suspense [syspɑ̃s] *nm* suspense.
suspension [syspɑ̃sjɔ̃] *nf* suspension; deferment; (*AUTO*) suspension; (*lustre*) pendant light fitting; **en ~** in suspension, suspended; **~ d'audience** adjournment.
suspicieux, euse [syspisjø, -øz] *adj* suspicious.
suspicion [syspisjɔ̃] *nf* suspicion.
sustentation [systɑ̃tɑsjɔ̃] *nf* (*AVIAT*) lift; **base** *ou* **polygone de ~** support polygon.
sustenter [systɑ̃te]: **se ~** *vi* to take sustenance.
susurrer [sysyʀe] *vt* to whisper.
sut [sy] *vb voir* **savoir**.
suture [sytyʀ] *nf*: **point de ~** stitch.
suturer [sytyʀe] *vt* to stitch up, suture.
suzeraineté [syzʀɛnte] *nf* suzerainty.
svelte [svɛlt(ə)] *adj* slender, svelte.
SVP *sigle* (= *s'il vous plaît*) please.
Swaziland [swazilɑ̃d] *nm*: **le ~** Swaziland.
syllabe [silab] *nf* syllable.
sylphide [silfid] *nf* (*fig*): **sa taille de ~** her sylph-like figure.
sylvestre [silvɛstʀ(ə)] *adj*: **pin ~** Scots pine, Scotch fir.
sylvicole [silvikɔl] *adj* forestry *cpd*.
sylviculteur [silvikyltœʀ] *nm* forester.
sylviculture [silvikyltyʀ] *nf* forestry, sylviculture.
symbole [sɛ̃bɔl] *nm* symbol; **~ graphique** (*INFORM*) icon.
symbolique [sɛ̃bɔlik] *adj* symbolic; (*geste, offrande*) token *cpd*; (*salaire, dommages-intérêts*) nominal.
symboliquement [sɛ̃bɔlikmɑ̃] *adv* symbolically.
symboliser [sɛ̃bɔlize] *vt* to symbolize.
symétrie [simetʀi] *nf* symmetry.
symétrique [simetʀik] *adj* symmetrical.
symétriquement [simetʀikmɑ̃] *adv* symmetrically.
sympa [sɛ̃pa] *adj inv* (= *sympathique*) nice; friendly; good.
sympathie [sɛ̃pati] *nf* (*inclination*) liking; (*affinité*) fellow feeling; (*condoléances*) sympathy; **accueillir avec ~** (*projet*) to receive favourably; **avoir de la ~ pour qn** to like sb, have a liking for sb; **témoignages de ~** expressions of sympathy; **croyez à toute ma ~** you have my deepest sympathy.
sympathique [sɛ̃patik] *adj* (*personne, figure*) nice, friendly, likeable; (*geste*) friendly; (*livre*) good; (*déjeuner*) nice; (*réunion, endroit*) pleasant, nice.
sympathisant, e [sɛ̃patizɑ̃, -ɑ̃t] *nm/f* sympathizer.
sympathiser [sɛ̃patize] *vi* (*voisins etc: s'entendre*) to get on (*BRIT*) *ou* along (*US*) (well); (*: se fréquenter*) to socialize, see each other; **~ avec** to get on *ou* along (well) with; to see, socialize with.
symphonie [sɛ̃fɔni] *nf* symphony.

symphonique [sɛ̃fɔnik] *adj* (*orchestre, concert*) symphony *cpd*; (*musique*) symphonic.
symposium [sɛ̃pozjɔm] *nm* symposium.
symptomatique [sɛ̃ptɔmatik] *adj* symptomatic.
symptôme [sɛ̃ptom] *nm* symptom.
synagogue [sinagɔg] *nf* synagogue.
synchrone [sɛ̃kʀɔn] *adj* synchronous.
synchronique [sɛ̃kʀɔnik] *adj*: **tableau ~** synchronic table of events.
synchronisation [sɛ̃kʀɔnizɑsjɔ̃] *nf* synchronization; (*AUTO*) **~ des vitesses** synchromesh.
synchronisé, e [sɛ̃kʀɔnize] *adj* synchronized.
synchroniser [sɛ̃kʀɔnize] *vt* to synchronize.
syncope [sɛ̃kɔp] *nf* (*MÉD*) blackout; (*MUS*) syncopation; **tomber en ~** to faint, pass out.
syncopé, e [sɛ̃kɔpe] *adj* syncopated.
syndic [sɛ̃dik] *nm* managing agent.
syndical, e, aux [sɛ̃dikal, -o] *adj* (trade-)union *cpd*; **centrale ~e** group of affiliated trade unions.
syndicalisme [sɛ̃dikalism(ə)] *nm* (*mouvement*) trade unionism; (*activités*) union(ist) activities *pl*.
syndicaliste [sɛ̃dikalist(ə)] *nm/f* trade unionist.
syndicat [sɛ̃dika] *nm* (*d'ouvriers, employés*) (trade(s)) union; (*autre association d'intérêts*) union, association; **~ d'initiative (SI)** tourist office *ou* bureau; **~ patronal** employers' syndicate, federation of employers; **~ de propriétaires** association of property owners.
syndiqué, e [sɛ̃dike] *adj* belonging to a (trade) union; **non ~** non-union.
syndiquer [sɛ̃dike]: **se ~** *vi* to form a trade union; (*adhérer*) to join a trade union.
syndrome [sɛ̃dʀom] *nm* syndrome; **~ prémenstruel** premenstrual syndrome (PMS).
synergie [sinɛʀʒi] *nf* synergy.
synode [sinɔd] *nm* synod.
synonyme [sinɔnim] *adj* synonymous ♦ *nm* synonym; **~ de** synonymous with.
synopsis [sinɔpsis] *nm ou nf* synopsis.
synoptique [sinɔptik] *adj*: **tableau ~** synoptic table.
synovie [sinɔvi] *nf* synovia; **épanchement de ~** water on the knee.
syntaxe [sɛ̃taks(ə)] *nf* syntax.
synthèse [sɛ̃tɛz] *nf* synthesis (*pl* -es); **faire la ~ de** to synthesize.
synthétique [sɛ̃tetik] *adj* synthetic.
synthétiser [sɛ̃tetize] *vt* to synthesize.
synthétiseur [sɛ̃tetizœʀ] *nm* (*MUS*) synthesizer.
syphilis [sifilis] *nf* syphilis.
Syrie [siʀi] *nf*: **la ~** Syria.
syrien, ne [siʀjɛ̃, -ɛn] *adj* Syrian ♦ *nm/f*: **S~, ne** Syrian.
systématique [sistematik] *adj* systematic.
systématiquement [sistematikmɑ̃] *adv* systematically.
systématiser [sistematize] *vt* to systematize.
système [sistɛm] *nm* system; **le ~ D** resourcefulness; **~ décimal** decimal system; **~ expert** expert system; **~ d'exploitation à disques** (*INFORM*) disk operating system; **~ immunitaire** immune system; **~ métrique** metric system; **~ solaire** solar system.

Tt

T, t [te] *nm inv* T, t ♦ *abr* (= *tonne*) t; **T comme Thérèse** T for Tommy.
t' [t(ə)] *pron voir* **te**.
ta [ta] *adj possessif voir* **ton**.
tabac [taba] *nm* tobacco; (*aussi*: **débit** *ou* **bureau de ~**) tobacconist's (shop) ♦ *adj inv*: **(couleur) ~** buff, tobacco *cpd*; **passer qn à ~** to beat sb up; **faire un ~** (*fam*) to be a big hit; **~ blond/brun** light/dark tobacco; **~ gris** shag; **~ à priser** snuff.
tabagie [tabaʒi] *nf* smoke den.
tabagisme [tabaʒism(ə)] *nm* nicotine addiction; **~ passif** passive smoking.
tabasser [tabase] *vt* to beat up.
tabatière [tabatjɛʀ] *nf* snuffbox.
tabernacle [tabɛʀnakl(ə)] *nm* tabernacle.
table [tabl(ə)] *nf* table; **avoir une bonne ~** to keep a good table; **à ~!** dinner *etc* is ready!; **se mettre à ~** to sit down to eat; (*fig*: *fam*) to come clean; **mettre** *ou* **dresser/desservir la ~** to lay *ou* set/clear the table; **faire ~ rase de** to make a clean sweep of; **~ basse** coffee table; **~ de cuisson** (*à l'électricité*) hotplate; (*au gas*) gas ring; **~ d'écoute** wire-tapping set; **~ d'harmonie** sounding board; **~ d'hôte** set menu; **~ de lecture** turntable; **~ des matières** (table of) contents *pl*; **~ de multiplication** multiplication table; **~ des négociations** negotiating table; **~ de nuit** *ou* **de chevet** bedside table; **~ ronde** (*débat*) round table; **~ roulante** (tea) trolley; **~ de toilette** washstand; **~ traçante** (*INFORM*) plotter.
tableau, x [tablo] *nm* (*ART*) painting; (*reproduction, fig*) picture; (*panneau*) board; (*schéma*) table, chart; **~ d'affichage** notice board; **~ de bord** dashboard; (*AVIAT*) instrument panel; **~ de chasse** tally; **~ de contrôle** console, control panel; **~ de maître** masterpiece; **~ noir** blackboard.
tablée [table] *nf* (*personnes*) table.
tabler [table] *vi*: **~ sur** to count *ou* bank on.
tablette [tablɛt] *nf* (*planche*) shelf (*pl* shelves); **~ de chocolat** bar of chocolate.
tableur [tablœʀ] *nm* (*INFORM*) spreadsheet.
tablier [tablije] *nm* apron; (*de pont*) roadway;

(*de cheminée*) (flue-)shutter.
tabou, e [tabu] *adj, nm* taboo.
tabouret [tabuʀɛ] *nm* stool.
tabulateur [tabylatœʀ] *nm* (*TECH*) tabulator.
TAC *sigle m* (= *train autos-couchettes*) car-sleeper train, ≈ Motorail ® (*BRIT*).
tac [tak] *nm*: **du ~ au ~** tit for tat.
tache [taʃ] *nf* (*saleté*) stain, mark; (*ART, de couleur, lumière*) spot; splash, patch; **faire ~ d'huile** to spread, gain ground; **~ de rousseur** *ou* **de son** freckle; **~ de vin** (*sur la peau*) strawberry mark.
tâche [tɑʃ] *nf* task; **travailler à la ~** to do piecework.
tacher [taʃe] *vt* to stain, mark; (*fig*) to sully, stain; **se ~** *vi* (*fruits*) to become marked.
tâcher [tɑʃe] *vi*: **~ de faire** to try to do, endeavour (*BRIT*) *ou* endeavor (*US*) to do.
tâcheron [tɑʃʀɔ̃] *nm* (*fig*) drudge.
tacheté, e [taʃte] *adj*: **~ de** speckled *ou* spotted with.
tachisme [taʃism(ə)] *nm* (*PEINTURE*) tachisme.
tachygraphe [takigʀaf] *nm* tachograph.
tachymètre [takimɛtʀ(ə)] *nm* tachometer.
tacite [tasit] *adj* tacit.
tacitement [tasitmɑ̃] *adv* tacitly.
taciturne [tasityʀn(ə)] *adj* taciturn.
tacot [tako] *nm* (*péj: voiture*) banger (*BRIT*), clunker (*US*).
tact [takt] *nm* tact; **avoir du ~** to be tactful, have tact.
tacticien, ne [taktisjɛ̃, -ɛn] *nm/f* tactician.
tactile [taktil] *adj* tactile.
tactique [taktik] *adj* tactical ♦ *nf* (*technique*) tactics *sg*; (*plan*) tactic.
Tadjikistan [tadʒikistɑ̃] *nm* Tajikistan.
taffetas [tafta] *nm* taffeta.
Tage [tɑʒ] *nm*: **le ~** the (river) Tagus.
Tahiti [taiti] *nf* Tahiti.
tahitien, ne [taisjɛ̃, -ɛn] *adj* Tahitian.
taie [tɛ] *nf*: **~ (d'oreiller)** pillowslip, pillowcase.
taillader [tɑjade] *vt* to gash.
taille [tɑj] *nf* cutting; pruning; (*milieu du corps*) waist; (*hauteur*) height; (*grandeur*) size; **de ~ à faire** capable of doing; **de ~** *adj* sizeable; **quelle ~ faites- vous?** what size are you?
taillé, e [tɑje] *adj* (*moustache, ongles, arbre*) trimmed; **~ pour** (*fait pour, apte à*) cut out for; tailor-made for; **~ en pointe** sharpened to a point.
taille-crayon(s) [tajkʀɛjɔ̃] *nm inv* pencil sharpener.
tailler [tɑje] *vt* (*pierre, diamant*) to cut; (*arbre, plante*) to prune; (*vêtement*) to cut out; (*crayon*) to sharpen; **se ~** *vt* (*ongles, barbe*) to trim, cut; (*fig: réputation*) to gain, win ♦ *vi* (*fam: s'enfuir*) to beat it; **~ dans** (*chair, bois*) to cut into; **~ grand/petit** to be on the large/small side.
tailleur [tɑjœʀ] *nm* (*couturier*) tailor; (*vêtement*) suit, costume; **en ~** (*assis*) cross-legged; **~ de diamants** diamond-cutter.
tailleur-pantalon [tɑjœʀpɑ̃talɔ̃] *nm* trouser (*BRIT*) *ou* pant(s) suit.
taillis [taji] *nm* copse.
tain [tɛ̃] *nm* silvering; **glace sans ~** two-way mirror.
taire [tɛʀ] *vt* to keep to o.s., conceal ♦ *vi*: **faire ~ qn** to make sb be quiet; (*fig*) to silence sb; **se ~** *vi* (*s'arrêter de parler*) to fall silent, stop talking; (*ne pas parler*) to be silent *ou* quiet; (*s'abstenir de s'exprimer*) to keep quiet; (*bruit, voix*) to disappear; **tais-toi!, taisez-vous!** be quiet!
Taiwan [tajwan] *nf* Taiwan.
talc [talk] *nm* talc, talcum powder.
talé, e [tale] *adj* (*fruit*) bruised.
talent [talɑ̃] *nm* talent; **avoir du ~** to be talented, have talent.
talentueux, euse [talɑ̃tɥø, -øz] *adj* talented.
talion [taljɔ̃] *nm*: **la loi du ~** an eye for an eye.
talisman [talismɑ̃] *nm* talisman.
talkie-walkie [tɔkiwɔki] *nm* walkie-talkie.
taloche [talɔʃ] *nf* (*fam: claque*) slap; (*TECH*) plaster float.
talon [talɔ̃] *nm* heel; (*de chèque, billet*) stub, counterfoil (*BRIT*); **~s plats/aiguilles** flat/stiletto heels; **être sur les ~s de qn** to be on sb's heels; **tourner les ~s** to turn on one's heel; **montrer les ~s** (*fig*) to show a clean pair of heels.
talonner [talɔne] *vt* to follow hard behind; (*fig*) to hound; (*RUGBY*) to heel.
talonnette [talɔnɛt] *nf* (*de chaussure*) heel-piece; (*de pantalon*) stirrup.
talquer [talke] *vt* to put talc(um powder) on.
talus [taly] *nm* embankment; **~ de remblai/déblai** embankment/excavation slope.
tamarin [tamaʀɛ̃] *nm* (*BOT*) tamarind.
tambour [tɑ̃buʀ] *nm* (*MUS, aussi TECH*) drum; (*musicien*) drummer; (*porte*) revolving door(s *pl*); **sans ~ ni trompette** unobtrusively.
tambourin [tɑ̃buʀɛ̃] *nm* tambourine.
tambouriner [tɑ̃buʀine] *vi*: **~ contre** to drum against *ou* on.
tambour-major, *pl* **tambours-majors** [tɑ̃buʀmaʒɔʀ] *nm* drum major.
tamis [tami] *nm* sieve.
Tamise [tamiz] *nf*: **la ~** the Thames.
tamisé, e [tamize] *adj* (*fig*) subdued, soft.
tamiser [tamize] *vt* to sieve, sift.
tampon [tɑ̃pɔ̃] *nm* (*de coton, d'ouate*) pad; (*aussi*: **~ hygiénique** *ou* **périodique**) tampon; (*amortisseur, INFORM: aussi*: **mémoire ~**) buffer; (*bouchon*) plug, stopper; (*cachet, timbre*) stamp; (*CHIMIE*) buffer; **~ buvard** blotter; **~ encreur** inking pad; **~ (à récurer)** scouring pad.
tamponné, e [tɑ̃pɔne] *adj*: **solution ~e** buffer solution.
tamponner [tɑ̃pɔne] *vt* (*timbres*) to stamp;

(*heurter*) to crash *ou* ram into; (*essuyer*) to mop up; **se ~** (*voitures*) to crash (into each other).
tamponneuse [tɑ̃pɔnøz] *adj f*: **autos ~s** dodgems, bumper cars.
tam-tam [tamtam] *nm* tomtom.
tancer [tɑ̃se] *vt* to scold.
tanche [tɑ̃ʃ] *nf* tench.
tandem [tɑ̃dɛm] *nm* tandem; (*fig*) duo, pair.
tandis [tɑ̃di]: **~ que** *conj* while.
tangage [tɑ̃gaʒ] *nm* pitching (and tossing).
tangent, e [tɑ̃ʒɑ̃, -ɑ̃t] *adj* (*MATH*): **~ à** tangential to; (*fam*: *de justesse*) close ♦ *nf* (*MATH*) tangent.
Tanger [tɑ̃ʒe] *n* Tangier.
tango [tɑ̃go] *nm* (*MUS*) tango ♦ *adj inv* (*couleur*) dark orange.
tanguer [tɑ̃ge] *vi* to pitch (and toss).
tanière [tanjɛʀ] *nf* lair, den.
tanin [tanɛ̃] *nm* tannin.
tank [tɑ̃k] *nm* tank.
tanker [tɑ̃kɛʀ] *nm* tanker.
tanné, e [tane] *adj* weather-beaten.
tanner [tane] *vt* to tan.
tannerie [tanʀi] *nf* tannery.
tanneur [tanœʀ] *nm* tanner.
tant [tɑ̃] *adv* so much; **~ de** (*sable, eau*) so much; (*gens, livres*) so many; **~ que** *conj* as long as; **~ que** (*comparatif*) as much as; **~ mieux** that's great; so much the better; **~ mieux pour lui** good for him; **~ pis** too bad; **un ~ soit peu** (*un peu*) a little bit; (*même un peu*) (even) remotely; **~ bien que mal** as well as can be expected; **~ s'en faut** far from it, not by a long way.
tante [tɑ̃t] *nf* aunt.
tantinet [tɑ̃tinɛ]: **un ~** *adv* a tiny bit.
tantôt [tɑ̃to] *adv* (*parfois*): **~ ... ~** now ... now; (*cet après-midi*) this afternoon.
Tanzanie [tɑ̃zani] *nf*: **la ~** Tanzania.
tanzanien, ne [tɑ̃zanjɛ̃, -ɛn] *adj* Tanzanian.
TAO *sigle f* (= *traduction assistée par ordinateur*) MAT (= *machine-aided translation*).
taon [tɑ̃] *nm* horsefly, gadfly.
tapage [tapaʒ] *nm* uproar, din; (*fig*) fuss, row; **~ nocturne** (*JUR*) disturbance of the peace (*at night*).
tapageur, euse [tapaʒœʀ, -øz] *adj* (*bruyant*: *enfants etc*) noisy; (*toilette*) loud, flashy; (*publicité*) obtrusive.
tape [tap] *nf* slap.
tape-à-l'œil [tapalœj] *adj inv* flashy, showy.
taper [tape] *vt* (*personne*) to clout; (*porte*) to bang, slam; (*dactylographier*) to type (out); (*INFORM*) to key(board); (*fam*: *emprunter*): **~ qn de 2 €** to touch sb for €2, cadge €2 off sb ♦ *vi* (*soleil*) to beat down; **se ~** *vt* (*fam*: *travail*) to get landed with; (*: boire, manger*) to down; **~ sur qn** to thump sb; (*fig*) to run sb down; **~ sur qch** (*clou etc*) to hit sth; (*table etc*) to bang on sth; **~ à** (*porte etc*) to knock on; **~ dans** (*se servir*) to dig into; **~ des mains/pieds** to clap one's hands/stamp one's feet; **~ (à la machine)** to type.
tapi, e [tapi] *adj*: **~ dans/derrière** (*blotti*) crouching *ou* cowering in/behind; (*caché*) hidden away in/behind.
tapinois [tapinwa]: **en ~** *adv* stealthily.
tapioca [tapjɔka] *nm* tapioca.
tapir [tapiʀ]: **se ~** *vi* to hide away.
tapis [tapi] *nm* carpet; (*de table*) cloth; **mettre sur le ~** (*fig*) to bring up for discussion; **aller au ~** (*BOXE*) to go down; **envoyer au ~** (*BOXE*) to floor; **~ roulant** conveyor belt; **~ de sol** (*de tente*) groundsheet; **~ de souris** (*INFORM*) mouse mat.
tapis-brosse [tapibʀɔs] *nm* doormat.
tapisser [tapise] *vt* (*avec du papier peint*) to paper; (*recouvrir*): **~ qch (de)** to cover sth (with).
tapisserie [tapisʀi] *nf* (*tenture, broderie*) tapestry; (*: travail*) tapestry-making; (*: ouvrage*) tapestry work; (*papier peint*) wallpaper; (*fig*): **faire ~** to sit out, be a wallflower.
tapissier, ière [tapisje, -jɛʀ] *nm/f*: **~(-décorateur)** upholsterer (and decorator).
tapoter [tapɔte] *vt* to pat, tap.
taquet [takɛ] *nm* (*cale*) wedge; (*cheville*) peg.
taquin, e [takɛ̃, -in] *adj* teasing.
taquiner [takine] *vt* to tease.
taquinerie [takinʀi] *nf* teasing *no pl*.
tarabiscoté, e [taʀabiskɔte] *adj* over-ornate, fussy.
tarabuster [taʀabyste] *vt* to bother, worry.
tarama [taʀama] *nm* (*CULIN*) taramasalata.
tarauder [taʀode] *vt* (*TECH*) to tap; to thread; (*fig*) to pierce.
tard [taʀ] *adv* late; **au plus ~** at the latest; **plus ~** later (on) ♦ *nm*: **sur le ~** (*à une heure avancée*) late in the day; (*vers la fin de la vie*) late in life.
tarder [taʀde] *vi* (*chose*) to be a long time coming; (*personne*): **~ à faire** to delay doing; **il me tarde d'être** I am longing to be; **sans (plus) ~** without (further) delay.
tardif, ive [taʀdif, -iv] *adj* (*heure, repas, fruit*) late; (*talent, goût*) late in developing.
tardivement [taʀdivmɑ̃] *adv* late.
tare [taʀ] *nf* (*COMM*) tare; (*fig*) defect; taint, blemish.
targette [taʀʒɛt] *nf* (*verrou*) bolt.
targuer [taʀge]: **se ~ de** *vt* to boast about.
tarif [taʀif] *nm* (*liste*) price list, tariff (*BRIT*); (*barème*) rate, rates *pl*, tariff (*BRIT*); (*: de taxis etc*) fares *pl*; **voyager à plein ~/à ~ réduit** to travel at full/reduced fare.
tarifaire [taʀifɛʀ] *adj* (*voir tarif*) relating to price lists *etc*.
tarifé, e [taʀife] *adj*: **~ 2 €** priced at €2.
tarifer [taʀife] *vt* to fix the price *ou* rate for.
tarification [taʀifikɑsjɔ̃] *nf fixing of a price scale*.
tarir [taʀiʀ] *vi* to dry up, run dry ♦ *vt* to dry up.

tarot(s) [taʀo] *nm(pl)* tarot cards.
tartare [taʀtaʀ] *adj (CULIN)* tartar(e).
tarte [taʀt(ə)] *nf* tart; ~ **aux pommes/à la crème** apple/custard tart.
tartelette [taʀtəlɛt] *nf* tartlet.
tartine [taʀtin] *nf* slice of bread (and butter (*ou* jam)); ~ **de miel** slice of bread and honey; ~ **beurrée** slice of bread and butter.
tartiner [taʀtine] *vt* to spread; **fromage à** ~ cheese spread.
tartre [taʀtʀ(ə)] *nm* (*des dents*) tartar; (*de chaudière*) fur, scale.
tas [tɑ] *nm* heap, pile; (*fig*): **un** ~ **de** heaps of, lots of; **en** ~ in a heap *ou* pile; **dans le** ~ (*fig*) in the crowd; among them; **formé sur le** ~ trained on the job.
Tasmanie [tasmani] *nf*: **la** ~ Tasmania.
tasmanien, ne [tasmanjɛ̃, -ɛn] *adj* Tasmanian.
tasse [tɑs] *nf* cup; **boire la** ~ (*en se baignant*) to swallow a mouthful; ~ **à café/thé** coffee/teacup.
tassé, e [tɑse] *adj*: **bien** ~ (*café etc*) strong.
tasseau, x [tɑso] *nm* length of wood.
tassement [tɑsmɑ̃] *nm* (*de vertèbres*) compression; (*ÉCON, POL: ralentissement*) fall-off, slowdown; (*BOURSE*) dullness.
tasser [tɑse] *vt* (*terre, neige*) to pack down; (*entasser*): ~ **qch dans** to cram sth into; (*INFORM*) to pack; **se** ~ *vi* (*terrain*) to settle; (*personne: avec l'âge*) to shrink; (*fig*) to sort itself out, settle down.
tâter [tɑte] *vt* to feel; (*fig*) to sound out; ~ **de** (*prison etc*) to have a taste of; **se** ~ (*hésiter*) to be in two minds; ~ **le terrain** (*fig*) to test the ground.
tatillon, ne [tatijɔ̃, -ɔn] *adj* pernickety.
tâtonnement [tɑtɔnmɑ̃] *nm*: **par** ~**s** (*fig*) by trial and error.
tâtonner [tɑtɔne] *vi* to grope one's way along; (*fig*) to grope around (in the dark).
tâtons [tɑtɔ̃]: **à** ~ *adv*: **chercher/avancer à** ~ to grope around for/grope one's way forward.
tatouage [tatwaʒ] *nm* tattooing; (*dessin*) tattoo.
tatouer [tatwe] *vt* to tattoo.
taudis [todi] *nm* hovel, slum.
taule [tol] *nf* (*fam*) nick (*BRIT*), jail.
taupe [top] *nf* mole; (*peau*) moleskin.
taupinière [topinjɛʀ] *nf* molehill.
taureau, x [tɔʀo] *nm* bull; (*signe*): **le T**~ Taurus, the Bull; **être du T**~ to be Taurus.
taurillon [tɔʀijɔ̃] *nm* bull-calf.
tauromachie [tɔʀɔmaʃi] *nf* bullfighting.
taux [to] *nm* rate; (*d'alcool*) level; ~ **d'escompte** discount rate; ~ **d'intérêt** interest rate; ~ **de mortalité** mortality rate.
tavelé, e [tavle] *adj* marked.
taverne [tavɛʀn(ə)] *nf* inn, tavern.
taxable [taksabl(ə)] *adj* taxable.
taxation [taksɑsjɔ̃] *nf* taxation; (*TÉL*) charges *pl*.
taxe [taks(ə)] *nf* tax; (*douanière*) duty; **toutes** ~**s comprises (TTC)** inclusive of tax; ~ **de base** (*TÉL*) unit charge; ~ **de séjour** tourist tax; ~ **à** *ou* **sur la valeur ajoutée (TVA)** value added tax (VAT) (*BRIT*).
taxer [takse] *vt* (*personne*) to tax; (*produit*) to put a tax on, tax; (*fig*): ~ **qn de** (*qualifier de*) to call sb + *attribut*; (*accuser de*) to accuse sb of, tax sb with.
taxi [taksi] *nm* taxi.
taxidermie [taksidɛʀmi] *nf* taxidermy.
taxidermiste [taksidɛʀmist(ə)] *nm/f* taxidermist.
taximètre [taksimɛtʀ(ə)] *nm* (taxi)meter.
taxiphone [taksifɔn] *nm* pay phone.
TB *abr* = *très bien, très bon.*
tbe *abr* (= *très bon état*) VGC, vgc.
TCA *sigle f* (= *taxe sur le chiffre d'affaires*) tax on turnover.
TCF *sigle m* (= *Touring Club de France*) ≈ AA *ou* RAC (*BRIT*), ≈ AAA (*US*).
Tchad [tʃad] *nm*: **le** ~ Chad.
tchadien, ne [tʃadjɛ̃, -ɛn] *adj* Chad(ian), of *ou* from Chad.
tchao [tʃao] *excl* (*fam*) bye(-bye)!
tchécoslovaque [tʃekɔslɔvak] *adj* Czechoslovak(ian) ♦ *nm/f*: **T**~ Czechoslovak(ian).
Tchécoslovaquie [tʃekɔslɔvaki] *nf*: **la** ~ Czechoslovakia.
tchèque [tʃɛk] *adj* Czech ♦ *nm* (*LING*) Czech ♦ *nm/f*: **T**~ Czech.
TCS *sigle m* (= *Touring Club de Suisse*) ≈ AA *ou* RAC (*BRIT*), ≈ AAA (*US*).
TD *sigle mpl* = **travaux dirigés**.
TDF *sigle f* (= *Télévision de France*) *French broadcasting authority.*
te, t' [t(ə)] *pron* you; (*réfléchi*) yourself.
té [te] *nm* T-square.
technicien, ne [tɛknisjɛ̃, -ɛn] *nm/f* technician.
technicité [tɛknisite] *nf* technical nature.
technico-commercial, e, aux [tɛknikokɔmɛʀsjal, -o] *adj*: **agent** ~ sales technician.
technique [tɛknik] *adj* technical ♦ *nf* technique.
techniquement [tɛknikmɑ̃] *adv* technically.
techno [tɛkno] *nf* (*MUS*) techno.
technocrate [tɛknɔkʀat] *nm/f* technocrat.
technocratie [tɛknɔkʀasi] *nf* technocracy.
technologie [tɛknɔlɔʒi] *nf* technology.
technologique [tɛknɔlɔʒik] *adj* technological.
technologue [tɛknɔlɔg] *nm/f* technologist.
teck [tɛk] *nm* teak.
teckel [tekɛl] *nm* dachshund.
TEE *sigle m* = *Trans-Europ-Express.*
tee-shirt [tiʃœʀt] *nm* T-shirt, tee-shirt.
Téhéran [teeʀɑ̃] *n* Teheran.
teigne [tɛɲ] *vb voir* **teindre** ♦ *nf* (*ZOOL*) moth; (*MÉD*) ringworm.
teigneux, euse [tɛɲø, -øz] *adj* (*péj*) nasty, scabby.
teindre [tɛ̃dʀ(ə)] *vt* to dye; **se** ~ **(les cheveux)**

to dye one's hair.

teint, e [tɛ̃, tɛ̃t] *pp de* **teindre** ♦ *adj* dyed ♦ *nm* (*du visage: permanent*) complexion, colouring (*BRIT*), coloring (*US*); (*momentané*) colour (*BRIT*), color (*US*) ♦ *nf* shade, colour, color; (*fig: petite dose*): **une ~e de** a hint of; **grand ~** *adj inv* colourfast; **bon ~** *adj inv* (*couleur*) fast; (*tissu*) colourfast; (*personne*) staunch, firm.

teinté, e [tɛ̃te] *adj* (*verres*) tinted; (*bois*) stained; **~ acajou** mahogany-stained; **~ de** (*fig*) tinged with.

teinter [tɛ̃te] *vt* to tint; (*bois*) to stain; (*fig: d'ironie etc*) to tinge.

teinture [tɛ̃tyʀ] *nf* dyeing; (*substance*) dye; (*MÉD*): **~ d'iode** tincture of iodine.

teinturerie [tɛ̃tyʀʀi] *nf* dry cleaner's.

teinturier, ière [tɛ̃tyʀje, -jɛʀ] *nm/f* dry cleaner.

tel, telle [tɛl] *adj* (*pareil*) such; (*comme*): **~ un/des** ... like a/like ...; (*indéfini*) such-and-such a, a given; (*intensif*): **un ~/de ~s** ... such (a)/such ...; **rien de ~** nothing like it, no such thing; **~ que** *conj* like, such as; **~ quel** as it is *ou* stands (*ou* was *etc*).

tél. *abr* = *téléphone*.

Tel Aviv [tɛlaviv] *n* Tel Aviv.

télé [tele] *nf* (= *télévision*) TV, telly (*BRIT*); **à la ~** on TV *ou* telly.

télébenne [telebɛn] *nm, nf* telecabine, gondola.

télécabine [telekabin] *nm, nf* telecabine, gondola.

télécarte [telekaʀt(ə)] *nf* phonecard.

télécharger [teleʃaʀʒe] *vt* (*INFORM*) to download.

TELECOM [telekɔm] *abr* (= *Télécommunications*) ≈ Telecom.

télécommande [telekɔmɑ̃d] *nf* remote control.

télécommander [telekɔmɑ̃de] *vt* to operate by remote control, radio-control.

télécommunications [telekɔmynikɑsjɔ̃] *nfpl* telecommunications.

téléconférence [telekɔ̃feʀɑ̃s] *nf* (*méthode*) teleconferencing; (*discussion*) conference call.

télécopie [telekɔpi] *nf* fax, telefax.

télécopieur [telekɔpjœʀ] *nm* fax (machine).

télédétection [teledetɛksjɔ̃] *nf* remote sensing.

télédiffuser [teledifyze] *vt* to broadcast (on television).

télédiffusion [teledifyzjɔ̃] *nf* television broadcasting.

télédistribution [teledistʀibysjɔ̃] *nf* cable TV.

téléenseignement [teleɑ̃sɛɲmɑ̃] *nm* distance teaching (*ou* learning).

téléférique [telefeʀik] *nm* = **téléphérique**.

téléfilm [telefilm] *nm* film made for TV.

télégramme [telegʀam] *nm* telegram.

télégraphe [telegʀaf] *nm* telegraph.

télégraphier [telegʀafje] *vt* to telegraph, cable.

télégraphique [telegʀafik] *adj* telegraph *cpd*, telegraphic; (*fig*) telegraphic.

téléguider [telegide] *vt* to operate by remote control, radio-control.

téléinformatique [teleɛ̃fɔʀmatik] *nf* remote access computing.

téléjournal, aux [teleʒuʀnal, -o] *nm* television news magazine programme.

télématique [telematik] *nf* telematics *sg* ♦ *adj* telematic.

téléobjectif [teleɔbʒɛktif] *nm* telephoto lens.

téléopérateur, trice [teleɔpeʀatœʀ, tʀis] *nm/f* call-centre operator.

télépathie [telepati] *nf* telepathy.

téléphérique [telefeʀik] *nm* cable-car.

téléphone [telefɔn] *nm* telephone; **avoir le ~** to be on the (tele)phone; **au ~** on the phone; **les T~s** the (tele)phone service *sg*; **~ arabe** bush telegraph; **~ à carte (magnétique)** cardphone; **~ cellulaire** cellphone, cellular phone; **~ portable** portable (tele)phone; **~ rouge** hotline.

téléphoner [telefɔne] *vt* to telephone ♦ *vi* to telephone; to make a phone call; **~ à** to phone up, ring up, call up.

téléphonie [telefɔni] *nf* telephony.

téléphonique [telefɔnik] *adj* telephone *cpd*, phone *cpd*; **cabine ~** call box (*BRIT*), (tele)phone box (*BRIT*) *ou* booth; **conversation/appel ~** (tele)phone conversation/call.

téléphoniste [telefɔnist(ə)] *nm/f* telephonist, telephone operator; (*d'entreprise*) switchboard operator.

téléport [telepɔʀ] *nm* teleport.

téléprospection [telepʀɔspɛksjɔ̃] *nf* telesales.

télescopage [telɛskɔpaʒ] *nm* crash.

télescope [telɛskɔp] *nm* telescope.

télescoper [telɛskɔpe] *vt* to smash up; **se ~** (*véhicules*) to collide, crash into each other.

télescopique [telɛskɔpik] *adj* telescopic.

téléscripteur [teleskʀiptœʀ] *nm* teleprinter.

télésiège [telesjɛʒ] *nm* chairlift.

téléski [teleski] *nm* ski-tow; **~ à archets** T-bar tow; **~ à perche** button lift.

téléspectateur, trice [telespɛktatœʀ, -tʀis] *nm/f* (television) viewer.

télétexte [teletɛkst] *nm* ® Teletext ®.

téléthon [teletɔ̃] *nm* telethon.

télétraitement [teletʀɛtmɑ̃] *nm* remote processing.

télétransmission [teletʀɑ̃smisjɔ̃] *nf* remote transmission.

télétravail [teletʀavaj] *nm* teleworking.

télétype [teletip] *nm* teleprinter.

télévente [televɑ̃t] *nf* telesales.

téléviser [televize] *vt* to televise.

téléviseur [televizœʀ] *nm* television set.

télévision [televizjɔ̃] *nf* television; **(poste de) ~** television (set); **avoir la ~** to have a television; **à la** ~ on television; ~ **par câble/satellite** cable/satellite television; ~ **en circuit fermé** closed-circuit television; ~ **numérique** digital TV.

télex [telɛks] *nm* telex.

télexer [telɛkse] *vt* to telex.

telle [tɛl] *adj f voir* **tel**.

tellement [tɛlmɑ̃] *adv* (*tant*) so much; (*si*) so; ~ **plus grand (que)** so much bigger (than); ~ **de** (*sable, eau*) so much; (*gens, livres*) so many; **il s'est endormi** ~ **il était fatigué** he was so tired (that) he fell asleep; **pas** ~ not really; **pas** ~ **fort/lentement** not (all) that strong/slowly; **il ne mange pas** ~ he doesn't eat (all that) much.

tellurique [telyʀik] *adj*: **secousse** ~ earth tremor.

téméraire [temeʀɛʀ] *adj* reckless, rash.

témérité [temeʀite] *nf* recklessness, rashness.

témoignage [temwaɲaʒ] *nm* (*JUR: déclaration*) testimony *no pl*, evidence *no pl*; (*: faits*) evidence *no pl*; (*gén: rapport, récit*) account; (*fig: d'affection etc*) token, mark; expression.

témoigner [temwaɲe] *vt* (*manifester: intérêt, gratitude*) to show ♦ *vi* (*JUR*) to testify, give evidence; ~ **que** to testify that; (*fig: démontrer*) to reveal that, testify to the fact that; ~ **de** *vt* (*confirmer*) to bear witness to.

témoin [temwɛ̃] *nm* witness; (*fig*) testimony; (*SPORT*) baton; (*CONSTR*) telltale ♦ *adj* control *cpd*, test *cpd*; ~ **le fait que ...** (as) witness the fact that ...; **appartement-**~ show flat (*BRIT*), model apartment (*US*); **être** ~ **de** (*voir*) to witness; **prendre à** ~ to call to witness; ~ **à charge** witness for the prosecution; **T**~ **de Jehovah** Jehovah's Witness; ~ **de moralité** character reference; ~ **oculaire** eyewitness.

tempe [tɑ̃p] *nf* (*ANAT*) temple.

tempérament [tɑ̃peʀamɑ̃] *nm* temperament, disposition; (*santé*) constitution; **à** ~ (*vente*) on deferred (payment) terms; (*achat*) by instalments, hire purchase *cpd*; **avoir du** ~ to be hot-blooded.

tempérance [tɑ̃peʀɑ̃s] *nf* temperance; **société de** ~ temperance society.

tempérant, e [tɑ̃peʀɑ̃, -ɑ̃t] *adj* temperate.

température [tɑ̃peʀatyʀ] *nf* temperature; **prendre la** ~ **de** to take the temperature of; (*fig*) to gauge the feeling of; **avoir** *ou* **faire de la** ~ to be running *ou* have a temperature.

tempéré, e [tɑ̃peʀe] *adj* temperate.

tempérer [tɑ̃peʀe] *vt* to temper.

tempête [tɑ̃pɛt] *nf* storm; ~ **de sable/neige** sand/snowstorm; **vent de** ~ gale.

tempêter [tɑ̃pete] *vi* to rant and rave.

temple [tɑ̃pl(ə)] *nm* temple; (*protestant*) church.

tempo [tɛmpo] *nm* tempo (*pl* -s).

temporaire [tɑ̃pɔʀɛʀ] *adj* temporary.

temporairement [tɑ̃pɔʀɛʀmɑ̃] *adv* temporarily.

temporel, le [tɑ̃pɔʀɛl] *adj* temporal.

temporisateur, trice [tɑ̃pɔʀizatœʀ, -tʀis] *adj* temporizing, delaying.

temporisation [tɑ̃pɔʀizɑsjɔ̃] *nf* temporizing, playing for time.

temporiser [tɑ̃pɔʀize] *vi* to temporize, play for time.

temps [tɑ̃] *nm* (*atmosphérique*) weather; (*durée*) time; (*époque*) time, times *pl*; (*LING*) tense; (*MUS*) beat; (*TECH*) stroke; **les** ~ **changent/sont durs** times are changing/hard; **il fait beau/mauvais** ~ the weather is fine/bad; **avoir le** ~**/tout le** ~**/juste le** ~ to have time/plenty of time/just enough time; **avoir fait son** ~ (*fig*) to have had its (*ou* his *etc*) day; **en** ~ **de paix/guerre** in peacetime/wartime; **en** ~ **utile** *ou* **voulu** in due time *ou* course; **de** ~ **en** ~, **de** ~ **à autre** from time to time, now and again; **en même** ~ at the same time; **à** ~ (*partir, arriver*) in time; **à plein/mi-**~ *adv, adj* full-/part-time; **à** ~ **partiel** *adv, adj* part-time; **dans le** ~ at one time; **de tout** ~ always; **du** ~ **que** at the time when, in the days when; **dans le** *ou* **du** *ou* **au** ~ **où** at the time when; **pendant ce** ~ in the meantime; ~ **d'accès** (*INFORM*) access time; ~ **d'arrêt** pause, halt; ~ **mort** (*SPORT*) stoppage (time); (*COMM*) slack period; ~ **partagé** (*INFORM*) time-sharing; ~ **réel** (*INFORM*) real time.

tenable [t(ə)nabl(ə)] *adj* bearable.

tenace [tənas] *adj* tenacious, persistent.

ténacité [tenasite] *nf* tenacity, persistence.

tenailler [tənaje] *vt* (*fig*) to torment, torture.

tenailles [tənaj] *nfpl* pincers.

tenais [t(ə)nɛ] *etc vb voir* **tenir**.

tenancier, ière [tənɑ̃sje, -jɛʀ] *nm/f* (*d'hôtel, de bistro*) manager/manageress.

tenant, e [tənɑ̃, -ɑ̃t] *adj f voir* **séance** ♦ *nm/f* (*SPORT*): ~ **du titre** title-holder ♦ *nm*: **d'un seul** ~ in one piece; **les** ~**s et les aboutissants** (*fig*) the ins and outs.

tendance [tɑ̃dɑ̃s] *nf* (*opinions*) leanings *pl*, sympathies *pl*; (*inclination*) tendency; (*évolution*) trend; ~ **à la hausse/baisse** upward/downward trend; **avoir** ~ **à** to have a tendency to, tend to.

tendancieux, euse [tɑ̃dɑ̃sjø, -øz] *adj* tendentious.

tendeur [tɑ̃dœʀ] *nm* (*de vélo*) chain-adjuster; (*de câble*) wire-strainer; (*de tente*) runner; (*attache*) elastic strap.

tendinite [tɑ̃dinit] *nf* tendinitis, tendonitis.

tendon [tɑ̃dɔ̃] *nm* tendon, sinew; ~ **d'Achille** Achilles' tendon.

tendre [tɑ̃dʀ(ə)] *adj* (*viande, légumes*) tender; (*bois, roche, couleur*) soft; (*affectueux*) tender, loving ♦ *vt* (*élastique, peau*) to stretch, draw tight; (*muscle*) to tense; (*donner*): ~ **qch à qn** to hold sth out to sb; to offer sb sth; (*fig: piège*) to set, lay; (*tapisserie*): **tendu de soie** hung with silk, with silk hangings; **se** ~ *vi* (*corde*) to tighten; (*relations*) to become

strained; ~ **à qch/à faire** to tend towards sth/to do; ~ **l'oreille** to prick up one's ears; ~ **la main/le bras** to hold out one's hand/ stretch out one's arm; ~ **la perche à qn** (*fig*) to throw sb a line.
tendrement [tɑ̃dʀəmɑ̃] *adv* tenderly, lovingly.
tendresse [tɑ̃dʀɛs] *nf* tenderness; ~**s** *nfpl* (*caresses etc*) tenderness *no pl*, caresses.
tendu, e [tɑ̃dy] *pp de* **tendre** ♦ *adj* tight; tensed; strained.
ténèbres [tenɛbʀ(ə)] *nfpl* darkness *sg*.
ténébreux, euse [tenebʀø, -øz] *adj* obscure, mysterious; (*personne*) saturnine.
Ténérife [teneʀif] *nf* Tenerife.
teneur [tənœʀ] *nf* content, substance; (*d'une lettre*) terms *pl*, content; ~ **en cuivre** copper content.
ténia [tenja] *nm* tapeworm.
tenir [təniʀ] *vt* to hold; (*magasin, hôtel*) to run; (*promesse*) to keep ♦ *vi* to hold; (*neige, gel*) to last; (*survivre*) to survive; **se** ~ *vi* (*avoir lieu*) to be held, take place; (*être: personne*) to stand; **se** ~ **droit** to stand up (*ou* sit up) straight; **bien se** ~ to behave well; **se** ~ **à qch** to hold on to sth; **s'en** ~ **à qch** to confine o.s. to sth; to stick to sth; ~ **à** *vt* to be attached to, care about (*ou* for); (*avoir pour cause*) to be due to, stem from; ~ **à faire** to want to do, be keen to do; ~ **à ce que qn fasse qch** to be anxious that sb should do sth; ~ **de** *vt* to partake of; (*ressembler à*) to take after; **ça ne tient qu'à lui** it is entirely up to him; ~ **qn pour** to take sb for; ~ **qch de qn** (*histoire*) to have heard *ou* learnt sth from sb; (*qualité, défaut*) to have inherited *ou* got sth from sb; ~ **les comptes** to keep the books; ~ **un rôle** to play a part; ~ **de la place** to take up space *ou* room; ~ **l'alcool** to be able to hold a drink; ~ **le coup** to hold out; ~ **bon** to stand *ou* hold fast; ~ **3 jours/2 mois** (*résister*) to hold out *ou* last 3 days/2 months; ~ **au chaud/à l'abri** to keep hot/ under shelter *ou* cover; ~ **prêt** to have ready; ~ **sa langue** (*fig*) to hold one's tongue; **tiens** (*ou* **tenez**), **voilà le stylo** there's the pen!; **tiens, Alain!** look, here's Alain!; **tiens?** (*surprise*) really?; **tiens-toi bien!** (*pour informer*) brace yourself!, take a deep breath!
tennis [tenis] *nm* tennis; (*aussi*: **court de** ~) tennis court ♦ *nmpl ou fpl* (*aussi*: **chaussures de** ~) tennis *ou* gym shoes; ~ **de table** table tennis.
tennisman [tenisman] *nm* tennis player.
ténor [tenɔʀ] *nm* tenor.
tension [tɑ̃sjɔ̃] *nf* tension; (*fig: des relations, de la situation*) tension; (*: concentration, effort*) strain; (*MÉD*) blood pressure; **faire** *ou* **avoir de la** ~ to have high blood pressure; ~ **nerveuse/raciale** nervous/racial tension.
tentaculaire [tɑ̃takylɛʀ] *adj* (*fig*) sprawling.
tentacule [tɑ̃takyl] *nm* tentacle.
tentant, e [tɑ̃tɑ̃, -ɑ̃t] *adj* tempting.
tentateur, trice [tɑ̃tatœʀ, -tʀis] *adj* tempting ♦ *nm* (*REL*) tempter.
tentation [tɑ̃tasjɔ̃] *nf* temptation.
tentative [tɑ̃tativ] *nf* attempt, bid; ~ **d'évasion** escape bid; ~ **de suicide** suicide attempt.
tente [tɑ̃t] *nf* tent; ~ **à oxygène** oxygen tent.
tenter [tɑ̃te] *vt* (*éprouver, attirer*) to tempt; (*essayer*): ~ **qch/de faire** to attempt *ou* try sth/ to do; **être tenté de** to be tempted to; ~ **sa chance** to try one's luck.
tenture [tɑ̃tyʀ] *nf* hanging.
tenu, e [təny] *pp de* **tenir** ♦ *adj* (*maison, comptes*): **bien** ~ well-kept; (*obligé*): ~ **de faire** under an obligation to do ♦ *nf* (*action de tenir*) running; keeping; holding; (*vêtements*) clothes *pl*, gear; (*allure*) dress *no pl*, appearance; (*comportement*) manners *pl*, behaviour (*BRIT*), behavior (*US*); **être en** ~**e** to be dressed (up); **se mettre en** ~**e** to dress (up); **en grande** ~**e** in full dress; **en petite** ~**e** scantily dressed *ou* clad; **avoir de la** ~**e** to have good manners; (*journal*) to have a high standard; ~**e de combat** combat gear *ou* dress; ~**e de pompier** fireman's uniform; ~**e de route** (*AUTO*) road-holding; ~**e de soirée** evening dress; ~**e de sport/voyage** sports/ travelling clothes *pl ou* gear *no pl*.
ténu, e [teny] *adj* (*indice, nuance*) tenuous, subtle; (*fil, objet*) fine; (*voix*) thin.
ter [tɛʀ] *adj*: **16** ~ 16b *ou* B.
térébenthine [teʀebɑ̃tin] *nf*: **(essence de)** ~ (oil of) turpentine.
tergal [tɛʀgal] *nm* ® Terylene ®.
tergiversations [tɛʀʒivɛʀsɑsjɔ̃] *nfpl* shilly-shallying *no pl*.
tergiverser [tɛʀʒivɛʀse] *vi* to shilly-shally.
terme [tɛʀm(ə)] *nm* term; (*fin*) end; **être en bons/mauvais** ~**s avec qn** to be on good/bad terms with sb; **vente/achat à** ~ (*COMM*) forward sale/purchase; **au** ~ **de** at the end of; **en d'autres** ~**s** in other words; **moyen** ~ (*solution intermédiare*) middle course; **à court/ long** ~ *adj* short-/long-term *ou* -range ♦ *adv* in the short/long term; **à** ~ *adj* (*MÉD*) full-term ♦ *adv* sooner or later, eventually; (*MÉD*) at term; **avant** ~ (*MÉD*) *adj* premature ♦ *adv* prematurely; **mettre un** ~ **à** to put an end *ou* a stop to; **toucher à son** ~ to be nearing its end.
terminaison [tɛʀminɛzɔ̃] *nf* (*LING*) ending.
terminal, e, aux [tɛʀminal, -o] *adj* (*partie, phase*) final; (*MÉD*) terminal ♦ *nm* terminal ♦ *nf* (*SCOL*) ≈ sixth form *ou* year (*BRIT*), ≈ twelfth grade (*US*).
terminer [tɛʀmine] *vt* to end; (*travail, repas*) to finish; **se** ~ *vi* to end; **se** ~ **par** to end with.
terminologie [tɛʀminɔlɔʒi] *nf* terminology.
terminus [tɛʀminys] *nm* terminus (*pl* -i); ~**!** all change!
termite [tɛʀmit] *nm* termite, white ant.

termitière [tɛʀmitjɛʀ] *nf* ant-hill.
ternaire [tɛʀnɛʀ] *adj* compound.
terne [tɛʀn(ə)] *adj* dull.
ternir [tɛʀniʀ] *vt* to dull; (*fig*) to sully, tarnish; **se** ~ *vi* to become dull.
terrain [tɛʀɛ̃] *nm* (*sol, fig*) ground; (*COMM*) land *no pl*, plot (of land); (*: à bâtir*) site; **sur le** ~ (*fig*) on the field; ~ **de football/rugby** football/rugby pitch (*BRIT*) *ou* field (*US*); ~ **d'atterrissage** landing strip; ~ **d'aviation** airfield; ~ **de camping** campsite; **un** ~ **d'entente** an area of agreement; ~ **de golf** golf course; ~ **de jeu** playground; (*SPORT*) games field; ~ **de sport** sports ground; ~ **vague** waste ground *no pl*.
terrasse [tɛʀas] *nf* terrace; (*de café*) pavement area, terrasse; **à la** ~ (*café*) outside.
terrassement [tɛʀasmɑ̃] *nm* earth-moving, earthworks *pl*; embankment.
terrasser [tɛʀase] *vt* (*adversaire*) to floor, bring down; (*suj: maladie etc*) to lay low.
terrassier [tɛʀasje] *nm* navvy, roadworker.
terre [tɛʀ] *nf* (*gén, aussi ÉLEC*) earth; (*substance*) soil, earth; (*opposé à mer*) land *no pl*; (*contrée*) land; ~**s** *nfpl* (*terrains*) lands, land *sg*; **travail de la** ~ work on the land; **en** ~ (*pipe, poterie*) clay *cpd*; **mettre en** ~ (*plante etc*) to plant; (*personne: enterrer*) to bury; **à** *ou* **par** ~ (*mettre, être*) on the ground (*ou* floor); (*jeter, tomber*) to the ground, down; ~ **à** ~ *adj inv* down-to-earth, matter-of-fact; **la T~ Adélie** Adélie Coast *ou* Land; ~ **de bruyère** (heath-) peat; ~ **cuite** earthenware; terracotta; **la** ~ **ferme** dry land, terra firma; **la T~ de Feu** Tierra del Fuego; ~ **glaise** clay; **la T~ promise** the Promised Land; **la T~ Sainte** the Holy Land.
terreau [tɛʀo] *nm* compost.
Terre-Neuve [tɛʀnœv] *nf*: **la** ~ (*aussi*: **l'île de** ~) Newfoundland.
terre-plein [tɛʀplɛ̃] *nm* platform.
terrer [tɛʀe]: **se** ~ *vi* to hide away; to go to ground.
terrestre [tɛʀɛstʀ(ə)] *adj* (*surface*) earth's, of the earth; (*BOT, ZOOL, MIL*) land *cpd*; (*REL*) earthly, worldly.
terreur [tɛʀœʀ] *nf* terror *no pl*, fear.
terreux, euse [tɛʀø, -øz] *adj* muddy; (*goût*) earthy.
terrible [tɛʀibl(ə)] *adj* terrible, dreadful; (*fam: fantastique*) terrific.
terriblement [tɛʀibləmɑ̃] *adv* (*très*) terribly, awfully.
terrien, ne [tɛʀjɛ̃, -ɛn] *adj*: **propriétaire** ~ landowner ♦ *nm/f* countryman/woman, man/woman of the soil; (*non martien etc*) earthling; (*non marin*) landsman.
terrier [tɛʀje] *nm* burrow, hole; (*chien*) terrier.
terrifiant, e [tɛʀifjɑ̃, -ɑ̃t] *adj* (*effrayant*) terrifying; (*extraordinaire*) terrible, awful.
terrifier [tɛʀifje] *vt* to terrify.
terril [tɛʀil] *nm* slag heap.
terrine [tɛʀin] *nf* (*récipient*) terrine; (*CULIN*) pâté.
territoire [tɛʀitwaʀ] *nm* territory; **T~ des Afars et des Issas** French Territory of Afars and Issas.
territorial, e, aux [tɛʀitɔʀjal, -o] *adj* territorial; **eaux ~es** territorial waters; **armée ~e** regional defence force, ≈ Territorial Army (*BRIT*); **collectivités ~es** local and regional authorities.
terroir [tɛʀwaʀ] *nm* (*AGR*) soil; (*région*) region; **accent du** ~ country *ou* rural accent.
terroriser [tɛʀɔʀize] *vt* to terrorize.
terrorisme [tɛʀɔʀism(ə)] *nm* terrorism.
terroriste [tɛʀɔʀist(ə)] *nm/f* terrorist.
tertiaire [tɛʀsjɛʀ] *adj* tertiary ♦ *nm* (*ÉCON*) tertiary sector, service industries *pl*.
tertiarisation [tɛʀsjaʀizɑsjɔ̃] *nf expansion or development of the service sector*.
tertre [tɛʀtʀ(ə)] *nm* hillock, mound.
tes [te] *adj possessif voir* **ton**.
tesson [tesɔ̃] *nm*: ~ **de bouteille** piece of broken bottle.
test [tɛst] *nm* test; ~ **de grossesse** pregnancy test.
testament [tɛstamɑ̃] *nm* (*JUR*) will; (*fig*) legacy; (*REL*): **T~** Testament; **faire son** ~ to make one's will.
testamentaire [tɛstamɑ̃tɛʀ] *adj* of a will.
tester [tɛste] *vt* to test.
testicule [tɛstikyl] *nm* testicle.
tétanie [tetani] *nf* tetany.
tétanos [tetanos] *nm* tetanus.
têtard [tɛtaʀ] *nm* tadpole.
tête [tɛt] *nf* head; (*cheveux*) hair *no pl*; (*visage*) face; (*longueur*): **gagner d'une (courte)** ~ to win by a (short) head; (*FOOTBALL*) header; **de** ~ *adj* (*wagon etc*) front *cpd*; (*concurrent*) leading ♦ *adv* (*calculer*) in one's head, mentally; **par** ~ (*par personne*) per head; **se mettre en** ~ **que** to get it into one's head that; **se mettre en** ~ **de faire** to take it into one's head to do; **prendre la** ~ **de qch** to take the lead in sth; **perdre la** ~ (*fig: s'affoler*) to lose one's head; (*: devenir fou*) to go off one's head; **ça ne va pas, la ~?** (*fam*) are you crazy?; **tenir** ~ **à qn** to stand up to *ou* defy sb; **la** ~ **en bas** with one's head down; **la** ~ **la première** (*tomber*) headfirst; **la** ~ **basse** hanging one's head; **avoir la** ~ **dure** (*fig*) to be thickheaded; **faire une** ~ (*FOOTBALL*) to head the ball; **faire la** ~ (*fig*) to sulk; **en** ~ (*SPORT*) in the lead; at the front *ou* head; **de la** ~ **aux pieds** from head to toe; ~ **d'affiche** (*THÉÂT etc*) top of the bill; ~ **de bétail** head *inv* of cattle; ~ **brulée** desperado; ~ **chercheuse** homing device; ~ **d'enregistrement** recording head; ~ **d'impression** printhead; ~ **de lecture** (playback) head; ~ **de ligne** (*TRANSPORTS*) start of the line; ~ **de liste** (*POL*) chief candidate; ~ **de mort** skull and crossbones; ~ **de pont**

(*MIL*) bridge- *ou* beachhead; ~ **de série** (*TENNIS*) seeded player, seed; ~ **de Turc** (*fig*) whipping boy (*BRIT*), butt; ~ **de veau** (*CULIN*) calf's head.
tête-à-queue [tɛtakø] *nm inv*: **faire un** ~ to spin round.
tête-à-tête [tɛtatɛt] *nm inv* tête-à-tête; (*service*) breakfast set for two; **en** ~ in private, alone together.
tête-bêche [tɛtbɛʃ] *adv* head to tail.
tétée [tete] *nf* (*action*) sucking; (*repas*) feed.
téter [tete] *vt*: ~ **(sa mère)** to suck at one's mother's breast, feed.
tétine [tetin] *nf* teat; (*sucette*) dummy (*BRIT*), pacifier (*US*).
téton [tetɔ̃] *nm* breast.
têtu, e [tety] *adj* stubborn, pigheaded.
texte [tɛkst(ə)] *nm* text; (*SCOL*: *d'un devoir*) subject, topic; **apprendre son** ~ (*THÉÂT*) to learn one's lines; **un** ~ **de loi** the wording of a law.
textile [tɛkstil] *adj* textile *cpd* ♦ *nm* textile; (*industrie*) textile industry.
Texto [tɛksto] *nm* ® text message.
textuel, le [tɛkstɥɛl] *adj* literal, word for word.
textuellement [tɛkstɥɛlmɑ̃] *adv* literally.
texture [tɛkstyʀ] *nf* texture; (*fig*: *d'un texte, livre*) feel.
TF1 *sigle f* (= *Télévision française 1*) *TV channel*.
TG *sigle f* = **Trésorerie générale.**
TGI *sigle m* = **tribunal de grande instance.**
TGV *sigle m* = **train à grande vitesse.**
thaï, e [tai] *adj* Thai ♦ *nm* (*LING*) Thai.
thaïlandais, e [tailɑ̃dɛ, -ɛz] *adj* Thai.
Thaïlande [tailɑ̃d] *nf*: **la** ~ Thailand.
thalassothérapie [talasɔteʀapi] *nf* sea-water therapy.
thé [te] *nm* tea; (*réunion*) tea party; **prendre le** ~ to have tea; ~ **au lait/citron** tea with milk/lemon.
théâtral, e, aux [teɑtʀal, -o] *adj* theatrical.
théâtre [teɑtʀ(ə)] *nm* theatre; (*techniques, genre*) drama, theatre; (*activité*) stage, theatre; (*œuvres*) plays *pl*, dramatic works *pl*; (*fig: lieu*): **le** ~ **de** the scene of; (*péj*) histrionics *pl*, playacting; **faire du** ~ to be on the stage; (*en amateur*) to do some acting; ~ **filmé** filmed stage productions *pl*.
thébain, e [tebɛ̃, -ɛn] *adj* Theban.
Thèbes [tɛb] *n* Thebes.
théière [tejɛʀ] *nf* teapot.
théine [tein] *nf* theine.
thématique [tematik] *adj* thematic.
thème [tɛm] *nm* theme; (*SCOL*: *traduction*) prose (composition); ~ **astral** birth chart.
théocratie [teɔkʀasi] *nf* theocracy.
théologie [teɔlɔʒi] *nf* theology.
théologien, ne [teɔlɔʒjɛ̃, -ɛn] *nm* theologian.
théologique [teɔlɔʒik] *adj* theological.
théorème [teɔʀɛm] *nm* theorem.
théoricien, ne [teɔʀisjɛ̃, -ɛn] *nm/f* theoretician, theorist.
théorie [teɔʀi] *nf* theory; **en** ~ in theory.
théorique [teɔʀik] *adj* theoretical.
théoriquement [teɔʀikmɑ̃] *adv* theoretically.
théoriser [teɔʀize] *vi* to theorize.
thérapeutique [teʀapøtik] *adj* therapeutic ♦ *nf* (*MÉD*: *branche*) therapeutics *sg*; (*: traitement*) therapy.
thérapie [teʀapi] *nf* therapy; ~ **de groupe** group therapy.
thermal, e, aux [tɛʀmal, -o] *adj* thermal; **station** ~**e** spa; **cure** ~**e** water cure.
thermes [tɛʀm(ə)] *nmpl* thermal baths; (*romains*) thermae *pl*.
thermique [tɛʀmik] *adj* (*énergie*) thermic; (*unité*) thermal.
thermodynamique [tɛʀmɔdinamik] *nf* thermodynamics *sg*.
thermoélectrique [tɛʀmoelɛktʀik] *adj* thermoelectric.
thermomètre [tɛʀmɔmɛtʀ(ə)] *nm* thermometer.
thermonucléaire [tɛʀmɔnykleɛʀ] *adj* thermonuclear.
thermos [tɛʀmos] *nm ou nf* ®: **(bouteille)** ~ vacuum *ou* Thermos ® flask (*BRIT*) *ou* bottle (*US*).
thermostat [tɛʀmɔsta] *nm* thermostat.
thésauriser [tezɔʀize] *vi* to hoard money.
thèse [tɛz] *nf* thesis (*pl* theses).
thessalien, ne [tɛsaljɛ̃, -ɛn] *adj* Thessalian.
thibaude [tibod] *nf* carpet underlay.
thon [tɔ̃] *nm* tuna (fish).
thonier [tɔnje] *nm* tuna boat.
thoracique [tɔʀasik] *adj* thoracic.
thorax [tɔʀaks] *nm* thorax.
thrombose [tʀɔ̃boz] *nf* thrombosis.
thym [tɛ̃] *nm* thyme.
thyroïde [tiʀɔid] *nf* thyroid (gland).
TI *sigle m* = **tribunal d'instance.**
tiare [tjaʀ] *nf* tiara.
Tibet [tibɛ] *nm*: **le** ~ Tibet.
tibétain, e [tibetɛ̃, -ɛn] *adj* Tibetan.
tibia [tibja] *nm* shin; (*os*) shinbone, tibia.
Tibre [tibʀ(ə)] *nm*: **le** ~ the Tiber.
TIC *sigle fpl* (= *technologies de l'information et de la communication*) ICT.
tic [tik] *nm* tic, (nervous) twitch; (*de langage etc*) mannerism.
ticket [tikɛ] *nm* ticket; ~ **de caisse** till receipt; ~ **modérateur** *patient's contribution towards medical costs*; ~ **de quai** platform ticket; ~ **repas** luncheon voucher.
tic-tac [tiktak] *nm inv* tick-tock.
tictaquer [tiktake] *vi* to tick (away).
tiède [tjɛd] *adj* (*bière etc*) lukewarm; (*thé, café etc*) tepid; (*bain, accueil, sentiment*) lukewarm; (*vent, air*) mild, warm ♦ *adv*: **boire** ~ to drink things lukewarm.
tièdement [tjɛdmɑ̃] *adv* coolly, half-heartedly.
tiédeur [tjedœʀ] *nf* lukewarmness; (*du vent, de*

l'air) mildness.
tiédir [tjediʀ] *vi* (*se réchauffer*) to grow warmer; (*refroidir*) to cool.
tien, tienne [tjɛ̃, tjɛn] *pron*: **le ~ (la tienne), les ~s (tiennes)** yours; **à la tienne!** cheers!
tiendrai [tjɛ̃dʀe] *etc vb voir* **tenir**.
tienne [tjɛn] *vb voir* **tenir** ♦ *pron voir* **tien**.
tiens [tjɛ̃] *vb, excl voir* **tenir**.
tierce [tjɛʀs(ə)] *adj f, nf voir* **tiers**.
tiercé [tjɛʀse] *nm system of forecast betting giving first three horses.*
tiers, tierce [tjɛʀ, tjɛʀs(ə)] *adj* third ♦ *nm* (*JUR*) third party; (*fraction*) third ♦ *nf* (*MUS*) third; (*CARTES*) tierce; **une tierce personne** a third party; **assurance au ~** third-party insurance; **le ~ monde** the third world; **~ payant** *direct payment by insurers of medical expenses*; **~ provisionnel** *interim payment of tax.*
tiersmondisme [tjɛʀmɔ̃dism(ə)] *nm* support for the Third World.
TIG *sigle m* = **travail d'intérêt général**.
tige [tiʒ] *nf* stem; (*baguette*) rod.
tignasse [tiɲas] *nf* (*péj*) shock *ou* mop of hair.
Tigre [tigʀ(ə)] *nm*: **le ~** the Tigris.
tigre [tigʀ(ə)] *nm* tiger.
tigré, e [tigʀe] *adj* (*rayé*) striped; (*tacheté*) spotted.
tigresse [tigʀɛs] *nf* tigress.
tilleul [tijœl] *nm* lime (tree), linden (tree); (*boisson*) lime(-blossom) tea.
tilt [tilt(ə)] *nm*: **faire ~** (*fig*: *échouer*) to miss the target; (*: inspirer*) to ring a bell.
timbale [tɛ̃bal] *nf* (metal) tumbler; **~s** *nfpl* (*MUS*) timpani, kettledrums.
timbrage [tɛ̃bʀaʒ] *nm*: **dispensé de ~** post(age) paid.
timbre [tɛ̃bʀ(ə)] *nm* (*tampon*) stamp; (*aussi*: **~-poste**) (postage) stamp; (*cachet de la poste*) postmark; (*sonnette*) bell; (*MUS*: *de voix, instrument*) timbre, tone; **~ anti-tabac** nicotine patch; **~ dateur** date stamp.
timbré, e [tɛ̃bʀe] *adj* (*enveloppe*) stamped; (*voix*) resonant; (*fam*: *fou*) cracked, nuts.
timbrer [tɛ̃bʀe] *vt* to stamp.
timide [timid] *adj* (*emprunté*) shy, timid; (*timoré*) timid, timorous.
timidement [timidmɑ̃] *adv* shyly; timidly.
timidité [timidite] *nf* shyness; timidity.
timonerie [timɔnʀi] *nf* wheelhouse.
timonier [timɔnje] *nm* helmsman.
timoré, e [timɔʀe] *adj* timorous.
tint [tɛ̃] *etc vb voir* **tenir**.
tintamarre [tɛ̃tamaʀ] *nm* din, uproar.
tintement [tɛ̃tmɑ̃] *nm* ringing, chiming; **~s d'oreilles** ringing in the ears.
tinter [tɛ̃te] *vi* to ring, chime; (*argent, clefs*) to jingle.
Tipp-Ex [tipɛks] *nm* ® Tipp-Ex ®.
tique [tik] *nf* tick (*insect*).
tiquer [tike] *vi* (*personne*) to make a face.
TIR *sigle mpl* (= *Transports internationaux routiers*) TIR.
tir [tiʀ] *nm* (*sport*) shooting; (*fait ou manière de tirer*) firing *no pl*; (*FOOTBALL*) shot; (*stand*) shooting gallery; **~ d'obus/de mitraillette** shell/machine gun fire; **~ à l'arc** archery; **~ de barrage** barrage fire; **~ au fusil** (rifle) shooting; **~ au pigeon** (*d'argile*) clay pigeon shooting.
tirade [tiʀad] *nf* tirade.
tirage [tiʀaʒ] *nm* (*action*) printing; (*PHOTO*) print; (*INFORM*) printout; (*de journal*) circulation; (*de livre*) (print-)run; edition; (*de cheminée*) draught (*BRIT*), draft (*US*); (*de loterie*) draw; (*fig*: *désaccord*) friction; **~ au sort** drawing lots.
tiraillement [tiʀajmɑ̃] *nm* (*douleur*) sharp pain; (*fig*: *doutes*) agony *no pl* of indecision; (*conflits*) friction *no pl*.
tirailler [tiʀaje] *vt* to pull at, tug at; (*fig*) to gnaw at ♦ *vi* to fire at random.
tirailleur [tiʀajœʀ] *nm* skirmisher.
tirant [tiʀɑ̃] *nm*: **~ d'eau** draught (*BRIT*), draft (*US*).
tire [tiʀ] *nf*: **vol à la ~** pickpocketing.
tiré [tiʀe] *adj* (*visage, traits*) drawn ♦ *nm* (*COMM*) drawee; **~ par les cheveux** far-fetched; **~ à part** off-print.
tire-au-flanc [tiʀoflɑ̃] *nm inv* (*péj*) skiver.
tire-bouchon [tiʀbuʃɔ̃] *nm* corkscrew.
tire-bouchonner [tiʀbuʃɔne] *vt* to twirl.
tire-d'aile [tiʀdɛl]: **à ~** *adv* swiftly.
tire-fesses [tiʀfɛs] *nm inv* ski-tow.
tire-lait [tiʀlɛ] *nm inv* breast-pump.
tire-larigot [tiʀlaʀigo]: **à ~** *adv* as much as one likes, to one's heart's content.
tirelire [tiʀliʀ] *nf* moneybox.
tirer [tiʀe] *vt* (*gén*) to pull; (*extraire*): **~ qch de** to take *ou* pull sth out of; to get sth out of; to extract sth from; (*tracer: ligne, trait*) to draw, trace; (*fermer: volet, porte, trappe*) to pull to, close; (*: rideau*) to draw; (*choisir: carte, conclusion, aussi COMM: chèque*) to draw; (*en faisant feu: balle, coup*) to fire; (*: animal*) to shoot; (*journal, livre, photo*) to print; (*FOOTBALL: corner etc*) to take ♦ *vi* (*faire feu*) to fire; (*faire du tir, FOOTBALL*) to shoot; (*cheminée*) to draw; **se ~** *vi* (*fam*) to push off; **s'en ~** to pull through; **~ sur** (*corde, poignée*) to pull on *ou* at; (*faire feu sur*) to shoot *ou* fire at; (*pipe*) to draw on; (*fig: avoisiner*) to verge *ou* border on; **~ 6 mètres** (*NAVIG*) to draw 6 metres of water; **~ son nom de** to take *ou* get its name from; **~ la langue** to stick out one's tongue; **~ qn de** (*embarras etc*) to help *ou* get sb out of; **~ à l'arc/la carabine** to shoot with a bow and arrow/with a rifle; **~ en longueur** to drag on; **~ à sa fin** to be drawing to an end; **~ les cartes** to read *ou* tell the cards.
tiret [tiʀɛ] *nm* dash; (*en fin de ligne*) hyphen.
tireur [tiʀœʀ] *nm* gunman; (*COMM*) drawer; **bon ~** good shot; **~ d'élite** marksman; **~ de**

cartes fortuneteller.
tiroir [tirwar] *nm* drawer.
tiroir-caisse [tirwarkɛs] *nm* till.
tisane [tizan] *nf* herb tea.
tison [tizɔ̃] *nm* brand.
tisonner [tizɔne] *vt* to poke.
tisonnier [tizɔnje] *nm* poker.
tissage [tisaʒ] *nm* weaving *no pl.*
tisser [tise] *vt* to weave.
tisserand, e [tisrɑ̃, -ɑ̃d] *nm/f* weaver.
tissu [tisy] *nm* fabric, material, cloth *no pl*; (*fig*) fabric; (*ANAT, BIO*) tissue; ~ **de mensonges** web of lies.
tissu, e [tisy] *adj*: ~ **de** woven through with.
tissu-éponge [tisyepɔ̃ʒ] *nm* (terry) towelling *no pl.*
titane [titan] *nm* titanium.
titanesque [titanɛsk(ə)] *adj* titanic.
titiller [titile] *vt* to titillate.
titrage [titraʒ] *nm* (*d'un film*) titling; (*d'un alcool*) *determination of alcohol content.*
titre [titr(ə)] *nm* (*gén*) title; (*de journal*) headline; (*diplôme*) qualification; (*COMM*) security; (*CHIMIE*) titre; **en** ~ (*champion, responsable*) official, recognized; **à juste** ~ with just cause, rightly; **à quel** ~**?** on what grounds?; **à aucun** ~ on no account; **au même** ~ **(que)** in the same way (as); **au** ~ **de la coopération** *etc* in the name of cooperation *etc*; **à** ~ **d'exemple** as an *ou* by way of an example; **à** ~ **exceptionnel** exceptionally; **à** ~ **d'information** for (your) information; **à** ~ **gracieux** free of charge; **à** ~ **d'essai** on a trial basis; **à** ~ **privé** in a private capacity; ~ **courant** running head; ~ **de propriété** title deed; ~ **de transport** ticket.
titré, e [titre] *adj* (*livre, film*) entitled; (*personne*) titled.
titrer [titre] *vt* (*CHIMIE*) to titrate; to assay; (*PRESSE*) to run as a headline; (*suj: vin*): ~ **10°** to be 10° proof.
titubant, e [titybɑ̃, -ɑ̃t] *adj* staggering, reeling.
tituber [titybe] *vi* to stagger *ou* reel (along).
titulaire [titylɛr] *adj* (*ADMIN*) appointed, with tenure ♦ *nm* (*ADMIN*) incumbent; **être** ~ **de** to hold.
titularisation [titylarizɑsjɔ̃] *nf* granting of tenure.
titulariser [titylarize] *vt* to give tenure to.
TNP *sigle m* = *Théâtre national populaire.*
TNT *sigle m* (= *Trinitrotoluène*) TNT.
toast [tost] *nm* slice *ou* piece of toast; (*de bienvenue*) (welcoming) toast; **porter un** ~ **à qn** to propose *ou* drink a toast to sb.
toboggan [tɔbɔgɑ̃] *nm* toboggan; (*jeu*) slide; (*AUTO*) temporary flyover (*BRIT*) *ou* overpass (*US*); ~ **de secours** (*AVIAT*) escape chute.
toc [tɔk] *nm*: **en** ~ imitation *cpd.*
tocsin [tɔksɛ̃] *nm* alarm (bell).
toge [tɔʒ] *nf* toga; (*de juge*) gown.
Togo [tɔgo] *nm*: **le** ~ Togo.
togolais, e [tɔgɔlɛ, -ɛz] *adj* Togolese.
tohu-bohu [tɔybɔy] *nm* (*désordre*) confusion; (*tumulte*) commotion.
toi [twa] *pron* you; ~**, tu l'as fait?** did YOU do it?
toile [twal] *nf* (*matériau*) cloth *no pl*; (*bâche*) piece of canvas; (*tableau*) canvas; **grosse** ~ canvas; **tisser sa** ~ (*araignée*) to spin its web; ~ **d'araignée** spider's web; (*au plafond etc: à enlever*) cobweb; ~ **cirée** oilcloth; ~ **émeri** emery cloth; ~ **de fond** (*fig*) backdrop; ~ **de jute** hessian; ~ **de lin** linen; ~ **de tente** canvas.
toilettage [twalɛtaʒ] *nm* grooming *no pl*; (*d'un texte*) tidying up.
toilette [twalɛt] *nf* wash; (*s'habiller et se préparer*) getting ready, washing and dressing; (*habits*) outfit; dress *no pl*; ~**s** *nfpl* toilet *sg*; **les** ~**s des dames/messieurs** the ladies'/gents' (toilets) (*BRIT*), the ladies'/mens' (rest)room (*US*); **faire sa** ~ to have a wash, get washed; **faire la** ~ **de** (*animal*) to groom; (*voiture etc*) to clean, wash; (*texte*) to tidy up; **articles de** ~ toiletries; ~ **intime** personal hygiene.
toi-même [twamɛm] *pron* yourself.
toise [twaz] *nf*: **passer à la** ~ to have one's height measured.
toiser [twaze] *vt* to eye up and down.
toison [twazɔ̃] *nf* (*de mouton*) fleece; (*cheveux*) mane.
toit [twa] *nm* roof; ~ **ouvrant** sun roof.
toiture [twatyr] *nf* roof.
Tokyo [tɔkjo] *n* Tokyo.
tôle [tol] *nf* sheet metal *no pl*; (*plaque*) steel (*ou* iron) sheet; ~**s** *nfpl* (*carosserie*) bodywork *sg* (*BRIT*), body *sg*; panels; ~ **d'acier** sheet steel *no pl*; ~ **ondulée** corrugated iron.
Tolède [tɔlɛd] *n* Toledo.
tolérable [tɔlerabl(ə)] *adj* tolerable, bearable.
tolérance [tɔlerɑ̃s] *nf* tolerance; (*hors taxe*) allowance.
tolérant, e [tɔlerɑ̃, -ɑ̃t] *adj* tolerant.
tolérer [tɔlere] *vt* to tolerate; (*ADMIN: hors taxe etc*) to allow.
tôlerie [tolri] *nf* sheet metal manufacture; (*atelier*) sheet metal workshop; (*ensemble des tôles*) panels *pl.*
tollé [tɔle] *nm*: **un** ~ **(de protestations)** a general outcry.
TOM [*parfois*: tɔm] *sigle m(pl)* = *territoire(s) d'outre-mer.*
tomate [tɔmat] *nf* tomato.
tombal, e [tɔ̃bal] *adj*: **pierre** ~**e** tombstone, gravestone.
tombant, e [tɔ̃bɑ̃, -ɑ̃t] *adj* (*fig*) drooping, sloping.
tombe [tɔ̃b] *nf* (*sépulture*) grave; (*avec monument*) tomb.
tombeau, x [tɔ̃bo] *nm* tomb; **à** ~ **ouvert** at breakneck speed.
tombée [tɔ̃be] *nf*: **à la** ~ **du jour** *ou* **de la nuit**

at the close of day, at nightfall.

tomber [tɔ̃be] *vi* to fall ♦ *vt*: ~ **la veste** to slip off one's jacket; **laisser** ~ to drop; ~ **sur** *vt* (*rencontrer*) to come across; (*attaquer*) to set about; ~ **de fatigue/sommeil** to drop from exhaustion/be falling asleep on one's feet; ~ **à l'eau** (*fig*: *projet etc*) to fall through; ~ **en panne** to break down; ~ **juste** (*opération, calcul*) to come out right; ~ **en ruine** to fall into ruins; **ça tombe bien/mal** (*fig*) that's come at the right/wrong time; **il est bien/mal tombé** (*fig*) he's been lucky/unlucky.

tombereau, x [tɔ̃bʀo] *nm* tipcart.

tombeur [tɔ̃bœʀ] *nm* (*péj*) Casanova.

tombola [tɔ̃bɔla] *nf* tombola.

Tombouctou [tɔ̃buktu] *n* Timbuktu.

tome [tɔm] *nm* volume.

tommette [tɔmɛt] *nf* hexagonal floor tile.

ton, ta, *pl* **tes** [tɔ̃, ta, te] *adj possessif* your.

ton [tɔ̃] *nm* (*gén*) tone; (*MUS*) key; (*couleur*) shade, tone; (*de la voix*: *hauteur*) pitch; **donner le** ~ to set the tone; **élever** *ou* **hausser le** ~ to raise one's voice; **de bon** ~ in good taste; **si vous le prenez sur ce** ~ if you're going to take it like that; ~ **sur** ~ in matching shades.

tonal, e [tɔnal] *adj* tonal.

tonalité [tɔnalite] *nf* (*au téléphone*) dialling tone; (*MUS*) tonality; (*: ton*) key; (*fig*) tone.

tondeuse [tɔ̃døz] *nf* (*à gazon*) (lawn)mower; (*du coiffeur*) clippers *pl*; (*pour la tonte*) shears *pl*.

tondre [tɔ̃dʀ(ə)] *vt* (*pelouse, herbe*) to mow; (*haie*) to cut, clip; (*mouton, toison*) to shear; (*cheveux*) to crop.

tondu, e [tɔ̃dy] *pp de* **tondre** ♦ *adj* (*cheveux*) cropped; (*mouton, crâne*) shorn.

Tonga [tɔ̃ga]: **les îles** ~ Tonga.

tonicité [tɔnisite] *nf* (*MÉD*: *des tissus*) tone; (*fig*: *de l'air, la mer*) bracing effect.

tonifiant, e [tɔnifjɑ̃, -ɑ̃t] *adj* invigorating, revivifying.

tonifier [tɔnifje] *vt* (*air, eau*) to invigorate; (*peau, organisme*) to tone up.

tonique [tɔnik] *adj* fortifying; (*personne*) dynamic ♦ *nm, nf* tonic.

tonitruant, e [tɔnitʀyɑ̃, -ɑ̃t] *adj*: **voix** ~**e** thundering voice.

Tonkin [tɔ̃kɛ̃] *nm*: **le** ~ Tonkin, Tongking.

tonkinois, e [tɔ̃kinwa, -waz] *adj* Tonkinese.

tonnage [tɔnaʒ] *nm* tonnage.

tonnant, e [tɔnɑ̃, -ɑ̃t] *adj* thunderous.

tonne [tɔn] *nf* metric ton, tonne.

tonneau, x [tɔno] *nm* (*à vin, cidre*) barrel; (*NAVIG*) ton; **faire des** ~**x** (*voiture, avion*) to roll over.

tonnelet [tɔnlɛ] *nm* keg.

tonnelier [tɔnəlje] *nm* cooper.

tonnelle [tɔnɛl] *nf* bower, arbour (*BRIT*), arbor (*US*).

tonner [tɔne] *vi* to thunder; (*parler avec véhémence*): ~ **contre qn/qch** to inveigh against sb/sth; **il tonne** it is thundering, there's some thunder.

tonnerre [tɔnɛʀ] *nm* thunder; **coup de** ~ (*fig*) thunderbolt, bolt from the blue; **un** ~ **d'applaudissements** thunderous applause; **du** ~ *adj* (*fam*) terrific.

tonsure [tɔ̃syʀ] *nf* bald patch; (*de moine*) tonsure.

tonte [tɔ̃t] *nf* shearing.

tonus [tɔnys] *nm* (*des muscles*) tone; (*d'une personne*) dynamism.

top [tɔp] *nm*: **au 3ème** ~ at the 3rd stroke ♦ *adj*: ~ **secret** top secret ♦ *excl* go!

topaze [tɔpɑz] *nf* topaz.

toper [tɔpe] *vi*: **tope-/topez-là** it's a deal!, you're on!

topinambour [tɔpinɑ̃buʀ] *nm* Jerusalem artichoke.

topo [tɔpo] *nm* (*discours, exposé*) talk; (*fam*) spiel.

topographie [tɔpɔgʀafi] *nf* topography.

topographique [tɔpɔgʀafik] *adj* topographical.

toponymie [tɔpɔnimi] *nf* study of place names, toponymy.

toquade [tɔkad] *nf* fad, craze.

toque [tɔk] *nf* (*de fourrure*) fur hat; ~ **de jockey/juge** jockey's/judge's cap; ~ **de cuisinier** chef's hat.

toqué, e [tɔke] *adj* (*fam*) touched, cracked.

torche [tɔʀʃ(ə)] *nf* torch; **se mettre en** ~ (*parachute*) to candle.

torcher [tɔʀʃe] *vt* (*fam*) to wipe.

torchère [tɔʀʃɛʀ] *nf* flare.

torchon [tɔʀʃɔ̃] *nm* cloth, duster; (*à vaisselle*) tea towel *ou* cloth.

tordre [tɔʀdʀ(ə)] *vt* (*chiffon*) to wring; (*barre, fig: visage*) to twist; **se** ~ *vi* (*barre*) to bend; (*roue*) to twist, buckle; (*ver, serpent*) to writhe; **se** ~ **le pied/bras** to twist one's foot/arm; **se** ~ **de douleur/rire** to writhe in pain/be doubled up with laughter.

tordu, e [tɔʀdy] *pp de* **tordre** ♦ *adj* (*fig*) warped, twisted.

torero [tɔʀeʀo] *nm* bullfighter.

tornade [tɔʀnad] *nf* tornado.

toron [tɔʀɔ̃] *nm* strand (of rope).

Toronto [tɔʀɔ̃to] *n* Toronto.

torontois, e [tɔʀɔ̃twa, -waz] *adj* Torontonian ♦ *nm/f*: **T**~, **e** Torontonian.

torpeur [tɔʀpœʀ] *nf* torpor, drowsiness.

torpille [tɔʀpij] *nf* torpedo.

torpiller [tɔʀpije] *vt* to torpedo.

torpilleur [tɔʀpijœʀ] *nm* torpedo boat.

torréfaction [tɔʀefaksjɔ̃] *nf* roasting.

torréfier [tɔʀefje] *vt* to roast.

torrent [tɔʀɑ̃] *nm* torrent, mountain stream; (*fig*): **un** ~ **de** a torrent *ou* flood of; **il pleut à** ~**s** the rain is lashing down.

torrentiel, le [tɔʀɑ̃sjɛl] *adj* torrential.

torride [tɔʀid] *adj* torrid.

tors, torse *ou* **torte** [tɔʀ, tɔʀs(ə) *ou* tɔʀt(ə)]

adj twisted.
torsade [tɔʀsad] *nf* twist; (*ARCHIT*) cable moulding (*BRIT*) *ou* molding (*US*).
torsader [tɔʀsade] *vt* to twist.
torse [tɔʀs(ə)] *nm* torso; (*poitrine*) chest.
torsion [tɔʀsjɔ̃] *nf* (*action*) twisting; (*TECH, PHYSIQUE*) torsion.
tort [tɔʀ] *nm* (*défaut*) fault; (*préjudice*) wrong *no pl*; **~s** *nmpl* (*JUR*) fault *sg*; **avoir ~** to be wrong; **être dans son ~** to be in the wrong; **donner ~ à qn** to lay the blame on sb; (*fig*) to prove sb wrong; **causer du ~ à** to harm; to be harmful *ou* detrimental to; **en ~** in the wrong, at fault; **à ~** wrongly; **à ~ ou à raison** rightly or wrongly; **à ~ et à travers** wildly.
torte [tɔʀt(ə)] *adj f voir* **tors**.
torticolis [tɔʀtikɔli] *nm* stiff neck.
tortiller [tɔʀtije] *vt* (*corde, mouchoir*) to twist; (*doigts*) to twiddle; **se ~** *vi* to wriggle, squirm.
tortionnaire [tɔʀsjɔnɛʀ] *nm* torturer.
tortue [tɔʀty] *nf* tortoise; (*fig*) slowcoach (*BRIT*), slowpoke (*US*).
tortueux, euse [tɔʀtɥø, -øz] *adj* (*rue*) twisting; (*fig*) tortuous.
torture [tɔʀtyʀ] *nf* torture.
torturer [tɔʀtyʀe] *vt* to torture; (*fig*) to torment.
torve [tɔʀv(ə)] *adj*: **regard ~** menacing *ou* grim look.
toscan, e [tɔskɑ̃, -an] *adj* Tuscan.
Toscane [tɔskan] *nf*: **la ~** Tuscany.
tôt [to] *adv* early; **~ ou tard** sooner or later; **si ~** so early; (*déjà*) so soon; **au plus ~** at the earliest, as soon as possible; **plus ~** earlier; **il eut ~ fait de faire ...** he soon did ....
total, e, aux [tɔtal, -o] *adj, nm* total; **au ~** in total *ou* all; (*fig*) all in all; **faire le ~** to work out the total.
totalement [tɔtalmɑ̃] *adv* totally, completely.
totalisateur [tɔtalizatœʀ] *nm* adding machine.
totaliser [tɔtalize] *vt* to total (up).
totalitaire [tɔtalitɛʀ] *adj* totalitarian.
totalitarisme [tɔtalitaʀism(ə)] *nm* totalitarianism.
totalité [tɔtalite] *nf*: **la ~ de**: **la ~ des élèves** all (of) the pupils; **la ~ de la population/classe** the whole population/class; **en ~** entirely.
totem [tɔtɛm] *nm* totem.
toubib [tubib] *nm* (*fam*) doctor.
touchant, e [tuʃɑ̃, -ɑ̃t] *adj* touching.
touche [tuʃ] *nf* (*de piano, de machine à écrire*) key; (*de violon*) fingerboard; (*de télécommande etc*) key, button; (*PEINTURE etc*) stroke, touch; (*fig: de couleur, nostalgie*) touch, hint; (*RUGBY*) line-out; (*FOOTBALL*: *aussi*: **remise en ~**) throw-in; (*aussi*: **ligne de ~**) touch-line; (*ESCRIME*) hit; **en ~** in (*ou* into) touch; **avoir une drôle de ~** to look a sight; **~ de commande/de fonction/de retour** (*INFORM*) control/function/return key; **~ à effleurement** *ou* **sensitive** touch-sensitive control *ou* key.
touche-à-tout [tuʃatu] *nm inv* (*péj*: *gén*: *enfant*) meddler; (: *fig*: *inventeur etc*) dabbler.
toucher [tuʃe] *nm* touch ♦ *vt* to touch; (*palper*) to feel; (*atteindre: d'un coup de feu etc*) to hit; (*affecter*) to touch, affect; (*concerner*) to concern, affect; (*contacter*) to reach, contact; (*recevoir: récompense*) to receive, get; (: *salaire*) to draw, get; (*chèque*) to cash; (*aborder*: *problème, sujet*) to touch on; **au ~** to the touch; by the feel; **se ~** (*être en contact*) to touch; **~ à** to touch; (*modifier*) to touch, tamper *ou* meddle with; (*traiter de, concerner*) to have to do with, concern; **je vais lui en ~ un mot** I'll have a word with him about it; **~ au but** (*fig*) to near one's goal; **~ à sa fin** to be drawing to a close.
touffe [tuf] *nf* tuft.
touffu, e [tufy] *adj* thick, dense; (*fig*) complex, involved.
toujours [tuʒuʀ] *adv* always; (*encore*) still; (*constamment*) forever; **depuis ~** always; **essaie ~** (you can) try anyway; **pour ~** forever; **~ est-il que** the fact remains that; **~ plus** more and more.
toulonnais, e [tulɔnɛ, -ɛz] of *ou* from Toulon.
toulousain, e [tuluzɛ̃, -ɛn] *adj* of *ou* from Toulouse.
toupet [tupɛ] *nm* quiff (*BRIT*), tuft; (*fam*) nerve, cheek (*BRIT*).
toupie [tupi] *nf* (spinning) top.
tour [tuʀ] *nf* tower; (*immeuble*) high-rise block (*BRIT*) *ou* building (*US*), tower block (*BRIT*); (*ÉCHECS*) castle, rook ♦ *nm* (*excursion: à pied*) stroll, walk; (: *en voiture etc*) run, ride; (: *plus long*) trip; (*SPORT*: *aussi*: **~ de piste**) lap; (*d'être servi ou de jouer etc, tournure, de vis ou clef*) turn; (*de roue etc*) revolution; (*circonférence*): **de 3 m de ~** 3 m round, with a circumference *ou* girth of 3 m; (*POL*: *aussi*: **~ de scrutin**) ballot; (*ruse, de prestidigitation, de cartes*) trick; (*de potier*) wheel; (*à bois, métaux*) lathe; **faire le ~ de** to go (a)round; (*à pied*) to walk (a)round; (*fig*) to review; **faire le ~ de l'Europe** to tour Europe; **faire un ~** to go for a walk; (*en voiture etc*) to go for a ride; **faire 2 ~s** to go (a)round twice; (*hélice etc*) to turn *ou* revolve twice; **fermer à double ~** *vi* to double-lock the door; **c'est au ~ de Renée** it's Renée's turn; **à ~ de rôle, ~ à ~** in turn; **à ~ de bras** with all one's strength; (*fig*) non-stop, relentlessly; **~ de taille/tête** waist/head measurement; **~ de chant** song recital; **~ de contrôle** *nf* control tower; **~ de garde** spell of duty; **~ d'horizon** (*fig*) general survey; **~ de lit** valance; **~ de main** dexterity, knack; **en un ~ de main** (as) quick as a flash; **~ de passe-passe** trick, sleight of hand; **~ de reins** sprained back; *see boxed note*.

TOUR DE FRANCE

The **Tour de France** *is an annual road race for professional cyclists. It takes about three weeks to complete and is divided into daily stages, or 'étapes', of approximately 175 km (110 miles) over terrain of varying levels of difficulty. The leading cyclist wears a yellow jersey, the 'maillot jaune'. The route varies; it is not usually confined to France but the race always ends in Paris. In addition, there are a number of time trials.*

tourangeau, elle, x [turɑ̃ʒo, -ɛl] *adj* (*de la région*) of *ou* from Touraine; (*de la ville*) of *ou* from Tours.
tourbe [turb(ə)] *nf* peat.
tourbière [turbjɛr] *nf* peat-bog.
tourbillon [turbijɔ̃] *nm* whirlwind; (*d'eau*) whirlpool; (*fig*) whirl, swirl.
tourbillonner [turbijɔne] *vi* to whirl, swirl; (*objet, personne*) to whirl *ou* twirl round.
tourelle [turɛl] *nf* turret.
tourisme [turism(ə)] *nm* tourism; **agence de** ~ tourist agency; **avion/voiture de** ~ private plane/car; **faire du** ~ to do some sightseeing, go touring.
touriste [turist(ə)] *nm/f* tourist.
touristique [turistik] *adj* tourist *cpd*; (*région*) touristic (*péj*), with tourist appeal.
tourment [turmɑ̃] *nm* torment.
tourmente [turmɑ̃t] *nf* storm.
tourmenté, e [turmɑ̃te] *adj* tormented, tortured; (*mer, période*) turbulent.
tourmenter [turmɑ̃te] *vt* to torment; **se** ~ *vi* to fret, worry o.s.
tournage [turnaʒ] *nm* (*d'un film*) shooting.
tournant, e [turnɑ̃, -ɑ̃t] *adj* (*feu, scène*) revolving; (*chemin*) winding; (*escalier*) spiral *cpd*; (*mouvement*) circling ♦ *nm* (*de route*) bend (*BRIT*), curve (*US*); (*fig*) turning point; *voir* **plaque, grève**.
tourné, e [turne] *adj* (*lait, vin*) sour, off; (*bois*) turned; (*fig: compliment*) well-phrased; **bien** ~ (*femme*) shapely; **mal** ~ (*lettre*) badly expressed; **avoir l'esprit mal** ~ to have a dirty mind.
tournebroche [turnəbrɔʃ] *nm* roasting spit.
tourne-disque [turnədisk(ə)] *nm* record player.
tournedos [turnədo] *nm* tournedos.
tournée [turne] *nf* (*du facteur etc*) round; (*d'artiste, politicien*) tour; (*au café*) round (of drinks); **faire la** ~ **de** to go (a)round.
tournemain [turnəmɛ̃]: **en un** ~ *adv* in a flash.
tourner [turne] *vt* to turn; (*sauce, mélange*) to stir; (*contourner*) to get (a)round; (*CINÉ*) to shoot; to make ♦ *vi* to turn; (*moteur*) to run; (*compteur*) to tick away; (*lait etc*) to turn (sour); (*fig: chance, vie*) to turn out; **se** ~ *vi* to turn (a)round; **se** ~ **vers** to turn to; to turn towards; **bien** ~ to turn out well; ~ **autour de** to go (a)round; (*planète*) to revolve (a)round; (*péj*) to hang (a)round; ~ **autour du pot** (*fig*) to go (a)round in circles; ~ **à/en** to turn into; ~ **à la pluie/au rouge** to turn rainy/red; ~ **en ridicule** to ridicule; ~ **le dos à** (*mouvement*) to turn one's back on; (*position*) to have one's back to; ~ **court** to come to a sudden end; **se** ~ **les pouces** to twiddle one's thumbs; ~ **la tête** to look away; ~ **la tête à qn** (*fig*) to go to sb's head; ~ **de l'œil** to pass out; ~ **la page** (*fig*) to turn the page.
tournesol [turnəsɔl] *nm* sunflower.
tourneur [turnœr] *nm* turner; lathe-operator.
tournevis [turnəvis] *nm* screwdriver.
tourniquer [turnike] *vi* to go round in circles.
tourniquet [turnikɛ] *nm* (*pour arroser*) sprinkler; (*portillon*) turnstile; (*présentoir*) revolving stand, spinner; (*CHIRURGIE*) tourniquet.
tournis [turni] *nm*: **avoir/donner le** ~ to feel/make dizzy.
tournoi [turnwa] *nm* tournament.
tournoyer [turnwaje] *vi* (*oiseau*) to wheel (a)round; (*fumée*) to swirl (a)round.
tournure [turnyr] *nf* (*LING: syntaxe*) turn of phrase; form; (*: d'une phrase*) phrasing; (*évolution*): **la** ~ **de qch** the way sth is developing; (*aspect*): **la** ~ **de** the look of; **la** ~ **des événements** the turn of events; **prendre** ~ to take shape.
tour-opérateur [turɔperatœr] *nm* tour operator.
tourte [turt(ə)] *nf* pie.
tourteau, x [turto] *nm* (*AGR*) oilcake, cattle-cake; (*ZOOL*) edible crab.
tourtereaux [turtəro] *nmpl* lovebirds.
tourterelle [turtərɛl] *nf* turtledove.
tourtière [turtjɛr] *nf* pie dish *ou* plate.
tous *dét* [tu], *pron* [tus] *voir* **tout**.
Toussaint [tusɛ̃] *nf*: **la** ~ All Saints' Day; *see boxed note*.

LA TOUSSAINT

La Toussaint, *1 November or All Saints' Day, is a public holiday in France. People traditionally visit the graves of friends and relatives to lay chrysanthemums on them.*

tousser [tuse] *vi* to cough.
toussoter [tusɔte] *vi* to have a slight cough; (*pour avertir*) to give a slight cough.

MOT-CLÉ

tout, e [tu, tut] (*mpl* **tous**, *fpl* **toutes**) *adj* **1** (*avec article singulier*) all; ~ **le lait** all the milk; ~**e la nuit** all night, the whole night; ~ **le livre** the whole book; ~ **un pain** a whole loaf; ~ **le temps** all the time, the whole time; **c'est** ~ **le contraire** it's quite the opposite; **c'est** ~**e une affaire** *ou* **histoire** it's quite a business, it's a whole rigmarole
2 (*avec article pluriel*) every; all; **tous les**

livres all the books; **~es les nuits** every night; **~es les fois** every time; **~es les trois/deux semaines** every third/other *ou* second week, every three/two weeks; **tous les deux** both *ou* each of us (*ou* them *ou* you); **~es les trois** all three of us (*ou* them *ou* you)
3 (*sans article*): **à ~ âge** at any age; **pour ~e nourriture, il avait ...** his only food was ...; **de tous côtés, de ~es parts** from everywhere, from every side
♦ *pron* everything, all; **il a ~ fait** he's done everything; **je les vois tous** I can see them all *ou* all of them; **nous y sommes tous allés** all of us went, we all went; **c'est ~** that's all; **en ~** in all; **en ~ et pour ~** all in all; **~ ce qu'il sait** all he knows; **c'était ~ ce qu'il y a de chic** it was the last word *ou* the ultimate in chic
♦ *nm* whole; **le ~** all of it (*ou* them); **le ~ est de ...** the main thing is to ...; **pas du ~** not at all; **elle a ~ d'une mère/d'une intrigante** she's a real *ou* true mother/schemer; **du ~ au ~** utterly
♦ *adv* **1** (*très, complètement*) very; **~ près** *ou* **à côté** very near; **le ~ premier** the very first; **~ seul** all alone; **il était ~ rouge** he was really *ou* all red; **parler ~ bas** to speak very quietly; **le livre ~ entier** the whole book; **~ en haut** right at the top; **~ droit** straight ahead
2: **~ en** while; **~ en travaillant** while working, as he *etc* works
3: **~ d'abord** first of all; **~ à coup** suddenly; **~ à fait** absolutely; **~ a fait!** exactly!; **~ à l'heure** a short while ago; (*futur*) in a short while, shortly; **à ~ à l'heure!** see you later!; **il répondit ~ court que non** he just answered no (and that was all); **~ de même** all the same; **~ le monde** everybody; **~ ou rien** all or nothing; **~ simplement** quite simply; **~ de suite** immediately, straight away

tout-à-l'égout [tutalegu] *nm inv* mains drainage.
toutefois [tutfwa] *adv* however.
toutou [tutu] *nm* (*fam*) doggie.
tout-petit [tup(ə)ti] *nm* toddler.
tout-puissant, toute-puissante [tupɥisɑ̃, tutpɥisɑ̃t] *adj* all-powerful, omnipotent.
tout-venant [tuvnɑ̃] *nm*: **le ~** everyday stuff.
toux [tu] *nf* cough.
toxémie [tɔksemi] *nf* toxaemia (*BRIT*), toxemia (*US*).
toxicité [tɔksisite] *nf* toxicity.
toxicologie [tɔksikɔlɔʒi] *nf* toxicology.
toxicomane [tɔksikɔman] *nm/f* drug addict.
toxicomanie [tɔksikɔmani] *nf* drug addiction.
toxine [tɔksin] *nf* toxin.
toxique [tɔksik] *adj* toxic, poisonous.
toxoplasmose [tɔksoplasmoz] *nf* toxoplasmosis.
TP *sigle mpl* = **travaux pratiques, travaux publics** ♦ *sigle m* = **trésor public**.
TPG *sigle m* = **Trésorier-payeur général**.
tps *abr* = **temps**.
trac [tʀak] *nm* nerves *pl*; (*THÉÂT*) stage fright; **avoir le ~** to get an attack of nerves; to have stage fright; **tout à ~** all of a sudden.
traçant, e [tʀasɑ̃, -ɑ̃t] *adj*: **table ~e** (*INFORM*) (graph) plotter.
tracas [tʀaka] *nm* bother *no pl*, worry *no pl*.
tracasser [tʀakase] *vt* to worry, bother; (*harceler*) to harass; **se ~** *vi* to worry o.s., fret.
tracasserie [tʀakasʀi] *nf* annoyance *no pl*; harassment *no pl*.
tracassier, ière [tʀakasje, -jɛʀ] *adj* irksome.
trace [tʀas] *nf* (*empreintes*) tracks *pl*; (*marques, aussi fig*) mark; (*restes, vestige*) trace; (*indice*) sign; **suivre à la ~** to track; **~s de pas** footprints.
tracé [tʀase] *nm* (*contour*) line; (*plan*) layout.
tracer [tʀase] *vt* to draw; (*mot*) to trace; (*piste*) to open up; (*fig*: *chemin*) to show.
traceur [tʀasœʀ] *nm* (*INFORM*) plotter.
trachée(-artère) [tʀaʃe(aʀtɛʀ)] *nf* windpipe, trachea.
trachéite [tʀakeit] *nf* tracheitis.
tract [tʀakt] *nm* tract, pamphlet; (*publicitaire*) handout.
tractations [tʀaktɑsjɔ̃] *nfpl* dealings, bargaining *sg*.
tracter [tʀakte] *vt* to tow.
tracteur [tʀaktœʀ] *nm* tractor.
traction [tʀaksjɔ̃] *nf* traction; (*GYM*) pull-up; **~ avant/arrière** front-wheel/rear-wheel drive; **~ électrique** electric(al) traction *ou* haulage.
trad. *abr* (= *traduit*) translated; (= *traduction*) translation; (= *traducteur*) translator.
tradition [tʀadisjɔ̃] *nf* tradition.
traditionalisme [tʀadisjɔnalism(ə)] *nm* traditionalism.
traditionaliste [tʀadisjɔnalist(ə)] *adj, nm/f* traditionalist.
traditionnel, le [tʀadisjɔnɛl] *adj* traditional.
traditionnellement [tʀadisjɔnɛlmɑ̃] *adv* traditionally.
traducteur, trice [tʀadyktœʀ, -tʀis] *nm/f* translator.
traduction [tʀadyksjɔ̃] *nf* translation.
traduire [tʀadɥiʀ] *vt* to translate; (*exprimer*) to render, convey; **se ~ par** to find expression in; **~ en français** to translate into French; **~ en justice** to bring before the courts.
traduis [tʀadɥi] *etc vb voir* **traduire**.
traduisible [tʀadɥizibl(ə)] *adj* translatable.
traduit, e [tʀadɥi, -it] *pp de* **traduire**.
trafic [tʀafik] *nm* traffic; **~ d'armes** arms dealing; **~ de drogue** drug peddling.
trafiquant, e [tʀafikɑ̃, -ɑ̃t] *nm/f* trafficker; dealer.
trafiquer [tʀafike] *vt* (*péj*) to doctor, tamper with ♦ *vi* to traffic, be engaged in traffick-

ing.

tragédie [tʀaʒedi] *nf* tragedy.

tragédien, ne [tʀaʒedjɛ̃, -ɛn] *nm/f* tragedian/ tragedienne.

tragi-comique [tʀaʒikɔmik] *adj* tragi-comic.

tragique [tʀaʒik] *adj* tragic ♦ *nm*: **prendre qch au** ~ to make a tragedy out of sth.

tragiquement [tʀaʒikmɑ̃] *adv* tragically.

trahir [tʀaiʀ] *vt* to betray; (*fig*) to give away, reveal; **se** ~ to betray o.s., give o.s. away.

trahison [tʀaizɔ̃] *nf* betrayal; (*JUR*) treason.

traie [tʀɛ] *etc vb voir* **traire**.

train [tʀɛ̃] *nm* (*RAIL*) train; (*allure*) pace; (*fig: ensemble*) set; **être en** ~ **de faire qch** to be doing sth; **mettre qch en** ~ to get sth under way; **mettre qn en** ~ to put sb in good spirits; **se mettre en** ~ (*commencer*) to get started; (*faire de la gymnastique*) to warm up; **se sentir en** ~ to feel in good form; **aller bon** ~ to make good progress; ~ **avant/arrière** front-wheel/rear-wheel axle unit; ~ **à grande vitesse (TGV)** high-speed train; ~ **d'atterrissage** undercarriage; ~ **autos-couchettes** car-sleeper train; ~ **électrique** (*jouet*) (electric) train set; ~ **de pneus** set of tyres *ou* tires; ~ **de vie** style of living.

traînailler [tʀɛnɑje] *vi* = **traînasser**.

traînant, e [tʀɛnɑ̃, -ɑ̃t] *adj* (*voix, ton*) drawling.

traînard, e [tʀɛnaʀ, -aʀd(ə)] *nm/f* (*péj*) slowcoach (*BRIT*), slowpoke (*US*).

traînasser [tʀɛnase] *vi* to dawdle.

traîne [tʀɛn] *nf* (*de robe*) train; **être à la** ~ to be in tow; (*en arrière*) to lag behind; (*en désordre*) to be lying around.

traineau, x [tʀɛno] *nm* sleigh, sledge.

traînée [tʀene] *nf* streak, trail; (*péj*) slut.

traîner [tʀene] *vt* (*remorque*) to pull; (*enfant, chien*) to drag *ou* trail along; (*maladie*): **il traine un rhume depuis l'hiver** he has a cold which has been dragging on since winter ♦ *vi* (*être en désordre*) to lie around; (*marcher lentement*) to dawdle (along); (*vagabonder*) to hang about; (*agir lentement*) to idle about; (*durer*) to drag on; **se** ~ *vi* (*ramper*) to crawl along; (*marcher avec difficulté*) to drag o.s. along; (*durer*) to drag on; **se** ~ **par terre** to crawl (on the ground); ~ **qn au cinéma** to drag sb to the cinema; ~ **les pieds** to drag one's feet; ~ **par terre** to trail on the ground; ~ **en longueur** to drag out.

training [tʀɛniŋ] *nm* (*pull*) tracksuit top; (*chaussure*) trainer (*BRIT*), sneaker (*US*).

train-train [tʀɛ̃tʀɛ̃] *nm* humdrum routine.

traire [tʀɛʀ] *vt* to milk.

trait, e [tʀɛ, -ɛt] *pp de* **traire** ♦ *nm* (*ligne*) line; (*de dessin*) stroke; (*caractéristique*) feature, trait; (*flèche*) dart, arrow; shaft; ~**s** *nmpl* (*du visage*) features; **d'un** ~ (*boire*) in one gulp; **de** ~ *adj* (*animal*) draught (*BRIT*), draft (*US*); **avoir** ~ **à** to concern; ~ **pour** ~ line for line; ~ **de caractère** characteristic, trait; ~ **d'esprit** flash of wit; ~ **de génie** brainwave; ~ **d'union** hyphen; (*fig*) link.

traitable [tʀɛtabl(ə)] *adj* (*personne*) accommodating; (*sujet*) manageable.

traitant, e [tʀɛtɑ̃, -ɑ̃t] *adj*: **votre médecin** ~ your usual *ou* family doctor; **shampooing** ~ medicated shampoo; **crème** ~**e** conditioning cream, conditioner.

traite [tʀɛt] *nf* (*COMM*) draft; (*AGR*) milking; (*trajet*) stretch; **d'une (seule)** ~ without stopping (once); **la** ~ **des noirs** the slave trade; **la** ~ **des blanches** the white slave trade.

traité [tʀete] *nm* treaty.

traitement [tʀɛtmɑ̃] *nm* treatment; processing; (*salaire*) salary; **suivre un** ~ to undergo treatment; **mauvais** ~ ill-treatment; ~ **de données** *ou* **de l'information** (*INFORM*) data processing; ~ **hormono-supplétif** hormone replacement therapy; ~ **par lots** (*INFORM*) batch processing; ~ **de texte** (*INFORM*) word processing.

traiter [tʀete] *vt* (*gén*) to treat; (*TECH: matériaux*) to process, treat; (*INFORM*) to process; (*affaire*) to deal with, handle; (*qualifier*): ~ **qn d'idiot** to call sb a fool ♦ *vi* to deal; ~ **de** *vt* to deal with; **bien/mal** ~ to treat well/ill-treat.

traiteur [tʀɛtœʀ] *nm* caterer.

traître, esse [tʀɛtʀ(ə), -tʀɛs] *adj* (*dangereux*) treacherous ♦ *nm* traitor; **prendre qn en** ~ to take sb off-guard.

traîtrise [tʀɛtʀiz] *nf* treachery.

trajectoire [tʀaʒɛktwaʀ] *nf* trajectory, path.

trajet [tʀaʒɛ] *nm* journey; (*itinéraire*) route; (*fig*) path, course.

tralala [tʀalala] *nm* (*péj*) fuss.

tram [tʀam] *nm* tram (*BRIT*), streetcar (*US*).

trame [tʀam] *nf* (*de tissu*) weft; (*fig*) framework; texture; (*TYPO*) screen.

tramer [tʀame] *vt* to plot, hatch.

trampoline [tʀɑ̃pɔlin], **trampolino** [tʀɑ̃pɔlino] *nm* trampoline; (*SPORT*) trampolining.

tramway [tʀamwɛ] *nm* tram(way); (*voiture*) tram(car) (*BRIT*), streetcar (*US*).

tranchant, e [tʀɑ̃ʃɑ̃, -ɑ̃t] *adj* sharp; (*fig: personne*) peremptory; (*: couleurs*) striking ♦ *nm* (*d'un couteau*) cutting edge; (*de la main*) edge; **à double** ~ (*argument, procédé*) double-edged.

tranche [tʀɑ̃ʃ] *nf* (*morceau*) slice; (*arête*) edge; (*partie*) section; (*série*) block; (*d'impôts, revenus etc*) bracket; (*loterie*) issue; ~ **d'âge** age bracket; ~ **(de silicium)** wafer.

tranché, e [tʀɑ̃ʃe] *adj* (*couleurs*) distinct, sharply contrasted; (*opinions*) clear-cut, definite ♦ *nf* trench.

trancher [tʀɑ̃ʃe] *vt* to cut, sever; (*fig: résoudre*) to settle ♦ *vi* to be decisive; (*entre deux choses*) to settle the argument; ~ **avec** to contrast sharply with.

tranchet [tʀɑ̃ʃɛ] *nm* knife.

tranchoir [tʀɑ̃ʃwaʀ] *nm* chopper.

tranquille [tʀɑ̃kil] *adj* calm, quiet; (*enfant,*

élève) quiet; (*rassuré*) easy in one's mind, with one's mind at rest; **se tenir** ~ (*enfant*) to be quiet; **avoir la conscience** ~ to have an easy conscience; **laisse-moi/laisse-ça** ~ leave me/it alone.

tranquillement [tʀɑ̃kilmɑ̃] *adv* calmly.

tranquillisant, e [tʀɑ̃kilizɑ̃, -ɑ̃t] *adj* (*nouvelle*) reassuring ♦ *nm* tranquillizer.

tranquilliser [tʀɑ̃kilize] *vt* to reassure; **se** ~ to calm (o.s.) down.

tranquillité [tʀɑ̃kilite] *nf* quietness; peace (and quiet); **en toute** ~ with complete peace of mind; ~ **d'esprit** peace of mind.

transaction [tʀɑ̃zaksjɔ̃] *nf* (*COMM*) transaction, deal.

transafricain, e [tʀɑ̃safʀikɛ̃, -ɛn] *adj* transafrican.

transalpin, e [tʀɑ̃zalpɛ̃, -in] *adj* transalpine.

transaméricain, e [tʀɑ̃zameʀikɛ̃, -ɛn] *adj* transamerican.

transat [tʀɑ̃zat] *nm* deckchair ♦ *nf* = *course transatlantique*.

transatlantique [tʀɑ̃zatlɑ̃tik] *adj* transatlantic ♦ *nm* transatlantic liner.

transborder [tʀɑ̃sbɔʀde] *vt* to tran(s)ship.

transcendant, e [tʀɑ̃sɑ̃dɑ̃, -ɑ̃t] *adj* (*PHILOSOPHIE*, *MATH*) transcendental; (*supérieur*) transcendent.

transcodeur [tʀɑ̃skɔdœʀ] *nm* compiler.

transcontinental, e, aux [tʀɑ̃skɔ̃tinɑ̃tal, -o] *adj* transcontinental.

transcription [tʀɑ̃skʀipsjɔ̃] *nf* transcription.

transcrire [tʀɑ̃skʀiʀ] *vt* to transcribe.

transe [tʀɑ̃s] *nf*: **entrer en** ~ to go into a trance; ~**s** *nfpl* agony *sg*.

transférable [tʀɑ̃sfeʀabl(ə)] *adj* transferable.

transfèrement [tʀɑ̃sfɛʀmɑ̃] *nm* transfer.

transférer [tʀɑ̃sfeʀe] *vt* to transfer.

transfert [tʀɑ̃sfɛʀ] *nm* transfer.

transfiguration [tʀɑ̃sfigyʀɑsjɔ̃] *nf* transformation, transfiguration.

transfigurer [tʀɑ̃sfigyʀe] *vt* to transform.

transfo [tʀɑ̃sfo] *nm* (= *transformateur*) transformer.

transformable [tʀɑ̃sfɔʀmabl(ə)] *adj* convertible.

transformateur [tʀɑ̃sfɔʀmatœʀ] *nm* transformer.

transformation [tʀɑ̃sfɔʀmɑsjɔ̃] *nf* transformation; (*RUGBY*) conversion; **industries de** ~ processing industries.

transformer [tʀɑ̃sfɔʀme] *vt* to transform, alter (*"alter" implique un changement moins radical*); (*matière première, appartement, RUGBY*) to convert; ~ **en** to transform into; to turn into; to convert into; **se** ~ *vi* to be transformed; to alter.

transfuge [tʀɑ̃sfyʒ] *nm* renegade.

transfuser [tʀɑ̃sfyze] *vt* to transfuse.

transfusion [tʀɑ̃sfyzjɔ̃] *nf*: ~ **sanguine** blood transfusion.

transgresser [tʀɑ̃sgʀese] *vt* to contravene, disobey.

transhumance [tʀɑ̃zymɑ̃s] *nf* transhumance, seasonal move to new pastures.

transi, e [tʀɑ̃zi] *adj* numb (with cold), chilled to the bone.

transiger [tʀɑ̃ziʒe] *vi* to compromise, come to an agreement; ~ **sur** *ou* **avec qch** to compromise on sth.

transistor [tʀɑ̃zistɔʀ] *nm* transistor.

transistorisé, e [tʀɑ̃zistɔʀize] *adj* transistorized.

transit [tʀɑ̃zit] *nm* transit; **de** ~ transit *cpd*; **en** ~ in transit.

transitaire [tʀɑ̃zitɛʀ] *nm/f* forwarding agent.

transiter [tʀɑ̃zite] *vi* to pass in transit.

transitif, ive [tʀɑ̃zitif, -iv] *adj* transitive.

transition [tʀɑ̃zisjɔ̃] *nf* transition; **de** ~ transitional.

transitoire [tʀɑ̃zitwaʀ] *adj* (*mesure, gouvernement*) transitional, provisional; (*fugitif*) transient.

translucide [tʀɑ̃slysid] *adj* translucent.

transmet [tʀɑ̃smɛ] *etc vb voir* **transmettre**.

transmettais [tʀɑ̃smɛtɛ] *etc vb voir* **transmettre**.

transmetteur [tʀɑ̃smɛtœʀ] *nm* transmitter.

transmettre [tʀɑ̃smɛtʀ(ə)] *vt* (*passer*): ~ **qch à qn** to pass sth on to sb; (*TECH*, *TÉL*, *MÉD*) to transmit; (*TV*, *RADIO*: *retransmettre*) to broadcast.

transmis, e [tʀɑ̃smi, -iz] *pp de* **transmettre**.

transmissible [tʀɑ̃smisibl(ə)] *adj* transmissible.

transmission [tʀɑ̃smisjɔ̃] *nf* transmission, passing on; (*AUTO*) transmission; ~**s** *nfpl* (*MIL*) ≈ signals corps *sg*; ~ **de données** (*INFORM*) data transmission; ~ **de pensée** thought transmission.

transocéanien, ne [tʀɑ̃zɔseanjɛ̃, -ɛn] *adj*, **transocéanique** [tʀɑ̃zɔseanik] *adj* transoceanic.

transparaître [tʀɑ̃spaʀɛtʀ(ə)] *vi* to show (through).

transparence [tʀɑ̃spaʀɑ̃s] *nf* transparence; **par** ~ (*regarder*) against the light; (*voir*) showing through.

transparent, e [tʀɑ̃spaʀɑ̃, -ɑ̃t] *adj* transparent.

transpercer [tʀɑ̃spɛʀse] *vt* to go through, pierce.

transpiration [tʀɑ̃spiʀɑsjɔ̃] *nf* perspiration.

transpirer [tʀɑ̃spiʀe] *vi* to perspire; (*information, nouvelle*) to come to light.

transplant [tʀɑ̃splɑ̃] *nm* transplant.

transplantation [tʀɑ̃splɑ̃tɑsjɔ̃] *nf* transplant.

transplanter [tʀɑ̃splɑ̃te] *vt* (*MÉD*, *BOT*) to transplant; (*personne*) to uproot, move.

transport [tʀɑ̃spɔʀ] *nm* transport; (*émotions*): ~ **de colère** fit of rage; ~ **de joie** transport of delight; ~ **de voyageurs/marchandises** passenger/goods transportation; ~**s en commun** public transport *sg*; ~**s routiers** haulage (*BRIT*), trucking (*US*).

transportable [tʀɑ̃spɔʀtabl(ə)] *adj* (*marchandises*) transportable; (*malade*) fit (enough) to be moved.
transporter [tʀɑ̃spɔʀte] *vt* to carry, move; (*COMM*) to transport; (*fig*): ~ **qn (de joie)** to send sb into raptures; **se ~ quelque part** (*fig*) to let one's imagination carry one away (somewhere).
transporteur [tʀɑ̃spɔʀtœʀ] *nm* haulage contractor (*BRIT*), trucker (*US*).
transposer [tʀɑ̃spoze] *vt* to transpose.
transposition [tʀɑ̃spozisjɔ̃] *nf* transposition.
transrhénan, e [tʀɑ̃sʀenɑ̃, -an] *adj* transrhenane.
transsaharien, ne [tʀɑ̃ssaaʀjɛ̃, -ɛn] *adj* trans-Saharan.
transsexuel, le [tʀɑ̃ssɛksɥɛl] *adj, nm/f* transsexual.
transsibérien, ne [tʀɑ̃ssibeʀjɛ̃, -ɛn] *adj* trans-Siberian.
transvaser [tʀɑ̃svaze] *vt* to decant.
transversal, e, aux [tʀɑ̃svɛʀsal, -o] *adj* transverse, cross(-); (*route etc*) cross-country; (*mur, chemin, rue*) running at right angles; (*AUTO*): **axe ~** main cross-country road (*BRIT*) *ou* highway (*US*).
transversalement [tʀɑ̃svɛʀsalmɑ̃] *adv* crosswise.
trapèze [tʀapɛz] *nm* (*GÉOM*) trapezium; (*au cirque*) trapeze.
trapéziste [tʀapezist(ə)] *nm/f* trapeze artist.
trappe [tʀap] *nf* (*de cave, grenier*) trap door; (*piège*) trap.
trappeur [tʀapœʀ] *nm* trapper, fur trader.
trapu, e [tʀapy] *adj* squat, stocky.
traquenard [tʀaknaʀ] *nm* trap.
traquer [tʀake] *vt* to track down; (*harceler*) to hound.
traumatisant, e [tʀomatizɑ̃, -ɑ̃t] traumatic.
traumatiser [tʀomatize] *vt* to traumatize.
traumatisme [tʀomatism(ə)] *nm* traumatism.
traumatologie [tʀomatɔlɔʒi] *nf branch of medicine concerned with accidents*.
travail, aux [tʀavaj, -o] *nm* (*gén*) work; (*tâche, métier*) work *no pl*, job; (*ÉCON, MÉD*) labour (*BRIT*), labor (*US*); (*INFORM*) job ♦ *nmpl* (*de réparation, agricoles etc*) work *sg*; (*sur route*) roadworks; (*de construction*) building (work) *sg*; **être/entrer en** ~ (*MÉD*) to be in/go into labour; **être sans** ~ (*employé*) to be out of work, be unemployed; ~ **d'intérêt général (TIG)** ≈ community service; ~ **(au) noir** moonlighting; ~ **posté** shiftwork; **travaux des champs** farmwork *sg*; **travaux dirigés (TD)** (*SCOL*) supervised practical work *sg*; **travaux forcés** hard labour *sg*; **travaux manuels** (*SCOL*) handicrafts; **travaux ménagers** housework *sg*; **travaux pratiques (TP)** (*gén*) practical work; (*en laboratoire*) lab work (*BRIT*), lab (*US*); **travaux publics (TP)** ≈ public works *sg*.
travaillé, e [tʀavaje] *adj* (*style*) polished.
travailler [tʀavaje] *vi* to work; (*bois*) to warp ♦ *vt* (*bois, métal*) to work; (*pâte*) to knead; (*objet d'art, discipline, fig: influencer*) to work on; **cela le travaille** it is on his mind; ~ **la terre** to work the land; ~ **son piano** to do one's piano practice; ~ **à** to work on; (*fig: contribuer à*) to work towards; ~ **à faire** to endeavour (*BRIT*) *ou* endeavor (*US*) to do.
travailleur, euse [tʀavajœʀ, -øz] *adj* hardworking ♦ *nm/f* worker; ~ **de force** labourer (*BRIT*), laborer (*US*); ~ **intellectuel** non-manual worker; ~ **social** social worker; **travailleuse familiale** home help.
travailliste [tʀavajist(ə)] *adj* ≈ Labour *cpd* ♦ *nm/f* member of the Labour party.
travée [tʀave] *nf* row; (*ARCHIT*) bay; span.
traveller's (chèque) [tʀavlœʀs(ʃɛk)] *nm* traveller's cheque.
travelling [tʀavliŋ] *nm* (*chariot*) dolly; (*technique*) tracking; ~ **optique** zoom shots *pl*.
travelo [tʀavlo] *nm* (*fam*) (drag) queen.
travers [tʀavɛʀ] *nm* fault, failing; **en ~ (de)** across; **au ~ (de)** through; **de ~** *adj* askew ♦ *adv* sideways; (*fig*) the wrong way; **à ~** through; **regarder de ~** (*fig*) to look askance at.
traverse [tʀavɛʀs(ə)] *nf* (*de voie ferrée*) sleeper; **chemin de ~** shortcut.
traversée [tʀavɛʀse] *nf* crossing.
traverser [tʀavɛʀse] *vt* (*gén*) to cross; (*ville, tunnel, aussi: percer, fig*) to go through; (*suj: ligne, trait*) to run across.
traversin [tʀavɛʀsɛ̃] *nm* bolster.
travesti [tʀavɛsti] *nm* (*costume*) fancy dress; (*artiste de cabaret*) female impersonator, drag artist; (*pervers*) transvestite.
travestir [tʀavɛstiʀ] *vt* (*vérité*) to misrepresent; **se ~** (*se costumer*) to dress up; (*artiste*) to put on drag; (*PSYCH*) to dress as a woman.
trayais [tʀɛjɛ] *etc vb voir* **traire**.
trayeuse [tʀɛjøz] *nf* milking machine.
trébucher [tʀebyʃe] *vi*: ~ **(sur)** to stumble (over), trip (over).
trèfle [tʀɛfl(ə)] *nm* (*BOT*) clover; (*CARTES: couleur*) clubs *pl*; (*: carte*) club; ~ **à quatre feuilles** four-leaf clover.
treillage [tʀɛjaʒ] *nm* lattice work.
treille [tʀɛj] *nf* (*tonnelle*) vine arbour (*BRIT*) *ou* arbor (*US*); (*vigne*) climbing vine.
treillis [tʀeji] *nm* (*métallique*) wire-mesh; (*toile*) canvas; (*MIL: tenue*) combat uniform; (*pantalon*) combat trousers *pl*.
treize [tʀɛz] *num* thirteen.
treizième [tʀɛzjɛm] *num* thirteenth; *see boxed note*.

TREIZIÈME MOIS

The **treizième mois** *is an end-of-year bonus roughly corresponding to one month's salary. For many employees it is a standard part of their salary package.*

tréma [tRema] *nm* diaeresis.
tremblant, e [tRɑ̃blɑ̃, -ɑ̃t] *adj* trembling, shaking.
tremble [tRɑ̃bl(ə)] *nm* (*BOT*) aspen.
tremblé, e [tRɑ̃ble] *adj* shaky.
tremblement [tRɑ̃bləmɑ̃] *nm* trembling *no pl*, shaking *no pl*, shivering *no pl*; ~ **de terre** earthquake.
trembler [tRɑ̃ble] *vi* to tremble, shake; ~ **de** (*froid, fièvre*) to shiver *ou* tremble with; (*peur*) to shake *ou* tremble with; ~ **pour qn** to fear for sb.
tremblotant, e [tRɑ̃blɔtɑ̃, -ɑ̃t] *adj* trembling.
trembloter [tRɑ̃blɔte] *vi* to tremble *ou* shake slightly.
trémolo [tRemɔlo] *nm* (*d'un instrument*) tremolo; (*de la voix*) quaver.
trémousser [tRemuse]: **se** ~ *vi* to jig about, wriggle about.
trempe [tRɑ̃p] *nf* (*fig*): **de cette/sa** ~ of this/his calibre (*BRIT*) *ou* caliber (*US*).
trempé, e [tRɑ̃pe] *adj* soaking (wet), drenched; (*TECH*): **acier** ~ tempered steel.
tremper [tRɑ̃pe] *vt* to soak, drench; (*aussi*: **faire ~, mettre à ~**) to soak; (*plonger*): ~ **qch dans** to dip sth in(to) ♦ *vi* to soak; (*fig*): ~ **dans** to be involved *ou* have a hand in; **se** ~ *vi* to have a quick dip; **se faire** ~ to get soaked *ou* drenched.
trempette [tRɑ̃pɛt] *nf*: **faire** ~ to go paddling.
tremplin [tRɑ̃plɛ̃] *nm* springboard; (*SKI*) ski jump.
trentaine [tRɑ̃tɛn] *nf* (*âge*): **avoir la** ~ to be around thirty; **une** ~ **(de)** thirty or so, about thirty.
trente [tRɑ̃t] *num* thirty; **voir** ~**-six chandelles** (*fig*) to see stars; **être/se mettre sur son** ~ **et un** to be/get dressed to kill; ~**-trois tours** *nm* long-playing record, LP.
trentième [tRɑ̃tjɛm] *num* thirtieth.
trépanation [tRepanasjɔ̃] *nf* trepan.
trépaner [tRepane] *vt* to trepan, trephine.
trépasser [tRepase] *vi* to pass away.
trépidant, e [tRepidɑ̃, -ɑ̃t] *adj* (*fig*: *rythme*) pulsating; (*: vie*) hectic.
trépidation [tRepidɑsjɔ̃] *nf* (*d'une machine, d'un moteur*) vibration; (*fig*: *de la vie*) whirl.
trépider [tRepide] *vi* to vibrate.
trépied [tRepje] *nm* (*d'appareil*) tripod; (*meuble*) trivet.
trépignement [tRepiɲmɑ̃] *nm* stamping (of feet).
trépigner [tRepiɲe] *vi* to stamp (one's feet).
très [tRɛ] *adv* very; much + *pp*, highly + *pp*; ~ **beau/bien** very beautiful/well; ~ **critiqué** much criticized; ~ **industrialisé** highly industrialized; **j'ai** ~ **faim** I'm very hungry.
trésor [tRezɔR] *nm* treasure; (*ADMIN*) finances *pl*; (*d'un organisation*) funds *pl*; ~ **(public) (TP)** public revenue; (*service*) public revenue office.
trésorerie [tRezɔRRi] *nf* (*fonds*) funds *pl*; (*gestion*) accounts *pl*; (*bureaux*) accounts department; (*poste*) treasurership; **difficultés de** ~ cash problems, shortage of cash *ou* funds; ~ **générale (TG)** *local government finance office*.
trésorier, ière [tRezɔRje, -jɛR] *nm/f* treasurer.
Trésorier-payeur [tRezɔRjepɛjœR] *nm*: ~ **général (TPG)** paymaster.
tressaillement [tResajmɑ̃] *nm* shiver, shudder; quiver.
tressaillir [tResajiR] *vi* (*de peur etc*) to shiver, shudder; (*de joie*) to quiver.
tressauter [tResote] *vi* to start, jump.
tresse [tRɛs] *nf* (*de cheveux*) braid, plait; (*cordon, galon*) braid.
tresser [tRese] *vt* (*cheveux*) to braid, plait; (*fil, jonc*) to plait; (*corbeille*) to weave; (*corde*) to twist.
tréteau, x [tReto] *nm* trestle; **les** ~**x** (*fig*: *THÉÂT*) the boards.
treuil [tRœj] *nm* winch.
trêve [tRɛv] *nf* (*MIL, POL*) truce; (*fig*) respite; **sans** ~ unremittingly; ~ **de ...** enough of this ...; **les États de la T**~ the Trucial States.
tri [tRi] *nm* (*voir trier*) sorting (out) *no pl*; selection; screening; (*INFORM*) sort; (*POSTES*: *action*) sorting; (*: bureau*) sorting office.
triage [tRijaʒ] *nm* (*RAIL*) shunting; (*gare*) marshalling yard.
trial [tRijal] *nm* (*SPORT*) scrambling.
triangle [tRijɑ̃gl(ə)] *nm* triangle; ~ **isocèle/équilatéral** isosceles/equilateral triangle; ~ **rectangle** right-angled triangle.
triangulaire [tRijɑ̃gylɛR] *adj* triangular.
triathlon [tRi(j)atlɔ̃] *nm* triathlon.
tribal, e, aux [tRibal, -o] *adj* tribal.
tribord [tRibɔR] *nm*: **à** ~ to starboard, on the starboard side.
tribu [tRiby] *nf* tribe.
tribulations [tRibylɑsjɔ̃] *nfpl* tribulations, trials.
tribunal, aux [tRibynal, -o] *nm* (*JUR*) court; (*MIL*) tribunal; ~ **de police/pour enfants** police/juvenile court; ~ **d'instance (TI)** ≈ magistrates' court (*BRIT*), ≈ district court (*US*); ~ **de grande instance (TGI)** ≈ High Court (*BRIT*), ≈ Supreme Court (*US*).
tribune [tRibyn] *nf* (*estrade*) platform, rostrum; (*débat*) forum; (*d'église, de tribunal*) gallery; (*de stade*) stand; ~ **libre** (*PRESSE*) opinion column.
tribut [tRiby] *nm* tribute.
tributaire [tRibytɛR] *adj*: **être** ~ **de** to be dependent on; (*GÉO*) to be a tributary of.
tricentenaire [tRisɑ̃tnɛR] *nm* tercentenary, tricentennial.
tricher [tRiʃe] *vi* to cheat.
tricherie [tRiʃRi] *nf* cheating *no pl*.
tricheur, euse [tRiʃœR, -øz] *nm/f* cheat.
trichromie [tRikRɔmi] *nf* three-colour (*BRIT*) *ou* -color (*US*) printing.
tricolore [tRikɔlɔR] *adj* three-coloured (*BRIT*),

three-colored (*US*); (*français: drapeau*) red, white and blue; (*: équipe etc*) French.
tricot [tʀiko] *nm* (*technique, ouvrage*) knitting *no pl*; (*tissu*) knitted fabric; (*vêtement*) jersey, sweater; ~ **de corps** vest (*BRIT*), undershirt (*US*).
tricoter [tʀikɔte] *vt* to knit; **machine/aiguille à** ~ knitting machine/needle (*BRIT*) *ou* pin (*US*).
trictrac [tʀiktʀak] *nm* backgammon.
tricycle [tʀisikl(ə)] *nm* tricycle.
tridimensionnel, le [tʀidimɑ̃sjɔnɛl] *adj* three-dimensional.
triennal, e, aux [tʀiɛnal, -o] *adj* (*prix, foire, élection*) three-yearly; (*charge, mandat, plan*) three-year.
trier [tʀije] *vt* (*classer*) to sort (out); (*choisir*) to select; (*visiteurs*) to screen; (*POSTES, INFORM*) to sort.
trieur, euse [tʀijœʀ, -øz] *nm/f* sorter.
trigonométrie [tʀigɔnɔmetʀi] *nf* trigonometry.
trigonométrique [tʀigɔnɔmetʀik] *adj* trigonometric.
trilingue [tʀilɛ̃g] *adj* trilingual.
trilogie [tʀilɔʒi] *nf* trilogy.
trimaran [tʀimaʀɑ̃] *nm* trimaran.
trimbaler [tʀɛ̃bale] *vt* to cart around, trail along.
trimer [tʀime] *vi* to slave away.
trimestre [tʀimɛstʀ(ə)] *nm* (*SCOL*) term; (*COMM*) quarter.
trimestriel, le [tʀimɛstʀijɛl] *adj* quarterly; (*SCOL*) end-of-term.
trimoteur [tʀimɔtœʀ] *nm* three-engined aircraft.
tringle [tʀɛ̃gl(ə)] *nf* rod.
Trinité [tʀinite] *nf* Trinity.
Trinité et Tobago [tʀiniteetɔbago] *nf* Trinidad and Tobago.
trinquer [tʀɛ̃ke] *vi* to clink glasses; (*fam*) to cop it; ~ **à qch/la santé de qn** to drink to sth/sb.
trio [tʀijo] *nm* trio.
triolet [tʀijɔlɛ] *nm* (*MUS*) triplet.
triomphal, e, aux [tʀijɔ̃fal, -o] *adj* triumphant, triumphal.
triomphalement [tʀijɔ̃falmɑ̃] *adv* triumphantly.
triomphant, e [tʀijɔ̃fɑ̃, -ɑ̃t] *adj* triumphant.
triomphateur, trice [tʀijɔ̃fatœʀ, -tʀis] *nm/f* (triumphant) victor.
triomphe [tʀijɔ̃f] *nm* triumph; **être reçu/porté en** ~ to be given a triumphant welcome/be carried shoulder-high in triumph.
triompher [tʀijɔ̃fe] *vi* to triumph; ~ **de** to triumph over, overcome.
triparti, e [tʀipaʀti] *adj* (*aussi*: **tripartite**: *réunion, assemblée*) tripartite, three-party.
triperie [tʀipʀi] *nf* tripe shop.
tripes [tʀip] *nfpl* (*CULIN*) tripe *sg*; (*fam*) guts.
triplace [tʀiplas] *adj* three-seater *cpd*.
triple [tʀipl(ə)] *adj* (*à trois élements*) triple; (*trois fois plus grand*) treble ♦ *nm*: **le** ~ **(de)** (*comparaison*) three times as much (as); **en** ~ **exemplaire** in triplicate; ~ **saut** (*SPORT*) triple jump.
triplé [tʀiple] *nm* hat-trick (*BRIT*), triple success.
triplement [tʀipləmɑ̃] *adv* (*à un degré triple*) three times over; (*de trois façons*) in three ways; (*pour trois raisons*) on three counts ♦ *nm* trebling, threefold increase.
tripler [tʀiple] *vi, vt* to triple, treble, increase threefold.
triplés, ées [tʀiple] *nm/fpl* triplets.
Tripoli [tʀipɔli] *n* Tripoli.
triporteur [tʀipɔʀtœʀ] *nm* delivery tricycle.
tripot [tʀipo] *nm* (*péj*) dive.
tripotage [tʀipɔtaʒ] *nm* (*péj*) jiggery-pokery.
tripoter [tʀipɔte] *vt* to fiddle with, finger ♦ *vi* (*fam*) to rummage about.
trique [tʀik] *nf* cudgel.
trisannuel, le [tʀizanɥɛl] *adj* triennial.
trisomie [tʀizɔmi] *nf* Down's syndrome.
triste [tʀist(ə)] *adj* sad; (*péj*): ~ **personnage/affaire** sorry individual/affair; **c'est pas** ~! (*fam*) it's something else!
tristement [tʀistəmɑ̃] *adv* sadly.
tristesse [tʀistɛs] *nf* sadness.
triton [tʀitɔ̃] *nm* triton.
triturer [tʀityʀe] *vt* (*pâte*) to knead; (*objets*) to manipulate.
trivial, e, aux [tʀivjal, -o] *adj* coarse, crude; (*commun*) mundane.
trivialité [tʀivjalite] *nf* coarseness, crudeness; mundaneness.
troc [tʀɔk] *nm* (*ÉCON*) barter; (*transaction*) exchange, swap.
troène [tʀɔɛn] *nm* privet.
troglodyte [tʀɔglɔdit] *nm/f* cave dweller, troglodyte.
trognon [tʀɔɲɔ̃] *nm* (*de fruit*) core; (*de légume*) stalk.
trois [tʀwɑ] *num* three.
trois-huit [tʀwɑɥit] *nmpl*: **faire les** ~ to work eight-hour shifts (round the clock).
troisième [tʀwɑzjɛm] *num* third; **le** ~ **âge** the years of retirement.
troisièmement [tʀwɑzjɛmmɑ̃] *adv* thirdly.
trois quarts [tʀwɑkaʀ] *nmpl*: **les** ~ **de** three-quarters of.
trolleybus [tʀɔlɛbys] *nm* trolley bus.
trombe [tʀɔ̃b] *nf* waterspout; **des ~s d'eau** a downpour; **en** ~ (*arriver, passer*) like a whirlwind.
trombone [tʀɔ̃bɔn] *nm* (*MUS*) trombone; (*de bureau*) paper clip; ~ **à coulisse** slide trombone.
tromboniste [tʀɔ̃bɔnist(ə)] *nm/f* trombonist.
trompe [tʀɔ̃p] *nf* (*d'éléphant*) trunk; (*MUS*) trumpet, horn; ~ **d'Eustache** Eustachian tube; **~s utérines** Fallopian tubes.
trompe-l'œil [tʀɔ̃plœj] *nm*: **en** ~ in trompe-

l'œil style.
tromper [tʀɔ̃pe] *vt* to deceive; (*fig: espoir, attente*) to disappoint; (*vigilance, poursuivants*) to elude; **se ~** *vi* to make a mistake, be mistaken; **se ~ de voiture/jour** to take the wrong car/get the day wrong; **se ~ de 3 cm/2 €** to be out by 3 cm/€2.
tromperie [tʀɔ̃pʀi] *nf* deception, trickery *no pl.*
trompette [tʀɔ̃pɛt] *nf* trumpet; **en ~** (*nez*) turned-up.
trompettiste [tʀɔ̃petist(ə)] *nm/f* trumpet player.
trompeur, euse [tʀɔ̃pœʀ, -øz] *adj* deceptive, misleading.
tronc [tʀɔ̃] *nm* (*BOT, ANAT*) trunk; (*d'église*) collection box; **~ d'arbre** tree trunk; **~ commun** (*SCOL*) common-core syllabus; **~ de cône** truncated cone.
tronche [tʀɔ̃ʃ] *nf* (*fam*) mug, face.
tronçon [tʀɔ̃sɔ̃] *nm* section.
tronçonner [tʀɔ̃sɔne] *vt* (*arbre*) to saw up; (*pierre*) to cut up.
tronçonneuse [tʀɔ̃sɔnøz] *nf* chain saw.
trône [tʀon] *nm* throne; **monter sur le ~** to ascend the throne.
trôner [tʀone] *vi* (*fig*) to have (*ou* take) pride of place (*BRIT*), have the place of honour (*BRIT*) *ou* honor (*US*).
tronquer [tʀɔ̃ke] *vt* to truncate; (*fig*) to curtail.
trop [tʀo] *adv vb +* too much; too *+ adjectif, adverbe*; **~ (nombreux)** too many; **~ peu (nombreux)** too few; **~ (souvent)** too often; **~ (longtemps)** (for) too long; **~ de** (*nombre*) too many; (*quantité*) too much; **de ~, en ~**: **des livres en ~** a few books too many, a few extra books; **du lait en ~** too much milk; **3 livres/1 € de ~** 3 books too many/€1 too much.
trophée [tʀɔfe] *nm* trophy.
tropical, e, aux [tʀɔpikal, -o] *adj* tropical.
tropique [tʀɔpik] *nm* tropic; **~s** *nmpl* tropics; **~ du Cancer/Capricorne** Tropic of Cancer/Capricorn.
trop-plein [tʀɔplɛ̃] *nm* (*tuyau*) overflow *ou* outlet (pipe); (*liquide*) overflow.
troquer [tʀɔke] *vt*: **~ qch contre** to barter *ou* trade sth for; (*fig*) to swap sth for.
trot [tʀo] *nm* trot; **aller au ~** to trot along; **partir au ~** to set off at a trot.
trotter [tʀɔte] *vi* to trot; (*fig*) to scamper along (*ou* about).
trotteuse [tʀɔtøz] *nf* (*de montre*) second hand.
trottiner [tʀɔtine] *vi* (*fig*) to scamper along (*ou* about).
trottinette [tʀɔtinɛt] *nf* (child's) scooter.
trottoir [tʀɔtwaʀ] *nm* pavement (*BRIT*), sidewalk (*US*); **faire le ~** (*péj*) to walk the streets; **~ roulant** moving pavement (*BRIT*) *ou* walkway.
trou [tʀu] *nm* hole; (*fig*) gap; (*COMM*) deficit; **~ d'aération** (air) vent; **~ d'air** air pocket; **~ de mémoire** blank, lapse of memory; **~ noir** black hole; **~ de la serrure** keyhole.
troublant, e [tʀublɑ̃, -ɑ̃t] *adj* disturbing.
trouble [tʀubl(ə)] *adj* (*liquide*) cloudy; (*image, mémoire*) indistinct, hazy; (*affaire*) shady, murky ♦ *adv* indistinctly ♦ *nm* (*désarroi*) distress, agitation; (*émoi sensuel*) turmoil, agitation; (*embarras*) confusion; (*zizanie*) unrest, discord; **~s** *nmpl* (*POL*) disturbances, troubles, unrest *sg*; (*MÉD*) trouble *sg*, disorders; **~s de la personnalité** personality problems; **~s de la vision** eye trouble.
trouble-fête [tʀubləfɛt] *nm/f inv* spoilsport.
troubler [tʀuble] *vt* (*embarrasser*) to confuse, disconcert; (*émouvoir*) to agitate; to disturb; to perturb; (*perturber: ordre etc*) to disrupt, disturb; (*liquide*) to make cloudy; **se ~** *vi* (*personne*) to become flustered *ou* confused; **~ l'ordre public** to cause a breach of the peace.
troué, e [tʀue] *adj* with a hole (*ou* holes) in it ♦ *nf* gap; (*MIL*) breach.
trouer [tʀue] *vt* to make a hole (*ou* holes) in; (*fig*) to pierce.
trouille [tʀuj] *nf* (*fam*): **avoir la ~** to be scared stiff, be scared out of one's wits.
troupe [tʀup] *nf* (*MIL*) troop; (*groupe*) troop, group; **la ~** (*MIL: l'armée*) the army; (*: les simples soldats*) the troops *pl*; **~ (de théâtre)** (theatrical) company; **~s de choc** shock troops.
troupeau, x [tʀupo] *nm* (*de moutons*) flock; (*de vaches*) herd.
trousse [tʀus] *nf* case, kit; (*d'écolier*) pencil case; (*de docteur*) instrument case; **aux ~s de** (*fig*) on the heels *ou* tail of; **~ à outils** toolkit; **~ de toilette** toilet *ou* sponge (*BRIT*) bag.
trousseau, x [tʀuso] *nm* (*de mariée*) trousseau; **~ de clefs** bunch of keys.
trouvaille [tʀuvaj] *nf* find; (*fig: idée, expression etc*) brainwave.
trouvé, e [tʀuve] *adj*: **tout ~** ready-made.
trouver [tʀuve] *vt* to find; (*rendre visite*): **aller/venir ~ qn** to go/come and see sb; **je trouve que** I find *ou* think that; **~ à boire/critiquer** to find something to drink/criticize; **~ asile/refuge** to find refuge/shelter; **se ~** *vi* (*être*) to be; (*être soudain*) to find o.s.; **se ~ être/avoir** to happen to be/have; **il se trouve que** it happens that, it turns out that; **se ~ bien** to feel well; **se ~ mal** to pass out.
truand [tʀyɑ̃] *nm* villain, crook.
truander [tʀyɑ̃de] *vi* (*fam*) to cheat, do.
trublion [tʀyblijɔ̃] *nm* troublemaker.
truc [tʀyk] *nm* (*astuce*) way, device; (*de cinéma, prestidigitateur*) trick effect; (*chose*) thing; (*machin*) thingumajig, whatsit (*BRIT*); **avoir le ~** to have the knack; **c'est pas son (ou mon etc) ~** (*fam*) it's not really his (*ou* my *etc*) thing.
truchement [tʀyʃmɑ̃] *nm*: **par le ~ de qn**

through (the intervention of) sb.
trucider [tʀyside] *vt* (*fam*) to do in, bump off.
truculence [tʀykylɑ̃s] *nf* colourfulness (*BRIT*), colorfulness (*US*).
truculent, e [tʀykylɑ̃, -ɑ̃t] *adj* colourful (*BRIT*), colorful (*US*).
truelle [tʀyɛl] *nf* trowel.
truffe [tʀyf] *nf* truffle; (*nez*) nose.
truffer [tʀyfe] *vt* (*CULIN*) to garnish with truffles; **truffé de** (*fig: citations*) peppered with; (*: pièges*) bristling with.
truie [tʀɥi] *nf* sow.
truite [tʀɥit] *nf* trout *inv*.
truquage [tʀykaʒ] *nm* fixing; (*CINÉ*) special effects *pl*.
truquer [tʀyke] *vt* (*élections, serrure, dés*) to fix; (*CINÉ*) to use special effects in.
trust [tʀœst] *nm* (*COMM*) trust.
truster [tʀœste] *vt* (*COMM*) to monopolize.
ts *abr* = **tous**.
tsar [dzaʀ] *nm* tsar.
tsé-tsé [tsetse] *nf*: **mouche ~** tsetse fly.
TSF *sigle f* (= *télégraphie sans fil*) wireless.
tsigane [tsigan] *adj, nm/f* = **tzigane**.
TSVP *abr* (= *tournez s'il vous plaît*) PTO.
tt *abr* = **tout**.
TT(A) *sigle m* (= *transit temporaire (autorisé)*) *vehicle registration for cars etc bought in France for export tax free by non-residents*.
TTC *abr* = **toutes taxes comprises**.
ttes *abr* = **toutes**.
TU *sigle m* = *temps universel*.
tu [ty] *pron* you ♦ *nm*: **employer le ~** to use the "tu" form.
tu, e [ty] *pp de* **taire**.
tuant, e [tɥɑ̃, -ɑ̃t] *adj* (*épuisant*) killing; (*énervant*) infuriating.
tuba [tyba] *nm* (*MUS*) tuba; (*SPORT*) snorkel.
tubage [tybaʒ] *nm* (*MÉD*) intubation.
tube [tyb] *nm* tube; (*de canalisation, métallique etc*) pipe; (*chanson, disque*) hit song *ou* record; **~ digestif** alimentary canal, digestive tract; **~ à essai** test tube.
tuberculeux, euse [tybɛʀkylø, -øz] *adj* tubercular ♦ *nm/f* tuberculosis *ou* TB patient.
tuberculose [tybɛʀkyloz] *nf* tuberculosis, TB.
tubulaire [tybylɛʀ] *adj* tubular.
tubulure [tybylyʀ] *nf* pipe; piping *no pl*; (*AUTO*): **~ d'échappement/d'admission** exhaust/inlet manifold.
TUC [tyk] *sigle m* (= *travail d'utilité collective*) *community work scheme for the young unemployed*.
tuciste [tysist(ə)] *nm/f* *young person on a community work scheme*.
tué, e [tɥe] *nm/f*: **5 ~s** 5 killed *ou* dead.
tue-mouche [tymuʃ] *adj*: **papier ~(s)** flypaper.
tuer [tɥe] *vt* to kill; **se ~** (*se suicider*) to kill o.s.; (*dans un accident*) to be killed; **se ~ au travail** (*fig*) to work o.s. to death.
tuerie [tyʀi] *nf* slaughter *no pl*, massacre.
tue-tête [tytɛt]: **à ~** *adv* at the top of one's voice.
tueur [tɥœʀ] *nm* killer; **~ à gages** hired killer.
tuile [tɥil] *nf* tile; (*fam*) spot of bad luck, blow.
tulipe [tylip] *nf* tulip.
tulle [tyl] *nm* tulle.
tuméfié, e [tymefje] *adj* puffy, swollen.
tumeur [tymœʀ] *nf* growth, tumour (*BRIT*), tumor (*US*).
tumulte [tymylt(ə)] *nm* commotion, hubbub.
tumultueux, euse [tymyltɥø, -øz] *adj* stormy, turbulent.
tuner [tynɛʀ] *nm* tuner.
tungstène [tœkstɛn] *nm* tungsten.
tunique [tynik] *nf* tunic; (*de femme*) smock, tunic.
Tunis [tynis] *n* Tunis.
Tunisie [tynizi] *nf*: **la ~** Tunisia.
tunisien, ne [tynizjɛ̃, -ɛn] *adj* Tunisian ♦ *nm/f*: **T~, ne** Tunisian.
tunisois, e [tynizwa, -waz] *adj* of *ou* from Tunis.
tunnel [tynɛl] *nm* tunnel; **le ~ sous la Manche** the Channel Tunnel, the Chunnel.
TUP *sigle m* (= *titre universel de paiement*) ≈ payment slip.
turban [tyʀbɑ̃] *nm* turban.
turbin [tyʀbɛ̃] *nm* (*fam*) work *no pl*.
turbine [tyʀbin] *nf* turbine.
turbo [tyʀbo] *nm* turbo; **un moteur ~** a turbo(-charged) engine.
turbomoteur [tyʀbɔmɔtœʀ] *nm* turbo(-boosted) engine.
turbopropulseur [tyʀbɔpʀɔpylsœʀ] *nm* turboprop.
turboréacteur [tyʀbɔʀeaktœʀ] *nm* turbojet.
turbot [tyʀbo] *nm* turbot.
turbotrain [tyʀbɔtʀɛ̃] *nm* turbotrain.
turbulences [tyʀbylɑ̃s] *nfpl* (*AVIAT*) turbulence *sg*.
turbulent, e [tyʀbylɑ̃, -ɑ̃t] *adj* boisterous, unruly.
turc, turque [tyʀk(ə)] *adj* Turkish; (*w.-c.*) seatless ♦ *nm* (*LING*) Turkish ♦ *nm/f*: **T~, Turque** Turk/Turkish woman; **à la turque** *adv* (*assis*) cross-legged.
turf [tyʀf] *nm* racing.
turfiste [tyʀfist(ə)] *nm/f* racegoer.
Turks et Caïques *ou* **Caicos** [tyʀkekaik(ɔs)] *nfpl* Turks and Caicos Islands.
turpitude [tyʀpityd] *nf* base act, baseness *no pl*.
turque [tyʀk(ə)] *adj f, nf voir* **turc**.
Turquie [tyʀki] *nf*: **la ~** Turkey.
turquoise [tyʀkwaz] *nf, adj inv* turquoise.
tut [ty] *etc vb voir* **taire**.
tutelle [tytɛl] *nf* (*JUR*) guardianship; (*POL*) trusteeship; **sous la ~ de** (*fig*) under the supervision of.
tuteur, trice [tytœʀ, -tʀis] *nm/f* (*JUR*) guardian; (*de plante*) stake, support.
tutoiement [tytwamɑ̃] *nm* use of familiar "tu" form.

tutoyer [tytwaje] *vt*: ~ **qn** to address sb as "tu".
tutti quanti [tutikwɑ̃ti] *nmpl*: **et** ~ and all the rest (of them).
tutu [tyty] *nm* (*DANSE*) tutu.
Tuvalu [tyvaly] *nm*: **le** ~ Tuvalu.
tuyau, x [tɥijo] *nm* pipe; (*flexible*) tube; (*fam*: *conseil*) tip; (*: mise au courant*) gen *no pl*; ~ **d'arrosage** hosepipe; ~ **d'échappement** exhaust pipe; ~ **d'incendie** fire hose.
tuyauté, e [tɥijote] *adj* fluted.
tuyauterie [tɥijotʀi] *nf* piping *no pl*.
tuyère [tɥijɛʀ] *nf* nozzle.
TV [teve] *nf* TV, telly (*BRIT*).
TVA *sigle f* = **taxe à** *ou* **sur la valeur ajoutée**.
tweed [twid] *nm* tweed.
tympan [tɛ̃pɑ̃] *nm* (*ANAT*) eardrum.
type [tip] *nm* type; (*personne, chose*: *représentant*) classic example, epitome; (*fam*) chap, guy ♦ *adj* typical, standard; **avoir le ~ nordique** to be Nordic-looking.
typé, e [tipe] *adj* ethnic (*euph*).
typhoïde [tifɔid] *nf* typhoid (fever).
typhon [tifɔ̃] *nm* typhoon.
typhus [tifys] *nm* typhus (fever).
typique [tipik] *adj* typical.
typiquement [tipikmɑ̃] *adv* typically.
typographe [tipɔgʀaf] *nm/f* typographer.
typographie [tipɔgʀafi] *nf* typography; (*procédé*) letterpress (printing).
typographique [tipɔgʀafik] *adj* typographical; letterpress *cpd*.
typologie [tipɔlɔʒi] *nf* typology.
tyran [tiʀɑ̃] *nm* tyrant.
tyrannie [tiʀani] *nf* tyranny.
tyrannique [tiʀanik] *adj* tyrannical.
tyranniser [tiʀanize] *vt* to tyrannize.
Tyrol [tiʀɔl] *nm*: **le** ~ the Tyrol.
tyrolien, ne [tiʀɔljɛ̃, -ɛn] *adj* Tyrolean.
tzar [dzaʀ] *nm* = **tsar**.
tzigane [dzigan] *adj* gipsy, tzigane ♦ *nm/f* (Hungarian) gipsy, Tzigane.

U u

U, u [y] *nm inv* U, u ♦ *abr* (= *unité*) *10,000 francs*; **maison à vendre 50 U** house for sale: 500,000 francs; **U comme Ursule** U for Uncle.
ubiquité [ybikɥite] *nf*: **avoir le don d'~** to be everywhere at once, be ubiquitous.
UDF *sigle f* (= *Union pour la démocratie française*) *political party*.
UE *sigle f* (= *Union européenne*) EU.
UEFA [yefa] *sigle f* (= *Union of European Football Associations*) UEFA.
UEM *sigle f* (= *Union économique et monétaire*) EMU.
UER *sigle f* (= *unité d'enseignement et de recherche*) *old title of UFR*; (= *Union européenne de radiodiffusion*) EBU (= *European Broadcasting Union*).
UFC *sigle f* (= *Union fédérale des consommateurs*) *national consumer group*.
UFR *sigle f* (= *unité de formation et de recherche*) ≈ university department.
UHF *sigle f* (= *ultra-haute fréquence*) UHF.
UHT *sigle* (= *ultra-haute température*) UHT.
UIT *sigle f* (= *Union internationale des télécommunications*) ITU (= *International Telecommunications Union*).
UJP *sigle f* (= *Union des jeunes pour le progrès*) *political party*.
Ukraine [ykʀɛn] *nf*: **l'~** the Ukraine.
ukrainien, ne [ykʀɛnjɛ̃, -ɛn] *adj* Ukrainian ♦ *nm* (*LING*) Ukrainian ♦ *nm/f*: **U~, ne** Ukrainian.
ulcère [ylsɛʀ] *nm* ulcer; ~ **à l'estomac** stomach ulcer.
ulcérer [ylseʀe] *vt* (*MÉD*) to ulcerate; (*fig*) to sicken, appal.
ulcéreux, euse [ylseʀø, -øz] *adj* (*plaie, lésion*) ulcerous; (*membre*) ulcerated.
ULM *sigle m* (= *ultra léger motorisé*) microlight.
ultérieur, e [ylteʀjœʀ] *adj* later, subsequent; **remis à une date ~e** postponed to a later date.
ultérieurement [ylteʀjœʀmɑ̃] *adv* later.
ultimatum [yltimatɔm] *nm* ultimatum.
ultime [yltim] *adj* final.
ultra... [yltʀa] *préfixe* ultra....
ultramoderne [yltʀamɔdɛʀn(ə)] *adj* ultramodern.
ultra-rapide [yltʀaʀapid] *adj* ultra-fast.
ultra-sensible [yltʀasɑ̃sibl(ə)] *adj* (*PHOTO*) high-speed.
ultra(-)son [yltʀasɔ̃] *nm* ultrasound *no pl*; **~s** *nmpl* ultrasonics.
ultra(-)violet, te [yltʀavjɔlɛ, -ɛt] *adj* ultraviolet ♦ *nm*: **les ~s** ultraviolet rays.
ululer [ylyle] *vi* = **hululer**.
UME *sigle f* (= *Union monétaire européenne*) EMU.

MOT-CLÉ

un, une [œ̃, yn] *art indéf* a; (*devant voyelle*) an; ~ **garçon/vieillard** a boy/an old man; **une fille** a girl
♦ *pron* one; **l'~ des meilleurs** one of the best; **l'~ ..., l'autre** (the) one ..., the other; **les ~s ..., les autres** some ..., others; **l'~ et l'autre** both (of them); **l'~ ou l'autre** either (of them); **l'~ l'autre, les ~s les autres** each other, one another; **pas ~ seul** not a single one; **~ par ~** one by one
♦ *num* one; **une pomme seulement** one apple

only
♦ *nf*: **la une** (*PRESSE*) the front page.

unanime [ynanim] *adj* unanimous; **ils sont ~s (à penser que)** they are unanimous (in thinking that).
unanimement [ynanimmɑ̃] *adv* (*par tous*) unanimously; (*d'un commun accord*) with one accord.
unanimité [ynanimite] *nf* unanimity; **à l'~** unanimously; **faire l'~** to be approved unanimously.
UNEF [ynɛf] *sigle f* = *Union nationale des étudiants de France.*
UNESCO [ynɛsko] *sigle f* (= *United Nations Educational, Scientific and Cultural Organization*) UNESCO.
Unetelle [yntɛl] *nf voir* **Untel**.
UNI *sigle f* = *Union nationale interuniversitaire.*
uni, e [yni] *adj* (*ton, tissu*) plain; (*surface*) smooth, even; (*famille*) close(-knit); (*pays*) united.
UNICEF [ynisɛf] *sigle m ou f* (= *United Nations International Children's Emergency Fund*) UNICEF.
unidirectionnel, le [ynidirɛksjɔnɛl] *adj* unidirectional, one-way.
unième [ynjɛm] *num*: **vingt/trente et ~** twenty-/thirty-first; **cent ~** (one) hundred and first.
unificateur, trice [ynifikatœr, -tris] *adj* unifying.
unification [ynifikɑsjɔ̃] *nf* uniting; unification; standardization.
unifier [ynifje] *vt* to unite, unify; (*systèmes*) to standardize, unify; **s'~** to become united.
uniforme [ynifɔrm(ə)] *adj* (*mouvement*) regular, uniform; (*surface, ton*) even; (*objets, maisons*) uniform; (*fig: vie, conduite*) unchanging ♦ *nm* uniform; **être sous l'~** (*MIL*) to be serving.
uniformément [ynifɔrmemɑ̃] *adv* uniformly.
uniformisation [ynifɔrmizɑsjɔ̃] *nf* standardization.
uniformiser [ynifɔrmize] *vt* to make uniform; (*systèmes*) to standardize.
uniformité [ynifɔrmite] *nf* regularity; uniformity; evenness.
unijambiste [ynizɑ̃bist(ə)] *nm/f* one-legged man/woman.
unilatéral, e, aux [ynilateral, -o] *adj* unilateral; **stationnement ~** parking on one side only.
unilatéralement [ynilateralmɑ̃] *adv* unilaterally.
uninominal, e, aux [yninɔminal, -o] *adj* uncontested.
union [ynjɔ̃] *nf* union; **~ conjugale** union of marriage; **~ de consommateurs** consumers' association; **~ libre** free love; **l'U~ des Républiques socialistes soviétiques (URSS)** the Union of Soviet Socialist Republics (USSR); **l'U~ soviétique** the Soviet Union.
unique [ynik] *adj* (*seul*) only; (*le même*): **un prix/système ~** a single price/system; (*exceptionnel*) unique; **ménage à salaire ~** one-salary family; **route à voie ~** single-lane road; **fils/fille ~** only son/daughter, only child; **~ en France** the only one of its kind in France.
uniquement [ynikmɑ̃] *adv* only, solely; (*juste*) only, merely.
unir [ynir] *vt* (*nations*) to unite; (*éléments, couleurs*) to combine; (*en mariage*) to unite, join together; **~ qch à** to unite sth with; to combine sth with; **s'~** to unite; (*en mariage*) to be joined together; **s'~ à** *ou* **avec** to unite with.
unisexe [ynisɛks] *adj* unisex.
unisson [ynisɔ̃]: **à l'~** *adv* in unison.
unitaire [ynitɛr] *adj* unitary; (*POL*) unitarian; **prix ~** unit price.
unité [ynite] *nf* (*harmonie, cohésion*) unity; (*COMM, MIL, de mesure, MATH*) unit; **~ centrale (de traitement)** central processing unit; **~ de valeur** (university) course, credit.
univers [ynivɛr] *nm* universe.
universalisation [ynivɛrsalizasjɔ̃] *nf* universalization.
universaliser [ynivɛrsalize] *vt* to universalize.
universalité [ynivɛrsalite] *nf* universality.
universel, le [ynivɛrsɛl] *adj* universal; (*esprit*) all-embracing.
universellement [ynivɛrsɛlmɑ̃] *adv* universally.
universitaire [ynivɛrsitɛr] *adj* university *cpd*; (*diplôme, études*) academic, university *cpd* ♦ *nm/f* academic.
université [ynivɛrsite] *nf* university.
univoque [ynivɔk] *adj* unambiguous; (*MATH*) one-to-one.
UNR *sigle f* (= *Union pour la nouvelle république*) *former political party.*
UNSS *sigle f* = *Union nationale de sport scolaire.*
Untel, Unetelle [œ̃tɛl, yntɛl] *nm/f*: **Monsieur ~** Mr so-and-so.
uranium [yranjɔm] *nm* uranium.
urbain, e [yrbɛ̃, -ɛn] *adj* urban, city *cpd*, town *cpd*; (*poli*) urbane.
urbanisation [yrbanizɑsjɔ̃] *nf* urbanization.
urbaniser [yrbanize] *vt* to urbanize.
urbanisme [yrbanism(ə)] *nm* town planning.
urbaniste [yrbanist(ə)] *nm/f* town planner.
urbanité [yrbanite] *nf* urbanity.
urée [yre] *nf* urea.
urémie [yremi] *nf* uraemia (*BRIT*), uremia (*US*).
urgence [yrʒɑ̃s] *nf* urgency; (*MÉD etc*) emergency; **d'~** *adj* emergency *cpd* ♦ *adv* as a matter of urgency; **en cas d'~** in case of emergency; **service des ~s** emergency service.
urgent, e [yrʒɑ̃, -ɑ̃t] *adj* urgent.
urinaire [yrinɛr] *adj* urinary.
urinal, aux [yrinal, -o] *nm* (bed) urinal.

urine [yʀin] *nf* urine.
uriner [yʀine] *vi* to urinate.
urinoir [yʀinwaʀ] *nm* (public) urinal.
urne [yʀn(ə)] *nf* (*électorale*) ballot box; (*vase*) urn; **aller aux ~s** (*voter*) to go to the polls.
urologie [yʀɔlɔʒi] *nf* urology.
URSS [*parfois*: yʀs] *sigle f* (= *Union des Républiques Socialistes Soviétiques*) USSR.
URSSAF [yʀsaf] *sigle f* (= *Union pour le recouvrement de la sécurité sociale et des allocations familiales*) *administrative body responsible for social security funds and payments*.
urticaire [yʀtikɛʀ] *nf* nettle rash, urticaria.
Uruguay [yʀygwɛ] *nm*: **l'~** Uruguay.
uruguayen, ne [yʀygwajɛ̃, -ɛn] *adj* Uruguayan ♦ *nm/f*: **U~, ne** Uruguayan.
us [ys] *nmpl*: **~ et coutumes** (habits and) customs.
US(A) *sigle mpl* (= *United States (of America)*) US(A).
usage [yzaʒ] *nm* (*emploi, utilisation*) use; (*coutume*) custom; (*éducation*) (good) manners *pl*, (good) breeding; (*LING*): **l'~** usage; **faire ~ de** (*pouvoir, droit*) to exercise; **avoir l'~ de** to have the use of; **à l'~** *adv* with use; **à l'~ de** (*pour*) for (use of); **en ~** in use; **hors d'~** out of service; **à ~ interne** to be taken; **à ~ externe** for external use only.
usagé, e [yzaʒe] *adj* (*usé*) worn; (*d'occasion*) used.
usager, ère [yzaʒe, -ɛʀ] *nm/f* user.
usé, e [yze] *adj* worn (down *ou* out *ou* away); ruined; (*banal*) hackneyed.
user [yze] *vt* (*outil*) to wear down; (*vêtement*) to wear out; (*matière*) to wear away; (*consommer: charbon etc*) to use; (*fig: santé*) to ruin; (*: personne*) to wear out; **s'~** *vi* to wear; to wear out; (*fig*) to decline; **s'~ à la tâche** to wear o.s. out with work; **~ de** *vt* (*moyen, procédé*) to use, employ; (*droit*) to exercise.
usine [yzin] *nf* factory; **~ atomique** nuclear power plant; **~ à gaz** gasworks *sg*; **~ marémotrice** tidal power station.
usiner [yzine] *vt* (*TECH*) to machine; (*fabriquer*) to manufacture.
usité, e [yzite] *adj* in common use, common; **peu ~** rarely used.
ustensile [ystɑ̃sil] *nm* implement; **~ de cuisine** kitchen utensil.
usuel, le [yzɥɛl] *adj* everyday, common.
usufruit [yzyfʀɥi] *nm* usufruct.
usuraire [yzyʀɛʀ] *adj* usurious.
usure [yzyʀ] *nf* wear; worn state; (*de l'usurier*) usury; **avoir qn à l'~** to wear sb down; **~ normale** fair wear and tear.
usurier, ière [yzyʀje, -jɛʀ] *nm/f* usurer.
usurpateur, trice [yzyʀpatœʀ, -tʀis] *nm/f* usurper.
usurpation [yzyʀpɑsjɔ̃] *nf* usurpation.
usurper [yzyʀpe] *vt* to usurp.
ut [yt] *nm* (*MUS*) C.
UTA *sigle f* = *Union des transporteurs aériens*.
utérin, e [yteʀɛ̃, -in] *adj* uterine.
utérus [yteʀys] *nm* uterus, womb.
utile [ytil] *adj* useful; **~ à qn/qch** of use to sb/sth.
utilement [ytilmɑ̃] *adv* usefully.
utilisable [ytilizabl(ə)] *adj* usable.
utilisateur, trice [ytilizatœʀ, -tʀis] *nm/f* user.
utilisation [ytilizɑsjɔ̃] *nf* use.
utiliser [ytilize] *vt* to use.
utilitaire [ytilitɛʀ] *adj* utilitarian; (*objets*) practical ♦ *nm* (*INFORM*) utility.
utilité [ytilite] *nf* usefulness *no pl*; use; **jouer les ~s** (*THÉÂT*) to play bit parts; **reconnu d'~ publique** state-approved; **c'est d'une grande ~** it's extremely useful; **il n'y a aucune ~ à** ... there's no use in ....
utopie [ytɔpi] *nf* (*idée, conception*) utopian idea *ou* view; (*société etc idéale*) utopia.
utopique [ytɔpik] *adj* utopian.
utopiste [ytɔpist(ə)] *nm/f* utopian.
UV *sigle f* (*SCOL*) = **unité de valeur**.
uvule [yvyl] *nf* uvula.

V v

V, v [ve] *nm inv* V, v ♦ *abr* (= *voir, verset*) v.; (= *vers: de poésie*) l.; (*: en direction de*) toward(s); **V comme Victor** V for Victor; **en ~** V-shaped; **encolure en ~** V-neck; **décolleté en ~** plunging neckline.
va [va] *vb voir* **aller**.
vacance [vakɑ̃s] *nf* (*ADMIN*) vacancy; **~s** *nfpl* holiday(s *pl*) (*BRIT*), vacation *sg* (*US*); **les grandes ~s** the summer holidays *ou* vacation; **prendre des/ses ~s** to take a holiday *ou* vacation/one's holiday(s) *ou* vacation; **aller en ~s** to go on holiday *ou* vacation.
vacancier, ière [vakɑ̃sje, -jɛʀ] *nm/f* holidaymaker (*BRIT*), vacationer (*US*).
vacant, e [vakɑ̃, -ɑ̃t] *adj* vacant.
vacarme [vakaʀm(ə)] *nm* row, din.
vacataire [vakatɛʀ] *nm/f* temporary (employee); (*enseignement*) supply (*BRIT*) *ou* substitute (*US*) teacher; (*UNIVERSITÉ*) part-time temporary lecturer.
vaccin [vaksɛ̃] *nm* vaccine; (*opération*) vaccination.
vaccination [vaksinɑsjɔ̃] *nf* vaccination.
vacciner [vaksine] *vt* to vaccinate; (*fig*) to make immune; **être vacciné** (*fig*) to be immune.
vache [vaʃ] *nf* (*ZOOL*) cow; (*cuir*) cowhide ♦ *adj* (*fam*) rotten, mean; **~ à eau** (canvas) water bag; **(manger de la) ~ enragée** (to go through) hard times; **~ à lait** (*péj*) mug,

sucker; ~ **laitière** dairy cow; **période des ~s maigres** lean times *pl*, lean period.

vachement [vaʃmɑ̃] *adv* (*fam*) damned, fantastically.

vacher, ère [vaʃe, -ɛʀ] *nm/f* cowherd.

vacherie [vaʃʀi] *nf* (*fam*) meanness *no pl*; (*action*) dirty trick; (*propos*) nasty remark.

vacherin [vaʃʀɛ̃] *nm* (*fromage*) vacherin cheese; (*gâteau*): ~ **glacé** vacherin (*type of cream gâteau*).

vachette [vaʃɛt] *nf* calfskin.

vacillant, e [vasijɑ̃, -ɑ̃t] *adj* wobbly; flickering; failing, faltering.

vaciller [vasije] *vi* to sway, wobble; (*bougie, lumière*) to flicker; (*fig*) to be failing, falter; ~ **dans ses réponses** to falter in one's replies; ~ **dans ses résolutions** to waver in one's resolutions.

vacuité [vakɥite] *nf* emptiness, vacuity.

vade-mecum [vademekɔm] *nm inv* pocketbook.

vadrouille [vadʀuj] *nf*: **être/partir en** ~ to be on/go for a wander.

vadrouiller [vadʀuje] *vi* to wander around *ou* about.

va-et-vient [vaevjɛ̃] *nm inv* (*de pièce mobile*) to and fro (*ou* up and down) movement; (*de personnes, véhicules*) comings and goings *pl*, to-ings and fro-ings *pl*; (*ELEC*) two-way switch.

vagabond, e [vagabɔ̃, -ɔ̃d] *adj* wandering; (*imagination*) roaming, roving ♦ *nm* (*rôdeur*) tramp, vagrant; (*voyageur*) wanderer.

vagabondage [vagabɔ̃daʒ] *nm* roaming, wandering; (*JUR*) vagrancy.

vagabonder [vagabɔ̃de] *vi* to roam, wander.

vagin [vaʒɛ̃] *nm* vagina.

vaginal, e, aux [vaʒinal, -o] *adj* vaginal.

vagissement [vaʒismɑ̃] *nm* cry (*of newborn baby*).

vague [vag] *nf* wave ♦ *adj* vague; (*regard*) faraway; (*manteau, robe*) loose(-fitting); (*quelconque*): **un ~ bureau/cousin** some office/cousin or other ♦ *nm*: **être dans le** ~ to be rather in the dark; **rester dans le** ~ to keep things rather vague; **regarder dans le** ~ to gaze into space; ~ **à l'âme** *nm* vague melancholy; ~ **d'assaut** *nf* (*MIL*) wave of assault; ~ **de chaleur** *nf* heatwave; ~ **de fond** *nf* ground swell; ~ **de froid** *nf* cold spell.

vaguelette [vaglɛt] *nf* ripple.

vaguement [vagmɑ̃] *adv* vaguely.

vaillamment [vajamɑ̃] *adv* bravely, gallantly.

vaillant, e [vajɑ̃, -ɑ̃t] *adj* (*courageux*) brave, gallant; (*robuste*) vigorous, hale and hearty; **n'avoir plus un sou** ~ to be penniless.

vaille [vaj] *vb voir* **valoir**.

vain, e [vɛ̃, vɛn] *adj* vain; **en** ~ *adv* in vain.

vaincre [vɛ̃kʀ(ə)] *vt* to defeat; (*fig*) to conquer, overcome.

vaincu, e [vɛ̃ky] *pp de* **vaincre** ♦ *nm/f* defeated party.

vainement [vɛnmɑ̃] *adv* vainly.

vainquais [vɛ̃kɛ] *etc vb voir* **vaincre**.

vainqueur [vɛ̃kœʀ] *nm* victor; (*SPORT*) winner ♦ *adj m* victorious.

vais [vɛ] *vb voir* **aller**.

vaisseau, x [vɛso] *nm* (*ANAT*) vessel; (*NAVIG*) ship, vessel; ~ **spatial** spaceship.

vaisselier [vɛsəlje] *nm* dresser.

vaisselle [vɛsɛl] *nf* (*service*) crockery; (*plats etc à laver*) (dirty) dishes *pl*; **faire la** ~ to do the washing-up (*BRIT*) *ou* the dishes.

val, vaux *ou* **vals** [val, vo] *nm* valley.

valable [valabl(ə)] *adj* valid; (*acceptable*) decent, worthwhile.

valablement [valabləmɑ̃] *adv* legitimately; (*de façon satisfaisante*) satisfactorily.

Valence [valɑ̃s] *n* (*en Espagne*) Valencia; (*en France*) Valence.

valent [val] *etc vb voir* **valoir**.

valet [valɛ] *nm* valet; (*péj*) lackey; (*CARTES*) jack, knave (*BRIT*); ~ **de chambre** manservant, valet; ~ **de ferme** farmhand; ~ **de pied** footman.

valeur [valœʀ] *nf* (*gén*) value; (*mérite*) worth, merit; (*COMM*: *titre*) security; **mettre en** ~ (*bien*) to exploit; (*terrain, région*) to develop; (*fig*) to highlight; to show off to advantage; **avoir de la** ~ to be valuable; **prendre de la** ~ to go up *ou* gain in value; **sans** ~ worthless; ~ **absolue** absolute value; ~ **d'échange** exchange value; ~ **nominale** face value; **~s mobilières** transferable securities.

valeureux, euse [valœʀø, -øz] *adj* valorous.

validation [validɑsjɔ̃] *nf* validation.

valide [valid] *adj* (*en bonne santé*) fit, well; (*indemne*) able-bodied, fit; (*valable*) valid.

valider [valide] *vt* to validate.

validité [validite] *nf* validity.

valions [valjɔ̃] *etc vb voir* **valoir**.

valise [valiz] *nf* (suit)case; **faire sa** ~ to pack one's (suit)case; **la ~ (diplomatique)** the diplomatic bag.

vallée [vale] *nf* valley.

vallon [valɔ̃] *nm* small valley.

vallonné, e [valɔne] *adj* undulating.

vallonnement [valɔnmɑ̃] *nm* undulation.

valoir [valwaʀ] *vi* (*être valable*) to hold, apply ♦ *vt* (*prix, valeur, effort*) to be worth; (*causer*): ~ **qch à qn** to earn sb sth; **se** ~ to be of equal merit; (*péj*) to be two of a kind; **faire** ~ (*droits, prérogatives*) to assert; (*domaine, capitaux*) to exploit; **faire ~ que** to point out that; **se faire** ~ to make the most of o.s.; **à** ~ on account; **à ~ sur** to be deducted from; **vaille que vaille** somehow or other; **cela ne me dit rien qui vaille** I don't like the look of it at all; **ce climat ne me vaut rien** this climate doesn't suit me; ~ **la peine** to be worth the trouble, be worth it; ~ **mieux**: **il vaut mieux se taire** it's better to say nothing; **il vaut mieux que je fasse/comme ceci** it's better if

I do/like this; **ça ne vaut rien** it's worthless; **que vaut ce candidat?** how good is this applicant?
valorisation [valɔRizasjɔ̃] *nf* (economic) development; increased standing.
valoriser [valɔRize] *vt* (*ÉCON*) to develop (the economy of); (*produit*) to increase the value of; (*PSYCH*) to increase the standing of; (*fig*) to highlight, bring out.
valse [vals(ə)] *nf* waltz; **c'est la ~ des étiquettes** the prices don't stay the same from one moment to the next.
valser [valse] *vi* to waltz; (*fig*): **aller ~** to go flying.
valu, e [valy] *pp de* **valoir**.
valve [valv(ə)] *nf* valve.
vamp [vɑ̃p] *nf* vamp.
vampire [vɑ̃piR] *nm* vampire.
van [vɑ̃] *nm* horse box (*BRIT*) *ou* trailer (*US*).
vandale [vɑ̃dal] *nm/f* vandal.
vandalisme [vɑ̃dalism(ə)] *nm* vandalism.
vanille [vanij] *nf* vanilla; **glace à la ~** vanilla ice cream.
vanillé, e [vanije] *adj* vanilla *cpd*.
vanité [vanite] *nf* vanity.
vaniteux, euse [vanitø, -øz] *adj* vain, conceited.
vanity-case [vaniti(e)kɛz] *nm* vanity case.
vanne [van] *nf* gate; (*fam*: *remarque*) dig, (nasty) crack; **lancer une ~ à qn** to have a go at sb (*BRIT*), knock sb.
vanneau, x [vano] *nm* lapwing.
vanner [vane] *vt* to winnow.
vannerie [vanRi] *nf* basketwork.
vantail, aux [vɑ̃taj, -o] *nm* door, leaf (*pl* leaves).
vantard, e [vɑ̃taR, -aRd(ə)] *adj* boastful.
vantardise [vɑ̃taRdiz] *nf* boastfulness *no pl*; boast.
vanter [vɑ̃te] *vt* to speak highly of, vaunt; **se ~** *vi* to boast, brag; **se ~ de** to pride o.s. on; (*péj*) to boast of.
Vanuatu [vanwatu] *nm*: **le ~** Vanuatu.
va-nu-pieds [vanypje] *nm/f inv* tramp, beggar.
vapeur [vapœR] *nf* steam; (*émanation*) vapour (*BRIT*), vapor (*US*), fumes *pl*; (*brouillard, buée*) haze; **~s** *nfpl* (*bouffées*) vapours, vapors; **à ~** steam-powered, steam *cpd*; **à toute ~** full steam ahead; (*fig*) at full tilt; **renverser la ~** to reverse engines; (*fig*) to backtrack, backpedal; **cuit à la ~** steamed.
vapocuiseur [vapɔkyizœR] *nm* pressure cooker.
vaporeux, euse [vapɔRø, -øz] *adj* (*flou*) hazy, misty; (*léger*) filmy, gossamer *cpd*.
vaporisateur [vapɔRizatœR] *nm* spray.
vaporiser [vapɔRize] *vt* (*CHIMIE*) to vaporize; (*parfum etc*) to spray.
vaquer [vake] *vi* (*ADMIN*) to be on vacation; **~ à ses occupations** to attend to one's affairs, go about one's business.
varappe [vaRap] *nf* rock climbing.
varappeur, euse [vaRapœR, -øz] *nm/f* (rock) climber.
varech [vaRɛk] *nm* wrack, varec.
vareuse [vaRøz] *nf* (*blouson*) pea jacket; (*d'uniforme*) tunic.
variable [vaRjabl(ə)] *adj* variable; (*temps, humeur*) changeable; (*TECH*: *à plusieurs positions etc*) adaptable; (*LING*) inflectional; (*divers: résultats*) varied, various ♦ *nf* (*INFORM, MATH*) variable.
variante [vaRjɑ̃t] *nf* variant.
variation [vaRjasjɔ̃] *nf* variation; changing *no pl*, change; (*MUS*) variation.
varice [vaRis] *nf* varicose vein.
varicelle [vaRisɛl] *nf* chickenpox.
varié, e [vaRje] *adj* varied; (*divers*) various; **hors-d'œuvre ~s** selection of hors d'œuvres.
varier [vaRje] *vi* to vary; (*temps, humeur*) to change ♦ *vt* to vary.
variété [vaRjete] *nf* variety; **spectacle de ~s** variety show.
variole [vaRjɔl] *nf* smallpox.
variqueux, euse [vaRikø, -øz] *adj* varicose.
Varsovie [vaRsɔvi] *n* Warsaw.
vas [va] *vb voir* **aller**; **~-y!** [vazi] go on!
vasculaire [vaskylɛR] *adj* vascular.
vase [vɑz] *nm* vase ♦ *nf* silt, mud; **en ~ clos** in isolation; **~ de nuit** chamberpot; **~s communicants** communicating vessels.
vasectomie [vazɛktɔmi] *nf* vasectomy.
vaseline [vazlin] *nf* Vaseline ®.
vaseux, euse [vɑzø, -øz] *adj* silty, muddy; (*fig: confus*) woolly, hazy; (*: fatigué*) peaky; (*: étourdi*) woozy.
vasistas [vazistɑs] *nm* fanlight.
vasque [vask(ə)] *nf* (*bassin*) basin; (*coupe*) bowl.
vassal, e, aux [vasal, -o] *nm/f* vassal.
vaste [vast(ə)] *adj* vast, immense.
Vatican [vatikɑ̃] *nm*: **le ~** the Vatican.
vaticiner [vatisine] *vi* (*péj*) to make pompous predictions.
va-tout [vatu] *nm*: **jouer son ~** to stake one's all.
vaudeville [vodvil] *nm* vaudeville, light comedy.
vaudrai [vodRe] *etc vb voir* **valoir**.
vau-l'eau [volo]: **à ~** *adv* with the current; **s'en aller à ~** (*fig: projets*) to be adrift.
vaurien, ne [voRjɛ̃, -ɛn] *nm/f* good-for-nothing, guttersnipe.
vaut [vo] *vb voir* **valoir**.
vautour [votuR] *nm* vulture.
vautrer [votRe]: **se ~** *vi*: **se ~ dans** to wallow in; **se ~ sur** to sprawl on.
vaux [vo] *pl de* **val** ♦ *vb voir* **valoir**.
va-vite [vavit]: **à la ~** *adv* in a rush.
vd *abr* = *vend*.
VDQS *abr* (= *vin délimité de qualité supérieure*) *label guaranteeing quality of wine*; *see boxed note*.

VDQS

VDQS *on a bottle of French wine indicates that it contains high-quality produce from an approved regional vineyard. It is the second-highest French wine classification after 'AOC' and is a step up from 'vin de pays'. In contrast, 'vin de table' or 'vin ordinaire' is table wine of unspecified origin, often blended.*

vds *abr* = *vends.*
veau, x [vo] *nm* (*ZOOL*) calf (*pl* calves); (*CULIN*) veal; (*peau*) calfskin; **tuer le ~ gras** to kill the fatted calf.
vecteur [vɛktœʀ] *nm* vector; (*MIL, BIO*) carrier.
vécu, e [veky] *pp de* **vivre** ♦ *adj* (*aventure*) real(-life).
vedettariat [vədɛtaʀja] *nm* stardom; (*attitude*) acting like a star.
vedette [vədɛt] *nf* (*artiste etc*) star; (*canot*) patrol boat; launch; **avoir la ~** to top the bill, get star billing; **mettre qn en ~** (*CINÉ etc*) to give sb the starring role; (*fig*) to push sb into the limelight; **voler la ~ à qn** to steal the show from sb.
végétal, e, aux [veʒetal, -o] *adj* vegetable ♦ *nm* vegetable, plant.
végétalien, ne [veʒetaljɛ̃, -ɛn] *adj, nm/f* vegan.
végétalisme [veʒetalism(ə)] *nm* veganism.
végétarien, ne [veʒetaʀjɛ̃, -ɛn] *adj, nm/f* vegetarian.
végétarisme [veʒetaʀism(ə)] *nm* vegetarianism.
végétatif, ive [veʒetatif, -iv] *adj*: **une vie ~ive** a vegetable existence.
végétation [veʒetɑsjɔ̃] *nf* vegetation; **~s** *nfpl* (*MÉD*) adenoids.
végéter [veʒete] *vi* (*fig*) to vegetate.
véhémence [veemɑ̃s] *nf* vehemence.
véhément, e [veemɑ̃, -ɑ̃t] *adj* vehement.
véhicule [veikyl] *nm* vehicle; **~ utilitaire** commercial vehicle.
véhiculer [veikyle] *vt* (*personnes, marchandises*) to transport, convey; (*fig: idées, substances*) to convey, serve as a vehicle for.
veille [vɛj] *nf* (*garde*) watch; (*PSYCH*) wakefulness; (*jour*): **la ~** the day before, the previous day; **la ~ au soir** the previous evening; **la ~ de** the day before; **à la ~ de** on the eve of; **l'état de ~** the waking state.
veillée [veje] *nf* (*soirée*) evening; (*réunion*) evening gathering; **~ d'armes** night before combat; (*fig*) vigil; **~ (mortuaire)** watch.
veiller [veje] *vi* (*rester debout*) to stay *ou* sit up; (*ne pas dormir*) to be awake; (*être de garde*) to be on watch; (*être vigilant*) to be watchful ♦ *vt* (*malade, mort*) to watch over, sit up with; **~ à** *vt* to attend to, see to; **~ à ce que** to make sure that, see to it that; **~ sur** *vt* to keep a watch *ou* an eye on.
veilleur [vɛjœʀ] *nm*: **~ de nuit** night watchman.
veilleuse [vɛjøz] *nf* (*lampe*) night light; (*AUTO*) sidelight; (*flamme*) pilot light; **en ~** *adj* (*lampe*) dimmed; (*fig: affaire*) shelved, set aside.
veinard, e [vɛnaʀ, -aʀd(ə)] *nm/f* (*fam*) lucky devil.
veine [vɛn] *nf* (*ANAT, du bois etc*) vein; (*filon*) vein, seam; (*fam: chance*): **avoir de la ~** to be lucky; (*inspiration*) inspiration.
veiné, e [vene] *adj* veined; (*bois*) grained.
veineux, euse [venø, -øz] *adj* venous.
Velcro [vɛlkʀo] *nm* ® Velcro ®.
vêler [vele] *vi* to calve.
vélin [velɛ̃] *nm*: **(papier) ~** vellum (paper).
véliplanchiste [veliplɑ̃ʃist(ə)] *nm/f* windsurfer.
velléitaire [veleitɛʀ] *adj* irresolute, indecisive.
velléités [veleite] *nfpl* vague impulses.
vélo [velo] *nm* bike, cycle; **faire du ~** to go cycling.
véloce [velɔs] *adj* swift.
vélocité [velɔsite] *nf* (*MUS*) nimbleness, swiftness; (*vitesse*) velocity.
vélodrome [velɔdʀɔm] *nm* velodrome.
vélomoteur [velɔmɔtœʀ] *nm* moped.
véloski [veloski] *nm* skibob.
velours [vəluʀ] *nm* velvet; **~ côtelé** corduroy.
velouté, e [vəlute] *adj* (*au toucher*) velvety; (*à la vue*) soft, mellow; (*au goût*) smooth, mellow ♦ *nm*: **~ d'asperges/de tomates** cream of asparagus/tomato soup.
velouteux, euse [vəlutø, -øz] *adj* velvety.
velu, e [vəly] *adj* hairy.
venais [vənɛ] *etc vb voir* **venir**.
venaison [vənɛzɔ̃] *nf* venison.
vénal, e, aux [venal, -o] *adj* venal.
vénalité [venalite] *nf* venality.
venant [vənɑ̃]: **à tout ~** *adv* to all and sundry.
vendable [vɑ̃dabl(ə)] *adj* saleable, marketable.
vendange [vɑ̃dɑ̃ʒ] *nf* (*opération, période: aussi:* **~s**) grape harvest; (*raisins*) grape crop, grapes *pl*.
vendanger [vɑ̃dɑ̃ʒe] *vi* to harvest the grapes.
vendangeur, euse [vɑ̃dɑ̃ʒœʀ, -øz] *nm/f* grape-picker.
vendéen, ne [vɑ̃deɛ̃, -ɛn] *adj* of *ou* from the Vendée.
vendeur, euse [vɑ̃dœʀ, -øz] *nm/f* (*de magasin*) shop *ou* sales assistant (*BRIT*), sales clerk (*US*); (*COMM*) salesman/woman ♦ *nm* (*JUR*) vendor, seller; **~ de journaux** newspaper seller.
vendre [vɑ̃dʀ(ə)] *vt* to sell; **~ qch à qn** to sell sb sth; **cela se vend à la douzaine** these are sold by the dozen; **"à ~"** "for sale".
vendredi [vɑ̃dʀədi] *nm* Friday; **V~ saint** Good Friday; *voir aussi* **lundi**.
vendu, e [vɑ̃dy] *pp de* **vendre** ♦ *adj* (*péj*) corrupt.
venelle [vənɛl] *nf* alley.
vénéneux, euse [venenø, -øz] *adj* poisonous.
vénérable [veneʀabl(ə)] *adj* venerable.

vénération [veneʀɑsjɔ̃] *nf* veneration.
vénérer [veneʀe] *vt* to venerate.
vénerie [vɛnʀi] *nf* hunting.
vénérien, ne [veneʀjɛ̃, -ɛn] *adj* venereal.
Venezuela [venezɥela] *nm*: **le** ~ Venezuela.
vénézuélien, ne [venezɥeljɛ̃, -ɛn] *adj* Venezuelan ♦ *nm/f*: **V~, ne** Venezuelan.
vengeance [vɑ̃ʒɑ̃s] *nf* vengeance *no pl*, revenge *no pl*; (*acte*) act of vengeance *ou* revenge.
venger [vɑ̃ʒe] *vt* to avenge; **se** ~ *vi* to avenge o.s.; (*par rancune*) to take revenge; **se ~ de qch** to avenge o.s. for sth; to take one's revenge for sth; **se ~ de qn** to take revenge on sb; **se ~ sur** to wreak vengeance upon; to take revenge on *ou* through; to take it out on.
vengeur, eresse [vɑ̃ʒœʀ, -ʒʀɛs] *adj* vengeful ♦ *nm/f* avenger.
véniel, le [venjɛl] *adj* venial.
venimeux, euse [vənimø, -øz] *adj* poisonous, venomous; (*fig: haineux*) venomous, vicious.
venin [vənɛ̃] *nm* venom, poison; (*fig*) venom.
venir [vəniʀ] *vi* to come; ~ **de** to come from; ~ **de faire**: **je viens d'y aller/de le voir** I've just been there/seen him; **s'il vient à pleuvoir** if it should rain, if it happens to rain; **en ~ à faire**: **j'en viens à croire que** I am coming to believe that; **où veux-tu en ~?** what are you getting at?; **il en est venu à mendier** he has been reduced to begging; **en ~ aux mains** to come to blows; **les années/générations à ~** the years/generations to come; **il me vient une idée** an idea has just occurred to me; **il me vient des soupçons** I'm beginning to be suspicious; **je te vois ~** I know what you're after; **faire ~** (*docteur, plombier*) to call (out); **d'où vient que ...?** how is it that ...?; **~ au monde** to come into the world.
Venise [vəniz] *n* Venice.
vénitien, ne [venisjɛ̃, -ɛn] *adj* Venetian.
vent [vɑ̃] *nm* wind; **il y a du** ~ it's windy; **c'est du** ~ it's all hot air; **au** ~ to windward; **sous le** ~ to leeward; **avoir le ~ debout/arrière** to head into the wind/have the wind astern; **dans le** ~ (*fam*) trendy; **prendre le** ~ (*fig*) to see which way the wind blows; **avoir ~ de** to get wind of; **contre ~s et marées** come hell or high water.
vente [vɑ̃t] *nf* sale; **la** ~ (*activité*) selling; (*secteur*) sales *pl*; **mettre en** ~ to put on sale; (*objets personnels*) to put up for sale; ~ **de charité** jumble (*BRIT*) *ou* rummage (*US*) sale; ~ **par correspondance (VPC)** mail-order selling; ~ **aux enchères** auction sale.
venté, e [vɑ̃te] *adj* windswept, windy.
venter [vɑ̃te] *vb impers*: **il vente** the wind is blowing.
venteux, euse [vɑ̃tø, -øz] *adj* windswept, windy.
ventilateur [vɑ̃tilatœʀ] *nm* fan.
ventilation [vɑ̃tilɑsjɔ̃] *nf* ventilation.
ventiler [vɑ̃tile] *vt* to ventilate; (*total, statistiques*) to break down.
ventouse [vɑ̃tuz] *nf* (*ampoule*) cupping glass; (*de caoutchouc*) suction pad; (*ZOOL*) sucker.
ventre [vɑ̃tʀ(ə)] *nm* (*ANAT*) stomach; (*fig*) belly; **prendre du** ~ to be getting a paunch; **avoir mal au** ~ to have (a) stomach ache.
ventricule [vɑ̃tʀikyl] *nm* ventricle.
ventriloque [vɑ̃tʀilɔk] *nm/f* ventriloquist.
ventripotent, e [vɑ̃tʀipɔtɑ̃, -ɑ̃t] *adj* potbellied.
ventru, e [vɑ̃tʀy] *adj* potbellied.
venu, e [vəny] *pp de* **venir** ♦ *adj*: **être mal ~ à** *ou* **de faire** to have no grounds for doing, be in no position to do; **mal** ~ ill-timed, unwelcome; **bien** ~ timely, welcome ♦ *nf* coming.
vêpres [vɛpʀ(ə)] *nfpl* vespers.
ver [vɛʀ] *nm voir aussi* **vers**; worm; (*des fruits etc*) maggot; (*du bois*) woodworm *no pl*; ~ **blanc** May beetle grub; ~ **luisant** glow-worm; ~ **à soie** silkworm; ~ **solitaire** tapeworm; ~ **de terre** earthworm.
véracité [veʀasite] *nf* veracity.
véranda [veʀɑ̃da] *nf* veranda(h).
verbal, e, aux [vɛʀbal, -o] *adj* verbal.
verbalement [vɛʀbalmɑ̃] *adv* verbally.
verbaliser [vɛʀbalize] *vi* (*POLICE*) to book *ou* report an offender; (*PSYCH*) to verbalize.
verbe [vɛʀb(ə)] *nm* (*LING*) verb; (*voix*): **avoir le ~ sonore** to have a sonorous tone (of voice); (*expression*): **la magie du** ~ the magic of language *ou* the word; (*REL*): **le V~** the Word.
verbeux, euse [vɛʀbø, -øz] *adj* verbose, wordy.
verbiage [vɛʀbjaʒ] *nm* verbiage.
verbosité [vɛʀbozite] *nf* verbosity.
verdâtre [vɛʀdɑtʀ(ə)] *adj* greenish.
verdeur [vɛʀdœʀ] *nf* (*vigueur*) vigour (*BRIT*), vigor (*US*), vitality; (*crudité*) forthrightness; (*défaut de maturité*) tartness, sharpness.
verdict [vɛʀdik(t)] *nm* verdict.
verdir [vɛʀdiʀ] *vi, vt* to turn green.
verdoyant, e [vɛʀdwajɑ̃, -ɑ̃t] *adj* green, verdant.
verdure [vɛʀdyʀ] *nf* (*arbres, feuillages*) greenery; (*légumes verts*) green vegetables *pl*, greens *pl*.
véreux, euse [veʀø, -øz] *adj* worm-eaten; (*malhonnête*) shady, corrupt.
verge [vɛʀʒ(ə)] *nf* (*ANAT*) penis; (*baguette*) stick, cane.
verger [vɛʀʒe] *nm* orchard.
vergeture [vɛʀʒətyʀ] *nf gén pl* stretch mark.
verglacé, e [vɛʀglase] *adj* icy, iced-over.
verglas [vɛʀgla] *nm* (black) ice.
vergogne [vɛʀgɔɲ]: **sans** ~ *adv* shamelessly.
véridique [veʀidik] *adj* truthful.
verificateur, trice [vɛʀifikatœʀ, -tʀis] *nm/f* controller, checker ♦ *nf* (*machine*) verifier; ~ **des comptes** (*FINANCE*) auditor.
vérification [veʀifikɑsjɔ̃] *nf* checking *no pl*, check; ~ **d'identité** identity check.
vérifier [veʀifje] *vt* to check; (*corroborer*) to

confirm, bear out; (*INFORM*) to verify; **se** ~ *vi* to be confirmed *ou* verified.
vérin [veʀɛ̃] *nm* jack.
véritable [veʀitabl(ə)] *adj* real; (*ami, amour*) true; **un ~ désastre** an absolute disaster.
véritablement [veʀitabləmɑ̃] *adv* (*effectivement*) really; (*absolument*) absolutely.
vérité [veʀite] *nf* truth; (*d'un portrait*) lifelikeness; (*sincérité*) truthfulness, sincerity; **en ~, à la ~** to tell the truth.
verlan [vɛʀlɑ̃] *nm* (back) slang; *see boxed note*.

VERLAN

Verlan *is a form of slang popularized in the 1950s. It consists of inverting a word's syllables, the term* **verlan** *itself coming from 'l'envers' ('à l'envers = back to front'). Typical examples are 'féca' ('café'), 'ripou' ('pourri'), 'meuf' ('femme'), and 'beur' ('Arabe').*

vermeil, le [vɛʀmɛj] *adj* bright red, ruby red ♦ *nm* (*substance*) vermeil.
vermicelles [vɛʀmisɛl] *nmpl* vermicelli *sg*.
vermifuge [vɛʀmifyʒ] *nm*: **poudre ~** worm powder.
vermillon [vɛʀmijɔ̃] *adj inv* vermilion, scarlet.
vermine [vɛʀmin] *nf* vermin *pl*.
vermoulu, e [vɛʀmuly] *adj* worm-eaten, with woodworm.
vermout(h) [vɛʀmut] *nm* vermouth.
verni, e [vɛʀni] *adj* varnished; glazed; (*fam*) lucky; **cuir ~** patent leather; **souliers ~s** patent (leather) shoes.
vernir [vɛʀniʀ] *vt* (*bois, tableau, ongles*) to varnish; (*poterie*) to glaze.
vernis [vɛʀni] *nm* (*enduit*) varnish; glaze; (*fig*) veneer; **~ à ongles** nail varnish (*BRIT*) *ou* polish.
vernissage [vɛʀnisaʒ] *nm* varnishing; glazing; (*d'une exposition*) preview.
vernisser [vɛʀnise] *vt* to glaze.
vérole [veʀɔl] *nf* (*variole*) smallpox; (*fam: syphilis*) pox.
Vérone [veʀɔn] *n* Verona.
verrai [vɛʀe] *etc vb voir* **voir**.
verre [vɛʀ] *nm* glass; (*de lunettes*) lens *sg*; **~s** *nmpl* (*lunettes*) glasses; **boire** *ou* **prendre un ~** to have a drink; **~ à vin/à liqueur** wine/liqueur glass; **~ à dents** tooth mug; **~ dépoli** frosted glass; **~ de lampe** lamp glass *ou* chimney; **~ de montre** watch glass; **~ à pied** stemmed glass; **~s de contact** contact lenses; **~s fumés** tinted lenses.
verrerie [vɛʀʀi] *nf* (*fabrique*) glassworks *sg*; (*activité*) glass-making, glass-working; (*objets*) glassware.
verrier [vɛʀje] *nm* glass-blower.
verrière [vɛʀjɛʀ] *nf* (*grand vitrage*) window; (*toit vitré*) glass roof.
verrons [vɛʀɔ̃] *etc vb voir* **voir**.
verroterie [vɛʀɔtʀi] *nf* glass beads *pl*, glass jewellery (*BRIT*) *ou* jewelry (*US*).
verrou [vɛʀu] *nm* (*targette*) bolt; (*fig*) constriction; **mettre le ~** to bolt the door; **mettre qn sous les ~s** to put sb behind bars.
verrouillage [vɛʀujaʒ] *nm* (*dispositif*) locking mechanism; (*AUTO*): **~ central** *ou* **centralisé** central locking.
verrouiller [vɛʀuje] *vt* to bolt; to lock; (*MIL: brèche*) to close.
verrue [vɛʀy] *nf* wart; (*plantaire*) verruca; (*fig*) eyesore.
vers [vɛʀ] *nm* line ♦ *nmpl* (*poésie*) verse *sg* ♦ *prép* (*en direction de*) toward(s); (*près de*) around (about); (*temporel*) about, around.
versant [vɛʀsɑ̃] *nm* slopes *pl*, side.
versatile [vɛʀsatil] *adj* fickle, changeable.
verse [vɛʀs(ə)]: **à ~** *adv*: **il pleut à ~** it's pouring (with rain).
versé, e [vɛʀse] *adj*: **être ~ dans** (*science*) to be (well-)versed in.
Verseau [vɛʀso] *nm*: **le ~** Aquarius, the water-carrier; **être du ~** to be Aquarius.
versement [vɛʀsəmɑ̃] *nm* payment; (*sur un compte*) deposit, remittance; **en 3 ~s** in 3 instalments.
verser [vɛʀse] *vt* (*liquide, grains*) to pour; (*larmes, sang*) to shed; (*argent*) to pay; (*soldat: affecter*): **~ qn dans** to assign sb to ♦ *vi* (*véhicule*) to overturn; (*fig*): **~ dans** to lapse into; **~ à un compte** to pay into an account.
verset [vɛʀsɛ] *nm* verse; versicle.
verseur [vɛʀsœʀ] *adj m voir* **bec, bouchon**.
versification [vɛʀsifikɑsjɔ̃] *nf* versification.
versifier [vɛʀsifje] *vt* to put into verse ♦ *vi* to versify, write verse.
version [vɛʀsjɔ̃] *nf* version; (*SCOL*) translation (*into the mother tongue*); **film en ~ originale** film in the original language.
verso [vɛʀso] *nm* back; **voir au ~** see over(leaf).
vert, e [vɛʀ, vɛʀt(ə)] *adj* green; (*vin*) young; (*vigoureux*) sprightly; (*cru*) forthright ♦ *nm* green; **dire des ~es (et des pas mûres)** to say some pretty spicy things; **il en a vu des ~es** he's seen a thing or two; **~ bouteille** *adj inv* bottle-green; **~ d'eau** *adj inv* sea-green; **~ pomme** *adj inv* apple-green.
vert-de-gris [vɛʀdəgʀi] *nm* verdigris ♦ *adj inv* grey(ish)-green.
vertébral, e, aux [vɛʀtebʀal, -o] *adj* back *cpd*; *voir* **colonne**.
vertèbre [vɛʀtɛbʀ(ə)] *nf* vertebra (*pl* -ae).
vertébré, e [vɛʀtebʀe] *adj, nm* vertebrate.
vertement [vɛʀtəmɑ̃] *adv* (*réprimander*) sharply.
vertical, e, aux [vɛʀtikal, -o] *adj, nf* vertical; **à la ~e** *adv* vertically.
verticalement [vɛʀtikalmɑ̃] *adv* vertically.
verticalité [vɛʀtikalite] *nf* verticalness, verticality.
vertige [vɛʀtiʒ] *nm* (*peur du vide*) vertigo; (*étourdissement*) dizzy spell; (*fig*) fever; **ça**

me donne le ~ it makes me dizzy; (*fig*) it makes my head spin *ou* reel.

vertigineux, euse [vɛʀtiʒinø, -øz] *adj* (*hausse, vitesse*) breathtaking; (*altitude, gorge*) breathtakingly high (*ou* deep).

vertu [vɛʀty] *nf* virtue; **une** ~ a saint, a paragon of virtue; **avoir la** ~ **de faire** to have the virtue of doing; **en** ~ **de** *prép* in accordance with.

vertueusement [vɛʀtɥøzmɑ̃] *adv* virtuously.

vertueux, euse [vɛʀtɥø, -øz] *adj* virtuous.

verve [vɛʀv(ə)] *nf* witty eloquence; **être en** ~ to be in brilliant form.

verveine [vɛʀvɛn] *nf* (*BOT*) verbena, vervain; (*infusion*) verbena tea.

vésicule [vezikyl] *nf* vesicle; ~ **biliaire** gall-bladder.

vespasienne [vɛspazjɛn] *nf* urinal.

vespéral, e, aux [vɛspeʀal, -o] *adj* vespertine, evening *cpd*.

vessie [vesi] *nf* bladder.

veste [vɛst(ə)] *nf* jacket; ~ **droite/croisée** single-/double-breasted jacket; **retourner sa** ~ (*fig*) to change one's colours.

vestiaire [vɛstjɛʀ] *nm* (*au théâtre etc*) cloak-room; (*de stade etc*) changing-room (*BRIT*), locker-room (*US*); (*métallique*): **(armoire)** ~ locker.

vestibule [vɛstibyl] *nm* hall.

vestige [vɛstiʒ] *nm* (*objet*) relic; (*fragment*) trace; (*fig*) remnant, vestige; ~**s** *nmpl* (*d'une ville*) remains; (*d'une civilisation, du passé*) remnants, relics.

vestimentaire [vɛstimɑ̃tɛʀ] *adj* (*dépenses*) clothing; (*détail*) of dress; (*élégance*) sartorial.

veston [vɛstɔ̃] *nm* jacket.

Vésuve [vezyv] *nm*: **le** ~ Vesuvius.

vêtais [vɛtɛ] *etc vb voir* **vêtir**.

vêtement [vɛtmɑ̃] *nm* garment, item of clothing; (*COMM*): **le** ~ the clothing industry; ~**s** *nmpl* clothes; ~**s de sport** sportswear *sg*, sports clothes.

vétéran [veteʀɑ̃] *nm* veteran.

vétérinaire [veteʀinɛʀ] *adj* veterinary ♦ *nm/f* vet, veterinary surgeon (*BRIT*), veterinarian (*US*).

vétille [vetij] *nf* trifle, triviality.

vétilleux, euse [vetijø, -øz] *adj* punctilious.

vêtir [vetiʀ] *vt* to clothe, dress; **se** ~ to dress (o.s.).

vêtit [veti] *etc vb voir* **vêtir**.

vétiver [vetivɛʀ] *nm* (*BOT*) vetiver.

veto [veto] *nm* veto; **droit de** ~ right of veto; **mettre** *ou* **opposer un** ~ **à** to veto.

vêtu, e [vɛty] *pp de* **vêtir** ♦ *adj*: ~ **de** dressed in, wearing; **chaudement** ~ warmly dressed.

vétuste [vetyst(ə)] *adj* ancient, timeworn.

vétusté [vetyste] *nf* age, delapidation.

veuf, veuve [vœf, vœv] *adj* widowed ♦ *nm* widower ♦ *nf* widow.

veuille [vœj], **veuillez** [vœje] *etc vb voir* **vouloir**.

veule [vøl] *adj* spineless.

veulent [vœl] *etc vb voir* **vouloir**.

veulerie [vølʀi] *nf* spinelessness.

veut [vø] *vb voir* **vouloir**.

veuvage [vœvaʒ] *nm* widowhood.

veuve [vœv] *adj f, nf voir* **veuf**.

veux [vø] *vb voir* **vouloir**.

vexant, e [vɛksɑ̃, -ɑ̃t] *adj* (*contrariant*) annoying; (*blessant*) upsetting.

vexations [vɛksɑsjɔ̃] *nfpl* humiliations.

vexatoire [vɛksatwaʀ] *adj*: **mesures** ~**s** harassment *sg*.

vexer [vɛkse] *vt* to hurt, upset; **se** ~ *vi* to be hurt, get upset.

VF *sigle f* (*CINÉ*) = *version française.*

VHF *sigle f* (= *Very High Frequency*) VHF.

via [vja] *prép* via.

viabiliser [vjabilize] *vt* to provide with services (*water etc*).

viabilité [vjabilite] *nf* viability; (*d'un chemin*) practicability.

viable [vjabl(ə)] *adj* viable.

viaduc [vjadyk] *nm* viaduct.

viager, ère [vjaʒe, -ɛʀ] *adj*: **rente** ~**ère** life annuity ♦ *nm*: **mettre en** ~ to sell in return for a life annuity.

viande [vjɑ̃d] *nf* meat.

viatique [vjatik] *nm* (*REL*) viaticum; (*fig*) provisions *pl ou* money for the journey.

vibrant, e [vibʀɑ̃, -ɑ̃t] *adj* vibrating; (*voix*) vibrant; (*émouvant*) emotive.

vibraphone [vibʀafɔn] *nm* vibraphone, vibes *pl*.

vibraphoniste [vibʀafɔnist(ə)] *nm/f* vibraphone player.

vibration [vibʀɑsjɔ̃] *nf* vibration.

vibratoire [vibʀatwaʀ] *adj* vibratory.

vibrer [vibʀe] *vi* to vibrate; (*son, voix*) to be vibrant; (*fig*) to be stirred; **faire** ~ to (cause to) vibrate; to stir, thrill.

vibromasseur [vibʀɔmasœʀ] *nm* vibrator.

vicaire [vikɛʀ] *nm* curate.

vice... [vis] *préfixe* vice-.

vice [vis] *nm* vice; (*défaut*) fault; ~ **caché** (*COMM*) latent *ou* inherent defect; ~ **de forme** legal flaw *ou* irregularity.

vice-consul [viskɔ̃syl] *nm* vice-consul.

vice-présidence [vispʀezidɑ̃s] *nf* (*d'un pays*) vice-presidency; (*d'une société*) vice-presidency, vice-chairmanship (*BRIT*).

vice-président, e [vispʀezidɑ̃, -ɑ̃t] *nm/f* vice-president; vice-chairman.

vice-roi [visʀwa] *nm* viceroy.

vice-versa [visevɛʀsa] *adv* vice versa.

vichy [viʃi] *nm* (*toile*) gingham; (*eau*) Vichy water; **carottes V**~ boiled carrots.

vichyssois, e [viʃiswa, -waz] *adj* of *ou* from Vichy, Vichy *cpd* ♦ *nf* (*soupe*) vichyssoise (soup), *cream of leek and potato soup* ♦ *nm/f*: **V**~**, e** native *ou* inhabitant of Vichy.

vicié, e [visje] *adj* (*air*) polluted, tainted; (*JUR*) invalidated.

vicier [visje] *vt* (*JUR*) to invalidate.

vicieux, euse [visjø, -øz] *adj* (*pervers*) dirty(-minded); (*méchant*) nasty; (*fautif*) incorrect, wrong.

vicinal, e, aux [visinal, -o] *adj*: **chemin ~** by-road, byway.

vicissitudes [visisityd] *nfpl* (trials and) tribulations.

vicomte [vikɔ̃t] *nm* viscount.

vicomtesse [vikɔ̃tɛs] *nf* viscountess.

victime [viktim] *nf* victim; (*d'accident*) casualty; **être (la) ~ de** to be the victim of; **être ~ d'une attaque/d'un accident** to suffer a stroke/be involved in an accident.

victoire [viktwaʀ] *nf* victory.

victorieusement [viktɔʀjøzmɑ̃] *adv* triumphantly, victoriously.

victorieux, euse [viktɔʀjø, -øz] *adj* victorious; (*sourire, attitude*) triumphant.

victuailles [viktɥɑj] *nfpl* provisions.

vidange [vidɑ̃ʒ] *nf* (*d'un fossé, réservoir*) emptying; (*AUTO*) oil change; (*de lavabo: bonde*) waste outlet; **~s** *nfpl* (*matières*) sewage *sg*; **faire la ~** (*AUTO*) to change the oil, do an oil change; **tuyau de ~** drainage pipe.

vidanger [vidɑ̃ʒe] *vt* to empty; **faire ~ la voiture** to have the oil changed in one's car.

vide [vid] *adj* empty ♦ *nm* (*PHYSIQUE*) vacuum; (*espace*) (empty) space, gap; (*sous soi: dans une falaise etc*) drop; (*futilité, néant*) void; **~ de** empty of; (*de sens etc*) devoid of; **sous ~** *adv* in a vacuum; **emballé sous ~** vacuum-packed; **regarder dans le ~** to stare into space; **avoir peur du ~** to be afraid of heights; **parler dans le ~** to waste one's breath; **faire le ~** (*dans son esprit*) to make one's mind go blank; **faire le ~ autour de qn** to isolate sb; **à ~** *adv* (*sans occupants*) empty; (*sans charge*) unladen; (*TECH*) without gripping *ou* being in gear.

vidé, e [vide] *adj* (*épuisé*) done in, all in.

vidéo [video] *nf, adj inv* video; **~ inverse** reverse video.

vidéocassette [videɔkasɛt] *nf* video cassette.

vidéoclub [videɔklœb] *nm* video club.

vidéodisque [videɔdisk] *nm* videodisc.

vide-ordures [vidɔʀdyʀ] *nm inv* (rubbish) chute.

vidéotex [videɔtɛks] *nm* ® teletext.

vide-poches [vidpɔʃ] *nm inv* tidy; (*AUTO*) glove compartment.

vide-pomme [vidpɔm] *nm inv* apple-corer.

vider [vide] *vt* to empty; (*CULIN: volaille, poisson*) to gut, clean out; (*régler: querelle*) to settle; (*fatiguer*) to wear out; (*fam: expulser*) to throw out, chuck out; **se ~** *vi* to empty; **~ les lieux** to quit *ou* vacate the premises.

videur [vidœʀ] *nm* (*de boîte de nuit*) bouncer.

vie [vi] *nf* life (*pl* lives); **être en ~** to be alive; **sans ~** lifeless; **à ~** for life; **membre à ~** life member; **dans la ~ courante** in everyday life; **avoir la ~ dure** to have nine lives; to die hard; **mener la ~ dure à qn** to make life a misery for sb.

vieil [vjɛj] *adj m voir* **vieux**.

vieillard [vjɛjaʀ] *nm* old man; **les ~s** old people, the elderly.

vieille [vjɛj] *adj f, nf voir* **vieux**.

vieilleries [vjɛjʀi] *nfpl* old things *ou* stuff *sg*.

vieillesse [vjɛjɛs] *nf* old age; (*vieillards*): **la ~** the old *pl*, the elderly *pl*.

vieilli, e [vjeji] *adj* (*marqué par l'âge*) aged; (*suranné*) dated.

vieillir [vjejiʀ] *vi* (*prendre de l'âge*) to grow old; (*population, vin*) to age; (*doctrine, auteur*) to become dated ♦ *vt* to age; **il a beaucoup vieilli** he has aged a lot; **se ~** to make o.s. older.

vieillissement [vjejismɑ̃] *nm* growing old; ageing.

vieillot, te [vjɛjo, -ɔt] *adj* antiquated, quaint.

vielle [vjɛl] *nf* hurdy-gurdy.

viendrai [vjɛ̃dʀe] *etc vb voir* **venir**.

Vienne [vjɛn] *n* (*en Autriche*) Vienna.

vienne [vjɛn], **viens** [vjɛ̃] *etc vb voir* **venir**.

viennois, e [vjɛnwa, -waz] *adj* Viennese.

vierge [vjɛʀʒ(ə)] *adj* virgin; (*film*) blank; (*page*) clean, blank; (*jeune fille*): **être ~** to be a virgin ♦ *nf* virgin; (*signe*): **la V~** Virgo, the Virgin; **être de la V~** to be Virgo; **~ de** (*sans*) free from, unsullied by.

Viêt-nam, Vietnam [vjɛtnam] *nm*: **le ~** Vietnam; **le ~ du Nord/du Sud** North/South Vietnam.

vietnamien, ne [vjɛtnamjɛ̃, -ɛn] *adj* Vietnamese ♦ *nm* (*LING*) Vietnamese ♦ *nm/f*: **V~, ne** Vietnamese; **V~, ne du Nord/Sud** North/South Vietnamese.

vieux (vieil), vieille [vjø, vjɛj] *adj* old ♦ *nm/f* old man/woman ♦ *nmpl*: **les ~** the old, old people; (*fam: parents*) the old folk *ou* ones; **un petit ~** a little old man; **mon ~/ma vieille** (*fam*) old man/girl; **pauvre ~** poor old soul; **prendre un coup de ~** to put years on; **se faire ~** to make o.s. look older; **un ~ de la vieille** one of the old brigade; **~ garçon** *nm* bachelor; **~ jeu** *adj inv* old-fashioned; **~ rose** *adj inv* old rose; **vieil or** *adj inv* old gold; **vieille fille** *nf* spinster.

vif, vive [vif, viv] *adj* (*animé*) lively; (*alerte*) sharp, quick; (*brusque*) sharp, brusque; (*aigu*) sharp; (*lumière, couleur*) brilliant; (*air*) crisp; (*vent, émotion*) keen; (*froid*) bitter; (*fort: regret, déception*) great, deep; (*vivant*): **brûlé ~** burnt alive; **eau vive** running water; **de vive voix** personally; **piquer qn au ~** to cut sb to the quick; **tailler dans le ~** to cut into the living flesh; **à ~** (*plaie*) open; **avoir les nerfs à ~** to be on edge; **sur le ~** (*ART*) from life; **entrer dans le ~ du sujet** to get to the very heart of the matter.

vif-argent [vifaʀʒɑ̃] *nm inv* quicksilver.

vigie [viʒi] *nf* (*matelot*) look-out; (*poste*) look-out post, crow's nest.

vigilance [viʒilɑ̃s] *nf* vigilance.
vigilant, e [viʒilɑ̃, -ɑ̃t] *adj* vigilant.
vigile [viʒil] *nm* (*veilleur de nuit*) (night) watchman; (*police privée*) vigilante.
vigne [viɲ] *nf* (*plante*) vine; (*plantation*) vineyard; ~ **vierge** Virginia creeper.
vigneron [viɲʀɔ̃] *nm* wine grower.
vignette [viɲɛt] *nf* (*motif*) vignette; (*de marque*) manufacturer's label *ou* seal; (*petite illustration*) (small) illustration; (*ADMIN*) ≈ (road) tax disc (*BRIT*), ≈ license plate sticker (*US*); (*: sur médicament*) price label (*on medicines for reimbursement by Social Security*).
vignoble [viɲɔbl(ə)] *nm* (*plantation*) vineyard; (*vignes d'une région*) vineyards *pl*.
vigoureusement [viguʀøzmɑ̃] *adv* vigorously.
vigoureux, euse [viguʀø, -øz] *adj* vigorous, robust.
vigueur [vigœʀ] *nf* vigour (*BRIT*), vigor (*US*); **être/entrer en** ~ to be in/come into force; **en** ~ current.
vil, e [vil] *adj* vile, base; **à** ~ **prix** at a very low price.
vilain, e [vilɛ̃, -ɛn] *adj* (*laid*) ugly; (*affaire, blessure*) nasty; (*pas sage: enfant*) naughty ♦ *nm* (*paysan*) villein, villain; **ça va tourner au** ~ things are going to turn nasty; ~ **mot** bad word.
vilainement [vilɛnmɑ̃] *adv* badly.
vilebrequin [vilbʀəkɛ̃] *nm* (*outil*) (bit-)brace; (*AUTO*) crankshaft.
vilenie [vilni] *nf* vileness *no pl*, baseness *no pl*.
vilipender [vilipɑ̃de] *vt* to revile, vilify.
villa [vila] *nf* (detached) house.
village [vilaʒ] *nm* village; ~ **de toile** tent village; ~ **de vacances** holiday village.
villageois, e [vilaʒwa, -waz] *adj* village *cpd* ♦ *nm/f* villager.
ville [vil] *nf* town; (*importante*) city; (*administration*): **la** ~ ≈ the Corporation; ≈ the (town) council; **aller en** ~ to go to town; **habiter en** ~ to live in town; ~ **nouvelle** new town.
ville-champignon, *pl* **villes-champignons** [vilʃɑ̃piɲɔ̃] *nf* boom town.
ville-dortoir, *pl* **villes-dortoirs** [vildɔʀtwaʀ] *nf* dormitory town.
villégiature [vileʒjatyʀ] *nf* (*séjour*) holiday; (*lieu*) (holiday) resort.
vin [vɛ̃] *nm* wine; **avoir le** ~ **gai/triste** to get happy/miserable after a few drinks; ~ **blanc/rosé/rouge** white/rosé/red wine; ~ **d'honneur** reception (*with wine and snacks*); ~ **de messe** altar wine; ~ **ordinaire** *ou* **de table** table wine; ~ **de pays** local wine; *voir aussi* **AOC**; **VDQS**.
vinaigre [vinɛgʀ(ə)] *nm* vinegar; **tourner au** ~ (*fig*) to turn sour; ~ **de vin/d'alcool** wine/spirit vinegar.
vinaigrette [vinɛgʀɛt] *nf* vinaigrette, French dressing.
vinaigrier [vinɛgʀije] *nm* (*fabricant*) vinegar-maker; (*flacon*) vinegar cruet *ou* bottle.
vinasse [vinas] *nf* (*péj*) cheap wine, plonk (*BRIT*).
vindicatif, ive [vɛ̃dikatif, -iv] *adj* vindictive.
vindicte [vɛ̃dikt(ə)] *nf*: **désigner qn à la** ~ **publique** to expose sb to public condemnation.
vineux, euse [vinø, -øz] *adj* win(e)y.
vingt [vɛ̃, vɛ̃t + *vowel and in 22, 23 etc*] *num* twenty; ~**-quatre heures sur** ~**-quatre** twenty-four hours a day, round the clock.
vingtaine [vɛ̃tɛn] *nf*: **une** ~ **(de)** around twenty, twenty or so.
vingtième [vɛ̃tjɛm] *num* twentieth.
vinicole [vinikɔl] *adj* (*production*) wine *cpd*; (*région*) wine-growing.
vinification [vinifikɑsjɔ̃] *nf* wine-making, wine production; (*des sucres*) vinification.
vinyle [vinil] *nm* vinyl.
viol [vjɔl] *nm* (*d'une femme*) rape; (*d'un lieu sacré*) violation.
violacé, e [vjɔlase] *adj* purplish, mauvish.
violation [vjɔlɑsjɔ̃] *nf* desecration; violation; (*d'un droit*) breach.
violemment [vjɔlamɑ̃] *adv* violently.
violence [vjɔlɑ̃s] *nf* violence; ~**s** *nfpl* acts of violence; **faire** ~ **à qn** to do violence to sb; **se faire** ~ to force o.s.
violent, e [vjɔlɑ̃, -ɑ̃t] *adj* violent; (*remède*) drastic; (*besoin, désir*) intense, urgent.
violenter [vjɔlɑ̃te] *vt* to assault (sexually).
violer [vjɔle] *vt* (*femme*) to rape; (*sépulture*) to desecrate, violate; (*loi, traité*) to violate.
violet, te [vjɔlɛ, -ɛt] *adj, nm* purple, mauve ♦ *nf* (*fleur*) violet.
violeur [vjɔlœʀ] *nm* rapist.
violine [vjɔlin] *nf* deep purple.
violon [vjɔlɔ̃] *nm* violin; (*dans la musique folklorique etc*) fiddle; (*fam: prison*) lock-up; **premier** ~ first violin; ~ **d'Ingres** (artistic) hobby.
violoncelle [vjɔlɔ̃sɛl] *nm* cello.
violoncelliste [vjɔlɔ̃selist(ə)] *nm/f* cellist.
violoniste [vjɔlɔnist(ə)] *nm/f* violinist, violin-player; (*folklorique etc*) fiddler.
VIP *sigle m* (= *Very Important Person*) VIP.
vipère [vipɛʀ] *nf* viper, adder.
virage [viʀaʒ] *nm* (*d'un véhicule*) turn; (*d'une route, piste*) bend; (*CHIMIE*) change in colour (*BRIT*) *ou* color (*US*); (*de cuti-réaction*) positive reaction; (*PHOTO*) toning; (*fig: POL*) about-turn; **prendre un** ~ to go into a bend, take a bend; ~ **sans visibilité** blind bend.
viral, e, aux [viʀal, -o] *adj* viral.
virée [viʀe] *nf* (*courte*) run; (*: à pied*) walk; (*longue*) trip; hike, walking tour.
virement [viʀmɑ̃] *nm* (*COMM*) transfer; ~ **bancaire** (bank) credit transfer, ≈ (bank) giro transfer (*BRIT*); ~ **postal** Post office credit transfer, ≈ Girobank ® transfer (*BRIT*).
virent [viʀ] *vb voir* **voir**.
virer [viʀe] *vt* (*COMM*): ~ **qch (sur)** to transfer sth (into); (*PHOTO*) to tone; (*fam: renvoyer*) to

sack, boot out ♦ *vi* to turn; (*CHIMIE*) to change colour (*BRIT*) *ou* color (*US*); (*cuti-réaction*) to come up positive; (*PHOTO*) to tone; ~ **au bleu** to turn blue; ~ **de bord** to tack; (*fig*) to change tack; ~ **sur l'aile** to bank.

virevolte [viʀvɔlt(ə)] *nf* twirl; (*d'avis, d'opinion*) about-turn.

virevolter [viʀvɔlte] *vi* to twirl around.

virginal, e, aux [viʀʒinal, -o] *adj* virginal.

virginité [viʀʒinite] *nf* virginity; (*fig*) purity.

virgule [viʀgyl] *nf* comma; (*MATH*) point; **4 ~ 2** 4 point 2; ~ **flottante** floating decimal.

viril, e [viʀil] *adj* (*propre à l'homme*) masculine; (*énergique, courageux*) manly, virile.

viriliser [viʀilize] *vt* to make (more) manly *ou* masculine.

virilité [viʀilite] *nf* (*attributs masculins*) masculinity; (*fermeté, courage*) manliness; (*sexuelle*) virility.

virologie [viʀɔlɔʒi] *nf* virology.

virtualité [viʀtɥalite] *nf* virtuality; potentiality.

virtuel, le [viʀtɥɛl] *adj* potential; (*théorique*) virtual.

virtuellement [viʀtɥɛlmɑ̃] *adj* potentially; (*presque*) virtually.

virtuose [viʀtɥoz] *nm/f* (*MUS*) virtuoso; (*gén*) master.

virtuosité [viʀtɥozite] *nf* virtuosity; masterliness, masterful skills *pl*.

virulence [viʀylɑ̃s] *nf* virulence.

virulent, e [viʀylɑ̃, -ɑ̃t] *adj* virulent.

virus [viʀys] *nm* virus.

vis *vb* [vi] *voir* **voir, vivre** ♦ *nf* [vis] screw; ~ **à tête plate/ronde** flat-headed/round-headed screw; ~ **platinées** (*AUTO*) (contact) points; ~ **sans fin** worm, endless screw.

visa [viza] *nm* (*sceau*) stamp; (*validation de passeport*) visa; ~ **de censure** (censor's) certificate.

visage [vizaʒ] *nm* face; **à ~ découvert** (*franchement*) openly.

visagiste [vizaʒist(ə)] *nm/f* beautician.

vis-à-vis [vizavi] *adv* face to face ♦ *nm* person opposite; house *etc* opposite; ~ **de** *prép* opposite; (*fig*) towards, vis-à-vis; **en** ~ facing *ou* opposite each other; **sans** ~ (*immeuble*) with an open outlook.

viscéral, e, aux [viseʀal, -o] *adj* (*fig*) deep-seated, deep-rooted.

viscères [visɛʀ] *nmpl* intestines, entrails.

viscose [viskoz] *nf* viscose.

viscosité [viskozite] *nf* viscosity.

visée [vize] *nf* (*avec une arme*) aiming; (*ARPENTAGE*) sighting; **~s** *nfpl* (*intentions*) designs; **avoir des ~s sur qn/qch** to have designs on sb/sth.

viser [vize] *vi* to aim ♦ *vt* to aim at; (*concerner*) to be aimed *ou* directed at; (*apposer un visa sur*) to stamp, visa; ~ **à qch/faire** to aim at sth/at doing *ou* to do.

viseur [vizœʀ] *nm* (*d'arme*) sights *pl*; (*PHOTO*) viewfinder.

visibilité [vizibilite] *nf* visibility; **sans** ~ (*pilotage, virage*) blind *cpd*.

visible [vizibl(ə)] *adj* visible; (*disponible*): **est-il ~?** can he see me?, will he see visitors?

visiblement [vizibləmɑ̃] *adv* visibly, obviously.

visière [vizjɛʀ] *nf* (*de casquette*) peak; (*qui s'attache*) eyeshade.

vision [vizjɔ̃] *nf* vision; (*sens*) (eye)sight, vision; (*fait de voir*): **la ~ de** the sight of; **première ~** (*CINÉ*) first showing.

visionnaire [vizjɔnɛʀ] *adj, nm/f* visionary.

visionner [vizjɔne] *vt* to view.

visionneuse [vizjɔnøz] *nf* viewer.

visiophone [vizjɔfɔn] *nm* videophone.

visite [vizit] *nf* visit; (*visiteur*) visitor; (*touristique: d'un musée etc*) tour; (*COMM: de représentant*) call; (*expertise, d'inspection*) inspection; (*médicale, à domicile*) visit, call; **la ~** (*MÉD*) medical examination; (*MIL: d'entrée*) medicals *pl*; (*: quotidienne*) sick parade; **faire une ~ à qn** to call on sb, pay sb a visit; **rendre ~ à qn** to visit sb, pay sb a visit; **être en ~ (chez qn)** to be visiting (sb); **heures de ~** (*hôpital, prison*) visiting hours; **le droit de ~** (*JUR: aux enfants*) right of access, access; ~ **de douane** customs inspection *ou* examination.

visiter [vizite] *vt* to visit; (*musée, ville*) to visit, go round.

visiteur, euse [vizitœʀ, -øz] *nm/f* visitor; ~ **des douanes** customs inspector; ~ **médical** medical rep(resentative); ~ **de prison** prison visitor.

vison [vizɔ̃] *nm* mink.

visqueux, euse [viskø, -øz] *adj* viscous; (*péj*) gooey; (*: manières*) slimy.

visser [vise] *vt*: ~ **qch** (*fixer, serrer*) to screw sth on.

visu [vizy]: **de ~** *adv* with one's own eyes.

visualisation [vizɥalizɑsjɔ̃] *nf* (*INFORM*) display; **écran de ~** visual display unit (VDU).

visualiser [vizɥalize] *vt* to visualize; (*INFORM*) to display, bring up on screen.

visuel, le [vizɥɛl] *adj* visual ♦ *nm* (visual) display; (*INFORM*) visual display unit (VDU).

visuellement [vizɥɛlmɑ̃] *adv* visually.

vit [vi] *vb voir* **vivre, voir**.

vital, e, aux [vital, -o] *adj* vital.

vitalité [vitalite] *nf* vitality.

vitamine [vitamin] *nf* vitamin.

vitaminé, e [vitamine] *adj* with (added) vitamins.

vitaminique [vitaminik] *adj* vitamin *cpd*.

vite [vit] *adv* (*rapidement*) quickly, fast; (*sans délai*) quickly; soon; **faire ~** (*agir rapidement*) to act fast; (*se dépêcher*) to be quick; **ce sera ~ fini** this will soon be finished; **viens ~** come quick(ly).

vitesse [vitɛs] *nf* speed; (*AUTO: dispositif*) gear;

faire de la ~ to drive fast *ou* at speed; **prendre qn de** ~ to outstrip sb, get ahead of sb; **prendre de la** ~ to pick up *ou* gather speed; **à toute** ~ at full *ou* top speed; **en perte de** ~ (*avion*) losing lift; (*fig*) losing momentum; **changer de** ~ (*AUTO*) to change gear; ~ **acquise** momentum; ~ **de croisière** cruising speed; ~ **de pointe** top speed; ~ **du son** speed of sound.

viticole [vitikɔl] *adj* (*industrie*) wine *cpd*; (*région*) wine-growing.

viticulteur [vitikyltœʀ] *nm* wine grower.

viticulture [vitikyltyʀ] *nf* wine growing.

vitrage [vitʀaʒ] *nm* (*cloison*) glass partition; (*toit*) glass roof; (*rideau*) net curtain.

vitrail, aux [vitʀaj, -o] *nm* stained-glass window.

vitre [vitʀ(ə)] *nf* (window) pane; (*de portière, voiture*) window.

vitré, e [vitʀe] *adj* glass *cpd*.

vitrer [vitʀe] *vt* to glaze.

vitreux, euse [vitʀø, -øz] *adj* vitreous; (*terne*) glassy.

vitrier [vitʀije] *nm* glazier.

vitrifier [vitʀifje] *vt* to vitrify; (*parquet*) to glaze.

vitrine [vitʀin] *nf* (*devanture*) (shop) window; (*étalage*) display; (*petite armoire*) display cabinet; **en** ~ in the window, on display; ~ **publicitaire** display case, showcase.

vitriol [vitʀijɔl] *nm* vitriol; **au** ~ (*fig*) vitriolic.

vitupérations [vitypeʀɑsjɔ̃] *nfpl* invective *sg*.

vitupérer [vitypeʀe] *vi* to rant and rave; ~ **contre** to rail against.

vivable [vivabl(ə)] *adj* (*personne*) livable-with; (*endroit*) fit to live in.

vivace *adj* [vivas] (*arbre, plante*) hardy; (*fig*) enduring ♦ *adv* [vivatʃe] (*MUS*) vivace.

vivacité [vivasite] *nf* (*voir vif*) liveliness, vivacity; sharpness; brilliance.

vivant, e [vivɑ̃, -ɑ̃t] *vb voir* **vivre** ♦ *adj* (*qui vit*) living, alive; (*animé*) lively; (*preuve, exemple*) living; (*langue*) modern ♦ *nm*: **du** ~ **de qn** in sb's lifetime; **les** ~**s et les morts** the living and the dead.

vivarium [vivaʀjɔm] *nm* vivarium.

vivats [viva] *nmpl* cheers.

vive [viv] *adj f voir* **vif** ♦ *vb voir* **vivre** ♦ *excl*: ~ **le roi!** long live the king!; ~ **les vacances!** hurrah for the holidays!

vivement [vivmɑ̃] *adv* vivaciously; sharply ♦ *excl*: ~ **les vacances!** I can't wait for the holidays!, roll on the holidays!

viveur [vivœʀ] *nm* (*péj*) high liver, pleasure-seeker.

vivier [vivje] *nm* (*au restaurant etc*) fish tank; (*étang*) fishpond.

vivifiant, e [vivifjɑ̃, -ɑ̃t] *adj* invigorating.

vivifier [vivifje] *vt* to invigorate; (*fig: souvenirs, sentiments*) to liven up, enliven.

vivipare [vivipaʀ] *adj* viviparous.

vivisection [vivisɛksjɔ̃] *nf* vivisection.

vivoter [vivɔte] *vi* (*personne*) to scrape a living, get by; (*fig: affaire etc*) to struggle along.

vivre [vivʀ(ə)] *vi, vt* to live ♦ *nm*: **le** ~ **et le logement** board and lodging ♦ ~**s** *nmpl* provisions, food supplies; **il vit encore** he is still alive; **se laisser** ~ to take life as it comes; **ne plus** ~ (*être anxieux*) to live on one's nerves; **il a vécu** (*eu une vie aventureuse*) he has seen life; **ce régime a vécu** this regime has had its day; **être facile à** ~ to be easy to get on with; **faire** ~ **qn** (*pourvoir à sa subsistance*) to provide (a living) for sb; ~ **mal** (*chichement*) to have a meagre existence; ~ **de** (*salaire etc*) to live on.

vivrier, ière [vivʀije, -jɛʀ] *adj* food-producing *cpd*.

vlan [vlɑ̃] *excl* wham!, bang!

VO *sigle f* (*CINÉ*: = *version originale*): **voir un film en** ~ to see a film in its original language.

v^o *abr* = **verso**.

vocable [vɔkabl(ə)] *nm* term.

vocabulaire [vɔkabylɛʀ] *nm* vocabulary.

vocal, e, aux [vɔkal, -o] *adj* vocal.

vocalique [vɔkalik] *adj* vocalic, vowel *cpd*.

vocalise [vɔkaliz] *nf* singing exercise.

vocaliser [vɔkalize] *vi* (*LING*) to vocalize; (*MUS*) to do one's singing exercises.

vocation [vɔkɑsjɔ̃] *nf* vocation, calling; **avoir la** ~ to have a vocation.

vociférations [vɔsifeʀɑsjɔ̃] *nfpl* cries of rage, screams.

vociférer [vɔsifeʀe] *vi, vt* to scream.

vodka [vɔdka] *nf* vodka.

vœu, x [vø] *nm* wish; (*à Dieu*) vow; **faire** ~ **de** to take a vow of; **avec tous nos** ~**x** with every good wish *ou* our best wishes; ~**x de bonheur** best wishes for your future happiness; ~**x de bonne année** best wishes for the New Year.

vogue [vɔg] *nf* fashion, vogue; **en** ~ in fashion, in vogue.

voguer [vɔge] *vi* to sail.

voici [vwasi] *prép* (*pour introduire, désigner*) here is + *sg*, here are + *pl*; **et** ~ **que** ... and now it (*ou* he) ...; **il est parti** ~ **3 ans** he left 3 years ago; ~ **une semaine que je l'ai vue** it's a week since I've seen her; **me** ~ here I am; *voir aussi* **voilà**.

voie [vwa] *vb voir* **voir** ♦ *nf* way; (*RAIL*) track, line; (*AUTO*) lane; **par** ~ **buccale** *ou* **orale** orally; **par** ~ **rectale** rectally; **suivre la** ~ **hiérarchique** to go through official channels; **ouvrir/montrer la** ~ to open up/show the way; **être en bonne** ~ to be shaping *ou* going well; **mettre qn sur la** ~ to put sb on the right track; **être en** ~ **d'achèvement/de rénovation** to be nearing completion/in the process of renovation; **à** ~ **étroite** narrow-gauge; **à** ~ **unique** single-track; **route à 2/3** ~**s** 2-/3-lane road; **par la** ~ **aérienne/ maritime** by air/sea; ~ **d'eau** (*NAVIG*) leak; ~ **express** expressway; ~ **de fait** (*JUR*) assault (and battery); ~ **ferrée** track; railway line (*BRIT*), railroad (*US*); **par ~ ferrée** by rail, by railroad; ~ **de garage** (*RAIL*) siding; **la ~ lactée** the Milky Way; ~ **navigable** waterway; ~ **prioritaire** (*AUTO*) road with right of way; ~ **privée** private road; **la ~ publique** the public highway.

voilà [vwala] *prép* (*en désignant*) there is + *sg*, there are + *pl*; **les ~** *ou* **voici** here *ou* there they are; **en ~** *ou* **voici un** here's one, there's one; ~ *ou* **voici deux ans** two years ago; ~ *ou* **voici deux ans que** it's two years since; **et ~!** there we are!; ~ **tout** that's all; **"~** *ou* **voici"** (*en offrant etc*) "there *ou* here you are".

voilage [vwalaʒ] *nm* (*rideau*) net curtain; (*tissu*) net.

voile [vwal] *nm* veil; (*tissu léger*) net ♦ *nf* sail; (*sport*) sailing; **prendre le ~** to take the veil; **mettre à la ~** to make way under sail; ~ **du palais** *nm* soft palate, velum; ~ **au poumon** *nm* shadow on the lung.

voiler [vwale] *vt* to veil; (*PHOTO*) to fog; (*fausser: roue*) to buckle; (*: bois*) to warp; **se ~** *vi* (*lune, regard*) to mist over; (*ciel*) to grow hazy; (*voix*) to become husky; (*roue, disque*) to buckle; (*planche*) to warp; **se ~ la face** to hide one's face.

voilette [vwalɛt] *nf* (hat) veil.

voilier [vwalje] *nm* sailing ship; (*de plaisance*) sailing boat.

voilure [vwalyʀ] *nf* (*de voilier*) sails *pl*; (*d'avion*) aerofoils *pl* (*BRIT*), airfoils *pl* (*US*); (*de parachute*) canopy.

voir [vwaʀ] *vi, vt* to see; **se ~**: **se ~ critiquer/transformer** to be criticized/transformed; **cela se voit** (*cela arrive*) it happens; (*c'est visible*) that's obvious, it shows; ~ **à faire qch** to see to it that sth is done; ~ **loin** (*fig*) to be far-sighted; ~ **venir** (*fig*) to wait and see; **faire ~ qch à qn** to show sb sth; **en faire ~ à qn** (*fig*) to give sb a hard time; **ne pas pouvoir ~ qn** (*fig*) not to be able to stand sb; **regardez ~** just look; **montrez ~** show (me); **dites ~** tell me; **voyons!** let's see now; (*indignation etc*) come (along) now!; **c'est à ~!** we'll see!; **c'est ce qu'on va ~!** we'll see about that!; **avoir quelque chose à ~ avec** to have something to do with; **ça n'a rien à ~ avec lui** that has nothing to do with him.

voire [vwaʀ] *adv* indeed; nay; or even.

voirie [vwaʀi] *nf* highway maintenance; (*administration*) highways department; (*enlèvement des ordures*) refuse (*BRIT*) *ou* garbage (*US*) collection.

vois [vwa] *vb voir* **voir**.

voisin, e [vwazɛ̃, -in] *adj* (*proche*) neighbouring (*BRIT*), neighboring (*US*); (*contigu*) next; (*ressemblant*) connected ♦ *nm/f* neighbo(u)r; (*de table, de dortoir etc*) person next to me (*ou* him *etc*); ~ **de palier** neighbo(u)r across the landing (*BRIT*) *ou* hall (*US*).

voisinage [vwazinaʒ] *nm* (*proximité*) proximity; (*environs*) vicinity; (*quartier, voisins*) neighbourhood (*BRIT*), neighborhood (*US*); **relations de bon ~** neighbo(u)rly terms.

voisiner [vwazine] *vi*: ~ **avec** to be side by side with.

voit [vwa] *vb voir* **voir**.

voiture [vwatyʀ] *nf* car; (*wagon*) coach, carriage; **en ~!** all aboard!; ~ **à bras** handcart; ~ **d'enfant** pram (*BRIT*), baby carriage (*US*); ~ **d'infirme** invalid carriage; ~ **de sport** sports car.

voiture-lit, *pl* **voitures-lits** [vwatyʀli] *nf* sleeper.

voiture-restaurant, *pl* **voitures-restaurants** [vwatyʀʀɛstɔʀɑ̃] *nf* dining car.

voix [vwa] *nf* voice; (*POL*) vote; **la ~ de la conscience/raison** the voice of conscience/reason; **à haute ~** aloud; **à ~ basse** in a low voice; **faire la grosse ~** to speak gruffly; **avoir de la ~** to have a good voice; **rester sans ~** to be speechless; ~ **de basse/ténor** *etc* bass/tenor *etc* voice; **à 2/4 ~** (*MUS*) in 2/4 parts; **avoir ~ au chapitre** to have a say in the matter; **mettre aux ~** to put to the vote; ~ **off** voice-over.

vol [vɔl] *nm* (*mode de locomotion*) flying; (*trajet, voyage, groupe d'oiseaux*) flight; (*mode d'appropriation*) theft, stealing; (*larcin*) theft; **à ~ d'oiseau** as the crow flies; **au ~**: **attraper qch au ~** to catch sth as it flies past; **saisir une remarque au ~** to pick up a passing remark; **prendre son ~** to take flight; **de haut ~** (*fig*) of the highest order; **en ~** in flight; ~ **avec effraction** breaking and entering *no pl*, break-in; ~ **à l'étalage** shoplifting *no pl*; ~ **libre** hang-gliding; ~ **à main armée** armed robbery; ~ **de nuit** night flight; ~ **plané** (*AVIAT*) glide, gliding *no pl*; ~ **à la tire** pickpocketing *no pl*; ~ **à voile** gliding.

vol. *abr* (= *volume*) vol.

volage [vɔlaʒ] *adj* fickle.

volaille [vɔlɑj] *nf* (*oiseaux*) poultry *pl*; (*viande*) poultry *no pl*; (*oiseau*) fowl.

volailler [vɔlɑje] *nm* poulterer.

volant, e [vɔlɑ̃, -ɑ̃t] *adj voir* **feuille** *etc* ♦ *nm* (*d'automobile*) (steering) wheel; (*de commande*) wheel; (*objet lancé*) shuttlecock; (*jeu*) battledore and shuttlecock; (*bande de tissu*) flounce; (*feuillet détachable*) tear-off portion; **le personnel ~, les ~s** (*AVIAT*) the flight staff; ~ **de sécurité** (*fig*) reserve, margin, safeguard.

volatil, e [vɔlatil] *adj* volatile.

volatile [vɔlatil] *nm* (*volaille*) bird; (*tout oiseau*) winged creature.

volatiliser [vɔlatilize]: **se ~** *vi* (*CHIMIE*) to volatilize; (*fig*) to vanish into thin air.

vol-au-vent [vɔlovɑ̃] *nm inv* vol-au-vent.

volcan [vɔlkɑ̃] *nm* volcano; (*fig: personne*) hothead.

volcanique [vɔlkanik] *adj* volcanic; (*fig: tem-

pérament) volatile.

volcanologie [vɔlkanɔlɔʒi] *nf* vulcanology.

volcanologue [vɔlkanɔlɔg] *nm/f* vulcanologist.

volée [vɔle] *nf* (*groupe d'oiseaux*) flight, flock; (*TENNIS*) volley; ~ **de coups/de flèches** volley of blows/arrows; **à la** ~: **rattraper à la** ~ to catch in midair; **lancer à la** ~ to fling about; **semer à la** ~ to (sow) broadcast; **à toute** ~ (*sonner les cloches*) vigorously; (*lancer un projectile*) with full force; **de haute** ~ (*fig*) of the highest order.

voler [vɔle] *vi* (*avion, oiseau, fig*) to fly; (*voleur*) to steal ♦ *vt* (*objet*) to steal; (*personne*) to rob; ~ **en éclats** to smash to smithereens; ~ **de ses propres ailes** (*fig*) to stand on one's own two feet; ~ **au vent** to fly in the wind; ~ **qch à qn** to steal sth from sb.

volet [vɔlɛ] *nm* (*de fenêtre*) shutter; (*AVIAT*) flap; (*de feuillet, document*) section; (*fig: d'un plan*) facet; **trié sur le** ~ hand-picked.

voleter [vɔlte] *vi* to flutter (about).

voleur, euse [vɔlœʀ, -øz] *nm/f* thief (*pl* thieves) ♦ *adj* thieving.

volière [vɔljɛʀ] *nf* aviary.

volley(-ball) [vɔlɛ(bol)] *nm* volleyball.

volleyeur, euse [vɔlɛjœʀ, -øz] *nm/f* volleyball player.

volontaire [vɔlɔ̃tɛʀ] *adj* (*acte, activité*) voluntary; (*délibéré*) deliberate; (*caractère, personne: décidé*) self-willed ♦ *nm/f* volunteer.

volontairement [vɔlɔ̃tɛʀmɑ̃] *adv* voluntarily; deliberately.

volontariat [vɔlɔ̃taʀja] *nm* voluntary service.

volontarisme [vɔlɔ̃taʀism(ə)] *nm* voluntarism.

volontariste [vɔlɔ̃taʀist(ə)] *adj, nm/f* voluntarist.

volonté [vɔlɔ̃te] *nf* (*faculté de vouloir*) will; (*énergie, fermeté*) will(power); (*souhait, désir*) wish; **se servir/boire à** ~ to take/drink as much as one likes; **bonne** ~ goodwill, willingness; **mauvaise** ~ lack of goodwill, unwillingness.

volontiers [vɔlɔ̃tje] *adv* (*de bonne grâce*) willingly; (*avec plaisir*) willingly, gladly; (*habituellement, souvent*) readily, willingly; **"~"** "with pleasure", "I'd be glad to".

volt [vɔlt] *nm* volt.

voltage [vɔltaʒ] *nm* voltage.

volte-face [vɔltəfas] *nf inv* about-turn; (*fig*) about-turn, U-turn; **faire** ~ to do an about-turn; to do a U-turn.

voltige [vɔltiʒ] *nf* (*ÉQUITATION*) trick riding; (*au cirque*) acrobatics *sg*; (*AVIAT*) (aerial) acrobatics *sg*; **numéro de haute** ~ acrobatic act.

voltiger [vɔltiʒe] *vi* to flutter (about).

voltigeur [vɔltiʒœʀ] *nm* (*au cirque*) acrobat; (*MIL*) light infantryman.

voltmètre [vɔltmɛtʀ(ə)] *nm* voltmeter.

volubile [vɔlybil] *adj* voluble.

volubilis [vɔlybilis] *nm* convolvulus.

volume [vɔlym] *nm* volume; (*GÉOM: solide*) solid.

volumineux, euse [vɔlyminø, -øz] *adj* voluminous, bulky.

volupté [vɔlypte] *nf* sensual delight *ou* pleasure.

voluptueusement [vɔlyptɥøzmɑ̃] *adv* voluptuously.

voluptueux, euse [vɔlyptɥø, -øz] *adj* voluptuous.

volute [vɔlyt] *nf* (*ARCHIT*) volute; ~ **de fumée** curl of smoke.

vomi [vɔmi] *nm* vomit.

vomir [vɔmiʀ] *vi* to vomit, be sick ♦ *vt* to vomit, bring up; (*fig*) to belch out, spew out; (*exécrer*) to loathe, abhor.

vomissement [vɔmismɑ̃] *nm* (*action*) vomiting *no pl*; **des ~s** vomit *sg*.

vomissure [vɔmisyʀ] *nf* vomit *no pl*.

vomitif [vɔmitif] *nm* emetic.

vont [vɔ̃] *vb voir* **aller**.

vorace [vɔʀas] *adj* voracious.

voracement [vɔʀasmɑ̃] *adv* voraciously.

voracité [vɔʀasite] *nf* voracity.

vos [vo] *adj possessif voir* **votre**.

Vosges [voʒ] *nfpl*: **les** ~ the Vosges.

vosgien, ne [voʒjɛ̃, -ɛn] *adj* of *ou* from the Vosges ♦ *nm/f* inhabitant *ou* native of the Vosges.

VOST *sigle f* (*CINÉ: = version originale sous-titrée*) *sub-titled version.*

votant, e [vɔtɑ̃, -ɑ̃t] *nm/f* voter.

vote [vɔt] *nm* vote; ~ **par correspondance/procuration** postal/proxy vote; ~ **à main levée** vote by show of hands; ~ **secret,** ~ **à bulletins secrets** secret ballot.

voter [vɔte] *vi* to vote ♦ *vt* (*loi, décision*) to vote for.

votre [vɔtʀ(ə)], *pl* **vos** [vo] *adj possessif* your.

vôtre [votʀ(ə)] *pron*: **le** ~, **la** ~, **les ~s** yours; **les ~s** (*fig*) your family *ou* folks; **à la** ~ (*toast*) your (good) health!

voudrai [vudʀe] *etc vb voir* **vouloir**.

voué, e [vwe] *adj*: ~ **à** doomed to, destined for.

vouer [vwe] *vt*: ~ **qch à** (*Dieu/un saint*) to dedicate sth to; ~ **sa vie/son temps à** (*étude, cause etc*) to devote one's life/time to; ~ **une haine/amitié éternelle à qn** to vow undying hatred/friendship to sb.

MOT-CLÉ

vouloir [vulwaʀ] *nm*: **le bon** ~ **de qn** sb's goodwill; sb's pleasure

♦ *vt* **1** (*exiger, désirer*) to want; ~ **faire/que qn fasse** to want to do/sb to do; **voulez-vous du thé?** would you like *ou* do you want some tea?; ~ **qch à qn** to wish sth for sb; **que me veut-il?** what does he want with me?; **que veux-tu que je te dise?** what do you want me to say?; **sans le** ~ (*involontairement*) without meaning to, unintentionally; **je voudrais ceci/faire** I would *ou* I'd like this/to do; **le**

hasard a voulu que ... as fate would have it, ...; **la tradition veut que ...** tradition demands that ...; ... **qui se veut moderne** ... which purports to be modern
2 (*consentir*): **je veux bien** (*bonne volonté*) I'll be happy to; (*concession*) fair enough, that's fine; **oui, si on veut** (*en quelque sorte*) yes, if you like; **comme tu veux** as you wish; (*en quelque sorte*) if you like; **veuillez attendre** please wait; **veuillez agréer ...** (*formule épistolaire*) yours faithfully
3: **en ~** (*être ambitieux*) to be out to win; **en ~ à qn** to bear sb a grudge; **je lui en veux d'avoir fait ça** I resent his having done that; **s'en ~ (de)** to be annoyed with o.s. (for); **il en veut à mon argent** he's after my money
4: **~ de** to want; **la compagnie ne veut plus de lui** the firm doesn't want him any more; **elle ne veut pas de son aide** she doesn't want his help
5: **~ dire** to mean.

voulu, e [vuly] *pp de* **vouloir** ♦ *adj* (*requis*) required, requisite; (*délibéré*) deliberate, intentional.
voulus [vuly] *etc vb voir* **vouloir**.
vous [vu] *pron* you; (*objet indirect*) (to) you; (*réfléchi*) yourself (*pl* yourselves); (*réciproque*) each other ♦ *nm*: **employer le ~** (*vouvoyer*) to use the "vous" form; **~-même** yourself; **~-mêmes** yourselves.
voûte [vut] *nf* vault; **la ~ céleste** the vault of heaven; **~ du palais** (*ANAT*) roof of the mouth; **~ plantaire** arch (of the foot).
voûté, e [vute] *adj* vaulted, arched; (*dos, personne*) bent, stooped.
voûter [vute] *vt* (*ARCHIT*) to arch, vault; **se ~** *vi* (*dos, personne*) to become stooped.
vouvoiement [vuvwamɑ̃] *nm* use of formal "vous" form.
vouvoyer [vuvwaje] *vt*: **~ qn** to address sb as "vous".
voyage [vwajaʒ] *nm* journey, trip; (*fait de voyager*): **le ~** travel(ling); **partir/être en ~** to go off/be away on a journey *ou* trip; **faire un ~** to go on *ou* make a trip *ou* journey; **faire bon ~** to have a good journey; **les gens du ~** travelling people; **~ d'agrément/d'affaires** pleasure/business trip; **~ de noces** honeymoon; **~ organisé** package tour.
voyager [vwajaʒe] *vi* to travel.
voyageur, euse [vwajaʒœʀ, -øz] *nm/f* traveller; (*passager*) passenger ♦ *adj* (*tempérament*) nomadic, wayfaring; **~ (de commerce)** commercial traveller.
voyagiste [vwajaʒist(ə)] *nm* tour operator.
voyais [vwajɛ] *etc vb voir* **voir**.
voyance [vwajɑ̃s] *nf* clairvoyance.
voyant, e [vwajɑ̃, -ɑ̃t] *adj* (*couleur*) loud, gaudy ♦ *nm/f* (*personne qui voit*) sighted person ♦ *nm* (*signal*) (warning) light ♦ *nf* clairvoyant.
voyelle [vwajɛl] *nf* vowel.
voyeur, euse [vwajœʀ, -øz] *nm/f* voyeur; peeping Tom.
voyeurisme [vwajœʀism(ə)] *nm* voyeurism.
voyons [vwajɔ̃] *etc vb voir* **voir**.
voyou [vwaju] *nm* lout, hoodlum; (*enfant*) guttersnipe.
VPC *sigle f* (= *vente par correspondance*) mail order selling.
vrac [vʀak]: **en ~** *adv* higgledy-piggledy; (*COMM*) in bulk.
vrai, e [vʀɛ] *adj* (*véridique: récit, faits*) true; (*non factice, authentique*) real ♦ *nm*: **le ~** the truth; **à ~ dire** to tell the truth; **il est ~ que** it is true that; **être dans le ~** to be right.
vraiment [vʀɛmɑ̃] *adv* really.
vraisemblable [vʀɛsɑ̃blabl(ə)] *adj* (*plausible*) likely, plausible; (*probable*) likely, probable.
vraisemblablement [vʀɛsɑ̃blabləmɑ̃] *adv* in all likelihood, very likely.
vraisemblance [vʀɛsɑ̃blɑ̃s] *nf* likelihood, plausibility; (*romanesque*) verisimilitude; **selon toute ~** in all likelihood.
vraquier [vʀakje] *nm* freighter.
vrille [vʀij] *nf* (*de plante*) tendril; (*outil*) gimlet; (*spirale*) spiral; (*AVIAT*) spin.
vriller [vʀije] *vt* to bore into, pierce.
vrombir [vʀɔ̃biʀ] *vi* to hum.
vrombissant, e [vʀɔ̃bisɑ̃, -ɑ̃t] *adj* humming.
vrombissement [vʀɔ̃bismɑ̃] *nm* hum(ming).
VRP *sigle m* (= *voyageur, représentant, placier*) (sales) rep.
VTT *sigle m* (= *vélo tout-terrain*) mountain bike.
vu [vy] *prép* (*en raison de*) in view of; **~ que** in view of the fact that.
vu, e [vy] *pp de* **voir** ♦ *adj*: **bien/mal ~** (*personne*) well/poorly thought of; (*conduite*) good/bad form ♦ *nm*: **au ~ et au su de tous** openly and publicly; **ni ~ ni connu** what the eye doesn't see ...!, no one will be any the wiser; **c'est tout ~** it's a foregone conclusion.
vue [vy] *nf* (*fait de voir*): **la ~ de** the sight of; (*sens, faculté*) (eye)sight; (*panorama, image, photo*) view; (*spectacle*) sight; **~s** *nfpl* (*idées*) views; (*dessein*) designs; **perdre la ~** to lose one's (eye)sight; **perdre de ~** to lose sight of; **à la ~ de tous** in full view of everybody; **hors de ~** out of sight; **à première ~** at first sight; **connaître de ~** to know by sight; **à ~** (*COMM*) at sight; **tirer à ~** to shoot on sight; **à ~ d'œil** *adv* visibly; (*à première vue*) at a quick glance; **avoir ~ sur** to have a view of; **en ~** (*visible*) in sight; (*COMM*) in the public eye; **avoir qch en ~** (*intentions*) to have one's sights on sth; **en ~ de faire** with the intention of doing, with a view to doing; **~ d'ensemble** overall view; **~ de l'esprit** theoretical view.
vulcanisation [vylkanizɑsjɔ̃] *nf* vulcanization.
vulcaniser [vylkanize] *vt* to vulcanize.
vulcanologie [vylkanɔlɔʒi] *nf* = **volcanologie**.
vulcanologue [vylkanɔlɔg] *nm/f* = **volcanolo-**

gue.
vulgaire [vylgɛʀ] *adj* (*grossier*) vulgar, coarse; (*trivial*) commonplace, mundane; (*péj*: *quelconque*): **de ~s touristes/chaises de cuisine** common tourists/kitchen chairs; (*BOT, ZOOL*: *non latin*) common.
vulgairement [vylgɛʀmɑ̃] *adv* vulgarly, coarsely; (*communément*) commonly.
vulgarisation [vylgaʀizɑsjɔ̃] *nf*: **ouvrage de ~** popularizing work, popularization.
vulgariser [vylgaʀize] *vt* to popularize.
vulgarité [vylgaʀite] *nf* vulgarity, coarseness.
vulnérabilité [vylneʀabilite] *nf* vulnerability.
vulnérable [vylneʀabl(ə)] *adj* vulnerable.
vulve [vylv(ə)] *nf* vulva.
vumètre [vymɛtʀ(ə)] *nm* recording level gauge.
Vve *abr* = **veuve**.
VVF *sigle m* (= *village vacances famille*) *state-subsidized holiday village*.
vx *abr* = **vieux**.

W w

W, w [dubləve] *nm inv* W, w ♦ *abr* (= *watt*) W; **W comme William** W for William.
wagon [vagɔ̃] *nm* (*de voyageurs*) carriage; (*de marchandises*) truck, wagon.
wagon-citerne, *pl* **wagons-citernes** [vagɔ̃sitɛʀn(ə)] *nm* tanker.
wagon-lit, *pl* **wagons-lits** [vagɔ̃li] *nm* sleeper, sleeping car.
wagonnet [vagɔnɛ] *nm* small truck.
wagon-poste, *pl* **wagons-postes** [vagɔ̃pɔst(ə)] *nm* mail van.
wagon-restaurant, *pl* **wagons-restaurants** [vagɔ̃ʀɛstɔʀɑ̃] *nm* restaurant *ou* dining car.
Walkman [wɔkman] *nm* ® Walkman ®, personal stereo.
Wallis et Futuna [walisefytyna]: **les îles ~** the Wallis and Futuna Islands.
wallon, ne [walɔ̃, -ɔn] *adj* Walloon ♦ *nm* (*LING*) Walloon ♦ *nm/f*: **W~, ne** Walloon.
Wallonie [walɔni] *nf*: **la ~** French-speaking (part of) Belgium.
water-polo [watɛʀpɔlo] *nm* water polo.
waters [watɛʀ] *nmpl* toilet *sg*, loo *sg* (*BRIT*).
watt [wat] *nm* watt.
w.-c. [vese] *nmpl* toilet *sg*, lavatory *sg*.
Web [wɛb] *nm inv*: **le ~** the (Worldwide) Web.
week-end [wikɛnd] *nm* weekend.
western [wɛstɛʀn] *nm* western.
Westphalie [vɛsfali] *nf*: **la ~** Westphalia.
whisky, *pl* **whiskies** [wiski] *nm* whisky.
white-spirit [wajtspiʀit] *nm* white spirit.
Winchester [wintʃɛstɛʀ]: **disque ~** Winchester disk.
wok [wɔk] *nm* wok.

X x

X, x [iks] *nm inv* X, x ♦ *sigle m* = (**École**) **polytechnique; plainte contre X** (*JUR*) action against person or persons unknown; **X comme Xavier** X for Xmas.
xénophobe [gzenɔfɔb] *adj* xenophobic ♦ *nm/f* xenophobe.
xénophobie [gzenɔfɔbi] *nf* xenophobia.
xérès [gzeʀɛs] *nm* sherry.
xylographie [ksilɔgʀafi] *nf* xylography; (*image*) xylograph.
xylophone [ksilɔfɔn] *nm* xylophone.

Y y

Y, y [igʀɛk] *nm inv* Y, y; **Y comme Yvonne** Y for Yellow (*BRIT*) *ou* Yoke (*US*).
y [i] *adv* (*à cet endroit*) there; (*dessus*) on it (*ou* them); (*dedans*) in it (*ou* them) ♦ *pron* (about *ou* on *ou* of) it : *vérifier la syntaxe du verbe employé*; **j'~ pense** I'm thinking about it; *voir aussi* **aller, avoir**.
yacht [jɔt] *nm* yacht.
yaourt [jauʀt] *nm* yoghurt.
yaourtière [jauʀtjɛʀ] *nf* yoghurt-maker.
Yémen [jemɛn] *nm*: **le ~** Yemen.
yéménite [jemenit] *adj* Yemeni.
yeux [jø] *pl de* **œil**.
yoga [jɔga] *nm* yoga.
yoghourt [jɔguʀt] *nm* = **yaourt**.
yole [jɔl] *nf* skiff.
yougoslave [jugɔslav] *adj* Yugoslav(ian) ♦ *nm/f*: **Y~** Yugoslav(ian).
Yougoslavie [jugɔslavi] *nf*: **la ~** Yugoslavia.
youyou [juju] *nm* dinghy.
yo-yo [jojo] *nm inv* yo-yo.
yucca [juka] *nm* yucca (tree *ou* plant).

Z z

Z, z [zɛd] *nm inv* Z, z; **Z comme Zoé** Z for Zebra.

ZAC [zak] *sigle f* (= *zone d'aménagement concerté*) urban development zone.

ZAD [zad] *sigle f* (= *zone d'aménagement différé*) future development zone.

Zaïre [zɑːˈɪəʳ] *nm*: **le** ~ Zaïre.

zaïrois, e [zaiʀwa, -waz] *adj* Zaïrese.

Zambèze [zɑ̃bɛz] *nm*: **le** ~ the Zambezi.

Zambie [zɑ̃bi] *nf*: **la** ~ Zambia.

zambien, ne [zɑ̃bjɛ̃, -ɛn] *adj* Zambian.

zapping [zapiŋ] *nm*: **faire du** ~ to flick through the channels.

zèbre [zɛbʀ(ə)] *nm* (*ZOOL*) zebra.

zébré, e [zebʀe] *adj* striped, streaked.

zébrure [zebʀyʀ] *nf* stripe, streak.

zélateur, trice [zelatœʀ, -tʀis] *nm/f* partisan, zealot.

zèle [zɛl] *nm* diligence, assiduousness; **faire du** ~ (*péj*) to be over-zealous.

zélé, e [zele] *adj* zealous.

zénith [zenit] *nm* zenith.

ZEP [zɛp] *sigle f* (= *zone d'éducation prioritaire*) *area targeted for special help in education.*

zéro [zeʀo] *nm* zero, nought (*BRIT*); **au-dessous de** ~ below zero (Centigrade), below freezing; **partir de** ~ to start from scratch; **réduire à** ~ to reduce to nothing; **trois (buts) à** ~ 3 (goals to) nil.

zeste [zɛst(ə)] *nm* peel, zest; **un** ~ **de citron** a piece of lemon peel.

zézaiement [zezɛmɑ̃] *nm* lisp.

zézayer [zezeje] *vi* to have a lisp.

ZI *sigle f* = **zone industrielle.**

zibeline [ziblin] *nf* sable.

ZIF [zif] *sigle f* (= *zone d'intervention foncière*) intervention zone.

zigouiller [ziguje] *vt* (*fam*) to do in.

zigzag [zigzag] *nm* zigzag.

zigzaguer [zigzage] *vi* to zigzag (along).

Zimbabwe [zimbabwe] *nm*: **le** ~ Zimbabwe.

zimbabwéen, ne [zimbabweɛ̃, -ɛn] *adj* Zimbabwean.

zinc [zɛ̃g] *nm* (*CHIMIE*) zinc; (*comptoir*) bar, counter.

zinguer [zɛ̃ge] *vt* to cover with zinc.

zircon [ziʀkɔ̃] *nm* zircon.

zizanie [zizani] *nf*: **semer la** ~ to stir up ill-feeling.

zizi [zizi] *nm* (*fam*) willy (*BRIT*), peter (*US*).

zodiacal, e, aux [zɔdjakal, -o] *adj* (*signe*) of the zodiac.

zodiaque [zɔdjak] *nm* zodiac.

zona [zona] *nm* shingles *sg*.

zonage [zonaʒ] *nm* (*ADMIN*) zoning.

zonard, e [zonaʀ, -aʀd] *nm/f* (*fam*) (young) hooligan *ou* thug.

zone [zon] *nf* zone, area; (*INFORM*) field; (*quartiers*): **la** ~ the slum belt; **de seconde** ~ (*fig*) second-rate; ~ **d'action** (*MIL*) sphere of activity; ~ **bleue** ≈ restricted parking area; ~ **d'extension** *ou* **d'urbanisation** urban development area; ~ **franche** free zone; ~ **industrielle (ZI)** industrial estate; ~ **résidentielle** residential area; ~ **tampon** buffer zone.

zoner [zone] *vi* (*fam*) to hang around.

zoo [zoo] *nm* zoo.

zoologie [zɔɔlɔʒi] *nf* zoology.

zoologique [zɔɔlɔʒik] *adj* zoological.

zoologiste [zɔɔlɔʒist(ə)] *nm/f* zoologist.

zoom [zum] *nm* (*PHOTO*) zoom (lens).

ZUP [zyp] *sigle f* (= *zone à urbaniser en priorité*) = **ZAC.**

Zurich [zyʀik] *n* Zürich.

zut [zyt] *excl* dash (it)! (*BRIT*), nuts! (*US*).

Aa

A, a [eɪ] *n* (*letter*) A, a *m*; (*SCOL*: *mark*) A; (*MUS*): **A** la *m*; **A for Andrew,** (*US*) **A for Able** A comme Anatole; **A road** *n* (*BRIT AUT*) route nationale; **A shares** *npl* (*BRIT STOCK EXCHANGE*) actions *fpl* prioritaires.

KEYWORD

a [eɪ, ə] (*before vowel or silent h:* **an**) *indef art* **1** un(e); ~ **book** un livre; **an apple** une pomme; **she's** ~ **doctor** elle est médecin
2 (*instead of the number "one"*) un(e); ~ **year ago** il y a un an; ~ **hundred/thousand** *etc* **pounds** cent/mille *etc* livres
3 (*in expressing ratios, prices etc*): **3** ~ **day/week** 3 par jour/semaine; **10 km an hour** 10 km à l'heure; **30p** ~ **kilo** 30p le kilo.

a. *abbr* = **acre.**
A2 *n* (*BRIT SCOL*) *deuxième partie de l'examen équivalent au baccalauréat.*
AA *n abbr* (*BRIT*: = *Automobile Association*) ≈ ACF *m*; (*US*: = *Associate in/of Arts*) *diplôme universitaire*; (= *Alcoholics Anonymous*) AA; (= *anti-aircraft*) AA.
AAA *n abbr* (= *American Automobile Association*) ≈ ACF *m*; (*BRIT*) = *Amateur Athletics Association.*
A & R *n abbr* (*MUS*: = *artists and repertoire*): ~ **man** découvreur *m* de talent.
AB *abbr* (*BRIT*) = **able-bodied seaman**; (*Canada*) = *Alberta.*
aback [ə'bæk] *adv*: **to be taken** ~ être décontenancé(e).
abacus, *pl* **abaci** ['æbəkəs, -saɪ] *n* boulier *m*.
abandon [ə'bændən] *vt* abandonner ♦ *n* abandon *m*; **to** ~ **ship** évacuer le navire.
abandoned [ə'bændənd] *adj* (*child, house etc*) abandonné(e); (*unrestrained*) sans retenue.
abase [ə'beɪs] *vt*: **to** ~ **o.s. (so far as to do)** s'abaisser (à faire).
abashed [ə'bæʃt] *adj* confus(e), embarrassé(e).
abate [ə'beɪt] *vi* s'apaiser, se calmer.
abatement [ə'beɪtmənt] *n*: **noise** ~ lutte *f* contre le bruit.
abattoir ['æbətwɑː*] *n* (*BRIT*) abattoir *m*.
abbey ['æbɪ] *n* abbaye *f*.
abbot ['æbət] *n* père supérieur.
abbreviate [ə'briːvɪeɪt] *vt* abréger.
abbreviation [əbriːvɪ'eɪʃən] *n* abréviation *f*.
ABC *n abbr* (= *American Broadcasting Company*) *chaîne de télévision.*
abdicate ['æbdɪkeɪt] *vt, vi* abdiquer.
abdication [æbdɪ'keɪʃən] *n* abdication *f*.
abdomen ['æbdəmən] *n* abdomen *m*.
abdominal [æb'dɔmɪnl] *adj* abdominal(e).
abduct [æb'dʌkt] *vt* enlever.
abduction [æb'dʌkʃən] *n* enlèvement *m*.
Aberdonian [æbə'dəunɪən] *adj* d'Aberdeen ♦ *n* habitant/e d'Aberdeen; natif/ive d'Aberdeen.
aberration [æbə'reɪʃən] *n* anomalie *f*; **in a moment of mental** ~ dans un moment d'égarement.
abet [ə'bɛt] *vt see* **aid.**
abeyance [ə'beɪəns] *n*: **in** ~ (*law*) en désuétude; (*matter*) en suspens.
abhor [əb'hɔː*] *vt* abhorrer, exécrer.
abhorrent [əb'hɔrənt] *adj* odieux(euse), exécrable.
abide [ə'baɪd] *vt* souffrir, supporter.
►**abide by** *vt fus* observer, respecter.
abiding [ə'baɪdɪŋ] *adj* (*memory etc*) durable.
ability [ə'bɪlɪtɪ] *n* compétence *f*, capacité *f*; (*skill*) talent *m*; **to the best of my** ~ de mon mieux.
abject ['æbdʒɛkt] *adj* (*poverty*) sordide; (*coward*) méprisable; **an** ~ **apology** les excuses les plus plates.
ablaze [ə'bleɪz] *adj* en feu, en flammes; ~ **with light** resplendissant de lumière.
able ['eɪbl] *adj* compétent(e); **to be** ~ **to do sth** pouvoir faire qch, être capable de faire qch.

able-bodied ['eɪbl'bɔdɪd] *adj* robuste; ~ **seaman** (*BRIT*) matelot breveté.
ably ['eɪblɪ] *adv* avec compétence *or* talent, habilement.
ABM *n abbr = anti-ballistic missile.*
abnormal [æb'nɔːməl] *adj* anormal(e).
abnormality [æbnɔː'mælɪtɪ] *n* (*condition*) caractère anormal; (*instance*) anomalie *f*.
aboard [ə'bɔːd] *adv* à bord ♦ *prep* à bord de; (*train*) dans.
abode [ə'bəud] *n* (*old*) demeure *f*; (*LAW*): **of no fixed** ~ sans domicile fixe.
abolish [ə'bɔlɪʃ] *vt* abolir.
abolition [æbə'lɪʃən] *n* abolition *f*.
abominable [ə'bɔmɪnəbl] *adj* abominable.
aborigine [æbə'rɪdʒɪnɪ] *n* aborigène *m/f*.
abort [ə'bɔːt] *vt* (*MED, fig*) faire avorter; (*COMPUT*) abandonner.
abortion [ə'bɔːʃən] *n* avortement *m*; **to have an** ~ se faire avorter.
abortionist [ə'bɔːʃənɪst] *n* avorteur/euse.
abortive [ə'bɔːtɪv] *adj* manqué(e).
abound [ə'baund] *vi* abonder; **to** ~ **in** abonder en, regorger de.

KEYWORD

about [ə'baut] *adv* **1** (*approximately*) environ, à peu près; ~ **a hundred/thousand** *etc* environ cent/mille *etc*, une centaine (de)/un millier (de) *etc*; **it takes** ~ **10 hours** ça prend environ *or* à peu près 10 heures; **at** ~ **2 o'clock** vers 2 heures; **I've just** ~ **finished** j'ai presque fini
2 (*referring to place*) çà et là, deci delà; **to run** ~ courir çà et là; **to walk** ~ se promener, aller et venir; **is Paul** ~**?** (*BRIT*) est-ce que Paul est là?; **it's** ~ **here** c'est par ici, c'est dans les parages; **they left all their things lying** ~ ils ont laissé traîner toutes leurs affaires
3: **to be** ~ **to do sth** être sur le point de faire qch; **I'm not** ~ **to do all that for nothing** (*col*) je ne vais quand même pas faire tout ça pour rien
4 (*opposite*): **it's the other way** ~ (*BRIT*) c'est l'inverse
♦ *prep* **1** (*relating to*) au sujet de, à propos de; **a book** ~ **London** un livre sur Londres; **what is it** ~**?** de quoi s'agit-il?; **we talked** ~ **it** nous en avons parlé; **do something** ~ **it!** faites quelque chose!; **what** *or* **how** ~ **doing this?** et si nous faisions ceci?
2 (*referring to place*) dans; **to walk** ~ **the town** se promener dans la ville.

about face, about turn *n* (*MIL*) demi-tour *m*; (*fig*) volte-face *f*.
above [ə'bʌv] *adv* au-dessus ♦ *prep* au-dessus de; **mentioned** ~ mentionné ci-dessus; **costing** ~ **£10** coûtant plus de 10 livres; ~ **all** par-dessus tout, surtout.
aboveboard [ə'bʌv'bɔːd] *adj* franc(franche), loyal(e); honnête.
abrasion [ə'breɪʒən] *n* frottement *m*; (*on skin*) écorchure *f*.
abrasive [ə'breɪzɪv] *adj* abrasif(ive); (*fig*) caustique, agressif(ive).
abreast [ə'brɛst] *adv* de front; **to keep** ~ **of** se tenir au courant de.
abridge [ə'brɪdʒ] *vt* abréger.
abroad [ə'brɔːd] *adv* à l'étranger; **there is a rumour** ~ **that ...** (*fig*) le bruit court que ....
abrupt [ə'brʌpt] *adj* (*steep, blunt*) abrupt(e); (*sudden, gruff*) brusque.
abscess ['æbsɪs] *n* abcès *m*.
abscond [əb'skɔnd] *vi* disparaître, s'enfuir.
absence ['æbsəns] *n* absence *f*; **in the** ~ **of** (*person*) en l'absence de; (*thing*) faute de.
absent ['æbsənt] *adj* absent(e); ~ **without leave (AWOL)** (*MIL*) en absence irrégulière.
absentee [æbsən'tiː] *n* absent/e.
absenteeism [æbsən'tiːɪzəm] *n* absentéisme *m*.
absent-minded ['æbsənt'maɪndɪd] *adj* distrait(e).
absent-mindedness ['æbsənt'maɪndɪdnɪs] *n* distraction *f*.
absolute ['æbsəluːt] *adj* absolu(e).
absolutely [æbsə'luːtlɪ] *adv* absolument.
absolve [əb'zɔlv] *vt*: **to** ~ **sb (from)** (*sin etc*) absoudre qn (de); **to** ~ **sb from** (*oath*) délier qn de.
absorb [əb'zɔːb] *vt* absorber; **to be** ~**ed in a book** être plongé(e) dans un livre.
absorbent [əb'zɔːbənt] *adj* absorbant(e).
absorbent cotton *n* (*US*) coton *m* hydrophile.
absorbing [əb'zɔːbɪŋ] *adj* absorbant(e); (*book, film etc*) captivant(e).
absorption [əb'sɔːpʃən] *n* absorption *f*.
abstain [əb'steɪn] *vi*: **to** ~ **(from)** s'abstenir (de).
abstemious [əb'stiːmɪəs] *adj* sobre, frugal(e).
abstention [əb'stɛnʃən] *n* abstention *f*.
abstinence ['æbstɪnəns] *n* abstinence *f*.
abstract *adj, n* ['æbstrækt] *adj* abstrait(e) ♦ *n* (*summary*) résumé *m* ♦ *vt* [æb'strækt] extraire.
absurd [əb'səːd] *adj* absurde.
absurdity [əb'səːdɪtɪ] *n* absurdité *f*.
ABTA ['æbtə] *n abbr = Association of British Travel Agents.*
Abu Dhabi ['æbuː'dɑːbɪ] *n* Ab(o)u Dhabî *m*.
abundance [ə'bʌndəns] *n* abondance *f*.
abundant [ə'bʌndənt] *adj* abondant(e).
abuse *n* [ə'bjuːs] insultes *fpl*, injures *fpl*; (*of power etc*) abus *m* ♦ *vt* [ə'bjuːz] abuser de; **to be open to** ~ se prêter à des abus.
abusive [ə'bjuːsɪv] *adj* grossier(ière), injurieux(euse).
abysmal [ə'bɪzməl] *adj* exécrable; (*ignorance etc*) sans bornes.
abyss [ə'bɪs] *n* abîme *m*, gouffre *m*.
AC *n abbr* (*US*) = *athletic club.*
a/c *abbr* (*BANKING etc*) = *account, account cur-*

rent.

academic [ækə'dɛmɪk] *adj* universitaire; (*pej: issue*) oiseux(euse), purement théorique ♦ *n* universitaire *m/f*; ~ **freedom** liberté *f* académique.

academic year *n* année *f* universitaire.

academy [ə'kædəmɪ] *n* (*learned body*) académie *f*; (*school*) collège *m*; **military/naval** ~ école militaire/navale; ~ **of music** conservatoire *m*.

ACAS ['eɪkæs] *n abbr* (*BRIT: = Advisory, Conciliation and Arbitration Service*) *organisme de conciliation et d'arbitrage des conflits du travail.*

accede [æk'siːd] *vi*: **to** ~ **to** (*request, throne*) accéder à.

accelerate [æk'sɛləreɪt] *vt, vi* accélérer.

acceleration [æksɛlə'reɪʃən] *n* accélération *f*.

accelerator [æk'sɛləreɪtə*] *n* accélérateur *m*.

accent ['æksɛnt] *n* accent *m*.

accentuate [æk'sɛntjueɪt] *vt* (*syllable*) accentuer; (*need, difference etc*) souligner.

accept [ək'sɛpt] *vt* accepter.

acceptable [ək'sɛptəbl] *adj* acceptable.

acceptance [ək'sɛptəns] *n* acceptation *f*; **to meet with general** ~ être favorablement accueilli par tous.

access ['æksɛs] *n* accès *m* ♦ *vt* (*COMPUT*) accéder à; **to have** ~ **to** (*information, library etc*) avoir accès à, pouvoir utiliser *or* consulter; (*person*) avoir accès auprès de; **the burglars gained** ~ **through a window** les cambrioleurs sont entrés par une fenêtre.

accessible [æk'sɛsəbl] *adj* accessible.

accession [æk'sɛʃən] *n* accession *f*; (*of king*) avènement *m*; (*to library*) acquisition *f*.

accessory [æk'sɛsərɪ] *n* accessoire *m*; **toilet accessories** (*BRIT*) articles *mpl* de toilette.

access road *n* voie *f* d'accès; (*to motorway*) bretelle *f* de raccordement.

access time *n* (*COMPUT*) temps *m* d'accès.

accident ['æksɪdənt] *n* accident *m*; (*chance*) hasard *m*; **to meet with** *or* **to have an** ~ avoir un accident; ~**s at work** accidents du travail; **by** ~ par hasard; (*not deliberately*) accidentellement.

accidental [æksɪ'dɛntl] *adj* accidentel(le).

accidentally [æksɪ'dɛntəlɪ] *adv* accidentellement.

accident insurance *n* assurance *f* accident.

accident-prone ['æksɪdənt'prəun] *adj* sujet(te) aux accidents.

acclaim [ə'kleɪm] *vt* acclamer ♦ *n* acclamation *f*.

acclamation [æklə'meɪʃən] *n* (*approval*) acclamation *f*; (*applause*) ovation *f*.

acclimatize [ə'klaɪmətaɪz], (*US*) **acclimate** [ə'klaɪmət] *vt*: **to become** ~**d** s'acclimater.

accolade ['ækəleɪd] *n* accolade *f*; (*fig*) marque *f* d'honneur.

accommodate [ə'kɔmədeɪt] *vt* loger, recevoir; (*oblige, help*) obliger; (*adapt*): **to** ~ **one's plans to** adapter ses projets à; **this car** ~**s 4 people comfortably** on tient confortablement à 4 dans cette voiture.

accommodating [ə'kɔmədeɪtɪŋ] *adj* obligeant(e), arrangeant(e).

accommodation, (*US*) **accommodations** [əkɔmə'deɪʃən(z)] *n(pl)* logement *m*; **he's found** ~ il a trouvé à se loger; **"~ to let"** (*BRIT*) "appartement (*or* studio *etc*) à louer"; **they have** ~ **for 500** ils peuvent recevoir 500 personnes, il y a de la place pour 500 personnes; **the hall has seating** ~ **for 600** (*BRIT*) la salle contient 600 places assises.

accompaniment [ə'kʌmpənɪmənt] *n* accompagnement *m*.

accompanist [ə'kʌmpənɪst] *n* accompagnateur/trice.

accompany [ə'kʌmpənɪ] *vt* accompagner.

accomplice [ə'kʌmplɪs] *n* complice *m/f*.

accomplish [ə'kʌmplɪʃ] *vt* accomplir.

accomplished [ə'kʌmplɪʃt] *adj* accompli(e).

accomplishment [ə'kʌmplɪʃmənt] *n* accomplissement *m*; (*achievement*) réussite *f*; ~**s** *npl* (*skills*) talents *mpl*.

accord [ə'kɔːd] *n* accord *m* ♦ *vt* accorder; **of his own** ~ de son plein gré; **with one** ~ d'un commun accord.

accordance [ə'kɔːdəns] *n*: **in** ~ **with** conformément à.

according [ə'kɔːdɪŋ]: ~ **to** *prep* selon; ~ **to plan** comme prévu.

accordingly [ə'kɔːdɪŋlɪ] *adv* en conséquence.

accordion [ə'kɔːdɪən] *n* accordéon *m*.

accost [ə'kɔst] *vt* accoster, aborder.

account [ə'kaunt] *n* (*COMM*) compte *m*; (*report*) compte rendu, récit *m*; ~**s** *npl* (*BOOKKEEPING*) comptabilité *f*, comptes; **"~ payee only"** (*BRIT*) "chèque non endossable"; **to keep an** ~ **of** noter; **to bring sb to** ~ **for sth/for having done sth** amener qn à rendre compte de qch/d'avoir fait qch; **by all** ~**s** au dire de tous; **of little** ~ de peu d'importance; **to pay £5 on** ~ verser un acompte de 5 livres; **to buy sth on** ~ acheter qch à crédit; **on no** ~ en aucun cas; **on** ~ **of** à cause de; **to take into** ~, **take** ~ **of** tenir compte de.

▸**account for** *vt fus* expliquer, rendre compte de; **all the children were** ~**ed for** aucun enfant ne manquait; **4 people are still not** ~**ed for** on n'a toujours pas retrouvé 4 personnes.

accountability [əkauntə'bɪlɪtɪ] *n* responsabilité *f*; (*financial, political*) transparence *f*.

accountable [ə'kauntəbl] *adj*: ~ **(for)** responsable (de).

accountancy [ə'kauntənsɪ] *n* comptabilité *f*.

accountant [ə'kauntənt] *n* comptable *m/f*.

accounting [ə'kauntɪŋ] *n* comptabilité *f*.

accounting period *n* exercice financier, période *f* comptable.

account number *n* numéro *m* de compte.

account payable *n* compte *m* fournisseurs.

account receivable *n* compte *m* clients.
accredited [ə'krɛdɪtɪd] *adj* (*person*) accrédité(e).
accretion [ə'kriːʃən] *n* accroissement *m*.
accrue [ə'kruː] *vi* s'accroître; (*mount up*) s'accumuler; **to ~ to** s'ajouter à; **~d interest** intérêt couru.
accumulate [ə'kjuːmjuleɪt] *vt* accumuler, amasser ♦ *vi* s'accumuler, s'amasser.
accumulation [əkjuːmju'leɪʃən] *n* accumulation *f*.
accuracy ['ækjurəsɪ] *n* exactitude *f*, précision *f*.
accurate ['ækjurɪt] *adj* exact(e), précis(e).
accurately ['ækjurɪtlɪ] *adv* avec précision.
accusation [ækju'zeɪʃən] *n* accusation *f*.
accusative [ə'kjuːzətɪv] *n* (*LING*) accusatif *m*.
accuse [ə'kjuːz] *vt* accuser.
accused [ə'kjuːzd] *n* accusé/e.
accuser [ə'kjuːzə*] *n* accusateur/trice.
accustom [ə'kʌstəm] *vt* accoutumer, habituer; **to ~ o.s. to sth** s'habituer à qch.
accustomed [ə'kʌstəmd] *adj* (*usual*) habituel(le); ~ **to** habitué(e) *or* accoutumé(e) à.
AC/DC *abbr* = **alternating current/direct current.**
ACE [eɪs] *n abbr* = *American Council on Education.*
ace [eɪs] *n* as *m*; **within an ~ of** (*BRIT*) à deux doigts *or* un cheveu de.
acerbic [ə'səːbɪk] *adj* (*also fig*) acerbe.
acetate ['æsɪteɪt] *n* acétate *m*.
ache [eɪk] *n* mal *m*, douleur *f* ♦ *vi* (*be sore*) faire mal, être douloureux(euse); (*yearn*): **to ~ to do sth** mourir d'envie de faire qch; **I've got stomach ~** *or* (*US*) **a stomach ~** j'ai mal à l'estomac; **my head ~s** j'ai mal à la tête; **I'm aching all over** j'ai mal partout.
achieve [ə'tʃiːv] *vt* (*aim*) atteindre; (*victory, success*) remporter, obtenir; (*task*) accomplir.
achievement [ə'tʃiːvmənt] *n* exploit *m*, réussite *f*; (*of aims*) réalisation *f*.
Achilles heel [ə'kɪliːz-] *n* talon *m* d'Achille.
acid ['æsɪd] *adj*, *n* acide (*m*).
acidity [ə'sɪdɪtɪ] *n* acidité *f*.
acid rain *n* pluies *fpl* acides.
acid test *n* (*fig*) épreuve décisive.
acknowledge [ək'nɔlɪdʒ] *vt* (*also*: **~ receipt of**) accuser réception de; (*fact*) reconnaître.
acknowledgement [ək'nɔlɪdʒmənt] *n* accusé *m* de réception; **~s** (*in book*) remerciements *mpl*.
ACLU *n abbr* (= *American Civil Liberties Union*) *ligue des droits de l'homme.*
acme ['ækmɪ] *n* point culminant.
acne ['æknɪ] *n* acné *m*.
acorn ['eɪkɔːn] *n* gland *m*.
acoustic [ə'kuːstɪk] *adj* acoustique.
acoustic coupler *n* (*COMPUT*) coupleur *m* acoustique.
acoustics [ə'kuːstɪks] *n*, *npl* acoustique *f*.
acquaint [ə'kweɪnt] *vt*: **to ~ sb with sth** mettre qn au courant de qch; **to be ~ed with** (*person*) connaître; (*fact*) savoir.
acquaintance [ə'kweɪntəns] *n* connaissance *f*; **to make sb's ~** faire la connaissance de qn.
acquiesce [ækwɪ'ɛs] *vi* (*agree*): **to ~ (in)** acquiescer (à).
acquire [ə'kwaɪə*] *vt* acquérir.
acquired [ə'kwaɪəd] *adj* acquis(e); **an ~ taste** un goût acquis.
acquisition [ækwɪ'zɪʃən] *n* acquisition *f*.
acquisitive [ə'kwɪzɪtɪv] *adj* qui a l'instinct de possession *or* le goût de la propriété.
acquit [ə'kwɪt] *vt* acquitter; **to ~ o.s. well** s'en tirer très honorablement.
acquittal [ə'kwɪtl] *n* acquittement *m*.
acre ['eɪkə*] *n* acre *f* (*= 4047 m²*).
acreage ['eɪkərɪdʒ] *n* superficie *f*.
acrid ['ækrɪd] *adj* (*smell*) âcre; (*fig*) mordant(e).
acrimonious [ækrɪ'məunɪəs] *adj* acrimonieux(euse), aigre.
acrobat ['ækrəbæt] *n* acrobate *m/f*.
acrobatic [ækrə'bætɪk] *adj* acrobatique.
acrobatics [ækrə'bætɪks] *n*, *npl* acrobatie *f*.
Acropolis [ə'krɔpəlɪs] *n*: **the ~** l'Acropole *f*.
across [ə'krɔs] *prep* (*on the other side*) de l'autre côté de; (*crosswise*) en travers de ♦ *adv* de l'autre côté; en travers; **to walk ~ (the road)** traverser (la route); **to take sb ~ the road** faire traverser la route à qn; **a road ~ the wood** une route qui traverse le bois; **the lake is 12 km ~** le lac fait 12 km de large; **~ from** en face de; **to get sth ~ (to sb)** faire comprendre qch (à qn).
acrylic [ə'krɪlɪk] *adj*, *n* acrylique (*m*).
ACT *n abbr* (= *American College Test*) *examen de fin d'études secondaires.*
act [ækt] *n* acte *m*, action *f*; (*THEAT*: *part of play*) acte; (*: of performer*) numéro *m*; (*LAW*) loi *f* ♦ *vi* agir; (*THEAT*) jouer; (*pretend*) jouer la comédie ♦ *vt* (*role*) jouer, tenir; **~ of God** (*LAW*) catastrophe naturelle; **to catch sb in the ~** prendre qn sur le fait *or* en flagrant délit; **it's only an ~** c'est du cinéma; **to ~ Hamlet** (*BRIT*) tenir *or* jouer le rôle d'Hamlet; **to ~ the fool** (*BRIT*) faire l'idiot; **to ~ as** servir de; **it ~s as a deterrent** cela a un effet dissuasif; **~ing in my capacity as chairman, I ...** en ma qualité de président, je ....
►**act on** *vt*: **to ~ on sth** agir sur la base de qch.
►**act out** *vt* (*event*) raconter en mimant; (*fantasies*) réaliser.
acting ['æktɪŋ] *adj* suppléant(e), par intérim ♦ *n* (*of actor*) jeu *m*; (*activity*): **to do some ~** faire du théâtre (*or* du cinéma); **he is the ~ manager** il remplace (provisoirement) le directeur.
action ['ækʃən] *n* action *f*; (*MIL*) combat(s) *m(pl)*; (*LAW*) procès *m*, action en justice; **to bring an ~ against sb** (*LAW*) poursuivre qn

en justice, intenter un procès contre qn; **killed in** ~ (*MIL*) tué au champ d'honneur; **out of** ~ hors de combat; (*machine etc*) hors d'usage; **to take** ~ agir, prendre des mesures; **to put a plan into** ~ mettre un projet à exécution.

action replay *n* (*BRIT TV*) retour *m* sur une séquence.

activate ['æktɪveɪt] *vt* (*mechanism*) actionner, faire fonctionner; (*CHEM, PHYSICS*) activer.

active ['æktɪv] *adj* actif(ive); (*volcano*) en activité; **to play an** ~ **part in** jouer un rôle actif dans.

active duty (AD) *n* (*US MIL*) campagne *f*.

actively ['æktɪvlɪ] *adv* activement.

active partner *n* (*COMM*) associé/e.

active service *n* (*BRIT MIL*) campagne *f*.

activist ['æktɪvɪst] *n* activiste *m/f*.

activity [æk'tɪvɪtɪ] *n* activité *f*.

actor ['æktə*] *n* acteur *m*.

actress ['æktrɪs] *n* actrice *f*.

actual ['æktjuəl] *adj* réel(le), véritable.

actually ['æktjuəlɪ] *adv* réellement, véritablement; (*in fact*) en fait.

actuary ['æktjuərɪ] *n* actuaire *m*.

actuate ['æktjueɪt] *vt* déclencher, actionner.

acuity [ə'kju:ɪtɪ] *n* acuité *f*.

acumen ['ækjumən] *n* perspicacité *f*; **business** ~ sens *m* des affaires.

acupuncture ['ækjupʌŋktʃə*] *n* acuponcture *f*.

acute [ə'kju:t] *adj* aigu(ë); (*mind, observer*) pénétrant(e).

AD *adv abbr* (= *Anno Domini*) ap. J.-C. ♦ *n abbr* (*US MIL*) = **active duty**.

ad [æd] *n abbr* = **advertisement**.

adamant ['ædəmənt] *adj* inflexible.

Adam's apple ['ædəmz-] *n* pomme *f* d'Adam.

adapt [ə'dæpt] *vt* adapter ♦ *vi*: **to** ~ **(to)** s'adapter (à).

adaptability [ədæptə'bɪlɪtɪ] *n* faculté *f* d'adaptation.

adaptable [ə'dæptəbl] *adj* (*device*) adaptable; (*person*) qui s'adapte facilement.

adaptation [ædæp'teɪʃən] *n* adaptation *f*.

adapter [ə'dæptə*] *n* (*ELEC*) adapteur *m*.

ADC *n abbr* (*MIL*) = *aide-de-camp*; (*US*: = *Aid to Dependent Children*) *aide pour enfants assistés*.

add [æd] *vt* ajouter; (*figures*) additionner ♦ *vi*: **to** ~ **to** (*increase*) ajouter à, accroître.

►**add on** *vt* ajouter.

►**add up** *vt* (*figures*) additionner ♦ *vi* (*fig*): **it doesn't** ~ **up** cela ne rime à rien; **it doesn't** ~ **up to much** ça n'est pas grand'chose.

adder ['ædə*] *n* vipère *f*.

addict ['ædɪkt] *n* toxicomane *m/f*; (*fig*) fanatique *m/f*; **heroin** ~ héroïnomane *m/f*; **drug** ~ drogué/e *m/f*.

addicted [ə'dɪktɪd] *adj*: **to be** ~ **to** (*drink etc*) être adonné(e) à; (*fig: football etc*) être un(e) fanatique de.

addiction [ə'dɪkʃən] *n* (*MED*) dépendance *f*.

adding machine ['ædɪŋ-] *n* machine *f* à calculer.

Addis Ababa ['ædɪs'æbəbə] *n* Addis Abeba, Addis Ababa.

addition [ə'dɪʃən] *n* addition *f*; **in** ~ de plus, de surcroît; **in** ~ **to** en plus de.

additional [ə'dɪʃənl] *adj* supplémentaire.

additive ['ædɪtɪv] *n* additif *m*.

addled ['ædld] *adj* (*BRIT: egg*) pourri(e).

address [ə'drɛs] *n* adresse *f*; (*talk*) discours *m*, allocution *f* ♦ *vt* adresser; (*speak to*) s'adresser à; **form of** ~ titre *m*; **what form of** ~ **do you use for ...?** comment s'adresse-t-on à ...?; **to** ~ **(o.s. to) sth** (*problem, issue*) aborder qch; **absolute/relative** ~ (*COMPUT*) adresse absolue/relative.

address book *n* carnet *m* d'adresses.

addressee [ædrɛ'si:] *n* destinataire *m/f*.

Aden ['eɪdən] *n*: **Gulf of** ~ Golfe *m* d'Aden.

adenoids ['ædɪnɔɪdz] *npl* végétations *fpl*.

adept ['ædɛpt] *adj*: ~ **at** expert(e) à *or* en.

adequate ['ædɪkwɪt] *adj* (*enough*) suffisant(e); **to feel** ~ **to the task** se sentir à la hauteur de la tâche.

adequately ['ædɪkwɪtlɪ] *adv* de façon adéquate.

adhere [əd'hɪə*] *vi*: **to** ~ **to** adhérer à; (*fig: rule, decision*) se tenir à.

adhesion [əd'hi:ʒən] *n* adhésion *f*.

adhesive [əd'hi:zɪv] *adj* adhésif(ive) ♦ *n* adhésif *m*; ~ **tape** (*BRIT*) ruban adhésif; (*US*) sparadrap *m*.

ad hoc [æd'hɔk] *adj* (*decision*) de circonstance; (*committee*) ad hoc.

ad infinitum ['ædɪnfɪ'naɪtəm] *adv* à l'infini.

adjacent [ə'dʒeɪsənt] *adj* adjacent(e), contigu(ë); ~ **to** adjacent à.

adjective ['ædʒɛktɪv] *n* adjectif *m*.

adjoin [ə'dʒɔɪn] *vt* jouxter.

adjoining [ə'dʒɔɪnɪŋ] *adj* voisin(e), adjacent(e), attenant(e) ♦ *prep* voisin de, adjacent à.

adjourn [ə'dʒə:n] *vt* ajourner ♦ *vi* suspendre la séance; lever la séance; clore la session; (*go*) se retirer; **to** ~ **a meeting till the following week** reporter une réunion à la semaine suivante; **they** ~**ed to the pub** (*BRIT col*) ils ont filé au pub.

adjournment [ə'dʒə:nmənt] *n* (*period*) ajournement *m*.

Adjt *abbr* (*MIL*: = *adjutant*) Adj.

adjudicate [ə'dʒu:dɪkeɪt] *vt* (*contest*) juger; (*claim*) statuer (sur) ♦ *vi* se prononcer.

adjudication [ədʒu:dɪ'keɪʃən] *n* (*LAW*) jugement *m*.

adjust [ə'dʒʌst] *vt* ajuster, régler; rajuster ♦ *vi*: **to** ~ **(to)** s'adapter (à).

adjustable [ə'dʒʌstəbl] *adj* réglable.

adjuster [ə'dʒʌstə*] *n see* **loss**.

adjustment [ə'dʒʌstmənt] *n* ajustage *m*, réglage *m*; (*of prices, wages*) rajustement *m*; (*of person*) adaptation *f*.

adjutant ['ædʒətənt] *n* adjudant *m*.
ad-lib [æd'lɪb] *vt, vi* improviser ♦ *n* improvisation *f* ♦ *adv*: **ad lib** à volonté, à discrétion.
adman ['ædmæn] *n* (*col*) publicitaire *m*.
admin ['ædmɪn] *n abbr* (*col*) = **administration**.
administer [əd'mɪnɪstə*] *vt* administrer; (*justice*) rendre.
administration [ədmɪnɪs'treɪʃən] *n* administration *f*; **the A~** (*US*) le gouvernement.
administrative [əd'mɪnɪstrətɪv] *adj* administratif(ive).
administrator [əd'mɪnɪstreɪtə*] *n* administrateur/trice.
admirable ['ædmərəbl] *adj* admirable.
admiral ['ædmərəl] *n* amiral *m*.
Admiralty ['ædmərəltɪ] *n* (*BRIT*: *also*: ~ **Board**) ministère *m* de la Marine.
admiration [ædmə'reɪʃən] *n* admiration *f*.
admire [əd'maɪə*] *vt* admirer.
admirer [əd'maɪərə*] *n* admirateur/trice.
admiring [əd'maɪərɪŋ] *adj* admiratif(ive).
admissible [əd'mɪsəbl] *adj* acceptable, admissible; (*evidence*) recevable.
admission [əd'mɪʃən] *n* admission *f*; (*to exhibition, night club etc*) entrée *f*; (*confession*) aveu *m*; **"~ free"**, **"free ~"** "entrée libre"; **by his own ~** de son propre aveu.
admit [əd'mɪt] *vt* laisser entrer; admettre; (*agree*) reconnaître, admettre; **"children not ~ted"** "entrée interdite aux enfants"; **this ticket ~s two** ce billet est valable pour deux personnes; **I must ~ that** ... je dois admettre *or* reconnaître que ....
▶**admit of** *vt fus* admettre, permettre.
▶**admit to** *vt fus* reconnaître, avouer.
admittance [əd'mɪtəns] *n* admission *f*, (droit *m* d')entrée *f*; **"no ~"** "défense d'entrer".
admittedly [əd'mɪtɪdlɪ] *adv* il faut en convenir.
admonish [əd'mɔnɪʃ] *vt* donner un avertissement à; réprimander.
ad nauseam [æd'nɔ:sɪæm] *adv* à satiété.
ado [ə'du:] *n*: **without (any) more ~** sans plus de cérémonies.
adolescence [ædəu'lɛsns] *n* adolescence *f*.
adolescent [ædəu'lɛsnt] *adj, n* adolescent(e).
adopt [ə'dɔpt] *vt* adopter.
adopted [ə'dɔptɪd] *adj* adoptif(ive), adopté(e).
adoption [ə'dɔpʃən] *n* adoption *f*.
adore [ə'dɔ:*] *vt* adorer.
adoring [ə'dɔ:rɪŋ] *adj*: **his ~ wife** sa femme qui est en adoration devant lui.
adoringly [ə'dɔ:rɪŋlɪ] *adv* avec adoration.
adorn [ə'dɔ:n] *vt* orner.
adornment [ə'dɔ:nmənt] *n* ornement *m*.
adrenalin [ə'drɛnəlɪn] *n* adrénaline *f*; **to get the ~ going** faire monter le taux d'adrénaline.
Adriatic (Sea) [eɪdrɪ'ætɪk-] *n* Adriatique *f*.
adrift [ə'drɪft] *adv* à la dérive; **to come ~** (*boat*) aller à la dérive; (*wire, rope, fastening etc*) se défaire.
adroit [ə'drɔɪt] *adj* adroit(e), habile.
ADT *abbr* (*US*: = *Atlantic Daylight Time*) *heure d'été de New York.*
adult ['ædʌlt] *n* adulte *m/f*.
adult education *n* éducation *f* des adultes.
adulterate [ə'dʌltəreɪt] *vt* frelater, falsifier.
adulterer [ə'dʌltərə*] *n* homme *m* adultère.
adulteress [ə'dʌltərɪs] *n* femme *f* adultère.
adultery [ə'dʌltərɪ] *n* adultère *m*.
adulthood ['ædʌlthud] *n* âge *m* adulte.
advance [əd'vɑ:ns] *n* avance *f* ♦ *vt* avancer ♦ *vi* s'avancer; **in ~** en avance, d'avance; **to make ~s to sb** (*gen*) faire des propositions à qn; (*amorously*) faire des avances à qn.
advanced [əd'vɑ:nst] *adj* avancé(e); (*SCOL*: *studies*) supérieur(e); **~ in years** d'un âge avancé.
Advanced Higher *n* (*SCOT SCOL*) ≈ baccalauréat *m*.
advancement [əd'vɑ:nsmənt] *n* avancement *m*.
advance notice *n* préavis *m*.
advantage [əd'vɑ:ntɪdʒ] *n* (*also TENNIS*) avantage *m*; **to take ~ of** profiter de; **it's to our ~** c'est notre intérêt; **it's to our ~ to ...** nous avons intérêt à ....
advantageous [ædvən'teɪdʒəs] *adj* avantageux(euse).
advent ['ædvənt] *n* avènement *m*, venue *f*; **A~** (*REL*) avent *m*.
Advent calendar *n* calendrier *m* de l'avent.
adventure [əd'vɛntʃə*] *n* aventure *f*.
adventure playground *n* aire *f* de jeux.
adventurous [əd'vɛntʃərəs] *adj* aventureux(euse).
adverb ['ædvə:b] *n* adverbe *m*.
adversary ['ædvəsərɪ] *n* adversaire *m/f*.
adverse ['ædvə:s] *adj* contraire, adverse; **~ to** hostile à; **in ~ circumstances** dans l'adversité.
adversity [əd'və:sɪtɪ] *n* adversité *f*.
advert ['ædvə:t] *n abbr* (*BRIT*) = **advertisement**.
advertise ['ædvətaɪz] *vi*(*vt*) faire de la publicité *or* de la réclame (pour); (*in classified ads etc*) mettre une annonce (pour vendre); **to ~ for** (*staff*) recruter par (voie d')annonce.
advertisement [əd'və:tɪsmənt] *n* (*COMM*) réclame *f*, publicité *f*; (*in classified ads etc*) annonce *f*.
advertiser ['ædvətaɪzə*] *n* annonceur *m*.
advertising ['ædvətaɪzɪŋ] *n* publicité *f*.
advertising agency *n* agence *f* de publicité.
advertising campaign *n* campagne *f* de publicité.
advice [əd'vaɪs] *n* conseils *mpl*; (*notification*) avis *m*; **piece of ~** conseil; **to ask (sb) for ~** demander conseil (à qn); **to take legal ~** consulter un avocat.
advice note *n* (*BRIT*) avis *m* d'expédition.
advisable [əd'vaɪzəbl] *adj* recommandable, indiqué(e).
advise [əd'vaɪz] *vt* conseiller; **to ~ sb of sth** aviser *or* informer qn de qch; **to ~ sb**

against sth déconseiller qch à qn; **to ~ sb against doing sth** conseiller à qn de ne pas faire qch; **you would be well/ill ~d to go** vous feriez mieux d'y aller/de ne pas y aller, vous auriez intérêt à y aller/à ne pas y aller.

advisedly [əd'vaɪzɪdlɪ] *adv* (*deliberately*) délibérément.

adviser, advisor [əd'vaɪzə*] *n* conseiller/ère.

advisory [əd'vaɪzərɪ] *adj* consultatif(ive); **in an ~ capacity** à titre consultatif.

advocate *n* ['ædvəkɪt] (*upholder*) défenseur *m*, avocat/e ♦ *vt* ['ædvəkeɪt] recommander, prôner; **to be an ~ of** être partisan/e de.

advt. *abbr* = **advertisement.**

AEA *n abbr* (*BRIT SCOL*: = *Advanced Extension Award*) *examen qui permet d'obtenir la mention très bien à l'équivalent du baccalauréat*; (*BRIT*: = *Atomic Energy Authority*) ≈ AEN *f* (= *Agence pour l'énergie nucléaire*).

AEC *n abbr* (*US*: = *Atomic Energy Commission*) CEA *m* (= *Commissariat à l'énergie atomique*).

Aegean (Sea) [iː'dʒiːən-] *n* mer *f* Égée.

aegis ['iːdʒɪs] *n*: **under the ~ of** sous l'égide de.

aeon ['iːən] *n* éternité *f*.

aerial ['ɛərɪəl] *n* antenne *f* ♦ *adj* aérien(ne).

aerie ['ɛərɪ] *n* (*US*) aire *f*.

aerobatics ['ɛərəu'bætɪks] *npl* acrobaties aériennes.

aerobics [ɛə'rəubɪks] *n* aérobic *m*.

aerodrome ['ɛərədrəum] *n* (*BRIT*) aérodrome *m*.

aerodynamic ['ɛərəudaɪ'næmɪk] *adj* aérodynamique.

aeronautics [ɛərə'nɔːtɪks] *n* aéronautique *f*.

aeroplane ['ɛərəpleɪn] *n* (*BRIT*) avion *m*.

aerosol ['ɛərəsɔl] *n* aérosol *m*.

aerospace industry ['ɛərəuspeɪs-] *n* (industrie) aérospatiale *f*.

aesthetic [ɪs'θɛtɪk] *adj* esthétique.

afar [ə'fɑː*] *adv*: **from ~** de loin.

AFB *n abbr* (*US*) = *Air Force Base*.

AFDC *n abbr* (*US*: = *Aid to Families with Dependent Children*) *aide pour enfants assistés*.

affable ['æfəbl] *adj* affable.

affair [ə'fɛə*] *n* affaire *f*; (*also*: **love ~**) liaison *f*; aventure *f*; **~s** (*business*) affaires.

affect [ə'fɛkt] *vt* affecter.

affectation [æfɛk'teɪʃən] *n* affectation *f*.

affected [ə'fɛktɪd] *adj* affecté(e).

affection [ə'fɛkʃən] *n* affection *f*.

affectionate [ə'fɛkʃənɪt] *adj* affectueux(euse).

affectionately [ə'fɛkʃənɪtlɪ] *adv* affectueusement.

affidavit [æfɪ'deɪvɪt] *n* (*LAW*) déclaration écrite sous serment.

affiliated [ə'fɪlɪeɪtɪd] *adj* affilié(e); **~ company** filiale *f*.

affinity [ə'fɪnɪtɪ] *n* affinité *f*.

affirm [ə'fəːm] *vt* affirmer.

affirmation [æfə'meɪʃən] *n* affirmation *f*, assertion *f*.

affirmative [ə'fəːmətɪv] *adj* affirmatif(ive) ♦ *n*: **in the ~** dans *or* par l'affirmative.

affix [ə'fɪks] *vt* apposer, ajouter.

afflict [ə'flɪkt] *vt* affliger.

affliction [ə'flɪkʃən] *n* affliction *f*.

affluence ['æfluəns] *n* aisance *f*, opulence *f*.

affluent ['æfluənt] *adj* opulent(e); (*person*) dans l'aisance, riche; **the ~ society** la société d'abondance.

afford [ə'fɔːd] *vt* (*goods etc*) avoir les moyens d'acheter *or* d'entretenir; (*behaviour*) se permettre; (*provide*) fournir, procurer; **can we ~ a car?** avons-nous de quoi acheter *or* les moyens d'acheter une voiture?; **I can't ~ the time** je n'ai vraiment pas le temps.

affordable [ə'fɔːdəbl] *adj* abordable.

affray [ə'freɪ] *n* (*BRIT LAW*) échauffourée *f*, rixe *f*.

affront [ə'frʌnt] *n* affront *m*.

affronted [ə'frʌntɪd] *adj* insulté(e).

Afghan ['æfgæn] *adj* afghan(e) ♦ *n* Afghan/e.

Afghanistan [æf'gænɪstæn] *n* Afghanistan *m*.

afield [ə'fiːld] *adv*: **far ~** loin.

AFL-CIO *n abbr* (= *American Federation of Labor and Congress of Industrial Organizations*) *confédération syndicale*.

afloat [ə'fləut] *adj* à flot ♦ *adv*: **to stay ~** surnager; **to keep/get a business ~** maintenir à flot/lancer une affaire.

afoot [ə'fut] *adv*: **there is something ~** il se prépare quelque chose.

aforementioned [ə'fɔːmɛnʃənd] *adj*, **aforesaid** [ə'fɔːsɛd] *adj* susdit(e), susmentionné(e).

afraid [ə'freɪd] *adj* effrayé(e); **to be ~ of** *or* **to** avoir peur de; **I am ~ that** je crains que + *sub*; **I'm ~ so/not** oui/non, malheureusement.

afresh [ə'frɛʃ] *adv* de nouveau.

Africa ['æfrɪkə] *n* Afrique *f*.

African ['æfrɪkən] *adj* africain(e) ♦ *n* Africain/e.

Afrikaans [æfrɪ'kɑːns] *n* afrikaans *m*.

Afrikaner [æfrɪ'kɑːnə*] *n* Afrikaner *m/f*.

Afro-American ['æfrəuə'mɛrɪkən] *adj* afro-américain(e).

AFT *n abbr* (= *American Federation of Teachers*) *syndicat enseignant*.

aft [ɑːft] *adv* à l'arrière, vers l'arrière.

after ['ɑːftə*] *prep, adv* après ♦ *conj* après que, après avoir *or* être + *pp*; **~ dinner** après (le) dîner; **the day ~ tomorrow** après demain; **quarter ~ two** (*US*) deux heures et quart; **what/who are you ~?** que/qui cherchez-vous?; **the police are ~ him** la police est à ses trousses; **~ you!** après vous!; **~ all** après tout.

afterbirth ['ɑːftəbəːθ] *n* placenta *m*.

aftercare ['ɑːftəkɛə*] *n* (*BRIT MED*) post-cure *f*.

after-effects ['ɑːftərɪfɛkts] *npl* répercussions *fpl*; (*of illness*) séquelles *fpl*, suites *fpl*.

afterlife ['ɑːftəlaɪf] *n* vie future.

aftermath ['ɑːftəmɑːθ] *n* conséquences *fpl*; **in the ~ of** dans les mois *or* années *etc* qui suivirent, au lendemain de.
afternoon ['ɑːftə'nuːn] *n* après-midi *m or f*; **good ~!** bonjour!; (*goodbye*) au revoir!
afters ['ɑːftəz] *n* (*BRIT col: dessert*) dessert *m*.
after-sales service [ɑːftə'seɪlz-] *n* service *m* après-vente, SAV *m*.
after-shave (lotion) ['ɑːftəʃeɪv-] *n* lotion *f* après-rasage.
aftershock ['ɑːftəʃɔk] *n* réplique *f* (sismique).
aftertaste ['ɑːftəteɪst] *n* arrière-goût *m*.
afterthought ['ɑːftəθɔːt] *n*: **I had an ~** il m'est venu une idée après coup.
afterwards ['ɑːftəwədz] *adv* après.
again [ə'gɛn] *adv* de nouveau, encore une fois; **to begin/see ~** recommencer/revoir; **not ... ~** ne ... plus; **~ and ~** à plusieurs reprises; **he's opened it ~** il l'a rouvert, il l'a de nouveau *or* l'a encore ouvert; **now and ~** de temps à autre.
against [ə'gɛnst] *prep* contre; **~ a blue background** sur un fond bleu; **(as) ~** (*BRIT*) contre.
age [eɪdʒ] *n* âge *m* ♦ *vt, vi* vieillir; **what ~ is he?** quel âge a-t-il?; **he is 20 years of ~** il a 20 ans; **under ~** mineur(e); **to come of ~** atteindre sa majorité; **it's been ~s since** ça fait une éternité que ... ne.
aged ['eɪdʒd] *adj* âgé(e); **~ 10** âgé de 10 ans; **the ~** ['eɪdʒɪd] *npl* les personnes âgées.
age group *n* tranche *f* d'âge; **the 40 to 50 ~** la tranche d'âge des 40 à 50 ans.
ageing ['eɪdʒɪŋ] *adj* vieillissant(e).
ageless ['eɪdʒlɪs] *adj* sans âge.
age limit *n* limite *f* d'âge.
agency ['eɪdʒənsɪ] *n* agence *f*; **through** *or* **by the ~ of** par l'entremise *or* l'action de.
agenda [ə'dʒɛndə] *n* ordre *m* du jour; **on the ~** à l'ordre du jour.
agent ['eɪdʒənt] *n* agent *m*.
aggravate ['ægrəveɪt] *vt* aggraver; (*annoy*) exaspérer, agacer.
aggravation [ægrə'veɪʃən] *n* agacements *mpl*.
aggregate ['ægrɪgɪt] *n* ensemble *m*, total *m*; **on ~** (*SPORT*) au total des points.
aggression [ə'grɛʃən] *n* agression *f*.
aggressive [ə'grɛsɪv] *adj* agressif(ive).
aggressiveness [ə'grɛsɪvnɪs] *n* agressivité *f*.
aggressor [ə'grɛsə*] *n* agresseur *m*.
aggrieved [ə'griːvd] *adj* chagriné(e), affligé(e).
aggro ['ægrəu] *n* (*col: physical*) grabuge *m*; (*: hassle*) embêtements *mpl*.
aghast [ə'gɑːst] *adj* consterné(e), atterré(e).
agile ['ædʒaɪl] *adj* agile.
agility [ə'dʒɪlɪtɪ] *n* agilité *f*, souplesse *f*.
agitate ['ædʒɪteɪt] *vt* rendre inquiet(ète) *or* agité(e) ♦ *vi* faire de l'agitation (politique); **to ~ for** faire campagne pour.
agitator ['ædʒɪteɪtə*] *n* agitateur/trice (politique).
AGM *n abbr* = **annual general meeting**.
ago [ə'gəu] *adv*: **2 days ~** il y a 2 jours; **not long ~** il n'y a pas longtemps; **as long ~ as 1960** déjà en 1960; **how long ~?** il y a combien de temps (de cela)?
agog [ə'gɔg] *adj*: **(all) ~** en émoi.
agonize ['ægənaɪz] *vi*: **he ~d over the problem** ce problème lui a causé bien du tourment.
agonizing ['ægənaɪzɪŋ] *adj* angoissant(e); (*cry*) déchirant(e).
agony ['ægənɪ] *n* grande souffrance *or* angoisse; **to be in ~** souffrir le martyre.
agony aunt *n* (*BRIT col*) *journaliste qui tient la rubrique du courrier du cœur*.
agony column *n* courrier *m* du cœur.
agree [ə'griː] *vt* (*price*) convenir de ♦ *vi*: **to ~ (with)** (*person*) être d'accord (avec); (*statements etc*) concorder (avec); (*LING*) s'accorder (avec); **to ~ to do** accepter de *or* consentir à faire; **to ~ to sth** consentir à qch; **to ~ that** (*admit*) convenir *or* reconnaître que; **it was ~d that ...** il a été convenu que ...; **they ~ on this** ils sont d'accord sur ce point; **they ~d on going/a price** ils se mirent d'accord pour y aller/sur un prix; **garlic doesn't ~ with me** je ne supporte pas l'ail.
agreeable [ə'griːəbl] *adj* (*pleasant*) agréable; (*willing*) consentant(e), d'accord; **are you ~ to this?** est-ce que vous êtes d'accord?
agreed [ə'griːd] *adj* (*time, place*) convenu(e); **to be ~** être d'accord.
agreement [ə'griːmənt] *n* accord *m*; **in ~** d'accord; **by mutual ~** d'un commun accord.
agricultural [ægrɪ'kʌltʃərəl] *adj* agricole.
agriculture ['ægrɪkʌltʃə*] *n* agriculture *f*.
aground [ə'graund] *adv*: **to run ~** s'échouer.
ahead [ə'hɛd] *adv* en avant; devant; **go right** *or* **straight ~** allez tout droit; **go ~!** (*fig*) allez-y!; **~ of** devant; (*fig: schedule etc*) en avance sur; **~ of time** en avance; **they were (right) ~ of us** ils nous précédaient (de peu), ils étaient (juste) devant nous.
AI *n abbr* = **Amnesty International**; (*COMPUT*) = **artificial intelligence**.
AIB *n abbr* (*BRIT: = Accident Investigation Bureau*) *commission d'enquête sur les accidents*.
AID *n abbr* (*= artificial insemination by donor*) IAD *f*; (*US: = Agency for International Development*) *agence pour le développement international*.
aid [eɪd] *n* aide *f* ♦ *vt* aider; **with the ~ of** avec l'aide de; **in ~ of** en faveur de; **to ~ and abet** (*LAW*) se faire le complice de.
aide [eɪd] *n* (*person*) assistant/e.
AIDS [eɪdz] *n abbr* (*= acquired immune* (*or immuno-*)*deficiency syndrome*) SIDA *m*.
AIH *n abbr* (*= artificial insemination by husband*) IAC *f*.
ailment ['eɪlmənt] *n* affection *f*.
aim [eɪm] *n* but *m* ♦ *vt*: **to ~ sth at** (*gun,*

camera) braquer *or* pointer qch sur, diriger qch contre; (*missile*) pointer qch vers *or* sur; (*remark, blow*) destiner *or* adresser qch à ♦ *vi* (*also*: **to take** ~) viser; **to** ~ **at** viser; (*fig*) viser (à); avoir pour but *or* ambition; **to** ~ **to do** avoir l'intention de faire.

aimless ['eɪmlɪs] *adj* sans but.

aimlessly ['eɪmlɪslɪ] *adv* sans but.

ain't [eɪnt] (*col*) = **am not, aren't, isn't**.

air [ɛə*] *n* air *m* ♦ *vt* aérer; (*idea, grievance, views*) mettre sur le tapis; (*knowledge*) faire étalage de ♦ *cpd* (*currents, attack etc*) aérien(ne); **by** ~ par avion; **to be on the** ~ (*RADIO, TV*: *programme*) être diffusé(e); (*: station*) émettre.

air bag *n* airbag *m*.

air base *n* base aérienne.

airbed ['ɛəbɛd] *n* (*BRIT*) matelas *m* pneumatique.

airborne ['ɛəbɔːn] *adj* (*plane*) en vol; (*troops*) aeroporté(e); (*particles*) dans l'air; **as soon as the plane was** ~ dès que l'avion eut décollé.

air cargo *n* fret aérien.

air-conditioned ['ɛəkən'dɪʃənd] *adj* climatisé(e), à air conditionné.

air conditioning [-kən'dɪʃnɪŋ] *n* climatisation *f*.

air-cooled ['ɛəkuːld] *adj* à refroidissement à air.

aircraft ['ɛəkrɑːft] *n* (*pl inv*) avion *m*.

aircraft carrier *n* porte-avions *m inv*.

air cushion *n* coussin *m* d'air.

airdrome ['ɛədrəum] *n* (*US*) aérodrome *m*.

airfield ['ɛəfiːld] *n* terrain *m* d'aviation.

Air Force *n* Armée *f* de l'air.

air freight *n* fret aérien.

airgun ['ɛəgʌn] *n* fusil *m* à air comprimé.

air hostess *n* (*BRIT*) hôtesse *f* de l'air.

airily ['ɛərɪlɪ] *adv* d'un air dégagé.

airing ['ɛərɪŋ] *n*: **to give an** ~ **to** aérer; (*fig: ideas, views etc*) mettre sur le tapis.

air letter *n* (*BRIT*) aérogramme *m*.

airlift ['ɛəlɪft] *n* pont aérien.

airline ['ɛəlaɪn] *n* ligne aérienne, compagnie aérienne.

airliner ['ɛəlaɪnə*] *n* avion *m* de ligne.

airlock ['ɛəlɔk] *n* sas *m*.

airmail ['ɛəmeɪl] *n*: **by** ~ par avion.

air mattress *n* matelas *m* pneumatique.

airplane ['ɛəpleɪn] *n* (*US*) avion *m*.

air pocket *n* trou *m* d'air.

airport ['ɛəpɔːt] *n* aéroport *m*.

air raid *n* attaque aérienne.

air rifle *n* carabine *f* à air comprimé.

airsick ['ɛəsɪk] *adj*: **to be** ~ avoir le mal de l'air.

airspeed ['ɛəspiːd] *n* vitesse relative.

airstrip ['ɛəstrɪp] *n* terrain *m* d'atterrissage.

air terminal *n* aérogare *f*.

airtight ['ɛətaɪt] *adj* hermétique.

air time *n* (*RADIO, TV*) temps *m* d'antenne.

air traffic control *n* contrôle *m* de la navigation aérienne.

air traffic controller *n* aiguilleur *m* du ciel.

airway ['ɛəweɪ] *n* (*AVIAT*) voie aérienne; ~**s** (*ANAT*) voies aériennes.

airy ['ɛərɪ] *adj* bien aéré(e); (*manners*) dégagé(e).

aisle [aɪl] *n* (*of church*) allée centrale; nef latérale; (*in theatre*) allée *f*; (*on plane*) couloir *m*.

ajar [ə'dʒɑː*] *adj* entrouvert(e).

AK *abbr* (*US*) = *Alaska*.

aka *abbr* (= *also known as*) alias.

akin [ə'kɪn] *adj*: ~ **to** semblable à, du même ordre que.

AL *abbr* (*US*) = *Alabama*.

ALA *n abbr* = *American Library Association*.

Ala. *abbr* (*US*) = *Alabama*.

alacrity [ə'lækrɪtɪ] *n*: **with** ~ avec empressement, promptement.

alarm [ə'lɑːm] *n* alarme *f* ♦ *vt* alarmer.

alarm clock *n* réveille-matin *m inv*, réveil *m*.

alarmed [ə'lɑːmd] *adj* (*frightened*) alarmé(e); (*protected by an alarm*) protégé(e) par un système d'alarme; **to become** ~ prendre peur.

alarming [ə'lɑːmɪŋ] *adj* alarmant(e).

alarmingly [ə'lɑːmɪŋlɪ] *adv* d'une manière alarmante; ~ **close** dangereusement proche; ~ **quickly** à une vitesse inquiétante.

alarmist [ə'lɑːmɪst] *n* alarmiste *m/f*.

alas [ə'læs] *excl* hélas.

Alas. *abbr* (*US*) = *Alaska*.

Alaska [ə'læskə] *n* Alaska *m*.

Albania [æl'beɪnɪə] *n* Albanie *f*.

Albanian [æl'beɪnɪən] *adj* albanais(e) ♦ *n* Albanais/e; (*LING*) albanais *m*.

albatross ['ælbətrɔs] *n* albatros *m*.

albeit [ɔːl'biːɪt] *conj* bien que + *sub*, encore que + *sub*.

album ['ælbəm] *n* album *m*.

albumen ['ælbjumɪn] *n* albumine *f*; (*of egg*) albumen *m*.

alchemy ['ælkɪmɪ] *n* alchimie *f*.

alcohol ['ælkəhɔl] *n* alcool *m*.

alcohol-free ['ælkəhɔlfriː] *adj* sans alcool.

alcoholic [ælkə'hɔlɪk] *adj*, *n* alcoolique (*m/f*).

alcoholism ['ælkəhɔlɪzəm] *n* alcoolisme *m*.

alcove ['ælkəuv] *n* alcôve *f*.

Ald. *abbr* = **alderman**.

alderman ['ɔːldəmən] *n* conseiller municipal (*en Angleterre*).

ale [eɪl] *n* bière *f*.

alert [ə'ləːt] *adj* alerte, vif(vive); (*watchful*) vigilant(e) ♦ *n* alerte *f* ♦ *vt*: **to** ~ **sb (to sth)** attirer l'attention de qn (sur qch); **to** ~ **sb to the dangers of sth** avertir qn des dangers de qch; **on the** ~ sur le qui-vive; (*MIL*) en état d'alerte.

Aleutian Islands [ə'luːʃən-] *npl* îles Aléoutiennes.

A levels *npl* ≈ baccalauréat *msg*.

Alexandria [ælɪg'zɑːndrɪə] *n* Alexandrie.
alfresco [æl'frɛskəu] *adj, adv* en plein air.
algebra ['ældʒɪbrə] *n* algèbre *m*.
Algeria [æl'dʒɪərɪə] *n* Algérie *f*.
Algerian [æl'dʒɪərɪən] *adj* algérien(ne) ♦ *n* Algérien/ne.
Algiers [æl'dʒɪəz] *n* Alger.
algorithm ['ælgərɪðəm] *n* algorithme *m*.
alias ['eɪlɪəs] *adv* alias ♦ *n* faux nom, nom d'emprunt.
alibi ['ælɪbaɪ] *n* alibi *m*.
alien ['eɪlɪən] *n* étranger/ère ♦ *adj*: ~ **(to)** étranger(ère) (à).
alienate ['eɪlɪəneɪt] *vt* aliéner; (*subj: person*) s'aliéner.
alienation [eɪlɪə'neɪʃən] *n* aliénation *f*.
alight [ə'laɪt] *adj, adv* en feu ♦ *vi* mettre pied à terre; (*passenger*) descendre; (*bird*) se poser.
align [ə'laɪn] *vt* aligner.
alignment [ə'laɪnmənt] *n* alignement *m*; **it's out of ~ (with)** ce n'est pas aligné (avec).
alike [ə'laɪk] *adj* semblable, pareil(le) ♦ *adv* de même; **to look ~** se ressembler.
alimony ['ælɪmənɪ] *n* (*payment*) pension *f* alimentaire.
alive [ə'laɪv] *adj* vivant(e); (*active*) plein(e) de vie; **~ with** grouillant(e) de; **~ to** sensible à.
alkali ['ælkəlaɪ] *n* alcali *m*.

KEYWORD

all [ɔːl] *adj* (*singular*) tout(e); (*plural*) tous(toutes); **~ day** toute la journée; **~ night** toute la nuit; **~ men** tous les hommes; **~ five** tous les cinq; **~ the food** toute la nourriture; **~ the books** tous les livres; **~ the time** tout le temps; **~ his life** toute sa vie
♦ *pron* **1** tout; **I ate it ~, I ate ~ of it** j'ai tout mangé; **~ of us went** nous y sommes tous allés; **~ of the boys went** tous les garçons y sont allés; **is that ~?** c'est tout?; (*in shop*) ce sera tout?
2 (*in phrases*): **above ~** surtout, par-dessus tout; **after ~** après tout; **at ~**: **not at ~** (*in answer to question*) pas du tout; (*in answer to thanks*) je vous en prie!; **I'm not at ~ tired** je ne suis pas du tout fatigué(e); **anything at ~ will do** n'importe quoi fera l'affaire; **~ in ~** tout bien considéré, en fin de compte
♦ *adv*: **~ alone** tout(e) seul(e); **it's not as hard as ~ that** ce n'est pas si difficile que ça; **~ the more/the better** d'autant plus/mieux; **~ but** presque, pratiquement; **to be ~ in** (*BRIT col*) être complètement à plat; **~ out** *adv* à fond; **the score is 2 ~** le score est de 2 partout.

all-around [ɔːlə'raund] *adj* (*US*) = **all-round**.
allay [ə'leɪ] *vt* (*fears*) apaiser, calmer.
all clear *n* (*also fig*) fin *f* d'alerte.
allegation [ælɪ'geɪʃən] *n* allégation *f*.
allege [ə'lɛdʒ] *vt* alléguer, prétendre; **he is ~d to have said** il aurait dit.
alleged [ə'lɛdʒd] *adj* prétendu(e).
allegedly [ə'lɛdʒɪdlɪ] *adv* à ce que l'on prétend, paraît-il.
allegiance [ə'liːdʒəns] *n* fidélité *f*, obéissance *f*.
allegory ['ælɪgərɪ] *n* allégorie *f*.
all-embracing ['ɔːlɪm'breɪsɪŋ] *adj* universel(le).
allergic [ə'ləːdʒɪk] *adj*: **~ to** allergique à.
allergy ['ælədʒɪ] *n* allergie *f*.
alleviate [ə'liːvɪeɪt] *vt* soulager, adoucir.
alley ['ælɪ] *n* ruelle *f*; (*in garden*) allée *f*.
alleyway ['ælɪweɪ] *n* ruelle *f*.
alliance [ə'laɪəns] *n* alliance *f*.
allied ['ælaɪd] *adj* allié(e).
alligator ['ælɪgeɪtə*] *n* alligator *m*.
all-important ['ɔːlɪm'pɔːtənt] *adj* capital(e), crucial(e).
all-in ['ɔːlɪn] *adj, adv* (*BRIT: charge*) tout compris.
all-in wrestling *n* (*BRIT*) catch *m*.
alliteration [əlɪtə'reɪʃən] *n* allitération *f*.
all-night ['ɔːl'naɪt] *adj* ouvert(e) *or* qui dure toute la nuit.
allocate ['æləkeɪt] *vt* (*share out*) répartir, distribuer; (*duties*): **to ~ sth to** assigner *or* attribuer qch à; (*sum, time*): **to ~ sth to** allouer qch à; **to ~ sth for** affecter qch à.
allocation [æləu'keɪʃən] *n* (*see vb*) répartition *f*; attribution *f*; allocation *f*; affectation *f*; (*money*) crédit(s) *m(pl)*, somme(s) allouée(s).
allot [ə'lɔt] *vt* (*share out*) répartir, distribuer; (*time*): **to ~ sth to** allouer qch à; (*duties*): **to ~ sth to** assigner qch à; **in the ~ted time** dans le temps imparti.
allotment [ə'lɔtmənt] *n* (*share*) part *f*; (*garden*) lopin *m* de terre (*loué à la municipalité*).
all-out ['ɔːlaut] *adj* (*effort etc*) total(e).
allow [ə'lau] *vt* (*practice, behaviour*) permettre, autoriser; (*sum to spend etc*) accorder, allouer; (*sum, time estimated*) compter, prévoir; (*concede*): **to ~ that** convenir que; **to ~ sb to do** permettre à qn de faire, autoriser qn à faire; **he is ~ed to ...** on lui permet de ...; **smoking is not ~ed** il est interdit de fumer; **we must ~ 3 days for the journey** il faut compter 3 jours pour le voyage.
►**allow for** *vt fus* tenir compte de.
allowance [ə'lauəns] *n* (*money received*) allocation *f*; (*: from parent etc*) subside *m*; (*: for expenses*) indemnité *f*; (*TAX*) somme *f* déductible du revenu imposable, abattement *m*; **to make ~s for** tenir compte de.
alloy ['ælɔɪ] *n* alliage *m*.
all right *adv* (*feel, work*) bien; (*as answer*) d'accord.
all-round ['ɔːl'raund] *adj* compétent(e) dans tous les domaines; (*athlete etc*) complet(ète).
all-rounder [ɔːl'raundə*] *n* (*BRIT*): **to be a good ~** être doué(e) en tout.
allspice ['ɔːlspaɪs] *n* poivre *m* de la Jamaïque.
all-time ['ɔːl'taɪm] *adj* (*record*) sans précédent, absolu(e).
allude [ə'luːd] *vi*: **to ~ to** faire allusion à.

alluring [ə'ljuərɪŋ] *adj* séduisant(e), alléchant(e).
allusion [ə'luːʒən] *n* allusion *f*.
alluvium [ə'luːvɪəm] *n* alluvions *fpl*.
ally *n* ['ælaɪ] allié *m* ♦ *vt* [ə'laɪ]: **to ~ o.s. with** s'allier avec.
almighty [ɔːl'maɪtɪ] *adj* tout-puissant.
almond ['ɑːmənd] *n* amande *f*.
almost ['ɔːlməust] *adv* presque; **he ~ fell** il a failli tomber.
alms [ɑːmz] *n* aumône(s) *f(pl)*.
aloft [ə'lɔft] *adv* en haut, en l'air; (*NAUT*) dans la mâture.
alone [ə'ləun] *adj*, *adv* seul(e); **to leave sb ~** laisser qn tranquille; **to leave sth ~** ne pas toucher à qch; **let ~** ... sans parler de ...; encore moins ....
along [ə'lɔŋ] *prep* le long de ♦ *adv*: **is he coming ~?** vient-il avec nous?; **he was hopping/limping ~** il venait *or* avançait en sautillant/boitant; **~ with** avec, en plus de; (*person*) en compagnie de.
alongside [ə'lɔŋ'saɪd] *prep* le long de; au côté de ♦ *adv* bord à bord; côte à côte; **we brought our boat ~** (*of a pier, shore etc*) nous avons accosté.
aloof [ə'luːf] *adj*, *adv* à distance, à l'écart; **to stand ~** se tenir à l'écart *or* à distance.
aloofness [ə'luːfnɪs] *n* réserve (hautaine), attitude distante.
aloud [ə'laud] *adv* à haute voix.
alphabet ['ælfəbɛt] *n* alphabet *m*.
alphabetical [ælfə'bɛtɪkl] *adj* alphabétique; **in ~ order** par ordre alphabétique.
alphanumeric [ælfənjuː'mɛrɪk] *adj* alphanumérique.
alpine ['ælpaɪn] *adj* alpin(e), alpestre; **~ hut** cabane *f or* refuge *m* de montagne; **~ pasture** pâturage *m* (de montagne).
Alps [ælps] *npl*: **the ~** les Alpes *fpl*.
already [ɔːl'rɛdɪ] *adv* déjà.
alright ['ɔːl'raɪt] *adv* (*BRIT*) = **all right.**
Alsace [æl'sæs] *n* Alsace *f*.
Alsatian [æl'seɪʃən] *adj* alsacien(ne), d'Alsace ♦ *n* Alsacien/ne; (*BRIT*: *dog*) berger allemand.
also ['ɔːlsəu] *adv* aussi.
Alta. *abbr* (*Canada*) = *Alberta.*
altar ['ɔltə*] *n* autel *m*.
alter ['ɔltə*] *vt*, *vi* changer, modifier.
alteration [ɔltə'reɪʃən] *n* changement *m*, modification *f*; **~s** (*SEWING*) retouches *fpl*; (*ARCHIT*) modifications *fpl*; **timetable subject to ~** horaires sujets à modifications.
altercation [ɔltə'keɪʃən] *n* altercation *f*.
alternate *adj* [ɔl'təːnɪt] alterné(e), alternant(e), alternatif(ive) ♦ *vi* ['ɔltəːneɪt] alterner; **on ~ days** un jour sur deux, tous les deux jours.
alternately [ɔl'təːnɪtlɪ] *adv* alternativement, en alternant.
alternating ['ɔltəːneɪtɪŋ] *adj* (*current*) alternatif(ive).
alternative [ɔl'təːnətɪv] *adj* (*solutions*) interchangeable, possible; (*solution*) autre, de remplacement; (*energy*) doux(douce); (*society*) parallèle ♦ *n* (*choice*) alternative *f*; (*other possibility*) autre possibilité *f*.
alternatively [ɔl'təːnətɪvlɪ] *adv*: **~ one could** une autre *or* l'autre solution serait de.
alternative medicine *n* médecines *fpl* parallèles *or* douces.
alternator ['ɔltəːneɪtə*] *n* (*AUT*) alternateur *m*.
although [ɔːl'ðəu] *conj* bien que + *sub*.
altitude ['æltɪtjuːd] *n* altitude *f*.
alto ['æltəu] *n* (*female*) contralto *m*; (*male*) haute-contre *f*.
altogether [ɔːltə'gɛðə*] *adv* entièrement, tout à fait; (*on the whole*) tout compte fait; (*in all*) en tout; **how much is that ~?** ça fait combien en tout?
altruism ['æltruɪzəm] *n* altruisme *m*.
altruistic [æltru'ɪstɪk] *adj* altruiste.
aluminium [ælju'mɪnɪəm], (*US*) **aluminum** [ə'luːmɪnəm] *n* aluminium *m*.
alumna, *pl* **alumnae** [ə'lʌmnə, -niː] *n* (*US*: *SCOL*) ancienne élève; (: *UNIVERSITY*) ancienne étudiante.
alumnus, *pl* **alumni** [ə'lʌmnəs, -naɪ] *n* (*US*: *SCOL*) ancien élève; (: *UNIVERSITY*) ancien étudiant.
always ['ɔːlweɪz] *adv* toujours.
Alzheimer's disease ['æltshaɪməz-] *n* maladie *f* d'Alzheimer.
AM *abbr* = *amplitude modulation* ♦ *n abbr* (= *Assembly Member*) député *m* au Parlement gallois.
am [æm] *vb see* **be**.
a.m. *adv abbr* (= *ante meridiem*) du matin.
AMA *n abbr* = *American Medical Association.*
amalgam [ə'mælgəm] *n* amalgame *m*.
amalgamate [ə'mælgəmeɪt] *vt*, *vi* fusionner.
amalgamation [əmælgə'meɪʃən] *n* fusion *f*; (*COMM*) fusionnement *m*.
amass [ə'mæs] *vt* amasser.
amateur ['æmətə*] *n* amateur *m* ♦ *adj* (*SPORT*) amateur *inv*; **~ dramatics** le théâtre amateur.
amateurish ['æmətərɪʃ] *adj* (*pej*) d'amateur, un peu amateur.
amaze [ə'meɪz] *vt* surprendre, étonner; **to be ~d (at)** être surpris *or* étonné (de).
amazement [ə'meɪzmənt] *n* surprise *f*, étonnement *m*.
amazing [ə'meɪzɪŋ] *adj* étonnant(e), incroyable; (*bargain, offer*) exceptionnel(le).
amazingly [ə'meɪzɪŋlɪ] *adv* incroyablement.
Amazon ['æməzən] *n* (*GEO, MYTHOLOGY*) Amazone *f* ♦ *cpd* amazonien(ne), de l'Amazone; **the ~ basin** le bassin de l'Amazone; **the ~ jungle** la forêt amazonienne.
Amazonian [æmə'zəunɪən] *adj* amazonien(ne).
ambassador [æm'bæsədə*] *n* ambassadeur *m*.
amber ['æmbə*] *n* ambre *m*; **at ~** (*BRIT AUT*) à l'orange.
ambidextrous [æmbɪ'dɛkstrəs] *adj* ambidex-

tre.
ambience ['æmbıəns] *n* ambiance *f*.
ambiguity [æmbı'gjuıtı] *n* ambiguïté *f*.
ambiguous [æm'bıgjuəs] *adj* ambigu(ë).
ambition [æm'bıʃən] *n* ambition *f*.
ambitious [æm'bıʃəs] *adj* ambitieux(euse).
ambivalent [æm'bıvələnt] *adj* (*attitude*) ambivalent(e).
amble ['æmbl] *vi* (*also*: **to ~ along**) aller d'un pas tranquille.
ambulance ['æmbjuləns] *n* ambulance *f*.
ambush ['æmbuʃ] *n* embuscade *f* ♦ *vt* tendre une embuscade à.
ameba [ə'mi:bə] *n* (*US*) = **amoeba**.
ameliorate [ə'mi:lıəreıt] *vt* améliorer.
amen ['ɑ:'mɛn] *excl* amen.
amenable [ə'mi:nəbl] *adj*: **~ to** (*advice etc*) disposé(e) à écouter *or* suivre; **~ to the law** responsable devant la loi.
amend [ə'mɛnd] *vt* (*law*) amender; (*text*) corriger; (*habits*) réformer ♦ *vi* s'amender, se corriger; **to make ~s** réparer ses torts, faire amende honorable.
amendment [ə'mɛndmənt] *n* (*to law*) amendement *m*; (*to text*) correction *f*.
amenities [ə'mi:nıtız] *npl* aménagements *mpl*, équipements *mpl*.
amenity [ə'mi:nıtı] *n* charme *m*, agrément *m*.
America [ə'mɛrıkə] *n* Amérique *f*.
American [ə'mɛrıkən] *adj* américain(e) ♦ *n* Américain/e.
americanize [ə'mɛrıkənaız] *vt* américaniser.
amethyst ['æmıθıst] *n* améthyste *f*.
Amex ['æmɛks] *n abbr* = *American Stock Exchange*.
amiable ['eımıəbl] *adj* aimable, affable.
amicable ['æmıkəbl] *adj* amical(e).
amicably ['æmıkəblı] *adv* amicalement.
amid(st) [ə'mıd(st)] *prep* parmi, au milieu de.
amiss [ə'mıs] *adj*, *adv*: **there's something ~** il y a quelque chose qui ne va pas *or* qui cloche; **to take sth ~** prendre qch mal *or* de travers.
ammo ['æməu] *n abbr* (*col*) = **ammunition**.
ammonia [ə'məunıə] *n* (*gas*) ammoniac *m*; (*liquid*) ammoniaque *f*.
ammunition [æmju'nıʃən] *n* munitions *fpl*; (*fig*) arguments *mpl*.
ammunition dump *n* dépôt *m* de munitions.
amnesia [æm'ni:zıə] *n* amnésie *f*.
amnesty ['æmnıstı] *n* amnistie *f*; **to grant an ~ to** accorder une amnistie à.
Amnesty International *n* Amnesty International.
amoeba, (*US*) **ameba** [ə'mi:bə] *n* amibe *f*.
amok [ə'mɔk] *adv*: **to run ~** être pris(e) d'un accès de folie furieuse.
among(st) [ə'mʌŋ(st)] *prep* parmi, entre.
amoral [æ'mɔrəl] *adj* amoral(e).
amorous ['æmərəs] *adj* amoureux(euse).
amorphous [ə'mɔ:fəs] *adj* amorphe.
amortization [əmɔ:taı'zeıʃən] *n* (*COMM*) amortissement *m*.
amount [ə'maunt] *n* (*sum of money*) somme *f*; (*total*) montant *m*; (*quantity*) quantité *f*; nombre *m* ♦ *vi*: **to ~ to** (*total*) s'élever à; (*be same as*) équivaloir à, revenir à; **this ~s to a refusal** cela équivaut à un refus; **the total ~** (*of money*) le montant total.
amp(ere) ['æmp(ɛə*)] *n* ampère *m*; **a 13 amp plug** une fiche de 13 A.
ampersand ['æmpəsænd] *n* signe &, "et" commercial.
amphetamine [æm'fɛtəmi:n] *n* amphétamine *f*.
amphibian [æm'fıbıən] *n* batracien *m*.
amphibious [æm'fıbıəs] *adj* amphibie.
amphitheatre, (*US*) **amphitheater** ['æmfıθıətə*] *n* amphithéâtre *m*.
ample ['æmpl] *adj* ample; spacieux(euse); (*enough*): **this is ~** c'est largement suffisant; **to have ~ time/room** avoir bien assez de temps/place, avoir largement le temps/la place.
amplifier ['æmplıfaıə*] *n* amplificateur *m*.
amplify ['æmplıfaı] *vt* amplifier.
amply ['æmplı] *adv* amplement, largement.
ampoule, (*US*) **ampule** ['æmpu:l] *n* (*MED*) ampoule *f*.
amputate ['æmpjuteıt] *vt* amputer.
amputee [æmpju'ti:] *n* amputé/e.
Amsterdam ['æmstədæm] *n* Amsterdam.
amt *abbr* = **amount**.
amuck [ə'mʌk] *adv* = **amok**.
amuse [ə'mju:z] *vt* amuser; **to ~ o.s. with sth/by doing sth** se divertir avec qch/à faire qch; **to be ~d at** être amusé par; **he was not ~d** il n'a pas apprécié.
amusement [ə'mju:zmənt] *n* amusement *m*.
amusement arcade *n* salle *f* de jeu.
amusement park *n* parc *m* d'attractions.
amusing [ə'mju:zıŋ] *adj* amusant(e), divertissant(e).
an [æn, ən, n] *indef art see* **a**.
ANA *n abbr* = *American Newspaper Association*; *American Nurses Association*.
anachronism [ə'nækrənızəm] *n* anachronisme *m*.
anaemia [ə'ni:mıə] *n* anémie *f*.
anaemic [ə'ni:mık] *adj* anémique.
anaesthetic [ænıs'θɛtık] *adj*, *n* anesthésique (*m*); **under the ~** sous anesthésie; **local/general ~** anesthésie locale/générale.
anaesthetist [æ'ni:sθıtıst] *n* anesthésiste *m/f*.
anagram ['ænəgræm] *n* anagramme *m*.
anal ['eınl] *adj* anal(e).
analgesic [ænæl'dʒi:sık] *adj*, *n* analgésique (*m*).
analogous [ə'næləgəs] *adj*: **~ (to** *or* **with)** analogue (à).
analog(ue) ['ænəlɔg] *adj* (*watch, computer*) analogique.
analogy [ə'nælədʒı] *n* analogie *f*; **to draw an ~ between** établir une analogie entre.
analyse ['ænəlaız] *vt* (*BRIT*) analyser.

analysis, *pl* **analyses** [ə'næləsɪs, -siːz] *n* analyse *f*; **in the last** ~ en dernière analyse.
analyst ['ænəlɪst] *n* (*political* ~ *etc*) analyste *m/f*; (*US*) psychanalyste *m/f*.
analytic(al) [ænə'lɪtɪk(əl)] *adj* analytique.
analyze ['ænəlaɪz] *vt* (*US*) = **analyse**.
anarchic [æ'nɑːkɪk] *adj* anarchique.
anarchist ['ænəkɪst] *adj, n* anarchiste *(m/f)*.
anarchy ['ænəkɪ] *n* anarchie *f*.
anathema [ə'næθɪmə] *n*: **it is** ~ **to him** il a cela en abomination.
anatomical [ænə'tɔmɪkəl] *adj* anatomique.
anatomy [ə'nætəmɪ] *n* anatomie *f*.
ANC *n abbr* (= *African National Congress*) ANC *m*.
ancestor ['ænsɪstə*] *n* ancêtre *m*, aïeul *m*.
ancestral [æn'sɛstrəl] *adj* ancestral(e).
ancestry ['ænsɪstrɪ] *n* ancêtres *mpl*; ascendance *f*.
anchor ['æŋkə*] *n* ancre *f* ♦ *vi* (*also*: **to drop** ~) jeter l'ancre, mouiller ♦ *vt* mettre à l'ancre.
anchorage ['æŋkərɪdʒ] *n* mouillage *m*, ancrage *m*.
anchor man, anchor woman *n* (*TV, RADIO*) présentateur/trice.
anchovy ['æntʃəvɪ] *n* anchois *m*.
ancient ['eɪnʃənt] *adj* ancien(ne), antique; (*fig*) d'un âge vénérable, antique; ~ **monument** monument *m* historique.
ancillary [æn'sɪlərɪ] *adj* auxiliaire.
and [ænd] *conj* et; ~ **so on** et ainsi de suite; **try** ~ **come** tâchez de venir; **come** ~ **sit here** venez vous asseoir ici; **better** ~ **better** de mieux en mieux; **more** ~ **more** de plus en plus.
Andes ['ændiːz] *npl*: **the** ~ les Andes *fpl*.
anecdote ['ænɪkdəut] *n* anecdote *f*.
anemia [ə'niːmɪə] *n* = **anaemia**.
anemic [ə'niːmɪk] *adj* = **anaemic**.
anemone [ə'nɛmənɪ] *n* (*BOT*) anémone *f*; **sea** ~ anémone de mer.
anesthesiologist [ænɪsθiːzɪ'ɔlədʒɪst] *n* (*US*) anesthésiste *m/f*.
anesthetic [ænɪs'θɛtɪk] *adj, n* = **anaesthetic**.
anesthetist [æ'niːsθɪtɪst] *n* = **anaesthetist**.
anew [ə'njuː] *adv* à nouveau.
angel ['eɪndʒəl] *n* ange *m*.
angel dust *n* poussière *f* d'ange.
anger ['æŋgə*] *n* colère *f* ♦ *vt* mettre en colère, irriter.
angina [æn'dʒaɪnə] *n* angine *f* de poitrine.
angle ['æŋgl] *n* angle *m* ♦ *vi*: **to** ~ **for** (*trout*) pêcher; (*compliments*) chercher, quêter; **from their** ~ de leur point de vue.
angler ['æŋglə*] *n* pêcheur/euse à la ligne.
Anglican ['æŋglɪkən] *adj, n* anglican(e).
anglicize ['æŋglɪsaɪz] *vt* angliciser.
angling ['æŋglɪŋ] *n* pêche *f* à la ligne.
Anglo- ['æŋgləu] *prefix* anglo(-).
Anglo-French ['æŋgləu'frɛntʃ] *adj* anglo-français(e).
Anglo-Saxon ['æŋgləu'sæksən] *adj, n* anglo-saxon(ne).
Angola [æŋ'gəulə] *n* Angola *m*.
Angolan [æŋ'gəulən] *adj* angolais(e) ♦ *n* Angolais/e.
angrily ['æŋgrɪlɪ] *adv* avec colère.
angry ['æŋgrɪ] *adj* en colère, furieux(euse); **to be** ~ **with sb/at sth** être furieux contre qn/de qch; **to get** ~ se fâcher, se mettre en colère; **to make sb** ~ mettre qn en colère.
anguish ['æŋgwɪʃ] *n* angoisse *f*.
anguished ['æŋgwɪʃt] *adj* (*mentally*) angoissé(e); (*physically*) plein(e) de souffrance.
angular ['æŋgjulə*] *adj* anguleux(euse).
animal ['ænɪməl] *n* animal *m* ♦ *adj* animal(e).
animal rights *npl* droits *mpl* de l'animal.
animate *vt* ['ænɪmeɪt] animer ♦ *adj* ['ænɪmɪt] animé(e), vivant(e).
animated ['ænɪmeɪtɪd] *adj* animé(e).
animation [ænɪ'meɪʃən] *n* (*of person*) entrain *m*; (*of street, CINE*) animation *f*.
animosity [ænɪ'mɔsɪtɪ] *n* animosité *f*.
aniseed ['ænɪsiːd] *n* anis *m*.
Ankara ['æŋkərə] *n* Ankara.
ankle ['æŋkl] *n* cheville *f*.
ankle socks *npl* socquettes *fpl*.
annex *n* ['ænɛks] (*also*: *BRIT*: **annexe**) annexe *f* ♦ *vt* [ə'nɛks] annexer.
annexation [ænɛks'eɪʃən] *n* annexion *f*.
annihilate [ə'naɪəleɪt] *vt* annihiler, anéantir.
annihilation [ənaɪə'leɪʃən] *n* anéantissement *m*.
anniversary [ænɪ'vəːsərɪ] *n* anniversaire *m*.
anniversary dinner *n* dîner commémoratif *or* anniversaire.
annotate ['ænəuteɪt] *vt* annoter.
announce [ə'nauns] *vt* annoncer; (*birth, death*) faire part de; **he** ~**d that he wasn't going** il a déclaré qu'il n'irait pas.
announcement [ə'naunsmənt] *n* annonce *f*; (*for births etc: in newspaper*) avis *m* de faire-part; (*: letter, card*) faire-part *m*; **I'd like to make an** ~ j'ai une communication à faire.
announcer [ə'naunsə*] *n* (*RADIO, TV*: *between programmes*) speaker/ine; (*: in a programme*) présentateur/trice.
annoy [ə'nɔɪ] *vt* agacer, ennuyer, contrarier; **to be** ~**ed (at sth/with sb)** être en colère *or* irrité (contre qch/qn); **don't get** ~**ed!** ne vous fâchez pas!
annoyance [ə'nɔɪəns] *n* mécontentement *m*, contrariété *f*.
annoying [ə'nɔɪɪŋ] *adj* ennuyeux(euse), agaçant(e), contrariant(e).
annual ['ænjuəl] *adj* annuel(le) ♦ *n* (*BOT*) plante annuelle; (*book*) album *m*.
annual general meeting (AGM) *n* (*BRIT*) assemblée générale annuelle (AGA).
annually ['ænjuəlɪ] *adv* annuellement.
annual report *n* rapport annuel.
annuity [ə'njuːɪtɪ] *n* rente *f*; **life** ~ rente viagère.
annul [ə'nʌl] *vt* annuler; (*law*) abroger.

annulment [ə'nʌlmənt] *n* (*see vb*) annulation *f*; abrogation *f*.
annum ['ænəm] *n see* **per annum**.
Annunciation [ənʌnsɪ'eɪʃən] *n* Annonciation *f*.
anode ['ænəud] *n* anode *f*.
anoint [ə'nɔɪnt] *vt* oindre.
anomalous [ə'nɔmələs] *adj* anormal(e).
anomaly [ə'nɔməlɪ] *n* anomalie *f*.
anon. [ə'nɔn] *abbr* = **anonymous**.
anonymity [ænə'nɪmɪtɪ] *n* anonymat *m*.
anonymous [ə'nɔnɪməs] *adj* anonyme; **to remain ~** garder l'anonymat.
anorak ['ænəræk] *n* anorak *m*.
anorexia [ænə'rɛksɪə] *n* (*also*: **~ nervosa**) anorexie *f*.
anorexic [ænə'rɛksɪk] *adj*, *n* anorexique (*m/f*).
another [ə'nʌðə*] *adj*: **~ book** (*one more*) un autre livre, encore un livre, un livre de plus; (*a different one*) un autre livre; **~ drink?** encore un verre?; **in ~ 5 years** dans 5 ans ♦ *pron* un(e) autre, encore un(e), un(e) de plus; *see also* **one**.
ANSI ['ænsɪ] *n abbr* (= *American National Standards Institution*) ANSI *m* (*Institut américain de normalisation*).
answer ['ɑːnsə*] *n* réponse *f*; (*to problem*) solution *f* ♦ *vi* répondre ♦ *vt* (*reply to*) répondre à; (*problem*) résoudre; (*prayer*) exaucer; **to ~ the phone** répondre (au téléphone); **in ~ to your letter** suite à *or* en réponse à votre lettre; **to ~ the bell** *or* **the door** aller *or* venir ouvrir (la porte).
►**answer back** *vi* répondre, répliquer.
►**answer for** *vt fus* répondre de, se porter garant de; (*crime, one's actions*) répondre de.
►**answer to** *vt fus* (*description*) répondre *or* correspondre à.
answerable ['ɑːnsərəbl] *adj*: **~ (to sb/for sth)** responsable (devant qn/de qch); **I am ~ to no-one** je n'ai de comptes à rendre à personne.
answering machine ['ɑːnsərɪŋ-] *n* répondeur *m*.
ant [ænt] *n* fourmi *f*.
ANTA *n abbr* = *American National Theater and Academy*.
antagonism [æn'tægənɪzəm] *n* antagonisme *m*.
antagonist [æn'tægənɪst] *n* antagoniste *m/f*, adversaire *m/f*.
antagonistic [æntægə'nɪstɪk] *adj* (*attitude, feelings*) hostile.
antagonize [æn'tægənaɪz] *vt* éveiller l'hostilité de, contrarier.
Antarctic [ænt'ɑːktɪk] *adj* antarctique, austral(e) ♦ *n*: **the ~** l'Antarctique *m*.
Antarctica [ænt'ɑːktɪkə] *n* Antarctique *m*, Terres Australes.
Antarctic Circle *n* cercle *m* Antarctique.
Antarctic Ocean *n* océan *m* Antarctique *or* Austral.
ante ['æntɪ] *n*: **to up the ~** faire monter les enjeux.
ante... ['æntɪ] *prefix* anté..., anti..., pré....
anteater ['æntiːtə*] *n* fourmilier *m*, tamanoir *m*.
antecedent [æntɪ'siːdənt] *n* antécédent *m*.
antechamber ['æntɪtʃeɪmbə*] *n* antichambre *f*.
antelope ['æntɪləup] *n* antilope *f*.
antenatal ['æntɪ'neɪtl] *adj* prénatal(e).
antenatal clinic *n* service *m* de consultation prénatale.
antenna, *pl* **~e** [æn'tɛnə, -niː] *n* antenne *f*.
anthem ['ænθəm] *n* motet *m*; **national ~** hymne national.
ant-hill ['ænthɪl] *n* fourmilière *f*.
anthology [æn'θɔlədʒɪ] *n* anthologie *f*.
anthropologist [ænθrə'pɔlədʒɪst] *n* anthropologue *m/f*.
anthropology [ænθrə'pɔlədʒɪ] *n* anthropologie *f*.
anti- ['æntɪ] *prefix* anti-.
anti-aircraft ['æntɪ'ɛəkrɑːft] *adj* anti-aérien(ne).
anti-aircraft defence *n* défense *f* contre avions, DCA *f*.
antiballistic ['æntɪbə'lɪstɪk] *adj* antibalistique.
antibiotic ['æntɪbaɪ'ɔtɪk] *adj*, *n* antibiotique (*m*).
antibody ['æntɪbɔdɪ] *n* anticorps *m*.
anticipate [æn'tɪsɪpeɪt] *vt* s'attendre à, prévoir; (*wishes, request*) aller au devant de, devancer; **this is worse than I ~d** c'est pire que je ne pensais; **as ~d** comme prévu.
anticipation [æntɪsɪ'peɪʃən] *n* attente *f*; **thanking you in ~** en vous remerciant d'avance, avec mes remerciements anticipés.
anticlimax ['æntɪ'klaɪmæks] *n réalisation décevante d'un événement que l'on escomptait important, intéressant etc.*
anticlockwise ['æntɪ'klɔkwaɪz] *adj* dans le sens inverse des aiguilles d'une montre.
antics ['æntɪks] *npl* singeries *fpl*.
anticyclone ['æntɪ'saɪkləun] *n* anticyclone *m*.
antidepressant ['æntɪdɪ'prɛsnt] *n* antidépresseur *m*.
antidote ['æntɪdəut] *n* antidote *m*, contrepoison *m*.
antifreeze ['æntɪfriːz] *n* antigel *m*.
anti-globalization ['æntɪgləubəlaɪzeɪʃən] *n* antimondialisation *f*.
antihistamine [æntɪ'hɪstəmɪn] *n* antihistaminique *m*.
Antilles [æn'tɪliːz] *npl*: **the ~** les Antilles *fpl*.
antipathy [æn'tɪpəθɪ] *n* antipathie *f*.
antiperspirant [æntɪ'pəːspɪrənt] *n* déodorant *m* anti-transpiration.
Antipodean [æntɪpə'diːən] *adj* australien(ne) et néozélandais(e), d'Australie et de Nouvelle-Zélande.
Antipodes [æn'tɪpədiːz] *npl*: **the ~** l'Australie *f* et la Nouvelle-Zélande.
antiquarian [æntɪ'kwɛərɪən] *adj*: **~ bookshop** librairie *f* d'ouvrages anciens ♦ *n* expert *m* en objets *or* livres anciens; amateur *m* d'antiquités.
antiquated ['æntɪkweɪtɪd] *adj* vieilli(e), suran-

né(e), vieillot(te).
antique [æn'tiːk] *n* objet *m* d'art ancien, meuble ancien *or* d'époque, antiquité *f* ♦ *adj* ancien(ne); (*pre-mediaeval*) antique.
antique dealer *n* antiquaire *m/f*.
antique shop *n* magasin *m* d'antiquités.
antiquity [æn'tɪkwɪtɪ] *n* antiquité *f*.
anti-Semitic ['æntɪsɪ'mɪtɪk] *adj* antisémite.
anti-Semitism ['æntɪ'sɛmɪtɪzəm] *n* antisémitisme *m*.
antiseptic [æntɪ'sɛptɪk] *adj, n* antiseptique *(m)*.
antisocial ['æntɪ'səuʃəl] *adj* peu liant(e), insociable; (*against society*) antisocial(e).
antitank [æntɪ'tæŋk] *adj* antichar.
antithesis, *pl* **antitheses** [æn'tɪθɪsɪs, -siːz] *n* antithèse *f*.
antitrust [æntɪ'trʌst] *adj*: ~ **legislation** loi *f* anti-trust.
antlers ['æntləz] *npl* bois *mpl*, ramure *f*.
Antwerp ['æntwəːp] *n* Anvers.
anus ['eɪnəs] *n* anus *m*.
anvil ['ænvɪl] *n* enclume *f*.
anxiety [æŋ'zaɪətɪ] *n* anxiété *f*; (*keenness*): ~ **to do** grand désir *or* impatience *f* de faire.
anxious ['æŋkʃəs] *adj* anxieux(euse), (très) inquiet(ète); (*keen*): ~ **to do/that** qui tient beaucoup à faire/à ce que; impatient(e) de faire/que; **I'm very** ~ **about you** je me fais beaucoup de souci pour toi.
anxiously ['æŋkʃəslɪ] *adv* anxieusement.

KEYWORD

any ['ɛnɪ] *adj* **1** (*in questions etc: singular*) du, de l', de la; (*in questions etc: plural*) des; **have you** ~ **butter/children/ink?** avez-vous du beurre/des enfants/de l'encre?
2 (*with negative*) de, d'; **I haven't** ~ **money/books** je n'ai pas d'argent/de livres; **without** ~ **difficulty** sans la moindre difficulté
3 (*no matter which*) n'importe quel(le), quelconque; (*each and every*) tout(e), chaque; **choose** ~ **book you like** vous pouvez choisir n'importe quel livre
4 (*in phrases*): **in** ~ **case** de toute façon; ~ **day now** d'un jour à l'autre; **at** ~ **moment** à tout moment, d'un instant à l'autre; **at** ~ **rate** en tout cas
♦ *pron* **1** (*in questions etc*) en; **have you got** ~**?** est-ce que vous en avez?; **can** ~ **of you sing?** est-ce que parmi vous il y en a qui savent chanter?
2 (*with negative*) en; **I haven't** ~ **(of them)** je n'en ai pas, je n'en ai aucun
3 (*no matter which one(s)*) n'importe lequel (*or* laquelle); (*anybody*) n'importe qui; **take** ~ **of those books (you like)** vous pouvez prendre n'importe lequel de ces livres
♦ *adv* **1** (*in questions etc*): **do you want** ~ **more soup/sandwiches?** voulez-vous encore de la soupe/des sandwichs?; **are you feeling** ~ **better?** est-ce que vous vous sentez mieux?
2 (*with negative*): **I can't hear him** ~ **more** je ne l'entends plus; **don't wait** ~ **longer** n'attendez pas plus longtemps.

anybody ['ɛnɪbɔdɪ] *pron* n'importe qui; (*in interrogative sentences*) quelqu'un; (*in negative sentences*): **I don't see** ~ je ne vois personne.
anyhow ['ɛnɪhau] *adv* quoi qu'il en soit; (*haphazardly*) n'importe comment; **I shall go** ~ j'irai de toute façon.
anyone ['ɛnɪwʌn] = **anybody**.
anyplace ['ɛnɪpleɪs] *adv* (*US*) = **anywhere**.
anything ['ɛnɪθɪŋ] *pron* n'importe quoi; (*in interrogative sentences*) quelque chose; (*in negative sentences*): **I don't want** ~ je ne veux rien; ~ **else?** (*in shop*) et avec ça?; **it can cost** ~ **between £15 and £20** (*BRIT*) ça peut coûter dans les 15 à 20 livres.
anytime ['ɛnɪtaɪm] *adv* n'importe quand.
anyway ['ɛnɪweɪ] *adv* de toute façon.
anywhere ['ɛnɪwɛə*] *adv* n'importe où; (*in interrogative sentences*) quelque part; (*in negative sentences*): **I don't see him** ~ je ne le vois nulle part.
Anzac ['ænzæk] *n abbr* (= *Australia-New Zealand Army Corps*) *soldat du corps ANZAC*.
Anzac Day *n voir encadré*.

ANZAC DAY

Anzac Day *est le 25 avril, jour férié en Australie et en Nouvelle-Zélande commémorant le débarquement des soldats du corps "ANZAC" à Gallipoli en 1915, pendant la Première Guerre mondiale. Ce fut la plus célèbre des campagnes du corps "ANZAC".*

apart [ə'pɑːt] *adv* (*to one side*) à part; de côté; à l'écart; (*separately*) séparément; **10 miles/a long way** ~ à 10 milles/très éloignés l'un de l'autre; ~ **from** *prep* à part, excepté.
apartheid [ə'pɑːteɪt] *n* apartheid *m*.
apartment [ə'pɑːtmənt] *n* (*US*) appartement *m*, logement *m*.
apartment building *n* (*US*) immeuble *m*; maison divisée en appartements.
apathetic [æpə'θɛtɪk] *adj* apathique, indifférent(e).
apathy ['æpəθɪ] *n* apathie *f*, indifférence *f*.
APB *n abbr* (*US: = all points bulletin*) *expression de la police signifiant "découvrir et appréhender le suspect"*.
ape [eɪp] *n* (grand) singe ♦ *vt* singer.
Apennines ['æpənaɪnz] *npl*: **the** ~ les Apennins *mpl*.
apéritif [ə'pɛrɪtiːf] *n* apéritif *m*.
aperture ['æpətʃjuə*] *n* orifice *m*, ouverture *f*; (*PHOT*) ouverture (du diaphragme).
APEX ['eɪpɛks] *n abbr* (*AVIAT: = advance purchase excursion*) APEX *m*.
apex ['eɪpɛks] *n* sommet *m*.
aphid ['eɪfɪd] *n* puceron *m*.

aphrodisiac [æfrəu'dɪzɪæk] *adj, n* aphrodisiaque *(m).*
API *n abbr = American Press Institute.*
apiece [ə'pi:s] *adv (for each person)* chacun(e), par tête; *(for each item)* chacun(e), (la) pièce.
aplomb [ə'plɔm] *n* sang-froid *m*, assurance *f.*
APO *n abbr (US: = Army Post Office) service postal de l'armée.*
apocalypse [ə'pɔkəlɪps] *n* apocalypse *f.*
apolitical [eɪpə'lɪtɪkl] *adj* apolitique.
apologetic [əpɔlə'dʒɛtɪk] *adj (tone, letter)* d'excuse; **to be very ~ about** s'excuser vivement de.
apologetically [əpɔlə'dʒɛtɪkəlɪ] *adv (say)* en s'excusant.
apologize [ə'pɔlədʒaɪz] *vi*: **to ~ (for sth to sb)** s'excuser (de qch auprès de qn), présenter des excuses (à qn pour qch).
apology [ə'pɔlədʒɪ] *n* excuses *fpl*; **to send one's apologies** envoyer une lettre *or* un mot d'excuse, s'excuser (de ne pas pouvoir venir); **please accept my apologies** vous voudrez bien m'excuser.
apoplectic [æpə'plɛktɪk] *adj (MED)* apoplectique; *(col)*: **~ with rage** fou(folle) de rage.
apoplexy ['æpəplɛksɪ] *n* apoplexie *f.*
apostle [ə'pɔsl] *n* apôtre *m.*
apostrophe [ə'pɔstrəfɪ] *n* apostrophe *f.*
appal [ə'pɔ:l] *vt* consterner, atterrer; horrifier.
Appalachian Mountains [æpə'leɪʃən-] *npl*: **the ~** les (monts *mpl*) Appalaches *mpl.*
appalling [ə'pɔ:lɪŋ] *adj* épouvantable; *(stupidity)* consternant(e); **she's an ~ cook** c'est une très mauvaise cuisinière.
apparatus [æpə'reɪtəs] *n* appareil *m*, dispositif *m*; *(in gymnasium)* agrès *mpl.*
apparel [ə'pærl] *n (US)* habillement *m*, confection *f.*
apparent [ə'pærənt] *adj* apparent(e); **it is ~ that** il est évident que.
apparently [ə'pærəntlɪ] *adv* apparemment.
apparition [æpə'rɪʃən] *n* apparition *f.*
appeal [ə'pi:l] *vi (LAW)* faire *or* interjeter appel ♦ *n (LAW)* appel *m*; *(request)* appel; prière *f*; *(charm)* attrait *m*, charme *m*; **to ~ for** demander (instamment); implorer; **to ~ to** *(subj: person)* faire appel à; *(subj: thing)* plaire à; **to ~ to sb for mercy** implorer la pitié de qn, prier *or* adjurer qn d'avoir pitié; **it doesn't ~ to me** cela ne m'attire pas; **right of ~** droit *m* de recours.
appealing [ə'pi:lɪŋ] *adj (nice)* attrayant(e); *(touching)* attendrissant(e).
appear [ə'pɪə*] *vi* apparaître, se montrer; *(LAW)* comparaître; *(publication)* paraître, sortir, être publié(e); *(seem)* paraître, sembler; **it would ~ that** il semble que; **to ~ in Hamlet** jouer dans Hamlet; **to ~ on TV** passer à la télé.
appearance [ə'pɪərəns] *n* apparition *f*, parution *f*; *(look, aspect)* apparence *f*, aspect *m*; **to put in** *or* **make an ~** faire acte de présence; *(THEAT)*: **by order of ~** par ordre d'entrée en scène; **to keep up ~s** sauver les apparences; **to all ~s** selon toute apparence.
appease [ə'pi:z] *vt* apaiser, calmer.
appeasement [ə'pi:zmənt] *n (POL)* apaisement *m.*
appellate court [ə'pɛlɪt-] *n (US)* cour *f* d'appel.
append [ə'pɛnd] *vt (COMPUT)* ajouter (à la fin d'un fichier).
appendage [ə'pɛndɪdʒ] *n* appendice *m.*
appendicitis [əpɛndɪ'saɪtɪs] *n* appendicite *f.*
appendix, *pl* **appendices** [ə'pɛndɪks, -si:z] *n* appendice *m*; **to have one's ~ out** se faire opérer de l'appendicite.
appetite ['æpɪtaɪt] *n* appétit *m*; **that walk has given me an ~** cette promenade m'a ouvert l'appétit.
appetizer ['æpɪtaɪzə*] *n (food)* amuse-gueule *m*; *(drink)* apéritif *m.*
appetizing ['æpɪtaɪzɪŋ] *adj* appétissant(e).
applaud [ə'plɔ:d] *vt, vi* applaudir.
applause [ə'plɔ:z] *n* applaudissements *mpl.*
apple ['æpl] *n* pomme *f*; *(also*: **~ tree)** pommier *m*; **it's the ~ of my eye** j'y tiens comme à la prunelle de mes yeux.
apple turnover *n* chausson *m* aux pommes.
appliance [ə'plaɪəns] *n* appareil *m*; **electrical ~s** l'électroménager *m.*
applicable [ə'plɪkəbl] *adj* applicable; **the law is ~ from January** la loi entre en vigueur au mois de janvier; **to be ~ to** valoir pour.
applicant ['æplɪkənt] *n*: **~ (for)** *(ADMIN: for benefit etc)* demandeur/euse (de); *(for post)* candidat/e (à).
application [æplɪ'keɪʃən] *n* application *f*; *(for a job, a grant etc)* demande *f*; candidature *f*; **on ~** sur demande.
application form *n* formulaire *m* de demande.
application program *n (COMPUT)* programme *m* d'application.
applications package *n (COMPUT)* progiciel *m* d'application.
applied [ə'plaɪd] *adj* appliqué(e); **~ arts** *npl* arts décoratifs.
apply [ə'plaɪ] *vt*: **to ~ (to)** *(paint, ointment)* appliquer (sur); *(theory, technique)* appliquer (à) ♦ *vi*: **to ~ to** *(ask)* s'adresser à; *(be suitable for, relevant to)* s'appliquer à, être valable pour; **to ~ (for)** *(permit, grant)* faire une demande (en vue d'obtenir); *(job)* poser sa candidature (pour), faire une demande d'emploi (concernant); **to ~ the brakes** actionner les freins, freiner; **to ~ o.s. to** s'appliquer à.
appoint [ə'pɔɪnt] *vt* nommer, engager; *(date, place)* fixer, désigner.
appointee [əpɔɪn'ti:] *n* personne nommée; candidat retenu.

appointment [ə'pɔɪntmənt] *n* (*to post*) nomination *f*; (*arrangement to meet*) rendez-vous *m*; **to make an ~ (with)** prendre rendez-vous (avec); **"~s (vacant)"** (*PRESS*) "offres d'emploi"; **by ~** sur rendez-vous.

apportion [ə'pɔːʃən] *vt* (*share out*) répartir, distribuer; **to ~ sth to sb** attribuer *or* assigner *or* allouer qch à qn.

appraisal [ə'preɪzl] *n* évaluation *f*.

appraise [ə'preɪz] *vt* (*value*) estimer; (*situation etc*) évaluer.

appreciable [ə'priːʃəbl] *adj* appréciable.

appreciably [ə'priːʃəblɪ] *adv* sensiblement, de façon appréciable.

appreciate [ə'priːʃɪeɪt] *vt* (*like*) apprécier, faire cas de; (*be grateful for*) être reconnaissant(e) de; (*assess*) évaluer; (*be aware of*) comprendre, se rendre compte de ♦ *vi* (*FINANCE*) prendre de la valeur; **I ~ your help** je vous remercie pour votre aide.

appreciation [əpriːʃɪ'eɪʃən] *n* appréciation *f*; (*gratitude*) reconnaissance *f*; (*FINANCE*) hausse *f*, valorisation *f*.

appreciative [ə'priːʃɪətɪv] *adj* (*person*) sensible; (*comment*) élogieux(euse).

apprehend [æprɪ'hɛnd] *vt* appréhender, arrêter; (*understand*) comprendre.

apprehension [æprɪ'hɛnʃən] *n* appréhension *f*, inquiétude *f*.

apprehensive [æprɪ'hɛnsɪv] *adj* inquiet(ète), appréhensif(ive).

apprentice [ə'prɛntɪs] *n* apprenti *m* ♦ *vt*: **to be ~d to** être en apprentissage chez.

apprenticeship [ə'prɛntɪsʃɪp] *n* apprentissage *m*; **to serve one's ~** faire son apprentissage.

appro. ['æprəu] *abbr* (*BRIT COMM*: *col*) = **approval**.

approach [ə'prəutʃ] *vi* approcher ♦ *vt* (*come near*) approcher de; (*ask, apply to*) s'adresser à; (*subject, passer-by*) aborder ♦ *n* approche *f*; accès *m*, abord *m*; démarche *f* (*auprès de qn*); démarche (*intellectuelle*); **to ~ sb about sth** aller *or* venir voir qn pour qch.

approachable [ə'prəutʃəbl] *adj* accessible.

approach road *n* voie *f* d'accès.

approbation [æprə'beɪʃən] *n* approbation *f*.

appropriate *vt* [ə'prəuprɪeɪt] (*take*) s'approprier; (*allot*): **to ~ sth for** affecter qch à ♦ *adj* [ə'prəuprɪɪt] qui convient, approprié(e); (*timely*) opportun(e); **~ for *or* to** approprié à; **it would not be ~ for me to comment** il ne me serait pas approprié de commenter.

appropriately [ə'prəuprɪɪtlɪ] *adv* pertinemment, avec à-propos.

appropriation [əprəuprɪ'eɪʃən] *n* dotation *f*, affectation *f*.

approval [ə'pruːvəl] *n* approbation *f*; **to meet with sb's ~** recueillir l'assentiment de qn; **on ~** (*COMM*) à l'examen.

approve [ə'pruːv] *vt* approuver.

►**approve of** *vt fus* approuver.

approved school [ə'pruːvd-] *n* (*BRIT*) centre *m* d'éducation surveillée.

approvingly [ə'pruːvɪŋlɪ] *adv* d'un air approbateur.

approx. *abbr* (= *approximately*) env.

approximate *adj* [ə'prɔksɪmɪt] approximatif(ive) ♦ *vt* [ə'prɔksɪmeɪt] se rapprocher de; être proche de.

approximation [ə'prɔksɪ'meɪʃən] *n* approximation *f*.

Apr. *abbr* = **April**.

apr *n abbr* (= *annual percentage rate*) taux (d'intérêt) annuel.

apricot ['eɪprɪkɔt] *n* abricot *m*.

April ['eɪprəl] *n* avril *m*; **~ fool!** poisson d'avril!; *for phrases see also* **July**.

April Fools' Day *n* le premier avril; *voir encadré*.

> **APRIL FOOLS' DAY**
>
> **April Fools' Day** *est le 1er avril, à l'occasion duquel on fait des farces de toutes sortes. Les victimes de ces farces sont les "April fools". Les médias britanniques se prennent aussi au jeu, diffusant de fausses nouvelles, comme la découverte d'îles de la taille de l'Irlande, ou faisant des reportages bidon, montrant par exemple la culture d'arbres à spaghettis en Italie.*

apron ['eɪprən] *n* tablier *m*; (*AVIAT*) aire *f* de stationnement.

apse [æps] *n* (*ARCHIT*) abside *f*.

APT *n abbr* (*BRIT*: = *advanced passenger train*) ≈ TGV *m*.

Apt. *abbr* (= *apartment*) appt.

apt [æpt] *adj* (*suitable*) approprié(e); (*able*): **~ (at)** doué(e) (pour); apte (à); (*likely*): **~ to do** susceptible de faire; ayant tendance à faire.

aptitude ['æptɪtjuːd] *n* aptitude *f*.

aptitude test *n* test *m* d'aptitude.

aptly ['æptlɪ] *adv* (fort) à propos.

aqualung ['ækwəlʌŋ] *n* scaphandre *m* autonome.

aquarium [ə'kwɛərɪəm] *n* aquarium *m*.

Aquarius [ə'kwɛərɪəs] *n* le Verseau; **to be ~** être du Verseau.

aquatic [ə'kwætɪk] *adj* aquatique; (*sport*) nautique.

aqueduct ['ækwɪdʌkt] *n* aqueduc *m*.

AR *abbr* (*US*) = *Arkansas*.

ARA *n abbr* (*BRIT*) = *Associate of the Royal Academy*.

Arab ['ærəb] *n* Arabe *m/f* ♦ *adj* arabe.

Arabia [ə'reɪbɪə] *n* Arabie *f*.

Arabian Desert *n* désert *m* d'Arabie.

Arabian Sea *n* mer *f* d'Arabie.

Arabic ['ærəbɪk] *adj, n* arabe (*m*).

Arabic numerals *npl* chiffres *mpl* arabes.

arable ['ærəbl] *adj* arable.

ARAM *n abbr* (*BRIT*) = *Associate of the Royal Academy of Music*.

arbiter ['ɑːbɪtə*] *n* arbitre *m*.
arbitrary ['ɑːbɪtrərɪ] *adj* arbitraire.
arbitrate ['ɑːbɪtreɪt] *vi* arbitrer; trancher.
arbitration [ɑːbɪ'treɪʃən] *n* arbitrage *m*; **the dispute went to** ~ le litige a été soumis à arbitrage.
arbitrator ['ɑːbɪtreɪtə*] *n* arbitre *m*, médiateur/trice.
ARC *n abbr = American Red Cross.*
arc [ɑːk] *n* arc *m*.
arcade [ɑː'keɪd] *n* arcade *f*; (*passage with shops*) passage *m*, galerie *f*.
arch [ɑːtʃ] *n* arche *f*; (*of foot*) cambrure *f*, voûte *f* plantaire ♦ *vt* arquer, cambrer ♦ *adj* malicieux(euse) ♦ *prefix*: ~(-) achevé(e); par excellence; **pointed** ~ ogive *f*.
archaeological [ɑːkɪə'lɔdʒɪkl] *adj* archéologique.
archaeologist [ɑːkɪ'ɔlədʒɪst] *n* archéologue *m/f*.
archaeology [ɑːkɪ'ɔlədʒɪ] *n* archéologie *f*.
archaic [ɑː'keɪɪk] *adj* archaïque.
archangel ['ɑːkeɪndʒəl] *n* archange *m*.
archbishop [ɑːtʃ'bɪʃəp] *n* archevêque *m*.
archenemy ['ɑːtʃ'ɛnɪmɪ] *n* ennemi *m* de toujours *or* par excellence.
archeology [ɑːkɪ'ɔlədʒɪ] *etc* (*US*) = **archaeology** *etc*.
archer ['ɑːtʃə*] *n* archer *m*.
archery ['ɑːtʃərɪ] *n* tir *m* à l'arc.
archetypal ['ɑːkɪtaɪpəl] *adj* archétype.
archetype ['ɑːkɪtaɪp] *n* prototype *m*, archétype *m*.
archipelago [ɑːkɪ'pɛlɪgəu] *n* archipel *m*.
architect ['ɑːkɪtɛkt] *n* architecte *m*.
architectural [ɑːkɪ'tɛktʃərəl] *adj* architectural(e).
architecture ['ɑːkɪtɛktʃə*] *n* architecture *f*.
archive ['ɑːkaɪv] *n* (*often pl*) archives *fpl*.
archive file *n* (*COMPUT*) fichier *m* d'archives.
archives ['ɑːkaɪvz] *npl* archives *fpl*.
archivist ['ɑːkɪvɪst] *n* archiviste *m/f*.
archway ['ɑːtʃweɪ] *n* voûte *f*, porche voûté *or* cintré.
ARCM *n abbr* (*BRIT*) = *Associate of the Royal College of Music.*
Arctic ['ɑːktɪk] *adj* arctique ♦ *n*: **the** ~ l'Arctique *m*.
Arctic Circle *n* cercle *m* Arctique.
Arctic Ocean *n* océan *m* Arctique.
ARD *n abbr* (*US MED*) = *acute respiratory disease.*
ardent ['ɑːdənt] *adj* fervent(e).
ardour, (*US*) **ardor** ['ɑːdə*] *n* ardeur *f*.
arduous ['ɑːdjuəs] *adj* ardu(e).
are [ɑː*] *vb see* **be**.
area ['ɛərɪə] *n* (*GEOM*) superficie *f*; (*zone*) région *f*; (*: smaller*) secteur *m*; **dining** ~ coin *m* salle à manger; **the London** ~ la région Londonienne.
area code *n* (*TEL*) indicatif *m* (téléphonique).
arena [ə'riːnə] *n* arène *f*.
aren't [ɑːnt] = **are not**.
Argentina [ɑːdʒən'tiːnə] *n* Argentine *f*.
Argentinian [ɑːdʒən'tɪnɪən] *adj* argentin(e) ♦ *n* Argentin/e.
arguable ['ɑːgjuəbl] *adj* discutable, contestable; **it is** ~ **whether** on peut se demander si.
arguably ['ɑːgjuəblɪ] *adv*: **it is** ~ ... on peut soutenir que c'est ....
argue ['ɑːgjuː] *vi* (*quarrel*) se disputer; (*reason*) argumenter ♦ *vt* (*debate: case, matter*) débattre; **to** ~ **about sth (with sb)** se disputer (avec qn) au sujet de qch; **to** ~ **that** objecter *or* alléguer que, donner comme argument que.
argument ['ɑːgjumənt] *n* (*reasons*) argument *m*; (*quarrel*) dispute *f*, discussion *f*; (*debate*) discussion, controverse *f*; ~ **for/against** argument pour/contre.
argumentative [ɑːgju'mɛntətɪv] *adj* ergoteur(euse), raisonneur(euse).
aria ['ɑːrɪə] *n* aria *f*.
ARIBA [ə'riːbə] *n abbr* (*BRIT*) = *Associate of the Royal Institute of British Architects.*
arid ['ærɪd] *adj* aride.
aridity [ə'rɪdɪtɪ] *n* aridité *f*.
Aries ['ɛərɪz] *n* le Bélier; **to be** ~ être du Bélier.
arise, pt arose, pp arisen [ə'raɪz, ə'rəuz, ə'rɪzn] *vi* survenir, se présenter; **to** ~ **from** résulter de; **should the need** ~ en cas de besoin.
aristocracy [ærɪs'tɔkrəsɪ] *n* aristocratie *f*.
aristocrat ['ærɪstəkræt] *n* aristocrate *m/f*.
aristocratic [ærɪstə'krætɪk] *adj* aristocratique.
arithmetic [ə'rɪθmətɪk] *n* arithmétique *f*.
arithmetical [ærɪθ'mɛtɪkl] *adj* arithmétique.
Ariz. *abbr* (*US*) = *Arizona.*
ark [ɑːk] *n*: **Noah's A**~ l'Arche *f* de Noé.
Ark. *abbr* (*US*) = *Arkansas.*
arm [ɑːm] *n* bras *m* ♦ *vt* armer; ~ **in** ~ bras dessus bras dessous.
armaments ['ɑːməmənts] *npl* (*weapons*) armement *m*.
armband ['ɑːmbænd] *n* brassard *m*.
armchair ['ɑːmtʃɛə*] *n* fauteuil *m*.
armed [ɑːmd] *adj* armé(e); **the** ~ **forces** les forces armées.
armed robbery *n* vol *m* à main armée.
Armenia [ɑː'miːnɪə] *n* Arménie *f*.
Armenian [ɑː'miːnɪən] *adj* arménien(ne) ♦ *n* Arménien/ne; (*LING*) arménien *m*.
armful ['ɑːmful] *n* brassée *f*.
armistice ['ɑːmɪstɪs] *n* armistice *m*.
armour, (*US*) **armor** ['ɑːmə*] *n* armure *f*; (*also*: ~**-plating**) blindage *m*; (*MIL: tanks*) blindés *mpl*.
armo(u)red car ['ɑːməd-] *n* véhicule blindé.
armo(u)ry ['ɑːmərɪ] *n* arsenal *m*.
armpit ['ɑːmpɪt] *n* aisselle *f*.
armrest ['ɑːmrɛst] *n* accoudoir *m*.
arms [ɑːmz] *npl* (*weapons, HERALDRY*) armes *fpl*.

arms control *n* contrôle *m* des armements.
arms race *n* course *f* aux armements.
army ['ɑːmɪ] *n* armée *f*.
aroma [ə'rəumə] *n* arôme *m*.
aromatherapy [ərəumə'θɛrəpɪ] *n* aromathérapie *f*.
aromatic [ærə'mætɪk] *adj* aromatique.
arose [ə'rəuz] *pt of* **arise**.
around [ə'raund] *adv* (tout) autour; (*nearby*) dans les parages ♦ *prep* autour de; (*fig: about*) environ; vers; **is he ~?** est-il dans les parages *or* là?
arousal [ə'rauzəl] *n* (*sexual*) excitation sexuelle, éveil *m*.
arouse [ə'rauz] *vt* (*sleeper*) éveiller; (*curiosity, passions*) éveiller, susciter; exciter.
arpeggio [ɑː'pɛdʒɪəu] *n* arpège *m*.
arrange [ə'reɪndʒ] *vt* arranger; (*programme*) arrêter, convenir de ♦ *vi*: **we have ~d for a car to pick you up** nous avons prévu qu'une voiture vienne vous prendre; **it was ~d that** ... il a été convenu que ..., il a été décidé que ...; **to ~ to do sth** prévoir de faire qch.
arrangement [ə'reɪndʒmənt] *n* arrangement *m*; (*plans etc*): **~s** dispositions *fpl*; **to come to an ~ (with sb)** se mettre d'accord (avec qn); **home deliveries by ~** livraison à domicile sur demande; **I'll make ~s for you to be met** je vous enverrai chercher.
arrant ['ærənt] *adj*: **he's talking ~ nonsense** il raconte vraiment n'importe quoi.
array [ə'reɪ] *n* (*of objects*) déploiement *m*, étalage *m*; (*MATH, COMPUT*) tableau *m*.
arrears [ə'rɪəz] *npl* arriéré *m*; **to be in ~ with one's rent** devoir un arriéré de loyer, être en retard pour le paiement de son loyer.
arrest [ə'rɛst] *vt* arrêter; (*sb's attention*) retenir, attirer ♦ *n* arrestation *f*; **under ~** en état d'arrestation.
arresting [ə'rɛstɪŋ] *adj* (*fig: beauty*) saisissant(e); (*: charm, candour*) désarmant(e).
arrival [ə'raɪvl] *n* arrivée *f*; (*COMM*) arrivage *m*; (*person*) arrivant/e; **new ~** nouveau venu/nouvelle venue.
arrive [ə'raɪv] *vi* arriver.
►**arrive at** *vt fus* (*fig*) parvenir à.
arrogance ['ærəgəns] *n* arrogance *f*.
arrogant ['ærəgənt] *adj* arrogant(e).
arrow ['ærəu] *n* flèche *f*.
arse [ɑːs] *n* (*BRIT col!*) cul *m* (*!*).
arsenal ['ɑːsɪnl] *n* arsenal *m*.
arsenic ['ɑːsnɪk] *n* arsenic *m*.
arson ['ɑːsn] *n* incendie criminel.
art [ɑːt] *n* art *m*; (*craft*) métier *m*; **work of ~** œuvre *f* d'art.
art and design *n* (*BRIT SCOL*) arts *mpl* plastiques.
artefact ['ɑːtɪfækt] *n* objet fabriqué.
arterial [ɑː'tɪərɪəl] *adj* (*ANAT*) artériel(le); (*road etc*) à grande circulation.
artery ['ɑːtərɪ] *n* artère *f*.
artful ['ɑːtful] *adj* rusé(e).
art gallery *n* musée *m* d'art; (*small and private*) galerie *f* de peinture.
arthritis [ɑː'θraɪtɪs] *n* arthrite *f*.
artichoke ['ɑːtɪtʃəuk] *n* artichaut *m*; **Jerusalem ~** topinambour *m*.
article ['ɑːtɪkl] *n* article *m*; (*BRIT LAW*): **~s** *npl* ≈ stage *m*; **~s of clothing** vêtements *mpl*.
articles of association *npl* (*COMM*) statuts *mpl* d'une société.
articulate *adj* [ɑː'tɪkjulɪt] (*person*) qui s'exprime clairement et aisément; (*speech*) bien articulé(e), prononcé(e) clairement ♦ *vi* [ɑː'tɪkjuleɪt] articuler, parler distinctement.
articulated lorry [ɑː'tɪkjuleɪtɪd-] *n* (*BRIT*) (camion *m*) semi-remorque *m*.
artifact ['ɑːtɪfækt] *n* (*US*) objet fabriqué.
artifice ['ɑːtɪfɪs] *n* ruse *f*.
artificial [ɑːtɪ'fɪʃəl] *adj* artificiel(le).
artificial insemination [-ɪnsɛmɪ'neɪʃən] *n* insémination artificielle.
artificial intelligence (A.I.) *n* intelligence artificielle (IA).
artificial respiration *n* respiration artificielle.
artillery [ɑː'tɪlərɪ] *n* artillerie *f*.
artisan ['ɑːtɪzæn] *n* artisan/e.
artist ['ɑːtɪst] *n* artiste *m/f*.
artistic [ɑː'tɪstɪk] *adj* artistique.
artistry ['ɑːtɪstrɪ] *n* art *m*, talent *m*.
artless ['ɑːtlɪs] *adj* naïf(naïve), simple, ingénu(e).
arts [ɑːts] *npl* (*SCOL*) lettres *fpl*.
art school *n* ≈ école *f* des beaux-arts.
artwork ['ɑːtwəːk] *n* maquette *f* (*prête pour la photogravure*).
ARV *n abbr* (= *American Revised Version*) *traduction américaine de la Bible*.
AS *n abbr* (*US SCOL: = Associate in/of Science*) *diplôme universitaire*.

KEYWORD

as [æz] *conj* **1** (*time: moment*) comme, alors que; à mesure que; (*: duration*) tandis que; **he came in ~ I was leaving** il est arrivé comme je partais; **~ the years went by** à mesure que les années passaient; **~ from tomorrow** à partir de demain
2 (*in comparisons*): **~ big ~** aussi grand que; **twice ~ big ~** deux fois plus grand que; **big ~ it is** si grand que ce soit; **much ~ I like them, I** ... je les aime bien, mais je ...; **~ much** *or* **many ~** autant que; **~ much money/many books** autant d'argent/de livres que; **~ soon ~** dès que
3 (*since, because*) comme, puisque; **~ he had to be home by 10** ... comme il *or* puisqu'il devait être de retour avant 10 h ...
4 (*referring to manner, way*) comme; **do ~ you wish** faites comme vous voudrez
5 (*concerning*): **~ for** *or* **to that** quant à cela, pour ce qui est de cela

6: ~ **if** *or* **though** comme si; **he looked ~ if he was ill** il avait l'air d'être malade; *see also* **long; such; well**
♦ *prep (in the capacity of)* en tant que, en qualité de; **he works ~ a driver** il travaille comme chauffeur; **~ chairman of the company, he ...** en tant que président de la société, il ...; **dressed up ~ a cowboy** déguisé en cowboy; **he gave me it ~ a present** il me l'a offert, il m'en a fait cadeau.

ASA *n abbr* (= *American Standards Association*) *association de normalisation.*
a.s.a.p. *abbr* = **as soon as possible.**
asbestos [æz'bɛstəs] *n* asbeste *m*, amiante *m*.
ascend [ə'sɛnd] *vt* gravir.
ascendancy [ə'sɛndənsɪ] *n* ascendant *m*.
ascendant [ə'sɛndənt] *n*: **to be in the ~** monter.
ascension [ə'sɛnʃən] *n*: **the A~** *(REL)* l'Ascension *f*.
Ascension Island *n* île *f* de l'Ascension.
ascent [ə'sɛnt] *n* ascension *f*.
ascertain [æsə'teɪn] *vt* s'assurer de, vérifier; établir.
ascetic [ə'sɛtɪk] *adj* ascétique.
asceticism [ə'sɛtɪsɪzəm] *n* ascétisme *m*.
ASCII ['æski:] *n abbr* (= *American Standard Code for Information Interchange*) ASCII.
ascribe [ə'skraɪb] *vt*: **to ~ sth to** attribuer qch à; *(blame)* imputer qch à.
ASCU *n abbr (US)* = *Association of State Colleges and Universities.*
ASE *n abbr* = *American Stock Exchange.*
ASH [æʃ] *n abbr (BRIT: = Action on Smoking and Health) ligue anti-tabac.*
ash [æʃ] *n (dust)* cendre *f*; *(also:* **~ tree***)* frêne *m*.
ashamed [ə'ʃeɪmd] *adj* honteux(euse), confus(e); **to be ~ of** avoir honte de; **to be ~ (of o.s.) for having done** avoir honte d'avoir fait.
ashen ['æʃən] *adj (pale)* cendreux(euse), blême.
ashore [ə'ʃɔ:*] *adv* à terre; **to go ~** aller à terre, débarquer.
ashtray ['æʃtreɪ] *n* cendrier *m*.
Ash Wednesday *n* mercredi *m* des Cendres.
Asia ['eɪʃə] *n* Asie *f*.
Asia Minor *n* Asie Mineure.
Asian ['eɪʃən] *n* Asiatique *m/f* ♦ *adj* asiatique.
Asiatic [eɪsɪ'ætɪk] *adj* asiatique.
aside [ə'saɪd] *adv* de côté; à l'écart ♦ *n* aparté *m*; **~ from** *prep* à part, excepté.
ask [ɑ:sk] *vt* demander; *(invite)* inviter; **to ~ sb sth/to do sth** demander à qn qch/de faire qch; **to ~ sb the time** demander l'heure à qn; **to ~ sb about sth** questionner qn au sujet de qch; se renseigner auprès de qn au sujet de qch; **to ~ about the price** s'informer du prix, se renseigner au sujet du prix; **to ~ (sb) a question** poser une question (à qn); **to ~ sb out to dinner** inviter qn au restaurant.
▸**ask after** *vt fus* demander des nouvelles de.
▸**ask for** *vt fus* demander; **it's just ~ing for trouble** *or* **for it** ce serait chercher des ennuis.
askance [ə'skɑ:ns] *adv*: **to look ~ at sb** regarder qn de travers *or* d'un œil désapprobateur.
askew [ə'skju:] *adv* de travers, de guingois.
asking price ['ɑ:skɪŋ-] *n* prix demandé.
asleep [ə'sli:p] *adj* endormi(e); **to be ~** dormir, être endormi; **to fall ~** s'endormir.
AS level *n abbr* (= *Advanced Subsidiary level*) *première partie de l'examen équivalent au baccalauréat.*
asp [æsp] *n* aspic *m*.
asparagus [əs'pærəgəs] *n* asperges *fpl*.
asparagus tips *npl* pointes *fpl* d'asperges.
ASPCA *n abbr* (= *American Society for the Prevention of Cruelty to Animals*) ≈ SPA *f*.
aspect ['æspɛkt] *n* aspect *m*; *(direction in which a building etc faces)* orientation *f*, exposition *f*.
aspersions [əs'pə:ʃənz] *npl*: **to cast ~ on** dénigrer.
asphalt ['æsfælt] *n* asphalte *m*.
asphyxiate [æs'fɪksɪeɪt] *vt* asphyxier.
asphyxiation [æsfɪksɪ'eɪʃən] *n* asphyxie *f*.
aspirate *vt* ['æspəreɪt] aspirer ♦ *adj* ['æspərɪt] aspiré(e).
aspiration [æspə'reɪʃən] *n* aspiration *f*.
aspire [əs'paɪə*] *vi*: **to ~ to** aspirer à.
aspirin ['æsprɪn] *n* aspirine *f*.
aspiring [əs'paɪərɪŋ] *adj (artist, writer)* en herbe; *(manager)* potentiel(le).
ass [æs] *n* âne *m*; *(col)* imbécile *m/f*; *(US col!)* cul *m (!)*.
assail [ə'seɪl] *vt* assaillir.
assailant [ə'seɪlənt] *n* agresseur *m*; assaillant *m*.
assassin [ə'sæsɪn] *n* assassin *m*.
assassinate [ə'sæsɪneɪt] *vt* assassiner.
assassination [əsæsɪ'neɪʃən] *n* assassinat *m*.
assault [ə'sɔ:lt] *n (MIL)* assaut *m*; *(gen: attack)* agression *f*; *(LAW)*: **~ (and battery)** voies *fpl* de fait, coups *mpl* et blessures *fpl* ♦ *vt* attaquer; *(sexually)* violenter.
assemble [ə'sɛmbl] *vt* assembler ♦ *vi* s'assembler, se rassembler.
assembly [ə'sɛmblɪ] *n (meeting)* rassemblement *m*; *(construction)* assemblage *m*.
assembly language *n (COMPUT)* langage *m* d'assemblage.
assembly line *n* chaîne *f* de montage.
assembly member *n* membre *m* de l'Assemblée.
assent [ə'sɛnt] *n* assentiment *m*, consentement *m* ♦ *vi*: **to ~ (to sth)** donner son assentiment (à qch), consentir (à qch).
assert [ə'sə:t] *vt* affirmer, déclarer; établir; **to ~ o.s.** s'imposer.
assertion [ə'sə:ʃən] *n* assertion *f*, affirmation *f*.

assertive [ə'sɜːtɪv] *adj* assuré(e); péremptoire.
assess [ə'sɛs] *vt* évaluer, estimer; (*tax, damages*) établir *or* fixer le montant de; (*property etc: for tax*) calculer la valeur imposable de.
assessment [ə'sɛsmənt] *n* évaluation *f*, estimation *f*; (*judgment*): ~ **(of)** jugement *m or* opinion *f* (sur).
assessor [ə'sɛsə*] *n* expert *m* (*en matière d'impôt et d'assurance*).
asset ['æsɛt] *n* avantage *m*, atout *m*; (*person*) atout; **~s** *npl* (*COMM*) capital *m*; avoir(s) *m(pl)*; actif *m*.
asset-stripping ['æsɛt'strɪpɪŋ] *n* (*COMM*) récupération *f* (et démantèlement *m*) d'une entreprise en difficulté.
assiduous [ə'sɪdjuəs] *adj* assidu(e).
assign [ə'saɪn] *vt* (*date*) fixer, arrêter; (*task*): **to ~ sth to** assigner qch à; (*resources*): **to ~ sth to** affecter qch à; (*cause, meaning*): **to ~ sth to** attribuer qch à.
assignment [ə'saɪnmənt] *n* tâche *f*, mission *f*.
assimilate [ə'sɪmɪleɪt] *vt* assimiler.
assimilation [əsɪmɪ'leɪʃən] *n* assimilation *f*.
assist [ə'sɪst] *vt* aider, assister; (*injured person etc*) secourir.
assistance [ə'sɪstəns] *n* aide *f*, assistance *f*; secours *mpl*.
assistant [ə'sɪstənt] *n* assistant/e, adjoint/e; (*BRIT*: *also*: **shop ~**) vendeur/euse.
assistant manager *n* sous-directeur *m*.
assizes [ə'saɪzɪz] *npl* assises *fpl*.
associate *adj, n* [ə'səuʃɪɪt] associé(e) ♦ *vb* [ə'səuʃɪeɪt] *vt* associer ♦ *vi*: **to ~ with sb** fréquenter qn; **~ director** directeur adjoint; **~d company** société affiliée.
association [əsəusɪ'eɪʃən] *n* association *f*; **in ~ with** en collaboration avec.
association football *n* (*BRIT*) football *m*.
assorted [ə'sɔːtɪd] *adj* assorti(e); **in ~ sizes** en plusieurs tailles.
assortment [ə'sɔːtmənt] *n* assortiment *m*.
Asst. *abbr* = **assistant**.
assuage [ə'sweɪdʒ] *vt* (*grief, pain*) soulager; (*thirst, appetite*) assouvir.
assume [ə'sjuːm] *vt* supposer; (*responsibilities etc*) assumer; (*attitude, name*) prendre, adopter.
assumed name [ə'sjuːmd-] *n* nom *m* d'emprunt.
assumption [ə'sʌmpʃən] *n* supposition *f*, hypothèse *f*; **on the ~ that** dans l'hypothèse où; (*on condition that*) à condition que.
assurance [ə'ʃuərəns] *n* assurance *f*; **I can give you no ~s** je ne peux rien vous garantir.
assure [ə'ʃuə*] *vt* assurer.
assured [ə'ʃuəd] *adj* assuré(e).
AST *abbr* (*US*: = *Atlantic Standard Time*) *heure d'hiver de New York*.
asterisk ['æstərɪsk] *n* astérisque *m*.
astern [ə'stəːn] *adv* à l'arrière.
asteroid ['æstərɔɪd] *n* astéroïde *m*.
asthma ['æsmə] *n* asthme *m*.
asthmatic [æs'mætɪk] *adj, n* asthmatique *(m/f)*.
astigmatism [ə'stɪgmətɪzəm] *n* astigmatisme *m*.
astir [ə'stəː*] *adv* en émoi.
astonish [ə'stɔnɪʃ] *vt* étonner, stupéfier.
astonishing [ə'stɔnɪʃɪŋ] *adj* étonnant(e), stupéfiant(e); **I find it ~ that ...** je trouve incroyable que ....
astonishingly [ə'stɔnɪʃɪŋlɪ] *adv* incroyablement.
astonishment [ə'stɔnɪʃmənt] *n* (grand) étonnement, stupéfaction *f*.
astound [ə'staund] *vt* stupéfier, sidérer.
astray [ə'streɪ] *adv*: **to go ~** s'égarer; (*fig*) quitter le droit chemin; **to go ~ in one's calculations** faire fausse route dans ses calculs.
astride [ə'straɪd] *adv* à cheval ♦ *prep* à cheval sur.
astringent [əs'trɪndʒənt] *adj* astringent(e) ♦ *n* astringent *m*.
astrologer [əs'trɔlədʒə*] *n* astrologue *m*.
astrology [əs'trɔlədʒɪ] *n* astrologie *f*.
astronaut ['æstrənɔːt] *n* astronaute *m/f*.
astronomer [əs'trɔnəmə*] *n* astronome *m*.
astronomical [æstrə'nɔmɪkl] *adj* astronomique.
astronomy [əs'trɔnəmɪ] *n* astronomie *f*.
astrophysics ['æstrəu'fɪzɪks] *n* astrophysique *f*.
astute [əs'tjuːt] *adj* astucieux(euse), malin(igne).
asunder [ə'sʌndə*] *adv*: **to tear ~** déchirer.
ASV *n abbr* (= *American Standard Version*) *traduction de la Bible*.
asylum [ə'saɪləm] *n* asile *m*; **to seek political ~** demander l'asile politique.
asymmetric(al) [eɪsɪ'mɛtrɪk(l)] *adj* asymétrique.

KEYWORD

at [æt] *prep* **1** (*referring to position, direction*) à; **~ the top** au sommet; **~ home/school** à la maison *or* chez soi/à l'école; **~ the baker's** à la boulangerie, chez le boulanger; **to look ~ sth** regarder qch
2 (*referring to time*): **~ 4 o'clock** à 4 heures; **~ Christmas** à Noël; **~ night** la nuit; **~ times** par moments, parfois
3 (*referring to rates, speed etc*) à; **~ £1 a kilo** une livre le kilo; **two ~ a time** deux à la fois; **~ 50 km/h** à 50 km/h; **~ full speed** à toute vitesse
4 (*referring to manner*): **~ a stroke** d'un seul coup; **~ peace** en paix
5 (*referring to activity*): **to be ~ work** être au travail, travailler; **to play ~ cowboys** jouer aux cowboys; **to be good ~ sth** être bon en qch
6 (*referring to cause*): **shocked/surprised/annoyed ~ sth** choqué par/étonné de/agacé

par qch; **I went ~ his suggestion** j'y suis allé sur son conseil.

ate [eɪt] *pt of* **eat**.
atheism ['eɪθɪɪzəm] *n* athéisme *m*.
atheist ['eɪθɪɪst] *n* athée *m/f*.
Athenian [ə'θiːnɪən] *adj* athénien(ne) ♦ *n* Athénien/ne.
Athens ['æθɪnz] *n* Athènes.
athlete ['æθliːt] *n* athlète *m/f*.
athletic [æθ'lɛtɪk] *adj* athlétique.
athletics [æθ'lɛtɪks] *n* athlétisme *m*.
Atlantic [ət'læntɪk] *adj* atlantique ♦ *n*: **the ~ (Ocean)** l'Atlantique *m*, l'océan *m* Atlantique.
atlas ['ætləs] *n* atlas *m*.
Atlas Mountains *npl*: **the ~** les monts *mpl* de l'Atlas, l'Atlas *m*.
ATM *abbr* (= *Automated Telling Machine*) guichet *m* automatique.
atmosphere ['ætməsfɪə*] *n* atmosphère *f*; (*air*) air *m*.
atmospheric [ætməs'fɛrɪk] *adj* atmosphérique.
atmospherics [ætməs'fɛrɪks] *n* (*RADIO*) parasites *mpl*.
atoll ['ætɔl] *n* atoll *m*.
atom ['ætəm] *n* atome *m*.
atomic [ə'tɔmɪk] *adj* atomique.
atom(ic) bomb *n* bombe *f* atomique.
atomizer ['ætəmaɪzə*] *n* atomiseur *m*.
atone [ə'təun] *vi*: **to ~ for** expier, racheter.
atonement [ə'təunmənt] *n* expiation *f*.
A to Z *n* ® guide *m* A à Z; (*map*) plan *m* des rues.
ATP *n abbr* (= *Association of Tennis Professionals*) ATP *f* (= *Association des tennismen professionnels*).
atrocious [ə'trəuʃəs] *adj* (*very bad*) atroce, exécrable.
atrocity [ə'trɔsɪtɪ] *n* atrocité *f*.
atrophy ['ætrəfɪ] *n* atrophie *f* ♦ *vt* atrophier ♦ *vi* s'atrophier.
attach [ə'tætʃ] *vt* (*gen*) attacher; (*document, letter*) joindre; (*employee, troops*) affecter; **to be ~ed to sb/sth** (*to like*) être attaché à qn/qch; **the ~ed letter** la lettre ci-jointe.
attaché [ə'tæʃeɪ] *n* attaché *m*.
attaché case *n* mallette *f*, attaché-case *m*.
attachment [ə'tætʃmənt] *n* (*tool*) accessoire *m*; (*love*): **~ (to)** affection *f* (pour), attachement *m* (à).
attack [ə'tæk] *vt* attaquer; (*task etc*) s'attaquer à ♦ *n* attaque *f*; (*also*: **heart ~**) crise *f* cardiaque.
attacker [ə'tækə*] *n* attaquant *m*; agresseur *m*.
attain [ə'teɪn] *vt* (*also*: **to ~ to**) parvenir à, atteindre; acquérir.
attainments [ə'teɪnmənts] *npl* connaissances *fpl*, résultats *mpl*.
attempt [ə'tɛmpt] *n* tentative *f* ♦ *vt* essayer, tenter; **~ed theft** *etc* (*LAW*) tentative de vol *etc*; **to make an ~ on sb's life** attenter à la vie de qn; **he made no ~ to help** il n'a rien fait pour m'aider (*or* l'aider *etc*).
attend [ə'tɛnd] *vt* (*course*) suivre; (*meeting, talk*) assister à; (*school, church*) aller à, fréquenter; (*patient*) soigner, s'occuper de; **to ~ (up)on** servir; être au service de.
▸**attend to** *vt fus* (*needs, affairs etc*) s'occuper de; (*customer*) s'occuper de, servir.
attendance [ə'tɛndəns] *n* (*being present*) présence *f*; (*people present*) assistance *f*.
attendant [ə'tɛndənt] *n* employé/e; gardien/ne ♦ *adj* concomitant(e), qui accompagne *or* s'ensuit.
attention [ə'tɛnʃən] *n* attention *f*; **~s** attentions *fpl*, prévenances *fpl*; **~!** (*MIL*) garde-à-vous!; **at ~** (*MIL*) au garde-à-vous; **for the ~ of** (*ADMIN*) à l'attention de; **it has come to my ~ that ...** je constate que ....
attentive [ə'tɛntɪv] *adj* attentif(ive); (*kind*) prévenant(e).
attentively [ə'tɛntɪvlɪ] *adv* attentivement, avec attention.
attenuate [ə'tɛnjueɪt] *vt* atténuer ♦ *vi* s'atténuer.
attest [ə'tɛst] *vi*: **to ~ to** témoigner de, attester (de).
attic ['ætɪk] *n* grenier *m*, combles *mpl*.
attire [ə'taɪə*] *n* habit *m*, atours *mpl*.
attitude ['ætɪtjuːd] *n* (*behaviour*) attitude *f*, manière *f*; (*posture*) pose *f*, attitude; (*view*): **~ (to)** attitude (envers).
attorney [ə'təːnɪ] *n* (*US*: *lawyer*) avocat *m*; (*having proxy*) mandataire *m*; **power of ~** procuration *f*.
Attorney General *n* (*BRIT*) ≈ procureur général; (*US*) ≈ garde *m* des Sceaux, ministre *m* de la Justice.
attract [ə'trækt] *vt* attirer.
attraction [ə'trækʃən] *n* (*gen pl: pleasant things*) attraction *f*, attrait *m*; (*PHYSICS*) attraction; (*fig: towards sth*) attirance *f*.
attractive [ə'træktɪv] *adj* séduisant(e), attrayant(e).
attribute *n* ['ætrɪbjuːt] attribut *m* ♦ *vt* [ə'trɪbjuːt]: **to ~ sth to** attribuer qch à.
attrition [ə'trɪʃən] *n*: **war of ~** guerre *f* d'usure.
Atty. Gen. *abbr* = **Attorney General**.
ATV *n abbr* (= *all terrain vehicle*) véhicule *m* tout-terrain.
atypical [eɪ'tɪpɪkl] *adj* atypique.
aubergine ['əubəʒiːn] *n* aubergine *f*.
auburn ['ɔːbən] *adj* auburn *inv*, châtain roux *inv*.
auction ['ɔːkʃən] *n* (*also*: **sale by ~**) vente *f* aux enchères ♦ *vt* (*also*: **to sell by ~**) vendre aux enchères; (*also*: **to put up for ~**) mettre aux enchères.
auctioneer [ɔːkʃə'nɪə*] *n* commissaire-priseur *m*.
auction room *n* salle *f* des ventes.

audacious [ɔː'deɪʃəs] *adj* impudent(e); audacieux(euse), intrépide.
audacity [ɔː'dæsɪtɪ] *n* impudence *f*; audace *f*.
audible ['ɔːdɪbl] *adj* audible.
audience ['ɔːdɪəns] *n* (*people*) assistance *f*, auditoire *m*; auditeurs *mpl*; spectateurs *mpl*; (*interview*) audience *f*.
audiotypist ['ɔːdɪəutaɪpɪst] *n* audiotypiste *m/f*.
audiovisual [ɔːdɪəu'vɪzjuəl] *adj* audiovisuel(le); ~ **aids** supports *or* moyens audiovisuels.
audit ['ɔːdɪt] *n* vérification *f* des comptes, apurement *m* ♦ *vt* vérifier, apurer.
audition [ɔː'dɪʃən] *n* audition *f* ♦ *vi* auditionner.
auditor ['ɔːdɪtə*] *n* vérificateur *m* des comptes.
auditorium [ɔːdɪ'tɔːrɪəm] *n* auditorium *m*, salle *f* de concert *or* de spectacle.
Aug. *abbr* = **August**.
augment [ɔːg'mɛnt] *vt, vi* augmenter.
augur ['ɔːgə*] *vt* (*be a sign of*) présager, annoncer ♦ *vi*: **it ~s well** c'est bon signe *or* de bon augure, cela s'annonce bien.
August ['ɔːgəst] *n* août *m*; *for phrases see also* **July**.
august [ɔː'gʌst] *adj* majestueux(euse), imposant(e).
aunt [ɑːnt] *n* tante *f*.
auntie, aunty ['ɑːntɪ] *n diminutive of* **aunt**.
au pair ['əu'pɛə*] *n* (*also*: ~ **girl**) jeune fille *f* au pair.
aura ['ɔːrə] *n* atmosphère *f*.
auspices ['ɔːspɪsɪz] *npl*: **under the ~ of** sous les auspices de.
auspicious [ɔːs'pɪʃəs] *adj* de bon augure, propice.
austere [ɔs'tɪə*] *adj* austère.
austerity [ɔs'tɛrɪtɪ] *n* austérité *f*.
Australasia [ɔːstrə'leɪzɪə] *n* Australasie *f*.
Australia [ɔs'treɪlɪə] *n* Australie *f*.
Australian [ɔs'treɪlɪən] *adj* australien(ne) ♦ *n* Australien/ne.
Austria ['ɔstrɪə] *n* Autriche *f*.
Austrian ['ɔstrɪən] *adj* autrichien(ne) ♦ *n* Autrichien/ne.
AUT *n abbr* (*BRIT*: = *Association of University Teachers*) *syndicat universitaire*.
authentic [ɔː'θɛntɪk] *adj* authentique.
authenticate [ɔː'θɛntɪkeɪt] *vt* établir l'authenticité de.
authenticity [ɔːθɛn'tɪsɪtɪ] *n* authenticité *f*.
author ['ɔːθə*] *n* auteur *m*.
authoritarian [ɔːθɔrɪ'tɛərɪən] *adj* autoritaire.
authoritative [ɔː'θɔrɪtətɪv] *adj* (*account*) digne de foi; (*study, treatise*) qui fait autorité; (*manner*) autoritaire.
authority [ɔː'θɔrɪtɪ] *n* autorité *f*; (*permission*) autorisation (formelle); **the authorities** les autorités, l'administration *f*; **to have ~ to do sth** être habilité à faire qch.
authorization [ɔːθəraɪ'zeɪʃən] *n* autorisation *f*.
authorize ['ɔːθəraɪz] *vt* autoriser.
authorized capital ['ɔːθəraɪzd-] *n* (*COMM*) capital social.
authorship ['ɔːθəʃɪp] *n* paternité *f* (*littéraire etc*).
autistic [ɔː'tɪstɪk] *adj* autistique.
auto ['ɔːtəu] *n* (*US*) auto *f*, voiture *f*.
autobiography [ɔːtəbaɪ'ɔgrəfɪ] *n* autobiographie *f*.
autocratic [ɔːtə'krætɪk] *adj* autocratique.
Autocue ['ɔːtəukjuː] *n* ® (télé)prompteur *m*.
autograph ['ɔːtəgrɑːf] *n* autographe *m* ♦ *vt* signer, dédicacer.
autoimmune [ɔːtəuɪ'mjuːn] *adj* auto-immune.
automat ['ɔːtəmæt] *n* (*vending machine*) distributeur *m* (automatique); (*US*: *place*) cafétéria *f* avec distributeurs automatiques.
automated ['ɔːtəmeɪtɪd] *adj* automatisé(e).
automatic [ɔːtə'mætɪk] *adj* automatique ♦ *n* (*gun*) automatique *m*; (*washing machine*) lave-linge *m* automatique; (*BRIT AUT*) voiture *f* à transmission automatique.
automatically [ɔːtə'mætɪklɪ] *adv* automatiquement.
automatic data processing (ADP) *n* traitement *m* automatique des données.
automation [ɔːtə'meɪʃən] *n* automatisation *f*.
automaton, *pl* **automata** [ɔː'tɔmətən, -tə] *n* automate *m*.
automobile ['ɔːtəməbiːl] *n* (*US*) automobile *f*.
autonomous [ɔː'tɔnəməs] *adj* autonome.
autonomy [ɔː'tɔnəmɪ] *n* autonomie *f*.
autopsy ['ɔːtɔpsɪ] *n* autopsie *f*.
autumn ['ɔːtəm] *n* automne *m*.
auxiliary [ɔːg'zɪlɪərɪ] *adj, n* auxiliaire (*m/f*).
AV *n abbr* (= *Authorized Version*) *traduction anglaise de la Bible* ♦ *abbr* = **audiovisual**.
Av. *abbr* (= *avenue*) Av.
avail [ə'veɪl] *vt*: **to ~ o.s. of** user de; profiter de ♦ *n*: **to no ~** sans résultat, en vain, en pure perte.
availability [əveɪlə'bɪlɪtɪ] *n* disponibilité *f*.
available [ə'veɪləbl] *adj* disponible; **every ~ means** tous les moyens possibles *or* à sa (*or* notre *etc*) disposition; **is the manager ~?** est-ce que le directeur peut (me) recevoir?; (*on phone*) pourrais-je parler au directeur?; **to make sth ~ to sb** mettre qch à la disposition de qn.
avalanche ['ævəlɑːnʃ] *n* avalanche *f*.
avant-garde ['ævɑ̃ŋ'gɑːd] *adj* d'avant-garde.
avaricious [ævə'rɪʃəs] *adj* âpre au gain.
avdp. *abbr* = *avoirdupoids*.
Ave. *abbr* (= *avenue*) Av.
avenge [ə'vɛndʒ] *vt* venger.
avenue ['ævənjuː] *n* avenue *f*.
average ['ævərɪdʒ] *n* moyenne *f* ♦ *adj* moyen(ne) ♦ *vt* (*a certain figure*) atteindre *or* faire *etc* en moyenne; **on ~** en moyenne; **above/below (the) ~** au-dessus/en-dessous de la moyenne.
►**average out** *vi*: **to ~ out at** représenter en

moyenne, donner une moyenne de.

averse [ə'vəːs] *adj*: **to be ~ to sth/doing** éprouver une forte répugnance envers qch/à faire; **I wouldn't be ~ to a drink** un petit verre ne serait pas de refus, je ne dirais pas non à un petit verre.

aversion [ə'vəːʃən] *n* aversion *f*, répugnance *f*.

avert [ə'vəːt] *vt* prévenir, écarter; (*one's eyes*) détourner.

aviary ['eɪvɪərɪ] *n* volière *f*.

aviation [eɪvɪ'eɪʃən] *n* aviation *f*.

avid ['ævɪd] *adj* avide.

avidly ['ævɪdlɪ] *adv* avidement, avec avidité.

avocado [ævə'kɑːdəu] *n* (*also*: BRIT: **~ pear**) avocat *m*.

avoid [ə'vɔɪd] *vt* éviter.

avoidable [ə'vɔɪdəbl] *adj* évitable.

avoidance [ə'vɔɪdəns] *n le fait d'éviter*.

avowed [ə'vaud] *adj* déclaré(e).

AVP *n abbr* (US) = *assistant vice-president*.

AWACS ['eɪwæks] *n abbr* (= *airborne warning and control system*) AWACS (*système aéroporté d'alerte et de contrôle*).

await [ə'weɪt] *vt* attendre; **~ing attention/delivery** (COMM) en souffrance; **long ~ed** tant attendu(e).

awake [ə'weɪk] *adj* éveillé(e); (*fig*) en éveil ♦ *vb* (*pt* **awoke** [ə'wəuk], *pp* **awoken** [ə'wəukən], **awaked**) *vt* éveiller ♦ *vi* s'éveiller; **~ to** conscient de; **he was still ~** il ne dormait pas encore.

awakening [ə'weɪknɪŋ] *n* réveil *m*.

award [ə'wɔːd] *n* récompense *f*, prix *m* ♦ *vt* (*prize*) décerner; (LAW: *damages*) accorder.

aware [ə'wɛə*] *adj*: **~ of** (*conscious*) conscient(e) de; (*informed*) au courant de; **to become ~ of** avoir conscience de, prendre conscience de; se rendre compte de; **politically/socially ~** sensibilisé(e) aux *or* ayant pris conscience des problèmes politiques/sociaux; **I am fully ~ that** je me rends parfaitement compte que.

awareness [ə'wɛənɪs] *n* conscience *f*, connaissance *f*; **to develop people's ~ (of)** sensibiliser le public (à).

awash [ə'wɔʃ] *adj* recouvert(e) (d'eau); **~ with** inondé(e) de.

away [ə'weɪ] *adj*, *adv* (au) loin; absent(e); **two kilometres ~** à (une distance de) deux kilomètres, à deux kilomètres de distance; **two hours ~ by car** à deux heures de voiture *or* de route; **the holiday was two weeks ~** il restait deux semaines jusqu'aux vacances; **~ from** loin de; **he's ~ for a week** il est parti (pour) une semaine; **he's ~ in Milan** il est (parti) à Milan; **to take ~** *vt* emporter; **to pedal/work/laugh** *etc* **~** *la particule indique la constance et l'énergie de l'action*: il pédalait *etc* tant qu'il pouvait; **to fade/wither** *etc* **~** *la particule renforce l'idée de la disparition, l'éloignement*.

away game *n* (SPORT) match *m* à l'extérieur.

awe [ɔː] *n* respect mêlé de crainte, effroi mêlé d'admiration.

awe-inspiring ['ɔːɪnspaɪərɪŋ], **awesome** ['ɔːsəm] *adj* impressionnant(e).

awestruck ['ɔːstrʌk] *adj* frappé(e) d'effroi.

awful ['ɔːfəl] *adj* affreux(euse); **an ~ lot of** énormément de.

awfully ['ɔːfəlɪ] *adv* (*very*) terriblement, vraiment.

awhile [ə'waɪl] *adv* un moment, quelque temps.

awkward ['ɔːkwəd] *adj* (*clumsy*) gauche, maladroit(e); (*inconvenient*) malaisé(e), d'emploi malaisé, peu pratique; (*embarrassing*) gênant(e).

awkwardness ['ɔːkwədnɪs] *n* (*embarrassment*) gêne *f*.

awl [ɔːl] *n* alêne *f*.

awning ['ɔːnɪŋ] *n* (*of tent*) auvent *m*; (*of shop*) store *m*; (*of hotel etc*) marquise *f* (de toile).

awoke [ə'wəuk] *pt of* **awake**.

awoken [ə'wəukən] *pp of* **awake**.

AWOL ['eɪwɔl] *abbr* (MIL) = **absent without leave**.

awry [ə'raɪ] *adv*, *adj* de travers; **to go ~** mal tourner.

axe, (US) **ax** [æks] *n* hache *f* ♦ *vt* (*employee*) renvoyer; (*project etc*) abandonner; (*jobs*) supprimer; **to have an ~ to grind** (*fig*) prêcher pour son saint.

axes ['æksiːz] *npl of* **axis**.

axiom ['æksɪəm] *n* axiome *m*.

axiomatic [æksɪəu'mætɪk] *adj* axiomatique.

axis, *pl* **axes** ['æksɪs, -siːz] *n* axe *m*.

axle ['æksl] *n* (*also*: **~-tree**) essieu *m*.

ay(e) [aɪ] *excl* (*yes*) oui ♦ *n*: **the ~s** les oui.

AYH *n abbr* = *American Youth Hostels*.

AZ *abbr* (US) = *Arizona*.

azalea [ə'zeɪlɪə] *n* azalée *f*.

Azerbaijan [æzəbaɪ'dʒɑːn] *n* Azerbaïdjan *m*.

Azerbaijani, Azeri [æzəbaɪ'dʒɑːnɪ, ə'zɛərɪ] *adj* azerbaïdjanais(e) ♦ *n* Azerbaïdjanais/e.

Azores [ə'zɔːz] *npl*: **the ~** les Açores *fpl*.

AZT *n abbr* (= *azidothymidine*) AZT *f*.

Aztec ['æztɛk] *adj* aztèque ♦ *n* Aztèque *m/f*.

azure ['eɪʒə*] *adj* azuré(e).

B b

B, b [biː] *n* (*letter*) B, b *m*; (*SCOL*: *mark*) B; (*MUS*): **B** si *m*; **B for Benjamin**, (*US*) **B for Baker** B comme Berthe; **B road** *n* (*BRIT AUT*) route départementale.
b. *abbr* = **born**.
BA *n abbr* = *British Academy*; (*SCOL*) – **Bachelor of Arts**.
babble ['bæbl] *vi* babiller ♦ *n* babillage *m*.
baboon [bə'buːn] *n* babouin *m*.
baby ['beɪbɪ] *n* bébé *m*.
baby carriage *n* (*US*) voiture *f* d'enfant.
baby grand *n* (*also*: ~ **piano**) (piano *m*) demi-queue *m*.
babyish ['beɪbɪɪʃ] *adj* enfantin(e), de bébé.
baby-sit ['beɪbɪsɪt] *vi* garder les enfants.
baby-sitter ['beɪbɪsɪtə*] *n* baby-sitter *m/f*.
bachelor ['bætʃələ*] *n* célibataire *m*; **B~ of Arts/Science (BA/BSc)** ≈ licencié/e ès *or* en lettres/sciences; **B~ of Arts/Science degree (BA/BSc)** *n* ≈ licence *f* ès *or* en lettres/sciences; *voir encadré*.

BACHELOR'S DEGREE

Un **Bachelor's degree** *est un diplôme accordé après trois ou quatre années d'université. Les Bachelor's degrees les plus courants sont le "BA" (Bachelor of Arts), le "BSc" (Bachelor of Science), le "BEd" (Bachelor of Education) et le "LLB" (Bachelor of Laws).*

bachelor party *n* (*US*) enterrement *m* de vie de garçon.
back [bæk] *n* (*of person, horse*) dos *m*; (*of hand*) dos, revers *m*; (*of house*) derrière *m*; (*of car, train*) arrière *m*; (*of chair*) dossier *m*; (*of page*) verso *m*; (*SPORT*) arrière *m*; **to have one's ~ to the wall** (*fig*) être au pied du mur; **to break the ~ of a job** (*BRIT*) faire le gros d'un travail; **~ to front** à l'envers ♦ *vt* (*financially*) soutenir (financièrement); (*candidate*: *also*: ~ **up**) soutenir, appuyer; (*horse*: *at races*) parier *or* miser sur ♦ *vi* reculer; (*car etc*) faire marche arrière ♦ *adj* (*in compounds*) de derrière, à l'arrière; ~ **seats/wheels** (*AUT*) sièges *mpl*/roues *fpl* arrière; ~ **payments/rent** arriéré *m* de paiements/loyer; ~ **garden/room** jardin/pièce sur l'arrière; **to take a ~ seat** (*fig*) se contenter d'un second rôle, être relégué(e) au second plan ♦ *adv* (*not forward*) en arrière; (*returned*): **he's ~** il est rentré, il est de retour; **when will you be ~?** quand seras-tu de retour?; **he ran ~** il est revenu en courant; (*restitution*): **throw the ball ~** renvoie la balle; **can I have it ~?** puis-je le ravoir?, peux-tu me le rendre?; (*again*): **he called ~** il a rappelé.
backbench ['bæk'bɛntʃ] *n* (*BRIT*) *banc des députés sans portefeuille*.
▸**back down** *vi* rabattre de ses prétentions.
▸**back on to** *vt fus*: **the house ~s on to the golf course** la maison donne derrière sur le terrain de golf.
▸**back out** *vi* (*of promise*) se dédire.
▸**back up** *vt* (*COMPUT*) faire une copie de sauvegarde de.
backache ['bækeɪk] *n* maux *mpl* de reins.
back benches *npl* (*BRIT*) *voir encadré*.

BACK BENCHES

Le terme **back benches** *désigne les bancs les plus éloignés de l'allée centrale de la Chambre des communes. Les députés qui occupent ces bancs sont les "backbenchers" et ils n'ont pas de portefeuille ministériel.*

backbiting ['bækbaɪtɪŋ] *n* médisance(s) *f(pl)*.
backbone ['bækbəun] *n* colonne vertébrale, épine dorsale; **he's the ~ of the organization** c'est sur lui que repose l'organisation.
backchat ['bæktʃæt] *n* (*BRIT col*) impertinences *fpl*.
back-cloth ['bækklɔθ] *n* (*BRIT*) toile *f* de fond.
backcomb ['bækkəum] *vt* (*BRIT*) crêper.
backdate [bæk'deɪt] *vt* (*letter*) antidater; **~d pay rise** augmentation *f* avec effet rétroactif.
backdrop ['bækdrɔp] *n* = **backcloth**.
backer ['bækə*] *n* partisan *m*; (*COMM*) commanditaire *m*.
backfire [bæk'faɪə*] *vi* (*AUT*) pétarader; (*plans*) mal tourner.
backgammon ['bækgæmən] *n* trictrac *m*.
background ['bækgraund] *n* arrière-plan *m*; (*of events*) situation *f*, conjoncture *f*; (*basic knowledge*) éléments *mpl* de base; (*experience*) formation *f* ♦ *cpd* (*noise, music*) de fond; ~ **reading** lecture(s) générale(s) (sur un sujet); **family ~** milieu familial.
backhand ['bækhænd] *n* (*TENNIS*: *also*: ~ **stroke**) revers *m*.
backhanded ['bæk'hændɪd] *adj* (*fig*) déloyal(e); équivoque.
backhander ['bæk'hændə*] *n* (*BRIT*: *bribe*) pot-de-vin *m*.
backing ['bækɪŋ] *n* (*fig*) soutien *m*, appui *m*; (*COMM*) soutien (financier); (*MUS*) accompagnement *m*.
backlash ['bæklæʃ] *n* contre-coup *m*, répercussion *f*.
backlog ['bæklɔg] *n*: ~ **of work** travail *m* en retard.
back number *n* (*of magazine etc*) vieux numéro.

backpack ['bækpæk] *n* sac *m* à dos.
backpacker ['bækpækə*] *n* randonneur/euse.
back pay *n* rappel *m* de salaire.
backpedal ['bækpɛdl] *vi* (*fig*) faire marche arrière.
backseat driver ['bæksiːt-] *n* *passager qui donne des conseils au conducteur*.
backside ['bæksaɪd] *n* (*col*) derrière *m*, postérieur *m*.
backslash ['bækslæʃ] *n* barre oblique inversée.
backslide ['bækslaɪd] *vi* retomber dans l'erreur.
backspace ['bækspeɪs] *vi* (*in typing*) appuyer sur la touche retour.
backstage [bæk'steɪdʒ] *adv* dans les coulisses.
back-street ['bækstriːt] *adj* (*abortion*) clandestin(e); ~ **abortionist** avorteur/euse (*clandestin*).
backstroke ['bækstrəuk] *n* dos crawlé.
backtrack ['bæktræk] *vi* (*fig*) = **backpedal**.
backup ['bækʌp] *adj* (*train, plane*) supplémentaire, de réserve; (*COMPUT*) de sauvegarde ♦ *n* (*support*) appui *m*, soutien *m*; (*COMPUT*: *also*: ~ **file**) sauvegarde *f*.
backward ['bækwəd] *adj* (*movement*) en arrière; (*measure*) rétrograde; (*person, country*) arriéré(e); attardé(e); (*shy*) hésitant(e); ~ **and forward movement** mouvement de va-et-vient.
backwards ['bækwədz] *adv* (*move, go*) en arrière; (*read a list*) à l'envers, à rebours; (*fall*) à la renverse; (*walk*) à reculons; (*in time*) en arrière, vers le passé; **to know sth** ~ *or* (*US*) ~ **and forwards** (*col*) connaître qch sur le bout des doigts.
backwater ['bækwɔːtə*] *n* (*fig*) coin reculé; bled perdu.
back yard *n* arrière-cour *f*.
bacon ['beɪkən] *n* bacon *m*, lard *m*.
bacteria [bæk'tɪərɪə] *npl* bactéries *fpl*.
bacteriology [bæktɪərɪ'ɔlədʒɪ] *n* bactériologie *f*.
bad [bæd] *adj* mauvais(e); (*child*) vilain(e); (*meat, food*) gâté(e), avarié(e); **his** ~ **leg** sa jambe malade; **to go** ~ (*meat, food*) se gâter; (*milk*) tourner; **to have a** ~ **time of it** traverser une mauvaise passe; **I feel** ~ **about it** (*guilty*) j'ai un peu mauvaise conscience; ~ **debt** créance douteuse; **in** ~ **faith** de mauvaise foi.
baddie, baddy ['bædɪ] *n* (*col*: *CINE etc*) méchant *m*.
bade [bæd] *pt of* **bid**.
badge [bædʒ] *n* insigne *m*; (*of policeman*) plaque *f*; (*stick-on, sew-on*) badge *m*.
badger ['bædʒə*] *n* blaireau *m* ♦ *vt* harceler.
badly ['bædlɪ] *adv* (*work, dress etc*) mal; ~ **wounded** grièvement blessé; **he needs it** ~ il en a absolument besoin; **things are going** ~ les choses vont mal; ~ **off** *adj, adv* dans la gêne.
bad-mannered ['bæd'mænəd] *adj* mal élevé(e).
badminton ['bædmɪntən] *n* badminton *m*.
bad-mouth ['bæd'mauθ] *vt* (*US col*) débiner.
bad-tempered ['bæd'tɛmpəd] *adj* (*by nature*) ayant mauvais caractère; (*on one occasion*) de mauvaise humeur.
baffle ['bæfl] *vt* (*puzzle*) déconcerter.
baffling ['bæflɪŋ] *adj* déroutant(e), déconcertant(e).
bag [bæg] *n* sac *m*; (*of hunter*) gibecière *f*, chasse *f* ♦ *vt* (*col*: *take*) empocher; s'approprier; (*TECH*) mettre en sacs; ~**s of** (*col*: *lots of*) des masses de; **to pack one's** ~**s** faire ses valises *or* bagages; ~**s under the eyes** poches *fpl* sous les yeux.
bagful ['bægful] *n* plein sac.
baggage ['bægɪdʒ] *n* bagages *mpl*.
baggage claim *n* (*at airport*) livraison *f* des bagages.
baggy ['bægɪ] *adj* avachi(e), qui fait des poches.
Baghdad [bæg'dæd] *n* Baghdâd, Bagdad.
bag lady *n* (*col*) clocharde *f*.
bagpipes ['bægpaɪps] *npl* cornemuse *f*.
bag-snatcher ['bægsnætʃə*] *n* (*BRIT*) voleur *m* à l'arraché.
bag-snatching ['bægsnætʃɪŋ] *n* (*BRIT*) vol *m* à l'arraché.
Bahamas [bə'hɑːməz] *npl*: **the** ~ les Bahamas *fpl*.
Bahrain [bɑː'reɪn] *n* Bahreïn *m*.
bail [beɪl] *n* caution *f* ♦ *vt* (*prisoner*: *also*: **grant** ~ **to**) mettre en liberté sous caution; (*boat*: *also*: ~ **out**) écoper; **to be released on** ~ être libéré(e) sous caution; *see* **bale**.
►**bail out** *vt* (*prisoner*) payer la caution de.
bailiff ['beɪlɪf] *n* huissier *m*.
bait [beɪt] *n* appât *m* ♦ *vt* appâter; (*fig*) tourmenter.
bake [beɪk] *vt* (faire) cuire au four ♦ *vi* (*bread etc*) cuire (au four); (*make cakes etc*) faire de la pâtisserie.
baked beans [beɪkt-] *npl* haricots blancs à la sauce tomate.
baker ['beɪkə*] *n* boulanger *m*.
bakery ['beɪkərɪ] *n* boulangerie *f*; boulangerie industrielle.
baking ['beɪkɪŋ] *n* cuisson *f*.
baking powder *n* levure *f* (chimique).
baking tin *n* (*for cake*) moule *m* à gâteaux; (*for meat*) plat *m* pour le four.
baking tray *n* plaque *f* à gâteaux.
balaclava [bælə'klɑːvə] *n* (*also*: ~ **helmet**) passe-montagne *m*.
balance ['bæləns] *n* équilibre *m*; (*COMM*: *sum*) solde *m*; (*scales*) balance *f* ♦ *vt* mettre *or* faire tenir en équilibre; (*pros and cons*) peser; (*budget*) équilibrer; (*account*) balancer; (*compensate*) compenser, contrebalancer; ~ **of trade/payments** balance commerciale/des comptes *or* paiements; ~ **carried for-**

ward solde *m* à reporter; ~ **brought forward** solde reporté; **to ~ the books** arrêter les comptes, dresser le bilan.
balanced ['bælənst] *adj* (*personality, diet*) équilibré(e).
balance sheet *n* bilan *m*.
balcony ['bælkənɪ] *n* balcon *m*.
bald [bɔːld] *adj* chauve; (*tyre*) lisse.
baldness ['bɔːldnɪs] *n* calvitie *f*.
bale [beɪl] *n* balle *f*, ballot *m*.
▶**bale out** *vi* (*of a plane*) sauter en parachute ♦ *vt* (*NAUT: water, boat*) écoper.
Balearic Islands [bælɪ'ærɪk-] *npl*: **the ~** les (îles *fpl*) Baléares *fpl*.
baleful ['beɪlful] *adj* funeste, maléfique.
balk [bɔːk] *vi*: **to ~ (at)** (*person*) regimber (contre); (*horse*) se dérober (devant).
Balkan ['bɔːlkən] *adj* balkanique ♦ *n*: **the ~s** les Balkans *mpl*.
ball [bɔːl] *n* boule *f*; (*football*) ballon *m*; (*for tennis, golf*) balle *f*; (*dance*) bal *m*; **to play ~ (with sb)** jouer au ballon (*or* à la balle) (avec qn); (*fig*) coopérer (avec qn); **to be on the ~** (*fig: competent*) être à la hauteur; (*: alert*) être éveillé(e), être vif(vive); **to start the ~ rolling** (*fig*) commencer; **the ~ is in their court** (*fig*) la balle est dans leur camp.
ballad ['bæləd] *n* ballade *f*.
ballast ['bæləst] *n* lest *m*.
ball bearing *n* roulement *m* à billes.
ball cock *n* robinet *m* à flotteur.
ballerina [bælə'riːnə] *n* ballerine *f*.
ballet ['bæleɪ] *n* ballet *m*; (*art*) danse *f* (classique).
ballet dancer *n* danseur/euse de ballet.
ballistic [bə'lɪstɪk] *adj* balistique.
ballistics [bə'lɪstɪks] *n* balistique *f*.
balloon [bə'luːn] *n* ballon *m*; (*in comic strip*) bulle *f* ♦ *vi* gonfler.
balloonist [bə'luːnɪst] *n* aéronaute *m/f*.
ballot ['bælət] *n* scrutin *m*.
ballot box *n* urne (électorale).
ballot paper *n* bulletin *m* de vote.
ballpark ['bɔːlpɑːk] *n* (*US*) stade *m* de baseball.
ballpark figure *n* (*col*) chiffre approximatif.
ball-point pen ['bɔːlpɔɪnt-] *n* stylo *m* à bille.
ballroom ['bɔːlrum] *n* salle *f* de bal.
balls [bɔːlz] *npl* (*col!*) couilles *fpl* (*!*).
balm [bɑːm] *n* baume *m*.
balmy ['bɑːmɪ] *adj* (*breeze, air*) doux(douce); (*BRIT col*) = **barmy**.
BALPA ['bælpə] *n abbr* (= *British Airline Pilots' Association*) *syndicat des pilotes de ligne*.
balsam ['bɔːlsəm] *n* baume *m*.
balsa (wood) ['bɔːlsə-] *n* balsa *m*.
Baltic [bɔːltɪk] *adj, n*: **the ~ (Sea)** la (mer) Baltique.
balustrade [bæləs'treɪd] *n* balustrade *f*.
bamboo [bæm'buː] *n* bambou *m*.
bamboozle [bæm'buːzl] *vt* (*col*) embobiner.
ban [bæn] *n* interdiction *f* ♦ *vt* interdire; **he was ~ned from driving** (*BRIT*) on lui a retiré le permis (de conduire).
banal [bə'nɑːl] *adj* banal(e).
banana [bə'nɑːnə] *n* banane *f*.
band [bænd] *n* bande *f*; (*at a dance*) orchestre *m*; (*MIL*) musique *f*, fanfare *f*.
▶**band together** *vi* se liguer.
B & B *n abbr* = **bed and breakfast**.
bandage ['bændɪdʒ] *n* bandage *m*, pansement *m* ♦ *vt* (*wound, leg*) mettre un pansement *or* un bandage sur; (*person*) mettre un pansement *or* un bandage à.
Band-Aid ['bændeɪd] *n* ® (*US*) pansement adhésif.
bandit ['bændɪt] *n* bandit *m*.
bandstand ['bændstænd] *n* kiosque *m* (à musique).
bandwagon ['bændwægən] *n*: **to jump on the ~** (*fig*) monter dans *or* prendre le train en marche.
bandy ['bændɪ] *vt* (*jokes, insults*) échanger.
▶**bandy about** *vt* employer à tout bout de champ *or* à tort et à travers.
bandy-legged ['bændɪ'lɛgɪd] *adj* aux jambes arquées.
bane [beɪn] *n*: **it (or he etc) is the ~ of my life** c'est (*or* il est *etc*) le drame de ma vie.
bang [bæŋ] *n* détonation *f*; (*of door*) claquement *m*; (*blow*) coup (violent) ♦ *vt* frapper (violemment); (*door*) claquer ♦ *vi* détoner; claquer ♦ *adv*: **to be ~ on time** (*BRIT col*) être à l'heure pile; **to ~ at the door** cogner à la porte; **to ~ into sth** se cogner contre qch.
banger ['bæŋə*] *n* (*BRIT: car: also:* **old ~**) (vieux) tacot; (*BRIT col: sausage*) saucisse *f*; (*firework*) pétard *m*.
Bangkok [bæŋ'kɔk] *n* Bangkok.
Bangladesh [bæŋglə'dɛʃ] *n* Bangladesh *m*.
bangle ['bæŋgl] *n* bracelet *m*.
bangs [bæŋz] *npl* (*US: fringe*) frange *f*.
banish ['bænɪʃ] *vt* bannir.
banister(s) ['bænɪstə(z)] *n(pl)* rampe *f* (d'escalier).
banjo, ~es *or* **~s** ['bændʒəu] *n* banjo *m*.
bank [bæŋk] *n* banque *f*; (*of river, lake*) bord *m*, rive *f*; (*of earth*) talus *m*, remblai *m* ♦ *vi* (*AVIAT*) virer sur l'aile; (*COMM*): **they ~ with Pitt's** leur banque *or* banquier est Pitt's.
▶**bank on** *vt fus* miser *or* tabler sur.
bank account *n* compte *m* en banque.
bank balance *n* solde *m* bancaire.
bank card *n* = **banker's card**.
bank charges *npl* (*BRIT*) frais *mpl* de banque.
bank draft *n* traite *f* bancaire.
banker ['bæŋkə*] *n* banquier *m*; **~'s card** (*BRIT*) carte *f* d'identité bancaire; **~'s order** (*BRIT*) ordre *m* de virement.
bank giro *n* paiement *m* par virement.
bank holiday *n* (*BRIT*) jour férié (*où les banques sont fermées*); *voir encadré*.

BANK HOLIDAY

Un **bank holiday** *en Grande-Bretagne est un lundi férié et donc l'occasion d'un week-end prolongé. La circulation sur les routes et le trafic dans les gares et les aéroports augmentent considérablement à ces périodes. Les principaux bank holidays, à part Pâques et Noël, se situent au mois de mai et fin août.*

banking ['bæŋkɪŋ] *n* opérations *fpl* bancaires; profession *f* de banquier.
banking hours *npl* heures *fpl* d'ouverture des banques.
bank loan *n* prêt *m* bancaire.
bank manager *n* directeur *m* d'agence (bancaire).
banknote ['bæŋknəut] *n* billet *m* de banque.
bank rate *n* taux *m* de l'escompte.
bankrupt ['bæŋkrʌpt] *n* failli/e ♦ *adj* en faillite; **to go ~** faire faillite.
bankruptcy ['bæŋkrʌptsɪ] *n* faillite *f*.
bank statement *n* relevé *m* de compte.
banned substance *n* substance *f* prohibée.
banner ['bænə*] *n* bannière *f*.
bannister(s) ['bænɪstə(z)] *n(pl)* = **banister(s)**.
banns [bænz] *npl* bans *mpl* (de mariage).
banquet ['bæŋkwɪt] *n* banquet *m*, festin *m*.
bantam-weight ['bæntəmweɪt] *n* poids *m* coq *inv*.
banter ['bæntə*] *n* badinage *m*.
BAOR *n abbr* (= *British Army of the Rhine*) *forces britanniques en Allemagne*.
baptism ['bæptɪzəm] *n* baptême *m*.
Baptist ['bæptɪst] *n* baptiste *m/f*.
baptize [bæp'taɪz] *vt* baptiser.
bar [bɑː*] *n* barre *f*; (*of window etc*) barreau *m*; (*of chocolate*) tablette *f*, plaque *f*; (*fig*) obstacle *m*; mesure *f* d'exclusion; (*pub*) bar *m*; (*counter: in pub*) comptoir *m*, bar; (*MUS*) mesure *f* ♦ *vt* (*road*) barrer; (*window*) munir de barreaux; (*person*) exclure; (*activity*) interdire; **~ of soap** savonnette *f*; **behind ~s** (*prisoner*) derrière les barreaux; **the B~** (*LAW*) le barreau; **~ none** sans exception.
Barbados [bɑː'beɪdɔs] *n* Barbade *f*.
barbaric [bɑː'bærɪk] *adj* barbare.
barbarous ['bɑːbərəs] *adj* barbare, cruel(le).
barbecue ['bɑːbɪkjuː] *n* barbecue *m*.
barbed wire ['bɑːbd-] *n* fil *m* de fer barbelé.
barber ['bɑːbə*] *n* coiffeur *m* (pour hommes).
barbiturate [bɑː'bɪtjurɪt] *n* barbiturique *m*.
Barcelona [bɑːsə'ləunə] *n* Barcelone.
bar chart *n* diagramme *m* en bâtons.
bar code *n* code *m* à barres.
bare [bɛə*] *adj* nu(e) ♦ *vt* mettre à nu, dénuder; (*teeth*) montrer; **the ~ essentials** le strict nécessaire.
bareback ['bɛəbæk] *adv* à cru, sans selle.
barefaced ['bɛəfeɪst] *adj* impudent(e), effronté(e).
barefoot ['bɛəfut] *adj, adv* nu-pieds, (les) pieds nus.
bareheaded [bɛə'hɛdɪd] *adj, adv* nu-tête, (la) tête nue.
barely ['bɛəlɪ] *adv* à peine.
Barents Sea ['bærənts-] *n*: **the ~** la mer de Barents.
bargain ['bɑːgɪn] *n* (*transaction*) marché *m*; (*good buy*) affaire *f*, occasion *f* ♦ *vi* (*haggle*) marchander; (*trade*) négocier, traiter; **into the ~** par-dessus le marché.
▶**bargain for** *vi* (*col*): **he got more than he ~ed for!** il en a eu pour son argent!
bargaining ['bɑːgənɪŋ] *n* marchandage *m*; négociations *fpl*.
bargaining position *n*: **to be in a weak/strong ~** être en mauvaise/bonne position pour négocier.
barge [bɑːdʒ] *n* péniche *f*.
▶**barge in** *vi* (*walk in*) faire irruption; (*interrupt talk*) intervenir mal à propos.
▶**barge into** *vt fus* rentrer dans.
baritone ['bærɪtəun] *n* baryton *m*.
barium meal ['bɛərɪəm-] *n* (bouillie *f* de) sulfate *m* de baryum.
bark [bɑːk] *n* (*of tree*) écorce *f*; (*of dog*) aboiement *m* ♦ *vi* aboyer.
barley ['bɑːlɪ] *n* orge *f*.
barley sugar *n* sucre *m* d'orge.
barmaid ['bɑːmeɪd] *n* serveuse *f* (de bar).
barman ['bɑːmən] *n* serveur *m* (de bar), barman *m*.
barmy ['bɑːmɪ] *adj* (*BRIT col*) timbré(e), cinglé(e).
barn [bɑːn] *n* grange *f*.
barnacle ['bɑːnəkl] *n* anatife *m*, bernache *f*.
barn owl *n* chouette-effraie *f*, chat-huant *m*.
barometer [bə'rɔmɪtə*] *n* baromètre *m*.
baron ['bærən] *n* baron *m*; **the press/oil ~s** les magnats *mpl or* barons *mpl* de la presse/du pétrole.
baroness ['bærənɪs] *n* baronne *f*.
barrack ['bærək] *vt* (*BRIT*) chahuter.
barracking ['bærəkɪŋ] *n* (*BRIT*): **to give sb a ~** chahuter qn.
barracks ['bærəks] *npl* caserne *f*.
barrage ['bærɑːʒ] *n* (*MIL*) tir *m* de barrage; (*dam*) barrage *m*; **a ~ of questions** un feu roulant de questions.
barrel ['bærəl] *n* tonneau *m*; (*of gun*) canon *m*.
barrel organ *n* orgue *m* de Barbarie.
barren ['bærən] *adj* stérile; (*hills*) aride.
barricade [bærɪ'keɪd] *n* barricade *f* ♦ *vt* barricader.
barrier ['bærɪə*] *n* barrière *f*; (*BRIT*: *also*: **crash ~**) rail *m* de sécurité.
barrier cream *n* (*BRIT*) crème protectrice.
barring ['bɑːrɪŋ] *prep* sauf.
barrister ['bærɪstə*] *n* (*BRIT*) avocat (plaidant); *voir encadré*.

BARRISTER

En Angleterre, un **barrister**, *que l'on appelle également "barrister-at-law", est un avocat qui représente ses clients devant la cour et plaide pour eux. Le client doit d'abord passer par l'intermédiaire d'un "solicitor". On obtient le diplôme de* **barrister** *après avoir fait des études dans l'une des "Inns of Court", les quatre écoles de droit londoniennes.*

barrow ['bærəu] *n* (*cart*) charrette *f* à bras.
barstool ['bɑːstuːl] *n* tabouret *m* de bar.
Bart. *abbr* (*BRIT*) = *baronet.*
bartender ['bɑːtɛndə*] *n* (*US*) serveur *m* (*de bar*), barman *m.*
barter ['bɑːtə*] *n* échange *m*, troc *m* ♦ *vt*: **to ~ sth for** échanger qch contre.
base [beɪs] *n* base *f* ♦ *vt* (*troops*): **to be ~d at** être basé(e) à; (*opinion, belief*): **to ~ sth on** baser *or* fonder qch sur ♦ *adj* vil(e), bas(se); **coffee-~d** à base de café; **a Paris-~d firm** une maison opérant de Paris; **I'm ~d in London** je suis basé(e) à Londres.
baseball ['beɪsbɔːl] *n* base-ball *m.*
baseboard ['beɪsbɔːd] *n* (*US*) plinthe *f.*
base camp *n* camp *m* de base.
Basel [bɑːl] *n* = **Basle**.
baseline ['beɪslaɪn] *n* (*TENNIS*) ligne *f* de fond.
basement ['beɪsmənt] *n* sous-sol *m.*
base rate *n* taux *m* de base.
bases ['beɪsiːz] *npl of* **basis**; ['beɪsɪz] *npl of* **base**.
bash [bæʃ] *vt* (*col*) frapper, cogner ♦ *n*: **I'll have a ~ (at it)** (*BRIT col*) je vais essayer un coup; **~ed in** *adj* enfoncé(e), défoncé(e).
▸**bash up** *vt* (*col*: *car*) bousiller; (*: BRIT*: *person*) tabasser.
bashful ['bæʃful] *adj* timide; modeste.
bashing ['bæʃɪŋ] *n* (*col*) raclée *f*; **Paki-~** ≈ ratonnade *f*; **queer-~** chasse *f* aux pédés.
BASIC ['beɪsɪk] *n* (*COMPUT*) BASIC *m.*
basic ['beɪsɪk] *adj* (*precautions, rules*) élémentaire; (*principles, research*) fondamental(e); (*vocabulary, salary*) de base; rudimentaire.
basically ['beɪsɪklɪ] *adv* (*really*) en fait; (*essentially*) fondamentalement.
basic rate *n* (*of tax*) première tranche d'imposition.
basil ['bæzl] *n* basilic *m.*
basin ['beɪsn] *n* (*vessel, also GEO*) cuvette *f*, bassin *m*; (*BRIT*: *for food*) bol *m*; (*: bigger*) saladier *m*; (*also*: **wash~**) lavabo *m.*
basis, *pl* **bases** ['beɪsɪs, -siːz] *n* base *f*; **on the ~ of what you've said** d'après *or* compte tenu de ce que vous dites.
bask [bɑːsk] *vi*: **to ~ in the sun** se chauffer au soleil.
basket ['bɑːskɪt] *n* corbeille *f*; (*with handle*) panier *m.*
basketball ['bɑːskɪtbɔːl] *n* basket-ball *m.*
basketball player *n* basketteur/euse.
Basle [bɑːl] *n* Bâle.
basmati rice [bəz'mætɪ-] *n* riz *m* basmati.
Basque [bæsk] *adj* basque ♦ *n* Basque *m/f.*
bass [beɪs] *n* (*MUS*) basse *f.*
bass clef *n* clé *f* de fa.
bassoon [bə'suːn] *n* basson *m.*
bastard ['bɑːstəd] *n* bâtard/e; (*col!*) salaud *m* (*!*).
baste [beɪst] *vt* (*CULIN*) arroser; (*SEWING*) bâtir, faufiler.
bat [bæt] *n* chauve-souris *f*; (*for baseball*) batte *f*; (*for table tennis*) raquette *f* ♦ *vt*: **he didn't ~ an eyelid** il n'a pas sourcillé *or* bronché; **off one's own ~** de sa propre initiative.
batch [bætʃ] *n* (*of bread*) fournée *f*; (*of papers*) liasse *f*; (*of applicants, letters*) paquet *m*; (*of work*) monceau *m*; (*of goods*) lot *m.*
batch processing *n* (*COMPUT*) traitement *m* par lot.
bated ['beɪtɪd] *adj*: **with ~ breath** en retenant son souffle.
bath [bɑːθ, *pl* bɑːðz] *n* bain *m*; (*bathtub*) baignoire *f* ♦ *vt* baigner, donner un bain à; **to have a ~** prendre un bain; *see also* **baths**.
Bath chair *n* (*BRIT*) fauteuil roulant.
bathe [beɪð] *vi* se baigner ♦ *vt* baigner; (*wound etc*) laver.
bather ['beɪðə*] *n* baigneur/euse.
bathing ['beɪðɪŋ] *n* baignade *f.*
bathing cap *n* bonnet *m* de bain.
bathing costume, (*US*) **bathing suit** *n* maillot *m* (de bain).
bathmat ['bɑːθmæt] *n* tapis *m* de bain.
bathrobe ['bɑːθrəub] *n* peignoir *m* de bain.
bathroom ['bɑːθrum] *n* salle *f* de bains.
baths [bɑːðz] *npl* établissement *m* de bains (-douches).
bath towel *n* serviette *f* de bain.
bathtub ['bɑːθtʌb] *n* baignoire *f.*
batman ['bætmən] *n* (*BRIT MIL*) ordonnance *f.*
baton ['bætən] *n* bâton *m*; (*MUS*) baguette *f*; (*club*) matraque *f.*
battalion [bə'tælɪən] *n* bataillon *m.*
batten ['bætn] *n* (*CARPENTRY*) latte *f*; (*NAUT*: *on sail*) latte de voile.
▸**batten down** *vt* (*NAUT*): **to ~ down the hatches** fermer les écoutilles.
batter ['bætə*] *vt* battre ♦ *n* pâte *f* à frire.
battered ['bætəd] *adj* (*hat, pan*) cabossé(e); **~ wife** épouse maltraitée *or* martyre.
battering ram ['bætərɪŋ-] *n* bélier *m* (*fig*).
battery ['bætərɪ] *n* batterie *f*; (*of torch*) pile *f.*
battery charger *n* chargeur *m.*
battery farming *n* élevage *m* en batterie.
battle ['bætl] *n* bataille *f*, combat *m* ♦ *vi* se battre, lutter; **that's half the ~** (*fig*) c'est déjà bien; **it's a** *or* **we're fighting a losing ~** (*fig*) c'est perdu d'avance, c'est peine perdue.
battle dress *n* tenue *f* de campagne *or* d'assaut.
battlefield ['bætlfiːld] *n* champ *m* de bataille.
battlements ['bætlmənts] *npl* remparts *mpl.*
battleship ['bætlʃɪp] *n* cuirassé *m.*

batty ['bætɪ] *adj* (*col*: *person*) toqué(e); (: *idea, behaviour*) loufoque.
bauble ['bɔːbl] *n* babiole *f*.
baud [bɔːd] *n* (*COMPUT*) baud *m*.
baud rate *n* (*COMPUT*) vitesse *f* de transmission.
baulk [bɔːlk] *vi* = **balk**.
Bavaria [bə'vɛərɪə] *n* Bavière *f*.
Bavarian [bə'vɛərɪən] *adj* bavarois(e) ♦ *n* Bavarois/e.
bawdy ['bɔːdɪ] *adj* paillard(e).
bawl [bɔːl] *vi* hurler, brailler.
bay [beɪ] *n* (*of sea*) baie *f*; (*BRIT*: *for parking*) place *f* de stationnement; (: *for loading*) aire *f* de chargement; (*horse*) bai/e *m/f*; **to hold sb at ~** tenir qn à distance *or* en échec.
bay leaf *n* laurier *m*.
bayonet ['beɪənɪt] *n* baïonnette *f*.
bay tree *n* laurier *m*.
bay window *n* baie vitrée.
bazaar [bə'zɑː*] *n* bazar *m*; vente *f* de charité.
BB *n abbr* (*BRIT*: = *Boys' Brigade*) *mouvement de garçons*.
BBB *n abbr* (*US*: = *Better Business Bureau*) *organisme de défense du consommateur*.
BBC *n abbr* (= *British Broadcasting Corporation*) *office de la radiodiffusion et télévision britannique*; *voir encadré*.

> **BBC**
>
> *La* **BBC** *est un organisme centralisé dont les membres, nommés par l'État, gèrent les chaînes de télévision publiques (BBC1, qui présente des émissions d'intérêt général, et BBC2, qui est plutôt orientée vers les émissions plus culturelles) et les stations de radio publiques. Bien que non contrôlée par l'État, la* **BBC** *est responsable devant le "Parliament" quant au contenu des émissions qu'elle diffuse. Par ailleurs, la* **BBC** *offre un service mondial de diffusion d'émissions, en anglais et dans 43 autres langues, appelé "BBC World Service". La* **BBC** *est financée par la redevance télévision et par l'exportation d'émissions.*

BC *adv abbr* (= *before Christ*) av. J.-C. ♦ *abbr* (*Canada*) = *British Columbia*.
BCG *n abbr* (= *Bacillus Calmette-Guérin*) BCG *m*.
BD *n abbr* (= *Bachelor of Divinity*) *diplôme universitaire*.
B/D *abbr* = **bank draft**.
BDS *n abbr* (= *Bachelor of Dental Surgery*) *diplôme universitaire*.

KEYWORD

be [biː] (*pt* **was, were**, *pp* **been**) *aux vb* **1** (*with present participle*: *forming continuous tenses*): **what are you doing?** que faites-vous?; **they're coming tomorrow** ils viennent demain; **I've been waiting for you for 2 hours** je t'attends depuis 2 heures
2 (*with pp*: *forming passives*) être; **to ~ killed** être tué(e); **he was nowhere to ~ seen** on ne le voyait nulle part
3 (*in tag questions*): **it was fun, wasn't it?** c'était drôle, n'est-ce pas?; **she's back, is she?** elle est rentrée, n'est-ce pas *or* alors?
4 (*+to +infinitive*): **the house is to ~ sold** la maison doit être vendue; **he's not to open it** il ne doit pas l'ouvrir; **am I to understand that ...?** dois-je comprendre que ...?; **he was to have come yesterday** il devait venir hier
5 (*possibility, supposition*): **if I were you, I ...** à votre place, je ..., si j'étais vous, je ...
♦ *vb + complement* **1** (*gen*) être; **I'm English** je suis anglais(e); **I'm tired** je suis fatigué(e); **I'm hot/cold** j'ai chaud/froid; **he's a doctor** il est médecin; **2 and 2 are 4** 2 et 2 font 4
2 (*of health*) aller; **how are you?** comment allez-vous?; **he's fine now** il va bien maintenant; **he's very ill** il est très malade
3 (*of age*) avoir; **how old are you?** quel âge avez-vous?; **I'm sixteen (years old)** j'ai seize ans
4 (*cost*) coûter; **how much was the meal?** combien a coûté le repas?; **that'll ~ £5, please** ça fera 5 livres, s'il vous plaît
♦ *vi* **1** (*exist, occur etc*) être, exister; **the prettiest girl that ever was** la fille la plus jolie qui ait jamais existé; **~ that as it may** quoi qu'il en soit; **so ~ it** soit
2 (*referring to place*) être, se trouver; **I won't ~ here tomorrow** je ne serai pas là demain; **Edinburgh is in Scotland** Édimbourg est *or* se trouve en Écosse
3 (*referring to movement*) aller; **where have you been?** où êtes-vous allé(s)?
♦ *impers vb* **1** (*referring to time, distance*) être; **it's 5 o'clock** il est 5 heures; **it's the 28th of April** c'est le 28 avril; **it's 10 km to the village** le village est à 10 km
2 (*referring to the weather*) faire; **it's too hot/cold** il fait trop chaud/froid; **it's windy** il y a du vent
3 (*emphatic*): **it's me/the postman** c'est moi/le facteur.

B/E *abbr* = **bill of exchange**.
beach [biːtʃ] *n* plage *f* ♦ *vt* échouer.
beachcomber ['biːtʃkəumə*] *n* ramasseur *m* d'épaves; (*fig*) bon/ne à rien.
beachwear ['biːtʃwɛə*] *n* tenues *fpl* de plage.
beacon ['biːkən] *n* (*lighthouse*) fanal *m*; (*marker*) balise *f*; (*also*: **radio ~**) radiophare *m*.
bead [biːd] *n* perle *f*; (*of dew, sweat*) goutte *f*; **~s** (*necklace*) collier *m*.
beady ['biːdɪ] *adj*: **~ eyes** yeux *mpl* de fouine.
beagle [biːgl] *n* beagle *m*.
beak [biːk] *n* bec *m*.
beaker ['biːkə*] *n* gobelet *m*.
beam [biːm] *n* poutre *f*; (*of light*) rayon *m*; (*RADIO*) faisceau *m* radio ♦ *vi* rayonner; **to**

drive on full *or* **main** *or* (*US*) **high** ~ rouler en pleins phares.
beaming ['biːmɪŋ] *adj* (*sun, smile*) radieux(euse).
bean [biːn] *n* haricot *m*; (*of coffee*) grain *m*.
beanpole ['biːnpəul] *n* (*col*) perche *f*.
bean sprouts *npl* pousses *fpl* (de soja).
bear [bɛə*] *n* ours *m*; (*STOCK EXCHANGE*) baissier *m* ♦ *vb* (*pt* **bore**, *pp* **borne** [bɔː*, bɔːn]) *vt* porter; (*endure*) supporter; (*traces, signs*) porter; (*COMM*: *interest*) rapporter ♦ *vi*: **to ~ right/left** obliquer à droite/gauche, se diriger vers la droite/gauche; **to ~ the responsibility of** assumer la responsabilité de; **to ~ comparison with** soutenir la comparaison avec; **I can't ~ him** je ne peux pas le supporter *or* souffrir; **to bring pressure to ~ on sb** faire pression sur qn.
►**bear out** *vt* (*theory, suspicion*) confirmer.
►**bear up** *vi* supporter, tenir le coup; **he bore up well** il a tenu le coup.
►**bear with** *vt fus* (*sb's moods, temper*) supporter; ~ **with me a minute** un moment, s'il vous plaît.
bearable ['bɛərəbl] *adj* supportable.
beard [bɪəd] *n* barbe *f*.
bearded ['bɪədɪd] *adj* barbu(e).
bearer ['bɛərə*] *n* porteur *m*; (*of passport etc*) titulaire *m/f*.
bearing ['bɛərɪŋ] *n* maintien *m*, allure *f*; (*connection*) rapport *m*; (*TECH*): **(ball) ~s** *npl* roulement *m* (à billes); **to take a ~** faire le point; **to find one's ~s** s'orienter.
beast [biːst] *n* bête *f*; (*col*). **he's a ~** c'est une brute.
beastly ['biːstlɪ] *adj* infect(e).
beat [biːt] *n* battement *m*; (*MUS*) temps *m*, mesure *f*; (*of policeman*) ronde *f* ♦ *vt* (*pt* **beat**, *pp* **beaten**) battre; **off the ~en track** hors des chemins *or* sentiers battus; **to ~ about the bush** tourner autour du pot; **that ~s everything!** c'est le comble!
►**beat down** *vt* (*door*) enfoncer; (*price*) faire baisser; (*seller*) faire descendre ♦ *vi* (*rain*) tambouriner; (*sun*) taper.
►**beat off** *vt* repousser.
►**beat up** *vt* (*eggs*) battre; (*col*: *person*) tabasser.
beater ['biːtə*] *n* (*for eggs, cream*) fouet *m*, batteur *m*.
beating ['biːtɪŋ] *n* raclée *f*.
beat-up ['biːt'ʌp] *adj* (*col*) déglingué(e).
beautician [bjuː'tɪʃən] *n* esthéticien/ne.
beautiful ['bjuːtɪful] *adj* beau(belle).
beautifully ['bjuːtɪflɪ] *adv* admirablement.
beautify ['bjuːtɪfaɪ] *vt* embellir.
beauty ['bjuːtɪ] *n* beauté *f*; **the ~ of it is that ...** le plus beau, c'est que ....
beauty contest *n* concours *m* de beauté.
beauty queen *n* reine *f* de beauté.
beauty salon *n* institut *m* de beauté.
beauty sleep *n*: **I need my ~** j'ai besoin de faire un gros dodo.
beauty spot *n* grain *m* de beauté; (*BRIT TOURISM*) site naturel (d'une grande beauté).
beaver ['biːvə*] *n* castor *m*.
becalmed [bɪ'kɑːmd] *adj* immobilisé(e) par le calme plat.
became [bɪ'keɪm] *pt of* **become**.
because [bɪ'kɔz] *conj* parce que; ~ **of** *prep* à cause de.
beck [bɛk] *n*: **to be at sb's ~ and call** être à l'entière disposition de qn.
beckon ['bɛkən] *vt* (*also*: ~ **to**) faire signe (de venir) à.
become [bɪ'kʌm] *vt* (*irreg*: *like* **come**) devenir; **to ~ fat/thin** grossir/maigrir; **to ~ angry** se mettre en colère; **it became known that** on apprit que; **what has ~ of him?** qu'est-il devenu?
becoming [bɪ'kʌmɪŋ] *adj* (*behaviour*) convenable, bienséant(e); (*clothes*) seyant(e).
BECTU ['bɛktu] *n abbr* (*BRIT*) = *Broadcasting, Entertainment, Cinematographic and Theatre Union*.
BEd *n abbr* (= *Bachelor of Education*) *diplôme d'aptitude à l'enseignement*.
bed [bɛd] *n* lit *m*; (*of flowers*) parterre *m*; (*of coal, clay*) couche *f*; (*of sea, lake*) fond *m*; **to go to ~** aller se coucher.
►**bed down** *vi* se coucher.
bed and breakfast (B & B) *n* (*terms*) chambre et petit déjeuner; (*place*) ≈ chambre *f* d'hôte; *voir encadré*.

BED AND BREAKFAST

Un **bed and breakfast** *est une petite pension dans une maison particulière ou une ferme où l'on peut louer une chambre avec petit déjeuner compris pour un prix modique par rapport à ce que l'on paierait dans un hôtel. Ces établissements sont communément appelés "B & B", et sont signalés par une pancarte dans le jardin ou au-dessus de la porte.*

bedbug ['bɛdbʌg] *n* punaise *f*.
bedclothes ['bɛdkləuðz] *npl* couvertures *fpl* et draps *mpl*.
bedcover ['bɛdkʌvə*] *n* couvre-lit *m*, dessus-de-lit *m*.
bedding ['bɛdɪŋ] *n* literie *f*.
bedevil [bɪ'dɛvl] *vt* (*harass*) harceler; **to be ~led by** être victime de.
bedfellow ['bɛdfɛləu] *n*: **they are strange ~s** (*fig*) ça fait un drôle de mélange.
bedlam ['bɛdləm] *n* chahut *m*, cirque *m*.
bedpan ['bɛdpæn] *n* bassin *m* (hygiénique).
bedpost ['bɛdpəust] *n* colonne *f* de lit.
bedraggled [bɪ'drægld] *adj* dépenaillé(e), les vêtements en désordre.
bedridden ['bɛdrɪdn] *adj* cloué(e) au lit.
bedrock ['bɛdrɔk] *n* (*fig*) principes essentiels *or* de base, essentiel *m*; (*GEO*) roche *f* en

place, socle *m*.
bedroom ['bɛdrum] *n* chambre *f* (à coucher).
Beds *abbr* (*BRIT*) = *Bedfordshire*.
bed settee *n* canapé-lit *m*.
bedside ['bɛdsaɪd] *n*: **at sb's ~** au chevet de qn ♦ *cpd* (*book, lamp*) de chevet.
bedsit(ter) ['bɛdsɪt(ə*)] *n* (*BRIT*) chambre meublée, studio *m*.
bedspread ['bɛdsprɛd] *n* couvre-lit *m*, dessus-de-lit *m*.
bedtime ['bɛdtaɪm] *n*: **it's ~** c'est l'heure de se coucher.
bee [bi:] *n* abeille *f*; **to have a ~ in one's bonnet (about sth)** être obnubilé(e) (par qch).
beech [bi:tʃ] *n* hêtre *m*.
beef [bi:f] *n* bœuf *m*.
▸**beef up** *vt* (*col*: *support*) renforcer; (: *essay*) étoffer.
beefburger ['bi:fbə:gə*] *n* hamburger *m*.
beefeater ['bi:fi:tə*] *n* hallebardier *m* (de la tour de Londres).
beehive ['bi:haɪv] *n* ruche *f*.
bee-keeping ['bi:ki:pɪŋ] *n* apiculture *f*.
beeline ['bi:laɪn] *n*: **to make a ~ for** se diriger tout droit vers.
been [bi:n] *pp of* **be**.
beep [bi:p] *n* bip *m*.
beeper ['bi:pə*] *n* (*pager*) bip *m*.
beer [bɪə*] *n* bière *f*.
beer belly *n* (*col*) bedaine *f* (*de buveur de bière*).
beer can *n* canette *f* de bière.
beetle ['bi:tl] *n* scarabée *m*, coléoptère *m*.
beetroot ['bi:tru:t] *n* (*BRIT*) betterave *f*.
befall [bɪ'fɔ:l] *vi*(*vt*) (*irreg: like* **fall**) advenir (à).
befit [bɪ'fɪt] *vt* seoir à.
before [bɪ'fɔ:*] *prep* (*of time*) avant; (*of space*) devant ♦ *conj* avant que + *sub*; avant de ♦ *adv* avant; **~ going** avant de partir; **~ she goes** avant qu'elle (ne) parte; **the week ~** la semaine précédente *or* d'avant; **I've seen it ~** je l'ai déjà vu; **I've never seen it ~** c'est la première fois que je le vois.
beforehand [bɪ'fɔ:hænd] *adv* au préalable, à l'avance.
befriend [bɪ'frɛnd] *vt* venir en aide à; traiter en ami.
befuddled [bɪ'fʌdld] *adj*: **to be ~** avoir les idées brouillées.
beg [bɛg] *vi* mendier ♦ *vt* mendier; (*favour*) quémander, solliciter; (*entreat*) supplier; **I ~ your pardon** (*apologising*) excusez-moi; (: *not hearing*) pardon?; **that ~s the question of ...** cela soulève la question de ..., cela suppose réglée la question de ....
began [bɪ'gæn] *pt of* **begin**.
beggar ['bɛgə*] *n* (*also*: **~man, ~woman**) mendiant/e.
begin, *pt* began, *pp* begun [bɪ'gɪn, -'gæn, -'gʌn] *vt, vi* commencer; **to ~ doing** *or* **to do sth** commencer à faire qch; **~ning (from) Monday** à partir de lundi; **I can't ~ to thank you** je ne saurais vous remercier; **to ~ with** d'abord, pour commencer.
beginner [bɪ'gɪnə*] *n* débutant/e.
beginning [bɪ'gɪnɪŋ] *n* commencement *m*, début *m*; **right from the ~** dès le début.
begrudge [bɪ'grʌdʒ] *vt*: **to ~ sb sth** envier qch à qn; donner qch à contrecœur *or* à regret à qn.
beguile [bɪ'gaɪl] *vt* (*enchant*) enjôler.
beguiling [bɪ'gaɪlɪŋ] *adj* (*charming*) séduisant(e), enchanteur(eresse).
begun [bɪ'gʌn] *pp of* **begin**.
behalf [bɪ'hɑ:f] *n*: **on ~ of**, (*US*) **in ~ of** de la part de; au nom de; pour le compte de.
behave [bɪ'heɪv] *vi* se conduire, se comporter; (*well*: *also*: **~ o.s.**) se conduire bien *or* comme il faut.
behaviour, (*US*) **behavior** [bɪ'heɪvjə*] *n* comportement *m*, conduite *f*.
behead [bɪ'hɛd] *vt* décapiter.
beheld [bɪ'hɛld] *pt, pp of* **behold**.
behind [bɪ'haɪnd] *prep* derrière; (*time*) en retard sur ♦ *adv* derrière; en retard ♦ *n* derrière *m*; **~ the scenes** dans les coulisses; **to leave sth ~** (*forget*) oublier de prendre qch; **to be ~ (schedule) with sth** être en retard dans qch.
behold [bɪ'həuld] *vt* (*irreg: like* **hold**) apercevoir, voir.
beige [beɪʒ] *adj* beige.
being ['bi:ɪŋ] *n* être *m*; **to come into ~** prendre naissance.
Beirut [beɪ'ru:t] *n* Beyrouth.
Belarus [bɛlə'rus] *n* Biélorussie *f*, Bélarus *m*.
Belarussian [bɛlə'rʌʃən] *adj* biélorusse ♦ *n* Biélorusse *m/f*; (*LING*) biélorusse *m*.
belated [bɪ'leɪtɪd] *adj* tardif(ive).
belch [bɛltʃ] *vi* avoir un renvoi, roter ♦ *vt* (*also*: **~ out**: *smoke etc*) vomir, cracher.
beleaguered [bɪ'li:gɪd] *adj* (*city*) assiégé(e); (*army*) cerné(e); (*fig*) sollicité(e) de toutes parts.
Belfast ['bɛlfɑ:st] *n* Belfast.
belfry ['bɛlfrɪ] *n* beffroi *m*.
Belgian ['bɛldʒən] *adj* belge, de Belgique ♦ *n* Belge *m/f*.
Belgium ['bɛldʒəm] *n* Belgique *f*.
Belgrade [bɛl'greɪd] *n* Belgrade.
belie [bɪ'laɪ] *vt* démentir; (*give false impression of*) occulter.
belief [bɪ'li:f] *n* (*opinion*) conviction *f*; (*trust, faith*) foi *f*; (*acceptance as true*) croyance *f*; **it's beyond ~** c'est incroyable; **in the ~ that** dans l'idée que.
believable [bɪ'li:vəbl] *adj* croyable.
believe [bɪ'li:v] *vt, vi* croire, estimer; **to ~ in** (*God*) croire en; (*ghosts, method*) croire à; **I don't ~ in corporal punishment** je ne suis pas partisan des châtiments corporels; **he is ~d to be abroad** il serait à l'étranger.
believer [bɪ'li:və*] *n* (*in idea, activity*): **~ in** partisan/e de; (*REL*) croyant/e.

belittle [bɪ'lɪtl] *vt* déprécier, rabaisser.
Belize [bɛ'li:z] *n* Bélize *m.*
bell [bɛl] *n* cloche *f*; (*small*) clochette *f*, grelot *m*; (*on door*) sonnette *f*; (*electric*) sonnerie *f*; **that rings a ~** (*fig*) cela me rappelle qch.
bell-bottoms ['bɛlbɔtəmz] *npl* pantalon *m* à pattes d'éléphant.
bellboy ['bɛlbɔɪ], (*US*) **bellhop** ['bɛlhɔp] *n* groom *m*, chasseur *m.*
belligerent [bɪ'lɪdʒərənt] *adj* (*at war*) belligérant(e); (*fig*) agressif(ive).
bellow ['bɛləu] *vi* mugir; beugler ♦ *vt* (*orders*) hurler.
bellows ['bɛləuz] *npl* soufflet *m.*
bell push *n* (*BRIT*) bouton *m* de sonnette.
belly ['bɛlɪ] *n* ventre *m.*
bellyache ['bɛlɪeɪk] (*col*) *n* colique *f* ♦ *vi* ronchonner.
bellybutton ['bɛlɪbʌtn] *n* nombril *m.*
bellyful ['bɛlɪful] *n* (*col*): **I've had a ~** j'en ai ras le bol.
belong [bɪ'lɔŋ] *vi*: **to ~ to** appartenir à; (*club etc*) faire partie de; **this book ~s here** ce livre va ici, la place de ce livre est ici.
belongings [bɪ'lɔŋɪŋz] *npl* affaires *fpl*, possessions *fpl*; **personal ~** effets personnels.
Belorussia [bɛlə'rʌʃə] *n* Biélorussie *f.*
Belorussian [bɛlə'rʌʃən] *adj*, *n* = **Belarussian.**
beloved [bɪ'lʌvɪd] *adj* (bien-)aimé(e), chéri(e) ♦ *n* bien-aimé/e.
below [bɪ'ləu] *prep* sous, au-dessous de ♦ *adv* en dessous; en contre-bas; **see ~** voir plus bas *or* plus loin *or* ci-dessous; **temperatures ~ normal** températures inférieures à la normale.
belt [bɛlt] *n* ceinture *f*; (*TECH*) courroie *f* ♦ *vt* (*thrash*) donner une raclée à ♦ *vi* (*BRIT col*) filer (à toutes jambes); **industrial ~** zone industrielle.
►**belt out** *vt* (*song*) chanter à tue-tête *or* à pleins poumons.
►**belt up** *vi* (*BRIT col*) la boucler.
beltway ['bɛltweɪ] *n* (*US AUT*) route *f* de ceinture; (*: motorway*) périphérique *m.*
bemoan [bɪ'məun] *vt* se lamenter sur.
bemused [bɪ'mju:zd] *adj* médusé(e).
bench [bɛntʃ] *n* banc *m*; (*in workshop*) établi *m*; **the B~** (*LAW*) la magistrature, la Cour.
bench mark *n* repère *m.*
bend [bɛnd] *vb* (*pt*, *pp* **bent** [bɛnt]) *vt* courber; (*leg, arm*) plier ♦ *vi* se courber ♦ *n* (*BRIT*: *in road*) virage *m*, tournant *m*; (*in pipe, river*) coude *m.*
►**bend down** *vi* se baisser.
►**bend over** *vi* se pencher.
bends [bɛndz] *npl* (*MED*) maladie *f* des caissons.
beneath [bɪ'ni:θ] *prep* sous, au-dessous de; (*unworthy of*) indigne de ♦ *adv* dessous, au-dessous, en bas.
benefactor ['bɛnɪfæktə*] *n* bienfaiteur *m.*
benefactress ['bɛnɪfæktrɪs] *n* bienfaitrice *f.*
beneficial [bɛnɪ'fɪʃəl] *adj*: **~ (to)** salutaire (pour), bénéfique (à).
beneficiary [bɛnɪ'fɪʃərɪ] *n* (*LAW*) bénéficiaire *m/f.*
benefit ['bɛnɪfɪt] *n* avantage *m*, profit *m*; (*allowance of money*) allocation *f* ♦ *vt* faire du bien à, profiter à ♦ *vi*: **he'll ~ from it** cela lui fera du bien, il y gagnera *or* s'en trouvera bien.
benefit performance *n* représentation *f or* gala *m* de bienfaisance.
Benelux ['bɛnɪlʌks] *n* Benelux *m.*
benevolent [bɪ'nɛvələnt] *adj* bienveillant(e).
BEng *n abbr* (= *Bachelor of Engineering*) *diplôme universitaire.*
benign [bɪ'naɪn] *adj* (*person, smile*) bienveillant(e), affable; (*MED*) bénin(igne).
bent [bɛnt] *pt, pp of* **bend** ♦ *n* inclination *f*, penchant *m* ♦ *adj* (*wire, pipe*) coudé(e); (*col*: *dishonest*) véreux(euse); **to be ~ on** être résolu(e) à.
bequeath [bɪ'kwi:ð] *vt* léguer.
bequest [bɪ'kwɛst] *n* legs *m.*
bereaved [bɪ'ri:vd] *n*: **the ~** la famille du disparu ♦ *adj* endeuillé(e).
bereavement [bɪ'ri:vmənt] *n* deuil *m.*
beret ['bɛreɪ] *n* béret *m.*
Bering Sea ['beɪrɪŋ-] *n*: **the ~** la mer de Béring.
berk [bə:k] *n* (*BRIT col*) andouille *m/f.*
Berks *abbr* (*BRIT*) = *Berkshire.*
Berlin [bə:'lɪn] *n* Berlin; **East/West ~** Berlin Est/Ouest.
berm [bə:m] *n* (*US AUT*) accotement *m.*
Bermuda [bə:'mju:də] *n* Bermudes *fpl.*
Bermuda shorts *npl* bermuda *m.*
Bern [bə:n] *n* Berne.
berry ['bɛrɪ] *n* baie *f.*
berserk [bə'sə:k] *adj*: **to go ~** être pris(e) d'une rage incontrôlable; se déchaîner.
berth [bə:θ] *n* (*bed*) couchette *f*; (*for ship*) poste *m* d'amarrage, mouillage *m* ♦ *vi* (*in harbour*) venir à quai; (*at anchor*) mouiller; **to give sb a wide ~** (*fig*) éviter qn.
beseech, *pt, pp* **besought** [bɪ'si:tʃ, -'sɔ:t] *vt* implorer, supplier.
beset, *pt, pp* **beset** [bɪ'sɛt] *vt* assaillir ♦ *adj*: **~ with** semé(e) de.
besetting [bɪ'sɛtɪŋ] *adj*: **his ~ sin** son vice, son gros défaut.
beside [bɪ'saɪd] *prep* à côté de; (*compared with*) par rapport à; **that's ~ the point** ça n'a rien à voir; **to be ~ o.s. (with anger)** être hors de soi.
besides [bɪ'saɪdz] *adv* en outre, de plus ♦ *prep* en plus de; (*except*) excepté.
besiege [bɪ'si:dʒ] *vt* (*town*) assiéger; (*fig*) assaillir.
besotted [bɪ'sɔtɪd] *adj* (*BRIT*): **~ with** entiché(e) de.
besought [bɪ'sɔ:t] *pt, pp of* **beseech.**
bespectacled [bɪ'spɛktɪkld] *adj* à lunettes.

bespoke [bɪ'spəuk] *adj* (*BRIT*: *garment*) fait(e) sur mesure; ~ **tailor** tailleur *m* à façon.
best [bɛst] *adj* meilleur(e) ♦ *adv* le mieux; **the ~ part of** (*quantity*) le plus clair de, la plus grande partie de; **at ~** au mieux; **to make the ~ of sth** s'accommoder de qch (du mieux que l'on peut); **to do one's ~** faire de son mieux; **to the ~ of my knowledge** pour autant que je sache; **to the ~ of my ability** du mieux que je pourrai; **he's not exactly patient at the ~ of times** il n'est jamais spécialement patient; **the ~ thing to do is ...** le mieux, c'est de ....
best man *n* garçon *m* d'honneur.
bestow [bɪ'stəu] *vt* accorder; (*title*) conférer.
bestseller ['bɛst'sɛlə*] *n* bestseller *m*, succès *m* de librairie.
bet [bɛt] *n* pari *m* ♦ *vt, vi* (*pt, pp* **bet** *or* **betted**) parier; **it's a safe ~** (*fig*) il y a de fortes chances.
Bethlehem ['bɛθlɪhɛm] *n* Bethléem.
betray [bɪ'treɪ] *vt* trahir.
betrayal [bɪ'treɪəl] *n* trahison *f*.
better ['bɛtə*] *adj* meilleur(e) ♦ *adv* mieux ♦ *vt* améliorer ♦ *n*: **to get the ~ of** triompher de, l'emporter sur; **a change for the ~** une amélioration; **I had ~ go** il faut que je m'en aille; **you had ~ do it** vous feriez mieux de le faire; **he thought ~ of it** il s'est ravisé; **to get ~** aller mieux; s'améliorer; **that's ~!** c'est mieux!; **~ off** *adj* plus à l'aise financièrement; (*fig*): **you'd be ~ off this way** vous vous en trouveriez mieux ainsi, ce serait mieux *or* plus pratique ainsi.
betting ['bɛtɪŋ] *n* paris *mpl*.
betting shop *n* (*BRIT*) bureau *m* de paris.
between [bɪ'twi:n] *prep* entre ♦ *adv* au milieu, dans l'intervalle; **the road ~ here and London** la route d'ici à Londres; **we only had 5 ~ us** nous n'en avions que 5 en tout.
bevel ['bɛvəl] *n* (*also*: **~ edge**) biseau *m*.
beverage ['bɛvərɪdʒ] *n* boisson *f* (*gén sans alcool*).
bevy ['bɛvɪ] *n*: **a ~ of** un essaim *or* une volée de.
bewail [bɪ'weɪl] *vt* se lamenter sur.
beware [bɪ'wɛə*] *vt, vi*: **to ~ (of)** prendre garde (à).
bewildered [bɪ'wɪldəd] *adj* dérouté(e), ahuri(e).
bewildering [bɪ'wɪldrɪŋ] *adj* déroutant(e), ahurissant(e).
bewitching [bɪ'wɪtʃɪŋ] *adj* enchanteur(teresse).
beyond [bɪ'jɔnd] *prep* (*in space*) au-delà de; (*exceeding*) au-dessus de ♦ *adv* au-delà; **~ doubt** hors de doute; **~ repair** irréparable.
b/f *abbr* = *brought forward*.
BFPO *n abbr* (= *British Forces Post Office*) *service postal de l'armée*.
bhp *n abbr* (*AUT*: = *brake horsepower*) puissance *f* aux freins.
bi... [baɪ] *prefix* bi....
biannual [baɪ'ænjuəl] *adj* semestriel(le).
bias ['baɪəs] *n* (*prejudice*) préjugé *m*, parti pris; (*preference*) prévention *f*.
bias(s)ed ['baɪəst] *adj* partial(e), montrant un parti pris; **to be ~ against** avoir un préjugé contre.
biathlon [baɪ'æθlən] *n* biathlon *m*.
bib [bɪb] *n* bavoir *m*, bavette *f*.
Bible ['baɪbl] *n* Bible *f*.
Bible Belt *n* (*US*): **the ~** *les États du Sud profondément protestants*.
bibliography [bɪblɪ'ɔgrəfɪ] *n* bibliographie *f*.
bicarbonate of soda [baɪ'kɑ:bənɪt-] *n* bicarbonate *m* de soude.
bicentenary [baɪsɛn'ti:nərɪ] *n*, **bicentennial** [baɪsɛn'tɛnɪəl] *n* bicentenaire *m*.
biceps ['baɪsɛps] *n* biceps *m*.
bicker ['bɪkə*] *vi* se chamailler.
bicycle ['baɪsɪkl] *n* bicyclette *f*.
bicycle path *n*, **bicycle track** *n* piste *f* cyclable.
bicycle pump *n* pompe *f* à vélo.
bid [bɪd] *n* offre *f*; (*at auction*) enchère *f*; (*attempt*) tentative *f* ♦ *vb* (*pt* **bid** *or* **bade** [bæd], *pp* **bid** *or* **bidden** ['bɪdn]) *vi* faire une enchère *or* offre ♦ *vt* faire une enchère *or* offre de; **to ~ sb good day** souhaiter le bonjour à qn.
bidder ['bɪdə*] *n*: **the highest ~** le plus offrant.
bidding ['bɪdɪŋ] *n* enchères *fpl*.
bide [baɪd] *vt*: **to ~ one's time** attendre son heure.
bidet ['bi:deɪ] *n* bidet *m*.
bidirectional ['baɪdɪ'rɛkʃənl] *adj* bidirectionnel(le).
biennial [baɪ'ɛnɪəl] *adj* biennal(e), bisannuel(le) ♦ *n* biennale *f*; (*plant*) plante bisannuelle.
bier [bɪə*] *n* bière *f* (*cercueil*).
bifocals [baɪ'fəuklz] *npl* lunettes *fpl* à double foyer.
big [bɪg] *adj* (*in height*: *person, building, tree*) grand(e); (*in bulk, amount*: *person, parcel, book*) gros(se); **to do things in a ~ way** faire les choses en grand.
bigamy ['bɪgəmɪ] *n* bigamie *f*.
big dipper [-'dɪpə*] *n* montagnes *fpl* russes.
big end *n* (*AUT*) tête *f* de bielle.
biggish ['bɪgɪʃ] *adj* (*see big*) assez grand(e); assez gros(se).
bigheaded ['bɪg'hɛdɪd] *adj* prétentieux(euse).
big-hearted ['bɪg'hɑ:tɪd] *adj* au grand cœur.
bigot ['bɪgət] *n* fanatique *m/f*, sectaire *m/f*.
bigoted ['bɪgətɪd] *adj* fanatique, sectaire.
bigotry ['bɪgətrɪ] *n* fanatisme *m*, sectarisme *m*.
big toe *n* gros orteil.
big top *n* grand chapiteau.
big wheel *n* (*at fair*) grande roue.
bigwig ['bɪgwɪg] *n* (*col*) grosse légume, huile *f*.

bike [baɪk] *n* vélo *m*, bécane *f*.
bike lane *n* piste *f* cyclable.
bikini [bɪ'kiːnɪ] *n* bikini *m*.
bilateral [baɪ'lætərl] *adj* bilatéral(e).
bile [baɪl] *n* bile *f*.
bilingual [baɪ'lɪŋgwəl] *adj* bilingue.
bilious ['bɪlɪəs] *adj* bilieux(euse); (*fig*) maussade, irritable.
bill [bɪl] *n* note *f*, facture *f*; (*POL*) projet *m* de loi; (*US*: *banknote*) billet *m* (de banque); (*in restaurant*) addition *f*, note *f*; (*notice*) affiche *f*; (*THEAT*): **on the** ~ à l'affiche; (*of bird*) bec *m* ♦ *vt* (*item*) facturer; (*customer*) remettre la facture à; **may I have the** ~ **please?** (est-ce que je peux avoir) l'addition, s'il vous plaît?; **"stick** *or* **post no** ~**s"** "défense d'afficher"; **to fit** *or* **fill the** ~ (*fig*) faire l'affaire; ~ **of exchange** lettre *f* de change; ~ **of lading** connaissement *m*; ~ **of sale** contrat *m* de vente.
billboard ['bɪlbɔːd] *n* panneau *m* d'affichage.
billet ['bɪlɪt] *n* cantonnement *m* (chez l'habitant) ♦ *vt* (*troops*) cantonner.
billfold ['bɪlfəuld] *n* (*US*) portefeuille *m*.
billiards ['bɪljədz] *n* (jeu *m* de) billard *m*.
billion ['bɪljən] *n* milliard *m*.
billow ['bɪləu] *n* nuage *m* ♦ *vi* (*smoke*) s'élever en nuage; (*sail*) se gonfler.
billy goat ['bɪlɪgəut] *n* bouc *m*.
bimbo ['bɪmbəu] *n* (*col*) ravissante idiote *f*.
bin [bɪn] *n* boîte *f*; (*BRIT*: *also*: **dust~, litter~**) poubelle *f*; (*for coal*) coffre *m*.
binary ['baɪnərɪ] *adj* binaire.
bind, *pt, pp* **bound** [baɪnd, baund] *vt* attacher; (*book*) relier; (*oblige*) obliger, contraindre.
▶**bind over** *vt* (*LAW*) mettre en liberté conditionnelle.
▶**bind up** *vt* (*wound*) panser; **to be bound up in** (*work, research etc*) être complètement absorbé par, être accroché par; **to be bound up with** (*person*) être accroché à.
binder ['baɪndə*] *n* (*file*) classeur *m*.
binding ['baɪndɪŋ] *n* (*of book*) reliure *f* ♦ *adj* (*contract*) qui constitue une obligation.
binge [bɪndʒ] *n* (*col*): **to go on a** ~ faire la bringue.
bingo ['bɪŋgəu] *n sorte de jeu de loto pratiqué dans des établissements publics.*
bin liner *n* sac *m* poubelle.
binoculars [bɪ'nɔkjuləz] *npl* jumelles *fpl*.
biochemistry [baɪə'kɛmɪstrɪ] *n* biochimie *f*.
biodegradable ['baɪəudɪ'greɪdəbl] *adj* biodégradable.
biodiversity ['baɪəudaɪ'vəːsɪtɪ] *n* biodiversité *f*.
biofuel ['baɪəufjuəl] *n* combustible *m* organique.
biographer [baɪ'ɔgrəfə*] *n* biographe *m/f*.
biographic(al) [baɪə'græfɪk(l)] *adj* biographique.
biography [baɪ'ɔgrəfɪ] *n* biographie *f*.
biological [baɪə'lɔdʒɪkl] *adj* biologique.
biological clock *n* horloge *f* physiologique.
biologist [baɪ'ɔlədʒɪst] *n* biologiste *m/f*.
biology [baɪ'ɔlədʒɪ] *n* biologie *f*.
biophysics ['baɪəu'fɪzɪks] *n* biophysique *f*.
biopic ['baɪəupɪk] *n* film *m* biographique.
biopsy ['baɪɔpsɪ] *n* biopsie *f*.
biosphere ['baɪəsfɪə*] *n* biosphère *f*.
biotechnology ['baɪəutɛk'nɔlədʒɪ] *n* biotechnologie *f*.
bioterrorism *n* bioterrorisme *m*.
birch [bəːtʃ] *n* bouleau *m*.
bird [bəːd] *n* oiseau *m*; (*BRIT col*: *girl*) nana *f*.
bird of prey *n* oiseau *m* de proie.
bird's-eye view ['bəːdzaɪ-] *n* vue *f* à vol d'oiseau; (*fig*) vue d'ensemble *or* générale.
bird watcher [-wɔtʃə*] *n* ornithologue *m/f* amateur.
Biro ['baɪərəu] *n* ® stylo *m* à bille.
birth [bəːθ] *n* naissance *f*; **to give** ~ **to** donner naissance à, mettre au monde; (*animal*) mettre bas.
birth certificate *n* acte *m* de naissance.
birth control *n* limitation *f* des naissances; méthode(s) contraceptive(s).
birthday ['bəːθdeɪ] *n* anniversaire *m*.
birthmark ['bəːθmɑːk] *n* envie *f*, tache *f* de vin.
birthplace ['bəːθpleɪs] *n* lieu *m* de naissance.
birth rate *n* (taux *m* de) natalité *f*.
Biscay ['bɪskeɪ] *n*: **the Bay of** ~ le golfe de Gascogne.
biscuit ['bɪskɪt] *n* (*BRIT*) biscuit *m*; (*US*) petit pain au lait.
bisect [baɪ'sɛkt] *vt* couper *or* diviser en deux.
bisexual ['baɪ'sɛksjuəl] *adj, n* bisexuel(le).
bishop ['bɪʃəp] *n* évêque *m*; (*CHESS*) fou *m*.
bistro ['biːstrəu] *n* petit restaurant *m*, bistrot *m*.
bit [bɪt] *pt of* **bite** ♦ *n* morceau *m*; (*of tool*) mèche *f*; (*of horse*) mors *m*; (*COMPUT*) bit *m*, élément *m* binaire; **a** ~ **of** un peu de; **a** ~ **mad/dangerous** un peu fou/risqué; ~ **by** ~ petit à petit; **to come to** ~**s** (*break*) tomber en morceaux, se déglinguer; **bring all your** ~**s and pieces** apporte toutes tes affaires; **to do one's** ~ y mettre du sien.
bitch [bɪtʃ] *n* (*dog*) chienne *f*; (*col!*) salope *f* (*!*), garce *f*.
bite [baɪt] *vt, vi* (*pt* **bit** [bɪt], *pp* **bitten** ['bɪtn]) mordre ♦ *n* morsure *f*; (*insect* ~) piqûre *f*; (*mouthful*) bouchée *f*; **let's have a** ~ **(to eat)** mangeons un morceau; **to** ~ **one's nails** se ronger les ongles.
biting ['baɪtɪŋ] *adj* mordant(e).
bit part *n* (*THEAT*) petit rôle.
bitten ['bɪtn] *pp of* **bite**.
bitter ['bɪtə*] *adj* amer(ère); (*criticism*) cinglant(e); (*icy: weather, wind*) glacial(e) ♦ *n* (*BRIT*: *beer*) bière *f* (*à forte teneur en houblon*); **to the** ~ **end** jusqu'au bout.
bitterly ['bɪtəlɪ] *adv* (*complain, weep*) amèrement; (*oppose, criticise*) durement, âprement; (*jealous, disappointed*) horriblement; **it's** ~ **cold** il fait un froid de loup.

bitterness ['bɪtənɪs] *n* amertume *f*; goût amer.
bittersweet ['bɪtəswiːt] *adj* aigre-doux(douce).
bitty ['bɪtɪ] *adj* (*BRIT col*) décousu(e).
bitumen ['bɪtjumɪn] *n* bitume *m*.
bivouac ['bɪvuæk] *n* bivouac *m*.
bizarre [bɪ'zɑː*] *adj* bizarre.
bk *abbr* = **bank, book**.
BL *n abbr* (*= Bachelor of Law(s), Bachelor of Letters*) *diplôme universitaire*; (*US*: *= Bachelor of Literature*) *diplôme universitaire*.
bl *abbr* = **bill of lading**.
blab [blæb] *vi* jaser, trop parler ♦ *vt* (*also*: ~ **out**) laisser échapper, aller raconter.
black [blæk] *adj* noir(e) ♦ *n* (*colour*) noir *m*; (*person*): **B~** noir/e ♦ *vt* (*shoes*) cirer; (*BRIT INDUSTRY*) boycotter; **to give sb a ~ eye** pocher l'œil à qn, faire un œil au beurre noir à qn; ~ **coffee** café noir; **there it is in ~ and white** (*fig*) c'est écrit noir sur blanc; **to be in the** ~ (*in credit*) avoir un compte créditeur; ~ **and blue** *adj* couvert(e) de bleus.
►**black out** *vi* (*faint*) s'évanouir.
black belt *n* (*JUDO etc*) ceinture noire; **he's a** ~ il est ceinture noire.
blackberry ['blækbərɪ] *n* mûre *f*.
blackbird ['blækbəːd] *n* merle *m*.
blackboard ['blækbɔːd] *n* tableau noir.
black box *n* (*AVIAT*) boîte noire.
Black Country *n* (*BRIT*): **the** ~ le Pays Noir (*dans les Midlands*).
blackcurrant ['blæk'kʌrənt] *n* cassis *m*.
black economy *n* (*BRIT*) travail *m* (au) noir.
blacken ['blækn] *vt* noircir.
Black Forest *n*: **the** ~ la Forêt Noire.
blackhead ['blækhɛd] *n* point noir.
black hole *n* (*ASTRONOMY*) trou noir.
black ice *n* verglas *m*.
blackjack ['blækdʒæk] *n* (*CARDS*) vingt-et-un *m*; (*US*: *truncheon*) matraque *f*.
blackleg ['blæklɛg] *n* (*BRIT*) briseur *m* de grève, jaune *m*.
blacklist ['blæklɪst] *n* liste noire ♦ *vt* mettre sur la liste noire.
blackmail ['blækmeɪl] *n* chantage *m* ♦ *vt* faire chanter, soumettre au chantage.
blackmailer ['blækmeɪlə*] *n* maître-chanteur *m*.
black market *n* marché noir.
blackout ['blækaut] *n* panne *f* d'électricité; (*in wartime*) black-out *m*; (*TV*) interruption *f* d'émission; (*fainting*) syncope *f*.
black pepper *n* poivre noir.
Black Sea *n*: **the** ~ la mer Noire.
black sheep *n* brebis galeuse.
blacksmith ['blæksmɪθ] *n* forgeron *m*.
black spot *n* (*AUT*) point noir.
bladder ['blædə*] *n* vessie *f*.
blade [bleɪd] *n* lame *f*; (*of oar*) plat *m*; ~ **of grass** brin *m* d'herbe.
blame [bleɪm] *n* faute *f*, blâme *m* ♦ *vt*: **to ~ sb/sth for sth** attribuer à qn/qch la responsabilité de qch; reprocher qch à qn/qch; **who's to ~?** qui est le fautif *or* coupable *or* responsable?; **I'm not to** ~ ce n'est pas ma faute.
blameless ['bleɪmlɪs] *adj* irréprochable.
blanch [blɑːntʃ] *vi* (*person, face*) blêmir ♦ *vt* (*CULIN*) blanchir.
bland [blænd] *adj* affable; (*taste*) doux(douce), fade.
blank [blæŋk] *adj* blanc(blanche); (*look*) sans expression, dénué(e) d'expression ♦ *n* espace *m* vide, blanc *m*; (*cartridge*) cartouche *f* à blanc; **we drew a** ~ (*fig*) nous n'avons abouti à rien.
blank cheque, (*US*) **blank check** *n* chèque *m* en blanc; **to give sb a ~ to do ...** (*fig*) donner carte blanche à qn pour faire ....
blanket ['blæŋkɪt] *n* couverture *f* ♦ *adj* (*statement, agreement*) global(e), de portée générale; **to give ~ cover** (*subj: insurance policy*) couvrir tous les risques.
blare [blɛə*] *vi* (*brass band, horns, radio*) beugler.
blarney ['blɑːnɪ] *n* boniment *m*.
blasé ['blɑːzeɪ] *adj* blasé(e).
blasphemous ['blæsfɪməs] *adj* (*words*) blasphématoire; (*person*) blasphémateur(trice).
blasphemy ['blæsfɪmɪ] *n* blasphème *m*.
blast [blɑːst] *n* explosion *f*; (*shock wave*) souffle *m*; (*of air, steam*) bouffée *f* ♦ *vt* faire sauter *or* exploser ♦ *excl* (*BRIT col*) zut!; **(at) full** ~ (*play music etc*) à plein volume.
►**blast off** *vi* (*SPACE*) décoller.
blast-off ['blɑːstɔf] *n* (*SPACE*) lancement *m*.
blatant ['bleɪtənt] *adj* flagrant(e), criant(e).
blatantly ['bleɪtəntlɪ] *adv* (*lie*) ouvertement; **it's ~ obvious** c'est l'évidence même.
blaze [bleɪz] *n* (*fire*) incendie *m*; (*flames: of fire, sun etc*) embrasement *m*; (*: in hearth*) flamme *f*, flambée *f*; (*fig*) flamboiement *m* ♦ *vi* (*fire*) flamber; (*fig*) flamboyer, resplendir ♦ *vt*: **to ~ a trail** (*fig*) montrer la voie; **in a ~ of publicity** à grand renfort de publicité.
blazer ['bleɪzə*] *n* blazer *m*.
bleach [bliːtʃ] *n* (*also*: **household** ~) eau *f* de Javel ♦ *vt* (*linen*) blanchir.
bleached [bliːtʃt] *adj* (*hair*) oxygéné(e), décoloré(e).
bleachers ['bliːtʃəz] *npl* (*US SPORT*) gradins *mpl* (*en plein soleil*).
bleak [bliːk] *adj* morne, désolé(e); (*weather*) triste, maussade; (*smile*) lugubre; (*prospect, future*) morose.
bleary-eyed ['blɪərɪ'aɪd] *adj* aux yeux pleins de sommeil.
bleat [bliːt] *n* bêlement *m* ♦ *vi* bêler.
bleed, *pt, pp* **bled** [bliːd, blɛd] *vt* saigner; (*brakes, radiator*) purger ♦ *vi* saigner; **my nose is ~ing** je saigne du nez.
bleep [bliːp] *n* (*RADIO, TV*) top *m*; (*of pocket device*) bip *m* ♦ *vi* émettre des signaux ♦ *vt* (*doctor etc*) appeler (*au moyen d'un bip*).

bleeper ['bli:pə*] *n* (*of doctor etc*) bip *m*.
blemish ['blɛmɪʃ] *n* défaut *m*; (*on reputation*) tache *f*.
blend [blɛnd] *n* mélange *m* ♦ *vt* mélanger ♦ *vi* (*colours etc*) se mélanger, se fondre, s'allier.
blender ['blɛndə*] *n* (*CULIN*) mixeur *m*.
bless, *pt, pp* **blessed** *or* **blest** [blɛs, blɛst] *vt* bénir; **to be ~ed with** avoir le bonheur de jouir de *or* d'avoir.
blessed ['blɛsɪd] *adj* (*REL: holy*) béni(e); (*happy*) bienheureux(euse); **it rains every ~ day** il ne se passe pas de jour sans qu'il ne pleuve.
blessing ['blɛsɪŋ] *n* bénédiction *f*; bienfait *m*; **to count one's ~s** s'estimer heureux; **it was a ~ in disguise** c'est un bien pour un mal.
blew [blu:] *pt of* **blow**.
blight [blaɪt] *n* (*of plants*) rouille *f* ♦ *vt* (*hopes etc*) anéantir, briser.
blimey ['blaɪmɪ] *excl* (*BRIT col*) mince alors!
blind [blaɪnd] *adj* aveugle ♦ *n* (*for window*) store *m* ♦ *vt* aveugler; **to turn a ~ eye (on** *or* **to)** fermer les yeux (sur).
blind alley *n* impasse *f*.
blind corner *n* (*BRIT*) virage *m* sans visibilité.
blind date *n* rendez-vous galant (avec un(e) inconnu(e)).
blindfold ['blaɪndfəuld] *n* bandeau *m* ♦ *adj, adv* les yeux bandés ♦ *vt* bander les yeux à.
blindly ['blaɪndlɪ] *adv* aveuglément.
blindness ['blaɪndnɪs] *n* cécité *f*; (*fig*) aveuglement *m*.
blind spot *n* (*AUT etc*) angle *m* aveugle; (*fig*) angle mort.
blink [blɪŋk] *vi* cligner des yeux; (*light*) clignoter ♦ *n*: **the TV's on the ~** (*col*) la télé ne va pas tarder à nous lâcher.
blinkers ['blɪŋkəz] *npl* œillères *fpl*.
blinking ['blɪŋkɪŋ] *adj* (*BRIT col*): **this ~ ...** ce fichu *or* sacré ....
blip [blɪp] *n* (*on radar etc*) spot *m*; (*on graph*) petite aberration; (*fig*) petite anomalie (passagère).
bliss [blɪs] *n* félicité *f*, bonheur *m* sans mélange.
blissful ['blɪsful] *adj* (*event, day*) merveilleux(euse); (*smile*) de bonheur; **a ~ sigh** un soupir d'aise; **in ~ ignorance** dans une ignorance béate.
blissfully ['blɪsfulɪ] *adv* (*smile*) béatement; (*happy*) merveilleusement.
blister ['blɪstə*] *n* (*on skin*) ampoule *f*, cloque *f*; (*on paintwork*) boursouflure *f* ♦ *vi* (*paint*) se boursoufler, se cloquer.
blithely ['blaɪðlɪ] *adv* (*unconcernedly*) tranquillement; (*joyfully*) gaiement.
blithering ['blɪðərɪŋ] *adj* (*col*): **this ~ idiot** cet espèce d'idiot.
BLit(t) *n abbr* (= *Bachelor of Literature*) *diplôme universitaire*.
blitz [blɪts] *n* bombardement (aérien); **to have a ~ on sth** (*fig*) s'attaquer à qch.
blizzard ['blɪzəd] *n* blizzard *m*, tempête *f* de neige.
BLM *n abbr* (*US*: = *Bureau of Land Management*) ≈ les domaines.
bloated ['bləutɪd] *adj* (*face*) bouffi(e); (*stomach*) gonflé(e).
blob [blɔb] *n* (*drop*) goutte *f*; (*stain, spot*) tache *f*.
bloc [blɔk] *n* (*POL*) bloc *m*.
block [blɔk] *n* bloc *m*; (*in pipes*) obstruction *f*; (*toy*) cube *m*; (*of buildings*) pâté *m* (de maisons) ♦ *vt* bloquer; (*COMPUT*) grouper; **~ of flats** (*BRIT*) immeuble (locatif); **3 ~s from here** à trois rues d'ici; **mental ~** blocage *m*; **~ and tackle** (*TECH*) palan *m*.
►**block up** *vt* boucher.
blockade [blɔ'keɪd] *n* blocus *m* ♦ *vt* faire le blocus de.
blockage ['blɔkɪdʒ] *n* obstruction *f*.
block booking *n* réservation *f* en bloc.
blockbuster ['blɔkbʌstə*] *n* (*film, book*) grand succès.
block capitals *npl* majuscules *fpl* d'imprimerie.
blockhead ['blɔkhɛd] *n* imbécile *m/f*.
block letters *npl* majuscules *fpl*.
block release *n* (*BRIT*) congé *m* de formation.
block vote *n* (*BRIT*) vote *m* de délégation.
bloke [bləuk] *n* (*BRIT col*) type *m*.
blonde [blɔnd] *adj, n* blond(e).
blood [blʌd] *n* sang *m*.
blood bank *n* banque *f* du sang.
blood count *n* numération *f* globulaire.
bloodcurdling ['blʌdkə:dlɪŋ] *adj* à vous glacer le sang.
blood donor *n* donneur/euse de sang.
blood group *n* groupe sanguin.
bloodhound ['blʌdhaund] *n* limier *m*.
bloodless ['blʌdlɪs] *adj* (*victory*) sans effusion de sang; (*pale*) anémié(e).
bloodletting ['blʌdlɛtɪŋ] *n* (*MED*) saignée *f*; (*fig*) effusion *f* de sang, représailles *fpl*.
blood poisoning *n* empoisonnement *m* du sang.
blood pressure *n* tension (artérielle); **to have high/low ~** faire de l'hypertension/l'hypotension.
bloodshed ['blʌdʃɛd] *n* effusion *f* de sang, carnage *m*.
bloodshot ['blʌdʃɔt] *adj*: **~ eyes** yeux injectés de sang.
bloodstained ['blʌdsteɪnd] *adj* taché(e) de sang.
bloodstream ['blʌdstri:m] *n* sang *m*, système sanguin.
blood test *n* analyse *f* de sang.
bloodthirsty ['blʌdθə:stɪ] *adj* sanguinaire.
blood transfusion *n* transfusion *f* de sang.
blood type *n* groupe sanguin.
blood vessel *n* vaisseau sanguin.
bloody ['blʌdɪ] *adj* sanglant(e); (*BRIT col!*): **this ~ ...** ce foutu ..., ce putain de ... (*!*); ~

strong/good (*col!*) vachement *or* sacrément fort/bon.
bloody-minded ['blʌdɪ'maɪndɪd] *adj* (*BRIT col*) contrariant(e), obstiné(e).
bloom [bluːm] *n* fleur *f*; (*fig*) épanouissement *m* ♦ *vi* être en fleur; (*fig*) s'épanouir; être florissant(e).
blooming ['bluːmɪŋ] *adj* (*col*): **this ~ ...** ce fichu *or* sacré ....
blossom ['blɔsəm] *n* fleur(s) *f(pl)* ♦ *vi* être en fleurs; (*fig*) s'épanouir; **to ~ into** (*fig*) devenir.
blot [blɔt] *n* tache *f* ♦ *vt* tacher; (*ink*) sécher; **to be a ~ on the landscape** gâcher le paysage; **to ~ one's copy book** (*fig*) faire un impair.
►**blot out** *vt* (*memories*) effacer; (*view*) cacher, masquer; (*nation, city*) annihiler.
blotchy ['blɔtʃɪ] *adj* (*complexion*) couvert(e) de marbrures.
blotter ['blɔtə*] *n*, **blotting paper** ['blɔtɪŋ-] *n* buvard *m*.
blotto ['blɔtəu] *adj* (*col*) bourré(e).
blouse [blauz] *n* (*feminine garment*) chemisier *m*, corsage *m*.
blow [bləu] *n* coup *m* ♦ *vb* (*pt* **blew**, *pp* **blown** [bluː, bləun]) *vi* souffler ♦ *vt* (*glass*) souffler; (*fuse*) faire sauter; **to ~ one's nose** se moucher; **to ~ a whistle** siffler; **to come to ~s** en venir aux coups.
►**blow away** *vi* s'envoler ♦ *vt* chasser, faire s'envoler.
►**blow down** *vt* faire tomber, renverser.
►**blow off** *vi* s'envoler ♦ *vt* (*hat*) emporter; (*ship*): **to ~ off course** faire dévier.
►**blow out** *vi* (*tyre*) éclater; (*fuse*) sauter.
►**blow over** *vi* s'apaiser.
►**blow up** *vi* exploser, sauter ♦ *vt* faire sauter; (*tyre*) gonfler; (*PHOT*) agrandir.
blow-dry ['bləudraɪ] *n* (*hairstyle*) brushing *m* ♦ *vt* faire un brushing à.
blowlamp ['bləulæmp] *n* (*BRIT*) chalumeau *m*.
blow-out ['bləuaut] *n* (*of tyre*) éclatement *m*; (*BRIT col: big meal*) gueuleton *m*.
blowtorch ['bləutɔːtʃ] *n* chalumeau *m*.
blowzy ['blauzɪ] *adj* (*BRIT*) peu soigné(e).
BLS *n abbr* (*US*) = *Bureau of Labor Statistics*.
blubber ['blʌbə*] *n* blanc *m* de baleine ♦ *vi* (*pej*) pleurer comme un veau.
bludgeon ['blʌdʒən] *n* gourdin *m*, trique *f*.
blue [bluː] *adj* bleu(e); **~ film/joke** film *m*/histoire *f* pornographique; **(only) once in a ~ moon** tous les trente-six du mois; **out of the ~** (*fig*) à l'improviste, sans qu'on si attende.
blue baby *n* enfant bleu(e).
bluebell ['bluːbɛl] *n* jacinthe *f* des bois.
blueberry ['bluːbərɪ] *n* myrtille *f*, airelle *f*.
bluebottle ['bluːbɔtl] *n* mouche *f* à viande.
blue cheese *n* (fromage) bleu *m*.
blue-chip ['bluːtʃɪp] *adj*: **~ investment** investissement *m* de premier ordre.
blue-collar worker ['bluːkɔlə*-] *n* ouvrier/ère, col bleu.
blue jeans *npl* blue-jeans *mpl*.
blueprint ['bluːprɪnt] *n* bleu *m*; (*fig*) projet *m*, plan directeur.
blues [bluːz] *npl*: **the ~** (*MUS*) le blues; **to have the ~** (*col: feeling*) avoir le cafard.
bluff [blʌf] *vi* bluffer ♦ *n* bluff *m*; (*cliff*) promontoire *m*, falaise *f* ♦ *adj* (*person*) bourru(e), brusque; **to call sb's ~** mettre qn au défi d'exécuter ses menaces.
blunder ['blʌndə*] *n* gaffe *f*, bévue *f* ♦ *vi* faire une gaffe *or* une bévue; **to ~ into sb/sth** buter contre qn/qch.
blunt [blʌnt] *adj* émoussé(e), peu tranchant(e); (*pencil*) mal taillé(e); (*person*) brusque, ne mâchant pas ses mots ♦ *vt* émousser; **~ instrument** (*LAW*) instrument contondant.
bluntly ['blʌntlɪ] *adv* carrément, sans prendre de gants.
bluntness ['blʌntnɪs] *n* (*of person*) brusquerie *f*, franchise brutale.
blur [bləː*] *n* tache *or* masse floue *or* confuse ♦ *vt* brouiller, rendre flou(e).
blurb [bləːb] *n* (*for book*) texte *m* de présentation; (*pej*) baratin *m*.
blurred [bləːd] *adj* flou(e).
blurt [bləːt]: **to ~ out** *vt* (*reveal*) lâcher; (*say*) balbutier, dire d'une voix entrecoupée.
blush [blʌʃ] *vi* rougir ♦ *n* rougeur *f*.
blusher ['blʌʃə*] *n* rouge *m* à joues.
bluster ['blʌstə*] *n* paroles *fpl* en l'air; (*boasting*) fanfaronnades *fpl*; (*threats*) menaces *fpl* en l'air ♦ *vi* parler en l'air; fanfaronner.
blustering ['blʌstərɪŋ] *adj* fanfaron(ne).
blustery ['blʌstərɪ] *adj* (*weather*) à bourrasques.
Blvd *abbr* (= *boulevard*) Bd.
BM *n abbr* = *British Museum*; (*SCOL: = Bachelor of Medicine*) *diplôme universitaire*.
BMA *n abbr* = *British Medical Association*.
BMJ *n abbr* = *British Medical Journal*.
BMus *n abbr* (= *Bachelor of Music*) *diplôme universitaire*.
BMX *n abbr* (= *bicycle motocross*) BMX *m*.
BO *n abbr* (*col: = body odour*) odeurs corporelles; (*US*) = **box office**.
boar [bɔː*] *n* sanglier *m*.
board [bɔːd] *n* planche *f*; (*on wall*) panneau *m*; (*for chess etc*) plateau *m*; (*committee*) conseil *m*, comité *m*; (*in firm*) conseil d'administration; (*NAUT, AVIAT*): **on ~** à bord ♦ *vt* (*ship*) monter à bord de; (*train*) monter dans; **full ~** (*BRIT*) pension complète; **half ~** (*BRIT*) demi-pension *f*; **~ and lodging** *n* chambre *f* avec pension; **with ~ and lodging** logé nourri; **above ~** (*fig*) régulier(ère); **across the ~** (*fig: ad*) systématiquement; (*: a*) de portée générale; **to go by the ~** être abandonné(e); (*be unimportant*) compter pour rien, n'avoir aucune importance.
►**board up** *vt* (*door*) condamner (*au moyen de planches, de tôle*).

boarder ['bɔːdə*] *n* pensionnaire *m/f*; (*SCOL*) interne *m/f*, pensionnaire.
board game *n* jeu *m* de société.
boarding card ['bɔːdɪŋ-] *n* (*AVIAT, NAUT*) carte *f* d'embarquement.
boarding house ['bɔːdɪŋ-] *n* pension *f*.
boarding party ['bɔːdɪŋ-] *n* section *f* d'abordage.
boarding pass ['bɔːdɪŋ-] *n* (*BRIT*) = **boarding card**.
boarding school ['bɔːdɪŋ-] *n* internat *m*, pensionnat *m*.
board meeting *n* réunion *f* du conseil d'administration.
board room *n* salle *f* du conseil d'administration.
boardwalk ['bɔːdwɔːk] *n* (*US*) cheminement *m* en planches.
boast [bəust] *vi*: **to ~ (about** *or* **of)** se vanter (de) ♦ *vt* s'enorgueillir de ♦ *n* vantardise *f*; sujet *m* d'orgueil *or* de fierté.
boastful ['bəustful] *adj* vantard(e).
boastfulness ['bəustfulnɪs] *n* vantardise *f*.
boat [bəut] *n* bateau *m*; (*small*) canot *m*; barque *f*; **to go by ~** aller en bateau; **to be in the same ~** (*fig*) être logé à la même enseigne.
boater ['bəutə*] *n* (*hat*) canotier *m*.
boating ['bəutɪŋ] *n* canotage *m*.
boat people *npl* boat people *mpl*.
boatswain ['bəusn] *n* maître *m* d'équipage.
bob [bɔb] *vi* (*boat, cork on water*: *also*: **~ up and down**) danser, se balancer ♦ *n* (*BRIT col*) = **shilling**.
▸**bob up** *vi* surgir *or* apparaître brusquement.
bobbin ['bɔbɪn] *n* bobine *f*; (*of sewing machine*) navette *f*.
bobby ['bɔbɪ] *n* (*BRIT col*) ≈ agent *m* (de police).
bobby pin *n* (*US*) pince *f* à cheveux.
bobsleigh ['bɔbsleɪ] *n* bob *m*.
bode [bəud] *vi*: **to ~ well/ill (for)** être de bon/mauvais augure (pour).
bodice ['bɔdɪs] *n* corsage *m*.
bodily ['bɔdɪlɪ] *adj* corporel(le); (*pain, comfort*) physique; (*needs*) matériel(le) ♦ *adv* (*carry, lift*) dans ses bras.
body ['bɔdɪ] *n* corps *m*; (*of car*) carrosserie *f*; (*of plane*) fuselage *m*; (*also*: **~ stocking**) body *m*, justaucorps *m*; (*fig: society*) organe *m*, organisme *m*; (*: quantity*) ensemble *m*, masse *f*; (*of wine*) corps; **ruling ~** organe directeur; **in a ~** en masse, ensemble; (*speak*) comme un seul et même homme.
body blow *n* (*fig*) coup dur, choc *m*.
body-building ['bɔdɪbɪldɪŋ] *n* body-building *m*, culturisme *m*.
bodyguard ['bɔdɪgɑːd] *n* garde *m* du corps.
body language *n* langage *m* du corps.
body repairs *npl* travaux *mpl* de carrosserie.
body search *n* fouille *f* (corporelle); **to carry out a ~ on sb** fouiller qn; **to submit to** *or* **undergo a ~** se faire fouiller.
bodywork ['bɔdɪwəːk] *n* carrosserie *f*.
boffin ['bɔfɪn] *n* (*BRIT*) savant *m*.
bog [bɔg] *n* tourbière *f* ♦ *vt*: **to get ~ged down (in)** (*fig*) s'enliser (dans).
boggle ['bɔgl] *vi*: **the mind ~s** c'est incroyable, on en reste sidéré.
bogie ['bəugɪ] *n* bogie *m*.
Bogotá [bəugə'tɑː] *n* Bogotá.
bogus ['bəugəs] *adj* bidon *inv*; fantôme.
Bohemia [bəu'hiːmɪə] *n* Bohême *f*.
Bohemian [bəu'hiːmɪən] *adj* bohémien(ne) ♦ *n* Bohémien/ne; (*gipsy*: *also*: **b~**) bohémien/ne.
boil [bɔɪl] *vt* (faire) bouillir ♦ *vi* bouillir ♦ *n* (*MED*) furoncle *m*; **to come to the** *or* (*US*) **a ~** bouillir; **to bring to the** *or* (*US*) **a ~** porter à ébullition; **~ed egg** œuf *m* à la coque; **~ed potatoes** pommes *fpl* à l'anglaise *or* à l'eau.
▸**boil down** *vi* (*fig*): **to ~ down to** se réduire *or* ramener à.
▸**boil over** *vi* déborder.
boiler ['bɔɪlə*] *n* chaudière *f*.
boiler suit *n* (*BRIT*) bleu *m* de travail, combinaison *f*.
boiling ['bɔɪlɪŋ] *adj*: **I'm ~ (hot)** (*col*) je crève de chaud.
boiling point *n* point *m* d'ébullition.
boil-in-the-bag [bɔɪlɪnðə'bæg] *adj* (*rice etc*) en sachet cuisson.
boisterous ['bɔɪstərəs] *adj* bruyant(e), tapageur(euse).
bold [bəuld] *adj* hardi(e), audacieux(euse); (*pej*) effronté(e); (*outline, colour*) franc(franche), tranché(e), marqué(e).
boldness ['bəuldnɪs] *n* hardiesse *f*, audace *f*; aplomb *m*, effronterie *f*.
bold type *n* (*TYP*) caractères *mpl* gras.
Bolivia [bə'lɪvɪə] *n* Bolivie *f*.
Bolivian [bə'lɪvɪən] *adj* bolivien(ne) ♦ *n* Bolivien/ne.
bollard ['bɔləd] *n* (*NAUT*) bitte *f* d'amarrage; (*BRIT AUT*) borne lumineuse *or* de signalisation.
bolshy ['bɔlʃɪ] *adj* râleur(euse); **to be in a ~ mood** être peu coopératif(ive).
bolster ['bəulstə*] *n* traversin *m*.
▸**bolster up** *vt* soutenir.
bolt [bəult] *n* verrou *m*; (*with nut*) boulon *m* ♦ *adv*: **~ upright** droit(e) comme un piquet ♦ *vt* verrouiller; (*food*) engloutir ♦ *vi* se sauver, filer (comme une flèche); **a ~ from the blue** (*fig*) un coup de tonnerre dans un ciel bleu.
bomb [bɔm] *n* bombe *f* ♦ *vt* bombarder.
bombard [bɔm'bɑːd] *vt* bombarder.
bombardment [bɔm'bɑːdmənt] *n* bombardement *m*.
bombastic [bɔm'bæstɪk] *adj* grandiloquent(e), pompeux(euse).
bomb disposal *n*: **~ unit** section *f* de déminage; **~ expert** artificier *m*.

bomber ['bɔmə*] *n* caporal *m* d'artillerie; (*AVIAT*) bombardier *m*; (*terrorist*) poseur *m* de bombes.
bombing ['bɔmɪŋ] *n* bombardement *m*.
bomb scare *n* alerte *f* à la bombe.
bombshell ['bɔmʃɛl] *n* obus *m*; (*fig*) bombe *f*.
bomb site *n* zone *f* de bombardement.
bona fide ['bəunə'faɪdɪ] *adj* de bonne foi; (*offer*) sérieux(euse).
bonanza [bə'nænzə] *n* filon *m*.
bond [bɔnd] *n* lien *m*; (*binding promise*) engagement *m*, obligation *f*; (*FINANCE*) obligation; **in** ~ (*of goods*) en entrepôt.
bondage ['bɔndɪdʒ] *n* esclavage *m*.
bonded warehouse ['bɔndɪd-] *n* entrepôt *m* sous douanes.
bone [bəun] *n* os *m*; (*of fish*) arête *f* ♦ *vt* désosser; ôter les arêtes de.
bone china *n* porcelaine *f* tendre.
bone-dry ['bəun'draɪ] *adj* absolument sec(sèche).
bone idle *adj* fainéant(e).
bone marrow *n* moelle osseuse.
boner ['bəunə*] *n* (*US*) gaffe *f*, bourde *f*.
bonfire ['bɔnfaɪə*] *n* feu *m* (de joie); (*for rubbish*) feu.
bonk [bɔŋk] (*col!*) *vt* s'envoyer (*!*), sauter (*!*) ♦ *vi* s'envoyer en l'air (*!*).
bonkers ['bɔŋkəz] *adj* (*BRIT col*) cinglé(e), dingue.
Bonn [bɔn] *n* Bonn.
bonnet ['bɔnɪt] *n* bonnet *m*; (*BRIT: of car*) capot *m*.
bonny [bɔnɪ] *adj* (*Scottish*) joli(e).
bonus ['bəunəs] *n* prime *f*, gratification *f*; (*on wages*) prime.
bony ['bəunɪ] *adj* (*arm, face, MED: tissue*) osseux(euse); (*thin: person*) squelettique; (*meat*) plein(e) d'os; (*fish*) plein d'arêtes.
boo [bu:] *excl* hou!, peuh! ♦ *vt* huer ♦ *n* huée *f*.
boob [bu:b] *n* (*col: breast*) nichon *m*; (*: BRIT: mistake*) gaffe *f*.
booby prize ['bu:bɪ-] *n* timbale *f* (*ironique*).
booby trap ['bu:bɪ-] *n* guet-apens *m*.
booby-trapped ['bu:bɪtræpt] *adj* piégé(e).
book [buk] *n* livre *m*; (*of stamps etc*) carnet *m*; (*COMM*): ~**s** comptes *mpl*, comptabilité *f* ♦ *vt* (*ticket*) prendre; (*seat, room, table*) réserver; (*driver*) dresser un procès-verbal à; (*football player*) prendre le nom de, donner un carton à; **to keep the** ~**s** tenir la comptabilité; **by the** ~ à la lettre, selon les règles; **to throw the** ~ **at sb** passer un savon à qn.
▶**book in** *vi* (*BRIT: at hotel*) prendre sa chambre.
▶**book up** *vt* réserver; **all seats are** ~**ed up** tout est pris, c'est complet; **the hotel is** ~**ed up** l'hôtel est complet.
bookable ['bukəbl] *adj*: **seats are** ~ on peut réserver ses places.
bookcase ['bukkeɪs] *n* bibliothèque *f* (*meuble*).
book ends *npl* serre-livres *m inv*.
booking ['bukɪŋ] *n* (*BRIT*) réservation *f*.
booking office *n* (*BRIT*) bureau *m* de location.
book-keeping ['buk'ki:pɪŋ] *n* comptabilité *f*.
booklet ['buklɪt] *n* brochure *f*.
bookmaker ['bukmeɪkə*] *n* bookmaker *m*.
bookseller ['buksɛlə*] *n* libraire *m/f*.
bookshelf ['bukʃɛlf] *n* (*single*) étagère *f* (à livres); **bookshelves** rayons *mpl* (de bibliothèque).
bookshop ['bukʃɔp] *n* librairie *f*.
bookstall ['bukstɔ:l] *n* kiosque *m* à journaux.
book token *n* bon-cadeau *m* (pour un livre).
book value *n* valeur *f* comptable.
bookworm ['bukwə:m] *n* dévoreur/euse de livres.
boom [bu:m] *n* (*noise*) grondement *m*; (*busy period*) boom *m*, vague *f* de prospérité ♦ *vi* gronder; prospérer.
boomerang ['bu:məræŋ] *n* boomerang *m*.
boom town *n* ville *f* en plein essor.
boon [bu:n] *n* bénédiction *f*, grand avantage.
boorish ['buərɪʃ] *adj* grossier(ère), rustre.
boost [bu:st] *n* stimulant *m*, remontant *m* ♦ *vt* stimuler; **to give a** ~ **to sb's spirits** *or* **to sb** remonter le moral à qn.
booster ['bu:stə*] *n* (*TV*) amplificateur *m* (de signal); (*ELEC*) survolteur *m*; (*also*: ~ **rocket**) booster *m*; (*MED: vaccine*) rappel *m*.
booster seat *n* (*AUT: for children*) siège *m* rehausseur.
boot [bu:t] *n* botte *f*; (*for hiking*) chaussure *f* (de marche); (*for football etc*) soulier *m*; (*ankle* ~) bottine *f*; (*BRIT: of car*) coffre *m* ♦ *vt* (*COMPUT*) lancer, mettre en route; **to** ~ (*in addition*) par-dessus le marché, en plus; **to give sb the** ~ (*col*) flanquer qn dehors, virer qn.
booth [bu:ð] *n* (*at fair*) baraque (foraine); (*of cinema, telephone etc*) cabine *f*; (*also*: **voting** ~) isoloir *m*.
bootleg ['bu:tlɛg] *adj* de contrebande; ~ **record** enregistrement *m* pirate.
booty ['bu:tɪ] *n* butin *m*.
booze [bu:z] (*col*) *n* boissons *fpl* alcooliques, alcool *m* ♦ *vi* boire, picoler.
boozer ['bu:zə*] *n* (*col: person*): **he's a** ~ il picole pas mal; (*BRIT col: pub*) pub *m*.
border ['bɔ:də*] *n* bordure *f*; bord *m*; (*of a country*) frontière *f*; **the B**~ *la frontière entre l'Écosse et l'Angleterre*; **the B**~**s** *la région frontière entre l'Écosse et l'Angleterre*.
▶**border on** *vt fus* être voisin(e) de, toucher à.
borderline ['bɔ:dəlaɪn] *n* (*fig*) ligne *f* de démarcation ♦ *adj*: ~ **case** cas *m* limite.
bore [bɔ:*] *pt of* **bear** ♦ *vt* (*hole*) percer; (*person*) ennuyer, raser ♦ *n* (*person*) raseur/euse; (*of gun*) calibre *m*; **he's** ~**d to tears** *or* ~**d to death** *or* ~**d stiff** il s'ennuie à mourir.
boredom ['bɔ:dəm] *n* ennui *m*.
boring ['bɔ:rɪŋ] *adj* ennuyeux(euse).
born [bɔ:n] *adj*: **to be** ~ naître; **I was** ~ **in 1960** je suis né en 1960; ~ **blind** aveugle de nais-

sance; **a ~ comedian** un comédien-né.

born-again [bɔːnə'gɛn] *adj*: **~ Christian** ≈ évangeliste *m/f*.

borne [bɔːn] *pp of* **bear**.

Borneo ['bɔːnɪəu] *n* Bornéo *f*.

borough ['bʌrə] *n* municipalité *f*.

borrow ['bɔrəu] *vt*: **to ~ sth (from sb)** emprunter qch (à qn); **may I ~ your car?** est-ce que je peux vous emprunter votre voiture?

borrower ['bɔrəuə*] *n* emprunteur/euse.

borrowing ['bɔrəuɪŋ] *n* emprunt(s) *m(pl)*.

borstal ['bɔːstl] *n (BRIT)* ≈ maison *f* de correction.

Bosnia ['bɔznɪə] *n* Bosnie *f*.

Bosnia-Herzegovina ['bɔznɪəhəːtsəgəu'viːnə] *n* (*also*: **Bosnia-Hercegovina**) Bosnie-Herzégovine *f*.

Bosnian ['bɔznɪən] *adj* bosniaque, bosnien(ne) ♦ *n* Bosniaque *m/f*, Bosnien/ne.

bosom ['buzəm] *n* poitrine *f*; (*fig*) sein *m*.

bosom friend *n* ami/e intime.

boss [bɔs] *n* patron/ne ♦ *vt* (*also*: **~ about, ~ around**) mener à la baguette.

bossy ['bɔsɪ] *adj* autoritaire.

bosun ['bəusn] *n* maître *m* d'équipage.

botanical [bə'tænɪkl] *adj* botanique.

botanist ['bɔtənɪst] *n* botaniste *m/f*.

botany ['bɔtənɪ] *n* botanique *f*.

botch [bɔtʃ] *vt* (*also*: **~ up**) saboter, bâcler.

both [bəuθ] *adj* les deux, l'un(e) et l'autre ♦ *pron*: **~ (of them)** les deux, tous(toutes) (les) deux, l'un(e) et l'autre; **~ of us went, we ~ went** nous y sommes allés tous les deux ♦ *adv*: **they sell ~ the fabric and the finished curtains** ils vendent (et) le tissu et les rideaux (finis), ils vendent à la fois le tissu et les rideaux (finis).

bother ['bɔðə*] *vt* (*worry*) tracasser; (*needle, bait*) importuner, ennuyer; (*disturb*) déranger ♦ *vi* (*also*: **~ o.s.**) se tracasser, se faire du souci ♦ *n*: **it is a ~ to have to do** c'est vraiment ennuyeux d'avoir à faire ♦ *excl* zut!; **to ~ doing** prendre la peine de faire; **I'm sorry to ~ you** excusez-moi de vous déranger; **please don't ~** ne vous dérangez pas; **don't ~** ce n'est pas la peine; **it's no ~** aucun problème.

Botswana [bɔt'swɑːnə] *n* Botswana *m*.

bottle ['bɔtl] *n* bouteille *f*; (*baby's*) biberon *m*; (*of perfume, medicine*) flacon *m* ♦ *vt* mettre en bouteille(s); **~ of wine/milk** bouteille de vin/lait; **wine/milk ~** bouteille à vin/lait.

►**bottle up** *vt* refouler, contenir.

bottle bank *n* conteneur *m* (de bouteilles).

bottleneck ['bɔtlnɛk] *n* (*in traffic*) bouchon *m*; (*in production*) goulet *m* d'étranglement.

bottle-opener ['bɔtləupnə*] *n* ouvre-bouteille *m*.

bottom ['bɔtəm] *n* (*of container, sea etc*) fond *m*; (*buttocks*) derrière *m*; (*of page, list*) bas *m*; (*of chair*) siège *m*; (*of mountain, tree, hill*) pied *m* ♦ *adj* du fond; du bas; **to get to the ~ of sth** (*fig*) découvrir le fin fond de qch.

bottomless ['bɔtəmlɪs] *adj* sans fond, insondable.

bottom line *n*: **the ~ is that ...** l'essentiel, c'est que ....

botulism ['bɔtjulɪzəm] *n* botulisme *m*.

bough [bau] *n* branche *f*, rameau *m*.

bought [bɔːt] *pt, pp of* **buy**.

boulder ['bəuldə*] *n* gros rocher (*gén lisse, arrondi*).

bounce [bauns] *vi* (*ball*) rebondir; (*cheque*) être refusé (*étant sans provision*); (*also*: **to ~ forward/out** *etc*) bondir, s'élancer ♦ *vt* faire rebondir ♦ *n* (*rebound*) rebond *m*; **he's got plenty of ~** (*fig*) il est plein d'entrain *or* d'allant.

bouncer ['baunsə*] *n* (*col*) videur *m*.

bouncy castle ['baunsɪ-] *n* ® château *m* gonflable.

bound [baund] *pt, pp of* **bind** ♦ *n* (*gen pl*) limite *f*; (*leap*) bond *m* ♦ *vt* (*leap*) bondir; (*limit*) borner ♦ *adj*: **to be ~ to do sth** (*obliged*) être obligé(e) *or* avoir obligation de faire qch; **he's ~ to fail** (*likely*) il est sûr d'échouer, son échec est inévitable *or* assuré; **~ for** à destination de; **out of ~s** dont l'accès est interdit.

boundary ['baundrɪ] *n* frontière *f*.

boundless ['baundlɪs] *adj* illimité(e), sans bornes.

bountiful ['bauntɪful] *adj* (*person*) généreux(euse); (*God*) bienfaiteur(trice); (*supply*) ample.

bounty ['bauntɪ] *n* (*generosity*) générosité *f*.

bouquet ['bukeɪ] *n* bouquet *m*.

bourbon ['buəbən] *n* (*US*: *also*: **~ whiskey**) bourbon *m*.

bourgeois ['buəʒwɑː] *adj, n* bourgeois(e).

bout [baut] *n* période *f*; (*of malaria etc*) accès *m*, crise *f*, attaque *f*; (*BOXING etc*) combat *m*, match *m*.

boutique [buː'tiːk] *n* boutique *f*.

bow[1] [bəu] *n* nœud *m*; (*weapon*) arc *m*; (*MUS*) archet *m*.

bow[2] [bau] *n* (*with body*) révérence *f*, inclination *f* (du buste *or* corps); (*NAUT*: *also*: **~s**) proue *f* ♦ *vi* faire une révérence, s'incliner; (*yield*): **to ~ to** *or* **before** s'incliner devant, se soumettre à; **to ~ to the inevitable** accepter l'inévitable *or* l'inéluctable.

bowels [bauəlz] *npl* intestins *mpl*; (*fig*) entrailles *fpl*.

bowl [bəul] *n* (*for eating*) bol *m*; (*for washing*) cuvette *f*; (*ball*) boule *f*; (*of pipe*) fourneau *m* ♦ *vi* (*CRICKET*) lancer (la balle).

►**bowl over** *vt* (*fig*) renverser.

bow-legged ['bəu'lɛgɪd] *adj* aux jambes arquées.

bowler ['bəulə*] *n* joueur *m* de boules; (*CRICKET*) lanceur *m* (de la balle); (*BRIT*: *also*: **~ hat**) (chapeau *m*) melon *m*.

bowling ['bəulɪŋ] *n* (*game*) jeu *m* de boules;

jeu de quilles.
bowling alley *n* bowling *m*.
bowling green *n* terrain *m* de boules (*gazonné et carré*).
bowls [bəulz] *n* (jeu *m* de) boules *fpl*.
bow tie [bəu-] *n* nœud *m* papillon.
box [bɔks] *n* boîte *f*; (*also*: **cardboard** ~) carton *m*; (*crate*) caisse *f*; (*THEAT*) loge *f*; (*BRIT AUT*) intersection *f* (*matérialisée par des marques au sol*) ♦ *vt* mettre en boîte; (*SPORT*) boxer avec ♦ *vi* boxer, faire de la boxe.
boxcar ['bɔkskɑ:*] *n* (*US RAIL*) wagon *m* (de marchandises) couvert.
boxer ['bɔksə*] *n* (*person*) boxeur *m*; (*dog*) boxer *m*.
boxing ['bɔksɪŋ] *n* (*sport*) boxe *f*.
Boxing Day *n* (*BRIT*) *le lendemain de Noël*; *voir encadré*.

BOXING DAY

Boxing Day *est le lendemain de Noël, férié en Grande-Bretagne. Si Noël tombe un samedi, le jour férié est reculé jusqu'au lundi suivant. Ce nom vient d'une coutume du XIXe siècle qui consistait à donner des cadeaux de Noël (dans des boîtes) à ses employés etc le 26 décembre.*

boxing gloves *npl* gants *mpl* de boxe.
boxing ring *n* ring *m*.
box number *n* (*for advertisements*) numéro *m* d'annonce.
box office *n* bureau *m* de location.
box room *n* débarras *m*; chambrette *f*.
boy [bɔɪ] *n* garçon *m*.
boycott ['bɔɪkɔt] *n* boycottage *m* ♦ *vt* boycotter.
boyfriend ['bɔɪfrɛnd] *n* (petit) ami.
boyish ['bɔɪɪʃ] *adj* d'enfant, de garçon; **to look** ~ (*man*: *appear youthful*) faire jeune.
Bp *abbr* = **bishop**.
BR *abbr* = **British Rail**.
Br. *abbr* (*REL*) = **brother**.
bra [brɑ:] *n* soutien-gorge *m*.
brace [breɪs] *n* attache *f*, agrafe *f*; (*on teeth*) appareil *m* (dentaire); (*tool*) vilbrequin *m* ♦ *vt* consolider, soutenir; **to** ~ **o.s.** (*fig*) se préparer mentalement.
bracelet ['breɪslɪt] *n* bracelet *m*.
braces ['breɪsɪz] *npl* (*BRIT*) bretelles *fpl*.
bracing ['breɪsɪŋ] *adj* tonifiant(e), tonique.
bracken ['brækən] *n* fougère *f*.
bracket ['brækɪt] *n* (*TECH*) tasseau *m*, support *m*; (*group*) classe *f*, tranche *f*; (*also*: **brace** ~) accolade *f*; (*also*: **round** ~) parenthèse *f*; (*also*: **square** ~) crochet *m* ♦ *vt* mettre entre parenthèses; (*fig*: *also*: ~ **together**) regrouper; **income** ~ tranche *f* des revenus; **in** ~**s** entre parenthèses (*or* crochets).
brackish ['brækɪʃ] *adj* (*water*) saumâtre.
brag [bræg] *vi* se vanter.
braid [breɪd] *n* (*trimming*) galon *m*; (*of hair*) tresse *f*, natte *f*.
Braille [breɪl] *n* braille *m*.
brain [breɪn] *n* cerveau *m*; ~**s** *npl* cervelle *f*; **he's got** ~**s** il est intelligent.
brainchild ['breɪntʃaɪld] *n* trouvaille (personnelle), invention *f*.
braindead ['breɪndɛd] *adj* (*MED*) dans un coma dépassé; (*col*) demeuré(e).
brainless ['breɪnlɪs] *adj* sans cervelle, stupide.
brainstorm ['breɪnstɔ:m] *n* (*fig*) moment *m* d'égarement; (*US*: *brainwave*) idée *f* de génie.
brainwash ['breɪnwɔʃ] *vt* faire subir un lavage de cerveau à.
brainwave ['breɪnweɪv] *n* idée *f* de génie.
brainy ['breɪnɪ] *adj* intelligent(e), doué(e).
braise [breɪz] *vt* braiser.
brake [breɪk] *n* frein *m* ♦ *vt*, *vi* freiner.
brake light *n* feu *m* de stop.
brake pedal *n* pédale *f* de frein.
bramble ['bræmbl] *n* ronces *fpl*; (*fruit*) mûre *f*.
bran [bræn] *n* son *m*.
branch [brɑ:ntʃ] *n* branche *f*; (*COMM*) succursale *f*; (*: bank*) agence *f*; (*of association*) section locale ♦ *vi* bifurquer.
►**branch out** *vi* diversifier ses activités; **to** ~ **out into** étendre ses activités à.
branch line *n* (*RAIL*) bifurcation *f*, embranchement *m*.
branch manager *n* directeur/trice de succursale (*or* d'agence).
brand [brænd] *n* marque (commerciale) ♦ *vt* (*cattle*) marquer (au fer rouge); (*fig*: *pej*): **to** ~ **sb a communist** *etc* traiter *or* qualifier qn de communiste *etc*.
brandish ['brændɪʃ] *vt* brandir.
brand name *n* nom *m* de marque.
brand-new ['brænd'nju:] *adj* tout(e) neuf(neuve), flambant neuf(neuve).
brandy ['brændɪ] *n* cognac *m*, fine *f*.
brash [bræʃ] *adj* effronté(e).
Brasilia [brə'zɪlɪə] *n* Brasilia.
brass [brɑ:s] *n* cuivre *m* (jaune), laiton *m*; **the** ~ (*MUS*) les cuivres.
brass band *n* fanfare *f*.
brassiere ['bræsɪə*] *n* soutien-gorge *m*.
brass tacks *npl*: **to get down to** ~ en venir au fait.
brat [bræt] *n* (*pej*) mioche *m/f*, môme *m/f*.
bravado [brə'vɑ:dəu] *n* bravade *f*.
brave [breɪv] *adj* courageux(euse), brave ♦ *n* guerrier indien ♦ *vt* braver, affronter.
bravery ['breɪvərɪ] *n* bravoure *f*, courage *m*.
brawl [brɔ:l] *n* rixe *f*, bagarre *f* ♦ *vi* se bagarrer.
brawn [brɔ:n] *n* muscle *m*; (*meat*) fromage *m* de tête.
brawny ['brɔ:nɪ] *adj* musclé(e), costaud(e).
bray [breɪ] *n* braiement *m* ♦ *vi* braire.
brazen ['breɪzn] *adj* impudent(e), effronté(e) ♦ *vt*: **to** ~ **it out** payer d'effronterie, crâner.
brazier ['breɪzɪə*] *n* brasero *m*.
Brazil [brə'zɪl] *n* Brésil *m*.

Brazilian [brə'zɪljən] *adj* brésilien(ne) ♦ *n* Brésilien/ne.
Brazil nut *n* noix *f* du Brésil.
breach [bri:tʃ] *vt* ouvrir une brèche dans ♦ *n* (*gap*) brèche *f*; (*estrangement*) brouille *f*; (*breaking*): ~ **of contract** rupture *f* de contrat; ~ **of the peace** attentat *m* à l'ordre pu- blic; ~ **of trust** abus *m* de confiance.
bread [brɛd] *n* pain *m*; (*col: money*) fric *m*; ~ **and butter** *n* tartines (beurrées); (*fig*) subsistance *f*; **to earn one's daily** ~ gagner son pain; **to know which side one's** ~ **is buttered (on)** savoir où est son avantage *or* intérêt.
breadbin ['brɛdbɪn] *n* (*BRIT*) boîte *f or* huche *f* à pain.
breadboard ['brɛdbɔ:d] *n* planche *f* à pain; (*COMPUT*) montage expérimental.
breadbox ['brɛdbɔks] *n* (*US*) boîte *f or* huche *f* à pain.
breadcrumbs ['brɛdkrʌmz] *npl* miettes *fpl* de pain; (*CULIN*) chapelure *f*, panure *f*.
breadline ['brɛdlaɪn] *n*: **to be on the** ~ être sans le sou *or* dans l'indigence.
breadth [brɛtθ] *n* largeur *f*.
breadwinner ['brɛdwɪnə*] *n* soutien *m* de famille.
break [breɪk] *vb* (*pt* **broke** [brəuk], *pp* **broken** ['brəukən]) *vt* casser, briser; (*promise*) rompre; (*law*) violer ♦ *vi* (se) casser, se briser; (*weather*) tourner ♦ *n* (*gap*) brèche *f*; (*fracture*) cassure *f*; (*rest*) interruption *f*, arrêt *m*; (*: short*) pause *f*; (*: at school*) récréation *f*; (*chance*) chance *f*, occasion *f* favorable; **to** ~ **one's leg** *etc* se casser la jambe *etc*; **to** ~ **a record** battre un record; **to** ~ **the news to sb** annoncer la nouvelle à qn; **to** ~ **with sb** rompre avec qn; **to** ~ **even** *vi* rentrer dans ses frais; **to** ~ **free** *or* **loose** *vi* se dégager, s'échapper; **to take a** ~ (*few minutes*) faire une pause, s'arrêter cinq minutes; (*holiday*) prendre un peu de repos; **without a** ~ sans interruption, sans arrêt.
►**break down** *vt* (*door etc*) enfoncer; (*resistance*) venir à bout de; (*figures, data*) décomposer, analyser ♦ *vi* s'effondrer; (*MED*) faire une dépression (nerveuse); (*AUT*) tomber en panne.
►**break in** *vt* (*horse etc*) dresser ♦ *vi* (*burglar*) entrer par effraction.
►**break into** *vt fus* (*house*) s'introduire *or* pénétrer par effraction dans.
►**break off** *vi* (*speaker*) s'interrompre; (*branch*) se rompre ♦ *vt* (*talks, engagement*) rompre.
►**break open** *vt* (*door etc*) forcer, fracturer.
►**break out** *vi* éclater, se déclarer; **to** ~ **out in spots** se couvrir de boutons.
►**break through** *vi*: **the sun broke through** le soleil a fait son apparition ♦ *vt fus* (*defences, barrier*) franchir; (*crowd*) se frayer un passage à travers.
►**break up** *vi* (*partnership*) cesser, prendre fin; (*marriage*) se briser; (*friends*) se séparer ♦ *vt* fracasser, casser; (*fight etc*) interrompre, faire cesser; (*marriage*) désunir.
breakable ['breɪkəbl] *adj* cassable, fragile ♦ *n*: ~**s** objets *mpl* fragiles.
breakage ['breɪkɪdʒ] *n* casse *f*; **to pay for** ~**s** payer la casse.
breakaway ['breɪkəweɪ] *adj* (*group etc*) dissident(e).
breakdown ['breɪkdaun] *n* (*AUT*) panne *f*; (*in communications*) rupture *f*; (*MED*: *also*: **nervous** ~) dépression (nerveuse); (*of figures*) ventilation *f*, répartition *f*.
breakdown service *n* (*BRIT*) service *m* de dépannage.
breakdown van *n* (*BRIT*) dépanneuse *f*.
breaker ['breɪkə*] *n* brisant *m*.
breakeven ['breɪk'i:vn] *cpd*: ~ **chart** graphique *m* de rentabilité; ~ **point** seuil *m* de rentabilité.
breakfast ['brɛkfəst] *n* petit déjeuner *m*.
breakfast cereal *n* céréales *fpl*.
break-in ['breɪkɪn] *n* cambriolage *m*.
breaking point ['breɪkɪŋ-] *n* limites *fpl*.
breakthrough ['breɪkθru:] *n* percée *f*.
break-up ['breɪkʌp] *n* (*of partnership, marriage*) rupture *f*.
break-up value *n* (*COMM*) valeur *f* de liquidation.
breakwater ['breɪkwɔ:tə*] *n* brise-lames *m inv*, digue *f*.
breast [brɛst] *n* (*of woman*) sein *m*; (*chest*) poitrine *f*.
breast-feed ['brɛstfi:d] *vt*, *vi* (*irreg: like* **feed**) allaiter.
breast pocket *n* poche *f* (de) poitrine.
breaststroke ['brɛststrəuk] *n* brasse *f*.
breath [brɛθ] *n* haleine *f*, souffle *m*; **to go out for a** ~ **of air** sortir prendre l'air; **out of** ~ à bout de souffle, essoufflé(e).
breathalyse ['brɛeəlaɪz] *vt* faire subir l'alcootest à.
Breathalyser ['brɛθəlaɪzə*] *n* ® alcootest *m*.
breathe [bri:ð] *vt*, *vi* respirer; **I won't** ~ **a word about it** je n'en soufflerai pas mot, je n'en dirai rien à personne.
►**breathe in** *vi* inspirer ♦ *vt* aspirer.
►**breathe out** *vt*, *vi* expirer.
breather ['bri:ðə*] *n* moment *m* de repos *or* de répit.
breathing ['bri:ðɪŋ] *n* respiration *f*.
breathing space *n* (*fig*) (moment *m* de) répit *m*.
breathless ['brɛθlɪs] *adj* essoufflé(e), haletant(e); oppressé(e); ~ **with excitement** le souffle coupé par l'émotion.
breath-taking ['brɛθteɪkɪŋ] *adj* stupéfiant(e), à vous couper le souffle.
breath test *n* alcootest *m*.
-bred [brɛd] *suffix*: **well/ill**~ bien/mal élevé(e).
breed [bri:d] (*pt*, *pp* **bred** [brɛd]) *vt* élever, faire l'élevage de; (*fig: hate, suspicion*) en-

gendrer ♦ *vi* se reproduire ♦ *n* race *f*, variété *f*.

breeder ['briːdə*] *n* (*person*) éleveur *m*; (*PHYSICS*: *also*: ~ **reactor**) (réacteur *m*) surrégénérateur *m*.

breeding ['briːdɪŋ] *n* reproduction *f*; élevage *m*; (*upbringing*) éducation *f*.

breeze [briːz] *n* brise *f*.

breezeblock ['briːzblɔk] *n* (*BRIT*) parpaing *m* (*de laitier*).

breezy ['briːzɪ] *adj* frais(fraîche); aéré(e); désinvolte, jovial(e).

Breton ['brɛtən] *adj* breton(ne) ♦ *n* Breton/ne; (*LING*) breton *m*.

brevity ['brɛvɪtɪ] *n* brièveté *f*.

brew [bruː] *vt* (*tea*) faire infuser; (*beer*) brasser; (*plot*) tramer, préparer ♦ *vi* (*tea*) infuser; (*beer*) fermenter; (*fig*) se préparer, couver.

brewer ['bruːə*] *n* brasseur *m*.

brewery ['bruːərɪ] *n* brasserie *f* (*fabrique*).

briar ['braɪə*] *n* (*thorny bush*) ronces *fpl*; (*wild rose*) églantine *f*.

bribe [braɪb] *n* pot-de-vin *m* ♦ *vt* acheter; soudoyer; **to ~ sb to do sth** soudoyer qn pour qu'il fasse qch.

bribery ['braɪbərɪ] *n* corruption *f*.

bric-a-brac ['brɪkəbræk] *n* bric-à-brac *m*.

brick [brɪk] *n* brique *f*.

bricklayer ['brɪkleɪə*] *n* maçon *m*.

brickwork ['brɪkwəːk] *n* briquetage *m*, maçonnerie *f*.

brickworks ['brɪkwəːks] *n* briqueterie *f*.

bridal ['braɪdl] *adj* nuptial(e); ~ **party** noce *f*.

bride [braɪd] *n* mariée *f*, épouse *f*.

bridegroom ['braɪdgruːm] *n* marié *m*, époux *m*.

bridesmaid ['braɪdzmeɪd] *n* demoiselle *f* d'honneur.

bridge [brɪdʒ] *n* pont *m*; (*NAUT*) passerelle *f* (de commandement); (*of nose*) arête *f*; (*CARDS*, *DENTISTRY*) bridge *m* ♦ *vt* (*river*) construire un pont sur; (*gap*) combler.

bridging loan ['brɪdʒɪŋ-] *n* (*BRIT*) prêt *m* relais.

bridle ['braɪdl] *n* bride *f* ♦ *vt* refréner, mettre la bride à; (*horse*) brider.

bridle path *n* piste *or* allée cavalière.

brief [briːf] *adj* bref(brève) ♦ *n* (*LAW*) dossier *m*, cause *f* ♦ *vt* (*MIL etc*) donner des instructions à; **in ~ ...** (en) bref ...; **to ~ sb (about sth)** mettre qn au courant (de qch).

briefcase ['briːfkeɪs] *n* serviette *f*; porte-documents *m inv*.

briefing ['briːfɪŋ] *n* instructions *fpl*.

briefly ['briːflɪ] *adv* brièvement; (*visit*) en coup de vent; **to glimpse ~** entrevoir.

briefness ['briːfnɪs] *n* brièveté *f*.

briefs [briːfs] *npl* slip *m*.

Brig. *abbr* = **brigadier**.

brigade [brɪ'geɪd] *n* (*MIL*) brigade *f*.

brigadier [brɪgə'dɪə*] *n* brigadier général.

bright [braɪt] *adj* brillant(e); (*room, weather*) clair(e); (*person*) intelligent(e), doué(e); (*colour*) vif(vive); **to look on the ~ side** regarder le bon côté des choses.

brighten ['braɪtn] (*also*: ~ **up**) *vt* (*room*) éclaircir; égayer ♦ *vi* s'éclaircir; (*person*) retrouver un peu de sa gaieté.

brightly ['braɪtlɪ] *adv* brillamment.

brill [brɪl] *adj* (*BRIT col*) super *inv*.

brilliance ['brɪljəns] *n* éclat *m*; (*fig: of person*) brio *m*.

brilliant ['brɪljənt] *adj* brillant(e).

brim [brɪm] *n* bord *m*.

brimful ['brɪm'ful] *adj* plein(e) à ras bord; (*fig*) débordant(e).

brine [braɪn] *n* eau salée; (*CULIN*) saumure *f*.

bring, *pt*, *pp* **brought** [brɪŋ, brɔːt] *vt* (*thing*) apporter; (*person*) amener; **to ~ sth to an end** mettre fin à qch; **I can't ~ myself to fire him** je ne peux me résoudre à le mettre à la porte.

►**bring about** *vt* provoquer, entraîner.

►**bring back** *vt* rapporter; (*person*) ramener.

►**bring down** *vt* (*lower*) abaisser; (*shoot down*) abattre; (*government*) faire s'effondrer.

►**bring forward** *vt* avancer; (*BOOK-KEEPING*) reporter.

►**bring in** *vt* (*person*) faire entrer; (*object*) rentrer; (*POL*: *legislation*) introduire; (*LAW*: *verdict*) rendre; (*produce: income*) rapporter.

►**bring off** *vt* (*task, plan*) réussir, mener à bien; (*deal*) mener à bien.

►**bring out** *vt* (*meaning*) faire ressortir, mettre en relief; (*new product, book*) sortir.

►**bring round**, **bring to** *vt* (*unconscious person*) ranimer.

►**bring up** *vt* élever; (*question*) soulever; (*food: vomit*) vomir, rendre.

brink [brɪŋk] *n* bord *m*; **on the ~ of doing** sur le point de faire, à deux doigts de faire; **she was on the ~ of tears** elle était au bord des larmes.

brisk [brɪsk] *adj* vif(vive); (*abrupt*) brusque; (*trade etc*) actif(ive); **to go for a ~ walk** se promener d'un bon pas; **business is ~** les affaires marchent (bien).

bristle ['brɪsl] *n* poil *m* ♦ *vi* se hérisser; **bristling with** hérissé(e) de.

bristly ['brɪslɪ] *adj* (*beard, hair*) hérissé(e); **your chin's all ~** ton menton gratte.

Brit [brɪt] *n abbr* (*col*: = *British person*) Britannique *m/f*.

Britain ['brɪtən] *n* (*also*: **Great ~**) la Grande-Bretagne; **in ~** en Grande-Bretagne.

British ['brɪtɪʃ] *adj* britannique; **the ~** *npl* les Britanniques *mpl*; **the ~ Isles** les îles *fpl* Britanniques.

British Rail (BR) *n compagnie ferroviaire britannique*, ≈ SNCF *f*.

British Summer Time *n* heure *f* d'été britannique.

Briton ['brɪtən] *n* Britannique *m/f*.
Brittany ['brɪtənɪ] *n* Bretagne *f*.
brittle ['brɪtl] *adj* cassant(e), fragile.
Bro. *abbr* (*REL*) = **brother**.
broach [brəutʃ] *vt* (*subject*) aborder.
broad [brɔːd] *adj* large; (*distinction*) général(e); (*accent*) prononcé(e) ♦ *n* (*US col*) nana *f*; ~ **hint** allusion transparente; **in ~ daylight** en plein jour; **the ~ outlines** les grandes lignes.
broad bean *n* fève *f*.
broadcast ['brɔːdkɑːst] *n* émission *f* ♦ *vb* (*pt*, *pp* **broadcast**) *vt* radiodiffuser; téléviser ♦ *vi* émettre.
broadcaster ['brɔːdkɑːstə*] *n* personnalité *f* de la radio *or* de la télévision.
broadcasting ['brɔːdkɑːstɪŋ] *n* radiodiffusion *f*; télévision *f*.
broadcasting station *n* station *f* de radio (*or* de télévision).
broaden ['brɔːdn] *vt* élargir ♦ *vi* s'élargir.
broadly ['brɔːdlɪ] *adv* en gros, généralement.
broad-minded ['brɔːd'maɪndɪd] *adj* large d'esprit.
broadsheet ['brɔːdʃiːt] *n* (*BRIT*) journal *m* grand format.
broccoli ['brɔkəlɪ] *n* brocoli *m*.
brochure ['brəuʃjuə*] *n* prospectus *m*, dépliant *m*.
brogue ['brəug] *n* (*accent*) accent régional; (*shoe*) *(sorte de) chaussure basse de cuir épais*.
broil [brɔɪl] *vt* rôtir.
broiler ['brɔɪlə*] *n* (*fowl*) poulet *m* (*à rôtir*).
broke [brəuk] *pt of* **break** ♦ *adj* (*col*) fauché(e); **to go ~** (*business*) faire faillite.
broken ['brəukn] *pp of* **break** ♦ *adj* (*stick, leg etc*) cassé(e); (*promise, vow*) rompu(e); **a ~ marriage** un couple dissocié; **a ~ home** un foyer désuni; **in ~ French/English** dans un français/anglais approximatif *or* hésitant.
broken-down ['brəukn'daun] *adj* (*car*) en panne; (*machine*) fichu(e); (*house*) en ruines.
broken-hearted ['brəukn'hɑːtɪd] *adj* (ayant) le cœur brisé.
broker ['brəukə*] *n* courtier *m*.
brokerage ['brəukrɪdʒ] *n* courtage *m*.
brolly ['brɔlɪ] *n* (*BRIT col*) pépin *m*, parapluie *m*.
bronchitis [brɔŋ'kaɪtɪs] *n* bronchite *f*.
bronze [brɔnz] *n* bronze *m*.
bronzed ['brɔnzd] *adj* bronzé(e), hâlé(e).
brooch [brəutʃ] *n* broche *f*.
brood [bruːd] *n* couvée *f* ♦ *vi* (*hen, storm*) couver; (*person*) méditer (sombrement), ruminer.
broody ['bruːdɪ] *adj* (*fig*) taciturne, mélancolique.
brook [bruk] *n* ruisseau *m*.
broom [brum] *n* balai *m*.
broomstick ['brumstɪk] *n* manche *m* à balai.
Bros. *abbr* (*COMM*: = *brothers*) Frères.
broth [brɔθ] *n* bouillon *m* de viande et de légumes.
brothel ['brɔθl] *n* maison close, bordel *m*.
brother ['brʌðə*] *n* frère *m*.
brotherhood ['brʌðəhud] *n* fraternité *f*.
brother-in-law ['brʌðərɪn'lɔː*] *n* beau-frère *m*.
brotherly ['brʌðəlɪ] *adj* fraternel(le).
brought [brɔːt] *pt*, *pp of* **bring**.
brow [brau] *n* front *m*; (*rare: gen:* **eye~**) sourcil *m*; (*of hill*) sommet *m*.
browbeat ['braubiːt] *vt* intimider, brusquer.
brown [braun] *adj* brun(e), marron *inv*; (*hair*) châtain *inv*; (*rice, bread, flour*) complet(ète) ♦ *n* (*colour*) brun *m*, marron *m* ♦ *vt* brunir; (*CULIN*) faire dorer, faire roussir; **to go ~** (*person*) bronzer; (*leaves*) jaunir.
brownie ['braunɪ] *n* jeannette *f*, éclaireuse (cadette).
brown paper *n* papier *m* d'emballage, papier kraft.
brown sugar *n* cassonade *f*.
browse [brauz] *vi* (*among books*) bouquiner, feuilleter les livres; (*animal*) paître; **to ~ through a book** feuilleter un livre.
browser ['brauzə*] *n* (*COMPUT*) navigateur *m*.
bruise [bruːz] *n* bleu *m*, ecchymose *f*, contusion *f* ♦ *vt* contusionner, meurtrir ♦ *vi* (*fruit*) se taler, se meurtrir; **to ~ one's arm** se faire un bleu au bras.
Brum [brʌm] *n abbr*, **Brummagem** ['brʌmədʒəm] *n* (*col*) = *Birmingham*.
Brummie ['brʌmɪ] *n* (*col*) habitant/e de Birmingham; natif/ive de Birmingham.
brunch [brʌntʃ] *n* brunch *m*.
brunette [bruː'nɛt] *n* (femme) brune.
brunt [brʌnt] *n*: **the ~ of** (*attack, criticism etc*) le plus gros de.
brush [brʌʃ] *n* brosse *f*; (*quarrel*) accrochage *m*, prise *f* de bec ♦ *vt* brosser; (*also*: ~ **past**, ~ **against**) effleurer, frôler; **to have a ~ with sb** s'accrocher avec qn; **to have a ~ with the police** avoir maille à partir avec la police.
►**brush aside** *vt* écarter, balayer.
►**brush up** *vt* (*knowledge*) rafraîchir, réviser.
brushed [brʌʃt] *adj* (*TECH*: *steel, chrome etc*) brossé(e); (*nylon, denim etc*) gratté(e).
brush-off ['brʌʃɔf] *n* (*col*): **to give sb the ~** envoyer qn promener.
brushwood ['brʌʃwud] *n* broussailles *fpl*.
brusque [bruːsk] *adj* (*person, manner*) brusque, cassant(e); (*tone*) sec(sèche), cassant(e).
Brussels ['brʌslz] *n* Bruxelles.
Brussels sprout *n* chou *m* de Bruxelles.
brutal ['bruːtl] *adj* brutal(e).
brutality [bruː'tælɪtɪ] *n* brutalité *f*.
brutalize ['bruːtəlaɪz] *vt* (*harden*) rendre brutal(e); (*ill-treat*) brutaliser.
brute [bruːt] *n* brute *f* ♦ *adj*: **by ~ force** par la force.
brutish ['bruːtɪʃ] *adj* grossier(ère), brutal(e).
BS *n abbr* (*US*: = *Bachelor of Science*) *diplôme universitaire*.

bs *abbr* = **bill of sale**.
BSA *n abbr* = *Boy Scouts of America*.
BSc *n abbr* = **Bachelor of Science**.
BSE *n abbr* (= *bovine spongiform encephalopathy*) ESB *f*, BSE *f*.
BSI *n abbr* (= *British Standards Institution*) *association de normalisation*.
BST *abbr* (= *British Summer Time*) heure *f* d'été.
Bt. *abbr* (*BRIT*) = *baronet*.
btu *n abbr* (= *British thermal unit*) btu.
bubble ['bʌbl] *n* bulle *f* ♦ *vi* bouillonner, faire des bulles; (*sparkle, fig*) pétiller.
bubble bath *n* bain moussant.
bubblejet printer ['bʌbldʒɛt-] *n* imprimante *f* à bulle d'encre.
bubbly ['bʌblɪ] *adj* (*drink*) pétillant(e); (*person*) plein(e) de vitalité ♦ *n* (*col*) champ *m*.
Bucharest [buːkə'rɛst] *n* Bucarest.
buck [bʌk] *n* mâle *m* (*d'un lapin etc*); (*US col*) dollar *m* ♦ *vi* ruer; **to pass the ~ (to sb)** se décharger de la responsabilité (sur qn).
►**buck up** *vi* (*cheer up*) reprendre du poil de la bête, se remonter ♦ *vt*: **to ~ one's ideas up** se reprendre.
bucket ['bʌkɪt] *n* seau *m* ♦ *vi* (*BRIT col*): **the rain is ~ing (down)** il pleut à verse
Buckingham Palace ['bʌkɪŋəm-] *n* le palais de Buckingham; *voir encadré*.

> **BUCKINGHAM PALACE**
>
> **Buckingham Palace** *est la résidence officielle londonienne du souverain britannique depuis 1762. Construit en 1703, il fut à l'origine le palais du duc de Buckingham. Il a été partiellement reconstruit au début du siècle.*

buckle ['bʌkl] *n* boucle *f* ♦ *vt* boucler, attacher; (*warp*) tordre, gauchir; (*: wheel*) voiler.
►**buckle down** *vi* s'y mettre.
Bucks [bʌks] *abbr* (*BRIT*) = *Buckinghamshire*.
bud [bʌd] *n* bourgeon *m*; (*of flower*) bouton *m* ♦ *vi* bourgeonner; (*flower*) éclore.
Buddha ['budə] *n* Bouddha *m*.
Buddhism ['budɪzəm] *n* bouddhisme *m*.
Buddhist ['budɪst] *adj* bouddhiste ♦ *n* Bouddhiste *m/f*.
budding ['bʌdɪŋ] *adj* (*flower*) en bouton; (*poet etc*) en herbe; (*passion etc*) naissant(e).
buddy ['bʌdɪ] *n* (*US*) copain *m*.
budge [bʌdʒ] *vt* faire bouger ♦ *vi* bouger.
budgerigar ['bʌdʒərɪgɑː*] *n* perruche *f*.
budget ['bʌdʒɪt] *n* budget *m* ♦ *vi*: **to ~ for sth** inscrire qch au budget; **I'm on a tight ~** je dois faire attention à mon budget.
budgie ['bʌdʒɪ] *n* = **budgerigar**.
buff [bʌf] *adj* (couleur *f*) chamois *m* ♦ *n* (*enthusiast*) mordu/e.
buffalo, *pl* ~ *or* **~es** ['bʌfələu] *n* buffle *m*; (*US*) bison *m*.
buffer ['bʌfə*] *n* tampon *m*; (*COMPUT*) mémoire *f* tampon.
buffering ['bʌfərɪŋ] *n* (*COMPUT*) mise *f* en mémoire tampon.
buffer state *n* état *m* tampon.
buffer zone *n* zone *f* tampon.
buffet *n* ['bufeɪ] (*food, BRIT: bar*) buffet *m* ♦ *vt* ['bʌfɪt] gifler, frapper; secouer, ébranler.
buffet car *n* (*BRIT RAIL*) voiture-bar *f*.
buffet lunch *n* lunch *m*.
buffoon [bə'fuːn] *n* buffon *m*, pitre *m*.
bug [bʌg] *n* (*insect*) punaise *f*; (*: gen*) insecte *m*, bestiole *f*; (*fig: germ*) virus *m*, microbe *m*; (*spy device*) dispositif *m* d'écoute (électronique), micro clandestin; (*COMPUT: of program*) erreur *f*; (*: of equipment*) défaut *m* ♦ *vt* (*room*) poser des micros dans; (*col: annoy*) embêter; **I've got the travel ~** (*fig*) j'ai le virus du voyage.
bugbear ['bʌgbɛə*] *n* cauchemar *m*, bête noire.
bugger ['bʌgə*] (*col!*) *n* salaud *m* (*!*); connard *m* (*!*) ♦ *vb*: **~ off!** tire-toi! (*!*); **~ (it)!** merde! (*!*).
bugle ['bjuːgl] *n* clairon *m*.
build [bɪld] *n* (*of person*) carrure *f*, charpente *f* ♦ *vt* (*pt, pp* **built** [bɪlt]) construire, bâtir.
►**build on** *vt fus* (*fig*) tirer parti de, partir de.
►**build up** *vt* accumuler, amasser; (*business*) développer; (*reputation*) bâtir.
builder ['bɪldə*] *n* entrepreneur *m*.
building ['bɪldɪŋ] *n* construction *f*; (*structure*) bâtiment *m*, construction; (*: residential, offices*) immeuble *m*.
building contractor *n* entrepreneur *m* (en bâtiment).
building industry *n* (industrie *f* du) bâtiment *m*.
building site *n* chantier *m* (de construction).
building society *n* (*BRIT*) société *f* de crédit immobilier; *voir encadré*.

> **BUILDING SOCIETY**
>
> *Une* **building society** *est une mutuelle dont les épargnants et emprunteurs sont les propriétaires. Ces mutuelles offrent deux services principaux: on peut y avoir un compte d'épargne duquel on peut retirer son argent sur demande ou moyennant un court préavis; et on peut également y faire des emprunts à long terme, par exemple pour acheter une maison. Les* **building societies** *ont eu jusqu'en 1985 le quasi-monopole des comptes d'épargne et des prêts immobiliers, mais les banques ont maintenant une part importante de ce marché.*

building trade *n* = **building industry**.
build-up ['bɪldʌp] *n* (*of gas etc*) accumulation *f*; (*publicity*): **to give sb/sth a good ~** faire de la pub pour qn/qch.
built [bɪlt] *pt, pp of* **build**.
built-in ['bɪlt'ɪn] *adj* (*cupboard*) encastré(e); (*device*) incorporé(e); intégré(e).
built-up area ['bɪltʌp-] *n* agglomération (ur-

baine); zone urbanisée.

bulb [bʌlb] *n* (*BOT*) bulbe *m*, oignon *m*; (*ELEC*) ampoule *f*.

bulbous ['bʌlbəs] *adj* bulbeux(euse).

Bulgaria [bʌl'gɛərɪə] *n* Bulgarie *f*.

Bulgarian [bʌl'gɛərɪən] *adj* bulgare ♦ *n* Bulgare *m/f*; (*LING*) bulgare *m*.

bulge [bʌldʒ] *n* renflement *m*, gonflement *m*; (*in birth rate, sales*) brusque augmentation *f* ♦ *vi* faire saillie; présenter un renflement; **to be bulging with** être plein(e) à craquer de.

bulimia [bə'lɪmɪə] *n* boulimie *f*.

bulk [bʌlk] *n* masse *f*, volume *m*; **in** ~ (*COMM*) en gros, en vrac; **the** ~ **of** la plus grande *or* grosse partie de.

bulk buying [-'baɪɪŋ] *n* achat *m* en gros.

bulk carrier *n* cargo *m*.

bulkhead ['bʌlkhɛd] *n* cloison *f* (étanche).

bulky ['bʌlkɪ] *adj* volumineux(euse), encombrant(e).

bull [bul] *n* taureau *m*; (*STOCK EXCHANGE*) haussier *m*; (*REL*) bulle *f*.

bulldog ['buldɔg] *n* bouledogue *m*.

bulldoze ['buldəuz] *vt* passer *or* raser au bulldozer; **I was ~d into doing it** (*fig*: *col*) on m'a forcé la main.

bulldozer ['buldəuzə*] *n* bulldozer *m*.

bullet ['bulɪt] *n* balle *f* (*de fusil etc*).

bulletin ['bulɪtɪn] *n* bulletin *m*, communiqué *m*.

bulletin board *n* (*COMPUT*) messagerie *f* (électronique).

bulletproof ['bulɪtpru:f] *adj* à l'épreuve des balles; ~ **vest** gilet *m* pare-balles.

bullfight ['bulfaɪt] *n* corrida *f*, course *f* de taureaux.

bullfighter ['bulfaɪtə*] *n* torero *m*.

bullfighting ['bulfaɪtɪŋ] *n* tauromachie *f*.

bullion ['buljən] *n* or *m or* argent *m* en lingots.

bullock ['bulək] *n* bœuf *m*.

bullring ['bulrɪŋ] *n* arène *f*.

bull's-eye ['bulzaɪ] *n* centre *m* (*de la cible*).

bullshit ['bulʃɪt] (*col!*) *n* connerie(s) *f(pl)* (*!*) ♦ *vt* raconter des conneries à (*!*) ♦ *vi* déconner (*!*).

bully ['bulɪ] *n* brute *f*, tyran *m* ♦ *vt* tyranniser, rudoyer; (*frighten*) intimider.

bullying ['bulɪɪŋ] *n* brimades *fpl*.

bum [bʌm] *n* (*col*: *backside*) derrière *m*; (*: tramp*) vagabond/e, traîne-savates *m/f inv*; (*: idler*) glandeur *m*.

►**bum around** *vi* (*col*) vagabonder.

bumblebee ['bʌmblbi:] *n* bourdon *m*.

bumf [bʌmf] *n* (*col*: *forms etc*) paperasses *fpl*.

bump [bʌmp] *n* (*blow*) coup *m*, choc *m*; (*jolt*) cahot *m*; (*on road etc, on head*) bosse *f* ♦ *vt* heurter, cogner; (*car*) emboutir.

►**bump along** *vi* avancer en cahotant.

►**bump into** *vt fus* rentrer dans; (*col*: *meet*) tomber sur.

bumper ['bʌmpə*] *n* pare-chocs *m inv* ♦ *adj*: ~ **crop/harvest** récolte/moisson exceptionnelle.

bumper cars *npl* (*US*) autos tamponneuses.

bumph [bʌmf] *n* = **bumf**.

bumptious ['bʌmpʃəs] *adj* suffisant(e), prétentieux(euse).

bumpy ['bʌmpɪ] *adj* cahoteux(euse); **it was a** ~ **flight/ride** on a été secoués dans l'avion/la voiture.

bun [bʌn] *n* petit pain au lait; (*of hair*) chignon *m*.

bunch [bʌntʃ] *n* (*of flowers*) bouquet *m*; (*of keys*) trousseau *m*; (*of bananas*) régime *m*; (*of people*) groupe *m*; ~ **of grapes** grappe *f* de raisin.

bundle ['bʌndl] *n* paquet *m* ♦ *vt* (*also*: ~ **up**) faire un paquet de; (*put*): **to** ~ **sth/sb into** fourrer *or* enfourner qch/qn dans.

►**bundle off** *vt* (*person*) faire sortir (en toute hâte); expédier.

►**bundle out** *vt* éjecter, sortir (sans ménagements).

bun fight *n* (*BRIT col*) réception *f*; (*tea party*) thé *m*.

bung [bʌŋ] *n* bonde *f*, bouchon *m* ♦ *vt* (*BRIT*: *throw*: *also*: ~ **into**) flanquer; (*also*: ~ **up**: *pipe, hole*) boucher; **my nose is ~ed up** j'ai le nez bouché.

bungalow ['bʌŋgələu] *n* bungalow *m*.

bungee jumping ['bʌndʒi:'dʒʌmpɪŋ] *n* saut *m* à l'élastique.

bungle ['bʌŋgl] *vt* bâcler, gâcher.

bunion ['bʌnjən] *n* oignon *m* (*au pied*).

bunk [bʌŋk] *n* couchette *f*; (*BRIT col*): **to do a** ~ mettre les bouts *or* les voiles.

►**bunk off** *vi* (*BRIT col*: *SCOL*) sécher (les cours); **I'll** ~ **off at 3 o'clock this afternoon** je vais mettre les bouts *or* les voiles à 3 heures cet après-midi.

bunk beds *npl* lits superposés.

bunker ['bʌŋkə*] *n* (*coal store*) soute *f* à charbon; (*MIL, GOLF*) bunker *m*.

bunny ['bʌnɪ] *n* (*also*: ~ **rabbit**) Jeannot *m* lapin.

bunny girl *n* (*BRIT*) *hôtesse de cabaret*.

bunny hill *n* (*US SKI*) piste *f* pour débutants.

bunting ['bʌntɪŋ] *n* pavoisement *m*, drapeaux *mpl*.

buoy [bɔɪ] *n* bouée *f*.

►**buoy up** *vt* faire flotter; (*fig*) soutenir, épauler.

buoyancy ['bɔɪənsɪ] *n* (*of ship*) flottabilité *f*.

buoyant ['bɔɪənt] *adj* (*ship*) flottable; (*carefree*) gai(e), plein(e) d'entrain; (*COMM*: *market*) actif(ive); (*: prices, currency*) soutenu(e).

burden ['bə:dn] *n* fardeau *m*, charge *f* ♦ *vt* charger; (*oppress*) accabler, surcharger; **to be a** ~ **to sb** être un fardeau pour qn.

bureau, *pl* **~x** ['bjuərəu, -z] *n* (*BRIT*: *writing desk*) bureau *m*, secrétaire *m*; (*US*: *chest of drawers*) commode *f*; (*office*) bureau, office *m*.

bureaucracy [bjuə'rɔkrəsɪ] *n* bureaucratie *f*.

bureaucrat ['bjuərəkræt] *n* bureaucrate *m/f*, rond-de-cuir *m*.
bureaucratic [bjuərə'krætɪk] *adj* bureaucratique.
burgeon ['bə:dʒən] *vi* (*fig*) être en expansion rapide.
burger ['bə:gə*] *n* hamburger *m*.
burglar ['bə:glə*] *n* cambrioleur *m*.
burglar alarm *n* sonnerie *f* d'alarme.
burglarize ['bə:gləraɪz] *vt* (*US*) cambrioler.
burglary ['bə:glərɪ] *n* cambriolage *m*.
burgle ['bə:gl] *vt* cambrioler.
Burgundy ['bə:gəndɪ] *n* Bourgogne *f*.
burial ['bɛrɪəl] *n* enterrement *m*.
burial ground *n* cimetière *m*.
burlesque [bə:'lɛsk] *n* caricature *f*, parodie *f*.
burly ['bə:lɪ] *adj* de forte carrure, costaud(e).
Burma ['bə:mə] *n* Birmanie *f*; *see also* **Myanmar**.
Burmese [bə:'mi:z] *adj* birman(e), de Birmanie ♦ *n* (*pl inv*) Birman/e; (*LING*) birman *m*.
burn [bə:n] *vt*, *vi* (*pt*, *pp* **burned** *or* **burnt** [bə:nt]) brûler ♦ *n* brûlure *f*; **the cigarette ~t a hole in her dress** la cigarette a fait un trou dans sa robe; **I've ~t myself!** je me suis brûlé(e)!
►**burn down** *vt* incendier, détruire par le feu.
►**burn out** *vt* (*subj: writer etc*): **to ~ o.s. out** s'user (à force de travailler).
burner ['bə:nə*] *n* brûleur *m*.
burning ['bə:nɪŋ] *adj* (*building, forest*) en flammes; (*issue, question*) brûlant(e).
burnish ['bə:nɪʃ] *vt* polir
Burns Night [bə:nz-] *n voir encadré*.

BURNS NIGHT

Burns Night *est une fête qui a lieu le 25 janvier, à la mémoire du poète écossais Robert Burns (1759-1796), à l'occasion de laquelle les Écossais partout dans le monde organisent un souper, en général arrosé de whisky. Le plat principal est toujours le haggis, servi avec de la purée de pommes de terre et de la purée de rutabagas. On apporte le haggis au son des cornemuses et au cours du repas on lit des poèmes de Burns et on chante ses chansons.*

burnt [bə:nt] *pt*, *pp of* **burn**.
burnt sugar *n* (*BRIT*) caramel *m*.
burp [bə:p] (*col*) *n* rot *m* ♦ *vi* roter.
burrow ['bʌrəu] *n* terrier *m* ♦ *vt* creuser.
bursar ['bə:sə*] *n* économe *m/f*; (*BRIT*: *student*) boursier/ère.
bursary ['bə:sərɪ] *n* (*BRIT*) bourse *f* (d'études).
burst [bə:st] *vb* (*pt*, *pp* **burst**) *vt* faire éclater ♦ *vi* éclater ♦ *n* explosion *f*; **~ of energy** activité soudaine; **~ of laughter** éclat *m* de rire; **a ~ of applause** une salve d'applaudissement; **a ~ of speed** une pointe de vitesse; **~ blood vessel** rupture *f* de vaisseau sanguin; **the river has ~ its banks** le cours d'eau est sorti de son lit; **to ~ into flames** s'enflammer soudainement; **to ~ out laughing** éclater de rire; **to ~ into tears** fondre en larmes; **to ~ open** *vi* s'ouvrir violemment *or* soudainement; **to be ~ing with** être plein(e) (à craquer) de; regorger de.
►**burst into** *vt fus* (*room etc*) faire irruption dans.
►**burst out of** *vt fus* sortir précipitamment de.
bury ['bɛrɪ] *vt* enterrer; **to ~ one's face in one's hands** se couvrir le visage de ses mains; **to ~ one's head in the sand** (*fig*) pratiquer la politique de l'autruche; **to ~ the hatchet** (*fig*) enterrer la hache de guerre.
bus, *pl* **~es** [bʌs, 'bʌsɪz] *n* autobus *m*.
busboy ['bʌsbɔɪ] *n* (*US*) aide-serveur *m*.
bush [buʃ] *n* buisson *m*; (*scrub land*) brousse *f*.
bushed [buʃt] *adj* (*col*) crevé(e), claqué(e).
bushel ['buʃl] *n* boisseau *m*.
bushfire ['buʃfaɪə*] *n* feu *m* de brousse.
bushy ['buʃɪ] *adj* broussailleux(euse), touffu(e).
busily ['bɪzɪlɪ] *adv*: **to be ~ doing sth** s'affairer à faire qch.
business ['bɪznɪs] *n* (*matter, firm*) affaire *f*; (*trading*) affaires *fpl*; (*job, duty*) travail *m*; **to be away on ~** être en déplacement d'affaires; **I'm here on ~** je suis là pour affaires; **he's in the insurance ~** il est dans les assurances; **to do ~ with sb** traiter avec qn; **it's none of my ~** cela ne me regarde pas, ce ne sont pas mes affaires; **he means ~** il ne plaisante pas, il est sérieux.
business address *n* adresse professionnelle *or* au bureau.
business card *n* carte *f* de visite (professionnelle).
businesslike ['bɪznɪslaɪk] *adj* sérieux(euse); efficace.
businessman ['bɪznɪsmən] *n* homme *m* d'affaires.
business trip *n* voyage *m* d'affaires.
businesswoman ['bɪznɪswumən] *n* femme *f* d'affaires.
busker ['bʌskə*] *n* (*BRIT*) artiste ambulant(e).
bus lane *n* (*BRIT*) voie réservée aux autobus.
bus shelter *n* abribus *m*.
bus station *n* gare routière.
bus stop *n* arrêt *m* d'autobus.
bust [bʌst] *n* buste *m* ♦ *adj* (*col*: *broken*) fichu(e), fini(e) ♦ *vt* (*col*: *POLICE*: *arrest*) pincer; **to go ~** faire faillite.
bustle ['bʌsl] *n* remue-ménage *m*, affairement *m* ♦ *vi* s'affairer, se démener.
bustling ['bʌslɪŋ] *adj* (*person*) affairé(e); (*town*) très animé(e).
bust-up ['bʌstʌp] *n* (*BRIT col*) engueulade *f*.
busty ['bʌstɪ] *adj* (*col*) à la poitrine plantureuse.
busy ['bɪzɪ] *adj* occupé(e); (*shop, street*) très fréquenté(e); (*US*: *telephone, line*) occupé

♦ *vt*: **to ~ o.s.** s'occuper; **he's a ~ man** (*normally*) c'est un homme très pris; (*temporarily*) il est très pris.
busybody ['bɪzɪbɔdɪ] *n* mouche *f* du coche, âme *f* charitable.
busy signal *n* (*US*) tonalité *f* occupé.

KEYWORD

but [bʌt] *conj* mais; **I'd love to come, ~ I'm busy** j'aimerais venir mais je suis occupé
♦ *prep* (*apart from, except*) sauf, excepté; **nothing ~** rien d'autre que; **we've had nothing ~ trouble** nous n'avons eu que des ennuis; **no-one ~ him can do it** lui seul peut le faire; **~ for you/your help** sans toi/ton aide; **anything ~ that** tout sauf *or* excepté ça, tout mais pas ça; **the last ~ one** (*BRIT*) l'avant-dernier(ère)
♦ *adv* (*just, only*) ne ... que; **she's ~ a child** elle n'est qu'une enfant; **had I ~ known** si seulement j'avais su; **all ~ finished** pratiquement terminé; **anything ~ finished** tout sauf fini, très loin d'être fini.

butane ['bju:teɪn] *n* (*also*: **~ gas**) butane *m*.
butch [butʃ] *adj* (*col*: *man*) costaud, viril; (*: woman*) costaude, masculine.
butcher ['butʃə*] *n* boucher *m* ♦ *vt* massacrer; (*cattle etc for meat*) tuer; **~'s (shop)** boucherie *f*.
butler ['bʌtlə*] *n* maître *m* d'hôtel.
butt [bʌt] *n* (*cask*) gros tonneau; (*thick end*) (gros) bout; (*of gun*) crosse *f*; (*of cigarette*) mégot *m*; (*BRIT fig: target*) cible *f* ♦ *vt* donner un coup de tête à.
►**butt in** *vi* (*interrupt*) interrompre.
butter ['bʌtə*] *n* beurre *m* ♦ *vt* beurrer.
buttercup ['bʌtəkʌp] *n* bouton *m* d'or.
butter dish *n* beurrier *m*.
butterfingers ['bʌtəfɪŋgəz] *n* (*col*) maladroit/e.
butterfly ['bʌtəflaɪ] *n* papillon *m*; (*SWIMMING*: *also*: **~ stroke**) brasse *f* papillon.
buttocks ['bʌtəks] *npl* fesses *fpl*.
button ['bʌtn] *n* bouton *m* ♦ *vt* (*also*: **~ up**) boutonner ♦ *vi* se boutonner.
buttonhole ['bʌtnhəul] *n* boutonnière *f* ♦ *vt* accrocher, arrêter, retenir.
buttress ['bʌtrɪs] *n* contrefort *m*.
buxom ['bʌksəm] *adj* aux formes avantageuses *or* épanouies, bien galbé(e).
buy [baɪ] *vb* (*pt, pp* **bought** [bɔ:t]) *vt* acheter; (*COMM*: *company*) (r)acheter ♦ *n*: **that was a good/bad ~** c'était un bon/mauvais achat; **to ~ sb sth/sth from sb** acheter qch à qn; **to ~ sb a drink** offrir un verre *or* à boire à qn.
►**buy back** *vt* racheter.
►**buy in** *vt* (*BRIT*: *goods*) acheter, faire venir.
►**buy into** *vt fus* (*BRIT COMM*) acheter des actions de.
►**buy off** *vt* (*bribe*) acheter.
►**buy out** *vt* (*partner*) désintéresser; (*business*) racheter.
►**buy up** *vt* acheter en bloc, rafler.
buyer ['baɪə*] *n* acheteur/euse; **~'s market** marché *m* favorable aux acheteurs.
buy-out ['baɪaut] *n* (*COMM*) rachat *m* (*d'entreprise*).
buzz [bʌz] *n* bourdonnement *m*; (*col*: *phone call*) coup *m* de fil ♦ *vi* bourdonner ♦ *vt* (*call on intercom*) appeler; (*with buzzer*) sonner; (*AVIAT*: *plane, building*) raser; **my head is ~ing** j'ai la tête qui bourdonne.
►**buzz off** *vi* (*col*) s'en aller, ficher le camp.
buzzard ['bʌzəd] *n* buse *f*.
buzzer ['bʌzə*] *n* timbre *m* électrique.
buzz word *n* (*col*) mot *m* à la mode *or* dans le vent.

KEYWORD

by [baɪ] *prep* **1** (*referring to cause, agent*) par, de; **killed ~ lightning** tué par la foudre; **surrounded ~ a fence** entouré d'une barrière; **a painting ~ Picasso** un tableau de Picasso
2 (*referring to method, manner, means*): **~ bus/car** en autobus/voiture; **~ train** par le *or* en train; **to pay ~ cheque** payer par chèque; **~ saving hard, he ...** à force d'économiser, il ...
3 (*via, through*) par; **we came ~ Dover** nous sommes venus par Douvres
4 (*close to, past*) à côté de; **the house ~ the school** la maison à côté de l'école; **a holiday ~ the sea** des vacances au bord de la mer; **she sat ~ his bed** elle était assise à son chevet; **she went ~ me** elle est passée à côté de moi; **I go ~ the post office every day** je passe devant la poste tous les jours
5 (*with time*: *not later than*) avant; (: *during*): **~ daylight** à la lumière du jour; **~ night** la nuit, de nuit; **~ 4 o'clock** avant 4 heures; **~ this time tomorrow** d'ici demain à la même heure; **~ the time I got here it was too late** lorsque je suis arrivé il était déjà trop tard
6 (*amount*) à; **~ the kilo/metre** au kilo/au mètre; **paid ~ the hour** payé à l'heure; **to increase** *etc* **~ the hour** augmenter *etc* d'heure en heure
7 (*MATH, measure*): **to divide/multiply ~ 3** diviser/multiplier par 3; **a room 3 metres ~ 4** une pièce de 3 mètres sur 4; **it's broader ~ a metre** c'est plus large d'un mètre; **the bullet missed him ~ inches** la balle est passée à quelques centimètres de lui; **one ~ one** un à un; **little ~ little** petit à petit, peu à peu
8 (*according to*) d'après, selon; **it's 3 o'clock ~ my watch** il est 3 heures à ma montre; **it's all right ~ me** je n'ai rien contre
9: **(all) ~ oneself** *etc* tout(e) seul(e)
10: **~ the way** au fait, à propos
♦ *adv* **1** *see* **go; pass** *etc*
2: **~ and ~** un peu plus tard, bientôt; **~ and large** dans l'ensemble.

bye(-bye) ['baɪ('baɪ)] *excl* au revoir!, salut!
by(e)-law ['baɪlɔː] *n* arrêté municipal.
by-election ['baɪɪlɛkʃən] *n* (*BRIT*) élection (législative) partielle.
Byelorussia [bjɛləu'rʌʃə] *n* Biélorussie *f*.
Byelorussian [bjɛləu'rʌʃən] *adj*, *n* = **Belorussian.**
bygone ['baɪgɔn] *adj* passé(e) ♦ *n*: **let ~s be ~s** passons l'éponge, oublions le passé.
bypass ['baɪpɑːs] *n* (route *f* de) contournement *m*; (*MED*) pontage *m* ♦ *vt* éviter.
by-product ['baɪprɔdʌkt] *n* sous-produit *m*, dérivé *m*; (*fig*) conséquence *f* secondaire, retombée *f*.
byre ['baɪə*] *n* (*BRIT*) étable *f* (à vaches).
bystander ['baɪstændə*] *n* spectateur/trice, badaud/e.
byte [baɪt] *n* (*COMPUT*) octet *m*.
byway ['baɪweɪ] *n* chemin détourné.
byword ['baɪwəːd] *n*: **to be a ~ for** être synonyme de (*fig*).
by-your-leave ['baɪjɔː'liːv] *n*: **without so much as a ~** sans même demander la permission.

C c

C, c [siː] *n* (*letter*) C, c *m*; (*SCOL*: *mark*) C; (*MUS*): **C** do *m*; **C for Charlie** C comme Célestin.
C *abbr* (= *Celsius, centigrade*) C.
c *abbr* (= *century*) s.; (= *circa*) v.; (*US etc*) = **cent(s).**
CA *n abbr* = **Central America**; (*BRIT*) = **chartered accountant** ♦ *abbr* (*US*) = *California*.
ca. *abbr* (= *circa*) v.
c/a *abbr* = **capital account, credit account, current account.**
CAA *n abbr* (*BRIT*: = *Civil Aviation Authority*, *US*: = *Civil Aeronautics Authority*) *direction de l'aviation civile*.
CAB *n abbr* (*BRIT*) = **Citizens' Advice Bureau.**
cab [kæb] *n* taxi *m*; (*of train, truck*) cabine *f*; (*horse-drawn*) fiacre *m*.
cabaret ['kæbəreɪ] *n* attractions *fpl*, spectacle *m* de cabaret.
cabbage ['kæbɪdʒ] *n* chou *m*.
cabbie, cabby ['kæbɪ] *n* (*col*), **cab driver** *n* taxi *m*, chauffeur *m* de taxi.
cabin ['kæbɪn] *n* cabane *f*, hutte *f*; (*on ship*) cabine *f*.
cabin cruiser *n* yacht *m* (à moteur).
cabinet ['kæbɪnɪt] *n* (*POL*) cabinet *m*; (*furniture*) petit meuble à tiroirs et rayons; (*also*: **display ~**) vitrine *f*, petite armoire vitrée.
cabinet-maker ['kæbɪnɪt'meɪkə*] *n* ébéniste *m*.
cabinet minister *n* ministre *m* (*membre du cabinet*).
cable ['keɪbl] *n* câble *m* ♦ *vt* câbler, télégraphier.
cable-car ['keɪblkɑː*] *n* téléphérique *m*.
cablegram ['keɪblgræm] *n* câblogramme *m*.
cable railway *n* (*BRIT*) funiculaire *m*.
cable television *n* télévision *f* par câble.
cache [kæʃ] *n* cachette *f*; **a ~ of food** *etc* un dépôt secret de provisions *etc*, une cachette contenant des provisions *etc*.
cackle ['kækl] *vi* caqueter.
cactus, *pl* **cacti** ['kæktəs, -taɪ] *n* cactus *m*.
CAD *n abbr* (= *computer-aided design*) CAO *f*.
caddie ['kædɪ] *n* caddie ® *m*.
cadet [kə'dɛt] *n* (*MIL*) élève *m* officier; **police ~** élève agent de police.
cadge [kædʒ] *vt* (*col*) se faire donner; **to ~ a meal (off sb)** se faire inviter à manger (par qn).
cadger ['kædʒə*] *n* pique-assiette *m/f inv*, tapeur/euse.
cadre ['kædrɪ] *n* cadre *m*.
Caesarean, (*US*) **Cesarean** [siː'zɛərɪən] *adj*: **~ (section)** césarienne *f*.
CAF *abbr* (*BRIT*: = *cost and freight*) C et F.
café ['kæfeɪ] *n* ≈ café(-restaurant) *m* (*sans alcool*).
cafeteria [kæfɪ'tɪərɪə] *n* cafeteria *f*.
caffein(e) ['kæfiːn] *n* caféine *f*.
cage [keɪdʒ] *n* cage *f* ♦ *vt* mettre en cage.
cagey ['keɪdʒɪ] *adj* (*col*) réticent(e); méfiant(e).
cagoule [kə'guːl] *n* K-way *m* ®.
cahoots [kə'huːts] *n*: **to be in ~ (with)** être de mèche (avec).
CAI *n abbr* (= *computer-aided instruction*) EAO *m*.
Cairo ['kaɪərəu] *n* Le Caire.
cajole [kə'dʒəul] *vt* couvrir de flatteries *or* de gentillesses.
cake [keɪk] *n* gâteau *m*; **~ of soap** savonnette *f*; **it's a piece of ~** (*col*) c'est un jeu d'enfant; **he wants to have his ~ and eat it (too)** (*fig*) il veut tout avoir.
caked [keɪkt] *adj*: **~ with** raidi(e) par, couvert(e) d'une croûte de.
cake shop *n* pâtisserie *f*.
Cal. *abbr* (*US*) = *California*.
calamitous [kə'læmɪtəs] *adj* catastrophique, désastreux(euse).
calamity [kə'læmɪtɪ] *n* calamité *f*, désastre *m*.
calcium ['kælsɪəm] *n* calcium *m*.
calculate ['kælkjuleɪt] *vt* calculer; (*estimate: chances, effect*) évaluer.
►**calculate on** *vt fus*: **to ~ on sth/on doing sth** compter sur qch/faire qch.
calculated ['kælkjuleɪtɪd] *adj* (*insult, action*) délibéré(e); **a ~ risk** un risque pris en toute connaissance de cause.

calculating ['kælkjuleɪtɪŋ] *adj* calculateur(trice).
calculation [kælkju'leɪʃən] *n* calcul *m*.
calculator ['kælkjuleɪtə*] *n* machine *f* à calculer, calculatrice *f*.
calculus ['kælkjuləs] *n* analyse *f* (mathématique), calcul infinitésimal; **integral/differential** ~ calcul intégral/différentiel.
calendar ['kæləndə*] *n* calendrier *m*.
calendar month *n* mois *m* (de calendrier).
calendar year *n* année civile.
calf, *pl* **calves** [kɑːf, kɑːvz] *n* (*of cow*) veau *m*; (*of other animals*) petit *m*; (*also*: ~**skin**) veau *m*, vachette *f*; (*ANAT*) mollet *m*.
caliber ['kælɪbə*] *n* (*US*) = **calibre**.
calibrate ['kælɪbreɪt] *vt* (*gun etc*) calibrer; (*scale of measuring instrument*) étalonner.
calibre, (*US*) **caliber** ['kælɪbə*] *n* calibre *m*.
calico ['kælɪkəu] *n* (*BRIT*) calicot *m*; (*US*) indienne *f*.
Calif. *abbr* (*US*) = *California*.
California [kælɪ'fɔːnɪə] *n* Californie *f*.
calipers ['kælɪpəz] *npl* (*US*) = **callipers**.
call [kɔːl] *vt* (*gen, also TEL*) appeler; (*announce: flight*) annoncer; (*meeting*) convoquer; (*strike*) lancer ♦ *vi* appeler; (*visit*: *also*: ~ **in**, ~ **round**): **to** ~ **(for)** passer (prendre) ♦ *n* (*shout*) appel *m*, cri *m*; (*summons: for flight etc, fig: lure*) appel; (*visit*) visite *f*; (*also*: **telephone** ~) coup *m* de téléphone; communication *f*; **to be on** ~ être de permanence; **she's** ~**ed Suzanne** elle s'appelle Suzanne; **who is** ~**ing?** (*TEL*) qui est à l'appareil?; **London** ~**ing** (*RADIO*) ici Londres, **please give me a** ~ **at 7** appelez-moi à 7 heures; **to make a** ~ téléphoner, passer un coup de fil; **to pay a** ~ **on sb** rendre visite à qn, passer voir qn; **there's not much** ~ **for these items** ces articles ne sont pas très demandés.
►**call at** *vt fus* (*subj: ship*) faire escale à; (*: train*) s'arrêter à.
►**call back** *vi* (*return*) repasser; (*TEL*) rappeler ♦ *vt* (*TEL*) rappeler.
►**call for** *vt fus* demander.
►**call in** *vt* (*doctor, expert, police*) appeler, faire venir.
►**call off** *vt* annuler; **the strike was** ~**ed off** l'ordre de grève a été rapporté.
►**call on** *vt fus* (*visit*) rendre visite à, passer voir; (*request*): **to** ~ **on sb to do** inviter qn à faire.
►**call out** *vi* pousser un cri *or* des cris ♦ *vt* (*doctor, police, troops*) appeler.
►**call up** *vt* (*MIL*) appeler, mobiliser.
Callanetics [kælə'netɪks] *n* ® stretching *m*.
callbox ['kɔːlbɔks] *n* (*BRIT*) cabine *f* téléphonique.
call centre *n* centre *m* d'appels.
caller ['kɔːlə*] *n* personne *f* qui appelle; visiteur *m*; **hold the line,** ~! (*TEL*) ne quittez pas, Monsieur (*or* Madame)!
call girl *n* call-girl *f*.
call-in ['kɔːlɪn] *n* (*US RADIO, TV*) programme *m* à ligne ouverte.
calling ['kɔːlɪŋ] *n* vocation *f*; (*trade, occupation*) état *m*.
calling card *n* (*US*) carte *f* de visite.
callipers, (*US*) **calipers** ['kælɪpəz] *npl* (*MATH*) compas *m*; (*MED*) appareil *m* orthopédique; gouttière *f*; étrier *m*.
callous ['kæləs] *adj* dur(e), insensible.
callousness ['kæləsnɪs] *n* dureté *f*, manque *m* de cœur, insensibilité *f*.
callow ['kæləu] *adj* sans expérience (de la vie).
calm [kɑːm] *adj* calme ♦ *n* calme *m* ♦ *vt* calmer, apaiser.
►**calm down** *vi* se calmer, s'apaiser ♦ *vt* calmer, apaiser.
calmly ['kɑːmlɪ] *adv* calmement, avec calme.
calmness ['kɑːmnɪs] *n* calme *m*.
Calor gas ['kælə*-] *n* ® (*BRIT*) butane *m*, butagaz *m* ®.
calorie ['kælərɪ] *n* calorie *f*; **low** ~ **product** produit *m* pauvre en calories.
calve [kɑːv] *vi* vêler, mettre bas.
calves [kɑːvz] *npl of* **calf**.
CAM *n abbr* (= *computer-aided manufacturing*) FAO *f*.
camber ['kæmbə*] *n* (*of road*) bombement *m*.
Cambodia [kæm'bəudjə] *n* Cambodge *m*.
Cambodian [kæm'bəudɪən] *adj* cambodgien(ne) ♦ *n* Cambodgien/ne.
Cambs *abbr* (*BRIT*) = *Cambridgeshire*.
camcorder ['kæmkɔːdə*] *n* caméscope *m*.
came [keɪm] *pt of* **come**.
camel ['kæməl] *n* chameau *m*.
cameo ['kæmɪəu] *n* camée *m*.
camera ['kæmərə] *n* appareil *m* photo; (*CINE, TV*) caméra *f*; **35mm** ~ appareil 24 x 36 *or* petit format; **in** ~ à huis clos, en privé.
cameraman ['kæmərəmæn] *n* caméraman *m*.
Cameroon, Cameroun [kæmə'ruːn] *n* Cameroun *m*.
camouflage ['kæməflɑːʒ] *n* camouflage *m* ♦ *vt* camoufler.
camp [kæmp] *n* camp *m* ♦ *vi* camper; **to go** ~**ing** faire du camping.
campaign [kæm'peɪn] *n* (*MIL, POL etc*) campagne *f* ♦ *vi* (*also fig*) faire campagne; **to** ~ **for/against** militer pour/contre.
campaigner [kæm'peɪnə*] *n*: ~ **for** partisan/e de; ~ **against** opposant/e à.
campbed ['kæmp'bed] *n* (*BRIT*) lit *m* de camp.
camper ['kæmpə*] *n* campeur/euse.
camping ['kæmpɪŋ] *n* camping *m*.
camp(ing) site *n* (terrain *m* de) camping *m*.
campus ['kæmpəs] *n* campus *m*.
camshaft ['kæmʃɑːft] *n* arbre *m* à came.
can[1] [kæn] *aux vb see keyword* ♦ *n* (*of milk, oil, water*) bidon *m*; (*tin*) boîte *f* (de conserve) ♦ *vt* mettre en conserve; **a** ~ **of beer** une canette de bière; **he had to carry the** ~ (*BRIT col*) on lui a fait porter le chapeau.

KEYWORD

can[2] [kæn] (*negative* **cannot, can't**; *conditional and pt* **could**) *aux vb* **1** (*be able to*) pouvoir; **you ~ do it if you try** vous pouvez le faire si vous essayez; **I ~'t hear you** je ne t'entends pas
2 (*know how to*) savoir; **I ~ swim/play tennis/drive** je sais nager/jouer au tennis/conduire; **~ you speak French?** parlez-vous français?
3 (*may*) pouvoir; **~ I use your phone?** puis-je me servir de votre téléphone?
4 (*expressing disbelief, puzzlement etc*): **it ~'t be true!** ce n'est pas possible!; **what CAN he want?** qu'est-ce qu'il peut bien vouloir?
5 (*expressing possibility, suggestion etc*): **he could be in the library** il est peut-être dans la bibliothèque; **she could have been delayed** il se peut qu'elle ait été retardée; **they could have forgotten** ils ont pu oublier.

Canada ['kænədə] *n* Canada *m*.
Canadian [kə'neɪdɪən] *adj* canadien(ne) ♦ *n* Canadien/ne.
canal [kə'næl] *n* canal *m*.
canary [kə'nɛərɪ] *n* canari *m*, serin *m*.
Canary Islands, Canaries [kə'nɛərɪz] *npl*: **the ~** les (îles *fpl*) Canaries *fpl*.
Canberra ['kænbərə] *n* Canberra.
cancel ['kænsəl] *vt* annuler; (*train*) supprimer; (*party, appointment*) décommander; (*cross out*) barrer, rayer; (*stamp*) oblitérer; (*cheque*) faire opposition à.
►**cancel out** *vt* annuler; **they ~ each other out** ils s'annulent.
cancellation [kænsə'leɪʃən] *n* annulation *f*; suppression *f*; oblitération *f*; (*TOURISM*) réservation annulée, client *etc* qui s'est décommandé.
cancer ['kænsə*] *n* cancer *m*; **C~** (*sign*) le Cancer; **to be C~** être du Cancer.
cancerous ['kænsrəs] *adj* cancéreux(euse).
cancer patient *n* cancéreux/euse.
cancer research *n* recherche *f* contre le cancer.
C and F *abbr* (*BRIT*: = *cost and freight*) C et F.
candid ['kændɪd] *adj* (très) franc(franche), sincère.
candidacy ['kændɪdəsɪ] *n* candidature *f*.
candidate ['kændɪdeɪt] *n* candidat/e.
candidature ['kændɪdətʃə*] *n* (*BRIT*) = **candidacy**.
candied ['kændɪd] *adj* confit(e); **~ apple** (*US*) pomme caramélisée.
candle ['kændl] *n* bougie *f*; (*of tallow*) chandelle *f*; (*in church*) cierge *m*.
candlelight ['kændllaɪt] *n*: **by ~** à la lumière d'une bougie; (*dinner*) aux chandelles.
candlestick ['kændlstɪk] *n* (*also*: **candle holder**) bougeoir *m*; (*bigger, ornate*) chandelier *m*.
candour, (*US*) candor ['kændə*] *n* (grande) franchise *or* sincérité.
C & W *n abbr* = **country and western (music)**.
candy ['kændɪ] *n* sucre candi; (*US*) bonbon *m*.
candy-floss ['kændɪflɔs] *n* (*BRIT*) barbe *f* à papa.
candy store *n* (*US*) confiserie *f*.
cane [keɪn] *n* canne *f*; (*for baskets, chairs etc*) rotin *m* ♦ *vt* (*BRIT SCOL*) administrer des coups de bâton à.
canine ['kænaɪn] *adj* canin(e).
canister ['kænɪstə*] *n* boîte *f* (*gén en métal*).
cannabis ['kænəbɪs] *n* (*drug*) cannabis *m*; (*also*: **~ plant**) chanvre indien.
canned ['kænd] *adj* (*food*) en boîte, en conserve; (*col: music*) enregistré(e); (*BRIT col: drunk*) bourré(e); (*US col: worker*) mis(e) à la porte.
cannibal ['kænɪbəl] *n* cannibale *m/f*, anthropophage *m/f*.
cannibalism ['kænɪbəlɪzəm] *n* cannibalisme *m*, anthropophagie *f*.
cannon, *pl* **~** *or* **~s** ['kænən] *n* (*gun*) canon *m*.
cannonball ['kænənbɔːl] *n* boulet *m* de canon.
cannon fodder *n* chair *f* à canon.
cannot ['kænɔt] = **can not**.
canny ['kænɪ] *adj* madré(e), finaud(e).
canoe [kə'nuː] *n* pirogue *f*; (*SPORT*) canoë *m*.
canoeing [kə'nuːɪŋ] *n* (*sport*) canoë *m*.
canoeist [kə'nuːɪst] *n* canoéiste *m/f*.
canon ['kænən] *n* (*clergyman*) chanoine *m*; (*standard*) canon *m*.
canonize ['kænənaɪz] *vt* canoniser.
can opener [-'əupnə*] *n* ouvre-boîte *m*.
canopy ['kænəpɪ] *n* baldaquin *m*; dais *m*.
cant [kænt] *n* jargon *m* ♦ *vt, vi* pencher.
can't [kænt] = **can not**.
Cantab. *abbr* (*BRIT*: = *cantabrigiensis*) *of Cambridge*.
cantankerous [kæn'tæŋkərəs] *adj* querelleur(euse), acariâtre.
canteen [kæn'tiːn] *n* cantine *f*; (*BRIT*: *of cutlery*) ménagère *f*.
canter ['kæntə*] *n* petit galop ♦ *vi* aller au petit galop.
cantilever ['kæntɪliːvə*] *n* porte-à-faux *m inv*.
canvas ['kænvəs] *n* (*gen*) toile *f*; **under ~** (*camping*) sous la tente; (*NAUT*) toutes voiles dehors.
canvass ['kænvəs] *vt* (*POL*: *district*) faire la tournée électorale dans; (*: person*) solliciter le suffrage de; (*COMM*: *district*) prospecter; (*citizens, opinions*) sonder.
canvasser ['kænvəsə*] *n* (*POL*) agent électoral; (*COMM*) démarcheur *m*.
canvassing ['kænvəsɪŋ] *n* (*POL*) prospection électorale, démarchage électoral; (*COMM*) démarchage, prospection.
canyon ['kænjən] *n* cañon *m*, gorge (profonde).
CAP *n abbr* (= *Common Agricultural Policy*) PAC *f*.
cap [kæp] *n* casquette *f*; (*for swimming*) bonnet

m de bain; (*of pen*) capuchon *m*; (*of bottle*) capsule *f*; (*BRIT*: *contraceptive*: *also*: **Dutch ~**) diaphragme *m*; (*: FOOTBALL*) sélection *f* pour l'équipe nationale ♦ *vt* capsuler; (*outdo*) surpasser; **~ped with** coiffé(e) de; **and to ~ it all, he ...** (*BRIT*) pour couronner le tout, il ....
capability [keɪpə'bɪlɪtɪ] *n* aptitude *f*, capacité *f*.
capable ['keɪpəbl] *adj* capable; **~ of** (*interpretation etc*) susceptible de.
capacious [kə'peɪʃəs] *adj* vaste.
capacity [kə'pæsɪtɪ] *n* (*of container*) capacité *f*, contenance *f*; (*ability*) aptitude *f*; **filled to ~** plein(e); **in his ~ as** en sa qualité de; **in an advisory ~** à titre consultatif; **to work at full ~** travailler à plein rendement.
cape [keɪp] *n* (*garment*) cape *f*; (*GEO*) cap *m*.
Cape of Good Hope *n* cap *m* de Bonne Espérance.
caper ['keɪpə*] *n* (*CULIN*: *also*: **~s**) câpre *f*.
Cape Town *n* Le Cap.
capita ['kæpɪtə] *see* **per capita**.
capital ['kæpɪtl] *n* (*also*: **~ city**) capitale *f*; (*money*) capital *m*; (*also*: **~ letter**) majuscule *f*.
capital account *n* balance *f* des capitaux; (*of country*) compte capital.
capital allowance *n* provision *f* pour amortissement.
capital assets *npl* immobilisations *fpl*.
capital expenditure *n* dépenses *fpl* d'équipement.
capital gains tax *n* impôt *m* sur les plus-values.
capital goods *n* biens *mpl* d'équipement.
capital-intensive ['kæpɪtlɪn'tɛnsɪv] *adj* à forte proportion de capitaux.
capitalism ['kæpɪtəlɪzəm] *n* capitalisme *m*.
capitalist ['kæpɪtəlɪst] *adj*, *n* capitaliste (*m/f*).
capitalize ['kæpɪtəlaɪz] *vt* (*provide with capital*) financer.
►**capitalize on** *vt fus* (*fig*) profiter de.
capital punishment *n* peine capitale.
capital transfer tax *n* (*BRIT*) impôt *m* sur le transfert de propriété.
Capitol ['kæpɪtl] *n*: **the ~** le Capitole; *voir encadré*.

CAPITOL

Le **Capitol** *est le siège du "Congress", à Washington. Il est situé sur Capitol Hill.*

capitulate [kə'pɪtjuleɪt] *vi* capituler.
capitulation [kəpɪtju'leɪʃən] *n* capitulation *f*.
capricious [kə'prɪʃəs] *adj* capricieux(euse), fantasque.
Capricorn ['kæprɪkɔ:n] *n* le Capricorne; **to be ~** être du Capricorne.
caps [kæps] *abbr* = **capital letters**.
capsize [kæp'saɪz] *vt* faire chavirer ♦ *vi* chavirer.
capstan ['kæpstən] *n* cabestan *m*.
capsule ['kæpsju:l] *n* capsule *f*.
Capt. *abbr* (= *captain*) Cne.
captain ['kæptɪn] *n* capitaine *m* ♦ *vt* commander, être le capitaine de.
caption ['kæpʃən] *n* légende *f*.
captivate ['kæptɪveɪt] *vt* captiver, fasciner.
captive ['kæptɪv] *adj*, *n* captif(ive).
captivity [kæp'tɪvɪtɪ] *n* captivité *f*.
captor ['kæptə*] *n* (*unlawful*) ravisseur *m*; (*lawful*): **his ~s** les gens (*or* ceux *etc*) qui l'ont arrêté.
capture ['kæptʃə*] *vt* capturer, prendre; (*attention*) capter ♦ *n* capture *f*.
car [kɑ:*] *n* voiture *f*, auto *f*; (*US RAIL*) wagon *m*, voiture; **by ~** en voiture.
carafe [kə'ræf] *n* carafe *f*.
carafe wine *n* (*in restaurant*) ≈ vin ouvert.
caramel ['kærəməl] *n* caramel *m*.
carat ['kærət] *n* carat *m*; **18 ~ gold** or *m* à 18 carats.
caravan ['kærəvæn] *n* caravane *f*.
caravan site *n* (*BRIT*) camping *m* pour caravanes.
caraway ['kærəweɪ] *n*: **~ seed** graine *f* de cumin, cumin *m*.
carbohydrates [kɑ:bəu'haɪdreɪts] *npl* (*foods*) aliments *mpl* riches en hydrate de carbone.
carbolic acid [kɑ:'bɔlɪk-] *n* phénol *m*.
car bomb *n* voiture piégée.
carbon ['kɑ:bən] *n* carbone *m*.
carbonated ['kɑ:bəneɪtɪd] *adj* (*drink*) gazeux(euse).
carbon copy *n* carbone *m*.
carbon dioxide *n* gaz *m* carbonique, dioxyde *m* de carbone.
carbon paper *n* papier *m* carbone.
carbon ribbon *n* ruban *m* carbone.
car boot sale *n* *marché aux puces où des particuliers vendent des objets entreposés dans le coffre de leur voiture.*
carburettor, (*US*) **carburetor** [kɑ:bju'rɛtə*] *n* carburateur *m*.
carcass ['kɑ:kəs] *n* carcasse *f*.
carcinogenic [kɑ:sɪnə'dʒɛnɪk] *adj* cancérigène.
card [kɑ:d] *n* carte *f*; (*membership ~*) carte d'adhérent; **to play ~s** jouer aux cartes.
cardamom ['kɑ:dəməm] *n* cardamome *f*.
cardboard ['kɑ:dbɔ:d] *n* carton *m*.
cardboard box *n* (boîte *f* en) carton *m*.
cardboard city *n* *endroit de la ville où dorment les SDF dans des boîtes en carton.*
card-carrying member ['kɑ:dkærɪɪŋ-] *n* membre actif.
card game *n* jeu *m* de cartes.
cardiac ['kɑ:dɪæk] *adj* cardiaque.
cardigan ['kɑ:dɪgən] *n* cardigan *m*.
cardinal ['kɑ:dɪnl] *adj* cardinal(e) ♦ *n* cardinal *m*.
card index *n* fichier *m* (alphabétique).
cardphone ['kɑ:dfəun] *n* téléphone *m* à carte (magnétique).

cardsharp [ˈkɑːdʃɑːp] *n* tricheur/euse professionnel(le).
card vote *n* (*BRIT*) vote *m* de délégués.
CARE [kɛə*] *n abbr* (= *Cooperative for American Relief Everywhere*) *association charitable*.
care [kɛə*] *n* soin *m*, attention *f*; (*worry*) souci *m* ♦ *vi*: **to ~ about** se soucier de, s'intéresser à; **in sb's ~** à la garde de qn, confié à qn; **~ of (c/o)** (*on letter*) aux bons soins de; **"with ~"** "fragile"; **to take ~ (to do)** faire attention (à faire); **to take ~ of** *vt* s'occuper de, prendre soin de; (*details, arrangements*) s'occuper de; **the child has been taken into ~** l'enfant a été placé en institution; **would you ~ to/for ...?** voulez-vous ...?; **I wouldn't ~ to do it** je n'aimerais pas le faire; **I don't ~** ça m'est bien égal, peu m'importe; **I couldn't ~ less** cela m'est complètement égal, je m'en fiche complètement.
►**care for** *vt fus* s'occuper de; (*like*) aimer.
careen [kəˈriːn] *vi* (*ship*) donner de la bande ♦ *vt* caréner, mettre en carène.
career [kəˈrɪə*] *n* carrière *f* ♦ *vi* (*also*: **~ along**) aller à toute allure.
career girl *n* jeune fille *f* (*or* femme *f*) qui veut faire carrière.
careers officer *n* conseiller/ère d'orientation (professionnelle).
carefree [ˈkɛəfriː] *adj* sans souci, insouciant(e).
careful [ˈkɛəful] *adj* soigneux(euse); (*cautious*) prudent(e); **(be) ~!** (fais) attention!; **to be ~ with one's money** regarder à la dépense.
carefully [ˈkɛəfəlɪ] *adv* avec soin, soigneusement; prudemment.
careless [ˈkɛəlɪs] *adj* négligent(e); (*heedless*) insouciant(e).
carelessly [ˈkɛəlɪslɪ] *adv* négligemment; avec insouciance.
carelessness [ˈkɛəlɪsnɪs] *n* manque *m* de soin, négligence *f*; insouciance *f*.
carer [ˈkɛərə*] *n personne qui s'occupe d'un proche qui est malade*.
caress [kəˈrɛs] *n* caresse *f* ♦ *vt* caresser.
caretaker [ˈkɛəteɪkə*] *n* gardien/ne, concierge *m/f*.
caretaker government *n* (*BRIT*) gouvernement *m* intérimaire.
car-ferry [ˈkɑːfɛrɪ] *n* (*on sea*) ferry(-boat) *m*; (*on river*) bac *m*.
cargo, *pl* **~es** [ˈkɑːgəu] *n* cargaison *f*, chargement *m*.
cargo boat *n* cargo *m*.
cargo plane *n* avion-cargo *m*.
car hire *n* (*BRIT*) location *f* de voitures.
Caribbean [kærɪˈbiːən] *adj* des Caraïbes; **the ~ (Sea)** la mer des Antilles *or* des Caraïbes.
caricature [ˈkærɪkətjuə*] *n* caricature *f*.
caring [ˈkɛərɪŋ] *adj* (*person*) bienveillant(e); (*society, organization*) humanitaire.
carnage [ˈkɑːnɪdʒ] *n* carnage *m*.
carnal [ˈkɑːnl] *adj* charnel(le).
carnation [kɑːˈneɪʃən] *n* œillet *m*.
carnival [ˈkɑːnɪvl] *n* (*public celebration*) carnaval *m*; (*US*: *funfair*) fête foraine.
carnivorous [kɑːˈnɪvərəs] *adj* carnivore, carnassier(ière).
carol [ˈkærəl] *n*: **(Christmas) ~** chant *m* de Noël.
carouse [kəˈrauz] *vi* faire la bringue.
carousel [kærəˈsɛl] *n* (*US*) manège *m*.
carp [kɑːp] *n* (*fish*) carpe *f*.
►**carp at** *vt fus* critiquer.
car park *n* parking *m*, parc *m* de stationnement.
carpenter [ˈkɑːpɪntə*] *n* charpentier *m*.
carpentry [ˈkɑːpɪntrɪ] *n* charpenterie *f*, métier *m* de charpentier; (*woodwork: at school etc*) menuiserie *f*.
carpet [ˈkɑːpɪt] *n* tapis *m* ♦ *vt* recouvrir (d'un tapis); **fitted ~** (*BRIT*) moquette *f*.
carpet bombing *n* bombardement intensif.
carpet slippers *npl* pantoufles *fpl*.
carpet sweeper [-ˈswiːpə*] *n* balai *m* mécanique.
car phone *n* téléphone *m* de voiture.
car rental *n* (*US*) location *f* de voitures.
carriage [ˈkærɪdʒ] *n* voiture *f*; (*of goods*) transport *m*; (*: cost*) port *m*; (*of typewriter*) chariot *m*; (*bearing*) maintien *m*, port *m*; **~ forward** port dû; **~ free** franco de port; **~ paid** (en) port payé.
carriage return *n* retour *m* à la ligne.
carriageway [ˈkærɪdʒweɪ] *n* (*BRIT*: *part of road*) chaussée *f*.
carrier [ˈkærɪə*] *n* transporteur *m*, camionneur *m*; (*MED*) porteur/euse; (*NAUT*) porte-avions *m inv*.
carrier bag *n* (*BRIT*) sac *m* en papier *or* en plastique.
carrier pigeon *n* pigeon voyageur.
carrion [ˈkærɪən] *n* charogne *f*.
carrot [ˈkærət] *n* carotte *f*.
carry [ˈkærɪ] *vt* (*subj: person*) porter; (*: vehicle*) transporter; (*a motion, bill*) voter, adopter; (*MATH*: *figure*) retenir; (*COMM*: *interest*) rapporter; (*involve: responsibilities etc*) comporter, impliquer ♦ *vi* (*sound*) porter; **to be carried away** (*fig*) s'emballer, s'enthousiasmer; **this loan carries 10% interest** ce prêt est à 10% (d'intérêt).
►**carry forward** *vt* (*gen, BOOK-KEEPING*) reporter.
►**carry on** *vi* (*continue*): **to ~ on with sth/doing** continuer qch/à faire; (*col*: *make a fuss*) faire des histoires ♦ *vt* entretenir, poursuivre.
►**carry out** *vt* (*orders*) exécuter; (*investigation*) effectuer; (*idea, threat*) mettre à exécution.
carrycot [ˈkærɪkɔt] *n* (*BRIT*) porte-bébé *m*.
carry-on [ˈkærɪˈɔn] *n* (*col*: *fuss*) histoires *fpl*; (*: annoying behaviour*) cirque *m*, cinéma *m*.
cart [kɑːt] *n* charrette *f* ♦ *vt* transporter.
carte blanche [ˈkɑːtˈblɔŋʃ] *n*: **to give sb ~**

donner carte blanche à qn.
cartel [kɑː'tɛl] *n* (*COMM*) cartel *m*.
cartilage ['kɑːtɪlɪdʒ] *n* cartilage *m*.
cartographer [kɑː'tɔgrəfə*] *n* cartographe *m/f*.
cartography [kɑː'tɔgrəfɪ] *n* cartographie *f*.
carton ['kɑːtən] *n* (*box*) carton *m*; (*of yogurt*) pot *m* (en carton); (*of cigarettes*) cartouche *f*.
cartoon [kɑː'tuːn] *n* (*PRESS*) dessin *m* (humoristique); (*satirical*) caricature *f*; (*comic strip*) bande dessinée; (*CINE*) dessin animé.
cartoonist [kɑː'tuːnɪst] *n* dessinateur/trice humoristique; caricaturiste *m/f*; auteur *m* de dessins animés; auteur de bandes dessinées.
cartridge ['kɑːtrɪdʒ] *n* (*for gun, pen*) cartouche *f*; (*for camera*) chargeur *m*; (*music tape*) cassette *f*; (*of record player*) cellule *f*.
cartwheel ['kɑːtwiːl] *n* roue *f*; **to turn a** ~ faire la roue.
carve [kɑːv] *vt* (*meat*: *also*: ~ **up**) découper; (*wood, stone*) tailler, sculpter.
carving ['kɑːvɪŋ] *n* (*in wood etc*) sculpture *f*.
carving knife *n* couteau *m* à découper.
car wash *n* station *f* de lavage (de voitures).
Casablanca [kæsə'blæŋkə] *n* Casablanca.
cascade [kæs'keɪd] *n* cascade *f* ♦ *vi* tomber en cascade.
case [keɪs] *n* cas *m*; (*LAW*) affaire *f*, procès *m*; (*box*) caisse *f*, boîte *f*, étui *m*; (*BRIT*: *also*: **suit**~) valise *f*; (*TYP*): **lower/upper** ~ minuscule *f*/majuscule *f*; **to have a good** ~ avoir de bons arguments; **there's a strong** ~ **for reform** il y aurait lieu d'engager une réforme; **in** ~ **of** en cas de; **in** ~ **he** au cas où il; **just in** ~ à tout hasard.
case history *n* (*MED*) dossier médical, antécédents médicaux.
case study *n* étude *f* de cas.
cash [kæʃ] *n* argent *m*; (*COMM*) argent liquide, numéraire *m*; liquidités *fpl*; (*: in payment*) argent comptant, espèces *fpl* ♦ *vt* encaisser; **to pay (in)** ~ payer (en argent) comptant *or* en espèces; ~ **with order/on delivery** (*COMM*) payable *or* paiement à la commande/livraison; **to be short of** ~ être à court d'argent.
▸**cash in** *vt* (*insurance policy etc*) toucher.
▸**cash in on** *vt fus* profiter de.
cash account *n* compte *m* caisse.
cash and carry *n* libre-service *m* de gros, cash and carry *m inv*.
cashbook ['kæʃbuk] *n* livre *m* de caisse.
cash box *n* caisse *f*.
cash card *n* carte de retrait *or* accréditive.
cash desk *n* (*BRIT*) caisse *f*.
cash discount *n* escompte *m* de caisse (pour paiement au comptant), remise *f* au comptant.
cash dispenser *n* distributeur *m* automatique de billets.
cashew [kæ'ʃuː] *n* (*also*: ~ **nut**) noix *f* de cajou.
cash flow *n* cash-flow *m*, marge brute d'autofinancement.
cashier [kæ'ʃɪə*] *n* caissier/ère ♦ *vt* (*MIL*) destituer, casser.
cashmere ['kæʃmɪə*] *n* cachemire *m*.
cash payment *n* paiement comptant, versement *m* en espèces.
cash price *n* prix comptant.
cash register *n* caisse enregistreuse.
cash sale *n* vente *f* au comptant.
casing ['keɪsɪŋ] *n* revêtement (protecteur), enveloppe (protectrice).
casino [kə'siːnəu] *n* casino *m*.
cask [kɑːsk] *n* tonneau *m*.
casket ['kɑːskɪt] *n* coffret *m*; (*US*: *coffin*) cercueil *m*.
Caspian Sea ['kæspɪən-] *n*: **the** ~ la mer Caspienne.
casserole ['kæsərəul] *n* cocotte *f*; (*food*) ragoût *m* (en cocotte).
cassette [kæ'sɛt] *n* cassette *f*, musicassette *f*.
cassette deck *n* platine *f* cassette.
cassette player *n* lecteur *m* de cassettes.
cassette recorder *n* magnétophone *m* à cassettes.
cast [kɑːst] *vb* (*pt, pp* **cast**) *vt* (*throw*) jeter; (*shed*) perdre; se dépouiller de; (*metal*) couler, fondre; (*THEAT*): **to** ~ **sb as Hamlet** attribuer à qn le rôle d'Hamlet ♦ *n* (*THEAT*) distribution *f*; (*mould*) moule *m*; (*also*: **plaster** ~) plâtre *m*; **to** ~ **one's vote** voter, exprimer son suffrage.
▸**cast aside** *vt* (*reject*) rejeter.
▸**cast off** *vi* (*NAUT*) larguer les amarres; (*KNITTING*) arrêter les mailles ♦ *vt* (*KNITTING*) arrêter.
▸**cast on** (*KNITTING*) *vt* monter ♦ *vi* monter les mailles.
castanets [kæstə'nɛts] *npl* castagnettes *fpl*.
castaway ['kɑːstəweɪ] *n* naufragé/e.
caste [kɑːst] *n* caste *f*, classe sociale.
caster sugar ['kɑːstə-] *n* (*BRIT*) sucre *m* semoule.
casting vote ['kɑːstɪŋ-] *n* (*BRIT*) voix prépondérante (*pour départager*).
cast iron *n* fonte *f* ♦ *adj*: **cast-iron** (*fig: will*) de fer; (*: alibi*) en béton.
castle ['kɑːsl] *n* château-fort *m*; (*manor*) château *m*.
cast-offs ['kɑːstɔfs] *npl* vêtements *mpl* dont on ne veut plus.
castor ['kɑːstə*] *n* (*wheel*) roulette *f*.
castor oil *n* huile *f* de ricin.
castrate [kæs'treɪt] *vt* châtrer.
casual ['kæʒjul] *adj* (*by chance*) de hasard, fait(e) au hasard, fortuit(e); (*irregular: work etc*) temporaire; (*unconcerned*) désinvolte; ~ **wear** vêtements *mpl* sport *inv*.
casual labour *n* main-d'œuvre *f* temporaire.
casually ['kæʒjulɪ] *adv* avec désinvolture, négligemment; (*by chance*) fortuitement.
casualty ['kæʒjultɪ] *n* accidenté/e, blessé/e;

(*dead*) victime *f*, mort/e; **heavy casualties** lourdes pertes.
casualty ward *n* (*BRIT*) service *m* des urgences.
cat [kæt] *n* chat *m*.
catacombs ['kætəku:mz] *npl* catacombes *fpl*.
catalogue, (*US*) **catalog** ['kætəlɔg] *n* catalogue *m* ♦ *vt* cataloguer.
catalyst ['kætəlɪst] *n* catalyseur *m*.
catalytic converter [kætə'lɪtɪkkən'və:tə*] *n* pot *m* catalytique.
catapult ['kætəpʌlt] *n* lance-pierres *m inv*, fronde *m*; (*HISTORY*) catapulte *f*.
cataract ['kætərækt] *n* (*also MED*) cataracte *f*.
catarrh [kə'tɑ:*] *n* rhume *m* chronique, catarrhe *f*.
catastrophe [kə'tæstrəfɪ] *n* catastrophe *f*.
catastrophic [kætə'strɔfɪk] *adj* catastrophique.
catcall ['kætkɔ:l] *n* (*at meeting etc*) sifflet *m*.
catch [kætʃ] *vb* (*pt, pp* **caught** [kɔ:t]) *vt* (*ball, train, thief, cold*) attraper; (*person: by surprise*) prendre, surprendre; (*understand*) saisir; (*get entangled*) accrocher ♦ *vi* (*fire*) prendre; (*get entangled*) s'accrocher ♦ *n* (*fish etc*) prise *f*; (*thief etc*) capture *f*; (*trick*) attrape *f*; (*TECH*) loquet *m*; cliquet *m*; **to ~ sb's attention** *or* **eye** attirer l'attention de qn; **to ~ fire** prendre feu; **to ~ sight of** apercevoir.
►**catch on** *vi* (*become popular*) prendre; (*understand*): **to ~ on (to sth)** saisir (qch).
►**catch out** *vt* (*BRIT fig: with trick question*) prendre en défaut.
►**catch up** *vi* se rattraper, combler son retard ♦ *vt* (*also*: **~ up with**) rattraper.
catching ['kætʃɪŋ] *adj* (*MED*) contagieux(euse).
catchment area ['kætʃmənt-] *n* (*BRIT SCOL*) aire *f* de recrutement; (*GEO*) bassin *m* hydrographique.
catch phrase *n* slogan *m*; expression toute faite.
catch-22 ['kætʃtwentɪ'tu:] *n*: **it's a ~ situation** c'est (une situation) sans issue.
catchy ['kætʃɪ] *adj* (*tune*) facile à retenir.
categoric(al) [kætɪ'gɔrɪk(l)] *adj* catégorique.
categorize ['kætɪgəraɪz] *vt* classer par catégories.
category ['kætɪgərɪ] *n* catégorie *f*.
cater ['keɪtə*] *vi* (*provide food*): **to ~ (for)** préparer des repas (pour).
►**cater for** *vt fus* (*BRIT: needs*) satisfaire, pourvoir à; (*: readers, consumers*) s'adresser à, pourvoir aux besoins de.
caterer ['keɪtərə*] *n* traiteur *m*; fournisseur *m*.
catering ['keɪtərɪŋ] *n* restauration *f*; approvisionnement *m*, ravitaillement *m*.
caterpillar ['kætəpɪlə*] *n* chenille *f* ♦ *cpd* (*vehicle*) à chenille; **~ track** *n* chenille *f*.
cat flap *n* chatière *f*.
cathedral [kə'θi:drəl] *n* cathédrale *f*.
cathode ['kæθəud] *n* cathode *f*.
cathode ray tube *n* tube *m* cathodique.
catholic ['kæθəlɪk] *adj* éclectique; universel(le); libéral(e); **C~** *adj, n* (*REL*) catholique (*m/f*).
cat's-eye ['kæts'aɪ] *n* (*BRIT AUT*) (clou *m* à) catadioptre *m*.
catsup ['kætsəp] *n* (*US*) ketchup *m*.
cattle ['kætl] *npl* bétail *m*, bestiaux *mpl*.
catty ['kætɪ] *adj* méchant(e).
catwalk ['kætwɔ:k] *n* passerelle *f*; (*for models*) podium *m* (*de défilé de mode*).
Caucasian [kɔ:'keɪzɪən] *adj, n* caucasien(ne).
Caucasus ['kɔ:kəsəs] *n* Caucase *m*.
caucus ['kɔ:kəs] *n* (*US POL*) comité électoral (pour désigner des candidats); (*BRIT POL: group*) comité local (*d'un parti politique*); *voir encadré*.

CAUCUS

Un ***caucus*** *aux États-Unis est une réunion restreinte des principaux dirigeants d'un parti politique, précédant souvent une assemblée générale, dans le but de choisir des candidats ou de définir une ligne d'action. Par extension, ce terme désigne également l'état-major d'un parti politique.*

caught [kɔ:t] *pt, pp of* **catch**.
cauliflower ['kɔlɪflauə*] *n* chou-fleur *m*.
cause [kɔ:z] *n* cause *f* ♦ *vt* causer; **there is no ~ for concern** il n'y a pas lieu de s'inquiéter; **to ~ sth to be done** faire faire qch; **to ~ sb to do sth** faire faire qch à qn.
causeway ['kɔ:zweɪ] *n* chaussée (surélevée).
caustic ['kɔ:stɪk] *adj* caustique.
caution ['kɔ:ʃən] *n* prudence *f*; (*warning*) avertissement *m* ♦ *vt* avertir, donner un avertissement à.
cautious ['kɔ:ʃəs] *adj* prudent(e).
cautiously ['kɔ:ʃəslɪ] *adv* prudemment, avec prudence.
cautiousness ['kɔ:ʃəsnɪs] *n* prudence *f*.
cavalier [kævə'lɪə*] *adj* cavalier(ère), désinvolte ♦ *n* (*knight*) cavalier *m*.
cavalry ['kævəlrɪ] *n* cavalerie *f*.
cave [keɪv] *n* caverne *f*, grotte *f* ♦ *vi*: **to go caving** faire de la spéléo(logie).
►**cave in** *vi* (*roof etc*) s'effondrer.
caveman ['keɪvmæn] *n* homme *m* des cavernes.
cavern ['kævən] *n* caverne *f*.
caviar(e) ['kævɪɑ:*] *n* caviar *m*.
cavity ['kævɪtɪ] *n* cavité *f*.
cavity wall insulation *n* isolation *f* des murs creux.
cavort [kə'vɔ:t] *vi* cabrioler, faire des cabrioles.
cayenne [keɪ'ɛn] *n* (*also*: **~ pepper**) poivre *m* de cayenne.
CB *n abbr* (*= Citizens' Band (Radio)*) CB *f*; (*BRIT: = Companion of (the Order of) the Bath*) *titre honorifique*.

CBC *n abbr* (= *Canadian Broadcasting Corporation*) *organisme de radiodiffusion.*
CBE *n abbr* (= *Companion of (the Order of) the British Empire*) *titre honorifique.*
CBI *n abbr* (= *Confederation of British Industry*) ≈ CNPF *m* (= *Conseil national du patronat français*).
CBS *n abbr* (*US*: = *Columbia Broadcasting System*) *chaîne de télévision.*
CC *abbr* (*BRIT*) = *county council.*
cc *abbr* (= *cubic centimetre*) cm³; (*on letter etc*) = **carbon copy**.
CCA *n abbr* (*US*: = *Circuit Court of Appeals*) cour d'appel itinérante.
CCTV *n abbr* = **closed-circuit television**.
CCU *n abbr* (*US*: = *coronary care unit*) unité *f* de soins cardiologiques.
CD *n abbr* (= *compact disc*) CD *m*; (*MIL*) = *Civil Defence (Corps)* (*BRIT*), *Civil Defense* (*US*) ♦ *abbr* (*BRIT*: = *Corps Diplomatique*) CD.
CDC *n abbr* (*US*) = *center for disease control.*
CD-I *n abbr* ® (= *Compact Disc Interactive*) CD-I *m*, disque compact interactif.
CD player *n* platine *f* laser.
Cdr. *abbr* (= *commander*) Cdt.
CD-ROM [siːdiːˈrɔm] *n abbr* (= *compact disc read-only memory*) CD-ROM *m inv*.
CDT *abbr* (*US*: = *Central Daylight Time*) *heure d'été du centre.*
CDW *n abbr* = **collision damage waiver**.
cease [siːs] *vt, vi* cesser.
ceasefire [ˈsiːsfaɪə*] *n* cessez-le-feu *m*.
ceaseless [ˈsiːslɪs] *adj* incessant(e), continuel(le).
CED *n abbr* (*US*) = *Committee for Economic Development.*
cedar [ˈsiːdə*] *n* cèdre *m*.
cede [siːd] *vt* céder.
cedilla [sɪˈdɪlə] *n* cédille *f*.
CEEB *n abbr* (*US*: = *College Entrance Examination Board*) *commission d'admission dans l'enseignement supérieur.*
ceilidh [ˈkeɪlɪ] *n* bal *m* folklorique écossais *or* irlandais.
ceiling [ˈsiːlɪŋ] *n* (*also fig*) plafond *m*.
celebrate [ˈsɛlɪbreɪt] *vt, vi* célébrer.
celebrated [ˈsɛlɪbreɪtɪd] *adj* célèbre.
celebration [sɛlɪˈbreɪʃən] *n* célébration *f*.
celebrity [sɪˈlɛbrɪtɪ] *n* célébrité *f*.
celeriac [səˈlɛrɪæk] *n* céleri(-rave) *m*.
celery [ˈsɛlərɪ] *n* céleri *m* (en branches).
celestial [sɪˈlɛstɪəl] *adj* céleste.
celibacy [ˈsɛlɪbəsɪ] *n* célibat *m*.
cell [sɛl] *n* (*gen*) cellule *f*; (*ELEC*) élément *m* (*de pile*).
cellar [ˈsɛlə*] *n* cave *f*.
'cellist [ˈtʃɛlɪst] *n* violoncelliste *m/f*.
'cello [ˈtʃɛləu] *n* violoncelle *m*.
cellophane [ˈsɛləfeɪn] *n* ® cellophane *f* ®.
cellphone [ˈsɛlfəun] *n* téléphone *m* cellulaire.
cellular [ˈsɛljulə*] *adj* cellulaire.
Celluloid [ˈsɛljulɔɪd] *n* ® celluloïd *m* ®.
cellulose [ˈsɛljuləus] *n* cellulose *f*.
Celsius [ˈsɛlsɪəs] *adj* Celsius *inv*.
Celt [kɛlt, sɛlt] *n* Celte *m/f*.
Celtic [ˈkɛltɪk, ˈsɛltɪk] *adj* celte, celtique ♦ *n* (*LING*) celtique *m*.
cement [səˈmɛnt] *n* ciment *m* ♦ *vt* cimenter.
cement mixer *n* bétonnière *f*.
cemetery [ˈsɛmɪtrɪ] *n* cimetière *m*.
cenotaph [ˈsɛnətɑːf] *n* cénotaphe *m*.
censor [ˈsɛnsə*] *n* censeur *m* ♦ *vt* censurer.
censorship [ˈsɛnsəʃɪp] *n* censure *f*.
censure [ˈsɛnʃə*] *vt* blâmer, critiquer.
census [ˈsɛnsəs] *n* recensement *m*.
cent [sɛnt] *n* (*US, euro*: *coin*) cent *m* (= *1:100 du dollar, de l'euro*); *see also* **per**.
centenary [sɛnˈtiːnərɪ], **centennial** [sɛnˈtɛnɪəl] *n* centenaire *m*.
center [ˈsɛntə*] *n, vt* (*US*) = **centre**.
centigrade [ˈsɛntɪgreɪd] *adj* centigrade.
centilitre, (*US*) **centiliter** [ˈsɛntɪliːtə*] *n* centilitre *m*.
centimetre, (*US*) **centimeter** [ˈsɛntɪmiːtə*] *n* centimètre *m*.
centipede [ˈsɛntɪpiːd] *n* mille-pattes *m inv*.
central [ˈsɛntrəl] *adj* central(e).
Central African Republic *n* République Centrafricaine.
Central America *n* Amérique centrale.
central heating *n* chauffage central.
centralize [ˈsɛntrəlaɪz] *vt* centraliser.
central processing unit (CPU) *n* (*COMPUT*) unité centrale (de traitement).
central reservation *n* (*BRIT AUT*) terre-plein central.
centre, (*US*) **center** [ˈsɛntə*] *n* centre *m* ♦ *vt* centrer; (*PHOT*) cadrer; (*concentrate*): **to ~ (on)** centrer (sur).
centrefold, (*US*) **centerfold** [ˈsɛntəfəuld] *n* (*PRESS*) pages centrales détachables (*avec photo de pin up*).
centre-forward [ˈsɛntəˈfɔːwəd] *n* (*SPORT*) avant-centre *m*.
centre-half [ˈsɛntəˈhɑːf] *n* (*SPORT*) demi-centre *m*.
centrepiece, (*US*) **centerpiece** [ˈsɛntəpiːs] *n* milieu *m* de table; (*fig*) pièce maîtresse.
centre spread *n* (*BRIT*) publicité *f* en double page.
centre-stage [sɛntəˈsteɪdʒ] *n*: **to take ~** occuper le centre de la scène.
centrifugal [sɛnˈtrɪfjugl] *adj* centrifuge.
century [ˈsɛntjurɪ] *n* siècle *m*; **in the twentieth ~** au vingtième siècle.
CEO *n abbr* (*US*) = **chief executive officer**.
ceramic [sɪˈræmɪk] *adj* céramique.
cereal [ˈsiːrɪəl] *n* céréale *f*.
cerebral [ˈsɛrɪbrəl] *adj* cérébral(e).
ceremonial [sɛrɪˈməunɪəl] *n* cérémonial *m*; (*rite*) rituel *m*.
ceremony [ˈsɛrɪmənɪ] *n* cérémonie *f*; **to stand on ~** faire des façons.
cert [səːt] *n* (*BRIT col*): **it's a dead ~** ça ne fait

pas un pli.

certain ['sə:tən] *adj* certain(e); **to make ~ of** s'assurer de; **for ~** certainement, sûrement.

certainly ['sə:tənlı] *adv* certainement.

certainty ['sə:təntı] *n* certitude *f*.

certificate [sə'tıfıkıt] *n* certificat *m*.

certified letter ['sə:tıfaıd-] *n* (*US*) lettre recommandée.

certified public accountant (CPA) ['sə:tıfaıd-] *n* (*US*) expert-comptable *m*.

certify ['sə:tıfaı] *vt* certifier ♦ *vi*: **to ~ to** attester.

cervical ['sə:vıkl] *adj*: **~ cancer** cancer *m* du col de l'utérus; **~ smear** frottis vaginal.

cervix ['sə:vıks] *n* col *m* de l'utérus.

Cesarean [si:'zεərıən] *adj, n* (*US*) = **Caesarean**.

cessation [sə'seıʃən] *n* cessation *f*, arrêt *m*.

cesspit ['sεspıt] *n* fosse *f* d'aisance.

CET *abbr* (= *Central European Time*) *heure d'Europe centrale*.

Ceylon [sı'lɔn] *n* Ceylan *m*.

cf. *abbr* (= *compare*) cf., voir.

c/f *abbr* (*COMM*) = *carried forward*.

CFC *n abbr* (= *chlorofluorocarbon*) CFC *m*.

CG *n abbr* (*US*) = **coastguard**.

cg *abbr* (= *centigram*) cg.

CH *n abbr* (*BRIT*: = *Companion of Honour*) *titre honorifique*.

ch *abbr* (*BRIT*: = *central heating*) c.c.

ch. *abbr* (= *chapter*) chap.

Chad [tʃæd] *n* Tchad *m*.

chafe [tʃeıf] *vt* irriter, frotter contre ♦ *vi* (*fig*): **to ~ against** se rebiffer contre, regimber contre.

chaffinch ['tʃæfıntʃ] *n* pinson *m*.

chagrin ['ʃægrın] *n* contrariété *f*, déception *f*.

chain [tʃeın] *n* (*gen*) chaîne *f* ♦ *vt* (*also*: **~ up**) enchaîner, attacher (avec une chaîne).

chain reaction *n* réaction *f* en chaîne.

chain-smoke ['tʃeınsməuk] *vi* fumer cigarette sur cigarette.

chain store *n* magasin *m* à succursales multiples.

chair [tʃεə*] *n* chaise *f*; (*armchair*) fauteuil *m*; (*of university*) chaire *f* ♦ *vt* (*meeting*) présider; **the ~** (*US*: *electric ~*) la chaise électrique.

chairlift ['tʃεəlıft] *n* télésiège *m*.

chairman ['tʃεəmən] *n* président *m*.

chairperson ['tʃεəpə:sn] *n* président/e.

chairwoman ['tʃεəwumən] *n* présidente *f*.

chalet ['ʃæleı] *n* chalet *m*.

chalice ['tʃælıs] *n* calice *m*.

chalk [tʃɔ:k] *n* craie *f*.

►**chalk up** *vt* écrire à la craie; (*fig: success etc*) remporter.

challenge ['tʃælındʒ] *n* défi *m* ♦ *vt* défier; (*statement, right*) mettre en question, contester; **to ~ sb to a fight/game** inviter qn à se battre/à jouer (*sous forme d'un défi*); **to ~ sb to do** mettre qn au défi de faire.

challenger ['tʃælındʒə*] *n* (*SPORT*) challenger *m*.

challenging ['tʃælındʒıŋ] *adj* de défi, provocateur(trice).

chamber ['tʃeımbə*] *n* chambre *f*; **~ of commerce** chambre de commerce.

chambermaid ['tʃeımbəmeıd] *n* femme *f* de chambre.

chamber music *n* musique *f* de chambre.

chamberpot ['tʃeımbəpɔt] *n* pot *m* de chambre.

chameleon [kə'mi:lıən] *n* caméléon *m*.

chamois ['ʃæmwɑ:] *n* chamois *m*.

chamois leather ['ʃæmı-] *n* peau *f* de chamois.

champagne [ʃæm'peın] *n* champagne *m*.

champers ['ʃæmpəz] *n* (*col*) champ *m*.

champion ['tʃæmpıən] *n* (*also of cause*) champion/ne ♦ *vt* défendre.

championship ['tʃæmpıənʃıp] *n* championnat *m*.

chance [tʃɑ:ns] *n* hasard *m*; (*opportunity*) occasion *f*, possibilité *f*; (*hope, likelihood*) chance *f* ♦ *vt* (*risk*): **to ~ it** risquer (le coup), essayer; (*happen*): **to ~ to do** faire par hasard ♦ *adj* fortuit(e), de hasard; **there is little ~ of his coming** il est peu probable *or* il y a peu de chances qu'il vienne; **to take a ~** prendre un risque; **it's the ~ of a lifetime** c'est une occasion unique; **by ~** par hasard.

►**chance (up)on** *vt fus* (*person*) tomber sur, rencontrer par hasard; (*thing*) trouver par hasard.

chancel ['tʃɑ:nsəl] *n* chœur *m*.

chancellor ['tʃɑ:nsələ*] *n* chancelier *m*; **C~ of the Exchequer** (*BRIT*) chancelier de l'Échiquier.

chandelier [ʃændə'lıə*] *n* lustre *m*.

change [tʃeındʒ] *vt* (*alter, replace, COMM: money*) changer; (*switch, substitute: gear, hands, trains, clothes, one's name etc*) changer de; (*transform*): **to ~ sb into** changer *or* transformer qn en ♦ *vi* (*gen*) changer; (*change clothes*) se changer; (*be transformed*): **to ~ into** se changer *or* transformer en ♦ *n* changement *m*; (*money*) monnaie *f*; **to ~ one's mind** changer d'avis; **she ~d into an old skirt** elle (s'est changée et) a enfilé une vieille jupe; **a ~ of clothes** des vêtements de rechange; **for a ~** pour changer; **small ~** petite monnaie; **to give sb ~ for** *or* **of £10** faire à qn la monnaie de 10 livres.

changeable ['tʃeındʒəbl] *adj* (*weather*) variable; (*person*) d'humeur changeante.

change machine *n* distributeur *m* de monnaie.

changeover ['tʃeındʒəuvə*] *n* (*to new system*) changement *m*, passage *m*.

changing ['tʃeındʒıŋ] *adj* changeant(e).

changing room *n* (*BRIT*: *in shop*) salon *m* d'essayage; (*: SPORT*) vestiaire *m*.

channel ['tʃænl] *n* (*TV*) chaîne *f*; (*waveband, groove, fig: medium*) canal *m*; (*of river, sea*) chenal *m* ♦ *vt* canaliser; (*fig: interest, ener-*

gies): **to ~ into** diriger vers; **through the usual ~s** en suivant la filière habituelle; **green/red ~** (*CUSTOMS*) couloir *m or* sortie *f* "rien à déclarer"/"marchandises à déclarer"; **the (English) C~** la Manche.
Channel Islands *npl*: **the ~** les îles de la Manche, les îles anglo-normandes.
Channel Tunnel *n*: **the ~** le tunnel sous la Manche.
chant [tʃɑːnt] *n* chant *m*; mélopée *f*; psalmodie *f* ♦ *vt* chanter, scander; psalmodier.
chaos ['keɪɔs] *n* chaos *m*.
chaos theory *n* théorie *f* du chaos.
chaotic [keɪ'ɔtɪk] *adj* chaotique.
chap [tʃæp] *n* (*BRIT col*: *man*) type *m*; (*term of address*): **old ~** mon vieux ♦ *vt* (*skin*) gercer, crevasser.
chapel ['tʃæpl] *n* chapelle *f*.
chaperon ['ʃæpərəun] *n* chaperon *m* ♦ *vt* chaperonner.
chaplain ['tʃæplɪn] *n* aumônier *m*.
chapter ['tʃæptə*] *n* chapitre *m*.
char [tʃɑː*] *vt* (*burn*) carboniser ♦ *vi* (*BRIT*: *cleaner*) faire des ménages ♦ *n* (*BRIT*) = **charlady**.
character ['kærɪktə*] *n* caractère *m*; (*in novel, film*) personnage *m*; (*eccentric*) numéro *m*, phénomène *m*; **a person of good ~** une personne bien.
character code *n* (*COMPUT*) code *m* de caractère.
characteristic ['kærɪktə'rɪstɪk] *adj*, *n* caractéristique (*f*).
characterize ['kærɪktəraɪz] *vt* caractériser; **to ~ (as)** définir (comme).
charade [ʃə'rɑːd] *n* charade *f*.
charcoal ['tʃɑːkəul] *n* charbon *m* de bois.
charge [tʃɑːdʒ] *n* accusation *f*; (*LAW*) inculpation *f*; (*cost*) prix (demandé); (*of gun, battery, MIL*: *attack*) charge *f* ♦ *vt* (*LAW*): **to ~ sb (with)** inculper qn (de); (*gun, battery, MIL*: *enemy*) charger; (*customer, sum*) faire payer ♦ *vi* (*gen with: up, along etc*) foncer; **~s** *npl*: **bank/labour ~s** frais *mpl* de banque/main-d'œuvre; **to ~ in/out** entrer/sortir en trombe; **to ~ down/up** dévaler/grimper à toute allure; **is there a ~?** doit-on payer?; **there's no ~** c'est gratuit, on ne fait pas payer; **extra ~** supplément *m*; **to take ~ of** se charger de; **to be in ~ of** être responsable de, s'occuper de; **to have ~ of sb** avoir la charge de qn; **they ~d us £10 for the meal** ils nous ont fait payer le repas 10 livres, ils nous ont compté 10 livres pour le repas; **how much do you ~ for this repair?** combien demandez-vous pour cette réparation?; **to ~ an expense (up) to sb** mettre une dépense sur le compte de qn; **~ it to my account** facturez-le sur mon compte.
charge account *n* compte *m* client.
charge card *n* carte *f* de client (*émise par un grand magasin*).
chargehand ['tʃɑːdʒhænd] *n* (*BRIT*) chef *m* d'équipe.
charger ['tʃɑːdʒə*] *n* (*also*: **battery ~**) chargeur *m*; (*old: warhorse*) cheval *m* de bataille.
charitable ['tʃærɪtəbl] *adj* charitable.
charity ['tʃærɪtɪ] *n* charité *f*; (*organization*) institution *f* charitable *or* de bienfaisance, œuvre *f* (de charité).
charlady ['tʃɑːleɪdɪ] *n* (*BRIT*) femme *f* de ménage.
charm [tʃɑːm] *n* charme *m* ♦ *vt* charmer, enchanter.
charm bracelet *n* bracelet *m* à breloques.
charming ['tʃɑːmɪŋ] *adj* charmant(e).
chart [tʃɑːt] *n* tableau *m*, diagramme *m*; graphique *m*; (*map*) carte marine; (*weather ~*) carte *f* du temps ♦ *vt* dresser *or* établir la carte de; (*sales, progress*) établir la courbe de; **to be in the ~s** (*record, pop group*) figurer au hit-parade.
charter ['tʃɑːtə*] *vt* (*plane*) affréter ♦ *n* (*document*) charte *f*; **on ~** (*plane*) affrété(e).
chartered accountant (CA) ['tʃɑːtəd-] *n* (*BRIT*) expert-comptable *m*.
charter flight *n* charter *m*.
charwoman ['tʃɑːwumən] *n* = **charlady**.
chase [tʃeɪs] *vt* poursuivre, pourchasser ♦ *n* poursuite *f*, chasse *f*.
►**chase down** *vt* (*US*) = **chase up**.
►**chase up** *vt* (*BRIT*: *person*) relancer; (*: information*) rechercher.
chasm ['kæzəm] *n* gouffre *m*, abîme *m*.
chassis ['ʃæsɪ] *n* châssis *m*.
chastened ['tʃeɪsnd] *adj* assagi(e), rappelé(e) à la raison.
chastening ['tʃeɪsnɪŋ] *adj* qui fait réfléchir.
chastise [tʃæs'taɪz] *vt* punir, châtier; corriger.
chastity ['tʃæstɪtɪ] *n* chasteté *f*.
chat [tʃæt] *vi* (*also*: **have a ~**) bavarder, causer ♦ *n* conversation *f*.
►**chat up** *vt* (*BRIT col*: *girl*) baratiner.
chatline ['tʃætlaɪn] *n numéro téléphonique qui permet de bavarder avec plusieurs personnes en même temps*.
chat show *n* (*BRIT*) entretien télévisé.
chattel ['tʃætl] *see* **goods**.
chatter ['tʃætə*] *vi* (*person*) bavarder, papoter ♦ *n* bavardage *m*, papotage *m*; **my teeth are ~ing** je claque des dents.
chatterbox ['tʃætəbɔks] *n* moulin *m* à paroles, babillard/e.
chattering classes ['tʃætərɪŋ-] *npl*: **the ~** (*col, pej*) les intellos *mpl*.
chatty ['tʃætɪ] *adj* (*style*) familier(ière); (*person*) enclin(e) à bavarder *or* au papotage.
chauffeur ['ʃəufə*] *n* chauffeur *m* (de maître).
chauvinism ['ʃəuvɪnɪzəm] *n* (*also*: **male ~**) phallocratie *f*, machisme *m*; (*nationalism*) chauvinisme *m*.
chauvinist ['ʃəuvɪnɪst] *n* (*also*: **male ~**) phallocrate *m*, macho *m*; (*nationalist*) chauvin/e.
ChE *abbr* = *chemical engineer*.

cheap [tʃiːp] *adj* bon marché *inv*, pas cher(chère); (*reduced: ticket*) à prix réduit; (*: fare*) réduit(e); (*joke*) facile, d'un goût douteux; (*poor quality*) à bon marché, de qualité médiocre ♦ *adv* à bon marché, pour pas cher; ~**er** *adj* moins cher(chère).

cheapen ['tʃiːpn] *vt* rabaisser, déprécier.

cheaply ['tʃiːplɪ] *adv* à bon marché, à bon compte.

cheat [tʃiːt] *vi* tricher; (*in exam*) copier ♦ *vt* tromper, duper; (*rob*) escroquer ♦ *n* tricheur/euse; escroc *m*; (*trick*) duperie *f*, tromperie *f*; **to ~ on sb** (*col: husband, wife etc*) tromper qn.

cheating ['tʃiːtɪŋ] *n* tricherie *f*.

check [tʃɛk] *vt* vérifier; (*passport, ticket*) contrôler; (*halt*) enrayer; (*restrain*) maîtriser ♦ *vi* (*official etc*) se renseigner ♦ *n* vérification *f*; contrôle *m*; (*curb*) frein *m*; (*bill*) addition *f*; (*pattern: gen pl*) carreaux *mpl*; (*US*) = **cheque** ♦ *adj* (*also: ~***ed**: *pattern, cloth*) à carreaux; **to ~ with sb** demander à qn; **to keep a ~ on sb/sth** surveiller qn/qch.

►**check in** *vi* (*in hotel*) remplir sa fiche (d'hôtel); (*at airport*) se présenter à l'enregistrement ♦ *vt* (*luggage*) (faire) enregistrer.

►**check off** *vt* cocher.

►**check out** *vi* (*in hotel*) régler sa note ♦ *vt* (*luggage*) retirer; (*investigate: story*) vérifier; (*person*) prendre des renseignements sur.

►**check up** *vi*: **to ~ up (on sth)** vérifier (qch); **to ~ up on sb** se renseigner sur le compte de qn.

checkered ['tʃɛkəd] *adj* (*US*) = **chequered**.

checkers ['tʃɛkəz] *n* (*US*) jeu *m* de dames.

check guarantee card *n* (*US*) carte *f* (d'identité) bancaire.

check-in ['tʃɛkin] *n* (*also: ~* **desk**: *at airport*) enregistrement *m*.

checking account ['tʃɛkɪŋ-] *n* (*US*) compte courant.

checklist ['tʃɛklɪst] *n* liste *f* de contrôle.

checkmate ['tʃɛkmeɪt] *n* échec et mat *m*.

checkout ['tʃɛkaut] *n* (*in supermarket*) caisse *f*.

checkpoint ['tʃɛkpɔɪnt] *n* contrôle *m*.

checkup ['tʃɛkʌp] *n* (*MED*) examen médical, check-up *m*.

cheek [tʃiːk] *n* joue *f*; (*impudence*) toupet *m*, culot *m*.

cheekbone ['tʃiːkbəun] *n* pommette *f*.

cheeky ['tʃiːkɪ] *adj* effronté(e), culotté(e).

cheep [tʃiːp] *n* (*of bird*) piaulement *m* ♦ *vi* piauler.

cheer [tʃɪə*] *vt* acclamer, applaudir; (*gladden*) réjouir, réconforter ♦ *vi* applaudir ♦ *n* (*gen pl*) acclamations *fpl*, applaudissements *mpl*; bravos *mpl*, hourras *mpl*; ~**s!** (à votre) santé!

►**cheer on** *vt* encourager (par des cris *etc*).

►**cheer up** *vi* se dérider, reprendre courage ♦ *vt* remonter le moral à *or* de, dérider, égayer.

cheerful ['tʃɪəful] *adj* gai(e), joyeux(euse).

cheerfulness ['tʃɪəfulnɪs] *n* gaieté *f*, bonne humeur.

cheerio [tʃɪərɪ'əu] *excl* (*BRIT*) salut!, au revoir!

cheerleader ['tʃɪəliːdə*] *n membre d'un groupe de majorettes qui chantent et dansent pour soutenir leur équipe pendant les matchs de football américain.*

cheerless ['tʃɪəlɪs] *adj* sombre, triste.

cheese [tʃiːz] *n* fromage *m*.

cheeseboard ['tʃiːzbɔːd] *n* plateau *m* à fromages; (*with cheese on it*) plateau *m* de fromages.

cheeseburger ['tʃiːzbəːgə*] *n* cheeseburger *m*.

cheesecake ['tʃiːzkeɪk] *n* tarte *f* au fromage.

cheetah ['tʃiːtə] *n* guépard *m*.

chef [ʃɛf] *n* chef (cuisinier).

chemical ['kɛmɪkl] *adj* chimique ♦ *n* produit *m* chimique.

chemist ['kɛmɪst] *n* (*BRIT: pharmacist*) pharmacien/ne; (*scientist*) chimiste *m/f*; ~**'s (shop)** *n* (*BRIT*) pharmacie *f*.

chemistry ['kɛmɪstrɪ] *n* chimie *f*.

chemotherapy [kiːməu'θɛrəpɪ] *n* chimiothérapie *f*.

cheque, (*US*) **check** [tʃɛk] *n* chèque *m*; **to pay by ~** payer par chèque.

chequebook, (*US*) **checkbook** ['tʃɛkbuk] *n* chéquier *m*, carnet *m* de chèques.

cheque card *n* (*BRIT*) carte *f* (d'identité) bancaire.

chequered, (*US*) **checkered** ['tʃɛkəd] *adj* (*fig*) varié(e).

cherish ['tʃɛrɪʃ] *vt* chérir; (*hope etc*) entretenir.

cheroot [ʃə'ruːt] *n* cigare *m* de Manille.

cherry ['tʃɛrɪ] *n* cerise *f*.

Ches *abbr* (*BRIT*) = *Cheshire*.

chess [tʃɛs] *n* échecs *mpl*.

chessboard ['tʃɛsbɔːd] *n* échiquier *m*.

chessman ['tʃɛsmən] *n* pièce *f* (de jeu d'échecs).

chessplayer ['tʃɛspleɪə*] *n* joueur/euse d'échecs.

chest [tʃɛst] *n* poitrine *f*; (*box*) coffre *m*, caisse *f*; **to get sth off one's ~** (*col*) vider son sac; ~ **of drawers** *n* commode *f*.

chest measurement *n* tour *m* de poitrine.

chestnut ['tʃɛsnʌt] *n* châtaigne *f*; (*also: ~* **tree**) châtaignier *m*; (*colour*) châtain *m* ♦ *adj* (*hair*) châtain *inv*; (*horse*) alezan.

chesty ['tʃɛstɪ] *adj* (*cough*) de poitrine.

chew [tʃuː] *vt* mâcher.

chewing gum ['tʃuːɪŋ-] *n* chewing-gum *m*.

chic [ʃiːk] *adj* chic *inv*, élégant(e).

chick [tʃɪk] *n* poussin *m*; (*US col*) pépée *f*.

chicken ['tʃɪkɪn] *n* poulet *m*; (*col: coward*) poule mouillée.

►**chicken out** *vi* (*col*) se dégonfler.

chicken feed *n* (*fig*) broutilles *fpl*, bagatelle *f*.

chickenpox ['tʃɪkɪnpɔks] *n* varicelle *f*.

chickpea ['tʃɪkpiː] *n* pois *m* chiche.
chicory ['tʃɪkərɪ] *n* chicorée *f*; (*salad*) endive *f*.
chide [tʃaɪd] *vt* réprimander, gronder.
chief [tʃiːf] *n* chef *m* ♦ *adj* principal(e); **C~ of Staff** (*MIL*) chef d'État-major.
chief constable *n* (*BRIT*) ≈ préfet *m* de police.
chief executive, (*US*) **chief executive officer** *n* directeur général.
chiefly ['tʃiːflɪ] *adv* principalement, surtout.
chiffon ['ʃɪfɔn] *n* mousseline *f* de soie.
chilblain ['tʃɪlbleɪn] *n* engelure *f*.
child, *pl* **~ren** [tʃaɪld, 'tʃɪldrən] *n* enfant *m/f*.
child benefit *n* (*BRIT*) ≈ allocations familiales.
childbirth ['tʃaɪldbəːθ] *n* accouchement *m*.
childhood ['tʃaɪldhud] *n* enfance *f*.
childish ['tʃaɪldɪʃ] *adj* puéril(e), enfantin(e).
childless ['tʃaɪldlɪs] *adj* sans enfants.
childlike ['tʃaɪldlaɪk] *adj* innocent(e), pur(e).
child minder *n* (*BRIT*) garde *f* d'enfants.
child prodigy *n* enfant *m/f* prodige.
children ['tʃɪldrən] *npl of* **child**.
children's home ['tʃɪldrənz-] *n* ≈ foyer *m* d'accueil (*pour enfants*).
Chile ['tʃɪlɪ] *n* Chili *m*.
Chilean ['tʃɪlɪən] *adj* chilien(ne) ♦ *n* Chilien/ne.
chill [tʃɪl] *n* froid *m*; (*MED*) refroidissement *m*, coup *m* de froid ♦ *adj* froid(e), glacial(e) ♦ *vt* faire frissonner; refroidir; (*CULIN*) mettre au frais, rafraîchir; **"serve ~ed"** "à servir frais".
►**chill out** *vi* (*col*: *esp US*) se relaxer.
chilli, (*US*) **chili** ['tʃɪlɪ] *n* piment *m* (rouge).
chilling ['tʃɪlɪŋ] *adj* (*wind*) frais(fraîche), froid(e); (*look, smile*) glacé(e); (*thought*) qui donne le frisson.
chilly ['tʃɪlɪ] *adj* froid(e), glacé(e); (*sensitive to cold*) frileux(euse); **to feel ~** avoir froid.
chime [tʃaɪm] *n* carillon *m* ♦ *vi* carillonner, sonner.
chimney ['tʃɪmnɪ] *n* cheminée *f*.
chimney sweep *n* ramoneur *m*.
chimpanzee [tʃɪmpæn'ziː] *n* chimpanzé *m*.
chin [tʃɪn] *n* menton *m*.
China ['tʃaɪnə] *n* Chine *f*.
china ['tʃaɪnə] *n* porcelaine *f*; (vaisselle *f* en) porcelaine.
Chinese [tʃaɪ'niːz] *adj* chinois(e) ♦ *n* (*pl inv*) Chinois/e; (*LING*) chinois *m*.
chink [tʃɪŋk] *n* (*opening*) fente *f*, fissure *f*; (*noise*) tintement *m*.
chinwag ['tʃɪnwæg] *n* (*BRIT col*): **to have a ~** tailler une bavette.
chip [tʃɪp] *n* (*gen pl*: *CULIN*) frite *f*; (: *US*: *also*: **potato ~**) chip *m*; (*of wood*) copeau *m*; (*of glass, stone*) éclat *m*; (*also*: **micro~**) puce *f*; (*in gambling*) fiche *f* ♦ *vt* (*cup, plate*) ébrécher; **when the ~s are down** (*fig*) au moment critique.
►**chip in** *vi* (*col*) mettre son grain de sel.
chipboard ['tʃɪpbɔːd] *n* aggloméré *m*, panneau *m* de particules.
chipmunk ['tʃɪpmʌŋk] *n* suisse *m* (*animal*).
chippings ['tʃɪpɪŋz] *npl*: **loose ~** gravillons *mpl*.
chip shop *n* (*BRIT*) friterie *f*; *voir encadré*.

CHIP SHOP

Un **chip shop**, *que l'on appelle également un "fish-and-chip shop", est un magasin où l'on vend des plats à emporter. Les* **chip shops** *sont d'ailleurs à l'origine des "takeaways". On y achète en particulier du poisson frit et des frites, mais on y trouve également des plats traditionnels britanniques ("steak pies", saucisses, etc). Tous les plats étaient à l'origine emballés dans du papier journal. Dans certains de ces magasins, on peut s'asseoir pour consommer sur place.*

chiropodist [kɪ'rɔpədɪst] *n* (*BRIT*) pédicure *m/f*.
chirp [tʃəːp] *n* pépiement *m*, gazouillis *m*; (*of crickets*) stridulation *f* ♦ *vi* pépier, gazouiller; chanter, striduler.
chirpy ['tʃəːpɪ] *adj* (*col*) plein(e) d'entrain, tout guilleret(te).
chisel ['tʃɪzl] *n* ciseau *m*.
chit [tʃɪt] *n* mot *m*, note *f*.
chitchat ['tʃɪttʃæt] *n* bavardage *m*, papotage *m*.
chivalrous ['ʃɪvəlrəs] *adj* chevaleresque.
chivalry ['ʃɪvəlrɪ] *n* chevalerie *f*; esprit *m* chevaleresque.
chives [tʃaɪvz] *npl* ciboulette *f*, civette *f*.
chloride ['klɔːraɪd] *n* chlorure *m*.
chlorinate ['klɔrɪneɪt] *vt* chlorer.
chlorine ['klɔːriːn] *n* chlore *m*.
chock [tʃɔk] *n* cale *f*.
chock-a-block ['tʃɔkə'blɔk], **chock-full** [tʃɔk'ful] *adj* plein(e) à craquer.
chocolate ['tʃɔklɪt] *n* chocolat *m*.
choice [tʃɔɪs] *n* choix *m* ♦ *adj* de choix; **by** *or* **from ~** par choix; **a wide ~** un grand choix.
choir ['kwaɪə*] *n* chœur *m*, chorale *f*.
choirboy ['kwaɪə'bɔɪ] *n* jeune choriste *m*, petit chanteur.
choke [tʃəuk] *vi* étouffer ♦ *vt* étrangler; étouffer; (*block*) boucher, obstruer ♦ *n* (*AUT*) starter *m*.
cholera ['kɔlərə] *n* choléra *m*.
cholesterol [kə'lɛstərɔl] *n* cholestérol *m*.
choose, *pt* **chose,** *pp* **chosen** [tʃuːz, tʃəuz, 'tʃəuzn] *vt* choisir ♦ *vi*: **to ~ between** choisir entre; **to ~ from** choisir parmi; **to ~ to do** décider de faire, juger bon de faire.
choosy ['tʃuːzɪ] *adj*: **(to be) ~** (faire le) difficile.
chop [tʃɔp] *vt* (*wood*) couper (à la hache); (*CULIN*: *also*: **~ up**) couper (fin), émincer, hacher (en morceaux) ♦ *n* coup *m* (*de hache, du tranchant de la main*); (*CULIN*) côtelette *f*; **to get the ~** (*BRIT col*: *project*) tomber à l'eau;

(*: person: be sacked*) se faire renvoyer.

►**chop down** *vt* (*tree*) abattre.

chopper ['tʃɔpə*] *n* (*helicopter*) hélicoptère *m*, hélico *m*.

choppy ['tʃɔpɪ] *adj* (*sea*) un peu agité(e).

chops [tʃɔps] *npl* (*jaws*) mâchoires *fpl*; babines *fpl*.

chopsticks ['tʃɔpstɪks] *npl* baguettes *fpl*.

choral ['kɔːrəl] *adj* choral(e), chanté(e) en chœur.

chord [kɔːd] *n* (*MUS*) accord *m*.

chore [tʃɔː*] *n* travail *m* de routine; **household ~s** travaux *mpl* du ménage.

choreographer [kɔrɪ'ɔgrəfə*] *n* chorégraphe *m/f*.

choreography [kɔrɪ'ɔgrəfɪ] *n* chorégraphie *f*.

chorister ['kɔrɪstə*] *n* choriste *m/f*.

chortle ['tʃɔːtl] *vi* glousser.

chorus ['kɔːrəs] *n* chœur *m*; (*repeated part of song, also fig*) refrain *m*.

chose [tʃəuz] *pt of* **choose**.

chosen ['tʃəuzn] *pp of* **choose**.

chow [tʃau] *n* (*dog*) chow-chow *m*.

chowder ['tʃaudə*] *n* soupe *f* de poisson.

Christ [kraɪst] *n* Christ *m*.

christen ['krɪsn] *vt* baptiser.

christening ['krɪsnɪŋ] *n* baptême *m*.

Christian ['krɪstɪən] *adj*, *n* chrétien(ne).

Christianity [krɪstɪ'ænɪtɪ] *n* christianisme *m*.

Christian name *n* prénom *m*.

Christmas ['krɪsməs] *n* Noël *m or f*; **happy** *or* **merry ~!** joyeux Noël!

Christmas card *n* carte *f* de Noël.

Christmas Day *n* le jour de Noël.

Christmas Eve *n* la veille de Noël; la nuit de Noël.

Christmas Island *n* île *f* Christmas.

Christmas tree *n* arbre *m* de Noël.

chrome [krəum] *n* = **chromium**.

chromium ['krəumɪəm] *n* chrome *m*; (*also*: ~ **plating**) chromage *m*.

chromosome ['krəuməsəum] *n* chromosome *m*.

chronic ['krɔnɪk] *adj* chronique; (*fig: liar, smoker*) invétéré(e).

chronicle ['krɔnɪkl] *n* chronique *f*.

chronological [krɔnə'lɔdʒɪkl] *adj* chronologique.

chrysanthemum [krɪ'sænθəməm] *n* chrysanthème *m*.

chubby ['tʃʌbɪ] *adj* potelé(e), rondelet(te).

chuck [tʃʌk] *vt* lancer, jeter; **to ~ (up** *or* **in)** *vt* (*BRIT: job*) lâcher; (*: person*) plaquer.

►**chuck out** *vt* flanquer dehors *or* à la porte.

chuckle ['tʃʌkl] *vi* glousser.

chuffed [tʃʌft] *adj* (*BRIT col*): **to be ~ about sth** être content(e) de qch.

chug [tʃʌg] *vi* faire teuf-teuf; souffler.

chum [tʃʌm] *n* copain/copine.

chump ['tʃʌmp] *n* (*col*) imbécile *m/f*, crétin/e.

chunk [tʃʌŋk] *n* gros morceau; (*of bread*) quignon *m*.

chunky ['tʃʌŋkɪ] *adj* (*furniture etc*) massif(ive); (*person*) trapu(e); (*knitwear*) en grosse laine.

Chunnel ['tʃʌnəl] *n* = **Channel Tunnel**.

church [tʃəːtʃ] *n* église *f*; **the C~ of England** l'Église anglicane.

churchyard ['tʃəːtʃjɑːd] *n* cimetière *m*.

churlish ['tʃəːlɪʃ] *adj* grossier(ère); hargneux(euse).

churn [tʃəːn] *n* (*for butter*) baratte *f*; (*for transport: also*: **milk** ~) (grand) bidon à lait.

►**churn out** *vt* débiter.

chute [ʃuːt] *n* glissoire *f*; (*also*: **rubbish** ~) vide-ordures *m inv*; (*BRIT: children's slide*) toboggan *m*.

chutney ['tʃʌtnɪ] *n* chutney *m*.

CIA *n abbr* (*US*: = *Central Intelligence Agency*) CIA *f*.

CID *n abbr* (*BRIT*: = *Criminal Investigation Department*) ≈ P.J. *f* (= *police judiciaire*).

cider ['saɪdə*] *n* cidre *m*.

CIF *abbr* (= *cost, insurance and freight*) CAF.

cigar [sɪ'gɑː*] *n* cigare *m*.

cigarette [sɪgə'rɛt] *n* cigarette *f*.

cigarette case *n* étui *m* à cigarettes.

cigarette end *n* mégot *m*.

cigarette holder *n* fume-cigarettes *m inv*.

C-in-C *abbr* = **commander-in-chief**.

cinch [sɪntʃ] *n* (*col*): **it's a ~** c'est du gâteau, c'est l'enfance de l'art.

cinder ['sɪndə*] *n* cendre *f*.

Cinderella [sɪndə'rɛlə] *n* Cendrillon.

cine-camera ['sɪnɪ'kæmərə] *n* (*BRIT*) caméra *f*.

cine-film ['sɪnɪfɪlm] *n* (*BRIT*) film *m*.

cinema ['sɪnəmə] *n* cinéma *m*.

cine-projector ['sɪnɪprə'dʒɛktə*] *n* (*BRIT*) projecteur *m* de cinéma.

cinnamon ['sɪnəmən] *n* cannelle *f*.

cipher ['saɪfə*] *n* code secret; (*fig: faceless employee etc*) numéro *m*; **in ~** codé(e).

circa ['səːkə] *prep* circa, environ.

circle ['səːkl] *n* cercle *m*; (*in cinema*) balcon *m* ♦ *vi* faire *or* décrire des cercles ♦ *vt* (*surround*) entourer, encercler; (*move round*) faire le tour de, tourner autour de.

circuit ['səːkɪt] *n* circuit *m*.

circuit board *n* plaquette *f*.

circuitous [səː'kjuɪtəs] *adj* indirect(e), qui fait un détour.

circular ['səːkjulə*] *adj* circulaire ♦ *n* circulaire *f*; (*as advertisement*) prospectus *m*.

circulate ['səːkjuleɪt] *vi* circuler ♦ *vt* faire circuler.

circulation [səːkju'leɪʃən] *n* circulation *f*; (*of newspaper*) tirage *m*.

circumcise ['səːkəmsaɪz] *vt* circoncire.

circumference [sə'kʌmfərəns] *n* circonférence *f*.

circumflex ['səːkəmflɛks] *n* (*also*: ~ **accent**) accent *m* circonflexe.

circumscribe ['səːkəmskraɪb] *vt* circonscrire.

circumspect ['səːkəmspɛkt] *adj* circonspect(e).

circumstances ['sə:kəmstənsɪz] *npl* circonstances *fpl*; (*financial condition*) moyens *mpl*, situation financière; **in the** ~ dans ces conditions; **under no** ~ en aucun cas, sous aucun prétexte.
circumstantial [sə:kəm'stænʃl] *adj* (*report, statement*) circonstancié(e); ~ **evidence** preuve indirecte.
circumvent [sə:kəm'vent] *vt* (*rule etc*) tourner.
circus ['sə:kəs] *n* cirque *m*; (*also*: **C**~: *in place names*) place *f*.
cirrhosis [sɪ'rəusɪs] *n* (*also*: ~ **of the liver**) cirrhose *f* (du foie).
CIS *n abbr* (= *Commonwealth of Independent States*) CEI *f*.
cissy ['sɪsɪ] *n* = **sissy**.
cistern ['sɪstən] *n* réservoir *m* (d'eau); (*in toilet*) réservoir de la chasse d'eau.
citation [saɪ'teɪʃən] *n* citation *f*; (*US*) P.-V. *m*.
cite [saɪt] *vt* citer.
citizen ['sɪtɪzn] *n* (*POL*) citoyen/ne; (*resident*): **the** ~**s of this town** les habitants de cette ville.
Citizens' Advice Bureau ['sɪtɪznz-] *n* (*BRIT*) ≈ Bureau *m* d'aide sociale.
citizenship ['sɪtɪznʃɪp] *n* citoyenneté *f*; (*BRIT SCOL*) éducation *f* civique.
citric ['sɪtrɪk] *adj*: ~ **acid** acide *m* citrique.
citrus fruit ['sɪtrəs-] *n* agrume *m*.
city ['sɪtɪ] *n* ville *f*, cité *f*; **the C**~ la Cité de Londres (*centre des affaires*).
city centre *n* centre-ville *m*.
City Hall *n* (*US*) ≈ hôtel *m* de ville.
City Technology College *n* (*BRIT*) établissement *m* d'enseignement technologique (*situé dans un quartier défavorisé*).
civic ['sɪvɪk] *adj* civique.
civic centre *n* (*BRIT*) centre administratif (municipal).
civil ['sɪvɪl] *adj* civil(e); (*polite*) poli(e), civil(e).
civil disobedience *n* désobéissance civile.
civil engineer *n* ingénieur civil.
civil engineering *n* génie civil, travaux publics.
civilian [sɪ'vɪlɪən] *adj, n* civil(e).
civilization [sɪvɪlaɪ'zeɪʃən] *n* civilisation *f*.
civilized ['sɪvɪlaɪzd] *adj* civilisé(e); (*fig*) où règnent les bonnes manières, empreint(e) d'une courtoisie de bon ton.
civil law *n* code civil; (*study*) droit civil.
civil liberties *npl* libertés *fpl* civiques.
civil rights *npl* droits *mpl* civiques.
civil servant *n* fonctionnaire *m/f*.
Civil Service *n* fonction publique, administration *f*.
civil war *n* guerre civile.
civvies ['sɪvɪz] *npl*: **in** ~ (*col*) en civil.
cl *abbr* (= *centilitre*) cl.
clad [klæd] *adj*: ~ **(in)** habillé(e) de, vêtu(e) de.
claim [kleɪm] *vt* (*rights etc*) revendiquer; (*compensation*) réclamer; **to** ~ **that/to be** prétendre que/être ♦ *vi* (*for insurance*) faire une déclaration de sinistre ♦ *n* revendication *f*; prétention *f*; (*right*) droit *m*; (*for expenses*) note *f* de frais; **(insurance)** ~ demande *f* d'indemnisation, déclaration *f* de sinistre; **to put in a** ~ **for** (*pay rise etc*) demander.
claimant ['kleɪmənt] *n* (*ADMIN, LAW*) requérant/e.
claim form *n* formulaire *m* de demande.
clairvoyant [klɛə'vɔɪənt] *n* voyant/e, extralucide *m/f*.
clam [klæm] *n* palourde *f*.
►**clam up** *vi* (*col*) la boucler.
clamber ['klæmbə*] *vi* grimper, se hisser.
clammy ['klæmɪ] *adj* humide et froid(e) (au toucher), moite.
clamour, (*US*) **clamor** ['klæmə*] *n* (*noise*) clameurs *fpl*; (*protest*) protestations bruyantes ♦ *vi*: **to** ~ **for sth** réclamer qch à grands cris.
clamp [klæmp] *n* étau *m* à main; agrafe *f*, crampon *m* ♦ *vt* serrer; cramponner.
►**clamp down on** *vt fus* sévir contre, prendre des mesures draconiennes à l'égard de.
clampdown ['klæmpdaun] *n*: **there has been a** ~ **on** ... des mesures énergiques ont été prises contre ....
clan [klæn] *n* clan *m*.
clandestine [klæn'destɪn] *adj* clandestin(e).
clang [klæŋ] *n* bruit *m or* fracas *m* métallique ♦ *vi* émettre un bruit *or* fracas métallique.
clanger ['klæŋə*] *n*: **to drop a** ~ (*BRIT col*) faire une boulette.
clansman ['klænzmən] *n* membre *m* d'un clan (écossais).
clap [klæp] *vi* applaudir ♦ *vt*: **to** ~ **(one's hands)** battre des mains ♦ *n* claquement *m*; tape *f*; **a** ~ **of thunder** un coup de tonnerre.
clapping ['klæpɪŋ] *n* applaudissements *mpl*.
claptrap ['klæptræp] *n* (*col*) baratin *m*.
claret ['klærət] *n* (vin *m* de) bordeaux *m* (rouge).
clarification [klærɪfɪ'keɪʃən] *n* (*fig*) clarification *f*, éclaircissement *m*.
clarify ['klærɪfaɪ] *vt* clarifier.
clarinet [klærɪ'net] *n* clarinette *f*.
clarity ['klærɪtɪ] *n* clarté *f*.
clash [klæʃ] *n* (*sound*) choc *m*, fracas *m*; (*with police*) affrontement *m*; (*fig*) conflit *m* ♦ *vi* se heurter; être *or* entrer en conflit; (*dates, events*) tomber en même temps.
clasp [klɑ:sp] *n* fermoir *m* ♦ *vt* serrer, étreindre.
class [klɑ:s] *n* (*gen*) classe *f*; (*group, category*) catégorie *f* ♦ *vt* classer, classifier.
class-conscious ['klɑ:s'kɔnʃəs] *adj* conscient(e) de son appartenance sociale.
class consciousness *n* conscience *f* de classe.
classic ['klæsɪk] *adj* classique ♦ *n* (*author*) classique *m*; (*race etc*) classique *f*.
classical ['klæsɪkl] *adj* classique.
classics ['klæsɪks] *npl* (*SCOL*) lettres *fpl* classi-

ques.

classification [klæsɪfɪ'keɪʃən] *n* classification *f*.

classified ['klæsɪfaɪd] *adj* (*information*) secret(ète); ~ **ads** petites annonces.

classify ['klæsɪfaɪ] *vt* classifier, classer.

classless society ['klɑːslɪs-] *n* société *f* sans classes.

classmate ['klɑːsmeɪt] *n* camarade *m/f* de classe.

classroom ['klɑːsrum] *n* (salle *f* de) classe *f*.

classroom assistant *n* aide-éducateur/trice *m/f*.

clatter ['klætə*] *n* cliquetis *m* ♦ *vi* cliqueter.

clause [klɔːz] *n* clause *f*; (*LING*) proposition *f*.

claustrophobia [klɔːstrə'fəubɪə] *n* claustrophobie *f*.

claustrophobic [klɔːstrə'fəubɪk] *adj* (*person*) claustrophobe; (*place*) claustrophobique.

claw [klɔː] *n* griffe *f*; (*of bird of prey*) serre *f*; (*of lobster*) pince *f* ♦ *vt* griffer; déchirer.

clay [kleɪ] *n* argile *f*.

clean [kliːn] *adj* propre; (*clear, smooth*) net(te) ♦ *vt* nettoyer ♦ *adv*: **he ~ forgot** il a complètement oublié; **to come ~** (*col*: *admit guilt*) se mettre à table; **to ~ one's teeth** (*BRIT*) se laver les dents; ~ **driving licence** *or* (*US*) **record** *permis où n'est portée aucune indication de contravention*.

►**clean off** *vt* enlever.

►**clean out** *vt* nettoyer (à fond).

►**clean up** *vt* nettoyer; (*fig*) remettre de l'ordre dans ♦ *vi* (*fig*: *make profit*): **to ~ up on** faire son beurre avec.

clean-cut ['kliːn'kʌt] *adj* (*man*) soigné; (*situation etc*) bien délimité(e), net(te), clair(e).

cleaner ['kliːnə*] *n* (*person*) nettoyeur/euse, femme *f* de ménage; (*also*: **dry ~er**) teinturier/ière; (*product*) détachant *m*.

cleaning ['kliːnɪŋ] *n* nettoyage *m*.

cleaning lady *n* femme *f* de ménage.

cleanliness ['klɛnlɪnɪs] *n* propreté *f*.

cleanly ['kliːnlɪ] *adv* proprement; nettement.

cleanse [klɛnz] *vt* nettoyer; purifier.

cleanser ['klɛnzə*] *n* détergent *m*; (*for face*) démaquillant *m*.

clean-shaven ['kliːn'ʃeɪvn] *adj* rasé(e) de près.

cleansing department ['klɛnzɪŋ-] *n* (*BRIT*) service *m* de voirie.

clean sweep *n*: **to make a ~** (*SPORT*) rafler tous les prix.

clean-up ['kliːnʌp] *n* nettoyage *m*.

clear [klɪə*] *adj* clair(e); (*road, way*) libre, dégagé(e); (*profit, majority*) net(te) ♦ *vt* dégager, déblayer, débarrasser; (*room etc*: *of people*) faire évacuer; (*woodland*) défricher; (*cheque*) compenser; (*COMM*: *goods*) liquider; (*LAW*: *suspect*) innocenter; (*obstacle*) franchir *or* sauter sans heurter ♦ *vi* (*weather*) s'éclaircir; (*fog*) se dissiper ♦ *adv*: ~ **of** à distance de, à l'écart de ♦ *n*: **to be in the ~** (*out of debt*) être dégagé(e) de toute dette; (*out of suspicion*) être lavé(e) de tout soupçon; (*out of danger*) être hors de danger; **to ~ the table** débarrasser la table, desservir; **to ~ one's throat** s'éclaircir la gorge; **to ~ a profit** faire un bénéfice net; **to make o.s. ~** se faire bien comprendre; **to make it ~ to sb that ...** bien faire comprendre à qn que ...; **I have a ~ day tomorrow** (*BRIT*) je n'ai rien de prévu demain; **to keep ~ of sb/sth** éviter qn/qch.

►**clear off** *vi* (*col*: *leave*) dégager.

►**clear up** *vi* s'éclaircir, se dissiper ♦ *vt* ranger, mettre en ordre; (*mystery*) éclaircir, résoudre.

clearance ['klɪərəns] *n* (*removal*) déblayage *m*; (*free space*) dégagement *m*; (*permission*) autorisation *f*.

clearance sale *n* (*COMM*) liquidation *f*.

clear-cut ['klɪə'kʌt] *adj* précis(e), nettement défini(e).

clearing ['klɪərɪŋ] *n* (*in forest*) clairière *f*; (*BRIT BANKING*) compensation *f*, clearing *m*.

clearing bank *n* (*BRIT*) banque *f* qui appartient à une chambre de compensation.

clearly ['klɪəlɪ] *adv* clairement; (*obviously*) de toute évidence.

clearway ['klɪəweɪ] *n* (*BRIT*) route *f* à stationnement interdit.

cleavage ['kliːvɪdʒ] *n* (*of dress*) décolleté *m*.

cleaver ['kliːvə*] *n* fendoir *m*, couperet *m*.

clef [klɛf] *n* (*MUS*) clé *f*.

cleft [klɛft] *n* (*in rock*) crevasse *f*, fissure *f*.

clemency ['klɛmənsɪ] *n* clémence *f*.

clement ['klɛmənt] *adj* (*weather*) clément(e).

clench [klɛntʃ] *vt* serrer.

clergy ['kləːdʒɪ] *n* clergé *m*.

clergyman ['kləːdʒɪmən] *n* ecclésiastique *m*.

clerical ['klɛrɪkl] *adj* de bureau, d'employé de bureau; (*REL*) clérical(e), du clergé.

clerk [klɑːk, (*US*) kləːrk] *n* employé/e de bureau; (*US*: *salesman/woman*) vendeur/euse; **C~ of Court** (*LAW*) greffier *m* (du tribunal).

clever ['klɛvə*] *adj* (*mentally*) intelligent(e); (*deft, crafty*) habile, adroit(e); (*device, arrangement*) ingénieux(euse), astucieux(euse).

cleverly ['klɛvəlɪ] *adv* (*skilfully*) habilement; (*craftily*) astucieusement.

cliché ['kliːʃeɪ] *n* cliché *m*.

click [klɪk] *vi* faire un bruit sec *or* un déclic ♦ *vt*: **to ~ one's tongue** faire claquer sa langue; **to ~ one's heels** claquer des talons.

client ['klaɪənt] *n* client/e.

clientele [kliːɑ̃ːn'tɛl] *n* clientèle *f*.

cliff [klɪf] *n* falaise *f*.

cliffhanger ['klɪfhæŋə*] *n* (*TV, fig*) histoire pleine de suspense.

climactic [klaɪ'mæktɪk] *adj* à son point culminant, culminant(e).

climate ['klaɪmɪt] *n* climat *m*.

climax ['klaɪmæks] *n* apogée *m*, point culminant; (*sexual*) orgasme *m*.

climb [klaɪm] *vi* grimper, monter; (*plane*)

prendre de l'altitude ♦ *vt* gravir, escalader, monter sur ♦ *n* montée *f*, escalade *f*; **to ~ over a wall** passer par dessus un mur.

►**climb down** *vi* (re)descendre; (*BRIT fig*) rabattre de ses prétentions.

climbdown ['klaımdaun] *n* (*BRIT*) reculade *f*.

climber ['klaımə*] *n* (*also*: **rock ~**) grimpeur/euse, varappeur/euse.

climbing ['klaımıŋ] *n* (*also*: **rock ~**) escalade *f*, varappe *f*.

clinch [klıntʃ] *vt* (*deal*) conclure, sceller.

clincher ['klıntʃə*] *n*: **that was the ~** c'est ce qui a fait pencher la balance.

cling, *pt, pp* **clung** [klıŋ, klʌŋ] *vi*: **to ~ (to)** se cramponner (à), s'accrocher (à); (*of clothes*) coller (à).

clingfilm ['klıŋfılm] *n* film *m* alimentaire.

clinic ['klınık] *n* clinique *f*; centre médical; (*session*: *MED*) consultation(s) *f(pl)*, séance(s) *f(pl)*; (: *SPORT*) séance(s) de perfectionnement.

clinical ['klınıkl] *adj* clinique; (*fig*) froid(e).

clink [klıŋk] *vi* tinter, cliqueter.

clip [klıp] *n* (*for hair*) barrette *f*; (*also*: **paper ~**) trombone *m*; (*BRIT*: *also*: **bulldog ~**) pince *f* de bureau; (*holding hose etc*) collier *m or* bague *f* (métallique) de serrage ♦ *vt* (*also*: **~ together**: *papers*) attacher; (*hair, nails*) couper; (*hedge*) tailler.

clippers ['klıpəz] *npl* tondeuse *f*; (*also*: **nail ~**) coupe-ongles *m inv*.

clipping ['klıpıŋ] *n* (*from newspaper*) coupure *f* de journal.

clique [kli:k] *n* clique *f*, coterie *f*.

cloak [kləuk] *n* grande cape.

cloakroom ['kləukrum] *n* (*for coats etc*) vestiaire *m*; (*BRIT*: *W.C.*) toilettes *fpl*.

clock [klɔk] *n* (*large*) horloge *f*; (*small*) pendule *f*; **round the ~** (*work etc*) vingt-quatre heures sur vingt-quatre; **to sleep round the ~** *or* **the ~ round** faire le tour du cadran; **30,000 on the ~** (*BRIT AUT*) 30 000 milles au compteur; **to work against the ~** faire la course contre la montre.

►**clock in, clock on** *vi* (*BRIT*) pointer (en arrivant).

►**clock off, clock out** *vi* (*BRIT*) pointer (en partant).

►**clock up** *vt* (*miles, hours etc*) faire.

clockwise ['klɔkwaız] *adv* dans le sens des aiguilles d'une montre.

clockwork ['klɔkwə:k] *n* mouvement *m* (d'horlogerie); rouages *mpl*, mécanisme *m* ♦ *adj* (*toy, train*) mécanique.

clog [klɔg] *n* sabot *m* ♦ *vt* boucher, encrasser ♦ *vi* se boucher, s'encrasser.

cloister ['klɔıstə*] *n* cloître *m*.

clone [kləun] *n* clone *m*.

close *adj, adv and derivatives* [kləus] *adj* (*near*): **~ (to)** près (de), proche (de); (*writing, texture*) serré(e); (*watch*) étroit(e), strict(e); (*examination*) attentif(ive), minutieux(euse); (*weather*) lourd(e), étouffant(e); (*room*) mal aéré(e) ♦ *adv* près, à proximité; **~ to** *prep* près de; **~ by, ~ at hand** *adj, adv* tout(e) près; **how ~ is Edinburgh to Glasgow?** combien de kilomètres y-a-t-il entre Édimbourg et Glasgow?; **a ~ friend** un ami intime; **to have a ~ shave** (*fig*) l'échapper belle; **at ~ quarters** tout près, à côté ♦ *vb and derivatives* [kləuz] *vt* fermer; (*bargain, deal*) conclure ♦ *vi* (*shop etc*) fermer; (*lid, door etc*) se fermer; (*end*) se terminer, se conclure ♦ *n* (*end*) conclusion *f*; **to bring sth to a ~** mettre fin à qch.

►**close down** *vt, vi* fermer (*définitivement*).

►**close in** *vi* (*hunters*) approcher; (*night, fog*) tomber; **the days are closing in** les jours raccourcissent; **to ~ in on sb** cerner qn.

►**close off** *vt* (*area*) boucler.

closed [kləuzd] *adj* (*shop etc*) fermé(e); (*road*) fermé à la circulation.

closed-circuit ['kləuzd'sə:kıt] *adj*: **~ television** télévision *f* en circuit fermé.

closed shop *n* organisation *f* qui n'admet que des travailleurs syndiqués.

close-knit ['kləus'nıt] *adj* (*family, community*) très uni(e).

closely ['kləuslı] *adv* (*examine, watch*) de près; **we are ~ related** nous sommes proches parents; **a ~ guarded secret** un secret bien gardé.

close season [kləus-] *n* (*BRIT: HUNTING*) fermeture *f* de la chasse/pêche; (: *FOOTBALL*) trêve *f*.

closet ['klɔzıt] *n* (*cupboard*) placard *m*, réduit *m*.

close-up ['kləusʌp] *n* gros plan.

closing ['kləuzıŋ] *adj* (*stages, remarks*) final(e); **~ price** (*STOCK EXCHANGE*) cours *m* de clôture; **~ time** heure *f* de fermeture.

closure ['kləuʒə*] *n* fermeture *f*.

clot [klɔt] *n* (*gen*: **blood ~**) caillot *m*; (*col*: *person*) ballot *m* ♦ *vi* (*blood*) former des caillots; (: *external bleeding*) se coaguler.

cloth [klɔθ] *n* (*material*) tissu *m*, étoffe *f*; (*BRIT*: *also*: **tea~**) torchon *m*; lavette *f*; (*also*: **table~**) nappe *f*.

clothe [kləuð] *vt* habiller, vêtir.

clothes [kləuðz] *npl* vêtements *mpl*, habits *mpl*; **to put one's ~ on** s'habiller; **to take one's ~ off** enlever ses vêtements.

clothes brush *n* brosse *f* à habits.

clothes line *n* corde *f* (à linge).

clothes peg, (*US*) **clothes pin** *n* pince *f* à linge.

clothing ['kləuðıŋ] *n* = **clothes.**

clotted cream ['klɔtıd-] *n* (*BRIT*) crème caillée.

cloud [klaud] *n* nuage *m* ♦ *vt* (*liquid*) troubler; **to ~ the issue** brouiller les cartes; **every ~ has a silver lining** (*proverb*) à quelque chose malheur est bon (*proverbe*).

►**cloud over** *vi* se couvrir; (*fig*) s'assombrir.

cloudburst ['klaudbə:st] *n* violente averse.
cloud-cuckoo-land ['klaud'kuku:'lænd] *n* (*BRIT*) monde *m* imaginaire.
cloudy ['klaudɪ] *adj* nuageux(euse), couvert(e); (*liquid*) trouble.
clout [klaut] *n* (*blow*) taloche *f*; (*fig*) pouvoir *m* ♦ *vt* flanquer une taloche à.
clove [kləuv] *n* clou *m* de girofle; ~ **of garlic** gousse *f* d'ail.
clover ['kləuvə*] *n* trèfle *m*.
cloverleaf ['kləuvəli:f] *n* feuille *f* de trèfle; (*AUT*) croisement *m* en trèfle.
clown [klaun] *n* clown *m* ♦ *vi* (*also*: ~ **about**, ~ **around**) faire le clown.
cloying ['klɔɪɪŋ] *adj* (*taste, smell*) écœurant(e).
club [klʌb] *n* (*society*) club *m*; (*weapon*) massue *f*, matraque *f*; (*also*: **golf** ~) club ♦ *vt* matraquer ♦ *vi*: **to** ~ **together** s'associer; ~**s** *npl* (*CARDS*) trèfle *m*.
club car *n* (*US RAIL*) wagon-restaurant *m*.
club class *n* (*AVIAT*) classe *f* club.
clubhouse ['klʌbhaus] *n* pavillon *m*.
club soda *n* (*US*) eau *f* de seltz.
cluck [klʌk] *vi* glousser.
clue [klu:] *n* indice *m*; (*in crosswords*) définition *f*; **I haven't a** ~ je n'en ai pas la moindre idée.
clued up, (*US*) **clued in** [klu:d-] *adj* (*col*) (vachement) calé(e).
clump [klʌmp] *n*: ~ **of trees** bouquet *m* d'arbres.
clumsy ['klʌmzɪ] *adj* (*person*) gauche, maladroit(e); (*object*) malcommode, peu maniable.
clung [klʌŋ] *pt, pp of* **cling**.
cluster ['klʌstə*] *n* (petit) groupe ♦ *vi* se rassembler.
clutch [klʌtʃ] *n* (*grip, grasp*) étreinte *f*, prise *f*; (*AUT*) embrayage *m* ♦ *vt* agripper, serrer fort; **to** ~ **at** se cramponner à.
clutter ['klʌtə*] *vt* (*also*: ~ **up**) encombrer ♦ *n* désordre *m*, fouillis *m*.
CM *abbr* (*US POST*) = *North Mariana Islands*.
cm *abbr* (= *centimetre*) cm.
CNAA *n abbr* (*BRIT*: = *Council for National Academic Awards*) *organisme non universitaire délivrant des diplômes*.
CND *n abbr* = *Campaign for Nuclear Disarmament*.
CO *n abbr* (= *commanding officer*) Cdt; (*BRIT*) = *Commonwealth Office* ♦ *abbr* (*US*) = *Colorado*.
Co. *abbr* = **company, county**.
c/o *abbr* (= *care of*) c/o, aux bons soins de.
coach [kəutʃ] *n* (*bus*) autocar *m*; (*horse-drawn*) diligence *f*; (*of train*) voiture *f*, wagon *m*; (*SPORT*: *trainer*) entraîneur/euse; (*school: tutor*) répétiteur/trice ♦ *vt* entraîner; donner des leçons particulières à.
coach trip *n* excursion *f* en car.
coagulate [kəu'ægjuleɪt] *vt* coaguler ♦ *vi* se coaguler.
coal [kəul] *n* charbon *m*.
coal face *n* front *m* de taille.
coalfield ['kəulfi:ld] *n* bassin houiller.
coalition [kəuə'lɪʃən] *n* coalition *f*.
coalman ['kəulmən] *n* charbonnier *m*, marchand *m* de charbon.
coal mine *n* mine *f* de charbon.
coal miner *n* mineur *m*.
coal mining *n* extraction *f* du charbon.
coarse [kɔ:s] *adj* grossier(ère), rude; (*vulgar*) vulgaire.
coast [kəust] *n* côte *f* ♦ *vi* (*with cycle etc*) descendre en roue libre.
coastal ['kəustl] *adj* côtier(ère).
coaster ['kəustə*] *n* (*NAUT*) caboteur *m*; (*for glass*) dessous *m* de verre.
coastguard ['kəustgɑ:d] *n* garde-côte *m*.
coastline ['kəustlaɪn] *n* côte *f*, littoral *m*.
coat [kəut] *n* manteau *m*; (*of animal*) pelage *m*, poil *m*; (*of paint*) couche *f* ♦ *vt* couvrir, enduire; ~ **of arms** *n* blason *m*, armoiries *fpl*.
coat hanger *n* cintre *m*.
coating ['kəutɪŋ] *n* couche *f*, enduit *m*.
co-author ['kəu'ɔ:θə*] *n* co-auteur *m*.
coax [kəuks] *vt* persuader par des cajoleries.
cob [kɔb] *n see* **corn**.
cobbler ['kɔblə*] *n* cordonnier *m*.
cobbles, cobblestones ['kɔblz, 'kɔblstəunz] *npl* pavés (ronds).
COBOL ['kəubɔl] *n* COBOL *m*.
cobra ['kəubrə] *n* cobra *m*.
cobweb ['kɔbwɛb] *n* toile *f* d'araignée.
cocaine [kə'keɪn] *n* cocaïne *f*.
cock [kɔk] *n* (*rooster*) coq *m*; (*male bird*) mâle *m* ♦ *vt* (*gun*) armer; **to** ~ **one's ears** (*fig*) dresser l'oreille.
cock-a-hoop [kɔkə'hu:p] *adj* jubilant(e).
cockerel ['kɔkərl] *n* jeune coq *m*.
cock-eyed ['kɔkaɪd] *adj* (*fig*) de travers; qui louche; qui ne tient pas debout (*fig*).
cockle ['kɔkl] *n* coque *f*.
cockney ['kɔknɪ] *n* cockney *m/f* (*habitant des quartiers populaires de l'East End de Londres*), ≈ faubourien/ne.
cockpit ['kɔkpɪt] *n* (*in aircraft*) poste *m* de pilotage, cockpit *m*.
cockroach ['kɔkrəutʃ] *n* cafard *m*, cancrelat *m*.
cocktail ['kɔkteɪl] *n* cocktail *m*; **prawn** ~, (*US*) **shrimp** ~ cocktail de crevettes.
cocktail cabinet *n* (meuble-)bar *m*.
cocktail party *n* cocktail *m*.
cocktail shaker [-'ʃeɪkə*] *n* shaker *m*.
cocky ['kɔkɪ] *adj* trop sûr(e) de soi.
cocoa ['kəukəu] *n* cacao *m*.
coconut ['kəukənʌt] *n* noix *f* de coco.
cocoon [kə'ku:n] *n* cocon *m*.
COD *abbr* = **cash on delivery, collect on delivery** (*US*).
cod [kɔd] *n* morue (fraîche), cabillaud *m*.
code [kəud] *n* code *m*; ~ **of behaviour** règles *fpl* de conduite; ~ **of practice** déontologie *f*.
codeine ['kəudi:n] *n* codéine *f*.

codger ['kɔdʒə*] *n*: **an old ~** (*BRIT col*) un drôle de vieux bonhomme.
codicil ['kɔdɪsɪl] *n* codicille *m*.
codify ['kəudɪfaɪ] *vt* codifier.
cod-liver oil ['kɔdlɪvər-] *n* huile *f* de foie de morue.
co-driver ['kəu'draɪvə*] *n* (*in race*) copilote *m*; (*of lorry*) deuxième chauffeur *m*.
co-ed ['kəu'ɛd] *adj abbr* = **coeducational** ♦ *n abbr* (*US*: *female student*) *étudiante d'une université mixte*; (*BRIT*: *school*) école *f* mixte.
coeducational ['kəuɛdju'keɪʃənl] *adj* mixte.
coerce [kəu'əːs] *vt* contraindre.
coercion [kəu'əːʃən] *n* contrainte *f*.
coexistence ['kəuɪg'zɪstəns] *n* coexistence *f*.
C. of C. *n abbr* = **chamber of commerce.**
C of E *abbr* = **Church of England.**
coffee ['kɔfɪ] *n* café *m*; **white ~**, (*US*) **~ with cream** (café-)crème *m*.
coffee bar *n* (*BRIT*) café *m*.
coffee bean *n* grain *m* de café.
coffee break *n* pause-café *f*.
coffeecake ['kɔfɪkeɪk] *n* (*US*) ≈ petit pain aux raisins.
coffee cup *n* tasse *f* à café.
coffeepot ['kɔfɪpɔt] *n* cafetière *f*.
coffee table *n* (petite) table basse.
coffin ['kɔfɪn] *n* cercueil *m*.
C of I *abbr* = *Church of Ireland.*
C of S *abbr* = *Church of Scotland.*
cog [kɔg] *n* dent *f* (d'engrenage).
cogent ['kəudʒənt] *adj* puissant(e), convaincant(e).
cognac ['kɔnjæk] *n* cognac *m*.
cogwheel ['kɔgwiːl] *n* roue dentée.
cohabit [kəu'hæbɪt] *vi* (*formal*): **to ~ (with sb)** cohabiter (avec qn).
coherent [kəu'hɪərənt] *adj* cohérent(e).
cohesion [kəu'hiːʒən] *n* cohésion *f*.
cohesive [kəu'hiːsɪv] *adj* (*fig*) cohésif(ive).
COI *n abbr* (*BRIT*: = *Central Office of Information*) *service d'information gouvernemental.*
coil [kɔɪl] *n* rouleau *m*, bobine *f*; (*one loop*) anneau *m*, spire *f*; (*of smoke*) volute *f*; (*contraceptive*) stérilet *m* ♦ *vt* enrouler.
coin [kɔɪn] *n* pièce *f* de monnaie ♦ *vt* (*word*) inventer.
coinage ['kɔɪnɪdʒ] *n* monnaie *f*, système *m* monétaire.
coin-box ['kɔɪnbɔks] *n* (*BRIT*) cabine *f* téléphonique.
coincide [kəuɪn'saɪd] *vi* coïncider.
coincidence [kəu'ɪnsɪdəns] *n* coïncidence *f*.
coin-operated ['kɔɪn'ɔpəreɪtɪd] *adj* (*machine, launderette*) automatique.
Coke [kəuk] *n* ® coca *m*.
coke [kəuk] *n* coke *m*.
Col. *abbr* (= *colonel*) Col; (*US*) = *Colorado.*
COLA *n abbr* (*US*: = *cost-of-living adjustment*) *réajustement (des salaires, indemnités etc) en fonction du coût de la vie.*
colander ['kɔləndə*] *n* passoire *f* (à légumes).
cold [kəuld] *adj* froid(e) ♦ *n* froid *m*; (*MED*) rhume *m*; **it's ~** il fait froid; **to be ~** avoir froid; **to catch ~** prendre *or* attraper froid; **to catch a ~** s'enrhumer, attraper un rhume; **in ~ blood** de sang-froid; **to have ~ feet** avoir froid aux pieds; (*fig*) avoir la frousse *or* la trouille; **to give sb the ~ shoulder** battre froid à qn.
cold-blooded ['kəuld'blʌdɪd] *adj* (*ZOOL*) à sang froid.
cold cream *n* crème *f* de soins.
coldly ['kəuldlɪ] *adv* froidement.
cold sore *n* bouton *m* de fièvre.
cold sweat *n*: **to be in a ~ (about sth)** avoir des sueurs froides (au sujet de qch).
cold turkey *n* (*col*) manque *m*; **to go ~** être en manque.
Cold War *n*: **the ~** la guerre froide.
coleslaw ['kəulslɔː] *n sorte de salade de chou cru.*
colic ['kɔlɪk] *n* colique(s) *f(pl)*.
colicky ['kɔlɪkɪ] *adj* qui souffre de coliques.
collaborate [kə'læbəreɪt] *vi* collaborer.
collaboration [kəlæbə'reɪʃən] *n* collaboration *f*.
collaborator [kə'læbəreɪtə*] *n* collaborateur/trice.
collage [kɔ'lɑːʒ] *n* (*ART*) collage *m*.
collagen ['kɔlədʒən] *n* collagène *m*.
collapse [kə'læps] *vi* s'effondrer, s'écrouler ♦ *n* effondrement *m*, écroulement *m*; (*of government*) chute *f*.
collapsible [kə'læpsəbl] *adj* pliant(e); télescopique.
collar ['kɔlə*] *n* (*of coat, shirt*) col *m*; (*for dog*) collier *m*; (*TECH*) collier, bague *f* ♦ *vt* (*col*: *person*) pincer.
collarbone ['kɔləbəun] *n* clavicule *f*.
collate [kɔ'leɪt] *vt* collationner.
collateral [kə'lætərl] *n* nantissement *m*.
collation [kə'leɪʃən] *n* collation *f*.
colleague ['kɔliːg] *n* collègue *m/f*.
collect [kə'lɛkt] *vt* rassembler; (*pick up*) ramasser; (*as a hobby*) collectionner; (*BRIT*: *call for*) (passer) prendre; (*mail*) faire la levée de, ramasser; (*money owed*) encaisser; (*donations, subscriptions*) recueillir ♦ *vi* (*people*) se rassembler; (*dust, dirt*) s'amasser; **to ~ one's thoughts** réfléchir, réunir ses idées; **~ on delivery (COD)** (*US COMM*) payable *or* paiement à la livraison; **to call ~** (*US TEL*) téléphoner en PCV.
collected [kə'lɛktɪd] *adj*: **~ works** œuvres complètes.
collection [kə'lɛkʃən] *n* collection *f*; (*of mail*) levée *f*; (*for money*) collecte *f*, quête *f*.
collective [kə'lɛktɪv] *adj* collectif(ive) ♦ *n* collectif *m*.
collective bargaining *n* convention collective.
collector [kə'lɛktə*] *n* collectionneur *m*; (*of taxes*) percepteur *m*; (*of rent, cash*) encais-

seur *m*; **~'s item** *or* **piece** pièce *f* de collection.
college ['kɔlɪdʒ] *n* collège *m*; (*of technology, agriculture etc*) institut *m*; **to go to ~** faire des études supérieures; **~ of education** ≈ école normale.
collide [kə'laɪd] *vi*: **to ~ (with)** entrer en collision (avec).
collie ['kɔlɪ] *n* (*dog*) colley *m*.
colliery ['kɔlɪərɪ] *n* (*BRIT*) mine *f* de charbon, houillère *f*.
collision [kə'lɪʒən] *n* collision *f*, heurt *m*; **to be on a ~ course** aller droit à la collision; (*fig*) aller vers l'affrontement.
collision damage waiver *n* (*INSURANCE*) rachat *m* de franchise.
colloquial [kə'ləukwɪəl] *adj* familier(ère).
collusion [kə'luːʒən] *n* collusion *f*; **in ~ with** en complicité avec.
Colo. *abbr* (*US*) = *Colorado.*
cologne [kə'ləun] *n* (*also*: **eau de ~**) eau *f* de cologne.
Colombia [kə'lɔmbɪə] *n* Colombie *f*.
Colombian [kə'lɔmbɪən] *adj* colombien(ne) ♦ *n* Colombien/ne.
colon ['kəulən] *n* (*sign*) deux-points *mpl*; (*MED*) côlon *m*.
colonel ['kəːnl] *n* colonel *m*.
colonial [kə'ləunɪəl] *adj* colonial(e).
colonize ['kɔlənaɪz] *vt* coloniser.
colony ['kɔlənɪ] *n* colonie *f*.
color *etc* ['kʌlə*] (*US*) = **colour** *etc*.
Colorado beetle [kɔlə'rɑːdəu-] *n* doryphore *m*.
colossal [kə'lɔsl] *adj* colossal(e).
colour, (*US*) **color** ['kʌlə*] *n* couleur *f* ♦ *vt* colorer; peindre; (*with crayons*) colorier; (*news*) fausser, exagérer ♦ *vi* rougir ♦ *cpd* (*film, photograph, television*) en couleur; **~s** *npl* (*of party, club*) couleurs *fpl*.
colo(u)r bar *n* discrimination raciale (*dans un établissement etc*).
colo(u)r-blind ['kʌləblaɪnd] *adj* daltonien(ne).
colo(u)red ['kʌləd] *adj* coloré(e); (*photo*) en couleur.
colo(u)rful ['kʌləful] *adj* coloré(e), vif(vive); (*personality*) pittoresque, haut(e) en couleurs.
colo(u)ring ['kʌlərɪŋ] *n* colorant *m*; (*complexion*) teint *m*.
colo(u)r scheme *n* combinaison *f* de(s) couleur(s).
colour supplement *n* (*BRIT PRESS*) supplément *m* magazine.
colt [kəult] *n* poulain *m*.
column ['kɔləm] *n* colonne *f*; (*fashion/sports ~ etc*) rubrique *f*; **the editorial ~** l'éditorial *m*.
columnist ['kɔləmnɪst] *n* rédacteur/trice d'une rubrique.
coma ['kəumə] *n* coma *m*.
comb [kəum] *n* peigne *m* ♦ *vt* (*hair*) peigner; (*area*) ratisser, passer au peigne fin.
combat ['kɔmbæt] *n* combat *m* ♦ *vt* combattre, lutter contre.
combination [kɔmbɪ'neɪʃən] *n* (*gen*) combinaison *f*.
combination lock *n* serrure *f* à combinaison.
combine *vb* [kəm'baɪn] *vt* combiner; (*one quality with another*): **to ~ sth with sth** joindre qch à qch, allier qch à qch ♦ *vi* s'associer; (*CHEM*) se combiner ♦ *n* ['kɔmbaɪn] association *f*; (*ECON*) trust *m*; **a ~d effort** un effort conjugué.
combine (harvester) *n* moissonneuse-batteuse(-lieuse) *f*.
combo ['kɔmbəu] *n* (*JAZZ etc*) groupe *m* de musiciens.
combustible [kəm'bʌstɪbl] *adj* combustible.
combustion [kəm'bʌstʃən] *n* combustion *f*.
come, *pt* **came,** *pp* **come** [kʌm, keɪm] *vi* venir; (*col: sexually*) jouir; **~ with me** suivez-moi; **we've just ~ from Paris** nous arrivons de Paris; ... **what might ~ of it** ... ce qui pourrait en résulter, ... ce qui pourrait advenir *or* se produire; **to ~ into sight** *or* **view** apparaître; **to ~ to** (*decision etc*) parvenir *or* arriver à; **to ~ undone/loose** se défaire/desserrer; **coming!** j'arrive!; **if it ~s to it** s'il le faut, dans le pire des cas.
►**come about** *vi* se produire, arriver.
►**come across** *vt fus* rencontrer par hasard, tomber sur ♦ *vi*: **to ~ across well/badly** faire une bonne/mauvaise impression.
►**come along** *vi* (*pupil, work*) faire des progrès, avancer; **~ along!** viens!; allons!, allez!; **if you ~ along on Thursday ...** si vous venez jeudi ...
►**come apart** *vi* s'en aller en morceaux; se détacher.
►**come away** *vi* partir, s'en aller; (*become detached*) se détacher.
►**come back** *vi* revenir; (*reply*): **can I ~ back to you on that one?** est-ce qu'on peut revenir là-dessus plus tard?
►**come by** *vt fus* (*acquire*) obtenir, se procurer.
►**come down** *vi* descendre; (*prices*) baisser; (*buildings*) s'écrouler; (*: be demolished*) être démoli(e).
►**come forward** *vi* s'avancer; (*make o.s. known*) se présenter, s'annoncer.
►**come from** *vt fus* venir de; (*place*) venir de, être originaire de.
►**come in** *vi* entrer.
►**come in for** *vt fus* (*criticism etc*) être l'objet de.
►**come into** *vt fus* (*money*) hériter de.
►**come off** *vi* (*button*) se détacher; (*stain*) s'enlever; (*attempt*) réussir.
►**come on** *vi* (*lights, electricity*) s'allumer; (*central heating*) se mettre en marche; (*pupil, work, project*) faire des progrès, avancer; **~ on!** viens!; allons!, allez!
►**come out** *vi* sortir; (*book*) paraître; (*strike*)

cesser le travail, se mettre en grève.
►**come over** *vt fus*: **I don't know what's ~ over him!** je ne sais pas ce qui lui a pris!
►**come round** *vi* (*after faint, operation*) revenir à soi, reprendre connaissance.
►**come through** *vi* (*survive*) s'en sortir; (*telephone call*): **the call came through** l'appel est bien parvenu.
►**come to** *vi* revenir à soi ♦ *vt* (*add up to: amount*): **how much does it ~ to?** ça fait combien?
►**come under** *vt fus* (*heading*) se trouver sous; (*influence*) subir.
►**come up** *vi* monter.
►**come up against** *vt fus* (*resistance, difficulties*) rencontrer.
►**come up to** *vt fus* arriver à; **the film didn't ~ up to our expectations** le film nous a déçu.
►**come up with** *vt fus*: **he came up with an idea** il a eu une idée, il a proposé quelque chose.
►**come upon** *vt fus* tomber sur.
comeback ['kʌmbæk] *n* (*reaction*) réaction *f*; (*response*) réponse *f*; (*THEAT etc*) rentrée *f*.
Comecon ['kɔmɪkɔn] *n abbr* (= *Council for Mutual Economic Aid*) COMECON *m*.
comedian [kə'miːdɪən] *n* (*in music hall etc*) comique *m*; (*THEAT*) comédien *m*.
comedienne [kəmiːdɪ'ɛn] *n* comique *f*.
comedown ['kʌmdaun] *n* déchéance *f*.
comedy ['kɔmɪdɪ] *n* comédie *f*.
comet ['kɔmɪt] *n* comète *f*.
comeuppance [kʌm'ʌpəns] *n*: **to get one's ~** recevoir ce qu'on mérite.
comfort ['kʌmfət] *n* confort *m*, bien-être *m*; (*solace*) consolation *f*, réconfort *m* ♦ *vt* consoler, réconforter.
comfortable ['kʌmfətəbl] *adj* confortable; **I don't feel very ~ about it** cela m'inquiète un peu.
comfortably ['kʌmfətəblɪ] *adv* (*sit*) confortablement; (*live*) à l'aise.
comforter ['kʌmfətə*] *n* (*US*) édredon *m*.
comforts ['kʌmfəts] *npl* aises *fpl*.
comfort station *n* (*US*) toilettes *fpl*.
comic ['kɔmɪk] *adj* comique ♦ *n* comique *m*; (*magazine*) illustré *m*.
comical ['kɔmɪkl] *adj* amusant(e).
comic strip *n* bande dessinée.
coming ['kʌmɪŋ] *n* arrivée *f* ♦ *adj* (*next*) prochain(e); (*future*) à venir; **in the ~ weeks** dans les prochaines semaines.
coming(s) and going(s) *n(pl)* va-et-vient *m inv*.
Comintern ['kɔmɪntəːn] *n* Comintern *m*.
comma ['kɔmə] *n* virgule *f*.
command [kə'maːnd] *n* ordre *m*, commandement *m*; (*MIL: authority*) commandement; (*mastery*) maîtrise *f*; (*COMPUT*) commande *f* ♦ *vt* (*troops*) commander; (*be able to get*) (pouvoir) disposer de, avoir à sa disposition; (*deserve*) avoir droit à; **to ~ sb to do** donner l'ordre *or* commander à qn de faire; **to have/take ~ of** avoir/prendre le commandement de; **to have at one's ~** (*money, resources etc*) disposer de.
command economy *n* économie planifiée.
commandeer [kɔmən'dɪə*] *vt* réquisitionner (par la force).
commander [kə'maːndə*] *n* chef *m*; (*MIL*) commandant *m*.
commander-in-chief [kə'maːndərɪn'tʃiːf] *n* (*MIL*) commandant *m* en chef.
commanding [kə'maːndɪŋ] *adj* (*appearance*) imposant(e); (*voice, tone*) autoritaire; (*lead, position*) dominant(e).
commanding officer *n* commandant *m*.
commandment [kə'maːndmənt] *n* (*REL*) commandement *m*.
command module *n* (*SPACE*) module *m* de commande.
commando [kə'maːndəu] *n* commando *m*; membre *m* d'un commando.
commemorate [kə'mɛməreɪt] *vt* commémorer.
commemoration [kəmɛmə'reɪʃən] *n* commémoration *f*.
commemorative [kə'mɛmərətɪv] *adj* commémoratif(ive).
commence [kə'mɛns] *vt, vi* commencer.
commend [kə'mɛnd] *vt* louer; recommander.
commendable [kə'mɛndəbl] *adj* louable.
commendation [kɔmɛn'deɪʃən] *n* éloge *m*; recommandation *f*.
commensurate [kə'mɛnʃərɪt] *adj*: **~ with/to** en rapport avec/selon.
comment ['kɔmɛnt] *n* commentaire *m* ♦ *vi* faire des remarques *or* commentaires; **to ~ on** faire des remarques sur; **to ~ that** faire remarquer que; **"no ~"** "je n'ai rien à déclarer".
commentary ['kɔməntərɪ] *n* commentaire *m*; (*SPORT*) reportage *m* (en direct).
commentator ['kɔmənteɪtə*] *n* commentateur *m*; (*SPORT*) reporter *m*.
commerce ['kɔməːs] *n* commerce *m*.
commercial [kə'məːʃəl] *adj* commercial(e) ♦ *n* (*RADIO, TV*) annonce *f* publicitaire, spot *m* (publicitaire).
commercial bank *n* banque *f* d'affaires.
commercial break *n* (*RADIO, TV*) spot *m* (publicitaire).
commercial college *n* école *f* de commerce.
commercialism [kə'məːʃəlɪzəm] *n* mercantilisme *m*.
commercial television *n* publicité *f* à la télévision; chaînes privées (financées par la publicité).
commercial traveller *n* voyageur *m* de commerce.
commercial vehicle *n* véhicule *m* utilitaire.
commiserate [kə'mɪzəreɪt] *vi*: **to ~ with sb** té-

moigner de la sympathie pour qn.

commission [kə'mɪʃən] *n* (*committee; fee: also for salesman*) commission *f*; (*order for work of art etc*) commande *f* ♦ *vt* (*MIL*) nommer (à un commandement); (*work of art*) commander, charger un artiste de l'exécution de; **out of ~** (*NAUT*) hors de service; (*machine*) hors service; **I get 10% ~** je reçois une commission de 10%; **~ of inquiry** (*BRIT*) commission d'enquête.

commissionaire [kəmɪʃə'nɛə*] *n* (*BRIT: at shop, cinema etc*) portier *m* (en uniforme).

commissioner [kə'mɪʃənə*] *n* membre *m* d'une commission; (*POLICE*) préfet *m* (de police).

commit [kə'mɪt] *vt* (*act*) commettre; (*to sb's care*) confier (à); **to ~ o.s. (to do)** s'engager (à faire); **to ~ suicide** se suicider; **to ~ to writing** coucher par écrit; **to ~ sb for trial** traduire qn en justice.

commitment [kə'mɪtmənt] *n* engagement *m*; (*obligation*) responsabilité(s) *f(pl)*.

committed [kə'mɪtɪd] *adj* (*writer, politician etc*) engagé(e).

committee [kə'mɪtɪ] *n* comité *m*; commission *f*; **to be on a ~** siéger dans un comité (*or* une commission).

committee meeting *n* réunion *f* de comité *or* commission.

commodity [kə'mɔdɪtɪ] *n* produit *m*, marchandise *f*, article *m*; (*food*) denrée *f*.

commodity exchange *n* bourse *f* de marchandises.

common ['kɔmən] *adj* (*gen, also pej*) commun(e); (*usual*) courant(e) ♦ *n* terrain communal; **in ~** en commun; **in ~ use** d'un usage courant; **it's ~ knowledge that** il est bien connu *or* notoire que; **to the ~ good** pour le bien de tous, dans l'intérêt général.

common cold *n*: **the ~** le rhume.

common denominator *n* dénominateur commun.

commoner ['kɔmənə*] *n* roturier/ière.

common ground *n* (*fig*) terrain *m* d'entente.

common land *n* terrain communal.

common law *n* droit coutumier.

common-law ['kɔmənlɔː] *adj*: **~ wife** épouse *f* de facto.

commonly ['kɔmənlɪ] *adv* communément, généralement; couramment.

Common Market *n* Marché commun.

commonplace ['kɔmənpleɪs] *adj* banal(e), ordinaire.

commonroom ['kɔmənrum] *n* salle commune; (*SCOL*) salle des professeurs.

Commons ['kɔmənz] *npl* (*BRIT POL*): **the (House of) ~** la chambre des Communes.

common sense *n* bon sens.

Commonwealth ['kɔmənwɛlθ] *n*: **the ~** le Commonwealth; *voir encadré*.

> **COMMONWEALTH**
>
> *Le* **Commonwealth** *regroupe 50 États indépendants et plusieurs territoires qui reconnaissent tous le souverain britannique comme chef de cette association.*

commotion [kə'məuʃən] *n* désordre *m*, tumulte *m*.

communal ['kɔmjuːnl] *adj* (*life*) communautaire; (*for common use*) commun(e).

commune *n* ['kɔmjuːn] (*group*) communauté *f* ♦ *vi* [kə'mjuːn]: **to ~ with** converser intimement avec; communier avec.

communicate [kə'mjuːnɪkeɪt] *vt* communiquer, transmettre ♦ *vi*: **to ~ (with)** communiquer (avec).

communication [kəmjuːnɪ'keɪʃən] *n* communication *f*.

communication cord *n* (*BRIT*) sonnette *f* d'alarme.

communications network *n* réseau *m* de communications.

communications satellite *n* satellite *m* de télécommunications.

communicative [kə'mjuːnɪkətɪv] *adj* communicatif(ive).

communion [kə'mjuːnɪən] *n* (*also*: **Holy C~**) communion *f*.

communism ['kɔmjunɪzəm] *n* communisme *m*.

communist ['kɔmjunɪst] *adj, n* communiste (*m/f*).

community [kə'mjuːnɪtɪ] *n* communauté *f*.

community centre *n* foyer socio-éducatif, centre *m* de loisirs.

community chest *n* (*US*) fonds commun.

community health centre *n* centre médico-social.

community service *n* ≈ travail *m* d'intérêt général, TIG *m*.

community spirit *n* solidarité *f*.

commutation ticket [kɔmju'teɪʃən-] *n* (*US*) carte *f* d'abonnement.

commute [kə'mjuːt] *vi* faire le trajet journalier (de son domicile à un lieu de travail assez éloigné) ♦ *vt* (*LAW*) commuer; (*MATH: terms etc*) opérer la commutation de.

commuter [kə'mjuːtə*] *n* banlieusard/e (qui ... *see vi*).

compact *adj* [kəm'pækt] compact(e) ♦ *n* ['kɔmpækt] contrat *m*, entente *f*; (*also*: **powder ~**) poudrier *m*.

compact disc *n* disque compact.

compact disc player *n* lecteur *m* de disques compacts.

companion [kəm'pænjən] *n* compagnon/compagne.

companionship [kəm'pænjənʃɪp] *n* camaraderie *f*.

companionway [kəm'pænjənweɪ] *n* (*NAUT*)

escalier *m* des cabines.
company ['kʌmpənɪ] *n* (*also COMM, MIL, THEAT*) compagnie *f*; **he's good** ~ il est d'une compagnie agréable; **we have** ~ nous avons de la visite; **to keep sb** ~ tenir compagnie à qn; **to part** ~ **with** se séparer de; **Smith and C**~ Smith et Compagnie.
company car *n* voiture *f* de fonction.
company director *n* administrateur/trice.
company secretary *n* (*BRIT COMM*) secrétaire général (*d'une société*).
comparable ['kɔmpərəbl] *adj* comparable.
comparative [kəm'pærətɪv] *adj* comparatif(ive); (*relative*) relatif(ive).
comparatively [kəm'pærətɪvlɪ] *adv* (*relatively*) relativement.
compare [kəm'pɛə*] *vt*: **to** ~ **sth/sb with/to** comparer qch/qn avec *or* et/à ♦ *vi*: **to** ~ **(with)** se comparer (à); être comparable (à); **how do the prices** ~**?** comment sont les prix?, est-ce que les prix sont comparables?; ~**d with** *or* **to** par rapport à.
comparison [kəm'pærɪsn] *n* comparaison *f*; **in** ~ **(with)** en comparaison (de).
compartment [kəm'pɑːtmənt] *n* (*also RAIL*) compartiment *m*.
compass ['kʌmpəs] *n* boussole *f*; **within the** ~ **of** dans les limites de.
compasses ['kʌmpəsɪz] *npl* compas *m*.
compassion [kəm'pæʃən] *n* compassion *f*, humanité *f*.
compassionate [kəm'pæʃənɪt] *adj* accessible à la compassion, au cœur charitable et bienveillant; **on** ~ **grounds** pour raisons personnelles *or* de famille.
compassionate leave *n* congé exceptionnel (*pour raisons de famille*).
compatibility [kəmpætɪ'bɪlɪtɪ] *n* compatibilité *f*.
compatible [kəm'pætɪbl] *adj* compatible.
compel [kəm'pɛl] *vt* contraindre, obliger.
compelling [kəm'pɛlɪŋ] *adj* (*fig: argument*) irrésistible.
compendium [kəm'pɛndɪəm] *n* (*summary*) abrégé *m*.
compensate ['kɔmpənseɪt] *vt* indemniser, dédommager ♦ *vi*: **to** ~ **for** compenser.
compensation [kɔmpən'seɪʃən] *n* compensation *f*; (*money*) dédommagement *m*, indemnité *f*.
compere ['kɔmpɛə*] *n* présentateur/trice, animateur/trice.
compete [kəm'piːt] *vi* (*take part*) concourir; (*vie*): **to** ~ **(with)** rivaliser (avec), faire concurrence (à).
competence ['kɔmpɪtəns] *n* compétence *f*, aptitude *f*.
competent ['kɔmpɪtənt] *adj* compétent(e), capable.
competing [kəm'piːtɪŋ] *adj* (*ideas, theories*) opposé(e); (*companies*) concurrent(e).
competition [kɔmpɪ'tɪʃən] *n* compétition *f*, concours *m*; (*ECON*) concurrence *f*; **in** ~ **with** en concurrence avec.
competitive [kəm'pɛtɪtɪv] *adj* (*ECON*) concurrentiel(le); (*sports*) de compétition.
competitive examination *n* concours *m*.
competitor [kəm'pɛtɪtə*] *n* concurrent/e.
compile [kəm'paɪl] *vt* compiler.
complacency [kəm'pleɪsnsɪ] *n* contentement *m* de soi, autosatisfaction *f*.
complacent [kəm'pleɪsnt] *adj* (trop) content(e) de soi.
complain [kəm'pleɪn] *vi*: **to** ~ **(about)** se plaindre (de); (*in shop etc*) réclamer (au sujet de).
►**complain of** *vt fus* (*MED*) se plaindre de.
complaint [kəm'pleɪnt] *n* plainte *f*; (*in shop etc*) réclamation *f*, (*MED*) affection *f*.
complement ['kɔmplɪmənt] *n* complément *m*; (*esp of ship's crew etc*) effectif complet ♦ *vt* compléter.
complementary [kɔmplɪ'mɛntərɪ] *adj* complémentaire.
complete [kəm'pliːt] *adj* complet(ète) ♦ *vt* achever, parachever; (*a form*) remplir.
completely [kəm'pliːtlɪ] *adv* complètement.
completion [kəm'pliːʃən] *n* achèvement *m*; **to be nearing** ~ être presque terminé; **on** ~ **of contract** dès signature du contrat.
complex ['kɔmplɛks] *adj* complexe ♦ *n* (*PSYCH, buildings etc*) complexe *m*.
complexion [kəm'plɛkʃən] *n* (*of face*) teint *m*; (*of event etc*) aspect *m*, caractère *m*.
complexity [kəm'plɛksɪtɪ] *n* complexité *f*.
compliance [kəm'plaɪəns] *n* (*submission*) docilité *f*; (*agreement*): ~ **with** le fait de se conformer à; **in** ~ **with** en conformité avec, conformément à.
compliant [kəm'plaɪənt] *adj* docile, très accommodant(e).
complicate ['kɔmplɪkeɪt] *vt* compliquer.
complicated ['kɔmplɪkeɪtɪd] *adj* compliqué(e).
complication [kɔmplɪ'keɪʃən] *n* complication *f*.
complicity [kəm'plɪsɪtɪ] *n* complicité *f*.
compliment *n* ['kɔmplɪmənt] compliment *m* ♦ *vt* ['kɔmplɪmɛnt] complimenter; ~**s** *npl* compliments *mpl*, hommages *mpl*; vœux *mpl*; **to pay sb a** ~ faire *or* adresser un compliment à qn; **to** ~ **sb (on sth/on doing sth)** féliciter qn (pour qch/de faire qch).
complimentary [kɔmplɪ'mɛntərɪ] *adj* flatteur(euse); (*free*) à titre gracieux.
complimentary ticket *n* billet *m* de faveur.
compliments slip *n* fiche *f* de transmission.
comply [kəm'plaɪ] *vi*: **to** ~ **with** se soumettre à, se conformer à.
component [kəm'pəunənt] *adj* composant(e), constituant(e) ♦ *n* composant *m*, élément *m*.
compose [kəm'pəuz] *vt* composer; **to** ~ **o.s.** se calmer, se maîtriser; prendre une contenance.
composed [kəm'pəuzd] *adj* calme, posé(e).

composer [kəm'pəuzə*] *n* (*MUS*) compositeur *m*.
composite ['kɔmpəzɪt] *adj* composite; (*BOT, MATH*) composé(e).
composition [kɔmpə'zɪʃən] *n* composition *f*.
compost ['kɔmpɔst] *n* compost *m*.
composure [kəm'pəuʒə*] *n* calme *m*, maîtrise *f* de soi.
compound ['kɔmpaund] *n* (*CHEM, LING*) composé *m*; (*enclosure*) enclos *m*, enceinte *f* ♦ *adj* composé(e) ♦ *vt* [kəm'paund] (*fig: problem etc*) aggraver.
compound fracture *n* fracture compliquée.
compound interest *n* intérêt composé.
comprehend [kɔmprɪ'hɛnd] *vt* comprendre.
comprehension [kɔmprɪ'hɛnʃən] *n* compréhension *f*.
comprehensive [kɔmprɪ'hɛnsɪv] *adj* (très) complet(ète).
comprehensive insurance policy *n* assurance *f* tous risques.
comprehensive (school) *n* (*BRIT*) *école secondaire non sélective avec libre circulation d'une section à l'autre*, ≈ CES *m*.
compress *vt* [kəm'prɛs] comprimer ♦ *n* ['kɔmprɛs] (*MED*) compresse *f*.
compression [kəm'prɛʃən] *n* compression *f*.
comprise [kəm'praɪz] *vt* (*also*: **be ~d of**) comprendre.
compromise ['kɔmprəmaɪz] *n* compromis *m* ♦ *vt* compromettre ♦ *vi* transiger, accepter un compromis ♦ *cpd* (*decision, solution*) de compromis.
compulsion [kəm'pʌlʃən] *n* contrainte *f*, force *f*; **under ~** sous la contrainte.
compulsive [kəm'pʌlsɪv] *adj* (*PSYCH*) compulsif(ive); **he's a ~ smoker** c'est un fumeur invétéré.
compulsory [kəm'pʌlsərɪ] *adj* obligatoire.
compulsory purchase *n* expropriation *f*.
compunction [kəm'pʌŋkʃən] *n* scrupule *m*; **to have no ~ about doing sth** n'avoir aucun scrupule à faire qch.
computer [kəm'pju:tə*] *n* ordinateur *m*; (*mechanical*) calculatrice *f*.
computer game *n* jeu *m* vidéo.
computerize [kəm'pju:təraɪz] *vt* traiter *or* automatiser par ordinateur.
computer language *n* langage *m* machine *or* informatique.
computer literate *adj* initié(e) à l'informatique.
computer peripheral *n* périphérique *m*.
computer program *n* programme *m* informatique.
computer programmer *n* programmeur/euse.
computer programming *n* programmation *f*.
computer science *n* informatique *f*.
computer scientist *n* informaticien/ne.
computing [kəm'pju:tɪŋ] *n* informatique *f*.
comrade ['kɔmrɪd] *n* camarade *m/f*.
comradeship ['kɔmrɪdʃɪp] *n* camaraderie *f*.
comsat ['kɔmsæt] *n abbr* = **communications satellite**.
con [kɔn] *vt* duper; escroquer ♦ *n* escroquerie *f*; **to ~ sb into doing sth** tromper qn pour lui faire faire qch.
concave ['kɔn'keɪv] *adj* concave.
conceal [kən'si:l] *vt* cacher, dissimuler.
concede [kən'si:d] *vt* concéder ♦ *vi* céder.
conceit [kən'si:t] *n* vanité *f*, suffisance *f*, prétention *f*.
conceited [kən'si:tɪd] *adj* vaniteux(euse), suffisant(e).
conceivable [kən'si:vəbl] *adj* concevable, imaginable; **it is ~ that** il est concevable que.
conceivably [kən'si:vəblɪ] *adv*: **he may ~ be right** il n'est pas impossible qu'il ait raison.
conceive [kən'si:v] *vt* concevoir ♦ *vi*: **to ~ of sth/of doing sth** imaginer qch/de faire qch.
concentrate ['kɔnsəntreɪt] *vi* se concentrer ♦ *vt* concentrer.
concentration [kɔnsən'treɪʃən] *n* concentration *f*.
concentration camp *n* camp *m* de concentration.
concentric [kɔn'sɛntrɪk] *adj* concentrique.
concept ['kɔnsɛpt] *n* concept *m*.
conception [kən'sɛpʃən] *n* conception *f*; (*idea*) idée *f*.
concern [kən'sə:n] *n* affaire *f*; (*COMM*) entreprise *f*, firme *f*; (*anxiety*) inquiétude *f*, souci *m* ♦ *vt* concerner; **to be ~ed (about)** s'inquiéter (de), être inquiet(ète) (au sujet de); **"to whom it may ~"** "à qui de droit"; **as far as I am ~ed** en ce qui me concerne; **to be ~ed with** (*person: involved with*) s'occuper de; **the department ~ed** (*under discussion*) le service en question; (*involved*) le service concerné.
concerning [kən'sə:nɪŋ] *prep* en ce qui concerne, à propos de.
concert ['kɔnsət] *n* concert *m*; **in ~** à l'unisson, en chœur; ensemble.
concerted [kən'sə:tɪd] *adj* concerté(e).
concert hall *n* salle *f* de concert.
concertina [kɔnsə'ti:nə] *n* concertina *m* ♦ *vi* se télescoper, se caramboler.
concerto [kən'tʃə:təu] *n* concerto *m*.
concession [kən'sɛʃən] *n* concession *f*.
concessionaire [kənsɛʃə'nɛə*] *n* concessionnaire *m/f*.
concessionary [kən'sɛʃənrɪ] *adj* (*ticket, fare*) à tarif réduit.
conciliation [kənsɪlɪ'eɪʃən] *n* conciliation *f*, apaisement *m*.
conciliatory [kən'sɪlɪətrɪ] *adj* conciliateur(trice); conciliant(e).
concise [kən'saɪs] *adj* concis(e).
conclave ['kɔnkleɪv] *n* assemblée secrète; (*REL*) conclave *m*.
conclude [kən'klu:d] *vt* conclure ♦ *vi* (*speaker*)

conclure; (*events*): **to ~ (with)** se terminer (par).
concluding [kən'klu:dɪŋ] *adj* (*remarks etc*) final(e).
conclusion [kən'klu:ʒən] *n* conclusion *f*; **to come to the ~ that** (en) conclure que.
conclusive [kən'klu:sɪv] *adj* concluant(e), définitif(ive).
concoct [kən'kɔkt] *vt* confectionner, composer.
concoction [kən'kɔkʃən] *n* (*food, drink*) mélange *m*.
concord ['kɔŋkɔ:d] *n* (*harmony*) harmonie *f*; (*treaty*) accord *m*.
concourse ['kɔŋkɔ:s] *n* (*hall*) hall *m*, salle *f* des pas perdus; (*crowd*) affluence *f*; multitude *f*.
concrete ['kɔŋkri:t] *n* béton *m* ♦ *adj* concret(ète); (*CONSTR*) en béton.
concrete mixer *n* bétonnière *f*.
concur [kən'kə:*] *vi* être d'accord.
concurrently [kən'kʌrntlɪ] *adv* simultanément.
concussion [kən'kʌʃən] *n* (*MED*) commotion (cérébrale).
condemn [kən'dɛm] *vt* condamner.
condemnation [kɔndɛm'neɪʃən] *n* condamnation *f*.
condensation [kɔndɛn'seɪʃən] *n* condensation *f*.
condense [kən'dɛns] *vi* se condenser ♦ *vt* condenser.
condensed milk [kən'dɛnst-] *n* lait concentré (sucré).
condescend [kɔndɪ'sɛnd] *vi* condescendre, s'abaisser; **to ~ to do sth** daigner faire qch.
condescending [kɔndɪ'sɛndɪŋ] *adj* condescendant(e).
condition [kən'dɪʃən] *n* condition *f*; (*disease*) maladie *f* ♦ *vt* déterminer, conditionner; **in good/poor ~** en bon/mauvais état; **a heart ~** une maladie cardiaque; **weather ~s** conditions *fpl* météorologiques; **on ~ that** à condition que *+ sub*, à condition de.
conditional [kən'dɪʃənl] *adj* conditionnel(le); **to be ~ upon** dépendre de.
conditioner [kən'dɪʃənə*] *n* (*for hair*) baume démêlant.
condo ['kɔndəu] *n abbr* (*US col*) = **condominium**.
condolences [kən'dəulənsɪz] *npl* condoléances *fpl*.
condom ['kɔndəm] *n* préservatif *m*.
condominium [kɔndə'mɪnɪəm] *n* (*US*: *building*) immeuble *m* (en copropriété); (*: rooms*) appartement *m* (dans un immeuble en copropriété).
condone [kən'dəun] *vt* fermer les yeux sur, approuver (tacitement).
conducive [kən'dju:sɪv] *adj*: **~ to** favorable à, qui contribue à.
conduct *n* ['kɔndʌkt] conduite *f* ♦ *vt* [kən'dʌkt] conduire; (*manage*) mener, diriger; (*MUS*) diriger; **to ~ o.s.** se conduire, se comporter.
conducted tour [kən'dʌktɪd-] *n* voyage organisé; (*of building*) visite guidée.
conductor [kən'dʌktə*] *n* (*of orchestra*) chef *m* d'orchestre; (*on bus*) receveur *m*; (*US*: *on train*) chef *m* de train; (*ELEC*) conducteur *m*.
conductress [kən'dʌktrɪs] *n* (*on bus*) receveuse *f*.
conduit ['kɔndɪt] *n* conduit *m*, tuyau *m*; tube *m*.
cone [kəun] *n* cône *m*; (*for ice-cream*) cornet *m*; (*BOT*) pomme *f* de pin, cône.
confectioner [kən'fɛkʃənə*] *n* (*of cakes*) pâtissier/ière; (*of sweets*) confiseur/euse; **~'s (shop)** confiserie(-pâtisserie) *f*.
confectionery [kən'fɛkʃənrɪ] *n* (*cakes*) pâtisserie *f*; (*sweets*) confiserie *f*.
confederate [kən'fɛdrɪt] *adj* confédéré(e) ♦ *n* (*pej*) acolyte *m*; (*US HISTORY*) confédéré/e.
confederation [kənfɛdə'reɪʃən] *n* confédération *f*.
confer [kən'fə:*] *vt*: **to ~ sth on** conférer qch à ♦ *vi* conférer, s'entretenir; **to ~ (with sb about sth)** s'entretenir (de qch avec qn).
conference ['kɔnfərns] *n* conférence *f*; **to be in ~** être en réunion *or* en conférence.
conference room *n* salle *f* de conférence.
confess [kən'fɛs] *vt* confesser, avouer ♦ *vi* se confesser.
confession [kən'fɛʃən] *n* confession *f*.
confessional [kən'fɛʃənl] *n* confessional *m*.
confessor [kən'fɛsə*] *n* confesseur *m*.
confetti [kən'fɛtɪ] *n* confettis *mpl*.
confide [kən'faɪd] *vi*: **to ~ in** s'ouvrir à, se confier à.
confidence ['kɔnfɪdns] *n* confiance *f*; (*also*: **self-~**) assurance *f*, confiance en soi; (*secret*) confidence *f*; **to have (every) ~ that** être certain que; **motion of no ~** motion *f* de censure; **to tell sb sth in strict ~** dire qch à qn en toute confidence.
confidence trick *n* escroquerie *f*.
confident ['kɔnfɪdənt] *adj* sûr(e), assuré(e).
confidential [kɔnfɪ'dɛnʃəl] *adj* confidentiel(le); (*secretary*) particulier(ère).
confidentiality ['kɔnfɪdɛnʃɪ'ælɪtɪ] *n* confidentialité *f*.
configuration [kən'fɪgju'reɪʃən] *n* (*also COMPUT*) configuration *f*.
confine [kən'faɪn] *vt* limiter, borner; (*shut up*) confiner, enfermer; **to ~ o.s. to doing sth/to sth** se contenter de faire qch/se limiter à qch.
confined [kən'faɪnd] *adj* (*space*) restreint(e), réduit(e).
confinement [kən'faɪnmənt] *n* emprisonnement *m*, détention *f*; (*MIL*) consigne *f* (au quartier); (*MED*) accouchement *m*.
confines ['kɔnfaɪnz] *npl* confins *mpl*, bornes *fpl*.
confirm [kən'fə:m] *vt* (*report, REL*) confirmer; (*appointment*) ratifier.
confirmation [kɔnfə'meɪʃən] *n* confirmation *f*; ratification *f*.

confirmed [kən'fə:md] *adj* invétéré(e), incorrigible.
confiscate ['kɔnfɪskeɪt] *vt* confisquer.
confiscation [kɔnfɪs'keɪʃən] *n* confiscation *f.*
conflagration [kɔnflə'greɪʃən] *n* incendie *m*; (*fig*) conflagration *f.*
conflict *n* ['kɔnflɪkt] conflit *m*, lutte *f* ♦ *vi* [kən'flɪkt] être *or* entrer en conflit; (*opinions*) s'opposer, se heurter.
conflicting [kən'flɪktɪŋ] *adj* contradictoire.
conform [kən'fɔ:m] *vi*: **to ~ (to)** se conformer (à).
conformist [kən'fɔ:mɪst] *n* (*gen, REL*) conformiste *m/f.*
confound [kən'faund] *vt* confondre; (*amaze*) rendre perplexe.
confounded [kən'faundɪd] *adj* maudit(e), sacré(e).
confront [kən'frʌnt] *vt* confronter, mettre en présence; (*enemy, danger*) affronter, faire face à.
confrontation [kɔnfrən'teɪʃən] *n* confrontation *f.*
confrontational [kɔnfrən'teɪʃənl] *adj* conflictuel(le).
confuse [kən'fju:z] *vt* embrouiller; (*one thing with another*) confondre.
confused [kən'fju:zd] *adj* (*person*) dérouté(e), désorienté(e); (*situation*) confus, embrouillé(e).
confusing [kən'fju:zɪŋ] *adj* peu clair(e), déroutant(e).
confusion [kən'fju:ʒən] *n* confusion *f.*
congeal [kən'dʒi:l] *vi* (*oil*) se figer; (*blood*) se coaguler.
congenial [kən'dʒi:nɪəl] *adj* sympathique, agréable.
congenital [kən'dʒenɪtl] *adj* congénital(e).
conger eel ['kɔŋgər-] *n* congre *m*, anguille *f* de roche.
congested [kən'dʒestɪd] *adj* (*MED*) congestionné(e); (*fig*) surpeuplé(e); congestionné; bloqué(e); (*telephone lines*) encombré(e).
congestion [kən'dʒestʃən] *n* congestion *f*; (*fig*) encombrement *m.*
congestion charge *n* péage *m* urbain.
conglomerate [kən'glɔmərɪt] *n* (*COMM*) conglomérat *m.*
conglomeration [kənglɔmə'reɪʃən] *n* groupement *m*; agglomération *f.*
Congo ['kɔŋgəu] *n* (république *f* du) Congo.
congratulate [kən'grætjuleɪt] *vt*: **to ~ sb (on)** féliciter qn (de).
congratulations [kəngrætju'leɪʃənz] *npl*: **~ (on)** félicitations *fpl* (pour) ♦ *excl*: **~!** (toutes mes) félicitations!
congregate ['kɔŋgrɪgeɪt] *vi* se rassembler, se réunir.
congregation [kɔŋgrɪ'geɪʃən] *n* assemblée *f* (des fidèles).
congress ['kɔŋgres] *n* congrès *m*; (*US POL*): **C~** Congrès *m*; *voir encadré.*

> **CONGRESS**
>
> *Le* **Congress** *est le parlement des États-Unis. Il comprend la "House of Representatives" et le "Senate". Représentants et sénateurs sont élus au suffrage universel direct. Le Congrès se réunit au "Capitol", à Washington.*

congressman ['kɔŋgresmən], **congresswoman** ['kɔŋgreswumən] *n* (*US*) membre *m* du Congrès.
conical ['kɔnɪkl] *adj* (de forme) conique.
conifer ['kɔnɪfə*] *n* conifère *m.*
coniferous [kə'nɪfərəs] *adj* de conifères.
conjecture [kən'dʒektʃə*] *n* conjecture *f* ♦ *vt, vi* conjecturer.
conjugal ['kɔndʒugl] *adj* conjugal(e).
conjugate ['kɔndʒugeɪt] *vt* conjuguer.
conjugation [kɔndʒə'geɪʃən] *n* conjugaison *f.*
conjunction [kən'dʒʌŋkʃən] *n* conjonction *f*; **in ~ with** (conjointement) avec.
conjunctivitis [kəndʒʌŋktɪ'vaɪtɪs] *n* conjonctivite *f.*
conjure ['kʌndʒə*] *vt* faire apparaître (par la prestidigitation); [kən'dʒuə*] conjurer, supplier ♦ *vi* faire des tours de passe-passe.
►**conjure up** *vt* (*ghost, spirit*) faire apparaître; (*memories*) évoquer.
conjurer ['kʌndʒərə*] *n* prestidigitateur *m*, illusionniste *m/f.*
conker ['kɔŋkə*] *n* (*BRIT*) marron *m* (d'Inde).
conk out [kɔŋk-] *vi* (*col*) tomber *or* rester en panne.
conman ['kɔnmæn] *n* escroc *m.*
Conn. *abbr* (*US*) = *Connecticut.*
connect [kə'nekt] *vt* joindre, relier; (*ELEC*) connecter; (*fig*) établir un rapport entre, faire un rapprochement entre ♦ *vi* (*train*): **to ~ with** assurer la correspondance avec; **to be ~ed with** avoir un rapport avec; (*have dealings with*) avoir des rapports avec, être en relation avec; **I am trying to ~ you** (*TEL*) j'essaie d'obtenir votre communication.
connection [kə'nekʃən] *n* relation *f*, lien *m*; (*ELEC*) connexion *f*; (*TEL*) communication *f*; (*train etc*) correspondance *f*; **in ~ with** à propos de; **what is the ~ between them?** quel est le lien entre eux?; **business ~s** relations d'affaires; **to miss/get one's ~** (*train etc*) rater/avoir sa correspondance.
connexion [kə'nekʃən] *n* (*BRIT*) = **connection.**
conning tower ['kɔnɪŋ-] *n* kiosque *m* (*de sous-marin*).
connive [kə'naɪv] *vi*: **to ~ at** se faire le complice de.
connoisseur [kɔnɪ'sə:*] *n* connaisseur *m.*
connotation [kɔnə'teɪʃən] *n* connotation *f*, implication *f.*
connubial [kə'nju:bɪəl] *adj* conjugal(e).
conquer ['kɔŋkə*] *vt* conquérir; (*feelings*) vaincre, surmonter.

conqueror ['kɔŋkərə*] *n* conquérant *m*, vainqueur *m*.
conquest ['kɔŋkwɛst] *n* conquête *f*.
cons [kɔnz] *npl see* **pro, convenience**.
conscience ['kɔnʃəns] *n* conscience *f*; **in all ~** en conscience.
conscientious [kɔnʃɪ'ɛnʃəs] *adj* consciencieux(euse); (*scruple, objection*) de conscience.
conscientious objector *n* objecteur *m* de conscience.
conscious ['kɔnʃəs] *adj* conscient(e); (*deliberate: insult, error*) délibéré(e); **to become ~ of sth/that** prendre conscience de qch/que.
consciousness ['kɔnʃəsnɪs] *n* conscience *f*; (*MED*) connaissance *f*; **to lose/regain ~** perdre/reprendre connaissance.
conscript ['kɔnskrɪpt] *n* conscrit *m*.
conscription [kən'skrɪpʃən] *n* conscription *f*.
consecrate ['kɔnsɪkreɪt] *vt* consacrer.
consecutive [kən'sɛkjutɪv] *adj* consécutif(ive); **on three ~ occasions** trois fois de suite.
consensus [kən'sɛnsəs] *n* consensus *m*; **the ~ (of opinion)** le consensus (d'opinion).
consent [kən'sɛnt] *n* consentement *m* ♦ *vi*: **to ~ (to)** consentir (à); **age of ~** âge nubile (légal); **by common ~** d'un commun accord.
consenting adults [kən'sɛntɪŋ-] *npl* personnes consentantes.
consequence ['kɔnsɪkwəns] *n* suites *fpl*, conséquence *f*; importance *f*; **in ~** en conséquence, par conséquent.
consequently ['kɔnsɪkwəntlɪ] *adv* par conséquent, donc.
conservation [kɔnsə'veɪʃən] *n* préservation *f*, protection *f*; (*also*: **nature ~**) défense *f* de l'environnement; **energy ~** économies *fpl* d'énergie.
conservationist [kɔnsə'veɪʃnɪst] *n* protecteur/trice de la nature.
conservative [kən'səːvətɪv] *adj* conservateur(trice); (*cautious*) prudent(e); **C~** *adj*, *n* (*BRIT POL*) conservateur(trice); **the C~ Party** le parti conservateur.
conservatory [kən'səːvətrɪ] *n* (*greenhouse*) serre *f*.
conserve [kən'səːv] *vt* conserver, préserver; (*supplies, energy*) économiser ♦ *n* confiture *f*, conserve *f* (de fruits).
consider [kən'sɪdə*] *vt* considérer, réfléchir à; (*take into account*) penser à, prendre en considération; (*regard, judge*) considérer, estimer; **to ~ doing sth** envisager de faire qch; **~ yourself lucky** estimez-vous heureux; **all things ~ed** (toute) réflexion faite.
considerable [kən'sɪdərəbl] *adj* considérable.
considerably [kən'sɪdərəblɪ] *adv* considérablement.
considerate [kən'sɪdərɪt] *adj* prévenant(e), plein(e) d'égards.
consideration [kənsɪdə'reɪʃən] *n* considération *f*; (*reward*) rétribution *f*, rémunération *f*; **out of ~ for** par égard pour; **under ~** à l'étude; **my first ~ is my family** ma famille passe avant tout le reste.
considered [kən'sɪdəd] *adj*: **it is my ~ opinion that ...** après avoir mûrement réfléchi, je pense que ....
considering [kən'sɪdərɪŋ] *prep*: **~ (that)** étant donné (que).
consign [kən'saɪn] *vt* expédier, livrer.
consignee [kɔnsaɪ'niː] *n* destinataire *m/f*.
consignment [kən'saɪnmənt] *n* arrivage *m*, envoi *m*.
consignment note *n* (*COMM*) bordereau *m* d'expédition.
consignor [kən'saɪnə*] *n* expéditeur/trice.
consist [kən'sɪst] *vi*: **to ~ of** consister en, se composer de.
consistency [kən'sɪstənsɪ] *n* consistance *f*; (*fig*) cohérence *f*.
consistent [kən'sɪstənt] *adj* logique, cohérent(e); **~ with** compatible avec, en accord avec.
consolation [kɔnsə'leɪʃən] *n* consolation *f*.
console *vt* [kən'səul] consoler ♦ *n* ['kɔnsəul] console *f*.
consolidate [kən'sɔlɪdeɪt] *vt* consolider.
consols ['kɔnsɔlz] *npl* (*BRIT STOCK EXCHANGE*) rente *f* d'État.
consommé [kən'sɔmeɪ] *n* consommé *m*.
consonant ['kɔnsənənt] *n* consonne *f*.
consort *n* ['kɔnsɔːt] époux/épouse; **prince ~** prince *m* consort ♦ *vi* [kən'sɔːt] (*often pej*): **to ~ with sb** frayer avec qn.
consortium [kən'sɔːtɪəm] *n* consortium *m*, comptoir *m*.
conspicuous [kən'spɪkjuəs] *adj* voyant(e), qui attire la vue *or* l'attention; **to make o.s. ~** se faire remarquer.
conspiracy [kən'spɪrəsɪ] *n* conspiration *f*, complot *m*.
conspiratorial [kən'spɪrə'tɔːrɪəl] *adj* (*behaviour*) de conspirateur; (*glance*) conspirateur(trice).
conspire [kən'spaɪə*] *vi* (*people*) conspirer, comploter.
constable ['kʌnstəbl] *n* (*BRIT*) ≈ agent *m* de police, gendarme *m*.
constabulary [kən'stæbjulərɪ] *n* ≈ police *f*, gendarmerie *f*.
constant ['kɔnstənt] *adj* constant(e); incessant(e).
constantly ['kɔnstəntlɪ] *adv* constamment, sans cesse.
constellation [kɔnstə'leɪʃən] *n* constellation *f*.
consternation [kɔnstə'neɪʃən] *n* consternation *f*.
constipated ['kɔnstɪpeɪtɪd] *adj* constipé(e).
constipation [kɔnstɪ'peɪʃən] *n* constipation *f*.
constituency [kən'stɪtjuənsɪ] *n* circonscription électorale; (*people*) électorat *m*; *voir encadré*.

CONSTITUENCY

Une **constituency** *est à la fois une région qui élit un député au parlement et l'ensemble des électeurs dans cette région. En Grande-Bretagne, les députés font régulièrement des "permanences" dans leur circonscription électorale lors desquelles les électeurs peuvent venir les voir pour parler de leurs problèmes de logement etc.*

constituency party *n* section locale (d'un parti).
constituent [kən'stɪtjuənt] *n* électeur/trice; (*part*) élément constitutif, composant *m*.
constitute ['kɔnstɪtju:t] *vt* constituer.
constitution [kɔnstɪ'tju:ʃən] *n* constitution *f*.
constitutional [kɔnstɪ'tju:ʃənl] *adj* constitutionnel(le).
constitutional monarchy *n* monarchie constitutionnelle.
constrain [kən'streɪn] *vt* contraindre, forcer.
constrained [kən'streɪnd] *adj* contraint(e), gêné(e).
constraint [kən'streɪnt] *n* contrainte *f*; (*embarrassment*) gêne *f*.
constrict [kən'strɪkt] *vt* rétrécir, resserrer; gêner, limiter.
construct [kən'strʌkt] *vt* construire.
construction [kən'strʌkʃən] *n* construction *f*; (*fig: interpretation*) interprétation *f*; **under ~** (*building etc*) en construction.
construction industry *n* (industrie *f* du) bâtiment.
constructive [kən'strʌktɪv] *adj* constructif(ive).
construe [kən'stru:] *vt* analyser, expliquer.
consul ['kɔnsl] *n* consul *m*.
consulate ['kɔnsjulɪt] *n* consulat *m*.
consult [kən'sʌlt] *vt* consulter.
consultancy [kən'sʌltənsɪ] *n* service *m* de conseils.
consultancy fee *n* honoraires *mpl* d'expert.
consultant [kən'sʌltənt] *n* (*MED*) médecin consultant; (*other specialist*) consultant *m*, (expert-)conseil *m* ♦ *cpd*: **~ engineer** *n* ingénieur-conseil *m*; **~ paediatrician** *n* pédiatre *m*; **legal/management ~** conseiller *m* juridique/en gestion.
consultation [kɔnsəl'teɪʃən] *n* consultation *f*; **in ~ with** en consultation avec.
consultative [kən'sʌltətɪv] *adj* consultatif(ive).
consulting room [kən'sʌltɪŋ-] *n* (*BRIT*) cabinet *m* de consultation.
consume [kən'sju:m] *vt* consommer.
consumer [kən'sju:mə*] *n* consommateur/trice; (*of electricity, gas etc*) usager *m*.
consumer credit *n* crédit *m* aux consommateurs.
consumer durables *npl* biens *mpl* de consommation durables.
consumer goods *npl* biens *mpl* de consommation.
consumerism [kən'sju:mərizəm] *n* (*consumer protection*) défense *f* du consommateur; (*ECON*) consumérisme *m*.
consumer society *n* société *f* de consommation.
consumer watchdog *n* organisme *m* pour la défense des consommateurs.
consummate ['kɔnsʌmeɪt] *vt* consommer.
consumption [kən'sʌmpʃən] *n* consommation *f*; **not fit for human ~** non comestible.
cont. *abbr* = **continued**.
contact ['kɔntækt] *n* contact *m*; (*person*) connaissance *f*, relation *f* ♦ *vt* se mettre en contact *or* en rapport avec; **to be in ~ with sb/sth** être en contact avec qn/qch; **business ~s** relations *fpl* d'affaires, contacts *mpl*.
contact lenses *npl* verres *mpl* de contact.
contagious [kən'teɪdʒəs] *adj* contagieux(euse).
contain [kən'teɪn] *vt* contenir; **to ~ o.s.** se contenir, se maîtriser.
container [kən'teɪnə*] *n* récipient *m*; (*for shipping etc*) conteneur *m*.
containerize [kən'teɪnəraɪz] *vt* conteneuriser.
container ship *n* porte-conteneurs *m inv*.
contaminate [kən'tæmɪneɪt] *vt* contaminer.
contamination [kəntæmɪ'neɪʃən] *n* contamination *f*.
cont'd *abbr* = **continued**.
contemplate ['kɔntəmpleɪt] *vt* contempler; (*consider*) envisager.
contemplation [kɔntəm'pleɪʃən] *n* contemplation *f*.
contemporary [kən'tɛmpərərɪ] *adj* contemporain(e); (*design, wallpaper*) moderne ♦ *n* contemporain/e.
contempt [kən'tɛmpt] *n* mépris *m*, dédain *m*; **~ of court** (*LAW*) outrage *m* à l'autorité de la justice.
contemptible [kən'tɛmptəbl] *adj* méprisable, vil(e).
contemptuous [kən'tɛmptjuəs] *adj* dédaigneux(euse), méprisant(e).
contend [kən'tɛnd] *vt*: **to ~ that** soutenir *or* prétendre que ♦ *vi*: **to ~ with** (*compete*) lutter avec; **to have to ~ with** (*be faced with*) avoir affaire à, être aux prises avec.
contender [kən'tɛndə*] *n* prétendant/e; candidat/e.
content [kən'tɛnt] *adj* content(e), satisfait(e) ♦ *vt* contenter, satisfaire ♦ *n* ['kɔntɛnt] contenu *m*; teneur *f*; **~s** *npl* contenu *m*; **(table of) ~s** table *f* des matières; **to be ~ with** se contenter de; **to ~ o.s. with sth/with doing sth** se contenter de qch/de faire qch.
contented [kən'tɛntɪd] *adj* content(e), satisfait(e).
contentedly [kən'tɛntɪdlɪ] *adv* avec un sentiment de (profonde) satisfaction.
contention [kən'tɛnʃən] *n* dispute *f*, contestation *f*; (*argument*) assertion *f*, affirmation *f*;

bone of ~ sujet *m* de discorde.
contentious [kən'tɛnʃəs] *adj* querelleur(euse); litigieux(euse).
contentment [kən'tɛntmənt] *n* contentement *m*, satisfaction *f*.
contest *n* ['kɔntɛst] combat *m*, lutte *f*; (*competition*) concours *m* ♦ *vt* [kən'tɛst] contester, discuter; (*compete for*) disputer; (*LAW*) attaquer.
contestant [kən'tɛstənt] *n* concurrent/e; (*in fight*) adversaire *m/f*.
context ['kɔntɛkst] *n* contexte *m*; **in/out of ~** dans le/hors contexte.
continent ['kɔntɪnənt] *n* continent *m*; **the C~** (*BRIT*) l'Europe continentale; **on the C~** en Europe (continentale).
continental [kɔntɪ'nɛntl] *adj* continental(e) ♦ *n* (*BRIT*) Européen/ne (continental(e)).
continental breakfast *n* café (*or* thé) complet.
continental quilt *n* (*BRIT*) couette *f*.
contingency [kən'tɪndʒənsɪ] *n* éventualité *f*, événement imprévu.
contingency plan *n* plan *m* d'urgence.
contingent [kən'tɪndʒənt] *adj* contingent(e) ♦ *n* contingent *m*; **to be ~ upon** dépendre de.
continual [kən'tɪnjuəl] *adj* continuel(le).
continually [kən'tɪnjuəlɪ] *adv* continuellement, sans cesse.
continuation [kəntɪnju'eɪʃən] *n* continuation *f*; (*after interruption*) reprise *f*; (*of story*) suite *f*.
continue [kən'tɪnju:] *vi* continuer ♦ *vt* continuer; (*start again*) reprendre; **to be ~d** (*story*) à suivre; **~d on page 10** suite page 10.
continuing education [kən'tɪnjuɪŋ-] *n* formation permanente *or* continue.
continuity [kɔntɪ'nju:ɪtɪ] *n* continuité *f*; (*CINE*) script *m*.
continuity girl *n* (*CINE*) script-girl *f*.
continuous [kən'tɪnjuəs] *adj* continu(e), permanent(e); **~ performance** (*CINE*) séance permanente; **~ stationery** (*COMPUT*) papier *m* en continu.
continuously [kən'tɪnjuəslɪ] *adv* (*repeatedly*) continuellement; (*uninterruptedly*) sans interruption.
contort [kən'tɔ:t] *vt* tordre, crisper.
contortion [kən'tɔ:ʃən] *n* crispation *f*, torsion *f*; (*of acrobat*) contorsion *f*.
contortionist [kən'tɔ:ʃənɪst] *n* contorsionniste *m/f*.
contour ['kɔntuə*] *n* contour *m*, profil *m*; (*also*: **~ line**) courbe *f* de niveau.
contraband ['kɔntrəbænd] *n* contrebande *f* ♦ *adj* de contrebande.
contraception [kɔntrə'sɛpʃən] *n* contraception *f*.
contraceptive [kɔntrə'sɛptɪv] *adj* contraceptif(ive), anticonceptionnel(le) ♦ *n* contraceptif *m*.
contract *n* ['kɔntrækt] contrat *m* ♦ *cpd* ['kɔntrækt] (*price, date*) contractuel(le); (*work*) à forfait ♦ *vb* [kən'trækt] *vi* (*become smaller*) se contracter, se resserrer; (*COMM*): **to ~ to do sth** s'engager (par contrat) à faire qch ♦ *vt* contracter; **~ of employment/service** contrat de travail/de service.
►**contract in** *vi* s'engager (par contrat); (*BRIT ADMIN*) s'affilier au régime de retraite complémentaire.
►**contract out** *vi* se dégager; (*BRIT ADMIN*) opter pour la non-affiliation au régime de retraite complémentaire.
contraction [kən'trækʃən] *n* contraction *f*; (*LING*) forme contractée.
contractor [kən'træktə*] *n* entrepreneur *m*.
contractual [kən'træktʃuəl] *adj* contractuel(le).
contradict [kɔntrə'dɪkt] *vt* contredire; (*be contrary to*) démentir, être en contradiction avec.
contradiction [kɔntrə'dɪkʃən] *n* contradiction *f*; **to be in ~ with** contredire, être en contradiction avec.
contradictory [kɔntrə'dɪktərɪ] *adj* contradictoire.
contralto [kən'træltəu] *n* contralto *m*.
contraption [kən'træpʃən] *n* (*pej*) machin *m*, truc *m*.
contrary[1] ['kɔntrərɪ] *adj* contraire, opposé(e) ♦ *n* contraire *m*; **on the ~** au contraire; **unless you hear to the ~** sauf avis contraire; **~ to what we thought** contrairement à ce que nous pensions.
contrary[2] [kən'trɛərɪ] *adj* (*perverse*) contrariant(e), entêté(e).
contrast *n* ['kɔntrɑ:st] contraste *m* ♦ *vt* [kən'trɑ:st] mettre en contraste, contraster; **in ~ to** *or* **with** contrairement à, par opposition à.
contrasting [kən'trɑ:stɪŋ] *adj* opposé(e), contrasté(e).
contravene [kɔntrə'vi:n] *vt* enfreindre, violer, contrevenir à.
contravention [kɔntrə'vɛnʃən] *n*: **~ (of)** infraction *f* (à).
contribute [kən'trɪbju:t] *vi* contribuer ♦ *vt*: **to ~ £10/an article to** donner 10 livres/un article à; **to ~ to** (*gen*) contribuer à; (*newspaper*) collaborer à; (*discussion*) prendre part à.
contribution [kɔntrɪ'bju:ʃən] *n* contribution *f*.
contributor [kən'trɪbjutə*] *n* (*to newspaper*) collaborateur/trice.
contributory [kən'trɪbjutərɪ] *adj* (*cause*) annexe; **it was a ~ factor in ...** ce facteur a contribué à ....
contributory pension scheme *n* (*BRIT*) régime *m* de retraite salariale.
contrite ['kɔntraɪt] *adj* contrit(e).
contrivance [kən'traɪvəns] *n* (*scheme*) machination *f*, combinaison *f*; (*device*) appareil *m*, dispositif *m*.
contrive [kən'traɪv] *vt* combiner, inventer ♦ *vi*: **to ~ to do** s'arranger pour faire, trouver le moyen de faire.

control [kən'trəul] *vt* maîtriser; (*check*) contrôler ♦ *n* maîtrise *f*; **~s** *npl* commandes *fpl*; **to take ~ of** se rendre maître de; (*COMM*) acquérir une participation majoritaire dans; **to be in ~ of** être maître de, maîtriser; (*in charge of*) être responsable de; **to ~ o.s.** se contrôler; **everything is under ~** j'ai (*or* il a *etc*) la situation en main; **the car went out of ~** j'ai (*or* il a *etc*) perdu le contrôle du véhicule; **beyond our ~** indépendant(e) de notre volonté.
control key *n* (*COMPUT*) touche *f* de commande.
controller [kən'trəulə*] *n* contrôleur *m*.
controlling interest [kən'trəulɪŋ-] *n* (*COMM*) participation *f* majoritaire.
control panel *n* (*on aircraft, ship, TV etc*) tableau *m* de commandes.
control point *n* (poste *m* de) contrôle *m*.
control room *n* (*NAUT, MIL*) salle *f* des commandes; (*RADIO, TV*) régie *f*.
control tower *n* (*AVIAT*) tour *f* de contrôle.
control unit *n* (*COMPUT*) unité *f* de contrôle.
controversial [kɔntrə'vəːʃl] *adj* discutable, controversé(e).
controversy ['kɔntrəvəːsɪ] *n* controverse *f*, polémique *f*.
conurbation [kɔnə'beɪʃən] *n* conurbation *f*.
convalesce [kɔnvə'lɛs] *vi* relever de maladie, se remettre (d'une maladie).
convalescence [kɔnvə'lɛsns] *n* convalescence *f*.
convalescent [kɔnvə'lɛsnt] *adj*, *n* convalescent(e).
convector [kən'vɛktə*] *n* radiateur *m* à convection, appareil *m* de chauffage par convection.
convene [kən'viːn] *vt* convoquer, assembler ♦ *vi* se réunir, s'assembler.
convener [kən'viːnə*] *n* organisateur *m*.
convenience [kən'viːnɪəns] *n* commodité *f*; **at your ~** quand *or* comme cela vous convient; **at your earliest ~** (*COMM*) dans les meilleurs délais, le plus tôt possible; **all modern ~s**, (*BRIT*) **all mod cons** avec tout le confort moderne, tout confort.
convenience foods *npl* plats cuisinés.
convenient [kən'viːnɪənt] *adj* commode; **if it is ~ to you** si cela vous convient, si cela ne vous dérange pas.
conveniently [kən'viːnɪəntlɪ] *adv* (*happen*) à pic; (*situated*) commodément.
convent ['kɔnvənt] *n* couvent *m*.
convention [kən'vɛnʃən] *n* convention *f*.
conventional [kən'vɛnʃənl] *adj* conventionnel(le).
convent school *n* couvent *m*.
converge [kən'vəːdʒ] *vi* converger.
conversant [kən'vəːsnt] *adj*: **to be ~ with** s'y connaître en; être au courant de.
conversation [kɔnvə'seɪʃən] *n* conversation *f*.
conversational [kɔnvə'seɪʃənl] *adj* de la conversation; (*COMPUT*) conversationnel(le).
conversationalist [kɔnvə'seɪʃnəlɪst] *n* brillant(e) causeur/euse.
converse *n* ['kɔnvəːs] contraire *m*, inverse *m* ♦ *vi* [kən'vəːs]: **to ~ (with sb about sth)** s'entretenir (avec qn de qch).
conversely [kɔn'vəːslɪ] *adv* inversement, réciproquement.
conversion [kən'vəːʃən] *n* conversion *f*; (*BRIT*: *of house*) transformation *f*, aménagement *m*.
conversion table *n* table *f* de conversion.
convert *vt* [kən'vəːt] (*REL, COMM*) convertir; (*alter*) transformer, aménager; (*RUGBY*) transformer ♦ *n* ['kɔnvəːt] converti/e.
convertible [kən'vəːtəbl] *adj* convertible ♦ *n* (voiture *f*) décapotable *f*.
convex ['kɔn'vɛks] *adj* convexe.
convey [kən'veɪ] *vt* transporter; (*thanks*) transmettre; (*idea*) communiquer.
conveyance [kən'veɪəns] *n* (*of goods*) transport *m* de marchandises; (*vehicle*) moyen *m* de transport.
conveyancing [kən'veɪənsɪŋ] *n* (*LAW*) rédaction *f* des actes de cession de propriété.
conveyor belt [kən'veɪə*-] *n* convoyeur *m*, tapis roulant.
convict *vt* [kən'vɪkt] déclarer (*or* reconnaître) coupable ♦ *n* ['kɔnvɪkt] forçat *m*, convict *m*.
conviction [kən'vɪkʃən] *n* condamnation *f*; (*belief*) conviction *f*.
convince [kən'vɪns] *vt* convaincre, persuader; **to ~ sb (of sth/that)** persuader qn (de qch/que).
convincing [kən'vɪnsɪŋ] *adj* persuasif(ive), convaincant(e).
convincingly [kən'vɪnsɪŋlɪ] *adv* de façon convaincante.
convivial [kən'vɪvɪəl] *adj* joyeux(euse), plein(e) d'entrain.
convoluted ['kɔnvəluːtɪd] *adj* (*shape*) tarabiscoté(e); (*argument*) compliqué(e).
convoy ['kɔnvɔɪ] *n* convoi *m*.
convulse [kən'vʌls] *vt* ébranler; **to be ~d with laughter** se tordre de rire.
convulsion [kən'vʌlʃən] *n* convulsion *f*.
coo [kuː] *vi* roucouler.
cook [kuk] *vt* (faire) cuire ♦ *vi* cuire; (*person*) faire la cuisine ♦ *n* cuisinier/ière.
►**cook up** *vt* (*col*: *excuse, story*) inventer.
cookbook ['kukbuk] *n* livre *m* de cuisine.
cooker ['kukə*] *n* cuisinière *f*.
cookery ['kukərɪ] *n* cuisine *f*.
cookery book *n* (*BRIT*) = **cookbook**.
cookie ['kukɪ] *n* (*US*) biscuit *m*, petit gâteau sec.
cooking ['kukɪŋ] *n* cuisine *f* ♦ *cpd* (*apples, chocolate*) à cuire; (*utensils, salt*) de cuisine.
cookout ['kukaut] *n* (*US*) barbecue *m*.
cool [kuːl] *adj* frais(fraîche); (*not afraid*) calme; (*unfriendly*) froid(e); (*impertinent*) effronté(e) ♦ *vt*, *vi* rafraîchir, refroidir; **it's ~** (*weather*) il fait frais; **to keep sth ~** *or* **in a ~**

place garder *or* conserver qch au frais.
►**cool down** *vi* refroidir; (*fig: person, situation*) se calmer.
coolant ['kuːlənt] *n* liquide *m* de refroidissement.
cool box, (*US*) **cooler** ['kuːlə*] *n* boîte *f* isotherme.
cooling ['kuːlɪŋ] *adj* (*breeze*) rafraîchissant(e).
cooling tower *n* refroidisseur *m*.
coolly ['kuːlɪ] *adv* (*calmly*) calmement; (*audaciously*) sans se gêner; (*unenthusiastically*) froidement.
coolness ['kuːlnɪs] *n* fraîcheur *f*; sang-froid *m*, calme *m*; froideur *f*.
coop [kuːp] *n* poulailler *m* ♦ *vt*: **to ~ up** (*fig*) cloîtrer, enfermer.
co-op ['kəuɔp] *n abbr* (= *cooperative (society)*) coop *f*.
cooperate [kəu'ɔpəreɪt] *vi* coopérer, collaborer.
cooperation [kəuɔpə'reɪʃən] *n* coopération *f*, collaboration *f*.
cooperative [kəu'ɔpərətɪv] *adj* coopératif(ive) ♦ *n* coopérative *f*.
coopt [kəu'ɔpt] *vt*: **to ~ sb onto a committee** coopter qn pour faire partie d'un comité.
coordinate *vt* [kəu'ɔːdɪneɪt] coordonner ♦ *n* [kəu'ɔdɪnət] (*MATH*) coordonnée *f*; **~s** *npl* (*clothes*) ensemble *m*, coordonnés *mpl*.
coordination [kəuɔːdɪ'neɪʃən] *n* coordination *f*.
coot [kuːt] *n* foulque *f*.
co-ownership ['kəu'əunəʃɪp] *n* copropriété *f*.
cop [kɔp] *n* (*col*) flic *m*.
cope [kəup] *vi* s'en sortir, tenir le coup; **to ~ with** faire face à; (*take care of*) s'occuper de.
Copenhagen ['kəupn'heɪgən] *n* Copenhague.
copier ['kɔpɪə*] *n* (*also*: **photo~**) copieur *m*.
co-pilot ['kəu'paɪlət] *n* copilote *m*.
copious ['kəupɪəs] *adj* copieux(euse), abondant(e).
copper ['kɔpə*] *n* cuivre *m*; (*col*: *policeman*) flic *m*; **~s** *npl* petite monnaie.
coppice ['kɔpɪs], **copse** [kɔps] *n* taillis *m*.
copulate ['kɔpjuleɪt] *vi* copuler.
copy ['kɔpɪ] *n* copie *f*; (*book etc*) exemplaire *m*; (*material: for printing*) copie ♦ *vt* copier; (*imitate*) imiter; **rough ~** (*gen*) premier jet; (*SCOL*) brouillon *m*; **fair ~** version définitive; propre *m*; **to make good ~** (*PRESS*) faire un bon sujet d'article.
►**copy out** *vt* copier.
copycat ['kɔpɪkæt] *n* (*pej*) copieur/euse.
copyright ['kɔpɪraɪt] *n* droit *m* d'auteur, copyright *m*; **~ reserved** tous droits (de reproduction) réservés.
copy typist *n* dactylo *m/f*.
copywriter ['kɔpɪraɪtə*] *n* rédacteur/trice publicitaire.
coral ['kɔrəl] *n* corail *m*.
coral reef *n* récif *m* de corail.
Coral Sea *n*: **the ~** la mer de Corail.
cord [kɔːd] *n* corde *f*; (*fabric*) velours côtelé; whipcord *m*; corde *f*; (*ELEC*) cordon *m* (d'alimentation), fil *m* (électrique); **~s** *npl* (*trousers*) pantalon *m* de velours côtelé.
cordial ['kɔːdɪəl] *adj* cordial(e), chaleureux(euse) ♦ *n* sirop *m*; cordial *m*.
cordless ['kɔːdlɪs] *adj* sans fil.
cordon ['kɔːdn] *n* cordon *m*.
►**cordon off** *vt* (*area*) interdire l'accès à; (*crowd*) tenir à l'écart.
corduroy ['kɔːdərɔɪ] *n* velours côtelé.
CORE [kɔː*] *n abbr* (*US*) = *Congress of Racial Equality*.
core [kɔː*] *n* (*of fruit*) trognon *m*, cœur *m*; (*TECH*: *also of earth*) noyau *m*; (*of nuclear reactor, fig: of problem etc*) cœur ♦ *vt* enlever le trognon *or* le cœur de; **rotten to the ~** complètement pourri.
Corfu [kɔː'fuː] *n* Corfou.
coriander [kɔrɪ'ændə*] *n* coriandre *f*.
cork [kɔːk] *n* liège *m*; (*of bottle*) bouchon *m*.
corkage ['kɔːkɪdʒ] *n droit payé par le client qui apporte sa propre bouteille de vin*.
corked [kɔːkt], (*US*) **corky** ['kɔːkɪ] *adj* (*wine*) qui sent le bouchon.
corkscrew ['kɔːkskruː] *n* tire-bouchon *m*.
cormorant ['kɔːmərnt] *n* cormorant *m*.
Corn *abbr* (*BRIT*) = *Cornwall*.
corn [kɔːn] *n* (*BRIT*: *wheat*) blé *m*; (*US*: *maize*) maïs *m*; (*on foot*) cor *m*; **~ on the cob** (*CULIN*) épi *m* de maïs au naturel.
cornea ['kɔːnɪə] *n* cornée *f*.
corned beef ['kɔːnd-] *n* corned-beef *m*.
corner ['kɔːnə*] *n* coin *m*; (*AUT*) tournant *m*, virage *m*; (*FOOTBALL*: *also*: **~ kick**) corner *m* ♦ *vt* acculer, mettre au pied du mur; coincer; (*COMM*: *market*) accaparer ♦ *vi* prendre un virage; **to cut ~s** (*fig*) prendre des raccourcis.
corner flag *n* (*FOOTBALL*) piquet *m* de coin.
corner kick *n* (*FOOTBALL*) corner *m*.
cornerstone ['kɔːnəstəun] *n* pierre *f* angulaire.
cornet ['kɔːnɪt] *n* (*MUS*) cornet *m* à pistons; (*BRIT*: *of ice-cream*) cornet (de glace).
cornflakes ['kɔːnfleɪks] *npl* cornflakes *mpl*.
cornflour ['kɔːnflauə*] *n* (*BRIT*) farine *f* de maïs, maïzena *f* ®.
cornice ['kɔːnɪs] *n* corniche *f*.
Cornish ['kɔːnɪʃ] *adj* de Cornouailles, cornouaillais(e).
corn oil *n* huile *f* de maïs.
cornstarch ['kɔːnstɑːtʃ] *n* (*US*) farine *f* de maïs, maïzena *f* ®.
cornucopia [kɔːnju'kəupɪə] *n* corne *f* d'abondance.
Cornwall ['kɔːnwəl] *n* Cornouailles *f*.
corny ['kɔːnɪ] *adj* (*col*) rebattu(e), galvaudé(e).
corollary [kə'rɔlərɪ] *n* corollaire *m*.
coronary ['kɔrənərɪ] *n*: **~ (thrombosis)** infarctus *m* (du myocarde), thrombose *f* coronaire.

coronation [kɔrə'neɪʃən] *n* couronnement *m*.
coroner ['kɔrənə*] *n* coroner *m*.
coronet ['kɔrənɪt] *n* couronne *f*.
Corp. *abbr* = **corporation**.
corporal ['kɔːpərl] *n* caporal *m*, brigadier *m* ♦ *adj*: ~ **punishment** châtiment corporel.
corporate ['kɔːpərɪt] *adj* en commun; (*COMM*) constitué(e) (en corporation).
corporate hospitality *n arrangement selon lequel une entreprise offre des places de théâtre, concert etc à ses clients*.
corporate identity, corporate image *n* (*of organization*) image *f* de l'entreprise.
corporation [kɔːpə'reɪʃən] *n* (*of town*) municipalité *f*, conseil municipal; (*COMM*) société *f*.
corporation tax *n* ≈ impôt *m* sur les bénéfices.
corps [kɔː*], *pl* **corps** [kɔːz] *n* corps *m*; **the press** ~ la presse.
corpse [kɔːps] *n* cadavre *m*.
corpuscle ['kɔːpʌsl] *n* corpuscule *m*.
corral [kə'rɑːl] *n* corral *m*.
correct [kə'rɛkt] *adj* (*accurate*) correct(e), exact(e); (*proper*) correct, convenable ♦ *vt* corriger; **you are** ~ vous avez raison.
correction [kə'rɛkʃən] *n* correction *f*.
correlate ['kɔrɪleɪt] *vt* mettre en corrélation ♦ *vi*: **to** ~ **with** correspondre à.
correlation [kɔrɪ'leɪʃən] *n* corrélation *f*.
correspond [kɔrɪs'pɔnd] *vi* correspondre.
correspondence [kɔrɪs'pɔndəns] *n* correspondance *f*.
correspondence course *n* cours *m* par correspondance.
correspondent [kɔrɪs'pɔndənt] *n* correspondant/e.
corridor ['kɔrɪdɔː*] *n* couloir *m*, corridor *m*.
corroborate [kə'rɔbəreɪt] *vt* corroborer, confirmer.
corrode [kə'rəud] *vt* corroder, ronger ♦ *vi* se corroder.
corrosion [kə'rəuʒən] *n* corrosion *f*.
corrosive [kə'rəuzɪv] *adj* corrosif(ive).
corrugated ['kɔrəgeɪtɪd] *adj* plissé(e); ondulé(e).
corrugated iron *n* tôle ondulée.
corrupt [kə'rʌpt] *adj* corrompu(e) ♦ *vt* corrompre; (*data*) altérer; ~ **practices** (*dishonesty, bribery*) malversation *f*.
corruption [kə'rʌpʃən] *n* corruption *f*; altération *f* (de données).
corset ['kɔːsɪt] *n* corset *m*.
Corsica ['kɔːsɪkə] *n* Corse *f*.
Corsican ['kɔːsɪkən] *adj* corse ♦ *n* Corse *m/f*.
cortège [kɔː'teɪʒ] *n* cortège *m* (*gén funèbre*).
cortisone ['kɔːtɪzəun] *n* cortisone *f*.
coruscating ['kɔrəskeɪtɪŋ] *adj* scintillant(e).
c.o.s. *abbr* (= *cash on shipment*) paiement *m* à l'expédition.
cosh [kɔʃ] *n* (*BRIT*) matraque *f*.
cosignatory ['kəu'sɪgnətərɪ] *n* cosignataire *m/f*.
cosiness ['kəuzɪnɪs] *n* atmosphère douillette, confort *m*.
cos lettuce ['kɔs-] *n* (laitue *f*) romaine *f*.
cosmetic [kɔz'mɛtɪk] *n* produit *m* de beauté, cosmétique *m* ♦ *adj* (*preparation*) cosmétique; (*surgery*) esthétique; (*fig: reforms*) symbolique, superficiel(le).
cosmic ['kɔzmɪk] *adj* cosmique.
cosmonaut ['kɔzmənɔːt] *n* cosmonaute *m/f*.
cosmopolitan [kɔzmə'pɔlɪtn] *adj* cosmopolite.
cosmos ['kɔzmɔs] *n* cosmos *m*.
cosset ['kɔsɪt] *vt* choyer, dorloter.
cost [kɔst] *n* coût *m* ♦ *vb* (*pt, pp* **cost**) *vi* coûter ♦ *vt* établir *or* calculer le prix de revient de; ~**s** *npl* (*LAW*) dépens *mpl*; **how much does it** ~? combien ça coûte?; **it** ~**s £5/too much** cela coûte 5 livres/trop cher; **what will it** ~ **to have it repaired?** combien cela coûtera de le faire réparer?; **it** ~ **him his life/job** ça lui a coûté la vie/son emploi; **the** ~ **of living** le coût de la vie; **at all** ~**s** coûte que coûte, à tout prix.
cost accountant *n* analyste *m/f* de coûts.
co-star ['kəustɑː*] *n* partenaire *m/f*.
Costa Rica ['kɔstə'riːkə] *n* Costa Rica *m*.
cost centre *n* centre *m* de coût.
cost control *n* contrôle *m* des coûts.
cost-effective ['kɔstɪ'fɛktɪv] *adj* rentable.
cost-effectiveness ['kɔstɪ'fɛktɪvnɪs] *n* rentabilité *f*.
costing ['kɔstɪŋ] *n* calcul *m* du prix de revient.
costly ['kɔstlɪ] *adj* coûteux(euse).
cost-of-living ['kɔstəv'lɪvɪŋ] *adj*: ~ **allowance** indemnité *f* de vie chère; ~ **index** indice *m* du coût de la vie.
cost price *n* (*BRIT*) prix coûtant *or* de revient.
costume ['kɔstjuːm] *n* costume *m*; (*lady's suit*) tailleur *m*; (*BRIT*: *also*: **swimming** ~) maillot *m* (de bain).
costume jewellery *n* bijoux *mpl* de fantaisie.
cosy, (*US*) **cozy** ['kəuzɪ] *adj* (*bed*) douillet(te); (*scarf, gloves*) bien chaud(e); (*atmosphere*) chaleureux(euse); (*room*) mignon(ne).
cot [kɔt] *n* (*BRIT*: *child's*) lit *m* d'enfant, petit lit; (*US*: *campbed*) lit de camp.
cot death *n* mort subite du nourrisson.
Cotswolds ['kɔtswəuldz] *npl*: **the** ~ *région de collines du Gloucestershire*.
cottage ['kɔtɪdʒ] *n* petite maison (à la campagne), cottage *m*.
cottage cheese *n* fromage blanc (*maigre*).
cottage industry *n* industrie familiale *or* artisanale.
cottage pie *n* ≈ hachis *m* Parmentier.
cotton ['kɔtn] *n* coton *m*; ~ **dress** *etc* robe *etc* en *or* de coton.
►**cotton on** *vi* (*col*): **to** ~ **on (to sth)** piger (qch).
cotton wool *n* (*BRIT*) ouate *f*, coton *m* hydrophile.
couch [kautʃ] *n* canapé *m*; divan *m*; (*doctor's*)

table *f* d'examen; (*psychiatrist's*) divan ♦ *vt* formuler, exprimer.
couchette [kuːˈʃɛt] *n* couchette *f*.
couch potato *n* (*col*) mollasson/ne (*qui passe son temps devant la télé*).
cough [kɔf] *vi* tousser ♦ *n* toux *f*.
cough drop *n* pastille *f* pour *or* contre la toux.
cough mixture, cough syrup *n* sirop *m* pour la toux.
could [kud] *pt of* **can**.
couldn't [ˈkudnt] = **could not**.
council [ˈkaunsl] *n* conseil *m*; **city** *or* **town** ~ conseil municipal; **C~ of Europe** Conseil de l'Europe.
council estate *n* (*BRIT*) (quartier *m or* zone *f* de) logements loués à/par la municipalité.
council house *n* (*BRIT*) maison *f* (à loyer modéré) louée par la municipalité.
councillor [ˈkaunslə*] *n* conseiller/ère.
council tax *n* (*BRIT*) impôts locaux.
counsel [ˈkaunsl] *n* consultation *f*, délibération *f*; (*person*) avocat/e ♦ *vt*: **to ~ sth/sb to do sth** conseiller qch/à qn de faire qch; **~ for the defence/the prosecution** (avocat de la) défense/avocat du ministère public.
counsellor, (*US*) **counselor** [ˈkaunslə*] *n* conseiller/ère; (*US LAW*) avocat *m*.
count [kaunt] *vt, vi* compter ♦ *n* compte *m*; (*nobleman*) comte *m*; **to ~ (up) to 10** compter jusqu'à 10; **to keep ~ of sth** tenir le compte de qch; **not ~ing the children** sans compter les enfants; **10 ~ing him** 10 avec lui, 10 en le comptant; **to ~ the cost of** établir le coût de; **it ~s for very little** cela n'a pas beaucoup d'importance; **~ yourself lucky** estimez-vous heureux.
▸**count on** *vt fus* compter sur; **to ~ on doing sth** compter faire qch.
▸**count up** *vt* compter, additionner.
countdown [ˈkauntdaun] *n* compte *m* à rebours.
countenance [ˈkauntɪnəns] *n* expression *f* ♦ *vt* approuver.
counter [ˈkauntə*] *n* comptoir *m*; (*in post office, bank*) guichet *m*; (*in game*) jeton *m* ♦ *vt* aller à l'encontre de, opposer; (*blow*) parer ♦ *adv*: **~ to** à l'encontre de; contrairement à; **to buy under the ~** (*fig*) acheter sous le manteau *or* en sous-main; **to ~ sth with sth/by doing sth** contrer *or* riposter à qch par qch/en faisant qch.
counteract [ˈkauntərˈækt] *vt* neutraliser, contrebalancer.
counterattack [ˈkauntərəˈtæk] *n* contre-attaque *f* ♦ *vi* contre-attaquer.
counterbalance [ˈkauntəˈbæləns] *vt* contrebalancer, faire contrepoids à.
counter-clockwise [ˈkauntəˈklɔkwaɪz] *adv* en sens inverse des aiguilles d'une montre.
counter-espionage [ˈkauntərˈɛspɪənɑːʒ] *n* contre-espionnage *m*.
counterfeit [ˈkauntəfɪt] *n* faux *m*, contrefaçon *f* ♦ *vt* contrefaire ♦ *adj* faux(fausse).
counterfoil [ˈkauntəfɔɪl] *n* talon *m*, souche *f*.
counterintelligence [ˈkauntərɪnˈtɛlɪdʒəns] *n* contre-espionnage *m*.
countermand [ˈkauntəmɑːnd] *vt* annuler.
countermeasure [ˈkauntəmɛʒə*] *n* contre-mesure *f*.
counteroffensive [ˈkauntərəˈfɛnsɪv] *n* contre-offensive *f*.
counterpane [ˈkauntəpeɪn] *n* dessus-de-lit *m*.
counterpart [ˈkauntəpɑːt] *n* (*of document etc*) double *m*; (*of person*) homologue *m/f*.
counterproductive [ˈkauntəprəˈdʌktɪv] *adj* contre-productif(ive).
counterproposal [ˈkauntəprəˈpəuzl] *n* contre-proposition *f*.
countersign [ˈkauntəsaɪn] *vt* contresigner.
countersink [ˈkauntəsɪŋk] *vt* (*hole*) fraiser.
countess [ˈkauntɪs] *n* comtesse *f*.
countless [ˈkauntlɪs] *adj* innombrable.
countrified [ˈkʌntrɪfaɪd] *adj* rustique, à l'air campagnard.
country [ˈkʌntrɪ] *n* pays *m*; (*native land*) patrie *f*; (*as opposed to town*) campagne *f*; (*region*) région *f*, pays; **in the ~** à la campagne; **mountainous ~** pays de montagne, région montagneuse.
country and western (music) *n* musique *f* country.
country dancing *n* (*BRIT*) danse *f* folklorique.
country house *n* manoir *m*, (petit) château.
countryman [ˈkʌntrɪmən] *n* (*national*) compatriote *m*; (*rural*) habitant *m* de la campagne, campagnard *m*.
countryside [ˈkʌntrɪsaɪd] *n* campagne *f*.
countrywide [ˈkʌntrɪˈwaɪd] *adj* s'étendant à l'ensemble du pays; (*problem*) à l'échelle nationale ♦ *adv* à travers *or* dans tout le pays.
county [ˈkauntɪ] *n* comté *m*.
county council *n* (*BRIT*) ≈ conseil régional.
county town *n* (*BRIT*) chef-lieu *m*.
coup, ~s [kuː, -z] *n* beau coup; (*also*: **~ d'état**) coup d'État.
coupé [kuːˈpeɪ] *n* (*AUT*) coupé *m*.
couple [ˈkʌpl] *n* couple *m* ♦ *vt* (*carriages*) atteler; (*TECH*) coupler; (*ideas, names*) associer; **a ~ of** deux; (*a few*) deux ou trois.
couplet [ˈkʌplɪt] *n* distique *m*.
coupling [ˈkʌplɪŋ] *n* (*RAIL*) attelage *m*.
coupon [ˈkuːpɔn] *n* (*voucher*) bon-prime *m*, bon-réclame *m*; (*detachable form*) coupon *m* détachable, coupon-réponse *m*; (*FINANCE*) coupon.
courage [ˈkʌrɪdʒ] *n* courage *m*.
courageous [kəˈreɪdʒəs] *adj* courageux(euse).
courgette [kuəˈʒɛt] *n* (*BRIT*) courgette *f*.
courier [ˈkurɪə*] *n* messager *m*, courrier *m*; (*for tourists*) accompagnateur/trice.
course [kɔːs] *n* cours *m*; (*of ship*) route *f*; (*for golf*) terrain *m*; (*part of meal*) plat *m*; **first ~** entrée *f*; **of ~** *adv* bien sûr; **(no) of ~ not!**

bien sûr que non!, évidemment que non!; **in the ~ of the next few days** au cours des prochains jours; **in due ~** en temps utile *or* voulu; **~ (of action)** parti *m*, ligne *f* de conduite; **the best ~ would be to ...** le mieux serait de ...; **we have no other ~ but to ...** nous n'avons pas d'autre solution que de ...; **~ of lectures** série *f* de conférences; **~ of treatment** (*MED*) traitement *m*.

court [kɔːt] *n* cour *f*; (*LAW*) cour, tribunal *m*; (*TENNIS*) court *m* ♦ *vt* (*woman*) courtiser, faire la cour à; (*fig: favour, popularity*) rechercher; (*: death, disaster*) courir après, flirter avec; **out of ~** (*LAW: settle*) à l'amiable; **to take to ~** actionner *or* poursuivre en justice; **~ of appeal** cour d'appel.

courteous ['kəːtɪəs] *adj* courtois(e), poli(e).

courtesan [kɔːtɪ'zæn] *n* courtisane *f*.

courtesy ['kəːtəsɪ] *n* courtoisie *f*, politesse *f*; **by ~ of** avec l'aimable autorisation de.

courtesy light *n* (*AUT*) plafonnier *m*.

court-house ['kɔːthaus] *n* (*US*) palais *m* de justice.

courtier ['kɔːtɪə*] *n* courtisan *m*, dame *f* de cour.

court martial, *pl* **courts martial** *n* cour martiale, conseil *m* de guerre.

courtroom ['kɔːtrum] *n* salle *f* de tribunal.

court shoe *n* escarpin *m*.

courtyard ['kɔːtjɑːd] *n* cour *f*.

cousin ['kʌzn] *n* cousin/e.

cove [kəuv] *n* petite baie, anse *f*.

covenant ['kʌvənənt] *n* contrat *m*, engagement *m* ♦ *vt*: **to ~ £200 per year to a charity** s'engager à verser 200 livres par an à une œuvre de bienfaisance.

Coventry ['kɔvəntrɪ] *n*: **to send sb to ~** (*fig*) mettre qn en quarantaine.

cover ['kʌvə*] *vt* couvrir; (*PRESS: report on*) faire un reportage sur ♦ *n* (*for bed, of book, COMM*) couverture *f*; (*of pan*) couvercle *m*; (*over furniture*) housse *f*; (*shelter*) abri *m*; **to take ~** se mettre à l'abri; **under ~** à l'abri; **under ~ of darkness** à la faveur de la nuit; **under separate ~** (*COMM*) sous pli séparé; **£10 will ~ everything** 10 livres suffiront (pour tout payer).

►**cover up** *vt* (*person, object*): **to ~ up (with)** couvrir (de); (*fig: truth, facts*) occulter; **to ~ up for sb** (*fig*) couvrir qn.

coverage ['kʌvərɪdʒ] *n* (*in media*) reportage *m*; (*INSURANCE*) couverture *f*.

cover charge *n* couvert *m* (*supplément à payer*).

covering ['kʌvərɪŋ] *n* couverture *f*, enveloppe *f*.

covering letter, (*US*) **cover letter** *n* lettre explicative.

cover note *n* (*INSURANCE*) police *f* provisoire.

cover price *n* prix *m* de l'exemplaire.

covert ['kʌvət] *adj* (*threat*) voilé(e), caché(e); (*attack*) indirect(e); (*glance*) furtif(ive).

cover-up ['kʌvərʌp] *n* tentative *f* pour étouffer une affaire.

covet ['kʌvɪt] *vt* convoiter.

cow [kau] *n* vache *f* ♦ *cpd* femelle ♦ *vt* effrayer, intimider.

coward ['kauəd] *n* lâche *m/f*.

cowardice ['kauədɪs] *n* lâcheté *f*.

cowardly ['kauədlɪ] *adj* lâche.

cowboy ['kaubɔɪ] *n* cow-boy *m*.

cower ['kauə*] *vi* se recroqueviller; trembler.

cowshed ['kauʃɛd] *n* étable *f*.

cowslip ['kauslɪp] *n* (*BOT*) (fleur *f* de) coucou *m*.

coxswain ['kɔksn] *n* (*abbr:* **cox**) barreur *m*; (*of ship*) patron *m*.

coy [kɔɪ] *adj* faussement effarouché(e) *or* timide.

coyote [kɔɪ'əutɪ] *n* coyote *m*.

cozy ['kəuzɪ] *adj* (*US*) = **cosy**.

CP *n abbr* (= *Communist Party*) PC *m*.

cp. *abbr* (= *compare*) cf.

c/p *abbr* (*BRIT*) = **carriage paid**.

CPA *n abbr* (*US*) = **certified public accountant**.

CPI *n abbr* (= *Consumer Price Index*) IPC *m*.

Cpl. *abbr* (= *corporal*) C/C.

CP/M *n abbr* (= *Central Program for Microprocessors*) CP/M *m*.

c.p.s. *abbr* (= *characters per second*) caractères/seconde.

CPSA *n abbr* (*BRIT: = Civil and Public Services Association*) *syndicat de la fonction publique*.

CPU *n abbr* = **central processing unit**.

cr. *abbr* = **credit; creditor**.

crab [kræb] *n* crabe *m*.

crab apple *n* pomme *f* sauvage.

crack [kræk] *n* fente *f*, fissure *f*; (*in bone, dish, glass*) fêlure *f*; (*in wall*) lézarde *f*; (*noise*) craquement *m*, coup (sec); (*joke*) plaisanterie *f*; (*col: attempt*): **to have a ~ (at sth)** essayer (qch); (*DRUGS*) crack *m* ♦ *vt* fendre, fissurer; fêler; lézarder; (*whip*) faire claquer; (*nut*) casser; (*solve*) résoudre, trouver la clef de; déchiffrer ♦ *cpd* (*athlete*) de première classe, d'élite; **to ~ jokes** (*col*) raconter des blagues; **to get ~ing** (*col*) s'y mettre, se magner.

►**crack down on** *vt fus* (*crime*) sévir contre, réprimer; (*spending*) mettre un frein à.

►**crack up** *vi* être au bout de son rouleau, flancher.

crackdown ['krækdaun] *n*: **~ (on)** (*on crime*) répression *f* (de); (*on spending*) restrictions *fpl* (de).

cracked [krækt] *adj* (*col*) toqué(e), timbré(e).

cracker ['krækə*] *n* pétard *m*; (*biscuit*) biscuit (salé), craquelin *m*; **a ~ of a ...** (*BRIT col*) un(e) ... formidable; **he's ~s** (*BRIT col*) il est cinglé.

crackle ['krækl] *vi* crépiter, grésiller.

crackling ['kræklɪŋ] *n* crépitement *m*, grésillement *m*; (*on radio, telephone*) grésillement, friture *f*; (*of pork*) couenne *f*.

crackpot ['krækpɔt] *n* (*col*) tordu/e.
cradle ['kreɪdl] *n* berceau *m* ♦ *vt* (*child*) bercer; (*object*) tenir dans ses bras.
craft [krɑːft] *n* métier (artisanal); (*cunning*) ruse *f*, astuce *f*; (*boat*) embarcation *f*, barque *f*.
craftsman ['krɑːftsmən] *n* artisan *m*, ouvrier (qualifié).
craftsmanship ['krɑːftsmənʃɪp] *n* métier *m*, habileté *f*.
crafty ['krɑːftɪ] *adj* rusé(e), malin(igne), astucieux(euse).
crag [kræg] *n* rocher escarpé.
craggy ['krægɪ] *adj* escarpé(e), rocheux(euse).
cram [kræm] *vt* (*fill*): **to ~ sth with** bourrer qch de; (*put*): **to ~ sth into** fourrer qch dans.
cramming ['kræmɪŋ] *n* (*for exams*) bachotage *m*.
cramp [kræmp] *n* crampe *f* ♦ *vt* gêner, entraver.
cramped [kræmpt] *adj* à l'étroit, très serré(e).
crampon ['kræmpən] *n* crampon *m*.
cranberry ['krænbərɪ] *n* canneberge *f*.
crane [kreɪn] *n* grue *f* ♦ *vt*, *vi*: **to ~ forward, to ~ one's neck** allonger le cou.
cranium, *pl* **crania** ['kreɪnɪəm, 'kreɪnɪə] *n* boîte crânienne.
crank [kræŋk] *n* manivelle *f*; (*person*) excentrique *m/f*.
crankshaft ['kræŋkʃɑːft] *n* vilebrequin *m*.
cranky ['kræŋkɪ] *adj* excentrique, loufoque; (*bad-tempered*) grincheux(euse), revêche.
cranny ['krænɪ] *n see* **nook**.
crap [kræp] *n* (*col!*) conneries *fpl* (*!*); **to have a ~** chier (*!*).
crappy ['kræpɪ] *adj* (*col*) merdique (*!*).
crash [kræʃ] *n* fracas *m*; (*of car, plane*) collision *f*; (*of business*) faillite *f*; (*STOCK EXCHANGE*) krach *m* ♦ *vt* (*plane*) écraser ♦ *vi* (*plane*) s'écraser; (*two cars*) se percuter, s'emboutir; (*fig*) s'effondrer; **to ~ into** se jeter *or* se fracasser contre; **he ~ed the car into a wall** il s'est écrasé contre un mur avec sa voiture.
crash barrier *n* (*BRIT AUT*) rail *m* de securité.
crash course *n* cours intensif.
crash helmet *n* casque (protecteur).
crash landing *n* atterrissage forcé *or* en catastrophe.
crass [kræs] *adj* grossier(ière), crasse.
crate [kreɪt] *n* cageot *m*.
crater ['kreɪtə*] *n* cratère *m*.
cravat [krə'væt] *n* foulard (*noué autour du cou*).
crave [kreɪv] *vt*, *vi*: **to ~ for** désirer violemment, avoir un besoin physiologique de, avoir une envie irrésistible de.
craving ['kreɪvɪŋ] *n*: **~ (for)** (*for food, cigarettes etc*) envie *f* irrésistible (de).
crawl [krɔːl] *vi* ramper; (*vehicle*) avancer au pas ♦ *n* (*SWIMMING*) crawl *m*; **to ~ on one's hands and knees** aller à quatre pattes; **to ~ to sb** (*col*) faire de la lèche à qn.
crawler lane ['krɔːlə-] *n* (*BRIT AUT*) file *f or* voie *f* pour véhicules lents.
crayfish ['kreɪfɪʃ] *n* (*pl inv*) (*freshwater*) écrevisse *f*; (*saltwater*) langoustine *f*.
crayon ['kreɪən] *n* crayon *m* (de couleur).
craze [kreɪz] *n* engouement *m*.
crazed [kreɪzd] *adj* (*look, person*) affolé(e); (*pottery, glaze*) craquelé(e).
crazy ['kreɪzɪ] *adj* fou(folle); **to go ~** devenir fou; **to be ~ about sb** (*col*) aimer qn à la folie; **he's ~ about skiing** (*col*) c'est un fana(tique) de ski.
crazy paving *n* (*BRIT*) dallage irrégulier (en pierres plates).
creak [kriːk] *vi* (*hinge*) grincer; (*floor, shoes*) craquer.
cream [kriːm] *n* crème *f* ♦ *adj* (*colour*) crème *inv*; **whipped ~** crème fouettée.
►**cream off** *vt* (*fig*) prélever.
cream cake *n* (petit) gâteau à la crème.
cream cheese *n* fromage *m* à la crème, fromage blanc.
creamery ['kriːmərɪ] *n* (*shop*) crémerie *f*; (*factory*) laiterie *f*.
creamy ['kriːmɪ] *adj* crémeux(euse).
crease [kriːs] *n* pli *m* ♦ *vt* froisser, chiffonner ♦ *vi* se froisser, se chiffonner.
crease-resistant ['kriːsrɪzɪstənt] *adj* infroissable.
create [kriː'eɪt] *vt* créer; (*impression, fuss*) faire.
creation [kriː'eɪʃən] *n* création *f*.
creative [kriː'eɪtɪv] *adj* créateur(trice).
creativity [kriːeɪ'tɪvɪtɪ] *n* créativité *f*.
creator [kriː'eɪtə*] *n* créateur/trice.
creature ['kriːtʃə*] *n* créature *f*.
creature comforts *npl* petit confort.
crèche [krɛʃ] *n* garderie *f*, crèche *f*.
credence ['kriːdns] *n* croyance *f*, foi *f*.
credentials [krɪ'dɛnʃlz] *npl* (*papers*) références *fpl*; (*letters of reference*) pièces justificatives.
credibility [krɛdɪ'bɪlɪtɪ] *n* crédibilité *f*.
credible ['krɛdɪbl] *adj* digne de foi, crédible.
credit ['krɛdɪt] *n* crédit *m*; (*SCOL*) unité *f* de valeur ♦ *vt* (*COMM*) créditer; (*believe*: *also*: **give ~ to**) ajouter foi à, croire; **to ~ sb with** (*fig*) prêter *or* attribuer à qn; **to ~ £5 to sb** créditer (le compte de) qn de 5 livres; **to be in ~** (*person, bank account*) être créditeur(trice); **on ~** à crédit; **to one's ~** à son honneur; à son actif; **to take the ~ for** s'attribuer le mérite de; **it does him ~** cela lui fait honneur.
creditable ['krɛdɪtəbl] *adj* honorable, estimable.
credit account *n* compte *m* client.
credit agency *n* (*BRIT*) agence *f* de renseignements commerciaux.
credit balance *n* solde créditeur.
credit bureau *n* (*US*) agence *f* de renseigne-

ments commerciaux.
credit card *n* carte *f* de crédit.
credit control *n* suivi *m* des factures.
credit facilities *npl* facilités *fpl* de paiement.
credit limit *n* limite *f* de crédit.
credit note *n* (*BRIT*) avoir *m*.
creditor ['krɛdɪtə*] *n* créancier/ière.
credits ['krɛdɪts] *npl* (*CINE*) générique *m*.
credit transfer *n* virement *m*.
creditworthy ['krɛdɪtwəːðɪ] *adj* solvable.
credulity [krɪ'djuːlɪtɪ] *n* crédulité *f*.
creed [kriːd] *n* croyance *f*; credo *m*, principes *mpl*.
creek [kriːk] *n* crique *f*, anse *f*; (*US*) ruisseau *m*, petit cours d'eau.
creel ['kriːl] *n* panier *m* de pêche; (*also*: **lobster** ~) panier à homards.
creep, *pt, pp* **crept** [kriːp, krɛpt] *vi* ramper; (*fig*) se faufiler, se glisser; (*plant*) grimper ♦ *n* (*col*) saligaud *m*; **he's a** ~ c'est un type puant; **it gives me the ~s** cela me fait froid dans le dos; **to ~ up on sb** s'approcher furtivement de qn.
creeper ['kriːpə*] *n* plante grimpante.
creepers ['kriːpəz] *npl* (*US*: *for baby*) barboteuse *f*.
creepy ['kriːpɪ] *adj* (*frightening*) qui fait frissonner, qui donne la chair de poule.
creepy-crawly ['kriːpɪ'krɔːlɪ] *n* (*col*) bestiole *f*.
cremate [krɪ'meɪt] *vt* incinérer.
cremation [krɪ'meɪʃən] *n* incinération *f*.
crematorium, *pl* **crematoria** [krɛmə'tɔːrɪəm, -'tɔːrɪə] *n* four *m* crématoire.
creosote ['krɪəsəut] *n* créosote *f*.
crepe [kreɪp] *n* crêpe *m*.
crepe bandage *n* (*BRIT*) bande *f* Velpeau ®.
crepe paper *n* papier *m* crépon.
crepe sole *n* semelle *f* de crêpe.
crept [krɛpt] *pt, pp of* **creep**.
crescendo [krɪ'ʃɛndəu] *n* crescendo *m*.
crescent ['krɛsnt] *n* croissant *m*; (*street*) rue *f* (*en arc de cercle*).
cress [krɛs] *n* cresson *m*.
crest [krɛst] *n* crête *f*; (*of helmet*) cimier *m*; (*of coat of arms*) timbre *m*.
crestfallen ['krɛstfɔːlən] *adj* déconfit(e), découragé(e).
Crete ['kriːt] *n* Crète *f*.
crevasse [krɪ'væs] *n* crevasse *f*.
crevice ['krɛvɪs] *n* fissure *f*, lézarde *f*, fente *f*.
crew [kruː] *n* équipage *m*; (*CINE*) équipe *f* (de tournage); (*gang*) bande *f*.
crew-cut ['kruːkʌt] *n*: **to have a** ~ avoir les cheveux en brosse.
crew-neck ['kruːnɛk] *n* col ras.
crib [krɪb] *n* lit *m* d'enfant ♦ *vt* (*col*) copier.
cribbage ['krɪbɪdʒ] *n sorte de jeu de cartes.*
crick [krɪk] *n* crampe *f*; ~ **in the neck** torticolis *m*.
cricket ['krɪkɪt] *n* (*insect*) grillon *m*, cri-cri *m inv*; (*game*) cricket *m*.
cricketer ['krɪkɪtə*] *n* joueur *m* de cricket.
crime [kraɪm] *n* crime *m*; **minor** ~ délit *m or* infraction *f* mineur(e).
crime wave *n* poussée *f* de la criminalité.
criminal ['krɪmɪnl] *adj, n* criminel(le).
crimp [krɪmp] *vt* friser, frisotter.
crimson ['krɪmzn] *adj* cramoisi(e).
cringe [krɪndʒ] *vi* avoir un mouvement de recul; (*fig*) s'humilier, ramper.
crinkle ['krɪŋkl] *vt* froisser, chiffonner.
cripple ['krɪpl] *n* boiteux/euse, infirme *m/f* ♦ *vt* estropier, paralyser; (*ship, plane*) immobiliser; (*production, exports*) paralyser; **~d with rheumatism** perclus(e) de rhumatismes.
crippling ['krɪplɪŋ] *adj* (*disease*) handicapant(e); (*taxation, debts*) écrasant(e).
crisis, *pl* **crises** ['kraɪsɪs, -siːz] *n* crise *f*.
crisp [krɪsp] *adj* croquant(e); (*fig*) vif(vive); brusque.
crisps [krɪsps] *npl* (*BRIT*) (pommes) chips *fpl*.
crisscross ['krɪskrɔs] *adj* entrecroisé(e), en croisillons ♦ *vt* sillonner; ~ **pattern** croisillons *mpl*.
criterion, *pl* **criteria** [kraɪ'tɪərɪən, -'tɪərɪə] *n* critère *m*.
critic ['krɪtɪk] *n* critique *m/f*.
critical ['krɪtɪkl] *adj* critique; **to be ~ of sb/sth** critiquer qn/qch.
critically ['krɪtɪklɪ] *adv* (*examine*) d'un œil critique; (*speak*) sévèrement; ~ **ill** gravement malade.
criticism ['krɪtɪsɪzəm] *n* critique *f*.
criticize ['krɪtɪsaɪz] *vt* critiquer.
croak [krəuk] *vi* (*frog*) coasser; (*raven*) croasser.
Croat ['krəuæt] *adj, n* = **Croatian**.
Croatia [krəu'eɪʃə] *n* Croatie *f*.
Croatian [krəu'eɪʃən] *adj* croate ♦ *n* Croate *m/f*; (*LING*) croate *m*.
crochet ['krəuʃeɪ] *n* travail *m* au crochet.
crock [krɔk] *n* cruche *f*; (*col*: *also*: **old** ~) épave *f*.
crockery ['krɔkərɪ] *n* vaisselle *f*.
crocodile ['krɔkədaɪl] *n* crocodile *m*.
crocus ['krəukəs] *n* crocus *m*.
croft [krɔft] *n* (*BRIT*) petite ferme.
crofter ['krɔftə*] *n* (*BRIT*) fermier *m*.
crone [krəun] *n* vieille bique, (vieille) sorcière.
crony ['krəunɪ] *n* copain/copine.
crook [kruk] *n* escroc *m*; (*of shepherd*) houlette *f*.
crooked ['krukɪd] *adj* courbé(e), tordu(e); (*action*) malhonnête.
crop [krɔp] *n* (*produce*) culture *f*; (*amount produced*) récolte *f*; (*riding* ~) cravache *f*; (*of bird*) jabot *m* ♦ *vt* (*hair*) tondre; (*subj: animals: grass*) brouter.
►**crop up** *vi* surgir, se présenter, survenir.
cropper ['krɔpə*] *n*: **to come a** ~ (*col*) faire la culbute, s'étaler.
crop spraying [-spreɪɪŋ] *n* pulvérisation *f* des cultures.
croquet ['krəukeɪ] *n* croquet *m*.

cross [krɔs] *n* croix *f*; (*BIOL*) croisement *m* ♦ *vt* (*street etc*) traverser; (*arms, legs, BIOL*) croiser; (*cheque*) barrer; (*thwart: person, plan*) contrarier ♦ *vi*: **the boat ~es from ... to ...** le bateau fait la traversée de ... à ... ♦ *adj* en colère, fâché(e); **to ~ o.s.** se signer, faire le signe de (la) croix; **we have a ~ed line** (*BRIT: on telephone*) il y a des interférences; **they've got their lines ~ed** (*fig*) il y a un malentendu entre eux; **to be/get ~ with sb (about sth)** être en colère/se fâcher contre qn (à propos de qch).
►**cross out** *vt* barrer, biffer.
►**cross over** *vi* traverser.
crossbar ['krɔsbɑː*] *n* barre transversale.
crossbow ['krɔsbəu] *n* arbalète *f*.
crossbreed ['krɔsbriːd] *n* hybride *m*, métis/se.
cross-Channel ferry ['krɔs'tʃænl-] *n* ferry *m* qui fait la traversée de la Manche.
cross-check ['krɔstʃɛk] *n* recoupement *m* ♦ *vi* vérifier par recoupement.
cross-country (race) ['krɔs'kʌntri-] *n* cross(-country) *m*.
cross-dressing [krɔs'drɛsiŋ] *n* travestisme *m*.
cross-examination ['krɔsigzæmi'neiʃən] *n* examen *m* contradictoire (*d'un témoin*).
cross-examine ['krɔsig'zæmin] *vt* (*LAW*) faire subir un examen contradictoire à.
cross-eyed ['krɔsaid] *adj* qui louche.
crossfire ['krɔsfaiə*] *n* feux croisés.
crossing ['krɔsiŋ] *n* croisement *m*, carrefour *m*; (*sea passage*) traversée *f*; (*also*: **pedestrian ~**) passage clouté.
crossing point *n* poste frontalier.
cross-purposes ['krɔs'pəːpəsiz] *npl*: **to be at ~ with sb** comprendre qn de travers; **we're (talking) at ~** on ne parle pas de la même chose.
cross-question ['krɔs'kwɛstʃən] *vt* faire subir un interrogatoire à.
cross-reference ['krɔs'rɛfrəns] *n* renvoi *m*, référence *f*.
crossroads ['krɔsrəudz] *n* carrefour *m*.
cross section *n* (*BIOL*) coupe transversale; (*in population*) échantillon *m*.
crosswalk ['krɔswɔːk] *n* (*US*) passage clouté.
crosswind ['krɔswind] *n* vent *m* de travers.
crosswise ['krɔswaiz] *adv* en travers.
crossword ['krɔswəːd] *n* mots *mpl* croisés.
crotch [krɔtʃ] *n* (*of garment*) entre-jambes *m inv*.
crotchet ['krɔtʃit] *n* (*MUS*) noire *f*.
crotchety ['krɔtʃiti] *adj* (*person*) grognon(ne), grincheux(euse).
crouch [krautʃ] *vi* s'accroupir; se tapir; se ramasser.
croup [kruːp] *n* (*MED*) croup *m*.
crouton ['kruːtɔn] *n* croûton *m*.
crow [krəu] *n* (*bird*) corneille *f*; (*of cock*) chant *m* du coq, cocorico *m* ♦ *vi* (*cock*) chanter; (*fig*) pavoiser, chanter victoire.
crowbar ['krəubɑː*] *n* levier *m*.
crowd [kraud] *n* foule *f* ♦ *vt* bourrer, remplir ♦ *vi* affluer, s'attrouper, s'entasser; **~s of people** une foule de gens.
crowded ['kraudid] *adj* bondé(e), plein(e); **~ with** plein de.
crowd scene *n* (*CINE, THEAT*) scène *f* de foule.
crown [kraun] *n* couronne *f*; (*of head*) sommet *m* de la tête, calotte crânienne; (*of hat*) fond *m*; (*of hill*) sommet *m* ♦ *vt* couronner.
crown court *n* (*BRIT*) ≈ Cour *f* d'assises; *voir encadré*.

CROWN COURT

En Angleterre et au Pays de Galles, une **crown court** *est une cour de justice où sont jugées les affaires très graves, telles que le meurtre, l'homicide, le viol et le vol, en présence d'un jury. Tous les crimes et délits, quel que soit leur degré de gravité, doivent d'abord passer devant une "magistrates' court". Il existe environ 90* **crown courts**.

crowning ['krauniŋ] *adj* (*achievement, glory*) suprême.
crown jewels *npl* joyaux *mpl* de la Couronne.
crown prince *n* prince héritier.
crow's-feet ['krəuzfiːt] *npl* pattes *fpl* d'oie (*fig*).
crow's-nest ['krəuznɛst] *n* (*on sailing-ship*) nid *m* de pie.
crucial ['kruːʃl] *adj* crucial(e), décisif(ive); **~ to** essentiel(le) à.
crucifix ['kruːsifiks] *n* crucifix *m*.
crucifixion [kruːsi'fikʃən] *n* crucifiement *m*, crucifixion *f*.
crucify ['kruːsifai] *vt* crucifier, mettre en croix; (*fig*) crucifier.
crude [kruːd] *adj* (*materials*) brut(e); non raffiné(e); (*basic*) rudimentaire, sommaire; (*vulgar*) cru(e), grossier(ière).
crude (oil) *n* (pétrole) brut *m*.
cruel ['kruəl] *adj* cruel(le).
cruelty ['kruəlti] *n* cruauté *f*.
cruet ['kruːit] *n* huilier *m*; vinaigrier *m*.
cruise [kruːz] *n* croisière *f* ♦ *vi* (*ship*) croiser; (*car*) rouler; (*aircraft*) voler; (*taxi*) être en maraude.
cruise missile *n* missile *m* de croisière.
cruiser ['kruːzə*] *n* croiseur *m*.
cruising speed ['kruːziŋ-] *n* vitesse *f* de croisière.
crumb [krʌm] *n* miette *f*.
crumble ['krʌmbl] *vt* émietter ♦ *vi* s'émietter; (*plaster etc*) s'effriter; (*land, earth*) s'ébouler; (*building*) s'écrouler, crouler; (*fig*) s'effondrer.
crumbly ['krʌmbli] *adj* friable.
crummy ['krʌmi] *adj* (*col*) minable; (*: unwell*) mal fichu(e), patraque.
crumpet ['krʌmpit] *n* petite crêpe (épaisse).
crumple ['krʌmpl] *vt* froisser, friper.

crunch [krʌntʃ] *vt* croquer; (*underfoot*) faire craquer, écraser; faire crisser ♦ *n* (*fig*) instant *m or* moment *m* critique, moment de vérité.
crunchy ['krʌntʃɪ] *adj* croquant(e), croustillant(e).
crusade [kruː'seɪd] *n* croisade *f* ♦ *vi* (*fig*): **to ~ for/against** partir en croisade pour/contre.
crusader [kruː'seɪdə*] *n* croisé *m*; (*fig*): **~ (for)** champion *m* (de).
crush [krʌʃ] *n* foule *f*, cohue *f*; (*love*): **to have a ~ on sb** avoir le béguin pour qn; (*drink*): **lemon ~** citron pressé ♦ *vt* écraser; (*crumple*) froisser; (*grind, break up: garlic, ice*) piler; (*: grapes*) presser.
crush barrier *n* (*BRIT*) barrière *f* de sécurité.
crushing ['krʌʃɪŋ] *adj* écrasant(e).
crust [krʌst] *n* croûte *f*.
crustacean [krʌs'teɪʃən] *n* crustacé *m*.
crusty ['krʌstɪ] *adj* (*bread*) croustillant(e); (*col: person*) revêche, bourru(e); (*: remark*) irrité(e).
crutch [krʌtʃ] *n* béquille *f*; (*TECH*) support *m*; (*also*: **crotch**) entrejambe *m*.
crux [krʌks] *n* point crucial.
cry [kraɪ] *vi* pleurer; (*shout*: *also*: **~ out**) crier ♦ *n* cri *m*; **what are you ~ing about?** pourquoi pleures-tu?; **to ~ for help** appeler à l'aide; **she had a good ~** elle a pleuré un bon coup; **it's a far ~ from ...** (*fig*) on est loin de ....
►**cry off** *vi* se dédire; se décommander.
crying ['kraɪɪŋ] *adj* (*fig*) criant(e), flagrant(e).
crypt [krɪpt] *n* crypte *f*.
cryptic ['krɪptɪk] *adj* énigmatique.
crystal ['krɪstl] *n* cristal *m*.
crystal-clear ['krɪstl'klɪə*] *adj* clair(e) comme de l'eau de roche.
crystallize ['krɪstəlaɪz] *vt* cristalliser ♦ *vi* (se) cristalliser; **~d fruits** (*BRIT*) fruits confits.
CSA *n abbr* = *Confederate States of America*; (*BRIT*: = *Child Support Agency*) *organisme pour la protection des enfants de parents séparés, qui contrôle le versement des pensions alimentaires*.
CSC *n abbr* (= *Civil Service Commission*) *commission de recrutement des fonctionnaires*.
CSE *n abbr* (*BRIT*: = *Certificate of Secondary Education*) ≈ BEPC *m*.
CS gas *n* (*BRIT*) gaz *m* C.S.
CST *abbr* (*US*: = *Central Standard Time*) *fuseau horaire*.
CT *abbr* (*US*) = *Connecticut*.
ct *abbr* = **carat**.
CTC *n abbr* (*BRIT*) = **city technology college.**
CT scanner *n abbr* (*MED*: = *computerized tomography scanner*) scanner *m*, tomodensitomètre *m*.
cu. *abbr* = **cubic**.
cub [kʌb] *n* petit *m* (*d'un animal*); (*also*: **~ scout**) louveteau *m*.
Cuba ['kjuːbə] *n* Cuba *m*.
Cuban ['kjuːbən] *adj* cubain(e) ♦ *n* Cubain/e.
cubbyhole ['kʌbɪhəul] *n* cagibi *m*.
cube [kjuːb] *n* cube *m* ♦ *vt* (*MATH*) élever au cube.
cube root *n* racine *f* cubique.
cubic ['kjuːbɪk] *adj* cubique; **~ metre** *etc* mètre *m etc* cube; **~ capacity** (*AUT*) cylindrée *f*.
cubicle ['kjuːbɪkl] *n* box *m*, cabine *f*.
cuckoo ['kukuː] *n* coucou *m*.
cuckoo clock *n* (pendule *f* à) coucou *m*.
cucumber ['kjuːkʌmbə*] *n* concombre *m*.
cud [kʌd] *n*: **to chew the ~** ruminer.
cuddle ['kʌdl] *vt* câliner, caresser ♦ *vi* se blottir l'un contre l'autre.
cuddly ['kʌdlɪ] *adj* câlin(e).
cudgel ['kʌdʒl] *n* gourdin *m* ♦ *vt*: **to ~ one's brains** se creuser la tête.
cue [kjuː] *n* queue *f* de billard; (*THEAT etc*) signal *m*.
cuff [kʌf] *n* (*of shirt, coat etc*) poignet *m*, manchette *f*; (*US*: *on trousers*) revers *m*; (*blow*) gifle *f* ♦ *vt* gifler; **off the ~** *adv* de chic, à l'improviste.
cufflink ['kʌflɪŋk] *n* bouton *m* de manchette.
cu. in. *abbr* = *cubic inches*.
cuisine [kwɪ'ziːn] *n* cuisine *f*, art *m* culinaire.
cul-de-sac ['kʌldəsæk] *n* cul-de-sac *m*, impasse *f*.
culinary ['kʌlɪnərɪ] *adj* culinaire.
cull [kʌl] *vt* sélectionner; (*kill selectively*) pratiquer l'abattage sélectif de.
culminate ['kʌlmɪneɪt] *vi*: **to ~ in** finir *or* se terminer par; (*lead to*) mener à.
culmination [kʌlmɪ'neɪʃən] *n* point culminant.
culottes [kjuː'lɔts] *npl* jupe-culotte *f*.
culpable ['kʌlpəbl] *adj* coupable.
culprit ['kʌlprɪt] *n* coupable *m/f*.
cult [kʌlt] *n* culte *m*.
cult figure *n* idole *f*.
cultivate ['kʌltɪveɪt] *vt* (*also fig*) cultiver.
cultivation [kʌltɪ'veɪʃən] *n* culture *f*.
cultural ['kʌltʃərəl] *adj* culturel(le).
culture ['kʌltʃə*] *n* (*also fig*) culture *f*.
cultured ['kʌltʃəd] *adj* cultivé(e) (*fig*).
cumbersome ['kʌmbəsəm] *adj* encombrant(e), embarrassant(e).
cumin ['kʌmɪn] *n* (*spice*) cumin *m*.
cumulative ['kjuːmjulətɪv] *adj* cumulatif(ive).
cunning ['kʌnɪŋ] *n* ruse *f*, astuce *f* ♦ *adj* rusé(e), malin(igne); (*clever: device, idea*) astucieux(euse).
cunt [kʌnt] *n* (*col!*) chatte *f* (*!*); (*insult*) salaud *m* (*!*), salope *f* (*!*).
cup [kʌp] *n* tasse *f*; (*prize, event*) coupe *f*; (*of bra*) bonnet *m*; **a ~ of tea** une tasse de thé.
cupboard ['kʌbəd] *n* placard *m*.
cup final *n* (*BRIT FOOTBALL*) finale *f* de la coupe.
Cupid ['kjuːpɪd] *n* Cupidon *m*; (*figurine*) amour *m*.
cupidity [kjuː'pɪdɪtɪ] *n* cupidité *f*.
cupola ['kjuːpələ] *n* coupole *f*.

cuppa ['kʌpə] *n* (*BRIT col*) tasse *f* de thé.
cup-tie ['kʌptaɪ] *n* (*BRIT FOOTBALL*) match *m* de coupe.
curable ['kjuərəbl] *adj* guérissable, curable.
curate ['kjuərɪt] *n* vicaire *m*.
curator [kjuə'reɪtə*] *n* conservateur *m* (*d'un musée etc*).
curb [kə:b] *vt* refréner, mettre un frein à; (*expenditure*) limiter, juguler ♦ *n* frein *m* (*fig*); (*US*) = **kerb**.
curd cheese *n* ≈ fromage blanc.
curdle ['kə:dl] *vi* (se) cailler.
curds [kə:dz] *npl* lait caillé.
cure [kjuə*] *vt* guérir; (*CULIN*) saler; fumer; sécher ♦ *n* remède *m*; **to be ~d of sth** être guéri de qch.
cure-all ['kjuərɔ:l] *n* (*also fig*) panacée *f*.
curfew ['kə:fju:] *n* couvre-feu *m*.
curio ['kjuərɪəu] *n* bibelot *m*, curiosité *f*.
curiosity [kjuərɪ'ɔsɪtɪ] *n* curiosité *f*.
curious ['kjuərɪəs] *adj* curieux(euse); **I'm ~ about him** il m'intrigue.
curiously ['kjuərɪəslɪ] *adv* curieusement; (*inquisitively*) avec curiosité; **~ enough, ...** bizarrement ....
curl [kə:l] *n* boucle *f* (de cheveux); (*of smoke etc*) volute *f* ♦ *vt*, *vi* boucler; (*tightly*) friser.
►**curl up** *vi* s'enrouler; se pelotonner.
curler ['kə:lə*] *n* bigoudi *m*, rouleau *m*; (*SPORT*) joueur/euse de curling.
curlew ['kə:lu:] *n* courlis *m*.
curling ['kə:lɪŋ] *n* (*sport*) curling *m*.
curling tongs, (*US*) **curling irons** *npl* fer *m* à friser.
curly ['kə:lɪ] *adj* bouclé(e); (*tightly curled*) frisé(e).
currant ['kʌrnt] *n* raisin *m* de Corinthe, raisin sec.
currency ['kʌrnsɪ] *n* monnaie *f*; **foreign ~** devises étrangères, monnaie étrangère; **to gain ~** (*fig*) s'accréditer.
current ['kʌrnt] *n* courant *m* ♦ *adj* courant(e); (*tendency, price, event*) actuel(le); **direct/alternating ~** (*ELEC*) courant continu/alternatif; **the ~ issue of a magazine** le dernier numéro d'un magazine; **in ~ use** d'usage courant.
current account *n* (*BRIT*) compte courant.
current affairs *npl* (questions *fpl* d')actualité *f*.
current assets *npl* (*COMM*) actif *m* disponible.
current liabilities *npl* (*COMM*) passif *m* exigible.
currently ['kʌrntlɪ] *adv* actuellement.
curriculum, *pl* **~s** *or* **curricula** [kə'rɪkjuləm, -lə] *n* programme *m* d'études.
curriculum vitae (CV) [-'vi:taɪ] *n* curriculum vitae (CV) *m*.
curry ['kʌrɪ] *n* curry *m* ♦ *vt*: **to ~ favour with** chercher à gagner la faveur *or* à s'attirer les bonnes grâces de; **chicken ~** curry de poulet, poulet *m* au curry.
curry powder *n* poudre *f* de curry.
curse [kə:s] *vi* jurer, blasphémer ♦ *vt* maudire ♦ *n* malédiction *f*; fléau *m*; (*swearword*) juron *m*.
cursor ['kə:sə*] *n* (*COMPUT*) curseur *m*.
cursory ['kə:sərɪ] *adj* superficiel(le), hâtif(ive).
curt [kə:t] *adj* brusque, sec(sèche).
curtail [kə:'teɪl] *vt* (*visit etc*) écourter; (*expenses etc*) réduire.
curtain ['kə:tn] *n* rideau *m*; **to draw the ~s** (*together*) fermer *or* tirer les rideaux; (*apart*) ouvrir les rideaux.
curtain call *n* (*THEAT*) rappel *m*.
curts(e)y ['kə:tsɪ] *n* révérence *f* ♦ *vi* faire une révérence.
curvature ['kə:vətʃə*] *n* courbure *f*.
curve [kə:v] *n* courbe *f*; (*in the road*) tournant *m*, virage *m* ♦ *vt* courber ♦ *vi* se courber; (*road*) faire une courbe.
curved [kə:vd] *adj* courbe.
cushion ['kuʃən] *n* coussin *m* ♦ *vt* (*seat*) rembourrer; (*shock*) amortir.
cushy ['kuʃɪ] *adj* (*col*): **a ~ job** un boulot de tout repos; **to have a ~ time** se la couler douce.
custard ['kʌstəd] *n* (*for pouring*) crème anglaise.
custard powder *n* (*BRIT*) ≈ crème pâtissière instantanée.
custodial sentence [kʌs'təudɪəl-] *n* peine *f* de prison.
custodian [kʌs'təudɪən] *n* gardien/ne; (*of collection etc*) conservateur/trice.
custody ['kʌstədɪ] *n* (*of child*) garde *f*; (*for offenders*) détention préventive; **to take sb into ~** placer qn en détention préventive; **in the ~ of** sous la garde de.
custom ['kʌstəm] *n* coutume *f*, usage *m*; (*LAW*) droit coutumier, coutume; (*COMM*) clientèle *f*.
customary ['kʌstəmərɪ] *adj* habituel(le); **it is ~ to do it** l'usage veut qu'on le fasse.
custom-built ['kʌstəm'bɪlt] *adj see* **custom-made**.
customer ['kʌstəmə*] *n* client/e; **he's an awkward ~** (*col*) ce n'est pas quelqu'un de facile.
customer profile *n* profil *m* du client.
customized ['kʌstəmaɪzd] *adj* personnalisé(e).
custom-made ['kʌstəm'meɪd] *adj* (*clothes*) fait(e) sur mesure; (*other goods*: *also*: **custom-built**) hors série, fait(e) sur commande.
customs ['kʌstəmz] *npl* douane *f*; **to go through (the) ~** passer la douane.
Customs and Excise *n* (*BRIT*) administration *f* des douanes.
customs officer *n* douanier *m*.
cut [kʌt] *vb* (*pt, pp* **cut**) *vt* couper; (*meat*) découper; (*shape, make*) tailler; couper; creuser; graver; (*reduce*) réduire; (*col*: *lecture, ap-*

pointment) manquer ♦ *vi* couper; (*intersect*) se couper ♦ *n* (*gen*) coupure *f*; (*of clothes*) coupe *f*; (*of jewel*) taille *f*; (*in salary etc*) réduction *f*; (*of meat*) morceau *m*; **cold ~s** *npl* (*US*) viandes froides; **to ~ teeth** (*baby*) faire ses dents; **to ~ a tooth** percer une dent; **to ~ one's finger** se couper le doigt; **to get one's hair ~** se faire couper les cheveux; **to ~ sth short** couper court à qch; **to ~ sb dead** ignorer (complètement) qn.

▸**cut back** *vt* (*plants*) tailler; (*production, expenditure*) réduire.

▸**cut down** *vt* (*tree*) abattre; (*reduce*) réduire; **to ~ sb down to size** (*fig*) remettre qn à sa place.

▸**cut down on** *vt fus* réduire.

▸**cut in** *vi* (*interrupt: conversation*): **to ~ in (on)** couper la parole (à); (*AUT*) faire une queue de poisson.

▸**cut off** *vt* couper; (*fig*) isoler; **we've been ~ off** (*TEL*) nous avons été coupés.

▸**cut out** *vt* (*picture etc*) découper; (*remove*) ôter; supprimer.

▸**cut up** *vt* découper.

cut-and-dried ['kʌtən'draɪd] *adj* (*also*: **cut-and-dry**) tout(e) fait(e), tout(e) décidé(e).

cutaway ['kʌtəweɪ] *adj, n*: **~ (drawing)** écorché *m*.

cutback ['kʌtbæk] *n* réduction *f*.

cute [kjuːt] *adj* mignon(ne), adorable; (*clever*) rusé(e), astucieux(euse).

cut glass *n* cristal taillé.

cuticle ['kjuːtɪkl] *n* (*on nail*): **~ remover** repousse-peaux *m inv*.

cutlery ['kʌtlərɪ] *n* couverts *mpl*; (*trade*) coutellerie *f*.

cutlet ['kʌtlɪt] *n* côtelette *f*.

cutoff ['kʌtɔf] *n* (*also*: **~ point**) seuil-limite *m*.

cutoff switch *n* interrupteur *m*.

cutout ['kʌtaut] *n* coupe-circuit *m inv*; (*paper figure*) découpage *m*.

cut-price ['kʌt'praɪs], (*US*) **cut-rate** ['kʌt'reɪt] *adj* au rabais, à prix réduit.

cutthroat ['kʌtθrəut] *n* assassin *m* ♦ *adj*: **~ competition** concurrence *f* sauvage.

cutting ['kʌtɪŋ] *adj* tranchant(e), coupant(e); (*fig*) cinglant(e), mordant(e) ♦ *n* (*BRIT*: *from newspaper*) coupure *f* (de journal); (: *RAIL*) tranchée *f*; (*CINE*) montage *m*.

cutting edge *n* (*of knife*) tranchant *m*; **on** *or* **at the ~ of** à la pointe de.

cuttlefish ['kʌtlfɪʃ] *n* seiche *f*.

cut-up ['kʌtʌp] *adj* affecté(e), démoralisé(e).

CV *n abbr* = **curriculum vitae**.

cwt. *abbr* = **hundredweight**.

cyanide ['saɪənaɪd] *n* cyanure *m*.

cybercafé ['saɪbəˌkæfeɪ] *n* cybercafé *m*.

cybernetics [saɪbə'nɛtɪks] *n* cybernétique *f*.

cyclamen ['sɪkləmən] *n* cyclamen *m*.

cycle ['saɪkl] *n* cycle *m* ♦ *vi* faire de la bicyclette.

cycle race *n* course *f* cycliste.

cycle rack *n* râtelier *m* à bicyclette.

cycling ['saɪklɪŋ] *n* cyclisme *m*; **to go on a ~ holiday** (*BRIT*) faire du cyclotourisme.

cyclist ['saɪklɪst] *n* cycliste *m/f*.

cyclone ['saɪkləun] *n* cyclone *m*.

cygnet ['sɪgnɪt] *n* jeune cygne *m*.

cylinder ['sɪlɪndə*] *n* cylindre *m*.

cylinder block *n* bloc-cylindres *m*.

cylinder capacity *n* cylindrée *f*.

cylinder head *n* culasse *f*.

cylinder-head gasket ['sɪlɪndəhɛd-] *n* joint *m* de culasse.

cymbals ['sɪmblz] *npl* cymbales *fpl*.

cynic ['sɪnɪk] *n* cynique *m/f*.

cynical ['sɪnɪkl] *adj* cynique.

cynicism ['sɪnɪsɪzəm] *n* cynisme *m*.

CYO *n abbr* (*US*: = *Catholic Youth Organization*) ≈ JC *f*.

cypress ['saɪprɪs] *n* cyprès *m*.

Cypriot ['sɪprɪət] *adj* cypriote, chypriote ♦ *n* Cypriote *m/f*, Chypriote *m/f*.

Cyprus ['saɪprəs] *n* Chypre *f*.

cyst [sɪst] *n* kyste *m*.

cystitis [sɪs'taɪtɪs] *n* cystite *f*.

CZ *n abbr* (*US*: = *Central Zone*) *zone du canal de Panama*.

czar [zɑː*] *n* tsar *m*.

Czech [tʃɛk] *adj* tchèque ♦ *n* Tchèque *m/f*; (*LING*) tchèque *m*; **the ~ Republic** la République tchèque.

Czechoslovak [tʃɛkə'sləuvæk] *adj, n* = **Czechoslovakian**.

Czechoslovakia [tʃɛkəslə'vækɪə] *n* Tchécoslovaquie *f*.

Czechoslovakian [tʃɛkəslə'vækɪən] *adj* tchécoslovaque ♦ *n* Tchécoslovaque *m/f*.

D d

D, d [diː] *n* (*letter*) D, d *m*; (*MUS*): **D** ré *m*; **D for David**, (*US*) **D for Dog** D comme Désirée.

D *abbr* (*US POL*) = **democrat(ic)**.

d *abbr* (*BRIT*: *old*) = **penny**.

d. *abbr* = *died*.

DA *n abbr* (*US*) = **district attorney**.

dab [dæb] *vt* (*eyes, wound*) tamponner; (*paint, cream*) appliquer (par petites touches *or* rapidement); **a ~ of paint** un petit coup de peinture.

dabble ['dæbl] *vi*: **to ~ in** faire *or* se mêler *or* s'occuper un peu de.

Dacca ['dækə] *n* Dacca.

dachshund ['dækshund] *n* teckel *m*.

dad, daddy [dæd, 'dædɪ] *n* papa *m*.

daddy-long-legs [dædɪ'lɔŋlɛgz] *n* tipule *f*;

faucheux *m*.
daffodil ['dæfədɪl] *n* jonquille *f*.
daft [dɑːft] *adj* (*col*) idiot(e), stupide; **to be ~ about** être toqué(e) *or* mordu(e) de.
dagger ['dægə*] *n* poignard *m*; **to be at ~s drawn with sb** être à couteaux tirés avec qn; **to look ~s at sb** foudroyer qn du regard.
dahlia ['deɪljə] *n* dahlia *m*.
daily ['deɪlɪ] *adj* quotidien(ne), journalier(ière) ♦ *n* quotidien *m*; (*BRIT*: *servant*) femme *f* de ménage (*à la journée*) ♦ *adv* tous les jours; **twice ~** deux fois par jour.
dainty ['deɪntɪ] *adj* délicat(e), mignon(ne).
dairy ['dɛərɪ] *n* (*shop*) crémerie *f*, laiterie *f*; (*on farm*) laiterie ♦ *adj* laitier(ière).
dairy cow *n* vache laitière.
dairy farm *n* exploitation *f* pratiquant l'élevage laitier.
dairy produce *n* produits laitiers.
dais ['deɪɪs] *n* estrade *f*.
daisy ['deɪzɪ] *n* pâquerette *f*.
daisy-wheel printer ['deɪzɪwiːl-] *n* imprimante *f* à marguerite.
Dakar ['dækə] *n* Dakar.
dale [deɪl] *n* vallon *m*.
dalmatian [dæl'meɪʃən] *n* (*dog*) dalmatien/ne.
dam [dæm] *n* barrage *m*; (*reservoir*) réservoir *m*, lac *m* de retenue ♦ *vt* endiguer.
damage ['dæmɪdʒ] *n* dégâts *mpl*, dommages *mpl*; (*fig*) tort *m* ♦ *vt* endommager, abîmer; (*fig*) faire du tort à; **~ to property** dégâts matériels.
damages ['dæmɪdʒɪz] *npl* (*LAW*) dommages-intérêts *mpl*; **to pay £5000 in ~** payer 5000 livres de dommages-intérêts.
damaging ['dæmɪdʒɪŋ] *adj*: **~ (to)** préjudiciable (à), nuisible (à).
Damascus [də'mɑːskəs] *n* Damas.
dame [deɪm] *n* (*title*) *titre porté par une femme décorée de l'ordre de l'Empire Britannique ou d'un ordre de chevalerie; titre porté par la femme ou la veuve d'un chevalier ou baronnet*; (*US col*) nana *f*; (*THEAT*) vieille dame (*rôle comique joué par un homme*).
damn [dæm] *vt* condamner; (*curse*) maudire ♦ *n* (*col*): **I don't give a ~** je m'en fous ♦ *adj* (*col*): **this ~** ... ce sacré *or* foutu ...; **~ (it)!** zut!
damnable ['dæmnəbl] *adj* (*col*: *behaviour*) odieux(euse), détestable; (*: weather*) épouvantable, abominable.
damnation [dæm'neɪʃən] *n* (*REL*) damnation *f* ♦ *excl* (*col*) malédiction!, merde!
damning ['dæmɪŋ] *adj* (*evidence*) accablant(e).
damp [dæmp] *adj* humide ♦ *n* humidité *f* ♦ *vt* (*also*: **~en**: *cloth, rag*) humecter; (*: enthusiasm etc*) refroidir.
dampcourse ['dæmpkɔːs] *n* couche isolante (contre l'humidité).
damper ['dæmpə*] *n* (*MUS*) étouffoir *m*; (*of fire*) registre *m*; **to put a ~ on** (*fig*: *atmosphere, enthusiasm*) refroidir.
dampness ['dæmpnɪs] *n* humidité *f*.
damson ['dæmzən] *n* prune *f* de Damas.
dance [dɑːns] *n* danse *f*; (*ball*) bal *m* ♦ *vi* danser; **to ~ about** sautiller, gambader.
dance hall *n* salle *f* de bal, dancing *m*.
dancer ['dɑːnsə*] *n* danseur/euse.
dancing ['dɑːnsɪŋ] *n* danse *f*.
D and C *n abbr* (*MED*: = *dilation and curettage*) curetage *m*.
dandelion ['dændɪlaɪən] *n* pissenlit *m*.
dandruff ['dændrəf] *n* pellicules *fpl*.
D and T *n abbr* (*BRIT SCOL* = *design and technology*) technologie *f*.
dandy ['dændɪ] *n* dandy *m*, élégant *m* ♦ *adj* (*US col*) fantastique, super.
Dane [deɪn] *n* Danois/e.
danger ['deɪndʒə*] *n* danger *m*; **there is a ~ of fire** il y a (un) risque d'incendie; **in ~** en danger; **he was in ~ of falling** il risquait de tomber; **out of ~** hors de danger.
danger list *n* (*MED*): **on the ~** dans un état critique.
danger money *n* (*BRIT*) prime *f* de risque.
dangerous ['deɪndʒrəs] *adj* dangereux(euse).
dangerously ['deɪndʒrəslɪ] *adv* dangereusement; **~ ill** très gravement malade, en danger de mort.
danger zone *n* zone dangereuse.
dangle ['dæŋgl] *vt* balancer; (*fig*) faire miroiter ♦ *vi* pendre, se balancer.
Danish ['deɪnɪʃ] *adj* danois(e) ♦ *n* (*LING*) danois *m*.
Danish pastry *n* feuilleté *m* (*recouvert d'un glaçage et fourré aux fruits etc*).
dank [dæŋk] *adj* froid(e) et humide.
Danube ['dænjuːb] *n*: **the ~** le Danube.
dapper ['dæpə*] *adj* pimpant(e).
Dardanelles [dɑːdə'nɛlz] *npl* Dardanelles *fpl*.
dare [dɛə*] *vt*: **to ~ sb to do** défier qn *or* mettre qn au défi de faire ♦ *vi*: **to ~ (to) do sth** oser faire qch; **I ~n't tell him** (*BRIT*) je n'ose pas le lui dire; **I ~ say he'll turn up** il est probable qu'il viendra.
daredevil ['dɛədɛvl] *n* casse-cou *m inv*.
Dar-es-Salaam ['dɑːrɛssə'lɑːm] *n* Dar-es-Salaam, Dar-es-Salam.
daring ['dɛərɪŋ] *adj* hardi(e), audacieux(euse) ♦ *n* audace *f*, hardiesse *f*.
dark [dɑːk] *adj* (*night, room*) obscur(e), sombre; (*colour, complexion*) foncé(e), sombre; (*fig*) sombre ♦ *n*: **in the ~** dans le noir; **in the ~ about** (*fig*) ignorant tout de; **after ~** après la tombée de la nuit; **it is/is getting ~** il fait nuit/commence à faire nuit.
darken [dɑːkn] *vt* obscurcir, assombrir ♦ *vi* s'obscurcir, s'assombrir.
dark glasses *npl* lunettes noires.
dark horse *n* (*fig*): **he's a ~** on ne sait pas grand-chose de lui.
darkly ['dɑːklɪ] *adv* (*gloomily*) mélancolique-

ment; (*in a sinister way*) lugubrement.
darkness ['dɑːknɪs] *n* obscurité *f*.
darkroom ['dɑːkrum] *n* chambre noire.
darling ['dɑːlɪŋ] *adj, n* chéri(e).
darn [dɑːn] *vt* repriser.
dart [dɑːt] *n* fléchette *f* ♦ *vi*: **to ~ towards** (*also*: **make a ~ towards**) se précipiter *or* s'élancer vers; **to ~ away/along** partir/passer comme une flèche.
dartboard ['dɑːtbɔːd] *n* cible *f* (de jeu de fléchettes).
darts [dɑːts] *n* jeu *m* de fléchettes.
dash [dæʃ] *n* (*sign*) tiret *m*; (*small quantity*) goutte *f*, larme *f* ♦ *vt* (*missile*) jeter *or* lancer violemment; (*hopes*) anéantir ♦ *vi*: **to ~ towards** (*also*: **make a ~ towards**) se précipiter *or* se ruer vers; **a ~ of soda** un peu d'eau gazeuse.
►**dash away** *vi* partir à toute allure.
dashboard ['dæʃbɔːd] *n* (*AUT*) tableau *m* de bord.
dashing ['dæʃɪŋ] *adj* fringant(e).
dastardly ['dæstədlɪ] *adj* lâche.
DAT *n abbr* (= *digital audio tape*) cassette *f* audio digitale.
data ['deɪtə] *npl* données *fpl*.
database ['deɪtəbeɪs] *n* base *f* de données.
data capture *n* saisie *f* de données.
data processing *n* traitement *m* (électronique) de l'information.
data transmission *n* transmission *f* de données.
date [deɪt] *n* date *f*; (*appointment*) rendez-vous *m*; (*fruit*) datte *f* ♦ *vt* dater; (*col*: *girl etc*) sortir avec; **what's the ~ today?** quelle date sommes-nous aujourd'hui?; **~ of birth** date de naissance; **closing ~** date de clôture; **to ~** *adv* à ce jour; **out of ~** périmé(e); **up to ~** à la page; mis(e) à jour; moderne; **to bring up to ~** (*correspondence, information*) mettre à jour; (*method*) moderniser; (*person*) mettre au courant; **letter ~d 5th July** *or* (*US*) **July 5th** lettre (datée) du 5 juillet.
dated ['deɪtɪd] *adj* démodé(e).
dateline ['deɪtlaɪn] *n* ligne *f* de changement de date.
date rape *n* viol *m* (*à l'issue d'un rendez-vous galant*).
date stamp *n* timbre-dateur *m*.
daub [dɔːb] *vt* barbouiller.
daughter ['dɔːtə*] *n* fille *f*.
daughter-in-law ['dɔːtərɪnlɔː] *n* belle-fille *f*, bru *f*.
daunt [dɔːnt] *vt* intimider, décourager.
daunting ['dɔːntɪŋ] *adj* décourageant(e), intimidant(e).
dauntless ['dɔːntlɪs] *adj* intrépide.
dawdle ['dɔːdl] *vi* traîner, lambiner; **to ~ over one's work** traînasser *or* lambiner sur son travail.
dawn [dɔːn] *n* aube *f*, aurore *f* ♦ *vi* (*day*) se lever, poindre; (*fig*) naître, se faire jour; **at ~** à l'aube; **from ~ to dusk** du matin au soir; **it ~ed on him that** ... il lui vint à l'esprit que ....
dawn chorus *n* (*BRIT*) chant *m* des oiseaux à l'aube.
day [deɪ] *n* jour *m*; (*as duration*) journée *f*; (*period of time, age*) époque *f*, temps *m*; **the ~ before** la veille, le jour précédent; **the ~ after, the following ~** le lendemain, le jour suivant; **the ~ before yesterday** avant-hier; **the ~ after tomorrow** après-demain; **(on) the ~ that** ... le jour où ...; **~ by ~** jour après jour; **by ~** de jour; **paid by the ~** payé(e) à la journée; **these ~s, in the present ~** de nos jours, à l'heure actuelle.
daybook ['deɪbuk] *n* (*BRIT*) main courante, brouillard *m*, journal *m*.
day boy *n* (*SCOL*) externe *m*.
daybreak ['deɪbreɪk] *n* point *m* du jour.
daycare centre ['deɪkɛə-] *n* garderie *f*.
daydream ['deɪdriːm] *n* rêverie *f* ♦ *vi* rêver (tout éveillé).
day girl *n* (*SCOL*) externe *f*.
daylight ['deɪlaɪt] *n* (lumière *f* du) jour *m*.
daylight robbery *n*: **it's ~** (*fig, col*) c'est du vol caractérisé *or* manifeste.
daylight saving time *n* (*US*) heure *f* d'été.
day release *n*: **to be on ~** avoir une journée de congé pour formation professionnelle.
day return (ticket) *n* (*BRIT*) billet *m* d'aller-retour (valable pour la journée).
day shift *n* équipe *f* de jour.
daytime ['deɪtaɪm] *n* jour *m*, journée *f*.
day-to-day ['deɪtə'deɪ] *adj* (*routine, expenses*) journalier(ière); **on a ~ basis** au jour le jour.
day trip *n* excursion *f* (d'une journée).
day tripper *n* excursionniste *m/f*.
daze [deɪz] *vt* (*subj: drug*) hébéter; (*: blow*) étourdir ♦ *n*: **in a ~** hébété(e); étourdi(e).
dazzle ['dæzl] *vt* éblouir, aveugler.
dazzling ['dæzlɪŋ] *adj* (*light*) aveuglant(e), éblouissant(e); (*fig*) éblouissant(e).
DC *abbr* (*ELEC*) = **direct current**; (*US*) = *District of Columbia*.
DCC *n abbr* ® (= *digital compact cassette*) DCC ®.
DD *n abbr* (= *Doctor of Divinity*) *titre universitaire*.
dd. *abbr* (*COMM*) = *delivered*.
D/D *abbr* = **direct debit**.
D-day ['diːdeɪ] *n* le jour J.
DDS *n abbr* (*US*: = *Doctor of Dental Science, Doctor of Dental Surgery*) *titres universitaires*.
DDT *n abbr* (= *dichlorodiphenyl trichloroethane*) DDT *m*.
DE *abbr* (*US*) = *Delaware*.
DEA *n abbr* (*US*: = *Drug Enforcement Administration*) ≈ brigade *f* des stupéfiants.
deacon ['diːkən] *n* diacre *m*.
dead [dɛd] *adj* mort(e); (*numb*) engourdi(e), insensible ♦ *adv* absolument, complètement;

the ~ *npl* les morts; **he was shot** ~ il a été tué d'un coup de revolver; ~ **on time** à l'heure pile; ~ **tired** éreinté(e), complètement fourbu(e); **to stop** ~ s'arrêter pile *or* net; **the line has gone** ~ (*TEL*) on n'entend plus rien.
dead beat *adj* (*col*) claqué(e), crevé(e).
deaden [dɛdn] *vt* (*blow, sound*) amortir; (*make numb*) endormir, rendre insensible.
dead end *n* impasse *f*.
dead-end ['dɛdɛnd] *adj*: **a** ~ **job** un emploi *or* poste sans avenir.
dead heat *n* (*SPORT*): **to finish in a** ~ terminer ex aequo.
dead-letter office [dɛd'lɛtər-] *n* ≈ centre *m* de recherche du courrier.
deadline ['dɛdlaɪn] *n* date *f or* heure *f* limite; **to work to a** ~ avoir des délais stricts à respecter.
deadlock ['dɛdlɔk] *n* impasse *f* (*fig*).
dead loss *n* (*col*): **to be a** ~ (*person*) n'être bon(bonne) à rien; (*thing*) ne rien valoir.
deadly ['dɛdlɪ] *adj* mortel(le); (*weapon*) meurtrier(ière); ~ **dull** ennuyeux(euse) à mourir, mortellement ennuyeux.
deadpan ['dɛdpæn] *adj* impassible; (*humour*) pince-sans-rire *inv*.
Dead Sea *n*: **the** ~ la mer Morte.
dead season *n* (*TOURISM*) morte saison.
deaf [dɛf] *adj* sourd(e); **to turn a** ~ **ear to sth** faire la sourde oreille à qch.
deaf-aid ['dɛfeɪd] *n* (*BRIT*) appareil auditif.
deaf-and-dumb ['dɛfən'dʌm] *adj* sourd(e)-muet(te); ~ **alphabet** alphabet *m* des sourds-muets.
deafen ['dɛfn] *vt* rendre sourd(e); (*fig*) assourdir.
deafening ['dɛfnɪŋ] *adj* assourdissant(e).
deaf-mute ['dɛfmjuːt] *n* sourd/e-muet/te.
deafness ['dɛfnɪs] *n* surdité *f*.
deal [diːl] *n* affaire *f*, marché *m* ♦ *vt* (*pt, pp* **dealt** [dɛlt]) (*blow*) porter; (*cards*) donner, distribuer; **to strike a** ~ **with sb** faire *or* conclure un marché avec qn; **it's a** ~! (*col*) marché conclu!, tope-là!, topez-là!; **he got a bad** ~ **from them** ils ont mal agi envers lui; **he got a fair** ~ **from them** ils ont agi loyalement envers lui; **a good** ~ (*a lot*) beaucoup; **a good** ~ **of, a great** ~ **of** beaucoup de, énormément de.
►**deal in** *vt fus* (*COMM*) faire le commerce de, être dans le commerce de.
►**deal with** *vt fus* (*COMM*) traiter avec; (*handle*) s'occuper *or* se charger de; (*be about: book etc*) traiter de.
dealer ['diːlə*] *n* marchand *m*.
dealership ['diːləʃɪp] *n* concession *f*.
dealings ['diːlɪŋz] *npl* (*in goods, shares*) opérations *fpl*, transactions *fpl*; (*relations*) relations *fpl*, rapports *mpl*.
dealt [dɛlt] *pt, pp of* **deal**.
dean [diːn] *n* (*REL, BRIT SCOL*) doyen *m*; (*US SCOL*) conseiller/ère (principal(e)) d'éducation.
dear [dɪə*] *adj* cher(chère); (*expensive*) cher, coûteux(euse) ♦ *n*: **my** ~ mon cher/ma chère; ~ **me!** mon Dieu!; **D**~ **Sir/Madam** (*in letter*) Monsieur/Madame; **D**~ **Mr/Mrs X** Cher Monsieur/Chère Madame X.
dearly ['dɪəlɪ] *adv* (*love*) tendrement; (*pay*) cher.
dearth [dəːθ] *n* disette *f*, pénurie *f*.
death [dɛθ] *n* mort *f*; (*ADMIN*) décès *m*.
deathbed ['dɛθbɛd] *n* lit *m* de mort.
death certificate *n* acte *m* de décès.
death duties *npl* (*BRIT*) droits *mpl* de succession.
deathly ['dɛθlɪ] *adj* de mort ♦ *adv* comme la mort.
death penalty *n* peine *f* de mort.
death rate *n* taux *m* de mortalité.
death row [-'rəu] *n* (*US*) quartier *m* des condamnés à mort; **to be on** ~ être condamné à la peine de mort.
death sentence *n* condamnation *f* à mort.
death squad *n* escadron *m* de la mort.
deathtrap ['dɛθtræp] *n* endroit (*or* véhicule *etc*) dangereux.
deb [dɛb] *n abbr* (*col*) = **debutante**.
debar [dɪ'bɑː*] *vt*: **to** ~ **sb from a club** *etc* exclure qn d'un club *etc*; **to** ~ **sb from doing** interdire à qn de faire.
debase [dɪ'beɪs] *vt* (*currency*) déprécier, dévaloriser; (*person*) abaisser, avilir.
debatable [dɪ'beɪtəbl] *adj* discutable, contestable; **it is** ~ **whether** ... il est douteux que ....
debate [dɪ'beɪt] *n* discussion *f*, débat *m* ♦ *vt* discuter, débattre ♦ *vi* (*consider*): **to** ~ **whether** se demander si.
debauchery [dɪ'bɔːtʃərɪ] *n* débauche *f*.
debenture [dɪ'bɛntʃə*] *n* (*COMM*) obligation *f*.
debilitate [dɪ'bɪlɪteɪt] *vt* débiliter.
debit ['dɛbɪt] *n* débit *m* ♦ *vt*: **to** ~ **a sum to sb** *or* **to sb's account** porter une somme au débit de qn, débiter qn d'une somme.
debit balance *n* solde débiteur.
debit note *n* note *f* de débit.
debrief [diː'briːf] *vt* demander un compte rendu de fin de mission à.
debriefing [diː'briːfɪŋ] *n* compte rendu *m*.
debris ['dɛbriː] *n* débris *mpl*, décombres *mpl*.
debt [dɛt] *n* dette *f*; **to be in** ~ avoir des dettes, être endetté(e); **bad** ~ créance *f* irrécouvrable.
debt collector *n* agent *m* de recouvrements.
debtor ['dɛtə*] *n* débiteur/trice.
debug ['diː'bʌg] *vt* (*COMPUT*) déverminer.
debunk [diː'bʌŋk] *vt* (*theory, claim*) montrer le ridicule de.
debut ['deɪbjuː] *n* début(s) *m(pl)*.
debutante ['dɛbjutænt] *n* débutante *f*.
Dec. *abbr* (= *December*) déc.
decade ['dɛkeɪd] *n* décennie *f*, décade *f*.
decadence ['dɛkədəns] *n* décadence *f*.

decadent ['dɛkədənt] *adj* décadent(e).
de-caff ['di:kæf] *n* (*col*) déca *m*.
decaffeinated [dɪ'kæfɪneɪtɪd] *adj* décaféiné(e).
decamp [dɪ'kæmp] *vi* (*col*) décamper, filer.
decant [dɪ'kænt] *vt* (*wine*) décanter.
decanter [dɪ'kæntə*] *n* carafe *f*.
decarbonize [di:'kɑ:bənaɪz] *vt* (*AUT*) décalaminer.
decathlon [dɪ'kæθlən] *n* décathlon *m*.
decay [dɪ'keɪ] *n* décomposition *f*, pourrissement *m*; (*fig*) déclin *m*, délabrement *m*; (*also*: **tooth** ~) carie *f* (dentaire) ♦ *vi* (*rot*) se décomposer, pourrir; (*fig*) se délabrer; décliner; se détériorer.
decease [dɪ'si:s] *n* décès *m*.
deceased [dɪ'si:st] *n*: **the** ~ le/la défunt/e.
deceit [dɪ'si:t] *n* tromperie *f*, supercherie *f*.
deceitful [dɪ'si:tful] *adj* trompeur(euse).
deceive [dɪ'si:v] *vt* tromper; **to** ~ **o.s.** s'abuser.
decelerate [di:'sɛləreɪt] *vt*, *vi* ralentir.
December [dɪ'sɛmbə*] *n* décembre *m*; *for phrases see also* **July**.
decency ['di:sənsɪ] *n* décence *f*.
decent ['di:sənt] *adj* décent(e), convenable; **they were very** ~ **about it** ils se sont montrés très chics.
decently ['di:səntlɪ] *adv* (*respectably*) décemment, convenablement; (*kindly*) décemment.
decentralization [di:sɛntrəlaɪ'zeɪʃən] *n* décentralisation *f*.
decentralize [di:'sɛntrəlaɪz] *vt* décentraliser.
deception [dɪ'sɛpʃən] *n* tromperie *f*.
deceptive [dɪ'sɛptɪv] *adj* trompeur(euse).
decibel ['dɛsɪbɛl] *n* décibel *m*.
decide [dɪ'saɪd] *vt* (*person*) décider; (*question, argument*) trancher, régler ♦ *vi* se décider, décider; **to** ~ **to do/that** décider de faire/que; **to** ~ **on** décider, se décider pour; **to** ~ **on doing** décider de faire; **to** ~ **against doing** décider de ne pas faire.
decided [dɪ'saɪdɪd] *adj* (*resolute*) résolu(e), décidé(e); (*clear, definite*) net(te), marqué(e).
decidedly [dɪ'saɪdɪdlɪ] *adv* résolument; incontestablement, nettement.
deciding [dɪ'saɪdɪŋ] *adj* décisif(ive).
deciduous [dɪ'sɪdjuəs] *adj* à feuilles caduques.
decimal ['dɛsɪməl] *adj* décimal(e) ♦ *n* décimale *f*; **to three** ~ **places** (jusqu')à la troisième décimale.
decimalize ['dɛsɪməlaɪz] *vt* (*BRIT*) décimaliser.
decimal point *n* ≈ virgule *f*.
decimate ['dɛsɪmeɪt] *vt* décimer.
decipher [dɪ'saɪfə*] *vt* déchiffrer.
decision [dɪ'sɪʒən] *n* décision *f*; **to make a** ~ prendre une décision.
decisive [dɪ'saɪsɪv] *adj* décisif(ive); (*influence*) décisif, déterminant(e); (*manner, person*) décidé(e), catégorique; (*reply*) ferme, catégorique.
deck [dɛk] *n* (*NAUT*) pont *m*; (*of bus*): **top** ~ impériale *f*; (*of cards*) jeu *m*; **to go up on** ~ monter sur le pont; **below** ~ dans l'entrepont; **record/cassette** ~ platine-disques/-cassettes *f*.
deckchair ['dɛktʃɛə*] *n* chaise longue.
deck hand *n* matelot *m*.
declaration [dɛklə'reɪʃən] *n* déclaration *f*.
declare [dɪ'klɛə*] *vt* déclarer.
declassify [di:'klæsɪfaɪ] *vt* rendre accessible au public *or* à tous.
decline [dɪ'klaɪn] *n* (*decay*) déclin *m*; (*lessening*) baisse *f* ♦ *vt* refuser, décliner ♦ *vi* décliner; être en baisse, baisser; ~ **in living standards** baisse du niveau de vie; **to** ~ **to do sth** refuser (poliment) de faire qch.
declutch ['di:'klʌtʃ] *vi* (*BRIT*) débrayer.
decode ['di:'kəud] *vt* décoder.
decoder [di:'kəudə*] *n* (*COMPUT, TV*) décodeur *m*.
decompose [di:kəm'pəuz] *vi* se décomposer.
decomposition [di:kɔmpə'zɪʃən] *n* décomposition *f*.
decompression [di:kəm'prɛʃən] *n* décompression *f*.
decompression chamber *n* caisson *m* de décompression.
decongestant [di:kən'dʒɛstənt] *n* décongestif *m*.
decontaminate [di:kən'tæmɪneɪt] *vt* décontaminer.
decontrol [di:kən'trəul] *vt* (*prices etc*) libérer.
décor ['deɪkɔ:*] *n* décor *m*.
decorate ['dɛkəreɪt] *vt* (*adorn, give a medal to*) décorer; (*paint and paper*) peindre et tapisser.
decoration [dɛkə'reɪʃən] *n* (*medal etc, adornment*) décoration *f*.
decorative ['dɛkərətɪv] *adj* décoratif(ive).
decorator ['dɛkəreɪtə*] *n* peintre *m* en bâtiment.
decorum [dɪ'kɔ:rəm] *n* décorum *m*, bienséance *f*.
decoy ['di:kɔɪ] *n* piège *m*; **they used him as a** ~ **for the enemy** ils se sont servis de lui pour attirer l'ennemi.
decrease *n* ['di:kri:s] diminution *f* ♦ *vt*, *vi* [di:'kri:s] diminuer; **to be on the** ~ diminuer, être en diminution.
decreasing [di:'kri:sɪŋ] *adj* en voie de diminution.
decree [dɪ'kri:] *n* (*POL, REL*) décret *m*; (*LAW*) arrêt *m*, jugement *m* ♦ *vt*: **to** ~ **(that)** décréter (que), ordonner (que); ~ **absolute** jugement définitif (de divorce); ~ **nisi** jugement provisoire de divorce.
decrepit [dɪ'krɛpɪt] *adj* (*person*) décrépit(e); (*building*) délabré(e).
decry [dɪ'kraɪ] *vt* condamner ouvertement, déplorer; (*disparage*) dénigrer, décrier.
dedicate ['dɛdɪkeɪt] *vt* consacrer; (*book etc*) dédier.
dedicated ['dɛdɪkeɪtɪd] *adj* (*person*) dévoué(e);

(*COMPUT*) spécialisé(e), dédié(e); ~ **word processor** station *f* de traitement de texte.
dedication [dɛdɪ'keɪʃən] *n* (*devotion*) dévouement *m*; (*in book*) dédicace *f*.
deduce [dɪ'djuːs] *vt* déduire, conclure.
deduct [dɪ'dʌkt] *vt*: **to ~ sth (from)** déduire qch (de), retrancher qch (de); (*from wage etc*) prélever qch (sur), retenir qch (sur).
deduction [dɪ'dʌkʃən] *n* (*deducting*) déduction *f*; (*from wage etc*) prélèvement *m*, retenue *f*; (*deducing*) déduction, conclusion *f*.
deed [diːd] *n* action *f*, acte *m*; (*LAW*) acte notarié, contrat *m*; ~ **of covenant** (acte *m* de) donation *f*.
deem [diːm] *vt* (*formal*) juger, estimer; **to ~ it wise to do** juger bon de faire.
deep [diːp] *adj* (*water, sigh, sorrow, thoughts*) profond(e); (*voice*) grave ♦ *adv*: ~ **in snow** recouvert(e) d'une épaisse couche de neige; **spectators stood 20 ~** il y avait 20 rangs de spectateurs; **knee-~ in water** dans l'eau jusqu'aux genoux; **4 metres ~** de 4 mètres de profondeur; **he took a ~ breath** il inspira profondément, il prit son souffle.
deepen [diːpn] *vt* (*hole*) approfondir ♦ *vi* s'approfondir; (*darkness*) s'épaissir.
deep-freeze ['diːp'friːz] *n* congélateur *m* ♦ *vt* surgeler.
deep-fry ['diːp'fraɪ] *vt* faire frire (dans une friteuse).
deeply ['diːplɪ] *adv* profondément; (*dig*) en profondeur; (*regret, interest*) vivement.
deep-rooted ['diːp'ruːtɪd] *adj* (*prejudice*) profondément enraciné(e); (*affection*) profond(e); (*habit*) invétéré(e).
deep-sea ['diːp'siː] *adj*: ~ **diver** plongeur sous-marin; ~ **diving** plongée sous-marine; ~ **fishing** pêche hauturière.
deep-seated ['diːp'siːtɪd] *adj* (*beliefs*) profondément enraciné(e).
deep-set ['diːpsɛt] *adj* (*eyes*) enfoncé(e).
deer [dɪə*] *n* (*pl inv*): **the ~** les cervidés *mpl* (*ZOOL*); **(red) ~** cerf *m*; **(fallow) ~** daim *m*; **(roe) ~** chevreuil *m*.
deerskin ['dɪəskɪn] *n* peau *f* de daim.
deerstalker ['dɪəstɔːkə*] *n* (*person*) chasseur *m* de cerf; (*hat*) casquette *f* à la Sherlock Holmes.
deface [dɪ'feɪs] *vt* dégrader; barbouiller; rendre illisible.
defamation [dɛfə'meɪʃən] *n* diffamation *f*.
defamatory [dɪ'fæmətrɪ] *adj* diffamatoire, diffamant(e).
default [dɪ'fɔːlt] *vi* (*LAW*) faire défaut; (*gen*) manquer à ses engagements ♦ *n* (*COMPUT*: *also*: ~ **value**) valeur *f* par défaut; **by ~** (*LAW*) par défaut, par contumace; (*SPORT*) par forfait; **to ~ on a debt** ne pas s'acquitter d'une dette.
defaulter [dɪ'fɔːltə*] *n* (*on debt*) débiteur défaillant.
default option *n* (*COMPUT*) option *f* par défaut.
defeat [dɪ'fiːt] *n* défaite *f* ♦ *vt* (*team, opponents*) battre; (*fig: plans, efforts*) faire échouer.
defeatism [dɪ'fiːtɪzəm] *n* défaitisme *m*.
defeatist [dɪ'fiːtɪst] *adj, n* défaitiste (*m/f*).
defecate ['dɛfəkeɪt] *vi* déféquer.
defect *n* ['diːfɛkt] défaut *m* ♦ *vi* [dɪ'fɛkt]: **to ~ to the enemy/the West** passer à l'ennemi/l'Ouest; **physical ~** malformation *f*, vice *m* de conformation; **mental ~** anomalie *or* déficience mentale.
defective [dɪ'fɛktɪv] *adj* défectueux(euse).
defector [dɪ'fɛktə*] *n* transfuge *m/f*.
defence, (*US*) **defense** [dɪ'fɛns] *n* défense *f*; **in ~ of** pour défendre; **witness for the ~** témoin *m* à décharge; **the Ministry of D~,** (*US*) **the Department of Defense** le ministère de la Défense nationale.
defenceless [dɪ'fɛnslɪs] *adj* sans défense.
defend [dɪ'fɛnd] *vt* défendre; (*decision, action, opinion*) justifier, défendre.
defendant [dɪ'fɛndənt] *n* défendeur/deresse; (*in criminal case*) accusé/e, prévenu/e.
defender [dɪ'fɛndə*] *n* défenseur *m*.
defending champion [dɪ'fɛndɪŋ-] *n* (*SPORT*) champion/ne en titre.
defending counsel [dɪ'fɛndɪŋ-] *n* (*LAW*) avocat *m* de la défense.
defense [dɪ'fɛns] *n* (*US*) = **defence**.
defensive [dɪ'fɛnsɪv] *adj* défensif(ive) ♦ *n* défensive *f*; **on the ~** sur la défensive.
defer [dɪ'fəː*] *vt* (*postpone*) différer, ajourner ♦ *vi* (*submit*): **to ~ to sb/sth** déférer à qn/qch, s'en remettre à qn/qch.
deference ['dɛfərəns] *n* déférence *f*, égards *mpl*; **out of** *or* **in ~ to** par déférence *or* égards pour.
defiance [dɪ'faɪəns] *n* défi *m*; **in ~ of** au mépris de.
defiant [dɪ'faɪənt] *adj* provocant(e), de défi.
defiantly [dɪ'faɪəntlɪ] *adv* d'un air (*or* d'un ton) de défi.
deficiency [dɪ'fɪʃənsɪ] *n* insuffisance *f*, déficience *f*; carence *f*; (*COMM*) déficit *m*, découvert *m*.
deficiency disease *n* maladie *f* de carence.
deficient [dɪ'fɪʃənt] *adj* insuffisant(e); défectueux(euse); déficient(e); **to be ~ in** manquer de.
deficit ['dɛfɪsɪt] *n* déficit *m*.
defile [dɪ'faɪl] *vt* souiller ♦ *vi* défiler ♦ *n* ['diːfaɪl] défilé *m*.
define [dɪ'faɪn] *vt* définir.
definite ['dɛfɪnɪt] *adj* (*fixed*) défini(e), (bien) déterminé(e); (*clear, obvious*) net(te), manifeste; (*LING*) défini(e); **he was ~ about it** il a été catégorique; il était sûr de son fait.
definitely ['dɛfɪnɪtlɪ] *adv* sans aucun doute.
definition [dɛfɪ'nɪʃən] *n* définition *f*.
definitive [dɪ'fɪnɪtɪv] *adj* définitif(ive).
deflate [diː'fleɪt] *vt* dégonfler; (*pompous person*) rabattre le caquet à; (*ECON*) provoquer

la déflation de; (: *prices*) faire tomber *or* baisser.
deflation [diːˈfleɪʃən] *n* (*ECON*) déflation *f*.
deflationary [diːˈfleɪʃənrɪ] *adj* (*ECON*) déflationniste.
deflect [dɪˈflɛkt] *vt* détourner, faire dévier.
defog [ˈdiːˈfɔg] *vt* (*US AUT*) désembuer.
defogger [ˈdiːˈfɔgə*] *n* (*US AUT*) dispositif *m* anti-buée *inv*.
deform [dɪˈfɔːm] *vt* déformer.
deformed [dɪˈfɔːmd] *adj* difforme.
deformity [dɪˈfɔːmɪtɪ] *n* difformité *f*.
defraud [dɪˈfrɔːd] *vt* frauder; **to ~ sb of sth** soutirer qch malhonnêtement à qn; escroquer qch à qn; frustrer qn de qch.
defray [dɪˈfreɪ] *vt*: **to ~ sb's expenses** défrayer qn (de ses frais), rembourser *or* payer à qn ses frais.
defrost [diːˈfrɔst] *vt* (*fridge*) dégivrer; (*frozen food*) décongeler.
deft [dɛft] *adj* adroit(e), preste.
defunct [dɪˈfʌŋkt] *adj* défunt(e).
defuse [diːˈfjuːz] *vt* désamorcer.
defy [dɪˈfaɪ] *vt* défier; (*efforts etc*) résister à.
degenerate *vi* [dɪˈdʒɛnəreɪt] dégénérer ♦ *adj* [dɪˈdʒɛnərɪt] dégénéré(e).
degradation [dɛgrəˈdeɪʃən] *n* dégradation *f*.
degrade [dɪˈgreɪd] *vt* dégrader.
degrading [dɪˈgreɪdɪŋ] *adj* dégradant(e).
degree [dɪˈgriː] *n* degré *m*; (*SCOL*) diplôme *m* (universitaire); **10 ~s below (zero)** 10 degrés au-dessous de zéro; **a (first) ~ in maths** (*BRIT*) une licence en maths; **a considerable ~ of risk** un considérable facteur *or* élément de risque; **by ~s** (*gradually*) par degrés; **to some ~, to a certain ~** jusqu'à un certain point, dans une certaine mesure.
dehydrated [diːhaɪˈdreɪtɪd] *adj* déshydraté(e); (*milk, eggs*) en poudre.
dehydration [diːhaɪˈdreɪʃən] *n* déshydratation *f*.
de-ice [ˈdiːˈaɪs] *vt* (*windscreen*) dégivrer.
de-icer [ˈdiːˈaɪsə*] *n* dégivreur *m*.
deign [deɪn] *vi*: **to ~ to do** daigner faire.
deity [ˈdiːɪtɪ] *n* divinité *f*; dieu *m*, déesse *f*.
déjà vu [deɪʒɑːˈvuː] *n*: **I had a sense of ~** j'ai eu une impression de déjà-vu.
dejected [dɪˈdʒɛktɪd] *adj* abattu(e), déprimé(e).
dejection [dɪˈdʒɛkʃən] *n* abattement *m*, découragement *m*.
Del. *abbr* (*US*) = *Delaware*.
del. *abbr* = **delete**.
delay [dɪˈleɪ] *vt* (*journey, operation*) retarder, différer; (*travellers, trains*) retarder; (*payment*) différer ♦ *vi* s'attarder ♦ *n* délai *m*, retard *m*; **without ~** sans délai, sans tarder.
delayed-action [dɪˈleɪdˈækʃən] *adj* à retardement.
delectable [dɪˈlɛktəbl] *adj* délicieux(euse).
delegate *n* [ˈdɛlɪgɪt] délégué/e ♦ *vt* [ˈdɛlɪgeɪt] déléguer; **to ~ sth to sb/sb to do sth** déléguer qch à qn/qn pour faire qch.
delegation [dɛlɪˈgeɪʃən] *n* délégation *f*.
delete [dɪˈliːt] *vt* rayer, supprimer; (*COMPUT*) effacer.
Delhi [ˈdɛlɪ] *n* Delhi.
deli [ˈdɛlɪ] *n* épicerie fine.
deliberate *adj* [dɪˈlɪbərɪt] (*intentional*) délibéré(e); (*slow*) mesuré(e) ♦ *vi* [dɪˈlɪbəreɪt] délibérer, réfléchir.
deliberately [dɪˈlɪbərɪtlɪ] *adv* (*on purpose*) exprès, délibérément.
deliberation [dɪlɪbəˈreɪʃən] *n* délibération *f*, réflexion *f*; (*gen pl: discussion*) délibérations, débats *mpl*.
delicacy [ˈdɛlɪkəsɪ] *n* délicatesse *f*; (*choice food*) mets fin *or* délicat, friandise *f*.
delicate [ˈdɛlɪkɪt] *adj* délicat(e).
delicately [ˈdɛlɪkɪtlɪ] *adv* délicatement; (*act, express*) avec délicatesse, avec tact.
delicatessen [dɛlɪkəˈtɛsn] *n* épicerie fine.
delicious [dɪˈlɪʃəs] *adj* délicieux(euse), exquis(e).
delight [dɪˈlaɪt] *n* (grande) joie, grand plaisir ♦ *vt* enchanter; **a ~ to the eyes** un régal *or* plaisir pour les yeux; **to take ~ in** prendre grand plaisir à; **to be the ~ of** faire les délices *or* la joie de.
delighted [dɪˈlaɪtɪd] *adj*: **~ (at** *or* **with sth)** ravi(e) (de qch); **to be ~ to do sth/that** être enchanté(e) *or* ravi(e) de faire qch/que; **I'd be ~** j'en serais enchanté *or* ravi.
delightful [dɪˈlaɪtful] *adj* (*person, child*) absolument charmant(e), adorable; (*evening, view*) merveilleux(euse); (*meal*) délicieux(euse).
delimit [diːˈlɪmɪt] *vt* délimiter.
delineate [dɪˈlɪnɪeɪt] *vt* tracer, esquisser; (*fig*) dépeindre, décrire.
delinquency [dɪˈlɪŋkwənsɪ] *n* délinquance *f*.
delinquent [dɪˈlɪŋkwənt] *adj, n* délinquant(e).
delirious [dɪˈlɪrɪəs] *adj* (*MED, fig*) délirant(e); **to be ~** délirer.
delirium [dɪˈlɪrɪəm] *n* délire *m*.
deliver [dɪˈlɪvə*] *vt* (*mail*) distribuer; (*goods*) livrer; (*message*) remettre; (*speech*) prononcer; (*warning, ultimatum*) lancer; (*free*) délivrer; (*MED*) accoucher; **to ~ the goods** (*fig*) tenir ses promesses.
deliverance [dɪˈlɪvrəns] *n* délivrance *f*, libération *f*.
delivery [dɪˈlɪvərɪ] *n* (*of mail*) distribution *f*; (*of goods*) livraison *f*; (*of speaker*) élocution *f*; (*MED*) accouchement *m*; **to take ~ of** prendre livraison de.
delivery note *n* bon *m* de livraison.
delivery van, (*US***) delivery truck** *n* fourgonnette *f or* camionnette *f* de livraison.
delouse [ˈdiːˈlaus] *vt* épouiller, débarrasser de sa (*or leur etc*) vermine.
delta [ˈdɛltə] *n* delta *m*.
delude [dɪˈluːd] *vt* tromper, leurrer; **to ~ o.s.** se leurrer, se faire des illusions.
deluge [ˈdɛljuːdʒ] *n* déluge *m* ♦ *vt* (*fig*): **to ~**

(with) inonder (de).
delusion [dɪ'luːʒən] *n* illusion *f*; **to have ~s of grandeur** être un peu mégalomane.
de luxe [də'lʌks] *adj* de luxe.
delve [dɛlv] *vi*: **to ~ into** fouiller dans.
Dem. *abbr* (*US POL*) = **democrat(ic)**.
demagogue ['dɛməgɔg] *n* démagogue *m/f*.
demand [dɪ'mɑːnd] *vt* réclamer, exiger; (*need*) exiger, requérir ♦ *n* exigence *f*; (*claim*) revendication *f*; (*ECON*) demande *f*; **to ~ sth (from** *or* **of sb)** exiger qch (de qn), réclamer qch (à qn); **in ~** demandé(e), recherché(e); **on ~** sur demande.
demanding [dɪ'mɑːndɪŋ] *adj* (*person*) exigeant(e); (*work*) astreignant(e).
demarcation [diːmɑː'keɪʃən] *n* démarcation *f*.
demarcation dispute *n* (*INDUSTRY*) conflit *m* d'attributions.
demean [dɪ'miːn] *vt*: **to ~ o.s.** s'abaisser.
demeanour, (*US*) **demeanor** [dɪ'miːnə*] *n* comportement *m*; maintien *m*.
demented [dɪ'mɛntɪd] *adj* dément(e), fou(folle).
demilitarized zone [diː'mɪlɪtəraɪzd-] *n* zone démilitarisée.
demise [dɪ'maɪz] *n* décès *m*.
demist [diː'mɪst] *vt* (*BRIT AUT*) désembuer.
demister [diː'mɪstə*] *n* (*BRIT AUT*) dispositif *m* anti-buée *inv*.
demo ['dɛməu] *n abbr* (*col*: = *demonstration*) manif *f*.
demobilize [diː'məubɪlaɪz] *vt* démobiliser.
democracy [dɪ'mɔkrəsɪ] *n* démocratie *f*.
democrat ['dɛməkræt] *n* démocrate *m/f*.
democratic [dɛmə'krætɪk] *adj* démocratique; **the D~ Party** (*US*) le parti démocrate.
demography [dɪ'mɔgrəfɪ] *n* démographie *f*.
demolish [dɪ'mɔlɪʃ] *vt* démolir.
demolition [dɛmə'lɪʃən] *n* démolition *f*.
demon ['diːmən] *n* démon *m* ♦ *cpd*: **a ~ squash player** un crack en squash; **a ~ driver** un fou du volant.
demonstrate ['dɛmənstreɪt] *vt* démontrer, prouver ♦ *vi*: **to ~ (for/against)** manifester (en faveur de/contre).
demonstration [dɛmən'streɪʃən] *n* démonstration *f*; (*POL etc*) manifestation *f*; **to hold a ~** (*POL etc*) organiser une manifestation, manifester.
demonstrative [dɪ'mɔnstrətɪv] *adj* démonstratif(ive).
demonstrator ['dɛmənstreɪtə*] *n* (*POL etc*) manifestant/e; (*COMM*: *sales person*) vendeur/euse; (*: car, computer etc*) modèle *m* de démonstration.
demoralize [dɪ'mɔrəlaɪz] *vt* démoraliser.
demote [dɪ'məut] *vt* rétrograder.
demotion [dɪ'məuʃən] *n* rétrogradation *f*.
demur [dɪ'məː*] *vi*: **to ~ (at sth)** hésiter (devant qch); (*object*) élever des objections (contre qch) ♦ *n*: **without ~** sans hésiter; sans faire de difficultés.
demure [dɪ'mjuə*] *adj* sage, réservé(e); d'une modestie affectée.
demurrage [dɪ'mʌrɪdʒ] *n* droits *mpl* de magasinage; surestarie *f*.
den [dɛn] *n* tanière *f*, antre *m*.
denationalization [diːnæʃnəlaɪ'zeɪʃən] *n* dénationalisation *f*.
denationalize [diː'næʃnəlaɪz] *vt* dénationaliser.
denial [dɪ'naɪəl] *n* (*of accusation*) démenti *m*; (*of rights, guilt, truth*) dénégation *f*.
denier ['dɛnɪə*] *n* denier *m*; **15 ~ stockings** bas de 15 deniers.
denigrate ['dɛnɪgreɪt] *vt* dénigrer.
denim ['dɛnɪm] *n* coton émerisé.
denim jacket *n* veste *f* en jean.
denims ['dɛnɪmz] *npl* (blue-)jeans *mpl*.
denizen ['dɛnɪzn] *n* (*inhabitant*) habitant/e; (*foreigner*) étranger/ère.
Denmark ['dɛnmɑːk] *n* Danemark *m*.
denomination [dɪnɔmɪ'neɪʃən] *n* (*money*) valeur *f*; (*REL*) confession *f*; culte *m*.
denominator [dɪ'nɔmɪneɪtə*] *n* dénominateur *m*.
denote [dɪ'nəut] *vt* dénoter.
denounce [dɪ'nauns] *vt* dénoncer.
dense [dɛns] *adj* dense; (*col*: *stupid*) obtus(e), dur(e) *or* lent(e) à la comprenette.
densely ['dɛnslɪ] *adv*: **~ wooded** couvert(e) d'épaisses forêts; **~ populated** à forte densité (de population), très peuplé(e).
density ['dɛnsɪtɪ] *n* densité *f*; **single/double ~ disk** (*COMPUT*) disquette *f* (à) simple/double densité.
dent [dɛnt] *n* bosse *f* ♦ *vt* (*also*: **make a ~ in**) cabosser; **to make a ~ in** (*fig*) entamer.
dental ['dɛntl] *adj* dentaire.
dental floss [-flɔs] *n* fil *m* dentaire.
dental surgeon *n* (chirurgien/ne) dentiste.
dentifrice ['dɛntɪfrɪs] *n* dentifrice *m*.
dentist ['dɛntɪst] *n* dentiste *m/f*; **~'s surgery** (*BRIT*) cabinet *m* de dentiste.
dentistry ['dɛntɪstrɪ] *n* art *m* dentaire.
denture(s) ['dɛntʃə(z)] *n(pl)* dentier *m*.
denunciation [dɪnʌnsɪ'eɪʃən] *n* dénonciation *f*.
deny [dɪ'naɪ] *vt* nier; (*refuse*) refuser; (*disown*) renier; **he denies having said it** il nie l'avoir dit.
deodorant [diː'əudərənt] *n* désodorisant *m*, déodorant *m*.
depart [dɪ'pɑːt] *vi* partir; **to ~ from** (*leave*) quitter, partir de; (*fig: differ from*) s'écarter de.
departed [dɪ'pɑːtɪd] *adj* (*dead*) défunt(e); **the (dear) ~** le défunt/la défunte/les défunts.
department [dɪ'pɑːtmənt] *n* (*COMM*) rayon *m*; (*SCOL*) section *f*; (*POL*) ministère *m*, département *m*; **that's not my ~** (*fig*) ce n'est pas mon domaine *or* ma compétence, ce n'est pas mon rayon; **D~ of State** (*US*) Département d'État.
departmental [diːpɑːt'mɛntl] *adj* d'une *or* de

la section; d'un *or* du ministère, d'un *or* du département; ~ **manager** chef *m* de service; (*in shop*) chef de rayon.

department store *n* grand magasin.

departure [dɪ'pɑːtʃə*] *n* départ *m*; (*fig*): ~ **from** écart *m* par rapport à; **a new** ~ une nouvelle voie.

departure lounge *n* salle *f* de départ.

depend [dɪ'pɛnd] *vi*: **to** ~ **(up)on** dépendre de; (*rely on*) compter sur; (*financially*) dépendre (financièrement) de, être à la charge de; **it** ~**s** cela dépend; ~**ing on the result** ... selon le résultat ....

dependable [dɪ'pɛndəbl] *adj* sûr(e), digne de confiance.

dependant [dɪ'pɛndənt] *n* personne *f* à charge.

dependence [dɪ'pɛndəns] *n* dépendance *f*.

dependent [dɪ'pɛndənt] *adj*: **to be** ~ **(on)** dépendre (de) ♦ *n* = **dependant**.

depict [dɪ'pɪkt] *vt* (*in picture*) représenter; (*in words*) (dé)peindre, décrire.

depilatory [dɪ'pɪlətrɪ] *n* (*also*: ~ **cream**) dépilatoire *m*, crème *f* à épiler.

depleted [dɪ'pliːtɪd] *adj* (considérablement) réduit(e) *or* diminué(e).

deplorable [dɪ'plɔːrəbl] *adj* déplorable, lamentable.

deplore [dɪ'plɔː*] *vt* déplorer.

deploy [dɪ'plɔɪ] *vt* déployer.

depopulate [diː'pɔpjuleɪt] *vt* dépeupler.

depopulation ['diːpɔpju'leɪʃən] *n* dépopulation *f*, dépeuplement *m*.

deport [dɪ'pɔːt] *vt* déporter, expulser.

deportation [diːpɔː'teɪʃən] *n* déportation *f*, expulsion *f*.

deportation order *n* arrêté *m* d'expulsion.

deportee [diːpɔː'tiː] *n* déporté/e.

deportment [dɪ'pɔːtmənt] *n* maintien *m*, tenue *f*.

depose [dɪ'pəuz] *vt* déposer.

deposit [dɪ'pɔzɪt] *n* (*CHEM, COMM, GEO*) dépôt *m*; (*of ore, oil*) gisement *m*; (*part payment*) arrhes *fpl*, acompte *m*; (*on bottle etc*) con- signe *f*; (*for hired goods etc*) cautionnement *m*, garantie *f* ♦ *vt* déposer; (*valuables*) mettre *or* laisser en dépôt; **to put down a** ~ **of £50** verser 50 livres d'arrhes *or* d'acompte; laisser 50 livres en garantie.

deposit account *n* compte *m* de dépôt.

depositor [dɪ'pɔzɪtə*] *n* déposant/e.

depository [dɪ'pɔzɪtərɪ] *n* (*person*) dépositaire *m/f*; (*place*) dépôt *m*.

depot ['dɛpəu] *n* dépôt *m*.

depraved [dɪ'preɪvd] *adj* dépravé(e), perverti(e).

depravity [dɪ'prævɪtɪ] *n* dépravation *f*.

deprecate ['dɛprɪkeɪt] *vt* désapprouver.

deprecating ['dɛprɪkeɪtɪŋ] *adj* (*disapproving*) désapprobateur(trice); (*apologetic*): **a** ~ **smile** un sourire d'excuse.

depreciate [dɪ'priːʃɪeɪt] *vt* déprécier ♦ *vi* se déprécier, se dévaloriser.

depreciation [dɪpriːʃɪ'eɪʃən] *n* dépréciation *f*.

depress [dɪ'prɛs] *vt* déprimer; (*press down*) appuyer sur, abaisser.

depressant [dɪ'prɛsnt] *n* (*MED*) dépresseur *m*.

depressed [dɪ'prɛst] *adj* (*person*) déprimé(e), abattu(e); (*area*) en déclin, touché(e) par le sous-emploi; (*COMM*: *market, trade*) maussade; **to get** ~ se démoraliser, se laisser abattre.

depressing [dɪ'prɛsɪŋ] *adj* déprimant(e).

depression [dɪ'prɛʃən] *n* (*also ECON*) dépression *f*.

deprivation [dɛprɪ'veɪʃən] *n* privation *f*; (*loss*) perte *f*.

deprive [dɪ'praɪv] *vt*: **to** ~ **sb of** priver qn de; enlever à qn.

deprived [dɪ'praɪvd] *adj* déshérité(e).

dept. *abbr* (= *department*) dép., dépt.

depth [dɛpθ] *n* profondeur *f*; **in the** ~**s of** au fond de; au cœur de; au plus profond de; **at a** ~ **of 3 metres** à 3 mètres de profondeur; **to be out of one's** ~ (*BRIT*: *swimmer*) ne plus avoir pied; (*fig*) être dépassé(e), nager; **to study sth in** ~ étudier qch en profondeur.

depth charge *n* grenade sous-marine.

deputation [dɛpju'teɪʃən] *n* députation *f*, délégation *f*.

deputize ['dɛpjutaɪz] *vi*: **to** ~ **for** assurer l'intérim de.

deputy ['dɛpjutɪ] *n* (*replacement*) suppléant/e, intérimaire *m/f*; (*second in command*) adjoint/e ♦ *adj*: ~ **chairman** vice-président *m*; ~ **head** (*SCOL*) directeur/trice adjoint(e), sous-directeur/trice; ~ **leader** (*BRIT POL*) vice-président/e, secrétaire adjoint(e).

derail [dɪ'reɪl] *vt* faire dérailler; **to be** ~**ed** dérailler.

derailment [dɪ'reɪlmənt] *n* déraillement *m*.

deranged [dɪ'reɪndʒd] *adj*: **to be (mentally)** ~ avoir le cerveau dérangé.

derby ['dəːrbɪ] *n* (*US*) (chapeau *m*) melon *m*.

Derbys *abbr* (*BRIT*) = *Derbyshire*.

deregulate [dɪ'rɛgjuleɪt] *vt* libérer, dérégler.

deregulation [dɪrɛgju'leɪʃən] *n* libération *f*, dérèglement *m*.

derelict ['dɛrɪlɪkt] *adj* abandonné(e), à l'abandon.

deride [dɪ'raɪd] *vt* railler.

derision [dɪ'rɪʒən] *n* dérision *f*.

derisive [dɪ'raɪsɪv] *adj* moqueur(euse), railleur(euse).

derisory [dɪ'raɪsərɪ] *adj* (*sum*) dérisoire; (*smile, person*) moqueur(euse), railleur(euse).

derivation [dɛrɪ'veɪʃən] *n* dérivation *f*.

derivative [dɪ'rɪvətɪv] *n* dérivé *m* ♦ *adj* dérivé(e).

derive [dɪ'raɪv] *vt*: **to** ~ **sth from** tirer qch de; trouver qch dans ♦ *vi*: **to** ~ **from** provenir de, dériver de.

dermatitis [dəːmə'taɪtɪs] *n* dermatite *f*.

dermatology [dəːmə'tɔlədʒɪ] *n* dermatologie

f.

derogatory [dɪ'rɔgətərɪ] *adj* désobligeant(e); péjoratif(ive).

derrick ['dɛrɪk] *n* mât *m* de charge; derrick *m*.

derv [dəːv] *n* (*BRIT*) gas-oil *m*, diesel *m*.

desalination [diːsælɪ'neɪʃən] *n* dessalement *m*, dessalage *m*.

descend [dɪ'sɛnd] *vt, vi* descendre; **to ~ from** descendre de, être issu(e) de; **in ~ing order of importance** par ordre d'importance décroissante.

►**descend on** *vt fus* (*subj: enemy, angry person*) tomber *or* sauter sur; (*: misfortune*) s'abattre sur; (*: gloom, silence*) envahir; **visitors ~ed (up)on us** des gens sont arrivés chez nous à l'improviste.

descendant [dɪ'sɛndənt] *n* descendant/e.

descent [dɪ'sɛnt] *n* descente *f*; (*origin*) origine *f*.

describe [dɪs'kraɪb] *vt* décrire.

description [dɪs'krɪpʃən] *n* description *f*; (*sort*) sorte *f*, espèce *f*; **of every ~** de toutes sortes.

descriptive [dɪs'krɪptɪv] *adj* descriptif(ive).

desecrate ['dɛsɪkreɪt] *vt* profaner.

desert *n* ['dɛzət] désert *m* ♦ *vb* [dɪ'zəːt] *vt* déserter, abandonner ♦ *vi* (*MIL*) déserter.

deserter [dɪ'zəːtə*] *n* déserteur *m*.

desertion [dɪ'zəːʃən] *n* désertion *f*.

desert island *n* île déserte

deserts [dɪ'zəːts] *npl*: **to get one's just ~** n'avoir que ce qu'on mérite.

deserve [dɪ'zəːv] *vt* mériter.

deservedly [dɪ'zəːvɪdlɪ] *adv* à juste titre, à bon droit.

deserving [dɪ'zəːvɪŋ] *adj* (*person*) méritant(e); (*action, cause*) méritoire.

desiccated ['dɛsɪkeɪtɪd] *adj* séché(e).

design [dɪ'zaɪn] *n* (*sketch*) plan *m*, dessin *m*; (*layout, shape*) conception *f*, ligne *f*; (*pattern*) dessin, motif(s) *m(pl)*; (*of dress, car*) modèle *m*; (*art*) design *m*, stylisme *m*; (*intention*) dessein *m* ♦ *vt* dessiner; (*plan*) concevoir; **to have ~s on** avoir des visées sur; **well-~ed** *adj* bien conçu(e); **industrial ~** esthétique industrielle.

design and technology *n* (*BRIT SCOL*) technologie *f*.

designate *vt* ['dɛzɪgneɪt] désigner ♦ *adj* ['dɛzɪgnɪt] désigné(e).

designation [dɛzɪg'neɪʃən] *n* désignation *f*.

designer [dɪ'zaɪnə*] *n* (*ARCHIT, ART*) dessinateur/trice; (*INDUSTRY*) concepteur *m*, designer *m*; (*FASHION*) modéliste *m/f*.

desirability [dɪzaɪərə'bɪlɪtɪ] *n* avantage *m*; attrait *m*.

desirable [dɪ'zaɪərəbl] *adj* désirable; **it is ~ that** il est souhaitable que.

desire [dɪ'zaɪə*] *n* désir *m* ♦ *vt* désirer, vouloir; **to ~ to do sth/that** désirer faire qch/que.

desirous [dɪ'zaɪərəs] *adj*: **~ of** désireux(euse) de.

desk [dɛsk] *n* (*in office*) bureau *m*; (*for pupil*) pupitre *m*; (*BRIT: in shop, restaurant*) caisse *f*; (*in hotel, at airport*) réception *f*.

desktop computer ['dɛsktɔp-] *n* ordinateur *m* de bureau *or* de table.

desktop publishing ['dɛsktɔp-] *n* publication assistée par ordinateur, PAO *f*.

desolate ['dɛsəlɪt] *adj* désolé(e).

desolation [dɛsə'leɪʃən] *n* désolation *f*.

despair [dɪs'pɛə*] *n* désespoir *m* ♦ *vi*: **to ~ of** désespérer de; **to be in ~** être au désespoir.

despatch [dɪs'pætʃ] *n, vt* = **dispatch**.

desperate ['dɛspərɪt] *adj* désespéré(e); (*fugitive*) prêt(e) à tout; (*measures*) désespéré, extrême; **we are getting ~** nous commençons à désespérer.

desperately ['dɛspərɪtlɪ] *adv* désespérément; (*very*) terriblement, extrêmement; **~ ill** très gravement malade.

desperation [dɛspə'reɪʃən] *n* désespoir *m*; **in ~** en désespoir de cause.

despicable [dɪs'pɪkəbl] *adj* méprisable.

despise [dɪs'paɪz] *vt* mépriser, dédaigner.

despite [dɪs'paɪt] *prep* malgré, en dépit de.

despondent [dɪs'pɔndənt] *adj* découragé(e), abattu(e).

despot ['dɛspɔt] *n* despote *m/f*.

dessert [dɪ'zəːt] *n* dessert *m*.

dessertspoon [dɪ'zəːtspuːn] *n* cuiller *f* à dessert.

destabilize [diː'steɪbɪlaɪz] *vt* déstabiliser.

destination [dɛstɪ'neɪʃən] *n* destination *f*.

destine ['dɛstɪn] *vt* destiner.

destined ['dɛstɪnd] *adj*: **to be ~ to do sth** être destiné(e) à faire qch; **~ for London** à destination de Londres.

destiny ['dɛstɪnɪ] *n* destinée *f*, destin *m*.

destitute ['dɛstɪtjuːt] *adj* indigent(e), dans le dénuement; **~ of** dépourvu(e) *or* dénué(e) de.

destroy [dɪs'trɔɪ] *vt* détruire.

destroyer [dɪs'trɔɪə*] *n* (*NAUT*) contre-torpilleur *m*.

destruction [dɪs'trʌkʃən] *n* destruction *f*.

destructive [dɪs'trʌktɪv] *adj* destructeur(trice).

desultory ['dɛsəltərɪ] *adj* (*reading, conversation*) décousu(e); (*contact*) irrégulier(ière).

detach [dɪ'tætʃ] *vt* détacher.

detachable [dɪ'tætʃəbl] *adj* amovible, détachable.

detached [dɪ'tætʃt] *adj* (*attitude*) détaché(e).

detached house *n* pavillon *m*, maison(nette) (individuelle).

detachment [dɪ'tætʃmənt] *n* (*MIL*) détachement *m*; (*fig*) détachement, indifférence *f*.

detail ['diːteɪl] *n* détail *m*; (*MIL*) détachement *m* ♦ *vt* raconter en détail, énumérer; (*MIL*): **to ~ sb (for)** affecter qn (à), détacher qn (pour); **in ~** en détail; **to go into ~(s)** entrer dans les détails.

detailed ['diːteɪld] *adj* détaillé(e).

detain [dɪ'teɪn] *vt* retenir; (*in captivity*) détenir; (*in hospital*) hospitaliser.
detainee [diːteɪ'niː] *n* détenu/e.
detect [dɪ'tɛkt] *vt* déceler, percevoir; (*MED, POLICE*) dépister; (*MIL, RADAR, TECH*) détecter.
detection [dɪ'tɛkʃən] *n* découverte *f*; (*MED, POLICE*) dépistage *m*; (*MIL, RADAR, TECH*) détection *f*; **to escape** ~ échapper aux recherches, éviter d'être découvert(e); (*mistake*) passer inaperçu(e); **crime** ~ le dépistage des criminels.
detective [dɪ'tɛktɪv] *n* agent *m* de la sûreté, policier *m*; **private** ~ détective privé.
detective story *n* roman policier.
detector [dɪ'tɛktə*] *n* détecteur *m*.
détente [deɪ'tɑːnt] *n* détente *f*.
detention [dɪ'tɛnʃən] *n* détention *f*; (*SCOL*) retenue *f*, consigne *f*.
deter [dɪ'təː*] *vt* dissuader.
detergent [dɪ'təːdʒənt] *n* détersif *m*, détergent *m*.
deteriorate [dɪ'tɪərɪəreɪt] *vi* se détériorer, se dégrader.
deterioration [dɪtɪərɪə'reɪʃən] *n* détérioration *f*.
determination [dɪtəːmɪ'neɪʃən] *n* détermination *f*.
determine [dɪ'təːmɪn] *vt* déterminer; **to ~ to do** résoudre de faire, se déterminer à faire.
determined [dɪ'təːmɪnd] *adj* (*person*) déterminé(e), décidé(e); (*quantity*) déterminé, établi(e); (*effort*) très gros(se).
deterrence [dɪ'tɛrns] *n* dissuasion *f*.
deterrent [dɪ'tɛrənt] *n* effet *m* de dissuasion; force *f* de dissuasion; **to act as a** ~ avoir un effet dissuasif.
detest [dɪ'tɛst] *vt* détester, avoir horreur de.
detestable [dɪ'tɛstəbl] *adj* détestable, odieux(euse).
detonate ['dɛtəneɪt] *vi* exploser ♦ *vt* faire exploser *or* détoner.
detonator ['dɛtəneɪtə*] *n* détonateur *m*.
detour ['diːtuə*] *n* détour *m*; (*US AUT: diversion*) déviation *f*.
detract [dɪ'trækt] *vt*: **to ~ from** (*quality, pleasure*) diminuer; (*reputation*) porter atteinte à.
detractor [dɪ'træktə*] *n* détracteur/trice.
detriment ['dɛtrɪmənt] *n*: **to the ~ of** au détriment de, au préjudice de; **without ~ to** sans porter atteinte *or* préjudice à, sans conséquences fâcheuses pour.
detrimental [dɛtrɪ'mɛntl] *adj*: ~ **to** préjudiciable *or* nuisible à.
deuce [djuːs] *n* (*TENNIS*) égalité *f*.
devaluation [dɪvælju'eɪʃən] *n* dévaluation *f*.
devalue ['diː'væljuː] *vt* dévaluer.
devastate ['dɛvəsteɪt] *vt* dévaster; **he was ~d by the news** cette nouvelle lui a porté un coup terrible.
devastating ['dɛvəsteɪtɪŋ] *adj* dévastateur(trice).
devastation [dɛvəs'teɪʃən] *n* dévastation *f*.
develop [dɪ'vɛləp] *vt* (*gen*) développer; (*habit*) contracter; (*resources*) mettre en valeur, exploiter; (*land*) aménager ♦ *vi* se développer; (*situation, disease: evolve*) évoluer; (*facts, symptoms: appear*) se manifester, se produire; **to ~ a taste for sth** prendre goût à qch; **to ~ into** devenir.
developer [dɪ'vɛləpə*] *n* (*PHOT*) révélateur *m*; (*of land*) promoteur *m*; (*also*: **property** ~) promoteur immobilier.
developing country [dɪ'vɛləpɪŋ-] *n* pays *m* en voie de développement.
development [dɪ'vɛləpmənt] *n* développement *m*; (*of affair, case*) rebondissement *m*, fait(s) nouveau(x).
development area *n* zone *f* à urbaniser.
deviate ['diːvɪeɪt] *vi*: **to ~ (from)** dévier (de).
deviation [diːvɪ'eɪʃən] *n* déviation *f*.
device [dɪ'vaɪs] *n* (*scheme*) moyen *m*, expédient *m*; (*apparatus*) engin *m*, dispositif *m*; **explosive** ~ engin explosif.
devil ['dɛvl] *n* diable *m*; démon *m*.
devilish ['dɛvlɪʃ] *adj* diabolique.
devil-may-care ['dɛvlmeɪ'kɛə*] *adj* je-m'en-foutiste.
devil's advocate *n*: **to play** ~ se faire avocat du diable.
devious ['diːvɪəs] *adj* (*means*) détourné(e); (*person*) sournois(e), dissimulé(e).
devise [dɪ'vaɪz] *vt* imaginer, concevoir.
devoid [dɪ'vɔɪd] *adj*: ~ **of** dépourvu(e) de, dénué(e) de.
devolution [diːvə'luːʃən] *n* (*POL*) décentralisation *f*.
devolve [dɪ'vɔlv] *vi*: **to ~ (up)on** retomber sur.
devote [dɪ'vəut] *vt*: **to ~ sth to** consacrer qch à.
devoted [dɪ'vəutɪd] *adj* dévoué(e); **to be ~ to** être dévoué(e) *or* très attaché(e) à; (*subj: book etc*) être consacré(e) à.
devotee [dɛvəu'tiː] *n* (*REL*) adepte *m/f*; (*MUS, SPORT*) fervent/e.
devotion [dɪ'vəuʃən] *n* dévouement *m*, attachement *m*; (*REL*) dévotion *f*, piété *f*.
devour [dɪ'vauə*] *vt* dévorer.
devout [dɪ'vaut] *adj* pieux(euse), dévot(e).
dew [djuː] *n* rosée *f*.
dexterity [dɛks'tɛrɪtɪ] *n* dextérité *f*, adresse *f*.
dext(e)rous ['dɛkstrəs] *adj* adroit(e).
dg *abbr* (= *decigram*) dg.
diabetes [daɪə'biːtiːz] *n* diabète *m*.
diabetic [daɪə'bɛtɪk] *n* diabétique *m/f* ♦ *adj* (*person*) diabétique; (*chocolate, jam*) pour diabétiques.
diabolical [daɪə'bɔlɪkl] *adj* diabolique; (*col: dreadful*) infernal(e), atroce.
diaeresis [daɪ'ɛrɪsɪs] *n* tréma *m*.
diagnose [daɪəg'nəuz] *vt* diagnostiquer.
diagnosis, *pl* **diagnoses** [daɪəg'nəusɪs, -siːz] *n*

diagnostic *m*.
diagonal [daɪ'ægənl] *adj* diagonal(e) ♦ *n* diagonale *f*.
diagram ['daɪəgræm] *n* diagramme *m*, schéma *m*.
dial ['daɪəl] *n* cadran *m* ♦ *vt* (*number*) faire, composer; **to ~ a wrong number** faire un faux numéro; **can I ~ London direct?** puis-je *or* est-ce-que je peux avoir Londres par l'automatique?
dialect ['daɪəlɛkt] *n* dialecte *m*.
dialling code ['daɪəlɪŋ-] *n* indicatif *m* (téléphonique).
dialling tone ['daɪəlɪŋ-], (*US*) **dial tone** *n* tonalité *f*.
dialogue ['daɪəlɔg] *n* dialogue *m*.
dialysis [daɪ'ælɪsɪs] *n* dialyse *f*.
diameter [daɪ'æmɪtə*] *n* diamètre *m*.
diametrically [daɪə'mɛtrɪklɪ] *adv*: **~ opposed (to)** diamétralement opposé(e) (à).
diamond ['daɪəmənd] *n* diamant *m*; (*shape*) losange *m*; **~s** *npl* (*CARDS*) carreau *m*.
diamond ring *n* bague *f* de diamant(s).
diaper ['daɪəpə*] *n* (*US*) couche *f*.
diaphragm ['daɪəfræm] *n* diaphragme *m*.
diarrhoea, (*US*) **diarrhea** [daɪə'ri:ə] *n* diarrhée *f*.
diary ['daɪərɪ] *n* (*daily account*) journal *m*; (*book*) agenda *m*; **to keep a ~** tenir un journal.
diatribe ['daɪətraɪb] *n* diatribe *f*.
dice [daɪs] *n* (*pl inv*) dé *m* ♦ *vt* (*CULIN*) couper en dés *or* en cubes.
dicey ['daɪsɪ] *adj* (*col*): **it's a bit ~** c'est un peu risqué.
dichotomy [daɪ'kɔtəmɪ] *n* dichotomie *f*.
dickhead ['dɪkhɛd] *n* (*BRIT col!*) tête *f* de nœud (*!*).
Dictaphone ['dɪktəfəun] *n* ® Dictaphone *m* ®.
dictate *vt* [dɪk'teɪt] dicter ♦ *vi*: **to ~ to** (*person*) imposer sa volonté à, régenter; **I won't be ~d to** je n'ai d'ordres à recevoir de personne ♦ *n* ['dɪkteɪt] injonction *f*.
dictation [dɪk'teɪʃən] *n* dictée *f*; **at ~ speed** à une vitesse de dictée.
dictator [dɪk'teɪtə*] *n* dictateur *m*.
dictatorship [dɪk'teɪtəʃɪp] *n* dictature *f*.
diction ['dɪkʃən] *n* diction *f*, élocution *f*.
dictionary ['dɪkʃənrɪ] *n* dictionnaire *m*.
did [dɪd] *pt of* **do**.
didactic [daɪ'dæktɪk] *adj* didactique.
didn't [dɪdnt] = **did not**.
die [daɪ] *n* (*pl*: **dice**) dé *m*; (*pl*: **dies**) coin *m*; matrice *f*; étampe *f* ♦ *vi*: **to ~ (of *or* from)** mourir (de); **to be dying** être mourant(e); **to be dying for sth** avoir une envie folle de qch; **to be dying to do sth** mourir d'envie de faire qch.
►**die away** *vi* s'éteindre.
►**die down** *vi* se calmer, s'apaiser.
►**die out** *vi* disparaître, s'éteindre.
diehard ['daɪhɑ:d] *n* réactionnaire *m/f*, jusqu'au-boutiste *m/f*.
diesel ['di:zl] *n* diesel *m*.
diesel engine *n* moteur *m* diesel.
diesel fuel, diesel oil *n* carburant *m* diesel.
diet ['daɪət] *n* alimentation *f*; (*restricted food*) régime *m* ♦ *vi* (*also*: **be on a ~**) suivre un régime; **to live on a ~ of** se nourrir de.
dietician [daɪə'tɪʃən] *n* diététicien/ne.
differ ['dɪfə*] *vi*: **to ~ from sth** être différent(e) de; différer de; **to ~ from sb over sth** ne pas être d'accord avec qn au sujet de qch.
difference ['dɪfrəns] *n* différence *f*; (*quarrel*) différend *m*, désaccord *m*; **it makes no ~ to me** cela m'est égal, cela m'est indifférent; **to settle one's ~s** résoudre la situation.
different ['dɪfrənt] *adj* différent(e).
differential [dɪfə'rɛnʃəl] *n* (*AUT*, *wages*) différentiel *m*.
differentiate [dɪfə'rɛnʃɪeɪt] *vt* différencier ♦ *vi* se différencier; **to ~ between** faire une différence entre.
differently ['dɪfrəntlɪ] *adv* différemment.
difficult ['dɪfɪkəlt] *adj* difficile; **~ to understand** difficile à comprendre.
difficulty ['dɪfɪkəltɪ] *n* difficulté *f*; **to have difficulties with** avoir des ennuis *or* problèmes avec; **to be in ~** avoir des difficultés, avoir des problèmes.
diffidence ['dɪfɪdəns] *n* manque *m* de confiance en soi, manque d'assurance.
diffident ['dɪfɪdənt] *adj* qui manque de confiance *or* d'assurance, peu sûr(e) de soi.
diffuse *adj* [dɪ'fju:s] diffus(e) ♦ *vt* [dɪ'fju:z] diffuser, répandre.
dig [dɪg] *vt* (*pt*, *pp* **dug** [dʌg]) (*hole*) creuser; (*garden*) bêcher ♦ *n* (*prod*) coup *m* de coude; (*fig*) coup de griffe *or* de patte; (*ARCHAEOLOGY*) fouille *f*; **to ~ into** (*snow, soil*) creuser; **to ~ into one's pockets for sth** fouiller dans ses poches pour chercher *or* prendre qch; **to ~ one's nails into** enfoncer ses ongles dans.
►**dig in** *vi* (*also*: **~ o.s. in**: *MIL*) se retrancher; (*: fig*) tenir bon, se braquer; (*col*: *eat*) attaquer (un repas *or* un plat *etc*) ♦ *vt* (*compost*) bien mélanger à la bêche; (*knife, claw*) enfoncer; **to ~ in one's heels** (*fig*) se braquer, se buter.
►**dig out** *vt* (*survivors, car from snow*) sortir *or* dégager (à coups de pelles *or* pioches).
►**dig up** *vt* déterrer.
digest *vt* [daɪ'dʒɛst] digérer ♦ *n* ['daɪdʒɛst] sommaire *m*, résumé *m*.
digestible [dɪ'dʒɛstəbl] *adj* digestible.
digestion [dɪ'dʒɛstʃən] *n* digestion *f*.
digestive [dɪ'dʒɛstɪv] *adj* digestif(ive).
digit ['dɪdʒɪt] *n* chiffre *m* (*de 0 à 9*); (*finger*) doigt *m*.
digital ['dɪdʒɪtl] *adj* digital(e); (*watch*) à affichage numérique *or* digital.
digital camera *n* appareil *m* photo numérique.

digital compact cassette *n* cassette *f* numérique.
digital TV *n* télévision *f* numérique.
dignified ['dɪgnɪfaɪd] *adj* digne.
dignitary ['dɪgnɪtərɪ] *n* dignitaire *m*.
dignity ['dɪgnɪtɪ] *n* dignité *f*.
digress [daɪ'grɛs] *vi*: **to ~ from** s'écarter de, s'éloigner de.
digression [daɪ'grɛʃən] *n* digression *f*.
digs [dɪgz] *npl* (*BRIT col*) chambre meublée.
dilapidated [dɪ'læpɪdeɪtɪd] *adj* délabré(e).
dilate [daɪ'leɪt] *vt* dilater ♦ *vi* se dilater.
dilatory ['dɪlətərɪ] *adj* dilatoire.
dilemma [daɪ'lɛmə] *n* dilemme *m*; **to be in a ~** être pris dans un dilemme.
diligent ['dɪlɪdʒənt] *adj* appliqué(e), assidu(e).
dill [dɪl] *n* aneth *m*.
dilly-dally ['dɪlɪ'dælɪ] *vi* hésiter, tergiverser; traînasser, lambiner.
dilute [daɪ'luːt] *vt* diluer ♦ *adj* dilué(e).
dim [dɪm] *adj* (*light, eyesight*) faible; (*memory, outline*) vague, indécis(e); (*stupid*) borné(e), obtus(e) ♦ *vt* (*light*) réduire, baisser; (*US AUT*) mettre en code, baisser; **to take a ~ view of sth** voir qch d'un mauvais œil.
dime [daɪm] *n* (*US*) = *10 cents*.
dimension [daɪ'mɛnʃən] *n* dimension *f*.
-dimensional [dɪ'mɛnʃənl] *adj suffix*: **two~** à deux dimensions.
diminish [dɪ'mɪnɪʃ] *vt, vi* diminuer.
diminished [dɪ'mɪnɪʃt] *adj*: **~ responsibility** (*LAW*) responsabilité atténuée.
diminutive [dɪ'mɪnjutɪv] *adj* minuscule, tout(e) petit(e) ♦ *n* (*LING*) diminutif *m*.
dimly ['dɪmlɪ] *adv* faiblement; vaguement.
dimmer ['dɪmə*] *n* (*also*: **~ switch**) variateur *m*; **~s** *npl* (*US AUT*: *dipped headlights*) phares *mpl* code *inv*; (: *parking lights*) feux *mpl* de position.
dimple ['dɪmpl] *n* fossette *f*.
dim-witted ['dɪm'wɪtɪd] *adj* (*col*) stupide, borné(e).
din [dɪn] *n* vacarme *m* ♦ *vt*: **to ~ sth into sb** (*col*) enfoncer qch dans la tête *or* la caboche de qn.
dine [daɪn] *vi* dîner.
diner ['daɪnə*] *n* (*person*) dîneur/euse; (*RAIL*) = **dining car**; (*US*: *eating place*) petit restaurant.
dinghy ['dɪŋgɪ] *n* youyou *m*; (*inflatable*) canot *m* pneumatique; (*also*: **sailing ~**) voilier *m*, dériveur *m*.
dingy ['dɪndʒɪ] *adj* miteux(euse), minable.
dining car ['daɪnɪŋ-] *n* voiture-restaurant *f*, wagon-restaurant *m*.
dining room ['daɪnɪŋ-] *n* salle *f* à manger.
dinner ['dɪnə*] *n* dîner *m*; (*public*) banquet *m*; **~'s ready!** à table!
dinner jacket *n* smoking *m*.
dinner party *n* dîner *m*.
dinner time *n* heure *f* du dîner.
dinosaur ['daɪnəsɔː*] *n* dinosaure *m*.
dint [dɪnt] *n*: **by ~ of (doing) sth** à force de (faire) qch.
diocese ['daɪəsɪs] *n* diocèse *m*.
dioxide [daɪ'ɔksaɪd] *n* dioxyde *m*.
Dip. *abbr* (*BRIT*) = **diploma.**
dip [dɪp] *n* déclivité *f*; (*in sea*) baignade *f*, bain *m* ♦ *vt* tremper, plonger; (*BRIT AUT*: *lights*) mettre en code, baisser ♦ *vi* plonger.
diphtheria [dɪf'θɪərɪə] *n* diphtérie *f*.
diphthong ['dɪfθɔŋ] *n* diphtongue *f*.
diploma [dɪ'pləumə] *n* diplôme *m*.
diplomacy [dɪ'pləuməsɪ] *n* diplomatie *f*.
diplomat ['dɪpləmæt] *n* diplomate *m*.
diplomatic [dɪplə'mætɪk] *adj* diplomatique; **to break off ~ relations (with)** rompre les relations diplomatiques (avec).
diplomatic corps *n* corps *m* diplomatique.
diplomatic immunity *n* immunité *f* diplomatique.
dipstick ['dɪpstɪk] *n* (*AUT*) jauge *f* de niveau d'huile.
dipswitch ['dɪpswɪtʃ] *n* (*BRIT AUT*) commutateur *m* de code.
dire [daɪə*] *adj* extrême, affreux(euse).
direct [daɪ'rɛkt] *adj* direct(e); (*manner, person*) direct, franc(franche) ♦ *vt* diriger, orienter; **can you ~ me to ...?** pouvez-vous m'indiquer le chemin de ...?; **to ~ sb to do sth** ordonner à qn de faire qch.
direct cost *n* (*COMM*) coût *m* variable.
direct current *n* (*ELEC*) courant continu.
direct debit *n* (*BANKING*) prélèvement *m* automatique.
direct dialling *n* (*TEL*) automatique *m*.
direct hit *n* (*MIL*) coup *m* au but, touché *m*.
direction [dɪ'rɛkʃən] *n* direction *f*; (*THEAT*) mise *f* en scène; (*CINE, TV*) réalisation *f*; **~s** *npl* (*instructions: to a place*) indications *fpl*; **~s for use** mode *m* d'emploi; **to ask for ~s** demander sa route *or* son chemin; **sense of ~** sens *m* de l'orientation; **in the ~ of** dans la direction de, vers.
directive [dɪ'rɛktɪv] *n* directive *f*; **a government ~** une directive du gouvernement.
direct labour *n* main-d'œuvre directe; employés municipaux.
directly [dɪ'rɛktlɪ] *adv* (*in straight line*) directement, tout droit; (*at once*) tout de suite, immédiatement.
direct mail *n* vente *f* par publicité directe.
direct mailshot *n* (*BRIT*) publicité postale.
directness [daɪ'rɛktnɪs] *n* (*of person, speech*) franchise *f*.
director [dɪ'rɛktə*] *n* directeur *m*; (*board member*) administrateur *m*; (*THEAT*) metteur *m* en scène; (*CINE, TV*) réalisateur/trice; **D~ of Public Prosecutions** (*BRIT*) ≈ procureur général.
directory [dɪ'rɛktərɪ] *n* annuaire *m*; (*also*: **street ~**) indicateur *m* de rues; (*also*: **trade ~**) annuaire du commerce; (*COMPUT*) répertoire *m*.
directory enquiries, (*US*) **directory assis-**

tance *n* (*TEL: service*) renseignements *mpl*.

dirt [dəːt] *n* saleté *f*; (*mud*) boue *f*; **to treat sb like ~** traiter qn comme un chien.

dirt-cheap ['dəːt'tʃiːp] *adj* (ne) coûtant presque rien.

dirt road *n* chemin non macadamisé *or* non revêtu.

dirty ['dəːtɪ] *adj* sale ♦ *vt* salir; **~ story** histoire cochonne; **~ trick** coup tordu.

disability [dɪsə'bɪlɪtɪ] *n* invalidité *f*, infirmité *f*.

disability allowance *n* allocation *f* d'invalidité *or* d'infirmité.

disable [dɪs'eɪbl] *vt* (*subj: illness, accident*) rendre *or* laisser infirme; (*tank, gun*) mettre hors d'action.

disabled [dɪs'eɪbld] *adj* infirme, invalide; (*maimed*) mutilé(e); (*through illness, old age*) impotent(e).

disadvantage [dɪsəd'vɑːntɪdʒ] *n* désavantage *m*, inconvénient *m*.

disadvantaged [dɪsəd'vɑːntɪdʒd] *adj* (*person*) désavantagé(e).

disadvantageous [dɪsædvɑːn'teɪdʒəs] *adj* désavantageux(euse).

disaffected [dɪsə'fɛktɪd] *adj*: **~ (to *or* towards)** mécontent(e) (de).

disaffection [dɪsə'fɛkʃən] *n* désaffection *f*, mécontentement *m*.

disagree [dɪsə'griː] *vi* (*differ*) ne pas concorder; (*be against, think otherwise*): **to ~ (with)** ne pas être d'accord (avec); **garlic ~s with me** l'ail ne me convient pas, je ne supporte pas l'ail.

disagreeable [dɪsə'griːəbl] *adj* désagréable.

disagreement [dɪsə'griːmənt] *n* désaccord *m*, différend *m*.

disallow ['dɪsə'lau] *vt* rejeter, désavouer; (*BRIT FOOTBALL: goal*) refuser.

disappear [dɪsə'pɪə*] *vi* disparaître.

disappearance [dɪsə'pɪərəns] *n* disparition *f*.

disappoint [dɪsə'pɔɪnt] *vt* décevoir.

disappointed [dɪsə'pɔɪntɪd] *adj* déçu(e).

disappointing [dɪsə'pɔɪntɪŋ] *adj* décevant(e).

disappointment [dɪsə'pɔɪntmənt] *n* déception *f*.

disapproval [dɪsə'pruːvəl] *n* désapprobation *f*.

disapprove [dɪsə'pruːv] *vi*: **to ~ of** désapprouver.

disapproving [dɪsə'pruːvɪŋ] *adj* désapprobateur(trice), de désapprobation.

disarm [dɪs'ɑːm] *vt* désarmer.

disarmament [dɪs'ɑːməmənt] *n* désarmement *m*.

disarming [dɪs'ɑːmɪŋ] *adj* (*smile*) désarmant(e).

disarray [dɪsə'reɪ] *n* désordre *m*, confusion *f*; **in ~** (*troops*) en déroute; (*thoughts*) embrouillé(e); (*clothes*) en désordre; **to throw into ~** semer la confusion *or* le désordre dans (*or* parmi).

disaster [dɪ'zɑːstə*] *n* catastrophe *f*, désastre *m*.

disastrous [dɪ'zɑːstrəs] *adj* désastreux(euse).

disband [dɪs'bænd] *vt* démobiliser; disperser ♦ *vi* se séparer; se disperser.

disbelief ['dɪsbə'liːf] *n* incrédulité *f*; **in ~** avec incrédulité.

disbelieve ['dɪsbə'liːv] *vt* (*person*) ne pas croire; (*story*) mettre en doute; **I don't ~ you** je veux bien vous croire.

disc [dɪsk] *n* disque *m*.

disc. *abbr* (*COMM*) = **discount**.

discard [dɪs'kɑːd] *vt* (*old things*) se défaire de, mettre au rencart *or* au rebut; (*fig*) écarter, renoncer à.

disc brake *n* frein *m* à disque.

discern [dɪ'səːn] *vt* discerner, distinguer.

discernible [dɪ'səːnəbl] *adj* discernable, perceptible; (*object*) visible.

discerning [dɪ'səːnɪŋ] *adj* judicieux(euse), perspicace.

discharge *vt* [dɪs'tʃɑːdʒ] (*duties*) s'acquitter de; (*settle: debt*) s'acquitter de, régler; (*waste etc*) déverser; décharger; (*ELEC, MED*) émettre; (*patient*) renvoyer (chez lui); (*employee, soldier*) congédier, licencier; (*defendant*) relaxer, élargir ♦ *n* ['dɪstʃɑːdʒ] (*ELEC, MED etc*) émission *f*; (*also*: **vaginal ~**) pertes blanches; (*dismissal*) renvoi *m*; licenciement *m*; élargissement *m*; **to ~ one's gun** faire feu; **~d bankrupt** failli/e réhabilité(e).

disciple [dɪ'saɪpl] *n* disciple *m*.

disciplinary ['dɪsɪplɪnərɪ] *adj* disciplinaire; **to take ~ action against sb** prendre des mesures disciplinaires à l'encontre de qn.

discipline ['dɪsɪplɪn] *n* discipline *f* ♦ *vt* discipliner; (*punish*) punir; **to ~ o.s. to do sth** s'imposer *or* s'astreindre à une discipline pour faire qch.

disc jockey (DJ) *n* disque-jockey *m* (DJ).

disclaim [dɪs'kleɪm] *vt* désavouer, dénier.

disclaimer [dɪs'kleɪmə*] *n* démenti *m*, dénégation *f*; **to issue a ~** publier un démenti.

disclose [dɪs'kləuz] *vt* révéler, divulguer.

disclosure [dɪs'kləuʒə*] *n* révélation *f*, divulgation *f*.

disco ['dɪskəu] *n abbr* = **discothèque**.

discolour, (*US*) **discolor** [dɪs'kʌlə*] *vt* décolorer; (*sth white*) jaunir ♦ *vi* se décolorer; jaunir.

discolo(u)ration [dɪskʌlə'reɪʃən] *n* décoloration *f*; jaunissement *m*.

discolo(u)red [dɪs'kʌləd] *adj* décoloré(e); jauni(e).

discomfort [dɪs'kʌmfət] *n* malaise *m*, gêne *f*; (*lack of comfort*) manque *m* de confort.

disconcert [dɪskən'səːt] *vt* déconcerter, décontenancer.

disconnect [dɪskə'nɛkt] *vt* détacher; (*ELEC, RADIO*) débrancher; (*gas, water*) couper.

disconnected [dɪskə'nɛktɪd] *adj* (*speech, thoughts*) décousu(e), peu cohérent(e).

disconsolate [dɪs'kɔnsəlɪt] *adj* inconsolable.

discontent [dɪskən'tɛnt] *n* mécontentement

m.

discontented [dɪskən'tɛntɪd] *adj* mécontent(e).

discontinue [dɪskən'tɪnjuː] *vt* cesser, interrompre; **"~d"** (*COMM*) "fin de série".

discord ['dɪskɔːd] *n* discorde *f*, dissension *f*; (*MUS*) dissonance *f*.

discordant [dɪs'kɔːdənt] *adj* discordant(e), dissonant(e).

discotheque ['dɪskəutɛk] *n* discothèque *f*.

discount *n* ['dɪskaunt] remise *f*, rabais *m* ♦ *vt* [dɪs'kaunt] (*report etc*) ne pas tenir compte de; **to give sb a ~ on sth** faire une remise *or* un rabais à qn sur qch; **~ for cash** escompte *f* au comptant; **at a ~** avec une remise *or* réduction, au rabais.

discount house *n* (*FINANCE*) banque *f* d'escompte; (*COMM*: *also*: **discount store**) magasin *m* de discount.

discount rate *n* taux *m* de remise.

discourage [dɪs'kʌrɪdʒ] *vt* décourager; (*dissuade, deter*) dissuader, décourager.

discouragement [dɪs'kʌrɪdʒmənt] *n* (*depression*) découragement *m*; **to act as a ~ to sb** dissuader qn.

discouraging [dɪs'kʌrɪdʒɪŋ] *adj* décourageant(e).

discourteous [dɪs'kəːtɪəs] *adj* incivil(e), discourtois(e).

discover [dɪs'kʌvə*] *vt* découvrir.

discovery [dɪs'kʌvərɪ] *n* découverte *f*.

discredit [dɪs'krɛdɪt] *vt* mettre en doute; discréditer ♦ *n* discrédit *m*.

discreet [dɪ'skriːt] *adj* discret(ète).

discreetly [dɪ'skriːtlɪ] *adv* discrètement.

discrepancy [dɪ'skrɛpənsɪ] *n* divergence *f*, contradiction *f*.

discretion [dɪ'skrɛʃən] *n* discrétion *f*; **use your own ~** à vous de juger.

discretionary [dɪ'skrɛʃənrɪ] *adj* (*powers*) discrétionnaire.

discriminate [dɪ'skrɪmɪneɪt] *vi*: **to ~ between** établir une distinction entre, faire la différence entre; **to ~ against** pratiquer une discrimination contre.

discriminating [dɪ'skrɪmɪneɪtɪŋ] *adj* qui a du discernement.

discrimination [dɪskrɪmɪ'neɪʃən] *n* discrimination *f*, (*judgment*) discernement *m*; **racial/sexual ~** discrimination raciale/sexuelle.

discus ['dɪskəs] *n* disque *m*.

discuss [dɪ'skʌs] *vt* discuter de; (*debate*) discuter.

discussion [dɪ'skʌʃən] *n* discussion *f*; **under ~** en discussion.

disdain [dɪs'deɪn] *n* dédain *m*.

disease [dɪ'ziːz] *n* maladie *f*.

diseased [dɪ'ziːzd] *adj* malade.

disembark [dɪsɪm'bɑːk] *vt, vi* débarquer.

disembarkation [dɪsɛmbɑː'keɪʃən] *n* débarquement *m*.

disembodied ['dɪsɪm'bɔdɪd] *adj* désincarné(e).

disembowel ['dɪsɪm'bauəl] *vt* éviscérer, étriper.

disenchanted ['dɪsɪn'tʃɑːntɪd] *adj*: **~ (with)** désenchanté(e) (de), désabusé(e) (de).

disenfranchise ['dɪsɪn'fræntʃaɪz] *vt* priver du droit de vote; (*COMM*) retirer la franchise à.

disengage [dɪsɪn'geɪdʒ] *vt* dégager; (*TECH*) déclencher; **to ~ the clutch** (*AUT*) débrayer.

disentangle [dɪsɪn'tæŋgl] *vt* démêler.

disfavour, (*US*) **disfavor** [dɪs'feɪvə*] *n* défaveur *f*; disgrâce *f*.

disfigure [dɪs'fɪgə*] *vt* défigurer.

disgorge [dɪs'gɔːdʒ] *vt* déverser.

disgrace [dɪs'greɪs] *n* honte *f*; (*disfavour*) disgrâce *f* ♦ *vt* déshonorer, couvrir de honte.

disgraceful [dɪs'greɪsful] *adj* scandaleux(euse), honteux(euse).

disgruntled [dɪs'grʌntld] *adj* mécontent(e).

disguise [dɪs'gaɪz] *n* déguisement *m* ♦ *vt* déguiser; (*voice*) déguiser, contrefaire; (*feelings etc*) masquer, dissimuler; **in ~** déguisé(e); **to ~ o.s. as** se déguiser en; **there's no disguising the fact that ...** on ne peut pas se dissimuler que ....

disgust [dɪs'gʌst] *n* dégoût *m*, aversion *f* ♦ *vt* dégoûter, écœurer.

disgusting [dɪs'gʌstɪŋ] *adj* dégoûtant(e), révoltant(e).

dish [dɪʃ] *n* plat *m*; **to do** *or* **wash the ~es** faire la vaisselle.

►**dish out** *vt* distribuer.

►**dish up** *vt* servir; (*facts, statistics*) sortir, débiter.

dishcloth ['dɪʃklɔθ] *n* (*for drying*) torchon *m*; (*for washing*) lavette *f*.

dishearten [dɪs'hɑːtn] *vt* décourager.

dishevelled, (*US*) **disheveled** [dɪ'ʃɛvəld] *adj* ébouriffé(e); décoiffé(e); débraillé(e).

dishonest [dɪs'ɔnɪst] *adj* malhonnête.

dishonesty [dɪs'ɔnɪstɪ] *n* malhonnêteté *f*.

dishonour, (*US*) **dishonor** [dɪs'ɔnə*] *n* déshonneur *m*.

dishono(u)rable [dɪs'ɔnərəbl] *adj* déshonorant(e).

dish soap *n* (*US*) produit *m* pour la vaisselle.

dishtowel ['dɪʃtauəl] *n* torchon *m* (à vaisselle).

dishwasher ['dɪʃwɔʃə*] *n* lave-vaisselle *m*; (*person*) plongeur/euse.

dishy ['dɪʃɪ] *adj* (*BRIT col*) séduisant(e), sexy *inv*.

disillusion [dɪsɪ'luːʒən] *vt* désabuser, désenchanter ♦ *n* désenchantement *m*; **to become ~ed (with)** perdre ses illusions (en ce qui concerne).

disillusionment [dɪsɪ'luːʒənmənt] *n* désillusionnement *m*, désillusion *f*.

disincentive [dɪsɪn'sɛntɪv] *n*: **it's a ~** c'est démotivant; **to be a ~ to sb** démotiver qn.

disinclined ['dɪsɪn'klaɪnd] *adj*: **to be ~ to do sth** être peu disposé(e) *or* peu enclin(e) à

faire qch.
disinfect [dɪsɪn'fɛkt] *vt* désinfecter.
disinfectant [dɪsɪn'fɛktənt] *n* désinfectant *m*.
disinflation [dɪsɪn'fleɪʃən] *n* désinflation *f*.
disinformation [dɪsɪnfə'meɪʃən] *n* désinformation *f*.
disinherit [dɪsɪn'hɛrɪt] *vt* déshériter.
disintegrate [dɪs'ɪntɪgreɪt] *vi* se désintégrer.
disinterested [dɪs'ɪntrəstɪd] *adj* désintéressé(e).
disjointed [dɪs'dʒɔɪntɪd] *adj* décousu(e), incohérent(e).
disk [dɪsk] *n* (*COMPUT*) disquette *f*; **single-/double-sided** ~ disquette une face/double face.
disk drive *n* lecteur *m* de disquette.
diskette [dɪs'kɛt] *n* (*COMPUT*) disquette *f*.
disk operating system (DOS) *n* système *m* d'exploitation à disques (DOS).
dislike [dɪs'laɪk] *n* aversion *f*, antipathie *f* ♦ *vt* ne pas aimer; **to take a** ~ **to sb/sth** prendre qn/qch en grippe; **I** ~ **the idea** l'idée me déplaît.
dislocate ['dɪsləkeɪt] *vt* disloquer, déboîter; (*services etc*) désorganiser; **he has** ~**d his shoulder** il s'est disloqué l'épaule.
dislodge [dɪs'lɔdʒ] *vt* déplacer, faire bouger; (*enemy*) déloger.
disloyal [dɪs'lɔɪəl] *adj* déloyal(e).
dismal ['dɪzml] *adj* lugubre, maussade.
dismantle [dɪs'mæntl] *vt* démonter; (*fort, warship*) démanteler.
dismast [dɪs'mɑːst] *vt* démâter.
dismay [dɪs'meɪ] *n* consternation *f* ♦ *vt* consterner; **much to my** ~ à ma grande consternation, à ma grande inquiétude.
dismiss [dɪs'mɪs] *vt* congédier, renvoyer; (*idea*) écarter; (*LAW*) rejeter ♦ *vi* (*MIL*) rompre les rangs.
dismissal [dɪs'mɪsl] *n* renvoi *m*.
dismount [dɪs'maunt] *vi* mettre pied à terre.
disobedience [dɪsə'biːdɪəns] *n* désobéissance *f*.
disobedient [dɪsə'biːdɪənt] *adj* désobéissant(e), indiscipliné(e).
disobey [dɪsə'beɪ] *vt* désobéir à; (*rule*) transgresser, enfreindre.
disorder [dɪs'ɔːdə*] *n* désordre *m*; (*rioting*) désordres *mpl*; (*MED*) troubles *mpl*.
disorderly [dɪs'ɔːdəlɪ] *adj* (*room*) en désordre; (*behaviour, retreat, crowd*) désordonné(e).
disorderly conduct *n* (*LAW*) conduite *f* contraire aux bonnes mœurs.
disorganized [dɪs'ɔːgənaɪzd] *adj* désorganisé(e).
disorientated [dɪs'ɔːrɪenteɪtɪd] *adj* désorienté(e).
disown [dɪs'əun] *vt* renier.
disparaging [dɪs'pærɪdʒɪŋ] *adj* désobligeant(e); **to be** ~ **about sb/sth** faire des remarques désobligeantes sur qn/qch.
disparate ['dɪspərɪt] *adj* disparate.
disparity [dɪs'pærɪtɪ] *n* disparité *f*.
dispassionate [dɪs'pæʃənət] *adj* calme, froid(e); impartial(e), objectif(ive).
dispatch [dɪs'pætʃ] *vt* expédier, envoyer; (*deal with: business*) régler, en finir avec ♦ *n* envoi *m*, expédition *f*; (*MIL, PRESS*) dépêche *f*.
dispatch department *n* service *m* des expéditions.
dispatch rider *n* (*MIL*) estafette *f*.
dispel [dɪs'pɛl] *vt* dissiper, chasser.
dispensary [dɪs'pɛnsərɪ] *n* pharmacie *f*; (*in chemist's*) officine *f*.
dispense [dɪs'pɛns] *vt* distribuer, administrer; (*medicine*) préparer (et vendre); **to** ~ **sb from** dispenser qn de.
►**dispense with** *vt fus* se passer de; (*make unnecessary*) rendre superflu(e).
dispenser [dɪs'pɛnsə*] *n* (*device*) distributeur *m*.
dispensing chemist [dɪs'pɛnsɪŋ-] *n* (*BRIT*) pharmacie *f*.
dispersal [dɪs'pəːsl] *n* dispersion *f*; (*ADMIN*) déconcentration *f*.
disperse [dɪs'pəːs] *vt* disperser; (*knowledge*) disséminer ♦ *vi* se disperser.
dispirited [dɪs'pɪrɪtɪd] *adj* découragé(e), déprimé(e).
displace [dɪs'pleɪs] *vt* déplacer.
displaced person [dɪs'pleɪst-] *n* (*POL*) personne déplacée.
displacement [dɪs'pleɪsmənt] *n* déplacement *m*.
display [dɪs'pleɪ] *n* (*of goods*) étalage *m*; affichage *m*; (*computer* ~*: information*) visualisation *f*; (*: device*) visuel *m*; (*of feeling*) manifestation *f*; (*pej*) ostentation *f*; (*show, spectacle*) spectacle *m*; (*military* ~) parade *f* militaire ♦ *vt* montrer; (*goods*) mettre à l'étalage, exposer; (*results, departure times*) afficher; (*pej*) faire étalage de; **on** ~ (*exhibits*) exposé(e), exhibé(e); (*goods*) à l'étalage.
display advertising *n* publicité rédactionnelle.
displease [dɪs'pliːz] *vt* mécontenter, contrarier; ~**d with** mécontent(e) de.
displeasure [dɪs'plɛʒə*] *n* mécontentement *m*.
disposable [dɪs'pəuzəbl] *adj* (*pack etc*) jetable; (*income*) disponible; ~ **nappy** (*BRIT*) couche *f* à jeter, couche-culotte *f*.
disposal [dɪs'pəuzl] *n* (*availability, arrangement*) disposition *f*; (*of property etc: by selling*) vente *f*; (*: by giving away*) cession *f*; (*of rubbish*) évacuation *f*, destruction *f*; **at one's** ~ à sa disposition; **to put sth at sb's** ~ mettre qch à la disposition de qn.
dispose [dɪs'pəuz] *vt* disposer.
►**dispose of** *vt fus* (*time, money*) disposer de; (*unwanted goods*) se débarrasser de, se défaire de; (*COMM: stock*) écouler, vendre; (*problem*) expédier.
disposed [dɪs'pəuzd] *adj*: ~ **to do** disposé(e) à faire.

disposition [dɪspəˈzɪʃən] *n* disposition *f*; (*temperament*) naturel *m*.
dispossess [ˈdɪspəˈzɛs] *vt*: **to ~ sb (of)** déposséder qn (de).
disproportion [dɪsprəˈpɔːʃən] *n* disproportion *f*.
disproportionate [dɪsprəˈpɔːʃənət] *adj* disproportionné(e).
disprove [dɪsˈpruːv] *vt* réfuter.
dispute [dɪsˈpjuːt] *n* discussion *f*; (*also*: **industrial** ~) conflit *m* ♦ *vt* contester; (*matter*) discuter; (*victory*) disputer; **to be in** *or* **under** ~ (*matter*) être en discussion; (*territory*) être contesté(e).
disqualification [dɪskwɔlɪfɪˈkeɪʃən] *n* disqualification *f*; ~ **(from driving)** (*BRIT*) retrait *m* du permis (de conduire).
disqualify [dɪsˈkwɔlɪfaɪ] *vt* (*SPORT*) disqualifier; **to ~ sb for sth/from doing** (*status, situation*) rendre qn inapte à qch/à faire; (*authority*) signifier à qn l'interdiction de faire; **to ~ sb (from driving)** (*BRIT*) retirer à qn son permis (de conduire).
disquiet [dɪsˈkwaɪət] *n* inquiétude *f*, trouble *m*.
disquieting [dɪsˈkwaɪətɪŋ] *adj* inquiétant(e), alarmant(e).
disregard [dɪsrɪˈgɑːd] *vt* ne pas tenir compte de ♦ *n* (*indifference*): ~ **(for)** (*feelings*) indifférence *f* (pour), insensibilité *f* (à); (*danger, money*) mépris *m* (pour).
disrepair [ˈdɪsrɪˈpɛə*] *n* mauvais état; **to fall into ~** (*building*) tomber en ruine; (*street*) se dégrader.
disreputable [dɪsˈrɛpjutəbl] *adj* (*person*) de mauvaise réputation, peu recommandable; (*behaviour*) déshonorant(e); (*area*) mal famé(e), louche.
disrepute [ˈdɪsrɪˈpjuːt] *n* déshonneur *m*, discrédit *m*; **to bring into ~** faire tomber dans le discrédit.
disrespectful [dɪsrɪˈspɛktful] *adj* irrespectueux(euse).
disrupt [dɪsˈrʌpt] *vt* (*plans, meeting, lesson*) perturber, déranger.
disruption [dɪsˈrʌpʃən] *n* perturbation *f*, dérangement *m*.
disruptive [dɪsˈrʌptɪv] *adj* perturbateur (trice).
dissatisfaction [dɪssætɪsˈfækʃən] *n* mécontentement *m*, insatisfaction *f*.
dissatisfied [dɪsˈsætɪsfaɪd] *adj*: ~ **(with)** mécontent(e) *or* insatisfait(e) (de).
dissect [dɪˈsɛkt] *vt* disséquer; (*fig*) disséquer, éplucher.
disseminate [dɪˈsɛmɪneɪt] *vt* disséminer.
dissent [dɪˈsɛnt] *n* dissentiment *m*, différence *f* d'opinion.
dissenter [dɪˈsɛntə*] *n* (*REL, POL etc*) dissident/e.
dissertation [dɪsəˈteɪʃən] *n* (*SCOL*) mémoire *m*.
disservice [dɪsˈsəːvɪs] *n*: **to do sb a ~** rendre un mauvais service à qn; desservir qn.
dissident [ˈdɪsɪdnt] *adj, n* dissident(e).
dissimilar [dɪˈsɪmɪlə*] *adj*: ~ **(to)** dissemblable (à), différent(e) (de).
dissipate [ˈdɪsɪpeɪt] *vt* dissiper; (*energy, efforts*) disperser.
dissipated [ˈdɪsɪpeɪtɪd] *adj* dissolu(e); débauché(e).
dissociate [dɪˈsəuʃɪeɪt] *vt* dissocier; **to ~ o.s. from** se désolidariser de.
dissolute [ˈdɪsəluːt] *adj* débauché(e), dissolu(e).
dissolution [dɪsəˈluːʃən] *n* dissolution *f*.
dissolve [dɪˈzɔlv] *vt* dissoudre ♦ *vi* se dissoudre, fondre; (*fig*) disparaître.
dissuade [dɪˈsweɪd] *vt*: **to ~ sb (from)** dissuader qn (de).
distaff [ˈdɪstɑːf] *n*: ~ **side** côté maternel.
distance [ˈdɪstns] *n* distance *f*; **what's the ~ to London?** à quelle distance se trouve Londres?; **it's within walking ~** on peut y aller à pied; **in the ~** au loin.
distant [ˈdɪstnt] *adj* lointain(e), éloigné(e); (*manner*) distant(e), froid(e).
distaste [dɪsˈteɪst] *n* dégoût *m*.
distasteful [dɪsˈteɪstful] *adj* déplaisant(e), désagréable.
Dist. Atty. *abbr* (*US*) = **district attorney**.
distemper [dɪsˈtɛmpə*] *n* (*paint*) détrempe *f*, badigeon *m*; (*of dogs*) maladie *f* de Carré.
distended [dɪsˈtɛndɪd] *adj* (*stomach*) dilaté(e).
distil, (*US*) **distill** [dɪsˈtɪl] *vt* distiller.
distillery [dɪsˈtɪlərɪ] *n* distillerie *f*.
distinct [dɪsˈtɪŋkt] *adj* distinct(e); (*preference, progress*) marqué(e); **as ~ from** par opposition à, en contraste avec.
distinction [dɪsˈtɪŋkʃən] *n* distinction *f*; (*in exam*) mention *f* très bien; **to draw a ~ between** faire une distinction entre; **a writer of ~** un écrivain réputé.
distinctive [dɪsˈtɪŋktɪv] *adj* distinctif(ive).
distinctly [dɪsˈtɪŋktlɪ] *adv* distinctement; (*specify*) expressément.
distinguish [dɪsˈtɪŋgwɪʃ] *vt* distinguer ♦ *vi*: **to ~ between** (*concepts*) distinguer entre, faire une distinction entre; **to ~ o.s.** se distinguer.
distinguished [dɪsˈtɪŋgwɪʃt] *adj* (*eminent, refined*) distingué(e); (*career*) remarquable, brillant(e).
distinguishing [dɪsˈtɪŋgwɪʃɪŋ] *adj* (*feature*) distinctif(ive), caractéristique.
distort [dɪsˈtɔːt] *vt* déformer.
distortion [dɪsˈtɔːʃən] *n* déformation *f*.
distract [dɪsˈtrækt] *vt* distraire, déranger.
distracted [dɪsˈtræktɪd] *adj* (*look etc*) éperdu(e), égaré(e).
distraction [dɪsˈtrækʃən] *n* distraction *f*, dérangement *m*; **to drive sb to ~** rendre qn fou(folle).
distraught [dɪsˈtrɔːt] *adj* éperdu(e).
distress [dɪsˈtrɛs] *n* détresse *f*, (*pain*) douleur *f*

♦ *vt* affliger; **in ~** (*ship*) en perdition; (*plane*) en détresse; **~ed area** (*BRIT*) zone sinistrée.
distressing [dɪs'trɛsɪŋ] *adj* douloureux(euse), pénible, affligeant(e).
distress signal *n* signal *m* de détresse.
distribute [dɪs'trɪbjuːt] *vt* distribuer.
distribution [dɪstrɪ'bjuːʃən] *n* distribution *f*.
distribution cost *n* coût *m* de distribution.
distributor [dɪs'trɪbjutə*] *n* (*gen, TECH*) distributeur *m*; (*COMM*) concessionnaire *m/f*.
district ['dɪstrɪkt] *n* (*of country*) région *f*; (*of town*) quartier *m*; (*ADMIN*) district *m*.
district attorney *n* (*US*) ≈ procureur *m* de la République.
district council *n* (*BRIT*) ≈ conseil municipal; *voir encadré*.

DISTRICT COUNCIL

En Grande-Bretagne, un **district council** *est une administration locale qui gère un "district". Les conseillers ("councillors") sont élus au niveau local, en général tous les 4 ans. Le* **district council** *est financé par des impôts locaux et par des subventions du gouvernement.*

district nurse *n* (*BRIT*) infirmière visiteuse.
distrust [dɪs'trʌst] *n* méfiance *f*, doute *m* ♦ *vt* se méfier de.
distrustful [dɪs'trʌstful] *adj* méfiant(e).
disturb [dɪs'təːb] *vt* troubler; (*inconvenience*) déranger; **sorry to ~ you** excusez-moi de vous déranger.
disturbance [dɪs'təːbəns] *n* dérangement *m*; (*political etc*) troubles *mpl*; (*by drunks etc*) tapage *m*; **to cause a ~** troubler l'ordre public; **~ of the peace** (*LAW*) tapage injurieux *or* nocturne.
disturbed [dɪs'təːbd] *adj* agité(e), troublé(e); **to be mentally/emotionally ~** avoir des problèmes psychologiques/affectifs.
disturbing [dɪs'təːbɪŋ] *adj* troublant(e), inquiétant(e).
disuse [dɪs'juːs] *n*: **to fall into ~** tomber en désuétude.
disused [dɪs'juːzd] *adj* désaffecté(e).
ditch [dɪtʃ] *n* fossé *m* ♦ *vt* (*col*) abandonner.
dither ['dɪðə*] *vi* hésiter.
ditto ['dɪtəu] *adv* idem.
divan [dɪ'væn] *n* divan *m*.
divan bed *n* divan-lit *m*.
dive [daɪv] *n* plongeon *m*; (*of submarine*) plongée *f*; (*AVIAT*) piqué *m*; (*pej: café, bar etc*) bouge *m* ♦ *vi* plonger.
diver ['daɪvə*] *n* plongeur *m*.
diverge [daɪ'vəːdʒ] *vi* diverger.
diverse [daɪ'vəːs] *adj* divers(e).
diversification [daɪvəːsɪfɪ'keɪʃən] *n* diversification *f*.
diversify [daɪ'vəːsɪfaɪ] *vt* diversifier.
diversion [daɪ'vəːʃən] *n* (*BRIT AUT*) déviation *f*; (*distraction, MIL*) diversion *f*.
diversionary tactics [daɪ'vəːʃənrɪ-] *npl* tactique *fsg* de diversion.
diversity [daɪ'vəːsɪtɪ] *n* diversité *f*, variété *f*.
divert [daɪ'vəːt] *vt* (*BRIT: traffic*) dévier; (*plane*) dérouter; (*train, river*) détourner; (*amuse*) divertir.
divest [daɪ'vɛst] *vt*: **to ~ sb of** dépouiller qn de.
divide [dɪ'vaɪd] *vt* diviser; (*separate*) séparer ♦ *vi* se diviser; **to ~ (between** *or* **among)** répartir *or* diviser (entre); **40 ~d by 5** 40 divisé par 5.
►**divide out** *vt*: **to ~ out (between** *or* **among)** distribuer *or* répartir (entre).
divided [dɪ'vaɪdɪd] *adj* (*fig: country, couple*) désuni(e); (*opinions*) partagé(e).
divided skirt *n* jupe-culotte *f*.
dividend ['dɪvɪdɛnd] *n* dividende *m*.
dividend cover *n* rapport *m* dividendes-résultat.
dividers [dɪ'vaɪdəz] *npl* compas *m* à pointes sèches; (*between pages*) feuillets *mpl* intercalaires.
divine [dɪ'vaɪn] *adj* divin(e) ♦ *vt* (*future*) prédire; (*truth*) deviner, entrevoir; (*water, metal*) détecter la présence de.
diving ['daɪvɪŋ] *n* plongée (sous-marine).
diving board *n* plongeoir *m*.
diving suit *n* scaphandre *m*.
divinity [dɪ'vɪnɪtɪ] *n* divinité *f*; (*as study*) théologie *f*.
division [dɪ'vɪʒən] *n* (*also BRIT FOOTBALL*) division *f*; (*separation*) séparation *f*; (*BRIT POL*) vote *m*; **~ of labour** division du travail.
divisive [dɪ'vaɪsɪv] *adj* qui entraîne la division, qui crée des dissensions.
divorce [dɪ'vɔːs] *n* divorce *m* ♦ *vt* divorcer d'avec.
divorced [dɪ'vɔːst] *adj* divorcé(e).
divorcee [dɪvɔː'siː] *n* divorcé/e.
divot ['dɪvət] *n* (*GOLF*) motte *f* de gazon.
divulge [daɪ'vʌldʒ] *vt* divulguer, révéler.
DIY *adj, n abbr* (*BRIT*) = **do-it-yourself**.
dizziness ['dɪzɪnɪs] *n* vertige *m*, étourdissement *m*.
dizzy ['dɪzɪ] *adj* (*height*) vertigineux(euse); **to make sb ~** donner le vertige à qn; **I feel ~** la tête me tourne, j'ai la tête qui tourne.
DJ *n abbr* = **disc jockey**.
d.j. *n abbr* = **dinner jacket**.
Djakarta [dʒə'kɑːtə] *n* Djakarta.
DJIA *n abbr* (*US STOCK EXCHANGE*) = *Dow-Jones Industrial Average*.
dl *abbr* (= *decilitre*) dl.
DLit(t) *n abbr* (= *Doctor of Literature, Doctor of Letters*) *titre universitaire*.
DLO *n abbr* = **dead-letter office**.
DMus *n abbr* (= *Doctor of Music*) *titre universitaire*.
DMZ *n abbr* = **demilitarized zone**.
DNA *n abbr* (= *deoxyribonucleic acid*) ADN *m*.
do *abbr* (= *ditto*) d°.

KEYWORD

do [duː] (*pt* **did,** *pp* **done**) *n* (*inf: party etc*) soirée *f*, fête *f*; (*: formal gathering*) réception *f*
♦ *vb* **1** (*in negative constructions*) *non traduit*; **I don't understand** je ne comprends pas
2 (*to form questions*) *non traduit*; **didn't you know?** vous ne le saviez pas?; **why didn't you come?** pourquoi n'êtes-vous pas venu?
3 (*for emphasis, in polite expressions*): **she does seem rather late** je trouve qu'elle est bien en retard; ~ **sit down/help yourself** asseyez-vous/servez-vous je vous en prie; **I DO wish I could go** j'aimerais tant y aller; **but I DO like it!** mais si, je l'aime!
4 (*used to avoid repeating vb*): **she swims better than I** ~ elle nage mieux que moi; ~ **you agree? — yes, I ~/no, I don't** vous êtes d'accord? — oui/non; **she lives in Glasgow — so ~ I** elle habite Glasgow — moi aussi; **who broke it? — I did** qui l'a cassé? — c'est moi
5 (*in question tags*): **he laughed, didn't he?** il a ri, n'est-ce pas?; **I don't know him, ~ I?** je ne crois pas le connaître
♦ *vt* (*gen: carry out, perform etc*) faire; (*visit: city, museum*) faire, visiter; **what are you ~ing tonight?** qu'est-ce que vous faites ce soir?; **what did he ~ with the cat?** qu'a t'il fait du chat?; **to ~ the cooking/washing-up** faire la cuisine/la vaisselle; **to ~ one's teeth/hair/nails** se brosser les dents/se coiffer/se faire les ongles; **the car was ~ing 100** la voiture faisait du 100 (à l'heure)
♦ *vi* **1** (*act, behave*) faire; ~ **as I** ~ faites comme moi
2 (*get on, fare*) marcher; **the firm is ~ing well** l'entreprise marche bien; **how ~ you ~?** comment allez-vous?; (*on being introduced*) enchanté(e)!
3 (*suit*) aller; **will it ~?** est-ce que ça ira?
4 (*be sufficient*) suffire, aller; **will £10 ~?** est-ce que 10 livres suffiront?; **that'll ~** ça suffit, ça ira; **that'll ~!** (*in annoyance*) ça va *or* suffit comme ça!; **to make ~ (with)** se contenter (de)

►**do away with** *vt fus* abolir; (*kill*) supprimer
►**do for** *vt fus* (*BRIT col: clean for*) faire le ménage chez
►**do up** *vt* (*laces, dress*) attacher; (*buttons*) boutonner; (*zip*) fermer; (*renovate: room*) refaire; (*: house*) remettre à neuf; **to ~ o.s. up** se faire beau(belle)
►**do with** *vt fus* (*need*): **I could ~ with a drink** quelque chose à boire ne serait pas de refus; **it could ~ with a wash** ça ne lui ferait pas de mal d'être lavé; (*be connected*): **that has nothing to ~ with you** cela ne vous concerne pas; **I won't have anything to ~ with it** je ne veux pas m'en mêler; **what has that got to ~ with it?** quel est le rapport?, qu'est-ce que cela vient faire là-dedans?
►**do without** *vi* s'en passer ♦ *vt fus* se passer de.

DOA *abbr* (= *dead on arrival*) décédé(e) à l'admission.
d.o.b. *abbr* = **date of birth**.
doc [dɔk] *n* (*col*) toubib *m*.
docile ['dəusaɪl] *adj* docile.
dock [dɔk] *n* dock *m*; (*wharf*) quai *m*; (*LAW*) banc *m* des accusés ♦ *vi* se mettre à quai ♦ *vt*: **they ~ed a third of his wages** ils lui ont retenu *or* décompté un tiers de son salaire.
dock dues *npl* droits *mpl* de bassin.
docker ['dɔkə*] *n* docker *m*.
docket ['dɔkɪt] *n* bordereau *m*; (*on parcel etc*) étiquette *f or* fiche *f* (*décrivant le contenu d'un paquet etc*).
dockyard ['dɔkjɑːd] *n* chantier *m* de construction navale.
doctor ['dɔktə*] *n* médecin *m*, docteur *m*; (*PhD etc*) docteur ♦ *vt* (*cat*) couper; (*interfere with: food*) altérer; (*: drink*) frelater; (*: text, document*) arranger; **~'s office** (*US*) cabinet *m* de consultation; **D~ of Philosophy (PhD)** doctorat *m*; titulaire *m/f* d'un doctorat.
doctorate ['dɔktərɪt] *n* doctorat *m*; *voir encadré*.

DOCTORATE

Le **doctorate** *est le diplôme universitaire le plus prestigieux. Il est le résultat d'au minimum trois années de recherches et est accordé après soutenance d'une thèse devant un jury. Le doctorat le plus courant est le "PhD" ("Doctor of Philosophy"), accordé en lettres, en sciences et en ingénierie, bien qu'il existe également d'autres doctorats spécialisés (en musique, en droit, etc); voir "Bachelor's degree", "Master's degree".*

docudrama ['dɔkjudrɑːmə] *n* (*TV*) docudrame *m*.
document *n* ['dɔkjumənt] document *m* ♦ *vt* ['dɔkjumɛnt] documenter.
documentary [dɔkju'mɛntərɪ] *adj, n* documentaire (*m*).
documentation [dɔkjumən'teɪʃən] *n* documentation *f*.
DOD *n abbr* (*US*) = **Department of Defense**.
doddering ['dɔdərɪŋ] *adj* (*senile*) gâteux(euse).
doddery ['dɔdərɪ] *adj* branlant(e).
doddle ['dɔdl] *n*: **it's a ~** (*col*) c'est simple comme bonjour, c'est du gâteau.
Dodecanese (Islands) [dəudɪkə'niːz-] *n(pl)* Dodécanèse *m*.
dodge [dɔdʒ] *n* truc *m*; combine *f* ♦ *vt* esquiver, éviter ♦ *vi* faire un saut de côté; (*SPORT*) faire une esquive; **to ~ out of the way** s'esquiver; **to ~ through the traffic** se faufiler *or* faire de savantes manœuvres entre les voitures.
dodgems ['dɔdʒəmz] *npl* (*BRIT*) autos tampon-

neuses.
dodgy ['dɔdʒɪ] *adj* (*col*: *uncertain*) douteux(euse); (*: shady*) louche.
DOE *n abbr* (*BRIT*) = *Department of the Environment*; (*US*) = *Department of Energy*.
doe [dəu] *n* (*deer*) biche *f*; (*rabbit*) lapine *f*.
does [dʌz] *see* **do**.
doesn't ['dʌznt] = **does not**.
dog [dɔg] *n* chien/ne ♦ *vt* (*follow closely*) suivre de près, ne pas lâcher d'une semelle; (*fig: memory etc*) poursuivre, harceler; **to go to the ~s** (*nation etc*) aller à vau-l'eau.
dog biscuits *npl* biscuits *mpl* pour chien.
dog collar *n* collier *m* de chien; (*fig*) faux-col *m* d'ecclésiastique.
dog-eared ['dɔgɪəd] *adj* corné(e).
dog food *n* nourriture *f* pour les chiens *or* le chien.
dogged ['dɔgɪd] *adj* obstiné(e), opiniâtre.
doggy ['dɔgɪ] *n* (*col*) toutou *m*.
doggy bag *n petit sac pour emporter les restes.*
dogma ['dɔgmə] *n* dogme *m*.
dogmatic [dɔg'mætɪk] *adj* dogmatique.
do-gooder [du:'gudə*] *n* (*pej*) faiseur/euse de bonnes œuvres.
dogsbody ['dɔgzbɔdɪ] *n* (*BRIT*) bonne *f* à tout faire, tâcheron *m*.
doily ['dɔɪlɪ] *n* dessus *m* d'assiette.
doing ['duɪŋ] *n*: **this is your ~** c'est votre travail, c'est vous qui avez fait ça.
doings ['duɪŋz] *npl* activités *fpl*.
do-it-yourself ['du:ɪtjɔ:'sɛlf] *n* bricolage *m*.
doldrums ['dɔldrəmz] *npl*: **to be in the ~** avoir le cafard; être dans le marasme.
dole [dəul] *n* (*BRIT*: *payment*) allocation *f* de chômage; **on the ~** au chômage.
►**dole out** *vt* donner au compte-goutte.
doleful ['dəulful] *adj* triste, lugubre.
doll [dɔl] *n* poupée *f*.
►**doll up** *vt*: **to ~ o.s. up** se faire beau(belle).
dollar ['dɔlə*] *n* dollar *m*.
dollop ['dɔləp] *n* (*of butter, cheese*) bon morceau; (*of cream*) bonne cuillerée.
dolly ['dɔlɪ] *n* poupée *f*.
dolphin ['dɔlfɪn] *n* dauphin *m*.
domain [də'meɪn] *n* (*also fig*) domaine *m*.
dome [dəum] *n* dôme *m*.
domestic [də'mɛstɪk] *adj* (*duty, happiness*) familial(e); (*policy, affairs, flights*) intérieur(e); (*news*) national(e); (*animal*) domestique.
domesticated [də'mɛstɪkeɪtɪd] *adj* domestiqué(e); (*pej*) d'intérieur; **he's very ~** il participe volontiers aux tâches ménagères; question ménage, il est très organisé.
domesticity [dəumɛs'tɪsɪtɪ] *n* vie *f* de famille.
domestic servant *n* domestique *m/f*.
domicile ['dɔmɪsaɪl] *n* domicile *m*.
dominant ['dɔmɪnənt] *adj* dominant(e).
dominate ['dɔmɪneɪt] *vt* dominer.
domination [dɔmɪ'neɪʃən] *n* domination *f*.
domineering [dɔmɪ'nɪərɪŋ] *adj* dominateur(trice), autoritaire.
Dominican Republic [də'mɪnɪkən-] *n* République Dominicaine.
dominion [də'mɪnɪən] *n* domination *f*; territoire *m*; dominion *m*.
domino, ~es ['dɔmɪnəu] *n* domino *m*; **~es** *n* (*game*) dominos *mpl*.
don [dɔn] *n* (*BRIT*) professeur *m* d'université ♦ *vt* revêtir.
donate [də'neɪt] *vt* faire don de, donner.
donation [də'neɪʃən] *n* donation *f*, don *m*.
done [dʌn] *pp of* **do**.
donkey ['dɔŋkɪ] *n* âne *m*.
donkey-work ['dɔŋkɪwə:k] *n* (*BRIT col*) le gros du travail, le plus dur (du travail).
donor ['dəunə*] *n* (*of blood etc*) donneur/euse; (*to charity*) donateur/trice.
donor card *n* carte *f* de don d'organes.
don't [dəunt] = **do not**.
doodle ['du:dl] *n* griffonnage *m*, gribouillage *m* ♦ *vi* griffonner, gribouiller.
doom [du:m] *n* (*fate*) destin *m*; (*ruin*) ruine *f* ♦ *vt*: **to be ~ed (to failure)** être voué(e) à l'échec.
doomsday ['du:mzdeɪ] *n* le Jugement dernier.
door [dɔ:*] *n* porte *f*; (*of vehicle*) portière *f*, porte; **to go from ~ to ~** aller de porte en porte.
doorbell ['dɔ:bɛl] *n* sonnette *f*.
door handle *n* poignée *f* de porte.
doorman ['dɔ:mən] *n* (*in hotel*) portier *m*; (*in block of flats*) concierge *m*.
doormat ['dɔ:mæt] *n* paillasson *m*.
doorpost ['dɔ:pəust] *n* montant *m* de porte.
doorstep ['dɔ:stɛp] *n* pas *m* de (la) porte, seuil *m*.
door-to-door ['dɔ:tə'dɔ:*] *adj*: **~ selling** vente *f* à domicile.
doorway ['dɔ:weɪ] *n* (embrasure *f* de) porte *f*.
dope [dəup] *n* (*col*) drogue *f*; (*: information*) tuyaux *mpl*, rancards *mpl* ♦ *vt* (*horse etc*) doper.
dopey ['dəupɪ] *adj* (*col*) à moitié endormi(e).
dormant ['dɔ:mənt] *adj* assoupi(e), en veilleuse; (*rule, law*) inappliqué(e).
dormer ['dɔ:mə*] *n* (*also*: **~ window**) lucarne *f*.
dormice ['dɔ:maɪs] *npl of* **dormouse**.
dormitory ['dɔ:mɪtrɪ] *n* dortoir *m*; (*US*: *hall of residence*) foyer *m* d'étudiants.
dormouse, *pl* **dormice** ['dɔ:maus, -maɪs] *n* loir *m*.
Dors *abbr* (*BRIT*) = *Dorset*.
DOS [dɔs] *n abbr* = **disk operating system**.
dosage ['dəusɪdʒ] *n* dose *f*; dosage *m*; (*on label*) posologie *f*.
dose [dəus] *n* dose *f*; (*BRIT*: *bout*) attaque *f* ♦ *vt*: **to ~ o.s.** se bourrer de médicaments; **a ~ of flu** une belle *or* bonne grippe.
dosser ['dɔsə*] *n* (*BRIT col*) clochard/e.
doss house ['dɔs-] *n* (*BRIT*) asile *m* de nuit.

DOT *n abbr* (*US*) = *Department of Transportation.*
dot [dɔt] *n* point *m* ♦ *vt*: **~ted with** parsemé(e) de; **on the ~** à l'heure tapante.
dot command *n* (*COMPUT*) commande précédée d'un point.
dote [dəut]: **to ~ on** *vt fus* être fou(folle) de.
dot-matrix printer [dɔt'meɪtrɪks-] *n* imprimante matricielle.
dotted line ['dɔtɪd-] *n* ligne pointillée; (*AUT*) ligne discontinue; **to sign on the ~** signer à l'endroit indiqué *or* sur la ligne pointillée; (*fig*) donner son consentement.
dotty ['dɔtɪ] *adj* (*col*) loufoque, farfelu(e).
double ['dʌbl] *adj* double ♦ *adv* (*fold*) en deux; (*twice*): **to cost ~ (sth)** coûter le double (de qch) *or* deux fois plus (que qch) ♦ *n* double *m*; (*CINE*) doublure *f* ♦ *vt* doubler; (*fold*) plier en deux ♦ *vi* doubler; (*have two uses*): **to ~ as** servir aussi de; **~ five two six (5526)** (*BRIT TEL*) cinquante-cinq - vingt-six; **it's spelt with a ~ "l"** ça s'écrit avec deux "l"; **on the ~**, (*BRIT*) **at the ~** au pas de course.
▶**double back** *vi* revenir sur ses pas.
▶**double up** *vi* (*bend over*) se courber, se plier; (*share room*) partager la chambre.
double bass *n* contrebasse *f*.
double bed *n* grand lit.
double-breasted ['dʌbl'brɛstɪd] *adj* croisé(e).
double-check ['dʌbl'tʃɛk] *vt, vi* revérifier.
double-click ['dʌbl'klɪk] *vi* (*COMPUT*) double-cliquer.
double-clutch ['dʌbl'klʌtʃ] *vi* (*US*) faire un double débrayage.
double cream *n* (*BRIT*) crème fraîche épaisse.
doublecross ['dʌbl'krɔs] *vt* doubler, trahir.
doubledecker ['dʌbl'dɛkə*] *n* autobus *m* à impériale.
double declutch *vi* (*BRIT*) faire un double débrayage.
double exposure *n* (*PHOT*) surimpression *f*.
double glazing *n* (*BRIT*) double vitrage *m*.
double-page ['dʌblpeɪdʒ] *adj*: **~ spread** publicité *f* en double page.
double parking *n* stationnement *m* en double file.
double room *n* chambre *f* pour deux.
doubles ['dʌblz] *n* (*TENNIS*) double *m*.
double whammy [-'wæmɪ] *n* (*col*) double contretemps *m*.
doubly ['dʌblɪ] *adv* doublement, deux fois plus.
doubt [daut] *n* doute *m* ♦ *vt* douter de; **without (a) ~** sans aucun doute; **beyond ~** *adv* indubitablement ♦ *adj* indubitable; **to ~ that** douter que; **I ~ it very much** j'en doute fort.
doubtful ['dautful] *adj* douteux(euse); (*person*) incertain(e); **to be ~ about sth** avoir des doutes sur qch, ne pas être convaincu de qch; **I'm a bit ~** je n'en suis pas certain *or* sûr.
doubtless ['dautlɪs] *adv* sans doute, sûrement.
dough [dəu] *n* pâte *f*; (*col*: *money*) fric *m*, pognon *m*.
doughnut ['dəunʌt] *n* beignet *m*.
dour [duə*] *adj* austère.
douse [dauz] *vt* (*with water*) tremper, inonder; (*flames*) éteindre.
dove [dʌv] *n* colombe *f*.
Dover ['dəuvə*] *n* Douvres.
dovetail ['dʌvteɪl] *n*: **~ joint** assemblage *m* à queue d'aronde ♦ *vi* (*fig*) concorder.
dowager ['dauədʒə*] *n* douairière *f*.
dowdy ['daudɪ] *adj* démodé(e); mal fagoté(e).
Dow-Jones average ['dau'dʒəunz-] *n* (*US*) indice *m* Dow-Jones.
down [daun] *n* (*fluff*) duvet *m*; (*hill*) colline (dénudée) ♦ *adv* en bas ♦ *prep* en bas de ♦ *vt* (*enemy*) abattre; (*col*: *drink*) siffler; **~ there** là-bas (en bas), là au fond; **~ here** ici en bas; **the price of meat is ~** le prix de la viande a baissé; **I've got it ~ in my diary** c'est inscrit dans mon agenda; **to pay £2 ~** verser 2 livres d'arrhes *or* en acompte; **England is two goals ~** l'Angleterre a deux buts de retard; **to ~ tools** (*BRIT*) cesser le travail; **~ with X!** à bas X!
down-and-out ['daunəndaut] *n* (*tramp*) clochard/e.
down-at-heel ['daunət'hiːl] *adj* (*fig*) miteux(euse).
downbeat ['daunbiːt] *n* (*MUS*) temps frappé ♦ *adj* sombre, négatif(ive).
downcast ['daunkɑːst] *adj* démoralisé(e).
downer ['daunə*] *n* (*col*: *drug*) tranquillisant *m*; **to be on a ~** (*depressed*) flipper.
downfall ['daunfɔːl] *n* chute *f*; ruine *f*.
downgrade ['daungreɪd] *vt* déclasser.
downhearted ['daun'hɑːtɪd] *adj* découragé(e).
downhill ['daun'hɪl] *adv* (*face, look*) en aval, vers l'aval; (*roll, go*) vers le bas, en bas ♦ *n* (*SKI*: *also*: **~ race**) descente *f*; **to go ~** descendre; (*business*) péricliter, aller à vau-l'eau.
Downing Street ['daunɪŋ-] *n* (*BRIT*): **10 ~** *résidence du Premier ministre*; *voir encadré*.

DOWNING STREET

Downing Street *est une rue de Westminster (à Londres) où se trouvent la résidence officielle du Premier ministre et celle du ministre des Finances. Le nom* **"Downing Street"** *est souvent utilisé pour désigner le gouvernement britannique.*

download ['daunləud] *vt* télécharger.
down-market ['daun'mɑːkɪt] *adj* (*product*) bas de gamme *inv*.
down payment *n* acompte *m*.
downplay ['daunpleɪ] *vt* (*US*) minimiser (l'importance de).
downpour ['daunpɔː*] *n* pluie torrentielle, déluge *m*.
downright ['daunraɪt] *adj* franc(franche); (*refusal*) catégorique.

Downs [daunz] *npl* (*BRIT*): **the ~** *collines crayeuses du sud-est de l'Angleterre.*
downsize [daun'saɪz] *vt* réduire l'effectif de.
Down's syndrome [daunz-] *n* mongolisme *m*, trisomie *f*; **a ~ baby** un bébé mongolien *or* trisomique.
downstairs ['daun'stɛəz] *adv* (*on or to ground floor*) au rez-de-chaussée; (*on or to floor below*) à l'étage inférieur; **to come ~, to go ~** descendre (l'escalier).
downstream ['daunstriːm] *adv* en aval.
downtime ['dauntaɪm] *n* (*of machine etc*) temps mort; (*of person*) temps d'arrêt.
down-to-earth ['dauntu'əːθ] *adj* terre à terre *inv*.
downtown ['daun'taun] *adv* en ville ♦ *adj* (*US*): **~ Chicago** le centre commerçant de Chicago.
downtrodden ['dauntrɔdn] *adj* opprimé(e).
down under *adv* en Australie (*or* Nouvelle Zélande).
downward ['daunwəd] *adj* vers le bas; **a ~ trend** une tendance à la baisse, une diminution progressive.
downward(s) ['daunwəd(z)] *adv* vers le bas.
dowry ['daurɪ] *n* dot *f*.
doz. *abbr* (= *dozen*) douz.
doze [dəuz] *vi* sommeiller.
►**doze off** *vi* s'assoupir.
dozen ['dʌzn] *n* douzaine *f*; **a ~ books** une douzaine de livres; **80p a ~** 80p la douzaine; **~s of times** des centaines de fois.
DPh, DPhil *n abbr* (= *Doctor of Philosophy*) *titre universitaire.*
DPP *n abbr* (*BRIT*) = **Director of Public Prosecutions.**
DPT *n abbr* (*MED*: = *diphtheria, pertussis, tetanus*) DCT *m*.
DPW *n abbr* (*US*) = *Department of Public Works.*
Dr *abbr* (= *doctor*) Dr.
Dr. *abbr* (= *doctor*) Dr; (*in street names*) = **drive**.
dr *abbr* (*COMM*) = **debtor**.
drab [dræb] *adj* terne, morne.
draft [drɑːft] *n* brouillon *m*; (*of contract, document*) version *f* préliminaire; (*COMM*) traite *f*; (*US MIL*) contingent *m*; (*: call-up*) conscription *f* ♦ *vt* faire le brouillon de; (*document, report*) rédiger une version préliminaire de; *see also* **draught**.
drag [dræg] *vt* traîner; (*river*) draguer ♦ *vi* traîner ♦ *n* (*AVIAT, NAUT*) résistance *f*; (*col: person*) raseur/euse; (*: task etc*) corvée *f*; (*women's clothing*): **in ~** (en) travesti.
►**drag away** *vt*: **to ~ away (from)** arracher *or* emmener de force (de).
►**drag on** *vi* s'éterniser.
dragnet ['drægnɛt] *n* drège *f*; (*fig*) piège *m*, filets *mpl*.
dragon ['drægn] *n* dragon *m*.
dragonfly ['drægənflaɪ] *n* libellule *f*.
dragoon [drə'guːn] *n* (*cavalryman*) dragon *m* ♦ *vt*: **to ~ sb into doing sth** (*BRIT*) forcer qn à faire qch.
drain [dreɪn] *n* égout *m*; (*on resources*) saignée *f* ♦ *vt* (*land, marshes*) drainer, assécher; (*vegetables*) égoutter; (*reservoir etc*) vider ♦ *vi* (*water*) s'écouler; **to feel ~ed (of energy** *or* **emotion)** être miné(e).
drainage ['dreɪnɪdʒ] *n* système *m* d'égouts.
draining board ['dreɪnɪŋ-], (*US*) **drainboard** ['dreɪnbɔːd] *n* égouttoir *m*.
drainpipe ['dreɪnpaɪp] *n* tuyau *m* d'écoulement.
drake [dreɪk] *n* canard *m* (mâle).
dram [dræm] *n* petit verre.
drama ['drɑːmə] *n* (*art*) théâtre *m*, art *m* dramatique; (*play*) pièce *f*; (*event*) drame *m*.
dramatic [drə'mætɪk] *adj* (*THEAT*) dramatique; (*impressive*) spectaculaire.
dramatically [drə'mætɪklɪ] *adv* de façon spectaculaire.
dramatist ['dræmətɪst] *n* auteur *m* dramatique.
dramatize ['dræmətaɪz] *vt* (*events etc*) dramatiser; (*adapt*) adapter pour la télévision (*or* pour l'écran).
drank [dræŋk] *pt of* **drink**.
drape [dreɪp] *vt* draper.
draper ['dreɪpə*] *n* (*BRIT*) marchand/e de nouveautés.
drapes [dreɪps] *npl* (*US*) rideaux *mpl*.
drastic ['dræstɪk] *adj* (*measures*) d'urgence, énergique; (*change*) radical(e).
drastically ['dræstɪklɪ] *adv* radicalement.
draught, (*US*) **draft** [drɑːft] *n* courant *m* d'air; (*of chimney*) tirage *m*; (*NAUT*) tirant *m* d'eau; **on ~** (*beer*) à la pression.
draught beer *n* bière *f* (à la) pression.
draughtboard ['drɑːftbɔːd] *n* (*BRIT*) damier *m*.
draughts [drɑːfts] *n* (*BRIT*) (jeu *m* de) dames *fpl*.
draughtsman, (*US*) **draftsman** ['drɑːftsmən] *n* dessinateur/trice (industriel(le)).
draughtsmanship, (*US*) **draftsmanship** ['drɑːftsmənʃɪp] *n* (*technique*) dessin industriel; (*art*) graphisme *m*.
draw [drɔː] *vb* (*pt* **drew**, *pp* **drawn** [druː, drɔːn]) *vt* tirer; (*attract*) attirer; (*picture*) dessiner; (*line, circle*) tracer; (*money*) retirer; (*comparison, distinction*): **to ~ (between)** faire (entre) ♦ *vi* (*SPORT*) faire match nul ♦ *n* match nul; (*lottery*) loterie *f*; (*: picking of ticket*) tirage *m* au sort; **to ~ to a close** toucher à *or* tirer à sa fin; **to ~ near** *vi* s'approcher; approcher.
►**draw back** *vi* (*move back*): **to ~ back (from)** reculer (de).
►**draw in** *vi* (*BRIT: car*) s'arrêter le long du trottoir; (*: train*) entrer en gare *or* dans la station.
►**draw on** *vt* (*resources*) faire appel à; (*imagination, person*) avoir recours à, faire appel à.
►**draw out** *vi* (*lengthen*) s'allonger ♦ *vt* (*money*) retirer.

►**draw up** *vi* (*stop*) s'arrêter ♦ *vt* (*document*) établir, dresser; (*plans*) formuler, dessiner.
drawback ['drɔːbæk] *n* inconvénient *m*, désavantage *m*.
drawbridge ['drɔːbrɪdʒ] *n* pont-levis *m*.
drawee [drɔː'iː] *n* tiré *m*.
drawer [drɔː*] *n* tiroir *m*; ['drɔːə*] (*of cheque*) tireur *m*.
drawing ['drɔːɪŋ] *n* dessin *m*.
drawing board *n* planche *f* à dessin.
drawing pin *n* (*BRIT*) punaise *f*.
drawing room *n* salon *m*.
drawl [drɔːl] *n* accent traînant.
drawn [drɔːn] *pp of* **draw** ♦ *adj* (*haggard*) tiré(e), crispé(e).
drawstring ['drɔːstrɪŋ] *n* cordon *m*.
dread [drɛd] *n* épouvante *f*, effroi *m* ♦ *vt* redouter, appréhender.
dreadful ['drɛdful] *adj* épouvantable, affreux(euse).
dream [driːm] *n* rêve *m* ♦ *vt*, *vi* (*pt*, *pp* **dreamed** *or* **dreamt** [drɛmt]) rêver; **to have a ~ about sb/sth** rêver à qn/qch; **sweet ~s!** faites de beaux rêves!
►**dream up** *vt* inventer.
dreamer ['driːmə*] *n* rêveur/euse.
dream world *n* monde *m* imaginaire.
dreamy ['driːmɪ] *adj* (*absent-minded*) rêveur(euse).
dreary ['drɪərɪ] *adj* triste; monotone.
dredge [drɛdʒ] *vt* draguer.
►**dredge up** *vt* draguer; (*fig: unpleasant facts*) (faire) ressortir.
dredger ['drɛdʒə*] *n* (*ship*) dragueur *m*; (*machine*) drague *f*; (*BRIT*: *also*: **sugar ~**) saupoudreuse *f*.
dregs [drɛgz] *npl* lie *f*.
drench [drɛntʃ] *vt* tremper; **~ed to the skin** trempé(e) jusqu'aux os.
dress [drɛs] *n* robe *f*; (*clothing*) habillement *m*, tenue *f* ♦ *vt* habiller; (*wound*) panser; (*food*) préparer ♦ *vi*: **she ~es very well** elle s'habille très bien; **to ~ o.s., to get ~ed** s'habiller; **to ~ a shop window** faire l'étalage *or* la vitrine.
►**dress up** *vi* s'habiller; (*in fancy dress*) se déguiser.
dress circle *n* premier balcon.
dress designer *n* modéliste *m/f*, dessinateur/trice de mode.
dresser ['drɛsə*] *n* (*THEAT*) habilleur/euse; (*also*: **window ~**) étalagiste *m/f*; (*furniture*) vaisselier *m*.
dressing ['drɛsɪŋ] *n* (*MED*) pansement *m*; (*CULIN*) sauce *f*, assaisonnement *m*.
dressing gown *n* (*BRIT*) robe *f* de chambre.
dressing room *n* (*THEAT*) loge *f*; (*SPORT*) vestiaire *m*.
dressing table *n* coiffeuse *f*.
dressmaker ['drɛsmeɪkə*] *n* couturière *f*.
dressmaking ['drɛsmeɪkɪŋ] *n* couture *f*; travaux *mpl* de couture.
dress rehearsal *n* (répétition *f*) générale *f*.
dress shirt *n* chemise *f* à plastron.
dressy ['drɛsɪ] *adj* (*col*: *clothes*) (qui fait) habillé(e).
drew [druː] *pt of* **draw**.
dribble ['drɪbl] *vi* tomber goutte à goutte; (*baby*) baver ♦ *vt* (*ball*) dribbler.
dried [draɪd] *adj* (*fruit, beans*) sec(sèche); (*eggs, milk*) en poudre.
drier ['draɪə*] *n* = **dryer**.
drift [drɪft] *n* (*of current etc*) force *f*; direction *f*; (*of sand etc*) amoncellement *m*; (*of snow*) rafale *f*; coulée *f*; (*: on ground*) congère *f*; (*general meaning*) sens général ♦ *vi* (*boat*) aller à la dérive, dériver; (*sand, snow*) s'amonceler, s'entasser; **to let things ~** laisser les choses aller à la dérive; **to ~ apart** (*friends, lovers*) s'éloigner l'un de l'autre; **I get** *or* **catch your ~** je vois en gros ce que vous voulez dire.
drifter ['drɪftə*] *n* personne *f* sans but dans la vie.
driftwood ['drɪftwud] *n* bois flotté.
drill [drɪl] *n* perceuse *f*; (*bit*) foret *m*; (*of dentist*) roulette *f*, fraise *f*; (*MIL*) exercice *m* ♦ *vt* percer; (*soldiers*) faire faire l'exercice à; (*pupils: in grammar*) faire faire des exercices à ♦ *vi* (*for oil*) faire un *or* des forage(s).
drilling ['drɪlɪŋ] *n* (*for oil*) forage *m*.
drilling rig *n* (*on land*) tour *f* (de forage), derrick *m*; (*at sea*) plate-forme *f* de forage.
drily ['draɪlɪ] *adv* = **dryly**.
drink [drɪŋk] *n* boisson *f* ♦ *vt*, *vi* (*pt* **drank**, *pp* **drunk** [dræŋk, drʌŋk]) boire; **to have a ~** boire quelque chose, boire un verre; **a ~ of water** un verre d'eau; **would you like something to ~?** aimeriez-vous boire quelque chose?; **we had ~s before lunch** on a pris l'apéritif.
►**drink in** *vt* (*fresh air*) inspirer profondément; (*story*) avaler, ne pas perdre une miette de; (*sight*) se remplir la vue de.
drinkable ['drɪŋkəbl] *adj* (*not dangerous*) potable; (*palatable*) buvable.
drink-driving ['drɪŋk'draɪvɪŋ] *n* conduite *f* en état d'ivresse.
drinker ['drɪŋkə*] *n* buveur/euse.
drinking ['drɪŋkɪŋ] *n* (*drunkenness*) boisson *f*, alcoolisme *m*.
drinking fountain *n* (*in park etc*) fontaine publique; (*in building*) jet *m* d'eau potable.
drinking water *n* eau *f* potable.
drip [drɪp] *n* goutte *f*; (*sound: of water etc*) bruit *m* de l'eau qui tombe goutte à goutte; (*MED*) goutte-à-goutte *m inv*, perfusion *f*; (*col*: *person*) lavette *f*, nouille *f* ♦ *vi* tomber goutte à goutte; (*washing*) s'égoutter; (*wall*) suinter.
drip-dry ['drɪp'draɪ] *adj* (*shirt*) sans repassage.
drip-feed ['drɪpfiːd] *vt* alimenter au goutte-à-goutte *or* par perfusion.
dripping ['drɪpɪŋ] *n* graisse *f* de rôti ♦ *adj*: **~ wet** trempé(e).
drive [draɪv] *n* promenade *f or* trajet *m* en voi-

ture; (*also*: ~**way**) allée *f*; (*energy*) dynamisme *m*, énergie *f*; (*PSYCH*) besoin *m*; pulsion *f*; (*push*) effort (concerté); campagne *f*; (*SPORT*) drive *m*; (*TECH*) entraînement *m*; traction *f*; transmission *f*; (*COMPUT*: *also*: **disk** ~) lecteur *m* de disquette ♦ *vb* (*pt* **drove**, *pp* **driven** [drəuv, 'drɪvn]) *vt* conduire; (*nail*) enfoncer; (*push*) chasser, pousser; (*TECH*: *motor*) actionner; entraîner ♦ *vi* (*be at the wheel*) conduire; (*travel by car*) aller en voiture; **to go for a** ~ aller faire une promenade en voiture; **it's 3 hours' ~ from London** Londres est à 3 heures de route; **left-/right-hand** ~ (*AUT*) conduite *f* à gauche/droite; **front-/rear-wheel** ~ (*AUT*) traction *f* avant/arrière; **to ~ sb to (do) sth** pousser *or* conduire qn à (faire) qch; **to ~ sb mad** rendre qn fou(folle).

▶**drive at** *vt fus* (*fig: intend, mean*) vouloir dire, en venir à.

▶**drive on** *vi* poursuivre sa route, continuer; (*after stopping*) reprendre sa route, repartir ♦ *vt* (*incite, encourage*) inciter.

drive-by ['draɪvbaɪ] *n* (*also*: ~ **shooting**) (*tentative d')assassinat par coups de feu tirés d'une voiture*.

drive-in ['draɪvɪn] *adj*, *n* (*esp US*) drive-in (*m*).

drive-in window *n* (*US*) guichet-auto *m*.

drivel ['drɪvl] *n* (*col*) idioties *fpl*, imbécillités *fpl*.

driven ['drɪvn] *pp of* **drive**.

driver ['draɪvə*] *n* conducteur/trice; (*of taxi, bus*) chauffeur *m*.

driver's license *n* (*US*) permis *m* de conduire.

driveway ['draɪvweɪ] *n* allée *f*.

driving ['draɪvɪŋ] *adj*: ~ **rain** *n* pluie battante ♦ *n* conduite *f*.

driving force *n* locomotive *f*, élément *m* dynamique.

driving instructor *n* moniteur *m* d'auto-école.

driving lesson *n* leçon *f* de conduite.

driving licence *n* (*BRIT*) permis *m* de conduire.

driving school *n* auto-école *f*.

driving test *n* examen *m* du permis de conduire.

drizzle ['drɪzl] *n* bruine *f*, crachin *m* ♦ *vi* bruiner.

droll [drəul] *adj* drôle.

dromedary ['drɔmədərɪ] *n* dromadaire *m*.

drone [drəun] *vi* (*bee*) bourdonner; (*engine etc*) ronronner; (*also*: ~ **on**) parler d'une voix monocorde ♦ *n* bourdonnement *m*; ronronnement *m*; (*male bee*) faux-bourdon *m*.

drool [dru:l] *vi* baver; **to ~ over sb/sth** (*fig*) baver d'admiration *or* être en extase devant qn/qch.

droop [dru:p] *vi* s'affaisser; tomber.

drop [drɔp] *n* goutte *f*; (*fall: also in price*) baisse *f*; (*: in salary*) réduction *f*; (*also*: **parachute** ~) saut *m*; (*of cliff*) dénivellation *f*; à-pic *m* ♦ *vt* laisser tomber; (*voice, eyes, price*) baisser; (*set down from car*) déposer ♦ *vi* (*wind, temperature, price, voice*) tomber; (*numbers, attendance*) diminuer; ~**s** *npl* (*MED*) gouttes; **cough ~s** pastilles *fpl* pour la toux; **a ~ of 10%** une baisse (*or* réduction) de 10%; **to ~ anchor** jeter l'ancre; **to ~ sb a line** mettre un mot à qn.

▶**drop in** *vi* (*col*: *visit*): **to ~ in (on)** faire un saut (chez), passer (chez).

▶**drop off** *vi* (*sleep*) s'assoupir ♦ *vt*: **to ~ sb off** déposer qn.

▶**drop out** *vi* (*withdraw*) se retirer; (*student etc*) abandonner, décrocher.

droplet ['drɔplɪt] *n* gouttelette *f*.

dropout ['drɔpaut] *n* (*from society*) marginal/e; (*from university*) drop-out *m/f*, dropé/e.

dropper ['drɔpə*] *n* (*MED etc*) compte-gouttes *m inv*.

droppings ['drɔpɪŋz] *npl* crottes *fpl*.

dross [drɔs] *n* déchets *mpl*; rebut *m*.

drought [draut] *n* sécheresse *f*.

drove [drəuv] *pt of* **drive** ♦ *n*: ~**s of people** une foule de gens.

drown [draun] *vt* noyer; (*also*: ~ **out**: *sound*) couvrir, étouffer ♦ *vi* se noyer.

drowse [drauz] *vi* somnoler.

drowsy ['drauzɪ] *adj* somnolent(e).

drudge [drʌdʒ] *n* bête *f* de somme (*fig*).

drudgery ['drʌdʒərɪ] *n* corvée *f*.

drug [drʌg] *n* médicament *m*; (*narcotic*) drogue *f* ♦ *vt* droguer; **he's on ~s** il se drogue; (*MED*) il est sous médication.

drug addict *n* toxicomane *m/f*.

druggist ['drʌgɪst] *n* (*US*) pharmacien/ne-droguiste.

drug peddler *n* revendeur/euse de drogue.

drugstore ['drʌgstɔ:*] *n* (*US*) pharmacie-droguerie *f*, drugstore *m*.

drum [drʌm] *n* tambour *m*; (*for oil, petrol*) bidon *m* ♦ *vt*: **to ~ one's fingers on the table** pianoter *or* tambouriner sur la table; ~**s** *npl* (*MUS*) batterie *f*.

▶**drum up** *vt* (*enthusiasm, support*) susciter, rallier.

drummer ['drʌmə*] *n* (joueur *m* de) tambour *m*.

drum roll *n* roulement *m* de tambour.

drumstick ['drʌmstɪk] *n* (*MUS*) baguette *f* de tambour; (*of chicken*) pilon *m*.

drunk [drʌŋk] *pp of* **drink** ♦ *adj* ivre, soûl(e) ♦ *n* soûlard/e; homme/femme soûl(e); **to get** ~ s'enivrer, se soûler.

drunkard ['drʌŋkəd] *n* ivrogne *m/f*.

drunken ['drʌŋkən] *adj* ivre, soûl(e); (*habitual*) ivrogne, d'ivrogne; ~ **driving** conduite *f* en état d'ivresse.

drunkenness ['drʌŋkənnɪs] *n* ivresse *f*; ivrognerie *f*.

dry [draɪ] *adj* sec(sèche); (*day*) sans pluie; (*humour*) pince-sans-rire; (*uninteresting*) aride, rébarbatif(ive) ♦ *vt* sécher; (*clothes*) faire sécher ♦ *vi* sécher; **on ~ land** sur la terre ferme; **to ~ one's hands/hair/eyes** se sécher les mains/les cheveux/les yeux.

▶**dry up** *vi* (*also fig: source of supply, imagination*) se tarir; (*: speaker*) sécher, rester sec.

dry-clean ['draɪ'kliːn] *vt* nettoyer à sec.

dry-cleaner ['draɪ'kliːnə*] *n* teinturier *m*.

dry-cleaner's ['draɪ'kliːnəz] *n* teinturerie *f*.

dry-cleaning ['draɪ'kliːnɪŋ] *n* nettoyage *m* à sec.

dry dock *n* (*NAUT*) cale sèche, bassin *m* de radoub.

dryer ['draɪə*] *n* séchoir *m*; (*spin-~*) essoreuse *f*.

dry goods *npl* (*COMM*) textiles *mpl*, mercerie *f*.

dry goods store *n* (*US*) magasin *m* de nouveautés.

dry ice *n* neige *f* carbonique.

dryly ['draɪlɪ] *adv* sèchement, d'un ton sec.

dryness ['draɪnɪs] *n* sécheresse *f*.

dry rot *n* pourriture sèche (*du bois*).

dry run *n* (*fig*) essai *m*.

dry ski slope *n* piste (de ski) artificielle.

DSc *n abbr* (= *Doctor of Science*) *titre universitaire*.

DSS *n abbr* (*BRIT*) = *Department of Social Security*.

DST *abbr* (*US*: = *Daylight Saving Time*) *heure d'été*.

DT *n abbr* (*COMPUT*) = **data transmission**.

DTI *n abbr* (*BRIT*) = *Department of Trade and Industry*.

DTP *n abbr* = **desktop publishing**.

DT's [diː'tiːz] *n abbr* (*col*: = *delirium tremens*) delirium tremens *m*.

dual ['djuəl] *adj* double.

dual carriageway *n* (*BRIT*) route *f* à quatre voies.

dual-control ['djuəlkən'trəul] *adj* à doubles commandes.

dual nationality *n* double nationalité *f*.

dual-purpose ['djuəl'pəːpəs] *adj* à double emploi.

dubbed [dʌbd] *adj* (*CINE*) doublé(e); (*nicknamed*) surnommé(e).

dubious ['djuːbɪəs] *adj* hésitant(e), incertain(e); (*reputation, company*) douteux(euse); **I'm very ~ about it** j'ai des doutes sur la question, je n'en suis pas sûr du tout.

Dublin ['dʌblɪn] *n* Dublin.

Dubliner ['dʌblɪnə*] *n* habitant/e de Dublin; originaire *m/f* de Dublin.

duchess ['dʌtʃɪs] *n* duchesse *f*.

duck [dʌk] *n* canard *m* ♦ *vi* se baisser vivement, baisser subitement la tête ♦ *vt* plonger dans l'eau.

duckling ['dʌklɪŋ] *n* caneton *m*.

duct [dʌkt] *n* conduite *f*, canalisation *f*; (*ANAT*) conduit *m*.

dud [dʌd] *n* (*shell*) obus non éclaté; (*object, tool*): **it's a ~** c'est de la camelote, ça ne marche pas ♦ *adj* (*BRIT*: *cheque*) sans provision; (*: note, coin*) faux(fausse).

due [djuː] *adj* dû(due); (*expected*) attendu(e); (*fitting*) qui convient ♦ *n* dû *m* ♦ *adv*: **~ north** droit vers le nord; **~s** *npl* (*for club, union*) cotisation *f*; (*in harbour*) droits *mpl* (de port); **in ~ course** en temps utile *or* voulu; (*in the end*) finalement; **~ to** dû à; causé par; **the rent is ~ on the 30th** il faut payer le loyer le 30; **the train is ~ at 8** le train est attendu à 8 h; **she is ~ back tomorrow** elle doit rentrer demain; **I am ~ 6 days' leave** j'ai droit à 6 jours de congé.

due date *n* date *f* d'échéance.

duel ['djuəl] *n* duel *m*.

duet [djuː'ɛt] *n* duo *m*.

duff [dʌf] *adj* (*BRIT col*) nullard(e), nul(le).

duffelbag, duffle bag ['dʌflbæg] *n* sac marin.

duffelcoat, duffle coat ['dʌflkəut] *n* duffel-coat *m*.

duffer ['dʌfə*] *n* (*col*) nullard/e.

dug [dʌg] *pt, pp of* **dig**.

dugout ['dʌgaut] *n* (*SPORT*) banc *m* de touche.

duke [djuːk] *n* duc *m*.

dull [dʌl] *adj* (*boring*) ennuyeux(euse); (*slow*) borné(e); (*lacklustre*) morne, terne; (*sound, pain*) sourd(e); (*weather, day*) gris(e), maussade; (*blade*) émoussé(e) ♦ *vt* (*pain, grief*) atténuer; (*mind, senses*) engourdir.

duly ['djuːlɪ] *adv* (*on time*) en temps voulu; (*as expected*) comme il se doit.

dumb [dʌm] *adj* muet(te); (*stupid*) bête; **to be struck ~** (*fig*) rester abasourdi(e), être sidéré(e).

dumbbell ['dʌmbɛl] *n* (*SPORT*) haltère *m*.

dumbfounded [dʌm'faundɪd] *adj* sidéré(e).

dummy ['dʌmɪ] *n* (*tailor's model*) mannequin *m*; (*SPORT*) feinte *f*; (*BRIT*: *for baby*) tétine *f* ♦ *adj* faux(fausse), factice.

dummy run *n* essai *m*.

dump [dʌmp] *n* tas *m* d'ordures; (*place*) décharge (publique); (*MIL*) dépôt *m*; (*COMPUT*) listage *m* (de la mémoire) ♦ *vt* (*put down*) déposer; déverser; (*get rid of*) se débarrasser de; (*COMPUT*) lister; (*COMM*: *goods*) vendre à perte (*sur le marché extérieur*); **to be (down) in the ~s** (*col*) avoir le cafard, broyer du noir.

dumping ['dʌmpɪŋ] *n* (*ECON*) dumping *m*; (*of rubbish*): **"no ~"** "décharge interdite".

dumpling ['dʌmplɪŋ] *n* boulette *f* (de pâte).

dumpy ['dʌmpɪ] *adj* courtaud(e), boulot(te).

dunce [dʌns] *n* âne *m*, cancre *m*.

dune [djuːn] *n* dune *f*.

dung [dʌŋ] *n* fumier *m*.

dungarees [dʌŋgə'riːz] *npl* bleu(s) *m(pl)*; (*for child, woman*) salopette *f*.

dungeon ['dʌndʒən] *n* cachot *m*.

dunk [dʌŋk] *vt* tremper.

Dunkirk [dʌn'kəːk] *n* Dunkerque.

duo ['djuːəu] *n* (*gen, MUS*) duo *m*.

duodenal [djuːəu'diːnl] *adj* duodénal(e); **~ ulcer** ulcère *m* du duodénum.

dupe [djuːp] *n* dupe *f* ♦ *vt* duper, tromper.
duplex ['djuːplɛks] *n* (*US*: *also*: ~ **apartment**) duplex *m*.
duplicate *n* ['djuːplɪkət] double *m*, copie exacte; (*copy of letter etc*) duplicata *m* ♦ *adj* (*copy*) en double ♦ *vt* ['djuːplɪkeɪt] faire un double de; (*on machine*) polycopier; **in** ~ en deux exemplaires, en double; ~ **key** double *m* de la (*or* d'une) clé.
duplicating machine ['djuːplɪkeɪtɪŋ-], **duplicator** ['djuːplɪkeɪtə*] *n* duplicateur *m*.
duplicity [djuː'plɪsɪtɪ] *n* duplicité *f*, fausseté *f*.
Dur *abbr* (*BRIT*) = *Durham*.
durability [djuərə'bɪlɪtɪ] *n* solidité *f*; durabilité *f*.
durable ['djuərəbl] *adj* durable; (*clothes, metal*) résistant(e), solide.
duration [djuə'reɪʃən] *n* durée *f*.
duress [djuə'rɛs] *n*: **under** ~ sous la contrainte.
Durex ['djuərɛks] *n* ® (*BRIT*) préservatif (masculin).
during ['djuərɪŋ] *prep* pendant, au cours de.
dusk [dʌsk] *n* crépuscule *m*.
dusky ['dʌskɪ] *adj* sombre.
dust [dʌst] *n* poussière *f* ♦ *vt* (*furniture*) essuyer, épousseter; (*cake etc*): **to** ~ **with** saupoudrer de.
►**dust off** *vt* (*also fig*) dépoussiérer.
dustbin ['dʌstbɪn] *n* (*BRIT*) poubelle *f*.
duster ['dʌstə*] *n* chiffon *m*.
dust jacket *n* jacquette *f*.
dustman ['dʌstmən] *n* (*BRIT*) boueux *m*, éboueur *m*.
dustpan ['dʌstpæn] *n* pelle *f* à poussière.
dusty ['dʌstɪ] *adj* poussiéreux(euse).
Dutch [dʌtʃ] *adj* hollandais(e), néerlandais(e) ♦ *n* (*LING*) hollandais *m*, néerlandais *m* ♦ *adv*: **to go** ~ *or* **d**~ partager les frais; **the** ~ *npl* les Hollandais, les Néerlandais.
Dutch auction *n* enchères *fpl* à la baisse.
Dutchman ['dʌtʃmən], **Dutchwoman** ['dʌtʃwumən] *n* Hollandais/e.
dutiable ['djuːtɪəbl] *adj* taxable; soumis(e) à des droits de douane.
dutiful ['djuːtɪful] *adj* (*child*) respectueux(euse); (*husband, wife*) plein(e) d'égards, prévenant(e); (*employee*) consciencieux(euse).
duty ['djuːtɪ] *n* devoir *m*; (*tax*) droit *m*, taxe *f*; **duties** *npl* fonctions *fpl*; **to make it one's** ~ **to do sth** se faire un devoir de faire qch; **to pay** ~ **on sth** payer un droit *or* une taxe sur qch; **on** ~ de service; (*at night etc*) de garde; **off** ~ libre, pas de service *or* de garde.
duty-free ['djuːtɪ'friː] *adj* exempté(e) de douane, hors-taxe; ~ **shop** boutique *f* hors-taxe.
duty officer *n* (*MIL etc*) officier *m* de permanence.
duvet ['duːveɪ] *n* (*BRIT*) couette *f*.
DV *abbr* (= *Deo volente*) si Dieu le veut.
DVD *n abbr* (= *digital versatile disc*) DVD *m*.
DVLA *n abbr* (*BRIT*: = *Driver and Vehicle Licensing Agency*) *service qui délivre les cartes grises et les permis de conduire*.
DVM *n abbr* (*US*: = *Doctor of Veterinary Medicine*) *titre universitaire*.
dwarf [dwɔːf] *n* nain/e ♦ *vt* écraser.
dwell, *pt, pp* **dwelt** [dwɛl, dwɛlt] *vi* demeurer.
►**dwell on** *vt fus* s'étendre sur.
dweller ['dwɛlə*] *n* habitant/e.
dwelling ['dwɛlɪŋ] *n* habitation *f*, demeure *f*.
dwindle ['dwɪndl] *vi* diminuer, décroître.
dwindling ['dwɪndlɪŋ] *adj* décroissant(e), en diminution.
dye [daɪ] *n* teinture *f* ♦ *vt* teindre; **hair** ~ teinture pour les cheveux.
dyestuffs ['daɪstʌfs] *npl* colorants *mpl*.
dying ['daɪɪŋ] *adj* mourant(e), agonisant(e).
dyke [daɪk] *n* (*embankment*) digue *f*.
dynamic [daɪ'næmɪk] *adj* dynamique.
dynamics [daɪ'næmɪks] *n or npl* dynamique *f*.
dynamite ['daɪnəmaɪt] *n* dynamite *f* ♦ *vt* dynamiter, faire sauter à la dynamite.
dynamo ['daɪnəməu] *n* dynamo *f*.
dynasty ['dɪnəstɪ] *n* dynastie *f*.
dysentery ['dɪsntrɪ] *n* dysenterie *f*.
dyslexia [dɪs'lɛksɪə] *n* dyslexie *f*.
dyslexic [dɪs'lɛksɪk] *adj, n* dyslexique *m/f*.
dyspepsia [dɪs'pɛpsɪə] *n* dyspepsie *f*.
dystrophy ['dɪstrəfɪ] *n* dystrophie *f*; **muscular** ~ dystrophie musculaire.

E e

E, e [iː] *n* (*letter*) E, e *m*; (*MUS*): **E** mi *m*; **E for Edward**, (*US*) **E for Easy** E comme Eugène.
E *abbr* (= *east*) E ♦ *n abbr* (*DRUGS*) = **ecstasy**.
E111 ['iːwʌnɪ'lɛvn] *n abbr* (*also*: **form** ~) formulaire *m* E111.
ea. *abbr* = **each**.
E.A. *n abbr* (*US*: = *educational age*) *niveau scolaire*.
each [iːtʃ] *adj* chaque ♦ *pron* chacun(e); ~ **one** chacun(e); ~ **other** se (*or* nous *etc*); **they hate** ~ **other** ils se détestent (mutuellement); **you are jealous of** ~ **other** vous êtes jaloux l'un de l'autre; ~ **day** chaque jour, tous les jours; **they have 2 books** ~ ils ont 2 livres chacun; **they cost £5** ~ ils coûtent 5 livres (la) pièce; ~ **of us** chacun(e) de nous.
eager ['iːgə*] *adj* impatient(e); avide; ardent(e), passionné(e); (*keen: pupil*) plein(e) d'enthousiasme, qui se passionne pour les études; **to be** ~ **to do sth** être impatient de faire qch, brûler de faire qch; désirer vivement faire qch; **to be** ~ **for** désirer vive-

ment, être avide de.

eagle ['iːgl] *n* aigle *m*.

E and OE *abbr* = **errors and omissions excepted**.

ear [ɪə*] *n* oreille *f*; (*of corn*) épi *m*; **up to one's ~s in debt** endetté(e) jusqu'au cou.

earache ['ɪəreɪk] *n* douleurs *fpl* aux oreilles.

eardrum ['ɪədrʌm] *n* tympan *m*.

earful ['ɪəful] *n* (*col*): **to give sb an ~** passer un savon à qn.

earl [əːl] *n* comte *m*.

earlier ['əːlɪə*] *adj* (*date etc*) plus rapproché(e); (*edition etc*) plus ancien(ne), antérieur(e) ♦ *adv* plus tôt.

early ['əːlɪ] *adv* tôt, de bonne heure; (*ahead of time*) en avance ♦ *adj* précoce; qui se manifeste (*or* se fait) tôt *or* de bonne heure; (*Christians, settlers*) premier(ière); **have an ~ night/start** couchez-vous/partez tôt *or* de bonne heure; **take the ~ train** prenez le premier train; **in the ~** *or* **~ in the spring/19th century** au début *or* commencement du printemps/19ème siècle; **you're ~!** tu es en avance!; **~ in the morning** tôt le matin; **she's in her ~ forties** elle a un peu plus de quarante ans *or* de la quarantaine; **at your earliest convenience** (*COMM*) dans les meilleurs délais.

early retirement *n* retraite anticipée.

early warning system *n* système *m* de première alerte.

earmark ['ɪəmɑːk] *vt*: **to ~ sth for** réserver *or* destiner qch à.

earn [əːn] *vt* gagner; (*COMM*: *yield*) rapporter; **to ~ one's living** gagner sa vie; **this ~ed him much praise, he ~ed much praise for this** ceci lui a valu de nombreux éloges; **he's ~ed his rest/reward** il mérite *or* a bien mérité *or* a bien gagné son repos/sa récompense.

earned income [əːnd-] *n* revenu *m* du travail.

earnest ['əːnɪst] *adj* sérieux(euse) ♦ *n* (*also*: **~ money**) acompte *m*, arrhes *fpl*; **in ~** *adv* sérieusement, pour de bon.

earnings ['əːnɪŋz] *npl* salaire *m*; gains *mpl*; (*of company etc*) profits *mpl*, bénéfices *mpl*.

ear, nose and throat specialist *n* oto-rhino-laryngologiste *m/f*.

earphones ['ɪəfəunz] *npl* écouteurs *mpl*.

earplugs ['ɪəplʌgz] *npl* boules *fpl* Quiès ®; (*to keep out water*) protège-tympans *mpl*.

earring ['ɪərɪŋ] *n* boucle *f* d'oreille.

earshot ['ɪəʃɔt] *n*: **out of/within ~** hors de portée/à portée de voix.

earth [əːθ] *n* (*gen, also BRIT ELEC*) terre *f*; (*of fox etc*) terrier *m* ♦ *vt* (*BRIT ELEC*) relier à la terre.

earthenware ['əːθnwɛə*] *n* poterie *f*; faïence *f* ♦ *adj* de *or* en faïence.

earthly ['əːθlɪ] *adj* terrestre; **~ paradise** paradis *m* terrestre; **there is no ~ reason to think ...** il n'y a absolument aucune raison *or* pas la moindre raison de penser ....

earthquake ['əːθkweɪk] *n* tremblement *m* de terre, séisme *m*.

earth-shattering ['əːθʃætərɪŋ] *adj* stupéfiant(e).

earth tremor *n* secousse *f* sismique.

earthworks ['əːθwəːks] *npl* travaux *mpl* de terrassement.

earthworm ['əːθwəːm] *n* ver *m* de terre.

earthy ['əːθɪ] *adj* (*fig*) terre à terre *inv*; truculent(e).

earwax ['ɪəwæks] *n* cérumen *m*.

earwig ['ɪəwɪg] *n* perce-oreille *m*.

ease [iːz] *n* facilité *f*, aisance *f* ♦ *vt* (*soothe*) calmer; (*loosen*) relâcher, détendre; (*help pass*): **to ~ sth in/out** faire pénétrer/sortir qch délicatement *or* avec douceur; faciliter la pénétration/la sortie de qch ♦ *vi* (*situation*) se détendre; **with ~** sans difficulté, aisément; **life of ~** vie oisive; **at ~** à l'aise; (*MIL*) au repos.

►**ease off, ease up** *vi* diminuer; (*slow down*) ralentir; (*relax*) se détendre.

easel ['iːzl] *n* chevalet *m*.

easily ['iːzɪlɪ] *adv* facilement.

easiness ['iːsɪnɪs] *n* facilité *f*; (*of manner*) aisance *f*; nonchalance *f*.

east [iːst] *n* est *m* ♦ *adj* d'est ♦ *adv* à l'est, vers l'est; **the E~** l'Orient *m*; (*POL*) les pays *mpl* de l'Est.

Easter ['iːstə*] *n* Pâques *fpl* ♦ *adj* (*holidays*) de Pâques, pascal(e).

Easter egg *n* œuf *m* de Pâques.

Easter Island *n* île *f* de Pâques.

easterly ['iːstəlɪ] *adj* d'est.

Easter Monday *n* le lundi de Pâques.

eastern ['iːstən] *adj* de l'est, oriental(e); **E~ Europe** l'Europe de l'Est; **the E~ bloc** (*POL*) les pays *mpl* de l'est.

Easter Sunday *n* le dimanche de Pâques.

East Germany *n* (*formerly*) Allemagne *f* de l'Est.

eastward(s) ['iːstwəd(z)] *adv* vers l'est, à l'est.

easy ['iːzɪ] *adj* facile; (*manner*) aisé(e) ♦ *adv*: **to take it** *or* **things ~** ne pas se fatiguer; (*not worry*) ne pas (trop) s'en faire; **payment on ~ terms** (*COMM*) facilités *fpl* de paiement; **that's easier said than done** c'est plus facile à dire qu'à faire, c'est vite dit; **I'm ~** (*col*) ça m'est égal.

easy chair *n* fauteuil *m*.

easy-going ['iːzɪ'gəuɪŋ] *adj* accommodant(e), facile à vivre.

easy touch *n* (*col*): **he's an ~** c'est une bonne poire.

eat, *pt* **ate,** *pp* **eaten** [iːt, eɪt, 'iːtn] *vt, vi* manger.

►**eat away** *vt* (*subj: sea*) saper, éroder; (*: acid*) ronger, corroder.

►**eat away at, eat into** *vt fus* ronger, attaquer.

►**eat out** *vi* manger au restaurant.
►**eat up** *vt* (*food*) finir (de manger); **it ~s up electricity** ça bouffe du courant, ça consomme beaucoup d'électricité.
eatable ['iːtəbl] *adj* mangeable; (*safe to eat*) comestible.
eau de Cologne ['əudəkə'ləun] *n* eau *f* de Cologne.
eaves [iːvz] *npl* avant-toit *m*.
eavesdrop ['iːvzdrɔp] *vi*: **to ~ (on)** écouter de façon indiscrète.
ebb [ɛb] *n* reflux *m* ♦ *vi* refluer; (*fig*: *also*: **~ away**) décliner; **the ~ and flow** le flux et le reflux; **to be at a low ~** (*fig*) être bien bas(se), ne pas aller bien fort.
ebb tide *n* marée descendante, reflux *m*.
ebony ['ɛbənɪ] *n* ébène *f*.
ebullient [ɪ'bʌlɪənt] *adj* exubérant(e).
e-business ['iːbɪznɪs] *n* entreprise *f* electronique, e-entreprise *f*.
EC *n abbr* (= *European Community*) CE *f* (= *Communauté européenne*).
ECB *n abbr* (= *European Central Bank*) BCE *f*.
eccentric [ɪk'sɛntrɪk] *adj*, *n* excentrique (*m/f*).
ecclesiastic(al) [ɪkliːzɪ'æstɪk(l)] *adj* ecclésiastique.
ECG *n abbr* = **electrocardiogram**.
ECGD *n abbr* (= *Export Credits Guarantee Department*) *service de garantie financière à l'exportation*.
echo, ~es ['ɛkəu] *n* écho *m* ♦ *vt* répéter; faire chorus avec ♦ *vi* résonner; faire écho.
éclair ['eɪklɛə*] *n* éclair *m* (*CULIN*).
eclipse [ɪ'klɪps] *n* éclipse *f* ♦ *vt* éclipser.
ECM *n abbr* (*US*) = *European Common Market*.
eco- ['iːkəu] *prefix* éco-.
eco-friendly [iːkəu'frɛndlɪ] *adj* non nuisible à *or* qui ne nuit pas à l'environnement.
ecological [iːkə'lɔdʒɪkəl] *adj* écologique.
ecologist [ɪ'kɔlədʒɪst] *n* écologiste *m/f*.
ecology [ɪ'kɔlədʒɪ] *n* écologie *f*.
e-commerce [iːkɔməːs] *n* commerce *m* électronique.
economic [iːkə'nɔmɪk] *adj* économique; (*profitable*) rentable.
economical [iːkə'nɔmɪkl] *adj* économique; (*person*) économe.
economically [iːkə'nɔmɪklɪ] *adv* économiquement.
economics [iːkə'nɔmɪks] *n* économie *f* politique ♦ *npl* côté *m or* aspect *m* économique.
economist [ɪ'kɔnəmɪst] *n* économiste *m/f*.
economize [ɪ'kɔnəmaɪz] *vi* économiser, faire des économies.
economy [ɪ'kɔnəmɪ] *n* économie *f*; **economies of scale** économies d'échelle.
economy class *n* (*AVIAT etc*) classe *f* touriste.
economy size *n* taille *f* économique.
ecosystem ['iːkəusɪstəm] *n* écosystème *m*.
eco-tourism [iːkəu'tuərɪzəm] *n* écotourisme *m*.
ECSC *n abbr* (= *European Coal & Steel Community*) CECA *f* (= *Communauté européenne du charbon et de l'acier*).
ecstasy ['ɛkstəsɪ] *n* extase *f*; (*DRUGS*) ecstasy *m*; **to go into ecstasies over** s'extasier sur.
ecstatic [ɛks'tætɪk] *adj* extatique, en extase.
ECT *n abbr* = **electroconvulsive therapy**.
Ecuador ['ɛkwədɔː*] *n* Équateur *m*.
ecumenical [iːkju'mɛnɪkl] *adj* œcuménique.
eczema ['ɛksɪmə] *n* eczéma *m*.
eddy ['ɛdɪ] *n* tourbillon *m*.
edge [ɛdʒ] *n* bord *m*; (*of knife etc*) tranchant *m*, fil *m* ♦ *vt* border ♦ *vi*: **to ~ forward** avancer petit à petit; **to ~ away from** s'éloigner furtivement de; **on ~** (*fig*) = **edgy**; **to have the ~ on** (*fig*) l'emporter (de justesse) sur, être légèrement meilleur que.
edgeways ['ɛdʒweɪz] *adv* latéralement; **he couldn't get a word in ~** il ne pouvait pas placer un mot.
edging ['ɛdʒɪŋ] *n* bordure *f*.
edgy ['ɛdʒɪ] *adj* crispé(e), tendu(e).
edible ['ɛdɪbl] *adj* comestible; (*meal*) mangeable.
edict ['iːdɪkt] *n* décret *m*.
edifice ['ɛdɪfɪs] *n* édifice *m*.
edifying ['ɛdɪfaɪɪŋ] *adj* édifiant(e).
Edinburgh ['ɛdɪnbərə] *n* Édimbourg.
edit ['ɛdɪt] *vt* éditer; (*magazine*) diriger; (*paper*) être le rédacteur *or* la rédactrice en chef de.
edition [ɪ'dɪʃən] *n* édition *f*.
editor ['ɛdɪtə*] *n* (*in newspaper*) rédacteur/trice; rédacteur/trice en chef; (*of sb's work*) éditeur/trice; (*also*: **film ~**) monteur/euse.
editorial [ɛdɪ'tɔːrɪəl] *adj* de la rédaction, éditorial(e) ♦ *n* éditorial *m*; **the ~ staff** la rédaction.
EDP *n abbr* = **electronic data processing**.
EDT *abbr* (*US*: = *Eastern Daylight Time*) *heure d'été de New York*.
educate ['ɛdjukeɪt] *vt* instruire; éduquer; **~d at ...** qui a fait ses études à ....
educated guess ['ɛdjukeɪtɪd-] *n* supposition éclairée.
education [ɛdju'keɪʃən] *n* éducation *f*; (*schooling*) enseignement *m*, instruction *f*; (*at university: subject etc*) pédagogie *f*; **primary** *or* (*US*) **elementary/secondary ~** instruction *f* primaire/secondaire.
educational [ɛdju'keɪʃənl] *adj* pédagogique; scolaire; (*useful*) instructif(ive); (*games, toys*) éducatif(ive); **~ technology** technologie *f* de l'enseignement.
Edwardian [ɛd'wɔːdɪən] *adj* de l'époque du roi Édouard VII, des années 1900.
EE *abbr* = **electrical engineer**.
EEC *n abbr* (= *European Economic Community*) C.E.E. *f* (= *Communauté économique européenne*).
EEG *n abbr* = **electroencephalogram**.
eel [iːl] *n* anguille *f*.
EENT *n abbr* (*US MED*) = *eye, ear, nose and throat*.
EEOC *n abbr* (*US*) = **Equal Employment Opportunity Commission**.

eerie ['ɪərɪ] *adj* inquiétant(e), spectral(e), surnaturel(le).
EET *abbr* (= *Eastern European Time*) HEO (= *heure d'Europe orientale*).
effect [ɪ'fɛkt] *n* effet *m* ♦ *vt* effectuer; **to take ~** (*LAW*) entrer en vigueur, prendre effet; (*drug*) agir, faire son effet; **to put into ~** (*plan*) mettre en application *or* à exécution; **to have an ~ on sb/sth** avoir *or* produire un effet sur qn/qch; **in ~** en fait; **his letter is to the ~ that** ... sa lettre nous apprend que ....
effective [ɪ'fɛktɪv] *adj* efficace; (*striking: display, outfit*) frappant(e), qui produit *or* fait de l'effet; **to become ~** (*LAW*) entrer en vigueur, prendre effet; **~ date** date *f* d'effet *or* d'entrée en vigueur.
effectively [ɪ'fɛktɪvlɪ] *adv* efficacement; (*strikingly*) d'une manière frappante, avec beaucoup d'effet; (*in reality*) effectivement, en fait.
effectiveness [ɪ'fɛktɪvnɪs] *n* efficacité *f*.
effects [ɪ'fɛkts] *npl* (*THEAT*) effets *mpl*; (*property*) effets, affaires *fpl*.
effeminate [ɪ'fɛmɪnɪt] *adj* efféminé(e).
effervescent [ɛfə'vɛsnt] *adj* effervescent(e).
efficacy ['ɛfɪkəsɪ] *n* efficacité *f*.
efficiency [ɪ'fɪʃənsɪ] *n* efficacité *f*; rendement *m*.
efficiency apartment *n* (*US*) studio *m* avec coin cuisine.
efficient [ɪ'fɪʃənt] *adj* efficace; (*machine, car*) d'un bon rendement.
efficiently [ɪ'fɪʃəntlɪ] *adv* efficacement.
effigy ['ɛfɪdʒɪ] *n* effigie *f*.
effluent ['ɛfluənt] *n* effluent *m*.
effort ['ɛfət] *n* effort *m*; **to make an ~ to do sth** faire *or* fournir un effort pour faire qch.
effortless ['ɛfətlɪs] *adj* sans effort, aisé(e).
effrontery [ɪ'frʌntərɪ] *n* effronterie *f*.
effusive [ɪ'fjuːsɪv] *adj* (*person*) expansif(ive); (*welcome*) chaleureux(euse).
EFL *n abbr* (*SCOL*) = *English as a Foreign Language*.
EFTA ['ɛftə] *n abbr* (= *European Free Trade Association*) AELE *f* (= *Association européenne de libre-échange*).
e.g. *adv abbr* (= *exempli gratia*) par exemple, p. ex.
egalitarian [ɪgælɪ'tɛərɪən] *adj* égalitaire.
egg [ɛg] *n* œuf *m*.
►**egg on** *vt* pousser.
eggcup ['ɛgkʌp] *n* coquetier *m*.
eggplant ['ɛgplɑːnt] *n* aubergine *f*.
eggshell ['ɛgʃɛl] *n* coquille *f* d'œuf ♦ *adj* (*colour*) blanc cassé *inv*.
egg-timer ['ɛgtaɪmə*] *n* sablier *m*.
egg white *n* blanc *m* d'œuf.
egg yolk *n* jaune *m* d'œuf.
ego ['iːgəu] *n* moi *m*.
egoism ['ɛgəuɪzəm] *n* égoïsme *m*.
egoist ['ɛgəuɪst] *n* égoïste *m/f*.
egotism ['ɛgəutɪzəm] *n* égotisme *m*.
egotist ['ɛgəutɪst] *n* égocentrique *m/f*.
ego trip *n*: **to be on an ~** être en plein délire d'autosatisfaction.
Egypt ['iːdʒɪpt] *n* Égypte *f*.
Egyptian [ɪ'dʒɪpʃən] *adj* égyptien(ne) ♦ *n* Egyptien/ne.
eiderdown ['aɪdədaun] *n* édredon *m*.
eight [eɪt] *num* huit.
eighteen [eɪ'tiːn] *num* dix-huit.
eighth [eɪtθ] *num* huitième.
eighty ['eɪtɪ] *num* quatre-vingt(s).
Eire ['ɛərə] *n* République *f* d'Irlande.
EIS *n abbr* (= *Educational Institute of Scotland*) *syndicat enseignant*.
either ['aɪðə*] *adj* l'un ou l'autre; (*both, each*) chaque; **on ~ side** de chaque côté ♦ *pron*: **~ (of them)** l'un ou l'autre; **I don't like ~** je n'aime ni l'un ni l'autre ♦ *adv* non plus; **no, I don't ~** moi non plus ♦ *conj*: **~ good or bad** ou bon ou mauvais, soit bon soit mauvais; **I haven't seen ~ one or the other** je n'ai vu ni l'un ni l'autre.
ejaculation [ɪdʒækju'leɪʃən] *n* (*PHYSIOL*) éjaculation *f*.
eject [ɪ'dʒɛkt] *vt* expulser; éjecter ♦ *vi* (*pilot*) s'éjecter.
ejector seat [ɪ'dʒɛktə-] *n* siège *m* éjectable.
eke [iːk]: **to ~ out** *vt* faire durer; augmenter.
EKG *n abbr* (*US*) = **electrocardiogram**.
el [ɛl] *n abbr* (*US col*) = **elevated railroad**.
elaborate *adj* [ɪ'læbərɪt] compliqué(e), recherché(e), minutieux(euse) ♦ *vb* [ɪ'læbəreɪt] *vt* élaborer ♦ *vi* entrer dans les détails.
elapse [ɪ'læps] *vi* s'écouler, passer.
elastic [ɪ'læstɪk] *adj*, *n* élastique (*m*).
elastic band *n* (*BRIT*) élastique *m*.
elasticity [ɪlæs'tɪsɪtɪ] *n* élasticité *f*.
elated [ɪ'leɪtɪd] *adj* transporté(e) de joie.
elation [ɪ'leɪʃən] *n* (grande) joie, allégresse *f*.
elbow ['ɛlbəu] *n* coude *m* ♦ *vt*: **to ~ one's way through the crowd** se frayer un passage à travers la foule (en jouant des coudes).
elbow grease *n*: **to use a bit of ~** mettre de l'huile de coude.
elder ['ɛldə*] *adj* aîné(e) ♦ *n* (*tree*) sureau *m*; **one's ~s** ses aînés.
elderly ['ɛldəlɪ] *adj* âgé(e) ♦ *npl*: **the ~** les personnes âgées.
elder statesman *n* vétéran *m* de la politique.
eldest ['ɛldɪst] *adj*, *n*: **the ~ (child)** l'aîné(e) (des enfants).
elect [ɪ'lɛkt] *vt* élire; (*choose*): **to ~ to do** choisir de faire ♦ *adj*: **the president ~** le président désigné.
election [ɪ'lɛkʃən] *n* élection *f*; **to hold an ~** procéder à une élection.
election campaign *n* campagne électorale.
electioneering [ɪlɛkʃə'nɪərɪŋ] *n* propagande électorale, manœuvres électorales.
elector [ɪ'lɛktə*] *n* électeur/trice.
electoral [ɪ'lɛktərəl] *adj* électoral(e).

electoral college *n* collège électoral.
electoral roll *n* (*BRIT*) liste électorale.
electorate [ɪ'lɛktərɪt] *n* électorat *m*.
electric [ɪ'lɛktrɪk] *adj* électrique.
electrical [ɪ'lɛktrɪkl] *adj* électrique.
electrical engineer *n* ingénieur électricien.
electrical failure *n* panne d'électricité *or* de courant.
electric blanket *n* couverture chauffante.
electric chair *n* chaise *f* électrique.
electric cooker *n* cuisinière *f* électrique.
electric current *n* courant *m* électrique.
electric fire *n* (*BRIT*) radiateur *m* électrique.
electrician [ɪlɛk'trɪʃən] *n* électricien *m*.
electricity [ɪlɛk'trɪsɪtɪ] *n* électricité *f*; **to switch on/off the ~** rétablir/couper le courant.
electricity board *n* (*BRIT*) ≈ agence régionale de l'E.D.F.
electric light *n* lumière *f* électrique.
electric shock *n* choc *m or* décharge *f* électrique.
electrify [ɪ'lɛktrɪfaɪ] *vt* (*RAIL*) électrifier; (*audience*) électriser.
electro... [ɪ'lɛktrəu] *prefix* électro....
electrocardiogram (ECG) [ɪ'lɛktrə 'kɑːdɪəgræm] *n* électrocardiogramme *m* (ECG).
electro-convulsive therapy [ɪ'lɛktrə kən'vʌlsɪv-] *n* électrochocs *mpl*.
electrocute [ɪ'lɛktrəkjuːt] *vt* électrocuter.
electrode [ɪ'lɛktrəud] *n* électrode *f*.
electroencephalogram (EEG) [ɪ'lɛktrəu ɛn'sɛfələgræm] *n* électroencéphalogramme *m* (EEG).
electrolysis [ɪlɛk'trɔlɪsɪs] *n* électrolyse *f*.
electromagnetic [ɪ'lɛktrəmæg'nɛtɪk] *adj* électromagnétique.
electron [ɪ'lɛktrɔn] *n* électron *m*.
electronic [ɪlɛk'trɔnɪk] *adj* électronique.
electronic data processing (EDP) *n* (*COMPUT*) traitement *m* électronique des données.
electronic mail *n* (*also*: **e-mail**) courrier *m* électronique.
electronics [ɪlɛk'trɔnɪks] *n* électronique *f*.
electronics engineer *n* électronicien/ne.
electron microscope *n* microscope *m* électronique.
electroplated [ɪ'lɛktrə'pleɪtɪd] *adj* plaqué(e) *or* doré(e) *or* argenté(e) par galvanoplastie.
electrotherapy [ɪ'lɛktrə'θɛrəpɪ] *n* électrothérapie *f*.
elegance ['ɛlɪgəns] *n* élégance *f*.
elegant ['ɛlɪgənt] *adj* élégant(e).
element ['ɛlɪmənt] *n* (*gen*) élément *m*; (*of heater, kettle etc*) résistance *f*.
elementary [ɛlɪ'mɛntərɪ] *adj* élémentaire; (*school, education*) primaire.
elementary school *n* (*US*) école *f* primaire; *voir encadré*.

ELEMENTARY SCHOOL

Aux États-Unis et au Canada, une ***elementary school*** *(également appelée "grade school" ou "grammar school" aux États-Unis) est une école publique où les enfants passent les six à huit premières années de leur scolarité.*

elephant ['ɛlɪfənt] *n* éléphant *m*.
elevate ['ɛlɪveɪt] *vt* élever.
elevated railroad ['ɛlɪveɪtɪd-] *n* (*US*) métro aérien.
elevation [ɛlɪ'veɪʃən] *n* élévation *f*; (*height*) altitude *f*.
elevator ['ɛlɪveɪtə*] *n* élévateur *m*, monte-charge *m inv*; (*US*: *lift*) ascenseur *m*.
eleven [ɪ'lɛvn] *num* onze.
elevenses [ɪ'lɛvnzɪz] *npl* (*BRIT*) ≈ pause-café *f*.
eleventh [ɪ'lɛvnθ] *adj* onzième; **at the ~ hour** (*fig*) à la dernière minute.
elf, *pl* **elves** [ɛlf, ɛlvz] *n* lutin *m*.
elicit [ɪ'lɪsɪt] *vt*: **to ~ (from)** obtenir (de); tirer (de).
eligible ['ɛlɪdʒəbl] *adj* éligible; (*for membership*) admissible; **~ for a pension** ayant droit à la retraite.
eliminate [ɪ'lɪmɪneɪt] *vt* éliminer.
elimination [ɪlɪmɪ'neɪʃən] *n* élimination *f*; **by process of ~** par élimination.
élitist [eɪ'liːtɪst] *adj* (*pej*) élitiste.
Elizabethan [ɪlɪzə'biːθən] *adj* élisabéthain(e).
elliptical [ɪ'lɪptɪkl] *adj* elliptique.
elm [ɛlm] *n* orme *m*.
elocution [ɛlə'kjuːʃən] *n* élocution *f*.
elongated ['iːlɔŋgeɪtɪd] *adj* étiré(e), allongé(e).
elope [ɪ'ləup] *vi* (*lovers*) s'enfuir (ensemble).
elopement [ɪ'ləupmənt] *n* fugue amoureuse.
eloquent ['ɛləkwənt] *adj* éloquent(e).
else [ɛls] *adv* d'autre; **something ~** quelque chose d'autre, autre chose; **somewhere ~** ailleurs, autre part; **everywhere ~** partout ailleurs; **everyone ~** tous les autres; **nothing ~** rien d'autre; **is there anything ~ I can do?** est-ce que je peux faire quelque chose d'autre?; **where ~?** à quel autre endroit?; **little ~** pas grand-chose d'autre.
elsewhere [ɛls'wɛə*] *adv* ailleurs, autre part.
ELT *n abbr* (*SCOL*) = *English Language Teaching*.
elucidate [ɪ'luːsɪdeɪt] *vt* élucider.
elude [ɪ'luːd] *vt* échapper à; (*question*) éluder.
elusive [ɪ'luːsɪv] *adj* insaisissable; (*answer*) évasif(ive).
elves [ɛlvz] *npl of* **elf**.
emaciated [ɪ'meɪsɪeɪtɪd] *adj* émacié(e), décharné(e).
E-mail, e-mail ['iːmeɪl] *n abbr* (= *electronic mail*) courrier *m* électronique ♦ *vt*: **to ~ sb** envoyer un message électronique à qn.
emanate ['ɛməneɪt] *vi*: **to ~ from** émaner de.
emancipate [ɪ'mænsɪpeɪt] *vt* émanciper.

emasculate [ɪ'mæskjuleɪt] *vt* émasculer.
embalm [ɪm'bɑːm] *vt* embaumer.
embankment [ɪm'bæŋkmənt] *n* (*of road, railway*) remblai *m*, talus *m*; (*riverside*) berge *f*, quai *m*; (*dyke*) digue *f*.
embargo, ~es [ɪm'bɑːgəu] *n* (*COMM, NAUT*) embargo *m* ♦ *vt* frapper d'embargo, mettre l'embargo sur; **to put an ~ on sth** mettre l'embargo sur qch.
embark [ɪm'bɑːk] *vi*: **to ~ (on)** (s')embarquer (à bord de *or* sur) ♦ *vt* embarquer; **to ~ on** (*journey etc*) commencer, entreprendre; (*fig*) se lancer *or* s'embarquer dans.
embarkation [ɛmbɑː'keɪʃən] *n* embarquement *m*.
embarkation card *n* carte *f* d'embarquement.
embarrass [ɪm'bærəs] *vt* embarrasser, gêner; **to be ~ed** être gêné(e).
embarrassing [ɪm'bærəsɪŋ] *adj* gênant(e), embarrassant(e).
embarrassment [ɪm'bærəsmənt] *n* embarras *m*, gêne *f*.
embassy ['ɛmbəsɪ] *n* ambassade *f*; **the French E~** l'ambassade de France.
embed [ɪm'bɛd] *vt* enfoncer; sceller.
embellish [ɪm'bɛlɪʃ] *vt* embellir; enjoliver.
embers ['ɛmbəz] *npl* braise *f*.
embezzle [ɪm'bɛzl] *vt* détourner.
embezzlement [ɪm'bɛzlmənt] *n* détournement *m* (de fonds).
embezzler [ɪm'bɛzlə*] *n* escroc *m*.
embitter [ɪm'bɪtə*] *vt* aigrir; envenimer.
emblem ['ɛmbləm] *n* emblème *m*.
embodiment [ɪm'bɔdɪmənt] *n* personification *f*, incarnation *f*.
embody [ɪm'bɔdɪ] *vt* (*features*) réunir, comprendre; (*ideas*) formuler, exprimer.
embolden [ɪm'bəuldn] *vt* enhardir.
embolism ['ɛmbəlɪzəm] *n* embolie *f*.
embossed [ɪm'bɔst] *adj* repoussé(e); gaufré(e); **~ with** où figure(nt) en relief.
embrace [ɪm'breɪs] *vt* embrasser, étreindre; (*include*) embrasser, couvrir, comprendre ♦ *vi* s'embrasser, s'étreindre ♦ *n* étreinte *f*.
embroider [ɪm'brɔɪdə*] *vt* broder; (*fig: story*) enjoliver.
embroidery [ɪm'brɔɪdərɪ] *n* broderie *f*.
embroil [ɪm'brɔɪl] *vt*: **to become ~ed (in sth)** se retrouver mêlé(e) (à qch), se laisser entraîner (dans qch).
embryo ['ɛmbrɪəu] *n* (*also fig*) embryon *m*.
emend [ɪ'mɛnd] *vt* (*text*) corriger.
emerald ['ɛmərəld] *n* émeraude *f*.
emerge [ɪ'məːdʒ] *vi* apparaître, surgir; **it ~s that** (*BRIT*) il ressort que.
emergence [ɪ'məːdʒəns] *n* apparition *f*; (*of nation*) naissance *f*.
emergency [ɪ'məːdʒənsɪ] *n* urgence *f*; **in an ~** en cas d'urgence; **state of ~** état *m* d'urgence.
emergency exit *n* sortie *f* de secours.
emergency landing *n* atterrissage forcé.
emergency lane *n* (*US AUT*) accotement stabilisé.
emergency road service *n* (*US*) service *m* de dépannage.
emergency service *n* service *m* d'urgence.
emergency stop *n* (*BRIT AUT*) arrêt *m* d'urgence.
emergent [ɪ'məːdʒənt] *adj*: **~ nation** pays *m* en voie de développement.
emery board ['ɛmərɪ-] *n* lime *f* à ongles (*en carton émerisé*).
emery paper ['ɛmərɪ-] *n* papier *m* (d')émeri.
emetic [ɪ'mɛtɪk] *n* vomitif *m*, émétique *m*.
emigrant ['ɛmɪgrənt] *n* émigrant/e.
emigrate ['ɛmɪgreɪt] *vi* émigrer.
emigration [ɛmɪ'greɪʃən] *n* émigration *f*.
émigré ['ɛmɪgreɪ] *n* émigré/e.
eminence ['ɛmɪnəns] *n* éminence *f*.
eminent ['ɛmɪnənt] *adj* éminent(e).
eminently ['ɛmɪnəntlɪ] *adv* éminemment, admirablement.
emission [ɪ'mɪʃən] *n* émission *f*.
emit [ɪ'mɪt] *vt* émettre.
emolument [ɪ'mɔljumənt] *n* (*often pl*: *formal*) émoluments *mpl*; (*fee*) honoraires *mpl*; (*salary*) traitement *m*.
emotion [ɪ'məuʃən] *n* sentiment *m*; (*as opposed to reason*) émotion *f*, sentiments.
emotional [ɪ'məuʃənl] *adj* (*person*) émotif(ive), très sensible; (*scene*) émouvant(e); (*tone, speech*) qui fait appel aux sentiments.
emotionally [ɪ'məuʃnəlɪ] *adv* (*behave*) émotivement; (*be involved*) affectivement; (*speak*) avec émotion; **~ disturbed** qui souffre de troubles de l'affectivité.
emotive [ɪ'məutɪv] *adj* émotif(ive); **~ power** capacité *f* d'émouvoir *or* de toucher.
empathy ['ɛmpəθɪ] *n* communion *f* d'idées *or* de sentiments; empathie *f*; **to feel ~ with sb** se mettre à la place de qn.
emperor ['ɛmpərə*] *n* empereur *m*.
emphasis, *pl* **-ases** ['ɛmfəsɪs, -siːz] *n* accent *m*; force *f*, insistance *f*; **to lay** *or* **place ~ on sth** (*fig*) mettre l'accent sur, insister sur; **the ~ is on reading** la lecture tient une place primordiale, on accorde une importance particulière à la lecture.
emphasize ['ɛmfəsaɪz] *vt* (*syllable, word, point*) appuyer *or* insister sur; (*feature*) souligner, accentuer.
emphatic [ɛm'fætɪk] *adj* (*strong*) énergique, vigoureux(euse); (*unambiguous, clear*) catégorique.
emphatically [ɛm'fætɪklɪ] *adv* avec vigueur *or* énergie; catégoriquement.
empire ['ɛmpaɪə*] *n* empire *m*.
empirical [ɛm'pɪrɪkl] *adj* empirique.
employ [ɪm'plɔɪ] *vt* employer; **he's ~ed in a bank** il est employé de banque, il travaille dans une banque.
employee [ɪmplɔɪ'iː] *n* employé/e.

employer [ɪm'plɔɪə*] *n* employeur/euse.
employment [ɪm'plɔɪmənt] *n* emploi *m*; **to find ~** trouver un emploi *or* du travail; **without ~** au chômage, sans emploi; **place of ~** lieu *m* de travail.
employment agency *n* agence *f or* bureau *m* de placement.
employment exchange *n* (*BRIT*) agence *f* pour l'emploi.
empower [ɪm'pauə*] *vt*: **to ~ sb to do** autoriser *or* habiliter qn à faire.
empress ['ɛmprɪs] *n* impératrice *f*.
emptiness ['ɛmptɪnɪs] *n* vide *m*.
empty ['ɛmptɪ] *adj* vide; (*street, area*) désert(e); (*threat, promise*) en l'air, vain(e) ♦ *n* (*bottle*) bouteille *f* vide ♦ *vt* vider ♦ *vi* se vider; (*liquid*) s'écouler; **on an ~ stomach** à jeun; **to ~ into** (*river*) se jeter dans, se déverser dans.
empty-handed ['ɛmptɪ'hændɪd] *adj* les mains vides.
empty-headed ['ɛmptɪ'hɛdɪd] *adj* écervelé(e), qui n'a rien dans la tête.
EMS *n abbr* (= *European Monetary System*) SME *m*.
EMT *n abbr* = *emergency medical technician*.
EMU *n abbr* (= *European Monetary Union*) UME *f*; (= *economic and monetary union*) UEM *f*.
emulate ['ɛmjuleɪt] *vt* rivaliser avec, imiter.
emulsion [ɪ'mʌlʃən] *n* émulsion *f*; (*also*: **~ paint**) peinture mate.
enable [ɪ'neɪbl] *vt*: **to ~ sb to do** permettre à qn de faire, donner à qn la possibilité de faire.
enact [ɪ'nækt] *vt* (*LAW*) promulguer; (*play, scene*) jouer, représenter.
enamel [ɪ'næməl] *n* émail *m*.
enamel paint *n* peinture émaillée.
enamoured [ɪ'næməd] *adj*: **~ of** amoureux(euse) de; (*idea*) enchanté(e) par.
encampment [ɪn'kæmpmənt] *n* campement *m*.
encased [ɪn'keɪst] *adj*: **~ in** enfermé(e) dans, recouvert(e) de.
enchant [ɪn'tʃɑːnt] *vt* enchanter.
enchanting [ɪn'tʃɑːntɪŋ] *adj* ravissant(e), enchanteur(eresse).
encircle [ɪn'səːkl] *vt* entourer, encercler.
enc(l). *abbr* (*on letters etc*: = *enclosed, enclosure*) PJ.
enclose [ɪn'kləuz] *vt* (*land*) clôturer; (*letter etc*): **to ~ (with)** joindre (à); **please find ~d** veuillez trouver ci-joint.
enclosure [ɪn'kləuʒə*] *n* enceinte *f*; (*in letter etc*) annexe *f*.
encoder [ɪn'kəudə*] *n* (*COMPUT*) encodeur *m*.
encompass [ɪn'kʌmpəs] *vt* encercler, entourer; (*include*) contenir, inclure.
encore [ɔŋ'kɔː*] *excl, n* bis (*m*).
encounter [ɪn'kauntə*] *n* rencontre *f* ♦ *vt* rencontrer.
encourage [ɪn'kʌrɪdʒ] *vt* encourager; (*industry, growth*) favoriser; **to ~ sb to do sth** encourager qn à faire qch.
encouragement [ɪn'kʌrɪdʒmənt] *n* encouragement *m*.
encouraging [ɪn'kʌrɪdʒɪŋ] *adj* encourageant(e).
encroach [ɪn'krəutʃ] *vi*: **to ~ (up)on** empiéter sur.
encrust [ɪn'krʌst] *vt* encroûter; (*with jewels etc*) incruster.
encrusted [ɪn'krʌstɪd] *adj*: **~ (with)** incrusté(e) (de).
encumber [ɪn'kʌmbə*] *vt*: **to be ~ed with** (*luggage*) être encombré(e) de; (*debts*) être grevé(e) de.
encyclop(a)edia [ɛnsaɪkləu'piːdɪə] *n* encyclopédie *f*.
end [ɛnd] *n* (*gen, also: aim*) fin *f*; (*of table, street, line, rope etc*) bout *m*, extrémité *f*; (*of pointed object*) pointe *f*; (*of town*) bout ♦ *vt* terminer; (*also*: **bring to an ~, put an ~ to**) mettre fin à ♦ *vi* se terminer, finir; **from ~ to ~** d'un bout à l'autre; **to come to an ~** prendre fin; **to be at an ~** être fini(e), être terminé(e); **in the ~** finalement; **on ~** (*object*) debout, dressé(e); **to stand on ~** (*hair*) se dresser sur la tête; **for 5 hours on ~** durant 5 heures d'affilée *or* de suite; **for hours on ~** pendant des heures (et des heures); **at the ~ of the day** (*BRIT fig*) en fin de compte; **to this ~, with this ~ in view** à cette fin, dans ce but.
►**end up** *vi*: **to ~ up in** finir *or* se terminer par; (*place*) finir *or* aboutir à.
endanger [ɪn'deɪndʒə*] *vt* mettre en danger; **an ~ed species** une espèce en voie de disparition.
endear [ɪn'dɪə*] *vt*: **to ~ o.s. to sb** se faire aimer de qn.
endearing [ɪn'dɪərɪŋ] *adj* attachant(e).
endearment [ɪn'dɪəmənt] *n*: **to whisper ~s** murmurer des mots *or* choses tendres; **term of ~** terme *m* d'affection.
endeavour, (*US*) **endeavor** [ɪn'dɛvə*] *n* tentative *f*, effort *m* ♦ *vi*: **to ~ to do** tenter *or* s'efforcer de faire.
endemic [ɛn'dɛmɪk] *adj* endémique.
ending ['ɛndɪŋ] *n* dénouement *m*, conclusion *f*; (*LING*) terminaison *f*.
endive ['ɛndaɪv] *n* (*curly*) chicorée *f*; (*smooth, flat*) endive *f*.
endless ['ɛndlɪs] *adj* sans fin, interminable; (*patience, resources*) inépuisable, sans limites; (*possibilities*) illimité(e).
endorse [ɪn'dɔːs] *vt* (*cheque*) endosser; (*approve*) appuyer, approuver, sanctionner.
endorsee [ɪndɔː'siː] *n* bénéficiaire *m/f*, endossataire *m/f*.
endorsement [ɪn'dɔːsmənt] *n* (*approval*) caution *f*, aval *m*; (*signature*) endossement *m*; (*BRIT*: *on driving licence*) contravention *f* (*portée au permis de conduire*).
endorser [ɪn'dɔːsə*] *n* avaliste *m*, endosseur *m*.

endow [ɪn'dau] *vt* (*provide with money*) faire une donation à, doter; (*equip*): **to ~ with** gratifier de, doter de.
endowment [ɪn'daumənt] *n* dotation *f*.
endowment mortgage *n hypothèque liée à une assurance-vie*.
endowment policy *n* assurance *f* à capital différé.
end product *n* (*INDUSTRY*) produit fini; (*fig*) résultat *m*, aboutissement *m*.
end result *n* résultat final.
endurable [ɪn'djuərəbl] *adj* supportable.
endurance [ɪn'djuərəns] *n* endurance *f*, résistance *f*; patience *f*.
endurance test *n* test *m* d'endurance.
endure [ɪn'djuə*] *vt* supporter, endurer ♦ *vi* durer.
end user *n* (*COMPUT*) utilisateur final.
enema ['ɛnɪmə] *n* (*MED*) lavement *m*.
enemy ['ɛnəmɪ] *adj, n* ennemi(e); **to make an ~ of sb** se faire un(e) ennemi(e) de qn, se mettre qn à dos.
energetic [ɛnə'dʒɛtɪk] *adj* énergique; (*activity*) très actif(ive), qui fait se dépenser (physiquement).
energy ['ɛnədʒɪ] *n* énergie *f*; **Department of E~** ministère *m* de l'Énergie.
energy crisis *n* crise *f* de l'énergie.
energy-saving ['ɛnədʒɪ'seɪvɪŋ] *adj* (*policy*) d'économie d'énergie; (*device*) qui permet de réaliser des économies d'énergie.
enervating ['ɛnəveɪtɪŋ] *adj* débilitant(e), affaiblissant(e).
enforce [ɪn'fɔːs] *vt* (*LAW*) appliquer, faire respecter.
enforced [ɪn'fɔːst] *adj* forcé(e).
enfranchise [ɪn'fræntʃaɪz] *vt* accorder le droit de vote à; (*set free*) affranchir.
engage [ɪn'geɪdʒ] *vt* engager; (*MIL*) engager le combat avec; (*lawyer*) prendre ♦ *vi* (*TECH*) s'enclencher, s'engrener; **to ~ in** se lancer dans; **to ~ sb in conversation** engager la conversation avec qn.
engaged [ɪn'geɪdʒd] *adj* (*BRIT: busy, in use*) occupé(e); (*betrothed*) fiancé(e); **to get ~** se fiancer; **he is ~ in research/a survey** il fait de la recherche/une enquête.
engaged tone *n* (*BRIT TEL*) tonalité *f* occupé *inv*.
engagement [ɪn'geɪdʒmənt] *n* obligation *f*, engagement *m*; (*appointment*) rendez-vous *m inv*; (*to marry*) fiançailles *fpl*; (*MIL*) combat *m*; **I have a previous ~** j'ai déjà un rendez-vous, je suis déjà prise(e).
engagement ring *n* bague *f* de fiançailles.
engaging [ɪn'geɪdʒɪŋ] *adj* engageant(e), attirant(e).
engender [ɪn'dʒɛndə*] *vt* produire, causer.
engine ['ɛndʒɪn] *n* (*AUT*) moteur *m*; (*RAIL*) locomotive *f*.
engine driver *n* (*BRIT: of train*) mécanicien *m*.
engineer [ɛndʒɪ'nɪə*] *n* ingénieur *m*; (*BRIT: for domestic appliances*) réparateur *m*; (*US RAIL*) mécanicien *m*; **civil/mechanical ~** ingénieur des Travaux Publics *or* des Ponts et Chaussées/mécanicien.
engineering [ɛndʒɪ'nɪərɪŋ] *n* engineering *m*, ingénierie *f*; (*of bridges, ships*) génie *m*; (*of machine*) mécanique *f* ♦ *cpd*: **~ works** *or* **factory** atelier *m* de construction mécanique.
engine failure *n* panne *f*.
engine trouble *n* ennuis *mpl* mécaniques.
England ['ɪŋglənd] *n* Angleterre *f*.
English ['ɪŋglɪʃ] *adj* anglais(e) ♦ *n* (*LING*) anglais *m*; **the ~** *npl* les Anglais; **an ~ speaker** un anglophone.
English Channel *n*: **the ~** la Manche.
Englishman ['ɪŋglɪʃmən], **Englishwoman** ['ɪŋglɪʃwumən] *n* Anglais/e.
English-speaking ['ɪŋglɪʃ'spiːkɪŋ] *adj* qui parle anglais; anglophone.
engrave [ɪn'greɪv] *vt* graver.
engraving [ɪn'greɪvɪŋ] *n* gravure *f*.
engrossed [ɪn'grəust] *adj*: **~ in** absorbé(e) par, plongé(e) dans.
engulf [ɪn'gʌlf] *vt* engloutir.
enhance [ɪn'hɑːns] *vt* rehausser, mettre en valeur; (*position*) améliorer; (*reputation*) accroître.
enigma [ɪ'nɪgmə] *n* énigme *f*.
enigmatic [ɛnɪg'mætɪk] *adj* énigmatique.
enjoy [ɪn'dʒɔɪ] *vt* aimer, prendre plaisir à; (*have benefit of: health, fortune*) jouir de; (*: success*) connaître; **to ~ o.s.** s'amuser.
enjoyable [ɪn'dʒɔɪəbl] *adj* agréable.
enjoyment [ɪn'dʒɔɪmənt] *n* plaisir *m*.
enlarge [ɪn'lɑːdʒ] *vt* accroître; (*PHOT*) agrandir ♦ *vi*: **to ~ on** (*subject*) s'étendre sur.
enlarged [ɪn'lɑːdʒd] *adj* (*edition*) augmenté(e); (*MED: organ, gland*) anormalement gros(se), hypertrophié(e).
enlargement [ɪn'lɑːdʒmənt] *n* (*PHOT*) agrandissement *m*.
enlighten [ɪn'laɪtn] *vt* éclairer.
enlightened [ɪn'laɪtnd] *adj* éclairé(e).
enlightening [ɪn'laɪtnɪŋ] *adj* instructif(ive), révélateur(trice).
enlightenment [ɪn'laɪtnmənt] *n* édification *f*; éclaircissements *mpl*; (*HISTORY*): **the E~** ≈ le Siècle des lumières.
enlist [ɪn'lɪst] *vt* recruter; (*support*) s'assurer ♦ *vi* s'engager; **~ed man** (*US MIL*) simple soldat *m*.
enliven [ɪn'laɪvn] *vt* animer, égayer.
enmity ['ɛnmɪtɪ] *n* inimitié *f*.
ennoble [ɪ'nəubl] *vt* (*with title*) anoblir.
enormity [ɪ'nɔːmɪtɪ] *n* énormité *f*.
enormous [ɪ'nɔːməs] *adj* énorme.
enormously [ɪ'nɔːməslɪ] *adv* (*increase*) dans des proportions énormes; (*rich*) extrêmement.
enough [ɪ'nʌf] *adj, n*: **~ time/books** assez *or* suffisamment de temps/livres ♦ *adv*: **big ~** assez *or* suffisamment grand; **have you got**

~? (en) avez-vous assez?; **will 5 be ~?** est-ce que 5 suffiront?, est-ce qu'il y en aura assez avec 5?; **that's ~!** ça suffit!, assez!; **that's ~, thanks** cela suffit *or* c'est assez, merci; **I've had ~!** je n'en peux plus!; **he has not worked ~** il n'a pas assez *or* suffisamment travaillé, il n'a pas travaillé assez *or* suffisamment; ~! assez!, ça suffit!; **it's hot ~ (as it is)!** il fait assez chaud comme ça!; **he was kind ~ to lend me the money** il a eu la gentillesse de me prêter l'argent; **... which, funnily ~ ...** qui, chose curieuse.
enquire [ɪn'kwaɪə*] *vt, vi* = **inquire**.
enrage [ɪn'reɪdʒ] *vt* mettre en fureur *or* en rage, rendre furieux(euse).
enrich [ɪn'rɪtʃ] *vt* enrichir.
enrol, (*US*) **enroll** [ɪn'rəul] *vt* inscrire ♦ *vi* s'inscrire.
enrol(l)ment [ɪn'rəulmənt] *n* inscription *f*.
en route [ɔn'ru:t] *adv* en route, en chemin; ~ **for** *or* **to** en route vers, à destination de.
ensconced [ɪn'skɔnst] *adj*: ~ **in** bien calé(e) dans.
enshrine [ɪn'ʃraɪn] *vt* (*fig*) préserver.
ensign *n* (*NAUT*) ['ɛnsən] enseigne *f*, pavillon *m*; (*MIL*) ['ɛnsaɪn] porte-étendard *m*.
enslave [ɪn'sleɪv] *vt* asservir.
ensue [ɪn'sju:] *vi* s'ensuivre, résulter.
ensure [ɪn'ʃuə*] *vt* assurer, garantir; **to ~ that** s'assurer que.
ENT *n abbr* (= *Ear, Nose and Throat*) ORL *f*.
entail [ɪn'teɪl] *vt* entraîner, nécessiter.
entangle [ɪn'tæŋgl] *vt* emmêler, embrouiller; **to become ~d in sth** (*fig*) se laisser entraîner *or* empêtrer dans qch.
enter ['ɛntə*] *vt* (*room*) entrer dans, pénétrer dans; (*club, army*) entrer à; (*profession*) embrasser; (*competition*) s'inscrire à *or* pour; (*sb for a competition*) (faire) inscrire; (*write down*) inscrire, noter; (*COMPUT*) entrer, introduire ♦ *vi* entrer.
►**enter for** *vt fus* s'inscrire à, se présenter pour *or* à.
►**enter into** *vt fus* (*explanation*) se lancer dans; (*negotiations*) entamer; (*debate*) prendre part à; (*agreement*) conclure.
►**enter up** *vt* inscrire.
►**enter (up)on** *vt fus* commencer.
enteritis [ɛntə'raɪtɪs] *n* entérite *f*.
enterprise ['ɛntəpraɪz] *n* (*company, undertaking*) entreprise *f*; (*initiative*) (esprit *m* d')initiative *f*.
enterprising ['ɛntəpraɪzɪŋ] *adj* entreprenant(e), dynamique.
entertain [ɛntə'teɪn] *vt* amuser, distraire; (*invite*) recevoir (à dîner); (*idea, plan*) envisager.
entertainer [ɛntə'teɪnə*] *n* artiste *m/f* de variétés.
entertaining [ɛntə'teɪnɪŋ] *adj* amusant(e), distrayant(e) ♦ *n*: **to do a lot of ~** beaucoup recevoir.
entertainment [ɛntə'teɪnmənt] *n* (*amusement*) distraction *f*, divertissement *m*, amusement *m*; (*show*) spectacle *m*.
entertainment allowance *n* frais *mpl* de représentation.
enthral [ɪn'θrɔ:l] *vt* captiver, passionner.
enthralling [ɪn'θrɔ:lɪŋ] *adj* captivant(e); enchanteur(eresse).
enthuse [ɪn'θu:z] *vi*: **to ~ about** *or* **over** parler avec enthousiasme de.
enthusiasm [ɪn'θu:zɪæzəm] *n* enthousiasme *m*.
enthusiast [ɪn'θu:zɪæst] *n* enthousiaste *m/f*; **a jazz** *etc* **~** un fervent *or* passionné du jazz *etc*.
enthusiastic [ɪnθu:zɪ'æstɪk] *adj* enthousiaste; **to be ~ about** être enthousiasmé(e) par.
entice [ɪn'taɪs] *vt* attirer, séduire.
enticing [ɪn'taɪsɪŋ] *adj* (*person, offer*) séduisant(e); (*food*) alléchant(e).
entire [ɪn'taɪə*] *adj* (tout) entier(ère).
entirely [ɪn'taɪəlɪ] *adv* entièrement, complètement.
entirety [ɪn'taɪərətɪ] *n*: **in its ~** dans sa totalité.
entitle [ɪn'taɪtl] *vt* (*allow*): **to ~ sb to do** donner (le) droit à qn de faire; **to ~ sb to sth** donner droit à qch à qn.
entitled [ɪn'taɪtld] *adj* (*book*) intitulé(e); **to be ~ to sth/to do sth** avoir droit à qch/le droit de faire qch.
entity ['ɛntɪtɪ] *n* entité *f*.
entrails ['ɛntreɪlz] *npl* entrailles *fpl*.
entrance *n* ['ɛntrns] entrée *f* ♦ *vt* [ɪn'trɑ:ns] enchanter, ravir; **to gain ~ to** (*university etc*) être admis à.
entrance examination *n* examen *m* d'entrée *or* d'admission.
entrance fee *n* droit *m* d'inscription; (*to museum etc*) prix *m* d'entrée.
entrance ramp *n* (*US AUT*) bretelle *f* d'accès.
entrancing [ɪn'trɑ:nsɪŋ] *adj* enchanteur(teresse), ravissant(e).
entrant ['ɛntrnt] *n* (*in race etc*) participant/e, concurrent/e; (*BRIT*: *in exam*) candidat/e.
entreat [ɛn'tri:t] *vt* supplier.
entreaty [ɛn'tri:tɪ] *n* supplication *f*, prière *f*.
entrée ['ɔntreɪ] *n* (*CULIN*) entrée *f*.
entrenched [ɛn'trɛntʃt] *adj* retranché(e).
entrepreneur ['ɔntrəprə'nə:*] *n* entrepreneur *m*.
entrepreneurial ['ɔntrəprə'nə:rɪəl] *adj* animé(e) d'un esprit d'entreprise.
entrust [ɪn'trʌst] *vt*: **to ~ sth to** confier qch à.
entry ['ɛntrɪ] *n* entrée *f*; (*in register, diary*) inscription *f*; (*in ledger*) écriture *f*; **"no ~"** "défense d'entrer", "entrée interdite"; (*AUT*) "sens interdit"; **single/double ~ bookkeeping** comptabilité *f* en partie simple/double.
entry form *n* feuille *f* d'inscription.
entry phone *n* (*BRIT*) interphone *m* (*à l'entrée d'un immeuble*).

entwine [ɪn'twaɪn] *vt* entrelacer.
E-number ['iːnʌmbə*] *n* additif *m* (alimentaire).
enumerate [ɪ'njuːməreɪt] *vt* énumérer.
enunciate [ɪ'nʌnsɪeɪt] *vt* énoncer; prononcer.
envelop [ɪn'vɛləp] *vt* envelopper.
envelope ['ɛnvələup] *n* enveloppe *f*.
enviable ['ɛnvɪəbl] *adj* enviable.
envious ['ɛnvɪəs] *adj* envieux(euse).
environment [ɪn'vaɪərnmənt] *n* milieu *m*; environnement *m*; **Department of the E~** (*BRIT*) *ministère de l'équipement et de l'aménagement du territoire*.
environmental [ɪnvaɪərn'mɛntl] *adj* écologique, relatif(ive) à l'environnement; **~ studies** (*in school etc*) écologie *f*.
environmentalist [ɪnvaɪərn'mɛntlɪst] *n* écologiste *m/f*.
environmentally [ɪnvaɪərn'mɛntlɪ] *adv*: **~ sound/friendly** qui ne nuit pas à l'environnement.
Environmental Protection Agency (EPA) *n* (*US*) ≈ ministère *m* de l'Environnement.
envisage [ɪn'vɪzɪdʒ] *vt* envisager; prévoir.
envision [ɪn'vɪʒən] *vt* envisager, concevoir.
envoy ['ɛnvɔɪ] *n* envoyé/e.
envy ['ɛnvɪ] *n* envie *f* ♦ *vt* envier; **to ~ sb sth** envier qch à qn.
enzyme ['ɛnzaɪm] *n* enzyme *m*.
EPA *n abbr* (*US*) = **Environmental Protection Agency**.
ephemeral [ɪ'fɛmərl] *adj* éphémère.
epic ['ɛpɪk] *n* épopée *f* ♦ *adj* épique.
epicentre, (*US*) **epicenter** ['ɛpɪsɛntə*] *n* épicentre *m*.
epidemic [ɛpɪ'dɛmɪk] *n* épidémie *f*.
epilepsy ['ɛpɪlɛpsɪ] *n* épilepsie *f*.
epileptic [ɛpɪ'lɛptɪk] *adj, n* épileptique (*m/f*).
epilogue ['ɛpɪlɔg] *n* épilogue *m*.
episcopal [ɪ'pɪskəpl] *adj* épiscopal(e).
episode ['ɛpɪsəud] *n* épisode *m*.
epistle [ɪ'pɪsl] *n* épître *f*.
epitaph ['ɛpɪtɑːf] *n* épitaphe *f*.
epithet ['ɛpɪθɛt] *n* épithète *f*.
epitome [ɪ'pɪtəmɪ] *n* (*fig*) quintessence *f*, type *m*.
epitomize [ɪ'pɪtəmaɪz] *vt* (*fig*) illustrer, incarner.
epoch ['iːpɔk] *n* époque *f*, ère *f*.
epoch-making ['iːpɔkmeɪkɪŋ] *adj* qui fait époque.
eponymous [ɪ'pɔnɪməs] *adj* de ce *or* du même nom, éponyme.
equable ['ɛkwəbl] *adj* égal(e); de tempérament égal.
equal ['iːkwl] *adj* égal(e) ♦ *n* égal/e ♦ *vt* égaler; **~ to** (*task*) à la hauteur de; **~ to doing** de taille à *or* capable de faire.
equality [iː'kwɔlɪtɪ] *n* égalité *f*.
equalize ['iːkwəlaɪz] *vt, vi* égaliser.
equalizer ['iːkwəlaɪzə*] *n* but égalisateur.
equally ['iːkwəlɪ] *adv* également; (*just as*) tout aussi; **they are ~ clever** ils sont tout aussi intelligents.
Equal Opportunities Commission, (*US*) **Equal Employment Opportunity Commission** *n commission pour la non discrimination dans l'emploi*.
equal(s) sign *n* signe *m* d'égalité.
equanimity [ɛkwə'nɪmɪtɪ] *n* égalité *f* d'humeur.
equate [ɪ'kweɪt] *vt*: **to ~ sth with** comparer qch à; assimiler qch à; **to ~ sth to** mettre qch en équation avec; égaler qch à.
equation [ɪ'kweɪʃən] *n* (*MATH*) équation *f*.
equator [ɪ'kweɪtə*] *n* équateur *m*.
equatorial [ɛkwə'tɔːrɪəl] *adj* équatorial(e).
Equatorial Guinea *n* Guinée équatoriale.
equestrian [ɪ'kwɛstrɪən] *adj* équestre ♦ *n* écuyer/ère, cavalier/ère.
equilibrium [iːkwɪ'lɪbrɪəm] *n* équilibre *m*.
equinox ['iːkwɪnɔks] *n* équinoxe *m*.
equip [ɪ'kwɪp] *vt* équiper; **to ~ sb/sth with** équiper *or* munir qn/qch de; **he is well ~ped for the job** il a les compétences *or* les qualités requises pour ce travail.
equipment [ɪ'kwɪpmənt] *n* équipement *m*; (*electrical etc*) appareillage *m*, installation *f*.
equitable ['ɛkwɪtəbl] *adj* équitable.
equities ['ɛkwɪtɪz] *npl* (*BRIT COMM*) actions cotées en Bourse.
equity ['ɛkwɪtɪ] *n* équité *f*.
equity capital *n* capitaux *mpl* propres.
equivalent [ɪ'kwɪvəlnt] *adj* équivalent(e) ♦ *n* équivalent *m*; **to be ~ to** équivaloir à, être équivalent(e) à.
equivocal [ɪ'kwɪvəkl] *adj* équivoque; (*open to suspicion*) douteux(euse).
equivocate [ɪ'kwɪvəkeɪt] *vi* user de fauxfuyants; éviter de répondre.
equivocation [ɪkwɪvə'keɪʃən] *n* équivoque *f*.
ER *abbr* (*BRIT*: = *Elizabeth Regina*) *la reine Élisabeth*.
ERA *n abbr* (*US POL*: = *Equal Rights Amendment*) *amendement sur l'égalité des droits des femmes*.
era ['ɪərə] *n* ère *f*, époque *f*.
eradicate [ɪ'rædɪkeɪt] *vt* éliminer.
erase [ɪ'reɪz] *vt* effacer.
eraser [ɪ'reɪzə*] *n* gomme *f*.
erect [ɪ'rɛkt] *adj* droit(e) ♦ *vt* construire; (*monument*) ériger, élever; (*tent etc*) dresser.
erection [ɪ'rɛkʃən] *n* (*PHYSIOL*) érection *f*; (*of building*) construction *f*; (*of machinery etc*) installation *f*.
ergonomics [əːgə'nɔmɪks] *n* ergonomie *f*.
ERISA *n abbr* (*US*: = *Employee Retirement Income Security Act*) *loi sur les pensions de retraite*.
Eritrea [ɛrɪ'treɪə] *n* Érythrée *f*.
ERM *n abbr* (= *Exchange Rate Mechanism*) MTC *m*.
ermine ['əːmɪn] *n* hermine *f*.
ERNIE ['əːnɪ] *n abbr* (*BRIT*: = *Electronic Random*

Number Indicator Equipment) ordinateur servant au tirage des bons à lots gagnants.
erode [ɪ'rəud] *vt* éroder; (*metal*) ronger.
erogenous zone [ɪ'rɔdʒənəs-] *n* zone *f* érogène.
erosion [ɪ'rəuʒən] *n* érosion *f*.
erotic [ɪ'rɔtɪk] *adj* érotique.
eroticism [ɪ'rɔtɪsɪzəm] *n* érotisme *m*.
err [əː*] *vi* se tromper; (*REL*) pécher.
errand ['ɛrnd] *n* course *f*, commission *f*; **to run ~s** faire des courses; **~ of mercy** mission *f* de charité, acte *m* charitable.
errand boy *n* garçon *m* de courses.
erratic [ɪ'rætɪk] *adj* irrégulier(ière); inconstant(e).
erroneous [ɪ'rəunɪəs] *adj* erroné(e).
error ['ɛrə*] *n* erreur *f*; **typing/spelling ~** faute *f* de frappe/d'orthographe; **in ~** par erreur, par méprise; **~s and omissions excepted** sauf erreur ou omission.
error message *n* (*COMPUT*) message *m* d'erreur.
erstwhile ['əːstwaɪl] *adj* précédent(e), d'autrefois.
erudite ['ɛrjudaɪt] *adj* savant(e).
erupt [ɪ'rʌpt] *vi* entrer en éruption; (*fig*) éclater, exploser.
eruption [ɪ'rʌpʃən] *n* éruption *f*; (*of anger, violence*) explosion *f*.
ESA *n abbr* (= *European Space Agency*) ASE *f* (= *Agence spatiale européenne*).
escalate ['ɛskəleɪt] *vi* s'intensifier; (*costs*) monter en flèche.
escalation [ɛskə'leɪʃən] *n* escalade *f*.
escalation clause *n* clause *f* d'indexation.
escalator ['ɛskəleɪtə*] *n* escalier roulant.
escapade [ɛskə'peɪd] *n* fredaine *f*; équipée *f*.
escape [ɪ'skeɪp] *n* évasion *f*, fuite *f*; (*of gas etc*) fuite; (*: TECH*) échappement *m* ♦ *vi* s'échapper, fuir; (*from jail*) s'évader; (*fig*) s'en tirer, en réchapper; (*leak*) fuir; s'échapper ♦ *vt* échapper à; **to ~ from** (*person*) échapper à; (*place*) s'échapper de; (*fig*) fuir; **to ~ to** (*another place*) fuir à, s'enfuir à; **to ~ to safety** se réfugier dans *or* gagner un endroit sûr; **to ~ notice** passer inaperçu(e).
escape artist *n* virtuose *m/f* de l'évasion.
escape clause *n* clause *f* dérogatoire.
escapee [ɪskeɪ'piː] *n* évadé/e.
escape key *n* (*COMPUT*) touche *f* d'échappement.
escape route *n* (*from fire*) issue *f* de secours; (*of prisoners etc*) voie empruntée pour s'échapper.
escapism [ɪ'skeɪpɪzəm] *n* évasion *f* (*fig*).
escapist [ɪ'skeɪpɪst] *adj* (*literature*) d'évasion ♦ *n* personne *f* qui se réfugie hors de la réalité.
escapologist [ɛskə'pɔlədʒɪst] *n* (*BRIT*) = **escape artist**.
escarpment [ɪs'kɑːpmənt] *n* escarpement *m*.
eschew [ɪs'tʃuː] *vt* éviter.
escort *vt* [ɪ'skɔːt] escorter ♦ *n* ['ɛskɔːt] escorte *f*; (*to dance etc*): **her ~** son compagnon *or* cavalier; **his ~** sa compagne.
escort agency *n* bureau *m* d'hôtesses.
Eskimo ['ɛskɪməu] *adj* esquimau(de), eskimo ♦ *n* Esquimau/de; (*LING*) esquimau *m*.
ESL *n abbr* (*SCOL*) = *English as a Second Language*.
esophagus [iː'sɔfəgəs] *n* (*US*) = **oesophagus**.
esoteric [ɛsə'tɛrɪk] *adj* ésotérique.
ESP *n abbr* = **extrasensory perception**; (*SCOL*) = *English for Special Purposes*.
esp. *abbr* = **especially**.
especially [ɪ'spɛʃlɪ] *adv* (*specifically*) spécialement, exprès; (*more than usually*) particulièrement; (*above all*) particulièrement, surtout.
espionage ['ɛspɪənɑːʒ] *n* espionnage *m*.
esplanade [ɛsplə'neɪd] *n* esplanade *f*.
espouse [ɪ'spauz] *vt* épouser, embrasser.
Esquire [ɪ'skwaɪə*] *n* (*BRIT*: *abbr* **Esq.**): **J. Brown, ~** Monsieur J. Brown.
essay ['ɛseɪ] *n* (*SCOL*) dissertation *f*; (*LITERATURE*) essai *m*; (*attempt*) tentative *f*.
essence ['ɛsns] *n* essence *f*; **in ~** en substance; **speed is of the ~** l'essentiel, c'est la rapidité.
essential [ɪ'sɛnʃl] *adj* essentiel(le); (*basic*) fondamental(e) ♦ *n* élément essentiel; **it is ~ that** il est essentiel *or* primordial que.
essentially [ɪ'sɛnʃlɪ] *adv* essentiellement.
EST *abbr* (*US*: = *Eastern Standard Time*) *heure d'hiver de New York*.
est. *abbr* = *established, estimate(d)*.
establish [ɪ'stæblɪʃ] *vt* établir; (*business*) fonder, créer; (*one's power etc*) asseoir, affermir.
establishment [ɪ'stæblɪʃmənt] *n* établissement *m*; création *f*; (*institution*) établissement; **the E~** les pouvoirs établis; l'ordre établi.
estate [ɪ'steɪt] *n* (*land*) domaine *m*, propriété *f*; (*LAW*) biens *mpl*, succession *f*; (*BRIT*: *also*: **housing ~**) lotissement *m*.
estate agency *n* (*BRIT*) agence immobilière.
estate agent *n* (*BRIT*) agent immobilier.
estate car *n* (*BRIT*) break *m*.
esteem [ɪ'stiːm] *n* estime *f* ♦ *vt* estimer; apprécier; **to hold sb in high ~** tenir qn en haute estime.
esthetic [ɪs'θɛtɪk] *adj* (*US*) = **aesthetic**.
estimate *n* ['ɛstɪmət] estimation *f*; (*COMM*) devis *m* ♦ *vb* ['ɛstɪmeɪt] *vt* estimer ♦ *vi* (*BRIT COMM*): **to ~ for** estimer, faire une estimation de; (*bid for*) faire un devis pour; **to give sb an ~ of** faire *or* donner un devis à qn pour; **at a rough ~** approximativement.
estimation [ɛstɪ'meɪʃən] *n* opinion *f*; estime *f*; **in my ~** à mon avis, selon moi.
Estonia [ɛ'stəunɪə] *n* Estonie *f*.
Estonian [ɛ'stəunɪən] *adj* estonien(ne) ♦ *n* Estonien/ne; (*LING*) estonien *m*.

estranged [ɪs'treɪndʒd] *adj* (*couple*) séparé(e); (*husband, wife*) dont on s'est séparé(e).
estrangement [ɪs'treɪndʒmənt] *n* (*from wife, family*) séparation *f*.
estrogen ['iːstrəudʒən] *n* (*US*) = **oestrogen**.
estuary ['ɛstjuərɪ] *n* estuaire *m*.
ET *abbr* (*US*: = *Eastern Time*) *heure de New York*.
ETA *n abbr* (= *estimated time of arrival*) HPA *f* (= *heure probable d'arrivée*).
et al. *abbr* (= *et alii: and others*) et coll.
etc. *abbr* (= *et cetera*) etc.
etch [ɛtʃ] *vt* graver à l'eau forte.
etching ['ɛtʃɪŋ] *n* eau-forte *f*.
ETD *n abbr* (= *estimated time of departure*) HPD *f* (= *heure probable de départ*).
eternal [ɪ'təːnl] *adj* éternel(le).
eternity [ɪ'təːnɪtɪ] *n* éternité *f*.
ether ['iːθə*] *n* éther *m*.
ethereal [ɪ'θɪərɪəl] *adj* éthéré(e).
ethical ['ɛθɪkl] *adj* moral(e).
ethics ['ɛθɪks] *n* éthique *f* ♦ *npl* moralité *f*.
Ethiopia [iːθɪ'əupɪə] *n* Éthiopie *f*.
Ethiopian [iːθɪ'əupɪən] *adj* éthiopien(ne) ♦ *n* Éthiopien/ne.
ethnic ['ɛθnɪk] *adj* ethnique; (*clothes, food*) *folklorique, exotique; propre aux minorités ethniques non-occidentales*.
ethnic cleansing [-'klɛnzɪŋ] *n* purification *f* ethnique.
ethnology [ɛθ'nɔlədʒɪ] *n* ethnologie *f*.
ethos ['iːθɔs] *n* (système *m* de) valeurs *fpl*.
etiquette ['ɛtɪkɛt] *n* convenances *fpl*, étiquette *f*.
ETV *n abbr* (*US*: = *Educational Television*) *télévision scolaire*.
etymology [ɛtɪ'mɔlədʒɪ] *n* étymologie *f*.
EU *n abbr* (= *European Union*) UE *f*.
eucalyptus [juːkə'lɪptəs] *n* eucalyptus *m*.
eulogy ['juːlədʒɪ] *n* éloge *m*.
euphemism ['juːfəmɪzəm] *n* euphémisme *m*.
euphemistic [juːfə'mɪstɪk] *adj* euphémique.
euphoria [juː'fɔːrɪə] *n* euphorie *f*.
Eurasia [juə'reɪʃə] *n* Eurasie *f*.
Eurasian [juə'reɪʃən] *adj* eurasien(ne); (*continent*) eurasiatique ♦ *n* Eurasien/ne.
Euratom [juə'rætəm] *n abbr* (= *European Atomic Energy Community*) EURATOM *f*.
euro ['juərəu] *n* (*currency*) euro *m*.
Euro- ['juərəu] *prefix* euro-.
Eurocheque ['juərəutʃɛk] *n* eurochèque *m*.
Eurocrat ['juərəukræt] *n* eurocrate *m/f*.
Eurodollar ['juərəudɔlə*] *n* eurodollar *m*.
Euroland ['juərəuˌlænd] *n* Euroland *m*.
Europe ['juərəp] *n* Europe *f*.
European [juərə'piːən] *adj* européen(ne) ♦ *n* Européen/ne.
European Court of Justice *n* Cour *f* de Justice de la CEE.
Euro-sceptic ['juərəuskeptɪk] *n* eurosceptique *m/f*.
euthanasia [juːθə'neɪzɪə] *n* euthanasie *f*.
evacuate [ɪ'vækjueɪt] *vt* évacuer.
evacuation [ɪvækju'eɪʃən] *n* évacuation *f*.
evacuee [ɪvækju'iː] *n* évacué/e.
evade [ɪ'veɪd] *vt* échapper à; (*question etc*) éluder; (*duties*) se dérober à.
evaluate [ɪ'væljueɪt] *vt* évaluer.
evangelist [ɪ'vændʒəlɪst] *n* évangéliste *m*.
evangelize [ɪ'vændʒəlaɪz] *vt* évangéliser, prêcher l'Évangile à.
evaporate [ɪ'væpəreɪt] *vi* s'évaporer ♦ *vt* faire évaporer.
evaporated milk [ɪ'væpəreɪtɪd-] *n* lait condensé (non sucré).
evaporation [ɪvæpə'reɪʃən] *n* évaporation *f*.
evasion [ɪ'veɪʒən] *n* dérobade *f*; (*excuse*) faux-fuyant *m*.
evasive [ɪ'veɪsɪv] *adj* évasif(ive).
eve [iːv] *n*: **on the ~ of** à la veille de.
even ['iːvn] *adj* régulier(ière), égal(e); (*number*) pair(e) ♦ *adv* même; ~ **if** même si + *indicative*; ~ **though** quand (bien) même + *conditional*, alors même que + *conditional*; ~ **more** encore plus; ~ **faster** encore plus vite; ~ **so** quand même; **not** ~ pas même; **to break** ~ s'y retrouver, équilibrer ses comptes; **to get** ~ **with sb** prendre sa revanche sur qn.
►**even out** *vi* s'égaliser.
even-handed [iːvn'hændɪd] *adj* équitable.
evening ['iːvnɪŋ] *n* soir *m*; (*as duration, event*) soirée *f*; **in the** ~ le soir; **this** ~ ce soir; **tomorrow/yesterday** ~ demain/hier soir.
evening class *n* cours *m* du soir.
evening dress *n* (*man's*) habit *m* de soirée, smoking *m*; (*woman's*) robe *f* de soirée.
evenly ['iːvnlɪ] *adv* uniformément, également; (*space*) régulièrement.
evensong ['iːvnsɔŋ] *n* office *m* du soir.
event [ɪ'vɛnt] *n* événement *m*; (*SPORT*) épreuve *f*; **in the course of ~s** par la suite; **in the ~ of** en cas de; **in the** ~ en réalité, en fait; **at all ~s** (*BRIT*), **in any** ~ en tout cas, de toute manière.
eventful [ɪ'vɛntful] *adj* mouvementé(e).
eventing [ɪ'vɛntɪŋ] *n* (*HORSE-RIDING*) concours complet (*équitation*).
eventual [ɪ'vɛntʃuəl] *adj* final(e).
eventuality [ɪvɛntʃu'ælɪtɪ] *n* possibilité *f*, éventualité *f*.
eventually [ɪ'vɛntʃuəlɪ] *adv* finalement.
ever ['ɛvə*] *adv* jamais; (*at all times*) toujours; **the best** ~ le meilleur qu'on ait jamais vu; **did you** ~ **meet him?** est-ce qu'il vous est arrivé de le rencontrer?; **have you** ~ **been there?** y êtes-vous déjà allé?; **for** ~ pour toujours; **hardly** ~ ne ... presque jamais; ~ **since** *adv* depuis ♦ *conj* depuis que; ~ **so pretty** si joli; **thank you** ~ **so much** merci mille fois;
Everest ['ɛvərɪst] *n* (*also*: **Mount** ~) le mont Everest, l'Everest *m*.
evergreen ['ɛvəgriːn] *n* arbre *m* à feuilles persistantes.

everlasting [ɛvə'lɑːstɪŋ] *adj* éternel(le).
every ['ɛvrɪ] *adj* chaque; ~ **day** tous les jours, chaque jour; ~ **other/third day** tous les deux/trois jours; ~ **other car** une voiture sur deux; ~ **now and then** de temps en temps; **I have** ~ **confidence in him** j'ai entièrement *or* pleinement confiance en lui.
everybody ['ɛvrɪbɔdɪ] *pron* tout le monde, tous *pl*; ~ **knows about it** tout le monde le sait; ~ **else** tous les autres.
everyday ['ɛvrɪdeɪ] *adj* (*expression*) courant(e), d'usage courant; (*use*) courant; (*occurrence, experience*) de tous les jours, ordinaire.
everyone ['ɛvrɪwʌn] = **everybody**.
everything ['ɛvrɪθɪŋ] *pron* tout; ~ **is ready** tout est prêt; **he did** ~ **possible** il a fait tout son possible.
everywhere ['ɛvrɪwɛə*] *adv* partout; ~ **you go you meet** ... où qu'on aille, on rencontre ....
evict [ɪ'vɪkt] *vt* expulser.
eviction [ɪ'vɪkʃən] *n* expulsion *f*.
eviction notice *n* préavis *m* d'expulsion.
evidence ['ɛvɪdns] *n* (*proof*) preuve(s) *f(pl)*; (*of witness*) témoignage *m*; (*sign*): **to show** ~ **of** donner des signes de; **to give** ~ témoigner, déposer; **in** ~ (*obvious*) en évidence; en vue.
evident ['ɛvɪdnt] *adj* évident(e).
evidently ['ɛvɪdntlɪ] *adv* de toute évidence.
evil ['iːvl] *adj* mauvais(e) ♦ *n* mal *m*.
evince [ɪ'vɪns] *vt* manifester.
evocative [ɪ'vɔkətɪv] *adj* évocateur(trice).
evoke [ɪ'vəuk] *vt* évoquer; (*admiration*) susciter.
evolution [iːvə'luːʃən] *n* évolution *f*.
evolve [ɪ'vɔlv] *vt* élaborer ♦ *vi* évoluer, se transformer.
ewe [juː] *n* brebis *f*.
ewer ['juːə*] *n* broc *m*.
ex- [ɛks] *prefix* (*former: husband, president etc*) ex-; (*out of*): **the price** ~ **works** le prix départ usine.
exacerbate [ɛks'æsəbeɪt] *vt* (*pain*) exacerber, accentuer; (*fig*) aggraver.
exact [ɪg'zækt] *adj* exact(e) ♦ *vt*: **to** ~ **sth (from)** extorquer qch (à); exiger qch (de).
exacting [ɪg'zæktɪŋ] *adj* exigeant(e); (*work*) fatigant(e).
exactitude [ɪg'zæktɪtjuːd] *n* exactitude *f*, précision *f*.
exactly [ɪg'zæktlɪ] *adv* exactement; ~! parfaitement!, précisément!
exaggerate [ɪg'zædʒəreɪt] *vt, vi* exagérer.
exaggeration [ɪgzædʒə'reɪʃən] *n* exagération *f*.
exalted [ɪg'zɔːltɪd] *adj* (*rank*) élevé(e); (*person*) haut placé(e); (*elated*) exalté(e).
exam [ɪg'zæm] *n abbr* (*SCOL*) = **examination**.
examination [ɪgzæmɪ'neɪʃən] *n* (*SCOL, MED*) examen *m*; **to take** *or* (*BRIT*) **sit an** ~ passer un examen; **the matter is under** ~ la question est à l'examen.
examine [ɪg'zæmɪn] *vt* (*gen*) examiner; (*SCOL, LAW: person*) interroger; (*inspect: machine, premises*) inspecter; (*passport*) contrôler; (*luggage*) fouiller.
examiner [ɪg'zæmɪnə*] *n* examinateur/trice.
example [ɪg'zɑːmpl] *n* exemple *m*; **for** ~ par exemple; **to set a good/bad** ~ donner le bon/mauvais exemple.
exasperate [ɪg'zɑːspəreɪt] *vt* exaspérer, agacer.
exasperation [ɪgzɑːspə'reɪʃən] *n* exaspération *f*, irritation *f*.
excavate ['ɛkskəveɪt] *vt* excaver; (*object*) mettre au jour.
excavation [ɛkskə'veɪʃən] *n* excavation *f*.
excavator ['ɛkskəveɪtə*] *n* excavateur *m*, excavatrice *f*.
exceed [ɪk'siːd] *vt* dépasser; (*one's powers*) outrepasser.
exceedingly [ɪk'siːdɪŋlɪ] *adv* excessivement.
excel [ɪk'sɛl] *vi* exceller ♦ *vt* surpasser; **to** ~ **o.s.** (*BRIT*) se surpasser.
excellence ['ɛksələns] *n* excellence *f*.
Excellency ['ɛksələnsɪ] *n*: **His** ~ son Excellence *f*.
excellent ['ɛksələnt] *adj* excellent(e).
except [ɪk'sɛpt] *prep* (*also*: ~ **for**, ~**ing**) sauf, excepté, à l'exception de ♦ *vt* excepter; ~ **if/when** sauf si/quand; ~ **that** excepté que, si ce n'est que.
exception [ɪk'sɛpʃən] *n* exception *f*; **to take** ~ **to** s'offusquer de; **with the** ~ **of** à l'exception de.
exceptional [ɪk'sɛpʃənl] *adj* exceptionnel(le).
excerpt ['ɛksəːpt] *n* extrait *m*.
excess [ɪk'sɛs] *n* excès *m*; **in** ~ **of** plus de.
excess baggage *n* excédent *m* de bagages.
excess fare *n* supplément *m*.
excessive [ɪk'sɛsɪv] *adj* excessif(ive).
excess supply *n* suroffre *f*, offre *f* excédentaire.
exchange [ɪks'tʃeɪndʒ] *n* échange *m*; (*also*: **telephone** ~) central *m* ♦ *vt*: **to** ~ **(for)** échanger (contre); **in** ~ **for** en échange de; **foreign** ~ (*COMM*) change *m*.
exchange control *n* contrôle *m* des changes.
exchange market *n* marché *m* des changes.
exchange rate *n* taux *m* de change.
exchequer [ɪks'tʃɛkə*] *n* (*BRIT*) Échiquier *m*, ≈ ministère *m* des Finances.
excisable [ɪk'saɪzəbl] *adj* taxable.
excise *n* ['ɛksaɪz] taxe *f* ♦ *vt* [ɛk'saɪz] exciser.
excise duties *npl* impôts indirects.
excitable [ɪk'saɪtəbl] *adj* excitable, nerveux(euse).
excite [ɪk'saɪt] *vt* exciter; **to get** ~**d** s'exciter.
excitement [ɪk'saɪtmənt] *n* excitation *f*.
exciting [ɪk'saɪtɪŋ] *adj* passionnant(e).
excl. *abbr* = **excluding, exclusive (of)**.
exclaim [ɪk'skleɪm] *vi* s'exclamer.
exclamation [ɛksklə'meɪʃən] *n* exclamation *f*.
exclamation mark *n* point *m* d'exclamation.

exclude [ɪk'sklu:d] *vt* exclure.
excluding [ɪk'sklu:dɪŋ] *prep*: ~ **VAT** la TVA non comprise.
exclusion [ɪk'sklu:ʒən] *n* exclusion *f*; **to the ~ of** à l'exclusion de.
exclusion clause *n* clause *f* d'exclusion.
exclusion zone *n* zone interdite.
exclusive [ɪk'sklu:sɪv] *adj* exclusif(ive); (*club, district*) sélect(e); (*item of news*) en exclusivité ♦ *adv* (*COMM*) exclusivement, non inclus; ~ **of VAT** TVA non comprise; ~ **of postage** (les) frais de poste non compris; **from 1st to 15th March** ~ du 1er au 15 mars exclusivement *or* exclu; ~ **rights** (*COMM*) exclusivité *f*.
exclusively [ɪk'sklu:sɪvlɪ] *adv* exclusivement.
excommunicate [ɛkskə'mju:nɪkeɪt] *vt* excommunier.
excrement ['ɛkskrəmənt] *n* excrément *m*.
excruciating [ɪk'skru:ʃɪeɪtɪŋ] *adj* atroce, déchirant(e).
excursion [ɪk'skə:ʃən] *n* excursion *f*.
excursion ticket *n* billet *m* tarif excursion.
excusable [ɪk'skju:zəbl] *adj* excusable.
excuse *n* [ɪk'skju:s] excuse *f* ♦ *vt* [ɪk'skju:z] excuser; (*justify*) excuser, justifier; **to ~ sb from** (*activity*) dispenser qn de; ~ **me!** excusez-moi!, pardon!; **now if you will ~ me,** ... maintenant, si vous (le) permettez ...; **to make ~s for sb** trouver des excuses à qn; **to ~ o.s. for sth/for doing sth** s'excuser de/d'avoir fait qch.
ex-directory ['ɛksdɪ'rɛktərɪ] *adj* (*BRIT*): ~ **(phone) number** numéro *m* (de téléphone) sur la liste rouge.
execute ['ɛksɪkju:t] *vt* exécuter.
execution [ɛksɪ'kju:ʃən] *n* exécution *f*.
executioner [ɛksɪ'kju:ʃnə*] *n* bourreau *m*.
executive [ɪg'zɛkjutɪv] *n* (*COMM*) cadre *m*; (*POL*) exécutif *m* ♦ *adj* exécutif(ive); (*position, job*) de cadre; (*secretary*) de direction; (*offices*) de la direction; (*car, plane*) de fonction.
executive director *n* administrateur/trice.
executor [ɪg'zɛkjutə*] *n* exécuteur/trice testamentaire.
exemplary [ɪg'zɛmplərɪ] *adj* exemplaire.
exemplify [ɪg'zɛmplɪfaɪ] *vt* illustrer.
exempt [ɪg'zɛmpt] *adj*: ~ **from** exempté(e) *or* dispensé(e) de ♦ *vt*: **to ~ sb from** exempter *or* dispenser qn de.
exemption [ɪg'zɛmpʃən] *n* exemption *f*, dispense *f*.
exercise ['ɛksəsaɪz] *n* exercice *m* ♦ *vt* exercer; (*patience etc*) faire preuve de; (*dog*) promener ♦ *vi* (*also*: **to take ~**) prendre de l'exercice.
exercise bike *n* vélo *m* d'appartement.
exercise book *n* cahier *m*.
exert [ɪg'zə:t] *vt* exercer, employer; (*strength, force*) employer; **to ~ o.s.** se dépenser.
exertion [ɪg'zə:ʃən] *n* effort *m*.
ex gratia ['ɛks'greɪʃə] *adj*: ~ **payment** gratification *f*.
exhale [ɛks'heɪl] *vt* expirer; exhaler ♦ *vi* expirer.
exhaust [ɪg'zɔ:st] *n* (*also*: ~ **fumes**) gaz *mpl* d'échappement; (*also*: ~ **pipe**) tuyau *m* d'échappement ♦ *vt* épuiser; **to ~ o.s.** s'épuiser.
exhausted [ɪg'zɔ:stɪd] *adj* épuisé(e).
exhausting [ɪg'zɔ:stɪŋ] *adj* épuisant(e).
exhaustion [ɪg'zɔ:stʃən] *n* épuisement *m*; **nervous ~** fatigue nerveuse.
exhaustive [ɪg'zɔ:stɪv] *adj* très complet(ète).
exhibit [ɪg'zɪbɪt] *n* (*ART*) pièce *f or* objet *m* exposé(e); (*LAW*) pièce à conviction ♦ *vt* exposer; (*courage, skill*) faire preuve de.
exhibition [ɛksɪ'bɪʃən] *n* exposition *f*; ~ **of temper** manifestation *f* de colère.
exhibitionist [ɛksɪ'bɪʃənɪst] *n* exhibitionniste *m/f*.
exhibitor [ɪg'zɪbɪtə*] *n* exposant/e.
exhilarating [ɪg'zɪləreɪtɪŋ] *adj* grisant(e); stimulant(e).
exhilaration [ɪgzɪlə'reɪʃən] *n* euphorie *f*, ivresse *f*.
exhort [ɪg'zɔ:t] *vt* exhorter.
exile ['ɛksaɪl] *n* exil *m*; (*person*) exilé/e ♦ *vt* exiler; **in ~** en exil.
exist [ɪg'zɪst] *vi* exister.
existence [ɪg'zɪstəns] *n* existence *f*; **to be in ~** exister.
existentialism [ɛgzɪs'tɛnʃlɪzəm] *n* existentialisme *m*.
existing [ɪg'zɪstɪŋ] *adj* (*laws*) existant(e); (*system, regime*) actuel(le).
exit ['ɛksɪt] *n* sortie *f* ♦ *vi* (*COMPUT, THEAT*) sortir.
exit poll *n* sondage *m* (*fait à la sortie de l'isoloir*).
exit ramp *n* (*US AUT*) bretelle *f* d'accès.
exit visa *n* visa *m* de sortie.
exodus ['ɛksədəs] *n* exode *m*.
ex officio ['ɛksə'fɪʃɪəu] *adj, adv* d'office, de droit.
exonerate [ɪg'zɔnəreɪt] *vt*: **to ~ from** disculper de.
exorbitant [ɪg'zɔ:bɪtnt] *adj* (*price*) exorbitant(e), excessif(ive); (*demands*) exorbitant, démesuré(e).
exorcize ['ɛksɔ:saɪz] *vt* exorciser.
exotic [ɪg'zɔtɪk] *adj* exotique.
expand [ɪk'spænd] *vt* (*area*) agrandir; (*quantity*) accroître; (*influence etc*) étendre ♦ *vi* (*population, production*) s'accroître; (*trade, influence etc*) se développer, s'étendre; (*gas, metal*) se dilater; **to ~ on** (*notes, story etc*) développer.
expanse [ɪk'spæns] *n* étendue *f*.
expansion [ɪk'spænʃən] *n* (*see* **expand**) développement *m*; accroissement *m*; extension *f*; dilatation *f*.
expansionism [ɪk'spænʃənɪzəm] *n* expansion-

nisme *m.*

expansionist [ɪk'spænʃənɪst] *adj* expansionniste.

expatriate *n* [ɛks'pætrɪət] expatrié/e ♦ *vt* [ɛks'pætrɪeɪt] expatrier, exiler.

expect [ɪk'spɛkt] *vt* (*anticipate*) s'attendre à, s'attendre à ce que *+ sub*; (*count on*) compter sur, escompter; (*hope for*) espérer; (*require*) demander, exiger; (*suppose*) supposer; (*await, also baby*) attendre ♦ *vi*: **to be ~ing** être enceinte; **to ~ sb to do** (*anticipate*) s'attendre à ce que qn fasse; (*demand*) attendre de qn qu'il fasse; **to ~ to do sth** penser *or* compter faire qch, s'attendre à faire qch; **as ~ed** comme prévu; **I ~ so** je crois que oui, je crois bien.

expectancy [ɪks'pɛktənsɪ] *n* attente *f*; **life ~** espérance *f* de vie.

expectant [ɪk'spɛktənt] *adj* qui attend (quelque chose); **~ mother** future maman.

expectantly [ɪk'spɛktəntlɪ] *adv* (*look, listen*) avec l'air d'attendre quelque chose.

expectation [ɛkspɛk'teɪʃən] *n* attente *f*, prévisions *fpl*; espérance(s) *f(pl)*; **in ~ of** dans l'attente de, en prévision de; **against** *or* **contrary to all ~(s)** contre toute attente, contrairement à ce qu'on attendait; **to come** *or* **live up to sb's ~s** répondre à l'attente *or* aux espérances de qn.

expedience, expediency [ɪk'spiːdɪəns, ɪk'spiːdɪənsɪ] *n* opportunité *f*; convenance *f* (du moment); **for the sake of ~** parce que c'est (*or* c'était) plus simple *or* plus commode.

expedient [ɪk'spiːdɪənt] *adj* indiqué(e), opportun(e); commode ♦ *n* expédient *m.*

expedite ['ɛkspədaɪt] *vt* hâter; expédier.

expedition [ɛkspə'dɪʃən] *n* expédition *f.*

expeditionary force [ɛkspə'dɪʃənrɪ-] *n* corps *m* expéditionnaire.

expeditious [ɛkspə'dɪʃəs] *adj* expéditif(ive), prompt(e).

expel [ɪk'spɛl] *vt* chasser, expulser; (*SCOL*) renvoyer, exclure.

expend [ɪk'spɛnd] *vt* consacrer; (*use up*) dépenser.

expendable [ɪk'spɛndəbl] *adj* remplaçable.

expenditure [ɪk'spɛndɪtʃə*] *n* dépense *f*; dépenses *fpl.*

expense [ɪk'spɛns] *n* (*cost*) coût *m*; (*spending*) dépense *f*, frais *mpl*; **~s** *npl* frais *mpl*; dépenses; **to go to the ~ of** faire la dépense de; **at great/little ~** à grands/peu de frais; **at the ~ of** aux frais de; (*fig*) aux dépens de.

expense account *n* (note *f* de) frais *mpl.*

expensive [ɪk'spɛnsɪv] *adj* cher(chère), coûteux(euse); **to be ~** coûter cher; **~ tastes** goûts *mpl* de luxe.

experience [ɪk'spɪərɪəns] *n* expérience *f* ♦ *vt* connaître; éprouver; **to know by ~** savoir par expérience.

experienced [ɪk'spɪərɪənst] *adj* expérimenté(e).

experiment [ɪk'spɛrɪmənt] *n* expérience *f* ♦ *vi* faire une expérience; **to ~ with** expérimenter; **to perform** *or* **carry out an ~** faire une expérience; **as an ~** à titre d'expérience.

experimental [ɪkspɛrɪ'mɛntl] *adj* expérimental(e).

expert ['ɛkspəːt] *adj* expert(e) ♦ *n* expert *m*; **~ in** *or* **at doing sth** spécialiste de qch; **an ~ on sth** un spécialiste de qch; **~ witness** (*LAW*) expert *m.*

expertise [ɛkspəː'tiːz] *n* (grande) compétence.

expire [ɪk'spaɪə*] *vi* expirer.

expiry [ɪk'spaɪərɪ] *n* expiration *f.*

explain [ɪk'spleɪn] *vt* expliquer.

►**explain away** *vt* justifier, excuser.

explanation [ɛksplə'neɪʃən] *n* explication *f*; **to find an ~ for sth** trouver une explication à qch.

explanatory [ɪk'splænətrɪ] *adj* explicatif(ive).

expletive [ɪk'spliːtɪv] *n* juron *m.*

explicit [ɪk'splɪsɪt] *adj* explicite; (*definite*) formel(le).

explode [ɪk'spləud] *vi* exploser ♦ *vt* faire exploser; (*fig: theory*) démolir; **to ~ a myth** détruire un mythe.

exploit *n* ['ɛksplɔɪt] exploit *m* ♦ *vt* [ɪk'splɔɪt] exploiter.

exploitation [ɛksplɔɪ'teɪʃən] *n* exploitation *f.*

exploration [ɛksplə'reɪʃən] *n* exploration *f.*

exploratory [ɪk'splɔrətrɪ] *adj* (*fig: talks*) préliminaire; **~ operation** (*MED*) intervention *f* (à visée) exploratrice.

explore [ɪk'splɔː*] *vt* explorer; (*possibilities*) étudier, examiner.

explorer [ɪk'splɔːrə*] *n* explorateur/trice.

explosion [ɪk'spləuʒən] *n* explosion *f.*

explosive [ɪk'spləusɪv] *adj* explosif(ive) ♦ *n* explosif *m.*

exponent [ɪk'spəunənt] *n* (*of school of thought etc*) interprète *m*, représentant *m*; (*MATH*) exposant *m.*

export *vt* [ɛk'spɔːt] exporter ♦ *n* ['ɛkspɔːt] exportation *f* ♦ *cpd* d'exportation.

exportation [ɛkspɔː'teɪʃən] *n* exportation *f.*

exporter [ɛk'spɔːtə*] *n* exportateur *m.*

export licence *n* licence *f* d'exportation.

expose [ɪk'spəuz] *vt* exposer; (*unmask*) démasquer, dévoiler; **to ~ o.s.** (*LAW*) commettre un outrage à la pudeur.

exposed [ɪk'spəuzd] *adj* (*land, house*) exposé(e); (*ELEC: wire*) à nu; (*pipe, beam*) apparent(e).

exposition [ɛkspə'zɪʃən] *n* exposition *f.*

exposure [ɪk'spəuʒə*] *n* exposition *f*; (*PHOT*) (temps *m* de) pose *f*; (*: shot*) pose; **suffering from ~** (*MED*) souffrant des effets du froid et de l'épuisement; **to die of ~** (*MED*) mourir de froid.

exposure meter *n* posemètre *m.*

expound [ɪk'spaund] *vt* exposer, expliquer.

express [ɪk'sprɛs] *adj* (*definite*) formel(le), exprès(esse); (*BRIT: letter etc*) exprès *inv* ♦ *n* (*train*) rapide *m* ♦ *adv* (*send*) exprès ♦ *vt* exprimer; **to ~ o.s.** s'exprimer.
expression [ɪk'sprɛʃən] *n* expression *f*.
expressionism [ɪk'sprɛʃənɪzəm] *n* expressionnisme *m*.
expressive [ɪk'sprɛsɪv] *adj* expressif(ive).
expressly [ɪk'sprɛslɪ] *adv* expressément, formellement.
expressway [ɪk'sprɛsweɪ] *n* (*US*) voie *f* express (à plusieurs files).
expropriate [ɛks'prəuprɪeɪt] *vt* exproprier.
expulsion [ɪk'spʌlʃən] *n* expulsion *f*; renvoi *m*.
exquisite [ɛk'skwɪzɪt] *adj* exquis(e).
ex-serviceman ['ɛks'səːvɪsmən] *n* ancien combattant.
ext. *abbr* (*TEL*) = **extension.**
extemporize [ɪk'stɛmpəraɪz] *vi* improviser.
extend [ɪk'stɛnd] *vt* (*visit, street*) prolonger; (*deadline*) reporter, remettre; (*building*) agrandir; (*offer*) présenter, offrir; (*COMM: credit*) accorder ♦ *vi* (*land*) s'étendre.
extension [ɪk'stɛnʃən] *n* (*see extend*) prolongation *f*, agrandissement *m*; (*building*) annexe *f*; (*to wire, table*) rallonge *f*; (*telephone: in offices*) poste *m*; (*: in private house*) téléphone *m* supplémentaire; **~ 3718** (*TEL*) poste 3718.
extension cable *n* (*ELEC*) rallonge *f*.
extensive [ɪk'stɛnsɪv] *adj* étendu(e), vaste; (*damage, alterations*) considérable; (*inquiries*) approfondi(e); (*use*) largement répandu(e).
extensively [ɪk'stɛnsɪvlɪ] *adv* (*altered, damaged etc*) considérablement; **he's travelled ~** il a beaucoup voyagé.
extent [ɪk'stɛnt] *n* étendue *f*; (*degree: of damage, loss*) importance *f*; **to some ~** dans une certaine mesure; **to a certain ~** dans une certaine mesure, jusqu'à un certain point; **to a large ~** en grande partie; **to what ~?** dans quelle mesure?, jusqu'à quel point?; **to such an ~ that ...** à tel point que ....
extenuating [ɪk'stɛnjueɪtɪŋ] *adj*: **~ circumstances** circonstances atténuantes.
exterior [ɛk'stɪərɪə*] *adj* extérieur(e), du dehors ♦ *n* extérieur *m*; dehors *m*.
exterminate [ɪk'stəːmɪneɪt] *vt* exterminer.
extermination [ɪkstəːmɪ'neɪʃən] *n* extermination *f*.
external [ɛk'stəːnl] *adj* externe ♦ *n*: **the ~s** les apparences *fpl*; **for ~ use only** (*MED*) à usage externe.
externally [ɛk'stəːnəlɪ] *adv* extérieurement.
extinct [ɪk'stɪŋkt] *adj* éteint(e).
extinction [ɪk'stɪŋkʃən] *n* extinction *f*.
extinguish [ɪk'stɪŋgwɪʃ] *vt* éteindre.
extinguisher [ɪk'stɪŋgwɪʃə*] *n* extincteur *m*.
extol, (*US*) **extoll** [ɪk'stəul] *vt* (*merits*) chanter, prôner; (*person*) chanter les louanges de.
extort [ɪk'stɔːt] *vt*: **to ~ sth (from)** extorquer qch (à).
extortion [ɪk'stɔːʃən] *n* extorsion *f*.
extortionate [ɪk'stɔːʃnɪt] *adj* exorbitant(e).
extra ['ɛkstrə] *adj* supplémentaire, de plus ♦ *adv* (*in addition*) en plus ♦ *n* supplément *m*; (*THEAT*) figurant/e; **wine will cost ~** le vin sera en supplément; **~ large sizes** très grandes tailles.
extra... ['ɛkstrə] *prefix* extra....
extract *vt* [ɪk'strækt] extraire; (*tooth*) arracher; (*money, promise*) soutirer ♦ *n* ['ɛkstrækt] extrait *m*.
extraction [ɪk'strækʃən] *n* (*also descent*) extraction *f*.
extractor fan [ɪk'stræktə-] *n* exhausteur *m*, ventilateur *m* extracteur.
extracurricular ['ɛkstrəkə'rɪkjulə*] *adj* (*SCOL*) parascolaire.
extradite ['ɛkstrədaɪt] *vt* extrader.
extradition [ɛkstrə'dɪʃən] *n* extradition *f*.
extramarital ['ɛkstrə'mærɪtl] *adj* extraconjugal(e).
extramural ['ɛkstrə'mjuərl] *adj* hors-faculté *inv*.
extraneous [ɛk'streɪnɪəs] *adj*: **~ to** étranger(ère) à.
extraordinary [ɪk'strɔːdnrɪ] *adj* extraordinaire; **the ~ thing is that ...** le plus étrange *or* étonnant c'est que ....
extraordinary general meeting *n* assemblée générale extraordinaire.
extrapolation [ɛkstræpə'leɪʃən] *n* extrapolation *f*.
extrasensory perception (ESP) ['ɛkstrə'sɛnsərɪ-] *n* perception extrasensorielle.
extra time *n* (*FOOTBALL*) prolongations *fpl*.
extravagance [ɪk'strævəgəns] *n* (*excessive spending*) prodigalités *fpl*; (*thing bought*) folie *f*, dépense excessive *or* exagérée.
extravagant [ɪk'strævəgənt] *adj* extravagant(e); (*in spending: person*) prodigue, dépensier(ière); (*: tastes*) dispendieux(euse).
extreme [ɪk'striːm] *adj, n* extrême (*m*); **the ~ left/right** (*POL*) l'extrême gauche *f*/droite *f*; **~s of temperature** différences *fpl* extrêmes de température.
extremely [ɪk'striːmlɪ] *adv* extrêmement.
extremist [ɪk'striːmɪst] *adj, n* extrémiste (*m/f*).
extremity [ɪk'strɛmɪtɪ] *n* extrémité *f*.
extricate ['ɛkstrɪkeɪt] *vt*: **to ~ sth (from)** dégager qch (de).
extrovert ['ɛkstrəvəːt] *n* extraverti/e.
exuberance [ɪg'zjuːbərns] *n* exubérance *f*.
exuberant [ɪg'zjuːbərnt] *adj* exubérant(e).
exude [ɪg'zjuːd] *vt* exsuder; (*fig*) respirer; **the charm** *etc* **he ~s** le charme *etc* qui émane de lui.
exult [ɪg'zʌlt] *vi* exulter, jubiler.
exultant [ɪg'zʌltənt] *adj* (*shout, expression*) de triomphe; **to be ~** jubiler, triompher.
exultation [ɛgzʌl'teɪʃən] *n* exultation *f*, jubilation *f*.

eye [aɪ] *n* œil *m* (*pl* yeux); (*of needle*) trou *m*, chas *m* ♦ *vt* examiner; **as far as the ~ can see** à perte de vue; **to keep an ~ on** surveiller; **to have an ~ for sth** avoir l'œil pour qch; **in the public ~** en vue; **with an ~ to doing sth** (*BRIT*) en vue de faire qch; **there's more to this than meets the ~** ce n'est pas aussi simple que cela paraît.
eyeball ['aɪbɔːl] *n* globe *m* oculaire.
eyebath ['aɪbɑːθ] *n* (*BRIT*) œillère *f* (*pour bains d'œil*).
eyebrow ['aɪbrau] *n* sourcil *m*.
eyebrow pencil *n* crayon *m* à sourcils.
eye-catching ['aɪkætʃɪŋ] *adj* voyant(e), accrocheur(euse).
eye cup *n* (*US*) = **eyebath**.
eyedrops ['aɪdrɔps] *npl* gouttes *fpl* pour les yeux.
eyeful ['aɪful] *n*: **to get an ~ (of sth)** se rincer l'œil (en voyant qch).
eyeglass ['aɪglɑːs] *n* monocle *m*.
eyelash ['aɪlæʃ] *n* cil *m*.
eyelet ['aɪlɪt] *n* œillet *m*.
eye-level ['aɪlɛvl] *adj* en hauteur.
eyelid ['aɪlɪd] *n* paupière *f*.
eyeliner ['aɪlaɪnə*] *n* eye-liner *m*.
eye-opener ['aɪəupnə*] *n* révélation *f*.
eyeshadow ['aɪʃædəu] *n* ombre *f* à paupières.
eyesight ['aɪsaɪt] *n* vue *f*.
eyesore ['aɪsɔː*] *n* horreur *f*, chose *f* qui dépare *or* enlaidit.
eyestrain ['aɪstreɪn] *adj*: **to get ~** se fatiguer la vue *or* les yeux.
eyetooth, *pl* **-teeth** ['aɪtuːθ, -tiːθ] *n* canine supérieure; **to give one's eyeteeth for sth/to do sth** (*fig*) donner n'importe quoi pour qch/pour faire qch.
eyewash ['aɪwɔʃ] *n* bain *m* d'œil; (*fig*) frime *f*.
eye witness *n* témoin *m* oculaire.
eyrie ['ɪərɪ] *n* aire *f*.

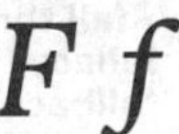

F, f [ɛf] *n* (*letter*) F, f *m*; (*MUS*): **F** fa *m*; **F for Frederick**, (*US*) **F for Fox** F comme François.
F *abbr* (= *Fahrenheit*) F.
FA *n abbr* (*BRIT*: = *Football Association*) *fédération de football*.
FAA *n abbr* (*US*) = *Federal Aviation Administration*.
fable ['feɪbl] *n* fable *f*.
fabric ['fæbrɪk] *n* tissu *m* ♦ *cpd*: **~ ribbon** *n* (*for typewriter*) ruban *m* (en) tissu.
fabricate ['fæbrɪkeɪt] *vt* fabriquer, inventer.
fabrication [fæbrɪ'keɪʃən] *n* fabrication *f*, invention *f*.
fabulous ['fæbjuləs] *adj* fabuleux(euse); (*col*: *super*) formidable, sensationnel(le).
façade [fə'sɑːd] *n* façade *f*.
face [feɪs] *n* visage *m*, figure *f*; expression *f*; grimace *f*; (*of clock*) cadran *m*; (*of building*) façade *f*; (*side, surface*) face *f* ♦ *vt* faire face à; (*facts etc*) accepter; **~ down** (*person*) à plat ventre; (*card*) face en dessous; **to lose/save ~** perdre/sauver la face; **to pull a ~** faire une grimace; **in the ~ of** (*difficulties etc*) face à, devant; **on the ~ of it** à première vue.
►**face up to** *vt fus* faire face à, affronter.
face cloth *n* (*BRIT*) gant *m* de toilette.
face cream *n* crème *f* pour le visage.
face lift *n* lifting *m*; (*of façade etc*) ravalement *m*, retapage *m*.
face powder *n* poudre *f* (pour le visage).
face-saving ['feɪsseɪvɪŋ] *adj* qui sauve la face.
facet ['fæsɪt] *n* facette *f*.
facetious [fə'siːʃəs] *adj* facétieux(euse).
face-to-face ['feɪstə'feɪs] *adv* face à face.
face value ['feɪs'væljuː] *n* (*of coin*) valeur nominale; **to take sth at ~** (*fig*) prendre qch pour argent comptant.
facia ['feɪʃə] *n* = **fascia**.
facial ['feɪʃl] *adj* facial(e) ♦ *n* soin complet du visage.
facile ['fæsaɪl] *adj* facile.
facilitate [fə'sɪlɪteɪt] *vt* faciliter.
facility [fə'sɪlɪtɪ] *n* facilité *f*; **facilities** *npl* installations *fpl*, équipement *m*; **credit facilities** facilités de paiement.
facing ['feɪsɪŋ] *prep* face à, en face de ♦ *n* (*of wall etc*) revêtement *m*; (*SEWING*) revers *m*.
facsimile [fæk'sɪmɪlɪ] *n* (*exact replica*) facsimilé *m*; (*also*: **~ machine**) télécopieur *m*; (*transmitted document*) télécopie *f*.
fact [fækt] *n* fait *m*; **in ~** en fait; **to know for a ~ that** ... savoir pertinemment que ....
fact-finding ['fæktfaɪndɪŋ] *adj*: **a ~ tour** *or* **mission** une mission d'enquête.
faction ['fækʃən] *n* faction *f*.
factional ['fækʃənl] *adj* de factions.
factor ['fæktə*] *n* facteur *m*; (*COMM*) factor *m*, société *f* d'affacturage; (*: agent*) dépositaire *m/f* ♦ *vi* faire du factoring; **safety ~** facteur de sécurité.
factory ['fæktərɪ] *n* usine *f*, fabrique *f*.
factory farming *n* (*BRIT*) élevage industriel.
factory floor *n*: **the ~** (*workers*) les ouvriers *mpl*; (*workshop*) l'usine *f*; **on the ~** dans les ateliers.
factory ship *n* navire-usine *m*.
factual ['fæktjuəl] *adj* basé(e) sur les faits.
faculty ['fækəltɪ] *n* faculté *f*; (*US*: *teaching staff*) corps enseignant.
fad [fæd] *n* (*col*) manie *f*, engouement *m*.
fade [feɪd] *vi* se décolorer, passer; (*light, sound, hope*) s'affaiblir, disparaître; (*flower*) se faner.

►**fade in** *vt* (*picture*) ouvrir en fondu; (*sound*) monter progressivement.
►**fade out** *vt* (*picture*) fermer en fondu; (*sound*) baisser progressivement.
faeces, (*US*) **feces** ['fi:si:z] *npl* fèces *fpl*.
fag [fæg] *n* (*BRIT col*: *cigarette*) sèche *f*; (*: chore*): **what a ~!** quelle corvée!; (*US col*: *homosexual*) pédé *m*.
fag end *n* (*BRIT col*) mégot *m*.
fagged out [fægd-] *adj* (*BRIT col*) crevé(e).
fail [feɪl] *vt* (*exam*) échouer à; (*candidate*) recaler; (*subj: courage, memory*) faire défaut à ♦ *vi* échouer; (*supplies*) manquer; (*eyesight, health, light*: *also*: **be ~ing**) baisser, s'affaiblir; (*brakes*) lâcher; **to ~ to do sth** (*neglect*) négliger de *or* ne pas faire qch; (*be unable*) ne pas arriver *or* parvenir à faire qch; **without ~** à coup sûr; sans faute.
failing ['feɪlɪŋ] *n* défaut *m* ♦ *prep* faute de; **~ that** à défaut, sinon.
failsafe ['feɪlseɪf] *adj* (*device etc*) à sûreté intégrée.
failure ['feɪljə*] *n* échec *m*; (*person*) raté/e; (*mechanical etc*) défaillance *f*; **his ~ to turn up** le fait de n'être pas venu *or* qu'il ne soit pas venu.
faint [feɪnt] *adj* faible; (*recollection*) vague; (*mark*) à peine visible; (*smell, breeze, trace*) léger(ère) ♦ *n* évanouissement *m* ♦ *vi* s'évanouir; **to feel ~** défaillir.
faintest ['feɪntɪst] *adj*: **I haven't the ~ idea** je n'en ai pas la moindre idée.
faint-hearted ['feɪnt'hɑ:tɪd] *adj* pusillanime.
faintly ['feɪntlɪ] *adv* faiblement; vaguement.
faintness ['feɪntnɪs] *n* faiblesse *f*.
fair [fɛə*] *adj* équitable, juste; (*reasonable*) correct(e), honnête; (*hair*) blond(e); (*skin, complexion*) pâle, blanc(blanche); (*weather*) beau(belle); (*good enough*) assez bon(ne) ♦ *adv*: **to play ~** jouer franc jeu ♦ *n* foire *f*; (*BRIT*: *funfair*) fête (foraine); (*also*: **trade ~**) foire(-exposition) commerciale; **it's not ~!** ce n'est pas juste!; **a ~ amount of** une quantité considérable de.
fair copy *n* copie *f* au propre; corrigé *m*.
fair game *n*: **to be ~ (for)** être une cible légitime (pour).
fairground ['fɛəgraund] *n* champ *m* de foire.
fair-haired [fɛə'hɛəd] *adj* (*person*) aux cheveux clairs, blond(e).
fairly ['fɛəlɪ] *adv* équitablement; (*quite*) assez; **I'm ~ sure** j'en suis quasiment *or* presque sûr.
fairness ['fɛənɪs] *n* (*of trial etc*) justice *f*, équité *f*; (*of person*) sens *m* de la justice; **in all ~** en toute justice.
fair play *n* fair play *m*.
fairy ['fɛərɪ] *n* fée *f*.
fairy godmother *n* bonne fée.
fairy lights *npl* (*BRIT*) guirlande *f* électrique.
fairy tale *n* conte *m* de fées.
faith [feɪθ] *n* foi *f*; (*trust*) confiance *f*; (*sect*) culte *m*, religion *f*; **to have ~ in sb/sth** avoir confiance en qn/qch.
faithful ['feɪθful] *adj* fidèle.
faithfully ['feɪθfəlɪ] *adv* fidèlement; **yours ~** (*BRIT*: *in letters*) veuillez agréer l'expression de mes salutations les plus distinguées.
faith healer [-hi:lə*] *n* guérisseur/euse.
fake [feɪk] *n* (*painting etc*) faux *m*; (*photo*) trucage *m*; (*person*) imposteur *m* ♦ *adj* faux(fausse) ♦ *vt* (*emotions*) simuler; (*photo*) truquer; (*story*) fabriquer; **his illness is a ~** sa maladie est une comédie *or* de la simulation.
falcon ['fɔ:lkən] *n* faucon *m*.
Falkland Islands ['fɔ:lklənd-] *npl*: **the ~** les Malouines *fpl*, les îles *fpl* Falkland.
fall [fɔ:l] *n* chute *f*; (*decrease*) baisse *f*; (*US*: *autumn*) automne *m* ♦ *vi* (*pt* **fell**, *pp* **fallen** [fɛl, 'fɔ:lən]) tomber; **~s** *npl* (*waterfall*) chute *f* d'eau, cascade *f*; **to ~ flat** *vi* (*on one's face*) tomber de tout son long, s'étaler; (*joke*) tomber à plat; (*plan*) échouer; **to ~ short of** (*sb's expectations*) ne pas répondre à; **a ~ of snow** (*BRIT*) une chute de neige.
►**fall apart** *vi* tomber en morceaux; (*col*: *emotionally*) craquer.
►**fall back** *vi* reculer, se retirer.
►**fall back on** *vt fus* se rabattre sur; **to have something to ~ back on** (*money etc*) avoir quelque chose en réserve; (*job etc*) avoir une solution de rechange.
►**fall behind** *vi* prendre du retard.
►**fall down** *vi* (*person*) tomber; (*building, hopes*) s'effondrer, s'écrouler.
►**fall for** *vt fus* (*trick*) se laisser prendre à; (*person*) tomber amoureux(euse) de.
►**fall in** *vi* s'effondrer; (*MIL*) se mettre en rangs.
►**fall in with** *vt fus* (*sb's plans etc*) accepter.
►**fall off** *vi* tomber; (*diminish*) baisser, diminuer.
►**fall out** *vi* (*friends etc*) se brouiller.
►**fall over** *vi* tomber (par terre).
►**fall through** *vi* (*plan, project*) tomber à l'eau.
fallacy ['fæləsɪ] *n* erreur *f*, illusion *f*.
fallback ['fɔ:lbæk] *adj*: **~ position** position *f* de repli.
fallen ['fɔ:lən] *pp of* **fall**.
fallible ['fæləbl] *adj* faillible.
fallopian tube [fə'ləupɪən-] *n* (*ANAT*) trompe *f* de Fallope.
fallout ['fɔ:laut] *n* retombées (radioactives).
fallout shelter *n* abri *m* anti-atomique.
fallow ['fæləu] *adj* en jachère; en friche.
false [fɔ:ls] *adj* faux(fausse); **under ~ pretences** sous un faux prétexte.
false alarm *n* fausse alerte.
falsehood ['fɔ:lshud] *n* mensonge *m*.
falsely ['fɔ:lslɪ] *adv* (*accuse*) à tort.
false teeth *npl* (*BRIT*) fausses dents.
falsify ['fɔ:lsɪfaɪ] *vt* falsifier; (*accounts*) maquiller.

falter ['fɔːltə*] *vi* chanceler, vaciller.
fame [feɪm] *n* renommée *f*, renom *m*.
familiar [fə'mɪlɪə*] *adj* familier(ière); **to be ~ with sth** connaître qch; **to make o.s. ~ with sth** se familiariser avec qch; **to be on ~ terms with sb** bien connaître qn.
familiarity [fəmɪlɪ'ærɪtɪ] *n* familiarité *f*.
familiarize [fə'mɪlɪəraɪz] *vt* familiariser.
family ['fæmɪlɪ] *n* famille *f*.
family allowance *n* (*BRIT*) allocations familiales.
family business *n* entreprise familiale.
family credit *n* (*BRIT*) complément familial.
family doctor *n* médecin *m* de famille.
family life *n* vie *f* de famille.
family man *n* père *m* de famille.
family planning clinic *n* centre *m* de planning familial.
family tree *n* arbre *m* généalogique.
famine ['fæmɪn] *n* famine *f*.
famished ['fæmɪʃt] *adj* affamé(e); **I'm ~!** (*col*) je meurs de faim!
famous ['feɪməs] *adj* célèbre.
famously ['feɪməslɪ] *adv* (*get on*) fameusement, à merveille.
fan [fæn] *n* (*folding*) éventail *m*; (*ELEC*) ventilateur *m*; (*person*) fan *m*, admirateur/trice; (: *SPORT*) supporter *m/f* ♦ *vt* éventer; (*fire, quarrel*) attiser.
►**fan out** *vi* se déployer (en éventail).
fanatic [fə'nætɪk] *n* fanatique *m/f*.
fanatical [fə'nætɪkl] *adj* fanatique.
fan belt *n* courroie *f* de ventilateur.
fancied ['fænsɪd] *adj* imaginaire.
fanciful ['fænsɪful] *adj* fantaisiste.
fan club *n* fan-club *m*.
fancy ['fænsɪ] *n* fantaisie *f*, envie *f*; imagination *f* ♦ *cpd* (de) fantaisie *inv* ♦ *vt* (*feel like, want*) avoir envie de; (*imagine*) imaginer; **to take a ~ to** se prendre d'affection pour; s'enticher de; **it took** *or* **caught my ~** ça m'a plu; **when the ~ takes him** quand ça lui prend; **to ~ that ...** se figurer *or* s'imaginer que ...; **he fancies her** elle lui plaît.
fancy dress *n* déguisement *m*, travesti *m*.
fancy-dress ball [fænsɪ'drɛs-] *n* bal masqué *or* costumé.
fancy goods *npl* articles *mpl* (de) fantaisie.
fanfare ['fænfɛə*] *n* fanfare *f* (*musique*).
fanfold paper ['fænfəuld-] *n* papier *m* à pliage accordéon.
fang [fæŋ] *n* croc *m*; (*of snake*) crochet *m*.
fan heater *n* (*BRIT*) radiateur soufflant.
fanlight ['fænlaɪt] *n* imposte *f*.
fanny ['fænɪ] *n* (*BRIT col!*) chatte *f* (*!*); (*US col*) cul *m* (*!*).
fantasize ['fæntəsaɪz] *vi* fantasmer.
fantastic [fæn'tæstɪk] *adj* fantastique.
fantasy ['fæntəsɪ] *n* imagination *f*, fantaisie *f*; fantasme *m*.
fanzine ['fænziːn] *n* fanzine *m*.
FAO *n abbr* (= *Food and Agriculture Organization*) FAO *f*.
FAQ *abbr* (= *free alongside quay*) FLQ.
far [fɑː*] *adj*: **the ~ side/end** l'autre côté/bout; **the ~ left/right** (*POL*) l'extrême gauche *f*/droite *f* ♦ *adv* loin; **is it ~ to London?** est-ce qu'on est loin de Londres?; **it's not ~ (from here)** ce n'est pas loin (d'ici); **~ away**, **~ off** au loin, dans le lointain; **~ better** beaucoup mieux; **~ from** loin de; **by ~** de loin, de beaucoup; **as ~ back as the 13th century** dès le 13e siècle; **go as ~ as the farm** allez jusqu'à la ferme; **as ~ as I know** pour autant que je sache; **as ~ as possible** dans la mesure du possible; **how ~ have you got with your work?** où en êtes-vous dans votre travail?
faraway ['fɑːrəweɪ] *adj* lointain(e); (*look*) absent(e).
farce [fɑːs] *n* farce *f*.
farcical ['fɑːsɪkl] *adj* grotesque.
fare [fɛə*] *n* (*on trains, buses*) prix *m* du billet; (*in taxi*) prix de la course; (*passenger in taxi*) client *m*; (*food*) table *f*, chère *f* ♦ *vi* se débrouiller.
Far East *n*: **the ~** l'Extrême-Orient *m*.
farewell [fɛə'wɛl] *excl, n* adieu (*m*) ♦ *cpd* (*party etc*) d'adieux.
far-fetched ['fɑː'fɛtʃt] *adj* exagéré(e), poussé(e).
farm [fɑːm] *n* ferme *f* ♦ *vt* cultiver.
►**farm out** *vt* (*work etc*) distribuer.
farmer ['fɑːmə*] *n* fermier/ière; cultivateur/trice.
farmhand ['fɑːmhænd] *n* ouvrier/ière agricole.
farmhouse ['fɑːmhaus] *n* (maison *f* de) ferme *f*.
farming ['fɑːmɪŋ] *n* agriculture *f*; **intensive ~** culture intensive; **sheep ~** élevage *m* du mouton.
farm labourer *n* = **farmhand**.
farmland ['fɑːmlænd] *n* terres cultivées *or* arables.
farm produce *n* produits *mpl* agricoles.
farm worker *n* = **farmhand**.
farmyard ['fɑːmjɑːd] *n* cour *f* de ferme.
Faroe Islands ['fɛərəu-] *npl*, **Faroes** ['fɛərəuz] *npl*: **the ~** les îles *fpl* Féroé *or* Faeroe.
far-reaching ['fɑː'riːtʃɪŋ] *adj* d'une grande portée.
far-sighted ['fɑː'saɪtɪd] *adj* presbyte; (*fig*) prévoyant(e), qui voit loin.
fart [fɑːt] (*col!*) *n* pet *m* ♦ *vi* péter.
farther ['fɑːðə*] *adv* plus loin ♦ *adj* plus eloigné(e), plus lointain(e).
farthest ['fɑːðɪst] *superlative of* **far**.
FAS *abbr* (*BRIT*: = *free alongside ship*) FLB.
fascia ['feɪʃə] *n* (*AUT*) (garniture *f* du) tableau *m* de bord.
fascinate ['fæsɪneɪt] *vt* fasciner, captiver.
fascinating ['fæsɪneɪtɪŋ] *adj* fascinant(e).
fascination [fæsɪ'neɪʃən] *n* fascination *f*.

fascism ['fæʃɪzəm] *n* fascisme *m*.
fascist ['fæʃɪst] *adj, n* fasciste *(m/f)*.
fashion ['fæʃən] *n* mode *f*; (*manner*) façon *f*, manière *f* ♦ *vt* façonner; **in** ~ à la mode; **out of** ~ démodé(e); **in the Greek** ~ à la grecque; **after a** ~ (*finish, manage etc*) tant bien que mal.
fashionable ['fæʃnəbl] *adj* à la mode.
fashion designer *n* (grand(e)) couturier/ière.
fashion show *n* défilé *m* de mannequins *or* de mode.
fast [fɑːst] *adj* rapide; (*clock*): **to be** ~ avancer; (*dye, colour*) grand *or* bon teint *inv* ♦ *adv* vite, rapidement; (*stuck, held*) solidement ♦ *n* jeûne *m* ♦ *vi* jeûner; **my watch is 5 minutes** ~ ma montre avance de 5 minutes; ~ **asleep** profondément endormi; **as** ~ **as I can** aussi vite que je peux; **to make a boat** ~ (*BRIT*) amarrer un bateau.
fasten ['fɑːsn] *vt* attacher, fixer; (*coat*) attacher, fermer ♦ *vi* se fermer, s'attacher.
►**fasten (up)on** *vt fus* (*idea*) se cramponner à.
fastener ['fɑːsnə*], **fastening** ['fɑːsnɪŋ] *n* fermeture *f*, attache *f*; (*BRIT*: *zip* ~) fermeture éclair *inv* ® *or* à glissière.
fast food *n* fast food *m*, restauration *f* rapide.
fastidious [fæs'tɪdɪəs] *adj* exigeant(e), difficile.
fast lane *n* (*AUT*: *in Britain*) voie *f* de droite.
fat [fæt] *adj* gros(se) ♦ *n* graisse *f*; (*on meat*) gras *m*; **to live off the** ~ **of the land** vivre grassement.
fatal ['feɪtl] *adj* fatal(e); (*leading to death*) mortel(le).
fatalism ['feɪtlɪzəm] *n* fatalisme *m*.
fatality [fə'tælɪtɪ] *n* (*road death etc*) victime *f*, décès *m*.
fatally ['feɪtəlɪ] *adv* fatalement; mortellement.
fate [feɪt] *n* destin *m*; (*of person*) sort *m*; **to meet one's** ~ trouver la mort.
fated ['feɪtɪd] *adj* (*person*) condamné(e); (*project*) voué(e) à l'échec.
fateful ['feɪtful] *adj* fatidique.
fat-free ['fæt'friː] *adj* sans matières grasses.
father ['fɑːðə*] *n* père *m*.
Father Christmas *n* le Père Noël.
fatherhood ['fɑːðəhud] *n* paternité *f*.
father-in-law ['fɑːðərənlɔː] *n* beau-père *m*.
fatherland ['fɑːðəlænd] *n* (mère *f*) patrie *f*.
fatherly ['fɑːðəlɪ] *adj* paternel(le).
fathom ['fæðəm] *n* brasse *f* (= *1828 mm*) ♦ *vt* (*mystery*) sonder, pénétrer.
fatigue [fə'tiːg] *n* fatigue *f*; (*MIL*) corvée *f*; **metal** ~ fatigue du métal.
fatness ['fætnɪs] *n* corpulence *f*, grosseur *f*.
fatten ['fætn] *vt, vi* engraisser; **chocolate is** ~**ing** le chocolat fait grossir.
fatty ['fætɪ] *adj* (*food*) gras(se) ♦ *n* (*col*) gros/grosse.
fatuous ['fætjuəs] *adj* stupide.
faucet ['fɔːsɪt] *n* (*US*) robinet *m*.
fault [fɔːlt] *n* faute *f*; (*defect*) défaut *m*; (*GEO*) faille *f* ♦ *vt* trouver des défauts à, prendre en défaut; **it's my** ~ c'est de ma faute; **to find** ~ **with** trouver à redire *or* à critiquer à; **at** ~ fautif(ive), coupable; **to a** ~ à l'excès.
faultless ['fɔːltlɪs] *adj* impeccable; irréprochable.
faulty ['fɔːltɪ] *adj* défectueux(euse).
fauna ['fɔːnə] *n* faune *f*.
faux pas ['fəu'pɑː] *n* impair *m*, bévue *f*, gaffe *f*.
favour, (*US*) **favor** ['feɪvə*] *n* faveur *f*; (*help*) service *m* ♦ *vt* (*proposition*) être en faveur de; (*pupil etc*) favoriser; (*team, horse*) donner gagnant; **to do sb a** ~ rendre un service à qn; **in** ~ **of** en faveur de; **to be in** ~ **of sth/of doing sth** être partisan de qch/de faire qch; **to find** ~ **with sb** trouver grâce aux yeux de qn.
favo(u)rable ['feɪvrəbl] *adj* favorable; (*price*) avantageux(euse).
favo(u)rably ['feɪvrəblɪ] *adv* favorablement.
favo(u)rite ['feɪvrɪt] *adj, n* favori(te).
favo(u)ritism ['feɪvrɪtɪzəm] *n* favoritisme *m*.
fawn [fɔːn] *n* faon *m* ♦ *adj* (*also*: ~**-coloured**) fauve ♦ *vi*: **to** ~ **(up)on** flatter servilement.
fax [fæks] *n* (*document*) télécopie *f*; (*machine*) télécopieur *m* ♦ *vt* envoyer par télécopie.
FBI *n abbr* (*US*: = *Federal Bureau of Investigation*) FBI *m*.
FCC *n abbr* (*US*) = *Federal Communications Commission*.
FCO *n abbr* (*BRIT*: = *Foreign and Commonwealth Office*) *ministère des Affaires étrangères et du Commonwealth*.
FD *n abbr* (*US*) = **fire department**.
FDA *n abbr* (*US*: = *Food and Drug Administration*) *office de contrôle des produits pharmaceutiques et alimentaires*.
FE *n abbr* = **further education**.
fear [fɪə*] *n* crainte *f*, peur *f* ♦ *vt* craindre ♦ *vi*: **to** ~ **for** craindre pour; **to** ~ **that** craindre que; ~ **of heights** vertige *m*; **for** ~ **of** de peur que *+ sub* or de *+ infinitive*.
fearful ['fɪəful] *adj* craintif(ive); (*sight, noise*) affreux(euse), épouvantable; **to be** ~ **of** avoir peur de, craindre.
fearfully ['fɪəfəlɪ] *adv* (*timidly*) craintivement; (*col*: *very*) affreusement.
fearless ['fɪəlɪs] *adj* intrépide, sans peur.
fearsome ['fɪəsəm] *adj* (*opponent*) redoutable; (*sight*) épouvantable.
feasibility [fiːzə'bɪlɪtɪ] *n* (*of plan*) possibilité *f* de réalisation, faisabilité *f*.
feasibility study *n* étude *f* de faisabilité.
feasible ['fiːzəbl] *adj* faisable, réalisable.
feast [fiːst] *n* festin *m*, banquet *m*; (*REL*: *also*: ~ **day**) fête *f* ♦ *vi* festoyer; **to** ~ **on** se régaler de.
feat [fiːt] *n* exploit *m*, prouesse *f*.
feather ['fɛðə*] *n* plume *f* ♦ *vt*: **to** ~ **one's nest**

(*fig*) faire sa pelote ♦ *cpd* (*bed etc*) de plumes.
feather-weight ['fɛðəweɪt] *n* poids *m* plume *inv*.
feature ['fiːtʃə*] *n* caractéristique *f*; (*article*) chronique *f*, rubrique *f* ♦ *vt* (*subj: film*) avoir pour vedette(s) ♦ *vi* figurer (en bonne place); **~s** *npl* (*of face*) traits *mpl*; **a (special) ~ on sth/sb** un reportage sur qch/qn; **it ~d prominently in** ... cela a figuré en bonne place sur *or* dans ....
feature film *n* long métrage.
featureless ['fiːtʃəlɪs] *adj* anonyme, sans traits distinctifs.
Feb. *abbr* (= *February*) fév.
February ['fɛbruərɪ] *n* février *m*; *for phrases see also* **July**.
feces ['fiːsiːz] *npl* (*US*) = **faeces**.
feckless ['fɛklɪs] *adj* inepte.
Fed *abbr* (*US*) = **federal; federation**.
fed [fɛd] *pt, pp of* **feed; to be ~ up** en avoir marre *or* plein le dos.
Fed. [fɛd] *n abbr* (*US col*) = **Federal Reserve Board**.
federal ['fɛdərəl] *adj* fédéral(e).
Federal Reserve Board *n* (*US*) *organe de contrôle de la banque centrale américaine*.
Federal Trade Commission (FTC) *n* (*US*) *organisme de protection contre les pratiques commerciales abusives*.
federation [fɛdə'reɪʃən] *n* fédération *f*.
fee [fiː] *n* rémunération *f*; (*of doctor, lawyer*) honoraires *mpl*; (*of school, college etc*) frais *mpl* de scolarité; (*for examination*) droits *mpl*; **entrance/membership ~** droit d'entrée/d'inscription; **for a small ~** pour une somme modique.
feeble ['fiːbl] *adj* faible.
feeble-minded ['fiːbl'maɪndɪd] *adj* faible d'esprit.
feed [fiːd] *n* (*of baby*) tétée *f*; (*of animal*) fourrage *m*; pâture *f*; (*on printer*) mécanisme *m* d'alimentation ♦ *vt* (*pt, pp* **fed** [fɛd]) nourrir; (*horse etc*) donner à manger à; (*machine*) alimenter; (*data etc*): **to ~ sth into** fournir qch à, introduire qch dans.
▶**feed back** *vt* (*results*) donner en retour.
▶**feed on** *vt fus* se nourrir de.
feedback ['fiːdbæk] *n* feed-back *m*; (*from person*) réactions *fpl*.
feeder ['fiːdə*] *n* (*bib*) bavette *f*.
feeding bottle ['fiːdɪŋ-] *n* (*BRIT*) biberon *m*.
feel [fiːl] *n* sensation *f* ♦ *vt* (*pt, pp* **felt** [fɛlt]) (*touch*) toucher; tâter, palper; (*cold, pain*) sentir; (*grief, anger*) ressentir, éprouver; (*think, believe*): **to ~ (that)** trouver que; **I ~ that you ought to do it** il me semble que vous devriez le faire; **to ~ hungry/cold** avoir faim/froid; **to ~ lonely/better** se sentir seul/mieux; **I don't ~ well** je ne me sens pas bien; **to ~ sorry for** avoir pitié de; **it ~s soft** c'est doux au toucher; **it ~s colder here** je trouve qu'il fait plus froid ici; **it ~s like velvet** on dirait du velours, ça ressemble au velours; **to ~ like** (*want*) avoir envie de; **to ~ about** *or* **around** fouiller, tâtonner; **to get the ~ of sth** (*fig*) s'habituer à qch.
feeler ['fiːlə*] *n* (*of insect*) antenne *f*; (*fig*): **to put out a ~** *or* **~s** tâter le terrain.
feeling ['fiːlɪŋ] *n* sensation *f*, sentiment *m*; (*impression*) sentiment; **to hurt sb's ~s** froisser qn; **~s ran high about it** cela a déchaîné les passions; **what are your ~s about the matter?** quel est votre sentiment sur cette question?; **my ~ is that** ... j'estime que ...; **I have a ~ that** ... j'ai l'impression que ....
fee-paying school ['fiːpeɪɪŋ-] *n* établissement (d'enseignement) privé.
feet [fiːt] *npl of* **foot**.
feign [feɪn] *vt* feindre, simuler.
felicitous [fɪ'lɪsɪtəs] *adj* heureux(euse).
fell [fɛl] *pt of* **fall** ♦ *vt* (*tree*) abattre ♦ *n* (*BRIT: mountain*) montagne *f*; (*: moorland*): **the ~s** la lande ♦ *adj*: **with one ~ blow** d'un seul coup.
fellow ['fɛləu] *n* type *m*; (*comrade*) compagnon *m*; (*of learned society*) membre *m*; (*of university*) universitaire *m/f* (*membre du conseil*) ♦ *cpd*: **their ~ prisoners/students** leurs camarades prisonniers/étudiants; **his ~ workers** ses collègues *mpl* (de travail).
fellow citizen *n* concitoyen/ne.
fellow countryman *n* compatriote *m*.
fellow feeling *n* sympathie *f*.
fellow men *npl* semblables *mpl*.
fellowship ['fɛləuʃɪp] *n* (*society*) association *f*; (*comradeship*) amitié *f*, camaraderie *f*; (*SCOL*) *sorte de bourse universitaire*.
fellow traveller *n* compagnon/compagne de route; (*POL*) communisant/e.
fell-walking ['fɛlwɔːkɪŋ] *n* (*BRIT*) randonnée *f* en montagne.
felon ['fɛlən] *n* (*LAW*) criminel/le.
felony ['fɛlənɪ] *n* (*LAW*) crime *m*, forfait *m*.
felt [fɛlt] *pt, pp of* **feel** ♦ *n* feutre *m*.
felt-tip pen ['fɛlttɪp-] *n* stylo-feutre *m*.
female ['fiːmeɪl] *n* (*ZOOL*) femelle *f*; (*pej: woman*) bonne femme ♦ *adj* (*BIOL, ELEC*) femelle; (*sex, character*) féminin(e); (*vote etc*) des femmes; (*child etc*) du sexe féminin; **male and ~ students** étudiants et étudiantes.
female impersonator *n* (*THEAT*) travesti *m*.
feminine ['fɛmɪnɪn] *adj* féminin(e) ♦ *n* féminin *m*.
femininity [fɛmɪ'nɪnɪtɪ] *n* féminité *f*.
feminism ['fɛmɪnɪzəm] *n* féminisme *m*.
feminist ['fɛmɪnɪst] *n* féministe *m/f*.
fen [fɛn] *n* (*BRIT*): **the F~s** les plaines *fpl* du Norfolk (*anciennement marécageuses*).
fence [fɛns] *n* barrière *f*; (*SPORT*) obstacle *m*; (*col: person*) receleur/euse ♦ *vt* (*also*: **~ in**) clôturer ♦ *vi* faire de l'escrime; **to sit on the ~** (*fig*) ne pas se mouiller.
fencing ['fɛnsɪŋ] *n* (*sport*) escrime *m*.

fend [fɛnd] *vi*: **to ~ for o.s.** se débrouiller (tout seul).
▶**fend off** *vt* (*attack etc*) parer.
fender ['fɛndə*] *n* (*of fireplace*) garde-feu *m inv*; (*on boat*) défense *f*; (*US*: *of car*) aile *f*.
fennel ['fɛnl] *n* fenouil *m*.
ferment *vi* [fə'mɛnt] fermenter ♦ *n* ['fəːmɛnt] agitation *f*, effervescence *f*.
fermentation [fəːmɛn'teɪʃən] *n* fermentation *f*.
fern [fəːn] *n* fougère *f*.
ferocious [fə'rəuʃəs] *adj* féroce.
ferocity [fə'rɔsɪtɪ] *n* férocité *f*.
ferret ['fɛrɪt] *n* furet *m*.
▶**ferret about, ferret around** *vi* fureter.
▶**ferret out** *vt* dénicher.
ferry ['fɛrɪ] *n* (*small*) bac *m*; (*large*: *also*: **~boat**) ferry(-boat *m*) *m* ♦ *vt* transporter; **to ~ sth/sb across** *or* **over** faire traverser qch/qn.
ferryman ['fɛrɪmən] *n* passeur *m*.
fertile ['fəːtaɪl] *adj* fertile; (*BIOL*) fécond(e); **~ period** période *f* de fécondité.
fertility [fə'tɪlɪtɪ] *n* fertilité *f*; fécondité *f*.
fertility drug *n* médicament *m* contre la stérilité.
fertilize ['fəːtɪlaɪz] *vt* fertiliser; féconder.
fertilizer ['fəːtɪlaɪzə*] *n* engrais *m*.
fervent ['fəːvənt] *adj* fervent(e), ardent(e).
fervour, (*US*) **fervor** ['fəːvə*] *n* ferveur *f*.
fester ['fɛstə*] *vi* suppurer.
festival ['fɛstɪvəl] *n* (*REL*) fête *f*; (*ART*, *MUS*) festival *m*.
festive ['fɛstɪv] *adj* de fête; **the ~ season** (*BRIT*: *Christmas*) la période des fêtes.
festivities [fɛs'tɪvɪtɪz] *npl* réjouissances *fpl*.
festoon [fɛs'tuːn] *vt*: **to ~ with** orner de.
fetch [fɛtʃ] *vt* aller chercher; (*BRIT*: *sell for*) se vendre; **how much did it ~?** ça a atteint quel prix?
▶**fetch up** *vi* (*BRIT*) se retrouver.
fetching ['fɛtʃɪŋ] *adj* charmant(e).
fête [feɪt] *n* fête *f*, kermesse *f*.
fetid ['fɛtɪd] *adj* fétide.
fetish ['fɛtɪʃ] *n* fétiche *m*.
fetter ['fɛtə*] *vt* entraver.
fetters ['fɛtəz] *npl* chaînes *fpl*.
fettle ['fɛtl] *n* (*BRIT*): **in fine ~** en bonne forme.
fetus ['fiːtəs] *n* (*US*) = **foetus**.
feud [fjuːd] *n* dispute *f*, dissension *f* ♦ *vi* se disputer, se quereller; **a family ~** une querelle de famille.
feudal ['fjuːdl] *adj* féodal(e).
feudalism ['fjuːdlɪzəm] *n* féodalité *f*.
fever ['fiːvə*] *n* fièvre *f*; **he has a ~** il a de la fièvre.
feverish ['fiːvərɪʃ] *adj* fiévreux(euse), fébrile.
few [fjuː] *adj* peu de ♦ *pron*: **~ succeed** il y en a peu qui réussissent, (bien) peu réussissent; **they were ~** ils étaient peu (nombreux), il y en avait peu; **a ~** ... quelques ...; **I know a ~** j'en connais quelques-uns; **quite a ~** ... un certain nombre de ..., pas mal de ...; **in the next ~ days** dans les jours qui viennent; **in the past ~ days** ces derniers jours; **every ~ days/months** tous les deux ou trois jours/mois; **a ~ more** ... encore quelques ..., quelques ... de plus.
fewer ['fjuːə*] *adj* moins de ♦ *pron* moins; **they are ~ now** il y en a moins maintenant, ils sont moins (nombreux) maintenant.
fewest ['fjuːɪst] *adj* le moins nombreux.
FFA *n abbr* = *Future Farmers of America*.
FH *abbr* (*BRIT*) = **fire hydrant**.
FHA *n abbr* (*US*: = *Federal Housing Administration*) *office fédéral du logement*.
fiancé [fɪ'ɑ̃ːŋseɪ] *n* fiancé *m*.
fiancée [fɪ'ɑ̃ːŋseɪ] *n* fiancée *f*.
fiasco [fɪ'æskəu] *n* fiasco *m*.
fib [fɪb] *n* bobard *m*.
fibre, (*US*) **fiber** ['faɪbə*] *n* fibre *f*.
fibreboard, (*US*) **fiberboard** ['faɪbəbɔːd] *n* panneau *m* de fibres.
fibre-glass, (*US*) **fiber-glass** ['faɪbəglɑːs] *n* fibre de verre.
fibrositis [faɪbrə'saɪtɪs] *n* aponévrosite *f*.
FICA *n abbr* (*US*) = *Federal Insurance Contributions Act*.
fickle ['fɪkl] *adj* inconstant(e), volage, capricieux(euse).
fiction ['fɪkʃən] *n* romans *mpl*, littérature *f* romanesque; (*invention*) fiction *f*.
fictional ['fɪkʃənl] *adj* fictif(ive).
fictionalize ['fɪkʃnəlaɪz] *vt* romancer.
fictitious [fɪk'tɪʃəs] *adj* fictif(ive), imaginaire.
fiddle ['fɪdl] *n* (*MUS*) violon *m*; (*cheating*) combine *f*; escroquerie *f* ♦ *vt* (*BRIT*: *accounts*) falsifier, maquiller; **tax ~** fraude fiscale, combine *f* pour échapper au fisc; **to work a ~** traficoter.
▶**fiddle with** *vt fus* tripoter.
fiddler ['fɪdlə*] *n* violoniste *m/f*.
fiddly ['fɪdlɪ] *adj* (*task*) minutieux(euse).
fidelity [fɪ'dɛlɪtɪ] *n* fidélité *f*.
fidget ['fɪdʒɪt] *vi* se trémousser, remuer.
fidgety ['fɪdʒɪtɪ] *adj* agité(e), qui a la bougeotte.
fiduciary [fɪ'djuːʃɪərɪ] *n* agent *m* fiduciaire.
field [fiːld] *n* champ *m*; (*fig*) domaine *m*, champ; (*SPORT*: *ground*) terrain *m*; (*COMPUT*) champ, zone *f*; **to lead the ~** (*SPORT*, *COMM*) dominer; **the children had a ~ day** (*fig*) c'était un grand jour pour les enfants.
field glasses *npl* jumelles *fpl*.
field hospital *n* antenne chirurgicale.
field marshal *n* maréchal *m*.
fieldwork ['fiːldwəːk] *n* travaux *mpl* pratiques (*or* recherches *fpl*) sur le terrain.
fiend [fiːnd] *n* démon *m*.
fiendish ['fiːndɪʃ] *adj* diabolique.
fierce [fɪəs] *adj* (*look*) féroce, sauvage; (*wind, attack*) (très) violent(e); (*fighting, enemy*) acharné(e).
fiery ['faɪərɪ] *adj* ardent(e), brûlant(e); fougueux(euse).

FIFA ['fi:fə] *n abbr* (= *Fédération internationale de Football Association*) FIFA *f*.
fifteen [fɪf'ti:n] *num* quinze.
fifth [fɪfθ] *num* cinquième.
fiftieth ['fɪftɪɪθ] *num* cinquantième.
fifty ['fɪftɪ] *num* cinquante.
fifty-fifty ['fɪftɪ'fɪftɪ] *adv*: **to share ~ with sb** partager moitié-moitié avec qn ♦ *adj*: **to have a ~ chance (of success)** avoir une chance sur deux (de réussir).
fig [fɪg] *n* figue *f*.
fight [faɪt] *n* bagarre *f*; (*MIL*) combat *m*; (*against cancer etc*) lutte *f* ♦ *vb* (*pt*, *pp* **fought** [fɔ:t]) *vt* se battre contre; (*cancer, alcoholism*) combattre, lutter contre; (*LAW*: *case*) défendre ♦ *vi* se battre; (*fig*): **to ~ (for/against)** lutter (pour/contre).
fighter ['faɪtə*] *n* lutteur *m* (*fig*); (*plane*) chasseur *m*.
fighter pilot *n* pilote *m* de chasse.
fighting ['faɪtɪŋ] *n* combats *mpl*; (*brawls*) bagarres *fpl*.
figment ['fɪgmənt] *n*: **a ~ of the imagination** une invention.
figurative ['fɪgjurətɪv] *adj* figuré(e).
figure ['fɪgə*] *n* (*DRAWING, GEOM*) figure *f*; (*number, cipher*) chiffre *m*; (*body, outline*) silhouette *f*, ligne *f*, formes *fpl*; (*person*) personnage *m* ♦ *vt* (*US*) supposer ♦ *vi* (*appear*) figurer; (*US*: *make sense*) s'expliquer; **public ~** personnalité *f*; **~ of speech** figure *f* de rhétorique.
▸**figure on** *vt fus* (*US*): **to ~ on doing** compter faire.
▸**figure out** *vt* arriver à comprendre; calculer.
figurehead ['fɪgəhɛd] *n* (*NAUT*) figure *f* de proue; (*pej*) prête-nom *m*.
figure skating *n* figures imposées (*en patinage*); patinage *m* artistique.
Fiji (Islands) ['fi:dʒi:-] *n(pl)* (îles *fpl*) Fi(d)ji *fpl*.
filament ['fɪləmənt] *n* filament *m*.
filch [fɪltʃ] *vt* (*col*: *steal*) voler, chiper.
file [faɪl] *n* (*tool*) lime *f*; (*dossier*) dossier *m*; (*folder*) dossier, chemise *f*; (: *binder*) classeur *m*; (*COMPUT*) fichier *m*; (*row*) file *f* ♦ *vt* (*nails, wood*) limer; (*papers*) classer; (*LAW*: *claim*) faire enregistrer; déposer ♦ *vi*: **to ~ in/out** entrer/sortir l'un derrière l'autre; **to ~ past** défiler devant; **to ~ a suit against sb** (*LAW*) intenter un procès à qn.
file name *n* (*COMPUT*) nom *m* de fichier.
filibuster ['fɪlɪbʌstə*] (*esp US POL*) *n* (*also*: **~er**) obstructionniste *m/f* ♦ *vi* faire de l'obstructionnisme.
filing ['faɪlɪŋ] *n* (travaux *mpl* de) classement *m*; **~s** *npl* limaille *f*.
filing cabinet *n* classeur *m* (*meuble*).
filing clerk *n* documentaliste *m/f*.
Filipino [fɪlɪ'pi:nəu] *n* (*person*) Philippin/e; (*LING*) tagalog *m*.
fill [fɪl] *vt* remplir; (*vacancy*) pourvoir à ♦ *n*: **to eat one's ~** manger à sa faim.
▸**fill in** *vt* (*hole*) boucher; (*form*) remplir; (*details, report*) compléter.
▸**fill out** *vt* (*form, receipt*) remplir.
▸**fill up** *vt* remplir ♦ *vi* (*AUT*) faire le plein; **~ it up, please** (*AUT*) le plein, s'il vous plaît.
fillet ['fɪlɪt] *n* filet *m* ♦ *vt* préparer en filets.
fillet steak *n* filet *m* de bœuf, tournedos *m*.
filling ['fɪlɪŋ] *n* (*CULIN*) garniture *f*, farce *f*; (*for tooth*) plombage *m*.
filling station *n* station *f* d'essence.
fillip ['fɪlɪp] *n* coup *m* de fouet (*fig*).
filly ['fɪlɪ] *n* pouliche *f*.
film [fɪlm] *n* film *m*; (*PHOT*) pellicule *f*, film ♦ *vt* (*scene*) filmer.
film star *n* vedette *f* de cinéma.
filmstrip ['fɪlmstrɪp] *n* (film *m* pour) projection *f* fixe.
film studio *n* studio *m* (de cinéma).
Filofax ['faɪləufæks] *n* ® Filofax *m* ®.
filter ['fɪltə*] *n* filtre *m* ♦ *vt* filtrer.
filter coffee *n* café *m* filtre.
filter lane *n* (*BRIT AUT*: *at traffic lights*) voie *f* de dégagement; (: *on motorway*) voie de sortie.
filter tip *n* bout *m* filtre.
filth [fɪlθ] *n* saleté *f*.
filthy ['fɪlθɪ] *adj* sale, dégoûtant(e); (*language*) ordurier(ière), grossier(ière).
fin [fɪn] *n* (*of fish*) nageoire *f*.
final ['faɪnl] *adj* final(e), dernier(ière); (*decision, answer*) définitif(ive) ♦ *n* (*SPORT*) finale *f*; **~s** *npl* (*SCOL*) examens *mpl* de dernière année; **~ demand** (*on invoice etc*) dernier rappel.
finale [fɪ'nɑ:lɪ] *n* finale *m*.
finalist ['faɪnəlɪst] *n* (*SPORT*) finaliste *m/f*.
finalize ['faɪnəlaɪz] *vt* mettre au point.
finally ['faɪnəlɪ] *adv* (*lastly*) en dernier lieu; (*eventually*) enfin, finalement; (*irrevocably*) définitivement.
finance [faɪ'næns] *n* finance *f* ♦ *vt* financer; **~s** *npl* finances *fpl*.
financial [faɪ'nænʃəl] *adj* financier(ière); **~ statement** bilan *m*, exercice financier.
financially [faɪ'nænʃəlɪ] *adv* financièrement.
financial year *n* année *f* budgétaire.
financier [faɪ'nænsɪə*] *n* financier *m*.
find [faɪnd] *vt* (*pt, pp* **found** [faund]) trouver; (*lost object*) retrouver ♦ *n* trouvaille *f*, découverte *f*; **to ~ sb guilty** (*LAW*) déclarer qn coupable; **to ~ (some) difficulty in doing sth** avoir du mal à faire qch.
▸**find out** *vt* se renseigner sur; (*truth, secret*) découvrir; (*person*) démasquer ♦ *vi*: **to ~ out about** se renseigner sur; (*by chance*) apprendre.
findings ['faɪndɪŋz] *npl* (*LAW*) conclusions *fpl*, verdict *m*; (*of report*) constatations *fpl*.
fine [faɪn] *adj* beau(belle); excellent(e); (*subtle, not coarse*) fin(e) ♦ *adv* (*well*) très bien; (*small*) fin, finement ♦ *n* (*LAW*) amende *f*; contravention *f* ♦ *vt* (*LAW*) condamner à une

amende; donner une contravention à; **he's ~** il va bien; **the weather is ~** il fait beau; **you're doing ~** c'est bien, vous vous débrouillez bien; **to cut it ~** calculer un peu juste.
fine arts *npl* beaux-arts *mpl*.
fine print *n*: **the ~** ce qui est imprimé en tout petit.
finery ['faɪnərɪ] *n* parure *f*.
finesse [fɪ'nɛs] *n* finesse *f*, élégance *f*.
fine-tooth comb ['faɪntuːθ-] *n*: **to go through sth with a ~** (*fig*) passer qch au peigne fin *or* au crible.
finger ['fɪŋgə*] *n* doigt *m* ♦ *vt* palper, toucher.
fingernail ['fɪŋgəneɪl] *n* ongle *m* (de la main).
fingerprint ['fɪŋgəprɪnt] *n* empreinte digitale ♦ *vt* (*person*) prendre les empreintes digitales de.
fingerstall ['fɪŋgəstɔːl] *n* doigtier *m*.
fingertip ['fɪŋgətɪp] *n* bout *m* du doigt; (*fig*): **to have sth at one's ~s** avoir qch à sa disposition; (*knowledge*) savoir qch sur le bout du doigt.
finicky ['fɪnɪkɪ] *adj* tatillon(ne), méticuleux(euse); minutieux(euse).
finish ['fɪnɪʃ] *n* fin *f*; (*SPORT*) arrivée *f*; (*polish etc*) finition *f* ♦ *vt* finir, terminer ♦ *vi* finir, se terminer; (*session*) s'achever; **to ~ doing sth** finir de faire qch; **to ~ third** arriver *or* terminer troisième.
►**finish off** *vt* finir, terminer; (*kill*) achever.
►**finish up** *vi*, *vt* finir.
finished product ['fɪnɪʃt-] *n* produit fini.
finishing line ['fɪnɪʃɪŋ-] *n* ligne *f* d'arrivée.
finishing school ['fɪnɪʃɪŋ-] *n* institution privée (*pour jeunes filles*).
finite ['faɪnaɪt] *adj* fini(e); (*verb*) conjugué(e).
Finland ['fɪnlənd] *n* Finlande *f*.
Finn [fɪn] *n* Finnois/e; Finlandais/e.
Finnish ['fɪnɪʃ] *adj* finnois(e); finlandais(e) ♦ *n* (*LING*) finnois *m*.
fiord [fjɔːd] *n* fjord *m*.
fir [fəː*] *n* sapin *m*.
fire ['faɪə*] *n* feu *m*; incendie *m* ♦ *vt* (*discharge*): **to ~ a gun** tirer un coup de feu; (*fig*) enflammer, animer; (*dismiss*) mettre à la porte, renvoyer ♦ *vi* tirer, faire feu ♦ *cpd*: **~ hazard, ~ risk**: **that's a ~ hazard** *or* **risk** cela présente un risque d'incendie; **on ~** en feu; **to set ~ to sth, set sth on ~** mettre le feu à qch; **insured against ~** assuré contre l'incendie.
fire alarm *n* avertisseur *m* d'incendie.
firearm ['faɪərɑːm] *n* arme *f* à feu.
fire brigade *n* (*BRIT*) (régiment *m* de sapeurs-)pompiers *mpl*.
fire chief *n* (*US*) = **fire master**.
fire department *n* (*US*) = **fire brigade**.
fire door *n* porte *f* coupe-feu.
fire engine *n* pompe *f* à incendie.
fire escape *n* escalier *m* de secours.
fire extinguisher *n* extincteur *m*.
fireguard ['faɪəgɑːd] *n* (*BRIT*) garde-feu *m inv*.
fire insurance *n* assurance *f* incendie.
fireman ['faɪəmən] *n* pompier *m*.
fire master *n* (*BRIT*) capitaine *m* des pompiers.
fireplace ['faɪəpleɪs] *n* cheminée *f*.
fireproof ['faɪəpruːf] *adj* ignifuge.
fire regulations *npl* consignes *fpl* en cas d'incendie.
fire screen *n* (*decorative*) écran *m* de cheminée; (*for protection*) garde-feu *m inv*.
fireside ['faɪəsaɪd] *n* foyer *m*, coin *m* du feu.
fire station *n* caserne *f* de pompiers.
firewood ['faɪəwud] *n* bois *m* de chauffage.
firework ['faɪəwəːk] *n* feu *m* d'artifice; **~s** *npl* (*display*) feu(x) d'artifice.
firing ['faɪərɪŋ] *n* (*MIL*) feu *m*, tir *m*.
firing squad *n* peloton *m* d'exécution.
firm [fəːm] *adj* ferme ♦ *n* compagnie *f*, firme *f*.
firmly ['fəːmlɪ] *adv* fermement.
firmness ['fəːmnɪs] *n* fermeté *f*.
first [fəːst] *adj* premier(ière) ♦ *adv* (*before others*) le premier, la première; (*before other things*) en premier, d'abord; (*when listing reasons etc*) en premier lieu, premièrement ♦ *n* (*person: in race*) premier/ière; (*BRIT SCOL*) mention *f* très bien; (*AUT*) première *f*; **the ~ of January** le premier janvier; **at ~** au commencement, au début; **~ of all** tout d'abord, pour commencer; **in the ~ instance** en premier lieu; **I'll do it ~ thing tomorrow** je le ferai tout de suite demain matin.
first aid *n* premiers secours *or* soins.
first-aid kit [fəːst'eɪd-] *n* trousse *f* à pharmacie.
first-class ['fəːst'klɑːs] *adj* de première classe.
first-class mail *n* courrier *m* rapide.
first-hand ['fəːst'hænd] *adj* de première main.
first lady *n* (*US*) femme *f* du président.
firstly ['fəːstlɪ] *adv* premièrement, en premier lieu.
first name *n* prénom *m*.
first night *n* (*THEAT*) première *f*.
first-rate ['fəːst'reɪt] *adj* excellent(e).
first-time buyer ['fəːsttaɪm-] *n* *personne achetant une maison ou un appartement pour la première fois*.
fir tree *n* sapin *m*.
FIS *n abbr* (*BRIT*: = *Family Income Supplement*) *complément familial*.
fiscal ['fɪskl] *adj* fiscal(e); **~ year** exercice financier.
fish [fɪʃ] *n* (*pl inv*) poisson *m*; poissons *mpl* ♦ *vt*, *vi* pêcher; **to ~ a river** pêcher dans une rivière; **to go ~ing** aller à la pêche.
fisherman ['fɪʃəmən] *n* pêcheur *m*.
fishery ['fɪʃərɪ] *n* pêcherie *f*.
fish factory *n* (*BRIT*) conserverie *f* de poissons.
fish farm *n* établissement *m* piscicole.
fish fingers *npl* (*BRIT*) bâtonnets de poisson (congelés).
fish hook *n* hameçon *m*.

fishing boat ['fɪʃɪŋ-] *n* barque *f* de pêche.
fishing industry ['fɪʃɪŋ-] *n* industrie *f* de la pêche.
fishing line ['fɪʃɪŋ-] *n* ligne *f* (de pêche).
fishing rod ['fɪʃɪŋ-] *n* canne *f* à pêche.
fishing tackle ['fɪʃɪŋ-] *n* attirail *m* de pêche.
fish market *n* marché *m* au poisson.
fishmonger ['fɪʃmʌŋgə*] *n* marchand *m* de poisson; **~'s (shop)** poissonnerie *f*.
fish slice *n* (*BRIT*) pelle *f* à poisson.
fish sticks *npl* (*US*) = **fish fingers**.
fishy ['fɪʃɪ] *adj* (*fig*) suspect(e), louche.
fission ['fɪʃən] *n* fission *f*; **atomic** *or* **nuclear ~** fission nucléaire.
fissure ['fɪʃə*] *n* fissure *f*.
fist [fɪst] *n* poing *m*.
fistfight ['fɪstfaɪt] *n* pugilat *m*, bagarre *f* (à coups de poing).
fit [fɪt] *adj* (*MED, SPORT*) en (bonne) forme; (*proper*) convenable; approprié(e) ♦ *vt* (*subj: clothes*) aller à; (*adjust*) ajuster; (*put in, attach*) installer, poser; adapter; (*equip*) équiper, garnir, munir ♦ *vi* (*clothes*) aller; (*parts*) s'adapter; (*in space, gap*) entrer, s'adapter ♦ *n* (*MED*) accès *m*, crise *f*; (*of coughing*) quinte *f*; **~ to** en état de; **~ for** digne de; apte à; **to keep ~** se maintenir en forme; **this dress is a tight/good ~** cette robe est un peu juste/(me) va très bien; **a ~ of anger** un accès de colère; **to have a ~** (*MED*) faire *or* avoir une crise; (*col*) piquer une crise; **by ~s and starts** par à-coups.
►**fit in** *vi* s'accorder; (*person*) s'adapter.
►**fit out** *vt* (*BRIT*: *also*: **fit up**) équiper.
fitful ['fɪtful] *adj* intermittent(e).
fitment ['fɪtmənt] *n* meuble encastré, élément *m*.
fitness ['fɪtnɪs] *n* (*MED*) forme *f* physique; (*of remark*) à-propos *m*, justesse *f*.
fitted kitchen ['fɪtɪd-] *n* (*BRIT*) cuisine équipée.
fitter ['fɪtə*] *n* monteur *m*; (*DRESSMAKING*) essayeur/euse.
fitting ['fɪtɪŋ] *adj* approprié(e) ♦ *n* (*of dress*) essayage *m*; (*of piece of equipment*) pose *f*, installation *f*.
fitting room *n* (*in shop*) cabine *f* d'essayage.
fittings ['fɪtɪŋz] *npl* installations *fpl*.
five [faɪv] *num* cinq.
five-day week ['faɪvdeɪ-] *n* semaine *f* de cinq jours.
fiver ['faɪvə*] *n* (*col*: *BRIT*) billet *m* de cinq livres; (*: US*) billet de cinq dollars.
fix [fɪks] *vt* fixer; (*sort out*) arranger; (*mend*) réparer; (*make ready: meal, drink*) préparer; (*col*: *game etc*) truquer ♦ *n*: **to be in a ~** être dans le pétrin.
►**fix up** *vt* (*meeting*) arranger; **to ~ sb up with sth** faire avoir qch à qn.
fixation [fɪk'seɪʃən] *n* (*PSYCH*) fixation *f*; (*fig*) obsession *f*.
fixed [fɪkst] *adj* (*prices etc*) fixe; **there's a ~ charge** il y a un prix forfaitaire; **how are you ~ for money?** (*col*) question fric, ça va?
fixed assets *npl* immobilisations *fpl*.
fixture ['fɪkstʃə*] *n* installation *f* (fixe); (*SPORT*) rencontre *f* (au programme).
fizz [fɪz] *vi* pétiller.
fizzle ['fɪzl] *vi* pétiller.
►**fizzle out** *vi* rater.
fizzy ['fɪzɪ] *adj* pétillant(e); gazeux(euse).
fjord [fjɔːd] *n* = **fiord**.
FL, Fla. *abbr* (*US*) = *Florida*.
flabbergasted ['flæbəgɑːstɪd] *adj* sidéré(e), ahuri(e).
flabby ['flæbɪ] *adj* mou(molle).
flag [flæg] *n* drapeau *m*; (*also*: **~stone**) dalle *f* ♦ *vi* faiblir; fléchir; **~ of convenience** pavillon *m* de complaisance.
►**flag down** *vt* héler, faire signe (de s'arrêter) à.
flagon ['flægən] *n* bonbonne *f*.
flagpole ['flægpəul] *n* mât *m*.
flagrant ['fleɪgrənt] *adj* flagrant(e).
flag stop *n* (*US*: *for bus*) arrêt facultatif.
flair [flɛə*] *n* flair *m*.
flak [flæk] *n* (*MIL*) tir antiaérien; (*col*: *criticism*) critiques *fpl*.
flake [fleɪk] *n* (*of rust, paint*) écaille *f*; (*of snow, soap powder*) flocon *m* ♦ *vi* (*also*: **~ off**) s'écailler.
flaky ['fleɪkɪ] *adj* (*paintwork*) écaillé(e); (*skin*) desquamé(e); (*pastry*) feuilleté(e).
flamboyant [flæm'bɔɪənt] *adj* flamboyant(e), éclatant(e); (*person*) haut(e) en couleur.
flame [fleɪm] *n* flamme *f*.
flamingo [flə'mɪŋgəu] *n* flamant *m* (rose).
flammable ['flæməbl] *adj* inflammable.
flan [flæn] *n* (*BRIT*) tarte *f*.
Flanders ['flɑːndəz] *n* Flandre(s) *f(pl)*.
flange [flændʒ] *n* boudin *m*; collerette *f*.
flank [flæŋk] *n* flanc *m* ♦ *vt* flanquer.
flannel ['flænl] *n* (*BRIT*: *also*: **face ~**) gant *m* de toilette; (*fabric*) flanelle *f*; (*BRIT col*) baratin *m*; **~s** *npl* pantalon *m* de flanelle.
flap [flæp] *n* (*of pocket, envelope*) rabat *m* ♦ *vt* (*wings*) battre (de) ♦ *vi* (*sail, flag*) claquer; (*col*: *also*: **be in a ~**) paniquer.
flapjack ['flæpdʒæk] *n* (*US*: *pancake*) ≈ crêpe *f*; (*BRIT*: *biscuit*) galette *f*.
flare [flɛə*] *n* fusée éclairante; (*in skirt etc*) évasement *m*.
►**flare up** *vi* s'embraser; (*fig: person*) se mettre en colère, s'emporter; (*: revolt*) éclater.
flared ['flɛəd] *adj* (*trousers*) à jambes évasées; (*skirt*) évasé(e).
flash [flæʃ] *n* éclair *m*; (*also*: **news ~**) flash *m* (d'information); (*PHOT*) flash ♦ *vt* (*switch on*) allumer (brièvement); (*direct*): **to ~ sth at** braquer qch sur; (*flaunt*) étaler, exhiber; (*send: message*) câbler ♦ *vi* briller; jeter des éclairs; (*light on ambulance etc*) clignoter; **in a ~** en un clin d'œil; **to ~ one's headlights**

faire un appel de phares; **he ~ed by** *or* **past** il passa (devant nous) comme un éclair.
flashback ['flæʃbæk] *n* flashback *m*, retour *m* en arrière.
flashbulb ['flæʃbʌlb] *n* ampoule *f* de flash.
flash card *n* (*SCOL*) carte *f* (*support visuel*).
flashcube ['flæʃkjuːb] *n* cube-flash *m*.
flasher ['flæʃə*] *n* (*AUT*) clignotant *m*.
flashlight ['flæʃlaɪt] *n* lampe *f* de poche.
flashpoint ['flæʃpɔɪnt] *n* point *m* d'ignition; (*fig*): **to be at ~** être sur le point d'exploser.
flashy ['flæʃɪ] *adj* (*pej*) tape-à-l'œil *inv*, tapageur(euse).
flask [flɑːsk] *n* flacon *m*, bouteille *f*; (*CHEM*) ballon *m*; (*also*: **vacuum ~**) bouteille *f* thermos ®.
flat [flæt] *adj* plat(e); (*tyre*) dégonflé(e), à plat; (*denial*) catégorique; (*MUS*) bémolisé(e); (*: voice*) faux(fausse) ♦ *n* (*BRIT*: *rooms*) appartement *m*; (*AUT*) crevaison *f*, pneu crevé; (*MUS*) bémol *m*; **~ out** (*work*) sans relâche; (*race*) à fond; **~ rate of pay** (*COMM*) (salaire *m*) fixe.
flat-footed ['flæt'futɪd] *adj*: **to be ~** avoir les pieds plats.
flatly ['flætlɪ] *adv* catégoriquement.
flatmate ['flætmeɪt] *n* (*BRIT*): **he's my ~** il partage l'appartement avec moi.
flatness ['flætnɪs] *n* (*of land*) absence *f* de relief, aspect plat.
flat-screen ['flætskriːn] *adj* à écran plat.
flatten ['flætn] *vt* (*also*: **~ out**) aplatir; (*house, city*) raser.
flatter ['flætə*] *vt* flatter.
flatterer ['flætərə*] *n* flatteur *m*.
flattering ['flætərɪŋ] *adj* flatteur(euse); (*clothes etc*) seyant(e).
flattery ['flætərɪ] *n* flatterie *f*.
flatulence ['flætjuləns] *n* flatulence *f*.
flaunt [flɔːnt] *vt* faire étalage de.
flavour, (*US*) **flavor** ['fleɪvə*] *n* goût *m*, saveur *f*; (*of ice cream etc*) parfum *m* ♦ *vt* parfumer, aromatiser; **vanilla-~ed** à l'arôme de vanille, vanillé(e); **to give** *or* **add ~ to** donner du goût à, relever.
flavo(u)ring ['fleɪvərɪŋ] *n* arôme *m* (synthétique).
flaw [flɔː] *n* défaut *m*.
flawless ['flɔːlɪs] *adj* sans défaut.
flax [flæks] *n* lin *m*.
flaxen ['flæksən] *adj* blond(e).
flea [fliː] *n* puce *f*.
flea market *n* marché *m* aux puces.
fleck [flɛk] *n* (*of dust*) particule *f*; (*of mud, paint, colour*) tacheture *f*, moucheture *f* ♦ *vt* tacher, éclabousser; **brown ~ed with white** brun moucheté de blanc.
fledg(e)ling ['flɛdʒlɪŋ] *n* oisillon *m*.
flee, *pt, pp* **fled** [fliː, flɛd] *vt* fuir, s'enfuir de ♦ *vi* fuir, s'enfuir.
fleece [fliːs] *n* toison *f* ♦ *vt* (*col*) voler, filouter.
fleecy ['fliːsɪ] *adj* (*blanket*) moelleux(euse); (*cloud*) floconneux(euse).
fleet [fliːt] *n* flotte *f*; (*of lorries, cars etc*) parc *m*; convoi *m*.
fleeting ['fliːtɪŋ] *adj* fugace, fugitif(ive); (*visit*) très bref(brève).
Flemish ['flɛmɪʃ] *adj* flamand(e) ♦ *n* (*LING*) flamand *m*; **the ~** *npl* les Flamands.
flesh [flɛʃ] *n* chair *f*.
flesh wound [-wuːnd] *n* blessure superficielle.
flew [fluː] *pt of* **fly**.
flex [flɛks] *n* fil *m or* câble *m* électrique (souple) ♦ *vt* fléchir; (*muscles*) tendre.
flexibility [flɛksɪ'bɪlɪtɪ] *n* flexibilité *f*.
flexible ['flɛksəbl] *adj* flexible; (*person, schedule*) souple.
flexitime ['flɛksɪtaɪm] *n* horaire *m* variable *or* à la carte.
flick [flɪk] *n* petite tape; chiquenaude *f*; sursaut *m*.
►**flick through** *vt fus* feuilleter.
flicker ['flɪkə*] *vi* vaciller ♦ *n* vacillement *m*; **a ~ of light** une brève lueur.
flick knife *n* (*BRIT*) couteau *m* à cran d'arrêt.
flicks [flɪks] *npl* (*col*) ciné *m*.
flier ['flaɪə*] *n* aviateur *m*.
flight [flaɪt] *n* vol *m*; (*escape*) fuite *f*; (*also*: **~ of steps**) escalier *m*; **to take ~** prendre la fuite; **to put to ~** mettre en fuite.
flight attendant *n* (*US*) steward *m*, hôtesse *f* de l'air.
flight crew *n* équipage *m*.
flight deck *n* (*AVIAT*) poste *m* de pilotage; (*NAUT*) pont *m* d'envol.
flight path *n* trajectoire *f* (de vol).
flight recorder *n* enregistreur *m* de vol.
flimsy ['flɪmzɪ] *adj* (*partition, fabric*) peu solide, mince; (*excuse*) pauvre, mince.
flinch [flɪntʃ] *vi* tressaillir; **to ~ from** se dérober à, reculer devant.
fling [flɪŋ] *vt* (*pt, pp* **flung** [flʌŋ]) jeter, lancer ♦ *n* (*love affair*) brève liaison, passade *f*.
flint [flɪnt] *n* silex *m*; (*in lighter*) pierre *f* (à briquet).
flip [flɪp] *n* chiquenaude *f* ♦ *vt* donner une chiquenaude à; (*US*: *pancake*) faire sauter ♦ *vi*: **to ~ for sth** (*US*) jouer qch à pile ou face.
►**flip through** *vt fus* feuilleter.
flippant ['flɪpənt] *adj* désinvolte, irrévérencieux(euse).
flipper ['flɪpə*] *n* (*of animal*) nageoire *f*; (*for swimmer*) palme *f*.
flip side *n* (*of record*) deuxième face *f*.
flirt [flɜːt] *vi* flirter ♦ *n* flirteuse *f*.
flirtation [flɜː'teɪʃən] *n* flirt *m*.
flit [flɪt] *vi* voleter.
float [fləut] *n* flotteur *m*; (*in procession*) char *m*; (*sum of money*) réserve *f* ♦ *vi* flotter; (*bather*) flotter, faire la planche ♦ *vt* faire flotter; (*loan, business, idea*) lancer.
floating ['fləutɪŋ] *adj* flottant(e); **~ vote** voix flottante; **~ voter** électeur indécis.

flock [flɔk] *n* troupeau *m*; (*of birds*) vol *m*; (*of people*) foule *f*.
floe [fləu] *n* (*also*: **ice** ~) iceberg *m*.
flog [flɔg] *vt* fouetter.
flood [flʌd] *n* inondation *f*; (*of words, tears etc*) flot *m*, torrent *m* ♦ *vt* inonder; (*AUT*: *carburettor*) noyer; **to** ~ **the market** (*COMM*) inonder le marché; **in** ~ en crue.
flooding ['flʌdɪŋ] *n* inondation *f*.
floodlight ['flʌdlaɪt] *n* projecteur *m* ♦ *vt* éclairer aux projecteurs, illuminer.
floodlit ['flʌdlɪt] *pt, pp of* **floodlight** ♦ *adj* illuminé(e).
flood tide *n* marée montante.
floodwater ['flʌdwɔːtə*] *n* eau *f* de la crue.
floor [flɔː*] *n* sol *m*; (*storey*) étage *m*; (*of sea, valley*) fond *m*; (*fig: at meeting*): **the** ~ l'assemblée *f*, les membres *mpl* de l'assemblée ♦ *vt* terrasser; (*baffle*) désorienter; **on the** ~ par terre; **ground** ~, (*US*) **first** ~ rez-de-chaussée *m*; **first** ~, (*US*) **second** ~ premier étage; **top** ~ dernier étage; **to have the** ~ (*speaker*) avoir la parole.
floorboard ['flɔːbɔːd] *n* planche *f* (*du plancher*).
flooring ['flɔːrɪŋ] *n* sol *m*; (*wooden*) plancher *m*; (*material to make floor*) matériau(x) *m(pl)* pour planchers; (*covering*) revêtement *m* de sol.
floor lamp *n* (*US*) lampadaire *m*.
floor show *n* spectacle *m* de variétés.
floorwalker ['flɔːwɔːkə*] *n* (*esp US*) surveillant *m* (de grand magasin).
flop [flɔp] *n* fiasco *m* ♦ *vi* (*fail*) faire fiasco.
floppy ['flɔpɪ] *adj* lâche, flottant(e); ~ **hat** chapeau *m* à bords flottants.
floppy disk *n* disquette *f*, disque *m* souple.
flora ['flɔːrə] *n* flore *f*.
floral ['flɔːrl] *adj* floral(e).
Florence ['flɔrəns] *n* Florence.
florid ['flɔrɪd] *adj* (*complexion*) fleuri(e); (*style*) plein(e) de fioritures.
florist ['flɔrɪst] *n* fleuriste *m/f*; ~**'s (shop)** magasin *m* or boutique *f* de fleuriste.
flotation [fləu'teɪʃən] *n* (*of shares*) émission *f*; (*of company*) lancement *m* (en Bourse).
flounce [flauns] *n* volant *m*.
►**flounce out** *vi* sortir dans un mouvement d'humeur.
flounder ['flaundə*] *n* (*ZOOL*) flet *m* ♦ *vi* patauger.
flour ['flauə*] *n* farine *f*.
flourish ['flʌrɪʃ] *vi* prospérer ♦ *vt* brandir ♦ *n* fioriture *f*; (*of trumpets*) fanfare *f*.
flourishing ['flʌrɪʃɪŋ] *adj* prospère, florissant(e).
flout [flaut] *vt* se moquer de, faire fi de.
flow [fləu] *n* (*of water, traffic etc*) écoulement *m*; (*tide, influx*) flux *m*; (*of orders, letters etc*) flot *m*; (*of blood, ELEC*) circulation *f*; (*of river*) courant *m* ♦ *vi* couler; (*traffic*) s'écouler; (*robes, hair*) flotter.
flow chart, flow diagram *n* organigramme *m*.
flower ['flauə*] *n* fleur *f* ♦ *vi* fleurir; **in** ~ en fleur.
flower bed *n* plate-bande *f*.
flowerpot ['flauəpɔt] *n* pot *m* (à fleurs).
flowery ['flauərɪ] *adj* fleuri(e).
flown [fləun] *pp of* **fly**.
flu [fluː] *n* grippe *f*.
fluctuate ['flʌktjueɪt] *vi* varier, fluctuer.
fluctuation [flʌktju'eɪʃən] *n* fluctuation *f*, variation *f*.
flue [fluː] *n* conduit *m*.
fluency ['fluːənsɪ] *n* facilité *f*, aisance *f*.
fluent ['fluːənt] *adj* (*speech, style*) coulant(e), aisé(e); **he's a** ~ **speaker/reader** il s'exprime/lit avec aisance *or* facilité; **he speaks** ~ **French, he's** ~ **in French** il parle le français couramment.
fluently ['fluːəntlɪ] *adv* couramment; avec aisance *or* facilité.
fluff [flʌf] *n* duvet *m*; peluche *f*.
fluffy ['flʌfɪ] *adj* duveteux(euse); pelucheux(euse); ~ **toy** jouet *m* en peluche.
fluid ['fluːɪd] *n* fluide *m*; (*in diet*) liquide *m* ♦ *adj* fluide.
fluid ounce *n* (*BRIT*) = *0.028 l; 0.05 pints.*
fluke [fluːk] *n* (*col*) coup *m* de veine.
flummox ['flʌməks] *vt* dérouter, déconcerter.
flung [flʌŋ] *pt, pp of* **fling**.
flunky ['flʌŋkɪ] *n* larbin *m*.
fluorescent [fluə'rɛsnt] *adj* fluorescent(e).
fluoride ['fluəraɪd] *n* fluor *m*.
fluorine ['fluəriːn] *n* fluor *m*.
flurry ['flʌrɪ] *n* (*of snow*) rafale *f*, bourrasque *f*; ~ **of activity/excitement** affairement *m*/excitation *f* soudain(e).
flush [flʌʃ] *n* rougeur *f*; (*fig*) éclat *m*; afflux *m* ♦ *vt* nettoyer à grande eau; (*also*: ~ **out**) débusquer ♦ *vi* rougir ♦ *adj* (*col*) en fonds; (*level*): ~ **with** au ras de, de niveau avec; **to** ~ **the toilet** tirer la chasse (d'eau); **hot** ~**es** (*MED*) bouffées *fpl* de chaleur.
flushed ['flʌʃt] *adj* (tout(e)) rouge.
fluster ['flʌstə*] *n* agitation *f*, trouble *m*.
flustered ['flʌstəd] *adj* énervé(e).
flute [fluːt] *n* flûte *f*.
fluted ['fluːtɪd] *adj* cannelé(e).
flutter ['flʌtə*] *n* agitation *f*; (*of wings*) battement *m* ♦ *vi* battre des ailes, voleter; (*person*) aller et venir dans une grande agitation.
flux [flʌks] *n*: **in a state of** ~ fluctuant sans cesse.
fly [flaɪ] *n* (*insect*) mouche *f*; (*on trousers*: *also*: **flies**) braguette *f* ♦ *vb* (*pt* **flew**, *pp* **flown** [fluː, fləun]) *vt* (*plane*) piloter; (*passengers, cargo*) transporter (par avion); (*distances*) parcourir ♦ *vi* voler; (*passengers*) aller en avion; (*escape*) s'enfuir, fuir; (*flag*) se déployer; **to** ~ **open** s'ouvrir brusquement; **to** ~ **off the handle** s'énerver, s'emporter.
►**fly away** *vi* s'envoler.

►**fly in** *vi* (*plane*) atterrir; (*person*): **he flew in yesterday** il est arrivé hier (par avion).
►**fly off** *vi* s'envoler.
►**fly out** *vi* (*see fly in*) s'envoler; partir (par avion).
fly-fishing ['flaɪfɪʃɪŋ] *n* pêche *f* à la mouche.
flying ['flaɪɪŋ] *n* (*activity*) aviation *f* ♦ *adj*: ~ **visit** visite *f* éclair *inv*; **with ~ colours** haut la main; **he doesn't like ~** il n'aime pas voyager en avion.
flying buttress *n* arc-boutant *m*.
flying picket *n* piquet *m* de grève volant.
flying saucer *n* soucoupe volante.
flying squad *n* (*POLICE*) brigade volante.
flying start *n*: **to get off to a ~** faire un excellent départ.
flyleaf ['flaɪli:f] *n* page *f* de garde.
flyover ['flaɪəuvə*] *n* (*BRIT AUT*) autopont *m*.
flypast ['flaɪpɑ:st] *n* défilé aérien.
flysheet ['flaɪʃi:t] *n* (*for tent*) double toit *m*.
flyweight ['flaɪweɪt] *n* (*SPORT*) poids *m* mouche.
flywheel ['flaɪwi:l] *n* volant *m* (de commande).
FM *abbr* (*BRIT MIL*) = **field marshal**; (*RADIO*) = **frequency modulation**.
FMB *n abbr* (*US*) = *Federal Maritime Board.*
FMCS *n abbr* (*US*: = *Federal Mediation and Conciliation Services*) *organisme de conciliation en cas de conflits du travail.*
FO *n abbr* (*BRIT*) = **Foreign Office**.
foal [fəul] *n* poulain *m*.
foam [fəum] *n* écume *f*; (*on beer*) mousse *f*; (*also*: **plastic ~**) mousse cellulaire *or* de plastique ♦ *vi* écumer; (*soapy water*) mousser.
foam rubber *n* caoutchouc *m* mousse.
FOB *abbr* (= *free on board*) fob.
fob [fɔb] *n* (*also*: **watch ~**) chaîne *f*, ruban *m* ♦ *vt*: **to ~ sb off with** refiler à qn; se débarrasser de qn avec.
foc *abbr* (*BRIT*) = **free of charge**.
focal ['fəukl] *adj* (*also fig*) focal(e).
focal point *n* foyer *m*; (*fig*) centre *m* de l'attention, point focal.
focus ['fəukəs] *n* (*pl*: **~es**) foyer *m*; (*of interest*) centre *m* ♦ *vt* (*field glasses etc*) mettre au point; (*light rays*) faire converger ♦ *vi*: **to ~ (on)** (*with camera*) régler la mise au point (sur); (*person*) fixer son regard (sur); **in ~** au point; **out of ~** pas au point.
fodder ['fɔdə*] *n* fourrage *m*.
FOE *n abbr* (= *Friends of the Earth*) AT *mpl* (= *Amis de la Terre*); (*US*: = *Fraternal Order of Eagles*) *organisation charitable.*
foe [fəu] *n* ennemi *m*.
foetus, (*US*) **fetus** ['fi:təs] *n* fœtus *m*.
fog [fɔg] *n* brouillard *m*.
fogbound ['fɔgbaund] *adj* bloqué(e) par le brouillard.
foggy ['fɔgɪ] *adj*: **it's ~** il y a du brouillard.
fog lamp, (*US*) **fog light** *n* (*AUT*) phare *m* anti-brouillard.
foible ['fɔɪbl] *n* faiblesse *f*.
foil [fɔɪl] *vt* déjouer, contrecarrer ♦ *n* feuille *f* de métal; (*kitchen ~*) papier *m* alu(minium); (*FENCING*) fleuret *m*; **to act as a ~ to** (*fig*) servir de repoussoir *or* de faire-valoir à.
foist [fɔɪst] *vt*: **to ~ sth on sb** imposer qch à qn.
fold [fəuld] *n* (*bend, crease*) pli *m*; (*AGR*) parc *m* à moutons; (*fig*) bercail *m* ♦ *vt* plier; **to ~ one's arms** croiser les bras.
►**fold up** *vi* (*map etc*) se plier, se replier; (*business*) fermer boutique ♦ *vt* (*map etc*) plier, replier.
folder ['fəuldə*] *n* (*for papers*) chemise *f*; (*: binder*) classeur *m*; (*brochure*) dépliant *m*; (*COMPUT*) répertoire *m*.
folding ['fəuldɪŋ] *adj* (*chair, bed*) pliant(e).
foliage ['fəulɪɪdʒ] *n* feuillage *m*.
folk [fəuk] *npl* gens *mpl* ♦ *cpd* folklorique; **~s** *npl* famille *f*, parents *mpl*.
folklore ['fəuklɔ:*] *n* folklore *m*.
folksong ['fəuksɔŋ] *n* chanson *f* folklorique; (*contemporary*) chanson folk *inv*.
follow ['fɔləu] *vt* suivre ♦ *vi* suivre; (*result*) s'ensuivre; **to ~ sb's advice** suivre les conseils de qn; **I don't quite ~ you** je ne vous suis plus; **to ~ in sb's footsteps** emboîter le pas à qn; (*fig*) suivre les traces de qn; **it ~s that ...** de ce fait, il s'ensuit que ...; **he ~ed suit** il fit de même.
►**follow out** *vt* (*idea, plan*) poursuivre, mener à terme.
►**follow through** *vt* = **follow out**.
►**follow up** *vt* (*victory*) tirer parti de; (*letter, offer*) donner suite à; (*case*) suivre.
follower ['fɔləuə*] *n* disciple *m/f*, partisan/e.
following ['fɔləuɪŋ] *adj* suivant(e) ♦ *n* partisans *mpl*, disciples *mpl*.
follow-up ['fɔləuʌp] *n* suite *f*; suivi *m*.
folly ['fɔlɪ] *n* inconscience *f*; sottise *f*; (*building*) folie *f*.
fond [fɔnd] *adj* (*memory, look*) tendre, affectueux(euse); **to be ~ of** aimer beaucoup.
fondle ['fɔndl] *vt* caresser.
fondly ['fɔndlɪ] *adv* (*lovingly*) tendrement; (*naïvely*) naïvement.
fondness ['fɔndnɪs] *n* (*for things*) attachement *m*; (*for people*) sentiments affectueux; **a special ~ for** une prédilection pour.
font [fɔnt] *n* (*REL*) fonts baptismaux; (*TYP*) police *f* de caractères.
food [fu:d] *n* nourriture *f*.
food chain *n* chaîne *f* alimentaire.
food mixer *n* mixeur *m*.
food poisoning *n* intoxication *f* alimentaire.
food processor *n* robot *m* de cuisine.
food stamp *n* (*US*) bon *m* de nourriture (*pour indigents*).
foodstuffs ['fu:dstʌfs] *npl* denrées *fpl* alimentaires.
fool [fu:l] *n* idiot/e; (*HIST*: *of king*) bouffon *m*, fou *m*; (*CULIN*) purée *f* de fruits à la crème

♦ *vt* berner, duper ♦ *vi* (*also*: ~ **around**) faire l'idiot *or* l'imbécile; **to make a ~ of sb** (*ridicule*) ridiculiser qn; (*trick*) avoir *or* duper qn; **to make a ~ of o.s.** se couvrir de ridicule; **you can't ~ me** vous (ne) me la ferez pas, on (ne) me la fait pas.
►**fool about, fool around** *vi* (*pej*: *waste time*) traînailler, glandouiller; (: *behave foolishly*) faire l'imbécile.
foolhardy ['fuːlhɑːdɪ] *adj* téméraire, imprudent(e).
foolish ['fuːlɪʃ] *adj* idiot(e), stupide; (*rash*) imprudent(e).
foolishly ['fuːlɪʃlɪ] *adv* stupidement.
foolishness ['fuːlɪʃnɪs] *n* idiotie *f*, stupidité *f*.
foolproof ['fuːlpruːf] *adj* (*plan etc*) infaillible.
foolscap ['fuːlskæp] *n* ≈ papier *m* ministre.
foot [fut] *n* (*pl*: **feet**) pied *m*; (*measure*) pied; (*of animal*) patte *f* ♦ *vt* (*bill*) casquer, payer; **on ~** à pied; **to find one's feet** (*fig*) s'acclimater; **to put one's ~ down** (*AUT*) appuyer sur le champignon; (*say no*) s'imposer.
footage ['futɪdʒ] *n* (*CINE*: *length*) ≈ métrage *m*; (: *material*) séquences *fpl*.
foot and mouth (disease) *n* fièvre aphteuse.
football ['futbɔːl] *n* ballon *m* (de football); (*sport*: *BRIT*) football *m*, foot *m*, (: *US*) football américain.
footballer ['futbɔːlə*] *n* (*BRIT*) = **football player**.
football ground *n* terrain *m* de football.
football match *n* (*BRIT*) match *m* de foot(ball).
football player *n* footballeur *m*, joueur *m* de football.
football pools *npl* (*BRIT*) ≈ loto *m* sportif, ≈ pronostics *mpl* (sur les matchs de football); *voir encadré*.

FOOTBALL POOLS

Les **football pools** *- ou plus familièrement les "***pools***" - sont une sorte de loto sportif britannique où l'on parie sur les matches de football qui se jouent tous les samedis. L'expression consacrée en anglais est "to do the pools". Les parieurs envoient à l'avance les fiches qu'ils ont complétées à l'organisme qui gère les paris et ils attendent les résultats, qui sont annoncés à 17 h le samedi. Les sommes gagnées se comptent parfois en milliers (ou même en millions) de livres sterling.*

footbridge ['futbrɪdʒ] *n* passerelle *f*.
foothills ['futhɪlz] *npl* contreforts *mpl*.
foothold ['futhəuld] *n* prise *f* (de pied).
footing ['futɪŋ] *n* (*fig*) position *f*; **to lose one's ~** perdre pied; **on an equal ~** sur pied d'égalité.
footlights ['futlaɪts] *npl* rampe *f*.
footman ['futmən] *n* laquais *m*.
footnote ['futnəut] *n* note *f* (en bas de page).
footpath ['futpɑːθ] *n* sentier *m*; (*in street*) trottoir *m*.
footprint ['futprɪnt] *n* trace *f* (de pied).
footrest ['futrɛst] *n* marchepied *m*.
footsie ['futsɪ] *n* (*col*): **to play ~ with sb** faire du pied à qn.
footsore ['futsɔː*] *adj*: **to be ~** avoir mal aux pieds.
footstep ['futstɛp] *n* pas *m*.
footwear ['futwɛə*] *n* chaussure(s) *f(pl)*.
FOR *abbr* (= *free on rail*) franco wagon.

KEYWORD

for [fɔː*] *prep* **1** (*indicating destination, intention, purpose*) pour; **the train ~ London** le train pour *or* (à destination) de Londres; **he went ~ the paper** il est allé chercher le journal; **it's time ~ lunch** c'est l'heure du déjeuner; **what's it ~?** ça sert à quoi?; **what ~?** (*why*) pourquoi?; (*to what end*) pour quoi faire?, à quoi bon?; **~ sale** à vendre
2 (*on behalf of, representing*) pour; **the MP ~ Hove** le député de Hove; **to work ~ sb/sth** travailler pour qn/qch; **G ~ George** G comme Georges
3 (*because of*) pour; **~ this reason** pour cette raison; **~ fear of being criticized** de peur d'être critiqué
4 (*with regard to*) pour; **it's cold ~ July** il fait froid pour juillet; **a gift ~ languages** un don pour les langues
5 (*in exchange for*): **I sold it ~ £5** je l'ai vendu 5 livres; **to pay 50 pence ~ a ticket** payer un billet 50 pence
6 (*in favour of*) pour; **are you ~ or against us?** êtes-vous pour ou contre nous?
7 (*referring to distance*) pendant, sur; **there are roadworks ~ 5 km** il y a des travaux sur 5 km; **we walked ~ miles** nous avons marché pendant des kilomètres
8 (*referring to time*) pendant; depuis; pour; **he was away ~ 2 years** il a été absent pendant 2 ans; **she will be away ~ a month** elle sera absente (pendant) un mois; **I have known her ~ years** je la connais depuis des années; **can you do it ~ tomorrow?** est-ce que tu peux le faire pour demain?
9 (*with infinitive clauses*): **it is not ~ me to decide** ce n'est pas à moi de décider; **it would be best ~ you to leave** le mieux serait que vous partiez; **there is still time ~ you to do it** vous avez encore le temps de le faire; **~ this to be possible ...** pour que cela soit possible ...
10 (*in spite of*): **~ all that** malgré cela, néanmoins; **~ all his work/efforts** malgré tout son travail/tous ses efforts; **~ all his complaints, he's very fond of her** il a beau se plaindre, il l'aime beaucoup
♦ *conj* (*since, as*: *rather formal*) car.

forage ['fɔrɪdʒ] *n* fourrage *m* ♦ *vi* fourrager, fouiller.
forage cap *n* calot *m*.
foray ['fɔreɪ] *n* incursion *f*.
forbad(e) [fə'bæd] *pt of* **forbid**.
forbearing [fɔː'bɛərɪŋ] *adj* patient(e), tolérant(e).
forbid, *pt* **forbad(e),** *pp* **forbidden** [fə'bɪd, -'bæd, -'bɪdn] *vt* défendre, interdire; **to ~ sb to do** défendre *or* interdire à qn de faire.
forbidden [fə'bɪdn] *adj* défendu(e).
forbidding [fə'bɪdɪŋ] *adj* d'aspect *or* d'allure sévère *or* sombre.
force [fɔːs] *n* force *f* ♦ *vt* forcer; **the F~s** *npl* (*BRIT*) l'armée *f*; **to ~ sb to do sth** forcer qn à faire qch; **in ~** en force; **to come into ~** entrer en vigueur; **a ~ 5 wind** un vent de force 5; **the sales ~** (*COMM*) la force de vente; **to join ~s** unir ses forces.
►**force back** *vt* (*crowd, enemy*) repousser; (*tears*) refouler.
►**force down** *vt* (*food*) se forcer à manger.
forced [fɔːst] *adj* forcé(e).
force-feed ['fɔːsfiːd] *vt* nourrir de force.
forceful ['fɔːsful] *adj* énergique, volontaire.
forcemeat ['fɔːsmiːt] *n* (*BRIT CULIN*) farce *f*.
forceps ['fɔːsɛps] *npl* forceps *m*.
forcibly ['fɔːsəblɪ] *adv* par la force, de force; (*vigorously*) énergiquement.
ford [fɔːd] *n* gué *m* ♦ *vt* passer à gué.
fore [fɔː*] *n*: **to the ~** en évidence.
forearm ['fɔːrɑːm] *n* avant-bras *m inv*.
forebear ['fɔːbɛə*] *n* ancêtre *m*.
foreboding [fɔː'bəudɪŋ] *n* pressentiment *m*.
forecast ['fɔːkɑːst] *n* prévision *f*; (*also*: **weather ~**) prévisions météorologiques, météo *f* ♦ *vt* (*irreg: like* **cast**) prévoir.
foreclose [fɔː'kləuz] *vt* (*LAW*: *also*: **~ on**) saisir.
foreclosure [fɔː'kləuʒə*] *n* saisie *f* du bien hypothéqué.
forecourt ['fɔːkɔːt] *n* (*of garage*) devant *m*.
forefathers ['fɔːfɑːðəz] *npl* ancêtres *mpl*.
forefinger ['fɔːfɪŋgə*] *n* index *m*.
forefront ['fɔːfrʌnt] *n*: **in the ~ of** au premier rang *or* plan de.
forego, *pt* **forewent,** *pp* **foregone** [fɔː'gəu, -'wɛnt, -'gɔn] *vt* renoncer à.
foregoing ['fɔːgəuɪŋ] *adj* susmentionné(e) ♦ *n*: **the ~** ce qui précède.
foregone ['fɔːgɔn] *adj*: **it's a ~ conclusion** c'est à prévoir, c'est couru d'avance.
foreground ['fɔːgraund] *n* premier plan ♦ *cpd* (*COMPUT*) prioritaire.
forehand ['fɔːhænd] *n* (*TENNIS*) coup droit.
forehead ['fɔrɪd] *n* front *m*.
foreign ['fɔrɪn] *adj* étranger(ère); (*trade*) extérieur(e).
foreign body *n* corps étranger.
foreign currency *n* devises étrangères.
foreigner ['fɔrɪnə*] *n* étranger/ère.
foreign exchange *n* (*system*) change *m*; (*money*) devises *fpl*.
foreign exchange market *n* marché *m* des devises.
foreign exchange rate *n* cours *m* des devises.
foreign investment *n* investissement *m* à l'étranger.
Foreign Office *n* (*BRIT*) ministère *m* des Affaires étrangères.
foreign secretary *n* (*BRIT*) ministre *m* des Affaires étrangères.
foreleg ['fɔːlɛg] *n* patte *f* de devant; jambe antérieure.
foreman ['fɔːmən] *n* contremaître *m*; (*LAW*: *of jury*) président *m* (du jury).
foremost ['fɔːməust] *adj* le(la) plus en vue; premier(ière) ♦ *adv*: **first and ~** avant tout, tout d'abord.
forename ['fɔːneɪm] *n* prénom *m*.
forensic [fə'rɛnsɪk] *adj*: **~ medicine** médecine légale; **~ expert** expert *m* de la police, expert légiste.
foreplay ['fɔːpleɪ] *n* stimulation *f* érotique, prélude *m*.
forerunner ['fɔːrʌnə*] *n* précurseur *m*.
foresee, *pt* **foresaw,** *pp* **foreseen** [fɔː'siː, -'sɔː, -'siːn] *vt* prévoir.
foreseeable [fɔː'siːəbl] *adj* prévisible.
foreshadow [fɔː'ʃædəu] *vt* présager, annoncer, laisser prévoir.
foreshorten [fɔː'ʃɔːtn] *vt* (*figure, scene*) réduire, faire en raccourci.
foresight ['fɔːsaɪt] *n* prévoyance *f*.
foreskin ['fɔːskɪn] *n* (*ANAT*) prépuce *m*.
forest ['fɔrɪst] *n* forêt *f*.
forestall [fɔː'stɔːl] *vt* devancer.
forestry ['fɔrɪstrɪ] *n* sylviculture *f*.
foretaste ['fɔːteɪst] *n* avant-goût *m*.
foretell, *pt, pp* **foretold** [fɔː'tɛl, -'təuld] *vt* prédire.
forethought ['fɔːθɔːt] *n* prévoyance *f*.
forever [fə'rɛvə*] *adv* pour toujours; (*fig*) continuellement.
forewarn [fɔː'wɔːn] *vt* avertir.
forewent [fɔː'wɛnt] *pt of* **forego**.
foreword ['fɔːwəːd] *n* avant-propos *m inv*.
forfeit ['fɔːfɪt] *n* prix *m*, rançon *f* ♦ *vt* perdre; (*one's life, health*) payer de.
forgave [fə'geɪv] *pt of* **forgive**.
forge [fɔːdʒ] *n* forge *f* ♦ *vt* (*signature*) contrefaire; (*wrought iron*) forger; **to ~ documents/a will** fabriquer de faux papiers/un faux testament; **to ~ money** (*BRIT*) fabriquer de la fausse monnaie.
►**forge ahead** *vi* pousser de l'avant, prendre de l'avance.
forger ['fɔːdʒə*] *n* faussaire *m*.
forgery ['fɔːdʒərɪ] *n* faux *m*, contrefaçon *f*.
forget, *pt* **forgot,** *pp* **forgotten** [fə'gɛt, -'gɔt, -'gɔtn] *vt, vi* oublier.
forgetful [fə'gɛtful] *adj* distrait(e), étourdi(e); **~ of** oublieux(euse) de.
forgetfulness [fə'gɛtfulnɪs] *n* tendance *f* aux

oublis; (*oblivion*) oubli *m*.
forget-me-not [fə'gɛtmɪnɔt] *n* myosotis *m*.
forgive, *pt* **forgave,** *pp* **forgiven** [fə'gɪv, -'geɪv, -'gɪvn] *vt* pardonner; **to ~ sb for sth/for doing sth** pardonner qch à qn/à qn de faire qch.
forgiveness [fə'gɪvnɪs] *n* pardon *m*.
forgiving [fə'gɪvɪŋ] *adj* indulgent(e).
forgo, *pt* **forwent,** *pp* **forgone** [fɔː'gəu, -'wɛnt, -'gɔn] *vt* = **forego**.
forgot [fə'gɔt] *pt of* **forget**.
forgotten [fə'gɔtn] *pp of* **forget**.
fork [fɔːk] *n* (*for eating*) fourchette *f*; (*for gardening*) fourche *f*; (*of roads*) bifurcation *f*; (*of railways*) embranchement *m* ♦ *vi* (*road*) bifurquer.
►**fork out** (*col*: *pay*) *vt* allonger, se fendre de ♦ *vi* casquer.
forked [fɔːkt] *adj* (*lightning*) en zigzags, ramifié(e).
fork-lift truck ['fɔːklɪft-] *n* chariot élévateur.
forlorn [fə'lɔːn] *adj* abandonné(e), délaissé(e); (*hope, attempt*) désespéré(e).
form [fɔːm] *n* forme *f*; (*SCOL*) classe *f*; (*questionnaire*) formulaire *m* ♦ *vt* former; **in the ~ of** sous forme de; **to ~ part of sth** faire partie de qch; **to be in good ~** (*SPORT, fig*) être en forme; **in top ~** en pleine forme.
formal ['fɔːməl] *adj* (*offer, receipt*) en bonne et due forme; (*person*) cérémonieux(euse), à cheval sur les convenances; (*occasion, dinner*) officiel(le); (*ART, PHILOSOPHY*) formel(le); **~ dress** tenue *f* de cérémonie; (*evening dress*) tenue de soirée.
formality [fɔː'mælɪtɪ] *n* formalité *f*, cérémonie(s) *f(pl)*.
formalize ['fɔːməlaɪz] *vt* officialiser.
formally ['fɔːməlɪ] *adv* officiellement; formellement; cérémonieusement.
format ['fɔːmæt] *n* format *m* ♦ *vt* (*COMPUT*) formater.
formation [fɔː'meɪʃən] *n* formation *f*.
formative ['fɔːmətɪv] *adj*: **~ years** années *fpl* d'apprentissage (*fig*) *or* de formation (*d'un enfant, d'un adolescent*).
former ['fɔːmə*] *adj* ancien(ne) (*before n*), précédent(e); **the ~ ... the latter** le premier ... le second, celui-là ... celui-ci; **the ~ president** l'ex-président; **the ~ Yugoslavia/Soviet Union** l'ex Yougoslavie/Union Soviétique.
formerly ['fɔːməlɪ] *adv* autrefois.
form feed *n* (*on printer*) alimentation *f* en feuilles.
formidable ['fɔːmɪdəbl] *adj* redoutable.
formula ['fɔːmjulə] *n* formule *f*; **F~ One** (*AUT*) Formule un.
formulate ['fɔːmjuleɪt] *vt* formuler.
fornicate ['fɔːnɪkeɪt] *vi* forniquer.
forsake, *pt* **forsook,** *pp* **forsaken** [fə'seɪk, -'suk, -'seɪkən] *vt* abandonner.
fort [fɔːt] *n* fort *m*; **to hold the ~** (*fig*) assurer la permanence.
forte ['fɔːtɪ] *n* (point) fort *m*.
forth [fɔːθ] *adv* en avant; **to go back and ~** aller et venir; **and so ~** et ainsi de suite.
forthcoming [fɔːθ'kʌmɪŋ] *adj* qui va paraître *or* avoir lieu prochainement; (*character*) ouvert(e), communicatif(ive).
forthright ['fɔːθraɪt] *adj* franc(franche), direct(e).
forthwith ['fɔːθ'wɪθ] *adv* sur le champ.
fortieth ['fɔːtɪɪθ] *num* quarantième.
fortification [fɔːtɪfɪ'keɪʃən] *n* fortification *f*.
fortified wine ['fɔːtɪfaɪd-] *n* vin liquoreux *or* de liqueur.
fortify ['fɔːtɪfaɪ] *vt* fortifier.
fortitude ['fɔːtɪtjuːd] *n* courage *m*, force *f* d'âme.
fortnight ['fɔːtnaɪt] *n* (*BRIT*) quinzaine *f*, quinze jours *mpl*; **it's a ~ since ...** il y a quinze jours que ....
fortnightly ['fɔːtnaɪtlɪ] *adj* bimensuel(le) ♦ *adv* tous les quinze jours.
FORTRAN ['fɔːtræn] *n* FORTRAN *m*.
fortress ['fɔːtrɪs] *n* forteresse *f*.
fortuitous [fɔː'tjuːɪtəs] *adj* fortuit(e).
fortunate ['fɔːtʃənɪt] *adj*: **to be ~** avoir de la chance; **it is ~ that** c'est une chance que, il est heureux que.
fortunately ['fɔːtʃənɪtlɪ] *adv* heureusement, par bonheur.
fortune ['fɔːtʃən] *n* chance *f*; (*wealth*) fortune *f*; **to make a ~** faire fortune.
fortuneteller ['fɔːtʃəntɛlə*] *n* diseuse *f* de bonne aventure.
forty ['fɔːtɪ] *num* quarante.
forum ['fɔːrəm] *n* forum *m*, tribune *f*.
forward ['fɔːwəd] *adj* (*movement, position*) en avant, vers l'avant; (*not shy*) effronté(e); (*COMM*: *delivery, sales, exchange*) à terme ♦ *adv* en avant ♦ *n* (*SPORT*) avant *m* ♦ *vt* (*letter*) faire suivre; (*parcel, goods*) expédier; (*fig*) promouvoir, contribuer au développement *or* à l'avancement de; **to move ~** avancer; **"please ~"** "prière de faire suivre"; **~ planning** planification *f* à long terme.
forwards ['fɔːwədz] *adv* en avant.
forwent [fɔː'wɛnt] *pt of* **forgo**.
fossil ['fɔsl] *adj*, *n* fossile (*m*); **~ fuel** combustible *m* fossile.
foster ['fɔstə*] *vt* encourager, favoriser.
foster brother *n* frère adoptif; frère de lait.
foster child *n* enfant adopté.
foster mother *n* mère adoptive; mère nourricière.
fought [fɔːt] *pt*, *pp of* **fight**.
foul [faul] *adj* (*weather, smell, food*) infect(e); (*language*) ordurier(ière); (*deed*) infâme ♦ *n* (*FOOTBALL*) faute *f* ♦ *vt* salir, encrasser; (*football player*) commettre une faute sur; (*entangle: anchor, propeller*) emmêler.
foul play *n* (*SPORT*) jeu déloyal; **~ is not suspected** la mort (*or* l'incendie *etc*) n'a pas de causes suspectes, on écarte l'hypothèse

d'un meurtre (*or* d'un acte criminel).

found [faund] *pt, pp of* **find** ♦ *vt (establish)* fonder.

foundation [faun'deɪʃən] *n (act)* fondation *f*; *(base)* fondement *m*; *(also*: ~ **cream)** fond *m* de teint; ~**s** *npl (of building)* fondations *fpl*; **to lay the ~s** *(fig)* poser les fondements.

foundation stone *n* première pierre.

founder ['faundə*] *n* fondateur *m* ♦ *vi* couler, sombrer.

founding ['faundɪŋ] *adj*: ~ **fathers** *(esp US)* pères *mpl* fondateurs; ~ **member** membre *m* fondateur.

foundry ['faundrɪ] *n* fonderie *f*.

fount [faunt] *n* source *f*; *(TYP)* fonte *f*.

fountain ['fauntɪn] *n* fontaine *f*.

fountain pen *n* stylo *m* (à encre).

four [fɔː*] *num* quatre; **on all ~s** à quatre pattes.

four-letter word ['fɔːlɛtə-] *n* obscénité *f*, gros mot.

four-poster ['fɔː'pəustə*] *n (also*: ~ **bed)** lit *m* à baldaquin.

foursome ['fɔːsəm] *n* partie *f* à quatre; sortie *f* à quatre.

fourteen ['fɔː'tiːn] *num* quatorze.

fourth ['fɔːθ] *num* quatrième ♦ *n (AUT*: *also*: ~ **gear)** quatrième *f*.

four-wheel drive ['fɔːwiːl-] *n (AUT)*: **with** ~ à quatre roues motrices.

fowl [faul] *n* volaille *f*.

fox [fɔks] *n* renard *m* ♦ *vt* mystifier.

fox fur *n* renard *m*.

foxglove ['fɔksglʌv] *n (BOT)* digitale *f*.

fox-hunting ['fɔkshʌntɪŋ] *n* chasse *f* au renard.

foyer ['fɔɪeɪ] *n* vestibule *m*; *(THEAT)* foyer *m*.

FP *n abbr (BRIT) = former pupil*; *(US) = fireplug*.

FPA *n abbr (BRIT) = Family Planning Association*.

Fr. *abbr (= father*: *REL)* P; *(= friar)* F.

fr. *abbr (= franc)* F.

fracas ['frækɑː] *n* bagarre *f*.

fraction ['frækʃən] *n* fraction *f*.

fractionally ['frækʃnəlɪ] *adv*: ~ **smaller** *etc* un poil plus petit *etc*.

fractious ['frækʃəs] *adj* grincheux(euse).

fracture ['fræktʃə*] *n* fracture *f* ♦ *vt* fracturer.

fragile ['frædʒaɪl] *adj* fragile.

fragment ['frægmənt] *n* fragment *m*.

fragmentary ['frægməntərɪ] *adj* fragmentaire.

fragrance ['freɪgrəns] *n* parfum *m*.

fragrant ['freɪgrənt] *adj* parfumé(e), odorant(e).

frail [freɪl] *adj* fragile, délicat(e).

frame [freɪm] *n (of building)* charpente *f*; *(of human, animal)* charpente, ossature *f*; *(of picture)* cadre *m*; *(of door, window)* encadrement *m*, chambranle *m*; *(of spectacles*: *also*: ~**s)** monture *f* ♦ *vt* encadrer; *(theory, plan)* construire, élaborer; **to ~ sb** *(col)* monter un coup contre qn; ~ **of mind** disposition *f* d'esprit.

framework ['freɪmwəːk] *n* structure *f*.

France [frɑːns] *n* la France; **in** ~ en France.

franchise ['fræntʃaɪz] *n (POL)* droit *m* de vote; *(COMM)* franchise *f*.

franchisee [fræntʃaɪ'ziː] *n* franchisé *m*.

franchiser ['fræntʃaɪzə*] *n* franchiseur *m*.

frank [fræŋk] *adj* franc(franche) ♦ *vt (letter)* affranchir.

Frankfurt ['fræŋkfəːt] *n* Francfort.

franking machine ['fræŋkɪŋ-] *n* machine *f* à affranchir.

frankly ['fræŋklɪ] *adv* franchement.

frankness ['fræŋknɪs] *n* franchise *f*.

frantic ['fræntɪk] *adj* frénétique; *(desperate: need, desire)* effréné(e); *(person)* hors de soi.

frantically ['fræntɪklɪ] *adv* frénétiquement.

fraternal [frə'təːnl] *adj* fraternel(le).

fraternity [frə'təːnɪtɪ] *n (club)* communauté *f*, confrérie *f*; *(spirit)* fraternité *f*.

fraternize ['frætənaɪz] *vi* fraterniser.

fraud [frɔːd] *n* supercherie *f*, fraude *f*, tromperie *f*; *(person)* imposteur *m*.

fraudulent ['frɔːdjulənt] *adj* frauduleux(euse).

fraught [frɔːt] *adj (tense: person)* très tendu(e); *(: situation)* pénible; ~ **with** *(difficulties etc)* chargé(e) de, plein(e) de.

fray [freɪ] *n* bagarre *f*; *(MIL)* combat *m* ♦ *vt* effilocher ♦ *vi* s'effilocher; **tempers were ~ed** les gens commençaient à s'énerver; **her nerves were ~ed** elle était à bout de nerfs.

FRB *n abbr (US)* = **Federal Reserve Board**.

FRCM *n abbr (BRIT) = Fellow of the Royal College of Music*.

FRCO *n abbr (BRIT) = Fellow of the Royal College of Organists*.

FRCP *n abbr (BRIT) = Fellow of the Royal College of Physicians*.

FRCS *n abbr (BRIT) = Fellow of the Royal College of Surgeons*.

freak [friːk] *n (also cpd)* phénomène *m*, *créature ou événement exceptionnel par sa rareté, son caractère d'anomalie*; *(pej: fanatic)*: **health** ~ fana *m/f or* obsédé/e de l'alimentation saine (*or* de la forme physique).

▸**freak out** *vi (col: drop out)* se marginaliser; *(: on drugs)* se défoncer.

freakish ['friːkɪʃ] *adj* insolite; anormal(e).

freckle ['frɛkl] *n* tache *f* de rousseur.

free [friː] *adj* libre; *(gratis)* gratuit(e); *(liberal)* généreux(euse), large ♦ *vt (prisoner etc)* libérer; *(jammed object or person)* dégager; **to give sb a ~ hand** donner carte blanche à qn; ~ **and easy** sans façon, décontracté(e); **admission** ~ entrée libre; ~ **(of charge)** *adv* gratuitement.

freebie ['friːbɪ] *n (col)*: **it's a** ~ c'est gratuit.

freedom ['friːdəm] *n* liberté *f*.

freedom fighter *n* combattant *m* de la liberté.

free enterprise *n* libre entreprise *f*.

Freefone ['friːfəun] *n* ® numéro vert.

free-for-all ['friːfərɔːl] *n* mêlée générale.
free gift *n* prime *f*.
freehold ['friːhəuld] *n* propriété foncière libre.
free kick *n* (*SPORT*) coup franc.
freelance ['friːlɑːns] *adj* (*journalist etc*) indépendant(e); (*work*) à la pige, à la tâche.
freeloader ['friːləudə*] *n* (*pej*) parasite *m*.
freely ['friːlɪ] *adv* librement; (*liberally*) libéralement.
free-market economy [friː'mɑːkɪt-] *n* économie *f* de marché.
freemason ['friːmeɪsn] *n* franc-maçon *m*.
freemasonry ['friːmeɪsnrɪ] *n* franc-maçonnerie *f*.
freepost ['friːpəust] *n* franchise postale.
free-range ['friː'reɪndʒ] *adj* (*eggs*) de ferme.
free sample *n* échantillon gratuit.
free speech *n* liberté *f* d'expression.
free trade *n* libre-échange *m*.
freeway ['friːweɪ] *n* (*US*) autoroute *f*.
freewheel [friː'wiːl] *vi* descendre en roue libre.
freewheeling [friː'wiːlɪŋ] *adj* indépendant(e), libre.
free will *n* libre arbitre *m*; **of one's own ~** de son plein gré.
freeze [friːz] *vb* (*pt* **froze**, *pp* **frozen** [frəuz, 'frəuzn]) *vi* geler ♦ *vt* geler; (*food*) congeler; (*prices, salaries*) bloquer, geler ♦ *n* gel *m*; blocage *m*.
▸**freeze over** *vi* (*river*) geler; (*windscreen*) se couvrir de givre *or* de glace.
▸**freeze up** *vi* geler.
freeze-dried ['friːzdraɪd] *adj* lyophilisé(e).
freezer ['friːzə*] *n* congélateur *m*.
freezing ['friːzɪŋ] *adj*: **~ (cold)** (*room etc*) glacial(e); (*person, hands*) gelé(e), glacé(e) ♦ *n*: **3 degrees below ~** 3 degrés au-dessous de zéro.
freezing point *n* point *m* de congélation.
freight [freɪt] *n* (*goods*) fret *m*, cargaison *f*; (*money charged*) fret, prix *m* du transport; **~ forward** port dû; **~ inward** port payé par le destinataire.
freighter ['freɪtə*] *n* (*NAUT*) cargo *m*.
freight forwarder [-fɔːwədə*] *n* transitaire *m*.
freight train *n* (*US*) train *m* de marchandises.
French [frɛntʃ] *adj* français(e) ♦ *n* (*LING*) français *m*; **the ~** *npl* les Français.
French bean *n* (*BRIT*) haricot vert.
French bread *n* pain *m* (*français*).
French Canadian *adj* canadien(ne) français(e) ♦ *n* Canadien/ne français(e).
French dressing *n* (*CULIN*) vinaigrette *f*.
French fried potatoes, (*US*) **French fries** *npl* (pommes de terre *fpl*) frites *fpl*.
French Guiana [-gaɪ'ænə] *n* Guyane française.
French loaf *n* ≈ pain *m*, ≈ parisien *m*.
Frenchman ['frɛntʃmən] *n* Français *m*.
French Riviera *n*: **the ~** la Côte d'Azur.
French stick *n* ≈ baguette *f*.
French window *n* porte-fenêtre *f*.
Frenchwoman ['frɛntʃwumən] *n* Française *f*.
frenetic [frə'nɛtɪk] *adj* frénétique.
frenzy ['frɛnzɪ] *n* frénésie *f*.
frequency ['friːkwənsɪ] *n* fréquence *f*.
frequency modulation (FM) *n* modulation *f* de fréquence (FM, MF).
frequent *adj* ['friːkwənt] fréquent(e) ♦ *vt* [frɪ'kwɛnt] fréquenter.
frequently ['friːkwəntlɪ] *adv* fréquemment.
fresco ['frɛskəu] *n* fresque *f*.
fresh [frɛʃ] *adj* frais(fraîche); (*new*) nouveau(nouvelle); (*cheeky*) familier(ière), culotté(e); **to make a ~ start** prendre un nouveau départ.
freshen ['frɛʃən] *vi* (*wind, air*) fraîchir.
▸**freshen up** *vi* faire un brin de toilette.
freshener ['frɛʃnə*] *n*: **skin ~** astringent *m*; **air ~** désodorisant *m*.
fresher ['frɛʃə*] *n* (*BRIT SCOL*: *col*) = **freshman**.
freshly ['frɛʃlɪ] *adv* nouvellement, récemment.
freshman ['frɛʃmən] *n* (*SCOL*) bizuth *m*, étudiant/e de première année.
freshness ['frɛʃnɪs] *n* fraîcheur *f*.
freshwater ['frɛʃwɔːtə*] *adj* (*fish*) d'eau douce.
fret [frɛt] *vi* s'agiter, se tracasser.
fretful ['frɛtful] *adj* (*child*) grincheux(euse).
Freudian ['frɔɪdɪən] *adj* freudien(ne); **~ slip** lapsus *m*.
FRG *n abbr* (= *Federal Republic of Germany*) RFA *f*.
Fri. *abbr* (= *Friday*) ve.
friar ['fraɪə*] *n* moine *m*, frère *m*.
friction ['frɪkʃən] *n* friction *f*, frottement *m*.
friction feed *n* (*on printer*) entraînement *m* par friction.
Friday ['fraɪdɪ] *n* vendredi *m*; *for phrases see also* **Tuesday**.
fridge [frɪdʒ] *n* (*BRIT*) frigo *m*, frigidaire *m* ®.
fridge-freezer ['frɪdʒ'friːzə*] *n* réfrigérateur-congélateur *m*.
fried [fraɪd] *pt, pp of* **fry** ♦ *adj* frit(e); **~ egg** œuf *m* sur le plat.
friend [frɛnd] *n* ami/e; **to make ~s with** se lier (d'amitié) avec.
friendliness ['frɛndlɪnɪs] *n* attitude amicale.
friendly ['frɛndlɪ] *adj* amical(e); (*kind*) sympathique, gentil(le); (*POL*: *country, government*) ami(e) ♦ *n* (*also*: **~ match**) match amical; **to be ~ with** être ami(e) avec; **to be ~ to** être bien disposé(e) à l'égard de.
friendly fire *n*: **they were killed by ~** ils sont morts sous les tirs de leur propre camp.
friendly society *n* société *f* mutualiste.
friendship ['frɛndʃɪp] *n* amitié *f*.
frieze [friːz] *n* frise *f*, bordure *f*.
frigate ['frɪgɪt] *n* (*NAUT*: *modern*) frégate *f*.
fright [fraɪt] *n* peur *f*, effroi *m*; **to take ~** prendre peur, s'effrayer; **she looks a ~** elle a l'air d'un épouvantail.

frighten ['fraɪtn] *vt* effrayer, faire peur à.
▸frighten away, frighten off *vt* (*birds, children etc*) faire fuir, effaroucher.
frightened ['fraɪtnd] *adj*: **to be ~ (of)** avoir peur (de).
frightening ['fraɪtnɪŋ] *adj* effrayant(e).
frightful ['fraɪtful] *adj* affreux(euse).
frightfully ['fraɪtfəlɪ] *adv* affreusement.
frigidity [frɪ'dʒɪdɪtɪ] *n* frigidité *f*.
frill [frɪl] *n* (*of dress*) volant *m*; (*of shirt*) jabot *m*; **without ~s** (*fig*) sans manières.
frilly ['frɪlɪ] *adj* à fanfreluches.
fringe [frɪndʒ] *n* frange *f*; (*edge: of forest etc*) bordure *f*; (*fig*): **on the ~** en marge.
fringe benefits *npl* avantages sociaux *or* en nature.
fringe theatre *n* théâtre *m* d'avant-garde.
Frisbee ['frɪzbɪ] *n* ® Frisbee *m* ®.
frisk [frɪsk] *vt* fouiller.
frisky ['frɪskɪ] *adj* vif(vive), sémillant(e).
fritter ['frɪtə*] *n* beignet *m*.
▸fritter away *vt* gaspiller.
frivolity [frɪ'vɔlɪtɪ] *n* frivolité *f*.
frivolous ['frɪvələs] *adj* frivole.
frizzy ['frɪzɪ] *adj* crépu(e).
fro [frəu] *see* **to**.
frock [frɔk] *n* robe *f*.
frog [frɔg] *n* grenouille *f*; **to have a ~ in one's throat** avoir un chat dans la gorge.
frogman ['frɔgmən] *n* homme-grenouille *m*.
frogmarch ['frɔgmɑːtʃ] *vt* (*BRIT*): **to ~ sb in/out** faire entrer/sortir qn de force.
frolic ['frɔlɪk] *n* ébats *mpl* ♦ *vi* folâtrer, batifoler.

KEYWORD

from [frɔm] *prep* **1** (*indicating starting place, origin etc*) de; **where do you come ~?, where are you ~?** d'où venez-vous?; **where has he come ~?** d'où arrive-t-il?; **~ London to Paris** de Londres à Paris; **a letter ~ my sister** une lettre de ma sœur; **to drink ~ the bottle** boire à (même) la bouteille
2 (*indicating time*) (à partir) de; **~ one o'clock to** *or* **until** *or* **till two** d'une heure à deux heures; **~ January (on)** à partir de janvier
3 (*indicating distance*) de; **the hotel is one kilometre ~ the beach** l'hôtel est à un kilomètre de la plage
4 (*indicating price, number etc*) de; **the interest rate was increased ~ 9% to 10%** le taux d'intérêt est passé de 9 à 10%
5 (*indicating difference*) de; **he can't tell red ~ green** il ne peut pas distinguer le rouge du vert
6 (*because of*): **~ what he says** d'après ce qu'il dit; **weak ~ hunger** affaibli par la faim.

frond [frɔnd] *n* fronde *f*.
front [frʌnt] *n* (*of house, dress*) devant *m*; (*of coach, train*) avant *m*; (*of book*) couverture *f*; (*promenade*: *also*: **sea ~**) bord *m* de mer; (*MIL, POL, METEOROLOGY*) front *m*; (*fig: appearances*) contenance *f*, façade *f* ♦ *adj* de devant; premier(ière) ♦ *vi*: **to ~ onto sth** donner sur qch; **in ~ (of)** devant.
frontage ['frʌntɪdʒ] *n* façade *f*; (*of shop*) devanture *f*.
frontal ['frʌntl] *adj* frontal(e).
front bench *n* (*BRIT POL*) voir encadré.

FRONT BENCH

Le **front bench** *est le banc du gouvernement, placé à la droite du "Speaker", ou celui du cabinet fantôme, placé à sa gauche. Ils se font face dans l'enceinte de la Chambre des communes. Par extension,* **front bench** *désigne les dirigeants des groupes parlementaires de la majorité et de l'opposition, qui sont appelés "frontbenchers" par opposition aux autres députés qui sont appelés "backbenchers".*

front desk *n* (*US*: *in hotel, at doctor's*) réception *f*.
front door *n* porte *f* d'entrée; (*of car*) portière *f* avant.
frontier ['frʌntɪə*] *n* frontière *f*.
frontispiece ['frʌntɪspiːs] *n* frontispice *m*.
front page *n* première page.
front room *n* (*BRIT*) pièce *f* de devant, salon *m*.
front runner *n* (*fig*) favori/te.
front-wheel drive ['frʌntwiːl-] *n* traction *f* avant.
frost [frɔst] *n* gel *m*, gelée *f*; (*also*: **hoar~**) givre *m*.
frostbite ['frɔstbaɪt] *n* gelures *fpl*.
frosted ['frɔstɪd] *adj* (*glass*) dépoli(e); (*esp US*: *cake*) glacé(e).
frosting ['frɔstɪŋ] *n* (*esp US*: *on cake*) glaçage *m*.
frosty ['frɔstɪ] *adj* (*window*) couvert(e) de givre; (*welcome*) glacial(e).
froth [frɔθ] *n* mousse *f*; écume *f*.
frown [fraun] *n* froncement *m* de sourcils ♦ *vi* froncer les sourcils.
▸frown on *vt* (*fig*) désapprouver.
froze [frəuz] *pt of* **freeze**.
frozen ['frəuzn] *pp of* **freeze** ♦ *adj* (*food*) congelé(e); (*COMM*: *assets*) gelé(e).
FRS *n abbr* (*BRIT*: *= Fellow of the Royal Society*) *membre de l'Académie des sciences*; (*US*: *= Federal Reserve System*) *banque centrale américaine*.
frugal ['fruːgl] *adj* frugal(e).
fruit [fruːt] *n* (*pl inv*) fruit *m*.
fruiterer ['fruːtərə*] *n* fruitier *m*, marchand/e de fruits; **~'s (shop)** fruiterie *f*.
fruit fly *n* mouche *f* du vinaigre, drosophile *f*.
fruitful ['fruːtful] *adj* fructueux(euse); (*plant, soil*) fécond(e).
fruition [fruː'ɪʃən] *n*: **to come to ~** se réaliser.

fruit juice *n* jus *m* de fruit.
fruitless ['fru:tlɪs] *adj* (*fig*) vain(e), infructueux(euse).
fruit machine *n* (*BRIT*) machine *f* à sous.
fruit salad *n* salade *f* de fruits.
frump [frʌmp] *n* mocheté *f*.
frustrate [frʌs'treɪt] *vt* frustrer; (*plot, plans*) faire échouer.
frustrated [frʌs'treɪtɪd] *adj* frustré(e).
frustrating [frʌs'treɪtɪŋ] *adj* (*job*) frustrant(e); (*day*) démoralisant(e).
frustration [frʌs'treɪʃən] *n* frustration *f*.
fry, *pt, pp* **fried** [fraɪ, -d] *vt* (faire) frire; **the small** ~ le menu fretin.
frying pan ['fraɪɪŋ-] *n* poêle *f* (à frire).
FT *n abbr* (*BRIT*: = *Financial Times*) *journal financier*.
ft. *abbr* = **foot, feet**.
FTC *n abbr* (*US*) = **Federal Trade Commission**.
FTSE 100 (Share) Index *n abbr* (= *Financial Times Stock Exchange 100 (Share) Index*) indice *m* Footsie, des cent grandes valeurs.
fuchsia ['fju:ʃə] *n* fuchsia *m*.
fuck [fʌk] *vt, vi* (*col!*) baiser (*!*); ~ **off!** fous le camp! (*!*).
fuddled ['fʌdld] *adj* (*muddled*) embrouillé(e), confus(e).
fuddy-duddy ['fʌdɪdʌdɪ] *adj* (*pej*) vieux jeu *inv*, ringard(e).
fudge [fʌdʒ] *n* (*CULIN*) *sorte de confiserie à base de sucre, de beurre et de lait* ♦ *vt* (*issue, problem*) esquiver.
fuel [fjuəl] *n* (*for heating*) combustible *m*; (*for propelling*) carburant *m*.
fuel oil *n* mazout *m*.
fuel pump *n* (*AUT*) pompe *f* d'alimentation.
fuel tank *n* cuve *f* à mazout, citerne *f*; (*in vehicle*) réservoir *m* de *or* à carburant.
fug [fʌg] *n* (*BRIT*) puanteur *f*, odeur *f* de renfermé.
fugitive ['fju:dʒɪtɪv] *n* fugitif/ive.
fulfil, (*US*) **fulfill** [ful'fɪl] *vt* (*function*) remplir; (*order*) exécuter; (*wish, desire*) satisfaire, réaliser.
fulfilled [ful'fɪld] *adj* (*person*) comblé(e), épanoui(e).
fulfil(l)ment [ful'fɪlmənt] *n* (*of wishes*) réalisation *f*.
full [ful] *adj* plein(e); (*details, information*) complet(ète); (*price*) fort(e), normal(e); (*skirt*) ample, large ♦ *adv*: **to know** ~ **well that** savoir fort bien que; ~ **(up)** (*hotel etc*) complet(ète); **I'm** ~ **(up)** j'ai bien mangé; ~ **employment/fare** plein emploi/tarif; **a** ~ **two hours** deux bonnes heures; **at** ~ **speed** à toute vitesse; **in** ~ (*reproduce, quote, pay*) intégralement; (*write name etc*) en toutes lettres.
fullback ['fulbæk] *n* (*RUGBY, FOOTBALL*) arrière *m*.
full-blooded ['ful'blʌdɪd] *adj* (*vigorous*) vigoureux(euse).
full-cream ['ful'kri:m] *adj*: ~ **milk** (*BRIT*) lait entier.
full-grown ['ful'grəun] *adj* arrivé(e) à maturité, adulte.
full-length ['ful'lɛŋθ] *adj* (*portrait*) en pied; ~ **film** long métrage.
full moon *n* pleine lune.
full-scale ['fulskeɪl] *adj* (*model*) grandeur nature *inv*; (*search, retreat*) complet(ète), total(e).
full-sized ['ful'saɪzd] *adj* (*portrait etc*) grandeur nature *inv*.
full stop *n* point *m*.
full-time ['ful'taɪm] *adj* (*work*) à plein temps ♦ *n* (*SPORT*) fin *f* du match.
fully ['fulɪ] *adv* entièrement, complètement; (*at least*): ~ **as big** au moins aussi grand.
fully-fledged ['fulɪ'flɛdʒd] *adj* (*teacher, barrister*) diplômé(e); (*citizen, member*) à part entière.
fulsome ['fulsəm] *adj* (*pej: praise*) excessif(ive); (*: manner*) exagéré(e).
fumble ['fʌmbl] *vi* fouiller, tâtonner ♦ *vt* (*ball*) mal réceptionner, cafouiller.
►**fumble with** *vt fus* tripoter.
fume [fju:m] *vi* rager; ~**s** *npl* vapeurs *fpl*, émanations *fpl*, gaz *mpl*.
fumigate ['fju:mɪgeɪt] *vt* désinfecter (par fumigation).
fun [fʌn] *n* amusement *m*, divertissement *m*; **to have** ~ s'amuser; **for** ~ pour rire; **it's not much** ~ ce n'est pas très drôle *or* amusant; **to make** ~ **of** se moquer de.
function ['fʌŋkʃən] *n* fonction *f*; (*reception, dinner*) cérémonie *f*, soirée officielle ♦ *vi* fonctionner; **to** ~ **as** faire office de.
functional ['fʌŋkʃənl] *adj* fonctionnel(le).
function key *n* (*COMPUT*) touche *f* de fonction.
fund [fʌnd] *n* caisse *f*, fonds *m*; (*source, store*) source *f*, mine *f*; ~**s** *npl* fonds *mpl*.
fundamental [fʌndə'mɛntl] *adj* fondamental(e); ~**s** *npl* principes *mpl* de base.
fundamentalism [fʌndə'mɛntəlɪzəm] *n* intégrisme *m*.
fundamentalist [fʌndə'mɛntəlɪst] intégriste *m/f*.
fundamentally [fʌndə'mɛntəlɪ] *adv* fondamentalement.
funding ['fʌndɪŋ] *n* financement *m*.
fund-raising ['fʌndreɪzɪŋ] *n* collecte *f* de fonds.
funeral ['fju:nərəl] *n* enterrement *m*, obsèques *fpl* (*more formal occasion*).
funeral director *n* entrepreneur *m* des pompes funèbres.
funeral parlour *n* dépôt *m* mortuaire.
funeral service *n* service *m* funèbre.
funereal [fju:'nɪərɪəl] *adj* lugubre, funèbre.
fun fair *n* (*BRIT*) fête (foraine).
fungus, *pl* **fungi** ['fʌŋgəs, -gaɪ] *n* champignon *m*; (*mould*) moisissure *f*.

funicular [fjuːˈnɪkjulə*] *n* (*also*: ~ **railway**) funiculaire *m*.
funky [ˈfʌŋkɪ] *adj* (*music*) funky *inv*; (*col*: *excellent*) super *inv*.
funnel [ˈfʌnl] *n* entonnoir *m*; (*of ship*) cheminée *f*.
funnily [ˈfʌnɪlɪ] *adv* (*see funny*) drôlement; curieusement.
funny [ˈfʌnɪ] *adj* amusant(e), drôle; (*strange*) curieux(euse), bizarre.
funny bone *n endroit sensible du coude.*
fun run *n* course *f* de fond (*pour amateurs*).
fur [fəː*] *n* fourrure *f*; (*BRIT*: *in kettle etc*) (dépôt *m* de) tartre *m*.
fur coat *n* manteau *m* de fourrure.
furious [ˈfjuərɪəs] *adj* furieux(euse); (*effort*) acharné(e); **to be ~ with sb** être dans une fureur noire contre qn.
furiously [ˈfjuərɪəslɪ] *adv* furieusement; avec acharnement.
furl [fəːl] *vt* rouler; (*NAUT*) ferler.
furlong [ˈfəːlɔŋ] *n* = *201.17 m* (*terme d'hippisme*).
furlough [ˈfəːləu] *n* permission *f*, congé *m*.
furnace [ˈfəːnɪs] *n* fourneau *m*.
furnish [ˈfəːnɪʃ] *vt* meubler; (*supply*) fournir; **~ed flat** *or* (*US*) **apartment** meublé *m*.
furnishings [ˈfəːnɪʃɪŋz] *npl* mobilier *m*, articles *mpl* d'ameublement.
furniture [ˈfəːnɪtʃə*] *n* meubles *mpl*, mobilier *m*; **piece of ~** meuble *m*.
furniture polish *n* encaustique *f*.
furore [fjuəˈrɔːrɪ] *n* (*protests*) protestations *fpl*.
furrier [ˈfʌrɪə*] *n* fourreur *m*.
furrow [ˈfʌrəu] *n* sillon *m*.
furry [ˈfəːrɪ] *adj* (*animal*) à fourrure; (*toy*) en peluche.
further [ˈfəːðə*] *adj* supplémentaire, autre; nouveau(nouvelle) ♦ *adv* plus loin; (*more*) davantage; (*moreover*) de plus ♦ *vt* faire avancer *or* progresser, promouvoir; **how much ~ is it?** quelle distance *or* combien reste-t-il à parcourir?; **until ~ notice** jusqu'à nouvel ordre *or* avis; **~ to your letter of ...** (*COMM*) suite à votre lettre du ....
further education *n* enseignement *m* postscolaire (*recyclage, formation professionnelle*).
furthermore [fəːðəˈmɔː*] *adv* de plus, en outre.
furthermost [ˈfəːðəməust] *adj* le(la) plus éloigné(e).
furthest [ˈfəːðɪst] *superlative of* **far**.
furtive [ˈfəːtɪv] *adj* furtif(ive).
furtively [ˈfəːtɪvlɪ] *adv* furtivement.
fury [ˈfjuərɪ] *n* fureur *f*.
fuse, (*US*) **fuze** [fjuːz] *n* fusible *m*; (*for bomb etc*) amorce *f*, détonateur *m* ♦ *vt*, *vi* (*metal*) fondre; (*fig*) fusionner; (*ELEC*): **to ~ the lights** faire sauter les fusibles *or* les plombs; **a ~ has blown** un fusible a sauté.
fuse box *n* boîte *f* à fusibles.
fuselage [ˈfjuːzəlɑːʒ] *n* fuselage *m*.
fuse wire *n* fusible *m*.
fusillade [fjuːzɪˈleɪd] *n* fusillade *f*; (*fig*) feu roulant.
fusion [ˈfjuːʒən] *n* fusion *f*.
fuss [fʌs] *n* (*anxiety, excitement*) chichis *mpl*, façons *fpl*; (*commotion*) tapage *m*; (*complaining, trouble*) histoire(s) *f(pl)* ♦ *vi* faire des histoires ♦ *vt* (*person*) embêter; **to make a ~** faire des façons (*or* des histoires); **to make a ~ of sb** dorloter qn.
►**fuss over** *vt fus* (*person*) dorloter.
fusspot [ˈfʌspɔt] *n* (*col*): **don't be such a ~!** ne fais pas tant d'histoires!
fussy [ˈfʌsɪ] *adj* (*person*) tatillon(ne), difficile; chichiteux(euse); (*dress, style*) tarabiscoté(e); **I'm not ~** (*col*) ça m'est égal.
fusty [ˈfʌstɪ] *adj* (*old-fashioned*) vieillot(te); (*smell*) de renfermé *or* moisi.
futile [ˈfjuːtaɪl] *adj* futile.
futility [fjuːˈtɪlɪtɪ] *n* futilité *f*.
futon [ˈfuːtɔn] *n* futon *m*.
future [ˈfjuːtʃə*] *adj* futur(e) ♦ *n* avenir *m*; (*LING*) futur *m*; **in (the) ~** à l'avenir; **in the near/immediate ~** dans un avenir proche/immédiat.
futures [ˈfjuːtʃəz] *npl* (*COMM*) opérations *fpl* à terme.
futuristic [fjuːtʃəˈrɪstɪk] *adj* futuriste.
fuze [fjuːz] *n, vt, vi* (*US*) = **fuse**.
fuzzy [ˈfʌzɪ] *adj* (*PHOT*) flou(e); (*hair*) crépu(e).
fwd. *abbr* = **forward**.
fwy *abbr* (*US*) = **freeway**.
FY *abbr* = **fiscal year**.
FYI *abbr* = *for your information.*

G g

G, g [dʒiː] *n* (*letter*) G, g *m*; (*MUS*): **G** sol *m*; **G for George** G comme Gaston.
G *n abbr* (*BRIT SCOL*: = *good*) b (= *bien*); (*US CINE*: = *general (audience)*) ≈ tous publics; **G7** (*POL*) G7 *m*.
g *abbr* (= *gram, gravity*) g.
GA *abbr* (*US*) = *Georgia*.
gab [gæb] *n* (*col*): **to have the gift of the ~** avoir la langue bien pendue.
gabble [ˈgæbl] *vi* bredouiller; jacasser.
gaberdine [gæbəˈdiːn] *n* gabardine *f*.
gable [ˈgeɪbl] *n* pignon *m*.
Gabon [gəˈbɔn] *n* Gabon *m*.
gad about [ˈgædəˈbaut] *vi* (*col*) se balader.
gadget [ˈgædʒɪt] *n* gadget *m*.
Gaelic [ˈgeɪlɪk] *adj*, *n* gaélique *(m)*.
gaffe [gæf] *n* gaffe *f*.
gaffer [ˈgæfə*] *n* (*BRIT*: *foreman*) contremaître *m*; (*BRIT col*: *boss*) patron *m*.

gag [gæg] *n* bâillon *m*; (*joke*) gag *m* ♦ *vt* (*prisoner etc*) bâillonner ♦ *vi* (*choke*) étouffer.
gaga ['gɑːgɑː] *adj*: **to go** ~ devenir gaga *or* gâteux(euse).
gaiety ['geɪɪtɪ] *n* gaieté *f*.
gaily ['geɪlɪ] *adv* gaiement.
gain [geɪn] *n* gain *m*, profit *m* ♦ *vt* gagner ♦ *vi* (*watch*) avancer; **to ~ in/by** gagner en/à; **to ~ 3lbs (in weight)** prendre 3 livres; **to ~ ground** gagner du terrain.
►**gain (up)on** *vt fus* rattraper.
gainful ['geɪnful] *adj* profitable, lucratif(ive).
gainfully ['geɪnfəlɪ] *adv*: **to be ~ employed** avoir un emploi rémunéré.
gainsay [geɪn'seɪ] *vt* (*irreg*: *like* **say**) contredire; nier.
gait [geɪt] *n* démarche *f*.
gal. *abbr* = **gallon.**
gala ['gɑːlə] *n* gala *m*; **swimming** ~ grand concours de natation.
Galápagos (Islands) [gə'læpəgəs-] *npl*: **the** ~ les (îles *fpl*) Galapagos *fpl*.
galaxy ['gæləksɪ] *n* galaxie *f*.
gale [geɪl] *n* coup *m* de vent; ~ **force 10** vent *m* de force 10.
gall [gɔːl] *n* (*ANAT*) bile *f*; (*fig*) effronterie *f* ♦ *vt* ulcérer, irriter.
gall. *abbr* = **gallon.**
gallant ['gælənt] *adj* vaillant(e), brave; (*towards ladies*) empressé(e), galant(e).
gallantry ['gæləntrɪ] *n* bravoure *f*, vaillance *f*; empressement *m*, galanterie *f*.
gall-bladder ['gɔːlblædə*] *n* vésicule *f* biliaire.
galleon ['gælɪən] *n* galion *m*.
gallery ['gælərɪ] *n* galerie *f*; (*for spectators*) tribune *f*; (*: in theatre*) dernier balcon; (*also*: **art** ~) musée *m*; (*: private*) galerie.
galley ['gælɪ] *n* (*ship's kitchen*) cambuse *f*; (*ship*) galère *f*; (*also*: ~ **proof**) placard *m*, galée *f*.
Gallic ['gælɪk] *adj* (*of Gaul*) gaulois(e); (*French*) français(e).
galling ['gɔːlɪŋ] *adj* irritant(e).
gallon ['gæln] *n* gallon *m* (*= 8 pints; BRIT* = 4.543 l; *US* = 3.785 l).
gallop ['gæləp] *n* galop *m* ♦ *vi* galoper; **~ing inflation** inflation galopante.
gallows ['gæləuz] *n* potence *f*.
gallstone ['gɔːlstəun] *n* calcul *m* (biliaire).
Gallup Poll ['gæləp-] *n* sondage *m* Gallup.
galore [gə'lɔː*] *adv* en abondance, à gogo.
galvanize ['gælvənaɪz] *vt* galvaniser; (*fig*): **to ~ sb into action** galvaniser qn.
Gambia ['gæmbɪə] *n* Gambie *f*.
gambit ['gæmbɪt] *n* (*fig*): **(opening)** ~ manœuvre *f* stratégique.
gamble ['gæmbl] *n* pari *m*, risque calculé ♦ *vt*, *vi* jouer; **to ~ on the Stock Exchange** jouer en *or* à la Bourse; **to ~ on** (*fig*) miser sur.
gambler ['gæmblə*] *n* joueur *m*.
gambling ['gæmblɪŋ] *n* jeu *m*.
gambol ['gæmbl] *vi* gambader.
game [geɪm] *n* jeu *m*; (*event*) match *m*; (*HUNTING*) gibier *m* ♦ *adj* brave; (*ready*): **to be ~ (for sth/to do)** être prêt(e) (à qch/à faire), se sentir de taille (à faire); **a ~ of football/tennis** une partie de football/tennis; **~s** (*SCOL*) sport *m*; **big** ~ gros gibier.
game bird *n* gibier *m* à plume.
gamekeeper ['geɪmkiːpə*] *n* garde-chasse *m*.
gamely ['geɪmlɪ] *adv* vaillamment.
game reserve *n* réserve animalière.
games console ['geɪmz-] *n* console *f* de jeux vidéo.
gameshow ['geɪmʃəu] *n* jeu télévisé.
gamesmanship ['geɪmzmənʃɪp] *n* roublardise *f*.
gaming ['geɪmɪŋ] *n* jeu *m*, jeux *mpl* d'argent.
gammon ['gæmən] *n* (*bacon*) quartier *m* de lard fumé; (*ham*) jambon fumé.
gamut ['gæmət] *n* gamme *f*.
gang [gæŋ] *n* bande *f*, groupe *m*.
►**gang up** *vi*: **to ~ up on sb** se liguer contre qn.
Ganges ['gændʒiːz] *n*: **the** ~ le Gange.
gangland ['gæŋlænd] *adj*: ~ **killer** tueur professionnel du milieu; ~ **boss** chef *m* de gang.
gangling ['gæŋglɪŋ], **gangly** ['gæŋglɪ] *adj* dégingandé(e).
gangplank ['gæŋplæŋk] *n* passerelle *f*.
gangrene ['gæŋgriːn] *n* gangrène *f*.
gangster ['gæŋstə*] *n* gangster *m*, bandit *m*.
gangway ['gæŋweɪ] *n* passerelle *f*; (*BRIT*: *of bus*) couloir central.
gantry ['gæntrɪ] *n* portique *m*; (*for rocket*) tour *f* de lancement.
GAO *n abbr* (*US*: *= General Accounting Office*) ≈ Cour *f* des comptes.
gaol [dʒeɪl] *n*, *vt* (*BRIT*) = **jail.**
gap [gæp] *n* trou *m*; (*in time*) intervalle *m*; (*fig*) lacune *f*; vide *m*.
gape [geɪp] *vi* être *or* rester bouche bée.
gaping ['geɪpɪŋ] *adj* (*hole*) béant(e).
garage ['gærɑːʒ] *n* garage *m*.
garb [gɑːb] *n* tenue *f*, costume *m*.
garbage ['gɑːbɪdʒ] *n* ordures *fpl*, détritus *mpl*; (*fig*: *col*) conneries *fpl*.
garbage can *n* (*US*) poubelle *f*, boîte *f* à ordures.
garbage collector *n* (*US*) éboueur *m*.
garbage disposal (unit) *n* (*US*) broyeur *m* d'ordures.
garbage truck *n* (*US*) camion *m* (du ramassage) des ordures, benne *f* à ordures.
garbled ['gɑːbld] *adj* déformé(e); faussé(e).
garden ['gɑːdn] *n* jardin *m* ♦ *vi* jardiner; **~s** *npl* (*public*) jardin public; (*private*) parc *m*.
garden centre *n* garden-centre *m*, pépinière *f*.
garden city *n* (*BRIT*) cité-jardin *f*.
gardener ['gɑːdnə*] *n* jardinier *m*.
gardening ['gɑːdnɪŋ] *n* jardinage *m*.
gargle ['gɑːgl] *vi* se gargariser ♦ *n* gargarisme

m.
gargoyle ['gɑːgɔɪl] *n* gargouille *f*.
garish ['gɛərɪʃ] *adj* criard(e), voyant(e).
garland ['gɑːlənd] *n* guirlande *f*; couronne *f*.
garlic ['gɑːlɪk] *n* ail *m*.
garment ['gɑːmənt] *n* vêtement *m*.
garner ['gɑːnə*] *vt* engranger, amasser.
garnish ['gɑːnɪʃ] *vt* garnir.
garret ['gærɪt] *n* mansarde *f*.
garrison ['gærɪsn] *n* garnison *f* ♦ *vt* mettre en garnison, stationner.
garrulous ['gærjuləs] *adj* volubile, loquace.
garter ['gɑːtə*] *n* jarretière *f*; (*US*: *suspender*) jarretelle *f*.
garter belt *n* (*US*) porte-jarretelles *m inv*.
gas [gæs] *n* gaz *m*; (*used as anaesthetic*): **to be given ~** se faire endormir; (*US*: *gasoline*) essence *f* ♦ *vt* asphyxier; (*MIL*) gazer.
Gascony ['gæskənɪ] *n* Gascogne *f*.
gas cooker *n* (*BRIT*) cuisinière *f* à gaz.
gas cylinder *n* bouteille *f* de gaz.
gaseous ['gæsɪəs] *adj* gazeux(euse).
gas fire *n* (*BRIT*) radiateur *m* à gaz.
gas-fired ['gæsfaɪəd] *adj* au gaz.
gash [gæʃ] *n* entaille *f*; (*on face*) balafre *f* ♦ *vt* taillader; balafrer.
gasket ['gæskɪt] *n* (*AUT*) joint *m* de culasse.
gas mask *n* masque *m* à gaz.
gas meter *n* compteur *m* à gaz.
gasoline ['gæsəliːn] *n* (*US*) essence *f*.
gasp [gɑːsp] *vi* haleter; (*fig*) avoir le souffle coupé.
►**gasp out** *vt* (*say*) dire dans un souffle *or* d'une voix entrecoupée.
gas ring *n* brûleur *m*.
gas station *n* (*US*) station-service *f*.
gas stove *n* réchaud *m* à gaz; (*cooker*) cuisinière *f* à gaz.
gassy ['gæsɪ] *adj* gazeux(euse).
gas tank *n* (*US AUT*) réservoir *m* d'essence.
gas tap *n* bouton *m* (de cuisinière à gaz); (*on pipe*) robinet *m* à gaz.
gastric ['gæstrɪk] *adj* gastrique.
gastric ulcer *n* ulcère *m* de l'estomac.
gastroenteritis ['gæstrəuɛntə'raɪtɪs] *n* gastroentérite *f*.
gastronomy [gæs'trɔnəmɪ] *n* gastronomie *f*.
gasworks ['gæswəːks] *n, npl* usine *f* à gaz.
gate [geɪt] *n* (*of garden*) portail *m*; (*of farm, at level crossing*) barrière *f*; (*of building, town, at airport*) porte *f*; (*of lock*) vanne *f*.
gâteau, *pl* **~x** ['gætəu, -z] *n* gros gâteau à la crème.
gatecrash ['geɪtkræʃ] *vt* s'introduire sans invitation dans.
gatecrasher ['geɪtkræʃə*] *n* intrus/e.
gatehouse ['geɪthaus] *n* loge *f*.
gateway ['geɪtweɪ] *n* porte *f*.
gather ['gæðə*] *vt* (*flowers, fruit*) cueillir; (*pick up*) ramasser; (*assemble*) rassembler, réunir; recueillir; (*understand*) comprendre ♦ *vi* (*assemble*) se rassembler; (*dust*) s'amasser; (*clouds*) s'amonceler; **to ~ (from/that)** conclure *or* déduire (de/que); **as far as I can ~** d'après ce que je comprends; **to ~ speed** prendre de la vitesse.
gathering ['gæðərɪŋ] *n* rassemblement *m*.
GATT [gæt] *n abbr* (= *General Agreement on Tariffs and Trade*) GATT *m*.
gauche [gəuʃ] *adj* gauche, maladroit(e).
gaudy ['gɔːdɪ] *adj* voyant(e).
gauge [geɪdʒ] *n* (*standard measure*) calibre *m*; (*RAIL*) écartement *m*; (*instrument*) jauge *f* ♦ *vt* jauger; (*fig: sb's capabilities, character*) juger de; **to ~ the right moment** calculer le moment propice; **petrol ~**, (*US*) **gas ~** jauge d'essence.
Gaul [gɔːl] *n* (*country*) Gaule *f*; (*person*) Gaulois/e.
gaunt [gɔːnt] *adj* décharné(e); (*grim, desolate*) désolé(e).
gauntlet ['gɔːntlɪt] *n* (*fig*): **to throw down the ~** jeter le gant; **to run the ~ through an angry crowd** se frayer un passage à travers une foule hostile *or* entre deux haies de manifestants *etc* hostiles.
gauze [gɔːz] *n* gaze *f*.
gave [geɪv] *pt of* **give**.
gavel ['gævl] *n* marteau *m*.
gawky ['gɔːkɪ] *adj* dégingandé(e), godiche.
gawp [gɔːp] *vi*: **to ~ at** regarder bouche bée.
gay [geɪ] *adj* (*homosexual*) homosexuel(le); (*slightly old-fashioned: cheerful*) gai(e), réjoui(e); (*colour*) gai, vif(vive).
gaze [geɪz] *n* regard *m* fixe ♦ *vi*: **to ~ at** *vt* fixer du regard.
gazelle [gə'zɛl] *n* gazelle *f*.
gazette [gə'zɛt] *n* (*newspaper*) gazette *f*; (*official publication*) journal officiel.
gazetteer [gæzə'tɪə*] *n* dictionnaire *m* géographique.
gazump [gə'zʌmp] *vi* (*BRIT*) *revenir sur une promesse de vente pour accepter un prix plus élevé*.
gazumping [gə'zʌmpɪŋ] *n le fait de revenir sur une promesse de vente pour accepter un prix plus élevé*.
GB *abbr* = **Great Britain**.
GBH *n abbr* (*BRIT LAW*: *col*) = **grievous bodily harm**.
GC *n abbr* (*BRIT*: = *George Cross*) *distinction honorifique*.
GCE *n abbr* (*BRIT*) = *General Certificate of Education*.
GCHQ *n abbr* (*BRIT*: = *Government Communications Headquarters*) *centre d'interception des télécommunications étrangères*.
GCSE *n abbr* (*BRIT*: = *General Certificate of Secondary Education*) *examen passé à l'âge de 16 ans sanctionnant les connaissances de l'élève*; **she's got eight ~s** elle a réussi dans huit matières aux épreuves du GCSE.
Gdns. *abbr* = *gardens*.
GDP *n abbr* = **gross domestic product**.

GDR *n abbr* (*old: = German Democratic Republic*) RDA *f*.
gear [gɪə*] *n* matériel *m*, équipement *m*; (*TECH*) engrenage *m*; (*AUT*) vitesse *f* ♦ *vt* (*fig: adapt*) adapter; **top** *or* (*US*) **high/low/bottom** ~ quatrième (*or* cinquième)/deuxième/première vitesse; **in** ~ en prise; **out of** ~ au point mort; **our service is ~ed to meet the needs of the disabled** notre service répond de façon spécifique aux besoins des handicapés.
►**gear up** *vi*: **to** ~ **up (to do)** se préparer (à faire).
gear box *n* boîte *f* de vitesse.
gear lever, (*US*) **gear shift** *n* levier *m* de vitesse.
GED *n abbr* (*US SCOL*) = *general educational development*.
geese [giːs] *npl of* **goose**.
geezer ['giːzə*] *n* (*BRIT col*) mec *m*.
Geiger counter ['gaɪgə-] *n* compteur *m* Geiger.
gel [dʒɛl] *n* gelée *f*; (*CHEMISTRY*) colloïde *m*.
gelatin(e) ['dʒɛlətiːn] *n* gélatine *f*.
gelignite ['dʒɛlɪgnaɪt] *n* plastic *m*.
gem [dʒɛm] *n* pierre précieuse.
Gemini ['dʒɛmɪnaɪ] *n* les Gémeaux *mpl*; **to be** ~ être des Gémeaux.
gen [dʒɛn] *n* (*BRIT col*): **to give sb the** ~ **on sth** mettre qn au courant de qch.
Gen. *abbr* (*MIL: = general*) Gal.
gen. *abbr* (*= general, generally*) gén.
gender ['dʒɛndə*] *n* genre *m*.
gene [dʒiːn] *n* (*BIOL*) gène *m*.
genealogy [dʒiːnɪ'ælədʒɪ] *n* généalogie *f*.
general ['dʒɛnərl] *n* général *m* ♦ *adj* général(e); **in** ~ en général; **the** ~ **public** le grand public; ~ **audit** (*COMM*) vérification annuelle.
general anaesthetic *n* anesthésie générale.
general election *n* élection(s) législative(s).
generalization ['dʒɛnrəlaɪ'zeɪʃən] *n* généralisation *f*.
generalize ['dʒɛnrəlaɪz] *vi* généraliser.
generally ['dʒɛnrəlɪ] *adv* généralement.
general manager *n* directeur général.
general practitioner (GP) *n* généraliste *m/f*; **who's your GP?** qui est votre médecin traitant?
general strike *n* grève générale.
generate ['dʒɛnəreɪt] *vt* engendrer; (*electricity*) produire.
generation [dʒɛnə'reɪʃən] *n* génération *f*; (*of electricity etc*) production *f*.
generator ['dʒɛnəreɪtə*] *n* générateur *m*.
generic [dʒɪ'nɛrɪk] *adj* générique.
generosity [dʒɛnə'rɔsɪtɪ] *n* générosité *f*.
generous ['dʒɛnərəs] *adj* généreux(euse); (*copious*) copieux(euse).
genesis ['dʒɛnɪsɪs] *n* genèse *f*.
genetic [dʒɪ'nɛtɪk] *adj* génétique.
genetic engineering *n* génie *m* génétique.
genetic fingerprinting [-'fɪŋgəprɪntɪŋ] *n* système *m* d'empreinte génétique.
genetics [dʒɪ'nɛtɪks] *n* génétique *f*.
Geneva [dʒɪ'niːvə] *n* Genève; **Lake** ~ le lac Léman.
genial ['dʒiːnɪəl] *adj* cordial(e), chaleureux(euse); (*climate*) clément(e).
genitals ['dʒɛnɪtlz] *npl* organes génitaux.
genitive ['dʒɛnɪtɪv] *n* génitif *m*.
genius ['dʒiːnɪəs] *n* génie *m*.
Genoa ['dʒɛnəuə] *n* Gênes.
genocide ['dʒɛnəusaɪd] *n* génocide *m*.
gent [dʒɛnt] *n abbr* (*BRIT col*) = **gentleman**.
genteel [dʒɛn'tiːl] *adj* de bon ton, distingué(e).
gentle ['dʒɛntl] *adj* doux(douce).
gentleman ['dʒɛntlmən] *n* monsieur *m*; (*well-bred man*) gentleman *m*; **~'s agreement** gentleman's agreement *m*.
gentlemanly ['dʒɛntlmənlɪ] *adj* bien élevé(e).
gentleness ['dʒɛntlnɪs] *n* douceur *f*.
gently ['dʒɛntlɪ] *adv* doucement.
gentry ['dʒɛntrɪ] *n* petite noblesse.
gents [dʒɛnts] *n* W.-C. *mpl* (pour hommes).
genuine ['dʒɛnjuɪn] *adj* véritable, authentique; (*person, emotion*) sincère.
genuinely ['dʒɛnjuɪnlɪ] *adv* sincèrement, vraiment.
geographer [dʒɪ'ɔgrəfə*] *n* géographe *m/f*.
geographic(al) [dʒɪə'græfɪk(l)] *adj* géographique.
geography [dʒɪ'ɔgrəfɪ] *n* géographie *f*.
geological [dʒɪə'lɔdʒɪkl] *adj* géologique.
geologist [dʒɪ'ɔlədʒɪst] *n* géologue *m/f*.
geology [dʒɪ'ɔlədʒɪ] *n* géologie *f*.
geometric(al) [dʒɪə'mɛtrɪk(l)] *adj* géométrique.
geometry [dʒɪ'ɔmətrɪ] *n* géométrie *f*.
Geordie ['dʒɔːdɪ] *n* (*col*) habitant/e de Tyneside; originaire *m/f* de Tyneside.
Georgia ['dʒɔːdʒə] *n* Géorgie *f*.
Georgian ['dʒɔːdʒən] *adj* (*GEO*) géorgien(ne) ♦ *n* Géorgien/ne; (*LING*) géorgien *m*.
geranium [dʒɪ'reɪnɪəm] *n* géranium *m*.
geriatric [dʒɛrɪ'ætrɪk] *adj* gériatrique.
germ [dʒəːm] *n* (*MED*) microbe *m*; (*BIO, fig*) germe *m*.
German ['dʒəːmən] *adj* allemand(e) ♦ *n* Allemand/e; (*LING*) allemand *m*.
germane [dʒəː'meɪn] *adj* (*formal*): ~ **(to)** se rapportant (à).
German measles *n* rubéole *f*.
Germany ['dʒəːmənɪ] *n* Allemagne *f*.
germination [dʒəːmɪ'neɪʃən] *n* germination *f*.
germ warfare *n* guerre *f* bactériologique.
gerrymandering ['dʒɛrɪmændərɪŋ] *n* tripotage *m* du découpage électoral.
gestation [dʒɛs'teɪʃən] *n* gestation *f*.
gesticulate [dʒɛs'tɪkjuleɪt] *vi* gesticuler.
gesture ['dʒɛstjə*] *n* geste *m*; **as a** ~ **of friendship** en témoignage d'amitié.

KEYWORD

get [gɛt] (*pt, pp* **got,** *pp* **gotten** (*US*)) *vi* **1** (*become, be*) devenir; **to ~ old/tired** devenir vieux/fatigué, vieillir/se fatiguer; **to ~ drunk** s'enivrer; **to ~ ready/washed/shaved** *etc* se préparer/laver/raser *etc*; **to ~ killed** se faire tuer; **when do I ~ paid?** quand est-ce que je serai payé?; **it's ~ting late** il se fait tard

2 (*go*): **to ~ to/from** aller à/de; **to ~ home** rentrer chez soi; **how did you ~ here?** comment es-tu arrivé ici?; **he got across the bridge/under the fence** il a traversé le pont/ est passé au-dessous de la barrière

3 (*begin*) commencer *or* se mettre à; **I'm ~ting to like him** je commence à l'apprécier; **let's ~ going** *or* **started** allons-y

4 (*modal aux vb*): **you've got to do it** il faut que vous le fassiez; **I've got to tell the police** je dois le dire à la police

♦ *vt* **1**: **to ~ sth done** (*do*) faire qch; (*have done*) faire faire qch; **to ~ sth/sb ready** préparer qch/qn; **to ~ one's hair cut** se faire couper les cheveux; **to ~ sb to do sth** faire faire qch à qn; **to ~ sb drunk** enivrer qn

2 (*obtain*: *money, permission, results*) obtenir, avoir; (*find*: *job, flat*) trouver; (*fetch*: *person, doctor, object*) aller chercher; **to ~ sth for sb** procurer qch à qn; **~ me Mr Jones, please** (*on phone*) passez-moi Mr Jones, s'il vous plaît; **can I ~ you a drink?** est-ce que je peux vous servir à boire?

3 (*receive*: *present, letter*) recevoir, avoir; (*acquire*: *reputation*) avoir; (: *prize*) obtenir; **what did you ~ for your birthday?** qu'est-ce que tu as eu pour ton anniversaire?

4 (*catch*) prendre, saisir, attraper; (*hit*: *target etc*) atteindre; **to ~ sb by the arm/throat** prendre *or* saisir *or* attraper qn par le bras/à la gorge; **~ him!** arrête-le!; **he really ~s me!** il me porte sur les nerfs!

5 (*take, move*) faire parvenir; **do you think we'll ~ it through the door?** on arrivera à le faire passer par la porte?; **I'll ~ you there somehow** je me débrouillerai pour t'y emmener

6 (*catch, take*: *plane, bus etc*) prendre

7 (*understand*) comprendre, saisir; (*hear*) entendre; **I've got it!** j'ai compris!; **I didn't ~ your name** je n'ai pas entendu votre nom

8 (*have, possess*): **to have got** avoir; **how many have you got?** vous en avez combien?

►**get about** *vi* se déplacer; (*news*) se répandre

►**get across** *vt*: **to ~ across (to)** (*message, meaning*) faire passer à ♦ *vi*: **to ~ across to** (*subj*: *speaker*) se faire comprendre (par)

►**get along** *vi* (*agree*) s'entendre; (*depart*) s'en aller; (*manage*) = **get by**

►**get at** *vt fus* (*attack*) s'en prendre à; (*reach*) attraper, atteindre; **what are you ~ting at?** à quoi voulez-vous en venir?

►**get away** *vi* partir, s'en aller; (*escape*) s'échapper

►**get away with** *vt fus* en être quitte pour; se faire passer *or* pardonner

►**get back** *vi* (*return*) rentrer ♦ *vt* récupérer, recouvrer; **to ~ back to** (*start again*) retourner *or* revenir à; (*contact again*) recontacter

►**get back at** *vt fus* (*col*): **to ~ back at sb** rendre la monnaie de sa pièce à qn

►**get by** *vi* (*pass*) passer; (*manage*) se débrouiller; **I can ~ by in Dutch** je me débrouille en hollandais

►**get down** *vi, vt fus* descendre ♦ *vt* descendre; (*depress*) déprimer

►**get down to** *vt fus* (*work*) se mettre à (faire); **to ~ down to business** passer aux choses sérieuses

►**get in** *vi* entrer; (*arrive home*) rentrer; (*train*) arriver ♦ *vt* (*bring in*: *harvest*) rentrer; (: *coal*) faire rentrer; (: *supplies*) faire des provisions de

►**get into** *vt fus* entrer dans; (*car, train etc*) monter dans; (*clothes*) mettre, enfiler, endosser; **to ~ into bed/a rage** se mettre au lit/en colère

►**get off** *vi* (*from train etc*) descendre; (*depart*: *person, car*) s'en aller; (*escape*) s'en tirer ♦ *vt* (*remove*: *clothes, stain*) enlever; (*send off*) expédier; (*have as leave*: *day, time*): **we got 2 days off** nous avons eu 2 jours de congé ♦ *vt fus* (*train, bus*) descendre de; **to ~ off to a good start** (*fig*) prendre un bon départ

►**get on** *vi* (*at exam etc*) se débrouiller; (*agree*): **to ~ on (with)** s'entendre (avec); **how are you ~ting on?** comment ça va? ♦ *vt fus* monter dans; (*horse*) monter sur

►**get on to** *vt fus* (*BRIT*: *deal with*: *problem*) s'occuper de; (*contact*: *person*) contacter

►**get out** *vi* sortir; (*of vehicle*) descendre; (*news etc*) s'ébruiter ♦ *vt* sortir

►**get out of** *vt fus* sortir de; (*duty etc*) échapper à, se soustraire à

►**get over** *vt fus* (*illness*) se remettre de ♦ *vt* (*communicate*: *idea etc*) communiquer; (*finish*): **let's ~ it over (with)** finissons-en

►**get round** *vi*: **to ~ round to doing sth** se mettre (finalement) à faire qch ♦ *vt fus* contourner; (*fig*: *person*) entortiller

►**get through** *vi* (*TEL*) avoir la communication; **to ~ through to sb** atteindre qn ♦ *vt fus* (*finish*: *work, book*) finir, terminer

►**get together** *vi* se réunir ♦ *vt* rassembler

►**get up** *vi* (*rise*) se lever ♦ *vt fus* monter

►**get up to** *vt fus* (*reach*) arriver à; (*prank etc*) faire.

getaway ['gɛtəweɪ] *n* fuite *f*.

getaway car *n* voiture prévue pour prendre la fuite.

get-together ['gɛttəgɛðə*] *n* petite réunion, petite fête.

get-up ['gɛtʌp] *n* (*col*: *outfit*) accoutrement *m*.
get-well card [gɛt'wɛl-] *n* carte *f* de vœux de bon rétablissement.
geyser ['giːzə*] *n* chauffe-eau *m inv*; (*GEO*) geyser *m*.
Ghana ['gɑːnə] *n* Ghana *m*.
Ghanaian [gɑː'neɪən] *adj* ghanéen(ne) ♦ *n* Ghanéen/ne.
ghastly ['gɑːstlɪ] *adj* atroce, horrible; (*pale*) livide, blême.
gherkin ['gəːkɪn] *n* cornichon *m*.
ghetto ['gɛtəu] *n* ghetto *m*.
ghetto blaster [-blɑːstə*] *n* (*col*) gros radio-cassette.
ghost [gəust] *n* fantôme *m*, revenant *m* ♦ *vt* (*sb else's book*) écrire.
ghostly ['gəustlɪ] *adj* fantomatique.
ghostwriter ['gəustraɪtə*] *n* nègre *m* (*fig*).
ghoul [guːl] *n* (*ghost*) vampire *m*.
ghoulish ['guːlɪʃ] *adj* (*tastes etc*) morbide.
GHQ *n abbr* (*MIL*: = *general headquarters*) GQG *m*.
GI *n abbr* (*US col*: = *government issue*) *soldat de l'armée américaine*, GI *m*.
giant ['dʒaɪənt] *n* géant/e ♦ *adj* géant(e), énorme; ~ **(size) packet** paquet géant.
giant killer *n* (*SPORT*) *équipe inconnue qui remporte un match contre une équipe renommée*.
gibber ['dʒɪbə*] *vi* émettre des sons inintelligibles.
gibberish ['dʒɪbərɪʃ] *n* charabia *m*.
gibe [dʒaɪb] *n* sarcasme *m* ♦ *vi*: **to ~ at** railler.
giblets ['dʒɪblɪts] *npl* abats *mpl*.
Gibraltar [dʒɪ'brɔːltə*] *n* Gibraltar *m*.
giddiness ['gɪdɪnɪs] *n* vertige *m*.
giddy ['gɪdɪ] *adj* (*dizzy*): **to be (or feel) ~** avoir le vertige; (*height*) vertigineux(euse); (*thoughtless*) sot(te), étourdi(e).
gift [gɪft] *n* cadeau *m*, présent *m*; (*donation*) don *m*; (*COMM*: *also*: **free ~**) cadeau(-réclame) *m*; (*talent*): **to have a ~ for sth** avoir des dons pour *or* le don de qch.
gifted ['gɪftɪd] *adj* doué(e).
gift token, gift voucher *n* bon *m* d'achat.
gig [gɪg] *n* (*col*: *of musician*) gig *f*.
gigabyte ['dʒɪgəbaɪt] *n* gigaoctet *m*.
gigantic [dʒaɪ'gæntɪk] *adj* gigantesque.
giggle ['gɪgl] *vi* pouffer, ricaner sottement ♦ *n* petit rire sot, ricanement *m*.
GIGO ['gaɪgəu] *abbr* (*COMPUT*: *col*: = *garbage in, garbage out*) qualité d'entrée = qualité de sortie.
gild [gɪld] *vt* dorer.
gill [dʒɪl] *n* (*measure*) = *0.25 pints* (*BRIT* = *0.148 l*; *US* = *0.118 l*).
gills [gɪlz] *npl* (*of fish*) ouïes *fpl*, branchies *fpl*.
gilt [gɪlt] *n* dorure *f* ♦ *adj* doré(e).
gilt-edged ['gɪltɛdʒd] *adj* (*stocks, securities*) de premier ordre.
gimlet ['gɪmlɪt] *n* vrille *f*.
gimmick ['gɪmɪk] *n* truc *m*; **sales ~** offre promotionnelle.
gin [dʒɪn] *n* gin *m*.
ginger ['dʒɪndʒə*] *n* gingembre *m*.
►**ginger up** *vt* secouer; animer.
ginger ale, ginger beer *n* boisson gazeuse au gingembre.
gingerbread ['dʒɪndʒəbrɛd] *n* pain *m* d'épices.
ginger group *n* (*BRIT*) groupe *m* de pression.
ginger-haired ['dʒɪndʒə'hɛəd] *adj* roux (rousse).
gingerly ['dʒɪndʒəlɪ] *adv* avec précaution.
gingham ['gɪŋəm] *n* vichy *m*.
ginseng ['dʒɪnsɛŋ] *n* ginseng *m*.
gipsy ['dʒɪpsɪ] *n* gitan/e, bohémien/ne ♦ *cpd*: ~ **caravan** *n* roulotte *f*.
giraffe [dʒɪ'rɑːf] *n* girafe *f*.
girder ['gəːdə*] *n* poutrelle *f*.
girdle ['gəːdl] *n* (*corset*) gaine *f* ♦ *vt* ceindre.
girl [gəːl] *n* fille *f*, fillette *f*; (*young unmarried woman*) jeune fille; (*daughter*) fille; **an English ~** une jeune Anglaise; **a little English ~** une petite Anglaise.
girlfriend ['gəːlfrɛnd] *n* (*of girl*) amie *f*; (*of boy*) petite amie.
girlish ['gəːlɪʃ] *adj* de jeune fille.
Girl Scout *n* (*US*) guide *f*.
Giro ['dʒaɪrəu] *n*: **the National ~** (*BRIT*) ≈ les comptes chèques postaux.
giro ['dʒaɪrəu] *n* (*bank ~*) virement *m* bancaire; (*post office ~*) mandat *m*.
girth [gəːθ] *n* circonférence *f*; (*of horse*) sangle *f*.
gist [dʒɪst] *n* essentiel *m*.
give [gɪv] *n* (*of fabric*) élasticité *f* ♦ *vb* (*pt* **gave**, *pp* **given** [geɪv, 'gɪvn]) *vt* donner ♦ *vi* (*break*) céder; (*stretch: fabric*) se prêter; **to ~ sb sth, ~ sth to sb** donner qch à qn; **to ~ a cry/sigh** pousser un cri/un soupir; **how much did you ~ for it?** combien (l')avez-vous payé?; **12 o'clock, ~ or take a few minutes** midi, à quelques minutes près; **to ~ way** *vi* céder; (*BRIT AUT*) donner la priorité.
►**give away** *vt* donner; (*give free*) faire cadeau de; (*betray*) donner, trahir; (*disclose*) révéler; (*bride*) conduire à l'autel.
►**give back** *vt* rendre.
►**give in** *vi* céder ♦ *vt* donner.
►**give off** *vt* dégager.
►**give out** *vt* (*food etc*) distribuer; (*news*) annoncer ♦ *vi* (*be exhausted: supplies*) s'épuiser; (*fail*) lâcher.
►**give up** *vi* renoncer ♦ *vt* renoncer à; **to ~ up smoking** arrêter de fumer; **to ~ o.s. up** se rendre.
give-and-take ['gɪvənd'teɪk] *n* concessions mutuelles.
giveaway ['gɪvəweɪ] *n* (*col*): **her expression was a ~** son expression la trahissait; **the exam was a ~!** cet examen, c'était du gâteau! ♦ *cpd*: ~ **prices** prix sacrifiés.
given ['gɪvn] *pp of* **give** ♦ *adj* (*fixed: time, amount*) donné(e), déterminé(e) ♦ *conj*: ~ **the**

circumstances ... étant donné les circonstances ..., vu les circonstances ...; ~ **that** ... étant donné que ....
glacial ['gleɪsɪəl] *adj* (*GEO*) glaciaire; (*wind, weather*) glacial(e).
glacier ['glæsɪə*] *n* glacier *m*.
glad [glæd] *adj* content(e); **to be ~ about sth/that** être heureux(euse) *or* bien content de qch/que; **I was ~ of his help** j'étais bien content de (pouvoir compter sur) son aide *or* qu'il m'aide.
gladden ['glædn] *vt* réjouir.
glade [gleɪd] *n* clairière *f*.
gladioli [glædɪ'əulaɪ] *npl* glaïeuls *mpl*.
gladly ['glædlɪ] *adv* volontiers.
glamorous ['glæmərəs] *adj* séduisant(e).
glamour ['glæmə*] *n* éclat *m*, prestige *m*.
glance [glɑːns] *n* coup *m* d'œil ♦ *vi*: **to ~ at** jeter un coup d'œil à.
►**glance off** *vt fus* (*bullet*) ricocher sur.
glancing ['glɑːnsɪŋ] *adj* (*blow*) oblique.
gland [glænd] *n* glande *f*.
glandular ['glændjulə*] *adj*: **~ fever** (*BRIT*) mononucléose infectieuse.
glare [glɛə*] *n* lumière éblouissante ♦ *vi* briller d'un éclat aveuglant; **to ~ at** lancer un *or* des regard(s) furieux à.
glaring ['glɛərɪŋ] *adj* (*mistake*) criant(e), qui saute aux yeux.
glasnost ['glæznɔst] *n* glasnost *f*.
glass [glɑːs] *n* verre *m*; (*also*: **looking ~**) miroir *m*.
glass-blowing ['glɑːsbləuɪŋ] *n* soufflage *m* (du verre).
glass ceiling *n* (*fig*) *plafond dans l'échelle hiérarchique au-dessus duquel les femmes ou les membres d'une minorité ethnique ne semblent pouvoir s'élever*.
glasses ['glɑːsəs] *npl* lunettes *fpl*.
glass fibre *n* fibre *f* de verre.
glasshouse ['glɑːshaus] *n* serre *f*.
glassware ['glɑːswɛə*] *n* verrerie *f*.
glassy ['glɑːsɪ] *adj* (*eyes*) vitreux(euse).
Glaswegian [glæs'wiːdʒən] *adj* de Glasgow ♦ *n* habitant/e de Glasgow; natif/ive de Glasgow.
glaze [gleɪz] *vt* (*door*) vitrer; (*pottery*) vernir; (*CULIN*) glacer ♦ *n* vernis *m*; (*CULIN*) glaçage *m*.
glazed [gleɪzd] *adj* (*eye*) vitreux(euse); (*pottery*) verni(e); (*tiles*) vitrifié(e).
glazier ['gleɪzɪə*] *n* vitrier *m*.
gleam [gliːm] *n* lueur *f* ♦ *vi* luire, briller; **a ~ of hope** une lueur d'espoir.
gleaming ['gliːmɪŋ] *adj* luisant(e).
glean [gliːn] *vt* (*information*) recueillir.
glee [gliː] *n* joie *f*.
gleeful ['gliːful] *adj* joyeux(euse).
glen [glɛn] *n* vallée *f*.
glib [glɪb] *adj* qui a du bagou; facile.
glide [glaɪd] *vi* glisser; (*AVIAT, bird*) planer ♦ *n* glissement *m*; vol plané.
glider ['glaɪdə*] *n* (*AVIAT*) planeur *m*.
gliding ['glaɪdɪŋ] *n* (*AVIAT*) vol *m* à voile.
glimmer ['glɪmə*] *vi* luire ♦ *n* lueur *f*.
glimpse [glɪmps] *n* vision passagère, aperçu *m* ♦ *vt* entrevoir, apercevoir; **to catch a ~ of** entrevoir.
glint [glɪnt] *n* éclair *m* ♦ *vi* étinceler.
glisten ['glɪsn] *vi* briller, luire.
glitter ['glɪtə*] *vi* scintiller, briller ♦ *n* scintillement *m*.
glitz [glɪts] *n* (*col*) clinquant *m*.
gloat [gləut] *vi*: **to ~ (over)** jubiler (à propos de).
global ['gləubl] *adj* (*world-wide*) mondial(e); (*overall*) global(e).
global warming [-'wɔːmɪŋ] *n* réchauffement *m* de la planète.
globe [gləub] *n* globe *m*.
globe-trotter ['gləubtrɔtə*] *n* globe-trotter *m*.
globule ['glɔbjuːl] *n* (*ANAT*) globule *m*; (*of water etc*) gouttelette *f*.
gloom [gluːm] *n* obscurité *f*; (*sadness*) tristesse *f*, mélancolie *f*.
gloomy ['gluːmɪ] *adj* sombre, triste, mélancolique; **to feel ~** avoir *or* se faire des idées noires.
glorification [glɔːrɪfɪ'keɪʃən] *n* glorification *f*.
glorify ['glɔːrɪfaɪ] *vt* glorifier.
glorious ['glɔːrɪəs] *adj* glorieux(euse); (*beautiful*) splendide.
glory ['glɔːrɪ] *n* gloire *f*; splendeur *f* ♦ *vi*: **to ~ in** se glorifier de.
glory hole *n* (*col*) capharnaüm *m*.
Glos *abbr* (*BRIT*) = *Gloucestershire*.
gloss [glɔs] *n* (*shine*) brillant *m*, vernis *m*; (*also*: **~ paint**) peinture brillante *or* laquée.
►**gloss over** *vt fus* glisser sur.
glossary ['glɔsərɪ] *n* glossaire *m*, lexique *m*.
glossy ['glɔsɪ] *adj* brillant(e), luisant(e) ♦ *n* (*also*: **~ magazine**) revue *f* de luxe.
glove [glʌv] *n* gant *m*.
glove compartment *n* (*AUT*) boîte *f* à gants, vide-poches *m inv*.
glow [gləu] *vi* rougeoyer; (*face*) rayonner ♦ *n* rougeoiement *m*.
glower ['glauə*] *vi* lancer des regards mauvais.
glowing ['gləuɪŋ] *adj* (*fire*) rougeoyant(e); (*complexion*) éclatant(e); (*report, description etc*) dithyrambique.
glow-worm ['gləuwəːm] *n* ver luisant.
glucose ['gluːkəus] *n* glucose *m*.
glue [gluː] *n* colle *f* ♦ *vt* coller.
glue-sniffing ['gluːsnɪfɪŋ] *n* inhalation *f* de colle.
glum [glʌm] *adj* maussade, morose.
glut [glʌt] *n* surabondance *f* ♦ *vt* rassasier; (*market*) encombrer.
glutinous ['gluːtɪnəs] *adj* visqueux(euse).
glutton ['glʌtn] *n* glouton/ne; **a ~ for work** un bourreau de travail.
gluttonous ['glʌtənəs] *adj* glouton(ne).

gluttony ['glʌtənɪ] *n* gloutonnerie *f*; (*sin*) gourmandise *f*.
glycerin(e) ['glɪsəri:n] *n* glycérine *f*.
gm *abbr* (= *gram*) g.
GMAT *n abbr* (*US*: = *Graduate Management Admissions Test*) *examen d'admission dans le 2e cycle de l'enseignement supérieur*.
GMO *abbr* (= *genetically modified organism*) OGM *m*.
GMT *abbr* (= *Greenwich Mean Time*) GMT.
gnarled [nɑ:ld] *adj* noueux(euse).
gnash [næʃ] *vt*: **to ~ one's teeth** grincer des dents.
gnat [næt] *n* moucheron *m*.
gnaw [nɔ:] *vt* ronger.
gnome [nəum] *n* gnome *m*, lutin *m*.
GNP *n abbr* = **gross national product**.
GNVQ *n abbr* (*BRIT*: = *General National Vocational Qualification*) *diplôme professionnel national*.
go [gəu] *vb* (*pt* **went**, *pp* **gone** [wɛnt, gɔn]) *vi* aller; (*depart*) partir, s'en aller; (*work*) marcher; (*be sold*): **to ~ for £10** se vendre 10 livres; (*fit, suit*): **to ~ with** aller avec; (*become*): **to ~ pale/mouldy** pâlir/moisir; (*break etc*) céder ♦ *n* (*pl*: **~es**): **to have a ~ (at)** essayer (de faire); **to be on the ~** être en mouvement; **whose ~ is it?** à qui est-ce de jouer?; **to ~ by car/on foot** aller en voiture/ à pied; **he's ~ing to do** il va faire, il est sur le point de faire; **to ~ for a walk** aller se promener; **to ~ dancing/shopping** aller danser/faire les courses; **to ~ looking for sb/sth** aller *or* partir à la recherche de qn/ qch; **to ~ to sleep** s'endormir; **to ~ and see sb, to ~ to see sb** aller voir qn; **how is it ~ing?** comment ça marche?; **how did it ~?** comment est-ce que ça s'est passé?; **to ~ round the back/by the shop** passer par derrière/devant le magasin; **my voice has gone** j'ai une extinction de voix; **the cake is all gone** il n'y a plus de gâteau; **I'll take whatever is ~ing** (*BRIT*) je prendrai ce qu'il y a (*or* ce que vous avez); **... to ~** (*US*: *food*) ... à emporter.
►**go about** *vi* (*also*: **~ around**) aller çà et là; (*: rumour*) se répandre ♦ *vt fus*: **how do I ~ about this?** comment dois-je m'y prendre (pour faire ceci)?; **to ~ about one's business** s'occuper de ses affaires.
►**go after** *vt fus* (*pursue*) poursuivre, courir après; (*job, record etc*) essayer d'obtenir.
►**go against** *vt fus* (*be unfavourable to*) être défavorable à; (*be contrary to*) être contraire à.
►**go ahead** *vi* (*make progress*) avancer; (*get going*) y aller.
►**go along** *vi* aller, avancer ♦ *vt fus* longer, parcourir; **as you ~ along (with your work)** au fur et à mesure (de votre travail); **to ~ along with** accompagner; (*agree with: idea*) être d'accord sur; (*: person*) suivre.
►**go away** *vi* partir, s'en aller.
►**go back** *vi* rentrer; revenir; (*go again*) retourner.
►**go back on** *vt fus* (*promise*) revenir sur.
►**go by** *vi* (*years, time*) passer, s'écouler ♦ *vt fus* s'en tenir à; (*believe*) en croire.
►**go down** *vi* descendre; (*ship*) couler; (*sun*) se coucher ♦ *vt fus* descendre; **that should ~ down well with him** ça devrait lui plaire.
►**go for** *vt fus* (*fetch*) aller chercher; (*like*) aimer; (*attack*) s'en prendre à; attaquer.
►**go in** *vi* entrer.
►**go in for** *vt fus* (*competition*) se présenter à; (*like*) aimer.
►**go into** *vt fus* entrer dans; (*investigate*) étudier, examiner; (*embark on*) se lancer dans.
►**go off** *vi* partir, s'en aller; (*food*) se gâter; (*bomb*) sauter; (*lights etc*) s'éteindre; (*event*) se dérouler ♦ *vt fus* ne plus aimer, ne plus avoir envie de; **the gun went off** le coup est parti; **to ~ off to sleep** s'endormir; **the party went off well** la fête s'est bien passée *or* était très réussie.
►**go on** *vi* continuer; (*happen*) se passer; (*lights*) s'allumer ♦ *vt fus* (*be guided by: evidence etc*) se fonder sur; **to ~ on doing** continuer à faire; **what's ~ing on here?** qu'est-ce qui se passe ici?
►**go on at** *vt fus* (*nag*) tomber sur le dos de.
►**go on with** *vt fus* poursuivre, continuer.
►**go out** *vi* sortir; (*fire, light*) s'éteindre; (*tide*) descendre; **to ~ out with sb** sortir avec qn.
►**go over** *vi* (*ship*) chavirer ♦ *vt fus* (*check*) revoir, vérifier; **to ~ over sth in one's mind** repasser qch dans son esprit.
►**go round** *vi* (*circulate: news, rumour*) circuler; (*revolve*) tourner; (*visit*): **to ~ round to sb's** passer chez qn; aller chez qn; (*make a detour*): **to ~ round (by)** faire un détour (par); (*suffice*) suffire (pour tout le monde).
►**go through** *vt fus* (*town etc*) traverser; (*search through*) fouiller; (*examine: list, book*) lire *or* regarder en détail, éplucher; (*perform: lesson*) réciter; (*: formalities*) remplir; (*: programme*) exécuter.
►**go through with** *vt fus* (*plan, crime*) aller jusqu'au bout de.
►**go under** *vi* (*sink: also fig*) couler; (*: person*) succomber.
►**go up** *vi* monter; (*price*) augmenter ♦ *vt fus* gravir; **to ~ up in flames** flamber, s'enflammer brusquement.
►**go without** *vt fus* se passer de.
goad [gəud] *vt* aiguillonner.
go-ahead ['gəuəhɛd] *adj* dynamique, entreprenant(e) ♦ *n* feu vert.
goal [gəul] *n* but *m*.
goal difference *n* différence *f* de buts.
goalie ['gəulɪ] *n* (*col*) goal *m*.
goalkeeper ['gəulki:pə*] *n* gardien *m* de but.
goal post *n* poteau *m* de but.
goat [gəut] *n* chèvre *f*.
gobble ['gɔbl] *vt* (*also*: **~ down, ~ up**) engloutir.

go-between ['gəubɪtwiːn] *n* médiateur *m*.
Gobi Desert ['gəubɪ-] *n* désert *m* de Gobi.
goblet ['gɔblɪt] *n* goblet *m*.
goblin ['gɔblɪn] *n* lutin *m*.
go-cart ['gəukɑːt] *n* kart *m* ♦ *cpd*: ~ **racing** *n* karting *m*.
god [gɔd] *n* dieu *m*; **G~** Dieu.
god-awful [gɔd'ɔːfəl] *adj* (*col*) franchement atroce.
godchild ['gɔdtʃaɪld] *n* filleul/e.
goddamn(ed) ['gɔddæm(d)] *excl* (*esp US col*): **goddamn (it)!** nom de Dieu! ♦ *adj* satané(e), sacré(e) ♦ *adv* sacrément.
goddaughter ['gɔddɔːtə*] *n* filleule *f*.
goddess ['gɔdɪs] *n* déesse *f*.
godfather ['gɔdfɑːðə*] *n* parrain *m*.
god-fearing ['gɔdfɪərɪŋ] *adj* croyant(e).
god-forsaken ['gɔdfəseɪkən] *adj* maudit(e).
godmother ['gɔdmʌðə*] *n* marraine *f*.
godparents ['gɔdpɛərənts] *npl*: **the** ~ le parrain et la marraine.
godsend ['gɔdsɛnd] *n* aubaine *f*.
godson ['gɔdsʌn] *n* filleul *m*.
goes [gəuz] *vb see* **go**.
gofer ['gəufə*] *n* coursier/ière.
go-getter ['gəugɛtə*] *n* arriviste *m/f*.
goggle ['gɔgl] *vi*: **to** ~ **at** regarder avec des yeux ronds.
goggles ['gɔglz] *npl* lunettes (protectrices) (*de motocycliste etc*).
going ['gəuɪŋ] *n* (*conditions*) état *m* du terrain ♦ *adj*: **the** ~ **rate** le tarif (en vigueur); **a** ~ **concern** une affaire prospère; **it was slow** ~ les progrès étaient lents, ça n'avançait pas vite.
going-over [gəuɪŋ'əuvə*] *n* vérification *f*, révision *f*; (*col: beating*) passage *m* à tabac.
goings-on ['gəuɪŋz'ɔn] *npl* (*col*) manigances *fpl*.
go-kart ['gəukɑːt] *n* = **go-cart**.
gold [gəuld] *n* or *m* ♦ *adj* en or; (*reserves*) d'or.
golden ['gəuldən] *adj* (*made of gold*) en or; (*gold in colour*) doré(e).
golden age *n* âge *m* d'or.
golden handshake *n* (*BRIT*) prime *f* de départ.
golden rule *n* règle *f* d'or.
goldfish ['gəuldfɪʃ] *n* poisson *m* rouge.
gold leaf *n* or *m* en feuille.
gold medal *n* (*SPORT*) médaille *f* d'or.
goldmine ['gəuldmaɪn] *n* mine *f* d'or.
gold-plated ['gəuld'pleɪtɪd] *adj* plaqué(e) or *inv*.
goldsmith ['gəuldsmɪθ] *n* orfèvre *m*.
gold standard *n* étalon-or *m*.
golf [gɔlf] *n* golf *m*.
golf ball *n* balle *f* de golf; (*on typewriter*) boule *f*.
golf club *n* club *m* de golf; (*stick*) club *m*, crosse *f* de golf.
golf course *n* terrain *m* de golf.
golfer ['gɔlfə*] *n* joueur/euse de golf.
golfing ['gɔlfɪŋ] *n* golf *m*.
gondola ['gɔndələ] *n* gondole *f*.
gondolier [gɔndə'lɪə*] *n* gondolier *m*.
gone [gɔn] *pp of* **go** ♦ *adj* parti(e).
goner ['gɔnə*] *n* (*col*): **to be a** ~ être fichu(e) *or* foutu(e).
gong [gɔŋ] *n* gong *m*.
good [gud] *adj* bon(ne); (*kind*) gentil(le); (*child*) sage ♦ *n* bien *m*; ~! bon!, très bien!; **to be** ~ **at** être bon en; **it's** ~ **for you** c'est bon pour vous; **it's a** ~ **thing you were there** heureusement que vous étiez là; **she is** ~ **with children/her hands** elle sait bien s'occuper des enfants/sait se servir de ses mains; **to feel** ~ se sentir bien; **it's** ~ **to see you** ça me fait plaisir de vous voir, je suis content de vous voir; **he's up to no** ~ il prépare quelque mauvais coup; **it's no** ~ **complaining** cela ne sert à rien de se plaindre; **for the common** ~ dans l'intérêt commun; **for** ~ (*for ever*) pour de bon, une fois pour toutes; **would you be** ~ **enough to ...?** auriez-vous la bonté *or* l'amabilité de ...?; **that's very** ~ **of you** c'est très gentil de votre part; **is this any** ~**?** (*will it do?*) est-ce que ceci fera l'affaire?, est-ce que cela peut vous rendre service?; (*what's it like?*) qu'est-ce que ça vaut?; **a** ~ **deal (of)** beaucoup (de); **a** ~ **many** beaucoup (de); ~ **morning/afternoon!** bonjour!; ~ **evening!** bonsoir!; ~ **night!** bonsoir!; (*on going to bed*) bonne nuit!
goodbye [gud'baɪ] *excl* au revoir!; **to say** ~ **to** dire au revoir à.
good faith *n* bonne foi.
good-for-nothing ['gudfənʌθɪŋ] *adj* bon(ne) *or* propre à rien.
Good Friday *n* Vendredi saint.
good-humoured ['gud'hjuːməd] *adj* (*person*) jovial(e); (*remark, joke*) sans malice.
good-looking ['gud'lukɪŋ] *adj* bien *inv*.
good-natured ['gud'neɪtʃəd] *adj* (*person*) qui a un bon naturel; (*discussion*) enjoué(e).
goodness ['gudnɪs] *n* (*of person*) bonté *f*; **for** ~ **sake!** je vous en prie!; ~ **gracious!** mon Dieu!
goods [gudz] *npl* marchandise *f*, articles *mpl*; (*COMM etc*) marchandises; ~ **and chattels** biens *mpl* et effets *mpl*.
goods train *n* (*BRIT*) train *m* de marchandises.
goodwill [gud'wɪl] *n* bonne volonté; (*COMM*) réputation *f* (auprès de la clientèle).
goody-goody ['gudɪgudɪ] *n* (*pej*) petit saint, sainte nitouche.
gooey ['guːɪ] *adj* (*BRIT col*) gluant(e).
goose, *pl* **geese** [guːs, giːs] *n* oie *f*.
gooseberry ['guzbərɪ] *n* groseille *f* à maquereau; **to play** ~ (*BRIT*) tenir la chandelle.
gooseflesh ['guːsflɛʃ] *n*, **goosepimples** ['guːspɪmplz] *npl* chair *f* de poule.
goose step *n* (*MIL*) pas *m* de l'oie.
GOP *n abbr* (*US POL*: *col*: = *Grand Old Party*) parti

républicain.
gopher ['gəufə*] *n* = **gofer**.
gore [gɔː*] *vt* encorner ♦ *n* sang *m*.
gorge [gɔːdʒ] *n* gorge *f* ♦ *vt*: **to ~ o.s. (on)** se gorger (de).
gorgeous ['gɔːdʒəs] *adj* splendide, superbe.
gorilla [gə'rɪlə] *n* gorille *m*.
gormless ['gɔːmlɪs] *adj* (*BRIT col*) lourdaud(e).
gorse [gɔːs] *n* ajoncs *mpl*.
gory ['gɔːrɪ] *adj* sanglant(e).
go-slow ['gəu'sləu] *n* (*BRIT*) grève perlée.
gospel ['gɔspl] *n* évangile *m*.
gossamer ['gɔsəmə*] *n* (*cobweb*) fils *mpl* de la vierge; (*light fabric*) étoffe très légère.
gossip ['gɔsɪp] *n* bavardages *mpl*; (*malicious*) commérage *m*, cancans *mpl*; (*person*) commère *f* ♦ *vi* bavarder; cancaner, faire des commérages; **a piece of ~** un ragot, un racontar.
gossip column *n* (*PRESS*) échos *mpl*.
got [gɔt] *pt*, *pp of* **get**.
Gothic ['gɔθɪk] *adj* gothique.
gotten ['gɔtn] (*US*) *pp of* **get**.
gouge [gaudʒ] *vt* (*also*: **~ out**: *hole etc*) évider; (*: initials*) tailler; **to ~ sb's eyes out** crever les yeux à qn.
gourd [guəd] *n* calebasse *f*, gourde *f*.
gourmet ['guəmeɪ] *n* gourmet *m*, gastronome *m/f*.
gout [gaut] *n* goutte *f*.
govern ['gʌvən] *vt* (*gen, LING*) gouverner.
governess ['gʌvənɪs] *n* gouvernante *f*.
governing ['gʌvənɪŋ] *adj* (*POL*) au pouvoir, au gouvernement; **~ body conseil** *m* d'administration.
government ['gʌvnmənt] *n* gouvernement *m*; (*BRIT: ministers*) ministère *m* ♦ *cpd* de l'État; **local ~** administration locale.
governmental [gʌvn'mɛntl] *adj* gouvernemental(e).
government housing *n* (*US*) logements sociaux.
government stock *n* titres *mpl* d'État.
governor ['gʌvənə*] *n* (*of colony, state, bank*) gouverneur *m*; (*of school, hospital etc*) administrateur/trice; (*BRIT: of prison*) directeur/trice.
Govt *abbr* (= *government*) gvt.
gown [gaun] *n* robe *f*; (*of teacher, BRIT: of judge*) toge *f*.
GP *n abbr* (*MED*) = **general practitioner**.
GPMU *n abbr* (*BRIT*) = *Graphical, Paper and Media Union.*
GPO *n abbr* (*BRIT: old*) = *General Post Office*; (*US*) = *Government Printing Office.*
gr. *abbr* (*COMM*) = **gross**.
grab [græb] *vt* saisir, empoigner; (*property, power*) se saisir de ♦ *vi*: **to ~ at** essayer de saisir.
grace [greɪs] *n* grâce *f* ♦ *vt* honorer; **5 days' ~** répit *m* de 5 jours; **to say ~** dire le bénédicité; (*after meal*) dire les grâces; **with a good/bad ~** de bonne/mauvaise grâce; **his sense of humour is his saving ~** il se rachète par son sens de l'humour.
graceful ['greɪsful] *adj* gracieux(euse), élégant(e).
gracious ['greɪʃəs] *adj* (*kind*) charmant(e), bienveillant(e); (*elegant*) plein(e) d'élégance, d'une grande élégance; (*formal: pardon etc*) miséricordieux(euse) ♦ *excl*: **(good) ~!** mon Dieu!
gradation [grə'deɪʃən] *n* gradation *f*.
grade [greɪd] *n* (*COMM*) qualité *f*; calibre *m*; catégorie *f*; (*in hierarchy*) grade *m*, échelon *m*; (*US: SCOL*) note *f*; classe *f*; (*: gradient*) pente *f* ♦ *vt* classer; calibrer; graduer; **to make the ~** (*fig*) réussir.
grade crossing *n* (*US*) passage *m* à niveau.
grade school *n* (*US*) école *f* primaire.
gradient ['greɪdɪənt] *n* inclinaison *f*, pente *f*; (*GEOM*) gradient *m*.
gradual ['grædjuəl] *adj* graduel(le), progressif(ive).
gradually ['grædjuəlɪ] *adv* peu à peu, graduellement.
graduate *n* ['grædjuɪt] diplômé/e d'université; (*US*) diplômé/e de fin d'études ♦ *vi* ['grædjueɪt] obtenir un diplôme d'université (*or* de fin d'études).
graduated pension ['grædjueɪtɪd-] *n* retraite calculée en fonction des derniers salaires.
graduation [grædju'eɪʃən] *n* cérémonie *f* de remise des diplômes.
graffiti [grə'fiːtɪ] *npl* graffiti *mpl*.
graft [grɑːft] *n* (*AGR, MED*) greffe *f*; (*bribery*) corruption *f* ♦ *vt* greffer; **hard ~** (*col*) boulot acharné.
grain [greɪn] *n* grain *m*; (*no pl: cereals*) céréales *fpl*; (*US: corn*) blé *m*; **it goes against the ~** cela va à l'encontre de sa (*or* ma *etc*) nature.
gram [græm] *n* gramme *m*.
grammar ['græmə*] *n* grammaire *f*.
grammar school *n* (*BRIT*) ≈ lycée *m*.
grammatical [grə'mætɪkl] *adj* grammatical(e).
gramme [græm] *n* = **gram**.
gramophone ['græməfəun] *n* (*BRIT*) gramophone *m*.
granary ['grænərɪ] *n* grenier *m*.
grand [grænd] *adj* splendide, imposant(e); (*terrific*) magnifique, formidable; (*also humorous: gesture etc*) noble ♦ *n* (*col: thousand*) mille livres *fpl* (*or* dollars *mpl*).
grandchildren ['græntʃɪldrən] *npl* petits-enfants *mpl*.
granddad ['grændæd] *n* grand-papa *m*.
granddaughter ['grændɔːtə*] *n* petite-fille *f*.
grandeur ['grændjə*] *n* magnificence *f*, splendeur *f*; (*of position etc*) éminence *f*.
grandfather ['grændfɑːðə*] *n* grand-père *m*.
grandiose ['grændɪəus] *adj* grandiose; (*pej*) pompeux(euse).
grand jury *n* (*US*) jury *m* d'accusation (*formé*

de 12 à 23 jurés).
grandma ['grænmɑː] *n* grand-maman *f*.
grandmother ['grænmʌðə*] *n* grand-mère *f*.
grandpa ['grænpɑː] *n* = **granddad**.
grandparent ['grændpɛərənt] *n* grand-père/grand-mère.
grand piano *n* piano *m* à queue.
Grand Prix ['grɑ̃ː'priː] *n* (*AUT*) grand prix automobile.
grandson ['grænsʌn] *n* petit-fils *m*.
grandstand ['grændstænd] *n* (*SPORT*) tribune *f*.
grand total *n* total général.
granite ['grænɪt] *n* granit *m*.
granny ['grænɪ] *n* grand-maman *f*.
grant [grɑːnt] *vt* accorder; (*a request*) accéder à; (*admit*) concéder ♦ *n* (*SCOL*) bourse *f*; (*ADMIN*) subside *m*, subvention *f*; **to take sth for ~ed** considérer qch comme acquis; **to ~ that** admettre que.
granulated ['grænjuleɪtɪd] *adj*: **~ sugar** sucre *m* en poudre.
granule ['grænjuːl] *n* granule *m*.
grape [greɪp] *n* raisin *m*; **a bunch of ~s** une grappe de raisin.
grapefruit ['greɪpfruːt] *n* pamplemousse *m*.
grapevine ['greɪpvaɪn] *n* vigne *f*; **I heard it on the ~** (*fig*) je l'ai appris par le téléphone arabe.
graph [grɑːf] *n* graphique *m*, courbe *f*.
graphic ['græfɪk] *adj* graphique; (*vivid*) vivant(e).
graphic designer *n* graphiste *m/f*.
graphic equalizer *n* égaliseur *m* graphique.
graphics ['græfɪks] *n* (*art*) arts *mpl* graphiques; (*process*) graphisme *m*; (*pl: drawings*) illustrations *fpl*.
graphite ['græfaɪt] *n* graphite *m*.
graph paper *n* papier millimétré.
grapple ['græpl] *vi*: **to ~ with** être aux prises avec.
grappling iron ['græplɪŋ-] *n* (*NAUT*) grappin *m*.
grasp [grɑːsp] *vt* saisir, empoigner; (*understand*) saisir, comprendre ♦ *n* (*grip*) prise *f*; (*fig*) compréhension *f*, connaissance *f*; **to have sth within one's ~** avoir qch à sa portée; **to have a good ~ of sth** (*fig*) bien comprendre qch.
►**grasp at** *vt fus* (*rope etc*) essayer de saisir; (*fig: opportunity*) sauter sur.
grasping ['grɑːspɪŋ] *adj* avide.
grass [grɑːs] *n* herbe *f*; (*BRIT col: informer*) mouchard/e; (*: ex-terrorist*) balanceur/euse.
grasshopper ['grɑːshɔpə*] *n* sauterelle *f*.
grassland ['grɑːslænd] *n* prairie *f*.
grass roots *npl* (*fig*) base *f*.
grass snake *n* couleuvre *f*.
grassy ['grɑːsɪ] *adj* herbeux(euse).
grate [greɪt] *n* grille *f* de cheminée ♦ *vi* grincer ♦ *vt* (*CULIN*) râper.
grateful ['greɪtful] *adj* reconnaissant(e).
gratefully ['greɪtfəlɪ] *adv* avec reconnaissance.
grater ['greɪtə*] *n* râpe *f*.
gratification [grætɪfɪ'keɪʃən] *n* satisfaction *f*.
gratify ['grætɪfaɪ] *vt* faire plaisir à; (*whim*) satisfaire.
gratifying ['grætɪfaɪɪŋ] *adj* agréable; satisfaisant(e).
grating ['greɪtɪŋ] *n* (*iron bars*) grille *f* ♦ *adj* (*noise*) grinçant(e).
gratitude ['grætɪtjuːd] *n* gratitude *f*.
gratuitous [grə'tjuːɪtəs] *adj* gratuit(e).
gratuity [grə'tjuːɪtɪ] *n* pourboire *m*.
grave [greɪv] *n* tombe *f* ♦ *adj* grave, sérieux(euse).
gravedigger ['greɪvdɪgə*] *n* fossoyeur *m*.
gravel ['grævl] *n* gravier *m*.
gravely ['greɪvlɪ] *adv* gravement, sérieusement; **~ ill** gravement malade.
gravestone ['greɪvstəun] *n* pierre tombale.
graveyard ['greɪvjɑːd] *n* cimetière *m*.
gravitate ['grævɪteɪt] *vi* graviter.
gravity ['grævɪtɪ] *n* (*PHYSICS*) gravité *f*; pesanteur *f*; (*seriousness*) gravité, sérieux *m*.
gravy ['greɪvɪ] *n* jus *m* (de viande); sauce *f* (au jus de viande).
gravy boat *n* saucière *f*.
gravy train *n* (*col*): **to ride the ~** avoir une bonne planque.
gray [greɪ] *adj* (*US*) = **grey**.
graze [greɪz] *vi* paître, brouter ♦ *vt* (*touch lightly*) frôler, effleurer; (*scrape*) écorcher ♦ *n* écorchure *f*.
grazing ['greɪzɪŋ] *n* (*pasture*) pâturage *m*.
grease [griːs] *n* (*fat*) graisse *f*; (*lubricant*) lubrifiant *m* ♦ *vt* graisser; lubrifier; **to ~ the skids** (*US: fig*) huiler les rouages.
grease gun *n* graisseur *m*.
greasepaint ['griːspeɪnt] *n* produits *mpl* de maquillage.
greaseproof paper ['griːspruːf-] *n* (*BRIT*) papier sulfurisé.
greasy ['griːsɪ] *adj* gras(se), graisseux(euse); (*hands, clothes*) graisseux; (*BRIT: road, surface*) glissant(e).
great [greɪt] *adj* grand(e); (*heat, pain etc*) très fort(e), intense; (*col*) formidable; **they're ~ friends** ils sont très amis, ce sont de grands amis; **we had a ~ time** nous nous sommes bien amusés; **it was ~!** c'était fantastique *or* super!; **the ~ thing is that** ... ce qu'il y a de vraiment bien c'est que ....
Great Barrier Reef *n*: **the ~** la Grande Barrière.
Great Britain *n* Grande-Bretagne *f*.
great-grandchild, *pl* **-children** [greɪt'græntʃaɪld, -tʃɪldrən] *n* arrière-petit(e)-enfant.
great-grandfather [greɪt'grænfɑːðə*] *n* arrière-grand-père *m*.
great-grandmother [greɪt'grænmʌðə*] *n* arrière-grand-mère *f*.
Great Lakes *npl*: **the ~** les Grands Lacs.

greatly ['greɪtlɪ] *adv* très, grandement; (*with verbs*) beaucoup.
greatness ['greɪtnɪs] *n* grandeur *f*.
Grecian ['gri:ʃən] *adj* grec(grecque).
Greece [gri:s] *n* Grèce *f*.
greed [gri:d] *n* (*also*: ~**iness**) avidité *f*; (*for food*) gourmandise *f*.
greedily ['gri:dɪlɪ] *adv* avidement; avec gourmandise.
greedy ['gri:dɪ] *adj* avide; gourmand(e).
Greek [gri:k] *adj* grec(grecque) ♦ *n* Grec/Grecque; (*LING*) grec *m*; **ancient/modern** ~ grec classique/moderne.
green [gri:n] *adj* vert(e); (*inexperienced*) (bien) jeune, naïf(ïve); (*ecological: product etc*) écologique ♦ *n* (*colour, of golf course*) vert *m*; (*stretch of grass*) pelouse *f*; (*also*: **village** ~) ≈ place *f* du village; ~**s** *npl* légumes verts; **to have** ~ **fingers** *or* (*US*) **a** ~ **thumb** (*fig*) avoir le pouce vert; **G**~ (*POL*) écologiste (*m/f*); **the G**~ **Party** le parti écologiste.
green belt *n* (*round town*) ceinture verte.
green card *n* (*AUT*) carte verte.
greenery ['gri:nərɪ] *n* verdure *f*.
greenfly ['gri:nflaɪ] *n* (*BRIT*) puceron *m*.
greengage ['gri:ngeɪdʒ] *n* reine-claude *f*.
greengrocer ['gri:ngrəusə*] *n* (*BRIT*) marchand *m* de fruits et légumes.
greenhouse ['gri:nhaus] *n* serre *f*.
greenhouse effect *n*: **the** ~ l'effet *m* de serre.
greenhouse gas *n* gaz *m* contribuant à l'effet de serre.
greenish ['gri:nɪʃ] *adj* verdâtre.
Greenland ['gri:nlənd] *n* Groenland *m*.
Greenlander ['gri:nləndə*] *n* Groenlandais/e.
green light *n*: **to give sb/sth the** ~ donner le feu vert à qn/qch.
green pepper *n* poivron (vert).
green pound *n* (*ECON*) livre verte.
greet [gri:t] *vt* accueillir.
greeting ['gri:tɪŋ] *n* salutation *f*; **Christmas/birthday** ~**s** souhaits *mpl* de Noël/de bon anniversaire.
greeting(s) card *n* carte *f* de vœux.
gregarious [grə'gɛərɪəs] *adj* grégaire; sociable.
grenade [grə'neɪd] *n* (*also*: **hand** ~) grenade *f*.
grew [gru:] *pt of* **grow**.
grey [greɪ] *adj* gris(e); (*dismal*) sombre; **to go** ~ (commencer à) grisonner.
grey-haired [greɪ'hɛəd] *adj* aux cheveux gris.
greyhound ['greɪhaund] *n* lévrier *m*.
grid [grɪd] *n* grille *f*; (*ELEC*) réseau *m*; (*US AUT*) intersection *f* (*matérialisée par des marques au sol*).
griddle [grɪdl] *n* (*on cooker*) plaque chauffante.
gridiron ['grɪdaɪən] *n* gril *m*.
gridlock ['grɪdlɔk] *n* (*traffic jam*) embouteillage *m*.
grief [gri:f] *n* chagrin *m*, douleur *f*; **to come to** ~ (*plan*) échouer; (*person*) avoir un malheur.
grievance ['gri:vəns] *n* doléance *f*, grief *m*; (*cause for complaint*) grief.
grieve [gri:v] *vi* avoir du chagrin; se désoler ♦ *vt* faire de la peine à, affliger; **to** ~ **at** se désoler de; pleurer.
grievous ['gri:vəs] *adj* grave; cruel(le); ~ **bodily harm** (*LAW*) coups *mpl* et blessures *fpl*.
grill [grɪl] *n* (*on cooker*) gril *m* ♦ *vt* (*BRIT*) griller; (*question*) interroger longuement, cuisiner.
grille [grɪl] *n* grillage *m*; (*AUT*) calandre *f*.
grill(room) ['grɪl(rum)] *n* rôtisserie *f*.
grim [grɪm] *adj* sinistre, lugubre.
grimace [grɪ'meɪs] *n* grimace *f* ♦ *vi* grimacer, faire une grimace.
grime [graɪm] *n* crasse *f*.
grimy ['graɪmɪ] *adj* crasseux(euse).
grin [grɪn] *n* large sourire *m* ♦ *vi* sourire; **to** ~ **(at)** faire un grand sourire (à).
grind [graɪnd] *vb* (*pt, pp* **ground** [graund]) *vt* écraser; (*coffee, pepper etc*) moudre; (*US: meat*) hacher; (*make sharp*) aiguiser; (*polish: gem, lens*) polir ♦ *vi* (*car gears*) grincer ♦ *n* (*work*) corvée *f*; **to** ~ **one's teeth** grincer des dents; **to** ~ **to a halt** (*vehicle*) s'arrêter dans un grincement de freins; (*fig*) s'arrêter, s'immobiliser; **the daily** ~ (*col*) le train-train quotidien.
grinder ['graɪndə*] *n* (*machine: for coffee*) moulin *m* (à café); (*: for waste disposal etc*) broyeur *m*.
grindstone ['graɪndstəun] *n*: **to keep one's nose to the** ~ travailler sans relâche.
grip [grɪp] *n* (*control, grasp*) étreinte *f*; (*hold*) prise *f*; (*handle*) poignée *f*; (*holdall*) sac *m* de voyage ♦ *vt* saisir, empoigner, étreindre; **to come to** ~**s with** se colleter avec, en venir aux prises avec; **to** ~ **the road** (*AUT*) adhérer à la route; **to lose one's** ~ lâcher prise; (*fig*) perdre les pédales, être dépassé(e).
gripe [graɪp] *n* (*MED*) coliques *fpl*; (*col: complaint*) ronchonnement *m*, rouspétance *f* ♦ *vi* (*col*) râler.
gripping ['grɪpɪŋ] *adj* prenant(e), palpitant(e).
grisly ['grɪzlɪ] *adj* sinistre, macabre.
grist [grɪst] *n* (*fig*): **it's (all)** ~ **to his mill** ça l'arrange, ça apporte de l'eau à son moulin.
gristle ['grɪsl] *n* cartilage *m* (*de poulet etc*).
grit [grɪt] *n* gravillon *m*; (*courage*) cran *m* ♦ *vt* (*road*) sabler; **to** ~ **one's teeth** serrer les dents; **to have a piece of** ~ **in one's eye** avoir une poussière *or* saleté dans l'œil.
grits [grɪts] *npl* (*US*) gruau *m* de maïs.
grizzle ['grɪzl] *vi* (*BRIT*) pleurnicher.
grizzly ['grɪzlɪ] *n* (*also*: ~ **bear**) grizzli *m*, ours gris.
groan [grəun] *n* gémissement *m*; grognement *m* ♦ *vi* gémir; grogner.
grocer ['grəusə*] *n* épicier *m*; **at the** ~**'s** à l'épicerie, chez l'épicier.
groceries ['grəusərɪz] *npl* provisions *fpl*.
grocery ['grəusərɪ] *n* (*shop*) épicerie *f*.

grog [grɔg] *n* grog *m*.
groggy ['grɔgɪ] *adj* groggy *inv*.
groin [grɔɪn] *n* aine *f*.
groom [gruːm] *n* palefrenier *m*; (*also*: **bride**~) marié *m* ♦ *vt* (*horse*) panser; (*fig*): **to ~ sb for** former qn pour.
groove [gruːv] *n* sillon *m*, rainure *f*.
grope [grəup] *vi* tâtonner; **to ~ for** *vt fus* chercher à tâtons.
gross [grəus] *adj* grossier(ière); (*COMM*) brut(e) ♦ *n* (*pl inv*) (*twelve dozen*) grosse *f* ♦ *vt* (*COMM*): **to ~ £500,000** gagner 500 000 livres avant impôt.
gross domestic product (GDP) *n* produit brut intérieur (PIB).
grossly ['grəuslɪ] *adv* (*greatly*) très, grandement.
gross national product (GNP) *n* produit national brut (PNB).
grotesque [grə'tɛsk] *adj* grotesque.
grotto ['grɔtəu] *n* grotte *f*.
grotty ['grɔtɪ] *adj* (*BRIT col*) minable.
grouch [grautʃ] (*col*) *vi* rouspéter ♦ *n* (*person*) rouspéteur/euse.
ground [graund] *pt, pp of* **grind** ♦ *n* sol *m*, terre *f*; (*land*) terrain *m*, terres *fpl*; (*SPORT*) terrain; (*reason: gen pl*) raison *f*; (*US*: *also*: **~ wire**) terre *f* ♦ *vt* (*plane*) empêcher de décoller, retenir au sol; (*US ELEC*) équiper d'une prise de terre, mettre à la terre ♦ *vi* (*ship*) s'échouer ♦ *adj* (*coffee etc*) moulu(e); (*US*: *meat*) haché(e); **~s** *npl* (*gardens etc*) parc *m*, domaine *m*; (*of coffee*) marc *m*; **on the ~, to the ~** par terre; **below ~** sous terre; **to gain/lose ~** gagner/perdre du terrain; **common ~** terrain d'entente; **he covered a lot of ~ in his lecture** sa conférence a traité un grand nombre de questions *or* la question en profondeur.
ground cloth *n* (*US*) = **groundsheet**.
ground control *n* (*AVIAT, SPACE*) centre *m* de contrôle (au sol).
ground floor *n* (*BRIT*) rez-de-chaussée *m*.
grounding ['graundɪŋ] *n* (*in education*) connaissances *fpl* de base.
groundless ['graundlɪs] *adj* sans fondement.
groundnut ['graundnʌt] *n* arachide *f*.
ground rent *n* (*BRIT*) fermage *m*.
ground rules *npl*: **the ~** les principes *mpl* de base.
groundsheet ['graundʃiːt] *n* (*BRIT*) tapis *m* de sol.
groundsman ['graundzmən], (*US*) **groundskeeper** ['graundzkiːpə*] *n* (*SPORT*) gardien *m* de stade.
ground staff *n* équipage *m* au sol.
groundswell ['graundswɛl] *n* lame *f or* vague *f* de fond.
ground-to-air ['grauntu'ɛə*] *adj* (*MIL*) sol-air *inv*.
ground-to-ground ['grauntə'graund] *adj* (*MIL*) sol-sol *inv*.
groundwork ['graundwəːk] *n* préparation *f*.
group [gruːp] *n* groupe *m* ♦ *vt* (*also*: **~ together**) grouper ♦ *vi* (*also*: **~ together**) se grouper.
groupie ['gruːpɪ] *n* groupie *f*.
group therapy *n* thérapie *f* de groupe.
grouse [graus] *n* (*pl inv*) (*bird*) grouse *f* (*sorte de coq de bruyère*) ♦ *vi* (*complain*) rouspéter, râler.
grove [grəuv] *n* bosquet *m*.
grovel ['grɔvl] *vi* (*fig*): **to ~ (before)** ramper (devant).
grow, *pt* **grew**, *pp* **grown** [grəu, gruː, grəun] *vi* (*plant*) pousser, croître; (*person*) grandir; (*increase*) augmenter, se développer; (*become*): **to ~ rich/weak** s'enrichir/s'affaiblir ♦ *vt* cultiver, faire pousser.
►**grow apart** *vi* (*fig*) se détacher (l'un de l'autre).
►**grow away from** *vt fus* (*fig*) s'éloigner de.
►**grow on** *vt fus*: **that painting is ~ing on me** je finirai par aimer ce tableau.
►**grow out of** *vt fus* (*clothes*) devenir trop grand pour; (*habit*) perdre (avec le temps); **he'll ~ out of it** ça lui passera.
►**grow up** *vi* grandir.
grower ['grəuə*] *n* producteur *m*; (*AGR*) cultivateur/trice.
growing ['grəuɪŋ] *adj* (*fear, amount*) croissant(e), grandissant(e); **~ pains** (*MED*) fièvre *f* de croissance; (*fig*) difficultés *fpl* de croissance.
growing pains *npl* (*fig*) difficultés *fpl* de croissance.
growl [graul] *vi* grogner.
grown [grəun] *pp of* **grow** ♦ *adj* adulte.
grown-up [grəun'ʌp] *n* adulte *m/f*, grande personne.
growth [grəuθ] *n* croissance *f*, développement *m*; (*what has grown*) pousse *f*, poussée *f*; (*MED*) grosseur *f*, tumeur *f*.
growth rate *n* taux *m* de croissance.
GRSM *n abbr* (*BRIT*) = *Graduate of the Royal Schools of Music*.
grub [grʌb] *n* larve *f*; (*col*: *food*) bouffe *f*.
grubby ['grʌbɪ] *adj* crasseux(euse).
grudge [grʌdʒ] *n* rancune *f* ♦ *vt*: **to ~ sb sth** donner qch à qn à contre-cœur; reprocher qch à qn; **to bear sb a ~ (for)** garder rancune *or* en vouloir à qn (de); **he ~s spending** il rechigne à dépenser.
grudgingly ['grʌdʒɪŋlɪ] *adv* à contre-cœur, de mauvaise grâce.
gruelling ['gruəlɪŋ] *adj* exténuant(e).
gruesome ['gruːsəm] *adj* horrible.
gruff [grʌf] *adj* bourru(e).
grumble ['grʌmbl] *vi* rouspéter, ronchonner.
grumpy ['grʌmpɪ] *adj* grincheux(euse).
grunge [grʌndʒ] *n* (*MUS, style*) grunge *m*.
grunt [grʌnt] *vi* grogner ♦ *n* grognement *m*.
G-string ['dʒiːstrɪŋ] *n* (*garment*) cache-sexe *m inv*.

GSUSA *n abbr* = *Girl Scouts of the United States of America.*
GU *abbr* (*US*) = *Guam.*
guarantee [gærən'tiː] *n* garantie *f* ♦ *vt* garantir; **he can't ~ (that) he'll come** il n'est pas absolument certain de pouvoir venir.
guarantor [gærən'tɔː*] *n* garant/e.
guard [gɑːd] *n* garde *f*, surveillance *f*; (*squad, BOXING, FENCING*) garde *f*; (*one man*) garde *m*; (*BRIT RAIL*) chef *m* de train; (*safety device: on machine*) dispositif *m* de sûreté; (*also*: **fire~**) garde-feu *m inv* ♦ *vt* garder, surveiller; (*protect*): **to ~ (against** *or* **from)** protéger (contre); **to be on one's ~** (*fig*) être sur ses gardes.
►**guard against** *vi*: **to ~ against doing sth** se garder de faire qch.
guard dog *n* chien *m* de garde.
guarded ['gɑːdɪd] *adj* (*fig*) prudent(e).
guardian ['gɑːdɪən] *n* gardien/ne; (*of minor*) tuteur/trice.
guard's van ['gɑːdz-] *n* (*BRIT RAIL*) fourgon *m*.
Guatemala [gwɑːtɪ'mɑːlə] *n* Guatémala *m*.
Guernsey ['gəːnzɪ] *n* Guernesey *m or f*.
guerrilla [gə'rɪlə] *n* guérillero *m*.
guerrilla warfare *n* guérilla *f*.
guess [gɛs] *vi* deviner ♦ *vt* deviner; (*US*) croire, penser ♦ *n* supposition *f*, hypothèse *f*; **to take** *or* **have a ~** essayer de deviner; **to keep sb ~ing** laisser qn dans le doute *or* l'incertitude, tenir qn en haleine.
guesstimate ['gɛstɪmɪt] *n* (*col*) estimation *f*.
guesswork ['gɛswəːk] *n* hypothèse *f*; **I got the answer by ~** j'ai deviné la réponse.
guest [gɛst] *n* invité/e; (*in hotel*) client/e; **be my ~** faites comme chez vous.
guest-house ['gɛsthaus] *n* pension *f*.
guest room *n* chambre *f* d'amis.
guff [gʌf] *n* (*col*) bêtises *fpl*.
guffaw [gʌ'fɔː] *n* gros rire ♦ *vi* pouffer de rire.
guidance ['gaɪdəns] *n* conseils *mpl*; **under the ~ of** conseillé(e) *or* encadré(e) par, sous la conduite de; **vocational ~** orientation professionnelle; **marriage ~** conseils conjugaux.
guide [gaɪd] *n* (*person, book etc*) guide *m*; (*also*: **girl ~**) guide *f* ♦ *vt* guider; **to be ~d by sb/sth** se laisser guider par qn/qch.
guidebook ['gaɪdbuk] *n* guide *m*.
guided missile ['gaɪdɪd-] *n* missile téléguidé.
guide dog *n* chien *m* d'aveugle.
guide lines *npl* (*fig*) instructions générales, conseils *mpl*.
guild [gɪld] *n* corporation *f*, cercle *m*, association *f*.
guildhall ['gɪldhɔːl] *n* (*BRIT*) hôtel *m* de ville.
guile [gaɪl] *n* astuce *f*.
guileless ['gaɪllɪs] *adj* candide.
guillotine ['gɪlətiːn] *n* guillotine *f*; (*for paper*) massicot *m*.
guilt [gɪlt] *n* culpabilité *f*.
guilty ['gɪltɪ] *adj* coupable; **to plead ~/not ~** plaider coupable/non coupable; **to feel ~ about doing sth** avoir mauvaise conscience à faire qch.
Guinea ['gɪnɪ] *n*: **Republic of ~** (République *f* de) Guinée *f*.
guinea ['gɪnɪ] *n* (*BRIT*) guinée *f* (*= 21 shillings: cette monnaie de compte ne s'emploie plus*).
guinea pig *n* cobaye *m*.
guise [gaɪz] *n* aspect *m*, apparence *f*.
guitar [gɪ'tɑː*] *n* guitare *f*.
guitarist [gɪ'tɑːrɪst] *n* guitariste *m/f*.
gulch [gʌltʃ] *n* (*US*) ravin *m*.
gulf [gʌlf] *n* golfe *m*; (*abyss*) gouffre *m*; **the (Persian) G~** le golfe Persique.
Gulf States *npl*: **the ~** (*in Middle East*) les pays *mpl* du Golfe.
Gulf Stream *n*: **the ~** le Gulf Stream.
gull [gʌl] *n* mouette *f*.
gullet ['gʌlɪt] *n* gosier *m*.
gullibility [gʌlɪ'bɪlɪtɪ] *n* crédulité *f*.
gullible ['gʌlɪbl] *adj* crédule.
gully ['gʌlɪ] *n* ravin *m*; ravine *f*; couloir *m*.
gulp [gʌlp] *vi* avaler sa salive; (*from emotion*) avoir la gorge serrée, s'étrangler ♦ *vt* (*also*: **~ down**) avaler ♦ *n* (*of drink*) gorgée *f*; **at one ~** d'un seul coup.
gum [gʌm] *n* (*ANAT*) gencive *f*; (*glue*) colle *f*; (*sweet*) boule *f* de gomme; (*also*: **chewing-~**) chewing-gum *m* ♦ *vt* coller.
►**gum up** *vt*: **to ~ up the works** (*col*) bousiller tout.
gumboil ['gʌmbɔɪl] *n* abcès *m* dentaire.
gumboots ['gʌmbuːts] *npl* (*BRIT*) bottes *fpl* en caoutchouc.
gumption ['gʌmpʃən] *n* bon sens, jugeote *f*.
gun [gʌn] *n* (*small*) revolver *m*, pistolet *m*; (*rifle*) fusil *m*, carabine *f*; (*cannon*) canon *m* ♦ *vt* (*also*: **~ down**) abattre; **to stick to one's ~s** (*fig*) ne pas en démordre.
gunboat ['gʌnbəut] *n* canonnière *f*.
gun dog *n* chien *m* de chasse.
gunfire ['gʌnfaɪə*] *n* fusillade *f*.
gunk [gʌŋk] *n* (*col*) saleté *f*.
gunman ['gʌnmən] *n* bandit armé.
gunner ['gʌnə*] *n* artilleur *m*.
gunpoint ['gʌnpɔɪnt] *n*: **at ~** sous la menace du pistolet (*or* fusil).
gunpowder ['gʌnpaudə*] *n* poudre *f* à canon.
gunrunner ['gʌnrʌnə*] *n* trafiquant *m* d'armes.
gunrunning ['gʌnrʌnɪŋ] *n* trafic *m* d'armes.
gunshot ['gʌnʃɔt] *n* coup *m* de feu; **within ~** à portée de fusil.
gunsmith ['gʌnsmɪθ] *n* armurier *m*.
gurgle ['gəːgl] *n* gargouillis *m* ♦ *vi* gargouiller.
guru ['guruː] *n* gourou *m*.
gush [gʌʃ] *n* jaillissement *m*, jet *m* ♦ *vi* jaillir; (*fig*) se répandre en effusions.
gushing ['gʌʃɪŋ] *adj* (*person*) trop exubérant(e) *or* expansif(ive); (*compliments*) exagéré(e).

gusset ['gʌsɪt] *n* gousset *m*, soufflet *m*; (*in tights, pants*) entre-jambes *m*.
gust [gʌst] *n* (*of wind*) rafale *f*.
gusto ['gʌstəu] *n* enthousiasme *m*.
gusty ['gʌstɪ] *adj* venteux(euse); ~ **winds** des rafales de vent.
gut [gʌt] *n* intestin *m*, boyau *m*; (*MUS etc*) boyau ♦ *vt* (*poultry, fish*) vider; (*building*) ne laisser que les murs de; ~**s** *npl* boyaux *mpl*; (*col: courage*) cran *m*; **to hate sb's ~s** ne pas pouvoir voir qn en peinture *or* sentir qn.
gut reaction *n* réaction instinctive.
gutsy ['gʌtsɪ] *adj* (*person*) qui a du cran; (*style*) qui a du punch.
gutted ['gʌtɪd] *adj*: **I was ~** (*col: disappointed*) j'étais carrément dégoûté.
gutter ['gʌtə*] *n* (*of roof*) gouttière *f*; (*in street*) caniveau *m*; (*fig*) ruisseau *m*.
gutter press *n*: **the ~** la presse de bas étage *or* à scandale.
guttural ['gʌtərl] *adj* guttural(e).
guy [gaɪ] *n* (*also*: ~**rope**) corde *f*; (*col*: *man*) type *m*; (*figure*) *effigie de Guy Fawkes*.
Guyana [gaɪ'ænə] *n* Guyane *f*.
Guy Fawkes Night [gaɪ'fɔːks-] *n voir encadré*.

GUY FAWKES NIGHT

Guy Fawkes Night, *que l'on appelle également "bonfire night", commémore l'échec du complot (le "Gunpowder Plot") contre James Ist et son parlement le 5 novembre 1605. L'un des conspirateurs, Guy Fawkes, avait été surpris dans les caves du parlement alors qu'il s'apprêtait à y mettre le feu. Chaque année pour le 5 novembre, les enfants préparent à l'avance une effigie de Guy Fawkes et ils demandent aux passants "un penny pour le guy" avec lequel ils pourront s'acheter des fusées de feu d'artifice. Beaucoup de gens font encore un feu dans leur jardin sur lequel ils brûlent le "guy".*

guzzle ['gʌzl] *vi* s'empiffrer ♦ *vt* avaler gloutonnement.
gym [dʒɪm] *n* (*also*: **gymnasium**) gymnase *m*; (*also*: **gymnastics**) gym *f*.
gymkhana [dʒɪm'kɑːnə] *n* gymkhana *m*.
gymnasium [dʒɪm'neɪzɪəm] *n* gymnase *m*.
gymnast ['dʒɪmnæst] *n* gymnaste *m/f*.
gymnastics [dʒɪm'næstɪks] *n*, *npl* gymnastique *f*.
gym shoes *npl* chaussures *fpl* de gym(nastique).
gym slip *n* (*BRIT*) tunique *f* (d'écolière).
gynaecologist, (*US*) **gynecologist** [gaɪnɪ'kɔlədʒɪst] *n* gynécologue *m/f*.
gynaecology, (*US*) **gynecology** [gaɪnə'kɔlədʒɪ] *n* gynécologie *f*.
gypsy ['dʒɪpsɪ] *n* = **gipsy**.
gyrate [dʒaɪ'reɪt] *vi* tournoyer.
gyroscope ['dʒaɪərəskəup] *n* gyroscope *m*.

H h

H, h [eɪtʃ] *n* (*letter*) H, h *m*; **H for Harry**, (*US*) **H for How** H comme Henri.
habeas corpus ['heɪbɪəs'kɔːpəs] *n* (*LAW*) habeas corpus *m*.
haberdashery [hæbə'dæʃərɪ] *n* (*BRIT*) mercerie *f*.
habit ['hæbɪt] *n* habitude *f*; (*costume*) habit *m*, tenue *f*; **to get out of/into the ~ of doing sth** perdre/prendre l'habitude de faire qch.
habitable ['hæbɪtəbl] *adj* habitable.
habitat ['hæbɪtæt] *n* habitat *m*.
habitation [hæbɪ'teɪʃən] *n* habitation *f*.
habitual [hə'bɪtjuəl] *adj* habituel(le); (*drinker, liar*) invétéré(e).
habitually [hə'bɪtjuəlɪ] *adv* habituellement, d'habitude.
hack [hæk] *vt* hacher, tailler ♦ *n* (*cut*) entaille *f*; (*blow*) coup *m*; (*pej: writer*) nègre *m*; (*old horse*) canasson *m*.
hackles ['hæklz] *npl*: **to make sb's ~ rise** (*fig*) mettre qn hors de soi.
hackney cab ['hæknɪ-] *n* fiacre *m*.
hackneyed ['hæknɪd] *adj* usé(e), rebattu(e).
hacksaw ['hæksɔː] *n* scie *f* à métaux.
had [hæd] *pt*, *pp of* **have**.
haddock, *pl* ~ *or* ~**s** ['hædək] *n* églefin *m*; **smoked ~** haddock *m*.
hadn't ['hædnt] = **had not**.
haematology, (*US*) **hematology** ['hiːmə'tɔlədʒɪ] *n* hématologie *f*.
haemoglobin, (*US*) **hemoglobin** ['hiːmə'gləubɪn] *n* hémoglobine *f*.
haemophilia, (*US*) **hemophilia** ['hiːmə'fɪlɪə] *n* hémophilie *f*.
haemorrhage, (*US*) **hemorrhage** ['hɛmərɪdʒ] *n* hémorragie *f*.
haemorrhoids, (*US*) **hemorrhoids** ['hɛmərɔɪdz] *npl* hémorroïdes *fpl*.
hag [hæg] *n* (*ugly*) vieille sorcière; (*nasty*) chameau *m*, harpie *f*; (*witch*) sorcière.
haggard ['hægəd] *adj* hagard(e), égaré(e).
haggis ['hægɪs] *n* haggis *m*.
haggle ['hægl] *vi* marchander; **to ~ over** chicaner sur.
haggling ['hæglɪŋ] *n* marchandage *m*.
Hague [heɪg] *n*: **The ~** La Haye.
hail [heɪl] *n* grêle *f* ♦ *vt* (*call*) héler; (*greet*) acclamer ♦ *vi* grêler; (*originate*): **he ~s from Scotland** il est originaire d'Écosse.
hailstone ['heɪlstəun] *n* grêlon *m*.
hailstorm ['heɪlstɔːm] *n* averse *f* de grêle.
hair [hɛə*] *n* cheveux *mpl*; (*on body*) poils *mpl*,

pilosité *f*; (*single hair: on head*) cheveu *m*; (*: on body*) poil *m*; **to do one's** ~ se coiffer.
hairbrush ['hɛəbrʌʃ] *n* brosse *f* à cheveux.
haircut ['hɛəkʌt] *n* coupe *f* (de cheveux).
hairdo ['hɛəduː] *n* coiffure *f*.
hairdresser ['hɛədrɛsə*] *n* coiffeur/euse.
hair-dryer ['hɛədraɪə*] *n* sèche-cheveux *m*.
-haired [hɛəd] *suffix*: **fair/long**~ aux cheveux blonds/longs.
hair gel *n* gel *m* pour cheveux.
hairgrip ['hɛəgrɪp] *n* pince *f* à cheveux.
hairline ['hɛəlaɪn] *n* naissance *f* des cheveux.
hairline fracture *n* fêlure *f*.
hairnet ['hɛənɛt] *n* résille *f*.
hair oil *n* huile *f* capillaire.
hairpiece ['hɛəpiːs] *n* postiche *m*.
hairpin ['hɛəpɪn] *n* épingle *f* à cheveux.
hairpin bend, (*US*) **hairpin curve** *n* virage *m* en épingle à cheveux.
hairraising ['hɛəreɪzɪŋ] *adj* à (vous) faire dresser les cheveux sur la tête.
hair remover *n* dépilateur *m*.
hair spray *n* laque *f* (pour les cheveux).
hairstyle ['hɛəstaɪl] *n* coiffure *f*.
hairy ['hɛərɪ] *adj* poilu(e); chevelu(e); (*fig*) effrayant(e).
Haiti ['heɪtɪ] *n* Haïti *m*.
hake [heɪk] *n* colin *m*, merlu *m*.
halcyon ['hælsɪən] *adj* merveilleux(euse).
hale [heɪl] *adj*: ~ **and hearty** robuste, en pleine santé.
half [hɑːf] *n* (*pl* **halves** [hɑːvz]) moitié *f*; (*SPORT*: *of match*) mi-temps *f*; (*: of ground*) moitié (du terrain) ♦ *adj* demi(e) ♦ *adv* (à) moitié, à demi; ~**-an-hour** une demi-heure; ~ **a dozen** une demi-douzaine; ~ **a pound** une demi-livre; **two and a** ~ deux et demi; **a week and a** ~ une semaine et demie; ~ **(of it)** la moitié; ~ **(of)** la moitié de; ~ **the amount of** la moitié de; **to cut sth in** ~ couper qch en deux; ~ **past three** trois heures et demie; ~ **empty** à moitié vide; **to go halves (with sb)** se mettre de moitié avec qn.
half-back ['hɑːfbæk] *n* (*SPORT*) demi *m*.
half-baked ['hɑːf'beɪkt] *adj* (*col*: *idea, scheme*) qui ne tient pas debout.
half-breed ['hɑːfbriːd] *n* = **halfcaste**.
half-brother ['hɑːfbrʌðə*] *n* demi-frère *m*.
half-caste ['hɑːfkɑːst] *n* métis/se.
half-hearted ['hɑːf'hɑːtɪd] *adj* tiède, sans enthousiasme.
half-hour [hɑːf'auə*] *n* demi-heure *f*.
half-mast ['hɑːf'mɑːst] *n*: **at** ~ (*flag*) en berne, à mi-mât.
halfpenny ['heɪpnɪ] *n* demi-penny *m*.
half-price ['hɑːf'praɪs] *adj* à moitié prix ♦ *adv* (*also*: **at** ~) à moitié prix.
half term *n* (*BRIT SCOL*) congé *m* de demi-trimestre.
half-time [hɑːf'taɪm] *n* mi-temps *f*.
halfway ['hɑːf'weɪ] *adv* à mi-chemin; **to meet sb** ~ (*fig*) parvenir à un compromis avec qn.
halfway house *n* (*hostel*) centre *m* de réadaptation (*pour anciens prisonniers, malades mentaux etc*); (*fig*): **a** ~ **(between)** une étape intermédiaire (entre).
half-wit ['hɑːfwɪt] *n* (*col*) idiot/e, imbécile *m/f*.
half-yearly [hɑːf'jɪəlɪ] *adv* deux fois par an ♦ *adj* semestriel(le).
halibut ['hælɪbət] *n* (*pl inv*) flétan *m*.
halitosis [hælɪ'təusɪs] *n* mauvaise haleine.
hall [hɔːl] *n* salle *f*; (*entrance way*) hall *m*, entrée *f*; (*corridor*) couloir *m*; (*mansion*) château *m*, manoir *m*; ~ **of residence** *n* (*BRIT*) pavillon *m or* résidence *f* universitaire.
hallmark ['hɔːlmɑːk] *n* poinçon *m*; (*fig*) marque *f*.
hallo [hə'ləu] *excl* = **hello**.
Hallowe'en [hæləu'iːn] *n* veille *f* de la Toussaint; *voir encadré*.

HALLOWE'EN

Selon la tradition, **Hallowe'en** *est la nuit des fantômes et des sorcières. En Écosse et aux États-Unis surtout (beaucoup moins en Angleterre) les enfants, pour fêter* **Hallowe'en**, *se déguisent ce soir-là et ils vont ainsi de porte en porte en demandant de petits cadeaux (du chocolat, une pomme etc).*

hallucination [həluːsɪ'neɪʃən] *n* hallucination *f*.
hallucinogenic [həluːsɪnəu'dʒɛnɪk] *adj* hallucinogène.
hallway ['hɔːlweɪ] *n* vestibule *m*; couloir *m*.
halo ['heɪləu] *n* (*of saint etc*) auréole *f*; (*of sun*) halo *m*.
halt [hɔːlt] *n* halte *f*, arrêt *m* ♦ *vt* faire arrêter ♦ *vi* faire halte, s'arrêter; **to call a** ~ **to sth** (*fig*) mettre fin à qch.
halter ['hɔːltə*] *n* (*for horse*) licou *m*.
halterneck ['hɔːltənɛk] *adj* (*dress*) (avec) dos nu *inv*.
halve [hɑːv] *vt* (*apple etc*) partager *or* diviser en deux; (*reduce by half*) réduire de moitié.
halves [hɑːvz] *npl of* **half**.
ham [hæm] *n* jambon *m*; (*col*: *also*: **radio** ~) radio-amateur *m*; (: *also*: ~ **actor**) cabotin/e.
Hamburg ['hæmbəːg] *n* Hambourg.
hamburger ['hæmbəːgə*] *n* hamburger *m*.
ham-fisted ['hæm'fɪstɪd], (*US*) **ham-handed** ['hæm'hændɪd] *adj* maladroit(e).
hamlet ['hæmlɪt] *n* hameau *m*.
hammer ['hæmə*] *n* marteau *m* ♦ *vt* (*fig*) éreinter, démolir ♦ *vi* (*at door*) frapper à coups redoublés; **to** ~ **a point home to sb** faire rentrer qch dans la tête de qn.
►**hammer out** *vt* (*metal*) étendre au marteau; (*fig: solution*) élaborer.
hammock ['hæmək] *n* hamac *m*.
hamper ['hæmpə*] *vt* gêner ♦ *n* panier *m* (d'osier).
hamstring ['hæmstrɪŋ] *n* (*ANAT*) tendon *m* du

jarret.

hand [hænd] *n* main *f*; (*of clock*) aiguille *f*; (*handwriting*) écriture *f*; (*at cards*) jeu *m*; (*measurement: of horse*) paume *f*; (*worker*) ouvrier/ière ♦ *vt* passer, donner; **to give sb a ~** donner un coup de main à qn; **at ~** à portée de la main; **in ~** en main; (*work*) en cours; **we have the situation in ~** nous avons la situation bien en main; **to be on ~** (*person*) être disponible; (*emergency services*) se tenir prêt(e) (à intervenir); **to ~** (*information etc*) sous la main, à portée de la main; **to force sb's ~** forcer la main à qn; **to have a free ~** avoir carte blanche; **to have sth in one's ~** tenir qch à la main; **on the one ~ ..., on the other ~** d'une part ..., d'autre part.

▸**hand down** *vt* passer; (*tradition, heirloom*) transmettre; (*US: sentence, verdict*) prononcer.

▸**hand in** *vt* remettre.

▸**hand out** *vt* distribuer.

▸**hand over** *vt* remettre; (*powers etc*) transmettre.

▸**hand round** *vt* (*BRIT: information*) faire circuler; (*: chocolates etc*) faire passer.

handbag ['hændbæg] *n* sac *m* à main.

hand baggage *n* bagages *mpl* à main; **one item of ~** un bagage à main.

handball ['hændbɔːl] *n* handball *m*.

handbasin ['hændbeɪsn] *n* lavabo *m*.

handbook ['hændbuk] *n* manuel *m*.

handbrake ['hændbreɪk] *n* frein *m* à main.

h & c *abbr* (*BRIT*) = *hot and cold (water)*.

hand cream *n* crème *f* pour les mains.

handcuffs ['hændkʌfs] *npl* menottes *fpl*.

handful ['hændful] *n* poignée *f*.

hand-held ['hænd'hɛld] *adj* à main.

handicap ['hændɪkæp] *n* handicap *m* ♦ *vt* handicaper; **mentally/physically ~ped** handicapé(e) mentalement/physiquement.

handicraft ['hændɪkrɑːft] *n* travail *m* d'artisanat, technique artisanale.

handiwork ['hændɪwəːk] *n* ouvrage *m*; **this looks like his ~** (*pej*) ça a tout l'air d'être son œuvre.

handkerchief ['hæŋkətʃɪf] *n* mouchoir *m*.

handle ['hændl] *n* (*of door etc*) poignée *f*; (*of cup etc*) anse *f*; (*of knife etc*) manche *m*; (*of saucepan*) queue *f*; (*for winding*) manivelle *f* ♦ *vt* toucher, manier; (*deal with*) s'occuper de; (*treat: people*) prendre; **"~ with care"** "fragile".

handlebar(s) ['hændlbɑː(z)] *n(pl)* guidon *m*.

handling ['hændlɪŋ] *n* (*AUT*) maniement *m*; (*treatment*): **his ~ of the matter** la façon dont il a traité l'affaire.

handling charges *npl* frais *mpl* de manutention; (*BANKING*) agios *mpl*.

hand-luggage ['hændlʌgɪdʒ] *n* bagages *mpl* à main.

handmade ['hænd'meɪd] *adj* fait(e) à la main.

handout ['hændaut] *n* documentation *f*, prospectus *m*; (*press ~*) communiqué *m* de presse.

hand-picked ['hænd'pɪkt] *adj* (*produce*) cueilli(e) à la main; (*staff etc*) trié(e) sur le volet.

handrail ['hændreɪl] *n* (*on staircase etc*) rampe *f*, main courante.

handset ['hændsɛt] *n* (*TEL*) combiné *m*.

handshake ['hændʃeɪk] *n* poignée *f* de main; (*COMPUT*) établissement *m* de la liaison.

handsome ['hænsəm] *adj* beau(belle); (*gift*) généreux(euse); (*profit*) considérable.

hands-on [hændz'ɔn] *adj* (*training, experience*) sur le tas; **she has a very ~ approach** sa politique est de mettre la main à la pâte.

handstand ['hændstænd] *n*: **to do a ~** faire l'arbre droit.

hand-to-mouth ['hændtə'mauθ] *adj* (*existence*) au jour le jour.

handwriting ['hændraɪtɪŋ] *n* écriture *f*.

handwritten ['hændrɪtn] *adj* manuscrit(e), écrit(e) à la main.

handy ['hændɪ] *adj* (*person*) adroit(e); (*close at hand*) sous la main; (*convenient*) pratique; **to come in ~** être (*or* s'avérer) utile.

handyman ['hændɪmæn] *n* bricoleur *m*; (*servant*) homme *m* à tout faire.

hang, *pt, pp* **hung** [hæŋ, hʌŋ] *vt* accrocher; (*criminal: pt, pp* **hanged**) pendre ♦ *vi* pendre; (*hair, drapery*) tomber ♦ *n*: **to get the ~ of (doing) sth** (*col*) attraper le coup pour faire qch.

▸**hang about** *vi* flâner, traîner.

▸**hang back** *vi* (*hesitate*): **to ~ back (from doing)** être réticent(e) (pour faire).

▸**hang on** *vi* (*wait*) attendre ♦ *vt fus* (*depend on*) dépendre de; **to ~ on to** (*keep hold of*) ne pas lâcher; (*keep*) garder.

▸**hang out** *vt* (*washing*) étendre (dehors) ♦ *vi* pendre; (*col: live*) habiter, percher.

▸**hang together** *vi* (*argument etc*) se tenir, être cohérent(e).

▸**hang up** *vi* (*TEL*) raccrocher ♦ *vt* accrocher, suspendre; **to ~ up on sb** (*TEL*) raccrocher au nez de qn.

hangar ['hæŋə*] *n* hangar *m*.

hangdog ['hæŋdɔg] *adj* (*look, expression*) de chien battu.

hanger ['hæŋə*] *n* cintre *m*, portemanteau *m*.

hanger-on [hæŋər'ɔn] *n* parasite *m*.

hang-glider ['hæŋglaɪdə*] *n* deltaplane *m*.

hang-gliding ['hæŋglaɪdɪŋ] *n* vol *m* libre *or* sur aile delta.

hanging ['hæŋɪŋ] *n* (*execution*) pendaison *f*.

hangman ['hæŋmən] *n* bourreau *m*.

hangover ['hæŋəuvə*] *n* (*after drinking*) gueule *f* de bois.

hang-up ['hæŋʌp] *n* complexe *m*.

hank [hæŋk] *n* écheveau *m*.

hanker ['hæŋkə*] *vi*: **to ~ after** avoir envie de.

hankering ['hæŋkərɪŋ] *n*: **to have a ~ for/to do sth** avoir une grande envie de/de faire qch.

hankie, hanky ['hæŋkɪ] *n abbr* = **handkerchief**.
Hants *abbr* (*BRIT*) = *Hampshire*.
haphazard [hæp'hæzəd] *adj* fait(e) au hasard, fait(e) au petit bonheur.
hapless ['hæplɪs] *adj* malheureux(euse).
happen ['hæpən] *vi* arriver, se passer, se produire; **what's ~ing?** que se passe-t-il?; **she ~ed to be free** il s'est trouvé (*or* se trouvait) qu'elle était libre; **if anything ~ed to him** s'il lui arrivait quoi que ce soit; **as it ~s** justement.
▶**happen (up)on** *vt fus* tomber sur.
happening ['hæpnɪŋ] *n* événement *m*.
happily ['hæpɪlɪ] *adv* heureusement.
happiness ['hæpɪnɪs] *n* bonheur *m*.
happy ['hæpɪ] *adj* heureux(euse); **~ with** (*arrangements etc*) satisfait(e) de; **yes, I'd be ~ to** oui, avec plaisir *or* (bien) volontiers; **~ birthday!** bon anniversaire!; **~ Christmas/New Year!** joyeux Noël/bonne année!
happy-go-lucky ['hæpɪgəu'lʌkɪ] *adj* insouciant(e).
happy hour *n* l'heure *f* de l'apéritif, *heure pendant laquelle les consommations sont à prix réduit*.
harangue [hə'ræŋ] *vt* haranguer.
harass ['hærəs] *vt* accabler, tourmenter.
harassed ['hærəst] *adj* tracassé(e).
harassment ['hærəsmənt] *n* tracasseries *fpl*.
harbour, (*US*) **harbor** ['hɑːbə*] *n* port *m* ♦ *vt* héberger, abriter; (*hopes, suspicions*) entretenir; **to ~ a grudge against sb** en vouloir à qn.
harbo(u)r dues *npl* droits *mpl* de port.
harbo(u)r master *n* capitaine *m* du port.
hard [hɑːd] *adj* dur(e) ♦ *adv* (*work*) dur; (*think, try*) sérieusement; **to look ~ at** regarder fixement; regarder de près; **to drink ~** boire sec; **~ luck!** pas de veine!; **no ~ feelings!** sans rancune!; **to be ~ of hearing** être dur(e) d'oreille; **to be ~ done by** être traité(e) injustement; **to be ~ on sb** être dur(e) avec qn; **I find it ~ to believe that ...** je n'arrive pas à croire que ....
hard-and-fast ['hɑːdən'fɑːst] *adj* strict(e), absolu(e).
hardback ['hɑːdbæk] *n* livre relié.
hardboard ['hɑːdbɔːd] *n* Isorel *m* ®.
hard-boiled egg ['hɑːd'bɔɪld-] *n* œuf dur.
hard cash *n* espèces *fpl*.
hard copy *n* (*COMPUT*) sortie *f or* copie *f* papier.
hard-core ['hɑːd'kɔː*] *adj* (*pornography*) (dit(e)) dur(e); (*supporters*) inconditionnel(le).
hard court *n* (*TENNIS*) court *m* en dur.
hard disk *n* (*COMPUT*) disque dur.
harden ['hɑːdn] *vt* durcir; (*steel*) tremper; (*fig*) endurcir ♦ *vi* (*substance*) durcir.
hardened ['hɑːdnd] *adj* (*criminal*) endurci(e); **to be ~ to sth** s'être endurci(e) à qch, être (devenu(e)) insensible à qch.
hardening ['hɑːdnɪŋ] *n* durcissement *m*.
hard-headed ['hɑːd'hɛdɪd] *adj* réaliste; décidé(e).
hard-hearted ['hɑːd'hɑːtɪd] *adj* dur(e), impitoyable.
hard-hitting ['hɑːd'hɪtɪŋ] *adj* (*speech, article*) sans complaisances.
hard labour *n* travaux forcés.
hardliner [hɑːd'laɪnə*] *n* intransigeant/e, dur/e.
hard-luck story [hɑːd'lʌk-] *n* histoire larmoyante.
hardly ['hɑːdlɪ] *adv* (*scarcely*) à peine; (*harshly*) durement; **it's ~ the case** ce n'est guère le cas; **~ anywhere/ever** presque nulle part/jamais; **I can ~ believe it** j'ai du mal à le croire.
hardness ['hɑːdnɪs] *n* dureté *f*.
hard-nosed ['hɑːd'nəuzd] *adj* impitoyable, dur(e).
hard-pressed ['hɑːd'prɛst] *adj* sous pression.
hard sell *n* vente agressive.
hardship ['hɑːdʃɪp] *n* épreuves *fpl*; privations *fpl*.
hard shoulder *n* (*BRIT AUT*) accotement stabilisé.
hard-up [hɑːd'ʌp] *adj* (*col*) fauché(e).
hardware ['hɑːdwɛə*] *n* quincaillerie *f*; (*COMPUT*) matériel *m*.
hardware shop *n* quincaillerie *f*.
hard-wearing [hɑːd'wɛərɪŋ] *adj* solide.
hard-won ['hɑːd'wʌn] *adj* (si) durement gagné(e).
hard-working [hɑːd'wəːkɪŋ] *adj* travailleur(euse), consciencieux(euse).
hardy ['hɑːdɪ] *adj* robuste; (*plant*) résistant(e) au gel.
hare [hɛə*] *n* lièvre *m*.
hare-brained ['hɛəbreɪnd] *adj* farfelu(e); écervelé(e).
harelip ['hɛəlɪp] *n* (*MED*) bec-de-lièvre *m*.
harem [hɑː'riːm] *n* harem *m*.
hark back [hɑːk-] *vi*: **to ~ to** (en) revenir toujours à.
harm [hɑːm] *n* mal *m*; (*wrong*) tort *m* ♦ *vt* (*person*) faire du mal *or* du tort à; (*thing*) endommager; **to mean no ~** ne pas avoir de mauvaises intentions; **there's no ~ in trying** on peut toujours essayer; **out of ~'s way** à l'abri du danger, en lieu sûr.
harmful ['hɑːmful] *adj* nuisible.
harmless [hɑːmlɪs] *adj* inoffensif(ive); sans méchanceté.
harmonic [hɑː'mɔnɪk] *adj* harmonique.
harmonica [hɑː'mɔnɪkə] *n* harmonica *m*.
harmonics [hɑː'mɔnɪks] *npl* harmoniques *mpl or fpl*.
harmonious [hɑː'məunɪəs] *adj* harmonieux(euse).
harmonium [hɑː'məunɪəm] *n* harmonium *m*.
harmonize ['hɑːmənaɪz] *vt* harmoniser ♦ *vi* s'harmoniser.

harmony ['hɑːmənɪ] *n* harmonie *f*.
harness ['hɑːnɪs] *n* harnais *m* ♦ *vt* (*horse*) harnacher; (*resources*) exploiter.
harp [hɑːp] *n* harpe *f* ♦ *vi*: **to ~ on about** parler tout le temps de.
harpist ['hɑːpɪst] *n* harpiste *m/f*.
harpoon [hɑː'puːn] *n* harpon *m*.
harpsichord ['hɑːpsɪkɔːd] *n* clavecin *m*.
harrow ['hærəu] *n* (*AGR*) herse *f*.
harrowing ['hærəuɪŋ] *adj* déchirant(e).
harry ['hærɪ] *vt* (*MIL, fig*) harceler.
harsh [hɑːʃ] *adj* (*hard*) dur(e), sévère; (*rough: surface*) rugueux(euse); (*: sound*) discordant(e); (*: taste*) âpre.
harshly ['hɑːʃlɪ] *adv* durement, sévèrement.
harshness ['hɑːʃnɪs] *n* dureté *f*, sévérité *f*.
harvest ['hɑːvɪst] *n* (*of corn*) moisson *f*; (*of fruit*) récolte *f*; (*of grapes*) vendange *f* ♦ *vi, vt* moissonner; récolter; vendanger.
harvester ['hɑːvɪstə*] *n* (*machine*) moissonneuse *f*; (*also*: **combine ~**) moissonneuse-batteuse(-lieuse *f*) *f*; (*person*) moissonneur/euse.
has [hæz] *vb see* **have**.
has-been ['hæzbiːn] *n* (*col*: *person*): **he/she's a ~** il/elle a fait son temps *or* est fini(e).
hash [hæʃ] *n* (*CULIN*) hachis *m*; (*fig: mess*) gâchis *m* ♦ *n abbr* (*col*) = **hashish**.
hashish ['hæʃɪʃ] *n* haschisch *m*.
hasn't ['hæznt] = **has not**.
hassle ['hæsl] *n* (*col*: *fuss*) histoire(s) *f(pl)*.
haste [heɪst] *n* hâte *f*, précipitation *f*; **in ~** à la hâte, précipitemment.
hasten ['heɪsn] *vt* hâter, accélérer ♦ *vi* se hâter, s'empresser; **I ~ to add that ...** je m'empresse d'ajouter que ....
hastily ['heɪstɪlɪ] *adv* à la hâte, précipitamment.
hasty ['heɪstɪ] *adj* hâtif(ive), précipité(e).
hat [hæt] *n* chapeau *m*.
hatbox ['hætbɔks] *n* carton *m* à chapeau.
hatch [hætʃ] *n* (*NAUT*: *also*: **~way**) écoutille *f*; (*BRIT*: *also*: **service ~**) passe-plats *m inv* ♦ *vi* éclore ♦ *vt* faire éclore; (*fig: scheme*) tramer, ourdir.
hatchback ['hætʃbæk] *n* (*AUT*) modèle *m* avec hayon arrière.
hatchet ['hætʃɪt] *n* hachette *f*.
hatchet job *n* (*col*) démolissage *m*.
hatchet man *n* (*col*) homme *m* de main.
hate [heɪt] *vt* haïr, détester ♦ *n* haine *f*; **to ~ to do** *or* **doing** détester faire; **I ~ to trouble you, but ...** désolé de vous déranger, mais ....
hateful ['heɪtful] *adj* odieux(euse), détestable.
hatred ['heɪtrɪd] *n* haine *f*.
hat trick *n* (*BRIT SPORT, also fig*): **to get a ~** réussir trois coups (*or* gagner trois matchs *etc*) consécutifs.
haughty ['hɔːtɪ] *adj* hautain(e), arrogant(e).
haul [hɔːl] *vt* traîner, tirer; (*by lorry*) camionner; (*NAUT*) haler ♦ *n* (*of fish*) prise *f*; (*of stolen goods etc*) butin *m*.
haulage ['hɔːlɪdʒ] *n* transport routier.
haulage contractor *n* (*BRIT*: *firm*) entreprise *f* de transport (routier); (*: person*) transporteur routier.
haulier ['hɔːlɪə*], (*US*) **hauler** ['hɔːlə*] *n* transporteur (routier), camionneur *m*.
haunch [hɔːntʃ] *n* hanche *f*; **~ of venison** cuissot *m* de chevreuil.
haunt [hɔːnt] *vt* (*subj: ghost, fear*) hanter; (*: person*) fréquenter ♦ *n* repaire *m*.
haunted ['hɔːntɪd] *adj* (*castle etc*) hanté(e); (*look*) égaré(e), hagard(e).
haunting ['hɔːntɪŋ] *adj* (*sight, music*) obsédant(e).
Havana [hə'vænə] *n* La Havane.

KEYWORD

have [hæv] (*pt, pp* **had**) *aux vb* **1** (*gen*) avoir; être; **to ~ arrived/gone** être arrivé(e)/allé(e); **to ~ eaten/slept** avoir mangé/dormi; **he has been promoted** il a eu une promotion
2 (*in tag questions*): **you've done it, ~n't you?** vous l'avez fait, n'est-ce pas?
3 (*in short answers and questions*): **no I ~n't!/yes we ~!** mais non!/mais si!; **so I ~!** ah oui!, oui c'est vrai!; **I've been there before, ~ you?** j'y suis déjà allé, et vous?
♦ *modal aux vb* (*be obliged*): **to ~ (got) to do sth** devoir faire qch; être obligé(e) de faire qch; **she has (got) to do it** elle doit le faire, il faut qu'elle le fasse; **you ~n't to tell her** vous n'êtes pas obligé de le lui dire; (*must not*) ne le lui dites surtout pas
♦ *vt* **1** (*possess, obtain*) avoir; **he has (got) blue eyes/dark hair** il a les yeux bleus/les cheveux bruns; **may I ~ your address?** puis-je avoir votre adresse?
2 (*+noun*: *take, hold etc*): **to ~ breakfast/a bath/a shower** prendre le petit déjeuner/un bain/une douche; **to ~ dinner/lunch** dîner/déjeuner; **to ~ a swim** nager; **to ~ a meeting** se réunir; **to ~ a party** organiser une fête; **let me ~ a try** laissez-moi essayer
3: **to ~ sth done** faire faire qch; **to ~ one's hair cut** se faire couper les cheveux; **to ~ sb do sth** faire faire qch à qn
4 (*experience, suffer*) avoir; **to ~ a cold/flu** avoir un rhume/la grippe; **to ~ an operation** se faire opérer; **I won't ~ it** cela ne se passera pas ainsi
5 (*inf*: *dupe*) avoir; **he's been had** il s'est fait avoir *or* rouler
▶**have out** *vt*: **to ~ it out with sb** (*settle a problem etc*) s'expliquer (franchement) avec qn.

haven ['heɪvn] *n* port *m*; (*fig*) havre *m*.
haversack ['hævəsæk] *n* sac *m* à dos.
haves [hævz] *npl* (*col*): **the ~ and have-nots** les riches et les pauvres.
havoc ['hævək] *n* ravages *mpl*, dégâts *mpl*;

to play ~ with (*fig*) désorganiser complètement; détraquer.
Hawaii [hə'waiiː] *n* (îles *fpl*) Hawaii *m*.
Hawaiian [hə'waɪjən] *adj* hawaïen(ne) ♦ *n* Hawaïen/ne; (*LING*) hawaïen *m*.
hawk [hɔːk] *n* faucon *m* ♦ *vt* (*goods for sale*) colporter.
hawker ['hɔːkə*] *n* colporteur *m*.
hawkish ['hɔːkɪʃ] *adj* belliciste.
hawthorn ['hɔːθɔːn] *n* aubépine *f*.
hay [heɪ] *n* foin *m*.
hay fever *n* rhume *m* des foins.
haystack ['heɪstæk] *n* meule *f* de foin.
haywire ['heɪwaɪə*] *adj* (*col*): **to go ~** perdre la tête; mal tourner.
hazard ['hæzəd] *n* (*chance*) hasard *m*, chance *f*; (*risk*) danger *m*, risque *m* ♦ *vt* risquer, hasarder; **to be a health/fire ~** présenter un risque d'incendie/pour la santé; **to ~ a guess** émettre *or* hasarder une hypothèse.
hazardous ['hæzədəs] *adj* hasardeux(euse), risqué(e).
hazard pay *n* (*US*) prime *f* de risque.
hazard warning lights *npl* (*AUT*) feux *mpl* de détresse.
haze [heɪz] *n* brume *f*.
hazel [heɪzl] *n* (*tree*) noisetier *m* ♦ *adj* (*eyes*) noisette *inv*.
hazelnut ['heɪzlnʌt] *n* noisette *f*.
hazy ['heɪzɪ] *adj* brumeux(euse); (*idea*) vague; (*photograph*) flou(e).
H-bomb ['eɪtʃbɔm] *n* bombe *f* H.
HE *abbr* = *high explosive*; (*REL, DIPLOMACY*) = *His (or Her) Excellency*.
he [hiː] *pron* il; **it is ~ who ...** c'est lui qui ...; **here ~ is** le voici; **~-bear** *etc* ours *etc* mâle.
head [hɛd] *n* tête *f*; (*leader*) chef *m* ♦ *vt* (*list*) être en tête de; (*group*) être à la tête de; **~s** (*on coin*) (le côté) face; **~s or tails** pile ou face; **~ over heels in love** follement *or* éperdument amoureux(euse); **to ~ the ball** faire une tête; **10 euros a** *or* **per ~** 10 euros par personne; **to sit at the ~ of the table** présider la tablée; **to have a ~ for business** avoir des dispositions pour les affaires; **to have no ~ for heights** être sujet(te) au vertige; **to come to a ~** (*fig: situation etc*) devenir critique.
►**head for** *vt fus* se diriger vers.
►**head off** *vt* (*threat, danger*) détourner.
headache ['hɛdeɪk] *n* mal *m* de tête; **to have a ~** avoir mal à la tête.
headband ['hɛdbænd] *n* bandeau *m*.
headboard ['hɛdbɔːd] *n* dosseret *m*.
head cold *n* rhume *m* de cerveau.
headdress ['hɛddrɛs] *n* coiffure *f*.
headed notepaper ['hɛdɪd-] *n* papier *m* à lettres à en-tête.
header ['hɛdə*] *n* (*BRIT col: FOOTBALL*) (coup *m* de) tête *f*; (*: fall*) chute *f* (*or* plongeon *m*) la tête la première.
head-first ['hɛd'fəːst] *adv* (*lit*) la tête la première.
headhunt ['hɛdhʌnt] *vt*: **she was ~ed** elle a été recrutée par un chasseur de têtes.
headhunter ['hɛdhʌntə*] *n* chasseur *m* de têtes.
heading ['hɛdɪŋ] *n* titre *m*; (*subject title*) rubrique *f*.
headlamp ['hɛdlæmp] *n* = **headlight**.
headland ['hɛdlənd] *n* promontoire *m*, cap *m*.
headlight ['hɛdlaɪt] *n* phare *m*.
headline ['hɛdlaɪn] *n* titre *m*.
headlong ['hɛdlɔŋ] *adv* (*fall*) la tête la première; (*rush*) tête baissée.
headmaster [hɛd'mɑːstə*] *n* directeur *m*, proviseur *m*.
headmistress [hɛd'mɪstrɪs] *n* directrice *f*.
head office *n* siège *m*, direction *f* (générale).
head-on [hɛd'ɔn] *adj* (*collision*) de plein fouet.
headphones ['hɛdfəunz] *npl* casque *m* (à écouteurs).
headquarters (HQ) ['hɛdkwɔːtəz] *npl* (*of business*) siège *m*, direction *f* (générale); (*MIL*) quartier général.
head-rest ['hɛdrɛst] *n* appui-tête *m*.
headroom ['hɛdrum] *n* (*in car*) hauteur *f* de plafond; (*under bridge*) hauteur limite; dégagement *m*.
headscarf ['hɛdskɑːf] *n* foulard *m*.
headset ['hɛdsɛt] *n* = **headphones**.
headstone ['hɛdstəun] *n* (*on grave*) pierre tombale.
headstrong ['hɛdstrɔŋ] *adj* têtu(e), entêté(e).
head waiter *n* maître *m* d'hôtel.
headway ['hɛdweɪ] *n*: **to make ~** avancer, faire des progrès.
headwind ['hɛdwɪnd] *n* vent *m* contraire.
heady ['hɛdɪ] *adj* capiteux(euse); enivrant(e).
heal [hiːl] *vt, vi* guérir.
health [hɛlθ] *n* santé *f*; **Department of H~** (*US*) ≈ ministère *m* de la Santé; **Department of H~ (DH)** (*BRIT*) ≈ ministère *m* de la Santé.
health care *n* services médicaux.
health centre *n* (*BRIT*) centre *m* de santé.
health food(s) *n(pl)* aliment(s) naturel(s).
health food shop *n* magasin *m* diététique.
health hazard *n* risque *m* pour la santé.
Health Service *n*: **the ~** (*BRIT*) ≈ la Sécurite Sociale.
healthy ['hɛlθɪ] *adj* (*person*) en bonne santé; (*climate, food, attitude etc*) sain(e).
heap [hiːp] *n* tas *m*, monceau *m* ♦ *vt* entasser, amonceler; **~s (of)** (*col: lots*) des tas (de); **to ~ favours/praise/gifts** *etc* **on sb** combler qn de faveurs/d'éloges/de cadeaux *etc*.
hear, *pt, pp* **heard** [hɪə*, həːd] *vt* entendre; (*news*) apprendre; (*lecture*) assister à, écouter ♦ *vi* entendre; **to ~ about** entendre parler de; (*have news of*) avoir des nouvelles de; **did you ~ about the move?** tu es au courant du déménagement?; **to ~ from sb** recevoir des nouvelles de qn; **I've never heard of that book** je n'ai jamais entendu parler de

ce livre.

▸**hear out** *vt* écouter jusqu'au bout.

hearing ['hɪərɪŋ] *n* (*sense*) ouïe *f*; (*of witnesses*) audition *f*; (*of a case*) audience *f*; (*of committee*) séance *f*; **to give sb a** ~ (*BRIT*) écouter ce que qn a à dire.

hearing aid *n* appareil *m* acoustique.

hearsay ['hɪəseɪ] *n* on-dit *mpl*, rumeurs *fpl*; **by** ~ *adv* par ouï-dire.

hearse [hə:s] *n* corbillard *m*.

heart [hɑ:t] *n* cœur *m*; ~**s** *npl* (*CARDS*) cœur; **at** ~ au fond; **by** ~ (*learn, know*) par cœur; **to have a weak** ~ avoir le cœur malade, avoir des problèmes de cœur; **to lose** ~ perdre courage, se décourager; **to take** ~ prendre courage; **to set one's** ~ **on sth/on doing sth** vouloir absolument qch/faire qch; **the** ~ **of the matter** le fond du problème.

heartache ['hɑ:teɪk] *n* chagrin *m*, douleur *f*.

heart attack *n* crise *f* cardiaque.

heartbeat ['hɑ:tbi:t] *n* battement *m* de cœur.

heartbreak ['hɑ:tbreɪk] *n* immense chagrin *m*.

heartbreaking ['hɑ:tbreɪkɪŋ] *adj* navrant(e), déchirant(e).

heartbroken ['hɑ:tbrəukən] *adj*: **to be** ~ avoir beaucoup de chagrin.

heartburn ['hɑ:tbə:n] *n* brûlures *fpl* d'estomac.

-hearted ['hɑ:tɪd] *suffix*: **kind**~ généreux(euse), qui a bon cœur.

heartening ['hɑ:tnɪŋ] *adj* encourageant(e), réconfortant(e).

heart failure *n* (*MED*) arrêt *m* du cœur.

heartfelt ['hɑ:tfɛlt] *adj* sincère.

hearth [hɑ:θ] *n* foyer *m*, cheminée *f*.

heartily ['hɑ:tɪlɪ] *adv* chaleureusement; (*laugh*) de bon cœur; (*eat*) de bon appétit; **to agree** ~ être entièrement d'accord; **to be** ~ **sick of** (*BRIT*) en avoir ras le bol de.

heartland ['hɑ:tlænd] *n* centre *m*, cœur *m*; **France's** ~**s** la France profonde.

heartless ['hɑ:tlɪs] *adj* sans cœur, insensible; cruel(le).

heartstrings ['hɑ:tstrɪŋz] *npl*: **to tug (at) sb's** ~ toucher *or* faire vibrer les cordes sensibles de qn.

heartthrob ['hɑ:tθrɔb] *n* idole *f*.

heart-to-heart ['hɑ:t'tə'hɑ:t] *adj, adv* à cœur ouvert.

heart transplant *n* greffe *f* du cœur.

heartwarming ['hɑ:twɔ:mɪŋ] *adj* réconfortant(e).

hearty ['hɑ:tɪ] *adj* chaleureux(euse); robuste; vigoureux(euse).

heat [hi:t] *n* chaleur *f*; (*fig*) ardeur *f*; feu *m*; (*SPORT*: *also*: **qualifying** ~) éliminatoire *f*; (*ZOOL*): **in** *or* (*BRIT*) **on** ~ en chaleur ♦ *vt* chauffer.

▸**heat up** *vi* (*liquids*) chauffer; (*room*) se réchauffer ♦ *vt* réchauffer.

heated ['hi:tɪd] *adj* chauffé(e); (*fig*) passionné(e); échauffé(e), excité(e).

heater ['hi:tə*] *n* appareil *m* de chauffage; radiateur *m*.

heath [hi:θ] *n* (*BRIT*) lande *f*.

heathen ['hi:ðn] *adj, n* païen(ne).

heather ['hɛðə*] *n* bruyère *f*.

heating ['hi:tɪŋ] *n* chauffage *m*.

heat-resistant ['hi:trɪzɪstənt] *adj* résistant(e) à la chaleur.

heat-seeking ['hi:tsi:kɪŋ] *adj* guidé(e) par infrarouge.

heatstroke ['hi:tstrəuk] *n* coup *m* de chaleur.

heatwave ['hi:tweɪv] *n* vague *f* de chaleur.

heave [hi:v] *vt* soulever (avec effort) ♦ *vi* se soulever; (*retch*) avoir des haut-le-cœur ♦ *n* (*push*) poussée *f*; **to** ~ **a sigh** pousser un gros soupir.

heaven ['hɛvn] *n* ciel *m*, paradis *m*; ~ **forbid!** surtout pas!; **thank** ~**!** Dieu merci!; **for** ~**'s sake!** (*pleading*) je vous en prie!; (*protesting*) mince alors!

heavenly ['hɛvnlɪ] *adj* céleste, divin(e).

heavily ['hɛvɪlɪ] *adv* lourdement; (*drink, smoke*) beaucoup; (*sleep, sigh*) profondément.

heavy ['hɛvɪ] *adj* lourd(e); (*work, rain, user, eater*) gros(se); (*drinker, smoker*) grand(e); **it's** ~ **going** ça ne va pas tout seul, c'est pénible.

heavy cream *n* (*US*) crème fraîche épaisse.

heavy-duty ['hɛvɪ'dju:tɪ] *adj* à usage intensif.

heavy goods vehicle (HGV) *n* (*BRIT*) poids lourd *m* (P.L.).

heavy-handed ['hɛvɪ'hændɪd] *adj* (*fig*) maladroit(e), qui manque de tact.

heavy metal *n* (*MUS*) heavy metal *m*.

heavy-set ['hɛvɪ'sɛt] *adj* (*esp US*) costaud(e).

heavyweight ['hɛvɪweɪt] *n* (*SPORT*) poids lourd.

Hebrew ['hi:bru:] *adj* hébraïque ♦ *n* (*LING*) hébreu *m*.

Hebrides ['hɛbrɪdi:z] *n*: **the** ~ les Hébrides *fpl*.

heck [hɛk] *n* (*col*): **why the** ~ **...?** pourquoi diable ...?; **a** ~ **of a lot** une sacrée quantité; **he has done a** ~ **of a lot for us** il a vraiment beaucoup fait pour nous.

heckle ['hɛkl] *vt* interpeller (*un orateur*).

heckler ['hɛklə*] *n* interrupteur *m*; élément perturbateur.

hectare ['hɛktɑ:*] *n* (*BRIT*) hectare *m*.

hectic ['hɛktɪk] *adj* agité(e), trépidant(e); (*busy*) trépidant.

hector ['hɛktə*] *vt* rudoyer, houspiller.

he'd [hi:d] = **he would, he had.**

hedge [hɛdʒ] *n* haie *f* ♦ *vi* se défiler ♦ *vt*: **to** ~ **one's bets** (*fig*) se couvrir; **as a** ~ **against inflation** pour se prémunir contre l'inflation.

▸**hedge in** *vt* entourer d'une haie.

hedgehog ['hɛdʒhɔg] *n* hérisson *m*.

hedgerow ['hɛdʒrəu] *n* haie(s) *f(pl)*.

hedonism ['hi:dənɪzəm] *n* hédonisme *m*.

heed [hi:d] *vt* (*also*: **take** ~ **of**) tenir compte de, prendre garde à.

heedless ['hi:dlɪs] *adj* insouciant(e).

heel [hiːl] *n* talon *m* ♦ *vt* (*shoe*) retalonner; **to bring to ~** (*dog*) faire venir à ses pieds; (*fig: person*) rappeler à l'ordre; **to take to one's ~s** prendre ses jambes à son cou.
hefty ['hɛftɪ] *adj* (*person*) costaud(e); (*parcel*) lourd(e); (*piece, price*) gros(se).
heifer ['hɛfə*] *n* génisse *f*.
height [haɪt] *n* (*of person*) taille *f*, grandeur *f*; (*of object*) hauteur *f*; (*of plane, mountain*) altitude *f*; (*high ground*) hauteur, éminence *f*; (*fig: of glory*) sommet *m*; (*: of stupidity*) comble *m*; **what ~ are you?** combien mesurez-vous?, quelle est votre taille?; **of average ~** de taille moyenne; **to be afraid of ~s** être sujet(te) au vertige; **it's the ~ of fashion** c'est le dernier cri.
heighten ['haɪtn] *vt* hausser, surélever; (*fig*) augmenter.
heinous ['heɪnəs] *adj* odieux(euse), atroce.
heir [ɛə*] *n* héritier *m*.
heir apparent *n* héritier présomptif.
heiress ['ɛərɛs] *n* héritière *f*.
heirloom ['ɛəluːm] *n* meuble *m* (*or* bijou *m or* tableau *m*) de famille.
heist [haɪst] *n* (*US col: hold-up*) casse *m*.
held [hɛld] *pt, pp of* **hold**.
helicopter ['hɛlɪkɔptə*] *n* hélicoptère *m*.
heliport ['hɛlɪpɔːt] *n* (*AVIAT*) héliport *m*.
helium ['hiːlɪəm] *n* hélium *m*.
hell [hɛl] *n* enfer *m*; **a ~ of a** (*col*) un(e) sacré(e) ...; **oh ~!** (*col*) merde!
he'll [hiːl] = **he will, he shall**.
hell-bent [hɛl'bɛnt] *adj* (*col*): **to be ~ on doing sth** vouloir à tout prix faire qch.
hellish ['hɛlɪʃ] *adj* infernal(e).
hello [hə'ləu] *excl* bonjour!; salut! (*to sb one addresses as "tu"*); (*surprise*) tiens!
helm [hɛlm] *n* (*NAUT*) barre *f*.
helmet ['hɛlmɪt] *n* casque *m*.
helmsman ['hɛlmzmən] *n* timonier *m*.
help [hɛlp] *n* aide *f*; (*charwoman*) femme *f* de ménage; (*assistant etc*) employé/e ♦ *vt* aider; **~!** au secours!; **~ yourself (to bread)** servez-vous (de pain); **can I ~ you?** (*in shop*) vous désirez?; **with the ~ of** (*person*) avec l'aide de; (*tool etc*) à l'aide de; **to be of ~ to sb** être utile à qn; **to ~ sb (to) do sth** aider qn à faire qch; **I can't ~ saying** je ne peux pas m'empêcher de dire; **he can't ~ it** il ne peut pas s'en empêcher.
helper ['hɛlpə*] *n* aide *m/f*, assistant/e.
helpful ['hɛlpful] *adj* serviable, obligeant(e); (*useful*) utile.
helping ['hɛlpɪŋ] *n* portion *f*.
helping hand *n* coup *m* de main; **to give sb a ~** prêter main-forte à qn.
helpless ['hɛlplɪs] *adj* impuissant(e); (*baby*) sans défense.
helplessly ['hɛlplɪslɪ] *adv* (*watch*) sans pouvoir rien faire.
helpline ['hɛlplaɪn] *n numéro téléphonique que l'on peut appeler pour obtenir une assistance sociale, médicale, judiciaire etc ou des renseignements sur un produit commercial.*
Helsinki ['hɛlsɪŋkɪ] *n* Helsinki.
helter-skelter ['hɛltə'skɛltə*] *n* (*BRIT: at amusement park*) toboggan *m*.
hem [hɛm] *n* ourlet *m* ♦ *vt* ourler.
▸**hem in** *vt* cerner; **to feel ~med in** (*fig*) avoir l'impression d'étouffer, se sentir oppressé(e) *or* écrasé(e).
he-man ['hiːmæn] *n* (*col*) macho *m*.
hematology ['hiːmə'tɔlədʒɪ] *n* (*US*) = **haematology**.
hemisphere ['hɛmɪsfɪə*] *n* hémisphère *m*.
hemlock ['hɛmlɔk] *n* cigüe *f*.
hemoglobin ['hiːmə'gləubɪn] *n* (*US*) = **haemoglobin**.
hemophilia ['hiːmə'fɪlɪə] *n* (*US*) = **haemophilia**.
hemorrhage ['hɛmərɪdʒ] *n* (*US*) = **haemorrhage**.
hemorrhoids ['hɛmərɔɪdz] *npl* (*US*) = **haemorrhoids**.
hemp [hɛmp] *n* chanvre *m*.
hen [hɛn] *n* poule *f*; (*female bird*) femelle *f*.
hence [hɛns] *adv* (*therefore*) d'où, de là; **2 years ~** d'ici 2 ans.
henceforth [hɛns'fɔːθ] *adv* dorénavant.
henchman ['hɛntʃmən] *n* (*pej*) acolyte *m*, séide *m*.
henna ['hɛnə] *n* henné *m*.
hen party *n* (*col*) réunion *f or* fête *f* entre femmes.
henpecked ['hɛnpɛkt] *adj* dominé par sa femme.
hepatitis [hɛpə'taɪtɪs] *n* hépatite *f*.
her [həː*] *pron* (*direct*) la, l' + *vowel or h mute*; (*indirect*) lui; (*stressed, after prep*) elle; *see note at* **she** ♦ *adj* son(sa), ses *pl*; **I see ~** je la vois; **give ~ a book** donne-lui un livre; **after ~** après elle.
herald ['hɛrəld] *n* héraut *m* ♦ *vt* annoncer.
heraldic [hɛ'rældɪk] *adj* héraldique.
heraldry ['hɛrəldrɪ] *n* héraldique *f*; (*coat of arms*) blason *m*.
herb [həːb] *n* herbe *f*; **~s** *npl* (*CULIN*) fines herbes.
herbaceous [həː'beɪʃəs] *adj* herbacé(e).
herbal ['həːbl] *adj* à base de plantes; **~ tea** tisane *f*.
herbicide ['həːbɪsaɪd] *n* herbicide *m*.
herd [həːd] *n* troupeau *m*; (*of wild animals, swine*) troupeau, troupe *f* ♦ *vt* (*drive: animals, people*) mener, conduire; (*gather*) rassembler; **~ed together** parqués (comme du bétail).
here [hɪə*] *adv* ici ♦ *excl* tiens!, tenez!; **~!** présent!; **~ is, ~ are** voici; **~'s my sister** voici ma sœur; **~ he/she is** le/la voici; **~ she comes** la voici qui vient; **come ~!** viens ici!; **~ and there** ici et là.
hereabouts ['hɪərə'bauts] *adv* par ici, dans les parages.

hereafter [hɪər'ɑːftə*] *adv* après, plus tard; ci-après ♦ *n*: **the** ~ l'au-delà *m*.
hereby [hɪə'baɪ] *adv* (*in letter*) par la présente.
hereditary [hɪ'rɛdɪtrɪ] *adj* héréditaire.
heredity [hɪ'rɛdɪtɪ] *n* hérédité *f*.
heresy ['hɛrəsɪ] *n* hérésie *f*.
heretic ['hɛrətɪk] *n* hérétique *m/f*.
heretical [hɪ'rɛtɪkl] *adj* hérétique.
herewith [hɪə'wɪð] *adv* avec ceci, ci-joint.
heritage ['hɛrɪtɪdʒ] *n* héritage *m*, patrimoine *m*; **our national** ~ notre patrimoine national.
hermetically [həː'mɛtɪklɪ] *adv* hermétiquement.
hermit ['həːmɪt] *n* ermite *m*.
hernia ['həːnɪə] *n* hernie *f*.
hero, *pl* **~es** ['hɪərəu] *n* héros *m*.
heroic [hɪ'rəuɪk] *adj* héroïque.
heroin ['hɛrəuɪn] *n* héroïne *f*.
heroin addict *n* héroïnomane *m/f*.
heroine ['hɛrəuɪn] *n* héroïne *f* (*femme*).
heroism ['hɛrəuɪzəm] *n* héroïsme *m*.
heron ['hɛrən] *n* héron *m*.
hero worship *n* culte *m* (du héros).
herring ['hɛrɪŋ] *n* hareng *m*.
hers [həːz] *pron* le(la) sien(ne), les siens(siennes); **a friend of** ~ un(e) ami(e) à elle, un(e) de ses ami(e)s.
herself [həː'sɛlf] *pron* (*reflexive*) se; (*emphatic*) elle-même; (*after prep*) elle.
Herts [hɑːts] *abbr* (*BRIT*) = *Hertfordshire*.
he's [hiːz] = **he is, he has**.
hesitant ['hɛzɪtənt] *adj* hésitant(e), indécis(e); **to be** ~ **about doing sth** hésiter à faire qch.
hesitate ['hɛzɪteɪt] *vi*: **to** ~ **(about/to do)** hésiter (sur/à faire).
hesitation [hɛzɪ'teɪʃən] *n* hésitation *f*; **I have no** ~ **in saying (that)** ... je n'hésiterai pas à dire (que) ....
hessian ['hɛsɪən] *n* (toile *f* de) jute *m*.
heterogeneous ['hɛtərə'dʒiːnɪəs] *adj* hétérogène.
heterosexual ['hɛtərəu'sɛksjuəl] *adj*, *n* hétérosexuel(le).
het up [hɛt'ʌp] *adj* (*col*) agité(e), excité(e).
HEW *n abbr* (*US*: = *Department of Health, Education and Welfare*) *ministère de la santé publique, de l'enseignement et du bien-être*.
hew [hjuː] *vt* tailler (*à la hache*).
hex [hɛks] (*US*) *n* sort *m* ♦ *vt* jeter un sort sur.
hexagon ['hɛksəgən] *n* hexagone *m*.
hexagonal [hɛk'sægənl] *adj* hexagonal(e).
hey [heɪ] *excl* hé!
heyday ['heɪdeɪ] *n*: **the** ~ **of** l'âge *m* d'or de.
HF *n abbr* (= *high frequency*) HF *f*.
HGV *n abbr* = **heavy goods vehicle**.
HI *abbr* (*US*) = *Hawaii*.
hi [haɪ] *excl* salut!
hiatus [haɪ'eɪtəs] *n* trou *m*, lacune *f*; (*LING*) hiatus *m*.
hibernate ['haɪbəneɪt] *vi* hiberner.
hibernation [haɪbə'neɪʃən] *n* hibernation *f*.
hiccough, hiccup ['hɪkʌp] *vi* hoqueter ♦ *n* hoquet *m*; **to have (the)** ~**s** avoir le hoquet.
hick [hɪk] *n* (*US col*) plouc *m*, péquenaud/e.
hid [hɪd] *pt of* **hide**.
hidden ['hɪdn] *pp of* **hide** ♦ *adj*: **there are no** ~ **extras** absolument tout est compris dans le prix; ~ **agenda** intentions non déclarées.
hide [haɪd] *n* (*skin*) peau *f* ♦ *vb* (*pt* **hid**, *pp* **hidden** [hɪd, 'hɪdn]) *vt*: **to** ~ **sth (from sb)** cacher qch (à qn); (*feelings, truth*) dissimuler qch (à qn) ♦ *vi*: **to** ~ **(from sb)** se cacher de qn.
hide-and-seek ['haɪdən'siːk] *n* cache-cache *m*.
hideaway ['haɪdəweɪ] *n* cachette *f*.
hideous ['hɪdɪəs] *adj* hideux(euse); atroce.
hide-out ['haɪdaut] *n* cachette *f*.
hiding ['haɪdɪŋ] *n* (*beating*) correction *f*, volée *f* de coups; **to be in** ~ (*hidden*) se tenir caché(e).
hiding place *n* cachette *f*.
hierarchy ['haɪərɑːkɪ] *n* hiérarchie *f*.
hieroglyphic [haɪərə'glɪfɪk] *adj* hiéroglyphique; **~s** *npl* hiéroglyphes *mpl*.
hi-fi ['haɪfaɪ] *adj*, *n abbr* (= *high fidelity*) hi-fi (*f*) *inv*.
higgledy-piggledy ['hɪgldɪ'pɪgldɪ] *adv* pêle-mêle, dans le plus grand désordre.
high [haɪ] *adj* haut(e); (*speed, respect, number*) grand(e); (*price*) élevé(e); (*wind*) fort(e), violent(e); (*voice*) aigu(aiguë); (*col*: *person: on drugs*) défoncé(e), fait(e); (*: on drink*) soûl(e), bourré(e); (*BRIT CULIN*: *meat, game*) faisandé(e); (*: spoilt*) avarié(e) ♦ *adv* haut, en haut ♦ *n*: **exports have reached a new** ~ les exportations ont atteint un nouveau record; **20 m** ~ haut(e) de 20 m; **to pay a** ~ **price for sth** payer cher pour qch.
highball ['haɪbɔːl] *n* (*US*) whisky *m* à l'eau avec des glaçons.
highboy ['haɪbɔɪ] *n* (*US*) grande commode.
highbrow ['haɪbrau] *adj*, *n* intellectuel(le).
highchair ['haɪtʃɛə*] *n* chaise haute (*pour enfant*).
high-class ['haɪ'klɑːs] *adj* (*neighbourhood, hotel*) chic *inv*, de grand standing; (*performance etc*) de haut niveau.
High Court *n* (*LAW*) cour *f* suprême; *voir encadré*.

HIGH COURT

La **High Court** *en Grande-Bretagne est la plus haute cour de justice à laquelle les affaires les plus graves telles que le meurtre et le viol sont soumises et où elles sont jugées devant un jury.*

higher ['haɪə*] *adj* (*form of life, study etc*) supérieur(e) ♦ *adv* plus haut ♦ *n* (*SCOT SCOL*): **H~** *première partie de l'examen équivalent au baccalauréat*.
higher education *n* études supérieures.
highfalutin [haɪfə'luːtɪn] *adj* (*col*) affecté(e).
high finance *n* la haute finance.
high-flier, high-flyer [haɪ'flaɪə*] *n* (*fig: ambitious*) ambitieux/euse; (*: gifted*) *personne particulièrement douée et promise à un*

avenir brillant.

high-flying [haɪ'flaɪɪŋ] *adj* (*fig*) ambitieux(euse), de haut niveau.

high-handed [haɪ'hændɪd] *adj* très autoritaire; très cavalier(ière).

high-heeled [haɪ'hiːld] *adj* à hauts talons.

highjack ['haɪdʒæk] *n, vt* = **hijack**.

high jump *n* (*SPORT*) saut *m* en hauteur.

highlands ['haɪləndz] *npl* région montagneuse; **the H~** (*in Scotland*) les Highlands *mpl*.

high-level ['haɪlɛvl] *adj* (*talks etc*) à un haut niveau; ~ **language** (*COMPUT*) langage évolué.

highlight ['haɪlaɪt] *n* (*fig: of event*) point culminant ♦ *vt* faire ressortir, souligner; **~s** *npl* (*hairstyle*) reflets *mpl*.

highlighter ['haɪlaɪtə*] *n* (*pen*) surligneur (lumineux).

highly ['haɪlɪ] *adv* très, fort, hautement; **to speak ~ of** dire beaucoup de bien de.

highly-strung ['haɪlɪ'strʌŋ] *adj* nerveux(euse), toujours tendu(e).

highness ['haɪnɪs] *n* hauteur *f*; **Her H~** son Altesse *f*.

high-pitched [haɪ'pɪtʃt] *adj* aigu(ë).

high point *n*: **the ~ (of)** le clou (de), le point culminant (de).

high-powered ['haɪ'pauəd] *adj* (*engine*) performant(e); (*fig: person*) dynamique; (*: job, businessman*) très important(e).

high-pressure ['haɪprɛʃə*] *adj* à haute pression.

high-rise block ['haɪraɪz-] *n* tour *f* (d'habitation).

high school *n* lycée *m*; (*US*) établissement *m* d'enseignement supérieur; *voir encadré*.

HIGH SCHOOL

Une **high school** *est un établissement d'enseignement secondaire. Aux États-Unis, il y a la "Junior High School", qui correspond au collège, et la "Senior High School", qui correspond au lycée. En Grande-Bretagne, c'est un nom que l'on donne parfois aux écoles secondaires; voir "elementary school".*

high season *n* (*BRIT*) haute saison.

high spirits *npl* pétulance *f*; **to be in ~** être plein(e) d'entrain.

high street *n* (*BRIT*) grand-rue *f*.

highway ['haɪweɪ] *n* grand'route *f*, route nationale; **the information ~** l'autoroute *f* de l'information.

Highway Code *n* (*BRIT*) code *m* de la route.

highwayman ['haɪweɪmən] *n* voleur *m* de grand chemin.

hijack ['haɪdʒæk] *vt* détourner (*par la force*) ♦ *n* (*also*: **~ing**) détournement *m* (d'avion).

hijacker ['haɪdʒækə*] *n* auteur *m* d'un détournement d'avion, pirate *m* de l'air.

hike [haɪk] *vi* aller à pied ♦ *n* excursion *f* à pied, randonnée *f*; (*col: in prices etc*) augmentation *f* ♦ *vt* (*col*) augmenter.

hiker ['haɪkə*] *n* promeneur/euse, excursionniste *m/f*.

hiking ['haɪkɪŋ] *n* excursions *fpl* à pied, randonnée *f*.

hilarious [hɪ'lɛərɪəs] *adj* (*behaviour, event*) désopilant(e).

hilarity [hɪ'lærɪtɪ] *n* hilarité *f*.

hill [hɪl] *n* colline *f*; (*fairly high*) montagne *f*; (*on road*) côte *f*.

hillbilly ['hɪlbɪlɪ] *n* (*US*) montagnard/e du sud des USA; (*pej*) péquenaud *m*.

hillock ['hɪlək] *n* petite colline, butte *f*.

hillside ['hɪlsaɪd] *n* (flanc *m* de) coteau *m*.

hill start *n* (*AUT*) démarrage *m* en côte.

hilly ['hɪlɪ] *adj* vallonné(e); montagneux(euse); (*road*) à fortes côtes.

hilt [hɪlt] *n* (*of sword*) garde *f*; **to the ~** (*fig: support*) à fond.

him [hɪm] *pron* (*direct*) le, l' + *vowel or h mute*; (*stressed, indirect, after prep*) lui; **I see ~** je le vois; **give ~ a book** donne-lui un livre; **after ~** après lui.

Himalayas [hɪmə'leɪəz] *npl*: **the ~** l'Himalaya *m*.

himself [hɪm'sɛlf] *pron* (*reflexive*) se; (*emphatic*) lui-même; (*after prep*) lui.

hind [haɪnd] *adj* de derrière ♦ *n* biche *f*.

hinder ['hɪndə*] *vt* gêner; (*delay*) retarder; (*prevent*): **to ~ sb from doing** empêcher qn de faire.

hindquarters ['haɪnd'kwɔːtəz] *npl* (*ZOOL*) arrière-train *m*.

hindrance ['hɪndrəns] *n* gêne *f*, obstacle *m*.

hindsight ['haɪndsaɪt] *n* bon sens après coup; **with the benefit of ~** avec du recul, rétrospectivement.

Hindu ['hɪnduː] *n* Hindou/e.

hinge [hɪndʒ] *n* charnière *f* ♦ *vi* (*fig*): **to ~ on** dépendre de.

hint [hɪnt] *n* allusion *f*; (*advice*) conseil *m* ♦ *vt*: **to ~ that** insinuer que ♦ *vi*: **to ~ at** faire une allusion à; **to drop a ~** faire une allusion *or* insinuation; **give me a ~** (*clue*) mettez-moi sur la voie, donnez-moi une indication.

hip [hɪp] *n* hanche *f*; (*BOT*) fruit *m* de l'églantier *or* du rosier.

hip flask *n* flacon *m* (pour la poche).

hip hop *n* hip hop *m*.

hippie, hippy ['hɪpɪ] *n* hippie *m/f*.

hip pocket *n* poche-revolver *f*.

hippopotamus, *pl* **~es** *or* **hippopotami** [hɪpə'pɔtəməs, -'pɔtəmaɪ] *n* hippopotame *m*.

hippy ['hɪpɪ] *n* = **hippie**.

hire ['haɪə*] *vt* (*BRIT: car, equipment*) louer; (*worker*) embaucher, engager ♦ *n* location *f*; **for ~** à louer; (*taxi*) libre; **on ~** en location.

►**hire out** *vt* louer.

hire(d) car ['haɪə(d)-] *n* (*BRIT*) voiture louée.

hire purchase (H.P.) *n* (*BRIT*) achat *m* (*or* vente *f*) à tempérament *or* crédit; **to buy sth**

on ~ acheter qch en location-vente.
his [hɪz] *pron* le(la) sien(ne), les siens(siennes) ♦ *adj* son(sa), ses *pl*; **this is** ~ c'est à lui, c'est le sien.
hiss [hɪs] *vi* siffler ♦ *n* sifflement *m*.
histogram ['hɪstəgræm] *n* histogramme *m*.
historian [hɪ'stɔːrɪən] *n* historien/ne.
historic(al) [hɪ'stɔrɪk(l)] *adj* historique.
history ['hɪstərɪ] *n* histoire *f*; **medical** ~ (*of patient*) passé médical.
histrionics [hɪstrɪ'ɔnɪks] *n* gestes *mpl* dramatiques, cinéma *m* (*fig*).
hit [hɪt] *vt* (*pt*, *pp* **hit**) frapper; (*knock against*) cogner; (*reach: target*) atteindre, toucher; (*collide with: car*) entrer en collision avec, heurter; (*fig: affect*) toucher; (*find*) tomber sur ♦ *n* coup *m*; (*success*) coup réussi; succès *m*; (*song*) chanson *f* à succès, tube *m*; **to** ~ **it off with sb** bien s'entendre avec qn; **to** ~ **the headlines** être à la une des journaux; **to** ~ **the road** (*col*) se mettre en route.
►**hit back** *vi*: **to** ~ **back at sb** prendre sa revanche sur qn.
►**hit out at** *vt fus* envoyer un coup à; (*fig*) attaquer.
►**hit (up)on** *vt fus* (*answer*) trouver (par hasard); (*solution*) tomber sur (par hasard).
hit-and-miss ['hɪtænd'mɪs] *adj* au petit bonheur (la chance).
hit-and-run driver ['hɪtænd'rʌn-] *n* chauffard *m*.
hitch [hɪtʃ] *vt* (*fasten*) accrocher, attacher; (*also*: ~ **up**) remonter d'une saccade ♦ *n* (*knot*) nœud *m*; (*difficulty*) anicroche *f*, contretemps *m*; **to** ~ **a lift** faire du stop; **technical** ~ incident *m* technique.
►**hitch up** *vt* (*horse, cart*) atteler; *see also* **hitch**.
hitch-hike ['hɪtʃhaɪk] *vi* faire de l'auto-stop.
hitch-hiker ['hɪtʃhaɪkə*] *n* auto-stoppeur/euse.
hi-tech ['haɪ'tɛk] *adj* de pointe ♦ *n* high-tech *m*.
hitherto [hɪðə'tuː] *adv* jusqu'ici, jusqu'à présent.
hit list *n* liste noire.
hitman ['hɪtmæn] *n* (*col*) tueur *m* à gages.
hit-or-miss ['hɪtə'mɪs] *adj* au petit bonheur (la chance); **it's** ~ **whether** ... il est loin d'être certain que ... + *sub*.
hit parade *n* hit parade *m*.
HIV *n abbr* (= *human immunodeficiency virus*) HIV *m*, VIH *m*; ~**-negative/-positive** séronégatif(ive)/séropositif(ive).
hive [haɪv] *n* ruche *f*; **the shop was a** ~ **of activity** (*fig*) le magasin était une véritable ruche.
►**hive off** *vt* (*col*) mettre à part, séparer.
hl *abbr* (= *hectolitre*) hl.
HM *abbr* (= *His (or Her) Majesty*) SM.
HMG *abbr* (*BRIT*) = *His (or Her) Majesty's Government*.
HMI *n abbr* (*BRIT SCOL*) = *His (or Her) Majesty's Inspector*.
HMO *n abbr* (*US*: = *health maintenance organization*) *organisme médical assurant un forfait entretien de santé*.
HMS *abbr* (*BRIT*) = *His (or Her) Majesty's Ship*.
HMSO *n abbr* (*BRIT*: = *His (or Her) Majesty's Stationery Office*) ≈ Imprimerie nationale.
HNC *n abbr* (*BRIT*: = *Higher National Certificate*) ≈ DUT *m*.
HND *n abbr* (*BRIT*: = *Higher National Diploma*) ≈ licence *f* de sciences et techniques.
hoard [hɔːd] *n* (*of food*) provisions *fpl*, réserves *fpl*; (*of money*) trésor *m* ♦ *vt* amasser.
hoarding ['hɔːdɪŋ] *n* (*BRIT*) panneau *m* d'affichage *or* publicitaire.
hoarfrost ['hɔːfrɔst] *n* givre *m*.
hoarse [hɔːs] *adj* enroué(e).
hoax [həuks] *n* canular *m*.
hob [hɔb] *n* plaque chauffante.
hobble ['hɔbl] *vi* boitiller.
hobby ['hɔbɪ] *n* passe-temps favori.
hobby-horse ['hɔbɪhɔːs] *n* cheval *m* à bascule; (*fig*) dada *m*.
hobnail(ed) boot ['hɔbneɪl(d)-] *n* chaussure (à semelle) cloutée.
hobnob ['hɔbnɔb] *vi*: **to** ~ **with** frayer avec, fréquenter.
hobo ['həubəu] *n* (*US*) vagabond *m*.
hock [hɔk] *n* (*BRIT*: *wine*) vin *m* du Rhin; (*of animal*, *CULIN*) jarret *m*; (*col*): **to be in** ~ (*person*) avoir des dettes; (*object*) être en gage *or* au clou.
hockey ['hɔkɪ] *n* hockey *m*.
hocus-pocus ['həukəs'pəukəs] *n* (*trickery*) supercherie *f*; (*words: of magician*) formules *fpl* magiques; (*: jargon*) galimatias *m*.
hod [hɔd] *n* oiseau *m*, hotte *f*.
hodgepodge ['hɔdʒpɔdʒ] *n* = **hotchpotch**.
hoe [həu] *n* houe *f*, binette *f* ♦ *vt* (*ground*) biner; (*plants etc*) sarcler.
hog [hɔg] *n* porc (châtré) ♦ *vt* (*fig*) accaparer; **to go the whole** ~ aller jusqu'au bout.
Hogmanay [hɔgmə'neɪ] *n* (*Scottish*) réveillon *m* du jour de l'An, Saint-Sylvestre *f*.
hogwash ['hɔgwɔʃ] *n* (*col*) foutaises *fpl*.
hoist [hɔɪst] *n* palan *m* ♦ *vt* hisser.
hoity-toity [hɔɪtɪ'tɔɪtɪ] *adj* (*col*) prétentieux(euse), qui se donne de grands airs.
hold [həuld] *vb* (*pt*, *pp* **held** [hɛld]) *vt* tenir; (*contain*) contenir; (*keep back*) retenir; (*believe*) maintenir; considérer; (*possess*) avoir; détenir ♦ *vi* (*withstand pressure*) tenir (bon); (*be valid*) valoir ♦ *n* prise *f*; (*fig*) influence *f*; (*NAUT*) cale *f*; **to catch** *or* **get (a)** ~ **of** saisir; **to get** ~ **of** (*fig*) trouver; **to get** ~ **of o.s.** se contrôler; ~ **the line!** (*TEL*) ne quittez pas!; **to** ~ **one's own** (*fig*) (bien) se défendre; **to** ~ **office** (*POL*) avoir un portefeuille; **to** ~ **firm** *or* **fast** tenir bon; **he** ~**s the view that** ... il pense *or* estime que ..., d'après lui ...; **to** ~ **sb responsible for sth** tenir qn pour responsable de qch.
►**hold back** *vt* retenir; (*secret*) cacher; **to** ~

sb back from doing sth empêcher qn de faire qch.
►**hold down** *vt* (*person*) maintenir à terre; (*job*) occuper.
►**hold forth** *vi* pérorer.
►**hold off** *vt* tenir à distance ♦ *vi* (*rain*): **if the rain ~s off** s'il ne pleut pas, s'il ne se met pas à pleuvoir.
►**hold on** *vi* tenir bon; (*wait*) attendre; ~ **on!** (*TEL*) ne quittez pas!
►**hold on to** *vt fus* se cramponner à; (*keep*) conserver, garder.
►**hold out** *vt* offrir ♦ *vi* (*resist*): **to ~ out (against)** résister (devant), tenir bon (devant).
►**hold over** *vt* (*meeting etc*) ajourner, reporter.
►**hold up** *vt* (*raise*) lever; (*support*) soutenir; (*delay*) retarder; (: *traffic*) ralentir; (*rob*) braquer.
holdall ['həuldɔːl] *n* (*BRIT*) fourre-tout *m inv*.
holder ['həuldə*] *n* (*of ticket, record*) détenteur/trice; (*of office, title, passport etc*) titulaire *m/f*.
holding ['həuldɪŋ] *n* (*share*) intérêts *mpl*; (*farm*) ferme *f*.
holding company *n* holding *m*.
holdup ['həuldʌp] *n* (*robbery*) hold-up *m*; (*delay*) retard *m*; (*BRIT*: *in traffic*) embouteillage *m*.
hole [həul] *n* trou *m* ♦ *vt* trouer, faire un trou dans; ~ **in the heart** (*MED*) communication *f* interventriculaire; **to pick ~s (in)** (*fig*) chercher des poux (dans).
►**hole up** *vi* se terrer.
holiday ['hɔlədɪ] *n* (*BRIT*: *vacation*) vacances *fpl*; (*day off*) jour *m* de congé; (*public*) jour férié; **to be on** ~ être en congé; **tomorrow is a** ~ demain c'est fête, on a congé demain.
holiday camp *n* (*BRIT*: *for children*) colonie *f* de vacances; (: *also*: **holiday centre**) camp *m* de vacances.
holidaymaker ['hɔlədɪmeɪkə*] *n* (*BRIT*) vacancier/ière.
holiday pay *n* paie *f* des vacances.
holiday resort *n* centre *m* de villégiature *or* de vacances.
holiday season *n* période *f* des vacances.
holiness ['həulɪnɪs] *n* sainteté *f*.
holistic [həu'lɪstɪk] *adj* holiste, holistique.
Holland ['hɔlənd] *n* Hollande *f*.
holler ['hɔlə*] *vi* (*col*) brailler.
hollow ['hɔləu] *adj* creux(euse); (*fig*) faux(fausse) ♦ *n* creux *m*; (*in land*) dépression *f* (de terrain), cuvette *f* ♦ *vt*: **to ~ out** creuser, évider.
holly ['hɔlɪ] *n* houx *m*.
hollyhock ['hɔlɪhɔk] *n* rose trémière.
holocaust ['hɔləkɔːst] *n* holocauste *m*.
hologram ['hɔləgræm] *n* hologramme *m*.
hols [hɔlz] *npl* (*col*) vacances *fpl*.
holster ['həulstə*] *n* étui *m* de revolver.
holy ['həulɪ] *adj* saint(e); (*bread, water*) bénit(e); (*ground*) sacré(e).
Holy Communion *n* la (sainte) communion.
Holy Ghost, Holy Spirit *n* Saint-Esprit *m*.
Holy Land *n*: **the** ~ la Terre Sainte.
holy orders *npl* ordres (majeurs).
homage ['hɔmɪdʒ] *n* hommage *m*; **to pay ~ to** rendre hommage à.
home [həum] *n* foyer *m*, maison *f*; (*country*) pays natal, patrie *f*; (*institution*) maison ♦ *adj* de famille; (*ECON, POL*) national(e), intérieur(e); (*SPORT*: *team*) qui reçoit; (: *match, win*) sur leur (*or* notre) terrain ♦ *adv* chez soi, à la maison; au pays natal; (*right in: nail etc*) à fond; **at** ~ chez soi, à la maison; **to go (or come)** ~ rentrer (chez soi), rentrer à la maison (*or* au pays); **make yourself at** ~ faites comme chez vous; **near my** ~ près de chez moi.
►**home in on** *vt fus* (*missiles*) se diriger automatiquement vers *or* sur.
home address *n* domicile permanent.
home-brew [həum'bruː] *n* vin *m* (*or* bière *f*) maison.
homecoming ['həumkʌmɪŋ] *n* retour *m* (au bercail).
home computer *n* ordinateur *m* domestique.
Home Counties *npl les comtés autour de Londres*.
home economics *n* économie *f* domestique.
home ground *n*: **to be on** ~ être sur son terrain.
home-grown ['həumgrəun] *adj* (*not foreign*) du pays; (*from garden*) du jardin.
home help *n* (*BRIT*) aide-ménagère *f*.
homeland ['həumlænd] *n* patrie *f*.
homeless ['həumlɪs] *adj* sans foyer, sans abri; **the** ~ *npl* les sans-abri *mpl*.
home loan *n* prêt *m* sur hypothèque.
homely ['həumlɪ] *adj* simple, sans prétention; accueillant(e).
home-made [həum'meɪd] *adj* fait(e) à la maison.
Home Office *n* (*BRIT*) ministère *m* de l'Intérieur.
homeopathy *etc* [həumɪ'ɔpəθɪ] (*US*) = **homoeopathy** *etc*.
homeowner ['həuməunə*] *n* propriétaire occupant.
home page *n* (*COMPUT*) page *f* d'accueil.
home rule *n* autonomie *f*.
Home Secretary *n* (*BRIT*) ministre *m* de l'Intérieur.
homesick ['həumsɪk] *adj*: **to be** ~ avoir le mal du pays; (*missing one's family*) s'ennuyer de sa famille.
homestead ['həumstɛd] *n* propriété *f*; (*farm*) ferme *f*.
home town *n* ville natale.
home truth *n*: **to tell sb a few ~s** dire ses quatre vérités à qn.
homeward ['həumwəd] *adj* (*journey*) du retour ♦ *adv* = **homewards**.

homewards ['həumwədz] *adv* vers la maison.
homework ['həumwə:k] *n* devoirs *mpl*.
homicidal [hɔmɪ'saɪdl] *adj* homicide.
homicide ['hɔmɪsaɪd] *n* (*US*) homicide *m*.
homily ['hɔmɪlɪ] *n* homélie *f*.
homing ['həumɪŋ] *adj* (*device, missile*) à tête chercheuse; ~ **pigeon** pigeon voyageur.
homoeopath, (*US*) **homeopath** ['həumɪəupæθ] *n* homéopathe *m/f*.
homoeopathy, (*US*) **homeopathy** [həumɪ'ɔpəθɪ] *n* homéopathie *f*.
homogeneous [hɔməu'dʒi:nɪəs] *adj* homogène.
homogenize [hə'mɔdʒənaɪz] *vt* homogénéiser.
homosexual [hɔməu'sɛksjuəl] *adj, n* homosexuel(le).
Hon. *abbr* (= *honourable, honorary*) *dans un titre*.
Honduras [hɔn'djuərəs] *n* Honduras *m*.
hone [həun] *n* pierre *f* à aiguiser ♦ *vt* affûter, aiguiser.
honest ['ɔnɪst] *adj* honnête; (*sincere*) franc(franche); **to be quite ~ with you ...** à dire vrai ....
honestly ['ɔnɪstlɪ] *adv* honnêtement; franchement.
honesty ['ɔnɪstɪ] *n* honnêteté *f*.
honey ['hʌnɪ] *n* miel *m*; (*col: darling*) chéri/e.
honeycomb ['hʌnɪkəum] *n* rayon *m* de miel; (*pattern*) nid *m* d'abeilles, motif alvéolé ♦ *vt* (*fig*): **to ~ with** cribler de.
honeymoon ['hʌnɪmu:n] *n* lune *f* de miel, voyage *m* de noces.
honeysuckle ['hʌnɪsʌkl] *n* chèvrefeuille *m*.
Hong Kong ['hɔŋ'kɔŋ] *n* Hong Kong.
honk [hɔŋk] *vi* klaxonner.
Honolulu [hɔnə'lu:lu:] *n* Honolulu.
honorary ['ɔnərərɪ] *adj* honoraire; (*duty, title*) honorifique.
honour, (*US*) **honor** ['ɔnə*] *vt* honorer ♦ *n* honneur *m*; **in ~ of** en l'honneur de.
hono(u)rable ['ɔnərəbl] *adj* honorable.
hono(u)r-bound ['ɔnə'baund] *adj*: **to be ~ to do** se devoir de faire.
honours degree ['ɔnəz-] *n* (*SCOL*) ≈ licence *f*; *voir encadré*.

HONOURS DEGREE

Un **honours degree** *est un diplôme universitaire que l'on reçoit après trois années d'études en Angleterre et quatre années en Écosse. Les mentions qui l'accompagnent sont, par ordre décroissant: "first class" (très bien/bien), "upper second class" (assez bien), "lower second class" (passable), et "third class" (diplôme sans mention). Le titulaire d'un* **honours degree** *a un titre qu'il peut mettre à la suite de son nom, par exemple: Peter Jones BA Hons; voir "ordinary degree".*

honours list *n* (*BRIT*): **the ~** *la liste des personnes auxquelles une distinction honorifique est conférée par le souverain; voir encadré*.

HONOURS LIST

*L'***honours list** *est la liste des citoyens du Royaume-Uni et du Commonwealth auxquels le souverain confère un titre ou une décoration. Cette liste est préparée par le Premier ministre et paraît deux fois par an, au Nouvel An et lors de l'anniversaire officiel du règne du souverain. Des personnes qui se sont distinguées dans le monde des affaires, des sports et des médias, ainsi que dans les forces armées, mais également des citoyens "ordinaires" qui se consacrent à des œuvres de charité sont ainsi récompensées.*

Hons. *abbr* (*SCOL*) = **honours degree**.
hood [hud] *n* capuchon *m*; (*BRIT AUT*) capote *f*; (*US AUT*) capot *m*; (*col*) truand *m*.
hoodlum ['hu:dləm] *n* truand *m*.
hoodwink ['hudwɪŋk] *vt* tromper.
hoof, *pl* **~s** *or* **hooves** [hu:f, hu:vz] *n* sabot *m*.
hook [huk] *n* crochet *m*; (*on dress*) agrafe *f*; (*for fishing*) hameçon *m* ♦ *vt* accrocher; (*dress*) agrafer; **~ and eye** agrafe; **by ~ or by crook** de gré ou de force, coûte que coûte; **to be ~ed (on)** (*col*) être accroché(e) (par); (*person*) être dingue (de).
►**hook up** *vt* (*RADIO, TV etc*) faire un duplex entre.
hooligan ['hu:lɪgən] *n* voyou *m*.
hoop [hu:p] *n* cerceau *m*; (*of barrel*) cercle *m*.
hoot [hu:t] *vi* (*AUT*) klaxonner; (*siren*) mugir; (*owl*) hululer ♦ *vt* (*jeer at*) huer ♦ *n* huée *f*; coup *m* de klaxon; mugissement *m*; hululement *m*; **to ~ with laughter** rire aux éclats.
hooter ['hu:tə*] *n* (*BRIT AUT*) klaxon *m*; (*NAUT, factory*) sirène *f*.
hoover ['hu:və*] *n* ® (*BRIT*) aspirateur *m* ♦ *vt* (*room*) passer l'aspirateur dans; (*carpet*) passer l'aspirateur sur.
hooves [hu:vz] *npl of* **hoof**.
hop [hɔp] *vi* sauter; (*on one foot*) sauter à cloche-pied ♦ *n* saut *m*.
hope [həup] *vt, vi* espérer ♦ *n* espoir *m*; **I ~ so** je l'espère; **I ~ not** j'espère que non.
hopeful ['həupful] *adj* (*person*) plein(e) d'espoir; (*situation*) prometteur(euse), encourageant(e); **I'm ~ that she'll manage to come** j'ai bon espoir qu'elle pourra venir.
hopefully ['həupfulɪ] *adv* avec espoir, avec optimisme; **~, they'll come back** espérons bien qu'ils reviendront.
hopeless ['həuplɪs] *adj* désespéré(e), sans espoir; (*useless*) nul(le).
hopelessly ['həuplɪslɪ] *adv* (*live etc*) sans espoir; **~ confused** *etc* complètement désorienté *etc*.
hopper ['hɔpə*] *n* (*chute*) trémie *f*.
hops [hɔps] *npl* houblon *m*.
horizon [hə'raɪzn] *n* horizon *m*.

horizontal [hɔrɪ'zɔntl] *adj* horizontal(e).
hormone ['hɔːməun] *n* hormone *f*.
hormone replacement therapy *n* hormonothérapie substitutive, traitement hormonosupplétif.
horn [hɔːn] *n* corne *f*; (*MUS*) cor *m*; (*AUT*) klaxon *m*.
horned [hɔːnd] *adj* (*animal*) à cornes.
hornet ['hɔːnɪt] *n* frelon *m*.
horny ['hɔːnɪ] *adj* corné(e); (*hands*) calleux(euse); (*col*: *aroused*) excité(e).
horoscope ['hɔrəskəup] *n* horoscope *m*.
horrendous [hə'rɛndəs] *adj* horrible, affreux(euse).
horrible ['hɔrɪbl] *adj* horrible, affreux(euse).
horrid ['hɔrɪd] *adj* méchant(e), désagréable.
horrific [hɔ'rɪfɪk] *adj* horrible.
horrify ['hɔrɪfaɪ] *vt* horrifier.
horrifying ['hɔrɪfaɪɪŋ] *adj* horrifiant(e).
horror ['hɔrə*] *n* horreur *f*.
horror film *n* film *m* d'épouvante.
horror-struck ['hɔrəstrʌk], **horror-stricken** ['hɔrəstrɪkn] *adj* horrifié(e).
hors d'œuvre [ɔː'dəːvrə] *n* hors d'œuvre *m*.
horse [hɔːs] *n* cheval *m*.
horseback ['hɔːsbæk]: **on ~** *adj*, *adv* à cheval.
horsebox ['hɔːsbɔks] *n* van *m*.
horse chestnut *n* marron *m* (d'Inde).
horse-drawn ['hɔːsdrɔːn] *adj* tiré(e) par des chevaux.
horsefly ['hɔːsflaɪ] *n* taon *m*.
horseman ['hɔːsmən] *n* cavalier *m*.
horsemanship ['hɔːsmənʃɪp] *n* talents *mpl* de cavalier.
horseplay ['hɔːspleɪ] *n* chahut *m* (*blagues etc*).
horsepower (hp) ['hɔːspauə*] *n* puissance *f* (en chevaux); cheval-vapeur *m* (CV).
horse-racing ['hɔːsreɪsɪŋ] *n* courses *fpl* de chevaux.
horseradish ['hɔːsrædɪʃ] *n* raifort *m*.
horseshoe ['hɔːsʃuː] *n* fer *m* à cheval.
horse show *n* concours *m* hippique.
horse-trading ['hɔːstreɪdɪŋ] *n* maquignonage *m*.
horse trials *npl* = **horse show**.
horsewhip ['hɔːswɪp] *vt* cravacher.
horsewoman ['hɔːswumən] *n* cavalière *f*.
horsey ['hɔːsɪ] *adj* féru(e) d'équitation *or* de cheval; (*appearance*) chevalin(e).
horticulture ['hɔːtɪkʌltʃə*] *n* horticulture *f*.
hose [həuz] *n* tuyau *m*; (*also*: **garden ~**) tuyau d'arrosage.
▸**hose down** *vt* laver au jet.
hosepipe ['həuzpaɪp] *n* tuyau *m*; (*in garden*) tuyau d'arrosage; (*for fire*) tuyau d'incendie.
hosiery ['həuzɪərɪ] *n* (*in shop*) (rayon *m* des) bas *mpl*.
hospice ['hɔspɪs] *n* hospice *m*.
hospitable ['hɔspɪtəbl] *adj* hospitalier(ière).
hospital ['hɔspɪtl] *n* hôpital *m*; **in ~**, (*US*) **in the ~** à l'hôpital.
hospitality [hɔspɪ'tælɪtɪ] *n* hospitalité *f*.
hospitalize ['hɔspɪtəlaɪz] *vt* hospitaliser.
host [həust] *n* hôte *m*; (*in hotel etc*) patron *m*; (*TV*, *RADIO*) présentateur/trice, animateur/trice; (*large number*): **a ~ of** une foule de; (*REL*) hostie *f* ♦ *vt* (*TV programme*) présenter, animer.
hostage ['hɔstɪdʒ] *n* otage *m*.
host country *n* pays *m* d'accueil, pays-hôte *m*.
hostel ['hɔstl] *n* foyer *m*; (*also*: **youth ~**) auberge *f* de jeunesse.
hostelling ['hɔstlɪŋ] *n*: **to go (youth) ~** faire une virée *or* randonnée en séjournant dans des auberges de jeunesse.
hostess ['həustɪs] *n* hôtesse *f*; (*AVIAT*) hôtesse de l'air; (*in nightclub*) entraîneuse *f*.
hostile ['hɔstaɪl] *adj* hostile.
hostility [hɔ'stɪlɪtɪ] *n* hostilité *f*.
hot [hɔt] *adj* chaud(e); (*as opposed to only warm*) très chaud; (*spicy*) fort(e); (*fig*) acharné(e); brûlant(e); violent(e), passionné(e); **to be ~** (*person*) avoir chaud; (*thing*) être (très) chaud; (*weather*) faire chaud.
▸**hot up** (*BRIT col*) *vi* (*situation*) devenir tendu(e); (*party*) s'animer ♦ *vt* (*pace*) accélérer, forcer; (*engine*) gonfler.
hot-air balloon [hɔt'ɛə-] *n* montgolfière *f*, ballon *m*.
hotbed ['hɔtbɛd] *n* (*fig*) foyer *m*, pépinière *f*.
hotchpotch ['hɔtʃpɔtʃ] *n* (*BRIT*) mélange *m* hétéroclite.
hot dog *n* hot-dog *m*.
hotel [həu'tɛl] *n* hôtel *m*.
hotelier [həu'tɛlɪə*] *n* hôtelier/ière.
hotel industry *n* industrie hôtelière.
hotel room *n* chambre *f* d'hôtel.
hot flush *n* (*BRIT*) bouffée *f* de chaleur.
hotfoot ['hɔtfut] *adv* à toute vitesse.
hothead ['hɔthɛd] *n* (*fig*) tête brûlée.
hotheaded [hɔt'hɛdɪd] *adj* impétueux(euse).
hothouse ['hɔthaus] *n* serre chaude.
hot line *n* (*POL*) téléphone *m* rouge, ligne directe.
hotly ['hɔtlɪ] *adv* passionnément, violemment.
hotplate ['hɔtpleɪt] *n* (*on cooker*) plaque chauffante.
hotpot ['hɔtpɔt] *n* (*BRIT CULIN*) ragoût *m*.
hot potato *n* (*BRIT col*) sujet brûlant; **to drop sb/sth like a ~** laisser tomber qn/qch brusquement.
hot seat *n* (*fig*) poste chaud.
hot spot *n* point chaud.
hot spring *n* source thermale.
hot-tempered ['hɔt'tɛmpəd] *adj* emporté(e).
hot-water bottle [hɔt'wɔːtə-] *n* bouillotte *f*.
hot-wire ['hɔtwaɪə*] *vt* (*col: car*) démarrer en faisant se toucher les fils de contact.
hound [haund] *vt* poursuivre avec acharnement ♦ *n* chien courant; **the ~s** la meute.
hour ['auə*] *n* heure *f*; **at 30 miles an ~** ≈ à 50 km à l'heure; **lunch ~** heure du déjeuner; **to pay sb by the ~** payer qn à l'heure.

hourly ['auəlɪ] *adj* toutes les heures; (*rate*) horaire; ~ **paid** *adj* payé(e) à l'heure.

house *n* [haus] (*pl*: ~**s** ['hauzɪz]) maison *f*; (*POL*) chambre *f*; (*THEAT*) salle *f*; auditoire *m* ♦ *vt* [hauz] (*person*) loger, héberger; **at** (*or* **to**) **my** ~ chez moi; **the H~ of Commons/of Lords** (*BRIT*) la Chambre des communes/des lords; *voir encadré*; **the H~ (of Representatives)** (*US*) la Chambre des représentants; *voir encadré*; **on the** ~ (*fig*) aux frais de la maison.

> **HOUSE OF COMMONS/LORDS**
>
> *Le parlement en Grande-Bretagne est constitué de deux assemblées:*
> *La* **House of Commons**, *présidée par le "Speaker" et composée de plus de 600 députés (les "MP") élus au suffrage universel direct. Ceux-ci reçoivent tous un salaire. La Chambre des communes siège environ 175 jours par an.*
> *La* **House of Lords**, *présidée par le "Lord Chancellor" et composée de membres du haut clergé et de lords séculiers dont le titre est, soit héréditaire, soit attribué par le souverain (dans ce dernier cas, il peut être héréditaire ou à vie); elle peut amender certains projets de loi votés par la Chambre des communes, mais elle n'est pas habilitée à débattre des projets de lois de finances. La Chambre des lords fait également office de la juridiction suprême en Angleterre et au Pays de Galles.*

> **HOUSE OF REPRESENTATIVES**
>
> *Aux États-Unis, le parlement, appelé le "Congress", est constitué du "Senate" et de la* **House of Representatives**. *Cette dernière comprend actuellement 435 membres, le nombre de représentants par État étant proportionnel à la densité de population de cet État. Ils sont élus pour deux ans au suffrage universel direct et siègent au "Capitol", à Washington D.C.*

house arrest *n* assignation *f* à domicile.

houseboat ['hausbəut] *n* bateau (aménagé en habitation).

housebound ['hausbaund] *adj* confiné(e) chez soi.

housebreaking ['hausbreɪkɪŋ] *n* cambriolage *m* (avec effraction).

house-broken ['hausbrəukn] *adj* (*US*) = **house-trained**.

housecoat ['hauskəut] *n* peignoir *m*.

household ['haushəuld] *n* ménage *m*; (*people*) famille *f*, maisonnée *f*; ~ **name** nom connu de tout le monde.

householder ['haushəuldə*] *n* propriétaire *m/f*; (*head of house*) chef *m* de ménage *or* de famille.

househunting ['haushʌntɪŋ] *n*: **to go** ~ se mettre en quête d'une maison.

housekeeper ['hauski:pə*] *n* gouvernante *f*.

housekeeping ['hauski:pɪŋ] *n* (*work*) ménage *m*; (*also*: ~ **money**) argent *m* du ménage.

houseman ['hausmən] *n* (*BRIT MED*) ≈ interne *m*.

house-owner ['hausəunə*] *n* propriétaire *m/f* (*de maison ou d'appartement*).

house-proud ['hauspraud] *adj* qui tient à avoir une maison impeccable.

house-to-house ['haustə'haus] *adj* (*enquiries*) chez tous les habitants (du quartier *etc*).

house-train ['haustreɪn] *vt* (*pet*) apprendre à être propre à.

house-trained ['haustreɪnd] *adj* (*pet*) propre.

house-warming ['hauswɔ:mɪŋ] *n* (*also*: ~ **party**) pendaison *f* de crémaillère.

housewife ['hauswaɪf] *n* ménagère *f*, femme *f* du foyer.

housework ['hauswə:k] *n* (travaux *mpl* du) ménage *m*.

housing ['hauzɪŋ] *n* logement *m* ♦ *cpd* (*problem, shortage*) de *or* du logement.

housing association *n* fondation *f* charitable fournissant des logements.

housing benefit *n* (*BRIT*) ≈ allocations *fpl* logement.

housing conditions *npl* conditions *fpl* de logement.

housing development, (*BRIT*) **housing estate** *n* cité *f*, lotissement *m*.

hovel ['hɔvl] *n* taudis *m*.

hover ['hɔvə*] *vi* planer; **to ~ round sb** rôder *or* tourner autour de qn.

hovercraft ['hɔvəkrɑ:ft] *n* aéroglisseur *m*.

hoverport ['hɔvəpɔ:t] *n* hoverport *m*.

how [hau] *adv* comment; ~ **are you?** comment allez-vous?; ~ **do you do?** bonjour; (*on being introduced*) enchanté(e); ~ **far is it to ...?** combien y a-t-il jusqu'à ...?; ~ **long have you been here?** depuis combien de temps êtes-vous là?; ~ **lovely!** que *or* comme c'est joli!; ~ **many/much?** combien?; ~ **old are you?** quel âge avez-vous?; ~**'s life?** (*col*) comment ça va?; ~ **about a drink?** si on buvait quelque chose?; ~ **is it that ...?** comment se fait-il que ... + *sub*?

however [hau'ɛvə*] *conj* pourtant, cependant ♦ *adv* de quelque façon *or* manière que + *sub*; (+ *adjective*) quelque *or* si ... que + *sub*; (*in questions*) comment.

howitzer ['hauɪtsə*] *n* (*MIL*) obusier *m*.

howl [haul] *n* hurlement *m* ♦ *vi* hurler.

howler ['haulə*] *n* gaffe *f*, bourde *f*.

howling ['haulɪŋ] *adj*: **a ~ wind** *or* **gale** un vent à décorner les bœufs.

HP *n abbr* (*BRIT*) = **hire purchase**.

hp *abbr* (*AUT*) = **horsepower**.

HQ *n abbr* (= *headquarters*) QG *m*.

HR *n abbr* (*US*) = **House of Representatives**.

HRH *abbr* (= *His (or Her) Royal Highness*) SAR.

hr(s) *abbr* (= *hour(s)*) h.

HRT *n abbr* = **hormone replacement therapy**.

HS *abbr* (*US*) = **high school**.
HST *abbr* (*US*: *= Hawaiian Standard Time*) *heure de Hawaii*.
hub [hʌb] *n* (*of wheel*) moyeu *m*; (*fig*) centre *m*, foyer *m*.
hubbub ['hʌbʌb] *n* brouhaha *m*.
hub cap *n* (*AUT*) enjoliveur *m*.
HUD *n abbr* (*US*: *= Department of Housing and Urban Development*) *ministère de l'urbanisme et du logement*.
huddle ['hʌdl] *vi*: **to ~ together** se blottir les uns contre les autres.
hue [hjuː] *n* teinte *f*, nuance *f*; **~ and cry** *n* tollé (général), clameur *f*.
huff [hʌf] *n*: **in a ~** fâché(e); **to take the ~** prendre la mouche.
huffy ['hʌfɪ] *adj* (*col*) froissé(e).
hug [hʌg] *vt* serrer dans ses bras; (*shore, kerb*) serrer ♦ *n* étreinte *f*; **to give sb a ~** serrer qn dans ses bras.
huge [hjuːdʒ] *adj* énorme, immense.
hulk [hʌlk] *n* (*ship*) vieux rafiot; (*car, building*) carcasse *f*; (*person*) mastodonte *m*, malabar *m*.
hulking ['hʌlkɪŋ] *adj* balourd(e).
hull [hʌl] *n* (*of ship, nuts*) coque *f*; (*of peas*) cosse *f*.
hullabaloo ['hʌləbə'luː] *n* (*col*: *noise*) tapage *m*, raffut *m*.
hullo [hə'ləu] *excl* = **hello**.
hum [hʌm] *vt* (*tune*) fredonner ♦ *vi* fredonner; (*insect*) bourdonner; (*plane, tool*) vrombir ♦ *n* fredonnement *m*; bourdonnement *m*; vrombissement *m*.
human ['hjuːmən] *adj* humain(e) ♦ *n* (*also*: **~ being**) être humain.
humane [hjuː'meɪn] *adj* humain(e), humanitaire.
humanism ['hjuːmənɪzəm] *n* humanisme *m*.
humanitarian [hjuːmænɪ'tɛərɪən] *adj* humanitaire.
humanity [hjuː'mænɪtɪ] *n* humanité *f*.
humanly ['hjuːmənlɪ] *adv* humainement.
humanoid ['hjuːmənɔɪd] *adj*, *n* humanoïde (*m/f*).
human rights *npl* droits *mpl* de l'homme.
humble ['hʌmbl] *adj* humble, modeste ♦ *vt* humilier.
humbly ['hʌmblɪ] *adv* humblement, modestement.
humbug ['hʌmbʌg] *n* fumisterie *f*; (*BRIT*: *sweet*) bonbon *m* à la menthe.
humdrum ['hʌmdrʌm] *adj* monotone, routinier(ière).
humid ['hjuːmɪd] *adj* humide.
humidifier [hjuː'mɪdɪfaɪə*] *n* humidificateur *m*.
humidity [hjuː'mɪdɪtɪ] *n* humidité *f*.
humiliate [hjuː'mɪlɪeɪt] *vt* humilier.
humiliation [hjuːmɪlɪ'eɪʃən] *n* humiliation *f*.
humility [hjuː'mɪlɪtɪ] *n* humilité *f*.
humorist ['hjuːmərɪst] *n* humoriste *m/f*.
humorous ['hjuːmərəs] *adj* humoristique; (*person*) plein(e) d'humour.
humour, (*US*) **humor** ['hjuːmə*] *n* humour *m*; (*mood*) humeur *f* ♦ *vt* (*person*) faire plaisir à; se prêter aux caprices de; **sense of ~** sens *m* de l'humour; **to be in a good/bad ~** être de bonne/mauvaise humeur.
humo(u)rless ['huːməlɪs] *adj* dépourvu(e) d'humour.
hump [hʌmp] *n* bosse *f*.
humpback ['hʌmpbæk] *n* bossu/e; (*BRIT*: *also*: **~ bridge**) dos-d'âne *m*.
humus ['hjuːməs] *n* humus *m*.
hunch [hʌntʃ] *n* bosse *f*; (*premonition*) intuition *f*; **I have a ~ that** j'ai (comme une vague) idée que.
hunchback ['hʌntʃbæk] *n* bossu/e.
hunched [hʌntʃt] *adj* arrondi(e), voûté(e).
hundred ['hʌndrəd] *num* cent; **about a ~ people** une centaine de personnes; **~s of people** des centaines de gens; **I'm a ~ per cent sure** j'en suis absolument certain.
hundredweight ['hʌndrɪdweɪt] *n* (*BRIT*) *= 50.8 kg; 112 lb*; (*US*) *= 45.3 kg; 100 lb*.
hung [hʌŋ] *pt*, *pp of* **hang**.
Hungarian [hʌŋ'gɛərɪən] *adj* hongrois(e) ♦ *n* Hongrois/e; (*LING*) hongrois *m*.
Hungary ['hʌŋgərɪ] *n* Hongrie *f*.
hunger ['hʌŋgə*] *n* faim *f* ♦ *vi*: **to ~ for** avoir faim de, désirer ardemment.
hunger strike *n* grève *f* de la faim.
hungover [hʌŋ'əuvə*] *adj* (*col*): **to be ~** avoir la gueule de bois.
hungrily ['hʌŋgrəlɪ] *adv* voracement; (*fig*) avidement.
hungry ['hʌŋgrɪ] *adj* affamé(e); **to be ~** avoir faim; **~ for** (*fig*) avide de.
hung up *adj* (*col*) complexé(e), bourré(e) de complexes.
hunk [hʌŋk] *n* gros morceau; (*col*: *man*) beau mec.
hunt [hʌnt] *vt* (*seek*) chercher; (*SPORT*) chasser ♦ *vi* chasser ♦ *n* chasse *f*.
▸**hunt down** *vt* pourchasser.
hunter ['hʌntə*] *n* chasseur *m*; (*BRIT*: *horse*) cheval *m* de chasse.
hunting ['hʌntɪŋ] *n* chasse *f*.
hurdle ['həːdl] *n* (*for fences*) claie *f*; (*SPORT*) haie *f*; (*fig*) obstacle *m*.
hurl [həːl] *vt* lancer (avec violence).
hurling ['həːlɪŋ] *n* (*SPORT*) *genre de hockey joué en Irlande*.
hurly-burly ['həːlɪ'bəːlɪ] *n* tohu-bohu *m inv*; brouhaha *m*.
hurrah, hurray [hu'rɑː, hu'reɪ] *n* hourra *m*.
hurricane ['hʌrɪkən] *n* ouragan *m*.
hurried ['hʌrɪd] *adj* pressé(e), précipité(e); (*work*) fait(e) à la hâte.
hurriedly ['hʌrɪdlɪ] *adv* précipitamment, à la hâte.
hurry ['hʌrɪ] *n* hâte *f*, précipitation *f* ♦ *vi* se presser, se dépêcher ♦ *vt* (*person*) faire

presser, faire se dépêcher; (*work*) presser; **to be in a ~** être pressé(e); **to do sth in a ~** faire qch en vitesse; **to ~ in/out** entrer/sortir précipitamment; **to ~ home** se dépêcher de rentrer.
▸**hurry along** *vi* marcher d'un pas pressé.
▸**hurry away, hurry off** *vi* partir précipitamment.
▸**hurry up** *vi* se dépêcher.
hurt [hə:t] *vb* (*pt, pp* **hurt**) *vt* (*cause pain to*) faire mal à; (*injure, fig*) blesser; (*damage: business, interests etc*) nuire à, faire du tort à ♦ *vi* faire mal ♦ *adj* blessé(e); **I ~ my arm** je me suis fait mal au bras; **where does it ~?** où avez-vous mal?, où est-ce que ça vous fait mal?
hurtful ['hə:tful] *adj* (*remark*) blessant(e).
hurtle ['hə:tl] *vt* lancer (de toutes ses forces) ♦ *vi*: **to ~ past** passer en trombe; **to ~ down** dégringoler.
husband ['hʌzbənd] *n* mari *m*.
hush [hʌʃ] *n* calme *m*, silence *m* ♦ *vt* faire taire; **~!** chut!
▸**hush up** *vt* (*fact*) étouffer.
hush-hush [hʌʃ'hʌʃ] *adj* (*col*) ultra-secret(ète).
husk [hʌsk] *n* (*of wheat*) balle *f*; (*of rice, maize*) enveloppe *f*; (*of peas*) cosse *f*.
husky ['hʌskɪ] *adj* rauque; (*burly*) costaud(e) ♦ *n* chien *m* esquimau *or* de traîneau.
hustings ['hʌstɪŋz] *npl* (*BRIT POL*) plate-forme électorale.
hustle ['hʌsl] *vt* pousser, bousculer ♦ *n* bousculade *f*; **~ and bustle** *n* tourbillon *m* (d'activité).
hut [hʌt] *n* hutte *f*; (*shed*) cabane *f*.
hutch [hʌtʃ] *n* clapier *m*.
hyacinth ['haɪəsɪnθ] *n* jacinthe *f*.
hybrid ['haɪbrɪd] *adj, n* hybride (*m*).
hydrant ['haɪdrənt] *n* prise *f* d'eau; (*also*: **fire ~**) bouche *f* d'incendie.
hydraulic [haɪ'drɔ:lɪk] *adj* hydraulique.
hydraulics [haɪ'drɔ:lɪks] *n* hydraulique *f*.
hydrochloric ['haɪdrəu'klɔrɪk] *adj*: **~ acid** acide *m* chlorhydrique.
hydroelectric ['haɪdrəuɪ'lɛktrɪk] *adj* hydro-électrique.
hydrofoil ['haɪdrəfɔɪl] *n* hydrofoil *m*.
hydrogen ['haɪdrədʒən] *n* hydrogène *m*.
hydrogen bomb *n* bombe *f* à hydrogène.
hydrophobia ['haɪdrə'fəubɪə] *n* hydrophobie *f*.
hydroplane ['haɪdrəpleɪn] *n* (*seaplane*) hydravion *m*; (*jetfoil*) hydroglisseur *m*.
hyena [haɪ'i:nə] *n* hyène *f*.
hygiene ['haɪdʒi:n] *n* hygiène *f*.
hygienic [haɪ'dʒi:nɪk] *adj* hygiénique.
hymn [hɪm] *n* hymne *m*; cantique *m*.
hype [haɪp] *n* (*col*) matraquage *m* publicitaire *or* médiatique.
hyperactive ['haɪpər'æktɪv] *adj* hyperactif(ive).
hypermarket ['haɪpəmɑ:kɪt] *n* (*BRIT*) hypermarché *m*.
hypertension ['haɪpə'tɛnʃən] *n* (*MED*) hypertension *f*.
hypertext ['haɪpə,tɛkst] *n* (*COMPUT*) hypertexte *m*.
hyphen ['haɪfn] *n* trait *m* d'union.
hypnosis [hɪp'nəusɪs] *n* hypnose *f*.
hypnotic [hɪp'nɔtɪk] *adj* hypnotique.
hypnotism ['hɪpnətɪzəm] *n* hypnotisme *m*.
hypnotist ['hɪpnətɪst] *n* hypnotiseur/euse.
hypnotize ['hɪpnətaɪz] *vt* hypnotiser.
hypoallergenic ['haɪpəuælə'dʒɛnɪk] *adj* hypoallergique.
hypochondriac [haɪpə'kɔndrɪæk] *n* hypocondriaque *m/f*.
hypocrisy [hɪ'pɔkrɪsɪ] *n* hypocrisie *f*.
hypocrite ['hɪpəkrɪt] *n* hypocrite *m/f*.
hypocritical [hɪpə'krɪtɪkl] *adj* hypocrite.
hypodermic [haɪpə'də:mɪk] *adj* hypodermique ♦ *n* (*syringe*) seringue *f* hypodermique.
hypotenuse [haɪ'pɔtɪnju:z] *n* hypoténuse *f*.
hypothermia [haɪpə'θə:mɪə] *n* hypothermie *f*.
hypothesis, *pl* **hypotheses** [haɪ'pɔθɪsɪs, -si:z] *n* hypothèse *f*.
hypothetic(al) [haɪpəu'θɛtɪk(l)] *adj* hypothétique.
hysterectomy [hɪstə'rɛktəmɪ] *n* hystérectomie *f*.
hysteria [hɪ'stɪərɪə] *n* hystérie *f*.
hysterical [hɪ'stɛrɪkl] *adj* hystérique; **to become ~** avoir une crise de nerfs.
hysterics [hɪ'stɛrɪks] *npl* (violente) crise de nerfs; (*laughter*) crise de rire; **to have ~** avoir une crise de nerfs; attraper un fou rire.
Hz *abbr* (= *hertz*) Hz.

I i

I, i [aɪ] *n* (*letter*) I, i *m*; **I for Isaac**, (*US*) **I for Item** I comme Irma.
I [aɪ] *pron* je; (*before vowel*) j'; (*stressed*) moi ♦ *abbr* (= *island, isle*) I.
IA, Ia. *abbr* (*US*) = *Iowa*.
IAEA *n abbr* = **International Atomic Energy Agency**.
IBA *n abbr* (*BRIT*: = *Independent Broadcasting Authority*) ≈ CNCL *f* (= *Commission nationale de la communication audio-visuelle*).
Iberian [aɪ'bɪərɪən] *adj* ibérique, ibérien(ne).
Iberian Peninsula *n*: **the ~** la péninsule Ibérique.
i/c *abbr* (*BRIT*) = **in charge**.
ICBM *n abbr* (= *intercontinental ballistic missile*) ICBM *m*, engin *m* balistique à portée inter-

continentale.
ICC *n abbr* (= *International Chamber of Commerce*) CCI *f*.
ice [aɪs] *n* glace *f*; (*on road*) verglas *m* ♦ *vt* (*cake*) glacer; (*drink*) faire rafraîchir ♦ *vi* (*also*: ~ **over**) geler; (*also*: ~ **up**) se givrer; **to put sth on** ~ (*fig*) mettre qch en attente.
Ice Age *n* ère *f* glaciaire.
ice axe *n* piolet *m*.
iceberg ['aɪsbəːg] *n* iceberg *m*; **the tip of the** ~ (*also fig*) la partie émergée de l'iceberg.
icebox ['aɪsbɔks] *n* (*US*) réfrigérateur *m*; (*BRIT*) compartiment *m* à glace; (*insulated box*) glacière *f*.
icebreaker ['aɪsbreɪkə*] *n* brise-glace *m*.
ice bucket *n* seau *m* à glace.
ice-cap ['aɪskæp] *n* calotte *f* glaciaire.
ice-cold [aɪs'kəuld] *adj* glacé(e).
ice cream *n* glace *f*.
ice cube *n* glaçon *m*.
iced [aɪst] *adj* (*drink*) frappé(e); (*coffee, tea, also cake*) glacé(e).
ice hockey *n* hockey *m* sur glace.
Iceland ['aɪslənd] *n* Islande *f*.
Icelander ['aɪsləndə*] *n* Islandais/e.
Icelandic [aɪs'lændɪk] *adj* islandais(e) ♦ *n* (*LING*) islandais *m*.
ice lolly [-'lɔlɪ] *n* (*BRIT*) esquimau *m*.
ice pick *n* pic *m* à glace.
ice rink *n* patinoire *f*.
ice-skate ['aɪsskeɪt] *n* patin *m* à glace ♦ *vi* faire du patin à glace.
ice-skating ['aɪsskeɪtɪŋ] *n* patinage *m* (sur glace).
icicle ['aɪsɪkl] *n* glaçon *m* (*naturel*).
icing ['aɪsɪŋ] *n* (*AVIAT etc*) givrage *m*; (*CULIN*) glaçage *m*.
icing sugar *n* (*BRIT*) sucre *m* glace.
ICJ *n abbr* = **International Court of Justice**.
icon ['aɪkɔn] *n* icône *f*.
ICR *n abbr* (*US*) = *Institute for Cancer Research*.
ICRC *n abbr* (= *International Committee of the Red Cross*) CICR *m*.
ICT *n* (= *information and communication technology*) TIC *fpl*.
ICU *n abbr* = **intensive care unit**.
icy ['aɪsɪ] *adj* glacé(e); (*road*) verglacé(e); (*weather, temperature*) glacial(e).
I'd [aɪd] = **I would, I had**.
Ida. *abbr* (*US*) = *Idaho*.
ID card *n* = **identity card**.
IDD *n abbr* (*BRIT TEL*: = *international direct dialling*) *automatique international*.
idea [aɪ'dɪə] *n* idée *f*; **good** ~! bonne idée!; **to have an** ~ **that** ... avoir idée que ...; **I haven't the least** ~ je n'ai pas la moindre idée.
ideal [aɪ'dɪəl] *n* idéal *m* ♦ *adj* idéal(e).
idealist [aɪ'dɪəlɪst] *n* idéaliste *m/f*.
ideally [aɪ'dɪəlɪ] *adv* idéalement, dans l'idéal; ~ **the book should have** ... l'idéal serait que le livre ait ....
identical [aɪ'dɛntɪkl] *adj* identique.
identification [aɪdɛntɪfɪ'keɪʃən] *n* identification *f*; **means of** ~ pièce *f* d'identité.
identify [aɪ'dɛntɪfaɪ] *vt* identifier ♦ *vi*: **to** ~ **with** s'identifier à.
Identikit [aɪ'dɛntɪkɪt] *n* ®: ~ **(picture)** portrait-robot *m*.
identity [aɪ'dɛntɪtɪ] *n* identité *f*.
identity card *n* carte *f* d'identité.
identity parade *n* (*BRIT*) parade *f* d'identification.
ideological [aɪdɪə'lɔdʒɪkl] *adj* idéologique.
ideology [aɪdɪ'ɔlədʒɪ] *n* idéologie *f*.
idiocy ['ɪdɪəsɪ] *n* idiotie *f*, stupidité *f*.
idiom ['ɪdɪəm] *n* langue *f*, idiome *m*; (*phrase*) expression *f* idiomatique.
idiomatic [ɪdɪə'mætɪk] *adj* idiomatique.
idiosyncrasy [ɪdɪəu'sɪŋkrəsɪ] *n* particularité *f*, caractéristique *f*.
idiot ['ɪdɪət] *n* idiot/e, imbécile *m/f*.
idiotic [ɪdɪ'ɔtɪk] *adj* idiot(e), bête, stupide.
idle ['aɪdl] *adj* sans occupation, désœuvré(e); (*lazy*) oisif(ive), paresseux(euse); (*unemployed*) au chômage; (*machinery*) au repos; (*question, pleasures*) vain(e), futile ♦ *vi* (*engine*) tourner au ralenti; **to lie** ~ être arrêté, ne pas fonctionner.
▶**idle away** *vt*: **to** ~ **away one's time** passer son temps à ne rien faire.
idleness ['aɪdlnɪs] *n* désœuvrement *m*; oisiveté *f*.
idler ['aɪdlə*] *n* désœuvré/e; oisif/ive.
idle time *n* (*COMM*) temps mort.
idol ['aɪdl] *n* idole *f*.
idolize ['aɪdəlaɪz] *vt* idolâtrer, adorer.
idyllic [ɪ'dɪlɪk] *adj* idyllique.
i.e. *abbr* (= *id est: that is*) c. à d., c'est-à-dire.
if [ɪf] *conj* si ♦ *n*: **there are a lot of** ~**s and buts** il y a beaucoup de si *mpl* et de mais *mpl*; **I'd be pleased** ~ **you could do it** je serais très heureux si vous pouviez le faire; ~ **necessary** si nécessaire, le cas échéant; ~ **only he were here** si seulement il était là; ~ **only to show him my gratitude** ne serait-ce que pour lui témoigner ma gratitude.
iffy ['ɪfɪ] *adj* (*col*) douteux(euse).
igloo ['ɪgluː] *n* igloo *m*.
ignite [ɪg'naɪt] *vt* mettre le feu à, enflammer ♦ *vi* s'enflammer.
ignition [ɪg'nɪʃən] *n* (*AUT*) allumage *m*; **to switch on/off the** ~ mettre/couper le contact.
ignition key *n* (*AUT*) clé *f* de contact.
ignoble [ɪg'nəubl] *adj* ignoble, indigne.
ignominious [ɪgnə'mɪnɪəs] *adj* honteux(euse), ignominieux(euse).
ignoramus [ɪgnə'reɪməs] *n* personne *f* ignare.
ignorance ['ɪgnərəns] *n* ignorance *f*; **to keep sb in** ~ **of sth** tenir qn dans l'ignorance de qch.
ignorant ['ɪgnərənt] *adj* ignorant(e); **to be** ~ **of** (*subject*) ne rien connaître en; (*events*) ne pas être au courant de.

ignore [ɪg'nɔː*] *vt* ne tenir aucun compte de, ne pas relever; (*person*) faire semblant de ne pas reconnaître, ignorer; (*fact*) méconnaître.
ikon ['aɪkɔn] *n* = **icon.**
IL *abbr* (*US*) = *Illinois.*
ILA *n abbr* (*US*: = *International Longshoremen's Association*) *syndicat international des dockers.*
ill [ɪl] *adj* (*sick*) malade; (*bad*) mauvais(e) ♦ *n* mal *m* ♦ *adv*: **to speak/think ~ of sb** dire/penser du mal de qn; **to take** *or* **be taken ~** tomber malade.
Ill. *abbr* (*US*) = *Illinois.*
I'll [aɪl] = **I will, I shall.**
ill-advised [ɪləd'vaɪzd] *adj* (*decision*) peu judicieux(euse); (*person*) malavisé(e).
ill-at-ease [ɪlət'iːz] *adj* mal à l'aise.
ill-considered [ɪlkən'sɪdəd] *adj* (*plan*) inconsidéré(e), irréfléchi(e).
ill-disposed [ɪldɪs'pəuzd] *adj*: **to be ~ towards sb/sth** être mal disposé(e) envers qn/qch.
illegal [ɪ'liːgl] *adj* illégal(e).
illegally [ɪ'liːgəlɪ] *adv* illégalement.
illegible [ɪ'lɛdʒɪbl] *adj* illisible.
illegitimate [ɪlɪ'dʒɪtɪmət] *adj* illégitime.
ill-fated [ɪl'feɪtɪd] *adj* malheureux(euse); (*day*) néfaste.
ill-favoured, (*US*) **ill-favored** [ɪl'feɪvəd] *adj* déplaisant(e).
ill feeling *n* ressentiment *m*, rancune *f*.
ill-gotten ['ɪlgɔtn] *adj* (*gains etc*) mal acquis(e).
ill health *n* mauvaise santé.
illicit [ɪ'lɪsɪt] *adj* illicite.
ill-informed [ɪlɪn'fɔːmd] *adj* (*judgment*) erroné(e); (*person*) mal renseigné(e).
illiterate [ɪ'lɪtərət] *adj* illettré(e); (*letter*) plein(e) de fautes.
ill-mannered [ɪl'mænəd] *adj* impoli(e), grossier(ière).
illness ['ɪlnɪs] *n* maladie *f*.
illogical [ɪ'lɔdʒɪkl] *adj* illogique.
ill-suited [ɪl'suːtɪd] *adj* (*couple*) mal assorti(e); **he is ~ to the job** il n'est pas vraiment fait pour ce travail.
ill-timed [ɪl'taɪmd] *adj* inopportun(e).
ill-treat [ɪl'triːt] *vt* maltraiter.
ill-treatment [ɪl'triːtmənt] *n* mauvais traitement.
illuminate [ɪ'luːmɪneɪt] *vt* (*room, street*) éclairer; (*building*) illuminer; **~d sign** enseigne lumineuse.
illuminating [ɪ'luːmɪneɪtɪŋ] *adj* éclairant(e).
illumination [ɪluːmɪ'neɪʃən] *n* éclairage *m*; illumination *f*.
illusion [ɪ'luːʒən] *n* illusion *f*; **to be under the ~ that** avoir l'illusion que.
illusive, illusory [ɪ'luːsɪv, ɪ'luːsərɪ] *adj* illusoire.
illustrate ['ɪləstreɪt] *vt* illustrer.
illustration [ɪlə'streɪʃən] *n* illustration *f*.
illustrator ['ɪləstreɪtə*] *n* illustrateur/trice.
illustrious [ɪ'lʌstrɪəs] *adj* illustre.
ill will *n* malveillance *f*.
ILO *n abbr* (= *International Labour Organization*) OIT *f*.
ILWU *n abbr* (*US*: = *International Longshoremen's and Warehousemen's Union*) *syndicat international des dockers et des magaziniers.*
I'm [aɪm] = **I am.**
image ['ɪmɪdʒ] *n* image *f*; (*public face*) image de marque.
imagery ['ɪmɪdʒərɪ] *n* images *fpl*.
imaginable [ɪ'mædʒɪnəbl] *adj* imaginable.
imaginary [ɪ'mædʒɪnərɪ] *adj* imaginaire.
imagination [ɪmædʒɪ'neɪʃən] *n* imagination *f*.
imaginative [ɪ'mædʒɪnətɪv] *adj* imaginatif(ive), plein(e) d'imagination.
imagine [ɪ'mædʒɪn] *vt* s'imaginer; (*suppose*) imaginer, supposer.
imbalance [ɪm'bæləns] *n* déséquilibre *m*.
imbecile ['ɪmbəsiːl] *n* imbécile *m/f*.
imbue [ɪm'bjuː] *vt*: **to ~ sth with** imprégner qch de.
IMF *n abbr* = **International Monetary Fund.**
imitate ['ɪmɪteɪt] *vt* imiter.
imitation [ɪmɪ'teɪʃən] *n* imitation *f*.
imitator ['ɪmɪteɪtə*] *n* imitateur/trice.
immaculate [ɪ'mækjulət] *adj* impeccable; (*REL*) immaculé(e).
immaterial [ɪmə'tɪərɪəl] *adj* sans importance, insignifiant(e).
immature [ɪmə'tjuə*] *adj* (*fruit*) qui n'est pas mûr(e); (*person*) qui manque de maturité.
immaturity [ɪmə'tjuərɪtɪ] *n* immaturité *f*.
immeasurable [ɪ'mɛʒrəbl] *adj* incommensurable.
immediacy [ɪ'miːdɪəsɪ] *n* (*of events etc*) caractère *or* rapport immédiat; (*of needs*) urgence *f*.
immediate [ɪ'miːdɪət] *adj* immédiat(e).
immediately [ɪ'miːdɪətlɪ] *adv* (*at once*) immédiatement; **~ next to** juste à côté de.
immense [ɪ'mɛns] *adj* immense; énorme.
immensity [ɪ'mɛnsɪtɪ] *n* immensité *f*.
immerse [ɪ'məːs] *vt* immerger, plonger; **to ~ sth in** plonger qch dans.
immersion heater [ɪ'məːʃən-] *n* (*BRIT*) chauffe-eau *m* électrique.
immigrant ['ɪmɪgrənt] *n* immigrant/e; (*already established*) immigré/e.
immigration [ɪmɪ'greɪʃən] *n* immigration *f*.
immigration authorities *npl* service *m* de l'immigration.
immigration laws *npl* lois *fpl* sur l'immigration.
imminent ['ɪmɪnənt] *adj* imminent(e).
immobile [ɪ'məubaɪl] *adj* immobile.
immobilize [ɪ'məubɪlaɪz] *vt* immobiliser.
immoderate [ɪ'mɔdərət] *adj* immodéré(e), démesuré(e).
immodest [ɪ'mɔdɪst] *adj* (*indecent*) indécent(e); (*boasting*) pas modeste, présomp-

tueux(euse).
immoral [ɪ'mɔrl] *adj* immoral(e).
immorality [ɪmɔ'rælɪtɪ] *n* immoralité *f*.
immortal [ɪ'mɔːtl] *adj*, *n* immortel(le).
immortalize [ɪ'mɔːtlaɪz] *vt* immortaliser.
immovable [ɪ'muːvəbl] *adj* (*object*) fixe; immobilier(ière); (*person*) inflexible; (*opinion*) immuable.
immune [ɪ'mjuːn] *adj*: ~ **(to)** immunisé(e) (contre).
immune system *n* système *m* immunitaire.
immunity [ɪ'mjuːnɪtɪ] *n* immunité *f*; **diplomatic** ~ immunité diplomatique.
immunization [ɪmjunaɪ'zeɪʃən] *n* immunisation *f*.
immunize ['ɪmjunaɪz] *vt* immuniser.
imp [ɪmp] *n* (*small devil*) lutin *m*; (*child*) petit diable.
impact ['ɪmpækt] *n* choc *m*, impact *m*; (*fig*) impact.
impair [ɪm'pɛə*] *vt* détériorer, diminuer.
impaired [ɪm'pɛəd] *adj* (*organ, vision*) abimé(e), détérioré(e); **his memory/circulation is** ~ il a des problèmes de mémoire/circulation; **visually** ~ malvoyant(e); **hearing** ~ malentendant(e); **mentally/physically** ~ intellectuellement/physiquement diminué(e).
impale [ɪm'peɪl] *vt* empaler.
impart [ɪm'pɑːt] *vt* (*make known*) communiquer, transmettre; (*bestow*) confier, donner.
impartial [ɪm'pɑːʃl] *adj* impartial(e).
impartiality [ɪmpɑːʃɪ'ælɪtɪ] *n* impartialité *f*.
impassable [ɪm'pɑːsəbl] *adj* infranchissable; (*road*) impraticable.
impasse [æm'pɑːs] *n* (*fig*) impasse *f*.
impassioned [ɪm'pæʃənd] *adj* passionné(e).
impassive [ɪm'pæsɪv] *adj* impassible.
impatience [ɪm'peɪʃəns] *n* impatience *f*.
impatient [ɪm'peɪʃənt] *adj* impatient(e); **to get** *or* **grow** ~ s'impatienter.
impeach [ɪm'piːtʃ] *vt* accuser, attaquer; (*public official*) mettre en accusation.
impeachment [ɪm'piːtʃmənt] *n* (*LAW*) (mise *f* en) accusation *f*.
impeccable [ɪm'pɛkəbl] *adj* impeccable, parfait(e).
impecunious [ɪmpɪ'kjuːnɪəs] *adj* sans ressources.
impede [ɪm'piːd] *vt* gêner.
impediment [ɪm'pɛdɪmənt] *n* obstacle *m*; (*also*: **speech** ~) défaut *m* d'élocution.
impel [ɪm'pɛl] *vt* (*force*): **to** ~ **sb (to do sth)** forcer qn (à faire qch).
impending [ɪm'pɛndɪŋ] *adj* imminent(e).
impenetrable [ɪm'pɛnɪtrəbl] *adj* impénétrable.
imperative [ɪm'pɛrətɪv] *adj* nécessaire; urgent(e), pressant(e); (*tone*) impérieux(euse) ♦ *n* (*LING*) impératif *m*.
imperceptible [ɪmpə'sɛptɪbl] *adj* imperceptible.
imperfect [ɪm'pəːfɪkt] *adj* imparfait(e); (*goods etc*) défectueux(euse) ♦ *n* (*LING*: *also*: ~ **tense**) imparfait *m*.
imperfection [ɪmpəː'fɛkʃən] *n* imperfection *f*; défectuosité *f*.
imperial [ɪm'pɪərɪəl] *adj* impérial(e); (*BRIT*: *measure*) légal(e).
imperialism [ɪm'pɪərɪəlɪzəm] *n* impérialisme *m*.
imperil [ɪm'pɛrɪl] *vt* mettre en péril.
imperious [ɪm'pɪərɪəs] *adj* impérieux(euse).
impersonal [ɪm'pəːsənl] *adj* impersonnel(le).
impersonate [ɪm'pəːsəneɪt] *vt* se faire passer pour; (*THEAT*) imiter.
impersonation [ɪmpəːsə'neɪʃən] *n* (*LAW*) usurpation *f* d'identité; (*THEAT*) imitation *f*.
impersonator [ɪm'pəːsəneɪtə*] *n* imposteur *m*; (*THEAT*) imitateur/trice.
impertinence [ɪm'pəːtɪnəns] *n* impertinence *f*, insolence *f*.
impertinent [ɪm'pəːtɪnənt] *adj* impertinent(e), insolent(e).
imperturbable [ɪmpə'təːbəbl] *adj* imperturbable.
impervious [ɪm'pəːvɪəs] *adj* imperméable; (*fig*): ~ **to** insensible à; inaccessible à.
impetuous [ɪm'pɛtjuəs] *adj* impétueux(euse), fougueux(euse).
impetus ['ɪmpətəs] *n* impulsion *f*; (*of runner*) élan *m*.
impinge [ɪm'pɪndʒ]: **to** ~ **on** *vt fus* (*person*) affecter, toucher; (*rights*) empiéter sur.
impish ['ɪmpɪʃ] *adj* espiègle.
implacable [ɪm'plækəbl] *adj* implacable.
implant [ɪm'plɑːnt] *vt* (*MED*) implanter; (*fig*) inculquer.
implausible [ɪm'plɔːzɪbl] *adj* peu plausible.
implement *n* ['ɪmplɪmənt] outil *m*, instrument *m*; (*for cooking*) ustensile *m* ♦ *vt* ['ɪmplɪmɛnt] exécuter, mettre à effet.
implicate ['ɪmplɪkeɪt] *vt* impliquer, compromettre.
implication [ɪmplɪ'keɪʃən] *n* implication *f*; **by** ~ indirectement.
implicit [ɪm'plɪsɪt] *adj* implicite; (*complete*) absolu(e), sans réserve.
implicitly [ɪm'plɪsɪtlɪ] *adv* implicitement; absolument, sans réserve.
implore [ɪm'plɔː*] *vt* implorer, supplier.
imply [ɪm'plaɪ] *vt* (*hint*) suggérer, laisser entendre; (*mean*) indiquer, supposer.
impolite [ɪmpə'laɪt] *adj* impoli(e).
imponderable [ɪm'pɔndərəbl] *adj* impondérable.
import *vt* [ɪm'pɔːt] importer ♦ *n* ['ɪmpɔːt] (*COMM*) importation *f*; (*meaning*) portée *f*, signification *f* ♦ *cpd* (*duty, licence etc*) d'importation.
importance [ɪm'pɔːtns] *n* importance *f*; **to be of great/little** ~ avoir beaucoup/peu d'importance.
important [ɪm'pɔːtnt] *adj* important(e); **it is** ~ **that** il importe que, il est important que; **it's**

not ~ c'est sans importance, ce n'est pas important.

importantly [ɪm'pɔːtntlɪ] *adv* (*with an air of importance*) d'un air important; (*essentially*): **but, more ~** ... mais, (ce qui est) plus important encore ....

importation [ɪmpɔː'teɪʃən] *n* importation *f*.

imported [ɪm'pɔːtɪd] *adj* importé(e), d'importation.

importer [ɪm'pɔːtə*] *n* importateur/trice.

impose [ɪm'pəuz] *vt* imposer ♦ *vi*: **to ~ on sb** abuser de la gentillesse de qn.

imposing [ɪm'pəuzɪŋ] *adj* imposant(e), impressionnant(e).

imposition [ɪmpə'zɪʃən] *n* (*of tax etc*) imposition *f*; **to be an ~ on** (*person*) abuser de la gentillesse *or* la bonté de.

impossibility [ɪmpɔsə'bɪlɪtɪ] *n* impossibilité *f*.

impossible [ɪm'pɔsɪbl] *adj* impossible; **it is ~ for me to leave** il m'est impossible de partir.

impostor [ɪm'pɔstə*] *n* imposteur *m*.

impotence ['ɪmpətns] *n* impuissance *f*.

impotent ['ɪmpətnt] *adj* impuissant(e).

impound [ɪm'paund] *vt* confisquer, saisir.

impoverished [ɪm'pɔvərɪʃt] *adj* pauvre, appauvri(e).

impracticable [ɪm'præktɪkəbl] *adj* impraticable.

impractical [ɪm'præktɪkl] *adj* pas pratique; (*person*) qui manque d'esprit pratique.

imprecise [ɪmprɪ'saɪs] *adj* imprécis(e).

impregnable [ɪm'prɛgnəbl] *adj* (*fortress*) imprenable; (*fig*) inattaquable; irréfutable.

impregnate ['ɪmprɛgneɪt] *vt* imprégner; (*fertilize*) féconder.

impresario [ɪmprɪ'sɑːrɪəu] *n* impresario *m*.

impress [ɪm'prɛs] *vt* impressionner, faire impression sur; (*mark*) imprimer, marquer; **to ~ sth on sb** faire bien comprendre qch à qn.

impression [ɪm'prɛʃən] *n* impression *f*; (*of stamp, seal*) empreinte *f*; **to make a good/bad ~ on sb** faire bonne/mauvaise impression sur qn; **to be under the ~ that** avoir l'impression que.

impressionable [ɪm'prɛʃnəbl] *adj* impressionnable, sensible.

impressionist [ɪm'prɛʃənɪst] *n* impressionniste *m/f*.

impressive [ɪm'prɛsɪv] *adj* impressionnant(e).

imprint ['ɪmprɪnt] *n* empreinte *f*; (*PUBLISHING*) notice *f*; (*: label*) nom *m* (de collection *or* d'éditeur).

imprinted [ɪm'prɪntɪd] *adj*: **~ on** imprimé(e) sur; (*fig*) imprimé(e) *or* gravé(e) dans.

imprison [ɪm'prɪzn] *vt* emprisonner, mettre en prison.

imprisonment [ɪm'prɪznmənt] *n* emprisonnement *m*.

improbable [ɪm'prɔbəbl] *adj* improbable; (*excuse*) peu plausible.

impromptu [ɪm'prɔmptjuː] *adj* impromptu(e) ♦ *adv* impromptu.

improper [ɪm'prɔpə*] *adj* (*wrong*) incorrect(e); (*unsuitable*) déplacé(e), de mauvais goût; indécent(e).

impropriety [ɪmprə'praɪətɪ] *n* inconvenance *f*; (*of expression*) impropriété *f*.

improve [ɪm'pruːv] *vt* améliorer ♦ *vi* s'améliorer; (*pupil etc*) faire des progrès.

►**improve (up)on** *vt fus* (*offer*) enchérir sur.

improvement [ɪm'pruːvmənt] *n* amélioration *f*; (*of pupil etc*) progrès *m*; **to make ~s to** apporter des améliorations à.

improvisation [ɪmprəvaɪ'zeɪʃən] *n* improvisation *f*.

improvise ['ɪmprəvaɪz] *vt, vi* improviser.

imprudence [ɪm'pruːdns] *n* imprudence *f*.

imprudent [ɪm'pruːdnt] *adj* imprudent(e).

impudent ['ɪmpjudnt] *adj* impudent(e).

impugn [ɪm'pjuːn] *vt* contester, attaquer.

impulse ['ɪmpʌls] *n* impulsion *f*; **on ~** impulsivement, sur un coup de tête.

impulse buy *n* achat *m* d'impulsion.

impulsive [ɪm'pʌlsɪv] *adj* impulsif(ive).

impunity [ɪm'pjuːnɪtɪ] *n*: **with ~** impunément.

impure [ɪm'pjuə*] *adj* impur(e).

impurity [ɪm'pjuərɪtɪ] *n* impureté *f*.

IN *abbr* (*US*) = *Indiana*.

KEYWORD

in [ɪn] *prep* **1** (*indicating place, position*) dans; **~ the house/the fridge** dans la maison/le frigo; **~ the garden** dans le *or* au jardin; **~ town** en ville; **~ the country** à la campagne; **~ school** à l'école; **~ here/there** ici/là

2 (*with place names: of town, region, country*): **~ London** à Londres; **~ England** en Angleterre; **~ Japan** au Japon; **~ the United States** aux États-Unis

3 (*indicating time: during*): **~ spring** au printemps; **~ summer** en été; **~ May/1992** en mai/1992; **~ the afternoon** (dans) l'après-midi; **at 4 o'clock ~ the afternoon** à 4 heures de l'après-midi

4 (*indicating time: in the space of*) en; (*: future*) dans; **I did it ~ 3 hours/days** je l'ai fait en 3 heures/jours; **I'll see you ~ 2 weeks** *or* **~ 2 weeks' time** je te verrai dans 2 semaines; **once ~ a hundred years** une fois tous les cent ans

5 (*indicating manner etc*) à; **~ a loud/soft voice** à voix haute/basse; **~ pencil** au crayon; **~ writing** par écrit; **~ French** en français; **to pay ~ dollars** payer en dollars; **the boy ~ the blue shirt** le garçon à *or* avec la chemise bleue

6 (*indicating circumstances*): **~ the sun** au soleil; **~ the shade** à l'ombre; **~ the rain** sous la pluie

7 (*indicating mood, state*): **~ tears** en larmes; **~ anger** sous le coup de la colère; **~ despair** au désespoir; **~ good condition** en bon état;

to live ~ luxury vivre dans le luxe
8 (*with ratios, numbers*): **1 ~ 10 (households), 1 (household) ~ 10** 1 (ménage) sur 10; **20 pence ~ the pound** 20 pence par livre sterling; **they lined up ~ twos** ils se mirent en rangs (deux) par deux; **~ hundreds** par centaines
9 (*referring to people, works*) chez; **the disease is common ~ children** c'est une maladie courante chez les enfants; **~ (the works of) Dickens** chez Dickens, dans (l'œuvre de) Dickens
10 (*indicating profession etc*) dans; **to be ~ teaching** être dans l'enseignement
11 (*after superlative*) de; **the best pupil ~ the class** le meilleur élève de la classe
12 (*with present participle*): **~ saying this** en disant ceci
♦ *adv*: **to be ~** (*person*: *at home, work*) être là; (*train, ship, plane*) être arrivé(e); (*in fashion*) être à la mode; **to ask sb ~** inviter qn à entrer; **to run/limp** *etc* **~** entrer en courant/boitant *etc*; **their party is ~** leur parti est au pouvoir
♦ *n*: **the ~s and outs (of)** (*of proposal, situation etc*) les tenants et aboutissants (de).

in. *abbr* = **inch(es)**.
inability [ɪnəˈbɪlɪtɪ] *n* incapacité *f*; **~ to pay** incapacité de payer.
inaccessible [ɪnəkˈsɛsɪbl] *adj* inaccessible.
inaccuracy [ɪnˈækjurəsɪ] *n* inexactitude *f*; manque *m* de précision.
inaccurate [ɪnˈækjurət] *adj* inexact(e); (*person*) qui manque de précision.
inaction [ɪnˈækʃən] *n* inaction *f*, inactivité *f*.
inactivity [ɪnækˈtɪvɪtɪ] *n* inactivité *f*.
inadequacy [ɪnˈædɪkwəsɪ] *n* insuffisance *f*.
inadequate [ɪnˈædɪkwət] *adj* insuffisant(e), inadéquat(e).
inadmissible [ɪnədˈmɪsəbl] *adj* (*behaviour*) inadmissible; (*LAW*: *evidence*) irrecevable.
inadvertent [ɪnədˈvəːtnt] *adj* (*mistake*) commis(e) par inadvertance.
inadvertently [ɪnədˈvəːtntlɪ] *adv* par mégarde.
inadvisable [ɪnədˈvaɪzəbl] *adj* à déconseiller; **it is ~ to** il est déconseillé de.
inane [ɪˈneɪn] *adj* inepte, stupide.
inanimate [ɪnˈænɪmət] *adj* inanimé(e).
inapplicable [ɪnˈæplɪkəbl] *adj* inapplicable.
inappropriate [ɪnəˈprəuprɪət] *adj* inopportun(e), mal à propos; (*word, expression*) impropre.
inapt [ɪnˈæpt] *adj* inapte; peu approprié(e).
inaptitude [ɪnˈæptɪtjuːd] *n* inaptitude *f*.
inarticulate [ɪnɑːˈtɪkjulət] *adj* (*person*) qui s'exprime mal; (*speech*) indistinct(e).
inasmuch [ɪnəzˈmʌtʃ] *adv*: **~ as** vu que, en ce sens que.
inattention [ɪnəˈtɛnʃən] *n* manque *m* d'attention.
inattentive [ɪnəˈtɛntɪv] *adj* inattentif(ive), distrait(e); négligent(e).
inaudible [ɪnˈɔːdɪbl] *adj* inaudible.
inaugural [ɪˈnɔːgjurəl] *adj* inaugural(e).
inaugurate [ɪˈnɔːgjureɪt] *vt* inaugurer; (*president, official*) investir de ses fonctions.
inauguration [ɪnɔːgjuˈreɪʃən] *n* inauguration *f*; investiture *f*.
inauspicious [ɪnɔːsˈpɪʃəs] *adj* peu propice.
in-between [ɪnbɪˈtwiːn] *adj* entre les deux.
inborn [ɪnˈbɔːn] *adj* (*feeling*) inné(e); (*defect*) congénital(e).
inbred [ɪnˈbrɛd] *adj* inné(e), naturel(le); (*family*) consanguin(e).
inbreeding [ɪnˈbriːdɪŋ] *n* croisement *m* d'animaux de même souche; unions consanguines.
Inc. *abbr* = **incorporated**.
Inca [ˈɪŋkə] *adj* (*also*: **~n**) inca *inv* ♦ *n* Inca *m/f*.
incalculable [ɪnˈkælkjuləbl] *adj* incalculable.
incapability [ɪnkeɪpəˈbɪlɪtɪ] *n* incapacité *f*.
incapable [ɪnˈkeɪpəbl] *adj*: **~ (of)** incapable (de).
incapacitate [ɪnkəˈpæsɪteɪt] *vt*: **to ~ sb from doing** rendre qn incapable de faire.
incapacitated [ɪnkəˈpæsɪteɪtɪd] *adj* (*LAW*) frappé(e) d'incapacité.
incapacity [ɪnkəˈpæsɪtɪ] *n* incapacité *f*.
incarcerate [ɪnˈkɑːsəreɪt] *vt* incarcérer.
incarnate *adj* [ɪnˈkɑːnɪt] incarné(e) ♦ *vt* [ˈɪnkɑːneɪt] incarner.
incarnation [ɪnkɑːˈneɪʃən] *n* incarnation *f*.
incendiary [ɪnˈsɛndɪərɪ] *adj* incendiaire ♦ *n* (*bomb*) bombe *f* incendiaire.
incense *n* [ˈɪnsɛns] encens *m* ♦ *vt* [ɪnˈsɛns] (*anger*) mettre en colère.
incense burner *n* encensoir *m*.
incentive [ɪnˈsɛntɪv] *n* encouragement *m*, raison *f* de se donner de la peine.
incentive scheme *n* système *m* de primes d'encouragement.
inception [ɪnˈsɛpʃən] *n* commencement *m*, début *m*.
incessant [ɪnˈsɛsnt] *adj* incessant(e).
incessantly [ɪnˈsɛsntlɪ] *adv* sans cesse, constamment.
incest [ˈɪnsɛst] *n* inceste *m*.
inch [ɪntʃ] *n* pouce *m* (= *25 mm; 12 in a foot*); **within an ~ of** à deux doigts de; **he wouldn't give an ~** (*fig*) il n'a pas voulu céder d'un pouce *or* faire la plus petite concession.
►**inch forward** *vi* avancer petit à petit.
inch tape *n* (*BRIT*) centimètre *m* (de couturière).
incidence [ˈɪnsɪdns] *n* (*of crime, disease*) fréquence *f*.
incident [ˈɪnsɪdnt] *n* incident *m*; (*in book*) péripétie *f*.
incidental [ɪnsɪˈdɛntl] *adj* accessoire; (*unplanned*) accidentel(le); **~ to** qui accompagne; **~ expenses** faux frais *mpl*.
incidentally [ɪnsɪˈdɛntəlɪ] *adv* (*by the way*) à propos.

incidental music *n* musique *f* de fond.
incident room *n* (*POLICE*) salle *f* d'opérations.
incinerate [ɪn'sɪnəreɪt] *vt* incinérer.
incinerator [ɪn'sɪnəreɪtə*] *n* incinérateur *m*.
incipient [ɪn'sɪpɪənt] *adj* naissant(e).
incision [ɪn'sɪʒən] *n* incision *f*.
incisive [ɪn'saɪsɪv] *adj* incisif(ive); mordant(e).
incisor [ɪn'saɪzə*] *n* incisive *f*.
incite [ɪn'saɪt] *vt* inciter, pousser.
incl. *abbr* = **including, inclusive (of)**.
inclement [ɪn'klɛmənt] *adj* inclément(e), rigoureux(euse).
inclination [ɪnklɪ'neɪʃən] *n* inclination *f*.
incline *n* ['ɪnklaɪn] pente *f*, plan incliné ♦ *vb* [ɪn'klaɪn] *vt* incliner ♦ *vi*: **to ~ to** avoir tendance à; **to be ~d to do** être enclin(e) à faire; (*have a tendency to do*) avoir tendance à faire; **to be well ~d towards sb** être bien disposé(e) à l'égard de qn.
include [ɪn'klu:d] *vt* inclure, comprendre; **the tip is/is not ~d** le service est compris/n'est pas compris.
including [ɪn'klu:dɪŋ] *prep* y compris; **~ tip** service compris.
inclusion [ɪn'klu:ʒən] *n* inclusion *f*.
inclusive [ɪn'klu:sɪv] *adj* inclus(e), compris(e); **£50 ~ of all surcharges** 50 livres tous frais compris.
inclusive terms *npl* (*BRIT*) prix tout compris.
incognito [ɪnkɔg'ni:təu] *adv* incognito.
incoherent [ɪnkəu'hɪərənt] *adj* incohérent(e).
income ['ɪnkʌm] *n* revenu *m*; **gross/net ~** revenu brut/net; **~ and expenditure account** compte *m* de recettes et de dépenses.
income support *n* (*BRIT*) ≈ revenu *m* minimum d'insertion, RMI *m*.
income tax *n* impôt *m* sur le revenu.
income tax inspector *n* inspecteur *m* des contributions directes.
income tax return *n* déclaration *f* des revenus.
incoming ['ɪnkʌmɪŋ] *adj* (*passengers, mail*) à l'arrivée; (*government, tenant*) nouveau(nouvelle); **~ tide** marée montante.
incommunicado ['ɪnkəmjunɪ'kɑ:dəu] *adj*: **to hold sb ~** tenir qn au secret.
incomparable [ɪn'kɔmpərəbl] *adj* incomparable.
incompatible [ɪnkəm'pætɪbl] *adj* incompatible.
incompetence [ɪn'kɔmpɪtns] *n* incompétence *f*, incapacité *f*.
incompetent [ɪn'kɔmpɪtnt] *adj* incompétent(e), incapable.
incomplete [ɪnkəm'pli:t] *adj* incomplet(ète).
incomprehensible [ɪnkɔmprɪ'hɛnsɪbl] *adj* incompréhensible.
inconceivable [ɪnkən'si:vəbl] *adj* inconcevable.
inconclusive [ɪnkən'klu:sɪv] *adj* peu concluant(e); (*argument*) peu convaincant(e).
incongruous [ɪn'kɔŋgruəs] *adj* peu approprié(e); (*remark, act*) incongru(e), déplacé(e).
inconsequential [ɪnkɔnsɪ'kwɛnʃl] *adj* sans importance.
inconsiderable [ɪnkən'sɪdərəbl] *adj*: **not ~** non négligeable.
inconsiderate [ɪnkən'sɪdərət] *adj* (*action*) inconsidéré(e); (*person*) qui manque d'égards.
inconsistency [ɪnkən'sɪstənsɪ] *n* (*of actions etc*) inconséquence *f*; (*of work*) irrégularité *f*; (*of statement etc*) incohérence *f*.
inconsistent [ɪnkən'sɪstnt] *adj* inconséquent(e); irregulier(ière); peu cohérent(e); **~ with** en contradiction avec.
inconsolable [ɪnkən'səuləbl] *adj* inconsolable.
inconspicuous [ɪnkən'spɪkjuəs] *adj* qui passe inaperçu(e); (*colour, dress*) discret(ète); **to make o.s. ~** ne pas se faire remarquer.
inconstant [ɪn'kɔnstnt] *adj* inconstant(e); variable.
incontinence [ɪn'kɔntɪnəns] *n* incontinence *f*.
incontinent [ɪn'kɔntɪnənt] *adj* incontinent(e).
incontrovertible [ɪnkɔntrə'və:təbl] *adj* irréfutable.
inconvenience [ɪnkən'vi:njəns] *n* inconvénient *m*; (*trouble*) dérangement *m* ♦ *vt* déranger; **don't ~ yourself** ne vous dérangez pas.
inconvenient [ɪnkən'vi:njənt] *adj* malcommode; (*time, place*) mal choisi(e), qui ne convient pas; **that time is very ~ for me** c'est un moment qui ne me convient pas du tout.
incorporate [ɪn'kɔ:pəreɪt] *vt* incorporer; (*contain*) contenir ♦ *vi* fusionner; (*two firms*) se constituer en société.
incorporated [ɪn'kɔ:pəreɪtɪd] *adj*: **~ company** (*US: abbr* **Inc.**) ≈ société *f* anonyme (S.A.).
incorrect [ɪnkə'rɛkt] *adj* incorrect(e); (*opinion, statement*) inexact(e).
incorrigible [ɪn'kɔrɪdʒɪbl] *adj* incorrigible.
incorruptible [ɪnkə'rʌptɪbl] *adj* incorruptible.
increase *n* ['ɪnkri:s] augmentation *f* ♦ *vi, vt* [ɪn'kri:s] augmenter; **an ~ of 5%** une augmentation de 5%; **to be on the ~** être en augmentation.
increasing [ɪn'kri:sɪŋ] *adj* croissant(e).
increasingly [ɪn'kri:sɪŋlɪ] *adv* de plus en plus.
incredible [ɪn'krɛdɪbl] *adj* incroyable.
incredulous [ɪn'krɛdjuləs] *adj* incrédule.
increment ['ɪnkrɪmənt] *n* augmentation *f*.
incriminate [ɪn'krɪmɪneɪt] *vt* incriminer, compromettre.
incriminating [ɪn'krɪmɪneɪtɪŋ] *adj* compromettant(e).
incrust [ɪn'krʌst] *vt* = **encrust**.
incubate ['ɪnkjubeɪt] *vt* (*egg*) couver, incuber ♦ *vi* (*eggs*) couver; (*disease*) couver.
incubation [ɪnkju'beɪʃən] *n* incubation *f*.
incubation period *n* période *f* d'incubation.
incubator ['ɪnkjubeɪtə*] *n* incubateur *m*; (*for babies*) couveuse *f*.
inculcate ['ɪnkʌlkeɪt] *vt*: **to ~ sth in sb** inculquer qch à qn.

incumbent [ɪn'kʌmbənt] *adj*: **it is ~ on him to ...** il lui appartient de ... ♦ *n* titulaire *m/f*.
incur [ɪn'kəː*] *vt* (*expenses*) encourir; (*anger, risk*) s'exposer à; (*debt*) contracter; (*loss*) subir.
incurable [ɪn'kjuərəbl] *adj* incurable.
incursion [ɪn'kəːʃən] *n* incursion *f*.
Ind. *abbr* (*US*) = *Indiana*.
indebted [ɪn'dɛtɪd] *adj*: **to be ~ to sb (for)** être redevable à qn (de).
indecent [ɪn'diːsnt] *adj* indécent(e), inconvenant(e).
indecent assault *n* (*BRIT*) attentat *m* à la pudeur.
indecent exposure *n* outrage *m* public à la pudeur.
indecipherable [ɪndɪ'saɪfərəbl] *adj* indéchiffrable.
indecision [ɪndɪ'sɪʒən] *n* indécision *f*.
indecisive [ɪndɪ'saɪsɪv] *adj* indécis(e); (*discussion*) peu concluant(e).
indeed [ɪn'diːd] *adv* en effet, effectivement; (*furthermore*) d'ailleurs; **yes ~!** certainement!
indefatigable [ɪndɪ'fætɪgəbl] *adj* infatigable.
indefensible [ɪndɪ'fɛnsɪbl] *adj* (*conduct*) indéfendable.
indefinable [ɪndɪ'faɪnəbl] *adj* indéfinissable.
indefinite [ɪn'dɛfɪnɪt] *adj* indéfini(e); (*answer*) vague; (*period, number*) indéterminé(e).
indefinitely [ɪn'dɛfɪnɪtlɪ] *adv* (*wait*) indéfiniment; (*speak*) vaguement, avec imprécision.
indelible [ɪn'dɛlɪbl] *adj* indélébile.
indelicate [ɪn'dɛlɪkɪt] *adj* (*tactless*) indélicat(e), grossier(ière); (*not polite*) inconvenant(e), malséant(e).
indemnify [ɪn'dɛmnɪfaɪ] *vt* indemniser, dédommager.
indemnity [ɪn'dɛmnɪtɪ] *n* (*insurance*) assurance *f*, garantie *f*; (*compensation*) indemnité *f*.
indent [ɪn'dɛnt] *vt* (*text*) commencer en retrait.
indentation [ɪndɛn'teɪʃən] *n* découpure *f*; (*TYP*) alinéa *m*; (*on metal*) bosse *f*.
indenture [ɪn'dɛntʃə*] *n* contrat *m* d'emploi-formation.
independence [ɪndɪ'pɛndns] *n* indépendance *f*.
Independence Day *n* (*US*) fête *f or* anniversaire *m* de l'Indépendance américaine; *voir encadré*.

INDEPENDENCE DAY

*L'***Independence Day** *est la fête nationale aux États-Unis, le 4 juillet. Il commémore l'adoption de la déclaration d'Indépendance, en 1776, écrite par Thomas Jefferson et proclamant la séparation des 13 colonies américaines de la Grande-Bretagne.*

independent [ɪndɪ'pɛndnt] *adj* indépendant(e); **to become ~** s'affranchir.
independently [ɪndɪ'pɛndntlɪ] *adv* de façon indépendante; **~ of** indépendamment de.
in-depth ['ɪndɛpθ] *adj* approfondi(e).
indescribable [ɪndɪ'skraɪbəbl] *adj* indescriptible.
indeterminate [ɪndɪ'təːmɪnɪt] *adj* indéterminé(e).
index ['ɪndɛks] *n* (*pl*: **~es**: *in book*) index *m*; (*: in library etc*) catalogue *m*; (*pl*: **indices** ['ɪndɪsiːz]) (*ratio, sign*) indice *m*.
index card *n* fiche *f*.
index finger *n* index *m*.
index-linked ['ɪndɛks'lɪŋkt], (*US*) **indexed** *adj* indexé(e) (sur le coût de la vie *etc*).
India ['ɪndɪə] *n* Inde *f*.
Indian ['ɪndɪən] *adj* indien(ne) ♦ *n* Indien/ne.
Indian ink *n* encre *f* de Chine.
Indian Ocean *n*: **the ~** l'océan Indien.
Indian summer *n* (*fig*) été indien, beaux jours en automne.
India rubber *n* gomme *f*.
indicate ['ɪndɪkeɪt] *vt* indiquer ♦ *vi* (*BRIT AUT*): **to ~ left** mettre son clignotant à gauche.
indication [ɪndɪ'keɪʃən] *n* indication *f*, signe *m*.
indicative [ɪn'dɪkətɪv] *adj* indicatif(ive) ♦ *n* (*LING*) indicatif *m*; **to be ~ of sth** être symptomatique de qch.
indicator ['ɪndɪkeɪtə*] *n* (*sign*) indicateur *m*; (*AUT*) clignotant *m*.
indices ['ɪndɪsiːz] *npl of* **index**.
indict [ɪn'daɪt] *vt* accuser.
indictable [ɪn'daɪtəbl] *adj* (*person*) passible de poursuites; **~ offence** délit *m* tombant sous le coup de la loi.
indictment [ɪn'daɪtmənt] *n* accusation *f*.
indifference [ɪn'dɪfrəns] *n* indifférence *f*.
indifferent [ɪn'dɪfrənt] *adj* indifférent(e); (*poor*) médiocre, quelconque.
indigenous [ɪn'dɪdʒɪnəs] *adj* indigène.
indigestible [ɪndɪ'dʒɛstɪbl] *adj* indigeste.
indigestion [ɪndɪ'dʒɛstʃən] *n* indigestion *f*, mauvaise digestion.
indignant [ɪn'dɪgnənt] *adj*: **~ (at sth/with sb)** indigné(e) (de qch/contre qn).
indignation [ɪndɪg'neɪʃən] *n* indignation *f*.
indignity [ɪn'dɪgnɪtɪ] *n* indignité *f*, affront *m*.
indigo ['ɪndɪgəu] *adj* indigo *inv* ♦ *n* indigo *m*.
indirect [ɪndɪ'rɛkt] *adj* indirect(e).
indirectly [ɪndɪ'rɛktlɪ] *adv* indirectement.
indiscreet [ɪndɪ'skriːt] *adj* indiscret(ète); (*rash*) imprudent(e).
indiscretion [ɪndɪ'skrɛʃən] *n* (*see indiscreet*) indiscrétion *f*; imprudence *f*.
indiscriminate [ɪndɪ'skrɪmɪnət] *adj* (*person*) qui manque de discernement; (*admiration*) aveugle; (*killings*) commis(e) au hasard.
indispensable [ɪndɪ'spɛnsəbl] *adj* indispensable.
indisposed [ɪndɪ'spəuzd] *adj* (*unwell*) indisposé(e), souffrant(e).

indisposition [ɪndɪspə'zɪʃən] *n* (*illness*) indisposition *f*, malaise *m*.
indisputable [ɪndɪ'spjuːtəbl] *adj* incontestable, indiscutable.
indistinct [ɪndɪ'stɪŋkt] *adj* indistinct(e); (*memory, noise*) vague.
indistinguishable [ɪndɪ'stɪŋgwɪʃəbl] *adj* impossible à distinguer.
individual [ɪndɪ'vɪdjuəl] *n* individu *m* ♦ *adj* individuel(le); (*characteristic*) particulier(ière), original(e).
individualist [ɪndɪ'vɪdjuəlɪst] *n* individualiste *m/f*.
individuality [ɪndɪvɪdju'ælɪtɪ] *n* individualité *f*.
individually [ɪndɪ'vɪdjuəlɪ] *adv* individuellement.
indivisible [ɪndɪ'vɪzɪbl] *adj* indivisible; (*MATH*) insécable.
Indo-China ['ɪndəu'tʃaɪnə] *n* Indochine *f*.
indoctrinate [ɪn'dɔktrɪneɪt] *vt* endoctriner.
indoctrination [ɪndɔktrɪ'neɪʃən] *n* endoctrinement *m*.
indolent ['ɪndələnt] *adj* indolent(e), nonchalant(e).
Indonesia [ɪndə'niːzɪə] *n* Indonésie *f*.
Indonesian [ɪndə'niːzɪən] *adj* indonésien(ne) ♦ *n* Indonésien/ne; (*LING*) indonésien *m*.
indoor ['ɪndɔː*] *adj* d'intérieur; (*plant*) d'appartement; (*swimming pool*) couvert(e); (*sport, games*) pratiqué(e) en salle.
indoors [ɪn'dɔːz] *adv* à l'intérieur; (*at home*) à la maison.
indubitable [ɪn'djuːbɪtəbl] *adj* indubitable, incontestable.
induce [ɪn'djuːs] *vt* persuader; (*bring about*) provoquer; **to ~ sb to do sth** inciter *or* pousser qn à faire qch.
inducement [ɪn'djuːsmənt] *n* incitation *f*; (*incentive*) but *m*; (*pej: bribe*) pot-de-vin *m*.
induct [ɪn'dʌkt] *vt* établir dans ses fonctions; (*fig*) initier.
induction [ɪn'dʌkʃən] *n* (*MED: of birth*) accouchement provoqué.
induction course *n* (*BRIT*) stage *m* de mise au courant.
indulge [ɪn'dʌldʒ] *vt* (*whim*) céder à, satisfaire; (*child*) gâter ♦ *vi*: **to ~ in sth** s'offrir qch, se permettre qch; se livrer à qch.
indulgence [ɪn'dʌldʒəns] *n* fantaisie *f* (que l'on s'offre); (*leniency*) indulgence *f*.
indulgent [ɪn'dʌldʒənt] *adj* indulgent(e).
industrial [ɪn'dʌstrɪəl] *adj* industriel(le); (*injury*) du travail; (*dispute*) ouvrier(ière).
industrial action *n* action revendicative.
industrial estate *n* (*BRIT*) zone industrielle.
industrialist [ɪn'dʌstrɪəlɪst] *n* industriel *m*.
industrialize [ɪn'dʌstrɪəlaɪz] *vt* industrialiser.
industrial park *n* (*US*) zone industrielle.
industrial relations *npl* relations *fpl* dans l'entreprise.
industrial tribunal *n* (*BRIT*) ≈ conseil *m* de prud'hommes.
industrial unrest *n* (*BRIT*) agitation sociale, conflits sociaux.
industrious [ɪn'dʌstrɪəs] *adj* travailleur(euse).
industry ['ɪndəstrɪ] *n* industrie *f*; (*diligence*) zèle *m*, application *f*.
inebriated [ɪ'niːbrɪeɪtɪd] *adj* ivre.
inedible [ɪn'ɛdɪbl] *adj* immangeable; (*plant etc*) non comestible.
ineffective [ɪnɪ'fɛktɪv], **ineffectual** [ɪnɪ'fɛktʃuəl] *adj* inefficace; incompétent(e).
inefficiency [ɪnɪ'fɪʃənsɪ] *n* inefficacité *f*.
inefficient [ɪnɪ'fɪʃənt] *adj* inefficace.
inelegant [ɪn'ɛlɪgənt] *adj* peu élégant(e), inélégant(e).
ineligible [ɪn'ɛlɪdʒɪbl] *adj* (*candidate*) inéligible; **to be ~ for sth** ne pas avoir droit à qch.
inept [ɪ'nɛpt] *adj* inepte.
ineptitude [ɪ'nɛptɪtjuːd] *n* ineptie *f*.
inequality [ɪnɪ'kwɔlɪtɪ] *n* inégalité *f*.
inequitable [ɪn'ɛkwɪtəbl] *adj* inéquitable, inique.
ineradicable [ɪnɪ'rædɪkəbl] *adj* indéracinable, tenace.
inert [ɪ'nəːt] *adj* inerte.
inertia [ɪ'nəːʃə] *n* inertie *f*.
inertia-reel seat belt [ɪ'nəːʃə'riːl-] *n* ceinture *f* de sécurité à enrouleur.
inescapable [ɪnɪ'skeɪpəbl] *adj* inéluctable, inévitable.
inessential [ɪnɪ'sɛnʃl] *adj* superflu(e).
inestimable [ɪn'ɛstɪməbl] *adj* inestimable, incalculable.
inevitable [ɪn'ɛvɪtəbl] *adj* inévitable.
inevitably [ɪn'ɛvɪtəblɪ] *adv* inévitablement, fatalement.
inexact [ɪnɪg'zækt] *adj* inexact(e).
inexcusable [ɪnɪks'kjuːzəbl] *adj* inexcusable.
inexhaustible [ɪnɪg'zɔːstɪbl] *adj* inépuisable.
inexorable [ɪn'ɛksərəbl] *adj* inexorable.
inexpensive [ɪnɪk'spɛnsɪv] *adj* bon marché *inv*.
inexperience [ɪnɪk'spɪərɪəns] *n* inexpérience *f*, manque *m* d'expérience.
inexperienced [ɪnɪk'spɪərɪənst] *adj* inexpérimenté(e); **to be ~ in sth** manquer d'expérience dans qch.
inexplicable [ɪnɪk'splɪkəbl] *adj* inexplicable.
inexpressible [ɪnɪk'sprɛsɪbl] *adj* inexprimable; indicible.
inextricable [ɪnɪk'strɪkəbl] *adj* inextricable.
infallibility [ɪnfælə'bɪlɪtɪ] *n* infaillibilité *f*.
infallible [ɪn'fælɪbl] *adj* infaillible.
infamous ['ɪnfəməs] *adj* infâme, abominable.
infamy ['ɪnfəmɪ] *n* infamie *f*.
infancy ['ɪnfənsɪ] *n* petite enfance, bas âge; (*fig*) enfance, débuts *mpl*.
infant ['ɪnfənt] *n* (*baby*) nourrisson *m*; (*young child*) petit(e) enfant.
infantile ['ɪnfəntaɪl] *adj* infantile.
infant mortality *n* mortalité *f* infantile.
infantry ['ɪnfəntrɪ] *n* infanterie *f*.
infantryman ['ɪnfəntrɪmən] *n* fantassin *m*.

infant school *n* (*BRIT*) classes *fpl* préparatoires (*entre 5 et 7 ans*).
infatuated [ɪn'fætjueɪtɪd] *adj*: ~ **with** entiché(e) de; **to become ~ (with sb)** s'enticher (de qn).
infatuation [ɪnfætju'eɪʃən] *n* toquade *f*; engouement *m*.
infect [ɪn'fɛkt] *vt* infecter, contaminer; (*fig*: *pej*) corrompre; **~ed with** (*illness*) atteint(e) de; **to become ~ed** (*wound*) s'infecter.
infection [ɪn'fɛkʃən] *n* infection *f*; contagion *f*.
infectious [ɪn'fɛkʃəs] *adj* infectieux(euse); (*also fig*) contagieux(euse).
infer [ɪn'fəː*] *vt*: **to ~ (from)** conclure (de), déduire (de).
inference ['ɪnfərəns] *n* conclusion *f*, déduction *f*.
inferior [ɪn'fɪərɪə*] *adj* inférieur(e); (*goods*) de qualité inférieure ♦ *n* inférieur/e; (*in rank*) subalterne *m/f*; **to feel ~** avoir un sentiment d'infériorité.
inferiority [ɪnfɪərɪ'ɔrətɪ] *n* infériorité *f*.
inferiority complex *n* complexe *m* d'infériorité.
infernal [ɪn'fəːnl] *adj* infernal(e).
inferno [ɪn'fəːnəu] *n* enfer *m*; brasier *m*.
infertile [ɪn'fəːtaɪl] *adj* stérile.
infertility [ɪnfəː'tɪlɪtɪ] *n* infertilité *f*, stérilité *f*.
infested [ɪn'fɛstɪd] *adj*: ~ **(with)** infesté(e) (de).
infidelity [ɪnfɪ'dɛlɪtɪ] *n* infidélité *f*.
in-fighting ['ɪnfaɪtɪŋ] *n* querelles *fpl* internes.
infiltrate ['ɪnfɪltreɪt] *vt* (*troops etc*) faire s'infiltrer; (*enemy line etc*) s'infiltrer dans ♦ *vi* s'infiltrer.
infinite ['ɪnfɪnɪt] *adj* infini(e); (*time, money*) illimité(e).
infinitely ['ɪnfɪnɪtlɪ] *adv* infiniment.
infinitesimal [ɪnfɪnɪ'tɛsɪməl] *adj* infinitésimal(e).
infinitive [ɪn'fɪnɪtɪv] *n* infinitif *m*.
infinity [ɪn'fɪnɪtɪ] *n* infinité *f*; (*also MATH*) infini *m*.
infirm [ɪn'fəːm] *adj* infirme.
infirmary [ɪn'fəːmərɪ] *n* hôpital *m*; (*in school, factory*) infirmerie *f*.
infirmity [ɪn'fəːmɪtɪ] *n* infirmité *f*.
inflamed [ɪn'fleɪmd] *adj* enflammé(e).
inflammable [ɪn'flæməbl] *adj* (*BRIT*) inflammable.
inflammation [ɪnflə'meɪʃən] *n* inflammation *f*.
inflammatory [ɪn'flæmətərɪ] *adj* (*speech*) incendiaire.
inflatable [ɪn'fleɪtəbl] *adj* gonflable.
inflate [ɪn'fleɪt] *vt* (*tyre, balloon*) gonfler; (*fig*) grossir; gonfler; faire monter.
inflated [ɪn'fleɪtɪd] *adj* (*style*) enflé(e); (*value*) exagéré(e).
inflation [ɪn'fleɪʃən] *n* (*ECON*) inflation *f*.
inflationary [ɪn'fleɪʃənərɪ] *adj* inflationniste.
inflection [ɪn'flɛkʃən] *n* inflexion *f*; (*ending*) désinence *f*.
inflexible [ɪn'flɛksɪbl] *adj* inflexible, rigide.
inflict [ɪn'flɪkt] *vt*: **to ~ on** infliger à.
infliction [ɪn'flɪkʃən] *n* infliction *f*; affliction *f*.
in-flight ['ɪnflaɪt] *adj* (*service etc*) à bord.
inflow ['ɪnfləu] *n* afflux *m*.
influence ['ɪnfluəns] *n* influence *f* ♦ *vt* influencer; **under the ~ of** sous l'effet de; **under the ~ of drink** en état d'ébriété.
influential [ɪnflu'ɛnʃl] *adj* influent(e).
influenza [ɪnflu'ɛnzə] *n* grippe *f*.
influx ['ɪnflʌks] *n* afflux *m*.
inform [ɪn'fɔːm] *vt*: **to ~ sb (of)** informer *or* avertir qn (de) ♦ *vi*: **to ~ on sb** dénoncer qn, informer contre qn; **to ~ sb about** renseigner qn sur, mettre qn au courant de.
informal [ɪn'fɔːml] *adj* (*person, manner*) simple, sans cérémonie; (*announcement, visit*) non officiel(le); **"dress ~"** "tenue de ville".
informality [ɪnfɔː'mælɪtɪ] *n* simplicité *f*, absence *f* de cérémonie; caractère non officiel.
informally [ɪn'fɔːməlɪ] *adv* sans cérémonie, en toute simplicité; non officiellement.
informant [ɪn'fɔːmənt] *n* informateur/trice.
information [ɪnfə'meɪʃən] *n* information(s) *f(pl)*; renseignements *mpl*; (*knowledge*) connaissances *fpl*; **to get ~ on** se renseigner sur; **a piece of ~** un renseignement; **for your ~** à titre d'information.
information and communication technology *n* (*BRIT*) informatique *f*; technologies *fpl* de l'information et de la communication.
information bureau *n* bureau *m* de renseignements.
information processing *n* traitement *m* de l'information.
information retrieval *n* recherche *f* (informatique) de renseignements.
information superhighway *n* autoroute *f* de l'information.
information technology (IT) *n* informatique *f*.
informative [ɪn'fɔːmətɪv] *adj* instructif(ive).
informed [ɪn'fɔːmd] *adj* (bien) informé(e); **an ~ guess** une hypothèse fondée sur la connaissance des faits.
informer [ɪn'fɔːmə*] *n* dénonciateur/trice; (*also*: **police ~**) indicateur/trice.
infra dig ['ɪnfrə'dɪg] *adj abbr* (*col*: = *infra dignitatem*) au-dessous de ma (*or* sa *etc*) dignité.
infra-red [ɪnfrə'rɛd] *adj* infrarouge.
infrastructure ['ɪnfrəstrʌktʃə*] *n* infrastructure *f*.
infrequent [ɪn'friːkwənt] *adj* peu fréquent(e), rare.
infringe [ɪn'frɪndʒ] *vt* enfreindre ♦ *vi*: **to ~ on** empiéter sur.
infringement [ɪn'frɪndʒmənt] *n*: **~ (of)** infraction *f* (à).
infuriate [ɪn'fjuərɪeɪt] *vt* mettre en fureur.
infuriating [ɪn'fjuərɪeɪtɪŋ] *adj* exaspérant(e).
infuse [ɪn'fjuːz] *vt*: **to ~ sb with sth** (*fig*) insuffler qch à qn.

infusion [ɪn'fjuːʒən] *n* (*tea etc*) infusion *f*.
ingenious [ɪn'dʒiːnjəs] *adj* ingénieux(euse).
ingenuity [ɪndʒɪ'njuːɪtɪ] *n* ingéniosité *f*.
ingenuous [ɪn'dʒɛnjuəs] *adj* franc(franche), ouvert(e).
ingot ['ɪŋgət] *n* lingot *m*.
ingrained [ɪn'greɪnd] *adj* enraciné(e).
ingratiate [ɪn'greɪʃɪeɪt] *vt*: **to ~ o.s. with** s'insinuer dans les bonnes grâces de, se faire bien voir de.
ingratiating [ɪn'greɪʃɪeɪtɪŋ] *adj* (*smile, speech*) insinuant(e); (*person*) patelin(e).
ingratitude [ɪn'grætɪtjuːd] *n* ingratitude *f*.
ingredient [ɪn'griːdɪənt] *n* ingrédient *m*; élément *m*.
ingrowing ['ɪngrəuɪŋ], **ingrown** ['ɪngrəun] *adj*: **~ toenail** ongle incarné.
inhabit [ɪn'hæbɪt] *vt* habiter.
inhabitable [ɪn'hæbɪtəbl] *adj* habitable.
inhabitant [ɪn'hæbɪtnt] *n* habitant/e.
inhale [ɪn'heɪl] *vt* inhaler; (*perfume*) respirer ♦ *vi* (*in smoking*) avaler la fumée.
inhaler [ɪn'heɪlə*] *n* inhalateur *m*.
inherent [ɪn'hɪərənt] *adj*: **~ (in** *or* **to)** inhérent(e) (à).
inherently [ɪn'hɪərəntlɪ] *adv* (*easy, difficult*) en soi; (*lazy*) fondamentalement.
inherit [ɪn'hɛrɪt] *vt* hériter (de).
inheritance [ɪn'hɛrɪtəns] *n* héritage *m*; **law of ~** droit *m* de la succession.
inhibit [ɪn'hɪbɪt] *vt* (*PSYCH*) inhiber; **to ~ sb from doing** empêcher *or* retenir qn de faire.
inhibited [ɪn'hɪbɪtɪd] *adj* (*person*) inhibé(e).
inhibiting [ɪn'hɪbɪtɪŋ] *adj* gênant(e).
inhibition [ɪnhɪ'bɪʃən] *n* inhibition *f*.
inhospitable [ɪnhɔs'pɪtəbl] *adj* inhospitalier(ière).
in-house ['ɪn'haus] *adj* (*system*) interne; (*training*) effectué(e) sur place *or* dans le cadre de la compagnie ♦ *adv* (*train, produce*) sur place.
inhuman [ɪn'hjuːmən] *adj* inhumain(e).
inhumane [ɪnhjuː'meɪn] *adj* inhumain(e).
inimitable [ɪ'nɪmɪtəbl] *adj* inimitable.
iniquity [ɪ'nɪkwɪtɪ] *n* iniquité *f*.
initial [ɪ'nɪʃl] *adj* initial(e) ♦ *n* initiale *f* ♦ *vt* parafer; **~s** *npl* initiales *fpl*; (*as signature*) parafe *m*.
initialize [ɪ'nɪʃəlaɪz] *vt* (*COMPUT*) initialiser.
initially [ɪ'nɪʃəlɪ] *adv* initialement, au début.
initiate [ɪ'nɪʃɪeɪt] *vt* (*start*) entreprendre; amorcer; lancer; (*person*) initier; **to ~ sb into a secret** initier qn à un secret; **to ~ proceedings against sb** (*LAW*) intenter une action à qn, engager des poursuites contre qn.
initiation [ɪnɪʃɪ'eɪʃən] *n* (*into secret etc*) initiation *f*.
initiative [ɪ'nɪʃətɪv] *n* initiative *f*; **to take the ~** prendre l'initiative.
inject [ɪn'dʒɛkt] *vt* (*liquid, fig: money*) injecter; (*person*) faire une piqûre à.
injection [ɪn'dʒɛkʃən] *n* injection *f*, piqûre *f*; **to have an ~** se faire faire une piqûre.
injudicious [ɪndʒu'dɪʃəs] *adj* peu judicieux(euse).
injunction [ɪn'dʒʌŋkʃən] *n* (*LAW*) injonction *f*, ordre *m*.
injure ['ɪndʒə*] *vt* blesser; (*wrong*) faire du tort à; (*damage: reputation etc*) compromettre; (*feelings*) heurter; **to ~ o.s.** se blesser.
injured ['ɪndʒəd] *adj* (*person, leg etc*) blessé(e); (*tone, feelings*) offensé(e); **~ party** (*LAW*) partie lésée.
injurious [ɪn'dʒuərɪəs] *adj*: **~ (to)** préjudiciable (à).
injury ['ɪndʒərɪ] *n* blessure *f*; (*wrong*) tort *m*; **to escape without ~** s'en sortir sain et sauf.
injury time *n* (*SPORT*) arrêts *mpl* de jeu.
injustice [ɪn'dʒʌstɪs] *n* injustice *f*; **you do me an ~** vous êtes injuste envers moi.
ink [ɪŋk] *n* encre *f*.
ink-jet printer ['ɪŋkdʒɛt-] *n* imprimante *f* à jet d'encre.
inkling ['ɪŋklɪŋ] *n* soupçon *m*, vague idée *f*.
inkpad ['ɪŋkpæd] *n* tampon *m* encreur.
inky ['ɪŋkɪ] *adj* taché(e) d'encre.
inlaid ['ɪnleɪd] *adj* incrusté(e); (*table etc*) marqueté(e).
inland *adj* ['ɪnlənd] intérieur(e) ♦ *adv* [ɪn'lænd] à l'intérieur, dans les terres; **~ waterways** canaux *mpl* et rivières *fpl*.
Inland Revenue *n* (*BRIT*) fisc *m*.
in-laws ['ɪnlɔːz] *npl* beaux-parents *mpl*; belle famille.
inlet ['ɪnlɛt] *n* (*GEO*) crique *f*.
inlet pipe *n* (*TECH*) tuyau *m* d'arrivée.
inmate ['ɪnmeɪt] *n* (*in prison*) détenu/e; (*in asylum*) interné/e.
inmost ['ɪnməust] *adj* le(la) plus profond(e).
inn [ɪn] *n* auberge *f*.
innards ['ɪnədz] *npl* (*col*) entrailles *fpl*.
innate [ɪ'neɪt] *adj* inné(e).
inner ['ɪnə*] *adj* intérieur(e).
inner city *n* (vieux quartiers du) centre urbain (*souffrant souvent de délabrement, d'embouteillages etc*).
innermost ['ɪnəməust] *adj* le(la) plus profond(e).
inner tube *n* (*of tyre*) chambre *f* à air.
innings ['ɪnɪŋz] *n* (*CRICKET*) tour *m* de batte; (*BRIT fig*): **he has had a good ~** il (en) a bien profité.
innocence ['ɪnəsns] *n* innocence *f*.
innocent ['ɪnəsnt] *adj* innocent(e).
innocuous [ɪ'nɔkjuəs] *adj* inoffensif(ive).
innovation [ɪnəu'veɪʃən] *n* innovation *f*.
innuendo, ~es [ɪnju'ɛndəu] *n* insinuation *f*, allusion (malveillante).
innumerable [ɪ'njuːmrəbl] *adj* innombrable.
inoculate [ɪ'nɔkjuleɪt] *vt*: **to ~ sb with sth** inoculer qch à qn; **to ~ sb against sth** vacciner qn contre qch.
inoculation [ɪnɔkju'leɪʃən] *n* inoculation *f*.
inoffensive [ɪnə'fɛnsɪv] *adj* inoffensif(ive).

inopportune [ɪn'ɔpətjuːn] *adj* inopportun(e).
inordinate [ɪ'nɔːdɪnət] *adj* démesuré(e).
inordinately [ɪ'nɔːdɪnətlɪ] *adv* démesurément.
inorganic [ɪnɔː'gænɪk] *adj* inorganique.
in-patient ['ɪnpeɪʃənt] *n* malade hospitalisé(e).
input ['ɪnput] *n* (*ELEC*) énergie *f*, puissance *f*; (*of machine*) consommation *f*; (*of computer*) information fournie ♦ *vt* (*COMPUT*) introduire, entrer.
inquest ['ɪnkwɛst] *n* enquête (criminelle).
inquire [ɪn'kwaɪə*] *vi* demander ♦ *vt* demander, s'informer de; **to ~ about** s'informer de, se renseigner sur; **to ~ when/where/whether** demander quand/où/si.
►**inquire after** *vt fus* demander des nouvelles de.
►**inquire into** *vt fus* faire une enquête sur.
inquiring [ɪn'kwaɪərɪŋ] *adj* (*mind*) curieux(euse), investigateur(trice).
inquiry [ɪn'kwaɪərɪ] *n* demande *f* de renseignements; (*LAW*) enquête *f*, investigation *f*; **to hold an ~ into sth** enquêter sur qch.
inquiry desk *n* (*BRIT*) guichet *m* de renseignements.
inquiry office *n* (*BRIT*) bureau *m* de renseignements.
inquisition [ɪnkwɪ'zɪʃən] *n* enquête *f*, investigation *f*; (*REL*): **the I~** l'Inquisition *f*.
inquisitive [ɪn'kwɪzɪtɪv] *adj* curieux(euse).
inroads ['ɪnrəudz] *npl*: **to make ~ into** (*savings, supplies*) entamer.
ins *abbr* = **inches**.
insane [ɪn'seɪn] *adj* fou(folle); (*MED*) aliéné(e).
insanitary [ɪn'sænɪtərɪ] *adj* insalubre.
insanity [ɪn'sænɪtɪ] *n* folie *f*; (*MED*) aliénation (mentale).
insatiable [ɪn'seɪʃəbl] *adj* insatiable.
inscribe [ɪn'skraɪb] *vt* inscrire; (*book etc*): **to ~ (to sb)** dédicacer (à qn).
inscription [ɪn'skrɪpʃən] *n* inscription *f*; (*in book*) dédicace *f*.
inscrutable [ɪn'skruːtəbl] *adj* impénétrable.
inseam ['ɪnsiːm] *n* (*US*): **~ measurement** hauteur *f* d'entre-jambe.
insect ['ɪnsɛkt] *n* insecte *m*.
insect bite *n* piqûre *f* d'insecte.
insecticide [ɪn'sɛktɪsaɪd] *n* insecticide *m*.
insect repellent *n* crème *f* anti-insectes.
insecure [ɪnsɪ'kjuə*] *adj* peu solide; peu sûr(e); (*person*) anxieux(euse).
insecurity [ɪnsɪ'kjuərɪtɪ] *n* insécurité *f*.
insensible [ɪn'sɛnsɪbl] *adj* insensible; (*unconscious*) sans connaissance.
insensitive [ɪn'sɛnsɪtɪv] *adj* insensible.
insensitivity [ɪnsɛnsɪ'tɪvɪtɪ] *n* insensibilité *f*.
inseparable [ɪn'sɛprəbl] *adj* inséparable.
insert *vt* [ɪn'səːt] insérer ♦ *n* ['ɪnsəːt] insertion *f*.
insertion [ɪn'səːʃən] *n* insertion *f*.
in-service ['ɪn'səːvɪs] *adj* (*training*) continu(e); (*course*) d'initiation; de perfectionnement; de recyclage.
inshore [ɪn'ʃɔː*] *adj* côtier(ière) ♦ *adv* près de la côte; vers la côte.
inside ['ɪn'saɪd] *n* intérieur *m*; (*of road*: *BRIT*) côté *m* gauche (*de la route*); (*: US, Europe etc*) côté droit (*de la route*) ♦ *adj* intérieur(e) ♦ *adv* à l'intérieur, dedans ♦ *prep* à l'intérieur de; (*of time*): **~ 10 minutes** en moins de 10 minutes; **~s** *npl* (*col*) intestins *mpl*; **~ out** *adv* à l'envers; **to turn sth ~ out** retourner qch; **to know sth ~ out** connaître qch à fond *or* comme sa poche; **~ information** renseignements *mpl* à la source; **~ story** histoire racontée par un témoin.
inside forward *n* (*SPORT*) intérieur *m*.
inside lane *n* (*AUT*: *in Britain*) voie *f* de gauche; (*: in US, Europe*) voie *f* de droite.
inside leg measurement *n* (*BRIT*) hauteur *f* d'entre-jambe.
insider [ɪn'saɪdə*] *n* initié/e.
insider dealing, insider trading *n* (*STOCK EXCHANGE*) délit *m* d'initiés.
insidious [ɪn'sɪdɪəs] *adj* insidieux(euse).
insight ['ɪnsaɪt] *n* perspicacité *f*; (*glimpse, idea*) aperçu *m*; **to gain (an) ~ into** parvenir à comprendre.
insignia [ɪn'sɪgnɪə] *npl* insignes *mpl*.
insignificant [ɪnsɪg'nɪfɪknt] *adj* insignifiant(e).
insincere [ɪnsɪn'sɪə*] *adj* hypocrite.
insincerity [ɪnsɪn'sɛrɪtɪ] *n* manque *m* de sincérité, hypocrisie *f*.
insinuate [ɪn'sɪnjueɪt] *vt* insinuer.
insinuation [ɪnsɪnju'eɪʃən] *n* insinuation *f*.
insipid [ɪn'sɪpɪd] *adj* insipide, fade.
insist [ɪn'sɪst] *vi* insister; **to ~ on doing** insister pour faire; **to ~ that** insister pour que; (*claim*) maintenir *or* soutenir que.
insistence [ɪn'sɪstəns] *n* insistance *f*.
insistent [ɪn'sɪstənt] *adj* insistant(e), pressant(e).
insofar [ɪnsəu'fɑː*]: **~ as** *conj* dans la mesure où.
insole ['ɪnsəul] *n* semelle intérieure; (*fixed part of shoe*) première *f*.
insolence ['ɪnsələns] *n* insolence *f*.
insolent ['ɪnsələnt] *adj* insolent(e).
insoluble [ɪn'sɔljubl] *adj* insoluble.
insolvency [ɪn'sɔlvənsɪ] *n* insolvabilité *f*; faillite *f*.
insolvent [ɪn'sɔlvənt] *adj* insolvable; (*bankrupt*) en faillite.
insomnia [ɪn'sɔmnɪə] *n* insomnie *f*.
insomniac [ɪn'sɔmnɪæk] *n* insomniaque *m/f*.
inspect [ɪn'spɛkt] *vt* inspecter; (*BRIT*: *ticket*) contrôler.
inspection [ɪn'spɛkʃən] *n* inspection *f*; contrôle *m*.
inspector [ɪn'spɛktə*] *n* inspecteur/trice; contrôleur/euse.
inspiration [ɪnspə'reɪʃən] *n* inspiration *f*.
inspire [ɪn'spaɪə*] *vt* inspirer.
inspired [ɪn'spaɪəd] *adj* (*writer, book etc*) inspi-

ré(e); **in an ~ moment** dans un moment d'inspiration.

inspiring [ɪn'spaɪərɪŋ] *adj* inspirant(e).

inst. *abbr* (*BRIT COMM*: = *instant*): **of the 16th ~** du 16 courant.

instability [ɪnstə'bɪlɪtɪ] *n* instabilité *f*.

install [ɪn'stɔːl] *vt* installer.

installation [ɪnstə'leɪʃən] *n* installation *f*.

installment plan *n* (*US*) achat *m* (*or* vente *f*) à tempérament *or* crédit.

instalment, (*US*) **installment** [ɪn'stɔːlmənt] *n* acompte *m*, versement partiel; (*of TV serial etc*) épisode *m*; **in ~s** (*pay*) à tempérament; (*receive*) en plusieurs fois.

instance ['ɪnstəns] *n* exemple *m*; **for ~** par exemple; **in many ~s** dans bien des cas; **in that ~** dans ce cas; **in the first ~** tout d'abord, en premier lieu.

instant ['ɪnstənt] *n* instant *m* ♦ *adj* immédiat(e); urgent(e); (*coffee, food*) instantané(e), en poudre; **the 10th ~** le 10 courant.

instantaneous [ɪnstən'teɪnɪəs] *adj* instantané(e).

instantly ['ɪnstəntlɪ] *adv* immédiatement, tout de suite.

instant replay *n* (*US TV*) retour *m* sur une séquence.

instead [ɪn'stɛd] *adv* au lieu de cela; **~ of** au lieu de; **~ of sb** à la place de qn.

instep ['ɪnstɛp] *n* cou-de-pied *m*; (*of shoe*) cambrure *f*.

instigate ['ɪnstɪgeɪt] *vt* (*rebellion, strike, crime*) inciter à; (*new ideas etc*) susciter.

instigation [ɪnstɪ'geɪʃən] *n* instigation *f*; **at sb's ~** à l'instigation de qn.

instil [ɪn'stɪl] *vt*: **to ~ (into)** inculquer (à); (*courage*) insuffler (à).

instinct ['ɪnstɪŋkt] *n* instinct *m*.

instinctive [ɪn'stɪŋktɪv] *adj* instinctif(ive).

instinctively [ɪn'stɪŋktɪvlɪ] *adv* instinctivement.

institute ['ɪnstɪtjuːt] *n* institut *m* ♦ *vt* instituer, établir; (*inquiry*) ouvrir; (*proceedings*) entamer.

institution [ɪnstɪ'tjuːʃən] *n* institution *f*; (*school*) établissement *m* (scolaire); (*for care*) établissement (psychiatrique *etc*).

institutional [ɪnstɪ'tjuːʃənl] *adj* institutionnel(le); **~ care** soins fournis par un établissement médico-social.

instruct [ɪn'strʌkt] *vt* instruire, former; **to ~ sb in sth** enseigner qch à qn; **to ~ sb to do** charger qn *or* ordonner à qn de faire.

instruction [ɪn'strʌkʃən] *n* instruction *f*; **~s** *npl* directives *fpl*; **~s for use** mode *m* d'emploi.

instruction book *n* manuel *m* d'instructions.

instructive [ɪn'strʌktɪv] *adj* instructif(ive).

instructor [ɪn'strʌktə*] *n* professeur *m*; (*for skiing, driving*) moniteur *m*.

instrument ['ɪnstrumənt] *n* instrument *m*.

instrumental [ɪnstru'mɛntl] *adj* (*MUS*) instrumental(e); **to be ~ in sth/in doing sth** contribuer à qch/à faire qch.

instrumentalist [ɪnstru'mɛntəlɪst] *n* instrumentiste *m/f*.

instrument panel *n* tableau *m* de bord.

insubordinate [ɪnsə'bɔːdənɪt] *adj* insubordonné(e).

insubordination [ɪnsəbɔːdə'neɪʃən] *n* insubordination *f*.

insufferable [ɪn'sʌfrəbl] *adj* insupportable.

insufficient [ɪnsə'fɪʃənt] *adj* insuffisant(e).

insufficiently [ɪnsə'fɪʃəntlɪ] *adv* insuffisamment.

insular ['ɪnsjulə*] *adj* insulaire; (*outlook*) étroit(e); (*person*) aux vues étroites.

insulate ['ɪnsjuleɪt] *vt* isoler; (*against sound*) insonoriser.

insulating tape ['ɪnsjuleɪtɪŋ-] *n* ruban isolant.

insulation [ɪnsju'leɪʃən] *n* isolation *f*; insonorisation *f*.

insulin ['ɪnsjulɪn] *n* insuline *f*.

insult *n* ['ɪnsʌlt] insulte *f*, affront *m* ♦ *vt* [ɪn'sʌlt] insulter, faire un affront à.

insulting [ɪn'sʌltɪŋ] *adj* insultant(e), injurieux(euse).

insuperable [ɪn'sjuːprəbl] *adj* insurmontable.

insurance [ɪn'ʃuərəns] *n* assurance *f*; **fire/life ~** assurance-incendie/-vie; **to take out ~ (against)** s'assurer (contre).

insurance agent *n* agent *m* d'assurances.

insurance broker *n* courtier *m* en assurances.

insurance policy *n* police *f* d'assurance.

insurance premium *n* prime *f* d'assurance.

insure [ɪn'ʃuə*] *vt* assurer; **to ~ sb/sb's life** assurer qn/la vie de qn; **to be ~d for £5000** être assuré(e) pour 5 000 livres.

insured [ɪn'ʃuəd] *n*: **the ~** l'assuré/e.

insurer [ɪn'ʃuərə*] *n* assureur *m*.

insurgent [ɪn'səːdʒənt] *adj, n* insurgé(e).

insurmountable [ɪnsə'mauntəbl] *adj* insurmontable.

insurrection [ɪnsə'rɛkʃən] *n* insurrection *f*.

intact [ɪn'tækt] *adj* intact(e).

intake ['ɪnteɪk] *n* (*TECH*) admission *f*, adduction *f*; (*of food*) consommation *f*; (*BRIT SCOL*): **an ~ of 200 a year** 200 admissions par an.

intangible [ɪn'tændʒɪbl] *adj* intangible; (*assets*) immatériel(le).

integral ['ɪntɪgrəl] *adj* intégral(e); (*part*) intégrant(e).

integrate ['ɪntɪgreɪt] *vt* intégrer ♦ *vi* s'intégrer.

integrated circuit ['ɪntɪgreɪtɪd-] *n* (*COMPUT*) circuit intégré.

integration [ɪntɪ'greɪʃən] *n* intégration *f*; **racial ~** intégration raciale.

integrity [ɪn'tɛgrɪtɪ] *n* intégrité *f*.

intellect ['ɪntəlɛkt] *n* intelligence *f*.

intellectual [ɪntə'lɛktjuəl] *adj, n* intellectuel(le).

intelligence [ɪn'tɛlɪdʒəns] *n* intelligence *f*; (*MIL etc*) informations *fpl*, renseignements *mpl*.

intelligence quotient (IQ) *n* quotient intellectuel (QI).
Intelligence Service *n* services *mpl* de renseignements.
intelligence test *n* test *m* d'intelligence.
intelligent [ɪn'tɛlɪdʒənt] *adj* intelligent(e).
intelligently [ɪn'tɛlɪdʒəntlɪ] *adv* intelligemment.
intelligible [ɪn'tɛlɪdʒɪbl] *adj* intelligible.
intemperate [ɪn'tɛmpərət] *adj* immodéré(e); (*drinking too much*) adonné(e) à la boisson.
intend [ɪn'tɛnd] *vt* (*gift etc*): **to ~ sth for** destiner qch à; **to ~ to do** avoir l'intention de faire.
intended [ɪn'tɛndɪd] *adj* (*insult*) intentionnel(le); (*journey*) projeté(e); (*effect*) voulu(e).
intense [ɪn'tɛns] *adj* intense; (*person*) véhément(e).
intensely [ɪn'tɛnslɪ] *adv* intensément; (*moving*) profondément.
intensify [ɪn'tɛnsɪfaɪ] *vt* intensifier.
intensity [ɪn'tɛnsɪtɪ] *n* intensité *f*.
intensive [ɪn'tɛnsɪv] *adj* intensif(ive).
intensive care *n*: **to be in ~** être en réanimation; **~ unit** *n* service *m* de réanimation.
intent [ɪn'tɛnt] *n* intention *f* ♦ *adj* attentif(ive), absorbé(e); **to all ~s and purposes** en fait, pratiquement; **to be ~ on doing sth** être (bien) décidé à faire qch.
intention [ɪn'tɛnʃən] *n* intention *f*.
intentional [ɪn'tɛnʃənl] *adj* intentionnel(le), délibéré(e).
intently [ɪn'tɛntlɪ] *adv* attentivement.
inter [ɪn'təː*] *vt* enterrer.
interact [ɪntər'ækt] *vi* avoir une action réciproque.
interaction [ɪntər'ækʃən] *n* interaction *f*.
interactive [ɪntər'æktɪv] *adj* (*group*) interactif(ive); (*COMPUT*) interactif, conversationnel(le).
intercede [ɪntə'siːd] *vi*: **to ~ with sb/on behalf of sb** intercéder auprès de qn/en faveur de qn.
intercept [ɪntə'sɛpt] *vt* intercepter; (*person*) arrêter au passage.
interception [ɪntə'sɛpʃən] *n* interception *f*.
interchange *n* ['ɪntətʃeɪndʒ] (*exchange*) échange *m*; (*on motorway*) échangeur *m* ♦ *vt* [ɪntə'tʃeɪndʒ] échanger; mettre à la place l'un(e) de l'autre.
interchangeable [ɪntə'tʃeɪndʒəbl] *adj* interchangeable.
intercity [ɪntə'sɪtɪ] *adj*: **~ (train)** train *m* rapide.
intercom ['ɪntəkɔm] *n* interphone *m*.
interconnect [ɪntəkə'nɛkt] *vi* (*rooms*) communiquer.
intercontinental ['ɪntəkɔntɪ'nɛntl] *adj* intercontinental(e).
intercourse ['ɪntəkɔːs] *n* rapports *mpl*; **sexual ~** rapports sexuels.
interdependent [ɪntədɪ'pɛndənt] *adj* interdépendant(e).
interest ['ɪntrɪst] *n* intérêt *m*; (*COMM*: *stake, share*) participation *f*, intérêts *mpl* ♦ *vt* intéresser; **compound/simple ~** intérêt composé/simple; **British ~s in the Middle East** les intérêts britanniques au Moyen-Orient; **his main ~ is ...** ce qui l'intéresse le plus est ....
interested ['ɪntrɪstɪd] *adj* intéressé(e); **to be ~ in** s'intéresser à.
interest-free ['ɪntrɪst'friː] *adj* sans intérêt.
interesting ['ɪntrɪstɪŋ] *adj* intéressant(e).
interest rate *n* taux *m* d'intérêt.
interface ['ɪntəfeɪs] *n* (*COMPUT*) interface *f*.
interfere [ɪntə'fɪə*] *vi*: **to ~ in** (*quarrel, other people's business*) se mêler à; **to ~ with** (*object*) tripoter, toucher à; (*plans*) contrecarrer; (*duty*) être en conflit avec; **don't ~** mêlez-vous de vos affaires.
interference [ɪntə'fɪərəns] *n* (*gen*) intrusion *f*; (*PHYSICS*) interférence *f*; (*RADIO, TV*) parasites *mpl*.
interfering [ɪntə'fɪərɪŋ] *adj* importun(e).
interim ['ɪntərɪm] *adj* provisoire; (*post*) intérimaire ♦ *n*: **in the ~** dans l'intérim.
interior [ɪn'tɪərɪə*] *n* intérieur *m* ♦ *adj* intérieur(e).
interior decorator, interior designer *n* décorateur/trice d'intérieur.
interjection [ɪntə'dʒɛkʃən] *n* interjection *f*.
interlock [ɪntə'lɔk] *vi* s'enclencher ♦ *vt* enclencher.
interloper ['ɪntələupə*] *n* intrus/e.
interlude ['ɪntəluːd] *n* intervalle *m*; (*THEAT*) intermède *m*.
intermarry [ɪntə'mærɪ] *vi* former des alliances entre familles (*or* tribus); former des unions consanguines.
intermediary [ɪntə'miːdɪərɪ] *n* intermédiaire *m/f*.
intermediate [ɪntə'miːdɪət] *adj* intermédiaire; (*SCOL*: *course, level*) moyen(ne).
interment [ɪn'təːmənt] *n* inhumation *f*, enterrement *m*.
interminable [ɪn'təːmɪnəbl] *adj* sans fin, interminable.
intermission [ɪntə'mɪʃən] *n* pause *f*; (*THEAT, CINE*) entracte *m*.
intermittent [ɪntə'mɪtnt] *adj* intermittent(e).
intermittently [ɪntə'mɪtntlɪ] *adv* par intermittence, par intervalles.
intern *vt* [ɪn'təːn] interner ♦ *n* ['ɪntəːn] (*US*) interne *m/f*.
internal [ɪn'təːnl] *adj* interne; (*dispute, reform etc*) intérieur(e); **~ injuries** lésions *fpl* internes.
internally [ɪn'təːnəlɪ] *adv* intérieurement; **"not to be taken ~"** "pour usage externe".
Internal Revenue (Service) (IRS) *n* (*US*) fisc *m*.
international [ɪntə'næʃənl] *adj* international(e) ♦ *n* (*BRIT SPORT*) international *m*.

International Atomic Energy Agency (IAEA) *n* Agence Internationale de l'Énergie Atomique (AIEA).
International Court of Justice (ICJ) *n* Cour internationale de justice (CIJ).
international date line *n* ligne *f* de changement de date.
internationally [ɪntə'næʃnəlɪ] *adv* dans le monde entier.
International Monetary Fund (IMF) *n* Fonds monétaire international (FMI).
international relations *npl* relations internationales.
internecine [ɪntə'ni:saɪn] *adj* mutuellement destructeur(trice).
internee [ɪntə:'ni:] *n* interné/e.
Internet ['ɪntə,nɛt] *n*: **the** ~ l'Internet *m*.
Internet café *n* cybercafé *m*.
Internet service provider *n* fournisseur *m* d'accès à Internet.
internment [ɪn'tə:nmənt] *n* internement *m*.
interplay ['ɪntəpleɪ] *n* effet *m* réciproque, jeu *m*.
Interpol ['ɪntəpɔl] *n* Interpol *m*.
interpret [ɪn'tə:prɪt] *vt* interpréter ♦ *vi* servir d'interprète.
interpretation [ɪntə:prɪ'teɪʃən] *n* interprétation *f*.
interpreter [ɪn'tə:prɪtə*] *n* interprète *m/f*.
interpreting [ɪn'tə:prɪtɪŋ] *n* (*profession*) interprétariat *m*.
interrelated [ɪntərɪ'leɪtɪd] *adj* en corrélation, en rapport étroit.
interrogate [ɪn'tɛrəugeɪt] *vt* interroger; (*suspect etc*) soumettre à un interrogatoire.
interrogation [ɪntɛrəu'geɪʃən] *n* interrogation *f*; interrogatoire *m*.
interrogative [ɪntə'rɔgətɪv] *adj* interrogateur(trice) ♦ *n* (*LING*) interrogatif *m*.
interrogator [ɪn'tɛrəgeɪtə*] *n* interrogateur/trice.
interrupt [ɪntə'rʌpt] *vt* interrompre.
interruption [ɪntə'rʌpʃən] *n* interruption *f*.
intersect [ɪntə'sɛkt] *vt* couper, croiser; (*MATH*) intersecter ♦ *vi* se croiser, se couper; s'intersecter.
intersection [ɪntə'sɛkʃən] *n* intersection *f*; (*of roads*) croisement *m*.
intersperse [ɪntə'spə:s] *vt*: **to ~ with** parsemer de.
intertwine [ɪntə'twaɪn] *vt* entrelacer ♦ *vi* s'entrelacer.
interval ['ɪntəvl] *n* intervalle *m*; (*BRIT: THEAT*) entracte *m*; **bright ~s** (*in weather*) éclaircies *fpl*; **at ~s** par intervalles.
intervene [ɪntə'vi:n] *vi* (*time*) s'écouler; (*event*) survenir; (*person*) intervenir.
intervention [ɪntə'vɛnʃən] *n* intervention *f*.
interview ['ɪntəvju:] *n* (*RADIO, TV etc*) interview *f*; (*for job*) entrevue *f* ♦ *vt* interviewer; avoir une entrevue avec.
interviewee [ɪntəvju'i:] *n* (*for job*) candidat *m* (*qui passe un entretien*); (*TV etc*) invité/e, personne interviewée.
interviewer ['ɪntəvjuə*] *n* interviewer *m*.
intestate [ɪn'tɛsteɪt] *adj* intestat *f inv*.
intestinal [ɪn'tɛstɪnl] *adj* intestinal(e).
intestine [ɪn'tɛstɪn] *n* intestin *m*; **large ~** gros intestin; **small ~** intestin grêle.
intimacy ['ɪntɪməsɪ] *n* intimité *f*.
intimate *adj* ['ɪntɪmət] intime; (*knowledge*) approfondi(e) ♦ *vt* ['ɪntɪmeɪt] suggérer, laisser entendre; (*announce*) faire savoir.
intimately ['ɪntɪmətlɪ] *adv* intimement.
intimation [ɪntɪ'meɪʃən] *n* annonce *f*.
intimidate [ɪn'tɪmɪdeɪt] *vt* intimider.
intimidation [ɪntɪmɪ'deɪʃən] *n* intimidation *f*.
into ['ɪntu] *prep* dans; **~ pieces/French** en morceaux/français; **to change pounds ~ dollars** changer des livres en dollars.
intolerable [ɪn'tɔlərəbl] *adj* intolérable.
intolerance [ɪn'tɔlərns] *n* intolérance *f*.
intolerant [ɪn'tɔlərnt] *adj*: **~ (of)** intolérant(e) (de); (*MED*) intolérant (à).
intonation [ɪntəu'neɪʃən] *n* intonation *f*.
intoxicate [ɪn'tɔksɪkeɪt] *vt* enivrer.
intoxicated [ɪn'tɔksɪkeɪtɪd] *adj* ivre.
intoxication [ɪntɔksɪ'keɪʃən] *n* ivresse *f*.
intractable [ɪn'træktəbl] *adj* (*child, temper*) indocile, insoumis(e); (*problem*) insoluble; (*illness*) incurable.
intranet ['ɪntrənɛt] *n* intranet *m*.
intransigent [ɪn'trænsɪdʒənt] *adj* intransigeant(e).
intransitive [ɪn'trænsɪtɪv] *adj* intransitif(ive).
intra-uterine device (IUD) ['ɪntrə'ju:təraɪn-] *n* dispositif intra-utérin (DIU), stérilet *m*.
intravenous [ɪntrə'vi:nəs] *adj* intraveineux(euse).
in-tray ['ɪntreɪ] *n* courrier *m* "arrivée".
intrepid [ɪn'trɛpɪd] *adj* intrépide.
intricacy ['ɪntrɪkəsɪ] *n* complexité *f*.
intricate ['ɪntrɪkət] *adj* complexe, compliqué(e).
intrigue [ɪn'tri:g] *n* intrigue *f* ♦ *vt* intriguer ♦ *vi* intriguer, comploter.
intriguing [ɪn'tri:gɪŋ] *adj* fascinant(e).
intrinsic [ɪn'trɪnsɪk] *adj* intrinsèque.
introduce [ɪntrə'dju:s] *vt* introduire; **to ~ sb (to sb)** présenter qn (à qn); **to ~ sb to** (*pastime, technique*) initier qn à; **may I ~ ...?** je vous présente ....
introduction [ɪntrə'dʌkʃən] *n* introduction *f*; (*of person*) présentation *f*; **a letter of ~** une lettre de recommendation.
introductory [ɪntrə'dʌktərɪ] *adj* préliminaire, introductif(ive); **~ remarks** remarques *fpl* liminaires; **an ~ offer** une offre de lancement.
introspective [ɪntrəu'spɛktɪv] *adj* introspectif(ive).
introvert ['ɪntrəuvə:t] *adj, n* introverti(e).
intrude [ɪn'tru:d] *vi* (*person*) être importun(e); **to ~ on** *or* **into** (*conversation etc*) s'immiscer dans; **am I intruding?** est-ce que je vous dé-

range?
intruder [ɪn'truːdə*] *n* intrus/e.
intrusion [ɪn'truːʒən] *n* intrusion *f*.
intrusive [ɪn'truːsɪv] *adj* importun(e), gênant(e).
intuition [ɪntjuː'ɪʃən] *n* intuition *f*.
intuitive [ɪn'tjuːɪtɪv] *adj* intuitif(ive).
inundate ['ɪnʌndeɪt] *vt*: **to ~ with** inonder de.
inure [ɪn'juə*] *vt*: **to ~ (to)** habituer (à).
invade [ɪn'veɪd] *vt* envahir.
invader [ɪn'veɪdə*] *n* envahisseur *m*.
invalid *n* ['ɪnvəlɪd] malade *m/f*; (*with disability*) invalide *m/f* ♦ *adj* [ɪn'vælɪd] (*not valid*) invalide, non valide.
invalidate [ɪn'vælɪdeɪt] *vt* invalider, annuler.
invalid chair ['ɪnvəlɪd-] *n* (*BRIT*) fauteuil *m* d'infirme.
invaluable [ɪn'væljuəbl] *adj* inestimable, inappréciable.
invariable [ɪn'veərɪəbl] *adj* invariable; (*fig*) immanquable.
invariably [ɪn'veərɪəblɪ] *adv* invariablement; **she is ~ late** elle est toujours en retard.
invasion [ɪn'veɪʒən] *n* invasion *f*.
invective [ɪn'vektɪv] *n* invective *f*.
inveigle [ɪn'viːgl] *vt*: **to ~ sb into (doing) sth** amener qn à (faire) qch (par la ruse *or* la flatterie).
invent [ɪn'vent] *vt* inventer.
invention [ɪn'venʃən] *n* invention *f*.
inventive [ɪn'ventɪv] *adj* inventif(ive).
inventiveness [ɪn'ventɪvnɪs] *n* esprit inventif *or* d'invention.
inventor [ɪn'ventə*] *n* inventeur/trice.
inventory ['ɪnvəntrɪ] *n* inventaire *m*.
inventory control *n* (*COMM*) contrôle *m* des stocks.
inverse [ɪn'vəːs] *adj* inverse ♦ *n* inverse *m*, contraire *m*; **in ~ proportion (to)** inversement proportionel(le) (à).
inversely [ɪn'vəːslɪ] *adv* inversement.
invert [ɪn'vəːt] *vt* intervertir; (*cup, object*) retourner.
invertebrate [ɪn'vəːtɪbrət] *n* invertébré *m*.
inverted commas [ɪn'vəːtɪd-] *npl* (*BRIT*) guillemets *mpl*.
invest [ɪn'vest] *vt* investir; (*endow*): **to ~ sb with sth** conférer qch à qn ♦ *vi* faire un investissement, investir; **to ~ in** placer de l'argent *or* investir dans; (*acquire*) s'offrir, faire l'acquisition de.
investigate [ɪn'vestɪgeɪt] *vt* étudier, examiner; (*crime*) faire une enquête sur.
investigation [ɪnvestɪ'geɪʃən] *n* examen *m*; (*of crime*) enquête *f*, investigation *f*.
investigative [ɪn'vestɪgeɪtɪv] *adj*: **~ journalism** enquête-reportage *f*, journalisme *m* d'enquête.
investigator [ɪn'vestɪgeɪtə*] *n* investigateur/trice; **private ~** détective privé.
investiture [ɪn'vestɪtʃə*] *n* investiture *f*.
investment [ɪn'vestmənt] *n* investissement *m*, placement *m*.
investment income *n* revenu *m* de placement.
investment trust *n* société *f* d'investissements.
investor [ɪn'vestə*] *n* épargnant/e; (*shareholder*) actionnaire *m/f*.
inveterate [ɪn'vetərət] *adj* invétéré(e).
invidious [ɪn'vɪdɪəs] *adj* injuste; (*task*) déplaisant(e).
invigilate [ɪn'vɪdʒɪleɪt] (*BRIT*) *vt* surveiller ♦ *vi* être de surveillance.
invigilator [ɪn'vɪdʒɪleɪtə*] *n* (*BRIT*) surveillant *m* (d'examen).
invigorating [ɪn'vɪgəreɪtɪŋ] *adj* vivifiant(e); stimulant(e).
invincible [ɪn'vɪnsɪbl] *adj* invincible.
inviolate [ɪn'vaɪələt] *adj* inviolé(e).
invisible [ɪn'vɪzɪbl] *adj* invisible.
invisible assets *npl* (*BRIT*) actif incorporel.
invisible ink *n* encre *f* sympathique.
invisible mending *n* stoppage *m*.
invitation [ɪnvɪ'teɪʃən] *n* invitation *f*; **by ~ only** sur invitation; **at sb's ~** à la demande de qn.
invite [ɪn'vaɪt] *vt* inviter; (*opinions etc*) demander; (*trouble*) chercher; **to ~ sb (to do)** inviter qn (à faire); **to ~ sb to dinner** inviter qn à dîner.
▶**invite out** *vt* inviter (à sortir).
▶**invite over** *vt* inviter (chez soi).
inviting [ɪn'vaɪtɪŋ] *adj* engageant(e), attrayant(e); (*gesture*) encourageant(e).
invoice ['ɪnvɔɪs] *n* facture *f* ♦ *vt* facturer; **to ~ sb for goods** facturer des marchandises à qn.
invoke [ɪn'vəuk] *vt* invoquer.
involuntary [ɪn'vɔləntrɪ] *adj* involontaire.
involve [ɪn'vɔlv] *vt* (*entail*) impliquer; (*concern*) concerner; (*require*) nécessiter; **to ~ sb in** (*theft etc*) impliquer qn dans; (*activity, meeting*) faire participer qn à.
involved [ɪn'vɔlvd] *adj* complexe; **to feel ~** se sentir concerné(e); **to become ~** (*in love etc*) s'engager.
involvement [ɪn'vɔlvmənt] *n* (*personal role*) participation *f*; (*of resources, funds*) mise *f* en jeu.
invulnerable [ɪn'vʌlnərəbl] *adj* invulnérable.
inward ['ɪnwəd] *adj* (*movement*) vers l'intérieur; (*thought, feeling*) profond(e), intime ♦ *adv* = **inwards**.
inwardly ['ɪnwədlɪ] *adv* (*feel, think etc*) secrètement, en son for intérieur.
inwards ['ɪnwədz] *adv* vers l'intérieur.
I/O *abbr* (*COMPUT*: = *input/output*) E/S.
IOC *n abbr* (= *International Olympic Committee*) CIO *m* (= *Comité international olympique*).
iodine ['aɪəudiːn] *n* iode *m*.
ion ['aɪən] *n* ion *m*.
Ionian Sea [aɪ'əunɪən-] *n*: **the ~** la mer Ionienne.

ioniser ['aɪənaɪzə*] *n* ioniseur *m*.
iota [aɪ'əutə] *n* (*fig*) brin *m*, grain *m*.
IOU *n abbr* (= *I owe you*) reconnaissance *f* de dette.
IOW *abbr* (*BRIT*) = *Isle of Wight*.
IPA *n abbr* (= *International Phonetic Alphabet*) A.P.I. *m*.
IQ *n abbr* = **intelligence quotient**.
IRA *n abbr* (= *Irish Republican Army*) IRA *f*; (*US*) = *individual retirement account*.
Iran [ɪ'rɑːn] *n* Iran *m*.
Iranian [ɪ'reɪnɪən] *adj* iranien(ne) ♦ *n* Iranien/ne; (*LING*) iranien *m*.
Iraq [ɪ'rɑːk] *n* Irak *m*.
Iraqi [ɪ'rɑːkɪ] *adj* irakien(ne) ♦ *n* Irakien/ne.
irate [aɪ'reɪt] *adj* courroucé(e).
Ireland ['aɪələnd] *n* Irlande *f*; **Republic of ~** République *f* d'Irlande.
iris, ~es ['aɪrɪs, -ɪz] *n* iris *m*.
Irish ['aɪrɪʃ] *adj* irlandais(e) ♦ *n* (*LING*) irlandais *m*; **the ~** *npl* les Irlandais.
Irishman ['aɪrɪʃmən] *n* Irlandais *m*.
Irish Sea *n*: **the ~** la mer d'Irlande.
Irishwoman ['aɪrɪʃwumən] *n* Irlandaise *f*.
irk [əːk] *vt* ennuyer.
irksome ['əːksəm] *adj* ennuyeux(euse).
IRN *n abbr* (= *Independent Radio News*) *agence de presse radiophonique*.
iron ['aɪən] *n* fer *m*; (*for clothes*) fer *m* à repasser ♦ *adj* de *or* en fer ♦ *vt* (*clothes*) repasser; **~s** *npl* (*chains*) fers *mpl*, chaînes *fpl*.
►**iron out** *vt* (*crease*) faire disparaître au fer; (*fig*) aplanir; faire disparaître.
Iron Curtain *n*: **the ~** le rideau de fer.
iron foundry *n* fonderie *f* de fonte.
ironic(al) [aɪ'rɔnɪk(l)] *adj* ironique.
ironically [aɪ'rɔnɪklɪ] *adv* ironiquement.
ironing ['aɪənɪŋ] *n* repassage *m*.
ironing board *n* planche *f* à repasser.
ironmonger ['aɪənmʌŋgə*] *n* (*BRIT*) quincailler *m*; **~'s (shop)** quincaillerie *f*.
iron ore *n* minerai *m* de fer.
ironworks ['aɪənwəːks] *n* usine *f* sidérurgique.
irony ['aɪrənɪ] *n* ironie *f*.
irrational [ɪ'ræʃənl] *adj* irrationnel(le); déraisonnable; qui manque de logique.
irreconcilable [ɪrɛkən'saɪləbl] *adj* irréconciliable; (*opinion*): **~ with** inconciliable avec.
irredeemable [ɪrɪ'diːməbl] *adj* (*COMM*) non remboursable.
irrefutable [ɪrɪ'fjuːtəbl] *adj* irréfutable.
irregular [ɪ'rɛgjulə*] *adj* irrégulier(ière).
irregularity [ɪrɛgju'lærɪtɪ] *n* irrégularité *f*.
irrelevance [ɪ'rɛləvəns] *n* manque *m* de rapport *or* d'à-propos.
irrelevant [ɪ'rɛləvənt] *adj* sans rapport, hors de propos.
irreligious [ɪrɪ'lɪdʒəs] *adj* irréligieux(euse).
irreparable [ɪ'rɛprəbl] *adj* irréparable.
irreplaceable [ɪrɪ'pleɪsəbl] *adj* irremplaçable.
irrepressible [ɪrɪ'prɛsəbl] *adj* irrépressible.
irreproachable [ɪrɪ'prəutʃəbl] *adj* irréprochable.
irresistible [ɪrɪ'zɪstɪbl] *adj* irrésistible.
irresolute [ɪ'rɛzəluːt] *adj* irrésolu(e), indécis(e).
irrespective [ɪrɪ'spɛktɪv]: **~ of** *prep* sans tenir compte de.
irresponsible [ɪrɪ'spɔnsɪbl] *adj* (*act*) irréfléchi(e); (*person*) qui n'a pas le sens des responsabilités.
irretrievable [ɪrɪ'triːvəbl] *adj* irréparable, irrémédiable; (*object*) introuvable.
irreverent [ɪ'rɛvərnt] *adj* irrévérencieux(euse).
irrevocable [ɪ'rɛvəkəbl] *adj* irrévocable.
irrigate ['ɪrɪgeɪt] *vt* irriguer.
irritable ['ɪrɪtəbl] *adj* irritable.
irritate ['ɪrɪteɪt] *vt* irriter.
irritation [ɪrɪ'teɪʃən] *n* irritation *f*.
IRS *n abbr* (*US*) = **Internal Revenue Service**.
is [ɪz] *vb see* **be**.
ISBN *n abbr* (= *International Standard Book Number*) ISBN *m*.
ISDN *n abbr* (= *Integrated Services Digital Network*) RNIS *m*.
island ['aɪlənd] *n* île *f*; (*also*: **traffic ~**) refuge *m* (pour piétons).
islander ['aɪləndə*] *n* habitant/e d'une île, insulaire *m/f*.
isle [aɪl] *n* île *f*.
isn't ['ɪznt] = **is not**.
isolate ['aɪsəleɪt] *vt* isoler.
isolated ['aɪsəleɪtɪd] *adj* isolé(e).
isolation [aɪsə'leɪʃən] *n* isolement *m*.
isolationism [aɪsə'leɪʃənɪzəm] *n* isolationnisme *m*.
ISP *n abbr* = **Internet service provider**.
Israel ['ɪzreɪl] *n* Israël *m*.
Israeli [ɪz'reɪlɪ] *adj* israélien(ne) ♦ *n* Israélien/ne.
issue ['ɪʃuː] *n* question *f*, problème *m*; (*outcome*) résultat *m*, issue *f*; (*of banknotes etc*) émission *f*; (*of newspaper etc*) numéro *m*; (*offspring*) descendance *f* ♦ *vt* (*rations, equipment*) distribuer; (*orders*) donner; (*book*) faire paraître, publier; (*banknotes, cheques, stamps*) émettre, mettre en circulation ♦ *vi*: **to ~ from** provenir de; **at ~** en jeu, en cause; **to avoid the ~** éluder le problème; **to take ~ with sb (over sth)** exprimer son désaccord avec qn (sur qch); **to make an ~ of sth** faire de qch un problème; **to confuse the ~** embrouiller la question.
Istanbul [ɪstæn'buːl] *n* Istamboul, Istanbul.
isthmus ['ɪsməs] *n* isthme *m*.
IT *n abbr* = **information technology**.

KEYWORD

it [ɪt] *pron* **1** (*specific*: *subject*) il(elle); (: *direct object*) le(la, l'); (: *indirect object*) lui; **~'s on the table** c'est *or* il (*or* elle) est sur la table;

about/from/of ~ en; **what did you learn from** ~**?** qu'est-ce que vous en avez retiré?; **I'm proud of** ~ j'en suis fier; **I've come from** ~ j'en viens; **in/to** ~ y; **put the book in** ~ mettez-y le livre; **it's on** ~ c'est dessus; **he agreed to** ~ il y a consenti; **did you go to** ~**?** (*party, concert etc*) est-ce que vous y êtes allé(s)?; **above** ~**, over** ~ (au-)dessus; **below** ~**, under** ~ (en-)dessous; **in front of/behind** ~ devant/derrière
2 (*impersonal*) il; ce, cela, ça; ~**'s raining** il pleut; ~**'s Friday tomorrow** demain c'est vendredi *or* nous sommes vendredi; ~**'s 6 o'clock** il est 6 heures; ~**'s 2 hours by train** c'est à 2 heures de train; **who is** ~**? —** ~**'s me** qui est-ce? — c'est moi.

ITA *n abbr* (*BRIT*: = *initial teaching alphabet*) *alphabet en partie phonétique utilisé pour l'enseignement de la lecture.*
Italian [ɪ'tæljən] *adj* italien(ne) ♦ *n* Italien/ne; (*LING*) italien *m*.
italic [ɪ'tælɪk] *adj* italique; ~**s** *npl* italique *m*.
Italy ['ɪtəlɪ] *n* Italie *f*.
itch [ɪtʃ] *n* démangeaison *f* ♦ *vi* (*person*) éprouver des démangeaisons; (*body*) démanger; **I'm** ~**ing to do** l'envie me démange de faire.
itchy ['ɪtʃɪ] *adj* qui démange; **my back is** ~ j'ai le dos qui me démange.
it'd ['ɪtd] = **it would, it had.**
item ['aɪtəm] *n* (*gen*) article *m*; (*on agenda*) question *f*, point *m*; (*in programme*) numéro *m*; (*also*: **news** ~) nouvelle *f*; ~**s of clothing** articles vestimentaires.
itemize ['aɪtəmaɪz] *vt* détailler, spécifier.
itemized bill ['aɪtəmaɪzd-] *n* facture détaillée.
itinerant [ɪ'tɪnərənt] *adj* itinérant(e); (*musician*) ambulant(e).
itinerary [aɪ'tɪnərərɪ] *n* itinéraire *m*.
it'll ['ɪtl] = **it will, it shall.**
ITN *n abbr* (*BRIT*: = *Independent Television News*) *chaîne de télévision commerciale.*
its [ɪts] *adj* son(sa), ses *pl* ♦ *pron* le(la) sien(ne), les siens(siennes).
it's [ɪts] = **it is, it has.**
itself [ɪt'sɛlf] *pron* (*emphatic*) lui-même(elle-même); (*reflexive*) se.
ITV *n abbr* (*BRIT*: = *Independent Television*) *chaîne de télévision commerciale*; *voir encadré.*

> **ITV**
>
> **ITV** *est une chaîne de télévision britannique financée par la publicité. Les actualités, documentaires, débats, etc, constituent environ un tiers des émissions de* **ITV**, *le reste étant partagé entre les sports, les films, les feuilletons, les jeux, les séries, etc. Des compagnies indépendantes fournissent des émissions au niveau régional.*

IUD *n abbr* = **intra-uterine device.**
IV, i.v. ['aɪ'viː] *abbr* (= *intravenous(ly)*) IV, iv.
I've [aɪv] = **I have.**
ivory ['aɪvərɪ] *n* ivoire *m*.
Ivory Coast *n* Côte *f* d'Ivoire.
ivy ['aɪvɪ] *n* lierre *m*.
Ivy League *n* (*US*) *les huit grandes universités privées du nord-est*; *voir encadré.*

> **IVY LEAGUE**
>
> *L'***Ivy League** *regroupe les huit universités les plus prestigieuses du nord-est des États-Unis, ainsi surnommées à cause de leurs murs recouverts de lierre. Elles organisent des compétitions sportives entre elles. Ces universités sont: Brown, Columbia, Cornell, Dartmouth College, Harvard, Princeton, l'université de Pennsylvanie et Yale.*

Jj

J, j [dʒeɪ] *n* (*letter*) J, j *m*; **J for Jack,** (*US*) **J for Jig** J comme Joseph.
JA *n abbr* = **judge advocate.**
jab [dʒæb] *vt*: **to** ~ **sth into** enfoncer *or* planter qch dans ♦ *n* coup *m* (*donné avec un objet pointu*); (*MED*: *col*) piqûre *f*.
jabber ['dʒæbə*] *vt, vi* bredouiller, baragouiner.
jack [dʒæk] *n* (*AUT*) cric *m*; (*BOWLS*) cochonnet *m*; (*CARDS*) valet *m*.
▸**jack in** *vt* (*col*) laisser tomber.
▸**jack up** *vt* soulever (au cric).
jackal ['dʒækl] *n* chacal *m*.
jackass ['dʒækæs] *n* (*also fig*) âne *m*.
jackdaw ['dʒækdɔː] *n* choucas *m*.
jacket ['dʒækɪt] *n* veste *f*, veston *m*; (*of boiler etc*) enveloppe *f*; (*of book*) couverture *f*, jaquette *f*.
jacket potato *n* pomme *f* de terre en robe des champs.
jack-in-the-box ['dʒækɪnðəbɔks] *n* diable *m* à ressort.
jack-knife ['dʒæknaɪf] *n* couteau *m* de poche ♦ *vi*: **the lorry** ~**d** la remorque (du camion) s'est mise en travers.
jack-of-all-trades ['dʒækəv'ɔːltreɪdz] *n* bricoleur *m*.
jack plug *n* (*BRIT*) jack *m*.
jackpot ['dʒækpɔt] *n* gros lot.
Jacuzzi [dʒə'kuːzɪ] *n* ® jacuzzi *m* ®.

jaded ['dʒeɪdɪd] *adj* éreinté(e), fatigué(e).
JAG *n abbr* = **Judge Advocate General**.
jagged ['dʒægɪd] *adj* dentelé(e).
jaguar ['dʒægjuə*] *n* jaguar *m*.
jail [dʒeɪl] *n* prison *f* ♦ *vt* emprisonner, mettre en prison.
jailbird ['dʒeɪlbə:d] *n* récidiviste *m/f*.
jailbreak ['dʒeɪlbreɪk] *n* évasion *f*.
jailer ['dʒeɪlə*] *n* geôlier/ière.
jalopy [dʒə'lɔpɪ] *n* (*col*) vieux clou.
jam [dʒæm] *n* confiture *f*; (*of shoppers etc*) cohue *f*; (*also*: **traffic** ~) embouteillage *m* ♦ *vt* (*passage etc*) encombrer, obstruer; (*mechanism, drawer etc*) bloquer, coincer; (*RADIO*) brouiller ♦ *vi* (*mechanism, sliding part*) se coincer, se bloquer; (*gun*) s'enrayer; **to get sb out of a** ~ (*col*) sortir qn du pétrin; **to** ~ **sth into** entasser *or* comprimer qch dans; enfoncer qch dans; **the telephone lines are** ~**med** les lignes (téléphoniques) sont encombrées.
Jamaica [dʒə'meɪkə] *n* Jamaïque *f*.
Jamaican [dʒə'meɪkən] *adj* jamaïquain(e) ♦ *n* Jamaïquain/e.
jamb ['dʒæm] *n* jambage *m*.
jam-packed [dʒæm'pækt] *adj*: ~ **(with)** bourré(e) (de).
jam session *n* jam session *f*.
Jan. *abbr* (= *January*) janv.
jangle ['dʒæŋgl] *vi* cliqueter.
janitor ['dʒænɪtə*] *n* (*caretaker*) huissier *m*; concierge *m*.
January ['dʒænjuərɪ] *n* janvier *m*; *for phrases see also* **July**.
Japan [dʒə'pæn] *n* Japon *m*.
Japanese [dʒæpə'ni:z] *adj* japonais(e) ♦ *n* (*pl inv*) Japonais/e; (*LING*) japonais *m*.
jar [dʒɑ:*] *n* (*container*) pot *m*, bocal *m* ♦ *vi* (*sound*) produire un son grinçant *or* discordant; (*colours etc*) détonner, jurer ♦ *vt* (*shake*) ébranler, secouer.
jargon ['dʒɑ:gən] *n* jargon *m*.
jarring ['dʒɑ:rɪŋ] *adj* (*sound, colour*) discordant(e).
Jas. *abbr* = *James*.
jasmin(e) ['dʒæzmɪn] *n* jasmin *m*.
jaundice ['dʒɔ:ndɪs] *n* jaunisse *f*.
jaundiced ['dʒɔ:ndɪst] *adj* (*fig*) envieux(euse), désapprobateur(trice).
jaunt [dʒɔ:nt] *n* balade *f*.
jaunty ['dʒɔ:ntɪ] *adj* enjoué(e); désinvolte.
Java ['dʒɑ:və] *n* Java *f*.
javelin ['dʒævlɪn] *n* javelot *m*.
jaw [dʒɔ:] *n* mâchoire *f*.
jawbone ['dʒɔ:bəun] *n* maxillaire *m*.
jay [dʒeɪ] *n* geai *m*.
jaywalker ['dʒeɪwɔ:kə*] *n* piéton indiscipliné.
jazz [dʒæz] *n* jazz *m*.
►**jazz up** *vt* animer, égayer.
jazz band *n* orchestre *m or* groupe *m* de jazz.
jazzy ['dʒæzɪ] *adj* bariolé(e), tapageur(euse); (*beat*) de jazz.
JCB *n* ® excavatrice *f*.
JCS *n abbr* (*US*) = *Joint Chiefs of Staff*.
JD *n abbr* (*US*: = *Doctor of Laws*) *titre universitaire*; (: = *Justice Department*) *ministère de la Justice*.
jealous ['dʒɛləs] *adj* jaloux(ouse).
jealously ['dʒɛləslɪ] *adv* jalousement.
jealousy ['dʒɛləsɪ] *n* jalousie *f*.
jeans [dʒi:nz] *npl* (blue-)jean *m*.
Jeep [dʒi:p] *n* ® jeep *f*.
jeer [dʒɪə*] *vi*: **to** ~ **(at)** huer; se moquer cruellement (de), railler.
jeering ['dʒɪərɪŋ] *adj* railleur(euse), moqueur(euse) ♦ *n* huées *fpl*.
jeers ['dʒɪəz] *npl* huées *fpl*; sarcasmes *mpl*.
jelly ['dʒɛlɪ] *n* gelée *f*.
jellyfish ['dʒɛlɪfɪʃ] *n* méduse *f*.
jeopardize ['dʒɛpədaɪz] *vt* mettre en danger *or* péril.
jeopardy ['dʒɛpədɪ] *n*: **in** ~ en danger *or* péril.
jerk [dʒə:k] *n* secousse *f*; saccade *f*; sursaut *m*, spasme *m*; (*col*) pauvre type *m* ♦ *vt* donner une secousse à ♦ *vi* (*vehicles*) cahoter.
jerkin ['dʒə:kɪn] *n* blouson *m*.
jerky ['dʒə:kɪ] *adj* saccadé(e); cahotant(e).
jerry-built ['dʒɛrɪbɪlt] *adj* de mauvaise qualité.
jerry can ['dʒɛrɪ-] *n* bidon *m*.
Jersey ['dʒə:zɪ] *n* Jersey *f*.
jersey ['dʒə:zɪ] *n* tricot *m*; (*fabric*) jersey *m*.
Jerusalem [dʒə'ru:sləm] *n* Jérusalem.
jest [dʒɛst] *n* plaisanterie *f*; **in** ~ en plaisantant.
jester ['dʒɛstə*] *n* (*HIST*) plaisantin *m*.
Jesus ['dʒi:zəs] *n* Jésus; ~ **Christ** Jésus-Christ.
jet [dʒɛt] *n* (*of gas, liquid*) jet *m*; (*AUT*) gicleur *m*; (*AVIAT*) avion *m* à réaction, jet *m*.
jet-black ['dʒɛt'blæk] *adj* (d'un noir) de jais.
jet engine *n* moteur *m* à réaction.
jet lag *n* décalage *m* horaire.
jetsam ['dʒɛtsəm] *n* objets jetés à la mer (et rejetés sur la côte).
jet-setter ['dʒɛtsɛtə*] *n* membre *m* du *or* de la jet set.
jettison ['dʒɛtɪsn] *vt* jeter par-dessus bord.
jetty ['dʒɛtɪ] *n* jetée *f*, digue *f*.
Jew [dʒu:] *n* Juif *m*.
jewel ['dʒu:əl] *n* bijou *m*, joyau *m*.
jeweller ['dʒu:ələ*] *n* bijoutier/ière, joaillier *m*; ~**'s (shop)** *n* bijouterie *f*, joaillerie *f*.
jewellery ['dʒu:əlrɪ] *n* bijoux *mpl*.
Jewess ['dʒu:ɪs] *n* Juive *f*.
Jewish ['dʒu:ɪʃ] *adj* juif(juive).
JFK *n abbr* (*US*) = *John Fitzgerald Kennedy International Airport*.
jib [dʒɪb] *n* (*NAUT*) foc *m*; (*of crane*) flèche *f* ♦ *vi* (*horse*) regimber; **to** ~ **at doing sth** rechigner à faire qch.
jibe [dʒaɪb] *n* sarcasme *m*.
jiffy ['dʒɪfɪ] *n* (*col*): **in a** ~ en un clin d'œil.
jig [dʒɪg] *n* (*dance, tune*) gigue *m*.
jigsaw ['dʒɪgsɔ:] *n* (*also*: ~ **puzzle**) puzzle *m*;

(*tool*) scie sauteuse.
jilt [dʒɪlt] *vt* laisser tomber, plaquer.
jingle ['dʒɪŋgl] *n* (*advertising* ~) couplet *m* publicitaire ♦ *vi* cliqueter, tinter.
jingoism ['dʒɪŋgəuɪzəm] *n* chauvinisme *m*.
jinx [dʒɪŋks] *n* (*col*) (mauvais) sort.
jitters ['dʒɪtəz] *npl* (*col*): **to get the** ~ avoir la trouille *or* la frousse.
jittery ['dʒɪtərɪ] *adj* (*col*) nerveux(euse); **to be** ~ avoir les nerfs en pelote.
jiujitsu [dʒuː'dʒɪtsuː] *n* jiu-jitsu *m*.
job [dʒɔb] *n* travail *m*; (*employment*) emploi *m*, poste *m*, place *f*; **a part-time/full-time** ~ un emploi à temps partiel/à plein temps; **he's only doing his** ~ il fait son boulot; **it's a good** ~ **that ...** c'est heureux *or* c'est une chance que ...; **just the** ~! (c'est) juste *or* exactement ce qu'il faut!
jobber ['dʒɔbə*] *n* (*BRIT STOCK EXCHANGE*) négociant *m* en titres.
jobbing ['dʒɔbɪŋ] *adj* (*BRIT*: *workman*) à la tâche, à la journée.
Jobcentre ['dʒɔbsɛntə*] *n* agence *f* pour l'emploi.
job creation scheme *n* plan *m* pour la création d'emplois.
job description *n* description *f* du poste.
jobless ['dʒɔblɪs] *adj* sans travail, au chômage ♦ *npl*: **the** ~ les sans-emploi *m inv*, les chômeurs *mpl*.
job lot *n* lot *m* (d'articles divers).
job satisfaction *n* satisfaction professionnelle.
job security *n* sécurité *f* de l'emploi.
job specification *n* caractéristiques *fpl* du poste.
Jock [dʒɔk] *n* (*col*: *Scotsman*) Écossais *m*.
jockey ['dʒɔkɪ] *n* jockey *m* ♦ *vi*: **to** ~ **for position** manœuvrer pour être bien placé.
jockey box *n* (*US AUT*) boîte *f* à gants, vide-poches *m inv*.
jockstrap ['dʒɔkstræp] *n* slip *m* de sport.
jocular ['dʒɔkjulə*] *adj* jovial(e), enjoué(e); facétieux(euse).
jog [dʒɔg] *vt* secouer ♦ *vi* (*SPORT*) faire du jogging; **to** ~ **along** cahoter; trotter; **to** ~ **sb's memory** rafraîchir la mémoire de qn.
jogger ['dʒɔgə*] *n* jogger *m/f*.
jogging ['dʒɔgɪŋ] *n* jogging *m*.
john [dʒɔn] *n* (*US col*): **the** ~ (*toilet*) les cabinets *mpl*.
join [dʒɔɪn] *vt* unir, assembler; (*become member of*) s'inscrire à; (*meet*) rejoindre, retrouver; se joindre à ♦ *vi* (*roads, rivers*) se rejoindre, se rencontrer ♦ *n* raccord *m*; **will you** ~ **us for dinner?** vous dînerez bien avec nous?; **I'll** ~ **you later** je vous rejoindrai plus tard; **to** ~ **forces (with)** s'associer (à).
▸**join in** *vi* se mettre de la partie ♦ *vt* se mêler à.
▸**join up** *vi* s'engager.
joiner ['dʒɔɪnə*] *n* menuisier *m*.
joinery ['dʒɔɪnərɪ] *n* menuiserie *f*.
joint [dʒɔɪnt] *n* (*TECH*) jointure *f*; joint *m*; (*ANAT*) articulation *f*, jointure; (*BRIT*: *CULIN*) rôti *m*; (*col*: *place*) boîte *f* ♦ *adj* commun(e); (*committee*) mixte, paritaire; ~ **responsibility** coresponsabilité *f*.
joint account (J/A) *n* compte joint.
jointly ['dʒɔɪntlɪ] *adv* ensemble, en commun.
joint ownership *n* copropriété *f*.
joint-stock company ['dʒɔɪntstɔk-] *n* société *f* par actions.
joint venture *n* entreprise commune.
joist [dʒɔɪst] *n* solive *f*.
joke [dʒəuk] *n* plaisanterie *f*; (*also*: **practical** ~) farce *f* ♦ *vi* plaisanter; **to play a** ~ **on** jouer un tour à, faire une farce à.
joker ['dʒəukə*] *n* plaisantin *m*, blagueur/euse; (*CARDS*) joker *m*.
joking ['dʒəukɪŋ] *n* plaisanterie *f*.
jollity ['dʒɔlɪtɪ] *n* réjouissances *fpl*, gaieté *f*.
jolly ['dʒɔlɪ] *adj* gai(e), enjoué(e) ♦ *adv* (*BRIT col*) rudement, drôlement ♦ *vt* (*BRIT*): **to** ~ **sb along** amadouer qn, convaincre *or* entraîner qn à force d'encouragements; ~ **good!** (*BRIT*) formidable!
jolt [dʒəult] *n* cahot *m*, secousse *f* ♦ *vt* cahoter, secouer.
Jordan [dʒɔːdən] *n* (*country*) Jordanie *f*; (*river*) Jourdain *m*.
Jordanian [dʒɔː'deɪnɪən] *adj* jordanien(ne) ♦ *n* Jordanien/ne.
joss stick ['dʒɔsstɪk] *n* bâton *m* d'encens.
jostle ['dʒɔsl] *vt* bousculer, pousser ♦ *vi* jouer des coudes.
jot [dʒɔt] *n*: **not one** ~ pas un brin.
▸**jot down** *vt* inscrire rapidement, noter.
jotter ['dʒɔtə*] *n* (*BRIT*) cahier *m* (de brouillon); bloc-notes *m*.
journal ['dʒəːnl] *n* journal *m*.
journalese [dʒəːnə'liːz] *n* (*pej*) style *m* journalistique.
journalism ['dʒəːnəlɪzəm] *n* journalisme *m*.
journalist ['dʒəːnəlɪst] *n* journaliste *m/f*.
journey ['dʒəːnɪ] *n* voyage *m*; (*distance covered*) trajet *m*; **a 5-hour** ~ un voyage de 5 heures ♦ *vi* voyager.
jovial ['dʒəuvɪəl] *adj* jovial(e).
jowl [dʒaul] *n* mâchoire *f* (*inférieure*); bajoue *f*.
joy [dʒɔɪ] *n* joie *f*.
joyful ['dʒɔɪful], **joyous** ['dʒɔɪəs] *adj* joyeux(euse).
joyride ['dʒɔɪraɪd] *vi*: **to go joyriding** *faire une virée dans une voiture volée.*
joyrider ['dʒɔɪraɪdə*] *n* voleur/euse de voiture (*qui fait une virée dans le véhicule volé*).
joystick ['dʒɔɪstɪk] *n* (*AVIAT*) manche *m* à balai; (*COMPUT*) manche à balai, manette *f* (de jeu).
JP *n abbr* = **Justice of the Peace.**
Jr. *abbr* = **junior.**
JTPA *n abbr* (*US*: = *Job Training Partnership Act*) *programme gouvernemental de formation.*

jubilant ['dʒuːbɪlnt] *adj* triomphant(e); réjoui(e).
jubilation [dʒuːbɪ'leɪʃən] *n* jubilation *f*.
jubilee ['dʒuːbɪliː] *n* jubilé *m*.
judge [dʒʌdʒ] *n* juge *m* ♦ *vt* juger; (*estimate: weight, size etc*) apprécier; (*consider*) estimer ♦ *vi*: **judging** *or* **to ~ by his expression** d'après son expression; **as far as I can ~** autant que je puisse en juger.
judge advocate (JA) *n* (*MIL*) magistrat *m* militaire.
judg(e)ment ['dʒʌdʒmənt] *n* jugement *m*; (*punishment*) châtiment *m*; **in my ~** à mon avis; **to pass ~ on** (*LAW*) prononcer un jugement (sur).
judicial [dʒuː'dɪʃl] *adj* judiciaire; (*fair*) impartial(e).
judiciary [dʒuː'dɪʃɪərɪ] *n* (pouvoir *m*) judiciaire *m*.
judicious [dʒuː'dɪʃəs] *adj* judicieux(euse).
judo ['dʒuːdəu] *n* judo *m*.
jug [dʒʌg] *n* pot *m*, cruche *f*.
jugged hare ['dʒʌgd-] *n* (*BRIT*) civet *m* de lièvre.
juggernaut ['dʒʌgənɔːt] *n* (*BRIT: huge truck*) mastodonte *m*.
juggle ['dʒʌgl] *vi* jongler.
juggler ['dʒʌglə*] *n* jongleur *m*.
Jugoslav ['juːgəu'slɑːv] *adj*, *n* = **Yugoslav**.
jugular ['dʒʌgjulə*] *adj*: **~ (vein)** veine *f* jugulaire.
juice [dʒuːs] *n* jus *m*; (*col: petrol*): **we've run out of ~** c'est la panne sèche.
juicy ['dʒuːsɪ] *adj* juteux(euse).
jukebox ['dʒuːkbɔks] *n* juke-box *m*.
Jul. *abbr* (= *July*) juil.
July [dʒuː'laɪ] *n* juillet *m*; **the first of ~** le premier juillet; **(on) the eleventh of ~** le onze juillet; **in the month of ~** au mois de juillet; **at the beginning/end of ~** au début/à la fin (du mois) de juillet, début/fin juillet; **in the middle of ~** au milieu (du mois) de juillet, à la mi-juillet; **during ~** pendant le mois de juillet; **in ~ of next year** en juillet de l'année prochaine; **each** *or* **every ~** tous les ans *or* chaque année en juillet; **~ was wet this year** il a beaucoup plu cette année en juillet.
jumble ['dʒʌmbl] *n* fouillis *m* ♦ *vt* (*also*: **~ up, ~ together**) mélanger, brouiller.
jumble sale *n* (*BRIT*) vente *f* de charité; *voir encadré*.

JUMBLE SALE

Les **jumble sales** *ont lieu dans les églises, salles des fêtes ou halls d'écoles, et l'on y vend des articles de toutes sortes, en général bon marché et surtout d'occasion, pour collecter des fonds pour une œuvre de charité, une école (par exemple, pour acheter un ordinateur), ou encore une église (pour réparer un toit etc).*

jumbo ['dʒʌmbəu] *adj*: **~ jet** (avion) gros porteur (à réaction); **~ size** format maxi *or* extra-grand.
jump [dʒʌmp] *vi* sauter, bondir; (*start*) sursauter; (*increase*) monter en flèche ♦ *vt* sauter, franchir ♦ *n* saut *m*, bond *m*; sursaut *m*; (*fence*) obstacle *m*; **to ~ the queue** (*BRIT*) passer avant son tour.
▸**jump about** *vi* sautiller.
▸**jump at** *vt fus* (*fig*) sauter sur; **he ~ed at the offer** il s'est empressé d'accepter la proposition.
▸**jump down** *vi* sauter (pour descendre).
▸**jump up** *vi* se lever (d'un bond).
jumped-up ['dʒʌmptʌp] *adj* (*BRIT pej*) parvenu(e).
jumper ['dʒʌmpə*] *n* (*BRIT: pullover*) pull-over *m*; (*US: pinafore dress*) robe-chasuble *f*; (*SPORT*) sauteur/euse.
jump leads, (*US*) **jumper cables** *npl* câbles *mpl* de démarrage.
jump-start ['dʒʌmpstɑːt] *vt* (*car: push*) démarrer en poussant; (*: with jump leads*) démarrer avec des câbles (de démarrage); (*fig: project, situation*) faire redémarrer promptement.
jumpy ['dʒʌmpɪ] *adj* nerveux(euse), agité(e).
Jun. *abbr* = **June**; **junior**.
Junr *abbr* = **junior**.
junction ['dʒʌŋkʃən] *n* (*BRIT: of roads*) carrefour *m*; (*of rails*) embranchement *m*.
juncture ['dʒʌŋktʃə*] *n*: **at this ~** à ce moment-là, sur ces entrefaites.
June [dʒuːn] *n* juin *m*; *for phrases see also* **July**.
jungle ['dʒʌŋgl] *n* jungle *f*.
junior ['dʒuːnɪə*] *adj*, *n*: **he's ~ to me (by 2 years), he's my ~ (by 2 years)** il est mon cadet (de 2 ans), il est plus jeune que moi (de 2 ans); **he's ~ to me** (*seniority*) il est en dessous de moi (dans la hiérarchie), j'ai plus d'ancienneté que lui.
junior executive *n* cadre moyen.
junior high school *n* (*US*) ≈ collège *m* d'enseignement secondaire.
junior minister *n* (*BRIT*) ministre *m* sous tutelle.
junior partner *n* associé(-adjoint) *m*.
junior school *n* (*BRIT*) école *f* primaire, cours moyen.
junior sizes *npl* (*COMM*) tailles *fpl* fillettes/garçonnets.
juniper ['dʒuːnɪpə*] *n*: **~ berry** baie *f* de genièvre.
junk [dʒʌŋk] *n* (*rubbish*) bric-à-brac *m inv*; (*ship*) jonque *f* ♦ *vt* (*col*) abandonner, mettre au rancart.
junk bond *n* (*COMM*) *obligation hautement spéculative utilisée dans les OPA agressives.*
junk dealer *n* brocanteur/euse.
junket ['dʒʌŋkɪt] *n* (*CULIN*) lait caillé; (*BRIT col*): **to go on a ~, go ~ing** voyager aux

frais de la princesse.
junk food *n* snacks vite prêts (*sans valeur nutritive*).
junkie ['dʒʌŋkɪ] *n* (*col*) junkie *m*, drogué/e.
junk mail *n* prospectus *mpl*.
junk room *n* (*US*) débarras *m*.
junk shop *n* (boutique *f* de) brocanteur *m*.
junta ['dʒʌntə] *n* junte *f*.
Jupiter ['dʒuːpɪtə*] *n* (*planet*) Jupiter *f*.
jurisdiction [dʒuərɪs'dɪkʃən] *n* juridiction *f*; **it falls** *or* **comes within/outside our** ~ cela est/n'est pas de notre compétence *or* ressort.
jurisprudence [dʒuərɪs'pruːdəns] *n* jurisprudence *f*.
juror ['dʒuərə*] *n* juré *m*.
jury ['dʒuərɪ] *n* jury *m*.
jury box *n* banc *m* des jurés.
juryman ['dʒuərɪmən] *n* = **juror**.
just [dʒʌst] *adj* juste ♦ *adv*: **he's** ~ **done it/left** il vient de le faire/partir; ~ **as I expected** exactement *or* précisément comme je m'y attendais; ~ **right/two o'clock** exactement *or* juste ce qu'il faut/deux heures; **we were** ~ **going** nous partions; **I was** ~ **about to phone** j'allais téléphoner; ~ **as he was leaving** au moment *or* à l'instant précis où il partait; ~ **before/enough/here** juste avant/assez/là; **it's** ~ **me/a mistake** ce n'est que moi/(rien) qu'une erreur; ~ **missed/caught** manqué/attrapé de justesse; ~ **listen to this!** écoutez un peu ça!; ~ **ask someone the way** vous n'avez qu'à demander votre chemin à quelqu'un; **it's** ~ **as good** c'est (vraiment) aussi bon; **it's** ~ **as well that you ...** heureusement que vous ...; **not** ~ **now** pas tout de suite; ~ **a minute!**, ~ **one moment!** un instant (s'il vous plaît)!
justice ['dʒʌstɪs] *n* justice *f*; **Lord Chief J**~ (*BRIT*) premier président de la cour d'appel; **this photo doesn't do you** ~ cette photo ne vous avantage pas.
Justice of the Peace (JP) *n* juge *m* de paix.
justifiable [dʒʌstɪ'faɪəbl] *adj* justifiable.
justifiably [dʒʌstɪ'faɪəblɪ] *adv* légitimement, à juste titre.
justification [dʒʌstɪfɪ'keɪʃən] *n* justification *f*.
justify ['dʒʌstɪfaɪ] *vt* justifier; **to be justified in doing sth** être en droit de faire qch.
justly ['dʒʌstlɪ] *adv* avec raison, justement.
justness ['dʒʌstnɪs] *n* justesse *f*.
jut [dʒʌt] *vi* (*also*: ~ **out**) dépasser, faire saillie.
jute [dʒuːt] *n* jute *m*.
juvenile ['dʒuːvənaɪl] *adj* juvénile; (*court, books*) pour enfants ♦ *n* adolescent/e.
juvenile delinquency *n* délinquance *f* juvénile.
juxtapose ['dʒʌkstəpəuz] *vt* juxtaposer.
juxtaposition ['dʒʌkstəpə'zɪʃən] *n* juxtaposition *f*.

K k

K, k [keɪ] *n* (*letter*) K, k *m*; **K for King** K comme Kléber.
K *abbr* (= *kilobyte*) Ko; (*BRIT*: = *Knight*) *titre honorifique* ♦ *n abbr* (= *one thousand*) K.
kaftan ['kæftæn] *n* cafetan *m*.
Kalahari Desert [kælə'hɑːrɪ-] *n* désert *m* de Kalahari.
kale [keɪl] *n* chou frisé.
kaleidoscope [kə'laɪdəskəup] *n* kaléidoscope *m*.
kamikaze [kæmɪ'kɑːzɪ] *adj* kamikaze.
Kampala [kæm'pɑːlə] *n* Kampala.
Kampuchea [kæmpu'tʃɪə] *n* Kampuchéa *m*.
kangaroo [kæŋgə'ruː] *n* kangourou *m*.
Kans. *abbr* (*US*) = *Kansas*.
kaput [kə'put] *adj* (*col*) kapout, capout.
karaoke [kɑːrə'əukɪ] *n* karaoke *m*.
karate [kə'rɑːtɪ] *n* karaté *m*.
Kashmir [kæʃ'mɪə*] *n* Cachemire *m*.
Kazakhstan [kɑːzɑːk'stæn] *n* Kazakhstan *m*.
KC *n abbr* (*BRIT LAW*: = *King's Counsel*) *titre donné à certains avocats*; *see also* **QC**.
kd *abbr* (*US*: = *knocked down*) en pièces détachées.
kebab [kə'bæb] *n* kébab *m*.
keel [kiːl] *n* quille *f*; **on an even** ~ (*fig*) à flot.
►**keel over** *vi* (*NAUT*) chavirer, dessaler; (*person*) tomber dans les pommes.
keen [kiːn] *adj* (*interest, desire, competition*) vif(vive); (*eye, intelligence*) pénétrant(e); (*edge*) effilé(e); (*eager*) plein(e) d'enthousiasme; **to be** ~ **to do** *or* **on doing sth** désirer vivement faire qch, tenir beaucoup à faire qch; **to be** ~ **on sth/sb** aimer beaucoup qch/qn; **I'm not** ~ **on going** je ne suis pas chaud pour aller, je n'ai pas très envie d'y aller.
keenly ['kiːnlɪ] *adv* (*enthusiastically*) avec enthousiasme; (*feel*) vivement, profondément; (*look*) intensément.
keenness ['kiːnnɪs] *n* (*eagerness*) enthousiasme *m*; ~ **to do** vif désir de faire.
keep [kiːp] *vb* (*pt, pp* **kept** [kɛpt]) *vt* (*retain, preserve*) garder; (*hold back*) retenir; (*a shop, the books, a diary*) tenir; (*feed: one's family etc*) entretenir, assurer la subsistance de; (*a promise*) tenir; (*chickens, bees, pigs etc*) élever ♦ *vi* (*food*) se conserver; (*remain: in a certain state or place*) rester ♦ *n* (*of castle*) donjon *m*; (*food etc*): **enough for his** ~ assez pour (assurer) sa subsistance; **to** ~ **doing sth** continuer à faire qch; faire qch continuelle-

ment; **to ~ sb from doing/sth from happening** empêcher qn de faire *or* que qn (ne) fasse/que qch (n')arrive; **to ~ sb happy/a place tidy** faire que qn soit content/qu'un endroit reste propre; **to ~ sb waiting** faire attendre qn; **to ~ an appointment** ne pas manquer un rendez-vous; **to ~ a record of sth** prendre note de qch; **to ~ sth to o.s.** garder qch pour soi, tenir qch secret; **to ~ sth (back) from sb** cacher qch à qn; **to ~ time** (*clock*) être à l'heure, ne pas retarder.

►**keep away** *vt*: **to ~ sth/sb away from sb** tenir qch/qn éloigné de qn ♦ *vi*: **to ~ away (from)** ne pas s'approcher (de).

►**keep back** *vt* (*crowds, tears, money*) retenir ♦ *vi* rester en arrière.

►**keep down** *vt* (*control: prices, spending*) empêcher d'augmenter, limiter; (*retain: food*) garder ♦ *vi* (*person*) rester assis(e); rester par terre.

►**keep in** *vt* (*invalid, child*) garder à la maison; (*SCOL*) consigner ♦ *vi* (*col*): **to ~ in with sb** rester en bons termes avec qn.

►**keep off** *vi* ne pas s'approcher; **"~ off the grass"** "pelouse interdite".

►**keep on** *vi* continuer; **to ~ on doing** continuer à faire.

►**keep out** *vt* empêcher d'entrer ♦ *vi* rester en dehors; **"~ out"** "défense d'entrer".

►**keep up** *vi* se maintenir; (*fig: in comprehension*) suivre ♦ *vt* continuer, maintenir; **to ~ up with** se maintenir au niveau de; **to ~ up with sb** (*in race etc*) aller aussi vite que qn, être du même niveau que qn.

keeper ['ki:pə*] *n* gardien/ne.

keep-fit [ki:p'fɪt] *n* gymnastique *f* de maintien.

keeping ['ki:pɪŋ] *n* (*care*) garde *f*; **in ~ with** à l'avenant de; en accord avec.

keeps [ki:ps] *n*: **for ~** (*col*) pour de bon, pour toujours.

keepsake ['ki:pseɪk] *n* souvenir *m*.

keg [kɛg] *n* barrique *f*, tonnelet *m*.

Ken. *abbr* (*US*) = *Kentucky*.

kennel ['kɛnl] *n* niche *f*; **~s** *npl* chenil *m*.

Kenya ['kɛnjə] *n* Kenya *m*.

Kenyan ['kɛnjən] *adj* kenyen(ne) ♦ *n* Kenyen/ne.

kept [kɛpt] *pt, pp of* **keep**.

kerb [kə:b] *n* (*BRIT*) bordure *f* du trottoir.

kerb crawler [-krɔ:lə*] *n personne qui accoste les prostitué(e)s en voiture*.

kernel ['kə:nl] *n* amande *f*; (*fig*) noyau *m*.

kerosene ['kɛrəsi:n] *n* kérosène *m*.

ketchup ['kɛtʃəp] *n* ketchup *m*.

kettle ['kɛtl] *n* bouilloire *f*.

kettle drums *npl* timbales *fpl*.

key [ki:] *n* (*gen, MUS*) clé *f*; (*of piano, typewriter*) touche *f*; (*on map*) légende *f* ♦ *cpd* (-)clé.

►**key in** *vt* (*text*) introduire au clavier.

keyboard ['ki:bɔ:d] *n* clavier *m* ♦ *vt* (*text*) saisir.

keyboarder ['ki:bɔ:də*] *n* claviste *m/f*.

keyed up [ki:d'ʌp] *adj*: **to be (all) ~** être surexcité(e).

keyhole ['ki:həul] *n* trou *m* de la serrure.

keyhole surgery *n chirurgie très minutieuse où l'incision est minimale*.

keynote ['ki:nəut] *n* (*MUS*) tonique *f*; (*fig*) note dominante.

keypad ['ki:pæd] *n* pavé *m* numérique.

key ring *n* porte-clés *m*.

keystroke ['ki:strəuk] *n* frappe *f*.

kg *abbr* (= *kilogram*) K.

KGB *n abbr* KGB *m*.

khaki ['kɑ:kɪ] *adj, n* kaki (*m*).

kibbutz [kɪ'buts] *n* kibboutz *m*.

kick [kɪk] *vt* donner un coup de pied à ♦ *vi* (*horse*) ruer ♦ *n* coup *m* de pied; (*of rifle*) recul *m*; (*col: thrill*): **he does it for ~s** il le fait parce que ça l'excite, il le fait pour le plaisir.

►**kick around** *vi* (*col*) traîner.

►**kick off** *vi* (*SPORT*) donner le coup d'envoi.

kick-off ['kɪkɔf] *n* (*SPORT*) coup *m* d'envoi.

kick-start ['kɪkstɑ:t] *n* (*also*: **~er**) lanceur *m* au pied.

kid [kɪd] *n* (*col: child*) gamin/e, gosse *m/f*; (*animal, leather*) chevreau *m* ♦ *vi* (*col*) plaisanter, blaguer.

kid gloves *npl*: **to treat sb with ~** traiter qn avec ménagement.

kidnap ['kɪdnæp] *vt* enlever, kidnapper.

kidnapper ['kɪdnæpə*] *n* ravisseur/euse.

kidnapping ['kɪdnæpɪŋ] *n* enlèvement *m*.

kidney ['kɪdnɪ] *n* (*ANAT*) rein *m*; (*CULIN*) rognon *m*.

kidney bean *n* haricot *m* rouge.

kidney machine *n* (*MED*) rein artificiel.

Kilimanjaro [kɪlɪmən'dʒɑ:rəu] *n*: **Mount ~** Kilimandjaro *m*.

kill [kɪl] *vt* tuer; (*fig*) faire échouer; détruire; supprimer ♦ *n* mise *f* à mort; **to ~ time** tuer le temps.

►**kill off** *vt* exterminer; (*fig*) éliminer.

killer ['kɪlə*] *n* tueur/euse; meurtrier/ière.

killer instinct *n* combativité *f*; **to have the ~** avoir un tempérament de battant.

killing ['kɪlɪŋ] *n* meurtre *m*; tuerie *f*, massacre *m*; (*col*): **to make a ~** se remplir les poches, réussir un beau coup ♦ *adj* (*col*) tordant(e).

kill-joy ['kɪldʒɔɪ] *n* rabat-joie *m inv*.

kiln [kɪln] *n* four *m*.

kilo ['ki:ləu] *n abbr* (= *kilogram*) kilo *m*.

kilobyte ['ki:ləubaɪt] *n* kilo-octet *m*.

kilogram(me) ['kɪləugræm] *n* kilogramme *m*.

kilometre, (*US*) **kilometer** ['kɪləmi:tə*] *n* kilomètre *m*.

kilowatt ['kɪləuwɔt] *n* kilowatt *m*.

kilt [kɪlt] *n* kilt *m*.

kilter ['kɪltə*] *n*: **out of ~** déréglé(e), détraqué(e).

kimono [kɪ'məunəu] *n* kimono *m*.

kin [kɪn] *n see* **next-of-kin, kith**.

kind [kaɪnd] *adj* gentil(le), aimable ♦ *n* sorte *f*, espèce *f*; (*species*) genre *m*; **to be two of a** ~ se ressembler; **would you be** ~ **enough to ...?, would you be so** ~ **as to ...?** auriez-vous la gentillesse *or* l'obligeance de ...?; **it's very** ~ **of you (to do)** c'est très aimable à vous (de faire); **in** ~ (*COMM*) en nature; (*fig*): **to repay sb in** ~ rendre la pareille à qn.

kindergarten ['kɪndəgɑːtn] *n* jardin *m* d'enfants.

kind-hearted [kaɪnd'hɑːtɪd] *adj* bon(bonne).

kindle ['kɪndl] *vt* allumer, enflammer.

kindling ['kɪndlɪŋ] *n* petit bois.

kindly ['kaɪndlɪ] *adj* bienveillant(e), plein(e) de gentillesse ♦ *adv* avec bonté; **will you** ~ ... auriez-vous la bonté *or* l'obligeance de ...; **he didn't take it** ~ il l'a mal pris.

kindness ['kaɪndnɪs] *n* bonté *f*, gentillesse *f*.

kindred ['kɪndrɪd] *adj* apparenté(e); ~ **spirit** âme *f* sœur.

kinetic [kɪ'nɛtɪk] *adj* cinétique.

king [kɪŋ] *n* roi *m*.

kingdom ['kɪŋdəm] *n* royaume *m*.

kingfisher ['kɪŋfɪʃə*] *n* martin-pêcheur *m*.

kingpin ['kɪŋpɪn] *n* (*TECH*) pivot *m*; (*fig*) cheville ouvrière.

king-size(d) ['kɪŋsaɪz(d)] *adj* (*cigarette*) (format) extra-long(longue).

kink [kɪŋk] *n* (*of rope*) entortillement *m*; (*in hair*) ondulation *f*; (*col: fig*) aberration *f*.

kinky ['kɪŋkɪ] *adj* (*fig*) excentrique; (*pej*) aux goûts spéciaux.

kinship ['kɪnʃɪp] *n* parenté *f*.

kinsman ['kɪnzmən] *n* parent *m*.

kinswoman ['kɪnzwumən] *n* parente *f*.

kiosk ['kiːɔsk] *n* kiosque *m*; (*BRIT*: *also*: **telephone** ~) cabine *f* (téléphonique); (*: also*: **newspaper** ~) kiosque à journaux.

kipper ['kɪpə*] *n* hareng fumé et salé.

Kirghizia [kəː'gɪzɪə] *n* Kirghizistan *m*.

kiss [kɪs] *n* baiser *m* ♦ *vt* embrasser; **to** ~ **(each other)** s'embrasser; **to** ~ **sb goodbye** dire au revoir à qn en l'embrassant; ~ **of life** *n* (*BRIT*) bouche à bouche *m*.

kissagram ['kɪsəgræm] *n* *baiser envoyé à l'occasion d'une célébration par l'intermédiaire d'une personne employée à cet effet.*

kit [kɪt] *n* équipement *m*, matériel *m*; (*set of tools etc*) trousse *f*; (*for assembly*) kit *m*; **tool** ~ nécessaire *m* à outils.

►**kit out** *vt* (*BRIT*) équiper.

kitbag ['kɪtbæg] *n* sac *m* de voyage *or* de marin.

kitchen ['kɪtʃɪn] *n* cuisine *f*.

kitchen garden *n* jardin *m* potager.

kitchen sink *n* évier *m*.

kitchen unit *n* (*BRIT*) élément *m* de cuisine.

kitchenware ['kɪtʃɪnwɛə*] *n* vaisselle *f*; ustensiles *mpl* de cuisine.

kite [kaɪt] *n* (*toy*) cerf-volant *m*; (*ZOOL*) milan *m*.

kith [kɪθ] *n*: ~ **and kin** parents et amis *mpl*.

kitten ['kɪtn] *n* petit chat, chaton *m*.

kitty ['kɪtɪ] *n* (*money*) cagnotte *f*.

kiwi ['kiːwiː] *n*: ~ **(fruit)** kiwi *m*.

KKK *n abbr* (*US*) = *Ku Klux Klan*.

Kleenex ['kliːnɛks] *n* ® Kleenex *m* ®.

kleptomaniac [klɛptəu'meɪnɪæk] *n* kleptomane *m/f*.

km *abbr* (= *kilometre*) km.

km/h *abbr* (= *kilometres per hour*) km/h.

knack [næk] *n*: **to have the** ~ **(of doing)** avoir le coup (pour faire); **there's a** ~ il y a un coup à prendre *or* une combine.

knackered ['nækəd] *adj* (*col*) crevé(e), nase.

knapsack ['næpsæk] *n* musette *f*.

knave [neɪv] *n* (*CARDS*) valet *m*.

knead [niːd] *vt* pétrir.

knee [niː] *n* genou *m*.

kneecap ['niːkæp] *n* rotule *f* ♦ *vt* tirer un coup de feu dans la rotule de.

knee-deep ['niː'diːp] *adj*: **the water was** ~ l'eau arrivait aux genoux.

kneel, *pt, pp* **knelt** [niːl, nɛlt] *vi* (*also*: ~ **down**) s'agenouiller.

kneepad ['niːpæd] *n* genouillère *f*.

knell [nɛl] *n* glas *m*.

knelt [nɛlt] *pt, pp of* **kneel**.

knew [njuː] *pt of* **know**.

knickers ['nɪkəz] *npl* (*BRIT*) culotte *f* (de femme).

knick-knack ['nɪknæk] *n* colifichet *m*.

knife [naɪf] *n* (*pl* **knives**) couteau *m* ♦ *vt* poignarder, frapper d'un coup de couteau; ~, **fork and spoon** couvert *m*.

knife-edge ['naɪfɛdʒ] *n*: **to be on a** ~ être sur le fil du rasoir.

knight [naɪt] *n* chevalier *m*; (*CHESS*) cavalier *m*.

knighthood ['naɪthud] *n* chevalerie *f*; (*title*): **to get a** ~ être fait chevalier.

knit [nɪt] *vt* tricoter; (*fig*): **to** ~ **together** unir ♦ *vi* (*broken bones*) se ressouder.

knitted ['nɪtɪd] *adj* en tricot.

knitting ['nɪtɪŋ] *n* tricot *m*.

knitting machine *n* machine *f* à tricoter.

knitting needle *n* aiguille *f* à tricoter.

knitting pattern *n* modèle *m* (pour tricot).

knitwear ['nɪtwɛə*] *n* tricots *mpl*, lainages *mpl*.

knives [naɪvz] *npl of* **knife**.

knob [nɔb] *n* bouton *m*; (*BRIT*): **a** ~ **of butter** une noix de beurre.

knobbly ['nɔblɪ], (*US*) **knobby** ['nɔbɪ] *adj* (*wood, surface*) noueux(euse); (*knees*) noueux.

knock [nɔk] *vt* frapper; (*make: hole etc*): **to** ~ **a hole in** faire un trou dans, trouer; (*force: nail etc*): **to** ~ **a nail into** enfoncer un clou dans; (*fig: col*) dénigrer ♦ *vi* (*engine*) cogner; (*at door etc*): **to** ~ **at/on** frapper à/sur ♦ *n* coup *m*; **he** ~**ed at the door** il frappa à la porte.

►**knock down** *vt* renverser; (*price*) réduire.

►**knock off** *vi* (*col: finish*) s'arrêter (de travailler) ♦ *vt* (*vase, object*) faire tomber; (*col: steal*) piquer; (*fig: from price etc*): **to ~ off £10** faire une remise de 10 livres.

▸**knock out** *vt* assommer; (*BOXING*) mettre k.-o.

▸**knock over** *vt* (*object*) faire tomber; (*pedestrian*) renverser.

knockdown ['nɔkdaun] *adj* (*price*) sacrifié(e).

knocker ['nɔkə*] *n* (*on door*) heurtoir *m*.

knocking ['nɔkıŋ] *n* coups *mpl*.

knock-kneed [nɔk'ni:d] *adj* aux genoux cagneux.

knockout ['nɔkaut] *n* (*BOXING*) knock-out *m*, K.-O. *m*.

knockout competition *n* (*BRIT*) compétition *f* avec épreuves éliminatoires.

knock-up ['nɔkʌp] *n* (*TENNIS*): **to have a ~** faire des balles.

knot [nɔt] *n* (*gen*) nœud *m* ♦ *vt* nouer; **to tie a ~** faire un nœud.

knotty ['nɔtı] *adj* (*fig*) épineux(euse).

know [nəu] *vt* (*pt* **knew**, *pp* **known** [nju:, nəun]) savoir; (*person, place*) connaître; **to ~ that** savoir que; **to ~ how to do** savoir faire; **to ~ about/of sth** être au courant de/connaître qch; **to get to ~ sth** (*fact*) apprendre qch; (*place*) apprendre à connaître qch; **to ~ right from wrong** savoir distinguer le bon du mauvais; **as far as I ~** ... à ma connaissance ..., autant que je sache ....

know-all ['nəuɔ:l] *n* (*BRIT pej*) je-sais-tout *m/f*.

know-how ['nəuhau] *n* savoir-faire *m*, technique *f*, compétence *f*.

knowing ['nəuıŋ] *adj* (*look etc*) entendu(e).

knowingly ['nəuıŋlı] *adv* sciemment; d'un air entendu.

know-it-all ['nəuıtɔ:l] *n* (*US*) = **know-all**.

knowledge ['nɔlıdʒ] *n* connaissance *f*; (*learning*) connaissances, savoir *m*; **to have no ~ of** ignorer; **not to my ~** pas à ma connaissance; **without my ~** à mon insu; **to have a working ~ of French** se débrouiller en français; **it is common ~ that** ... chacun sait que ...; **it has come to my ~ that** ... j'ai appris que ....

knowledgeable ['nɔlıdʒəbl] *adj* bien informé(e).

known [nəun] *pp of* **know** ♦ *adj* (*thief, facts*) notoire; (*expert*) célèbre.

knuckle ['nʌkl] *n* articulation *f* (des phalanges), jointure *f*.

▸**knuckle down** *vi* (*col*) s'y mettre.

▸**knuckle under** *vi* (*col*) céder.

knuckleduster ['nʌkldʌstə*] *n* coup-de-poing américain.

KO *abbr* (= *knock out*) *n* K.-O. *m* ♦ *vt* mettre K.-O.

koala [kəu'ɑ:lə] *n* (*also*: **~ bear**) koala *m*.

kook [ku:k] *n* (*US col*) loufoque *m/f*.

Koran [kɔ'rɑ:n] *n* Coran *m*.

Korea [kə'rıə] *n* Corée *f*; **North/South ~** Corée du Nord/Sud.

Korean [kə'rıən] *adj* coréen(ne) ♦ *n* Coréen/ne.

kosher ['kəuʃə*] *adj* kascher *inv*.

Kosovo ['kɔsɔvəu] *n* Kosovo *m*.

kowtow ['kau'tau] *vi*: **to ~ to sb** s'aplatir devant qn.

Kremlin ['krεmlın] *n*: **the ~** le Kremlin.

KS *abbr* (*US*) = *Kansas*.

Kt *abbr* (*BRIT*: = *Knight*) *titre honorifique*.

Kuala Lumpur ['kwɑ:lə'lumpuə*] *n* Kuala Lumpur.

kudos ['kju:dɔs] *n* gloire *f*, lauriers *mpl*.

Kurd [kə:d] *n* Kurde *m/f*.

Kuwait [ku'weıt] *n* Koweït *f*, Kuweit *f*.

Kuwaiti [ku'weıtı] *adj* koweïtien(ne) ♦ *n* Koweïtien/ne.

kW *abbr* (= *kilowatt*) kW.

KY, Ky. *abbr* (*US*) = *Kentucky*.

L l

L, l [εl] *n* (*letter*) L, l *m*; **L for Lucy**, (*US*) **L for Love** L comme Louis.

L *abbr* (= *lake, large*) L; (= *left*) g; (*BRIT AUT*: = *learner*) *signale un conducteur débutant*.

l *abbr* (= *litre*) l.

LA *n abbr* (*US*) = *Los Angeles* ♦ *abbr* (*US*) = *Louisiana*.

La. *abbr* (*US*) = *Louisiana*.

lab [læb] *n abbr* (= *laboratory*) labo *m*.

Lab. *abbr* (*Canada*) = *Labrador*.

label ['leıbl] *n* étiquette *f*; (*brand: of record*) marque *f* ♦ *vt* étiqueter; **to ~ sb a** ... qualifier qn de ....

labor *etc* ['leıbə*] (*US*) = **labour** *etc*.

laboratory [lə'bɔrətərı] *n* laboratoire *m*.

Labor Day *n* (*US, Canada*) fête *f* du travail (*le premier lundi de septembre*).

laborious [lə'bɔ:rıəs] *adj* laborieux(euse).

labor union *n* (*US*) syndicat *m*.

Labour ['leıbə*] *n* (*BRIT POL*: *also*: **the ~ Party**) le parti travailliste, les travaillistes *mpl*.

labour, (*US*) **labor** ['leıbə*] *n* (*task*) travail *m*; (*workmen*) main-d'œuvre *f*; (*MED*) travail, accouchement *m* ♦ *vi*: **to ~ (at)** travailler dur (à), peiner (sur); **in ~** (*MED*) en travail.

labo(u)r camp *n* camp *m* de travaux forcés.

labo(u)r cost *n* coût *m* de la main-d'œuvre; coût de la façon.

labo(u)red ['leıbəd] *adj* lourd(e), laborieux(euse); (*breathing*) difficile, pénible; (*style*) lourd, embarrassé(e).

labo(u)rer ['leıbərə*] *n* manœuvre *m*; (*on farm*) ouvrier *m* agricole.

labo(u)r force *n* main-d'œuvre *f*.

labo(u)r-intensive [leıbərın'tεnsıv] *adj* inten-

sif(ive) en main-d'œuvre.
labo(u)r market *n* marché *m* du travail.
labo(u)r pains *npl* douleurs *fpl* de l'accouchement.
labo(u)r relations *npl* relations *fpl* dans l'entreprise.
labo(u)r-saving ['leɪbəseɪvɪŋ] *adj* qui simplifie le travail.
labo(u)r unrest *n* agitation sociale.
labyrinth ['læbɪrɪnθ] *n* labyrinthe *m*, dédale *m*.
lace [leɪs] *n* dentelle *f*; (*of shoe etc*) lacet *m* ♦ *vt* (*shoe*) lacer; (*drink*) arroser, corser.
lacemaking ['leɪsmeɪkɪŋ] *n* fabrication *f* de dentelle.
laceration [læsə'reɪʃən] *n* lacération *f*.
lace-up ['leɪsʌp] *adj* (*shoes etc*) à lacets.
lack [læk] *n* manque *m* ♦ *vt* manquer de; **through** *or* **for ~ of** faute de, par manque de; **to be ~ing** manquer, faire défaut; **to be ~ing in** manquer de.
lackadaisical [lækə'deɪzɪkl] *adj* nonchalant(e), indolent(e).
lackey ['lækɪ] *n* (*also fig*) laquais *m*.
lacklustre ['læklʌstə*] *adj* terne.
laconic [lə'kɔnɪk] *adj* laconique.
lacquer ['lækə*] *n* laque *f*.
lacy ['leɪsɪ] *adj* comme de la dentelle, qui ressemble à de la dentelle.
lad [læd] *n* garçon *m*, gars *m*; (*BRIT*: *in stable etc*) lad *m*.
ladder ['lædə*] *n* échelle *f*; (*BRIT*: *in tights*) maille filée ♦ *vt*, *vi* (*BRIT*: *tights*) filer.
laden ['leɪdn] *adj*: ~ **(with)** chargé(e) (de); **fully ~** (*truck, ship*) en pleine charge.
ladle ['leɪdl] *n* louche *f*.
lady ['leɪdɪ] *n* dame *f*; **L~ Smith** lady Smith; **the ladies' (room)** les toilettes *fpl* des dames; **a ~ doctor** une doctoresse, une femme médecin.
ladybird ['leɪdɪbə:d], (*US*) **ladybug** ['leɪdɪbʌg] *n* coccinelle *f*.
lady-in-waiting ['leɪdɪɪn'weɪtɪŋ] *n* dame *f* d'honneur.
ladykiller ['leɪdɪkɪlə*] *n* don Juan *m*.
ladylike ['leɪdɪlaɪk] *adj* distingué(e).
ladyship ['leɪdɪʃɪp] *n*: **your L~** Madame la comtesse (*or* la baronne *etc*).
lag [læg] *n* = **time ~** ♦ *vi* (*also*: ~ **behind**) rester en arrière, traîner ♦ *vt* (*pipes*) calorifuger.
lager ['lɑ:gə*] *n* bière blonde.
lager lout *n* (*BRIT col*) jeune voyou *m* (*porté sur la boisson*).
lagging ['lægɪŋ] *n* enveloppe isolante, calorifuge *m*.
lagoon [lə'gu:n] *n* lagune *f*.
Lagos ['leɪgɔs] *n* Lagos.
laid [leɪd] *pt*, *pp of* **lay**.
laid-back [leɪd'bæk] *adj* (*col*) relaxe, décontracté(e).
lain [leɪn] *pp of* **lie**.
lair [lɛə*] *n* tanière *f*, gîte *m*.
laissez-faire [lɛseɪ'fɛə*] *n* libéralisme *m*.
laity ['leɪətɪ] *n* laïques *mpl*.
lake [leɪk] *n* lac *m*.
Lake District *n*: **the ~** (*BRIT*) la région des lacs.
lamb [læm] *n* agneau *m*.
lamb chop *n* côtelette *f* d'agneau.
lambskin ['læmskɪn] *n* (peau *f* d')agneau *m*.
lambswool ['læmzwul] *n* laine *f* d'agneau.
lame [leɪm] *adj* boiteux(euse); ~ **duck** (*fig*) canard boiteux.
lamely ['leɪmlɪ] *adv* (*fig*) sans conviction.
lament [lə'mɛnt] *n* lamentation *f* ♦ *vt* pleurer, se lamenter sur.
lamentable ['læməntəbl] *adj* déplorable, lamentable.
laminated ['læmɪneɪtɪd] *adj* laminé(e); (*windscreen*) (en verre) feuilleté.
lamp [læmp] *n* lampe *f*.
lamplight ['læmplaɪt] *n*: **by ~** à la lumière de la (*or* d'une) lampe.
lampoon [læm'pu:n] *n* pamphlet *m*.
lamppost ['læmppəust] *n* (*BRIT*) réverbère *m*.
lampshade ['læmpʃeɪd] *n* abat-jour *m inv*.
lance [lɑ:ns] *n* lance *f* ♦ *vt* (*MED*) inciser.
lance corporal *n* (*BRIT*) (soldat *m* de) première classe *m*.
lancet ['lɑ:nsɪt] *n* (*MED*) bistouri *m*.
Lancs [læŋks] *abbr* (*BRIT*) = *Lancashire*.
land [lænd] *n* (*as opposed to sea*) terre *f* (ferme); (*country*) pays *m*; (*soil*) terre; terrain *m*; (*estate*) terre(s), domaine(s) *m(pl)* ♦ *vi* (*from ship*) débarquer; (*AVIAT*) atterrir; (*fig: fall*) (re)tomber ♦ *vt* (*passengers, goods*) débarquer; (*obtain*) décrocher; **to go/travel by ~** se déplacer par voie de terre; **to own ~** être propriétaire foncier; **to ~ on one's feet** (*also fig*) retomber sur ses pieds.
►**land up** *vi* atterrir, (finir par) se retrouver.
landed gentry ['lændɪd-] *n* (*BRIT*) propriétaires terriens *or* fonciers.
landfill site ['lændfɪl-] *n* centre *m* d'enfouissement des déchets.
landing ['lændɪŋ] *n* (*from ship*) débarquement *m*; (*AVIAT*) atterrissage *m*; (*of staircase*) palier *m*.
landing card *n* carte *f* de débarquement.
landing craft *n* péniche *f* de débarquement.
landing gear *n* train *m* d'atterrissage.
landing stage *n* (*BRIT*) débarcadère *m*, embarcadère *m*.
landing strip *n* piste *f* d'atterrissage.
landlady ['lændleɪdɪ] *n* propriétaire *f*, logeuse *f*.
landlocked ['lændlɔkt] *adj* entouré(e) de terre(s), sans accès à la mer.
landlord ['lændlɔ:d] *n* propriétaire *m*, logeur *m*; (*of pub etc*) patron *m*.
landlubber ['lændlʌbə*] *n* terrien/ne.
landmark ['lændmɑ:k] *n* (point *m* de) repère *m*; **to be a ~** (*fig*) faire date *or* époque.
landowner ['lændəunə*] *n* propriétaire foncier *or* terrien.

landscape ['lænskeɪp] *n* paysage *m*.
landscape architect, landscape gardener *n* paysagiste *m/f*.
landscape painting *n* (*ART*) paysage *m*.
landslide ['lændslaɪd] *n* (*GEO*) glissement *m* (de terrain); (*fig*: *POL*) raz-de-marée (électoral).
lane [leɪn] *n* (*in country*) chemin *m*; (*in town*) ruelle *f*; (*AUT*) voie *f*; file *f*; (*in race*) couloir *m*; **shipping** ~ route *f* maritime *or* de navigation.
language ['læŋgwɪdʒ] *n* langue *f*; (*way one speaks*) langage *m*; **bad** ~ grossièretés *fpl*, langage grossier.
language laboratory *n* laboratoire *m* de langues.
languid ['læŋgwɪd] *adj* languissant(e); langoureux(euse).
languish ['læŋgwɪʃ] *vi* languir.
lank [læŋk] *adj* (*hair*) raide et terne.
lanky ['læŋkɪ] *adj* grand(e) et maigre, efflanqué(e).
lanolin(e) ['lænəlɪn] *n* lanoline *f*.
lantern ['læntn] *n* lanterne *f*.
Laos [laus] *n* Laos *m*.
lap [læp] *n* (*of track*) tour *m* (de piste); (*of body*): **in** *or* **on one's** ~ sur les genoux ♦ *vt* (*also*: ~ **up**) laper ♦ *vi* (*waves*) clapoter.
▸**lap up** *vt* (*fig*) boire comme du petit-lait, se gargariser de; (*: lies etc*) gober.
La Paz [læ'pæz] *n* La Paz.
lapdog ['læpdɔg] *n* chien *m* d'appartement.
lapel [lə'pɛl] *n* revers *m*.
Lapland ['læplænd] *n* Laponie *f*.
lapse [læps] *n* défaillance *f*; (*in behaviour*) écart *m* (de conduite) ♦ *vi* (*LAW*) cesser d'être en vigueur; se périmer; **to** ~ **into bad habits** prendre de mauvaises habitudes; ~ **of time** laps *m* de temps, intervalle *m*; **a** ~ **of memory** un trou de mémoire.
laptop ['læptɔp] *n* (*also*: ~ **computer**) ordinateur portatif.
larceny ['lɑːsənɪ] *n* vol *m*.
lard [lɑːd] *n* saindoux *m*.
larder ['lɑːdə*] *n* garde-manger *m inv*.
large [lɑːdʒ] *adj* grand(e); (*person, animal*) gros(grosse); **to make** ~**r** agrandir; **a** ~ **number of people** beaucoup de gens; **by and** ~ en général; **on a** ~ **scale** sur une grande échelle; **at** ~ (*free*) en liberté; (*generally*) en général; pour la plupart.
largely ['lɑːdʒlɪ] *adv* en grande partie.
large-scale ['lɑːdʒ'skeɪl] *adj* (*map, drawing etc*) à grande échelle; (*fig*) important(e).
lark [lɑːk] *n* (*bird*) alouette *f*; (*joke*) blague *f*, farce *f*.
▸**lark about** *vi* faire l'idiot, rigoler.
larva, *pl* **larvae** ['lɑːvə, -iː] *n* larve *f*.
laryngitis [lærɪn'dʒaɪtɪs] *n* laryngite *f*.
larynx ['lærɪŋks] *n* larynx *m*.
lasagne [lə'zænjə] *n* lasagne *f*.
lascivious [lə'sɪvɪəs] *adj* lascif(ive).
laser ['leɪzə*] *n* laser *m*.
laser beam *n* rayon *m* laser.
laser printer *n* imprimante *f* laser.
lash [læʃ] *n* coup *m* de fouet; (*also*: **eye**~) cil *m* ♦ *vt* fouetter; (*tie*) attacher.
▸**lash down** *vt* attacher; amarrer; arrimer ♦ *vi* (*rain*) tomber avec violence.
▸**lash out** *vi*: **to** ~ **out (at** *or* **against sb/sth)** attaquer violemment (qn/qch); **to** ~ **out (on sth)** (*col*: *spend*) se fendre (de qch).
lashing ['læʃɪŋ] *n*: ~**s of** (*BRIT col*: *cream etc*) des masses de.
lass [læs] *n* (jeune) fille *f*.
lasso [læ'suː] *n* lasso *m* ♦ *vt* prendre au lasso.
last [lɑːst] *adj* dernier(ière) ♦ *adv* en dernier ♦ *vi* durer; ~ **week** la semaine dernière; ~ **night** hier soir; la nuit dernière; **at** ~ enfin; ~ **but one** avant-dernier(ière); **the** ~ **time** la dernière fois; **it** ~**s (for) 2 hours** ça dure 2 heures.
last-ditch ['lɑːst'dɪtʃ] *adj* ultime, désespéré(e).
lasting ['lɑːstɪŋ] *adj* durable.
lastly ['lɑːstlɪ] *adv* en dernier lieu, pour finir.
last-minute ['lɑːstmɪnɪt] *adj* de dernière minute.
latch [lætʃ] *n* loquet *m*.
▸**latch on to** *vt* (*cling to: person*) s'accrocher à; (*: idea*) trouver bon(ne).
latchkey ['lætʃkiː] *n* clé *f* (de la porte d'entrée).
late [leɪt] *adj* (*not on time*) en retard; (*far on in day etc*) dernier(ière); tardif(ive); (*recent*) récent(e), dernier; (*former*) ancien(ne); (*dead*) défunt(e) ♦ *adv* tard; (*behind time, schedule*) en retard; **to be** ~ avoir du retard; **to be 10 minutes** ~ avoir 10 minutes de retard; **to work** ~ travailler tard; ~ **in life** sur le tard, à un âge avancé; **of** ~ dernièrement; **in** ~ **May** vers la fin (du mois) de mai, fin mai; **the** ~ **Mr X** feu M. X.
latecomer ['leɪtkʌmə*] *n* retardataire *m/f*.
lately ['leɪtlɪ] *adv* récemment.
lateness ['leɪtnɪs] *n* (*of person*) retard *m*; (*of event*) heure tardive.
latent ['leɪtnt] *adj* latent(e); ~ **defect** vice caché.
later ['leɪtə*] *adj* (*date etc*) ultérieur(e); (*version etc*) plus récent(e) ♦ *adv* plus tard; ~ **on today** plus tard dans la journée.
lateral ['lætərl] *adj* latéral(e).
latest ['leɪtɪst] *adj* tout(e) dernier(ière); **the** ~ **news** les dernières nouvelles; **at the** ~ au plus tard.
latex ['leɪtɛks] *n* latex *m*.
lath, ~s [læθ, læðz] *n* latte *f*.
lathe [leɪð] *n* tour *m*.
lather ['lɑːðə*] *n* mousse *f* (de savon) ♦ *vt* savonner ♦ *vi* mousser.
Latin ['lætɪn] *n* latin *m* ♦ *adj* latin(e).
Latin America *n* Amérique latine.
Latin American *adj* latino-américain(e), d'Amérique latine ♦ *n* Latino-Américain/e.

latitude ['lætɪtju:d] *n* (*also fig*) latitude *f*.
latrine [lə'tri:n] *n* latrines *fpl*.
latter ['lætə*] *adj* deuxième, dernier(ière) ♦ *n*: **the ~** ce dernier, celui-ci.
latterly ['lætəlɪ] *adv* dernièrement, récemment.
lattice ['lætɪs] *n* treillis *m*; treillage *m*.
lattice window *n* fenêtre treillissée, fenêtre à croisillons.
Latvia ['lætvɪə] *n* Lettonie *f*.
Latvian ['lætvɪən] *adj* letton(ne) ♦ *n* Letton/ne; (*LING*) letton *m*.
laudable ['lɔ:dəbl] *adj* louable.
laudatory ['lɔ:dətrɪ] *adj* élogieux(euse).
laugh [lɑ:f] *n* rire *m* ♦ *vi* rire.
▸**laugh at** *vt fus* se moquer de; (*joke*) rire de.
▸**laugh off** *vt* écarter *or* rejeter par une plaisanterie *or* par une boutade.
laughable ['lɑ:fəbl] *adj* risible, ridicule.
laughing ['lɑ:fɪŋ] *adj* rieur(euse); **this is no ~ matter** il n'y a pas de quoi rire, ça n'a rien d'amusant.
laughing gas *n* gaz hilarant.
laughing stock *n*: **the ~ of** la risée de.
laughter ['lɑ:ftə*] *n* rire *m*; (*people laughing*) rires *mpl*.
launch [lɔ:ntʃ] *n* lancement *m*; (*boat*) chaloupe *f*; (*also*: **motor ~**) vedette *f* ♦ *vt* (*ship, rocket, plan*) lancer.
▸**launch out** *vi*: **to ~ out (into)** se lancer (dans).
launching ['lɔ:ntʃɪŋ] *n* lancement *m*.
launch(ing) pad *n* rampe *f* de lancement.
launder ['lɔ:ndə*] *vt* blanchir.
Launderette [lɔ:n'drɛt], (*US*) **Laundromat** ['lɔ:ndrəmæt] *n* ® laverie *f* (automatique).
laundry ['lɔ:ndrɪ] *n* blanchisserie *f*; (*clothes*) linge *m*; **to do the ~** faire la lessive.
laureate ['lɔ:rɪət] *adj see* **poet laureate**.
laurel ['lɔrl] *n* laurier *m*; **to rest on one's ~s** se reposer sur ses lauriers.
lava ['lɑ:və] *n* lave *f*.
lavatory ['lævətərɪ] *n* toilettes *fpl*.
lavatory paper *n* (*BRIT*) papier *m* hygiénique.
lavender ['lævəndə*] *n* lavande *f*.
lavish ['lævɪʃ] *adj* copieux(euse); somptueux(euse); (*giving freely*): **~ with** prodigue de ♦ *vt*: **to ~ sth on sb** prodiguer qch à qn.
lavishly ['lævɪʃlɪ] *adv* (*give, spend*) sans compter; (*furnished*) luxueusement.
law [lɔ:] *n* loi *f*; (*science*) droit *m*; **against the ~** contraire à la loi; **to study ~** faire du droit; **to go to ~** (*BRIT*) avoir recours à la justice; **~ and order** *n* l'ordre public.
law-abiding ['lɔ:əbaɪdɪŋ] *adj* respectueux(euse) des lois.
lawbreaker ['lɔ:breɪkə*] *n* personne *f* qui transgresse la loi.
law court *n* tribunal *m*, cour *f* de justice.
lawful ['lɔ:ful] *adj* légal(e); permis(e).
lawfully ['lɔ:fəlɪ] *adv* légalement.
lawless ['lɔ:lɪs] *adj* sans loi.
Law Lord *n* (*BRIT*) *juge siégant à la Chambre des Lords*.
lawmaker ['lɔ:meɪkə*] *n* législateur/trice.
lawn [lɔ:n] *n* pelouse *f*.
lawnmower ['lɔ:nməuə*] *n* tondeuse *f* à gazon.
lawn tennis *n* tennis *m*.
law school *n* faculté *f* de droit.
law student *n* étudiant/e en droit.
lawsuit ['lɔ:su:t] *n* procès *m*; **to bring a ~ against** engager des poursuites contre.
lawyer ['lɔ:jə*] *n* (*consultant, with company*) juriste *m*; (*for sales, wills etc*) ≈ notaire *m*; (*partner, in court*) ≈ avocat *m*.
lax [læks] *adj* relâché(e).
laxative ['læksətɪv] *n* laxatif *m*.
laxity ['læksɪtɪ] *n* relâchement *m*.
lay [leɪ] *pt of* **lie** ♦ *adj* laïque; profane ♦ *vt* (*pt, pp* **laid** [leɪd]) poser, mettre; (*eggs*) pondre; (*trap*) tendre; (*plans*) élaborer; **to ~ the table** mettre la table; **to ~ the facts/one's proposals before sb** présenter les faits/ses propositions à qn; **to get laid** (*col!*) baiser (*!*); se faire baiser (*!*).
▸**lay aside**, **lay by** *vt* mettre de côté.
▸**lay down** *vt* poser; **to ~ down the law** (*fig*) faire la loi.
▸**lay in** *vt* accumuler, s'approvisionner en.
▸**lay into** *vi* (*col*: *attack*) tomber sur; (*: scold*) passer une engueulade a.
▸**lay off** *vt* (*workers*) licencier.
▸**lay on** *vt* (*water, gas*) mettre, installer; (*provide: meal etc*) fournir; (*paint*) étaler.
▸**lay out** *vt* (*design*) dessiner, concevoir; (*display*) disposer; (*spend*) dépenser.
▸**lay up** *vt* (*to store*) amasser; (*car*) remiser; (*ship*) désarmer; (*subj: illness*) forcer à s'aliter.
layabout ['leɪəbaut] *n* fainéant/e.
lay-by ['leɪbaɪ] *n* (*BRIT*) aire *f* de stationnement (sur le bas-côté).
lay days *npl* (*NAUT*) estarie *f*.
layer ['leɪə*] *n* couche *f*.
layette [leɪ'ɛt] *n* layette *f*.
layman ['leɪmən] *n* laïque *m*; profane *m*.
lay-off ['leɪɔf] *n* licenciement *m*.
layout ['leɪaut] *n* disposition *f*, plan *m*, agencement *m*; (*PRESS*) mise *f* en page.
laze [leɪz] *vi* paresser.
laziness ['leɪzɪnɪs] *n* paresse *f*.
lazy ['leɪzɪ] *adj* paresseux(euse).
LB *abbr* (*Canada*) = *Labrador*.
lb. *abbr* (= *libra: pound*) *unité de poids*.
lbw *abbr* (*CRICKET*: = *leg before wicket*) *faute dans laquelle le joueur a la jambe devant le guichet*.
LC *n abbr* (*US*) = *Library of Congress*.
lc *abbr* (*TYP*: = *lower case*) b.d.c.
L/C *abbr* = **letter of credit**.
LCD *n abbr* = **liquid crystal display**.
Ld *abbr* (*BRIT*: = *lord*) *titre honorifique*.
LDS *n abbr* (= *Licentiate in Dental Surgery*) di-

plôme universitaire; (= *Latter-day Saints*) *Église de Jésus-Christ des Saints du dernier jour*.

LEA *n abbr* (*BRIT*: = *local education authority*) *services locaux de l'enseignement*.

lead¹ [li:d] *n* (*front position*) tête *f*; (*distance, time ahead*) avance *f*; (*clue*) piste *f*; (*to battery*) raccord *m*; (*ELEC*) fil *m*; (*for dog*) laisse *f*; (*THEAT*) rôle principal ♦ *vb* (*pt, pp* **led** [lɛd]) *vt* mener, conduire; (*induce*) amener; (*be leader of*) être à la tête de; (*SPORT*) être en tête de; (*orchestra*: *BRIT*) être le premier violon de; (*: US*) diriger ♦ *vi* mener, être en tête; **to ~ to** mener à; (*result in*) conduire à; aboutir à; **to ~sb astray** détourner qn du droit chemin; **to be in the ~** (*SPORT*: *in race*) mener, être en tête; (*: match*) mener (à la marque); **to take the ~** (*SPORT*) passer en tête, prendre la tête; mener; (*fig*) prendre l'initiative; **to ~ sb to believe that ...** amener qn à croire que ...; **to ~ sb to do sth** amener qn à faire qch.

►**lead away** *vt* emmener.

►**lead back** *vt* ramener.

►**lead off** *vi* (*in game etc*) commencer.

►**lead on** *vt* (*tease*) faire marcher; **to ~ sb on to** (*induce*) amener qn à.

►**lead up to** *vt* conduire à.

lead² [lɛd] *n* (*chemical*) plomb *m*; (*in pencil*) mine *f*.

leaded ['lɛdɪd] *adj* (*windows*) à petits carreaux.

leaden ['lɛdn] *adj* de *or* en plomb.

leader ['li:də*] *n* (*of team*) chef *m*; (*of party etc*) dirigeant/e, leader *m*; (*in newspaper*) éditorial *m*; **they are ~s in their field** (*fig*) ils sont à la pointe du progrès dans leur domaine; **the L~ of the House** (*BRIT*) le chef de la majorité ministérielle.

leadership ['li:dəʃɪp] *n* direction *f*; **under the ~ of ...** sous la direction de ...; **qualities of ~** qualités *fpl* de chef *or* de meneur.

lead-free ['lɛdfri:] *adj* sans plomb.

leading ['li:dɪŋ] *adj* de premier plan; (*main*) principal(e); **a ~ question** une question tendancieuse; **~ role** rôle prépondérant *or* de premier plan.

leading lady *n* (*THEAT*) vedette (féminine).

leading light *n* (*person*) sommité *f*, personnalité *f* de premier plan.

leading man *n* (*THEAT*) vedette (masculine).

lead pencil [lɛd-] *n* crayon noir *or* à papier.

lead poisoning [lɛd-] *n* saturnisme *m*.

lead time [li:d-] *n* (*COMM*) délai *m* de livraison.

lead weight [lɛd-] *n* plomb *m*.

leaf, *pl* **leaves** [li:f, li:vz] *n* feuille *f*; (*of table*) rallonge *f*; **to turn over a new ~** (*fig*) changer de conduite *or* d'existence; **to take a ~ out of sb's book** (*fig*) prendre exemple sur qn.

►**leaf through** *vt* (*book*) feuilleter.

leaflet ['li:flɪt] *n* prospectus *m*, brochure *f*; (*POL, REL*) tract *m*.

leafy ['li:fɪ] *adj* feuillu(e).

league [li:g] *n* ligue *f*; (*FOOTBALL*) championnat *m*; (*measure*) lieue *f*; **to be in ~ with** avoir partie liée avec, être de mèche avec.

league table *n* classement *m*.

leak [li:k] *n* (*out, also fig*) fuite *f*; (*in*) infiltration *f* ♦ *vi* (*pipe, liquid etc*) fuir; (*shoes*) prendre l'eau ♦ *vt* (*liquid*) répandre; (*information*) divulguer.

►**leak out** *vi* fuir; (*information*) être divulgué(e).

leakage ['li:kɪdʒ] *n* (*also fig*) fuite *f*.

leaky ['li:kɪ] *adj* (*pipe, bucket*) qui fuit, percé(e); (*roof*) qui coule; (*shoe*) qui prend l'eau; (*boat*) qui fait eau.

lean [li:n] *adj* maigre ♦ *n* (*of meat*) maigre *m* ♦ *vb* (*pt, pp* **leaned** *or* **leant** [lɛnt]) *vt*: **to ~ sth on** appuyer qch sur ♦ *vi* (*slope*) pencher; (*rest*): **to ~ against** s'appuyer contre; être appuyé(e) contre; **to ~ on** s'appuyer sur.

►**lean back** *vi* se pencher en arrière.

►**lean forward** *vi* se pencher en avant.

►**lean out** *vi*: **to ~ out (of)** se pencher au dehors (de).

►**lean over** *vi* se pencher.

leaning ['li:nɪŋ] *adj* penché(e) ♦ *n*: **~ (towards)** penchant *m* (pour); **the L~ Tower of Pisa** la tour penchée de Pise.

leant [lɛnt] *pt, pp of* **lean**.

lean-to ['li:ntu:] *n* appentis *m*.

leap [li:p] *n* bond *m*, saut *m* ♦ *vi* (*pt, pp* **leaped** *or* **leapt** [lɛpt]) bondir, sauter; **to ~ at an offer** saisir une offre.

►**leap up** *vi* (*person*) faire un bond; se lever d'un bond.

leapfrog ['li:pfrɔg] *n* jeu *m* de saute-mouton.

leapt [lɛpt] *pt, pp of* **leap**.

leap year *n* année *f* bissextile.

learn, *pt, pp* **learned** *or* **learnt** [lə:n, -t] *vt, vi* apprendre; **to ~ how to do sth** apprendre à faire qch; **we were sorry to ~ that ...** nous apprenons avec regret que ...; **to ~ about sth** (*SCOL*) étudier qch; (*hear*) apprendre qch.

learned ['lə:nɪd] *adj* érudit(e), savant(e).

learner ['lə:nə*] *n* débutant/e; (*BRIT*: *also*: **~ driver**) (conducteur/trice) débutant(e).

learning ['lə:nɪŋ] *n* savoir *m*.

lease [li:s] *n* bail *m* ♦ *vt* louer à bail; **on ~** en location.

►**lease back** *vt* vendre en cession-bail.

leaseback ['li:sbæk] *n* cession-bail *f*.

leasehold ['li:shəuld] *n* (*contract*) bail *m* ♦ *adj* loué(e) à bail.

leash [li:ʃ] *n* laisse *f*.

least [li:st] *adj*: **the ~** + *noun* le(la) plus petit(e), le(la) moindre; (*smallest amount of*) le moins de; **the ~** + *adjective* le(la) moins; **the ~ money** le moins d'argent; **the ~ expensive** le moins cher; **at ~** au moins; **not in the ~** pas le moins du monde.

leather ['lɛðə*] *n* cuir *m* ♦ *cpd* en *or* de cuir.
leave [liːv] *vb* (*pt, pp* **left** [lɛft]) *vt* laisser; (*go away from*) quitter ♦ *vi* partir, s'en aller ♦ *n* (*time off*) congé *m*; (*MIL, also: consent*) permission *f*; **to be left** rester; **there's some milk left over** il reste du lait; **to ~ school** quitter l'école, terminer sa scolarité; **~ it to me!** laissez-moi faire!, je m'en occupe!; **on ~** en permission; **to take one's ~ of** prendre congé de; **~ of absence** *n* congé exceptionnel; (*MIL*) permission spéciale.
►**leave behind** *vt* (*also fig*) laisser; (*opponent in race*) distancer; (*forget*) laisser, oublier.
►**leave off** *vt* (*cover, lid, heating*) ne pas (re)mettre; (*light*) ne pas (r)allumer, laisser éteint(e); (*BRIT col: stop*): **to ~ off (doing sth)** s'arrêter (de faire qch).
►**leave on** *vt* (*coat etc*) garder, ne pas enlever; (*lid*) laisser dessus; (*light, fire, cooker*) laisser allumé(e).
►**leave out** *vt* oublier, omettre.
leaves [liːvz] *npl of* **leaf**.
leavetaking ['liːvteɪkɪŋ] *n* adieux *mpl*.
Lebanese [lɛbə'niːz] *adj* libanais(e) ♦ *n* (*pl inv*) Libanais/e.
Lebanon ['lɛbənən] *n* Liban *m*.
lecherous ['lɛtʃərəs] *adj* lubrique.
lectern ['lɛktəːn] *n* lutrin *m*, pupitre *m*.
lecture ['lɛktʃə*] *n* conférence *f*; (*SCOL*) cours (magistral) ♦ *vi* donner des cours; enseigner ♦ *vt* (*reprove*) sermonner, réprimander; **to ~ on** faire un cours (*or* son cours) sur; **to give a ~ (on)** faire une conférence (sur); faire un cours (sur).
lecture hall *n* amphithéâtre *m*.
lecturer ['lɛktʃərə*] *n* (*speaker*) conférencier/ière; (*BRIT: at university*) professeur *m* (d'université), ≈ maître assistant, maître de conférences; **assistant ~** (*BRIT*) ≈ assistant/e; **senior ~** (*BRIT*) ≈ chargé/e d'enseignement.
lecture theatre *n* = **lecture hall**.
LED *n abbr* (= *light-emitting diode*) LED *f*, diode électroluminescente.
led [lɛd] *pt, pp of* **lead[1]**.
ledge [lɛdʒ] *n* (*of window, on wall*) rebord *m*; (*of mountain*) saillie *f*, corniche *f*.
ledger ['lɛdʒə*] *n* registre *m*, grand livre.
lee [liː] *n* côté *m* sous le vent; **in the ~ of** à l'abri de.
leech [liːtʃ] *n* sangsue *f*.
leek [liːk] *n* poireau *m*.
leer [lɪə*] *vi*: **to ~ at sb** regarder qn d'un air mauvais *or* concupiscent, lorgner qn.
leeward ['liːwəd] *adj, adv* sous le vent ♦ *n* côté *m* sous le vent; **to ~** sous le vent.
leeway ['liːweɪ] *n* (*fig*): **to make up ~** rattraper son retard; **to have some ~** avoir une certaine liberté d'action.
left [lɛft] *pt, pp of* **leave** ♦ *adj* gauche ♦ *adv* à gauche ♦ *n* gauche *f*; **on the ~, to the ~** à gauche; **the L~** (*POL*) la gauche.
left-click *vi* faire un clic gauche ♦ *vt* faire un clic gauche sur.
left-hand drive ['lɛfthænd-] *n* (*BRIT*) conduite *f* à gauche.
left-handed [lɛft'hændɪd] *adj* gaucher(ère); (*scissors etc*) pour gauchers.
left-hand side ['lɛfthænd-] *n* gauche *f*, côté *m* gauche.
leftie ['lɛftɪ] *n* (*col*) gaucho *m/f*, gauchiste *m/f*.
leftist ['lɛftɪst] *adj* (*POL*) gauchiste, de gauche.
left-luggage (office) [lɛft'lʌgɪdʒ(-)] *n* (*BRIT*) consigne *f*.
left-overs ['lɛftəuvəz] *npl* restes *mpl*.
left wing *n* (*MIL, SPORT*) aile *f* gauche; (*POL*) gauche *f* ♦ *adj*: **left-wing** (*POL*) de gauche.
left-winger ['lɛft'wɪŋgə*] *n* (*POL*) membre *m* de la gauche; (*SPORT*) ailier *m* gauche.
lefty ['lɛftɪ] *n* (*col*) = **leftie**.
leg [lɛg] *n* jambe *f*; (*of animal*) patte *f*; (*of furniture*) pied *m*; (*CULIN: of chicken*) cuisse *f*; **lst/2nd ~** (*SPORT*) match *m* aller/retour; (*of journey*) 1ère/2ème étape; **~ of lamb** (*CULIN*) gigot *m* d'agneau; **to stretch one's ~s** se dégourdir les jambes.
legacy ['lɛgəsɪ] *n* (*also fig*) héritage *m*, legs *m*.
legal ['liːgl] *adj* légal(e); **to take ~ action** *or* **proceedings against sb** poursuivre qn en justice.
legal adviser *n* conseiller/ère juridique.
legality [lɪ'gælɪtɪ] *n* légalité *f*.
legalize ['liːgəlaɪz] *vt* légaliser.
legally ['liːgəlɪ] *adv* légalement; **~ binding** juridiquement contraignant(e).
legal tender *n* monnaie légale.
legation [lɪ'geɪʃən] *n* légation *f*.
legend ['lɛdʒənd] *n* légende *f*.
legendary ['lɛdʒəndərɪ] *adj* légendaire.
-legged ['lɛgɪd] *suffix*: **two~** à deux pattes (*or* jambes *or* pieds).
leggings ['lɛgɪŋz] *npl* jambières *fpl*, guêtres *fpl*.
leggy ['lɛgɪ] *adj* aux longues jambes.
legibility [lɛdʒɪ'bɪlɪtɪ] *n* lisibilité *f*.
legible ['lɛdʒəbl] *adj* lisible.
legibly ['lɛdʒəblɪ] *adv* lisiblement.
legion ['liːdʒən] *n* légion *f*.
legionnaire [liːdʒə'nɛə*] *n* légionnaire *m*; **~'s disease** maladie *f* du légionnaire.
legislate ['lɛdʒɪsleɪt] *vi* légiférer.
legislation [lɛdʒɪs'leɪʃən] *n* législation *f*; **a piece of ~** un texte de loi.
legislative ['lɛdʒɪslətɪv] *adj* législatif(ive).
legislator ['lɛdʒɪsleɪtə*] *n* législateur/trice.
legislature ['lɛdʒɪslətʃə*] *n* corps législatif.
legitimacy [lɪ'dʒɪtɪməsɪ] *n* légitimité *f*.
legitimate [lɪ'dʒɪtɪmət] *adj* légitime.
legitimize [lɪ'dʒɪtɪmaɪz] *vt* légitimer.
legless ['lɛglɪs] *adj* (*BRIT col*) bourré(e).
leg-room ['lɛgruːm] *n* place *f* pour les jambes.
leisure ['lɛʒə*] *n* (*time*) loisir *m*, temps *m*; (*free time*) temps libre, loisirs *mpl*; **at ~** (tout) à loisir; à tête reposée.

leisure centre *n* centre *m* de loisirs.
leisurely ['lɛʒəlɪ] *adj* tranquille; fait(e) sans se presser.
leisure suit *n* (*BRIT*) survêtement *m* (mode).
lemon ['lɛmən] *n* citron *m*.
lemonade [lɛmə'neɪd] *n* limonade *f*.
lemon cheese *n*, **lemon curd** *n* crème *f* de citron.
lemon juice *n* jus *m* de citron.
lemon squeezer [-skwiːzə*] *n* presse-citron *m inv*.
lemon tea *n* thé *m* au citron.
lend, *pt, pp* **lent** [lɛnd, lɛnt] *vt*: **to ~ sth (to sb)** prêter qch (à qn); **to ~ a hand** donner un coup de main.
lender ['lɛndə*] *n* prêteur/euse.
lending library ['lɛndɪŋ-] *n* bibliothèque *f* de prêt.
length [lɛŋθ] *n* longueur *f*; (*section: of road, pipe etc*) morceau *m*, bout *m*; **~ of time** durée *f*; **what ~ is it?** quelle longueur fait-il?; **it is 2 metres in ~** cela fait 2 mètres de long; **to fall full ~** tomber de tout son long; **at ~** (*at last*) enfin, à la fin; (*lengthily*) longuement; **to go to any ~(s) to do sth** faire n'importe quoi pour faire qch, ne reculer devant rien pour faire qch.
lengthen ['lɛŋθn] *vt* allonger, prolonger ♦ *vi* s'allonger.
lengthways ['lɛŋθweɪz] *adv* dans le sens de la longueur, en long.
lengthy ['lɛŋθɪ] *adj* (très) long(longue).
leniency ['liːnɪənsɪ] *n* indulgence *f*, clémence *f*.
lenient ['liːnɪənt] *adj* indulgent(e), clément(e).
leniently ['liːnɪəntlɪ] *adv* avec indulgence *or* clémence.
lens [lɛnz] *n* lentille *f*; (*of spectacles*) verre *m*; (*of camera*) objectif *m*.
Lent [lɛnt] *n* carême *m*.
lent [lɛnt] *pt, pp of* **lend**.
lentil ['lɛntl] *n* lentille *f*.
Leo ['liːəu] *n* le Lion; **to be ~** être du Lion.
leopard ['lɛpəd] *n* léopard *m*.
leotard ['liːətɑːd] *n* maillot *m* (*de danseur etc*).
leper ['lɛpə*] *n* lépreux/euse.
leper colony *n* léproserie *f*.
leprosy ['lɛprəsɪ] *n* lèpre *f*.
lesbian ['lɛzbɪən] *n* lesbienne *f* ♦ *adj* lesbien(ne).
lesion ['liːʒən] *n* (*MED*) lésion *f*.
Lesotho [lɪ'suːtuː] *n* Lesotho *m*.
less [lɛs] *adj* moins de ♦ *pron, adv* moins; **~ than that/you** moins que cela/vous; **~ than half** moins de la moitié; **~ than one/a kilo/3 metres** moins de un/d'un kilo/de 3 mètres; **~ and ~** de moins en moins; **the ~ he works ...** moins il travaille ....
lessee [lɛ'siː] *n* locataire *m/f* (à bail), preneur/euse du bail.
lessen ['lɛsn] *vi* diminuer, s'amoindrir, s'atténuer ♦ *vt* diminuer, réduire, atténuer.
lesser ['lɛsə*] *adj* moindre; **to a ~ extent** *or* **degree** à un degré moindre.
lesson ['lɛsn] *n* leçon *f*; **a maths ~** une leçon *or* un cours de maths; **to give ~s in** donner des cours de; **it taught him a ~** (*fig*) cela lui a servi de leçon.
lessor ['lɛsɔː*, lɛ'sɔː*] *n* bailleur/eresse.
lest [lɛst] *conj* de peur de + *infinitive*, de peur que + *sub*.
let, *pt, pp* **let** [lɛt] *vt* laisser; (*BRIT*: *lease*) louer; **to ~ sb do sth** laisser qn faire qch; **to ~ sb know sth** faire savoir qch à qn, prévenir qn de qch; **he ~ me go** il m'a laissé partir; **~ the water boil and ...** faites bouillir l'eau et ...; **~'s go** allons-y; **~ him come** qu'il vienne; **"to ~"** (*BRIT*) "à louer".
►**let down** *vt* (*lower*) baisser; (*dress*) rallonger; (*hair*) défaire; (*BRIT*: *tyre*) dégonfler; (*disappoint*) décevoir.
►**let go** *vi* lâcher prise ♦ *vt* lâcher.
►**let in** *vt* laisser entrer; (*visitor etc*) faire entrer; **what have you ~ yourself in for?** à quoi t'es-tu engagé?
►**let off** *vt* (*allow to leave*) laisser partir; (*not punish*) ne pas punir; (*subj: taxi driver, bus driver*) déposer; (*firework etc*) faire partir; (*smell etc*) dégager; **to ~ off steam** (*fig*: *col*) se défouler, décharger sa rate *or* bile.
►**let on** *vi* (*col*): **to ~ on that ...** révéler que ..., dire que ....
►**let out** *vt* laisser sortir; (*dress*) élargir; (*scream*) laisser échapper; (*rent out*) louer.
►**let up** *vi* diminuer, s'arrêter.
let-down ['lɛtdaun] *n* (*disappointment*) déception *f*.
lethal ['liːθl] *adj* mortel(le), fatal(e).
lethargic [lɛ'θɑːdʒɪk] *adj* léthargique.
lethargy ['lɛθədʒɪ] *n* léthargie *f*.
letter ['lɛtə*] *n* lettre *f*; **~s** *npl* (*LITERATURE*) lettres; **small/capital ~** minuscule *f*/majuscule *f*; **~ of credit** lettre *f* de crédit.
letter bomb *n* lettre piégée.
letterbox ['lɛtəbɔks] *n* (*BRIT*) boîte *f* aux *or* à lettres.
letterhead ['lɛtəhɛd] *n* en-tête *m*.
lettering ['lɛtərɪŋ] *n* lettres *fpl*; caractères *mpl*.
letter opener *n* coupe-papier *m*.
letterpress ['lɛtəprɛs] *n* (*method*) typographie *f*.
letter quality *n* qualité *f* "courrier".
letters patent *npl* brevet *m* d'invention.
lettuce ['lɛtɪs] *n* laitue *f*, salade *f*.
let-up ['lɛtʌp] *n* répit *m*, détente *f*.
leukaemia, (*US*) **leukemia** [luː'kiːmɪə] *n* leucémie *f*.
level ['lɛvl] *adj* plat(e), plan(e), uni(e); horizontal(e) ♦ *n* niveau *m*; (*flat place*) terrain plat; (*also*: **spirit ~**) niveau à bulle ♦ *vt* niveler, aplanir; (*gun*) pointer, braquer; (*accusation*): **to ~ (against)** lancer *or* porter (contre) ♦ *vi* (*col*): **to ~ with sb** être franc(franche) avec qn; **"A" ~s** *npl* (*BRIT*: *for-*

merly) ≈ baccalauréat *m*; **"O" ~s** *npl* (*BRIT: formerly*) *examens passés à l'âge de 16 ans sanctionnant les connaissances de l'élève*, ≈ brevet *m* des collèges; **a ~ spoonful** (*CULIN*) une cuillerée à raser; **to be ~ with** être au même niveau que; **to draw ~ with** (*team*) arriver à égalité de points avec, égaliser avec; arriver au même classement que; (*runner, car*) arriver à la hauteur de, rattra- per; **on the ~** à l'horizontale; (*fig: honest*) régulier(ière).

▸**level off**, **level out** *vi* (*prices etc*) se stabiliser ♦ *vt* (*ground*) aplanir, niveler.

level crossing *n* (*BRIT*) passage *m* à niveau.

level-headed [lɛvl'hɛdɪd] *adj* équilibré(e).

levelling, (*US*) **leveling** ['lɛvlɪŋ] *adj* (*process, effect*) de nivellement.

level playing field *n*: **to compete on a ~** jouer sur un terrain d'égalité.

lever ['liːvə*] *n* levier *m* ♦ *vt*: **to ~ up/out** soulever/extraire au moyen d'un levier.

leverage ['liːvərɪdʒ] *n*: **~ (on or with)** prise *f* (sur).

levity ['lɛvɪtɪ] *n* manque *m* de sérieux, légèreté *f*.

levy ['lɛvɪ] *n* taxe *f*, impôt *m* ♦ *vt* prélever, imposer; percevoir.

lewd [luːd] *adj* obscène, lubrique.

lexicographer [lɛksɪ'kɔgrəfə*] *n* lexicographe *m/f*.

lexicography [lɛksɪ'kɔgrəfɪ] *n* lexicographie *f*.

LGV *n abbr* (= *Large Goods Vehicle*) poids lourd.

LI *abbr* (*US*) = *Long Island*.

liabilities [laɪə'bɪlətɪz] *npl* (*COMM*) obligations *fpl*, engagements *mpl*; (*on balance sheet*) passif *m*.

liability [laɪə'bɪlətɪ] *n* responsabilité *f*; (*handicap*) handicap *m*.

liable ['laɪəbl] *adj* (*subject*): **~ to** sujet(te) à; passible de; (*responsible*): **~ (for)** responsable (de); (*likely*): **~ to do** susceptible de faire; **to be ~ to a fine** être passible d'une amende.

liaise [liː'eɪz] *vi*: **to ~ with** rester en liaison avec.

liaison [liː'eɪzɔn] *n* liaison *f*.

liar ['laɪə*] *n* menteur/euse.

libel ['laɪbl] *n* écrit *m* diffamatoire; diffamation *f* ♦ *vt* diffamer.

libellous ['laɪbləs] *adj* diffamatoire.

liberal ['lɪbərl] *adj* libéral(e); (*generous*): **~ with** prodigue de, généreux(euse) avec ♦ *n*: **L~** (*POL*) libéral/e.

Liberal Democrat *n* démocrate *m/f*.

liberality [lɪbə'rælɪtɪ] *n* (*generosity*) générosité *f*, libéralité *f*.

liberalize ['lɪbərəlaɪz] *vt* libéraliser.

liberal-minded ['lɪbərl'maɪndɪd] *adj* libéral(e), tolérant(e).

liberate ['lɪbəreɪt] *vt* libérer.

liberation [lɪbə'reɪʃən] *n* libération *f*.

liberation theology *n* théologie *f* de libération.

Liberia [laɪ'bɪərɪə] *n* Libéria *m*, Liberia *m*.

Liberian [laɪ'bɪərɪən] *adj* libérien(ne) ♦ *n* Libérien/ne.

liberty ['lɪbətɪ] *n* liberté *f*; **at ~ to do** libre de faire; **to take the ~ of** prendre la liberté de, se permettre de.

libido [lɪ'biːdəu] *n* libido *f*.

Libra ['liːbrə] *n* la Balance; **to be ~** être de la Balance.

librarian [laɪ'brɛərɪən] *n* bibliothécaire *m/f*.

library ['laɪbrərɪ] *n* bibliothèque *f*.

library book *n* livre *m* de bibliothèque.

libretto [lɪ'brɛtəu] *n* livret *m*.

Libya ['lɪbɪə] *n* Libye *f*.

Libyan ['lɪbɪən] *adj* libyen(ne), de Libye ♦ *n* Libyen/ne.

lice [laɪs] *npl of* **louse**.

licence, (*US*) **license** ['laɪsns] *n* autorisation *f*, permis *m*; (*COMM*) licence *f*; (*RADIO, TV*) redevance *f*; (*also*: **driving ~**, (*US*) **driver's ~**) permis *m* (de conduire); (*excessive freedom*) licence; **import ~** licence d'importation; **produced under ~** fabriqué(e) sous licence.

licence number *n* (*BRIT AUT*) numéro *m* d'immatriculation.

license ['laɪsns] *n* (*US*) = **licence** ♦ *vt* donner une licence à; (*car*) acheter la vignette de; délivrer la vignette de.

licensed ['laɪsnst] *adj* (*for alcohol*) patenté(e) pour la vente des spiritueux, qui a une patente de débit de boissons.

licensee [laɪsən'siː] *n* (*BRIT: of pub*) patron/ne, gérant/e.

license plate *n* (*esp US AUT*) plaque *f* minéralogique.

licentious [laɪ'sɛnʃəs] *adj* licentieux(euse).

lichen ['laɪkən] *n* lichen *m*.

lick [lɪk] *vt* lécher; (*col: defeat*) écraser, flanquer une piquette *or* raclée à ♦ *n* coup *m* de langue; **a ~ of paint** un petit coup de peinture.

licorice ['lɪkərɪs] *n* = **liquorice**.

lid [lɪd] *n* couvercle *m*; **to take the ~ off sth** (*fig*) exposer *or* étaler qch au grand jour.

lido ['laɪdəu] *n* piscine *f* en plein air; complexe *m* balnéaire.

lie [laɪ] *n* mensonge *m* ♦ *vi* mentir; (*pt* **lay**, *pp* **lain** [leɪ, leɪn]) (*rest*) être étendu(e) *or* allongé(e) *or* couché(e); (*in grave*) être enterré(e), reposer; (*of object: be situated*) se trouver, être; **to ~ low** (*fig*) se cacher, rester caché(e); **to tell ~s** mentir.

▸**lie about**, **lie around** *vi* (*things*) traîner; (*person*) traînasser, flemmarder.

▸**lie back** *vi* se renverser en arrière.

▸**lie down** *vi* se coucher, s'étendre.

▸**lie up** *vi* (*hide*) se cacher.

Liechtenstein ['lɪktənstaɪn] *n* Liechtenstein *m*.

lie detector *n* détecteur *m* de mensonges.

lie-down ['laɪdaun] *n* (*BRIT*): **to have a ~** s'al-

longer, se reposer.
lie-in ['laɪɪn] *n* (*BRIT*): **to have a** ~ faire la grasse matinée.
lieu [luː]: **in** ~ **of** *prep* au lieu de, à la place de.
Lieut. *abbr* (= *lieutenant*) Lt.
lieutenant [lɛf'tɛnənt, (*US*) luː'tɛnənt] *n* lieutenant *m*.
lieutenant-colonel [lɛf'tɛnənt'kəːnl, (*US*) luː'tɛnənt'kəːnl] *n* lieutenant-colonel *m*.
life, *pl* **lives** [laɪf, laɪvz] *n* vie *f* ♦ *cpd* de vie; de la vie; à vie; **true to** ~ réaliste, fidèle à la réalité; **to paint from** ~ peindre d'après nature; **to be sent to prison for** ~ être condamné(e) (à la réclusion criminelle) à perpétuité; **country/city** ~ la vie à la campagne/à la ville.
life annuity *n* pension *f*, rente viagère.
life assurance *n* (*BRIT*) = **life insurance**.
lifebelt ['laɪfbɛlt] *n* (*BRIT*) bouée *f* de sauvetage.
lifeblood ['laɪfblʌd] *n* (*fig*) élément moteur.
lifeboat ['laɪfbəut] *n* canot *m or* chaloupe *f* de sauvetage.
lifebuoy ['laɪfbɔɪ] *n* bouée *f* de sauvetage.
life expectancy *n* espérance *f* de vie.
lifeguard ['laɪfgɑːd] *n* surveillant *m* de baignade.
life imprisonment *n* prison *f* à vie; (*LAW*) réclusion *f* à perpétuité.
life insurance *n* assurance-vie *f*.
life jacket *n* gilet *m or* ceinture *f* de sauvetage.
lifeless ['laɪflɪs] *adj* sans vie, inanimé(e); (*dull*) qui manque de vie *or* de vigueur.
lifelike ['laɪflaɪk] *adj* qui semble vrai(e) *or* vivant(e); ressemblant(e).
lifeline ['laɪflaɪn] *n* corde *f* de sauvetage.
lifelong ['laɪflɔŋ] *adj* de toute une vie, de toujours.
life preserver [-prɪ'zəːvə*] *n* (*US*) gilet *m or* ceinture *f* de sauvetage.
lifer ['laɪfə*] *n* (*col*) condamné/e à perpète.
life-raft ['laɪfrɑːft] *n* radeau *m* de sauvetage.
life-saver ['laɪfseɪvə*] *n* surveillant *m* de baignade.
life sentence *n* condamnation *f* à vie *or* à perpétuité.
life-sized ['laɪfsaɪzd] *adj* grandeur nature *inv*.
life span *n* (durée *f* de) vie *f*.
life style *n* style *m* de vie.
life support system *n* (*MED*) respirateur artificiel.
lifetime ['laɪftaɪm] *n*: **in his** ~ de son vivant; **the chance of a** ~ la chance de ma (*or* sa *etc*) vie, une occasion unique.
lift [lɪft] *vt* soulever, lever; (*steal*) prendre, voler ♦ *vi* (*fog*) se lever ♦ *n* (*BRIT*: *elevator*) ascenseur *m*; **to give sb a** ~ (*BRIT*) emmener *or* prendre qn en voiture.
►**lift off** *vi* (*rocket, helicopter*) décoller.
►**lift out** *vt* sortir; (*troops, evacuees etc*) évacuer par avion *or* hélicoptère.
►**lift up** *vt* soulever.
lift-off ['lɪftɔf] *n* décollage *m*.
ligament ['lɪgəmənt] *n* ligament *m*.
light [laɪt] *n* lumière *f*; (*daylight*) lumière, jour *m*; (*lamp*) lampe *f*; (*AUT*: *traffic* ~, *rear* ~) feu *m*; (: *headlamp*) phare *m*; (*for cigarette etc*): **have you got a** ~? avez-vous du feu? ♦ *vt* (*pt, pp* **lighted** *or* **lit** [lɪt]) (*candle, cigarette, fire*) allumer; (*room*) éclairer ♦ *adj* (*room, colour*) clair(e); (*not heavy, also fig*) léger(ère) ♦ *adv* (*travel*) avec peu de bagages; **to turn the** ~ **on/off** allumer/éteindre; **to cast** *or* **shed** *or* **throw** ~ **on** éclaircir; **to come to** ~ être dévoilé(e) *or* découvert(e); **in the** ~ **of** à la lumière de; étant donné; **to make** ~ **of sth** (*fig*) prendre qch à la légère, faire peu de cas de qch.
►**light up** *vi* s'allumer; (*face*) s'éclairer ♦ *vt* (*illuminate*) éclairer, illuminer.
light bulb *n* ampoule *f*.
lighten ['laɪtn] *vi* s'éclairer ♦ *vt* (*give light to*) éclairer; (*make lighter*) éclaircir; (*make less heavy*) alléger.
lighter ['laɪtə*] *n* (*also*: **cigarette** ~) briquet *m*; (: *in car*) allume-cigare *m inv*; (*boat*) péniche *f*.
light-fingered [laɪt'fɪŋgəd] *adj* chapardeur(euse).
light-headed [laɪt'hɛdɪd] *adj* étourdi(e), écervelé(e).
light-hearted [laɪt'hɑːtɪd] *adj* gai(e), joyeux(euse), enjoué(e).
lighthouse ['laɪthaus] *n* phare *m*.
lighting ['laɪtɪŋ] *n* (*on road*) éclairage *m*; (*in theatre*) éclairages.
lighting-up time [laɪtɪŋ'ʌp-] *n* (*BRIT*) *heure officielle de la tombée du jour*.
lightly ['laɪtlɪ] *adv* légèrement; **to get off** ~ s'en tirer à bon compte.
light meter *n* (*PHOT*) photomètre *m*, cellule *f*.
lightness ['laɪtnɪs] *n* clarté *f*; (*in weight*) légèreté *f*.
lightning ['laɪtnɪŋ] *n* éclair *m*, foudre *f*.
lightning conductor, (*US*) **lightning rod** *n* paratonnerre *m*.
lightning strike *n* (*BRIT*) grève *f* surprise.
light pen *n* crayon *m* optique.
lightship ['laɪtʃɪp] *n* bateau-phare *m*.
lightweight ['laɪtweɪt] *adj* (*suit*) léger(ère); (*boxer*) poids léger *inv*.
light year ['laɪtjɪə*] *n* année-lumière *f*.
like [laɪk] *vt* aimer (bien) ♦ *prep* comme ♦ *adj* semblable, pareil(le) ♦ *n*: **the** ~ un(e) pareil(le) *or* semblable; le(la) pareil(le); (*pej*) (d')autres du même genre *or* acabit; **his** ~**s and dislikes** ses goûts *mpl or* préférences *fpl*; **I would** ~, **I'd** ~ je voudrais, j'aimerais; **would you** ~ **a coffee?** voulez-vous du café?; **to be/look** ~ **sb/sth** ressembler à qn/qch; **what's he** ~? comment est-il?; **what's the weather** ~? quel temps fait-il?; **that's just** ~ **him** c'est bien de lui, ça lui ressemble; **something** ~ **that** quelque chose comme ça;

I feel ~ a drink je boirais bien quelque chose; **if you ~** si vous voulez; **there's nothing ~ ...** il n'y a rien de tel que ....
likeable ['laɪkəbl] *adj* sympathique, agréable.
likelihood ['laɪklɪhud] *n* probabilité *f*; **in all ~** selon toute vraisemblance.
likely ['laɪklɪ] *adj* (*result, outcome*) probable; (*excuse*) plausible; **he's ~ to leave** il va sûrement partir, il risque fort de partir; **not ~!** (*col*) pas de danger!
like-minded ['laɪk'maɪndɪd] *adj* de même opinion.
liken ['laɪkən] *vt*: **to ~ sth to** comparer qch à.
likeness ['laɪknɪs] *n* ressemblance *f*.
likewise ['laɪkwaɪz] *adv* de même, pareillement.
liking ['laɪkɪŋ] *n* affection *f*, penchant *m*; goût *m*; **to take a ~ to sb** se prendre d'amitié pour qn; **to be to sb's ~** être au goût de qn, plaire à qn.
lilac ['laɪlək] *n* lilas *m* ♦ *adj* lilas *inv*.
Lilo ['laɪləu] *n* ® matelas *m* pneumatique.
lilt [lɪlt] *n* rythme *m*, cadence *f*.
lilting ['lɪltɪŋ] *adj* aux cadences mélodieuses; chantant(e).
lily ['lɪlɪ] *n* lis *m*; **~ of the valley** muguet *m*.
Lima ['li:mə] *n* Lima.
limb [lɪm] *n* membre *m*; **to be out on a ~** (*fig*) être isolé(e).
limber ['lɪmbə*]: **to ~ up** *vi* se dégourdir, se mettre en train.
limbo ['lɪmbəu] *n*: **to be in ~** (*fig*) être tombé(e) dans l'oubli.
lime [laɪm] *n* (*tree*) tilleul *m*; (*fruit*) citron vert, lime *f*; (*GEO*) chaux *f*.
lime juice *n* jus *m* de citron vert.
limelight ['laɪmlaɪt] *n*: **in the ~** (*fig*) en vedette, au premier plan.
limerick ['lɪmərɪk] *n* petit poème humoristique.
limestone ['laɪmstəun] *n* pierre *f* à chaux; (*GEO*) calcaire *m*.
limit ['lɪmɪt] *n* limite *f* ♦ *vt* limiter; **weight/speed ~** limite de poids/de vitesse.
limitation [lɪmɪ'teɪʃən] *n* limitation *f*, restriction *f*.
limited ['lɪmɪtɪd] *adj* limité(e), restreint(e); **~ edition** édition *f* à tirage limité.
limited (liability) company (Ltd) *n* (*BRIT*) ≈ société *f* anonyme (SA).
limitless ['lɪmɪtlɪs] *adj* illimité(e).
limousine ['lɪməzi:n] *n* limousine *f*.
limp [lɪmp] *n*: **to have a ~** boiter ♦ *vi* boiter ♦ *adj* mou(molle).
limpet ['lɪmpɪt] *n* patelle *f*; **like a ~** (*fig*) comme une ventouse.
limpid ['lɪmpɪd] *adj* limpide.
linchpin ['lɪntʃpɪn] *n* esse *f*; (*fig*) pivot *m*.
Lincs [lɪŋks] *abbr* (*BRIT*) = *Lincolnshire*.
line [laɪn] *n* (*gen*) ligne *f*; (*rope*) corde *f*; (*wire*) fil *m*; (*of poem*) vers *m*; (*row, series*) rangée *f*; file *f*, queue *f*; (*COMM: series of goods*) article(s) *m(pl)*, ligne de produits ♦ *vt* (*clothes*): **to ~ (with)** doubler (de); (*box*): **to ~ (with)** garnir *or* tapisser (de); (*subj: trees, crowd*) border; **to cut in ~** (*US*) passer avant son tour; **in his ~ of business** dans sa partie, dans son rayon; **on the right ~s** sur la bonne voie; **a new ~ in cosmetics** une nouvelle ligne de produits de beauté; **hold the ~ please** (*BRIT TEL*) ne quittez pas; **to be in ~ for sth** (*fig*) être en lice pour qch; **in ~ with** en accord avec, en conformité avec; **to bring sth into ~ with sth** aligner qch sur qch; **to draw the ~ at (doing) sth** (*fig*) se refuser à (faire) qch; ne pas tolérer *or* admettre (qu'on fasse) qch; **to take the ~ that ...** être d'avis *or* de l'opinion que ....
►**line up** *vi* s'aligner, se mettre en rang(s) ♦ *vt* aligner; (*set up, have ready*) prévoir; trouver; **to have sb/sth ~d up** avoir qn/qch en vue *or* de prévu(e).
linear ['lɪnɪə*] *adj* linéaire.
lined [laɪnd] *adj* (*paper*) réglé(e); (*face*) marqué(e), ridé(e); (*clothes*) doublé(e).
line feed *n* (*COMPUT*) interligne *m*.
lineman ['laɪnmən] *n* (*US: RAIL*) poseur *m* de rails; (*: TEL*) ouvrier *m* de ligne; (*: FOOTBALL*) avant *m*.
linen ['lɪnɪn] *n* linge *m* (de corps *or* de maison); (*cloth*) lin *m*.
line printer *n* imprimante *f* (ligne par) ligne.
liner ['laɪnə*] *n* paquebot *m* de ligne.
linesman ['laɪnzmən] *n* (*TENNIS*) juge *m* de ligne; (*FOOTBALL*) juge de touche.
line-up ['laɪnʌp] *n* file *f*; (*also*: **police ~**) parade *f* d'identification; (*SPORT*) (composition *f* de l')équipe *f*.
linger ['lɪŋgə*] *vi* s'attarder; traîner; (*smell, tradition*) persister.
lingerie ['lænʒəri:] *n* lingerie *f*.
lingering ['lɪŋgərɪŋ] *adj* persistant(e); qui subsiste; (*death*) lent(e).
lingo, ~es ['lɪŋgəu] *n* (*pej*) jargon *m*.
linguist ['lɪŋgwɪst] *n* linguiste *m/f*; personne douée pour les langues.
linguistic [lɪŋ'gwɪstɪk] *adj* linguistique.
linguistics [lɪŋ'gwɪstɪks] *n* linguistique *f*.
lining ['laɪnɪŋ] *n* doublure *f*; (*TECH*) revêtement *m*; (*: of brakes*) garniture *f*.
link [lɪŋk] *n* (*of a chain*) maillon *m*; (*connection*) lien *m*, rapport *m* ♦ *vt* relier, lier, unir; **rail ~** liaison *f* ferroviaire.
►**link up** *vt* relier ♦ *vi* se rejoindre; s'associer.
links [lɪŋks] *npl* (terrain *m* de) golf *m*.
link-up ['lɪŋkʌp] *n* lien *m*, rapport *m*; (*of roads*) jonction *f*, raccordement *m*; (*of spaceships*) arrimage *m*; (*RADIO, TV*) liaison *f*; (*: programme*) duplex *m*.
linoleum [lɪ'nəulɪəm] *n* linoléum *m*.
linseed oil ['lɪnsi:d-] *n* huile *f* de lin.
lint [lɪnt] *n* tissu ouaté (*pour pansements*).
lintel ['lɪntl] *n* linteau *m*.
lion ['laɪən] *n* lion *m*.

lion cub *n* lionceau *m*.
lioness ['laɪənɪs] *n* lionne *f*.
lip [lɪp] *n* lèvre *f*; (*of cup etc*) rebord *m*; (*insolence*) insolences *fpl*.
liposuction ['lɪpəusʌkʃən] *n* liposuccion *f*.
lipread ['lɪpri:d] *vi* lire sur les lèvres.
lip salve [-sælv] *n* pommade *f* pour les lèvres, pommade rosat.
lip service *n*: **to pay ~ to sth** ne reconnaître le mérite de qch que pour la forme *or* qu'en paroles.
lipstick ['lɪpstɪk] *n* rouge *m* à lèvres.
liquefy ['lɪkwɪfaɪ] *vt* liquéfier ♦ *vi* se liquéfier.
liqueur [lɪ'kjuə*] *n* liqueur *f*.
liquid ['lɪkwɪd] *n* liquide *m* ♦ *adj* liquide.
liquid assets *npl* liquidités *fpl*, disponibilités *fpl*.
liquidate ['lɪkwɪdeɪt] *vt* liquider.
liquidation [lɪkwɪ'deɪʃən] *n* liquidation *f*; **to go into ~** déposer son bilan.
liquidator ['lɪkwɪdeɪtə*] *n* liquidateur *m*.
liquid crystal display (LCD) *n* affichage *m* à cristaux liquides.
liquidize ['lɪkwɪdaɪz] *vt* (*BRIT CULIN*) passer au mixer.
liquidizer ['lɪkwɪdaɪzə*] *n* (*BRIT CULIN*) mixer *m*.
liquor ['lɪkə*] *n* spiritueux *m*, alcool *m*.
liquorice ['lɪkərɪs] *n* (*BRIT*) réglisse *m*.
Lisbon ['lɪzbən] *n* Lisbonne.
lisp [lɪsp] *n* zézaiement *m*.
lissom ['lɪsəm] *adj* souple, agile.
list [lɪst] *n* liste *f*; (*of ship*) inclinaison *f* ♦ *vt* (*write down*) inscrire; faire la liste de; (*enumerate*) énumérer; (*COMPUT*) lister ♦ *vi* (*ship*) gîter, donner de la bande; **shopping ~** liste des courses.
listed building ['lɪstɪd-] *n* monument classé.
listed company ['lɪstɪd-] *n* société cotée en Bourse.
listen ['lɪsn] *vi* écouter; **to ~ to** écouter.
listener ['lɪsnə*] *n* auditeur/trice.
listeria [lɪs'tɪərɪə] *n* listéria *f*.
listing ['lɪstɪŋ] *n* (*COMPUT*) listage *m*; (*: hard copy*) liste *f*, listing *m*.
listless ['lɪstlɪs] *adj* indolent(e), apathique.
listlessly ['lɪstlɪslɪ] *adv* avec indolence *or* apathie.
list price *n* prix *m* de catalogue.
lit [lɪt] *pt, pp of* **light**.
litany ['lɪtənɪ] *n* litanie *f*.
liter ['li:tə*] *n* (*US*) = **litre**.
literacy ['lɪtərəsɪ] *n* degré *m* d'alphabétisation, fait *m* de savoir lire et écrire; (*BRIT SCOL*) éducation littéraire *f*.
literal ['lɪtərl] *adj* littéral(e).
literally ['lɪtrəlɪ] *adv* littéralement.
literary ['lɪtərərɪ] *adj* littéraire.
literate ['lɪtərət] *adj* qui sait lire et écrire, instruit(e).
literature ['lɪtrɪtʃə*] *n* littérature *f*, (*brochures etc*) copie *f* publicitaire, prospectus *mpl*.
lithe [laɪð] *adj* agile, souple.
lithography [lɪ'θɔgrəfɪ] *n* lithographie *f*.
Lithuania [lɪθju'eɪnɪə] *n* Lituanie *f*.
Lithuanian [lɪθju'eɪnɪən] *adj* lituanien(ne) ♦ *n* Lituanien/ne; (*LING*) lituanien *m*.
litigate ['lɪtɪgeɪt] *vt* mettre en litige ♦ *vi* plaider.
litigation [lɪtɪ'geɪʃən] *n* litige *m*; contentieux *m*.
litmus ['lɪtməs] *n*: **~ paper** papier *m* de tournesol.
litre, (*US*) **liter** ['li:tə*] *n* litre *m*.
litter ['lɪtə*] *n* (*rubbish*) détritus *mpl*, ordures *fpl*; (*young animals*) portée *f* ♦ *vt* éparpiller; laisser des détritus dans; **~ed with** jonché(e) de, couvert(e) de.
litter bin *n* (*BRIT*) boîte *f* à ordures, poubelle *f*.
litter lout, (*US*) **litterbug** ['lɪtəbʌg] *n personne qui jette des détritus par terre*.
little ['lɪtl] *adj* (*small*) petit(e); (*not much*): **it's ~** c'est peu ♦ *adv* peu; **~ milk** peu de lait; **a ~** un peu (de); **a ~ milk** un peu de lait; **for a ~ while** pendant un petit moment; **with ~ difficulty** sans trop de difficulté; **as ~ as possible** le moins possible; **~ by ~** petit à petit, peu à peu; **to make ~ of** faire peu de cas de.
little-known ['lɪtl'nəun] *adj* peu connu(e).
liturgy ['lɪtədʒɪ] *n* liturgie *f*.
live *vi* [lɪv] vivre; (*reside*) vivre, habiter ♦ *adj* [laɪv] (*animal*) vivant(e), en vie; (*wire*) sous tension; (*broadcast*) (transmis(e)) en direct; (*issue*) d'actualité, brûlant(e); (*unexploded*) non explosé(e); **to ~ in London** habiter (à) Londres; **to ~ together** vivre ensemble, cohabiter; **~ ammunition** munitions *fpl* de combat.
▸**live down** *vt* faire oublier (avec le temps).
▸**live in** *vi* être logé(e) et nourri(e); être interne.
▸**live off** *vt* (*land, fish etc*) vivre de; (*pej: parents etc*) vivre aux crochets de.
▸**live on** *vt fus* (*food*) vivre de ♦ *vi* survivre; **to ~ on £50 a week** vivre avec 50 livres par semaine.
▸**live out** *vi* (*BRIT: students*) être externe ♦ *vt*: **to ~ out one's days** *or* **life** passer sa vie.
▸**live up** *vt*: **to ~ it up** (*col*) faire la fête; mener la grande vie.
▸**live up to** *vt fus* se montrer à la hauteur de.
live-in ['lɪvɪn] *adj* (*nanny*) à demeure; **~ partner** concubin/e.
livelihood ['laɪvlɪhud] *n* moyens *mpl* d'existence.
liveliness ['laɪvlɪnəs] *n* vivacité *f*, entrain *m*.
lively ['laɪvlɪ] *adj* vif(vive), plein(e) d'entrain.
liven up ['laɪvn-] *vt* (*room etc*) égayer; (*discussion, evening*) animer.
liver ['lɪvə*] *n* foie *m*.
liverish ['lɪvərɪʃ] *adj* qui a mal au foie; (*fig*) grincheux(euse).
Liverpudlian [lɪvə'pʌdlɪən] *adj* de Liverpool

♦ *n* habitant/e de Liverpool; natif/ive de Liverpool.
livery ['lɪvərɪ] *n* livrée *f*.
lives [laɪvz] *npl of* **life**.
livestock ['laɪvstɔk] *n* cheptel *m*, bétail *m*.
live wire [laɪv-] *n* (*col, fig*): **to be a (real)** ~ péter le feu.
livid ['lɪvɪd] *adj* livide, blafard(e); (*furious*) furieux(euse), furibond(e).
living ['lɪvɪŋ] *adj* vivant(e), en vie ♦ *n*: **to earn** *or* **make a** ~ gagner sa vie; **cost of** ~ coût *m* de la vie; **within** ~ **memory** de mémoire d'homme.
living conditions *npl* conditions *fpl* de vie.
living expenses *npl* dépenses courantes.
living room *n* salle *f* de séjour.
living wage *n* salaire *m* permettant de vivre (décemment).
lizard ['lɪzəd] *n* lézard *m*.
llama ['lɑːmə] *n* lama *m*.
LLB *n abbr* (= *Bachelor of Laws*) *titre universitaire*.
LLD *n abbr* (= *Doctor of Laws*) *titre universitaire*.
LMT *abbr* (*US*: = *Local Mean Time*) *heure locale*.
load [ləud] *n* (*weight*) poids *m*; (*thing carried*) chargement *m*, charge *f*; (*ELEC, TECH*) charge ♦ *vt* (*lorry, ship*): **to** ~ **(with)** charger (de); (*gun, camera*): **to** ~ **(with)** charger (avec); (*COMPUT*) charger; **a** ~ **of,** ~**s of** (*fig*) un *or* des tas de, des masses de.
loaded ['ləudɪd] *adj* (*dice*) pipé(e); (*question*) insidieux(euse); (*col*: *rich*) bourré(e) de fric; (: *drunk*) bourré.
loading bay ['ləudɪŋ-] *n* aire *f* de chargement.
loaf, loaves [ləuf, ləuvz] *n* pain *m*, miche *f* ♦ *vi* (*also*: ~ **about,** ~ **around**) fainéanter, traîner.
loam [ləum] *n* terreau *m*.
loan [ləun] *n* prêt *m* ♦ *vt* prêter; **on** ~ prêté(e), en prêt; **public** ~ emprunt public.
loan account *n* compte *m* de prêt.
loan capital *n* capital-obligations *m*.
loan shark *n* (*col, pej*) usurier *m*.
loath [ləuθ] *adj*: **to be** ~ **to do** répugner à faire.
loathe [ləuð] *vt* détester, avoir en horreur.
loathing ['ləuðɪŋ] *n* dégoût *m*, répugnance *f*.
loathsome ['ləuðsəm] *adj* répugnant(e), détestable.
loaves [ləuvz] *npl of* **loaf**.
lob [lɔb] *vt* (*ball*) lober.
lobby ['lɔbɪ] *n* hall *m*, entrée *f*; (*POL*) groupe *m* de pression, lobby *m* ♦ *vt* faire pression sur.
lobbyist ['lɔbɪɪst] *n* membre *m/f* d'un groupe de pression.
lobe [ləub] *n* lobe *m*.
lobster ['lɔbstə*] *n* homard *m*.
lobster pot *n* casier *m* à homards.
local ['ləukl] *adj* local(e) ♦ *n* (*BRIT*: *pub*) pub *m* *or* café *m* du coin; **the** ~**s** *npl* les gens *mpl* du pays *or* du coin.
local anaesthetic *n* anesthésie locale.
local authority *n* collectivité locale, municipalité *f*.
local call *n* (*TEL*) communication urbaine.
local government *n* administration locale *or* municipale.
locality [ləu'kælɪtɪ] *n* région *f*, environs *mpl*; (*position*) lieu *m*.
localize ['ləukəlaɪz] *vt* localiser.
locally ['ləukəlɪ] *adv* localement; dans les environs *or* la région.
locate [ləu'keɪt] *vt* (*find*) trouver, repérer; (*situate*) situer.
location [ləu'keɪʃən] *n* emplacement *m*; **on** ~ (*CINE*) en extérieur.
loch [lɔx] *n* lac *m*, loch *m*.
lock [lɔk] *n* (*of door, box*) serrure *f*; (*of canal*) écluse *f*; (*of hair*) mèche *f*, boucle *f* ♦ *vt* (*with key*) fermer à clé; (*immobilize*) bloquer ♦ *vi* (*door etc*) fermer à clé; (*wheels*) se bloquer; ~ **stock and barrel** (*fig*) en bloc; **on full** ~ (*BRIT AUT*) le volant tourné à fond.
►**lock away** *vt* (*valuables*) mettre sous clé; (*criminal*) mettre sous les verrous, enfermer.
►**lock out** *vt* enfermer dehors; (*on purpose*) mettre à la porte; (: *workers*) lock-outer.
►**lock up** *vi* tout fermer (à clé).
locker ['lɔkə*] *n* casier *m*.
locket ['lɔkɪt] *n* médaillon *m*.
lockjaw ['lɔkdʒɔː] *n* tétanos *m*.
lockout ['lɔkaut] *n* (*INDUSTRY*) lock-out *m*, grève patronale.
locksmith ['lɔksmɪθ] *n* serrurier *m*.
lock-up ['lɔkʌp] *n* (*prison*) prison *f*; (*cell*) cellule *f* provisoire; (*also*: ~ **garage**) box *m*.
locomotive [ləukə'məutɪv] *n* locomotive *f*.
locum ['ləukəm] *n* (*MED*) suppléant/e (de médecin).
locust ['ləukəst] *n* locuste *f*, sauterelle *f*.
lodge [lɔdʒ] *n* pavillon *m* (de gardien); (*FREEMASONRY*) loge *f* ♦ *vi* (*person*): **to** ~ **with** être logé(e) chez, être en pension chez ♦ *vt* (*appeal etc*) présenter; déposer; **to** ~ **a complaint** porter plainte; **to** ~ **(itself) in/between** se loger dans/entre.
lodger ['lɔdʒə*] *n* locataire *m/f*; (*with room and meals*) pensionnaire *m/f*.
lodging ['lɔdʒɪŋ] *n* logement *m*; *see also* **board**.
lodging house *n* (*BRIT*) pension *f* de famille.
lodgings ['lɔdʒɪŋz] *npl* chambre *f*, meublé *m*.
loft [lɔft] *n* grenier *m*; (*US*) grenier aménagé (en appartement) (*gén dans ancien entrepôt ou fabrique*).
lofty ['lɔftɪ] *adj* élevé(e); (*haughty*) hautain(e); (*sentiments, aims*) noble.
log [lɔg] *n* (*of wood*) bûche *f*; (*book*) = **logbook** ♦ *n abbr* (= *logarithm*) log *m* ♦ *vt* enregistrer.
►**log in, log on** *vi* (*COMPUT*) ouvrir une session, entrer dans le système.
►**log off, log out** *vi* (*COMPUT*) clore une session, sortir du système.

logarithm ['lɔgərɪðm] *n* logarithme *m*.
logbook ['lɔgbuk] *n* (*NAUT*) livre *m or* journal *m* de bord; (*AVIAT*) carnet *m* de vol; (*of lorry driver*) carnet de route; (*of movement of goods etc*) registre *m*; (*of car*) ≈ carte grise.
log cabin *n* cabane *f* en rondins.
logger ['lɔgə*] *n* bûcheron *m*.
loggerheads ['lɔgəhɛdz] *npl*: **at ~ (with)** à couteaux tirés (avec).
logic ['lɔdʒɪk] *n* logique *f*.
logical ['lɔdʒɪkl] *adj* logique.
logically ['lɔdʒɪkəlɪ] *adv* logiquement.
logistics [lɔ'dʒɪstɪks] *n* logistique *f*.
logjam ['lɔgdʒæm] *n*: **to break the ~** créer une ouverture dans l'impasse.
logo ['ləugəu] *n* logo *m*.
loin [lɔɪn] *n* (*CULIN*) filet *m*, longe *f*; **~s** *npl* reins *mpl*.
loin cloth *n* pagne *m*.
loiter ['lɔɪtə*] *vi* s'attarder; **to ~ (about)** traîner, musarder; (*pej*) rôder.
loll [lɔl] *vi* (*also*: **~ about**) se prélasser, fainéanter.
lollipop ['lɔlɪpɔp] *n* sucette *f*.
lollipop lady *n* (*BRIT*) voir encadré.
lollipop man *n* (*BRIT*) voir encadré.

LOLLIPOP LADIES/MEN

Les **lollipop ladies/men** *sont employés pour aider les enfants à traverser la rue à proximité des écoles à l'heure où ils entrent en classe et à la sortie. On les repère facilement à cause de leur long ciré blanc et ils portent une pancarte ronde pour faire signe aux automobilistes de s'arrêter. On les appelle ainsi car la forme circulaire de cette pancarte rappelle une sucette.*

lollop ['lɔləp] *vi* (*BRIT*) avancer (*or* courir) maladroitement.
lolly ['lɔlɪ] *n* (*col*: *ice*) esquimau *m*; (*: lollipop*) sucette *f*; (*: money*) fric *m*.
Lombardy ['lɔmbədɪ] *n* Lombardie *f*.
London ['lʌndən] *n* Londres.
Londoner ['lʌndənə*] *n* Londonien/ne.
lone [ləun] *adj* solitaire.
loneliness ['ləunlɪnɪs] *n* solitude *f*, isolement *m*.
lonely ['ləunlɪ] *adj* seul(e); (*childhood etc*) solitaire; (*place*) solitaire, isolé(e).
lonely hearts *adj*: **~ ad** petite annonce (personnelle); **~ club** club *m* de rencontres (*pour personnes seules*).
lone parent *n* parent *m* unique.
loner ['ləunə*] *n* solitaire *m/f*.
lonesome ['ləunsəm] *adj* seul(e); solitaire.
long [lɔŋ] *adj* long(longue) ♦ *adv* longtemps ♦ *n*: **the ~ and the short of it is that ...** (*fig*) le fin mot de l'histoire c'est que ... ♦ *vi*: **to ~ for sth/to do** avoir très envie de qch/de faire; attendre qch avec impatience/impatience de faire; **he had ~ understood that ...** il avait compris depuis longtemps que ...; **how ~ is this river/course?** quelle est la longueur de ce fleuve/la durée de ce cours?; **6 metres ~** (long) de 6 mètres; **6 months ~** qui dure 6 mois, de 6 mois; **all night ~** toute la nuit; **he no ~er comes** il ne vient plus; **~ before** longtemps avant; **before ~** (*+ future*) avant peu, dans peu de temps; (*+ past*) peu de temps après; **~ ago** il y a longtemps; **don't be ~!** fais vite!, dépêche-toi!; **I shan't be ~** je n'en ai pas pour longtemps; **at ~ last** enfin; **in the ~ run** à la longue; finalement; **so** *or* **as ~ as** pourvu que.
long-distance [lɔŋ'dɪstəns] *adj* (*race*) de fond; (*call*) interurbain(e).
long-haired ['lɔŋ'hɛəd] *adj* (*person*) aux cheveux longs; (*animal*) aux longs poils.
longhand ['lɔŋhænd] *n* écriture normale *or* courante.
longing ['lɔŋɪŋ] *n* désir *m*, envie *f*, nostalgie *f* ♦ *adj* plein(e) d'envie *or* de nostalgie.
longingly ['lɔŋɪŋlɪ] *adv* avec désir *or* nostalgie.
longitude ['lɔŋgɪtju:d] *n* longitude *f*.
long johns [-dʒɔnz] *npl* caleçons longs.
long jump *n* saut *m* en longueur.
long-lost ['lɔŋlɔst] *adj* perdu(e) depuis longtemps.
long-playing ['lɔŋpleɪɪŋ] *adj*: **~ record (LP)** (disque *m*) 33 tours *m inv*.
long-range ['lɔŋ'reɪndʒ] *adj* à longue portée; (*weather forecast*) à long terme.
longshoreman ['lɔŋʃɔ:mən] *n* (*US*) docker *m*, débardeur *m*.
long-sighted ['lɔŋ'saɪtɪd] *adj* (*BRIT*) presbyte; (*fig*) prévoyant(e).
long-standing ['lɔŋ'stændɪŋ] *adj* de longue date.
long-suffering [lɔŋ'sʌfərɪŋ] *adj* empreint(e) d'une patience résignée; extrêmement patient(e).
long-term ['lɔŋtə:m] *adj* à long terme.
long wave *n* (*RADIO*) grandes ondes, ondes longues.
long-winded [lɔŋ'wɪndɪd] *adj* intarissable, interminable.
loo [lu:] *n* (*BRIT col*) w.-c. *mpl*, petit coin.
loofah ['lu:fə] *n sorte d'éponge végétale*.
look [luk] *vi* regarder; (*seem*) sembler, paraître, avoir l'air; (*building etc*): **to ~ south/on to the sea** donner au sud/sur la mer ♦ *n* regard *m*; (*appearance*) air *m*, allure *f*, aspect *m*; **~s** *npl* physique *m*, beauté *f*; **to ~ like** ressembler à; **it ~s like him** on dirait que c'est lui; **it ~s about 4 metres long** je dirais que ça fait 4 mètres de long; **it ~s all right to me** ça me paraît bien; **to have a ~ at sth** jeter un coup d'œil à qch; **to have a ~ for sth** chercher qch; **to ~ ahead** regarder devant soi; (*fig*) envisager l'avenir.
▸**look after** *vt fus* s'occuper de, prendre soin de; (*luggage etc: watch over*) garder, surveiller.

►**look around** *vi* regarder autour de soi.
►**look at** *vt fus* regarder.
►**look back** *vi*: **to ~ back at sth/sb** se retourner pour regarder qch/qn; **to look back on** (*event, period*) évoquer, repenser à.
►**look down on** *vt fus* (*fig*) regarder de haut, dédaigner.
►**look for** *vt fus* chercher.
►**look forward to** *vt fus* attendre avec impatience; **I'm not ~ing forward to it** cette perspective ne me réjouit guère; **~ing forward to hearing from you** (*in letter*) dans l'attente de vous lire.
►**look in** *vi*: **to ~ in on sb** passer voir qn.
►**look into** *vt fus* (*matter, possibility*) examiner, étudier.
►**look on** *vi* regarder (en spectateur).
►**look out** *vi* (*beware*): **to ~ out (for)** prendre garde (à), faire attention (à).
►**look out for** *vt fus* être à la recherche de; guetter.
►**look over** *vt* (*essay*) jeter un coup d'œil à; (*town, building*) visiter (rapidement); (*person*) jeter un coup d'œil à; examiner de la tête aux pieds.
►**look round** *vi* (*turn*) regarder derrière soi, se retourner; **to ~ round for sth** chercher qch.
►**look through** *vt fus* (*papers, book*) examiner; (*: briefly*) parcourir; (*telescope*) regarder à travers.
►**look to** *vt fus* veiller à; (*rely on*) compter sur.
►**look up** *vi* lever les yeux; (*improve*) s'améliorer ♦ *vt* (*word*) chercher; (*friend*) passer voir.
►**look up to** *vt fus* avoir du respect pour.
look-out ['lukaut] *n* poste *m* de guet; guetteur *m*; **to be on the ~ (for)** guetter.
look-up table ['lukʌp-] *n* (*COMPUT*) table *f* à consulter.
LOOM *n abbr* (*US*: = *Loyal Order of Moose*) *association charitable*.
loom [lu:m] *n* métier *m* à tisser ♦ *vi* surgir; (*fig*) menacer, paraître imminent(e).
loony ['lu:nɪ] *adj, n* (*col*) timbré(e), cinglé(e) (*m/f*).
loop [lu:p] *n* boucle *f*; (*contraceptive*) stérilet *m*.
loophole ['lu:phəul] *n* porte *f* de sortie (*fig*); échappatoire *f*.
loose [lu:s] *adj* (*knot, screw*) desserré(e); (*stone*) branlant(e); (*clothes*) vague, ample, lâche; (*animal*) en liberté, échappé(e); (*life*) dissolu(e); (*morals, discipline*) relâché(e); (*thinking*) peu rigoureux(euse), vague; (*translation*) approximatif(ive) ♦ *vt* (*free: animal*) lâcher; (*: prisoner*) relâcher, libérer; (*slacken*) détendre, relâcher; desserrer; défaire; donner du mou a; donner du ballant à; (*BRIT: arrow*) tirer; **~ connection** (*ELEC*) mauvais contact; **to be at a ~ end** *or* (*US*) **at ~ ends** (*fig*) ne pas trop savoir quoi faire; **to tie up ~ ends** (*fig*) mettre au point *or* régler les derniers détails.
loose change *n* petite monnaie.
loose-fitting ['lu:sfɪtɪŋ] *adj* (*clothes*) ample.
loose-leaf ['lu:sli:f] *adj*: **~ binder** *or* **folder** classeur *m* à feuilles *or* feuillets mobiles.
loose-limbed [lu:s'lɪmd] *adj* agile, souple.
loosely ['lu:slɪ] *adv* sans serrer; approximativement.
loosely-knit ['lu:slɪ'nɪt] *adj* élastique.
loosen ['lu:sn] *vt* desserrer, relâcher, défaire.
►**loosen up** *vi* (*before game*) s'échauffer; (*col: relax*) se détendre, se laisser aller.
loot [lu:t] *n* butin *m* ♦ *vt* piller.
looter ['lu:tə*] *n* pillard *m*, casseur *m*.
looting ['lu:tɪŋ] *n* pillage *m*.
lop [lɔp]: **to ~ off** *vt* couper, trancher.
lop-sided ['lɔp'saɪdɪd] *adj* de travers, asymétrique.
lord [lɔ:d] *n* seigneur *m*; **L~ Smith** lord Smith; **the L~** (*REL*) le Seigneur; **the (House of) L~s** (*BRIT*) la Chambre des Lords.
lordly ['lɔ:dlɪ] *adj* noble, majestueux(euse); (*arrogant*) hautain(e).
lordship ['lɔ:dʃɪp] *n* (*BRIT*): **your L~** Monsieur le comte (*or* le baron *or* le Juge).
lore [lɔ:*] *n* tradition(s) *f(pl)*.
lorry ['lɔrɪ] *n* (*BRIT*) camion *m*.
lorry driver *n* (*BRIT*) camionneur *m*, routier *m*.
lose, *pt, pp* **lost** [lu:z, lɔst] *vt* perdre; (*opportunity*) manquer, perdre; (*pursuers*) distancer, semer ♦ *vi* perdre; **to ~ (time)** (*clock*) retarder; **to ~ no time (in doing sth)** ne pas perdre de temps (à faire qch); **to get lost** *vi* (*person*) se perdre; **my watch has got lost** ma montre est perdue.
loser ['lu:zə*] *n* perdant/e; **to be a good/bad ~** être beau/mauvais joueur.
loss [lɔs] *n* perte *f*; **to cut one's ~es** limiter les dégâts; **to make a ~** enregistrer une perte; **to sell sth at a ~** vendre qch à perte; **to be at a ~** être perplexe *or* embarrassé(e); **to be at a ~ to do** se trouver incapable de faire.
loss adjuster *n* (*INSURANCE*) responsable *m/f* de l'évaluation des dommages.
loss leader *n* (*COMM*) article sacrifié.
lost [lɔst] *pt, pp of* **lose** ♦ *adj* perdu(e); **~ in thought** perdu dans ses pensées; **~ and found property** *n* (*US*) objets trouvés; **~ and found** *n* (*US*) (bureau *m* des) objets trouvés.
lost property *n* (*BRIT*) objets trouvés; **~ office** *or* **department** (bureau *m* des) objets trouvés.
lot [lɔt] *n* (*at auctions*) lot *m*; (*destiny*) sort *m*, destinée *f*; **the ~** le tout; tous *mpl*, toutes *fpl*; **a ~** beaucoup; **a ~ of** beaucoup de; **~s of** des tas de; **to draw ~s (for sth)** tirer (qch) au sort.
lotion ['ləuʃən] *n* lotion *f*.
lottery ['lɔtərɪ] *n* loterie *f*.
loud [laud] *adj* bruyant(e), sonore, fort(e); (*gaudy*) voyant(e), tapageur(euse) ♦ *adv*

(*speak etc*) fort; **out** ~ tout haut.
loudhailer [laud'heɪlə*] *n* porte-voix *m inv*.
loudly ['laudlɪ] *adv* fort, bruyamment.
loudspeaker [laud'spiːkə*] *n* haut-parleur *m*.
lounge [laundʒ] *n* salon *m*; (*of airport*) salle *f* ♦ *vi* se prélasser, paresser.
lounge bar *n* (salle *f* de) bar *m*.
lounge suit *n* (*BRIT*) complet *m*; (*: on invitation*) "tenue de ville".
louse, *pl* **lice** [laus, laɪs] *n* pou *m*.
▸**louse up** *vt* (*col*) gâcher.
lousy ['lauzɪ] *adj* (*fig*) infect(e), moche.
lout [laut] *n* rustre *m*, butor *m*.
louvre, (*US*) **louver** ['luːvə*] *adj* (*door, window*) à claire-voie.
lovable ['lʌvəbl] *adj* très sympathique; adorable.
love [lʌv] *n* amour *m* ♦ *vt* aimer; aimer beaucoup; **to ~ to do** aimer beaucoup *or* adorer faire; **I'd ~ to come** cela me ferait très plaisir (de venir); **"15 ~"** (*TENNIS*) "15 à rien *or* zéro"; **to be/fall in ~ with** être/tomber amoureux(euse) de; **to make ~** faire l'amour; **~ at first sight** le coup de foudre; **to send one's ~ to sb** adresser ses amitiés à qn; **~ from Anne, ~, Anne** affectueusement, Anne.
love affair *n* liaison (amoureuse).
love child *n* enfant *m/f* illégitime *or* naturel(le).
loved ones ['lʌvdwʌnz] *npl* proches *mpl* et amis chers.
love-hate relationship [lʌv'heɪt-] *n* rapport ambigu; **they have a ~** ils s'aiment et se détestent à la fois.
love letter *n* lettre *f* d'amour.
love life *n* vie sentimentale.
lovely ['lʌvlɪ] *adj* (*pretty*) ravissant(e); (*friend, wife*) charmant(e); (*holiday, surprise*) très agréable, merveilleux(euse); **we had a ~ time** c'était vraiment très bien.
lover ['lʌvə*] *n* amant *m*; (*amateur*): **a ~ of** un(e) ami(e) de, un(e) amoureux(euse) de.
lovesick ['lʌvsɪk] *adj* qui se languit d'amour.
lovesong ['lʌvsɔŋ] *n* chanson *f* d'amour.
loving ['lʌvɪŋ] *adj* affectueux(euse), tendre, aimant(e).
low [ləu] *adj* bas(basse) ♦ *adv* bas ♦ *n* (*METEOROLOGY*) dépression *f* ♦ *vi* (*cow*) mugir; **to feel ~** se sentir déprimé(e); **he's very ~** (*ill*) il est bien bas *or* très affaibli; **to turn (down) ~** *vt* baisser; **to reach a new *or* an all-time ~** tomber au niveau le plus bas.
low-alcohol [ləu'ælkəhɔl] *adj* à faible teneur en alcool, peu alcoolisé(e).
lowbrow ['ləubrau] *adj* sans prétentions intellectuelles.
low-calorie ['ləu'kælərɪ] *adj* hypocalorique.
low-cut ['ləukʌt] *adj* (*dress*) décolleté(e).
low-down ['ləudaun] *n* (*col*): **he gave me the ~ (on it)** il m'a mis au courant ♦ *adj* (*mean*) méprisable.
lower ['ləuə*] *adj, adv comparative of* **low** ♦ *vt* baisser; (*resistance*) diminuer ♦ *vi* ['lauə*] (*person*): **to ~ at sb** jeter un regard mauvais *or* noir à qn; (*sky, clouds*) être menaçant.
low-fat ['ləu'fæt] *adj* maigre.
low-key ['ləu'kiː] *adj* modéré(e); discret(ète).
lowland ['ləulənd] *n* plaine *f*.
low-level ['ləulɛvl] *adj* bas(basse); (*flying*) à basse altitude.
low-loader ['ləuləudə*] *n* semi-remorque *f* à plate-forme surbaissée.
lowly ['ləulɪ] *adj* humble, modeste.
low-lying [ləu'laɪɪŋ] *adj* à faible altitude.
low-paid [ləu'peɪd] *adj* mal payé(e), aux salaires bas.
low-rise ['ləuraɪz] *adj* bas(se), de faible hauteur.
low-tech ['ləutɛk] *adj* sommaire.
loyal ['lɔɪəl] *adj* loyal(e), fidèle.
loyalist ['lɔɪəlɪst] *n* loyaliste *m/f*.
loyalty ['lɔɪəltɪ] *n* loyauté *f*, fidélité *f*.
loyalty card *n* carte *f* de fidélité.
lozenge ['lɔzɪndʒ] *n* (*MED*) pastille *f*; (*GEOM*) losange *m*.
LP *n abbr* = **long-playing record.**
L-plates ['ɛlpleɪts] *npl* (*BRIT*) plaques *fpl* (obligatoires) d'apprenti conducteur; *voir encadré*.

L-PLATES

Les **L-plates** *sont des carrés blancs portant un "L" rouge que l'on met à l'avant et à l'arrière de sa voiture pour montrer qu'on n'a pas encore son permis de conduire. Jusqu'à l'obtention du permis, l'apprenti conducteur a un permis provisoire et n'a le droit de conduire que si un conducteur qualifié est assis à côté de lui. Il est interdit aux apprentis conducteurs de circuler sur les autoroutes, même s'ils sont accompagnés.*

LPN *n abbr* (*US: = Licensed Practical Nurse*) infirmier/ière diplômé(e).
LRAM *n abbr* (*BRIT*) = *Licentiate of the Royal Academy of Music.*
LSAT *n abbr* (*US*) = *Law School Admissions Test.*
LSD *n abbr* (= *lysergic acid diethylamide*) LSD *m*; (*BRIT: = pounds, shillings and pence*) *système monétaire en usage en GB jusqu'en 1971.*
LSE *n abbr* = *London School of Economics.*
LT *abbr* (*ELEC: = low tension*) BT.
Lt. *abbr* (= *lieutenant*) Lt.
Ltd *abbr* (*COMM*) = **limited**.
lubricant ['luːbrɪkənt] *n* lubrifiant *m*.
lubricate ['luːbrɪkeɪt] *vt* lubrifier, graisser.
lucid ['luːsɪd] *adj* lucide.
lucidity [luː'sɪdɪtɪ] *n* lucidité *f*.
luck [lʌk] *n* chance *f*; **bad ~** malchance *f*, malheur *m*; **to be in ~** avoir de la chance; **to be out of ~** ne pas avoir de chance; **good ~!** bonne chance!
luckily ['lʌkɪlɪ] *adv* heureusement, par bon-

heur.

luckless ['lʌklɪs] *adj* (*person*) malchanceux(euse); (*trip*) marqué(e) par la malchance.

lucky ['lʌkɪ] *adj* (*person*) qui a de la chance; (*coincidence*) heureux(euse); (*number etc*) qui porte bonheur.

lucrative ['lu:krətɪv] *adj* lucratif(ive), rentable, qui rapporte.

ludicrous ['lu:dɪkrəs] *adj* ridicule, absurde.

ludo ['lu:dəu] *n* jeu *m* des petits chevaux.

lug [lʌg] *vt* traîner, tirer.

luggage ['lʌgɪdʒ] *n* bagages *mpl*.

luggage lockers *npl* consigne *f* automatique.

luggage rack *n* (*in train*) porte-bagages *m inv*; (*: made of string*) filet *m* à bagages; (*on car*) galerie *f*.

luggage van, (*US*) **luggage car** *n* (*RAIL*) fourgon *m* (à bagages).

lugubrious [lu'gu:brɪəs] *adj* lugubre.

lukewarm ['lu:kwɔ:m] *adj* tiède.

lull [lʌl] *n* accalmie *f* ♦ *vt* (*child*) bercer; (*person, fear*) apaiser, calmer.

lullaby ['lʌləbaɪ] *n* berceuse *f*.

lumbago [lʌm'beɪgəu] *n* lumbago *m*.

lumber ['lʌmbə*] *n* bric-à-brac *m inv* ♦ *vt* (*BRIT col*): **to ~ sb with sth/sb** coller *or* refiler qch/qn à qn ♦ *vi* (*also*: **~ about, ~ along**) marcher pesamment.

lumberjack ['lʌmbədʒæk] *n* bûcheron *m*.

lumber room *n* (*BRIT*) débarras *m*.

lumber yard *n* entrepôt *m* de bois.

luminous ['lu:mɪnəs] *adj* lumineux(euse).

lump [lʌmp] *n* morceau *m*; (*in sauce*) grumeau *m*; (*swelling*) grosseur *f* ♦ *vt* (*also*: **~ together**) réunir, mettre en tas.

lump sum *n* somme globale *or* forfaitaire.

lumpy ['lʌmpɪ] *adj* (*sauce*) qui a des grumeaux.

lunacy ['lu:nəsɪ] *n* démence *f*, folie *f*.

lunar ['lu:nə*] *adj* lunaire.

lunatic ['lu:nətɪk] *n* fou/folle, dément/e ♦ *adj* fou(folle), dément(e).

lunatic asylum *n* asile *m* d'aliénés.

lunch [lʌntʃ] *n* déjeuner *m* ♦ *vi* déjeuner; **it is his ~ hour** c'est l'heure où il déjeune; **to invite sb to** *or* **for ~** inviter qn à déjeuner.

luncheon ['lʌntʃən] *n* déjeuner *m*.

luncheon meat *n sorte de saucisson.*

luncheon voucher *n* chèque-repas *m*, ticket-repas *m*.

lunchtime ['lʌntʃtaɪm] *n* l'heure *f* du déjeuner.

lung [lʌŋ] *n* poumon *m*.

lung cancer *n* cancer *m* du poumon.

lunge [lʌndʒ] *vi* (*also*: **~ forward**) faire un mouvement brusque en avant; **to ~ at sb** envoyer *or* assener un coup à qn.

lupin ['lu:pɪn] *n* lupin *m*.

lurch [lə:tʃ] *vi* vaciller, tituber ♦ *n* écart *m* brusque, embardée *f*; **to leave sb in the ~** laisser qn se débrouiller *or* se dépêtrer tout(e) seul(e).

lure [luə*] *n* appât *m*, leurre *m* ♦ *vt* attirer *or* persuader par la ruse.

lurid ['luərɪd] *adj* affreux(euse), atroce.

lurk [lə:k] *vi* se tapir, se cacher.

luscious ['lʌʃəs] *adj* succulent(e); appétissant(e).

lush [lʌʃ] *adj* luxuriant(e).

lust [lʌst] *n* luxure *f*; lubricité *f*; désir *m*; (*fig*): **~ for** soif *f* de.

►**lust after** *vt fus* convoiter, désirer.

luster ['lʌstə*] *n* (*US*) = **lustre.**

lustful ['lʌstful] *adj* lascif(ive).

lustre, (*US*) **luster** ['lʌstə*] *n* lustre *m*, brillant *m*.

lusty ['lʌstɪ] *adj* vigoureux(euse), robuste.

lute [lu:t] *n* luth *m*.

Luxembourg ['lʌksəmbə:g] *n* Luxembourg *m*.

luxuriant [lʌg'zjuərɪənt] *adj* luxuriant(e).

luxurious [lʌg'zjuərɪəs] *adj* luxueux(euse).

luxury ['lʌkʃərɪ] *n* luxe *m* ♦ *cpd* de luxe.

LV *n abbr* (*BRIT*) = **luncheon voucher.**

LW *abbr* (*RADIO*: = *long wave*) GO.

Lycra ['laɪkrə] *n* ® Lycra *m* ®.

lying ['laɪɪŋ] *n* mensonge(s) *m(pl)* ♦ *adj* (*statement, story*) mensonger(ère), faux(fausse); (*person*) menteur(euse).

lynch [lɪntʃ] *vt* lyncher.

lynx [lɪŋks] *n* lynx *m inv*.

Lyons ['laɪənz] *n* Lyon.

lyre ['laɪə*] *n* lyre *f*.

lyric ['lɪrɪk] *adj* lyrique; **~s** *npl* (*of song*) paroles *fpl*.

lyrical ['lɪrɪkl] *adj* lyrique.

lyricism ['lɪrɪsɪzəm] *n* lyrisme *m*.

M m

M, m [ɛm] *n* (*letter*) M, m *m*; **M for Mary,** (*US*) **M for Mike** M comme Marcel.

M *n abbr* (*BRIT*: = *motorway*): **the M8** ≈ l'A8 ♦ *abbr* (= *medium*) M.

m *abbr* (= *metre*) m; (= *million*) M; (= *mile*) mi.

MA *n abbr* (*SCOL*) = **Master of Arts** ♦ *abbr* (*US*) = *military academy*; (*US*) = *Massachusetts*.

mac [mæk] *n* (*BRIT*) imper(méable *m*) *m*.

macabre [mə'kɑ:brə] *adj* macabre.

macaroni [mækə'rəunɪ] *n* macaronis *mpl*.

macaroon [mækə'ru:n] *n* macaron *m*.

mace [meɪs] *n* masse *f*; (*spice*) macis *m*.

Macedonia [mæsɪ'dəunɪə] *n* Macédoine *f*.

Macedonian [mæsɪ'dəunɪən] *adj* macédonien(ne) ♦ *n* Macédonien/ne; (*LING*) macédonien *m*.

machinations [mækɪ'neɪʃənz] *npl* machina-

tions *fpl*, intrigues *fpl*.
machine [mə'ʃiːn] *n* machine *f* ♦ *vt* (*dress etc*) coudre à la machine; (*TECH*) usiner.
machine code *n* (*COMPUT*) code *m* machine.
machine gun *n* mitrailleuse *f*.
machine language *n* (*COMPUT*) langage *m* machine.
machine-readable [mə'ʃiːnriːdəbl] *adj* (*COMPUT*) exploitable par une machine.
machinery [mə'ʃiːnərɪ] *n* machinerie *f*, machines *fpl*; (*fig*) mécanisme(s) *m(pl)*.
machine shop *n* atelier *m* d'usinage.
machine tool *n* machine-outil *f*.
machine washable *adj* (*garment*) lavable en machine.
machinist [mə'ʃiːnɪst] *n* machiniste *m/f*.
macho ['mætʃəu] *adj* macho *inv*.
mackerel ['mækrl] *n* (*pl inv*) maquereau *m*.
mackintosh ['mækɪntɔʃ] *n* (*BRIT*) imperméable *m*.
macro... ['mækrəu] *prefix* macro....
macro-economics ['mækrəuiːkə'nɔmɪks] *n* macro-économie *f*.
mad [mæd] *adj* fou(folle); (*foolish*) insensé(e); (*angry*) furieux(euse); **to go ~** devenir fou; **to be ~ (keen) about** *or* **on sth** (*col*) être follement passionné de qch, être fou de qch.
madam ['mædəm] *n* madame *f*; **yes ~** oui Madame; **M~ Chairman** Madame la Présidente.
madcap ['mædkæp] *adj* (*col*) écervelé(e).
mad cow disease *n* maladie *f* des vaches folles.
madden ['mædn] *vt* exaspérer.
maddening ['mædnɪŋ] *adj* exaspérant(e).
made [meɪd] *pt, pp of* **make**.
Madeira [mə'dɪərə] *n* (*GEO*) Madère *f*; (*wine*) madère *m*.
made-to-measure ['meɪdtə'mɛʒə*] *adj* (*BRIT*) fait(e) sur mesure.
madhouse ['mædhaus] *n* (*also fig*) maison *f* de fous.
madly ['mædlɪ] *adv* follement.
madman ['mædmən] *n* fou *m*, aliéné *m*.
madness ['mædnɪs] *n* folie *f*.
Madrid [mə'drɪd] *n* Madrid.
Mafia ['mæfɪə] *n* maf(f)ia *f*.
mag. [mæg] *n abbr* (*BRIT col*) = **magazine** (*PRESS*).
magazine [mægə'ziːn] *n* (*PRESS*) magazine *m*, revue *f*; (*MIL: store*) dépôt *m*, arsenal *m*; (*of firearm*) magasin *m*.
maggot ['mægət] *n* ver *m*, asticot *m*.
magic ['mædʒɪk] *n* magie *f* ♦ *adj* magique.
magical ['mædʒɪkl] *adj* magique.
magician [mə'dʒɪʃən] *n* magicien/ne.
magistrate ['mædʒɪstreɪt] *n* magistrat *m*; juge *m*; **~s' court** (*BRIT*) ≈ tribunal *m* d'instance.
magnanimous [mæg'nænɪməs] *adj* magnanime.
magnate ['mægneɪt] *n* magnat *m*.
magnesium [mæg'niːzɪəm] *n* magnésium *m*.
magnet ['mægnɪt] *n* aimant *m*.
magnetic [mæg'nɛtɪk] *adj* magnétique.
magnetic disk *n* (*COMPUT*) disque *m* magnétique.
magnetic tape *n* bande *f* magnétique.
magnetism ['mægnɪtɪzəm] *n* magnétisme *m*.
magnification [mægnɪfɪ'keɪʃən] *n* grossissement *m*.
magnificence [mæg'nɪfɪsns] *n* magnificence *f*.
magnificent [mæg'nɪfɪsnt] *adj* superbe, magnifique.
magnify ['mægnɪfaɪ] *vt* grossir; (*sound*) amplifier.
magnifying glass ['mægnɪfaɪɪŋ-] *n* loupe *f*.
magnitude ['mægnɪtjuːd] *n* ampleur *f*.
magnolia [mæg'nəulɪə] *n* magnolia *m*.
magpie ['mægpaɪ] *n* pie *f*.
mahogany [mə'hɔgənɪ] *n* acajou *m* ♦ *cpd* en (bois d')acajou.
maid [meɪd] *n* bonne *f*; **old ~** (*pej*) vieille fille.
maiden ['meɪdn] *n* jeune fille *f* ♦ *adj* (*aunt etc*) non mariée; (*speech, voyage*) inaugural(e).
maiden name *n* nom *m* de jeune fille.
mail [meɪl] *n* poste *f*; (*letters*) courrier *m* ♦ *vt* envoyer (par la poste); **by ~** par la poste.
mailbag ['meɪlbæg] *n* (*US*) sac postal; (*postman's*) sacoche *f*.
mailbox ['meɪlbɔks] *n* (*US: for letters etc; COMPUT*) boîte *f* aux lettres.
mailing list ['meɪlɪŋ-] *n* liste *f* d'adresses.
mailman ['meɪlmæn] *n* (*US*) facteur *m*.
mail-order ['meɪlɔːdə*] *n* vente *f or* achat *m* par correspondance ♦ *cpd*: **~ firm** *or* **house** maison *f* de vente par correspondance.
mailshot ['meɪlʃɔt] *n* (*BRIT*) mailing *m*.
mail train *n* train postal.
mail truck *n* (*US AUT*) = **mail van**.
mail van *n* (*BRIT: AUT*) voiture *f or* fourgonnette *f* des postes; (*: RAIL*) wagon-poste *m*.
maim [meɪm] *vt* mutiler.
main [meɪn] *adj* principal(e) ♦ *n* (*pipe*) conduite principale, canalisation *f*; **the ~s** (*ELEC*) le secteur; **the ~ thing** l'essentiel *m*; **in the ~** dans l'ensemble.
main course *n* (*CULIN*) plat *m* de résistance.
mainframe ['meɪnfreɪm] *n* (*also:* **~ computer**) (gros) ordinateur, unité centrale.
mainland ['meɪnlənd] *n* continent *m*.
mainline ['meɪnlaɪn] *adj* (*RAIL*) de grande ligne ♦ *vb* (*drugs slang*) *vt* se shooter à ♦ *vi* se shooter.
main line *n* (*RAIL*) grande ligne.
mainly ['meɪnlɪ] *adv* principalement, surtout.
main road *n* grand axe, route nationale.
mainstay ['meɪnsteɪ] *n* (*fig*) pilier *m*.
mainstream ['meɪnstriːm] *n* (*fig*) courant principal.
maintain [meɪn'teɪn] *vt* entretenir; (*continue*) maintenir, préserver; (*affirm*) soutenir; **to ~ that ...** soutenir que ....
maintenance ['meɪntənəns] *n* entretien *m*; (*LAW: alimony*) pension *f* alimentaire.
maintenance contract *n* contrat *m*

d'entretien.
maintenance order *n* (*LAW*) obligation *f* alimentaire.
maisonette [meɪzə'nɛt] *n* (*BRIT*) appartement *m* en duplex.
maize [meɪz] *n* maïs *m*.
Maj. *abbr* (*MIL*) = **major**.
majestic [mə'dʒɛstɪk] *adj* majestueux(euse).
majesty ['mædʒɪstɪ] *n* majesté *f*.
major ['meɪdʒə*] *n* (*MIL*) commandant *m* ♦ *adj* important(e), principal(e); (*MUS*) majeur(e) ♦ *vi* (*US SCOL*): **to ~ (in)** se spécialiser (en); **a ~ operation** (*MED*) une grosse opération.
Majorca [mə'jɔːkə] *n* Majorque *f*.
major general *n* (*MIL*) général *m* de division.
majority [mə'dʒɔrɪtɪ] *n* majorité *f* ♦ *cpd* (*verdict, holding*) majoritaire.
make [meɪk] *vt* (*pt, pp* **made** [meɪd]) faire; (*manufacture*) faire, fabriquer; (*cause to be*): **to ~ sb sad** *etc* rendre qn triste *etc*; (*force*): **to ~ sb do sth** obliger qn à faire qch, faire faire qch à qn; (*equal*): **2 and 2 ~ 4** 2 et 2 font 4 ♦ *n* fabrication *f*; (*brand*) marque *f*; **to ~ it** (*in time etc*) y arriver; (*succeed*) réussir; **what time do you ~ it?** quelle heure avez-vous?; **to ~ good** *vi* (*succeed*) faire son chemin, réussir ♦ *vt* (*deficit*) combler; (*losses*) compenser; **to ~ do with** se contenter de; se débrouiller avec.
►**make for** *vt fus* (*place*) se diriger vers.
►**make off** *vi* filer.
►**make out** *vt* (*write out*) écrire; (*understand*) comprendre; (*see*) distinguer; (*claim, imply*) prétendre, vouloir faire croire; **to ~ out a case for sth** présenter des arguments solides en faveur de qch.
►**make over** *vt* (*assign*): **to ~ over (to)** céder (à), transférer (au nom de).
►**make up** *vt* (*invent*) inventer, imaginer; (*parcel*) faire ♦ *vi* se réconcilier; (*with cosmetics*) se maquiller, se farder; **to be made up of** se composer de.
►**make up for** *vt fus* compenser; racheter.
make-believe ['meɪkbɪliːv] *n*: **a world of ~** un monde de chimères *or* d'illusions; **it's just ~** c'est de la fantaisie; c'est une illusion.
maker ['meɪkə*] *n* fabricant *m*.
makeshift ['meɪkʃɪft] *adj* provisoire, improvisé(e).
make-up ['meɪkʌp] *n* maquillage *m*.
make-up bag *n* trousse *f* de maquillage.
make-up remover *n* démaquillant *m*.
making ['meɪkɪŋ] *n* (*fig*): **in the ~** en formation *or* gestation; **he has the ~s of an actor** il a l'étoffe d'un acteur.
maladjusted [mælə'dʒʌstɪd] *adj* inadapté(e).
malaise [mæ'leɪz] *n* malaise *m*.
malaria [mə'lɛərɪə] *n* malaria *f*, paludisme *m*.
Malawi [mə'lɑːwɪ] *n* Malawi *m*.
Malay [mə'leɪ] *adj* malais(e) ♦ *n* (*person*) Malais/e; (*language*) malais *m*.
Malaya [mə'leɪə] *n* Malaisie *f*.
Malayan [mə'leɪən] *adj, n* = **Malay**.
Malaysia [mə'leɪzɪə] *n* Malaisie *f*.
Malaysian [mə'leɪzɪən] *adj* malaisien(ne) ♦ *n* Malaisien/ne.
Maldives ['mɔːldaɪvz] *npl*: **the ~** les Maldives *fpl*.
male [meɪl] *n* (*BIOL, ELEC*) mâle *m* ♦ *adj* (*sex, attitude*) masculin(e); mâle; (*child etc*) du sexe masculin; **~ and female students** étudiants et étudiantes.
male chauvinist *n* phallocrate *m*.
male nurse *n* infirmier *m*.
malevolence [mə'lɛvələns] *n* malveillance *f*.
malevolent [mə'lɛvələnt] *adj* malveillant(e).
malfunction [mæl'fʌŋkʃən] *n* fonctionnement défectueux.
malice ['mælɪs] *n* méchanceté *f*, malveillance *f*.
malicious [mə'lɪʃəs] *adj* méchant(e), malveillant(e); (*LAW*) avec intention criminelle.
malign [mə'laɪn] *vt* diffamer, calomnier.
malignant [mə'lɪgnənt] *adj* (*MED*) malin(igne).
malingerer [mə'lɪŋgərə*] *n* simulateur/trice.
mall [mɔːl] *n* (*also*: **shopping ~**) centre commercial.
malleable ['mælɪəbl] *adj* malléable.
mallet ['mælɪt] *n* maillet *m*.
malnutrition [mælnjuː'trɪʃən] *n* malnutrition *f*.
malpractice [mæl'præktɪs] *n* faute professionnelle; négligence *f*.
malt [mɔːlt] *n* malt *m* ♦ *cpd* (*whisky*) pur malt.
Malta ['mɔːltə] *n* Malte *f*.
Maltese [mɔːl'tiːz] *adj* maltais(e) ♦ *n* (*pl inv*) Maltais/e; (*LING*) maltais *m*.
maltreat [mæl'triːt] *vt* maltraiter.
mammal ['mæml] *n* mammifère *m*.
mammoth ['mæməθ] *n* mammouth *m* ♦ *adj* géant(e), monstre.
man, *pl* **men** [mæn, mɛn] *n* homme *m*; (*CHESS*) pièce *f*; (*DRAUGHTS*) pion *m* ♦ *vt* garnir d'hommes; servir, assurer le fonctionnement de; être de service à; **an old ~** un vieillard; **~ and wife** mari et femme.
Man. *abbr* (*Canada*) = *Manitoba*.
manacles ['mænəklz] *npl* menottes *fpl*.
manage ['mænɪdʒ] *vi* se débrouiller; y arriver, réussir ♦ *vt* (*business*) gérer; (*team, operation*) diriger; (*device, things to do, carry etc*) arriver à se débrouiller avec, s'en tirer avec; **to ~ to do** se débrouiller pour faire; (*succeed*) réussir à faire.
manageable ['mænɪdʒəbl] *adj* maniable; (*task etc*) faisable.
management ['mænɪdʒmənt] *n* administration *f*, direction *f*; (*persons: of business, firm*) dirigeants *mpl*, cadres *mpl*; (*: of hotel, shop, theatre*) direction; **"under new ~"** "changement de gérant", "changement de propriétaire".
management accounting *n* comptabilité *f* de gestion.
management consultant *n* conseiller/ère

de direction.
manager ['mænɪdʒə*] *n* (*of business*) directeur *m*; (*of institution etc*) administrateur *m*; (*of department, unit*) responsable *m/f*, chef *m*; (*of hotel etc*) gérant *m*; (*of artist*) impresario *m*; **sales** ~ responsable *or* chef des ventes.
manageress [mænɪdʒə'rɛs] *n* directrice *f*; (*of hotel etc*) gérante *f*.
managerial [mænɪ'dʒɪərɪəl] *adj* directorial(e); ~ **staff** cadres *mpl*.
managing director (MD) ['mænɪdʒɪŋ-] *n* directeur général.
Mancunian [mæŋ'kjuːnɪən] *adj* de Manchester ♦ *n* habitant/e de Manchester; natif/ive de Manchester.
mandarin ['mændərɪn] *n* (*also*: ~ **orange**) mandarine *f*; (*person*) mandarin *m*.
mandate ['mændeɪt] *n* mandat *m*.
mandatory ['mændətərɪ] *adj* obligatoire; (*powers etc*) mandataire.
mandolin(e) ['mændəlɪn] *n* mandoline *f*.
mane [meɪn] *n* crinière *f*.
maneuver *etc* [mə'nuːvə*] (*US*) = **manoeuvre** *etc*.
manfully ['mænfəlɪ] *adv* vaillamment.
manganese [mæŋgə'niːz] *n* manganèse *m*.
mangetout ['mɔnʒ'tuː] *n* mange-tout *m inv*.
mangle ['mæŋgl] *vt* déchiqueter; mutiler ♦ *n* essoreuse *f*; calandre *f*.
mango, ~es ['mæŋgəu] *n* mangue *f*.
mangrove ['mæŋgrəuv] *n* palétuvier *m*.
mangy ['meɪndʒɪ] *adj* galeux(euse).
manhandle ['mænhændl] *vt* (*mistreat*) maltraiter, malmener; (*move by hand*) manutentionner.
manhole ['mænhəul] *n* trou *m* d'homme.
manhood ['mænhud] *n* âge *m* d'homme; virilité *f*.
man-hour ['mænauə*] *n* heure-homme *f*, heure *f* de main-d'œuvre.
manhunt ['mænhʌnt] *n* chasse *f* à l'homme.
mania ['meɪnɪə] *n* manie *f*.
maniac ['meɪnɪæk] *n* maniaque *m/f*.
manic ['mænɪk] *adj* maniaque.
manic-depressive ['mænɪkdɪ'prɛsɪv] *adj*, *n* (*PSYCH*) maniaco-dépressif(ive).
manicure ['mænɪkjuə*] *n* manucure *f* ♦ *vt* (*person*) faire les mains à.
manicure set *n* trousse *f* à ongles.
manifest ['mænɪfɛst] *vt* manifester ♦ *adj* manifeste, évident(e) ♦ *n* (*AVIAT*, *NAUT*) manifeste *m*.
manifestation [mænɪfɛs'teɪʃən] *n* manifestation *f*.
manifesto [mænɪ'fɛstəu] *n* manifeste *m* (*POL*).
manifold ['mænɪfəuld] *adj* multiple, varié(e) ♦ *n* (*AUT etc*): **exhaust** ~ collecteur *m* d'échappement.
Manila [mə'nɪlə] *n* Manille, Manila.
manila [mə'nɪlə] *adj*: ~ **paper** papier *m* bulle.
manipulate [mə'nɪpjuleɪt] *vt* manipuler.
manipulation [mənɪpju'leɪʃən] *n* manipulation *f*.
mankind [mæn'kaɪnd] *n* humanité *f*, genre humain.
manliness ['mænlɪnɪs] *n* virilité *f*.
manly ['mænlɪ] *adj* viril(e); courageux(euse).
man-made ['mæn'meɪd] *adj* artificiel(le).
manna ['mænə] *n* manne *f*.
mannequin ['mænɪkɪn] *n* mannequin *m*.
manner ['mænə*] *n* manière *f*, façon *f*; **(good) ~s** (bonnes) manières; **bad ~s** mauvaises manières; **all ~ of** toutes sortes de.
mannerism ['mænərɪzəm] *n* particularité *f* de langage (*or* de comportement), tic *m*.
mannerly ['mænəlɪ] *adj* poli(e), courtois(e).
manoeuvrable, (*US*) **maneuverable** [mə'nuːvrəbl] *adj* facile à manœuvrer.
manoeuvre, (*US*) **maneuver** [mə'nuːvə*] *vt*, *vi* manœuvrer ♦ *n* manœuvre *f*; **to ~ sb into doing sth** manipuler qn pour lui faire faire qch.
manor ['mænə*] *n* (*also*: ~ **house**) manoir *m*.
manpower ['mænpauə*] *n* main-d'œuvre *f*.
manservant, *pl* **menservants** ['mænsəːvənt, 'mɛn-] *n* domestique *m*.
mansion ['mænʃən] *n* château *m*, manoir *m*.
manslaughter ['mænslɔːtə*] *n* homicide *m* involontaire.
mantelpiece ['mæntlpiːs] *n* cheminée *f*.
mantle ['mæntl] *n* cape *f*; (*fig*) manteau *m*.
man-to-man ['mæntə'mæn] *adj*, *adv* d'homme à homme.
manual ['mænjuəl] *adj* manuel(le) ♦ *n* manuel *m*.
manual worker *n* travailleur manuel.
manufacture [mænju'fæktʃə*] *vt* fabriquer ♦ *n* fabrication *f*.
manufactured goods [mænju'fæktʃəd-] *npl* produits manufacturés.
manufacturer [mænju'fæktʃərə*] *n* fabricant *m*.
manufacturing industries [mænju'fæktʃərɪŋ-] *npl* industries *fpl* de transformation.
manure [mə'njuə*] *n* fumier *m*; (*artificial*) engrais *m*.
manuscript ['mænjuskrɪpt] *n* manuscrit *m*.
many ['mɛnɪ] *adj* beaucoup de, de nombreux(euses) ♦ *pron* beaucoup, un grand nombre; **how ~?** combien?; **a great ~** un grand nombre (de); **too ~ difficulties** trop de difficultés; **twice as ~** deux fois plus; **~ a** ... bien des ..., plus d'un(e) ....
Maori ['maurɪ] *n* Maori/e ♦ *adj* maori(e).
map [mæp] *n* carte *f* ♦ *vt* dresser la carte de.
►**map out** *vt* tracer; (*fig: career, holiday*) organiser, préparer (à l'avance); (*: essay*) faire le plan de.
maple ['meɪpl] *n* érable *m*.
Mar. *abbr* = **March**.
mar [mɑː*] *vt* gâcher, gâter.
marathon ['mærəθən] *n* marathon *m* ♦ *adj*: **a ~ session** une séance-marathon.

marathon runner *n* coureur/euse de marathon, marathonien/ne.
marauder [mə'rɔːdə*] *n* maraudeur/euse.
marble ['mɑːbl] *n* marbre *m*; (*toy*) bille *f*; **~s** *n* (*game*) billes.
March [mɑːtʃ] *n* mars *m*; *for phrases see also* **July**.
march [mɑːtʃ] *vi* marcher au pas; (*demonstrators*) défiler ♦ *n* marche *f*; (*demonstration*) rallye *m*; **to ~ out of/into** *etc* sortir de/entrer dans *etc* (*de manière décidée ou impulsive*).
marcher ['mɑːtʃə*] *n* (*demonstrator*) manifestant/e, marcheur/euse.
marching ['mɑːtʃɪŋ] *n*: **to give sb his ~ orders** (*fig*) renvoyer qn; envoyer promener qn.
march-past ['mɑːtʃpɑːst] *n* défilé *m*.
mare [mɛə*] *n* jument *f*.
marg. [mɑːdʒ] *n abbr* (*col*) = **margarine**.
margarine [mɑːdʒə'riːn] *n* margarine *f*.
margin ['mɑːdʒɪn] *n* marge *f*.
marginal ['mɑːdʒɪnl] *adj* marginal(e); **~ seat** (*POL*) siège disputé.
marginally ['mɑːdʒɪnəlɪ] *adv* très légèrement, sensiblement.
marigold ['mærɪgəuld] *n* souci *m*.
marijuana [mærɪ'wɑːnə] *n* marijuana *f*.
marina [mə'riːnə] *n* marina *f*.
marinade *n* [mærɪ'neɪd] marinade *f* ♦ *vt* ['mærɪneɪd] = **marinate**.
marinate ['mærɪneɪt] *vt* (faire) mariner.
marine [mə'riːn] *adj* marin(e) ♦ *n* fusilier marin; (*US*) marine *m*.
marine insurance *n* assurance *f* maritime.
marital ['mærɪtl] *adj* matrimonial(e); **~ status** situation *f* de famille.
maritime ['mærɪtaɪm] *adj* maritime.
maritime law *n* droit *m* maritime.
marjoram ['mɑːdʒərəm] *n* marjolaine *f*.
mark [mɑːk] *n* marque *f*; (*of skid etc*) trace *f*; (*BRIT SCOL*) note *f*; (*SPORT*) cible *f*; (*currency*) mark *m*; (*BRIT TECH*): **M~ 2/3** 2ème/3ème série *f or* version *f* ♦ *vt* (*also SPORT*: *player*) marquer; (*stain*) tacher; (*BRIT SCOL*) noter; corriger; **punctuation ~s** signes *mpl* de ponctuation; **to ~ time** marquer le pas; **to be quick off the ~ (in doing)** (*fig*) ne pas perdre de temps (pour faire); **up to the ~** (*in efficiency*) à la hauteur.
▶**mark down** *vt* (*prices, goods*) démarquer, réduire le prix de.
▶**mark off** *vt* (*tick off*) cocher, pointer.
▶**mark out** *vt* désigner.
▶**mark up** *vt* (*price*) majorer.
marked [mɑːkt] *adj* marqué(e), net(te).
markedly ['mɑːkɪdlɪ] *adv* visiblement, manifestement.
marker ['mɑːkə*] *n* (*sign*) jalon *m*; (*bookmark*) signet *m*.
market ['mɑːkɪt] *n* marché *m* ♦ *vt* (*COMM*) commercialiser; **to be on the ~** être sur le marché; **on the open ~** en vente libre; **to play the ~** jouer à la *or* spéculer en Bourse.
marketable ['mɑːkɪtəbl] *adj* commercialisable.
market analysis *n* analyse *f* de marché.
market day *n* jour *m* de marché.
market demand *n* besoins *mpl* du marché.
market economy *n* économie *f* de marché.
market forces *npl* tendances *fpl* du marché.
market garden *n* (*BRIT*) jardin maraîcher.
marketing ['mɑːkɪtɪŋ] *n* marketing *m*.
marketplace ['mɑːkɪtpleɪs] *n* place *f* du marché; (*COMM*) marché *m*.
market price *n* prix marchand.
market research *n* étude *f* de marché.
market value *n* valeur marchande; valeur du marché.
marking ['mɑːkɪŋ] *n* (*on animal*) marque *f*, tache *f*; (*on road*) signalisation *f*.
marksman ['mɑːksmən] *n* tireur *m* d'élite.
marksmanship ['mɑːksmənʃɪp] *n* adresse *f* au tir.
mark-up ['mɑːkʌp] *n* (*COMM*: *margin*) marge *f* (bénéficiaire); (*: increase*) majoration *f*.
marmalade ['mɑːməleɪd] *n* confiture *f* d'oranges.
maroon [mə'ruːn] *vt* (*fig*): **to be ~ed (in** *or* **at)** être bloqué(e) (à) ♦ *adj* bordeaux *inv*.
marquee [mɑː'kiː] *n* chapiteau *m*.
marquess, marquis ['mɑːkwɪs] *n* marquis *m*.
Marrakech, Marrakesh [mærə'kɛʃ] *n* Marrakech.
marriage ['mærɪdʒ] *n* mariage *m*.
marriage bureau *n* agence matrimoniale.
marriage certificate *n* extrait *m* d'acte de mariage.
marriage guidance, (*US*) **marriage counseling** *n* conseils conjugaux.
marriage of convenience *n* mariage *m* de convenance.
married ['mærɪd] *adj* marié(e); (*life, love*) conjugal(e).
marrow ['mærəu] *n* moelle *f*; (*vegetable*) courge *f*.
marry ['mærɪ] *vt* épouser, se marier avec; (*subj: father, priest etc*) marier ♦ *vi* (*also*: **get married**) se marier.
Mars [mɑːz] *n* (*planet*) Mars *f*.
Marseilles [mɑː'seɪlz] *n* Marseille.
marsh [mɑːʃ] *n* marais *m*, marécage *m*.
marshal ['mɑːʃl] *n* maréchal *m*; (*US*: *fire, police*) ≈ capitaine *m*; (*for demonstration, meeting*) membre *m* du service d'ordre ♦ *vt* rassembler.
marshalling yard ['mɑːʃlɪŋ-] *n* (*RAIL*) gare *f* de triage.
marshmallow [mɑːʃ'mæləu] *n* (*BOT*) guimauve *f*; (*sweet*) (pâte *f* de) guimauve.
marshy ['mɑːʃɪ] *adj* marécageux(euse).
marsupial [mɑː'suːpɪəl] *adj* marsupial(e) ♦ *n* marsupial *m*.
martial ['mɑːʃl] *adj* martial(e).
martial arts *npl* arts martiaux.
martial law *n* loi martiale.
Martian ['mɑːʃən] *n* Martien/ne.

martin ['mɑːtɪn] *n* (*also*: **house** ~) martinet *m*.
martyr ['mɑːtə*] *n* (*REL, fig*) martyr/e ♦ *vt* martyriser.
martyrdom ['mɑːtədəm] *n* martyre *m*.
marvel ['mɑːvl] *n* merveille *f* ♦ *vi*: **to ~ (at)** s'émerveiller (de).
marvellous, (*US*) **marvelous** ['mɑːvləs] *adj* merveilleux(euse).
Marxism ['mɑːksɪzəm] *n* marxisme *m*.
Marxist ['mɑːksɪst] *adj, n* marxiste (*m/f*).
marzipan ['mɑːzɪpæn] *n* pâte *f* d'amandes.
mascara [mæs'kɑːrə] *n* mascara *m*.
mascot ['mæskət] *n* mascotte *f*.
masculine ['mæskjulɪn] *adj* masculin(e) ♦ *n* masculin *m*.
masculinity [mæskju'lɪnɪtɪ] *n* masculinité *f*.
MASH [mæʃ] *n abbr* (*US MIL*) = *mobile army surgical hospital*.
mash [mæʃ] *vt* (*CULIN*) faire une purée de.
mashed [mæʃt] *adj*: ~ **potatoes** purée *f* de pommes de terre.
mask [mɑːsk] *n* masque *m* ♦ *vt* masquer.
masochism ['mæsəukɪzəm] *n* masochisme *m*.
masochist ['mæsəukɪst] *n* masochiste *m/f*.
mason ['meɪsn] *n* (*also*: **stone**~) maçon *m*; (*also*: **free**~) franc-maçon *m*.
masonic [mə'sɔnɪk] *adj* maçonnique.
masonry ['meɪsnrɪ] *n* maçonnerie *f*.
masquerade [mæskə'reɪd] *n* bal masqué; (*fig*) mascarade *f* ♦ *vi*: **to ~ as** se faire passer pour.
mass [mæs] *n* multitude *f*, masse *f*; (*PHYSICS*) masse; (*REL*) messe *f* ♦ *vi* se masser; **the ~es** les masses; **to go to** ~ aller à la messe.
Mass. *abbr* (*US*) = *Massachusetts*.
massacre ['mæsəkə*] *n* massacre *m* ♦ *vt* massacrer.
massage ['mæsɑːʒ] *n* massage *m* ♦ *vt* masser.
massive ['mæsɪv] *adj* énorme, massif(ive).
mass market *n* marché *m* grand public.
mass media *npl* mass-media *mpl*.
mass meeting *n* rassemblement *m* de masse.
mass-produce ['mæsprə'djuːs] *vt* fabriquer en série.
mass production *n* production *f or* fabrication *f* en série.
mast [mɑːst] *n* mât *m*; (*RADIO, TV*) pylône *m*.
mastectomy [mæs'tɛktəmɪ] *n* (*MED*) mastectomie *f*.
master ['mɑːstə*] *n* maître *m*; (*in secondary school*) professeur *m*; (*title for boys*): **M~ X** Monsieur X ♦ *vt* maîtriser; (*learn*) apprendre à fond; (*understand*) posséder parfaitement *or* à fond; ~ **of ceremonies (MC)** *n* maître des cérémonies; **M~ of Arts/Science (MA/MSc)** *n* ≈ titulaire *m/f* d'une maîtrise (en lettres/science); **M~ of Arts/Science degree (MA/MSc)** *n* ≈ maîtrise *f*; **M~'s degree** *n* ≈ maîtrise; *voir encadré*.

MASTER'S DEGREE

Le **Master's degree** *est un diplôme que l'on prépare en général après le "Bachelor's degree", bien que certaines universités décernent un* **Master's** *au lieu d'un "Bachelor's". Pour l'obtenir, il faut soit suivre des cours, soit rédiger un mémoire à partir d'une recherche personnelle, soit encore les deux. Les principaux masters sont le "MA" (Master of Arts), et le "MSc (Master of Science)", qui comprennent cours et mémoire, et le "MLitt (Master of Letters)" et le "MPhil (Master of Philosophy)", qui reposent sur le mémoire; voir "doctorate".*

master disk *n* (*COMPUT*) disque original.
masterful ['mɑːstəful] *adj* autoritaire, impérieux(euse).
master key *n* passe-partout *m inv*.
masterly ['mɑːstəlɪ] *adj* magistral(e).
mastermind ['mɑːstəmaɪnd] *n* esprit supérieur ♦ *vt* diriger, être le cerveau de.
masterpiece ['mɑːstəpiːs] *n* chef-d'œuvre *m*.
master plan *n* stratégie *f* d'ensemble.
master stroke *n* coup *m* de maître.
mastery ['mɑːstərɪ] *n* maîtrise *f*; connaissance parfaite.
masturbate ['mæstəbeɪt] *vi* se masturber.
mat [mæt] *n* petit tapis; (*also*: **door**~) paillasson *m* ♦ *adj* = **matt**.
match [mætʃ] *n* allumette *f*; (*game*) match *m*, partie *f*; (*fig*) égal/e; mariage *m*; parti *m* ♦ *vt* assortir; (*go well with*) aller bien avec, s'assortir à; (*equal*) égaler, valoir ♦ *vi* être assorti(e); **to be a good** ~ être bien assorti(e).
►**match up** *vt* assortir.
matchbox ['mætʃbɔks] *n* boîte *f* d'allumettes.
matching ['mætʃɪŋ] *adj* assorti(e).
matchless ['mætʃlɪs] *adj* sans égal.
mate [meɪt] *n* camarade *m/f*; (*col*) copain/copine; (*animal*) mâle/femelle; (*in merchant navy*) second *m* ♦ *vi* s'accoupler ♦ *vt* accoupler.
material [mə'tɪərɪəl] *n* (*substance*) matière *f*, matériau *m*; (*cloth*) tissu *m* ♦ *adj* matériel(le); (*important*) essentiel(le); **~s** *npl* matériaux *mpl*; **reading** ~ de quoi lire, de la lecture.
materialistic [mətɪərɪə'lɪstɪk] *adj* matérialiste.
materialize [mə'tɪərɪəlaɪz] *vi* se matérialiser, se réaliser.
materially [mə'tɪərɪəlɪ] *adv* matériellement; essentiellement.
maternal [mə'təːnl] *adj* maternel(le).
maternity [mə'təːnɪtɪ] *n* maternité *f* ♦ *cpd* de maternité, de grossesse.
maternity benefit *n* prestation *f* de maternité.
maternity hospital *n* maternité *f*.
matey ['meɪtɪ] *adj* (*BRIT col*) copain-copain *inv*.
math. [mæθ] *n abbr* (*US*: = *mathematics*) maths *fpl*.
mathematical [mæθə'mætɪkl] *adj* mathémati-

que.

mathematician [mæθəmə'tɪʃən] *n* mathématicien/ne.

mathematics [mæθə'mætɪks] *n* mathématiques *fpl*.

maths [mæθs] *n abbr* (*BRIT*: = *mathematics*) maths *fpl*.

matinée ['mætɪneɪ] *n* matinée *f*.

mating ['meɪtɪŋ] *n* accouplement *m*.

mating call *n* appel *m* du mâle.

mating season *n* saison *f* des amours.

matriarchal [meɪtrɪ'ɑːkl] *adj* matriarcal(e).

matrices ['meɪtrɪsiːz] *npl of* **matrix**.

matriculation [mətrɪkju'leɪʃən] *n* inscription *f*.

matrimonial [mætrɪ'məunɪəl] *adj* matrimonial(e), conjugal(e).

matrimony ['mætrɪmənɪ] *n* mariage *m*.

matrix, *pl* **matrices** ['meɪtrɪks, 'meɪtrɪsiːz] *n* matrice *f*.

matron ['meɪtrən] *n* (*in hospital*) infirmière-chef *f*; (*in school*) infirmière *f*.

matronly ['meɪtrənlɪ] *adj* de matrone; imposant(e).

matt [mæt] *adj* mat(e).

matted ['mætɪd] *adj* emmêlé(e).

matter ['mætə*] *n* question *f*; (*PHYSICS*) matière *f*, substance *f*; (*content*) contenu *m*, fond *m*; (*MED*: *pus*) pus *m* ♦ *vi* importer; **it doesn't** ~ cela n'a pas d'importance; (*I don't mind*) cela ne fait rien; **what's the ~?** qu'est-ce qu'il y a?, qu'est-ce qui ne va pas?; **no ~ what** quoiqu'il arrive; **that's another ~** c'est une autre affaire; **as a ~ of course** tout naturellement; **as a ~ of fact** en fait; **it's a ~ of habit** c'est une question d'habitude; **printed ~** imprimés *mpl*; **reading ~** (*BRIT*) de quoi lire, de la lecture.

matter-of-fact ['mætərəv'fækt] *adj* terre à terre, neutre.

matting ['mætɪŋ] *n* natte *f*.

mattress ['mætrɪs] *n* matelas *m*.

mature [mə'tjuə*] *adj* mûr(e); (*cheese*) fait(e) ♦ *vi* mûrir; se faire.

mature student *n étudiant/e plus âgé(e) que la moyenne*.

maturity [mə'tjuərɪtɪ] *n* maturité *f*.

maudlin ['mɔːdlɪn] *adj* larmoyant(e).

maul [mɔːl] *vt* lacérer.

Mauritania [mɔːrɪ'teɪnɪə] *n* Mauritanie *f*.

Mauritius [mə'rɪʃəs] *n* l'île *f* Maurice.

mausoleum [mɔːsə'lɪəm] *n* mausolée *m*.

mauve [məuv] *adj* mauve.

maverick ['mævrɪk] *n* (*fig*) franc-tireur *m*, non-conformiste *m/f*.

mawkish ['mɔːkɪʃ] *adj* mièvre; fade.

max. *abbr* = **maximum**.

maxim ['mæksɪm] *n* maxime *f*.

maxima ['mæksɪmə] *npl of* **maximum**.

maximize ['mæksɪmaɪz] *vt* (*profits etc, chances*) maximiser.

maximum ['mæksɪməm] *adj* maximum ♦ *n* (*pl* **maxima** ['mæksɪmə]) maximum *m*.

May [meɪ] *n* mai *m*; *for phrases see also* **July**.

may [meɪ] *vi* (*conditional*: **might**) (*indicating possibility*): **he ~ come** il se peut qu'il vienne; (*be allowed to*): **~ I smoke?** puis-je fumer?; (*wishes*): **~ God bless you!** (que) Dieu vous bénisse!; **~ I sit here?** vous permettez que je m'assoie ici?; **he might be there** il pourrait bien y être, il se pourrait qu'il y soit; **I might as well go** je ferais aussi bien d'y aller, autant y aller; **you might like to try** vous pourriez (peut-être) essayer.

maybe ['meɪbiː] *adv* peut-être; **~ he'll** ... peut-être qu'il ...; **~ not** peut-être pas.

May Day *n* le Premier mai.

mayday ['meɪdeɪ] *n* S.O.S. *m*.

mayhem ['meɪhɛm] *n* grabuge *m*.

mayonnaise [meɪə'neɪz] *n* mayonnaise *f*.

mayor [mɛə*] *n* maire *m*.

mayoress ['mɛərɛs] *n* maire *m*; épouse *f* du maire.

maypole ['meɪpəul] *n* mât enrubanné (*autour duquel on danse*).

maze [meɪz] *n* labyrinthe *m*, dédale *m*.

MB *abbr* (*COMPUT*) = **megabyte**; (*Canada*) = *Manitoba*.

MBA *n abbr* (= *Master of Business Administration*) *titre universitaire*.

MBBS, MBChB *n abbr* (*BRIT*: = *Bachelor of Medicine and Surgery*) *titre universitaire*.

MBE *n abbr* (*BRIT*: = *Member of the Order of the British Empire*) *titre honorifique*.

MC *n abbr* = **master of ceremonies**.

MCAT *n abbr* (*US*) = *Medical College Admissions Test*.

MCP *n abbr* (*BRIT col*: = *male chauvinist pig*) phallocrate *m*.

MD *n abbr* (= *Doctor of Medicine*) *titre universitaire*; (*COMM*) = **managing director** ♦ *abbr* (*US*) = *Maryland*.

Md. *abbr* (*US*) = *Maryland*.

MDT *abbr* (*US*: = *Mountain Daylight Time*) *heure d'été des Montagnes Rocheuses*.

ME *n abbr* (*US*: = *medical examiner*) médecin légiste *m/f*; (*MED*: = *myalgic encephalomyelitis*) encéphalomyélite *f* myalgique ♦ *abbr* (*US*) = *Maine*.

me [miː] *pron* me, m' + *vowel*; (*stressed, after prep*) moi; **it's** ~ c'est moi; **it's for** ~ c'est pour moi.

meadow ['mɛdəu] *n* prairie *f*, pré *m*.

meagre, (*US*) **meager** ['miːgə*] *adj* maigre.

meal [miːl] *n* repas *m*; (*flour*) farine *f*; **to go out for a ~** sortir manger.

meals on wheels *npl* (*BRIT*) *repas livrés à domicile aux personnes âgées ou handicapées*.

mealtime ['miːltaɪm] *n* heure *f* du repas.

mealy-mouthed ['miːlɪmauðd] *adj* mielleux(euse).

mean [miːn] *adj* (*with money*) avare, radin(e); (*unkind*) mesquin(e), méchant(e); (*US col*: *animal*) méchant, vicieux(euse); (*: person*)

vache; (*average*) moyen(ne) ♦ *vt* (*pt*, *pp* **meant** [mɛnt]) (*signify*) signifier, vouloir dire; (*intend*): **to ~ to do** avoir l'intention de faire ♦ *n* moyenne *f*; **to be meant for** être destiné(e) à; **do you ~ it?** vous êtes sérieux?; **what do you ~?** que voulez-vous dire?
meander [mɪ'ændə*] *vi* faire des méandres; (*fig*) flâner.
meaning ['mi:nɪŋ] *n* signification *f*, sens *m*.
meaningful ['mi:nɪŋful] *adj* significatif(ive); (*relationship*) valable.
meaningless ['mi:nɪŋlɪs] *adj* dénué(e) de sens.
meanness ['mi:nnɪs] *n* avarice *f*; mesquinerie *f*.
means [mi:nz] *npl* moyens *mpl*; **by ~ of** par l'intermédiaire de; au moyen de; **by all ~** je vous en prie.
means test *n* (*ADMIN*) contrôle *m* des conditions de ressources.
meant [mɛnt] *pt*, *pp of* **mean**.
meantime ['mi:ntaɪm] *adv*, **meanwhile** ['mi:nwaɪl] *adv* (*also*: **in the ~**) pendant ce temps.
measles ['mi:zlz] *n* rougeole *f*.
measly ['mi:zlɪ] *adj* (*col*) minable.
measurable ['mɛʒərəbl] *adj* mesurable.
measure ['mɛʒə*] *vt*, *vi* mesurer ♦ *n* mesure *f*; (*ruler*) règle (graduée); **a litre ~** un litre; **some ~ of success** un certain succès; **to take ~s to do sth** prendre des mesures pour faire qch.
▸**measure up** *vi*: **to ~ up (to)** être à la hauteur (de).
measured ['mɛʒəd] *adj* mesuré(e).
measurement ['mɛʒəmənt] *n*: **chest/hip ~** tour *m* de poitrine/hanches; **~s** *npl* mesures *fpl*; **to take sb's ~s** prendre les mesures de qn.
meat [mi:t] *n* viande *f*; **cold ~s** (*BRIT*) viandes froides; **crab ~** crabe *f*.
meatball ['mi:tbɔ:l] *n* boulette *f* de viande.
meat pie *n* pâté *m* en croûte.
meaty ['mi:tɪ] *adj* (*flavour*) de viande; (*fig: argument, book*) étoffé(e), substantiel(le).
Mecca ['mɛkə] *n* La Mecque; (*fig*): **a ~ (for)** la Mecque (de).
mechanic [mɪ'kænɪk] *n* mécanicien *m*.
mechanical [mɪ'kænɪkl] *adj* mécanique.
mechanical engineering *n* (*science*) mécanique *f*; (*industry*) construction *f* mécanique.
mechanics [mə'kænɪks] *n* mécanique *f* ♦ *npl* mécanisme *m*.
mechanism ['mɛkənɪzəm] *n* mécanisme *m*.
mechanization [mɛkənaɪ'zeɪʃən] *n* mécanisation *f*.
MEd *n abbr* (= *Master of Education*) *titre universitaire*.
medal ['mɛdl] *n* médaille *f*.
medallion [mɪ'dælɪən] *n* médaillon *m*.
medallist, (*US*) **medalist** ['mɛdlɪst] *n* (*SPORT*) médaillé/e.
meddle ['mɛdl] *vi*: **to ~ in** se mêler de, s'occuper de; **to ~ with** toucher à.
meddlesome ['mɛdlsəm], **meddling** ['mɛdlɪŋ] *adj* indiscret(ète), qui se mêle de ce qui ne le (*or* la) regarde pas; touche-à-tout *inv*.
media ['mi:dɪə] *npl* media *mpl*.
media circus *n* (*event*) battage *m* médiatique; (*group of journalists*) cortège *m* médiatique.
mediaeval [mɛdɪ'i:vl] *adj* = **medieval**.
median ['mi:dɪən] *n* (*US*: *also*: **~ strip**) bande médiane.
media research *n* étude *f* de l'audience.
mediate ['mi:dɪeɪt] *vi* s'interposer; servir d'intermédiaire.
mediation [mi:dɪ'eɪʃən] *n* médiation *f*.
mediator ['mi:dɪeɪtə*] *n* médiateur/trice.
Medicaid ['mɛdɪkeɪd] *n* (*US*) *assistance médicale aux indigents*.
medical ['mɛdɪkl] *adj* médical(e) ♦ *n* (*also*: **~ examination**) visite médicale; examen médical.
medical certificate *n* certificat médical.
medical student *n* étudiant/e en médecine.
Medicare ['mɛdɪkɛə*] *n* (*US*) *régime d'assurance maladie*.
medicated ['mɛdɪkeɪtɪd] *adj* traitant(e), médicamenteux(euse).
medication [mɛdɪ'keɪʃən] *n* (*drugs etc*) médication *f*.
medicinal [mɛ'dɪsɪnl] *adj* médicinal(e).
medicine ['mɛdsɪn] *n* médecine *f*; (*drug*) médicament *m*.
medicine chest *n* pharmacie *f* (*murale ou portative*).
medicine man *n* sorcier *m*.
medieval [mɛdɪ'i:vl] *adj* médiéval(e).
mediocre [mi:dɪ'əukə*] *adj* médiocre.
mediocrity [mi:dɪ'ɔkrɪtɪ] *n* médiocrité *f*.
meditate ['mɛdɪteɪt] *vi*: **to ~ (on)** méditer (sur).
meditation [mɛdɪ'teɪʃən] *n* méditation *f*.
Mediterranean [mɛdɪtə'reɪnɪən] *adj* méditerranéen(ne); **the ~ (Sea)** la (mer) Méditerranée.
medium ['mi:dɪəm] *adj* moyen(ne) ♦ *n* (*pl* **media**) (*means*) moyen *m*; (*pl* **mediums**) (*person*) médium *m*; **the happy ~** le juste milieu.
medium-dry ['mi:dɪəm'draɪ] *adj* demi-sec.
medium-sized ['mi:dɪəm'saɪzd] *adj* de taille moyenne.
medium wave *n* (*RADIO*) ondes moyennes, petites ondes.
medley ['mɛdlɪ] *n* mélange *m*.
meek [mi:k] *adj* doux(douce), humble.
meet, *pt*, *pp* **met** [mi:t, mɛt] *vt* rencontrer; (*by arrangement*) retrouver, rejoindre; (*for the first time*) faire la connaissance de; (*go and fetch*): **I'll ~ you at the station** j'irai te chercher à la gare; (*problem*) faire face à; (*requirements*) satisfaire à, répondre à; (*bill, expenses*) régler, honorer ♦ *vi* se rencontrer; se retrouver; (*in session*) se réunir; (*join: objects*) se joindre ♦ *n* (*BRIT*: *HUNTING*) rendez-

vous *m* de chasse; (*US SPORT*) rencontre *f*, meeting *m*; **pleased to ~ you!** enchanté!
►**meet up** *vi*: **to ~ up with sb** rencontrer qn.
►**meet with** *vt fus* rencontrer.
meeting ['mi:tɪŋ] *n* rencontre *f*; (*session: of club etc*) réunion *f*; (*formal*) assemblée *f*; (*SPORT: rally*) rencontre, meeting *m*; (*interview*) entrevue *f*; **she's at a ~** (*COMM*) elle est en conférence; **to call a ~** convoquer une réunion.
meeting place *n* lieu *m* de (la) réunion; (*for appointment*) lieu de rendez-vous.
megabyte ['mɛgəbaɪt] *n* méga-octet *m*.
megaphone ['mɛgəfəun] *n* porte-voix *m inv*.
melancholy ['mɛlənkəlɪ] *n* mélancolie *f* ♦ *adj* mélancolique.
mellow ['mɛləu] *adj* velouté(e); doux(douce); (*colour*) riche et profond(e); (*fruit*) mûr(e) ♦ *vi* (*person*) s'adoucir.
melodious [mɪ'ləudɪəs] *adj* mélodieux(euse).
melodrama ['mɛləudrɑ:mə] *n* mélodrame *m*.
melodramatic [mɛlədrə'mætɪk] *adj* mélodramatique.
melody ['mɛlədɪ] *n* mélodie *f*.
melon ['mɛlən] *n* melon *m*.
melt [mɛlt] *vi* fondre; (*become soft*) s'amollir; (*fig*) s'attendrir ♦ *vt* faire fondre.
►**melt away** *vi* fondre complètement.
►**melt down** *vt* fondre.
meltdown ['mɛltdaun] *n* fusion *f* (du cœur d'un réacteur nucléaire).
melting point ['mɛltɪŋ-] *n* point *m* de fusion.
melting pot ['mɛltɪŋ-] *n* (*fig*) creuset *m*; **to be in the ~** être encore en discussion.
member ['mɛmbə*] *n* membre *m*; (*of club, political party*) membre, adhérent/e ♦ *cpd*: **~ country/state** *n* pays *m*/état *m* membre; **M~ of Parliament (MP)** *n* (*BRIT*) député *m*; **M~ of the European Parliament (MEP)** *n* Eurodéputé *m*; **M~ of the House of Representatives (MHR)** *n* (*US*) membre de la Chambre des représentants.
membership ['mɛmbəʃɪp] *n* (*becoming a member*) adhésion *f*; admission *f*; (*being a member*) qualité *f* de membre, fait *m* d'être membre; (*the members*) membres *mpl*, adhérents *mpl*; (*number of members*) nombre *m* des membres *or* adhérents.
membership card *n* carte *f* de membre.
membrane ['mɛmbreɪn] *n* membrane *f*.
memento [mə'mɛntəu] *n* souvenir *m*.
memo ['mɛməu] *n* note *f* (de service).
memoir ['mɛmwɑ:*] *n* mémoire *m*, étude *f*; **~s** *npl* mémoires.
memo pad *n* bloc-notes *m*.
memorable ['mɛmərəbl] *adj* mémorable.
memorandum, *pl* **memoranda** [mɛmə'rændəm, -də] *n* note *f* (de service); (*DIPLOMACY*) mémorandum *m*.
memorial [mɪ'mɔ:rɪəl] *n* mémorial *m* ♦ *adj* commémoratif(ive); *voir encadré*.
Memorial Day *n* (*US*) le jour des morts au champ d'honneur; *voir encadré*.

MEMORIAL DAY

Memorial Day *est un jour férié aux États-Unis, le dernier lundi de mai dans la plupart des États, à la mémoire des soldats américains morts au combat.*

memorize ['mɛməraɪz] *vt* apprendre *or* retenir par cœur.
memory ['mɛmərɪ] *n* mémoire *f*; (*recollection*) souvenir *m*; **to have a good/bad ~** avoir une bonne/mauvaise mémoire; **loss of ~** perte *f* de mémoire; **in ~ of** à la mémoire de.
men [mɛn] *npl of* **man**.
menace ['mɛnɪs] *n* menace *f*; (*col: nuisance*) peste *f*, plaie *f* ♦ *vt* menacer; **a public ~** un danger public.
menacing ['mɛnɪsɪŋ] *adj* menaçant(e).
menagerie [mɪ'nædʒərɪ] *n* ménagerie *f*.
mend [mɛnd] *vt* réparer; (*darn*) raccommoder, repriser ♦ *n* reprise *f*; **on the ~** en voie de guérison.
mending ['mɛndɪŋ] *n* raccommodages *mpl*.
menial ['mi:nɪəl] *adj* de domestique, inférieur(e); subalterne.
meningitis [mɛnɪn'dʒaɪtɪs] *n* méningite *f*.
menopause ['mɛnəupɔ:z] *n* ménopause *f*.
menservants ['mɛnsə:vənts] *npl of* **manservant**.
men's room *n*: **the ~** (*esp US*) les toilettes *fpl* pour hommes.
menstruate ['mɛnstrueɪt] *vi* avoir ses règles.
menstruation [mɛnstru'eɪʃən] *n* menstruation *f*.
menswear ['mɛnzwɛə*] *n* vêtements *mpl* d'hommes.
mental ['mɛntl] *adj* mental(e); **~ illness** maladie mentale.
mental hospital *n* hôpital *m* psychiatrique.
mentality [mɛn'tælɪtɪ] *n* mentalité *f*.
mentally ['mɛntlɪ] *adv*: **to be ~ handicapped** être handicapé/e mental(e).
menthol ['mɛnθɔl] *n* menthol *m*.
mention ['mɛnʃən] *n* mention *f* ♦ *vt* mentionner, faire mention de; **don't ~ it!** je vous en prie, il n'y a pas de quoi!; **I need hardly ~ that ...** est-il besoin de rappeler que ...?; **not to ~ ..., without ~ing ...** sans parler de ..., sans compter ....
mentor ['mɛntɔ:*] *n* mentor *m*.
menu ['mɛnju:] *n* (*in restaurant, COMPUT*) menu *m*; (*printed*) carte *f*.
menu-driven ['mɛnju:drɪvn] *adj* (*COMPUT*) piloté(e) par menu.
MEP *n abbr* = **Member of the European Parliament.**
mercantile ['mə:kəntaɪl] *adj* marchand(e); (*law*) commercial(e).
mercenary ['mə:sɪnərɪ] *adj* mercantile ♦ *n* mercenaire *m*.

merchandise ['mə:tʃəndaɪz] *n* marchandises *fpl* ♦ *vt* commercialiser.
merchandiser ['mə:tʃəndaɪzə*] *n* marchandiseur *m*.
merchant ['mə:tʃənt] *n* négociant *m*, marchand *m*; **timber/wine** ~ négociant en bois/vins, marchand de bois/vins.
merchant bank *n* (*BRIT*) banque *f* d'affaires.
merchantman ['mə:tʃəntmən] *n* navire marchand.
merchant navy, (*US*) **merchant marine** *n* marine marchande.
merciful ['mə:sɪful] *adj* miséricordieux(euse), clément(e).
mercifully ['mə:sɪflɪ] *adv* avec clémence; (*fortunately*) par bonheur, Dieu merci.
merciless ['mə:sɪlɪs] *adj* impitoyable, sans pitié.
mercurial [mə:'kjuərɪəl] *adj* changeant(e); (*lively*) vif(vive).
mercury ['mə:kjurɪ] *n* mercure *m*.
mercy ['mə:sɪ] *n* pitié *f*, merci *f*; (*REL*) miséricorde *f*; **to have** ~ **on sb** avoir pitié de qn; **at the** ~ **of** à la merci de.
mercy killing *n* euthanasie *f*.
mere [mɪə*] *adj* simple.
merely ['mɪəlɪ] *adv* simplement, purement.
merge [mə:dʒ] *vt* unir; (*COMPUT*) fusionner, interclasser ♦ *vi* se fondre; (*COMM*) fusionner.
merger ['mə:dʒə*] *n* (*COMM*) fusion *f*.
meridian [mə'rɪdɪən] *n* méridien *m*.
meringue [mə'ræŋ] *n* meringue *f*.
merit ['mɛrɪt] *n* mérite *m*, valeur *f* ♦ *vt* mériter.
meritocracy [mɛrɪ'tɔkrəsɪ] *n* méritocratie *f*.
mermaid ['mə:meɪd] *n* sirène *f*.
merrily ['mɛrɪlɪ] *adv* joyeusement, gaiement.
merriment ['mɛrɪmənt] *n* gaieté *f*.
merry ['mɛrɪ] *adj* gai(e); **M~ Christmas!** joyeux Noël!
merry-go-round ['mɛrɪgəuraund] *n* manège *m*.
mesh [mɛʃ] *n* maille *f*; filet *m* ♦ *vi* (*gears*) s'engrener; **wire** ~ grillage *m* (métallique), treillis *m* (métallique).
mesmerize ['mɛzməraɪz] *vt* hypnotiser; fasciner.
mess [mɛs] *n* désordre *m*, fouillis *m*, pagaille *f*; (*MIL*) mess *m*, cantine *f*; **to be (in) a** ~ être en désordre; **to be/get o.s. in a** ~ (*fig*) être/se mettre dans le pétrin.
►**mess about**, **mess around** *vi* (*col*) perdre son temps.
►**mess about** *or* **around with** *vt fus* (*col*) chambarder, tripoter.
►**mess up** *vt* salir; chambarder; gâcher.
message ['mɛsɪdʒ] *n* message *m*; **to get the** ~ (*fig: col*) saisir, piger.
message switching [-swɪtʃɪŋ] *n* (*COMPUT*) commutation *f* de messages.
messenger ['mɛsɪndʒə*] *n* messager *m*.
Messiah [mɪ'saɪə] *n* Messie *m*.
Messrs, Messrs. ['mɛsəz] *abbr* (*on letters*: = *messieurs*) MM.
messy ['mɛsɪ] *adj* sale; en désordre.
Met [mɛt] *n abbr* (*US*) = *Metropolitan Opera*.
met [mɛt] *pt, pp of* **meet** ♦ *adj abbr* (= *meteorological*) météo *inv*.
metabolism [mɛ'tæbəlɪzəm] *n* métabolisme *m*.
metal ['mɛtl] *n* métal *m* ♦ *vt* empierrer.
metallic [mɛ'tælɪk] *adj* métallique.
metallurgy [mɛ'tælədʒɪ] *n* métallurgie *f*.
metalwork ['mɛtlwə:k] *n* (*craft*) ferronnerie *f*.
metamorphosis, *pl* **-ses** [mɛtə'mɔ:fəsɪs, -si:z] *n* métamorphose *f*.
metaphor ['mɛtəfə*] *n* métaphore *f*.
metaphysics [mɛtə'fɪzɪks] *n* métaphysique *f*.
mete [mi:t]: **to** ~ **out** *vt fus* infliger.
meteor ['mi:tɪə*] *n* météore *m*.
meteoric [mi:tɪ'ɔrɪk] *adj* (*fig*) fulgurant(e).
meteorite ['mi:tɪəraɪt] *n* météorite *m or f*.
meteorological [mi:tɪərə'lɔdʒɪkl] *adj* météorologique.
meteorology [mi:tɪə'rɔlədʒɪ] *n* météorologie *f*.
meter ['mi:tə*] *n* (*instrument*) compteur *m*; (*also*: **parking** ~) parc(o)mètre *m*; (*US*) = **metre**.
methane ['mi:θeɪn] *n* méthane *m*.
method ['mɛθəd] *n* méthode *f*; ~ **of payment** mode *m or* modalité *f* de paiement.
methodical [mɪ'θɔdɪkl] *adj* méthodique.
Methodist ['mɛθədɪst] *adj, n* méthodiste (*m/f*).
methylated spirit ['mɛθɪleɪtɪd-] *n* (*BRIT*: *also*: **meths**) alcool *m* à brûler.
meticulous [mɛ'tɪkjuləs] *adj* méticuleux(euse).
metre, (*US*) **meter** ['mi:tə*] *n* mètre *m*.
metric ['mɛtrɪk] *adj* métrique; **to go** ~ adopter le système métrique.
metrical ['mɛtrɪkl] *adj* métrique.
metrication [mɛtrɪ'keɪʃən] *n* conversion *f* au système métrique.
metric system *n* système *m* métrique.
metric ton *n* tonne *f*.
metronome ['mɛtrənəum] *n* métronome *m*.
metropolis [mɪ'trɔpəlɪs] *n* métropole *f*.
metropolitan [mɛtrə'pɔlɪtən] *adj* métropolitain(e).
Metropolitan Police *n* (*BRIT*): **the** ~ la police londonienne.
mettle ['mɛtl] *n* courage *m*.
mew [mju:] *vi* (*cat*) miauler.
mews [mju:z] *n* (*BRIT*): ~ **cottage** *maisonnette aménagée dans une ancienne écurie ou remise*.
Mexican ['mɛksɪkən] *adj* mexicain(e) ♦ *n* Mexicain/e.
Mexico ['mɛksɪkəu] *n* Mexique *m*.
Mexico City *n* Mexico.
mezzanine ['mɛtsəni:n] *n* mezzanine *f*; (*of shops, offices*) entresol *m*.
MFA *n abbr* (*US*: = *Master of Fine Arts*) *titre universitaire*.
mfr *abbr* = **manufacture, manufacturer**.
mg *abbr* (= *milligram*) mg.

Mgr *abbr* (= *Monseigneur, Monsignor*) Mgr; (= *manager*) dir.
MHR *n abbr* (*US*) = **Member of the House of Representatives.**
MHz *abbr* (= *megahertz*) MHz.
MI *abbr* (*US*) = *Michigan.*
MI5 *n abbr* (*BRIT*: = *Military Intelligence 5*) ≈ DST *f.*
MI6 *n abbr* (*BRIT*: = *Military Intelligence 6*) ≈ DGSE *f.*
MIA *abbr* (= *missing in action*) disparu au combat.
miaow [miː'au] *vi* miauler.
mice [maɪs] *npl of* **mouse.**
Mich. *abbr* (*US*) = *Michigan.*
microbe ['maɪkrəub] *n* microbe *m.*
microbiology [maɪkrəbaɪ'ɔlədʒɪ] *n* microbiologie *f.*
microchip ['maɪkrəutʃɪp] *n* (*ELEC*) puce *f.*
micro(computer) ['maɪkrəu(kəm'pjuːtə*)] *n* micro(-ordinateur *m*) *m.*
microcosm ['maɪkrəukɔzəm] *n* microcosme *m.*
microeconomics ['maɪkrəuiːkə'nɔmɪks] *n* micro-économie *f.*
microfiche ['maɪkrəufiːʃ] *n* microfiche *f.*
microfilm ['maɪkrəufɪlm] *n* microfilm *m* ♦ *vt* microfilmer.
microlight ['maɪkrəulaɪt] *n* ULM *m.*
micrometer [maɪ'krɔmɪtə*] *n* palmer *m*, micromètre *m.*
microphone ['maɪkrəfəun] *n* microphone *m.*
microprocessor ['maɪkrəu'prəusesə*] *n* microprocesseur *m.*
microscope ['maɪkrəskəup] *n* microscope *m*; **under the** ~ au microscope.
microscopic [maɪkrə'skɔpɪk] *adj* microscopique.
microwave ['maɪkrəuweɪv] *n* (*also*: ~ **oven**) four *m* à micro-ondes.
mid [mɪd] *adj*: ~ **May** la mi-mai; ~ **afternoon** le milieu de l'après-midi; **in** ~ **air** en plein ciel; **he's in his** ~ **thirties** il a dans les trente-cinq ans.
midday [mɪd'deɪ] *n* midi *m.*
middle ['mɪdl] *n* milieu *m*; (*waist*) ceinture *f*, taille *f* ♦ *adj* du milieu; **in the** ~ **of the night** au milieu de la nuit; **I'm in the** ~ **of reading it** je suis (justement) en train de le lire.
middle age *n tranche d'âge aux limites floues, entre la quarantaine et le début du troisième âge.*
middle-aged [mɪdl'eɪdʒd] *adj* (*people*: *see middle age*) d'un certain âge, ni vieux ni jeune; (*pej*: *values, outlook*) conventionnel(le), rassis(e).
Middle Ages *npl*: **the** ~ le moyen âge.
middle class *n*: **the** ~**(es)** ≈ les classes moyennes ♦ *adj* (*also*: **middle-class**) ≈ (petit(e)-)bourgeois(e).
Middle East *n*: **the** ~ le Proche-Orient, le Moyen-Orient.
middleman ['mɪdlmæn] *n* intermédiaire *m.*
middle management *n* cadres moyens.
middle name *n* second prénom.
middle-of-the-road ['mɪdləvðə'rəud] *adj* (*policy*) modéré(e), du juste milieu; (*music etc*) plutôt classique, assez traditionnel(le).
middleweight ['mɪdlweɪt] *n* (*BOXING*) poids moyen.
middling ['mɪdlɪŋ] *adj* moyen(ne).
Middx *abbr* (*BRIT*) = *Middlesex.*
midge [mɪdʒ] *n* moucheron *m.*
midget ['mɪdʒɪt] *n* nain/e ♦ *adj* minuscule.
midi system ['mɪdɪ-] *n* chaîne *f* midi.
Midlands ['mɪdləndz] *npl comtés du centre de l'Angleterre.*
midnight ['mɪdnaɪt] *n* minuit *m*; **at** ~ à minuit.
midriff ['mɪdrɪf] *n* estomac *m*, taille *f.*
midst [mɪdst] *n*: **in the** ~ **of** au milieu de.
midsummer [mɪd'sʌmə*] *n* milieu *m* de l'été.
midway [mɪd'weɪ] *adj, adv*: ~ **(between)** à mi-chemin (entre).
midweek [mɪd'wiːk] *adj* du milieu de la semaine ♦ *adv* au milieu de la semaine, en pleine semaine.
midwife, midwives ['mɪdwaɪf, -vz] *n* sage-femme *f.*
midwifery ['mɪdwɪfərɪ] *n* obstétrique *f.*
midwinter [mɪd'wɪntə*] *n* milieu *m* de l'hiver.
miffed [mɪft] *adj* (*col*) fâché(e), vexé(e).
might [maɪt] *vb see* **may** ♦ *n* puissance *f*, force *f.*
mighty ['maɪtɪ] *adj* puissant(e) ♦ *adv* (*col*) rudement.
migraine ['miːgreɪn] *n* migraine *f.*
migrant ['maɪgrənt] *n* (*bird, animal*) migrateur *m*; (*person*) migrant/e; nomade *m/f* ♦ *adj* migrateur(trice); migrant(e); nomade; (*worker*) saisonnier(ière).
migrate [maɪ'greɪt] *vi* émigrer.
migration [maɪ'greɪʃən] *n* migration *f.*
mike [maɪk] *n abbr* (= *microphone*) micro *m.*
Milan [mɪ'læn] *n* Milan.
mild [maɪld] *adj* doux(douce); (*reproach*) léger(ère); (*illness*) bénin(igne) ♦ *n* bière légère.
mildew ['mɪldjuː] *n* mildiou *m.*
mildly ['maɪldlɪ] *adv* doucement; légèrement; **to put it** ~ (*col*) c'est le moins qu'on puisse dire.
mildness ['maɪldnɪs] *n* douceur *f.*
mile [maɪl] *n* mil(l)e *m* (= *1609 m*); **to do 30** ~**s per gallon** ≈ faire 9,4 litres aux cent.
mileage ['maɪlɪdʒ] *n* distance *f* en milles, ≈ kilométrage *m.*
mileage allowance *n* ≈ indemnité *f* kilométrique.
mileometer [maɪ'lɔmɪtə*] *n* (*BRIT*) = **milometer.**
milestone ['maɪlstəun] *n* borne *f*; (*fig*) jalon *m.*
milieu ['miːljəː] *n* milieu *m.*
militant ['mɪlɪtnt] *adj, n* militant(e).
militarism ['mɪlɪtərɪzəm] *n* militarisme *m.*

militaristic [mɪlɪtə'rɪstɪk] *adj* militariste.
military ['mɪlɪtərɪ] *adj* militaire ♦ *n*: **the** ~ l'armée *f*, les militaires *mpl*.
military service *n* service *m* (militaire *ou* national).
militate ['mɪlɪteɪt] *vi*: **to ~ against** militer contre.
militia [mɪ'lɪʃə] *n* milice *f*.
milk [mɪlk] *n* lait *m* ♦ *vt* (*cow*) traire; (*fig*) dépouiller, plumer.
milk chocolate *n* chocolat *m* au lait.
milk float *n* (*BRIT*) voiture *f or* camionnette *f* du *or* de laitier.
milking ['mɪlkɪŋ] *n* traite *f*.
milkman ['mɪlkmən] *n* laitier *m*.
milk shake *n* milk-shake *m*.
milk tooth *n* dent *f* de lait.
milk truck *n* (*US*) = **milk float**.
milky ['mɪlkɪ] *adj* lacté(e); (*colour*) laiteux(euse).
Milky Way *n* Voie lactée.
mill [mɪl] *n* moulin *m*; (*factory*) usine *f*, fabrique *f*; (*spinning* ~) filature *f*; (*flour* ~) minoterie *f* ♦ *vt* moudre, broyer ♦ *vi* (*also*: ~ **about**) grouiller.
millennium, *pl* **~s** *or* **millennia** [mɪ'lɛnɪəm, -'lɛnɪə] *n* millénaire *m*.
millennium bug *n* bogue *m or* bug *m* de l'an 2000.
miller ['mɪlə*] *n* meunier *m*.
millet ['mɪlɪt] *n* millet *m*.
milli... ['mɪlɪ] *prefix* milli....
milligram(me) ['mɪlɪgræm] *n* milligramme *m*.
millilitre, (*US*) **milliliter** ['mɪlɪli:tə*] *n* millilitre *m*.
millimetre, (*US*) **millimeter** ['mɪlɪmi:tə*] *n* millimètre *m*.
milliner ['mɪlɪnə*] *n* modiste *f*.
millinery ['mɪlɪnərɪ] *n* modes *fpl*.
million ['mɪljən] *n* million *m*.
millionaire [mɪljə'nɛə*] *n* millionnaire *m*.
millipede ['mɪlɪpi:d] *n* mille-pattes *m inv*.
millstone ['mɪlstəun] *n* meule *f*.
millwheel ['mɪlwi:l] *n* roue *f* de moulin.
milometer [maɪ'lɔmɪtə*] *n* (*BRIT*) ≈ compteur *m* kilométrique.
mime [maɪm] *n* mime *m* ♦ *vt, vi* mimer.
mimic ['mɪmɪk] *n* imitateur/trice ♦ *vt, vi* imiter, contrefaire.
mimicry ['mɪmɪkrɪ] *n* imitation *f*; (*ZOOL*) mimétisme *m*.
Min. *abbr* (*BRIT POL*) = **ministry**.
min. *abbr* (= *minute*) mn.; (= *minimum*) min.
minaret [mɪnə'rɛt] *n* minaret *m*.
mince [mɪns] *vt* hacher ♦ *vi* (*in walking*) marcher à petits pas maniérés ♦ *n* (*BRIT CULIN*) viande hachée, hachis *m*; **he does not ~ (his) words** il ne mâche pas ses mots.
mincemeat ['mɪnsmi:t] *n hachis de fruits secs utilisés en pâtisserie*.
mince pie *n sorte de tarte aux fruits secs*.
mincer ['mɪnsə*] *n* hachoir *m*.
mincing ['mɪnsɪŋ] *adj* affecté(e).
mind [maɪnd] *n* esprit *m* ♦ *vt* (*attend to, look after*) s'occuper de; (*be careful*) faire attention à; (*object to*): **I don't ~ the noise** je ne crains pas le bruit, le bruit ne me dérange pas; **do you ~ if ...?** est-ce que cela vous gêne si ...?; **I don't ~** cela ne me dérange pas; **~ you, ...** remarquez, ...; **never ~** peu importe, ça ne fait rien; **it is on my ~** cela me préoccupe; **to change one's ~** changer d'avis; **to be in two ~s about sth** (*BRIT*) être indécis(e) *or* irrésolu(e) en ce qui concerne qch; **to my ~** à mon avis, selon moi; **to be out of one's ~** ne plus avoir toute sa raison; **to keep sth in ~** ne pas oublier qch; **to bear sth in ~** tenir compte de qch; **to have sb/sth in ~** avoir qn/qch en tête; **to have in ~ to do** avoir l'intention de faire; **it went right out of my ~** ça m'est complètement sorti de la tête; **to bring** *or* **call sth to ~** se rappeler qch; **to make up one's ~** se décider; **"~ the step"** "attention à la marche".
mind-boggling ['maɪndbɔglɪŋ] *adj* (*col*) époustouflant(e), ahurissant(e).
-minded ['maɪndɪd] *adj*: **fair~** impartial(e); **an industrially~ nation** une nation orientée vers l'industrie.
minder ['maɪndə*] *n* (*child* ~) gardienne *f*; (*bodyguard*) ange gardien (*fig*).
mindful ['maɪndful] *adj*: **~ of** attentif(ive) à, soucieux(euse) de.
mindless ['maɪndlɪs] *adj* irréfléchi(e); (*violence, crime*) insensé(e).
mine [maɪn] *pron* le(la) mien(ne), les miens(miennes); **this book is ~** ce livre est à moi ♦ *n* mine *f* ♦ *vt* (*coal*) extraire; (*ship, beach*) miner.
mine detector *n* détecteur *m* de mines.
minefield ['maɪnfi:ld] *n* champ *m* de mines.
miner ['maɪnə*] *n* mineur *m*.
mineral ['mɪnərəl] *adj* minéral(e) ♦ *n* minéral *m*; **~s** *npl* (*BRIT*: *soft drinks*) boissons gazeuses (sucrées).
mineralogy [mɪnə'rælədʒɪ] *n* minéralogie *f*.
mineral water *n* eau minérale.
minesweeper ['maɪnswi:pə*] *n* dragueur *m* de mines.
mingle ['mɪŋgl] *vt* mêler, mélanger ♦ *vi*: **to ~ with** se mêler à.
mingy ['mɪndʒɪ] *adj* (*col*) radin(e).
miniature ['mɪnətʃə*] *adj* (en) miniature ♦ *n* miniature *f*.
minibus ['mɪnɪbʌs] *n* minibus *m*.
minicab ['mɪnɪkæb] *n* (*BRIT*) minitaxi *m*.
minim ['mɪnɪm] *n* (*MUS*) blanche *f*.
minima ['mɪnɪmə] *npl of* **minimum**.
minimal ['mɪnɪml] *adj* minimal(e).
minimalist ['mɪnɪməlɪst] *adj, n* minimaliste (*m/f*).
minimize ['mɪnɪmaɪz] *vt* minimiser.
minimum ['mɪnɪməm] *n* (*pl*: **minima** ['mɪnɪmə]) minimum *m* ♦ *adj* minimum; **to reduce to a ~**

réduire au minimum.
minimum lending rate (MLR) *n* (*ECON*) taux *m* de crédit minimum.
mining ['maɪnɪŋ] *n* exploitation minière ♦ *adj* minier(ière); de mineurs.
minion ['mɪnjən] *n* (*pej*) laquais *m*; favori/te.
mini-series ['mɪnɪsɪəri:z] *n* téléfilm *m* en plusieurs parties.
miniskirt ['mɪnɪskə:t] *n* mini-jupe *f*.
minister ['mɪnɪstə*] *n* (*BRIT POL*) ministre *m*; (*REL*) pasteur *m* ♦ *vi*: **to ~ to sb** donner ses soins à qn; **to ~ to sb's needs** pourvoir aux besoins de qn.
ministerial [mɪnɪs'tɪərɪəl] *adj* (*BRIT POL*) ministériel(le).
ministry ['mɪnɪstrɪ] *n* (*BRIT POL*) ministère *m*; (*REL*): **to go into the ~** devenir pasteur.
mink [mɪŋk] *n* vison *m*.
mink coat *n* manteau *m* de vison.
Minn. *abbr* (*US*) = *Minnesota*.
minnow ['mɪnəu] *n* vairon *m*.
minor ['maɪnə*] *adj* petit(e), de peu d'importance; (*MUS*) mineur(e) ♦ *n* (*LAW*) mineur/e.
Minorca [mɪ'nɔ:kə] *n* Minorque *f*.
minority [maɪ'nɔrɪtɪ] *n* minorité *f*; **to be in a ~** être en minorité.
minster ['mɪnstə*] *n* église abbatiale.
minstrel ['mɪnstrəl] *n* trouvère *m*, ménestrel *m*.
mint [mɪnt] *n* (*plant*) menthe *f*; (*sweet*) bonbon *m* à la menthe ♦ *vt* (*coins*) battre; **the (Royal) M~**, (*US*) **the (US) M~** ≈ l'hôtel *m* de la Monnaie; **in ~ condition** à l'état de neuf.
mint sauce *n* sauce *f* à la menthe.
minuet [mɪnju'ɛt] *n* menuet *m*.
minus ['maɪnəs] *n* (*also*: **~ sign**) signe *m* moins ♦ *prep* moins.
minuscule ['mɪnəskju:l] *adj* minuscule.
minute *adj* [maɪ'nju:t] minuscule; (*detailed*) minutieux(euse) ♦ *n* ['mɪnɪt] minute *f*; (*official record*) procès-verbal *m*, compte rendu; **~s** *npl* procès-verbal; **it is 5 ~s past 3** il est 3 heures 5; **wait a ~!** (attendez) un instant!; **at the last ~** à la dernière minute; **up to the ~** (*fashion*) dernier cri; (*news*) de dernière minute; (*machine, technology*) de pointe; **in ~ detail** par le menu.
minute book *n* registre *m* des procès-verbaux.
minute hand *n* aiguille *f* des minutes.
minutely [maɪ'nju:tlɪ] *adv* (*by a small amount*) de peu, de manière infime; (*in detail*) minutieusement, dans les moindres détails.
minutiae [mɪ'nju:ʃɪi:] *npl* menus détails.
miracle ['mɪrəkl] *n* miracle *m*.
miraculous [mɪ'rækjuləs] *adj* miraculeux(euse).
mirage ['mɪrɑ:ʒ] *n* mirage *m*.
mire ['maɪə*] *n* bourbe *f*, boue *f*.
mirror ['mɪrə*] *n* miroir *m*, glace *f* ♦ *vt* refléter.
mirror image *n* image inversée.
mirth [mə:θ] *n* gaieté *f*.
misadventure [mɪsəd'vɛntʃə*] *n* mésaventure *f*; **death by ~** (*BRIT*) décès accidentel.
misanthropist [mɪ'zænθrəpɪst] *n* misanthrope *m/f*.
misapply [mɪsə'plaɪ] *vt* mal employer.
misapprehension ['mɪsæprɪ'hɛnʃən] *n* malentendu *m*, méprise *f*.
misappropriate [mɪsə'prəuprɪeɪt] *vt* détourner.
misappropriation ['mɪsəprəuprɪ'eɪʃən] *n* escroquerie *f*, détournement *m*.
misbehave [mɪsbɪ'heɪv] *vi* mal se conduire.
misbehaviour, (*US*) **misbehavior** [mɪsbɪ'heɪvjə*] *n* mauvaise conduite.
misc. *abbr* = **miscellaneous**.
miscalculate [mɪs'kælkjuleɪt] *vt* mal calculer.
miscalculation ['mɪskælkju'leɪʃən] *n* erreur *f* de calcul.
miscarriage ['mɪskærɪdʒ] *n* (*MED*) fausse couche; **~ of justice** erreur *f* judiciaire.
miscarry [mɪs'kærɪ] *vi* (*MED*) faire une fausse couche; (*fail: plans*) échouer, mal tourner.
miscellaneous [mɪsɪ'leɪnɪəs] *adj* (*items, expenses*) divers(es); (*selection*) varié(e).
miscellany [mɪ'sɛlənɪ] *n* recueil *m*.
mischance [mɪs'tʃɑ:ns] *n* malchance *f*; **by (some) ~** par malheur.
mischief ['mɪstʃɪf] *n* (*naughtiness*) sottises *fpl*; (*harm*) mal *m*, dommage *m*; (*maliciousness*) méchanceté *f*.
mischievous ['mɪstʃɪvəs] *adj* (*naughty*) coquin(e), espiègle; (*harmful*) méchant(e).
misconception ['mɪskən'sɛpʃən] *n* idée fausse.
misconduct [mɪs'kɔndʌkt] *n* inconduite *f*; **professional ~** faute professionnelle.
misconstrue [mɪskən'stru:] *vt* mal interpréter.
miscount [mɪs'kaunt] *vt, vi* mal compter.
misdeed ['mɪs'di:d] *n* méfait *m*.
misdemeanour, (*US*) **misdemeanor** [mɪsdɪ'mi:nə*] *n* écart *m* de conduite; infraction *f*.
misdirect [mɪsdɪ'rɛkt] *vt* (*person*) mal renseigner; (*letter*) mal adresser.
miser ['maɪzə*] *n* avare *m/f*.
miserable ['mɪzərəbl] *adj* malheureux(euse); (*wretched*) misérable; **to feel ~** avoir le cafard.
miserably ['mɪzərəblɪ] *adv* (*smile, answer*) tristement; (*live, pay*) misérablement; (*fail*) lamentablement.
miserly ['maɪzəlɪ] *adj* avare.
misery ['mɪzərɪ] *n* (*unhappiness*) tristesse *f*; (*pain*) souffrances *fpl*; (*wretchedness*) misère *f*.
misfire [mɪs'faɪə*] *vi* rater; (*car engine*) avoir des ratés.
misfit ['mɪsfɪt] *n* (*person*) inadapté/e.
misfortune [mɪs'fɔ:tʃən] *n* malchance *f*, malheur *m*.
misgiving(s) [mɪs'gɪvɪŋ(z)] *n(pl)* craintes *fpl*,

soupçons *mpl*; **to have ~s about sth** avoir des doutes quant à qch.
misguided [mɪs'gaɪdɪd] *adj* malavisé(e).
mishandle [mɪs'hændl] *vt* (*treat roughly*) malmener; (*mismanage*) mal s'y prendre pour faire *or* résoudre *etc*.
mishap ['mɪshæp] *n* mésaventure *f*.
mishear [mɪs'hɪə*] *vt, vi irreg* mal entendre.
mishmash ['mɪʃmæʃ] *n* (*col*) fatras *m*, méli-mélo *m*.
misinform [mɪsɪn'fɔːm] *vt* mal renseigner.
misinterpret [mɪsɪn'təːprɪt] *vt* mal interpréter.
misinterpretation ['mɪsɪntəːprɪ'teɪʃən] *n* interprétation erronée, contresens *m*.
misjudge [mɪs'dʒʌdʒ] *vt* méjuger, se méprendre sur le compte de.
mislay [mɪs'leɪ] *vt irreg* égarer.
mislead [mɪs'liːd] *vt irreg* induire en erreur.
misleading [mɪs'liːdɪŋ] *adj* trompeur(euse).
misled [mɪs'lɛd] *pt, pp of* **mislead**.
mismanage [mɪs'mænɪdʒ] *vt* mal gérer; mal s'y prendre pour faire *or* résoudre *etc*.
mismanagement [mɪs'mænɪdʒmənt] *n* mauvaise gestion.
misnomer [mɪs'nəumə*] *n* terme *or* qualificatif trompeur *or* peu approprié.
misogynist [mɪ'sɔdʒɪnɪst] *n* misogyne *m/f*.
misplace [mɪs'pleɪs] *vt* égarer; **to be ~d** (*trust etc*) être mal placé(e).
misprint ['mɪsprɪnt] *n* faute *f* d'impression.
mispronounce [mɪsprə'nauns] *vt* mal prononcer.
misquote ['mɪs'kwəut] *vt* citer erronément *or* inexactement.
misread [mɪs'riːd] *vt irreg* mal lire.
misrepresent [mɪsrɛprɪ'zɛnt] *vt* présenter sous un faux jour.
Miss [mɪs] *n* Mademoiselle; **Dear ~ Smith** Chère Mademoiselle Smith.
miss [mɪs] *vt* (*fail to get*) manquer, rater; (*appointment, class*) manquer; (*escape, avoid*) échapper à, éviter; (*notice loss of: money etc*) s'apercevoir de l'absence de; (*regret the absence of*): **I ~ him/it** il/cela me manque ♦ *vi* manquer ♦ *n* (*shot*) coup manqué; **the bus just ~ed the wall** le bus a évité le mur de justesse; **you're ~ing the point** vous êtes à côté de la question.
►**miss out** *vt* (*BRIT*) oublier.
►**miss out on** *vt fus* (*fun, party*) rater, manquer; (*chance, bargain*) laisser passer.
Miss. *abbr* (*US*) = *Mississippi*.
missal ['mɪsl] *n* missel *m*.
misshapen [mɪs'ʃeɪpən] *adj* difforme.
missile ['mɪsaɪl] *n* (*AVIAT*) missile *m*; (*object thrown*) projectile *m*.
missile base *n* base *f* de missiles.
missile launcher [-lɔːntʃə*] *n* lance-missiles *m*.
missing ['mɪsɪŋ] *adj* manquant(e); (*after escape, disaster: person*) disparu(e); **to go ~** disparaître; **~ person** personne disparue, disparu/e.
mission ['mɪʃən] *n* mission *f*; **on a ~ to sb** en mission auprès de qn.
missionary ['mɪʃənrɪ] *n* missionnaire *m/f*.
missive ['mɪsɪv] *n* missive *f*.
misspell ['mɪs'spɛl] *vt* (*irreg: like* **spell**) mal orthographier.
misspent ['mɪs'spɛnt] *adj*: **his ~ youth** sa folle jeunesse.
mist [mɪst] *n* brume *f* ♦ *vi* (*also*: **~ over, ~ up**) devenir brumeux(euse); (*BRIT: windows*) s'embuer.
mistake [mɪs'teɪk] *n* erreur *f*, faute *f* ♦ *vt* (*irreg: like* **take**) (*meaning*) mal comprendre; (*intentions*) se méprendre sur; **to ~ for** prendre pour; **by ~** par erreur, par inadvertance; **to make a ~** (*in writing*) faire une faute; (*in calculating etc*) faire une erreur; **to make a ~ about sb/sth** se tromper sur le compte de qn/sur qch.
mistaken [mɪs'teɪkən] *pp of* **mistake** ♦ *adj* (*idea etc*) erroné(e); **to be ~** faire erreur, se tromper.
mistaken identity *n* erreur *f* d'identité.
mistakenly [mɪs'teɪkənlɪ] *adv* par erreur, par mégarde.
mister ['mɪstə*] *n* (*col*) Monsieur *m*; *see* **Mr**.
mistletoe ['mɪsltəu] *n* gui *m*.
mistook [mɪs'tuk] *pt of* **mistake**.
mistranslation [mɪstræns'leɪʃən] *n* erreur *f* de traduction, contresens *m*.
mistreat [mɪs'triːt] *vt* maltraiter.
mistress ['mɪstrɪs] *n* maîtresse *f*; (*BRIT: in primary school*) institutrice *f*; *see* **Mrs**.
mistrust [mɪs'trʌst] *vt* se méfier de ♦ *n*: **~ (of)** méfiance *f* (à l'égard de).
mistrustful [mɪs'trʌstful] *adj*: **~ (of)** méfiant(e) (à l'égard de).
misty ['mɪstɪ] *adj* brumeux(euse).
misty-eyed ['mɪstɪ'aɪd] *adj* les yeux embués de larmes; (*fig*) sentimental(e).
misunderstand [mɪsʌndə'stænd] *vt, vi irreg* mal comprendre.
misunderstanding ['mɪsʌndə'stændɪŋ] *n* méprise *f*, malentendu *m*.
misunderstood [mɪsʌndə'stud] *pt, pp of* **misunderstand**.
misuse *n* [mɪs'juːs] mauvais emploi; (*of power*) abus *m* ♦ *vt* [mɪs'juːz] mal employer; abuser de.
MIT *n abbr* (*US*) = *Massachusetts Institute of Technology*.
mite [maɪt] *n* (*small quantity*) grain *m*, miette *f*; (*BRIT: small child*) petit/e.
mitigate ['mɪtɪgeɪt] *vt* atténuer; **mitigating circumstances** circonstances atténuantes.
mitigation [mɪtɪ'geɪʃən] *n* atténuation *f*.
mitre, (*US*) **miter** ['maɪtə*] *n* mitre *f*; (*CARPENTRY*) onglet *m*.
mitt(en) ['mɪt(n)] *n* mitaine *f*; moufle *f*.
mix [mɪks] *vt* mélanger ♦ *vi* se mélanger ♦ *n*

mélange *m*; dosage *m*; **to ~ sth with sth** mélanger qch à qch; **to ~ business with pleasure** unir l'utile à l'agréable; **cake ~** préparation *f* pour gâteau.
▸**mix in** *vt* incorporer, mélanger.
▸**mix up** *vt* mélanger; (*confuse*) confondre; **to be ~ed up in sth** être mêlé(e) à qch *or* impliqué(e) dans qch.
mixed [mɪkst] *adj* (*assorted*) assortis(ies); (*school etc*) mixte.
mixed-ability ['mɪkstə'bɪlɪtɪ] *adj* (*class etc*) sans groupes de niveaux.
mixed bag *n*: **it's a (bit of a) ~** il y a (un peu) de tout.
mixed blessing *n*: **it's a ~** cela a du bon et du mauvais.
mixed doubles *npl* (*SPORT*) double *m* mixte.
mixed economy *n* économie *f* mixte.
mixed grill *n* (*BRIT*) assortiment *m* de grillades.
mixed marriage *n* mariage *m* mixte.
mixed-up [mɪkst'ʌp] *adj* (*person*) désorienté(e) (*fig*).
mixer ['mɪksə*] *n* (*for food*) batteur *m*, mixeur *m*; (*person*): **he is a good ~** il est très sociable.
mixer tap *n* (robinet *m*) mélangeur *m*.
mixture ['mɪkstʃə*] *n* assortiment *m*, mélange *m*; (*MED*) préparation *f*.
mix-up ['mɪksʌp] *n* confusion *f*.
MK *abbr* (*BRIT TECH*) = **mark**.
mk *abbr* = **mark** (*currency*).
mkt *abbr* = **market**.
MLitt *n abbr* (= *Master of Literature, Master of Letters*) *titre universitaire*.
MLR *n abbr* (*BRIT*) = **minimum lending rate**.
mm *abbr* (= *millimetre*) mm.
MN *abbr* (*BRIT*) = **Merchant Navy**; (*US*) = *Minnesota*.
MO *n abbr* (*MED*) = *medical officer*; (*US col*: = *modus operandi*) méthode *f* ♦ *abbr* (*US*) = *Missouri*.
Mo. *abbr* (*US*) = *Missouri*.
m.o. *abbr* = **money order**.
moan [məun] *n* gémissement *m* ♦ *vi* gémir; (*col*: *complain*): **to ~ (about)** se plaindre (de).
moaner ['məunə*] *n* (*col*) rouspéteur/euse, râleur/euse.
moaning ['məunɪŋ] *n* gémissements *mpl*.
moat [məut] *n* fossé *m*, douves *fpl*.
mob [mɔb] *n* foule *f*; (*disorderly*) cohue *f*; (*pej*): **the ~** la populace ♦ *vt* assaillir.
mobile ['məubaɪl] *adj* mobile ♦ *n* (*ART*) mobile *m*; **applicants must be ~** (*BRIT*) les candidats devront être prêts à accepter tout déplacement.
mobile home *n* caravane *f*.
mobile phone *n* téléphone portatif.
mobile shop *n* (*BRIT*) camion *m* magasin.
mobility [məu'bɪlɪtɪ] *n* mobilité *f*.
mobilize ['məubɪlaɪz] *vt, vi* mobiliser.
moccasin ['mɔkəsɪn] *n* mocassin *m*.
mock [mɔk] *vt* ridiculiser, se moquer de ♦ *adj* faux(fausse).
mockery ['mɔkərɪ] *n* moquerie *f*, raillerie *f*; **to make a ~ of** ridiculiser, tourner en dérision.
mocking ['mɔkɪŋ] *adj* moqueur(euse).
mockingbird ['mɔkɪŋbə:d] *n* moqueur *m*.
mock-up ['mɔkʌp] *n* maquette *f*.
MOD *n abbr* (*BRIT*) = **Ministry of Defence**; *see* **defence**.
mod cons ['mɔd'kɔnz] *npl abbr* (*BRIT*) = **modern conveniences**; *see* **convenience**.
mode [məud] *n* mode *m*; (*of transport*) moyen *m*.
model ['mɔdl] *n* modèle *m*; (*person: for fashion*) mannequin *m*; (*: for artist*) modèle ♦ *vt* modeler ♦ *vi* travailler comme mannequin ♦ *adj* (*railway: toy*) modèle réduit *inv*; (*child, factory*) modèle; **to ~ clothes** présenter des vêtements; **to ~ sb/sth on** modeler qn/qch sur.
modeller, (*US*) **modeler** ['mɔdlə*] *n* modeleur *m*; (*model maker*) maquettiste *m/f*; fabricant *m* de modèles réduits.
modem ['məudɛm] *n* modem *m*.
moderate *adj, n* ['mɔdərət] *adj* modéré(e) ♦ *n* (*POL*) modéré/e ♦ *vb* ['mɔdəreɪt] *vi* se modérer, se calmer ♦ *vt* modérer.
moderately ['mɔdərətlɪ] *adv* (*act*) avec modération *or* mesure; (*expensive, difficult*) moyennement; (*pleased, happy*) raisonnablement, assez; **~ priced** à un prix raisonnable.
moderation [mɔdə'reɪʃən] *n* modération *f*, mesure *f*; **in ~** à dose raisonnable, pris(e) *or* pratiqué(e) modérément.
moderator ['mɔdəreɪtə*] *n* (*REL*): **M~** président *m* (*de l'Assemblée générale de l'Église presbytérienne*); (*POL*) modérateur *m*.
modern ['mɔdən] *adj* moderne; **~ languages** langues vivantes.
modernization [mɔdənaɪ'zeɪʃən] *n* modernisation *f*.
modernize ['mɔdənaɪz] *vt* moderniser.
modest ['mɔdɪst] *adj* modeste.
modesty ['mɔdɪstɪ] *n* modestie *f*.
modicum ['mɔdɪkəm] *n*: **a ~ of** un minimum de.
modification [mɔdɪfɪ'keɪʃən] *n* modification *f*; **to make ~s** faire *or* apporter des modifications.
modify ['mɔdɪfaɪ] *vt* modifier.
modish ['məudɪʃ] *adj* à la mode.
Mods [mɔdz] *n abbr* (*BRIT*: = *(Honour) Moderations*) *premier examen universitaire (à Oxford)*.
modular ['mɔdjulə*] *adj* (*filing, unit*) modulaire.
modulate ['mɔdjuleɪt] *vt* moduler.
modulation [mɔdju'leɪʃən] *n* modulation *f*.
module ['mɔdju:l] *n* module *m*.
mogul ['məugl] *n* (*fig*) nabab *m*; (*SKI*) bosse *f*.
MOH *n abbr* (*BRIT*) = *Medical Officer of Health*.

mohair ['məuhɛə*] *n* mohair *m*.
Mohammed [mə'hæmɛd] *n* Mahomet *m*.
moist [mɔɪst] *adj* humide, moite.
moisten ['mɔɪsn] *vt* humecter, mouiller légèrement.
moisture ['mɔɪstʃə*] *n* humidité *f*; (*on glass*) buée *f*.
moisturize ['mɔɪstʃəraɪz] *vt* (*skin*) hydrater.
moisturizer ['mɔɪstʃəraɪzə*] *n* produit hydratant.
molar ['məulə*] *n* molaire *f*.
molasses [məu'læsɪz] *n* mélasse *f*.
mold [məuld] *n, vt* (*US*) = **mould**.
Moldavia [mɔl'deɪvɪə], **Moldova** [mɔl'dəuvə] *n* Moldavie *f*.
Moldavian [mɔl'deɪvɪən], **Moldovan** [mɔl-'dəuvən] *adj* moldave.
mole [məul] *n* (*animal*) taupe *f*; (*spot*) grain *m* de beauté.
molecule ['mɔlɪkju:l] *n* molécule *f*.
molehill ['məulhɪl] *n* taupinière *f*.
molest [məu'lɛst] *vt* tracasser; molester.
mollusc ['mɔləsk] *n* mollusque *m*.
mollycoddle ['mɔlɪkɔdl] *vt* chouchouter, couver.
Molotov cocktail ['mɔlətɔf-] *n* cocktail *m* Molotov.
molt [məult] *vi* (*US*) = **moult**.
molten ['məultən] *adj* fondu(e).
mom [mɔm] *n* (*US*) = **mum**.
moment ['məumənt] *n* moment *m*, instant *m*; (*importance*) importance *f*; **at the ~** en ce moment; **for the ~** pour l'instant; **in a ~** dans un instant; **"one ~ please"** (*TEL*) "ne quittez pas".
momentarily ['məuməntrɪlɪ] *adv* momentanément; (*US: soon*) bientôt.
momentary ['məuməntərɪ] *adj* momentané(e), passager(ère).
momentous [məu'mɛntəs] *adj* important(e), capital(e).
momentum [məu'mɛntəm] *n* élan *m*, vitesse acquise; **to gather ~** prendre de la vitesse.
mommy ['mɔmɪ] *n* (*US: mother*) maman *f*.
Mon. *abbr* (= *Monday*) l.
Monaco ['mɔnəkəu] *n* Monaco *f*.
monarch ['mɔnək] *n* monarque *m*.
monarchist ['mɔnəkɪst] *n* monarchiste *m/f*.
monarchy ['mɔnəkɪ] *n* monarchie *f*.
monastery ['mɔnəstərɪ] *n* monastère *m*.
monastic [mə'næstɪk] *adj* monastique.
Monday ['mʌndɪ] *n* lundi *m*; *for phrases see also* **Tuesday**.
monetarist ['mʌnɪtərɪst] *n* monétariste *m/f*.
monetary ['mʌnɪtərɪ] *adj* monétaire.
money ['mʌnɪ] *n* argent *m*; **to make ~** (*person*) gagner de l'argent; (*business*) rapporter; **I've got no ~ left** je n'ai plus d'argent, je n'ai plus un sou.
moneyed ['mʌnɪd] *adj* riche.
moneylender ['mʌnɪlɛndə*] *n* prêteur/euse.
moneymaker ['mʌnɪmeɪkə*] *n* (*BRIT col: business*) affaire lucrative.
moneymaking ['mʌnɪmeɪkɪŋ] *adj* lucratif(ive), qui rapporte (de l'argent).
money market *n* marché financier.
money order *n* mandat *m*.
money-spinner ['mʌnɪspɪnə*] *n* (*col*) mine *f* d'or (*fig*).
money supply *n* masse *f* monétaire.
Mongol ['mɔŋgəl] *n* Mongol/e; (*LING*) mongol *m*.
mongol ['mɔŋgəl] *adj, n* (*MED*) mongolien(ne).
Mongolia [mɔŋ'gəulɪə] *n* Mongolie *f*.
Mongolian [mɔŋ'gəulɪən] *adj* mongol(e) ♦ *n* Mongol/e; (*LING*) mongol *m*.
mongoose ['mɔŋgu:s] *n* mangouste *f*.
mongrel ['mʌŋgrəl] *n* (*dog*) bâtard *m*.
monitor ['mɔnɪtə*] *n* (*BRIT SCOL*) chef *m* de classe; (*US SCOL*) surveillant *m* (d'examen); (*TV, COMPUT*) écran *m*, moniteur *m* ♦ *vt* contrôler; (*foreign station*) être à l'écoute de.
monk [mʌŋk] *n* moine *m*.
monkey ['mʌŋkɪ] *n* singe *m*.
monkey nut *n* (*BRIT*) cacahuète *f*.
monkey wrench *n* clé *f* à molette.
mono ['mɔnəu] *adj* mono *inv*.
mono... ['mɔnəu] *prefix* mono....
monochrome ['mɔnəkrəum] *adj* monochrome.
monocle ['mɔnəkl] *n* monocle *m*.
monogamous [mɔ'nɔgəməs] *adj* monogame.
monogamy [mɔ'nɔgəmɪ] *n* monogamie *f*.
monogram ['mɔnəgræm] *n* monogramme *m*.
monolith ['mɔnəlɪθ] *n* monolithe *m*.
monologue ['mɔnəlɔg] *n* monologue *m*.
monoplane ['mɔnəpleɪn] *n* monoplan *m*.
monopolize [mə'nɔpəlaɪz] *vt* monopoliser.
monopoly [mə'nɔpəlɪ] *n* monopole *m*; **Monopolies and Mergers Commission** (*BRIT*) *commission britannique d'enquête sur les monopoles*.
monorail ['mɔnəureɪl] *n* monorail *m*.
monosodium glutamate [mɔnə'səudɪəm 'glu:təmeɪt] *n* glutamate *m* de sodium.
monosyllabic [mɔnəsɪ'læbɪk] *adj* monosyllabique; (*person*) laconique.
monosyllable ['mɔnəsɪləbl] *n* monosyllabe *m*.
monotone ['mɔnətəun] *n* ton *m* (*or* voix *f*) monocorde; **to speak in a ~** parler sur un ton monocorde.
monotonous [mə'nɔtənəs] *adj* monotone.
monotony [mə'nɔtənɪ] *n* monotonie *f*.
monoxide [mɔ'nɔksaɪd] *n*: **carbon ~** oxyde *m* de carbone.
monsoon [mɔn'su:n] *n* mousson *f*.
monster ['mɔnstə*] *n* monstre *m*.
monstrosity [mɔns'trɔsɪtɪ] *n* monstruosité *f*, atrocité *f*.
monstrous ['mɔnstrəs] *adj* (*huge*) gigantesque; (*atrocious*) monstrueux(euse), atroce.
Mont. *abbr* (*US*) = *Montana*.
montage [mɔn'tɑ:ʒ] *n* montage *m*.
Mont Blanc [mɔ̃blɑ̃] *n* Mont Blanc *m*.
month [mʌnθ] *n* mois *m*; **every ~** tous les

mois; **300 dollars a** ~ 300 dollars par mois.
monthly ['mʌnθlɪ] *adj* mensuel(le) ♦ *adv* mensuellement ♦ *n* (*magazine*) mensuel *m*, publication mensuelle; **twice** ~ deux fois par mois.
Montreal [mɔntrɪ'ɔːl] *n* Montréal.
monument ['mɔnjumənt] *n* monument *m*.
monumental [mɔnju'mɛntl] *adj* monumental(e).
monumental mason *n* marbrier *m*.
moo [muː] *vi* meugler, beugler.
mood [muːd] *n* humeur *f*, disposition *f*; **to be in a good/bad** ~ être de bonne/mauvaise humeur; **to be in the** ~ **for** être d'humeur à, avoir envie de.
moody ['muːdɪ] *adj* (*variable*) d'humeur changeante, lunatique; (*sullen*) morose, maussade.
moon [muːn] *n* lune *f*.
moonbeam ['muːnbiːm] *n* rayon *m* de lune.
moon landing *n* alunissage *m*.
moonlight ['muːnlaɪt] *n* clair *m* de lune ♦ *vi* travailler au noir.
moonlighting ['muːnlaɪtɪŋ] *n* travail *m* au noir.
moonlit ['muːnlɪt] *adj* éclairé(e) par la lune; **a** ~ **night** une nuit de lune.
moonshot ['muːnʃɔt] *n* (*SPACE*) tir *m* lunaire.
moonstruck ['muːnstrʌk] *adj* fou(folle), dérangé(e).
moony ['muːnɪ] *adj*: **to have** ~ **eyes** avoir l'air dans la lune *or* rêveur.
Moor [muə*] *n* Maure/Mauresque.
moor [muə*] *n* lande *f* ♦ *vt* (*ship*) amarrer ♦ *vi* mouiller.
moorings ['muərɪŋz] *npl* (*chains*) amarres *fpl*; (*place*) mouillage *m*.
Moorish ['muərɪʃ] *adj* maure(mauresque).
moorland ['muələnd] *n* lande *f*.
moose [muːs] *n* (*pl inv*) élan *m*.
moot [muːt] *vt* soulever ♦ *adj*: ~ **point** point *m* discutable.
mop [mɔp] *n* balai *m* à laver ♦ *vt* éponger, essuyer; ~ **of hair** tignasse *f*.
►**mop up** *vt* éponger.
mope [məup] *vi* avoir le cafard, se morfondre.
►**mope about, mope around** *vi* broyer du noir, se morfondre.
moped ['məupɛd] *n* cyclomoteur *m*.
moquette [mɔ'kɛt] *n* moquette *f*.
MOR *adj abbr* (*MUS*: = *middle-of-the-road*) tous publics.
moral ['mɔrl] *adj* moral(e) ♦ *n* morale *f*; **~s** *npl* moralité *f*.
morale [mɔ'rɑːl] *n* moral *m*.
morality [mə'rælɪtɪ] *n* moralité *f*.
moralize ['mɔrəlaɪz] *vi*: **to** ~ **(about)** moraliser (sur).
morally ['mɔrəlɪ] *adv* moralement.
moral victory *n* victoire morale.
morass [mə'ræs] *n* marais *m*, marécage *m*.
moratorium [mɔrə'tɔːrɪəm] *n* moratoire *m*.
morbid ['mɔːbɪd] *adj* morbide.

KEYWORD

more [mɔː*] *adj* **1** (*greater in number etc*) plus (de), davantage; ~ **people/work (than)** plus de gens/de travail (que)
2 (*additional*) encore (de); **do you want (some)** ~ **tea?** voulez-vous encore du thé?; **I have no** *or* **I don't have any** ~ **money** je n'ai plus d'argent; **it'll take a few** ~ **weeks** ça prendra encore quelques semaines
♦ *pron* plus, davantage; ~ **than 10** plus de 10; **it cost** ~ **than we expected** cela a coûté plus que prévu; **I want** ~ j'en veux plus *or* davantage; **is there any** ~**?** est-ce qu'il en reste?; **there's no** ~ il n'y en a plus; **a little** ~ un peu plus; **many/much** ~ beaucoup plus, bien davantage
♦ *adv*: ~ **dangerous/easily (than)** plus dangereux/facilement (que); ~ **and** ~ **expensive** de plus en plus cher; ~ **or less** plus ou moins; ~ **than ever** plus que jamais; **once** ~ encore une fois, une fois de plus; **and what's** ~ ... et de plus ..., et qui plus est ...

moreover [mɔː'rəuvə*] *adv* de plus.
morgue [mɔːg] *n* morgue *f*.
MORI ['mɔːrɪ] *n abbr* (*BRIT*: = *Market & Opinion Research Institute*) *institut de sondage*.
moribund ['mɔrɪbʌnd] *adj* moribond(e).
morning ['mɔːnɪŋ] *n* matin *m*; (*as duration*) matinée *f*; **in the** ~ le matin; **7 o'clock in the** ~ 7 heures du matin, **this** ~ ce matin.
morning-after pill ['mɔːnɪŋ'ɑːftə-] *n* pilule *f* du lendemain.
morning sickness *n* nausées matinales.
Moroccan [mə'rɔkən] *adj* marocain(e) ♦ *n* Marocain/e.
Morocco [mə'rɔkəu] *n* Maroc *m*.
moron ['mɔːrɔn] *n* idiot/e, minus *m/f*.
moronic [mə'rɔnɪk] *adj* idiot(e), imbécile.
morose [mə'rəus] *adj* morose, maussade.
morphine ['mɔːfiːn] *n* morphine *f*.
morris dancing ['mɔrɪs-] *n* (*BRIT*) *danses folkloriques anglaises*.
Morse [mɔːs] *n* (*also*: ~ **code**) morse *m*.
morsel ['mɔːsl] *n* bouchée *f*.
mortal ['mɔːtl] *adj, n* mortel(le).
mortality [mɔː'tælɪtɪ] *n* mortalité *f*.
mortality rate *n* (taux *m* de) mortalité *f*.
mortar ['mɔːtə*] *n* mortier *m*.
mortgage ['mɔːgɪdʒ] *n* hypothèque *f*; (*loan*) prêt *m* (*or* crédit *m*) hypothécaire ♦ *vt* hypothéquer; **to take out a** ~ prendre une hypothèque, faire un emprunt.
mortgage company *n* (*US*) société *f* de crédit immobilier.
mortgagee [mɔːgə'dʒiː] *n* prêteur/euse (sur hypothèque).
mortgagor ['mɔːgədʒə*] *n* emprunteur/euse (sur hypothèque).

mortician [mɔːˈtɪʃən] *n* (*US*) entrepreneur *m* de pompes funèbres.
mortified [ˈmɔːtɪfaɪd] *adj* mortifié(e).
mortise lock [ˈmɔːtɪs-] *n* serrure encastrée.
mortuary [ˈmɔːtjuərɪ] *n* morgue *f*.
mosaic [məuˈzeɪɪk] *n* mosaïque *f*.
Moscow [ˈmɔskəu] *n* Moscou.
Moslem [ˈmɔzləm] *adj*, *n* = **Muslim**.
mosque [mɔsk] *n* mosquée *f*.
mosquito, ~es [mɔsˈkiːtəu] *n* moustique *m*.
mosquito net *n* moustiquaire *f*.
moss [mɔs] *n* mousse *f*.
mossy [ˈmɔsɪ] *adj* moussu(e).
most [məust] *adj* la plupart de; le plus de ♦ *pron* la plupart ♦ *adv* le plus; (*very*) très, extrêmement; **the ~** (*also: + adjective*) le plus; **~ fish** la plupart des poissons; **~ of** la plus grande partie de; **~ of them** la plupart d'entre eux; **I saw ~** j'en ai vu la plupart; c'est moi qui en ai vu le plus; **at the (very) ~** au plus; **to make the ~ of** profiter au maximum de.
mostly [ˈməustlɪ] *adv* surtout, principalement.
MOT *n abbr* (*BRIT*: = *Ministry of Transport*): **the ~ (test)** *visite technique (annuelle) obligatoire des véhicules à moteur*.
motel [məuˈtɛl] *n* motel *m*.
moth [mɔθ] *n* papillon *m* de nuit; mite *f*.
mothball [ˈmɔθbɔːl] *n* boule *f* de naphtaline.
moth-eaten [ˈmɔθiːtn] *adj* mité(e).
mother [ˈmʌðə*] *n* mère *f* ♦ *vt* (*care for*) dorloter.
mother board *n* (*COMPUT*) carte-mère *f*.
motherhood [ˈmʌðəhud] *n* maternité *f*.
mother-in-law [ˈmʌðərɪnlɔː] *n* belle-mère *f*.
motherly [ˈmʌðəlɪ] *adj* maternel(le).
mother-of-pearl [ˈmʌðərəvˈpəːl] *n* nacre *f*.
mother's help *n* aide *f or* auxiliaire *f* familiale.
mother-to-be [ˈmʌðətəˈbiː] *n* future maman.
mother tongue *n* langue maternelle.
mothproof [ˈmɔθpruːf] *adj* traité(e) à l'antimite.
motif [məuˈtiːf] *n* motif *m*.
motion [ˈməuʃən] *n* mouvement *m*; (*gesture*) geste *m*; (*at meeting*) motion *f*; (*BRIT*: *also*: **bowel ~**) selles *fpl* ♦ *vt*, *vi*: **to ~ (to) sb to do** faire signe à qn de faire; **to be in ~** (*vehicle*) être en marche; **to set in ~** mettre en marche; **to go through the ~s of doing sth** (*fig*) faire qch machinalement *or* sans conviction.
motionless [ˈməuʃənlɪs] *adj* immobile, sans mouvement.
motion picture *n* film *m*.
motivate [ˈməutɪveɪt] *vt* motiver.
motivated [ˈməutɪveɪtɪd] *adj* motivé(e).
motivation [məutɪˈveɪʃən] *n* motivation *f*.
motive [ˈməutɪv] *n* motif *m*, mobile *m* ♦ *adj* moteur(trice); **from the best (of) ~s** avec les meilleures intentions (du monde).
motley [ˈmɔtlɪ] *adj* hétéroclite; bigarré(e), bariolé(e).
motor [ˈməutə*] *n* moteur *m*; (*BRIT col*: *vehicle*) auto *f* ♦ *adj* moteur(trice).
motorbike [ˈməutəbaɪk] *n* moto *f*.
motorboat [ˈməutəbəut] *n* bateau *m* à moteur.
motorcade [ˈməutəkeɪd] *n* cortège *m* d'automobiles *or* de voitures.
motorcar [ˈməutəkɑː] *n* (*BRIT*) automobile *f*.
motorcoach [ˈməutəkəutʃ] *n* (*BRIT*) car *m*.
motorcycle [ˈməutəsaɪkl] *n* vélomoteur *m*.
motorcyclist [ˈməutəsaɪklɪst] *n* motocycliste *m/f*.
motoring [ˈməutərɪŋ] (*BRIT*) *n* tourisme *m* automobile ♦ *adj* (*accident*) de voiture, de la route; **~ holiday** vacances *fpl* en voiture; **~ offence** infraction *f* au code de la route.
motorist [ˈməutərɪst] *n* automobiliste *m/f*.
motorize [ˈməutəraɪz] *vt* motoriser.
motor oil *n* huile *f* de graissage.
motor racing *n* (*BRIT*) course *f* automobile.
motor scooter *n* scooter *m*.
motor vehicle *n* véhicule *m* automobile.
motorway [ˈməutəweɪ] *n* (*BRIT*) autoroute *f*.
mottled [ˈmɔtld] *adj* tacheté(e), marbré(e).
motto, ~es [ˈmɔtəu] *n* devise *f*.
mould, (*US*) **mold** [məuld] *n* moule *m*; (*mildew*) moisissure *f* ♦ *vt* mouler, modeler; (*fig*) façonner.
mo(u)lder [ˈməuldə*] *vi* (*decay*) moisir.
mo(u)lding [ˈməuldɪŋ] *n* (*ARCHIT*) moulure *f*.
mo(u)ldy [ˈməuldɪ] *adj* moisi(e).
moult, (*US*) **molt** [məult] *vi* muer.
mound [maund] *n* monticule *m*, tertre *m*.
mount [maunt] *n* mont *m*, montagne *f*; (*horse*) monture *f*; (*for jewel etc*) monture ♦ *vt* monter; (*exhibition*) organiser, monter; (*picture*) monter sur carton; (*stamp*) coller dans un album ♦ *vi* (*also*: **~ up**) s'élever, monter.
mountain [ˈmauntɪn] *n* montagne *f* ♦ *cpd* de (la) montagne; **to make a ~ out of a molehill** (*fig*) se faire une montagne d'un rien.
mountain bike *n* VTT *m*, vélo *m* tout terrain.
mountaineer [mauntɪˈnɪə*] *n* alpiniste *m/f*.
mountaineering [mauntɪˈnɪərɪŋ] *n* alpinisme *m*; **to go ~** faire de l'alpinisme.
mountainous [ˈmauntɪnəs] *adj* montagneux(euse).
mountain range *n* chaîne *f* de montagnes.
mountain rescue team *n* colonne *f* de secours.
mountainside [ˈmauntɪnsaɪd] *n* flanc *m or* versant *m* de la montagne.
mounted [ˈmauntɪd] *adj* monté(e).
Mount Everest *n* le mont Everest.
mourn [mɔːn] *vt* pleurer ♦ *vi*: **to ~ (for)** se lamenter (sur).
mourner [ˈmɔːnə*] *n* parent/e *or* ami/e du défunt; personne *f* en deuil *or* venue rendre hommage au défunt.
mournful [ˈmɔːnful] *adj* triste, lugubre.
mourning [ˈmɔːnɪŋ] *n* deuil *m* ♦ *cpd* (*dress*) de deuil; **in ~** en deuil.

mouse, *pl* **mice** [maus, mais] *n* (*also COMPUT*) souris *f*.
mouse mat *n* (*COMPUT*) tapis *m* de souris.
mousetrap ['maustræp] *n* souricière *f*.
moussaka [mu'sɑːkə] *n* moussaka *f*.
mousse [muːs] *n* mousse *f*.
moustache [məs'tɑːʃ] *n* moustache(s) *f(pl)*.
mousy ['mausɪ] *adj* (*person*) effacé(e); (*hair*) d'un châtain terne.
mouth, ~**s** [mauθ, -ðz] *n* bouche *f*; (*of dog, cat*) gueule *f*; (*of river*) embouchure *f*; (*of bottle*) goulot *m*; (*opening*) orifice *m*.
mouthful ['mauθful] *n* bouchée *f*.
mouth organ *n* harmonica *m*.
mouthpiece ['mauθpiːs] *n* (*of musical instrument*) bec *m*, embouchure *f*; (*spokesman*) porte-parole *m inv*.
mouth-to-mouth ['mauθtə'mauθ] *adj*: ~ **resuscitation** bouche à bouche *m*.
mouthwash ['mauθwɔʃ] *n* eau *f* dentifrice.
mouth-watering ['mauθwɔːtərɪŋ] *adj* qui met l'eau à la bouche.
movable ['muːvəbl] *adj* mobile.
move [muːv] *n* (*movement*) mouvement *m*; (*in game*) coup *m*; (*: turn to play*) tour *m*; (*change of house*) déménagement *m* ♦ *vt* déplacer, bouger; (*emotionally*) émouvoir; (*POL: resolution etc*) proposer ♦ *vi* (*gen*) bouger, remuer; (*traffic*) circuler; (*also*: ~ **house**) déménager; **to** ~ **towards** se diriger vers; **to** ~ **sb to do sth** pousser *or* inciter qn à faire qch; **to get a** ~ **on** se dépêcher, se remuer.
▸**move about, move around** *vi* (*fidget*) remuer; (*travel*) voyager, se déplacer.
▸**move along** *vi* se pousser.
▸**move away** *vi* s'en aller, s'éloigner.
▸**move back** *vi* revenir, retourner.
▸**move forward** *vi* avancer ♦ *vt* avancer; (*people*) faire avancer.
▸**move in** *vi* (*to a house*) emménager.
▸**move off** *vi* s'éloigner, s'en aller.
▸**move on** *vi* se remettre en route ♦ *vt* (*onlookers*) faire circuler.
▸**move out** *vi* (*of house*) déménager.
▸**move over** *vi* se pousser, se déplacer.
▸**move up** *vi* avancer; (*employee*) avoir de l'avancement.
movement ['muːvmənt] *n* mouvement *m*; ~ **(of the bowels)** (*MED*) selles *fpl*.
mover ['muːvə*] *n* auteur *m* d'une proposition.
movie ['muːvɪ] *n* film *m*; **the** ~**s** le cinéma.
movie camera *n* caméra *f*.
moviegoer ['muːvɪgəuə*] *n* (*US*) cinéphile *m/f*.
moving ['muːvɪŋ] *adj* en mouvement; (*touching*) émouvant(e) ♦ *n* (*US*) déménagement *m*.
mow, *pt* **mowed,** *pp* **mowed** *or* **mown** [məu, -n] *vt* faucher; (*lawn*) tondre.
▸**mow down** *vt* faucher.
mower ['məuə*] *n* (*also*: **lawn**~) tondeuse *f* à gazon.
Mozambique [məuzəm'biːk] *n* Mozambique *m*.
MP *n abbr* (= *Military Police*) PM; (*BRIT*) = **Member of Parliament**; (*Canada*) = *Mounted Police*.
mpg *n abbr* = *miles per gallon (30 mpg = 9,4 l. aux 100 km)*.
mph *abbr* = *miles per hour (60 mph = 96 km/h)*.
MPhil *n abbr* (*US*: = *Master of Philosophy*) *titre universitaire*.
MPS *n abbr* (*BRIT*) = *Member of the Pharmaceutical Society*.
Mr, Mr. ['mɪstə*] *n*: ~ **X** Monsieur X, M. X.
MRC *n abbr* (*BRIT*: = *Medical Research Council*) *conseil de la recherche médicale*.
MRCP *n abbr* (*BRIT*) = *Member of the Royal College of Physicians*.
MRCS *n abbr* (*BRIT*) = *Member of the Royal College of Surgeons*.
MRCVS *n abbr* (*BRIT*) = *Member of the Royal College of Veterinary Surgeons*.
Mrs, Mrs. ['mɪsɪz] *n*: ~ **X** Madame X, Mme X.
MS *n abbr* (= *manuscript*) ms; (= *multiple sclerosis*) SEP *f*; (*US*: = *Master of Science*) *titre universitaire* ♦ *abbr* (*US*) = *Mississippi*.
Ms, Ms. [mɪz] *n* (= *Miss or Mrs*): ~ **X** Madame X, Mme X.
MSA *n abbr* (*US*: = *Master of Science in Agriculture*) *titre universitaire*.
MSc *n abbr* = **Master of Science**.
MSG *n abbr* = **monosodium glutamate**.
MSP *n abbr* (= *Member of the Scottish Parliament*) député *m* au Parlement écossais.
MST *abbr* (*US*: = *Mountain Standard Time*) *heure d'hiver des Montagnes Rocheuses*.
MT *n abbr* (= *machine translation*) TM ♦ *abbr* (*US*) = *Montana*.
Mt *abbr* (*GEO*: = *mount*) Mt.
MTV *n abbr* = *music television*.
much [mʌtʃ] *adj* beaucoup de ♦ *adv, n or pron* beaucoup; ~ **milk** beaucoup de lait; **how** ~ **is it?** combien est-ce que ça coûte?; **it's not** ~ ce n'est pas beaucoup; **too** ~ trop (de); **so** ~ tant (de); **I like it very/so** ~ j'aime beaucoup/tellement ça; **thank you very** ~ merci beaucoup; ~ **to my amazement** ... à mon grand étonnement ....
muck [mʌk] *n* (*mud*) boue *f*; (*dirt*) ordures *fpl*.
▸**muck about** *vi* (*col*) faire l'imbécile; (*: waste time*) traînasser; (*: tinker*) bricoler; tripoter.
▸**muck in** *vi* (*BRIT col*) donner un coup de main.
▸**muck out** *vt* (*stable*) nettoyer.
▸**muck up** *vt* (*col: ruin*) gâcher, esquinter; (*: dirty*) salir.
muckraking ['mʌkreɪkɪŋ] *n* (*fig: col*) déterrement *m* d'ordures.
mucky ['mʌkɪ] *adj* (*dirty*) boueux(euse), sale.
mucus ['mjuːkəs] *n* mucus *m*.
mud [mʌd] *n* boue *f*.
muddle ['mʌdl] *n* pagaille *f*, désordre *m*, fouillis *m* ♦ *vt* (*also*: ~ **up**) brouiller, embrouiller; **to be in a** ~ (*person*) ne plus savoir ou l'on

en est; **to get in a ~** (*while explaining etc*) s'embrouiller.
▸muddle along *vi* aller son chemin tant bien que mal.
▸muddle through *vi* se débrouiller.
muddle-headed [mʌdl'hɛdɪd] *adj* (*person*) à l'esprit embrouillé *or* confus, dans le brouillard.
muddy ['mʌdɪ] *adj* boueux(euse).
mud flats *npl* plage *f* de vase.
mudguard ['mʌdgɑːd] *n* garde-boue *m inv*.
mudpack ['mʌdpæk] *n* masque *m* de beauté.
mud-slinging ['mʌdslɪŋɪŋ] *n* médisance *f*, dénigrement *m*.
muesli ['mjuːzlɪ] *n* muesli *m*.
muff [mʌf] *n* manchon *m* ♦ *vt* (*col*: *shot, catch etc*) rater, louper; **to ~ it** rater *or* louper son coup.
muffin ['mʌfɪn] *n petit pain rond et plat*.
muffle ['mʌfl] *vt* (*sound*) assourdir, étouffer; (*against cold*) emmitoufler.
muffled ['mʌfld] *adj* étouffé(e), voilé(e).
muffler ['mʌflə*] *n* (*scarf*) cache-nez *m inv*; (*US AUT*) silencieux *m*.
mufti ['mʌftɪ] *n*: **in ~** en civil.
mug [mʌg] *n* (*cup*) tasse *f* (*sans soucoupe*); (*: for beer*) chope *f*; (*col*: *face*) bouille *f*; (*: fool*) poire *f* ♦ *vt* (*assault*) agresser; **it's a ~'s game** (*BRIT*) c'est bon pour les imbéciles.
▸mug up *vt* (*BRIT col*: *also*: **~ up on**) bosser, bûcher.
mugger ['mʌgə*] *n* agresseur *m*.
mugging ['mʌgɪŋ] *n* agression *f*.
muggins ['mʌgɪnz] *n* (*col*) ma pomme.
muggy ['mʌgɪ] *adj* lourd(e), moite.
mug shot *n* (*col*: *POLICE*) photo *f* de criminel; (: *gen*: *photo*) photo d'identité.
mulatto, ~es [mjuː'lætəu] *n* mulâtre/esse.
mulberry ['mʌlbrɪ] *n* (*fruit*) mûre *f*; (*tree*) mûrier *m*.
mule [mjuːl] *n* mule *f*.
mull [mʌl]: **to ~ over** *vt* réfléchir à, ruminer.
mulled [mʌld] *adj*: **~ wine** vin chaud.
multi... ['mʌltɪ] *prefix* multi....
multi-access ['mʌltɪ'æksɛs] *adj* (*COMPUT*) à accès multiple.
multicoloured, (*US*) **multicolored** ['mʌltɪkʌləd] *adj* multicolore.
multifarious [mʌltɪ'fɛərɪəs] *adj* divers(es); varié(e).
multilateral [mʌltɪ'lætərl] *adj* (*POL*) multilatéral(e).
multi-level ['mʌltɪlɛvl] *adj* (*US*) = **multistorey**.
multimillionaire [mʌltɪmɪljə'nɛə*] *n* milliardaire *m/f*.
multinational [mʌltɪ'næʃənl] *n* multinationale *f* ♦ *adj* multinational(e).
multiple ['mʌltɪpl] *adj* multiple ♦ *n* multiple *m*; (*BRIT*: *also*: **~ store**) magasin *m* à succursales (multiples).
multiple choice *adj* à choix multiple.
multiple crash *n* carambolage *m*.
multiple sclerosis *n* sclérose *f* en plaques.
multiplex ['mʌltɪplɛks] *n* (*also*: **~ cinema**) (cinéma *m*) multisalles *m*.
multiplication [mʌltɪplɪ'keɪʃən] *n* multiplication *f*.
multiplication table *n* table *f* de multiplication.
multiplicity [mʌltɪ'plɪsɪtɪ] *n* multiplicité *f*.
multiply ['mʌltɪplaɪ] *vt* multiplier ♦ *vi* se multiplier.
multiracial [mʌltɪ'reɪʃl] *adj* multiracial(e).
multistorey ['mʌltɪ'stɔːrɪ] *adj* (*BRIT*: *building*) à étages; (*: car park*) à étages *or* niveaux multiples.
multitude ['mʌltɪtjuːd] *n* multitude *f*.
mum [mʌm] *n* (*BRIT*) maman *f* ♦ *adj*: **to keep ~** ne pas souffler mot; **~'s the word!** motus et bouche cousue!
mumble ['mʌmbl] *vt, vi* marmotter, marmonner.
mumbo jumbo ['mʌmbəu-] *n* (*col*) baragouin *m*, charabia *m*.
mummify ['mʌmɪfaɪ] *vt* momifier.
mummy ['mʌmɪ] *n* (*BRIT*: *mother*) maman *f*; (*embalmed*) momie *f*.
mumps [mʌmps] *n* oreillons *mpl*.
munch [mʌntʃ] *vt, vi* mâcher.
mundane [mʌn'deɪn] *adj* banal(e), terre à terre *inv*.
municipal [mjuː'nɪsɪpl] *adj* municipal(e).
municipality [mjuːnɪsɪ'pælɪtɪ] *n* municipalité *f*.
munitions [mjuː'nɪʃənz] *npl* munitions *fpl*.
mural ['mjuərl] *n* peinture murale.
murder ['məːdə*] *n* meurtre *m*, assassinat *m* ♦ *vt* assassiner; **to commit ~** commettre un meurtre.
murderer ['məːdərə*] *n* meurtrier *m*, assassin *m*.
murderess ['məːdərɪs] *n* meurtrière *f*.
murderous ['məːdərəs] *adj* meurtrier(ière).
murk [məːk] *n* obscurité *f*.
murky ['məːkɪ] *adj* sombre, ténébreux(euse).
murmur ['məːmə*] *n* murmure *m* ♦ *vt, vi* murmurer; **heart ~** (*MED*) souffle *m* au cœur.
MusB(ac) *n abbr* (= *Bachelor of Music*) *titre universitaire*.
muscle ['mʌsl] *n* muscle *m*.
▸muscle in *vi* s'imposer, s'immiscer.
muscular ['mʌskjulə*] *adj* musculaire; (*person, arm*) musclé(e).
muscular dystrophy *n* dystrophie *f* musculaire.
MusD(oc) *n abbr* (= *Doctor of Music*) *titre universitaire*.
muse [mjuːz] *vi* méditer, songer ♦ *n* muse *f*.
museum [mjuː'zɪəm] *n* musée *m*.
mush [mʌʃ] *n* bouillie *f*; (*pej*) sentimentalité *f* à l'eau de rose.
mushroom ['mʌʃrum] *n* champignon *m* ♦ *vi* (*fig*) pousser comme un (*or* des) champignon(s).

mushy ['mʌʃɪ] *adj* (*vegetables, fruit*) en bouillie; (*movie etc*) à l'eau de rose.
music ['mju:zɪk] *n* musique *f*.
musical ['mju:zɪkl] *adj* musical(e); (*person*) musicien(ne) ♦ *n* (*show*) comédie musicale.
music(al) box *n* boîte *f* à musique.
musical chairs *npl* chaises musicales; (*fig*) **to play** ~ faire des permutations.
musical instrument *n* instrument *m* de musique.
music centre *n* chaîne compacte.
music hall *n* music-hall *m*.
musician [mju:'zɪʃən] *n* musicien/ne.
music stand *n* pupitre *m* à musique.
musk [mʌsk] *n* musc *m*.
musket ['mʌskɪt] *n* mousquet *m*.
muskrat ['mʌskræt] *n* rat musqué.
musk rose *n* (*BOT*) rose *f* muscade.
Muslim ['mʌzlɪm] *adj, n* musulman(e).
muslin ['mʌzlɪn] *n* mousseline *f*.
musquash ['mʌskwɔʃ] *n* loutre *f*; (*fur*) rat *m* d'Amérique, ondatra *m*.
mussel ['mʌsl] *n* moule *f*.
must [mʌst] *aux vb* (*obligation*): **I ~ do it** je dois le faire, il faut que je le fasse; (*probability*): **he ~ be there by now** il doit y être maintenant, il y est probablement maintenant; **I ~ have made a mistake** j'ai dû me tromper ♦ *n* nécessité *f*, impératif *m*; **it's a ~** c'est indispensable.
mustache ['mʌstæʃ] *n* (*US*) = **moustache**.
mustard ['mʌstəd] *n* moutarde *f*.
mustard gas *n* ypérite *f*, gaz *m* moutarde.
muster ['mʌstə*] *vt* rassembler; (*also*: **~ up**: *strength, courage*) rassembler.
mustiness ['mʌstɪnɪs] *n* goût *m* de moisi; odeur *f* de moisi *or* de renfermé.
mustn't ['mʌsnt] = **must not**.
musty ['mʌstɪ] *adj* qui sent le moisi *or* le renfermé.
mutant ['mju:tənt] *adj* mutant(e) ♦ *n* mutant *m*.
mutate [mju:'teɪt] *vi* subir une mutation.
mutation [mju:'teɪʃən] *n* mutation *f*.
mute [mju:t] *adj, n* muet(te).
muted ['mju:tɪd] *adj* (*noise*) sourd(e), assourdi(e); (*criticism*) voilé(e); (*MUS*) en sourdine; (*: trumpet*) bouché(e).
mutilate ['mju:tɪleɪt] *vt* mutiler.
mutilation [mju:tɪ'leɪʃən] *n* mutilation *f*.
mutinous ['mju:tɪnəs] *adj* (*troops*) mutiné(e); (*attitude*) rebelle.
mutiny ['mju:tɪnɪ] *n* mutinerie *f* ♦ *vi* se mutiner.
mutter ['mʌtə*] *vt, vi* marmonner, marmotter.
mutton ['mʌtn] *n* mouton *m*.
mutual ['mju:tʃuəl] *adj* mutuel(le), réciproque.
mutually ['mju:tʃuəlɪ] *adv* mutuellement, réciproquement.
Muzak ['mju:zæk] *n* ® (*often pej*) musique *f* d'ambiance.
muzzle ['mʌzl] *n* museau *m*; (*protective device*) muselière *f*; (*of gun*) gueule *f* ♦ *vt* museler.
MVP *n abbr* (*US SPORT*) = *most valuable player*.
MW *abbr* (= *medium wave*) PO.
my [maɪ] *adj* mon(ma), mes *pl*.
Myanmar ['maɪænmɑ:*] *n* Myanmar *m*.
myopic [maɪ'ɔpɪk] *adj* myope.
myriad ['mɪrɪəd] *n* myriade *f*.
myself [maɪ'sɛlf] *pron* (*reflexive*) me; (*emphatic*) moi-même; (*after prep*) moi.
mysterious [mɪs'tɪərɪəs] *adj* mystérieux(euse).
mystery ['mɪstərɪ] *n* mystère *m*.
mystery story *n* roman *m* à suspense.
mystic ['mɪstɪk] *n* mystique *m/f* ♦ *adj* (*mysterious*) ésotérique.
mystical ['mɪstɪkl] *adj* mystique.
mystify ['mɪstɪfaɪ] *vt* mystifier; (*puzzle*) ébahir.
mystique [mɪs'ti:k] *n* mystique *f*.
myth [mɪθ] *n* mythe *m*.
mythical ['mɪθɪkl] *adj* mythique.
mythological [mɪθə'lɔdʒɪkl] *adj* mythologique.
mythology [mɪ'θɔlədʒɪ] *n* mythologie *f*.

N n

N, n [ɛn] *n* (*letter*) N, n *m*; **N for Nellie**, (*US*) **N for Nan** N comme Nicolas.
N *abbr* (= *north*) N.
NA *n abbr* (*US*: = *Narcotics Anonymous*) *association d'aide aux drogués*; (*US*) = *National Academy*.
n/a *abbr* (= *not applicable*) n.a.; (*COMM etc*) = *no account*.
NAACP *n abbr* (*US*) = *National Association for the Advancement of Colored People*.
NAAFI ['næfɪ] *n abbr* (*BRIT*: = *Navy, Army & Air Force Institute*) *organisme responsable des magasins et cantines de l'armée*.
nab [næb] *vt* (*col*) pincer, attraper.
NACU *n abbr* (*US*) = *National Association of Colleges and Universities*.
nadir ['neɪdɪə*] *n* (*ASTRONOMY*) nadir *m*; (*fig*) fond *m*, point *m* extrême.
nag [næg] *vt* (*person*) être toujours après, reprendre sans arrêt ♦ *n* (*pej*: *horse*) canasson *m*; (*person*): **she's an awful ~** elle est constamment après lui (*or* eux *etc*), elle est terriblement casse-pieds.
nagging ['nægɪŋ] *adj* (*doubt, pain*) persistant(e) ♦ *n* remarques continuelles.
nail [neɪl] *n* (*human*) ongle *m*; (*metal*) clou *m* ♦ *vt* clouer; **to ~ sb down to a date/price** contraindre qn à accepter *or* donner une

date/un prix; **to pay cash on the ~** (*BRIT*) payer rubis sur l'ongle.
nailbrush ['neɪlbrʌʃ] *n* brosse *f* à ongles.
nailfile ['neɪlfaɪl] *n* lime *f* à ongles.
nail polish *n* vernis *m* à ongles.
nail polish remover *n* dissolvant *m*.
nail scissors *npl* ciseaux *mpl* à ongles.
nail varnish *n* (*BRIT*) = **nail polish**.
Nairobi [naɪ'rəubɪ] *n* Nairobi.
naïve [naɪ'i:v] *adj* naïf(ïve).
naïveté [naɪ'i:vteɪ], **naivety** [naɪ'i:vɪtɪ] *n* naïveté *f*.
naked ['neɪkɪd] *adj* nu(e); **with the ~ eye** à l'œil nu.
nakedness ['neɪkɪdnɪs] *n* nudité *f*.
NAM *n abbr* (*US*) = *National Association of Manufacturers*.
name [neɪm] *n* nom *m*; (*reputation*) réputation *f* ♦ *vt* nommer; citer; (*price, date*) fixer, donner; **by ~** par son nom; de nom; **in the ~ of** au nom de; **what's your ~?** quel est votre nom?; **my ~ is Peter** je m'appelle Peter; **to take sb's ~ and address** relever l'identité de qn *or* les nom et adresse de qn; **to make a ~ for o.s.** se faire un nom; **to get (o.s.) a bad ~** se faire une mauvaise réputation; **to call sb ~s** traiter qn de tous les noms.
name dropping *n mention (pour se faire valoir) du nom de personnalités qu'on connaît (ou prétend connaître)*.
nameless ['neɪmlɪs] *adj* sans nom; (*witness, contributor*) anonyme.
namely ['neɪmlɪ] *adv* à savoir.
nameplate ['neɪmpleɪt] *n* (*on door etc*) plaque *f*.
namesake ['neɪmseɪk] *n* homonyme *m*.
nan bread [nɑ:n-] *n* nan *m*.
nanny ['nænɪ] *n* bonne *f* d'enfants.
nanny goat *n* chèvre *f*.
nap [næp] *n* (*sleep*) (petit) somme ♦ *vi*: **to be caught ~ping** être pris(e) à l'improviste *or* en défaut.
NAPA *n abbr* (*US*: = *National Association of Performing Artists*) *syndicat des gens du spectacle*.
napalm ['neɪpɑ:m] *n* napalm *m*.
nape [neɪp] *n*: **~ of the neck** nuque *f*.
napkin ['næpkɪn] *n* serviette *f* (de table).
Naples ['neɪplz] *n* Naples.
Napoleonic [nəpəulɪ'ɔnɪk] *adj* napoléonien(ne).
nappy ['næpɪ] *n* (*BRIT*) couche *f* (*gen pl*).
nappy liner *n* (*BRIT*) protège-couche *m*.
narcissistic [nɑ:sɪ'sɪstɪk] *adj* narcissique.
narcissus, *pl* **narcissi** [nɑ:'sɪsəs, -saɪ] *n* narcisse *m*.
narcotic [nɑ:'kɔtɪk] *n* (*MED*) narcotique *m*; **~s** *npl* (*drugs*) stupéfiants *mpl*.
nark [nɑ:k] *vt* (*BRIT col*) mettre en rogne.
narrate [nə'reɪt] *vt* raconter, narrer.
narration [nə'reɪʃən] *n* narration *f*.
narrative ['nærətɪv] *n* récit *m* ♦ *adj* narratif(ive).
narrator [nə'reɪtə*] *n* narrateur/trice.
narrow ['nærəu] *adj* étroit(e); (*fig*) restreint(e), limité(e) ♦ *vi* devenir plus étroit, se rétrécir; **to have a ~ escape** l'échapper belle; **to ~ sth down to** réduire qch à.
narrow gauge *adj* (*RAIL*) à voie étroite.
narrowly ['nærəulɪ] *adv*: **he ~ missed injury/the tree** il a failli se blesser/rentrer dans l'arbre; **he only ~ missed the target** il a manqué la cible de peu *or* de justesse.
narrow-minded [nærəu'maɪndɪd] *adj* à l'esprit étroit, borné(e).
NAS *n abbr* (*US*) = *National Academy of Sciences*.
NASA ['næsə] *n abbr* (*US*: = *National Aeronautics and Space Administration*) NASA *f*.
nasal ['neɪzl] *adj* nasal(e).
Nassau ['næsɔ:] *n* (*in Bahamas*) Nassau.
nastily ['nɑ:stɪlɪ] *adv* (*say, act*) méchamment.
nastiness ['nɑ:stɪnɪs] *n* (*of person, remark*) méchanceté *f*.
nasturtium [nəs'tə:ʃəm] *n* capucine *f*.
nasty ['nɑ:stɪ] *adj* (*person*) méchant(e); très désagréable; (*smell*) dégoûtant(e); (*wound, situation*) mauvais(e), vilain(e); (*weather*) affreux(euse); **to turn ~** (*situation*) mal tourner; (*weather*) se gâter; (*person*) devenir méchant; **it's a ~ business** c'est une sale affaire.
NAS/UWT *n abbr* (*BRIT*: = *National Association of Schoolmasters/Union of Women Teachers*) *syndicat enseignant*.
nation ['neɪʃən] *n* nation *f*.
national ['næʃənl] *adj* national(e) ♦ *n* (*abroad*) ressortissant/e; (*when home*) national/e.
national anthem *n* hymne national.
National Curriculum *n* (*BRIT*) *programme scolaire commun à toutes les écoles publiques en Angleterre et au Pays de Galles comprenant dix disciplines*.
national debt *n* dette publique.
national dress *n* costume national.
National Guard *n* (*US*) milice *f* (*de volontaires dans chaque État*).
National Health Service (NHS) *n* (*BRIT*) *service national de santé*, ≈ Sécurité Sociale.
National Insurance *n* (*BRIT*) ≈ Sécurité Sociale.
nationalism ['næʃnəlɪzəm] *n* nationalisme *m*.
nationalist ['næʃnəlɪst] *adj*, *n* nationaliste (*m/f*).
nationality [næʃə'nælɪtɪ] *n* nationalité *f*.
nationalization [næʃnəlaɪ'zeɪʃən] *n* nationalisation *f*.
nationalize ['næʃnəlaɪz] *vt* nationaliser.
nationally ['næʃnəlɪ] *adv* du point de vue national; dans le pays entier.
national park *n* parc national.
national press *n* presse nationale.
National Security Council *n* (*US*) conseil national de sécurité.
national service *n* (*MIL*) service *m* militaire.

National Trust *n* (*BRIT*) ≈ Caisse *f* nationale des monuments historiques et des sites; *voir encadré*.

> **NATIONAL TRUST**
>
> *Le* **National Trust** *est un organisme indépendant, à but non lucratif, dont la mission est de protéger et de mettre en valeur les monuments et les sites britanniques en raison de leur intérêt historique ou de leur beauté naturelle.*

nation-wide ['neɪʃənwaɪd] *adj* s'étendant à l'ensemble du pays; (*problem*) à l'échelle du pays entier ♦ *adv* à travers *or* dans tout le pays.
native ['neɪtɪv] *n* habitant/e du pays, autochtone *m/f*; (*in colonies*) indigène *m/f* ♦ *adj* du pays, indigène; (*country*) natal(e); (*language*) maternel(le); (*ability*) inné(e); **a ~ of Russia** une personne originaire de Russie; **a ~ speaker of French** une personne de langue maternelle française.
Native American *n* Indien/ne d'Amérique.
Nativity [nə'tɪvɪtɪ] *n* (*REL*): **the ~** la Nativité.
nativity play *n* mystère *m or* miracle *m* de la Nativité.
NATO ['neɪtəu] *n abbr* (= *North Atlantic Treaty Organization*) OTAN *f*.
natter ['nætə*] *vi* (*BRIT*) bavarder.
natural ['nætʃrəl] *adj* naturel(le); **to die of ~ causes** mourir d'une mort naturelle.
natural childbirth *n* accouchement *m* sans douleur.
natural gas *n* gaz naturel.
natural history *n* histoire naturelle.
naturalist ['nætʃrəlɪst] *n* naturaliste *m/f*.
naturalization ['nætʃrəlaɪ'zeɪʃən] *n* naturalisation *f*; acclimatation *f*.
naturalize ['nætʃrəlaɪz] *vt* naturaliser; (*plant*) acclimater; **to become ~d** (*person*) se faire naturaliser.
naturally ['nætʃrəlɪ] *adv* naturellement.
natural resources *npl* ressources naturelles.
natural selection *n* sélection naturelle.
natural wastage *n* (*INDUSTRY*) départs naturels et volontaires.
nature ['neɪtʃə*] *n* nature *f*; **by ~** par tempérament, de nature; **documents of a confidential ~** documents à caractère confidentiel.
-natured ['neɪtʃəd] *suffix*: **ill~** qui a mauvais caractère.
nature reserve *n* (*BRIT*) réserve naturelle.
nature trail *n sentier de découverte de la nature.*
naturist ['neɪtʃərɪst] *n* naturiste *m/f*.
naught [nɔːt] *n* = **nought**.
naughtiness ['nɔːtɪnɪs] *n* (*of child*) désobéissance *f*; (*of story etc*) grivoiserie *f*.
naughty ['nɔːtɪ] *adj* (*child*) vilain(e), pas sage; (*story, film*) grivois(e).
nausea ['nɔːsɪə] *n* nausée *f*.
nauseate ['nɔːsɪeɪt] *vt* écœurer, donner la nausée à.
nauseating ['nɔːsɪeɪtɪŋ] *adj* écœurant(e), dégoûtant(e).
nauseous ['nɔːsɪəs] *adj* nauséabond(e), écœurant(e); (*feeling sick*): **to be ~** avoir des nausées.
nautical ['nɔːtɪkl] *adj* nautique.
nautical mile *n* mille marin (= *1853 m*).
naval ['neɪvl] *adj* naval(e).
naval officer *n* officier *m* de marine.
nave [neɪv] *n* nef *f*.
navel ['neɪvl] *n* nombril *m*.
navigable ['nævɪgəbl] *adj* navigable.
navigate ['nævɪgeɪt] *vt* diriger, piloter ♦ *vi* naviguer; (*AUT*) indiquer la route à suivre.
navigation [nævɪ'geɪʃən] *n* navigation *f*.
navigator ['nævɪgeɪtə*] *n* navigateur *m*.
navvy ['nævɪ] *n* (*BRIT*) terrassier *m*.
navy ['neɪvɪ] *n* marine *f*; **Department of the N~** (*US*) ministère *m* de la Marine.
navy(-blue) ['neɪvɪ('bluː)] *adj* bleu marine *inv*.
Nazi ['nɑːtsɪ] *adj* nazi(e) ♦ *n* Nazi/e.
NB *abbr* (= *nota bene*) NB; (*Canada*) = *New Brunswick*.
NBA *n abbr* (*US*) = *National Basketball Association, National Boxing Association.*
NBC *n abbr* (*US*: = *National Broadcasting Company*) *chaîne de télévision.*
NBS *n abbr* (*US*: = *National Bureau of Standards*) *office de normalisation.*
NC *abbr* (*COMM etc*) = *no charge*; (*US*) = *North Carolina.*
NCC *n abbr* (*BRIT*: = *Nature Conservancy Council*) *organisme de protection de la nature*; (*US*) = *National Council of Churches.*
NCCL *n abbr* (*BRIT*: = *National Council for Civil Liberties*) *association de défense des libertés publiques.*
NCO *n abbr* = **non-commissioned officer**.
ND, N. Dak. *abbr* (*US*) = *North Dakota.*
NE *abbr* (*US*) = *Nebraska, New England.*
NEA *n abbr* (*US*) = *National Education Association.*
neap [niːp] *n* (*also*: **~tide**) mortes-eaux *fpl*.
near [nɪə*] *adj* proche ♦ *adv* près ♦ *prep* (*also*: **~ to**) près de ♦ *vt* approcher de; **~ here/there** près d'ici/non loin de là; **£25,000 or ~est offer** (*BRIT*) 25 000 livres à débattre; **in the ~ future** dans un proche avenir; **to come ~** *vi* s'approcher.
nearby [nɪə'baɪ] *adj* proche ♦ *adv* tout près, à proximité.
Near East *n*: **the ~** le Proche-Orient.
nearer ['nɪərə*] *adj* plus proche ♦ *adv* plus près.
nearly ['nɪəlɪ] *adv* presque; **I ~ fell** j'ai failli tomber; **it's not ~ big enough** ce n'est vraiment pas assez grand, c'est loin d'être assez grand.
near miss *n* collision évitée de justesse; (*when aiming*) coup manqué de peu *or* de

justesse.

nearness ['nɪənɪs] *n* proximité *f*.

nearside ['nɪəsaɪd] (*AUT*) *n* (*right-hand drive*) côté *m* gauche; (*left-hand drive*) côté droit ♦ *adj* de gauche; de droite.

near-sighted [nɪə'saɪtɪd] *adj* myope.

neat [niːt] *adj* (*person, work*) soigné(e); (*room etc*) bien tenu(e) *or* rangé(e); (*solution, plan*) habile; (*spirits*) pur(e); **I drink it ~** je le bois sec *or* sans eau.

neatly ['niːtlɪ] *adv* avec soin *or* ordre; habilement.

neatness ['niːtnɪs] *n* (*tidiness*) netteté *f*; (*skilfulness*) habileté *f*.

Nebr. *abbr* (*US*) = *Nebraska*.

nebulous ['nɛbjuləs] *adj* nébuleux(euse).

necessarily ['nɛsɪsrɪlɪ] *adv* nécessairement; **not ~** pas nécessairement *or* forcément.

necessary ['nɛsɪsrɪ] *adj* nécessaire; **if ~** si besoin est, le cas échéant.

necessitate [nɪ'sɛsɪteɪt] *vt* nécessiter.

necessity [nɪ'sɛsɪtɪ] *n* nécessité *f*; chose nécessaire *or* essentielle; **in case of ~** en cas d'urgence.

neck [nɛk] *n* cou *m*; (*of horse, garment*) encolure *f*; (*of bottle*) goulot *m* ♦ *vi* (*col*) se peloter; **~ and ~** à égalité; **to stick one's ~ out** (*col*) se mouiller.

necklace ['nɛklɪs] *n* collier *m*.

neckline ['nɛklaɪn] *n* encolure *f*.

necktie ['nɛktaɪ] *n* (*esp US*) cravate *f*.

nectar ['nɛktə*] *n* nectar *m*.

nectarine ['nɛktərɪn] *n* brugnon *m*, nectarine *f*.

NEDC *n abbr* (*BRIT*: = *National Economic Development Council*) *conseil national pour le développement économique*.

Neddy ['nɛdɪ] *n abbr* (*BRIT col*) = **NEDC**.

née [neɪ] *adj*: **~ Scott** née Scott.

need [niːd] *n* besoin *m* ♦ *vt* avoir besoin de; **to ~ to do** devoir faire; avoir besoin de faire; **you don't ~ to go** vous n'avez pas besoin *or* vous n'êtes pas obligé de partir; **a signature is ~ed** il faut une signature; **to be in ~ of** *or* **have ~ of** avoir besoin de; **£10 will meet my immediate ~s** 10 livres suffiront pour mes besoins immédiats; **in case of ~** en cas de besoin, au besoin; **there's no ~ to do ...** il n'y a pas lieu de faire ..., il n'est pas nécessaire de faire ...; **there's no ~ for that** ce n'est pas la peine, cela n'est pas nécessaire.

needle ['niːdl] *n* aiguille *f*; (*on record player*) saphir *m* ♦ *vt* (*col*) asticoter, tourmenter.

needlecord ['niːdlkɔːd] *n* (*BRIT*) velours *m* milleraies.

needless ['niːdlɪs] *adj* inutile; **~ to say, ...** inutile de dire que ....

needlessly ['niːdlɪslɪ] *adv* inutilement.

needlework ['niːdlwəːk] *n* (*activity*) travaux *mpl* d'aiguille; (*object*) ouvrage *m*.

needn't ['niːdnt] = **need not**.

needy ['niːdɪ] *adj* nécessiteux(euse).

negation [nɪ'geɪʃən] *n* négation *f*.

negative ['nɛgətɪv] *n* (*PHOT, ELEC*) négatif *m*; (*LING*) terme *m* de négation ♦ *adj* négatif(ive); **to answer in the ~** répondre par la négative.

negative equity *n situation dans laquelle la valeur d'une maison est inférieure à celle de l'emprunt-logement contracté pour la payer*.

neglect [nɪ'glɛkt] *vt* négliger ♦ *n* (*of person, duty, garden*) le fait de négliger; **(state of) ~** abandon *m*; **to ~ to do sth** négliger *or* omettre de faire qch.

neglected [nɪ'glɛktɪd] *adj* négligé(e), à l'abandon.

neglectful [nɪ'glɛktful] *adj* (*gen*) négligent(e); **to be ~ of sb/sth** négliger qn/qch.

negligee ['nɛglɪʒeɪ] *n* déshabillé *m*.

negligence ['nɛglɪdʒəns] *n* négligence *f*.

negligent ['nɛglɪdʒənt] *adj* négligent(e).

negligently ['nɛglɪdʒəntlɪ] *adv* par négligence; (*offhandedly*) négligemment.

negligible ['nɛglɪdʒɪbl] *adj* négligeable.

negotiable [nɪ'gəuʃɪəbl] *adj* négociable; **not ~** (*cheque*) non négociable.

negotiate [nɪ'gəuʃɪeɪt] *vi* négocier ♦ *vt* (*COMM*) négocier; (*obstacle*) franchir, négocier; (*bend in road*) négocier; **to ~ with sb for sth** négocier avec qn en vue d'obtenir qch.

negotiating table [nɪ'gəuʃɪeɪtɪŋ-] *n* table *f* des négociations.

negotiation [nɪgəuʃɪ'eɪʃən] *n* négociation *f*, pourparlers *mpl*; **to enter into ~s with sb** engager des négociations avec qn.

negotiator [nɪ'gəuʃɪeɪtə*] *n* négociateur/trice.

Negress ['niːgrɪs] *n* négresse *f*.

Negro ['niːgrəu] *adj* (*gen*) noir(e); (*music, arts*) nègre, noir ♦ *n* (*pl*: **~es**) Noir/e.

neigh [neɪ] *vi* hennir.

neighbour, (*US*) **neighbor** ['neɪbə*] *n* voisin/e.

neighbo(u)rhood ['neɪbəhud] *n* quartier *m*; voisinage *m*.

neighbourhood watch *n* (*BRIT*: *also*: **~ scheme**) *système de surveillance, assuré par les habitants d'un même quartier*.

neighbo(u)ring ['neɪbərɪŋ] *adj* voisin(e), avoisinant(e).

neighbo(u)rly ['neɪbəlɪ] *adj* obligeant(e); (*relations*) de bon voisinage.

neither ['naɪðə*] *adj, pron* aucun(e) (des deux), ni l'un(e) ni l'autre ♦ *conj*: **I didn't move and ~ did Claude** je n'ai pas bougé, (et) Claude non plus ♦ *adv*: **~ good nor bad** ni bon ni mauvais; **..., ~ did I refuse** ..., (et *or* mais) je n'ai pas non plus refusé.

neo... ['niːəu] *prefix* néo-.

neolithic [niːəu'lɪθɪk] *adj* néolithique.

neologism [nɪ'ɔlədʒɪzəm] *n* néologisme *m*.

neon ['niːɔn] *n* néon *m*.

neon light *n* lampe *f* au néon.

neon sign *n* enseigne (lumineuse) au néon.

Nepal [nɪ'pɔːl] *n* Népal *m*.

nephew ['nɛvjuː] *n* neveu *m*.
nepotism ['nɛpətɪzəm] *n* népotisme *m*.
nerd [nəːd] *n* (*col*) pauvre mec *m*, ballot *m*.
nerve [nəːv] *n* nerf *m*; (*bravery*) sang-froid *m*, courage *m*; (*cheek*) aplomb *m*, toupet *m*; **he gets on my ~s** il m'énerve; **to have a fit of ~s** avoir le trac; **to lose one's ~** (*self-confidence*) perdre son sang-froid.
nerve centre *n* (*ANAT*) centre nerveux; (*fig*) centre névralgique.
nerve gas *n* gaz *m* neuroplégique.
nerve-racking ['nəːvrækɪŋ] *adj* angoissant(e).
nervous ['nəːvəs] *adj* nerveux(euse); (*apprehensive*) inquiet(ète), plein(e) d'appréhension.
nervous breakdown *n* dépression nerveuse.
nervously ['nəːvəslɪ] *adv* nerveusement.
nervousness ['nəːvəsnɪs] *n* nervosité *f*; inquiétude *f*, appréhension *f*.
nervous wreck *n*: **to be a ~** être une boule de nerfs.
nervy ['nəːvɪ] *adj*: **he's very ~** il a les nerfs à fleur de peau *or* à vif.
nest [nɛst] *n* nid *m* ♦ *vi* (se) nicher, faire son nid; **~ of tables** table *f* gigogne.
nest egg *n* (*fig*) bas *m* de laine, magot *m*.
nestle ['nɛsl] *vi* se blottir.
nestling ['nɛstlɪŋ] *n* oisillon *m*.
net [nɛt] *n* (*also fabric*) filet *m*; **the N~** (*Internet*) le Net ♦ *adj* net(te) ♦ *vt* (*fish etc*) prendre au filet; (*money: subj: person*) toucher; (*: deal, sale*) rapporter; **~ of tax** net d'impôt; **he earns £10,000 ~ per year** il gagne 10 000 livres net par an.
netball ['nɛtbɔːl] *n* netball *m*.
net curtains *npl* voilages *mpl*.
Netherlands ['nɛðələndz] *npl*: **the ~** les Pays-Bas *mpl*.
net profit *n* bénéfice net.
nett [nɛt] *adj* = **net**.
netting ['nɛtɪŋ] *n* (*for fence etc*) treillis *m*, grillage *m*; (*fabric*) voile *m*.
nettle ['nɛtl] *n* ortie *f*.
network ['nɛtwəːk] *n* réseau *m* ♦ *vt* (*RADIO, TV*) diffuser sur l'ensemble du réseau; (*computers*) interconnecter.
neuralgia [njuə'rældʒə] *n* névralgie *f*.
neurological [njuərə'lɔdʒɪkl] *adj* neurologique.
neurosis, *pl* **neuroses** [njuə'rəusɪs, -siːz] *n* névrose *f*.
neurotic [njuə'rɔtɪk] *adj, n* névrosé(e).
neuter ['njuːtə*] *adj, n* neutre (*m*) ♦ *vt* (*cat etc*) châtrer, couper.
neutral ['njuːtrəl] *adj* neutre ♦ *n* (*AUT*) point mort.
neutrality [njuː'trælɪtɪ] *n* neutralité *f*.
neutralize ['njuːtrəlaɪz] *vt* neutraliser.
Nev. *abbr* (*US*) = *Nevada*.
never ['nɛvə*] *adv* (ne ...) jamais; **~ again** plus jamais; **~ in my life** jamais de ma vie; *see also* **mind**.
never-ending [nɛvər'ɛndɪŋ] *adj* interminable.
nevertheless [nɛvəðə'lɛs] *adv* néanmoins, malgré tout.
new [njuː] *adj* nouveau(nouvelle); (*brand new*) neuf(neuve); **as good as ~** comme neuf.
New Age *n* New Age *m*.
newborn ['njuːbɔːn] *adj* nouveau-né(e).
newcomer ['njuːkʌmə*] *n* nouveau venu/nouvelle venue.
new-fangled ['njuːfæŋgld] *adj* (*pej*) ultramoderne (et farfelu(e)).
new-found ['njuːfaund] *adj* de fraîche date; (*friend*) nouveau(nouvelle).
Newfoundland ['njuːfənlənd] *n* Terre-Neuve *f*.
New Guinea *n* Nouvelle-Guinée *f*.
newly ['njuːlɪ] *adv* nouvellement, récemment.
newly-weds ['njuːlɪwɛdz] *npl* jeunes mariés *mpl*.
new moon *n* nouvelle lune.
newness ['njuːnɪs] *n* nouveauté *f*; (*of fabric, clothes etc*) état neuf.
New Orleans [-'ɔːliːənz] *n* la Nouvelle-Orléans.
news [njuːz] *n* nouvelle(s) *f(pl)*; (*RADIO, TV*) informations *fpl*; **a piece of ~** une nouvelle; **good/bad ~** bonne/mauvaise nouvelle; **financial ~** (*PRESS, RADIO, TV*) page financière.
news agency *n* agence *f* de presse.
newsagent ['njuːzeɪdʒənt] *n* (*BRIT*) marchand *m* de journaux.
news bulletin *n* (*RADIO, TV*) bulletin *m* d'informations.
newscaster ['njuːzkɑːstə*] *n* (*RADIO, TV*) présentateur/trice.
newsdealer ['njuːzdiːlə*] *n* (*US*) = **newsagent**.
news flash *n* flash *m* d'information.
newsletter ['njuːzlɛtə*] *n* bulletin *m*.
newspaper ['njuːzpeɪpə*] *n* journal *m*; **daily ~** quotidien *m*; **weekly ~** hebdomadaire *m*.
newsprint ['njuːzprɪnt] *n* papier *m* (de) journal.
newsreader ['njuːzriːdə*] *n* = **newscaster**.
newsreel ['njuːzriːl] *n* actualités (filmées).
newsroom ['njuːzruːm] *n* (*PRESS*) salle *f* de rédaction; (*RADIO, TV*) studio *m*.
news stand *n* kiosque *m* à journaux.
newsworthy ['njuːzwəːðɪ] *adj*: **to be ~** valoir la peine d'être publié.
newt [njuːt] *n* triton *m*.
new town *n* (*BRIT*) ville nouvelle.
New Year *n* Nouvel An; **Happy ~!** Bonne Année!; **to wish sb a happy ~** souhaiter la Bonne Année à qn.
New Year's Day *n* le jour de l'An.
New Year's Eve *n* la Saint-Sylvestre.
New York [-'jɔːk] *n* New York; (*also*: **~ State**) New York *m*.
New Zealand [-'ziːlənd] *n* Nouvelle-Zélande *f* ♦ *adj* néo-zélandais(e).

New Zealander [-'zi:ləndə*] *n* Néo-Zélandais/e.
next [nɛkst] *adj* (*seat, room*) voisin(e), d'à côté; (*meeting, bus stop*) suivant(e); prochain(e) ♦ *adv* la fois suivante; la prochaine fois; (*afterwards*) ensuite; ~ **to** *prep* à côté de; ~ **to nothing** presque rien; ~ **time** *adv* la prochaine fois; **the** ~ **day** le lendemain, le jour suivant *or* d'après; ~ **week** la semaine prochaine; **the** ~ **week** la semaine suivante; ~ **year** l'année prochaine; **"turn to the ~ page"** "voir page suivante"; **who's ~?** c'est à qui?; **the week after** ~ dans deux semaines; **when do we meet ~?** quand nous revoyons-nous?
next door *adv* à côté.
next-of-kin ['nɛkstəv'kɪn] *n* parent *m* le plus proche.
NF *n abbr* (*BRIT POL*: = *National Front*) ≈ FN ♦ *abbr* (*Canada*) = *Newfoundland.*
NFL *n abbr* (*US*) = *National Football League.*
Nfld. *abbr* (*Canada*) = *Newfoundland.*
NG *abbr* (*US*) = **National Guard.**
NGO *n abbr* (*US*: = *non-governmental organization*) ONG *f.*
NH *abbr* (*US*) = *New Hampshire.*
NHL *n abbr* (*US*) = *National Hockey League.*
NHS *n abbr* (*BRIT*) = **National Health Service.**
NI *abbr* = **Northern Ireland**; (*BRIT*) = **National Insurance.**
Niagara Falls [naɪ'ægərə-] *npl*: **the** ~ les chutes *fpl* du Niagara.
nib [nɪb] *n* (*of pen*) (bec *m* de) plume *f.*
nibble ['nɪbl] *vt* grignoter.
Nicaragua [nɪkə'rægjuə] *n* Nicaragua *m.*
Nicaraguan [nɪkə'rægjuən] *adj* nicaraguayen(ne) ♦ *n* Nicaraguayen/ne.
nice [naɪs] *adj* (*holiday, trip, taste*) agréable; (*flat, picture*) joli(e); (*person*) gentil(le); (*distinction, point*) subtil(e).
nice-looking ['naɪslukɪŋ] *adj* joli(e).
nicely ['naɪslɪ] *adv* agréablement; joliment; gentiment; subtilement; **that will do** ~ ce sera parfait.
niceties ['naɪsɪtɪz] *npl* subtilités *fpl.*
niche [ni:ʃ] *n* (*ARCHIT*) niche *f.*
nick [nɪk] *n* encoche *f*; (*BRIT col*): **in good** ~ en bon état ♦ *vt* (*cut*): **to** ~ **o.s.** se couper; (*col*: *steal*) faucher, piquer; (*: BRIT*: *arrest*) choper, pincer; **in the** ~ **of time** juste à temps.
nickel ['nɪkl] *n* nickel *m*; (*US*) pièce *f* de 5 cents.
nickname ['nɪkneɪm] *n* surnom *m* ♦ *vt* surnommer.
Nicosia [nɪkə'si:ə] *n* Nicosie.
nicotine ['nɪkəti:n] *n* nicotine *f.*
nicotine patch *n* timbre *m* anti-tabac, patch *m.*
niece [ni:s] *n* nièce *f.*
nifty ['nɪftɪ] *adj* (*col*: *car, jacket*) qui a du chic *or* de la classe; (*: gadget, tool*) astucieux(euse).
Niger ['naɪdʒə*] *n* (*country, river*) Niger *m.*
Nigeria [naɪ'dʒɪərɪə] *n* Nigéria *m or f.*
Nigerian [naɪ'dʒɪərɪən] *adj* nigérien(ne) ♦ *n* Nigérien/ne.
niggardly ['nɪgədlɪ] *adj* (*person*) parcimonieux(euse), pingre; (*allowance, amount*) misérable.
nigger ['nɪgə*] *n* (*col*: *highly offensive*) nègre/négresse.
niggle ['nɪgl] *vt* tracasser ♦ *vi* (*find fault*) trouver toujours à redire; (*fuss*) n'être jamais content(e).
niggling ['nɪglɪŋ] *adj* tatillon(ne); (*detail*) insignifiant(e); (*doubt, pain*) persistant(e).
night [naɪt] *n* nuit *f*; (*evening*) soir *m*; **at** ~ la nuit; **by** ~ de nuit; **in the** ~, **during the** ~ pendant la nuit; **the** ~ **before last** avant-hier soir.
night-bird ['naɪtbə:d] *n* oiseau *m* nocturne; (*fig*) couche-tard *m inv*, noctambule *m/f.*
nightcap ['naɪtkæp] *n* *boisson prise avant le coucher.*
night club *n* boîte *f* de nuit.
nightdress ['naɪtdrɛs] *n* chemise *f* de nuit.
nightfall ['naɪtfɔ:l] *n* tombée *f* de la nuit.
nightie ['naɪtɪ] *n* chemise *f* de nuit.
nightingale ['naɪtɪŋgeɪl] *n* rossignol *m.*
night life *n* vie *f* nocturne.
nightly ['naɪtlɪ] *adj* de chaque nuit *or* soir; (*by night*) nocturne ♦ *adv* chaque nuit *or* soir; nuitamment.
nightmare ['naɪtmɛə*] *n* cauchemar *m.*
night porter *n* gardien *m* de nuit, concierge *m* de service la nuit.
night safe *n* coffre *m* de nuit.
night school *n* cours *mpl* du soir.
nightshade ['naɪtʃeɪd] *n*: **deadly** ~ (*BOT*) belladone *f.*
nightshift ['naɪtʃɪft] *n* équipe *f* de nuit.
night-time ['naɪttaɪm] *n* nuit *f.*
night watchman *n* veilleur *m* de nuit; poste *m* de nuit.
nihilism ['naɪɪlɪzəm] *n* nihilisme *m.*
nil [nɪl] *n* rien *m*; (*BRIT SPORT*) zéro *m.*
Nile [naɪl] *n*: **the** ~ le Nil.
nimble ['nɪmbl] *adj* agile.
nine [naɪn] *num* neuf.
nineteen ['naɪn'ti:n] *num* dix-neuf.
ninety ['naɪntɪ] *num* quatre-vingt-dix.
ninth [naɪnθ] *num* neuvième.
nip [nɪp] *vt* pincer ♦ *vi* (*BRIT col*): **to** ~ **out/down/up** sortir/descendre/monter en vitesse ♦ *n* pincement *m*; (*drink*) petit verre; **to** ~ **into a shop** faire un saut dans un magasin.
nipple ['nɪpl] *n* (*ANAT*) mamelon *m*, bout *m* du sein.
nippy ['nɪpɪ] *adj* (*BRIT*: *person*) alerte, leste; (*: car*) nerveux(euse).
nit [nɪt] *n* (*in hair*) lente *f*; (*col*: *idiot*) imbécile *m/f*, crétin/e.
nit-pick ['nɪtpɪk] *vi* (*col*) être tatillon(ne).
nitrogen ['naɪtrədʒən] *n* azote *m.*

nitroglycerin(e) ['naɪtrəu'glɪsəriːn] *n* nitroglycérine *f*.
nitty-gritty ['nɪtɪ'grɪtɪ] *n* (*fam*): **to get down to the ~** en venir au fond du problème.
nitwit ['nɪtwɪt] *n* (*col*) nigaud/e.
NJ *abbr* (*US*) = *New Jersey*.
NLF *n abbr* (= *National Liberation Front*) FLN *m*.
NLQ *abbr* (= *near letter quality*) qualité *f* courrier.
NLRB *n abbr* (*US*: = *National Labor Relations Board*) *organisme de protection des travailleurs*.
NM, N. Mex. *abbr* (*US*) = *New Mexico*.

KEYWORD

no [nəu] (*pl* **~es**) *adv* (*opposite of "yes"*) non; **are you coming? — ~ (I'm not)** est-ce que vous venez? — non; **would you like some more? — ~ thank you** vous en voulez encore? — non merci
♦ *adj* (*not any*) pas de, aucun(e) (*used with "ne"*); **I have ~ money/books** je n'ai pas d'argent/de livres; **~ student would have done it** aucun étudiant ne l'aurait fait; **"~ smoking"** "défense de fumer"; **"~ dogs"** "les chiens ne sont pas admis"
♦ *n* non *m*; **I won't take ~ for an answer** il n'est pas question de refuser.

no. *abbr* (= *number*) n°.
nobble ['nɔbl] *vt* (*BRIT col*: *bribe*: *person*) soudoyer, acheter; (*: person: to speak to*) mettre le grappin sur; (*RACING*: *horse, dog*) droguer (*pour l'empêcher de gagner*).
Nobel prize [nəu'bɛl-] *n* prix *m* Nobel.
nobility [nəu'bɪlɪtɪ] *n* noblesse *f*.
noble ['nəubl] *adj* noble.
nobleman ['nəublmən] *n* noble *m*.
nobly ['nəublɪ] *adv* noblement.
nobody ['nəubədɪ] *pron* personne (*with negative*).
no-claims bonus ['nəukleɪmz-] *n* bonus *m*.
nocturnal [nɔk'təːnl] *adj* nocturne.
nod [nɔd] *vi* faire un signe de (la) tête (*affirmatif ou amical*); (*sleep*) somnoler ♦ *vt*: **to ~ one's head** faire un signe de (la) tête; (*in agreement*) faire signe que oui ♦ *n* signe *m* de (la) tête; **they ~ded their agreement** ils ont acquiescé d'un signe de la tête.
►**nod off** *vi* s'assoupir.
no-fly zone [nəu'flaɪ-] *n* zone interdite (*aux avions et hélicoptères*).
noise [nɔɪz] *n* bruit *m*.
noiseless ['nɔɪzlɪs] *adj* silencieux(euse).
noisily ['nɔɪzɪlɪ] *adv* bruyamment.
noisy ['nɔɪzɪ] *adj* bruyant(e).
nomad ['nəumæd] *n* nomade *m/f*.
nomadic [nəu'mædɪk] *adj* nomade.
no man's land *n* no man's land *m*.
nominal ['nɔmɪnl] *adj* (*rent, fee*) symbolique; (*value*) nominal(e).
nominate ['nɔmɪneɪt] *vt* (*propose*) proposer; (*elect*) nommer.
nomination [nɔmɪ'neɪʃən] *n* nomination *f*.
nominee [nɔmɪ'niː] *n* candidat agréé; personne nommée.
non- [nɔn] *prefix* non-.
nonalcoholic [nɔnælkə'hɔlɪk] *adj* non-alcoolisé(e).
nonbreakable [nɔn'breɪkəbl] *adj* incassable.
nonce word ['nɔns-] *n* mot créé pour l'occasion.
nonchalant ['nɔnʃələnt] *adj* nonchalant(e).
noncommissioned [nɔnkə'mɪʃənd] *adj*: **~ officer** sous-officier *m*.
noncommittal [nɔnkə'mɪtl] *adj* évasif(ive).
nonconformist [nɔnkən'fɔːmɪst] *n* non-conformiste *m/f* ♦ *adj* non-conformiste, dissident(e).
noncontributory [nɔnkən'trɪbjutərɪ] *adj*: **~ pension scheme** *or* (*US*) **plan** *régime de retraite payée par l'employeur*.
noncooperation ['nɔnkəuɔpə'reɪʃən] *n* refus *m* de coopérer, non-coopération *f*.
nondescript ['nɔndɪskrɪpt] *adj* quelconque, indéfinissable.
none [nʌn] *pron* aucun/e; **~ of you** aucun d'entre vous, personne parmi vous; **I have ~** je n'en ai pas; **I have ~ left** je n'en ai plus; **~ at all** (*not one*) aucun(e); **how much milk? — ~ at all** combien de lait? — pas du tout; **he's ~ the worse for it** il ne s'en porte pas plus mal.
nonentity [nɔ'nɛntɪtɪ] *n* personne insignifiante.
nonessential [nɔnɪ'sɛnʃl] *adj* accessoire, superflu(e) ♦ *n*: **~s** le superflu.
nonetheless ['nʌnðə'lɛs] *adv* néanmoins.
nonevent [nɔnɪ'vɛnt] *n* événement manqué.
nonexecutive [nɔnɪg'zɛkjutɪv] *adj*: **~ director** administrateur/trice, conseiller/ère de direction.
nonexistent [nɔnɪg'zɪstənt] *adj* inexistant(e).
nonfiction [nɔn'fɪkʃən] *n* littérature *f* non-romanesque.
nonflammable [nɔn'flæməbl] *adj* ininflammable.
nonintervention ['nɔnɪntə'vɛnʃən] *n* non-intervention *f*.
no-no ['nəunəu] *n* (*col*): **it's a ~** il n'en est pas question.
non obst. *abbr* (= *non obstante: notwithstanding*) nonobstant.
no-nonsense [nəu'nɔnsəns] *adj* (*manner, person*) plein(e) de bon sens.
nonpayment [nɔn'peɪmənt] *n* non-paiement *m*.
nonplussed [nɔn'plʌst] *adj* perplexe.
non-profit-making [nɔn'prɔfɪtmeɪkɪŋ] *adj* à but non lucratif.
nonsense ['nɔnsəns] *n* absurdités *fpl*, idioties *fpl*; **~!** ne dites pas d'idioties!; **it is ~ to say that ...** il est absurde de dire que ....
nonsensical [nɔn'sɛnsɪkl] *adj* absurde, qui n'a

pas de sens.
nonshrink [nɔn'ʃrɪŋk] *adj* (*BRIT*) irrétrécissable.
nonskid [nɔn'skɪd] *adj* antidérapant(e).
nonsmoker ['nɔn'sməukə*] *n* non-fumeur *m*.
nonstarter [nɔn'stɑːtə*] *n*: **it's a ~** c'est voué à l'échec.
nonstick ['nɔn'stɪk] *adj* qui n'attache pas.
nonstop ['nɔn'stɔp] *adj* direct(e), sans arrêt (*or* escale) ♦ *adv* sans arrêt.
nontaxable [nɔn'tæksəbl] *adj*: ~ **income** revenu *m* non imposable.
non-U ['nɔnjuː] *adj abbr* (*BRIT col*: = *non-upper class*) qui ne se dit (*or* se fait) pas.
nonvolatile [nɔn'vɔlətaɪl] *adj*: ~ **memory** (*COMPUT*) mémoire rémanente *or* non volatile.
nonvoting [nɔn'vəutɪŋ] *adj*: ~ **shares** actions *fpl* sans droit de vote.
non-white ['nɔn'waɪt] *adj* de couleur ♦ *n* personne *f* de couleur.
no-win situation [nəu'wɪn-] *n* impasse *f*; **we're in a ~** nous sommes dans l'impasse.
noodles ['nuːdlz] *npl* nouilles *fpl*.
nook [nuk] *n*: **~s and crannies** recoins *mpl*.
noon [nuːn] *n* midi *m*.
no one ['nəuwʌn] *pron* = **nobody**.
noose [nuːs] *n* nœud coulant; (*hangman's*) corde *f*.
nor [nɔː*] *conj* = **neither** ♦ *adv see* **neither**.
Norf *abbr* (*BRIT*) = *Norfolk*.
norm [nɔːm] *n* norme *f*.
normal ['nɔːml] *adj* normal(e) ♦ *n*: **to return to ~** redevenir normal(e).
normality [nɔː'mælɪtɪ] *n* normalité *f*.
normally ['nɔːməlɪ] *adv* normalement.
Normandy ['nɔːməndɪ] *n* Normandie *f*.
north [nɔːθ] *n* nord *m* ♦ *adj* du nord, nord *inv* ♦ *adv* au *or* vers le nord.
North Africa *n* Afrique *f* du Nord.
North African *adj* nord-africain(e), d'Afrique du Nord ♦ *n* Nord-Africain/e.
North America *n* Amérique *f* du Nord.
North American *n* Nord-Américain/e ♦ *adj* nord-américain(e), d'Amérique du Nord.
Northants [nɔː'θænts] *abbr* (*BRIT*) = *Northamptonshire*.
northbound ['nɔːθbaund] *adj* (*traffic*) en direction du nord; (*carriageway*) nord *inv*.
Northd *abbr* (*BRIT*) = *Northumberland*.
north-east [nɔːθ'iːst] *n* nord-est *m*.
northerly ['nɔːðəlɪ] *adj* (*wind, direction*) du nord.
northern ['nɔːðən] *adj* du nord, septentrional(e).
Northern Ireland *n* Irlande *f* du Nord.
North Pole *n*: **the ~** le pôle Nord.
North Sea *n*: **the ~** la mer du Nord.
North Sea oil *n* pétrole *m* de la mer du Nord.
northward(s) ['nɔːθwəd(z)] *adv* vers le nord.
north-west [nɔːθ'wɛst] *n* nord-ouest *m*.
Norway ['nɔːweɪ] *n* Norvège *f*.
Norwegian [nɔː'wiːdʒən] *adj* norvégien(ne) ♦ *n* Norvégien/ne; (*LING*) norvégien *m*.
nos. *abbr* (= *numbers*) n^{o}.
nose [nəuz] *n* nez *m*; (*fig*) flair *m* ♦ *vi* (*also*: ~ **one's way**) avancer précautionneusement; **to pay through the ~ (for sth)** (*col*) payer un prix excessif (pour qch).
▶**nose about, nose around** *vi* fouiner *or* fureter (partout).
nosebleed ['nəuzbliːd] *n* saignement *m* de nez.
nose-dive ['nəuzdaɪv] *n* (descente *f* en) piqué *m*.
nose drops *npl* gouttes *fpl* pour le nez.
nosey ['nəuzɪ] *adj* curieux(euse).
nostalgia [nɔs'tældʒɪə] *n* nostalgie *f*.
nostalgic [nɔs'tældʒɪk] *adj* nostalgique.
nostril ['nɔstrɪl] *n* narine *f*; (*of horse*) naseau *m*.
nosy ['nəuzɪ] *adj* = **nosey**.
not [nɔt] *adv* (ne ...) pas; **I hope ~** j'espère que non; ~ **at all** pas du tout; (*after thanks*) de rien; **you must ~** *or* **mustn't do this** tu ne dois pas faire ça; **he isn't ...** il n'est pas ....
notable ['nəutəbl] *adj* notable.
notably ['nəutəblɪ] *adv* en particulier.
notary ['nəutərɪ] *n* (*also*: ~ **public**) notaire *m*.
notation [nəu'teɪʃən] *n* notation *f*.
notch [nɔtʃ] *n* encoche *f*.
▶**notch up** *vt* (*score*) marquer; (*victory*) remporter.
note [nəut] *n* note *f*; (*letter*) mot *m*; (*banknote*) billet *m* ♦ *vt* (*also*: ~ **down**) noter; (*notice*) constater; **just a quick ~ to let you know ...** juste un mot pour vous dire ...; **to take ~s** prendre des notes; **to compare ~s** (*fig*) échanger des (*or* leurs *etc*) impressions; **to take ~ of** prendre note de; **a person of ~** une personne éminente.
notebook ['nəutbuk] *n* carnet *m*; (*for shorthand etc*) bloc-notes *m*.
note-case ['nəutkeɪs] *n* (*BRIT*) porte-feuille *m*.
noted ['nəutɪd] *adj* réputé(e).
notepad ['nəutpæd] *n* bloc-notes *m*.
notepaper ['nəutpeɪpə*] *n* papier *m* à lettres.
noteworthy ['nəutwəːðɪ] *adj* remarquable.
nothing ['nʌθɪŋ] *n* rien *m*; **he does ~** il ne fait rien; ~ **new** rien de nouveau; **for ~** (*free*) pour rien, gratuitement; ~ **at all** rien du tout.
notice ['nəutɪs] *n* avis *m*; (*of leaving*) congé *m*; (*BRIT*: *review: of play etc*) critique *f*, compte rendu *m* ♦ *vt* remarquer, s'apercevoir de; **without ~** sans préavis; **advance ~** préavis *m*; **to give sb ~ of sth** notifier qn de qch; **at short ~** dans un délai très court; **until further ~** jusqu'à nouvel ordre; **to give ~, hand in one's ~** (*subj: employee*) donner sa démission, démissionner; **to take ~ of** prêter attention à; **to bring sth to sb's ~** porter qch à la connaissance de qn; **it has come to my ~ that ...** on m'a signalé que ...; **to escape** *or* **avoid ~** (essayer de) passer inaperçu *or* ne pas se faire remarquer.

noticeable ['nəutɪsəbl] *adj* visible.
notice board *n* (*BRIT*) panneau *m* d'affichage.
notification [nəutɪfɪ'keɪʃən] *n* notification *f*.
notify ['nəutɪfaɪ] *vt*: **to ~ sth to sb** notifier qch à qn; **to ~ sb of sth** avertir qn de qch.
notion ['nəuʃən] *n* idée *f*; (*concept*) notion *f*.
notions ['nəuʃənz] *npl* (*US*: *haberdashery*) mercerie *f*.
notoriety [nəutə'raɪətɪ] *n* notoriété *f*.
notorious [nəu'tɔːrɪəs] *adj* notoire (*souvent en mal*).
notoriously [nəu'tɔːrɪəslɪ] *adj* notoirement.
Notts [nɔts] *abbr* (*BRIT*) = *Nottinghamshire*.
notwithstanding [nɔtwɪθ'stændɪŋ] *adv* néanmoins ♦ *prep* en dépit de.
nougat ['nuːgɑː] *n* nougat *m*.
nought [nɔːt] *n* zéro *m*.
noun [naun] *n* nom *m*.
nourish ['nʌrɪʃ] *vt* nourrir.
nourishing ['nʌrɪʃɪŋ] *adj* nourrissant(e).
nourishment ['nʌrɪʃmənt] *n* nourriture *f*.
Nov. *abbr* (= *November*) nov.
Nova Scotia ['nəuvə'skəuʃə] *n* Nouvelle-Écosse *f*.
novel ['nɔvl] *n* roman *m* ♦ *adj* nouveau(nouvelle), original(e).
novelist ['nɔvəlɪst] *n* romancier *m*.
novelty ['nɔvəltɪ] *n* nouveauté *f*.
November [nəu'vɛmbə*] *n* novembre *m*; *for phrases see also* **July**.
novice ['nɔvɪs] *n* novice *m/f*.
NOW [nau] *n abbr* (*US*) = *National Organization for Women*.
now [nau] *adv* maintenant ♦ *conj*: **~ (that)** maintenant (que); **right ~** tout de suite; **by ~** à l'heure qu'il est; **just ~**: **that's the fashion just ~** c'est la mode en ce moment *or* maintenant; **I saw her just ~** je viens de la voir, je l'ai vue à l'instant; **I'll read it just ~** je vais le lire à l'instant *or* dès maintenant; **~ and then, ~ and again** de temps en temps; **from ~ on** dorénavant; **in 3 days from ~** dans *or* d'ici trois jours; **between ~ and Monday** d'ici (à) lundi; **that's all for ~** c'est tout pour l'instant.
nowadays ['nauədeɪz] *adv* de nos jours.
nowhere ['nəuwɛə*] *adv* nulle part; **~ else** nulle part ailleurs.
noxious ['nɔkʃəs] *adj* toxique.
nozzle ['nɔzl] *n* (*of hose*) jet *m*, lance *f*.
NP *n abbr* = **notary public**.
NS *abbr* (*Canada*) = *Nova Scotia*.
NSC *n abbr* (*US*) = **National Security Council**.
NSF *n abbr* (*US*) = *National Science Foundation*.
NSPCC *n abbr* (*BRIT*) = *National Society for the Prevention of Cruelty to Children*.
NSW *abbr* (*Australia*) = *New South Wales*.
NT *n abbr* (= *New Testament*) NT *m* ♦ *abbr* (*Canada*) = *Northwest Territories*.
nth [ɛnθ] *adj*: **for the ~ time** (*col*) pour la énième fois.
nuance ['njuːɑ̃ːns] *n* nuance *f*.
nubile ['njuːbaɪl] *adj* nubile; (*attractive*) jeune et désirable.
nuclear ['njuːklɪə*] *adj* nucléaire.
nuclear disarmament *n* désarmement *m* nucléaire.
nuclear family *n* famille *f* nucléaire.
nuclear-free zone ['njuːklɪə'friː-] *n* zone *f* où le nucléaire est interdit.
nucleus, *pl* **nuclei** ['njuːklɪəs, 'njuːklɪaɪ] *n* noyau *m*.
NUCPS *n abbr* (*BRIT*: = *National Union of Civil and Public Servants*) *syndicat des fonctionnaires*.
nude [njuːd] *adj* nu(e) ♦ *n* (*ART*) nu *m*; **in the ~** (tout(e)) nu(e).
nudge [nʌdʒ] *vt* donner un (petit) coup de coude à.
nudist ['njuːdɪst] *n* nudiste *m/f*.
nudist colony *n* colonie *f* de nudistes.
nudity ['njuːdɪtɪ] *n* nudité *f*.
nugget ['nʌgɪt] *n* pépite *f*.
nuisance ['njuːsns] *n*: **it's a ~** c'est (très) ennuyeux *or* gênant; **he's a ~** il est assommant *or* casse-pieds; **what a ~!** quelle barbe!
NUJ *n abbr* (*BRIT*: = *National Union of Journalists*) *syndicat des journalistes*.
nuke [njuːk] *n* (*col*) bombe *f* atomique.
null [nʌl] *adj*: **~ and void** nul(le) et non avenu(e).
nullify ['nʌlɪfaɪ] *vt* invalider.
NUM *n abbr* (*BRIT*: = *National Union of Mineworkers*) *syndicat des mineurs*.
numb [nʌm] *adj* engourdi(e) ♦ *vt* engourdir; **~ with cold** engourdi(e) par le froid, transi(e) (de froid); **~ with fear** transi de peur, paralysé(e) par la peur.
number ['nʌmbə*] *n* nombre *m*; (*numeral*) chiffre *m*; (*of house, car, telephone, newspaper*) numéro *m* ♦ *vt* numéroter; (*include*) compter; **a ~ of** un certain nombre de; **to be ~ed among** compter parmi; **the staff ~s 20** le nombre d'employés s'élève à *or* est de 20; **wrong ~** (*TEL*) mauvais numéro.
numbered account ['nʌmbəd-] *n* (*in bank*) compte numéroté.
number plate *n* (*BRIT AUT*) plaque *f* minéralogique *or* d'immatriculation.
Number Ten *n* (*BRIT*: = *10 Downing Street*) *résidence du Premier ministre*.
numbness ['nʌmnɪs] *n* torpeur *f*; (*due to cold*) engourdissement *m*.
numbskull ['nʌmskʌl] *n* (*col*) gourde *f*.
numeral ['njuːmərəl] *n* chiffre *m*.
numerate ['njuːmərɪt] *adj* (*BRIT*): **to be ~** avoir des notions d'arithmétique.
numerical [njuː'mɛrɪkl] *adj* numérique.
numerous ['njuːmərəs] *adj* nombreux(euse).
nun [nʌn] *n* religieuse *f*, sœur *f*.
nunnery ['nʌnərɪ] *n* couvent *m*.
nuptial ['nʌpʃəl] *adj* nuptial(e).
nurse [nəːs] *n* infirmière *f*; (*also*: **~maid**) bon-

ne *f* d'enfants ♦ *vt* (*patient, cold*) soigner; (*baby*: *BRIT*) bercer (dans ses bras); (*: US*) allaiter, nourrir; (*hope*) nourrir *m*.

nursery ['nəːsərɪ] *n* (*room*) nursery *f*; (*institution*) pouponnière *f*; (*for plants*) pépinière *f*.

nursery rhyme *n* comptine *f*, chansonnette *f* pour enfants.

nursery school *n* école maternelle.

nursery slope *n* (*BRIT SKI*) piste *f* pour débutants.

nursing ['nəːsɪŋ] *n* (*profession*) profession *f* d'infirmière ♦ *adj* (*mother*) qui allaite.

nursing home *n* clinique *f*; maison *f* de convalescence.

nurture ['nəːtʃə*] *vt* élever.

NUS *n abbr* (*BRIT*: = *National Union of Students*) *syndicat des étudiants*.

NUT *n abbr* (*BRIT*: = *National Union of Teachers*) *syndicat enseignant*.

nut [nʌt] *n* (*of metal*) écrou *m*; (*fruit*) noix *f*, noisette *f*, cacahuète *f* (*terme générique en anglais*) ♦ *adj* (*chocolate etc*) aux noisettes; **he's ~s** (*col*) il est dingue.

nutcase ['nʌtkeɪs] *n* (*col*) dingue *m/f*.

nutcrackers ['nʌtkrækəz] *npl* casse-noix *m inv*, casse-noisette(s) *m*.

nutmeg ['nʌtmɛg] *n* (noix *f*) muscade *f*.

nutrient ['njuːtrɪənt] *adj* nutritif(ive) ♦ *n* substance nutritive.

nutrition [njuː'trɪʃən] *n* nutrition *f*, alimentation *f*.

nutritionist [njuː'trɪʃənɪst] *n* nutritionniste *m/f*.

nutritious [njuː'trɪʃəs] *adj* nutritif(ive), nourrissant(e).

nutshell ['nʌtʃɛl] *n* coquille *f* de noix; **in a ~** en un mot.

nutty ['nʌtɪ] *adj* (*flavour*) à la noisette; (*col: person*) cinglé(e), dingue.

nuzzle ['nʌzl] *vi*: **to ~ up to** fourrer son nez contre.

NV *abbr* (*US*) = *Nevada*.

NVQ *n abbr* (*BRIT*: = *National Vocational Qualification*) CAP *m*.

NWT *abbr* (*Canada*) = *Northwest Territories*.

NY *abbr* (*US*) = *New York*.

NYC *abbr* (*US*) = *New York City*.

nylon ['naɪlɔn] *n* nylon *m* ♦ *adj* de *or* en nylon; **~s** *npl* bas *mpl* nylon.

nymph [nɪmf] *n* nymphe *f*.

nymphomaniac ['nɪmfəu'meɪnɪæk] *adj*, *n* nymphomane (*f*).

NYSE *n abbr* (*US*) = *New York Stock Exchange*.

NZ *abbr* = **New Zealand**.

O o

O, o [əu] *n* (*letter*) O, o *m*; (*US SCOL*: = *outstanding*) tb (= *très bien*); **O for Oliver**, (*US*) **O for Oboe** O comme Oscar.

oaf [əuf] *n* balourd *m*.

oak [əuk] *n* chêne *m* ♦ *cpd* de *or* en (bois de) chêne.

O&M *n abbr* = *organization and method*.

OAP *n abbr* (*BRIT*) = **old age pensioner**.

oar [ɔː*] *n* aviron *m*, rame *f*; **to put** *or* **shove one's ~ in** (*fig: col*) mettre son grain de sel.

oarsman ['ɔːzmən], **oarswoman** ['ɔːzwumən] *n* rameur/euse; (*NAUT, SPORT*) nageur/euse.

OAS *n abbr* (= *Organization of American States*) OEA *f* (= *Organisation des États américains*).

oasis, *pl* **oases** [əu'eɪsɪs, əu'eɪsiːz] *n* oasis *f*.

oath [əuθ] *n* serment *m*; (*swear word*) juron *m*; **to take the ~** prêter serment; **on** (*BRIT*) *or* **under ~** sous serment; assermenté(e).

oatmeal ['əutmiːl] *n* flocons *mpl* d'avoine.

oats [əuts] *n* avoine *f*.

OAU *n abbr* (= *Organization of African Unity*) OUA *f* (= *Organisation de l'unité africaine*).

obdurate ['ɔbdjurɪt] *adj* obstiné(e); impénitent(e); intraitable.

OBE *n abbr* (*BRIT*: = *Order of the British Empire*) *distinction honorifique*.

obedience [ə'biːdɪəns] *n* obéissance *f*; **in ~ to** conformément à.

obedient [ə'biːdɪənt] *adj* obéissant(e); **to be ~ to sb/sth** obéir à qn/qch.

obelisk ['ɔbɪlɪsk] *n* obélisque *m*.

obese [əu'biːs] *adj* obèse.

obesity [əu'biːsɪtɪ] *n* obésité *f*.

obey [ə'beɪ] *vt* obéir à; (*instructions, regulations*) se conformer à ♦ *vi* obéir.

obituary [ə'bɪtjuərɪ] *n* nécrologie *f*.

object *n* ['ɔbdʒɪkt] objet *m*; (*purpose*) but *m*, objet; (*LING*) complément *m* d'objet ♦ *vi* [əb'dʒɛkt]: **to ~ to** (*attitude*) désapprouver; (*proposal*) protester contre, élever une objection contre; **I ~!** je proteste!; **he ~ed that ...** il a fait valoir *or* a objecté que ...; **do you ~ to my smoking?** est-ce que cela vous gêne si je fume?; **what's the ~ of doing that?** quel est l'intérêt de faire cela?; **money is no ~** l'argent n'est pas un problème.

objection [əb'dʒɛkʃən] *n* objection *f*; (*drawback*) inconvénient *m*; **if you have no ~** si vous n'y voyez pas d'inconvénient; **to make** *or* **raise an ~** élever une objection.

objectionable [əb'dʒɛkʃənəbl] *adj* très dés-

agréable; choquant(e).
objective [əb'dʒɛktɪv] *n* objectif *m* ♦ *adj* objectif(ive).
objectivity [ɔbdʒɪk'tɪvɪtɪ] *n* objectivité *f*.
object lesson *n* (*fig*) (bonne) illustration.
objector [əb'dʒɛktə*] *n* opposant/e.
obligation [ɔblɪ'geɪʃən] *n* obligation *f*, devoir *m*; (*debt*) dette *f* (de reconnaissance); **"without ~"** "sans engagement".
obligatory [ə'blɪgətərɪ] *adj* obligatoire.
oblige [ə'blaɪdʒ] *vt* (*force*): **to ~ sb to do** obliger *or* forcer qn à faire; (*do a favour*) rendre service à, obliger; **to be ~d to sb for sth** être obligé(e) à qn de qch; **anything to ~!** (*col*) (toujours prêt à rendre) service!
obliging [ə'blaɪdʒɪŋ] *adj* obligeant(e), serviable.
oblique [ə'bliːk] *adj* oblique; (*allusion*) indirect(e) ♦ *n* (*BRIT TYP*): **~ (stroke)** barre *f* oblique.
obliterate [ə'blɪtəreɪt] *vt* effacer.
oblivion [ə'blɪvɪən] *n* oubli *m*.
oblivious [ə'blɪvɪəs] *adj*: **~ of** oublieux(euse) de.
oblong ['ɔblɔŋ] *adj* oblong(ue) ♦ *n* rectangle *m*.
obnoxious [əb'nɔkʃəs] *adj* odieux(euse); (*smell*) nauséabond(e).
o.b.o. *abbr* (*US: = or best offer: in classified ads*) ≈ à débattre.
oboe ['əubəu] *n* hautbois *m*.
obscene [əb'siːn] *adj* obscène.
obscenity [əb'sɛnɪtɪ] *n* obscénité *f*.
obscure [əb'skjuə*] *adj* obscur(e) ♦ *vt* obscurcir; (*hide: sun*) cacher.
obscurity [əb'skjuərɪtɪ] *n* obscurité *f*.
obsequious [əb'siːkwɪəs] *adj* obséquieux(euse).
observable [əb'zəːvəbl] *adj* observable; (*appreciable*) notable.
observance [əb'zəːvns] *n* observance *f*, observation *f*; **religious ~s** observances religieuses.
observant [əb'zəːvnt] *adj* observateur(trice).
observation [ɔbzə'veɪʃən] *n* observation *f*; (*by police etc*) surveillance *f*.
observation post *n* (*MIL*) poste *m* d'observation.
observatory [əb'zəːvətrɪ] *n* observatoire *m*.
observe [əb'zəːv] *vt* observer; (*remark*) faire observer *or* remarquer.
observer [əb'zəːvə*] *n* observateur/trice.
obsess [əb'sɛs] *vt* obséder; **to be ~ed by** *or* **with sb/sth** être obsédé(e) par qn/qch.
obsession [əb'sɛʃən] *n* obsession *f*.
obsessive [əb'sɛsɪv] *adj* obsédant(e).
obsolescence [ɔbsə'lɛsns] *n* vieillissement *m*; obsolescence *f*; **built-in** *or* **planned ~** (*COMM*) désuétude calculée.
obsolescent [ɔbsə'lɛsnt] *adj* obsolescent(e), en voie d'être périmé(e).
obsolete ['ɔbsəliːt] *adj* dépassé(e), périmé(e).
obstacle ['ɔbstəkl] *n* obstacle *m*.
obstacle race *n* course *f* d'obstacles.
obstetrician [ɔbstə'trɪʃən] *n* obstétricien/ne.
obstetrics [ɔb'stɛtrɪks] *n* obstétrique *f*.
obstinacy ['ɔbstɪnəsɪ] *n* obstination *f*.
obstinate ['ɔbstɪnɪt] *adj* obstiné(e); (*pain, cold*) persistant(e).
obstreperous [əb'strɛpərəs] *adj* turbulent(e).
obstruct [əb'strʌkt] *vt* (*block*) boucher, obstruer; (*halt*) arrêter; (*hinder*) entraver.
obstruction [əb'strʌkʃən] *n* obstruction *f*; obstacle *m*.
obstructive [əb'strʌktɪv] *adj* obstructionniste.
obtain [əb'teɪn] *vt* obtenir ♦ *vi* avoir cours.
obtainable [əb'teɪnəbl] *adj* qu'on peut obtenir.
obtrusive [əb'truːsɪv] *adj* (*person*) importun(e); (*smell*) pénétrant(e); (*building etc*) trop en évidence.
obtuse [əb'tjuːs] *adj* obtus(e).
obverse ['ɔbvəːs] *n* (*of medal, coin*) côté *m* face; (*fig*) contrepartie *f*.
obviate ['ɔbvɪeɪt] *vt* parer à, obvier à.
obvious ['ɔbvɪəs] *adj* évident(e), manifeste.
obviously ['ɔbvɪəslɪ] *adv* manifestement; (*of course*): **~, he ...** *or* **he ~ ...** il est bien évident qu'il ...; **~!** bien sûr!; **~ not!** évidemment pas!, bien sûr que non!
OCAS *n abbr* (= *Organization of Central American States*) ODEAC *f* (= *Organisation des États d'Amérique centrale*).
occasion [ə'keɪʒən] *n* occasion *f*; (*event*) événement *m* ♦ *vt* occasionner, causer; **on that ~** à cette occasion; **to rise to the ~** se montrer à la hauteur de la situation.
occasional [ə'keɪʒənl] *adj* pris(e) (*or* fait(e) *etc*) de temps en temps; occasionnel(le).
occasionally [ə'keɪʒənəlɪ] *adv* de temps en temps; **very ~** (assez) rarement.
occasional table *n* table décorative.
occult [ɔ'kʌlt] *adj* occulte ♦ *n*: **the ~** le surnaturel.
occupancy ['ɔkjupənsɪ] *n* occupation *f*.
occupant ['ɔkjupənt] *n* occupant *m*.
occupation [ɔkju'peɪʃən] *n* occupation *f*; (*job*) métier *m*, profession *f*; **unfit for ~** (*house*) impropre à l'habitation.
occupational [ɔkju'peɪʃənl] *adj* (*accident, disease*) du travail; (*hazard*) du métier.
occupational guidance *n* (*BRIT*) orientation professionnelle.
occupational pension *n* retraite professionnelle.
occupational therapy *n* ergothérapie *f*.
occupier ['ɔkjupaɪə*] *n* occupant/e.
occupy ['ɔkjupaɪ] *vt* occuper; **to ~ o.s. with** *or* **by doing** s'occuper à faire; **to be occupied with sth** être occupé avec qch.
occur [ə'kəː*] *vi* se produire; (*difficulty, opportunity*) se présenter; (*phenomenon, error*) se rencontrer; **to ~ to sb** venir à l'esprit de qn.
occurrence [ə'kʌrəns] *n* présence *f*, existence *f*; cas *m*, fait *m*.
ocean ['əuʃən] *n* océan *m*; **~s of** (*col*) des mas-

ses de.
ocean bed *n* fond (sous-)marin.
ocean-going ['əuʃəngəuɪŋ] *adj* de haute mer.
Oceania [əuʃɪ'eɪnɪə] *n* Océanie *f.*
ocean liner *n* paquebot *m.*
ochre ['əukə*] *adj* ocre.
o'clock [ə'klɔk] *adv*: **it is 5 ~** il est 5 heures.
OCR *n abbr* = **optical character reader, optical character recognition.**
Oct. *abbr* (= *October*) oct.
octagonal [ɔk'tægənl] *adj* octogonal(e).
octane ['ɔkteɪn] *n* octane *m*; **high-~ petrol** *or* (*US*) **gas** essence *f* à indice d'octane élevé.
octave ['ɔktɪv] *n* octave *f.*
October [ɔk'təubə*] *n* octobre *m*; *for phrases see also* **July.**
octogenarian ['ɔktəudʒɪ'nɛərɪən] *n* octogénaire *m/f.*
octopus ['ɔktəpəs] *n* pieuvre *f.*
odd [ɔd] *adj* (*strange*) bizarre, curieux(euse); (*number*) impair(e); (*left over*) qui reste, en plus; (*not of a set*) dépareillé(e); **60-~** 60 et quelques; **at ~ times** de temps en temps; **the ~ one out** l'exception *f.*
oddball ['ɔdbɔːl] *n* (*col*) excentrique *m/f.*
oddity ['ɔdɪtɪ] *n* bizarrerie *f*; (*person*) excentrique *m/f.*
odd-job man [ɔd'dʒɔb-] *n* homme *m* à tout faire.
odd jobs *npl* petits travaux divers.
oddly ['ɔdlɪ] *adv* bizarrement, curieusement.
oddments ['ɔdmənts] *npl* (*BRIT COMM*) fins *fpl* de série.
odds [ɔdz] *npl* (*in betting*) cote *f*; **the ~ are against his coming** il y a peu de chances qu'il vienne; **it makes no ~** cela n'a pas d'importance; **to succeed against all the ~** réussir contre toute attente; **~ and ends** de petites choses; **at ~** en désaccord.
odds-on [ɔdz'ɔn] *adj*: **the ~ favourite** le grand favori; **it's ~ that he'll come** il y a toutes les chances *or* gros à parier qu'il vienne.
ode [əud] *n* ode *f.*
odious ['əudɪəs] *adj* odieux(euse), détestable.
odometer [ɔ'dɔmɪtə*] *n* odomètre *m.*
odour, (*US*) **odor** ['əudə*] *n* odeur *f.*
odo(u)rless ['əudəlɪs] *adj* inodore.
OECD *n abbr* (= *Organization for Economic Cooperation and Development*) OCDE *f* (= *Organisation de coopération et de développement économique*).
oesophagus, (*US*) **esophagus** [iː'sɔfəgəs] *n* œsophage *m.*
oestrogen, (*US*) **estrogen** ['iːstrəudʒən] *n* œstrogène *m.*

KEYWORD

of [ɔv, əv] *prep* **1** (*gen*) de; **a friend ~ ours** un de nos amis; **a boy ~ 10** un garçon de 10 ans; **that was kind ~ you** c'était gentil de votre part
2 (*expressing quantity, amount, dates etc*) de; **a kilo ~ flour** un kilo de farine; **how much ~ this do you need?** combien vous en faut-il?; **there were 3 ~ them** (*people*) ils étaient 3; (*objects*) il y en avait 3; **3 ~ us went** 3 d'entre nous y sont allé(e)s; **the 5th ~ July** le 5 juillet; **a quarter ~ 4** (*US*) 4 heures moins le quart
3 (*from, out of*) en, de; **a statue ~ marble** une statue de *or* en marbre; **made ~ wood** (fait) en bois.

off [ɔf] *adj, adv* (*engine*) coupé(e); (*tap*) fermé(e); (*BRIT: food*) mauvais(e), avancé(e); (*: milk*) tourné(e); (*absent*) absent(e); (*cancelled*) annulé(e); (*removed*): **the lid was ~** le couvercle était retiré *or* n'était pas mis ♦ *prep* de; sur; **to be ~** (*to leave*) partir, s'en aller; **I must be ~** il faut que je file; **to be ~ sick** être absent pour cause de maladie; **a day ~** un jour de congé; **to have an ~ day** n'être pas en forme; **he had his coat ~** il avait enlevé son manteau; **the hook is ~** le crochet s'est détaché; le crochet n'est pas mis; **10% ~** (*COMM*) 10% de rabais; **5 km ~ (the road)** à 5 km (de la route); **~ the coast** au large de la côte; **a house ~ the main road** une maison à l'écart de la grand-route; **it's a long way ~** c'est loin (d'ici); **I'm ~ meat** je ne mange plus de viande; je n'aime plus la viande; **on the ~ chance** à tout hasard; **to be well/badly ~** être bien/mal loti; (*financially*) être aisé/dans la gêne; **~ and on, on and ~** de temps à autre; **I'm afraid the chicken is ~** (*BRIT: not available*) je regrette, il n'y a plus de poulet; **that's a bit ~** (*fig: col*) c'est un peu fort.
offal ['ɔfl] *n* (*CULIN*) abats *mpl.*
offbeat ['ɔfbiːt] *adj* excentrique.
off-centre [ɔf'sɛntə*] *adj* décentré(e), excentré(e).
off-colour ['ɔf'kʌlə*] *adj* (*BRIT: ill*) malade, mal fichu(e); **to feel ~** être mal fichu.
offence, (*US*) **offense** [ə'fɛns] *n* (*crime*) délit *m*, infraction *f*; **to give ~ to** blesser, offenser; **to take ~ at** se vexer de, s'offenser de; **to commit an ~** commettre une infraction.
offend [ə'fɛnd] *vt* (*person*) offenser, blesser ♦ *vi*: **to ~ against** (*law, rule*) contrevenir à, enfreindre.
offender [ə'fɛndə*] *n* délinquant/e; (*against regulations*) contrevenant/e.
offending [ə'fɛndɪŋ] *adj* incriminé(e).
offense [ə'fɛns] *n* (*US*) = **offence.**
offensive [ə'fɛnsɪv] *adj* offensant(e), choquant(e); (*smell etc*) très déplaisant(e); (*weapon*) offensif(ive) ♦ *n* (*MIL*) offensive *f.*
offer ['ɔfə*] *n* offre *f*, proposition *f* ♦ *vt* offrir, proposer; **to make an ~ for sth** faire une offre pour qch; **to ~ sth to sb, ~ sb sth** offrir qch à qn; **to ~ to do sth** proposer de faire qch; **"on special ~"** (*COMM*) "en promotion".

offering ['ɔfərɪŋ] *n* offrande *f*.
offhand [ɔf'hænd] *adj* désinvolte ♦ *adv* spontanément; **I can't tell you** ~ je ne peux pas vous le dire comme ça.
office ['ɔfɪs] *n* (*place*) bureau *m*; (*position*) charge *f*, fonction *f*; **doctor's** ~ (*US*) cabinet (médical); **to take** ~ entrer en fonctions; **through his good** ~**s** (*fig*) grâce à ses bons offices; **O**~ **of Fair Trading** (*BRIT*) *organisme de protection contre les pratiques commerciales abusives*.
office automation *n* bureautique *f*.
office bearer *n* (*of club etc*) membre *m* du bureau.
office block, (*US*) **office building** *n* immeuble *m* de bureaux.
office boy *n* garçon *m* de bureau.
office hours *npl* heures *fpl* de bureau; (*US MED*) heures de consultation.
office manager *n* responsable administratif(ive).
officer ['ɔfɪsə*] *n* (*MIL etc*) officier *m*; (*of organization*) membre *m* du bureau directeur; (*also*: **police** ~) agent *m* (de police).
office work *n* travail *m* de bureau.
office worker *n* employé/e de bureau.
official [ə'fɪʃl] *adj* (*authorized*) officiel(le) ♦ *n* officiel *m*; (*civil servant*) fonctionnaire *m/f*; employé/e.
officialdom [ə'fɪʃldəm] *n* bureaucratie *f*.
officially [ə'fɪʃəlɪ] *adv* officiellement.
official receiver *n* administrateur *m* judiciaire, syndic *m* de faillite.
officiate [ə'fɪʃɪeɪt] *vi* (*REL*) officier; **to** ~ **as Mayor** exercer les fonctions de maire; **to** ~ **at a marriage** célébrer un mariage.
officious [ə'fɪʃəs] *adj* trop empressé(e).
offing ['ɔfɪŋ] *n*: **in the** ~ (*fig*) en perspective.
off-key [ɔf'kiː] *adj* faux(fausse) ♦ *adv* faux.
off-licence ['ɔflaɪsns] *n* (*BRIT*: *shop*) débit *m* de vins et de spiritueux; *voir encadré*.

> **OFF-LICENCE**
>
> *Un* **off-licence** *est un magasin où l'on vend de l'alcool (à emporter) aux heures où les pubs sont fermés. On peut également y acheter des boissons non alcoolisées, des cigarettes, des chips, des bonbons, des chocolats etc.*

off-limits [ɔf'lɪmɪts] *adj* (*esp US*) dont l'accès est interdit.
off line *adj* (*COMPUT*) (en mode) autonome; (*: switched off*) non connecté(e).
off-load ['ɔfləud] *vt*: **to** ~ **sth (onto)** (*goods*) décharger qch (sur); (*job*) se décharger de qch (sur).
off-peak ['ɔf'piːk] *adj* aux heures creuses.
off-putting ['ɔfputɪŋ] *adj* (*BRIT*) rébarbatif(ive); rebutant(e), peu engageant(e).
off-season ['ɔf'siːzn] *adj, adv* hors-saison (*inv*).
offset ['ɔfsɛt] *vt irreg* contrebalancer, compenser ♦ *n* (*also*: ~ **printing**) offset *m*.
offshoot ['ɔfʃuːt] *n* (*fig*) ramification *f*, antenne *f*; (*: of discussion etc*) conséquence *f*.
offshore [ɔf'ʃɔː*] *adj* (*breeze*) de terre; (*island*) proche du littoral; (*fishing*) côtier(ière); ~ **oilfield** gisement *m* pétrolifère en mer.
offside ['ɔf'saɪd] *n* (*AUT*: *with right-hand drive*) côté droit; (*: with left-hand drive*) côté gauche ♦ *adj* (*AUT*) de droite; de gauche; (*SPORT*) hors jeu.
offspring ['ɔfsprɪŋ] *n* progéniture *f*.
offstage [ɔf'steɪdʒ] *adv* dans les coulisses.
off-the-cuff [ɔfðə'kʌf] *adv* au pied levé; de chic.
off-the-job ['ɔfðə'dʒɔb] *adj*: ~ **training** formation professionnelle extérieure.
off-the-peg ['ɔfðə'pɛg], (*US*) **off-the-rack** ['ɔfðə'ræk] *adv* en prêt-à-porter.
off-the-record ['ɔfðə'rɛkɔːd] *adj* (*remark*) confidentiel(le), sans caractère officiel ♦ *adv* officieusement.
off-white ['ɔfwaɪt] *adj* blanc cassé *inv*.
Ofgas ['ɔfgæs] *n* (*BRIT*: = *Office of Gas Supply*) *organisme qui surveille les activités des compagnies de gaz*.
Oftel ['ɔftɛl] *n* (*BRIT*: = *Office of Telecommunications*) *organisme qui supervise les télécommunications*.
often ['ɔfn] *adv* souvent; **how** ~ **do you go?** vous y allez tous les combien?; **as** ~ **as not** la plupart du temps.
Ofwat ['ɔfwɔt] *n* (*BRIT*: = *Office of Water Services*) *organisme qui surveille les activités des compagnies des eaux*.
ogle ['əugl] *vt* lorgner.
ogre ['əugə*] *n* ogre *m*.
OH *abbr* (*US*) = *Ohio*.
oh [əu] *excl* ô!, oh!, ah!
OHMS *abbr* (*BRIT*) = *On His (or Her) Majesty's Service*.
oil [ɔɪl] *n* huile *f*; (*petroleum*) pétrole *m*; (*for central heating*) mazout *m* ♦ *vt* (*machine*) graisser.
oilcan ['ɔɪlkæn] *n* burette *f* de graissage; (*for storing*) bidon *m* à huile.
oil change *n* vidange *f*.
oilfield ['ɔɪlfiːld] *n* gisement *m* de pétrole.
oil filter *n* (*AUT*) filtre *m* à huile.
oil-fired ['ɔɪlfaɪəd] *adj* au mazout.
oil gauge *n* jauge *f* de niveau d'huile.
oil industry *n* industrie pétrolière.
oil level *n* niveau *m* d'huile.
oil painting *n* peinture *f* à l'huile.
oil refinery *n* raffinerie *f* de pétrole.
oil rig *n* derrick *m*; (*at sea*) plate-forme pétrolière.
oilskins ['ɔɪlskɪnz] *npl* ciré *m*.
oil slick *n* nappe *f* de mazout.
oil tanker *n* pétrolier *m*.
oil well *n* puits *m* de pétrole.
oily ['ɔɪlɪ] *adj* huileux(euse); (*food*) gras(se).
ointment ['ɔɪntmənt] *n* onguent *m*.

OK *abbr (US) = Oklahoma.*
O.K., okay ['əu'keɪ] (*col*) *excl* d'accord! ♦ *vt* approuver, donner son accord à ♦ *n*: **to give sth one's** ~ donner son accord à qch ♦ *adj* en règle; en bon état; sain et sauf; acceptable; **is it ~?, are you ~?** ça va?; **are you ~ for money?** ça va *or* ira question argent?; **it's ~ with** *or* **by me** ça me va, c'est d'accord en ce qui me concerne.
Okla. *abbr (US) = Oklahoma.*
old [əuld] *adj* vieux(vieille); (*person*) vieux, âgé(e); (*former*) ancien(ne), vieux; **how ~ are you?** quel âge avez-vous?; **he's 10 years ~** il a 10 ans, il est âgé de 10 ans; **~er brother/sister** frère/sœur aîné(e); **any ~ thing will do** n'importe quoi fera l'affaire.
old age *n* vieillesse *f*.
old age pensioner (OAP) *n (BRIT)* retraité/e.
old-fashioned ['əuld'fæʃnd] *adj* démodé(e); (*person*) vieux jeu *inv*.
old maid *n* vieille fille.
old people's home *n* maison *f* de retraite.
old-style ['əuldstaɪl] *adj* à l'ancienne (mode).
old-time ['əuld'taɪm] *adj* du temps jadis, d'autrefois.
old-timer [əuld'taɪmə*] *n* ancien *m*.
old wives' tale *n* conte *m* de bonne femme.
O-level ['əulɛvl] *n* (*in England and Wales*: *formerly*) *examen passé à l'âge de 16 ans sanctionnant les connaissances de l'élève*, ≈ brevet *m* des collèges.
olive ['ɔlɪv] *n* (*fruit*) olive *f*; (*tree*) olivier *m* ♦ *adj* (*also*: **~-green**) (vert) olive *inv*.
olive oil *n* huile *f* d'olive.
Olympic [əu'lɪmpɪk] *adj* olympique; **the ~ Games, the ~s** les Jeux *mpl* olympiques.
OM *n abbr (BRIT: = Order of Merit) titre honorifique.*
Oman [əu'mɑːn] *n* Oman *m*.
OMB *n abbr (US: = Office of Management and Budget) service conseillant le président en matière budgétaire.*
omelet(te) ['ɔmlɪt] *n* omelette *f*; **ham/cheese ~** omelette au jambon/fromage.
omen ['əumən] *n* présage *m*.
ominous ['ɔmɪnəs] *adj* menaçant(e), inquiétant(e); (*event*) de mauvais augure.
omission [əu'mɪʃən] *n* omission *f*.
omit [əu'mɪt] *vt* omettre; **to ~ to do sth** négliger de faire qch.
omnivorous [ɔm'nɪvrəs] *adj* omnivore.
ON *abbr (Canada) = Ontario.*

KEYWORD

on [ɔn] *prep* **1** (*indicating position*) sur; **~ the table** sur la table; **~ the wall** sur le *or* au mur; **~ the left** à gauche; **I haven't any money ~ me** je n'ai pas d'argent sur moi
2 (*indicating means, method, condition etc*): **~ foot** à pied; **~ the train/plane** (*be*) dans le train/l'avion; (*go*) en train/avion; **~ the telephone/radio/television** au téléphone/à la radio/à la télévision; **to be ~ drugs** se droguer; **~ holiday,** (*US*) **~ vacation** en vacances; **~ the continent** sur le continent
3 (*referring to time*): **~ Friday** vendredi; **~ Fridays** le vendredi; **~ June 20th** le 20 juin; **a week ~ Friday** vendredi en huit; **~ arrival** à l'arrivée; **~ seeing this** en voyant cela
4 (*about, concerning*) sur, de; **a book ~ Balzac/physics** un livre sur Balzac/de physique
5 (*at the expense of*): **this round is ~ me** c'est ma tournée
♦ *adv* **1** (*referring to dress, covering*): **to have one's coat ~** avoir (mis) son manteau; **to put one's coat ~** mettre son manteau; **what's she got ~?** qu'est-ce qu'elle porte?; **screw the lid ~ tightly** vissez bien le couvercle
2 (*further, continuously*): **to walk** *etc* **~** continuer à marcher *etc*; **~ and off** de temps à autre; **from that day ~** depuis ce jour
♦ *adj* **1** (*in operation*: *machine*) en marche; (: *radio, TV, light*) allumé(e); (: *tap, gas*) ouvert(e); (: *brakes*) mis(e); **is the meeting still ~?** (*not cancelled*) est-ce que la réunion a bien lieu?; (*in progress*) la réunion dure-t-elle encore?; **it was well ~ in the evening** c'était tard dans la soirée; **when is this film ~?** quand passe ce film?
2 (*col*): **that's not ~!** (*not acceptable*) cela ne se fait pas!; (*not possible*) pas question!

ONC *n abbr (BRIT: = Ordinary National Certificate)* ≈ BT *m*.
once [wʌns] *adv* une fois; (*formerly*) autrefois ♦ *conj* une fois que; **~ he had left/it was done** une fois qu'il fut parti/que ce fut terminé; **at ~** tout de suite, immédiatement; (*simultaneously*) à la fois; **all at ~** *adv* tout d'un coup; **~ a week** une fois par semaine; **~ more** encore une fois; **I knew him ~** je l'ai connu autrefois; **~ and for all** une fois pour toutes; **~ upon a time there was ...** il y avait une fois ..., il était une fois ....
oncoming ['ɔnkʌmɪŋ] *adj* (*traffic*) venant en sens inverse.
OND *n abbr (BRIT: = Ordinary National Diploma)* ≈ BTS *m*.

KEYWORD

one [wʌn] *num* un(e); **~ hundred and fifty** cent cinquante; **~ day** un jour
♦ *adj* **1** (*sole*) seul(e), unique; **the ~ book which** l'unique *or* le seul livre qui; **the ~ man who** le seul (homme) qui
2 (*same*) même; **they came in the ~ car** ils sont venus dans la même voiture
♦ *pron* **1**: **this ~** celui-ci(celle-ci); **that ~** celui-là(celle-là); **I've already got ~/a red ~** j'en ai déjà un(e)/un(e) rouge; **~ by ~** un(e) à *or* par un(e); **which ~ do you want?** lequel voulez-vous?

2: ~ **another** l'un(e) l'autre; **to look at ~ another** se regarder
3 (*impersonal*) on; ~ **never knows** on ne sait jamais; **to cut ~'s finger** se couper le doigt
4 (*phrases*): **to be ~ up on sb** avoir l'avantage sur qn; **to be at ~ (with sb)** être d'accord (avec qn).

one-armed bandit ['wʌnɑːmd-] *n* machine *f* à sous.
one-day excursion ['wʌndeɪ-] *n* (*US*) billet *m* d'aller-retour (valable pour la journée).
One-hundred share index ['wʌnhʌndrəd-] *n* indice *m* Footsie des cent grandes valeurs.
one-man ['wʌn'mæn] *adj* (*business*) dirigé(e) *etc* par un seul homme.
one-man band *n* homme-orchestre *m*.
one-off [wʌn'ɔf] (*BRIT col*) *n* exemplaire *m* unique ♦ *adj* unique.
one-parent family ['wʌnpɛərənt-] *n* famille monoparentale.
one-piece ['wʌnpiːs] *adj*: ~ **bathing suit** maillot *m* une pièce.
onerous ['ɔnərəs] *adj* (*task, duty*) pénible; (*responsibility*) lourd(e).
oneself [wʌn'sɛlf] *pron* se; (*after prep, also emphatic*) soi-même; **by ~** tout seul.
one-sided [wʌn'saɪdɪd] *adj* (*decision*) unilatéral(e); (*contest*) inégal(e).
one-time ['wʌntaɪm] *adj* d'autrefois.
one-to-one ['wʌntəwʌn] *adj* (*relationship*) univoque.
one-upmanship [wʌn'ʌpmənʃɪp] *n*: **the art of ~** l'art de faire mieux que les autres.
one-way ['wʌnweɪ] *adj* (*street, traffic*) à sens unique.
ongoing ['ɔngəuɪŋ] *adj* en cours; suivi(e).
onion ['ʌnjən] *n* oignon *m*.
on line *adj* (*COMPUT*) en ligne; (*: switched on*) connecté(e).
onlooker ['ɔnlukə*] *n* spectateur/trice.
only ['əunlɪ] *adv* seulement ♦ *adj* seul(e), unique ♦ *conj* seulement, mais; **not ~** non seulement; **I ~ took one** j'en ai seulement pris un, je n'en ai pris qu'un; **I saw her ~ yesterday** je l'ai vue hier encore; **I'd be ~ too pleased to help** je ne serais que trop content de vous aider; **I would come, ~ I'm very busy** je viendrais bien mais j'ai beaucoup à faire.
ono *abbr* (*BRIT: = or nearest offer*) ≈ à débattre.
onset ['ɔnsɛt] *n* début *m*; (*of winter, old age*) approche *f*.
onshore ['ɔnʃɔː*] *adj* (*wind*) du large.
onslaught ['ɔnslɔːt] *n* attaque *f*, assaut *m*.
Ont. *abbr* (*Canada*) = *Ontario*.
on-the-job ['ɔnðə'dʒɔb] *adj*: ~ **training** formation *f* sur place.
onto ['ɔntu] *prep* = *on to*.
onus ['əunəs] *n* responsabilité.
onward(s) ['ɔnwəd(z)] *adv* (*move*) en avant.
oops [ups] *excl* houp!; **~-a-daisy!** houp-là!
ooze [uːz] *vi* suinter.
opal ['əupl] *n* opale *f*.
opaque [əu'peɪk] *adj* opaque.
OPEC ['əupɛk] *n abbr* (= *Organization of Petroleum-Exporting Countries*) OPEP *f*.
open ['əupn] *adj* ouvert(e); (*car*) découvert(e); (*road, view*) dégagé(e); (*meeting*) public(ique); (*admiration*) manifeste; (*question*) non résolu(e); (*enemy*) déclaré(e) ♦ *vt* ouvrir ♦ *vi* (*flower, eyes, door, debate*) s'ouvrir; (*shop, bank, museum*) ouvrir; (*book etc: commence*) commencer, débuter; **in the ~ (air)** en plein air; **the ~ sea** le large; **~ ground** (*among trees*) clairière *f*; (*waste ground*) terrain *m* vague; **to have an ~ mind (on sth)** avoir l'esprit ouvert (sur qch).
►**open on to** *vt fus* (*subj: room, door*) donner sur.
►**open out** *vt* ouvrir ♦ *vi* s'ouvrir.
►**open up** *vt* ouvrir; (*blocked road*) dégager ♦ *vi* s'ouvrir.
open-air [əupn'ɛə*] *adj* en plein air.
open-and-shut ['əupnən'ʃʌt] *adj*: ~ **case** cas *m* limpide.
open day *n* journée *f* portes ouvertes.
open-ended [əupn'ɛndɪd] *adj* (*fig*) non limité(e).
opener ['əupnə*] *n* (*also*: **can ~, tin ~**) ouvre-boîtes *m*.
open-heart surgery [əupn'hɑːt-] *n* chirurgie *f* à cœur ouvert.
opening ['əupnɪŋ] *n* ouverture *f*; (*opportunity*) occasion *f*; débouché *m*; (*job*) poste vacant.
opening night *n* (*THEAT*) première *f*.
open learning centre *n centre ouvert à tous où l'on dispense un enseignement général à temps partiel.*
openly ['əupnlɪ] *adv* ouvertement.
open-minded [əupn'maɪndɪd] *adj* à l'esprit ouvert.
open-necked ['əupnnɛkt] *adj* à col ouvert.
openness ['əupnnɪs] *n* (*frankness*) franchise *f*.
open-plan ['əupn'plæn] *adj* sans cloisons.
open prison *n* prison ouverte.
open sandwich *n* canapé *m*.
open shop *n entreprise qui admet les travailleurs non syndiqués.*
Open University *n* (*BRIT*) *cours universitaires par correspondance*; voir encadré.

OPEN UNIVERSITY

*L'***Open University** *a été fondée en 1969. L'enseignement comprend des cours (certaines plages horaires sont réservées à cet effet à la télévision et à la radio), des devoirs qui sont envoyés par l'étudiant à son directeur ou sa directrice d'études, et un stage obligatoire en université d'été. Il faut préparer un certain nombre d'unités de valeur pendant une période de temps déterminée et obtenir la moyenne à un certain nombre d'entre elles pour recevoir le diplôme visé.*

opera ['ɔpərə] *n* opéra *m*.
opera glasses *npl* jumelles *fpl* de théâtre.
opera house *n* opéra *m*.
opera singer *n* chanteur/euse d'opéra.
operate ['ɔpəreɪt] *vt* (*machine*) faire marcher, faire fonctionner; (*system*) pratiquer ♦ *vi* fonctionner; (*drug*) faire effet; **to ~ on sb (for)** (*MED*) opérer qn (de).
operatic [ɔpə'rætɪk] *adj* d'opéra.
operating ['ɔpəreɪtɪŋ] *adj* (*COMM*: *costs, profit*) d'exploitation; (*MED*): ~ **table/theatre** table *f*/salle *f* d'opération.
operating room *n* (*US*: *MED*) salle *f* d'opération.
operating system *n* (*COMPUT*) système *m* d'exploitation.
operation [ɔpə'reɪʃən] *n* opération *f*; (*of machine*) fonctionnement *m*; **to have an ~ (for)** se faire opérer (de); **to be in ~** (*machine*) être en service; (*system*) être en vigueur.
operational [ɔpə'reɪʃənl] *adj* opérationnel(le); (*ready for use or action*) en état de marche; **when the service is fully ~** lorsque le service fonctionnera pleinement.
operative ['ɔpərətɪv] *adj* (*measure*) en vigueur ♦ *n* (*in factory*) ouvrier/ière; **the ~ word** le mot clef.
operator ['ɔpəreɪtə*] *n* (*of machine*) opérateur/trice; (*TEL*) téléphoniste *m/f*.
operetta [ɔpə'rɛtə] *n* opérette *f*.
ophthalmologist [ɔfθæl'mɔlədʒɪst] *n* ophtalmologiste *m/f*, ophtalmologue *m/f*.
opinion [ə'pɪnjən] *n* opinion *f*, avis *m*; **in my ~** à mon avis; **to seek a second ~** demander un deuxième avis.
opinionated [ə'pɪnjəneɪtɪd] *adj* aux idées bien arrêtées.
opinion poll *n* sondage *m* d'opinion.
opium ['əupɪəm] *n* opium *m*.
opponent [ə'pəunənt] *n* adversaire *m/f*.
opportune ['ɔpətju:n] *adj* opportun(e).
opportunist [ɔpə'tju:nɪst] *n* opportuniste *m/f*.
opportunity [ɔpə'tju:nɪtɪ] *n* occasion *f*; **to take the ~ to do** *or* **of doing** profiter de l'occasion pour faire.
oppose [ə'pəuz] *vt* s'opposer à; **~d to** *adj* opposé(e) à; **as ~d to** par opposition à.
opposing [ə'pəuzɪŋ] *adj* (*side*) opposé(e).
opposite ['ɔpəzɪt] *adj* opposé(e); (*house etc*) d'en face ♦ *adv* en face ♦ *prep* en face de ♦ *n* opposé *m*, contraire *m*; (*of word*) contraire; **"see ~ page"** "voir ci-contre".
opposite number *n* (*BRIT*) homologue *m/f*.
opposite sex *n*: **the ~** l'autre sexe.
opposition [ɔpə'zɪʃən] *n* opposition *f*.
oppress [ə'prɛs] *vt* opprimer.
oppression [ə'prɛʃən] *n* oppression *f*.
oppressive [ə'prɛsɪv] *adj* oppressif(ive).
opprobrium [ə'prəubrɪəm] *n* (*formal*) opprobre *m*.
opt [ɔpt] *vi*: **to ~ for** opter pour; **to ~ to do** choisir de faire.
►**opt out** *vi* (*school, hospital*) devenir autonome; (*health service*) devenir privé(e); **to ~ out of** choisir de quitter.
optical ['ɔptɪkl] *adj* optique; (*instrument*) d'optique.
optical character reader/recognition (OCR) *n* lecteur *m*/lecture *f* optique.
optical fibre *n* fibre *f* optique.
optician [ɔp'tɪʃən] *n* opticien/ne.
optics ['ɔptɪks] *n* optique *f*.
optimism ['ɔptɪmɪzəm] *n* optimisme *m*.
optimist ['ɔptɪmɪst] *n* optimiste *m/f*.
optimistic [ɔptɪ'mɪstɪk] *adj* optimiste.
optimum ['ɔptɪməm] *adj* optimum.
option ['ɔpʃən] *n* choix *m*, option *f*; (*SCOL*) matière *f* à option; (*COMM*) option; **to keep one's ~s open** (*fig*) ne pas s'engager; **I have no ~** je n'ai pas le choix.
optional ['ɔpʃənl] *adj* facultatif(ive); (*COMM*) en option; ~ **extras** accessoires *mpl* en option, options *fpl*.
opulence ['ɔpjuləns] *n* opulence *f*; abondance *f*.
opulent ['ɔpjulənt] *adj* opulent(e); abondant(e).
OR *abbr* (*US*) = *Oregon*.
or [ɔ:*] *conj* ou; (*with negative*): **he hasn't seen ~ heard anything** il n'a rien vu ni entendu; ~ **else** sinon; ou bien, ou alors.
oracle ['ɔrəkl] *n* oracle *m*.
oral ['ɔ:rəl] *adj* oral(e) ♦ *n* oral *m*.
orange ['ɔrɪndʒ] *n* (*fruit*) orange *f* ♦ *adj* orange *inv*.
orangeade [ɔrɪndʒ'eɪd] *n* orangeade *f*.
oration [ɔ:'reɪʃən] *n* discours solennel.
orator ['ɔrətə*] *n* orateur/trice.
oratorio [ɔrə'tɔ:rɪəu] *n* oratorio *m*.
orb [ɔ:b] *n* orbe *m*.
orbit ['ɔ:bɪt] *n* orbite *f* ♦ *vt* décrire une *or* des orbite(s) autour de; **to be in/go into ~ (round)** être/entrer en orbite (autour de).
orbital ['ɔ:bɪtl] *n* (*also*: ~ **motorway**) périphérique *f*.
orchard ['ɔ:tʃəd] *n* verger *m*; **apple ~** verger de pommiers.
orchestra ['ɔ:kɪstrə] *n* orchestre *m*; (*US*: *seating*) (fauteils *mpl* d')orchestre.
orchestral [ɔ:'kɛstrəl] *adj* orchestral(e); (*concert*) symphonique.
orchestrate ['ɔ:kɪstreɪt] *vt* (*MUS, fig*) orchestrer.
orchid ['ɔ:kɪd] *n* orchidée *f*.
ordain [ɔ:'deɪn] *vt* (*REL*) ordonner; (*decide*) décréter.
ordeal [ɔ:'di:l] *n* épreuve *f*.
order ['ɔ:də*] *n* ordre *m*; (*COMM*) commande *f* ♦ *vt* ordonner; (*COMM*) commander; **in ~** en ordre; (*of document*) en règle; **out of ~** hors service; (*telephone*) en dérangement; **a machine in working ~** une machine en état de marche; **in ~ of size** par ordre de grandeur; **in ~ to do/that** pour faire/que + *sub*; **to**

~ **sb to do** ordonner à qn de faire; **to place an** ~ **for sth with sb** commander qch auprès de qn, passer commande de qch à qn; **to be on** ~ être en commande; **made to** ~ fait sur commande; **to be under** ~**s to do sth** avoir ordre de faire qch; **a point of** ~ un point de procédure; **to the** ~ **of** (*BANKING*) à l'ordre de.

order book *n* carnet *m* de commandes.

order form *n* bon *m* de commande.

orderly ['ɔːdəlɪ] *n* (*MIL*) ordonnance *f* ♦ *adj* (*room*) en ordre; (*mind*) méthodique; (*person*) qui a de l'ordre.

order number *n* (*COMM*) numéro *m* de commande.

ordinal ['ɔːdɪnl] *adj* (*number*) ordinal(e).

ordinary ['ɔːdnrɪ] *adj* ordinaire, normal(e); (*pej*) ordinaire, quelconque; **out of the** ~ exceptionnel(le).

ordinary degree *n* (*SCOL*) ≈ licence *f* libre; *voir encadré*.

ORDINARY DEGREE

Un **ordinary degree** *est un diplôme inférieur à l'"honours degree" que l'on obtient en général après trois années d'études universitaires. Il peut aussi être décerné en cas d'échec à l'honours degree.*

ordinary seaman (OS) *n* (*BRIT*) matelot *m*.

ordinary shares *npl* actions *fpl* ordinaires.

ordination [ɔːdɪ'neɪʃən] *n* ordination *f*.

ordnance ['ɔːdnəns] *n* (*MIL: unit*) service *m* du matériel.

Ordnance Survey map *n* (*BRIT*) ≈ carte *f* d'État-major.

ore [ɔː*] *n* minerai *m*.

Ore(g). *abbr* (*US*) = *Oregon*.

organ ['ɔːgən] *n* organe *m*; (*MUS*) orgue *m*, orgues *fpl*.

organic [ɔː'gænɪk] *adj* organique; (*crops etc*) biologique, naturel(le).

organism ['ɔːgənɪzəm] *n* organisme *m*.

organist ['ɔːgənɪst] *n* organiste *m/f*.

organization [ɔːgənaɪ'zeɪʃən] *n* organisation *f*.

organization chart *n* organigramme *m*.

organize ['ɔːgənaɪz] *vt* organiser; **to get** ~**d** s'organiser.

organized crime ['ɔːgənaɪzd-] *n* crime organisé, grand banditisme.

organized labour ['ɔːgənaɪzd-] *n* main-d'œuvre syndiquée.

organizer ['ɔːgənaɪzə*] *n* organisateur/trice.

orgasm ['ɔːgæzəm] *n* orgasme *m*.

orgy ['ɔːdʒɪ] *n* orgie *f*.

Orient ['ɔːrɪənt] *n*: **the** ~ l'Orient *m*.

oriental [ɔːrɪ'ɛntl] *adj* oriental(e) ♦ *n* Oriental/e.

orientate ['ɔːrɪənteɪt] *vt* orienter.

orifice ['ɔrɪfɪs] *n* orifice *m*.

origin ['ɔrɪdʒɪn] *n* origine *f*; **country of** ~ pays *m* d'origine.

original [ə'rɪdʒɪnl] *adj* original(e); (*earliest*) originel(le) ♦ *n* original *m*.

originality [ərɪdʒɪ'nælɪtɪ] *n* originalité *f*.

originally [ə'rɪdʒɪnəlɪ] *adv* (*at first*) à l'origine.

originate [ə'rɪdʒɪneɪt] *vi*: **to** ~ **from** être originaire de; (*suggestion*) provenir de; **to** ~ **in** prendre naissance dans; avoir son origine dans.

originator [ə'rɪdʒɪneɪtə*] *n* auteur *m*.

Orkneys ['ɔːknɪz] *npl*: **the** ~ (*also*: **the Orkney Islands**) les Orcades *fpl*.

ornament ['ɔːnəmənt] *n* ornement *m*; (*trinket*) bibelot *m*.

ornamental [ɔːnə'mɛntl] *adj* décoratif(ive); (*garden*) d'agrément.

ornamentation [ɔːnəmɛn'teɪʃən] *n* ornementation *f*.

ornate [ɔː'neɪt] *adj* très orné(e).

ornithologist [ɔːnɪ'θɔlədʒɪst] *n* ornithologue *m/f*.

ornithology [ɔːnɪ'θɔlədʒɪ] *n* ornithologie *f*.

orphan ['ɔːfn] *n* orphelin/e ♦ *vt*: **to be** ~**ed** devenir orphelin.

orphanage ['ɔːfənɪdʒ] *n* orphelinat *m*.

orthodox ['ɔːθədɔks] *adj* orthodoxe.

orthopaedic, (*US*) **orthopedic** [ɔːθə'piːdɪk] *adj* orthopédique.

OS *abbr* (*BRIT*: = *Ordnance Survey*) ≈ IGN *m* (= *Institut géographique national*); (: *NAUT*) = **ordinary seaman**; (: *DRESS*) = **outsize**.

O/S *abbr* = **out of stock**.

Oscar ['ɔskə*] *n* oscar *m*.

oscillate ['ɔsɪleɪt] *vi* osciller.

OSHA *n abbr* (*US*: = *Occupational Safety and Health Administration*) *office de l'hygiène et de la sécurité au travail*.

Oslo ['ɔzləu] *n* Oslo.

ostensible [ɔs'tɛnsɪbl] *adj* prétendu(e); apparent(e).

ostensibly [ɔs'tɛnsɪblɪ] *adv* en apparence.

ostentation [ɔstɛn'teɪʃən] *n* ostentation *f*.

ostentatious [ɔstɛn'teɪʃəs] *adj* prétentieux(euse); ostentatoire.

osteopath ['ɔstɪəpæθ] *n* ostéopathe *m/f*.

ostracize ['ɔstrəsaɪz] *vt* frapper d'ostracisme.

ostrich ['ɔstrɪtʃ] *n* autruche *f*.

OT *n abbr* (= *Old Testament*) AT *m*.

OTB *n abbr* (*US*: = *off-track betting*) *paris pris en dehors du champ de course*.

O.T.E. *abbr* (= *on-target earnings*) primes *fpl* sur objectifs inclus.

other ['ʌðə*] *adj* autre ♦ *pron*: **the** ~ **(one)** l'autre; ~**s** (~ *people*) d'autres; **some** ~ **people have still to arrive** on attend encore quelques personnes; **the** ~ **day** l'autre jour; ~ **than** autrement que; à part; **some actor or** ~ un certain acteur, je ne sais quel acteur; **somebody or** ~ quelqu'un; **the car was none** ~ **than John's** la voiture n'était autre que celle de John.

otherwise ['ʌðəwaɪz] *adv, conj* autrement; **an ~ good piece of work** par ailleurs, un beau travail.

OTT *abbr (col)* = **over the top**; *see* **top**.

otter ['ɔtə*] *n* loutre *f*.

OU *n abbr (BRIT)* = **Open University**.

ouch [autʃ] *excl* aïe!

ought, *pt* **ought** [ɔ:t] *aux vb*: **I ~ to do it** je devrais le faire, il faudrait que je le fasse; **this ~ to have been corrected** cela aurait dû être corrigé; **he ~ to win** il devrait gagner; **you ~ to go and see it** vous devriez aller le voir.

ounce [auns] *n* once *f (= 28.35g; 16 in a pound)*.

our ['auə*] *adj* notre, nos *pl*.

ours [auəz] *pron* le(la) nôtre, les nôtres.

ourselves [auə'sɛlvz] *pron pl (reflexive, after preposition)* nous; *(emphatic)* nous-mêmes; **we did it (all) by ~** nous avons fait ça tout seuls.

oust [aust] *vt* évincer.

out [aut] *adv* dehors; *(published, not at home etc)* sorti(e); *(light, fire)* éteint(e); *(on strike)* en grève ♦ *vt*: **to ~ sb** révéler l'homosexualité de qn; **~ here** ici; **~ there** là-bas; **he's ~** *(absent)* il est sorti; *(unconscious)* il est sans connaissance; **to be ~ in one's calculations** s'être trompé dans ses calculs; **to run/back** *etc* **~** sortir en courant/en reculant *etc*; **to be ~ and about** *or (US)* **around again** être de nouveau sur pied; **before the week was ~** avant la fin de la semaine; **the journey ~** l'aller *m*; **the boat was 10 km ~** le bateau était à 10 km du rivage; **~ loud** *adv* à haute voix; **~ of** *prep (outside)* en dehors de; *(because of: anger etc)* par; *(from among)*: **~ of 10** sur 10; *(without)*: **~ of petrol** sans essence, à court d'essence; **made ~ of wood** en *or* de bois; **~ of order** *(machine)* en panne; *(TEL: line)* en dérangement; **~ of stock** *(COMM: article)* épuisé(e); *(: shop)* en rupture de stock.

outage ['autɪdʒ] *n (esp US: power failure)* panne *f or* coupure *f* de courant.

out-and-out ['autəndaut] *adj* véritable.

outback ['autbæk] *n* campagne isolée; *(in Australia)* intérieur *m*.

outbid [aut'bɪd] *irreg vt* surenchérir.

outboard ['autbɔ:d] *n*: **~ (motor)** (moteur *m*) hors-bord *m*.

outbound ['autbaund] *adj*: **~ (from/for)** en partance (de/pour).

outbreak ['autbreɪk] *n* éruption *f*, explosion *f*; *(start)* déclenchement *m*.

outbuilding ['autbɪldɪŋ] *n* dépendance *f*.

outburst ['autbə:st] *n* explosion *f*, accès *m*.

outcast ['autkɑ:st] *n* exilé/e; *(socially)* paria *m*.

outclass [aut'klɑ:s] *vt* surclasser.

outcome ['autkʌm] *n* issue *f*, résultat *m*.

outcrop ['autkrɔp] *n* affleurement *m*.

outcry ['autkraɪ] *n* tollé (général).

outdated [aut'deɪtɪd] *adj* démodé(e).

outdistance [aut'dɪstəns] *vt* distancer.

outdo [aut'du:] *vt irreg* surpasser.

outdoor [aut'dɔ:*] *adj* de *or* en plein air.

outdoors [aut'dɔ:z] *adv* dehors; au grand air.

outer ['autə*] *adj* extérieur(e); **~ suburbs** grande banlieue.

outer space *n* espace *m* cosmique.

outfit ['autfɪt] *n* équipement *m*; *(clothes)* tenue *f*; *(col: COMM)* organisation *f*, boîte *f*.

outfitter ['autfɪtə*] *n (BRIT)*: **"(gent's) ~'s"** "confection pour hommes".

outgoing ['autgəuɪŋ] *adj (president, tenant)* sortant(e); *(character)* ouvert(e), extraverti(e).

outgoings ['autgəuɪŋz] *npl (BRIT: expenses)* dépenses *fpl*.

outgrow [aut'grəu] *vt irreg (clothes)* devenir trop grand(e) pour.

outhouse ['authaus] *n* appentis *m*, remise *f*.

outing ['autɪŋ] *n* sortie *f*; excursion *f*.

outlandish [aut'lændɪʃ] *adj* étrange.

outlast [aut'lɑ:st] *vt* survivre à.

outlaw ['autlɔ:] *n* hors-la-loi *m inv* ♦ *vt (person)* mettre hors la loi; *(practice)* proscrire.

outlay ['autleɪ] *n* dépenses *fpl*; *(investment)* mise *f* de fonds.

outlet ['autlɛt] *n (for liquid etc)* issue *f*, sortie *f*; *(for emotion)* exutoire *m*; *(for goods)* débouché *m*; *(also*: **retail ~**) point *m* de vente; *(US: ELEC)* prise *f* de courant.

outline ['autlaɪn] *n (shape)* contour *m*; *(summary)* esquisse *f*, grandes lignes.

outlive [aut'lɪv] *vt* survivre à.

outlook ['autluk] *n* perspective *f*.

outlying ['autlaɪɪŋ] *adj* écarté(e).

outmanoeuvre [autmə'nu:və*] *vt (rival etc)* avoir au tournant.

outmoded [aut'məudɪd] *adj* démodé(e); dépassé(e).

outnumber [aut'nʌmbə*] *vt* surpasser en nombre.

out-of-court [autəv'kɔ:t] *adj, adv* à l'aimable.

out-of-date [autəv'deɪt] *adj (passport, ticket)* périmé(e); *(theory, idea)* dépassé(e); *(custom)* désuet(ète); *(clothes)* démodé(e).

out-of-the-way ['autəvðə'weɪ] *adj* loin de tout; *(fig)* insolite.

outpatient ['autpeɪʃənt] *n* malade *m/f* en consultation externe.

outpost ['autpəust] *n* avant-poste *m*.

outpouring ['autpɔ:rɪŋ] *n (fig)* épanchement(s) *m(pl)*.

output ['autput] *n* rendement *m*, production *f* ♦ *vt (COMPUT)* sortir.

outrage ['autreɪdʒ] *n* atrocité *f*, acte *m* de violence; scandale *m* ♦ *vt* outrager.

outrageous [aut'reɪdʒəs] *adj* atroce; scandaleux(euse).

outrider ['autraɪdə*] *n (on motorcycle)* motard *m*.

outright *adv* [aut'raɪt] complètement; catégoriquement; carrément; sur le coup ♦ *adj* ['autraɪt] complet(ète); catégorique.

outrun [aut'rʌn] *vt irreg* dépasser.

outset ['autsɛt] *n* début *m*.
outshine [aut'ʃaɪn] *vt irreg* (*fig*) éclipser.
outside [aut'saɪd] *n* extérieur *m* ♦ *adj* extérieur(e); (*remote, unlikely*): **an ~ chance** une (très) faible chance ♦ *adv* (au) dehors, à l'extérieur ♦ *prep* hors de, à l'extérieur de; **at the ~** (*fig*) au plus *or* maximum; **~ left/right** *n* (*FOOTBALL*) ailier gauche/droit.
outside broadcast *n* (*RADIO, TV*) reportage *m*.
outside lane *n* (*AUT: in Britain*) voie *f* de droite; (*: in US, Europe*) voie de gauche.
outside line *n* (*TEL*) ligne extérieure.
outsider [aut'saɪdə*] *n* (*in race etc*) outsider *m*; (*stranger*) étranger/ère.
outsize ['autsaɪz] *adj* énorme; (*clothes*) grande taille *inv*.
outskirts ['autskəːts] *npl* faubourgs *mpl*.
outsmart [aut'smɑːt] *vt* se montrer plus malin(igne) *or* futé(e) que.
outspoken [aut'spəukən] *adj* très franc(franche).
outspread [aut'sprɛd] *adj* (*wings*) déployé(e).
outstanding [aut'stændɪŋ] *adj* remarquable, exceptionnel(le); (*unfinished*) en suspens; en souffrance; non réglé(e); **your account is still ~** vous n'avez pas encore tout remboursé.
outstay [aut'steɪ] *vt*: **to ~ one's welcome** abuser de l'hospitalité de son hôte.
outstretched [aut'strɛtʃt] *adj* (*hand*) tendu(e); (*body*) étendu(e).
outstrip [aut'strɪp] *vt* (*also fig*) dépasser.
out-tray ['auttreɪ] *n* courrier *m* "départ".
outvote [aut'vəut] *vt*: **to ~ sb (by)** mettre qn en minorité (par); **to ~ sth (by)** rejeter qch (par).
outward ['autwəd] *adj* (*sign, appearances*) extérieur(e); (*journey*) (d')aller.
outwardly ['autwədlɪ] *adv* extérieurement; en apparence.
outweigh [aut'weɪ] *vt* l'emporter sur.
outwit [aut'wɪt] *vt* se montrer plus malin que.
oval ['əuvl] *adj*, *n* ovale (*m*).
Oval Office *n* (*US POL*) *voir encadré*.

OVAL OFFICE

*L'***Oval Office** *est le bureau personnel du président des États-Unis à la Maison-Blanche, ainsi appelé du fait de sa forme ovale. Par extension, ce terme désigne la présidence elle-même.*

ovarian [əu'vɛərɪən] *adj* ovarien(ne); (*cancer*) des ovaires.
ovary ['əuvərɪ] *n* ovaire *m*.
ovation [əu'veɪʃən] *n* ovation *f*.
oven ['ʌvn] *n* four *m*.
ovenproof ['ʌvnpruːf] *adj* allant au four.
oven-ready ['ʌvnrɛdɪ] *adj* prêt(e) à cuire.
ovenware ['ʌvnwɛə*] *n* plats *mpl* allant au four.
over ['əuvə*] *adv* (par-)dessus; (*excessively*) trop ♦ *adj (or adv)* (*finished*) fini(e), terminé(e); (*too much*) en plus ♦ *prep* sur; par-dessus; (*above*) au-dessus de; (*on the other side of*) de l'autre côté de; (*more than*) plus de; (*during*) pendant; (*about, concerning*): **they fell out ~ money/her** ils se sont brouillés pour des questions d'argent/à cause d'elle; **~ here** ici; **~ there** là-bas; **all ~** (*everywhere*) partout; (*finished*) fini(e); **~ and ~ (again)** à plusieurs reprises; **~ and above** en plus de; **to ask sb ~** inviter qn (à passer); **to go ~ to sb's** passer chez qn; **now ~ to our Paris correspondent** nous passons l'antenne à notre correspondant à Paris; **the world ~** dans le monde entier; **she's not ~ intelligent** (*BRIT*) elle n'est pas particulièrement intelligente.
over... ['əuvə*] *prefix*: **~abundant** surabondant(e).
overact [əuvər'ækt] *vi* (*THEAT*) outrer son rôle.
overall *adj*, *n* ['əuvərɔːl] *adj* (*length*) total(e); (*study*) d'ensemble ♦ *n* (*BRIT*) blouse *f* ♦ *adv* [əuvər'ɔːl] dans l'ensemble, en général; **~s** *npl* bleus *mpl* (de travail).
overall majority *n* majorité absolue.
overanxious [əuvər'æŋkʃəs] *adj* trop anxieux(euse).
overawe [əuvər'ɔː] *vt* impressionner.
overbalance [əuvə'bæləns] *vi* basculer.
overbearing [əuvə'bɛərɪŋ] *adj* impérieux(euse), autoritaire.
overboard ['əuvəbɔːd] *adv* (*NAUT*) par-dessus bord; **to go ~ for sth** (*fig*) s'emballer (pour qch).
overbook [əuvə'buk] *vt* faire du surbooking.
overcapitalize [əuvə'kæpɪtəlaɪz] *vt* surcapitaliser.
overcast ['əuvəkɑːst] *adj* couvert(e).
overcharge [əuvə'tʃɑːdʒ] *vt*: **to ~ sb for sth** faire payer qch trop cher à qn.
overcoat ['əuvəkəut] *n* pardessus *m*.
overcome [əuvə'kʌm] *vt irreg* triompher de; surmonter ♦ *adj* (*emotionally*) bouleversé(e); **~ with grief** accablé(e) de douleur.
overconfident [əuvə'kɔnfɪdənt] *adj* trop sûr(e) de soi.
overcrowding [əuvə'kraudɪŋ] *n* surpeuplement *m*; (*in bus*) encombrement *m*.
overdo [əuvə'duː] *vt irreg* exagérer; (*overcook*) trop cuire; **to ~ it, to ~ things** (*work too hard*) en faire trop, se surmener.
overdose ['əuvədəus] *n* dose excessive.
overdraft ['əuvədrɑːft] *n* découvert *m*.
overdrawn [əuvə'drɔːn] *adj* (*account*) à découvert.
overdrive ['əuvədraɪv] *n* (*AUT*) (vitesse *f*) surmultipliée *f*.
overdue [əuvə'djuː] *adj* en retard; (*bill*) impayé(e); **that change was long ~** ce changement n'avait que trop tardé.
overemphasis [əuvər'ɛmfəsɪs] *n*: **to put an ~ on** accorder trop d'importance à.
overestimate [əuvər'ɛstɪmeɪt] *vt* surestimer.

overexcited [əuvərɪk'saɪtɪd] *adj* surexcité(e).
overexertion [əuvərɪg'zəːʃən] *n* surmenage *m* (physique).
overexpose [əuvərɪk'spəuz] *vt* (*PHOT*) surexposer.
overflow *vi* [əuvə'fləu] déborder ♦ *n* ['əuvəfləu] trop-plein *m*; (*also*: ~ **pipe**) tuyau *m* d'écoulement, trop-plein *m*.
overfly [əuvə'flaɪ] *vt irreg* survoler.
overgenerous [əuvə'dʒɛnərəs] *adj* (*person*) prodigue; (*offer*) excessif(ive).
overgrown [əuvə'grəun] *adj* (*garden*) envahi(e) par la végétation; **he's just an ~ schoolboy** (*fig*) c'est un écolier attardé.
overhang ['əuvə'hæŋ] *irreg vt* surplomber ♦ *vi* faire saillie.
overhaul *vt* [əuvə'hɔːl] réviser ♦ *n* ['əuvəhɔːl] révision *f*.
overhead *adv* [əuvə'hɛd] au-dessus ♦ *adj*, *n* ['əuvəhɛd] *adj* aérien(ne); (*lighting*) vertical(e) ♦ *n* (*US*) = **overheads**.
overheads ['əuvəhɛdz] *npl* (*BRIT*) frais généraux.
overhear [əuvə'hɪə*] *vt irreg* entendre (par hasard).
overheat [əuvə'hiːt] *vi* devenir surchauffé(e); (*engine*) chauffer.
overjoyed [əuvə'dʒɔɪd] *adj* ravi(e), enchanté(e).
overkill ['əuvəkɪl] *n* (*fig*): **it would be ~** ce serait de trop.
overland ['əuvəlænd] *adj*, *adv* par voie de terre.
overlap *vi* [əuvə'læp] se chevaucher ♦ *n* ['əuvəlæp] chevauchement *m*.
overleaf [əuvə'liːf] *adv* au verso.
overload [əuvə'ləud] *vt* surcharger.
overlook [əuvə'luk] *vt* (*have view of*) donner sur; (*miss*) oublier, négliger; (*forgive*) fermer les yeux sur.
overlord ['əuvəlɔːd] *n* chef *m* suprême.
overmanning [əuvə'mænɪŋ] *n* sureffectif *m*, main-d'œuvre *f* pléthorique.
overnight *adv* [əuvə'naɪt] (*happen*) durant la nuit; (*fig*) soudain ♦ *adj* ['əuvənaɪt] d'une (*or* de) nuit; soudain(e); **he stayed there ~** il y a passé la nuit; **if you travel ~ ...** si tu fais le voyage de nuit ...; **he'll be away ~** il ne rentrera pas ce soir.
overpass ['əuvəpɑːs] *n* pont autoroutier; (*US*) passerelle *f*, pont *m*.
overpay [əuvə'peɪ] *vt*: **to ~ sb by £50** donner à qn 50 livres de trop.
overplay [əuvə'pleɪ] *vt* exagérer; **to ~ one's hand** trop présumer de sa situation.
overpower [əuvə'pauə*] *vt* vaincre; (*fig*) accabler.
overpowering [əuvə'pauərɪŋ] *adj* irrésistible; (*heat, stench*) suffocant(e).
overproduction ['əuvəprə'dʌkʃən] *n* surproduction *f*.
overrate [əuvə'reɪt] *vt* surestimer.
overreact [əuvəriː'ækt] *vi* réagir de façon excessive.
override [əuvə'raɪd] *vt* (*irreg*: *like* **ride**) (*order, objection*) passer outre à; (*decision*) annuler.
overriding [əuvə'raɪdɪŋ] *adj* prépondérant(e).
overrule [əuvə'ruːl] *vt* (*decision*) annuler; (*claim*) rejeter.
overrun [əuvə'rʌn] *irreg vt* (*MIL*: *country etc*) occuper; (*time limit etc*) dépasser ♦ *vi* dépasser le temps imparti; **the town is ~ with tourists** la ville est envahie de touristes.
overseas [əuvə'siːz] *adv* outre-mer; (*abroad*) à l'étranger ♦ *adj* (*trade*) extérieur(e); (*visitor*) étranger(ère).
oversee [əuvə'siː] *vt irreg* surveiller.
overseer ['əuvəsɪə*] *n* (*in factory*) contremaître *m*.
overshadow [əuvə'ʃædəu] *vt* (*fig*) éclipser.
overshoot [əuvə'ʃuːt] *vt irreg* dépasser.
oversight ['əuvəsaɪt] *n* omission *f*, oubli *m*; **due to an ~** par suite d'une inadvertance.
oversimplify [əuvə'sɪmplɪfaɪ] *vt* simplifier à l'excès.
oversleep [əuvə'sliːp] *vi irreg* se réveiller (trop) tard.
overspend [əuvə'spɛnd] *vi irreg* dépenser de trop; **we have overspent by 5,000 dollars** nous avons dépassé notre budget de 5 000 dollars, nous avons dépensé 5 000 dollars de trop.
overspill ['əuvəspɪl] *n* excédent *m* de population.
overstaffed [əuvə'stɑːft] *adj*: **to be ~** avoir trop de personnel, être en surnombre.
overstate [əuvə'steɪt] *vt* exagérer.
overstatement [əuvə'steɪtmənt] *n* exagération *f*.
overstay [əuvə'steɪ] *vt*: **to ~ one's welcome (at sb's)** abuser de l'hospitalité de qn.
overstep [əuvə'stɛp] *vt*: **to ~ the mark** dépasser la mesure.
overstock [əuvə'stɔk] *vt* stocker en surabondance.
overstretched [əuvə'strɛtʃt] *adj* (*person*) débordé(e); **my budget is ~** j'ai atteint les limites de mon budget.
overstrike *n* ['əuvəstraɪk] (*on printer*) superposition *f*, double frappe *f* ♦ *vt irreg* [əuvə'straɪk] surimprimer.
overt [əu'vəːt] *adj* non dissimulé(e).
overtake [əuvə'teɪk] *vt irreg* dépasser; (*AUT*) dépasser, doubler.
overtaking [əuvə'teɪkɪŋ] *n* (*AUT*) dépassement *m*.
overtax [əuvə'tæks] *vt* (*ECON*) surimposer; (*fig: strength, patience*) abuser de; **to ~ o.s.** se surmener.
overthrow [əuvə'θrəu] *vt irreg* (*government*) renverser.
overtime ['əuvətaɪm] *n* heures *fpl* supplémentaires; **to do** *or* **work ~** faire des heures supplémentaires.

overtime ban *n* refus *m* de faire des heures supplémentaires.
overtone ['əuvətəun] *n* (*also*: ~**s**) note *f*, sous-entendus *mpl*.
overture ['əuvətʃuə*] *n* (*MUS, fig*) ouverture *f*.
overturn [əuvə'tə:n] *vt* renverser ♦ *vi* se retourner.
overview ['əuvəvju:] *n* vue *f* d'ensemble.
overweight [əuvə'weıt] *adj* (*person*) trop gros(se); (*luggage*) trop lourd(e).
overwhelm [əuvə'wɛlm] *vt* accabler; submerger; écraser.
overwhelming [əuvə'wɛlmıŋ] *adj* (*victory, defeat*) écrasant(e); (*desire*) irrésistible; **one's ~ impression is of heat** on a une impression dominante de chaleur.
overwhelmingly [əuvə'wɛlmıŋlı] *adv* (*vote*) en masse; (*win*) d'une manière écrasante.
overwork [əuvə'wə:k] *n* surmenage *m* ♦ *vt* surmener ♦ *vi* se surmener.
overwrite [əuvə'raıt] *vt irreg* (*COMPUT*) écraser.
overwrought [əuvə'rɔ:t] *adj* excédé(e).
ovulation [ɔvju'leıʃən] *n* ovulation *f*.
owe [əu] *vt* devoir; **to ~ sb sth, to ~ sth to sb** devoir qch à qn.
owing to ['əuıŋtu:] *prep* à cause de, en raison de.
owl [aul] *n* hibou *m*.
own [əun] *vt* posséder ♦ *vi* (*BRIT*): **to ~ to sth** reconnaître *or* avouer qch; **to ~ to having done sth** avouer avoir fait qch ♦ *adj* propre; **a room of my ~** une chambre à moi, ma propre chambre; **can I have it for my (very) ~?** puis-je l'avoir pour moi (tout) seul?; **to get one's ~ back** prendre sa revanche; **on one's ~** tout(e) seul(e); **to come into one's ~** trouver sa voie; trouver sa justification.
►**own up** *vi* avouer.
own brand *n* (*COMM*) marque *f* de distributeur.
owner ['əunə*] *n* propriétaire *m/f*.
owner-occupier ['əunər'ɔkjupaıə*] *n* propriétaire occupant.
ownership ['əunəʃıp] *n* possession *f*; **it's under new ~** (*shop etc*) il y a eu un changement de propriétaire.
own goal *n*: **he scored an ~** (*SPORT*) il a marqué un but contre son camp; (*fig*) cela s'est retourné contre lui.
ox, *pl* **oxen** [ɔks, 'ɔksn] *n* bœuf *m*.
Oxbridge ['ɔksbrıdʒ] *n* (*BRIT*) *voir encadré*.

> **OXBRIDGE**
>
> **Oxbridge**, *nom formé à partir des mots Ox(ford) et (Cam)bridge, s'utilise pour parler de ces deux universités comme formant un tout, dans la mesure où elles sont toutes deux les universités britanniques les plus prestigieuses et mondialement connues.*

Oxfam ['ɔksfæm] *n abbr* (*BRIT*: = *Oxford Committee for Famine Relief*) *association humanitaire*.
oxide ['ɔksaıd] *n* oxyde *m*.
Oxon. ['ɔksn] *abbr* (*BRIT*: = *Oxoniensis*) = *of Oxford*.
oxtail ['ɔksteıl] *n*: **~ soup** soupe *f* à la queue de bœuf.
oxygen ['ɔksıdʒən] *n* oxygène *m*.
oxygen mask *n* masque *m* à oxygène.
oxygen tent *n* tente *f* à oxygène.
oyster ['ɔıstə*] *n* huître *f*.
oz. *abbr* = **ounce**.
ozone ['əuzəun] *n* ozone *m*.

P p

P, p [pi:] *n* (*letter*) P, p *m*; **P for Peter** P comme Pierre.
P *abbr* = **president, prince**.
p *abbr* (= *page*) p; (*BRIT*) = **penny, pence**.
PA *n abbr* = **personal assistant, public address system** ♦ *abbr* (*US*) = *Pennsylvania*.
pa [pɑ:] *n* (*col*) papa *m*.
Pa. *abbr* (*US*) = *Pennsylvania*.
p.a. *abbr* = **per annum**.
PAC *n abbr* (*US*) = *political action committee*.
pace [peıs] *n* pas *m*; (*speed*) allure *f*; vitesse *f* ♦ *vi*: **to ~ up and down** faire les cent pas; **to keep ~ with** aller à la même vitesse que; (*events*) se tenir au courant de; **to set the ~** (*running*) donner l'allure; (*fig*) donner le ton; **to put sb through his ~s** (*fig*) mettre qn à l'épreuve.
pacemaker ['peısmeıkə*] *n* (*MED*) stimulateur *m* cardiaque.
pacific [pə'sıfık] *adj* pacifique ♦ *n*: **the P~ (Ocean)** le Pacifique, l'océan *m* Pacifique.
pacification [pæsıfı'keıʃən] *n* pacification *f*.
pacifier ['pæsıfaıə*] *n* (*US*: *dummy*) tétine *f*.
pacifist ['pæsıfıst] *n* pacifiste *m/f*.
pacify ['pæsıfaı] *vt* pacifier; (*soothe*) calmer.
pack [pæk] *n* paquet *m*; ballot *m*; (*of hounds*) meute *f*; (*of thieves, wolves etc*) bande *f*; (*of cards*) jeu *m* ♦ *vt* (*goods*) empaqueter, emballer; (*in suitcase etc*) emballer; (*box*) remplir; (*cram*) entasser; (*press down*) tasser; damer; (*COMPUT*) grouper, tasser ♦ *vi*: **to ~ (one's bags)** faire ses bagages; **to ~ into** (*room, stadium*) s'entasser dans; **to send sb ~ing** (*col*) envoyer promener qn.
►**pack in** (*BRIT col*) *vi* (*machine*) tomber en panne ♦ *vt* (*boyfriend*) plaquer; **~ it in!** laisse tomber!
►**pack off** *vt* (*person*) envoyer (promener),

expédier.
▸**pack up** *vi* (*BRIT col: machine*) tomber en panne; (*: person*) se tirer ♦ *vt* (*belongings*) ranger; (*goods, presents*) empaqueter, emballer.
package ['pækɪdʒ] *n* paquet *m*; (*of goods*) emballage *m*, conditionnement *m*; (*also*: ~ **deal**) marché global; forfait *m*; (*COMPUT*) progiciel *m* ♦ *vt* (*goods*) conditionner.
package holiday *n* (*BRIT*) vacances organisées.
package tour *n* voyage organisé.
packaging ['pækɪdʒɪŋ] *n* conditionnement *m*.
packed [pækt] *adj* (*crowded*) bondé(e); ~ **lunch** (*BRIT*) repas froid.
packer ['pækə*] *n* (*person*) emballeur/euse; conditionneur/euse.
packet ['pækɪt] *n* paquet *m*.
packet switching [-swɪtʃɪŋ] *n* (*COMPUT*) commutation *f* de paquets.
pack ice ['pækaɪs] *n* banquise *f*.
packing ['pækɪŋ] *n* emballage *m*.
packing case *n* caisse *f* (d'emballage).
pact [pækt] *n* pacte *m*, traité *m*.
pad [pæd] *n* bloc(-notes *m*) *m*; (*for inking*) tampon *m* encreur; (*col: flat*) piaule *f* ♦ *vt* rembourrer ♦ *vi*: **to** ~ **in/about** *etc* entrer/aller et venir *etc* à pas feutrés.
padded cell ['pædɪd-] *n* cellule capitonnée.
padding ['pædɪŋ] *n* rembourrage *m*; (*fig*) délayage *m*.
paddle ['pædl] *n* (*oar*) pagaie *f* ♦ *vi* barboter, faire trempette ♦ *vt*: **to** ~ **a canoe** *etc* pagayer.
paddle steamer *n* bateau *m* à aubes.
paddling pool ['pædlɪŋ-] *n* petit bassin.
paddock ['pædək] *n* enclos *m*; paddock *m*.
paddy ['pædɪ] *n* (*also*: ~ **field**) rizière *f*.
padlock ['pædlɔk] *n* cadenas *m* ♦ *vt* cadenasser.
padre ['pɑːdrɪ] *n* aumônier *m*.
paediatrician, (*US*) **pediatrician** [piːdɪə'trɪʃən] *n* pédiatre *m/f*.
paediatrics, (*US*) **pediatrics** [piːdɪ'ætrɪks] *n* pédiatrie *f*.
paedophile, (*US*) **pedophile** ['piːdəufaɪl] *n* pédophile *m*.
pagan ['peɪgən] *adj*, *n* païen(ne).
page [peɪdʒ] *n* (*of book*) page *f*; (*also*: ~ **boy**) groom *m*, chasseur *m*; (*at wedding*) garçon *m* d'honneur ♦ *vt* (*in hotel etc*) (faire) appeler.
pageant ['pædʒənt] *n* spectacle *m* historique; grande cérémonie.
pageantry ['pædʒəntrɪ] *n* apparat *m*, pompe *f*.
page break *n* fin *f or* saut *m* de page.
pager ['peɪdʒə*] *n* système *m* de téléappel, bip *m*.
paginate ['pædʒɪneɪt] *vt* paginer.
pagination [pædʒɪ'neɪʃən] *n* pagination *f*.
pagoda [pə'gəudə] *n* pagode *f*.
paid [peɪd] *pt*, *pp of* **pay** ♦ *adj* (*work, official*) rémunéré(e); **to put** ~ **to** (*BRIT*) mettre fin à, mettre par terre.
paid-up ['peɪdʌp], (*US*) **paid-in** ['peɪdɪn] *adj* (*member*) à jour de sa cotisation; (*shares*) libéré(e); ~ **capital** capital versé.
pail [peɪl] *n* seau *m*.
pain [peɪn] *n* douleur *f*; **to be in** ~ souffrir, avoir mal; **to have a** ~ **in** avoir mal à *or* une douleur à *or* dans; **to take** ~**s to do** se donner du mal pour faire; **on** ~ **of death** sous peine de mort.
pained ['peɪnd] *adj* peiné(e), chagrin(e).
painful ['peɪnful] *adj* douloureux(euse); (*difficult*) difficile, pénible.
painfully ['peɪnfəlɪ] *adv* (*fig: very*) terriblement.
painkiller ['peɪnkɪlə*] *n* calmant *m*.
painless ['peɪnlɪs] *adj* indolore.
painstaking ['peɪnzteɪkɪŋ] *adj* (*person*) soigneux(euse); (*work*) soigné(e).
paint [peɪnt] *n* peinture *f* ♦ *vt* peindre; (*fig*) dépeindre; **to** ~ **the door blue** peindre la porte en bleu; **to** ~ **in oils** faire de la peinture à l'huile.
paintbox ['peɪntbɔks] *n* boîte *f* de couleurs.
paintbrush ['peɪntbrʌʃ] *n* pinceau *m*.
painter ['peɪntə*] *n* peintre *m*.
painting ['peɪntɪŋ] *n* peinture *f*; (*picture*) tableau *m*.
paint-stripper ['peɪntstrɪpə*] *n* décapant *m*.
paintwork ['peɪntwəːk] *n* (*BRIT*) peintures *fpl*; (*: of car*) peinture *f*.
pair [pɛə*] *n* (*of shoes, gloves etc*) paire *f*; (*couple*) couple *m*; (*twosome*) duo *m*; ~ **of scissors** (paire de) ciseaux *mpl*; ~ **of trousers** pantalon *m*.
▸**pair off** *vi* se mettre par deux.
pajamas [pə'dʒɑːməz] *npl* (*US*) pyjama(s) *m(pl)*.
Pakistan [pɑːkɪ'stɑːn] *n* Pakistan *m*.
Pakistani [pɑːkɪ'stɑːnɪ] *adj* pakistanais(e) ♦ *n* Pakistanais/e.
PAL [pæl] *n abbr* (*TV*: = *phase alternation line*) PAL *m*.
pal [pæl] *n* (*col*) copain/copine.
palace ['pæləs] *n* palais *m*.
palatable ['pælɪtəbl] *adj* bon(bonne), agréable au goût.
palate ['pælɪt] *n* palais *m* (*ANAT*).
palatial [pə'leɪʃəl] *adj* grandiose, magnifique.
palaver [pə'lɑːvə*] *n* palabres *fpl or mpl*; histoire(s) *f(pl)*.
pale [peɪl] *adj* pâle ♦ *vi* pâlir ♦ *n*: **to be beyond the** ~ être au ban de la société; **to grow** *or* **turn** ~ (*person*) pâlir; ~ **blue** *adj* bleu pâle *inv*; **to** ~ **into insignificance (beside)** perdre beaucoup d'importance (par rapport à).
paleness ['peɪlnɪs] *n* pâleur *f*.
Palestine ['pælɪstaɪn] *n* Palestine *f*.
Palestinian [pælɪs'tɪnɪən] *adj* palestinien(ne) ♦ *n* Palestinien/ne.
palette ['pælɪt] *n* palette *f*.
paling ['peɪlɪŋ] *n* (*stake*) palis *m*; (*fence*) palissade *f*.

palisade [pælɪ'seɪd] *n* palissade *f.*
pall [pɔːl] *n* (*of smoke*) voile *m* ♦ *vi*: **to ~ (on)** devenir lassant (pour).
pallet ['pælɪt] *n* (*for goods*) palette *f.*
pallid ['pælɪd] *adj* blême.
pallor ['pælə*] *n* pâleur *f.*
pally ['pælɪ] *adj* (*col*) copain(copine).
palm [pɑːm] *n* (*ANAT*) paume *f*; (*also*: **~ tree**) palmier *m*; (*leaf, symbol*) palme *f* ♦ *vt*: **to ~ sth off on sb** (*col*) refiler qch à qn.
palmist ['pɑːmɪst] *n* chiromancien/ne.
Palm Sunday *n* le dimanche des Rameaux.
palpable ['pælpəbl] *adj* évident(e), manifeste.
palpitation [pælpɪ'teɪʃən] *n* palpitation *f.*
paltry ['pɔːltrɪ] *adj* dérisoire; piètre.
pamper ['pæmpə*] *vt* gâter, dorloter.
pamphlet ['pæmflət] *n* brochure *f*; (*political etc*) tract *m.*
pan [pæn] *n* (*also*: **sauce~**) casserole *f*; (*also*: **frying ~**) poêle *f*; (*of lavatory*) cuvette *f* ♦ *vi* (*CINE*) faire un panoramique ♦ *vt* (*col*: *book, film*) éreinter; **to ~ for gold** laver du sable aurifère.
panacea [pænə'sɪə] *n* panacée *f.*
Panama ['pænəmɑː] *n* Panama *m.*
Panama canal *n* canal *m* de Panama.
pancake ['pænkeɪk] *n* crêpe *f.*
Pancake Day *n* (*BRIT*) mardi gras.
pancake roll *n* rouleau *m* de printemps.
pancreas ['pæŋkrɪəs] *n* pancréas *m.*
panda ['pændə] *n* panda *m.*
panda car *n* (*BRIT*) ≈ voiture *f* pie *inv.*
pandemonium [pændɪ'məunɪəm] *n* tohu-bohu *m.*
pander ['pændə*] *vi*: **to ~ to** flatter bassement; obéir servilement à.
p&h *abbr* (*US: = postage and handling*) frais *mpl* de port.
P&L *abbr = profit and loss.*
p&p *abbr* (*BRIT: = postage and packing*) frais *mpl* de port.
pane [peɪn] *n* carreau *m* (de fenêtre).
panel ['pænl] *n* (*of wood, cloth etc*) panneau *m*; (*RADIO, TV*) panel *m*, invités *mpl*; (*of experts*) table ronde, comité *m.*
panel game *n* (*BRIT*) jeu *m* (radiophonique/télévisé).
panelling, (*US*) **paneling** ['pænəlɪŋ] *n* boiseries *fpl.*
panellist, (*US*) **panelist** ['pænəlɪst] *n* invité/e (*d'un panel*), membre d'un panel.
pang [pæŋ] *n*: **~s of remorse** pincements *mpl* de remords; **~s of hunger/conscience** tiraillements *mpl* d'estomac/de la conscience.
panhandler ['pænhændlə*] *n* (*US col*) mendiant/e.
panic ['pænɪk] *n* panique *f*, affolement *m* ♦ *vi* s'affoler, paniquer.
panic buying [-baɪɪŋ] *n* achats *mpl* de précaution.
panicky ['pænɪkɪ] *adj* (*person*) qui panique *or* s'affole facilement.
panic-stricken ['pænɪkstrɪkən] *adj* affolé(e).
pannier ['pænɪə*] *n* (*on animal*) bât *m*; (*on bicycle*) sacoche *f.*
panorama [pænə'rɑːmə] *n* panorama *m.*
panoramic [pænə'ræmɪk] *adj* panoramique.
pansy ['pænzɪ] *n* (*BOT*) pensée *f*; (*col*) pédé *m.*
pant [pænt] *vi* haleter.
pantechnicon [pæn'tɛknɪkən] *n* (*BRIT*) (grand) camion de déménagement.
panther ['pænθə*] *n* panthère *f.*
panties ['pæntɪz] *npl* slip *m*, culotte *f.*
pantihose ['pæntɪhəuz] *n* (*US*) collant *m.*
pantomime ['pæntəmaɪm] *n* (*BRIT*: *also*: **panto**) spectacle *m* de Noël; *voir encadré.*

PANTOMIME

*Une **pantomime** (à ne pas confondre avec le mot tel qu'on l'utilise en français), que l'on appelle également de façon familière "panto", est un genre de farce où le personnage principal est souvent un jeune garçon et où il y a toujours une "dame", c'est-à-dire une vieille femme jouée par un homme, et un méchant. La plupart du temps, l'histoire est basée sur un conte de fées comme Cendrillon ou Le Chat botté, et le public est encouragé à participer en prévenant le héros d'un danger imminent. Ce genre de spectacle, qui s'adresse surtout aux enfants, vise également un public d'adultes au travers des nombreuses plaisanteries faisant allusion à des faits d'actualité.*

pantry ['pæntrɪ] *n* garde-manger *m inv*; (*room*) office *m.*
pants [pænts] *n* (*BRIT*: *woman's*) culotte *f*, slip *m*; (*: man's*) slip, caleçon *m*; (*US*: *trousers*) pantalon *m.*
pantsuit ['pæntsuːt] *n* (*US*) tailleur-pantalon *m.*
papacy ['peɪpəsɪ] *n* papauté *f.*
papal ['peɪpəl] *adj* papal(e), pontifical(e).
paparazzi [pæpə'rætsiː] *npl* paparazzi *mpl.*
paper ['peɪpə*] *n* papier *m*; (*also*: **wall~**) papier peint; (*also*: **news~**) journal *m*; (*study, article*) article *m*; (*exam*) épreuve écrite ♦ *adj* en *or* de papier ♦ *vt* tapisser (de papier peint); **a piece of ~** (*odd bit*) un bout de papier; (*sheet*) une feuille de papier; **to put sth down on ~** mettre qch par écrit.
paper advance *n* (*on printer*) avance *f* (du) papier.
paperback ['peɪpəbæk] *n* livre *m* de poche; livre broché *or* non relié ♦ *adj*: **~ edition** édition brochée.
paper bag *n* sac *m* en papier.
paperboy ['peɪpəbɔɪ] *n* (*selling*) vendeur *m* de journaux; (*delivering*) livreur *m* de journaux.
paper clip *n* trombone *m.*
paper handkerchief *n* mouchoir *m* en papier.
paper mill *n* papeterie *f.*
paper money *n* papier-monnaie *m.*

paper profit *n* profit *m* théorique.
papers ['peɪpəz] *npl* (*also*: **identity** ~) papiers *mpl* (d'identité).
paper shop *n* (*BRIT*) marchand *m* de journaux.
paperweight ['peɪpəweɪt] *n* presse-papiers *m inv*.
paperwork ['peɪpəwə:k] *n* paperasserie *f*.
papier-mâché ['pæpɪeɪ'mæʃeɪ] *n* papier mâché.
paprika ['pæprɪkə] *n* paprika *m*.
Pap test, Pap smear ['pæp-] *n* (*MED*) frottis *m*.
par [pɑ:*] *n* pair *m*; (*GOLF*) normale *f* du parcours; **on a** ~ **with** à égalité avec, au même niveau que; **at** ~ au pair; **above/below** ~ au-dessus/au-dessous du pair; **to feel below** *or* **under** *or* **not up to** ~ ne pas se sentir en forme.
parable ['pærəbl] *n* parabole *f* (*REL*).
parabola [pə'ræbələ] *n* parabole *f* (*MATH*).
parachute ['pærəʃu:t] *n* parachute *m* ♦ *vi* sauter en parachute.
parachute jump *n* saut *m* en parachute.
parachutist ['pærəʃu:tɪst] *n* parachutiste *m/f*.
parade [pə'reɪd] *n* défilé *m*; (*inspection*) revue *f*; (*street*) boulevard *m* ♦ *vt* (*fig*) faire étalage de ♦ *vi* défiler; **a fashion** ~ (*BRIT*) un défilé de mode.
parade ground *n* terrain *m* de manœuvre.
paradise ['pærədaɪs] *n* paradis *m*.
paradox ['pærədɔks] *n* paradoxe *m*.
paradoxical [pærə'dɔksɪkl] *adj* paradoxal(e).
paradoxically [pærə'dɔksɪklɪ] *adv* paradoxalement.
paraffin ['pærəfɪn] *n* (*BRIT*): ~ **(oil)** pétrole (lampant); **liquid** ~ huile *f* de paraffine.
paraffin heater *n* (*BRIT*) poêle *m* à mazout.
paraffin lamp *n* (*BRIT*) lampe *f* à pétrole.
paragon ['pærəgən] *n* parangon *m*.
paragraph ['pærəgrɑ:f] *n* paragraphe *m*; **to begin a new** ~ aller à la ligne.
Paraguay ['pærəgwaɪ] *n* Paraguay *m*.
Paraguayan [pærə'gwaɪən] *adj* paraguayen(ne) ♦ *n* Paraguayen/ne.
parallel ['pærəlɛl] *adj*: ~ **(with** *or* **to)** parallèle (à); (*fig*) analogue (à) ♦ *n* (*line*) parallèle *f*; (*fig*, *GEO*) parallèle *m*.
paralysis, *pl* **paralyses** [pə'rælɪsɪs, -si:z] *n* paralysie *f*.
paralytic [pærə'lɪtɪk] *adj* paralytique; (*BRIT col*: *drunk*) ivre mort(e).
paralyze ['pærəlaɪz] *vt* paralyser.
paramedic [pærə'mɛdɪk] *n* auxiliaire *m/f* médical(e).
parameter [pə'ræmɪtə*] *n* paramètre *m*.
paramilitary [pærə'mɪlɪtərɪ] *adj* paramilitaire.
paramount ['pærəmaunt] *adj*: **of** ~ **importance** de la plus haute *or* grande importance.
paranoia [pærə'nɔɪə] *n* paranoïa *f*.
paranoid ['pærənɔɪd] *adj* (*PSYCH*) paranoïaque; (*neurotic*) paranoïde.
paranormal [pærə'nɔ:ml] *adj* paranormal(e).
paraphernalia [pærəfə'neɪlɪə] *n* attirail *m*, affaires *fpl*.
paraphrase ['pærəfreɪz] *vt* paraphraser.
paraplegic [pærə'pli:dʒɪk] *n* paraplégique *m/f*.
parapsychology [pærəsaɪ'kɔlədʒɪ] *n* parapsychologie *f*.
parasite ['pærəsaɪt] *n* parasite *m*.
parasol ['pærəsɔl] *n* ombrelle *f*; (*at café etc*) parasol *m*.
paratrooper ['pærətru:pə*] *n* parachutiste *m* (*soldat*).
parcel ['pɑ:sl] *n* paquet *m*, colis *m* ♦ *vt* (*also*: ~ **up**) empaqueter.
►**parcel out** *vt* répartir.
parcel bomb *n* (*BRIT*) colis piégé.
parcel post *n* service *m* de colis postaux.
parch [pɑ:tʃ] *vt* dessécher.
parched [pɑ:tʃt] *adj* (*person*) assoiffé(e).
parchment ['pɑ:tʃmənt] *n* parchemin *m*.
pardon ['pɑ:dn] *n* pardon *m*; grâce *f* ♦ *vt* pardonner à; (*LAW*) gracier; ~**!** pardon!; ~ **me!** excusez-moi!; **I beg your** ~**!** pardon!, je suis désolé!; **(I beg your)** ~**?**, (*US*) ~ **me?** pardon?
pare [pɛə*] *vt* (*BRIT*: *nails*) couper; (*fruit etc*) peler; (*fig*: *costs etc*) réduire.
parent ['pɛərənt] *n* père *m or* mère *f*; ~**s** *npl* parents *mpl*.
parentage ['pɛərəntɪdʒ] *n* naissance *f*; **of unknown** ~ de parents inconnus.
parental [pə'rɛntl] *adj* parental(e), des parents.
parent company *n* société *f* mère.
parenthesis, *pl* **parentheses** [pə'rɛnθɪsɪs, -si:z] *n* parenthèse *f*; **in parentheses** entre parenthèses.
parenthood ['pɛərənthud] *n* paternité *f or* maternité *f*.
parenting ['pɛərəntɪŋ] *n* le métier de parent, le travail d'un parent.
Paris ['pærɪs] *n* Paris.
parish ['pærɪʃ] *n* paroisse *f*; (*civil*) ≈ commune *f* ♦ *adj* paroissial(e).
parish council *n* (*BRIT*) ≈ conseil municipal.
parishioner [pə'rɪʃənə*] *n* paroissien/ne.
Parisian [pə'rɪzɪən] *adj* parisien(ne) ♦ *n* Parisien/ne.
parity ['pærɪtɪ] *n* parité *f*.
park [pɑ:k] *n* parc *m*, jardin public ♦ *vt* garer ♦ *vi* se garer.
parka ['pɑ:kə] *n* parka *m*.
parking ['pɑ:kɪŋ] *n* stationnement *m*; **"no ~"** "stationnement interdit".
parking lights *npl* feux *mpl* de stationnement.
parking lot *n* (*US*) parking *m*, parc *m* de stationnement.
parking meter *n* parc(o)mètre *m*.
parking offence, (*US*) **parking violation** *n* infraction *f* au stationnement.
parking place *n* place *f* de stationnement.
parking ticket *n* P.-V. *m*.
Parkinson's ['pɑ:kɪnsənz] *n* (*also*: ~ **disease**)

maladie *f* de Parkinson, parkinson *m*.
parkway ['pɑːkweɪ] *n* (*US*) route *f* express (*en site vert ou aménagé*).
parlance ['pɑːləns] *n*: **in common/modern ~** dans le langage courant/actuel.
parliament ['pɑːləmənt] *n* parlement *m*; *voir encadré*.

PARLIAMENT

Le **Parliament** *est l'assemblée législative britannique; elle est composée de deux chambres: la "House of Commons" et la "House of Lords". Ses bureaux sont les "Houses of Parliament" au palais de Westminster à Londres. Chaque Parliament est en général élu pour cinq ans. Les débats du Parliament sont maintenant retransmis à la télévision.*

parliamentary [pɑːlə'mɛntərɪ] *adj* parlementaire.
parlour, (*US*) **parlor** ['pɑːlə*] *n* salon *m*.
parlous ['pɑːləs] *adj* (*formal*) précaire.
Parmesan [pɑːmɪ'zæn] *n* (*also*: **~ cheese**) Parmesan *m*.
parochial [pə'rəukɪəl] *adj* paroissial(e); (*pej*) à l'esprit de clocher.
parody ['pærədɪ] *n* parodie *f*.
parole [pə'rəul] *n*: **on ~** en liberté conditionnelle.
paroxysm ['pærəksɪzəm] *n* (*MED, of grief*) paroxysme *m*; (*of anger*) accès *m*.
parquet ['pɑːkeɪ] *n*: **~ floor(ing)** parquet *m*.
parrot ['pærət] *n* perroquet *m*.
parrot fashion *adv* comme un perroquet.
parry ['pærɪ] *vt* esquiver, parer à.
parsimonious [pɑːsɪ'məunɪəs] *adj* parcimonieux(euse).
parsley ['pɑːslɪ] *n* persil *m*.
parsnip ['pɑːsnɪp] *n* panais *m*.
parson ['pɑːsn] *n* ecclésiastique *m*; (*Church of England*) pasteur *m*.
parsonage ['pɑːsnɪdʒ] *n* presbytère *m*.
part [pɑːt] *n* partie *f*; (*of machine*) pièce *f*; (*THEAT etc*) rôle *m*; (*MUS*) voix *f*; partie ♦ *adj* partiel(le) ♦ *adv* = **partly** ♦ *vt* séparer ♦ *vi* (*people*) se séparer; (*roads*) se diviser; **to take ~ in** participer à, prendre part à; **to take sb's ~** prendre le parti de qn, prendre parti pour qn; **on his ~** de sa part; **for my ~** en ce qui me concerne; **for the most ~** en grande partie; dans la plupart des cas; **for the better ~ of the day** pendant la plus grande partie de la journée; **to be ~ and parcel of** faire partie de; **to take sth in good/bad ~** prendre qch du bon/mauvais côté; **~ of speech** (*LING*) partie *f* du discours.
►**part with** *vt fus* se séparer de; se défaire de.
partake [pɑː'teɪk] *vi irreg* (*formal*): **to ~ of sth** prendre part à qch, partager qch.
part exchange *n* (*BRIT*): **in ~** en reprise.
partial ['pɑːʃl] *adj* partiel(le); (*unjust*) partial(e); **to be ~ to** aimer, avoir un faible pour.
partially ['pɑːʃəlɪ] *adv* en partie, partiellement; partialement.
participate [pɑː'tɪsɪpeɪt] *vi*: **to ~ (in)** participer (à), prendre part (à).
participation [pɑːtɪsɪ'peɪʃən] *n* participation *f*.
participle ['pɑːtɪsɪpl] *n* participe *m*.
particle ['pɑːtɪkl] *n* particule *f*.
particular [pə'tɪkjulə*] *adj* (*specific*) particulier(ière); (*special*) particulier, spécial(e); (*fussy*) difficile, exigeant(e); **~s** *npl* détails *mpl*; (*information*) renseignements *mpl*; **in ~** surtout, en particulier.
particularly [pə'tɪkjuləlɪ] *adv* particulièrement; (*in particular*) en particulier.
parting ['pɑːtɪŋ] *n* séparation *f*; (*BRIT: in hair*) raie *f* ♦ *adj* d'adieu; **his ~ shot was ...** il lança en partant ....
partisan [pɑːtɪ'zæn] *n* partisan/e ♦ *adj* partisan(e); de parti.
partition [pɑː'tɪʃən] *n* (*POL*) partition *f*, division *f*; (*wall*) cloison *f*.
partly ['pɑːtlɪ] *adv* en partie, partiellement.
partner ['pɑːtnə*] *n* (*COMM*) associé/e; (*SPORT*) partenaire *m/f*; (*at dance*) cavalier/ière ♦ *vt* être l'associé *or* le partenaire *or* le cavalier de.
partnership ['pɑːtnəʃɪp] *n* association *f*; **to go into ~ (with), form a ~ (with)** s'associer (avec).
part payment *n* acompte *m*.
partridge ['pɑːtrɪdʒ] *n* perdrix *f*.
part-time ['pɑːt'taɪm] *adj*, *adv* à mi-temps, à temps partiel.
part-timer [pɑːt'taɪmə*] *n* (*also*: **part-time worker**) travailleur/euse à temps partiel.
party ['pɑːtɪ] *n* (*POL*) parti *m*; (*team*) équipe *f*; groupe *m*; (*LAW*) partie *f*; (*celebration*) réception *f*; soirée *f*; réunion *f*, fête *f*; **dinner ~** dîner *m*; **to give** *or* **throw a ~** donner une réception; **we're having a ~ next Saturday** nous organisons une soirée *or* réunion entre amis samedi prochain; **it's for our son's birthday ~** c'est pour la fête (*or* le goûter) d'anniversaire de notre garçon; **to be a ~ to a crime** être impliqué(e) dans un crime.
party line *n* (*POL*) ligne *f* politique; (*TEL*) ligne partagée.
party piece *n* numéro habituel.
party political broadcast *n émission réservée à un parti politique*.
pass [pɑːs] *vt* (*time, object*) passer; (*place*) passer devant; (*car, friend*) croiser; (*exam*) être reçu(e) à, réussir; (*candidate*) admettre; (*overtake, surpass*) dépasser; (*approve*) approuver, accepter; (*law*) promulguer ♦ *vi* passer; (*SCOL*) être reçu(e) *or* admis(e), réussir ♦ *n* (*permit*) laissez-passer *m inv*; carte *f* d'accès *or* d'abonnement; (*in mountains*) col *m*; (*SPORT*) passe *f*; (*SCOL*: *also*: **~ mark**): **to get a ~** être reçu(e) (sans mention); **she**

could ~ for 25 on lui donnerait 25 ans; **to ~ sth through a ring** *etc* (faire) passer qch dans un anneau *etc*; **could you ~ the vegetables round?** pourriez-vous faire passer les légumes?; **things have come to a pretty ~** (*BRIT*) voilà où on en est!; **to make a ~ at sb** (*col*) faire des avances à qn.
►**pass away** *vi* mourir.
►**pass by** *vi* passer ♦ *vt* négliger.
►**pass down** *vt* (*customs, inheritance*) transmettre.
►**pass on** *vi* (*die*) s'éteindre, décéder ♦ *vt* (*hand on*): **to ~ on (to)** transmettre (à); (*: illness*) passer (à); (*: price rises*) répercuter (sur).
►**pass out** *vi* s'évanouir; (*BRIT MIL*) sortir (*d'une école militaire*).
►**pass over** *vt* (*ignore*) passer sous silence.
►**pass up** *vt* (*opportunity*) laisser passer.
passable ['pɑːsəbl] *adj* (*road*) praticable; (*work*) acceptable.
passage ['pæsɪdʒ] *n* (*also*: **~way**) couloir *m*; (*gen, in book*) passage *m*; (*by boat*) traversée *f*.
passenger ['pæsɪndʒə*] *n* passager/ère.
passer-by [pɑːsə'baɪ] *n* passant/e.
passing ['pɑːsɪŋ] *adj* (*fig*) passager(ère); **in ~** en passant.
passing place *n* (*AUT*) aire *f* de croisement.
passion ['pæʃən] *n* passion *f*; **to have a ~ for sth** avoir la passion de qch.
passionate ['pæʃənɪt] *adj* passionné(e).
passion fruit *n* fruit *m* de la passion.
passion play *n* mystère *m* de la Passion.
passive ['pæsɪv] *adj* (*also LING*) passif(ive).
passive smoking *n* tabagisme passif.
passkey ['pɑːskiː] *n* passe *m*.
Passover ['pɑːsəuvə*] *n* Pâque juive.
passport ['pɑːspɔːt] *n* passeport *m*.
passport control *n* contrôle *m* des passeports.
password ['pɑːswəːd] *n* mot *m* de passe.
past [pɑːst] *prep* (*further than*) au delà de, plus loin que; après; (*later than*) après ♦ *adj* passé(e); (*president etc*) ancien(ne) ♦ *n* passé *m*; **quarter/half ~ four** quatre heures et quart/demie; **ten/twenty ~ four** quatre heures dix/vingt; **he's ~ forty** il a dépassé la quarantaine, il a plus de *or* passé quarante ans; **it's ~ midnight** il est plus de minuit, il est passé minuit; **for the ~ few/3 days** depuis quelques/3 jours; ces derniers/3 derniers jours; **to run ~** passer en courant; **he ran ~ me** il m'a dépassé en courant; il a passé devant moi en courant; **in the ~** (*gen*) dans le temps, autrefois; (*LING*) au passé; **I'm ~ caring** je ne m'en fais plus; **to be ~ it** (*BRIT col*: *person*) avoir passé l'âge.
pasta ['pæstə] *n* pâtes *fpl*.
paste [peɪst] *n* (*glue*) colle *f* (de pâte); (*jewellery*) strass *m*; (*CULIN*) pâté *m* (à tartiner); pâte *f* ♦ *vt* coller; **tomato ~** concentré *m* de tomate, purée *f* de tomate.
pastel ['pæstl] *adj* pastel *inv*.
pasteurized ['pæstəraɪzd] *adj* pasteurisé(e).
pastille ['pæstl] *n* pastille *f*.
pastime ['pɑːstaɪm] *n* passe-temps *m inv*, distraction *f*.
past master *n* (*BRIT*): **to be a ~ at** être expert en.
pastor ['pɑːstə*] *n* pasteur *m*.
pastoral ['pɑːstərl] *adj* pastoral(e).
pastry ['peɪstrɪ] *n* pâte *f*; (*cake*) pâtisserie *f*.
pasture ['pɑːstʃə*] *n* pâturage *m*.
pasty *n* ['pæstɪ] petit pâté (en croûte) ♦ *adj* ['peɪstɪ] pâteux(euse); (*complexion*) terreux(euse).
pat [pæt] *vt* donner une petite tape à ♦ *n*: **a ~ of butter** une noisette de beurre; **to give sb/o.s. a ~ on the back** (*fig*) congratuler qn/se congratuler; **he knows it (off) ~**, (*US*) **he has it down ~** il sait cela sur le bout des doigts.
patch [pætʃ] *n* (*of material*) pièce *f*; (*spot*) tache *f*; (*of land*) parcelle *f* ♦ *vt* (*clothes*) rapiécer; **a bad ~** (*BRIT*) une période difficile.
►**patch up** *vt* réparer.
patchwork ['pætʃwəːk] *n* patchwork *m*.
patchy ['pætʃɪ] *adj* inégal(e).
pate [peɪt] *n*: **a bald ~** un crâne chauve *or* dégarni.
pâté ['pæteɪ] *n* pâté *m*, terrine *f*.
patent ['peɪtnt, (*US*) 'pætənt] *n* brevet *m* (d'invention) ♦ *vt* faire breveter ♦ *adj* patent(e), manifeste.
patent leather *n* cuir verni.
patently ['peɪtntlɪ] *adv* manifestement.
patent medicine *n* spécialité *f* pharmaceutique.
patent office *n* bureau *m* des brevets.
paternal [pə'təːnl] *adj* paternel(le).
paternity [pə'təːnɪtɪ] *n* paternité *f*.
paternity suit *n* (*LAW*) action *f* en recherche de paternité.
path [pɑːθ] *n* chemin *m*, sentier *m*; allée *f*; (*of planet*) course *f*; (*of missile*) trajectoire *f*.
pathetic [pə'θɛtɪk] *adj* (*pitiful*) pitoyable; (*very bad*) lamentable, minable; (*moving*) pathétique.
pathological [pæθə'lɔdʒɪkl] *adj* pathologique.
pathologist [pə'θɔlədʒɪst] *n* pathologiste *m/f*.
pathology [pə'θɔlədʒɪ] *n* pathologie *f*.
pathos ['peɪθɔs] *n* pathétique *m*.
pathway ['pɑːθweɪ] *n* chemin *m*, sentier *m*.
patience ['peɪʃns] *n* patience *f*; (*BRIT*: *CARDS*) réussite *f*; **to lose (one's) ~** perdre patience.
patient ['peɪʃnt] *n* patient/e; (*in hospital*) malade *m/f* ♦ *adj* patient(e).
patiently ['peɪʃntlɪ] *adv* patiemment.
patio ['pætɪəu] *n* patio *m*.
patriot ['peɪtrɪət] *n* patriote *m/f*.
patriotic [pætrɪ'ɔtɪk] *adj* patriotique; (*person*) patriote.
patriotism ['pætrɪətɪzəm] *n* patriotisme *m*.
patrol [pə'trəul] *n* patrouille *f* ♦ *vt* patrouiller

dans; **to be on ~** être de patrouille.
patrol boat *n* patrouilleur *m.*
patrol car *n* voiture *f* de police.
patrolman [pəˈtrəulmən] *n* (*US*) agent *m* de police.
patron [ˈpeɪtrən] *n* (*in shop*) client/e; (*of charity*) patron/ne; **~ of the arts** mécène *m.*
patronage [ˈpætrənɪdʒ] *n* patronage *m*, appui *m.*
patronize [ˈpætrənaɪz] *vt* être (un) client *or* un habitué de; (*fig*) traiter avec condescendance.
patronizing [ˈpætrənaɪzɪŋ] *adj* condescendant(e).
patron saint *n* saint(e) patron/ne.
patter [ˈpætə*] *n* crépitement *m*, tapotement *m*; (*sales talk*) boniment *m* ♦ *vi* crépiter, tapoter.
pattern [ˈpætən] *n* modèle *m*; (*SEWING*) patron *m*; (*design*) motif *m*; (*sample*) échantillon *m*; **behaviour ~** mode *m* de comportement.
patterned [ˈpætənd] *adj* à motifs.
paucity [ˈpɔːsɪtɪ] *n* pénurie *f*, carence *f.*
paunch [pɔːntʃ] *n* gros ventre, bedaine *f.*
pauper [ˈpɔːpə*] *n* indigent/e; **~'s grave** fosse commune.
pause [pɔːz] *n* pause *f*, arrêt *m*; (*MUS*) silence *m* ♦ *vi* faire une pause, s'arrêter; **to ~ for breath** reprendre son souffle; (*fig*) faire une pause.
pave [peɪv] *vt* paver, daller; **to ~ the way for** ouvrir la voie à.
pavement [ˈpeɪvmənt] *n* (*BRIT*) trottoir *m*; (*US*) chaussée *f.*
pavilion [pəˈvɪlɪən] *n* pavillon *m*; tente *f*; (*SPORT*) stand *m.*
paving [ˈpeɪvɪŋ] *n* pavage *m*, dallage *m.*
paving stone *n* pavé *m.*
paw [pɔː] *n* patte *f* ♦ *vt* donner un coup de patte à; (*subj: person: pej*) tripoter.
pawn [pɔːn] *n* gage *m*; (*CHESS, also fig*) pion *m* ♦ *vt* mettre en gage.
pawnbroker [ˈpɔːnbrəukə*] *n* prêteur *m* sur gages.
pawnshop [ˈpɔːnʃɔp] *n* mont-de-piété *m.*
pay [peɪ] *n* salaire *m*; (*of manual worker*) paie *f* ♦ *vb* (*pt, pp* **paid** [peɪd]) *vt* payer; (*be profitable to: also fig*) rapporter à ♦ *vi* payer; (*be profitable*) être rentable; **how much did you ~ for it?** combien l'avez-vous payé?, vous l'avez payé combien?; **I paid £5 for that record** j'ai payé ce disque 5 livres; **to ~ one's way** payer sa part; (*company*) couvrir ses frais; **to ~ dividends** (*fig*) porter ses fruits, s'avérer rentable; **it won't ~ you to do that** vous ne gagnerez rien à faire cela; **to ~ attention (to)** prêter attention (à).
►**pay back** *vt* rembourser.
►**pay in** *vt* verser.
►**pay off** *vt* (*debts*) régler, acquitter; (*creditor, mortgage*) rembourser; (*workers*) licencier ♦ *vi* (*plan, patience*) se révéler payant(e); **to ~ sth off in instalments** payer qch à tempérament.
►**pay out** *vt* (*money*) payer, sortir de sa poche; (*rope*) laisser filer.
►**pay up** *vt* (*debts*) régler; (*amount*) payer.
payable [ˈpeɪəbl] *adj* payable; **to make a cheque ~ to sb** établir un chèque à l'ordre de qn.
pay award *n* augmentation *f.*
pay day *n* jour *m* de paie.
PAYE *n abbr* (*BRIT*: = *pay as you earn*) *système de retenue des impôts à la source.*
payee [peɪˈiː] *n* bénéficiaire *m/f.*
pay envelope *n* (*US*) (enveloppe *f* de) paie *f.*
paying [ˈpeɪɪŋ] *adj* payant(e); **~ guest** hôte payant.
payload [ˈpeɪləud] *n* charge *f* utile.
payment [ˈpeɪmənt] *n* paiement *m*; (*of bill*) règlement *m*; (*of deposit, cheque*) versement *m*; **advance ~** (*part sum*) acompte *m*; (*total sum*) paiement anticipé; **deferred ~, ~ by instalments** paiement par versements échelonnés; **monthly ~** mensualité *f*; **in ~ for, in ~ of** en règlement de; **on ~ of £5** pour 5 livres.
pay packet *n* (*BRIT*) paie *f.*
payphone [ˈpeɪfəun] *n* cabine *f* téléphonique, téléphone public.
payroll [ˈpeɪrəul] *n* registre *m* du personnel; **to be on a firm's ~** être employé par une entreprise.
pay slip *n* (*BRIT*) bulletin *m* de paie, feuille *f* de paie.
pay station *n* (*US*) cabine *f* téléphonique.
PBS *n abbr* (*US*: = *Public Broadcasting Service*) *groupement d'aide à la réalisation d'émissions pour la TV publique.*
PC *n abbr* = **personal computer**; (*BRIT*) = **police constable** ♦ *adj abbr* = **politically correct** ♦ *abbr* (*BRIT*) = *Privy Councillor.*
pc *abbr* = **per cent, postcard.**
p/c *abbr* = **petty cash.**
PCB *n abbr* = **printed circuit board.**
PD *n abbr* (*US*) = **police department.**
pd *abbr* = **paid.**
PDSA *n abbr* (*BRIT*) = *People's Dispensary for Sick Animals.*
PDT *abbr* (*US*: = *Pacific Daylight Time*) *heure d'été du Pacifique.*
PE *n abbr* (= *physical education*) EPS *f* ♦ *abbr* (*Canada*) = *Prince Edward Island.*
pea [piː] *n* (petit) pois.
peace [piːs] *n* paix *f*; (*calm*) calme *m*, tranquillité *f*; **to be at ~ with sb/sth** être en paix avec qn/qch; **to keep the ~** (*subj: policeman*) assurer le maintien de l'ordre; (*: citizen*) ne pas troubler l'ordre.
peaceable [ˈpiːsəbl] *adj* paisible, pacifique.
peaceful [ˈpiːsful] *adj* paisible, calme.
peacekeeper [ˈpiːskiːpə*] *n* (*force*) force gardienne de la paix.
peacekeeping [ˈpiːskiːpɪŋ] *n* maintien *m* de la

paix.
peacekeeping force *n* forces *fpl* qui assurent le maintien de la paix.
peace offering *n* gage *m* de réconciliation; (*humorous*) gage de paix.
peach [pi:tʃ] *n* pêche *f*.
peacock ['pi:kɔk] *n* paon *m*.
peak [pi:k] *n* (*mountain*) pic *m*, cime *f*; (*fig: highest level*) maximum *m*; (*: of career, fame*) apogée *m*.
peak-hour ['pi:kauə*] *adj* (*traffic etc*) de pointe.
peak hours *npl* heures *fpl* d'affluence.
peak period *n* période *f* de pointe.
peak rate *n* plein tarif.
peaky ['pi:kɪ] *adj* (*BRIT col*) fatigué(e).
peal [pi:l] *n* (*of bells*) carillon *m*; **~s of laughter** éclats *mpl* de rire.
peanut ['pi:nʌt] *n* arachide *f*, cacahuète *f*.
peanut butter *n* beurre *m* de cacahuète.
pear [pɛə*] *n* poire *f*.
pearl [pə:l] *n* perle *f*.
peasant ['pɛznt] *n* paysan/ne.
peat [pi:t] *n* tourbe *f*.
pebble ['pɛbl] *n* galet *m*, caillou *m*.
peck [pɛk] *vt* (*also*: **~ at**) donner un coup de bec à; (*food*) picorer ♦ *n* coup *m* de bec; (*kiss*) bécot *m*.
pecking order ['pɛkɪŋ-] *n* ordre *m* hiérarchique.
peckish ['pɛkɪʃ] *adj* (*BRIT col*): **I feel ~** je mangerais bien quelque chose, j'ai la dent.
peculiar [pɪ'kju:lɪə*] *adj* (*odd*) étrange, bizarre, curieux(euse); (*particular*) particulier(ière); **~ to** particulier à.
peculiarity [pɪkju:lɪ'ærɪtɪ] *n* bizarrerie *f*, particularité *f*.
pecuniary [pɪ'kju:nɪərɪ] *adj* pécuniaire.
pedal ['pɛdl] *n* pédale *f* ♦ *vi* pédaler.
pedal bin *n* (*BRIT*) poubelle *f* à pédale.
pedantic [pɪ'dæntɪk] *adj* pédant(e).
peddle ['pɛdl] *vt* colporter; (*drugs*) faire le trafic de.
peddler ['pɛdlə*] *n* colporteur *m*; camelot *m*.
pedestal ['pɛdəstl] *n* piédestal *m*.
pedestrian [pɪ'dɛstrɪən] *n* piéton *m* ♦ *adj* piétonnier(ière); (*fig*) prosaïque, terre à terre *inv*.
pedestrian crossing *n* (*BRIT*) passage clouté.
pedestrian precinct *n* (*BRIT*) zone piétonne.
pediatrics [pi:dɪ'ætrɪks] *n* (*US*) = **paediatrics**.
pedigree ['pɛdɪgri:] *n* ascendance *f*; (*of animal*) pedigree *m* ♦ *cpd* (*animal*) de race.
pedlar ['pɛdlə*] *n* = **peddler**.
pee [pi:] *vi* (*col*) faire pipi, pisser.
peek [pi:k] *vi* jeter un coup d'œil (furtif).
peel [pi:l] *n* pelure *f*, épluchure *f*; (*of orange, lemon*) écorce *f* ♦ *vt* peler, éplucher ♦ *vi* (*paint etc*) s'écailler; (*wallpaper*) se décoller.
►**peel back** *vt* décoller.
peeler ['pi:lə*] *n* (*potato etc ~*) éplucheur *m*.
peelings ['pi:lɪŋz] *npl* pelures *fpl*, épluchures *fpl*.
peep [pi:p] *n* (*BRIT: look*) coup d'œil furtif; (*sound*) pépiement *m* ♦ *vi* (*BRIT*) jeter un coup d'œil (furtif).
►**peep out** *vi* (*BRIT*) se montrer (furtivement).
peephole ['pi:phəul] *n* judas *m*.
peer [pɪə*] *vi*: **to ~ at** regarder attentivement, scruter ♦ *n* (*noble*) pair *m*; (*equal*) pair, égal/e.
peerage ['pɪərɪdʒ] *n* pairie *f*.
peerless ['pɪəlɪs] *adj* incomparable, sans égal.
peeved [pi:vd] *adj* irrité(e), ennuyé(e).
peevish ['pi:vɪʃ] *adj* grincheux(euse), maussade.
peg [pɛg] *n* cheville *f*; (*for coat etc*) patère *f*; (*BRIT: also*: **clothes ~**) pince *f* à linge ♦ *vt* (*clothes*) accrocher; (*BRIT: groundsheet*) fixer (avec des piquets); (*fig: prices, wages*) contrôler, stabiliser.
pejorative [pɪ'dʒɔrətɪv] *adj* péjoratif(ive).
Pekin [pi:'kɪn] *n*, **Peking** [pi:'kɪŋ] *n* Pékin.
pekingese [pi:kɪ'ni:z] *n* pékinois *m*.
pelican ['pɛlɪkən] *n* pélican *m*.
pelican crossing *n* (*BRIT AUT*) feu *m* à commande manuelle.
pellet ['pɛlɪt] *n* boulette *f*; (*of lead*) plomb *m*.
pell-mell ['pɛl'mɛl] *adv* pêle-mêle.
pelmet ['pɛlmɪt] *n* cantonnière *f*; lambrequin *m*.
pelt [pɛlt] *vt*: **to ~ sb (with)** bombarder qn (de) ♦ *vi* (*rain*) tomber à seaux ♦ *n* peau *f*.
pelvis ['pɛlvɪs] *n* bassin *m*.
pen [pɛn] *n* (*for writing*) stylo *m*; (*for sheep*) parc *m*; (*US col: prison*) taule *f*; **to put ~ to paper** prendre la plume.
penal ['pi:nl] *adj* pénal(e).
penalize ['pi:nəlaɪz] *vt* pénaliser; (*fig*) désavantager.
penal servitude [-'sə:vɪtju:d] *n* travaux forcés.
penalty ['pɛnltɪ] *n* pénalité *f*, sanction *f*, (*fine*) amende *f*; (*SPORT*) pénalisation *f*; (*FOOTBALL: also*: **~ kick**) penalty *m*.
penalty area *n* (*BRIT SPORT*) surface *f* de réparation.
penalty clause *n* clause pénale.
penalty kick *n* (*FOOTBALL*) penalty *m*.
penalty shoot-out [-'ʃu:taut] *n* (*FOOTBALL*) épreuve *f* des penalties.
penance ['pɛnəns] *n* pénitence *f*.
pence [pɛns] *npl* (*BRIT*) *see* **penny**.
penchant ['pã:ʃã:ŋ] *n* penchant *m*.
pencil ['pɛnsl] *n* crayon *m* ♦ *vt*: **to ~ sth in** noter qch provisoirement.
pencil case *n* trousse *f* (d'écolier).
pencil sharpener *n* taille-crayon(s) *m inv*.
pendant ['pɛndnt] *n* pendentif *m*.
pending ['pɛndɪŋ] *prep* en attendant ♦ *adj* en suspens.
pendulum ['pɛndjuləm] *n* pendule *m*; (*of clock*) balancier *m*.
penetrate ['pɛnɪtreɪt] *vt* pénétrer dans; péné-

trer.
penetrating ['pɛnɪtreɪtɪŋ] *adj* pénétrant(e).
penetration [pɛnɪ'treɪʃən] *n* pénétration *f*.
penfriend ['pɛnfrɛnd] *n* (*BRIT*) correspondant/e.
penguin ['pɛŋgwɪn] *n* pingouin *m*.
penicillin [pɛnɪ'sɪlɪn] *n* pénicilline *f*.
peninsula [pə'nɪnsjulə] *n* péninsule *f*.
penis ['pi:nɪs] *n* pénis *m*, verge *f*.
penitence ['pɛnɪtns] *n* repentir *m*.
penitent ['pɛnɪtnt] *adj* repentant(e).
penitentiary [pɛnɪ'tɛnʃərɪ] *n* (*US*) prison *f*.
penknife ['pɛnnaɪf] *n* canif *m*.
Penn(a). *abbr* (*US*) = *Pennsylvania*.
pen name *n* nom *m* de plume, pseudonyme *m*.
pennant ['pɛnənt] *n* flamme *f*, banderole *f*.
penniless ['pɛnɪlɪs] *adj* sans le sou.
Pennines ['pɛnaɪnz] *npl*: **the** ~ les Pennines *fpl*.
penny, *pl* **pennies** *or* **pence** (*BRIT*) ['pɛnɪ, 'pɛnɪz, pɛns] *n* penny *m* (*pl* pennies) (*new: 100 in a pound; old: 12 in a shilling; on tend à employer "pennies" ou "two-pence piece" etc pour les pièces, "pence" pour la valeur*).
penpal ['pɛnpæl] *n* correspondant/e.
penpusher ['pɛnpuʃɛ*] *n* (*pej*) gratte-papier *m inv*.
pension ['pɛnʃən] *n* retraite *f*; (*MIL*) pension *f*.
►**pension off** *vt* mettre à la retraite.
pensionable ['pɛnʃnəbl] *adj* qui a droit à une retraite.
pensioner ['pɛnʃənə*] *n* (*BRIT*) retraité/e.
pension fund *n* caisse *f* de retraite.
pensive ['pɛnsɪv] *adj* pensif(ive).
pentagon ['pɛntəgən] *n* pentagone *m*; **the P~** (*US POL*) le Pentagone; *voir encadré*.

> **PENTAGON**
>
> *Le* **Pentagon** *est le nom donné aux bureaux du ministère de la Défense américain, situés à Arlington en Virginie, à cause de la forme pentagonale du bâtiment dans lequel ils se trouvent. Par extension, ce terme est également utilisé en parlant du ministère lui-même.*

Pentecost ['pɛntɪkɔst] *n* Pentecôte *f*.
penthouse ['pɛnthaus] *n* appartement *m* (de luxe) en attique.
pent-up ['pɛntʌp] *adj* (*feelings*) refoulé(e).
penultimate [pɪ'nʌltɪmət] *adj* pénultième, avant-dernier(ière).
penury ['pɛnjurɪ] *n* misère *f*.
people ['pi:pl] *npl* gens *mpl*; personnes *fpl*; (*citizens*) peuple *m* ♦ *n* (*nation, race*) peuple *m* ♦ *vt* peupler; **I know ~ who ...** je connais des gens qui ...; **the room was full of ~** la salle était pleine de monde *or* de gens; **~ say that ...** on dit *or* les gens disent que ...; **old ~** les personnes âgées; **young ~** les jeunes; **a man of the ~** un homme du peuple.
PEP [pɛp] *n* (= *personal equity plan*) ≈ CEA *m* (= *compte d'épargne en actions*)
pep [pɛp] *n* (*col*) entrain *m*, dynamisme *m*.
►**pep up** *vt* (*col*) remonter.
pepper ['pɛpə*] *n* poivre *m*; (*vegetable*) poivron *m* ♦ *vt* poivrer.
peppermint ['pɛpəmɪnt] *n* (*plant*) menthe poivrée; (*sweet*) pastille *f* de menthe.
pepperoni [pɛpə'rəunɪ] *n* *saucisson sec de porc et de bœuf très poivré*.
pepperpot ['pɛpəpɔt] *n* poivrière *f*.
peptalk ['pɛptɔ:k] *n* (*col*) (petit) discours d'encouragement.
per [pə:*] *prep* par; ~ **hour** (*miles etc*) à l'heure; (*fee*) (de) l'heure; ~ **kilo** *etc* le kilo *etc*; ~ **day** par jour; **as ~ your instructions** conformément à vos instructions.
per annum *adv* par an.
per capita *adj, adv* par habitant, par personne.
perceive [pə'si:v] *vt* percevoir; (*notice*) remarquer, s'apercevoir de.
per cent *adv* pour cent; **a 20 ~ discount** une réduction de 20 pour cent.
percentage [pə'sɛntɪdʒ] *n* pourcentage *m*; **on a ~ basis** au pourcentage.
percentage point *n*: **ten ~s** dix pour cent.
perceptible [pə'sɛptɪbl] *adj* perceptible.
perception [pə'sɛpʃən] *n* perception *f*; (*insight*) sensibilité *f*.
perceptive [pə'sɛptɪv] *adj* (*remark, person*) perspicace.
perch [pə:tʃ] *n* (*fish*) perche *f*; (*for bird*) perchoir *m* ♦ *vi* (se) percher.
percolate ['pə:kəleɪt] *vt, vi* passer.
percolator ['pə:kəleɪtə*] *n* percolateur *m*; cafetière *f* électrique.
percussion [pə'kʌʃən] *n* percussion *f*.
peremptory [pə'rɛmptərɪ] *adj* péremptoire.
perennial [pə'rɛnɪəl] *adj* perpétuel(le); (*BOT*) vivace ♦ *n* plante *f* vivace.
perfect *adj, n* ['pə:fɪkt] *adj* parfait(e) ♦ *n* (*also*: ~ **tense**) parfait *m* ♦ *vt* [pə'fɛkt] parfaire; mettre au point; **he's a ~ stranger to me** il m'est totalement inconnu.
perfection [pə'fɛkʃən] *n* perfection *f*.
perfectionist [pə'fɛkʃənɪst] *n* perfectionniste *m/f*.
perfectly ['pə:fɪktlɪ] *adv* parfaitement; **I'm ~ happy with the situation** cette situation me convient parfaitement; **you know ~ well** vous le savez très bien.
perforate ['pə:fəreɪt] *vt* perforer, percer.
perforated ulcer ['pə:fəreɪtɪd-] *n* (*MED*) ulcère perforé.
perforation [pə:fə'reɪʃən] *n* perforation *f*; (*line of holes*) pointillé *m*.
perform [pə'fɔ:m] *vt* (*carry out*) exécuter, remplir; (*concert etc*) jouer, donner ♦ *vi* jouer.
performance [pə'fɔ:məns] *n* représentation *f*, spectacle *m*; (*of an artist*) interprétation *f*; (*of player etc*) prestation *f*; (*of car, engine*) performance *f*; **the team put up a good ~**

l'équipe a bien joué.
performer [pə'fɔːmə*] *n* artiste *m/f*.
performing [pə'fɔːmɪŋ] *adj* (*animal*) savant(e).
performing arts *npl*: **the ~** les arts *mpl* du spectacle.
perfume ['pəːfjuːm] *n* parfum *m* ♦ *vt* parfumer.
perfunctory [pə'fʌŋktərɪ] *adj* négligent(e), pour la forme.
perhaps [pə'hæps] *adv* peut-être; **~ he'll ...** peut-être qu'il ...; **~ so/not** peut-être que oui/que non.
peril ['pɛrɪl] *n* péril *m*.
perilous ['pɛrɪləs] *adj* périlleux(euse).
perilously ['pɛrɪləslɪ] *adv*: **they came ~ close to being caught** ils ont été à deux doigts de se faire prendre.
perimeter [pə'rɪmɪtə*] *n* périmètre *m*.
perimeter wall *n* mur *m* d'enceinte.
period ['pɪərɪəd] *n* période *f*; (*HISTORY*) époque *f*; (*SCOL*) cours *m*; (*full stop*) point *m*; (*MED*) règles *fpl* ♦ *adj* (*costume, furniture*) d'époque; **for a ~ of three weeks** pour (une période de) trois semaines; **the holiday ~** (*BRIT*) la période des vacances.
periodic [pɪərɪ'ɔdɪk] *adj* périodique.
periodical [pɪərɪ'ɔdɪkl] *adj* périodique ♦ *n* périodique *m*.
periodically [pɪərɪ'ɔdɪklɪ] *adv* périodiquement.
period pains *npl* (*BRIT*) douleurs menstruelles.
peripatetic [pɛrɪpə'tɛtɪk] *adj* (*salesman*) ambulant(e); (*BRIT*: *teacher*) qui travaille dans plusieurs établissements.
peripheral [pə'rɪfərəl] *adj* périphérique ♦ *n* (*COMPUT*) périphérique *m*.
periphery [pə'rɪfərɪ] *n* périphérie *f*.
periscope ['pɛrɪskəup] *n* périscope *m*.
perish ['pɛrɪʃ] *vi* périr, mourir; (*decay*) se détériorer.
perishable ['pɛrɪʃəbl] *adj* périssable.
perishables ['pɛrɪʃəblz] *npl* denrées *fpl* périssables.
perishing ['pɛrɪʃɪŋ] *adj* (*BRIT col*: *cold*) glacial(e).
peritonitis [pɛrɪtə'naɪtɪs] *n* péritonite *f*.
perjure ['pəːdʒə*] *vt*: **to ~ o.s.** se parjurer.
perjury ['pəːdʒərɪ] *n* (*LAW*: *in court*) faux témoignage; (*breach of oath*) parjure *m*.
perk [pəːk] *n* (*col*) avantage *m*, à-côté *m*.
►**perk up** *vi* (*col*: *cheer up*) se ragaillardir.
perky ['pəːkɪ] *adj* (*cheerful*) guilleret(te), gai(e).
perm [pəːm] *n* (*for hair*) permanente *f* ♦ *vt*: **to have one's hair ~ed** se faire faire une permanente.
permanence ['pəːmənəns] *n* permanence *f*.
permanent ['pəːmənənt] *adj* permanent(e); (*job, position*) permanent(e), fixe; (*dye, ink*) indélébile; **I'm not ~ here** je ne suis pas ici à titre définitif; **~ address** adresse habituelle.
permanently ['pəːmənəntlɪ] *adv* de façon permanente.
permeable ['pəːmɪəbl] *adj* perméable.
permeate ['pəːmɪeɪt] *vi* s'infiltrer ♦ *vt* s'infiltrer dans; pénétrer.
permissible [pə'mɪsɪbl] *adj* permis(e), acceptable.
permission [pə'mɪʃən] *n* permission *f*, autorisation *f*; **to give sb ~ to do sth** donner à qn la permission de faire qch.
permissive [pə'mɪsɪv] *adj* tolérant(e); **the ~ society** la société de tolérance.
permit *n* ['pəːmɪt] permis *m*; (*entrance pass*) autorisation *f*, laisser-passer *m*; (*for goods*) licence *f* ♦ *vt* [pə'mɪt] permettre; **to ~ sb to do** autoriser qn à faire, permettre à qn de faire; **weather ~ting** si le temps le permet.
permutation [pəːmju'teɪʃən] *n* permutation *f*.
pernicious [pəː'nɪʃəs] *adj* pernicieux(euse), nocif(ive).
pernickety [pə'nɪkɪtɪ] *adj* (*col*) pointilleux(euse), tatillon(ne); (*task*) minutieux(euse).
perpendicular [pəːpən'dɪkjulə*] *adj, n* perpendiculaire (*f*).
perpetrate ['pəːpɪtreɪt] *vt* perpétrer, commettre.
perpetual [pə'pɛtjuəl] *adj* perpétuel(le).
perpetuate [pə'pɛtjueɪt] *vt* perpétuer.
perpetuity [pəːpɪ'tjuːɪtɪ] *n*: **in ~** à perpétuité.
perplex [pə'plɛks] *vt* rendre perplexe; (*complicate*) embrouiller.
perplexing [pəː'plɛksɪŋ] *adj* embarrassant(e).
perquisites ['pəːkwɪzɪts] *npl* (*also*: **perks**) avantages *mpl* annexes.
persecute ['pəːsɪkjuːt] *vt* persécuter.
persecution [pəːsɪ'kjuːʃən] *n* persécution *f*.
perseverance [pəːsɪ'vɪərns] *n* persévérance *f*, ténacité *f*.
persevere [pəːsɪ'vɪə*] *vi* persévérer.
Persia ['pəːʃə] *n* Perse *f*.
Persian ['pəːʃən] *adj* persan(e) ♦ *n* (*LING*) persan *m*; **the (~) Gulf** le golfe Persique.
Persian cat *n* chat persan.
persist [pə'sɪst] *vi*: **to ~ (in doing)** persister (à faire), s'obstiner (à faire).
persistence [pə'sɪstəns] *n* persistance *f*, obstination *f*; opiniâtreté *f*.
persistent [pə'sɪstənt] *adj* persistant(e), tenace; (*lateness, rain*) persistant; **~ offender** (*LAW*) multirécidiviste *m/f*.
persnickety [pə'snɪkɪtɪ] *adj* (*US col*) = **pernickety**.
person ['pəːsn] *n* personne *f*; **in ~** en personne; **on** *or* **about one's ~** sur soi; **~ to ~ call** (*TEL*) appel *m* avec préavis.
personable ['pəːsnəbl] *adj* de belle prestance, au physique attrayant.
personal ['pəːsnl] *adj* personnel(le); **~ belongings, ~ effects** effets personnels; **~ hygiene** hygiène *f* intime; **a ~ interview** un entretien.
personal allowance *n* (*TAX*) part *f* du revenu

non imposable.
personal assistant (PA) *n* secrétaire personnel(le).
personal call *n* (*TEL*) communication *f* avec préavis.
personal column *n* annonces personnelles.
personal computer (PC) *n* ordinateur individuel, PC *m*.
personal details *npl* (*on form etc*) coordonnées *fpl*.
personal identification number (PIN) *n* (*COMPUT, BANKING*) numéro *m* d'identification personnel.
personality [pəːsəˈnælɪtɪ] *n* personnalité *f*.
personally [ˈpəːsnəlɪ] *adv* personnellement.
personal organizer *n* agenda (personnel) (*style Filofax*); (*electronic*) agenda électronique.
personal property *n* biens personnels.
Personal, Social and Health Education *n* (*BRIT SCOL*) ≈ éducation *f* civique.
personal stereo *n* walkman *m* ®, baladeur *m*.
personify [pəːˈsɔnɪfaɪ] *vt* personnifier.
personnel [pəːsəˈnɛl] *n* personnel *m*.
personnel department *n* service *m* du personnel.
personnel manager *n* chef *m* du personnel.
perspective [pəˈspɛktɪv] *n* perspective *f*; **to get sth into** ~ ramener qch à sa juste mesure.
perspex [ˈpəːspɛks] *n* ® (*BRIT*) Plexiglas *m* ®.
perspicacity [pəːspɪˈkæsɪtɪ] *n* perspicacité *f*.
perspiration [pəːspɪˈreɪʃən] *n* transpiration *f*.
perspire [pəˈspaɪə*] *vi* transpirer.
persuade [pəˈsweɪd] *vt*: **to ~ sb to do sth** persuader qn de faire qch, amener *or* décider qn à faire qch; **to ~ sb of sth/that** persuader qn de qch/que.
persuasion [pəˈsweɪʒən] *n* persuasion *f*; (*creed*) conviction *f*.
persuasive [pəˈsweɪsɪv] *adj* persuasif(ive).
pert [pəːt] *adj* coquin(e), mutin(e).
pertaining [pəːˈteɪnɪŋ]: **~ to** *prep* relatif(ive) à.
pertinent [ˈpəːtɪnənt] *adj* pertinent(e).
perturb [pəˈtəːb] *vt* troubler, inquiéter.
perturbing [pəˈtəːbɪŋ] *adj* troublant(e).
Peru [pəˈruː] *n* Pérou *m*.
perusal [pəˈruːzl] *n* lecture (attentive).
Peruvian [pəˈruːvjən] *adj* péruvien(ne) ♦ *n* Péruvien/ne.
pervade [pəˈveɪd] *vt* se répandre dans, envahir.
pervasive [pəˈveɪsɪv] *adj* (*smell*) pénétrant(e); (*influence*) insidieux(euse); (*gloom, ideas*) diffus(e).
perverse [pəˈvəːs] *adj* pervers(e); (*stubborn*) entêté(e), contrariant(e).
perversion [pəˈvəːʃən] *n* perversion *f*.
perversity [pəˈvəːsɪtɪ] *n* perversité *f*.
pervert *n* [ˈpəːvəːt] perverti/e ♦ *vt* [pəˈvəːt] pervertir.
pessimism [ˈpɛsɪmɪzəm] *n* pessimisme *m*.
pessimist [ˈpɛsɪmɪst] *n* pessimiste *m/f*.
pessimistic [pɛsɪˈmɪstɪk] *adj* pessimiste.
pest [pɛst] *n* animal *m* (*or* insecte *m*) nuisible; (*fig*) fléau *m*.
pest control *n* lutte *f* contre les nuisibles.
pester [ˈpɛstə*] *vt* importuner, harceler.
pesticide [ˈpɛstɪsaɪd] *n* pesticide *m*.
pestilence [ˈpɛstɪləns] *n* peste *f*.
pestle [ˈpɛsl] *n* pilon *m*.
pet [pɛt] *n* animal familier; (*favourite*) chouchou *m* ♦ *vt* choyer ♦ *vi* (*col*) se peloter; ~ **lion** *etc* lion *etc* apprivoisé.
petal [ˈpɛtl] *n* pétale *m*.
peter [ˈpiːtə*]: **to ~ out** *vi* s'épuiser; s'affaiblir.
petite [pəˈtiːt] *adj* menu(e).
petition [pəˈtɪʃən] *n* pétition *f* ♦ *vt* adresser une pétition à ♦ *vi*: **to ~ for divorce** demander le divorce.
pet name *n* (*BRIT*) petit nom.
petrified [ˈpɛtrɪfaɪd] *adj* (*fig*) mort(e) de peur.
petrify [ˈpɛtrɪfaɪ] *vt* pétrifier.
petrochemical [pɛtrəˈkɛmɪkl] *adj* pétrochimique.
petrodollars [ˈpɛtrəudɔləz] *npl* pétrodollars *mpl*.
petrol [ˈpɛtrəl] *n* (*BRIT*) essence *f*.
petrol bomb *n* cocktail *m* Molotov.
petrol can *n* (*BRIT*) bidon *m* à essence.
petrol engine *n* (*BRIT*) moteur *m* à essence.
petroleum [pəˈtrəulɪəm] *n* pétrole *m*.
petroleum jelly *n* vaseline *f*.
petrol pump *n* (*BRIT: in car, at garage*) pompe *f* à essence.
petrol station *n* (*BRIT*) station-service *f*.
petrol tank *n* (*BRIT*) réservoir *m* d'essence.
petticoat [ˈpɛtɪkəut] *n* jupon *m*.
pettifogging [ˈpɛtɪfɔgɪŋ] *adj* chicanier(ière).
pettiness [ˈpɛtɪnɪs] *n* mesquinerie *f*.
petty [ˈpɛtɪ] *adj* (*mean*) mesquin(e); (*unimportant*) insignifiant(e), sans importance.
petty cash *n* caisse *f* des dépenses courantes, petite caisse.
petty officer *n* second-maître *m*.
petulant [ˈpɛtjulənt] *adj* irritable.
pew [pjuː] *n* banc *m* (d'église).
pewter [ˈpjuːtə*] *n* étain *m*.
Pfc *abbr* (*US MIL*) = *private first class*.
PG *n abbr* (*CINE*: = *parental guidance*) *avis des parents recommandé*.
PGA *n abbr* = *Professional Golfers Association*.
PH *n abbr* (*US MIL*: = *Purple Heart*) *décoration accordée aux blessés de guerre*.
phallic [ˈfælɪk] *adj* phallique.
phantom [ˈfæntəm] *n* fantôme *m*; (*vision*) fantasme *m*.
Pharaoh [ˈfɛərəu] *n* pharaon *m*.
pharmaceutical [fɑːməˈsjuːtɪkl] *adj* pharmaceutique ♦ *n*: **~s** produits *mpl* pharmaceutiques.
pharmacist [ˈfɑːməsɪst] *n* pharmacien/ne.

pharmacy ['fɑːməsɪ] *n* pharmacie *f*.
phase [feɪz] *n* phase *f*, période *f* ♦ *vt*: **to ~ sth in/out** introduire/supprimer qch progressivement.
PhD *abbr* (= *Doctor of Philosophy*) *title* ≈ Docteur *m* en Droit *or* Lettres *etc* ♦ *n* ≈ doctorat *m*; titulaire *m* d'un doctorat; *see also* **doctorate**.
pheasant ['fɛznt] *n* faisan *m*.
phenomenon, *pl* **phenomena** [fə'nɔmɪnən, -nə] *n* phénomène *m*.
phew [fjuː] *excl* ouf!
phial ['faɪəl] *n* fiole *f*.
philanderer [fɪ'lændərə*] *n* don Juan *m*.
philanthropic [fɪlən'θrɔpɪk] *adj* philanthropique.
philanthropist [fɪ'lænθrəpɪst] *n* philanthrope *m/f*.
philatelist [fɪ'lætəlɪst] *n* philatéliste *m/f*.
philately [fɪ'lætəlɪ] *n* philatélie *f*.
Philippines ['fɪlɪpiːnz] *npl* (*also*: **Philippine Islands**): **the ~** les Philippines *fpl*.
philosopher [fɪ'lɔsəfə*] *n* philosophe *m*.
philosophical [fɪlə'sɔfɪkl] *adj* philosophique.
philosophy [fɪ'lɔsəfɪ] *n* philosophie *f*.
phlegm [flɛm] *n* flegme *m*.
phlegmatic [flɛg'mætɪk] *adj* flegmatique.
phobia ['fəubjə] *n* phobie *f*.
phone [fəun] *n* téléphone *m* ♦ *vt* téléphoner à ♦ *vi* téléphoner; **to be on the ~** avoir le téléphone; (*be calling*) être au téléphone.
►**phone back** *vt, vi* rappeler.
phone book *n* annuaire *m*.
phone box, phone booth *n* cabine *f* téléphonique.
phone call *n* coup *m* de fil *or* de téléphone.
phonecard ['fəunkɑːd] *n* télécarte *f*.
phone-in ['fəunɪn] *n* (*BRIT RADIO, TV*) programme *m* à ligne ouverte.
phone tapping [-tæpɪŋ] *n* mise *f* sur écoutes téléphoniques.
phonetics [fə'nɛtɪks] *n* phonétique *f*.
phoney ['fəunɪ] *adj* faux(fausse), factice ♦ *n* (*person*) charlatan *m*; fumiste *m/f*.
phonograph ['fəunəgrɑːf] *n* (*US*) électrophone *m*.
phony ['fəunɪ] *adj, n* = **phoney**.
phosphate ['fɔsfeɪt] *n* phosphate *m*.
phosphorus ['fɔsfərəs] *n* phosphore *m*.
photo ['fəutəu] *n* photo *f*.
photo... ['fəutəu] *prefix* photo....
photocall ['fəutəukɔːl] *n* séance *f* de photos pour la presse.
photocopier ['fəutəukɔpɪə*] *n* copieur *m*.
photocopy ['fəutəukɔpɪ] *n* photocopie *f* ♦ *vt* photocopier.
photoelectric [fəutəuɪ'lɛktrɪk] *adj* photoélectrique; **~ cell** cellule *f* photoélectrique.
Photofit ['fəutəufɪt] *n* ® portrait-robot *m*.
photogenic [fəutəu'dʒɛnɪk] *adj* photogénique.
photograph ['fəutəgræf] *n* photographie *f* ♦ *vt* photographier; **to take a ~ of sb** prendre qn en photo.
photographer [fə'tɔgrəfə*] *n* photographe *m/f*.
photographic [fəutə'græfɪk] *adj* photographique.
photography [fə'tɔgrəfɪ] *n* photographie *f*.
photo opportunity *n occasion, souvent arrangée, pour prendre des photos d'une personnalité*.
Photostat ['fəutəustæt] *n* ® photocopie *f*, photostat *m*.
photosynthesis [fəutəu'sɪnθəsɪs] *n* photosynthèse *f*.
phrase [freɪz] *n* expression *f*; (*LING*) locution *f* ♦ *vt* exprimer; (*letter*) rédiger.
phrasebook ['freɪzbuk] *n* recueil *m* d'expressions (pour touristes).
physical ['fɪzɪkl] *adj* physique; **~ examination** examen médical; **~ education** éducation physique; **~ exercises** gymnastique *f*.
physically ['fɪzɪklɪ] *adv* physiquement.
physician [fɪ'zɪʃən] *n* médecin *m*.
physicist ['fɪzɪsɪst] *n* physicien/ne.
physics ['fɪzɪks] *n* physique *f*.
physiological [fɪzɪə'lɔdʒɪkl] *adj* physiologique.
physiology [fɪzɪ'ɔlədʒɪ] *n* physiologie *f*.
physiotherapist [fɪzɪəu'θɛrəpɪst] *n* kinésithérapeute *m/f*.
physiotherapy [fɪzɪəu'θɛrəpɪ] *n* kinésithérapie *f*.
physique [fɪ'ziːk] *n* (*appearance*) physique *m*; (*health etc*) constitution *f*.
pianist ['piːənɪst] *n* pianiste *m/f*.
piano [pɪ'ænəu] *n* piano *m*.
piano accordion *n* (*BRIT*) accordéon *m* à touches.
Picardy ['pɪkədɪ] *n* Picardie *f*.
piccolo ['pɪkələu] *n* piccolo *m*.
pick [pɪk] *n* (*tool*: *also*: **~-axe**) pic *m*, pioche *f* ♦ *vt* choisir; (*gather*) cueillir; (*scab, spot*) gratter, écorcher; **take your ~** faites votre choix; **the ~ of** le(la) meilleur(e) de; **to ~ a bone** ronger un os; **to ~ one's nose** se mettre le doigt dans le nez; **to ~ one's teeth** se curer les dents; **to ~ sb's brains** faire appel aux lumières de qn; **to ~ pockets** pratiquer le vol à la tire; **to ~ a quarrel/fight with sb** chercher querelle à/la bagarre avec qn.
►**pick off** *vt* (*kill*) (viser soigneusement et) abattre.
►**pick on** *vt fus* (*person*) harceler.
►**pick out** *vt* choisir; (*distinguish*) distinguer.
►**pick up** *vi* (*improve*) remonter, s'améliorer ♦ *vt* ramasser; (*telephone*) décrocher; (*collect*) passer prendre; (*AUT*: *give lift to*) prendre; (*learn*) apprendre; (*RADIO, TV, TEL*) capter; **to ~ up speed** prendre de la vitesse; **to ~ o.s. up** se relever; **to ~ up where one left off** reprendre là où l'on s'est arrêté.
pickaxe, (*US*) **pickax** ['pɪkæks] *n* pioche *f*.
picket ['pɪkɪt] *n* (*in strike*) gréviste *m/f* participant à un piquet de grève; piquet *m* de grève ♦ *vt* mettre un piquet de grève de-

vant.
picket line *n* piquet *m* de grève.
pickings ['pɪkɪŋz] *npl*: **there are rich ~ to be had in ...** il y a gros à gagner dans ....
pickle ['pɪkl] *n* (*also*: **~s**: *as condiment*) pickles *mpl*; (*fig*): **in a ~** dans le pétrin ♦ *vt* conserver dans du vinaigre *or* dans de la saumure.
pick-me-up ['pɪkmiːʌp] *n* remontant *m*.
pickpocket ['pɪkpɔkɪt] *n* pickpocket *m*.
pickup ['pɪkʌp] *n* (also: **~ truck, ~ van**) camionnette *f*.
picnic ['pɪknɪk] *n* pique-nique *m* ♦ *vi* pique-niquer.
picnicker ['pɪknɪkə*] *n* pique-niqueur/euse.
pictorial [pɪk'tɔːrɪəl] *adj* illustré(e).
picture ['pɪktʃə*] *n* (*also TV*) image *f*; (*painting*) peinture *f*, tableau *m*; (*photograph*) photo(graphie) *f*; (*drawing*) dessin *m*; (*film*) film *m* ♦ *vt* se représenter; (*describe*) dépeindre, représenter; **the ~s** (*BRIT*) le cinéma; **to take a ~ of sb/sth** prendre qn/qch en photo; **the overall ~** le tableau d'ensemble; **to put sb in the ~** mettre qn au courant.
picture book *n* livre *m* d'images.
picture messaging *n* envoi *m* de photos numériques.
picturesque [pɪktʃə'rɛsk] *adj* pittoresque.
picture window *n* baie vitrée, fenêtre *f* panoramique.
piddling ['pɪdlɪŋ] *adj* (*col*) insignifiant(e).
pidgin ['pɪdʒɪn] *adj*: **~ English** pidgin *m*.
pie [paɪ] *n* tourte *f*; (*of meat*) pâté *m* en croûte.
piebald ['paɪbɔːld] *adj* pie *inv*.
piece [piːs] *n* morceau *m*; (*of land*) parcelle *f*; (*item*): **a ~ of furniture/advice** un meuble/conseil; (*DRAUGHTS etc*) pion *m* ♦ *vt*: **to ~ together** rassembler; **in ~s** (*broken*) en morceaux, en miettes; (*not yet assembled*) en pièces détachées; **to take to ~s** démonter; **in one ~** (*object*) intact(e); **to get back all in one ~** (*person*) rentrer sain et sauf; **a 10p ~** (*BRIT*) une pièce de 10p; **~ by ~** morceau par morceau; **a six-~ band** un orchestre de six musiciens; **to say one's ~** réciter son morceau.
piecemeal ['piːsmiːl] *adv* par bouts.
piece rate *n* taux *m or* tarif *m* à la pièce.
piecework ['piːswəːk] *n* travail *m* aux pièces *or* à la pièce.
pie chart *n* graphique *m* à secteurs, camembert *m*.
Piedmont ['piːdmɔnt] *n* Piémont *m*.
pier [pɪə*] *n* jetée *f*; (*of bridge etc*) pile *f*.
pierce [pɪəs] *vt* percer, transpercer; **to have one's ears ~d** se faire percer les oreilles.
piercing ['pɪəsɪŋ] *adj* (*cry*) perçant(e).
piety ['paɪətɪ] *n* piété *f*.
piffling ['pɪflɪŋ] *adj* insignifiant(e).
pig [pɪg] *n* cochon *m*, porc *m*.
pigeon ['pɪdʒən] *n* pigeon *m*.
pigeonhole ['pɪdʒənhəul] *n* casier *m*.
pigeon-toed ['pɪdʒəntəud] *adj* marchant les pieds en dedans.
piggy bank ['pɪgɪ-] *n* tirelire *f*.
pigheaded ['pɪg'hɛdɪd] *adj* entêté(e), têtu(e).
piglet ['pɪglɪt] *n* petit cochon, porcelet *m*.
pigment ['pɪgmənt] *n* pigment *m*.
pigmentation [pɪgmən'teɪʃən] *n* pigmentation *f*.
pigmy ['pɪgmɪ] *n* = **pygmy**.
pigskin ['pɪgskɪn] *n* (peau *f* de) porc *m*.
pigsty ['pɪgstaɪ] *n* porcherie *f*.
pigtail ['pɪgteɪl] *n* natte *f*, tresse *f*.
pike [paɪk] *n* (*spear*) pique *f*; (*fish*) brochet *m*.
pilchard ['pɪltʃəd] *n* pilchard *m* (*sorte de sardine*).
pile [paɪl] *n* (*pillar, of books*) pile *f*; (*heap*) tas *m*; (*of carpet*) épaisseur *f* ♦ *vb* (*also*: **~ up**) *vt* empiler, entasser ♦ *vi* s'entasser; **in a ~** en tas.
►**pile on** *vt*: **to ~ it on** (*col*) exagérer.
piles [paɪlz] *npl* hémorroïdes *fpl*.
pileup ['paɪlʌp] *n* (*AUT*) télescopage *m*, collision *f* en série.
pilfer ['pɪlfə*] *vt* chaparder ♦ *vi* commettre des larcins.
pilfering ['pɪlfərɪŋ] *n* chapardage *m*.
pilgrim ['pɪlgrɪm] *n* pèlerin *m*.
pilgrimage ['pɪlgrɪmɪdʒ] *n* pèlerinage *m*.
pill [pɪl] *n* pilule *f*; **the ~** la pilule; **to be on the ~** prendre la pilule.
pillage ['pɪlɪdʒ] *vt* piller.
pillar ['pɪlə*] *n* pilier *m*.
pillar box *n* (*BRIT*) boîte *f* aux lettres (*publique*).
pillion ['pɪljən] *n* (*of motor cycle*) siège *m* arrière; **to ride ~** être derrière; (*on horse*) être en croupe.
pillory ['pɪlərɪ] *n* pilori *m* ♦ *vt* mettre au pilori.
pillow ['pɪləu] *n* oreiller *m*.
pillowcase ['pɪləukeɪs], **pillowslip** ['pɪləuslɪp] *n* taie *f* d'oreiller.
pilot ['paɪlət] *n* pilote *m* ♦ *cpd* (*scheme etc*) pilote, expérimental(e) ♦ *vt* piloter.
pilot boat *n* bateau-pilote *m*.
pilot light *n* veilleuse *f*.
pimento [pɪ'mɛntəu] *n* piment *m*.
pimp [pɪmp] *n* souteneur *m*, maquereau *m*.
pimple ['pɪmpl] *n* bouton *m*.
pimply ['pɪmplɪ] *adj* boutonneux(euse).
PIN *n abbr* = **personal identification number**.
pin [pɪn] *n* épingle *f*; (*TECH*) cheville *f*; (*BRIT*: *drawing ~*) punaise *f*; (*in grenade*) goupille *f*; (*BRIT ELEC*: *of plug*) broche *f* ♦ *vt* épingler; **~s and needles** fourmis *fpl*; **to ~ sb against/to** clouer qn contre/à; **to ~ sth on sb** (*fig*) mettre qch sur le dos de qn.
►**pin down** *vt* (*fig*): **to ~ sb down** obliger qn à répondre; **there's something strange here but I can't quite ~ it down** il y a quelque chose d'étrange ici, mais je n'arrive pas exactement à savoir quoi.
pinafore ['pɪnəfɔː*] *n* tablier *m*.
pinafore dress *n* robe-chasuble *f*.
pinball ['pɪnbɔːl] *n* flipper *m*.
pincers ['pɪnsəz] *npl* tenailles *fpl*.

pinch [pɪntʃ] *n* pincement *m*; (*of salt etc*) pincée *f* ♦ *vt* pincer; (*col: steal*) piquer, chiper ♦ *vi* (*shoe*) serrer; **at a** ~ à la rigueur; **to feel the** ~ (*fig*) se ressentir des restrictions (*or* de la récession *etc*).
pinched [pɪntʃt] *adj* (*drawn*) tiré(e); ~ **with cold** transi(e) de froid; ~ **for** (*short of*): ~ **for money** à court d'argent; ~ **for space** à l'étroit.
pincushion ['pɪnkuʃən] *n* pelote *f* à épingles.
pine [paɪn] *n* (*also*: ~ **tree**) pin *m* ♦ *vi*: **to** ~ **for** aspirer à, désirer ardemment.
►**pine away** *vi* dépérir.
pineapple ['paɪnæpl] *n* ananas *m*.
pine cone *n* pomme *f* de pin.
pine needle *n* aiguille *f* de pin.
ping [pɪŋ] *n* (*noise*) tintement *m*.
Ping-Pong ['pɪŋpɔŋ] *n* ® ping-pong *m* ®.
pink [pɪŋk] *adj* rose ♦ *n* (*colour*) rose *m*; (*BOT*) œillet *m*, mignardise *f*.
pinking shears ['pɪŋkɪŋ-] *npl* ciseaux *mpl* à denteler.
pin money *n* (*BRIT*) argent *m* de poche.
pinnacle ['pɪnəkl] *n* pinacle *m*.
pinpoint ['pɪnpɔɪnt] *vt* indiquer (avec précision).
pinstripe ['pɪnstraɪp] *n* rayure très fine.
pint [paɪnt] *n* pinte *f* (*BRIT = 0.57 l; US = 0.47 l*); (*BRIT col*) ≈ demi *m*, ≈ pot *m*.
pinup ['pɪnʌp] *n* pin-up *f inv*.
pioneer [paɪə'nɪə*] *n* explorateur/trice; (*early settler*) pionnier *m*; (*fig*) pionnier, précurseur *m* ♦ *vt* être un pionnier de.
pious ['paɪəs] *adj* pieux(euse).
pip [pɪp] *n* (*seed*) pépin *m*; (*BRIT: time signal on radio*) top *m*.
pipe [paɪp] *n* tuyau *m*, conduite *f*; (*for smoking*) pipe *f*; (*MUS*) pipeau *m* ♦ *vt* amener par tuyau; ~**s** *npl* (*also*: **bag**~**s**) cornemuse *f*.
►**pipe down** *vi* (*col*) se taire.
pipe cleaner *n* cure-pipe *m*.
piped music [paɪpt-] *n* musique *f* de fond.
pipe dream *n* chimère *f*, utopie *f*.
pipeline ['paɪplaɪn] *n* (*for gas*) gazoduc *m*, pipeline *m*; (*for oil*) oléoduc *m*, pipeline; **it is in the** ~ (*fig*) c'est en route, ça va se faire.
piper ['paɪpə*] *n* joueur/euse de pipeau (*or* de cornemuse).
pipe tobacco *n* tabac *m* pour la pipe.
piping ['paɪpɪŋ] *adv*: ~ **hot** très chaud(e).
piquant ['pi:kənt] *adj* piquant(e).
pique [pi:k] *n* dépit *m*.
piracy ['paɪərəsɪ] *n* piraterie *f*.
pirate ['paɪərət] *n* pirate *m* ♦ *vt* (*record, video, book*) pirater.
pirate radio *n* (*BRIT*) radio *f* pirate.
pirouette [pɪru'ɛt] *n* pirouette *f* ♦ *vi* faire une *or* des pirouette(s).
Pisces ['paɪsi:z] *n* les Poissons *mpl*; **to be** ~ être des Poissons.
piss [pɪs] *vi* (*col!*) pisser (*!*); ~ **off!** tire-toi! (*!*).
pissed [pɪst] *adj* (*BRIT col: drunk*) bourré(e).
pistol ['pɪstl] *n* pistolet *m*.
piston ['pɪstən] *n* piston *m*.
pit [pɪt] *n* trou *m*, fosse *f*; (*also*: **coal** ~) puits *m* de mine; (*also*: **orchestra** ~) fosse d'orchestre ♦ *vt*: **to** ~ **sb against sb** opposer qn à qn; **to** ~ **o.s. against** se mesurer à; ~**s** *npl* (*in motor racing*) aire *f* de service.
pitapat ['pɪtə'pæt] *adv* (*BRIT*): **to go** ~ (*heart*) battre la chamade; (*rain*) tambouriner.
pitch [pɪtʃ] *n* (*throw*) lancement *m*; (*MUS*) ton *m*; (*of voice*) hauteur *f*; (*fig: degree*) degré *m*; (*also*: **sales** ~) baratin *m*, boniment *m*; (*BRIT SPORT*) terrain *m*; (*NAUT*) tangage *m*; (*tar*) poix *f* ♦ *vt* (*throw*) lancer; (*tent*) dresser; (*set: price, message*) adapter, positionner ♦ *vi* (*NAUT*) tanguer; (*fall*): **to** ~ **into/off** tomber dans/de; **to be** ~**ed forward** être projeté(e) en avant; **at this** ~ à ce rythme.
pitch-black ['pɪtʃ'blæk] *adj* noir(e) comme poix.
pitched battle [pɪtʃt-] *n* bataille rangée.
pitcher ['pɪtʃə*] *n* cruche *f*.
pitchfork ['pɪtʃfɔ:k] *n* fourche *f*.
piteous ['pɪtɪəs] *adj* pitoyable.
pitfall ['pɪtfɔ:l] *n* trappe *f*, piège *m*.
pith [pɪθ] *n* (*of plant*) moelle *f*; (*of orange*) intérieur *m* de l'écorce; (*fig*) essence *f*; vigueur *f*.
pithead ['pɪthɛd] *n* (*BRIT*) bouche *f* de puits.
pithy ['pɪθɪ] *adj* piquant(e); vigoureux(euse).
pitiable ['pɪtɪəbl] *adj* pitoyable.
pitiful ['pɪtɪful] *adj* (*touching*) pitoyable; (*contemptible*) lamentable.
pitifully ['pɪtɪfəlɪ] *adv* pitoyablement; lamentablement.
pitiless ['pɪtɪlɪs] *adj* impitoyable.
pittance ['pɪtns] *n* salaire *m* de misère.
pitted ['pɪtɪd] *adj*: ~ **with** (*chickenpox*) grêlé(e) par; (*rust*) piqué(e) de.
pity ['pɪtɪ] *n* pitié *f* ♦ *vt* plaindre; **what a** ~! quel dommage!; **it is a** ~ **that you can't come** c'est dommage que vous ne puissiez venir; **to have** *or* **take** ~ **on sb** avoir pitié de qn.
pitying ['pɪtɪɪŋ] *adj* compatissant(e).
pivot ['pɪvət] *n* pivot *m* ♦ *vi* pivoter.
pixel ['pɪksl] *n* (*COMPUT*) pixel *m*.
pixie ['pɪksɪ] *n* lutin *m*.
pizza ['pi:tsə] *n* pizza *f*.
placard ['plækɑ:d] *n* affiche *f*.
placate [plə'keɪt] *vt* apaiser, calmer.
placatory [plə'keɪtərɪ] *adj* d'apaisement, lénifiant(e).
place [pleɪs] *n* endroit *m*, lieu *m*; (*proper position, rank, seat*) place *f*; (*house*) maison *f*, logement *m*; (*in street names*): **Laurel** ~ ≈ rue des Lauriers; (*home*): **at/to his** ~ chez lui ♦ *vt* (*position*) placer, mettre; (*identify*) situer; reconnaître; **to take** ~ avoir lieu; (*occur*) se produire; **from** ~ **to** ~ d'un endroit à l'autre; **all over the** ~ partout; **out of** ~ (*not suitable*) déplacé(e), inopportun(e); **I feel out of** ~ **here** je ne me sens pas à ma place ici;

in the first ~ d'abord, en premier; **to put sb in his** ~ (*fig*) remettre qn à sa place; **he's going** ~**s** (*fig*: *col*) il fait son chemin; **it is not my** ~ **to do it** ce n'est pas à moi de le faire; **to** ~ **an order with sb (for)** (*COMM*) passer commande à qn (de); **to be** ~**d** (*in race, exam*) se placer; **how are you** ~**d next week?** comment ça se présente pour la semaine prochaine?

placebo [plə'si:bəu] *n* placebo *m*.

place mat *n* set *m* de table; (*in linen etc*) napperon *m*.

placement ['pleɪsmənt] *n* placement *m*; poste *m*.

place name *n* nom *m* de lieu.

placenta [plə'sɛntə] *n* placenta *m*.

placid ['plæsɪd] *adj* placide.

placidity [plə'sɪdɪtɪ] *n* placidité *f*.

plagiarism ['pleɪdʒjərɪzəm] *n* plagiat *m*.

plagiarist ['pleɪdʒjərɪst] *n* plagiaire *m/f*.

plagiarize ['pleɪdʒjəraɪz] *vt* plagier.

plague [pleɪg] *n* fléau *m*; (*MED*) peste *f* ♦ *vt* (*fig*) tourmenter; **to** ~ **sb with questions** harceler qn de questions.

plaice [pleɪs] *n* (*pl inv*) carrelet *m*.

plaid [plæd] *n* tissu écossais.

plain [pleɪn] *adj* (*clear*) clair(e), évident(e); (*simple*) simple, ordinaire; (*frank*) franc(franche); (*not handsome*) quelconque, ordinaire; (*cigarette*) sans filtre; (*without seasoning etc*) nature *inv*; (*in one colour*) uni(e) ♦ *adv* franchement, carrément ♦ *n* plaine *f*; **in** ~ **clothes** (*police*) en civil; **to make sth** ~ **to sb** faire clairement comprendre qch à qn.

plain chocolate *n* chocolat *m* à croquer.

plainly ['pleɪnlɪ] *adv* clairement; (*frankly*) carrément, sans détours.

plainness ['pleɪnnɪs] *n* simplicité *f*.

plain speaking *n* propos *mpl* sans équivoque; **she has a reputation for** ~ elle est bien connue pour son franc parler *or* sa franchise.

plaintiff ['pleɪntɪf] *n* plaignant/e.

plaintive ['pleɪntɪv] *adj* plaintif(ive).

plait [plæt] *n* tresse *f*, natte *f* ♦ *vt* tresser, natter.

plan [plæn] *n* plan *m*; (*scheme*) projet *m* ♦ *vt* (*think in advance*) projeter; (*prepare*) organiser ♦ *vi* faire des projets; **to** ~ **to do** projeter de faire; **how long do you** ~ **to stay?** combien de temps comptez-vous rester?

plane [pleɪn] *n* (*AVIAT*) avion *m*; (*tree*) platane *m*; (*tool*) rabot *m*; (*ART, MATH etc*) plan *m* ♦ *adj* plan(e), plat(e) ♦ *vt* (*with tool*) raboter.

planet ['plænɪt] *n* planète *f*.

planetarium [plænɪ'tɛərɪəm] *n* planétarium *m*.

plank [plæŋk] *n* planche *f*; (*POL*) point *m* d'un programme.

plankton ['plæŋktən] *n* plancton *m*.

planned economy [plænd-] *n* économie planifiée.

planner ['plænə*] *n* planificateur/trice; (*chart*) planning *m*; **town** *or* (*US*) **city** ~ urbaniste *m/f*.

planning ['plænɪŋ] *n* planification *f*; **family** ~ planning familial.

planning permission *n* (*BRIT*) permis *m* de construire.

plant [plɑ:nt] *n* plante *f*; (*machinery*) matériel *m*; (*factory*) usine *f* ♦ *vt* planter; (*bomb*) déposer, poser.

plantation [plæn'teɪʃən] *n* plantation *f*.

plant pot *n* (*BRIT*) pot *m* de fleurs.

plaque [plæk] *n* plaque *f*.

plasma ['plæzmə] *n* plasma *m*.

plaster ['plɑ:stə*] *n* plâtre *m*; (*BRIT*: *also*: **sticking** ~) pansement adhésif ♦ *vt* plâtrer; (*cover*): **to** ~ **with** couvrir de; **in** ~ (*BRIT*: *leg etc*) dans le plâtre; ~ **of Paris** plâtre à mouler.

plasterboard ['plɑ:stəbɔ:d] *n* Placoplâtre *m* ®.

plaster cast *n* (*MED*) plâtre *m*; (*model, statue*) moule *m*.

plastered ['plɑ:stəd] *adj* (*col*) soûl(e).

plasterer ['plɑ:stərə*] *n* plâtrier *m*.

plastic ['plæstɪk] *n* plastique *m* ♦ *adj* (*made of plastic*) en plastique; (*flexible*) plastique, malléable; (*art*) plastique.

plastic bag *n* sac *m* en plastique.

plastic bullet *n* balle *f* de plastique.

plastic explosive *n* plastic *m*.

plasticine ['plæstɪsi:n] *n* ® pâte *f* à modeler.

plastic surgery *n* chirurgie *f* esthétique.

plate [pleɪt] *n* (*dish*) assiette *f*; (*sheet of metal, on door, PHOT*) plaque *f*; (*TYP*) cliché *m*; (*in book*) gravure *f*; (*AUT*: *number* ~) plaque minéralogique; **gold/silver** ~ (*dishes*) vaisselle *f* d'or/d'argent.

plateau, ~**s** *or* ~**x** ['plætəu, -z] *n* plateau *m*.

plateful ['pleɪtful] *n* assiette *f*, assiettée *f*.

plate glass *n* verre *m* à vitre, vitre *f*.

platen ['plætən] *n* (*on typewriter, printer*) rouleau *m*.

plate rack *n* égouttoir *m*.

platform ['plætfɔ:m] *n* (*at meeting*) tribune *f*; (*BRIT*: *of bus*) plate-forme *f*; (*stage*) estrade *f*; (*RAIL*) quai *m*; **the train leaves from** ~ **7** le train part de la voie 7.

platform ticket *n* (*BRIT*) billet *m* de quai.

platinum ['plætɪnəm] *n* platine *m*.

platitude ['plætɪtju:d] *n* platitude *f*, lieu commun.

platoon [plə'tu:n] *n* peloton *m*.

platter ['plætə*] *n* plat *m*.

plaudits ['plɔ:dɪts] *npl* applaudissements *mpl*.

plausible ['plɔ:zɪbl] *adj* plausible; (*person*) convaincant(e).

play [pleɪ] *n* jeu *m*; (*THEAT*) pièce *f* (de théâtre) ♦ *vt* (*game*) jouer à; (*team, opponent*) jouer contre; (*instrument*) jouer de; (*part, piece of music, note*) jouer ♦ *vi* jouer; **to bring** *or* **call into** ~ faire entrer en jeu; ~ **on words** jeu de mots; **to** ~ **a trick on sb** jouer un tour à qn; **they're** ~**ing at soldiers** ils jouent aux soldats; **to** ~ **for time** (*fig*) chercher à gagner du temps; **to** ~ **into sb's hands** (*fig*) faire le jeu de qn.

►**play about, play around** *vi* (*person*) s'amuser.

►**play along** *vi* (*fig*): **to ~ along with** (*person*) entrer dans le jeu de ♦ *vt* (*fig*): **to ~ sb along** faire marcher qn.

►**play back** *vt* repasser, réécouter.

►**play down** *vt* minimiser.

►**play on** *vt fus* (*sb's feelings, credulity*) jouer sur; **to ~ on sb's nerves** porter sur les nerfs de qn.

►**play up** *vi* (*cause trouble*) faire des siennes.

playact ['pleɪækt] *vi* jouer la comédie.

playboy ['pleɪbɔɪ] *n* playboy *m*.

played-out ['pleɪd'aut] *adj* épuisé(e).

player ['pleɪə*] *n* joueur/euse; (*THEAT*) acteur/trice; (*MUS*) musicien/ne.

playful ['pleɪful] *adj* enjoué(e).

playgoer ['pleɪgəuə*] *n* amateur/trice de théâtre, habitué/e des théâtres.

playground ['pleɪgraund] *n* cour *f* de récréation.

playgroup ['pleɪgru:p] *n* garderie *f*.

playing card ['pleɪɪŋ-] *n* carte *f* à jouer.

playing field ['pleɪɪŋ-] *n* terrain *m* de sport.

playmaker ['pleɪmeɪkə*] *n* (*SPORT*) *joueur qui crée des occasions de marquer des buts pour ses coéquipiers*.

playmate ['pleɪmeɪt] *n* camarade *m/f*, copain/copine.

play-off ['pleɪɔf] *n* (*SPORT*) belle *f*.

playpen ['pleɪpɛn] *n* parc *m* (pour bébé).

playroom ['pleɪru:m] *n* salle *f* de jeux.

plaything ['pleɪθɪŋ] *n* jouet *m*.

playtime ['pleɪtaɪm] *n* (*SCOL*) récréation *f*.

playwright ['pleɪraɪt] *n* dramaturge *m*.

plc *abbr* (*BRIT*) = **public limited company**.

plea [pli:] *n* (*request*) appel *m*; (*excuse*) excuse *f*; (*LAW*) défense *f*.

plea bargaining *n* (*LAW*) *négociations entre le procureur, l'avocat de la défense et parfois le juge, pour réduire la gravité des charges*.

plead [pli:d] *vt* plaider; (*give as excuse*) invoquer ♦ *vi* (*LAW*) plaider; (*beg*): **to ~ with sb (for sth)** implorer qn (d'accorder qch); **to ~ for sth** implorer qch; **to ~ guilty/not guilty** plaider coupable/non coupable.

pleasant ['plɛznt] *adj* agréable.

pleasantly ['plɛzntlɪ] *adv* agréablement.

pleasantry ['plɛzntrɪ] *n* (*joke*) plaisanterie *f*; **pleasantries** *npl* (*polite remarks*) civilités *fpl*.

please [pli:z] *vt* plaire à ♦ *vi* (*think fit*): **do as you ~** faites comme il vous plaira; **~!** s'il te (*or* vous) plaît; **my bill, ~** l'addition, s'il vous plaît; **~ don't cry!** je t'en prie, ne pleure pas!; **~ yourself!** (faites) comme vous voulez!

pleased [pli:zd] *adj*: **~ (with)** content(e) (de); **~ to meet you** enchanté (de faire votre connaissance); **we are ~ to inform you that ...** nous sommes heureux de vous annoncer que ....

pleasing ['pli:zɪŋ] *adj* plaisant(e), qui fait plaisir.

pleasurable ['plɛʒərəbl] *adj* très agréable.

pleasure ['plɛʒə*] *n* plaisir *m*; **"it's a ~"** "je vous en prie"; **with ~** avec plaisir; **is this trip for business or ~?** est-ce un voyage d'affaires ou d'agrément?

pleasure cruise *n* croisière *f*.

pleat [pli:t] *n* pli *m*.

plebiscite ['plɛbɪsɪt] *n* plébiscite *m*.

plebs [plɛbz] *npl* (*pej*) bas peuple.

plectrum ['plɛktrəm] *n* plectre *m*.

pledge [plɛdʒ] *n* gage *m*; (*promise*) promesse *f* ♦ *vt* engager; promettre; **to ~ support for sb** s'engager à soutenir qn; **to ~ sb to secrecy** faire promettre à qn de garder le secret.

plenary ['pli:nərɪ] *adj*: **in ~ session** en séance plénière.

plentiful ['plɛntɪful] *adj* abondant(e), copieux(euse).

plenty ['plɛntɪ] *n* abondance *f*; **~ of** beaucoup de; (*sufficient*) (bien) assez de; **we've got ~ of time** nous avons largement le temps.

pleurisy ['pluərɪsɪ] *n* pleurésie *f*.

Plexiglas ['plɛksɪglɑ:s] *n* ® (*US*) Plexiglas *m* ®.

pliable ['plaɪəbl] *adj* flexible; (*person*) malléable.

pliers ['plaɪəz] *npl* pinces *fpl*.

plight [plaɪt] *n* situation *f* critique.

plimsolls ['plɪmsəlz] *npl* (*BRIT*) (chaussures *fpl*) tennis *fpl*.

plinth [plɪnθ] *n* socle *m*.

PLO *n abbr* (= *Palestine Liberation Organization*) OLP *f*.

plod [plɔd] *vi* avancer péniblement; (*fig*) peiner.

plodder ['plɔdə*] *n* bûcheur/euse.

plodding ['plɔdɪŋ] *adj* pesant(e).

plonk [plɔŋk] (*col*) *n* (*BRIT: wine*) pinard *m*, piquette *f* ♦ *vt*: **to ~ sth down** poser brusquement qch.

plot [plɔt] *n* complot *m*, conspiration *f*; (*of story, play*) intrigue *f*; (*of land*) lot *m* de terrain, lopin *m* ♦ *vt* (*mark out*) pointer; relever; (*conspire*) comploter ♦ *vi* comploter; **a vegetable ~** (*BRIT*) un carré de légumes.

plotter ['plɔtə*] *n* conspirateur/trice; (*COMPUT*) traceur *m*.

plough, (*US*) **plow** [plau] *n* charrue *f* ♦ *vt* (*earth*) labourer.

►**plough back** *vt* (*COMM*) réinvestir.

►**plough through** *vt fus* (*snow etc*) avancer péniblement dans.

ploughing, (*US*) **plowing** ['plauɪŋ] *n* labourage *m*.

ploughman, (*US*) **plowman** ['plaumən] *n* laboureur *m*; **~'s lunch** (*BRIT*) *repas sommaire de pain et de fromage*.

ploy [plɔɪ] *n* stratagème *m*.

pluck [plʌk] *vt* (*fruit*) cueillir; (*musical instru-*

ment) pincer; (*bird*) plumer ♦ *n* courage *m*, cran *m*; **to ~ one's eyebrows** s'épiler les sourcils; **to ~ up courage** prendre son courage à deux mains.

plucky ['plʌkɪ] *adj* courageux(euse).

plug [plʌg] *n* bouchon *m*, bonde *f*; (*ELEC*) prise *f* de courant; (*AUT*: *also*: **spark(ing)** ~) bougie *f* ♦ *vt* (*hole*) boucher; (*col*: *advertise*) faire du battage pour, matraquer; **to give sb/sth a ~** (*col*) faire de la pub pour qn/qch.

►**plug in** (*ELEC*) *vt* brancher ♦ *vi* se brancher.

plughole ['plʌghəul] *n* (*BRIT*) trou *m* (d'écoulement).

plum [plʌm] *n* (*fruit*) prune *f* ♦ *adj*: ~ **job** (*col*) travail *m* en or.

plumb [plʌm] *adj* vertical(e) ♦ *n* plomb *m* ♦ *adv* (*exactly*) en plein ♦ *vt* sonder.

►**plumb in** *vt* (*washing machine*) faire le raccordement de.

plumber ['plʌmə*] *n* plombier *m*.

plumbing ['plʌmɪŋ] *n* (*trade*) plomberie *f*; (*piping*) tuyauterie *f*.

plumbline ['plʌmlaɪn] *n* fil *m* à plomb.

plume [plu:m] *n* plume *f*, plumet *m*.

plummet ['plʌmɪt] *vi* plonger, dégringoler.

plump [plʌmp] *adj* rondelet(te), dodu(e), bien en chair ♦ *vt*: **to ~ sth (down) on** laisser tomber qch lourdement sur.

►**plump for** *vt fus* (*col*: *choose*) se décider pour.

►**plump up** *vt* (*cushion*) battre (pour lui redonner forme).

plunder ['plʌndə*] *n* pillage *m* ♦ *vt* piller.

plunge [plʌndʒ] *n* plongeon *m* ♦ *vt* plonger ♦ *vi* (*fall*) tomber, dégringoler; **to take the ~** se jeter à l'eau.

plunger ['plʌndʒə*] *n* piston *m*; (*for blocked sink*) (débouchoir *m* à) ventouse *f*.

plunging ['plʌndʒɪŋ] *adj* (*neckline*) plongeant(e).

pluperfect [plu:'pə:fɪkt] *n* plus-que-parfait *m*.

plural ['pluərl] *adj* pluriel(le) ♦ *n* pluriel *m*.

plus [plʌs] *n* (*also*: ~ **sign**) signe *m* plus ♦ *prep* plus; **ten/twenty ~** plus de dix/vingt; **it's a ~** c'est un atout.

plus fours *npl* pantalon *m* (de) golf.

plush [plʌʃ] *adj* somptueux(euse) ♦ *n* peluche *f*.

plutonium [plu:'təunɪəm] *n* plutonium *m*.

ply [plaɪ] *n* (*of wool*) fil *m*; (*of wood*) feuille *f*, épaisseur *f* ♦ *vt* (*tool*) manier; (*a trade*) exercer ♦ *vi* (*ship*) faire la navette; **three ~ (wool)** *n* laine *f* trois fils; **to ~ sb with drink** donner continuellement à boire à qn.

plywood ['plaɪwud] *n* contreplaqué *m*.

PM *n abbr* (*BRIT*) = **prime minister**.

p.m. *adv abbr* (= *post meridiem*) de l'après-midi.

PMS *n abbr* (= *premenstrual syndrome*) syndrome prémenstruel.

PMT *n abbr* = **premenstrual tension**.

pneumatic [nju:'mætɪk] *adj* pneumatique; ~ **drill** marteau-piqueur *m*.

pneumonia [nju:'məunɪə] *n* pneumonie *f*.

PO *n abbr* (= *Post Office*) PTT *fpl*; (*MIL*) = **petty officer**.

po *abbr* = **postal order**.

POA *n abbr* (*BRIT*) = *Prison Officers' Association*.

poach [pəutʃ] *vt* (*cook*) pocher; (*steal*) pêcher (*or* chasser) sans permis ♦ *vi* braconner.

poached [pəutʃt] *adj* (*egg*) poché(e).

poacher ['pəutʃə*] *n* braconnier *m*.

poaching ['pəutʃɪŋ] *n* braconnage *m*.

PO box *n abbr* = **post office box**.

pocket ['pɔkɪt] *n* poche *f* ♦ *vt* empocher; **to be (£5) out of ~** (*BRIT*) en être de sa poche (pour 5 livres).

pocketbook ['pɔkɪtbuk] *n* (*wallet*) portefeuille *m*; (*notebook*) carnet *m*; (*US*: *handbag*) sac *m* à main.

pocket knife *n* canif *m*.

pocket money *n* argent *m* de poche.

pockmarked ['pɔkmɑ:kt] *adj* (*face*) grêlé(e).

pod [pɔd] *n* cosse *f* ♦ *vt* écosser.

podgy ['pɔdʒɪ] *adj* rondelet(te).

podiatrist [pɔ'di:ətrɪst] *n* (*US*) pédicure *m/f*.

podiatry [pɔ'di:ətrɪ] *n* (*US*) pédicurie *f*.

podium ['pəudɪəm] *n* podium *m*.

POE *n abbr* = *port of embarkation, port of entry*.

poem ['pəuɪm] *n* poème *m*.

poet ['pəuɪt] *n* poète *m*.

poetic [pəu'ɛtɪk] *adj* poétique.

poet laureate *n* poète lauréat; *voir encadré*.

POET LAUREATE

En Grande-Bretagne, le **poet laureate** *est un poète qui reçoit un traitement en tant que poète de la cour et qui est officier de la maison royale à vie. Le premier d'entre eux fut Ben Jonson, en 1616. Jadis, le poète lauréat écrivait des poèmes lors des grandes occasions, mais cette tradition n'est plus guère observée.*

poetry ['pəuɪtrɪ] *n* poésie *f*.

poignant ['pɔɪnjənt] *adj* poignant(e); (*sharp*) vif(vive).

point [pɔɪnt] *n* (*tip*) pointe *f*; (*in time*) moment *m*; (*in space*) endroit *m*; (*GEOM, SCOL, SPORT, on scale*) point *m*; (*subject, idea*) point, sujet *m*; (*also*: **decimal** ~): **2 ~ 3 (2.3)** 2 virgule 3 (2,3); (*BRIT ELEC*: *also*: **power** ~) prise *f* (de courant) ♦ *vt* (*show*) indiquer; (*wall, window*) jointoyer; (*gun etc*): **to ~ sth at** braquer *or* diriger qch sur ♦ *vi* montrer du doigt; **to ~ to** montrer du doigt; (*fig*) signaler; **~s** *npl* (*AUT*) vis platinées; (*RAIL*) aiguillage *m*; **good ~s** qualités *fpl*; **the train stops at Carlisle and all ~s south** le train dessert Carlisle et toutes les gares vers le sud; **to make a ~** faire une remarque; **to make a ~ of doing sth** ne pas manquer de faire qch; **to make one's ~** se faire comprendre; **to get the ~** comprendre, saisir; **to come to the ~** en venir au fait; **when it comes to the ~** le moment

venu; **there's no ~ (in doing)** cela ne sert à rien (de faire); **to be on the ~ of doing sth** être sur le point de faire qch; **that's the whole ~!** précisément!; **to be beside the ~** être à côté de la question; **you've got a ~ there!** (c'est) juste!; **in ~ of fact** en fait, en réalité; **~ of departure** (*also fig*) point de départ; **~ of order** point de procédure; **~ of sale** (*COMM*) point de vente; **~ of view** point de vue.
►**point out** *vt* faire remarquer, souligner.
point-blank ['pɔɪnt'blæŋk] *adv* (*also*: **at ~ range**) à bout portant ♦ *adj* (*fig*) catégorique.
point duty *n* (*BRIT*): **to be on ~** diriger la circulation.
pointed ['pɔɪntɪd] *adj* (*shape*) pointu(e); (*remark*) plein(e) de sous-entendus.
pointedly ['pɔɪntɪdlɪ] *adv* d'une manière significative.
pointer ['pɔɪntə*] *n* (*stick*) baguette *f*; (*needle*) aiguille *f*; (*dog*) chien *m* d'arrêt; (*clue*) indication *f*; (*advice*) tuyau *m*.
pointless ['pɔɪntlɪs] *adj* inutile, vain(e).
poise [pɔɪz] *n* (*balance*) équilibre *m*; (*of head, body*) port *m*; (*calmness*) calme *m* ♦ *vt* placer en équilibre; **to be ~d for** (*fig*) être prêt à.
poison ['pɔɪzn] *n* poison *m* ♦ *vt* empoisonner.
poisoning ['pɔɪznɪŋ] *n* empoisonnement *m*.
poisonous ['pɔɪznəs] *adj* (*snake*) venimeux(euse); (*substance etc*) vénéneux(euse); (*fumes*) toxique; (*fig*) pernicieux(euse).
poke [pəuk] *vt* (*fire*) tisonner; (*jab with finger, stick etc*) piquer; pousser du doigt; (*put*): **to ~ sth into** fourrer *or* enfoncer qch dans ♦ *n* (*jab*) (petit) coup; (*to fire*) coup *m* de tisonnier; **to ~ one's head out of the window** passer la tête par la fenêtre; **to ~ fun at sb** se moquer de qn.
►**poke about** *vi* fureter.
poker ['pəukə*] *n* tisonnier *m*; (*CARDS*) poker *m*.
poker-faced ['pəukə'feɪst] *adj* au visage impassible.
poky ['pəukɪ] *adj* exigu(ë).
Poland ['pəulənd] *n* Pologne *f*.
polar ['pəulə*] *adj* polaire.
polar bear *n* ours blanc.
polarize ['pəuləraɪz] *vt* polariser.
Pole [pəul] *n* Polonais/e.
pole [pəul] *n* (*of wood*) mât *m*, perche *f*; (*ELEC*) poteau *m*; (*GEO*) pôle *m*.
poleaxe ['pəulæks] *vt* (*fig*) terrasser.
pole bean *n* (*US*) haricot *m* (à rames).
polecat ['pəulkæt] *n* putois *m*.
Pol. Econ. ['pɔlɪkɔn] *n abbr* = *political economy*.
polemic [pɔ'lɛmɪk] *n* polémique *f*.
pole star ['pəulstɑː*] *n* étoile *f* polaire.
pole vault ['pəulvɔːlt] *n* saut *m* à la perche.
police [pə'liːs] *npl* police *f* ♦ *vt* maintenir l'ordre dans; **a large number of ~ were hurt** de nombreux policiers ont été blessés.
police car *n* voiture *f* de police.
police constable *n* (*BRIT*) agent *m* de police.
police department *n* (*US*) services *mpl* de police.
police force *n* police *f*, forces *fpl* de l'ordre.
policeman [pə'liːsmən] *n* agent *m* de police, policier *m*.
police officer *n* agent *m* de police.
police record *n* casier *m* judiciaire.
police state *n* état policier.
police station *n* commissariat *m* de police.
policewoman [pə'liːswumən] *n* femme-agent *f*.
policy ['pɔlɪsɪ] *n* politique *f*; (*also*: **insurance ~**) police *f* (d'assurance); (*of newspaper, company*) politique générale; **to take out a ~** (*INSURANCE*) souscrire une police d'assurance.
policy holder *n* assuré/e.
policy-making ['pɔlɪsɪmeɪkɪŋ] *n* élaboration *f* de nouvelles lignes d'action.
polio ['pəulɪəu] *n* polio *f*.
Polish ['pəulɪʃ] *adj* polonais(e) ♦ *n* (*LING*) polonais *m*.
polish ['pɔlɪʃ] *n* (*for shoes*) cirage *m*; (*for floor*) cire *f*, encaustique *f*; (*for nails*) vernis *m*; (*shine*) éclat *m*, poli *m*; (*fig: refinement*) raffinement *m* ♦ *vt* (*put polish on: shoes, wood*) cirer; (*make shiny*) astiquer, faire briller; (*fig: improve*) perfectionner.
►**polish off** *vt* (*work*) expédier; (*food*) liquider.
polished ['pɔlɪʃt] *adj* (*fig*) raffiné(e).
polite [pə'laɪt] *adj* poli(e); **it's not ~ to do that** ça ne se fait pas.
politely [pə'laɪtlɪ] *adv* poliment.
politeness [pə'laɪtnɪs] *n* politesse *f*.
politic ['pɔlɪtɪk] *adj* diplomatique.
political [pə'lɪtɪkl] *adj* politique.
political asylum *n* asile *m* politique.
politically [pə'lɪtɪklɪ] *adv* politiquement.
politically correct *adj* politiquement correct(e).
politician [pɔlɪ'tɪʃən] *n* homme/femme politique, politicien/ne.
politics ['pɔlɪtɪks] *n* politique *f*.
polka ['pɔlkə] *n* polka *f*.
polka dot *n* pois *m*.
poll [pəul] *n* scrutin *m*, vote *m*; (*also*: **opinion ~**) sondage *m* (d'opinion) ♦ *vt* obtenir; **to go to the ~s** (*voters*) aller aux urnes; (*government*) tenir des élections.
pollen ['pɔlən] *n* pollen *m*.
pollen count *n* taux *m* de pollen.
pollination [pɔlɪ'neɪʃən] *n* pollinisation *f*.
polling ['pəulɪŋ] *n* (*BRIT POL*) élections *fpl*; (*TEL*) invitation *f* à émettre.
polling booth *n* (*BRIT*) isoloir *m*.
polling day *n* (*BRIT*) jour *m* des élections.
polling station *n* (*BRIT*) bureau *m* de vote.
pollster ['pəulstə*] *n* sondeur *m*, enquêteur/euse.
poll tax *n* (*BRIT*: *formerly*) ≈ impôts locaux.
pollutant [pə'luːtənt] *n* polluant *m*.

pollute [pə'lu:t] *vt* polluer.
pollution [pə'lu:ʃən] *n* pollution *f*.
polo ['pəuləu] *n* polo *m*.
poloneck ['pəuləunɛk] *n* col roulé ♦ *adj* à col roulé.
poly ['pɔlɪ] *n abbr* (*BRIT*) = **polytechnic**.
poly bag *n* (*BRIT col*) sac *m* en plastique.
polyester [pɔlɪ'ɛstə*] *n* polyester *m*.
polygamy [pə'lɪgəmɪ] *n* polygamie *f*.
polygraph ['pɔlɪgrɑ:f] *n* détecteur *m* de mensonges.
Polynesia [pɔlɪ'ni:zɪə] *n* Polynésie *f*.
Polynesian [pɔlɪ'ni:zɪən] *adj* polynésien(ne) ♦ *n* Polynésien/ne.
polyp ['pɔlɪp] *n* (*MED*) polype *m*.
polystyrene [pɔlɪ'staɪri:n] *n* polystyrène *m*.
polytechnic [pɔlɪ'tɛknɪk] *n* (*college*) IUT *m*, Institut *m* universitaire de technologie.
polythene ['pɔlɪθi:n] *n* polyéthylène *m*.
polythene bag *n* sac *m* en plastique.
polyurethane [pɔlɪ'juərɪθeɪn] *n* polyuréthane *m*.
pomegranate ['pɔmɪgrænɪt] *n* grenade *f*.
pommel ['pɔml] *n* pommeau *m* ♦ *vt* = **pummel**.
pomp [pɔmp] *n* pompe *f*, faste *f*, apparat *m*.
pompom ['pɔmpɔm] *n* pompon *m*.
pompous ['pɔmpəs] *adj* pompeux(euse).
pond [pɔnd] *n* étang *m*; (*stagnant*) mare *f*.
ponder ['pɔndə*] *vi* réfléchir ♦ *vt* considérer, peser.
ponderous ['pɔndərəs] *adj* pesant(e), lourd(e).
pong [pɔŋ] (*BRIT col*) *n* puanteur *f* ♦ *vi* schlinguer.
pontiff ['pɔntɪf] *n* pontife *m*.
pontificate [pɔn'tɪfɪkeɪt] *vi* (*fig*): **to ~ (about)** pontifier (sur).
pontoon [pɔn'tu:n] *n* ponton *m*; (*BRIT*: *CARDS*) vingt-et-un *m*.
pony ['pəunɪ] *n* poney *m*.
ponytail ['pəunɪteɪl] *n* queue *f* de cheval.
pony trekking [-trɛkɪŋ] *n* (*BRIT*) randonnée *f* équestre *or* à cheval.
poodle ['pu:dl] *n* caniche *m*.
pooh-pooh ['pu:'pu:] *vt* dédaigner.
pool [pu:l] *n* (*of rain*) flaque *f*; (*pond*) mare *f*; (*artificial*) bassin *m*; (*also*: **swimming ~**) piscine *f*; (*sth shared*) fonds commun; (*money at cards*) cagnotte *f*; (*billiards*) poule *f*; (*COMM*: *consortium*) pool *m*; (*US*: *monopoly trust*) trust *m* ♦ *vt* mettre en commun; **typing ~**, (*US*) **secretary ~** pool *m* dactylographique; **to do the (football) ~s** (*BRIT*) ≈ jouer au loto sportif; *see also* **football pools**.
poor [puə*] *adj* pauvre; (*mediocre*) médiocre, faible, mauvais(e) ♦ *npl*: **the ~** les pauvres *mpl*.
poorly ['puəlɪ] *adv* pauvrement; médiocrement ♦ *adj* souffrant(e), malade.
pop [pɔp] *n* (*noise*) bruit sec; (*MUS*) musique *f* pop; (*col*: *drink*) soda *m*; (*US col*: *father*) papa *m* ♦ *vt* (*put*) fourrer, mettre (rapidement) ♦ *vi* éclater; (*cork*) sauter; **she ~ped her head out of the window** elle passa la tête par la fenêtre.
▸**pop in** *vi* entrer en passant.
▸**pop out** *vi* sortir.
▸**pop up** *vi* apparaître, surgir.
pop concert *n* concert *m* pop.
popcorn ['pɔpkɔ:n] *n* pop-corn *m*.
pope [pəup] *n* pape *m*.
poplar ['pɔplə*] *n* peuplier *m*.
poplin ['pɔplɪn] *n* popeline *f*.
popper ['pɔpə*] *n* (*BRIT*) bouton-pression *m*.
poppy ['pɔpɪ] *n* coquelicot *m*; pavot *m*.
poppycock ['pɔpɪkɔk] *n* (*col*) balivernes *fpl*.
Popsicle ['pɔpsɪkl] *n* ® (*US*) esquimau *m* (*glace*).
populace ['pɔpjuləs] *n* peuple *m*.
popular ['pɔpjulə*] *adj* populaire; (*fashionable*) à la mode; **to be ~ (with)** (*person*) avoir du succès (auprès de); (*decision*) être bien accueilli(e) (par).
popularity [pɔpju'lærɪtɪ] *n* popularité *f*.
popularize ['pɔpjuləraɪz] *vt* populariser; (*science*) vulgariser.
populate ['pɔpjuleɪt] *vt* peupler.
population [pɔpju'leɪʃən] *n* population *f*.
population explosion *n* explosion *f* démographique.
populous ['pɔpjuləs] *adj* populeux(euse).
porcelain ['pɔ:slɪn] *n* porcelaine *f*.
porch [pɔ:tʃ] *n* porche *m*.
porcupine ['pɔ:kjupaɪn] *n* porc-épic *m*.
pore [pɔ:*] *n* pore *m* ♦ *vi*: **to ~ over** s'absorber dans, être plongé(e) dans.
pork [pɔ:k] *n* porc *m*.
pork chop *n* côte *f* de porc.
porn [pɔ:n] *adj*, *n* (*col*) porno (*m*).
pornographic [pɔ:nə'græfɪk] *adj* pornographique.
pornography [pɔ:'nɔgrəfɪ] *n* pornographie *f*.
porous ['pɔ:rəs] *adj* poreux(euse).
porpoise ['pɔ:pəs] *n* marsouin *m*.
porridge ['pɔrɪdʒ] *n* porridge *m*.
port [pɔ:t] *n* (*harbour*) port *m*; (*opening in ship*) sabord *m*; (*NAUT*: *left side*) bâbord *m*; (*wine*) porto *m*; (*COMPUT*) port *m*, accès *m* ♦ *cpd* portuaire, du port; **to ~** (*NAUT*) à bâbord; **~ of call** (port d')escale *f*.
portable ['pɔ:təbl] *adj* portatif(ive).
portal ['pɔ:tl] *n* portail *m*.
portcullis [pɔ:t'kʌlɪs] *n* herse *f*.
portend [pɔ:'tɛnd] *vt* présager, annoncer.
portent ['pɔ:tɛnt] *n* présage *m*.
porter ['pɔ:tə*] *n* (*for luggage*) porteur *m*; (*doorkeeper*) gardien/ne; portier *m*.
portfolio [pɔ:t'fəulɪəu] *n* portefeuille *m*; (*of artist*) portfolio *m*.
porthole ['pɔ:thəul] *n* hublot *m*.
portico ['pɔ:tɪkəu] *n* portique *m*.
portion ['pɔ:ʃən] *n* portion *f*, part *f*.
portly ['pɔ:tlɪ] *adj* corpulent(e).
portrait ['pɔ:treɪt] *n* portrait *m*.
portray [pɔ:'treɪ] *vt* faire le portrait de; (*in*

writing) dépeindre, représenter.
portrayal [pɔː'treɪəl] *n* portrait *m*, représentation *f*.
Portugal ['pɔːtjugl] *n* Portugal *m*.
Portuguese [pɔːtju'giːz] *adj* portugais(e) ♦ *n* (*pl inv*) Portugais/e; (*LING*) portugais *m*.
Portuguese man-of-war [-mænəv'wɔː*] *n* (*jellyfish*) galère *f*.
pose [pəuz] *n* pose *f*; (*pej*) affectation *f* ♦ *vi* poser; (*pretend*): **to ~ as** se poser en ♦ *vt* poser, créer; **to strike a ~** poser (pour la galerie).
poser ['pəuzə*] *n* question difficile *or* embarrassante; (*person*) = **poseur**.
poseur [pəu'zəː*] *n* (*pej*) poseur/euse.
posh [pɔʃ] *adj* (*col*) chic *inv*; **to talk ~** parler d'une manière affectée.
position [pə'zɪʃən] *n* position *f*; (*job*) situation *f* ♦ *vt* mettre en place *or* en position; **to be in a ~ to do sth** être en mesure de faire qch.
positive ['pɔzɪtɪv] *adj* positif(ive); (*certain*) sûr(e), certain(e); (*definite*) formel(le), catégorique; (*clear*) indéniable, réel(le).
posse ['pɔsɪ] *n* (*US*) détachement *m*.
possess [pə'zɛs] *vt* posséder; **like one ~ed** comme un fou; **whatever can have ~ed you?** qu'est-ce qui vous a pris?
possession [pə'zɛʃən] *n* possession *f*; **to take ~ of sth** prendre possession de qch.
possessive [pə'zɛsɪv] *adj* possessif(ive).
possessiveness [pə'zɛsɪvnɪs] *n* possessivité *f*.
possessor [pə'zɛsə*] *n* possesseur *m*.
possibility [pɔsɪ'bɪlɪtɪ] *n* possibilité *f*, éventualité *f*; **he's a ~ for the part** c'est un candidat possible pour le rôle.
possible ['pɔsɪbl] *adj* possible; (*solution*) envisageable, éventuel(le); **it is ~ to do it** il est possible de le faire; **as far as ~** dans la mesure du possible, autant que possible; **if ~** si possible; **as big as ~** aussi gros que possible.
possibly ['pɔsɪblɪ] *adv* (*perhaps*) peut-être; **if you ~ can** si cela vous est possible; **I cannot ~ come** il m'est impossible de venir.
post [pəust] *n* (*BRIT*: *mail*) poste *f*; (*: collection*) levée *f*; (*: letters, delivery*) courrier *m*; (*job, situation*) poste *m*; (*pole*) poteau *m*; (*trading ~*) comptoir (commercial) ♦ *vt* (*BRIT*: *send by post*, *MIL*) poster; (*BRIT*: *appoint*): **to ~ to** affecter à; (*notice*) afficher; **by ~** (*BRIT*) par la poste; **by return of ~** (*BRIT*) par retour du courrier; **to keep sb ~ed** tenir qn au courant.
post... [pəust] *prefix* post...; **~ 1990** *adj* d'après 1990 ♦ *adv* après 1990.
postage ['pəustɪdʒ] *n* affranchissement *m*; **~ paid** port payé; **~ prepaid** (*US*) franco (de port).
postage stamp *n* timbre-poste *m*.
postal ['pəustl] *adj* postal(e).
postal order *n* mandat(-poste *m*) *m*.
postbag ['pəustbæg] *n* (*BRIT*) sac postal; (*postman's*) sacoche *f*.
postbox ['pəustbɔks] *n* (*BRIT*) boîte *f* aux lettres (*publique*).
postcard ['pəustkɑːd] *n* carte postale.
postcode ['pəustkəud] *n* (*BRIT*) code postal.
postdate ['pəust'deɪt] *vt* (*cheque*) postdater.
poster ['pəustə*] *n* affiche *f*.
poste restante [pəust'rɛstɑ̃ːnt] *n* (*BRIT*) poste restante.
posterior [pɔs'tɪərɪə*] *n* (*col*) postérieur *m*, derrière *m*.
posterity [pɔs'tɛrɪtɪ] *n* postérité *f*.
poster paint *n* gouache *f*.
post exchange (PX) *n* (*US MIL*) magasin *m* de l'armée.
post-free [pəust'friː] *adj* (*BRIT*) franco (de port).
postgraduate ['pəust'grædjuət] *n* ≈ étudiant/e de troisième cycle.
posthumous ['pɔstjuməs] *adj* posthume.
posthumously ['pɔstjuməslɪ] *adv* après la mort de l'auteur, à titre posthume.
posting ['pəustɪŋ] *n* (*BRIT*) affectation *f*.
postman ['pəustmən] *n* facteur *m*.
postmark ['pəustmɑːk] *n* cachet *m* (de la poste).
postmaster ['pəustmɑːstə*] *n* receveur *m* des postes.
Postmaster General *n* ≈ ministre *m* des Postes et Télécommunications.
postmistress ['pəustmɪstrɪs] *n* receveuse *f* des postes.
post-mortem [pəust'mɔːtəm] *n* autopsie *f*.
postnatal ['pəust'neɪtl] *adj* post-natal(e).
post office *n* (*building*) poste *f*; (*organization*) postes *fpl*.
post office box (PO box) *n* boîte postale (B.P.).
post-paid ['pəust'peɪd] *adj* (*BRIT*) port payé.
postpone [pəs'pəun] *vt* remettre (à plus tard), reculer.
postponement [pəs'pəunmənt] *n* ajournement *m*, renvoi *m*.
postscript ['pəustskrɪpt] *n* post-scriptum *m*.
postulate ['pɔstjuleɪt] *vt* postuler.
posture ['pɔstʃə*] *n* posture *f*, attitude *f* ♦ *vi* poser.
postwar [pəust'wɔː*] *adj* d'après-guerre.
posy ['pəuzɪ] *n* petit bouquet.
pot [pɔt] *n* (*for cooking*) marmite *f*; casserole *f*; (*for plants, jam*) pot *m*; (*piece of pottery*) poterie *f*; (*col*: *marijuana*) herbe *f* ♦ *vt* (*plant*) mettre en pot; **to go to ~** aller à vau-l'eau; **~s of** (*BRIT col*) beaucoup de, plein de.
potash ['pɔtæʃ] *n* potasse *f*.
potassium [pə'tæsɪəm] *n* potassium *m*.
potato, ~es [pə'teɪtəu] *n* pomme *f* de terre.
potato crisps, (*US*) **potato chips** *npl* chips *mpl*.
potato flour *n* fécule *f*.
potato peeler *n* épluche-légumes *m*.
potbellied ['pɔtbɛlɪd] *adj* (*from overeating*) bedonnant(e); (*from malnutrition*) au ventre

ballonné.

potency ['pəutnsɪ] *n* puissance *f*, force *f*; (*of drink*) degré *m* d'alcool.

potent ['pəutnt] *adj* puissant(e); (*drink*) fort(e), très alcoolisé(e).

potentate ['pəutnteɪt] *n* potentat *m*.

potential [pə'tɛnʃl] *adj* potentiel(le) ♦ *n* potentiel *m*; **to have ~** être prometteur(euse); ouvrir des possibilités.

potentially [pə'tɛnʃəlɪ] *adv* potentiellement; **it's ~ dangerous** ça pourrait se révéler dangereux, il y a possibilité de danger.

pothole ['pɔthəul] *n* (*in road*) nid *m* de poule; (*BRIT: underground*) gouffre *m*, caverne *f*.

potholer ['pɔthəulə*] *n* (*BRIT*) spéléologue *m/f*.

potholing ['pɔthəulɪŋ] *n* (*BRIT*): **to go ~** faire de la spéléologie.

potion ['pəuʃən] *n* potion *f*.

potluck [pɔt'lʌk] *n*: **to take ~** tenter sa chance.

potpourri [pəu'puriː] *n* pot-pourri *m*.

pot roast *n* rôti *m* à la cocotte.

potshot ['pɔtʃɔt] *n*: **to take ~s at** canarder.

potted ['pɔtɪd] *adj* (*food*) en conserve; (*plant*) en pot; (*fig: shortened*) abrégé(e).

potter ['pɔtə*] *n* potier *m* ♦ *vi* (*BRIT*): **to ~ around, ~ about** bricoler; **~'s wheel** tour *m* de potier.

pottery ['pɔtərɪ] *n* poterie *f*; **a piece of ~** une poterie.

potty ['pɔtɪ] *adj* (*BRIT col: mad*) dingue ♦ *n* (*child's*) pot *m*.

potty-training ['pɔtɪtreɪnɪŋ] *n* apprentissage *m* de la propreté.

pouch [pautʃ] *n* (*ZOOL*) poche *f*; (*for tobacco*) blague *f*.

pouf(fe) [puːf] *n* (*stool*) pouf *m*.

poultice ['pəultɪs] *n* cataplasme *m*.

poultry ['pəultrɪ] *n* volaille *f*.

poultry farm *n* élevage *m* de volaille.

poultry farmer *n* aviculteur *m*.

pounce [pauns] *vi*: **to ~ (on)** bondir (sur), fondre (sur) ♦ *n* bond *m*, attaque *f*.

pound [paund] *n* livre *f* (*weight = 453g, 16 ounces; money = 100 pence*); (*for dogs, cars*) fourrière *f* ♦ *vt* (*beat*) bourrer de coups, marteler; (*crush*) piler, pulvériser; (*with guns*) pilonner ♦ *vi* (*beat*) battre violemment, taper; **half a ~ (of)** une demi-livre (de); **a five-~ note** un billet de cinq livres.

pounding ['paundɪŋ] *n*: **to take a ~** (*fig*) prendre une râclée.

pound sterling *n* livre *f* sterling.

pour [pɔː*] *vt* verser ♦ *vi* couler à flots; (*rain*) pleuvoir à verse; **to come ~ing in** (*water*) entrer à flots; (*letters*) arriver par milliers; (*cars, people*) affluer.

►**pour away, pour off** *vt* vider.

►**pour in** *vi* (*people*) affluer, se précipiter.

►**pour out** *vi* (*people*) sortir en masse ♦ *vt* vider; déverser; (*serve: a drink*) verser.

pouring ['pɔːrɪŋ] *adj*: **~ rain** pluie torrentielle.

pout [paut] *n* moue *f* ♦ *vi* faire la moue.

poverty ['pɔvətɪ] *n* pauvreté *f*, misère *f*.

poverty line *n* seuil *m* de pauvreté.

poverty-stricken ['pɔvətɪstrɪkn] *adj* pauvre, déshérité(e).

poverty trap *n* (*BRIT*) piège *m* de la pauvreté.

POW *n abbr* = **prisoner of war**.

powder ['paudə*] *n* poudre *f* ♦ *vt* poudrer; **to ~ one's nose** se poudrer; (*euphemism*) aller à la salle de bain; **~ed milk** lait *m* en poudre.

powder compact *n* poudrier *m*.

powder keg *n* (*fig*) poudrière *f*.

powder puff *n* houppette *f*.

powder room *n* toilettes *fpl* (pour dames).

powdery ['paudərɪ] *adj* poudreux(euse).

power ['pauə*] *n* (*strength*) puissance *f*, force *f*; (*ability, POL: of party, leader*) pouvoir *m*; (*MATH*) puissance; (*of speech, thought*) faculté *f*; (*ELEC*) courant *m* ♦ *vt* faire marcher, actionner; **to do all in one's ~ to help sb** faire tout ce qui est en son pouvoir pour aider qn; **the world ~s** les grandes puissances; **to be in ~** être au pouvoir.

powerboat ['pauəbəut] *n* (*BRIT*) hors-bord *m*.

power cut *n* (*BRIT*) coupure *f* de courant.

powered ['pauəd] *adj*: **~ by** actionné(e) par, fonctionnant à; **nuclear-~ submarine** sous-marin *m* (à propulsion) nucléaire.

power failure *n* panne *f* de courant.

powerful ['pauəful] *adj* puissant(e).

powerhouse ['pauəhaus] *n* (*fig: person*) fonceur *m*; **a ~ of ideas** une mine d'idées.

powerless ['pauəlɪs] *adj* impuissant(e).

power line *n* ligne *f* électrique.

power of attorney *n* procuration *f*.

power point *n* (*BRIT*) prise *f* de courant.

power station *n* centrale *f* électrique.

power steering *n* direction assistée.

powwow ['pauwau] *n* conciliabule *m*.

pox [pɔks] *n see* **chickenpox**.

pp *abbr* (= *per procurationem: by proxy*) p.p.

PPE *n abbr* (*BRIT SCOL*) = *philosophy, politics and economics*.

PPS *n abbr* (= *post postscriptum*) PPS; (*BRIT*: = *parliamentary private secretary*) *parlementaire chargé de mission auprès d'un ministre*.

PQ *abbr* (*Canada*: = *Province of Quebec*) PQ.

PR *n abbr* = **proportional representation, public relations** ♦ *abbr* (*US*) = *Puerto Rico*.

Pr. *abbr* (= *prince*) Pce.

practicability [præktɪkə'bɪlɪtɪ] *n* possibilité *f* de réalisation.

practicable ['præktɪkəbl] *adj* (*scheme*) réalisable.

practical ['præktɪkl] *adj* pratique.

practicality [præktɪ'kælɪtɪ] *n* (*of plan*) aspect *m* pratique; (*of person*) sens *m* pratique; **practicalities** *npl* détails *mpl* pratiques.

practical joke *n* farce *f*.

practically ['præktɪklɪ] *adv* (*almost*) pratiquement.

practice ['præktɪs] *n* pratique *f*; (*of profession*)

exercice *m*; (*at football etc*) entraînement *m*; (*business*) cabinet *m*; clientèle *f* ♦ *vt*, *vi* (*US*) = **practise**; **in** ~ (*in reality*) en pratique; **out of** ~ rouillé(e); **2 hours' piano** ~ 2 heures de travail *or* d'exercices au piano; **target** ~ exercices de tir; **it's common** ~ c'est courant, ça se fait couramment; **to put sth into** ~ mettre qch en pratique.

practice match *n* match *m* d'entraînement.

practise, (*US*) **practice** ['præktɪs] *vt* (*work at: piano, one's backhand etc*) s'exercer à, travailler; (*train for: skiing, running etc*) s'entraîner à; (*a sport, religion, method*) pratiquer; (*profession*) exercer ♦ *vi* s'exercer, travailler; (*train*) s'entraîner; **to** ~ **for a match** s'entraîner pour un match.

practised, (*US*) **practiced** ['præktɪst] *adj* (*person*) expérimenté(e); (*performance*) impeccable; (*liar*) invétéré(e); **with a** ~ **eye** d'un œil exercé.

practising, (*US*) **practicing** ['præktɪsɪŋ] *adj* (*Christian etc*) pratiquant(e); (*lawyer*) en exercice; (*homosexual*) déclaré.

practitioner [præk'tɪʃənə*] *n* praticien/ne.

pragmatic [præg'mætɪk] *adj* pragmatique.

Prague [prɑːg] *n* Prague.

prairie ['prɛərɪ] *n* savane *f*; (*US*): **the** ~**s** la Prairie.

praise [preɪz] *n* éloge(s) *m(pl)*, louange(s) *f(pl)* ♦ *vt* louer, faire l'éloge de.

praiseworthy ['preɪzwəːðɪ] *adj* digne de louanges.

pram [præm] *n* (*BRIT*) landau *m*, voiture *f* d'enfant.

prance [prɑːns] *vi* (*horse*) caracoler.

prank [præŋk] *n* farce *f*.

prat [præt] *n* (*BRIT col*) imbécile *m*, andouille *f*.

prattle ['prætl] *vi* jacasser.

prawn [prɔːn] *n* crevette *f* (rose).

pray [preɪ] *vi* prier.

prayer [prɛə*] *n* prière *f*.

prayer book *n* livre *m* de prières.

pre... ['priː] *prefix* pré...; ~**-1970** *adj* d'avant 1970 ♦ *adv* avant 1970.

preach [priːtʃ] *vt*, *vi* prêcher; **to** ~ **at sb** faire la morale à qn.

preacher ['priːtʃə*] *n* prédicateur *m*; (*US: clergyman*) pasteur *m*.

preamble [prɪ'æmbl] *n* préambule *m*.

prearranged [priːə'reɪndʒd] *adj* organisé(e) *or* fixé(e) à l'avance.

precarious [prɪ'kɛərɪəs] *adj* précaire.

precaution [prɪ'kɔːʃən] *n* précaution *f*.

precautionary [prɪ'kɔːʃənrɪ] *adj* (*measure*) de précaution.

precede [prɪ'siːd] *vt*, *vi* précéder.

precedence ['prɛsɪdəns] *n* préséance *f*.

precedent ['prɛsɪdənt] *n* précédent *m*; **to establish** *or* **set a** ~ créer un précédent.

preceding [prɪ'siːdɪŋ] *adj* qui précède (*or* précédait).

precept ['priːsɛpt] *n* précepte *m*.

precinct ['priːsɪŋkt] *n* (*round cathedral*) pourtour *m*, enceinte *f*; (*US: district*) circonscription *f*, arrondissement *m*; ~**s** *npl* (*neighbourhood*) alentours *mpl*, environs *mpl*; **pedestrian** ~ zone piétonne; **shopping** ~ (*BRIT*) centre commercial.

precious ['prɛʃəs] *adj* précieux(euse) ♦ *adv* (*col*): ~ **little** *or* **few** fort peu; **your** ~ **dog** (*ironic*) ton chien chéri, ton chéri chien.

precipice ['prɛsɪpɪs] *n* précipice *m*.

precipitate *adj* [prɪ'sɪpɪtɪt] (*hasty*) précipité(e) ♦ *vt* [prɪ'sɪpɪteɪt] précipiter.

precipitation [prɪsɪpɪ'teɪʃən] *n* précipitation *f*.

precipitous [prɪ'sɪpɪtəs] *adj* (*steep*) abrupt(e), à pic.

précis, *pl* **précis** ['preɪsiː, -z] *n* résumé *m*.

precise [prɪ'saɪs] *adj* précis(e).

precisely [prɪ'saɪslɪ] *adv* précisément.

precision [prɪ'sɪʒən] *n* précision *f*.

preclude [prɪ'kluːd] *vt* exclure, empêcher; **to** ~ **sb from doing** empêcher qn de faire.

precocious [prɪ'kəuʃəs] *adj* précoce.

preconceived [priːkən'siːvd] *adj* (*idea*) préconçu(e).

preconception [priːkən'sɛpʃən] *n* idée préconçue.

precondition [priːkən'dɪʃən] *n* condition *f* nécessaire.

precursor [priː'kəːsə*] *n* précurseur *m*.

predate [priː'deɪt] *vt* (*precede*) antidater.

predator ['prɛdətə*] *n* prédateur *m*, rapace *m*.

predatory ['prɛdətərɪ] *adj* rapace.

predecessor ['priːdɪsɛsə*] *n* prédécesseur *m*.

predestination [priːdɛstɪ'neɪʃən] *n* prédestination *f*.

predetermine [priːdɪ'təːmɪn] *vt* déterminer à l'avance.

predicament [prɪ'dɪkəmənt] *n* situation *f* difficile.

predicate ['prɛdɪkɪt] *n* (*LING*) prédicat *m*.

predict [prɪ'dɪkt] *vt* prédire.

predictable [prɪ'dɪktəbl] *adj* prévisible.

predictably [prɪ'dɪktəblɪ] *adv* (*behave, react*) de façon prévisible; ~ **she didn't arrive** comme on pouvait s'y attendre, elle n'est pas venue.

prediction [prɪ'dɪkʃən] *n* prédiction *f*.

predispose [priːdɪs'pəuz] *vt* prédisposer.

predominance [prɪ'dɔmɪnəns] *n* prédominance *f*.

predominant [prɪ'dɔmɪnənt] *adj* prédominant(e).

predominantly [prɪ'dɔmɪnəntlɪ] *adv* en majeure partie; surtout.

predominate [prɪ'dɔmɪneɪt] *vi* prédominer.

pre-eminent [priː'ɛmɪnənt] *adj* prééminent(e).

pre-empt [priː'ɛmt] *vt* (*BRIT*) acquérir par droit de préemption; (*fig*) anticiper sur; **to** ~ **the issue** conclure avant même d'ouvrir les débats.

pre-emptive [prɪ'ɛmtɪv] *adj*: ~ **strike** attaque (*or* action) préventive.

preen [priːn] *vt*: **to ~ itself** (*bird*) se lisser les plumes; **to ~ o.s.** s'admirer.
prefab ['priːfæb] *n abbr* (= *prefabricated building*) (bâtiment) préfabriqué *m*.
prefabricated [priː'fæbrɪkeɪtɪd] *adj* préfabriqué(e).
preface ['prɛfəs] *n* préface *f*.
prefect ['priːfɛkt] *n* (*BRIT*: *in school*) *élève chargé de certaines fonctions de discipline*; (*in France*) préfet *m*.
prefer [prɪ'fəː*] *vt* préférer; (*LAW*): **to ~ charges** procéder à une inculpation; **to ~ coffee to tea** préférer le café au thé.
preferable ['prɛfrəbl] *adj* préférable.
preferably ['prɛfrəblɪ] *adv* de préférence.
preference ['prɛfrəns] *n* préférence *f*; **in ~ to sth** plutôt que qch, de préférence à qch.
preference shares *npl* (*BRIT*) actions privilégiées.
preferential [prɛfə'rɛnʃəl] *adj* préférentiel(le); **~ treatment** traitement *m* de faveur.
preferred stock [prɪ'fəːd-] *npl* (*US*) = **preference shares**.
prefix ['priːfɪks] *n* préfixe *m*.
pregnancy ['prɛgnənsɪ] *n* grossesse *f*.
pregnancy test *n* test *m* de grossesse.
pregnant ['prɛgnənt] *adj* enceinte *adj f*; **3 months ~** enceinte de 3 mois.
prehistoric ['priːhɪs'tɔrɪk] *adj* préhistorique.
prehistory [priː'hɪstərɪ] *n* préhistoire *f*.
prejudge [priː'dʒʌdʒ] *vt* préjuger de.
prejudice ['prɛdʒudɪs] *n* préjugé *m*; (*harm*) tort *m*, préjudice *m* ♦ *vt* porter préjudice à; (*bias*): **to ~ sb in favour of/against** prévenir qn en faveur de/contre.
prejudiced ['prɛdʒudɪst] *adj* (*person*) plein(e) de préjugés; (*view*) préconçu(e), partial(e); **to be ~ against sb/sth** avoir un parti-pris contre qn/qch; **to be racially ~** avoir des préjugés raciaux.
prelate ['prɛlət] *n* prélat *m*.
preliminaries [prɪ'lɪmɪnərɪz] *npl* préliminaires *mpl*.
preliminary [prɪ'lɪmɪnərɪ] *adj* préliminaire.
prelude ['prɛljuːd] *n* prélude *m*.
premarital ['priː'mærɪtl] *adj* avant le mariage; **~ contract** contrat *m* de mariage.
premature ['prɛmətʃuə*] *adj* prématuré(e); **to be ~ (in doing sth)** aller un peu (trop) vite (en faisant qch).
premeditated [priː'mɛdɪteɪtɪd] *adj* prémédité(e).
premeditation [priːmɛdɪ'teɪʃən] *n* préméditation *f*.
premenstrual [priː'mɛnstruəl] *adj* prémenstruel(le).
premenstrual tension *n* irritabilité *f* avant les règles.
premier ['prɛmɪə*] *adj* premier(ière), principal(e) ♦ *n* (*POL*: *Prime Minister*) premier ministre; (: *President*) chef *m* de l'État.
premiere ['prɛmɪɛə*] *n* première *f*.
premise ['prɛmɪs] *n* prémisse *f*.
premises ['prɛmɪsɪz] *npl* locaux *mpl*; **on the ~** sur les lieux; sur place; **business ~** locaux commerciaux.
premium ['priːmɪəm] *n* prime *f*; **to be at a ~** (*fig: housing etc*) être très demandé(e), être rarissime; **to sell at a ~** (*shares*) vendre au-dessus du pair.
premium bond *n* (*BRIT*) obligation *f* à prime, bon *m* à lots.
premium deal *n* (*COMM*) offre spéciale.
premium fuel (*BRIT*), **premium gasoline** (*US*) *n* super(carburant) *m*.
premonition [prɛmə'nɪʃən] *n* prémonition *f*.
preoccupation [priːɔkju'peɪʃən] *n* préoccupation *f*.
preoccupied [priː'ɔkjupaɪd] *adj* préoccupé(e).
prep [prɛp] *adj abbr*: **~ school = preparatory school** ♦ *n abbr* (*SCOL*: = *preparation*) étude *f*.
prepackaged [priː'pækɪdʒd] *adj* préempaqueté(e).
prepaid [priː'peɪd] *adj* payé(e) d'avance.
preparation [prɛpə'reɪʃən] *n* préparation *f*; **~s** (*for trip, war*) préparatifs *mpl*; **in ~ for** en vue de.
preparatory [prɪ'pærətərɪ] *adj* préparatoire; **~ to sth/to doing sth** en prévision de qch/avant de faire qch.
preparatory school *n* école primaire privée; (*US*) lycée privé; *voir encadré*.

PREPARATORY SCHOOL

En Grande-Bretagne, une **preparatory school** *- ou, plus familièrement, une "prep school" - est une école payante qui prépare les enfants de 7 à 13 ans aux "public schools".*

prepare [prɪ'pɛə*] *vt* préparer ♦ *vi*: **to ~ for** se préparer à.
prepared [prɪ'pɛəd] *adj*: **~ for** préparé(e) à; **~ to** prêt(e) à.
preponderance [prɪ'pɔndərns] *n* prépondérance *f*.
preposition [prɛpə'zɪʃən] *n* préposition *f*.
prepossessing [priːpə'zɛsɪŋ] *adj* avenant(e), engageant(e).
preposterous [prɪ'pɔstərəs] *adj* ridicule, grotesque.
prep school *n* = **preparatory school**.
prerecord ['priːrɪ'kɔːd] *vt*: **~ed broadcast** émission *f* en différé; **~ed cassette** cassette enregistrée.
prerequisite [priː'rɛkwɪzɪt] *n* condition *f* préalable.
prerogative [prɪ'rɔgətɪv] *n* prérogative *f*.
presbyterian [prɛzbɪ'tɪərɪən] *adj, n* presbytérien(ne).
presbytery ['prɛzbɪtərɪ] *n* presbytère *m*.
preschool ['priː'skuːl] *adj* préscolaire; (*child*) d'âge préscolaire.
prescribe [prɪ'skraɪb] *vt* prescrire; **~d books**

(*BRIT SCOL*) œuvres *fpl* au programme.
prescription [prɪ'skrɪpʃən] *n* prescription *f*; (*MED*) ordonnance *f*; **to make up** *or* (*US*) **fill a ~** faire une ordonnance; **"only available on ~"** "uniquement sur ordonnance".
prescription charges *npl* (*BRIT*) participation *f* fixe au coût de l'ordonnance.
prescriptive [prɪ'skrɪptɪv] *adj* normatif(ive).
presence ['prɛzns] *n* présence *f*; **~ of mind** présence d'esprit.
present ['prɛznt] *adj* présent(e) ♦ *n* cadeau *m*; (*also*: **~ tense**) présent *m* ♦ *vt* [prɪ'zɛnt] présenter; (*give*): **to ~ sb with sth** offrir qch à qn; **to be ~ at** assister à; **those ~** les présents; **at ~** en ce moment; **to give sb a ~** offrir un cadeau à qn; **to ~ sb (to sb)** présenter qn (à qn).
presentable [prɪ'zɛntəbl] *adj* présentable.
presentation [prɛzn'teɪʃən] *n* présentation *f*; (*gift*) cadeau *m*, présent *m*; (*ceremony*) remise *f* du cadeau; **on ~ of** (*voucher etc*) sur présentation de.
present-day ['prɛzntdeɪ] *adj* contemporain(e), actuel(le).
presenter [prɪ'zɛntə*] *n* (*BRIT RADIO, TV*) présentateur/trice.
presently ['prɛzntlɪ] *adv* (*soon*) tout à l'heure, bientôt; (*at present*) en ce moment; (*US*: *now*) maintenant.
preservation [prɛzə'veɪʃən] *n* préservation *f*, conservation *f*.
preservative [prɪ'zə:vətɪv] *n* agent *m* de conservation.
preserve [prɪ'zə:v] *vt* (*keep safe*) préserver, protéger; (*maintain*) conserver, garder; (*food*) mettre en conserve ♦ *n* (*for game, fish*) réserve *f*; (*often pl*: *jam*) confiture *f*; (*: fruit*) fruits *mpl* en conserve.
preshrunk [pri:'ʃrʌŋk] *adj* irrétrécissable.
preside [prɪ'zaɪd] *vi* présider.
presidency ['prɛzɪdənsɪ] *n* présidence *f*.
president ['prɛzɪdənt] *n* président/e; (*US*: *of company*) président-directeur général, PDG *m*.
presidential [prɛzɪ'dɛnʃl] *adj* présidentiel(le).
press [prɛs] *n* (*tool, machine, newspapers*) presse *f*; (*for wine*) pressoir *m*; (*crowd*) cohue *f*, foule *f* ♦ *vt* (*push*) appuyer sur; (*squeeze*) presser, serrer; (*clothes: iron*) repasser; (*pursue*) talonner; (*insist*): **to ~ sth on sb** presser qn d'accepter qch; (*urge, entreat*): **to ~ sb to do** *or* **into doing sth** pousser qn à faire qch ♦ *vi* appuyer, peser; se presser; **we are ~ed for time** le temps nous manque; **to ~ for sth** faire pression pour obtenir qch; **to ~ sb for an answer** presser qn de répondre; **to ~ charges against sb** (*LAW*) engager des poursuites contre qn; **to go to ~** (*newspaper*) aller à l'impression; **to be in the ~** (*being printed*) être sous presse; (*in the newspapers*) être dans le journal.
►**press ahead** *vi* = **press on**.
►**press on** *vi* continuer.
press agency *n* agence *f* de presse.
press clipping *n* coupure *f* de presse.
press conference *n* conférence *f* de presse.
press cutting *n* = **press clipping**.
press-gang ['prɛsgæŋ] *vt* (*fig*): **to ~ sb into doing sth** faire pression sur qn pour qu'il fasse qch.
pressing ['prɛsɪŋ] *adj* urgent(e), pressant(e) ♦ *n* repassage *m*.
press officer *n* attaché/e de presse.
press release *n* communiqué *m* de presse.
press stud *n* (*BRIT*) bouton-pression *m*.
press-up ['prɛsʌp] *n* (*BRIT*) traction *f*.
pressure ['prɛʃə*] *n* pression *f*; (*stress*) tension *f* ♦ *vt* = **to put ~ on**; **to put ~ on sb (to do sth)** faire pression sur qn (pour qu'il fasse qch).
pressure cooker *n* cocotte-minute *f*.
pressure gauge *n* manomètre *m*.
pressure group *n* groupe *m* de pression.
pressurize ['prɛʃəraɪz] *vt* pressuriser; (*BRIT fig*): **to ~ sb (into doing sth)** faire pression sur qn (pour qu'il fasse qch).
pressurized ['prɛʃəraɪzd] *adj* pressurisé(e).
Prestel ['prɛstɛl] *n* ® ≈ Minitel *m* ®.
prestige [prɛs'ti:ʒ] *n* prestige *m*.
prestigious [prɛs'tɪdʒəs] *adj* prestigieux(euse).
presumably [prɪ'zju:məblɪ] *adv* vraisemblablement; **~ he did it** c'est sans doute lui (qui a fait cela).
presume [prɪ'zju:m] *vt* présumer, supposer; **to ~ to do** (*dare*) se permettre de faire.
presumption [prɪ'zʌmpʃən] *n* supposition *f*, présomption *f*; (*boldness*) audace *f*.
presumptuous [prɪ'zʌmpʃəs] *adj* présomptueux(euse).
presuppose [pri:sə'pəuz] *vt* présupposer.
pre-tax [pri:'tæks] *adj* avant impôt(s).
pretence, (*US*) **pretense** [prɪ'tɛns] *n* (*claim*) prétention *f*; (*pretext*) prétexte *m*; **she is devoid of all ~** elle n'est pas du tout prétentieuse; **to make a ~ of doing** faire semblant de faire; **on** *or* **under the ~ of doing sth** sous prétexte de faire qch.
pretend [prɪ'tɛnd] *vt* (*feign*) feindre, simuler ♦ *vi* (*feign*) faire semblant; (*claim*): **to ~ to sth** prétendre à qch; **to ~ to do** faire semblant de faire.
pretense [prɪ'tɛns] *n* (*US*) = **pretence**.
pretension [prɪ'tɛnʃən] *n* (*claim*) prétention *f*; **to have no ~s to sth/to being sth** n'avoir aucune prétention à qch/à être qch.
pretentious [prɪ'tɛnʃəs] *adj* prétentieux(euse).
preterite ['prɛtərɪt] *n* prétérit *m*.
pretext ['pri:tɛkst] *n* prétexte *m*; **on** *or* **under the ~ of doing sth** sous prétexte de faire qch.
pretty ['prɪtɪ] *adj* joli(e) ♦ *adv* assez.
prevail [prɪ'veɪl] *vi* (*win*) l'emporter, prévaloir; (*be usual*) avoir cours; (*persuade*): **to ~ (up)on sb to do** persuader qn de faire.
prevailing [prɪ'veɪlɪŋ] *adj* dominant(e).

prevalent ['prɛvələnt] *adj* répandu(e), courant(e); (*fashion*) en vogue.
prevarication [prɪværɪ'keɪʃən] *n* (usage *m* de) faux-fuyants *mpl*.
prevent [prɪ'vɛnt] *vt*: **to ~ (from doing)** empêcher (de faire).
preventable [prɪ'vɛntəbl] *adj* évitable.
preventative [prɪ'vɛntətɪv] *adj* préventif(ive).
prevention [prɪ'vɛnʃən] *n* prévention *f*.
preventive [prɪ'vɛntɪv] *adj* préventif(ive).
preview ['priːvjuː] *n* (*of film*) avant-première *f*; (*fig*) aperçu *m*.
previous ['priːvɪəs] *adj* (*last*) précédent(e); (*earlier*) antérieur(e); (*question, experience*) préalable; **I have a ~ engagement** je suis déjà pris(e); **~ to doing** avant de faire.
previously ['priːvɪəslɪ] *adv* précédemment, auparavant.
prewar [priː'wɔː*] *adj* d'avant-guerre.
prey [preɪ] *n* proie *f* ♦ *vi*: **to ~ on** s'attaquer à; **it was ~ing on his mind** ça le rongeait *or* minait.
price [praɪs] *n* prix *m*; (*BETTING*: *odds*) cote *f* ♦ *vt* (*goods*) fixer le prix de; tarifer; **what is the ~ of ...?** combien coûte ...?, quel est le prix de ...?; **to go up** *or* **rise in ~** augmenter; **to put a ~ on sth** chiffrer qch; **what ~ his promises now?** (*BRIT*) que valent maintenant toutes ses promesses?; **he regained his freedom, but at a ~** il a retrouvé sa liberté, mais cela lui a coûté cher.
price control *n* contrôle *m* des prix.
price-cutting ['praɪskʌtɪŋ] *n* réductions *fpl* de prix.
priceless ['praɪslɪs] *adj* sans prix, inestimable; (*col*: *amusing*) impayable.
price list *n* tarif *m*.
price range *n* gamme *f* de prix; **it's within my ~** c'est dans mes prix.
price tag *n* étiquette *f*.
price war *n* guerre *f* des prix.
pricey ['praɪsɪ] *adj* (*col*) chérot *inv*.
prick [prɪk] *n* piqûre *f*; (*col!*) bitte *f* (*!*); connard *m* (*!*) ♦ *vt* piquer; **to ~ up one's ears** dresser *or* tendre l'oreille.
prickle ['prɪkl] *n* (*of plant*) épine *f*; (*sensation*) picotement *m*.
prickly ['prɪklɪ] *adj* piquant(e), épineux(euse); (*fig: person*) irritable.
prickly heat *n* fièvre *f* miliaire.
prickly pear *n* figue *f* de Barbarie.
pride [praɪd] *n* (*feeling proud*) fierté *f*; (*: pej*) orgueil *m*; (*self-esteem*) amour-propre *m* ♦ *vt*: **to ~ o.s. on** se flatter de; s'enorgueillir de; **to take (a) ~ in** être (très) fier(ère) de; **to take a ~ in doing** mettre sa fierté à faire; **to have ~ of place** (*BRIT*) avoir la place d'honneur.
priest [priːst] *n* prêtre *m*.
priestess ['priːstɪs] *n* prêtresse *f*.
priesthood ['priːsthud] *n* prêtrise *f*, sacerdoce *m*.
prig [prɪg] *n* poseur/euse, fat *m*.
prim [prɪm] *adj* collet monté *inv*, guindé(e).
prima facie ['praɪmə'feɪʃɪ] *adj*: **to have a ~ case** (*LAW*) avoir une affaire recevable.
primal ['praɪməl] *adj* (*first in time*) primitif(ive); (*first in importance*) primordial(e).
primarily ['praɪmərɪlɪ] *adv* principalement, essentiellement.
primary ['praɪmərɪ] *adj* primaire; (*first in importance*) premier(ière), primordial(e) ♦ *n* (*US*: *election*) (élection *f*) primaire *f*; *voir encadré*.

PRIMARIES

Aux États-Unis, les **primaries** *constituent un processus de sélection préliminaire des candidats qui seront choisis par les principaux partis lors de la campagne électorale pour l'élection présidentielle. Elles ont lieu dans 35 États, de février à juin, l'année de l'élection. Chaque État envoie en juillet - août des "delegates" aux conventions démocrate et républicaine chargées de désigner leur candidat à la présidence. Ces "delegates" sont généralement choisis en fonction du nombre de voix obtenu par les candidats lors des* **primaries**.

primary colour *n* couleur fondamentale.
primary school *n* (*BRIT*) école *f* primaire; *voir encadré*.

PRIMARY SCHOOL

Les **primary schools** *en Grande-Bretagne accueillent les enfants de 5 à 11 ans. Elles marquent le début du cycle scolaire obligatoire et elles comprennent deux sections: la section des petits ("infant school") et la section des grands ("junior school"); voir "secondary school".*

primate *n* (*REL*) ['praɪmɪt] primat *m*; (*ZOOL*) ['praɪmeɪt] primate *m*.
prime [praɪm] *adj* primordial(e), fondamental(e); (*excellent*) excellent(e) ♦ *vt* (*gun, pump*) amorcer; (*fig*) mettre au courant; **in the ~ of life** dans la fleur de l'âge.
prime minister *n* Premier ministre.
primer ['praɪmə*] *n* (*book*) premier livre, manuel *m* élémentaire; (*paint*) apprêt *m*.
prime time *n* (*RADIO, TV*) heure(s) *f(pl)* de grande écoute.
primeval [praɪ'miːvl] *adj* primitif(ive).
primitive ['prɪmɪtɪv] *adj* primitif(ive).
primrose ['prɪmrəuz] *n* primevère *f*.
primus (stove) ['praɪməs-] *n* ® (*BRIT*) réchaud *m* de camping.
prince [prɪns] *n* prince *m*.
princess [prɪn'sɛs] *n* princesse *f*.
principal ['prɪnsɪpl] *adj* principal(e) ♦ *n* (*headmaster*) directeur *m*, principal *m*; (*in play*) rôle principal; (*money*) principal *m*.

principality [prɪnsɪ'pælɪtɪ] *n* principauté *f*.
principally ['prɪnsɪplɪ] *adv* principalement.
principle ['prɪnsɪpl] *n* principe *m*; **in** ~ en principe; **on** ~ par principe.
print [prɪnt] *n* (*mark*) empreinte *f*; (*letters*) caractères *mpl*; (*fabric*) imprimé *m*; (*ART*) gravure *f*, estampe *f*; (*PHOT*) épreuve *f* ♦ *vt* imprimer; (*publish*) publier; (*write in capitals*) écrire en majuscules; **out of** ~ épuisé(e).
►**print out** *vt* (*COMPUT*) imprimer.
printed circuit board (PCB) ['prɪntɪd-] *n* carte *f* à circuit imprimé.
printed matter ['prɪntɪd-] *n* imprimés *mpl*.
printer ['prɪntə*] *n* imprimeur *m*; (*machine*) imprimante *f*.
printhead ['prɪnthɛd] *n* tête *f* d'impression.
printing ['prɪntɪŋ] *n* impression *f*.
printing press *n* presse *f* typographique.
printout ['prɪntaut] *n* copie *f* papier, tirage *m*.
print wheel *n* marguerite *f*.
prior ['praɪə*] *adj* antérieur(e), précédent(e) ♦ *n* (*REL*) prieur *m*; ~ **to doing** avant de faire; **without** ~ **notice** sans préavis; **to have a** ~ **claim to sth** avoir priorité pour qch.
priority [praɪ'ɔrɪtɪ] *n* priorité *f*; **to have** *or* **take** ~ **over sth/sb** avoir la priorité sur qch/qn.
priory ['praɪərɪ] *n* prieuré *m*.
prise [praɪz] *vt*: **to** ~ **open** forcer.
prism ['prɪzəm] *n* prisme *m*.
prison ['prɪzn] *n* prison *f*.
prison camp *n* camp *m* de prisonniers.
prisoner ['prɪznə*] *n* prisonnier/ière; **the** ~ **at the bar** l'accusé/e; **to take sb** ~ faire qn prisonnier; ~ **of war** prisonnier de guerre.
prissy ['prɪsɪ] *adj* bégueule.
pristine ['prɪstiːn] *adj* virginal(e).
privacy ['prɪvəsɪ] *n* intimité *f*, solitude *f*.
private ['praɪvɪt] *adj* (*not public*) privé(e); (*personal*) personnel(le); (*house, car, lesson*) particulier(ière) ♦ *n* soldat *m* de deuxième classe; **"~"** (*on envelope*) "personnelle"; **in** ~ en privé; **in (his)** ~ **life** dans sa vie privée; **he is a very** ~ **person** il est très secret; **to be in** ~ **practice** être médecin non conventionné; ~ **hearing** (*LAW*) audience *f* à huis-clos.
private enterprise *n* entreprise privée.
private eye *n* détective privé.
private limited company *n* (*BRIT*) société *f* à participation restreinte (*non cotée en Bourse*).
privately ['praɪvɪtlɪ] *adv* en privé; (*within oneself*) intérieurement.
private parts *npl* parties (génitales).
private property *n* propriété privée.
private school *n* école privée.
privatize ['praɪvɪtaɪz] *vt* privatiser.
privet ['prɪvɪt] *n* troène *m*.
privilege ['prɪvɪlɪdʒ] *n* privilège *m*.
privileged ['prɪvɪlɪdʒd] *adj* privilégié(e); **to be** ~ **to do sth** avoir le privilège de faire qch.
privy ['prɪvɪ] *adj*: **to be** ~ **to** être au courant de.
privy council *n* conseil privé; *voir encadré*.

PRIVY COUNCIL

Le **privy council** *existe en Angleterre depuis l'avènement des Normands. À l'époque, ses membres étaient les conseillers privés du roi, mais en 1688 le cabinet les a supplantés. Les ministres du cabinet sont aujourd'hui automatiquement conseillers du roi, et ce titre est également accordé aux personnes qui ont occupé de hautes fonctions en politique, dans le clergé ou dans les milieux juridiques. Les pouvoirs de ces conseillers en tant que tels sont maintenant limités.*

prize [praɪz] *n* prix *m* ♦ *adj* (*example, idiot*) parfait(e); (*bull, novel*) primé(e) ♦ *vt* priser, faire grand cas de.
prize-fighter ['praɪzfaɪtə*] *n* boxeur professionnel.
prize giving *n* distribution *f* des prix.
prize money *n* argent *m* du prix.
prizewinner ['praɪzwɪnə*] *n* gagnant/e.
prizewinning ['praɪzwɪnɪŋ] *adj* gagnant(e); (*novel, essay etc*) primé(e).
PRO *n abbr* = **public relations officer**.
pro [prəu] *n* (*SPORT*) professionnel/le; **the ~s and cons** le pour et le contre.
pro- [prəu] *prefix* (*in favour of*) pro-.
pro-active [prəu'æktɪv] *adj* dynamique.
probability [prɔbə'bɪlɪtɪ] *n* probabilité *f*; **in all** ~ très probablement.
probable ['prɔbəbl] *adj* probable; **it is ~/hardly ~ that ...** il est probable/peu probable que ....
probably ['prɔbəblɪ] *adv* probablement.
probate ['prəubɪt] *n* (*LAW*) validation *f*, homologation *f*.
probation [prə'beɪʃən] *n* (*in employment*) (période *f* d')essai *m*; (*LAW*) liberté surveillée; (*REL*) noviciat *m*, probation *f*; **on** ~ (*employee*) à l'essai; (*LAW*) en liberté surveillée.
probationary [prə'beɪʃənrɪ] *adj* (*period*) d'essai.
probe [prəub] *n* (*MED, SPACE*) sonde *f*; (*enquiry*) enquête *f*, investigation *f* ♦ *vt* sonder, explorer.
probity ['prəubɪtɪ] *n* probité *f*.
problem ['prɔbləm] *n* problème *m*; **to have ~s with the car** avoir des ennuis avec la voiture; **what's the ~?** qu'y a-t-il?, quel est le problème?; **I had no** ~ **in finding her** je n'ai pas eu de mal à la trouver; **no ~!** pas de problème!
problematic [prɔblə'mætɪk] *adj* problématique.
problem-solving ['prɔbləmsɔlvɪŋ] *n* résolution *f* de problèmes; **an approach to** ~ une approche en matière de résolution de problèmes.
procedure [prə'siːdʒə*] *n* (*ADMIN, LAW*) procé-

dure *f*; (*method*) marche *f* à suivre, façon *f* de procéder.

proceed [prə'si:d] *vi* (*go forward*) avancer; (*go about it*) procéder; (*continue*): **to ~ (with)** continuer, poursuivre; **to ~ to** aller à; passer à; **to ~ to do** se mettre à faire; **I am not sure how to ~** je ne sais pas exactement comment m'y prendre; **to ~ against sb** (*LAW*) intenter des poursuites contre qn.

proceedings [prə'si:dɪŋz] *npl* mesures *fpl*; (*LAW*) poursuites *fpl*; (*meeting*) réunion *f*, séance *f*; (*records*) compte rendu; actes *mpl*.

proceeds ['prəusi:dz] *npl* produit *m*, recette *f*.

process ['prəusɛs] *n* processus *m*; (*method*) procédé *m* ♦ *vt* traiter ♦ *vi* [prə'sɛs] (*BRIT formal: go in procession*) défiler; **in ~** en cours; **we are in the ~ of doing** nous sommes en train de faire.

processed cheese ['prəusɛst-] *n* ≈ fromage fondu.

processing ['prəusɛsɪŋ] *n* traitement *m*.

procession [prə'sɛʃən] *n* défilé *m*, cortège *m*; **funeral ~** cortège funèbre, convoi *m* mortuaire.

pro-choice [prəu'tʃɔɪs] *adj* en faveur de l'avortement.

proclaim [prə'kleɪm] *vt* déclarer, proclamer.

proclamation [prɔklə'meɪʃən] *n* proclamation *f*.

proclivity [prə'klɪvɪtɪ] *n* inclination *f*.

procrastination [prəukræstɪ'neɪʃən] *n* procrastination *f*.

procreation [prəukrɪ'eɪʃən] *n* procréation *f*.

Procurator Fiscal ['prɔkjureɪtə-] *n* (*Scottish*) ≈ procureur *m* (*de la République*).

procure [prə'kjuə*] *vt* (*for o.s.*) se procurer; (*for sb*) procurer.

procurement [prə'kjuəmənt] *n* achat *m*, approvisionnement *m*.

prod [prɔd] *vt* pousser ♦ *n* (*push, jab*) petit coup, poussée *f*.

prodigal ['prɔdɪgl] *adj* prodigue.

prodigious [prə'dɪdʒəs] *adj* prodigieux(euse).

prodigy ['prɔdɪdʒɪ] *n* prodige *m*.

produce *n* ['prɔdju:s] (*AGR*) produits *mpl* ♦ *vt* [prə'dju:s] produire; (*to show*) présenter; (*cause*) provoquer, causer; (*THEAT*) monter, mettre en scène.

producer [prə'dju:sə*] *n* (*THEAT*) metteur *m* en scène; (*AGR, CINE*) producteur *m*.

product ['prɔdʌkt] *n* produit *m*.

production [prə'dʌkʃən] *n* production *f*; (*THEAT*) mise *f* en scène; **to put into ~** (*goods*) entreprendre la fabrication de.

production agreement *n* (*US*) accord *m* de productivité.

production line *n* chaîne *f* (de fabrication).

production manager *n* directeur/trice de la production.

productive [prə'dʌktɪv] *adj* productif(ive).

productivity [prɔdʌk'tɪvɪtɪ] *n* productivité *f*.

productivity agreement *n* (*BRIT*) accord *m* de productivité.

productivity bonus *n* prime *f* de rendement.

Prof. [prɔf] *abbr* (= *professor*) Prof.

profane [prə'feɪn] *adj* sacrilège; (*lay*) profane.

profess [prə'fɛs] *vt* professer; **I do not ~ to be an expert** je ne prétends pas être spécialiste.

professed [prə'fɛst] *adj* (*self-declared*) déclaré(e).

profession [prə'fɛʃən] *n* profession *f*; **the ~s** les professions libérales.

professional [prə'fɛʃənl] *n* (*SPORT*) professionnel/le ♦ *adj* professionnel(le); (*work*) de professionnel; **he's a ~ man** il exerce une profession libérale; **to take ~ advice** consulter un spécialiste.

professionalism [prə'fɛʃnəlɪzəm] *n* professionnalisme *m*.

professionally [prə'fɛʃnəlɪ] *adv* professionnellement; (*SPORT: play*) en professionnel; **I only know him ~** je n'ai avec lui que des relations de travail.

professor [prə'fɛsə*] *n* professeur *m* (*titulaire d'une chaire*); (*US: teacher*) professeur *m*.

professorship [prə'fɛsəʃɪp] *n* chaire *f*.

proffer ['prɔfə*] *vt* (*hand*) tendre; (*remark*) faire; (*apologies*) présenter.

proficiency [prə'fɪʃənsɪ] *n* compétence *f*, aptitude *f*.

proficient [prə'fɪʃənt] *adj* compétent(e), capable.

profile ['prəufaɪl] *n* profil *m*; **to keep a high/low ~** (*fig*) rester *or* être très en évidence/discret(ète).

profit ['prɔfɪt] *n* (*from trading*) bénéfice *m*; (*advantage*) profit *m* ♦ *vi*: **to ~ (by *or* from)** profiter (de); **~ and loss account** compte *m* de profits et pertes; **to make a ~** faire un *or* des bénéfice(s); **to sell sth at a ~** vendre qch à profit.

profitability [prɔfɪtə'bɪlɪtɪ] *n* rentabilité *f*.

profitable ['prɔfɪtəbl] *adj* lucratif(ive), rentable; (*fig: beneficial*) avantageux(euse); (*: meeting*) fructueux(euse).

profit centre *n* centre *m* de profit.

profiteering [prɔfɪ'tɪərɪŋ] *n* (*pej*) mercantilisme *m*.

profit-making ['prɔfɪtmeɪkɪŋ] *adj* à but lucratif.

profit margin *n* marge *f* bénéficiaire.

profit-sharing ['prɔfɪtʃɛərɪŋ] *n* intéressement *m* aux bénéfices.

profits tax *n* (*BRIT*) impôt *m* sur les bénéfices.

profligate ['prɔflɪgɪt] *adj* (*behaviour, act*) dissolu(e); (*person*) débauché(e); (*extravagant*): **~ (with)** prodigue (de).

pro forma ['prəu'fɔ:mə] *adj*: **~ invoice** facture *f* pro-forma.

profound [prə'faund] *adj* profond(e).

profuse [prə'fju:s] *adj* abondant(e).

profusely [prə'fju:slɪ] *adv* abondamment; (*thank etc*) avec effusion.

profusion [prə'fju:ʒən] *n* profusion *f*, abondance *f*.

progeny ['prɔdʒɪnɪ] *n* progéniture *f*; descendants *mpl*.

programme, (*US, also: BRIT COMPUT*) **program** ['prəugræm] *n* programme *m*; (*RADIO, TV*) émission *f* ♦ *vt* programmer.

program(m)er ['prəugræmə*] *n* programmeur/euse.

program(m)ing ['prəugræmɪŋ] *n* programmation *f*.

program(m)ing language *n* langage *m* de programmation.

progress *n* ['prəugrɛs] progrès *m* ♦ *vi* [prə'grɛs] progresser, avancer; **in** ~ en cours; **to make** ~ progresser, faire des progrès, être en progrès; **as the match** ~**ed** au fur et à mesure que la partie avançait.

progression [prə'grɛʃən] *n* progression *f*.

progressive [prə'grɛsɪv] *adj* progressif(ive); (*person*) progressiste.

progressively [prə'grɛsɪvlɪ] *adv* progressivement.

progress report *n* (*MED*) bulletin *m* de santé; (*ADMIN*) rapport *m* d'activité; rapport sur l'état (d'avancement) des travaux.

prohibit [prə'hɪbɪt] *vt* interdire, défendre; **to** ~ **sb from doing sth** défendre *or* interdire à qn de faire qch; **"smoking** ~**ed"** "défense de fumer".

prohibition [prəuɪ'bɪʃən] *n* prohibition *f*.

prohibitive [prə'hɪbɪtɪv] *adj* (*price etc*) prohibitif(ive).

project *n* ['prɔdʒɛkt] (*plan*) projet *m*, plan *m*; (*venture*) opération *f*, entreprise *f*; (*gen SCOL: research*) étude *f*, dossier *m* ♦ *vb* [prə'dʒɛkt] *vt* projeter ♦ *vi* (*stick out*) faire saillie, s'avancer.

projectile [prə'dʒɛktaɪl] *n* projectile *m*.

projection [prə'dʒɛkʃən] *n* projection *f*; (*overhang*) saillie *f*.

projectionist [prə'dʒɛkʃənɪst] *n* (*CINE*) projectionniste *m/f*.

projection room *n* (*CINE*) cabine *f* de projection.

projector [prə'dʒɛktə*] *n* (*CINE*) projecteur *m*.

proletarian [prəulɪ'tɛərɪən] *adj* prolétarien(ne) ♦ *n* prolétaire *m/f*.

proletariat [prəulɪ'tɛərɪət] *n* prolétariat *m*.

pro-life [prəu'laɪf] *adj* contre l'avortement.

proliferate [prə'lɪfəreɪt] *vi* proliférer.

proliferation [prəlɪfə'reɪʃən] *n* prolifération *f*.

prolific [prə'lɪfɪk] *adj* prolifique.

prologue ['prəulɔg] *n* prologue *m*.

prolong [prə'lɔŋ] *vt* prolonger.

prom [prɔm] *n abbr* = **promenade, promenade concert**; (*US: ball*) bal *m* d'étudiants; *voir encadré*.

promenade [prɔmə'nɑːd] *n* (*by sea*) esplanade *f*, promenade *f*.

promenade concert *n* concert *m* (de musique classique); *voir encadré*.

PROM

En Grande-Bretagne, un **promenade concert** *(ou* **prom***) est un concert de musique classique, ainsi appelé car, à l'origine, le public restait debout et se promenait au lieu de rester assis. De nos jours, une partie du public reste debout, mais il y a également des places assises (plus chères). Les Proms les plus connus sont les Proms londoniens. La dernière séance ("the Last Night of the Proms") est un grand événement médiatique où se jouent des airs traditionnels et patriotiques.*

Aux États-Unis et au Canada, le **prom** *ou* **promenade** *est un bal organisé par le lycée.*

promenade deck *n* (*NAUT*) pont *m* promenade.

prominence ['prɔmɪnəns] *n* proéminence *f*; importance *f*.

prominent ['prɔmɪnənt] *adj* (*standing out*) proéminent(e); (*important*) important(e); **he is** ~ **in the field of** ... il est très connu dans le domaine de ....

prominently ['prɔmɪnəntlɪ] *adv* (*display, set*) bien en évidence; **he figured** ~ **in the case** il a joué un rôle important dans l'affaire.

promiscuity [prɔmɪs'kjuːɪtɪ] *n* (*sexual*) légèreté *f* de mœurs.

promiscuous [prə'mɪskjuəs] *adj* (*sexually*) de mœurs légères.

promise ['prɔmɪs] *n* promesse *f* ♦ *vt, vi* promettre; **to make sb a** ~ faire une promesse à qn; **a young man of** ~ un jeune homme plein d'avenir; **to** ~ **well** *vi* promettre.

promising ['prɔmɪsɪŋ] *adj* prometteur(euse).

promissory note ['prɔmɪsərɪ-] *n* billet *m* à ordre.

promontory ['prɔməntrɪ] *n* promontoire *m*.

promote [prə'məut] *vt* promouvoir; (*venture, event*) organiser, mettre sur pied; (*new product*) lancer; **the team was** ~**d to the second division** (*BRIT FOOTBALL*) l'équipe est montée en 2e division.

promoter [prə'məutə*] *n* (*of event*) organisateur/trice.

promotion [prə'məuʃən] *n* promotion *f*.

prompt [prɔmpt] *adj* rapide ♦ *n* (*COMPUT*) message *m* (de guidage) ♦ *vt* inciter; (*cause*) entraîner, provoquer; (*THEAT*) souffler (son rôle *or* ses répliques) à; **they're very** ~ (*punctual*) ils sont ponctuels; **at 8 o'clock** ~ à 8 heures précises; **he was** ~ **to accept** il a tout de suite accepté; **to** ~ **sb to do** inciter *or* pousser qn à faire.

prompter ['prɔmptə*] *n* (*THEAT*) souffleur *m*.

promptly ['prɔmptlɪ] *adv* rapidement, sans délai; ponctuellement.

promptness ['prɔmptnɪs] *n* rapidité *f*; promptitude *f*; ponctualité *f*.

promulgate ['prɔməlgeɪt] *vt* promulguer.
prone [prəun] *adj* (*lying*) couché(e) (face contre terre); (*liable*): ~ **to** enclin(e) à; **to be ~ to illness** être facilement malade; **to be ~ to an illness** être sujet à une maladie; **she is ~ to burst into tears if** ... elle a tendance à tomber en larmes si ....
prong [prɔŋ] *n* pointe *f*; (*of fork*) dent *f*.
pronoun ['prəunaun] *n* pronom *m*.
pronounce [prə'nauns] *vt* prononcer ♦ *vi*: **to ~ (up)on** se prononcer sur; **they ~d him unfit to drive** ils l'ont déclaré inapte à la conduite.
pronounced [prə'naunst] *adj* (*marked*) prononcé(e).
pronouncement [prə'naunsmənt] *n* déclaration *f*.
pronunciation [prənʌnsɪ'eɪʃən] *n* prononciation *f*.
proof [pru:f] *n* preuve *f*; (*test, of book, PHOT*) épreuve *f*; (*of alcohol*) degré *m* ♦ *adj*: ~ **against** à l'épreuve de ♦ *vt* (*BRIT*: *tent, anorak*) imperméabiliser; **to be 70° ~** ≈ titrer 40 degrés.
proofreader ['pru:fri:də*] *n* correcteur/trice (d'épreuves).
prop [prɔp] *n* support *m*, étai *m* ♦ *vt* (*also*: ~ **up**) étayer, soutenir; (*lean*): **to ~ sth against** appuyer qch contre *or* à.
Prop. *abbr* (*COMM*) = **proprietor**.
propaganda [prɔpə'gændə] *n* propagande *f*.
propagation [prɔpə'geɪʃən] *n* propagation *f*.
propel [prə'pɛl] *vt* propulser, faire avancer.
propeller [prə'pɛlə*] *n* hélice *f*.
propelling pencil [prə'pɛlɪŋ-] *n* (*BRIT*) portemine *m inv*.
propensity [prə'pɛnsɪtɪ] *n* propension *f*.
proper ['prɔpə*] *adj* (*suited, right*) approprié(e), bon(bonne); (*seemly*) correct(e), convenable; (*authentic*) vrai(e), véritable; (*col*: *real*) fini(e), vrai(e); **to go through the ~ channels** (*ADMIN*) passer par la voie officielle.
properly ['prɔpəlɪ] *adv* correctement, convenablement; (*really*) bel et bien.
proper noun *n* nom *m* propre.
property ['prɔpətɪ] *n* (*possessions*) biens *mpl*; (*house etc*) propriété *f*; (*land*) terres *fpl*, domaine *m*; (*CHEM etc*: *quality*) propriété *f*; **it's their ~** cela leur appartient, c'est leur propriété.
property developer *n* (*BRIT*) promoteur immobilier.
property owner *n* propriétaire *m*.
property tax *n* impôt foncier.
prophecy ['prɔfɪsɪ] *n* prophétie *f*.
prophesy ['prɔfɪsaɪ] *vt* prédire ♦ *vi* prophétiser.
prophet ['prɔfɪt] *n* prophète *m*.
prophetic [prə'fɛtɪk] *adj* prophétique.
proportion [prə'pɔ:ʃən] *n* proportion *f*; (*share*) part *f*; partie *f* ♦ *vt* proportionner; **to be in/out of ~ to** *or* **with sth** être à la mesure de/hors de proportion avec qch; **to see sth in ~** (*fig*) ramener qch à de justes proportions.
proportional [prə'pɔ:ʃənl], **proportionate** [prə'pɔ:ʃənɪt] *adj* proportionnel(le).
proportional representation (PR) *n* (*POL*) représentation proportionnelle.
proposal [prə'pəuzl] *n* proposition *f*, offre *f*; (*plan*) projet *m*; (*of marriage*) demande *f* en mariage.
propose [prə'pəuz] *vt* proposer, suggérer; (*have in mind*): **to ~ sth/to do** *or* **doing sth** envisager qch/de faire qch ♦ *vi* faire sa demande en mariage; **to ~ to do** avoir l'intention de faire.
proposer [prə'pəuzə*] *n* (*BRIT*: *of motion etc*) auteur *m*.
proposition [prɔpə'zɪʃən] *n* proposition *f*; **to make sb a ~** faire une proposition à qn.
propound [prə'paund] *vt* proposer, soumettre.
proprietary [prə'praɪətərɪ] *adj* de marque déposée; ~ **article** article *m or* produit *m* de marque; ~ **brand** marque déposée.
proprietor [prə'praɪətə*] *n* propriétaire *m/f*.
propriety [prə'praɪətɪ] *n* (*seemliness*) bienséance *f*, convenance *f*.
propulsion [prə'pʌlʃən] *n* propulsion *f*.
pro rata [prəu'rɑ:tə] *adv* au prorata.
prosaic [prəu'zeɪɪk] *adj* prosaïque.
Pros. Atty. *abbr* (*US*) = **prosecuting attorney**.
proscribe [prə'skraɪb] *vt* proscrire.
prose [prəuz] *n* prose *f*; (*SCOL*: *translation*) thème *m*.
prosecute ['prɔsɪkju:t] *vt* poursuivre.
prosecuting attorney (Pros. Atty.) ['prɔsɪkju:tɪŋ-] *n* (*US*) procureur *m*.
prosecution [prɔsɪ'kju:ʃən] *n* poursuites *fpl* judiciaires; (*accusing side*) accusation *f*.
prosecutor ['prɔsɪkju:tə*] *n* procureur *m*; (*also*: **public ~**) ministère public.
prospect *n* ['prɔspɛkt] perspective *f*; (*hope*) espoir *m*, chances *fpl* ♦ *vt, vi* [prə'spɛkt] prospecter; **we are faced with the ~ of leaving** nous risquons de devoir partir; **there is every ~ of an early victory** tout laisse prévoir une victoire rapide.
prospecting [prə'spɛktɪŋ] *n* prospection *f*.
prospective [prə'spɛktɪv] *adj* (*possible*) éventuel(le); (*future*) futur(e).
prospector [prə'spɛktə*] *n* prospecteur *m*; **gold ~** chercheur *m* d'or.
prospects ['prɔspɛkts] *npl* (*for work etc*) possibilités *fpl* d'avenir, débouchés *mpl*.
prospectus [prə'spɛktəs] *n* prospectus *m*.
prosper ['prɔspə*] *vi* prospérer.
prosperity [prɔ'spɛrɪtɪ] *n* prospérité *f*.
prosperous ['prɔspərəs] *adj* prospère.
prostate ['prɔsteɪt] *n* (*also*: ~ **gland**) prostate *f*.
prostitute ['prɔstɪtju:t] *n* prostituée *f*; **male ~** prostitué *m*.
prostitution [prɔstɪ'tju:ʃən] *n* prostitution *f*.

prostrate *adj* ['prɔstreɪt] prosterné(e); (*fig*) prostré(e) ♦ *vt* [prə'streɪt]: **to ~ o.s. (before sb)** se prosterner (devant qn).
protagonist [prə'tægənɪst] *n* protagoniste *m*.
protect [prə'tɛkt] *vt* protéger.
protection [prə'tɛkʃən] *n* protection *f*; **to be under sb's ~** être sous la protection de qn.
protectionism [prə'tɛkʃənɪzəm] *n* protectionnisme *m*.
protection racket *n* racket *m*.
protective [prə'tɛktɪv] *adj* protecteur(trice); **~ custody** (*LAW*) détention préventive.
protector [prə'tɛktə*] *n* protecteur/trice.
protégé ['prəutɛʒeɪ] *n* protégé *m*.
protégée ['prəutɛʒeɪ] *n* protégée *f*.
protein ['prəutiːn] *n* protéine *f*.
pro tem [prəu'tɛm] *adv abbr* (= *pro tempore: for the time being*) provisoirement.
protest *n* ['prəutɛst] protestation *f* ♦ *vb* [prə'tɛst] *vi*: **to ~ against/about** protester contre/à propos de ♦ *vt* protester de.
Protestant ['prɔtɪstənt] *adj, n* protestant(e).
protester, protestor [prə'tɛstə*] *n* (*in demonstration*) manifestant/e.
protest march *n* manifestation *f*.
protocol ['prəutəkɔl] *n* protocole *m*.
prototype ['prəutətaɪp] *n* prototype *m*.
protracted [prə'træktɪd] *adj* prolongé(e).
protractor [prə'træktə*] *n* rapporteur *m*.
protrude [prə'truːd] *vi* avancer, dépasser.
protuberance [prə'tjuːbərəns] *n* protubérance *f*.
proud [praud] *adj* fier(ère); (*pej*) orgueilleux(euse); **to be ~ to do sth** être fier de faire qch; **to do sb ~** (*col*) faire honneur à qn; **to do o.s. ~** (*col*) ne se priver de rien.
proudly ['praudlɪ] *adv* fièrement.
prove [pruːv] *vt* prouver, démontrer ♦ *vi*: **to ~ correct** *etc* s'avérer juste *etc*; **to ~ o.s.** montrer ce dont on est capable; **to ~ o.s./itself (to be) useful** *etc* se montrer *or* se révéler utile *etc*; **he was ~d right in the end** il s'est avéré qu'il avait raison.
proverb ['prɔvəːb] *n* proverbe *m*.
proverbial [prə'vəːbɪəl] *adj* proverbial(e).
provide [prə'vaɪd] *vt* fournir; **to ~ sb with sth** fournir qch à qn; **to be ~d with** (*person*) disposer de; (*thing*) être équipé(e) *or* muni(e) de.
►**provide for** *vt fus* (*person*) subvenir aux besoins de; (*emergency*) prévoir.
provided [prə'vaɪdɪd] *conj*: **~ (that)** à condition que + *sub*.
Providence ['prɔvɪdəns] *n* la Providence.
providing [prə'vaɪdɪŋ] *conj* à condition que + *sub*.
province ['prɔvɪns] *n* province *f*.
provincial [prə'vɪnʃəl] *adj* provincial(e).
provision [prə'vɪʒən] *n* (*supply*) provision *f*; (*supplying*) fourniture *f*; approvisionnement *m*; (*stipulation*) disposition *f*; **~s** *npl* (*food*) provisions *fpl*; **to make ~ for** (*one's future*) assurer; (*one's family*) assurer l'avenir de; **there's no ~ for this in the contract** le contrat ne prévoit pas cela.
provisional [prə'vɪʒənl] *adj* provisoire ♦ *n*: **P~** (*Irish POL*) Provisional *m* (*membre de la tendance activiste de l'IRA*).
provisional licence *n* (*BRIT AUT*) permis *m* provisoire.
provisionally [prə'vɪʒnəlɪ] *adv* provisoirement.
proviso [prə'vaɪzəu] *n* condition *f*; **with the ~ that** à la condition (expresse) que.
provocation [prɔvə'keɪʃən] *n* provocation *f*.
provocative [prə'vɔkətɪv] *adj* provocateur(trice), provocant(e).
provoke [prə'vəuk] *vt* provoquer; **to ~ sb to sth/to do** *or* **into doing sth** pousser qn à qch/à faire qch.
provoking [prə'vəukɪŋ] *adj* énervant(e), exaspérant(e).
provost ['prɔvəst] *n* (*BRIT: of university*) principal *m*; (*Scottish*) maire *m*.
prow [prau] *n* proue *f*.
prowess ['prauɪs] *n* prouesse *f*.
prowl [praul] *vi* (*also*: **~ about, ~ around**) rôder ♦ *n*: **to be on the ~** rôder.
prowler ['praulə*] *n* rôdeur/euse.
proximity [prɔk'sɪmɪtɪ] *n* proximité *f*.
proxy ['prɔksɪ] *n* procuration *f*; **by ~** par procuration.
PRP *n abbr* (= *performance related pay*) salaire *m* au rendement.
prude [pruːd] *n* prude *f*.
prudence ['pruːdns] *n* prudence *f*.
prudent ['pruːdnt] *adj* prudent(e).
prudish ['pruːdɪʃ] *adj* prude, pudibond(e).
prune [pruːn] *n* pruneau *m* ♦ *vt* élaguer.
pry [praɪ] *vi*: **to ~ into** fourrer son nez dans.
PS *n abbr* (= *postscript*) PS *m*.
psalm [sɑːm] *n* psaume *m*.
PSAT *n abbr* (*US*) = *Preliminary Scholastic Aptitude Test*.
PSBR *n abbr* (*BRIT: = public sector borrowing requirement*) besoins *mpl* d'emprunts des pouvoirs publics.
pseud [sjuːd] *n* (*BRIT col: intellectually*) pseudo-intello *m*; (*: socially*) snob *m/f*.
pseudo- ['sjuːdəu] *prefix* pseudo-.
pseudonym ['sjuːdənɪm] *n* pseudonyme *m*.
PSHE *n abbr* (*BRIT SCOL: = personal, social and health education*) ≈ éducation *f* civique.
PST *abbr* (*US: = Pacific Standard Time*) *heure d'hiver du Pacifique*.
PSV *n abbr* (*BRIT*) = **public service vehicle**.
psyche ['saɪkɪ] *n* psychisme *m*.
psychiatric [saɪkɪ'ætrɪk] *adj* psychiatrique.
psychiatrist [saɪ'kaɪətrɪst] *n* psychiatre *m/f*.
psychiatry [saɪ'kaɪətrɪ] *n* psychiatrie *f*.
psychic ['saɪkɪk] *adj* (*also*: **~al**) (méta)psychique; (*person*) doué(e) de télépathie *or* d'un sixième sens.
psycho ['saɪkəu] *n* (*col*) psychopathe *m/f*.

psychoanalysis, *pl* **-ses** [saɪkəuə'næləsɪs, -si:z] *n* psychanalyse *f*.
psychoanalyst [saɪkəu'ænəlɪst] *n* psychanalyste *m/f*.
psychological [saɪkə'lɔdʒɪkl] *adj* psychologique.
psychologist [saɪ'kɔlədʒɪst] *n* psychologue *m/f*.
psychology [saɪ'kɔlədʒɪ] *n* psychologie *f*.
psychopath ['saɪkəupæθ] *n* psychopathe *m/f*.
psychosis, *pl* **psychoses** [saɪ'kəusɪs, -si:z] *n* psychose *f*.
psychosomatic [saɪkəusə'mætɪk] *adj* psychosomatique.
psychotherapy [saɪkəu'θɛrəpɪ] *n* psychothérapie *f*.
psychotic [saɪ'kɔtɪk] *adj, n* psychotique (*m/f*).
PT *n abbr* (*BRIT*: = *physical training*) EPS *f*.
Pt. *abbr* (*in place names*: = *Point*) Pte.
pt *abbr* = **pint, point**.
PTA *n abbr* = *Parent-Teacher Association*.
Pte. *abbr* (*BRIT MIL*) = **private**.
PTO *abbr* (= *please turn over*) TSVP (= *tournez s'il vous plaît*).
pub [pʌb] *n abbr* (= *public house*) pub *m*; *voir encadré*.

PUB

Un **pub** *comprend en général deux salles: l'une ("the lounge") est plutôt confortable, avec des fauteuils et des bancs capitonnés, tandis que l'autre ("the public bar") est simplement un bar où les consommations sont en général moins chères. Cette dernière est souvent aussi une salle de jeux, les jeux les plus courants étant les fléchettes, les dominos et le billard. Il y a parfois aussi une petite arrière-salle douillette appelée "the snug". Beaucoup de pubs servent maintenant des repas, surtout à l'heure du déjeuner, et c'est alors le seul moment où les enfants sont acceptés, à condition d'être accompagnés. Les pubs sont en général ouverts de 11 h à 23 h, mais cela peut varier selon leur licence; certains pubs ferment l'après-midi.*

pub crawl *n* (*BRIT col*): **to go on a ~** faire la tournée des bars.
puberty ['pju:bətɪ] *n* puberté *f*.
pubic ['pju:bɪk] *adj* pubien(ne), du pubis.
public ['pʌblɪk] *adj* public(ique) ♦ *n* public *m*; **in ~** en public; **the general ~** le grand public; **to be ~ knowledge** être de notoriété publique; **to go ~** (*COMM*) être coté(e) en Bourse.
public address system (PA) *n* (système *m* de) sonorisation *f*, sono *f* (*col*).
publican ['pʌblɪkən] *n* patron *m or* gérant *m* de pub.
publication [pʌblɪ'keɪʃən] *n* publication *f*.
public company *n* société *f* anonyme.
public convenience *n* (*BRIT*) toilettes *fpl*.
public holiday *n* (*BRIT*) jour férié.
public house *n* (*BRIT*) pub *m*.
publicity [pʌb'lɪsɪtɪ] *n* publicité *f*.
publicize ['pʌblɪsaɪz] *vt* faire connaître, rendre public.
public limited company (plc) *n* ≈ société *f* anonyme (SA) (*cotée en Bourse*).
publicly ['pʌblɪklɪ] *adv* publiquement, en public.
public opinion *n* opinion publique.
public ownership *n*: **to be taken into ~** être nationalisé(e), devenir propriété de l'État.
public prosecutor *n* ≈ procureur *m* (*de la République*); **~'s office** parquet *m*.
public relations (PR) *n or npl* relations publiques (RP).
public relations officer *n* responsable *m/f* des relations publiques.
public school *n* (*BRIT*) école privée; (*US*) école publique; *voir encadré*.

PUBLIC SCHOOL

Une **public school** *est un établissement d'enseignement secondaire privé. Bon nombre d'entre elles sont des pensionnats. Beaucoup ont également une école primaire qui leur est rattachée (une "prep" ou "preparatory school") pour préparer les élèves au cycle secondaire. Ces écoles sont en général prestigieuses, et les frais de scolarité sont très élevés dans les plus connues (Westminster, Eton, Harrow). Beaucoup d'élèves vont ensuite à l'université, et un grand nombre entre à Oxford ou à Cambridge. Les grands industriels, les députés et les hauts fonctionnaires sortent souvent de ces écoles. En Écosse et aux États-Unis, le terme "public school" désigne tout simplement une école publique gratuite.*

public sector *n* secteur public.
public service vehicle (PSV) *n* (*BRIT*) véhicule affecté au transport de personnes.
public-spirited [pʌblɪk'spɪrɪtɪd] *adj* qui fait preuve de civisme.
public transport, (*US*) **public transportation** *n* transports *mpl* en commun.
public utility *n* service public.
public works *npl* travaux publics.
publish ['pʌblɪʃ] *vt* publier.
publisher ['pʌblɪʃə*] *n* éditeur *m*.
publishing ['pʌblɪʃɪŋ] *n* (*industry*) édition *f*; (*of a book*) publication *f*.
publishing company *n* maison *f* d'édition.
puce [pju:s] *adj* puce.
puck [pʌk] *n* (*elf*) lutin *m*; (*ICE HOCKEY*) palet *m*.
pucker ['pʌkə*] *vt* plisser.
pudding ['pudɪŋ] *n* (*BRIT*: *sweet*) dessert *m*, entremets *m*; (*sausage*) boudin *m*; **rice ~** ≈ riz *m* au lait; **black ~**, (*US*) **blood ~** boudin (noir).

puddle ['pʌdl] *n* flaque *f* d'eau.
puerile ['pjuəraɪl] *adj* puéril(e).
Puerto Rico ['pwəːtəu'riːkəu] *n* Porto Rico *f*.
puff [pʌf] *n* bouffée *f* ♦ *vt*: **to ~ one's pipe** tirer sur sa pipe; (*also*: **~ out**: *sails, cheeks*) gonfler ♦ *vi* sortir par bouffées; (*pant*) haleter; **to ~ out smoke** envoyer des bouffées de fumée.
puffed [pʌft] *adj* (*col*: *out of breath*) tout(e) essoufflé(e).
puffin ['pʌfɪn] *n* macareux *m*.
puff pastry, (*US*) **puff paste** *n* pâte feuilletée.
puffy ['pʌfɪ] *adj* bouffi(e), boursouflé(e).
pugnacious [pʌg'neɪʃəs] *adj* pugnace, batailleur(euse).
pull [pul] *n* (*of moon, magnet, the sea etc*) attraction *f*; (*fig*) influence *f* ♦ *vt* tirer; (*strain: muscle, tendon*) se claquer ♦ *vi* tirer; **to give sth a ~** (*tug*) tirer sur qch; **to ~ a face** faire une grimace; **to ~ to pieces** mettre en morceaux; **to ~ one's punches** (*also fig*) ménager son adversaire; **to ~ one's weight** y mettre du sien; **to ~ o.s. together** se ressaisir; **to ~ sb's leg** (*fig*) faire marcher qn; **to ~ strings (for sb)** intervenir (en faveur de qn).
►**pull about** *vt* (*BRIT*: *handle roughly: object*) maltraiter; (*: person*) malmener.
►**pull apart** *vt* séparer; (*break*) mettre en pièces, démantibuler.
►**pull down** *vt* baisser, abaisser; (*house*) démolir; (*tree*) abattre.
►**pull in** *vi* (*AUT*) se ranger; (*RAIL*) entrer en gare.
►**pull off** *vt* enlever, ôter; (*deal etc*) conclure.
►**pull out** *vi* démarrer, partir; (*withdraw*) se retirer; (*AUT*: *come out of line*) déboîter ♦ *vt* sortir; arracher; (*withdraw*) retirer.
►**pull over** *vi* (*AUT*) se ranger.
►**pull round** *vi* (*unconscious person*) revenir à soi; (*sick person*) se rétablir.
►**pull through** *vi* s'en sortir.
►**pull up** *vi* (*stop*) s'arrêter ♦ *vt* remonter; (*uproot*) déraciner, arracher; (*stop*) arrêter.
pulley ['pulɪ] *n* poulie *f*.
pull-out ['pulaut] *n* (*of forces etc*) retrait *m* ♦ *cpd* (*magazine, pages*) détachable.
pullover ['puləuvə*] *n* pull-over *m*, tricot *m*.
pulp [pʌlp] *n* (*of fruit*) pulpe *f*; (*for paper*) pâte *f* à papier; (*pej*: *also*: **~ magazines** *etc*) presse *f* à sensation *or* de bas étage; **to reduce sth to (a) ~** réduire qch en purée.
pulpit ['pulpɪt] *n* chaire *f*.
pulsate [pʌl'seɪt] *vi* battre, palpiter; (*music*) vibrer.
pulse [pʌls] *n* (*of blood*) pouls *m*; (*of heart*) battement *m*; (*of music, engine*) vibrations *fpl*; **to feel** *or* **take sb's ~** prendre le pouls à qn.
pulses ['pʌlsəz] *npl* (*CULIN*) légumineuses *fpl*.
pulverize ['pʌlvəraɪz] *vt* pulvériser.
puma ['pjuːmə] *n* puma *m*.
pumice ['pʌmɪs] *n* (*also*: **~ stone**) pierre *f* ponce.
pummel ['pʌml] *vt* rouer de coups.
pump [pʌmp] *n* pompe *f*; (*shoe*) escarpin *m* ♦ *vt* pomper; (*fig: col*) faire parler; **to ~ sb for information** essayer de soutirer des renseignements à qn.
►**pump up** *vt* gonfler.
pumpkin ['pʌmpkɪn] *n* potiron *m*, citrouille *f*.
pun [pʌn] *n* jeu *m* de mots, calembour *m*.
punch [pʌntʃ] *n* (*blow*) coup *m* de poing; (*fig: force*) vivacité *f*, mordant *m*; (*tool*) poinçon *m*; (*drink*) punch *m* ♦ *vt* (*make a hole*) poinçonner, perforer; (*hit*): **to ~ sb/sth** donner un coup de poing à qn/sur qch; **to ~ a hole (in)** faire un trou (dans).
►**punch in** *vi* (*US*) pointer (en arrivant).
►**punch out** *vi* (*US*) pointer (en partant).
punch-drunk ['pʌntʃdrʌŋk] *adj* (*BRIT*) sonné(e).
punch(ed) card [pʌntʃ(t)-] *n* carte perforée.
punch line *n* (*of joke*) conclusion *f*.
punch-up ['pʌntʃʌp] *n* (*BRIT col*) bagarre *f*.
punctual ['pʌŋktjuəl] *adj* ponctuel(le).
punctuality [pʌŋktju'ælɪtɪ] *n* ponctualité *f*.
punctually ['pʌŋktjuəlɪ] *adv* ponctuellement; **it will start ~ at 6** cela commencera à 6 heures précises.
punctuate ['pʌŋktjueɪt] *vt* ponctuer.
punctuation [pʌŋktju'eɪʃən] *n* ponctuation *f*.
punctuation mark *n* signe *m* de ponctuation.
puncture ['pʌŋktʃə*] *n* (*BRIT*) crevaison *f* ♦ *vt* crever; **I have a ~** (*AUT*) j'ai (un pneu) crevé.
pundit ['pʌndɪt] *n* individu *m* qui pontifie, pontife *m*.
pungent ['pʌndʒənt] *adj* piquant(e); (*fig*) mordant(e), caustique.
punish ['pʌnɪʃ] *vt* punir; **to ~ sb for sth/for doing sth** punir qn de qch/d'avoir fait qch.
punishable ['pʌnɪʃəbl] *adj* punissable.
punishing ['pʌnɪʃɪŋ] *adj* (*fig: exhausting*) épuisant(e) ♦ *n* punition *f*.
punishment ['pʌnɪʃmənt] *n* punition *f*, châtiment *m*; (*fig*: *col*): **to take a lot of ~** (*boxer*) encaisser; (*car, person etc*) être mis(e) à dure épreuve.
punk [pʌŋk] *n* (*person*: *also*: **~ rocker**) punk *m/f*; (*music*: *also*: **~ rock**) le punk; (*US col*: *hoodlum*) voyou *m*.
punt [pʌnt] *n* (*boat*) bachot *m*; (*IRELAND*) livre irlandaise ♦ *vi* (*BRIT*: *bet*) parier.
punter ['pʌntə*] *n* (*BRIT*: *gambler*) parieur/euse; (: *col*) Monsieur *m* tout le monde; type *m*.
puny ['pjuːnɪ] *adj* chétif(ive).
pup [pʌp] *n* chiot *m*.
pupil ['pjuːpl] *n* élève *m/f*; (*of eye*) pupille *f*.
puppet ['pʌpɪt] *n* marionnette *f*, pantin *m*.
puppet government *n* gouvernement *m* fantoche.
puppy ['pʌpɪ] *n* chiot *m*, petit chien.
purchase ['pəːtʃɪs] *n* achat *m*; (*grip*) prise *f* ♦ *vt*

acheter; **to get a ~ on** trouver appui sur.
purchase order *n* ordre *m* d'achat.
purchase price *n* prix *m* d'achat.
purchaser ['pəːtʃɪsə*] *n* acheteur/euse.
purchase tax *n* (*BRIT*) taxe *f* à l'achat.
purchasing power ['pəːtʃɪsɪŋ-] *n* pouvoir *m* d'achat.
pure [pjuə*] *adj* pur(e); **a ~ wool jumper** un pull en pure laine; **~ and simple** pur(e) et simple.
purebred ['pjuəbrɛd] *adj* de race.
purée ['pjuəreɪ] *n* purée *f*.
purely ['pjuəlɪ] *adv* purement.
purge [pəːdʒ] *n* (*MED*) purge *f*; (*POL*) épuration *f*, purge ♦ *vt* purger; (*fig*) épurer, purger.
purification [pjuərɪfɪ'keɪʃən] *n* purification *f*.
purify ['pjuərɪfaɪ] *vt* purifier, épurer.
purist ['pjuərɪst] *n* puriste *m/f*.
puritan ['pjuərɪtən] *n* puritain/e.
puritanical [pjuərɪ'tænɪkl] *adj* puritain(e).
purity ['pjuərɪtɪ] *n* pureté *f*.
purl [pəːl] *n* maille *f* à l'envers ♦ *vt* tricoter à l'envers.
purloin [pəː'lɔɪn] *vt* dérober.
purple ['pəːpl] *adj* violet(te); cramoisi(e).
purport [pəː'pɔːt] *vi*: **to ~ to be/do** prétendre être/faire.
purpose ['pəːpəs] *n* intention *f*, but *m*; **on ~** exprès; **for illustrative ~s** à titre d'illustration; **for teaching ~s** dans un but pédagogique; **for the ~s of this meeting** pour cette réunion; **to no ~** en pure perte.
purpose-built ['pəːpəs'bɪlt] *adj* (*BRIT*) fait(e) sur mesure.
purposeful ['pəːpəsful] *adj* déterminé(e), résolu(e).
purposely ['pəːpəslɪ] *adv* exprès.
purr [pəː*] *n* ronronnement *m* ♦ *vi* ronronner.
purse [pəːs] *n* porte-monnaie *m inv*, bourse *f*; (*US: handbag*) sac *m* (à main) ♦ *vt* serrer, pincer.
purser ['pəːsə*] *n* (*NAUT*) commissaire *m* du bord.
purse snatcher [-'snætʃə*] *n* (*US*) voleur *m* à l'arraché.
pursue [pə'sjuː] *vt* poursuivre; (*pleasures*) rechercher; (*inquiry, matter*) approfondir.
pursuer [pə'sjuːə*] *n* poursuivant/e.
pursuit [pə'sjuːt] *n* poursuite *f*; (*occupation*) occupation *f*, activité *f*; **scientific ~s** recherches *fpl* scientifiques; **in (the) ~ of sth** à la recherche de qch.
purveyor [pə'veɪə*] *n* fournisseur *m*.
pus [pʌs] *n* pus *m*.
push [puʃ] *n* poussée *f*; (*effort*) gros effort; (*drive*) énergie *f* ♦ *vt* pousser; (*button*) appuyer sur; (*thrust*): **to ~ sth (into)** enfoncer qch (dans); (*fig*) mettre en avant, faire de la publicité pour ♦ *vi* pousser; appuyer; **to ~ a door open/shut** pousser une porte (pour l'ouvrir/pour la fermer); **"~"** (*on door*) "pousser"; (*on bell*) "appuyer"; **to ~ for** (*better pay, conditions*) réclamer; **to be ~ed for time/money** être à court de temps/d'argent; **she is ~ing fifty** (*col*) elle frise la cinquantaine; **at a ~** (*BRIT col*) à la limite, à la rigueur.
►**push aside** *vt* écarter.
►**push in** *vi* s'introduire de force.
►**push off** *vi* (*col*) filer, ficher le camp.
►**push on** *vi* (*continue*) continuer.
►**push over** *vt* renverser.
►**push through** *vt* (*measure*) faire voter.
►**push up** *vt* (*total, prices*) faire monter.
push-bike ['puʃbaɪk] *n* (*BRIT*) vélo *m*.
push-button ['puʃbʌtn] *n* bouton(-poussoir *m*) *m*.
pushchair ['puʃtʃɛə*] *n* (*BRIT*) poussette *f*.
pusher ['puʃə*] *n* (*also*: **drug ~**) revendeur/euse (de drogue), ravitailleur/euse (en drogue).
pushover ['puʃəuvə*] *n* (*col*): **it's a ~** c'est un jeu d'enfant.
push-up ['puʃʌp] *n* (*US*) traction *f*.
pushy ['puʃɪ] *adj* (*pej*) arriviste.
puss, pussy(-cat) [pus, 'pusɪ(kæt)] *n* minet *m*.
put, *pt, pp* **put** [put] *vt* mettre; (*place*) poser, placer; (*say*) dire, exprimer; (*a question*) poser; (*estimate*) estimer; **to ~ sb in a good/bad mood** mettre qn de bonne/mauvaise humeur; **to ~ sb to bed** mettre qn au lit, coucher qn; **to ~ sb to a lot of trouble** déranger qn; **how shall I ~ it?** comment dirais-je?, comment dire?; **to ~ a lot of time into sth** passer beaucoup de temps à qch; **to ~ money on a horse** miser sur un cheval; **I ~ it to you that ...** (*BRIT*) je (vous) suggère que ..., je suis d'avis que ...; **to stay ~** ne pas bouger.
►**put about** *vi* (*NAUT*) virer de bord ♦ *vt* (*rumour*) faire courir.
►**put across** *vt* (*ideas etc*) communiquer; faire comprendre.
►**put aside** *vt* mettre de côté.
►**put away** *vt* (*store*) ranger.
►**put back** *vt* (*replace*) remettre, replacer; (*postpone*) remettre; (*delay, also: watch, clock*) retarder; **this will ~ us back ten years** cela nous ramènera dix ans en arrière.
►**put by** *vt* (*money*) mettre de côté, économiser.
►**put down** *vt* (*parcel etc*) poser, déposer; (*pay*) verser; (*in writing*) mettre par écrit, inscrire; (*suppress: revolt etc*) réprimer, écraser; (*attribute*) attribuer.
►**put forward** *vt* (*ideas*) avancer, proposer; (*date, watch, clock*) avancer.
►**put in** *vt* (*gas, electricity*) installer; (*application, complaint*) faire.
►**put in for** *vt fus* (*job*) poser sa candidature pour; (*promotion*) solliciter.
►**put off** *vt* (*light etc*) éteindre; (*postpone*) remettre à plus tard, ajourner; (*discourage*) dissuader.

►**put on** *vt* (*clothes, lipstick etc*) mettre; (*light etc*) allumer; (*play etc*) monter; (*extra bus, train etc*) mettre en service; (*food, meal*) servir; (*weight*) prendre; (*assume: accent, manner*) prendre; (*: airs*) se donner, prendre; (*brake*) mettre; (*col: tease*) faire marcher; (*inform, indicate*): **to ~ sb on to sb/sth** indiquer qn/qch à qn.

►**put out** *vt* mettre dehors; (*one's hand*) tendre; (*news, rumour*) faire courir, répandre; (*light etc*) éteindre; (*person: inconvenience*) déranger, gêner; (*BRIT: dislocate*) se démettre ♦ *vi* (*NAUT*): **to ~ out to sea** prendre le large; **to ~ out from Plymouth** quitter Plymouth.

►**put through** *vt* (*caller*) mettre en communication; (*call*) passer; **~ me through to Miss Blair** passez-moi Miss Blair.

►**put together** *vt* mettre ensemble; (*assemble: furniture, toy etc*) monter, assembler; (*meal*) préparer.

►**put up** *vt* (*raise*) lever, relever, remonter; (*pin up*) afficher; (*hang*) accrocher; (*build*) construire, ériger; (*a tent*) monter; (*increase*) augmenter; (*accommodate*) loger; (*incite*): **to ~ sb up to doing sth** pousser qn à faire qch; **to ~ sth up for sale** mettre qch en vente.

►**put upon** *vt fus*: **to be ~ upon** (*imposed on*) se laisser faire.

►**put up with** *vt fus* supporter.

putrid ['pjuːtrɪd] *adj* putride.

putt [pʌt] *vt, vi* putter ♦ *n* putt *m*.

putter ['pʌtə*] *n* (*GOLF*) putter *m*.

putting green ['pʌtɪŋ-] *n* green *m*.

putty ['pʌtɪ] *n* mastic *m*.

put-up ['putʌp] *adj*: **~ job** coup monté.

puzzle ['pʌzl] *n* énigme *f*, mystère *m*; (*jigsaw*) puzzle *m*; (*also*: **crossword ~**) problème *m* de mots croisés ♦ *vt* intriguer, rendre perplexe ♦ *vi* se creuser la tête; **to ~ over** chercher à comprendre; **to be ~d about sth** être perplexe au sujet de qch.

puzzling ['pʌzlɪŋ] *adj* déconcertant(e), inexplicable.

PVC *n abbr* (= *polyvinyl chloride*) PVC *m*.

Pvt. *abbr* (*US MIL*) = **private**.

pw *abbr* (= *per week*) p.sem.

PX *n abbr* (*US MIL*) = **post exchange**.

pygmy ['pɪgmɪ] *n* pygmée *m/f*.

pyjamas [pɪ'dʒɑːməz] *npl* (*BRIT*) pyjama *m*; **a pair of ~** un pyjama.

pylon ['paɪlən] *n* pylône *m*.

pyramid ['pɪrəmɪd] *n* pyramide *f*.

Pyrenean [pɪrə'niːən] *adj* pyrénéen(ne), des Pyrénées.

Pyrenees [pɪrə'niːz] *npl*: **the ~** les Pyrénées *fpl*.

Pyrex ['paɪrɛks] *n* ® Pyrex *m* ® ♦ *cpd*: **~ dish** plat *m* en Pyrex.

python ['paɪθən] *n* python *m*.

Q q

Q, q [kjuː] *n* (*letter*) Q, q *m*; **Q for Queen** Q comme Quintal.

Qatar [kæ'tɑː*] *n* Qatar *m*, Katar *m*.

QC [ˌkjuː'siː] *n abbr* (*BRIT JUR*) (= *Queen's Counsel*); *voir encadré*.

> **QC**
>
> *En Angleterre, un* **QC** *ou "Queen's Counsel" (ou "KC" pour "King's Counsel", sous le règne d'un roi) est un avocat qui reçoit un poste de haut fonctionnaire sur recommandation du "Lord Chancellor". Il fait alors souvent suivre son nom des lettres QC, et lorsqu'il va au tribunal, il est toujours accompagné par un autre avocat (un "junior barrister").*

QCA *n abbr* (*BRIT*: = *Qualifications and Curriculum Authority*) *autorité régulant les diplômes et les programmes scolaires.*

QED *abbr* (= *quod erat demonstrandum*) CQFD.

q.t. *n abbr* (*col*: = *quiet*): **on the ~** discrètement.

qty *abbr* (= *quantity*) qté.

quack [kwæk] *n* (*of duck*) coin-coin *m inv*; (*pej: doctor*) charlatan *m* ♦ *vi* faire coin-coin.

quad [kwɔd] *n abbr* = **quadruplet, quadrangle**.

quadrangle ['kwɔdræŋgl] *n* (*MATH*) quadrilatère *m*; (*courtyard: abbr*: **quad**) cour *f*.

quadruped ['kwɔdrupɛd] *n* quadrupède *m*.

quadruple [kwɔ'druːpl] *adj, n* quadruple (*m*) ♦ *vt, vi* quadrupler.

quadruplet [kwɔ'druːplɪt] *n* quadruplé(e) *m(f)*.

quagmire ['kwægmaɪə*] *n* bourbier *m*.

quail [kweɪl] *n* (*ZOOL*) caille *f*.

quaint [kweɪnt] *adj* bizarre; (*old-fashioned*) désuet(ète); au charme vieillot, pittoresque.

quake [kweɪk] *vi* trembler ♦ *n abbr* = **earthquake**.

Quaker ['kweɪkə*] *n* quaker/esse.

qualification [kwɔlɪfɪ'keɪʃən] *n* (*degree etc*) diplôme *m*; (*ability*) compétence *f*, qualification *f*; (*limitation*) réserve *f*, restriction *f*; **what are your ~s?** qu'avez-vous comme diplômes?; quelles sont vos qualifications?

qualified ['kwɔlɪfaɪd] *adj* diplômé(e); (*able*) compétent(e), qualifié(e); (*limited*) conditionnel(le); **it was a ~ success** ce fut un succès mitigé; **~ for/to do** qui a les diplômes requis pour/pour faire; qualifié pour/pour faire.

qualify ['kwɔlɪfaɪ] *vt* qualifier; (*limit: statement*) apporter des réserves à ♦ *vi*: **to ~ (as)** obtenir son diplôme (de); **to ~ (for)** remplir les

conditions requises (pour); (*SPORT*) se qualifier (pour).
qualifying ['kwɔlɪfaɪɪŋ] *adj*: ~ **exam** examen *m* d'entrée; ~ **round** éliminatoires *fpl*.
qualitative ['kwɔlɪtətɪv] *adj* qualitatif(ive).
quality ['kwɔlɪtɪ] *n* qualité *f* ♦ *cpd* de qualité; **of good/poor** ~ de bonne/mauvaise qualité.
quality control *n* contrôle *m* de qualité.
quality press *n* (*BRIT*): **the** ~ la presse d'information; *voir encadré*.

QUALITY PRESS

La **quality press** *(ou les "quality (news) papers") englobent les journaux sérieux, quotidiens ou hebdomadaires, par opposition aux journaux populaires ("tabloid press"). Ces journaux visent un public qui souhaite des informations détaillées sur un éventail très vaste de sujets et qui est prêt à consacrer beaucoup de temps à leur lecture. Les quality newspapers sont en général de grand format.*

qualm [kwɑːm] *n* doute *m*; scrupule *m*; **to have ~s about sth** avoir des doutes sur qch; éprouver des scrupules à propos de qch.
quandary ['kwɔndrɪ] *n*: **in a** ~ devant un dilemme, dans l'embarras.
quango ['kwæŋgəu] *n abbr* (*BRIT*: = *quasi-autonomous non-governmental organization*) commission nommée par le gouvernement.
quantitative ['kwɔntɪtətɪv] *adj* quantitatif(ive).
quantity ['kwɔntɪtɪ] *n* quantité *f*; **in** ~ en grande quantité.
quantity surveyor *n* (*BRIT*) métreur vérificateur.
quantum leap ['kwɔntəm-] *n* (*fig*) bond *m* en avant.
quarantine ['kwɔrntiːn] *n* quarantaine *f*.
quark [kwɑːk] *n* quark *m*.
quarrel ['kwɔrl] *n* querelle *f*, dispute *f* ♦ *vi* se disputer, se quereller; **to have a ~ with sb** se quereller avec qn; **I've no ~ with him** je n'ai rien contre lui; **I can't ~ with that** je ne vois rien à redire à cela.
quarrelsome ['kwɔrəlsəm] *adj* querelleur(euse).
quarry ['kwɔrɪ] *n* (*for stone*) carrière *f*; (*animal*) proie *f*, gibier *m* ♦ *vt* (*marble etc*) extraire.
quart [kwɔːt] *n* ≈ litre *m*.
quarter ['kwɔːtə*] *n* quart *m*; (*of year*) trimestre *m*; (*district*) quartier *m*; (*US, Canada*: *25 cents*) (pièce *f* de) vingt-cinq cents *mpl* ♦ *vt* partager en quartiers *or* en quatre; (*MIL*) caserner, cantonner; **~s** *npl* logement *m*; (*MIL*) quartiers *mpl*, cantonnement *m*; **a ~ of an hour** un quart d'heure; **it's a ~ to 3**, (*US*) **it's a ~ of 3** il est 3 heures moins le quart; **it's a ~ past 3**, (*US*) **it's a ~ after 3** il est 3 heures et quart; **from all ~s** de tous côtés.
quarterback ['kwɔːtəbæk] *n* (*US FOOTBALL*) quarterback *m/f*.
quarter-deck ['kwɔːtədɛk] *n* (*NAUT*) plage *f* arrière.
quarter final *n* quart *m* de finale.
quarterly ['kwɔːtəlɪ] *adj* trimestriel(le) ♦ *adv* tous les trois mois ♦ *n* (*PRESS*) revue trimestrielle.
quartermaster ['kwɔːtəmɑːstə*] *n* (*MIL*) intendant *m* militaire de troisième classe; (*NAUT*) maître *m* de manœuvre.
quartet(te) [kwɔː'tɛt] *n* quatuor *m*; (*jazz players*) quartette *m*.
quarto ['kwɔːtəu] *adj*, *n* in-quarto *(m) inv*.
quartz [kwɔːts] *n* quartz *m* ♦ *cpd* de *or* en quartz; (*watch, clock*) à quartz.
quash [kwɔʃ] *vt* (*verdict*) annuler, casser.
quasi- ['kweɪzaɪ] *prefix* quasi- + *noun*; quasi, presque + *adjective*.
quaver ['kweɪvə*] *n* (*BRIT MUS*) croche *f* ♦ *vi* trembler.
quay [kiː] *n* (*also*: **~side**) quai *m*.
Que. *abbr* (*Canada*) = *Quebec*.
queasy ['kwiːzɪ] *adj* (*stomach*) délicat(e); **to feel** ~ avoir mal au cœur.
Quebec [kwɪ'bɛk] *n* Québec *m*.
queen [kwiːn] *n* (*gen*) reine *f*; (*CARDS etc*) dame *f*.
queen mother *n* reine mère *f*.
Queen's Speech *n* (*BRIT*) discours *m* de la reine; *voir encadré*.

QUEEN'S SPEECH

Le **Queen's Speech** *(ou "King's Speech") est le discours lu par le souverain à l'ouverture du "Parliament" dans la "House of Lords", en présence des lords et des députés. Il contient le programme de politique générale que propose le gouvernement pour la session, et il est préparé par le Premier ministre en consultation avec le cabinet.*

queer [kwɪə*] *adj* étrange, curieux(euse); (*suspicious*) louche; (*BRIT*: *sick*): **I feel** ~ je ne me sens pas bien ♦ *n* (*col*) homosexuel *m*.
quell [kwɛl] *vt* réprimer, étouffer.
quench [kwɛntʃ] *vt* (*flames*) éteindre; **to ~ one's thirst** se désaltérer.
querulous ['kwɛruləs] *adj* (*person*) récriminateur(trice); (*voice*) plaintif(ive).
query ['kwɪərɪ] *n* question *f*; (*doubt*) doute *m*; (*question mark*) point *m* d'interrogation ♦ *vt* (*disagree with, dispute*) mettre en doute.
quest [kwɛst] *n* recherche *f*, quête *f*.
question ['kwɛstʃən] *n* question *f* ♦ *vt* (*person*) interroger; (*plan, idea*) mettre en question *or* en doute; **to ask sb a ~, to put a ~ to sb** poser une question à qn; **to bring** *or* **call sth into** ~ remettre qch en question; **the ~ is ...** la question est de savoir ...; **it's a ~ of doing** il s'agit de faire; **there's some ~ of doing** il est question de faire; **beyond** ~ sans aucun doute; **out of the** ~ hors de question.
questionable ['kwɛstʃənəbl] *adj* discutable.
questioner ['kwɛstʃənə*] *n* personne *f* qui pose

une question (*or* qui a posé la question *etc*).
questioning ['kwɛstʃənɪŋ] *adj* interrogateur(trice) ♦ *n* interrogatoire *m*.
question mark *n* point *m* d'interrogation.
questionnaire [kwɛstʃə'nɛə*] *n* questionnaire *m*.
queue [kjuː] (*BRIT*) *n* queue *f*, file *f* ♦ *vi* faire la queue; **to jump the** ~ passer avant son tour.
quibble ['kwɪbl] *vi* ergoter, chicaner.
quick [kwɪk] *adj* rapide; (*reply*) prompt(e), rapide; (*mind*) vif(vive) ♦ *adv* vite, rapidement ♦ *n*: **cut to the** ~ (*fig*) touché(e) au vif; **be** ~! dépêche-toi!; **to be** ~ **to act** agir tout de suite.
quicken ['kwɪkən] *vt* accélérer, presser; (*rouse*) stimuler ♦ *vi* s'accélérer, devenir plus rapide.
quick fix *n* solution *f* de fortune.
quicklime ['kwɪklaɪm] *n* chaux vive.
quickly ['kwɪklɪ] *adv* (*fast*) vite, rapidement; (*immediately*) tout de suite.
quickness ['kwɪknɪs] *n* rapidité *f*, promptitude *f*; (*of mind*) vivacité *f*.
quicksand ['kwɪksænd] *n* sables mouvants.
quickstep ['kwɪkstɛp] *n* fox-trot *m*.
quick-tempered [kwɪk'tɛmpəd] *adj* emporté(e).
quick-witted [kwɪk'wɪtɪd] *adj* à l'esprit vif.
quid [kwɪd] *n* (*pl inv*: *BRIT col*) livre *f*.
quid pro quo ['kwɪdprəu'kwəu] *n* contrepartie *f*.
quiet ['kwaɪət] *adj* tranquille, calme; (*not noisy: engine*) silencieux(euse); (*reserved*) réservé(e); (*not busy: day, business*) calme; (*ceremony, colour*) discret(ète) ♦ *n* tranquillité *f*, calme *m* ♦ *vt*, *vi* (*US*) = **quieten**; **keep** ~! taistoi!; **on the** ~ en secret, discrètement; **I'll have a** ~ **word with him** je lui en parlerai discrètement.
quieten ['kwaɪətn] (*also*: ~ **down**) *vi* se calmer, s'apaiser ♦ *vt* calmer, apaiser.
quietly ['kwaɪətlɪ] *adv* tranquillement, calmement; discrètement.
quietness ['kwaɪətnɪs] *n* tranquillité *f*, calme *m*; silence *m*.
quill [kwɪl] *n* plume *f* (d'oie).
quilt [kwɪlt] *n* édredon *m*; (*continental* ~) couette *f*.
quin [kwɪn] *n abbr* = **quintuplet**.
quince [kwɪns] *n* coing *m*; (*tree*) cognassier *m*.
quinine [kwɪ'niːn] *n* quinine *f*.
quintet(te) [kwɪn'tɛt] *n* quintette *m*.
quintuplet [kwɪn'tjuːplɪt] *n* quintuplé/e.
quip [kwɪp] *n* remarque piquante *or* spirituelle, pointe *f* ♦ *vt*: ... **he** ~**ped** ... lança-t-il.
quire ['kwaɪə*] *n* ≈ main *f* (*de papier*).
quirk [kwəːk] *n* bizarrerie *f*; **by some** ~ **of fate** par un caprice du hasard.
quit, *pt*, *pp* **quit** *or* **quitted** [kwɪt] *vt* quitter ♦ *vi* (*give up*) abandonner, renoncer; (*resign*) démissionner; **to** ~ **doing** arrêter de faire; ~ **stalling!** (*US col*) arrête de te dérober!; **notice to** ~ (*BRIT*) congé *m* (*signifié au locataire*).
quite [kwaɪt] *adv* (*rather*) assez, plutôt; (*entirely*) complètement, tout à fait; ~ **new** plutôt neuf; tout à fait neuf; **she's** ~ **pretty** elle est plutôt jolie; **I** ~ **understand** je comprends très bien; ~ **a few of them** un assez grand nombre d'entre eux; **that's not** ~ **right** ce n'est pas tout à fait juste; **not** ~ **as many as last time** pas tout à fait autant que la dernière fois; ~ **(so)!** exactement!
Quito ['kiːtəu] *n* Quito.
quits [kwɪts] *adj*: ~ **(with)** quitte (envers); **let's call it** ~ restons-en là.
quiver ['kwɪvə*] *vi* trembler, frémir ♦ *n* (*for arrows*) carquois *m*.
quiz [kwɪz] *n* (*on TV*) jeu-concours *m* (télévisé); (*in magazine etc*) test *m* de connaissances ♦ *vt* interroger.
quizzical ['kwɪzɪkl] *adj* narquois(e).
quoits [kwɔɪts] *npl* jeu *m* du palet.
quorum ['kwɔːrəm] *n* quorum *m*.
quota ['kwəutə] *n* quota *m*.
quotation [kwəu'teɪʃən] *n* citation *f*; (*of shares etc*) cote *f*, cours *m*; (*estimate*) devis *m*.
quotation marks *npl* guillemets *mpl*.
quote [kwəut] *n* citation *f* ♦ *vt* (*sentence, author*) citer; (*price*) donner, soumettre; (*shares*) coter ♦ *vi*: **to** ~ **from** citer; **to** ~ **for a job** établir un devis pour des travaux; ~**s** *npl* (*col*) = **quotation marks**; **in** ~**s** entre guillemets; ~ ... **unquote** (*in dictation*) ouvrez les guillemets ... fermez les guillemets.
quotient ['kwəuʃənt] *n* quotient *m*.
qv *abbr* (= *quod vide: which see*) voir.
qwerty keyboard ['kwəːtɪ-] *n* clavier *m* QWERTY.

R r

R, r [ɑː*] *n* (*letter*) R, r *m*; **R for Robert**, (*US*) **R for Roger** R comme Raoul.
R *abbr* (= *right*) dr; (= *river*) riv., fl.; (= *Réaumur (scale)*) R; (*US CINE*: = *restricted*) *interdit aux moins de 17 ans*; (*US POL*) = **republican**; (*BRIT*) = *Rex, Regina*.
RA *abbr* = **rear admiral** ♦ *n abbr* (*BRIT*) = **Royal Academy**, *Royal Academician*.
RAAF *n abbr* = *Royal Australian Air Force*.
Rabat [rə'bɑːt] *n* Rabat.
rabbi ['ræbaɪ] *n* rabbin *m*.
rabbit ['ræbɪt] *n* lapin *m* ♦ *vi*: **to** ~ **(on)** (*BRIT*) parler à n'en plus finir.
rabbit hole *n* terrier *m* (de lapin).
rabbit hutch *n* clapier *m*.

rabble ['ræbl] *n (pej)* populace *f*.
rabid ['ræbɪd] *adj* enragé(e).
rabies ['reɪbiːz] *n* rage *f*.
RAC *n abbr (BRIT: = Royal Automobile Club)* ≈ ACF *m*.
ra(c)coon [rə'kuːn] *n* raton *m* laveur.
race [reɪs] *n* race *f*; (*competition, rush*) course *f* ♦ *vt* (*person*) faire la course avec; (*horse*) faire courir; (*engine*) emballer ♦ *vi* courir; (*engine*) s'emballer; **the human ~** la race humaine; **to ~ in/out** *etc* entrer/sortir *etc* à toute vitesse.
race car *n (US)* = **racing car**.
race car driver *n (US)* = **racing driver**.
racecourse ['reɪskɔːs] *n* champ *m* de courses.
racehorse ['reɪshɔːs] *n* cheval *m* de course.
race relations *npl* rapports *mpl* entre les races.
racetrack ['reɪstræk] *n* piste *f*.
racial ['reɪʃl] *adj* racial(e).
racialism ['reɪʃlɪzəm] *n* racisme *m*.
racialist ['reɪʃlɪst] *adj, n* raciste *(m/f)*.
racing ['reɪsɪŋ] *n* courses *fpl*.
racing car *n (BRIT)* voiture *f* de course.
racing driver *n (BRIT)* pilote *m* de course.
racism ['reɪsɪzəm] *n* racisme *m*.
racist ['reɪsɪst] *adj, n (pej)* raciste *(m/f)*.
rack [ræk] *n* (*also*: **luggage ~**) filet *m* à bagages; (*also*: **roof ~**) galerie *f* ♦ *vt* tourmenter; **magazine ~** porte-revues *m inv*; **shoe ~** étagère *f* à chaussures; **toast ~** porte-toast *m*; **to ~ one's brains** se creuser la cervelle; **to go to ~ and ruin** (*building*) tomber en ruine; (*business*) péricliter.
►**rack up** *vt* accumuler.
racket ['rækɪt] *n* (*for tennis*) raquette *f*; (*noise*) tapage *m*, vacarme *m*; (*swindle*) escroquerie *f*; (*organized crime*) racket *m*.
racketeer [rækɪ'tɪə*] *n (esp US)* racketteur *m*.
racquet ['rækɪt] *n* raquette *f*.
racy ['reɪsɪ] *adj* plein(e) de verve; osé(e).
RADA [rɑːdə] *n abbr (BRIT) = Royal Academy of Dramatic Art.*
radar ['reɪdɑː*] *n* radar *m* ♦ *cpd* radar *inv*.
radar trap *n (AUT, Police)* contrôle *m* radar.
radial ['reɪdɪəl] *adj* (*also*: **~-ply**) à carcasse radiale.
radiance ['reɪdɪəns] *n* éclat *m*, rayonnement *m*.
radiant ['reɪdɪənt] *adj* rayonnant(e); (*PHYSICS*) radiant(e).
radiate ['reɪdɪeɪt] *vt* (*heat*) émettre, dégager ♦ *vi* (*lines*) rayonner.
radiation [reɪdɪ'eɪʃən] *n* rayonnement *m*; (*radioactive*) radiation *f*.
radiation sickness *n* mal *m* des rayons.
radiator ['reɪdɪeɪtə*] *n* radiateur *m*.
radiator cap *n* bouchon *m* de radiateur.
radiator grill *n (AUT)* calandre *f*.
radical ['rædɪkl] *adj* radical(e).
radii ['reɪdɪaɪ] *npl of* **radius**.
radio ['reɪdɪəu] *n* radio *f* ♦ *vi*: **to ~ to sb** envoyer un message radio à qn ♦ *vt* (*information*) transmettre par radio; (*one's position*) signaler par radio; (*person*) appeler par radio; **on the ~** à la radio.
radioactive ['reɪdɪəu'æktɪv] *adj* radioactif(ive).
radioactivity ['reɪdɪəuæk'tɪvɪtɪ] *n* radioactivité *f*.
radio announcer *n* annonceur *m*.
radio-controlled ['reɪdɪəukən'trəuld] *adj* radioguidé(e).
radiographer [reɪdɪ'ɔgrəfə*] *n* radiologue *m/f* (*technicien*).
radiography [reɪdɪ'ɔgrəfɪ] *n* radiographie *f*.
radiologist [reɪdɪ'ɔlədʒɪst] *n* radiologue *m/f* (*médecin*).
radiology [reɪdɪ'ɔlədʒɪ] *n* radiologie *f*.
radio station *n* station *f* de radio.
radio taxi *n* radio-taxi *m*.
radiotelephone ['reɪdɪəu'tɛlɪfəun] *n* radiotéléphone *m*.
radiotherapist ['reɪdɪəu'θɛrəpɪst] *n* radiothérapeute *m/f*.
radiotherapy ['reɪdɪəu'θɛrəpɪ] *n* radiothérapie *f*.
radish ['rædɪʃ] *n* radis *m*.
radium ['reɪdɪəm] *n* radis *m*.
radius, *pl* **radii** ['reɪdɪəs, -ɪaɪ] *n* rayon *m*; (*ANAT*) radius *m*; **within a ~ of 50 miles** dans un rayon de 50 milles.
RAF *n abbr (BRIT)* = **Royal Air Force**.
raffia ['ræfɪə] *n* raphia *m*.
raffish ['ræfɪʃ] *adj* dissolu(e); canaille.
raffle ['ræfl] *n* tombola *f* ♦ *vt* mettre comme lot dans une tombola.
raft [rɑːft] *n* (*craft*; *also*: **life ~**) radeau *m*; (*logs*) train *m* de flottage.
rafter ['rɑːftə*] *n* chevron *m*.
rag [ræg] *n* chiffon *m*; (*pej*: *newspaper*) feuille *f*, torchon *m*; (*for charity*) *attractions organisées par les étudiants au profit d'œuvres de charité* ♦ *vt (BRIT)* chahuter, mettre en boîte; **~s** *npl* haillons *mpl*; **in ~s** (*person*) en haillons; (*clothes*) en lambeaux.
rag-and-bone man [rægən'bəunmæn] *n* chiffonnier *m*.
ragbag ['rægbæg] *n (fig)* ramassis *m*.
rag doll *n* poupée *f* de chiffon.
rage [reɪdʒ] *n* (*fury*) rage *f*, fureur *f* ♦ *vi* (*person*) être fou(folle) de rage; (*storm*) faire rage, être déchaîné(e); **to fly into a ~** se mettre en rage; **it's all the ~** cela fait fureur.
ragged ['rægɪd] *adj* (*edge*) inégal(e), qui accroche; (*cuff*) effiloché(e); (*appearance*) déguenillé(e).
raging ['reɪdʒɪŋ] *adj* (*sea, storm*) en furie; (*fever, pain*) violent(e); **~ toothache** rage *f* de dents; **in a ~ temper** dans une rage folle.
rag trade *n (col)*: **the ~** la confection.
Rag Week *n voir encadré.*

RAG WEEK

Rag Week *est une semaine où les étudiants se déguisent et collectent de l'argent pour les œuvres de charité. Toutes sortes d'animations sont organisées à cette occasion (marches sponsorisées, spectacles de rue etc). Des magazines (les "rag mags") contenant des plaisanteries osées sont vendus dans les rues, également au profit des œuvres. Enfin, la plupart des universités organisent un bal (le "rag ball").*

raid [reɪd] *n* (*MIL*) raid *m*; (*criminal*) hold-up *m inv*; (*by police*) descente *f*, rafle *f* ♦ *vt* faire un raid sur *or* un hold-up dans *or* une descente dans.
raider ['reɪdə*] *n* malfaiteur *m*.
rail [reɪl] *n* (*on stair*) rampe *f*; (*on bridge, balcony*) balustrade *f*; (*of ship*) bastingage *m*; (*for train*) rail *m*; ~**s** *npl* rails *mpl*, voie ferrée; **by** ~ par chemin de fer, par le train.
railcard ['reɪlkɑːd] *n* (*BRIT*) carte *f* de chemin de fer; **young person's** ~ carte *f* jeune.
railing(s) ['reɪlɪŋ(z)] *n(pl)* grille *f*.
railway ['reɪlweɪ], (*US*) **railroad** ['reɪlrəud] *n* chemin *m* de fer.
railway engine *n* locomotive *f*.
railway line *n* ligne *f* de chemin de fer; (*track*) voie ferrée.
railwayman ['reɪlweɪmən] *n* cheminot *m*.
railway station *n* gare *f*.
rain [reɪn] *n* pluie *f* ♦ *vi* pleuvoir; **in the** ~ sous la pluie; **it's** ~**ing** il pleut; **it's** ~**ing cats and dogs** il pleut à torrents.
rainbow ['reɪnbəu] *n* arc-en-ciel *m*.
raincoat ['reɪnkəut] *n* imperméable *m*.
raindrop ['reɪndrɔp] *n* goutte *f* de pluie.
rainfall ['reɪnfɔːl] *n* chute *f* de pluie; (*measurement*) hauteur *f* des précipitations.
rainforest ['reɪnfɔrɪst] *n* forêt tropicale.
rainproof ['reɪnpruːf] *adj* imperméable.
rainstorm ['reɪnstɔːm] *n* pluie torrentielle.
rainwater ['reɪnwɔːtə*] *n* eau *f* de pluie.
rainy ['reɪnɪ] *adj* pluvieux(euse).
raise [reɪz] *n* augmentation *f* ♦ *vt* (*lift*) lever; hausser; (*end: siege, embargo*) lever; (*build*) ériger; (*increase*) augmenter; (*a protest, doubt*) provoquer, causer; (*a question*) soulever; (*cattle, family*) élever; (*crop*) faire pousser; (*army, funds*) rassembler; (*loan*) obtenir; **to** ~ **one's glass to sb/sth** porter un toast en l'honneur de qn/qch; **to** ~ **one's voice** élever la voix; **to** ~ **sb's hopes** donner de l'espoir à qn; **to** ~ **a laugh/a smile** faire rire/sourire.
raisin ['reɪzn] *n* raisin sec.
Raj [rɑːdʒ] *n*: **the** ~ l'empire *m* (*aux Indes*).
rajah ['rɑːdʒə] *n* radja(h) *m*.
rake [reɪk] *n* (*tool*) râteau *m*; (*person*) débauché *m* ♦ *vt* (*garden*) ratisser; (*fire*) tisonner; (*with machine gun*) balayer ♦ *vi*: **to** ~ **through** (*fig: search*) fouiller (dans).
rake-off ['reɪkɔf] *n* (*col*) pourcentage *m*.
rakish ['reɪkɪʃ] *adj* dissolu(e); cavalier(ière).
rally ['rælɪ] *n* (*POL etc*) meeting *m*, rassemblement *m*; (*AUT*) rallye *m*; (*TENNIS*) échange *m* ♦ *vt* rassembler, rallier ♦ *vi* se rallier; (*sick person*) aller mieux; (*Stock Exchange*) reprendre.
►**rally round** *vi* venir en aide ♦ *vt fus* se rallier à; venir en aide à.
rallying point ['rælɪɪŋ-] *n* (*MIL*) point *m* de ralliement.
RAM [ræm] *n abbr* (*COMPUT*) = **random access memory**.
ram [ræm] *n* bélier *m* ♦ *vt* enfoncer; (*soil*) tasser; (*crash into*) emboutir; percuter; éperonner.
ramble ['ræmbl] *n* randonnée *f* ♦ *vi* (*pej*: *also*: ~ **on**) discourir, pérorer.
rambler ['ræmblə*] *n* promeneur/euse, randonneur/euse; (*BOT*) rosier grimpant.
rambling ['ræmblɪŋ] *adj* (*speech*) décousu(e); (*house*) plein(e) de coins et de recoins; (*BOT*) grimpant(e).
RAMC *n abbr* (*BRIT*) = *Royal Army Medical Corps*.
ramification [ræmɪfɪ'keɪʃən] *n* ramification *f*.
ramp [ræmp] *n* (*incline*) rampe *f*; dénivellation *f*; (*in garage*) pont *m*.
rampage [ræm'peɪdʒ] *n*: **to be on the** ~ se déchaîner ♦ *vi*: **they went rampaging through the town** ils ont envahi les rues et ont tout saccagé sur leur passage.
rampant ['ræmpənt] *adj* (*disease etc*) qui sévit.
rampart ['ræmpɑːt] *n* rempart *m*.
ram raiding [-reɪdɪŋ] *n* *pillage d'un magasin en enfonçant la vitrine avec une voiture volée.*
ramshackle ['ræmʃækl] *adj* (*house*) délabré(e); (*car etc*) déglingué(e).
RAN *n abbr* = *Royal Australian Navy*.
ran [ræn] *pt of* **run**.
ranch [rɑːntʃ] *n* ranch *m*.
rancher ['rɑːntʃə*] *n* (*owner*) propriétaire *m* de ranch; (*ranch hand*) cowboy *m*.
rancid ['rænsɪd] *adj* rance.
rancour, (*US*) **rancor** ['ræŋkə*] *n* rancune *f*, rancœur *f*.
R&B *n abbr* = *rhythm and blues*.
R&D *n abbr* (= *research and development*) R-D *f*.
random ['rændəm] *adj* fait(e) *or* établi(e) au hasard; (*COMPUT, MATH*) aléatoire ♦ *n*: **at** ~ au hasard.
random access memory (RAM) *n* (*COMPUT*) mémoire vive, RAM *f*.
R&R *n abbr* (*US MIL*) = *rest and recreation*.
randy ['rændɪ] *adj* (*BRIT col*) excité(e); lubrique.
rang [ræŋ] *pt of* **ring**.
range [reɪndʒ] *n* (*of mountains*) chaîne *f*; (*of missile, voice*) portée *f*; (*of products*) choix *m*, gamme *f*; (*also*: **shooting** ~) champ *m* de tir; (*: indoor*) stand *m* de tir; (*also*: **kitchen** ~) fourneau *m* (de cuisine) ♦ *vt* (*place*) mettre en rang, placer; (*roam*) parcourir ♦ *vi*: **to** ~ **over** couvrir; **to** ~ **from ... to** aller de ... à;

price ~ éventail *m* des prix; **do you have anything else in this price ~?** avez-vous autre chose dans ces prix?; **within (firing) ~** à portée (de tir); **~d left/right** (*text*) justifié à gauche/à droite.
ranger ['reɪndʒə*] *n* garde *m* forestier.
Rangoon [ræŋ'guːn] *n* Rangoon.
rank [ræŋk] *n* rang *m*; (*MIL*) grade *m*; (*BRIT*: *also*: **taxi ~**) station *f* de taxis ♦ *vi*: **to ~ among** compter *or* se classer parmi ♦ *vt*: **I ~ him sixth** je le place sixième ♦ *adj* (*smell*) nauséabond(e); (*hypocrisy, injustice etc*) flagrant(e); **he's a ~ outsider** il n'est vraiment pas dans la course; **the ~s** (*MIL*) la troupe; **the ~ and file** (*fig*) la masse, la base; **to close ~s** (*MIL, fig*) serrer les rangs.
rankle ['ræŋkl] *vi* (*insult*) rester sur le cœur.
ransack ['rænsæk] *vt* fouiller (à fond); (*plunder*) piller.
ransom ['rænsəm] *n* rançon *f*; **to hold sb to ~** (*fig*) exercer un chantage sur qn.
rant [rænt] *vi* fulminer.
ranting ['ræntɪŋ] *n* invectives *fpl*.
rap [ræp] *n* petit coup sec; tape *f* ♦ *vt* frapper sur *or* à; taper sur.
rape [reɪp] *n* viol *m*; (*BOT*) colza *m* ♦ *vt* violer.
rape(seed) oil ['reɪp(siːd)-] *n* huile *f* de colza.
rapid ['ræpɪd] *adj* rapide.
rapidity [rə'pɪdɪtɪ] *n* rapidité *f*.
rapidly ['ræpɪdlɪ] *adv* rapidement.
rapids ['ræpɪdz] *npl* (*GEO*) rapides *mpl*.
rapist ['reɪpɪst] *n* auteur *m* d'un viol.
rapport [ræ'pɔː*] *n* entente *f*.
rapt [ræpt] *adj* (*attention*) extrême; **to be ~ in contemplation** être perdu(e) dans la contemplation.
rapture ['ræptʃə*] *n* extase *f*, ravissement *m*; **to go into ~s over** s'extasier sur.
rapturous ['ræptʃərəs] *adj* extasié(e); frénétique.
rare [rɛə*] *adj* rare; (*CULIN*: *steak*) saignant(e).
rarebit ['rɛəbɪt] *n see* **Welsh rarebit**.
rarefied ['rɛərɪfaɪd] *adj* (*air, atmosphere*) raréfié(e).
rarely ['rɛəlɪ] *adv* rarement.
raring ['rɛərɪŋ] *adj*: **to be ~ to go** (*col*) être très impatient(e) de commencer.
rarity ['rɛərɪtɪ] *n* rareté *f*.
rascal ['rɑːskl] *n* vaurien *m*.
rash [ræʃ] *adj* imprudent(e), irréfléchi(e) ♦ *n* (*MED*) rougeur *f*, éruption *f*; **to come out in a ~** avoir une éruption.
rasher ['ræʃə*] *n* fine tranche (de lard).
rasp [rɑːsp] *n* (*tool*) lime *f* ♦ *vt* (*speak*: *also*: **~ out**) dire d'une voix grinçante.
raspberry ['rɑːzbərɪ] *n* framboise *f*.
raspberry bush *n* framboisier *m*.
rasping ['rɑːspɪŋ] *adj*: **~ noise** grincement *m*.
Rastafarian [ræstə'fɛərɪən] *adj*, *n* rastafari (*m/f*).
rat [ræt] *n* rat *m*.
ratable ['reɪtəbl] *adj* = **rateable**.
ratchet ['rætʃɪt] *n*: **~ wheel** roue *f* à rochet.
rate [reɪt] *n* (*ratio*) taux *m*, pourcentage *m*; (*speed*) vitesse *f*, rythme *m*; (*price*) tarif *m* ♦ *vt* classer; évaluer; **to ~ sb/sth as** considérer qn/qch comme; **to ~ sb/sth among** classer qn/qch parmi; **to ~ sb/sth highly** avoir une haute opinion de qn/qch; **at a ~ of 60 kph** à une vitesse de 60 km/h; **~ of exchange** taux *or* cours *m* du change; **~ of flow** débit *m*; **~ of return** (taux de) rendement *m*; **pulse ~** fréquence *f* des pulsations.
rateable value ['reɪtəbl-] *n* (*BRIT*) valeur locative imposable.
ratepayer ['reɪtpeɪə*] *n* (*BRIT*) contribuable *m/f* (*payant les impôts locaux*).
rates [reɪts] *npl* (*BRIT*) impôts locaux.
rather ['rɑːðə*] *adv* (*somewhat*) assez, plutôt; (*to some extent*) un peu; **it's ~ expensive** c'est assez cher; (*too much*) c'est un peu cher; **there's ~ a lot** il y en a beaucoup; **I would** *or* **I'd ~ go** j'aimerais mieux *or* je préférerais partir; **I had ~ go** il vaudrait mieux que je parte; **I'd ~ not leave** j'aimerais mieux ne pas partir; **or ~** (*more accurately*) ou plutôt; **I ~ think he won't come** je crois bien qu'il ne viendra pas.
ratification [rætɪfɪ'keɪʃən] *n* ratification *f*.
ratify ['rætɪfaɪ] *vt* ratifier.
rating ['reɪtɪŋ] *n* classement *m*; cote *f*; (*NAUT*: *category*) classe *f*; (*: sailor*: *BRIT*) matelot *m*; **~s** *npl* (*RADIO, TV*) indice(s) *m(pl)* d'écoute.
ratio ['reɪʃɪəu] *n* proportion *f*; **in the ~ of 100 to 1** dans la proportion de 100 contre 1.
ration ['ræʃən] *n* (*gen pl*) ration(s) *f(pl)* ♦ *vt* rationner.
rational ['ræʃənl] *adj* raisonnable, sensé(e); (*solution, reasoning*) logique; (*MED*) lucide.
rationale [ræʃə'nɑːl] *n* raisonnement *m*; justification *f*.
rationalization [ræʃnəlaɪ'zeɪʃən] *n* rationalisation *f*.
rationalize ['ræʃnəlaɪz] *vt* rationaliser; (*conduct*) essayer d'expliquer *or* de motiver.
rationally ['ræʃnəlɪ] *adv* raisonnablement; logiquement.
rationing ['ræʃnɪŋ] *n* rationnement *m*.
ratpack ['rætpæk] *n* (*BRIT col*) journalistes *mpl* de la presse à sensation.
rat poison *n* mort-aux-rats *f inv*.
rat race *n* foire *f* d'empoigne.
rattan [ræ'tæn] *n* rotin *m*.
rattle ['rætl] *n* cliquetis *m*; (*louder*) bruit *m* de ferraille; (*object*: *of baby*) hochet *m*; (*: of sports fan*) crécelle *f* ♦ *vi* cliqueter; faire un bruit de ferraille *or* du bruit ♦ *vt* agiter (bruyamment); (*col*: *disconcert*) décontenancer; (*: annoy*) embêter.
rattlesnake ['rætlsneɪk] *n* serpent *m* à sonnettes.
ratty ['rætɪ] *adj* (*col*) en rogne.
raucous ['rɔːkəs] *adj* rauque.
raucously ['rɔːkəslɪ] *adv* d'une voix rauque.
raunchy ['rɔːntʃɪ] *adj* (*col*: *voice, image, act*)

sexy; (:*scenes, film*) lubrique.
ravage ['rævɪdʒ] *vt* ravager.
ravages ['rævɪdʒɪz] *npl* ravages *mpl*.
rave [reɪv] *vi* (*in anger*) s'emporter; (*with enthusiasm*) s'extasier; (*MED*) délirer ♦ *n*: **a ~ (party)** une rave, une soirée techno ♦ *adj* (*scene, culture, music*) rave, techno ♦ *cpd*: **~ review** (*col*) critique *f* dithyrambique.
raven ['reɪvən] *n* grand corbeau.
ravenous ['rævənəs] *adj* affamé(e).
ravine [rə'viːn] *n* ravin *m*.
raving ['reɪvɪŋ] *adj*: **~ lunatic** *n* fou furieux/folle furieuse.
ravings ['reɪvɪŋz] *npl* divagations *fpl*.
ravioli [rævɪ'əulɪ] *n* ravioli *mpl*.
ravish ['rævɪʃ] *vt* ravir.
ravishing ['rævɪʃɪŋ] *adj* enchanteur(eresse).
raw [rɔː] *adj* (*uncooked*) cru(e); (*not processed*) brut(e); (*sore*) à vif, irrité(e); (*inexperienced*) inexpérimenté(e); **~ deal** (*col: bad bargain*) sale coup *m*; (*: unfair treatment*): **to get a ~ deal** être traité(e) injustement.
Rawalpindi [rɔːl'pɪndɪ] *n* Rawalpindi.
raw material *n* matière première.
ray [reɪ] *n* rayon *m*; **~ of hope** lueur *f* d'espoir.
rayon ['reɪɔn] *n* rayonne *f*.
raze [reɪz] *vt* (*also*: **~ to the ground**) raser.
razor ['reɪzə*] *n* rasoir *m*.
razor blade *n* lame *f* de rasoir.
razzle(-dazzle) ['ræzl('dæzl)] *n* (*BRIT col*): **to go on the ~** faire la bringue.
razzmatazz ['ræzmə'tæz] *n* (*col*) tralala *m*, tapage *m*.
RC *abbr* = **Roman Catholic**.
RCAF *n abbr* = *Royal Canadian Air Force*.
RCMP *n abbr* = *Royal Canadian Mounted Police*.
RCN *n abbr* = *Royal Canadian Navy*.
RD *abbr* (*US*) = *rural delivery*.
Rd *abbr* = **road**.
RE *n abbr* (*BRIT*) = *religious education*; (*BRIT MIL*) = *Royal Engineers*.
re [riː] *prep* concernant.
reach [riːtʃ] *n* portée *f*, atteinte *f*; (*of river etc*) étendue *f* ♦ *vt* atteindre, arriver à ♦ *vi* s'étendre; (*stretch out hand*): **to ~ up/down/out** *etc* **(for sth)** lever/baisser/allonger *etc* le bras (pour prendre qch); **to ~ sb by phone** joindre qn par téléphone; **out of/within ~** (*object*) hors de/à portée; **within easy ~ (of)** (*place*) à proximité (de), proche (de).
react [riː'ækt] *vi* réagir.
reaction [riː'ækʃən] *n* réaction *f*.
reactionary [riː'ækʃənrɪ] *adj, n* réactionnaire (*m/f*).
reactor [riː'æktə*] *n* réacteur *m*.
read, *pt, pp* **read** [riːd, rɛd] *vi* lire ♦ *vt* lire; (*understand*) comprendre, interpréter; (*study*) étudier; (*subj: instrument etc*) indiquer, marquer; **to take sth as read** (*fig*) considérer qch comme accepté; **do you ~ me?** (*TEL*) est-ce que vous me recevez?
►**read out** *vt* lire à haute voix.
►**read over** *vt* relire.
►**read through** *vt* (*quickly*) parcourir; (*thoroughly*) lire jusqu'au bout.
►**read up** *vt*, **read up on** *vt fus* étudier.
readable ['riːdəbl] *adj* facile *or* agréable à lire.
reader ['riːdə*] *n* lecteur/trice; (*book*) livre *m* de lecture; (*BRIT: at university*) maître *m* de conférences.
readership ['riːdəʃɪp] *n* (*of paper etc*) (nombre *m* de) lecteurs *mpl*.
readily ['rɛdɪlɪ] *adv* volontiers, avec empressement; (*easily*) facilement.
readiness ['rɛdɪnɪs] *n* empressement *m*; **in ~** (*prepared*) prêt(e).
reading ['riːdɪŋ] *n* lecture *f*; (*understanding*) interprétation *f*; (*on instrument*) indications *fpl*.
reading lamp *n* lampe *f* de bureau.
reading room *n* salle *f* de lecture.
readjust [riːə'dʒʌst] *vt* rajuster; (*instrument*) régler de nouveau ♦ *vi* (*person*): **to ~ (to)** se réadapter (à).
ready ['rɛdɪ] *adj* prêt(e); (*willing*) prêt, disposé(e); (*quick*) prompt(e); (*available*) disponible ♦ *n*: **at the ~** (*MIL*) prêt à faire feu; (*fig*) tout(e) prêt(e); **~ for use** prêt à l'emploi; **to be ~ to do sth** être prêt à faire qch; **to get ~** *vi* se préparer ♦ *vt* préparer.
ready cash *n* (argent *m*) liquide *m*.
ready-made ['rɛdɪ'meɪd] *adj* tout(e) fait(e).
ready-mix ['rɛdɪmɪks] *n* (*for cakes etc*) préparation *f* en sachet.
ready reckoner [-'rɛknə*] *n* (*BRIT*) barème *m*.
ready-to-wear ['rɛdɪtə'wɛə*] *adj* (en) prêt-à-porter.
reagent [riː'eɪdʒənt] *n* réactif *m*.
real [rɪəl] *adj* réel(le); (*genuine*) véritable; (*proper*) vrai(e) ♦ *adv* (*US col: very*) vraiment; **in ~ life** dans la réalité.
real ale *n* bière traditionnelle.
real estate *n* biens fonciers *or* immobiliers.
realism ['rɪəlɪzəm] *n* réalisme *m*.
realist ['rɪəlɪst] *n* réaliste *m/f*.
realistic [rɪə'lɪstɪk] *adj* réaliste.
reality [riː'ælɪtɪ] *n* réalité *f*; **in ~** en réalité, en fait.
reality TV *n* télé-réalité *f*.
realization [rɪəlaɪ'zeɪʃən] *n* prise *f* de conscience; réalisation *f*.
realize ['rɪəlaɪz] *vt* (*understand*) se rendre compte de, prendre conscience de; (*a project, COMM: asset*) réaliser.
really ['rɪəlɪ] *adv* vraiment.
realm [rɛlm] *n* royaume *m*.
real-time ['riːltaɪm] *adj* (*COMPUT*) en temps réel.
Realtor ['rɪəltɔː*] *n* ® (*US*) agent immobilier.
ream [riːm] *n* rame *f* (*de papier*); **~s** *npl* (*fig: col*) des pages et des pages.
reap [riːp] *vt* moissonner; (*fig*) récolter.
reaper ['riːpə*] *n* (*machine*) moissonneuse *f*.
reappear [riːə'pɪə*] *vi* réapparaître, reparaître.

reappearance [riːə'pɪərəns] *n* réapparition *f*.
reapply [riːə'plaɪ] *vi*: **to ~ for** (*job*) faire une nouvelle demande d'emploi concernant; reposer sa candidature à; (*loan, grant*) faire une nouvelle demande de.
reappraisal [riːə'preɪzl] *n* réévaluation *f*.
rear [rɪə*] *adj* de derrière, arrière *inv*; (*AUT*: *wheel etc*) arrière ♦ *n* arrière *m*, derrière *m* ♦ *vt* (*cattle, family*) élever ♦ *vi* (*also*: **~ up**: *animal*) se cabrer.
rear admiral (RA) *n* vice-amiral *m*.
rear-engined ['rɪər'ɛndʒɪnd] *adj* (*AUT*) avec moteur à l'arrière.
rearguard ['rɪəgɑːd] *n* arrière-garde *f*.
rearmament [riː'ɑːməmənt] *n* réarmement *m*.
rearrange [riːə'reɪndʒ] *vt* réarranger.
rear-view ['rɪəvjuː]: **~ mirror** *n* (*AUT*) rétroviseur *m*.
reason ['riːzn] *n* raison *f* ♦ *vi*: **to ~ with sb** raisonner qn, faire entendre raison à qn; **the ~ for/why** la raison de/pour laquelle; **to have ~ to think** avoir lieu de penser; **it stands to ~ that** il va sans dire que; **she claims with good ~ that** ... elle affirme à juste titre que ...; **all the more ~ why** raison de plus pour + *infinitive or* pour que + *sub*.
reasonable ['riːznəbl] *adj* raisonnable; (*not bad*) acceptable.
reasonably ['riːznəblɪ] *adv* (*to behave*) raisonnablement; (*fairly*) assez; **one can ~ assume that** ... on est fondé à *or* il est permis de supposer que ....
reasoned ['riːznd] *adj* (*argument*) raisonné(e).
reasoning ['riːznɪŋ] *n* raisonnement *m*.
reassemble [riːə'sɛmbl] *vt* rassembler; (*machine*) remonter.
reassert [riːə'səːt] *vt* réaffirmer.
reassurance [riːə'ʃuərəns] *n* assurance *f*, garantie *f*; (*comfort*) réconfort *m*.
reassure [riːə'ʃuə*] *vt* rassurer; **to ~ sb of** donner à qn l'assurance répétée de.
reassuring [riːə'ʃuərɪŋ] *adj* rassurant(e).
reawakening [riːə'weɪknɪŋ] *n* réveil *m*.
rebate ['riːbeɪt] *n* (*on product*) rabais *m*; (*on tax etc*) dégrèvement *m*; (*repayment*) remboursement *m*.
rebel *n* ['rɛbl] rebelle *m/f* ♦ *vi* [rɪ'bɛl] se rebeller, se révolter.
rebellion [rɪ'bɛljən] *n* rébellion *f*, révolte *f*.
rebellious [rɪ'bɛljəs] *adj* rebelle.
rebirth [riː'bəːθ] *n* renaissance *f*.
rebound *vi* [rɪ'baund] (*ball*) rebondir ♦ *n* ['riːbaund] rebond *m*.
rebuff [rɪ'bʌf] *n* rebuffade *f* ♦ *vt* repousser.
rebuild [riː'bɪld] *vt irreg* reconstruire.
rebuke [rɪ'bjuːk] *n* réprimande *f*, reproche *m* ♦ *vt* réprimander.
rebut [rɪ'bʌt] *vt* réfuter.
rebuttal [rɪ'bʌtl] *n* réfutation *f*.
recalcitrant [rɪ'kælsɪtrənt] *adj* récalcitrant(e).
recall [rɪ'kɔːl] *vt* rappeler; (*remember*) se rappeler, se souvenir de ♦ *n* rappel *m*; **beyond ~** *adj* irrévocable.
recant [rɪ'kænt] *vi* se rétracter; (*REL*) abjurer.
recap ['riːkæp] *n* récapitulation *f* ♦ *vt, vi* récapituler.
recapitulate [riːkə'pɪtjuleɪt] *vt, vi* récapituler.
recapture [riː'kæptʃə*] *vt* reprendre; (*atmosphere*) recréer.
recd. *abbr = received.*
recede [rɪ'siːd] *vi* s'éloigner; reculer.
receding [rɪ'siːdɪŋ] *adj* (*forehead, chin*) fuyant(e); **~ hairline** front dégarni.
receipt [rɪ'siːt] *n* (*document*) reçu *m*; (*for parcel etc*) accusé *m* de réception; (*act of receiving*) réception *f*; **~s** *npl* (*COMM*) recettes *fpl*; **to acknowledge ~ of** accuser réception de; **we are in ~ of** ... nous avons reçu ....
receivable [rɪ'siːvəbl] *adj* (*COMM*) recevable; (*: owing*) à recevoir.
receive [rɪ'siːv] *vt* recevoir; (*guest*) recevoir, accueillir; **"~d with thanks"** (*COMM*) "pour acquit"; **R~d Pronunciation** *voir encadré.*

RECEIVED PRONUNCIATION

En Grande-Bretagne, la **received pronunciation** *ou "RP" est une prononciation de la langue anglaise qui, récemment encore, était surtout associée à l'aristocratie et à la bourgeoisie, mais qui maintenant est en général considérée comme la prononciation correcte.*

receiver [rɪ'siːvə*] *n* (*TEL*) récepteur *m*; (*RADIO*) récepteur; (*of stolen goods*) receleur *m*; (*COMM*) administrateur *m* judiciaire.
receivership [rɪ'siːvəʃɪp] *n*: **to go into ~** être placé sous administration judiciaire.
recent ['riːsnt] *adj* récent(e); **in ~ years** au cours de ces dernières années.
recently ['riːsntlɪ] *adv* récemment; **as ~ as** pas plus tard que; **until ~** jusqu'à il y a peu de temps encore.
receptacle [rɪ'sɛptɪkl] *n* récipient *m*.
reception [rɪ'sɛpʃən] *n* réception *f*; (*welcome*) accueil *m*, réception.
reception centre *n* (*BRIT*) centre *m* d'accueil.
reception desk *n* réception *f*.
receptionist [rɪ'sɛpʃənɪst] *n* réceptionniste *m/f*.
receptive [rɪ'sɛptɪv] *adj* réceptif(ive).
recess [rɪ'sɛs] *n* (*in room*) renfoncement *m*; (*for bed*) alcôve *f*; (*secret place*) recoin *m*; (*POL etc*: *holiday*) vacances *fpl*; (*US*: *LAW*: *short break*) suspension *f* d'audience; (*SCOL*: *esp US*) récréation *f*.
recession [rɪ'sɛʃən] *n* (*ECON*) récession *f*.
recharge [riː'tʃɑːdʒ] *vt* (*battery*) recharger.
rechargeable [riː'tʃɑːdʒəbl] *adj* rechargeable.
recipe ['rɛsɪpɪ] *n* recette *f*.
recipient [rɪ'sɪpɪənt] *n* bénéficiaire *m/f*; (*of letter*) destinataire *m/f*.
reciprocal [rɪ'sɪprəkl] *adj* réciproque.

reciprocate [rɪ'sɪprəkeɪt] *vt* retourner, offrir en retour ♦ *vi* en faire autant.
recital [rɪ'saɪtl] *n* récital *m*.
recite [rɪ'saɪt] *vt* (*poem*) réciter; (*complaints etc*) énumérer.
reckless ['rɛkləs] *adj* (*driver etc*) imprudent(e); (*spender etc*) insouciant(e).
recklessly ['rɛkləslɪ] *adv* imprudemment; avec insouciance.
reckon ['rɛkən] *vt* (*count*) calculer, compter; (*consider*) considérer, estimer; (*think*): **I ~ (that)** ... je pense (que) ..., j'estime (que) ... ♦ *vi*: **he is somebody to be ~ed with** il ne faut pas le sous-estimer; **to ~ without sb/sth** ne pas tenir compte de qn/qch.
►**reckon on** *vt fus* compter sur, s'attendre à.
reckoning ['rɛknɪŋ] *n* compte *m*, calcul *m*; estimation *f*; **the day of ~** le jour du Jugement.
reclaim [rɪ'kleɪm] *vt* (*land*) amender; (*: from sea*) assécher; (*: from forest*) défricher; (*demand back*) réclamer (le remboursement *or* la restitution de).
reclamation [rɛklə'meɪʃən] *n* (*of land*) amendement *m*; assèchement *m*; défrichement *m*.
recline [rɪ'klaɪn] *vi* être allongé(e) *or* étendu(e).
reclining [rɪ'klaɪnɪŋ] *adj* (*seat*) à dossier réglable.
recluse [rɪ'klu:s] *n* reclus/e, ermite *m*.
recognition [rɛkəg'nɪʃən] *n* reconnaissance *f*; **in ~ of** en reconnaissance de; **to gain ~** être reconnu(e); **transformed beyond ~** méconnaissable.
recognizable ['rɛkəgnaɪzəbl] *adj*: **~ (by)** reconnaissable (à).
recognize ['rɛkəgnaɪz] *vt*: **to ~ (by/as)** reconnaître (à/comme étant).
recoil [rɪ'kɔɪl] *vi* (*person*): **to ~ (from)** reculer (devant) ♦ *n* (*of gun*) recul *m*.
recollect [rɛkə'lɛkt] *vt* se rappeler, se souvenir de.
recollection [rɛkə'lɛkʃən] *n* souvenir *m*; **to the best of my ~** autant que je m'en souvienne.
recommend [rɛkə'mɛnd] *vt* recommander; **she has a lot to ~ her** elle a beaucoup de choses en sa faveur.
recommendation [rɛkəmɛn'deɪʃən] *n* recommandation *f*.
recommended retail price (RRP) [rɛkə'mɛndɪd-] *n* (*BRIT*) prix conseillé.
recompense ['rɛkəmpɛns] *vt* récompenser; (*compensate*) dédommager ♦ *n* récompense *f*; dédommagement *m*.
reconcilable ['rɛkənsaɪləbl] *adj* (*ideas*) conciliable.
reconcile ['rɛkənsaɪl] *vt* (*two people*) réconcilier; (*two facts*) concilier, accorder; **to ~ o.s. to** se résigner à.
reconciliation [rɛkənsɪlɪ'eɪʃən] *n* réconciliation *f*; conciliation *f*.
recondite [rɪ'kɔndaɪt] *adj* abstrus(e), obscur(e).
recondition [ri:kən'dɪʃən] *vt* remettre à neuf; réviser entièrement.
reconnaissance [rɪ'kɔnɪsns] *n* (*MIL*) reconnaissance *f*.
reconnoitre, (*US*) **reconnoiter** [rɛkə'nɔɪtə*] (*MIL*) *vt* reconnaître ♦ *vi* faire une reconnaissance.
reconsider [ri:kən'sɪdə*] *vt* reconsidérer.
reconstitute [ri:'kɔnstɪtju:t] *vt* reconstituer.
reconstruct [ri:kən'strʌkt] *vt* (*building*) reconstruire; (*crime*) reconstituer.
reconstruction [ri:kən'strʌkʃən] *n* reconstruction *f*; reconstitution *f*.
reconvene [ri:kən'vi:n] *vt* reconvoquer ♦ *vi* se réunir *or* s'assembler de nouveau.
record *n* ['rɛkɔ:d] rapport *m*, récit *m*; (*of meeting etc*) procès-verbal *m*; (*register*) registre *m*; (*file*) dossier *m*; (*COMPUT*) article *m*; (*also*: **police ~**) casier *m* judiciaire; (*MUS*: *disc*) disque *m*; (*SPORT*) record *m* ♦ *vt* [rɪ'kɔ:d] (*set down*) noter; (*relate*) rapporter; (*MUS*: *song etc*) enregistrer; **in ~ time** dans un temps record *inv*; **public ~s** archives *fpl*; **to keep a ~ of** noter; **to keep the ~ straight** (*fig*) mettre les choses au point; **he is on ~ as saying that** ... il a déclaré en public que ...; **Italy's excellent ~** les excellents résultats obtenus par l'Italie; **off the ~** *adj* officieux(euse) ♦ *adv* officieusement.
record card *n* (*in file*) fiche *f*.
recorded delivery letter [rɪ'kɔ:dɪd-] *n* (*BRIT POST*) ≈ lettre recommandée.
recorder [rɪ'kɔ:də*] *n* (*LAW*) *avocat nommé à la fonction de juge*; (*MUS*) flûte *f* à bec.
record holder *n* (*SPORT*) détenteur/trice du record.
recording [rɪ'kɔ:dɪŋ] *n* (*MUS*) enregistrement *m*.
recording studio *n* studio *m* d'enregistrement.
record library *n* discothèque *f*.
record player *n* électrophone *m*.
recount [rɪ'kaunt] *vt* raconter.
re-count *n* ['ri:kaunt] (*POL*: *of votes*) nouveau décompte (des suffrages) ♦ *vt* [ri:'kaunt] recompter.
recoup [rɪ'ku:p] *vt*: **to ~ one's losses** récupérer ce qu'on a perdu, se refaire.
recourse [rɪ'kɔ:s] *n* recours *m*; expédient *m*; **to have ~ to** recourir à, avoir recours à.
recover [rɪ'kʌvə*] *vt* récupérer ♦ *vi* (*from illness*) se rétablir; (*from shock*) se remettre; (*country*) se redresser.
re-cover [ri:'kʌvə*] *vt* (*chair etc*) recouvrir.
recovery [rɪ'kʌvərɪ] *n* récupération *f*; rétablissement *m*; redressement *m*.
recreate [ri:krɪ'eɪt] *vt* recréer.
recreation [rɛkrɪ'eɪʃən] *n* récréation *f*, détente *f*.
recreational [rɛkrɪ'eɪʃənl] *adj* pour la détente, récréatif(ive).

recreational drug *n* drogue *f* euphorisante.
recreational vehicle (RV) *n* (*US*) camping-car *m*.
recrimination [rɪkrɪmɪ'neɪʃən] *n* récrimination *f*.
recruit [rɪ'kru:t] *n* recrue *f* ♦ *vt* recruter.
recruiting office [rɪ'kru:tɪŋ-] *n* bureau *m* de recrutement.
recruitment [rɪ'kru:tmənt] *n* recrutement *m*.
rectangle ['rɛktæŋgl] *n* rectangle *m*.
rectangular [rɛk'tæŋgjulə*] *adj* rectangulaire.
rectify ['rɛktɪfaɪ] *vt* (*error*) rectifier, corriger; (*omission*) réparer.
rector ['rɛktə*] *n* (*REL*) pasteur *m*; (*in Scottish universities*) *personnalité élue par les étudiants pour les représenter*.
rectory ['rɛktərɪ] *n* presbytère *m*.
rectum ['rɛktəm] *n* (*ANAT*) rectum *m*.
recuperate [rɪ'kju:pəreɪt] *vi* se rétablir.
recur [rɪ'kə:*] *vi* se reproduire; (*idea, opportunity*) se retrouver; (*symptoms*) réapparaître.
recurrence [rɪ'kə:rns] *n* répétition *f*; réapparition *f*.
recurrent [rɪ'kə:rnt] *adj* périodique, fréquent(e).
recurring [rɪ'kə:rɪŋ] *adj* (*MATH*) périodique.
recycle [ri:'saɪkl] *vt*, *vi* recycler.
red [rɛd] *n* rouge *m*; (*POL*: *pej*) rouge *m/f* ♦ *adj* rouge; **in the ~** (*account*) à découvert; (*business*) en déficit.
red alert *n* alerte *f* rouge.
red-blooded [rɛd'blʌdɪd] *adj* (*col*) viril(e), vigoureux(euse).
redbrick university ['rɛdbrɪk-] *n voir encadré*.

REDBRICK UNIVERSITY

Une **redbrick university**, *ainsi nommée à cause du matériau de construction répandu à l'époque (la brique), est une université britannique provinciale construite assez récemment, en particulier fin XIXe-début XXe siècle. Il y en a notamment une à Manchester, une à Liverpool et une à Bristol. Ce terme est utilisé pour établir une distinction avec les universités les plus anciennes et traditionnelles.*

red carpet treatment *n* réception *f* en grande pompe.
Red Cross *n* Croix-Rouge *f*.
redcurrant ['rɛdkʌrənt] *n* groseille *f* (rouge).
redden ['rɛdn] *vt*, *vi* rougir.
reddish ['rɛdɪʃ] *adj* rougeâtre; (*hair*) plutôt roux(rousse).
redecorate [ri:'dɛkəreɪt] *vt* refaire à neuf, repeindre et retapisser.
redecoration [ri:dɛkə'reɪʃən] *n* remise *f* à neuf.
redeem [rɪ'di:m] *vt* (*debt*) rembourser; (*sth in pawn*) dégager; (*fig, also REL*) racheter.
redeemable [rɪ'di:məbl] *adj* rachetable; remboursable, amortissable.
redeeming [rɪ'di:mɪŋ] *adj* (*feature*) qui sauve, qui rachète (le reste).
redefine [ri:dɪ'faɪn] *vt* redéfinir.
redemption [rɪ'dɛmʃən] *n* (*REL*) rédemption *f*; **past** *or* **beyond ~** (*situation*) irrémédiable; (*place*) qui ne peut plus être sauvé(e); (*person*) irrécupérable.
redeploy [ri:dɪ'plɔɪ] *vt* (*MIL*) redéployer; (*staff, resources*) reconvertir.
redeployment [ri:dɪ'plɔɪmənt] *n* redéploiement *m*; reconversion *f*.
redevelop [ri:dɪ'vɛləp] *vt* rénover.
redevelopment [ri:dɪ'vɛləpmənt] *n* rénovation *f*, reconstruction *f*.
red-handed [rɛd'hændɪd] *adj*: **to be caught ~** être pris(e) en flagrant délit *or* la main dans le sac.
redhead ['rɛdhɛd] *n* roux/rousse.
red herring *n* (*fig*) diversion *f*, fausse piste.
red-hot [rɛd'hɔt] *adj* chauffé(e) au rouge, brûlant(e).
redirect [ri:daɪ'rɛkt] *vt* (*mail*) faire suivre.
redistribute [ri:dɪ'strɪbju:t] *vt* redistribuer.
red-letter day ['rɛdlɛtə-] *n* grand jour, jour mémorable.
red light *n*: **to go through a ~** (*AUT*) brûler un feu rouge.
red-light district ['rɛdlaɪt-] *n* quartier réservé.
red meat *n* viande *f* rouge.
redness ['rɛdnɪs] *n* rougeur *f*; (*of hair*) rousseur *f*.
redo [ri:'du:] *vt irreg* refaire.
redolent ['rɛdələnt] *adj*: **~ of** qui sent; (*fig*) qui évoque.
redouble [ri:'dʌbl] *vt*: **to ~ one's efforts** redoubler d'efforts.
redraft [ri:'drɑ:ft] *vt* remanier.
redress [rɪ'drɛs] *n* réparation *f* ♦ *vt* redresser; **to ~ the balance** rétablir l'équilibre.
Red Sea *n*: **the ~** la mer Rouge.
redskin ['rɛdskɪn] *n* Peau-Rouge *m/f*.
red tape *n* (*fig*) paperasserie (administrative).
reduce [rɪ'dju:s] *vt* réduire; (*lower*) abaisser; **"~ speed now"** (*AUT*) "ralentir"; **to ~ sth by/to** réduire qch de/à; **to ~ sb to tears** faire pleurer qn.
reduced [rɪ'dju:st] *adj* réduit(e); **"greatly ~ prices"** "gros rabais"; **at a ~ price** (*goods*) au rabais; (*ticket etc*) à prix réduit.
reduction [rɪ'dʌkʃən] *n* réduction *f*; (*of price*) baisse *f*; (*discount*) rabais *m*; réduction.
redundancy [rɪ'dʌndənsɪ] *n* (*BRIT*) licenciement *m*, mise *f* au chômage; **compulsory ~** licenciement; **voluntary ~** départ *m* volontaire.
redundancy payment *n* (*BRIT*) indemnité *f* de licenciement.
redundant [rɪ'dʌndnt] *adj* (*BRIT*: *worker*) licencié(e), mis(e) au chômage; (*detail, object*) superflu(e); **to be made ~** (*worker*) être li-

cencié, être mis au chômage.
reed [riːd] *n* (*BOT*) roseau *m*; (*MUS*: *of clarinet etc*) anche *f*.
re-educate [riːˈedjukeɪt] *vt* rééduquer.
reedy [ˈriːdɪ] *adj* (*voice, instrument*) ténu(e).
reef [riːf] *n* (*at sea*) récif *m*, écueil *m*.
reek [riːk] *vi*: **to ~ (of)** puer, empester.
reel [riːl] *n* bobine *f*; (*TECH*) dévidoir *m*; (*FISHING*) moulinet *m*; (*CINE*) bande *f* ♦ *vt* (*TECH*) bobiner; (*also*: **~ up**) enrouler ♦ *vi* (*sway*) chanceler; **my head is ~ing** j'ai la tête qui tourne.
►**reel off** *vt* (*say*) énumérer, débiter.
re-election [riːɪˈlɛkʃən] *n* réélection *f*.
re-enter [riːˈɛntə*] *vt* (*also SPACE*) rentrer dans.
re-entry [riːˈɛntrɪ] *n* (*also SPACE*) rentrée *f*.
re-export *vt* [ˈriːɪksˈpɔːt] réexporter ♦ *n* [riːˈɛkspɔːt] marchandise réexportée; (*act*) réexportation *f*.
ref [rɛf] *n abbr* (*col*: = *referee*) arbitre *m*.
ref. *abbr* (*COMM*: = *with reference to*) réf.
refectory [rɪˈfɛktərɪ] *n* réfectoire *m*.
refer [rɪˈfəː*] *vt*: **to ~ sth to** (*dispute, decision*) soumettre qch à; **to ~ sb to** (*inquirer: for information*) adresser *or* envoyer qn à; (*reader: to text*) renvoyer qn à; **he ~red me to the manager** il m'a dit de m'adresser au directeur.
►**refer to** *vt fus* (*allude to*) parler de, faire allusion à; (*apply to*) s'appliquer à; (*consult*) se reporter à; **~ring to your letter** (*COMM*) en réponse à votre lettre.
referee [rɛfəˈriː] *n* arbitre *m*; (*TENNIS*) juge-arbitre *m*; (*BRIT*: *for job application*) répondant/e ♦ *vt* arbitrer.
reference [ˈrɛfrəns] *n* référence *f*, renvoi *m*; (*mention*) allusion *f*, mention *f*; (*for job application: letter*) références; lettre *f* de recommandation; (*: person*) répondant/e; **with ~ to** en ce qui concerne; (*COMM*: *in letter*) me référant à; **"please quote this ~"** (*COMM*) "prière de rappeler cette référence".
reference book *n* ouvrage *m* de référence.
reference library *n* bibliothèque *f* d'ouvrages à consulter.
reference number *n* (*COMM*) numéro *m* de référence.
referendum, *pl* **referenda** [rɛfəˈrɛndəm, -də] *n* référendum *m*.
referral [rɪˈfəːrəl] *n* soumission *f*; **she got a ~ to a specialist** elle a été adressée à un spécialiste.
refill *vt* [riːˈfɪl] remplir à nouveau; (*pen, lighter etc*) recharger ♦ *n* [ˈriːfɪl] (*for pen etc*) recharge *f*.
refine [rɪˈfaɪn] *vt* (*sugar, oil*) raffiner; (*taste*) affiner.
refined [rɪˈfaɪnd] *adj* (*person, taste*) raffiné(e).
refinement [rɪˈfaɪnmənt] *n* (*of person*) raffinement *m*.
refinery [rɪˈfaɪnərɪ] *n* raffinerie *f*.
refit (*NAUT*) *n* [ˈriːfɪt] remise *f* en état ♦ *vt* [riːˈfɪt] remettre en état.
reflate [riːˈfleɪt] *vt* (*economy*) relancer.
reflation [riːˈfleɪʃən] *n* relance *f*.
reflationary [riːˈfleɪʃənrɪ] *adj* de relance.
reflect [rɪˈflɛkt] *vt* (*light, image*) réfléchir, refléter; (*fig*) refléter ♦ *vi* (*think*) réfléchir, méditer.
►**reflect on** *vt fus* (*discredit*) porter atteinte à, faire tort à.
reflection [rɪˈflɛkʃən] *n* réflexion *f*; (*image*) reflet *m*; (*criticism*): **~ on** critique *f* de; atteinte *f* à; **on ~** réflexion faite.
reflector [rɪˈflɛktə*] *n* (*also AUT*) réflecteur *m*.
reflex [ˈriːflɛks] *adj*, *n* réflexe (*m*).
reflexive [rɪˈflɛksɪv] *adj* (*LING*) réfléchi(e).
reform [rɪˈfɔːm] *n* réforme *f* ♦ *vt* réformer.
reformat [riːˈfɔːmæt] *vt* (*COMPUT*) reformater.
Reformation [rɛfəˈmeɪʃən] *n*: **the ~** la Réforme.
reformatory [rɪˈfɔːmətərɪ] *n* (*US*) centre *m* d'éducation surveillée.
reformed [rɪˈfɔːmd] *adj* amendé(e), assagi(e).
reformer [rɪˈfɔːmə*] *n* réformateur/trice.
refrain [rɪˈfreɪn] *vi*: **to ~ from doing** s'abstenir de faire ♦ *n* refrain *m*.
refresh [rɪˈfrɛʃ] *vt* rafraîchir; (*subj: food, sleep etc*) redonner des forces à.
refresher course [rɪˈfrɛʃə-] *n* (*BRIT*) cours *m* de recyclage.
refreshing [rɪˈfrɛʃɪŋ] *adj* rafraîchissant(e); (*sleep*) réparateur(trice); (*fact, idea etc*) qui réjouit par son originalité *or* sa rareté.
refreshment [rɪˈfrɛʃmənt] *n*: **for some ~** (*eating*) pour se restaurer *or* sustenter; **in need of ~** (*resting etc*) ayant besoin de refaire ses forces; **~(s)** rafraîchissement(s) *m(pl)*.
refrigeration [rɪfrɪdʒəˈreɪʃən] *n* réfrigération *f*.
refrigerator [rɪˈfrɪdʒəreɪtə*] *n* réfrigérateur *m*, frigidaire *m*.
refuel [riːˈfjuəl] *vt* ravitailler en carburant ♦ *vi* se ravitailler en carburant.
refuge [ˈrɛfjuːdʒ] *n* refuge *m*; **to take ~ in** se réfugier dans.
refugee [rɛfjuˈdʒiː] *n* réfugié/e.
refugee camp *n* camp *m* de réfugiés.
refund *n* [ˈriːfʌnd] remboursement *m* ♦ *vt* [rɪˈfʌnd] rembourser.
refurbish [riːˈfəːbɪʃ] *vt* remettre à neuf.
refurnish [riːˈfəːnɪʃ] *vt* remeubler.
refusal [rɪˈfjuːzəl] *n* refus *m*; **to have first ~ on sth** avoir droit de préemption sur qch.
refuse *n* [ˈrɛfjuːs] ordures *fpl*, détritus *mpl* ♦ *vt*, *vi* [rɪˈfjuːz] refuser; **to ~ to do sth** refuser de faire qch.
refuse collection *n* ramassage *m* d'ordures.
refuse disposal *n* élimination *f* des ordures.
refusenik [rɪˈfjuːznɪk] *n* refuznik *m/f*.
refute [rɪˈfjuːt] *vt* réfuter.
regain [rɪˈgeɪn] *vt* regagner; retrouver.
regal [ˈriːgl] *adj* royal(e).

regale [rɪ'geɪl] *vt*: **to ~ sb with sth** régaler qn de qch.
regalia [rɪ'geɪlɪə] *n* insignes *mpl* de la royauté.
regard [rɪ'gɑːd] *n* respect *m*, estime *f*, considération *f* ♦ *vt* considérer; **to give one's ~s to** faire ses amitiés à; **"with kindest ~s"** "bien amicalement"; **as ~s, with ~ to** en ce qui concerne.
regarding [rɪ'gɑːdɪŋ] *prep* en ce qui concerne.
regardless [rɪ'gɑːdlɪs] *adv* quand même; **~ of** sans se soucier de.
regatta [rɪ'gætə] *n* régate *f*.
regency ['riːdʒənsɪ] *n* régence *f*.
regenerate [rɪ'dʒɛnəreɪt] *vt* régénérer ♦ *vi* se régénérer.
regent ['riːdʒənt] *n* régent/e.
reggae ['rɛgeɪ] *n* reggae *m*.
régime [reɪ'ʒiːm] *n* régime *m*.
regiment *n* ['rɛdʒɪmənt] régiment *m* ♦ *vt* ['rɛdʒɪmɛnt] imposer une discipline trop stricte à.
regimental [rɛdʒɪ'mɛntl] *adj* d'un régiment.
regimentation [rɛdʒɪmɛn'teɪʃən] *n* réglementation excessive.
region ['riːdʒən] *n* région *f*; **in the ~ of** (*fig*) aux alentours de.
regional ['riːdʒənl] *adj* régional(e).
regional council *n* BRIT) ≈ conseil *m* général; *voir encadré*.

REGIONAL COUNCIL

En Écosse, le **regional council** *est une assemblée délibérante régionale dont les membres sont élus tous les quatre ans. Elle est responsable, entre autres, de l'urbanisme, des transports, de l'éducation, de la police et des pompiers; voir "district council".*

regional development *n* aménagement *m* du territoire.
register ['rɛdʒɪstə*] *n* registre *m*; (*also*: **electoral ~**) liste électorale ♦ *vt* enregistrer, inscrire; (*birth*) déclarer; (*vehicle*) immatriculer; (*luggage*) enregistrer; (*letter*) envoyer en recommandé; (*subj: instrument*) marquer ♦ *vi* se faire inscrire; (*at hotel*) signer le registre; (*make impression*) être (bien) compris(e); **to ~ for a course** s'inscrire à un cours; **to ~ a protest** protester.
registered ['rɛdʒɪstəd] *adj* (*design*) déposé(e); (BRIT: *letter*) recommandé(e); (*student, voter*) inscrit(e).
registered company *n* société immatriculée.
registered nurse *n* (US) infirmier/ière diplômé(e) d'État.
registered office *n* siège social.
registered trademark *n* marque déposée.
registrar ['rɛdʒɪstrɑː*] *n* officier *m* de l'état civil; secrétaire (général).
registration [rɛdʒɪs'treɪʃən] *n* (*act*) enregistrement *m*; inscription *f*; (BRIT AUT: *also*: **~ number**) numéro *m* d'immatriculation.
registry ['rɛdʒɪstrɪ] *n* bureau *m* de l'enregistrement.
registry office *n* (BRIT) bureau *m* de l'état civil; **to get married in a ~** ≈ se marier à la mairie.
regret [rɪ'grɛt] *n* regret *m* ♦ *vt* regretter; **to ~ that** regretter que + *sub*; **we ~ to inform you that ...** nous sommes au regret de vous informer que ....
regretfully [rɪ'grɛtfəlɪ] *adv* à *or* avec regret.
regrettable [rɪ'grɛtəbl] *adj* regrettable, fâcheux(euse).
regrettably [rɪ'grɛtəblɪ] *adv* (*drunk, late*) fâcheusement; **~, he ...** malheureusement, il ....
regroup [riː'gruːp] *vt* regrouper ♦ *vi* se regrouper.
regt *abbr* = **regiment**.
regular ['rɛgjulə*] *adj* régulier(ière); (*usual*) habituel(le), normal(e); (*listener, reader*) fidèle; (*soldier*) de métier; (COMM: *size*) ordinaire ♦ *n* (*client etc*) habitué/e.
regularity [rɛgju'lærɪtɪ] *n* régularité *f*.
regularly ['rɛgjuləlɪ] *adv* régulièrement.
regulate ['rɛgjuleɪt] *vt* régler.
regulation [rɛgju'leɪʃən] *n* (*rule*) règlement *m*; (*adjustment*) réglage *m* ♦ *cpd* réglementaire.
rehabilitate [riːə'bɪlɪteɪt] *vt* (*criminal*) réinsérer; (*drug addict*) désintoxiquer; (*invalid*) rééduquer.
rehabilitation ['riːəbɪlɪ'teɪʃən] *n* (*of offender*) réhabilitation *f*; (*of disabled*) rééducation *f*, réadaptation *f*.
rehash [riː'hæʃ] *vt* (*col*) remanier.
rehearsal [rɪ'həːsəl] *n* répétition *f*; **dress ~** (répétition) générale *f*.
rehearse [rɪ'həːs] *vt* répéter.
rehouse [riː'hauz] *vt* reloger.
reign [reɪn] *n* règne *m* ♦ *vi* régner.
reigning ['reɪnɪŋ] *adj* (*monarch*) régnant(e); (*champion*) actuel(le).
reimburse [riːɪm'bəːs] *vt* rembourser.
rein [reɪn] *n* (*for horse*) rêne *f*; **to give sb free ~** (*fig*) donner carte blanche à qn.
reindeer ['reɪndɪə*] *n* (*pl inv*) renne *m*.
reinforce [riːɪn'fɔːs] *vt* renforcer.
reinforced concrete *n* béton armé.
reinforcement [riːɪn'fɔːsmənt] *n* (*action*) renforcement *m*; **~s** *npl* (MIL) renfort(s) *m(pl)*.
reinstate [riːɪn'steɪt] *vt* rétablir, réintégrer.
reinstatement [riːɪn'steɪtmənt] *n* réintégration *f*.
reissue [riː'ɪʃjuː] *vt* (*book*) rééditer; (*film*) ressortir.
reiterate [riː'ɪtəreɪt] *vt* réitérer, répéter.
reject *n* ['riːdʒɛkt] (COMM) article *m* de rebut ♦ *vt* [rɪ'dʒɛkt] refuser; (COMM: *goods*) mettre au rebut; (*idea*) rejeter.
rejection [rɪ'dʒɛkʃən] *n* rejet *m*, refus *m*.
rejoice [rɪ'dʒɔɪs] *vi*: **to ~ (at *or* over)** se réjouir

(de).
rejoinder [rɪ'dʒɔɪndə*] *n* (*retort*) réplique *f*.
rejuvenate [rɪ'dʒu:vəneɪt] *vt* rajeunir.
rekindle [ri:'kɪndl] *vt* rallumer; (*fig*) raviver.
relapse [rɪ'læps] *n* (*MED*) rechute *f*.
relate [rɪ'leɪt] *vt* (*tell*) raconter; (*connect*) établir un rapport entre ♦ *vi*: **to ~ to** (*connect*) se rapporter à; (*interact*) établir un rapport *or* une entente avec.
related [rɪ'leɪtɪd] *adj* apparenté(e).
relating [rɪ'leɪtɪŋ]: ~ **to** *prep* concernant.
relation [rɪ'leɪʃən] *n* (*person*) parent/e; (*link*) rapport *m*, lien *m*; **diplomatic/international ~s** relations diplomatiques/internationales; **in ~ to** en ce qui concerne; par rapport à; **to bear no ~ to** être sans rapport avec.
relationship [rɪ'leɪʃənʃɪp] *n* rapport *m*, lien *m*; (*personal ties*) relations *fpl*, rapports; (*also*: **family ~**) lien de parenté; (*affair*) liaison *f*; **they have a good ~** ils s'entendent bien.
relative ['rɛlətɪv] *n* parent/e ♦ *adj* relatif(ive); (*respective*) respectif(ive); **all her ~s** toute sa famille.
relatively ['rɛlətɪvlɪ] *adv* relativement.
relax [rɪ'læks] *vi* se relâcher; (*person: unwind*) se détendre; (*calm down*) se calmer ♦ *vt* relâcher; (*mind, person*) détendre.
relaxation [ri:læk'seɪʃən] *n* relâchement *m*; détente *f*; (*entertainment*) distraction *f*.
relaxed [rɪ'lækst] *adj* relâché(e); détendu(e).
relaxing [rɪ'læksɪŋ] *adj* délassant(e).
relay ['ri:leɪ] *n* (*SPORT*) course *f* de relais ♦ *vt* (*message*) retransmettre, relayer.
release [rɪ'li:s] *n* (*from prison, obligation*) libération *f*; (*of gas etc*) émission *f*; (*of film etc*) sortie *f*; (*record*) disque *m*; (*device*) déclencheur *m* ♦ *vt* (*prisoner*) libérer; (*book, film*) sortir; (*report, news*) rendre public, publier; (*gas etc*) émettre, dégager; (*free: from wreckage etc*) dégager; (*TECH: catch, spring etc*) déclencher; (*let go*) relâcher; lâcher; desserrer; **to ~ one's grip** *or* **hold** lâcher prise; **to ~ the clutch** (*AUT*) débrayer.
relegate ['rɛləgeɪt] *vt* reléguer; (*SPORT*): **to be ~d** descendre dans une division inférieure.
relent [rɪ'lɛnt] *vi* se laisser fléchir.
relentless [rɪ'lɛntlɪs] *adj* implacable.
relevance ['rɛləvəns] *n* pertinence *f*; **~ of sth to sth** rapport *m* entre qch et qch.
relevant ['rɛləvənt] *adj* approprié(e); (*fact*) significatif(ive); (*information*) utile, pertinent(e); **~ to** ayant rapport à, approprié à.
reliability [rɪlaɪə'bɪlɪtɪ] *n* sérieux *m*; fiabilité *f*.
reliable [rɪ'laɪəbl] *adj* (*person, firm*) sérieux(euse), fiable; (*method, machine*) fiable.
reliably [rɪ'laɪəblɪ] *adv*: **to be ~ informed** savoir de source sûre.
reliance [rɪ'laɪəns] *n*: ~ **(on)** (*trust*) confiance *f* (en); (*dependence*) besoin *m* (de), dépendance *f* (de).
reliant [rɪ'laɪənt] *adj*: **to be ~ on sth/sb** dépendre de qch/qn.
relic ['rɛlɪk] *n* (*REL*) relique *f*; (*of the past*) vestige *m*.
relief [rɪ'li:f] *n* (*from pain, anxiety*) soulagement *m*; (*help, supplies*) secours *m(pl)*; (*of guard*) relève *f*; (*ART, GEO*) relief *m*; **by way of light ~** pour faire diversion.
relief map *n* carte *f* en relief.
relief road *n* (*BRIT*) route *f* de délestage.
relieve [rɪ'li:v] *vt* (*pain, patient*) soulager; (*bring help*) secourir; (*take over from: gen*) relayer; (*: guard*) relever; **to ~ sb of sth** débarrasser qn de qch; **to ~ sb of his command** (*MIL*) relever qn de ses fonctions; **to ~ o.s.** (*euphemism*) se soulager, faire ses besoins.
relieved [rɪ'li:vd] *adj* soulagé(e); **to be ~ that** ... être soulagé que ...; **I'm ~ to hear it** je suis soulagé de l'entendre.
religion [rɪ'lɪdʒən] *n* religion *f*.
religious [rɪ'lɪdʒəs] *adj* religieux(euse); (*book*) de piété.
religious education *n* instruction religieuse.
relinquish [rɪ'lɪŋkwɪʃ] *vt* abandonner; (*plan, habit*) renoncer à.
relish ['rɛlɪʃ] *n* (*CULIN*) condiment *m*; (*enjoyment*) délectation *f* ♦ *vt* (*food etc*) savourer; **to ~ doing** se délecter à faire.
relive [ri:'lɪv] *vt* revivre.
reload [ri:'ləud] *vt* recharger.
relocate [ri:ləu'keɪt] *vt* (*business*) transférer ♦ *vi* se transférer, s'installer *or* s'établir ailleurs; **to ~ in** (déménager et) s'installer *or* s'établir à, se transférer à.
reluctance [rɪ'lʌktəns] *n* répugnance *f*.
reluctant [rɪ'lʌktənt] *adj* peu disposé(e), qui hésite; **to be ~ to do sth** hésiter à faire qch.
reluctantly [rɪ'lʌktəntlɪ] *adv* à contrecœur, sans enthousiasme.
rely [rɪ'laɪ]: **to ~ on** *vt fus* compter sur; (*be dependent*) dépendre de.
remain [rɪ'meɪn] *vi* rester; **to ~ silent** garder le silence; **I ~, yours faithfully** (*BRIT: in letters*) je vous prie d'agréer, Monsieur (*etc*), l'assurance de mes sentiments distingués.
remainder [rɪ'meɪndə*] *n* reste *m*; (*COMM*) fin *f* de série.
remaining [rɪ'meɪnɪŋ] *adj* qui reste.
remains [rɪ'meɪnz] *npl* restes *mpl*.
remand [rɪ'mɑ:nd] *n*: **on ~** en détention préventive ♦ *vt*: **to ~ in custody** écrouer; renvoyer en détention provisoire.
remand home *n* (*BRIT*) centre *m* d'éducation surveillée.
remark [rɪ'mɑ:k] *n* remarque *f*, observation *f* ♦ *vt* (faire) remarquer, dire; (*notice*) remarquer; **to ~ on sth** faire une *or* des remarque(s) sur qch.
remarkable [rɪ'mɑ:kəbl] *adj* remarquable.
remarry [ri:'mærɪ] *vi* se remarier.
remedial [rɪ'mi:dɪəl] *adj* (*tuition, classes*) de rattrapage.
remedy ['rɛmədɪ] *n*: ~ **(for)** remède *m* (contre

or à) ♦ *vt* remédier à.

remember [rɪ'mɛmbə*] *vt* se rappeler, se souvenir de; **I ~ seeing it, I ~ having seen it** je me rappelle l'avoir vu *or* que je l'ai vu; **she ~ed to do it** elle a pensé à le faire; **~ me to your wife** rappelez-moi au bon souvenir de votre femme.

remembrance [rɪ'mɛmbrəns] *n* souvenir *m*; mémoire *f*.

Remembrance Day *n* (BRIT) ≈ (le jour de) l'Armistice *m*, ≈ le 11 Novembre; *voir encadré*.

REMEMBRANCE DAY

Remembrance Day *ou* **Remembrance Sunday** *est le dimanche le plus proche du 11 novembre, jour où la Première Guerre mondiale a officiellement pris fin. Il rend hommage aux victimes des deux guerres mondiales. À cette occasion, on observe deux minutes de silence à 11 h, heure de la signature de l'armistice avec l'Allemagne en 1918; certains membres de la famille royale et du gouvernement déposent des gerbes de coquelicots au cénotaphe de Whitehall, et des couronnes sont placées sur les monuments aux morts dans toute la Grande-Bretagne; par ailleurs, les gens portent des coquelicots artificiels fabriqués et vendus par des membres de la légion britannique blessés au combat, au profit des blessés de guerre et de leur famille.*

remind [rɪ'maɪnd] *vt*: **to ~ sb of sth** rappeler qch à qn; **to ~ sb to do** faire penser à qn à faire, rappeler à qn qu'il doit faire; **that ~s me!** j'y pense!

reminder [rɪ'maɪndə*] *n* rappel *m*; (*note etc*) pense-bête *m*.

reminisce [rɛmɪ'nɪs] *vi*: **to ~ (about)** évoquer ses souvenirs (de).

reminiscences [rɛmɪ'nɪsnsɪz] *npl* réminiscences *fpl*, souvenirs *mpl*.

reminiscent [rɛmɪ'nɪsnt] *adj*: **~ of** qui rappelle, qui fait penser à.

remiss [rɪ'mɪs] *adj* négligent(e); **it was ~ of me** c'était une négligence de ma part.

remission [rɪ'mɪʃən] *n* rémission *f*; (*of debt, sentence*) remise *f*; (*of fee*) exemption *f*.

remit [rɪ'mɪt] *vt* (*send: money*) envoyer.

remittance [rɪ'mɪtns] *n* envoi *m*, paiement *m*.

remnant ['rɛmnənt] *n* reste *m*, restant *m*; **~s** *npl* (COMM) coupons *mpl*; fins *fpl* de série.

remonstrate ['rɛmənstreɪt] *vi*: **to ~ (with sb about sth)** se plaindre (à qn de qch).

remorse [rɪ'mɔːs] *n* remords *m*.

remorseful [rɪ'mɔːsful] *adj* plein(e) de remords.

remorseless [rɪ'mɔːslɪs] *adj* (*fig*) impitoyable.

remote [rɪ'məut] *adj* éloigné(e), lointain(e); (*person*) distant(e); **there is a ~ possibility that ...** il est tout juste possible que ....

remote control *n* télécommande *f*.

remote-controlled [rɪ'məutkən'trəuld] *adj* téléguidé(e).

remotely [rɪ'məutlɪ] *adv* au loin; (*slightly*) très vaguement.

remould ['riːməuld] *n* (BRIT: *tyre*) pneu rechapé.

removable [rɪ'muːvəbl] *adj* (*detachable*) amovible.

removal [rɪ'muːvəl] *n* (*taking away*) enlèvement *m*; suppression *f*; (BRIT: *from house*) déménagement *m*; (*from office: dismissal*) renvoi *m*; (MED) ablation *f*.

removal man *n* (BRIT) déménageur *m*.

removal van *n* (BRIT) camion *m* de déménagement.

remove [rɪ'muːv] *vt* enlever, retirer; (*stain*) faire partir; (*doubt*) supprimer; **first cousin once ~d** cousin/e au deuxième degré.

remover [rɪ'muːvə*] *n* (*for paint*) décapant *m*; (*for varnish*) dissolvant *m*; **make-up ~** démaquillant *m*.

remunerate [rɪ'mjuːnəreɪt] *vt* rémunérer.

remuneration [rɪmjuːnə'reɪʃən] *n* rémunération *f*.

rename [riː'neɪm] *vt* rebaptiser.

rend, *pt, pp* **rent** [rɛnd, rɛnt] *vt* déchirer.

render ['rɛndə*] *vt* rendre; (CULIN: *fat*) clarifier.

rendering ['rɛndərɪŋ] *n* (MUS *etc*) interprétation *f*.

rendez-vous ['rɔndɪvuː] *n* rendez-vous *m inv* ♦ *vi* opérer une jonction, se rejoindre; **to ~ with sb** rejoindre qn.

renegade ['rɛnɪgeɪd] *n* rénégat/e.

renew [rɪ'njuː] *vt* renouveler; (*negotiations*) reprendre; (*acquaintance*) renouer.

renewable [rɪ'njuːəbl] *adj* renouvelable; **~ energy, ~s** énergies renouvelables.

renewal [rɪ'njuːəl] *n* renouvellement *m*; reprise *f*.

renounce [rɪ'nauns] *vt* renoncer à; (*disown*) renier.

renovate ['rɛnəveɪt] *vt* rénover; (*work of art*) restaurer.

renovation [rɛnə'veɪʃən] *n* rénovation *f*; restauration *f*.

renown [rɪ'naun] *n* renommée *f*.

renowned [rɪ'naund] *adj* renommé(e).

rent [rɛnt] *pt, pp of* **rend** ♦ *n* loyer *m* ♦ *vt* louer; (*car, TV*) louer, prendre en location; (*also*: **~ out**: *car, TV*) louer, donner en location.

rental ['rɛntl] *n* (*for television, car*) (prix *m* de) location *f*.

rent boy *n* (BRIT *col*) jeune prostitué.

renunciation [rɪnʌnsɪ'eɪʃən] *n* renonciation *f*; (*self-denial*) renoncement *m*.

reopen [riː'əupən] *vt* rouvrir.

reorder [riː'ɔːdə*] *vt* commander de nouveau; (*rearrange*) réorganiser.

reorganize [riː'ɔːgənaɪz] *vt* réorganiser.

rep [rɛp] *n abbr* (COMM) = **representative**; (THEAT) = **repertory**.

Rep. *abbr* (US POL) = **representative, republi-**

can.
repair [rɪ'pɛə*] *n* réparation *f* ♦ *vt* réparer; **in good/bad** ~ en bon/mauvais état; **under** ~ en réparation.
repair kit *n* trousse *f* de réparations.
repair man *n* réparateur *m*.
repair shop *n* (*AUT etc*) atelier *m* de réparations.
repartee [rɛpɑː'tiː] *n* repartie *f*.
repast [rɪ'pɑːst] *n* (*formal*) repas *m*.
repatriate [riː'pætrɪeɪt] *vt* rapatrier.
repay [riː'peɪ] *vt irreg* (*money, creditor*) rembourser; (*sb's efforts*) récompenser.
repayment [riː'peɪmənt] *n* remboursement *m*; récompense *f*.
repeal [rɪ'piːl] *n* (*of law*) abrogation *f*; (*of sentence*) annulation *f* ♦ *vt* abroger; annuler.
repeat [rɪ'piːt] *n* (*RADIO, TV*) reprise *f* ♦ *vt* répéter; (*pattern*) reproduire; (*promise, attack, also COMM: order*) renouveler; (*SCOL: a class*) redoubler ♦ *vi* répéter.
repeatedly [rɪ'piːtɪdlɪ] *adv* souvent, à plusieurs reprises.
repel [rɪ'pɛl] *vt* repousser.
repellent [rɪ'pɛlənt] *adj* repoussant(e) ♦ *n*: **insect** ~ insectifuge *m*; **moth** ~ produit *m* antimite(s).
repent [rɪ'pɛnt] *vi*: **to** ~ **(of)** se repentir (de).
repentance [rɪ'pɛntəns] *n* repentir *m*.
repercussion [riːpə'kʌʃən] *n* (*consequence*) répercussion *f*.
repertoire ['rɛpətwɑː*] *n* répertoire *m*.
repertory ['rɛpətərɪ] *n* (*also*: ~ **theatre**) théâtre *m* de répertoire.
repertory company *n* troupe théâtrale permanente.
repetition [rɛpɪ'tɪʃən] *n* répétition *f*.
repetitious [rɛpɪ'tɪʃəs] *adj* (*speech*) plein(e) de redites.
repetitive [rɪ'pɛtɪtɪv] *adj* (*movement, work*) répétitif(ive); (*speech*) plein(e) de redites.
replace [rɪ'pleɪs] *vt* (*put back*) remettre, replacer; (*take the place of*) remplacer; (*TEL*): **"~ the receiver"** "raccrochez".
replacement [rɪ'pleɪsmənt] *n* replacement *m*; remplacement *m*; (*person*) remplaçant/e.
replacement part *n* pièce *f* de rechange.
replay ['riːpleɪ] *n* (*of match*) match rejoué; (*of tape, film*) répétition *f*.
replenish [rɪ'plɛnɪʃ] *vt* (*glass*) remplir (de nouveau); (*stock etc*) réapprovisionner.
replete [rɪ'pliːt] *adj* rempli(e); (*well-fed*): ~ **(with)** rassasié(e) (de).
replica ['rɛplɪkə] *n* réplique *f*, copie exacte.
reply [rɪ'plaɪ] *n* réponse *f* ♦ *vi* répondre; **in** ~ **(to)** en réponse (à); **there's no** ~ (*TEL*) ça ne répond pas.
reply coupon *n* coupon-réponse *m*.
report [rɪ'pɔːt] *n* rapport *m*; (*PRESS etc*) reportage *m*; (*BRIT: also*: **school** ~) bulletin *m* (scolaire); (*of gun*) détonation *f* ♦ *vt* rapporter, faire un compte rendu de; (*PRESS etc*) faire un reportage sur; (*bring to notice: occurrence*) signaler; (*: person*) dénoncer ♦ *vi* (*make a report*): **to** ~ **(on)** faire un rapport (sur); (*for newspaper*) faire un reportage (sur); (*present o.s.*): **to** ~ **(to sb)** se présenter (chez qn); **it is ~ed that** on dit *or* annonce que; **it is ~ed from Berlin that** on nous apprend de Berlin que.
report card *n* (*US, Scottish*) bulletin *m* (scolaire).
reportedly [rɪ'pɔːtɪdlɪ] *adv*: **she is** ~ **living in Spain** elle habiterait en Espagne; **he** ~ **ordered them to ...** il leur aurait ordonné de ....
reported speech *n* (*LING*) discours indirect.
reporter [rɪ'pɔːtə*] *n* reporter *m*.
repose [rɪ'pəuz] *n*: **in** ~ en *or* au repos.
repossess [riːpə'zɛs] *vt* saisir.
repossession order [riːpə'zɛʃən-] *n* ordre *m* de reprise de possession.
reprehensible [rɛprɪ'hɛnsɪbl] *adj* répréhensible.
represent [rɛprɪ'zɛnt] *vt* représenter; (*explain*): **to** ~ **to sb that** expliquer à qn que.
representation [rɛprɪzɛn'teɪʃən] *n* représentation *f*; **~s** *npl* (*protest*) démarche *f*.
representative [rɛprɪ'zɛntətɪv] *n* représentant/e; (*COMM*) représentant/e (de commerce); (*US POL*) député *m* ♦ *adj*: ~ **(of)** représentatif(ive) (de), caractéristique (de).
repress [rɪ'prɛs] *vt* réprimer.
repression [rɪ'prɛʃən] *n* répression *f*.
repressive [rɪ'prɛsɪv] *adj* répressif(ive).
reprieve [rɪ'priːv] *n* (*LAW*) grâce *f*; (*fig*) sursis *m*, délai *m* ♦ *vt* gracier; accorder un sursis *or* un délai à.
reprimand ['rɛprɪmɑːnd] *n* réprimande *f* ♦ *vt* réprimander.
reprint *n* ['riːprɪnt] réimpression *f* ♦ *vt* [riː'prɪnt] réimprimer.
reprisal [rɪ'praɪzl] *n* représailles *fpl*; **to take ~s** user de représailles.
reproach [rɪ'prəutʃ] *n* reproche *m* ♦ *vt*: **to** ~ **sb with sth** reprocher qch à qn; **beyond** ~ irréprochable.
reproachful [rɪ'prəutʃful] *adj* de reproche.
reproduce [riːprə'djuːs] *vt* reproduire ♦ *vi* se reproduire.
reproduction [riːprə'dʌkʃən] *n* reproduction *f*.
reproductive [riːprə'dʌktɪv] *adj* reproducteur(trice).
reproof [rɪ'pruːf] *n* reproche *m*.
reprove [rɪ'pruːv] *vt* (*action*) réprouver; (*person*): **to** ~ **(for)** blâmer (de).
reproving [rɪ'pruːvɪŋ] *adj* réprobateur(trice).
reptile ['rɛptaɪl] *n* reptile *m*.
Repub. *abbr* (*US POL*) = **republican.**
republic [rɪ'pʌblɪk] *n* république *f*.
republican [rɪ'pʌblɪkən] *adj, n* républicain(e).
repudiate [rɪ'pjuːdɪeɪt] *vt* (*ally, behaviour*) désavouer; (*accusation*) rejeter; (*wife*) répu-

dier.

repugnant [rɪ'pʌgnənt] *adj* répugnant(e).

repulse [rɪ'pʌls] *vt* repousser.

repulsion [rɪ'pʌlʃən] *n* répulsion *f*.

repulsive [rɪ'pʌlsɪv] *adj* repoussant(e), répulsif(ive).

reputable ['rɛpjutəbl] *adj* de bonne réputation; (*occupation*) honorable.

reputation [rɛpju'teɪʃən] *n* réputation *f*; **to have a ~ for** être réputé(e) pour; **he has a ~ for being awkward** il a la réputation de ne pas être commode.

repute [rɪ'pjuːt] *n* (bonne) réputation.

reputed [rɪ'pjuːtɪd] *adj* réputé(e); **he is ~ to be rich/intelligent** *etc* on dit qu'il est riche/intelligent *etc*.

reputedly [rɪ'pjuːtɪdlɪ] *adv* d'après ce qu'on dit.

request [rɪ'kwɛst] *n* demande *f*; (*formal*) requête *f* ♦ *vt*: **to ~ (of** *or* **from sb)** demander (à qn); **at the ~ of** à la demande de.

request stop *n* (*BRIT*: *for bus*) arrêt facultatif.

requiem ['rɛkwɪəm] *n* requiem *m*.

require [rɪ'kwaɪə*] *vt* (*need: subj: person*) avoir besoin de; (*: thing, situation*) nécessiter, demander; (*demand*) exiger, requérir; (*order*): **to ~ sb to do sth/sth of sb** exiger que qn fasse qch/qch de qn; **if ~d** s'il le faut; **what qualifications are ~d?** quelles sont les qualifications requises?; **~d by law** requis par la loi.

required [ri'kwaɪəd] *adj* requis(e), voulu(e).

requirement [rɪ'kwaɪəmənt] *n* exigence *f*; besoin *m*; condition *f* (requise).

requisite ['rɛkwɪzɪt] *n* chose *f* nécessaire ♦ *adj* requis(e), nécessaire; **toilet ~s** accessoires *mpl* de toilette.

requisition [rɛkwɪ'zɪʃən] *n*: **~ (for)** demande *f* (de) ♦ *vt* (*MIL*) réquisitionner.

reroute [riː'ruːt] *vt* (*train etc*) dérouter.

resale ['riː'seɪl] *n* revente *f*.

resale price maintenance (RPM) *n vente au détail à prix imposé*.

rescind [rɪ'sɪnd] *vt* annuler; (*law*) abroger; (*judgment*) rescinder.

rescue ['rɛskjuː] *n* sauvetage *m*; (*help*) secours *mpl* ♦ *vt* sauver; **to come to sb's ~** venir au secours de qn.

rescue party *n* équipe *f* de sauvetage.

rescuer ['rɛskjuə*] *n* sauveteur *m*.

research [rɪ'səːtʃ] *n* recherche(s) *f(pl)* ♦ *vt* faire des recherches sur ♦ *vi*: **to ~ (into sth)** faire des recherches (sur qch); **a piece of ~** un travail de recherche; **~ and development (R & D)** recherche-développement (R-D).

researcher [rɪ'səːtʃə*] *n* chercheur/euse.

research work *n* recherches *fpl*.

resell [riː'sɛl] *vt irreg* revendre.

resemblance [rɪ'zɛmbləns] *n* ressemblance *f*; **to bear a strong ~ to** ressembler beaucoup à.

resemble [rɪ'zɛmbl] *vt* ressembler à.

resent [rɪ'zɛnt] *vt* éprouver du ressentiment de, être contrarié(e) par.

resentful [rɪ'zɛntful] *adj* irrité(e), plein(e) de ressentiment.

resentment [rɪ'zɛntmənt] *n* ressentiment *m*.

reservation [rɛzə'veɪʃən] *n* (*booking*) réservation *f*; (*doubt*; *protected area*) réserve *f*; (*BRIT AUT*: *also*: **central ~**) bande médiane; **to make a ~ (in an hotel/a restaurant/on a plane)** réserver *or* retenir une chambre/une table/une place; **with ~s** (*doubts*) avec certaines réserves.

reservation desk *n* (*US*: *in hotel*) réception *f*.

reserve [rɪ'zəːv] *n* réserve *f*; (*SPORT*) remplaçant/e ♦ *vt* (*seats etc*) réserver, retenir; **~s** *npl* (*MIL*) réservistes *mpl*; **in ~** en réserve.

reserve currency *n* monnaie *f* de réserve.

reserved [rɪ'zəːvd] *adj* réservé(e).

reserve price *n* (*BRIT*) mise *f* à prix, prix *m* de départ.

reserve team *n* (*BRIT SPORT*) deuxième équipe *f*.

reservist [rɪ'zəːvɪst] *n* (*MIL*) réserviste *m*.

reservoir ['rɛzəvwɑː*] *n* réservoir *m*.

reset [riː'sɛt] *vt irreg* remettre; (*clock, watch*) mettre à l'heure; (*COMPUT*) remettre à zéro.

reshape [riː'ʃeɪp] *vt* (*policy*) réorganiser.

reshuffle [riː'ʃʌfl] *n*: **Cabinet ~** (*POL*) remaniement ministériel.

reside [rɪ'zaɪd] *vi* résider.

residence ['rɛzɪdəns] *n* résidence *f*; **to take up ~** s'installer; **in ~** (*queen etc*) en résidence; (*doctor*) résidant(e).

residence permit *n* (*BRIT*) permis *m* de séjour.

resident ['rɛzɪdənt] *n* résident/e ♦ *adj* résidant(e).

residential [rɛzɪ'dɛnʃəl] *adj* de résidence; (*area*) résidentiel(le).

residue ['rɛzɪdjuː] *n* reste *m*; (*CHEM, PHYSICS*) résidu *m*.

resign [rɪ'zaɪn] *vt* (*one's post*) se démettre de ♦ *vi*: **to ~ (from)** démissionner (de); **to ~ o.s. to** (*endure*) se résigner à.

resignation [rɛzɪg'neɪʃən] *n* démission *f*; résignation *f*; **to tender one's ~** donner sa démission.

resigned [rɪ'zaɪnd] *adj* résigné(e).

resilience [rɪ'zɪlɪəns] *n* (*of material*) élasticité *f*; (*of person*) ressort *m*.

resilient [rɪ'zɪlɪənt] *adj* (*person*) qui réagit, qui a du ressort.

resin ['rɛzɪn] *n* résine *f*.

resist [rɪ'zɪst] *vt* résister à.

resistance [rɪ'zɪstəns] *n* résistance *f*.

resistant [rɪ'zɪstənt] *adj*: **~ (to)** résistant(e) (à).

resolute ['rɛzəluːt] *adj* résolu(e).

resolution [rɛzə'luːʃən] *n* résolution *f*; **to make a ~** prendre une résolution.

resolve [rɪ'zɔlv] *n* résolution *f* ♦ *vt* (*decide*): **to ~ to do** résoudre *or* décider de faire; (*problem*) résoudre.
resolved [rɪ'zɔlvd] *adj* résolu(e).
resonance ['rɛzənəns] *n* résonance *f*.
resonant ['rɛzənənt] *adj* résonnant(e).
resort [rɪ'zɔːt] *n* (*town*) station *f* (de vacances); (*recourse*) recours *m* ♦ *vi*: **to ~ to** avoir recours à; **seaside/winter sports ~** station balnéaire/de sports d'hiver; **in the last ~** en dernier ressort.
resound [rɪ'zaund] *vi*: **to ~ (with)** retentir (de).
resounding [rɪ'zaundɪŋ] *adj* retentissant(e).
resource [rɪ'sɔːs] *n* ressource *f*; **~s** *npl* ressources; **natural ~s** ressources naturelles; **to leave sb to his (*or* her) own ~s** (*fig*) livrer qn à lui-même (*or* elle-même).
resourceful [rɪ'sɔːsful] *adj* plein(e) de ressource, débrouillard(e).
resourcefulness [rɪ'sɔːsfəlnɪs] *n* ressource *f*.
respect [rɪs'pɛkt] *n* respect *m*; (*point, detail*): **in some ~s** à certains égards ♦ *vt* respecter; **~s** *npl* respects, hommages *mpl*; **to have *or* show ~ for sb/sth** respecter qn/qch; **out of ~ for** par respect pour; **with ~ to** en ce qui concerne; **in ~ of** sous le rapport de, quant à; **in this ~** sous ce rapport, à cet égard; **with due ~ I** ... malgré le respect que je vous dois, je ....
respectability [rɪspɛktə'bɪlɪtɪ] *n* respectabilité *f*.
respectable [rɪs'pɛktəbl] *adj* respectable; (*quite good: result etc*) honorable; (*player*) assez bon(bonne).
respectful [rɪs'pɛktful] *adj* respectueux(euse).
respective [rɪs'pɛktɪv] *adj* respectif(ive).
respectively [rɪs'pɛktɪvlɪ] *adv* respectivement.
respiration [rɛspɪ'reɪʃən] *n* respiration *f*.
respirator ['rɛspɪreɪtə*] *n* respirateur *m*.
respiratory ['rɛspərətərɪ] *adj* respiratoire.
respite ['rɛspaɪt] *n* répit *m*.
resplendent [rɪs'plɛndənt] *adj* resplendissant(e).
respond [rɪs'pɔnd] *vi* répondre; (*to treatment*) réagir.
respondent [rɪs'pɔndənt] *n* (*LAW*) défendeur/deresse.
response [rɪs'pɔns] *n* réponse *f*; (*to treatment*) réaction *f*; **in ~ to** en réponse à.
responsibility [rɪspɔnsɪ'bɪlɪtɪ] *n* responsabilité *f*; **to take ~ for sth/sb** accepter la responsabilité de qch/d'être responsable de qn.
responsible [rɪs'pɔnsɪbl] *adj* (*liable*): **~ (for)** responsable (de); (*person*) digne de confiance; (*job*) qui comporte des responsabilités; **to be ~ to sb (for sth)** être responsable devant qn (de qch).
responsibly [rɪs'pɔnsɪblɪ] *adv* avec sérieux.
responsive [rɪs'pɔnsɪv] *adj* qui n'est pas réservé(e) *or* indifférent(e).
rest [rɛst] *n* repos *m*; (*stop*) arrêt *m*, pause *f*; (*MUS*) silence *m*; (*support*) support *m*, appui *m*; (*remainder*) reste *m*, restant *m* ♦ *vi* se reposer; (*be supported*): **to ~ on** appuyer *or* reposer sur; (*remain*) rester ♦ *vt* (*lean*): **to ~ sth on/against** appuyer qch sur/contre; **the ~ of them** les autres; **to set sb's mind at ~** tranquilliser qn; **it ~s with him to** c'est à lui de; **~ assured that** ... soyez assuré que ....
restart [riː'stɑːt] *vt* (*engine*) remettre en marche; (*work*) reprendre.
restaurant ['rɛstərɔŋ] *n* restaurant *m*.
restaurant car *n* (*BRIT*) wagon-restaurant *m*.
rest cure *n* cure *f* de repos.
restful ['rɛstful] *adj* reposant(e).
rest home *n* maison *f* de repos.
restitution [rɛstɪ'tjuːʃən] *n* (*act*) restitution *f*; (*reparation*) réparation *f*.
restive ['rɛstɪv] *adj* agité(e), impatient(e); (*horse*) rétif(ive).
restless ['rɛstlɪs] *adj* agité(e); **to get ~** s'impatienter.
restlessly ['rɛstlɪslɪ] *adv* avec agitation.
restock [riː'stɔk] *vt* réapprovisionner.
restoration [rɛstə'reɪʃən] *n* restauration *f*; restitution *f*.
restorative [rɪ'stɔrətɪv] *adj* reconstituant(e) ♦ *n* reconstituant *m*.
restore [rɪ'stɔː*] *vt* (*building*) restaurer; (*sth stolen*) restituer; (*peace, health*) rétablir.
restorer [rɪ'stɔːrə*] *n* (*ART etc*) restaurateur/trice (d'œuvres d'art).
restrain [rɪs'treɪn] *vt* (*feeling*) contenir; (*person*): **to ~ (from doing)** retenir (de faire).
restrained [rɪs'treɪnd] *adj* (*style*) sobre; (*manner*) mesuré(e).
restraint [rɪs'treɪnt] *n* (*restriction*) contrainte *f*; (*moderation*) retenue *f*; (*of style*) sobriété *f*; **wage ~** limitations salariales.
restrict [rɪs'trɪkt] *vt* restreindre, limiter.
restricted area [rɪs'trɪktɪd-] *n* (*AUT*) zone *f* à vitesse limitée.
restriction [rɪs'trɪkʃən] *n* restriction *f*, limitation *f*.
restrictive [rɪs'trɪktɪv] *adj* restrictif(ive).
restrictive practices *npl* (*INDUSTRY*) pratiques *fpl* entravant la libre concurrence.
rest room *n* (*US*) toilettes *fpl*.
restructure [riː'strʌktʃə*] *vt* restructurer.
result [rɪ'zʌlt] *n* résultat *m* ♦ *vi*: **to ~ (from)** résulter (de); **to ~ in** aboutir à, se terminer par; **as a ~ it is too expensive** il en résulte que c'est trop cher; **as a ~ of** à la suite de.
resultant [rɪ'zʌltənt] *adj* résultant(e).
resume [rɪ'zjuːm] *vt* (*work, journey*) reprendre; (*sum up*) résumer ♦ *vi* (*work etc*) reprendre.
résumé ['reɪzjuːmeɪ] *n* (*summary*) résumé *m*; (*US: curriculum vitae*) curriculum vitae *m inv*.
resumption [rɪ'zʌmpʃən] *n* reprise *f*.
resurgence [rɪ'səːdʒəns] *n* réapparition *f*.
resurrection [rɛzə'rɛkʃən] *n* résurrection *f*.

resuscitate [rɪ'sʌsɪteɪt] *vt* (*MED*) réanimer.
resuscitation [rɪsʌsɪ'teɪʃən] *n* réanimation *f*.
retail ['riːteɪl] *n* (vente *f* au) détail *m* ♦ *cpd* de *or* au détail ♦ *vt* vendre au détail ♦ *vi*: **to ~ at 10 euros** se vendre au détail à 10 euros.
retailer ['riːteɪlə*] *n* détaillant/e.
retail outlet *n* point *m* de vente.
retail price *n* prix *m* de détail.
retail price index *n* ≈ indice *m* des prix.
retain [rɪ'teɪn] *vt* (*keep*) garder, conserver; (*employ*) engager.
retainer [rɪ'teɪnə*] *n* (*servant*) serviteur *m*; (*fee*) acompte *m*, provision *f*.
retaliate [rɪ'tælɪeɪt] *vi*: **to ~ (against)** se venger (de); **to ~ (on sb)** rendre la pareille (à qn).
retaliation [rɪtælɪ'eɪʃən] *n* représailles *fpl*, vengeance *f*; **in ~ for** par représailles pour.
retaliatory [rɪ'tælɪətərɪ] *adj* de représailles.
retarded [rɪ'tɑːdɪd] *adj* retardé(e).
retch [rɛtʃ] *vi* avoir des haut-le-cœur.
retentive [rɪ'tɛntɪv] *adj*: **~ memory** excellente mémoire.
rethink ['riː'θɪŋk] *vt* repenser.
reticence ['rɛtɪsns] *n* réticence *f*.
reticent ['rɛtɪsnt] *adj* réticent(e).
retina ['rɛtɪnə] *n* rétine *f*.
retinue ['rɛtɪnjuː] *n* suite *f*, cortège *m*.
retire [rɪ'taɪə*] *vi* (*give up work*) prendre sa retraite; (*withdraw*) se retirer, partir; (*go to bed*) (aller) se coucher.
retired [rɪ'taɪəd] *adj* (*person*) retraité(e).
retirement [rɪ'taɪəmənt] *n* retraite *f*.
retirement age *n* âge *m* de la retraite.
retiring [rɪ'taɪərɪŋ] *adj* (*person*) réservé(e); (*chairman etc*) sortant(e).
retort [rɪ'tɔːt] *n* (*reply*) riposte *f*; (*container*) cornue *f* ♦ *vi* riposter.
retrace [riː'treɪs] *vt* reconstituer; **to ~ one's steps** revenir sur ses pas.
retract [rɪ'trækt] *vt* (*statement, claws*) rétracter; (*undercarriage, aerial*) rentrer, escamoter ♦ *vi* se rétracter; rentrer.
retractable [rɪ'træktəbl] *adj* escamotable.
retrain [riː'treɪn] *vt* recycler ♦ *vi* se recycler.
retraining [riː'treɪnɪŋ] *n* recyclage *m*.
retread *vt* [riː'trɛd] (*AUT*: *tyre*) rechaper ♦ *n* ['riːtrɛd] pneu rechapé.
retreat [rɪ'triːt] *n* retraite *f* ♦ *vi* battre en retraite; (*flood*) reculer; **to beat a hasty ~** (*fig*) partir avec précipitation.
retrial [riː'traɪəl] *n* nouveau procès.
retribution [rɛtrɪ'bjuːʃən] *n* châtiment *m*.
retrieval [rɪ'triːvəl] *n* récupération *f*; réparation *f*; recherche *f* et extraction *f*.
retrieve [rɪ'triːv] *vt* (*sth lost*) récupérer; (*situation, honour*) sauver; (*error, loss*) réparer; (*COMPUT*) rechercher.
retriever [rɪ'triːvə*] *n* chien *m* d'arrêt.
retroactive [rɛtrəu'æktɪv] *adj* rétroactif(ive).
retrograde ['rɛtrəgreɪd] *adj* rétrograde.
retrospect ['rɛtrəspɛkt] *n*: **in ~** rétrospectivement, après coup.
retrospective [rɛtrə'spɛktɪv] *adj* (*law*) rétroactif(ive) ♦ *n* (*ART*) rétrospective *f*.
return [rɪ'təːn] *n* (*going or coming back*) retour *m*; (*of sth stolen etc*) restitution *f*; (*recompense*) récompense *f*; (*FINANCE*: *from land, shares*) rapport *m*; (*report*) relevé *m*, rapport ♦ *cpd* (*journey*) de retour; (*BRIT*: *ticket*) aller et retour; (*match*) retour ♦ *vi* (*person etc*: *come back*) revenir; (*: go back*) retourner ♦ *vt* rendre; (*bring back*) rapporter; (*send back*) renvoyer; (*put back*) remettre; (*POL*: *candidate*) élire; **~s** *npl* (*COMM*) recettes *fpl*; bénéfices *mpl*; (*: ~ed goods*) marchandises renvoyées; **many happy ~s (of the day)!** bon anniversaire!; **by ~ (of post)** par retour (du courrier); **in ~ (for)** en échange (de).
returnable [rɪ'təːnəbl] *adj* (*bottle etc*) consigné(e).
returner [rɪ'təːnə*] *n femme qui reprend un travail après avoir élevé ses enfants*.
returning officer [rɪ'təːnɪŋ-] *n* (*BRIT POL*) président *m* de bureau de vote.
return key *n* (*COMPUT*) touche *f* de retour.
reunion [riː'juːnɪən] *n* réunion *f*.
reunite [riːjuː'naɪt] *vt* réunir.
rev [rɛv] *n abbr* (= *revolution*: *AUT*) tour *m* ♦ *vb* (*also* **~ up**) *vt* emballer ♦ *vi* s'emballer.
Rev. *abbr* = **reverend.**
revaluation [riːvælju'eɪʃən] *n* réévaluation *f*.
revamp [riː'væmp] *vt* (*house*) retaper; (*firm*) réorganiser.
rev counter *n* (*BRIT*) compte-tours *m inv*.
Revd. *abbr* = **reverend.**
reveal [rɪ'viːl] *vt* (*make known*) révéler; (*display*) laisser voir.
revealing [rɪ'viːlɪŋ] *adj* révélateur(trice); (*dress*) au décolleté généreux *or* suggestif.
reveille [rɪ'vælɪ] *n* (*MIL*) réveil *m*.
revel ['rɛvl] *vi*: **to ~ in sth/in doing** se délecter de qch/à faire.
revelation [rɛvə'leɪʃən] *n* révélation *f*.
reveller ['rɛvlə*] *n* fêtard *m*.
revelry ['rɛvlrɪ] *n* festivités *fpl*.
revenge [rɪ'vɛndʒ] *n* vengeance *f*; (*in game etc*) revanche *f* ♦ *vt* venger; **to take ~** se venger.
revengeful [rɪ'vɛndʒful] *adj* vengeur(eresse); vindicatif(ive).
revenue ['rɛvənjuː] *n* revenu *m*.
reverberate [rɪ'vəːbəreɪt] *vi* (*sound*) retentir, se répercuter; (*light*) se réverbérer.
reverberation [rɪvəːbə'reɪʃən] *n* répercussion *f*; réverbération *f*.
revere [rɪ'vɪə*] *vt* vénérer, révérer.
reverence ['rɛvərəns] *n* vénération *f*, révérence *f*.
reverend ['rɛvərənd] *adj* vénérable; **the R~ John Smith** (*Anglican*) le révérend John Smith; (*Catholic*) l'abbé John Smith; (*Protestant*) le pasteur John Smith.
reverent ['rɛvərənt] *adj* respectueux(euse).
reverie ['rɛvərɪ] *n* rêverie *f*.

reversal [rɪ'vəːsl] *n* (*of opinion*) revirement *m*.
reverse [rɪ'vəːs] *n* contraire *m*, opposé *m*; (*back*) dos *m*, envers *m*; (*AUT*: *also*: ~ **gear**) marche *f* arrière ♦ *adj* (*order, direction*) opposé(e), inverse ♦ *vt* (*turn*) renverser, retourner; (*change*) renverser, changer complètement; (*LAW*: *judgment*) réformer ♦ *vi* (*BRIT AUT*) faire marche arrière; **to go into** ~ faire marche arrière; **in ~ order** en ordre inverse.
reversed charge call [rɪ'vəːst-] *n* (*BRIT TEL*) communication *f* en PCV.
reverse video *n* vidéo *m* inverse.
reversible [rɪ'vəːsəbl] *adj* (*garment*) réversible; (*procedure*) révocable.
reversing lights [rɪ'vəːsɪŋ-] *npl* (*BRIT AUT*) feux *mpl* de marche arrière *or* de recul.
reversion [rɪ'vəːʃən] *n* retour *m*.
revert [rɪ'vəːt] *vi*: **to ~ to** revenir à, retourner à.
review [rɪ'vjuː] *n* revue *f*; (*of book, film*) critique *f* ♦ *vt* passer en revue; faire la critique de; **to come under** ~ être révisé(e).
reviewer [rɪ'vjuːə*] *n* critique *m*.
revile [rɪ'vaɪl] *vt* injurier.
revise [rɪ'vaɪz] *vt* (*manuscript*) revoir, corriger; (*opinion*) réviser, modifier; (*study: subject, notes*) réviser; **~d edition** édition revue et corrigée.
revision [rɪ'vɪʒən] *n* révision *f*; (*revised version*) version corrigée.
revitalize [riː'vaɪtəlaɪz] *vt* revitaliser.
revival [rɪ'vaɪvəl] *n* reprise *f*; rétablissement *m*; (*of faith*) renouveau *m*.
revive [rɪ'vaɪv] *vt* (*person*) ranimer; (*custom*) rétablir; (*hope, courage*) redonner; (*play, fashion*) reprendre ♦ *vi* (*person*) reprendre connaissance; (*hope*) renaître; (*activity*) reprendre.
revoke [rɪ'vəuk] *vt* révoquer; (*promise, decision*) revenir sur.
revolt [rɪ'vəult] *n* révolte *f* ♦ *vi* se révolter, se rebeller.
revolting [rɪ'vəultɪŋ] *adj* dégoûtant(e).
revolution [rɛvə'luːʃən] *n* révolution *f*; (*of wheel etc*) tour *m*, révolution.
revolutionary [rɛvə'luːʃənrɪ] *adj, n* révolutionnaire (*m/f*).
revolutionize [rɛvə'luːʃənaɪz] *vt* révolutionner.
revolve [rɪ'vɔlv] *vi* tourner.
revolver [rɪ'vɔlvə*] *n* revolver *m*.
revolving [rɪ'vɔlvɪŋ] *adj* (*chair*) pivotant(e); (*light*) tournant(e).
revolving door *n* (porte *f* à) tambour *m*.
revue [rɪ'vjuː] *n* (*THEAT*) revue *f*.
revulsion [rɪ'vʌlʃən] *n* dégoût *m*, répugnance *f*.
reward [rɪ'wɔːd] *n* récompense *f* ♦ *vt*: **to ~ (for)** récompenser (de).
rewarding [rɪ'wɔːdɪŋ] *adj* (*fig*) qui (en) vaut la peine, gratifiant(e); **financially** ~ financièrement intéressant(e).
rewind [riː'waɪnd] *vt irreg* (*watch*) remonter; (*ribbon etc*) réembobiner.
rewire [riː'waɪə*] *vt* (*house*) refaire l'installation électrique de.
reword [riː'wəːd] *vt* formuler *or* exprimer différemment.
rewrite [riː'raɪt] *vt irreg* récrire.
Reykjavik ['reɪkjəviːk] *n* Reykjavik.
RFD *abbr* (*US POST*) = *rural free delivery*.
Rh *abbr* (= *rhesus*) Rh.
rhapsody ['ræpsədɪ] *n* (*MUS*) rhapsodie *f*; (*fig*) éloge délirant.
rhesus negative ['riːsəs-] *adj* (*MED*) de rhésus négatif.
rhesus positive ['riːsəs-] *adj* (*MED*) de rhésus positif.
rhetoric ['rɛtərɪk] *n* rhétorique *f*.
rhetorical [rɪ'tɔrɪkl] *adj* rhétorique.
rheumatic [ruː'mætɪk] *adj* rhumatismal(e).
rheumatism ['ruːmətɪzəm] *n* rhumatisme *m*.
rheumatoid arthritis ['ruːmətɔɪd-] *n* polyarthrite *f* chronique.
Rhine [raɪn] *n*: **the** ~ le Rhin.
rhinestone ['raɪnstəun] *n* faux diamant.
rhinoceros [raɪ'nɔsərəs] *n* rhinocéros *m*.
Rhodes [rəudz] *n* Rhodes *f*.
Rhodesia [rəu'diːʒə] *n* Rhodésie *f*.
Rhodesian [rəu'diːʒən] *adj* rhodésien(ne) ♦ *n* Rhodésien/ne.
rhododendron [rəudə'dɛndrn] *n* rhododendron *m*.
Rhône [rəun] *n*: **the** ~ le Rhône.
rhubarb ['ruːbɑːb] *n* rhubarbe *f*.
rhyme [raɪm] *n* rime *f*; (*verse*) vers *mpl* ♦ *vi*: **to ~ (with)** rimer (avec); **without ~ or reason** sans rime ni raison.
rhythm ['rɪðm] *n* rythme *m*.
rhythmic(al) ['rɪðmɪk(l)] *adj* rythmique.
rhythmically ['rɪðmɪklɪ] *adv* avec rythme.
rhythm method *n* méthode *f* des températures.
RI *n abbr* (*BRIT*) = *religious instruction* ♦ *abbr* (*US*) = *Rhode Island*.
rib [rɪb] *n* (*ANAT*) côte *f* ♦ *vt* (*mock*) taquiner.
ribald ['rɪbəld] *adj* paillard(e).
ribbed [rɪbd] *adj* (*knitting*) à côtes; (*shell*) strié(e).
ribbon ['rɪbən] *n* ruban *m*; **in ~s** (*torn*) en lambeaux.
rice [raɪs] *n* riz *m*.
ricefield ['raɪsfiːld] *n* rizière *f*.
rice pudding *n* riz *m* au lait.
rich [rɪtʃ] *adj* riche; (*gift, clothes*) somptueux(euse); **the** ~ *npl* les riches *mpl*; **~es** *npl* richesses *fpl*; **to be ~ in sth** être riche en qch.
richly ['rɪtʃlɪ] *adv* richement; (*deserved, earned*) largement, grandement.
richness ['rɪtʃnɪs] *n* richesse *f*.
rickets ['rɪkɪts] *n* rachitisme *m*.
rickety ['rɪkɪtɪ] *adj* branlant(e).

rickshaw ['rɪkʃɔː] *n* pousse(-pousse) *m inv.*
ricochet ['rɪkəʃeɪ] *n* ricochet *m* ♦ *vi* ricocher.
rid, *pt, pp* **rid** [rɪd] *vt*: **to ~ sb of** débarrasser qn de; **to get ~ of** se débarrasser de.
riddance ['rɪdns] *n*: **good ~!** bon débarras!
ridden ['rɪdn] *pp of* **ride.**
riddle ['rɪdl] *n* (*puzzle*) énigme *f* ♦ *vt*: **to be ~d with** être criblé(e) de.
ride [raɪd] *n* promenade *f*, tour *m*; (*distance covered*) trajet *m* ♦ *vb* (*pt* **rode**, *pp* **ridden** [rəud, 'rɪdn]) *vi* (*as sport*) monter (à cheval), faire du cheval; (*go somewhere: on horse, bicycle*) aller (à cheval *or* bicyclette *etc*); (*journey: on bicycle, motor cycle, bus*) rouler ♦ *vt* (*a certain horse*) monter; (*distance*) parcourir, faire; **we rode all day/all the way** nous sommes restés toute la journée en selle/ avons fait tout le chemin en selle *or* à cheval; **to ~ a horse/bicycle/camel** monter à cheval/à bicyclette/à dos de chameau; **can you ~ a bike?** est-ce que tu sais monter à bicyclette?; **to ~ at anchor** (*NAUT*) être à l'ancre; **horse/car ~** promenade *or* tour à cheval/en voiture; **to go for a ~** faire une promenade (en voiture *or* à bicyclette *etc*); **to take sb for a ~** (*fig*) faire marcher qn; rouler qn.
►**ride out** *vt*: **to ~ out the storm** (*fig*) surmonter les difficultés.
rider ['raɪdə*] *n* cavalier/ière; (*in race*) jockey *m*; (*on bicycle*) cycliste *m/f*; (*on motorcycle*) motocycliste *m/f*; (*in document*) annexe *f*, clause additionnelle.
ridge [rɪdʒ] *n* (*of hill*) faîte *m*; (*of roof, mountain*) arête *f*; (*on object*) strie *f*.
ridicule ['rɪdɪkjuːl] *n* ridicule *m*; dérision *f* ♦ *vt* ridiculiser, tourner en dérision; **to hold sb/ sth up to ~** tourner qn/qch en ridicule.
ridiculous [rɪ'dɪkjuləs] *adj* ridicule.
riding ['raɪdɪŋ] *n* équitation *f*.
riding school *n* manège *m*, école *f* d'équitation.
rife [raɪf] *adj* répandu(e); **~ with** abondant(e) en.
riffraff ['rɪfræf] *n* racaille *f*.
rifle ['raɪfl] *n* fusil *m* (à canon rayé) ♦ *vt* vider, dévaliser.
►**rifle through** *vt fus* fouiller dans.
rifle range *n* champ *m* de tir; (*indoor*) stand *m* de tir.
rift [rɪft] *n* fente *f*, fissure *f*; (*fig*) désaccord *m*.
rig [rɪg] *n* (*also*: **oil ~**: *on land*) derrick *m*; (*: at sea*) plate-forme pétrolière ♦ *vt* (*election etc*) truquer.
►**rig out** *vt* (*BRIT*) habiller; (*: pej*) fringuer, attifer.
►**rig up** *vt* arranger, faire avec des moyens de fortune.
rigging ['rɪgɪŋ] *n* (*NAUT*) gréement *m*.
right [raɪt] *adj* (*true*) juste, exact(e); (*correctly chosen: answer, road etc*) bon(bonne); (*suitable*) approprié(e), convenable; (*just*) juste, équitable; (*morally good*) bien *inv*; (*not left*) droit(e) ♦ *n* (*title, claim*) droit *m*; (*not left*) droite *f* ♦ *adv* (*answer*) correctement; (*not on the left*) à droite ♦ *vt* redresser ♦ *excl* bon!; **the ~ time** (*precise*) l'heure exacte; (*not wrong*) la bonne heure; **to be ~** (*person*) avoir raison; (*answer*) être juste *or* correct(e); **to get sth ~** ne pas se tromper sur qch; **let's get it ~ this time!** essayons de ne pas nous tromper cette fois-ci!; **you did the ~ thing** vous avez bien fait; **to put a mistake ~** (*BRIT*) rectifier une erreur; **~ now** en ce moment même; tout de suite; **~ before/after** juste avant/après; **~ against the wall** tout contre le mur; **~ ahead** tout droit; droit devant; **~ in the middle** en plein milieu; **~ away** immédiatement; **to go ~ to the end of sth** aller jusqu'au bout de qch; **by ~s** en toute justice; **on the ~** à droite; **~ and wrong** le bien et le mal; **to be in the ~** avoir raison; **film ~s** droits d'adaptation cinématographique; **~ of way** droit *m* de passage; (*AUT*) priorité *f*.
right angle *n* angle droit.
right-click *vi* faire un clic droit ♦ *vt* faire un clic droit sur.
righteous ['raɪtʃəs] *adj* droit(e), vertueux(euse); (*anger*) justifié(e).
righteousness ['raɪtʃəsnɪs] *n* droiture *f*, vertu *f*.
rightful ['raɪtful] *adj* (*heir*) légitime.
rightfully ['raɪtfəlɪ] *adv* à juste titre, légitimement.
right-handed [raɪt'hændɪd] *adj* droitier(ière).
right-hand man ['raɪthænd-] *n* bras droit (*fig*).
right-hand side ['raɪthænd-] *n* côté droit.
rightly ['raɪtlɪ] *adv* bien, correctement; (*with reason*) à juste titre; **if I remember ~** (*BRIT*) si je me souviens bien.
right-minded ['raɪt'maɪndɪd] *adj* sensé(e), sain(e) d'esprit.
rights issue *n* (*STOCK EXCHANGE*) émission préférentielle *or* de droit de souscription.
right wing *n* (*MIL, SPORT*) aile droite; (*POL*) droite *f* ♦ *adj*: **right-wing** (*POL*) de droite.
right-winger [raɪt'wɪŋə*] *n* (*POL*) membre *m* de la droite; (*SPORT*) ailier droit.
rigid ['rɪdʒɪd] *adj* rigide; (*principle*) strict(e).
rigidity [rɪ'dʒɪdɪtɪ] *n* rigidité *f*.
rigidly ['rɪdʒɪdlɪ] *adv* rigidement; (*behave*) inflexiblement.
rigmarole ['rɪgmərəul] *n* galimatias *m*, comédie *f*.
rigor ['rɪgə*] *n* (*US*) = **rigour.**
rigor mortis ['rɪgə'mɔːtɪs] *n* rigidité *f* cadavérique.
rigorous ['rɪgərəs] *adj* rigoureux(euse).
rigorously ['rɪgərəslɪ] *adv* rigoureusement.
rigour, (*US*) **rigor** ['rɪgə*] *n* rigueur *f*.
rig-out ['rɪgaut] *n* (*BRIT col*) tenue *f*.
rile [raɪl] *vt* agacer.

rim [rɪm] *n* bord *m*; (*of spectacles*) monture *f*; (*of wheel*) jante *f*.
rimless ['rɪmlɪs] *adj* (*spectacles*) à monture invisible.
rind [raɪnd] *n* (*of bacon*) couenne *f*; (*of lemon etc*) écorce *f*.
ring [rɪŋ] *n* anneau *m*; (*on finger*) bague *f*; (*also*: **wedding** ~) alliance *f*; (*for napkin*) rond *m*; (*of people, objects*) cercle *m*; (*of spies*) réseau *m*; (*of smoke etc*) rond; (*arena*) piste *f*, arène *f*; (*for boxing*) ring *m*; (*sound of bell*) sonnerie *f*; (*telephone call*) coup *m* de téléphone ♦ *vb* (*pt* **rang**, *pp* **rung** [ræŋ, rʌŋ]) *vi* (*person, bell*) sonner; (*also*: ~ **out**: *voice, words*) retentir; (*TEL*) téléphoner ♦ *vt* (*BRIT TEL*: *also*: ~ **up**) téléphoner à; **to** ~ **the bell** sonner; **to give sb a** ~ (*TEL*) passer un coup de téléphone *or* de fil à qn; **that has the** ~ **of truth about it** cela sonne vrai; **the name doesn't** ~ **a bell (with me)** ce nom ne me dit rien.
►**ring back** *vt, vi* (*BRIT TEL*) rappeler.
►**ring off** *vi* (*BRIT TEL*) raccrocher.
ring binder *n* classeur *m* à anneaux.
ring finger *n* annulaire *m*.
ringing ['rɪŋɪŋ] *n* (*of bell*) tintement *m*; (*louder, also of telephone*) sonnerie *f*; (*in ears*) bourdonnement *m*.
ringing tone *n* (*BRIT TEL*) sonnerie *f*.
ringleader ['rɪŋliːdə*] *n* (*of gang*) chef *m*, meneur *m*.
ringlets ['rɪŋlɪts] *npl* anglaises *fpl*.
ring road *n* (*BRIT*) route *f* de ceinture.
rink [rɪŋk] *n* (*also*: **ice** ~) patinoire *f*; (*for roller-skating*) skating *m*.
rinse [rɪns] *n* rinçage *m* ♦ *vt* rincer.
Rio (de Janeiro) ['riːəu(dədʒə'nɪərəu)] *n* Rio de Janeiro.
riot ['raɪət] *n* émeute *f*, bagarres *fpl* ♦ *vi* manifester avec violence; **a** ~ **of colours** une débauche *or* orgie de couleurs; **to run** ~ se déchaîner.
rioter ['raɪətə*] *n* émeutier/ière, manifestant/e.
riot gear *n*: **in** ~ casqué et portant un bouclier.
riotous ['raɪətəs] *adj* tapageur(euse); tordant(e).
riotously ['raɪətəslɪ] *adv*: ~ **funny** tordant(e).
riot police *n* forces *fpl* de police intervenant en cas d'émeute; **hundreds of** ~ des centaines de policiers casqués et armés.
RIP *abbr* (= *rest in peace*) RIP.
rip [rɪp] *n* déchirure *f* ♦ *vt* déchirer ♦ *vi* se déchirer.
►**rip up** *vt* déchirer.
ripcord ['rɪpkɔːd] *n* poignée *f* d'ouverture.
ripe [raɪp] *adj* (*fruit*) mûr(e); (*cheese*) fait(e).
ripen ['raɪpn] *vt* mûrir ♦ *vi* mûrir; se faire.
ripeness ['raɪpnɪs] *n* maturité *f*.
rip-off ['rɪpɔf] *n* (*col*): **it's a** ~! c'est du vol manifeste!
riposte [rɪ'pɔst] *n* riposte *f*.
ripple ['rɪpl] *n* ride *f*, ondulation *f*; égrènement *m*, cascade *f* ♦ *vi* se rider, onduler ♦ *vt* rider, faire onduler.
rise [raɪz] *n* (*slope*) côte *f*, pente *f*; (*hill*) élévation *f*; (*increase: in wages*: *BRIT*) augmentation *f*; (*: in prices, temperature*) hausse *f*, augmentation; (*fig*) ascension *f* ♦ *vi* (*pt* **rose**, *pp* **risen** [rəuz, rɪzn]) s'élever, monter; (*prices*) augmenter, monter; (*waters, river*) monter; (*sun, wind, person: from chair, bed*) se lever; (*also*: ~ **up**: *rebel*) se révolter; se rebeller; ~ **to power** montée *f* au pouvoir; **to give** ~ **to** donner lieu à; **to** ~ **to the occasion** se montrer à la hauteur.
rising ['raɪzɪŋ] *adj* (*increasing: number, prices*) en hausse; (*tide*) montant(e); (*sun, moon*) levant(e) ♦ *n* (*uprising*) soulèvement *m*, insurrection *f*.
rising damp *n* humidité *f* (montant des fondations).
rising star *n* (*also fig*) étoile montante.
risk [rɪsk] *n* risque *m*, danger *m*; (*deliberate*) risque ♦ *vt* risquer; **to take** *or* **run the** ~ **of doing** courir le risque de faire; **at** ~ en danger; **at one's own** ~ à ses risques et périls; **it's a fire/health** ~ cela présente un risque d'incendie/pour la santé; **I'll** ~ **it** je vais risquer le coup.
risk capital *n* capital-risques *m*.
risky ['rɪskɪ] *adj* risqué(e).
risqué ['riːskeɪ] *adj* (*joke*) risqué(e).
rissole ['rɪsəul] *n* croquette *f*.
rite [raɪt] *n* rite *m*; **the last** ~**s** les derniers sacrements.
ritual ['rɪtjuəl] *adj* rituel(le) ♦ *n* rituel *m*.
rival ['raɪvl] *n* rival/e; (*in business*) concurrent/e ♦ *adj* rival(e); qui fait concurrence ♦ *vt* être en concurrence avec; **to** ~ **sb/sth in** rivaliser avec qn/qch de.
rivalry ['raɪvlrɪ] *n* rivalité *f*, concurrence *f*.
river ['rɪvə*] *n* rivière *f*; (*major, also fig*) fleuve *m* ♦ *cpd* (*port, traffic*) fluvial(e); **up/down** ~ en amont/aval.
riverbank ['rɪvəbæŋk] *n* rive *f*, berge *f*.
riverbed ['rɪvəbɛd] *n* lit *m* (de rivière *or* de fleuve).
riverside ['rɪvəsaɪd] *n* bord *m* de la rivière *or* du fleuve.
rivet ['rɪvɪt] *n* rivet *m* ♦ *vt* riveter; (*fig*) river, fixer.
riveting ['rɪvɪtɪŋ] *adj* (*fig*) fascinant(e).
Riviera [rɪvɪ'ɛərə] *n*: **the (French)** ~ la Côte d'Azur; **the Italian** ~ la Riviera (italienne).
Riyadh [rɪ'jɑːd] *n* Riyad.
RMT *n abbr* (= *Rail, Maritime and Transport*) *syndicat des transports*.
RN *n abbr* (*BRIT*) = **Royal Navy**; (*US*) = **registered nurse**.
RNA *n abbr* (= *ribonucleic acid*) ARN *m*.
RNLI *n abbr* (*BRIT*: = *Royal National Lifeboat Institution*) ≈ SNSM *f*.
RNZAF *n abbr* = *Royal New Zealand Air Force*.

RNZN *n abbr* = *Royal New Zealand Navy.*
road [rəud] *n* route *f*; (*in town*) rue *f*; (*fig*) chemin, voie *f*; **main** ~ grande route; **major** ~ route principale *or* à priorité; **minor** ~ voie secondaire; **it takes four hours by** ~ il y a quatre heures de route; **"~ up"** (*BRIT*) "attention travaux".
roadblock ['rəudblɔk] *n* barrage routier.
road haulage *n* transports routiers.
roadhog ['rəudhɔg] *n* chauffard *m*.
road map *n* carte routière.
road safety *n* sécurité routière.
roadside ['rəudsaɪd] *n* bord *m* de la route, bas-côté *m* ♦ *cpd* (situé(e) *etc*) au bord de la route; **by the** ~ au bord de la route.
roadsign ['rəudsaɪn] *n* panneau *m* de signalisation.
roadsweeper ['rəudswiːpə*] *n* (*BRIT*: *person*) balayeur/euse.
road user *n* usager *m* de la route.
roadway ['rəudweɪ] *n* chaussée *f*.
roadworks ['rəudwəːks] *npl* travaux *mpl* (de réfection des routes).
roadworthy ['rəudwəːðɪ] *adj* en bon état de marche.
roam [rəum] *vi* errer, vagabonder ♦ *vt* parcourir, errer par.
roar [rɔː*] *n* rugissement *m*; (*of crowd*) hurlements *mpl*; (*of vehicle, thunder, storm*) grondement *m* ♦ *vi* rugir; hurler; gronder; **to** ~ **with laughter** rire à gorge déployée.
roaring ['rɔːrɪŋ] *adj*: **a** ~ **fire** une belle flambée; **a** ~ **success** un succès fou; **to do a** ~ **trade** faire des affaires d'or.
roast [rəust] *n* rôti *m* ♦ *vt* (*meat*) (faire) rôtir.
roast beef *n* rôti *m* de bœuf, rosbif *m*.
roasting ['rəustɪŋ] *n* (*col*): **to give sb a** ~ sonner les cloches à qn.
rob [rɔb] *vt* (*person*) voler; (*bank*) dévaliser; **to** ~ **sb of sth** voler *or* dérober qch à qn; (*fig: deprive*) priver qn de qch.
robber ['rɔbə*] *n* bandit *m*, voleur *m*.
robbery ['rɔbərɪ] *n* vol *m*.
robe [rəub] *n* (*for ceremony etc*) robe *f*; (*also*: **bath**~) peignoir *m* ♦ *vt* revêtir (d'une robe).
robin ['rɔbɪn] *n* rouge-gorge *m*.
robot ['rəubɔt] *n* robot *m*.
robotics [rə'bɔtɪks] *n* robotique *m*.
robust [rəu'bʌst] *adj* robuste; (*material, appetite*) solide.
rock [rɔk] *n* (*substance*) roche *f*, roc *m*; (*boulder*) rocher *m*; roche; (*BRIT*: *sweet*) ≈ sucre *m* d'orge ♦ *vt* (*swing gently: cradle*) balancer; (*: child*) bercer; (*shake*) ébranler, secouer ♦ *vi* (se) balancer; être ébranlé(e) *or* secoué(e); **on the ~s** (*drink*) avec des glaçons; (*ship*) sur les écueils; (*marriage etc*) en train de craquer; **to** ~ **the boat** (*fig*) jouer les trouble-fête.
rock and roll *n* rock (and roll) *m*, rock'n'roll *m*.
rock bottom ['rɔk'bɔtəm] *n* (*fig*) niveau le plus bas ♦ *adj*: **rock-bottom** (*fig: prices*) sacrifié(e); **to reach** *or* **touch rock bottom** (*price, person*) tomber au plus bas.
rock climber *n* varappeur/euse.
rock climbing *n* varappe *f*.
rockery ['rɔkərɪ] *n* (jardin *m* de) rocaille *f*.
rocket ['rɔkɪt] *n* fusée *f*; (*MIL*) fusée, roquette *f* ♦ *vi* (*prices*) monter en flèche.
rocket launcher [-lɔːnʃə*] *n* lance-roquettes *m inv*.
rock face *n* paroi rocheuse.
rock fall *n* chute *f* de pierres.
rocking chair ['rɔkɪŋ-] *n* fauteuil *m* à bascule.
rocking horse ['rɔkɪŋ-] *n* cheval *m* à bascule.
rocky ['rɔkɪ] *adj* (*hill*) rocheux(euse); (*path*) rocailleux(euse); (*unsteady: table*) branlant(e).
Rocky Mountains *npl*: **the** ~ les (montagnes *fpl*) Rocheuses *fpl*.
rod [rɔd] *n* (*metallic*) tringle *f*; (*TECH*) tige *f*; (*wooden*) baguette *f*; (*also*: **fishing** ~) canne *f* à pêche.
rode [rəud] *pt of* **ride**.
rodent ['rəudnt] *n* rongeur *m*.
rodeo ['rəudɪəu] *n* rodéo *m*.
roe [rəu] *n* (*species*: *also*: ~ **deer**) chevreuil *m*; (*of fish*: *also*: **hard** ~) œufs *mpl* de poisson; **soft** ~ laitance *f*.
roe deer *n* chevreuil *m*; chevreuil femelle.
rogue [rəug] *n* coquin/e.
roguish ['rəugɪʃ] *adj* coquin(e).
role [rəul] *n* rôle *m*.
role model *n* modèle *m* à émuler.
role play, role playing *n* jeu *m* de rôle.
roll [rəul] *n* rouleau *m*; (*of banknotes*) liasse *f*; (*also*: **bread** ~) petit pain; (*register*) liste *f*; (*sound: of drums etc*) roulement *m*; (*movement: of ship*) roulis *m* ♦ *vt* rouler; (*also*: ~ **up**: *string*) enrouler; (*also*: ~ **out**: *pastry*) étendre au rouleau ♦ *vi* rouler; (*wheel*) tourner; **cheese** ~ ≈ sandwich *m* au fromage (*dans un petit pain*).
▸**roll about, roll around** *vi* rouler çà et là; (*person*) se rouler par terre.
▸**roll by** *vi* (*time*) s'écouler, passer.
▸**roll in** *vi* (*mail, cash*) affluer.
▸**roll over** *vi* se retourner.
▸**roll up** *vi* (*col*: *arrive*) arriver, s'amener ♦ *vt* (*carpet, cloth, map*) rouler; (*sleeves*) retrousser; **to** ~ **o.s. up into a ball** se rouler en boule.
roll call *n* appel *m*.
rolled-gold ['rəuldgəuld] *adj* plaqué or *inv*.
roller ['rəulə*] *n* rouleau *m*; (*wheel*) roulette *f*.
roller blind *n* (*BRIT*) store *m*.
roller coaster *n* montagnes *fpl* russes.
roller skates *npl* patins *mpl* à roulettes.
rollicking ['rɔlɪkɪŋ] *adj* bruyant(e) et joyeux(euse); (*play*) bouffon(ne); **to have a** ~ **time** s'amuser follement.
rolling ['rəulɪŋ] *adj* (*landscape*) onduleux(euse).
rolling mill *n* laminoir *m*.

rolling pin *n* rouleau *m* à pâtisserie.
rolling stock *n* (*RAIL*) matériel roulant.
roll-on-roll-off ['rəulɔn'rəulɔf] *adj* (*BRIT: ferry*) transroulier(ière).
roly-poly ['rəulɪ'pəulɪ] *n* (*BRIT CULIN*) roulé *m* à la confiture.
ROM [rɔm] *n abbr* (*COMPUT: = read-only memory*) mémoire morte, ROM *f*.
Roman ['rəumən] *adj* romain(e) ♦ *n* Romain/e.
Roman Catholic *adj, n* catholique (*m/f*).
romance [rə'mæns] *n* histoire *f* (*or* film *m or* aventure *f*) romanesque; (*charm*) poésie *f*; (*love affair*) idylle *f*.
Romanesque [rəumə'nɛsk] *adj* roman(e).
Romania [rəu'meɪnɪə] *n* Roumanie *f*.
Romanian [rəu'meɪnɪən] *adj* roumain(e) ♦ *n* Roumain/e; (*LING*) roumain *m*.
Roman numeral *n* chiffre romain.
romantic [rə'mæntɪk] *adj* romantique; (*play, attachment*) sentimental(e).
romanticism [rə'mæntɪsɪzəm] *n* romantisme *m*.
Romany ['rɔmənɪ] *adj* de bohémien ♦ *n* bohémien/ne; (*LING*) romani *m*.
Rome [rəum] *n* Rome.
romp [rɔmp] *n* jeux bruyants ♦ *vi* (*also*: ~ **about**) s'ébattre, jouer bruyamment; **to ~ home** (*horse*) arriver bon premier.
rompers ['rɔmpəz] *npl* barboteuse *f*.
rondo ['rɔndəu] *n* (*MUS*) rondeau *m*.
roof [ru:f] *n* toit *m*; (*of tunnel, cave*) plafond *m* ♦ *vt* couvrir (d'un toit); **the ~ of the mouth** la voûte du palais.
roof garden *n* toit-terrasse *m*.
roofing ['ru:fɪŋ] *n* toiture *f*.
roof rack *n* (*AUT*) galerie *f*.
rook [ruk] *n* (*bird*) freux *m*; (*CHESS*) tour *f* ♦ *vt* (*col: cheat*) rouler, escroquer.
rookie ['rukɪ] *n* (*col: esp MIL*) bleu *m*.
room [ru:m] *n* (*in house*) pièce *f*; (*also*: **bed~**) chambre *f* (à coucher); (*in school etc*) salle *f*; (*space*) place *f*; **~s** *npl* (*lodging*) meublé *m*; **"~s to let"**, (*US*) **"~s for rent"** "chambres à louer"; **is there ~ for this?** est-ce qu'il y a de la place pour ceci?; **to make ~ for sb** faire de la place à qn; **there is ~ for improvement** on peut faire mieux.
rooming house ['ru:mɪŋ-] *n* (*US*) maison *f* de rapport.
roommate ['ru:mmeɪt] *n* camarade *m/f* de chambre.
room service *n* service *m* des chambres (*dans un hôtel*).
room temperature *n* température ambiante; **"serve at ~"** (*wine*) "servir chambré".
roomy ['ru:mɪ] *adj* spacieux(euse); (*garment*) ample.
roost [ru:st] *n* juchoir *m* ♦ *vi* se jucher.
rooster ['ru:stə*] *n* coq *m*.
root [ru:t] *n* (*BOT, MATH*) racine *f*; (*fig: of problem*) origine *f*, fond *m* ♦ *vi* (*plant*) s'enraciner; **to take ~** (*plant, idea*) prendre racine.
▸**root about** *vi* (*fig*) fouiller.
▸**root for** *vt fus* (*col*) applaudir.
▸**root out** *vt* extirper.
root beer *n* (*US*) *sorte de limonade à base d'extraits végétaux*.
rope [rəup] *n* corde *f*; (*NAUT*) cordage *m* ♦ *vt* (*box*) corder; (*climbers*) encorder; **to ~ sb in** (*fig*) embringuer qn; **to know the ~s** (*fig*) être au courant, connaître les ficelles.
rope ladder *n* échelle *f* de corde.
ropey ['rəupɪ] *adj* (*col*) pas fameux(euse) *or* brillant(e); **I feel a bit ~ today** c'est pas la forme aujourd'hui.
rosary ['rəuzərɪ] *n* chapelet *m*.
rose [rəuz] *pt of* **rise** ♦ *n* rose *f*; (*also*: **~bush**) rosier *m*; (*on watering can*) pomme *f* ♦ *adj* rose.
rosé ['rəuzeɪ] *n* rosé *m*.
rosebed ['rəuzbɛd] *n* massif *m* de rosiers.
rosebud ['rəuzbʌd] *n* bouton *m* de rose.
rosebush ['rəuzbuʃ] *n* rosier *m*.
rosemary ['rəuzmərɪ] *n* romarin *m*.
rosette [rəu'zɛt] *n* rosette *f*; (*larger*) cocarde *f*.
ROSPA ['rɔspə] *n abbr* (*BRIT*) = *Royal Society for the Prevention of Accidents*.
roster ['rɔstə*] *n*: **duty ~** tableau *m* de service.
rostrum ['rɔstrəm] *n* tribune *f* (*pour un orateur etc*).
rosy ['rəuzɪ] *adj* rose; **a ~ future** un bel avenir.
rot [rɔt] *n* (*decay*) pourriture *f*; (*fig: pej*) idioties *fpl*, balivernes *fpl* ♦ *vt, vi* pourrir; **to stop the ~** (*BRIT fig*) rétablir la situation; **dry ~** pourriture sèche (*du bois*); **wet ~** pourriture (du bois).
rota ['rəutə] *n* liste *f*, tableau *m* de service; **on a ~ basis** par roulement.
rotary ['rəutərɪ] *adj* rotatif(ive).
rotate [rəu'teɪt] *vt* (*revolve*) faire tourner; (*change round: crops*) alterner; (*: jobs*) faire à tour de rôle ♦ *vi* (*revolve*) tourner.
rotating [rəu'teɪtɪŋ] *adj* (*movement*) tournant(e).
rotation [rəu'teɪʃən] *n* rotation *f*; **in ~** à tour de rôle.
rote [rəut] *n*: **by ~** machinalement, par cœur.
rotor ['rəutə*] *n* rotor *m*.
rotten ['rɔtn] *adj* (*decayed*) pourri(e); (*dishonest*) corrompu(e); (*col: bad*) mauvais(e), moche; **to feel ~** (*ill*) être mal fichu(e).
rotting ['rɔtɪŋ] *adj* pourrissant(e).
rotund [rəu'tʌnd] *adj* rondelet(te); arrondi(e).
rouble, (*US*) **ruble** ['ru:bl] *n* rouble *m*.
rouge [ru:ʒ] *n* rouge *m* (à joues).
rough [rʌf] *adj* (*cloth, skin*) rêche, rugueux(euse); (*terrain*) accidenté(e); (*path*) rocailleux(euse); (*voice*) rauque, rude; (*person, manner: coarse*) rude, fruste; (*: violent*) brutal(e); (*district, weather*) mauvais(e); (*plan*) ébauché(e); (*guess*) approximatif(ive) ♦ *n* (*GOLF*) rough *m* ♦ *vt*: **to ~ it** vivre à la

dure; **the sea is ~ today** la mer est agitée aujourd'hui; **to have a ~ time (of it)** en voir de dures; **~ estimate** approximation *f*; **to play ~** jouer avec brutalité; **to sleep ~** (*BRIT*) coucher à la dure; **to feel ~** (*BRIT*) être mal fichu(e).

►**rough out** *vt* (*draft*) ébaucher.

roughage ['rʌfɪdʒ] *n* fibres *fpl* diététiques.

rough-and-ready ['rʌfən'rɛdɪ] *adj* (*accommodation, method*) rudimentaire.

rough-and-tumble ['rʌfən'tʌmbl] *n* agitation *f*.

roughcast ['rʌfkɑːst] *n* crépi *m*.

rough copy, rough draft *n* brouillon *m*.

roughen ['rʌfn] *vt* (*a surface*) rendre rude *or* rugueux(euse).

rough justice *n* justice *f* sommaire.

roughly ['rʌflɪ] *adv* (*handle*) rudement, brutalement; (*make*) grossièrement; (*approximately*) à peu près, en gros; **~ speaking** en gros.

roughness ['rʌfnɪs] *n* (*of cloth, skin*) rugosité *f*; (*of person*) rudesse *f*; brutalité *f*.

roughshod ['rʌfʃɔd] *adv*: **to ride ~ over** ne tenir aucun compte de.

rough work *n* (*at school etc*) brouillon *m*.

Roumania *etc* [ruː'meɪnɪə] = **Romania** *etc*.

round [raund] *adj* rond(e) ♦ *n* rond *m*, cercle *m*; (*BRIT: of toast*) tranche *f*; (*duty: of policeman, milkman etc*) tournée *f*; (*: of doctor*) visites *fpl*; (*game: of cards, in competition*) partie *f*; (*BOXING*) round *m*; (*of talks*) série *f* ♦ *vt* (*corner*) tourner; (*bend*) prendre; (*cape*) doubler ♦ *prep* autour de ♦ *adv*: **right ~, all ~** tout autour; **the long way ~** (par) le chemin le plus long; **all the year ~** toute l'année; **in ~ figures** en chiffres ronds; **it's just ~ the corner** c'est juste après le coin; (*fig*) c'est tout près; **to ask sb ~** inviter qn (chez soi); **I'll be ~ at 6 o'clock** je serai là à 6 heures; **to go ~** faire le tour *or* un détour; **to go ~ to sb's (house)** aller chez qn; **to go ~ an obstacle** contourner un obstacle; **go ~ the back** passez par derrière; **to go ~ a house** visiter une maison, faire le tour d'une maison; **enough to go ~** assez pour tout le monde; **she arrived ~ (about) noon** (*BRIT*) elle est arrivée vers midi; **~ the clock** 24 heures sur 24; **to go the ~s** (*disease, story*) circuler; **the daily ~** (*fig*) la routine quotidienne; **~ of ammunition** cartouche *f*; **~ of applause** applaudissements *mpl*; **~ of drinks** tournée *f*; **~ of sandwiches** (*BRIT*) *sandwich de pain de mie*.

►**round off** *vt* (*speech etc*) terminer.

►**round up** *vt* rassembler; (*criminals*) effectuer une rafle de; (*prices*) arrondir (au chiffre supérieur).

roundabout ['raundəbaut] *n* (*BRIT AUT*) rond-point *m* (à sens giratoire); (*at fair*) manège *m* ♦ *adj* (*route, means*) détourné(e).

rounded ['raundɪd] *adj* arrondi(e); (*style*) harmonieux(euse).

rounders ['raundəz] *npl* (*game*) ≈ balle *f* au camp.

roundly ['raundlɪ] *adv* (*fig*) tout net, carrément.

round-robin ['raundrɔbɪn] *n* (*SPORT*) *tournoi où tous les joueurs se rencontrent*.

round-shouldered *adj* au dos rond.

round trip *n* (voyage *m*) aller et retour *m*.

roundup ['raundʌp] *n* rassemblement *m*; (*of criminals*) rafle *f*; **a ~ of the latest news** un rappel des derniers événements.

rouse [rauz] *vt* (*wake up*) réveiller; (*stir up*) susciter; provoquer; éveiller.

rousing ['rauzɪŋ] *adj* (*welcome*) enthousiaste.

rout [raut] *n* (*MIL*) déroute *f* ♦ *vt* mettre en déroute.

route [ruːt] *n* itinéraire *m*; (*of bus*) parcours *m*; (*of trade, shipping*) route *f*; **"all ~s"** (*AUT*) "toutes directions"; **the best ~ to London** le meilleur itinéraire pour aller à Londres.

route map *n* (*BRIT: for journey*) croquis *m* d'itinéraire; (*for trains etc*) carte *f* du réseau.

routine [ruː'tiːn] *adj* (*work*) de routine; (*procedure*) d'usage ♦ *n* routine *f*; (*THEAT*) numéro *m*; **daily ~** occupations journalières.

roving ['rəuvɪŋ] *adj* (*life*) vagabond(e).

roving reporter *n* reporter volant.

row[1] [rəu] *n* (*line*) rangée *f*; (*of people, seats, KNITTING*) rang *m*; (*behind one another: of cars, people*) file *f* ♦ *vi* (*in boat*) ramer; (*as sport*) faire de l'aviron ♦ *vt* (*boat*) faire aller à la rame *or* à l'aviron; **in a ~** (*fig*) d'affilée.

row[2] [rau] *n* (*noise*) vacarme *m*; (*dispute*) dispute *f*, querelle *f*; (*scolding*) réprimande *f*, savon *m* ♦ *vi* (*also*: **to have a ~**) se disputer, se quereller.

rowboat ['rəubəut] *n* (*US*) canot *m* (à rames).

rowdiness ['raudɪnɪs] *n* tapage *m*, chahut *m*; (*fighting*) bagarre *f*.

rowdy ['raudɪ] *adj* chahuteur(euse); bagarreur(euse) ♦ *n* voyou *m*.

rowdyism ['raudɪɪzəm] *n* tapage *m*, chahut *m*.

rowing ['rəuɪŋ] *n* canotage *m*; (*as sport*) aviron *m*.

rowing boat *n* (*BRIT*) canot *m* (à rames).

rowlock ['rɔlək] *n* (*BRIT*) dame *f* de nage, tolet *m*.

royal ['rɔɪəl] *adj* royal(e).

Royal Academy (of Arts) *n* (*BRIT*) l'Académie *f* royale des Beaux-Arts; *voir encadré*.

ROYAL ACADEMY (OF ARTS)

La **Royal Academy** *ou* **Royal Academy of Arts**, *fondée en 1768 par George III pour encourager la peinture, la sculpture et l'architecture, est située à Burlington House, sur Piccadilly. Une exposition des œuvres d'artistes contemporains a lieu tous les étés. L'Académie dispense également des cours en peinture, sculpture et architecture.*

Royal Air Force (RAF) *n* (*BRIT*) *armée de l'air britannique*.
royal blue *adj* bleu roi *inv*.
royalist ['rɔɪəlɪst] *adj, n* royaliste (*m/f*).
Royal Navy (RN) *n* (*BRIT*) *marine de guerre britannique*.
royalty ['rɔɪəltɪ] *n* (*royal persons*) (membres *mpl* de la) famille royale; (*payment: to author*) droits *mpl* d'auteur; (*: to inventor*) royalties *fpl*.
RP *n abbr* (*BRIT*: = *received pronunciation*) prononciation *f* standard.
rpm *abbr* (= *revolutions per minute*) t/mn (= *tours/minute*).
RR *abbr* (*US*) = **railroad**.
RSA *n abbr* (*BRIT*) = *Royal Society of Arts, Royal Scottish Academy*.
RSI *n abbr* (*MED*: = *repetitive strain injury*) microtraumatisme permanent.
RSPB *n abbr* (*BRIT*: = *Royal Society for the Protection of Birds*) ≈ LPO *f*.
RSPCA *n abbr* (*BRIT*: = *Royal Society for the Prevention of Cruelty to Animals*) ≈ SPA *f*.
RSVP *abbr* (= *répondez s'il vous plaît*) RSVP.
RTA *n abbr* (= *road traffic accident*) accident *m* de la route.
Rt Hon. *abbr* (*BRIT*: = *Right Honourable*) *titre donné aux députés de la Chambre des communes*.
Rt Rev. *abbr* (= *Right Reverend*) très révérend.
rub [rʌb] *n* (*with cloth*) coup *m* de chiffon *or* de torchon; (*on person*) friction *f* ♦ *vt* frotter; frictionner; **to ~ sb up** *or* (*US*) **~ sb the wrong way** prendre qn à rebrousse-poil.
▶**rub down** *vt* (*body*) frictionner; (*horse*) bouchonner.
▶**rub in** *vt* (*ointment*) faire pénétrer.
▶**rub off** *vi* partir; **to ~ off on** déteindre sur.
▶**rub out** *vt* effacer ♦ *vi* s'effacer.
rubber ['rʌbə*] *n* caoutchouc *m*; (*BRIT*: *eraser*) gomme *f* (à effacer).
rubber band *n* élastique *m*.
rubber bullet *n* balle *f* en caoutchouc.
rubber plant *n* caoutchouc *m* (*plante verte*).
rubber ring *n* (*for swimming*) bouée *f* (de natation).
rubber solution *n* dissolution *f*.
rubber stamp *n* tampon *m*.
rubber-stamp [rʌbə'stæmp] *vt* (*fig*) approuver sans discussion.
rubber tree *n* arbre *m* à gomme, hévéa *m*.
rubbery ['rʌbərɪ] *adj* caoutchouteux(euse).
rubbish ['rʌbɪʃ] *n* (*from household*) ordures *fpl*; (*fig*: *pej*) choses *fpl* sans valeur; camelote *f*; (*nonsense*) bêtises *fpl*, idioties *fpl* ♦ *vt* (*BRIT col*) dénigrer, rabaisser; **what you've just said is ~** tu viens de dire une bêtise.
rubbish bin *n* (*BRIT*) boîte *f* à ordures, poubelle *f*.
rubbish dump *n* (*in town*) décharge publique, dépotoir *m*.
rubbishy ['rʌbɪʃɪ] *adj* (*BRIT col*) qui ne vaut rien, moche.
rubble ['rʌbl] *n* décombres *mpl*; (*smaller*) gravats *mpl*.
ruble ['ru:bl] *n* (*US*) = **rouble**.
ruby ['ru:bɪ] *n* rubis *m*.
RUC *n abbr* (*BRIT*: *POLICE*) = *Royal Ulster Constabulary*.
rucksack ['rʌksæk] *n* sac *m* à dos.
ructions ['rʌkʃənz] *npl* grabuge *m*.
rudder ['rʌdə*] *n* gouvernail *m*.
ruddy ['rʌdɪ] *adj* (*face*) coloré(e); (*col*: *damned*) sacré(e), fichu(e).
rude [ru:d] *adj* (*impolite: person*) impoli(e); (*: word, manners*) grossier(ière); (*shocking*) indécent(e), inconvenant(e); **to be ~ to sb** être grossier envers qn.
rudely ['ru:dlɪ] *adv* impoliment; grossièrement.
rudeness ['ru:dnɪs] *n* impolitesse *f*; grossièreté *f*.
rudiment ['ru:dɪmənt] *n* rudiment *m*.
rudimentary [ru:dɪ'mɛntərɪ] *adj* rudimentaire.
rue [ru:] *vt* se repentir de, regretter amèrement.
rueful ['ru:ful] *adj* triste.
ruff [rʌf] *n* fraise *f*, collerette *f*.
ruffian ['rʌfɪən] *n* brute *f*, voyou *m*.
ruffle ['rʌfl] *vt* (*hair*) ébouriffer; (*clothes*) chiffonner; (*water*) agiter; (*fig: person*) émouvoir, faire perdre son flegme à.
rug [rʌg] *n* petit tapis; (*BRIT*: *for knees*) couverture *f*.
rugby ['rʌgbɪ] *n* (*also*: **~ football**) rugby *m*.
rugged ['rʌgɪd] *adj* (*landscape*) accidenté(e); (*features, kindness, character*) rude; (*determination*) farouche.
rugger ['rʌgə*] *n* (*BRIT col*) rugby *m*.
ruin ['ru:ɪn] *n* ruine *f* ♦ *vt* ruiner; (*spoil: clothes*) abîmer; **~s** *npl* ruine(s); **in ~s** en ruine.
ruination [ru:ɪ'neɪʃən] *n* ruine *f*.
ruinous ['ru:ɪnəs] *adj* ruineux(euse).
rule [ru:l] *n* règle *f*; (*regulation*) règlement *m*; (*government*) autorité *f*, gouvernement *m*; (*dominion etc*): **under British ~** sous l'autorité britannique ♦ *vt* (*country*) gouverner; (*person*) dominer; (*decide*) décider ♦ *vi* commander; décider; (*LAW*): **to ~ against/in favour of/on** statuer contre/en faveur de/sur; **to ~ that** (*umpire, judge etc*) décider que; **it's against the ~s** c'est contraire au règlement; **by ~ of thumb** à vue de nez; **as a ~** normalement, en règle générale.
▶**rule out** *vt* exclure; **murder cannot be ~d out** l'hypothèse d'un meurtre ne peut être exclue.
ruled [ru:ld] *adj* (*paper*) réglé(e).
ruler ['ru:lə*] *n* (*sovereign*) souverain/e; (*leader*) chef *m* (d'État); (*for measuring*) règle *f*.
ruling ['ru:lɪŋ] *adj* (*party*) au pouvoir; (*class*) dirigeant(e) ♦ *n* (*LAW*) décision *f*.
rum [rʌm] *n* rhum *m* ♦ *adj* (*BRIT col*) bizarre.

Rumania *etc* [ruːˈmeɪnɪə] = **Romania** *etc*.
rumble *n* grondement *m*; gargouillement *m* ♦ *vi* gronder; (*stomach, pipe*) gargouiller.
rumbustious [rʌmˈbʌstʃəs], (*US*) **rumbunctious** [rʌmˈbʌŋkʃəs] *adj* (*person*) exubérant(e).
rummage [ˈrʌmɪdʒ] *vi* fouiller.
rumour, (*US*) **rumor** [ˈruːmə*] *n* rumeur *f*, bruit *m* (qui court) ♦ *vt*: **it is ~ed that** le bruit court que.
rump [rʌmp] *n* (*of animal*) croupe *f*; (*also*: ~ **steak**) romsteck *m*.
rumple [ˈrʌmpl] *vt* (*hair*) ébouriffer; (*clothes*) chiffonner, friper.
rumpus [ˈrʌmpəs] *n* (*col*) tapage *m*, chahut *m*; (*quarrel*) prise *f* de bec; **to kick up a ~** faire toute une histoire.
run [rʌn] *n* (*race etc*) course *f*; (*outing*) tour *m* *or* promenade *f* (en voiture); (*journey*) parcours *m*, trajet *m*; (*series*) suite *f*, série *f*; (*THEAT*) série de représentations; (*SKI*) piste *f*; (*in tights, stockings*) maille filée, échelle *f* ♦ *vb* (*pt* **ran**, *pp* **run** [ræn, rʌn]) *vt* (*business*) diriger; (*competition, course*) organiser; (*hotel, house*) tenir; (*COMPUT*: *program*) exécuter; (*force through: rope, pipe*): **to ~ sth through** faire passer qch à travers; (*to pass: hand, finger*): **to ~ sth over** promener *or* passer qch sur; (*water, bath*) faire couler ♦ *vi* courir; (*pass: road etc*) passer; (*work: machine, factory*) marcher; (*bus, train*) circuler; (*continue: play*) se jouer, être à l'affiche; (*: contract*) être valide *or* en vigueur; (*slide: drawer etc*) glisser; (*flow: river, bath*) couler; (*colours, washing*) déteindre; (*in election*) être candidat, se présenter; **to go for a ~** aller courir *or* faire un peu de course à pied; (*in car*) faire un tour *or* une promenade (en voiture); **to break into a ~** se mettre à courir; **a ~ of luck** une série de coups de chance; **to have the ~ of sb's house** avoir la maison de qn à sa disposition; **there was a ~ on** (*meat, tickets*) les gens se sont rués sur; **in the long ~** à longue échéance; à la longue; en fin de compte; **in the short ~** à brève échéance, à court terme; **on the ~** en fuite; **to make a ~ for it** s'enfuir; **I'll ~ you to the station** je vais vous emmener *or* conduire à la gare; **to ~ errands** faire des commissions; **the train ~s between Gatwick and Victoria** le train assure le service entre Gatwick et Victoria; **the bus ~s every 20 minutes** il y a un autobus toutes les 20 minutes; **it's very cheap to ~** (*car, machine*) c'est très économique; **to ~ on petrol** *or* (*US*) **gas/on diesel/off batteries** marcher à l'essence/au diesel/sur piles; **to ~ for president** être candidat à la présidence; **their losses ran into millions** leurs pertes se sont élevées à plusieurs millions; **to be ~ off one's feet** (*BRIT*) ne plus savoir où donner de la tête.
►**run about** *vi* (*children*) courir çà et là.
►**run across** *vt fus* (*find*) trouver par hasard.
►**run away** *vi* s'enfuir.
►**run down** *vi* (*clock*) s'arrêter (faute d'avoir été remonté) ♦ *vt* (*AUT*) renverser; (*BRIT*: *reduce: production*) réduire progressivement; (*: factory/shop*) réduire progressivement la production/l'activité de; (*criticize*) critiquer, dénigrer; **to be ~ down** être fatigué(e) *or* à plat.
►**run in** *vt* (*BRIT*: *car*) roder.
►**run into** *vt fus* (*meet: person*) rencontrer par hasard; (*: trouble*) se heurter à; (*collide with*) heurter; **to ~ into debt** contracter des dettes.
►**run off** *vi* s'enfuir ♦ *vt* (*water*) laisser s'écouler.
►**run out** *vi* (*person*) sortir en courant; (*liquid*) couler; (*lease*) expirer; (*money*) être épuisé(e).
►**run out of** *vt fus* se trouver à court de; **I've ~ out of petrol** *or* (*US*) **gas** je suis en panne d'essence.
►**run over** *vt* (*AUT*) écraser ♦ *vt fus* (*revise*) revoir, reprendre.
►**run through** *vt fus* (*instructions*) reprendre, revoir.
►**run up** *vt* (*debt*) laisser accumuler; **to ~ up against** (*difficulties*) se heurter à.
runaround [ˈrʌnəraund] *n* (*col*): **to give sb the ~** rester très évasif.
runaway [ˈrʌnəweɪ] *adj* (*horse*) emballé(e); (*truck*) fou(folle); (*inflation*) galopant(e).
rundown [ˈrʌndaun] *n* (*BRIT*: *of industry etc*) réduction progressive.
rung [rʌŋ] *pp of* **ring** ♦ *n* (*of ladder*) barreau *m*.
run-in [ˈrʌnɪn] *n* (*col*) accrochage *m*, prise *f* de bec.
runner [ˈrʌnə*] *n* (*in race: person*) coureur/euse; (*: horse*) partant *m*; (*on sledge*) patin *m*; (*for drawer etc*) coulisseau *m*; (*carpet: in hall etc*) chemin *m*.
runner bean *n* (*BRIT*) haricot *m* (à rames).
runner-up [rʌnərˈʌp] *n* second/e.
running [ˈrʌnɪŋ] *n* (*in race etc*) course *f*; (*of business*) direction *f*; (*of event*) organisation *f*; (*of machine etc*) marche *f*, fonctionnement *m* ♦ *adj* (*water*) courant(e); (*commentary*) suivi(e); **6 days ~** 6 jours de suite; **to be in/out of the ~ for sth** être/ne pas être sur les rangs pour qch.
running costs *npl* (*of business*) frais *mpl* de gestion; (*of car*): **the ~ are high** elle revient cher.
running head *n* (*TYP, WORD PROCESSING*) titre courant.
running mate *n* (*US POL*) *candidat à la vice-présidence*.
runny [ˈrʌnɪ] *adj* qui coule.
run-off [ˈrʌnɔf] *n* (*in contest, election*) deuxième tour *m*; (*extra race etc*) épreuve *f* supplémentaire.

run-of-the-mill ['rʌnəvðə'mɪl] *adj* ordinaire, banal(e).
runt [rʌnt] *n* (*also pej*) avorton *m*.
run-through ['rʌnθruː] *n* répétition *f*, essai *m*.
run-up ['rʌnʌp] *n* (*BRIT*): ~ **to sth** période *f* précédant qch.
runway ['rʌnweɪ] *n* (*AVIAT*) piste *f* (d'envol *or* d'atterrissage).
rupee [ruː'piː] *n* roupie *f*.
rupture ['rʌptʃə*] *n* (*MED*) hernie *f* ♦ *vt*: **to ~ o.s.** se donner une hernie.
rural ['ruərl] *adj* rural(e).
ruse [ruːz] *n* ruse *f*.
rush [rʌʃ] *n* course précipitée; (*of crowd*) ruée *f*, bousculade *f*; (*hurry*) hâte *f*, bousculade; (*current*) flot *m*; (*BOT*) jonc *m*; (*for chair*) paille *f* ♦ *vt* transporter *or* envoyer d'urgence; (*attack: town etc*) prendre d'assaut; (*BRIT col: overcharge*) estamper; faire payer ♦ *vi* se précipiter; **don't ~ me!** laissez-moi le temps de souffler!; **to ~ sth off** (*do quickly*) faire qch à la hâte; (*send*) envoyer d'urgence; **is there any ~ for this?** est-ce urgent?; **we've had a ~ of orders** nous avons reçu une avalanche de commandes; **I'm in a ~ (to do)** je suis vraiment pressé (de faire); **gold ~** ruée vers l'or.
►**rush through** *vt fus* (*work*) exécuter à la hâte ♦ *vt* (*COMM: order*) exécuter d'urgence.
rush hour *n* heures *fpl* de pointe *or* d'affluence.
rush job *n* travail urgent.
rush matting *n* natte *f* de paille.
rusk [rʌsk] *n* biscotte *f*.
Russia ['rʌʃə] *n* Russie *f*.
Russian ['rʌʃən] *adj* russe ♦ *n* Russe *m/f*; (*LING*) russe *m*.
rust [rʌst] *n* rouille *f* ♦ *vi* rouiller.
rustic ['rʌstɪk] *adj* rustique ♦ *n* (*pej*) rustaud/e.
rustle ['rʌsl] *vi* bruire, produire un bruissement ♦ *vt* (*paper*) froisser; (*US: cattle*) voler.
rustproof ['rʌstpruːf] *adj* inoxydable.
rustproofing ['rʌstpruːfɪŋ] *n* traitement *m* antirouille.
rusty ['rʌstɪ] *adj* rouillé(e).
rut [rʌt] *n* ornière *f*; (*ZOOL*) rut *m*; **to be in a ~** (*fig*) suivre l'ornière, s'encroûter.
rutabaga [ruːtə'beɪgə] *n* (*US*) rutabaga *m*.
ruthless ['ruːθlɪs] *adj* sans pitié, impitoyable.
ruthlessness ['ruːθlɪsnɪs] *n* dureté *f*, cruauté *f*.
RV *abbr* (= *revised version*) *traduction anglaise de la Bible de 1885* ♦ *n abbr* (*US*) = **recreational vehicle**.
rye [raɪ] *n* seigle *m*.
rye bread *n* pain *m* de seigle.

S s

S, s [ɛs] *n* (*letter*) S, s *m*; (*US SCOL*: = *satisfactory*) ≈ assez bien; **S for Sugar** S comme Suzanne.
S *abbr* (= *south, small*) S; (= *saint*) St.
SA *n abbr* = **South Africa, South America**.
Sabbath ['sæbəθ] *n* (*Jewish*) sabbat *m*; (*Christian*) dimanche *m*.
sabbatical [sə'bætɪkl] *adj*: ~ **year** année *f* sabbatique.
sabotage ['sæbətɑːʒ] *n* sabotage *m* ♦ *vt* saboter.
saccharin(e) ['sækərɪn] *n* saccharine *f*.
sachet ['sæʃeɪ] *n* sachet *m*.
sack [sæk] *n* (*bag*) sac *m* ♦ *vt* (*dismiss*) renvoyer, mettre à la porte; (*plunder*) piller, mettre à sac; **to give sb the ~** renvoyer qn, mettre qn à la porte; **to get the ~** être renvoyé(e) *or* mis(e) à la porte.
sackful ['sækful] *n*: **a ~ of** un (plein) sac de.
sacking ['sækɪŋ] *n* toile *f* à sac; (*dismissal*) renvoi *m*.
sacrament ['sækrəmənt] *n* sacrement *m*.
sacred ['seɪkrɪd] *adj* sacré(e).
sacred cow *n* (*fig*) chose sacro-sainte.
sacrifice ['sækrɪfaɪs] *n* sacrifice *m* ♦ *vt* sacrifier; **to make ~s (for sb)** se sacrifier *or* faire des sacrifices (pour qn).
sacrilege ['sækrɪlɪdʒ] *n* sacrilège *m*.
sacrosanct ['sækrəusæŋkt] *adj* sacro-saint(e).
sad [sæd] *adj* (*unhappy*) triste; (*deplorable*) triste, fâcheux(euse).
sadden ['sædn] *vt* attrister, affliger.
saddle ['sædl] *n* selle *f* ♦ *vt* (*horse*) seller; **to be ~d with sth** (*col*) avoir qch sur les bras.
saddlebag ['sædlbæg] *n* sacoche *f*.
sadism ['seɪdɪzəm] *n* sadisme *m*.
sadist ['seɪdɪst] *n* sadique *m/f*.
sadistic [sə'dɪstɪk] *adj* sadique.
sadly ['sædlɪ] *adv* tristement; (*regrettably*) malheureusement.
sadness ['sædnɪs] *n* tristesse *f*.
sado-masochism [seɪdəu'mæsəkɪzəm] *n* sadomasochisme *m*.
sae *abbr* (*BRIT*: = *stamped addressed envelope*) *enveloppe affranchie pour la réponse*.
safari [sə'fɑːrɪ] *n* safari *m*.
safari park *n* réserve *f*.
safe [seɪf] *adj* (*out of danger*) hors de danger, en sécurité; (*not dangerous*) sans danger; (*cautious*) prudent(e); (*sure: bet etc*) assuré(e) ♦ *n* coffre-fort *m*; ~ **from** à l'abri de; ~ **and sound** sain(e) et sauf(sauve); **(just) to**

be on the ~ side pour plus de sûreté, par précaution; **to play ~** ne prendre aucun risque; **it is ~ to say that ...** on peut dire sans crainte que ...; **~ journey!** bon voyage!
safe bet *n*: **it was a ~** ça ne comportait pas trop de risques; **it's a ~ that he'll be late** il y a toutes les chances pour qu'il soit en retard.
safe-breaker ['seɪfbreɪkə*] *n* (*BRIT*) perceur *m* de coffre-fort.
safe-conduct [seɪf'kɔndʌkt] *n* sauf-conduit *m*.
safe-cracker ['seɪfkrækə*] *n* = **safe-breaker**.
safe-deposit ['seɪfdɪpɔzɪt] *n* (*vault*) dépôt *m* de coffres-forts; (*box*) coffre-fort *m*.
safeguard ['seɪfgɑːd] *n* sauvegarde *f*, protection *f* ♦ *vt* sauvegarder, protéger.
safe haven *n* zone *f* de sécurité.
safekeeping ['seɪf'kiːpɪŋ] *n* bonne garde.
safely ['seɪflɪ] *adv* sans danger, sans risque; (*without mishap*) sans accident; **I can ~ say ...** je peux dire à coup sûr ....
safe passage *n*: **to grant sb ~** accorder un laissez-passer à qn.
safe sex *n* rapports sexuels protégés.
safety ['seɪftɪ] *n* sécurité *f*; **~ first!** la sécurité d'abord!
safety belt *n* ceinture *f* de sécurité.
safety catch *n* cran *m* de sûreté *or* sécurité.
safety net *n* filet *m* de sécurité.
safety pin *n* épingle *f* de sûreté *or* de nourrice.
safety valve *n* soupape *f* de sûreté.
saffron ['sæfrən] *n* safran *m*.
sag [sæg] *vi* s'affaisser, fléchir; pendre.
saga ['sɑːgə] *n* saga *f*; (*fig*) épopée *f*.
sage [seɪdʒ] *n* (*herb*) sauge *f*; (*man*) sage *m*.
Sagittarius [sædʒɪ'tɛərɪəs] *n* le Sagittaire; **to be ~** être du Sagittaire.
sago ['seɪgəu] *n* sagou *m*.
Sahara [sə'hɑːrə] *n*: **the ~ (Desert)** le (désert du) Sahara *m*.
Sahel [sæ'hɛl] *n* Sahel *m*.
said [sɛd] *pt, pp of* **say**.
Saigon [saɪ'gɔn] *n* Saigon.
sail [seɪl] *n* (*on boat*) voile *f*; (*trip*): **to go for a ~** faire un tour en bateau ♦ *vt* (*boat*) manœuvrer, piloter ♦ *vi* (*travel: ship*) avancer, naviguer; (*: passenger*) aller *or* se rendre (en bateau); (*set off*) partir, prendre la mer; (*SPORT*) faire de la voile; **they ~ed into Le Havre** ils sont entrés dans le port du Havre.
▸**sail through** *vi, vt fus* (*fig*) réussir haut la main.
sailboat ['seɪlbəut] *n* (*US*) bateau *m* à voiles, voilier *m*.
sailing ['seɪlɪŋ] *n* (*SPORT*) voile *f*; **to go ~** faire de la voile.
sailing boat *n* bateau *m* à voiles, voilier *m*.
sailing ship *n* grand voilier.
sailor ['seɪlə*] *n* marin *m*, matelot *m*.
saint [seɪnt] *n* saint/e.
saintly ['seɪntlɪ] *adj* saint(e), plein(e) de bonté.
sake [seɪk] *n*: **for the ~ of** (*out of concern for*) pour, dans l'intérêt de; (*out of consideration for*) par égard pour; (*in order to achieve*) pour plus de, par souci de; **arguing for arguing's ~** discuter pour (le plaisir de) discuter; **for the ~ of argument** à titre d'exemple; **for heaven's ~!** pour l'amour du ciel!
salad ['sæləd] *n* salade *f*; **tomato ~** salade de tomates.
salad bowl *n* saladier *m*.
salad cream *n* (*BRIT*) (sorte *f* de) mayonnaise *f*.
salad dressing *n* vinaigrette *f*.
salad oil *n* huile *f* de table.
salami [sə'lɑːmɪ] *n* salami *m*.
salaried ['sælərɪd] *adj* (*staff*) salarié(e), qui touche un traitement.
salary ['sælərɪ] *n* salaire *m*, traitement *m*.
salary scale *n* échelle *f* des traitements.
sale [seɪl] *n* vente *f*; (*at reduced prices*) soldes *mpl*; **"for ~"** "à vendre"; **on ~** en vente; **on ~ or return** vendu(e) avec faculté de retour; **closing-down** *or* (*US*) **liquidation ~** liquidation *f* (*avant fermeture*); **~ and lease back** *n* cession-bail *f*.
saleroom ['seɪlruːm] *n* salle *f* des ventes.
sales assistant *n* (*BRIT*) vendeur/euse.
sales clerk *n* (*US*) vendeur/euse.
sales conference *n* réunion *f* de vente.
sales drive *n* campagne commerciale, animation *f* des ventes.
sales force *n* (ensemble *m* du) service des ventes.
salesman ['seɪlzmən] *n* vendeur *m*; (*representative*) représentant *m* de commerce.
sales manager *n* directeur commercial.
salesmanship ['seɪlzmənʃɪp] *n* art *m* de la vente.
sales tax *n* (*US*) taxe *f* à l'achat.
saleswoman ['seɪlzwumən] *n* vendeuse *f*.
salient ['seɪlɪənt] *adj* saillant(e).
saline ['seɪlaɪn] *adj* salin(e).
saliva [sə'laɪvə] *n* salive *f*.
sallow ['sæləu] *adj* cireux(euse).
sally forth, sally out ['sælɪ-] *vi* partir plein(e) d'entrain.
salmon ['sæmən] *n* (*pl inv*) saumon *m*.
salmon trout *n* truite saumonée.
saloon [sə'luːn] *n* (*US*) bar *m*; (*BRIT AUT*) berline *f*; (*ship's lounge*) salon *m*.
SALT [sɔːlt] *n abbr* (= *Strategic Arms Limitation Talks/Treaty*) SALT *m*.
salt [sɔːlt] *n* sel *m* ♦ *vt* saler ♦ *cpd* de sel; (*CULIN*) salé(e); **an old ~** un vieux loup de mer.
▸**salt away** *vt* mettre de côté.
salt cellar *n* salière *f*.
salt-free ['sɔːlt'friː] *adj* sans sel.
saltwater ['sɔːlt'wɔːtə*] *adj* (*fish etc*) (d'eau) de mer.
salty ['sɔːltɪ] *adj* salé(e).
salubrious [sə'luːbrɪəs] *adj* salubre.

salutary ['sæljutərɪ] *adj* salutaire.
salute [sə'lu:t] *n* salut *m* ♦ *vt* saluer.
salvage ['sælvɪdʒ] *n* (*saving*) sauvetage *m*; (*things saved*) biens sauvés *or* récupérés ♦ *vt* sauver, récupérer.
salvage vessel *n* bateau *m* de sauvetage.
salvation [sæl'veɪʃən] *n* salut *m*.
Salvation Army *n* Armée *f* du Salut.
salver ['sælvə*] *n* plateau *m* de métal.
salvo ['sælvəu] *n* salve *f*.
Samaritan [sə'mærɪtən] *n*: **the ~s** (*organization*) ≈ S.O.S. Amitié.
same [seɪm] *adj* même ♦ *pron*: **the ~** le(la) même, les mêmes; **the ~ book as** le même livre que; **on the ~ day** le même jour; **at the ~ time** en même temps; **all** *or* **just the ~** tout de même, quand même; **they're one and the ~** (*person/thing*) c'est une seule et même personne/chose; **to do the ~** faire de même, en faire autant; **to do the ~ as sb** faire comme qn; **and the ~ to you!** et à vous de même!; (*after insult*) toi-même!; **~ here!** moi aussi!; **the ~ again!** la même chose!
sample ['sɑ:mpl] *n* échantillon *m*; (*MED*) prélèvement *m* ♦ *vt* (*food, wine*) goûter; **to take a ~** prélever un échantillon; **free ~** échantillon gratuit.
sanatorium, *pl* **sanatoria** [sænə'tɔ:rɪəm, -rɪə] *n* sanatorium *m*.
sanctify ['sæŋktɪfaɪ] *vt* sanctifier.
sanctimonious [sæŋktɪ'məunɪəs] *adj* moralisateur(trice).
sanction ['sæŋkʃən] *n* sanction *f* ♦ *vt* cautionner, sanctionner; **to impose economic ~s on** *or* **against** prendre des sanctions économiques contre.
sanctity ['sæŋktɪtɪ] *n* sainteté *f*, caractère sacré.
sanctuary ['sæŋktjuərɪ] *n* (*holy place*) sanctuaire *m*; (*refuge*) asile *m*; (*for wild life*) réserve *f*.
sand [sænd] *n* sable *m* ♦ *vt* sabler; (*also*: **~ down**: *wood etc*) poncer.
sandal ['sændl] *n* sandale *f*.
sandbag ['sændbæg] *n* sac *m* de sable.
sandblast ['sændblɑ:st] *vt* décaper à la sableuse.
sandbox ['sændbɔks] *n* (*US*: *for children*) tas *m* de sable.
sandcastle ['sændkɑ:sl] *n* château *m* de sable.
sand dune *n* dune *f* de sable.
sander ['sændə*] *n* ponceuse *f*.
S&M *n abbr* (= *sadomasochism*) sadomasochisme *m*.
sandpaper ['sændpeɪpə*] *n* papier *m* de verre.
sandpit ['sændpɪt] *n* (*BRIT*: *for children*) tas *m* de sable.
sands [sændz] *npl* plage *f* (de sable).
sandstone ['sændstəun] *n* grès *m*.
sandstorm ['sændstɔ:m] *n* tempête *f* de sable.
sandwich ['sændwɪtʃ] *n* sandwich *m* ♦ *vt* (*also*: **~ in**) intercaler; **~ed between** pris en sandwich entre; **cheese/ham ~** sandwich au fromage/jambon.
sandwich board *n* panneau *m* publicitaire (porté par un homme-sandwich).
sandwich course *n* (*BRIT*) cours *m* de formation professionnelle.
sandy ['sændɪ] *adj* sablonneux(euse); couvert(e) de sable; (*colour*) sable *inv*, blond roux *inv*.
sane [seɪn] *adj* (*person*) sain(e) d'esprit; (*outlook*) sensé(e), sain(e).
sang [sæŋ] *pt of* **sing**.
sanguine ['sæŋgwɪn] *adj* optimiste.
sanitarium, *pl* **sanitaria** [sænɪ'tɛərɪəm, -rɪə] *n* (*US*) = **sanatorium**.
sanitary ['sænɪtərɪ] *adj* (*system, arrangements*) sanitaire; (*clean*) hygiénique.
sanitary towel, (*US*) **sanitary napkin** *n* serviette *f* hygiénique.
sanitation [sænɪ'teɪʃən] *n* (*in house*) installations *fpl* sanitaires; (*in town*) système *m* sanitaire.
sanitation department *n* (*US*) service *m* de voirie.
sanity ['sænɪtɪ] *n* santé mentale; (*common sense*) bon sens.
sank [sæŋk] *pt of* **sink**.
San Marino ['sænmə'ri:nəu] *n* Saint-Marin *m*.
Santa Claus [sæntə'klɔ:z] *n* le Père Noël.
Santiago [sæntɪ'ɑ:gəu] *n* (*also*: **~ de Chile**) Santiago (du Chili).
sap [sæp] *n* (*of plants*) sève *f* ♦ *vt* (*strength*) saper, miner.
sapling ['sæplɪŋ] *n* jeune arbre *m*.
sapphire ['sæfaɪə*] *n* saphir *m*.
sarcasm ['sɑ:kæzm] *n* sarcasme *m*, raillerie *f*.
sarcastic [sɑ:'kæstɪk] *adj* sarcastique.
sarcophagus, *pl* **sarcophagi** [sɑ:'kɔfəgəs, -gaɪ] *n* sarcophage *m*.
sardine [sɑ:'di:n] *n* sardine *f*.
Sardinia [sɑ:'dɪnɪə] *n* Sardaigne *f*.
Sardinian [sɑ:'dɪnɪən] *adj* sarde ♦ *n* Sarde *m/f*; (*LING*) sarde *m*.
sardonic [sɑ:'dɔnɪk] *adj* sardonique.
sari ['sɑ:rɪ] *n* sari *m*.
SARS [sɑ:z] *n abbr* (= *severe acute respiratory syndrome*) pneumonie *f* atypique, SRAS *m*.
sartorial [sɑ:'tɔ:rɪəl] *adj* vestimentaire.
SAS *n abbr* (*BRIT MIL*: = *Special Air Service*) ≈ GIGN *m*.
SASE *n abbr* (*US*: = *self-addressed stamped envelope*) *enveloppe affranchie pour la réponse*.
sash [sæʃ] *n* écharpe *f*.
sash window *n* fenêtre *f* à guillotine.
SAT *n abbr* (*US*) = *Scholastic Aptitude Test*.
sat [sæt] *pt, pp of* **sit**.
Sat. *abbr* (= *Saturday*) sa.
Satan ['seɪtn] *n* Satan *m*.
satanic [sə'tænɪk] *adj* satanique, démoniaque.
satchel ['sætʃl] *n* cartable *m*.
sated ['seɪtɪd] *adj* repu(e); blasé(e).
satellite ['sætəlaɪt] *adj, n* satellite (*m*).

satellite television *n* télévision *f* par satellite.

satiate ['seɪʃɪeɪt] *vt* rassasier.

satin ['sætɪn] *n* satin *m* ♦ *adj* en *or* de satin, satiné(e); **with a ~ finish** satiné(e).

satire ['sætaɪə*] *n* satire *f*.

satirical [sə'tɪrɪkl] *adj* satirique.

satirist ['sætɪrɪst] *n* (*writer*) auteur *m* satirique; (*cartoonist*) caricaturiste *m/f*.

satirize ['sætɪraɪz] *vt* faire la satire de, satiriser.

satisfaction [sætɪs'fækʃən] *n* satisfaction *f*.

satisfactory [sætɪs'fæktərɪ] *adj* satisfaisant(e).

satisfied ['sætɪsfaɪd] *adj* satisfait(e); **to be ~ with sth** être satisfait de qch.

satisfy ['sætɪsfaɪ] *vt* satisfaire, contenter; (*convince*) convaincre, persuader; **to ~ the requirements** remplir les conditions; **to ~ sb (that)** convaincre qn (que); **to ~ o.s. of sth** vérifier qch, s'assurer de qch.

satisfying ['sætɪsfaɪɪŋ] *adj* satisfaisant(e).

satsuma [sæt'suːmə] *n* satsuma *f*.

saturate ['sætʃəreɪt] *vt*: **to ~ (with)** saturer (de).

saturated fat ['sætʃəreɪtɪd-] *n* graisse saturée.

saturation [sætʃə'reɪʃən] *n* saturation *f*.

Saturday ['sætədɪ] *n* samedi *m*; *for phrases see also* **Tuesday**.

sauce [sɔːs] *n* sauce *f*.

saucepan ['sɔːspən] *n* casserole *f*.

saucer ['sɔːsə*] *n* soucoupe *f*.

saucy ['sɔːsɪ] *adj* impertinent(e).

Saudi Arabia ['saudɪ-] *n* Arabie *f* Saoudite *or* Séoudite.

Saudi (Arabian) ['saudi-] *adj* saoudien(ne) ♦ *n* Saoudien/ne.

sauna ['sɔːnə] *n* sauna *m*.

saunter ['sɔːntə*] *vi*: **to ~ to** aller en flânant *or* se balader jusqu'à.

sausage ['sɔsɪdʒ] *n* saucisse *f*; (*salami etc*) saucisson *m*.

sausage roll *n* friand *m*.

sauté ['səuteɪ] *adj* (*CULIN*: *potatoes*) sauté(e); (*: onions*) revenu(e) ♦ *vt* faire sauter; faire revenir.

savage ['sævɪdʒ] *adj* (*cruel, fierce*) brutal(e), féroce; (*primitive*) primitif(ive), sauvage ♦ *n* sauvage *m/f* ♦ *vt* attaquer férocement.

savagery ['sævɪdʒrɪ] *n* sauvagerie *f*, brutalité *f*, férocité *f*.

save [seɪv] *vt* (*person, belongings*) sauver; (*money*) mettre de côté, économiser; (*time*) (faire) gagner; (*food*) garder; (*COMPUT*) sauvegarder; (*avoid: trouble*) éviter ♦ *vi* (*also*: **~ up**) mettre de l'argent de côté ♦ *n* (*SPORT*) arrêt *m* (du ballon) ♦ *prep* sauf, à l'exception de; **it will ~ me an hour** ça me fera gagner une heure; **to ~ face** sauver la face; **God ~ the Queen!** vive la Reine!

saving ['seɪvɪŋ] *n* économie *f* ♦ *adj*: **the ~ grace of** ce qui rachète; **~s** *npl* économies *fpl*; **to make ~s** faire des économies.

savings account *n* compte *m* d'épargne.

savings bank *n* caisse *f* d'épargne.

saviour, (*US*) **savior** ['seɪvjə*] *n* sauveur *m*.

savour, (*US*) **savor** ['seɪvə*] *n* saveur *f*, goût *m* ♦ *vt* savourer.

savo(u)ry ['seɪvərɪ] *adj* savoureux(euse); (*dish*: *not sweet*) salé(e).

savvy ['sævɪ] *n* (*col*) jugeote *f*.

saw [sɔː] *pt of* **see** ♦ *n* (*tool*) scie *f* ♦ *vt* (*pt* **sawed**, *pp* **sawed** *or* **sawn** [sɔːn]) scier; **to ~ sth up** débiter qch à la scie.

sawdust ['sɔːdʌst] *n* sciure *f*.

sawmill ['sɔːmɪl] *n* scierie *f*.

sawn-off ['sɔːnɔf], (*US*) **sawed-off** ['sɔːdɔf] *adj*: **~ shotgun** carabine *f* à canon scié.

saxophone ['sæksətəun] *n* saxophone *m*.

say [seɪ] *n*: **to have one's ~** dire ce qu'on a à dire ♦ *vt* (*pt, pp* **said** [sɛd]) dire; **to have a ~** avoir voix au chapitre; **could you ~ that again?** pourriez-vous répéter ceci?; **to ~ yes/no** dire oui/non; **she said (that) I was to give you this** elle m'a chargé de vous remettre ceci; **my watch ~s 3 o'clock** ma montre indique 3 heures, il est 3 heures à ma montre; **shall we ~ Tuesday?** disons mardi?; **that doesn't ~ much for him** ce n'est pas vraiment à son honneur; **when all is said and done** en fin de compte, en définitive; **there is something** *or* **a lot to be said for it** cela a des avantages; **that is to ~** c'est-à-dire; **to ~ nothing of** sans compter; **~ that** ... mettons *or* disons que ...; **that goes without ~ing** cela va sans dire, cela va de soi.

saying ['seɪɪŋ] *n* dicton *m*, proverbe *m*.

SBA *n abbr* (*US*: = *Small Business Administration*) *organisme d'aide aux PME*.

SC *n abbr* (*US*) = **supreme court** ♦ *abbr* (*US*) = *South Carolina*.

s/c *abbr* = **self-contained**.

scab [skæb] *n* croûte *f*; (*pej*) jaune *m*.

scabby ['skæbɪ] *adj* croûteux(euse).

scaffold ['skæfəld] *n* échafaud *m*.

scaffolding ['skæfəldɪŋ] *n* échafaudage *m*.

scald [skɔːld] *n* brûlure *f* ♦ *vt* ébouillanter.

scalding ['skɔːldɪŋ] *adj* (*also*: **~ hot**) brûlant(e), bouillant(e).

scale [skeɪl] *n* (*of fish*) écaille *f*; (*MUS*) gamme *f*; (*of ruler, thermometer etc*) graduation *f*, échelle (graduée); (*of salaries, fees etc*) barème *m*; (*of map, also size, extent*) échelle ♦ *vt* (*mountain*) escalader; (*fish*) écailler; **pay ~** échelle des salaires; **~ of charges** tarif *m* (des consultations *or* prestations *etc*); **on a large ~** sur une grande échelle, en grand; **to draw sth to ~** dessiner qch à l'échelle; **small-~ model** modèle réduit.

►**scale down** *vt* réduire.

scaled-down [skeɪld'daun] *adj* à échelle réduite.

scale drawing *n* dessin *m* à l'échelle.

scale model *n* modèle *m* à l'échelle.
scales [skeɪlz] *npl* balance *f*; (*larger*) bascule *f*.
scallion ['skæljən] *n* oignon *m*; (*US*: *shallot*) échalote *f*; (*: leek*) poireau *m*.
scallop ['skɔləp] *n* coquille *f* Saint-Jacques.
scalp [skælp] *n* cuir chevelu ♦ *vt* scalper.
scalpel ['skælpl] *n* scalpel *m*.
scalper ['skælpə*] *n* (*US col*: *of tickets*) revendeur *m* de billets.
scam [skæm] *n* (*col*) arnaque *f*.
scamp [skæmp] *vt* bâcler.
scamper ['skæmpə*] *vi*: **to ~ away, ~ off** détaler.
scampi ['skæmpɪ] *npl* langoustines (frites), scampi *mpl*.
scan [skæn] *vt* scruter, examiner; (*glance at quickly*) parcourir; (*poetry*) scander; (*TV, RADAR*) balayer ♦ *n* (*MED*) scanographie *f*.
scandal ['skændl] *n* scandale *m*; (*gossip*) ragots *mpl*.
scandalize ['skændəlaɪz] *vt* scandaliser, indigner.
scandalous ['skændələs] *adj* scandaleux(euse).
Scandinavia [skændɪ'neɪvɪə] *n* Scandinavie *f*.
Scandinavian [skændɪ'neɪvɪən] *adj* scandinave ♦ *n* Scandinave *m/f*.
scanner ['skænə*] *n* (*RADAR, MED*) scanner *m*, scanographe *m*.
scant [skænt] *adj* insuffisant(e).
scantily ['skæntɪlɪ] *adv*: **~ clad** *or* **dressed** vêtu(e) du strict minimum.
scanty ['skæntɪ] *adj* peu abondant(e), insuffisant(e), maigre.
scapegoat ['skeɪpgəut] *n* bouc *m* émissaire.
scar [skɑ:] *n* cicatrice *f* ♦ *vt* laisser une cicatrice *or* une marque à.
scarce [skɛəs] *adj* rare, peu abondant(e).
scarcely ['skɛəslɪ] *adv* à peine, presque pas; **~ anybody** pratiquement personne; **I can ~ believe it** j'ai du mal à le croire.
scarcity ['skɛəsɪtɪ] *n* rareté *f*, manque *m*.
scarcity value *n* valeur *f* de rareté.
scare [skɛə*] *n* peur *f*, panique *f* ♦ *vt* effrayer, faire peur à; **to ~ sb stiff** faire une peur bleue à qn; **bomb ~** alerte *f* à la bombe.
►**scare away, scare off** *vt* faire fuir.
scarecrow ['skɛəkrəu] *n* épouvantail *m*.
scared ['skɛəd] *adj*: **to be ~** avoir peur.
scaremonger ['skɛəmʌŋgə*] *n* alarmiste *m/f*.
scarf, *pl* **scarves** [skɑ:f, skɑ:vz] *n* (*long*) écharpe *f*; (*square*) foulard *m*.
scarlet ['skɑ:lɪt] *adj* écarlate.
scarlet fever *n* scarlatine *f*.
scarper ['skɑ:pə*] *vi* (*BRIT col*) ficher le camp.
SCART socket ['skɑ:t-] *n* prise *f* péritel.
scarves [skɑ:vz] *npl of* **scarf**.
scary ['skɛərɪ] *adj* (*col*) qui fiche la frousse.
scathing ['skeɪðɪŋ] *adj* cinglant(e), acerbe; **to be ~ about sth** être très critique vis-à-vis de qch.
scatter ['skætə*] *vt* éparpiller, répandre; (*crowd*) disperser ♦ *vi* se disperser.
scatterbrained ['skætəbreɪnd] *adj* écervelé(e), étourdi(e).
scattered ['skætəd] *adj* épars(e), dispersé(e).
scatty ['skætɪ] *adj* (*BRIT col*) loufoque.
scavenge ['skævəndʒ] *vi* (*person*): **to ~ (for)** faire les poubelles (pour trouver); **to ~ for food** (*hyenas etc*) se nourrir de charognes.
scavenger ['skævəndʒə*] *n* éboueur *m*.
SCE *n abbr = Scottish Certificate of Education.*
scenario [sɪ'nɑ:rɪəu] *n* scénario *m*.
scene [si:n] *n* (*THEAT, fig etc*) scène *f*; (*of crime, accident*) lieu(x) *m(pl)*, endroit *m*; (*sight, view*) spectacle *m*, vue *f*; **behind the ~s** (*also fig*) dans les coulisses; **to make a ~** (*col*: *fuss*) faire une scène *or* toute une histoire; **to appear on the ~** (*also fig*) faire son apparition, arriver; **the political ~** la situation politique.
scenery ['si:nərɪ] *n* (*THEAT*) décor(s) *m(pl)*; (*landscape*) paysage *m*.
scenic ['si:nɪk] *adj* scénique; offrant de beaux paysages *or* panoramas.
scent [sɛnt] *n* parfum *m*, odeur *f*; (*fig: track*) piste *f*; (*sense of smell*) odorat *m* ♦ *vt* parfumer; (*smell, also fig*) flairer; **to put** *or* **throw sb off the ~** (*fig*) mettre *or* lancer qn sur une mauvaise piste.
sceptic, (*US*) **skeptic** ['skɛptɪk] *n* sceptique *m/f*.
sceptical, (*US*) **skeptical** ['skɛptɪkl] *adj* sceptique.
scepticism, (*US*) **skepticism** ['skɛptɪsɪzəm] *n* scepticisme *m*.
sceptre, (*US*) **scepter** ['sɛptə*] *n* sceptre *m*.
schedule ['ʃɛdju:l, (*US*) 'skɛdju:l] *n* programme *m*, plan *m*; (*of trains*) horaire *m*; (*of prices etc*) barème *m*, tarif *m* ♦ *vt* prévoir; **as ~d** comme prévu; **on ~** à l'heure (prévue); à la date prévue; **to be ahead of/behind ~** avoir de l'avance/du retard; **we are working to a very tight ~** notre programme de travail est très serré *or* intense; **everything went according to ~** tout s'est passé comme prévu.
scheduled ['ʃɛdju:ld, (*US*) 'skɛdju:ld] *adj* (*date, time*) prévu(e), indiqué(e); (*visit, event*) programmé(e), prévu; (*train, bus, stop, flight*) régulier(ière).
schematic [skɪ'mætɪk] *adj* schématique.
scheme [ski:m] *n* plan *m*, projet *m*; (*method*) procédé *m*; (*dishonest plan, plot*) complot *m*, combine *f*; (*arrangement*) arrangement *m*, classification *f*; (*pension ~ etc*) régime *m* ♦ *vt, vi* comploter, manigancer; **colour ~** combinaison *f* de(s) couleurs.
scheming ['ski:mɪŋ] *adj* rusé(e), intrigant(e) ♦ *n* manigances *fpl*, intrigues *fpl*.
schism ['skɪzəm] *n* schisme *m*.
schizophrenia [skɪtsə'fri:nɪə] *n* schizophrénie *f*.
schizophrenic [skɪtsə'frɛnɪk] *adj* schizophrène.

scholar ['skɔlə*] *n* érudit/e.
scholarly ['skɔləlɪ] *adj* érudit(e), savant(e).
scholarship ['skɔləʃɪp] *n* érudition *f*; (*grant*) bourse *f* (d'études).
school [sku:l] *n* (*gen*) école *f*; (*in university*) faculté *f*; (*secondary school*) collège *m*, lycée *m*; (*of fish*) banc *m* ♦ *cpd* scolaire ♦ *vt* (*animal*) dresser.
school age *n* âge *m* scolaire.
schoolbook ['sku:lbuk] *n* livre *m* scolaire *or* de classe.
schoolboy ['sku:lbɔɪ] *n* écolier *m*; collégien *m*, lycéen *m*.
schoolchild, *pl* **-children** ['sku:ltʃaɪld, -'tʃɪldrən] *n* écolier/ière, collégien/ne, lycéen/ne.
schooldays ['sku:ldeɪz] *npl* années *fpl* de scolarité.
schoolgirl ['sku:lgə:l] *n* écolière *f*; collégienne *f*, lycéenne *f*.
schooling ['sku:lɪŋ] *n* instruction *f*, études *fpl*.
school-leaver ['sku:lli:və*] *n* (*BRIT*) *jeune qui vient de terminer ses études secondaires*.
schoolmaster ['sku:lmɑ:stə*] *n* (*primary*) instituteur *m*; (*secondary*) professeur *m*.
schoolmistress ['sku:lmɪstrɪs] *n* (*primary*) institutrice *f*; (*secondary*) professeur *m*.
school report *n* (*BRIT*) bulletin *m* (scolaire).
schoolroom ['sku:lru:m] *n* (salle *f* de) classe *f*.
schoolteacher ['sku:lti:tʃə*] *n* (*primary*) instituteur/trice; (*secondary*) professeur *m*.
schoolyard ['sku:ljɑ:d] *n* (*US*) cour *f* de récréation.
schooner ['sku:nə*] *n* (*ship*) schooner *m*, goélette *f*; (*glass*) grand verre (à xérès).
sciatica [saɪ'ætɪkə] *n* sciatique *f*.
science ['saɪəns] *n* science *f*; **the ~s** les sciences; (*SCOL*) les matières *fpl* scientifiques.
science fiction *n* science-fiction *f*.
scientific [saɪən'tɪfɪk] *adj* scientifique.
scientist ['saɪəntɪst] *n* scientifique *m/f*.
sci-fi ['saɪfaɪ] *n abbr* (*col*: = *science fiction*) SF *f*.
Scilly Isles ['sɪlɪ'aɪlz] *npl*, **Scillies** ['sɪlɪz] *npl*: **the ~** les Sorlingues *fpl*, les îles *fpl* Scilly.
scintillating ['sɪntɪleɪtɪŋ] *adj* scintillant(e), étincelant(e); (*wit etc*) brillant(e).
scissors ['sɪzəz] *npl* ciseaux *mpl*; **a pair of ~** une paire de ciseaux.
sclerosis [sklɪ'rəusɪs] *n* sclérose *f*.
scoff [skɔf] *vt* (*BRIT col*: *eat*) avaler, bouffer ♦ *vi*: **to ~ (at)** (*mock*) se moquer (de).
scold [skəuld] *vt* gronder, attraper, réprimander.
scolding ['skəuldɪŋ] *n* réprimande *f*.
scone [skɔn] *n sorte de petit pain rond au lait*.
scoop [sku:p] *n* pelle *f* (à main); (*for ice cream*) boule *f* à glace; (*PRESS*) reportage exclusif *or* à sensation.
►**scoop out** *vt* évider, creuser.
►**scoop up** *vt* ramasser.
scooter ['sku:tə*] *n* (*motor cycle*) scooter *m*; (*toy*) trottinette *f*.
scope [skəup] *n* (*capacity: of plan, undertaking*) portée *f*, envergure *f*; (*: of person*) compétence *f*, capacités *fpl*; (*opportunity*) possibilités *fpl*; **within the ~ of** dans les limites de; **there is plenty of ~ for improvement** (*BRIT*) cela pourrait être beaucoup mieux.
scorch [skɔ:tʃ] *vt* (*clothes*) brûler (légèrement), roussir; (*earth, grass*) dessécher, brûler.
scorched earth policy ['skɔ:tʃt-] *n* politique *f* de la terre brûlée.
scorcher ['skɔ:tʃə*] *n* (*col*: *hot day*) journée *f* torride.
scorching ['skɔ:tʃɪŋ] *adj* torride, brûlant(e).
score [skɔ:*] *n* score *m*, décompte *m* des points; (*MUS*) partition *f*; (*twenty*) vingt ♦ *vt* (*goal, point*) marquer; (*success*) remporter; (*cut: leather, wood, card*) entailler, inciser ♦ *vi* marquer des points; (*FOOTBALL*) marquer un but; (*keep score*) compter les points; **on that ~** sur ce chapitre, à cet égard; **to have an old ~ to settle with sb** (*fig*) avoir un (vieux) compte à régler avec qn; **~s of** (*fig*) des tas de; **to ~ well/6 out of 10** obtenir un bon résultat/6 sur 10.
►**score out** *vt* rayer, barrer, biffer.
scoreboard ['skɔ:bɔ:d] *n* tableau *m*.
scorecard ['skɔ:kɑ:d] *n* (*SPORT*) carton *m*, feuille *f* de marque.
scoreline ['skɔ:laɪn] *n* (*SPORT*) score *m*.
scorer ['skɔ:rə*] *n* (*FOOTBALL*) auteur *m* du but; buteur *m*; (*keeping score*) marqueur *m*.
scorn [skɔ:n] *n* mépris *m*, dédain *m* ♦ *vt* mépriser, dédaigner.
scornful ['skɔ:nful] *adj* méprisant(e), dédaigneux(euse).
Scorpio ['skɔ:pɪəu] *n* le Scorpion; **to be ~** être du Scorpion.
scorpion ['skɔ:pɪən] *n* scorpion *m*.
Scot [skɔt] *n* Écossais/e.
Scotch [skɔtʃ] *n* whisky *m*, scotch *m*.
scotch [skɔtʃ] *vt* faire échouer; enrayer; étouffer.
Scotch tape *n* ® scotch *m* ®, ruban adhésif.
scot-free ['skɔt'fri:] *adj*: **to get off ~** s'en tirer sans être puni(e); s'en sortir indemne.
Scotland ['skɔtlənd] *n* Écosse *f*.
Scots [skɔts] *adj* écossais(e).
Scotsman ['skɔtsmən] *n* Écossais *m*.
Scotswoman ['skɔtswumən] *n* Écossaise *f*.
Scottish ['skɔtɪʃ] *adj* écossais(e); **the ~ National Party** le parti national écossais.
Scottish Parliament *n* Parlement *m* écossais.
scoundrel ['skaundrl] *n* vaurien *m*.
scour ['skauə*] *vt* (*clean*) récurer; frotter; décaper; (*search*) battre, parcourir.
scourer ['skauərə*] *n* tampon abrasif *or* à récurer; (*powder*) poudre *f* à récurer.
scourge [skə:dʒ] *n* fléau *m*.
scouring pad ['skauərɪŋ-] *n* tampon abrasif *or* à récurer.

scout [skaut] *n* (*MIL*) éclaireur *m*; (*also*: **boy ~**) scout *m*.
►scout around *vi* chercher.
scowl [skaul] *vi* se renfrogner, avoir l'air maussade; **to ~ at** regarder de travers.
scrabble ['skræbl] *vi* (*claw*): **to ~ (at)** gratter; **to ~ about** *or* **around for sth** chercher qch à tâtons ♦ *n*: **S~** ® Scrabble *m* ®.
scraggy ['skrægɪ] *adj* décharné(e), efflanqué(e), famélique.
scram [skræm] *vi* (*col*) ficher le camp.
scramble ['skræmbl] *n* bousculade *f*, ruée *f* ♦ *vi* avancer tant bien que mal (à quatre pattes *or* en grimpant); **to ~ for** se bousculer *or* se disputer pour (avoir); **to go scrambling** (*SPORT*) faire du trial.
scrambled eggs ['skræmbld-] *npl* œufs brouillés.
scrap [skræp] *n* bout *m*, morceau *m*; (*fight*) bagarre *f*; (*also*: **~ iron**) ferraille *f* ♦ *vt* jeter, mettre au rebut; (*fig*) abandonner, laisser tomber; **~s** *npl* (*waste*) déchets *mpl*; **to sell sth for ~** vendre qch à la casse *or* à la ferraille.
scrapbook ['skræpbuk] *n* album *m*.
scrap dealer *n* marchand *m* de ferraille.
scrape [skreɪp] *vt*, *vi* gratter, racler ♦ *n*: **to get into a ~** s'attirer des ennuis.
►scrape through *vi* (*in exam etc*) réussir de justesse.
scraper ['skreɪpə*] *n* grattoir *m*, racloir *m*.
scrap heap *n* tas *m* de ferraille; (*fig*): **on the ~** au rancart *or* rebut.
scrap merchant *n* (*BRIT*) marchand *m* de ferraille.
scrap metal *n* ferraille *f*.
scrap paper *n* papier *m* brouillon.
scrappy ['skræpɪ] *adj* fragmentaire, décousu(e).
scrap yard *n* parc *m* à ferrailles; (*for cars*) cimetière *m* de voitures.
scratch [skrætʃ] *n* égratignure *f*, rayure *f*; éraflure *f*; (*from claw*) coup *m* de griffe ♦ *adj*: **~ team** équipe de fortune *or* improvisée ♦ *vt* (*record*) rayer; (*paint etc*) érafler; (*with claw, nail*) griffer; (*COMPUT*) effacer ♦ *vi* (se) gratter; **to start from ~** partir de zéro; **to be up to ~** être à la hauteur.
scrawl [skrɔːl] *n* gribouillage *m* ♦ *vi* gribouiller.
scrawny ['skrɔːnɪ] *adj* décharné(e).
scream [skriːm] *n* cri perçant, hurlement *m* ♦ *vi* crier, hurler; **to be a ~** (*col*) être impayable; **to ~ at sb to do sth** crier *or* hurler à qn de faire qch.
scree [skriː] *n* éboulis *m*.
screech [skriːtʃ] *n* cri strident, hurlement *m*; (*of tyres, brakes*) crissement *m*, grincement *m* ♦ *vi* hurler; crisser, grincer.
screen [skriːn] *n* écran *m*, paravent *m*; (*CINE, TV*) écran; (*fig*) écran, rideau *m* ♦ *vt* masquer, cacher; (*from the wind etc*) abriter, protéger; (*film*) projeter; (*candidates etc*) filtrer; (*for illness*): **to ~ sb for sth** faire subir un test de dépistage de qch à qn.
screen editing [-'ɛdɪtɪŋ] *n* (*COMPUT*) édition *f* *or* correction *f* sur écran.
screening ['skriːnɪŋ] *n* (*of film*) projection *f*; (*MED*) test *m* (*or* tests) de dépistage; (*for security*) filtrage *m*.
screen memory *n* (*COMPUT*) mémoire *f* écran.
screenplay ['skriːnpleɪ] *n* scénario *m*.
screen saver *n* (*COMPUT*) économiseur *m* d'écran.
screen test *n* bout *m* d'essai.
screw [skruː] *n* vis *f*; (*propeller*) hélice *f* ♦ *vt* visser; (*col!*: *woman*) baiser (*!*); **to ~ sth to the wall** visser qch au mur; **to have one's head ~ed on** (*fig*) avoir la tête sur les épaules.
►screw up *vt* (*paper, material*) froisser; (*col*: *ruin*) bousiller; **to ~ up one's face** faire la grimace.
screwdriver ['skruːdraɪvə*] *n* tournevis *m*.
screwed-up ['skruːd'ʌp] *adj* (*col*): **to be ~** être paumé(e).
screwy ['skruːɪ] *adj* (*col*) dingue, cinglé(e).
scribble ['skrɪbl] *n* gribouillage *m* ♦ *vt* gribouiller, griffonner; **to ~ sth down** griffonner qch.
scribe [skraɪb] *n* scribe *m*.
script [skrɪpt] *n* (*CINE etc*) scénario *m*, texte *m*; (*in exam*) copie *f*; (*writing*) (écriture *f*) script *m*.
Scripture ['skrɪptʃə*] *n* Écriture sainte.
scriptwriter ['skrɪptraɪtə*] *n* scénariste *m/f*, dialoguiste *m/f*.
scroll [skrəul] *n* rouleau *m* ♦ *vt* (*COMPUT*) faire défiler (sur l'écran).
scrotum ['skrəutəm] *n* scrotum *m*.
scrounge [skraundʒ] (*col*) *vt*: **to ~ sth (off** *or* **from sb)** se faire payer qch (par qn), emprunter qch (à qn) ♦ *vi*: **to ~ on sb** vivre aux crochets de qn.
scrounger ['skraundʒə*] *n* parasite *m*.
scrub [skrʌb] *n* (*clean*) nettoyage *m* (à la brosse); (*land*) broussailles *fpl* ♦ *vt* (*floor*) nettoyer à la brosse; (*pan*) récurer; (*washing*) frotter; (*reject*) annuler.
scrubbing brush ['skrʌbɪŋ-] *n* brosse dure.
scruff [skrʌf] *n*: **by the ~ of the neck** par la peau du cou.
scruffy ['skrʌfɪ] *adj* débraillé(e).
scrum(mage) ['skrʌm(ɪdʒ)] *n* mêlée *f*.
scruple ['skruːpl] *n* scrupule *m*; **to have no ~s about doing sth** n'avoir aucun scrupule à faire qch.
scrupulous ['skruːpjuləs] *adj* scrupuleux(euse).
scrupulously ['skruːpjuləslɪ] *adv* scrupuleusement; **to be ~ honest** être d'une honnêteté scrupuleuse.
scrutinize ['skruːtɪnaɪz] *vt* scruter, examiner

minutieusement.
scrutiny ['skru:tɪnɪ] *n* examen minutieux; **under the ~ of sb** sous la surveillance de qn.
scuba ['sku:bə] *n* scaphandre *m* (autonome).
scuba diving *n* plongée sous-marine (autonome).
scuff [skʌf] *vt* érafler.
scuffle ['skʌfl] *n* échauffourée *f*, rixe *f*.
scull [skʌl] *n* aviron *m*.
scullery ['skʌlərɪ] *n* arrière-cuisine *f*.
sculptor ['skʌlptə*] *n* sculpteur *m*.
sculpture ['skʌlptʃə*] *n* sculpture *f*.
scum [skʌm] *n* écume *f*, mousse *f*; (*pej*: *people*) rebut *m*, lie *f*.
scupper ['skʌpə*] *vt* (*BRIT*) saborder.
scurrilous ['skʌrɪləs] *adj* haineux(euse), virulent(e); calomnieux(euse).
scurry ['skʌrɪ] *vi* filer à toute allure; **to ~ off** détaler, se sauver.
scurvy ['skə:vɪ] *n* scorbut *m*.
scuttle ['skʌtl] *n* (*NAUT*) écoutille *f*; (*also*: **coal ~**) seau *m* (à charbon) ♦ *vt* (*ship*) saborder ♦ *vi* (*scamper*): **to ~ away, ~ off** détaler.
scythe [saɪð] *n* faux *f*.
SD, S. Dak. *abbr* (*US*) = *South Dakota*.
SDI *n abbr* (= *Strategic Defense Initiative*) IDS *f*.
SDLP *n abbr* (*BRIT POL*) = *Social Democratic and Labour Party*.
SDP *n abbr* (*BRIT POL*) = *Social Democratic Party*.
sea [si:] *n* mer *f* ♦ *cpd* marin(e), de (la) mer, maritime; **on the ~** (*boat*) en mer; (*town*) au bord de la mer; **by** *or* **beside the ~** (*holiday*) au bord de la mer; (*village*) près de la mer; **by ~** par mer, en bateau; **out to ~** au large; **(out) at ~** en mer; **heavy** *or* **rough ~(s)** grosse mer, mer agitée; **a ~ of faces** (*fig*) une multitude de visages; **to be all at ~** (*fig*) nager complètement.
sea bed *n* fond *m* de la mer.
sea bird *n* oiseau *m* de mer.
seaboard ['si:bɔ:d] *n* côte *f*.
sea breeze *n* brise *f* de mer.
seafarer ['si:fɛərə*] *n* marin *m*.
seafaring ['si:fɛərɪŋ] *adj* (*life*) de marin; **~ people** les gens *mpl* de mer.
seafood ['si:fu:d] *n* fruits *mpl* de mer.
sea front *n* bord *m* de mer.
seagoing ['si:gəuɪŋ] *adj* (*ship*) de haute mer.
seagull ['si:gʌl] *n* mouette *f*.
seal [si:l] *n* (*animal*) phoque *m*; (*stamp*) sceau *m*, cachet *m*; (*impression*) cachet, estampille *f* ♦ *vt* sceller; (*envelope*) coller; (*: with seal*) cacheter; (*decide: sb's fate*) décider (de); (*: bargain*) conclure; **~ of approval** approbation *f*.
►**seal off** *vt* (*close*) condamner; (*forbid entry to*) interdire l'accès de.
sea level *n* niveau *m* de la mer.
sealing wax ['si:lɪŋ-] *n* cire *f* à cacheter.
sea lion *n* lion *m* de mer.
sealskin ['si:lskɪn] *n* peau *f* de phoque.
seam [si:m] *n* couture *f*; (*of coal*) veine *f*, filon *m*; **the hall was bursting at the ~s** la salle était pleine à craquer.
seaman ['si:mən] *n* marin *m*.
seamanship ['si:mənʃɪp] *n* qualités *fpl* de marin.
seamless ['si:mlɪs] *adj* sans couture(s).
seamy ['si:mɪ] *adj* louche, mal famé(e).
seance ['seɪɔns] *n* séance *f* de spiritisme.
seaplane ['si:pleɪn] *n* hydravion *m*.
seaport ['si:pɔ:t] *n* port *m* de mer.
search [sə:tʃ] *n* (*for person, thing*) recherche(s) *f(pl)*; (*of drawer, pockets*) fouille *f*; (*LAW*: *at sb's home*) perquisition *f* ♦ *vt* fouiller; (*examine*) examiner minutieusement; scruter ♦ *vi*: **to ~ for** chercher; **in ~ of** à la recherche de; **"~ and replace"** (*COMPUT*) "rechercher et remplacer".
►**search through** *vt fus* fouiller.
searcher ['sə:tʃə*] *n* chercheur/euse.
searching ['sə:tʃɪŋ] *adj* (*look, question*) pénétrant(e); (*examination*) minutieux(euse).
searchlight ['sə:tʃlaɪt] *n* projecteur *m*.
search party *n* expédition *f* de secours.
search warrant *n* mandat *m* de perquisition.
searing ['sɪərɪŋ] *adj* (*heat*) brûlant(e); (*pain*) aigu(ë).
seashore ['si:ʃɔ:*] *n* rivage *m*, plage *f*, bord *m* de (la) mer; **on the ~** sur le rivage.
seasick ['si:sɪk] *adj*: **to be ~** avoir le mal de mer.
seaside ['si:saɪd] *n* bord *m* de la mer.
seaside resort *n* station *f* balnéaire.
season ['si:zn] *n* saison *f* ♦ *vt* assaisonner, relever; **to be in/out of ~** être/ne pas être de saison; **the busy ~** (*for shops*) la période de pointe; (*for hotels etc*) la pleine saison; **the open ~** (*HUNTING*) la saison de la chasse.
seasonal ['si:znl] *adj* saisonnier(ière).
seasoned ['si:znd] *adj* (*wood*) séché(e); (*fig: worker, actor, troops*) expérimenté(e); **a ~ campaigner** un vieux militant, un vétéran.
seasoning ['si:znɪŋ] *n* assaisonnement *m*.
season ticket *n* carte *f* d'abonnement.
seat [si:t] *n* siège *m*; (*in bus, train: place*) place *f*; (*PARLIAMENT*) siège; (*buttocks*) postérieur *m*; (*of trousers*) fond *m* ♦ *vt* faire asseoir, placer; (*have room for*) avoir des places assises pour, pouvoir accueillir; **are there any ~s left?** est-ce qu'il reste des places?; **to take one's ~** prendre place; **to be ~ed** être assis; **please be ~ed** veuillez vous asseoir.
seat belt *n* ceinture *f* de sécurité.
seating capacity ['si:tɪŋ-] *n* nombre *m* de places assises.
SEATO ['si:təu] *n abbr* (= *Southeast Asia Treaty Organization*) OTASE *f* (= *Organisation du traité de l'Asie du Sud-Est*).
sea urchin *n* oursin *m*.
sea water *n* eau *f* de mer.
seaweed ['si:wi:d] *n* algues *fpl*.
seaworthy ['si:wə:ðɪ] *adj* en état de naviguer.
SEC *n abbr* (*US*: = *Securities and Exchange*

Commission) ≈ COB *f* (= *Commission des opérations de Bourse*).

sec. *abbr* (= *second*) sec.

secateurs [sɛkə'təːz] *npl* sécateur *m*.

secede [sɪ'siːd] *vi* faire sécession.

secluded [sɪ'kluːdɪd] *adj* retiré(e), à l'écart.

seclusion [sɪ'kluːʒən] *n* solitude *f*.

second[1] ['sɛkənd] *num* deuxième, second(e) ♦ *adv* (*in race etc*) en seconde position ♦ *n* (*unit of time*) seconde *f*; (*in series, position*) deuxième *m/f*, second/e; (*BRIT SCOL*) ≈ licence *f* avec mention bien *or* assez bien; (*AUT*: *also*: ~ **gear**) seconde *f*; (*COMM*: *imperfect*) article *m* de second choix ♦ *vt* (*motion*) appuyer; **Charles the S~** Charles II; **just a ~!** une seconde!, un instant!; (*stopping sb*) pas si vite!; ~ **floor** (*BRIT*) deuxième (étage) *m*; (*US*) premier (étage) *m*; **to ask for a ~ opinion** (*MED*) demander l'avis d'un autre médecin; **to have ~ thoughts (about doing sth)** changer d'avis (à propos de faire qch); **on ~ thoughts** *or* (*US*) **thought** à la réflexion.

second[2] [sɪ'kɔnd] *vt* (*employee*) détacher, mettre en détachement.

secondary ['sɛkəndərɪ] *adj* secondaire.

secondary school *n* collège *m*, lycée *m*; *voir encadré*.

> **SECONDARY SCHOOL**
>
> *Une* **secondary school** *est un établissement d'enseignement pour les élèves de 11 à 18 ans, certains d'entre eux pouvant décider d'arrêter leurs études à 16 ans. La plupart de ces écoles sont des "comprehensive schools" sans examen d'entrée; mais certaines sont encore à recrutement sélectif;* voir *"primary school".*

second-best [sɛkənd'bɛst] *n* deuxième choix *m*; **as a ~** faute de mieux.

second-class ['sɛkənd'klɑːs] *adj* de deuxième classe ♦ *adv*: **to send sth ~** envoyer qch à tarif réduit; **to travel ~** voyager en seconde; ~ **citizen** citoyen/ne de deuxième classe.

second cousin *n* cousin/e issu(e) de germains.

seconder ['sɛkəndə*] *n* personne *f* qui appuie une motion.

second-guess ['sɛkənd'gɛs] *vt* (*predict*) (essayer d')anticiper; **they're still trying to ~ his motives** ils essaient toujours de comprendre ses raisons.

second hand *n* (*on clock*) trotteuse *f*.

secondhand ['sɛkənd'hænd] *adj* d'occasion ♦ *adv* (*buy*) d'occasion; **to hear sth ~** apprendre qch indirectement.

second-in-command ['sɛkəndɪnkə'mɑːnd] *n* (*MIL*) commandant *m* en second; (*ADMIN*) adjoint/e, sous-chef *m*.

secondly ['sɛkəndlɪ] *adv* deuxièmement; **firstly ... ~ ...** d'abord ... ensuite ... *or* de plus ...

secondment [sɪ'kɔndmənt] *n* (*BRIT*) détachement *m*.

second-rate ['sɛkənd'reɪt] *adj* de deuxième ordre, de qualité inférieure.

secrecy ['siːkrəsɪ] *n* secret *m*; **in ~** en secret.

secret ['siːkrɪt] *adj* secret(ète) ♦ *n* secret *m*; **in ~** *adv* en secret, secrètement, en cachette; **to keep sth ~ from sb** cacher qch à qn, ne pas révéler qch à qn; **keep it ~** n'en parle à personne; **to make no ~ of sth** ne pas cacher qch.

secret agent *n* agent secret.

secretarial [sɛkrɪ'tɛərɪəl] *adj* de secrétaire, de secrétariat.

secretariat [sɛkrɪ'tɛərɪət] *n* secrétariat *m*.

secretary ['sɛkrətrɪ] *n* secrétaire *m/f*; (*COMM*) secrétaire général; **S~ of State** (*US POL*) ≈ ministre *m* des Affaires étrangères; **S~ of State (for)** (*BRIT POL*) ministre *m* (de).

secretary-general ['sɛkrətrɪ'dʒɛnərl] *n* secrétaire général.

secrete [sɪ'kriːt] *vt* (*ANAT, BIOL, MED*) sécréter; (*hide*) cacher.

secretion [sɪ'kriːʃən] *n* sécrétion *f*.

secretive ['siːkrətɪv] *adj* réservé(e); (*pej*) cachottier(ière), dissimulé(e).

secretly ['siːkrɪtlɪ] *adv* en secret, secrètement, en cachette.

secret police *n* police secrète.

secret service *n* services secrets.

sect [sɛkt] *n* secte *f*.

sectarian [sɛk'tɛərɪən] *adj* sectaire.

section ['sɛkʃən] *n* coupe *f*, section *f*; (*department*) section; (*COMM*) rayon *m*; (*of document*) section, article *m*, paragraphe *m* ♦ *vt* sectionner; **the business** *etc* ~ (*PRESS*) la page des affaires *etc*.

sectional ['sɛkʃənl] *adj* (*drawing*) en coupe.

sector ['sɛktə*] *n* secteur *m*.

secular ['sɛkjulə*] *adj* profane; laïque; séculier(ière).

secure [sɪ'kjuə*] *adj* (*free from anxiety*) sans inquiétude, sécurisé(e); (*firmly fixed*) solide, bien attaché(e) (*or* fermé(e) *etc*); (*in safe place*) en lieu sûr, en sûreté ♦ *vt* (*fix*) fixer, attacher; (*get*) obtenir, se procurer; (*COMM*: *loan*) garantir; **to make sth ~** bien fixer *or* attacher qch; **to ~ sth for sb** obtenir qch pour qn, procurer qch à qn.

secured creditor [sɪ'kjuəd-] *n* créancier/ière privilégié(e).

security [sɪ'kjuərɪtɪ] *n* sécurité *f*, mesures *fpl* de sécurité; (*for loan*) caution *f*, garantie *f*; **securities** *npl* (*STOCK EXCHANGE*) valeurs *fpl*, titres *mpl*; **to increase** *or* **tighten ~** renforcer les mesures de sécurité; ~ **of tenure** stabilité *f* d'un emploi, titularisation *f*.

Security Council *n*: **the ~** le Conseil de sécurité.

security forces *npl* forces *fpl* de sécurité.

security guard *n* garde chargé de la sécurité; (*transporting money*) convoyeur *m* de fonds.

security risk *n* menace *f* pour la sécurité de l'état (*or* d'une entreprise *etc*).
secy *abbr* (= *secretary*) secr.
sedan [sə'dæn] *n* (*US AUT*) berline *f*.
sedate [sɪ'deɪt] *adj* calme; posé(e) ♦ *vt* donner des sédatifs à.
sedation [sɪ'deɪʃən] *n* (*MED*) sédation *f*; **to be under ~** être sous calmants.
sedative ['sɛdɪtɪv] *n* calmant *m*, sédatif *m*.
sedentary ['sɛdntrɪ] *adj* sédentaire.
sediment ['sɛdɪmənt] *n* sédiment *m*, dépôt *m*.
sedition [sɪ'dɪʃən] *n* sédition *f*.
seduce [sɪ'djuːs] *vt* séduire.
seduction [sɪ'dʌkʃən] *n* séduction *f*.
seductive [sɪ'dʌktɪv] *adj* séduisant(e), séducteur(trice).
see [siː] *vb* (*pt* **saw**, *pp* **seen** [sɔː, siːn]) *vt* (*gen*) voir; (*accompany*): **to ~ sb to the door** reconduire *or* raccompagner qn jusqu'à la porte ♦ *vi* voir ♦ *n* évêché *m*; **to ~ that** (*ensure*) veiller à ce que + *sub*, faire en sorte que + *sub*, s'assurer que; **there was nobody to be ~n** il n'y avait pas un chat; **let me ~** (*show me*) fais(-moi) voir; (*let me think*) voyons (un peu); **to go and ~ sb** aller voir qn; **~ for yourself** voyez vous-même; **I don't know what she ~s in him** je ne sais pas ce qu'elle lui trouve; **as far as I can ~** pour autant que je puisse en juger; **~ you!** au revoir!, à bientôt!; **~ you soon/later/tomorrow!** à bientôt/plus tard/demain!
►**see about** *vt fus* (*deal with*) s'occuper de.
►**see off** *vt* accompagner (à la gare *or* à l'aéroport *etc*).
►**see through** *vt* mener à bonne fin ♦ *vt fus* voir clair dans.
►**see to** *vt fus* s'occuper de, se charger de.
seed [siːd] *n* graine *f*; (*fig*) germe *m*; (*TENNIS etc*) tête *f* de série; **to go to ~** monter en graine; (*fig*) se laisser aller.
seedless ['siːdlɪs] *adj* sans pépins.
seedling ['siːdlɪŋ] *n* jeune plant *m*, semis *m*.
seedy ['siːdɪ] *adj* (*shabby*) minable, miteux(euse).
seeing ['siːɪŋ] *conj*: **~ (that)** vu que, étant donné que.
seek, *pt, pp* **sought** [siːk, sɔːt] *vt* chercher, rechercher; **to ~ advice/help from sb** demander conseil/de l'aide à qn.
►**seek out** *vt* (*person*) chercher.
seem [siːm] *vi* sembler, paraître; **there ~s to be** ... il semble qu'il y a ..., on dirait qu'il y a ...; **it ~s (that)** ... il semble que ...; **what ~s to be the trouble?** qu'est-ce qui ne va pas?
seemingly ['siːmɪŋlɪ] *adv* apparemment.
seen [siːn] *pp of* **see**.
seep [siːp] *vi* suinter, filtrer.
seer [sɪə*] *n* prophète/prophétesse, voyant/e.
seersucker ['sɪəsʌkə*] *n* cloqué *m*, étoffe cloquée.
seesaw ['siːsɔː] *n* (jeu *m* de) bascule *f*.
seethe [siːð] *vi* être en effervescence; **to ~ with anger** bouillir de colère.
see-through ['siːθruː] *adj* transparent(e).
segment ['sɛgmənt] *n* segment *m*.
segregate ['sɛgrɪgeɪt] *vt* séparer, isoler.
segregation [sɛgrɪ'geɪʃən] *n* ségrégation *f*.
Seine [seɪn] *n*: **the ~** la Seine.
seismic ['saɪzmɪk] *adj* sismique.
seize [siːz] *vt* (*grasp*) saisir, attraper; (*take possession of*) s'emparer de; (*LAW*) saisir.
►**seize up** *vi* (*TECH*) se gripper.
►**seize (up)on** *vt fus* saisir, sauter sur.
seizure ['siːʒə*] *n* (*MED*) crise *f*, attaque *f*; (*LAW*) saisie *f*.
seldom ['sɛldəm] *adv* rarement.
select [sɪ'lɛkt] *adj* choisi(e), d'élite; (*hotel, restaurant, club*) chic *inv*, sélect *inv* ♦ *vt* sélectionner, choisir; **a ~ few** quelques privilégiés.
selection [sɪ'lɛkʃən] *n* sélection *f*, choix *m*.
selection committee *n* comité *m* de sélection.
selective [sɪ'lɛktɪv] *adj* sélectif(ive); (*school*) à recrutement sélectif.
selector [sɪ'lɛktə*] *n* (*person*) sélectionneur/euse; (*TECH*) sélecteur *m*.
self [sɛlf] *n* (*pl* **selves** [sɛlvz]): **the ~** le moi *inv* ♦ *prefix* auto-.
self-addressed ['sɛlfə'drɛst] *adj*: **~ envelope** enveloppe *f* à mon (*or* votre *etc*) nom.
self-adhesive [sɛlfəd'hiːzɪv] *adj* autocollant(e).
self-assertive [sɛlfə'səːtɪv] *adj* autoritaire.
self-assurance [sɛlfə'ʃuərəns] *n* assurance *f*.
self-assured [sɛlfə'ʃuəd] *adj* sûr(e) de soi, plein(e) d'assurance.
self-catering [sɛlf'keɪtərɪŋ] *adj* (*BRIT*: *flat*) avec cuisine, où l'on peut faire sa cuisine; (: *holiday*) en appartement (*or* chalet *etc*) loué.
self-centred, (*US*) **self-centered** [sɛlf'sɛntəd] *adj* égocentrique.
self-cleaning [sɛlf'kliːnɪŋ] *adj* autonettoyant(e).
self-confessed [sɛlfkən'fɛst] *adj* (*alcoholic etc*) déclaré(e), qui ne s'en cache pas.
self-confidence [sɛlf'kɔnfɪdns] *n* confiance *f* en soi.
self-conscious [sɛlf'kɔnʃəs] *adj* timide, qui manque d'assurance.
self-contained [sɛlfkən'teɪnd] *adj* (*BRIT*: *flat*) avec entrée particulière, indépendant(e).
self-control [sɛlfkən'trəul] *n* maîtrise *f* de soi.
self-defeating [sɛlfdɪ'fiːtɪŋ] *adj* qui a un effet contraire à l'effet recherché.
self-defence, (*US*) **self-defense** [sɛlfdɪ'fɛns] *n* légitime défense *f*.
self-discipline [sɛlf'dɪsɪplɪn] *n* discipline personnelle.
self-employed [sɛlfɪm'plɔɪd] *adj* qui travaille à son compte.
self-esteem [sɛlfɪ'stiːm] *n* amour-propre *m*.
self-evident [sɛlf'ɛvɪdnt] *adj* évident(e), qui va de soi.
self-explanatory [sɛlfɪk'splænətrɪ] *adj* qui se

passe d'explication.
self-governing [sɛlf'gʌvənɪŋ] *adj* autonome.
self-help ['sɛlf'hɛlp] *n* initiative personnelle, efforts personnels.
self-importance [sɛlfɪm'pɔːtns] suffisance *f*.
self-indulgent [sɛlfɪn'dʌldʒənt] *adj* qui ne se refuse rien.
self-inflicted [sɛlfɪn'flɪktɪd] *adj* volontaire.
self-interest [sɛlf'ɪntrɪst] *n* intérêt personnel.
selfish ['sɛlfɪʃ] *adj* égoïste.
selfishness ['sɛlfɪʃnɪs] *n* égoïsme *m*.
selfless ['sɛlflɪs] *adj* désintéressé(e).
selflessly ['sɛlflɪslɪ] *adv* sans penser à soi.
self-made man ['sɛlfmeɪd-] *n* self-made man *m*.
self-pity [sɛlf'pɪtɪ] *n* apitoiement *m* sur soi-même.
self-portrait [sɛlf'pɔːtreɪt] *n* autoportrait *m*.
self-possessed [sɛlfpə'zɛst] *adj* assuré(e).
self-preservation ['sɛlfprɛzə'veɪʃən] *n* instinct *m* de conservation.
self-raising [sɛlf'reɪzɪŋ], (*US*) **self-rising** [sɛlf'raɪzɪŋ] *adj*: ~ **flour** farine *f* pour gâteaux (*avec levure incorporée*).
self-reliant [sɛlfrɪ'laɪənt] *adj* indépendant(e).
self-respect [sɛlfrɪs'pɛkt] *n* respect *m* de soi.
self-respecting [sɛlfrɪs'pɛktɪŋ] *adj* qui se respecte.
self-righteous [sɛlf'raɪtʃəs] *adj* satisfait(e) de soi, pharisaïque.
self-rising [sɛlf'raɪzɪŋ] *adj* (*US*) = **self-raising**.
self-sacrifice [sɛlf'sækrɪfaɪs] *n* abnégation *f*.
self-same ['sɛlfseɪm] *adj* même.
self-satisfied [sɛlf'sætɪsfaɪd] *adj* content(e) de soi, suffisant(e).
self-sealing [sɛlf'siːlɪŋ] *adj* (*envelope*) autocollant(e).
self-service [sɛlf'səːvɪs] *adj*, *n* libre-service (*m*), self-service (*m*).
self-styled ['sɛlfstaɪld] *adj* soi-disant *inv*.
self-sufficient [sɛlfsə'fɪʃənt] *adj* indépendant(e).
self-supporting [sɛlfsə'pɔːtɪŋ] *adj* financièrement indépendant(e).
self-tanning ['sɛlf'tænɪŋ] *adj*: ~ **cream**, ~ **lotion** autobronzant *m*.
self-taught [sɛlf'tɔːt] *adj* autodidacte.
sell, *pt*, *pp* **sold** [sɛl, səuld] *vt* vendre ♦ *vi* se vendre; **to** ~ **at** *or* **for 10 €** se vendre €10; **to** ~ **sb an idea** (*fig*) faire accepter une idée à qn.
►**sell off** *vt* liquider.
►**sell out** *vi*: **to** ~ **out (to)** (*COMM*) vendre son fonds *or* son affaire (à) ♦ *vt* vendre tout son stock de; **the tickets are all sold out** il ne reste plus de billets.
►**sell up** *vi* vendre son fonds *or* son affaire.
sell-by date ['sɛlbaɪ-] *n* date *f* limite de vente.
seller ['sɛlə*] *n* vendeur/euse, marchand/e; ~**'s market** marché *m* à la hausse.
selling price ['sɛlɪŋ-] *n* prix *m* de vente.
Sellotape ['sɛləuteɪp] *n* ® (*BRIT*) papier collant, scotch *m* ®.
sellout ['sɛlaut] *n* trahison *f*, capitulation *f*; (*of tickets*): **it was a** ~ tous les billets ont été vendus.
selves [sɛlvz] *npl of* **self**.
semantic [sɪ'mæntɪk] *adj* sémantique.
semantics [sɪ'mæntɪks] *n* sémantique *f*.
semaphore ['sɛməfɔː*] *n* signaux *mpl* à bras; (*RAIL*) sémaphore *m*.
semblance ['sɛmblns] *n* semblant *m*.
semen ['siːmən] *n* sperme *m*.
semester [sɪ'mɛstə*] *n* (*esp US*) semestre *m*.
semi... ['sɛmɪ] *prefix* semi-, demi-; à demi, à moitié ♦ *n*: **semi** = **semidetached (house)**.
semi-breve ['sɛmɪbriːv] *n* (*BRIT*) ronde *f*.
semicircle ['sɛmɪsəːkl] *n* demi-cercle *m*.
semicircular ['sɛmɪ'səːkjulə*] *adj* en demi-cercle, semi-circulaire.
semicolon [sɛmɪ'kəulən] *n* point-virgule *m*.
semiconductor [sɛmɪkən'dʌktə*] *n* semi-conducteur *m*.
semiconscious [sɛmɪ'kɔnʃəs] *adj* à demi conscient(e).
semidetached (house) [sɛmɪdɪ'tætʃt-] *n* (*BRIT*) maison jumelée *or* jumelle.
semifinal [sɛmɪ'faɪnl] *n* demi-finale *f*.
seminar ['sɛmɪnɑː*] *n* séminaire *m*.
seminary ['sɛmɪnərɪ] *n* (*REL*) séminaire *m*.
semiprecious [sɛmɪ'prɛʃəs] *adj* semi-précieux(euse).
semiquaver ['sɛmɪkweɪvə*] *n* (*BRIT*) double croche *f*.
semiskilled [sɛmɪ'skɪld] *adj*: ~ **worker** ouvrier/ière spécialisé(e).
semi-skimmed ['sɛmɪ'skɪmd] *adj* demi-écrémé(e).
semitone ['sɛmɪtəun] *n* (*MUS*) demi-ton *m*.
semolina [sɛmə'liːnə] *n* semoule *f*.
SEN *n abbr* (*BRIT*) = *State Enrolled Nurse*.
Sen., sen. *abbr* = **senator, senior**.
senate ['sɛnɪt] *n* sénat *m*; (*US*): **the S**~ le Sénat; *voir encadré*.

SENATE

Le **Senate** *est la chambre haute du "Congress", le parlement des États-Unis. Il est composé de 100 sénateurs, 2 par État, élus au suffrage universel direct tous les 6 ans, un tiers d'entre eux étant renouvelé tous les 2 ans.*

senator ['sɛnɪtə*] *n* sénateur *m*.
send, *pt*, *pp* **sent** [sɛnd, sɛnt] *vt* envoyer; **to** ~ **by post** *or* (*US*) **mail** envoyer *or* expédier par la poste; **to** ~ **sb for sth** envoyer qn chercher qch; **to** ~ **word that ...** faire dire que ...; **she** ~**s (you) her love** elle vous adresse ses amitiés; **to** ~ **sb to Coventry** (*BRIT*) mettre qn en quarantaine; **to** ~ **sb to sleep** endormir qn; **to** ~ **sb into fits of laughter** faire rire qn aux éclats; **to** ~ **sth flying** envoyer valser qch.
►**send away** *vt* (*letter, goods*) envoyer, expé-

dier.
►**send away for** *vt fus* commander par correspondance, se faire envoyer.
►**send back** *vt* renvoyer.
►**send for** *vt fus* envoyer chercher; faire venir; (*by post*) se faire envoyer, commander par correspondance.
►**send in** *vt* (*report, application, resignation*) remettre.
►**send off** *vt* (*goods*) envoyer, expédier; (*BRIT SPORT: player*) expulser *or* renvoyer du terrain.
►**send on** *vt* (*BRIT: letter*) faire suivre; (*luggage etc: in advance*) (faire) expédier à l'avance.
►**send out** *vt* (*invitation*) envoyer (par la poste); (*emit: light, heat, signals*) émettre.
►**send round** *vt* (*letter, document etc*) faire circuler.
►**send up** *vt* (*person, price*) faire monter; (*BRIT: parody*) mettre en boîte, parodier.
sender ['sɛndə*] *n* expéditeur/trice.
send-off ['sɛndɔf] *n*: **a good** ~ des adieux chaleureux.
Senegal [sɛnɪ'gɔːl] *n* Sénégal *m*.
Senegalese [sɛnɪgə'liːz] *adj* sénégalais(e) ♦ *n* (*pl inv*) Sénégalais/e.
senile ['siːnaɪl] *adj* sénile.
senility [sɪ'nɪlɪtɪ] *n* sénilité *f*.
senior ['siːnɪə*] *adj* (*older*) aîné(e), plus âgé(e); (*of higher rank*) supérieur(e) ♦ *n* aîné/e; (*in service*) personne *f* qui a plus d'ancienneté; **P. Jones** ~ P. Jones père.
senior citizen *n* personne âgée.
senior high school *n* (*US*) ≈ lycée *m*.
seniority [siːnɪ'ɔrɪtɪ] *n* priorité *f* d'âge, ancienneté *f*; (*in rank*) supériorité *f* (hiérarchique).
sensation [sɛn'seɪʃən] *n* sensation *f*; **to create a** ~ faire sensation.
sensational [sɛn'seɪʃənl] *adj* qui fait sensation; (*marvellous*) sensationnel(le).
sense [sɛns] *n* sens *m*; (*feeling*) sentiment *m*; (*meaning*) signification *f*; (*wisdom*) bon sens ♦ *vt* sentir, pressentir; ~**s** *npl* raison *f*; **it makes** ~ c'est logique; ~ **of humour** sens de l'humour; **there is no** ~ **in (doing) that** cela n'a pas de sens; **to come to one's** ~**s** (*regain consciousness*) reprendre conscience; (*become reasonable*) revenir à la raison; **to take leave of one's** ~**s** perdre la tête.
senseless ['sɛnslɪs] *adj* insensé(e), stupide; (*unconscious*) sans connaissance.
sensibility [sɛnsɪ'bɪlɪtɪ] *n* sensibilité *f*; **sensibilities** *npl* susceptibilité *f*.
sensible ['sɛnsɪbl] *adj* sensé(e), raisonnable; (*shoes etc*) pratique.
sensitive ['sɛnsɪtɪv] *adj*: ~ **(to)** sensible (à); **he is very** ~ **about it** c'est un point très sensible (chez lui).
sensitivity [sɛnsɪ'tɪvɪtɪ] *n* sensibilité *f*.
sensual ['sɛnsjuəl] *adj* sensuel(le).
sensuous ['sɛnsjuəs] *adj* voluptueux(euse), sensuel(le).
sent [sɛnt] *pt, pp of* **send**.
sentence ['sɛntns] *n* (*LING*) phrase *f*; (*LAW: judgment*) condamnation *f*, sentence *f*; (*: punishment*) peine *f* ♦ *vt*: **to** ~ **sb to death/to 5 years** condamner qn à mort/à 5 ans; **to pass** ~ **on sb** prononcer une peine contre qn.
sentiment ['sɛntɪmənt] *n* sentiment *m*; (*opinion*) opinion *f*, avis *m*.
sentimental [sɛntɪ'mɛntl] *adj* sentimental(e).
sentimentality [sɛntɪmɛn'tælɪtɪ] *n* sentimentalité *f*, sensiblerie *f*.
sentry ['sɛntrɪ] *n* sentinelle *f*, factionnaire *m*.
sentry duty *n*: **to be on** ~ être de faction.
Seoul [səul] *n* Séoul.
separable ['sɛprəbl] *adj* séparable.
separate *adj* ['sɛprɪt] séparé(e), indépendant(e), différent(e) ♦ *vb* ['sɛpəreɪt] *vt* séparer ♦ *vi* se séparer; ~ **from** distinct(e) de; **under** ~ **cover** (*COMM*) sous pli séparé; **to** ~ **into** diviser en.
separately ['sɛprɪtlɪ] *adv* séparément.
separates ['sɛprɪts] *npl* (*clothes*) coordonnés *mpl*.
separation [sɛpə'reɪʃən] *n* séparation *f*.
Sept. *abbr* (= *September*) sept.
September [sɛp'tɛmbə*] *n* septembre *m*; *for phrases see also* **July**.
septic ['sɛptɪk] *adj* septique; (*wound*) infecté(e); **to go** ~ s'infecter.
septicaemia [sɛptɪ'siːmɪə] *n* septicémie *f*.
septic tank *n* fosse *f* septique.
sequel ['siːkwl] *n* conséquence *f*; séquelles *fpl*; (*of story*) suite *f*.
sequence ['siːkwəns] *n* ordre *m*, suite *f*; **in** ~ par ordre, dans l'ordre, les uns après les autres; ~ **of tenses** concordance *f* des temps.
sequential [sɪ'kwɛnʃəl] *adj*: ~ **access** (*COMPUT*) accès séquentiel.
sequin ['siːkwɪn] *n* paillette *f*.
Serb [səːb] *adj, n* = **Serbian**.
Serbia ['səːbɪə] *n* Serbie *f*.
Serbian ['səːbɪən] *adj* serbe ♦ *n* Serbe *m/f*; (*LING*) serbe *m*.
Serbo-Croat ['səːbəu'krəuæt] *n* (*LING*) serbo-croate *m*.
serenade [sɛrə'neɪd] *n* sérénade *f* ♦ *vt* donner une sérénade à.
serene [sɪ'riːn] *adj* serein(e), calme, paisible.
serenity [sə'rɛnɪtɪ] *n* sérénité *f*, calme *m*.
sergeant ['sɑːdʒənt] *n* sergent *m*; (*POLICE*) brigadier *m*.
sergeant major *n* sergent-major *m*.
serial ['sɪərɪəl] *n* feuilleton *m* ♦ *adj* (*COMPUT: interface, printer*) série *inv*; (*: access*) séquentiel(le).
serialize ['sɪərɪəlaɪz] *vt* publier (*or* adapter) en feuilleton.
serial killer *n* meurtrier *m* tuant en série.
serial number *n* numéro *m* de série.
series ['sɪərɪz] *n* série *f*, (*PUBLISHING*) collec-

tion *f*.

serious ['sɪərɪəs] *adj* sérieux(euse); (*accident etc*) grave; **are you ~ (about it?)** parlez-vous sérieusement?

seriously ['sɪərɪəslɪ] *adv* sérieusement, gravement; **~ rich/difficult** (*col: extremely*) drôlement riche/difficile; **to take sth/sb ~** prendre qch/qn au sérieux.

seriousness ['sɪərɪəsnɪs] *n* sérieux *m*, gravité *f*.

sermon ['səːmən] *n* sermon *m*.

serrated [sɪ'reɪtɪd] *adj* en dents de scie.

serum ['sɪərəm] *n* sérum *m*.

servant ['səːvənt] *n* domestique *m/f*; (*fig*) serviteur/servante.

serve [səːv] *vt* (*employer etc*) servir, être au service de; (*purpose*) servir à; (*customer, food, meal*) servir; (*apprenticeship*) faire, accomplir; (*prison term*) faire; purger ♦ *vi* (*also TENNIS*) servir; (*be useful*): **to ~ as/for/to do** servir de/à/à faire ♦ *n* (*TENNIS*) service *m*; **are you being ~d?** est-ce qu'on s'occupe de vous?; **to ~ on a committee/jury** faire partie d'un comité/jury; **it ~s him right** c'est bien fait pour lui; **it ~s my purpose** cela fait mon affaire.

►**serve out, serve up** *vt* (*food*) servir.

service ['səːvɪs] *n* (*gen*) service *m*; (*AUT: maintenance*) révision *f*; (*REL*) office *m* ♦ *vt* (*car, washing machine*) réviser; **the S~s** *npl* les forces armées; **to be of ~ to sb, to do sb a ~** rendre service à qn; **to put one's car in for ~** donner sa voiture à réviser; **dinner ~** service de table.

serviceable ['səːvɪsəbl] *adj* pratique, commode.

service area *n* (*on motorway*) aire *f* de services.

service charge *n* (*BRIT*) service *m*.

service industries *npl* les industries *fpl* de service, les services *mpl*.

serviceman ['səːvɪsmən] *n* militaire *m*.

service station *n* station-service *f*.

serviette [səːvɪ'ɛt] *n* (*BRIT*) serviette *f* (de table).

servile ['səːvaɪl] *adj* servile.

session ['sɛʃən] *n* (*sitting*) séance *f*; (*SCOL*) année *f* scolaire (*or* universitaire); **to be in ~** siéger, être en session *or* en séance.

session musician *n* musicien/ne de studio.

set [sɛt] *n* série *f*, assortiment *m*; (*of tools etc*) jeu *m*; (*RADIO, TV*) poste *m*; (*TENNIS*) set *m*; (*group of people*) cercle *m*, milieu *m*; (*CINE*) plateau *m*; (*THEAT: stage*) scène *f*; (*: scenery*) décor *m*; (*MATH*) ensemble *m*; (*HAIRDRESSING*) mise *f* en plis ♦ *adj* (*fixed*) fixe, déterminé(e); (*ready*) prêt(e) ♦ *vb* (*pt, pp* **set**) *vt* (*place*) mettre, poser, placer; (*fix, establish*) fixer; (*: record*) établir; (*assign: task, homework*) donner; (*adjust*) régler; (*decide: rules etc*) fixer, choisir; (*TYP*) composer ♦ *vi* (*sun*) se coucher; (*jam, jelly, concrete*) prendre; **to be ~ on doing** être résolu(e) à faire; **to be all ~ to do** être (fin) prêt(e) pour faire; **to be (dead) ~ against** être (totalement) opposé à; **he's ~ in his ways** il n'est pas très souple, il tient à ses habitudes; **to ~ to music** mettre en musique; **to ~ on fire** mettre le feu à; **to ~ free** libérer; **to ~ sth going** déclencher qch; **to ~ the alarm clock for 7 o'clock** mettre le réveil à sonner à sept heures; **to ~ sail** partir, prendre la mer; **a ~ phrase** une expression toute faite, une locution; **a ~ of false teeth** un dentier; **a ~ of dining-room furniture** une salle à manger.

►**set about** *vt fus* (*task*) entreprendre, se mettre à; **to ~ about doing sth** se mettre à faire qch.

►**set aside** *vt* mettre de côté.

►**set back** *vt* (*in time*): **to ~ back (by)** retarder (de); (*place*): **a house ~ back from the road** une maison située en retrait de la route.

►**set in** *vi* (*infection, bad weather*) s'installer; (*complications*) survenir, surgir; **the rain has ~ in for the day** c'est parti pour qu'il pleuve toute la journée.

►**set off** *vi* se mettre en route, partir ♦ *vt* (*bomb*) faire exploser; (*cause to start*) déclencher; (*show up well*) mettre en valeur, faire valoir.

►**set out** *vi*: **to ~ out to do** entreprendre de faire; avoir pour but *or* intention de faire ♦ *vt* (*arrange*) disposer; (*state*) présenter, exposer; **to ~ out (from)** partir (de).

►**set up** *vt* (*organization*) fonder, constituer; (*monument*) ériger; **to ~ up shop** (*fig*) s'établir, s'installer.

setback ['sɛtbæk] *n* (*hitch*) revers *m*, contretemps *m*; (*in health*) rechute *f*.

set menu *n* menu *m*.

set square *n* équerre *f*.

settee [sɛ'tiː] *n* canapé *m*.

setting ['sɛtɪŋ] *n* cadre *m*; (*of jewel*) monture *f*.

setting lotion *n* lotion *f* pour mise en plis.

settle ['sɛtl] *vt* (*argument, matter, account*) régler; (*problem*) résoudre; (*MED: calm*) calmer; (*colonize: land*) coloniser ♦ *vi* (*bird, dust etc*) se poser; (*sediment*) se déposer; (*also:* **~ down**) s'installer, se fixer; (*: become calmer*) se calmer; se ranger; **to ~ to sth** se mettre sérieusement à qch; **to ~ for sth** accepter qch, se contenter de qch; **to ~ on sth** opter *or* se décider pour qch; **that's ~d then** alors, c'est d'accord!; **to ~ one's stomach** calmer des maux d'estomac.

►**settle in** *vi* s'installer.

►**settle up** *vi*: **to ~ up with sb** régler (ce que l'on doit à) qn.

settlement ['sɛtlmənt] *n* (*payment*) règlement *m*; (*agreement*) accord *m*; (*colony*) colonie *f*; (*village etc*) établissement *m*; hameau *m*; **in ~ of our account** (*COMM*) en règlement de notre compte.

settler ['sɛtlə*] *n* colon *m*.

setup ['sɛtʌp] *n* (*arrangement*) manière *f* dont les choses sont organisées; (*situation*) situation *f*, allure *f* des choses.
seven ['sɛvn] *num* sept.
seventeen [sɛvn'tiːn] *num* dix-sept.
seventh ['sɛvnθ] *num* septième.
seventy ['sɛvntɪ] *num* soixante-dix.
sever ['sɛvə*] *vt* couper, trancher; (*relations*) rompre.
several ['sɛvərl] *adj, pron* plusieurs (*m/fpl*); ~ **of us** plusieurs d'entre nous; ~ **times** plusieurs fois.
severance ['sɛvərəns] *n* (*of relations*) rupture *f*.
severance pay *n* indemnité *f* de licenciement.
severe [sɪ'vɪə*] *adj* sévère, strict(e); (*serious*) grave, sérieux(euse); (*hard*) rigoureux(euse), dur(e); (*plain*) sévère, austère.
severely [sɪ'vɪəlɪ] *adv* sévèrement; (*wounded, ill*) gravement.
severity [sɪ'vɛrɪtɪ] *n* sévérité *f*; gravité *f*; rigueur *f*.
sew, *pt* **sewed,** *pp* **sewn** [səu, səud, səun] *vt, vi* coudre.
►**sew up** *vt* (re)coudre; **it is all sewn up** (*fig*) c'est dans le sac *or* dans la poche.
sewage ['suːɪdʒ] *n* vidange(s) *f(pl)*.
sewage works *n* champ *m* d'épandage.
sewer ['suːə*] *n* égout *m*.
sewing ['səuɪŋ] *n* couture *f*.
sewing machine *n* machine *f* à coudre.
sewn [səun] *pp of* **sew**.
sex [sɛks] *n* sexe *m*; **to have ~ with** avoir des rapports (sexuels) avec.
sex act *n* acte sexuel.
sex appeal *n* sex-appeal *m*.
sex education *n* éducation sexuelle.
sexism ['sɛksɪzəm] *n* sexisme *m*.
sexist ['sɛksɪst] *adj* sexiste.
sex life *n* vie sexuelle.
sex object *n* femme-objet *f*, objet sexuel.
sextet [sɛks'tɛt] *n* sextuor *m*.
sexual ['sɛksjuəl] *adj* sexuel(le); ~ **assault** attentat *m* à la pudeur; ~ **harassment** harcèlement sexuel; ~ **intercourse** rapports sexuels.
sexy ['sɛksɪ] *adj* sexy *inv*.
Seychelles [seɪ'ʃɛl(z)] *npl*: **the** ~ les Seychelles *fpl*.
SF *n abbr* (= *science fiction*) SF *f*.
SG *n abbr* (*US*) = **Surgeon General**.
Sgt *abbr* (= *sergeant*) Sgt.
shabbiness ['ʃæbɪnɪs] *n* aspect miteux; mesquinerie *f*.
shabby ['ʃæbɪ] *adj* miteux(euse); (*behaviour*) mesquin(e), méprisable.
shack [ʃæk] *n* cabane *f*, hutte *f*.
shackles ['ʃæklz] *npl* chaînes *fpl*, entraves *fpl*.
shade [ʃeɪd] *n* ombre *f*; (*for lamp*) abat-jour *m inv*; (*of colour*) nuance *f*, ton *m*; (*US*: *window* ~) store *m*; (*small quantity*): **a ~ of** un soupçon de ♦ *vt* abriter du soleil, ombrager; **~s** *npl* (*US*: *sunglasses*) lunettes *fpl* de soleil; **in the** ~ à l'ombre; **a ~ smaller** un tout petit peu plus petit.
shadow ['ʃædəu] *n* ombre *f* ♦ *vt* (*follow*) filer; **without** *or* **beyond a ~ of doubt** sans l'ombre d'un doute.
shadow cabinet *n* (*BRIT POL*) *cabinet parallèle formé par le parti qui n'est pas au pouvoir*.
shadowy ['ʃædəuɪ] *adj* ombragé(e); (*dim*) vague, indistinct(e).
shady ['ʃeɪdɪ] *adj* ombragé(e); (*fig: dishonest*) louche, véreux(euse).
shaft [ʃɑːft] *n* (*of arrow, spear*) hampe *f*; (*AUT, TECH*) arbre *m*; (*of mine*) puits *m*; (*of lift*) cage *f*; (*of light*) rayon *m*, trait *m*; **ventilator** ~ conduit *m* d'aération *or* de ventilation.
shaggy ['ʃægɪ] *adj* hirsute; en broussaille.
shake [ʃeɪk] *vb* (*pt* **shook**, *pp* **shaken** [ʃuk, 'ʃeɪkn]) *vt* secouer; (*bottle, cocktail*) agiter; (*house, confidence*) ébranler ♦ *vi* trembler ♦ *n* secousse *f*; **to ~ one's head** (*in refusal etc*) dire *or* faire non de la tête; (*in dismay*) secouer la tête; **to ~ hands with sb** serrer la main à qn.
►**shake off** *vt* secouer; (*fig*) se débarrasser de.
►**shake up** *vt* secouer.
shake-up ['ʃeɪkʌp] *n* grand remaniement.
shakily ['ʃeɪkɪlɪ] *adv* (*reply*) d'une voix tremblante; (*walk*) d'un pas mal assuré; (*write*) d'une main tremblante.
shaky ['ʃeɪkɪ] *adj* (*hand, voice*) tremblant(e); (*building*) branlant(e), peu solide; (*memory*) chancelant(e); (*knowledge*) incertain(e).
shale [ʃeɪl] *n* schiste argileux.
shall [ʃæl] *aux vb*: **I ~ go** j'irai.
shallot [ʃə'lɔt] *n* (*BRIT*) échalote *f*.
shallow ['ʃæləu] *adj* peu profond(e); (*fig*) superficiel(le), qui manque de profondeur.
sham [ʃæm] *n* frime *f*; (*jewellery, furniture*) imitation *f* ♦ *adj* feint(e), simulé(e) ♦ *vt* feindre, simuler.
shambles ['ʃæmblz] *n* confusion *f*, pagaïe *f*, fouillis *m*; **the economy is (in) a complete ~** l'économie est dans la confusion la plus totale.
shambolic [ʃæm'bɔlɪk] *adj* (*col*) bordélique.
shame [ʃeɪm] *n* honte *f* ♦ *vt* faire honte à; **it is a ~ (that/to do)** c'est dommage (que + *sub*/de faire); **what a ~!** quel dommage!; **to put sb/sth to ~** (*fig*) faire honte à qn/qch.
shamefaced ['ʃeɪmfeɪst] *adj* honteux(euse), penaud(e).
shameful ['ʃeɪmful] *adj* honteux(euse), scandaleux(euse).
shameless ['ʃeɪmlɪs] *adj* éhonté(e), effronté(e); (*immodest*) impudique.
shampoo [ʃæm'puː] *n* shampooing *m* ♦ *vt* faire un shampooing à; **~ and set** shampooing et mise *f* en plis.
shamrock ['ʃæmrɔk] *n* trèfle *m* (*emblème natio-*

nal de l'Irlande).
shandy ['ʃændɪ] *n* bière panachée.
shan't [ʃɑːnt] = **shall not.**
shantytown ['ʃæntɪtaun] *n* bidonville *m.*
SHAPE [ʃeɪp] *n abbr (= Supreme Headquarters Allied Powers, Europe) quartier général des forces alliées en Europe.*
shape [ʃeɪp] *n* forme *f* ♦ *vt* façonner, modeler; (*clay, stone*) donner forme à; (*statement*) formuler; (*sb's ideas, character*) former; (*sb's life*) déterminer; (*course of events*) influer sur le cours de ♦ *vi* (*also*: ~ **up**: *events*) prendre tournure; (*: person*) faire des progrès, s'en sortir; **to take** ~ prendre forme *or* tournure; **in the** ~ **of a heart** en forme de cœur; **I can't bear gardening in any** ~ **or form** je déteste le jardinage sous quelque forme que ce soit; **to get o.s. into** ~ (re)trouver la forme.
-shaped [ʃeɪpt] *suffix*: **heart-**~ en forme de cœur.
shapeless ['ʃeɪplɪs] *adj* informe, sans forme.
shapely ['ʃeɪplɪ] *adj* bien proportionné(e), beau(belle).
share [ʃɛə*] *n* (*thing received, contribution*) part *f*; (*COMM*) action *f* ♦ *vt* partager; (*have in common*) avoir en commun; **to** ~ **out (among** *or* **between)** partager (entre); **to** ~ **in** (*joy, sorrow*) prendre part à; (*profits*) participer à, avoir part à; (*work*) partager.
share capital *n* capital social.
share certificate *n* certificat *m or* titre *m* d'action.
shareholder ['ʃɛəhəuldə*] *n* actionnaire *m/f.*
share index *n* indice *m* de la Bourse.
shark [ʃɑːk] *n* requin *m.*
sharp [ʃɑːp] *adj* (*razor, knife*) tranchant(e), bien aiguisé(e); (*point*) aigu(ë); (*nose, chin*) pointu(e); (*outline*) net(te); (*curve, bend*) brusque; (*cold, pain*) vif(vive); (*MUS*) dièse; (*voice*) coupant(e); (*person: quick-witted*) vif(vive), éveillé(e); (*: unscrupulous*) malhonnête ♦ *n* (*MUS*) dièse *m* ♦ *adv*: **at 2 o'clock** ~ à 2 heures pile *or* tapantes; **turn** ~ **left** tournez immédiatement à gauche; **to be** ~ **with sb** être brusque avec qn; **look** ~! dépêche-toi!
sharpen ['ʃɑːpn] *vt* aiguiser; (*pencil*) tailler; (*fig*) aviver.
sharpener ['ʃɑːpnə*] *n* (*also*: **pencil** ~) taille-crayon(s) *m inv*; (*also*: **knife** ~) aiguisoir *m.*
sharp-eyed [ʃɑːp'aɪd] *adj* à qui rien n'échappe.
sharpish ['ʃɑːpɪʃ] *adv* (*BRIT col*: *quickly*) en vitesse.
sharply ['ʃɑːplɪ] *adv* (*abruptly*) brusquement; (*clearly*) nettement; (*harshly*) sèchement, vertement.
sharp-tempered [ʃɑːp'tɛmpəd] *adj* prompt(e) à se mettre en colère.
sharp-witted [ʃɑːp'wɪtɪd] *adj* à l'esprit vif, malin(igne).
shatter ['ʃætə*] *vt* fracasser, briser, faire voler en éclats; (*fig: upset*) bouleverser; (*: ruin*) briser, ruiner ♦ *vi* voler en éclats, se briser, se fracasser.
shattered ['ʃætəd] *adj* (*overwhelmed, grief-stricken*) bouleversé(e); (*col*: *exhausted*) éreinté(e).
shatterproof ['ʃætəpruːf] *adj* incassable.
shave [ʃeɪv] *vt* raser ♦ *vi* se raser ♦ *n*: **to have a** ~ se raser.
shaven ['ʃeɪvn] *adj* (*head*) rasé(e).
shaver ['ʃeɪvə*] *n* (*also*: **electric** ~) rasoir *m* électrique.
shaving ['ʃeɪvɪŋ] *n* (*action*) rasage *m*; ~**s** *npl* (*of wood etc*) copeaux *mpl.*
shaving brush *n* blaireau *m.*
shaving cream *n* crème *f* à raser.
shaving soap *n* savon *m* à barbe.
shawl [ʃɔːl] *n* châle *m.*
she [ʃiː] *pron* elle; **there** ~ **is** la voilà; ~-**elephant** *etc* éléphant *m etc* femelle; *NB: for ships, countries follow the gender of your translation.*
sheaf, *pl* **sheaves** [ʃiːf, ʃiːvz] *n* gerbe *f.*
shear [ʃɪə*] *vt* (*pt* ~**ed**, *pp* ~**ed** *or* **shorn** [ʃɔːn]) (*sheep*) tondre.
►**shear off** *vt* tondre; (*branch*) élaguer.
shears ['ʃɪəz] *npl* (*for hedge*) cisaille(s) *f(pl).*
sheath [ʃiːθ] *n* gaine *f*, fourreau *m*, étui *m*; (*contraceptive*) préservatif *m.*
sheathe [ʃiːð] *vt* gainer; (*sword*) rengainer.
sheath knife *n* couteau *m* à gaine.
sheaves [ʃiːvz] *npl of* **sheaf.**
shed [ʃɛd] *n* remise *f*, resserre *f*; (*INDUSTRY, RAIL*) hangar *m* ♦ *vt* (*pt, pp* **shed**) (*leaves, fur etc*) perdre; (*tears*) verser, répandre; **to** ~ **light on** (*problem, mystery*) faire la lumière sur.
she'd [ʃiːd] = **she had, she would.**
sheen [ʃiːn] *n* lustre *m.*
sheep [ʃiːp] *n* (*pl inv*) mouton *m.*
sheepdog ['ʃiːpdɔg] *n* chien *m* de berger.
sheep farmer *n* éleveur *m* de moutons.
sheepish ['ʃiːpɪʃ] *adj* penaud(e), timide.
sheepskin ['ʃiːpskɪn] *n* peau *f* de mouton.
sheepskin jacket *n* canadienne *f.*
sheer [ʃɪə*] *adj* (*utter*) pur(e), pur et simple; (*steep*) à pic, abrupt(e); (*almost transparent*) extrêmement fin(e) ♦ *adv* à pic, abruptement; **by** ~ **chance** par pur hasard.
sheet [ʃiːt] *n* (*on bed*) drap *m*; (*of paper*) feuille *f*; (*of glass, metal*) feuille, plaque *f.*
sheet feed *n* (*on printer*) alimentation *f* en papier (feuille à feuille).
sheet lightning *n* éclair *m* en nappe(s).
sheet metal *n* tôle *f.*
sheet music *n* partition(s) *f(pl).*
sheik(h) [ʃeɪk] *n* cheik *m.*
shelf, *pl* **shelves** [ʃɛlf, ʃɛlvz] *n* étagère *f*, rayon *m*; **set of shelves** rayonnage *m.*
shelf life *n* (*COMM*) durée *f* de conservation (avant la vente).
shell [ʃɛl] *n* (*on beach*) coquillage *m*; (*of egg,*

nut etc) coquille *f*; (*explosive*) obus *m*; (*of building*) carcasse *f* ♦ *vt* (*crab, prawn etc*) décortiquer; (*peas*) écosser; (*MIL*) bombarder (d'obus).
▸**shell out** *vi* (*col*): **to ~ out (for)** casquer (pour).
she'll [ʃiːl] = **she will, she shall**.
shellfish ['ʃɛlfɪʃ] *n* (*pl inv*) (*crab etc*) crustacé *m*; (*scallop etc*) coquillage *m*; (*pl: as food*) crustacés; coquillages.
shellsuit ['ʃɛlsuːt] *n* survêtement *m*.
shelter ['ʃɛltə*] *n* abri *m*, refuge *m* ♦ *vt* abriter, protéger; (*give lodging to*) donner asile à ♦ *vi* s'abriter, se mettre à l'abri; **to take ~ (from)** s'abriter (de).
sheltered ['ʃɛltəd] *adj* (*life*) retiré(e), à l'abri des soucis; (*spot*) abrité(e).
shelve [ʃɛlv] *vt* (*fig*) mettre en suspens *or* en sommeil.
shelves ['ʃɛlvz] *npl of* **shelf**.
shelving ['ʃɛlvɪŋ] *n* (*shelves*) rayonnage(s) *m(pl)*.
shepherd ['ʃɛpəd] *n* berger *m* ♦ *vt* (*guide*) guider, escorter.
shepherdess ['ʃɛpədɪs] *n* bergère *f*.
shepherd's pie ['ʃɛpədz-] *n* ≈ hachis *m* Parmentier.
sherbet ['ʃəːbət] *n* (*BRIT: powder*) poudre acidulée; (*US: water ice*) sorbet *m*.
sheriff ['ʃɛrɪf] *n* shérif *m*.
sherry ['ʃɛrɪ] *n* xérès *m*, sherry *m*.
she's [ʃiːz] = **she is, she has**.
Shetland ['ʃɛtlənd] *n* (*also*: **the ~s, the ~ Isles** *or* **Islands**) les îles *fpl* Shetland.
Shetland pony *n* poney *m* des îles Shetland.
shield [ʃiːld] *n* bouclier *m* ♦ *vt*: **to ~ (from)** protéger (de *or* contre).
shift [ʃɪft] *n* (*change*) changement *m*; (*of workers*) équipe *f*, poste *m* ♦ *vt* déplacer, changer de place; (*remove*) enlever ♦ *vi* changer de place, bouger; **the wind has ~ed to the south** le vent a tourné au sud; **a ~ in demand** (*COMM*) un déplacement de la demande.
shift key *n* (*on typewriter*) touche *f* de majuscule.
shiftless ['ʃɪftlɪs] *adj* fainéant(e).
shift work *n* travail *m* par roulement; **to do ~** travailler par roulement.
shifty ['ʃɪftɪ] *adj* sournois(e); (*eyes*) fuyant(e).
Shiite ['ʃiːaɪt] *n* Chiite *m/f* ♦ *adj* chiite.
shilling ['ʃɪlɪŋ] *n* (*BRIT*) shilling *m* (*= 12 old pence; 20 in a pound*).
shilly-shally ['ʃɪlɪʃælɪ] *vi* tergiverser, atermoyer.
shimmer ['ʃɪmə*] *n* miroitement *m*, chatoiement *m* ♦ *vi* miroiter, chatoyer.
shin [ʃɪn] *n* tibia *m* ♦ *vi*: **to ~ up/down a tree** grimper dans un/descendre d'un arbre.
shindig ['ʃɪndɪg] *n* (*col*) bamboula *f*.
shine [ʃaɪn] *n* éclat *m*, brillant *m* ♦ *vb* (*pt, pp* **shone** [ʃɔn]) *vi* briller ♦ *vt* faire briller *or* reluire; (*torch*): **to ~ on** braquer sur.
shingle ['ʃɪŋgl] *n* (*on beach*) galets *mpl*; (*on roof*) bardeau *m*.
shingles ['ʃɪŋglz] *n* (*MED*) zona *m*.
shining ['ʃaɪnɪŋ] *adj* brillant(e).
shiny ['ʃaɪnɪ] *adj* brillant(e).
ship [ʃɪp] *n* bateau *m*; (*large*) navire *m* ♦ *vt* transporter (par mer); (*send*) expédier (par mer); (*load*) charger, embarquer; **on board ~** à bord.
shipbuilder ['ʃɪpbɪldə*] *n* constructeur *m* de navires.
shipbuilding ['ʃɪpbɪldɪŋ] *n* construction navale.
ship canal *n* canal *m* maritime *or* de navigation.
ship chandler [-'tʃɑːndlə*] *n* fournisseur *m* maritime, shipchandler *m*.
shipment ['ʃɪpmənt] *n* cargaison *f*.
shipowner ['ʃɪpəunə*] *n* armateur *m*.
shipper ['ʃɪpə*] *n* affréteur *m*, expéditeur *m*.
shipping ['ʃɪpɪŋ] *n* (*ships*) navires *mpl*; (*traffic*) navigation *f*.
shipping agent *n* agent *m* maritime.
shipping company *n* compagnie *f* de navigation.
shipping lane *n* couloir *m* de navigation.
shipping line *n* = **shipping company**.
shipshape ['ʃɪpʃeɪp] *adj* en ordre impeccable.
shipwreck ['ʃɪprɛk] *n* épave *f*; (*event*) naufrage *m* ♦ *vt*: **to be ~ed** faire naufrage.
shipyard ['ʃɪpjɑːd] *n* chantier naval.
shire ['ʃaɪə*] *n* (*BRIT*) comté *m*.
shirk [ʃəːk] *vt* esquiver, se dérober à.
shirt [ʃəːt] *n* chemise *f*; **in ~ sleeves** en bras de chemise.
shirty ['ʃəːtɪ] *adj* (*BRIT col*) de mauvais poil.
shit [ʃɪt] *excl* (*col!*) merde (*!*).
shiver ['ʃɪvə*] *n* frisson *m* ♦ *vi* frissonner.
shoal [ʃəul] *n* (*of fish*) banc *m*.
shock [ʃɔk] *n* (*impact*) choc *m*, heurt *m*; (*ELEC*) secousse *f*, décharge *f*; (*emotional*) choc; (*MED*) commotion *f*, choc ♦ *vt* (*scandalize*) choquer, scandaliser; (*upset*) bouleverser; **suffering from ~** (*MED*) commotionné(e); **it gave us a ~** ça nous a fait un choc; **it came as a ~ to hear that** ... nous avons appris avec stupeur que ....
shock absorber [-əbzɔːbə*] *n* amortisseur *m*.
shocker ['ʃɔkə*] *n* (*col*): **the news was a real ~ to him** il a vraiment été choqué par cette nouvelle.
shocking ['ʃɔkɪŋ] *adj* choquant(e), scandaleux(euse); (*weather, handwriting*) épouvantable.
shockproof ['ʃɔkpruːf] *adj* anti-choc *inv*.
shock therapy, shock treatment *n* (*MED*) (traitement *m* par) électrochoc(s) *m(pl)*.
shock wave *n* (*also fig*) onde *f* de choc.
shod [ʃɔd] *pt, pp of* **shoe**; **well-~** bien chaussé(e).
shoddy ['ʃɔdɪ] *adj* de mauvaise qualité, mal

fait(e).

shoe [ʃuː] *n* chaussure *f*, soulier *m*; (*also*: **horse**~) fer *m* à cheval; (*also*: **brake** ~) mâchoire *f* de frein ⧫ *vt* (*pt*, *pp* **shod** [ʃɔd]) (*horse*) ferrer.

shoebrush [ˈʃuːbrʌʃ] *n* brosse *f* à chaussures.

shoehorn [ˈʃuːhɔːn] *n* chausse-pied *m*.

shoelace [ˈʃuːleɪs] *n* lacet *m* (de soulier).

shoemaker [ˈʃuːmeɪkə*] *n* cordonnier *m*, fabricant *m* de chaussures.

shoe polish *n* cirage *m*.

shoeshop [ˈʃuːʃɔp] *n* magasin *m* de chaussures.

shoestring [ˈʃuːstrɪŋ] *n*: **on a** ~ (*fig*) avec un budget dérisoire; avec des moyens très restreints.

shoetree [ˈʃuːtriː] *n* embauchoir *m*.

shone [ʃɔn] *pt*, *pp of* **shine**.

shoo [ʃuː] *excl* (allez,) ouste! ⧫ *vt* (*also*: ~ **away**, ~ **off**) chasser.

shook [ʃuk] *pt of* **shake**.

shoot [ʃuːt] *n* (*on branch, seedling*) pousse *f*; (*shooting party*) partie *f* de chasse ⧫ *vb* (*pt*, *pp* **shot** [ʃɔt]) *vt* (*game*: *BRIT*) chasser; tirer; abattre; (*person*) blesser (*or* tuer) d'un coup de fusil (*or* de revolver); (*execute*) fusiller; (*CINE*) tourner ⧫ *vi* (*with gun, bow*): **to** ~ **(at)** tirer (sur); (*FOOTBALL*) shooter, tirer; **to** ~ **past sb** passer en flèche devant qn; **to** ~ **in/out** entrer/sortir comme une flèche.

►**shoot down** *vt* (*plane*) abattre.

►**shoot up** *vi* (*fig*) monter en flèche.

shooting [ˈʃuːtɪŋ] *n* (*shots*) coups *mpl* de feu; (*attack*) fusillade *f*; (*: murder*) homicide *m* (*à l'aide d'une arme à feu*); (*HUNTING*) chasse *f*; (*CINE*) tournage *m*.

shooting range *n* stand *m* de tir.

shooting star *n* étoile filante.

shop [ʃɔp] *n* magasin *m*; (*workshop*) atelier *m* ⧫ *vi* (*also*: **go** ~**ping**) faire ses courses *or* ses achats; **repair** ~ atelier de réparations; **to talk** ~ (*fig*) parler boutique.

►**shop around** *vi* faire le tour des magasins (pour comparer les prix); (*fig*) se renseigner avant de choisir *or* décider.

shopaholic [ʃɔpəˈhɔlɪk] *n* (*col*) *personne qui achète sans pouvoir s'arrêter*.

shop assistant *n* (*BRIT*) vendeur/euse.

shop floor *n* (*BRIT*: *fig*) ouvriers *mpl*.

shopkeeper [ˈʃɔpkiːpə*] *n* marchand/e, commerçant/e.

shoplift [ˈʃɔplɪft] *vi* voler à l'étalage.

shoplifter [ˈʃɔplɪftə*] *n* voleur/euse à l'étalage.

shoplifting [ˈʃɔplɪftɪŋ] *n* vol *m* à l'étalage.

shopper [ˈʃɔpə*] *n* personne *f* qui fait ses courses, acheteur/euse.

shopping [ˈʃɔpɪŋ] *n* (*goods*) achats *mpl*, provisions *fpl*.

shopping bag *n* sac *m* (à provisions).

shopping centre *n* centre commercial.

shopping mall *n* centre commercial.

shop-soiled [ˈʃɔpsɔɪld] *adj* défraîchi(e), qui a fait la vitrine.

shop steward *n* (*BRIT INDUSTRY*) délégué/e syndical(e).

shop window *n* vitrine *f*.

shore [ʃɔː*] *n* (*of sea, lake*) rivage *m*, rive *f* ⧫ *vt*: **to** ~ **(up)** étayer; **on** ~ à terre.

shore leave *n* (*NAUT*) permission *f* à terre.

shorn [ʃɔːn] *pp of* **shear** ⧫ *adj*: ~ **of** dépouillé(e) de.

short [ʃɔːt] *adj* (*not long*) court(e); (*soon finished*) court, bref(brève); (*person, step*) petit(e); (*curt*) brusque, sec(sèche); (*insufficient*) insuffisant(e) ⧫ *n* (*also*: ~ **film**) court métrage; **to be** ~ **of sth** être à court de *or* manquer de qch; **to be in** ~ **supply** manquer, être difficile à trouver; **I'm 3** ~ il m'en manque 3; **in** ~ bref; en bref; ~ **of doing** à moins de faire; **everything** ~ **of** tout sauf; **it is** ~ **for** c'est l'abréviation *or* le diminutif de; **a** ~ **time ago** il y a peu de temps; **in the** ~ **term** à court terme; **to cut** ~ (*speech, visit*) abréger, écourter; (*person*) couper la parole à; **to fall** ~ **of** ne pas être à la hauteur de; **to stop** ~ s'arrêter net; **to stop** ~ **of** ne pas aller jusqu'à.

shortage [ˈʃɔːtɪdʒ] *n* manque *m*, pénurie *f*.

shortbread [ˈʃɔːtbrɛd] *n* ≈ sablé *m*.

short-change [ʃɔːtˈtʃeɪndʒ] *vt*: **to** ~ **sb** ne pas rendre assez à qn.

short-circuit [ʃɔːtˈsəːkɪt] *n* court-circuit *m* ⧫ *vt* court-circuiter ⧫ *vi* se mettre en court-circuit.

shortcoming [ˈʃɔːtkʌmɪŋ] *n* défaut *m*.

short(crust) pastry [ˈʃɔːt(krʌst)-] *n* (*BRIT*) pâte brisée.

shortcut [ˈʃɔːtkʌt] *n* raccourci *m*.

shorten [ˈʃɔːtn] *vt* raccourcir; (*text, visit*) abréger.

shortening [ˈʃɔːtnɪŋ] *n* (*CULIN*) matière grasse.

shortfall [ˈʃɔːtfɔːl] *n* déficit *m*.

shorthand [ˈʃɔːthænd] *n* (*BRIT*) sténo(graphie) *f*; **to take sth down in** ~ prendre qch en sténo.

shorthand notebook *n* bloc *m* sténo.

shorthand typist *n* (*BRIT*) sténodactylo *m/f*.

short list *n* (*BRIT*: *for job*) liste *f* des candidats sélectionnés.

short-lived [ˈʃɔːtˈlɪvd] *adj* de courte durée.

shortly [ˈʃɔːtlɪ] *adv* bientôt, sous peu.

shortness [ˈʃɔːtnɪs] *n* brièveté *f*.

shorts [ʃɔːts] *npl* (*also*: **a pair of** ~) un short.

short-sighted [ʃɔːtˈsaɪtɪd] *adj* (*BRIT*) myope; (*fig*) qui manque de clairvoyance.

short-staffed [ʃɔːtˈstɑːft] *adj* à court de personnel.

short story *n* nouvelle *f*.

short-tempered [ʃɔːtˈtɛmpəd] *adj* qui s'emporte facilement.

short-term [ˈʃɔːttəːm] *adj* (*effect*) à court terme.

short time *n*: **to work ~, to be on ~** (*INDUSTRY*) être en chômage partiel, travailler à horaire réduit.

short wave *n* (*RADIO*) ondes courtes.

shot [ʃɔt] *pt, pp of* **shoot** ♦ *n* coup *m* (de feu); (*shotgun pellets*) plombs *mpl*; (*person*) tireur *m*; (*try*) coup, essai *m*; (*injection*) piqûre *f*; (*PHOT*) photo *f*; **to fire a ~ at sb/sth** tirer sur qn/qch; **to have a ~ at (doing) sth** essayer de faire qch; **like a ~** comme une flèche; (*very readily*) sans hésiter; **to get ~ of sb/sth** (*col*) se débarrasser de qn/qch; **a big ~** (*col*) un gros bonnet.

shotgun ['ʃɔtgʌn] *n* fusil *m* de chasse.

should [ʃud] *aux vb*: **I ~ go now** je devrais partir maintenant; **he ~ be there now** il devrait être arrivé maintenant; **I ~ go if I were you** si j'étais vous j'irais; **I ~ like to** j'aimerais bien, volontiers; **~ he phone ...** si jamais il téléphone ....

shoulder ['ʃəuldə*] *n* épaule *f*; (*BRIT*: *of road*): **hard ~** accotement *m* ♦ *vt* (*fig*) endosser, se charger de; **to look over one's ~** regarder derrière soi (en tournant la tête); **to rub ~s with sb** (*fig*) côtoyer qn; **to give sb the cold ~** (*fig*) battre froid à qn.

shoulder bag *n* sac *m* à bandoulière.

shoulder blade *n* omoplate *f*.

shoulder strap *n* bretelle *f*.

shouldn't ['ʃudnt] = **should not**.

shout [ʃaut] *n* cri *m* ♦ *vt* crier ♦ *vi* crier, pousser des cris; **to give sb a ~** appeler qn.

►**shout down** *vt* huer.

shouting ['ʃautɪŋ] *n* cris *mpl*.

shouting match *n* (*col*) engueulade *f*, empoignade *f*.

shove [ʃʌv] *vt* pousser; (*col*: *put*): **to ~ sth in** fourrer *or* ficher qch dans ♦ *n* poussée *f*; **he ~d me out of the way** il m'a écarté en me poussant.

►**shove off** *vi* (*NAUT*) pousser au large; (*fig*: *col*) ficher le camp.

shovel ['ʃʌvl] *n* pelle *f* ♦ *vt* pelleter, enlever (*or* enfourner) à la pelle.

show [ʃəu] *n* (*of emotion*) manifestation *f*, démonstration *f*; (*semblance*) semblant *m*, apparence *f*; (*exhibition*) exposition *f*, salon *m*; (*THEAT*) spectacle *m*, représentation *f*; (*CINE*) séance *f* ♦ *vb* (*pt* **~ed**, *pp* **shown** [ʃəun]) *vt* montrer; (*courage etc*) faire preuve de, manifester; (*exhibit*) exposer ♦ *vi* se voir, être visible; **to ask for a ~ of hands** demander que l'on vote à main levée; **to be on ~** être exposé(e); **it's just for ~** c'est juste pour l'effet; **who's running the ~ here?** (*col*) qui est-ce qui commande ici?; **to ~ sb to his seat/to the door** accompagner qn jusqu'à sa place/la porte; **to ~ a profit/ loss** (*COMM*) indiquer un bénéfice/une perte; **it just goes to ~ that ...** ça prouve bien que ....

►**show in** *vt* faire entrer.

►**show off** *vi* (*pej*) crâner ♦ *vt* (*display*) faire valoir; (*pej*) faire étalage de.

►**show out** *vt* reconduire à la porte.

►**show up** *vi* (*stand out*) ressortir; (*col*: *turn up*) se montrer ♦ *vt* démontrer; (*unmask*) démasquer, dénoncer.

showbiz ['ʃəubɪz] *n* (*col*) showbiz *m*.

show business *n* le monde du spectacle.

showcase ['ʃəukeɪs] *n* vitrine *f*.

showdown ['ʃəudaun] *n* épreuve *f* de force.

shower ['ʃauə*] *n* (*also*: **~ bath**) douche *f*; (*rain*) averse *f*; (*of stones etc*) pluie *f*, grêle *f*; (*US*: *party*) *réunion organisée pour la remise de cadeaux* ♦ *vi* prendre une douche, se doucher ♦ *vt*: **to ~ sb with** (*gifts etc*) combler qn de; (*abuse etc*) accabler qn de; (*missiles*) bombarder qn de; **to have** *or* **take a ~** prendre une douche, se doucher.

shower cap *n* bonnet *m* de douche.

showerproof ['ʃauəpru:f] *adj* imperméable.

showery ['ʃauərɪ] *adj* (*weather*) pluvieux(euse).

showground ['ʃəugraund] *n* champ *m* de foire.

showing ['ʃəuɪŋ] *n* (*of film*) projection *f*.

show jumping [-dʒʌmpɪŋ] *n* concours *m* hippique.

showman ['ʃəumən] *n* (*at fair, circus*) forain *m*; (*fig*) comédien *m*.

showmanship ['ʃəumənʃɪp] *n* art *m* de la mise en scène.

shown [ʃəun] *pp of* **show**.

show-off ['ʃəuɔf] *n* (*col*: *person*) crâneur/euse, m'as-tu-vu/e.

showpiece ['ʃəupi:s] *n* (*of exhibition etc*) joyau *m*, clou *m*; **that hospital is a ~** cet hôpital est un modèle du genre.

showroom ['ʃəurum] *n* magasin *m or* salle *f* d'exposition.

show trial *n* grand procès *m* médiatique (*qui fait un exemple*).

showy ['ʃəuɪ] *adj* tapageur(euse).

shrank [ʃræŋk] *pt of* **shrink**.

shrapnel ['ʃræpnl] *n* éclats *mpl* d'obus.

shred [ʃrɛd] *n* (*gen pl*) lambeau *m*, petit morceau; (*fig*: *of truth, evidence*) parcelle *f* ♦ *vt* mettre en lambeaux, déchirer; (*documents*) détruire; (*CULIN*) râper; couper en lanières.

shredder ['ʃrɛdə*] *n* (*for vegetables*) râpeur *m*; (*for documents, papers*) déchiqueteuse *f*.

shrewd [ʃru:d] *adj* astucieux(euse), perspicace.

shrewdness ['ʃru:dnɪs] *n* perspicacité *f*.

shriek [ʃri:k] *n* cri perçant *or* aigu, hurlement *m* ♦ *vt, vi* hurler, crier.

shrift [ʃrɪft] *n*: **to give sb short ~** expédier qn sans ménagements.

shrill [ʃrɪl] *adj* perçant(e), aigu(ë), strident(e).

shrimp [ʃrɪmp] *n* crevette grise.

shrine [ʃraɪn] *n* châsse *f*; (*place*) lieu *m* de pèlerinage.

shrink, *pt* **shrank**, *pp* **shrunk** [ʃrɪŋk, ʃræŋk, ʃrʌŋk] *vi* rétrécir; (*fig*) se réduire; se

contracter ♦ *vt* (*wool*) (faire) rétrécir ♦ *n* (*col*: *pej*) psychanalyste *m/f*; **to ~ from (doing) sth** reculer devant (la pensée de faire) qch.
shrinkage ['ʃrɪŋkɪdʒ] *n* (*of clothes*) rétrécissement *m*.
shrink-wrap ['ʃrɪŋkræp] *vt* emballer sous film plastique.
shrivel ['ʃrɪvl] (*also*: ~ **up**) *vt* ratatiner, flétrir ♦ *vi* se ratatiner, se flétrir.
shroud [ʃraud] *n* linceul *m* ♦ *vt*: **~ed in mystery** enveloppé(e) de mystère.
Shrove Tuesday ['ʃrəuv-] *n* (le) Mardi gras.
shrub [ʃrʌb] *n* arbuste *m*.
shrubbery ['ʃrʌbərɪ] *n* massif *m* d'arbustes.
shrug [ʃrʌg] *n* haussement *m* d'épaules ♦ *vt, vi*: **to ~ (one's shoulders)** hausser les épaules.
►**shrug off** *vt* faire fi de; (*cold, illness*) se débarrasser de.
shrunk [ʃrʌŋk] *pp of* **shrink**.
shrunken ['ʃrʌŋkn] *adj* ratatiné(e).
shudder ['ʃʌdə*] *n* frisson *m*, frémissement *m* ♦ *vi* frissonner, frémir.
shuffle ['ʃʌfl] *vt* (*cards*) battre; **to ~ (one's feet)** traîner les pieds.
shun [ʃʌn] *vt* éviter, fuir.
shunt [ʃʌnt] *vt* (*RAIL*: *direct*) aiguiller; (*: divert*) détourner ♦ *vi*: **to ~ (to and fro)** faire la navette.
shunting yard ['ʃʌntɪŋ-] *n* voies *fpl* de garage *or* de triage.
shush [ʃuʃ] *excl* chut!
shut, *pt, pp* **shut** [ʃʌt] *vt* fermer ♦ *vi* (se) fermer.
►**shut down** *vt* fermer définitivement; (*machine*) arrêter ♦ *vi* fermer définitivement.
►**shut off** *vt* couper, arrêter.
►**shut out** *vt* (*person, cold*) empêcher d'entrer; (*noise*) éviter d'entendre; (*block: view*) boucher; (*: memory of sth*) chasser de son esprit.
►**shut up** *vi* (*col*: *keep quiet*) se taire ♦ *vt* (*close*) fermer; (*silence*) faire taire.
shutdown ['ʃʌtdaun] *n* fermeture *f*.
shutter ['ʃʌtə*] *n* volet *m*; (*PHOT*) obturateur *m*.
shuttle ['ʃʌtl] *n* navette *f*; (*also*: ~ **service**) (service *m* de) navette *f* ♦ *vi* (*vehicle, person*) faire la navette ♦ *vt* (*passengers*) transporter par un système de navette.
shuttlecock ['ʃʌtlkɔk] *n* volant *m* (*de badminton*).
shuttle diplomacy *n* navettes *fpl* diplomatiques.
shy [ʃaɪ] *adj* timide; **to fight ~ of** se dérober devant; **to be ~ of doing sth** hésiter à faire qch, ne pas oser faire qch ♦ *vi*: **to ~ away from doing sth** (*fig*) craindre de faire qch.
shyness ['ʃaɪnɪs] *n* timidité *f*.
Siam [saɪ'æm] *n* Siam *m*.
Siamese [saɪə'miːz] *adj*: ~ **cat** chat siamois *mpl*; ~ **twins** (frères *mpl*) siamois *mpl*, (sœurs *fpl*) siamoises *fpl*.
Siberia [saɪ'bɪərɪə] *n* Sibérie *f*.
siblings ['sɪblɪŋz] *npl* (*formal*) enfants *mpl* d'un même couple.
Sicilian [sɪ'sɪlɪən] *adj* sicilien(ne) ♦ *n* Sicilien/ne.
Sicily ['sɪsɪlɪ] *n* Sicile *f*.
sick [sɪk] *adj* (*ill*) malade; (*vomiting*): **to be ~** vomir; (*humour*) noir(e), macabre; **to feel ~** avoir envie de vomir, avoir mal au cœur; **to fall ~** tomber malade; **to be (off) ~** être absent(e) pour cause de maladie; **a ~ person** un(e) malade; **to be ~ of** (*fig*) en avoir assez de.
sickbag ['sɪkbæg] *n* sac *m* vomitoire.
sick bay *n* infirmerie *f*.
sick building syndrome *n maladie dûe à la climatisation, l'éclairage artificiel etc des bureaux*.
sicken ['sɪkn] *vt* écœurer ♦ *vi*: **to be ~ing for sth** (*cold, flu etc*) couver qch.
sickening ['sɪknɪŋ] *adj* (*fig*) écœurant(e), révoltant(e), répugnant(e).
sickle ['sɪkl] *n* faucille *f*.
sick leave *n* congé *m* de maladie.
sickle-cell anaemia ['sɪklsel-] *n* anémie *f* à hématies falciformes, drépanocytose *f*.
sickly ['sɪklɪ] *adj* maladif(ive), souffreteux(euse); (*causing nausea*) écœurant(e).
sickness ['sɪknɪs] *n* maladie *f*; (*vomiting*) vomissement(s) *m(pl)*.
sickness benefit *n* (prestations *fpl* de l')assurance-maladie *f*.
sick pay *n* indemnité *f* de maladie (*versée par l'employeur*).
sickroom ['sɪkruːm] *n* infirmerie *f*.
side [saɪd] *n* côté *m*; (*of animal*) flanc *m*; (*of lake, road*) bord *m*; (*of mountain*) versant *m*; (*fig: aspect*) côté, aspect *m*; (*team*: *SPORT*) équipe *f* ♦ *cpd* (*door, entrance*) latéral(e) ♦ *vi*: **to ~ with sb** prendre le parti de qn, se ranger du côté de qn; **by the ~ of** au bord de; **~ by ~** côte à côte; **the right/ wrong ~** le bon/mauvais côté, l'endroit/l'envers *m*; **they are on our ~** ils sont avec nous; **from all ~s** de tous côtés; **to take ~s (with)** prendre parti (pour); **a ~ of beef** ≈ un quartier de bœuf.
sideboard ['saɪdbɔːd] *n* buffet *m*.
sideboards ['saɪdbɔːdz] (*BRIT*), **sideburns** ['saɪdbəːnz] *npl* (*whiskers*) pattes *fpl*.
sidecar ['saɪdkɑː*] *n* side-car *m*.
side dish *n* (plat *m* d')accompagnement *m*.
side drum *n* (*MUS*) tambour plat, caisse claire.
side effect *n* (*MED*) effet *m* secondaire.
sidekick ['saɪdkɪk] *n* (*col*) sous-fifre *m*.
sidelight ['saɪdlaɪt] *n* (*AUT*) veilleuse *f*.
sideline ['saɪdlaɪn] *n* (*SPORT*) (ligne *f* de) touche *f*; (*fig*) activité *f* secondaire.
sidelong ['saɪdlɔŋ] *adj*: **to give sb a ~ glance** regarder qn du coin de l'œil.
side plate *n* petite assiette.

side road *n* petite route, route transversale.
sidesaddle ['saɪdsædl] *adv* en amazone.
side show *n* attraction *f*.
sidestep ['saɪdstɛp] *vt* (*question*) éluder; (*problem*) éviter ♦ *vi* (*BOXING etc*) esquiver.
side street *n* rue transversale.
sidetrack ['saɪdtræk] *vt* (*fig*) faire dévier de son sujet.
sidewalk ['saɪdwɔːk] *n* (*US*) trottoir *m*.
sideways ['saɪdweɪz] *adv* de côté.
siding ['saɪdɪŋ] *n* (*RAIL*) voie *f* de garage.
sidle ['saɪdl] *vi*: **to ~ up (to)** s'approcher furtivement (de).
SIDS [sɪdz] *n abbr* (= *sudden infant death syndrome*) mort subite du nourrisson, mort *f* au berceau.
siege [siːdʒ] *n* siège *m*; **to lay ~ to** assiéger.
siege economy *n* économie *f* de (temps de) siège.
Sierra Leone [sɪ'ɛrəlɪ'əun] *n* Sierra Leone *f*.
sieve [sɪv] *n* tamis *m*, passoire *f* ♦ *vt* tamiser, passer (au tamis).
sift [sɪft] *vt* passer au tamis *or* au crible; (*fig*) passer au crible ♦ *vi* (*fig*): **to ~ through** passer en revue.
sigh [saɪ] *n* soupir *m* ♦ *vi* soupirer, pousser un soupir.
sight [saɪt] *n* (*faculty*) vue *f*; (*spectacle*) spectacle *m*; (*on gun*) mire *f* ♦ *vt* apercevoir; **in ~** visible; (*fig*) en vue; **out of ~** hors de vue; **at ~** (*COMM*) à vue; **at first ~** à première vue, au premier abord; **I know her by ~** je la connais de vue; **to catch ~ of sb/sth** apercevoir qn/qch; **to lose ~ of sb/sth** perdre qn/qch de vue; **to set one's ~s on sth** jeter son dévolu sur qch.
sighted ['saɪtɪd] *adj* qui voit; **partially ~** qui a un certain degré de vision.
sightseeing ['saɪtsiːɪŋ] *n* tourisme *m*; **to go ~** faire du tourisme.
sightseer ['saɪtsiːə*] *n* touriste *m/f*.
sign [saɪn] *n* (*gen*) signe *m*; (*with hand etc*) signe, geste *m*; (*notice*) panneau *m*, écriteau *m*; (*also*: **road ~**) panneau de signalisation ♦ *vt* signer; **as a ~ of** en signe de; **it's a good/bad ~** c'est bon/mauvais signe; **plus/minus ~** signe plus/moins; **there's no ~ of a change of mind** rien ne laisse présager un revirement; **he was showing ~s of improvement** il commençait visiblement à faire des progrès; **to ~ one's name** signer.
►**sign away** *vt* (*rights etc*) renoncer officiellement à.
►**sign in** *vi* signer le registre (en arrivant).
►**sign off** *vi* (*RADIO, TV*) terminer l'émission.
►**sign on** *vi* (*MIL*) s'engager; (*as unemployed*) s'inscrire au chômage; (*enrol*): **to ~ on for a course** s'inscrire pour un cours ♦ *vt* (*MIL*) engager; (*employee*) embaucher.
►**sign out** *vi* signer le registre (en partant).
►**sign over** *vt*: **to ~ sth over to sb** céder qch par écrit à qn.
►**sign up** (*MIL*) *vt* engager ♦ *vi* s'engager.
signal ['sɪgnl] *n* signal *m* ♦ *vi* (*AUT*) mettre son clignotant ♦ *vt* (*person*) faire signe à; (*message*) communiquer par signaux; **to ~ a left/right turn** (*AUT*) indiquer *or* signaler que l'on tourne à gauche/droite; **to ~ to sb (to do sth)** faire signe à qn (de faire qch).
signal box *n* (*RAIL*) poste *m* d'aiguillage.
signalman [sɪgnlmən] *n* (*RAIL*) aiguilleur *m*.
signatory ['sɪgnətərɪ] *n* signataire *m/f*.
signature ['sɪgnətʃə*] *n* signature *f*.
signature tune *n* indicatif musical.
signet ring ['sɪgnət-] *n* chevalière *f*.
significance [sɪg'nɪfɪkəns] *n* signification *f*; importance *f*; **that is of no ~** ceci n'a pas d'importance.
significant [sɪg'nɪfɪkənt] *adj* significatif(ive); (*important*) important(e), considérable.
significantly [sɪg'nɪfɪkəntlɪ] *adv* (*improve, increase*) sensiblement; (*smile*) d'un air entendu, éloquemment; **~, ...** fait significatif, ...
signify ['sɪgnɪfaɪ] *vt* signifier.
sign language *n* langage *m* par signes.
signpost ['saɪnpəust] *n* poteau indicateur.
silage ['saɪlɪdʒ] *n* (*fodder*) fourrage vert; (*method*) ensilage *m*.
silence ['saɪlns] *n* silence *m* ♦ *vt* faire taire, réduire au silence.
silencer ['saɪlənsə*] *n* (*on gun, BRIT AUT*) silencieux *m*.
silent ['saɪlnt] *adj* silencieux(euse); (*film*) muet(te); **to keep** *or* **remain ~** garder le silence, ne rien dire.
silently ['saɪlntlɪ] *adv* silencieusement.
silent partner *n* (*COMM*) bailleur *m* de fonds, commanditaire *m*.
silhouette [sɪluː'ɛt] *n* silhouette *f* ♦ *vt*: **~d against** se profilant sur, se découpant contre.
silicon ['sɪlɪkən] *n* silicium *m*.
silicon chip *n* puce *f* électronique.
silicone ['sɪlɪkəun] *n* silicone *f*.
silk [sɪlk] *n* soie *f* ♦ *cpd* de *or* en soie.
silky ['sɪlkɪ] *adj* soyeux(euse).
sill [sɪl] *n* (*also*: **window~**) rebord *m* (de la fenêtre); (*of door*) seuil *m*; (*AUT*) bas *m* de marche.
silly ['sɪlɪ] *adj* stupide, sot(te), bête; **to do something ~** faire une bêtise.
silo ['saɪləu] *n* silo *m*.
silt [sɪlt] *n* vase *f*; limon *m*.
silver ['sɪlvə*] *n* argent *m*; (*money*) monnaie *f* (en pièces d'argent); (*also*: **~ware**) argenterie *f* ♦ *cpd* d'argent, en argent.
silver paper (*BRIT*), **silver foil** *n* papier *m* d'argent *or* d'étain.
silver-plated [sɪlvə'pleɪtɪd] *adj* plaqué(e) argent.
silversmith ['sɪlvəsmɪθ] *n* orfèvre *m/f*.
silverware ['sɪlvəwɛə*] *n* argenterie *f*.
silver wedding (anniversary) *n* noces *fpl* d'argent.

silvery ['sɪlvrɪ] *adj* argenté(e).
similar ['sɪmɪlə*] *adj*: ~ **(to)** semblable (à).
similarity [sɪmɪ'lærɪtɪ] *n* ressemblance *f*, similarité *f*.
similarly ['sɪmɪləlɪ] *adv* de la même façon, de même.
simile ['sɪmɪlɪ] *n* comparaison *f*.
simmer ['sɪmə*] *vi* cuire à feu doux, mijoter.
►**simmer down** *vi* (*fig: col*) se calmer.
simper ['sɪmpə*] *vi* minauder.
simpering ['sɪmprɪŋ] *adj* stupide.
simple ['sɪmpl] *adj* simple; **the ~ truth** la vérité pure et simple.
simple interest *n* (*MATH, COMM*) intérêts *mpl* simples.
simple-minded [sɪmpl'maɪndɪd] *adj* simplet(te), simple d'esprit.
simpleton ['sɪmpltən] *n* nigaud/e, niais/e.
simplicity [sɪm'plɪsɪtɪ] *n* simplicité *f*.
simplification [sɪmplɪfɪ'keɪʃən] *n* simplification *f*.
simplify ['sɪmplɪfaɪ] *vt* simplifier.
simply ['sɪmplɪ] *adv* simplement; (*without fuss*) avec simplicité.
simulate ['sɪmjuleɪt] *vt* simuler, feindre.
simulation [sɪmju'leɪʃən] *n* simulation *f*.
simultaneous [sɪməl'teɪnɪəs] *adj* simultané(e).
simultaneously [sɪməl'teɪnɪəslɪ] *adv* simultanément.
sin [sɪn] *n* péché *m* ♦ *vi* pécher.
Sinai ['saɪneɪaɪ] *n* Sinaï *m*.
since [sɪns] *adv*, *prep* depuis ♦ *conj* (*time*) depuis que; (*because*) puisque, étant donné que, comme; ~ **then** depuis ce moment-là; ~ **Monday** depuis lundi; **(ever) ~ I arrived** depuis mon arrivée, depuis que je suis arrivé.
sincere [sɪn'sɪə*] *adj* sincère.
sincerely [sɪn'sɪəlɪ] *adv* sincèrement; **Yours ~** (*at end of letter*) veuillez agréer, Monsieur (*or* Madame), l'expression de mes sentiments distingués *or* les meilleurs.
sincerity [sɪn'sɛrɪtɪ] *n* sincérité *f*.
sine [saɪn] *n* (*MATH*) sinus *m*.
sinew ['sɪnjuː] *n* tendon *m*; **~s** *npl* muscles *mpl*.
sinful ['sɪnful] *adj* coupable.
sing, *pt* **sang**, *pp* **sung** [sɪŋ, sæŋ, sʌŋ] *vt*, *vi* chanter.
Singapore [sɪŋgə'pɔː*] *n* Singapour *m*.
singe [sɪndʒ] *vt* brûler légèrement; (*clothes*) roussir.
singer ['sɪŋə*] *n* chanteur/euse.
Singhalese [sɪŋə'liːz] *adj* = **Sinhalese**.
singing ['sɪŋɪŋ] *n* (*of person, bird*) chant *m*; façon *f* de chanter; (*of kettle, bullet, in ears*) sifflement *m*.
single ['sɪŋgl] *adj* seul(e), unique; (*unmarried*) célibataire; (*not double*) simple ♦ *n* (*BRIT: also*: ~ **ticket**) aller *m* (simple); (*record*) 45 tours *m*; **not a ~ one was left** il n'en est pas resté un(e) seul(e); **every ~ day** chaque jour sans exception.
►**single out** *vt* choisir; distinguer.
single bed *n* lit *m* à une place.
single-breasted ['sɪŋglbrɛstɪd] *adj* droit(e).
Single European Market *n*: **the ~** le marché unique européen.
single file *n*: **in ~** en file indienne.
single-handed [sɪŋgl'hændɪd] *adv* tout(e) seul(e), sans (aucune) aide.
single-minded [sɪŋgl'maɪndɪd] *adj* résolu(e), tenace.
single parent *n* parent unique (*or* célibataire).
single room *n* chambre *f* à un lit *or* pour une personne.
singles ['sɪŋglz] *npl* (*TENNIS*) simple *m*; (*US: single people*) célibataires *m/fpl*.
singles bar *n* (*esp US*) bar *m* de rencontres pour célibataires.
single-sex school [sɪŋgl'sɛks-] *n* école *f* non mixte.
singlet ['sɪŋglɪt] *n* tricot *m* de corps.
singly ['sɪŋglɪ] *adv* séparément.
singsong ['sɪŋsɔŋ] *adj* (*tone*) chantant(e) ♦ *n* (*songs*): **to have a ~** chanter quelque chose (ensemble).
singular ['sɪŋgjulə*] *adj* singulier(ière); (*odd*) singulier, étrange; (*LING*) (au) singulier, du singulier ♦ *n* (*LING*) singulier *m*; **in the feminine ~** au féminin singulier.
singularly ['sɪŋgjuləlɪ] *adv* singulièrement; étrangement.
Sinhalese [sɪnhə'liːz] *adj* cingalais(e).
sinister ['sɪnɪstə*] *adj* sinistre.
sink [sɪŋk] *n* évier *m* ♦ *vb* (*pt* **sank**, *pp* **sunk** [sæŋk, sʌŋk]) *vt* (*ship*) (faire) couler, faire sombrer; (*foundations*) creuser; (*piles etc*): **to ~ sth into** enfoncer qch dans ♦ *vi* couler, sombrer; (*ground etc*) s'affaisser; **he sank into a chair/the mud** il s'est enfoncé dans un fauteuil/la boue; **a ~ing feeling** un serrement de cœur.
►**sink in** *vi* s'enfoncer, pénétrer; (*explanation*): **it took a long time to ~ in** il a fallu longtemps pour que ça rentre.
sinking ['sɪŋkɪŋ] *adj*: **that ~ feeling** un serrement de cœur.
sinking fund *n* fonds *mpl* d'amortissement.
sink unit *n* bloc-évier *m*.
sinner ['sɪnə*] *n* pécheur/eresse.
Sinn Féin [ʃɪn'feɪn] *n* Sinn Féin *m* (*parti politique irlandais qui soutient l'IRA*).
Sino- ['saɪnəu] *prefix* sino-.
sinuous ['sɪnjuəs] *adj* sinueux(euse).
sinus ['saɪnəs] *n* (*ANAT*) sinus *m inv*.
sip [sɪp] *n* petite gorgée ♦ *vt* boire à petites gorgées.
siphon ['saɪfən] *n* siphon *m* ♦ *vt* (*also*: ~ **off**) siphonner; (*: fig: funds*) transférer; (*: illegally*) détourner.
sir [sə*] *n* monsieur *m*; **S~ John Smith** sir John Smith; **yes ~** oui Monsieur; **Dear S~** (*in letter*) Monsieur.
siren ['saɪərn] *n* sirène *f*.

sirloin ['sɜːlɔɪn] *n* aloyau *m*.
sirloin steak *n* bifteck *m* dans l'aloyau.
sirocco [sɪ'rɔkəu] *n* sirocco *m*.
sisal ['saɪsəl] *n* sisal *m*.
sissy ['sɪsɪ] *n* (*col*: *coward*) poule mouillée.
sister ['sɪstə*] *n* sœur *f*; (*nun*) religieuse *f*, (bonne) sœur; (*BRIT*: *nurse*) infirmière *f* en chef ♦ *cpd*: ~ **organization** organisation *f* sœur; ~ **ship** sister(-)ship *m*.
sister-in-law ['sɪstərɪnlɔː] *n* belle-sœur *f*.
sit, *pt, pp* **sat** [sɪt, sæt] *vi* s'asseoir; (*assembly*) être en séance, siéger; (*for painter*) poser; (*dress etc*) tomber ♦ *vt* (*exam*) passer, se présenter à; **to ~ on a committee** faire partie d'un comité; **to ~ tight** ne pas bouger.
►**sit about**, **sit around** *vi* être assis(e) *or* rester à ne rien faire.
►**sit back** *vi* (*in seat*) bien s'installer, se carrer.
►**sit down** *vi* s'asseoir; **to be ~ting down** être assis(e).
►**sit in** *vi*: **to ~ in on a discussion** assister à une discussion.
►**sit up** *vi* s'asseoir; (*not go to bed*) rester debout, ne pas se coucher.
sitcom ['sɪtkɔm] *n abbr* (*TV*: = *situation comedy*) série *f* comique.
sit-down ['sɪtdaun] *adj*: **a ~ strike** une grève sur le tas; **a ~ meal** un repas assis.
site [saɪt] *n* emplacement *m*, site *m*; (*also*: **building ~**) chantier *m* ♦ *vt* placer.
sit-in ['sɪtɪn] *n* (*demonstration*) sit-in *m inv*, occupation *f* de locaux.
siting ['saɪtɪŋ] *n* (*location*) emplacement *m*.
sitter ['sɪtə*] *n* (*for painter*) modèle *m*; (*also*: **baby~**) baby-sitter *m/f*.
sitting ['sɪtɪŋ] *n* (*of assembly etc*) séance *f*; (*in canteen*) service *m*.
sitting member *n* (*POL*) parlementaire *m/f* en exercice.
sitting room *n* salon *m*.
sitting tenant *n* (*BRIT*) locataire occupant(e).
situate ['sɪtjueɪt] *vt* situer.
situated ['sɪtjueɪtɪd] *adj* situé(e).
situation [sɪtju'eɪʃən] *n* situation *f*; **"~s vacant/wanted"** (*BRIT*) "offres/demandes d'emploi".
situation comedy *n* (*THEAT*) comédie *f* de situation.
six [sɪks] *num* six.
six-pack ['sɪkspæk] *n* (*esp US*) pack *m* de six canettes.
sixteen [sɪks'tiːn] *num* seize.
sixth ['sɪksθ] *adj* sixième; **the upper/lower ~** (*BRIT SCOL*) la terminale/la première.
sixty ['sɪkstɪ] *num* soixante.
size [saɪz] *n* dimensions *fpl*; (*of person*) taille *f*; (*of estate, area*) étendue *f*; (*of problem*) ampleur *f*; (*of company*) importance *f*; (*of clothing*) taille; (*of shoes*) pointure *f*; (*glue*) colle *f*; **I take ~ 14** (*of dress etc*) ≈ je prends du 42 *or* la taille 42; **the small/large ~** (*of soap powder etc*) le petit/grand modèle; **it's the ~ of** ... c'est de la taille (*or* grosseur) de ..., c'est grand (*or* gros) comme ...; **cut to ~** découpé(e) aux dimensions voulues.
►**size up** *vt* juger, jauger.
sizeable ['saɪzəbl] *adj* assez grand(e) *or* gros(se); assez important(e).
sizzle ['sɪzl] *vi* grésiller.
SK *abbr* (*Canada*) = *Saskatchewan*.
skate [skeɪt] *n* patin *m*; (*fish: pl inv*) raie *f* ♦ *vi* patiner.
►**skate over**, **skate around** *vt* (*problem, issue*) éluder.
skateboard ['skeɪtbɔːd] *n* skateboard *m*, planche *f* à roulettes.
skater ['skeɪtə*] *n* patineur/euse.
skating ['skeɪtɪŋ] *n* patinage *m*.
skating rink *n* patinoire *f*.
skeleton ['skɛlɪtn] *n* squelette *m*; (*outline*) schéma *m*.
skeleton key *n* passe-partout *m*.
skeleton staff *n* effectifs réduits.
skeptic *etc* ['skɛptɪk] (*US*) = **sceptic** *etc*.
sketch [skɛtʃ] *n* (*drawing*) croquis *m*, esquisse *f*; (*THEAT*) sketch *m*, saynète *f* ♦ *vt* esquisser, faire un croquis *or* une esquisse de.
sketch book *n* carnet *m* à dessin.
sketch pad *n* bloc *m* à dessin.
sketchy ['skɛtʃɪ] *adj* incomplet(ète), fragmentaire.
skew [skjuː] *n* (*BRIT*): **on the ~** de travers, en biais.
skewer ['skjuːə*] *n* brochette *f*.
ski [skiː] *n* ski *m* ♦ *vi* skier, faire du ski.
ski boot *n* chaussure *f* de ski.
skid [skɪd] *n* dérapage *m* ♦ *vi* déraper; **to go into a ~** déraper.
skid mark *n* trace *f* de dérapage.
skier ['skiːə*] *n* skieur/euse.
skiing ['skiːɪŋ] *n* ski *m*; **to go ~** (aller) faire du ski.
ski instructor *n* moniteur/trice de ski.
ski jump *n* (*ramp*) tremplin *m*; (*event*) saut *m* à skis.
skilful, (*US*) **skillful** ['skɪlful] *adj* habile, adroit(e).
ski lift *n* remonte-pente *m inv*.
skill [skɪl] *n* (*ability*) habileté *f*, adresse *f*, talent *m*; (*art, craft*) technique(s) *f(pl)*, compétences *fpl*.
skilled [skɪld] *adj* habile, adroit(e); (*worker*) qualifié(e).
skillet ['skɪlɪt] *n* poêlon *m*.
skillful *etc* ['skɪlful] (*US*) = **skilful** *etc*.
skil(l)fully ['skɪlfəlɪ] *adv* habilement, adroitement.
skim [skɪm] *vt* (*milk*) écrémer; (*soup*) écumer; (*glide over*) raser, effleurer ♦ *vi*: **to ~ through** (*fig*) parcourir.
skimmed milk [skɪmd-] *n* lait écrémé.
skimp [skɪmp] *vt* (*work*) bâcler, faire à la va-vite; (*cloth etc*) lésiner sur.

skimpy ['skɪmpɪ] *adj* étriqué(e); maigre.
skin [skɪn] *n* peau *f* ♦ *vt* (*fruit etc*) éplucher; (*animal*) écorcher; **wet** *or* **soaked to the ~** trempé(e) jusqu'aux os.
skin cancer *n* cancer *m* de la peau.
skin-deep ['skɪn'diːp] *adj* superficiel(le).
skin diver *n* plongeur/euse sous-marin(e).
skin diving *n* plongée sous-marine.
skinflint ['skɪnflɪnt] *n* grippe-sou *m*.
skin graft *n* greffe *f* de peau.
skinhead ['skɪnhɛd] *n* skinhead *m*.
skinny ['skɪnɪ] *adj* maigre, maigrichon(ne).
skin test *n* cuti(-réaction *f*) *f*.
skintight ['skɪntaɪt] *adj* (*dress etc*) collant(e), ajusté(e).
skip [skɪp] *n* petit bond *or* saut; (*container*) benne *f* ♦ *vi* gambader, sautiller; (*with rope*) sauter à la corde ♦ *vt* (*pass over*) sauter; **to ~ school** (*esp US*) faire l'école buissonnière.
ski pants *npl* pantalon *m* de ski.
ski pole *n* bâton *m* de ski.
skipper ['skɪpə*] *n* (*NAUT, SPORT*) capitaine *m* ♦ *vt* (*boat*) commander; (*team*) être le chef de.
skipping rope ['skɪpɪŋ-] *n* (*BRIT*) corde *f* à sauter.
ski resort *n* station *f* de sports d'hiver.
skirmish ['skəːmɪʃ] *n* escarmouche *f*, accrochage *m*.
skirt [skəːt] *n* jupe *f* ♦ *vt* longer, contourner.
skirting board ['skəːtɪŋ-] *n* (*BRIT*) plinthe *f*.
ski run *n* piste *f* de ski.
ski suit *n* combinaison *f* de ski.
skit [skɪt] *n* sketch *m* satirique.
ski tow *n* = **ski lift**.
skittle ['skɪtl] *n* quille *f*; **~s** (*game*) (jeu *m* de) quilles *fpl*.
skive [skaɪv] *vi* (*BRIT col*) tirer au flanc.
skulk [skʌlk] *vi* rôder furtivement.
skull [skʌl] *n* crâne *m*.
skullcap ['skʌlkæp] *n* calotte *f*.
skunk [skʌŋk] *n* mouffette *f*; (*fur*) sconse *m*.
sky [skaɪ] *n* ciel *m*; **to praise sb to the skies** porter qn aux nues.
sky-blue [skaɪ'bluː] *adj* bleu ciel *inv*.
skydiving ['skaɪdaɪvɪŋ] *n* parachutisme *m* (*en chute libre*).
sky-high ['skaɪ'haɪ] *adv* très haut ♦ *adj* exorbitant(e); **prices are ~** les prix sont exorbitants.
skylark ['skaɪlɑːk] *n* (*bird*) alouette *f* (des champs).
skylight ['skaɪlaɪt] *n* lucarne *f*.
skyline ['skaɪlaɪn] *n* (*horizon*) (ligne *f* d')horizon *m*; (*of city*) ligne des toits.
skyscraper ['skaɪskreɪpə*] *n* gratte-ciel *m inv*.
slab [slæb] *n* plaque *f*; dalle *f*; (*of wood*) bloc *m*; (*of meat, cheese*) tranche épaisse.
slack [slæk] *adj* (*loose*) lâche, desserré(e); (*slow*) stagnant(e); (*careless*) négligent(e), peu sérieux(euse) *or* conscientieux(euse); (*COMM: market*) peu actif(ive); (*: demand*) faible; (*period*) creux(euse) ♦ *n* (*in rope etc*) mou *m*; **business is ~** les affaires vont mal.
slacken ['slækn] (*also*: **~ off**) *vi* ralentir, diminuer ♦ *vt* relâcher.
slacks [slæks] *npl* pantalon *m*.
slag [slæg] *n* scories *fpl*.
slag heap *n* crassier *m*.
slain [sleɪn] *pp of* **slay**.
slake [sleɪk] *vt* (*one's thirst*) étancher.
slalom ['slɑːləm] *n* slalom *m*.
slam [slæm] *vt* (*door*) (faire) claquer; (*throw*) jeter violemment, flanquer; (*criticize*) éreinter, démolir ♦ *vi* claquer.
slammer ['slæmə*] *n* (*col*): **the ~** la taule.
slander ['slɑːndə*] *n* calomnie *f*; (*LAW*) diffamation *f* ♦ *vt* calomnier; diffamer.
slanderous ['slɑːndrəs] *adj* calomnieux(euse); diffamatoire.
slang [slæŋ] *n* argot *m*.
slanging match ['slæŋɪŋ-] *n* (*BRIT col*) engueulade *f*, empoignade *f*.
slant [slɑːnt] *n* inclinaison *f*; (*fig*) angle *m*, point *m* de vue.
slanted ['slɑːntɪd] *adj* tendancieux(euse).
slanting ['slɑːntɪŋ] *adj* en pente, incliné(e); couché(e).
slap [slæp] *n* claque *f*, gifle *f*; (*on the back*) tape *f* ♦ *vt* donner une claque *or* une gifle (*or* une tape) à ♦ *adv* (*directly*) tout droit, en plein.
slapdash ['slæpdæʃ] *adj* (*work*) fait(e) sans soin *or* à la va-vite; (*person*) insouciant(e), négligent(e).
slaphead ['slæphɛd] *n* (*BRIT col*) abruti/e, taré/e.
slapstick ['slæpstɪk] *n* (*comedy*) grosse farce (*style tarte à la crème*).
slap-up ['slæpʌp] *adj* (*BRIT*): **a ~ meal** un repas extra *or* fameux.
slash [slæʃ] *vt* entailler, taillader; (*fig: prices*) casser.
slat [slæt] *n* (*of wood*) latte *f*, lame *f*.
slate [sleɪt] *n* ardoise *f* ♦ *vt* (*fig: criticize*) éreinter, démolir.
slaughter ['slɔːtə*] *n* carnage *m*, massacre *m*; (*of animals*) abattage *m* ♦ *vt* (*animal*) abattre; (*people*) massacrer.
slaughterhouse ['slɔːtəhaus] *n* abattoir *m*.
Slav [slɑːv] *adj* slave.
slave [sleɪv] *n* esclave *m/f* ♦ *vi* (*also*: **~ away**) trimer, travailler comme un forçat; **to ~ (away) at sth/at doing sth** se tuer à qch/à faire qch.
slave driver *n* (*col, pej*) négrier/ière.
slave labour *n* travail *m* d'esclave; **it's just ~** (*fig*) c'est de l'esclavage.
slaver ['slævə*] *vi* (*dribble*) baver.
slavery ['sleɪvərɪ] *n* esclavage *m*.
Slavic ['slævɪk] *adj* slave.
slavish ['sleɪvɪʃ] *adj* servile.
slavishly ['sleɪvɪʃlɪ] *adv* (*copy*) servilement.
Slavonic [slə'vɔnɪk] *adj* slave.
slay, *pt* **slew,** *pp* **slain** [sleɪ, sluː, sleɪn] *vt* (*lite-*

rary) tuer.
sleazy ['sli:zɪ] *adj* miteux(euse), minable.
sledge [slɛdʒ] *n* luge *f*.
sledgehammer ['slɛdʒhæmə*] *n* marteau *m* de forgeron.
sleek [sli:k] *adj* (*hair, fur*) brillant(e), luisant(e); (*car, boat*) aux lignes pures *or* élégantes.
sleep [sli:p] *n* sommeil *m* ♦ *vi* (*pt, pp* **slept** [slɛpt]) dormir; (*spend night*) dormir, coucher ♦ *vt*: **we can ~ 4** on peut coucher *or* loger 4 personnes; **to go to ~** s'endormir; **to have a good night's ~** passer une bonne nuit; **to put to ~** (*patient*) endormir; (*animal: euphemism: kill*) piquer; **to ~ lightly** avoir le sommeil léger; **to ~ with sb** (*euphemism*) coucher avec qn.
►**sleep in** *vi* (*lie late*) faire la grasse matinée; (*oversleep*) se réveiller trop tard.
sleeper ['sli:pə*] *n* (*person*) dormeur/euse; (*BRIT RAIL*: *on track*) traverse *f*; (*: train*) train *m* de voitures-lits; (*: carriage*) wagon-lits *m*, voiture-lits *f*; (*: berth*) couchette *f*.
sleepily ['sli:pɪlɪ] *adv* d'un air endormi.
sleeping ['sli:pɪŋ] *adj* qui dort, endormi(e).
sleeping bag *n* sac *m* de couchage.
sleeping car *n* wagon-lits *m*, voiture-lits *f*.
sleeping partner *n* (*BRIT COMM*) = **silent partner**.
sleeping pill *n* somnifère *m*.
sleeping sickness *n* maladie *f* du sommeil.
sleepless ['sli:plɪs] *adj*: **a ~ night** une nuit blanche.
sleeplessness ['sli:plɪsnɪs] *n* insomnie *f*.
sleepwalk ['sli:pwɔ:k] *vi* marcher en dormant.
sleepwalker ['sli:pwɔ:kə*] *n* somnambule *m/f*.
sleepy ['sli:pɪ] *adj* qui a envie de dormir; (*fig*) endormi(e); **to be** *or* **feel ~** avoir sommeil, avoir envie de dormir.
sleet [sli:t] *n* neige fondue.
sleeve [sli:v] *n* manche *f*; (*of record*) pochette *f*.
sleeveless ['sli:vlɪs] *adj* (*garment*) sans manches.
sleigh [sleɪ] *n* traîneau *m*.
sleight [slaɪt] *n*: **~ of hand** tour *m* de passe-passe.
slender ['slɛndə*] *adj* svelte, mince; (*fig*) faible, ténu(e).
slept [slɛpt] *pt, pp of* **sleep**.
sleuth [slu:θ] *n* (*col*) détective (privé).
slew [slu:] *vi* (*also*: **~ round**) virer, pivoter ♦ *pt of* **slay**.
slice [slaɪs] *n* tranche *f*; (*round*) rondelle *f* ♦ *vt* couper en tranches (*or* en rondelles); **~d bread** pain *m* en tranches.
slick [slɪk] *adj* brillant(e) en apparence; mielleux(euse) ♦ *n* (*also*: **oil ~**) nappe *f* de pétrole, marée noire.
slid [slɪd] *pt, pp of* **slide**.
slide [slaɪd] *n* (*in playground*) toboggan *m*; (*PHOT*) diapositive *f*; (*BRIT*: *also*: **hair ~**) barrette *f*; (*microscope ~*) (lame *f*) porte-objet *m*; (*in prices*) chute *f*, baisse *f* ♦ *vb* (*pt, pp* **slid** [slɪd]) *vt* (faire) glisser ♦ *vi* glisser; **to let things ~** (*fig*) laisser les choses aller à la dérive.
slide projector *n* (*PHOT*) projecteur *m* de diapositives.
slide rule *n* règle *f* à calcul.
sliding ['slaɪdɪŋ] *adj* (*door*) coulissant(e); **~ roof** (*AUT*) toit ouvrant.
sliding scale *n* échelle *f* mobile.
slight [slaɪt] *adj* (*slim*) mince, menu(e); (*frail*) frêle; (*trivial*) faible, insignifiant(e); (*small*) petit(e), léger(ère) (*before n*) ♦ *n* offense *f*, affront *m* ♦ *vt* (*offend*) blesser, offenser; **the ~est** le (*or* la) moindre; **not in the ~est** pas le moins du monde, pas du tout.
slightly ['slaɪtlɪ] *adv* légèrement, un peu; **~ built** fluet(te).
slim [slɪm] *adj* mince ♦ *vi* maigrir, suivre un régime amaigrissant.
slime [slaɪm] *n* vase *f*; substance visqueuse.
slimming [slɪmɪŋ] *n* amaigrissement *m* ♦ *adj* (*diet, pills*) amaigrissant(e), pour maigrir.
slimy ['slaɪmɪ] *adj* visqueux(euse), gluant(e); (*covered with mud*) vaseux(euse).
sling [slɪŋ] *n* (*MED*) écharpe *f* ♦ *vt* (*pt, pp* **slung** [slʌŋ]) lancer, jeter; **to have one's arm in a ~** avoir le bras en écharpe.
slink, *pt, pp* **slunk** [slɪŋk, slʌŋk] *vi*: **to ~ away** *or* **off** s'en aller furtivement.
slinky ['slɪŋkɪ] *adj* (*clothes*) moulant(e).
slip [slɪp] *n* faux pas; (*mistake*) erreur *f*, bévue *f*; (*underskirt*) combinaison *f*; (*of paper*) petite feuille, fiche *f* ♦ *vt* (*slide*) glisser ♦ *vi* (*slide*) glisser; (*move smoothly*): **to ~ into/out of** se glisser *or* se faufiler dans/hors de; (*decline*) baisser; **to let a chance ~ by** laisser passer une occasion; **to ~ sth on/off** enfiler/enlever qch; **it ~ped from her hand** cela lui a glissé des mains; **to give sb the ~** fausser compagnie à qn; **a ~ of the tongue** un lapsus.
►**slip away** *vi* s'esquiver.
►**slip in** *vt* glisser.
►**slip out** *vi* sortir.
slip-on ['slɪpɔn] *adj* facile à enfiler; **~ shoes** mocassins *mpl*.
slipped disc [slɪpt-] *n* hernie discale.
slipper ['slɪpə*] *n* pantoufle *f*.
slippery ['slɪpərɪ] *adj* glissant(e); (*fig: person*) insaisissable.
slip road *n* (*BRIT*: *to motorway*) bretelle *f* d'accès.
slipshod ['slɪpʃɔd] *adj* négligé(e), peu soigné(e).
slip-up ['slɪpʌp] *n* bévue *f*.
slipway ['slɪpweɪ] *n* cale *f* (de construction *or* de lancement).
slit [slɪt] *n* fente *f*; (*cut*) incision *f*; (*tear*) déchirure *f* ♦ *vt* (*pt, pp* **slit**) fendre; couper; inciser; déchirer; **to ~ sb's throat** trancher la gorge à qn.

slither ['slɪðə*] *vi* glisser, déraper.
sliver ['slɪvə*] *n* (*of glass, wood*) éclat *m*; (*of cheese, sausage*) petit morceau.
slob [slɔb] *n* (*col*) rustaud/e.
slog [slɔg] *n* (*BRIT*) gros effort; tâche fastidieuse ♦ *vi* travailler très dur.
slogan ['sləugən] *n* slogan *m*.
slop [slɔp] *vi* (*also*: ~ **over**) se renverser; déborder ♦ *vt* répandre; renverser.
slope [sləup] *n* pente *f*; (*side of mountain*) versant *m*; (*slant*) inclinaison *f* ♦ *vi*: **to ~ down** être *or* descendre en pente; **to ~ up** monter.
sloping ['sləupɪŋ] *adj* en pente, incliné(e); (*handwriting*) penché(e).
sloppy ['slɔpɪ] *adj* (*work*) peu soigné(e), bâclé(e); (*appearance*) négligé(e), débraillé(e); (*film etc*) sentimental(e).
slosh [slɔʃ] *vi* (*col*): **to ~ about** *or* **around** (*children*) patauger; (*liquid*) clapoter.
sloshed [slɔʃt] *adj* (*col: drunk*) bourré(e).
slot [slɔt] *n* fente *f*; (*fig: in timetable, RADIO, TV*) créneau *m*, plage *f* ♦ *vt*: **to ~ into** encastrer *or* insérer dans ♦ *vi*: **to ~ into** s'encastrer *or* s'insérer dans.
sloth [sləuθ] *n* (*vice*) paresse *f*; (*ZOOL*) paresseux *m*.
slot machine *n* (*BRIT: vending machine*) distributeur *m* (automatique), machine *f* à sous; (*for gambling*) appareil *m or* machine à sous.
slot meter *n* (*BRIT*) compteur *m* à pièces.
slouch [slautʃ] *vi* avoir le dos rond, être voûté(e).
►**slouch about, slouch around** *vi* traîner à ne rien faire.
Slovak ['sləuvæk] *adj* slovaque ♦ *n* Slovaque *m/f*; (*LING*) slovaque *m*; **the ~ Republic** la République slovaque.
Slovakia [sləu'vækɪə] *n* Slovaquie *f*.
Slovakian [sləu'vækɪən] *adj, n* = **Slovak**.
Slovene [sləu'vi:n] *adj* slovène ♦ *n* Slovène *m/f*; (*LING*) slovène *m*.
Slovenia [sləu'vi:nɪə] *n* Slovénie *f*.
Slovenian [sləu'vi:nɪən] *adj, n* = **Slovene**.
slovenly ['slʌvənlɪ] *adj* sale, débraillé(e), négligé(e).
slow [sləu] *adj* lent(e); (*watch*): **to be ~** retarder ♦ *adv* lentement ♦ *vt, vi* (*also*: ~ **down**, ~ **up**) ralentir; **"~"** (*road sign*) "ralentir"; **at a ~ speed** à petite vitesse; **to be ~ to act/decide** être lent à agir/décider; **my watch is 20 minutes ~** ma montre retarde de 20 minutes; **business is ~** les affaires marchent au ralenti; **to go ~** (*driver*) rouler lentement; (*in industrial dispute*) faire la grève perlée.
slow-acting [sləu'æktɪŋ] *adj* qui agit lentement, à action lente.
slowcoach ['sləukəutʃ] *n* (*BRIT col*) lambin/e.
slowly ['sləulɪ] *adv* lentement.
slow motion *n*: **in ~** au ralenti.
slowness ['sləunɪs] *n* lenteur *f*.
slowpoke ['sləupəuk] *n* (*US col*) = **slowcoach**.
sludge [slʌdʒ] *n* boue *f*.
slug [slʌg] *n* limace *f*; (*bullet*) balle *f*.
sluggish ['slʌgɪʃ] *adj* mou(molle), lent(e); (*business, sales*) stagnant(e).
sluice [slu:s] *n* écluse *f*; (*also*: ~ **gate**) vanne *f* ♦ *vt*: **to ~ down** *or* **out** laver à grande eau.
slum [slʌm] *n* taudis *m*.
slumber ['slʌmbə*] *n* sommeil *m*.
slump [slʌmp] *n* baisse soudaine, effondrement *m*; crise *f* ♦ *vi* s'effondrer, s'affaisser.
slung [slʌŋ] *pt, pp of* **sling**.
slunk [slʌŋk] *pt, pp of* **slink**.
slur [slə:*] *n* bredouillement *m*; (*smear*): ~ **(on)** atteinte *f* (à); insinuation *f* (contre) ♦ *vt* mal articuler; **to be a ~ on** porter atteinte à.
slurp [slə:p] *vt, vi* boire à grand bruit.
slurred [slə:d] *adj* (*pronunciation*) inarticulé(e), indistinct(e).
slush [slʌʃ] *n* neige fondue.
slush fund *n* caisse noire, fonds secrets.
slushy ['slʌʃɪ] *adj* (*snow*) fondu(e); (*street*) couvert(e) de neige fondue; (*BRIT: fig*) à l'eau de rose.
slut [slʌt] *n* souillon *f*.
sly [slaɪ] *adj* rusé(e); sournois(e); **on the ~** en cachette.
smack [smæk] *n* (*slap*) tape *f*; (*on face*) gifle *f* ♦ *vt* donner une tape à; gifler; (*child*) donner la fessée à ♦ *vi*: **to ~ of** avoir des relents de, sentir ♦ *adv* (*col*): **it fell ~ in the middle** c'est tombé en plein milieu *or* en plein dedans; **to ~ one's lips** se lécher les babines.
smacker ['smækə*] *n* (*col: kiss*) bisou *m or* bise *f* sonore; (*: BRIT: pound note*) livre *f*; (*: US: dollar bill*) dollar *m*.
small [smɔ:l] *adj* petit(e); (*letter*) minuscule ♦ *n*: **the ~ of the back** le creux des reins; **to get** *or* **grow ~er** diminuer; **to make ~er** (*amount, income*) diminuer; (*object, garment*) rapetisser; **a ~ shopkeeper** un petit commerçant.
small ads *npl* (*BRIT*) petites annonces.
small arms *npl* armes individuelles.
small business *n* petit commerce, petite affaire.
small change *n* petite *or* menue monnaie.
smallholder ['smɔ:lhəuldə*] *n* (*BRIT*) petit cultivateur.
smallholding ['smɔ:lhəuldɪŋ] *n* (*BRIT*) petite ferme.
small hours *npl*: **in the ~** au petit matin.
smallish ['smɔ:lɪʃ] *adj* plutôt *or* assez petit(e).
small-minded [smɔ:l'maɪndɪd] *adj* mesquin(e).
smallpox ['smɔ:lpɔks] *n* variole *f*.
small print *n* (*in contract etc*) clause(s) imprimée(s) en petits caractères.
small-scale ['smɔ:lskeɪl] *adj* (*map, model*) à échelle réduite, à petite échelle; (*business, farming*) peu important(e), modeste.
small talk *n* menus propos.
small-time ['smɔ:ltaɪm] *adj* (*farmer etc*) petit(e); **a ~ thief** un voleur à la petite semaine.

small-town ['smɔːltaun] *adj* provincial(e).
smarmy ['smɑːmɪ] *adj* (*BRIT pej*) flagorneur(euse), lécheur(euse).
smart [smɑːt] *adj* élégant(e), chic *inv*; (*clever*) intelligent(e); (*pej*) futé(e); (*quick*) vif(vive), prompt(e) ♦ *vi* faire mal, brûler; **the ~ set** le beau monde; **to look ~** être élégant(e); **my eyes are ~ing** j'ai les yeux irrités *or* qui me piquent.
smartcard ['smɑːtkɑːd] *n* carte *f* à puce.
smarten up ['smɑːtn-] *vi* devenir plus élégant(e), se faire beau(belle) ♦ *vt* rendre plus élégant(e).
smash [smæʃ] *n* (*also*: **~-up**) collision *f*, accident *m*; (*sound*) fracas *m* ♦ *vt* casser, briser, fracasser; (*opponent*) écraser; (*hopes*) ruiner, détruire, (*SPORT*: *record*) pulvériser ♦ *vi* se briser, se fracasser; s'écraser.
►**smash up** *vt* (*car*) bousiller; (*room*) tout casser dans.
smash hit *n* (grand) succès.
smashing ['smæʃɪŋ] *adj* (*col*) formidable.
smattering ['smætərɪŋ] *n*: **a ~ of** quelques notions de.
smear [smɪə*] *n* tache *f*, salissure *f*; trace *f*; (*MED*) frottis *m*; (*insult*) calomnie *f* ♦ *vt* enduire; (*fig*) porter atteinte à; **his hands were ~ed with oil/ink** il avait les mains maculées de cambouis/d'encre.
smear campaign *n* campagne *f* de dénigrement.
smear test *n* (*BRIT MED*) frottis *m*.
smell [smɛl] *n* odeur *f*; (*sense*) odorat *m* ♦ *vb* (*pt, pp* **smelt** *or* **smelled** [smɛlt, smɛld]) *vt* sentir ♦ *vi* (*food etc*): **to ~ (of)** sentir; (*pej*) sentir mauvais; **it ~s good** ça sent bon.
smelly ['smɛlɪ] *adj* qui sent mauvais, malodorant(e).
smelt [smɛlt] *pt, pp of* **smell** ♦ *vt* (*ore*) fondre.
smile [smaɪl] *n* sourire *m* ♦ *vi* sourire.
smiling ['smaɪlɪŋ] *adj* souriant(e).
smirk [smɔːk] *n* petit sourire suffisant *or* affecté.
smith [smɪθ] *n* maréchal-ferrant *m*; forgeron *m*.
smithy ['smɪðɪ] *n* forge *f*.
smitten ['smɪtn] *adj*: **~ with** pris(e) de; frappé(e) de.
smock [smɔk] *n* blouse *f*, sarrau *m*.
smog [smɔg] *n* brouillard mêlé de fumée.
smoke [sməuk] *n* fumée *f* ♦ *vt, vi* fumer; **to have a ~** fumer une cigarette; **do you ~?** est-ce que vous fumez?; **to go up in ~** (*house etc*) brûler; (*fig*) partir en fumée.
smoked ['sməukt] *adj* (*bacon, glass*) fumé(e).
smokeless fuel ['sməuklɪs-] *n* combustible non polluant.
smokeless zone ['sməuklɪs-] *n* (*BRIT*) zone *f* où l'usage du charbon est réglementé.
smoker ['sməukə*] *n* (*person*) fumeur/euse; (*RAIL*) wagon *m* fumeurs.
smoke screen *n* rideau *m or* écran *m* de fumée; (*fig*) paravent *m*.
smoke shop *n* (*US*) (bureau *m* de) tabac *m*.
smoking ['sməukɪŋ] *n*: **"no ~"** (*sign*) "défense de fumer"; **he's given up ~** il a arrêté de fumer.
smoking compartment, (*US*) **smoking car** *n* wagon *m* fumeurs.
smoking room *n* fumoir *m*.
smoky ['sməukɪ] *adj* enfumé(e).
smolder ['sməuldə*] *vi* (*US*) = **smoulder**.
smoochy ['smuːtʃɪ] *adj* (*col*) langoureux(euse).
smooth [smuːð] *adj* lisse; (*sauce*) onctueux(euse); (*flavour, whisky*) moelleux(euse); (*cigarette*) doux(douce); (*movement*) régulier(ière), sans à-coups *or* heurts; (*landing, takeoff*) en douceur; (*flight*) sans secousses; (*person*) doucereux(euse), mielleux(euse) ♦ *vt* lisser, défroisser; (*also*: **~ out**: *creases, difficulties*) faire disparaître.
►**smooth over** *vt*: **to ~ things over** (*fig*) arranger les choses.
smoothly ['smuːðlɪ] *adv* (*easily*) facilement, sans difficulté(s); **everything went ~** tout s'est bien passé.
smother ['smʌðə*] *vt* étouffer.
smoulder, (*US*) **smolder** ['sməuldə*] *vi* couver.
smudge [smʌdʒ] *n* tache *f*, bavure *f* ♦ *vt* salir, maculer.
smug [smʌg] *adj* suffisant(e), content(e) de soi.
smuggle ['smʌgl] *vt* passer en contrebande *or* en fraude; **to ~ in/out** (*goods etc*) faire entrer/sortir clandestinement *or* en fraude.
smuggler ['smʌglə*] *n* contrebandier/ière.
smuggling ['smʌglɪŋ] *n* contrebande *f*.
smut [smʌt] *n* (*grain of soot*) grain *m* de suie; (*mark*) tache *f* de suie; (*in conversation etc*) obscénités *fpl*.
smutty ['smʌtɪ] *adj* (*fig*) grossier(ière), obscène.
snack [snæk] *n* casse-croûte *m inv*; **to have a ~** prendre un en-cas, manger quelque chose (de léger).
snack bar *n* snack(-bar) *m*.
snag [snæg] *n* inconvénient *m*, difficulté *f*.
snail [sneɪl] *n* escargot *m*.
snake [sneɪk] *n* serpent *m*.
snap [snæp] *n* (*sound*) claquement *m*, bruit sec; (*photograph*) photo *f*, instantané *m*; (*game*) *sorte de jeu de bataille* ♦ *adj* subit(e); fait(e) sans réfléchir ♦ *vt* faire claquer; (*break*) casser net; (*photograph*) prendre un instantané de ♦ *vi* se casser net *or* avec un bruit sec; (*fig: person*) craquer; **to ~ at sb** (*subj: person*) parler d'un ton brusque à qn; (*: dog*) essayer de mordre qn; **to ~ open/shut** s'ouvrir/se refermer brusquement; **to ~ one's fingers at** (*fig*) se moquer de; **a cold ~** (*of weather*) un refroidissement soudain de la température.

►**snap off** *vt* (*break*) casser net.
►**snap up** *vt* sauter sur, saisir.
snap fastener *n* bouton-pression *m*.
snappy ['snæpɪ] *adj* prompt(e); (*slogan*) qui a du punch; **make it ~!** (*col: hurry up*) grouille-toi!, magne-toi!
snapshot ['snæpʃɔt] *n* photo *f*, instantané *m*.
snare [snɛə*] *n* piège *m* ♦ *vt* attraper, prendre au piège.
snarl [snɑːl] *n* grondement *m* or grognement *m* féroce ♦ *vi* gronder ♦ *vt*: **to get ~ed up** (*wool, plans*) s'emmêler; (*traffic*) se bloquer.
snatch [snætʃ] *n* (*fig*) vol *m*; (*BRIT: small amount*): **~es of** des fragments *mpl* or bribes *fpl* de ♦ *vt* saisir (*d'un geste vif*); (*steal*) voler ♦ *vi*: **don't ~!** doucement!; **to ~ a sandwich** manger or avaler un sandwich à la hâte; **to ~ some sleep** arriver à dormir un peu.
►**snatch up** *vt* saisir, s'emparer de.
snazzy ['snæzɪ] *adj* (*col: clothes*) classe *inv*, chouette.
sneak [sniːk] *vi*: **to ~ in/out** entrer/sortir furtivement or à la dérobée ♦ *vt*: **to ~ a look at sth** regarder furtivement qch.
sneakers ['sniːkəz] *npl* chaussures *fpl* de tennis or basket.
sneaking ['sniːkɪŋ] *adj*: **to have a ~ feeling** or **suspicion that ...** avoir la vague impression que ....
sneaky ['sniːkɪ] *adj* sournois(e).
sneer [snɪə*] *n* ricanement *m* ♦ *vi* ricaner, sourire d'un air sarcastique; **to ~ at sb/sth** se moquer de qn/qch avec mépris.
sneeze [sniːz] *n* éternuement *m* ♦ *vi* éternuer.
snide [snaɪd] *adj* sarcastique, narquois(e).
sniff [snɪf] *n* reniflement *m* ♦ *vi* renifler ♦ *vt* renifler, flairer; (*glue, drug*) sniffer, respirer.
►**sniff at** *vt fus*: **it's not to be ~ed at** il ne faut pas cracher dessus, ce n'est pas à dédaigner.
sniffer dog ['snɪfə-] *n* (*POLICE*) *chien dressé pour la recherche d'explosifs et de stupéfiants*.
snigger ['snɪgə*] *n* ricanement *m*; rire moqueur ♦ *vi* ricaner; pouffer de rire.
snip [snɪp] *n* petit bout; (*bargain*) (bonne) occasion or affaire ♦ *vt* couper.
sniper ['snaɪpə*] *n* (*marksman*) tireur embusqué.
snippet ['snɪpɪt] *n* bribes *fpl*.
snivelling ['snɪvlɪŋ] *adj* larmoyant(e), pleurnicheur(euse).
snob [snɔb] *n* snob *m/f*.
snobbery ['snɔbərɪ] *n* snobisme *m*.
snobbish ['snɔbɪʃ] *adj* snob *inv*.
snog [snɔg] *vi* (*col*) se bécoter.
snooker ['snuːkə*] *n sorte de jeu de billard*.
snoop [snuːp] *vi*: **to ~ on sb** espionner qn; **to ~ about somewhere** fourrer son nez quelque part.
snooper ['snuːpə*] *n* fureteur/euse.
snooty ['snuːtɪ] *adj* snob *inv*, prétentieux(euse).
snooze [snuːz] *n* petit somme ♦ *vi* faire un petit somme.
snore [snɔː*] *vi* ronfler ♦ *n* ronflement *m*.
snoring ['snɔːrɪŋ] *n* ronflement(s) *m(pl)*.
snorkel ['snɔːkl] *n* (*of swimmer*) tuba *m*.
snort [snɔːt] *n* grognement *m* ♦ *vi* grogner; (*horse*) renâcler ♦ *vt* (*col: drugs*) sniffer.
snotty ['snɔtɪ] *adj* morveux(euse).
snout [snaut] *n* museau *m*.
snow [snəu] *n* neige *f* ♦ *vi* neiger ♦ *vt*: **to be ~ed under with work** être débordé(e) de travail.
snowball ['snəubɔːl] *n* boule *f* de neige.
snowbound ['snəubaund] *adj* enneigé(e), bloqué(e) par la neige.
snow-capped ['snəukæpt] *adj* (*peak, mountain*) couvert(e) de neige.
snowdrift ['snəudrɪft] *n* congère *f*.
snowdrop ['snəudrɔp] *n* perce-neige *m*.
snowfall ['snəufɔːl] *n* chute *f* de neige.
snowflake ['snəufleɪk] *n* flocon *m* de neige.
snowman ['snəumæn] *n* bonhomme *m* de neige.
snowplough, (*US*) **snowplow** ['snəuplau] *n* chasse-neige *m inv*.
snowshoe ['snəuʃuː] *n* raquette *f* (*pour la neige*).
snowstorm ['snəustɔːm] *n* tempête *f* de neige.
snowy ['snəuɪ] *adj* neigeux(euse); (*covered with snow*) enneigé(e).
SNP *n abbr* (*BRIT POL*) = **Scottish National Party**.
snub [snʌb] *vt* repousser, snober ♦ *n* rebuffade *f*.
snub-nosed [snʌb'nəuzd] *adj* au nez retroussé.
snuff [snʌf] *n* tabac *m* à priser ♦ *vt* (*also*: **~ out**: *candle*) moucher.
snuff movie *n* (*col*) *film pornographique qui se termine par le meurtre réel de l'un des acteurs*.
snug [snʌg] *adj* douillet(te), confortable; **it's a ~ fit** c'est bien ajusté(e).
snuggle ['snʌgl] *vi*: **to ~ down in bed/up to sb** se pelotonner dans son lit/contre qn.
SO *abbr* (*BANKING*) = **standing order**.

KEYWORD

so [səu] *adv* **1** (*thus, likewise*) ainsi, de cette façon; **if ~** si oui; **~ do** or **have I** moi aussi; **it's 5 o'clock — ~ it is!** il est 5 heures — en effet! or c'est vrai!; **I hope/think ~** je l'espère/le crois; **~ far** jusqu'ici, jusqu'à maintenant; (*in past*) jusque-là; **quite ~!** exactement!, c'est bien ça!; **even ~** quand même, tout de même
2 (*in comparisons etc: to such a degree*) si, tellement; **~ big (that)** si or tellement grand (que); **she's not ~ clever as her brother** elle n'est pas aussi intelligente que son frère
3: **~ much** *adj, adv* tant (de); **I've got ~ much**

work j'ai tant de travail; **I love you ~ much** je vous aime tant; ~ **many** tant (de)
4 (*phrases*): **10 or** ~ à peu près *or* environ 10; ~ **long!** (*inf. goodbye*) au revoir!, à un de ces jours!; ~ **to speak** pour ainsi dire; ~ **(what)?** (*col*) (bon) et alors?, et après?
♦ *conj* **1** (*expressing purpose*): ~ **as to do** pour faire, afin de faire; ~ **(that)** pour que *or* afin que *+sub*
2 (*expressing result*) donc, par conséquent; ~ **that** si bien que, de (telle) sorte que; ~ **that's the reason!** c'est donc (pour) ça!

soak [səuk] *vt* faire *or* laisser tremper ♦ *vi* tremper; **to be ~ed through** être trempé jusqu'aux os.
►**soak in** *vi* pénétrer, être absorbé(e).
►**soak up** *vt* absorber.
soaking ['səukɪŋ] *adj* (*also*: ~ **wet**) trempé(e).
so and so *n* un tel/une telle.
soap [səup] *n* savon *m*.
soapbox ['səupbɔks] *n* tribune improvisée (en plein air).
soapflakes ['səupfleɪks] *npl* paillettes *fpl* de savon.
soap opera *n* feuilleton télévisé (*quotidienneté réaliste ou embellie*).
soap powder *n* lessive *f*, détergent *m*.
soapsuds ['səupsʌds] *npl* mousse *f* de savon.
soapy ['səupɪ] *adj* savonneux(euse).
soar [sɔː*] *vi* monter (en flèche), s'élancer; **~ing prices** prix qui grimpent.
sob [sɔb] *n* sanglot *m* ♦ *vi* sangloter.
s.o.b. *n abbr* (*US col!*: *= son of a bitch*) salaud *m* (*!*).
sober ['səubə*] *adj* qui n'est pas (*or* plus) ivre; (*sedate*) sérieux(euse), sensé(e); (*moderate*) mesuré(e); (*colour, style*) sobre, discret(ète).
►**sober up** *vt* dégriser ♦ *vi* se dégriser.
sobriety [sə'braɪətɪ] *n* (*not being drunk*) sobriété *f*; (*seriousness, sedateness*) sérieux *m*.
sob story *n* (*col, pej*) histoire larmoyante.
Soc. *abbr* (*= society*) Soc.
so-called ['səu'kɔːld] *adj* soi-disant *inv*.
soccer ['sɔkə*] *n* football *m*.
soccer pitch *n* terrain *m* de football.
soccer player *n* footballeur *m*.
sociable ['səuʃəbl] *adj* sociable.
social ['səuʃl] *adj* social(e) ♦ *n* (petite) fête.
social climber *n* arriviste *m/f*.
social club *n* amicale *f*, foyer *m*.
Social Democrat *n* social-démocrate *m/f*.
social insurance *n* (*US*) sécurité sociale.
socialism ['səuʃəlɪzəm] *n* socialisme *m*.
socialist ['səuʃəlɪst] *adj*, *n* socialiste (*m/f*).
socialite ['səuʃəlaɪt] *n* personnalité mondaine.
socialize ['səuʃəlaɪz] *vi* voir *or* rencontrer des gens, se faire des amis; **to ~ with** fréquenter; lier connaissance *or* parler avec.
social life *n* vie sociale; **how's your ~?** est-ce que tu sors beaucoup?
socially ['səuʃəlɪ] *adv* socialement, en société.
social science *n* sciences humaines.
social security *n* aide sociale.
social services *npl* services sociaux.
social welfare *n* sécurité sociale.
social work *n* assistance sociale.
social worker *n* assistant/e social(e).
society [sə'saɪətɪ] *n* société *f*; (*club*) société, association *f*; (*also*: **high** ~) (haute) société, grand monde ♦ *cpd* (*party*) mondain(e).
socio-economic ['səusɪəuiːkə'nɔmɪk] *adj* socioéconomique.
sociological [səusɪə'lɔdʒɪkl] *adj* sociologique.
sociologist [səusɪ'ɔlədʒɪst] *n* sociologue *m/f*.
sociology [səusɪ'ɔlədʒɪ] *n* sociologie *f*.
sock [sɔk] *n* chaussette *f* ♦ *vt* (*col*: *hit*) flanquer un coup à; **to pull one's ~s up** (*fig*) se secouer (les puces).
socket ['sɔkɪt] *n* cavité *f*; (*ELEC*: *also*: **wall** ~) prise *f* de courant; (*: for light bulb*) douille *f*.
sod [sɔd] *n* (*of earth*) motte *f*; (*BRIT col!*) con *m* (*!*); salaud *m* (*!*).
►**sod off** *vi*: ~ **off!** (*BRIT col!*) fous le camp!, va te faire foutre! (*!*).
soda ['səudə] *n* (*CHEM*) soude *f*; (*also*: ~ **water**) eau *f* de Seltz; (*US*: *also*: ~ **pop**) soda *m*.
sodden ['sɔdn] *adj* trempé(e); détrempé(e).
sodium ['səudɪəm] *n* sodium *m*.
sodium chloride *n* chlorure *m* de sodium.
sofa ['səufə] *n* sofa *m*, canapé *m*.
Sofia ['səufɪə] *n* Sofia.
soft [sɔft] *adj* (*not rough*) doux(douce); (*not hard*) doux; mou(molle); (*not loud*) doux, léger(ère); (*kind*) doux, gentil(le); (*weak*) indulgent(e); (*stupid*) stupide, débile.
soft-boiled ['sɔftbɔɪld] *adj* (*egg*) à la coque.
soft drink *n* boisson non alcoolisée.
soft drugs *npl* drogues douces.
soften ['sɔfn] *vt* (r)amollir; adoucir; atténuer ♦ *vi* se ramollir; s'adoucir; s'atténuer.
softener ['sɔfnə*] *n* (*water* ~) adoucisseur *m*; (*fabric* ~) produit assouplissant.
soft fruit *n* (*BRIT*) baies *fpl*.
soft furnishings *npl* tissus *mpl* d'ameublement.
soft-hearted [sɔft'hɑːtɪd] *adj* au cœur tendre.
softly ['sɔftlɪ] *adv* doucement; légèrement; gentiment.
softness ['sɔftnɪs] *n* douceur *f*.
soft option *n* solution *f* de facilité.
soft sell *n* promotion *f* de vente discrète.
soft target *n* cible *f* facile.
soft toy *n* jouet *m* en peluche.
software ['sɔftwɛə*] *n* logiciel *m*, software *m*.
software package *n* progiciel *m*.
soggy ['sɔgɪ] *adj* trempé(e); détrempé(e).
soil [sɔɪl] *n* (*earth*) sol *m*, terre *f* ♦ *vt* salir; (*fig*) souiller.
soiled [sɔɪld] *adj* sale; (*COMM*) défraîchi(e).
sojourn ['sɔdʒəːn] *n* (*formal*) séjour *m*.
solace ['sɔlɪs] *n* consolation *f*, réconfort *m*.
solar ['səulə*] *adj* solaire.
solarium, *pl* **solaria** [sə'lɛərɪəm, -rɪə] *n* sola-

rium *m*.
solar panel *n* panneau *m* solaire.
solar plexus [-'plɛksəs] *n* (*ANAT*) plexus *m* solaire.
solar power *n* énergie *f* solaire.
sold [səuld] *pt, pp of* **sell**.
solder ['səuldə*] *vt* souder (*au fil à souder*) ♦ *n* soudure *f*.
soldier ['səuldʒə*] *n* soldat *m*, militaire *m* ♦ *vi*: **to ~ on** persévérer, s'accrocher; **toy ~** petit soldat.
sold out *adj* (*COMM*) épuisé(e).
sole [səul] *n* (*of foot*) plante *f*; (*of shoe*) semelle *f*; (*fish: pl inv*) sole *f* ♦ *adj* seul(e), unique; **the ~ reason** la seule et unique raison.
solely ['səullɪ] *adv* seulement, uniquement; **I will hold you ~ responsible** je vous en tiendrai pour seul responsable.
solemn ['sɔləm] *adj* solennel(le); sérieux(euse), grave.
sole trader *n* (*COMM*) chef *m* d'entreprise individuelle.
solicit [sə'lɪsɪt] *vt* (*request*) solliciter ♦ *vi* (*prostitute*) racoler.
solicitor [sə'lɪsɪtə*] *n* (*BRIT: for wills etc*) ≈ notaire *m*; (*: in court*) ≈ avocat *m*.
solid ['sɔlɪd] *adj* (*not hollow*) plein(e), compact(e), massif(ive); (*strong, sound, reliable, not liquid*) solide; (*meal*) consistant(e), substantiel(le); (*vote*) unanime ♦ *n* solide *m*; **to be on ~ ground** être sur la terre ferme; (*fig*) être en terrain sûr; **we waited 2 ~ hours** nous avons attendu deux heures entières.
solidarity [sɔlɪ'dærɪtɪ] *n* solidarité *f*.
solid fuel *n* combustible *m* solide.
solidify [sə'lɪdɪfaɪ] *vi* se solidifier ♦ *vt* solidifier.
solidity [sə'lɪdɪtɪ] *n* solidité *f*.
solid-state ['sɔlɪdsteɪt] *adj* (*ELEC*) à circuits intégrés.
soliloquy [sə'lɪləkwɪ] *n* monologue *m*.
solitaire [sɔlɪ'tɛə*] *n* (*gem, BRIT: game*) solitaire *m*; (*US: card game*) réussite *f*.
solitary ['sɔlɪtərɪ] *adj* solitaire.
solitary confinement *n* (*LAW*) isolement *m* (cellulaire).
solitude ['sɔlɪtju:d] *n* solitude *f*.
solo ['səuləu] *n* solo *m*.
soloist ['səuləuɪst] *n* soliste *m/f*.
Solomon Islands ['sɔləmən-] *npl*: **the ~** les (îles *fpl*) Salomon *fpl*.
solstice ['sɔlstɪs] *n* solstice *m*.
soluble ['sɔljubl] *adj* soluble.
solution [sə'lu:ʃən] *n* solution *f*.
solve [sɔlv] *vt* résoudre.
solvency ['sɔlvənsɪ] *n* (*COMM*) solvabilité *f*.
solvent ['sɔlvənt] *adj* (*COMM*) solvable ♦ *n* (*CHEM*) (dis)solvant *m*.
solvent abuse *n* usage *m* de solvants hallucinogènes.
Som. *abbr* (*BRIT*) = *Somerset*.
Somali [səu'mɑ:lɪ] *adj* somali(e), somalien(ne) ♦ *n* Somali/e, Somalien/ne.
Somalia [səu'mɑ:lɪə] *n* (République *f* de) Somalie *f*.
Somaliland [səu'mɑ:lɪlænd] *n* Somaliland *m*.
sombre, (*US*) **somber** ['sɔmbə*] *adj* sombre, morne.

KEYWORD

some [sʌm] *adj* **1** (*a certain amount or number of*): **~ tea/water/ice cream** du thé/de l'eau/de la glace; **~ children/apples** des enfants/pommes
2 (*certain: in contrasts*): **~ people say that ...** il y a des gens qui disent que ...; **~ films were excellent, but most ...** certains films étaient excellents, mais la plupart ...
3 (*unspecified*): **~ woman was asking for you** il y avait une dame qui vous demandait; **he was asking for ~ book (or other)** il demandait un livre quelconque; **~ day** un de ces jours; **~ day next week** un jour la semaine prochaine; **after ~ time** après un certain temps; **at ~ length** assez longuement; **in ~ form or other** sous une forme ou une autre, sous une forme quelconque
♦ *pron* **1** (*a certain number*) quelques-un(e)s, certain(e)s; **I've got ~** (*books etc*) j'en ai (quelques-uns); **~ (of them) have been sold** certains ont été vendus
2 (*a certain amount*) un peu; **I've got ~** (*money, milk*) j'en ai (un peu); **would you like ~?** est-ce que vous en voulez?, en voulez-vous?
♦ *adv*: **~ 10 people** quelque 10 personnes, 10 personnes environ.

somebody ['sʌmbədɪ] *pron* quelqu'un; **~ or other** quelqu'un, je ne sais qui.
someday ['sʌmdeɪ] *adv* un de ces jours, un jour ou l'autre.
somehow ['sʌmhau] *adv* d'une façon ou d'une autre; (*for some reason*) pour une raison ou une autre.
someone ['sʌmwʌn] *pron* = **somebody**.
someplace ['sʌmpleɪs] *adv* (*US*) = **somewhere**.
somersault ['sʌməsɔ:lt] *n* culbute *f*, saut périlleux ♦ *vi* faire la culbute *or* un saut périlleux; (*car*) faire un tonneau.
something ['sʌmθɪŋ] *pron* quelque chose *m*; **~ interesting** quelque chose d'intéressant; **~ to do** quelque chose à faire; **he's ~ like me** il est un peu comme moi; **it's ~ of a problem** il y a là un problème.
sometime ['sʌmtaɪm] *adv* (*in future*) un de ces jours, un jour ou l'autre; (*in past*): **~ last month** au cours du mois dernier.
sometimes ['sʌmtaɪmz] *adv* quelquefois, parfois.
somewhat ['sʌmwɔt] *adv* quelque peu, un peu.
somewhere ['sʌmwɛə*] *adv* quelque part; **~ else** ailleurs, autre part.

son [sʌn] *n* fils *m*.
sonar ['səunɑː*] *n* sonar *m*.
sonata [sə'nɑːtə] *n* sonate *f*.
song [sɔŋ] *n* chanson *f*.
songbook ['sɔŋbuk] *n* chansonnier *m*.
songwriter ['sɔŋraɪtə*] *n* auteur-compositeur *m*.
sonic ['sɔnɪk] *adj* (*boom*) supersonique.
son-in-law ['sʌnɪnlɔː] *n* gendre *m*, beau-fils *m*.
sonnet ['sɔnɪt] *n* sonnet *m*.
sonny ['sʌnɪ] *n* (*col*) fiston *m*.
soon [suːn] *adv* bientôt; (*early*) tôt; ~ **afterwards** peu après; **quite** ~ sous peu; **how** ~ **can you do it?** combien de temps vous faut-il pour le faire, au plus pressé?; **how** ~ **can you come back?** quand *or* dans combien de temps pouvez-vous revenir, au plus tôt; **see you** ~! à bientôt!; *see also* **as.**
sooner ['suːnə*] *adv* (*time*) plus tôt; (*preference*): **I would** ~ **do** j'aimerais autant *or* je préférerais faire; ~ **or later** tôt ou tard; **no** ~ **said than done** sitôt dit, sitôt fait; **the** ~ **the better** le plus tôt sera le mieux; **no** ~ **had we left than** ... à peine étions-nous partis que ....
soot [sut] *n* suie *f*.
soothe [suːð] *vt* calmer, apaiser.
soothing ['suːðɪŋ] *adj* (*ointment etc*) lénitif(ive), lénifiant(e); (*tone, words etc*) apaisant(e); (*drink, bath*) relaxant(e).
SOP *n abbr* = *standard operating procedure.*
sop [sɔp] *n*: **that's only a** ~ c'est pour nous (*or* les *etc*) amadouer.
sophisticated [sə'fɪstɪkeɪtɪd] *adj* raffiné(e), sophistiqué(e); (*system etc*) très perfectionné(e), sophistiqué.
sophistication [səfɪstɪ'keɪʃən] *n* raffinement *m*; (niveau *m* de) perfectionnement *m*.
sophomore ['sɔfəmɔː*] *n* (*US*) étudiant/e de seconde année.
soporific [sɔpə'rɪfɪk] *adj* soporifique ♦ *n* somnifère *m*.
sopping ['sɔpɪŋ] *adj* (*also*: ~ **wet**) tout(e) trempé(e).
soppy ['sɔpɪ] *adj* (*pej*) sentimental(e).
soprano [sə'prɑːnəu] *n* (*voice*) soprano *m*; (*singer*) soprano *m/f*.
sorbet ['sɔːbeɪ] *n* sorbet *m*.
sorcerer ['sɔːsərə*] *n* sorcier *m*.
sordid ['sɔːdɪd] *adj* sordide.
sore [sɔː*] *adj* (*painful*) douloureux(euse), sensible; (*offended*) contrarié(e), vexé(e) ♦ *n* plaie *f*; **to have a** ~ **throat** avoir mal à la gorge; **it's a** ~ **point** (*fig*) c'est un point délicat.
sorely ['sɔːlɪ] *adv* (*tempted*) fortement.
sorrel ['sɔrəl] *n* oseille *f*.
sorrow ['sɔrəu] *n* peine *f*, chagrin *m*.
sorrowful ['sɔrəuful] *adj* triste.
sorry ['sɔrɪ] *adj* désolé(e); (*condition, excuse, tale*) triste, déplorable; (*sight*) désolant(e); ~! pardon!, excusez-moi!; **to feel** ~ **for sb** plaindre qn; **I'm** ~ **to hear that** ... je suis désolé(e) *or* navré(e) d'apprendre que ...; **to be** ~ **about sth** regretter qch.
sort [sɔːt] *n* genre *m*, espèce *f*, sorte *f*; (*make: of coffee, car etc*) marque *f* ♦ *vt* (*also*: ~ **out**: *papers*) trier; classer; ranger; (*: letters etc*) trier; (*: problems*) résoudre, régler; (*COMPUT*) trier; **what** ~ **do you want?** quelle sorte *or* quel genre voulez-vous?; **what** ~ **of car?** quelle marque de voiture?; **I'll do nothing of the** ~! je ne ferai rien de tel!; **it's** ~ **of awkward** (*col*) c'est plutôt gênant.
sortie ['sɔːtɪ] *n* sortie *f*.
sorting office ['sɔːtɪŋ-] *n* (*POST*) bureau *m* de tri.
SOS *n abbr* (= *save our souls*) SOS *m*.
so-so ['səusəu] *adv* comme ci comme ça.
soufflé ['suːfleɪ] *n* soufflé *m*.
sought [sɔːt] *pt, pp of* **seek.**
sought-after ['sɔːtɑːftə*] *adj* recherché(e).
soul [səul] *n* âme *f*; **the poor** ~ **had nowhere to sleep** le pauvre n'avait nulle part où dormir; **I didn't see a** ~ je n'ai vu (absolument) personne.
soul-destroying ['səuldɪstrɔɪɪŋ] *adj* démoralisant(e).
soulful ['səulful] *adj* plein(e) de sentiment.
soulless ['səullɪs] *adj* sans cœur, inhumain(e).
soul mate *n* âme *f* sœur.
soul-searching ['səulsəːtʃɪŋ] *n*: **after much** ~, **I decided** ... j'ai longuement réfléchi avant de décider ....
sound [saund] *adj* (*healthy*) en bonne santé, sain(e); (*safe, not damaged*) solide, en bon état; (*reliable, not superficial*) sérieux(euse), solide; (*sensible*) sensé(e) ♦ *adv*: ~ **asleep** dormant d'un profond sommeil ♦ *n* (*noise*) son *m*; bruit *m*; (*GEO*) détroit *m*, bras *m* de mer ♦ *vt* (*alarm*) sonner; (*also*: ~ **out**: *opinions*) sonder ♦ *vi* sonner, retentir; (*fig: seem*) sembler (être); **to be of** ~ **mind** être sain(e) d'esprit; **I don't like the** ~ **of it** ça ne me dit rien qui vaille; **to** ~ **one's horn** (*AUT*) klaxonner, actionner son avertisseur; **to** ~ **like** ressembler à; **it** ~**s as if** ... il semblerait que ..., j'ai l'impression que ....
►**sound off** *vi* (*col*): **to** ~ **off (about)** la ramener (sur).
sound barrier *n* mur *m* du son.
soundbite ['saundbaɪt] *n* phrase toute faite (*pour être citée dans les médias*).
sound effects *npl* bruitage *m*.
sound engineer *n* ingénieur *m* du son.
sounding ['saundɪŋ] *n* (*NAUT etc*) sondage *m*.
sounding board *n* (*MUS*) table *f* d'harmonie; (*fig*): **to use sb as a** ~ **for one's ideas** essayer ses idées sur qn.
soundly ['saundlɪ] *adv* (*sleep*) profondément; (*beat*) complètement, à plate couture.
soundproof ['saundpruːf] *vt* insonoriser ♦ *adj* insonorisé(e).
sound system *n* sono(risation) *f*.

soundtrack ['saundtræk] *n* (*of film*) bande *f* sonore.
sound wave *n* (*PHYSICS*) onde *f* sonore.
soup [su:p] *n* soupe *f*, potage *m*; **in the ~** (*fig*) dans le pétrin.
soup course *n* potage *m*.
soup kitchen *n* soupe *f* populaire.
soup plate *n* assiette creuse *or* à soupe.
soupspoon ['su:pspu:n] *n* cuiller *f* à soupe.
sour ['sauə*] *adj* aigre, acide; (*milk*) tourné(e), aigre; (*fig*) acerbe, aigre; revêche; **to go** *or* **turn ~** (*milk, wine*) tourner; (*fig: relationship, plans*) mal tourner; **it's ~ grapes** c'est du dépit.
source [sɔ:s] *n* source *f*; **I have it from a reliable ~ that** je sais de source sûre que.
south [sauθ] *n* sud *m* ♦ *adj* sud *inv*, du sud ♦ *adv* au sud, vers le sud; **(to the) ~ of** au sud de; **to travel ~** aller en direction du sud; **the S~ of France** le Sud de la France, le Midi.
South Africa *n* Afrique *f* du Sud.
South African *adj* sud-africain(e) ♦ *n* Sud-Africain/e.
South America *n* Amérique *f* du Sud.
South American *adj* sud-américain(e) ♦ *n* Sud-Américain/e.
southbound ['sauθbaund] *adj* en direction du sud; (*carriageway*) sud *inv*.
south-east [sauθ'i:st] *n* sud-est *m*.
South-East Asia *n* le Sud-Est asiatique.
southerly ['sʌðəlı] *adj* du sud; au sud.
southern ['sʌðən] *adj* (du) sud; méridional(e); **with a ~ aspect** orienté(e) *or* exposé(e) au sud; **the ~ hemisphere** l'hémisphère sud *or* austral.
South Pole *n* Pôle *m* Sud.
South Sea Islands *npl*: **the ~** l'Océanie *f*.
South Seas *npl*: **the ~** les mers *fpl* du Sud.
South Vietnam *n* Viêt-Nam *m* du Sud.
southward(s) ['sauθwəd(z)] *adv* vers le sud.
south-west [sauθ'wɛst] *n* sud-ouest *m*.
souvenir [su:və'nıə*] *n* souvenir *m* (*objet*).
sovereign ['sɔvrın] *adj*, *n* souverain(e).
sovereignty ['sɔvrıntı] *n* souveraineté *f*.
soviet ['səuvıət] *adj* soviétique.
Soviet Union *n*: **the ~** l'Union *f* soviétique.
sow *n* [sau] truie *f* ♦ *vt* [səu] (*pt* **~ed**, *pp* **sown** [səun]) semer.
soya ['sɔıə], (*US*) **soy** [sɔı] *n*: **~ bean** graine *f* de soja; **~ sauce** sauce *f* au soja.
sozzled ['sɔzld] *adj* (*BRIT col*) paf *inv*.
spa [spɑ:] *n* (*town*) station thermale; (*US*: *also*: **health ~**) établissement *m* de cure de rajeunissement.
space [speıs] *n* (*gen*) espace *m*; (*room*) place *f*; espace; (*length of time*) laps *m* de temps ♦ *cpd* spatial(e) ♦ *vt* (*also*: **~ out**) espacer; **to clear a ~ for sth** faire de la place pour qch; **in a confined ~** dans un espace réduit *or* restreint; **in a short ~ of time** dans peu de temps; **(with)in the ~ of an hour** en l'espace d'une heure.
space bar *n* (*on typewriter*) barre *f* d'espacement.
spacecraft ['speıskrɑ:ft] *n* engin spatial.
spaceman ['speısmæn] *n* astronaute *m*, cosmonaute *m*.
spaceship ['speısʃıp] *n* engin *or* vaisseau spatial.
space shuttle *n* navette spatiale.
spacesuit ['speıssu:t] *n* combinaison spatiale.
spacewoman ['speıswumən] *n* astronaute *f*, cosmonaute *f*.
spacing ['speısıŋ] *n* espacement *m*; **single/double ~** interligne *m* simple/double.
spacious ['speıʃəs] *adj* spacieux(euse), grand(e).
spade [speıd] *n* (*tool*) bêche *f*, pelle *f*; (*child's*) pelle; **~s** *npl* (*CARDS*) pique *m*.
spadework ['speıdwə:k] *n* (*fig*) gros *m* du travail.
spaghetti [spə'gɛtı] *n* spaghetti *mpl*.
Spain [speın] *n* Espagne *f*.
spam [spæm] *n* spam *m* ♦ *vt* spammer.
span [spæn] *n* (*of bird, plane*) envergure *f*; (*of arch*) portée *f*; (*in time*) espace *m* de temps, durée *f* ♦ *vt* enjamber, franchir; (*fig*) couvrir, embrasser.
Spaniard ['spænjəd] *n* Espagnol/e.
spaniel ['spænjəl] *n* épagneul *m*.
Spanish ['spænıʃ] *adj* espagnol(e), d'Espagne ♦ *n* (*LING*) espagnol *m*; **the ~** *npl* les Espagnols; **~ omelette** omelette *f* à l'espagnole.
spank [spæŋk] *vt* donner une fessée à.
spanner ['spænə*] *n* (*BRIT*) clé *f* (de mécanicien).
spar [spɑ:*] *n* espar *m* ♦ *vi* (*BOXING*) s'entraîner.
spare [spɛə*] *adj* de réserve, de rechange; (*surplus*) de *or* en trop, de reste ♦ *n* (*part*) pièce *f* de rechange, pièce détachée ♦ *vt* (*do without*) se passer de; (*afford to give*) donner, accorder, passer; (*refrain from hurting*) épargner; (*refrain from using*) ménager; **to ~** (*surplus*) en surplus, de trop; **there are 2 going ~** (*BRIT*) il y en a 2 de disponible; **to ~ no expense** ne pas reculer devant la dépense; **can you ~ the time?** est-ce que vous avez le temps?; **there is no time to ~** il n'y a pas de temps à perdre; **I've a few minutes to ~** je dispose de quelques minutes.
spare part *n* pièce *f* de rechange, pièce détachée.
spare room *n* chambre *f* d'ami.
spare time *n* moments *mpl* de loisir.
spare tyre *n* (*AUT*) pneu *m* de rechange.
spare wheel *n* (*AUT*) roue *f* de secours.
sparing ['spɛərıŋ] *adj*: **to be ~ with** ménager.
sparingly ['spɛərıŋlı] *adv* avec modération.
spark [spɑ:k] *n* étincelle *f*; (*fig*) étincelle, lueur *f*.
spark(ing) plug ['spɑ:k(ıŋ)-] *n* bougie *f*.
sparkle ['spɑ:kl] *n* scintillement *m*, étincellement *m*, éclat *m* ♦ *vi* étinceler, scintiller;

(*bubble*) pétiller.
sparkler ['spɑːklə*] *n* cierge *m* magique.
sparkling ['spɑːklɪŋ] *adj* étincelant(e), scintillant(e); (*wine*) mousseux(euse), pétillant(e).
sparring partner ['spɑːrɪŋ-] *n* sparring-partner *m*; (*fig*) vieil(le) ennemi/e.
sparrow ['spærəu] *n* moineau *m*.
sparse [spɑːs] *adj* clairsemé(e).
spartan ['spɑːtən] *adj* (*fig*) spartiate.
spasm ['spæzəm] *n* (*MED*) spasme *m*; (*fig*) accès *m*.
spasmodic [spæz'mɔdɪk] *adj* (*fig*) intermittent(e).
spastic ['spæstɪk] *n* handicapé/e moteur.
spat [spæt] *pt, pp of* **spit** ♦ *n* (*US*) prise *f* de bec.
spate [speɪt] *n* (*fig*): ~ **of** avalanche *f or* torrent *m* de; **in** ~ (*river*) en crue.
spatial ['speɪʃl] *adj* spatial(e).
spatter ['spætə*] *n* éclaboussure(s) *f(pl)* ♦ *vt* éclabousser ♦ *vi* gicler.
spatula ['spætjulə] *n* spatule *f*.
spawn [spɔːn] *vt* pondre; (*pej*) engendrer ♦ *vi* frayer ♦ *n* frai *m*.
SPCA *n abbr* (*US*: = *Society for the Prevention of Cruelty to Animals*) ≈ SPA *f*.
SPCC *n abbr* (*US*) = *Society for the Prevention of Cruelty to Children*.
speak, *pt* **spoke,** *pp* **spoken** [spiːk, spəuk, 'spəukn] *vt* (*language*) parler; (*truth*) dire ♦ *vi* parler; (*make a speech*) prendre la parole; **to ~ to sb/of** *or* **about sth** parler à qn/de qch; **~ing!** (*on telephone*) c'est moi-même!; **to ~ one's mind** dire ce que l'on pense; **it ~s for itself** c'est évident; **~ up!** parle plus fort!, **he has no money to ~ of** il n'a pas d'argent.
►**speak for** *vt fus*: **to ~ for sb** parler pour qn; **that picture is already spoken for** (*in shop*) ce tableau est déjà réservé.
speaker ['spiːkə*] *n* (*in public*) orateur *m*; (*also*: **loud~**) haut-parleur *m*; (*POL*): **the S~** *le président de la Chambre des communes* (*BRIT*) *or des représentants* (*US*); **are you a Welsh ~?** parlez-vous gallois?
speaking ['spiːkɪŋ] *adj* parlant(e); **French-~ people** les francophones; **to be on ~ terms** se parler.
spear [spɪə*] *n* lance *f* ♦ *vt* transpercer.
spearhead ['spɪəhɛd] *n* fer *m* de lance; (*MIL*) colonne *f* d'attaque ♦ *vt* (*attack etc*) mener.
spearmint ['spɪəmɪnt] *n* (*BOT etc*) menthe verte.
spec [spɛk] *n* (*BRIT col*): **on ~** à tout hasard; **to buy on ~** acheter avec l'espoir de faire une bonne affaire.
special ['spɛʃl] *adj* spécial(e) ♦ *n* (*train*) train spécial; **take ~ care** soyez particulièrement prudents; **nothing ~** rien de spécial; **today's ~** (*at restaurant*) le plat du jour.
special agent *n* agent secret.
special correspondent *n* envoyé spécial.
special delivery *n* (*POST*): **by ~** en exprès.
special effects *npl* (*CINE*) effets spéciaux.
specialist ['spɛʃəlɪst] *n* spécialiste *m/f*; **heart ~** cardiologue *m/f*.
speciality [spɛʃɪ'ælɪtɪ] *n* spécialité *f*.
specialize ['spɛʃəlaɪz] *vi*: **to ~ (in)** se spécialiser (dans).
specially ['spɛʃlɪ] *adv* spécialement, particulièrement.
special offer *n* (*COMM*) réclame *f*.
specialty ['spɛʃəltɪ] *n* (*US*) = **speciality**.
species ['spiːʃiːz] *n* (*pl inv*) espèce *f*.
specific [spə'sɪfɪk] *adj* (*not vague*) précis(e), explicite; (*particular*) particulier(ière); (*BOT, CHEM etc*) spécifique; **to be ~ to** être particulier à, être le *or* un caractère (*or* les caractères) spécifique(s) de.
specifically [spə'sɪfɪklɪ] *adv* explicitement, précisément; (*intend, ask, design*) expressément, spécialement; (*exclusively*) exclusivement, spécifiquement.
specification [spɛsɪfɪ'keɪʃən] *n* spécification *f*; stipulation *f*; **~s** *npl* (*of car, building etc*) spécification.
specify ['spɛsɪfaɪ] *vt* spécifier, préciser; **unless otherwise specified** sauf indication contraire.
specimen ['spɛsɪmən] *n* spécimen *m*, échantillon *m*; (*MED*) prélèvement *m*.
specimen copy *n* spécimen *m*.
specimen signature *n* spécimen *m* de signature.
speck [spɛk] *n* petite tache, petit point; (*particle*) grain *m*.
speckled ['spɛkld] *adj* tacheté(e), moucheté(e).
specs [spɛks] *npl* (*col*) lunettes *fpl*.
spectacle ['spɛktəkl] *n* spectacle *m*.
spectacle case *n* (*BRIT*) étui *m* à lunettes.
spectacles ['spɛktəklz] *npl* (*BRIT*) lunettes *fpl*.
spectacular [spɛk'tækjulə*] *adj* spectaculaire ♦ *n* (*CINE etc*) superproduction *f*.
spectator [spɛk'teɪtə*] *n* spectateur/trice.
spectator sport *n*: **football is a great ~** le football est un sport qui passionne les foules.
spectra ['spɛktrə] *npl of* **spectrum**.
spectre, (*US*) **specter** ['spɛktə*] *n* spectre *m*, fantôme *m*.
spectrum, *pl* **spectra** ['spɛktrəm, -rə] *n* spectre *m*; (*fig*) gamme *f*.
speculate ['spɛkjuleɪt] *vi* spéculer; (*try to guess*): **to ~ about** s'interroger sur.
speculation [spɛkju'leɪʃən] *n* spéculation *f*; conjectures *fpl*.
speculative ['spɛkjulətɪv] *adj* spéculatif(ive).
speculator ['spɛkjuleɪtə*] *n* spéculateur/trice.
speech [spiːtʃ] *n* (*faculty*) parole *f*; (*talk*) discours *m*, allocution *f*; (*manner of speaking*) façon *f* de parler, langage *m*; (*language*) langage *m*; (*enunciation*) élocution *f*.
speech day *n* (*BRIT SCOL*) distribution *f* des prix.
speech impediment *n* défaut *m* d'élocution.

speechless ['spi:tʃlɪs] *adj* muet(te).
speech therapy *n* orthophonie *f*.
speed [spi:d] *n* vitesse *f*; (*promptness*) rapidité *f* ♦ *vi* (*pt, pp* **sped** [spɛd]): **to ~ along/by** *etc* aller/passer *etc* à toute vitesse; (*AUT: exceed ~ limit*) faire un excès de vitesse; **at ~** (*BRIT*) rapidement; **at full** *or* **top ~** à toute vitesse *or* allure; **at a ~ of 70 km/h** à une vitesse de 70 km/h; **shorthand/typing ~s** nombre *m* de mots à la minute en sténographie/dactylographie; **a five-~ gearbox** une boîte cinq vitesses.
►**speed up**, *pt, pp* **~ed up** *vi* aller plus vite, accélérer ♦ *vt* accélérer.
speedboat ['spi:dbəut] *n* vedette *f*, hors-bord *m inv*.
speedily ['spi:dɪlɪ] *adv* rapidement, promptement.
speeding ['spi:dɪŋ] *n* (*AUT*) excès *m* de vitesse.
speed limit *n* limitation *f* de vitesse, vitesse maximale permise.
speedometer [spɪ'dɔmɪtə*] *n* compteur *m* (de vitesse).
speed trap *n* (*AUT*) piège *m* de police pour contrôle de vitesse.
speedway *n* (*SPORT*) piste *f* de vitesse pour motos; (*: also:* **~ racing**) épreuve(s) *f(pl)* de vitesse de motos.
speedy [spi:dɪ] *adj* rapide, prompt(e).
speleologist [spɛlɪ'ɔlədʒɪst] *n* spéléologue *m/f*.
spell [spɛl] *n* (*also:* **magic ~**) sortilège *m*, charme *m*; (*period of time*) (courte) période ♦ *vt* (*pt, pp* **spelt** *or* **~ed** [spɛlt, spɛld]) (*in writing*) écrire, orthographier; (*aloud*) épeler; (*fig*) signifier; **to cast a ~ on sb** jeter un sort à qn; **he can't ~** il fait des fautes d'orthographe; **how do you ~ your name?** comment écrivez-vous votre nom?; **can you ~ it for me?** pouvez-vous me l'épeler?
spellbound ['spɛlbaund] *adj* envoûté(e), subjugué(e).
spelling ['spɛlɪŋ] *n* orthographe *f*.
spelt [spɛlt] *pt, pp of* **spell**.
spend, *pt, pp* **spent** [spɛnd, spɛnt] *vt* (*money*) dépenser; (*time, life*) passer; (*devote*): **to ~ time/money/effort on sth** consacrer du temps/de l'argent/de l'énergie à qch.
spending ['spɛndɪŋ] *n* dépenses *fpl*; **government ~** les dépenses publiques.
spending money *n* argent *m* de poche.
spending power *n* pouvoir *m* d'achat.
spendthrift ['spɛndθrɪft] *n* dépensier/ière.
spent [spɛnt] *pt, pp of* **spend** ♦ *adj* (*patience*) épuisé(e), à bout; (*cartridge, bullets*) vide; **~ matches** vieilles allumettes.
sperm [spə:m] *n* spermatozoïde *m*; (*semen*) sperme *m*.
sperm bank *n* banque *f* du sperme.
sperm whale *n* cachalot *m*.
spew [spju:] *vt* vomir.
sphere [sfɪə*] *n* sphère *f*; (*fig*) sphère, domaine *m*.
spherical ['sfɛrɪkl] *adj* sphérique.
sphinx [sfɪŋks] *n* sphinx *m*.
spice [spaɪs] *n* épice *f* ♦ *vt* épicer.
spick-and-span ['spɪkən'spæn] *adj* impeccable.
spicy ['spaɪsɪ] *adj* épicé(e), relevé(e); (*fig*) piquant(e).
spider ['spaɪdə*] *n* araignée *f*; **~'s web** toile *f* d'araignée.
spiel [spi:l] *n* laïus *m inv*.
spike [spaɪk] *n* pointe *f*; (*ELEC*) pointe de tension; **~s** *npl* (*SPORT*) chaussures *fpl* à pointes.
spike heel *n* (*US*) talon *m* aiguille.
spiky ['spaɪkɪ] *adj* (*bush, branch*) épineux(euse); (*animal*) plein(e) de piquants.
spill, *pt, pp* **spilt** *or* **~ed** [spɪl, -t, -d] *vt* renverser; répandre ♦ *vi* se répandre; **to ~ the beans** (*col*) vendre la mèche; (*: confess*) lâcher le morceau.
►**spill out** *vi* sortir à flots, se répandre.
►**spill over** *vi* déborder.
spillage ['spɪlɪdʒ] *n* (*of oil*) déversement *m* (accidentel).
spin [spɪn] *n* (*revolution of wheel*) tour *m*; (*AVIAT*) (chute *f* en) vrille *f*; (*trip in car*) petit tour, balade *f* ♦ *vb* (*pt, pp* **spun** [spʌn]) *vt* (*wool etc*) filer; (*wheel*) faire tourner; (*BRIT: clothes*) essorer ♦ *vi* tourner, tournoyer; **to ~ a yarn** débiter une longue histoire; **to ~ a coin** (*BRIT*) jouer à pile ou face.
►**spin out** *vt* faire durer.
spina bifida ['spaɪnə'bɪfɪdə] *n* spina-bifida *m inv*.
spinach ['spɪnɪtʃ] *n* épinard *m*; (*as food*) épinards.
spinal ['spaɪnl] *adj* vertébral(e), spinal(e).
spinal column *n* colonne vertébrale.
spinal cord *n* moelle épinière.
spindly ['spɪndlɪ] *adj* grêle, filiforme.
spin doctor *n* (*col*) *personne employée pour présenter un parti politique sous un jour favorable.*
spin-dry ['spɪn'draɪ] *vt* essorer.
spin-dryer [spɪn'draɪə*] *n* (*BRIT*) essoreuse *f*.
spine [spaɪn] *n* colonne vertébrale; (*thorn*) épine *f*, piquant *m*.
spine-chilling ['spaɪntʃɪlɪŋ] *adj* terrifiant(e).
spineless ['spaɪnlɪs] *adj* invertébré(e); (*fig*) mou(molle), sans caractère.
spinner ['spɪnə*] *n* (*of thread*) fileur/euse.
spinning ['spɪnɪŋ] *n* (*of thread*) filage *m*; (*by machine*) filature *f*.
spinning top *n* toupie *f*.
spinning wheel *n* rouet *m*.
spin-off ['spɪnɔf] *n* sous-produit *m*; avantage inattendu.
spinster ['spɪnstə*] *n* célibataire *f*; vieille fille.
spiral ['spaɪərl] *n* spirale *f* ♦ *adj* en spirale ♦ *vi* (*fig: prices etc*) monter en flèche; **the inflationary ~** la spirale inflationniste.
spiral staircase *n* escalier *m* en colimaçon.
spire ['spaɪə*] *n* flèche *f*, aiguille *f*.

spirit ['spɪrɪt] *n* (*soul*) esprit *m*, âme *f*; (*ghost*) esprit, revenant *m*; (*mood*) esprit, état *m* d'esprit; (*courage*) courage *m*, énergie *f*; **~s** *npl* (*drink*) spiritueux *mpl*, alcool *m*; **in good ~s** de bonne humeur; **in low ~s** démoralisé(e); **community ~** solidarité *f*; **public ~** civisme *m*.
spirit duplicator *n* duplicateur *m* à alcool.
spirited ['spɪrɪtɪd] *adj* vif(vive), fougueux(euse), plein(e) d'allant.
spirit level *n* niveau *m* à bulle.
spiritual ['spɪrɪtjuəl] *adj* spirituel(le); religieux(euse) ♦ *n* (*also*: **Negro ~**) spiritual *m*.
spiritualism ['spɪrɪtjuəlɪzəm] *n* spiritisme *m*.
spit [spɪt] *n* (*for roasting*) broche *f*; (*spittle*) crachat *m*; (*saliva*) salive *f* ♦ *vi* (*pt, pp* **spat** [spæt]) cracher; (*sound*) crépiter.
spite [spaɪt] *n* rancune *f*, dépit *m* ♦ *vt* contrarier, vexer; **in ~ of** en dépit de, malgré.
spiteful ['spaɪtful] *adj* malveillant(e), rancunier(ière).
spitroast ['spɪt'rəust] *vt* faire rôtir à la broche.
spitting ['spɪtɪŋ] *n*: **"~ prohibited"** "défense de cracher" ♦ *adj*: **to be the ~ image of sb** être le portrait tout craché de qn.
spittle ['spɪtl] *n* salive *f*; bave *f*; crachat *m*.
spiv [spɪv] *n* (*BRIT col*) chevalier *m* d'industrie, aigrefin *m*.
splash [splæʃ] *n* éclaboussement *m*; (*of colour*) tache *f* ♦ *excl* (*sound*) plouf! ♦ *vt* éclabousser ♦ *vi* (*also*: **~ about**) barboter, patauger.
splashdown ['splæʃdaun] *n* amerrissage *m*.
splay [spleɪ] *adj*: **~footed** marchant les pieds en dehors.
spleen [spli:n] *n* (*ANAT*) rate *f*.
splendid ['splɛndɪd] *adj* splendide, superbe, magnifique.
splendour, (*US*) splendor ['splɛndə*] *n* splendeur *f*, magnificence *f*.
splice [splaɪs] *vt* épisser.
splint [splɪnt] *n* attelle *f*, éclisse *f*.
splinter ['splɪntə*] *n* (*wood*) écharde *f*; (*metal*) éclat *m* ♦ *vi* se fragmenter.
splinter group *n* groupe dissident.
split [splɪt] *n* fente *f*, déchirure *f*; (*fig*: *POL*) scission *f* ♦ *vb* (*pt, pp* **split**) *vt* fendre, déchirer; (*party*) diviser; (*work, profits*) partager, répartir ♦ *vi* (*break*) se fendre, se briser; (*divide*) se diviser; **let's ~ the difference** coupons la poire en deux; **to do the ~s** faire le grand écart.
►**split up** *vi* (*couple*) se séparer, rompre; (*meeting*) se disperser.
split-level ['splɪtlɛvl] *adj* (*house*) à deux *or* plusieurs niveaux.
split peas *npl* pois cassés.
split personality *n* double personnalité *f*.
split second *n* fraction *f* de seconde.
splitting ['splɪtɪŋ] *adj*: **a ~ headache** un mal de tête atroce.
splutter ['splʌtə*] *vi* bafouiller; postillonner.
spoil, *pt, pp* **spoilt** *or* **~ed** [spɔɪl, -t, -d] *vt* (*damage*) abîmer; (*mar*) gâcher; (*child*) gâter; (*ballot paper*) rendre nul ♦ *vi*: **to be ~ing for a fight** chercher la bagarre.
spoils [spɔɪlz] *npl* butin *m*.
spoilsport ['spɔɪlspɔ:t] *n* trouble-fête *m/f inv*, rabat-joie *m inv*.
spoilt [spɔɪlt] *pt, pp of* **spoil** ♦ *adj* (*child*) gâté(e); (*ballot paper*) nul(le).
spoke [spəuk] *pt of* **speak** ♦ *n* rayon *m*.
spoken ['spəukn] *pp of* **speak**.
spokesman ['spəuksmən], **spokeswoman** [-wumən] *n* porte-parole *m inv*.
spokesperson ['spəukspə:sn] *n* porte-parole *m inv*.
sponge [spʌndʒ] *n* éponge *f*; (*CULIN*: *also*: **~ cake**) ≈ biscuit *m* de Savoie ♦ *vt* éponger ♦ *vi*: **to ~ on** *or* (*US*) **off of** vivre aux crochets de.
sponge bag *n* (*BRIT*) trousse *f* de toilette.
sponge cake *n* ≈ biscuit *m* de Savoie.
sponger ['spʌndʒə*] *n* (*pej*) parasite *m*.
spongy ['spʌndʒɪ] *adj* spongieux(euse).
sponsor ['spɔnsə*] *n* sponsor *m*, personne *f* (*or* organisme *m*) qui assure le parrainage; (*of new member*) parrain *m*/marraine *f* ♦ *vt* (*programme, competition etc*) parrainer, patronner, sponsoriser; (*POL*: *bill*) présenter; (*new member*) parrainer; **I ~ed him at 3p a mile** (*in fund-raising race*) je me suis engagé à lui donner 3p par mile.
sponsorship ['spɔnsəʃɪp] *n* patronage *m*, parrainage *m*.
spontaneity [spɔntə'neɪɪtɪ] *n* spontanéité *f*.
spontaneous [spɔn'teɪnɪəs] *adj* spontané(e).
spoof [spu:f] *n* (*parody*) parodie *f*; (*trick*) canular *m*.
spooky ['spu:kɪ] *adj* qui donne la chair de poule.
spool [spu:l] *n* bobine *f*.
spoon [spu:n] *n* cuiller *f*.
spoon-feed ['spu:nfi:d] *vt* nourrir à la cuiller; (*fig*) mâcher le travail à.
spoonful ['spu:nful] *n* cuillerée *f*.
sporadic [spə'rædɪk] *adj* sporadique.
sport [spɔ:t] *n* sport *m*; (*amusement*) divertissement *m*; (*person*) chic type/chic fille ♦ *vt* arborer; **indoor/outdoor ~s** sports en salle/de plein air; **to say sth in ~** dire qch pour rire.
sporting ['spɔ:tɪŋ] *adj* sportif(ive); **to give sb a ~ chance** donner sa chance à qn.
sport jacket *n* (*US*) = **sports jacket**.
sports car *n* voiture *f* de sport.
sports ground *n* terrain *m* de sport.
sports jacket *n* veste *f* de sport.
sportsman ['spɔ:tsmən] *n* sportif *m*.
sportsmanship ['spɔ:tsmənʃɪp] *n* esprit sportif, sportivité *f*.
sports page *n* page *f* des sports.
sportswear ['spɔ:tswɛə*] *n* vêtements *mpl* de sport.

sportswoman ['spɔːtswumən] *n* sportive *f*.
sporty ['spɔːtɪ] *adj* sportif(ive).
spot [spɔt] *n* tache *f*; (*dot: on pattern*) pois *m*; (*pimple*) bouton *m*; (*place*) endroit *m*, coin *m*; (*also*: ~ **advertisement**) message *m* publicitaire; (*small amount*): **a ~ of** un peu de ♦ *vt* (*notice*) apercevoir, repérer; **on the ~** sur place, sur les lieux; (*immediately*) sur le champ; **to put sb on the ~** (*fig*) mettre qn dans l'embarras; **to come out in ~s** se couvrir de boutons, avoir une éruption de boutons.
spot check *n* contrôle intermittent.
spotless ['spɔtlɪs] *adj* immaculé(e).
spotlight ['spɔtlaɪt] *n* projecteur *m*; (*AUT*) phare *m* auxiliaire.
spot-on [spɔt'ɔn] *adj* (*BRIT col*) en plein dans le mille.
spot price *n* prix *m* sur place.
spotted ['spɔtɪd] *adj* tacheté(e), moucheté(e); à pois; ~ **with** tacheté(e) de.
spotty ['spɔtɪ] *adj* (*face*) boutonneux(euse).
spouse [spauz] *n* époux/épouse.
spout [spaut] *n* (*of jug*) bec *m*; (*of liquid*) jet *m* ♦ *vi* jaillir.
sprain [spreɪn] *n* entorse *f*, foulure *f* ♦ *vt*: **to ~ one's ankle** se fouler *or* se tordre la cheville.
sprang [spræŋ] *pt of* **spring**.
sprawl [sprɔːl] *vi* s'étaler ♦ *n*: **urban ~** expansion urbaine; **to send sb ~ing** envoyer qn rouler par terre.
spray [spreɪ] *n* jet *m* (en fines gouttelettes); (*container*) vaporisateur *m*, bombe *f*; (*of flowers*) petit bouquet ♦ *vt* vaporiser, pulvériser; (*crops*) traiter ♦ *cpd* (*deodorant etc*) en bombe *or* atomiseur.
spread [sprɛd] *n* (*distribution*) répartition *f*; (*CULIN*) pâte *f* à tartiner; (*PRESS, TYP: two pages*) double page *f* ♦ *vb* (*pt, pp* **spread**) *vt* (*paste, contents*) étendre, étaler; (*rumour, disease*) répandre, propager; (*repayments*) échelonner, étaler; (*wealth*) répartir ♦ *vi* s'étendre; se répandre; se propager; **middle-age ~** embonpoint *m* (pris avec l'âge).
spread-eagled ['sprɛdiːgld] *adj*: **to be** *or* **lie ~** être étendu(e) bras et jambes écartés.
spreadsheet ['sprɛdʃiːt] *n* (*COMPUT*) tableur *m*.
spree [spriː] *n*: **to go on a ~** faire la fête.
sprig [sprɪg] *n* rameau *m*.
sprightly ['spraɪtlɪ] *adj* alerte.
spring [sprɪŋ] *n* (*leap*) bond *m*, saut *m*; (*coiled metal*) ressort *m*; (*bounciness*) élasticité *f*; (*season*) printemps *m*; (*of water*) source *f* ♦ *vb* (*pt* **sprang**, *pp* **sprung** [spræŋ, sprʌŋ]) *vi* bondir, sauter ♦ *vt*: **to ~ a leak** (*pipe etc*) se mettre à fuir; **he sprang the news on me** il m'a annoncé la nouvelle de but en blanc; **in ~, in the ~** au printemps; **to ~ from** provenir de; **to ~ into action** passer à l'action; **to walk with a ~ in one's step** marcher d'un pas souple.
►**spring up** *vi* (*problem*) se présenter, surgir.
springboard ['sprɪŋbɔːd] *n* tremplin *m*.
spring-clean [sprɪŋ'kliːn] *n* (*also*: **~ing**) grand nettoyage de printemps.
spring onion *n* (*BRIT*) ciboule *f*, cive *f*.
spring roll *n* rouleau *m* de printemps.
springtime ['sprɪŋtaɪm] *n* printemps *m*.
springy ['sprɪŋɪ] *adj* élastique, souple.
sprinkle ['sprɪŋkl] *vt* (*pour*) répandre; verser; **to ~ water** *etc* **on, ~ with water** *etc* asperger d'eau *etc*; **to ~ sugar** *etc* **on, ~ with sugar** *etc* saupoudrer de sucre *etc*; **~d with** (*fig*) parsemé(e) de.
sprinkler ['sprɪŋklə*] *n* (*for lawn etc*) arroseur *m*; (*to put out fire*) diffuseur *m* d'extincteur automatique d'incendie.
sprinkling ['sprɪŋklɪŋ] *n* (*of water*) quelques gouttes *fpl*; (*of salt*) pincée *f*; (*of sugar*) légère couche.
sprint [sprɪnt] *n* sprint *m* ♦ *vi* sprinter.
sprinter ['sprɪntə*] *n* sprinteur/euse.
sprite [spraɪt] *n* lutin *m*.
spritzer ['sprɪtsə*] *n* *boisson à base de vin blanc et d'eau de Seltz.*
sprocket ['sprɔkɪt] *n* (*on printer etc*) picot *m*.
sprout [spraut] *vi* germer, pousser.
sprouts [sprauts] *npl* (*also*: **Brussels ~**) choux *mpl* de Bruxelles.
spruce [spruːs] *n* épicéa *m* ♦ *adj* net(te), pimpant(e).
►**spruce up** *vt* (*smarten up: room etc*) apprêter; **to ~ o.s. up** se faire beau(belle).
sprung [sprʌŋ] *pp of* **spring**.
spry [spraɪ] *adj* alerte, vif(vive).
SPUC *n abbr* = *Society for the Protection of Unborn Children.*
spud [spʌd] *n* (*col: potato*) patate *f*.
spun [spʌn] *pt, pp of* **spin**.
spur [spəː*] *n* éperon *m*; (*fig*) aiguillon *m* ♦ *vt* (*also*: ~ **on**) éperonner; aiguillonner; **on the ~ of the moment** sous l'impulsion du moment.
spurious ['spjuərɪəs] *adj* faux(fausse).
spurn [spəːn] *vt* repousser avec mépris.
spurt [spəːt] *n* jet *m*; (*of energy*) sursaut *m* ♦ *vi* jaillir, gicler; **to put in** *or* **on a ~** (*runner*) piquer un sprint; (*fig: in work etc*) donner un coup de collier.
sputter ['spʌtə*] *vi* = **splutter**.
spy [spaɪ] *n* espion/ne ♦ *vi*: **to ~ on** espionner, épier ♦ *vt* (*see*) apercevoir ♦ *cpd* (*film, story*) d'espionnage.
spying ['spaɪɪŋ] *n* espionnage *m*.
Sq. *abbr* (*in address*) = **square**.
sq. *abbr* (*MATH etc*) = **square**.
squabble ['skwɔbl] *n* querelle *f*, chamaillerie *f* ♦ *vi* se chamailler.
squad [skwɔd] *n* (*MIL, POLICE*) escouade *f*, groupe *m*; (*FOOTBALL*) contingent *m*; **flying ~** (*POLICE*) brigade volante.

squad car *n* (*BRIT POLICE*) voiture *f* de police.
squaddie ['skwɔdɪ] *n* (*MIL col*) troufion *m*, bidasse *m*.
squadron ['skwɔdrn] *n* (*MIL*) escadron *m*; (*AVIAT, NAUT*) escadrille *f*.
squalid ['skwɔlɪd] *adj* sordide, ignoble.
squall [skwɔːl] *n* rafale *f*, bourrasque *f*.
squalor ['skwɔlə*] *n* conditions *fpl* sordides.
squander ['skwɔndə*] *vt* gaspiller, dilapider.
square [skwɛə*] *n* carré *m*; (*in town*) place *f*; (*US*: *block of houses*) îlot *m*, pâté *m* de maisons; (*instrument*) équerre *f* ♦ *adj* carré(e); (*honest*) honnête, régulier(ière); (*col*: *ideas, tastes*) vieux jeu *inv*, qui retarde ♦ *vt* (*arrange*) régler; arranger; (*MATH*) élever au carré; (*reconcile*) concilier ♦ *vi* (*agree*) cadrer, s'accorder; **all** ~ quitte; à égalité; **a ~ meal** un repas convenable; **2 metres ~** (de) 2 mètres sur 2; **1 ~ metre** 1 mètre carré; **we're back to ~ one** (*fig*) on se retrouve à la case départ.
►**square up** *vi* (*BRIT*: *settle*) régler; **to ~ up with sb** régler ses comptes avec qn.
square bracket *n* (*TYP*) crochet *m*.
squarely ['skwɛəlɪ] *adv* carrément; (*honestly, fairly*) honnêtement, équitablement.
square root *n* racine carrée.
squash [skwɔʃ] *n* (*BRIT*: *drink*): **lemon/orange ~** citronnade/orangeade *f*; (*SPORT*) squash *m*; (*vegetable*) courge *f* ♦ *vt* écraser.
squat [skwɔt] *adj* petit(e) et épais(se), ramassé(e) ♦ *vi* s'accroupir; (*on property*) squatter, squattériser.
squatter ['skwɔtə*] *n* squatter *m*.
squawk [skwɔːk] *vi* pousser un *or* des gloussement(s).
squeak [skwiːk] *n* (*of hinge, wheel etc*) grincement *m*; (*of shoes*) craquement *m*; (*of mouse etc*) petit cri aigu ♦ *vi* grincer, crier.
squeaky ['skwiːkɪ] *adj* grinçant(e); **to be ~ clean** (*fig*) être au-dessus de tout soupçon.
squeal [skwiːl] *vi* pousser un *or* des cri(s) aigu(s) *or* perçant(s).
squeamish ['skwiːmɪʃ] *adj* facilement dégoûté(e); facilement scandalisé(e).
squeeze [skwiːz] *n* pression *f*; (*also*: **credit ~**) encadrement *m* du crédit, restrictions *fpl* de crédit ♦ *vt* presser; (*hand, arm*) serrer ♦ *vi*: **to ~ past/under sth** se glisser avec (beaucoup de) difficulté devant/sous qch; **a ~ of lemon** quelques gouttes de citron.
►**squeeze out** *vt* exprimer; (*fig*) soutirer.
squelch [skwɛltʃ] *vi* faire un bruit de succion; patauger.
squib [skwɪb] *n* pétard *m*.
squid [skwɪd] *n* calmar *m*.
squiggle ['skwɪgl] *n* gribouillis *m*.
squint [skwɪnt] *vi* loucher ♦ *n*: **he has a ~** il louche, il souffre de strabisme; **to ~ at sth** regarder qch du coin de l'œil; (*quickly*) jeter un coup d'œil à qch.
squire ['skwaɪə*] *n* (*BRIT*) propriétaire terrien.
squirm [skwəːm] *vi* se tortiller.
squirrel ['skwɪrəl] *n* écureuil *m*.
squirt [skwəːt] *n* jet *m* ♦ *vi* jaillir, gicler.
Sr *abbr* = **senior, sister** (*REL*).
SRC *n abbr* (*BRIT*: = *Students' Representative Council*) ≈ CROUS *m*.
Sri Lanka [srɪ'læŋkə] *n* Sri Lanka *m or f*.
SRN *n abbr* (*BRIT*) = *State Registered Nurse*.
SRO *abbr* (*US*) = *standing room only*.
SS *abbr* (= *steamship*) S/S.
SSA *n abbr* (*US*: = *Social Security Administration*) *organisme de sécurité sociale*.
SST *n abbr* (*US*) = *supersonic transport*.
ST *abbr* (*US*: = *Standard Time*) *heure officielle*.
St *abbr* (= *saint*) St; (= *street*) R.
stab [stæb] *n* (*with knife etc*) coup *m* (de couteau *etc*); (*col*: *try*): **to have a ~ at (doing) sth** s'essayer à (faire) qch ♦ *vt* poignarder; **to ~ sb to death** tuer qn à coups de couteau.
stabbing ['stæbɪŋ] *n*: **there's been a ~** quelqu'un a été attaqué à coups de couteau ♦ *adj* (*pain, ache*) lancinant(e).
stability [stə'bɪlɪtɪ] *n* stabilité *f*.
stabilization [steɪbəlaɪ'zeɪʃən] *n* stabilisation *f*.
stabilize ['steɪbəlaɪz] *vt* stabiliser ♦ *vi* se stabiliser.
stabilizer ['steɪbəlaɪzə*] *n* stabilisateur *m*.
stable ['steɪbl] *n* écurie *f* ♦ *adj* stable; **riding ~s** centre *m* d'équitation.
staccato [stə'kɑːtəu] *adv* staccato ♦ *adj* (*MUS*) piqué(e); (*noise, voice*) saccadé(e).
stack [stæk] *n* tas *m*, pile *f* ♦ *vt* empiler, entasser; **there's ~s of time** (*BRIT col*) on a tout le temps.
stadium ['steɪdɪəm] *n* stade *m*.
staff [stɑːf] *n* (*work force*) personnel *m*; (*BRIT SCOL*: *also*: **teaching ~**) professeurs *mpl*, enseignants *mpl*, personnel enseignant; (*servants*) domestiques *mpl*; (*MIL*) état-major *m*; (*stick*) perche *f*, bâton *m* ♦ *vt* pourvoir en personnel.
staffroom ['stɑːfruːm] *n* salle *f* des professeurs.
Staffs *abbr* (*BRIT*) = *Staffordshire*.
stag [stæg] *n* cerf *m*; (*BRIT STOCK EXCHANGE*) loup *m*.
stage [steɪdʒ] *n* scène *f*; (*profession*): **the ~** le théâtre; (*point*) étape *f*, stade *m*; (*platform*) estrade *f* ♦ *vt* (*play*) monter, mettre en scène; (*demonstration*) organiser; (*fig: recovery etc*) effectuer; **in ~s** par étapes, par degrés; **to go through a difficult ~** traverser une période difficile; **in the early ~s** au début; **in the final ~s** à la fin.
stagecoach ['steɪdʒkəutʃ] *n* diligence *f*.
stage door *n* entrée *f* des artistes.
stage fright *n* trac *m*.
stagehand ['steɪdʒhænd] *n* machiniste *m*.
stage-manage ['steɪdʒmænɪdʒ] *vt* (*fig*) orchestrer.
stage manager *n* régisseur *m*.

stagger ['stægə*] *vi* chanceler, tituber ♦ *vt* (*person*) stupéfier; bouleverser; (*hours, holidays*) étaler, échelonner.
staggering ['stægərɪŋ] *adj* (*amazing*) stupéfiant(e), renversant(e).
staging post ['steɪdʒɪŋ-] *n* relais *m*.
stagnant ['stægnənt] *adj* stagnant(e).
stagnate [stæg'neɪt] *vi* stagner, croupir.
stagnation [stæg'neɪʃən] *n* stagnation *f*.
stag night, stag party *n* enterrement *m* de vie de garçon.
staid [steɪd] *adj* posé(e), rassis(e).
stain [steɪn] *n* tache *f*; (*colouring*) colorant *m* ♦ *vt* tacher; (*wood*) teindre.
stained glass window [steɪnd-] *n* vitrail *m*.
stainless ['steɪnlɪs] *adj* (*steel*) inoxydable.
stain remover *n* détachant *m*.
stair [stɛə*] *n* (*step*) marche *f*; **~s** *npl* escalier *m*; **on the ~s** dans l'escalier.
staircase ['stɛəkeɪs], **stairway** ['stɛəweɪ] *n* escalier *m*.
stairwell ['stɛəwɛl] *n* cage *f* d'escalier.
stake [steɪk] *n* pieu *m*, poteau *m*; (*BETTING*) enjeu *m* ♦ *vt* risquer, jouer; (*also*: **~ out**: *area*) marquer, délimiter; **to be at ~** être en jeu; **to have a ~ in sth** avoir des intérêts (en jeu) dans qch; **to ~ a claim (to sth)** revendiquer (qch).
stakeout ['steɪkaut] *n* surveillance *f*; **to be on a ~** effectuer une surveillance.
stalactite ['stæləktaɪt] *n* stalactite *f*.
stalagmite ['stæləgmaɪt] *n* stalagmite *f*.
stale [steɪl] *adj* (*bread*) rassis(e); (*beer*) éventé(e); (*smell*) de renfermé.
stalemate ['steɪlmeɪt] *n* pat *m*; (*fig*) impasse *f*.
stalk [stɔːk] *n* tige *f* ♦ *vt* traquer ♦ *vi*: **to ~ in/out** *etc* entrer/sortir *etc* avec raideur.
stall [stɔːl] *n* (*BRIT*: *in street, market etc*) éventaire *m*, étal *m*; (*in stable*) stalle *f* ♦ *vt* (*AUT*) caler ♦ *vi* (*AUT*) caler; (*fig*) essayer de gagner du temps; **~s** *npl* (*BRIT*: *in cinema, theatre*) orchestre *m*; **a newspaper/flower ~** un kiosque à journaux/de fleuriste.
stallholder ['stɔːlhəuldə*] *n* (*BRIT*) marchand/e en plein air.
stallion ['stæljən] *n* étalon *m* (*cheval*).
stalwart ['stɔːlwət] *n* partisan *m* fidèle.
stamen ['steɪmɛn] *n* étamine *f*.
stamina ['stæmɪnə] *n* vigueur *f*, endurance *f*.
stammer ['stæmə*] *n* bégaiement *m* ♦ *vi* bégayer.
stamp [stæmp] *n* timbre *m*; (*mark, also fig*) empreinte *f*; (*on document*) cachet *m* ♦ *vi* (*also*: **~ one's foot**) taper du pied ♦ *vt* tamponner (*letter*) timbrer; **~ed addressed envelope (s.a.e.)** enveloppe affranchie pour la réponse.
►**stamp out** *vt* (*fire*) piétiner; (*crime*) éradiquer; (*opposition*) éliminer.
stamp album *n* album *m* de timbres(-poste).
stamp collecting [-kəlɛktɪŋ] *n* philatélie *f*.
stamp duty *n* (*BRIT*) droit *m* de timbre.
stampede [stæm'piːd] *n* ruée *f*; (*of cattle*) débandade *f*.
stamp machine *n* distributeur *m* de timbres-poste.
stance [stæns] *n* position *f*.
stand [stænd] *n* (*position*) position *f*; (*MIL*) résistance *f*; (*structure*) guéridon *m*; support *m*; (*COMM*) étalage *m*, stand *m*; (*SPORT*) tribune *f*; (*also*: **music ~**) pupitre *m* ♦ *vb* (*pt, pp* **stood** [stud]) *vi* être *or* se tenir (debout); (*rise*) se lever, se mettre debout; (*be placed*) se trouver ♦ *vt* (*place*) mettre, poser; (*tolerate, withstand*) supporter; **to make a ~** prendre position; **to take a ~ on an issue** prendre position sur un problème; **to ~ for parliament** (*BRIT*) se présenter aux élections (*comme candidat à la députation*); **to ~ guard** *or* **watch** (*MIL*) monter la garde; **it ~s to reason** c'est logique; cela va de soi; **as things ~** dans l'état actuel des choses; **to ~ sb a drink/meal** payer à boire/à manger à qn; **I can't ~ him** je ne peux pas le voir.
►**stand aside** *vi* s'écarter.
►**stand by** *vi* (*be ready*) se tenir prêt(e) ♦ *vt fus* (*opinion*) s'en tenir à.
►**stand down** *vi* (*withdraw*) se retirer; (*LAW*) renoncer à ses droits.
►**stand for** *vt fus* (*signify*) représenter, signifier; (*tolerate*) supporter, tolérer.
►**stand in for** *vt fus* remplacer.
►**stand out** *vi* (*be prominent*) ressortir.
►**stand up** *vi* (*rise*) se lever, se mettre debout.
►**stand up for** *vt fus* défendre.
►**stand up to** *vt fus* tenir tête à, résister à.
stand-alone ['stændələun] *adj* (*COMPUT*) autonome.
standard ['stændəd] *n* (*reference*) norme *f*; (*level*) niveau *m*; (*flag*) étendard *m* ♦ *adj* (*size etc*) ordinaire, normal(e); (*model, feature*) standard *inv*; (*practice*) courant(e); (*text*) de base; **~s** *npl* (*morals*) morale *f*, principes *mpl*; **to be** *or* **come up to ~** être du niveau voulu *or* à la hauteur; **to apply a double ~** avoir *or* appliquer deux poids deux mesures; **~ of living** niveau de vie.
Standard Grade *n* (*SCOT SCOL*) *examen passé à l'âge de 16 ans.*
standardization [stændədaɪ'zeɪʃən] *n* standardisation *f*.
standardize ['stændədaɪz] *vt* standardiser.
standard lamp *n* (*BRIT*) lampadaire *m*.
standard time *n* heure légale.
stand-by ['stændbaɪ] *n* remplaçant/e ♦ *adj* (*provisions*) de réserve; **to be on ~** se tenir prêt(e); (*doctor*) être de garde.
stand-by generator *n* générateur *m* de secours.
stand-by passenger *n* passager/ère en stand-by *or* en attente.
stand-by ticket *n* billet *m* stand-by.
stand-in ['stændɪn] *n* remplaçant/e; (*CINE*) doublure *f*.

standing ['stændɪŋ] *adj* debout *inv*; (*permanent: rule*) immuable; (*army*) de métier; (*grievance*) constant(e), de longue date ♦ *n* réputation *f*, rang *m*, standing *m*; (*duration*): **of 6 months'** ~ qui dure depuis 6 mois; **of many years'** ~ qui dure *or* existe depuis longtemps; **he was given a ~ ovation** on s'est levé pour l'acclamer; **it's a ~ joke** c'est un vieux sujet de plaisanterie; **a man of some** ~ un homme estimé.
standing committee *n* commission permanente.
standing order *n* (*BRIT*: *at bank*) virement permanent; **~s** *npl* (*MIL*) règlement *m*.
standing room *n* places *fpl* debout.
stand-off ['stændɔf] *n* (*esp US*: *stalemate*) impasse *f*.
stand-offish [stænd'ɔfɪʃ] *adj* distant(e), froid(e).
standpat ['stændpæt] *adj* (*US*) inflexible, rigide.
standpipe ['stændpaɪp] *n* colonne *f* d'alimentation.
standpoint ['stændpɔɪnt] *n* point *m* de vue.
standstill ['stændstɪl] *n*: **at a** ~ à l'arrêt; (*fig*) au point mort; **to come to a** ~ s'immobiliser, s'arrêter.
stank [stæŋk] *pt of* **stink**.
stanza ['stænzə] *n* strophe *f*; couplet *m*.
staple ['steɪpl] *n* (*for papers*) agrafe *f*; (*chief product*) produit *m* de base ♦ *adj* (*food, crop, industry etc*) de base, principal(e) ♦ *vt* agrafer.
stapler ['steɪplə*] *n* agrafeuse *f*.
star [stɑː*] *n* étoile *f*; (*celebrity*) vedette *f* ♦ *vi*: **to ~ (in)** être la vedette (de) ♦ *vt* (*CINE*) avoir pour vedette; **4-~ hotel** hôtel *m* 4 étoiles; **2-~ petrol** (*BRIT*) essence *f* ordinaire; **4-~ petrol** (*BRIT*) super *m*.
star attraction *n* grande attraction.
starboard ['stɑːbəd] *n* tribord *m*; **to ~** à tribord.
starch [stɑːtʃ] *n* amidon *m*.
starched ['stɑːtʃt] *adj* (*collar*) amidonné(e), empesé(e).
starchy ['stɑːtʃɪ] *adj* riche en féculents; (*person*) guindé(e).
stardom ['stɑːdəm] *n* célébrité *f*.
stare [stɛə*] *n* regard *m* fixe ♦ *vi*: **to ~ at** regarder fixement.
starfish ['stɑːfɪʃ] *n* étoile *f* de mer.
stark [stɑːk] *adj* (*bleak*) désolé(e), morne; (*simplicity, colour*) austère; (*reality, poverty*) nu(e) ♦ *adv*: **~ naked** complètement nu(e).
starkers ['stɑːkəz] *adj*: **to be ~** (*BRIT col*) être à poil.
starlet ['stɑːlɪt] *n* (*CINE*) starlette *f*.
starlight ['stɑːlaɪt] *n*: **by ~** à la lumière des étoiles.
starling ['stɑːlɪŋ] *n* étourneau *m*.
starlit ['stɑːlɪt] *adj* étoilé(e); illuminé(e) par les étoiles.
starry ['stɑːrɪ] *adj* étoilé(e).
starry-eyed [stɑːrɪ'aɪd] *adj* (*innocent*) ingénu(e).
Stars and Stripes *npl*: **the ~** la bannière étoilée.
star sign *n* signe zodiacal *or* du zodiaque.
star-studded ['stɑːstʌdɪd] *adj*: **a ~ cast** une distribution prestigieuse.
start [stɑːt] *n* commencement *m*, début *m*; (*of race*) départ *m*; (*sudden movement*) sursaut *m*; (*advantage*) avance *f* ♦ *vt* commencer; (*found: business, newspaper*) lancer, créer ♦ *vi* partir, se mettre en route; (*jump*) sursauter; **at the ~** au début; **for a ~** d'abord, pour commencer; **to make an early ~** partir *or* commencer de bonne heure; **to ~ doing sth** se mettre à faire qch; **to ~ (off) with ...** (*firstly*) d'abord ...; (*at the beginning*) au commencement ....
►**start off** *vi* commencer; (*leave*) partir.
►**start over** *vi* (*US*) recommencer.
►**start up** *vi* commencer; (*car*) démarrer ♦ *vt* déclencher; (*car*) mettre en marche.
starter ['stɑːtə*] *n* (*AUT*) démarreur *m*; (*SPORT*: *official*) starter *m*; (*: runner, horse*) partant *m*; (*BRIT CULIN*) entrée *f*.
starting handle ['stɑːtɪŋ-] *n* (*BRIT*) manivelle *f*.
starting point ['stɑːtɪŋ-] *n* point *m* de départ.
starting price ['stɑːtɪŋ-] *n* prix initial.
startle ['stɑːtl] *vt* faire sursauter; donner un choc à.
startling ['stɑːtlɪŋ] *adj* surprenant(e), saisissant(e).
star turn *n* (*BRIT*) vedette *f*.
starvation [stɑː'veɪʃən] *n* faim *f*, famine *f*; **to die of ~** mourir de faim *or* d'inanition.
starve [stɑːv] *vi* mourir de faim; être affamé(e) ♦ *vt* affamer; **I'm starving** je meurs de faim.
stash [stæʃ] *vt* (*col*): **to ~ sth away** planquer qch.
state [steɪt] *n* état *m*; (*pomp*): **in ~** en grande pompe ♦ *vt* (*declare*) déclarer, affirmer; (*specify*) indiquer, spécifier; **to be in a ~** être dans tous ses états; **~ of emergency** état d'urgence; **~ of mind** état d'esprit; **the ~ of the art** l'état actuel de la technologie (*or* des connaissances).
state control *n* contrôle *m* de l'État.
stated ['steɪtɪd] *adj* fixé(e), prescrit(e).
State Department *n* (*US*) Département *m* d'État, ≈ ministère *m* des Affaires étrangères.
state education *n* (*BRIT*) enseignement public.
stateless ['steɪtlɪs] *adj* apatride.
stately ['steɪtlɪ] *adj* majestueux(euse), imposant(e).
statement ['steɪtmənt] *n* déclaration *f*; (*LAW*) déposition *f*; (*ECON*) relevé *m*; **official ~** communiqué officiel; **~ of account, bank ~**

relevé de compte.
state-owned ['steɪtəund] *adj* étatisé(e).
States [steɪts] *npl*: **the** ~ les États-Unis *mpl*.
state school *n* école publique.
state secret *n* secret *m* d'État.
statesman ['steɪtsmən] *n* homme *m* d'État.
statesmanship ['steɪtsmənʃɪp] *n* qualités *fpl* d'homme d'État.
static ['stætɪk] *n* (*RADIO*) parasites *mpl*; (*also*: ~ **electricity**) électricité *f* statique ♦ *adj* statique.
station ['steɪʃən] *n* gare *f*; (*MIL, POLICE*) poste *m* (militaire *or* de police *etc*); (*rank*) condition *f*, rang *m* ♦ *vt* placer, poster; **action ~s** postes de combat; **to be ~ed in** (*MIL*) être en garnison à.
stationary ['steɪʃnərɪ] *adj* à l'arrêt, immobile.
stationer ['steɪʃənə*] *n* papetier/ière; **~'s (shop)** papeterie *f*.
stationery ['steɪʃnərɪ] *n* papier *m* à lettres, petit matériel de bureau.
station master *n* (*RAIL*) chef *m* de gare.
station wagon *n* (*US*) break *m*.
statistic [stə'tɪstɪk] *n* statistique *f*.
statistical [stə'tɪstɪkl] *adj* statistique.
statistics [stə'tɪstɪks] *n* (*science*) statistique *f*.
statue ['stætjuː] *n* statue *f*.
statuesque [stætju'ɛsk] *adj* sculptural(e).
statuette [stætju'ɛt] *n* statuette *f*.
stature ['stætʃə*] *n* stature *f*; (*fig*) envergure *f*.
status ['steɪtəs] *n* position *f*, situation *f*; (*prestige*) prestige *m*; (*ADMIN, official position*) statut *m*.
status quo [-'kwəu] *n*: **the** ~ le statu quo.
status symbol *n* marque *f* de standing, signe extérieur de richesse.
statute ['stætjuːt] *n* loi *f*; **~s** *npl* (*of club etc*) statuts *mpl*.
statute book *n* ≈ code *m*, textes *mpl* de loi.
statutory ['stætjutrɪ] *adj* statutaire, prévu(e) par un article de loi; ~ **meeting** assemblée constitutive *or* statutaire.
staunch [stɔːntʃ] *adj* sûr(e), loyal(e) ♦ *vt* étancher.
stave [steɪv] *n* (*MUS*) portée *f* ♦ *vt*: **to ~ off** (*attack*) parer; (*threat*) conjurer.
stay [steɪ] *n* (*period of time*) séjour *m*; (*LAW*): ~ **of execution** sursis *m* à statuer ♦ *vi* rester; (*reside*) loger; (*spend some time*) séjourner; **to ~ put** ne pas bouger; **to ~ with friends** loger chez des amis; **to ~ the night** passer la nuit.
►**stay behind** *vi* rester en arrière.
►**stay in** *vi* (*at home*) rester à la maison.
►**stay on** *vi* rester.
►**stay out** *vi* (*of house*) ne pas rentrer; (*strikers*) rester en grève.
►**stay up** *vi* (*at night*) ne pas se coucher.
staying power ['steɪɪŋ-] *n* endurance *f*.
STD *n abbr* (*BRIT*: = *subscriber trunk dialling*) l'automatique *m*; (= *sexually transmitted disease*) MST *f*.
stead [stɛd] *n* (*BRIT*): **in sb's** ~ à la place de qn; **to stand sb in good** ~ être très utile *or* servir beaucoup à qn.
steadfast ['stɛdfɑːst] *adj* ferme, résolu(e).
steadily ['stɛdɪlɪ] *adv* régulièrement; fermement; d'une voix *etc* ferme.
steady ['stɛdɪ] *adj* stable, solide, ferme; (*regular*) constant(e), régulier(ière); (*person*) calme, pondéré(e) ♦ *vt* assurer, stabiliser; (*voice*) assurer; **to ~ oneself** reprendre son aplomb.
steak [steɪk] *n* (*meat*) bifteck *m*, steak *m*; (*fish*) tranche *f*.
steakhouse ['steɪkhaus] *n* ≈ grill-room *m*.
steal, *pt* **stole,** *pp* **stolen** [stiːl, stəul, 'stəuln] *vt, vi* voler.
►**steal away, steal off** *vi* s'esquiver.
stealth [stɛlθ] *n*: **by** ~ furtivement.
stealthy ['stɛlθɪ] *adj* furtif(ive).
steam [stiːm] *n* vapeur *f* ♦ *vt* passer à la vapeur; (*CULIN*) cuire à la vapeur ♦ *vi* fumer; (*ship*): **to ~ along** filer; **under one's own** ~ (*fig*) par ses propres moyens; **to run out of** ~ (*fig: person*) caler; être à bout; **to let off** ~ (*fig: col*) se défouler.
►**steam up** *vi* (*window*) se couvrir de buée; **to get ~ed up about sth** (*fig: col*) s'exciter à propos de qch.
steam engine *n* locomotive *f* à vapeur.
steamer ['stiːmə*] *n* (bateau *m* à) vapeur *m*; (*CULIN*) ≈ couscoussier *m*.
steam iron *n* fer *m* à repasser à vapeur.
steamroller ['stiːmrəulə*] *n* rouleau compresseur.
steamy ['stiːmɪ] *adj* embué(e), humide.
steed [stiːd] *n* (*literary*) coursier *m*.
steel [stiːl] *n* acier *m* ♦ *cpd* d'acier.
steel band *n* steel band *m*.
steel industry *n* sidérurgie *f*.
steel mill *n* aciérie *f*, usine *f* sidérurgique.
steelworks ['stiːlwəːks] *n* aciérie *f*.
steely ['stiːlɪ] *adj* (*determination*) inflexible; (*eyes, gaze*) d'acier.
steep [stiːp] *adj* raide, escarpé(e); (*price*) très élevé(e), excessif(ive) ♦ *vt* (faire) tremper.
steeple ['stiːpl] *n* clocher *m*.
steeplechase ['stiːpltʃeɪs] *n* steeple(-chase) *m*.
steeplejack ['stiːpldʒæk] *n* réparateur *m* de clochers et de hautes cheminées.
steeply ['stiːplɪ] *adv* en pente raide.
steer [stɪə*] *n* bœuf *m* ♦ *vt* diriger, gouverner; (*lead*) guider ♦ *vi* tenir le gouvernail; **to ~ clear of sb/sth** (*fig*) éviter qn/qch.
steering ['stɪərɪŋ] *n* (*AUT*) conduite *f*.
steering column *n* (*AUT*) colonne *f* de direction.
steering committee *n* comité *m* d'organisation.
steering wheel *n* volant *m*.
stellar ['stɛlə*] *adj* stellaire.
stem [stɛm] *n* (*of plant*) tige *f*; (*of leaf, fruit*)

queue *f*; (*of glass*) pied *m* ♦ *vt* contenir, endiguer, juguler.
▸**stem from** *vt fus* provenir de, découler de.
stench [stɛntʃ] *n* puanteur *f*.
stencil ['stɛnsl] *n* stencil *m*; pochoir *m* ♦ *vt* polycopier.
stenographer [stɛ'nɔgrəfə*] *n* (*US*) sténographe *m/f*.
stenography [stɛ'nɔgrəfɪ] *n* (*US*) sténo(graphie) *f*.
step [stɛp] *n* pas *m*; (*stair*) marche *f*; (*action*) mesure *f*, disposition *f* ♦ *vi*: **to ~ forward** faire un pas en avant, avancer; **~s** *npl* (*BRIT*) = **stepladder**; **~ by ~** pas à pas; (*fig*) petit à petit; **to be in ~ (with)** (*fig*) aller dans le sens (de); **to be out of ~ (with)** (*fig*) être déphasé(e) (par rapport à).
▸**step down** *vi* (*fig*) se retirer, se désister.
▸**step in** *vi* (*fig*) intervenir.
▸**step off** *vt fus* descendre de.
▸**step over** *vt fus* enjamber.
▸**step up** *vt* augmenter; intensifier.
step aerobics *npl* ® step *m* ®.
stepbrother ['stɛpbrʌðə*] *n* demi-frère *m*.
stepchild ['stɛptʃaɪld] *n* beau-fils/belle-fille.
stepdaughter ['stɛpdɔːtə*] *n* belle-fille *f*.
stepfather ['stɛpfɑːðə*] *n* beau-père *m*.
stepladder ['stɛplædə*] *n* (*BRIT*) escabeau *m*.
stepmother ['stɛpmʌðə*] *n* belle-mère *f*.
stepping stone ['stɛpɪŋ-] *n* pierre *f* de gué; (*fig*) tremplin *m*.
step Reebok [-'riːbɔk] *n* ® step *m* ®.
stepsister ['stɛpsɪstə*] *n* demi-sœur *f*.
stepson ['stɛpsʌn] *n* beau-fils *m*.
stereo ['stɛrɪəu] *n* (*system*) stéréo *f*; (*record player*) chaîne *f* stéréo ♦ *adj* (*also*: **~phonic**) stéréophonique; **in ~** en stéréo.
stereotype ['stɪərɪətaɪp] *n* stéréotype *m* ♦ *vt* stéréotyper.
sterile ['stɛraɪl] *adj* stérile.
sterility [stɛ'rɪlɪtɪ] *n* stérilité *f*.
sterilization [stɛrɪlaɪ'zeɪʃən] *n* stérilisation *f*.
sterilize ['stɛrɪlaɪz] *vt* stériliser.
sterling ['stəːlɪŋ] *adj* sterling *inv*; (*silver*) de bon aloi, fin(e); (*fig*) à toute épreuve, excellent(e) ♦ *n* (*currency*) livre *f* sterling *inv*; **a pound ~** une livre sterling.
sterling area *n* zone *f* sterling *inv*.
stern [stəːn] *adj* sévère ♦ *n* (*NAUT*) arrière *m*, poupe *f*.
sternum ['stəːnəm] *n* sternum *m*.
steroid ['stɪərɔɪd] *n* stéroïde *m*.
stethoscope ['stɛθəskəup] *n* stéthoscope *m*.
stevedore ['stiːvədɔː*] *n* docker *m*, débardeur *m*.
stew [stjuː] *n* ragoût *m* ♦ *vt, vi* cuire à la casserole; **~ed tea** thé trop infusé; **~ed fruit** fruits cuits *or* en compote.
steward ['stjuːəd] *n* (*AVIAT, NAUT, RAIL*) steward *m*; (*in club etc*) intendant *m*; (*also*: **shop ~**) délégué syndical.
stewardess ['stjuədɛs] *n* hôtesse *f*.
stewardship ['stjuədʃɪp] *n* intendance *f*.
stewing steak ['stjuːɪŋ-], (*US*) **stew meat** *n* bœuf *m* à braiser.
St. Ex. *abbr* = **stock exchange**.
stg *abbr* = **sterling**.
stick [stɪk] *n* bâton *m*; (*of chalk etc*) morceau *m* ♦ *vb* (*pt, pp* **stuck** [stʌk]) *vt* (*glue*) coller; (*thrust*): **to ~ sth into** piquer *or* planter *or* enfoncer qch dans; (*col*: *put*) mettre, fourrer; (*: tolerate*) supporter ♦ *vi* (*adhere*) coller; (*remain*) rester; (*get jammed: door, lift*) se bloquer; **to get hold of the wrong end of the ~** (*BRIT fig*) comprendre de travers; **to ~ to** (*one's word, promise*) s'en tenir à; (*principles*) rester fidèle à.
▸**stick around** *vi* (*col*) rester (dans les parages).
▸**stick out** *vi* dépasser, sortir ♦ *vt*: **to ~ it out** (*col*) tenir le coup.
▸**stick up** *vi* dépasser, sortir.
▸**stick up for** *vt fus* défendre.
sticker ['stɪkə*] *n* auto-collant *m*.
sticking plaster ['stɪkɪŋ-] *n* sparadrap *m*, pansement adhésif.
sticking point ['stɪkɪŋ-] *n* (*fig*) point *m* de friction.
stickleback ['stɪklbæk] *n* épinoche *f*.
stickler ['stɪklə*] *n*: **to be a ~ for** être pointilleux(euse) sur.
stick shift *n* (*US AUT*) levier *m* de vitesses.
stick-up ['stɪkʌp] *n* (*col*) braquage *m*, hold-up *m*.
sticky ['stɪkɪ] *adj* poisseux(euse); (*label*) adhésif(ive).
stiff [stɪf] *adj* (*gen*) raide, rigide; (*door, brush*) dur(e); (*difficult*) difficile, ardu(e); (*cold*) froid(e), distant(e); (*strong, high*) fort(e), élevé(e); **to be** *or* **feel ~** (*person*) avoir des courbatures; **to have a ~ back** avoir mal au dos; **~ upper lip** (*BRIT*: *fig*) flegme *m* (*typiquement britannique*).
stiffen ['stɪfn] *vt* raidir, renforcer ♦ *vi* se raidir; se durcir.
stiffness ['stɪfnɪs] *n* raideur *f*.
stifle ['staɪfl] *vt* étouffer, réprimer.
stifling ['staɪflɪŋ] *adj* (*heat*) suffocant(e).
stigma, *pl* (*BOT, MED, REL*) **~ta**, (*fig*) **~s** ['stɪgmə, stɪg'mɑːtə] *n* stigmate *m*.
stile [staɪl] *n* échalier *m*.
stiletto [stɪ'lɛtəu] *n* (*BRIT*: *also*: **~ heel**) talon *m* aiguille.
still [stɪl] *adj* (*motionless*) immobile; (*calm*) calme, tranquille; (*BRIT*: *orange drink etc*) non gazeux(euse) ♦ *adv* (*up to this time*) encore, toujours; (*even*) encore; (*nonetheless*) quand même, tout de même ♦ *n* (*CINE*) photo *f*; **to stand ~** rester immobile, ne pas bouger; **keep ~!** ne bouge pas!; **he ~ hasn't arrived** il n'est pas encore arrivé, il n'est toujours pas arrivé.
stillborn ['stɪlbɔːn] *adj* mort-né(e).
still life *n* nature morte.

stilt [stɪlt] *n* échasse *f*; (*pile*) pilotis *m*.
stilted ['stɪltɪd] *adj* guindé(e), emprunté(e).
stimulant ['stɪmjulənt] *n* stimulant *m*.
stimulate ['stɪmjuleɪt] *vt* stimuler.
stimulating ['stɪmjuleɪtɪŋ] *adj* stimulant(e).
stimulation [stɪmju'leɪʃən] *n* stimulation *f*.
stimulus, *pl* **stimuli** ['stɪmjuləs, 'stɪmjulaɪ] *n* stimulant *m*; (*BIOL, PSYCH*) stimulus *m*.
sting [stɪŋ] *n* piqûre *f*; (*organ*) dard *m*; (*col: confidence trick*) arnaque *m* ♦ *vt* (*pt, pp* **stung** [stʌŋ]) piquer ♦ *vi* piquer; **my eyes are ~ing** j'ai les yeux qui piquent.
stingy ['stɪndʒɪ] *adj* avare, pingre, chiche.
stink [stɪŋk] *n* puanteur *f* ♦ *vi* (*pt* **stank,** *pp* **stunk** [stæŋk, stʌŋk]) puer, empester.
stinker ['stɪŋkə*] *n* (*col: problem, exam*) vacherie *f*; (*: person*) dégueulasse *m/f*.
stinking ['stɪŋkɪŋ] *adj* (*fig: col*) infect(e); **~ rich** bourré(e) de pognon.
stint [stɪnt] *n* part *f* de travail ♦ *vi*: **to ~ on** lésiner sur, être chiche de.
stipend ['staɪpɛnd] *n* (*of vicar etc*) traitement *m*.
stipendiary [staɪ'pɛndɪərɪ] *adj*: **~ magistrate** juge *m* de tribunal d'instance.
stipulate ['stɪpjuleɪt] *vt* stipuler.
stipulation [stɪpju'leɪʃən] *n* stipulation *f*, condition *f*.
stir [stəː*] *n* agitation *f*, sensation *f* ♦ *vt* remuer ♦ *vi* remuer, bouger; **to give sth a ~** remuer qch; **to cause a ~** faire sensation.
►**stir up** *vt* exciter.
stir-fry ['stəː'fraɪ] *vt* faire sauter ♦ *n*: **vegetable ~** légumes sautés à la poêle.
stirring [stəːrɪŋ] *adj* excitant(e); émouvant(e).
stirrup ['stɪrəp] *n* étrier *m*.
stitch [stɪtʃ] *n* (*SEWING*) point *m*; (*KNITTING*) maille *f*; (*MED*) point de suture; (*pain*) point de côté ♦ *vt* coudre, piquer; suturer.
stoat [stəut] *n* hermine *f* (*avec son pelage d'été*).
stock [stɔk] *n* réserve *f*, provision *f*; (*COMM*) stock *m*; (*AGR*) cheptel *m*, bétail *m*; (*CULIN*) bouillon *m*; (*FINANCE*) valeurs *fpl*, titres *mpl*; (*RAIL: also:* **rolling ~**) matériel roulant; (*descent, origin*) souche *f* ♦ *adj* (*fig: reply etc*) courant(e); classique ♦ *vt* (*have in stock*) avoir, vendre; **well-~ed** bien approvisionné(e) *or* fourni(e); **in ~** en stock, en magasin; **out of ~** épuisé(e); **to take ~** (*fig*) faire le point; **~s and shares** valeurs (mobilières), titres; **government ~** fonds publics.
►**stock up** *vi*: **to ~ up (with)** s'approvisionner (en).
stockade [stɔ'keɪd] *n* palissade *f*.
stockbroker ['stɔkbrəukə*] *n* agent *m* de change.
stock control *n* (*COMM*) gestion *f* des stocks.
stock cube *n* (*BRIT CULIN*) bouillon-cube *m*.
stock exchange *n* Bourse *f* (des valeurs).
stockholder ['stɔkhəuldə*] *n* actionnaire *m/f*.
Stockholm ['stɔkhəum] *n* Stockholm.
stocking ['stɔkɪŋ] *n* bas *m*.
stock-in-trade ['stɔkɪn'treɪd] *n* (*fig*): **it's his ~** c'est sa spécialité.
stockist ['stɔkɪst] *n* (*BRIT*) stockiste *m*.
stock market *n* (*BRIT*) Bourse *f*, marché financier.
stock phrase *n* cliché *m*.
stockpile ['stɔkpaɪl] *n* stock *m*, réserve *f* ♦ *vt* stocker, accumuler.
stockroom ['stɔkruːm] *n* réserve *f*, magasin *m*.
stocktaking ['stɔkteɪkɪŋ] *n* (*BRIT COMM*) inventaire *m*.
stocky ['stɔkɪ] *adj* trapu(e), râblé(e).
stodgy ['stɔdʒɪ] *adj* bourratif(ive), lourd(e).
stoic ['stəuɪk] *n* stoïque *m/f*.
stoical ['stəuɪkl] *adj* stoïque.
stoke [stəuk] *vt* garnir, entretenir; chauffer.
stoker ['stəukə*] *n* (*RAIL, NAUT etc*) chauffeur *m*.
stole [stəul] *pt of* **steal** ♦ *n* étole *f*.
stolen ['stəuln] *pp of* **steal**.
stolid ['stɔlɪd] *adj* impassible, flegmatique.
stomach ['stʌmək] *n* estomac *m*; (*abdomen*) ventre *m* ♦ *vt* supporter, digérer.
stomach ache *n* mal *m* à l'estomac *or* au ventre.
stomach pump *n* pompe stomacale.
stomach ulcer *n* ulcère *m* à l'estomac.
stomp [stɔmp] *vi*: **to ~ in/out** entrer/sortir d'un pas bruyant.
stone [stəun] *n* pierre *f*; (*pebble*) caillou *m*, galet *m*; (*in fruit*) noyau *m*; (*MED*) calcul *m*; (*BRIT: weight*) *= 6.348 kg; 14 pounds* ♦ *cpd* de *or* en pierre ♦ *vt* dénoyauter; **within a ~'s throw of the station** à deux pas de la gare.
Stone Age *n*: **the ~** l'âge *m* de pierre.
stone-cold ['stəun'kəuld] *adj* complètement froid(e).
stoned [stəund] *adj* (*col: drunk*) bourré(e); (*: on drugs*) défoncé(e).
stone-deaf ['stəun'dɛf] *adj* sourd(e) comme un pot.
stonemason ['stəunmeɪsn] *n* tailleur *m* de pierre(s).
stonewall [stəun'wɔːl] *vi* faire de l'obstruction ♦ *vt* faire obstruction à.
stonework ['stəunwəːk] *n* maçonnerie *f*.
stony ['stəunɪ] *adj* pierreux(euse), rocailleux(euse).
stood [stud] *pt, pp of* **stand**.
stooge [stuːdʒ] *n* (*col*) larbin *m*.
stool [stuːl] *n* tabouret *m*.
stoop [stuːp] *vi* (*also:* **have a ~**) être voûté(e); (*bend*) se baisser, se courber; (*fig*): **to ~ to sth/doing sth** s'abaisser jusqu'à qch/jusqu'à faire qch.
stop [stɔp] *n* arrêt *m*; (*short stay*) halte *f*; (*in punctuation*) point *m* ♦ *vt* arrêter; (*break off*) interrompre; (*also:* **put a ~ to**) mettre fin à; (*prevent*) empêcher ♦ *vi* s'arrêter; (*rain, noise etc*) cesser, s'arrêter; **to ~ doing sth** cesser

or arrêter de faire qch; **to ~ sb (from) doing sth** empêcher qn de faire qch; **to ~ dead** *vi* s'arrêter net; **~ it!** arrête!

▸**stop by** *vi* s'arrêter (au passage).

▸**stop off** *vi* faire une courte halte.

▸**stop up** *vt* (*hole*) boucher.

stopcock ['stɔpkɔk] *n* robinet *m* d'arrêt.

stopgap ['stɔpgæp] *n* (*person*) bouche-trou *m*; (*also*: **~ measure**) mesure *f* intérimaire.

stoplights ['stɔplaɪts] *npl* (*AUT*) signaux *mpl* de stop, feux *mpl* arrière.

stopover ['stɔpəuvə*] *n* halte *f*; (*AVIAT*) escale *f*.

stoppage ['stɔpɪdʒ] *n* arrêt *m*; (*of pay*) retenue *f*; (*strike*) arrêt de travail.

stopper ['stɔpə*] *n* bouchon *m*.

stop press *n* nouvelles *fpl* de dernière heure.

stopwatch ['stɔpwɔtʃ] *n* chronomètre *m*.

storage ['stɔːrɪdʒ] *n* emmagasinage *m*; (*of nuclear waste etc*) stockage *m*; (*in house*) rangement *m*; (*COMPUT*) mise *f* en mémoire *or* réserve.

storage heater *n* (*BRIT*) radiateur *m* électrique par accumulation.

store [stɔː*] *n* provision *f*, réserve *f*; (*depot*) entrepôt *m*; (*BRIT*: *large shop*) grand magasin; (*US*: *shop*) magasin *m* ♦ *vt* emmagasiner; (*nuclear waste etc*) stocker; (*in filing system*) classer, ranger; (*COMPUT*) mettre en mémoire; **~s** *npl* provisions; **who knows what is in ~ for us?** qui sait ce que l'avenir nous réserve *or* ce qui nous attend?; **to set great/little ~ by sth** faire grand cas/peu de cas de qch.

▸**store up** *vt* mettre en réserve, emmagasiner.

storehouse ['stɔːhaus] *n* entrepôt *m*.

storekeeper ['stɔːkiːpə*] *n* (*US*) commerçant/e.

storeroom ['stɔːruːm] *n* réserve *f*, magasin *m*.

storey, (*US*) **story** ['stɔːrɪ] *n* étage *m*.

stork [stɔːk] *n* cigogne *f*.

storm [stɔːm] *n* tempête *f*; (*also*: **electric ~**) orage *m* ♦ *vi* (*fig*) fulminer ♦ *vt* prendre d'assaut.

storm cloud *n* nuage *m* d'orage.

storm door *n* double-porte (extérieure).

stormy ['stɔːmɪ] *adj* orageux(euse).

story ['stɔːrɪ] *n* histoire *f*; récit *m*; (*PRESS*: *article*) article *m*; (*: subject*) affaire *f*; (*US*) = **storey**.

storybook ['stɔːrɪbuk] *n* livre *m* d'histoires *or* de contes.

storyteller ['stɔːrɪtɛlə*] *n* conteur/euse.

stout [staut] *adj* solide; (*brave*) intrépide; (*fat*) gros(se), corpulent(e) ♦ *n* bière brune.

stove [stəuv] *n* (*for cooking*) fourneau *m*; (*: small*) réchaud *m*; (*for heating*) poêle *m*; **gas/electric ~** (*cooker*) cuisinière *f* à gaz/électrique.

stow [stəu] *vt* ranger; cacher.

stowaway ['stəuəweɪ] *n* passager/ère clandestin(e).

straddle ['strædl] *vt* enjamber, être à cheval sur.

strafe [strɑːf] *vt* mitrailler.

straggle ['strægl] *vi* être (*or* marcher) en désordre; **~d along the coast** disséminé(e) tout au long de la côte.

straggler [stræglə*] *n* traînard/e.

straggling ['stræglɪŋ], **straggly** ['stræglɪ] *adj* (*hair*) en désordre.

straight [streɪt] *adj* droit(e); (*frank*) honnête, franc(franche); (*plain, uncomplicated*) simple; (*THEAT*: *part, play*) sérieux(euse); (*col*: *heterosexual*) hétéro *inv* ♦ *adv* (tout) droit; (*drink*) sec, sans eau ♦ *n*: **the ~** (*SPORT*) la ligne droite; **to put** *or* **get ~** mettre en ordre, mettre de l'ordre dans; **let's get this ~** mettons les choses au point; **10 ~ wins** 10 victoires d'affilée; **to go ~ home** rentrer directement à la maison; **~ away**, **~ off** (*at once*) tout de suite; **~ off**, **~ out** sans hésiter.

straighten ['streɪtn] *vt* (*also*: **~ out**) redresser; **to ~ things out** arranger les choses.

straight-faced [streɪt'feɪst] *adj* impassible ♦ *adv* en gardant son sérieux.

straightforward [streɪt'fɔːwəd] *adj* simple; (*frank*) honnête, direct(e).

strain [streɪn] *n* (*TECH*) tension *f*; pression *f*; (*physical*) effort *m*; (*mental*) tension (nerveuse); (*MED*) entorse *f*; (*streak, trace*) tendance *f*; élément *m*; (*breed*) variété *f*; (*of virus*) souche *f*; **~s** *npl* (*of music*) accents *mpl*, accords *mpl* ♦ *vt* tendre fortement; mettre à l'épreuve; (*filter*) passer, filtrer ♦ *vi* peiner, fournir un gros effort; **he's been under a lot of ~** il a traversé des moments très difficiles, il est très éprouvé nerveusement.

strained [streɪnd] *adj* (*laugh etc*) forcé(e), contraint(e); (*relations*) tendu(e).

strainer ['streɪnə*] *n* passoire *f*.

strait [streɪt] *n* (*GEO*) détroit *m*; **to be in dire ~s** (*fig*) être dans une situation désespérée.

straitjacket ['streɪtdʒækɪt] *n* camisole *f* de force.

strait-laced [streɪt'leɪst] *adj* collet monté *inv*.

strand [strænd] *n* (*of thread*) fil *m*, brin *m* ♦ *vt* (*boat*) échouer.

stranded ['strændɪd] *adj* en rade, en plan.

strange [streɪndʒ] *adj* (*not known*) inconnu(e); (*odd*) étrange, bizarre.

strangely ['streɪndʒlɪ] *adv* étrangement, bizarrement.

stranger ['streɪndʒə*] *n* (*unknown*) inconnu/e; (*from somewhere else*) étranger/ère; **I'm a ~ here** je ne suis pas d'ici.

strangle ['stræŋgl] *vt* étrangler.

stranglehold ['stræŋglhəuld] *n* (*fig*) emprise totale, mainmise *f*.

strangulation [stræŋgju'leɪʃən] *n* strangulation *f*.

strap [stræp] *n* lanière *f*, courroie *f*, sangle *f*; (*of slip, dress*) bretelle *f* ♦ *vt* attacher (avec

une courroie *etc*).
straphanging ['stræphæŋɪŋ] *n* (fait *m* de) voyager debout (dans le métro *etc*).
strapless ['stræplɪs] *adj* (*bra, dress*) sans bretelles.
strapped [stræpt] *adj*: **to be ~ for cash** (*col*) être à court d'argent.
strapping ['stræpɪŋ] *adj* bien découplé(e), costaud(e).
strappy ['stræpɪ] *adj* (*dress*) à bretelles; (*sandals*) à lanières.
Strasbourg ['stræzbəːg] *n* Strasbourg.
strata ['strɑːtə] *npl of* **stratum.**
stratagem ['strætɪdʒəm] *n* stratagème *m*.
strategic [strə'tiːdʒɪk] *adj* stratégique.
strategist ['strætɪdʒɪst] *n* stratège *m*.
strategy ['strætɪdʒɪ] *n* stratégie *f*.
stratosphere ['strætəsfɪə*] *n* stratosphère *f*.
stratum, *pl* **strata** ['strɑːtəm, 'strɑːtə] *n* strate *f*, couche *f*.
straw [strɔː] *n* paille *f*; **that's the last ~!** ça c'est le comble!
strawberry ['strɔːbərɪ] *n* fraise *f*; (*plant*) fraisier *m*.
stray [streɪ] *adj* (*animal*) perdu(e), errant(e) ♦ *vi* s'égarer; **~ bullet** balle perdue.
streak [striːk] *n* raie *f*, bande *f*, filet *m*; (*fig: of madness etc*): **a ~ of** une *or* des tendance(s) à ♦ *vt* zébrer, strier ♦ *vi*: **to ~ past** passer à toute allure; **to have ~s in one's hair** s'être fait faire des mèches; **a winning/losing ~** une bonne/mauvaise série *or* période.
streaker ['striːkə*] *n* streaker/euse.
streaky ['striːkɪ] *adj* zébré(e), strié(e).
streaky bacon *n* (*BRIT*) ≈ lard *m* (maigre).
stream [striːm] *n* (*brook*) ruisseau *m*; (*current*) courant *m*, flot *m*; (*of people*) défilé ininterrompu, flot ♦ *vt* (*SCOL*) répartir par niveau ♦ *vi* ruisseler; **to ~ in/out** entrer/sortir à flots; **against the ~** à contre courant; **on ~** (*new power plant etc*) en service.
streamer ['striːmə*] *n* serpentin *m*, banderole *f*.
stream feed *n* (*on photocopier etc*) alimentation *f* en continu.
streamline ['striːmlaɪn] *vt* donner un profil aérodynamique à; (*fig*) rationaliser.
streamlined ['striːmlaɪnd] *adj* (*AVIAT*) fuselé(e), profilé(e); (*AUT*) aérodynamique; (*fig*) rationalisé(e).
street [striːt] *n* rue *f*; **the back ~s** les quartiers pauvres; **to be on the ~s** (*homeless*) être à la rue *or* sans abri.
streetcar ['striːtkɑː*] *n* (*US*) tramway *m*.
street cred [-krɛd] *n* (*col*): **to have ~** être branché(e).
street lamp *n* réverbère *m*.
street lighting *n* éclairage public.
street map, street plan *n* plan *m* des rues.
street market *n* marché *m* à ciel ouvert.
streetwise ['striːtwaɪz] *adj* (*col*) futé(e), réaliste.
strength [strɛŋθ] *n* force *f*; (*of girder, knot etc*) solidité *f*; (*of chemical solution*) titre *m*; (*of wine*) degré *m* d'alcool; **on the ~ of** en vertu de; **at full ~** au grand complet; **below ~** à effectifs réduits.
strengthen ['strɛŋθn] *vt* renforcer; (*muscle*) fortifier.
strenuous ['strɛnjuəs] *adj* vigoureux(euse), énergique; (*tiring*) ardu(e), fatigant(e).
stress [strɛs] *n* (*force, pressure*) pression *f*; (*mental strain*) tension (nerveuse); (*accent*) accent *m*; (*emphasis*) insistance *f* ♦ *vt* insister sur, souligner; **to lay great ~ on sth** insister beaucoup sur qch; **to be under ~** être stressé(e).
stressful ['strɛsful] *adj* (*job*) stressant(e).
stretch [strɛtʃ] *n* (*of sand etc*) étendue *f*; (*of time*) période *f* ♦ *vi* s'étirer; (*extend*): **to ~ to** *or* **as far as** s'étendre jusqu'à; (*be enough: money, food*): **to ~ to** aller pour ♦ *vt* tendre, étirer; (*spread*) étendre; (*fig*) pousser (au maximum); **at a ~** sans discontinuer, sans interruption; **to ~ a muscle** se distendre un muscle; **to ~ one's legs** se dégourdir les jambes.
►**stretch out** *vi* s'étendre ♦ *vt* (*arm etc*) allonger, tendre; (*to spread*) étendre; **to ~ out for sth** allonger la main pour prendre qch.
stretcher ['strɛtʃə*] *n* brancard *m*, civière *f*.
stretcher-bearer ['strɛtʃəbɛərə*] *n* brancardier *m*.
stretch marks *npl* (*on skin*) vergetures *fpl*.
strewn [struːn] *adj*: **~ with** jonché(e) de.
stricken ['strɪkən] *adj* très éprouvé(e); dévasté(e); (*ship*) très endommagé(e); **~ with** frappé(e) *or* atteint(e) de.
strict [strɪkt] *adj* strict(e); **in ~ confidence** tout à fait confidentiellement.
strictly [strɪktlɪ] *adv* strictement; **~ confidential** strictement confidentiel(le); **~ speaking** à strictement parler.
strictness ['strɪktnɪs] *n* sévérité *f*.
stride [straɪd] *n* grand pas, enjambée *f* ♦ *vi* (*pt* **strode,** *pp* **stridden** [strəud, 'strɪdn]) marcher à grands pas; **to take in one's ~** (*fig: changes etc*) accepter sans sourciller.
strident ['straɪdnt] *adj* strident(e).
strife [straɪf] *n* conflit *m*, dissensions *fpl*.
strike [straɪk] *n* grève *f*; (*of oil etc*) découverte *f*; (*attack*) raid *m* ♦ *vb* (*pt, pp* **struck** [strʌk]) *vt* frapper; (*oil etc*) trouver, découvrir; (*make: agreement, deal*) conclure ♦ *vi* faire grève; (*attack*) attaquer; (*clock*) sonner; **to go on** *or* **come out on ~** se mettre en grève, faire grève; **to ~ a match** frotter une allumette; **to ~ a balance** (*fig*) trouver un juste milieu.
►**strike back** *vi* (*MIL, fig*) contre-attaquer.
►**strike down** *vt* (*fig*) terrasser.
►**strike off** *vt* (*from list*) rayer; (*: doctor etc*) radier.
►**strike out** *vt* rayer.
►**strike up** *vt* (*MUS*) se mettre à jouer; **to ~**

up a friendship with se lier d'amitié avec.
strikebreaker ['straɪkbreɪkə*] *n* briseur *m* de grève.
striker ['straɪkə*] *n* gréviste *m/f*; (*SPORT*) buteur *m*.
striking ['straɪkɪŋ] *adj* frappant(e), saisissant(e).
strimmer ['strɪmə*] *n* ® (*BRIT*) coupe-bordures *m*.
string [strɪŋ] *n* ficelle *f*, fil *m*; (*row: of beads*) rang *m*; (*: of onions, excuses*) chapelet *m*; (*: of people, cars*) file *f*; (*MUS*) corde *f*; (*COMPUT*) chaîne *f* ♦ *vt* (*pt, pp* **strung** [strʌŋ]): **to ~ out** échelonner; **to ~ together** enchaîner; **the ~s** (*MUS*) les instruments *mpl* à cordes; **to get a job by pulling ~s** obtenir un emploi en faisant jouer le piston; **with no ~s attached** (*fig*) sans conditions.
string bean *n* haricot vert.
string(ed) instrument [strɪŋ(d)-] *n* (*MUS*) instrument *m* à cordes.
stringent ['strɪndʒənt] *adj* rigoureux(euse); (*need*) impérieux(euse).
string quartet *n* quatuor *m* à cordes.
strip [strɪp] *n* bande *f*; (*SPORT*): **wearing the Celtic ~** en tenue du Celtic ♦ *vt* déshabiller; (*fig*) dégarnir, dépouiller; (*also*: **~ down**: *machine*) démonter ♦ *vi* se déshabiller.
strip cartoon *n* bande dessinée.
stripe [straɪp] *n* raie *f*, rayure *f*.
striped ['straɪpt] *adj* rayé(e), à rayures.
strip light *n* (*BRIT*) (tube *m* au) néon *m*.
stripper ['strɪpə*] *n* strip-teaseuse *f*.
strip-search ['strɪpsəːtʃ] *n* fouille corporelle (*en faisant se déshabiller la personne*) ♦ *vt*: **to ~ sb** fouiller qn (*en le faisant se déshabiller*).
striptease ['strɪptiːz] *n* strip-tease *m*.
strive, *pt* **strove,** *pp* **striven** [straɪv, strəuv, 'strɪvn] *vi*: **to ~ to do** s'efforcer de faire.
strobe [strəub] *n* (*also*: **~ light**) stroboscope *m*.
strode [strəud] *pt of* **stride**.
stroke [strəuk] *n* coup *m*; (*MED*) attaque *f*; (*caress*) caresse *f*; (*SWIMMING: style*) (sorte *f* de) nage *f*; (*of piston*) course *f* ♦ *vt* caresser; **at a ~** d'un (seul) coup; **on the ~ of 5** à 5 heures sonnantes; **a ~ of luck** un coup de chance; **a 2-~ engine** un moteur à 2 temps.
stroll [strəul] *n* petite promenade ♦ *vi* flâner, se promener nonchalamment; **to go for a ~** aller se promener *or* faire un tour.
stroller ['strəulə*] *n* (*US*) poussette *f*.
strong [strɔŋ] *adj* (*gen*) fort(e); (*healthy*) vigoureux(euse); (*object, material*) solide; (*distaste, desire*) vif(vive); (*drugs, chemicals*) puissant(e) ♦ *adv*: **to be going ~** (*company*) marcher bien; (*person*) être toujours solide; **they are 50 ~** ils sont au nombre de 50.
strong-arm ['strɔŋɑːm] *adj* (*tactics, methods*) musclé(e).
strongbox ['strɔŋbɔks] *n* coffre-fort *m*.
stronghold ['strɔŋhəuld] *n* bastion *m*.
strongly ['strɔŋlɪ] *adv* fortement, avec force; vigoureusement; solidement; **I feel ~ about it** c'est une question qui me tient particulièrement à cœur; (*negatively*) j'y suis profondément opposé(e).
strongman ['strɔŋmæn] *n* hercule *m*, colosse *m*; (*fig*) homme *m* à poigne.
strongroom ['strɔŋruːm] *n* chambre forte.
stroppy ['strɔpɪ] *adj* (*BRIT col*) contrariant(e), difficile.
strove [strəuv] *pt of* **strive**.
struck [strʌk] *pt, pp of* **strike**.
structural ['strʌktʃrəl] *adj* structural(e); (*CONSTR*) de construction; affectant les parties portantes.
structurally ['strʌktʃrəlɪ] *adv* du point de vue de la construction.
structure ['strʌktʃə*] *n* structure *f*; (*building*) construction *f*.
struggle ['strʌgl] *n* lutte *f* ♦ *vi* lutter, se battre; **to have a ~ to do sth** avoir beaucoup de mal à faire qch.
strum [strʌm] *vt* (*guitar*) gratter de.
strung [strʌŋ] *pt, pp of* **string**.
strut [strʌt] *n* étai *m*, support *m* ♦ *vi* se pavaner.
strychnine ['strɪkniːn] *n* strychnine *f*.
stub [stʌb] *n* bout *m*; (*of ticket etc*) talon *m* ♦ *vt*: **to ~ one's toe (on sth)** se heurter le doigt de pied (contre qch).
►**stub out** *vt* écraser.
stubble ['stʌbl] *n* chaume *m*; (*on chin*) barbe *f* de plusieurs jours.
stubborn ['stʌbən] *adj* têtu(e), obstiné(e), opiniâtre.
stubby ['stʌbɪ] *adj* trapu(e); gros(se) et court(e).
stucco ['stʌkəu] *n* stuc *m*.
stuck [stʌk] *pt, pp of* **stick** ♦ *adj* (*jammed*) bloqué(e), coincé(e); **to get ~** se bloquer *or* coincer.
stuck-up [stʌk'ʌp] *adj* prétentieux(euse).
stud [stʌd] *n* clou *m* (à grosse tête); (*collar ~*) bouton *m* de col; (*of horses*) écurie *f*, haras *m*; (*also*: **~ horse**) étalon *m* ♦ *vt* (*fig*): **~ded with** parsemé(e) *or* criblé(e) de.
student ['stjuːdənt] *n* étudiant/e ♦ *cpd* estudiantin(e); universitaire; d'étudiant; **law/medical ~** étudiant en droit/médecine.
student driver *n* (*US*) (conducteur/trice) débutant(e).
students' union *n* (*BRIT: association*) ≈ union *f* des étudiants; (*: building*) ≈ foyer *m* des étudiants.
studied ['stʌdɪd] *adj* étudié(e), calculé(e).
studio ['stjuːdɪəu] *n* studio *m*, atelier *m*.
studio flat, (*US*) **studio apartment** *n* studio *m*.
studious ['stjuːdɪəs] *adj* studieux(euse), appliqué(e); (*studied*) étudié(e).
studiously ['stjuːdɪəslɪ] *adv* (*carefully*) soigneusement.
study ['stʌdɪ] *n* étude *f*; (*room*) bureau *m* ♦ *vt*

étudier ♦ *vi* étudier, faire ses études; **to make a ~ of sth** étudier qch, faire une étude de qch; **to ~ for an exam** préparer un examen.
stuff [stʌf] *n* (*gen*) chose(s) *f(pl)*, truc *m*; (*belongings*) affaires *fpl*, trucs; (*substance*) substance *f* ♦ *vt* rembourrer; (*CULIN*) farcir; (*animal: for exhibition*) empailler; **my nose is ~ed up** j'ai le nez bouché; **get ~ed!** (*col!*) va te faire foutre! (*!*); **~ed toy** jouet *m* en peluche.
stuffing ['stʌfɪŋ] *n* bourre *f*, rembourrage *m*; (*CULIN*) farce *f*.
stuffy ['stʌfɪ] *adj* (*room*) mal ventilé(e) *or* aéré(e); (*ideas*) vieux jeu *inv*.
stumble ['stʌmbl] *vi* trébucher.
►**stumble across** *vt fus* (*fig*) tomber sur.
stumbling block ['stʌmblɪŋ-] *n* pierre *f* d'achoppement.
stump [stʌmp] *n* souche *f*; (*of limb*) moignon *m* ♦ *vt*: **to be ~ed** sécher, ne pas savoir que répondre.
stun [stʌn] *vt* (*subj*: *blow*) étourdir; (: *news*) abasourdir, stupéfier.
stung [stʌŋ] *pt, pp of* **sting**.
stunk [stʌŋk] *pp of* **stink**.
stunning ['stʌnɪŋ] *adj* étourdissant(e); (*fabulous*) stupéfiant(e), sensationnel(le).
stunt [stʌnt] *n* tour *m* de force; truc *m* publicitaire; (*AVIAT*) acrobatie *f* ♦ *vt* retarder, arrêter.
stunted ['stʌntɪd] *adj* rabougri(e).
stuntman ['stʌntmæn] *n* cascadeur *m*.
stupefaction [stju:pɪ'fækʃən] *n* stupéfaction *f*, stupeur *f*.
stupefy ['stju:pɪfaɪ] *vt* étourdir; abrutir; (*fig*) stupéfier.
stupendous [stju:'pɛndəs] *adj* prodigieux(euse), fantastique.
stupid ['stju:pɪd] *adj* stupide, bête.
stupidity [stju:'pɪdɪtɪ] *n* stupidité *f*, bêtise *f*.
stupidly ['stju:pɪdlɪ] *adv* stupidement, bêtement.
stupor ['stju:pə*] *n* stupeur *f*.
sturdy ['stə:dɪ] *adj* robuste, vigoureux(euse); solide.
sturgeon ['stə:dʒən] *n* esturgeon *m*.
stutter ['stʌtə*] *n* bégaiement *m* ♦ *vi* bégayer.
sty [staɪ] *n* (*of pigs*) porcherie *f*.
stye [staɪ] *n* (*MED*) orgelet *m*.
style [staɪl] *n* style *m*; (*of dress etc*) genre *m*; (*distinction*) allure *f*, cachet *m*, style; **in the latest ~** à la dernière mode; **hair ~** coiffure *f*.
stylish ['staɪlɪʃ] *adj* élégant(e), chic *inv*.
stylist ['staɪlɪst] *n* (*hair ~*) coiffeur/euse; (*literary ~*) styliste *m/f*.
stylized ['staɪlaɪzd] *adj* stylisé(e).
stylus, *pl* **styli** *or* **styluses** ['staɪləs, -laɪ] *n* (*of record player*) pointe *f* de lecture.
Styrofoam ['staɪrəfəum] *n* ® (*US*) polystyrène expansé ♦ *adj* en polystyrène.
suave [swɑ:v] *adj* doucereux(euse), onctueux(euse).
sub [sʌb] *n abbr* = **submarine, subscription.**
sub... [sʌb] *prefix* sub..., sous-.
subcommittee ['sʌbkəmɪtɪ] *n* sous-comité *m*.
subconscious [sʌb'kɔnʃəs] *adj* subconscient(e) ♦ *n* subconscient *m*.
subcontinent [sʌb'kɔntɪnənt] *n*: **the (Indian) ~** le sous-continent indien.
subcontract *n* ['sʌb'kɔntrækt] contrat *m* de sous-traitance ♦ *vt* [sʌbkən'trækt] sous-traiter.
subcontractor ['sʌbkən'træktə*] *n* sous-traitant *m*.
subdivide [sʌbdɪ'vaɪd] *vt* subdiviser.
subdivision ['sʌbdɪvɪʒən] *n* subdivision *f*.
subdue [səb'dju:] *vt* subjuguer, soumettre.
subdued [səb'dju:d] *adj* contenu(e), atténué(e); (*light*) tamisé(e); (*person*) qui a perdu de son entrain.
sub-editor ['sʌb'ɛdɪtə*] *n* (*BRIT*) secrétaire *m/f* de (la) rédaction.
subject *n* ['sʌbdʒɪkt] sujet *m*; (*SCOL*) matière *f* ♦ *vt* [səb'dʒɛkt]: **to ~ to** soumettre à; exposer à; **to be ~ to** (*law*) être soumis(e) à; (*disease*) être sujet(te) à; **~ to confirmation in writing** sous réserve de confirmation écrite; **to change the ~** changer de conversation.
subjection [səb'dʒɛkʃən] *n* soumission *f*, sujétion *f*.
subjective [səb'dʒɛktɪv] *adj* subjectif(ive).
subject matter *n* sujet *m*; contenu *m*.
sub judice [sʌb'dju:dɪsɪ] *adj* (*LAW*) devant les tribunaux.
subjugate ['sʌbdʒugeɪt] *vt* subjuguer.
subjunctive [səb'dʒʌŋktɪv] *adj* subjonctif(ive) ♦ *n* subjonctif *m*.
sublet [sʌb'lɛt] *vt* sous-louer.
sublime [sə'blaɪm] *adj* sublime.
subliminal [sʌb'lɪmɪnl] *adj* subliminal(e).
submachine gun ['sʌbmə'ʃi:n-] *n* mitraillette *f*.
submarine [sʌbmə'ri:n] *n* sous-marin *m*.
submerge [səb'mə:dʒ] *vt* submerger; immerger ♦ *vi* plonger.
submersion [səb'mə:ʃən] *n* submersion *f*; immersion *f*.
submission [səb'mɪʃən] *n* soumission *f*; (*to committee etc*) présentation *f*.
submissive [səb'mɪsɪv] *adj* soumis(e).
submit [səb'mɪt] *vt* soumettre ♦ *vi* se soumettre.
subnormal [sʌb'nɔ:ml] *adj* au-dessous de la normale; (*person*) arriéré(e).
subordinate [sə'bɔ:dɪnət] *adj*, *n* subordonné(e).
subpoena [səb'pi:nə] (*LAW*) *n* citation *f*, assignation *f* ♦ *vt* citer *or* assigner (à comparaître).
subroutine [sʌbru:'ti:n] *n* (*COMPUT*) sous-programme *m*.
subscribe [səb'skraɪb] *vi* cotiser; **to ~ to** (*opinion, fund*) souscrire à; (*newspaper*) s'abon-

ner à; être abonné(e) à.
subscriber [səb'skraɪbə*] *n* (*to periodical, telephone*) abonné/e.
subscript ['sʌbskrɪpt] *n* (*TYP*) indice inférieur.
subscription [səb'skrɪpʃən] *n* (*to fund*) souscription *f*; (*to magazine etc*) abonnement *m*; (*membership dues*) cotisation *f*; **to take out a ~ to** s'abonner à.
subsequent ['sʌbsɪkwənt] *adj* ultérieur(e), suivant(e); ~ **to** *prep* à la suite de.
subsequently ['sʌbsɪkwəntlɪ] *adv* par la suite.
subservient [səb'sə:vɪənt] *adj* obséquieux(euse).
subside [səb'saɪd] *vi* s'affaisser; (*flood*) baisser; (*wind*) tomber.
subsidence [səb'saɪdns] *n* affaissement *m*.
subsidiarity [səbsɪdɪ'ærɪtɪ] *n* (*POL*) subsidiarité *f*.
subsidiary [səb'sɪdɪərɪ] *adj* subsidiaire; accessoire; (*BRIT SCOL: subject*) complémentaire ♦ *n* filiale *f*.
subsidize ['sʌbsɪdaɪz] *vt* subventionner.
subsidy ['sʌbsɪdɪ] *n* subvention *f*.
subsist [səb'sɪst] *vi*: **to ~ on sth** (arriver à) vivre avec *or* subsister avec qch.
subsistence [səb'sɪstəns] *n* existence *f*, subsistance *f*.
subsistence allowance *n* indemnité *f* de séjour.
subsistence level *n* niveau *m* de vie minimum.
substance ['sʌbstəns] *n* substance *f*; (*fig*) essentiel *m*; **a man of ~** un homme jouissant d'une certaine fortune; **to lack ~** être plutôt mince (*fig*).
substance abuse *n* abus *m* de substances toxiques.
substandard [sʌb'stændəd] *adj* (*goods*) de qualité inférieure, qui laisse à désirer; (*housing*) inférieur(e) aux normes requises.
substantial [səb'stænʃl] *adj* substantiel(le); (*fig*) important(e).
substantially [səb'stænʃəlɪ] *adv* considérablement; en grande partie.
substantiate [səb'stænʃɪeɪt] *vt* étayer, fournir des preuves à l'appui de.
substitute ['sʌbstɪtju:t] *n* (*person*) remplaçant/e; (*thing*) succédané *m* ♦ *vt*: **to ~ sth/sb for** substituer qch/qn à, remplacer par qch/qn.
substitute teacher *n* (*US*) suppléant/e.
substitution [sʌbstɪ'tju:ʃən] *n* substitution *f*.
subterfuge ['sʌbtəfju:dʒ] *n* subterfuge *m*.
subterranean [sʌbtə'reɪnɪən] *adj* souterrain(e).
subtitle ['sʌbtaɪtl] *n* (*CINE*) sous-titre *m*.
subtle ['sʌtl] *adj* subtil(e).
subtlety ['sʌtltɪ] *n* subtilité *f*.
subtly ['sʌtlɪ] *adv* subtilement.
subtotal [sʌb'təutl] *n* total partiel.
subtract [səb'trækt] *vt* soustraire, retrancher.
subtraction [səb'trækʃən] *n* soustraction *f*.
subtropical [sʌb'trɔpɪkl] *adj* subtropical(e).
suburb ['sʌbə:b] *n* faubourg *m*; **the ~s** la banlieue.
suburban [sə'bə:bən] *adj* de banlieue, suburbain(e).
suburbia [sə'bə:bɪə] *n* la banlieue.
subvention [səb'vɛnʃən] *n* (*subsidy*) subvention *f*.
subversion [səb'və:ʃən] *n* subversion *f*.
subversive [səb'və:sɪv] *adj* subversif(ive).
subway ['sʌbweɪ] *n* (*US*) métro *m*; (*BRIT*) passage souterrain.
sub-zero [sʌb'zɪərəu] *adj* au-dessous de zéro.
succeed [sək'si:d] *vi* réussir ♦ *vt* succéder à; **to ~ in doing** réussir à faire.
succeeding [sək'si:dɪŋ] *adj* suivant(e), qui suit (*or* suivent *or* suivront *etc*).
success [sək'sɛs] *n* succès *m*; réussite *f*.
successful [sək'sɛsful] *adj* qui a du succès; (*candidate*) choisi(e), agréé(e); (*business*) prospère, qui réussit; (*attempt*) couronné(e) de succès; **to be ~ (in doing)** réussir (à faire).
successfully [sək'sɛsfəlɪ] *adv* avec succès.
succession [sək'sɛʃən] *n* succession *f*; **in ~** successivement; **3 years in ~** 3 ans de suite.
successive [sək'sɛsɪv] *adj* successif(ive); **on 3 ~ days** 3 jours de suite *or* consécutifs.
successor [sək'sɛsə*] *n* successeur *m*.
succinct [sək'sɪŋkt] *adj* succinct(e), bref(brève).
succulent ['sʌkjulənt] *adj* succulent(e) ♦ *n* (*BOT*): **~s** plantes grasses.
succumb [sə'kʌm] *vi* succomber.
such [sʌtʃ] *adj* tel(telle); (*of that kind*): **~ a book** un livre de ce genre *or* pareil, un tel livre ♦ *adv* si; **~ books** des livres de ce genre *or* pareils, de tels livres; (*so much*): **~ courage** un tel courage; **~ a long trip** un si long voyage; **~ good books** de si bons livres; **~ a long trip that** un voyage si *or* tellement long que; **~ a lot of** tellement *or* tant de; **making ~ a noise that** faisant un tel bruit que *or* tellement de bruit que; **~ a long time ago** il y a si *or* tellement longtemps; **~ as** (*like*) tel(telle) que, comme; **a noise ~ as to** un bruit de nature à; **~ books as I have** les quelques livres que j'ai; **as ~** *adv* en tant que tel(telle), à proprement parler.
such-and-such ['sʌtʃənsʌtʃ] *adj* tel(telle) ou tel(telle).
suchlike ['sʌtʃlaɪk] *pron* (*col*): **and ~** et le reste.
suck [sʌk] *vt* sucer; (*breast, bottle*) téter; (*subj: pump, machine*) aspirer.
sucker ['sʌkə*] *n* (*BOT, ZOOL, TECH*) ventouse *f*; (*col*) naïf/ïve, poire *f*.
suckle ['sʌkl] *vt* allaiter.
sucrose ['su:krəuz] *n* saccharose *m*.
suction ['sʌkʃən] *n* succion *f*.
suction pump *n* pompe aspirante.

Sudan [su'dɑːn] *n* Soudan *m*.
Sudanese [suːdə'niːz] *adj* soudanais(e) ♦ *n* Soudanais/e.
sudden ['sʌdn] *adj* soudain(e), subit(e); **all of a ~** soudain, tout à coup.
sudden-death [sʌdn'dɛθ] *n*: **~ play-off** *partie supplémentaire pour départager les adversaires*.
suddenly ['sʌdnlɪ] *adv* brusquement, tout à coup, soudain.
suds [sʌdz] *npl* eau savonneuse.
sue [suː] *vt* poursuivre en justice, intenter un procès à ♦ *vi*: **to ~ (for)** intenter un procès (pour); **to ~ for divorce** engager une procédure de divorce; **to ~ sb for damages** poursuivre qn en dommages-intérêts.
suede [sweɪd] *n* daim *m*, cuir suédé ♦ *cpd* de daim.
suet ['suɪt] *n* graisse *f* de rognon *or* de bœuf.
Suez Canal ['suːɪz-] *n* canal *m* de Suez.
Suff. *abbr* (*BRIT*) = *Suffolk*.
suffer ['sʌfə*] *vt* souffrir, subir; (*bear*) tolérer, supporter, subir ♦ *vi* souffrir; **to ~ from** (*illness*) souffrir de, avoir; **to ~ from the effects of alcohol/a fall** se ressentir des effets de l'alcool/des conséquences d'une chute.
sufferance ['sʌfərns] *n*: **he was only there on ~** sa présence était seulement tolérée.
sufferer ['sʌfərə*] *n* malade *m/f*; victime *m/f*.
suffering ['sʌfərɪŋ] *n* souffrance(s) *f(pl)*.
suffice [sə'faɪs] *vi* suffire.
sufficient [sə'fɪʃənt] *adj* suffisant(e); **~ money** suffisamment d'argent.
sufficiently [sə'fɪʃəntlɪ] *adv* suffisamment, assez.
suffix ['sʌfɪks] *n* suffixe *m*.
suffocate ['sʌfəkeɪt] *vi* suffoquer; étouffer.
suffocation [sʌfə'keɪʃən] *n* suffocation *f*; (*MED*) asphyxie *f*.
suffrage ['sʌfrɪdʒ] *n* suffrage *m*; droit *m* de suffrage *or* de vote.
suffuse [sə'fjuːz] *vt* baigner, imprégner; **the room was ~d with light** la pièce baignait dans la lumière *or* était imprégnée de lumière.
sugar ['ʃugə*] *n* sucre *m* ♦ *vt* sucrer.
sugar beet *n* betterave sucrière.
sugar bowl *n* sucrier *m*.
sugar cane *n* canne *f* à sucre.
sugar-coated ['ʃugə'kəutɪd] *adj* dragéifié(e).
sugar lump *n* morceau *m* de sucre.
sugar refinery *n* raffinerie *f* de sucre.
sugary ['ʃugərɪ] *adj* sucré(e).
suggest [sə'dʒɛst] *vt* suggérer, proposer; (*indicate*) laisser supposer, suggérer; **what do you ~ I do?** que vous me suggérez de faire?
suggestion [sə'dʒɛstʃən] *n* suggestion *f*.
suggestive [sə'dʒɛstɪv] *adj* suggestif(ive).
suicidal [suɪ'saɪdl] *adj* suicidaire.
suicide ['suɪsaɪd] *n* suicide *m*; **to commit ~** se suicider.
suicide attempt, suicide bid *n* tentative *f* de suicide.
suit [suːt] *n* (*man's*) costume *m*, complet *m*; (*woman's*) tailleur *m*, ensemble *m*; (*CARDS*) couleur *f*; (*law~*) procès *m* ♦ *vt* aller à; convenir à; (*adapt*): **to ~ sth to** adapter *or* approprier qch à; **to be ~ed to sth** (*suitable for*) être adapté(e) *or* approprié(e) à qch; **well ~ed** (*couple*) faits l'un pour l'autre, très bien assortis; **to bring a ~ against sb** intenter un procès contre qn; **to follow ~** (*fig*) faire de même.
suitable ['suːtəbl] *adj* qui convient; approprié(e), adéquat(e); **would tomorrow be ~?** est-ce que demain vous convien- drait?; **we found somebody ~** nous avons trouvé la personne qu'il nous faut.
suitably ['suːtəblɪ] *adv* comme il se doit (*or* se devait *etc*), convenablement.
suitcase ['suːtkeɪs] *n* valise *f*.
suite [swiːt] *n* (*of rooms, also MUS*) suite *f*; (*furniture*): **bedroom/dining room ~** (ensemble *m* de) chambre *f* à coucher/salle *f* à manger; **a three-piece ~** un salon (canapé et deux fauteuils).
suitor ['suːtə*] *n* soupirant *m*, prétendant *m*.
sulfate ['sʌlfeɪt] *n* (*US*) = **sulphate**.
sulfur *etc* ['sʌlfə*] (*US*) = **sulphur** *etc*.
sulk [sʌlk] *vi* bouder.
sulky ['sʌlkɪ] *adj* boudeur(euse), maussade.
sullen ['sʌlən] *adj* renfrogné(e), maussade; morne.
sulphate, (*US*) sulfate ['sʌlfeɪt] *n* sulfate *m*; **copper ~** sulfate de cuivre.
sulphur, (*US*) sulfur ['sʌlfə*] *n* soufre *m*.
sulphur dioxide *n* anhydride sulfureux.
sulphuric, (*US*) sulfuric [sʌl'fjuərɪk] *adj*: **~ acid** acide *m* sulfurique.
sultan ['sʌltən] *n* sultan *m*.
sultana [sʌl'tɑːnə] *n* (*fruit*) raisin (sec) de Smyrne.
sultry ['sʌltrɪ] *adj* étouffant(e).
sum [sʌm] *n* somme *f*; (*SCOL etc*) calcul *m*.
►**sum up** *vt* résumer; (*evaluate rapidly*) récapituler ♦ *vi* résumer.
Sumatra [su'mɑːtrə] *n* Sumatra.
summarize ['sʌməraɪz] *vt* résumer.
summary ['sʌmərɪ] *n* résumé *m* ♦ *adj* (*justice*) sommaire.
summer ['sʌmə*] *n* été *m* ♦ *cpd* d'été, estival(e); **in (the) ~** en été, pendant l'été.
summer camp *n* (*US*) colonie *f* de vacances.
summerhouse ['sʌməhaus] *n* (*in garden*) pavillon *m*.
summertime ['sʌmətaɪm] *n* (*season*) été *m*.
summer time *n* (*by clock*) heure *f* d'été.
summery ['sʌmərɪ] *adj* estival(e); d'été.
summing-up [sʌmɪŋ'ʌp] *n* résumé *m*, récapitulation *f*.
summit ['sʌmɪt] *n* sommet *m*; (*also*: **~ conference**) (conférence *f* au) sommet *m*.
summon ['sʌmən] *vt* appeler, convoquer; **to ~ a witness** citer *or* assigner un témoin.

►**summon up** *vt* rassembler, faire appel à.
summons ['sʌmənz] *n* citation *f*, assignation *f* ♦ *vt* citer, assigner; **to serve a ~ on sb** remettre une assignation à qn.
sumo ['suːməu] *n*: ~ **wrestling** sumo *m*.
sump [sʌmp] *n* (*BRIT AUT*) carter *m*.
sumptuous ['sʌmptjuəs] *adj* somptueux(euse).
sun [sʌn] *n* soleil *m*; **in the ~** au soleil; **to catch the ~** prendre le soleil; **everything under the ~** absolument tout.
Sun. *abbr* (= *Sunday*) dim.
sunbathe ['sʌnbeɪð] *vi* prendre un bain de soleil.
sunbeam ['sʌnbiːm] *n* rayon *m* de soleil.
sunbed ['sʌnbɛd] *n* lit pliant; (*with sun lamp*) lit à ultra-violets.
sunburn ['sʌnbəːn] *n* coup *m* de soleil.
sunburnt ['sʌnbəːnt], **sunburned** ['sʌnbəːnd] *adj* bronzé(e), hâlé(e); (*painfully*) brûlé(e) par le soleil.
sun cream *n* crème *f* (anti-)solaire.
sundae ['sʌndeɪ] *n* sundae *m*, coupe glacée.
Sunday ['sʌndɪ] *n* dimanche *m*; *for phrases see also* **Tuesday**.
Sunday paper *n* journal *m* du dimanche; *voir encadré*.

SUNDAY PAPER

Les **Sunday papers** *sont une véritable institution en Grande-Bretagne. Il y a des "quality" Sunday papers et des "popular" Sunday papers, et la plupart des quotidiens ont un journal du dimanche qui leur est associé, bien que leurs équipes de rédacteurs soient différentes. Les quality Sunday papers ont plusieurs suppléments et magazines; voir "quality press" et "tabloid press".*

Sunday school *n* ≈ catéchisme *m*.
sundial ['sʌndaɪəl] *n* cadran *m* solaire.
sundown ['sʌndaun] *n* coucher *m* du soleil.
sundries ['sʌndrɪz] *npl* articles divers.
sundry ['sʌndrɪ] *adj* divers(e), différent(e); **all and ~** tout le monde, n'importe qui.
sunflower ['sʌnflauə*] *n* tournesol *m*.
sung [sʌŋ] *pp of* **sing**.
sunglasses ['sʌnglɑːsɪz] *npl* lunettes *fpl* de soleil.
sunk [sʌŋk] *pp of* **sink**.
sunken ['sʌŋkn] *adj* (*rock, ship*) submergé(e); (*cheeks*) creux(euse); (*bath*) encastré(e).
sunlamp ['sʌnlæmp] *n* lampe *f* à rayons ultraviolets.
sunlight ['sʌnlaɪt] *n* (lumière *f* du) soleil *m*.
sunlit ['sʌnlɪt] *adj* ensoleillé(e).
sunny ['sʌnɪ] *adj* ensoleillé(e); (*fig*) épanoui(e), radieux(euse); **it is ~** il fait (du) soleil, il y a du soleil.
sunrise ['sʌnraɪz] *n* lever *m* du soleil.
sun roof *n* (*AUT*) toit ouvrant.
sunscreen ['sʌnskriːn] *n* crème *f* solaire.
sunset ['sʌnsɛt] *n* coucher *m* du soleil.
sunshade ['sʌnʃeɪd] *n* (*lady's*) ombrelle *f*; (*over table*) parasol *m*.
sunshine ['sʌnʃaɪn] *n* (lumière *f* du) soleil *m*.
sunspot ['sʌnspɔt] *n* tache *f* solaire.
sunstroke ['sʌnstrəuk] *n* insolation *f*, coup *m* de soleil.
suntan ['sʌntæn] *n* bronzage *m*.
suntanned ['sʌntænd] *adj* bronzé(e).
suntan oil *n* huile *f* solaire.
suntrap ['sʌntræp] *n* coin très ensoleillé.
super ['suːpə*] *adj* (*col*) formidable.
superannuation [suːpərænju'eɪʃən] *n* cotisations *fpl* pour la pension.
superb [suː'pəːb] *adj* superbe, magnifique.
Super Bowl *n* (*US SPORT*) Super Bowl *m*.
supercilious [suːpə'sɪlɪəs] *adj* hautain(e), dédaigneux(euse).
superconductor [suːpəkən'dʌktə*] *n* supraconducteur *m*.
superficial [suːpə'fɪʃəl] *adj* superficiel(le).
superficially [suːpə'fɪʃəlɪ] *adv* superficiellement.
superfluous [su'pəːfluəs] *adj* superflu(e).
superglue ['suːpəgluː] *n* colle forte.
superhighway ['suːpəhaɪweɪ] *n* (*US*) voie *f* express (à plusieurs files); **the information ~** la super-autoroute de l'information.
superhuman [suːpə'hjuːmən] *adj* surhumain(e).
superimpose ['suːpərɪm'pəuz] *vt* superposer.
superintend [suːpərɪn'tɛnd] *vt* surveiller.
superintendent [suːpərɪn'tɛndənt] *n* directeur/trice; (*POLICE*) ≈ commissaire *m*.
superior [su'pɪərɪə*] *adj* supérieur(e); (*COMM: goods, quality*) de qualité supérieure; (*smug*) condescendant(e), méprisant(e) ♦ *n* supérieur/e.
superiority [supɪərɪ'ɔrɪtɪ] *n* supériorité *f*.
superlative [su'pəːlətɪv] *adj* sans pareil(le), suprême ♦ *n* (*LING*) superlatif *m*.
superman ['suːpəmæn] *n* surhomme *m*.
supermarket ['suːpəmɑːkɪt] *n* supermarché *m*.
supermodel ['suːpəmɔdl] *n* top model *m*.
supernatural [suːpə'nætʃərəl] *adj* surnaturel(le).
supernova [suːpə'nəuvə] *n* supernova *f*.
superpower ['suːpəpauə*] *n* (*POL*) superpuissance *f*.
supersede [suːpə'siːd] *vt* remplacer, supplanter.
supersonic ['suːpə'sɔnɪk] *adj* supersonique.
superstar ['suːpəstɑː*] *n* (*CINE etc*) superstar *f*; (*SPORT*) superchampion/ne ♦ *adj* (*status, lifestyle*) de superstar.
superstition [suːpə'stɪʃən] *n* superstition *f*.
superstitious [suːpə'stɪʃəs] *adj* superstitieux(euse).
superstore ['suːpəstɔː*] *n* (*BRIT*) hypermarché *m*, grand surface.

supertanker ['su:pətæŋkə*] *n* pétrolier géant, superpétrolier *m*.
supertax ['su:pətæks] *n* tranche supérieure de l'impôt.
supervise ['su:pəvaɪz] *vt* (*children etc*) surveiller; (*organization, work*) diriger.
supervision [su:pə'vɪʒən] *n* surveillance *f*; direction *f*; **under medical ~** sous contrôle du médecin.
supervisor ['su:pəvaɪzə*] *n* surveillant/e; (*in shop*) chef *m* de rayon; (*SCOL*) directeur/trice de thèse.
supervisory ['su:pəvaɪzərɪ] *adj* de surveillance.
supine ['su:paɪn] *adj* couché(e) *or* étendu(e) sur le dos.
supper ['sʌpə*] *n* dîner *m*; (*late*) souper *m*; **to have ~** dîner; souper.
supplant [sə'plɑ:nt] *vt* supplanter.
supple ['sʌpl] *adj* souple.
supplement *n* ['sʌplɪmənt] supplément *m* ♦ *vt* [sʌplɪ'mɛnt] ajouter à, compléter.
supplementary [sʌplɪ'mɛntərɪ] *adj* supplémentaire.
supplementary benefit *n* (*BRIT*) allocation *f* supplémentaire d'aide sociale.
supplier [sə'plaɪə*] *n* fournisseur *m*.
supply [sə'plaɪ] *vt* (*goods*): **to ~ sth (to sb)** fournir qch (à qn); (*people, organization*): **to ~ sb (with sth)** approvisionner *or* ravitailler qn (en qch); fournir qn (en qch), fournir qch à qn; (*system, machine*): **to ~ sth (with sth)** alimenter qch (en qch); (*a need*) répondre à ♦ *n* provision *f*, réserve *f*; (*supplying*) approvisionnement *m*; (*TECH*) alimentation *f*; **supplies** *npl* (*food*) vivres *mpl*; (*MIL*) subsistances *fpl*; **office supplies** fournitures *fpl* de bureau; **to be in short ~** être rare, manquer; **the electricity/water/gas ~** l'alimentation en électricité/eau/gaz; **~ and demand** l'offre *f* et la demande; **it comes supplied with an adaptor** il (*or* elle) est pourvu(e) d'un adaptateur.
supply teacher *n* (*BRIT*) suppléant/e.
support [sə'pɔ:t] *n* (*moral, financial etc*) soutien *m*, appui *m*; (*TECH*) support *m*, soutien ♦ *vt* soutenir, supporter; (*financially*) subvenir aux besoins de; (*uphold*) être pour, être partisan de, appuyer; (*SPORT: team*) être pour; **to ~ o.s.** (*financially*) gagner sa vie.
supporter [sə'pɔ:tə*] *n* (*POL etc*) partisan/e; (*SPORT*) supporter *m*.
supporting [sə'pɔ:tɪŋ] *adj* (*wall*) d'appui.
supporting actor/actress *n* second rôle *m/f*.
supporting role *n* second rôle *m*.
supportive [sə'pɔ:tɪv] *adj*: **my family were very ~** ma famille m'a été d'un grand soutien.
suppose [sə'pəuz] *vt, vi* supposer; imaginer; **to be ~d to do/be** être censé(e) faire/être; **I don't ~ she'll come** je suppose qu'elle ne viendra pas, cela m'étonnerait qu'elle vienne.
supposedly [sə'pəuzɪdlɪ] *adv* soi-disant.
supposing [sə'pəuzɪŋ] *conj* si, à supposer que + *sub*.
supposition [sʌpə'zɪʃən] *n* supposition *f*, hypothèse *f*.
suppository [sə'pɔzɪtrɪ] *n* suppositoire *m*.
suppress [sə'prɛs] *vt* (*revolt, feeling*) réprimer; (*publication*) supprimer; (*scandal*) étouffer.
suppression [sə'prɛʃən] *n* suppression *f*, répression *f*.
suppressor [sə'prɛsə*] *n* (*ELEC etc*) dispositif *m* antiparasite.
supremacy [su'prɛməsɪ] *n* suprématie *f*.
supreme [su'pri:m] *adj* suprême.
Supreme Court *n* (*US*) Cour *f* suprême.
supremo [su'pri:məu] *n* grand chef.
Supt. *abbr* (*POLICE*) = **superintendent**.
surcharge ['sə:tʃɑ:dʒ] *n* surcharge *f*; (*extra tax*) surtaxe *f*.
sure [ʃuə*] *adj* (*gen*) sûr(e); (*definite, convinced*) sûr, certain(e) ♦ *adv* (*col: esp US*): **that ~ is pretty, that's ~ pretty** c'est drôlement joli(e); **~!** (*of course*) bien sûr!; **~ enough** effectivement; **I'm not ~ how/why/ when** je ne sais pas très bien comment/pourquoi/quand; **to be ~ of o.s.** être sûr de soi; **to make ~ of** s'assurer de; vérifier.
sure-fire ['ʃuəfaɪə*] *adj* (*col*) certain(e), infaillible.
sure-footed [ʃuə'futɪd] *adj* au pied sûr.
surely ['ʃuəlɪ] *adv* sûrement; certainement; **~ you don't mean that!** vous ne parlez pas sérieusement!
surety ['ʃuərətɪ] *n* caution *f*; **to go** *or* **stand ~ for sb** se porter caution pour qn.
surf [sə:f] *n* ressac *m*.
surface ['sə:fɪs] *n* surface *f* ♦ *vt* (*road*) poser le revêtement de ♦ *vi* remonter à la surface; faire surface; **on the ~** (*fig*) au premier abord.
surface area *n* superficie *f*, aire *f*.
surface mail *n* courrier *m* par voie de terre (*or* maritime).
surface-to-surface ['sə:fɪstə'sə:fɪs] *adj* (*MIL*) sol-sol *inv*.
surfboard ['sə:fbɔ:d] *n* planche *f* de surf.
surfeit ['sə:fɪt] *n*: **a ~ of** un excès de; une indigestion de.
surfer ['sə:fə*] *n* surfiste *m/f*.
surfing ['sə:fɪŋ] *n* surf *m*.
surge [sə:dʒ] *n* vague *f*, montée *f*; (*ELEC*) pointe *f* de courant ♦ *vi* déferler; **to ~ forward** se précipiter (en avant).
surgeon ['sə:dʒən] *n* chirurgien *m*.
Surgeon General *n* (*US*) chef *m* du service fédéral de la santé publique.
surgery ['sə:dʒərɪ] *n* chirurgie *f*; (*BRIT: room*) cabinet *m* (de consultation); (*: session*) consultation *f*; (*: of MP etc*) permanence *f* (*où le député etc reçoit les électeurs etc*); **to undergo ~** être opéré(e).

surgery hours *npl* (*BRIT*) heures *fpl* de consultation.
surgical ['sə:dʒɪkl] *adj* chirurgical(e).
surgical spirit *n* (*BRIT*) alcool *m* à 90°.
surly ['sə:lɪ] *adj* revêche, maussade.
surmise [sə:'maɪz] *vt* présumer, conjecturer.
surmount [sə:'maunt] *vt* surmonter.
surname ['sə:neɪm] *n* nom *m* de famille.
surpass [sə:'pɑ:s] *vt* surpasser, dépasser.
surplus ['sə:pləs] *n* surplus *m*, excédent *m* ♦ *adj* en surplus, de trop; **it is ~ to our requirements** cela dépasse nos besoins; **~ stock** surplus *m*.
surprise [sə'praɪz] *n* (*gen*) surprise *f*; (*astonishment*) étonnement *m* ♦ *vt* surprendre; étonner; **to take by ~** (*person*) prendre au dépourvu; (*MIL*) prendre par surprise.
surprising [sə'praɪzɪŋ] *adj* surprenant(e), étonnant(e).
surprisingly [sə'praɪzɪŋlɪ] *adv* (*easy, helpful*) étonnamment, étrangement; **(somewhat) ~, he agreed** curieusement, il a accepté.
surrealism [sə'rɪəlɪzəm] *n* surréalisme *m*.
surrealist [sə'rɪəlɪst] *adj, n* surréaliste (*m/f*).
surrender [sə'rɛndə*] *n* reddition *f*, capitulation *f* ♦ *vi* se rendre, capituler ♦ *vt* (*claim, right*) renoncer à.
surrender value *n* valeur *f* de rachat.
surreptitious [sʌrəp'tɪʃəs] *adj* subreptice, furtif(ive).
surrogate ['sʌrəgɪt] *n* (*BRIT*: *substitute*) substitut *m* ♦ *adj* de substitution, de remplacement; **a food ~** un succédané alimentaire; **~ coffee** ersatz *m* or succédané *m* de café.
surrogate mother *n* mère porteuse *or* de substitution.
surround [sə'raund] *vt* entourer; (*MIL etc*) encercler.
surrounding [sə'raundɪŋ] *adj* environnant(e).
surroundings [sə'raundɪŋz] *npl* environs *mpl*, alentours *mpl*.
surtax ['sə:tæks] *n* surtaxe *f*.
surveillance [sə:'veɪləns] *n* surveillance *f*.
survey *n* ['sə:veɪ] enquête *f*, étude *f*; (*in house buying etc*) inspection *f*, (rapport *m* d')expertise *f*; (*of land*) levé *m*; (*comprehensive view: of situation etc*) vue *f* d'ensemble ♦ *vt* [sə:'veɪ] passer en revue; enquêter sur; inspecter; (*building*) expertiser; (*land*) faire le levé de.
surveying [sə'veɪɪŋ] *n* arpentage *m*.
surveyor [sə'veɪə*] *n* (*of building*) expert *m*; (*of land*) (arpenteur *m*) géomètre *m*.
survival [sə'vaɪvl] *n* survie *f*; (*relic*) vestige *m* ♦ *cpd* (*course, kit*) de survie.
survive [sə'vaɪv] *vi* survivre; (*custom etc*) subsister ♦ *vt* survivre à, réchapper de; (*person*) survivre à.
survivor [sə'vaɪvə*] *n* survivant/e.
susceptible [sə'sɛptəbl] *adj*: **~ (to)** sensible (à); (*disease*) prédisposé(e) (à).
suspect *adj, n* ['sʌspɛkt] suspect(e) ♦ *vt* [səs'pɛkt] soupçonner, suspecter.
suspected [səs'pɛktɪd] *adj*: **a ~ terrorist** une personne soupçonnée de terrorisme; **he had a ~ broken arm** il avait une supposée fracture du bras.
suspend [səs'pɛnd] *vt* suspendre.
suspended animation [səs'pɛndɪd-] *n*: **in a state of ~** en hibernation.
suspended sentence [səs'pɛndɪd-] *n* condamnation *f* avec sursis.
suspender belt [səs'pɛndə-] *n* (*BRIT*) porte-jarretelles *m inv*.
suspenders [səs'pɛndəz] *npl* (*BRIT*) jarretelles *fpl*; (*US*) bretelles *fpl*.
suspense [səs'pɛns] *n* attente *f*; (*in film etc*) suspense *m*.
suspension [səs'pɛnʃən] *n* (*gen, AUT*) suspension *f*; (*of driving licence*) retrait *m* provisoire.
suspension bridge *n* pont suspendu.
suspicion [səs'pɪʃən] *n* soupçon(s) *m(pl)*; **to be under ~** être considéré(e) comme suspect(e), être suspecté(e); **arrested on ~ of murder** arrêté sur présomption de meurtre.
suspicious [səs'pɪʃəs] *adj* (*suspecting*) soupçonneux(euse), méfiant(e); (*causing suspicion*) suspect(e); **to be ~ of** *or* **about sb/sth** avoir des doutes à propos de qn/sur qch, trouver qn/qch suspect(e).
suss out ['sʌs'aut] *vt* (*BRIT col*: *discover*) supputer; (*: understand*) piger.
sustain [səs'teɪn] *vt* supporter; soutenir; corroborer; (*suffer*) subir; recevoir.
sustainable [səs'teɪnəbl] *adj* (*rate, growth*) qui peut être maintenu(e), (*agriculture, development*) durable.
sustained [səs'teɪnd] *adj* (*effort*) soutenu(e), prolongé(e).
sustenance ['sʌstɪnəns] *n* nourriture *f*; moyens *mpl* de subsistance.
suture ['su:tʃə*] *n* suture *f*.
SVQ *n abbr* (= *Scottish Vocational Qualification*) CAP *m*.
SW *abbr* (= *short wave*) OC.
swab [swɔb] *n* (*MED*) tampon *m*; prélèvement *m* ♦ *vt* (*NAUT*: *also*: **~ down**) nettoyer.
swagger ['swægə*] *vi* plastronner, parader.
swallow ['swɔləu] *n* (*bird*) hirondelle *f*; (*of food etc*) gorgée *f* ♦ *vt* avaler; (*fig*) gober.
►**swallow up** *vt* engloutir.
swam [swæm] *pt of* **swim**.
swamp [swɔmp] *n* marais *m*, marécage *m* ♦ *vt* submerger.
swampy ['swɔmpɪ] *adj* marécageux(euse).
swan [swɔn] *n* cygne *m*.
swank [swæŋk] *vi* (*col*) faire de l'épate.
swan song *n* (*fig*) chant *m* du cygne.
swap [swɔp] *n* échange *m*, troc *m* ♦ *vt*: **to ~ (for)** échanger (contre), troquer (contre).
SWAPO ['swɑ:pəu] *n abbr* (= *South-West Africa People's Organization*) SWAPO *f*.
swarm [swɔ:m] *n* essaim *m* ♦ *vi* essaimer; fourmiller, grouiller.

swarthy ['swɔːðɪ] *adj* basané(e), bistré(e).
swashbuckling ['swɔʃbʌklɪŋ] *adj* (*film*) de cape et d'épée.
swastika ['swɔstɪkə] *n* croix gammée.
SWAT *n abbr* (*US*: = *Special Weapons and Tactics*) ≈ CRS *f*.
swat [swɔt] *vt* écraser ♦ *n* (*BRIT*: *also*: **fly** ~) tapette *f*.
swathe [sweɪð] *vt*: **to ~ in** (*bandages, blankets*) embobiner de.
swatter ['swɔtə*] *n* (*also*: **fly** ~) tapette *f*.
sway [sweɪ] *vi* se balancer, osciller; tanguer ♦ *vt* (*influence*) influencer ♦ *n* (*rule, power*): ~ **(over)** emprise *f* (sur); **to hold ~ over sb** avoir de l'emprise sur qn.
Swaziland ['swɑːzɪlænd] *n* Swaziland *m*.
swear, *pt* **swore,** *pp* **sworn** [swɛə*, swɔː*, swɔːn] *vi* jurer; **to ~ to sth** jurer de qch; **to ~ an oath** prêter serment.
▶**swear in** *vt* assermenter.
swearword ['swɛəwəːd] *n* gros mot, juron *m*.
sweat [swɛt] *n* sueur *f*, transpiration *f* ♦ *vi* suer; **in a ~** en sueur.
sweatband ['swɛtbænd] *n* (*SPORT*) bandeau *m*.
sweater ['swɛtə*] *n* tricot *m*, pull *m*.
sweatshirt ['swɛtʃəːt] *n* sweat-shirt *m*.
sweatshop ['swɛtʃɔp] *n* atelier *m* où les ouvriers sont exploités.
sweaty ['swɛtɪ] *adj* en sueur, moite *or* mouillé(e) de sueur.
Swede [swiːd] *n* Suédois/e.
swede [swiːd] *n* (*BRIT*) rutabaga *m*.
Sweden ['swiːdn] *n* Suède *f*.
Swedish ['swiːdɪʃ] *adj* suédois(e) ♦ *n* (*LING*) suédois *m*.
sweep [swiːp] *n* coup *m* de balai; (*curve*) grande courbe; (*range*) champ *m*; (*also*: **chimney** ~) ramoneur *m* ♦ *vb* (*pt, pp* **swept** [swɛpt]) *vt* balayer; (*fashion, craze*) se répandre dans ♦ *vi* avancer majestueusement *or* rapidement; s'élancer; s'étendre.
▶**sweep away** *vt* balayer; entraîner; emporter.
▶**sweep past** *vi* passer majestueusement *or* rapidement.
▶**sweep up** *vt, vi* balayer.
sweeper ['swiːpə*] *n* (*person*) balayeur *m*; (*machine*) balayeuse *f*; (*FOOTBALL*) libéro *m*.
sweeping ['swiːpɪŋ] *adj* (*gesture*) large; circulaire; (*changes, reforms*) radical(e); **a ~ statement** une généralisation hâtive.
sweepstake ['swiːpsteɪk] *n* sweepstake *m*.
sweet [swiːt] *n* (*BRIT*) dessert *m*; (*candy*) bonbon *m* ♦ *adj* doux(douce); (*not savoury*) sucré(e); (*fresh*) frais(fraîche), pur(e); (*kind*) gentil(le); (*cute*) mignon(ne) ♦ *adv*: **to smell ~** sentir bon; **to taste ~** avoir un goût sucré; **~ and sour** *adj* aigre-doux(douce).
sweetbread ['swiːtbrɛd] *n* ris *m* de veau.
sweetcorn ['swiːtkɔːn] *n* maïs doux.
sweeten ['swiːtn] *vt* sucrer; (*fig*) adoucir.
sweetener ['swiːtnə*] *n* (*CULIN*) édulcorant *m*.
sweetheart ['swiːthɑːt] *n* amoureux/euse.
sweetly ['swiːtlɪ] *adv* (*smile*) gentiment; (*sing, play*) mélodieusement.
sweetness ['swiːtnɪs] *n* douceur *f*; (*of taste*) goût sucré.
sweet pea *n* pois *m* de senteur.
sweet potato *n* patate douce.
sweetshop ['swiːtʃɔp] *n* (*BRIT*) confiserie *f*.
sweet tooth *n*: **to have a ~** aimer les sucreries.
swell [swɛl] *n* (*of sea*) houle *f* ♦ *adj* (*col*: *excellent*) chouette ♦ *vb* (*pt* **~ed**, *pp* **swollen** *or* **~ed** ['swəulən]) *vt* augmenter; grossir ♦ *vi* grossir, augmenter; (*sound*) s'enfler; (*MED*) enfler.
swelling ['swɛlɪŋ] *n* (*MED*) enflure *f*; grosseur *f*.
sweltering ['swɛltərɪŋ] *adj* étouffant(e), oppressant(e).
swept [swɛpt] *pt, pp of* **sweep**.
swerve [swəːv] *vi* faire une embardée *or* un écart; dévier.
swift [swɪft] *n* (*bird*) martinet *m* ♦ *adj* rapide, prompt(e).
swiftly ['swɪftlɪ] *adv* rapidement, vite.
swiftness ['swɪftnɪs] *n* rapidité *f*.
swig [swɪg] *n* (*col*: *drink*) lampée *f*.
swill [swɪl] *n* pâtée *f* ♦ *vt* (*also*: **~ out**, **~ down**) laver à grande eau.
swim [swɪm] *n*: **to go for a ~** aller nager *or* se baigner ♦ *vb* (*pt* **swam**, *pp* **swum** [swæm, swʌm]) *vi* nager; (*SPORT*) faire de la natation; (*fig: head, room*) tourner ♦ *vt* traverser (à la nage); (*distance*) faire (à la nage); **to ~ a length** nager une longueur; **to go ~ming** aller nager.
swimmer ['swɪmə*] *n* nageur/euse.
swimming ['swɪmɪŋ] *n* nage *f*, natation *f*.
swimming baths *npl* (*BRIT*) piscine *f*.
swimming cap *n* bonnet *m* de bain.
swimming costume *n* (*BRIT*) maillot *m* (de bain).
swimmingly ['swɪmɪŋlɪ] *adv*: **to go ~** (*wonderfully*) se dérouler à merveille.
swimming pool *n* piscine *f*.
swimming trunks *npl* maillot *m* de bain.
swimsuit ['swɪmsuːt] *n* maillot *m* (de bain).
swindle ['swɪndl] *n* escroquerie *f* ♦ *vt* escroquer.
swindler ['swɪndlə*] *n* escroc *m*.
swine [swaɪn] *n* (*pl inv*) pourceau *m*, porc *m*; (*col!*) salaud *m* (*!*).
swing [swɪŋ] *n* balançoire *f*; (*movement*) balancement *m*, oscillations *fpl*; (*MUS*) swing *m*; rythme *m* ♦ *vb* (*pt, pp* **swung** [swʌŋ]) *vt* balancer, faire osciller; (*also*: **~ round**) tourner, faire virer ♦ *vi* se balancer, osciller; (*also*: **~ round**) virer, tourner; **a ~ to the left** (*POL*) un revirement en faveur de la gauche; **to be in full ~** battre son plein; **to get into the ~ of things** se mettre dans le bain; **the road ~s south** la route prend la direction sud.

swing bridge *n* pont tournant.
swing door *n* (*BRIT*) porte battante.
swingeing ['swɪndʒɪŋ] *adj* (*BRIT*) écrasant(e); considérable.
swinging ['swɪŋɪŋ] *adj* rythmé(e); entraînant(e); (*fig*) dans le vent; ~ **door** (*US*) porte battante.
swipe [swaɪp] *n* grand coup; gifle *f* ♦ *vt* (*hit*) frapper à toute volée; gifler; (*col*: *steal*) piquer; (*credit card etc*) faire passer (dans la machine).
swirl [swəːl] *n* tourbillon *m* ♦ *vi* tourbillonner, tournoyer.
swish [swɪʃ] *adj* (*BRIT col*: *smart*) rupin(e) ♦ *vi* (*whip*) siffler; (*skirt, long grass*) bruire.
Swiss [swɪs] *adj* suisse ♦ *n* (*pl inv*) Suisse/esse.
Swiss French *adj* suisse romand(e).
Swiss German *adj* suisse-allemand(e).
Swiss roll *n* gâteau roulé.
switch [swɪtʃ] *n* (*for light, radio etc*) bouton *m*; (*change*) changement *m*, revirement *m* ♦ *vt* (*change*) changer; (*exchange*) intervertir; (*invert*): **to ~ (round** *or* **over)** changer de place.
▸**switch off** *vt* éteindre; (*engine*) arrêter.
▸**switch on** *vt* allumer; (*engine, machine*) mettre en marche; (*BRIT*: *water supply*) ouvrir.
switchback ['swɪtʃbæk] *n* (*BRIT*) montagnes *fpl* russes.
switchblade ['swɪtʃbleɪd] *n* (*also*: ~ **knife**) couteau *m* à cran d'arrêt.
switchboard ['swɪtʃbɔːd] *n* (*TEL*) standard *m*.
switchboard operator *n* (*TEL*) standardiste *m/f*.
Switzerland ['swɪtsələnd] *n* Suisse *f*.
swivel ['swɪvl] *vi* (*also*: ~ **round**) pivoter, tourner.
swollen ['swəulən] *pp of* **swell** ♦ *adj* (*ankle etc*) enflé(e).
swoon [swuːn] *vi* se pâmer.
swoop [swuːp] *n* (*by police etc*) rafle *f*, descente *f*; (*of bird etc*) descente *f* en piqué ♦ *vi* (*also*: ~ **down**) descendre en piqué, piquer.
swop [swɔp] *n*, *vt* = **swap**.
sword [sɔːd] *n* épée *f*.
swordfish ['sɔːdfɪʃ] *n* espadon *m*.
swore [swɔː*] *pt of* **swear**.
sworn [swɔːn] *pp of* **swear**.
swot [swɔt] *vt*, *vi* bûcher, potasser.
swum [swʌm] *pp of* **swim**.
swung [swʌŋ] *pt*, *pp of* **swing**.
sycamore ['sɪkəmɔː*] *n* sycomore *m*.
sycophant ['sɪkəfænt] *n* flagorneur/euse.
sycophantic [sɪkə'fæntɪk] *adj* flagorneur(euse).
Sydney ['sɪdnɪ] *n* Sydney.
syllable ['sɪləbl] *n* syllabe *f*.
syllabus ['sɪləbəs] *n* programme *m*; **on the ~** au programme.
symbol ['sɪmbl] *n* symbole *m*.
symbolic(al) [sɪm'bɔlɪk(l)] *adj* symbolique.
symbolism ['sɪmbəlɪzəm] *n* symbolisme *m*.
symbolize ['sɪmbəlaɪz] *vt* symboliser.
symmetrical [sɪ'mɛtrɪkl] *adj* symétrique.
symmetry ['sɪmɪtrɪ] *n* symétrie *f*.
sympathetic [sɪmpə'θɛtɪk] *adj* (*showing pity*) compatissant(e); (*understanding*) bienveillant(e), compréhensif(ive); ~ **towards** bien disposé(e) envers.
sympathetically [sɪmpə'θɛtɪklɪ] *adv* avec compassion (*or* bienveillance).
sympathize ['sɪmpəθaɪz] *vi*: **to ~ with sb** (*in grief*) être de tout cœur avec qn, compatir à la douleur de qn; (*in predicament*) partager les sentiments de qn; **to ~ with** (*sb's feelings*) comprendre.
sympathizer ['sɪmpəθaɪzə*] *n* (*POL*) sympathisant/e.
sympathy ['sɪmpəθɪ] *n* compassion *f*; **in ~ with** en accord avec; (*strike*) en *or* par solidarité avec; **with our deepest ~** en vous priant d'accepter nos sincères condoléances.
symphonic [sɪm'fɔnɪk] *adj* symphonique.
symphony ['sɪmfənɪ] *n* symphonie *f*.
symphony orchestra *n* orchestre *m* symphonique.
symposium [sɪm'pəuzɪəm] *n* symposium *m*.
symptom ['sɪmptəm] *n* symptôme *m*; indice *m*.
symptomatic [sɪmptə'mætɪk] *adj* symptomatique.
synagogue ['sɪnəgɔg] *n* synagogue *f*.
sync [sɪŋk] *n* (*col*): **in/out of ~** bien/mal synchronisé(e); **they're in ~ with each other** (*fig*) le courant passe bien entre eux.
synchromesh [sɪŋkrəu'mɛʃ] *n* (*AUT*) synchronisation *f*.
synchronize ['sɪŋkrənaɪz] *vt* synchroniser ♦ *vi*: **to ~ with** se produire en même temps que.
synchronized swimming ['sɪŋkrənaɪzd-] *n* natation synchronisée.
syncopated ['sɪŋkəpeɪtɪd] *adj* syncopé(e).
syndicate ['sɪndɪkɪt] *n* syndicat *m*, coopérative *f*; (*PRESS*) agence *f* de presse.
syndrome ['sɪndrəum] *n* syndrome *m*.
synonym ['sɪnənɪm] *n* synonyme *m*.
synonymous [sɪ'nɔnɪməs] *adj*: ~ **(with)** synonyme (de).
synopsis, *pl* **synopses** [sɪ'nɔpsɪs, -siːz] *n* résumé *m*, synopsis *m or f*.
syntax ['sɪntæks] *n* syntaxe *f*.
synthesis, *pl* **syntheses** ['sɪnθəsɪs, -siːz] *n* synthèse *f*.
synthesizer ['sɪnθəsaɪzə*] *n* (*MUS*) synthétiseur *m*.
synthetic [sɪn'θɛtɪk] *adj* synthétique ♦ *n* matière *f* synthétique; **~s** *npl* textiles artificiels.
syphilis ['sɪfɪlɪs] *n* syphilis *f*.
syphon ['saɪfən] *n*, *vb* = **siphon**.
Syria ['sɪrɪə] *n* Syrie *f*.
Syrian ['sɪrɪən] *adj* syrien(ne) ♦ *n* Syrien/ne.
syringe [sɪ'rɪndʒ] *n* seringue *f*.

syrup ['sɪrəp] *n* sirop *m*; (*BRIT*: *also*: **golden ~**) mélasse raffinée.
syrupy ['sɪrəpɪ] *adj* sirupeux(euse).
system ['sɪstəm] *n* système *m*; (*order*) méthode *f*; (*ANAT*) organisme *m*.
systematic [sɪstə'mætɪk] *adj* systématique; méthodique.
system disk *n* (*COMPUT*) disque *m* système.
systems analyst *n* analyste-programmeur *m/f*.

T t

T, t [tiː] *n* (*letter*) T, t *m*; **T for Tommy** T comme Thérèse.
TA *n abbr* (*BRIT*) = *Territorial Army*.
ta [tɑː] *excl* (*BRIT col*) merci!
tab [tæb] *n abbr* = **tabulator** ♦ *n* (*loop on coat etc*) attache *f*; (*label*) étiquette *f*; **to keep ~s on** (*fig*) surveiller.
tabby ['tæbɪ] *n* (*also*: **~ cat**) chat/te tigré(e).
table ['teɪbl] *n* table *f* ♦ *vt* (*BRIT*: *motion etc*) présenter; **to lay** *or* **set the ~** mettre le couvert *or* la table; **to clear the ~** débarrasser la table; **league ~** (*BRIT FOOTBALL, RUGBY*) classement *m* (du championnat); **~ of contents** table des matières.
tablecloth ['teɪblklɔθ] *n* nappe *f*.
table d'hôte [tɑːbl'dəut] *adj* (*meal*) à prix fixe.
table football *n* baby-foot *m*.
table lamp *n* lampe décorative.
tablemat ['teɪblmæt] *n* (*for plate*) napperon *m*, set *m*; (*for hot dish*) dessous-de-plat *m inv*.
table salt *n* sel fin *or* de table.
tablespoon ['teɪblspuːn] *n* cuiller *f* de service; (*also*: **~ful**: *as measurement*) cuillerée *f* à soupe.
tablet ['tæblɪt] *n* (*MED*) comprimé *m*; (*: for sucking*) pastille *f*; (*of stone*) plaque *f*; **~ of soap** (*BRIT*) savonnette *f*.
table tennis *n* ping-pong *m*, tennis *m* de table.
table wine *n* vin *m* de table.
tabloid ['tæblɔɪd] *n* (*newspaper*) tabloïde *m*; **the ~s** les journaux *mpl* populaires; *voir encadré*.
tabloid press *n voir encadré*.

TABLOID PRESS

Le terme **tabloid press** *désigne les journaux populaires de demi-format où l'on trouve beaucoup de photos et qui adoptent un style très concis. Ce type de journaux vise des lecteurs s'intéressant aux faits divers ayant un parfum de scandale; voir "quality press".*

taboo [tə'buː] *adj, n* tabou (*m*).
tabulate ['tæbjuleɪt] *vt* (*data, figures*) mettre sous forme de table(s).
tabulator ['tæbjuleɪtə*] *n* tabulateur *m*.
tachograph ['tækəgrɑːf] *n* tachygraphe *m*.
tachometer [tæ'kɔmɪtə*] *n* tachymètre *m*.
tacit ['tæsɪt] *adj* tacite.
taciturn ['tæsɪtəːn] *adj* taciturne.
tack [tæk] *n* (*nail*) petit clou; (*stitch*) point *m* de bâti; (*NAUT*) bord *m*, bordée *f* ♦ *vt* clouer; bâtir ♦ *vi* tirer un *or* des bord(s); **to change ~** virer de bord; **on the wrong ~** (*fig*) sur la mauvaise voie; **to ~ sth on to (the end of) sth** (*of letter, book*) rajouter qch à la fin de qch.
tackle ['tækl] *n* matériel *m*, équipement *m*; (*for lifting*) appareil *m* de levage; (*FOOTBALL, RUGBY*) plaquage *m* ♦ *vt* (*difficulty*) s'attaquer à; (*FOOTBALL, RUGBY*) plaquer.
tacky ['tækɪ] *adj* collant(e); pas sec(sèche); (*col*: *shabby*) moche.
tact [tækt] *n* tact *m*.
tactful ['tæktful] *adj* plein(e) de tact.
tactfully ['tæktfəlɪ] *adv* avec tact.
tactical ['tæktɪkl] *adj* tactique; **~ error** erreur *f* de tactique.
tactical voting *n* vote *m* tactique.
tactician [tæk'tɪʃən] *n* tacticien/ne.
tactics ['tæktɪks] *n, npl* tactique *f*.
tactless ['tæktlɪs] *adj* qui manque de tact.
tactlessly ['tæktlɪslɪ] *adv* sans tact.
tadpole ['tædpəul] *n* têtard *m*.
Tadzhikistan [tædʒɪkɪ'stɑːn] *n* = **Tajikistan**.
taffy ['tæfɪ] *n* (*US*) (bonbon *m* au) caramel *m*.
tag [tæg] *n* étiquette *f*; **price/name ~** étiquette (portant le prix/le nom).
►**tag along** *vi* suivre.
Tahiti [tɑː'hiːtɪ] *n* Tahiti *m*.
tail [teɪl] *n* queue *f*; (*of shirt*) pan *m* ♦ *vt* (*follow*) suivre, filer; **to turn ~** se sauver à toutes jambes; *see also* **head**.
►**tail away, tail off** *vi* (*in size, quality etc*) baisser peu à peu.
tailback ['teɪlbæk] *n* (*BRIT*) bouchon *m*.
tail coat *n* habit *m*.
tail end *n* bout *m*, fin *f*.
tailgate ['teɪlgeɪt] *n* (*AUT*) hayon *m* arrière.
tail light *n* (*AUT*) feu *m* arrière.
tailor ['teɪlə*] *n* tailleur *m* (*artisan*) ♦ *vt*: **to ~ sth (to)** adapter qch exactement (à).
tailoring ['teɪlərɪŋ] *n* (*cut*) coupe *f*.
tailor-made ['teɪlə'meɪd] *adj* fait(e) sur mesure; (*fig*) conçu(e) spécialement.
tailwind ['teɪlwɪnd] *n* vent *m* arrière *inv*.
taint [teɪnt] *vt* (*meat, food*) gâter; (*fig: reputation*) salir.
tainted ['teɪntɪd] *adj* (*food*) gâté(e); (*water, air*) infecté(e); (*fig*) souillé(e).
Taiwan ['taɪ'wɑːn] *n* Taiwan (*no article*).
Tajikistan [tædʒɪkɪ'stɑːn] *n* Tadjikistan *m/f*.
take [teɪk] *vb* (*pt* **took**, *pp* **taken** [tuk, 'teɪkn]) *vt* prendre; (*gain: prize*) remporter; (*require: ef-*

fort, courage) demander; (*tolerate*) accepter, supporter; (*hold: passengers etc*) contenir; (*accompany*) emmener, accompagner; (*bring, carry*) apporter, emporter; (*exam*) passer, se présenter à; (*conduct: meeting*) présider ♦ *vi* (*dye, fire etc*) prendre ♦ *n* (*CINE*) prise *f* de vues; **to ~ sth from** (*drawer etc*) prendre qch dans; (*person*) prendre qch à; **I ~ it that** je suppose que; **I took him for a doctor** je l'ai pris pour un docteur; **to ~ sb's hand** prendre qn par la main; **to ~ for a walk** (*child, dog*) emmener promener; **to be taken ill** tomber malade; **to ~ it upon o.s. to do sth** prendre sur soi de faire qch; **~ the first (street) on the left** prenez la première à gauche; **it won't ~ long** ça ne prendra pas longtemps; **I was quite taken with her/it** elle/cela m'a beaucoup plu.

▸**take after** *vt fus* ressembler à.

▸**take apart** *vt* démonter.

▸**take away** *vt* emporter; (*remove*) enlever; (*subtract*) soustraire ♦ *vi*: **to ~ away from** diminuer.

▸**take back** *vt* (*return*) rendre, rapporter; (*one's words*) retirer.

▸**take down** *vt* (*building*) démolir; (*dismantle: scaffolding*) démonter; (*letter etc*) prendre, écrire.

▸**take in** *vt* (*deceive*) tromper, rouler; (*understand*) comprendre, saisir; (*include*) couvrir, inclure; (*lodger*) prendre; (*orphan, stray dog*) recueillir; (*dress, waistband*) reprendre.

▸**take off** *vi* (*AVIAT*) décoller ♦ *vt* (*remove*) enlever; (*imitate*) imiter, pasticher.

▸**take on** *vt* (*work*) accepter, se charger de; (*employee*) prendre, embaucher; (*opponent*) accepter de se battre contre.

▸**take out** *vt* sortir; (*remove*) enlever; (*licence*) prendre, se procurer; **to ~ sth out of** enlever qch de; prendre qch dans; **don't ~ it out on me!** ne t'en prends pas à moi!

▸**take over** *vt* (*business*) reprendre ♦ *vi*: **to ~ over from sb** prendre la relève de qn.

▸**take to** *vt fus* (*person*) se prendre d'amitié pour; (*activity*) prendre goût à; **to ~ to doing sth** prendre l'habitude de faire qch.

▸**take up** *vt* (*one's story, a dress*) reprendre; (*occupy: time, space*) prendre, occuper; (*engage in: hobby etc*) se mettre à; (*accept: offer, challenge*) accepter; (*absorb: liquids*) absorber ♦ *vi*: **to ~ up with sb** se lier d'amitié avec qn.

takeaway ['teɪkəweɪ] (*BRIT*) *adj* (*food*) à emporter ♦ *n* (*shop, restaurant*) ≈ traiteur *m* (*qui vend des plats à emporter*).

take-home pay ['teɪkhəum-] *n* salaire net.

taken ['teɪkən] *pp of* **take**.

takeoff ['teɪkɔf] *n* (*AVIAT*) décollage *m*.

takeout ['teɪkaut] *adj* (*US*) = **takeaway**.

takeover ['teɪkəuvə*] *n* (*COMM*) rachat *m*.

takeover bid *n* offre publique d'achat, OPA *f*.

takings ['teɪkɪŋz] *npl* (*COMM*) recette *f*.

talc [tælk] *n* (*also*: **~um powder**) talc *m*.

tale [teɪl] *n* (*story*) conte *m*, histoire *f*; (*account*) récit *m*; (*pej*) histoire; **to tell ~s** (*fig*) rapporter.

talent ['tælnt] *n* talent *m*, don *m*.

talented ['tæləntɪd] *adj* doué(e), plein(e) de talent.

talent scout *n* découvreur *m* de vedettes (*or* joueurs *etc*).

talisman ['tælɪzmən] *n* talisman *m*.

talk [tɔːk] *n* propos *mpl*; (*gossip*) racontars *mpl* (*pej*); (*conversation*) discussion *f*; (*interview*) entretien *m*; (*a speech*) causerie *f*, exposé *m* ♦ *vi* (*chatter*) bavarder; **~s** *npl* (*POL etc*) entretiens *mpl*; conférence *f*; **to give a ~** faire un exposé; **to ~ about** parler de; (*converse*) s'entretenir *or* parler de; **~ing of films, have you seen ...?** à propos de films, avez-vous vu ...?; **to ~ sb out of/into doing** persuader qn de ne pas faire/de faire; **to ~ shop** parler métier *or* affaires.

▸**talk over** *vt* discuter (de).

talkative ['tɔːkətɪv] *adj* bavard(e).

talker ['tɔːkə*] *n* causeur/euse; (*pej*) bavard/e.

talking point ['tɔːkɪŋ-] *n* sujet *m* de conversation.

talking-to ['tɔːkɪŋtu] *n*: **to give sb a good ~** passer un savon à qn.

talk show *n* (*TV, RADIO*) causerie (télévisée *or* radiodiffusée).

tall [tɔːl] *adj* (*person*) grand(e); (*building, tree*) haut(e); **to be 6 feet ~** ≈ mesurer 1 mètre 80; **how ~ are you?** combien mesurez-vous?

tallboy ['tɔːlbɔɪ] *n* (*BRIT*) grande commode.

tallness ['tɔːlnɪs] *n* grande taille; hauteur *f*.

tall story *n* histoire *f* invraisemblable.

tally ['tælɪ] *n* compte *m* ♦ *vi*: **to ~ (with)** correspondre (à); **to keep a ~ of sth** tenir le compte de qch.

talon ['tælən] *n* griffe *f*; (*of eagle*) serre *f*.

tambourine [tæmbə'riːn] *n* tambourin *m*.

tame [teɪm] *adj* apprivoisé(e); (*fig: story, style*) insipide.

Tamil ['tæmɪl] *adj* tamoul(e) *or* tamil(e) ♦ *n* Tamoul/e *or* Tamil/e; (*LING*) tamoul *m or* tamil *m*.

tamper ['tæmpə*] *vi*: **to ~ with** toucher à (*en cachette ou sans permission*).

tampon ['tæmpən] *n* tampon *m* hygiénique *or* périodique.

tan [tæn] *n* (*also*: **sun~**) bronzage *m* ♦ *vt*, *vi* bronzer, brunir ♦ *adj* (*colour*) brun roux *inv*; **to get a ~** bronzer.

tandem ['tændəm] *n* tandem *m*.

tandoori [tæn'duərɪ] *adj* tandouri.

tang [tæŋ] *n* odeur (*or* saveur) piquante.

tangent ['tændʒənt] *n* (*MATH*) tangente *f*; **to go off at a ~** (*fig*) changer complètement de direction.

tangerine [tændʒə'riːn] *n* mandarine *f*.

tangible ['tændʒəbl] *adj* tangible; **~ assets** biens réels.

Tangier [tæn'dʒɪə*] *n* Tanger.
tangle ['tæŋgl] *n* enchevêtrement *m* ♦ *vt* enchevêtrer; **to get in(to) a ~** s'emmêler.
tango ['tæŋgəu] *n* tango *m*.
tank [tæŋk] *n* réservoir *m*; (*for processing*) cuve *f*; (*for fish*) aquarium *m*; (*MIL*) char *m* d'assaut, tank *m*.
tankard ['tæŋkəd] *n* chope *f*.
tanker ['tæŋkə*] *n* (*ship*) pétrolier *m*, tanker *m*; (*truck*) camion-citerne *m*; (*RAIL*) wagon-citerne *m*.
tanned [tænd] *adj* bronzé(e).
tannin ['tænɪn] *n* tanin *m*.
tanning ['tænɪŋ] *n* (*of leather*) tannage *m*.
tannoy ['tænɔɪ] *n* ® (*BRIT*) haut-parleur *m*; **over the ~** par haut-parleur.
tantalizing ['tæntəlaɪzɪŋ] *adj* (*smell*) extrêmement appétissant(e); (*offer*) terriblement tentant(e).
tantamount ['tæntəmaunt] *adj*: **~ to** qui équivaut à.
tantrum ['tæntrəm] *n* accès *m* de colère; **to throw a ~** piquer une colère.
Tanzania [tænzə'nɪə] *n* Tanzanie *f*.
Tanzanian [tænzə'nɪən] *adj* tanzanien(ne) ♦ *n* Tanzanien/ne.
tap [tæp] *n* (*on sink etc*) robinet *m*; (*gentle blow*) petite tape ♦ *vt* frapper *or* taper légèrement; (*resources*) exploiter, utiliser; (*telephone*) mettre sur écoute; **on ~** (*beer*) en tonneau; (*fig: resources*) disponible.
tap-dancing ['tæpdɑːnsɪŋ] *n* claquettes *fpl*.
tape [teɪp] *n* ruban *m*; (*also*: **magnetic ~**) bande *f* (magnétique) ♦ *vt* (*record*) enregistrer (au magnétophone *or* sur bande); **on ~** (*song etc*) enregistré(e).
tape deck *n* platine *f* d'enregistrement.
tape measure *n* mètre *m* à ruban.
taper ['teɪpə*] *n* cierge *m* ♦ *vi* s'effiler.
tape-record ['teɪprɪkɔːd] *vt* enregistrer (au magnétophone *or* sur bande).
tape recorder *n* magnétophone *m*.
tape recording *n* enregistrement *m* (au magnétophone).
tapered ['teɪpəd], **tapering** ['teɪpərɪŋ] *adj* fuselé(e), effilé(e).
tapestry ['tæpɪstrɪ] *n* tapisserie *f*.
tape-worm ['teɪpwəːm] *n* ver *m* solitaire, ténia *m*.
tapioca [tæpɪ'əukə] *n* tapioca *m*.
tappet ['tæpɪt] *n* (*AUT*) poussoir *m* (de soupape).
tar [tɑː] *n* goudron *m*; **low-/middle-~ cigarettes** cigarettes *fpl* à faible/moyenne teneur en goudron.
tarantula [tə'ræntjulə] *n* tarentule *f*.
tardy ['tɑːdɪ] *adj* tardif(ive).
target ['tɑːgɪt] *n* cible *f*; (*fig: objective*) objectif *m*; **to be on ~** (*project*) progresser comme prévu.
target practice *n* exercices *mpl* de tir (à la cible).
tariff ['tærɪf] *n* (*COMM*) tarif *m*; (*taxes*) tarif douanier.
tariff barrier *n* barrière douanière.
tarmac ['tɑːmæk] *n* (*BRIT*: *on road*) macadam *m*; (*AVIAT*) aire *f* d'envol ♦ *vt* (*BRIT*) goudronner.
tarnish ['tɑːnɪʃ] *vt* ternir.
tarot ['tærəu] *n* tarot *m*.
tarpaulin [tɑː'pɔːlɪn] *n* bâche goudronnée.
tarragon ['tærəgən] *n* estragon *m*.
tart [tɑːt] *n* (*CULIN*) tarte *f*; (*BRIT col*: *pej*: *woman*) poule *f* ♦ *adj* (*flavour*) âpre, aigrelet(te).
►**tart up** *vt* (*col*): **to ~ o.s. up** se faire beau(belle); (*: pej*) s'attifer.
tartan ['tɑːtn] *n* tartan *m* ♦ *adj* écossais(e).
tartar ['tɑːtə*] *n* (*on teeth*) tartre *m*.
tartar sauce *n* sauce *f* tartare.
task [tɑːsk] *n* tâche *f*; **to take to ~** prendre à partie.
task force *n* (*MIL, POLICE*) détachement spécial.
taskmaster ['tɑːskmɑːstə*] *n*: **he's a hard ~** il est très exigeant dans le travail.
Tasmania [tæz'meɪnɪə] *n* Tasmanie *f*.
tassel ['tæsl] *n* gland *m*; pompon *m*.
taste [teɪst] *n* goût *m*; (*fig: glimpse, idea*) idée *f*, aperçu *m* ♦ *vt* goûter ♦ *vi*: **to ~ of** (*fish etc*) avoir le *or* un goût de; **it ~s like fish** ça a un *or* le goût de poisson, on dirait du poisson; **what does it ~ like?** quel goût ça a?; **you can ~ the garlic (in it)** on sent bien l'ail; **can I have a ~ of this wine?** puis-je goûter un peu de ce vin?; **to have a ~ of sth** goûter (à) qch; **to have a ~ for sth** aimer qch, avoir un penchant pour qch; **to be in good/bad** *or* **poor ~** être de bon/mauvais goût.
taste bud *n* papille *f*.
tasteful ['teɪstful] *adj* de bon goût.
tastefully ['teɪstfəlɪ] *adv* avec goût.
tasteless ['teɪstlɪs] *adj* (*food*) qui n'a aucun goût; (*remark*) de mauvais goût.
tasty ['teɪstɪ] *adj* savoureux(euse), délicieux(euse).
tattered ['tætəd] *adj see* **tatters**.
tatters ['tætəz] *npl*: **in ~** (*also*: **tattered**) en lambeaux.
tattoo [tə'tuː] *n* tatouage *m*; (*spectacle*) parade *f* militaire ♦ *vt* tatouer.
tatty ['tætɪ] *adj* (*BRIT col*) défraîchi(e), en piteux état.
taught [tɔːt] *pt, pp of* **teach**.
taunt [tɔːnt] *n* raillerie *f* ♦ *vt* railler.
Taurus ['tɔːrəs] *n* le Taureau; **to be ~** être du Taureau.
taut [tɔːt] *adj* tendu(e).
tavern ['tævən] *n* taverne *f*.
tawdry ['tɔːdrɪ] *adj* (d'un mauvais goût) criard.
tawny ['tɔːnɪ] *adj* fauve (*couleur*).
tax [tæks] *n* (*on goods etc*) taxe *f*; (*on income*) impôts *mpl*, contributions *fpl* ♦ *vt* taxer; imposer; (*fig: strain: patience etc*) mettre à

l'épreuve; **before/after** ~ avant/après l'impôt; **free of** ~ exonéré(e) d'impôt.
taxable ['tæksəbl] *adj* (*income*) imposable.
tax allowance *n* part *f* du revenu non imposable, abattement *m* à la base.
taxation [tæk'seɪʃən] *n* taxation *f*; impôts *mpl*, contributions *fpl*; **system of** ~ système fiscal.
tax avoidance *n* évasion fiscale.
tax collector *n* percepteur *m*.
tax disc *n* (*BRIT AUT*) vignette *f* (automobile).
tax evasion *n* fraude fiscale.
tax exemption *n* exonération fiscale, exemption *f* d'impôts.
tax exile *n personne qui s'expatrie pour raisons fiscales*.
tax-free ['tæksfriː] *adj* exempt(e) d'impôts.
tax haven *n* paradis fiscal.
taxi ['tæksɪ] *n* taxi *m* ♦ *vi* (*AVIAT*) rouler (lentement) au sol.
taxidermist ['tæksɪdəːmɪst] *n* empailleur/euse (*d'animaux*).
taxi driver *n* chauffeur *m* de taxi.
tax inspector *n* (*BRIT*) percepteur *m*.
taxi rank (*BRIT*), **taxi stand** *n* station *f* de taxis.
tax payer [-peɪə*] *n* contribuable *m/f*.
tax rebate *n* ristourne *f* d'impôt.
tax relief *n* dégrèvement *or* allègement fiscal, réduction *f* d'impôt.
tax return *n* déclaration *f* d'impôts *or* de revenus.
tax year *n* année fiscale.
TB *n abbr* = **tuberculosis**.
tbc *n abbr* (= *to be confirmed*) à confirmer, sous réserve.
TD *n abbr* (*US*) = **Treasury Department**; (: *FOOTBALL*) = **touchdown**.
tea [tiː] *n* thé *m*; (*BRIT: snack: for children*) goûter *m*; **high** ~ (*BRIT*) *collation combinant goûter et dîner*.
tea bag *n* sachet *m* de thé.
tea break *n* (*BRIT*) pause-thé *f*.
teacake ['tiːkeɪk] *n* (*BRIT*) ≈ petit pain aux raisins.
teach, *pt, pp* **taught** [tiːtʃ, tɔːt] *vt*: **to** ~ **sb sth**, ~ **sth to sb** apprendre qch à qn; (*in school etc*) enseigner qch à qn ♦ *vi* enseigner; **it taught him a lesson** (*fig*) ça lui a servi de leçon.
teacher ['tiːtʃə*] *n* (*in secondary school*) professeur *m*; (*in primary school*) instituteur/trice; **French** ~ professeur de français.
teacher training college *n* (*for primary schools*) ≈ école normale d'instituteurs; (*for secondary schools*) collège *m* de formation pédagogique (*pour l'enseignement secondaire*).
teaching ['tiːtʃɪŋ] *n* enseignement *m*.
teaching aids *npl* supports *mpl* pédagogiques.
teaching hospital *n* (*BRIT*) C.H.U. *m*, centre *m* hospitalo-universitaire.
teaching staff *n* (*BRIT*) enseignants *mpl*.
tea cosy *n* couvre-théière *m*.
teacup ['tiːkʌp] *n* tasse *f* à thé.
teak [tiːk] *n* teck *m* ♦ *adj* en *or* de teck.
tea leaves *npl* feuilles *fpl* de thé.
team [tiːm] *n* équipe *f*; (*of animals*) attelage *m*.
▶**team up** *vi*: **to** ~ **up (with)** faire équipe (avec).
team games *npl* jeux *mpl* d'équipe.
teamwork ['tiːmwəːk] *n* travail *m* d'équipe.
tea party *n* thé *m* (*réception*).
teapot ['tiːpɔt] *n* théière *f*.
tear[1] *n* [tɛə*] déchirure *f* ♦ *vb* (*pt* **tore**, *pp* **torn** [tɔː*, tɔːn]) *vt* déchirer ♦ *vi* se déchirer; **to** ~ **to pieces** *or* **to bits** *or* **to shreds** mettre en pièces; (*fig*) démolir.
▶**tear along** *vi* (*rush*) aller à toute vitesse.
▶**tear apart** *vt* (*also fig*) déchirer.
▶**tear away** *vt*: **to** ~ **o.s. away (from sth)** (*fig*) s'arracher (de qch).
▶**tear out** *vt* (*sheet of paper, cheque*) arracher.
▶**tear up** *vt* (*sheet of paper etc*) déchirer, mettre en morceaux *or* pièces.
tear[2] ['tɪə*] *n* larme *f*; **in** ~**s** en larmes; **to burst into** ~**s** fondre en larmes.
tearaway ['tɛərəweɪ] *n* (*col*) casse-cou *m inv*.
teardrop ['tɪədrɔp] *n* larme *f*.
tearful ['tɪəful] *adj* larmoyant(e).
tear gas ['tɪə-] *n* gaz *m* lacrymogène.
tearoom ['tiːruːm] *n* salon *m* de thé.
tease [tiːz] *n* taquin/e ♦ *vt* taquiner; (*unkindly*) tourmenter.
tea set *n* service *m* à thé.
teashop ['tiːʃɔp] *n* (*BRIT*) pâtisserie-salon de thé *f*.
teaspoon ['tiːspuːn] *n* petite cuiller; (*also*: ~**ful**: *as measurement*) ≈ cuillerée *f* à café.
tea strainer *n* passoire *f* (à thé).
teat [tiːt] *n* tétine *f*.
teatime ['tiːtaɪm] *n* l'heure *f* du thé.
tea towel *n* (*BRIT*) torchon *m* (à vaisselle).
tea urn *n* fontaine *f* à thé.
tech [tɛk] *n abbr* (*col*) = **technology, technical college**.
technical ['tɛknɪkl] *adj* technique.
technical college *n* C.E.T. *m*, collège *m* d'enseignement technique.
technicality [tɛknɪ'kælɪtɪ] *n* technicité *f*; (*detail*) détail *m* technique; **on a legal** ~ à cause de (*or* grâce à) l'application à la lettre d'une subtilité juridique; pour vice de forme.
technically ['tɛknɪklɪ] *adv* techniquement; (*strictly speaking*) en théorie, en principe.
technician [tɛk'nɪʃən] *n* technicien/ne.
technique [tɛk'niːk] *n* technique *f*.
techno ['tɛknəu] *n* (*MUS*) techno *f*.
technocrat ['tɛknəkræt] *n* technocrate *m/f*.
technological [tɛknə'lɔdʒɪkl] *adj* technologique.
technologist [tɛk'nɔlədʒɪst] *n* technologue *m/f*.
technology [tɛk'nɔlədʒɪ] *n* technologie *f*.
teddy (bear) ['tɛdɪ-] *n* ours *m* (en peluche).

tedious ['tiːdɪəs] *adj* fastidieux(euse).
tedium ['tiːdɪəm] *n* ennui *m*.
tee [tiː] *n* (*GOLF*) tee *m*.
teem [tiːm] *vi*: **to ~ (with)** grouiller (de); **it is ~ing (with rain)** il pleut à torrents.
teenage ['tiːneɪdʒ] *adj* (*fashions etc*) pour jeunes, pour adolescents.
teenager ['tiːneɪdʒə*] *n* jeune *m/f*, adolescent/e.
teens [tiːnz] *npl*: **to be in one's ~** être adolescent(e).
tee-shirt ['tiːʃəːt] *n* = **T-shirt**.
teeter ['tiːtə*] *vi* chanceler, vaciller.
teeth [tiːθ] *npl of* **tooth**.
teethe [tiːð] *vi* percer ses dents.
teething ring ['tiːðɪŋ-] *n* anneau *m* (*pour bébé qui perce ses dents*).
teething troubles ['tiːðɪŋ-] *npl* (*fig*) difficultés initiales.
teetotal ['tiː'təutl] *adj* (*person*) qui ne boit jamais d'alcool.
teetotaller, (*US*) **teetotaler** ['tiː'təutlə*] *n* personne *f* qui ne boit jamais d'alcool.
TEFL ['tɛfl] *n abbr* = *Teaching of English as a Foreign Language*.
Teflon ['tɛflɔn] *n* ® Téflon *m* ®.
Teheran [tɛə'rɑːn] *n* Téhéran.
tel. *abbr* (= *telephone*) tél.
Tel Aviv ['tɛlə'viːv] *n* Tel Aviv.
telecast ['tɛlɪkɑːst] *vt* télédiffuser, téléviser.
telecommunications ['tɛlɪkəmjuːnɪ'keɪʃənz] *n* télécommunications *fpl*.
teleconferencing ['tɛlɪkɒnfərənsɪŋ] *n* téléconférence *f*.
telegram ['tɛlɪgræm] *n* télégramme *m*.
telegraph ['tɛlɪgrɑːf] *n* télégraphe *m*.
telegraphic [tɛlɪ'græfɪk] *adj* télégraphique.
telegraph pole *n* poteau *m* télégraphique.
telegraph wire *n* fil *m* télégraphique.
telepathic [tɛlɪ'pæθɪk] *adj* télépathique.
telepathy [tə'lɛpəθɪ] *n* télépathie *f*.
telephone ['tɛlɪfəun] *n* téléphone *m* ♦ *vt* (*person*) téléphoner à; (*message*) téléphoner; **to have a ~**, (*BRIT*) **to be on the ~** (*subscriber*) être abonné(e) au téléphone; **to be on the ~** (*be speaking*) être au téléphone.
telephone booth, (*BRIT*) **telephone box** *n* cabine *f* téléphonique.
telephone call *n* appel *m* téléphonique, communication *f* téléphonique.
telephone directory *n* annuaire *m* (du téléphone).
telephone number *n* numéro *m* de téléphone.
telephone operator *n* téléphoniste *m/f*, standardiste *m/f*.
telephone tapping [-tæpɪŋ] *n* mise *f* sur écoute.
telephonist [tə'lɛfənɪst] *n* (*BRIT*) téléphoniste *m/f*.
telephoto ['tɛlɪfəutəu] *adj*: **~ lens** téléobjectif *m*.
teleprinter ['tɛlɪprɪntə*] *n* téléscripteur *m*.
Teleprompter ['tɛlɪprɔmptə*] *n* ® (*US*) prompteur *m*.
telesales ['tɛlɪseɪlz] *npl* télévente *f*.
telescope ['tɛlɪskəup] *n* télescope *m* ♦ *vi* se télescoper ♦ *vt* télescoper.
telescopic [tɛlɪ'skɔpɪk] *adj* télescopique; (*umbrella*) à manche télescopique.
Teletext ['tɛlɪtɛkst] *n* ® télétexte *m*.
telethon ['tɛlɪθɔn] *n* téléthon *m*.
televise ['tɛlɪvaɪz] *vt* téléviser.
television ['tɛlɪvɪʒən] *n* télévision *f*.
television licence *n* (*BRIT*) redevance *f* (de l'audio-visuel).
television programme *n* émission *f* de télévision.
television set *n* poste *m* de télévision, téléviseur *m*.
teleworking ['tɛlɪwɜːkɪŋ] *n* télétravail *m*.
telex ['tɛlɛks] *n* télex *m* ♦ *vt* (*message*) envoyer par télex; (*person*) envoyer un télex à ♦ *vi* envoyer un télex.
tell, *pt, pp* **told** [tɛl, təuld] *vt* dire; (*relate: story*) raconter; (*distinguish*): **to ~ sth from** distinguer qch de ♦ *vi* (*talk*): **to ~ (of)** parler (de); (*have effect*) se faire sentir, se voir; **to ~ sb to do** dire à qn de faire; **to ~ sb about sth** (*place, object etc*) parler de qch à qn; (*what happened etc*) raconter qch à qn; **to ~ the time** (*know how to*) savoir lire l'heure; **can you ~ me the time?** pourriez-vous me dire l'heure?; **(I) ~ you what ...** écoute, ...; **I can't ~ them apart** je n'arrive pas à les distinguer.
►**tell off** *vt* réprimander, gronder.
►**tell on** *vt fus* (*inform against*) dénoncer, rapporter contre.
teller ['tɛlə*] *n* (*in bank*) caissier/ière.
telling ['tɛlɪŋ] *adj* (*remark, detail*) révélateur(trice).
telltale ['tɛlteɪl] *n* rapporteur/euse ♦ *adj* (*sign*) éloquent(e), révélateur(trice).
telly ['tɛlɪ] *n abbr* (*BRIT col*: = *television*) télé *f*.
temerity [tə'mɛrɪtɪ] *n* témérité *f*.
temp [tɛmp] *abbr* (*BRIT col*: = *temporary*) *n* intérimaire *m/f* ♦ *vi* travailler comme intérimaire.
temper ['tɛmpə*] *n* (*nature*) caractère *m*; (*mood*) humeur *f*; (*fit of anger*) colère *f* ♦ *vt* (*moderate*) tempérer, adoucir; **to be in a ~** être en colère; **to lose one's ~** se mettre en colère; **to keep one's ~** rester calme.
temperament ['tɛmprəmənt] *n* (*nature*) tempérament *m*.
temperamental [tɛmprə'mɛntl] *adj* capricieux(euse).
temperance ['tɛmpərns] *n* modération *f*; (*in drinking*) tempérance *f*.
temperate ['tɛmprət] *adj* modéré(e); (*climate*) tempéré(e).
temperature ['tɛmprətʃə*] *n* température *f*; **to have** *or* **run a ~** avoir de la fièvre.
temperature chart *n* (*MED*) feuille *f* de tem-

pérature.
tempered ['tɛmpəd] *adj* (*steel*) trempé(e).
tempest ['tɛmpɪst] *n* tempête *f*.
tempestuous [tɛm'pɛstjuəs] *adj* (*fig*) orageux(euse); (*: person*) passionné(e).
tempi ['tɛmpiː] *npl of* **tempo**.
template ['tɛmplɪt] *n* patron *m*.
temple ['tɛmpl] *n* (*building*) temple *m*; (*ANAT*) tempe *f*.
templet ['tɛmplɪt] *n* = **template**.
tempo, ~s *or* **tempi** ['tɛmpəu, 'tɛmpiː] *n* tempo *m*; (*fig: of life etc*) rythme *m*.
temporal ['tɛmpərl] *adj* temporel(le).
temporarily ['tɛmpərərɪlɪ] *adv* temporairement; provisoirement.
temporary ['tɛmpərərɪ] *adj* temporaire, provisoire; (*job, worker*) temporaire; ~ **secretary** (secrétaire *f*) intérimaire *f*; **a ~ teacher** un professeur remplaçant *or* suppléant.
temporize ['tɛmpəraɪz] *vi* atermoyer; transiger.
tempt [tɛmpt] *vt* tenter; **to ~ sb into doing** induire qn à faire; **to be ~ed to do sth** être tenté(e) de faire qch.
temptation [tɛmp'teɪʃən] *n* tentation *f*.
tempting ['tɛmptɪŋ] *adj* tentant(e).
ten [tɛn] *num* dix ♦ *n*: **~s of thousands** des dizaines *fpl* de milliers.
tenable ['tɛnəbl] *adj* défendable.
tenacious [tə'neɪʃəs] *adj* tenace.
tenacity [tə'næsɪtɪ] *n* ténacité *f*.
tenancy ['tɛnənsɪ] *n* location *f*; état *m* de locataire.
tenant ['tɛnənt] *n* locataire *m/f*.
tend [tɛnd] *vt* s'occuper de; (*sick etc*) soigner ♦ *vi*: **to ~ to do** avoir tendance à faire; (*colour*): **to ~ to** tirer sur.
tendency ['tɛndənsɪ] *n* tendance *f*.
tender ['tɛndə*] *adj* tendre; (*delicate*) délicat(e); (*sore*) sensible; (*affectionate*) tendre, doux(douce) ♦ *n* (*COMM: offer*) soumission *f*; (*money*): **legal ~** cours légal ♦ *vt* offrir; **to ~ one's resignation** donner *or* remettre sa démission; **to put in a ~ (for)** faire une soumission (pour); **to put work out to ~** (*BRIT*) mettre un contrat en adjudication.
tenderize ['tɛndəraɪz] *vt* (*CULIN*) attendrir.
tenderly ['tɛndəlɪ] *adv* tendrement.
tenderness ['tɛndənɪs] *n* tendresse *f*; (*of meat*) tendreté *f*.
tendon ['tɛndən] *n* tendon *m*.
tenement ['tɛnəmənt] *n* immeuble *m* (de rapport).
Tenerife [tɛnə'riːf] *n* Ténérife *f*.
tenet ['tɛnət] *n* principe *m*.
Tenn. *abbr* (*US*) = *Tennessee*.
tenner ['tɛnə*] *n* (*BRIT col*) billet *m* de dix livres.
tennis ['tɛnɪs] *n* tennis *m* ♦ *cpd* (*club, match, racket, player*) de tennis.
tennis ball *n* balle *f* de tennis.
tennis court *n* (court *m* de) tennis *m*.
tennis elbow *n* (*MED*) synovite *f* du coude.
tennis shoes *npl* (chaussures *fpl* de) tennis *mpl*.
tenor ['tɛnə*] *n* (*MUS*) ténor *m*; (*of speech etc*) sens général.
tenpin bowling ['tɛnpɪn-] *n* (*BRIT*) bowling *m* (*à 10 quilles*).
tense [tɛns] *adj* tendu(e); (*person*) tendu, crispé(e) ♦ *n* (*LING*) temps *m* ♦ *vt* (*tighten: muscles*) tendre.
tenseness ['tɛnsnɪs] *n* tension *f*.
tension ['tɛnʃən] *n* tension *f*.
tent [tɛnt] *n* tente *f*.
tentacle ['tɛntəkl] *n* tentacule *m*.
tentative ['tɛntətɪv] *adj* timide, hésitant(e); (*conclusion*) provisoire.
tenterhooks ['tɛntəhuks] *npl*: **on ~** sur des charbons ardents.
tenth [tɛnθ] *num* dixième.
tent peg *n* piquet *m* de tente.
tent pole *n* montant *m* de tente.
tenuous ['tɛnjuəs] *adj* ténu(e).
tenure ['tɛnjuə*] *n* (*of property*) bail *m*; (*of job*) période *f* de jouissance; statut *m* de titulaire.
tepid ['tɛpɪd] *adj* tiède.
Ter. *abbr* = **terrace**.
term [təːm] *n* (*limit*) terme *m*; (*word*) terme, mot *m*; (*SCOL*) trimestre *m*; (*LAW*) session *f* ♦ *vt* appeler; **~s** *npl* (*conditions*) conditions *fpl*; (*COMM*) tarif *m*; **~ of imprisonment** peine *f* de prison; **his ~ of office** la période où il était en fonction; **in the short/long ~** à court/long terme; **"easy ~s"** (*COMM*) "facilités de paiement"; **to come to ~s with** (*problem*) faire face à; **to be on good ~s with** bien s'entendre avec, être en bons termes avec.
terminal ['təːmɪnl] *adj* terminal(e); (*disease*) dans sa phase terminale ♦ *n* (*ELEC*) borne *f*; (*for oil, ore etc, also COMPUT*) terminal *m*; (*also*: **air ~**) aérogare *f*; (*BRIT: also*: **coach ~**) gare routière.
terminate ['təːmɪneɪt] *vt* mettre fin à ♦ *vi*: **to ~ in** finir en *or* par.
termination [təːmɪ'neɪʃən] *n* fin *f*; cessation *f*; (*of contract*) résiliation *f*; **~ of pregnancy** (*MED*) interruption *f* de grossesse.
termini ['təːmɪnaɪ] *npl of* **terminus**.
terminology [təːmɪ'nɔlədʒɪ] *n* terminologie *f*.
terminus, *pl* **termini** ['təːmɪnəs, 'təːmɪnaɪ] *n* terminus *m inv*.
termite ['təːmaɪt] *n* termite *m*.
term paper *n* (*US UNIVERSITY*) dissertation trimestrielle.
Terr. *abbr* = **terrace**.
terrace ['tɛrəs] *n* terrasse *f*; (*BRIT: row of houses*) rangée *f* de maisons (*attenantes les unes aux autres*); **the ~s** (*BRIT SPORT*) les gradins *mpl*.
terraced ['tɛrəst] *adj* (*garden*) en terrasses; (*in a row: house, cottage etc*) attenant(e) aux

maisons voisines.
terracotta ['tɛrə'kɔtə] *n* terre cuite.
terrain [tɛ'reɪn] *n* terrain *m* (*sol*).
terrible ['tɛrɪbl] *adj* terrible, atroce; (*weather, work*) affreux(euse), épouvantable.
terribly ['tɛrɪblɪ] *adv* terriblement; (*very badly*) affreusement mal.
terrific [tə'rɪfɪk] *adj* fantastique, incroyable, terrible; (*wonderful*) formidable, sensationnel(le).
terrify ['tɛrɪfaɪ] *vt* terrifier.
territorial [tɛrɪ'tɔːrɪəl] *adj* territorial(e).
territorial waters *npl* eaux territoriales.
territory ['tɛrɪtərɪ] *n* territoire *m*.
terror ['tɛrə*] *n* terreur *f*.
terror attack *n* attentat *m*.
terrorism ['tɛrərɪzəm] *n* terrorisme *m*.
terrorist ['tɛrərɪst] *n* terroriste *m/f*.
terrorize ['tɛrəraɪz] *vt* terroriser.
terse [təːs] *adj* (*style*) concis(e); (*reply*) laconique.
tertiary ['təːʃərɪ] *adj* tertiaire; ~ **education** (*BRIT*) enseignement *m* postscolaire.
Terylene ['tɛrɪliːn] *n* ® (*BRIT*) tergal *m* ®.
TESL ['tɛsl] *n abbr = Teaching of English as a Second Language.*
TESSA ['tɛsə] *n abbr* (*BRIT*: *= Tax Exempt Special Savings Account*) *compte de dépôt aux intérêts exempts d'impôts si le capital reste bloqué.*
test [tɛst] *n* (*trial, check*) essai *m*; (*: of goods in factory*) contrôle *m*; (*of courage etc*) épreuve *f*; (*MED*) examens *mpl*; (*CHEM*) analyses *fpl*; (*exam: of intelligence etc*) test *m* (d'aptitude); (*: in school*) interrogation *f* de contrôle; (*also*: **driving** ~) (examen du) permis *m* de conduire ♦ *vt* essayer; contrôler; mettre à l'épreuve; examiner; analyser; tester; faire subir une interrogation (de contrôle) à; **to put sth to the** ~ mettre qch à l'épreuve.
testament ['tɛstəmənt] *n* testament *m*; **the Old/New T**~ l'Ancien/le Nouveau Testament.
test ban *n* (*also*: **nuclear** ~) interdiction *f* des essais nucléaires.
test case *n* (*LAW, fig*) affaire-test *f*.
testes ['tɛstiːz] *npl* testicules *mpl*.
test flight *n* vol *m* d'essai.
testicle ['tɛstɪkl] *n* testicule *m*.
testify ['tɛstɪfaɪ] *vi* (*LAW*) témoigner, déposer; **to** ~ **to sth** (*LAW*) attester qch; (*gen*) témoigner de qch.
testimonial [tɛstɪ'məunɪəl] *n* (*BRIT*: *reference*) recommandation *f*; (*gift*) témoignage *m* d'estime.
testimony ['tɛstɪmənɪ] *n* (*LAW*) témoignage *m*, déposition *f*.
testing ['tɛstɪŋ] *adj* (*situation, period*) difficile.
test match *n* (*CRICKET, RUGBY*) match international.
testosterone [tɛs'tɔstərəun] *n* testostérone *f*.
test paper *n* (*SCOL*) interrogation écrite.
test pilot *n* pilote *m* d'essai.
test tube *n* éprouvette *f*.
test-tube baby ['tɛsttjuːb-] *n* bébé-éprouvette *m*.
testy ['tɛstɪ] *adj* irritable.
tetanus ['tɛtənəs] *n* tétanos *m*.
tetchy ['tɛtʃɪ] *adj* hargneux(euse).
tether ['tɛðə*] *vt* attacher ♦ *n*: **at the end of one's** ~ à bout (de patience).
Tex. *abbr* (*US*) = *Texas*.
text [tɛkst] *n* texte *m*; ~ **message** message *m* SMS ♦ *vt* envoyer un message SMS à ♦ *vi* envoyer des messages SMS.
textbook ['tɛkstbuk] *n* manuel *m*.
textile ['tɛkstaɪl] *n* textile *m*.
textual ['tɛkstjuəl] *adj* textuel(le).
texture ['tɛkstʃə*] *n* texture *f*; (*of skin, paper etc*) grain *m*.
Thai [taɪ] *adj* thaïlandais(e) ♦ *n* Thaïlandais/e; (*LING*) thaï *m*.
Thailand ['taɪlænd] *n* Thaïlande *f*.
thalidomide [θə'lɪdəmaɪd] *n* ® thalidomide *f* ®.
Thames [tɛmz] *n*: **the** ~ la Tamise.
than [ðæn, ðən] *conj* que; (*with numerals*): **more** ~ **10/once** plus de 10/d'une fois; **I have more/less** ~ **you** j'en ai plus/moins que toi; **she has more apples** ~ **pears** elle a plus de pommes que de poires; **it is better to phone** ~ **to write** il vaut mieux téléphoner (plutôt) qu'écrire; **no sooner did he leave** ~ **the phone rang** il venait de partir quand le téléphone a sonné.
thank [θæŋk] *vt* remercier, dire merci à; ~ **you (very much)** merci (beaucoup); ~ **heavens,** ~ **God** Dieu merci.
thankful ['θæŋkful] *adj*: ~ **(for)** reconnaissant(e) (de); ~ **for/that** (*relieved*) soulagé(e) de/que.
thankfully ['θæŋkfəlɪ] *adv* avec reconnaissance; avec soulagement; ~ **there were few victims** il y eut fort heureusement peu de victimes.
thankless ['θæŋklɪs] *adj* ingrat(e).
thanks [θæŋks] *npl* remerciements *mpl* ♦ *excl* merci!; ~ **to** *prep* grâce à.
Thanksgiving (Day) ['θæŋksgɪvɪŋ-] *n* jour *m* d'action de grâce; *voir encadré*.

THANKSGIVING DAY

Thanksgiving (Day) *est un jour de congé aux États-Unis, le quatrième jeudi du mois de novembre, commémorant la bonne récolte que les Pèlerins venus de Grande-Bretagne ont eue en 1621; traditionnellement, c'était un jour où l'on remerciait Dieu et où l'on organisait un grand festin.*
Une fête semblable, mais qui n'a aucun rapport avec les Pères Pèlerins, a lieu au Canada le deuxième lundi d'octobre.

KEYWORD

that [ðæt] *adj* (*demonstrative*: *pl* **those**) ce, cet *+vowel or h mute*, *f* cette; ~ **man/woman/book** cet homme/cette femme/ce livre; (*not this*) cet homme-là/cette femme-là/ce livre-là; ~ **one** celui-là(celle-là)
⧫ *pron* **1** (*demonstrative*: *pl* **those**) ce; (*not this one*) cela, ça; (*the one*) celui(celle); **who's ~?** qui est-ce?; **what's ~?** qu'est-ce que c'est?; **is ~ you?** c'est toi?; **I prefer this to ~** je préfère ceci à cela *or* ça; **~'s what he said** c'est *or* voilà ce qu'il a dit; **all ~** tout cela, tout ça; **~ is (to say)** c'est-à-dire, à savoir; **at** *or* **with ~, she ...** là-dessus, elle ...; **do it like ~** fais-le comme ça
2 (*relative*: *subject*) qui; (: *object*) que; (: *indirect*) lequel(laquelle), lesquels(lesquelles) *pl*; **the book ~ I read** le livre que j'ai lu; **the books ~ are in the library** les livres qui sont dans la bibliothèque; **all ~ I have** tout ce que j'ai; **the box ~ I put it in** la boîte dans laquelle je l'ai mis; **the people ~ I spoke to** les gens auxquels *or* à qui j'ai parlé; **not ~ I know of** pas à ma connaissance
3 (*relative*: *of time*) où; **the day ~ he came** le jour où il est venu
⧫ *conj* que; **he thought ~ I was ill** il pensait que j'étais malade
⧫ *adv* (*demonstrative*): **I can't work ~ much** je ne peux pas travailler autant que cela; **I didn't know it was ~ bad** je ne savais pas que c'était si *or* aussi mauvais; **~ high** aussi haut; si haut; **it's about ~ high** c'est à peu près de cette hauteur.

thatched [θætʃt] *adj* (*roof*) de chaume; **~ cottage** chaumière *f*.
Thatcherism ['θætʃərɪzəm] *n* thatchérisme *m*.
thaw [θɔː] *n* dégel *m* ⧫ *vi* (*ice*) fondre; (*food*) dégeler ⧫ *vt* (*food*) (faire) dégeler; **it's ~ing** (*weather*) il dégèle.

KEYWORD

the [ðiː, ðə] *def art* **1** (*gen*) le, la *f*, l' *+vowel or h mute*, les *pl*; (NB: *à +le(s)* = au(x); *de + le* = du; *de +les* = des); **~ boy/girl/ink** le garçon/la fille/l'encre; **~ children** les enfants; **~ history of ~ world** l'histoire du monde; **give it to ~ postman** donne-le au facteur; **to play ~ piano/flute** jouer du piano/de la flûte; **~ rich and ~ poor** les riches et les pauvres
2 (*in titles*): **Elizabeth ~ First** Elisabeth première; **Peter ~ Great** Pierre le Grand
3 (*in comparisons*): **~ more he works, ~ more he earns** plus il travaille, plus il gagne de l'argent; **~ sooner ~ better** le plus tôt sera le mieux.

theatre, (*US*) **theater** ['θɪətə*] *n* théâtre *m*.
theatre-goer ['θɪətəgəuə*] *n* habitué/e du théâtre.
theatrical [θɪ'ætrɪkl] *adj* théâtral(e); **~ company** troupe *f* de théâtre.
theft [θɛft] *n* vol *m* (*larcin*).
their [ðɛə*] *adj* leur, leurs *pl*.
theirs [ðɛəz] *pron* le(la) leur, les leurs; **it is ~** c'est à eux; **a friend of ~** un de leurs amis.
them [ðɛm, ðəm] *pron* (*direct*) les; (*indirect*) leur; (*stressed, after prep*) eux(elles); **I see ~** je les vois; **give ~ the book** donne-leur le livre; **give me a few of ~** donnez m'en quelques uns (*or* quelques unes).
theme [θiːm] *n* thème *m*.
theme park *n* parc *m* à thème.
theme song *n* chanson principale.
themselves [ðəm'sɛlvz] *pl pron* (*reflexive*) se; (*emphatic*) eux-mêmes(elles-mêmes); **between ~** entre eux(elles).
then [ðɛn] *adv* (*at that time*) alors, à ce moment-là; (*next*) puis, ensuite; (*and also*) et puis ⧫ *conj* (*therefore*) alors, dans ce cas ⧫ *adj*: **the ~ president** le président d'alors *or* de l'époque; **by ~** (*past*) à ce moment-là; (*future*) d'ici là; **from ~ on** dès lors; **before ~** avant; **until ~** jusqu'à ce moment-là, jusque-là; **and ~ what?** et puis après?; **what do you want me to do ~?** (*afterwards*) que veux-tu que je fasse ensuite?; (*in that case*) bon alors, qu'est-ce que je fais?
theologian [θɪə'ləudʒən] *n* théologien/ne.
theological [θɪə'lɔdʒɪkl] *adj* théologique.
theology [θɪ'ɔlədʒɪ] *n* théologie *f*.
theorem ['θɪərəm] *n* théorème *m*.
theoretical [θɪə'rɛtɪkl] *adj* théorique.
theorize ['θɪəraɪz] *vi* élaborer une théorie; (*pej*) faire des théories.
theory ['θɪərɪ] *n* théorie *f*.
therapeutic(al) [θɛrə'pjuːtɪk(l)] *adj* thérapeutique.
therapist ['θɛrəpɪst] *n* thérapeute *m/f*.
therapy ['θɛrəpɪ] *n* thérapie *f*.

KEYWORD

there [ðɛə*] *adv* **1**: **~ is, ~ are** il y a; **~ are 3 of them** (*people, things*) il y en a 3; **~ has been an accident** il y a eu un accident
2 (*referring to place*) là, là-bas; **it's ~** c'est là(-bas); **in/on/up/down ~** là-dedans/là-dessus/là-haut/en bas; **he went ~ on Friday** il y est allé vendredi; **to go ~ and back** faire l'aller-retour; **I want that book ~** je veux ce livre-là; **~ he is!** le voilà!
3: **~, ~** (*esp to child*) allons, allons!

thereabouts ['ðɛərə'bauts] *adv* (*place*) par là, près de là; (*amount*) environ, à peu près.
thereafter [ðɛər'ɑːftə*] *adv* par la suite.
thereby ['ðɛəbaɪ] *adv* ainsi.
therefore ['ðɛəfɔː*] *adv* donc, par conséquent.
there's ['ðɛəz] = **there is, there has**.
thereupon [ðɛərə'pɔn] *adv* (*at that point*) sur ce; (*formal: on that subject*) à ce sujet.
thermal ['θəːml] *adj* thermique; **~ paper/**

printer papier *m*/imprimante *f* thermique.
thermodynamics ['θəːmədaɪ'næmɪks] *n* thermodynamique *f*.
thermometer [θə'mɔmɪtə*] *n* thermomètre *m*.
thermonuclear ['θəːməu'njuːklɪə*] *adj* thermonucléaire.
Thermos ['θəːməs] *n* ® (*also*: ~ **flask**) thermos *m or f inv* ®.
thermostat ['θəːməustæt] *n* thermostat *m*.
thesaurus [θɪ'sɔːrəs] *n* dictionnaire *m* synonymique.
these [ðiːz] *pl pron* ceux-ci(celles-ci) ♦ *pl adj* ces; (*not those*): ~ **books** ces livres-ci.
thesis, *pl* **theses** ['θiːsɪs, 'θiːsiːz] *n* thèse *f*.
they [ðeɪ] *pl pron* ils(elles); (*stressed*) eux(elles); ~ **say that ...** (*it is said that*) on dit que ....
they'd [ðeɪd] = **they had, they would.**
they'll [ðeɪl] = **they shall, they will.**
they're [ðɛə*] = **they are.**
they've [ðeɪv] = **they have.**
thick [θɪk] *adj* épais(se); (*crowd*) dense; (*stupid*) bête, borné(e) ♦ *n*: **in the ~ of** au beau milieu de, en plein cœur de; **it's 20 cm ~** ça a 20 cm d'épaisseur.
thicken ['θɪkn] *vi* s'épaissir ♦ *vt* (*sauce etc*) épaissir.
thicket ['θɪkɪt] *n* fourré *m*, hallier *m*.
thickly ['θɪklɪ] *adv* (*spread*) en couche épaisse; (*cut*) en tranches épaisses; ~ **populated** à forte densité de population.
thickness ['θɪknɪs] *n* épaisseur *f*.
thickset [θɪk'sɛt] *adj* trapu(e), costaud(e).
thickskinned [θɪk'skɪnd] *adj* (*fig*) peu sensible.
thief, *pl* **thieves** [θiːf, θiːvz] *n* voleur/euse.
thieving ['θiːvɪŋ] *n* vol *m* (*larcin*).
thigh [θaɪ] *n* cuisse *f*.
thighbone ['θaɪbəun] *n* fémur *m*.
thimble ['θɪmbl] *n* dé *m* (à coudre).
thin [θɪn] *adj* mince; (*person*) maigre; (*soup*) peu épais(se); (*hair, crowd*) clairsemé(e); (*fog*) léger(ère) ♦ *vt* (*hair*) éclaircir; (*also*: ~ **down**: *sauce, paint*) délayer ♦ *vi* (*fog*) s'éclaircir; (*also*: ~ **out**: *crowd*) se disperser; **his hair is ~ning** il se dégarnit.
thing [θɪŋ] *n* chose *f*; (*object*) objet *m*; (*contraption*) truc *m*; **~s** *npl* (*belongings*) affaires *fpl*; **first ~ (in the morning)** à la première heure, tout de suite (le matin); **last ~ (at night), he** ... juste avant de se coucher, il ...; **the ~ is ...** c'est que ...; **for one ~** d'abord; **the best ~ would be to** le mieux serait de; **how are ~s?** comment ça va?; **she's got a ~ about ...** elle déteste ...; **poor ~!** le (*or* la) pauvre!
think, *pt, pp* **thought** [θɪŋk, θɔːt] *vi* penser, réfléchir ♦ *vt* penser, croire; (*imagine*) s'imaginer; **to ~ of** penser à; **what do you ~ of it?** qu'en pensez-vous?; **what did you ~ of them?** qu'avez-vous pensé d'eux?; **to ~ about sth/sb** penser à qch/qn; **I'll ~ about it** je vais y réfléchir; **to ~ of doing** avoir l'idée de faire; **I ~ so/not** je crois *or* pense que oui/non; **to ~ well of** avoir une haute opinion de; ~ **again!** attention, réfléchis bien!; **to ~ aloud** penser tout haut.
▸**think out** *vt* (*plan*) bien réfléchir à; (*solution*) trouver.
▸**think over** *vt* bien réfléchir à; **I'd like to ~ things over** (*offer, suggestion*) j'aimerais bien y réfléchir un peu.
▸**think through** *vt* étudier dans tous les détails.
▸**think up** *vt* inventer, trouver.
thinking ['θɪŋkɪŋ] *n*: **to my (way of) ~** selon moi.
think tank *n* groupe *m* de réflexion.
thinly ['θɪnlɪ] *adv* (*cut*) en tranches fines; (*spread*) en couche mince.
thinness ['θɪnnɪs] *n* minceur *f*; maigreur *f*.
third [θəːd] *num* troisième ♦ *n* troisième *m/f*; (*fraction*) tiers *m*; (*BRIT SCOL*: *degree*) ≈ licence *f* avec mention passable; **a ~ of** le tiers de.
third-degree burns ['θəːddɪgriː-] *npl* brûlures *fpl* au troisième degré.
thirdly ['θəːdlɪ] *adv* troisièmement.
third party insurance *n* (*BRIT*) assurance *f* au tiers.
third-rate ['θəːd'reɪt] *adj* de qualité médiocre.
Third World *n*: **the ~** le Tiers-Monde.
thirst [θəːst] *n* soif *f*.
thirsty ['θəːstɪ] *adj* qui a soif, assoiffé(e); **to be ~** avoir soif.
thirteen [θəː'tiːn] *num* treize.
thirtieth ['θəːtɪɪθ] *num* trentième.
thirty ['θəːtɪ] *num* trente.

KEYWORD

this [ðɪs] *adj* (*demonstrative*: *pl* **these**) ce, cet *+vowel or h mute*, cette *f*; ~ **man/woman/book** cet homme/cette femme/ce livre; (*not that*) cet homme-ci/cette femme-ci/ce livre-ci; ~ **one** celui-ci(celle-ci); ~ **time** cette fois-ci; ~ **time last year** l'année dernière à la même époque; ~ **way** (*in this direction*) par ici; (*in this fashion*) de cette façon, ainsi
♦ *pron* (*demonstrative*: *pl* **these**) ce; (*not that one*) celui-ci(celle-ci), ceci; **who's ~?** qui est-ce?; **what's ~?** qu'est-ce que c'est?; **I prefer ~ to that** je préfère ceci à cela; **they were talking of ~ and that** ils parlaient de choses et d'autres; **~ is what he said** voici ce qu'il a dit; **~ is Mr Brown** (*in introductions*) je vous présente Mr Brown; (*in photo*) c'est Mr Brown; (*on telephone*) ici Mr Brown
♦ *adv* (*demonstrative*): **it was about ~ big** c'était à peu près de cette grandeur *or* grand comme ça; **I didn't know it was ~ bad** je ne savais pas que c'était si *or* aussi mauvais.

thistle ['θɪsl] *n* chardon *m*.
thong [θɔŋ] *n* lanière *f*.
thorn [θɔːn] *n* épine *f*.

thorny ['θɔːnɪ] *adj* épineux(euse).
thorough ['θʌrə] *adj* (*search*) minutieux(euse); (*knowledge, research*) approfondi(e); (*work*) consciencieux(euse); (*cleaning*) à fond.
thoroughbred ['θʌrəbrɛd] *n* (*horse*) pur-sang *m inv*.
thoroughfare ['θʌrəfɛə*] *n* rue *f*; **"no ~"** (*BRIT*) "passage interdit".
thoroughgoing ['θʌrəgəuɪŋ] *adj* (*analysis*) approfondi(e); (*reform*) profond(e).
thoroughly ['θʌrəlɪ] *adv* minutieusement; en profondeur; à fond; **he ~ agreed** il était tout à fait d'accord.
thoroughness ['θʌrənɪs] *n* soin (méticuleux).
those [ðəuz] *pl pron* ceux-là(celles-là) ♦ *pl adj* ces; (*not these*): ~ **books** ces livres-là.
though [ðəu] *conj* bien que + *sub*, quoique + *sub* ♦ *adv* pourtant; **even ~** quand bien même + *conditional*; **it's not easy, ~** pourtant, ce n'est pas facile.
thought [θɔːt] *pt, pp of* **think** ♦ *n* pensée *f*; (*opinion*) avis *m*; (*intention*) intention *f*; **after much ~** après mûre réflexion; **I've just had a ~** je viens de penser à quelque chose; **to give sth some ~** réfléchir à qch.
thoughtful ['θɔːtful] *adj* pensif(ive); (*considerate*) prévenant(e).
thoughtfully ['θɔːtfəlɪ] *adv* pensivement; avec prévenance.
thoughtless ['θɔːtlɪs] *adj* étourdi(e); qui manque de considération.
thoughtlessly ['θɔːtlɪslɪ] *adv* inconsidérément.
thought-provoking ['θɔːtprəvəukɪŋ] *adj* stimulant(e).
thousand ['θauzənd] *num* mille; **one ~** mille; **~s of** des milliers de.
thousandth ['θauzəntθ] *num* millième.
thrash [θræʃ] *vt* rouer de coups; donner une correction à; (*defeat*) battre à plate(s) couture(s).
►**thrash about** *vi* se débattre.
►**thrash out** *vt* débattre de.
thrashing ['θræʃɪŋ] *n*: **to give sb a ~ = to thrash sb.**
thread [θrɛd] *n* fil *m*; (*of screw*) pas *m*, filetage *m* ♦ *vt* (*needle*) enfiler; **to ~ one's way between** se faufiler entre.
threadbare ['θrɛdbɛə*] *adj* râpé(e), élimé(e).
threat [θrɛt] *n* menace *f*; **to be under ~ of** être menacé(e) de.
threaten ['θrɛtn] *vi* (*storm*) menacer ♦ *vt*: **to ~ sb with sth/to do** menacer qn de qch/de faire.
threatening ['θrɛtnɪŋ] *adj* menaçant(e).
three [θriː] *num* trois.
three-dimensional [θriːdɪ'mɛnʃənl] *adj* à trois dimensions; (*film*) en relief.
threefold ['θriːfəuld] *adv*: **to increase ~** tripler.
three-piece ['θriːpiːs]: **~ suit** *n* complet *m* (avec gilet); **~ suite** *n* salon *m* comprenant un canapé et deux fauteuils assortis.
three-ply [θriː'plaɪ] *adj* (*wood*) à trois épaisseurs; (*wool*) trois fils *inv*.
three-quarters [θriː'kwɔːtəz] *npl* trois-quarts *mpl*; **~ full** aux trois-quarts plein.
three-wheeler [θriː'wiːlə*] *n* (*car*) voiture *f* à trois roues.
thresh [θrɛʃ] *vt* (*AGR*) battre.
threshing machine ['θrɛʃɪŋ-] *n* batteuse *f*.
threshold ['θrɛʃhəuld] *n* seuil *m*; **to be on the ~ of** (*fig*) être au seuil de.
threshold agreement *n* (*ECON*) accord *m* d'indexation des salaires.
threw [θruː] *pt of* **throw**.
thrift [θrɪft] *n* économie *f*.
thrifty ['θrɪftɪ] *adj* économe.
thrill [θrɪl] *n* frisson *m*, émotion *f* ♦ *vi* tressaillir, frissonner ♦ *vt* (*audience*) électriser; **to be ~ed** (*with gift etc*) être ravi(e).
thriller ['θrɪlə*] *n* film *m* (*or* roman *m or* pièce *f*) à suspense.
thrilling ['θrɪlɪŋ] *adj* (*book, play etc*) saisissant(e); (*news, discovery*) excitant(e).
thrive, *pt* **thrived, throve,** *pp* **thrived, thriven** [θraɪv, θrəuv, 'θrɪvn] *vi* pousser *or* se développer bien; (*business*) prospérer; **he ~s on it** cela lui réussit.
thriving ['θraɪvɪŋ] *adj* vigoureux(euse); (*industry etc*) prospère.
throat [θrəut] *n* gorge *f*; **to have a sore ~** avoir mal à la gorge.
throb [θrɔb] *n* (*of heart*) pulsation *f*; (*of engine*) vibration *f*; (*of pain*) élancement *m* ♦ *vi* (*heart*) palpiter; (*engine*) vibrer; (*pain*) lanciner; (*wound*) causer des élancements; **my head is ~bing** j'ai des élancements dans la tête.
throes [θrəuz] *npl*: **in the ~ of** au beau milieu de; en proie à; **in the ~ of death** à l'agonie.
thrombosis [θrɔm'bəusɪs] *n* thrombose *f*.
throne [θrəun] *n* trône *m*.
throng ['θrɔŋ] *n* foule *f* ♦ *vt* se presser dans.
throttle ['θrɔtl] *n* (*AUT*) accélérateur *m* ♦ *vt* étrangler.
through [θruː] *prep* à travers; (*time*) pendant, durant; (*by means of*) par, par l'intermédiaire de; (*owing to*) à cause de ♦ *adj* (*ticket, train, passage*) direct(e) ♦ *adv* à travers; **(from) Monday ~ Friday** (*US*) de lundi à vendredi; **to let sb ~** laisser passer qn; **to put sb ~ to sb** (*TEL*) passer qn à qn; **to be ~** (*TEL*) avoir la communication; (*have finished*) avoir fini; **"no ~ traffic"** (*US*) "passage interdit"; **"no ~ way"** (*BRIT*) "impasse".
throughout [θruː'aut] *prep* (*place*) partout dans; (*time*) durant tout(e) le(la) ♦ *adv* partout.
throughput ['θruːput] *n* (*of goods, materials*) quantité de matières premières utilisée; (*COMPUT*) débit *m*.
throve [θrəuv] *pt of* **thrive**.
throw [θrəu] *n* jet *m*; (*SPORT*) lancer *m* ♦ *vt* (*pt* **threw,** *pp* **thrown** [θruː, θrəun]) lancer, jeter;

(*SPORT*) lancer; (*rider*) désarçonner; (*fig*) décontenancer; (*pottery*) tourner; **to ~ a party** donner une réception.
▸**throw about, throw around** *vt* (*litter etc*) éparpiller.
▸**throw away** *vt* jeter.
▸**throw off** *vt* se débarrasser de.
▸**throw out** *vt* jeter dehors; (*reject*) rejeter.
▸**throw together** *vt* (*clothes, meal etc*) assembler à la hâte; (*essay*) bâcler.
▸**throw up** *vi* vomir.
throwaway ['θrəuəweɪ] *adj* à jeter.
throwback ['θrəubæk] *n*: **it's a ~ to** ça nous *etc* ramène à.
throw-in ['θrəuɪn] *n* (*SPORT*) remise *f* en jeu.
thru [θru:] *prep, adj, adv* (*US*) = **through**.
thrush [θrʌʃ] *n* (*ZOOL*) grive *f*; (*MED*: *esp in children*) muguet *m*; (: *BRIT*: *in women*) muguet vaginal.
thrust [θrʌst] *n* (*TECH*) poussée *f* ♦ *vt* (*pt, pp* **thrust**) pousser brusquement; (*push in*) enfoncer.
thrusting ['θrʌstɪŋ] *adj* dynamique; qui se met trop en avant.
thud [θʌd] *n* bruit sourd.
thug [θʌg] *n* voyou *m*.
thumb [θʌm] *n* (*ANAT*) pouce *m* ♦ *vt* (*book*) feuilleter; **to ~ a lift** faire de l'auto-stop, arrêter une voiture; **to give sb/sth the ~s up/~s down** donner/refuser de donner le feu vert à qn/qch.
thumb index *n* répertoire *m* (à onglets).
thumbnail ['θʌmneɪl] *n* ongle *m* du pouce.
thumbnail sketch *n* croquis *m*.
thumbtack ['θʌmtæk] *n* (*US*) punaise *f* (*clou*).
thump [θʌmp] *n* grand coup; (*sound*) bruit sourd ♦ *vt* cogner sur ♦ *vi* cogner, frapper.
thunder ['θʌndə*] *n* tonnerre *m* ♦ *vi* tonner; (*train etc*): **to ~ past** passer dans un grondement *or* un bruit de tonnerre.
thunderbolt ['θʌndəbəult] *n* foudre *f*.
thunderclap ['θʌndəklæp] *n* coup *m* de tonnerre.
thunderous ['θʌndrəs] *adj* étourdissant(e).
thunderstorm ['θʌndəstɔːm] *n* orage *m*.
thunderstruck ['θʌndəstrʌk] *adj* (*fig*) abasourdi(e).
thundery ['θʌndərɪ] *adj* orageux(euse).
Thur(s). *abbr* (= *Thursday*) jeu.
Thursday ['θəːzdɪ] *n* jeudi *m*; *for phrases see also* **Tuesday**.
thus [ðʌs] *adv* ainsi.
thwart [θwɔːt] *vt* contrecarrer.
thyme [taɪm] *n* thym *m*.
thyroid ['θaɪrɔɪd] *n* thyroïde *f*.
tiara [tɪ'ɑːrə] *n* (*woman's*) diadème *m*.
Tibet [tɪ'bɛt] *n* Tibet *m*.
Tibetan [tɪ'bɛtən] *adj* tibétain(e) ♦ *n* Tibétain/e; (*LING*) tibétain *m*.
tibia ['tɪbɪə] *n* tibia *m*.
tic [tɪk] *n* tic (nerveux).
tick [tɪk] *n* (*sound: of clock*) tic-tac *m*; (*mark*) coche *f*; (*ZOOL*) tique *f*; (*BRIT col*): **in a ~** dans un instant; (*BRIT col: credit*): **to buy sth on ~** acheter qch à crédit ♦ *vi* faire tic-tac ♦ *vt* cocher; **to put a ~ against sth** cocher qch.
▸**tick off** *vt* cocher; (*person*) réprimander, attraper.
▸**tick over** *vi* (*BRIT*: *engine*) tourner au ralenti; (: *fig*) aller *or* marcher doucettement.
ticker tape ['tɪkə-] *n* bande *f* de téléscripteur; (*US*: *in celebrations*) ≈ serpentin *m*.
ticket ['tɪkɪt] *n* billet *m*; (*for bus, tube*) ticket *m*; (*in shop: on goods*) étiquette *f*; (: *from cash register*) reçu *m*, ticket; (*for library*) carte *f*; (*US POL*) liste électorale (*soutenue par un parti*); **to get a (parking) ~** (*AUT*) attraper une contravention (pour stationnement illégal).
ticket agency *n* (*THEAT*) agence *f* de spectacles.
ticket collector *n* contrôleur/euse.
ticket holder *n* personne munie d'un billet.
ticket inspector *n* contrôleur/euse.
ticket office *n* guichet *m*, bureau *m* de vente des billets.
tickle ['tɪkl] *n* chatouillement *m* ♦ *vt* chatouiller; (*fig*) plaire à; faire rire.
ticklish ['tɪklɪʃ] *adj* (*person*) chatouilleux(euse); (*which tickles: blanket*) qui chatouille; (: *cough*) qui irrite.
tidal ['taɪdl] *adj* à marée.
tidal wave *n* raz-de-marée *m inv*.
tidbit ['tɪdbɪt] *n* (*esp US*) = **titbit**.
tiddlywinks ['tɪdlɪwɪŋks] *n* jeu *m* de puce.
tide [taɪd] *n* marée *f*; (*fig: of events*) cours *m* ♦ *vt*: **to ~ sb over** dépanner qn; **high/low ~** marée haute/basse.
tidily ['taɪdɪlɪ] *adv* avec soin, soigneusement.
tidiness ['taɪdɪnɪs] *n* bon ordre; goût *m* de l'ordre.
tidy ['taɪdɪ] *adj* (*room*) bien rangé(e); (*dress, work*) net(nette), soigné(e); (*person*) ordonné(e), qui a de l'ordre; (: *in character*) soigneux(euse); (*mind*) méthodique ♦ *vt* (*also*: **~ up**) ranger; **to ~ o.s. up** s'arranger.
tie [taɪ] *n* (*string etc*) cordon *m*; (*BRIT*: *also*: **neck~**) cravate *f*; (*fig: link*) lien *m*; (*SPORT*: *draw*) égalité *f* de points; match nul; (: *match*) rencontre *f*; (*US RAIL*) traverse *f* ♦ *vt* (*parcel*) attacher; (*ribbon*) nouer ♦ *vi* (*SPORT*) faire match nul; finir à égalité de points; **"black/white ~"** "smoking/habit de rigueur"; **family ~s** liens de famille; **to ~ sth in a bow** faire un nœud à *or* avec qch; **to ~ a knot in sth** faire un nœud à qch.
▸**tie down** *vt* attacher; (*fig*): **to ~ sb down to** contraindre qn à accepter.
▸**tie in** *vi*: **to ~ in (with)** (*correspond*) correspondre (à).
▸**tie on** *vt* (*BRIT*: *label etc*) attacher (avec une ficelle).
▸**tie up** *vt* (*parcel*) ficeler; (*dog, boat*) attacher; (*arrangements*) conclure; **to be ~d up** (*busy*) être pris *or* occupé.

tie-break(er) ['taɪbreɪk(ə*)] *n* (*TENNIS*) tie-break *m*; (*in quiz*) question *f* subsidiaire.
tie-on ['taɪɔn] *adj* (*BRIT*: *label*) qui s'attache.
tie-pin ['taɪpɪn] *n* (*BRIT*) épingle *f* de cravate.
tier [tɪə*] *n* gradin *m*; (*of cake*) étage *m*.
Tierra del Fuego [tɪ'ɛrədɛl'fweɪgəu] *n* Terre *f* de Feu.
tie tack *n* (*US*) épingle *f* de cravate.
tiff [tɪf] *n* petite querelle.
tiger ['taɪgə*] *n* tigre *m*.
tight [taɪt] *adj* (*rope*) tendu(e), raide; (*clothes*) étroit(e), très juste; (*budget, programme, bend*) serré(e); (*control*) strict(e), sévère; (*col*: *drunk*) ivre, rond(e) ♦ *adv* (*squeeze*) très fort; (*shut*) à bloc, hermétiquement; **to be packed ~** (*suitcase*) être bourré(e); (*people*) être serré(e); **everybody hold ~!** accrochez-vous bien!
tighten ['taɪtn] *vt* (*rope*) tendre; (*screw*) resserrer; (*control*) renforcer ♦ *vi* se tendre; se resserrer.
tight-fisted [taɪt'fɪstɪd] *adj* avare.
tight-lipped ['taɪt'lɪpt] *adj*: **to be ~ (about sth)** (*silent*) ne pas desserrer les lèvres *or* les dents (au sujet de qch); **she was ~ with anger** elle pinçait les lèvres de colère.
tightly ['taɪtlɪ] *adv* (*grasp*) bien, très fort.
tight-rope ['taɪtrəup] *n* corde *f* raide.
tight-rope walker *n* funambule *m/f*.
tights [taɪts] *npl* (*BRIT*) collant *m*.
tigress ['taɪgrɪs] *n* tigresse *f*.
tilde ['tɪldə] *n* tilde *m*.
tile [taɪl] *n* (*on roof*) tuile *f*; (*on wall or floor*) carreau *m* ♦ *vt* (*floor, bathroom etc*) carreler.
tiled [taɪld] *adj* en tuiles; carrelé(e).
till [tɪl] *n* caisse (enregistreuse) ♦ *vt* (*land*) cultiver ♦ *prep, conj* = **until**.
tiller ['tɪlə*] *n* (*NAUT*) barre *f* (du gouvernail).
tilt [tɪlt] *vt* pencher, incliner ♦ *vi* pencher, être incliné(e) ♦ *n* (*slope*) inclinaison *f*; **to wear one's hat at a ~** porter son chapeau incliné sur le côté; **(at) full ~** à toute vitesse.
timber ['tɪmbə*] *n* (*material*) bois *m* de construction; (*trees*) arbres *mpl*.
time [taɪm] *n* temps *m*; (*epoch: often pl*) époque *f*, temps; (*by clock*) heure *f*; (*moment*) moment *m*; (*occasion, also MATH*) fois *f*; (*MUS*) mesure *f* ♦ *vt* (*race*) chronométrer; (*programme*) minuter; (*remark etc*) choisir le moment de; **a long ~** un long moment, longtemps; **for the ~ being** pour le moment; **from ~ to ~** de temps en temps; **~ after ~, ~ and again** bien des fois; **in ~** (*soon enough*) à temps; (*after some time*) avec le temps, à la longue; (*MUS*) en mesure; **in a week's ~** dans une semaine; **in no ~** en un rien de temps; **on ~** à l'heure; **to be 30 minutes behind/ahead of ~** avoir 30 minutes de retard/d'avance; **by the ~ he arrived** quand il est arrivé, le temps qu'il arrive *sub*; **5 ~s 5** 5 fois 5; **what ~ is it?** quelle heure est-il?; **what ~ do you make it?** quelle heure avez-vous?; **to have a good ~** bien s'amuser; **we** (*or* **they** *etc*) **had a hard ~** ça a été difficile *or* pénible; **~'s up!** c'est l'heure!; **I've no ~ for it** (*fig*) cela m'agace; **he'll do it in his own (good) ~** (*without being hurried*) il le fera quand il en aura le temps; **he'll do it in** *or* (*US*) **on his own ~** (*out of working hours*) il le fera à ses heures perdues; **to be behind the ~s** retarder (sur son temps).
time-and-motion study ['taɪmənd'məuʃən-] *n* étude *f* des cadences.
time bomb *n* bombe *f* à retardement.
time clock *n* horloge pointeuse.
time-consuming ['taɪmkənsju:mɪŋ] *adj* qui prend beaucoup de temps.
time difference *n* décalage *m* horaire.
time frame *n* délais *mpl*.
time-honoured, (*US*) **time-honored** ['taɪmɔnəd] *adj* consacré(e).
timekeeper ['taɪmki:pə*] *n* (*SPORT*) chronomètre *m*.
time lag *n* (*BRIT*) décalage *m*; (*: in travel*) décalage horaire.
timeless ['taɪmlɪs] *adj* éternel(le).
time limit *n* limite *f* de temps, délai *m*.
timely ['taɪmlɪ] *adj* opportun(e).
time off *n* temps *m* libre.
timer ['taɪmə*] *n* (*in kitchen*) compte-minutes *m inv*; (*TECH*) minuteur *m*.
time-saving ['taɪmseɪvɪŋ] *adj* qui fait gagner du temps.
time scale *n* délais *mpl*.
time-sharing ['taɪmʃɛərɪŋ] *n* (*COMPUT*) temps partagé.
time sheet *n* feuille *f* de présence.
time signal *n* signal *m* horaire.
time switch *n* (*BRIT*) minuteur *m*; (*: for lighting*) minuterie *f*.
timetable ['taɪmteɪbl] *n* (*RAIL*) (indicateur *m*) horaire *m*; (*SCOL*) emploi *m* du temps; (*programme of events etc*) programme *m*.
time zone *n* fuseau *m* horaire.
timid ['tɪmɪd] *adj* timide; (*easily scared*) peureux(euse).
timidity [tɪ'mɪdɪtɪ] *n* timidité *f*.
timing ['taɪmɪŋ] *n* minutage *m*; chronométrage *m*; **the ~ of his resignation** le moment choisi pour sa démission.
timing device *n* (*on bomb*) mécanisme *m* de retardement.
timpani ['tɪmpənɪ] *npl* timbales *fpl*.
tin [tɪn] *n* étain *m*; (*also*: **~ plate**) fer-blanc *m*; (*BRIT*: *can*) boîte *f* (de conserve); (*: for baking*) moule *m* (à gâteau); **a ~ of paint** un pot de peinture.
tin foil *n* papier *m* d'étain.
tinge [tɪndʒ] *n* nuance *f* ♦ *vt*: **~d with** teinté(e) de.
tingle ['tɪŋgl] *n* picotement *m*; frisson *m* ♦ *vi* picoter.
tinker ['tɪŋkə*] *n* rétameur ambulant; (*gipsy*) romanichel *m*.

▸**tinker with** *vt fus* bricoler, rafistoler.
tinkle ['tɪŋkl] *vi* tinter ♦ *n* (*col*): **to give sb a ~** passer un coup de fil à qn.
tin mine *n* mine *f* d'étain.
tinned [tɪnd] *adj* (*BRIT*: *food*) en boîte, en conserve.
tinnitus ['tɪnɪtəs] *n* (*MED*) acouphène *m*.
tinny ['tɪnɪ] *adj* métallique.
tin opener [-'əupnə*] *n* (*BRIT*) ouvre-boîte(s) *m*.
tinsel ['tɪnsl] *n* guirlandes *fpl* de Noël (*argentées*).
tint [tɪnt] *n* teinte *f*; (*for hair*) shampooing colorant ♦ *vt* (*hair*) faire un shampooing colorant à.
tinted ['tɪntɪd] *adj* (*hair*) teint(e); (*spectacles, glass*) teinté(e).
tiny ['taɪnɪ] *adj* minuscule.
tip [tɪp] *n* (*end*) bout *m*; (*protective: on umbrella etc*) embout *m*; (*gratuity*) pourboire *m*; (*BRIT*: *for coal*) terril *m*; (*: for rubbish*) décharge *f*; (*advice*) tuyau *m* ♦ *vt* (*waiter*) donner un pourboire à; (*tilt*) incliner; (*overturn*: *also*: **~ over**) renverser; (*empty*: *also*: **~ out**) déverser; (*predict: winner etc*) pronostiquer; **he ~ped out the contents of the box** il a vidé le contenu de la boîte.
▸**tip off** *vt* prévenir, avertir.
tip-off ['tɪpɔf] *n* (*hint*) tuyau *m*.
tipped ['tɪpt] *adj* (*BRIT*: *cigarette*) (à bout) filtre *inv*; **steel-~** à bout métallique, à embout de métal.
Tipp-Ex ['tɪpɛks] *n* ® (*BRIT*) Tipp-Ex *m* ®.
tipple ['tɪpl] (*BRIT*) *vi* picoler ♦ *n*: **to have a ~** boire un petit coup.
tipster ['tɪpstə*] *n* (*RACING*) pronostiqueur *m*.
tipsy ['tɪpsɪ] *adj* un peu ivre, éméché(e).
tiptoe ['tɪptəu] *n*: **on ~** sur la pointe des pieds.
tiptop ['tɪptɔp] *adj*: **in ~ condition** en excellent état.
tirade [taɪ'reɪd] *n* diatribe *f*.
tire ['taɪə*] *n* (*US*) = **tyre** ♦ *vt* fatiguer ♦ *vi* se fatiguer.
▸**tire out** *vt* épuiser.
tired ['taɪəd] *adj* fatigué(e); **to be/feel/look ~** être/se sentir/avoir l'air fatigué; **to be ~ of** en avoir assez de, être las(lasse) de.
tiredness ['taɪədnɪs] *n* fatigue *f*.
tireless ['taɪəlɪs] *adj* infatigable, inlassable.
tiresome ['taɪsəm] *adj* ennuyeux(euse).
tiring ['taɪərɪŋ] *adj* fatigant(e).
tissue ['tɪʃuː] *n* tissu *m*; (*paper handkerchief*) mouchoir *m* en papier, kleenex *m* ®.
tissue paper *n* papier *m* de soie.
tit [tɪt] *n* (*bird*) mésange *f*; (*col*: *breast*) nichon *m*; **to give ~ for tat** rendre coup pour coup.
titanium [tɪ'teɪnɪəm] *n* titane *m*.
titbit ['tɪtbɪt] *n* (*food*) friandise *f*; (*before meal*) amuse-gueule *m inv*; (*news*) potin *m*.
titillate ['tɪtɪleɪt] *vt* titiller, exciter.
titivate ['tɪtɪveɪt] *vt* pomponner.
title ['taɪtl] *n* titre *m*; (*LAW*: *right*): **~ (to)** droit *m* (à).
title deed *n* (*LAW*) titre (constitutif) de propriété.
title page *n* page *f* de titre.
title role *n* rôle principal.
titter ['tɪtə*] *vi* rire (bêtement).
tittle-tattle ['tɪtltætl] *n* bavardages *mpl*.
titular ['tɪtjulə*] *adj* (*in name only*) nominal(e).
tizzy ['tɪzɪ] *n*: **to be in a ~** être dans tous ses états.
T-junction ['tiː'dʒʌŋkʃən] *n* croisement *m* en T.
TM *n abbr* = **trademark, transcendental meditation**.
TN *abbr* (*US*) = *Tennessee*.
TNT *n abbr* (= *trinitrotoluene*) TNT *m*.

KEYWORD

to [tuː, tə] *prep* **1** (*direction*) à; (*towards*) vers; envers; **to go ~ France/Portugal/London/school** aller en France/au Portugal/à Londres/à l'école; **to go ~ Claude's/the doctor's** aller chez Claude/le docteur; **the road ~ Edinburgh** la route d'Édimbourg
2 (*as far as*) (jusqu')à; **to count ~ 10** compter jusqu'à 10; **from 40 ~ 50 people** de 40 à 50 personnes
3 (*with expressions of time*): **a quarter ~ 5** 5 heures moins le quart; **it's twenty ~ 3** il est 3 heures moins vingt
4 (*for, of*) de; **the key ~ the front door** la clé de la porte d'entrée; **a letter ~ his wife** une lettre (adressée) à sa femme
5 (*expressing indirect object*) à; **to give sth ~ sb** donner qch à qn; **to talk ~ sb** parler à qn; **it belongs ~ him** cela lui appartient, c'est à lui
6 (*in relation to*) à; **3 goals ~ 2** 3 (buts) à 2; **30 miles ~ the gallon** ≈ 9,4 litres aux cent (km)
7 (*purpose, result*): **to come ~ sb's aid** venir au secours de qn, porter secours à qn; **to sentence sb ~ death** condamner qn à mort; **~ my surprise** à ma grande surprise
♦ *with vb* **1** (*simple infinitive*): **~ go/eat** aller/manger
2 (*following another vb*): **to want/try/start ~ do** vouloir/essayer de/commencer à faire
3 (*with vb omitted*): **I don't want ~** je ne veux pas
4 (*purpose, result*) pour; **I did it ~ help you** je l'ai fait pour vous aider
5 (*equivalent to relative clause*): **I have things ~ do** j'ai des choses à faire; **the main thing is ~ try** l'important est d'essayer
6 (*after adjective etc*): **ready ~ go** prêt(e) à partir; **too old/young ~ ...** trop vieux/jeune pour ...
♦ *adv*: **push/pull the door ~** tirez/poussez la porte; **to go ~ and fro** aller et venir.

toad [təud] *n* crapaud *m*.
toadstool ['təudstu:l] *n* champignon (vénéneux).
toady ['təudɪ] *vi* flatter bassement.
toast [təust] *n* (*CULIN*) pain grillé, toast *m*; (*drink, speech*) toast ♦ *vt* (*CULIN*) faire griller; (*drink to*) porter un toast à; **a piece** *or* **slice of** ~ un toast.
toaster ['təustə*] *n* grille-pain *m inv*.
toastmaster ['təustmɑ:stə*] *n* animateur *m* pour réceptions.
toast rack *n* porte-toast *m inv*.
tobacco [tə'bækəu] *n* tabac *m*; **pipe** ~ tabac à pipe.
tobacconist [tə'bækənɪst] *n* marchand/e de tabac; **~'s (shop)** (bureau *m* de) tabac *m*.
Tobago [tə'beɪgəu] *n see* **Trinidad and Tobago**.
toboggan [tə'bɔgən] *n* toboggan *m*; (*child's*) luge *f*.
today [tə'deɪ] *adv*, *n* (*also fig*) aujourd'hui *(m)*; **what day is it** ~? quel jour sommes-nous aujourd'hui?; **what date is it** ~? quelle est la date aujourd'hui?; ~ **is the 4th of March** aujourd'hui nous sommes le 4 mars; **a week ago** ~ il y a huit jours aujourd'hui.
toddler ['tɔdlə*] *n* enfant *m/f* qui commence à marcher, bambin *m*.
toddy ['tɔdɪ] *n* grog *m*.
to-do [tə'du:] *n* (*fuss*) histoire *f*, affaire *f*.
toe [təu] *n* doigt *m* de pied, orteil *m*; (*of shoe*) bout *m* ♦ *vt*: **to** ~ **the line** (*fig*) obéir, se conformer; **big** ~ gros orteil; **little** ~ petit orteil.
TOEFL *n abbr* = *Test(ing) of English as a Foreign Language*.
toehold ['təuhəuld] *n* prise *f*.
toenail ['təuneɪl] *n* ongle *m* de l'orteil.
toffee ['tɔfɪ] *n* caramel *m*.
toffee apple *n* (*BRIT*) pomme caramélisée.
tofu ['təufu:] *n* fromage *m* de soja.
toga ['təugə] *n* toge *f*.
together [tə'gɛðə*] *adv* ensemble; (*at same time*) en même temps; ~ **with** *prep* avec.
togetherness [tə'gɛðənɪs] *n* camaraderie *f*; intimité *f*.
toggle switch ['tɔgl-] *n* (*COMPUT*) interrupteur *m* à bascule.
Togo ['təugəu] *n* Togo *m*.
togs [tɔgz] *npl* (*col*: *clothes*) fringues *fpl*.
toil [tɔɪl] *n* dur travail, labeur *m* ♦ *vi* travailler dur; peiner.
toilet ['tɔɪlət] *n* (*BRIT*: *lavatory*) toilettes *fpl*, cabinets *mpl* ♦ *cpd* (*bag, soap etc*) de toilette; **to go to the** ~ aller aux toilettes.
toilet bag *n* (*BRIT*) nécessaire *m* de toilette.
toilet bowl *n* cuvette *f* des W.-C.
toilet paper *n* papier *m* hygiénique.
toiletries ['tɔɪlətrɪz] *npl* articles *mpl* de toilette.
toilet roll *n* rouleau *m* de papier hygiénique.
toilet water *n* eau *f* de toilette.
to-ing and fro-ing ['tu:ɪŋən'frəuɪŋ] *n* (*BRIT*) allées et venues *fpl*.
token ['təukən] *n* (*sign*) marque *f*, témoignage *m*; (*voucher*) bon *m*, coupon *m* ♦ *cpd* (*fee, strike*) symbolique; **by the same** ~ (*fig*) de même; **book/record** ~ (*BRIT*) chèque-livre/-disque *m*.
tokenism ['təukənɪzəm] *n* (*POL*): **it's just** ~ c'est une politique de pure forme.
Tokyo ['təukjəu] *n* Tokyo.
told [təuld] *pt, pp of* **tell**.
tolerable ['tɔlərəbl] *adj* (*bearable*) tolérable; (*fairly good*) passable.
tolerably ['tɔlərəblɪ] *adv*: ~ **good** tolérable.
tolerance ['tɔlərns] *n* (*also TECH*) tolérance *f*.
tolerant ['tɔlərnt] *adj*: ~ **(of)** tolérant(e) (à l'égard de).
tolerate ['tɔləreɪt] *vt* supporter; (*MED, TECH*) tolérer.
toleration [tɔlə'reɪʃən] *n* tolérance *f*.
toll [təul] *n* (*tax, charge*) péage *m* ♦ *vi* (*bell*) sonner; **the accident** ~ **on the roads** le nombre des victimes de la route.
tollbridge ['təulbrɪdʒ] *n* pont *m* à péage.
toll call *n* (*US TEL*) appel *m* (à) longue distance.
toll-free ['təul'fri:] *adj* (*US*) gratuit(e) ♦ *adv* gratuitement.
tomato, ~es [tə'mɑ:təu] *n* tomate *f*.
tomb [tu:m] *n* tombe *f*.
tombola [tɔm'bəulə] *n* tombola *f*.
tomboy ['tɔmbɔɪ] *n* garçon manqué.
tombstone ['tu:mstəun] *n* pierre tombale.
tomcat ['tɔmkæt] *n* matou *m*.
tomorrow [tə'mɔrəu] *adv*, *n* (*also fig*) demain *(m)*; **the day after** ~ après-demain; **a week** ~ demain en huit; ~ **morning** demain matin.
ton [tʌn] *n* tonne *f* (*Brit: = 1016 kg; US = 907 kg; metric = 1000 kg*); (*NAUT*: *also*: **register** ~) tonneau *m* (*= 2.83 cu.m*); **~s of** (*col*) des tas de.
tonal ['təunl] *adj* tonal(e).
tone [təun] *n* ton *m*; (*of radio, BRIT TEL*) tonalité *f* ♦ *vi* s'harmoniser.
▸**tone down** *vt* (*colour, criticism*) adoucir; (*sound*) baisser.
▸**tone up** *vt* (*muscles*) tonifier.
tone-deaf [təun'dɛf] *adj* qui n'a pas d'oreille.
toner ['təunə*] *n* (*for photocopier*) encre *f*.
Tonga [tɔŋə] *n* îles *fpl* Tonga.
tongs [tɔŋz] *npl* pinces *fpl*; (*for coal*) pincettes *fpl*; (*for hair*) fer *m* à friser.
tongue [tʌŋ] *n* langue *f*; ~ **in cheek** *adv* ironiquement.
tongue-tied ['tʌŋtaɪd] *adj* (*fig*) muet(te).
tongue-twister ['tʌŋtwɪstə*] *n* phrase *f* très difficile à prononcer.
tonic ['tɔnɪk] *n* (*MED*) tonique *m*; (*MUS*) tonique *f*; (*also*: ~ **water**) tonic *m*.
tonight [tə'naɪt] *adv*, *n* cette nuit; (*this evening*) ce soir; **(I'll) see you** ~! à ce soir!
tonnage ['tʌnɪdʒ] *n* (*NAUT*) tonnage *m*.
tonne [tʌn] *n* (*BRIT*: *metric ton*) tonne *f*.
tonsil ['tɔnsl] *n* amygdale *f*; **to have one's ~s**

out se faire opérer des amygdales.
tonsillitis [tɔnsɪ'laɪtɪs] *n* amygdalite *f*; **to have** ~ avoir une angine *or* une amygdalite.
too [tuː] *adv* (*excessively*) trop; (*also*) aussi; **it's** ~ **sweet** c'est trop sucré; **I went** ~ moi aussi, j'y suis allé; ~ **much** *adv* trop ♦ *adj* trop de; ~ **many** *adj* trop de; ~ **bad!** tant pis!
took [tuk] *pt of* **take**.
tool [tuːl] *n* outil *m*; (*fig*) instrument *m* ♦ *vt* travailler, ouvrager.
tool box *n* boîte *f* à outils.
tool kit *n* trousse *f* à outils.
toot [tuːt] *n* coup *m* de sifflet (*or* de klaxon) ♦ *vi* siffler; (*with car-horn*) klaxonner.
tooth, *pl* **teeth** [tuːθ, tiːθ] *n* (*ANAT, TECH*) dent *f*; **to have a** ~ **out** *or* (*US*) **pulled** se faire arracher une dent; **to brush one's teeth** se laver les dents; **by the skin of one's teeth** (*fig*) de justesse.
toothache ['tuːθeɪk] *n* mal *m* de dents; **to have** ~ avoir mal aux dents.
toothbrush ['tuːθbrʌʃ] *n* brosse *f* à dents.
toothpaste ['tuːθpeɪst] *n* (pâte *f*) dentifrice *m*.
toothpick ['tuːθpɪk] *n* cure-dent *m*.
tooth powder *n* poudre *f* dentifrice.
top [tɔp] *n* (*of mountain, head*) sommet *m*; (*of page, ladder*) haut *m*; (*of list, queue*) commencement *m*; (*of box, cupboard, table*) dessus *m*; (*lid: of box, jar*) couvercle *m*; (*: of bottle*) bouchon *m*; (*toy*) toupie *f*; (*DRESS*: *blouse etc*) haut; (*of pyjamas*) veste *f* ♦ *adj* du haut; (*in rank*) premier(ière); (*best*) meilleur(e) ♦ *vt* (*exceed*) dépasser; (*be first in*) être en tête de; **the** ~ **of the milk** (*BRIT*) la crème du lait; **at the** ~ **of the stairs/ page/street** en haut de l'escalier/de la page/de la rue; **on** ~ **of** sur; (*in addition to*) en plus de; **from** ~ **to toe** (*BRIT*) de la tête aux pieds; **at the** ~ **of the list** en tête de liste; **at the** ~ **of one's voice** à tue-tête; **at** ~ **speed** à toute vitesse; **over the** ~ (*col*: *behaviour etc*) qui dépasse les limites.
▸**top up**, (*US*) **top off** *vt* remplir.
topaz ['təupæz] *n* topaze *f*.
top-class ['tɔp'klɑːs] *adj* de première classe; (*SPORT*) de haute compétition.
topcoat ['tɔpkəut] *n* pardessus *m*.
topflight ['tɔpflaɪt] *adj* excellent(e).
top floor *n* dernier étage.
top hat *n* haut-de-forme *m*.
top-heavy [tɔp'hɛvɪ] *adj* (*object*) trop lourd(e) du haut.
topic ['tɔpɪk] *n* sujet *m*, thème *m*.
topical ['tɔpɪkl] *adj* d'actualité.
topless ['tɔplɪs] *adj* (*bather etc*) aux seins nus; ~ **swimsuit** monokini *m*.
top-level ['tɔplɛvl] *adj* (*talks*) à l'échelon le plus élevé.
topmost ['tɔpməust] *adj* le(la) plus haut(e).
top-notch ['tɔp'nɔtʃ] *adj* (*col*) de premier ordre.
topography [tə'pɔgrəfɪ] *n* topographie *f*.
topping ['tɔpɪŋ] *n* (*CULIN*) *couche de crème, fromage etc qui recouvre un plat*.
topple ['tɔpl] *vt* renverser, faire tomber ♦ *vi* basculer; tomber.
top-ranking ['tɔpræŋkɪŋ] *adj* très haut placé(e).
top-secret ['tɔp'siːkrɪt] *adj* ultra-secret(ète).
top-security ['tɔpsə'kjuərɪtɪ] *adj* (*BRIT*) de haute sécurité.
topsy-turvy ['tɔpsɪ'təːvɪ] *adj, adv* sens dessus-dessous.
top-up ['tɔpʌp] *n*: **would you like a** ~**?** je vous en remets *or* rajoute?
top-up loan *n* (*BRIT*) prêt *m* complémentaire.
torch [tɔːtʃ] *n* torche *f*; (*BRIT*: *electric*) lampe *f* de poche.
tore [tɔː*] *pt of* **tear**.
torment *n* ['tɔːmɛnt] tourment *m* ♦ *vt* [tɔː'mɛnt] tourmenter; (*fig: annoy*) agacer.
torn [tɔːn] *pp of* **tear** ♦ *adj*: ~ **between** (*fig*) tiraillé(e) entre.
tornado, ~**es** [tɔː'neɪdəu] *n* tornade *f*.
torpedo, ~**es** [tɔː'piːdəu] *n* torpille *f*.
torpedo boat *n* torpilleur *m*.
torpor ['tɔːpə*] *n* torpeur *f*.
torrent ['tɔrnt] *n* torrent *m*.
torrential [tɔ'rɛnʃl] *adj* torrentiel(le).
torrid ['tɔrɪd] *adj* torride; (*fig*) ardent(e).
torso ['tɔːsəu] *n* torse *m*.
tortoise ['tɔːtəs] *n* tortue *f*.
tortoiseshell ['tɔːtəʃɛl] *adj* en écaille.
tortuous ['tɔːtjuəs] *adj* tortueux(euse).
torture ['tɔːtʃə*] *n* torture *f* ♦ *vt* torturer.
torturer ['tɔːtʃərə*] *n* tortionnaire *m*.
Tory ['tɔːrɪ] *adj* (*BRIT POL*) tory (*pl* tories), conservateur(trice) ♦ *n* tory *m/f*, conservateur/trice.
toss [tɔs] *vt* lancer, jeter; (*BRIT*: *pancake*) faire sauter; (*head*) rejeter en arrière ♦ *vi*: **to** ~ **up for sth** (*BRIT*) jouer qch à pile ou face ♦ *n* (*movement: of head etc*) mouvement soudain; (*of coin*) tirage *m* à pile ou face; **to** ~ **a coin** jouer à pile ou face; **to** ~ **and turn** (*in bed*) se tourner et se retourner; **to win/lose the** ~ gagner/perdre à pile ou face; (*SPORT*) gagner/perdre le tirage au sort.
tot [tɔt] *n* (*BRIT*: *drink*) petit verre; (*child*) bambin *m*.
▸**tot up** *vt* (*BRIT*: *figures*) additionner.
total ['təutl] *adj* total(e) ♦ *n* total *m* ♦ *vt* (*add up*) faire le total de, totaliser; (*amount to*) s'élever à; **in** ~ au total.
totalitarian [təutælɪ'tɛərɪən] *adj* totalitaire.
totality [təu'tælɪtɪ] *n* totalité *f*.
totally ['təutəlɪ] *adv* totalement.
tote bag [təut-] *n* fourre-tout *m inv*.
totem pole ['təutəm-] *n* mât *m* totémique.
totter ['tɔtə*] *vi* chanceler; (*object, government*) être chancelant(e).
touch [tʌtʃ] *n* contact *m*, toucher *m*; (*sense, also skill: of pianist etc*) toucher; (*fig: note, also FOOTBALL*) touche *f* ♦ *vt* (*gen*) toucher; (*tamper with*) toucher à; **the personal** ~ la petite

note personnelle; **to put the finishing ~es to sth** mettre la dernière main à qch; **a ~ of** (*fig*) un petit peu de; une touche de; **in ~ with** en contact *or* rapport avec; **to get in ~ with** prendre contact avec; **I'll be in ~** je resterai en contact; **to lose ~** (*friends*) se perdre de vue; **to be out of ~ with events** ne pas être au courant de ce qui se passe.
▸**touch on** *vt fus* (*topic*) effleurer, toucher.
▸**touch up** *vt* (*paint*) retoucher.
touch-and-go ['tʌtʃən'gəu] *adj* incertain(e); **it was ~ whether we did it** nous avons failli ne pas le faire.
touchdown ['tʌtʃdaun] *n* atterrissage *m*; (*on sea*) amerrissage *m*; (*US FOOTBALL*) essai *m*.
touched [tʌtʃt] *adj* touché(e); (*col*) cinglé(e).
touching ['tʌtʃıŋ] *adj* touchant(e), attendrissant(e).
touchline ['tʌtʃlaın] *n* (*SPORT*) (ligne *f* de) touche *f*.
touch-sensitive ['tʌtʃsɛnsıtıv] *adj* (*keypad*) à effleurement; (*screen*) tactile.
touch-type ['tʌtʃtaıp] *vi* taper au toucher.
touchy ['tʌtʃı] *adj* (*person*) susceptible.
tough [tʌf] *adj* dur(e); (*resistant*) résistant(e), solide; (*meat*) dur, coriace; (*journey*) pénible; (*task, problem, situation*) difficile; (*rough*) dur ♦ *n* (*gangster etc*) dur *m*; **~ luck!** pas de chance!; tant pis!
toughen ['tʌfn] *vt* rendre plus dur(e) (*or* plus résistant(e) *or* plus solide).
toughness ['tʌfnıs] *n* dureté *f*; résistance *f*; solidité *f*.
toupee ['tu:peı] *n* postiche *m*.
tour ['tuə*] *n* voyage *m*; (*also*: **package ~**) voyage organisé; (*of town, museum*) tour *m*, visite *f*; (*by artist*) tournée *f* ♦ *vt* visiter; **to go on a ~ of** (*museum, region*) visiter; **to go on ~** partir en tournée.
touring ['tuərıŋ] *n* voyages *mpl* touristiques, tourisme *m*.
tourism ['tuərızm] *n* tourisme *m*.
tourist ['tuərıst] *n* touriste *m/f* ♦ *adv* (*travel*) en classe touriste ♦ *cpd* touristique; **the ~ trade** le tourisme.
tourist class *n* (*AVIAT*) classe *f* touriste.
tourist office *n* syndicat *m* d'initiative.
tournament ['tuənəmənt] *n* tournoi *m*.
tourniquet ['tuənıkeı] *n* (*MED*) garrot *m*.
tour operator *n* (*BRIT*) organisateur *m* de voyages, tour-opérateur *m*.
tousled ['tauzld] *adj* (*hair*) ébouriffé(e).
tout [taut] *vi*: **to ~ for** essayer de raccrocher, racoler; **to ~ sth (around)** (*BRIT*) essayer de placer *or* (re)vendre qch ♦ *n* (*BRIT*: *ticket ~*) revendeur *m* de billets.
tow [təu] *n*: **to give sb a ~** (*AUT*) remorquer qn ♦ *vt* remorquer; **"on ~"**, (*US*) **"in ~"** (*AUT*) "véhicule en remorque".
toward(s) [tə'wɔ:d(z)] *prep* vers; (*of attitude*) envers, à l'égard de; (*of purpose*) pour; **~ noon/the end of the year** vers midi/la fin de l'année; **to feel friendly ~ sb** être bien disposé envers qn.
towel ['tauəl] *n* serviette *f* (de toilette); (*also*: **tea ~**) torchon *m*; **to throw in the ~** (*fig*) jeter l'éponge.
towelling ['tauəlıŋ] *n* (*fabric*) tissu-éponge *m*.
towel rail, (*US*) **towel rack** *n* porte-serviettes *m inv*.
tower ['tauə*] *n* tour *f* ♦ *vi* (*building, mountain*) se dresser (majestueusement); **to ~ above** *or* **over sb/sth** dominer qn/qch.
tower block *n* (*BRIT*) tour *f* (d'habitation).
towering ['tauərıŋ] *adj* très haut(e), imposant(e).
towline ['təulaın] *n* (câble *m* de) remorque *f*.
town [taun] *n* ville *f*; **to go to ~** aller en ville; (*fig*) y mettre le paquet; **in the ~** dans la ville, en ville; **to be out of ~** (*person*) être en déplacement.
town centre *n* centre *m* de la ville, centre-ville *m*.
town clerk *n* ≈ secrétaire *m/f* de mairie.
town council *n* conseil municipal.
town crier [-'kraıə*] *n* (*BRIT*) crieur public.
town hall *n* ≈ mairie *f*.
townie ['taunı] *n* (*BRIT col*) citadin/e.
town plan *n* plan *m* de ville.
town planner *n* urbaniste *m/f*.
town planning *n* urbanisme *m*.
township ['taunʃıp] *n* banlieue noire (*établie sous le régime de l'apartheid*).
townspeople ['taunzpi:pl] *npl* citadins *mpl*.
towpath ['təupɑ:θ] *n* (chemin *m* de) halage *m*.
towrope ['təurəup] *n* (câble *m* de) remorque *f*.
tow truck *n* (*US*) dépanneuse *f*.
toxic ['tɔksık] *adj* toxique.
toxin ['tɔksın] *n* toxine *f*.
toy [tɔı] *n* jouet *m*.
▸**toy with** *vt fus* jouer avec; (*idea*) caresser.
toyshop ['tɔıʃɔp] *m* magasin *m* de jouets.
trace [treıs] *n* trace *f* ♦ *vt* (*draw*) tracer, dessiner; (*follow*) suivre la trace de; (*locate*) retrouver; **without ~** (*disappear*) sans laisser de traces; **there was no ~ of it** il n'y en avait pas trace.
trace element *n* oligo-élément *m*.
trachea [trə'kıə] *n* (*ANAT*) trachée *f*.
tracing paper ['treısıŋ-] *n* papier-calque *m*.
track [træk] *n* (*mark*) trace *f*; (*path: gen*) chemin *m*, piste *f*; (*: of bullet etc*) trajectoire *f*; (*: of suspect, animal*) piste; (*RAIL*) voie ferrée, rails *mpl*; (*on tape, COMPUT, SPORT*) piste; (*on record*) plage *f* ♦ *vt* suivre la trace *or* la piste de; **to keep ~ of** suivre; **to be on the right ~** (*fig*) être sur la bonne voie.
▸**track down** *vt* (*prey*) trouver et capturer; (*sth lost*) finir par retrouver.
tracked [trækt] *adj* (*AUT*) à chenille.
tracker dog ['trækə-] *n* (*BRIT*) *chien dressé pour suivre une piste*.
track events *npl* (*SPORT*) épreuves *fpl* sur piste.

tracking station ['trækɪŋ-] *n* (*SPACE*) centre *m* d'observation de satellites.
track meet *n* (*US*) réunion sportive sur piste.
track record *n*: **to have a good** ~ (*fig*) avoir fait ses preuves.
track suit *n* survêtement *m*.
tract [trækt] *n* (*GEO*) étendue *f*, zone *f*; (*pamphlet*) tract *m*; **respiratory** ~ (*ANAT*) système *m* respiratoire.
traction ['trækʃən] *n* traction *f*.
tractor ['træktə*] *n* tracteur *m*.
trade [treɪd] *n* commerce *m*; (*skill, job*) métier *m* ♦ *vi* faire du commerce; **to** ~ **with/in** faire du commerce avec/le commerce de; **foreign** ~ commerce extérieur; **Department of T~ and Industry (DTI)** (*BRIT*) ministère *m* du Commerce et de l'Industrie.
►**trade in** *vt* (*old car etc*) faire reprendre.
trade barrier *n* barrière commerciale.
trade deficit *n* déficit extérieur.
Trade Descriptions Act *n* (*BRIT*) *loi contre les appellations et la publicité mensongères*.
trade discount *n* remise *f* au détaillant.
trade fair *n* foire(-exposition) commerciale.
trade-in ['treɪdɪn] *n* reprise *f*.
trade-in price *n* prix *m* à la reprise.
trademark ['treɪdmɑːk] *n* marque *f* de fabrique.
trade mission *n* mission commerciale.
trade name *n* marque déposée.
trade-off ['treɪdɔf] *n* (*exchange*) échange *f*; (*balancing*) équilibre *m*.
trader ['treɪdə*] *n* commerçant/e, négociant/e.
trade secret *n* secret *m* de fabrication.
tradesman ['treɪdzmən] *n* (*shopkeeper*) commerçant *m*; (*skilled worker*) ouvrier qualifié.
trade union *n* syndicat *m*.
trade unionist [-'juːnjənɪst] *n* syndicaliste *m/f*.
trade wind *n* alizé *m*.
trading ['treɪdɪŋ] *n* affaires *fpl*, commerce *m*.
trading estate *n* (*BRIT*) zone industrielle.
trading stamp *n* timbre-prime *m*.
tradition [trə'dɪʃən] *n* tradition *f*; **~s** *npl* coutumes *fpl*, traditions.
traditional [trə'dɪʃənl] *adj* traditionnel(le).
traffic ['træfɪk] *n* trafic *m*; (*cars*) circulation *f* ♦ *vi*: **to** ~ **in** (*pej*: *liquor, drugs*) faire le trafic de.
traffic calming [-'kɑːmɪŋ] *n* ralentissement *m* de la circulation.
traffic circle *n* (*US*) rond-point *m*.
traffic island *n* refuge *m* (pour piétons).
traffic jam *n* embouteillage *m*.
trafficker ['træfɪkə*] *n* trafiquant/e.
traffic lights *npl* feux *mpl* (de signalisation).
traffic offence *n* (*BRIT*) infraction *f* au code de la route.
traffic sign *n* panneau *m* de signalisation.
traffic violation *n* (*US*) = **traffic offence**.
traffic warden *n* contractuel/le.
tragedy ['trædʒədɪ] *n* tragédie *f*.
tragic ['trædʒɪk] *adj* tragique.
trail [treɪl] *n* (*tracks*) trace *f*, piste *f*; (*path*) chemin *m*, piste; (*of smoke etc*) traînée *f* ♦ *vt* traîner, tirer; (*follow*) suivre ♦ *vi* traîner; **to be on sb's** ~ être sur la piste de qn.
►**trail away, trail off** *vi* (*sound, voice*) s'évanouir; (*interest*) disparaître.
►**trail behind** *vi* traîner, être à la traîne.
trailer ['treɪlə*] *n* (*AUT*) remorque *f*; (*US*) caravane *f*; (*CINE*) bande-annonce *f*.
trailer truck *n* (*US*) (camion *m*) semi-remorque *m*.
train [treɪn] *n* train *m*; (*in underground*) rame *f*; (*of dress*) traîne *f*; (*BRIT*: *series*): ~ **of events** série *f* d'événements ♦ *vt* (*apprentice, doctor etc*) former; (*sportsman*) entraîner; (*dog*) dresser; (*memory*) exercer; (*point: gun etc*): **to** ~ **sth on** braquer qch sur ♦ *vi* recevoir sa formation; s'entraîner; **one's** ~ **of thought** le fil de sa pensée; **to go by** ~ voyager par le train *or* en train; **to** ~ **sb to do sth** apprendre à qn à faire qch; (*employee*) former qn à faire qch.
train attendant *n* (*US*) employé/e des wagons-lits.
trained [treɪnd] *adj* qualifié(e), qui a reçu une formation; dressé(e).
trainee [treɪ'niː] *n* stagiaire *m/f*; (*in trade*) apprenti/e.
trainer ['treɪnə*] *n* (*SPORT*) entraîneur/euse; (*of dogs etc*) dresseur/euse; **~s** *npl* (*shoes*) chaussures *fpl* de sport.
training ['treɪnɪŋ] *n* formation *f*; entraînement *m*; dressage *m*; **in** ~ (*SPORT*) à l'entraînement; (*fit*) en forme.
training college *n* école professionnelle; (*for teachers*) ≈ école normale.
training course *n* cours *m* de formation professionnelle.
traipse [treɪps] *vi* (se) traîner, déambuler.
trait [treɪt] *n* trait *m* (de caractère).
traitor ['treɪtə*] *n* traître *m*.
trajectory [trə'dʒɛktərɪ] *n* trajectoire *f*.
tram [træm] *n* (*BRIT*: *also*: **~car**) tram(way) *m*.
tramline ['træmlaɪn] *n* ligne *f* de tram(way).
tramp [træmp] *n* (*person*) vagabond/e, clochard/e; (*col*: *pej*: *woman*): **to be a** ~ être coureuse ♦ *vi* marcher d'un pas lourd ♦ *vt* (*walk through: town, streets*) parcourir à pied.
trample ['træmpl] *vt*: **to** ~ **(underfoot)** piétiner; (*fig*) bafouer.
trampoline ['træmpəliːn] *n* trampolino *m*.
trance [trɑːns] *n* transe *f*; (*MED*) catalepsie *f*; **to go into a** ~ entrer en transe.
tranquil ['træŋkwɪl] *adj* tranquille.
tranquillity [træŋ'kwɪlɪtɪ] *n* tranquillité *f*.
tranquillizer ['træŋkwɪlaɪzə*] *n* (*MED*) tranquillisant *m*.
transact [træn'zækt] *vt* (*business*) traiter.
transaction [træn'zækʃən] *n* transaction *f*; **~s** *npl* (*minutes*) actes *mpl*; **cash** ~ transaction au comptant.

transatlantic ['trænzət'læntık] *adj* transatlantique.
transcend [træn'sɛnd] *vt* transcender; (*excel over*) surpasser.
transcendental [trænsɛn'dɛntl] *adj*: ~ **meditation** méditation transcendantale.
transcribe [træn'skraıb] *vt* transcrire.
transcript ['trænskrıpt] *n* transcription *f* (*texte*).
transcription [træn'skrıpʃən] *n* transcription *f*.
transept ['trænsɛpt] *n* transept *m*.
transfer *n* ['trænsfə*] (*gen, also SPORT*) transfert *m*; (*POL: of power*) passation *f*; (*of money*) virement *m*; (*picture, design*) décalcomanie *f*; (*: stick-on*) autocollant *m* ♦ *vt* [træns'fə:*] transférer; passer; virer; décalquer; **to ~ the charges** (*BRIT TEL*) téléphoner en P.C.V.; **by bank ~** par virement bancaire.
transferable [træns'fə:rəbl] *adj* transmissible, transférable; **"not ~"** "personnel".
transfix [træns'fıks] *vt* transpercer; (*fig*): **~ed with fear** paralysé(e) par la peur.
transform [træns'fɔ:m] *vt* transformer.
transformation [trænsfə'meıʃən] *n* transformation *f*.
transformer [træns'fɔ:mə*] *n* (*ELEC*) transformateur *m*.
transfusion [træns'fju:ʒən] *n* transfusion *f*.
transgress [træns'grɛs] *vt* transgresser.
transient ['trænzıənt] *adj* transitoire, éphémère.
transistor [træn'zıstə*] *n* (*ELEC; also*: **~ radio**) transistor *m*.
transit ['trænzıt] *n*: **in ~** en transit.
transit camp *n* camp *m* de transit.
transition [træn'zıʃən] *n* transition *f*.
transitional [træn'zıʃənl] *adj* transitoire.
transitive ['trænzıtıv] *adj* (*LING*) transitif(ive).
transit lounge *n* (*AVIAT*) salle *f* de transit.
transitory ['trænzıtərı] *adj* transitoire.
translate [trænz'leıt] *vt*: **to ~ (from/into)** traduire (du/en).
translation [trænz'leıʃən] *n* traduction *f*; (*SCOL: as opposed to prose*) version *f*.
translator [trænz'leıtə*] *n* traducteur/trice.
translucent [trænz'lu:snt] *adj* translucide.
transmission [trænz'mıʃən] *n* transmission *f*.
transmit [trænz'mıt] *vt* transmettre; (*RADIO, TV*) émettre.
transmitter [trænz'mitə*] *n* émetteur *m*.
transparency [træns'pɛərnsı] *n* (*BRIT PHOT*) diapositive *f*.
transparent [træns'pærnt] *adj* transparent(e).
transpire [træns'paıə*] *vi* (*become known*): **it finally ~d that ...** on a finalement appris que ...; (*happen*) arriver.
transplant *vt* [træns'plɑ:nt] transplanter; (*seedlings*) repiquer ♦ *n* ['trænsplɑ:nt] (*MED*) transplantation *f*; **to have a heart ~** subir une greffe du cœur.
transport *n* ['trænspɔ:t] transport *m* ♦ *vt* [træns'pɔ:t] transporter; **public ~** transports en commun; **Department of T~** (*BRIT*) ministère *m* des Transports.
transportation [trænspɔ:'teıʃən] *n* (moyen *m* de) transport *m*; (*of prisoners*) transportation *f*; **Department of T~** (*US*) ministère *m* des Transports.
transport café *n* (*BRIT*) ≈ routier *m*.
transpose [træns'pəuz] *vt* transposer.
transsexual [trænz'sɛksjuəl] *adj, n* transsexuel(le).
transverse ['trænzvə:s] *adj* transversal(e).
transvestite [trænz'vɛstaıt] *n* travesti/e.
trap [træp] *n* (*snare, trick*) piège *m*; (*carriage*) cabriolet *m* ♦ *vt* prendre au piège; (*immobilize*) bloquer; (*jam*) coincer; **to set** *or* **lay a ~ (for sb)** tendre un piège (à qn); **to shut one's ~** (*col*) la fermer.
trap door *n* trappe *f*.
trapeze [trə'pi:z] *n* trapèze *m*.
trapper ['træpə*] *n* trappeur *m*.
trappings ['træpıŋz] *npl* ornements *mpl*; attributs *mpl*.
trash [træʃ] *n* (*pej: goods*) camelote *f*; (*: nonsense*) sottises *fpl*; (*US: rubbish*) ordures *fpl*.
trash can *n* (*US*) boîte *f* à ordures.
trashy ['træʃı] *adj* (*col*) de camelote, qui ne vaut rien.
trauma ['trɔ:mə] *n* traumatisme *m*.
traumatic [trɔ:'mætık] *adj* traumatisant(e).
travel ['trævl] *n* voyage(s) *m(pl)* ♦ *vi* voyager; (*move*) aller, se déplacer ♦ *vt* (*distance*) parcourir; **this wine doesn't ~ well** ce vin voyage mal.
travel agency *n* agence *f* de voyages.
travel agent *n* agent *m* de voyages.
travel brochure *n* brochure *f* touristique.
traveller, (*US*) **traveler** ['trævlə*] *n* voyageur/euse; (*COMM*) représentant *m* de commerce.
traveller's cheque, (*US*) **traveler's check** *n* chèque *m* de voyage.
travelling, (*US*) **traveling** ['trævlıŋ] *n* voyage(s) *m(pl)* ♦ *adj* (*circus, exhibition*) ambulant(e) ♦ *cpd* (*bag, clock*) de voyage; (*expenses*) de déplacement.
travel(l)ing salesman *n* voyageur *m* de commerce.
travelogue ['trævəlɔg] *n* (*book, talk*) récit *m* de voyage; (*film*) documentaire *m* de voyage.
travel sickness *n* mal *m* de la route (*or* de mer *or* de l'air).
traverse ['trævəs] *vt* traverser.
travesty ['trævəstı] *n* parodie *f*.
trawler ['trɔ:lə*] *n* chalutier *m*.
tray [treı] *n* (*for carrying*) plateau *m*; (*on desk*) corbeille *f*.
treacherous ['trɛtʃərəs] *adj* traître(sse); **road conditions are ~** l'état des routes est dangereux.
treachery ['trɛtʃərı] *n* traîtrise *f*.
treacle ['tri:kl] *n* mélasse *f*.

tread [trɛd] *n* pas *m*; (*sound*) bruit *m* de pas; (*of tyre*) chape *f*, bande *f* de roulement ♦ *vi* (*pt* **trod**, *pp* **trodden** [trɔd, 'trɔdn]) marcher.
▸**tread on** *vt fus* marcher sur.
treadle ['trɛdl] *n* pédale *f* (*de machine*).
treas. *abbr* = **treasurer**.
treason ['tri:zn] *n* trahison *f*.
treasure ['trɛʒə*] *n* trésor *m* ♦ *vt* (*value*) tenir beaucoup à; (*store*) conserver précieusement.
treasure hunt *n* chasse *f* au trésor.
treasurer ['trɛʒərə*] *n* trésorier/ière.
treasury ['trɛʒərɪ] *n* trésorerie *f*; **the T~**, (*US*) **the T~ Department** ≈ le ministère des Finances.
treasury bill *n* bon *m* du Trésor.
treat [tri:t] *n* petit cadeau, petite surprise ♦ *vt* traiter; **it was a ~** ça m'a (*or* nous a *etc*) vraiment fait plaisir; **to ~ sb to sth** offrir qch à qn; **to ~ sth as a joke** prendre qch à la plaisanterie.
treatise ['tri:tɪz] *n* traité *m* (*ouvrage*).
treatment ['tri:tmənt] *n* traitement *m*; **to have ~ for sth** (*MED*) suivre un traitement pour qch.
treaty ['tri:tɪ] *n* traité *m*.
treble ['trɛbl] *adj* triple ♦ *n* (*MUS*) soprano *m* ♦ *vt, vi* tripler.
treble clef *n* clé *f* de sol.
tree [tri:] *n* arbre *m*.
tree-lined ['tri:laɪnd] *adj* bordé(e) d'arbres.
treetop ['tri:tɔp] *n* cime *f* d'un arbre.
tree trunk *n* tronc *m* d'arbre.
trek [trɛk] *n* voyage *m*; randonnée *f*; (*tiring walk*) tirée *f* ♦ *vi* (*as holiday*) faire de la randonnée.
trellis ['trɛlɪs] *n* treillis *m*, treillage *m*.
tremble ['trɛmbl] *vi* trembler.
trembling ['trɛmblɪŋ] *n* tremblement *m* ♦ *adj* tremblant(e).
tremendous [trɪ'mɛndəs] *adj* énorme, formidable; (*excellent*) fantastique, formidable.
tremendously [trɪ'mɛndəslɪ] *adv* énormément, extrêmement + *adjective*; formidablement.
tremor ['trɛmə*] *n* tremblement *m*; (*also*: **earth ~**) secousse *f* sismique.
trench [trɛntʃ] *n* tranchée *f*.
trench coat *n* trench-coat *m*.
trench warfare *n* guerre *f* de tranchées.
trend [trɛnd] *n* (*tendency*) tendance *f*; (*of events*) cours *m*; (*fashion*) mode *f*; **~ towards/away from doing** tendance à faire/à ne pas faire; **to set the ~** donner le ton; **to set a ~** lancer une mode.
trendy ['trɛndɪ] *adj* (*idea*) dans le vent; (*clothes*) dernier cri *inv*.
trepidation [trɛpɪ'deɪʃən] *n* vive agitation.
trespass ['trɛspəs] *vi*: **to ~ on** s'introduire sans permission dans; (*fig*) empiéter sur; **"no ~ing"** "propriété privée", "défense d'entrer".
trespasser ['trɛspəsə*] *n* intrus/e; **"~s will be prosecuted"** "interdiction d'entrer sous peine de poursuites".
tress [trɛs] *n* boucle *f* de cheveux.
trestle ['trɛsl] *n* tréteau *m*.
trestle table *n* table *f* à tréteaux.
trial ['traɪəl] *n* (*LAW*) procès *m*, jugement *m*; (*test: of machine etc*) essai *m*; (*hardship*) épreuve *f*; (*worry*) souci *m*; **~s** *npl* (*SPORT*) épreuves éliminatoires; **horse ~s** concours *m* hippique; **~ by jury** jugement par jury; **to be sent for ~** être traduit(e) en justice; **to be on ~** passer en jugement; **by ~ and error** par tâtonnements.
trial balance *n* (*COMM*) balance *f* de vérification.
trial basis *n*: **on a ~** pour une période d'essai.
trial run *n* essai *m*.
triangle ['traɪæŋgl] *n* (*MATH, MUS*) triangle *m*.
triangular [traɪ'æŋgjulə*] *adj* triangulaire.
triathlon [traɪ'æθlən] *n* triathlon *m*.
tribal ['traɪbl] *adj* tribal(e).
tribe [traɪb] *n* tribu *f*.
tribesman ['traɪbzmən] *n* membre *m* de la tribu.
tribulation [trɪbju'leɪʃən] *n* tribulation *f*, malheur *m*.
tribunal [traɪ'bju:nl] *n* tribunal *m*.
tributary ['trɪbjutərɪ] *n* (*river*) affluent *m*.
tribute ['trɪbju:t] *n* tribut *m*, hommage *m*; **to pay ~ to** rendre hommage à.
trice [traɪs] *n*: **in a ~** en un clin d'œil.
trick [trɪk] *n* ruse *f*; (*clever act*) astuce *f*; (*joke*) tour *m*; (*CARDS*) levée *f* ♦ *vt* attraper, rouler; **to play a ~ on sb** jouer un tour à qn; **to ~ sb into doing sth** persuader qn par la ruse de faire qch; **to ~ sb out of sth** obtenir qch de qn par la ruse; **it's a ~ of the light** c'est une illusion d'optique causée par la lumière; **that should do the ~** (*col*) ça devrait faire l'affaire.
trickery ['trɪkərɪ] *n* ruse *f*.
trickle ['trɪkl] *n* (*of water etc*) filet *m* ♦ *vi* couler en un filet *or* goutte à goutte; **to ~ in/out** (*people*) entrer/sortir par petits groupes.
trick question *n* question-piège *f*.
trickster ['trɪkstə*] *n* arnaqueur/euse, filou *m*.
tricky ['trɪkɪ] *adj* difficile, délicat(e).
tricycle ['traɪsɪkl] *n* tricycle *m*.
trifle ['traɪfl] *n* bagatelle *f*; (*CULIN*) ≈ diplomate *m* ♦ *adv*: **a ~ long** un peu long ♦ *vi*: **to ~ with** traiter à la légère.
trifling ['traɪflɪŋ] *adj* insignifiant(e).
trigger ['trɪgə*] *n* (*of gun*) gâchette *f*.
▸**trigger off** *vt* déclencher.
trigonometry [trɪgə'nɔmətrɪ] *n* trigonométrie *f*.
trilby ['trɪlbɪ] *n* (*BRIT*: *also*: **~ hat**) chapeau mou, feutre *m*.
trill [trɪl] *n* (*of bird, MUS*) trille *m*.
trilogy ['trɪlədʒɪ] *n* trilogie *f*.
trim [trɪm] *adj* net(te); (*house, garden*) bien

tenu(e); (*figure*) svelte ♦ *n* (*haircut etc*) légère coupe; (*embellishment*) finitions *fpl*; (*on car*) garnitures *fpl* ♦ *vt* couper légèrement; (*decorate*): **to ~ (with)** décorer (de); (*NAUT*: *a sail*) gréer; **to keep in (good) ~** maintenir en (bon) état.
trimmings ['trɪmɪŋz] *npl* décorations *fpl*; (*extras*: *gen CULIN*) garniture *f*.
Trinidad and Tobago ['trɪnɪdæd-] *n* Trinité et Tobago *f*.
Trinity ['trɪnɪtɪ] *n*: **the ~** la Trinité.
trinket ['trɪŋkɪt] *n* bibelot *m*; (*piece of jewellery*) colifichet *m*.
trio ['triːəu] *n* trio *m*.
trip [trɪp] *n* voyage *m*; (*excursion*) excursion *f*; (*stumble*) faux pas ♦ *vi* faire un faux pas, trébucher; (*go lightly*) marcher d'un pas léger; **on a ~** en voyage.
►**trip up** *vi* trébucher ♦ *vt* faire un croc-en-jambe à.
tripartite [traɪ'pɑːtaɪt] *adj* triparti(e).
tripe [traɪp] *n* (*CULIN*) tripes *fpl*; (*pej*: *rubbish*) idioties *fpl*.
triple ['trɪpl] *adj* triple ♦ *adv*: **~ the distance/the speed** trois fois la distance/la vitesse.
triple jump *n* triple saut *m*.
triplets ['trɪplɪts] *npl* triplés/ées.
triplicate ['trɪplɪkət] *n*: **in ~** en trois exemplaires.
tripod ['traɪpɔd] *n* trépied *m*.
Tripoli ['trɪpəlɪ] *n* Tripoli.
tripper ['trɪpə*] *n* (*BRIT*) touriste *m/f*; excursionniste *m/f*.
tripwire ['trɪpwaɪə*] *n* fil *m* de déclenchement.
trite [traɪt] *adj* banal(e).
triumph ['traɪʌmf] *n* triomphe *m* ♦ *vi*: **to ~ (over)** triompher (de).
triumphal [traɪ'ʌmfl] *adj* triomphal(e).
triumphant [traɪ'ʌmfənt] *adj* triomphant(e).
trivia ['trɪvɪə] *npl* futilités *fpl*.
trivial ['trɪvɪəl] *adj* insignifiant(e); (*commonplace*) banal(e).
triviality [trɪvɪ'ælɪtɪ] *n* caractère insignifiant; banalité *f*.
trivialize ['trɪvɪəlaɪz] *vt* rendre banal(e).
trod [trɔd] *pt of* **tread**.
trodden [trɔdn] *pp of* **tread**.
trolley ['trɔlɪ] *n* chariot *m*.
trolley bus *n* trolleybus *m*.
trollop ['trɔləp] *n* prostituée *f*.
trombone [trɔm'bəun] *n* trombone *m*.
troop [truːp] *n* bande *f*, groupe *m* ♦ *vi*: **to ~ in/out** entrer/sortir en groupe; **~ing the colour** (*BRIT*: *ceremony*) le salut au drapeau.
troop carrier *n* (*plane*) avion *m* de transport de troupes; (*NAUT*: *also*: **troopship**) transport *m* (*navire*).
trooper ['truːpə*] *n* (*MIL*) soldat *m* de cavalerie; (*US*: *policeman*) ≈ gendarme *m*.
troops [truːps] *npl* (*MIL*) troupes *fpl*; (*: men*) hommes *mpl*, soldats *mpl*.
troopship ['truːpʃɪp] *n* transport *m* (*navire*).
trophy ['trəufɪ] *n* trophée *m*.
tropic ['trɔpɪk] *n* tropique *m*; **in the ~s** sous les tropiques; **T~ of Cancer/Capricorn** tropique du Cancer/Capricorne.
tropical ['trɔpɪkl] *adj* tropical(e).
trot [trɔt] *n* trot *m* ♦ *vi* trotter; **on the ~** (*BRIT*: *fig*) d'affilée.
►**trot out** *vt* (*excuse, reason*) débiter; (*names, facts*) réciter les uns après les autres.
trouble ['trʌbl] *n* difficulté(s) *f(pl)*, problème(s) *m(pl)*; (*worry*) ennuis *mpl*, soucis *mpl*; (*bother, effort*) peine *f*; (*POL*) conflit(s) *m(pl)*, troubles *mpl*; (*MED*): **stomach** *etc* **~** troubles gastriques *etc* ♦ *vt* déranger, gêner; (*worry*) inquiéter ♦ *vi*: **to ~ to do** prendre la peine de faire; **~s** *npl* (*POL etc*) troubles; **to be in ~** avoir des ennuis; (*ship, climber etc*) être en difficulté; **to have ~ doing sth** avoir du mal à faire qch; **to go to the ~ of doing** se donner le mal de faire; **it's no ~!** je vous en prie!; **please don't ~ yourself** je vous en prie, ne vous dérangez pas!; **the ~ is ...** le problème, c'est que ...; **what's the ~?** qu'est-ce qui ne va pas?
troubled [trʌbld] *adj* (*person*) inquiet(ète); (*epoch, life*) agité(e).
trouble-free ['trʌblfriː] *adj* sans problèmes *or* ennuis.
troublemaker ['trʌblmeɪkə*] *n* élément perturbateur, fauteur *m* de troubles.
troubleshooter ['trʌblʃuːtə*] *n* (*in conflict*) conciliateur *m*.
troublesome ['trʌblsəm] *adj* ennuyeux(euse), gênant(e).
trouble spot *n* point chaud (*fig*).
troubling ['trʌblɪŋ] *adj* (*times, thought*) inquiétant(e).
trough [trɔf] *n* (*also*: **drinking ~**) abreuvoir *m*; (*also*: **feeding ~**) auge *f*; (*channel*) chenal *m*; **~ of low pressure** (*METEOROLOGY*) dépression *f*.
trounce [trauns] *vt* (*defeat*) battre à plates coutures.
troupe [truːp] *n* troupe *f*.
trouser press *n* presse-pantalon *m inv*.
trousers ['trauzəz] *npl* pantalon *m*; **short ~** (*BRIT*) culottes courtes.
trouser suit *n* (*BRIT*) tailleur-pantalon *m*.
trousseau, *pl* **~x** *or* **~s** ['truːsəu, -z] *n* trousseau *m*.
trout [traut] *n* (*pl inv*) truite *f*.
trowel ['trauəl] *n* truelle *f*.
truant ['truənt] *n*: **to play ~** (*BRIT*) faire l'école buissonnière.
truce [truːs] *n* trêve *f*.
truck [trʌk] *n* camion *m*; (*RAIL*) wagon *m* à plate-forme; (*for luggage*) chariot *m* (à bagages).
truck driver *n* camionneur *m*.
trucker ['trʌkə*] *n* (*esp US*) camionneur *m*.
truck farm *n* (*US*) jardin maraîcher.
trucking ['trʌkɪŋ] *n* (*esp US*) transport routier.

trucking company *n* (*US*) entreprise *f* de transport (routier).
truck stop (*US*) routier *m*, restaurant *m* de routiers.
truculent ['trʌkjulənt] *adj* agressif(ive).
trudge [trʌdʒ] *vi* marcher lourdement, se traîner.
true [tru:] *adj* vrai(e); (*accurate*) exact(e); (*genuine*) vrai, véritable; (*faithful*) fidèle; (*wall*) d'aplomb; (*beam*) droit(e); (*wheel*) dans l'axe; **to come** ~ se réaliser; ~ **to life** réaliste.
truffle ['trʌfl] *n* truffe *f*.
truly ['tru:lɪ] *adv* vraiment, réellement; (*truthfully*) sans mentir; (*faithfully*) fidèlement; **yours** ~ (*in letter*) je vous prie d'agréer, Monsieur (*or* Madame *etc*), l'expression de mes sentiments respectueux.
trump [trʌmp] *n* atout *m*; **to turn up ~s** (*fig*) faire des miracles.
trump card *n* atout *m*; (*fig*) carte maîtresse *f*.
trumped-up [trʌmpt'ʌp] *adj* inventé(e) (de toutes pièces).
trumpet ['trʌmpɪt] *n* trompette *f*.
truncated [trʌŋ'keɪtɪd] *adj* tronqué(e).
truncheon ['trʌntʃən] *n* bâton *m* (d'agent de police); matraque *f*.
trundle ['trʌndl] *vt, vi*: **to ~ along** rouler bruyamment.
trunk [trʌŋk] *n* (*of tree, person*) tronc *m*; (*of elephant*) trompe *f*; (*case*) malle *f*; (*US AUT*) coffre *m*.
trunk call *n* (*BRIT TEL*) communication interurbaine.
trunk road *n* (*BRIT*) ≈ (route *f*) nationale *f*.
trunks [trʌŋks] *npl* (*also*: **swimming** ~) maillot *m or* slip *m* de bain.
truss [trʌs] *n* (*MED*) bandage *m* herniaire ♦ *vt*: **to ~ (up)** (*CULIN*) brider.
trust [trʌst] *n* confiance *f*; (*LAW*) fidéicommis *m*; (*COMM*) trust *m* ♦ *vt* (*rely on*) avoir confiance en; (*entrust*): **to ~ sth to sb** confier qch à qn; (*hope*): **to ~ (that)** espérer (que); **to take sth on** ~ accepter qch sans garanties (*or* sans preuves); **in** ~ (*LAW*) par fidéicommis.
trust company *n* société *f* fiduciaire.
trusted ['trʌstɪd] *adj* en qui l'on a confiance.
trustee [trʌs'ti:] *n* (*LAW*) fidéicommissaire *m/f*; (*of school etc*) administrateur/trice.
trustful ['trʌstful] *adj* confiant(e).
trust fund *n* fonds *m* en fidéicommis.
trusting ['trʌstɪŋ] *adj* confiant(e).
trustworthy ['trʌstwə:ðɪ] *adj* digne de confiance.
trusty ['trʌstɪ] *adj* fidèle.
truth, ~s [tru:θ, tru:ðz] *n* vérité *f*.
truthful ['tru:θful] *adj* (*person*) qui dit la vérité; (*description*) exact(e), vrai(e).
truthfully ['tru:θfəlɪ] *adv* sincèrement, sans mentir.
truthfulness ['tru:θfəlnɪs] *n* véracité *f*.
try [traɪ] *n* essai *m*, tentative *f*; (*RUGBY*) essai ♦ *vt* (*LAW*) juger; (*test: sth new*) essayer, tester; (*strain*) éprouver ♦ *vi* essayer; **to ~ to do** essayer de faire; (*seek*) chercher à faire; **to ~ one's (very) best** *or* **one's (very) hardest** faire de son mieux; **to give sth a** ~ essayer qch.
▸**try on** *vt* (*clothes*) essayer; **to ~ it on** (*fig*) tenter le coup, bluffer.
▸**try out** *vt* essayer, mettre à l'essai.
trying ['traɪɪŋ] *adj* pénible.
tsar [zɑ:*] *n* tsar *m*.
T-shirt ['ti:ʃə:t] *n* tee-shirt *m*.
T-square ['ti:skwɛə*] *n* équerre *f* en T.
TT *adj abbr* (*BRIT col*) = **teetotal** ♦ *abbr* (*US*) = *Trust Territory*.
tub [tʌb] *n* cuve *f*; baquet *m*; (*bath*) baignoire *f*.
tuba ['tju:bə] *n* tuba *m*.
tubby ['tʌbɪ] *adj* rondelet(te).
tube [tju:b] *n* tube *m*; (*BRIT: underground*) métro *m*; (*for tyre*) chambre *f* à air; (*col: television*): **the** ~ la télé.
tubeless ['tju:blɪs] *adj* (*tyre*) sans chambre à air.
tuber ['tju:bə*] *n* (*BOT*) tubercule *m*.
tuberculosis [tjubə:kju'ləusɪs] *n* tuberculose *f*.
tube station *n* (*BRIT*) station *f* de métro.
tubing ['tju:bɪŋ] *n* tubes *mpl*; **a piece of** ~ un tube.
tubular ['tju:bjulə*] *adj* tubulaire.
TUC *n abbr* (*BRIT: = Trades Union Congress*) confédération *f* des syndicats britanniques.
tuck [tʌk] *n* (*SEWING*) pli *m*, rempli *m* ♦ *vt* (*put*) mettre.
▸**tuck away** *vt* cacher, ranger.
▸**tuck in** *vt* rentrer; (*child*) border ♦ *vi* (*eat*) manger de bon appétit; attaquer le repas.
▸**tuck up** *vt* (*child*) border.
tuck shop *n* (*BRIT SCOL*) boutique *f* à provisions.
Tue(s). *abbr* (= *Tuesday*) ma.
Tuesday ['tju:zdɪ] *n* mardi *m*; **(the date) today is ~ 23rd March** nous sommes aujourd'hui le mardi 23 mars; **on** ~ mardi; **on ~s** le mardi; **every** ~ tous les mardis, chaque mardi; **every other** ~ un mardi sur deux; **last/next** ~ mardi dernier/prochain; ~ **next** mardi qui vient; **the following** ~ le mardi suivant; **a week/fortnight on** ~, ~ **week/fortnight** mardi en huit/quinze; **the ~ before last** l'autre mardi; **the ~ after next** mardi en huit; ~ **morning/lunchtime/afternoon/evening** mardi matin/midi/après-midi/soir; ~ **night** mardi soir; (*overnight*) la nuit de mardi (à mercredi); **~'s newspaper** le journal de mardi.
tuft [tʌft] *n* touffe *f*.
tug [tʌg] *n* (*ship*) remorqueur *m* ♦ *vt* tirer (sur).
tug-of-love [tʌgəv'lʌv] *n lutte acharnée entre parents divorcés pour avoir la garde d'un enfant*.

tug-of-war [tʌgəv'wɔː*] *n* lutte *f* à la corde.
tuition [tjuː'ɪʃən] *n* (*BRIT*: *lessons*) leçons *fpl*; (*US*: *fees*) frais *mpl* de scolarité.
tulip ['tjuːlɪp] *n* tulipe *f*.
tumble ['tʌmbl] *n* (*fall*) chute *f*, culbute *f* ♦ *vi* tomber, dégringoler; (*somersault*) faire une *or* des culbute(s) ♦ *vt* renverser, faire tomber; **to ~ to sth** (*col*) réaliser qch.
tumbledown ['tʌmbldaun] *adj* délabré(e).
tumble dryer *n* (*BRIT*) séchoir *m* (à linge) à air chaud.
tumbler ['tʌmblə*] *n* verre (droit), gobelet *m*.
tummy ['tʌmɪ] *n* (*col*) ventre *m*.
tumour, (*US*) **tumor** ['tjuːmə*] *n* tumeur *f*.
tumult ['tjuːmʌlt] *n* tumulte *m*.
tumultuous [tjuː'mʌltjuəs] *adj* tumultueux(euse).
tuna ['tjuːnə] *n* (*pl inv*) (*also*: **~ fish**) thon *m*.
tune [tjuːn] *n* (*melody*) air *m* ♦ *vt* (*MUS*) accorder; (*RADIO, TV, AUT*) régler, mettre au point; **to be in/out of ~** (*instrument*) être accordé/désaccordé; (*singer*) chanter juste/faux; **to be in/out of ~ with** (*fig*) être en accord/désaccord avec; **she was robbed to the ~ of £10,000** (*fig*) on lui a volé la jolie somme de 10 000 livres.
►**tune in** *vi* (*RADIO, TV*): **to ~ in (to)** se mettre à l'écoute (de).
►**tune up** *vi* (*musician*) accorder son instrument.
tuneful ['tjuːnful] *adj* mélodieux(euse).
tuner ['tjuːnə*] *n* (*radio set*) radio-préamplificateur *m*; **piano ~** accordeur *m* de pianos.
tuner amplifier *n* radio-ampli *m*.
tungsten ['tʌŋstn] *n* tungstène *m*.
tunic ['tjuːnɪk] *n* tunique *f*.
tuning ['tjuːnɪŋ] *n* réglage *m*.
tuning fork *n* diapason *m*.
Tunis ['tjuːnɪs] *n* Tunis.
Tunisia [tjuː'nɪzɪə] *n* Tunisie *f*.
Tunisian [tjuː'nɪzɪən] *adj* tunisien(ne) ♦ *n* Tunisien/ne.
tunnel ['tʌnl] *n* tunnel *m*; (*in mine*) galerie *f* ♦ *vi* creuser un tunnel (*or* une galerie).
tunnel vision *n* (*MED*) rétrécissement *m* du champ visuel; (*fig*) vision étroite des choses.
tunny ['tʌnɪ] *n* thon *m*.
turban ['təːbən] *n* turban *m*.
turbid ['təːbɪd] *adj* boueux(euse).
turbine ['təːbaɪn] *n* turbine *f*.
turbo ['təːbəu] *n* turbo *m*.
turbojet [təːbəu'dʒɛt] *n* turboréacteur *m*.
turboprop [təːbəu'prɔp] *n* (*engine*) turbopropulseur *m*.
turbot ['təːbət] *n* (*pl inv*) turbot *m*.
turbulence ['təːbjuləns] *n* (*AVIAT*) turbulence *f*.
turbulent ['təːbjulənt] *adj* turbulent(e); (*sea*) agité(e).
tureen [tə'riːn] *n* soupière *f*.
turf [təːf] *n* gazon *m*; (*clod*) motte *f* (de gazon) ♦ *vt* gazonner; **the T~** le turf, les courses *fpl*.
►**turf out** *vt* (*col*) jeter; jeter dehors.
turf accountant *n* (*BRIT*) bookmaker *m*.
turgid ['təːdʒɪd] *adj* (*speech*) pompeux(euse).
Turin [tjuə'rɪn] *n* Turin.
Turk [təːk] *n* Turc/Turque.
Turkey ['təːkɪ] *n* Turquie *f*.
turkey ['təːkɪ] *n* dindon *m*, dinde *f*.
Turkish ['təːkɪʃ] *adj* turc(turque) ♦ *n* (*LING*) turc *m*.
Turkish bath *n* bain turc.
Turkish delight *n* loukoum *m*.
turmeric ['təːmərɪk] *n* curcuma *m*.
turmoil ['təːmɔɪl] *n* trouble *m*, bouleversement *m*.
turn [təːn] *n* tour *m*; (*in road*) tournant *m*; (*tendency: of mind, events*) tournure *f*; (*performance*) numéro *m*; (*MED*) crise *f*, attaque *f* ♦ *vt* tourner; (*collar, steak*) retourner; (*milk*) faire tourner; (*change*): **to ~ sth into** changer qch en; (*shape: wood, metal*) tourner ♦ *vi* tourner; (*person: look back*) se (re)tourner; (*reverse direction*) faire demi-tour; (*change*) changer; (*become*) devenir; **to ~ into** se changer en, se transformer en; **a good ~** un service; **a bad ~** un mauvais tour; **it gave me quite a ~** ça m'a fait un coup; **"no left ~"** (*AUT*) "défense de tourner à gauche"; **it's your ~** c'est (à) votre tour; **in ~** à son tour; à tour de rôle; **to take ~s** se relayer; **to take ~s at** faire à tour de rôle; **at the ~ of the year/ century** à la fin de l'année/du siècle; **to take a ~ for the worse** (*situation, events*) empirer; **his health** *or* **he has taken a ~ for the worse** son état s'est aggravé.
►**turn about** *vi* faire demi-tour; faire un demi-tour.
►**turn away** *vi* se détourner, tourner la tête ♦ *vt* (*reject: person*) renvoyer; (*: business*) refuser.
►**turn back** *vi* revenir, faire demi-tour.
►**turn down** *vt* (*refuse*) rejeter, refuser; (*reduce*) baisser; (*fold*) rabattre.
►**turn in** *vi* (*col: go to bed*) aller se coucher ♦ *vt* (*fold*) rentrer.
►**turn off** *vi* (*from road*) tourner ♦ *vt* (*light, radio etc*) éteindre; (*engine*) arrêter.
►**turn on** *vt* (*light, radio etc*) allumer; (*engine*) mettre en marche.
►**turn out** *vt* (*light, gas*) éteindre; (*produce: goods, novel, good pupils*) produire ♦ *vi* (*appear, attend: troops, doctor etc*) être présent(e); **to ~ out to be ...** s'avérer ..., se révéler ....
►**turn over** *vi* (*person*) se retourner ♦ *vt* (*object*) retourner; (*page*) tourner.
►**turn round** *vi* faire demi-tour; (*rotate*) tourner.
►**turn up** *vi* (*person*) arriver, se pointer; (*lost object*) être retrouvé(e) ♦ *vt* (*collar*) remonter; (*increase: sound, volume etc*) mettre plus

fort.
turnabout ['tə:nəbaut], **turnaround** ['tə:nəraund] *n* volte-face *f inv.*
turncoat ['tə:nkəut] *n* rénégat/e.
turned-up ['tə:ndʌp] *adj* (*nose*) retroussé(e).
turning ['tə:nɪŋ] *n* (*in road*) tournant *m*; **the first ~ on the right** la première (rue *or* route) à droite.
turning circle *n* (*BRIT*) rayon *m* de braquage.
turning point *n* (*fig*) tournant *m*, moment décisif.
turning radius *n* (*US*) = **turning circle**.
turnip ['tə:nɪp] *n* navet *m*.
turnout ['tə:naut] *n* (nombre *m* de personnes dans l')assistance *f*.
turnover ['tə:nəuvə*] *n* (*COMM*: *amount of money*) chiffre *m* d'affaires; (*: of goods*) roulement *m*; (*CULIN*) *sorte de chausson*; **there is a rapid ~ in staff** le personnel change souvent.
turnpike ['tə:npaɪk] *n* (*US*) autoroute *f* à péage.
turnstile ['tə:nstaɪl] *n* tourniquet *m* (*d'entrée*).
turntable ['tə:nteɪbl] *n* (*on record player*) platine *f*.
turn-up ['tə:nʌp] *n* (*BRIT*: *on trousers*) revers *m*.
turpentine ['tə:pəntaɪn] *n* (*also*: **turps**) (essence *f* de) térébenthine *f*.
turquoise ['tə:kwɔɪz] *n* (*stone*) turquoise *f* ♦ *adj* turquoise *inv*.
turret ['tʌrɪt] *n* tourelle *f*.
turtle ['tə:tl] *n* tortue marine.
turtleneck (sweater) ['tə:tlnɛk-] *n* pullover *m* à col montant.
Tuscany ['tʌskənɪ] *n* Toscane *f*.
tusk [tʌsk] *n* défense *f* (*d'éléphant*).
tussle ['tʌsl] *n* bagarre *f*, mêlée *f*.
tutor ['tju:tə*] *n* (*BRIT SCOL*) directeur/trice d'études; (*private teacher*) précepteur/trice.
tutorial [tju:'tɔ:rɪəl] *n* (*SCOL*) (séance *f* de) travaux *mpl* pratiques.
tuxedo [tʌk'si:dəu] *n* (*US*) smoking *m*.
TV [ti:'vi:] *n abbr* (= *television*) télé *f*, TV *f*.
TV dinner *n* plateau-repas surgelé.
twaddle ['twɔdl] *n* balivernes *fpl*.
twang [twæŋ] *n* (*of instrument*) son vibrant; (*of voice*) ton nasillard ♦ *vi* vibrer ♦ *vt* (*guitar*) pincer les cordes de.
tweak [twi:k] *vt* (*nose*) tordre; (*ear, hair*) tirer.
tweed [twi:d] *n* tweed *m*.
tweezers ['twi:zəz] *npl* pince *f* à épiler.
twelfth [twɛlfθ] *num* douzième.
Twelfth Night *n* la fête des Rois.
twelve [twɛlv] *num* douze; **at ~ (o'clock)** à midi; (*midnight*) à minuit.
twentieth ['twɛntɪɪθ] *num* vingtième.
twenty ['twɛntɪ] *num* vingt.
twerp [twə:p] *n* (*col*) imbécile *m/f*.
twice [twaɪs] *adv* deux fois; **~ as much** deux fois plus; **~ a week** deux fois par semaine; **she is ~ your age** elle a deux fois ton âge.
twiddle ['twɪdl] *vt*, *vi*: **to ~ (with) sth** tripoter qch; **to ~ one's thumbs** (*fig*) se tourner les pouces.
twig [twɪg] *n* brindille *f* ♦ *vt*, *vi* (*col*) piger.
twilight ['twaɪlaɪt] *n* crépuscule *m*; (*morning*) aube *f*; **in the ~** dans la pénombre.
twill [twɪl] *n* sergé *m*.
twin [twɪn] *adj*, *n* jumeau(elle) ♦ *vt* jumeler.
twin(-bedded) room ['twɪn('bɛdɪd)-] *n* chambre *f* à deux lits.
twin beds *npl* lits *mpl* jumeaux.
twin-carburettor ['twɪnkɑ:bju'rɛtə*] *adj* à double carburateur.
twine [twaɪn] *n* ficelle *f* ♦ *vi* (*plant*) s'enrouler.
twin-engined [twɪn'ɛndʒɪnd] *adj* bimoteur; **~ aircraft** bimoteur *m*.
twinge [twɪndʒ] *n* (*of pain*) élancement *m*; (*of conscience*) remords *m*.
twinkle ['twɪŋkl] *n* scintillement *m*; pétillement *m* ♦ *vi* scintiller; (*eyes*) pétiller.
twin town *n* ville jumelée.
twirl [twə:l] *n* tournoiement *m* ♦ *vt* faire tournoyer ♦ *vi* tournoyer.
twist [twɪst] *n* torsion *f*, tour *m*; (*in wire, flex*) tortillon *m*; (*bend: in road*) tournant *m*; (*in story*) coup *m* de théâtre ♦ *vt* tordre; (*weave*) entortiller; (*roll around*) enrouler; (*fig*) déformer ♦ *vi* s'entortiller; s'enrouler; (*road*) serpenter; **to ~ one's ankle/wrist** (*MED*) se tordre la cheville/le poignet.
twisted ['twɪstɪd] *adj* (*wire, rope*) entortillé(e); (*ankle, wrist*) tordu(e), foulé(e); (*fig: logic, mind*) tordu.
twit [twɪt] *n* (*col*) crétin/e.
twitch [twɪtʃ] *n* saccade *f*; (*nervous*) tic *m* ♦ *vi* se convulser; avoir un tic.
two [tu:] *num* deux; **~ by ~, in ~s** par deux; **to put ~ and ~ together** (*fig*) faire le rapport.
two-bit [tu:'bɪt] *adj* (*esp US col, pej*) de pacotille.
two-door [tu:'dɔ:*] *adj* (*AUT*) à deux portes.
two-faced [tu:'feɪst] *adj* (*pej*: *person*) faux(fausse).
twofold ['tu:fəuld] *adv*: **to increase ~** doubler ♦ *adj* (*increase*) de cent pour cent; (*reply*) en deux parties.
two-piece ['tu:'pi:s] *n* (*also*: **~ suit**) (costume *m*) deux-pièces *m inv*; (*also*: **~ swimsuit**) (maillot *m* de bain) deux-pièces.
two-seater [tu:'si:tə*] *n* (*plane*) (avion *m*) biplace *m*; (*car*) voiture *f* à deux places.
twosome ['tu:səm] *n* (*people*) couple *m*.
two-stroke ['tu:strəuk] *n* (*also*: **~ engine**) moteur *m* à deux temps ♦ *adj* à deux temps.
two-tone ['tu:'təun] *adj* (*in colour*) à deux tons.
two-way ['tu:weɪ] *adj* (*traffic*) dans les deux sens; **~ radio** émetteur-récepteur *m*.
TX *abbr* (*US*) = *Texas*.
tycoon [taɪ'ku:n] *n*: **(business) ~** gros homme d'affaires.
type [taɪp] *n* (*category*) genre *m*, espèce *f*; (*model*) modèle *m*; (*example*) type *m*; (*TYP*) type,

caractère *m* ♦ *vt* (*letter etc*) taper (à la machine); **what ~ do you want?** quel genre voulez-vous?; **in bold/italic ~** en caractères gras/en italiques.
typecast ['taɪpkɑːst] *adj* condamné(e) à toujours jouer le même rôle.
typeface ['taɪpfeɪs] *n* police *f* (de caractères).
typescript ['taɪpskrɪpt] *n* texte dactylographié.
typeset ['taɪpsɛt] *vt* composer (*en imprimerie*).
typesetter ['taɪpsɛtə*] *n* compositeur *m*.
typewriter ['taɪpraɪtə*] *n* machine *f* à écrire.
typewritten ['taɪprɪtn] *adj* dactylographié(e).
typhoid ['taɪfɔɪd] *n* typhoïde *f*.
typhoon [taɪ'fuːn] *n* typhon *m*.
typhus ['taɪfəs] *n* typhus *m*.
typical ['tɪpɪkl] *adj* typique, caractéristique.
typify ['tɪpɪfaɪ] *vt* être caractéristique de.
typing ['taɪpɪŋ] *n* dactylo(graphie) *f*.
typing error *n* faute *f* de frappe.
typing pool *n* pool *m* de dactylos.
typist ['taɪpɪst] *n* dactylo *m/f*.
typo ['taɪpəu] *n abbr* (*col*: = *typographical error*) coquille *f*.
typography [taɪ'pɔgrəfɪ] *n* typographie *f*.
tyranny ['tɪrənɪ] *n* tyrannie *f*.
tyrant ['taɪərnt] *n* tyran *m*.
tyre, (*US*) **tire** ['taɪə*] *n* pneu *m*.
tyre pressure *n* pression *f* (de gonflage).
Tyrol [tɪ'rəul] *n* Tyrol *m*.
Tyrolean [tɪrə'liːən], **Tyrolese** [tɪrə'liːz] *adj* tyrolien(ne) ♦ *n* Tyrolien/ne.
Tyrrhenian Sea [tɪ'riːnɪən-] *n*: **the ~** la mer Tyrrhénienne.
tzar [zɑː*] *n* = **tsar**.

U u

U, u [juː] *n* (*letter*) U, u *m*; **U for Uncle** U comme Ursule.
U *n abbr* (*BRIT CINE*: = *universal*) ≈ tous publics.
UAW *n abbr* (*US*: = *United Automobile Workers*) *syndicat des ouvriers de l'automobile*.
UB40 *n abbr* (*BRIT*: = *unemployment benefit form 40*) *numéro de référence d'un formulaire d'inscription au chômage*: *par extension, le bénéficiaire*.
U-bend ['juːbɛnd] *n* (*BRIT AUT*) coude *m*, virage *m* en épingle à cheveux; (*in pipe*) coude.
ubiquitous [juː'bɪkwɪtəs] *adj* doué(e) d'ubiquité, omniprésent(e).
UCAS ['juːkæs] *n abbr* (*BRIT*) = *Universities and Colleges Admissions Service*.
UDA *n abbr* (*BRIT*) = *Ulster Defence Association*.
UDC *n abbr* (*BRIT*) = *Urban District Council*.
udder ['ʌdə*] *n* pis *m*, mamelle *f*.
UDI *n abbr* (*BRIT POL*) = *unilateral declaration of independence*.
UDR *n abbr* (*BRIT*) = *Ulster Defence Regiment*.
UEFA [juː'eɪfə] *n abbr* (= *Union of European Football Associations*) UEFA *f*.
UFO ['juːfəu] *n abbr* (= *unidentified flying object*) ovni *m* (= *objet volant non identifié*).
Uganda [juː'gændə] *n* Ouganda *m*.
Ugandan [juː'gændən] *adj* ougandais(e) ♦ *n* Ougandais/e.
UGC *n abbr* (*BRIT*: = *University Grants Committee*) *commission d'attribution des dotations aux universités*.
ugh [əːh] *excl* pouah!
ugliness ['ʌglɪnɪs] *n* laideur *f*.
ugly ['ʌglɪ] *adj* laid(e), vilain(e); (*fig*) répugnant(e).
UHF *abbr* (= *ultra-high frequency*) UHF.
UHT *adj abbr* (= *ultra-heat treated*): **~ milk** lait *m* UHT *or* longue conservation.
UK *n abbr* = **United Kingdom**.
Ukraine [juː'kreɪn] *n* Ukraine *f*.
Ukrainian [juː'kreɪnɪən] *adj* ukrainien(ne) ♦ *n* Ukrainien/ne; (*LING*) ukrainien *m*.
ulcer ['ʌlsə*] *n* ulcère *m*; **mouth ~** aphte *f*.
Ulster ['ʌlstə*] *n* Ulster *m*.
ulterior [ʌl'tɪərɪə*] *adj* ultérieur(e); **~ motive** arrière-pensée *f*.
ultimate ['ʌltɪmət] *adj* ultime, final(e); (*authority*) suprême ♦ *n*: **the ~ in luxury** le summum du luxe.
ultimately ['ʌltɪmətlɪ] *adv* (*in the end*) en fin de compte; (*at last*) finalement; (*eventually*) par la suite.
ultimatum, *pl* **~s** *or* **ultimata** [ʌltɪ'meɪtəm, -tə] *n* ultimatum *m*.
ultrasonic [ʌltrə'sɔnɪk] *adj* ultrasonique.
ultrasound ['ʌltrəsaund] *n* (*MED*) ultrason *m*.
ultraviolet ['ʌltrə'vaɪəlɪt] *adj* ultraviolet(te).
umbilical [ʌmbɪ'laɪkl] *adj*: **~ cord** cordon ombilical.
umbrage ['ʌmbrɪdʒ] *n*: **to take ~** prendre ombrage, se froisser.
umbrella [ʌm'brɛlə] *n* parapluie *m*; (*fig*): **under the ~ of** sous les auspices de; chapeauté(e) par.
umlaut ['umlaut] *n* tréma *m*.
umpire ['ʌmpaɪə*] *n* arbitre *m*; (*TENNIS*) juge *m* de chaise ♦ *vt* arbitrer.
umpteen [ʌmp'tiːn] *adj* je ne sais combien de; **for the ~th time** pour la nième fois.
UMW *n abbr* (= *United Mineworkers of America*) *syndicat des mineurs*.
UN *n abbr* = **United Nations**.
unabashed [ʌnə'bæʃt] *adj* nullement intimidé(e).
unabated [ʌnə'beɪtɪd] *adj* non diminué(e).
unable [ʌn'eɪbl] *adj*: **to be ~ to** ne (pas) pouvoir, être dans l'impossibilité de; (*not capable*) être incapable de.
unabridged [ʌnə'brɪdʒd] *adj* complet(ète), in-

tégral(e).
unacceptable [ʌnək'sɛptəbl] *adj* (*behaviour*) inadmissible; (*price, proposal*) inacceptable.
unaccompanied [ʌnə'kʌmpənɪd] *adj* (*child, lady*) non accompagné(e); (*singing, song*) sans accompagnement.
unaccountably [ʌnə'kauntəblɪ] *adv* inexplicablement.
unaccounted [ʌnə'kauntɪd] *adj*: **two passengers are ~ for** on est sans nouvelles de deux passagers.
unaccustomed [ʌnə'kʌstəmd] *adj* inaccoutumé(e), inhabituel(le); **to be ~ to sth** ne pas avoir l'habitude de qch.
unacquainted [ʌnə'kweɪntɪd] *adj*: **to be ~ with** ne pas connaître.
unadulterated [ʌnə'dʌltəreɪtɪd] *adj* pur(e), naturel(le).
unaffected [ʌnə'fɛktɪd] *adj* (*person, behaviour*) naturel(le); (*emotionally*): **to be ~ by** ne pas être touché(e) par.
unafraid [ʌnə'freɪd] *adj*: **to be ~** ne pas avoir peur.
unaided [ʌn'eɪdɪd] *adj* sans aide, tout(e) seul(e).
unanimity [juːnə'nɪmɪtɪ] *n* unanimité *f*.
unanimous [juː'nænɪməs] *adj* unanime.
unanimously [juː'nænɪməslɪ] *adv* à l'unanimité.
unanswered [ʌn'ɑːnsəd] *adj* (*question, letter*) sans réponse.
unappetizing [ʌn'æpɪtaɪzɪŋ] *adj* peu appétissant(e).
unappreciative [ʌnə'priːʃɪətɪv] *adj* indifférent(e).
unarmed [ʌn'ɑːmd] *adj* (*person*) non armé(e); (*combat*) sans armes.
unashamed [ʌnə'ʃeɪmd] *adj* sans honte; impudent(e).
unassisted [ʌnə'sɪstɪd] *adj* non assisté(e) ♦ *adv* sans aide, tout(e) seul(e).
unassuming [ʌnə'sjuːmɪŋ] *adj* modeste, sans prétentions.
unattached [ʌnə'tætʃt] *adj* libre, sans attaches.
unattended [ʌnə'tɛndɪd] *adj* (*car, child, luggage*) sans surveillance.
unattractive [ʌnə'træktɪv] *adj* peu attrayant(e).
unauthorized [ʌn'ɔːθəraɪzd] *adj* non autorisé(e), sans autorisation.
unavailable [ʌnə'veɪləbl] *adj* (*article, room, book*) (qui n'est) pas disponible; (*person*) (qui n'est) pas libre.
unavoidable [ʌnə'vɔɪdəbl] *adj* inévitable.
unavoidably [ʌnə'vɔɪdəblɪ] *adv* inévitablement.
unaware [ʌnə'wɛə*] *adj*: **to be ~ of** ignorer, ne pas savoir, être inconscient(e) de.
unawares [ʌnə'wɛəz] *adv* à l'improviste, au dépourvu.
unbalanced [ʌn'bælənst] *adj* déséquilibré(e).
unbearable [ʌn'bɛərəbl] *adj* insupportable.
unbeatable [ʌn'biːtəbl] *adj* imbattable.
unbeaten [ʌn'biːtn] *adj* invaincu(e); (*record*) non battu(e).
unbecoming [ʌnbɪ'kʌmɪŋ] *adj* (*unseemly: language, behaviour*) malséant(e), inconvenant(e); (*unflattering: garment*) peu seyant(e).
unbeknown(st) [ʌnbɪ'nəun(st)] *adv*: **~ to** à l'insu de.
unbelief [ʌnbɪ'liːf] *n* incrédulité *f*.
unbelievable [ʌnbɪ'liːvəbl] *adj* incroyable.
unbelievingly [ʌnbɪ'liːvɪŋlɪ] *adv* avec incrédulité.
unbend [ʌn'bɛnd] *vb* (*irreg*) *vi* se détendre ♦ *vt* (*wire*) redresser, détordre.
unbending [ʌn'bɛndɪŋ] *adj* (*fig*) inflexible.
unbias(s)ed [ʌn'baɪəst] *adj* impartial(e).
unblemished [ʌn'blɛmɪʃt] *adj* impeccable.
unblock [ʌn'blɔk] *vt* (*pipe*) déboucher; (*road*) dégager.
unborn [ʌn'bɔːn] *adj* à naître.
unbounded [ʌn'baundɪd] *adj* sans bornes, illimité(e).
unbreakable [ʌn'breɪkəbl] *adj* incassable.
unbridled [ʌn'braɪdld] *adj* débridé(e), déchaîné(e).
unbroken [ʌn'brəukn] *adj* intact(e); (*line*) continu(e); (*record*) non battu(e).
unbuckle [ʌn'bʌkl] *vt* déboucler.
unburden [ʌn'bəːdn] *vt*: **to ~ o.s.** s'épancher, se livrer.
unbutton [ʌn'bʌtn] *vt* déboutonner.
uncalled-for [ʌn'kɔːldfɔː*] *adj* déplacé(e), injustifié(e).
uncanny [ʌn'kænɪ] *adj* étrange, troublant(e).
unceasing [ʌn'siːsɪŋ] *adj* incessant(e), continu(e).
unceremonious [ʌnsɛrɪ'məunɪəs] *adj* (*abrupt, rude*) brusque.
uncertain [ʌn'səːtn] *adj* incertain(e); **we were ~ whether ...** nous ne savions pas vraiment si ...; **in no ~ terms** sans équivoque possible.
uncertainty [ʌn'səːtntɪ] *n* incertitude *f*, doutes *mpl*.
unchallenged [ʌn'tʃælɪndʒd] *adj* (*gen*) incontesté(e); (*information*) non contesté(e); **to go ~** ne pas être contesté.
unchanged [ʌn'tʃeɪndʒd] *adj* inchangé(e).
uncharitable [ʌn'tʃærɪtəbl] *adj* peu charitable.
uncharted [ʌn'tʃɑːtɪd] *adj* inexploré(e).
unchecked [ʌn'tʃɛkt] *adj* non réprimé(e).
uncivilized [ʌn'sɪvɪlaɪzd] *adj* non civilisé(e); (*fig*) barbare.
uncle ['ʌŋkl] *n* oncle *m*.
unclear [ʌn'klɪə*] *adj* (qui n'est) pas clair(e) *or* évident(e); **I'm still ~ about what I'm supposed to do** je ne sais pas encore exactement ce que je dois faire.
uncoil [ʌn'kɔɪl] *vt* dérouler ♦ *vi* se dérouler.
uncomfortable [ʌn'kʌmfətəbl] *adj* inconfortable; (*uneasy*) mal à l'aise, gêné(e); (*situation*) désagréable.

uncomfortably [ʌn'kʌmfətəblɪ] *adv* inconfortablement; d'un ton *etc* gêné *or* embarrassé; désagréablement.
uncommitted [ʌnkə'mɪtɪd] *adj* (*attitude, country*) non engagé(e).
uncommon [ʌn'kɔmən] *adj* rare, singulier(ière), peu commun(e).
uncommunicative [ʌnkə'mju:nɪkətɪv] *adj* réservé(e).
uncomplicated [ʌn'kɔmplɪkeɪtɪd] *adj* simple, peu compliqué(e).
uncompromising [ʌn'kɔmprəmaɪzɪŋ] *adj* intransigeant(e), inflexible.
unconcerned [ʌnkən'sə:nd] *adj* (*unworried*): **to be ~ (about)** ne pas s'inquiéter (de).
unconditional [ʌnkən'dɪʃənl] *adj* sans conditions.
uncongenial [ʌnkən'dʒi:nɪəl] *adj* peu agréable.
unconnected [ʌnkə'nɛktɪd] *adj* (*unrelated*): **~ (with)** sans rapport (avec).
unconscious [ʌn'kɔnʃəs] *adj* sans connaissance, évanoui(e); (*unaware*) inconscient(e) ♦ *n*: **the ~** l'inconscient *m*; **to knock sb ~** assommer qn.
unconsciously [ʌn'kɔnʃəslɪ] *adv* inconsciemment.
unconstitutional [ʌnkɔnstɪ'tju:ʃənl] *adj* anticonstitutionnel(le).
uncontested [ʌnkən'tɛstɪd] *adj* (*champion*) incontesté(e); (*POL: seat*) non disputé(e).
uncontrollable [ʌnkən'trəuləbl] *adj* (*child, dog*) indiscipliné(e); (*emotion*) irrépressible.
uncontrolled [ʌnkən'trəuld] *adj* (*laughter, price rises*) incontrôlé(e).
unconventional [ʌnkən'vɛnʃənl] *adj* non conventionnel(le).
unconvinced [ʌnkən'vɪnst] *adj*: **to be ~** ne pas être convaincu(e).
unconvincing [ʌnkən'vɪnsɪŋ] *adj* peu convaincant(e).
uncork [ʌn'kɔ:k] *vt* déboucher.
uncorroborated [ʌnkə'rɔbəreɪtɪd] *adj* non confirmé(e).
uncouth [ʌn'ku:θ] *adj* grossier(ière), fruste.
uncover [ʌn'kʌvə*] *vt* découvrir.
unctuous ['ʌŋktjuəs] *adj* onctueux(euse), mielleux(euse).
undamaged [ʌn'dæmɪdʒd] *adj* (*goods*) intact(e), en bon état; (*fig: reputation*) intact.
undaunted [ʌn'dɔ:ntɪd] *adj* non intimidé(e), inébranlable.
undecided [ʌndɪ'saɪdɪd] *adj* indécis(e), irrésolu(e).
undelivered [ʌndɪ'lɪvəd] *adj* non remis(e), non livré(e).
undeniable [ʌndɪ'naɪəbl] *adj* indéniable, incontestable.
under ['ʌndə*] *prep* sous; (*less than*) (de) moins de; au-dessous de; (*according to*) selon, en vertu de ♦ *adv* au-dessous; en dessous; **from ~ sth** de dessous *or* de sous qch; **~ there** là-dessous; **in ~ 2 hours** en moins de 2 heures; **~ anaesthetic** sous anesthésie; **~ discussion** en discussion; **~ the circumstances** étant donné les circonstances; **~ repair** en (cours de) réparation.
under... ['ʌndə*] *prefix* sous-.
under-age [ʌndər'eɪdʒ] *adj* qui n'a pas l'âge réglementaire.
underarm ['ʌndərɑ:m] *adv* par en-dessous ♦ *adj* (*throw*) par en-dessous; (*deodorant*) pour les aisselles.
undercapitalized [ʌndə'kæpɪtəlaɪzd] *adj* sous-capitalisé(e).
undercarriage ['ʌndəkærɪdʒ] *n* (*BRIT AVIAT*) train *m* d'atterrissage.
undercharge [ʌndə'tʃɑ:dʒ] *vt* ne pas faire payer assez à.
underclass ['ʌndəklɑ:s] *n* ≈ quart-monde *m*.
underclothes ['ʌndəkləuðz] *npl* sous-vêtements *mpl*; (*women's only*) dessous *mpl*.
undercoat ['ʌndəkəut] *n* (*paint*) couche *f* de fond.
undercover [ʌndə'kʌvə*] *adj* secret(ète), clandestin(e).
undercurrent ['ʌndəkʌrnt] *n* courant sous-jacent.
undercut [ʌndə'kʌt] *vt irreg* vendre moins cher que.
underdeveloped ['ʌndədɪ'vɛləpt] *adj* sous-développé(e).
underdog ['ʌndədɔg] *n* opprimé *m*.
underdone [ʌndə'dʌn] *adj* (*food*) pas assez cuit(e).
underemployment [ʌndərɪm'plɔɪmənt] *n* sous-emploi *m*.
underestimate ['ʌndər'ɛstɪmeɪt] *vt* sous-estimer, mésestimer.
underexposed ['ʌndərɪks'pəuzd] *adj* (*PHOT*) sous-exposé(e).
underfed [ʌndə'fɛd] *adj* sous-alimenté(e).
underfoot [ʌndə'fut] *adv* sous les pieds.
under-funded ['ʌndə'fʌndɪd] *adj*: **to be ~** (*organization*) ne pas être doté(e) de fonds suffisants.
undergo [ʌndə'gəu] *vt irreg* subir; (*treatment*) suivre; **the car is ~ing repairs** la voiture est en réparation.
undergraduate [ʌndə'grædjuɪt] *n* étudiant/e (qui prépare la licence) ♦ *cpd*: **~ courses** cours *mpl* préparant à la licence.
underground ['ʌndəgraund] *adj* souterrain(e); (*fig*) clandestin(e) ♦ *n* (*BRIT*) métro *m*; (*POL*) clandestinité *f*.
undergrowth ['ʌndəgrəuθ] *n* broussailles *fpl*, sous-bois *m*.
underhand(ed) [ʌndə'hænd(ɪd)] *adj* (*fig*) sournois(e), en dessous.
underinsured [ʌndərɪn'ʃuəd] *adj* sous-assuré(e).
underlie [ʌndə'laɪ] *vt irreg* être à la base de; **the underlying cause** la cause sous-jacente.
underline [ʌndə'laɪn] *vt* souligner.

underling ['ʌndəlɪŋ] *n (pej)* sous-fifre *m*, subalterne *m*.
undermanning [ʌndə'mænɪŋ] *n* pénurie *f* de main-d'œuvre.
undermentioned [ʌndə'mɛnʃənd] *adj* mentionné(e) ci-dessous.
undermine [ʌndə'maɪn] *vt* saper, miner.
underneath [ʌndə'ni:θ] *adv* (en) dessous ♦ *prep* sous, au-dessous de.
undernourished [ʌndə'nʌrɪʃt] *adj* sous-alimenté(e).
underpaid [ʌndə'peɪd] *adj* sous-payé(e).
underpants ['ʌndəpænts] *npl* caleçon *m*, slip *m*.
underpass ['ʌndəpɑ:s] *n (BRIT)* passage souterrain; *(: on motorway)* passage inférieur.
underpin [ʌndə'pɪn] *vt (argument, case)* étayer.
underplay [ʌndə'pleɪ] *vt (BRIT)* minimiser.
underpopulated [ʌndə'pɔpjuleɪtɪd] *adj* sous-peuplé(e).
underprice [ʌndə'praɪs] *vt* vendre à un prix trop bas.
underprivileged [ʌndə'prɪvɪlɪdʒd] *adj* défavorisé(e), déshérité(e).
underrate [ʌndə'reɪt] *vt* sous-estimer, mésestimer.
underscore [ʌndə'skɔ:*] *vt* souligner.
underseal [ʌndə'si:l] *vt (BRIT)* traiter contre la rouille.
undersecretary ['ʌndə'sɛkrətrɪ] *n* sous-secrétaire *m*.
undersell [ʌndə'sɛl] *vt (competitors)* vendre moins cher que.
undershirt ['ʌndəʃə:t] *n (US)* tricot *m* de corps.
undershorts ['ʌndəʃɔ:ts] *npl (US)* caleçon *m*, slip *m*.
underside ['ʌndəsaɪd] *n* dessous *m*.
undersigned ['ʌndə'saɪnd] *adj, n* soussigné(e) *(m/f)*.
underskirt ['ʌndəskə:t] *n (BRIT)* jupon *m*.
understaffed [ʌndə'stɑ:ft] *adj* qui manque de personnel.
understand [ʌndə'stænd] *vb (irreg: like* **stand***) vt, vi* comprendre; **I ~ that ...** je me suis laissé dire que ...; je crois comprendre que ...; **to make o.s. understood** se faire comprendre.
understandable [ʌndə'stændəbl] *adj* compréhensible.
understanding [ʌndə'stændɪŋ] *adj* compréhensif(ive) ♦ *n* compréhension *f*; *(agreement)* accord *m*; **to come to an ~ with sb** s'entendre avec qn; **on the ~ that ...** à condition que ....
understate [ʌndə'steɪt] *vt* minimiser.
understatement ['ʌndəsteɪtmənt] *n*: **that's an ~** c'est (bien) peu dire, le terme est faible.
understood [ʌndə'stud] *pt, pp of* **understand** ♦ *adj* entendu(e); *(implied)* sous-entendu(e).
understudy ['ʌndəstʌdɪ] *n* doublure *f*.
undertake [ʌndə'teɪk] *vt irreg (job, task)* entreprendre; *(duty)* se charger de; **to ~ to do sth** s'engager à faire qch.
undertaker ['ʌndəteɪkə*] *n* entrepreneur *m* des pompes funèbres, croque-mort *m*.
undertaking ['ʌndəteɪkɪŋ] *n* entreprise *f*; *(promise)* promesse *f*.
undertone ['ʌndətəun] *n (low voice)*: **in an ~** à mi-voix; *(of criticism etc)* nuance cachée.
undervalue [ʌndə'vælju:] *vt* sous-estimer.
underwater [ʌndə'wɔ:tə*] *adv* sous l'eau ♦ *adj* sous-marin(e).
underwear ['ʌndəwɛə*] *n* sous-vêtements *mpl*; *(women's only)* dessous *mpl*.
underweight [ʌndə'weɪt] *adj* d'un poids insuffisant; *(person)* (trop) maigre.
underworld ['ʌndəwə:ld] *n (of crime)* milieu *m*, pègre *f*.
underwrite [ʌndə'raɪt] *vt (FINANCE)* garantir; *(INSURANCE)* souscrire.
underwriter ['ʌndəraɪtə*] *n (INSURANCE)* souscripteur *m*.
undeserving [ʌndɪ'zə:vɪŋ] *adj*: **to be ~ of** ne pas mériter.
undesirable [ʌndɪ'zaɪərəbl] *adj* peu souhaitable; indésirable.
undeveloped [ʌndɪ'vɛləpt] *adj (land, resources)* non exploité(e).
undies ['ʌndɪz] *npl (col)* dessous *mpl*, lingerie *f*.
undiluted ['ʌndaɪ'lu:tɪd] *adj* pur(e), non dilué(e).
undiplomatic ['ʌndɪplə'mætɪk] *adj* peu diplomatique, maladroit(e).
undischarged ['ʌndɪs'tʃɑ:dʒd] *adj*: **~ bankrupt** failli/e non réhabilité(e).
undisciplined [ʌn'dɪsɪplɪnd] *adj* indiscipliné(e).
undisguised ['ʌndɪs'gaɪzd] *adj (dislike, amusement etc)* franc(franche).
undisputed ['ʌndɪs'pju:tɪd] *adj* incontesté(e).
undistinguished ['ʌndɪs'tɪŋgwɪʃt] *adj* médiocre, quelconque.
undisturbed [ʌndɪs'tə:bd] *adj (sleep)* tranquille, paisible; **to leave ~** ne pas déranger.
undivided [ʌndɪ'vaɪdɪd] *adj*: **can I have your ~ attention?** puis-je avoir toute votre attention?
undo [ʌn'du:] *vt irreg* défaire.
undoing [ʌn'du:ɪŋ] *n* ruine *f*, perte *f*.
undone [ʌn'dʌn] *pp of* **undo**; **to come ~** se défaire.
undoubted [ʌn'dautɪd] *adj* indubitable, certain(e).
undoubtedly [ʌn'dautɪdlɪ] *adv* sans aucun doute.
undress [ʌn'drɛs] *vi* se déshabiller ♦ *vt* déshabiller.
undrinkable [ʌn'drɪŋkəbl] *adj (unpalatable)* imbuvable; *(poisonous)* non potable.
undue [ʌn'dju:] *adj* indu(e), excessif(ive).
undulating ['ʌndjuleɪtɪŋ] *adj* ondoyant(e), onduleux(euse).
unduly [ʌn'dju:lɪ] *adv* trop, excessivement.

undying [ʌn'daiiŋ] *adj* éternel(le).
unearned [ʌn'ə:nd] *adj* (*praise, respect*) immérité(e); ~ **income** rentes *fpl*.
unearth [ʌn'ə:θ] *vt* déterrer; (*fig*) dénicher.
unearthly [ʌn'ə:θlɪ] *adj* surnaturel(le); (*hour*) indu(e), impossible.
uneasy [ʌn'i:zɪ] *adj* mal à l'aise, gêné(e); (*worried*) inquiet(ète); **to feel ~ about doing sth** se sentir mal à l'aise à l'idée de faire qch.
uneconomic(al) ['ʌni:kə'nɔmɪk(l)] *adj* peu économique; peu rentable.
uneducated [ʌn'ɛdjukeɪtɪd] *adj* sans éducation.
unemployed [ʌnɪm'plɔɪd] *adj* sans travail, au chômage ♦ *n*: **the** ~ les chômeurs *mpl*.
unemployment [ʌnɪm'plɔɪmənt] *n* chômage *m*.
unemployment benefit, (*US*) **unemployment compensation** *n* allocation *f* de chômage.
unending [ʌn'ɛndɪŋ] *adj* interminable.
unenviable [ʌn'ɛnvɪəbl] *adj* peu enviable.
unequal [ʌn'i:kwəl] *adj* inégal(e).
unequalled, (*US*) **unequaled** [ʌn'i:kwəld] *adj* inégalé(e).
unequivocal [ʌnɪ'kwɪvəkl] *adj* (*answer*) sans équivoque; (*person*) catégorique.
unerring [ʌn'ə:rɪŋ] *adj* infaillible, sûr(e).
UNESCO [ju:'nɛskəu] *n abbr* (= *United Nations Educational, Scientific and Cultural Organization*) UNESCO *f*.
unethical [ʌn'ɛθɪkl] *adj* (*methods*) immoral(e); (*doctor's behaviour*) qui ne respecte pas l'éthique.
uneven [ʌn'i:vn] *adj* inégal(e); irrégulier(ière).
uneventful [ʌnɪ'vɛntful] *adj* tranquille, sans histoires.
unexceptional [ʌnɪk'sɛpʃənl] *adj* banal(e), quelconque.
unexciting [ʌnɪk'saɪtɪŋ] *adj* pas passionnant(e).
unexpected [ʌnɪk'spɛktɪd] *adj* inattendu(e), imprévu(e).
unexpectedly [ʌnɪk'spɛktɪdlɪ] *adv* contre toute attente; (*arrive*) à l'improviste.
unexplained [ʌnɪk'spleɪnd] *adj* inexpliqué(e).
unexploded [ʌnɪk'spləudɪd] *adj* non explosé(e) *or* éclaté(e).
unfailing [ʌn'feɪlɪŋ] *adj* inépuisable; infaillible.
unfair [ʌn'fɛə*] *adj*: ~ **(to)** injuste (envers); **it's ~ that** ... il n'est pas juste que ....
unfair dismissal *n* licenciement abusif.
unfairly [ʌn'fɛəlɪ] *adv* injustement.
unfaithful [ʌn'feɪθful] *adj* infidèle.
unfamiliar [ʌnfə'mɪlɪə*] *adj* étrange, inconnu(e); **to be ~ with sth** mal connaître qch.
unfashionable [ʌn'fæʃnəbl] *adj* (*clothes*) démodé(e); (*district*) déshérité(e), pas à la mode.
unfasten [ʌn'fɑ:sn] *vt* défaire; détacher.
unfathomable [ʌn'fæðəməbl] *adj* insondable.
unfavourable, (*US*) **unfavorable** [ʌn'feɪvrəbl] *adj* défavorable.
unfavo(u)rably [ʌn'feɪvrəblɪ] *adv*: **to look ~ upon** ne pas être favorable à.
unfeeling [ʌn'fi:lɪŋ] *adj* insensible, dur(e).
unfinished [ʌn'fɪnɪʃt] *adj* inachevé(e).
unfit [ʌn'fɪt] *adj* (*physically*) pas en forme; (*incompetent*): ~ **(for)** impropre (à); (*work, service*) inapte (à).
unflagging [ʌn'flægɪŋ] *adj* infatigable, inlassable.
unflappable [ʌn'flæpəbl] *adj* imperturbable.
unflattering [ʌn'flætərɪŋ] *adj* (*dress, hairstyle*) qui n'avantage pas; (*remark*) peu flatteur(euse).
unflinching [ʌn'flɪntʃɪŋ] *adj* stoïque.
unfold [ʌn'fəuld] *vt* déplier; (*fig*) révéler, exposer ♦ *vi* se dérouler.
unforeseeable [ʌnfɔ:'si:əbl] *adj* imprévisible.
unforeseen ['ʌnfɔ:'si:n] *adj* imprévu(e).
unforgettable [ʌnfə'gɛtəbl] *adj* inoubliable.
unforgivable [ʌnfə'gɪvəbl] *adj* impardonnable.
unformatted [ʌn'fɔ:mætɪd] *adj* (*disk, text*) non formaté(e).
unfortunate [ʌn'fɔ:tʃnət] *adj* malheureux(euse); (*event, remark*) malencontreux(euse).
unfortunately [ʌn'fɔ:tʃnətlɪ] *adv* malheureusement.
unfounded [ʌn'faundɪd] *adj* sans fondement.
unfriendly [ʌn'frɛndlɪ] *adj* froid(e), inamical(e).
unfulfilled [ʌnful'fɪld] *adj* (*ambition, prophecy*) non réalisé(e); (*desire*) insatisfait(e); (*promise*) non tenu(e); (*terms of contract*) non rempli(e); (*person*) qui n'a pas su se réaliser.
unfurl [ʌn'fə:l] *vt* déployer.
unfurnished [ʌn'fə:nɪʃt] *adj* non meublé(e).
ungainly [ʌn'geɪnlɪ] *adj* gauche, dégingandé(e).
ungodly [ʌn'gɔdlɪ] *adj* impie; **at an ~ hour** à une heure indue.
ungrateful [ʌn'greɪtful] *adj* qui manque de reconnaissance, ingrat(e).
unguarded [ʌn'gɑ:dɪd] *adj*: ~ **moment** moment *m* d'inattention.
unhappily [ʌn'hæpɪlɪ] *adv* tristement; (*unfortunately*) malheureusement.
unhappiness [ʌn'hæpɪnɪs] *n* tristesse *f*, peine *f*.
unhappy [ʌn'hæpɪ] *adj* triste, malheureux(euse); (*unfortunate*: *remark etc*) malheureux(euse); (*not pleased*): ~ **with** mécontent(e) de, peu satisfait(e) de.
unharmed [ʌn'hɑ:md] *adj* indemne, sain(e) et sauf(sauve).
UNHCR *n abbr* (= *United Nations High Commission for Refugees*) HCR *m*.
unhealthy [ʌn'hɛlθɪ] *adj* (*gen*) malsain(e); (*person*) maladif(ive).
unheard-of [ʌn'hə:dɔv] *adj* inouï(e), sans précédent.

unhelpful [ʌn'hɛlpful] *adj* (*person*) peu serviable; (*advice*) peu utile.
unhesitating [ʌn'hɛzɪteɪtɪŋ] *adj* (*loyalty*) spontané(e); (*reply, offer*) immédiat(e).
unholy [ʌn'həulɪ] *adj*: **an ~ alliance** une alliance contre nature; **he got home at an ~ hour** il est rentré à une heure impossible.
unhook [ʌn'huk] *vt* décrocher; dégrafer.
unhurt [ʌn'hə:t] *adj* indemne, sain(e) et sauf(sauve).
unhygienic ['ʌnhaɪ'dʒi:nɪk] *adj* antihygiénique.
UNICEF ['ju:nɪsɛf] *n abbr* (= *United Nations Children's Fund*) UNICEF *m*, FISE *m*.
unicorn ['ju:nɪkɔ:n] *n* licorne *f*.
unidentified [ʌnaɪ'dɛntɪfaɪd] *adj* non identifié(e).
uniform ['ju:nɪfɔ:m] *n* uniforme *m* ♦ *adj* uniforme.
uniformity [ju:nɪ'fɔ:mɪtɪ] *n* uniformité *f*.
unify ['ju:nɪfaɪ] *vt* unifier.
unilateral [ju:nɪ'lætərəl] *adj* unilatéral(e).
unimaginable [ʌnɪ'mædʒɪnəbl] *adj* inimaginable, inconcevable.
unimaginative [ʌnɪ'mædʒɪnətɪv] *adj* sans imagination.
unimpaired [ʌnɪm'pɛəd] *adj* intact(e).
unimportant [ʌnɪm'pɔ:tənt] *adj.* sans importance.
unimpressed [ʌnɪm'prɛst] *adj* pas impressionné(e).
uninhabited [ʌnɪn'hæbɪtɪd] *adj* inhabité(e).
uninhibited [ʌnɪn'hɪbɪtɪd] *adj* sans inhibitions; sans retenue.
uninjured [ʌn'ɪndʒəd] *adj* indemne.
uninspiring [ʌnɪn'spaɪərɪŋ] *adj* peu inspirant(e).
unintelligent [ʌnɪn'tɛlɪdʒənt] *adj* inintelligent(e).
unintentional [ʌnɪn'tɛnʃənəl] *adj* involontaire.
unintentionally [ʌnɪn'tɛnʃnəlɪ] *adv* sans le vouloir.
uninvited [ʌnɪn'vaɪtɪd] *adj* (*guest*) qui n'a pas été invité(e).
uninviting [ʌnɪn'vaɪtɪŋ] *adj* (*place*) peu attirant(e); (*food*) peu appétissant(e).
union ['ju:njən] *n* union *f*; (*also*: **trade ~**) syndicat *m* ♦ *cpd* du syndicat, syndical(e).
unionize ['ju:njənaɪz] *vt* syndiquer.
Union Jack *n drapeau du Royaume-Uni.*
Union of Soviet Socialist Republics (USSR) *n* (*formerly*) Union *f* des républiques socialistes soviétiques (URSS).
union shop *n entreprise où tous les travailleurs doivent être syndiqués.*
unique [ju:'ni:k] *adj* unique.
unisex ['ju:nɪsɛks] *adj* unisexe.
UNISON ['ju:nɪsn] *n* (*trade union*) *grand syndicat des services publics en Grande-Bretagne.*
unison ['ju:nɪsn] *n*: **in ~** à l'unisson, en chœur.
unit ['ju:nɪt] *n* unité *f*; (*section: of furniture etc*) élément *m*, bloc *m*; (*team, squad*) groupe *m*, service *m*; **production ~** atelier *m* de fabrication; **sink ~** bloc-évier *m*.
unit cost *n* coût *m* unitaire.
unite [ju:'naɪt] *vt* unir ♦ *vi* s'unir.
united [ju:'naɪtɪd] *adj* uni(e); unifié(e); (*efforts*) conjugué(e).
United Arab Emirates *npl* Émirats Arabes Unis.
United Kingdom (UK) *n* Royaume-Uni *m* (R.U.).
United Nations (Organization) (UN, UNO) *n* (Organisation *f* des) Nations unies (ONU).
United States (of America) (US, USA) *n* États-Unis *mpl*.
unit price *n* prix *m* unitaire.
unit trust *n* (*BRIT COMM*) fonds commun de placement, FCP *m*.
unity ['ju:nɪtɪ] *n* unité *f*.
Univ. *abbr* = **university**.
universal [ju:nɪ'və:sl] *adj* universel(le).
universe ['ju:nɪvə:s] *n* univers *m*.
university [ju:nɪ'və:sɪtɪ] *n* université *f* ♦ *cpd* (*student, professor*) d'université; (*education, year, degree*) universitaire.
unjust [ʌn'dʒʌst] *adj* injuste.
unjustifiable ['ʌndʒʌstɪ'faɪəbl] *adj* injustifiable.
unjustified [ʌn'dʒʌstɪfaɪd] *adj* injustifié(e); (*text*) non justifié(e).
unkempt [ʌn'kɛmpt] *adj* mal tenu(e), débraillé(e); mal peigné(e).
unkind [ʌn'kaɪnd] *adj* peu gentil(le), méchant(e).
unkindly [ʌn'kaɪndlɪ] *adv* (*treat, speak*) avec méchanceté.
unknown [ʌn'nəun] *adj* inconnu(e); **~ to me** sans que je le sache; **~ quantity** (*MATH, fig*) inconnue *f*.
unladen [ʌn'leɪdn] *adj* (*ship, weight*) à vide.
unlawful [ʌn'lɔ:ful] *adj* illégal(e).
unleaded [ʌn'lɛdɪd] *n* (*also*: **~ petrol**) essence *f* sans plomb.
unleash [ʌn'li:ʃ] *vt* détacher; (*fig*) déchaîner, déclencher.
unleavened [ʌn'lɛvnd] *adj* sans levain.
unless [ʌn'lɛs] *conj*: **~ he leaves** à moins qu'il (ne) parte; **~ we leave** à moins de partir, à moins que nous (ne) partions; **~ otherwise stated** sauf indication contraire; **~ I am mistaken** si je ne me trompe.
unlicensed [ʌn'laɪsnst] *adj* (*BRIT*) non patenté(e) pour la vente des spiritueux.
unlike [ʌn'laɪk] *adj* dissemblable, différent(e) ♦ *prep* à la différence de, contrairement à.
unlikelihood [ʌn'laɪklɪhud] *adj* improbabilité *f*.
unlikely [ʌn'laɪklɪ] *adj* (*result, event*) improbable; (*explanation*) invraisemblable.
unlimited [ʌn'lɪmɪtɪd] *adj* illimité(e).
unlisted ['ʌn'lɪstɪd] *adj* (*US TEL*) sur la liste rouge; (*STOCK EXCHANGE*) non coté(e) en

Bourse.
unlit [ʌn'lɪt] *adj* (*room*) non éclairé(e).
unload [ʌn'ləud] *vt* décharger.
unlock [ʌn'lɔk] *vt* ouvrir.
unlucky [ʌn'lʌkɪ] *adj* malchanceux(euse); (*object, number*) qui porte malheur; **to be ~** (*person*) ne pas avoir de chance.
unmanageable [ʌn'mænɪdʒəbl] *adj* (*unwieldy: tool, vehicle*) peu maniable; (*: situation*) inextricable.
unmanned [ʌn'mænd] *adj* sans équipage.
unmannerly [ʌn'mænəlɪ] *adj* mal élevé(e), impoli(e).
unmarked [ʌn'mɑːkt] *adj* (*unstained*) sans marque; ~ **police car** voiture de police banalisée.
unmarried [ʌn'mærɪd] *adj* célibataire.
unmask [ʌn'mɑːsk] *vt* démasquer.
unmatched [ʌn'mætʃt] *adj* sans égal(e).
unmentionable [ʌn'mɛnʃnəbl] *adj* (*topic*) dont on ne parle pas; (*word*) qui ne se dit pas.
unmerciful [ʌn'məːsɪful] *adj* sans pitié.
unmistakable [ʌnmɪs'teɪkəbl] *adj* indubitable; qu'on ne peut pas ne pas reconnaître.
unmitigated [ʌn'mɪtɪgeɪtɪd] *adj* non mitigé(e), absolu(e), pur(e).
unnamed [ʌn'neɪmd] *adj* (*nameless*) sans nom; (*anonymous*) anonyme.
unnatural [ʌn'nætʃrəl] *adj* non naturel(le); contre nature.
unnecessary [ʌn'nɛsəsərɪ] *adj* inutile, superflu(e).
unnerve [ʌn'nəːv] *vt* faire perdre son sang-froid à.
unnoticed [ʌn'nəutɪst] *adj* inaperçu(e); **to go ~** passer inaperçu.
UNO ['juːnəu] *n abbr* = **United Nations Organization.**
unobservant [ʌnəb'zəːvnt] *adj* pas observateur(trice).
unobtainable [ʌnəb'teɪnəbl] *adj* (*TEL*) impossible à obtenir.
unobtrusive [ʌnəb'truːsiv] *adj* discret(ète).
unoccupied [ʌn'ɔkjupaɪd] *adj* (*seat, table, also MIL*) libre; (*house*) inoccupé(e).
unofficial [ʌnə'fɪʃl] *adj* non officiel(le); (*strike*) ≈ non sanctionné(e) par la centrale.
unopposed [ʌnə'pəuzd] *adj* sans opposition.
unorthodox [ʌn'ɔːθədɔks] *adj* peu orthodoxe.
unpack [ʌn'pæk] *vi* défaire sa valise, déballer ses affaires.
unpaid [ʌn'peɪd] *adj* (*bill*) impayé(e); (*holiday*) non-payé(e), sans salaire; (*work*) non rétribué(e); (*worker*) bénévole.
unpalatable [ʌn'pælətəbl] *adj* (*truth*) désagréable (à entendre).
unparalleled [ʌn'pærəlɛld] *adj* incomparable, sans égal.
unpatriotic ['ʌnpætrɪ'ɔtɪk] *adj* (*person*) manquant de patriotisme; (*speech, attitude*) antipatriotique.
unplanned [ʌn'plænd] *adj* (*visit*) imprévu(e); (*baby*) non prévu(e).
unpleasant [ʌn'plɛznt] *adj* déplaisant(e), désagréable.
unplug [ʌn'plʌg] *vt* débrancher.
unpolluted [ʌnpə'luːtɪd] *adj* non pollué(e).
unpopular [ʌn'pɔpjulə*] *adj* impopulaire; **to make o.s. ~ (with)** se rendre impopulaire (auprès de).
unprecedented [ʌn'prɛsɪdɛntɪd] *adj* sans précédent.
unpredictable [ʌnprɪ'dɪktəbl] *adj* imprévisible.
unprejudiced [ʌn'prɛdʒudɪst] *adj* (*not biased*) impartial(e); (*having no prejudices*) qui n'a pas de préjugés.
unprepared [ʌnprɪ'pɛəd] *adj* (*person*) qui n'est pas suffisamment préparé(e); (*speech*) improvisé(e).
unprepossessing ['ʌnpriːpə'zɛsɪŋ] *adj* peu avenant(e).
unpretentious [ʌnprɪ'tɛnʃəs] *adj* sans prétention(s).
unprincipled [ʌn'prɪnsɪpld] *adj* sans principes.
unproductive [ʌnprə'dʌktɪv] *adj* improductif(ive); (*discussion*) stérile.
unprofessional [ʌnprə'fɛʃənl] *adj* (*conduct*) contraire à la déontologie.
unprofitable [ʌn'prɔfɪtəbl] *adj* non rentable.
UNPROFOR [ʌn'prəufɔː*] *n abbr* (= *United Nations Protection Force*) FORPRONU *f*.
unprotected ['ʌnprə'tɛktɪd] *adj* (*sex*) non protégé(e).
unprovoked [ʌnprə'vəukt] *adj* (*attack*) sans provocation.
unpunished [ʌn'pʌnɪʃt] *adj* impuni(e); **to go ~** rester impuni.
unqualified [ʌn'kwɔlɪfaɪd] *adj* (*teacher*) non diplômé(e), sans titres; (*success*) sans réserve, total(e).
unquestionably [ʌn'kwɛstʃənəblɪ] *adv* incontestablement.
unquestioning [ʌn'kwɛstʃənɪŋ] *adj* (*obedience, acceptance*) inconditionnel(le).
unravel [ʌn'rævl] *vt* démêler.
unreal [ʌn'rɪəl] *adj* irréel(le).
unrealistic ['ʌnrɪə'lɪstɪk] *adj* (*idea*) irréaliste; (*estimate*) peu réaliste.
unreasonable [ʌn'riːznəbl] *adj* qui n'est pas raisonnable; **to make ~ demands on sb** exiger trop de qn.
unrecognizable [ʌn'rɛkəgnaɪzəbl] *adj* pas reconnaissable.
unrecognized [ʌn'rɛkəgnaɪzd] *adj* (*talent, genius*) méconnu(e); (*POL: régime*) non reconnu(e).
unrecorded [ʌnrɪ'kɔːdɪd] *adj* non enregistré(e).
unrefined [ʌnrɪ'faɪnd] *adj* (*sugar, petroleum*) non raffiné(e).
unrehearsed [ʌnrɪ'həːst] *adj* (*THEAT etc*) qui n'a pas été répété(e); (*spontaneous*) spontané(e).

unrelated [ʌnrɪ'leɪtɪd] *adj* sans rapport; sans lien de parenté.
unrelenting [ʌnrɪ'lɛntɪŋ] *adj* implacable; acharné(e).
unreliable [ʌnrɪ'laɪəbl] *adj* sur qui (*or* quoi) on ne peut pas compter, peu fiable.
unrelieved [ʌnrɪ'liːvd] *adj* (*monotony*) constant(e), uniforme.
unremitting [ʌnrɪ'mɪtɪŋ] *adj* inlassable, infatigable, acharné(e).
unrepeatable [ʌnrɪ'piːtəbl] *adj* (*offer*) unique, exceptionnel(le).
unrepentant [ʌnrɪ'pɛntənt] *adj* impénitent(e).
unrepresentative ['ʌnrɛprɪ'zɛntətɪv] *adj*: ~ **(of)** peu représentatif(ive) (de).
unreserved [ʌnrɪ'zəːvd] *adj* (*seat*) non réservé(e); (*approval, admiration*) sans réserve.
unresponsive [ʌnrɪs'pɔnsɪv] *adj* insensible.
unrest [ʌn'rɛst] *n* agitation *f*, troubles *mpl*.
unrestricted [ʌnrɪ'strɪktɪd] *adj* illimité(e); **to have ~ access to** avoir librement accès *or* accès en tout temps à.
unrewarded [ʌnrɪ'wɔːdɪd] *adj* pas récompensé(e).
unripe [ʌn'raɪp] *adj* pas mûr(e).
unrivalled, (*US*) **unrivaled** [ʌn'raɪvəld] *adj* sans égal, incomparable.
unroll [ʌn'rəul] *vt* dérouler.
unruffled [ʌn'rʌfld] *adj* (*person*) imperturbable; (*hair*) qui n'est pas ébouriffé(e).
unruly [ʌn'ruːlɪ] *adj* indiscipliné(e).
unsafe [ʌn'seɪf] *adj* (*machine, wiring*) dangereux(euse); (*method*) hasardeux(euse); ~ **to drink/eat** non potable/comestible.
unsaid [ʌn'sɛd] *adj*: **to leave sth** ~ passer qch sous silence.
unsaleable, (*US*) **unsalable** [ʌn'seɪləbl] *adj* invendable.
unsatisfactory ['ʌnsætɪs'fæktərɪ] *adj* qui laisse à désirer.
unsavoury, (*US*) **unsavory** [ʌn'seɪvərɪ] *adj* (*fig*) peu recommandable, répugnant(e).
unscathed [ʌn'skeɪðd] *adj* indemne.
unscientific ['ʌnsaɪən'tɪfɪk] *adj* non scientifique.
unscrew [ʌn'skruː] *vt* dévisser.
unscrupulous [ʌn'skruːpjuləs] *adj* sans scrupules.
unseat [ʌn'siːt] *vt* (*rider*) désarçonner; (*fig: official*) faire perdre son siège à.
unsecured ['ʌnsɪ'kjuəd] *adj*: ~ **creditor** créancier/ière sans garantie.
unseeded [ʌn'siːdɪd] *adj* (*SPORT*) non classé(e).
unseemly [ʌn'siːmlɪ] *adj* inconvenant(e).
unseen [ʌn'siːn] *adj* (*person*) invisible; (*danger*) imprévu(e).
unselfish [ʌn'sɛlfɪʃ] *adj* désintéressé(e).
unsettled [ʌn'sɛtld] *adj* (*restless*) perturbé(e); (*unpredictable*) instable; incertain(e); (*not finalized*) non résolu(e).
unsettling [ʌn'sɛtlɪŋ] *adj* qui a un effet perturbateur.
unshak(e)able [ʌn'ʃeɪkəbl] *adj* inébranlable.
unshaven [ʌn'ʃeɪvn] *adj* non *or* mal rasé(e).
unsightly [ʌn'saɪtlɪ] *adj* disgracieux(euse), laid(e).
unskilled [ʌn'skɪld] *adj*: ~ **worker** manœuvre *m*.
unsociable [ʌn'səuʃəbl] *adj* (*person*) peu sociable; (*behaviour*) qui manque de sociabilité.
unsocial [ʌn'səuʃl] *adj* (*hours*) en dehors de l'horaire normal.
unsold [ʌn'səuld] *adj* invendu(e), non vendu(e).
unsolicited [ʌnsə'lɪsɪtɪd] *adj* non sollicité(e).
unsophisticated [ʌnsə'fɪstɪkeɪtɪd] *adj* simple, naturel(le).
unsound [ʌn'saund] *adj* (*health*) chancelant(e); (*floor, foundations*) peu solide; (*policy, advice*) peu judicieux(euse).
unspeakable [ʌn'spiːkəbl] *adj* indicible; (*awful*) innommable.
unspoken [ʌn'spəukn] *adj* (*word*) qui n'est pas prononcé(e); (*agreement, approval*) tacite.
unsteady [ʌn'stɛdɪ] *adj* mal assuré(e), chancelant(e), instable.
unstinting [ʌn'stɪntɪŋ] *adj* (*support*) total(e), sans réserve; (*generosity*) sans limites.
unstuck [ʌn'stʌk] *adj*: **to come** ~ se décoller; (*fig*) faire fiasco.
unsubstantiated ['ʌnsəb'stænʃɪeɪtɪd] *adj* (*rumour*) qui n'est pas confirmé(e); (*accusation*) sans preuve.
unsuccessful [ʌnsək'sɛsful] *adj* (*attempt*) infructueux(euse); (*writer, proposal*) qui n'a pas de succès; (*marriage*) malheureux(euse), qui ne réussit pas; **to be** ~ (*in attempting sth*) ne pas réussir; ne pas avoir de succès; (*application*) ne pas être retenu(e).
unsuccessfully [ʌnsək'sɛsfəlɪ] *adv* en vain.
unsuitable [ʌn'suːtəbl] *adj* qui ne convient pas, peu approprié(e); inopportun(e).
unsuited [ʌn'suːtɪd] *adj*: **to be ~ for** *or* **to** être inapte *or* impropre à.
unsung ['ʌnsʌŋ] *adj*: **an ~ hero** un héros méconnu.
unsupported [ʌnsə'pɔːtɪd] *adj* (*claim*) non soutenu(e); (*theory*) qui n'est pas corroboré(e).
unsure [ʌn'ʃuə*] *adj* pas sûr(e); **to be ~ of o.s.** ne pas être sûr de soi, manquer de confiance en soi.
unsuspecting [ʌnsə'spɛktɪŋ] *adj* qui ne se méfie pas.
unsweetened [ʌn'swiːtnd] *adj* non sucré(e).
unswerving [ʌn'swəːvɪŋ] *adj* inébranlable.
unsympathetic ['ʌnsɪmpə'θɛtɪk] *adj* hostile; (*unpleasant*) antipathique; ~ **to** indifférent(e) à.
untangle [ʌn'tæŋgl] *vt* démêler, débrouiller.
untapped [ʌn'tæpt] *adj* (*resources*) inexploité(e).
untaxed [ʌn'tækst] *adj* (*goods*) non taxé(e); (*income*) non imposé(e).

unthinkable [ʌn'θɪŋkəbl] *adj* impensable, inconcevable.
unthinkingly [ʌn'θɪŋkɪŋlɪ] *adv* sans réfléchir.
untidy [ʌn'taɪdɪ] *adj* (*room*) en désordre; (*appearance*) désordonné(e), débraillé(e); (*person*) sans ordre, désordonné; débraillé; (*work*) peu soigné(e).
untie [ʌn'taɪ] *vt* (*knot, parcel*) défaire; (*prisoner, dog*) détacher.
until [ən'tɪl] *prep* jusqu'à; (*after negative*) avant ♦ *conj* jusqu'à ce que *+ sub*, en attendant que *+ sub*; (*in past, after negative*) avant que *+ sub*; ~ **now** jusqu'à présent, jusqu'ici; ~ **then** jusque-là; **from morning** ~ **night** du matin au soir *or* jusqu'au soir.
untimely [ʌn'taɪmlɪ] *adj* inopportun(e); (*death*) prématuré(e).
untold [ʌn'təuld] *adj* incalculable; indescriptible.
untouched [ʌn'tʌtʃt] *adj* (*not used etc*) tel(le) quel(le), intact(e); (*safe: person*) indemne; (*unaffected*): ~ **by** indifférent(e) à.
untoward [ʌntə'wɔːd] *adj* fâcheux(euse), malencontreux(euse).
untrained ['ʌn'treɪnd] *adj* (*worker*) sans formation; (*troops*) sans entraînement; **to the** ~ **eye** à l'œil non exercé.
untrammelled [ʌn'træmld] *adj* sans entraves.
untranslatable [ʌntrænz'leɪtəbl] *adj* intraduisible.
untrue [ʌn'truː] *adj* (*statement*) faux(fausse).
untrustworthy [ʌn'trʌstwəːðɪ] *adj* (*person*) pas digne de confiance, peu sûr(e).
unusable [ʌn'juːzəbl] *adj* inutilisable.
unused *adj* [ʌn'juːzd] (*new*) neuf(neuve); [ʌn'juːst]: **to be** ~ **to sth/to doing sth** ne pas avoir l'habitude de qch/de faire qch.
unusual [ʌn'juːʒuəl] *adj* insolite, exceptionnel(le), rare.
unusually [ʌn'juːʒuəlɪ] *adv* exceptionnellement, particulièrement.
unveil [ʌn'veɪl] *vt* dévoiler.
unwanted [ʌn'wɔntɪd] *adj* non désiré(e).
unwarranted [ʌn'wɔrəntɪd] *adj* injustifié(e).
unwary [ʌn'wɛərɪ] *adj* imprudent(e).
unwavering [ʌn'weɪvərɪŋ] *adj* inébranlable.
unwelcome [ʌn'wɛlkəm] *adj* importun(e); **to feel** ~ se sentir de trop.
unwell [ʌn'wɛl] *adj* indisposé(e), souffrant(e); **to feel** ~ ne pas se sentir bien.
unwieldy [ʌn'wiːldɪ] *adj* difficile à manier.
unwilling [ʌn'wɪlɪŋ] *adj*: **to be** ~ **to do** ne pas vouloir faire.
unwillingly [ʌn'wɪlɪŋlɪ] *adv* à contrecœur, contre son gré.
unwind [ʌn'waɪnd] *vb* (*irreg*) *vt* dérouler ♦ *vi* (*relax*) se détendre.
unwise [ʌn'waɪz] *adj* imprudent(e), peu judicieux(euse).
unwitting [ʌn'wɪtɪŋ] *adj* involontaire.
unworkable [ʌn'wəːkəbl] *adj* (*plan etc*) inexploitable.
unworthy [ʌn'wəːðɪ] *adj* indigne.
unwrap [ʌn'ræp] *vt* défaire; ouvrir.
unwritten [ʌn'rɪtn] *adj* (*agreement*) tacite.
unzip [ʌn'zɪp] *vt* ouvrir (la fermeture éclair de).

KEYWORD

up [ʌp] *prep*: **he went** ~ **the stairs/the hill** il a monté l'escalier/la colline; **the cat was** ~ **a tree** le chat était dans un arbre; **they live further** ~ **the street** ils habitent plus haut dans la rue
♦ *vi* (*col*): **she** ~**ped and left** elle a fichu le camp sans plus attendre
♦ *adv* **1** en haut; en l'air; (*upwards, higher*): ~ **in the sky/the mountains** (là-haut) dans le ciel/les montagnes; **put it a bit higher** ~ mettez-le un peu plus haut; ~ **there** là-haut; ~ **above** au-dessus; **"this side** ~**"** "haut"
2: **to be** ~ (*out of bed*) être levé(e); (*prices*) avoir augmenté *or* monté; (*finished*): **when the year was** ~ à la fin de l'année; **time's** ~ c'est l'heure
3: ~ **to** (*as far as*) jusqu'à; ~ **to now** jusqu'à présent
4: **to be** ~ **to** (*depending on*): **it's** ~ **to you** c'est à vous de décider; (*equal to*): **he's not** ~ **to it** (*job, task etc*) il n'en est pas capable; (*inf: be doing*): **what is he** ~ **to?** qu'est-ce qu'il peut bien faire?
5 (*phrases*): **he's well** ~ **in** *or* **on ...** (*BRIT: knowledgeable*) il s'y connaît en ...; ~ **with Leeds United!** vive Leeds United!; **what's** ~**?** (*col*) qu'est-ce qui ne va pas?; **what's** ~ **with him?** (*col*) qu'est-ce qui lui arrive?
♦ *n*: ~**s and downs** hauts et bas *mpl*.

up-and-coming [ʌpənd'kʌmɪŋ] *adj* plein(e) d'avenir *or* de promesses.
upbeat ['ʌpbiːt] *n* (*MUS*) levé *m*; (*in economy, prosperity*) amélioration *f* ♦ *adj* (*optimistic*) optimiste.
upbraid [ʌp'breɪd] *vt* morigéner.
upbringing ['ʌpbrɪŋɪŋ] *n* éducation *f*.
upcoming ['ʌpkʌmɪŋ] *adj* tout(e) prochain(e).
update [ʌp'deɪt] *vt* mettre à jour.
upend [ʌp'ɛnd] *vt* mettre debout.
up-front [ʌp'frʌnt] *adj* franc(franche) ♦ *adv* (*pay*) d'avance.
upgrade [ʌp'greɪd] *vt* (*person*) promouvoir; (*job*) revaloriser; (*property, equipment*) moderniser.
upheaval [ʌp'hiːvl] *n* bouleversement *m*; branle-bas *m*; crise *f*.
uphill [ʌp'hɪl] *adj* qui monte; (*fig: task*) difficile, pénible ♦ *adv* (*face, look*) en amont, vers l'amont; (*go, move*) vers le haut, en haut; **to go** ~ monter.
uphold [ʌp'həuld] *vt irreg* maintenir; soutenir.
upholstery [ʌp'həulstərɪ] *n* rembourrage *m*; (*of car*) garniture *f*.
upkeep ['ʌpkiːp] *n* entretien *m*.

up-market [ʌp'mɑːkɪt] *adj* (*product*) haut de gamme *inv*.
upon [ə'pɔn] *prep* sur.
upper ['ʌpə*] *adj* supérieur(e); du dessus ♦ *n* (*of shoe*) empeigne *f*.
upper class *n*: **the ~** ≈ la haute bourgeoisie ♦ *adj*: **upper-class** (*district*) élégant(e), huppé(e); (*accent, attitude*) caractéristique des classes supérieures.
uppercut ['ʌpəkʌt] *n* uppercut *m*.
upper hand *n*: **to have the ~** avoir le dessus.
Upper House *n*: **the ~** (*in Britain*) la Chambre des Lords, la Chambre haute; (*in France, in the US etc*) le Sénat.
uppermost ['ʌpəməust] *adj* le(la) plus haut(e); en dessus; **it was ~ in my mind** j'y pensais avant tout autre chose.
Upper Volta [-'vɔltə] *n* Haute Volta.
upright ['ʌpraɪt] *adj* droit(e); vertical(e); (*fig*) droit, honnête ♦ *n* montant *m*.
uprising ['ʌpraɪzɪŋ] *n* soulèvement *m*, insurrection *f*.
uproar ['ʌprɔː*] *n* tumulte *m*, vacarme *m*.
uproarious [ʌp'rɔːrɪəs] *adj* (*event etc*) désopilant(e); **~ laughter** un brouhaha de rires.
uproot [ʌp'ruːt] *vt* déraciner.
upset *n* ['ʌpsɛt] dérangement *m* ♦ *vt* [ʌp'sɛt] (*irreg: like* **set**) (*glass etc*) renverser; (*plan*) déranger; (*person: offend*) contrarier; (*: grieve*) faire de la peine à; bouleverser ♦ *adj* [ʌp'sɛt] contrarié(e); peiné(e); (*stomach*) détraqué(e), dérangé(e); **to get ~** (*sad*) devenir triste; (*offended*) se vexer; **to have a stomach ~** (*BRIT*) avoir une indigestion.
upset price *n* (*US, Scottish*) mise *f* à prix, prix *m* de départ.
upsetting [ʌp'sɛtɪŋ] *adj* (*offending*) vexant(e); (*annoying*) ennuyeux(euse).
upshot ['ʌpʃɔt] *n* résultat *m*; **the ~ of it all was that ...** il a résulté de tout cela que ....
upside down ['ʌpsaɪd-] *adv* à l'envers.
upstage ['ʌp'steɪdʒ] *vt*: **to ~ sb** souffler la vedette à qn.
upstairs [ʌp'stɛəz] *adv* en haut ♦ *adj* (*room*) du dessus, d'en haut ♦ *n*: **there's no ~** il n'y a pas d'étage.
upstart ['ʌpstɑːt] *n* parvenu/e.
upstream [ʌp'striːm] *adv* en amont.
upsurge ['ʌpsəːdʒ] *n* (*of enthusiasm etc*) vague *f*.
uptake ['ʌpteɪk] *n*: **he is quick/slow on the ~** il comprend vite/est lent à comprendre.
uptight [ʌp'taɪt] *adj* (*col*) très tendu(e), crispé(e).
up-to-date ['ʌptə'deɪt] *adj* moderne; très récent(e).
upturn ['ʌptəːn] *n* (*in economy*) reprise *f*.
upturned ['ʌptəːnd] *adj* (*nose*) retroussé(e).
upward ['ʌpwəd] *adj* ascendant(e); vers le haut ♦ *adv see* **upwards**.
upwardly-mobile ['ʌpwədlɪ'məubaɪl] *adj* à mobilité sociale ascendante.
upwards ['ʌpwədz] *adv* vers le haut; **and ~** et plus, et au-dessus.
URA *n abbr* (*US*) = *Urban Renewal Administration.*
Ural Mountains ['juərəl-] *npl*: **the ~** (*also*: **the Urals**) les monts *mpl* Oural, l'Oural *m*.
uranium [juə'reɪnɪəm] *n* uranium *m*.
Uranus [juə'reɪnəs] *n* Uranus *f*.
urban ['əːbən] *adj* urbain(e).
urbane [əː'beɪn] *adj* urbain(e), courtois(e).
urbanization [əːbənaɪ'zeɪʃən] *n* urbanisation *f*.
urchin ['əːtʃɪn] *n* gosse *m*, garnement *m*.
Urdu ['uəduː] *n* ourdou *m*.
urge [əːdʒ] *n* besoin (impératif), envie (pressante) ♦ *vt* (*caution etc*) recommander avec insistance; (*person*): **to ~ sb to do** presser qn de faire, recommander avec insistance à qn de faire.
►**urge on** *vt* pousser, presser.
urgency ['əːdʒənsɪ] *n* urgence *f*; (*of tone*) insistance *f*.
urgent ['əːdʒənt] *adj* urgent(e); (*plea, tone*) pressant(e).
urgently ['əːdʒəntlɪ] *adv* d'urgence, de toute urgence; (*need*) sans délai.
urinal ['juərɪnl] *n* (*BRIT*) urinoir *m*.
urinate ['juərɪneɪt] *vi* uriner.
urine ['juərɪn] *n* urine *f*.
urn [əːn] *n* urne *f*; (*also*: **tea ~**) fontaine *f* à thé.
Uruguay ['juərəgwaɪ] *n* Uruguay *m*.
Uruguayan [juərə'gwaɪən] *adj* uruguayen(ne) ♦ *n* Uruguayen/ne.
US *n abbr* = **United States**.
us [ʌs] *pron* nous.
USA *n abbr* = **United States of America**; (*MIL*) = *United States Army.*
usable ['juːzəbl] *adj* utilisable.
USAF *n abbr* = *United States Air Force.*
usage ['juːzɪdʒ] *n* usage *m*.
USCG *n abbr* = *United States Coast Guard.*
USDA *n abbr* = *United States Department of Agriculture.*
USDAW ['ʌzdɔː] *n abbr* (*BRIT*: = *Union of Shop, Distributive and Allied Workers*) *syndicat du commerce de détail et de la distribution.*
USDI *n abbr* = *United States Department of the Interior.*
use *n* [juːs] emploi *m*, utilisation *f*; usage *m* ♦ *vt* [juːz] se servir de, utiliser, employer; **in ~** en usage; **out of ~** hors d'usage; **to be of ~** servir, être utile; **to make ~ of sth** utiliser qch; **ready for ~** prêt à l'emploi; **it's no ~** ça ne sert à rien; **to have the ~ of** avoir l'usage de; **what's this ~d for?** à quoi est-ce que ça sert?; **she ~d to do it** elle le faisait (autrefois), elle avait coutume de le faire; **to be ~d to** avoir l'habitude de, être habitué(e) à; **to get ~d to** s'habituer à.
►**use up** *vt* finir, épuiser; (*food*) consommer.
used [juːzd] *adj* (*car*) d'occasion.

useful ['juːsful] *adj* utile; **to come in ~** être utile.
usefulness ['juːsfəlnɪs] *n* utilité *f*.
useless ['juːslɪs] *adj* inutile.
user ['juːzə*] *n* utilisateur/trice, usager *m*.
user-friendly ['juːzə'frɛndlɪ] *adj* convivial(e), facile d'emploi.
USES *n abbr* = *United States Employment Service*.
usher ['ʌʃə*] *n* placeur *m* ♦ *vt*: **to ~ sb in** faire entrer qn.
usherette [ʌʃə'rɛt] *n* (*in cinema*) ouvreuse *f*.
USIA *n abbr* = *United States Information Agency*.
USM *n abbr* = *United States Mail, United States Mint*.
USN *n abbr* = *United States Navy*.
USPHS *n abbr* = *United States Public Health Service*.
USPO *n abbr* = *United States Post Office*.
USS *abbr* = *United States Ship (or Steamer)*.
USSR *n abbr* = **Union of Soviet Socialist Republics**.
usu. *abbr* = **usually**.
usual ['juːʒuəl] *adj* habituel(le); **as ~** comme d'habitude.
usually ['juːʒuəlɪ] *adv* d'habitude, d'ordinaire.
usurer ['juːʒərə*] *n* usurier/ière.
usurp [juː'zəːp] *vt* usurper.
UT *abbr* (*US*) = *Utah*.
utensil [juː'tɛnsl] *n* ustensile *m*; **kitchen ~s** batterie *f* de cuisine.
uterus ['juːtərəs] *n* utérus *m*.
utilitarian [juːtɪlɪ'tɛərɪən] *adj* utilitaire.
utility [juː'tɪlɪtɪ] *n* utilité *f*; (*also*: **public ~**) service public.
utility room *n* buanderie *f*.
utilization [juːtɪlaɪ'zeɪʃən] *n* utilisation *f*.
utilize ['juːtɪlaɪz] *vt* utiliser; exploiter.
utmost ['ʌtməust] *adj* extrême, le(la) plus grand(e) ♦ *n*: **to do one's ~** faire tout son possible; **of the ~ importance** d'une importance capitale, de la plus haute importance.
utter ['ʌtə*] *adj* total(e), complet(ète) ♦ *vt* prononcer, proférer; émettre.
utterance ['ʌtrns] *n* paroles *fpl*.
utterly ['ʌtəlɪ] *adv* complètement, totalement.
U-turn ['juː'təːn] *n* demi-tour *m*; (*fig*) volte-face *f inv*.
Uzbekistan [ʌżbɛkɪ'stɑːn] *n* Ouzbékistan *m*.

V v

V, v [viː] *n* (*letter*) V, v *m*; **V for Victor** V comme Victor.
v *abbr* (= *verse*, = *vide: see*) v.; (= *versus*) c.; (= *volt*) V.
VA, Va. *abbr* (*US*) = *Virginia*.
vac [væk] *n abbr* (*BRIT col*) = **vacation**.
vacancy ['veɪkənsɪ] *n* (*BRIT*: *job*) poste vacant; (*room*) chambre *f* disponible; **"no vacancies"** "complet".
vacant ['veɪkənt] *adj* (*post*) vacant(e); (*seat etc*) libre, disponible; (*expression*) distrait(e).
vacant lot *n* terrain inoccupé; (*for sale*) terrain à vendre.
vacate [və'keɪt] *vt* quitter.
vacation [və'keɪʃən] *n* (*esp US*) vacances *fpl*; **to take a ~** prendre des vacances; **on ~** en vacances.
vacation course *n* cours *mpl* de vacances.
vaccinate ['væksɪneɪt] *vt* vacciner.
vaccination [væksɪ'neɪʃən] *n* vaccination *f*.
vaccine ['væksiːn] *n* vaccin *m*.
vacuum ['vækjum] *n* vide *m*.
vacuum bottle *n* (*US*) = **vacuum flask**.
vacuum cleaner *n* aspirateur *m*.
vacuum flask *n* (*BRIT*) bouteille *f* thermos ®.
vacuum-packed ['vækjumpækt] *adj* emballé(e) sous vide.
vagabond ['vægəbɔnd] *n* vagabond/e; (*tramp*) chemineau *m*, clochard/e.
vagary ['veɪgərɪ] *n* caprice *m*.
vagina [və'dʒaɪnə] *n* vagin *m*.
vagrancy ['veɪgrənsɪ] *n* vagabondage *m*.
vagrant ['veɪgrənt] *n* vagabond/e, mendiant/e.
vague [veɪg] *adj* vague, imprécis(e); (*blurred: photo, memory*) flou(e); **I haven't the ~st idea** je n'en ai pas la moindre idée.
vaguely ['veɪglɪ] *adv* vaguement.
vain [veɪn] *adj* (*useless*) vain(e); (*conceited*) vaniteux(euse); **in ~** en vain.
valance ['væləns] *n* (*of bed*) tour *m* de lit.
valedictory [vælɪ'dɪktərɪ] *adj* d'adieu.
valentine ['væləntaɪn] *n* (*also*: **~ card**) carte *f* de la Saint-Valentin.
valet ['vælɪt] *n* valet *m* de chambre.
valet parking *n* parcage *m* par les soins du personnel (de l'hôtel *etc*).
valet service *n* (*for clothes*) pressing *m*; (*for car*) nettoyage complet.
valiant ['vælɪənt] *adj* vaillant(e), courageux(euse).
valid ['vælɪd] *adj* valide, valable; (*excuse*) valable.

validate ['vælɪdeɪt] *vt* (*contract, document*) valider; (*argument, claim*) prouver la justesse de, confirmer.
validity [və'lɪdɪtɪ] *n* validité *f*.
valise [və'li:z] *n* sac *m* de voyage.
valley ['vælɪ] *n* vallée *f*.
valour, (*US*) **valor** ['vælə*] *n* courage *m*.
valuable ['væljuəbl] *adj* (*jewel*) de grande valeur; (*time*) précieux(euse); **~s** *npl* objets *mpl* de valeur.
valuation [vælju'eɪʃən] *n* évaluation *f*, expertise *f*.
value ['vælju:] *n* valeur *f* ♦ *vt* (*fix price*) évaluer, expertiser; (*cherish*) tenir à; **you get good ~ (for money) in that shop** vous en avez pour votre argent dans ce magasin; **to lose (in) ~** (*currency*) baisser; (*property*) se déprécier; **to gain (in) ~** (*currency*) monter; (*property*) prendre de la valeur; **to be of great ~ to sb** (*fig*) être très utile à qn.
value added tax (VAT) [-'ædɪd-] *n* (*BRIT*) taxe *f* à la valeur ajoutée (TVA).
valued ['vælju:d] *adj* (*appreciated*) estimé(e).
valuer ['væljuə*] *n* expert *m* (en estimations).
valve [vælv] *n* (*in machine*) soupape *f*; (*on tyre*) valve *f*; (*in radio*) lampe *f*.
vampire ['væmpaɪə*] *n* vampire *m*.
van [væn] *n* (*AUT*) camionnette *f*; (*BRIT RAIL*) fourgon *m*.
V and A *n abbr* (*BRIT*) = *Victoria and Albert Museum*.
vandal ['vændl] *n* vandale *m/f*.
vandalism ['vændəlɪzəm] *n* vandalisme *m*.
vandalize ['vændəlaɪz] *vt* saccager.
vanguard ['vængɑ:d] *n* avant-garde *m*.
vanilla [və'nɪlə] *n* vanille *f* ♦ *cpd* (*ice cream*) à la vanille.
vanish ['vænɪʃ] *vi* disparaître.
vanity ['vænɪtɪ] *n* vanité *f*.
vanity case *n* sac *m* de toilette.
vantage ['vɑ:ntɪdʒ] *n*: **~ point** bonne position.
vaporize ['veɪpəraɪz] *vt* vaporiser ♦ *vi* se vaporiser.
vapour, (*US*) **vapor** ['veɪpə*] *n* vapeur *f*; (*on window*) buée *f*.
vapo(u)r trail *n* (*AVIAT*) traînée *f* de condensation.
variable ['vɛərɪəbl] *adj* variable; (*mood*) changeant(e) ♦ *n* variable *f*.
variance ['vɛərɪəns] *n*: **to be at ~ (with)** être en désaccord (avec); (*facts*) être en contradiction (avec).
variant ['vɛərɪənt] *n* variante *f*.
variation [vɛərɪ'eɪʃən] *n* variation *f*; (*in opinion*) changement *m*.
varicose ['værɪkəus] *adj*: **~ veins** varices *fpl*.
varied ['vɛərɪd] *adj* varié(e), divers(e).
variety [və'raɪətɪ] *n* variété *f*; (*quantity*): **a wide ~ of** ... une quantité *or* un grand nombre de ... (différent(e)s *or* divers(es)); **for a ~ of reasons** pour diverses raisons.
variety show *n* (spectacle *m* de) variétés *fpl*.
various ['vɛərɪəs] *adj* divers(e), différent(e); (*several*) divers, plusieurs; **at ~ times** (*different*) en diverses occasions; (*several*) à plusieurs reprises.
varnish ['vɑ:nɪʃ] *n* vernis *m*; (*for nails*) vernis (à ongles) ♦ *vt* vernir; **to ~ one's nails** se vernir les ongles.
vary ['vɛərɪ] *vt, vi* varier, changer; **to ~ with** *or* **according to** varier selon.
varying ['vɛərɪɪŋ] *adj* variable.
vase [vɑ:z] *n* vase *m*.
vasectomy [væ'sɛktəmɪ] *n* vasectomie *f*.
Vaseline ['væsɪli:n] *n* ® vaseline *f*.
vast [vɑ:st] *adj* vaste, immense; (*amount, success*) énorme.
vastly ['vɑ:stlɪ] *adv* infiniment, extrêmement.
vastness ['vɑ:stnɪs] *n* immensité *f*.
VAT [væt] *n abbr* (*BRIT*) = **value added tax**.
vat [væt] *n* cuve *f*.
Vatican ['vætɪkən] *n*: **the ~** le Vatican.
vatman ['vætmæn] *n* (*BRIT col*) contrôleur *m* de la T.V.A.
vault [vɔ:lt] *n* (*of roof*) voûte *f*; (*tomb*) caveau *m*; (*in bank*) salle *f* des coffres; chambre forte; (*jump*) saut *m* ♦ *vt* (*also*: **~ over**) sauter (d'un bond).
vaunted ['vɔ:ntɪd] *adj*: **much-~** tant célébré(e).
VC *n abbr* = **vice-chairman**; (*BRIT*: = *Victoria Cross*) *distinction militaire*.
VCR *n abbr* = **video cassette recorder**.
VD *n abbr* = **venereal disease**.
VDU *n abbr* = **visual display unit**.
veal [vi:l] *n* veau *m*.
veer [vɪə*] *vi* tourner; virer.
veg. [vɛdʒ] *n abbr* (*BRIT col*) = **vegetable(s)**.
vegan ['vi:gən] *n* végétalien/ne.
vegeburger ['vɛdʒɪbə:gə*] *n* burger végétarien.
vegetable ['vɛdʒtəbl] *n* légume *m* ♦ *adj* végétal(e).
vegetable garden *n* (jardin *m*) potager *m*.
vegetarian [vɛdʒɪ'tɛərɪən] *adj, n* végétarien(ne).
vegetate ['vɛdʒɪteɪt] *vi* végéter.
vegetation [vɛdʒɪ'teɪʃən] *n* végétation *f*.
vegetative ['vɛdʒɪtətɪv] *adj* (*lit*) végétal(e); (*fig*) végétatif(ive).
veggieburger ['vɛdʒɪbə:gə*] *n* = **vegeburger**.
vehemence ['vi:ɪməns] *n* véhémence *f*, violence *f*.
vehement ['vi:ɪmənt] *adj* violent(e), impétueux(euse); (*impassioned*) ardent(e).
vehicle ['vi:ɪkl] *n* véhicule *m*.
vehicular [vɪ'hɪkjulə*] *adj*: **"no ~ traffic"** "interdit à tout véhicule".
veil [veɪl] *n* voile *m* ♦ *vt* voiler; **under a ~ of secrecy** (*fig*) dans le plus grand secret.
veiled [veɪld] *adj* voilé(e).
vein [veɪn] *n* veine *f*; (*on leaf*) nervure *f*; (*fig: mood*) esprit *m*.
Velcro ['vɛlkrəu] *n* ® velcro *m* ®.

vellum ['vɛləm] *n* (*writing paper*) vélin *m*.
velocity [vɪ'lɔsɪtɪ] *n* vitesse *f*, vélocité *f*.
velour(s) [və'luə*] *n* velours *m*.
velvet ['vɛlvɪt] *n* velours *m*.
vending machine ['vɛndɪŋ-] *n* distributeur *m* automatique.
vendor ['vɛndə*] *n* vendeur/euse; **street ~** marchand ambulant.
veneer [və'nɪə*] *n* placage *m* de bois; (*fig*) vernis *m*.
venerable ['vɛnərəbl] *adj* vénérable.
venereal [vɪ'nɪərɪəl] *adj*: **~ disease (VD)** maladie vénérienne.
Venetian [vɪ'ni:ʃən] *adj*: **~ blind** store vénitien.
Venezuela [vɛnɛ'zweɪlə] *n* Venezuela *m*.
Venezuelan [vɛnɛ'zweɪlən] *adj* vénézuélien(ne) ♦ *n* Vénézuélien/ne.
vengeance ['vɛndʒəns] *n* vengeance *f*; **with a ~** (*fig*) vraiment, pour de bon.
vengeful ['vɛndʒful] *adj* vengeur(geresse).
Venice ['vɛnɪs] *n* Venise.
venison ['vɛnɪsn] *n* venaison *f*.
venom ['vɛnəm] *n* venin *m*.
venomous ['vɛnəməs] *adj* venimeux(euse).
vent [vɛnt] *n* conduit *m* d'aération; (*in dress, jacket*) fente *f* ♦ *vt* (*fig: one's feelings*) donner libre cours à.
ventilate ['vɛntɪleɪt] *vt* (*room*) ventiler, aérer.
ventilation [vɛntɪ'leɪʃən] *n* ventilation *f*, aération *f*.
ventilation shaft *n* conduit *m* de ventilation *or* d'aération.
ventilator ['vɛntɪleɪtə*] *n* ventilateur *m*.
ventriloquist [vɛn'trɪləkwɪst] *n* ventriloque *m/f*.
venture ['vɛntʃə*] *n* entreprise *f* ♦ *vt* risquer, hasarder ♦ *vi* s'aventurer, se risquer; **a business ~** une entreprise commerciale; **to ~ to do sth** se risquer à faire qch.
venture capital *n* capital-risques *m*.
venue ['vɛnju:] *n* (*of conference etc*) lieu *m* de la réunion (*or* manifestation *etc*); (*of match*) lieu de la rencontre.
Venus ['vi:nəs] *n* (*planet*) Vénus *f*.
veracity [və'ræsɪtɪ] *n* véracité *f*.
veranda(h) [və'rændə] *n* véranda *f*.
verb [və:b] *n* verbe *m*.
verbal ['və:bl] *adj* verbal(e); (*translation*) littéral(e).
verbally ['və:bəlɪ] *adv* verbalement.
verbatim [və:'beɪtɪm] *adj*, *adv* mot pour mot.
verbose [və:'bəus] *adj* verbeux(euse).
verdict ['və:dɪkt] *n* verdict *m*; **~ of guilty/not guilty** verdict de culpabilité/de non-culpabilité.
verge [və:dʒ] *n* bord *m*; **"soft ~s"** (*BRIT*) "accotements non stabilisés"; **on the ~ of doing** sur le point de faire.
►**verge on** *vt fus* approcher de.
verger ['və:dʒə*] *n* (*REL*) bedeau *m*.
verification [vɛrɪfɪ'keɪʃən] *n* vérification *f*.
verify ['vɛrɪfaɪ] *vt* vérifier.
veritable ['vɛrɪtəbl] *adj* véritable.
vermin ['və:mɪn] *npl* animaux *mpl* nuisibles; (*insects*) vermine *f*.
vermouth ['və:məθ] *n* vermouth *m*.
vernacular [və'nækjulə*] *n* langue *f* vernaculaire, dialecte *m*.
versatile ['və:sətaɪl] *adj* polyvalent(e).
verse [və:s] *n* vers *mpl*; (*stanza*) strophe *f*; (*in bible*) verset *m*; **in ~** en vers.
versed [və:st] *adj*: **(well-)~ in** versé(e) dans.
version ['və:ʃən] *n* version *f*.
versus ['və:səs] *prep* contre.
vertebra, *pl* **~e** ['və:tɪbrə, -bri:] *n* vertèbre *f*.
vertebrate ['və:tɪbrɪt] *n* vertébré *m*.
vertical ['və:tɪkl] *adj* vertical(e) ♦ *n* verticale *f*.
vertically ['və:tɪklɪ] *adv* verticalement.
vertigo ['və:tɪgəu] *n* vertige *m*; **to suffer from ~** avoir des vertiges.
verve [və:v] *n* brio *m*; enthousiasme *m*.
very ['vɛrɪ] *adv* très ♦ *adj*: **the ~ book which** le livre même que; **the ~ thought (of it)** ... rien que d'y penser ...; **at the ~ end** tout à la fin; **the ~ last** le tout dernier; **at the ~ least** au moins; **~ well** très bien; **~ little** très peu; **~ much** beaucoup.
vespers ['vɛspəz] *npl* vêpres *fpl*.
vessel ['vɛsl] *n* (*ANAT*, *NAUT*) vaisseau *m*; (*container*) récipient *m*.
vest [vɛst] *n* (*BRIT*) tricot *m* de corps; (*US*) gilet *m* ♦ *vt*: **to ~ sb with sth, to ~ sth in sb** investir qn de qch.
vested interest *n*: **to have a ~ in doing** avoir tout intérêt à faire; **~s** *npl* (*COMM*) droits acquis.
vestibule ['vɛstɪbju:l] *n* vestibule *m*.
vestige ['vɛstɪdʒ] *n* vestige *m*.
vestry ['vɛstrɪ] *n* sacristie *f*.
Vesuvius [vɪ'su:vɪəs] *n* Vésuve *m*.
vet [vɛt] *n abbr* (= *veterinary surgeon*) vétérinaire *m/f* ♦ *vt* examiner minutieusement; (*text*) revoir; (*candidate*) se renseigner soigneusement sur, soumettre à une enquête approfondie.
veteran ['vɛtərn] *n* vétéran *m*; (*also*: **war ~**) ancien combattant ♦ *adj*: **she's a ~ campaigner for ...** cela fait très longtemps qu'elle lutte pour ....
veteran car *n* voiture *f* d'époque.
veterinarian [vɛtrɪ'nɛərɪən] *n* (*US*) = **veterinary surgeon**.
veterinary ['vɛtrɪnərɪ] *adj* vétérinaire.
veterinary surgeon *n* (*BRIT*) vétérinaire *m/f*.
veto ['vi:təu] *n* (*pl* **~es**) veto *m* ♦ *vt* opposer son veto à; **to put a ~ on** mettre (*or* opposer) son veto à.
vetting ['vɛtɪŋ] *n*: **positive ~** enquête *f* de sécurité.
vex [vɛks] *vt* fâcher, contrarier.
vexed [vɛkst] *adj* (*question*) controversé(e).
VFD *n abbr* (*US*) = *voluntary fire department*.
VG *n abbr* (*BRIT*: *SCOL etc*: = *very good*) tb (= *très*

bien).
VHF *abbr* (= *very high frequency*) VHF.
VI *abbr* (*US*) = *Virgin Islands*.
via ['vaɪə] *prep* par, via.
viability [vaɪə'bɪlɪtɪ] *n* viabilité *f*.
viable ['vaɪəbl] *adj* viable.
viaduct ['vaɪədʌkt] *n* viaduc *m*.
vial ['vaɪəl] *m* fiole *f*.
vibes [vaɪbz] *npl* (*col*): **I get good/bad ~ about it** je le sens bien/ne le sens pas; **there are good/bad ~ between us** entre nous le courant passe bien/ne passe pas.
vibrant ['vaɪbrnt] *adj* (*sound, colour*) vibrant(e).
vibraphone ['vaɪbrəfəun] *n* vibraphone *m*.
vibrate [vaɪ'breɪt] *vi*: **to ~ (with)** vibrer (de); (*resound*) retentir (de).
vibration [vaɪ'breɪʃən] *n* vibration *f*.
vibrator [vaɪ'breɪtə*] *n* vibromasseur *m*.
vicar ['vɪkə*] *n* pasteur *m* (*de l'Église anglicane*).
vicarage ['vɪkərɪdʒ] *n* presbytère *m*.
vicarious [vɪ'kɛərɪəs] *adj* (*pleasure, experience*) indirect(e).
vice [vaɪs] *n* (*evil*) vice *m*; (*TECH*) étau *m*.
vice- [vaɪs] *prefix* vice-.
vice-chairman [vaɪs'tʃɛəmən] *n* vice-président/e.
vice-chancellor [vaɪs'tʃɑːnsələ*] *n* (*BRIT*) ≈ président/e d'université.
vice-president [vaɪs'prɛzɪdənt] *n* vice-président/e.
viceroy ['vaɪsrɔɪ] *n* vice-roi *m*.
vice squad *n* ≈ brigade mondaine.
vice versa ['vaɪsɪ'vəːsə] *adv* vice versa.
vicinity [vɪ'sɪnɪtɪ] *n* environs *mpl*, alentours *mpl*.
vicious ['vɪʃəs] *adj* (*remark*) cruel(le), méchant(e); (*blow*) brutal(e); **a ~ circle** un cercle vicieux.
viciousness ['vɪʃəsnɪs] *n* méchanceté *f*, cruauté *f*; brutalité *f*.
vicissitudes [vɪ'sɪsɪtjuːdz] *npl* vicissitudes *fpl*.
victim ['vɪktɪm] *n* victime *f*; **to be the ~ of** être victime de.
victimization [vɪktɪmaɪ'zeɪʃən] *n* brimades *fpl*; représailles *fpl*.
victimize ['vɪktɪmaɪz] *vt* brimer; exercer des représailles sur.
victor ['vɪktə*] *n* vainqueur *m*.
Victorian [vɪk'tɔːrɪən] *adj* victorien(ne).
victorious [vɪk'tɔːrɪəs] *adj* victorieux(euse).
victory ['vɪktərɪ] *n* victoire *f*; **to win a ~ over sb** remporter une victoire sur qn.
video ['vɪdɪəu] *n* (~ *film*) vidéo *f*; (*also*: ~ **cassette**) vidéocassette *f*; (*also*: ~ **cassette recorder**) magnétoscope *m* ♦ *vt* (*with recorder*) enregistrer; (*with camera*) filmer ♦ *cpd* vidéo *inv*.
video camera *n* caméra *f* vidéo *inv*.
video cassette *n* vidéocassette *f*.
video (cassette) recorder *n* magnétoscope *m*.
videodisc ['vɪdɪəudɪsk] *n* vidéodisque *m*.
video game *n* jeu *m* vidéo *inv*.
video nasty *n* *vidéo à caractère violent ou pornographique*.
videophone ['vɪdɪəufəun] *n* visiophone *m*, vidéophone *m*.
video recording *n* enregistrement *m* (en) vidéo *inv*.
video tape *n* bande *f* vidéo *inv*; (*cassette*) vidéocassette *f*.
vie [vaɪ] *vi*: **to ~ with** lutter avec, rivaliser avec.
Vienna [vɪ'ɛnə] *n* Vienne.
Vietnam, Viet Nam ['vjɛt'næm] *n* Viêt-nam *or* Vietnam *m*.
Vietnamese [vjɛtnə'miːz] *adj* vietnamien(ne) ♦ *n* (*pl inv*) Vietnamien/ne; (*LING*) vietnamien *m*.
view [vjuː] *n* vue *f*; (*opinion*) avis *m*, vue ♦ *vt* (*situation*) considérer; (*house*) visiter; **on ~** (*in museum etc*) exposé(e); **in full ~ of sb** sous les yeux de qn; **to be within ~ (of sth)** être à portée de vue (de qch); **an overall ~ of the situation** une vue d'ensemble de la situation; **in my ~** à mon avis; **in ~ of the fact that** étant donné que; **with a ~ to doing sth** dans l'intention de faire qch.
viewdata ['vjuːdeɪtə] *n* (*BRIT*) télétexte *m* (*version téléphonique*).
viewer ['vjuːə*] *n* (*viewfinder*) viseur *m*; (*small projector*) visionneuse *f*; (*TV*) téléspectateur/trice.
viewfinder ['vjuːfaɪndə*] *n* viseur *m*.
viewpoint ['vjuːpɔɪnt] *n* point *m* de vue.
vigil ['vɪdʒɪl] *n* veille *f*; **to keep ~** veiller.
vigilance ['vɪdʒɪləns] *n* vigilance *f*.
vigilance committee *n* comité *m* d'autodéfense.
vigilant ['vɪdʒɪlənt] *adj* vigilant(e).
vigilante [vɪdʒɪ'læntɪ] *n* *justicier ou membre d'un groupe d'autodéfense*.
vigorous ['vɪgərəs] *adj* vigoureux(euse).
vigour, (*US*) **vigor** ['vɪgə*] *n* vigueur *f*.
vile [vaɪl] *adj* (*action*) vil(e); (*smell*) abominable; (*temper*) massacrant(e).
vilify ['vɪlɪfaɪ] *vt* calomnier, vilipender.
villa ['vɪlə] *n* villa *f*.
village ['vɪlɪdʒ] *n* village *m*.
villager ['vɪlɪdʒə*] *n* villageois/e.
villain ['vɪlən] *n* (*scoundrel*) scélérat *m*; (*criminal*) bandit *m*; (*in novel etc*) traître *m*.
VIN *n abbr* (*US*) = *vehicle identification number*.
vinaigrette [vɪneɪ'grɛt] *n* vinaigrette *f*.
vindicate ['vɪndɪkeɪt] *vt* défendre avec succès; justifier.
vindication [vɪndɪ'keɪʃən] *n*: **in ~ of** pour justifier.
vindictive [vɪn'dɪktɪv] *adj* vindicatif(ive), rancunier(ière).
vine [vaɪn] *n* vigne *f*; (*climbing plant*) plante grimpante.
vinegar ['vɪnɪgə*] *n* vinaigre *m*.

vine grower *n* viticulteur *m*.
vine-growing ['vaɪngrəuɪŋ] *adj* viticole ♦ *n* viticulture *f*.
vineyard ['vɪnjɑːd] *n* vignoble *m*.
vintage ['vɪntɪdʒ] *n* (*year*) année *f*, millésime *m*; **the 1970 ~** le millésime 1970.
vintage car *n* voiture ancienne.
vintage wine *n* vin *m* de grand cru.
vinyl ['vaɪnl] *n* vinyle *m*.
viola [vɪ'əulə] *n* alto *m*.
violate ['vaɪəleɪt] *vt* violer.
violation [vaɪə'leɪʃən] *n* violation *f*; **in ~ of** (*rule, law*) en infraction à, en violation de.
violence ['vaɪələns] *n* violence *f*; (*POL etc*) incidents violents.
violent ['vaɪələnt] *adj* violent(e); **a ~ dislike of sb/sth** une aversion profonde pour qn/qch.
violently ['vaɪələntlɪ] *adv* violemment; (*ill, angry*) terriblement.
violet ['vaɪələt] *adj* (*colour*) violet(te) ♦ *n* (*plant*) violette *f*.
violin [vaɪə'lɪn] *n* violon *m*.
violinist [vaɪə'lɪnɪst] *n* violoniste *m/f*.
VIP *n abbr* (= *very important person*) VIP *m*.
viper ['vaɪpə*] *n* vipère *f*.
viral ['vaɪərəl] *adj* viral(e).
virgin ['vəːdʒɪn] *n* vierge *f* ♦ *adj* vierge; **she is a ~** elle est vierge; **the Blessed V~** la Sainte Vierge.
virginity [vəː'dʒɪnɪtɪ] *n* virginité *f*.
Virgo ['vəːgəu] *n* la Vierge; **to be ~** être de la Vierge.
virile ['vɪraɪl] *adj* viril(e).
virility [vɪ'rɪlɪtɪ] *n* virilité *f*.
virtual ['vəːtjuəl] *adj* (*COMPUT, PHYSICS*) virtuel(le); (*in effect*): **it's a ~ impossibility** c'est quasiment impossible; **the ~ leader** le chef dans la pratique.
virtually ['vəːtjuəlɪ] *adv* (*almost*) pratiquement; **it is ~ impossible** c'est quasiment impossible.
virtual reality *n* réalité virtuelle.
virtue ['vəːtjuː] *n* vertu *f*; (*advantage*) mérite *m*, avantage *m*; **by ~ of** par le fait de.
virtuosity [vəːtju'ɔsɪtɪ] *n* virtuosité *f*.
virtuoso [vəːtju'əuzəu] *n* virtuose *m/f*.
virtuous ['vəːtjuəs] *adj* vertueux(euse).
virulent ['vɪrulənt] *adj* virulent(e).
virus ['vaɪərəs] *n* virus *m*.
visa ['viːzə] *n* visa *m*.
vis-à-vis [viːzə'viː] *prep* vis-à-vis de.
viscount ['vaɪkaunt] *n* vicomte *m*.
viscous ['vɪskəs] *adj* visqueux(euse), gluant(e).
vise [vaɪs] *n* (*US TECH*) = **vice**.
visibility [vɪzɪ'bɪlɪtɪ] *n* visibilité *f*.
visible ['vɪzəbl] *adj* visible; **~ exports/imports** exportations/importations *fpl* visibles.
visibly ['vɪzəblɪ] *adv* visiblement.
vision ['vɪʒən] *n* (*sight*) vue *f*, vision *f*; (*foresight, in dream*) vision.
visionary ['vɪʒənrɪ] *n* visionnaire *m/f*.
visit ['vɪzɪt] *n* visite *f*; (*stay*) séjour *m* ♦ *vt* (*person*) rendre visite à; (*place*) visiter; **on a private/official ~** en visite privée/officielle.
visiting ['vɪzɪtɪŋ] *adj* (*speaker, team*) invité(e), de l'extérieur.
visiting card *n* carte *f* de visite.
visiting hours *npl* heures *fpl* de visite.
visiting professor *n* ≈ professeur associé.
visitor ['vɪzɪtə*] *n* visiteur/euse; (*in hotel*) client/e.
visitors' book *n* livre *m* d'or; (*in hotel*) registre *m*.
visor ['vaɪzə*] *n* visière *f*.
VISTA ['vɪstə] *n abbr* (= *Volunteers in Service to America*) *programme d'assistance bénévole aux régions pauvres*.
vista ['vɪstə] *n* vue *f*, perspective *f*.
visual ['vɪzjuəl] *adj* visuel(le).
visual aid *n* support visuel (pour l'enseignement).
visual arts *npl* arts *mpl* plastiques.
visual display unit (VDU) *n* console *f* de visualisation, visuel *m*.
visualize ['vɪzjuəlaɪz] *vt* se représenter; (*foresee*) prévoir.
visually ['vɪzjuəlɪ] *adv* visuellement; **~ handicapped** handicapé(e) visuel(le).
vital ['vaɪtl] *adj* vital(e); **of ~ importance (to sb/sth)** d'une importance capitale (pour qn/qch).
vitality [vaɪ'tælɪtɪ] *n* vitalité *f*.
vitally ['vaɪtəlɪ] *adv* extrêmement.
vital statistics *npl* (*of population*) statistiques *fpl* démographiques; (*col: woman's*) mensurations *fpl*.
vitamin ['vɪtəmɪn] *n* vitamine *f*.
vitiate ['vɪʃɪeɪt] *vt* vicier.
vitreous ['vɪtrɪəs] *adj* (*china*) vitreux(euse); (*enamel*) vitrifié(e).
vitriolic [vɪtrɪ'ɔlɪk] *adj* (*fig*) venimeux(euse).
viva ['vaɪvə] *n* (*also*: **~ voce**) (examen) oral.
vivacious [vɪ'veɪʃəs] *adj* animé(e), qui a de la vivacité.
vivacity [vɪ'væsɪtɪ] *n* vivacité *f*.
vivid ['vɪvɪd] *adj* (*account*) frappant(e); (*light, imagination*) vif(vive).
vividly ['vɪvɪdlɪ] *adv* (*describe*) d'une manière vivante; (*remember*) de façon précise.
vivisection [vɪvɪ'sɛkʃən] *n* vivisection *f*.
vixen ['vɪksn] *n* renarde *f*; (*pej: woman*) mégère *f*.
viz [vɪz] *abbr* (= *vide licet: namely*) à savoir, c. à d.
VLF *abbr* = *very low frequency*.
V-neck ['viːnɛk] *n* décolleté *m* en V.
VOA *n abbr* (= *Voice of America*) voix *f* de l'Amérique (*émissions de radio à destination de l'étranger*).
vocabulary [vəu'kæbjulərɪ] *n* vocabulaire *m*.
vocal ['vəukl] *adj* vocal(e); (*articulate*) qui n'hésite pas à s'exprimer, qui sait faire entendre ses opinions; **~s** *npl* voix *fpl*.

vocal cords *npl* cordes vocales.
vocalist ['vəukəlɪst] *n* chanteur/euse.
vocation [vəu'keɪʃən] *n* vocation *f*.
vocational [vəu'keɪʃənl] *adj* professionnel(le); ~ **guidance/training** orientation/formation professionnelle.
vociferous [və'sɪfərəs] *adj* bruyant(e).
vodka ['vɔdkə] *n* vodka *f*.
vogue [vəug] *n* mode *f*; (*popularity*) vogue *f*; **to be in** ~ être en vogue *or* à la mode.
voice [vɔɪs] *n* voix *f*; (*opinion*) avis *m* ♦ *vt* (*opinion*) exprimer, formuler; **in a loud/soft** ~ à voix haute/basse; **to give** ~ **to** exprimer.
voice mail *n* (*system*) messagerie *f* vocale; (*device*) boîte *f* vocale.
voice-over ['vɔɪsəuvə*] *n* voix off *f*.
void [vɔɪd] *n* vide *m* ♦ *adj* (*invalid*) nul(le); (*empty*): ~ **of** vide de, dépourvu(e) de.
voile [vɔɪl] *n* voile *m* (*tissu*).
vol. *abbr* (= *volume*) vol.
volatile ['vɔlətaɪl] *adj* volatil(e); (*fig*) versatile.
volcanic [vɔl'kænɪk] *adj* volcanique.
volcano, ~es [vɔl'keɪnəu] *n* volcan *m*.
volition [və'lɪʃən] *n*: **of one's own** ~ de son propre gré.
volley ['vɔlɪ] *n* (*of gunfire*) salve *f*; (*of stones etc*) pluie *f*, volée *f*; (*TENNIS etc*) volée.
volleyball ['vɔlɪbɔːl] *n* volley(-ball) *m*.
volt [vəult] *n* volt *m*.
voltage ['vəultɪdʒ] *n* tension *f*, voltage *m*; **high/low** ~ haute/basse tension.
voluble ['vɔljubl] *adj* volubile.
volume ['vɔljuːm] *n* volume *m*; (*of tank*) capacité *f*; ~ **one/two** (*of book*) tome un/deux; **his expression spoke ~s** son expression en disait long.
volume control *n* (*RADIO, TV*) bouton *m* de réglage du volume.
voluminous [və'luːmɪnəs] *adj* volumineux(euse).
voluntarily ['vɔləntrɪlɪ] *adv* volontairement; bénévolement.
voluntary ['vɔləntərɪ] *adj* volontaire; (*unpaid*) bénévole.
voluntary liquidation *n* (*COMM*) dépôt *m* de bilan.
voluntary redundancy *n* (*BRIT*) départ *m* volontaire (*en cas de licenciements*).
volunteer [vɔlən'tɪə*] *n* volontaire *m/f* ♦ *vi* (*MIL*) s'engager comme volontaire; **to** ~ **to do** se proposer pour faire.
voluptuous [və'lʌptjuəs] *adj* voluptueux(euse).
vomit ['vɔmɪt] *n* vomissure *f* ♦ *vt, vi* vomir.
voracious [və'reɪʃəs] *adj* vorace; (*reader*) avide.
vote [vəut] *n* vote *m*, suffrage *m*; (*cast*) voix *f*, vote; (*franchise*) droit *m* de vote ♦ *vt* (*bill*) voter; (*chairman*) élire ♦ *vi* voter; **to put sth to the** ~, **to take a** ~ **on sth** mettre qch aux voix, procéder à un vote sur qch; ~ **for** *or* **in favour of/against** vote pour/contre; **to** ~ **to do sth** voter en faveur de faire qch; ~ **of censure** motion *f* de censure; ~ **of thanks** discours *m* de remerciement.
voter ['vəutə*] *n* électeur/trice.
voting ['vəutɪŋ] *n* scrutin *m*.
voting paper *n* (*BRIT*) bulletin *m* de vote.
voting right *n* droit *m* de vote.
vouch [vautʃ]: **to** ~ **for** *vt fus* se porter garant de.
voucher ['vautʃə*] *n* (*for meal, petrol*) bon *m*; (*receipt*) reçu *m*; **travel** ~ bon *m* de transport.
vow [vau] *n* vœu *m*, serment *m* ♦ *vi* jurer; **to take** *or* **make a** ~ **to do sth** faire le vœu de faire qch.
vowel ['vauəl] *n* voyelle *f*.
voyage ['vɔɪɪdʒ] *n* voyage *m* par mer, traversée *f*.
voyeur [vwɑːjəː*] *n* voyeur *m*.
VP *n abbr* = **vice-president**.
vs *abbr* (= *versus*) c.
VSO *n abbr* (*BRIT*: = *Voluntary Service Overseas*) ≈ coopération civile.
VT, Vt. *abbr* (*US*) = *Vermont*.
vulgar ['vʌlgə*] *adj* vulgaire.
vulgarity [vʌl'gærɪtɪ] *n* vulgarité *f*.
vulnerability [vʌlnərə'bɪlɪtɪ] *n* vulnérabilité *f*.
vulnerable ['vʌlnərəbl] *adj* vulnérable.
vulture ['vʌltʃə*] *n* vautour *m*.

W w

W, w ['dʌbljuː] *n* (*letter*) W, w *m*; **W for William** W comme William.
W *abbr* (= *west*) O; (*ELEC*: = *watt*) W.
WA *abbr* (*US*) = *Washington*.
wad [wɔd] *n* (*of cotton wool, paper*) tampon *m*; (*of banknotes etc*) liasse *f*.
wadding ['wɔdɪŋ] *n* rembourrage *m*.
waddle ['wɔdl] *vi* se dandiner.
wade [weɪd] *vi*: **to** ~ **through** marcher dans, patauger dans ♦ *vt* passer à gué.
wafer ['weɪfə*] *n* (*CULIN*) gaufrette *f*; (*REL*) pain *m* d'hostie; (*COMPUT*) tranche *f* (de silicium).
wafer-thin ['weɪfə'θɪn] *adj* ultra-mince, mince comme du papier à cigarette.
waffle ['wɔfl] *n* (*CULIN*) gaufre *f*; (*col*) rabâchage *m*; remplissage *m* ♦ *vi* parler pour ne rien dire; faire du remplissage.
waffle iron *n* gaufrier *m*.
waft [wɔft] *vt* porter ♦ *vi* flotter.
wag [wæg] *vt* agiter, remuer ♦ *vi* remuer; **the dog ~ged its tail** le chien a remué la queue.
wage [weɪdʒ] *n* (*also*: ~**s**) salaire *m*, paye *f* ♦ *vt*: **to** ~ **war** faire la guerre; **a day's ~s** un

jour de salaire.
wage claim *n* demande *f* d'augmentation de salaire.
wage differential *n* éventail *m* des salaires.
wage earner [-ə:nə*] *n* salarié/e; (*breadwinner*) soutien *m* de famille.
wage freeze *n* blocage *m* des salaires.
wage packet *n* (*BRIT*) (enveloppe *f* de) paye *f*.
wager ['weɪdʒə*] *n* pari *m* ♦ *vt* parier.
waggle ['wægl] *vt, vi* remuer.
wag(g)on ['wægən] *n* (*horse-drawn*) chariot *m*; (*BRIT RAIL*) wagon *m* (de marchandises).
wail [weɪl] *n* gémissement *m*; (*of siren*) hurlement *m* ♦ *vi* gémir; hurler.
waist [weɪst] *n* taille *f*, ceinture *f*.
waistcoat ['weɪskəut] *n* (*BRIT*) gilet *m*.
waistline ['weɪstlaɪn] *n* (tour *m* de) taille *f*.
wait [weɪt] *n* attente *f* ♦ *vi* attendre; **to ~ for sb/sth** attendre qn/qch; **to keep sb ~ing** faire attendre qn; **~ a minute!** un instant!; **"repairs while you ~"** "réparations minute"; **I can't ~ to ...** (*fig*) je meurs d'envie de ...; **to lie in ~ for** guetter.
►**wait behind** *vi* rester (à attendre).
►**wait on** *vt fus* servir.
►**wait up** *vi* attendre, ne pas se coucher; **don't ~ up for me** ne m'attendez pas pour aller vous coucher.
waiter ['weɪtə*] *n* garçon *m* (de café), serveur *m*.
waiting ['weɪtɪŋ] *n*: **"no ~"** (*BRIT AUT*) "stationnement interdit".
waiting list *n* liste *f* d'attente.
waiting room *n* salle *f* d'attente.
waitress ['weɪtrɪs] *n* serveuse *f*.
waive [weɪv] *vt* renoncer à, abandonner.
waiver ['weɪvə*] *n* dispense *f*.
wake [weɪk] *vb* (*pt* **woke, ~d**, *pp* **woken, ~d** [wəuk, 'wəukn]) *vt* (*also*: **~ up**) réveiller ♦ *vi* (*also*: **~ up**) se réveiller ♦ *n* (*for dead person*) veillée *f* mortuaire; (*NAUT*) sillage *m*; **to ~ up to sth** (*fig*) se rendre compte de qch; **in the ~ of** (*fig*) à la suite de; **to follow in sb's ~** (*fig*) marcher sur les traces de qn.
waken ['weɪkn] *vt, vi* = **wake**.
Wales [weɪlz] *n* pays *m* de Galles.
walk [wɔ:k] *n* promenade *f*; (*short*) petit tour; (*gait*) démarche *f*; (*pace*): **at a quick ~** d'un pas rapide; (*path*) chemin *m*; (*in park etc*) allée *f* ♦ *vi* marcher; (*for pleasure, exercise*) se promener ♦ *vt* (*distance*) faire à pied; (*dog*) promener; **10 minutes' ~ from** à 10 minutes de marche de; **to go for a ~** se promener; faire un tour; **I'll ~ you home** je vais vous raccompagner chez vous; **from all ~s of life** de toutes conditions sociales.
►**walk out** *vi* (*go out*) sortir; (*as protest*) partir (en signe de protestation); (*strike*) se mettre en grève; **to ~ out on sb** quitter qn.
walkabout ['wɔ:kəbaut] *n*: **to go (on a) ~** (*VIP*) prendre un bain de foule.
walker ['wɔ:kə*] *n* (*person*) marcheur/euse.
walkie-talkie ['wɔ:kɪ'tɔ:kɪ] *n* talkie-walkie *m*.
walking ['wɔ:kɪŋ] *n* marche *f* à pied; **it's within ~ distance** on peut y aller à pied.
walking holiday *n* vacances passées à faire de la randonnée.
walking shoes *npl* chaussures *fpl* de marche.
walking stick *n* canne *f*.
Walkman ['wɔ:kmən] *n* ® Walkman *m* ®.
walk-on ['wɔ:kɔn] *adj* (*THEAT*: *part*) de figurant/e.
walkout ['wɔ:kaut] *n* (*of workers*) grève-surprise *f*.
walkover ['wɔ:kəuvə*] *n* (*col*) victoire *f* or examen *m* *etc* facile.
walkway ['wɔ:kweɪ] *n* promenade *f*, cheminement piéton.
wall [wɔ:l] *n* mur *m*; (*of tunnel, cave*) paroi *f*; **to go to the ~** (*fig: firm etc*) faire faillite.
►**wall in** *vt* (*garden etc*) entourer d'un mur.
wall cupboard *n* placard mural.
walled [wɔ:ld] *adj* (*city*) fortifié(e).
wallet ['wɔlɪt] *n* portefeuille *m*.
wallflower ['wɔ:lflauə*] *n* giroflée *f*; **to be a ~** (*fig*) faire tapisserie.
wall hanging *n* tenture (murale), tapisserie *f*.
wallop ['wɔləp] *vt* (*BRIT col*) taper sur, cogner.
wallow ['wɔləu] *vi* se vautrer; **to ~ in one's grief** se complaire à sa douleur.
wallpaper ['wɔ:lpeɪpə*] *n* papier peint.
wall-to-wall ['wɔ:ltə'wɔ:l] *adj*: **~ carpeting** moquette *f*.
wally [wɔlɪ] *n* (*col*) imbécile *m/f*.
walnut ['wɔ:lnʌt] *n* noix *f*; (*tree*) noyer *m*.
walrus, *pl* **~** *or* **~es** ['wɔ:lrəs] *n* morse *m*.
waltz [wɔ:lts] *n* valse *f* ♦ *vi* valser.
wan [wɔn] *adj* pâle; triste.
wand [wɔnd] *n* (*also*: **magic ~**) baguette *f* (magique).
wander ['wɔndə*] *vi* (*person*) errer, aller sans but; (*thoughts*) vagabonder; (*river*) serpenter ♦ *vt* errer dans.
wanderer ['wɔndərə*] *n* vagabond/e.
wandering ['wɔndrɪŋ] *adj* (*tribe*) nomade; (*minstrel, actor*) ambulant(e).
wane [weɪn] *vi* (*moon*) décroître; (*reputation*) décliner.
wangle ['wæŋgl] (*BRIT col*) *vt* se débrouiller pour avoir; carotter ♦ *n* combine *f*, magouille *f*.
wanker ['wæŋkə*] *n* (*col!*) branleur *m* (*!*).
want [wɔnt] *vt* vouloir; (*need*) avoir besoin de; (*lack*) manquer de ♦ *n* (*poverty*) pauvreté *f*, besoin *m*; **~s** *npl* (*needs*) besoins *mpl*; **for ~ of** par manque de, faute de; **to ~ to do** vouloir faire; **to ~ sb to do** vouloir que qn fasse; **you're ~ed on the phone** on vous demande au téléphone; **"cook ~ed"** "on demande un cuisinier".
want ads *npl* (*US*) petites annonces.
wanting ['wɔntɪŋ] *adj*: **to be ~ (in)** manquer (de); **to be found ~** ne pas être à la hau-

teur.

wanton ['wɔntn] *adj* capricieux(euse); dévergondé(e).

war [wɔː*] *n* guerre *f*; **to go to ~** se mettre en guerre.

warble ['wɔːbl] *n* (*of bird*) gazouillis *m* ♦ *vi* gazouiller.

war cry *n* cri *m* de guerre.

ward [wɔːd] *n* (*in hospital*) salle *f*; (*POL*) section électorale; (*LAW: child*) pupille *m/f*.

▸**ward off** *vt* parer, éviter.

warden ['wɔːdn] *n* (*BRIT: of institution*) directeur/trice; (*of park, game reserve*) gardien/ne; (*BRIT: also:* **traffic ~**) contractuel/le.

warder ['wɔːdə*] *n* (*BRIT*) gardien *m* de prison.

wardrobe ['wɔːdrəub] *n* (*cupboard*) armoire *f*; (*clothes*) garde-robe *f*; (*THEAT*) costumes *mpl*.

warehouse ['wɛəhaus] *n* entrepôt *m*.

wares [wɛəz] *npl* marchandises *fpl*.

warfare ['wɔːfɛə*] *n* guerre *f*.

war game *n* jeu *m* de stratégie militaire.

warhead ['wɔːhɛd] *n* (*MIL*) ogive *f*.

warily ['wɛərılı] *adv* avec prudence, avec précaution.

warlike ['wɔːlaık] *adj* guerrier(ière).

warm [wɔːm] *adj* chaud(e); (*person, greeting, welcome, applause*) chaleureux(euse); (*supporter*) ardent(e), enthousiaste; **it's ~** il fait chaud; **I'm ~** j'ai chaud; **to keep sth ~** tenir qch au chaud; **with my ~est thanks/congratulations** avec mes remerciements/mes félicitations les plus sincères.

▸**warm up** *vi* (*person, room*) se réchauffer; (*water*) chauffer; (*athlete, discussion*) s'échauffer ♦ *vt* réchauffer; chauffer; (*engine*) faire chauffer.

warm-blooded ['wɔːm'blʌdıd] *adj* (*ZOOL*) à sang chaud.

war memorial *n* monument *m* aux morts.

warm-hearted [wɔːm'hɑːtıd] *adj* affectueux(euse).

warmly ['wɔːmlı] *adv* chaudement; chaleureusement.

warmonger ['wɔːmʌŋgə*] *n* belliciste *m/f*.

warmongering ['wɔːmʌŋgrıŋ] *n* propagande *f* belliciste, bellicisme *m*.

warmth [wɔːmθ] *n* chaleur *f*.

warm-up ['wɔːmʌp] *n* (*SPORT*) période *f* d'échauffement.

warn [wɔːn] *vt* avertir, prévenir; **to ~ sb not to do sth** *or* **against doing sth** prévenir qn de ne pas faire qch.

warning ['wɔːnıŋ] *n* avertissement *m*; (*notice*) avis *m*; **without (any) ~** (*suddenly*) inopinément; (*without notifying*) sans prévenir; **gale ~** (*METEOROLOGY*) avis de grand vent.

warning light *n* avertisseur lumineux.

warning triangle *n* (*AUT*) triangle *m* de présignalisation.

warp [wɔːp] *n* (*TEXTILES*) chaîne *f* ♦ *vi* (*wood*) travailler, se voiler *or* gauchir ♦ *vt* voiler; (*fig*) pervertir.

warpath ['wɔːpɑːθ] *n*: **to be on the ~** (*fig*) être sur le sentier de la guerre.

warped [wɔːpt] *adj* (*wood*) gauchi(e); (*fig*) perverti(e).

warrant ['wɔrnt] *n* (*guarantee*) garantie *f*; (*LAW: to arrest*) mandat *m* d'arrêt; (*: to search*) mandat de perquisition ♦ *vt* (*justify, merit*) justifier.

warrant officer *n* (*MIL*) adjudant *m*; (*NAUT*) premier-maître *m*.

warranty ['wɔrəntı] *n* garantie *f*; **under ~** (*COMM*) sous garantie.

warren ['wɔrən] *n* (*of rabbits*) terriers *mpl*, garenne *f*.

warring ['wɔːrıŋ] *adj* (*nations*) en guerre; (*interests etc*) contradictoire, opposé(e).

warrior ['wɔrıə*] *n* guerrier/ière.

Warsaw ['wɔːsɔː] *n* Varsovie.

warship ['wɔːʃıp] *n* navire *m* de guerre.

wart [wɔːt] *n* verrue *f*.

wartime ['wɔːtaım] *n*: **in ~** en temps de guerre.

wary ['wɛərı] *adj* prudent(e); **to be ~ about** *or* **of doing sth** hésiter beaucoup à faire qch.

was [wɔz] *pt of* **be**.

wash [wɔʃ] *vt* laver; (*sweep, carry: sea etc*) emporter, entraîner; (*: ashore*) rejeter ♦ *vi* se laver ♦ *n* (*paint*) badigeon *m*; (*washing programme*) lavage *m*; (*of ship*) sillage *m*; **to give sth a ~** laver qch; **to have a ~** se laver, faire sa toilette; **he was ~ed overboard** il a été emporté par une vague.

▸**wash away** *vt* (*stain*) enlever au lavage; (*subj: river etc*) emporter.

▸**wash down** *vt* laver; laver à grande eau.

▸**wash off** *vi* partir au lavage.

▸**wash up** *vi* faire la vaisselle; (*US: have a wash*) se débarbouiller.

Wash. *abbr* (*US*) = *Washington*.

washable ['wɔʃəbl] *adj* lavable.

washbasin ['wɔʃbeısn] *n* lavabo *m*.

washcloth ['wɔʃklɔθ] *n* (*US*) gant *m* de toilette.

washer ['wɔʃə*] *n* (*TECH*) rondelle *f*, joint *m*.

washing ['wɔʃıŋ] *n* (*BRIT: linen etc*) lessive *f*.

washing line *n* (*BRIT*) corde *f* à linge.

washing machine *n* machine *f* à laver.

washing powder *n* (*BRIT*) lessive *f* (en poudre).

Washington ['wɔʃıŋtən] *n* (*city, state*) Washington *m*.

washing-up [wɔʃıŋ'ʌp] *n* (*BRIT*) vaisselle *f*.

washing-up liquid *n* (*BRIT*) produit *m* pour la vaisselle.

wash-out ['wɔʃaut] *n* (*col*) désastre *m*.

washroom ['wɔʃrum] *n* toilettes *fpl*.

wasn't ['wɔznt] = **was not**.

Wasp, WASP [wɔsp] *n abbr* (*US col: = White Anglo-Saxon Protestant*) *surnom, souvent péjoratif, donné à l'américain de souche anglo-saxonne, aisé et de tendance conser-*

vatrice.

wasp [wɔsp] *n* guêpe *f*.

waspish ['wɔspɪʃ] *adj* irritable.

wastage ['weɪstɪdʒ] *n* gaspillage *m*; (*in manufacturing, transport etc*) déchet *m*.

waste [weɪst] *n* gaspillage *m*; (*of time*) perte *f*; (*rubbish*) déchets *mpl*; (*also*: **household ~**) ordures *fpl* ♦ *adj* (*material*) de rebut; (*energy, heat*) perdu(e); (*food*) inutilisé(e); (*land, ground: in city*) à l'abandon; (*: in country*) inculte, en friche ♦ *vt* gaspiller; (*time, opportunity*) perdre; **~s** *npl* étendue *f* désertique; **it's a ~ of money** c'est de l'argent jeté en l'air; **to go to ~** être gaspillé(e); **to lay ~** (*destroy*) dévaster.

►**waste away** *vi* dépérir.

wastebasket ['weɪstbɑːskɪt] *n* = **wastepaper basket**.

waste disposal (unit) *n* (*BRIT*) broyeur *m* d'ordures.

wasteful ['weɪstful] *adj* gaspilleur(euse); (*process*) peu économique.

waste ground *n* (*BRIT*) terrain *m* vague.

wasteland ['weɪstlənd] *n* terres *fpl* à l'abandon; (*in town*) terrain(s) *m(pl)* vague(s).

wastepaper basket ['weɪstpeɪpə-] *n* corbeille *f* à papier.

waste pipe *n* (tuyau *m* de) vidange *f*.

waste products *npl* (*INDUSTRY*) déchets *mpl* (de fabrication).

waster ['weɪstə*] *n* (*col*) bon/ne à rien.

watch [wɔtʃ] *n* montre *f*; (*act of watching*) surveillance *f*; guet *m*; (*guard*: *MIL*) sentinelle *f*; (*: NAUT*) homme *m* de quart; (*NAUT*: *spell of duty*) quart *m* ♦ *vt* (*look at*) observer; (*: match, programme*) regarder; (*spy on, guard*) surveiller; (*be careful of*) faire attention à ♦ *vi* regarder; (*keep guard*) monter la garde; **to keep a close ~ on sb/sth** surveiller qn/qch de près; **~ what you're doing** fais attention à ce que tu fais.

►**watch out** *vi* faire attention.

watchband ['wɔtʃbænd] *n* (*US*) bracelet *m* de montre.

watchdog ['wɔtʃdɔg] *n* chien *m* de garde; (*fig*) gardien/ne.

watchful ['wɔtʃful] *adj* attentif(ive), vigilant(e).

watchmaker ['wɔtʃmeɪkə*] *n* horloger/ère.

watchman ['wɔtʃmən] *n* gardien *m*; (*also*: **night ~**) veilleur *m* de nuit.

watch stem *n* (*US*) remontoir *m*.

watch strap *n* bracelet *m* de montre.

watchword ['wɔtʃwəːd] *n* mot *m* de passe.

water ['wɔːtə*] *n* eau *f* ♦ *vt* (*plant*) arroser ♦ *vi* (*eyes*) larmoyer; **a drink of ~** un verre d'eau; **in British ~s** dans les eaux territoriales Britanniques; **to pass ~** uriner; **to make sb's mouth ~** mettre l'eau à la bouche de qn.

►**water down** *vt* (*milk*) couper d'eau; (*fig: story*) édulcorer.

water closet *n* (*BRIT*) w.-c. *mpl*, waters *mpl*.

watercolour, (*US*) **watercolor** ['wɔːtəkʌlə*] *n* aquarelle *f*; **~s** *npl* couleurs *fpl* pour aquarelle.

water-cooled ['wɔːtəkuːld] *adj* à refroidissement par eau.

watercress ['wɔːtəkrɛs] *n* cresson *m* (de fontaine).

waterfall ['wɔːtəfɔːl] *n* chute *f* d'eau.

waterfront ['wɔːtəfrʌnt] *n* (*seafront*) front *m* de mer; (*at docks*) quais *mpl*.

water heater *n* chauffe-eau *m*.

water hole *n* mare *f*.

water ice *n* (*BRIT*) sorbet *m*.

watering can ['wɔːtərɪŋ-] *n* arrosoir *m*.

water level *n* niveau *m* de l'eau; (*of flood*) niveau des eaux.

water lily *n* nénuphar *m*.

waterline ['wɔːtəlaɪn] *n* (*NAUT*) ligne *f* de flottaison.

waterlogged ['wɔːtəlɔgd] *adj* détrempé(e); imbibé(e) d'eau.

water main *n* canalisation *f* d'eau.

watermark ['wɔːtəmɑːk] *n* (*on paper*) filigrane *m*.

watermelon ['wɔːtəmɛlən] *n* pastèque *f*.

water polo *n* water-polo *m*.

waterproof ['wɔːtəpruːf] *adj* imperméable.

water-repellent ['wɔːtərɪ'pɛlnt] *adj* hydrofuge.

watershed ['wɔːtəʃɛd] *n* (*GEO*) ligne *f* de partage des eaux; (*fig*) moment *m* critique, point décisif.

water-skiing ['wɔːtəskiːɪŋ] *n* ski *m* nautique.

water softener *n* adoucisseur *m* d'eau.

water tank *n* réservoir *m* d'eau.

watertight ['wɔːtətaɪt] *adj* étanche.

water vapour *n* vapeur *f* d'eau.

waterway ['wɔːtəweɪ] *n* cours *m* d'eau navigable.

waterworks ['wɔːtəwəːks] *npl* station *f* hydraulique.

watery ['wɔːtərɪ] *adj* (*colour*) délavé(e); (*coffee*) trop faible.

watt [wɔt] *n* watt *m*.

wattage ['wɔtɪdʒ] *n* puissance *f or* consommation *f* en watts.

wattle ['wɔtl] *n* clayonnage *m*.

wave [weɪv] *n* vague *f*; (*of hand*) geste *m*, signe *m*; (*RADIO*) onde *f*; (*in hair*) ondulation *f*; (*fig: of enthusiasm, strikes etc*) vague ♦ *vi* faire signe de la main; (*flag*) flotter au vent ♦ *vt* (*handkerchief*) agiter; (*stick*) brandir; (*hair*) onduler; **to ~ goodbye to sb** dire au revoir de la main à qn; **short/medium ~** (*RADIO*) ondes courtes/moyennes; **long ~** (*RADIO*) grandes ondes; **the new ~** (*CINE, MUS*) la nouvelle vague.

►**wave aside, wave away** *vt* (*person*): **to ~ sb aside** faire signe à qn de s'écarter; (*fig: suggestion, objection*) rejeter, repousser; (*: doubts*) chasser.

waveband ['weɪvbænd] *n* bande *f* de fréquences.

wavelength ['weɪvlɛŋθ] *n* longueur *f* d'ondes.

waver ['weɪvə*] *vi* vaciller; (*voice*) trembler; (*person*) hésiter.

wavy ['weɪvɪ] *adj* ondulé(e); onduleux(euse).

wax [wæks] *n* cire *f*; (*for skis*) fart *m* ♦ *vt* cirer; (*car*) lustrer ♦ *vi* (*moon*) croître.

waxen [wæksn] *adj* cireux(euse).

waxworks ['wækswə:ks] *npl* personnages *mpl* de cire; musée *m* de cire.

way [weɪ] *n* chemin *m*, voie *f*; (*path, access*) passage *m*; (*distance*) distance *f*; (*direction*) chemin, direction *f*; (*manner*) façon *f*, manière *f*; (*habit*) habitude *f*, façon; (*condition*) état *m*; **which ~? — this ~** par où *or* de quel côté? — par ici; **to crawl one's ~ to ...** ramper jusqu'à ...; **to lie one's ~ out of it** s'en sortir par un mensonge; **to lose one's ~** perdre son chemin; **on the ~ (to)** en route (pour); **to be on one's ~** être en route; **to be in the ~** bloquer le passage; (*fig*) gêner; **to keep out of sb's ~** éviter qn; **it's a long ~ away** c'est loin d'ici; **the village is rather out of the ~** le village est plutôt à l'écart *or* isolé; **to go out of one's ~ to do** (*fig*) se donner beaucoup de mal pour faire; **to be under ~** (*work, project*) être en cours; **to make ~ (for sb/sth)** faire place (à qn/qch), s'écarter pour laisser passer (qn/qch); **to get one's own ~** arriver à ses fins; **put it the right ~ up** (*BRIT*) mettez-le dans le bon sens; **to be the wrong ~ round** être à l'envers, ne pas être dans le bon sens; **he's in a bad ~** il va mal; **in a ~** d'un côté; **in some ~s** à certains égards; d'un côté; **in the ~ of** en fait de, comme; **by ~ of** (*through*) en passant par, via; (*as a sort of*) en guise de; **"~ in"** (*BRIT*) "entrée"; **"~ out"** (*BRIT*) "sortie"; **the ~ back** le chemin du retour; **this ~ and that** par-ci par-là; **"give ~"** (*BRIT AUT*) "cédez la priorité"; **no ~!** (*col*) pas question!

waybill ['weɪbɪl] *n* (*COMM*) récépissé *m*.

waylay [weɪ'leɪ] *vt irreg* attaquer; (*fig*): **I got waylaid** quelqu'un m'a accroché.

wayside ['weɪsaɪd] *n* bord *m* de la route; **to fall by the ~** (*fig*) abandonner; (*morally*) quitter le droit chemin.

way station *n* (*US RAIL*) petite gare.

wayward ['weɪwəd] *adj* capricieux(euse), entêté(e).

WC *n abbr* (*BRIT: = water closet*) w.-c. *mpl*, waters *mpl*.

WCC *n abbr* (*= World Council of Churches*) COE *m* (*= Conseil œcuménique des Églises*).

we [wi:] *pl pron* nous.

weak [wi:k] *adj* faible; (*health*) fragile; (*beam etc*) peu solide; (*tea, coffee*) léger(ère); **to grow ~(er)** s'affaiblir, faiblir.

weaken ['wi:kn] *vi* faiblir ♦ *vt* affaiblir.

weak-kneed ['wi:k'ni:d] *adj* (*fig*) lâche, faible.

weakling ['wi:klɪŋ] *n* gringalet *m*; faible *m/f*.

weakly ['wi:klɪ] *adj* chétif(ive) ♦ *adv* faiblement.

weakness ['wi:knɪs] *n* faiblesse *f*; (*fault*) point *m* faible.

wealth [wɛlθ] *n* (*money, resources*) richesse(s) *f(pl)*; (*of details*) profusion *f*.

wealth tax *n* impôt *m* sur la fortune.

wealthy ['wɛlθɪ] *adj* riche.

wean [wi:n] *vt* sevrer.

weapon ['wɛpən] *n* arme *f*; **~s of mass destruction** armes de destruction massive.

wear [wɛə*] *n* (*use*) usage *m*; (*deterioration through use*) usure *f*; (*clothing*): **sports/baby~** vêtements *mpl* de sport/pour bébés; **town/evening ~** tenue *f* de ville/de soirée ♦ *vb* (*pt* **wore**, *pp* **worn** [wɔ:*, wɔ:n]) *vt* (*clothes*) porter; (*beard etc*) avoir; (*damage: through use*) user ♦ *vi* (*last*) faire de l'usage; (*rub etc through*) s'user; **~ and tear** usure *f*; **to ~ a hole in sth** faire (à la longue) un trou dans qch.

▸**wear away** *vt* user, ronger ♦ *vi* s'user, être rongé(e).

▸**wear down** *vt* user; (*strength*) épuiser.

▸**wear off** *vi* disparaître.

▸**wear on** *vi* se poursuivre; passer.

▸**wear out** *vt* user; (*person, strength*) épuiser.

wearily ['wɪərɪlɪ] *adv* avec lassitude.

weariness ['wɪərɪnɪs] *n* épuisement *m*, lassitude *f*.

wearisome ['wɪərɪsəm] *adj* (*tiring*) fatigant(e); (*boring*) ennuyeux(euse).

weary ['wɪərɪ] *adj* (*tired*) épuisé(e); (*dispirited*) las(lasse); abattu(e) ♦ *vt* lasser ♦ *vi*: **to ~ of** se lasser de.

weasel ['wi:zl] *n* (*ZOOL*) belette *f*.

weather ['wɛðə*] *n* temps *m* ♦ *vt* (*wood*) faire mûrir; (*tempest, crisis*) essuyer, être pris(e) dans; survivre à, tenir le coup durant; **what's the ~ like?** quel temps fait-il?; **under the ~** (*fig: ill*) mal fichu(e).

weather-beaten ['wɛðəbi:tn] *adj* (*person*) hâlé(e); (*building*) dégradé(e) par les intempéries.

weather cock *n* girouette *f*.

weather forecast *n* prévisions *fpl* météorologiques, météo *f*.

weatherman ['wɛðəmæn] *n* météorologue *m*.

weatherproof ['wɛðəpru:f] *adj* (*garment*) imperméable; (*building*) étanche.

weather report *n* bulletin *m* météo, météo *f*.

weather vane [-veɪn] *n* = **weather cock**.

weave, *pt* **wove**, *pp* **woven** [wi:v, wəuv, 'wəuvn] *vt* (*cloth*) tisser; (*basket*) tresser ♦ *vi* (*fig: pt, pp* **~d**: *move in and out*) se faufiler.

weaver ['wi:və*] *n* tisserand/e.

weaving ['wi:vɪŋ] *n* tissage *m*.

web [wɛb] *n* (*of spider*) toile *f*; (*on foot*) palmure *f*; (*fabric, also fig*) tissu *m*; **the (World Wide) W~** le Web.

webbed ['wɛbd] *adj* (*foot*) palmé(e).

webbing ['wɛbɪŋ] *n* (*on chair*) sangles *fpl*.

website ['wɛbsaɪt] *n* (*COMPUT*) site *m* Web.
wed [wɛd] *vt* (*pt, pp* **wedded**) épouser ♦ *n*: **the newly-~s** les jeunes mariés.
Wed. *abbr* (= *Wednesday*) me.
we'd [wi:d] = **we had, we would**.
wedded ['wɛdɪd] *pt, pp of* **wed**.
wedding ['wɛdɪŋ] *n* mariage *m*.
wedding anniversary *n* anniversaire *m* de mariage; **silver/golden ~** noces *fpl* d'argent/d'or.
wedding day *n* jour *m* du mariage.
wedding dress *n* robe *f* de mariée.
wedding present *n* cadeau *m* de mariage.
wedding ring *n* alliance *f*.
wedge [wɛdʒ] *n* (*of wood etc*) coin *m*; (*under door etc*) cale *f*; (*of cake*) part *f* ♦ *vt* (*fix*) caler; (*push*) enfoncer, coincer.
wedge-heeled shoes ['wɛdʒhi:ld-] *npl* chaussures *fpl* à semelles compensées.
wedlock ['wɛdlɔk] *n* (union *f* du) mariage *m*.
Wednesday ['wɛdnzdɪ] *n* mercredi *m*; *for phrases see also* **Tuesday**.
wee [wi:] *adj* (*Scottish*) petit(e); tout(e) petit(e).
weed [wi:d] *n* mauvaise herbe ♦ *vt* désherber.
►**weed out** *vt* éliminer.
weed-killer ['wi:dkɪlə*] *n* désherbant *m*.
weedy ['wi:dɪ] *adj* (*man*) gringalet.
week [wi:k] *n* semaine *f*; **once/twice a ~** une fois/deux fois par semaine; **in two ~s' time** dans quinze jours; **Tuesday ~, a ~ on Tuesday** mardi en huit.
weekday ['wi:kdeɪ] *n* jour *m* de semaine; (*COMM*) jour ouvrable; **on ~s** en semaine.
weekend [wi:k'ɛnd] *n* week-end *m*.
weekend case *n* sac *m* de voyage.
weekly ['wi:klɪ] *adv* une fois par semaine, chaque semaine ♦ *adj, n* hebdomadaire (*m*).
weep, *pt, pp* **wept** [wi:p, wɛpt] *vi* (*person*) pleurer; (*MED*: *wound etc*) suinter.
weeping willow ['wi:pɪŋ-] *n* saule pleureur.
weepy ['wi:pɪ] *n* (*col*: *film*) mélo *m*.
weft [wɛft] *n* (*TEXTILES*) trame *f*.
weigh [weɪ] *vt, vi* peser; **to ~ anchor** lever l'ancre; **to ~ the pros and cons** peser le pour et le contre.
►**weigh down** *vt* (*branch*) faire plier; (*fig*: *with worry*) accabler.
►**weigh out** *vt* (*goods*) peser.
►**weigh up** *vt* examiner.
weighbridge ['weɪbrɪdʒ] *n* pont-bascule *m*.
weighing machine ['weɪɪŋ-] *n* balance *f*, bascule *f*.
weight [weɪt] *n* poids *m* ♦ *vt* alourdir; (*fig*: *factor*) pondérer; **sold by ~** vendu au poids; **to put on/lose ~** grossir/maigrir; **~s and measures** poids et mesures.
weighting ['weɪtɪŋ] *n*: **~ allowance** indemnité *f* de résidence.
weightlessness ['weɪtlɪsnɪs] *n* apesanteur *f*.
weightlifter ['weɪtlɪftə*] *n* haltérophile *m*.
weight training *n* musculation *f*.
weighty ['weɪtɪ] *adj* lourd(e).
weir [wɪə*] *n* barrage *m*.
weird [wɪəd] *adj* bizarre; (*eerie*) surnaturel(le).
weirdo ['wɪədəu] *n* (*col*) type *m* bizarre.
welcome ['wɛlkəm] *adj* bienvenu(e) ♦ *n* accueil *m* ♦ *vt* accueillir; (*also*: **bid ~**) souhaiter la bienvenue à; (*be glad of*) se réjouir de; **to be ~** être le(la) bienvenu(e); **to make sb ~** faire bon accueil à qn; **you're ~ to try** vous pouvez essayer si vous voulez; **you're ~!** (*after thanks*) de rien, il n'y a pas de quoi.
welcoming ['wɛlkəmɪŋ] *adj* accueillant(e); (*speech*) d'accueil.
weld [wɛld] *n* soudure *f* ♦ *vt* souder.
welder ['wɛldə*] *n* (*person*) soudeur *m*.
welding ['wɛldɪŋ] *n* soudure *f* (autogène).
welfare ['wɛlfɛə*] *n* bien-être *m*.
welfare state *n* État-providence *m*.
welfare work *n* travail social.
well [wɛl] *n* puits *m* ♦ *adv* bien ♦ *adj*: **to be ~** aller bien ♦ *excl* eh bien!; bon!; enfin!; **~ done!** bravo!; **I don't feel ~** je ne me sens pas bien; **get ~ soon!** remets-toi vite!; **to do ~ in sth** bien réussir en *or* dans qch; **to think ~ of sb** penser du bien de qn; **as ~** (*in addition*) aussi, également; **you might as ~ tell me** tu ferais aussi bien de me le dire; **as ~ as** aussi bien que *or* de; en plus de; **~, as I was saying ...** donc, comme je disais ....
►**well up** *vi* (*tears, emotions*) monter.
we'll [wi:l] = **we will, we shall**.
well-behaved ['wɛlbɪ'heɪvd] *adj* sage, obéissant(e).
well-being ['wɛl'bi:ɪŋ] *n* bien-être *m*.
well-bred ['wɛl'brɛd] *adj* bien élevé(e).
well-built ['wɛl'bɪlt] *adj* (*house*) bien construit(e); (*person*) bien bâti(e).
well-chosen ['wɛl'tʃəuzn] *adj* bien choisi(e).
well-developed ['wɛldɪ'vɛləpt] *adj* (*girl*) bien fait(e).
well-disposed ['wɛldɪs'pəuzd] *adj*: **~ to(wards)** bien disposé(e) envers.
well-dressed ['wɛl'drɛst] *adj* bien habillé(e), bien vêtu(e).
well-earned ['wɛl'ə:nd] *adj* (*rest*) bien mérité(e).
well-groomed ['wɛl'gru:md] *adj* très soigné(e) de sa personne.
well-heeled ['wɛl'hi:ld] *adj* (*col*: *wealthy*) fortuné(e), riche.
well-informed ['wɛlɪn'fɔ:md] *adj* (*having knowledge of sth*) bien renseigné(e); (*having general knowledge*) cultivé(e).
Wellington ['wɛlɪŋtən] *n* Wellington.
wellingtons ['wɛlɪŋtənz] *npl* (*also*: **wellington boots**) bottes *fpl* de caoutchouc.
well-kept ['wɛl'kɛpt] *adj* (*house, grounds*) bien tenu(e), bien entretenu(e); (*secret*) bien gardé(e); (*hair, hands*) soigné(e).
well-known ['wɛl'nəun] *adj* (*person*) bien connu(e).

well-mannered ['wɛl'mænəd] *adj* bien élevé(e).
well-meaning ['wɛl'miːnɪŋ] *adj* bien intentionné(e).
well-nigh ['wɛl'naɪ] *adv*: ~ **impossible** pratiquement impossible.
well-off ['wɛl'ɔf] *adj* aisé(e), assez riche.
well-read ['wɛl'rɛd] *adj* cultivé(e).
well-spoken ['wɛl'spəukn] *adj* (*person*) qui parle bien; (*words*) bien choisi(e).
well-stocked ['wɛl'stɔkt] *adj* bien approvisionné(e).
well-timed ['wɛl'taɪmd] *adj* opportun(e).
well-to-do ['wɛltə'duː] *adj* aisé(e), assez riche.
well-wisher ['wɛlwɪʃə*] *n* ami/e, admirateur/trice; **scores of ~s had gathered** de nombreux amis et admirateurs s'étaient rassemblés; **letters from ~s** des lettres d'encouragement.
well-woman clinic ['wɛlwumən-] *n centre prophylactique et thérapeutique pour femmes.*
Welsh [wɛlʃ] *adj* gallois(e) ♦ *n* (*LING*) gallois *m*; **the** ~ *npl* les Gallois.
Welsh Assembly *n* Parlement *m* gallois.
Welshman, Welshwoman ['wɛlʃmən, -wumən] *n* Gallois/e.
Welsh rarebit *n* croûte *f* au fromage.
welter ['wɛltə*] *n* fatras *m*.
went [wɛnt] *pt of* **go**.
wept [wɛpt] *pt, pp of* **weep**.
were [wəː*] *pt of* **be**.
we're [wɪə*] = **we are**.
weren't [wəːnt] = **were not**.
werewolf, *pl* **-wolves** ['wɪəwulf, -wulvz] *n* loup-garou *m*.
west [wɛst] *n* ouest *m* ♦ *adj* ouest *inv*, de *or* à l'ouest ♦ *adv* à *or* vers l'ouest; **the W~** l'Occident *m*, l'Ouest.
westbound ['wɛstbaund] *adj* (*traffic*) en direction de l'ouest; (*carriageway*) ouest *inv*.
West Country *n*: **the** ~ le sud-ouest de l'Angleterre.
westerly ['wɛstəlɪ] *adj* (*situation*) à l'ouest; (*wind*) d'ouest.
western ['wɛstən] *adj* occidental(e), de *or* à l'ouest ♦ *n* (*CINE*) western *m*.
westerner ['wɛstənə*] *n* occidental/e.
westernized ['wɛstənaɪzd] *adj* occidentalisé(e).
West German (*formerly*) *adj* ouest-allemand(e) ♦ *n* Allemand/e de l'Ouest.
West Germany *n* (*formerly*) Allemagne *f* de l'Ouest.
West Indian *adj* antillais(e) ♦ *n* Antillais/e.
West Indies [-'ɪndɪz] *npl*: **the** ~ les Antilles *fpl*.
Westminster ['wɛstmɪnstə*] *n* (*BRIT PARLIAMENT*) Westminster *m*.
westward(s) ['wɛstwəd(z)] *adv* vers l'ouest.
wet [wɛt] *adj* mouillé(e); (*damp*) humide; (*soaked*) trempé(e); (*rainy*) pluvieux(euse) ♦ *vt*: **to ~ one's pants** *or* **o.s.** mouiller sa culotte, faire pipi dans sa culotte; **to get ~** se mouiller; **"~ paint"** "attention peinture fraîche".
wet blanket *n* (*fig*) rabat-joie *m inv*.
wetness ['wɛtnɪs] *n* humidité *f*.
wet suit *n* combinaison *f* de plongée.
we've [wiːv] = **we have**.
whack [wæk] *vt* donner un grand coup à.
whacked [wækt] *adj* (*BRIT col*: *tired*) crevé(e).
whale [weɪl] *n* (*ZOOL*) baleine *f*.
whaler ['weɪlə*] *n* (*ship*) baleinier *m*.
whaling ['weɪlɪŋ] *n* pêche *f* à la baleine.
wharf, *pl* **wharves** [wɔːf, wɔːvz] *n* quai *m*.

KEYWORD

what [wɔt] *adj* quel(le); ~ **size is he?** quelle taille fait-il?; ~ **colour is it?** de quelle couleur est-ce?; ~ **books do you need?** quels livres vous faut-il?; ~ **a mess!** quel désordre!

♦ *pron* **1** (*interrogative*) que, *prep* +quoi; ~ **are you doing?** que faites-vous?, qu'est-ce que vous faites?; ~ **is happening?** qu'est-ce qui se passe?, que se passe-t-il?; ~ **are you talking about?** de quoi parlez-vous?; ~ **is it called?** comment est-ce que ça s'appelle?; ~ **about me?** et moi?; ~ **about doing ...?** et si on faisait ...?

2 (*relative*: *subject*) ce qui; (: *direct object*) ce que; (: *indirect object*) ce +*prep* +quoi, ce dont; **I saw ~ you did/was on the table** j'ai vu ce que vous avez fait/ce qui était sur la table; **tell me ~ you remember** dites-moi ce dont vous vous souvenez; ~ **I want is a cup of tea** ce que je veux, c'est une tasse de thé

♦ *excl* (*disbelieving*) quoi!, comment!

whatever [wɔt'ɛvə*] *adj*: ~ **book** quel que soit le livre que (*or* qui) + *sub*; n'importe quel livre ♦ *pron*: **do ~ is necessary** faites (tout) ce qui est nécessaire; ~ **happens** quoi qu'il arrive; **no reason ~** *or* **whatsoever** pas la moindre raison; **nothing ~** *or* **whatsoever** rien du tout.
whatsoever [wɔtsəu'ɛvə*] *adj see* **whatever**.
wheat [wiːt] *n* blé *m*, froment *m*.
wheatgerm ['wiːtdʒəːm] *n* germe *m* de blé.
wheatmeal ['wiːtmiːl] *n* farine bise.
wheedle ['wiːdl] *vt*: **to ~ sb into doing sth** cajoler *or* enjôler qn pour qu'il fasse qch; **to ~ sth out of sb** obtenir qch de qn par des cajoleries.
wheel [wiːl] *n* roue *f*; (*AUT*: *also*: **steering ~**) volant *m*; (*NAUT*) gouvernail *m* ♦ *vt* pousser, rouler ♦ *vi* (*also*: ~ **round**) tourner.
wheelbarrow ['wiːlbærəu] *n* brouette *f*.
wheelbase ['wiːlbeɪs] *n* empattement *m*.
wheelchair ['wiːltʃɛə*] *n* fauteuil roulant.
wheel clamp *n* (*AUT*) sabot *m* (de Denver).
wheeler-dealer ['wiːlə'diːlə*] *n* (*pej*) combinard/e, affairiste *m/f*.
wheelie-bin ['wiːlɪbɪn] *n* (*BRIT*) poubelle *f* à roulettes.

wheeling ['wi:lɪŋ] *n*: ~ **and dealing** (*pej*) manigances *fpl*, magouilles *fpl*.
wheeze [wi:z] *n* respiration bruyante (*d'asthmatique*) ♦ *vi* respirer bruyamment.
wheezy ['wi:zɪ] *adj* sifflant(e).

KEYWORD

when [wen] *adv* quand; ~ **did he go?** quand est-ce qu'il est parti?
♦ *conj* **1** (*at, during, after the time that*) quand, lorsque; **she was reading ~ I came in** elle lisait quand *or* lorsque je suis entré
2 (*on, at which*): **on the day ~ I met him** le jour où je l'ai rencontré
3 (*whereas*) alors que; **I thought I was wrong ~ in fact I was right** j'ai cru que j'avais tort alors qu'en fait j'avais raison.

whenever [wɛn'ɛvə*] *adv* quand donc ♦ *conj* quand; (*every time that*) chaque fois que; **I go ~ I can** j'y vais quand *or* chaque fois que je le peux.
where [wɛə*] *adv, conj* où; **this is ~** c'est là que; ~ **are you from?** d'où venez vous?
whereabouts ['wɛərəbauts] *adv* où donc ♦ *n*: **sb's ~** l'endroit où se trouve qn.
whereas [wɛər'æz] *conj* alors que.
whereby [wɛə'baɪ] *adv* (*formal*) par lequel (*or* laquelle *etc*).
whereupon [wɛərə'pɔn] *adv* sur quoi, et sur ce.
wherever [wɛər'ɛvə*] *adv* où donc ♦ *conj* où que + *sub*; **sit ~ you like** asseyez-vous (là) où vous voulez.
wherewithal ['wɛəwɪðɔ:l] *n*: **the ~ (to do sth)** les moyens *mpl* (de faire qch).
whet [wɛt] *vt* aiguiser.
whether ['wɛðə*] *conj* si; **I don't know ~ to accept or not** je ne sais pas si je dois accepter ou non; **it's doubtful ~** il est peu probable que; ~ **you go or not** que vous y alliez ou non.
whey ['weɪ] *n* petit-lait *m*.

KEYWORD

which [wɪtʃ] *adj* **1** (*interrogative*: *direct, indirect*) quel(le); ~ **picture do you want?** quel tableau voulez-vous?; ~ **one?** lequel(laquelle)?
2: **in ~ case** auquel cas
♦ *pron* **1** (*interrogative*) lequel(laquelle), lesquels(lesquelles) *pl*; **I don't mind ~** peu importe lequel; ~ **(of these) are yours?** lesquels sont à vous?; **tell me ~ you want** dites-moi lesquels *or* ceux que vous voulez
2 (*relative*: *subject*) qui; (: *object*) que, *prep* +lequel(laquelle); (NB: *à + lequel* = auquel; *de + lequel* = duquel); **the apple ~ you ate/~ is on the table** la pomme que vous avez mangée/qui est sur la table; **the chair on ~ you are sitting** la chaise sur laquelle vous êtes assis; **the book of ~ you spoke** le livre dont vous avez parlé; **he knew, ~ is true/I feared** il le savait, ce qui est vrai/ce que je craignais; **after ~** après quoi.

whichever [wɪtʃ'ɛvə*] *adj*: **take ~ book you prefer** prenez le livre que vous préférez, peu importe lequel; ~ **book you take** quel que soit le livre que vous preniez; ~ **way you** de quelque façon que vous + *sub*.
whiff [wɪf] *n* bouffée *f*; **to catch a ~ of sth** sentir l'odeur de qch.
while [waɪl] *n* moment *m* ♦ *conj* pendant que; (*as long as*) tant que; (*as, whereas*) alors que; (*though*) quoique + *sub*; **for a ~** pendant quelque temps; **in a ~** dans un moment; **all the ~** pendant tout ce temps-là; **we'll make it worth your ~** nous vous récompenserons de votre peine.
►**while away** *vt* (*time*) (faire) passer.
whilst [waɪlst] *conj* = **while**.
whim [wɪm] *n* caprice *m*.
whimper ['wɪmpə*] *n* geignement *m* ♦ *vi* geindre.
whimsical ['wɪmzɪkl] *adj* (*person*) capricieux(euse); (*look*) étrange.
whine [waɪn] *n* gémissement *m* ♦ *vi* gémir, geindre; pleurnicher.
whip [wɪp] *n* fouet *m*; (*for riding*) cravache *f*; (*POL*: *person*) chef *m* de file (*assurant la discipline dans son groupe parlementaire*); *voir encadré* ♦ *vt* fouetter; (*snatch*) enlever (*or* sortir) brusquement.
►**whip up** *vt* (*cream*) fouetter; (*col*: *meal*) préparer en vitesse; (*stir up*: *support*) stimuler; (: *feeling*) attiser, aviver.

WHIP

Un **whip** *est un député dont le rôle est, entre autres, de s'assurer que les membres de son parti sont régulièrement présents à la "House of Commons", surtout lorsque les votes ont lieu. Les convocations que les* **whips** *envoient se distinguent, selon leur degré d'importance, par le fait qu'elles sont soulignées 1, 2 ou 3 fois (les "1-, 2-, ou 3-line whips").*

whiplash ['wɪplæʃ] *n* (*MED*: *also*: ~ **injury**) coup *m* du lapin.
whipped cream [wɪpt-] *n* crème fouettée.
whipping boy ['wɪpɪŋ-] *n* (*fig*) bouc *m* émissaire.
whip-round ['wɪpraund] *n* (*BRIT*) collecte *f*.
whirl [wə:l] *n* tourbillon *m* ♦ *vt* faire tourbillonner; faire tournoyer ♦ *vi* tourbillonner.
whirlpool ['wə:lpu:l] *n* tourbillon *m*.
whirlwind ['wə:lwɪnd] *n* tornade *f*.
whirr [wə:*] *vi* bruire; ronronner; vrombir.
whisk [wɪsk] *n* (*CULIN*) fouet *m* ♦ *vt* fouetter, battre; **to ~ sb away** *or* **off** emmener qn rapidement.
whiskers ['wɪskəz] *npl* (*of animal*) moustaches *fpl*; (*of man*) favoris *mpl*.

whisky, (*Irish, US*) **whiskey** ['wɪskɪ] *n* whisky *m*.
whisper ['wɪspə*] *n* chuchotement *m*; (*fig: of leaves*) bruissement *m*; (*rumour*) rumeur *f* ♦ *vt, vi* chuchoter; **to ~ sth to sb** chuchoter.
whispering ['wɪspərɪŋ] *n* chuchotement(s) *m(pl)*.
whist [wɪst] *n* (*BRIT*) whist *m*.
whistle ['wɪsl] *n* (*sound*) sifflement *m*; (*object*) sifflet *m* ♦ *vi* siffler ♦ *vt* siffler, siffloter.
whistle-stop ['wɪslstɔp] *adj*: **to make a ~ tour of** (*POL*) faire la tournée électorale des petits patelins de.
Whit [wɪt] *n* la Pentecôte.
white [waɪt] *adj* blanc(blanche); (*with fear*) blême ♦ *n* blanc *m*; (*person*) blanc/blanche; **to turn** *or* **go ~** (*person*) pâlir, blêmir; (*hair*) blanchir; **the ~s** (*washing*) le linge blanc; **tennis ~s** tenue *f* de tennis.
whitebait ['waɪtbeɪt] *n* blanchaille *f*.
white coffee *n* (*BRIT*) café *m* au lait, (café) crème *m*.
white-collar worker ['waɪtkɔlə-] *n* employé/e de bureau.
white elephant *n* (*fig*) objet *m* superflu.
white goods *npl* (*appliances*) (gros) électroménager *m*; (*linen etc*) linge *m* de maison.
white-hot [waɪt'hɔt] *adj* incandescent(e).
White House *n* (*US*): **the ~** la Maison-Blanche; *voir encadré*.

WHITE HOUSE

La **White House** *est un grand bâtiment blanc situé à Washington D.C. où réside le président des États-Unis. Par extension, ce terme désigne l'exécutif américain.*

white lie *n* pieux mensonge.
whiteness ['waɪtnɪs] *n* blancheur *f*.
white noise *n* son *m* blanc.
whiteout ['waɪtaut] *n* jour blanc.
white paper *n* (*POL*) livre blanc.
whitewash ['waɪtwɔʃ] *n* (*paint*) lait *m* de chaux ♦ *vt* blanchir à la chaux; (*fig*) blanchir.
whiting ['waɪtɪŋ] *n* (*pl inv*) (*fish*) merlan *m*.
Whit Monday *n* le lundi de Pentecôte.
Whitsun ['wɪtsn] *n* la Pentecôte.
whittle ['wɪtl] *vt*: **to ~ away, ~ down** (*costs*) réduire, rogner.
whizz [wɪz] *vi* aller (*or* passer) à toute vitesse.
whizz kid *n* (*col*) petit prodige.
WHO *n abbr* (= *World Health Organization*) OMS *f* (= *Organisation mondiale de la Santé*).
who [hu:] *pron* qui.
whodunit [hu:'dʌnɪt] *n* (*col*) roman policier.
whoever [hu:'ɛvə*] *pron*: **~ finds it** celui(celle) qui le trouve (, qui que ce soit), quiconque le trouve; **ask ~ you like** demandez à qui vous voulez; **~ he marries** qui que ce soit *or* quelle que soit la personne qu'il épouse; **~ told you that?** qui a bien pu vous dire ça?, qui donc vous a dit ça?
whole [həul] *adj* (*complete*) entier(ière), tout(e); (*not broken*) intact(e), complet(ète) ♦ *n* (*total*) totalité *f*; (*sth not broken*) tout *m*; **the ~ lot (of it)** tout; **the ~ lot (of them)** tous (sans exception); **the ~ of the time** tout le temps; **the ~ of the town** la ville tout entière; **on the ~, as a ~** dans l'ensemble.
wholehearted [həul'ha:tɪd] *adj* sans réserve(s), sincère.
wholemeal ['həulmi:l] *adj* (*BRIT: flour, bread*) complet(ète).
whole note *n* (*US*) ronde *f*.
wholesale ['həulseɪl] *n* (vente *f* en) gros *m* ♦ *adj* de gros; (*destruction*) systématique.
wholesaler ['həulseɪlə*] *n* grossiste *m/f*.
wholesome ['həulsəm] *adj* sain(e); (*advice*) salutaire.
wholewheat ['həulwi:t] *adj* = **wholemeal**.
wholly ['həulɪ] *adv* entièrement, tout à fait.

KEYWORD

whom [hu:m] *pron* **1** (*interrogative*) qui; **~ did you see?** qui avez-vous vu?; **to ~ did you give it?** à qui l'avez-vous donné?

2 (*relative*) que, *prep* + qui; **the man ~ I saw/to ~ I spoke** l'homme que j'ai vu/à qui j'ai parlé.

whooping cough ['hu:pɪŋ-] *n* coqueluche *f*.
whoops [wu:ps] *excl* (*also*: **~-a-daisy**) oups!, houp-là!
whoosh [wuʃ] *n, vi*: **the skiers ~ed past, the skiers came by with a ~** les skieurs passèrent dans un glissement rapide.
whopper ['wɔpə*] *n* (*col: lie*) gros bobard; (*: large thing*) monstre *m*, phénomène *m*.
whopping ['wɔpɪŋ] *adj* (*col: big*) énorme.
whore [hɔ:*] *n* (*col: pej*) putain *f*.

KEYWORD

whose [hu:z] *adj* **1** (*possessive: interrogative*): **~ book is this?** à qui est ce livre?; **~ pencil have you taken?** à qui est le crayon que vous avez pris?, c'est le crayon de qui que vous avez pris?; **~ daughter are you?** de qui êtes-vous la fille?

2 (*possessive: relative*): **the man ~ son you rescued** l'homme dont *or* de qui vous avez sauvé le fils; **the girl ~ sister you were speaking to** la fille à la sœur de qui *or* de laquelle vous parliez; **the woman ~ car was stolen** la femme dont la voiture a été volée

♦ *pron* à qui; **~ is this?** à qui est ceci?; **I know ~ it is** je sais à qui c'est.

Who's Who ['hu:z'hu:] *n* ≈ Bottin Mondain.
why [waɪ] *adv* pourquoi ♦ *excl* eh bien!, tiens!; **the reason ~** la raison pour laquelle; **~ is he**

late? pourquoi est-il en retard?
whyever [waɪ'ɛvə*] *adv* pourquoi donc, mais pourquoi.
WI *n abbr (BRIT: = Women's Institute) amicale de femmes au foyer* ♦ *abbr (GEO)* = **West Indies**; *(US) = Wisconsin.*
wick [wɪk] *n* mèche *f (de bougie).*
wicked ['wɪkɪd] *adj* foncièrement mauvais(e), inique; *(mischievous: grin, look)* espiègle, malicieux(euse); *(terrible: prices, weather)* épouvantable.
wicker ['wɪkə*] *n* osier *m*; *(also:* **~work**) vannerie *f.*
wicket ['wɪkɪt] *n (CRICKET)* guichet *m*; espace compris entre les deux guichets.
wicket keeper *n (CRICKET)* gardien *m* de guichet.
wide [waɪd] *adj* large; *(region, knowledge)* vaste, très étendu(e); *(choice)* grand(e) ♦ *adv*: **to open ~** ouvrir tout grand; **to shoot ~** tirer à côté; **it is 3 metres ~** cela fait 3 mètres de large.
wide-angle lens ['waɪdæŋgl-] *n* objectif *m* grand-angulaire.
wide-awake [waɪdə'weɪk] *adj* bien éveillé(e).
wide-eyed [waɪd'aɪd] *adj* aux yeux écarquillés; *(fig)* naïf(ïve), crédule.
widely ['waɪdlɪ] *adv (different)* radicalement; *(spaced)* sur une grande étendue; *(believed)* généralement; **to be ~ read** *(author)* être beaucoup lu(e); *(reader)* avoir beaucoup lu, être cultivé(e).
widen ['waɪdn] *vt* élargir.
wideness ['waɪdnɪs] *n* largeur *f.*
wide open *adj* grand(e) ouvert(e).
wide-ranging [waɪd'reɪndʒɪŋ] *adj (survey, report)* vaste; *(interests)* divers(e).
widespread ['waɪdsprɛd] *adj (belief etc)* très répandu(e).
widow ['wɪdəu] *n* veuve *f.*
widowed ['wɪdəud] *adj* (qui est devenu(e)) veuf(veuve).
widower ['wɪdəuə*] *n* veuf *m.*
width [wɪdθ] *n* largeur *f*; **it's 7 metres in ~** cela fait 7 mètres de large.
widthways ['wɪdθweɪz] *adv* en largeur.
wield [wi:ld] *vt (sword)* manier; *(power)* exercer.
wife, *pl* **wives** [waɪf, waɪvz] *n* femme (mariée), épouse *f.*
wig [wɪg] *n* perruque *f.*
wigging ['wɪgɪŋ] *n (BRIT col)* savon *m*, engueulade *f.*
wiggle ['wɪgl] *vt* agiter, remuer ♦ *vi (loose screw etc)* branler; *(worm)* se tortiller.
wiggly ['wɪglɪ] *adj (line)* ondulé(e).
wild [waɪld] *adj* sauvage; *(sea)* déchaîné(e); *(idea, life)* fou(folle); extravagant(e); *(col: angry)* hors de soi, furieux(euse); *(: enthusiastic)*: **to be ~ about** être fou(folle) *or* dingue de ♦ *n*: **the ~** la nature; **~s** *npl* régions *fpl* sauvages.
wild card *n (COMPUT)* caractère *m* de remplacement.
wildcat ['waɪldkæt] *n* chat *m* sauvage.
wildcat strike *n* grève *f* sauvage.
wilderness ['wɪldənɪs] *n* désert *m*, région *f* sauvage.
wildfire ['waɪldfaɪə*] *n*: **to spread like ~** se répandre comme une traînée de poudre.
wild-goose chase [waɪld'gu:s-] *n (fig)* fausse piste.
wildlife ['waɪldlaɪf] *n* faune *f* (et flore *f*) sauvage(s).
wildly ['waɪldlɪ] *adv (applaud)* frénétiquement; *(hit, guess)* au hasard; *(happy)* follement.
wiles [waɪlz] *npl* ruses *fpl*, artifices *mpl.*
wilful, *(US)* **willful** ['wɪlful] *adj (person)* obstiné(e); *(action)* délibéré(e); *(crime)* prémédité(e).

KEYWORD

will [wɪl] *(vt: pt, pp* **willed**) *aux vb* **1** *(forming future tense)*: **I ~ finish it tomorrow** je le finirai demain; **I ~ have finished it by tomorrow** je l'aurai fini d'ici demain; **~ you do it? — yes I ~/no I won't** le ferez-vous? — oui/non; **you won't lose it, ~ you?** vous ne le perdrez pas, n'est-ce pas?
2 *(in conjectures, predictions)*: **he ~** *or* **he'll be there by now** il doit être arrivé à l'heure qu'il est; **that ~ be the postman** ça doit être le facteur
3 *(in commands, requests, offers)*: **~ you be quiet!** voulez-vous bien vous taire!; **~ you help me?** est-ce que vous pouvez m'aider?; **~ you have a cup of tea?** voulez-vous une tasse de thé?; **I won't put up with it!** je ne le tolérerai pas!
♦ *vt*: **to ~ sb to do** souhaiter ardemment que qn fasse; **he ~ed himself to go on** par un suprême effort de volonté, il continua
♦ *n* volonté *f*; testament *m*; **to do sth of one's own free ~** faire qch de son propre gré; **against one's ~** à contre-cœur.

willful ['wɪlful] *adj (US)* = **wilful.**
willing ['wɪlɪŋ] *adj* de bonne volonté, serviable ♦ *n*: **to show ~** faire preuve de bonne volonté; **he's ~ to do it** il est disposé à le faire, il veut bien le faire.
willingly ['wɪlɪŋlɪ] *adv* volontiers.
willingness ['wɪlɪŋnɪs] *n* bonne volonté.
will-o'-the-wisp ['wɪləðə'wɪsp] *n (also fig)* feu follet *m.*
willow ['wɪləu] *n* saule *m.*
will power *n* volonté *f.*
willy-nilly ['wɪlɪ'nɪlɪ] *adv* bon gré mal gré.
wilt [wɪlt] *vi* dépérir.
Wilts [wɪlts] *abbr (BRIT) = Wiltshire.*
wily ['waɪlɪ] *adj* rusé(e).
wimp [wɪmp] *n (col)* mauviette *f.*
win [wɪn] *n (in sports etc)* victoire *f* ♦ *vb (pt, pp* **won** [wʌn]) *vt (battle, money)* gagner; *(prize,*

contract) remporter; (*popularity*) acquérir ♦ *vi* gagner.
▸**win over**, (*BRIT*) **win round** *vt* gagner, se concilier.
wince [wɪns] *n* tressaillement *m* ♦ *vi* tressaillir.
winch [wɪntʃ] *n* treuil *m*.
Winchester disk ['wɪntʃɪstə-] *n* (*COMPUT*) disque *m* Winchester.
wind[1] [wɪnd] *n* (*also MED*) vent *m* ♦ *vt* (*take breath away*) couper le souffle à; **the** ~**(s)** (*MUS*) les instruments *mpl* à vent; **into** *or* **against the** ~ contre le vent; **to get** ~ **of sth** (*fig*) avoir vent de qch; **to break** ~ avoir des gaz.
wind[2], *pt, pp* **wound** [waɪnd, waund] *vt* enrouler; (*wrap*) envelopper; (*clock, toy*) remonter ♦ *vi* (*road, river*) serpenter
▸**wind down** *vt* (*car window*) baisser; (*fig: production, business*) réduire progressivement.
▸**wind up** *vt* (*clock*) remonter; (*debate*) terminer, clôturer.
windbreak ['wɪndbreɪk] *n* brise-vent *m inv*.
windcheater ['wɪndtʃiːtə*], (*US*) **windbreaker** ['wɪndbreɪkə*] *n* anorak *m*.
winder ['waɪndə*] *n* (*BRIT*: *on watch*) remontoir *m*.
windfall ['wɪndfɔːl] *n* coup *m* de chance.
winding ['waɪndɪŋ] *adj* (*road*) sinueux(euse); (*staircase*) tournant(e).
wind instrument *n* (*MUS*) instrument *m* à vent.
windmill ['wɪndmɪl] *n* moulin *m* à vent.
window ['wɪndəu] *n* fenêtre *f*; (*in car, train, also*: ~**pane**) vitre *f*; (*in shop etc*) vitrine *f*.
window box *n* jardinière *f*.
window cleaner *n* (*person*) laveur/euse de vitres.
window dressing *n* arrangement *m* de la vitrine.
window envelope *n* enveloppe *f* à fenêtre.
window frame *n* châssis *m* de fenêtre.
window ledge *n* rebord *m* de la fenêtre.
window pane *n* vitre *f*, carreau *m*.
window-shopping ['wɪndəuʃɔpɪŋ] *n*: **to go** ~ faire du lèche-vitrines.
windowsill ['wɪndəusɪl] *n* (*inside*) appui *m* de la fenêtre; (*outside*) rebord *m* de la fenêtre.
windpipe ['wɪndpaɪp] *n* gosier *m*.
wind power *n* énergie éolienne.
windscreen ['wɪndskriːn], (*US*) **windshield** ['wɪndʃiːld] *n* pare-brise *m inv*.
windscreen washer *n* lave-glace *m inv*.
windscreen wiper [-waɪpə*] *n* essuie-glace *m inv*.
windsurfing ['wɪndsəːfɪŋ] *n* planche *f* à voile.
windswept ['wɪndswɛpt] *adj* balayé(e) par le vent.
wind tunnel *n* soufflerie *f*.
windy ['wɪndɪ] *adj* venté(e), venteux(euse); **it's** ~ il y a du vent.
wine [waɪn] *n* vin *m* ♦ *vt*: **to** ~ **and dine sb** offrir un dîner bien arrosé à qn.
wine bar *n* bar *m* à vin.
wine cellar *n* cave *f* à vins.
wine glass *n* verre *m* à vin.
wine list *n* carte *f* des vins.
wine merchant *n* marchand/e de vins.
wine tasting [-teɪstɪŋ] *n* dégustation *f* (de vins).
wine waiter *n* sommelier *m*.
wing [wɪŋ] *n* aile *f*; (*in air force*) groupe *m* d'escadrilles; ~**s** *npl* (*THEAT*) coulisses *fpl*.
winger ['wɪŋə*] *n* (*SPORT*) ailier *m*.
wing mirror *n* (*BRIT*) rétroviseur latéral.
wing nut *n* papillon *m*, écrou *m* à ailettes.
wingspan ['wɪŋspæn] *n*, **wingspread** ['wɪŋsprɛd] *n* envergure *f*.
wink [wɪŋk] *n* clin *m* d'œil ♦ *vi* faire un clin d'œil; (*blink*) cligner des yeux.
winkle [wɪŋkl] *n* bigorneau *m*.
winner ['wɪnə*] *n* gagnant/e.
winning ['wɪnɪŋ] *adj* (*team*) gagnant(e); (*goal*) décisif(ive); (*charming*) charmeur(euse).
winning post *n* poteau *m* d'arrivée.
winnings ['wɪnɪŋz] *npl* gains *mpl*.
winsome ['wɪnsəm] *adj* avenant(e), engageant(e).
winter ['wɪntə*] *n* hiver *m* ♦ *vi* hiverner.
winter sports *npl* sports *mpl* d'hiver.
wintry ['wɪntrɪ] *adj* hivernal(e).
wipe [waɪp] *n* coup *m* de torchon (*or* de chiffon *or* d'éponge) ♦ *vt* essuyer; **to give sth a** ~ donner un coup de torchon à qch; **to** ~ **one's nose** se moucher.
▸**wipe off** *vt* essuyer.
▸**wipe out** *vt* (*debt*) régler; (*memory*) oublier; (*destroy*) anéantir.
▸**wipe up** *vt* essuyer.
wire ['waɪə*] *n* fil *m* (de fer); (*ELEC*) fil électrique; (*TEL*) télégramme *m* ♦ *vt* (*fence*) grillager; (*house*) faire l'installation électrique de; (*also*: ~ **up**) brancher.
wire brush *n* brosse *f* métallique.
wire cutters [-kʌtəz] *npl* cisaille *f*.
wireless ['waɪəlɪs] *n* (*BRIT*) télégraphie *f* sans fil; (*set*) T.S.F. *f*.
wire netting *n* treillis *m* métallique, grillage *m*.
wire service *n* (*US*) revue *f* de presse (*par téléscripteur*).
wire-tapping ['waɪə'tæpɪŋ] *n* écoute *f* téléphonique.
wiring ['waɪərɪŋ] *n* (*ELEC*) installation *f* électrique.
wiry ['waɪərɪ] *adj* noueux(euse), nerveux(euse).
Wis. *abbr* (*US*) = *Wisconsin*.
wisdom ['wɪzdəm] *n* sagesse *f*; (*of action*) prudence *f*.
wisdom tooth *n* dent *f* de sagesse.
wise [waɪz] *adj* sage, prudent(e), judicieux(euse); **I'm none the** ~**r** je ne suis pas

plus avancé(e) pour autant.
▸**wise up** *vi* (*col*): **to ~ up to** commencer à se rendre compte de.
...wise [waɪz] *suffix*: **time~** en ce qui concerne le temps, question temps.
wisecrack ['waɪzkræk] *n* sarcasme *m*.
wish [wɪʃ] *n* (*desire*) désir *m*; (*specific desire*) souhait *m*, vœu *m* ♦ *vt* souhaiter, désirer, vouloir; **best ~es** (*on birthday etc*) meilleurs vœux; **with best ~es** (*in letter*) bien amicalement; **give her my best ~es** faites-lui mes amitiés; **to ~ sb goodbye** dire au revoir à qn; **he ~ed me well** il me souhaitait de réussir; **to ~ to do/sb to do** désirer *or* vouloir faire/que qn fasse; **to ~ for** souhaiter; **to ~ sth on sb** souhaiter qch à qn.
wishbone ['wɪʃbəun] *n* fourchette *f*.
wishful ['wɪʃful] *adj*: **it's ~ thinking** c'est prendre ses désirs pour des réalités.
wishy-washy ['wɪʃɪ'wɔʃɪ] *adj* (*col*: *person*) qui manque de caractère, falot(e); (*: ideas, thinking*) faiblard(e).
wisp [wɪsp] *n* fine mèche (*de cheveux*); (*of smoke*) mince volute *f*; **a ~ of straw** un fétu de paille.
wistful ['wɪstful] *adj* mélancolique.
wit [wɪt] *n* (*gen pl: intelligence*) intelligence *f*, esprit *m*; (*presence of mind*) présence *f* d'esprit; (*wittiness*) esprit; (*person*) homme/femme d'esprit; **to be at one's ~s' end** (*fig*) ne plus savoir que faire; **to have one's ~s about one** avoir toute sa présence d'esprit, ne pas perdre la tête; **to ~** *adv* à savoir.
witch [wɪtʃ] *n* sorcière *f*.
witchcraft ['wɪtʃkrɑːft] *n* sorcellerie *f*.
witch doctor *n* sorcier *m*.
witch-hunt ['wɪtʃhʌnt] *n* chasse *f* aux sorcières.

KEYWORD

with [wɪð, wɪθ] *prep* **1** (*in the company of*) avec; (*at the home of*) chez; **we stayed ~ friends** nous avons logé chez des amis; **I'll be ~ you in a minute** je suis à vous dans un instant
2 (*descriptive*): **a room ~ a view** une chambre avec vue; **the man ~ the grey hat/blue eyes** l'homme au chapeau gris/aux yeux bleus
3 (*indicating manner, means, cause*): **~ tears in her eyes** les larmes aux yeux; **to walk ~ a stick** marcher avec une canne; **red ~ anger** rouge de colère; **to shake ~ fear** trembler de peur; **to fill sth ~ water** remplir qch d'eau
4: **I'm ~ you** (*I understand*) je vous suis; **to be ~ it** (*col*: *up-to-date*) être dans le vent.

withdraw [wɪθ'drɔː] *irreg vt* retirer ♦ *vi* se retirer; (*go back on promise*) se rétracter; **to ~ into o.s.** se replier sur soi-même.
withdrawal [wɪθ'drɔːəl] *n* retrait *m*; (*MED*) état *m* de manque.
withdrawal symptoms *npl*: **to have ~** être en état de manque, présenter les symptômes *mpl* de sevrage.
withdrawn [wɪθ'drɔːn] *pp of* **withdraw** ♦ *adj* (*person*) renfermé(e).
wither ['wɪðə*] *vi* se faner.
withered ['wɪðəd] *adj* fané(e), flétri(e); (*limb*) atrophié(e).
withhold [wɪθ'həuld] *vt irreg* (*money*) retenir; (*decision*) remettre; (*permission*): **to ~ (from)** refuser (à); (*information*): **to ~ (from)** cacher (à).
within [wɪð'ɪn] *prep* à l'intérieur de ♦ *adv* à l'intérieur; **~ sight of** en vue de; **~ a mile of** à moins d'un mille de; **~ the week** avant la fin de la semaine; **~ an hour from now** d'ici une heure; **to be ~ the law** être légal(e) *or* dans les limites de la légalité.
without [wɪð'aut] *prep* sans; **~ anybody knowing** sans que personne le sache; **to go** *or* **do ~ sth** se passer de qch.
withstand [wɪθ'stænd] *vt irreg* résister à.
witness ['wɪtnɪs] *n* (*person*) témoin *m*; (*evidence*) témoignage *m* ♦ *vt* (*event*) être témoin de; (*document*) attester l'authenticité de; **to bear ~ to sth** témoigner de qch; **~ for the prosecution/defence** témoin à charge/à décharge; **to ~ to sth/having seen sth** témoigner de qch/d'avoir vu qch.
witness box, (*US*) **witness stand** *n* barre *f* des témoins.
witticism ['wɪtɪsɪzəm] *n* mot *m* d'esprit.
witty ['wɪtɪ] *adj* spirituel(le), plein(e) d'esprit.
wives [waɪvz] *npl of* **wife**.
wizard ['wɪzəd] *n* magicien *m*.
wizened ['wɪznd] *adj* ratatiné(e).
wk *abbr* = **week**.
Wm. *abbr* = *William*.
WO *n abbr* = **warrant officer**.
wobble ['wɔbl] *vi* trembler; (*chair*) branler.
wobbly ['wɔblɪ] *adj* tremblant(e); branlant(e).
woe [wəu] *n* malheur *m*.
woeful ['wəuful] *adj* (*sad*) malheureux(euse); (*terrible*) affligeant(e).
wok [wɔk] *n* wok *m*.
woke [wəuk] *pt of* **wake**.
woken ['wəukn] *pp of* **wake**.
wolf, *pl* **wolves** [wulf, wulvz] *n* loup *m*.
woman, *pl* **women** ['wumən, 'wɪmɪn] *n* femme *f* ♦ *cpd*: **~ doctor** femme *f* médecin; **~ friend** amie *f*; **~ teacher** professeur *m* femme; **young ~** jeune femme; **women's page** (*PRESS*) page *f* des lectrices.
womanize ['wumənaɪz] *vi* jouer les séducteurs.
womanly ['wumənlɪ] *adj* féminin(e).
womb [wuːm] *n* (*ANAT*) utérus *m*.
women ['wɪmɪn] *npl of* **woman**.
Women's (Liberation) Movement *n* (*also*: **women's lib**) mouvement *m* de libération de la femme, MLF *m*.
won [wʌn] *pt, pp of* **win**.

wonder ['wʌndə*] *n* merveille *f*, miracle *m*; (*feeling*) émerveillement *m* ♦ *vi*: **to ~ whether** se demander si; **to ~ at** s'étonner de; s'émerveiller de; **to ~ about** songer à; **it's no ~ that** il n'est pas étonnant que + *sub*.
wonderful ['wʌndəful] *adj* merveilleux(euse).
wonderfully ['wʌndəfəlı] *adv* (+ *adj*) merveilleusement; (+ *vb*) à merveille.
wonky ['wɔŋkı] *adj* (*BRIT col*) qui ne va *or* ne marche pas très bien.
wont [wəunt] *n*: **as is his/her ~** comme de coutume.
won't [wəunt] = **will not**.
woo [wu:] *vt* (*woman*) faire la cour à.
wood [wud] *n* (*timber, forest*) bois *m* ♦ *cpd* de bois, en bois.
wood carving *n* sculpture *f* en *or* sur bois.
wooded ['wudıd] *adj* boisé(e).
wooden ['wudn] *adj* en bois; (*fig*) raide; inexpressif(ive).
woodland ['wudlənd] *n* forêt *f*, région boisée.
woodpecker ['wudpɛkə*] *n* pic *m* (*oiseau*).
wood pigeon *n* ramier *m*.
woodwind ['wudwınd] *n* (*MUS*) bois *m*; **the ~** (*MUS*) les bois.
woodwork ['wudwə:k] *n* menuiserie *f*.
woodworm ['wudwə:m] *n* ver *m* du bois; **the table has got ~** la table est piquée des vers.
woof [wuf] *n* (*of dog*) aboiement *m* ♦ *vi* aboyer; **~, ~!** oua, oua!
wool [wul] *n* laine *f*; **to pull the ~ over sb's eyes** (*fig*) en faire accroire à qn.
woollen, (*US*) **woolen** ['wulən] *adj* de laine; (*industry*) lainier(ière) ♦ *n*: **~s** lainages *mpl*.
woolly, (*US*) **wooly** ['wulı] *adj* laineux(euse); (*fig: ideas*) confus(e).
woozy ['wu:zı] *adj* (*col*) dans les vapes.
word [wə:d] *n* mot *m*; (*spoken*) mot, parole *f*; (*promise*) parole; (*news*) nouvelles *fpl* ♦ *vt* rédiger, formuler; **~ for ~** (*repeat*) mot pour mot; (*translate*) mot à mot; **what's the ~ for "pen" in French?** comment dit-on "pen" en français?; **to put sth into ~s** exprimer qch; **in other ~s** en d'autres termes; **to have a ~ with sb** toucher un mot à qn; **to have ~s with sb** (*quarrel with*) avoir des mots avec qn; **to break/keep one's ~** manquer à/tenir sa parole; **I'll take your ~ for it** je vous crois sur parole; **to send ~ of** prévenir de; **to leave ~ (with sb/for sb) that** ... laisser un mot (à qn/pour qn) disant que ....
wording ['wə:dıŋ] *n* termes *mpl*, langage *m*; libellé *m*.
word of mouth *n*: **by** *or* **through ~** de bouche à oreille.
word-perfect ['wə:d'pə:fıkt] *adj*: **he was ~ (in his speech** *etc*), **his speech** *etc* **was ~** il savait son discours *etc* sur le bout du doigt.
word processing *n* traitement *m* de texte.
word processor [-prəusɛsə*] *n* machine *f* de traitement de texte.
wordwrap ['wə:dræp] *n* (*COMPUT*) retour *m* (automatique) à la ligne.
wordy ['wə:dı] *adj* verbeux(euse).
wore [wɔ:*] *pt of* **wear**.
work [wə:k] *n* travail *m*; (*ART, LITERATURE*) œuvre *f* ♦ *vi* travailler; (*mechanism*) marcher, fonctionner; (*plan etc*) marcher; (*medicine*) agir ♦ *vt* (*clay, wood etc*) travailler; (*mine etc*) exploiter; (*machine*) faire marcher *or* fonctionner; **to go to ~** aller travailler; **to set to ~, to start ~** se mettre à l'œuvre; **to be at ~ (on sth)** travailler (sur qch); **to be out of ~** être au chômage; **to ~ hard** travailler dur; **to ~ loose** se défaire, se desserrer.
►**work on** *vt fus* travailler à; (*principle*) se baser sur.
►**work out** *vi* (*plans etc*) marcher; (*SPORT*) s'entraîner ♦ *vt* (*problem*) résoudre; (*plan*) élaborer; **it ~s out at £100** ça fait 100 livres.
workable ['wə:kəbl] *adj* (*solution*) réalisable.
workaholic [wə:kə'hɔlık] *n* bourreau *m* de travail.
workbench ['wə:kbɛntʃ] *n* établi *m*.
worked up [wə:kt-] *adj*: **to get ~** se mettre dans tous ses états.
worker ['wə:kə*] *n* travailleur/euse, ouvrier/ière; **office ~** employé/e de bureau.
work force *n* main-d'œuvre *f*.
work-in ['wə:kın] *n* (*BRIT*) occupation *f* d'usine *etc* (*sans arrêt de la production*).
working ['wə:kıŋ] *adj* (*day, tools etc, conditions*) de travail; (*wife*) qui travaille; (*partner, population*) actif(ive); **in ~ order** en état de marche; **a ~ knowledge of English** une connaissance toute pratique de l'anglais.
working capital *n* (*COMM*) fonds *mpl* de roulement.
working class *n* classe ouvrière ♦ *adj*: **working-class** ouvrier(ière), de la classe ouvrière.
working man *n* travailleur *m*.
working party *n* (*BRIT*) groupe *m* de travail.
working week *n* semaine *f* de travail.
work-in-progress ['wə:kın'prəugrɛs] *n* (*COMM*) en-cours *m inv*; (*: value*) valeur *f* des en-cours.
workload ['wə:kləud] *n* charge *f* de travail.
workman ['wə:kmən] *n* ouvrier *m*.
workmanship ['wə:kmənʃıp] *n* métier *m*, habileté *f*; facture *f*.
workmate ['wə:kmeıt] *n* collègue *m/f*.
workout ['wə:kaut] *n* (*SPORT*) séance *f* d'entraînement.
work permit *n* permis *m* de travail.
works [wə:ks] *n* (*BRIT: factory*) usine *f* ♦ *npl* (*of clock, machine*) mécanisme *m*; **road ~** travaux *mpl* (d'entretien des routes).
works council *n* comité *m* d'entreprise.
work sheet *n* (*COMPUT*) feuille *f* de programmation.
workshop ['wə:kʃɔp] *n* atelier *m*.
work station *n* poste *m* de travail.

work study *n* étude *f* du travail.
worktop ['wəːktɔp] *n* plan *m* de travail.
work-to-rule ['wəːktə'ruːl] *n* (*BRIT*) grève *f* du zèle.
world [wəːld] *n* monde *m* ♦ *cpd* (*champion*) du monde; (*power, war*) mondial(e); **all over the ~** dans le monde entier, partout dans le monde; **to think the ~ of sb** (*fig*) ne jurer que par qn; **what in the ~ is he doing?** qu'est-ce qu'il peut bien être en train de faire?; **to do sb a ~ of good** faire le plus grand bien à qn; **W~ War One/Two, the First/Second W~ War** la Première/ Deuxième Guerre mondiale; **out of this ~** *adj* extraordinaire.
World Cup *n*: **the ~** (*FOOTBALL*) la Coupe du monde.
world-famous [wəːld'feɪməs] *adj* de renommée mondiale.
worldly ['wəːldlɪ] *adj* de ce monde.
world music *n* world music *f*.
World Series *n*: **the ~** (*US: BASEBALL*) le championnat national de baseball.
world-wide ['wəːld'waɪd] *adj* universel(le) ♦ *adv* dans le monde entier.
worm [wəːm] *n* ver *m*.
worn [wɔːn] *pp of* **wear** ♦ *adj* usé(e).
worn-out ['wɔːnaut] *adj* (*object*) complètement usé(e); (*person*) épuisé(e).
worried ['wʌrɪd] *adj* inquiet(ète); **to be ~ about sth** être inquiet au sujet de qch.
worrier ['wʌrɪə*] *n* inquiet/ète.
worrisome ['wʌrɪsəm] *adj* inquiétant(e).
worry ['wʌrɪ] *n* souci *m* ♦ *vt* inquiéter ♦ *vi* s'inquiéter, se faire du souci; **to ~ about** *or* **over sth/sb** se faire du souci pour *or* à propos de qch/qn.
worrying ['wʌrɪɪŋ] *adj* inquiétant(e).
worse [wəːs] *adj* pire, plus mauvais(e) ♦ *adv* plus mal ♦ *n* pire *m*; **to get ~** (*condition, situation*) empirer, se dégrader; **a change for the ~** une détérioration; **he is none the ~ for it** il ne s'en porte pas plus mal; **so much the ~ for you!** tant pis pour vous!
worsen ['wəːsn] *vt, vi* empirer.
worse off *adj* moins à l'aise financièrement; (*fig*): **you'll be ~ this way** ça ira moins bien de cette façon; **he is now ~ than before** il se retrouve dans une situation pire qu'auparavant.
worship ['wəːʃɪp] *n* culte *m* ♦ *vt* (*God*) rendre un culte à; (*person*) adorer; **Your W~** (*BRIT: to mayor*) Monsieur le Maire; (*: to judge*) Monsieur le Juge.
worshipper ['wəːʃɪpə*] *n* adorateur/trice; (*in church*) fidèle *m/f*.
worst [wəːst] *adj* le(la) pire, le(la) plus mauvais(e) ♦ *adv* le plus mal ♦ *n* pire *m*; **at ~** au pis aller; **if the ~ comes to the ~** si le pire doit arriver.
worst-case ['wəːstkeɪs] *adj*: **the ~ scenario** le pire scénario *or* cas de figure.
worsted ['wustɪd] *n*: **(wool) ~** laine peignée.
worth [wəːθ] *n* valeur *f* ♦ *adj*: **to be ~** valoir; **how much is it ~?** ça vaut combien?; **it's ~ it** cela en vaut la peine; **50 pence ~ of apples** (pour) 50 pence de pommes.
worthless ['wəːθlɪs] *adj* qui ne vaut rien.
worthwhile ['wəːθ'waɪl] *adj* (*activity*) qui en vaut la peine; (*cause*) louable; **a ~ book** un livre qui vaut la peine d'être lu.
worthy ['wəːðɪ] *adj* (*person*) digne; (*motive*) louable; **~ of** digne de.

KEYWORD

would [wud] *aux vb* **1** (*conditional tense*): **if you asked him he ~ do it** si vous le lui demandiez, il le ferait; **if you had asked him he ~ have done it** si vous le lui aviez demandé, il l'aurait fait
2 (*in offers, invitations, requests*): **~ you like a biscuit?** voulez-vous un biscuit?; **~ you close the door please?** voulez-vous fermer la porte, s'il vous plaît?
3 (*in indirect speech*): **I said I ~ do it** j'ai dit que je le ferais
4 (*emphatic*): **it WOULD have to snow today!** naturellement il neige aujourd'hui! *or* il fallait qu'il neige aujourd'hui!
5 (*insistence*): **she ~n't do it** elle n'a pas voulu *or* elle a refusé de le faire
6 (*conjecture*): **it ~ have been midnight** il devait être minuit
7 (*indicating habit*): **he ~ go there on Mondays** il y allait le lundi.

would-be ['wudbiː] *adj* (*pej*) soi-disant.
wound *vb* [waund] *pt, pp of* **wind** ♦ *n, vt* [wuːnd] *n* blessure *f* ♦ *vt* blesser; **~ed in the leg** blessé à la jambe.
wove [wəuv] *pt of* **weave**.
woven ['wəuvn] *pp of* **weave**.
WP *n abbr* = **word processing, word processor** ♦ *abbr* (*BRIT col*) = *weather permitting*.
WPC *n abbr* (*BRIT*) = *woman police constable*.
wpm *abbr* (= *words per minute*) mots/minute.
WRAC *n abbr* (*BRIT: = Women's Royal Army Corps*) *auxiliaires féminines de l'armée de terre*.
WRAF *n abbr* (*BRIT: = Women's Royal Air Force*) *auxiliaires féminines de l'armée de l'air*.
wrangle ['ræŋgl] *n* dispute *f* ♦ *vi* se disputer.
wrap [ræp] *n* (*stole*) écharpe *f*; (*cape*) pèlerine *f* ♦ *vt* (*also*: **~ up**) envelopper; **under ~s** (*fig: plan, scheme*) secret(ète).
wrapper ['ræpə*] *n* (*BRIT: of book*) couverture *f*; (*on chocolate etc*) papier *m*.
wrapping paper ['ræpɪŋ-] *n* papier *m* d'emballage; (*for gift*) papier cadeau.
wrath [rɔθ] *n* courroux *m*.
wreak [riːk] *vt* (*destruction*) entraîner; **to ~ havoc** faire des ravages; **to ~ vengeance on** se venger de, exercer sa vengeance sur.
wreath, ~s [riːθ, riːðz] *n* couronne *f*.

wreck [rɛk] *n* (*sea disaster*) naufrage *m*; (*ship*) épave *f*; (*pej*: *person*) loque (humaine) ♦ *vt* démolir; (*ship*) provoquer le naufrage de; (*fig*) briser, ruiner.

wreckage ['rɛkɪdʒ] *n* débris *mpl*; (*of building*) décombres *mpl*; (*of ship*) naufrage *m*.

wrecker ['rɛkə*] *n* (*US*: *breakdown van*) dépanneuse *f*.

WREN [rɛn] *n abbr* (*BRIT*) *membre du WRNS*.

wren [rɛn] *n* (*ZOOL*) troglodyte *m*.

wrench [rɛntʃ] *n* (*TECH*) clé *f* (à écrous); (*tug*) violent mouvement de torsion; (*fig*) arrachement *m* ♦ *vt* tirer violemment sur, tordre; **to ~ sth from** arracher qch (violemment) à *or* de.

wrest [rɛst] *vt*: **to ~ sth from sb** arracher *or* ravir qch à qn.

wrestle ['rɛsl] *vi*: **to ~ (with sb)** lutter (avec qn); **to ~ with** (*fig*) se débattre avec, lutter contre.

wrestler ['rɛslə*] *n* lutteur/euse.

wrestling ['rɛslɪŋ] *n* lutte *f*; (*also*: **all-in ~**: *BRIT*) catch *m*.

wrestling match *n* rencontre *f* de lutte (*or* de catch).

wretch [rɛtʃ] *n* pauvre malheureux/euse; **little ~!** (*often humorous*) petit(e) misérable!

wretched ['rɛtʃɪd] *adj* misérable; (*col*) maudit(e).

wriggle ['rɪgl] *n* tortillement *m* ♦ *vi* se tortiller.

wring, *pt, pp* **wrung** [rɪŋ, rʌŋ] *vt* tordre; (*wet clothes*) essorer; (*fig*): **to ~ sth out of** arracher qch à.

wringer ['rɪŋə*] *n* essoreuse *f*.

wringing ['rɪŋɪŋ] *adj* (*also*: **~ wet**) tout mouillé(e), trempé(e).

wrinkle ['rɪŋkl] *n* (*on skin*) ride *f*; (*on paper etc*) pli *m* ♦ *vt* rider, plisser ♦ *vi* se plisser.

wrinkled ['rɪŋkld] *adj*, **wrinkly** ['rɪŋklɪ] *adj* (*fabric, paper*) froissé(e), plissé(e); (*surface*) plissé; (*skin*) ridé(e), plissé.

wrist [rɪst] *n* poignet *m*.

wristband ['rɪstbænd] *n* (*BRIT*: *of shirt*) poignet *m*; (*: of watch*) bracelet *m*.

wrist watch *n* montre-bracelet *f*.

writ [rɪt] *n* acte *m* judiciaire; **to issue a ~ against sb, serve a ~ on sb** assigner qn en justice.

write, *pt* **wrote,** *pp* **written** [raɪt, rəut, 'rɪtn] *vt, vi* écrire; **to ~ sb a letter** écrire une lettre à qn.

▸**write away** *vi*: **to ~ away for** (*information*) (écrire pour) demander; (*goods*) (écrire pour) commander.

▸**write down** *vt* noter; (*put in writing*) mettre par écrit.

▸**write off** *vt* (*debt*) passer aux profits et pertes; (*depreciate*) amortir; (*smash up: car etc*) démolir complètement.

▸**write out** *vt* écrire; (*copy*) recopier.

▸**write up** *vt* rédiger.

write-off ['raɪtɔf] *n* perte totale; **the car is a ~** la voiture est bonne pour la casse.

write-protect ['raɪtprə'tɛkt] *vt* (*COMPUT*) protéger contre l'écriture.

writer ['raɪtə*] *n* auteur *m*, écrivain *m*.

write-up ['raɪtʌp] *n* (*review*) critique *f*.

writhe [raɪð] *vi* se tordre.

writing ['raɪtɪŋ] *n* écriture *f*; (*of author*) œuvres *fpl*; **in ~** par écrit; **in my own ~** écrit(e) de ma main.

writing case *n* nécessaire *m* de correspondance.

writing desk *n* secrétaire *m*.

writing paper *n* papier *m* à lettres.

written ['rɪtn] *pp of* **write**.

WRNS *n abbr* (*BRIT*: *= Women's Royal Naval Service*) *auxiliaires féminines de la marine*.

wrong [rɔŋ] *adj* faux(fausse); (*incorrectly chosen: number, road etc*) mauvais(e); (*not suitable*) qui ne convient pas; (*wicked*) mal; (*unfair*) injuste ♦ *adv* faux ♦ *n* tort *m* ♦ *vt* faire du tort à, léser; **to be ~** (*answer*) être faux(fausse); (*in doing/saying*) avoir tort (de dire/faire); **you are ~ to do it** tu as tort de le faire; **it's ~ to steal, stealing is ~** c'est mal de voler; **you are ~ about that, you've got it ~** tu te trompes; **to be in the ~** avoir tort; **what's ~?** qu'est-ce qui ne va pas?; **there's nothing ~** tout va bien; **what's ~ with the car?** qu'est-ce qu'elle a, la voiture?; **to go ~** (*person*) se tromper; (*plan*) mal tourner; (*machine*) se détraquer.

wrongdoer ['rɔŋduːə*] *n* malfaiteur *m*.

wrong-foot [rɔŋ'fut] *vt* (*SPORT*) prendre à contre-pied; (*fig*) prendre au dépourvu.

wrongful ['rɔŋful] *adj* injustifié(e); **~ dismissal** (*INDUSTRY*) licenciement abusif.

wrongly ['rɔŋlɪ] *adv* à tort; (*answer, do, count*) mal, incorrectement; (*treat*) injustement.

wrong number *n* (*TEL*): **you have the ~** vous vous êtes trompé de numéro.

wrong side *n* (*of cloth*) envers *m*.

wrote [rəut] *pt of* **write**.

wrought [rɔːt] *adj*: **~ iron** fer forgé.

wrung [rʌŋ] *pt, pp of* **wring**.

WRVS *n abbr* (*BRIT*: *= Women's Royal Voluntary Service*) *auxiliaires féminines bénévoles au service de la collectivité*.

wry [raɪ] *adj* désabusé(e).

wt. *abbr* (*= weight*) pds.

WV, W. Va. *abbr* (*US*) *= West Virginia*.

WWW *n abbr* (*= World Wide Web*): **the ~** le Web.

WY, Wyo. *abbr* (*US*) *= Wyoming*.

WYSIWYG ['wɪzɪwɪg] *abbr* (*COMPUT*: *= what you see is what you get*) ce que vous voyez est ce que vous aurez.

X *x*

X, x [ɛks] *n* (*letter*) X, x *m*; (*BRIT CINE: formerly*) film interdit aux moins de 18 ans; **X for Xmas** X comme Xavier.
Xerox ['zɪərɔks] *n* ® (*also*: ~ **machine**) photocopieuse *f*; (*photocopy*) photocopie *f* ♦ *vt* photocopier.
XL *abbr* (= *extra large*) XL.
Xmas ['ɛksməs] *n abbr* = **Christmas**.
X-rated ['ɛks'reɪtɪd] *adj* (*US*: *film*) interdit(e) aux moins de 18 ans.
X-ray ['ɛksreɪ] *n* rayon *m* X; (*photograph*) radio(graphie) *f* ♦ *vt* radiographier.
xylophone ['zaɪləfəun] *n* xylophone *m*.

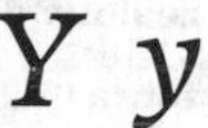

Y, y [waɪ] *n* (*letter*) Y, y *m*; **Y for Yellow**, (*US*) **Y for Yoke** Y comme Yvonne.
Y2K *n abbr* (= *year 2000*) l'an *m* 2000.
yacht [jɔt] *n* voilier *m*; (*motor, luxury* ~) yacht *m*.
yachting ['jɔtɪŋ] *n* yachting *m*, navigation *f* de plaisance.
yachtsman ['jɔtsmən] *n* yacht(s)man *m*.
yam [jæm] *n* igname *f*.
Yank [jæŋk], **Yankee** ['jæŋkɪ] *n* (*pej*) Amerloque *m/f*, Ricain/e.
yank [jæŋk] *vt* tirer d'un coup sec.
yap [jæp] *vi* (*dog*) japper.
yard [jɑːd] *n* (*of house etc*) cour *f*; (*US*: *garden*) jardin *m*; (*measure*) yard *m* (= *914 mm; 3 feet*); **builder's** ~ chantier *m*.
yardstick ['jɑːdstɪk] *n* (*fig*) mesure *f*, critère *m*.
yarn [jɑːn] *n* fil *m*; (*tale*) longue histoire.
yawn [jɔːn] *n* bâillement *m* ♦ *vi* bâiller.
yawning ['jɔːnɪŋ] *adj* (*gap*) béant(e).
yd *abbr* = **yard**.
yeah [jɛə] *adv* (*col*) ouais.
year [jɪə*] *n* an *m*, année *f*; (*SCOL etc*) année; **every** ~ tous les ans, chaque année; **this** ~ cette année; **a** *or* **per** ~ par an; ~ **in**, ~ **out** année après année; **to be 8** ~**s old** avoir 8 ans; **an eight-**~**-old child** un enfant de huit ans.
yearbook ['jɪəbuk] *n* annuaire *m*.
yearly ['jɪəlɪ] *adj* annuel(le) ♦ *adv* annuellement; **twice** ~ deux fois par an.
yearn [jəːn] *vi*: **to** ~ **for sth/to do** aspirer à qch/à faire, languir après qch.
yearning ['jəːnɪŋ] *n* désir ardent, envie *f*.
yeast [jiːst] *n* levure *f*.
yell [jɛl] *n* hurlement *m*, cri *m* ♦ *vi* hurler.
yellow ['jɛləu] *adj*, *n* jaune (*m*).
yellow fever *n* fièvre *f* jaune.
yellowish ['jɛləuɪʃ] *adj* qui tire sur le jaune, jaunâtre (*pej*).
Yellow Pages *npl* ® pages *fpl* jaunes.
Yellow Sea *n*: **the** ~ la mer Jaune.
yelp [jɛlp] *n* jappement *m*; glapissement *m* ♦ *vi* japper; glapir.
Yemen ['jɛmən] *n* Yémen *m*.
yen [jɛn] *n* (*currency*) yen *m*; (*craving*): ~ **for/to do** grand(e) envie *f or* désir *m* de/de faire.
yeoman ['jəumən] *n*: **Y**~ **of the Guard** hallebardier *m* de la garde royale.
yes [jɛs] *adv* oui; (*answering negative question*) si ♦ *n* oui *m*; **to say** ~ **(to)** dire oui (à).
yesterday ['jɛstədɪ] *adv*, *n* hier (*m*); ~ **morning/evening** hier matin/soir; **the day before** ~ avant-hier; **all day** ~ toute la journée d'hier.
yet [jɛt] *adv* encore; déjà ♦ *conj* pourtant, néanmoins; **it is not finished** ~ ce n'est pas encore fini *or* toujours pas fini; **must you go just** ~? dois-tu déjà partir?; **the best** ~ le meilleur jusqu'ici *or* jusque-là; **as** ~ jusqu'ici, encore; **a few days** ~ encore quelques jours; ~ **again** une fois de plus.
yew [juː] *n* if *m*.
Y-fronts ['waɪfrʌnts] *npl* ® (*BRIT*) slip *m* kangourou.
YHA *n abbr* (*BRIT*) = *Youth Hostels Association*.
Yiddish ['jɪdɪʃ] *n* yiddish *m*.
yield [jiːld] *n* production *f*, rendement *m*; (*FINANCE*) rapport *m* ♦ *vt* produire, rendre, rapporter; (*surrender*) céder ♦ *vi* céder; (*US AUT*) céder la priorité; **a** ~ **of 5%** un rendement de 5%.
YMCA *n abbr* (= *Young Men's Christian Association*) ≈ union chrétienne de jeunes gens (UCJG).
yob(bo) ['jɔb(əu)] *n* (*BRIT col*) loubar(d) *m*.
yodel ['jəudl] *vi* faire des tyroliennes, jodler.
yoga ['jəugə] *n* yoga *m*.
yog(h)ourt, yog(h)urt ['jəugət] *n* yaourt *m*.
yoke [jəuk] *n* joug *m* ♦ *vt* (*also*: ~ **together**: *oxen*) accoupler.
yolk [jəuk] *n* jaune *m* (d'œuf).
yonder ['jɔndə*] *adv* là(-bas).
yonks [jɔŋks] *npl* (*col*): **for** ~ très longtemps; **we've been here for** ~ ça fait une éternité qu'on est ici; **we were there for** ~ on est resté là pendant des lustres.
Yorks [jɔːks] *abbr* (*BRIT*) = *Yorkshire*.

KEYWORD

you [juː] *pron* **1** (*subject*) tu; (*polite form*) vous; (*plural*) vous; ~ **French enjoy your food** vous autres Français, vous aimez bien manger; ~ **and I will go** toi et moi *or* vous et moi, nous irons
2 (*object: direct, indirect*) te, t' *+vowel*; vous; **I know** ~ je te *or* vous connais; **I gave it to** ~, je vous l'ai donné, je te l'ai donné
3 (*stressed*) toi; vous; **I told YOU to do it** c'est à toi *or* vous que j'ai dit de le faire
4 (*after prep, in comparisons*) toi; vous; **it's for** ~ c'est pour toi *or* vous; **she's younger than** ~ elle est plus jeune que toi *or* vous
5 (*impersonal: one*) on; **fresh air does** ~ **good** l'air frais fait du bien; ~ **never know** on ne sait jamais.

you'd [juːd] = **you had, you would.**
you'll [juːl] = **you will, you shall.**
young [jʌŋ] *adj* jeune ♦ *npl* (*of animal*) petits *mpl*; (*people*): **the** ~ les jeunes, la jeunesse; **a** ~ **man** un jeune homme; **a** ~ **lady** (*unmarried*) une jeune fille, une demoiselle; (*married*) une jeune femme *or* dame; **my** ~**er brother** mon frère cadet; **the** ~**er generation** la jeune génération.
youngish ['jʌŋɪʃ] *adj* assez jeune.
youngster ['jʌŋstə*] *n* jeune *m/f*; (*child*) enfant *m/f*.
your [jɔː*] *adj* ton(ta), tes *pl*; (*polite form, pl*) votre, vos *pl*.
you're [juə*] = **you are.**
yours [jɔːz] *pron* le(la) tien(ne), les tiens(tiennes); (*polite form, pl*) le(la) vôtre, les vôtres; **is it** ~**?** c'est à toi (*or* à vous)?; **a friend of** ~ un(e) de tes (*or* de vos) amis.
yourself [jɔː'sɛlf] *pron* (*reflexive*) te; (*: polite form*) vous; (*after prep*) toi; vous; (*emphatic*) toi-même; vous-même; **you** ~ **told me** c'est vous qui me l'avez dit, vous me l'avez dit vous-même.
yourselves [jɔː'sɛlvz] *pl pron* vous; (*emphatic*) vous-mêmes.
youth [juːθ] *n* jeunesse *f*; (*young man: pl* ~**s** [juːðz]) jeune homme *m*; **in my** ~ dans ma jeunesse, quand j'étais jeune.
youth club *n* centre *m* de jeunes.
youthful ['juːθful] *adj* jeune; (*enthusiasm etc*) juvénile; (*misdemeanour*) de jeunesse.
youthfulness ['juːθfəlnɪs] *n* jeunesse *f*.
youth hostel *n* auberge *f* de jeunesse.
youth movement *n* mouvement *m* de jeunes.
you've [juːv] = **you have.**
yowl [jaul] *n* hurlement *m*; miaulement *m* ♦ *vi* hurler; miauler.
YT *abbr* (*Canada*) = *Yukon Territory.*
Yugoslav ['juːgəuslɑːv] *adj* yougoslave ♦ *n* Yougoslave *m/f*.
Yugoslavia [juːgəu'slɑːvɪə] *n* Yougoslavie *f*.
Yugoslavian [juːgəu'slɑːvɪən] *adj* yougoslave.
Yule [juːl]: ~ **log** *n* bûche *f* de Noël.
yuppie ['jʌpɪ] *n* yuppie *m/f*.
YWCA *n abbr* (= *Young Women's Christian Association*) union chrétienne féminine.

Z z

Z, z [zɛd, (*US*) ziː] *n* (*letter*) Z, z *m*; **Z for Zebra** Z comme Zoé.
Zaïre [zɑː'iːə*] *n* Zaïre *m*.
Zambia ['zæmbɪə] *n* Zambie *f*.
Zambian ['zæmbɪən] *adj* zambien(ne) ♦ *n* Zambien/ne.
zany ['zeɪnɪ] *adj* farfelu(e), loufoque.
zap [zæp] *vt* (*COMPUT*) effacer.
zeal [ziːl] *n* (*revolutionary etc*) ferveur *f*; (*keenness*) ardeur *f*, zèle *m*.
zealot ['zɛlət] *n* fanatique *m/f*.
zealous ['zɛləs] *adj* fervent(e); ardent(e), zélé(e).
zebra ['ziːbrə] *n* zèbre *m*.
zebra crossing *n* (*BRIT*) passage *m* pour piétons.
zenith ['zɛnɪθ] *n* (*ASTRONOMY*) zénith *m*; (*fig*) zénith, apogée *m*.
zero ['zɪərəu] *n* zéro *m* ♦ *vi*: **to** ~ **in on** (*target*) se diriger droit sur; **5° below** ~ 5 degrés au-dessous de zéro.
zero hour *n* l'heure *f* H.
zero option *n* (*POL*): **the** ~ l'option *f* zéro.
zero-rated ['ziːrəureɪtɪd] *adj* (*BRIT*) exonéré(e) de TVA.
zest [zɛst] *n* entrain *m*, élan *m*; (*of lemon etc*) zeste *m*.
zigzag ['zɪgzæg] *n* zigzag *m* ♦ *vi* zigzaguer, faire des zigzags.
Zimbabwe [zɪm'bɑːbwɪ] *n* Zimbabwe *m*.
Zimbabwean [zɪm'bɑːbwɪən] *adj* zimbabwéen(ne) ♦ *n* Zimbabwéen/ne.
Zimmer ['zɪmə*] *n* ® (*also*: ~ **frame**) déambulateur *m*.
zinc [zɪŋk] *n* zinc *m*.
Zionism ['zaɪənɪzəm] *n* sionisme *m*.
Zionist ['zaɪənɪst] *adj* sioniste ♦ *n* Sioniste *m/f*.
zip [zɪp] *n* (*also*: ~ **fastener,** (*US*) ~**per**) fermeture *f* éclair ® *or* à glissière; (*energy*) entrain *m* ♦ *vt* (*also*: ~ **up**) fermer (avec une fermeture éclair ®).
zip code *n* (*US*) code postal.
zither ['zɪðə*] *n* cithare *f*.
zodiac ['zəudɪæk] *n* zodiaque *m*.
zombie ['zɔmbɪ] *n* (*fig*): **like a** ~ avec l'air d'un zombie, comme un automate.
zone [zəun] *n* zone *f*.

zonked [zɔŋkt] *adj* (*col*) crevé(e), claqué(e).
zoo [zuː] *n* zoo *m*.
zoological [zuə'lɔdʒɪkl] *adj* zoologique.
zoologist [zu'ɔlədʒɪst] *n* zoologiste *m/f*.
zoology [zuː'ɔlədʒɪ] *n* zoologie *f*.
zoom [zuːm] *vi*: **to ~ past** passer en trombe; **to ~ in (on sb/sth)** (*PHOT*, *CINE*) zoomer (sur qn/qch).
zoom lens *n* zoom *m*, objectif *m* à focale variable.
zucchini [zuː'kiːnɪ] *n(pl)* (*US*) courgette(s) *f(pl)*.
Zulu ['zuːluː] *adj* zoulou ♦ *n* Zoulou *m/f*.
Zürich ['zjuərɪk] *n* Zurich.

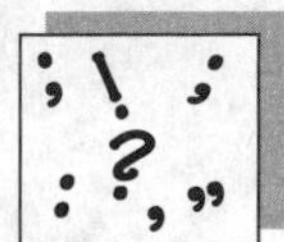

Grammar
Grammaire

USING THE GRAMMAR

The Grammar section deals systematically and comprehensively with all the information you will need in order to communicate accurately in French. The user-friendly layout explains the grammar point on a lefthand page, leaving the facing page free for illustrative examples. The boxed numbers, → 1 etc, direct you to the relevant example in every case.

The Grammar section also provides invaluable guidance on the danger of translating English structures by identical structures in French. Use of Numbers and Punctuation are important areas covered towards the end of the section. Finally, the index lists the main words and grammatical terms in both English and French.

ABBREVIATIONS

ctd.	continued	**p(p)**	page(s)	**qu**	quelqu'un
fem.	feminine	**perf.**	perfect	**sb**	somebody
infin.	infinitive	**plur.**	plural	**sing.**	singular
masc.	masculine	**qch**	quelque chose	**sth**	something

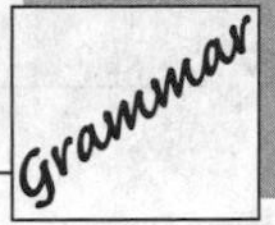

CONTENTS

		Page
VERBS	Simple tenses: formation	6
	first conjugation	8
	second conjugation	10
	third conjugation	12
	First conjugation spelling irregularities	14
	The imperative	20
	Compound tenses: formation	22
	Reflexive verbs	30
	The passive	36
	Impersonal verbs	40
	The infinitive	44
	The present participle	48
	Past participle agreement	50
	Modal auxiliary verbs	52
	Use of tenses	54
	The subjunctive: when to use it	58
	Verbs governing **à** and **de**	64
	Irregular verbs	74
NOUNS	The gender of nouns	132
	Formation of feminines	134
	Regular feminine endings	136
	Formation of plurals	138
ARTICLES	The definite article	140
	The partitive article	144
	The indefinite article	146
ADJECTIVES	Formation of feminines and plurals	148
	Regular feminine endings	150
	Irregular feminine forms	152
	Comparatives and superlatives	154
	Demonstrative adjectives	156
	Interrogative and exclamatory adjectives	158
	Possessive adjectives	160
	Position of adjectives	162

CONTENTS

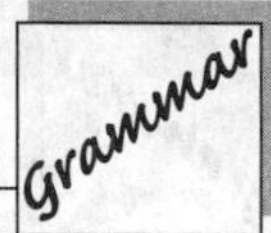

		Page
PRONOUNS	Personal pronouns	164
	The pronoun **en**	174
	The pronoun **y**	176
	Indefinite pronouns	178
	Relative pronouns	180
	Interrogative pronouns	186
	Possessive pronouns	192
	Demonstrative pronouns	194
ADVERBS	Formation	198
	Irregular adverbs	198
	Position	200
	Comparatives and superlatives	200
	Common adverbs and their usage	202
PREPOSITIONS		204
CONJUNCTIONS		212
SENTENCE STRUCTURE	Word order	214
	Negatives	216
	Question forms	220
USE OF NUMBERS	Cardinal and ordinal numbers	224
	Calendar	227
	The time	228
TRANSLATION PROBLEMS		230
PRONUNCIATION		236
	From spelling to sounds	240
	Pronunciation of feminines and plurals	244
ALPHABET		246
INDEX		247

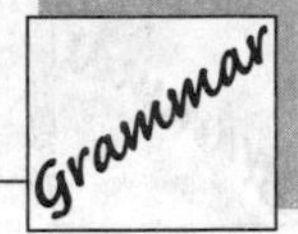

❒ Simple Tenses: formation

In French the simple tenses are:

Present → [1]
Imperfect → [2]
Future → [3]
Conditional → [4]
Past Historic → [5]
Present Subjunctive → [6]
Imperfect Subjunctive → [7]

They are formed by adding endings to a verb stem. The endings show the number and person of the subject of the verb → [8]

The stem and endings of regular verbs are totally predictable. The following sections show all the patterns for regular verbs. For irregular verbs see pp 74 ff.

❒ Regular Verbs

There are three regular verb patterns (called conjugations), each identifiable by the ending of the infinitive:

- First conjugation verbs end in **-er** e.g. **donner** to give
- Second conjugation verbs end in **-ir** e.g. **finir** to finish
- Third conjugation verbs end in **-re** e.g. **vendre** to sell

These three conjugations are treated in order on the following pages.

7 Examples

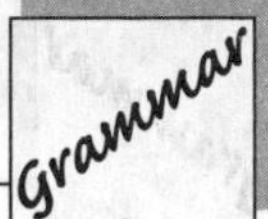

[1]	**je donne**	I give I am giving I do give
[2]	**je donnais**	I gave I was giving I used to give
[3]	**je donnerai**	I shall give I shall be giving
[4]	**je donnerais**	I should/would give I should/would be giving
[5]	**je donnai**	I gave
[6]	**(que) je donne**	(that) I give/gave
[7]	**(que) je donnasse**	(that) I gave
[8]	**je donne** **nous donnons** **je donnerais** **nous donnerions**	I give we give I would give we would give

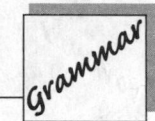

❐ Simple Tenses: First Conjugation

- The stem is formed as follows:

TENSE	FORMATION	EXAMPLE
Present Imperfect Past Historic Present Subjunctive Imperfect Subjunctive	infinitive minus **-er**	**donn-**
Future Conditional	infinitive	**donner-**

- To the appropriate stem add the following endings:

		PRESENT → 1	IMPERFECT → 2	PAST HISTORIC → 3
sing.	1st person	**-e**	**-ais**	**-ai**
	2nd person	**-es**	**-ais**	**-as**
	3rd person	**-e**	**-ait**	**-a**
plur.	1st person	**-ons**	**-ions**	**-âmes**
	2nd person	**-ez**	**-iez**	**-âtes**
	3rd person	**-ent**	**-aient**	**-èrent**

		PRESENT SUBJUNCTIVE → 4	IMPERFECT SUBJUNCTIVE → 5
sing.	1st person	**-e**	**-asse**
	2nd person	**-es**	**-asses**
	3rd person	**-e**	**-ât**
plur.	1st person	**-ions**	**-assions**
	2nd person	**-iez**	**-assiez**
	3rd person	**-ent**	**-assent**

		FUTURE → 6	CONDITIONAL → 7
sing.	1st person	**-ai**	**-ais**
	2nd person	**-as**	**-ais**
	3rd person	**-a**	**-ait**
plur.	1st person	**-ons**	**-ions**
	2nd person	**-ez**	**-iez**
	3rd person	**-ont**	**-aient**

Examples

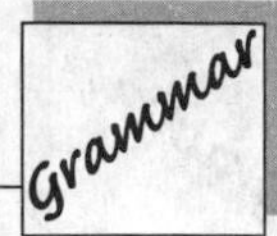

	1 PRESENT		2 IMPERFECT		3 PAST HISTORIC
je	donn**e**	je	donn**ais**	je	donn**ai**
tu	donn**es**	tu	donn**ais**	tu	donn**as**
il	donn**e**	il	donn**ait**	il	donn**a**
elle	donn**e**	elle	donn**ait**	elle	donn**a**
nous	donn**ons**	nous	donn**ions**	nous	donn**âmes**
vous	donn**ez**	vous	donn**iez**	vous	donn**âtes**
ils	donn**ent**	ils	donn**aient**	ils	donn**èrent**
elles	donn**ent**	elles	donn**aient**	elles	donn**èrent**

	4 PRESENT SUBJUNCTIVE		5 IMPERFECT SUBJUNCTIVE
je	donn**e**	je	donn**asse**
tu	donn**es**	tu	donn**asses**
il	donn**e**	il	donn**ât**
elle	donn**e**	elle	donn**ât**
nous	donn**ions**	nous	donn**assions**
vous	donn**iez**	vous	donn**assiez**
ils	donn**ent**	ils	donn**assent**
elles	donn**ent**	elles	donn**assent**

	6 FUTURE		7 CONDITIONAL
je	donner**ai**	je	donner**ais**
tu	donner**as**	tu	donner**ais**
il	donner**a**	il	donner**ait**
elle	donner**a**	elle	donner**ait**
nous	donner**ons**	nous	donner**ions**
vous	donner**ez**	vous	donner**iez**
ils	donner**ont**	ils	donner**aient**
elles	donner**ont**	elles	donner**aient**

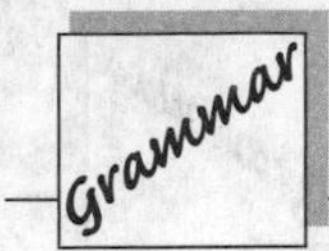

❒ Simple Tenses: Second Conjugation

◆ The stem is formed as follows:

TENSE	FORMATION	EXAMPLE
Present Imperfect Past Historic Present Subjunctive Imperfect Subjunctive	infinitive minus **-ir**	**fin-**
Future Conditional	infinitive	**finir-**

◆ To the appropriate stem add the following endings:

		PRESENT → 1	IMPERFECT → 2	PAST HISTORIC → 3
sing.	1st person	**-is**	**-issais**	**-is**
	2nd person	**-is**	**-issais**	**-is**
	3rd person	**-it**	**-issait**	**-it**
plur.	1st person	**-issons**	**-issions**	**-îmes**
	2nd person	**-issez**	**-issiez**	**-îtes**
	3rd person	**-issent**	**-issaient**	**-irent**

		PRESENT SUBJUNCTIVE → 4	IMPERFECT SUBJUNCTIVE → 5
sing.	1st person	**-isse**	**-isse**
	2nd person	**-isses**	**-isses**
	3rd person	**-isse**	**-ît**
plur.	1st person	**-issions**	**-issions**
	2nd person	**-issiez**	**-issiez**
	3rd person	**-issent**	**-issent**

		FUTURE → 6	CONDITIONAL → 7
sing.	1st person	**-ai**	**-ais**
	2nd person	**-as**	**-ais**
	3rd person	**-a**	**-ait**
plur.	1st person	**-ons**	**-ions**
	2nd person	**-ez**	**-iez**
	3rd person	**-ont**	**-aient**

Examples

	1 PRESENT		2 IMPERFECT		3 PAST HISTORIC
je	fin**is**	je	fin**issais**	je	fin**is**
tu	fin**is**	tu	fin**issais**	tu	fin**is**
il	fin**it**	il	fin**issait**	il	fin**it**
elle	fin**it**	elle	fin**issait**	elle	fin**it**
nous	fin**issons**	nous	fin**issions**	nous	fin**îmes**
vous	fin**issez**	vous	fin**issiez**	vous	fin**îtes**
ils	fin**issent**	ils	fin**issaient**	ils	fin**irent**
elles	fin**issent**	elles	fin**issaient**	elles	fin**irent**

	4 PRESENT SUBJUNCTIVE		5 IMPERFECT SUBJUNCTIVE
je	fin**isse**	je	fin**isse**
tu	fin**isses**	tu	fin**isses**
il	fin**isse**	il	fin**ît**
elle	fin**isse**	elle	fin**ît**
nous	fin**issions**	nous	fin**issions**
vous	fin**issiez**	vous	fin**issiez**
ils	fin**issent**	ils	fin**issent**
elles	fin**issent**	elles	fin**issent**

	6 FUTURE		7 CONDITIONAL
je	finir**ai**	je	finir**ais**
tu	finir**as**	tu	finir**ais**
il	finir**a**	il	finir**ait**
elle	finir**a**	elle	finir**ait**
nous	finir**ons**	nous	finir**ions**
vous	finir**ez**	vous	finir**iez**
ils	finir**ont**	ils	finir**aient**
elles	finir**ont**	elles	finir**aient**

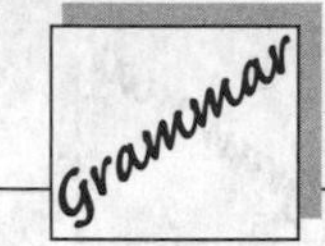

❒ Simple Tenses: Third Conjugation

- The stem is formed as follows:

TENSE	FORMATION	EXAMPLE
Present Imperfect Past Historic Present Subjunctive Imperfect Subjunctive	infinitive minus **-re**	**vend-**
Future Conditional	infinitive minus **-e**	**vendr-**

- To the appropriate stem add the following endings:

		PRESENT → 1	IMPERFECT → 2	PAST HISTORIC → 3
	1st person	**-s**	**-ais**	**-is**
sing.	2nd person	**-s**	**-ais**	**-is**
	3rd person	–	**-ait**	**-it**
	1st person	**-ons**	**-ions**	**-îmes**
plur.	2nd person	**-ez**	**-iez**	**-îtes**
	3rd person	**-ent**	**-aient**	**-irent**

		PRESENT SUBJUNCTIVE → 4	IMPERFECT SUBJUNCTIVE → 5
	1st person	**-e**	**-isse**
sing.	2nd person	**-es**	**-isses**
	3rd person	**-e**	**-ît**
	1st person	**-ions**	**-issions**
plur.	2nd person	**-iez**	**-issiez**
	3rd person	**-ent**	**-issent**

		FUTURE → 6	CONDITIONAL → 7
	1st person	**-ai**	**-ais**
sing.	2nd person	**-as**	**-ais**
	3rd person	**-a**	**-ait**
	1st person	**-ons**	**-ions**
plur.	2nd person	**-ez**	**-iez**
	3rd person	**-ont**	**-aient**

Examples

	1 PRESENT		2 IMPERFECT		3 PAST HISTORIC
je	vend**s**	je	vend**ais**	je	vend**is**
tu	vend**s**	tu	vend**ais**	tu	vend**is**
il	vend	il	vend**ait**	il	vend**it**
elle	vend	elle	vend**ait**	elle	vend**it**
nous	vend**ons**	nous	vend**ions**	nous	vend**îmes**
vous	vend**ez**	vous	vend**iez**	vous	vend**îtes**
ils	vend**ent**	ils	vend**aient**	ils	vend**irent**
elles	vend**ent**	elles	vend**aient**	elles	vend**irent**

	4 PRESENT SUBJUNCTIVE		5 IMPERFECT SUBJUNCTIVE
je	vend**e**	je	vend**isse**
tu	vend**es**	tu	vend**isses**
il	vend**e**	il	vend**ît**
elle	vend**e**	elle	vend**ît**
nous	vend**ions**	nous	vend**issions**
vous	vend**iez**	vous	vend**issiez**
ils	vend**ent**	ils	vend**issent**
elles	vend**ent**	elles	vend**issent**

	6 FUTURE		7 CONDITIONAL
je	vendr**ai**	je	vendr**ais**
tu	vendr**as**	tu	vendr**ais**
il	vendr**a**	il	vendr**ait**
elle	vendr**a**	elle	vendr**ait**
nous	vendr**ons**	nous	vendr**ions**
vous	vendr**ez**	vous	vendr**iez**
ils	vendr**ont**	ils	vendr**aient**
elles	vendr**ont**	elles	vendr**aient**

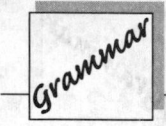

❒ First Conjugation Spelling Irregularities

Before certain endings, the stems of some **'-er'** verbs may change slightly.

Below, and on subsequent pages, the verb types are identified, and the changes described are illustrated by means of a representative verb.

Verbs ending:	**-cer**
Change:	**c** becomes **ç** before **a** or **o**
Tenses affected:	Present, Imperfect, Past Historic, Imperfect Subjunctive, Present Participle
Model:	**lancer** *to throw* → 1

- Why the change occurs:
  A cedilla is added to the **c** to retain its soft [s] pronunciation before the vowels **a** and **o**.

Verbs ending:	**-ger**
Change:	**g** becomes **ge** before **a** or **o**
Tenses affected:	Present, Imperfect, Past Historic, Imperfect Subjunctive, Present Participle
Model:	**manger** *to eat* → 2

- Why the change occurs:
  An **e** is added after the **g** to retain its soft [ʒ] pronunciation before the vowels **a** and **o**.

Examples

1

	INFINITIVE		PRESENT PARTICIPLE
	lancer		**lançant**

PRESENT		IMPERFECT	
je	lance	**je**	**lançais**
tu	lances	**tu**	**lançais**
il/elle	lance	**il/elle**	**lançait**
nous	**lançons**	nous	lancions
vous	lancez	vous	lanciez
ils/elles	lancent	**ils/elles**	**lançaient**

PAST HISTORIC		IMPERFECT SUBJUNCTIVE	
je	**lançai**	**je**	**lançasse**
tu	**lanças**	**tu**	**lançasses**
il/elle	**lança**	**il/elle**	**lançât**
nous	**lançâmes**	**nous**	**lançassions**
vous	**lançâtes**	**vous**	**lançassiez**
ils/elles	lancèrent	**ils/elles**	**lançassent**

2

	INFINITIVE		PRESENT PARTICIPLE
	manger		**mangeant**

PRESENT		IMPERFECT	
je	mange	**je**	**mangeais**
tu	manges	**tu**	**mangeais**
il/elle	mange	**il/elle**	**mangeait**
nous	**mangeons**	nous	mangions
vous	mangez	vous	mangiez
ils/elles	mangent	**ils/elles**	**mangeaient**

PAST HISTORIC		IMPERFECT SUBJUNCTIVE	
je	**mangeai**	**je**	**mangeasse**
tu	**mangeas**	**tu**	**mangeasses**
il/elle	**mangea**	**il/elle**	**mangeât**
nous	**mangeâmes**	**nous**	**mangeassions**
vous	**mangeâtes**	**vous**	**mangeassiez**
ils/elles	mangèrent	**ils/elles**	**mangeassent**

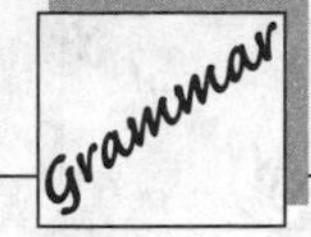

❐ First Conjugation Spelling Irregularities

(Continued)

Verbs ending: **-eler**
Change: **-l** doubles before **-e**, **-es**, **-ent** and throughout the Future and Conditional tenses
Tenses affected: Present, Present Subjunctive, Future, Conditional
Model: **appeler** *to call* → [1]

◆ EXCEPTIONS: **geler** *to freeze*, **peler** *to peel* } like **mener** (p 18)

Verbs ending: **-eter**
Change: **-t** doubles before **-e**, **-es**, **-ent** and throughout the Future and Conditional tenses
Tenses affected: Present, Present Subjunctive, Future, Conditional
Model: **jeter** *to throw* → [2]

◆ EXCEPTIONS: **acheter** *to buy*, **haleter** *to pant* } like **mener** (p 18)

Verbs ending: **-yer**
Change: **y** changes to **i** before **-e**, **-es**, **-ent** and throughout the Future and Conditional tenses
Tenses affected: Present, Present Subjunctive, Future, Conditional
Model: **essuyer** *to wipe* → [3]

◆ The change described is optional for verbs ending in **-ayer** e.g. **payer** *to pay*, **essayer** *to try*.

Examples

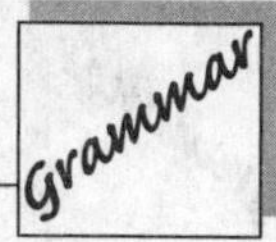

1 PRESENT (+ SUBJUNCTIVE)

	j'appelle
tu	**appelles**
il/elle	**appelle**
nous	appelons
	(appelions)
vous	appelez
	(appeliez)
ils/elles	**appellent**

FUTURE

	j'appellerai
tu	**appelleras**
il	**appellera** *etc*

CONDITIONAL

	j'appellerais
tu	**appellerais**
il	**appellerait** *etc*

2 PRESENT (+ SUBJUNCTIVE)

je	**jette**
tu	**jettes**
il/elle	**jette**
nous	jetons
	(jetions)
vous	jetez
	(jetiez)
ils/elles	**jettent**

FUTURE

je	**jetterai**
tu	**jetteras**
il	**jettera** *etc*

CONDITIONAL

je	**jetterais**
tu	**jetterais**
il	**jetterait** *etc*

3 PRESENT (+ SUBJUNCTIVE)

	j'essuie
tu	**essuies**
il/elle	**essuie**
nous	essuyons
	(essuyions)
vous	essuyez
	(essuyiez)
ils/elles	**essuient**

FUTURE

	j'essuierai
tu	**essuieras**
il	**essuiera** *etc*

CONDITIONAL

	j'essuierais
tu	**essuierais**
il	**essuierait** *etc*

❐ First Conjugation Spelling Irregularities

(Continued)

Verbs ending	**mener, peser, lever** etc
Change:	**e** changes to **è**, before **-e, -es, -ent** and throughout the Future and Conditional tenses
Tenses affected:	Present, Present Subjunctive, Future, Conditional
Model:	**mener** *to lead* → 1
Verbs like:	**céder, régler, espérer** etc
Change:	**é** changes to **è** before **-e, -es, -ent**
Tenses affected:	Present, Present Subjunctive
Model:	**céder** *to yield* → 2

Examples

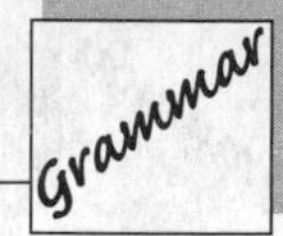

①	PRESENT (+ SUBJUNCTIVE)
je	**mène**
tu	**mènes**
il/elle	**mène**
nous	menons (menions)
vous	menez (meniez)
ils/elles	**mènent**

FUTURE

je	**mènerai**
tu	**mèneras**
il	**mènera** *etc*

CONDITIONAL

je	**mènerais**
tu	**mènerais**
il	**mènerait** *etc*

②	PRESENT (+ SUBJUNCTIVE)
je	**cède**
tu	**cèdes**
il/elle	**cède**
nous	cédons (cédions)
vous	cédez (cédiez)
ils/elles	**cèdent**

❐ The Imperative

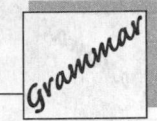

The imperative is the form of the verb used to give commands or orders. It can be used politely, as in English 'Shut the door, please'.

The imperative is the same as the present tense **tu, nous** and **vous** forms without the subject pronouns:

donne*	**finis**	**vends**
give	*finish*	*sell*

*The final 's' of the present tense of first conjugation verbs is dropped, except before **y** and **en** → 1

donnons	**finissons**	**vendons**
let's give	*let's finish*	*let's sell*
donnez	**finissez**	**vendez**
give	*finish*	*sell*

- The imperative of irregular verbs is given in the verb tables, pp 74 ff.
- Position of object pronouns with the imperative:
  in POSITIVE commands: they follow the verb and are attached to it by hyphens → 2
  in NEGATIVE commands: they precede the verb and are not attached to it → 3
- For the order of object pronouns, see p 170.
- For reflexive verbs – e.g. **se lever** *to get up* – the object pronoun is the reflexive pronoun → 4

Examples

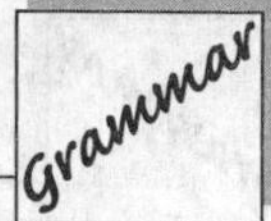

[1] Compare: **Tu donnes de l'argent à Paul**
You give (some) money to Paul
and: **Donne de l'argent à Paul**
Give (some) money to Paul

[2] **Excusez-moi**
Excuse me
Crois-nous
Believe us
Attendons-la
Let's wait for her/it

Envoyons-les-leur
Let's send them to them
Expliquez-le-moi
Explain it to me
Rends-la-lui
Give it back to him/her

[3] **Ne me dérange pas**
Don't disturb me
Ne les négligeons pas
Let's not neglect them
Ne leur répondez pas
Don't answer them

Ne leur en parlons pas
Let's not speak to them about it
N'y pense plus
Don't think about it any more
Ne la lui rends pas
Don't give it back to him/her

[4] **Lève-toi**
Get up
Dépêchons-nous
Let's hurry
Levez-vous
Get up

Ne te lève pas
Don't get up
Ne nous affolons pas
Let's not panic
Ne vous levez pas
Don't get up

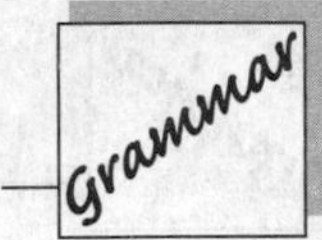

❐ Compound Tenses: formation

In French the compound tenses are:

Perfect → [1]
Pluperfect → [2]
Future Perfect → [3]
Conditional Perfect → [4]
Past Anterior → [5]
Perfect Subjunctive → [6]
Pluperfect Subjunctive → [7]

They consist of the past participle of the verb together with an auxiliary verb. Most verbs take the auxiliary **avoir,** but some take **être** (see p 28).

Compound tenses are formed in exactly the same way for both regular and irregular verbs, the only difference being that irregular verbs may have an irregular past participle.

❐ The Past Participle

For all compound tenses you need to know how to form the past participle of the verb. For regular verbs this is as follows:

- 1st conjugation: replace the -**er** of the infinitive by -**é** → [8]
- 2nd conjugation: replace the -**ir** of the infinitive by -**i** → [9]
- 3rd conjugation: replace the -**re** of the infinitive by -**u** → [10]
- See p 50 for agreement of past participles.

Examples

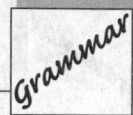

	with **avoir**	with **être**
1	**j'ai donné** I gave, have given	**je suis tombé** I fell, have fallen
2	**j'avais donné** I had given	**j'étais tombé** I had fallen
3	**j'aurai donné** I shall have given	**je serai tombé** I shall have fallen
4	**j'aurais donné** I should /would have given	**je serais tombé** I should/would have fallen
5	**j'eus donné** I had given	**je fus tombé** I had fallen
6	**(que) j'aie donné** (that) I gave, have given	**(que) je sois tombé** (that) I fell, have fallen
7	**(que) j'eusse donné** (that) I had given	**(que) je fusse tombé** (that) I had fallen

8	**donner** → **donné** to give given	
9	**finir** → **fini** to finish finished	
10	**vendre** → **vendu** to sell sold	

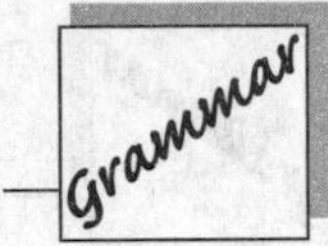

❒ Compound Tenses: formation (Continued)

Verbs taking the auxiliary avoir

Perfect tense:	the present tense of **avoir** plus the past participle → [1]
Pluperfect tense:	the imperfect tense of **avoir** plus the past participle → [2]
Future Perfect:	the future tense of **avoir** plus the past participle → [3]
Conditional Perfect:	the conditional of **avoir** plus the past participle → [4]
Past Anterior:	the past historic of **avoir** plus the past participle → [5]
Perfect Subjunctive:	the present subjunctive of **avoir** plus the past participle → [6]
Pluperfect Subjunctive:	the imperfect subjunctive of **avoir** plus the past participle → [7]

- For how to form the past participle of regular verbs see p 22. The past participle of irregular verbs is given for each verb in the verb tables, pp 74 ff.
- The past participle must agree in number and in gender with any preceding direct object (see p 50).

Examples

1 PERFECT

j'ai donné **nous avons donné**
tu as donné **vous avez donné**
il/elle a donné **ils/elles ont donné**

2 PLUPERFECT

j'avais donné **nous avions donné**
tu avais donné **vous aviez donné**
il/elle avait donné **ils/elles avaient donné**

3 FUTURE PERFECT

j'aurai donné **nous aurons donné**
tu auras donné **vous aurez donné**
il/elle aura donné **ils/elles auront donné**

4 CONDITIONAL PERFECT

j'aurais donné **nous aurions donné**
tu aurais donné **vous auriez donné**
il/elle aurait donné **ils/elles auraient donné**

5 PAST ANTERIOR

j'eus donné **nous eûmes donné**
tu eus donné **vous eûtes donné**
il/elle eut donné **ils/elles eurent donné**

6 PERFECT SUBJUNCTIVE

j'aie donné **nous ayons donné**
tu aies donné **vous ayez donné**
il/elle ait donné **ils/elles aient donné**

7 PLUPERFECT SUBJUNCTIVE

j'eusse donné **nous eussions donné**
tu eusses donné **vous eussiez donné**
il/elle eût donné **ils/elles eussent donné**

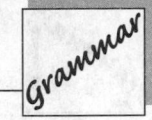

❒ Compound Tenses: formation (Continued)

Verbs taking the auxiliary être

Perfect tense: the present tense of **être** plus the past participle → 1

Pluperfect tense: the imperfect tense of **être** plus the past participle → 2

Future Perfect: the future tense of **être** plus the past participle → 3

Conditional Perfect: the conditional of **être** plus the past participle → 4

Past Anterior: the past historic of **être** plus the past participle → 5

Perfect Subjunctive: the present subjunctive of **être** plus the past participle → 6

Pluperfect Subjunctive: the imperfect subjunctive of **être** plus the past participle → 7

- For how to form the past participle of regular verbs see p 22. The past participle of irregular verbs is given for each verb in the verb tables, pp 74 ff.
- For agreement of past participles, see p 50.
- For a list of verbs and verb types that take the auxiliary **être,** see p 28.

Examples

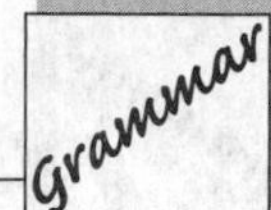

1 PERFECT

je suis tombé(e)	**nous sommes tombé(e)s**
tu es tombé(e)	**vous êtes tombé(e)(s)**
il est tombé	**ils sont tombés**
elle est tombée	**elles sont tombées**

2 PLUPERFECT

j'étais tombé(e)	**nous étions tombé(e)s**
tu étais tombé(e)	**vous étiez tombé(e)(s)**
il était tombé	**ils étaient tombés**
elle était tombée	**elles étaient tombées**

3 FUTURE PERFECT

je serai tombé(e)	**nous serons tombé(e)s**
tu seras tombé(e)	**vous serez tombé(e)(s)**
il sera tombé	**ils seront tombés**
elle sera tombée	**elles seront tombées**

4 CONDITIONAL PERFECT

je serais tombé(e)	**nous serions tombé(e)s**
tu serais tombé(e)	**vous seriez tombé(e)(s)**
il serait tombé	**ils seraient tombés**
elle serait tombée	**elles seraient tombées**

5 PAST ANTERIOR

je fus tombé(e)	**nous fûmes tombé(e)s**
tu fus tombé(e)	**vous fûtes tombé(e)(s)**
il fut tombé	**ils furent tombés**
elle fut tombée	**elles furent tombées**

6 PERFECT SUBJUNCTIVE

je sois tombé(e)	**nous soyons tombé(e)s**
tu sois tombé(e)	**vous soyez tombé(e)(s)**
il soit tombé	**ils soient tombés**
elle soit tombée	**elles soient tombées**

7 PLUPERFECT SUBJUNCTIVE

je fusse tombé(e)	**nous fussions tombé(e)s**
tu fusses tombé(e)	**vous fussiez tombé(e)(s)**
il fût tombé	**ils fussent tombés**
elle fût tombée	**elles fussent tombées**

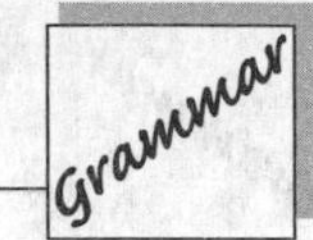

❐ Compound Tenses (Continued)

The following verbs take the auxiliary être

- Reflexive verbs (see p 30) → [1]
- The following intransitive verbs (i.e. verbs which cannot take a direct object), largely expressing motion or a change of state:

aller	*to go* → [2]	**passer**	*to pass*
arriver	*to arrive; to happen*	**rentrer**	*to go back/in*
descendre	*to go/come down*	**rester**	*to stay* → [5]
devenir	*to become*	**retourner**	*to go back*
entrer	*to go/come in*	**revenir**	*to come back*
monter	*to go/come up*	**sortir**	*to go/come out*
mourir	*to die* → [3]	**tomber**	*to fall*
naître	*to be born*	**venir**	*to come* → [6]
partir	*to leave* → [4]		

- Of these, the following are conjugated with **avoir** when used transitively (i.e. with a direct object):

descendre	*to bring/take down*
entrer	*to bring/take in*
monter	*to bringl/take up* → [7]
passer	*to pass; to spend* → [8]
rentrer	*to bring/take in*
retourner	*to turn over*
sortir	*to bring/take out* → [9]

⚠ NOTE that the past participle must show an agreement in number and gender whenever the auxiliary is **être** EXCEPT FOR REFLEXIVE VERBS WHERE THE REFLEXIVE PRONOUN IS THE INDIRECT OBJECT (see p 50).

Examples

1 **je me suis arrêté(e)**
I stopped
tu t'es levé(e)
you got up

elle s'est trompée
she made a mistake
ils s'étaient battus
they had fought (one another)

2 **elle est allée**
she went

3 **ils sont morts**
they died

4 **vous êtes partie**
you left *(addressing a female person)*
vous êtes parties
you left *(addressing more than one female person)*

5 **nous sommes resté(e)s**
we stayed

6 **elles étaient venues**
they [female] had come

7 **Il a monté les valises**
He's taken up the cases

8 **Nous avons passé trois semaines chez elle**
We spent three weeks at her place

9 **Avez-vous sorti la voiture?**
Have you taken the car out?

❒ Reflexive Verbs

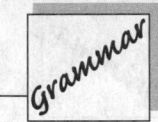

A reflexive verb is one accompanied by a reflexive pronoun, e.g. **se lever** *to get up;* **se laver** *to wash (oneself).* The pronouns are:

PERSON	SINGULAR	PLURAL
1st	**me (m')**	**nous**
2nd	**te (t')**	**vous**
3rd	**se (s')**	**se (s')**

The forms shown in brackets are used before a vowel, an **h** 'mute', or the pronoun **y** → 1

- In positive commands, **te** changes to **toi** → 2
- The reflexive pronoun 'reflects back' to the subject, but it is not always translated in English → 3

  The plural pronouns are sometimes translated as *one another, each other* (the 'reciprocal' meaning) → 4

  The reciprocal meaning may be emphasized by **l'un(e) l'autre (les un(e)s les autres)** → 5
- Simple tenses of reflexive verbs are conjugated in exactly the same way as those of non-reflexive verbs except that the reflexive pronoun is always used. Compound tenses are formed with the auxiliary **être.** A sample reflexive verb is conjugated in full on pp 34 and 35.

  For agreement of past participles, see p 32.

Position of Reflexive Pronouns

- In constructions other than the imperative affirmative the pronoun comes before the verb → 6
- In the imperative affirmative, the pronoun follows the verb and is attached to it by a hyphen → 7

Examples

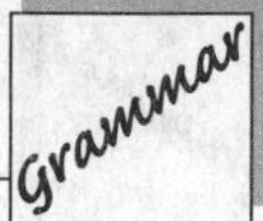

1 **Je m'ennuie**
I'm bored
Elle s'habille
She's getting dressed
Ils s'y intéressent
They are interested in it

2 **Assieds-toi**
Sit down
Tais-toi
Be quiet

3 **Je me prépare**
I'm getting (myself) ready
Nous nous lavons
We're washing (ourselves)
Elle se lève
She gets up

4 **Nous nous parlons**
We speak to each other
Ils se ressemblent
They resemble one another

5 **Ils se regardent l'un l'autre**
They are looking at each other

6 **Je me couche tôt**
I go to bed early
Comment vous appelez-vous?
What is your name?
Il ne s'est pas rasé
He hasn't shaved
Ne te dérange pas pour nous
Don't put yourself out on our account

7 **Dépêche-toi**
Hurry (up)
Renseignons-nous
Let's find out
Asseyez-vous
Sit down

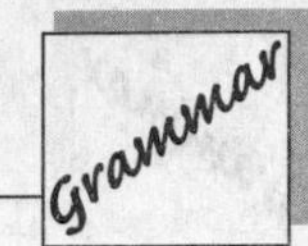

❐ Reflexive Verbs (Continued)

Past Participle Agreement

- In most reflexive verbs the reflexive pronoun is a DIRECT object pronoun → [1]
- When a direct object accompanies the reflexive verb the pronoun is then the INDIRECT object → [2]
- The past participle of a reflexive verb agrees in number and gender with a direct object which *precedes* the verb (usually, but not always, the reflexive pronoun) → [3]

  The past participle does not change if the direct object follows the verb → [4]

Here are some common reflexive verbs:

s'en aller	*to go away*	**se hâter**	*to hurry*
s'amuser	*to enjoy oneself*	**se laver**	*to wash (oneself)*
s'appeler	*to be called*	**se lever**	*to get up*
s'arrêter	*to stop*	**se passer**	*to happen*
s'asseoir	*to sit (down)*	**se promener**	*to go for a walk*
se baigner	*to go swimming*	**se rappeler**	*to remember*
se blesser	*to hurt oneself*	**se ressembler**	*to resemble each other*
se coucher	*to go to bed*	**se retourner**	*to turn round*
se demander	*to wonder*	**se réveiller**	*to wake up*
se dépêcher	*to hurry*	**se sauver**	*to run away*
se diriger	*to make one's way*	**se souvenir de**	*to remember*
s'endormir	*to fall asleep*	**se taire**	*to be quiet*
s'ennuyer	*to be/get bored*	**se tromper**	*to be mistaken*
se fâcher	*to get angry*	**se trouver**	*to be (situated)*
s'habiller	*to dress (oneself)*		

Examples

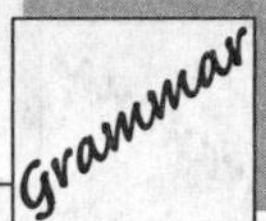

1 **Je m'appelle**
I'm called *(literally: I call myself)*
Asseyez-vous
Sit down *(literally: Seat yourself)*
Ils se lavent
They wash (themselves)

2 **Elle se lave les mains**
She's washing her hands *(literally: She's washing to herself the hands)*
Je me brosse les dents
I brush my teeth
Nous nous envoyons des cadeaux à Noël
We send presents to each other at Christmas

3 **'Je me suis endormi' s'est-il excusé**
'I fell asleep', he apologized
Pauline s'est dirigée vers la sortie
Pauline made her way towards the exit
Ils se sont levés vers dix heures
They got up around ten o'clock
Elles se sont excusées de leur erreur
They apologized for their mistake
Est-ce que tu t'es blessée, Cécile?
Have you hurt yourself, Cécile?

4 **Elle s'est lavé les cheveux**
She (has) washed her hair
Nous nous sommes serré la main
We shook hands
Christine s'est cassé la jambe
Christine has broken her leg

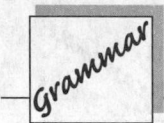

❒ Reflexive Verbs (Continued)

Conjugation of: **se laver** *to wash (oneself)*

I SIMPLE TENSES

PRESENT

je me lave	**nous nous lavons**
tu te laves	**vous vous lavez**
il/elle se lave	**ils/elles se lavent**

IMPERFECT

je me lavais	**nous nous lavions**
tu te lavais	**vous vous laviez**
il/elle se lavait	**ils/elles se lavaient**

FUTURE

je me laverai	**nous nous laverons**
tu te laveras	**vous vous laverez**
il/elle se lavera	**ils/elles se laveront**

CONDITIONAL

je me laverais	**nous nous laverions**
tu te laverais	**vous vous laveriez**
il/elle se laverait	**ils/elles se laveraient**

PAST HISTORIC

je me lavai	**nous nous lavâmes**
tu te lavas	**vous vous lavâtes**
il/elle se lava	**ils/elles se lavèrent**

PRESENT SUBJUNCTIVE

je me lave	**nous nous lavions**
tu te laves	**vous vous laviez**
il/elle se lave	**ils/elles se lavent**

IMPERFECT SUBJUNCTIVE

je me lavasse	**nous nous lavassions**
tu te lavasses	**vous vous lavassiez**
il/elle se lavât	**ils/elles se lavassent**

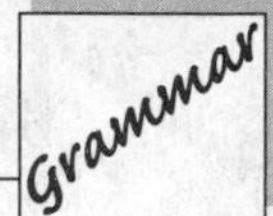

❐ Reflexive Verbs (Continued)

Conjugation of: se **laver** *to wash (oneself)*

II COMPOUND TENSES

PERFECT

je me suis lavé(e)	**nous nous sommes lavé(e)s**
tu t'es lavé(e)	**vous vous êtes lavé(e)(s)**
il/elle s'est lavé(e)	**ils/elles se sont lavé(e)s**

PLUPERFECT

je m'étais lavé(e)	**nous nous étions lavé(e)s**
tu t'étais lavé(e)	**vous vous étiez lavé(e)(s)**
il/elle s'était lavé(e)	**ils/elles s'étaient lavé(e)s**

FUTURE PERFECT

je me serai lavé(e)	**nous nous serons lavé(e)s**
tu te seras lavé(e)	**vous vous serez lavé(e)(s)**
il/elle se sera lavé(e)	**ils/elles se seront lavé(e)s**

CONDITIONAL PERFECT

je me serais lavé(e)	**nous nous serions lavé(e)s**
tu te serais lavé(e)	**vous vous seriez lavé(e)(s)**
il/elle se serait lavé(e)	**ils/elles se seraient lavé(e)s**

PAST ANTERIOR

je me fus lavé(e)	**nous nous fûmes lavé(e)s**
tu te fus lavé(e)	**vous vous fûtes lavé(e)(s)**
il/elle se fut lavé(e)	**ils/elles se furent lavé(e)s**

PERFECT SUBJUNCTIVE

je me sois lavé(e)	**nous nous soyons lavé(e)s**
tu te sois lavé(e)	**vous vous soyez lavé(e)(s)**
il/elle se soit lavé(e)	**ils/elles se soient lavé(e)s**

PLUPERFECT SUBJUNCTIVE

je me fusse lavé(e)	**nous nous fussions lavé(e)s**
tu te fusses lavé(e)	**vous vous fussiez lavé(e)(s)**
il/elle se fût lavé(e)	**ils/elles se fussent lavé(e)s**

❒ The Passive

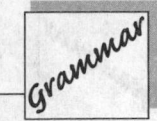

In the passive, the subject *receives* the action (e.g. *I was hit)* as opposed to *performing* it (e.g. *I hit him).* In English the verb 'to be' is used with the past participle. In French the passive is formed in exactly the same way, i.e.:
a tense of **être** + past participle.

The past participle agrees in number and gender with the subject → 1

A sample verb is conjugated in the passive voice on pp 38 and 39.

- The indirect object in French cannot become the subject in the passive:

  in **quelqu'un m'a donné un livre** the indirect object **m'** cannot become the subject of a passive verb (unlike English: *someone gave me a book→ I was given a book).*

- The passive meaning is often expressed in French by:

  – **on** plus a verb in the active voice → 2
  – a reflexive verb (see p 30) → 3

1 **Philippe a été récompensé**
Phillip has been rewarded
Cette peinture est très admirée
This painting is greatly admired
Ils le feront pourvu qu'ils soient payés
They'll do it provided they're paid
Les enfants seront félicités
The children will be congratulated
Cette mesure aurait été critiquée si ...
This measure would have been criticized if ...
Les portes avaient été fermées
The doors had been closed

2 **On leur a envoyé une lettre**
They were sent a letter
On nous a montré le jardin
We were shown the garden
On m'a dit que ...
I was told that ...

3 **Ils se vendent 3 euros (la) pièce**
They are sold for 3 euros each
Ce mot ne s'emploie plus
This word is no longer used

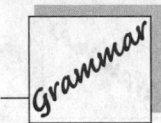

❒ The Passive (Continued)

Conjugation of: **être aimé** to *be liked*

PRESENT

je suis aimé(e)	**nous sommes aimé(e)s**
tu es aimé(e)	**vous êtes aimé(e)(s)**
il/elle est aimé(e)	**ils/elles sont aimé(e)s**

IMPERFECT

j'étais aimé(e)	**nous étions aimé(e)s**
tu étais aimé(e)	**vous étiez aimé(e)(s)**
il/elle était aimé(e)	**ils/elles étaient aimé(e)s**

FUTURE

je serai aimé(e)	**nous serons aimé(e)s**
tu seras aimé(e)	**vous serez aimé(e)(s)**
il/elle sera aimé(e)	**ils/elles seront aimé(e)s**

CONDITIONAL

je serais aimé(e)	**nous serions aimé(e)s**
tu serais aimé(e)	**vous seriez aimé(e)(s)**
il/elle serait aimé(e)	**ils/elles seraient aimé(e)s**

PAST HISTORIC

je fus aimé(e)	**nous fûmes aimé(e)s**
tu fus aimé(e)	**vous fûtes aimé(e)(s)**
il/elle fut aimé(e)	**ils/elles furent aimé(e)s**

PRESENT SUBJUNCTIVE

je sois aimé(e)	**nous soyons aimé(e)s**
tu sois aimé(e)	**vous soyez aimé(e)(s)**
il/elle soit aimé(e)	**ils/elles soient aimé(e)s**

IMPERFECT SUBJUNCTIVE

je fusse aimé(e)	**nous fussions aimé(e)s**
tu fusses aimé(e)	**vous fussiez aimé(e)(s)**
il/elle fût aimé(e)	**ils/elles fussent aimé(e)s**

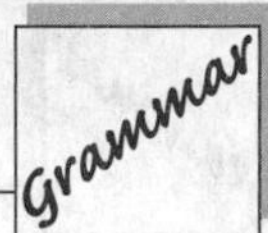

❒ The Passive (Continued)

Conjugation of: **être aimé** to *be liked*

PERFECT	
j'ai été aimé(e)	**nous avons été aimé(e)s**
tu as été aimé(e)	**vous avez été aimé(e)(s)**
il/elle a été aimé(e)	**ils/elles ont été aimé(e)s**
PLUPERFECT	
j'avais été aimé(e)	**nous avions été aimé(e)s**
tu avais été aimé(e)	**vous aviez été aimé(e)(s)**
il/elle avait été aimé(e)	**ils/elles avaient été aimé(e)s**
FUTURE PERFECT	
j'aurai été aimé(e)	**nous aurons été aimé(e)s**
tu auras été aimé(e)	**vous aurez été aimé(e)(s)**
il/elle aura été aimé(e)	**ils/elles auront été aimé(e)s**
CONDITIONAL PERFECT	
j'aurals été aimé(e)	**nous aurions été aimé(e)s**
tu aurais été aimé(e)	**vous auriez été aimé(e)(s)**
il/elle aurait été aimé(e)	**ils/elles auraient été aimé(e)s**
PAST ANTERIOR	
j'eus été aimé(e)	**nous eûmes été aimé(e)s**
tu eus été aimé(e)	**vous eûtes été aimé(e)(s)**
il/elle eut été aimé(e)	**ils/elles eurent été aimé(e)s**
PERFECT SUBJUNCTIVE	
j'aie été aimé(e)	**nous ayons été aimé(e)s**
tu aies été aimé(e)	**vous ayez été aimé(e)(s)**
il/elle ait été aimé(e)	**ils/elles aient été aimé(e)s**
PLUPERFECT SUBJUNCTIVE	
j'eusse été aimé(e)	**nous eussions été aimé(e)s**
tu eusses été aimé(e)	**vous eussiez été aimé(e)(s)**
il/elle eût été aimé(e)	**ils/elles eussent été aimé(e)s**

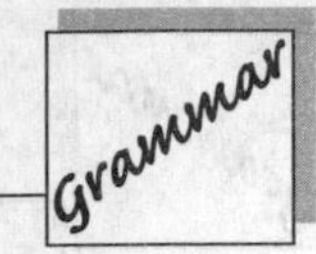

❒ Impersonal Verbs

Impersonal verbs are used only in the infinitive and in the third person singular with the subject pronoun **il**, generally translated *it.*

e.g. **il pleut**
it's raining
il est facile de dire que ...
it's easy to say that ...

The most common impersonal verbs are:

INFINITIVE	CONSTRUCTIONS
s'agir	**il s'agit de** + noun → 1 *it's a question/matter of something, it's about something* **il s'agit de** + infinitive → 2 *it's a question/matter of doing; somebody must do*
falloir	**il faut** + noun object (+ indirect object) → 3 *(somebody) needs something, something is necessary (to somebody)* **il faut** + infinitive (+ indirect object) → 4 *it is necessary to do* **il faut que** + subjunctive → 5 *it is necessary to do, somebody must do*
grêler	**il grêle** *it's hailing* → 6
neiger	**il neige** *it's snowing* → 6
pleuvoir	**il pleut** *it's raining* → 6
tonner	**il tonne** *it's thundering* → 6
valoir mieux	**il vaut mieux** + infinitive → 7 *it's better to do* **il vaut mieux que** + subjunctive → 8 *it's better to do/that somebody does*

Examples

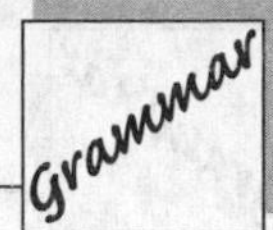

1 **Il ne s'agit pas d'argent**
It isn't a question/matter of money
De quoi s'agit-il?
What is it about?
Il s'agit de la vie d'une famille au début du siècle
It's about the life of a family at the turn of the century

2 **Il s'agit de faire vite**
We must act quickly

3 **Il faut du courage pour faire ça**
One needs courage to do that; Courage is needed to do that
Il me faut une chaise de plus
I need an extra chair

4 **Il faut partir**
It is necessary to leave; We/I/You must leave*
Il me fallait prendre une décision
I had to make a decision

5 **Il faut que vous partiez**
You have to leave/You must leave
Il faudrait que je fasse mes valises
I should have to/ought to pack my cases

6 **Il pleuvait à verse**
It was raining heavily/It was pouring

7 **Il vaut mieux refuser**
It's better to refuse; You/He/I had better refuse*
Il vaudrait mieux rester
You/We/She had better stay*

8 **Il vaudrait mieux que nous ne venions pas**
It would be better if we didn't come; We'd better not come

** The translation here obviously depends on context*

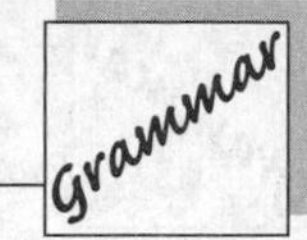

❒ Impersonal Verbs (Continued)

The following verbs are also commonly used in impersonal constructions:

INFINITIVE	CONSTRUCTIONS
avoir	**il y a** + noun → 1 *there is/are*
être	**il est** + noun → 2 *it is, there are* (very literary style) **il est** + adjective + **de** + infinitive → 3 *it is*
faire	**il fait** + adjective of weather → 4 *it is* **il fait** + noun depicting weather/dark/light etc *it is* → 5
manquer	**il manque** + noun (+ indirect object) → 6 *there is/are … missing, something is missing/lacking*
paraître	**il paraît que** + subjunctive → 7 *it seems/appears that* **il paraît** + indirect object + **que** + indicative → 8 *it seems/appears to somebody that*
rester	**il reste** + noun (+ indirect object) → 9 *there is/are … left, (somebody) has something left*
sembler	**il semble que** + subjunctive → 10 *it seems/appears that* **il semble** + indirect object + **que** + indicative → 11 *it seems/appears to somebody that*
suffire	**il suffit de** + infinitive → 12 *it is enough to do* **il suffit de** + noun → 13 *something is enough, it only takes something*

Examples

1 **Il y a du pain (qui reste)**
There is some bread (left)
Il n'y avait pas de lettres ce matin
There were no letters this morning

2 **Il est dix heures**
It's ten o'clock
Il est des gens qui …
There are (some) people who …

3 **Il était inutile de protester**
It was useless to protest
Il est facile de critiquer
Criticizing is easy

4 **Il fait beau/mauvais**
It's lovely/horrible weather

5 **Il faisait du soleil/du vent**
It was sunny/windy
Il fait jour/nuit
It's light/dark

6 **Il manque deux tasses**
There are two cups missing; Two cups are missing
Il manquait un bouton à sa chemise
His shirt had a button missing

7 **Il paraît qu'ils partent demain**
It appears they are leaving tomorrow

8 **Il nous paraît certain qu'il aura du succès**
It seems certain to us that he'll be successful

9 **Il reste deux miches de pain**
There are two loaves left
Il lui restait cinquante euros
He/She had fifty euros left

10 **Il semble que vous ayez raison**
It seems that you are right

11 **Il me semblait qu'il conduisait trop vite**
It seemed to me (that) he was driving too fast

12 **Il suffit de téléphoner pour réserver une place**
You need only phone to reserve a seat

13 **Il suffit d'une seule erreur pour tout gâcher**
One single error is enough to ruin everything

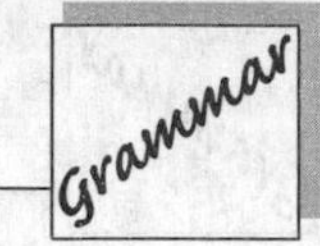

❐ The Infinitive

The infinitive is the form of the verb found in dictionary entries meaning 'to … ', e.g. **donner** *to give*, **vivre** *to live*.

There are three main types of verbal construction involving the infinitive:

- with no linking preposition → [1]
- with the linking preposition **à** → [2] (see also p 64)
- with the linking preposition **de** → [3] (see also p 64)

Verbs followed by an infinitive with no linking preposition

- **devoir, pouvoir, savoir, vouloir** and **falloir** (i.e. modal auxiliary verbs: p 52 → [1]).
- **valoir mieux**: see Impersonal Verbs, p 40.
- verbs of seeing or hearing e.g. **voir** *to see*, **entendre** *to hear* → [4]
- intransitive verbs of motion e.g. **aller** *to go*, **descendre** *to come/go down* → [5]
- **envoyer** *to send* → [6]
- **faillir** → [7]
- **faire** → [8]
- **laisser** *to let, allow* → [9]
- The following common verbs:

adorer	*to love*
aimer	*to like, love* → [10]
aimer mieux	*to prefer* → [11]
compter	*to expect*
désirer	*to wish, want* → [12]
détester	*to hate* → [13]
espérer	*to hope* → [14]
oser	*to dare* → [15]
préférer	*to prefer*
sembler	*to seem* → [16]
souhaiter	*to wish*

Examples

1 **Voulez-vous attendre?**
Would you like to wait?

2 **J'apprends à nager**
I'm learning to swim

3 **Essayez de venir**
Try to come

4 **Il nous a vus arriver**
He saw us arriving
On les entend chanter
You can hear them singing

5 **Allez voir Nicolas**
Go and see Nicholas
Descends leur demander
Go down and ask them

6 **Je l'ai envoyé les voir**
I sent him to see them

7 **J'ai failli tomber**
I almost fell

8 **Ne me faites pas rire!**
Don't make me laugh!
J'ai fait réparer ma valise
I've had my case repaired

9 **Laissez-moi passer**
Let me pass

10 **Il aime nous accompagner**
He likes to come with us

11 **J'aimerais mieux le choisir moi-même**
I'd rather choose it myself

12 **Elle ne désire pas venir**
She doesn't wish to come

13 **Je déteste me lever le matin**
I hate getting up in the morning

14 **Espérez-vous aller en vacances?**
Are you hoping to go on holiday?

15 **Nous n'avons pas osé y retourner**
We haven't dared go back

16 **Vous semblez être inquiet**
You seem to be worried

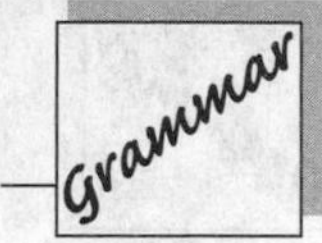

❒ The Infinitive: Set Expressions

The following are set in French with the meaning shown:

aller chercher	*to go for, to go and get*	→ [1]
envoyer chercher	*to send for*	→ [2]
entendre dire que	*to hear it said that*	→ [3]
entendre parler de	*to hear of/about*	→ [4]
faire entrer	*to show in*	→ [5]
faire sortir	*to let out*	→ [6]
faire venir	*to send for*	→ [7]
laisser tomber	*to drop*	→ [8]
vouloir dire	*to mean*	→ [9]

The Perfect Infinitive

- The perfect infinitive is formed using the auxiliary verb **avoir** or **être** as appropriate with the past participle of the verb → [10]

- The perfect infinitive is found:

  – following the preposition **après** *after* → [11]
  – following certain verbal constructions → [12]

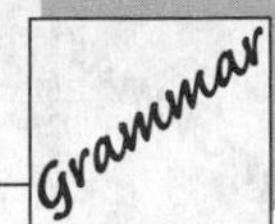

1 **Va chercher tes photos**
Go and get your photos
Il est allé chercher Alexandre
He's gone to get Alexander

2 **J'ai envoyé chercher un médecin**
I've sent for a doctor

3 **J'ai entendu dire qu'il est malade**
I've heard it said that he's ill

4 **Je n'ai plus entendu parler de lui**
I didn't hear anything more (said) of him

5 **Fais entrer nos invités**
Show our guests in

6 **J'ai fait sortir le chat**
I've let the cat out

7 **Je vous ai fait venir parce que ...**
I sent for you because ...

8 **Il a laissé tomber le vase**
He dropped the vase

9 **Qu'est-ce que cela veut dire?**
What does that mean?

10 **avoir fini**
to have finished

être allé	**s'être levé**
to have gone	to have got up

11 **Après avoir pris cette décision, il nous a appelé**
After making/having made that decision, he called us
Après être sorties, elles se sont dirigées vers le parking
After leaving/having left, they headed for the car park
Après nous être levé(e)s, nous avons lu les journaux
After getting up/having got up, we read the papers

12 **pardonner à qn d'avoir fait**
to forgive sb for doing/having done
remercier qn d'avoir fait
to thank sb for doing/having done
regretter d'avoir fait
to be sorry for doing/having done

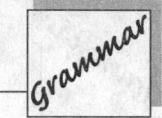

❒ The Present Participle

Formation

- 1st conjugation
  Replace the **-er** of the infinitive by **-ant** → [1]

  – Verbs ending in **-cer**: **c** changes to **ç** → [2]
  – Verbs ending in **-ger**: **g** changes to **ge** → [3]

- 2nd conjugation
  Replace the **-ir** of the infinitive by **-issant** → [4]

- 3rd conjugation
  Replace the **-re** of the infinitive by **-ant** → [5]

- For irregular present participles, see irregular verbs, p 74 ff.

Uses

The present participle has a more restricted use in French than in English.

- Used as a verbal form, the present participle is invariable. It is found:

  – on its own, where it corresponds to the English present participle → [6]
  – following the preposition **en** → [7]

   NOTE, in particular, the construction:

  verb + **en** + present participle

  which is often translated by an English phrasal verb, i.e. one followed by a preposition like *to run down, to bring up* → [8]

- Used as an adjective, the present participle agrees in number and gender with the noun or pronoun → [9]

  NOTE, in particular, the use of **ayant** and **étant** – the present participles of the auxiliary verbs **avoir** and **être** – with a past participle → [10]

Examples

1 **donner** → **donnant**
to give giving

2 **lancer** → **lançant**
to throw throwing

3 **manger** → **mangeant**
to eat eating

4 **finir** → **finissant**
to finish finishing

5 **vendre** → **vendant**
to sell selling

6 **David, habitant près de Paris, a la possibilité de ...**
David, living near Paris, has the opportunity of...
Elle, pensant que je serais fâché, a dit '...'
She, thinking that I would be angry, said '...'
Ils m'ont suivi, criant à tue-tête
They followed me, shouting at the top of their voices

7 **En attendant sa sœur, Richard s'est endormi**
While waiting for his sister, Richard fell asleep
Téléphone-nous an arrivant chez toi
Telephone us when you get home
En appuyant sur ce bouton, on peut ...
By pressing this button, you can ...
Il s'est blessé en essayant de sauver un chat
He hurt himself trying to rescue a cat

8 **sortir en courant**
to run out *(literally: to go out running)*
avancer en boîtant
to limp along *(literally: to go forward limping)*

9 **le soleil couchant** — **une lumière éblouissante**
the setting sun — a dazzling light
ils sont déroutants — **elles étaient étonnantes**
they are disconcerting — they were surprising

10 **Ayant mangé plus tôt, il a pu ...**
Having eaten earlier, he was able to ...
Étant arrivée en retard, elle a dû ...
Having arrived late, she had to ...

❒ Past Participle Agreement

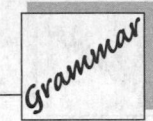

Like adjectives, a past participle must sometimes agree in number and gender with a noun or pronoun. For the rules of agreement, see below. Example: **donné**

	MASCULINE	FEMININE
SING.	donné	donné**e**
PLUR.	donné**s**	donné**es**

- When the masculine singular form already ends in **-s**, no further **s** is added in the masculine plural, e.g. **pris** *taken*.

Rules of Agreement in Compound Tenses

- When the auxiliary verb is **avoir**

  The past participle remains in the masculine singular form, unless a direct object precedes the verb. The past participle then agrees in number and gender with the preceding direct object → 1

- When the auxiliary verb is **être**

  The past participle of a non-reflexive verb agrees in number and gender with the subject → 2

  The past participle of a reflexive verb agrees in number and gender with the reflexive pronoun, if the pronoun is a direct object → 3

  No agreement is made if the reflexive pronoun is an indirect object → 4

The Past Participle as an adjective

The past participle agrees in number and gender with the noun or pronoun → 5

Examples

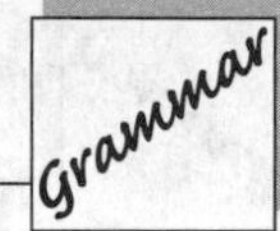

1 **Voici le livre que vous avez demandé**
Here's the book you asked for
Laquelle avaient-elles choisie?
Which one had they chosen?
Ces amis? Je les ai rencontrés à Édimbourg
Those friends? I met them in Edinburgh
Il a gardé toutes les lettres qu'elle a écrites
He has kept all the letters she wrote

2 **Est-ce que ton frère est allé à l'étranger?**
Did your brother go abroad?
Elle était restée chez elle
She had stayed at home
Ils sont partis dans la matinée
They left in the morning
Mes cousines sont revenues hier
My cousins came back yesterday

3 **Tu t'es rappelé d'acheter du pain, Georges?**
Did you remember to buy bread, George?
Martine s'est demandée pourquoi il l'appelait
Martine wondered why he was calling her
'Lui at moi nous nous sommes cachés' a-t-elle dit
'He and I hid,' she said
Les vendeuses se sont mises en grève
Shop assistants have gone on strike
Vous vous êtes brouillés?
Have you fallen out with each other?
Les ouvrières s'étaient entraidées
The workers had helped one another

4 **Elle s'est lavé les mains**
She washed her hands
Ils se sont parlé pendant des heures
They talked to each other for hours

5 **à un moment donné**
at a given time
ils sont bien connus
they are well-known
la porte ouverte
the open door
elles semblent fatiguées
they seem tired

❐ Modal Auxiliary Verbs

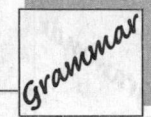

- In French, the modal auxiliary verbs are: **devoir**, **pouvoir**, **savoir**, **vouloir** and **falloir**.

- They are followed by a verb in the infinitive and have the following meanings:

devoir	*to have to, must* → [1] *to be due to* → [2] in the conditional/conditional perfect: *should/should have, ought/ought to have* → [3]
pouvoir	*to be able to, can* → [4] *to be allowed to, can, may* → [5] indicating possibility: *may/might/could* → [6]
savoir	*to know how to, can* → [7]
vouloir	*to want/wish to* → [8] *to be willing to, will* → [9] in polite phrases → [10]
falloir	*to be necessary:* see Impersonal Verbs, p 40.

Examples

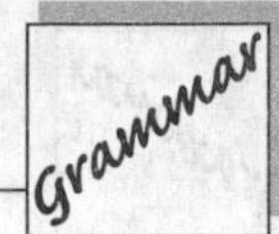

1 **Je dois leur rendre visite**
I must visit them
Elle a dû partir
She (has) had to leave
Il a dû regretter d'avoir parlé
He must have been sorry he spoke

2 **Vous devez revenir demain**
You're due (to come) back tomorrow
Je devais attraper le train de neuf heures mais ...
I was (supposed) to catch the nine o'clock train but ...

3 **Je devrais le faire**
I ought to do it
J'aurais dû m'excuser
I ought to have apologized

4 **Il ne peut pas lever le bras**
He can't raise his arm
Pouvez-vous réparer cette montre?
Can you mend this watch?

5 **Puis-je les accompagner?**
May I go with them?

6 **Il peut encore changer d'avis**
He may change his mind yet
Cela pourrait être vrai
It could/might be true

7 **Savez-vous conduire?**
Can you drive?
Je ne sais pas faire une omelette
I don't know how to make an omelette

8 **Elle veut rester encore un jour**
She wants to stay another day

9 **Ils ne voulaient pas le faire**
They wouldn't do it/They weren't willing to do it
Ma voiture ne veut pas démarrer
My car won't start

10 **Voulez-vous boire quelque chose?**
Would you like something to drink?

❒ Use of Tenses

The Present

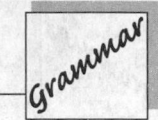

- Unlike English, French does not distinguish between the simple present (e.g. *I smoke, he reads, we live*) and the continuous present (e.g. *I am smoking, he is reading, we are living*) → 1

- To emphasize continuity, the following constructions may be used:

  être en train de faire
  être à faire } *to be doing* → 2

- French uses the present tense where English uses the perfect in the following cases:

  – with certain prepositions of time – notably **depuis** *for/since* – when an action begun in the past is continued in the present → 3
  Note, however, that the perfect is used as in English when the verb is negative or the action has been completed → 4

  – in the construction **venir de faire** *to have just done* → 5

The Future

The future is generally used as in English, but note the following:

- Immediate future time is often expressed by means of the present tense of **aller** plus an infinitive → 6

- In time clauses expressing future action, French uses the future where English uses the present → 7

The Future Perfect

- Used as in English to mean *shall/will have done* → 8

- In time clauses expressing future action, where English uses the perfect tense → 9

Examples

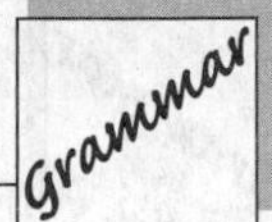

1 **Je fume**
I smoke OR I am smoking
Il lit
He reads OR He is reading
Nous habitons
We live OR We are living

2 **Il est en train de travailler**
He's (busy) working

3 **Paul apprend à nager depuis six mois**
Paul's been learning to swim for six months *(and still is)*
Je suis debout depuis sept heures
I've been up since seven
Il y a longtemps que vous attendez?
Have you been waiting long?
Voilà deux semaines que nous sommes ici
That's two weeks we've been here (now)

4 **Ils ne se sont pas vus depuis des mois**
They haven't seen each other for months
Elle est revenue il y a un an
She came back a year ago

5 **Elisabeth vient de partir**
Elizabeth has just left

6 **Tu vas tomber si tu ne fais pas attention**
You'll fall if you're not careful
Il va manquer le train
He's going to miss the train
Ça va prendre une demi-heure
It'll take half an hour

7 **Quand il viendra vous serez en vacances**
When he comes you'll be on holiday
Faites-nous savoir aussitôt qu'elle arrivera
Let us know as soon as she arrives

8 **J'aurai fini dans une heure**
I shall have finished in an hour

9 **Quand tu auras lu ce roman, rends-le-moi**
When you've read the novel, give it back to me
Je partirai dès que j'aurai fini
I'll leave as soon as I've finished

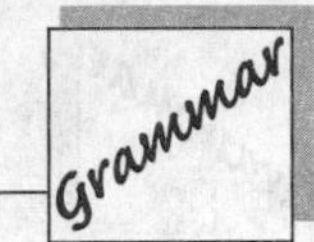

❒ Use of Tenses (Continued)

The Imperfect

- The imperfect describes:
  – an action (or state) in the past without definite limits in time → 1
  – habitual action(s) in the past (often translated by means of *would* or *used to*) → 2
- French uses the imperfect tense where English uses the pluperfect in the following cases:
  – with certain prepositions of time – notably **depuis** *for/since* – when an action begun in the remoter past was continued in the more recent past → 3
  Note, however, that the pluperfect *is* used as in English, when the verb is negative or the action has been completed → 4
  – in the construction **venir de faire** *to have just done* → 5

The Perfect

- The perfect is used to recount a completed action or event in the past. Note that this corresponds to a perfect tense or a simple past tense in English → 6

The Past Historic

- Only ever used in *written, literary* French, the past historic recounts a completed action in the past, corresponding to a simple past tense in English → 7

The Past Anterior

This tense is used instead of the pluperfect when a verb in another part of the sentence is in the past historic. That is

- in time clauses, after conjunctions like: **quand**, **lorsque** *when*, **dès que**, **aussitôt que** *as soon as*, **après que** *after* → 8
- after **à peine** *hardly, scarcely* → 9

The Subjunctive

- In spoken French, the present subjunctive generally replaces the imperfect subjunctive. See also pp 58 ff.

Examples

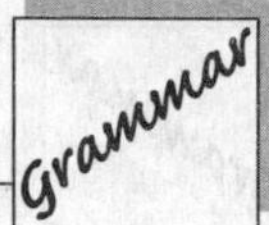

1 **Elle regardait par la fenêtre**
She was looking out of the window
Il pleuvait quand je suis sorti de chez moi
It was raining when I left the house
Nos chambres donnaient sur la plage
Our rooms overlooked the beach

2 **Dans sa jeunesse, il se levait à l'aube**
In his youth he got up at dawn
Nous causions des heures entières
We would talk for hours on end
Elle te taquinait, n'est-ce pas?
She used to tease you, didn't she?

3 **Nous habitions à Londres depuis deux ans**
We had been living in London for two years *(and still were)*
Il était malade depuis 1985
He had been ill since 1985
Il y avait assez longtemps qu'il le faisait
He had been doing it for quite a long time

4 **Voilà un an que je ne l'avais pas vu**
I hadn't seen him for a year
Il y avait une heure qu'elle était arrivée
She had arrived one hour before

5 **Je venais de les rencontrer**
I had just met them

6 **Nous sommes allés au bord de la mer**
We went/have been to the seaside
Il a refusé de nous aider
He (has) refused to help us
La voiture ne s'est pas arrêtée
The car didn't stop/hasn't stopped

7 **Le roi mourut en 1592**
The king died in 1592

8 **Quand il eut fini, il se leva**
When he had finished, he got up

9 **À peine eut-il parlé qu'on frappa à la porte**
He had scarcely spoken when there was a knock at the door

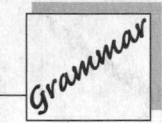

❒ The Subjunctive: when to use it

(For how to form the subjunctive see pp 6 ff.)

◆ After certain conjunctions

quoique / **bien que**	*although* → 1
pour que / **afin que**	*so that* → 2
pourvu que	*provided that* → 3
jusqu'à ce que	*until* → 4
avant que (... ne)	*before* → 5
à moins que (... ne)	*unless* → 6
de peur que (... ne) / **de crainte que (... ne)**	*for fear that, lest* → 7

⚠ NOTE that the **ne** following the conjunctions in examples 5 to 7 has no translation value. It is often omitted in spoken informal French.

◆ After the conjunctions

de sorte que / **de façon que** / **de manière que**	*so that* (indicating a *purpose*) → 8

When these conjunctions introduce a *result* and not a *purpose*, the subjunctive is not used → 9

◆ After impersonal constructions which express necessity, possibility etc

il faut que / **il est nécessaire que**	*it is necessary that* → 10
il est possible que	*it is possible that* → 11
il semble que	*it seems that* → 12
il vaut mieux que	*it is better that* → 13
il est dommage que	*it's a pity that* → 14

Examples

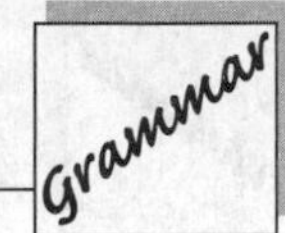

1 **Bien qu'il fasse beaucoup d'efforts, il est peu récompensé**
Although he makes a lot of effort, he isn't rewarded for it

2 **Demandez un reçu afin que vous puissiez être remboursé**
Ask for a receipt so that you can get a refund

3 **Nous partirons ensemble pourvu que Sylvie soit d'accord**
We'll leave together provided Sylvie agrees

4 **Reste ici jusqu'à ce que nous revenions**
Stay here until we come back

5 **Je le ferai avant que tu ne partes**
I'll do it before you leave

6 **Ce doit être Paul, à moins que je ne me trompe**
That must be Paul, unless I'm mistaken

7 **Parlez bas de peur qu'on ne vous entende**
Speak softly lest anyone hears you

8 **Retournez-vous de sorte que je vous voie**
Turn round so that I can see you

9 **Il refuse de le faire de sorte que je dois le faire moi-même**
He refuses to do it so that I have to do it myself

10 **Il faut que je vous parle immédiatement**
I must speak to you right away/It is necessary that I speak …

11 **Il est possible qu'ils aient raison**
They may be right/It's possible that they are right

12 **Il semble qu'elle ne soit pas venue**
It appears that she hasn't come

13 **Il vaut mieux que vous restiez chez vous**
It's better that you stay at home

14 **Il est dommage qu'elle ait perdu cette adresse**
It's a shame/a pity that she's lost the address

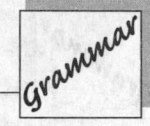

❐ The Subjunctive: when to use it (Continued)

- After verbs of:
  – 'wishing'
  vouloir que
  désirer que
  souhaiter que] *to wish that, want* → 1

  – 'fearing'
  craindre que
  avoir peur que } *to be afraid that* → 2

  ⚠ NOTE that **ne** in the first phrase of example 2 has no translation value. It is often omitted in spoken informal French.

  – 'ordering', 'forbidding', 'allowing'
  ordonner que *to order that* → 3
  défendre que *to forbid that* → 4
  permettre que *to allow that* → 5

  – opinion, expressing uncertainty
  croire que
  penser que } *to think that* → 6
  douter que *to doubt that* → 7

  – emotion (e.g. regret, shame, pleasure)
  regretter que *to be sorry that* → 8
  être content/surpris etc **que** *to be pleased/surprised* etc *that* → 9

- After a superlative → 10

- After certain adjectives expressing some sort of 'uniqueness'

dernier ... qui/que	*last ... who/that*	→ 11
premier ... qui/que	*first ... who/that*	
meilleur ... qui/que	*best ... who/that*	
seul / **unique** } **... qui/que**	*only ... who/that*	

Examples

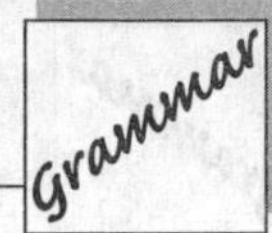

1 **Nous voulons qu'elle soit contente**
We want her to be happy *(literally: We want that she is happy)*
Désirez-vous que je le fasse?
Do you want me to do it?

2 **Il craint qu'il ne soit trop tard**
He's afraid it may be too late
Avez-vous peur qu'il ne revienne pas?
Are you afraid that he won't come back?

3 **Il a ordonné qu'ils soient désormais à l'heure**
He has ordered that they be on time from now on

4 **Elle défend que vous disiez cela**
She forbids you to say that

5 **Permettez que nous vous aidions**
Allow us to help you

6 **Je ne pense pas qu'ils soient venus**
I don't think they came

7 **Nous doutons qu'il ait dit la vérité**
We doubt that he told the truth

8 **Je regrette que vous ne puissiez pas venir**
I'm sorry that you cannot come

9 **Je suis content que vous les aimiez**
I'm pleased that you like them

10 **la personne la plus sympathique que je connaisse**
the nicest person I know
l'article le moins cher que j'aie jamais acheté
the cheapest item I have ever bought

11 **Voici la dernière lettre qu'elle m'ait écrite**
This is the last letter she wrote to me
David est la seule personne qui puisse me conseiller
David is the only person who can advise me

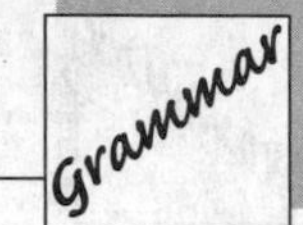

❒ The Subjunctive: when to use it (Continued)

- After **si (…) que** *however* → 1
  qui que *whoever* → 2
  quoi que *whatever* → 3

- After **que** in the following:
  – to form the 3rd person imperative or to express a wish → 4
  – when **que** has the meaning *if*, replacing **si** in a clause → 5
  – when **que** has the meaning *whether* → 6

- In relative clauses following certain types of indefinite and negative construction → 7/8

- In set expressions → 9

Examples

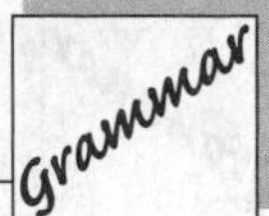

1 **si courageux qu'il soit**
however brave he may be
si peu que ce soit
however little it is

2 **Qui que vous soyez, allez-vous-en!**
Whoever you are, go away!

3 **Quoi que nous fassions, ...**
Whatever we do, ...

4 **Qu'il entre!**
Let him come in!
Que cela vous serve de leçon!
Let that be a lesson to you!

5 **S'il fait beau et que tu te sentes mieux, nous irons ...**
If it's nice and you're feeling better, we'll go ...

6 **Que tu viennes ou non, je ...**
Whether you come or not, I ...

7 **Il cherche une maison qui ait deux caves**
He's looking for a house which has two cellars
(subjunctive used since such a house may or may not exist)
J'ai besoin d'un livre qui décrive l'art du mime
I need a book which describes the art of mime
(subjunctive used since such a book may or may not exist)

8 **Je n'ai rencontré personne qui la connaisse**
I haven't met anyone who knows her
Il n'y a rien qui puisse vous empêcher de ...
There's nothing that can prevent you from ...

9 **Vive le roi!**
Long live the king!
Que Dieu vous bénisse!
God bless you!

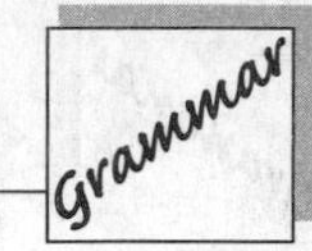

❒ Verbs governing à and de

The following lists (pp 64 to 72) contain common verbal constructions using the prepositions **à** and **de**

Note the following abbreviations:

infin.	infinitive
perf. infin.	perfect infinitive*
qch	quelque chose
qn	quelqu'un
sb	somebody
sth	something

*For formation see p 46

accuser qn de qch/de + perf. infin.	*to accuse sb of sth/of doing, having done* → 1
accoutumer qn à qch/à + infin.	*to accustom sb to sth/to doing*
acheter qch à qn	*to buy sth from sb/for sb* → 2
achever de + infin.	*to end up doing*
aider qn à + infin.	*to help sb to do* → 3
s'amuser à + infin.	*to have fun doing*
s'apercevoir de qch	*to notice sth* → 4
apprendre qch à qn	*to teach sb sth*
apprendre à + infin.	*to learn to do* → 5
apprendre à qn à + infin.	*to teach sb to do* → 6
s'approcher de qn/qch	*to approach sb/sth* → 7
arracher qch à qn	*to snatch sth from sb* → 8
(s')arrêter de + infin.	*to stop doing* → 9
arriver à + infin.	*to manage to do* → 10
assister à qch	*to attend sth, be at sth*
s'attendre à + infin.	*to expect to do* → 11
blâmer qn de qch/de + perf. infin.	*to blame sb for sth/for having done* → 12
cacher qch à qn	*to hide sth from sb* → 13
cesser de + infin.	*to stop doing* → 14

Examples

1 **Il m'a accusé d'avoir menti**
He accused me of lying

2 **Marie-Christine leur a acheté deux billets**
Marie-Christine bought two tickets from/for them

3 **Aidez-moi à porter ces valises**
Help me to carry these cases

4 **Il ne s'est pas aperçu de son erreur**
He didn't notice his mistake

5 **Elle apprend à lire**
She's learning to read

6 **Je lui apprends à nager**
I'm teaching him/her to swim

7 **Elle s'est approchée de moi, en disant '...'**
She came up to me, saying '...'

8 **Le voleur lui a arraché l'argent**
The thief snatched the money from him/her

9 **Arrêtez de faire du bruit!**
Stop being (so) noisy!

10 **Je n'arrive pas à le comprendre**
I can't understand it

11 **Est-ce qu'elle s'attendait à le voir?**
Was she expecting to see him?

12 **Je ne la blâme pas de l'avoir fait**
I don't blame her for doing it

13 **Cache-les-leur!**
Hide them from them!

14 **Est-ce qu'il a cessé de pleuvoir?**
Has it stopped raining?

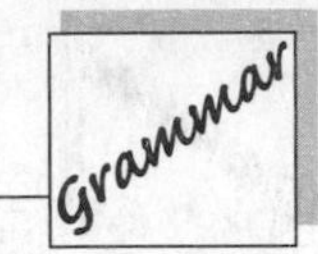

❒ Verbs governing à and de (Continued)

changer de qch	*to change sth* → 1
se charger de qch/de + infin.	*to see to sth/undertake to do*
chercher à + infin.	*to try to do*
commander à qn de + infin.	*to order sb to do* → 2
commencer à/de + infin.	*to begin to do* → 3
conseiller à qn de + infin.	*to advise sb to do* → 4
consentir à qch/à + infin.	*to agree to sth/to do* → 5
continuer à/de + infin.	*to continue to do*
craindre de + infin.	*to be afraid to do/of doing*
décider de + infin.	*to decide to* → 6
se décider à + infin.	*to make up one's mind to do*
défendre à qn de + infin.	*to forbid sb to do* → 7
demander qch à qn	*to ask sb sth/for sth* → 8
demander à qn de + infin.	*to ask sb to do* → 9
se dépêcher de + infin.	*to hurry to do*
dépendre de qn/qch	*to depend on sb/sth*
déplaire à qn	*to displease sb* → 10
désobéir à qn	*to disobey sb* → 11
dire à qn de + infin.	*to tell sb to do* → 12
dissuader qn de + infin.	*to dissuade sb from doing*
douter de qch	*to doubt sth*
se douter de qch	*to suspect sth*
s'efforcer de + infin.	*to strive to do*
empêcher qn de + infin.	*to prevent sb from doing* → 13
emprunter qch à qn	*to borrow sth from sb* → 14
encourager qn à + infin.	*to encourage sb to do* → 15
enlever qch à qn	*to take sth away from sb*
enseigner qch à qn	*to teach sb sth*
enseigner à qn à + infin.	*to teach sb to do*
entreprendre de + infin.	*to undertake to do*
essayer de + infin.	*to try to do* → 16
eviter de + infin.	*to avoid doing* → 17

Examples

1 **J'ai changé d'avis/de robe**
I changed my mind/my dress
Il faut changer de train à Toulouse
You have to change trains at Toulouse

2 **Il leur a commandé de tirer**
He ordered them to shoot

3 **Il commence à neiger**
It's starting to snow

4 **Il leur a conseillé d'attendre**
He advised them to wait

5 **Je n'ai pas consenti à l'aider**
I haven't agreed to help him/her

6 **Qu'est-ce que vous avez décidé de faire?**
What have you decided to do?

7 **Je leur ai défendu de sortir**
I've forbidden them to go out

8 **Je lui ai demandé l'heure**
I asked him/her the time
Il lui a demandé un livre
He asked him/her for a book

9 **Demande à Alain de le faire**
Ask Alan to do it

10 **Leur attitude lui déplaît**
He/She doesn't like their attitude

11 **Ils lui désobéissent souvent**
They often disobey him/her

12 **Dites-leur de se taire**
Tell them to be quiet

13 **Le bruit m'empêche de travailler**
The noise is preventing me from working

14 **Puis-je vous emprunter ce stylo?**
May I borrow this pen from you?

15 **Elle encourage ses enfants à être indépendants**
She encourages her children to be independent

16 **Essayez d'arriver à l'heure**
Try to arrive on time

17 **Il évite de lui parler**
He avoids speaking to him/her

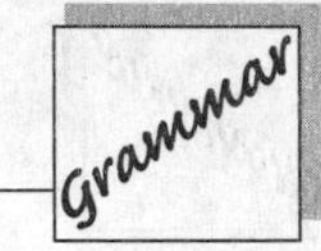

❒ Verbs governing à and de (Continued)

s'excuser de qch/de + (perf.) infin.	*to apologize for sth/for doing, having done* → 1
exceller à + infin.	*to excel at doing*
se fâcher de qch	*to be annoyed at sth*
feindre de + infin.	*to pretend to do* → 2
féliciter qn de qch/de + (perf.) infin.	*to congratulate sb on sth/on doing, having done* → 3
se fier à qn	*to trust sb* → 4
finir de + infin.	*to finish doing* → 5
forcer qn à + infin.	*to force sb to do*
habituer qn à + infin.	*to accustom sb to doing*
s'habituer à + infin.	*to get/be used to doing* → 6
se hâter de + infin.	*to hurry to do*
hésiter à + infin.	*to hesitate to do*
interdire à qn de + infin.	*to forbid sb to do* → 7
s'intéresser à qn/qch/à + infin.	*to be interested in sb/sth/in doing* → 8
inviter qn à + infin.	*to invite sb to do* → 9
jouer à (+ sports, games)	*to play* → 10
jouer de (+ musical instruments)	*to play* → 11
jouir de qch	*to enjoy sth* → 12
jurer de + infin.	*to swear to do*
louer qn de qch	*to praise sb for sth*
manquer à qn	*to be missed by sb* → 13
manquer de qch	*to lack sth*
manquer de + infin.	*to fail to do* → 14
se marier à qn	*to marry sb*
se méfier de qn	*to distrust sb*
menacer de + infin.	*to threaten to do* → 15
mériter de + infin.	*to deserve to do* → 16
se mettre à + infin.	*to begin to do*
se moquer de qn/qch	*to make fun of sb/sth*
négliger de + infin.	*to fail to do*

Examples

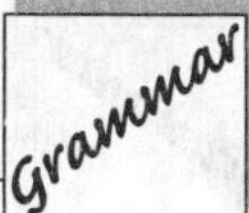

1 **Je m'excuse d'être (arrivé) en retard**
I apologize for being/arriving late

2 **Elle feint de dormir**
She's pretending to be asleep

3 **Je l'ai félicitée d'avoir gagné**
I congratulated her on winning

4 **Je ne me fie pas à ces gens-là**
I don't trust those people

5 **Avez-vous fini de lire ce journal?**
Have you finished reading this newspaper?

6 **Il s'est habitué à boire moins de café**
He got used to drinking less coffee

7 **Il a interdit aux enfants de jouer avec des allumettes**
He's forbidden the children to play with matches

8 **Elle s'intéresse beaucoup au sport**
She's very interested in sport

9 **Il m'a invitée à danser**
He asked me to dance

10 **Elle joue au tennis et au hockey**
She plays tennis and hockey

11 **Il joue du piano et de la guitare**
He plays the piano and the guitar

12 **Il jouit d'une santé solide**
He enjoys good health

13 **Tu manques à tes parents**
Your parents miss you

14 **Je ne manquerai pas de le lui dire**
I'll be sure to tell him/her about it

15 **Elle a menacé de démissionner tout de suite**
She threatened to resign at once

16 **Ils méritent d'être promus**
They deserve to be promoted

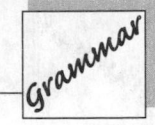

❐ Verbs governing à and de (Continued)

nuire à qch	*to harm sth* → 1
obéir à qn	*to obey sb*
obliger qn à + infin.	*to oblige sb to do* → 2
s'occuper de qch/qn	*to look after sth/sb* → 3
offrir de + infin.	*to offer to do* → 4
omettre de + infin.	*to fail to do*
ordonner à qn de + infin.	*to order sb to do* → 5
ôter qch à qn	*to take sth away from sb*
oublier de + infin.	*to forget to do*
pardonner qch à qn	*to forgive sb for sth*
pardonner à qn de + perf. infin.	*to forgive sb for having done* → 6
parvenir à + infin.	*to manage to do*
se passer de qch	*to do/go without sth* → 7
penser à qn/qch	*to think about sb/sth* → 8
permettre qch à qn	*to allow sb sth*
permettre à qn de + infin.	*to allow sb to do* → 9
persister à + infin.	*to persist in doing*
persuader qn de + infin.	*to persuade sb to do* → 10
se plaindre de qch	*to complain about sth*
plaire à qn	*to please sb* → 11
pousser qn à + infin.	*to urge sb to do*
prendre qch à qn	*to take sth from sb* → 12
préparer qn à + infin.	*to prepare sb to do*
se préparer à + infin.	*to get ready to do*
prier qn de + infin.	*to beg sb to do*
profiter de qch/de + infin.	*to take advantage of sth/of doing*
promettre à qn de + infin.	*to promise sb to do* → 13
proposer de + infin.	*to suggest doing* → 14
punir qn de qch	*to punish sb for sth* → 15
récompenser qn de qch	*to reward sb for sth*
réfléchir à qch	*to think about sth*
refuser de + infin.	*to refuse to do* → 16

Examples

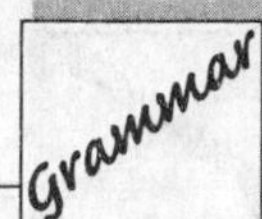

1 **Ce mode de vie va nuire à sa santé**
This lifestyle will damage her health

2 **Il les a obligés à faire la vaisselle**
He made them do the washing-up

3 **Je m'occupe de ma nièce**
I'm looking after my niece

4 **Stuart a offert de nous accompagner**
Stuart has offered to go with us

5 **Les soldats leur ont ordonné de se rendre**
The soldiers ordered them to give themselves up

6 **Est-ce que tu as pardonné à Charles de t'avoir menti?**
Have you forgiven Charles for lying to you?

7 **Nous nous sommes passés d'électricité pendant plusieurs jours**
We did without electricity for several days

8 **Je pense souvent à toi**
I often think about you

9 **Permettez-moi de continuer, s'il vous plaît**
Allow me to go on, please

10 **Elle nous a persuadés de rester**
She persuaded us to stay

11 **Est-ce que ce genre de film lui plaît?**
Does he/she like this kind of film?

12 **Je lui ai pris son baladeur**
I took his personal stereo from him

13 **Ils ont promis à Pascale de venir**
They promised Pascale that they would come

14 **J'ai proposé de les inviter**
I suggested inviting them

15 **Il a été puni de sa malhonnêteté**
He has been punished for his dishonesty

16 **Il a refusé de coopérer**
He has refused to cooperate

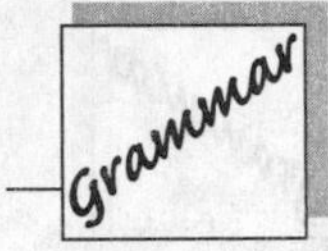

❐ Verbs governing à and de (Continued)

regretter de + perf. infin.	*to regret doing, having done* → 1
remercier qn de qch/de + perf. infin.	*to thank sb for sth/for doing, having done* → 2
renoncer à qch/à + infin.	*to give sth up/give up doing*
reprocher qch à qn	*to reproach sb with/for sth* → 3
résister à qch	*to resist sth* → 4
résoudre de + infin.	*to resolve to do*
ressembler à qn/qch	*to look/be like sb/sth* → 5
réussir à + infin.	*to manage to do* → 6
rire de qn/qch	*to laugh at sb/sth*
risquer de + infin.	*to risk doing* → 7
servir à qch/à + infin.	*to be used for sth/for doing* → 8
se servir de qch	*to use sth; to help oneself to sth* → 9
songer à + infin.	*to think of doing*
se souvenir de qn/qch/de + perf. infin.	*to remember sb/sth/doing, having done* → 10
succéder à qn	*to succeed sb*
survivre à qn	*to outlive sb* → 11
tâcher de + infin.	*to try to do* → 12
tarder à + infin.	*to delay doing* → 13
tendre à + infin.	*to tend to do*
tenir à + infin.	*to be keen to do* → 14
tenter de + infin.	*to try to do* → 15
se tromper de qch	*to be wrong about sth* → 16
venir de* + infin.	*to have just done* → 17
vivre de qch	*to live on sth*
voler qch à qn	*to steal sth from sb*

*See also Use of Tenses, pp 54 and 56

Examples

1 **Je regrette de ne pas vous avoir écrit plus tôt**
I'm sorry for not writing to you sooner

2 **Nous les avons remerciés de leur gentillesse**
We thanked them for their kindness

3 **On lui reproche son manque d'enthousiasme**
They're reproaching him for his lack of enthusiasm

4 **Comment résistez-vous à la tentation?**
How do you resist temptation?

5 **Elles ressemblent beaucoup à leur mère**
They look very like their mother

6 **Vous avez réussi à me convaincre**
You've managed to convince me

7 **Vous risquez de tomber en faisant cela**
You risk falling doing that

8 **Ce bouton sert à régler le volume**
This knob is (used) for adjusting the volume

9 **Il s'est servi d'un tournevis pour l'ouvrir**
He used a screwdriver to open it

10 **Vous vous souvenez de Lucienne?**
Do you remember Lucienne?
Il ne se souvient pas de l'avoir perdu
He doesn't remember losing it

11 **Elle a survécu à son mari**
She outlived her husband

12 **Tâchez de ne pas être en retard!**
Try not to be late!

13 **Il n'a pas tardé à prendre une décision**
He was not long in taking a decision

14 **Elle tient à le faire elle-même**
She's keen to do it herself

15 **J'ai tenté de la comprendre**
I've tried to understand her

16 **Je me suis trompé de route**
I took the wrong road

17 **Mon père vient de téléphoner**
My father's just phoned
Nous venions d'arriver
We had just arrived

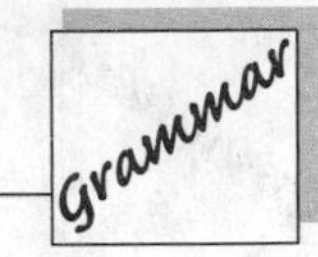

❒ Irregular Verbs

The verbs listed opposite and conjugated on pp 76 to 131 provide the main patterns for irregular verbs. The verbs are grouped opposite according to their infinitive ending (except **avoir** and **être**), and are shown in the following tables in alphabetical order.

In the tables, the most important irregular verbs are given in their most common simple tenses, together with the imperative and the present participle.

The auxiliary (**avoir** or **être**) is also shown for each verb, together with the past participle, to enable you to form all the compound tenses, as on pp 24 and 26.

- For a fuller list of irregular verbs, the reader is referred to Collins Gem French Verb Tables, which shows you how to conjugate some 2000 French verbs.

VERBS: IRREGULAR

avoir
être

'-er': **aller**
envoyer

'-ir': **acquérir**
bouillir
courir
cueillir
dormir
fuir
haïr
mourir
ouvrir
partir
sentir
servir
sortir
tenir
venir
vêtir

'-oir': **s'asseoir**
devoir
falloir
pleuvoir
pouvoir
recevoir
savoir
valoir
voir
vouloir

'-re': **battre**
boire
connaître
coudre
craindre
croire
croître
cuire
dire
écrire
faire
lire
mettre
moudre
naître
paraître
plaire
prendre
résoudre
rire
rompre
suffire
suivre
se taire
vaincre
vivre

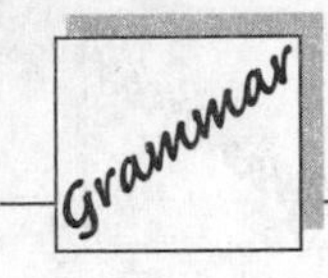

acquérir *to acquire* — Auxiliary: **avoir**

PAST PARTICIPLE	IMPERATIVE
acquis	**acquiers**
PRESENT PARTICIPLE	**acquérons**
acquérant	**acquérez**

PRESENT	IMPERFECT
j'acquiers	**j'acquérais**
tu acquiers	**tu acquérais**
il acquiert	**il acquérait**
nous acquérons	**nous acquérions**
vous acquérez	**vous acquériez**
ils acquierent	**ils acquéraient**
FUTURE	CONDITIONAL
j'acquerrai	**j'acquerrais**
tu acquerras	**tu acquerrais**
il acquerra	**il acquerrait**
nous acquerrons	**nous acquerrions**
vous acquerrez	**vous acquerriez**
ils acquerront	**ils acquerraient**
PRESENT SUBJUNCTIVE	PAST HISTORIC
j'acquière	**j'acquis**
tu acquières	**tu acquis**
il acquière	**il acquit**
nous acquérions	**nous acquîmes**
vous acquériez	**vous acquîtes**
ils acquièrent	**ils acquirent**

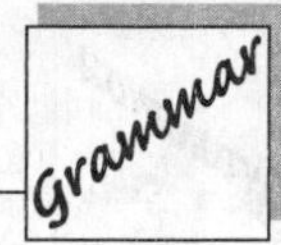

aller *to go* Auxiliary: **être**

PAST PARTICIPLE
allé

PRESENT PARTICIPLE
allant

IMPERATIVE
va
allons
allez

PRESENT	IMPERFECT
je vais	j'allais
tu vas	tu allais
il va	il allait
nous allons	nous allions
vous allez	vous alliez
ils vont	ils allaient

FUTURE	CONDITIONAL
j'irai	**j'irais**
tu iras	**tu irais**
il ira	**il irait**
nous irons	**nous irions**
vous irez	**vous iriez**
ils iront	**ils iraient**

PRESENT SUBJUNCTIVE	PAST HISTORIC
j'aille	j'allai
tu ailles	tu allas
il aille	il alla
nous allions	nous allâmes
vous alliez	vous allâtes
ils aillent	ils allèrent

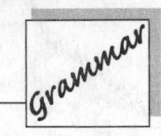

s'asseoir *to sit down* Auxiliary: **être**

PAST PARTICIPLE

assis

PRESENT PARTICIPLE

s'asseyant

IMPERATIVE

assieds-toi
asseyons-nous
asseyez-vous

PRESENT	IMPERFECT
je m'assieds *or* **assois** **tu t'assieds** *or* **assois** **il s'assied** *or* **assoit** **nous nous asseyons** *or* **assoyons** **vous vous asseyez** *or* **assoyez** **ils s'asseyent** *or* **assoient**	**je m'asseyais** **tu t'asseyais** **il s'asseyait** **nous nous asseyions** **vous vous asseyiez** **ils s'asseyaient**
FUTURE	CONDITIONAL
je m'assiérai **tu t'assiéras** **il s'assiéra** **nous nous assiérons** **vous vous assiérez** **ils s'assiéront**	**je m'assiérais** **tu t'assiérais** **il s'assiérait** **nous nous assiérions** **vous vous assiériez** **ils s'assiéraient**
PRESENT SUBJUNCTIVE	PAST HISTORIC
je m'asseye **tu t'asseyes** **il s'asseye** **nous nous asseyions** **vous vous asseyiez** **ils s'asseyent**	**je m'assis** **tu t'assis** **il s'assit** **nous nous assîmes** **vous vous assîtes** **ils s'assirent**

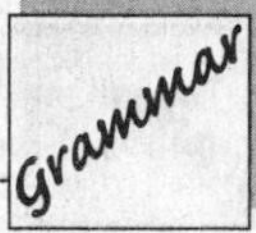

avoir *to have*	Auxiliary: **avoir**
PAST PARTICIPLE **eu** PRESENT PARTICIPLE **ayant**	IMPERATIVE **aie** **ayons** **ayez**

PRESENT	IMPERFECT
j'ai **tu as** **il a** **nous avons** **vous avez** **ils ont**	**j'avais** **tu avais** **il avait** **nous avions** **vous aviez** **ils avaient**
FUTURE	CONDITIONAL
j'aurai **tu auras** **il aura** **nous aurons** **vous aurez** **ils auront**	**j'aurais** **tu aurais** **il aurait** **nous aurions** **vous auriez** **ils auraient**
PRESENT SUBJUNCTIVE	PAST HISTORIC
j'aie **tu aies** **il ait** **nous ayons** **vous ayez** **ils aient**	**j'eus** **tu eus** **il eut** **nous eûmes** **vous eûtes** **ils eurent**

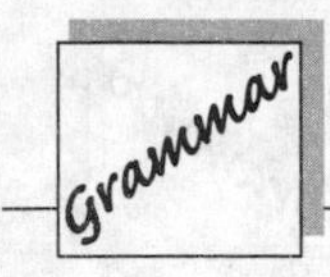

battre *to beat* Auxiliary: **avoir**

PAST PARTICIPLE

battu

PRESENT PARTICIPLE

battant

IMPERATIVE

bats
battons
battez

PRESENT	IMPERFECT
je bats	je battais
tu bats	tu battais
il bat	il battait
nous battons	nous battions
vous battez	vous battiez
ils battent	ils battaient
FUTURE	CONDITIONAL
je battrai	je battrais
tu battras	tu battrais
il battra	il battrait
nous battrons	nous battrions
vous battrez	vous battriez
ils battront	ils battraient
PRESENT SUBJUNCTIVE	PAST HISTORIC
je batte	je battis
tu battes	tu battis
il batte	il battit
nous battions	nous battîmes
vous battiez	vous battîtes
ils battent	ils battirent

VERBS: IRREGULAR

boire *to drink* Auxiliary: **avoir**

PAST PARTICIPLE
bu

PRESENT PARTICIPLE
buvant

IMPERATIVE
bois
buvons
buvez

PRESENT		IMPERFECT	
je	bois	**je**	**buvais**
tu	bois	**tu**	**buvais**
il	boit	**il**	**buvait**
nous	**buvons**	**nous**	**buvions**
vous	**buvez**	**vous**	**buviez**
ils	**boivent**	**ils**	**buvaient**
FUTURE		CONDITIONAL	
je	boirai	je	boirais
tu	boiras	tu	boirais
il	boira	il	boirait
nous	boirons	nous	boirions
vous	boirez	vous	boiriez
ils	boiront	ils	boiraient
PRESENT SUBJUNCTIVE		PAST HISTORIC	
je	**boive**	**je**	**bus**
tu	**boives**	**tu**	**bus**
il	**boive**	**il**	**but**
nous	**buvions**	**nous**	**bûmes**
vous	**buviez**	**vous**	**bûtes**
ils	**boivent**	**ils**	**burent**

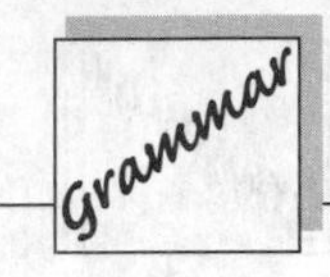

bouillir *to boil* Auxiliary: **avoir**

PAST PARTICIPLE

bouilli

PRESENT PARTICIPLE

bouillant

IMPERATIVE

bous
bouillons
bouillez

PRESENT		IMPERFECT	
je	**bous**	**je**	**bouillais**
tu	**bous**	**tu**	**bouillais**
il	**bout**	**il**	**bouillait**
nous	**bouillons**	**nous**	**bouillions**
vous	**bouillez**	**vous**	**bouilliez**
ils	**bouillent**	**ils**	**bouillaient**

FUTURE		CONDITIONAL	
je	bouillirai	je	bouillirais
tu	bouilliras	tu	bouillirais
il	bouillira	il	bouillirait
nous	bouillirons	nous	bouillirions
vous	bouillirez	vous	bouilliriez
ils	bouilliront	ils	bouilliraient

PRESENT SUBJUNCTIVE		PAST HISTORIC	
je	**bouille**	je	bouillis
tu	**bouilles**	tu	bouillis
il	**bouille**	il	bouillit
nous	**bouillions**	nous	bouillîmes
vous	**bouilliez**	vous	bouillîtes
ils	**bouillent**	ils	bouillirent

connaître *to know* Auxiliary: **avoir**

PAST PARTICIPLE	IMPERATIVE
connu	**connais**
PRESENT PARTICIPLE	**connaissons**
connaissant	**connaissez**

PRESENT		IMPERFECT	
je	**connais**	**je**	**connaissais**
tu	**connais**	**tu**	**connaissais**
il	connaît	**il**	**connaissait**
nous	**connaissons**	**nous**	**connaissions**
vous	**connaissez**	**vous**	**connaissiez**
ils	**connaissent**	**ils**	**connaissaient**
FUTURE		CONDITIONAL	
je	connaîtrai	je	connaîtrais
tu	connaîtras	tu	connaîtrais
il	connaîtra	il	connaîtrait
nous	connaîtrons	nous	connaîtrions
vous	connaîtrez	vous	connaîtriez
ils	connaîtront	ils	connaîtraient
PRESENT SUBJUNCTIVE		PAST HISTORIC	
je	**connaisse**	**je**	**connus**
tu	**connaisses**	**tu**	**connus**
il	**connaisse**	**il**	**connut**
nous	**connaissions**	**nous**	**connûmes**
vous	**connaissiez**	**vous**	**connûtes**
ils	**connaissent**	**ils**	**connurent**

coudre *to sew* Auxiliary: **avoir**

PAST PARTICIPLE
cousu

PRESENT PARTICIPLE
cousant

IMPERATIVE
couds
cousons
cousez

PRESENT	IMPERFECT
je couds	**je cousais**
tu couds	**tu cousais**
il coud	**il cousait**
nous cousons	**nous cousions**
vous cousez	**vous cousiez**
ils cousent	**ils cousaient**

FUTURE	CONDITIONAL
je coudrai	je coudrais
tu coudras	tu coudrais
il coudra	il coudrait
nous coudrons	nous coudrions
vous coudrez	vous coudriez
ils coudront	ils coudraient

PRESENT SUBJUNCTIVE	PAST HISTORIC
je couse	**je cousis**
tu couses	**tu cousis**
il couse	**il cousit**
nous cousions	**nous cousîmes**
vous cousiez	**vous cousîtes**
ils cousent	**ils cousirent**

courir *to run* — Auxiliary: **avoir**

PAST PARTICIPLE	IMPERATIVE
couru	**cours**
	courons
PRESENT PARTICIPLE	**courez**
courant	

PRESENT	IMPERFECT
je cours	**je courais**
tu cours	**tu courais**
il court	**il courait**
nous courons	**nous courions**
vous courez	**vous couriez**
ils courent	**ils couraient**

FUTURE	CONDITIONAL
je courrai	**je courrais**
tu courras	**tu courrais**
il courra	**il courrait**
nous courrons	**nous courrions**
vous courrez	**vous courriez**
ils courront	**ils courraient**

PRESENT SUBJUNCTIVE	PAST HISTORIC
je coure	**je courus**
tu coures	**tu courus**
il coure	**il courut**
nous courions	**nous courûmes**
vous couriez	**vous courûtes**
ils courent	**ils coururent**

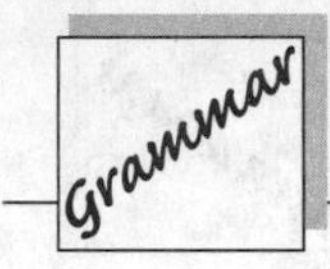

craindre *to fear* Auxiliary: **avoir**

PAST PARTICIPLE
craint

PRESENT PARTICIPLE
craignant

IMPERATIVE
crains
craignons
craignez

PRESENT		IMPERFECT	
je	**crains**	**je**	**craignais**
tu	**crains**	**tu**	**craignais**
il	**craint**	**il**	**craignait**
nous	**craignons**	**nous**	**craignions**
vous	**craignez**	**vous**	**craigniez**
ils	**craignent**	**ils**	**craignaient**
FUTURE		CONDITIONAL	
je	craindrai	je	craindrais
tu	craindras	tu	craindrais
il	craindra	il	craindrait
nous	craindrons	nous	craindrions
vous	craindrez	vous	craindriez
ils	craindront	ils	craindraient
PRESENT SUBJUNCTIVE		PAST HISTORIC	
je	**craigne**	**je**	**craignis**
tu	**craignes**	**tu**	**craignis**
il	**craigne**	**il**	**craignit**
nous	**craignions**	**nous**	**craignîmes**
vous	**craigniez**	**vous**	**craignîtes**
ils	**craignent**	**ils**	**craignirent**

Verbs ending in **-eindre** and **-oindre** are conjugated similarly

VERBS: IRREGULAR

croire *to believe* Auxiliary: **avoir**

PAST PARTICIPLE
cru

PRESENT PARTICIPLE
croyant

IMPERATIVE
crois
croyons
croyez

PRESENT		IMPERFECT	
je	crois	**je**	**croyais**
tu	crois	**tu**	**croyais**
il	**croit**	**il**	**croyait**
nous	**croyons**	**nous**	**croyions**
vous	**croyez**	**vous**	**croyiez**
ils	croient	**ils**	**croyaient**

FUTURE		CONDITIONAL	
je	croirai	je	croirais
tu	croiras	tu	croirais
il	croira	il	croirait
nous	croirons	nous	croirions
vous	croirez	vous	croiriez
ils	croiront	ils	croiraient

PRESENT SUBJUNCTIVE		PAST HISTORIC	
je	croie	**je**	**crus**
tu	croies	**tu**	**crus**
il	croie	**il**	**crut**
nous	**croyions**	**nous**	**crûmes**
vous	**croyiez**	**vous**	**crûtes**
ils	croient	**ils**	**crurent**

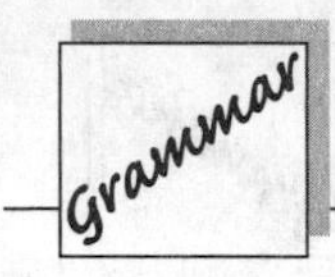

croître *to grow* Auxiliary: **avoir**

PAST PARTICIPLE

crû

PRESENT PARTICIPLE

croissant

IMPERATIVE

croîs
croissons
croissez

PRESENT		IMPERFECT	
je	**croîs**	**je**	**croissais**
tu	**croîs**	**tu**	**croissais**
il	croît	**il**	**croissait**
nous	**croissons**	**nous**	**croissions**
vous	**croissez**	**vous**	**croissiez**
ils	**croissent**	**ils**	**croissaient**
FUTURE		CONDITIONAL	
je	croîtrai	je	croîtrais
tu	croîtras	tu	croîtrais
il	croîtra	il	croîtrait
nous	croîtrons	nous	croîtrions
vous	croîtrez	vous	croîtriez
ils	croîtront	ils	croîtraient
PRESENT SUBJUNCTIVE		PAST HISTORIC	
je	**croisse**	**je**	**crûs**
tu	**croisses**	**tu**	**crûs**
il	**croisse**	**il**	**crût**
nous	**croissions**	**nous**	**crûmes**
vous	**croissiez**	**vous**	**crûtes**
ils	**croissent**	**ils**	**crûrent**

cueillir *to pick* Auxiliary: **avoir**

PAST PARTICIPLE	IMPERATIVE
cueilli	**cueille**
PRESENT PARTICIPLE	**cueillons**
cueillant	**cueillez**

PRESENT		IMPERFECT	
je	**cueille**	**je**	**cueillais**
tu	**cueilles**	**tu**	**cueillais**
il	**cueille**	**il**	**cueillait**
nous	**cueillons**	**nous**	**cueillions**
vous	**cueillez**	**vous**	**cueilliez**
ils	**cueillent**	**ils**	**cueillaient**
FUTURE		CONDITIONAL	
je	**cueillerai**	**je**	**cueillerais**
tu	**cueilleras**	**tu**	**cueillerais**
il	**cueillera**	**il**	**cueillerait**
nous	**cueillerons**	**nous**	**cueillerions**
vous	**cueillerez**	**vous**	**cueilleriez**
ils	**cueilleront**	**ils**	**cueilleraient**
PRESENT SUBJUNCTIVE		PAST HISTORIC	
je	**cueille**	je	cueillis
tu	**cueilles**	tu	cueillis
il	**cueille**	il	cueillit
nous	**cueillions**	nous	cueillîmes
vous	**cueilliez**	vous	cueillîtes
ils	**cueillent**	ils	cueillirent

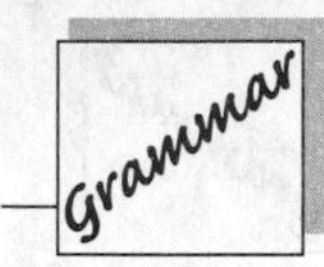

cuire *to cook* — Auxiliary: **avoir**

PAST PARTICIPLE
cuit

PRESENT PARTICIPLE
cuisant

IMPERATIVE
cuis
cuisons
cuisez

PRESENT	IMPERFECT
je cuis	**je cuisais**
tu cuis	**tu cuisais**
il cuit	**il cuisait**
nous cuisons	**nous cuisions**
vous cuisez	**vous cuisiez**
ils cuisent	**ils cuisaient**
FUTURE	**CONDITIONAL**
je cuirai	je cuirais
tu cuiras	tu cuirais
il cuira	il cuirait
nous cuirons	nous cuirions
vous cuirez	vous cuiriez
ils cuiront	ils cuiraient
PRESENT SUBJUNCTIVE	**PAST HISTORIC**
je cuise	**je cuisis**
tu cuises	**tu cuisis**
il cuise	**il cuisit**
nous cuisions	**nous cuisîmes**
vous cuisiez	**vous cuisîtes**
ils cuisent	**ils cuisirent**

nuire *to harm*, conjugated similarly, but past participle **nui**

VERBS: IRREGULAR

devoir *to have to; to owe* Auxiliary: **avoir**

PAST PARTICIPLE
dû

PRESENT PARTICIPLE
devant

IMPERATIVE
dois
devons
devez

PRESENT		IMPERFECT	
je	**dois**	**je**	**devais**
tu	**dois**	**tu**	**devais**
il	**doit**	**il**	**devait**
nous	**devons**	**nous**	**devions**
vous	**devez**	**vous**	**deviez**
ils	**doivent**	**ils**	**devaient**
FUTURE		CONDITIONAL	
je	**devrai**	**je**	**devrais**
tu	**devras**	**tu**	**devrais**
il	**devra**	**il**	**devrait**
nous	**devrons**	**nous**	**devrions**
vous	**devrez**	**vous**	**devriez**
ils	**devront**	**ils**	**devraient**
PRESENT SUBJUNCTIVE		PAST HISTORIC	
je	**doive**	**je**	**dus**
tu	**doives**	**tu**	**dus**
il	**doive**	**il**	**dut**
nous	**devions**	**nous**	**dûmes**
vous	**deviez**	**vous**	**dûtes**
ils	**doivent**	**ils**	**durent**

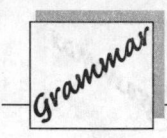

dire *to say, tell* — Auxiliary: **avoir**

PAST PARTICIPLE
dit

PRESENT PARTICIPLE
disant

IMPERATIVE
dis
disons
dites

PRESENT	IMPERFECT
je dis	**je disais**
tu dis	**tu disais**
il dit	**il disait**
nous disons	**nous disions**
vous dites	**vous disiez**
ils disent	**ils disaient**

FUTURE	CONDITIONAL
je dirai	je dirais
tu diras	tu dirais
il dira	il dirait
nous dirons	nous dirions
vous direz	vous diriez
ils diront	ils diraient

PRESENT SUBJUNCTIVE	PAST HISTORIC
je dise	**je dis**
tu dises	**tu dis**
il dise	**il dit**
nous disions	**nous dîmes**
vous disiez	**vous dîtes**
ils disent	**ils dirent**

interdire *to forbid,* conjugated similarly, but 2nd person plural of the present tense is **vous interdisez**

dormir *to sleep* Auxiliary: **avoir**

PAST PARTICIPLE	IMPERATIVE
dormi	**dors**
	dormons
PRESENT PARTICIPLE	**dormez**
dormant	

PRESENT	IMPERFECT
je dors	**je dormais**
tu dors	**tu dormais**
il dort	**il dormait**
nous dormons	**nous dormions**
vous dormez	**vous dormiez**
ils dorment	**ils dormaient**
FUTURE	CONDITIONAL
je dormirai	je dormirais
tu dormiras	tu dormirais
il dormira	il dormirait
nous dormirons	nous dormirions
vous dormirez	vous dormiriez
ils dormiront	ils dormiraient
PRESENT SUBJUNCTIVE	PAST HISTORIC
je dorme	je dormis
tu dormes	tu dormis
il dorme	il dormit
nous dormions	nous dormîmes
vous dormiez	vous dormîtes
ils dorment	ils dormirent

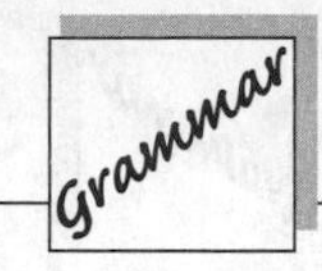

écrire *to write* — Auxiliary: **avoir**

PAST PARTICIPLE
écrit

PRESENT PARTICIPLE
écrivant

IMPERATIVE
écris
écrivons
écrivez

PRESENT		IMPERFECT	
	j'écris		**j'écrivais**
tu	écris	**tu**	**écrivais**
il	écrit	**il**	**écrivait**
nous	**écrivons**	**nous**	**écrivions**
vous	**écrivez**	**vous**	**écriviez**
ils	**écrivent**	**ils**	**écrivaient**
FUTURE		CONDITIONAL	
	j'écrirai		j'écrirais
tu	écriras	tu	écrirais
il	écrira	il	écrirait
nous	écrirons	nous	écririons
vous	écrirez	vous	écririez
ils	écriront	ils	écriraient
PRESENT SUBJUNCTIVE		PAST HISTORIC	
	j'écrive		**j'écrivis**
tu	**écrives**	**tu**	**écrivis**
il	**écrive**	**il**	**écrivit**
nous	**écrivions**	**nous**	**écrivîmes**
vous	**écriviez**	**vous**	**écrivîtes**
ils	**écrivent**	**ils**	**écrivirent**

envoyer *to send* Auxiliary: **avoir**

PAST PARTICIPLE
envoyé

PRESENT PARTICIPLE
envoyant

IMPERATIVE
envoie
envoyons
envoyez

PRESENT		IMPERFECT	
	j'envoie		j'envoyais
tu	envoies	tu	envoyais
il	envoie	il	envoyait
nous	envoyons	nous	envoyions
vous	envoyez	vous	envoyiez
ils	envoient	ils	envoyaient
FUTURE		**CONDITIONAL**	
	j'enverrai		**j'enverrais**
tu	**enverras**	**tu**	**enverrais**
il	**enverra**	**il**	**enverrait**
nous	**enverrons**	**nous**	**enverrions**
vous	**enverrez**	**vous**	**enverriez**
ils	**enverront**	**ils**	**enverraient**
PRESENT SUBJUNCTIVE		**PAST HISTORIC**	
	j'envoie		j'envoyai
tu	envoies	tu	envoyas
il	envoie	il	envoya
nous	envoyions	nous	envoyâmes
vous	envoyiez	vous	envoyâtes
ils	envoient	ils	envoyèrent

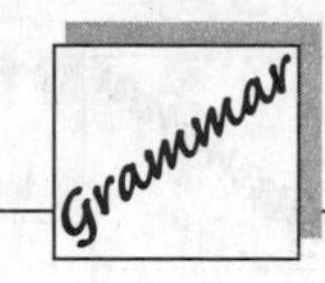

être *to be* Auxiliary: **avoir**

PAST PARTICIPLE

été

PRESENT PARTICIPLE

étant

IMPERATIVE

sois
soyons
soyez

PRESENT	IMPERFECT
je suis	**j'étais**
tu es	**tu étais**
il est	**il était**
nous sommes	**nous étions**
vous êtes	**vous étiez**
ils sont	**ils étaient**

FUTURE	CONDITIONAL
je serai	**je serais**
tu seras	**tu serais**
il sera	**il serait**
nous serons	**nous serions**
vous serez	**vous seriez**
ils seront	**ils seraient**

PRESENT SUBJUNCTIVE	PAST HISTORIC
je sois	**je fus**
tu sois	**tu fus**
il soit	**il fut**
nous soyons	**nous fûmes**
vous soyez	**vous fûtes**
ils soient	**ils furent**

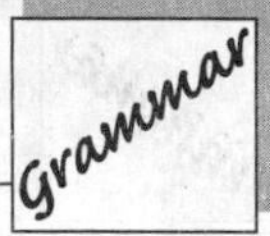

faire *to do; to make* Auxiliary: **avoir**

PAST PARTICIPLE
fait

PRESENT PARTICIPLE
faisant

IMPERATIVE
fais
faisons
faites

PRESENT	IMPERFECT
je fais	**je faisais**
tu fais	**tu faisais**
il fait	**il faisait**
nous faisons	**nous faisions**
vous faites	**vous faisiez**
ils font	**ils faisaient**

FUTURE	CONDITIONAL
je ferai	**je ferais**
tu feras	**tu ferais**
il fera	**il ferait**
nous ferons	**nous ferions**
vous ferez	**vous feriez**
ils feront	**ils feraient**

PRESENT SUBJUNCTIVE	PAST HISTORIC
je fasse	**je fis**
tu fasses	**tu fis**
il fasse	**il fit**
nous fassions	**nous fîmes**
vous fassiez	**vous fîtes**
ils fassent	**ils firent**

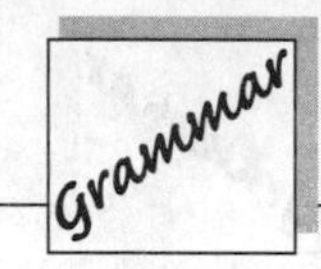

falloir *to be necessary* Auxiliary: **avoir**

PAST PARTICIPLE

fallu

PRESENT PARTICIPLE

not used

IMPERATIVE

not used

PRESENT	IMPERFECT
il faut	**il fallait**
FUTURE	CONDITIONAL
il faudra	**il faudrait**
PRESENT SUBJUNCTIVE	PAST HISTORIC
il faille	**il fallut**

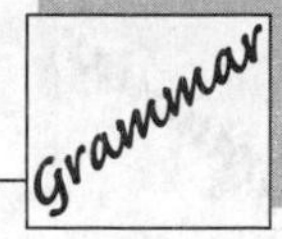

fuir *to flee* — Auxiliary: **avoir**

PAST PARTICIPLE
fui

PRESENT PARTICIPLE
fuyant

IMPERATIVE
fuis
fuyons
fuyez

PRESENT		IMPERFECT	
je	fuis	**je**	**fuyais**
tu	fuis	**tu**	**fuyais**
il	fuit	**il**	**fuyait**
nous	**fuyons**	**nous**	**fuyions**
vous	**fuyez**	**vous**	**fuyiez**
ils	**fuient**	**ils**	**fuyaient**
FUTURE		**CONDITIONAL**	
je	fuirai	je	fuirais
tu	fuiras	tu	fuirais
il	fuira	il	fuirait
nous	fuirons	nous	fuirions
vous	fuirez	vous	fuiriez
ils	fuiront	ils	fuiraient
PRESENT SUBJUNCTIVE		**PAST HISTORIC**	
je	**fuie**	je	fuis
tu	**fuies**	tu	fuis
il	**fuie**	il	fuit
nous	**fuyions**	nous	fuîmes
vous	**fuyiez**	vous	fuîtes
ils	**fuient**	ils	fuirent

haïr *to hate* Auxiliary: **avoir**

PAST PARTICIPLE

haï

PRESENT PARTICIPLE

haïssant

IMPERATIVE

hais
haïssons
haïssez

PRESENT		IMPERFECT	
je	hais	**je**	**haïssais**
tu	hais	**tu**	**haïssais**
il	hait	**il**	**haïssait**
nous	**haïssons**	**nous**	**haïssions**
vous	**haïssez**	**vous**	**haïssiez**
ils	**haïssent**	**ils**	**haïssaient**
FUTURE		CONDITIONAL	
je	haïrai	je	haïrais
tu	haïras	tu	haïrais
il	haïra	il	haïrait
nous	haïrons	nous	haïrions
vous	haïrez	vous	haïriez
ils	haïront	ils	haïraient
PRESENT SUBJUNCTIVE		PAST HISTORIC	
je	**haïsse**	**je**	**haïs**
tu	**haïsses**	**tu**	**haïs**
il	**haïsse**	**il**	**haït**
nous	**haïssions**	**nous**	**haïmes**
vous	**haïssiez**	**vous**	**haïtes**
ils	**haïssent**	**ils**	**haïrent**

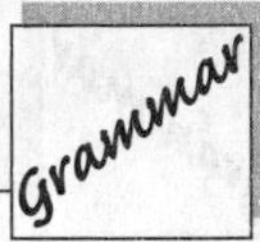

lire *to read*	Auxiliary: **avoir**
PAST PARTICIPLE **lu** PRESENT PARTICIPLE **lisant**	IMPERATIVE lis **lisons** **lisez**

PRESENT	IMPERFECT
je lis	**je lisais**
tu lis	**tu lisais**
il lit	**il lisait**
nous lisons	**nous lisions**
vous lisez	**vous lisiez**
ils lisent	**ils lisaient**
FUTURE	**CONDITIONAL**
je lirai	je lirais
tu liras	tu lirais
il lira	il lirait
nous lirons	nous lirions
vous lirez	vous liriez
ils liront	ils liraient
PRESENT SUBJUNCTIVE	**PAST HISTORIC**
je lise	**je lus**
tu lises	**tu lus**
il lise	**il lut**
nous lisions	**nous lûmes**
vous lisiez	**vous lûtes**
ils lisent	**ils lurent**

mettre *to put* Auxiliary: **avoir**

PAST PARTICIPLE

mis

PRESENT PARTICIPLE

mettant

IMPERATIVE

mets
mettons
mettez

PRESENT		IMPERFECT	
je	**mets**	je	mettais
tu	**mets**	tu	mettais
il	**met**	il	mettait
nous	mettons	nous	mettions
vous	mettez	vous	mettiez
ils	mettent	ils	mettaient
FUTURE		**CONDITIONAL**	
je	mettrai	je	mettrais
tu	mettras	tu	mettrais
il	mettra	il	mettrait
nous	mettrons	nous	mettrions
vous	mettrez	vous	mettriez
ils	mettront	ils	mettraient
PRESENT SUBJUNCTIVE		**PAST HISTORIC**	
je	mette	**je**	**mis**
tu	mettes	**tu**	**mis**
il	mette	**il**	**mit**
nous	mettions	**nous**	**mîmes**
vous	mettiez	**vous**	**mîtes**
ils	mettent	**ils**	**mirent**

VERBS: IRREGULAR

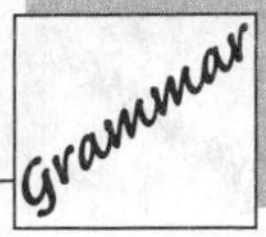

moudre *to grind* — Auxiliary: **avoir**

PAST PARTICIPLE	IMPERATIVE
moulu	mouds
PRESENT PARTICIPLE	**moulons**
moulant	**moulez**

PRESENT	IMPERFECT
je mouds	**je moulais**
tu mouds	**tu moulais**
il moud	**il moulait**
nous moulons	**nous moulions**
vous moulez	**vous mouliez**
ils moulent	**ils moulaient**
FUTURE	**CONDITIONAL**
je moudrai	je moudrais
tu moudras	tu moudrais
il moudra	il moudrait
nous moudrons	nous moudrions
vous moudrez	vous moudriez
ils moudront	ils moudraient
PRESENT SUBJUNCTIVE	**PAST HISTORIC**
je moule	**je moulus**
tu moules	**tu moulus**
il moule	**il moulut**
nous moulions	**nous moulûmes**
vous mouliez	**vous moulûtes**
ils moulent	**ils moulurent**

mourir *to die* Auxiliary: **être**

PAST PARTICIPLE

mort

PRESENT PARTICIPLE

mourant

IMPERATIVE

meurs
mourons
mourez

PRESENT		IMPERFECT	
je	**meurs**	**je**	**mourais**
tu	**meurs**	**tu**	**mourais**
il	**meurt**	**il**	**mourait**
nous	**mourons**	**nous**	**mourions**
vous	**mourez**	**vous**	**mouriez**
ils	**meurent**	**ils**	**mouraient**
FUTURE		CONDITIONAL	
je	**mourrai**	**je**	**mourrais**
tu	**mourras**	**tu**	**mourrais**
il	**mourra**	**il**	**mourrait**
nous	**mourrons**	**nous**	**mourrions**
vous	**mourrez**	**vous**	**mourriez**
ils	**mourront**	**ils**	**mourraient**
PRESENT SUBJUNCTIVE		PAST HISTORIC	
je	**meure**	**je**	**mourus**
tu	**meures**	**tu**	**mourus**
il	**meure**	**il**	**mourut**
nous	**mourions**	**nous**	**mourûmes**
vous	**mouriez**	**vous**	**mourûtes**
ils	**meurent**	**ils**	**moururent**

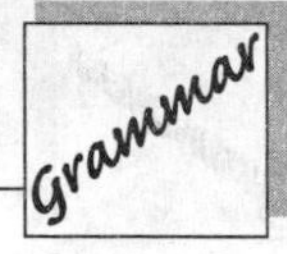

naître *to be born* Auxiliary: **être**

PAST PARTICIPLE	IMPERATIVE
né	**nais**
PRESENT PARTICIPLE	**naissons**
naissant	**naissez**

PRESENT	IMPERFECT
je nais	**je naissais**
tu nais	**tu naissais**
il naît	**il naissait**
nous naissons	**nous naissions**
vous naissez	**vous naissiez**
ils naissent	**ils naissaient**
FUTURE	CONDITIONAL
je naîtrai	je naîtrais
tu naîtras	tu naîtrais
il naîtra	il naîtrait
nous naîtrons	nous naîtrions
vous naîtrez	vous naîtriez
ils naîtront	ils naîtraient
PRESENT SUBJUNCTIVE	PAST HISTORIC
je naisse	je naquis
tu naisses	tu naquis
il naisse	il naquit
nous naissions	nous naquîmes
vous naissiez	vous naquîtes
ils naissent	ils naquirent

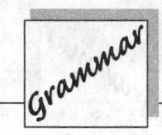

ouvrir *to open* Auxiliary: **avoir**

PAST PARTICIPLE	IMPERATIVE
ouvert	**ouvre**
	ouvrons
PRESENT PARTICIPLE	**ouvrez**
ouvrant	

PRESENT	IMPERFECT
j'ouvre	**j'ouvrais**
tu ouvres	**tu ouvrais**
il ouvre	**il ouvrait**
nous ouvrons	**nous ouvrions**
vous ouvrez	**vous ouvriez**
ils ouvrent	**ils ouvraient**

FUTURE	CONDITIONAL
j'ouvrirai	j'ouvrirais
tu ouvriras	tu ouvrirais
il ouvrira	il ouvrirait
nous ouvrirons	nous ouvririons
vous ouvrirez	vous ouvririez
ils ouvriront	ils ouvriraient

PRESENT SUBJUNCTIVE	PAST HISTORIC
j'ouvre	j'ouvris
tu ouvres	tu ouvris
il ouvre	il ouvrit
nous ouvrions	nous ouvrîmes
vous ouvriez	vous ouvrîtes
ils ouvrent	ils ouvrirent

offrir *to offer*, **souffrir** *to suffer* are conjugated similarly

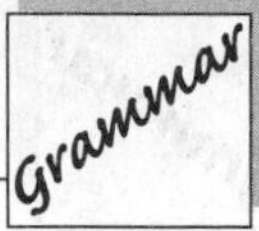

paraître *to appear* — Auxiliary: **avoir**

PAST PARTICIPLE

paru

PRESENT PARTICIPLE

paraissant

IMPERATIVE

parais
paraissons
paraissez

PRESENT		IMPERFECT	
je	**parais**	**je**	**paraissais**
tu	**parais**	**tu**	**paraissais**
il	paraît	**il**	**paraissait**
nous	**paraissons**	**nous**	**paraissions**
vous	**paraissez**	**vous**	**paraissiez**
ils	**paraissent**	**ils**	**paraissaient**

FUTURE		CONDITIONAL	
je	paraîtrai	je	paraîtrais
tu	paraîtras	tu	paraîtrais
il	paraîtra	il	paraîtrait
nous	paraîtrons	nous	paraîtrions
vous	paraîtrez	vous	paraîtriez
ils	paraîtront	ils	paraîtraient

PRESENT SUBJUNCTIVE		PAST HISTORIC	
je	**paraisse**	**je**	**parus**
tu	**paraisses**	**tu**	**parus**
il	**paraisse**	**il**	**parut**
nous	**paraissions**	**nous**	**parûmes**
vous	**paraissiez**	**vous**	**parûtes**
ils	**paraissent**	**ils**	**parurent**

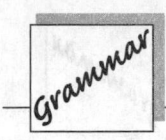

partir *to leave* — Auxiliary: **être**

PAST PARTICIPLE

parti

PRESENT PARTICIPLE

partant

IMPERATIVE

pars
partons
partez

PRESENT		IMPERFECT	
je	**pars**	**je**	**partais**
tu	**pars**	**tu**	**partais**
il	**part**	**il**	**partait**
nous	**partons**	**nous**	**partions**
vous	**partez**	**vous**	**partiez**
ils	**partent**	**ils**	**partaient**
FUTURE		CONDITIONAL	
je	partirai	je	partirais
tu	partiras	tu	partirais
il	partira	il	partirait
nous	partirons	nous	partirions
vous	partirez	vous	partiriez
ils	partiront	ils	partiraient
PRESENT SUBJUNCTIVE		PAST HISTORIC	
je	**parte**	je	partis
tu	**partes**	tu	partis
il	**parte**	il	partit
nous	**partions**	nous	partîmes
vous	**partiez**	vous	partîtes
ils	**partent**	ils	partirent

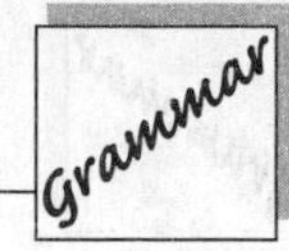

plaire *to please* Auxiliary: **avoir**

PAST PARTICIPLE

plu

PRESENT PARTICIPLE

plaisant

IMPERATIVE

plais
plaisons
plaisez

PRESENT		IMPERFECT	
je	plais	**je**	**plaisais**
tu	plais	**tu**	**plaisais**
il	**plaît**	**il**	**plaisait**
nous	**plaisons**	**nous**	**plaisions**
vous	**plaisez**	**vous**	**plaisiez**
ils	**plaisent**	**ils**	**plaisaient**

FUTURE		CONDITIONAL	
je	plairai	je	plairais
tu	plairas	tu	plairais
il	plaira	il	plairait
nous	plairons	nous	plairions
vous	plairez	vous	plairiez
ils	plairont	ils	plairaient

PRESENT SUBJUNCTIVE		PAST HISTORIC	
je	**plaise**	**je**	**plus**
tu	**plaises**	**tu**	**plus**
il	**plaise**	**il**	**plut**
nous	**plaisions**	**nous**	**plûmes**
vous	**plaisiez**	**vous**	**plûtes**
ils	**plaisent**	**ils**	**plurent**

pleuvoir *to rain* Auxiliary: **avoir**

PAST PARTICIPLE
plu

PRESENT PARTICIPLE
pleuvant

IMPERATIVE
not used

PRESENT	IMPERFECT
il pleut	**il pleuvait**

FUTURE	CONDITIONAL
il pleuvra	**il pleuvrait**

PRESENT SUBJUNCTIVE	PAST HISTORIC
il pleuve	**il plut**

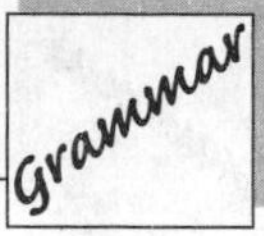

pouvoir *to be able to* Auxiliary: **avoir**

PAST PARTICIPLE
pu

PRESENT PARTICIPLE
pouvant

IMPERATIVE
not used

PRESENT	IMPERFECT
je peux*	**je pouvais**
tu peux	**tu pouvais**
il peut	**il pouvait**
nous pouvons	**nous pouvions**
vous pouvez	**vous pouviez**
ils peuvent	**ils pouvaient**
FUTURE	CONDITIONAL
je pourrai	**je pourrais**
tu pourras	**tu pourrais**
il pourra	**il pourrait**
nous pourrons	**nous pourrions**
vous pourrez	**vous pourriez**
ils pourront	**ils pourraient**
PRESENT SUBJUNCTIVE	PAST HISTORIC
je puisse	**je pus**
tu puisses	**tu pus**
il puisse	**il put**
nous puissions	**nous pûmes**
vous puissiez	**vous pûtes**
ils puissent	**ils purent**

*In questions: **puis-je?**

prendre *to take*	Auxiliary: **avoir**
PAST PARTICIPLE **pris** PRESENT PARTICIPLE **prenant**	IMPERATIVE prends **prenons** **prenez**

PRESENT	IMPERFECT
je prends tu prends il prend **nous prenons** **vous prenez** **ils prennent**	**je prenais** **tu prenais** **il prenait** **nous prenions** **vous preniez** **ils prenaient**
FUTURE	CONDITIONAL
je prendrai tu prendras il prendra nous prendrons vous prendrez ils prendront	je prendrais tu prendrais il prendrait nous prendrions vous prendriez ils prendraient
PRESENT SUBJUNCTIVE	PAST HISTORIC
je prenne **tu prennes** **il prenne** **nous prenions** **vous preniez** **ils prennent**	**je pris** **tu pris** **il prit** **nous prîmes** **vous prîtes** **ils prirent**

recevoir *to receive* Auxiliary: **avoir**

PAST PARTICIPLE

reçu

PRESENT PARTICIPLE

recevant

IMPERATIVE

reçois
recevons
recevez

PRESENT		IMPERFECT	
je	**reçois**	**je**	**recevais**
tu	**reçois**	**tu**	**recevais**
il	**reçoit**	**il**	**recevait**
nous	**recevons**	**nous**	**recevions**
vous	**recevez**	**vous**	**receviez**
ils	**reçoivent**	**ils**	**recevaient**

FUTURE		CONDITIONAL	
je	**recevrai**	**je**	**recevrais**
tu	**recevras**	**tu**	**recevrais**
il	**recevra**	**il**	**recevrait**
nous	**recevrons**	**nous**	**recevrions**
vous	**recevrez**	**vous**	**recevriez**
ils	**recevront**	**ils**	**recevraient**

PRESENT SUBJUNCTIVE		PAST HISTORIC	
je	**reçoive**	**je**	**reçus**
tu	**reçoives**	**tu**	**reçus**
il	**reçoive**	**il**	**reçut**
nous	**recevions**	**nous**	**reçûmes**
vous	**receviez**	**vous**	**reçûtes**
ils	**reçoivent**	**ils**	**reçurent**

résoudre *to solve* Auxiliary: **avoir**

PAST PARTICIPLE
résolu

PRESENT PARTICIPLE
résolvant

IMPERATIVE
résous
résolvons
résolvez

PRESENT		IMPERFECT	
je	**résous**	**je**	**résolvais**
tu	**résous**	**tu**	**résolvais**
il	**résout**	**il**	**résolvait**
nous	**résolvons**	**nous**	**résolvions**
vous	**résolvez**	**vous**	**résolviez**
ils	**résolvent**	**ils**	**résolvaient**

FUTURE		CONDITIONAL	
je	résoudrai	je	résoudrais
tu	résoudras	tu	résoudrais
il	résoudra	il	résoudrait
nous	résoudrons	nous	résoudrions
vous	résoudrez	vous	résoudriez
ils	résoudront	ils	résoudraient

PRESENT SUBJUNCTIVE		PAST HISTORIC	
je	**résolve**	**je**	**résolus**
tu	**résolves**	**tu**	**résolus**
il	**résolve**	**il**	**résolut**
nous	**résolvions**	**nous**	**résolûmes**
vous	**résolviez**	**vous**	**résolûtes**
ils	**résolvent**	**ils**	**résolurent**

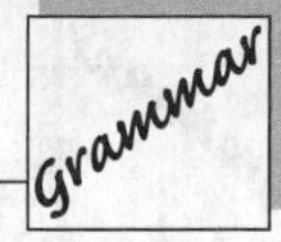

rire *to laugh* Auxiliary: **avoir**

PAST PARTICIPLE

ri

PRESENT PARTICIPLE

riant

IMPERATIVE

ris
rions
riez

PRESENT		IMPERFECT	
je	ris	je	riais
tu	ris	tu	riais
il	**rit**	il	riait
nous	rions	nous	riions
vous	riez	vous	riiez
ils	rient	ils	riaient

FUTURE		CONDITIONAL	
je	rirai	je	rirais
tu	riras	tu	rirais
il	rira	il	rirait
nous	rirons	nous	ririons
vous	rirez	vous	ririez
ils	riront	ils	riraient

PRESENT SUBJUNCTIVE		PAST HISTORIC	
je	rie	**je**	**ris**
tu	ries	**tu**	**ris**
il	rie	**il**	**rit**
nous	riions	**nous**	**rîmes**
vous	riiez	**vous**	**rîtes**
ils	rient	**ils**	**rirent**

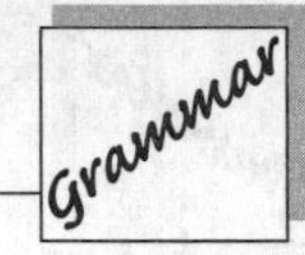

rompre *to break* Auxiliary: **avoir**

PAST PARTICIPLE

rompu

PRESENT PARTICIPLE

rompant

IMPERATIVE

romps
rompons
rompez

PRESENT		IMPERFECT	
je	romps	je	rompais
tu	romps	tu	rompais
il	**rompt**	il	rompait
nous	rompons	nous	rompions
vous	rompez	vous	rompiez
ils	rompent	ils	rompaient
FUTURE		**CONDITIONAL**	
je	romprai	je	romprais
tu	rompras	tu	romprais
il	rompra	il	romprait
nous	romprons	nous	romprions
vous	romprez	vous	rompriez
ils	rompront	ils	rompraient
PRESENT SUBJUNCTIVE		**PAST HISTORIC**	
je	rompe	je	rompis
tu	rompes	tu	rompis
il	rompe	il	rompit
nous	rompions	nous	rompîmes
vous	rompiez	vous	rompîtes
ils	rompent	ils	rompirent

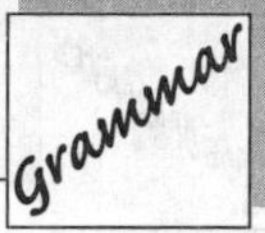

savoir *to know* Auxiliary: **avoir**

PAST PARTICIPLE

su

PRESENT PARTICIPLE

sachant

IMPERATIVE

sache
sachons
sachez

PRESENT		IMPERFECT	
je	**sais**	**je**	**savais**
tu	**sais**	**tu**	**savais**
il	**sait**	**il**	**savait**
nous	**savons**	**nous**	**savions**
vous	**savez**	**vous**	**saviez**
ils	**savent**	**ils**	**savaient**

FUTURE		CONDITIONAL	
je	**saurai**	**je**	**saurais**
tu	**sauras**	**tu**	**saurais**
il	**saura**	**il**	**saurait**
nous	**saurons**	**nous**	**saurions**
vous	**saurez**	**vous**	**sauriez**
ils	**sauront**	**ils**	**sauraient**

PRESENT SUBJUNCTIVE		PAST HISTORIC	
je	**sache**	**je**	**sus**
tu	**saches**	**tu**	**sus**
il	**sache**	**il**	**sut**
nous	**sachions**	**nous**	**sûmes**
vous	**sachiez**	**vous**	**sûtes**
ils	**sachent**	**ils**	**surent**

sentir *to feel, to smell* Auxiliary: **avoir**

PAST PARTICIPLE

senti

PRESENT PARTICIPLE

sentant

IMPERATIVE

sens
sentons
sentez

PRESENT		IMPERFECT	
je	**sens**	**je**	**sentais**
tu	**sens**	**tu**	**sentais**
il	**sent**	**il**	**sentait**
nous	**sentons**	**nous**	**sentions**
vous	**sentez**	**vous**	**sentiez**
ils	**sentent**	**ils**	**sentaient**
FUTURE		CONDITIONAL	
je	sentirai	je	sentirais
tu	sentiras	tu	sentirais
il	sentira	il	sentirait
nous	sentirons	nous	sentirions
vous	sentirez	vous	sentiriez
ils	sentiront	ils	sentiraient
PRESENT SUBJUNCTIVE		PAST HISTORIC	
je	**sente**	je	sentis
tu	**sentes**	tu	sentis
il	**sente**	il	sentit
nous	**sentions**	nous	sentîmes
vous	**sentiez**	vous	sentîtes
ils	**sentent**	ils	sentirent

servir *to serve* Auxiliary: **avoir**

PAST PARTICIPLE	IMPERATIVE
servi	
	sers
PRESENT PARTICIPLE	**servons**
	servez
servant	

PRESENT	IMPERFECT
je sers	**je servais**
tu sers	**tu servais**
il sert	**il servait**
nous servons	**nous servions**
vous servez	**vous serviez**
ils servent	**ils servaient**
FUTURE	CONDITIONAL
je servirai	je servirais
tu serviras	tu servirais
il servira	il servirait
nous servirons	nous servirions
vous servirez	vous serviriez
ils serviront	ils serviraient
PRESENT SUBJUNCTIVE	PAST HISTORIC
je serve	je servis
tu serves	tu servis
il serve	il servit
nous servions	nous servîmes
vous serviez	vous servîtes
ils servent	ils servirent

sortir *to go/come out* Auxiliary: **être**

PAST PARTICIPLE
sorti

PRESENT PARTICIPLE
sortant

IMPERATIVE
sors
sortons
sortez

PRESENT	IMPERFECT
je sors	**je sortais**
tu sors	**tu sortais**
il sort	**il sortait**
nous sortons	**nous sortions**
vous sortez	**vous sortiez**
ils sortent	**ils sortaient**
FUTURE	**CONDITIONAL**
je sortirai	je sortirais
tu sortiras	tu sortirais
il sortira	il sortirait
nous sortirons	nous sortirions
vous sortirez	vous sortiriez
ils sortiront	ils sortiraient
PRESENT SUBJUNCTIVE	**PAST HISTORIC**
je sorte	je sortis
tu sortes	tu sortis
il sorte	il sortit
nous sortions	nous sortîmes
vous sortiez	vous sortîtes
ils sortent	ils sortirent

suffire *to be enough* Auxiliary: **avoir**

PAST PARTICIPLE
suffi

PRESENT PARTICIPLE
suffisant

IMPERATIVE
suffis
suffisons
suffisez

PRESENT		IMPERFECT	
je	suffis	**je**	**suffisais**
tu	suffis	**tu**	**suffisais**
il	suffit	**il**	**suffisait**
nous	**suffisons**	**nous**	**suffisions**
vous	**suffisez**	**vous**	**suffisiez**
ils	**suffisent**	**ils**	**suffisaient**
FUTURE		CONDITIONAL	
je	suffirai	je	suffirais
tu	suffiras	tu	suffirais
il	suffira	il	suffirait
nous	suffirons	nous	suffirions
vous	suffirez	vous	suffiriez
ils	suffiront	ils	suffiraient
PRESENT SUBJUNCTIVE		PAST HISTORIC	
je	**suffise**	**je**	**suffis**
tu	**suffises**	**tu**	**suffis**
il	**suffise**	**il**	**suffit**
nous	**suffisions**	**nous**	**suffîmes**
vous	**suffisiez**	**vous**	**suffîtes**
ils	**suffisent**	**ils**	**suffirent**

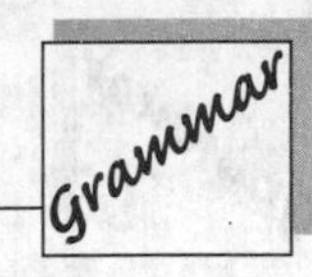

suivre *to follow* Auxiliary: **avoir**

PAST PARTICIPLE
suivi

PRESENT PARTICIPLE
suivant

IMPERATIVE
suis
suivons
suivez

PRESENT		IMPERFECT	
je	**suis**	je	suivais
tu	**suis**	tu	suivais
il	**suit**	il	suivait
nous	suivons	nous	suivions
vous	suivez	vous	suiviez
ils	suivent	ils	suivaient

FUTURE		CONDITIONAL	
je	suivrai	je	suivrais
tu	suivras	tu	suivrais
il	suivra	il	suivrait
nous	suivrons	nous	suivrions
vous	suivrez	vous	suivriez
ils	suivront	ils	suivraient

PRESENT SUBJUNCTIVE		PAST HISTORIC	
je	suive	je	suivis
tu	suives	tu	suivis
il	suive	il	suivit
nous	suivions	nous	suivîmes
vous	suiviez	vous	suivîtes
ils	suivent	ils	suivirent

123 VERBS: IRREGULAR

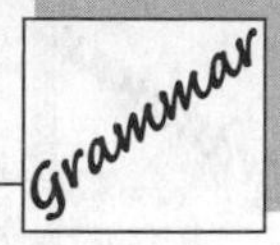

se taire *to stop talking*	Auxiliary: **être**
PAST PARTICIPLE **tu** PRESENT PARTICIPLE **se taisant**	IMPERATIVE tais-toi **taisons-nous** **taisez-vous**

PRESENT		IMPERFECT	
je	me tais	**je**	**me taisais**
tu	te tais	**tu**	**te taisais**
il	se tait	**il**	**se taisait**
nous	**nous taisons**	**nous**	**nous taisions**
vous	**vous taisez**	**vous**	**vous taisiez**
ils	**se taisent**	**ils**	**se taisaient**

FUTURE		CONDITIONAL	
je	me tairai	je	me tairais
tu	te tairas	tu	te tairais
il	se taira	il	se tairait
nous	nous tairons	nous	nous tairions
vous	vous tairez	vous	vous tairiez
ils	se tairont	ils	se tairaient

PRESENT SUBJUNCTIVE		PAST HISTORIC	
je	**me taise**	**je**	**me tus**
tu	**te taises**	**tu**	**te tus**
il	**se taise**	**il**	**se tut**
nous	**nous taisions**	**nous**	**nous tûmes**
vous	**vous taisiez**	**vous**	**vous tûtes**
ils	**se taisent**	**ils**	**se turent**

tenir *to hold* — Auxiliary: **avoir**

PAST PARTICIPLE

tenu

PRESENT PARTICIPLE

tenant

IMPERATIVE

tiens
tenons
tenez

PRESENT		IMPERFECT	
je	**tiens**	**je**	**tenais**
tu	**tiens**	**tu**	**tenais**
il	**tient**	**il**	**tenait**
nous	**tenons**	**nous**	**tenions**
vous	**tenez**	**vous**	**teniez**
ils	**tiennent**	**ils**	**tenaient**
FUTURE		CONDITIONAL	
je	**tiendrai**	**je**	**tiendrais**
tu	**tiendras**	**tu**	**tiendrais**
il	**tiendra**	**il**	**tiendrait**
nous	**tiendrons**	**nous**	**tiendrions**
vous	**tiendrez**	**vous**	**tiendriez**
ils	**tiendront**	**ils**	**tiendraient**
PRESENT SUBJUNCTIVE		PAST HISTORIC	
je	**tienne**	**je**	**tins**
tu	**tiennes**	**tu**	**tins**
il	**tienne**	**il**	**tint**
nous	**tenions**	**nous**	**tînmes**
vous	**teniez**	**vous**	**tîntes**
ils	**tiennent**	**ils**	**tinrent**

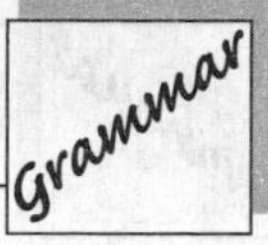

vaincre *to defeat*	Auxiliary: **avoir**
PAST PARTICIPLE vaincu PRESENT PARTICIPLE **vainquant**	IMPERATIVE vaincs **vainquons** **vainquez**

PRESENT	IMPERFECT
je vaincs	**je vainquais**
tu vaincs	**tu vainquais**
il vainc	**il vainquait**
nous vainquons	**nous vainquions**
vous vainquez	**vous vainquiez**
ils vainquent	**ils vainquaient**
FUTURE	**CONDITIONAL**
je vaincrai	je vaincrais
tu vaincras	tu vaincrais
il vaincra	il vaincrait
nous vaincrons	nous vaincrions
vous vaincrez	vous vaincriez
ils vaincront	ils vaincraient
PRESENT SUBJUNCTIVE	**PAST HISTORIC**
je vainque	**je vainquis**
tu vainques	**tu vainquis**
il vainque	**il vainquit**
nous vainquions	**nous vainquîmes**
vous vainquiez	**vous vainquîtes**
ils vainquent	**ils vainquirent**

valoir *to be worth* Auxiliary: **avoir**

PAST PARTICIPLE

valu

PRESENT PARTICIPLE

valant

IMPERATIVE

vaux
valons
valez

PRESENT	IMPERFECT
je vaux	**je valais**
tu vaux	**tu valais**
il vaut	**il valait**
nous valons	**nous valions**
vous valez	**vous valiez**
ils valent	**ils valaient**
FUTURE	CONDITIONAL
je vaudrai	**je vaudrais**
tu vaudras	**tu vaudrais**
il vaudra	**il vaudrait**
nous vaudrons	**nous vaudrions**
vous vaudrez	**vous vaudriez**
ils vaudront	**ils vaudraient**
PRESENT SUBJUNCTIVE	PAST HISTORIC
je vaille	**je valus**
tu vailles	**tu valus**
il vaille	**il valut**
nous valions	**nous valûmes**
vous valiez	**vous valûtes**
ils vaillent	**ils valurent**

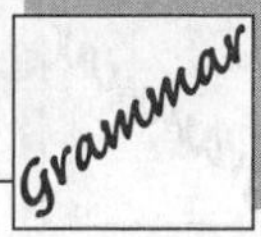

venir *to come*	Auxiliary: **être**
PAST PARTICIPLE **venu** PRESENT PARTICIPLE **venant**	IMPERATIVE **viens** **venons** **venez**

PRESENT	IMPERFECT
je viens **tu viens** **il vient** **nous venons** **vous venez** **ils viennent**	**je venais** **tu venais** **il venait** **nous venions** **vous veniez** **ils venaient**
FUTURE	CONDITIONAL
je viendrai **tu viendras** **il viendra** **nous viendrons** **vous viendrez** **ils viendront**	**je viendrais** **tu viendrais** **il viendrait** **nous viendrions** **vous viendriez** **ils viendraient**
PRESENT SUBJUNCTIVE	PAST HISTORIC
je vienne **tu viennes** **il vienne** **nous venions** **vous veniez** **ils viennent**	**je vins** **tu vins** **il vint** **nous vînmes** **vous vîntes** **ils vinrent**

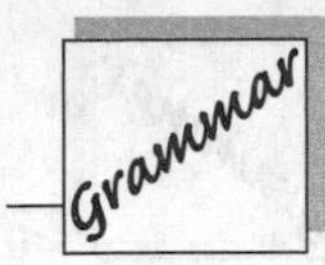

vêtir *to dress* — Auxiliary: **avoir**

PAST PARTICIPLE

vêtu

PRESENT PARTICIPLE

vêtant

IMPERATIVE

vêts
vêtons
vêtez

PRESENT		IMPERFECT	
je	**vêts**	**je**	**vêtais**
tu	**vêts**	**tu**	**vêtais**
il	**vêt**	**il**	**vêtait**
nous	**vêtons**	**nous**	**vêtions**
vous	**vêtez**	**vous**	**vêtiez**
ils	**vêtent**	**ils**	**vêtaient**

FUTURE		CONDITIONAL	
je	vêtirai	je	vêtirais
tu	vêtiras	tu	vêtirais
il	vêtira	il	vêtirait
nous	vêtirons	nous	vêtirions
vous	vêtirez	vous	vêtiriez
ils	vêtiront	ils	vêtiraient

PRESENT SUBJUNCTIVE		PAST HISTORIC	
je	**vête**	je	vêtis
tu	**vêtes**	tu	vêtis
il	**vête**	il	vêtit
nous	**vêtions**	nous	vêtîmes
vous	**vêtiez**	vous	vêtîtes
ils	**vêtent**	ils	vêtirent

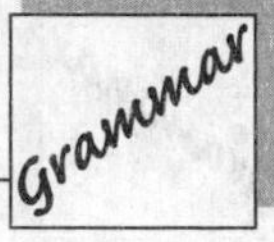

vivre *to live* — Auxiliary: **avoir**

PAST PARTICIPLE
vécu

PRESENT PARTICIPLE
vivant

IMPERATIVE
vis
vivons
vivez

PRESENT		IMPERFECT	
je	**vis**	je	vivais
tu	**vis**	tu	vivais
il	**vit**	il	vivait
nous	vivons	nous	vivions
vous	vivez	vous	viviez
ils	vivent	ils	vivaient
FUTURE		**CONDITIONAL**	
je	vivrai	je	vivrais
tu	vivras	tu	vivrais
il	vivra	il	vivrait
nous	vivrons	nous	vivrions
vous	vivrez	vous	vivriez
ils	vivront	ils	vivraient
PRESENT SUBJUNCTIVE		**PAST HISTORIC**	
je	vive	**je**	**vécus**
tu	vives	**tu**	**vécus**
il	vive	**il**	**vécut**
nous	vivions	**nous**	**vécûmes**
vous	viviez	**vous**	**vécûtes**
ils	vivent	**ils**	**vécurent**

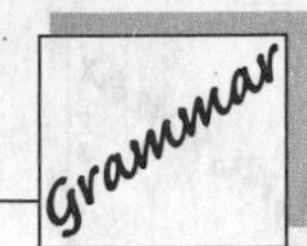

voir *to see* Auxiliary: **avoir**

PAST PARTICIPLE

vu

PRESENT PARTICIPLE

voyant

IMPERATIVE

vois
voyons
voyez

PRESENT	IMPERFECT
je vois	**je voyais**
tu vois	**tu voyais**
il voit	**il voyait**
nous voyons	**nous voyions**
vous voyez	**vous voyiez**
ils voient	**ils voyaient**

FUTURE	CONDITIONAL
je verrai	**je verrais**
tu verras	**tu verrais**
il verra	**il verrait**
nous verrons	**nous verrions**
vous verrez	**vous verriez**
ils verront	**ils verraient**

PRESENT SUBJUNCTIVE	PAST HISTORIC
je voie	**je vis**
tu voies	**tu vis**
il voie	**il vit**
nous voyions	**nous vîmes**
vous voyiez	**vous vîtes**
ils voient	**ils virent**

vouloir *to wish, want* Auxiliary: **avoir**

PAST PARTICIPLE	IMPERATIVE
voulu	**veuille**
PRESENT PARTICIPLE	**veuillons**
voulant	**veuillez**

PRESENT	IMPERFECT
je veux	**je voulais**
tu veux	**tu voulais**
il veut	**il voulait**
nous voulons	**nous voulions**
vous voulez	**vous vouliez**
ils veulent	**ils voulaient**
FUTURE	CONDITIONAL
je voudrai	**je voudrais**
tu voudras	**tu voudrais**
il voudra	**il voudrait**
nous voudrons	**nous voudrions**
vous voudrez	**vous voudriez**
ils voudront	**ils voudraient**
PRESENT SUBJUNCTIVE	PAST HISTORIC
je veuille	**je voulus**
tu veuilles	**tu voulus**
il veuille	**il voulut**
nous voulions	**nous voulûmes**
vous vouliez	**vous voulûtes**
ils veuillent	**ils voulurent**

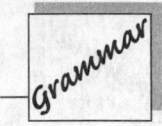

❒ The Gender of Nouns

In French, all nouns are either masculine or feminine, whether denoting people, animals or things. Unlike English, there is no neuter gender for inanimate objects and abstract nouns.

Gender is largely unpredictable and has to be learnt for each noun. However, the following guidelines will help you determine the gender for certain types of nouns.

- Nouns denoting male people and animals are usually – but not always – masculine, e.g.

un homme *a man*	**un taureau** *a bull*
un infirmier *a (male) nurse*	**un cheval** *a horse*

- Nouns denoting female people and animals are usually – but not always – feminine, e.g.

une fille *a girl*	**une vache** *a cow*
une infirmière *a nurse*	**une brebis** *a ewe*

- Some nouns are masculine OR feminine depending on the sex of the person to whom they refer, e.g.

un camarade *a (male) friend*	**une camarade** *a (female) friend*
un Belge *a Belgian (man)*	**une Belge** *a Belgian (woman)*

- Other nouns referring to either men or women have only one gender which applies to both, e.g.

un professeur *a teacher*	**une personne** *a person*	**une sentinelle** *a sentry*
un témoin *a witness*	**une victime** *a victim*	**une recrue** *a recruit*

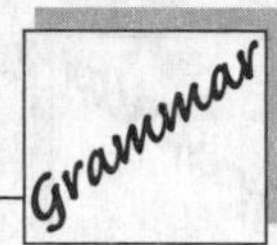

◆ Sometimes the ending of the noun indicates its gender. Shown below are some of the most important to guide you:

Masculine endings

-age	**le courage** *courage*, **le rinçage** *rinsing* EXCEPTIONS: **une cage** *a cage*, **une image** *a picture*, **la nage** *swimming*, **une page** *a page*, **une plage** *a beach*, **une rage** *a rage*
-ment	**le commencement** *the beginning* EXCEPTION: **une jument** *a mare*
-oir	**un couloir** *a corridor*, **un miroir** *a mirror*
-sme	**le pessimisme** *pessimism*, **l'enthousiasme** *enthusiasm*

Feminine endings

-ance, anse	**la confiance** *confidence*, **la danse** *dancing*
-ence, -ense	**la prudence** *caution*, **la défense** *defence* EXCEPTION: **le silence** *silence*
-ion	**une région** *a region*, **une addition** *a bill* EXCEPTIONS: **un pion** *a pawn*, **un espion** *a spy*
-oire	**une baignoire** *a bath(tub)*
-té, -tié	**la beauté** *beauty*, **la moitié** *half*

◆ Suffixes which differentiate between male and female are shown on pp 134 and 136.

◆ The following words have different meanings depending on gender:

le crêpe	*crêpe*	**la crêpe**	*pancake*
le livre	*book*	**la livre**	*pound*
le manche	*handle*	**la manche**	*sleeve*
le mode	*method*	**la mode**	*fashion*
le moule	*mould*	**la moule**	*mussel*
le page	*page(boy)*	**la page**	*page (in* book)
le physique	*physique*	**la physique**	*physics*
le poêle	*stove*	**la poêle**	*frying pan*
le somme	*nap*	**la somme**	*sum*
le tour	*turn*	**la tour**	*tower*
le voile	*veil*	**la voile**	*sail*

❐ Gender: the Formation of Feminines

As in English, male and female are sometimes differentiated by the use of two quite separate words, e.g.

mon oncle *my uncle*	**ma tante** *my aunt*
un taureau *a bull*	**une vache** *a cow*

There are, however, some words in French which show this distinction by the form of their ending.

- Some nouns add an **e** to the masculine singular form to form the feminine → [1]
- If the masculine singular form already ends in -**e**, no further **e** is added in the feminine → [2]
- Some nouns undergo a further change when **e** is added. These changes occur regularly and are shown on p 136.

Feminine forms to note

MASCULINE	FEMININE	
un âne	**une ânesse**	*donkey*
le comte	**la comtesse**	*count/countess*
le duc	**la duchesse**	*duke/duchess*
un Esquimau	**une Esquimaude**	*Eskimo*
le fou	**la folle**	*madman/madwoman*
le Grec	**la Grecque**	*Greek*
un hôte	**une hôtesse**	*host/hostess*
le jumeau	**la jumelle**	*twin*
le maître	**la maîtresse**	*master/mistress*
le prince	**la princesse**	*prince/princess*
le tigre	**la tigresse**	*tiger/tigress*
le traître	**la traîtresse**	*traitor*
le Turc	**la Turque**	*Turk*
le vieux	**la vieille**	*old man/old woman*

Examples

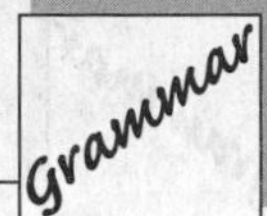

1 **un ami**
a (male) friend
un employé
a (male) employee
un Français
a Frenchman

une amie
a (female) friend
une employée
a (female) employee
une Française
a Frenchwoman

2 **un élève**
a (male) pupil
un collègue
a (male) colleague
un camarade
a (male) friend

une élève
a (female) pupil
une collègue
a (female) colleague
une camarade
a (female) friend

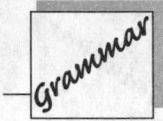

❒ Regular feminine endings

MASC. SING.	FEM. SING.	
-f	**-ve**	→ 1
-x	**-se**	→ 2
-eur	**-euse**	→ 3
-teur	{ **-teuse**	→ 4
	{ **-trice**	→ 5

Some nouns double the final consonant before adding **e:**

MASC. SING.	FEM. SING.	
-an	**-anne**	→ 6
-en	**-enne**	→ 7
-on	**-onne**	→ 8
-et	**-ette**	→ 9
-el	**-elle**	→ 10

Some nouns add an accent to the final syllable before adding **e**:

MASC. SING.	FEM. SING.	
-er	**-ère**	→ 11

Pronunciation and feminine endings

This is dealt with on p 244.

Examples

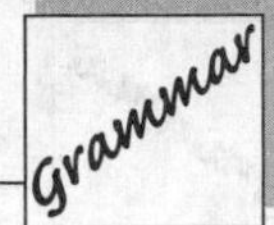

1	**un sportif** a sportsman	**une sportive** a sportswoman
	un veuf a widower	**une veuve** a widow
2	**un époux** a husband	**une épouse** a wife
	un amoureux a man in love	**une amoureuse** a woman in love
3	**un danseur** a dancer	**une danseuse** a dancer
	un voleur a thief	**une voleuse** a thief
4	**un menteur** a liar	**une menteuse** a liar
	un chanteur a singer	**une chanteuse** a singer
5	**un acteur** an actor	**une actrice** an actress
	un conducteur a driver	**une conductrice** a driver
6	**un paysan** a countryman	**une paysanne** a countrywoman
7	**un Parisien** a Parisian	**une Parisienne** a Parisian (woman)
8	**un baron** a baron	**une baronne** a baroness
9	**le cadet** the youngest (child)	**la cadette** the youngest (child)
10	**un intellectuel** an intellectual	**une intellectuelle** an intellectual
11	**un étranger** a foreigner	**une étrangère** a foreigner
	le dernier the last (one)	**la dernière** the last (one)

❒ The Formation of Plurals

◆ Most nouns add **s** to the singular form → [1]

◆ When the singular form already ends in -**s**, -**x** or -**z**, no further **s** is added → [2]

◆ For nouns ending in -**au**, -**eau** or -**eu**, the plural ends in -**aux**, -**eaux** or -**eux** → [3]

EXCEPTIONS:	**pneu**	*tyre*	(plur: **pneus**)
	bleu	*bruise*	(plur: **bleus**)

◆ For nouns ending in -**al** or -**ail**, the plural ends in -**aux** → [4]

EXCEPTIONS:	**bal**	*ball*	(plur: **bals**)
	festival	*festival*	(plur: **festivals**)
	chandail	*sweater*	(plur: **chandails**)
	détail	*detail*	(plur: **détails**)

◆ Forming the plural of compound nouns is complicated and you are advised to check each one individually in a dictionary.

Irregular plural forms

◆ Some masculine nouns ending in -**ou** add **x** in the plural. These are:

bijou	*jewel*	**genou**	*knee*	**joujou**	*toy*
caillou	*pebble*	**hibou**	*owl*	**pou**	*louse*
chou	*cabbage*				

◆ Some other nouns are totally unpredictable. Chief among these are:

SINGULAR		PLURAL
œil	*eye*	**yeux**
ciel	*sky*	**cieux**
Monsieur	*Mr*	**Messieurs**
Madame	*Mrs*	**Mesdames**
Mademoiselle	*Miss*	**Mesdemoiselles**

Pronunciation of plural forms

This is dealt with on p 244.

Examples

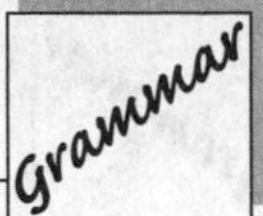

1	**le jardin** the garden	**les jardins** the gardens
	une voiture a car	**des voitures** (some) cars
	l'hôtel the hotel	**les hôtels** the hotels
2	**un tas** a heap	**des tas** (some) heaps
	une voix a voice	**des voix** (some) voices
	le gaz the gas	**les gaz** the gases
3	**un tuyau** a pipe	**des tuyaux** (some) pipes
	le chapeau the hat	**les chapeaux** the hats
	le feu the fire	**les feux** the fires
4	**le journal** the newspaper	**les journaux** the newspapers
	un travail a job	**des travaux** (some) jobs

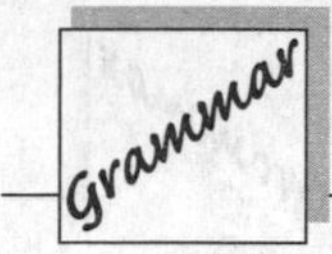

❒ The Definite Article

	WITH MASC. NOUN	WITH FEM. NOUN	
SING.	**le (l')**	**la (l')**	*the*
PLUR.	**les**	**les**	*the*

- The gender and number of the noun determines the form of the article → 1
- **le** and **la** change to **l'** before a vowel or an **h** 'mute' → 2
- For uses of the definite article see p 142.
- **à + le/la (l'), à + les**

	WITH MASC. NOUN	WITH FEM. NOUN	
SING.	**au (à l')**	**à la (à l')**	→ 3
PLUR.	**aux**	**aux**	

- The definite article combines with the preposition **à**, as shown above. You should pay particular attention to the masculine singular form **au,** and both plural forms **aux,** since these are not visually the sum of their parts.
- **de + le/la (l'), de + les**

	WITH MASC. NOUN	WITH FEM. NOUN	
SING.	**du (de l')**	**de la (de l')**	→ 4
PLUR.	**des**	**des**	

- The definite article combines with the preposition **de**, as shown above. You should pay particular attention to the masculine singular form **du**, and both plural forms **des**, since these are not visually the sum of their parts.

Examples

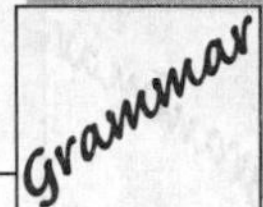

	MASCULINE	FEMININE
1	**le train** the train	**la gare** the station
	le garçon the boy	**la fille** the girl
	les hôtels the hotels	**les écoles** the schools
	les professeurs the teachers	**les femmes** the women
2	**l'acteur** the actor	**l'actrice** the actress
	l'effet the effect	**l'eau** the water
	l'ingrédient the ingredient	**l'idée** the idea
	l'objet the object	**l'ombre** the shadow
	l'univers the universe	**l'usine** the factory
	l'hôpital the hospital	**l'heure** the time
3	**au cinéma** at/to the cinema	**à la bibliothèque** at/to the library
	à l'employé to the employee	**à l'infirmière** to the nurse
	à l'hôpital at/to the hospital	**à l'hôtesse** to the hostess
	aux étudiants to the students	**aux maisons** to the houses
4	**du bureau** from/of the office	**de la réunion** from/of the meeting
	de l'auteur from/of the author	**de l'Italienne** from/of the Italian woman
	de l'hôte from/of the host	**de l'horloge** of the clock
	des États-Unis from/of the United States	**des vendeuses** from/of the saleswomen

❒ Uses of the Definite Article

While the definite article is used in much the same way in French as it is in English, its use is more widespread in French. Unlike English the definite article is also used:

- with abstract nouns, except when following certain prepositions → 1
- in generalizations, especially with plural or uncountable* nouns → 2
- with names of countries → 3
  EXCEPTIONS: no article with countries following **en** *to/in* → 4
- with parts of the body → 5
  'Ownership' is often indicated by an indirect object pronoun or a reflexive pronoun → 6
- in expressions of quantity/rate/price → 7
- with titles/ranks/professions followed by a proper name → 8
- The definite article is NOT used with nouns in apposition → 9

*An uncountable noun is one which cannot be used in the plural or with an indefinite article, e.g. **l'acier** *steel,* **le lait** *milk.*

Examples

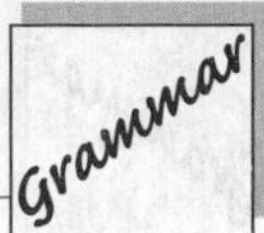

1 **Les prix montent**
Prices are rising
L'amour rayonne dans ses yeux
Love shines in his eyes
BUT **avec plaisir** with pleasure — **sans espoir** without hope

2 **Je n'aime pas le café**
I don't like coffee
Les enfants ont besoin d'être aimés
Children need to be loved

3 **le Japon** Japan — **la France** France — **l'Italie** Italy — **les Pays-Bas** The Netherlands

4 **aller en Écosse** to go to Scotland — **Il travaille en Allemagne** He works in Germany

5 **Tournez la tête à gauche**
Turn your head to the left
j'ai mal à la gorge
My throat is sore, I have a sore throat

6 **La tête me tourne**
My head is spinning
Elle s'est brossé les dents
She brushed her teeth

7 **4 euros le mètre/le kilo/la douzaine/la pièce**
4 euros a metre/a kilo/a dozen/each
rouler à 80 km à l'heure
to go at 50 m.p.h.
payé à l'heure/au jour/au mois
paid by the hour/by the day/by the month

8 **le roi Georges III** King George III — **le capitaine Darbeau** Captain Darbeau
le docteur Rousseau Dr Rousseau — **Monsieur le président** Mr Chairman/President

9 **Victor Hugo, grand écrivain du dix-neuvième siècle**
Victor Hugo, a great author of the nineteenth century
Joseph Leblanc, inventeur et entrepreneur, a été le premier ...
Joseph Leblanc, an inventor and entrepreneur, was the first...

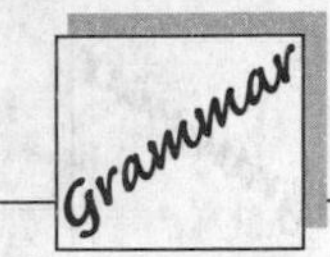

❒ The Partitive Article

The partitive article has the sense of *some* or *any*, although the French is not always translated in English.

Forms of the partitive

	WITH MASC. NOUN	WITH FEM. NOUN	
SING.	**du (de l')**	**de la (de l')**	*some, any*
PLUR.	**des**	**des**	*some, any*

- The gender and number of the noun determines the form of the partitive → 1
- The forms shown in brackets are used before a vowel or an **h** 'mute' → 2
- **des** becomes **de** (**d'** + vowel) before an adjective → 3, unless the adjective and noun are seen as forming one unit → 4
- In negative sentences **de** (**d'** + vowel) is used for both genders, singular and plural → 5
  EXCEPTION: after **ne ... que** *only*, the positive forms above are used → 6

Examples

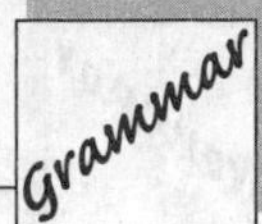

1 **Avez-vous du sucre?**
Have you any sugar?
J'ai acheté de la farine et de la margarine
I bought (some) flour and margarine
Il a mangé des gâteaux
He ate some cakes
Est-ce qu'il y a des lettres pour moi?
Are there (any) letters for me?

2 **Il me doit de l'argent**
He owes me (some) money
C'est de l'histoire ancienne
That's ancient history

3 **Il a fait de gros efforts pour nous aider**
He made a great effort to help us
Cette région a de belles églises
This region has some beautiful churches

4 **des grandes vacances** — summer holidays
des jeunes gens — young people

5 **Je n'ai pas de nourriture/d'argent**
I don't have any food/money
Vous n'avez pas de timbres/d'œufs?
Have you no stamps/eggs?
Je ne mange jamais de viande/d'omelettes
I never eat meat/omelettes
Il ne veut plus de visiteurs/d'eau
He doesn't want any more visitors/water

6 **Il ne boit que du thé/de la bière/de l'eau**
He only drinks tea/beer/water
Je n'ai que des problèmes avec cette machine
I have nothing but problems with this machine

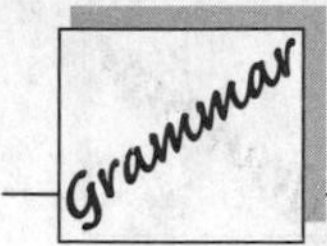

❐ The Indefinite Article

	WITH MASC. NOUN	WITH FEM. NOUN	
SING.	**un**	**une**	*a*
PLUR.	**des**	**des**	*some*

- **des** is also the plural of the partitive article (see p 144).
- In negative sentences, **de** (**d'** + vowel) is used for both singular and plural → 1
- The indefinite article is used in French largely as it is in English EXCEPT:

  – there is no article when a person's profession is being stated → 2
  The article *is* present however, following **ce** (**c'** + vowel) → 3

  – the English article is not translated by **un**/**une** in constructions like *what a surprise, what an idiot* → 4

  – in structures of the type given in example 5 the article **un**/**une** is used in French and not translated in English → 5

Examples

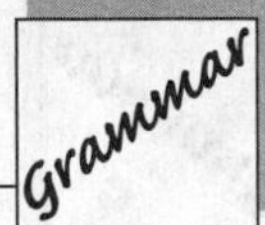

1 **Je n'ai pas de livre/d'enfants**
I don't have a book/(any) children

2 **Il est professeur**
He's a teacher

Ma mère est infirmière
My mother's a nurse

3 **C'est un médecin**
He's/She's a doctor

Ce sont des acteurs
They're actors

4 **Quelle surprise!**
What a surprise!

Quel dommage!
What a shame!

5 **avec une grande sagesse/un courage admirable**
with great wisdom /admirable courage
Il a fait preuve d'un sang-froid incroyable
He showed incredible coolness
Un produit d'une qualité incomparable
A product of incomparable quality

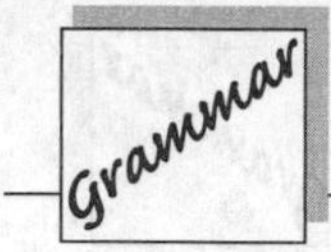

❐ Adjectives

Most adjectives agree in number and in gender with the noun or pronoun.

The formation of feminines

- Most adjectives add an **e** to the masculine singular form → [1]
- If the masculine singular form already ends in **-e,** no further **e** is added → [2]
- Some adjectives undergo a further change when **e** is added. These changes occur regularly and are shown on p 150.
- Irregular feminine forms are shown on p 152.

The formation of plurals

- The plural of both regular and irregular adjectives is formed by adding an **s** to the masculine or feminine singular form, as appropriate → [3]
- When the masculine singular form already ends in **-s** or **-x**, no further **s** is added → [4]
- For masculine singulars ending in **-au** and **-eau**, the masculine plural is **-aux** and **-eaux** → [5]
- For masculine singulars ending in **-al**, the masculine plural is **-aux** → [6]

EXCEPTIONS: **final** (masculine plural **finals**)
fatal (masculine plural **fatals**)
naval (masculine plural **navals**)

Pronunciation of feminine and plural adjectives

This is dealt with on p 244.

Examples

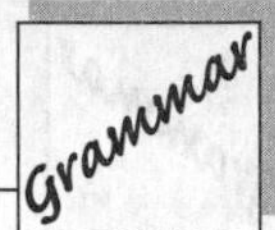

1 **mon frère aîné**
my elder brother
ma sœur aînée
my elder sister
le petit garçon
the little boy
la petite fille
the little girl
un sac gris
a grey bag
une chemise grise
a grey shirt
un bruit fort
a loud noise
une voix forte
a loud voice

2 **un jeune homme**
a young man
une jeune femme
a young woman
l'autre verre
the other glass
l'autre assiette
the other plate

3 **le dernier train**
the last train
les derniers trains
the last trains
une vieille maison
an old house
de vieilles maisons
old houses
un long voyage
a long journey
de longs voyages
long journeys
la rue étroite
the narrow street
les rues étroites
the narrow streets

4 **un diplomate français**
a French diplomat
des diplomates français
French diplomats
un homme dangereux
a dangerous man
des hommes dangereux
dangerous men

5 **le nouveau professeur**
the new teacher
les nouveaux professeurs
the new teachers
un chien esquimau
a husky (Fr. = an Eskimo dog)
des chiens esquimaux
huskies (Fr. = Eskimo dogs)

6 **un ami loyal**
a loyal friend
des amis loyaux
loyal friends
un geste amical
a friendly gesture
des gestes amicaux
friendly gestures

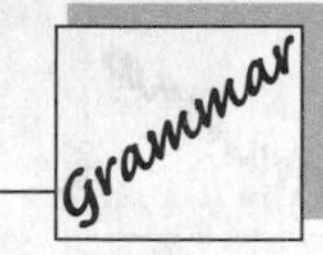

❐ Regular feminine endings

MASC. SING.	FEM. SING.	EXAMPLES	
-f	**-ve**	**neuf, vif**	→ 1
-x	**-se**	**heureux, jaloux**	→ 2
-eur	**-euse**	**travailleur, flâneur**	→ 3
-teur	{ **-teuse**	**flatteur, menteur**	→ 4
	-trice	**destructeur, séducteur**	→ 5

EXCEPTIONS:

bref: see p 152
doux, faux, roux, vieux: see p 152
extérieur, **inférieur**, **intérieur**, **meilleur**, **supérieur**: all add **e** to the masculine
enchanteur: fem. = **enchanteresse**

MASC. SING.	FEM. SING.	EXAMPLES	
-an	**-anne**	**paysan**	→ 6
-en	**-enne**	**ancien, parisien**	→ 7
-on	**-onne**	**bon, breton**	→ 8
-as	**-asse**	**bas, las**	→ 9
-et*	**-ette**	**muet, violet**	→ 10
-el	**-elle**	**annuel, mortel**	→ 11
-eil	**-eille**	**pareil, vermeil**	→ 12

EXCEPTION:

ras: fem. = **rase**

MASC. SING.	FEM. SING.	EXAMPLES	
-et*	**-ète**	**secret, complet**	→ 13
-er	**-ère**	**étranger, fier**	→ 14

*Note that there are two feminine endings for masculine adjectives ending in **-et**.

Examples

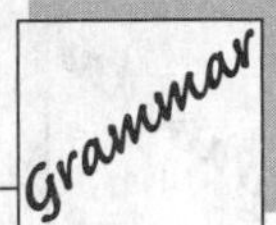

1	**un résultat positif** a positive result	**une attitude positive** a positive attitude
2	**d'un ton sérieux** in a serious tone (of voice)	**une voix sérieuse** a serious voice
3	**un enfant trompeur** a deceitful child	**une déclaration trompeuse** a misleading statement
4	**un tableau flatteur** a flattering picture	**une comparaison flatteuse** a flattering comparison
5	**un geste protecteur** a protective gesture	**une couche protectrice** a protective layer
6	**un problème paysan** a farming problem	**la vie paysanne** country life
7	**un avion égyptien** an Egyptian plane	**une statue égyptienne** an Egyptian statue
8	**un bon repas** a good meal	**de bonne humeur** in a good mood
9	**un plafond bas** a low ceiling	**à voix basse** in a low voice
10	**un travail net** a clean piece of work	**une explication nette** a clear explanation
11	**un homme cruel** a cruel man	**une remarque cruelle** a cruel remark
12	**un livre pareil** such a book	**en pareille occasion** on such an occasion
13	**un regard inquiet** an anxious look	**une attente inquiète** an anxious wait
14	**un goût amer** a bitter taste	**une amère déception** a bitter disappointment

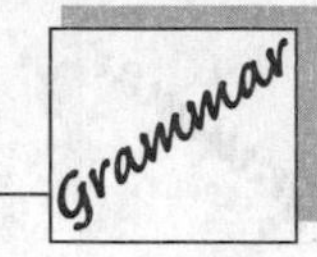

❒ Adjectives with irregular feminine forms

MASC. SING.	FEM. SING.		
aigu	**aiguë**	*sharp; high-pitched*	→ 1
ambigu	**ambiguë**	*ambiguous*	
beau (bel)*	**belle**	*beautiful*	
bénin	**bénigne**	*benign*	
blanc	**blanche**	*white*	
bref	**brève**	*brief, short*	→ 2
doux	**douce**	*soft; sweet*	
épais	**épaisse**	*thick*	
esquimau	**esquimaude**	*Eskimo*	
faux	**fausse**	*wrong*	
favori	**favorite**	*favourite*	→ 3
fou (fol*)	**folle**	*mad*	
frais	**fraîche**	*fresh*	→ 4
franc	**franche**	*frank*	
gentil	**gentille**	*kind*	
grec	**grecque**	*Greek*	
gros	**grosse**	*big*	
jumeau	**jumelle**	*twin*	→ 5
long	**longue**	*long*	
malin	**maligne**	*malignant*	
mou (mol*)	**molle**	*soft*	
nouveau (nouvel)*	**nouvelle**	*new*	
nul	**nulle**	*no*	
public	**publique**	*public*	→ 6
roux	**rousse**	*red-haired*	
sec	**sèche**	*dry*	
sot	**sotte**	*foolish*	
turc	**turque**	*Turkish*	
vieux (vieil)*	**vieille**	*old*	

*This form is used when the following word begins with a vowel or an **h** 'mute' → 7

Examples

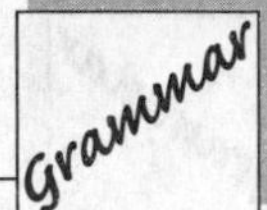

1 **un son aigu**
a high-pitched sound

une douleur aiguë
a sharp pain

2 **un bref discours**
a short speech

une brève rencontre
a short meeting

3 **mon sport favori**
my favourite sport

ma chanson favorite
my favourite song

4 **du pain frais**
fresh bread

de la crème fraîche
fresh cream

5 **mon frère jumeau**
my twin brother

ma sœur jumelle
my twin sister

6 **un jardin public**
a (public) park

l'opinion publique
public opinion

7 **un bel appartement**
a beautiful flat
le nouvel inspecteur
the new inspector
un vieil arbre
an old tree

un bel habit
a beautiful outfit
un nouvel harmonica
a new harmonica
un vieil hôtel
an old hotel

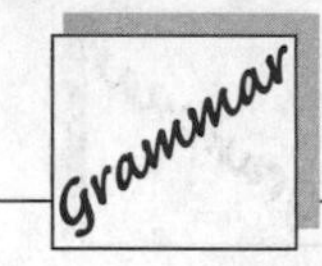

❒ Comparatives and Superlatives

Comparatives

These are formed using the following constructions:

plus … (que)	*more … (than)*	→ 1
moins … (que)	*less … (than)*	→ 2
aussi … que	*as … as*	→ 3
si … que*	*as … as*	→ 4

*used mainly after a negative

Superlatives

These are formed using the following constructions:

le/la/les plus … (que)	*the most … (that)*	→ 5
le/la/les moins … (que)	*the least … (that)*	→ 6

- When the possessive adjective is present, two constructions are possible → 7
- After a superlative the preposition **de** is often translated as *in* → 8
- If a clause follows a superlative, the verb is in the subjunctive → 9

Adjectives with irregular comparatives/superlatives

ADJECTIVE	COMPARATIVE	SUPERLATIVE
bon *good*	**meilleur** *better*	**le meilleur** *the best*
mauvais *bad*	**pire** OR **plus mauvais** *worse*	**le pire** OR **le plus mauvais** *the worst*
petit *small*	**moindre*** OR **plus petit** *smaller;* *lesser*	**le moindre*** OR **le plus petit** *the smallest;* *the least*

*used only with abstract nouns

- Comparative and superlative adjectives agree in number and in gender with the noun, just like any other adjective → 10

Examples

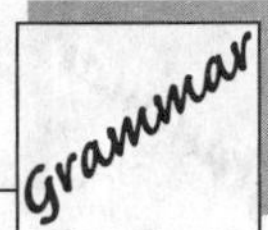

1 **une raison plus grave**
a more serious reason
Elle est plus petite que moi
She is smaller than me

2 **un film moins connu**
a less well-known film
C'est moins cher qu'il ne pense
It's cheaper than he thinks

3 **Robert était aussi inquiet que moi**
Robert was as worried as I was
Cette ville n'est pas aussi grande que Bordeaux
This town isn't as big as Bordeaux

4 **Ils ne sont pas si contents que ça**
They aren't as happy as all that

5 **le guide le plus utile**
the most useful guidebook
la voiture la plus petite
the smallest car
les plus grandes maisons
the biggest houses

6 **le mois le moins agréable**
the least pleasant month
la fille la moins forte
the weakest girl
les moins belles peintures
the least attractive paintings

7 **Mon désir le plus cher** } **est de voyager**
Mon plus cher désir }
My dearest wish is to travel

8 **la plus grande gare de Londres**
the biggest station in London
l'habitant le plus âgé du village/de la région
the oldest inhabitant in the village/in the area

9 **la personne la plus gentille que je connaisse**
the nicest person I know

10 **les moindres difficultés**
the least difficulties
la meilleure qualité
the best quality

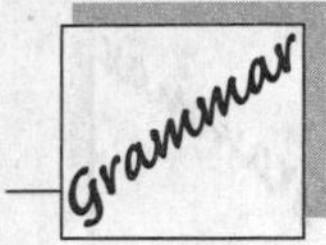

❐ Demonstrative Adjectives

	MASCULINE	FEMININE	
SING.	**ce (cet)**	**cette**	*this; that*
PLUR.	**ces**	**ces**	*these; those*

- Demonstrative adjectives agree in number and gender with the noun → 1
- **cet** is used when the following word begins with a vowel or an **h** 'mute' → 2
- For emphasis or in order to distinguish between people or objects, **-ci** or **-là** is added to the noun: **-ci** indicates proximity (usually translated *this)* and **là** distance *(that)* → 3

Examples

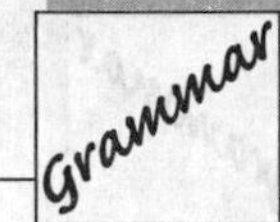

1 **Ce stylo ne marche pas**
This/That pen isn't working
Comment s'appelle cette entreprise?
What's this/that company called?
Ces livres sont les miens
These/Those books are mine
Ces couleurs sont plus jolies
These/Those colours are nicer

2 **cet oiseau**
this/that bird
cet article
this/that article
cet homme
this/that man

3 **Combien coûte ce manteau-ci?**
How much is this coat?
Je voudrais cinq de ces pommes-là
I'd like five of those apples
Est-ce que tu reconnais cette personne-là?
Do you recognize that person?
Mettez ces vêtements-ci dans cette valise-là
Put these clothes in that case
Ce garçon-là appartient à ce groupe-ci
That boy belongs to this group

❒ Interrogative Adjectives

	MASCULINE	FEMININE	
SING.	**quel?**	**quelle?**	*what?; which?*
PLUR.	**quels?**	**quelles?**	*what?; which?*

- Interrogative adjectives agree in number and gender with the noun → [1]

- The forms shown above are also used in indirect questions → [2]

❒ Exclamatory Adjectives

	MASCULINE	FEMININE	
SING.	**quel!**	**quelle!**	*what (a)!*
PLUR.	**quels!**	**quelles!**	*what!*

- Exclamatory adjectives agree in number and gender with the noun → [3]

- For other exclamations, see p 214.

Examples

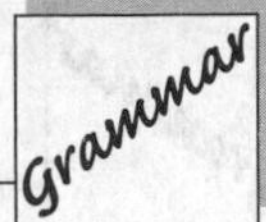

1 **Quel genre d'homme est-ce?**
What type of man is he?
Quelle est leur décision?
What is their decision?
Vous jouez de quels instruments?
What instruments do you play?
Quelles offres avez-vous reçues?
What offers have you received?
Quel vin recommandez-vous?
Which wine do you recommend?
Quelles couleurs préférez-vous?
Which colours do you prefer?

2 **Je ne sais pas à quelle heure il est arrivé**
I don't know what time he arrived
Dites-moi quels sont les livres les plus intéressants
Tell me which books are the most interesting

3 **Quel dommage!**
What a pity!
Quelle idée!
What an idea!
Quels beaux livres vous avez!
What fine books you have!
Quelles jolies fleurs!
What nice flowers!

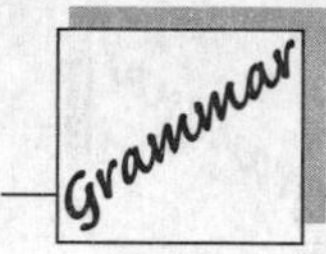

❐ Possessive Adjectives

WITH SING. NOUN		WITH PLUR. NOUN	
MASC.	FEM.	MASC./FEM.	
mon	**ma (mon)**	**mes**	*my*
ton	**ta (ton)**	**tes**	*your*
son	**sa (son)**	**ses**	*his; her; its*
notre	**notre**	**nos**	*our*
votre	**votre**	**vos**	*your*
leur	**leur**	**leurs**	*their*

- Possessive adjectives agree in number and gender with the noun, NOT WITH THE OWNER → 1
- The forms shown in brackets are used when the following word begins with a vowel or an **h** 'mute' → 2
- **son**, **sa**, **ses** have the additional meaning of *one's* → 3

Examples

1 **Catherine a oublié son parapluie**
Catherine has left her umbrella
Paul cherche sa montre
Paul's looking for his watch
Mon frère et ma sœur habitent à Glasgow
My brother and sister live in Glasgow
Est-ce que tes voisins ont vendu leur voiture?
Did your neighbours sell their car?
Rangez vos affaires
Put your things away

2 **mon appareil-photo**
my camera
ton histoire
your story
son erreur
his/her mistake
mon autre sœur
my other sister

3 **perdre son équilibre**
to lose one's balance
présenter ses excuses
to offer one's apologies

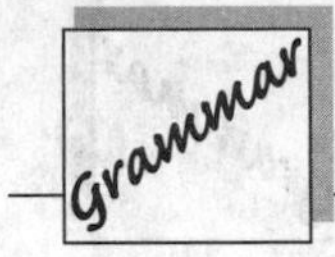

❒ Position of Adjectives

- French adjectives usually follow the noun → 1
- Adjectives of colour or nationality *always* follow the noun → 2
- As in English, demonstrative, possessive, numerical and interrogative adjectives precede the noun → 3
- The adjectives **autre** *other* and **chaque** *each, every* precede the noun → 4
- The following common adjectives can precede the noun:

beau	*beautiful*	**jeune**	*young*
bon	*good*	**joli**	*pretty*
court	*short*	**long**	*long*
dernier	*last*	**mauvais**	*bad*
grand	*great*	**petit**	*small*
gros	*big*	**tel**	*such (a)*
haut	*high*	**vieux**	*old*

- The meaning of the following adjectives varies according to their position:

	BEFORE NOUN	AFTER NOUN	
ancien	*former*	*old, ancient*	→ 5
brave	*good*	*brave*	→ 6
cher	*dear (beloved)*	*expensive*	→ 7
grand	*great*	*tall*	→ 8
même	*same*	*very*	→ 9
pauvre	*poor (wretched)*	*poor (not rich)*	→ 10
propre	*own*	*clean*	→ 11
seul	*single, sole*	*on one's own*	→ 12
simple	*mere, simple*	*simple, easy*	→ 13
vrai	*real*	*true*	→ 14

Adjectives following the noun are linked by **et** → 15

163 Examples

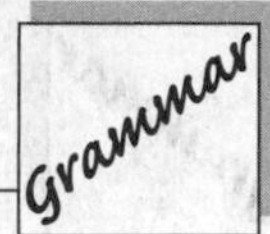

1	**le chapitre suivant** the following chapter	**l'heure exacte** the right time
2	**une cravate rouge** a red tie	**un mot français** a French word
3	**ce dictionnaire** this dictionary	**mon père** my father
	le premier étage the first floor	**deux exemples** two examples
	quel homme? which man?	
4	**une autre fois** another time	**chaque jour** every day
5	**un ancien collègue** a former colleague	**l'histoire ancienne** ancient history
6	**un brave homme** a good man	**un homme brave** a brave man
7	**mes chers amis** my dear friends	**une robe chère** an expensive dress
8	**un grand peintre** a great painter	**un homme grand** a tall man
9	**la même réponse** the same answer	**vos paroles mêmes** your very words
10	**cette pauvre femme** that poor woman	**une nation pauvre** a poor nation
11	**ma propre vie** my own life	**une chemise propre** a clean shirt
12	**une seule réponse** a single reply	**une femme seule** a woman on her own
13	**un simple regard** a mere look	**un problème simple** a simple problem
14	**la vraie raison** the real reason	**les faits vrais** the true facts
15	**un acte lâche et trompeur** a cowardly, deceitful act	
	un acte lâche, trompeur et ignoble a cowardly, deceitful and ignoble act	

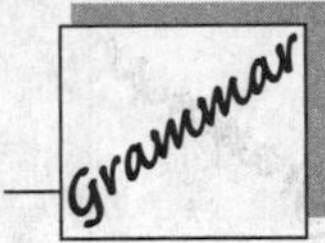

❒ Personal Pronouns

SUBJECT PRONOUNS		
PERSON	SINGULAR	PLURAL
1st	**je (j')** *I*	**nous** *we*
2nd	**tu** *you*	**vous** *you*
3rd (masc.)	**il** *he; it*	**ils** *they*
(fem.)	**elle** *she; it*	**elles** *they*

je changes to j' before a vowel, an **h** 'mute', or the pronoun **y** → 1

◆ **tu/vous**

Vous, as well as being the second person plural, is also used when addressing one person. As a general rule, use **tu** only when addressing a friend, a child, a relative, someone you know very well, or when invited to do so. In all other cases use **vous**. For singular and plural uses of **vous**, see example 2

◆ **il/elle; ils/elles**

The form of the 3rd person pronouns reflects the number and gender of the noun(s) they replace, referring to animals and things as well as to people. **Ils** also replaces a combination of masculine and feminine nouns → 3

◆ Sometimes stressed pronouns replace the subject pronouns, see p 172.

Examples

1 **J'arrive!**
I'm just coming!
J'en ai trois
I've got 3 of them
J'hésite à le déranger
I hesitate to disturb him
J'y pense souvent
I often think about it

2 Compare: **Vous êtes certain, Monsieur Leclerc?**
Are you sure, Mr Leclerc?
and: **Vous êtes certains, les enfants?**
Are you sure, children?
Compare: **Vous êtes partie quand, Estelle?**
When did you leave, Estelle?
and: **Estelle et Sophie – vous êtes parties quand?**
Estelle and Sophie – when did you leave?

3 **Où logent ton père et ta mère quand ils vont à Rome?**
Where do your father and mother stay when they go to Rome?
Donne-moi le journal et les lettres quand ils arriveront
Give me the newspaper and the letters when they arrive

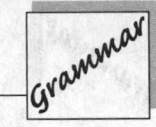

❐ Personal Pronouns (Continued)

	DIRECT OBJECT PRONOUNS	
PERSON	SINGULAR	PLURAL
1st	**me (m')** *me*	**nous** *us*
2nd	**te (t')** *you*	**vous** *you*
3rd (masc.)	**le (l')** *him; it*	**les** *them*
(fem.)	**la (l')** *her; it*	**les** *them*

The forms shown in brackets are used before a vowel, an **h** 'mute', or the pronoun **y** → 1

- In positive commands **me** and **te** change to **moi** and **toi** except before **en** or **y** → 2
- **le** sometimes functions as a 'neuter' pronoun, referring to an idea or information contained in a previous statement or question. It is often not translated → 3

Position of direct object pronouns

- In constructions other than the imperative affirmative the pronoun comes before the verb → 4

  The same applies when the verb is in the infinitive → 5

  In the imperative affirmative, the pronoun follows the verb and is attached to it by a hyphen → 6
- For further information, see Order of Object Pronouns, p 170.

Reflexive Pronouns

These are dealt with under reflexive verbs, p 30.

Examples

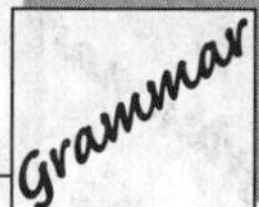

1 **Il m'a vu**
He saw me
Je ne t'oublierai jamais
I'll never forget you
Ça l'habitue à travailler seul
That gets him/her used to working on his/her own
Je veux l'y accoutumer
I want to accustom him/her to it

2 **Avertis-moi de ta décision → Avertis-m'en**
Inform me of your decision — Inform me of it

3 **Il n'est pas là. – Je le sais bien.**
He isn't there. – I know that.
Aidez-moi si vous le pouvez
Help me if you can
Elle viendra demain. – Je l'espère bien.
She'll come tomorrow. – I hope so.

4 **Je t'aime**
I love you
Les voyez-vous?
Can you see them?
Elle ne nous connaît pas
She doesn't know us
Est-ce que tu ne les aimes pas?
Don't you like them?
Ne me faites pas rire
Don't make me laugh

5 **Puis-je vous aider?**
May I help you?

6 **Aidez-moi** — **Suivez-nous**
Help me — Follow us

❒ Personal Pronouns (Continued)

INDIRECT OBJECT PRONOUNS		
PERSON	SINGULAR	PLURAL
1st	**me (m')**	**nous**
2nd	**te (t')**	**vous**
3rd (masc.)	**lui**	**leur**
(fem.)	**lui**	**leur**

me and **te** change to **m'** and **t'** before a vowel or an **h** 'mute' → 1

- In positive commands, **me** and **te** change to **moi** and **toi** except before **en** → 2
- The pronouns shown in the above table replace the preposition **à** + noun, where the noun is a person or an animal → 3
- The verbal construction affects the translation of the pronoun → 4

Position of indirect object pronouns

- In constructions other than the imperative affirmative, the pronoun comes before the verb → 5
  The same applies when the verb is in the infinitive → 6
  In the imperative affirmative, the pronoun follows the verb and is attached to it by a hyphen → 7
- For further information, see Order of Object Pronouns, p 170.

Reflexive Pronouns

These are dealt with under reflexive verbs, p 30.

Examples

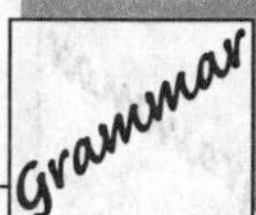

1 **Tu m'as donné ce livre**
You gave me this book
Ils t'ont caché les faits
They hid the facts from you

2 **Donnez-moi du sucre** → **Donnez-m'en**
Give me some sugar — Give me some
Garde-toi assez d'argent → **Garde-t'en assez**
Keep enough money for yourself — Keep enough for yourself

3 **J'écris à Suzanne** → **Je lui écris**
I'm writing to Suzanne — I'm writing to her
Donne du lait au chat → **Donne-lui du lait**
Give the cat some milk — Give it some milk

4 **arracher qch à qn** to snatch sth from sb:
Un voleur m'a arraché mon porte-monnaie
A thief snatched my purse from me
promettre qch à qn to promise sb sth:
Il leur a promis un cadeau
He promised them a present
demander à qn de faire to ask sb to do:
Elle nous avait demandé de revenir
She had asked us to come back

5 **Elle vous a écrit** — **Vous a-t-elle écrit?**
She's written to you — Has she written to you?
Il ne nous parle pas
He doesn't speak to us
Est-ce que cela ne vous intéresse pas?
Doesn't it interest you?
Ne leur répondez pas
Don't answer them

6 **Voulez-vous leur envoyer l'adresse?**
Do you want to send them the address?

7 **Répondez-moi** — **Donnez-nous la réponse**
Answer me — Tell us the answer

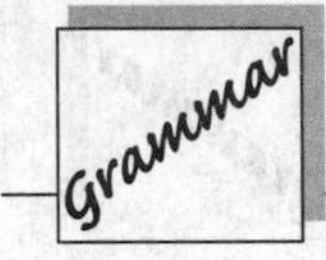

❐ Personal Pronouns (Continued)

Order of object pronouns

- When two object pronouns of different persons come before the verb, the order is: indirect before direct, i.e.

me **te** **nous** **vous**	before	**le** **la** **les**	→ 1

- When two 3rd person object pronouns come before the verb, the order is: direct before indirect, i.e.

le **la** **les**	before	**lui** **leur**	→ 2

- When two object pronouns come after the verb (i.e. in the imperative affirmative), the order is: direct before indirect, i.e.

le **la** **les**	before	**moi** **toi** **lui** **nous** **vous** **leur**	→ 3

- The pronouns **y** and **en** (see pp 176 and 174) always come last → 4

Examples

1 **Dominique vous l'envoie demain**
Dominique's sending it to you tomorrow
Est-ce qu'il te les a montrés?
Has he shown them to you?
Ne me le dis pas
Don't tell me (it)
Il ne veut pas nous la prêter
He won't lend it to us

2 **Elle le leur a emprunté**
She borrowed it from them
Je les lui ai lus
I read them to him/her
Ne la leur donne pas
Don't give it to them
Je voudrais les lui rendre
I'd like to give them back to him/ her

3 **Rends-les-moi**
Give them back to me
Donnez-le-nous
Give it to us
Apportons-les-leur
Let's take them to them

4 **Donnez-leur-en**
Give them some
Je l'y ai déposé
I dropped him there
Ne nous en parlez plus
Don't speak to us about it any more

❐ Personal Pronouns (Continued)

STRESSED OR DISJUNCTIVE PRONOUNS		
PERSON	SINGULAR	PLURAL
1st	**moi**	**nous**
	me	*us*
2nd	**toi**	**vous**
	you	*you*
3rd (masc.)	**lui**	**eux**
	him; it	*them*
(fem.)	**elle**	**elles**
	her; it	*them*
('reflexive')	**soi**	
	oneself	

- These pronouns are used:

  – after prepositions → 1
  – on their own → 2
  – following **c'est, ce sont** *it is* → 3
  – for emphasis, especially where contrast is involved → 4
  – when the subject consists of two or more pronouns → 5
  – when the subject consists of a pronoun and a noun → 6
  – in comparisons → 7
  – before relative pronouns → 8

- For particular emphasis **-même** (singular) or **-mêmes** (plural) is added to the pronoun → 9

moi-même	*myself*	**nous-mêmes**	*ourselves*
toi-même	*yourself*	**vous-même**	*yourself*
lui-même	*himself; itself*	**vous-mêmes**	*yourselves*
elle-même	*herself; itself*	**eux-mêmes**	*themselves*
soi-même	*oneself*	**elles-mêmes**	*themselves*

Examples

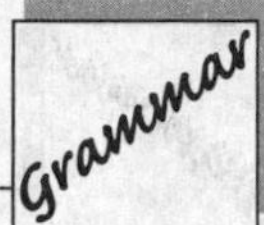

1 **Je pense à toi**
I think about you
C'est pour elle
This is for her
Venez avec moi
Come with me
Partez sans eux
Leave without them
Assieds-toi à côté de lui
Sit beside him
Il a besoin de nous
He needs us

2 **Qui a fait cela? – Lui.**
Who did that? – He did.
Qui est-ce qui gagne? – Moi
Who's winning? – Me

3 **C'est toi, Simon? – Non, c'est moi, David.**
Is that you, Simon? – No, it's me, David.
Qui est-ce? – Ce sont eux.
Who is it? – It's them.

4 **Ils voyagent séparément: lui par le train, elle en autobus**
They travel separately: he by train and she by bus
Toi, tu ressembles à ton père, eux pas
You look like your father, *they* don't
Il n'a pas l'air de s'ennuyer, lui!
He doesn't look bored!

5 **Lui et moi partons demain**
He and I are leaving tomorrow
Ni vous ni elles ne pouvez rester
Neither you nor they can stay

6 **Mon père et elle ne s'entendent pas**
My father and she don't get on

7 **plus jeune que moi**
younger than me
Il est moins grand que toi
He's smaller than you (are)

8 **Moi, qui étais malade, je n'ai pas pu les accompagner**
I, who was ill, couldn't go with them
Ce sont eux qui font du bruit, pas nous
They're the ones making the noise, not us

9 **Je l'ai fait moi-même**
I did it myself

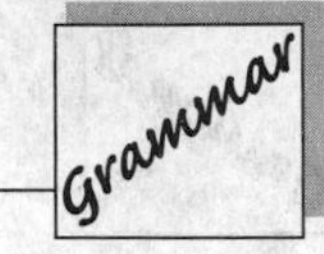

❐ The pronoun en

- **en** replaces the preposition **de** + noun → 1
  The verbal construction can affect the translation → 2

- **en** also replaces the partitive article *(English = some, any)* + noun → 3

In expressions of quantity **en** represents the noun → 4

- Position:

  en comes before the verb, except in positive commands when it follows and is attached to the verb by a hyphen → 5

- **en** follows other object pronouns → 6

Examples

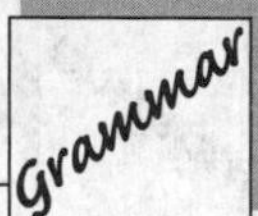

1 **Il est fier de son succès** → **Il en est fier**
He's proud of his success — He's proud of it
Elle est sortie du cinéma → **Elle en est sortie**
She came out of the cinema — She came out (of it)
Je suis couvert de peinture → **J'en suis couvert**
I'm covered in paint — I'm covered in it
Il a beaucoup d'amis → **Il en a beaucoup**
He has lots of friends — He has lots (of them)

2 **avoir besoin de qch** to need sth:
J'en ai besoin
I need it/them
avoir peur de qch to be afraid of sth:
J'en ai peur
I'm afraid of it/them

3 **Avez-vous de l'argent?** → **En avez-vous?**
Have you any money? — Do you have any?
Je veux acheter des timbres → **Je veux en acheter**
I want to buy some stamps — I want to buy some

4 **J'ai deux crayons** → **J'en ai deux**
I've two pencils — I've two (of them)
Combien de sœurs as-tu? – J'en ai trois.
How many sisters do you have? – I have three.

5 **Elle en a discuté avec moi**
She discussed it with me
En êtes-vous content?
Are you pleased with it/them?
Je veux an garder trois
I want to keep three of them
N'en parlez plus
Don't talk about it any more
Prenez-en — **Soyez-en fier**
Take some — Be proud of it/them

6 **Donnez-leur-en** — **Il m'en a parlé**
Give them some — He spoke to me about it

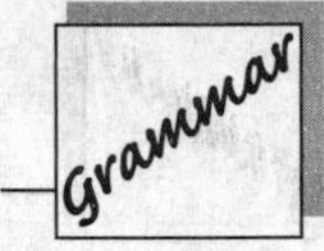

❒ The pronoun y

- **y** replaces the preposition **à** + noun → 1
  The verbal construction can affect the translation → 2
- **y** also replaces the prepositions **dans** and **sur** + noun → 3
- **y** can also mean *there* → 4
- Position:
  y comes before the verb, except in positive commands when it follows and is attached to the verb by a hyphen → 5
- **y** follows other object pronouns → 6

Examples

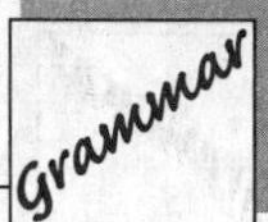

1 **Ne touchez pas à ce bouton** → **N'y touchez pas**
Don't touch this switch — Don't touch it
Il participe aux concerts → **Il y participe**
He takes part in the concerts — He takes part (in them)

2 **penser à qch** to think about sth:
J'y pense souvent
I often think about it
consentir à qch to agree to sth:
Tu y as consenti?
Have you agreed to it?

3 **Mettez-les dans la boîte** → **Mettez-les-y**
Put them in the box — Put them in it
Il les a mis sur les étagères → **Il les y a mis**
He put them on the shelves — He put them on them
J'ai placé de l'argent sur ce compte → **J'y ai placé de l'argent**
I've put money into this account — I've put money into it

4 **Elle y passe tout l'été**
She spends the whole summer there

5 **Il y a ajouté du sucre**
He added sugar to it
Elle n'y a pas écrit son nom
She hasn't written her name on it
Comment fait-on pour y aller?
How do you get there?
N'y pense plus!
Don't give it another thought!
Restez-y — **Réfléchissez-y**
Stay there — Think it over

6 **Elle m'y a conduit** — **Menez-nous-y**
She drove me there — Take us there

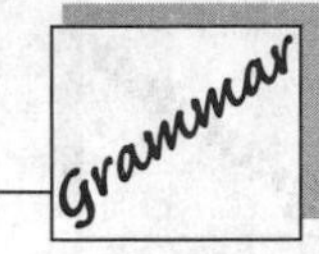

❒ Indefinite Pronouns

aucun(e)	*none, not any*	→ [1]
certain(e)s	*some, certain*	→ [2]
chacun(e)	*each (one)* *everybody*	→ [3]
on	*one, you* *somebody* *they, people* *we* (informal use)	→ [4]
personne	*nobody*	→ [5]
plusieurs	*several*	→ [6]
quelque chose	*something; anything*	→ [7]
quelques-un(e)s	*some, a few*	→ [8]
quelqu'un	*somebody; anybody*	→ [9]
rien	*nothing*	→ [10]
tout	*all; everything*	→ [11]
tous (toutes)	*all*	→ [12]
l'un(e) ... l'autre	*(the) one ... the other*	
les un(e)s ... les autres	*some ... others*	→ [13]

◆ **aucun(e), personne, rien**

When used as subject or object of the verb, these require the word **ne** placed immediately before the verb. Note that **aucun** further needs the pronoun **en** when used as an object → [14]

◆ **quelque chose, rien**

When qualified by an adjective, these pronouns require the preposition **de** before the adjective → [15]

Examples

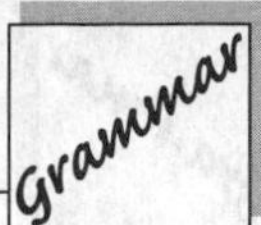

1	**Combien en avez-vous? – Aucun** How many have you got? – None	
2	**Certains pensent que ...** Some (people) think that ...	
3	**Chacune de ces boîtes est pleine** Each of these boxes is full	**Chacun son tour!** Everybody in turn!
4	**On voit l'église de cette fenêtre** You can see the church from this window **À la campagne on se couche tôt** In the country they/we go to bed early **Est-ce qu'on lui a permis de rester?** Was he/she allowed to stay?	
5	**Qui voyez-vous? – Personne** Who can you see? – Nobody	
6	**Ils sont plusieurs** There are several of them	
7	**Mange donc quelque chose!** Eat something!	**Tu as vu quelque chose?** Did you see anything?
8	**Je connais quelques-uns de ses amis** I know some of his/her friends	
9	**Quelqu'un a appelé** Somebody called (out)	**Tu as vu quelqu'un?** Did you see anybody?
10	**Qu'est-ce que tu as dans la main? – Rien** What have you got in your hand? – Nothing	
11	**Il a tout gâché** He has spoiled everything	**Tout va bien** All's well
12	**Tu les as tous?** Do you have all of them?	**Elles sont toutes venues** They all came
13	**Les uns sont satisfaits, les autres pas** Some are satisfied, (the) others aren't	
14	**Je ne vois personne** I can't see anyone **Aucune des entreprises ne veut ...** None of the companies wants ...	**Rien ne lui plaît** Nothing pleases him/her **Il n'en a aucun** He hasn't any (of them)
15	**quelque chose de grand** something big	**rien d'intéressant** nothing interesting

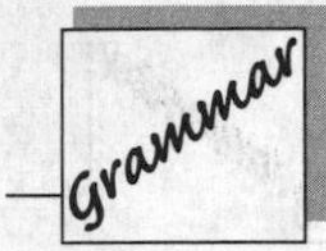

❒ Relative Pronouns

qui *who; which*
que *who(m); which*

These are subject and direct object pronouns that introduce a clause and refer to people or things.

	PEOPLE	THINGS
SUBJECT	**qui** → 1	**qui** → 3
	who, that	*which, that*
DIRECT OBJECT	**que (qu')** → 2	**que (qu')** → 4
	who(m), that	*which, that*

- **que** changes to **qu'** before a vowel → 2/4
- You cannot omit the object relative pronoun in French as you can in English → 2/4

After a preposition:
- When referring to people, use **qui** → 5
  EXCEPTIONS: after **parmi** *among* and **entre** *between* use **lesquels/lesquelles** (see below) → 6
- When referring to things, use forms of **lequel:**

	MASCULINE	FEMININE	
SING.	**lequel**	**laquelle**	*which*
PLUR.	**lesquels**	**lesquelles**	*which*

The pronoun agrees in number and gender with the noun → 7

- After the prepositions **à** and **de, lequel** and **lesquel(le)s** contract as follows:
  à + lequel → auquel
  à + lesquels → auxquels → 8
  à + lesquelles → auxquelles

  de + lequel → duquel
  de + lesquels → desquels → 9
  de + lesquelles → desquelles

Examples

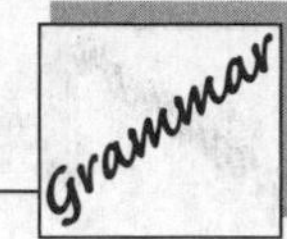

1 **Mon frère, qui a vingt ans, est à l'université**
My brother, who's twenty, is at university

2 **Les amis que je vois le plus sont ...**
The friends (that) I see most are ...
Lucienne, qu'il connaît depuis longtemps, est ...
Lucienne, whom he has known for a long time, is ...

3 **Il y a un escalier qui mène au toit**
There's a staircase which leads to the roof

4 **La maison que nous avons achetée a ...**
The house (which) we've bought has ...
Voici le cadeau qu'elle m'a envoyé
This is the present (that) she sent me

5 **la personne à qui il parle**
the person he's talking to
la personne avec qui je voyage
the person with whom I travel
les enfants pour qui je l'ai acheté
the children for whom I bought it

6 **Il y avait des jeunes, parmi lesquels Robert**
There were some young people, Robert among them
les filles entre lesquelles j'étais assis
the girls between whom I was sitting

7 **le torchon avec lequel il l'essuie**
the cloth he's wiping it with
la table sur laquelle je l'ai mis
the table on which I put it
les moyens par lesquels il l'accomplit
the means by which he achieves it
les pièces pour lesquelles elle est connue
the plays for which she is famous

8 **le magasin auquel il livre ces marchandises**
the shop to which he delivers these goods

9 **les injustices desquelles il se plaint**
the injustices he's complaining about

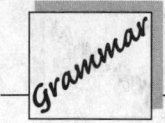

❒ Relative Pronouns (Continued)

quoi *which, what*

- When the relative pronoun does not refer to a specific noun, **quoi** is used after a preposition → 1

dont *whose, of whom, of which*

- **dont** often (but not always) replaces **de qui**, **duquel**, **de laquelle**, and **desquel(le)s** → 2
- It cannot replace **de qui**, **duquel** etc in the construction preposition + noun + **de qui/duquel** → 3

Examples

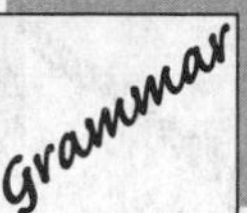

1 **C'est en quoi vous vous trompez**
That's where you're wrong
À quoi, j'ai répondu '...'
To which I replied, '...'

2 **la femme dont (= de qui) la voiture est garée en face**
the woman whose car is parked opposite
un prix dont (= de qui) je suis fier
an award I am proud of
un ami dont (= de qui) je connais le frère
a friend whose brother I know
les enfants dont (= de qui) vous vous occupez
the children you look after
le film dont (= duquel) il a parlé
the film of which he spoke
la fenêtre dont (= de laquelle) les rideaux sont tirés
the window whose curtains are drawn
des livres dont (= desquels) j'ai oublié les titres
books whose titles I've forgotten
les maladies dont (= desquelles) il souffre
the illnesses he suffers from

3 **une personne sur l'aide de qui on peut compter**
a person whose help one can rely on
les enfants aux parents de qui j'écris
the children to whose parents I'm writing
la maison dans le jardin de laquelle il y a ...
the house in whose garden there is ...

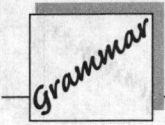

❒ Relative Pronouns (Continued)

ce qui, ce que *that which, what*

These are used when the relative pronoun does not refer to a specific noun, and they are often translated as *what* (literally: *that which*)

ce qui is used as the subject → [1]
ce que* is used as the direct object → [2]

***que** changes to **qu'** before a vowel → [2]

◆ Note the construction

tout ce qui }
tout ce que } *everything/all that* → [3]

◆ **de + ce que → ce dont** → [4]

◆ preposition + **ce que** → **ce** + preposition + **quoi** → [5]

◆ When **ce qui**, **ce que** etc, refers to a previous CLAUSE the translation is *which* → [6]

Examples

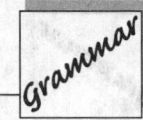

1 **Ce qui m'intéresse ne l'intéresse pas forcément**
What interests me doesn't necessarily interest him
Je n'ai pas vu ce qui s'est passé
I didn't see what happened

2 **Ce que j'aime c'est la musique classique**
What I like is classical music
Montrez-moi ce qu'il vous a donné
Show me what he gave you

3 **Tout ce qui reste c'est ...**
All that's left is ...
Donnez-moi tout ce que vous avez
Give me everything you have

4 **Il risque de perdre ce dont il est si fier**
He risks losing what he's so proud of
Voilà ce dont il s'agit
That's what it's about

5 **Ce n'est pas ce à quoi je m'attendais**
It's not what I was expecting
Ce à quoi je m'intéresse particulièrement c'est ...
What I'm particularly interested in is ...

6 **Il est d'accord, ce qui m'étonne**
He agrees, which surprises me
Il a dit qu'elle ne venait pas, ce que nous savions déjà
He said she wasn't coming, which we already knew

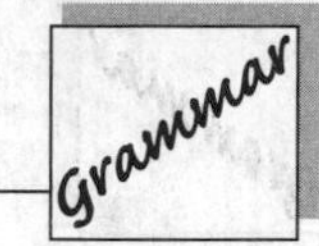

❒ Interrogative Pronouns

qui?	*who; whom?*
que?	*what?*
quoi?	*what?*

These pronouns are used in direct questions.
The form of the pronoun depends on:
- whether it refers to people or to things
- whether it is the subject or object of the verb, or if it comes after a preposition

Qui and **que** have longer forms, as shown in the tables below.

◆ Referring to people:

SUBJECT	**qui?** **qui est-ce qui?** *who?*	→ [1]
OBJECT	**qui?** **qui est-ce que*?** *who(m)?*	→ [2]
AFTER PREPOSITIONS	**qui?** *who(m)?*	→ [3]

◆ Referring to things:

SUBJECT	**qu'est-ce qui?** *what?*	→ [4]
OBJECT	**que*?** **qu'est-ce que*?** *what?*	→ [5]
AFTER PREPOSITIONS	**quoi?** *what?*	→ [6]

***que** changes to **qu'** before a vowel → [2], [5]

Examples

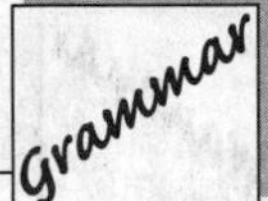

1 **Qui vient?**
Qui est-ce qui vient?
Who's coming?

2 **Qui vois-tu?**
Qui est-ce que tu vois?
Who(m) can you see?
Qui a-t-elle rencontré?
Qui est-ce qu'elle a rencontré?
Who(m) did she meet?

3 **De qui parle-t-il?**
Who's he talking about?
Pour qui est ce livre?
Who's this book for?
À qui avez-vous écrit?
To whom did you write?

4 **Qu'est-ce qui se passe?**
What's happening?
Qu'est-ce qui a vexé Paul?
What upset Paul?

5 **Que faites-vous?**
Qu'est-ce que vous faites?
What are you doing?
Qu'a-t-il dit?
Qu'est-ce qu'il a dit?
What did he say?

6 **À quoi cela sert-il?**
What's that used for?
De quoi a-t-on parlé?
What was the discussion about?
Sur quoi vous basez-vous?
What do you base it on?

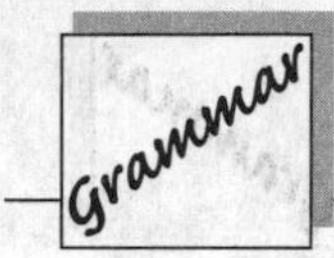

❒ Interrogative Pronouns (Continued)

qui	*who; whom*
ce qui	*what*
ce que	*what*
quoi	*what*

These pronouns are used in indirect questions.
The form of the pronoun depends on:

- whether it refers to people or to things
- whether it is the subject or object of the verb, or if it comes after a preposition

◆ Referring to people: use **qui** in all instances → 1

◆ Referring to things:

SUBJECT	**ce qui** *what*	→ 2
OBJECT	**ce que*** *what*	→ 3
AFTER PREPOSITIONS	**quoi** *what*	→ 4

*__que__ changes to **qu'** before a vowel → 3

Examples

1 **Demande-lui qui est venu**
Ask him who came
Je me demande qui ils ont vu
I wonder who they saw
Dites-moi qui vous préférez
Tell me who you prefer
Elle ne sait pas à qui s'adresser
She doesn't know who to apply to
Demandez-leur pour qui elles travaillent
Ask them who they work for

2 **Il se demande ce qui se passe**
He's wondering what's happening
Je ne sais pas ce qui vous fait croire que ...
I don't know what makes you think that ...

3 **Raconte-nous ce que tu as fait**
Tell us what you did
Je me demande ce qu'elle pense
I wonder what she's thinking

4 **On ne sait pas de quoi vivent ces animaux**
We don't know what these animals live on
Je vais lui demander à quoi il fait allusion
I'm going to ask him what he's hinting at

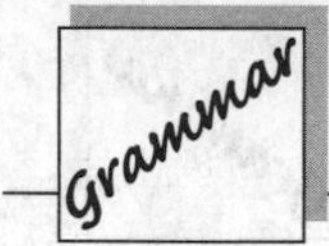

❐ Interrogative Pronouns (Continued)

lequel?, laquelle?; lesquels?, lesquelles?

	MASCULINE	FEMININE	
SING.	**lequel?**	**laquelle?**	*which (one)?*
PLUR.	**lesquels?**	**lesquelles?**	*which (ones)?*

- The pronoun agrees in number and gender with the noun it refers to → 1
- The same forms are used in indirect questions → 2
- After the prepositions **à** and **de**, **lequel** and **lesquel(le)s** contract as follows:

à + lequel? → auquel?
à + lesquels? → auxquels?
à + lesquelles? → auxquelles?

de + lequel? → duquel?
de + lesquels? → desquels?
de + lesquelles? → desquelles?

1 **J'ai choisi un livre. – Lequel?**
I've chosen a book. – Which one?
Laquelle de ces valises est la vôtre?
Which of these cases is yours?
Amenez quelques amis. – Lesquels?
Bring some friends. – Which ones?
Lesquelles de vos sœurs sont mariées?
Which of your sisters are married?

2 **Je me demande laquelle des maisons est la leur**
I wonder which is their house
Dites-moi lesquels d'entre eux étaient là
Tell me which of them were there

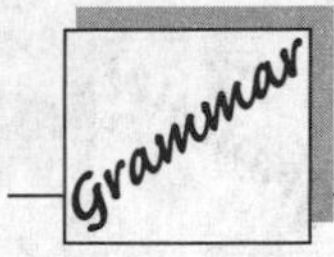

❒ Possessive Pronouns

SINGULAR		
MASCULINE	FEMININE	
le mien	**la mienne**	*mine*
le tien	**la tienne**	*yours*
le sien	**la sienne**	*his; hers; its*
le nôtre	**la nôtre**	*ours*
le vôtre	**la vôtre**	*yours*
le leur	**la leur**	*theirs*

PLURAL		
MASCULINE	FEMININE	
les miens	**les miennes**	*mine*
les tiens	**les tiennes**	*yours*
les siens	**les siennes**	*his; hers; its*
les nôtres	**les nôtres**	*ours*
les vôtres	**les vôtres**	*yours*
les leurs	**les leurs**	*theirs*

- The pronoun agrees in number and gender with the noun it replaces, NOT WITH THE OWNER → [1]

- Alternative translations are *my own, your own* etc; **le sien, la sienne** etc may also mean *one's own* → [2]

- After the prepositions **à** and **de** the articles **le** and **les** are contracted in the normal way (see p 140):

  à + le mien → au mien
  à + les miens → aux miens → [3]
  à + les miennes → aux miennes

  de + le mien → du mien
  de + les miens → des miens → [4]
  de + les miennes → des miennes

Examples

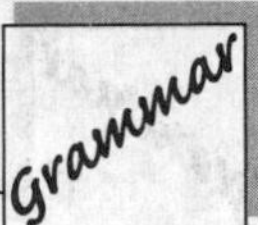

1 **Demandez à Carole si ce stylo est le sien**
Ask Carole if this pen is hers
Quelle équipe a gagné – la leur ou la nôtre?
Which team won – theirs or ours?
Mon stylo marche mieux que le tien
My pen writes better than yours
Richard a pris mes affaires pour les siennes
Richard mistook my belongings for his
Si tu n'as pas de disques, emprunte les miens
If you don't have any records, borrow mine
Nos maisons sont moins grandes que les vôtres
Our houses are smaller than yours

2 **Est-ce que leur entreprise est aussi grande que la vôtre?**
Is their company as big as your own?
Leurs prix sont moins élevés que les nôtres
Their prices are lower than our own
Le bonheur des autres importe plus que le sien
Other people's happiness matters more than one's own

3 **Pourquoi préfères-tu ce manteau au mien?**
Why do you prefer this coat to mine?
Quelles maisons ressemblent aux leurs?
Which houses resemble theirs?

4 **Leur car est garé**
Their coach is parked
Vos livres sont au-dessus des miens
Your books are on top of mine

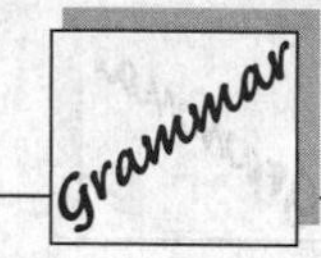

❒ Demonstrative Pronouns

celui, celle; ceux, celles

	MASCULINE	FEMININE	
SING.	**celui**	**celle**	*the one*
PLUR.	**ceux**	**celles**	*the ones*

- The pronoun agrees in number and gender with the noun it replaces → 1
- Uses:

  – preceding a relative pronoun, meaning *the one(s) who/which* → 1
  – preceding the preposition **de**, meaning *the one(s) belonging to, the one(s) of* → 2
  – with **-ci** and **-là**, for emphasis or to distinguish between two things:

	MASCULINE	FEMININE		
SING.	**celui-ci**	**celle-ci**	*this (one)*	→ 3
PLUR.	**ceux-ci**	**celles-ci**	*these (ones)*	
	MASCULINE	FEMININE		
SING.	**celui-là**	**celle-là**	*that(one)*	→ 3
PLUR.	**ceux-là**	**celles-là**	*those (ones)*	

  – an additional meaning of **celui-ci/celui-là** etc is *the former/the latter.*

Examples

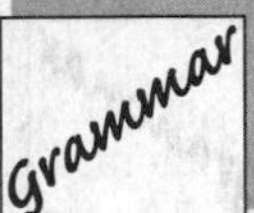

1 **Lequel?-Celui qui parle à Anne**
Which man? – The one who's talking to Anne
Quelle robe désirez-vous? – Celle qui est en vitrine
Which dress do you want? – The one which is in the window
Est-ce que ces livres sont ceux qu'il t'a donnés?
Are these the books that he gave you?
Quelles filles? – Celles que nous avons vues hier
Which girls? – The ones we saw yesterday
Cet article n'est pas celui dont vous m'avez parlé
This article isn't the one you spoke to me about

2 **Ce jardin est plus grand que celui de mes parents**
This garden is bigger than my parents' (garden)
Est-ce que ta fille est plus âgée que celle de Gabrielle?
Is your daughter older than Gabrielle's (daughter)?
Je préfère les enfants de Paul à ceux de Roger
I prefer Paul's children to Roger's (children)
Comparez vos réponses à celles de votre voisin
Compare your answers with your neighbour's (answers)
les montagnes d'Écosse et celles du pays de Galles
the mountains of Scotland and those of Wales

3 **Quel tailleur préférez-vous: celui-ci ou celui-là?**
Which suit do you prefer: this one or that one?
Cette chemise a deux poches mais celle-la n'en a pas
This shirt has two pockets but that one has none
Quels œufs choisirais-tu: ceux-ci ou ceux-là?
Which eggs would you choose: these (ones) or those (ones)?
De toutes mes jupes, celle-ci me va le mieux
Of all my skirts, this one fits me best

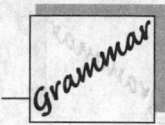

❐ Demonstrative Pronouns (Continued)

ce (c') *it, that*

- Usually used with **être**, in the expressions **c'est**, **c'était**, **ce sont** etc → 1
- Note the spelling **ç** when followed by the letter **a** → 2
- Uses:
  – to identify a person or object → 3
  – for emphasis → 4
  – as a neuter pronoun, referring to a statement, idea etc → 5

ce qui, ce que, ce dont etc: see Relative Pronouns (p 184), Interrogative Pronouns (p 188).

cela, ça *it, that*

- **cela** and **ça** are used as 'neuter' pronouns, referring to a statement, an idea, an object → 6
- In everyday spoken language **ça** is used in preference to **cela**

ceci *this* → 7

- **ceci** is not used as often as 'this' in English; **cela**, **ça** are often used where we use 'this'.

Examples

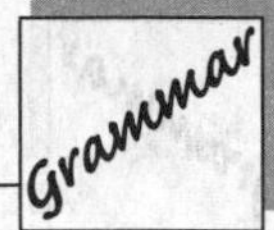

1 **C'est …**
It's/That's …

C'était moi
It was me

2 **Ç'a été la cause de …**
it has been cause of…

3 **Qui est-ce?**
Who is it?; Who's this/that?; Who's he/she?

C'est lui/mon frère/nous
It's/That's him/my brother/us

Ce sont eux
It's them

C'est une infirmière*
She's a nurse

Ce sont des professeurs*
They're teachers

Qu'est-ce que c'est?
What's this/that?

Qu'est-ce que c'est que ça?
What's that?

C'est une agrafeuse
it's a stapler

Ce sont des trombones
They're paper clips

4 **C'est moi qui ai téléphoné**
it was me who phoned
Ce sont les enfants qui importent le plus
It's the children who matter most

5 **C'est très intéressant**
That's/It's very interesting
Ce serait dangereux
That/It would be dangerous

6 **Ça ne fait rien**
It doesn't matter
À quoi bon faire ça?
What's the use of doing that?
Cela ne compte pas
That doesn't count
Cela demande du temps
It/That takes time

7 **À qui est ceci?**
Whose is this?

Ouvrez-le comme ceci
Open it like this

*See pp 146 and 147 for the use of the article when stating a person's profession

❒ Adverbs

Formation

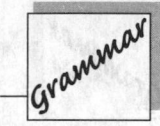

- Most adverbs are formed by adding **-ment** to the feminine form of the adjective → [1]
- **-ment** is added to the *masculine* form when the masculine form ends in **-é**, **-i** or **-u** → [2]
  EXCEPTION: **gai** → [3]
  Occasionally the **u** changes to **û** before **-ment** is added → [4]
- If the adjective ends in **-ant** or **-ent**, the adverb ends in **-amment** or **-emment** → [5]
  EXCEPTIONS: **lent**, **présent** → [6]

Irregular Adverbs

ADJECTIVE		ADVERB		
aveugle	*blind*	**aveuglément**	blindly	
bon	*good*	**bien**	well	→ [7]
bref	*brief*	**brièvement**	briefly	
énorme	*enormous*	**énormément**	enormously	
exprès	*express*	**expressément**	expressly	→ [8]
gentil	*kind*	**gentiment**	kindly	
mauvais	*bad*	**mal**	badly	→ [9]
meilleur	*better*	**mieux**	better	
pire	*worse*	**pis**	worse	
précis	*precise*	**précisément**	precisely	
profond	*deep*	**profondément**	deeply	→ [10]
traître	*treacherous*	**traîtreusement**	treacherously	

Adjectives used as adverbs

Certain adjectives are used adverbially. These include: **bas, bon, cher, clair, court, doux, droit, dur, faux, ferme, fort, haut, mauvais** and **net** → [11]

Examples

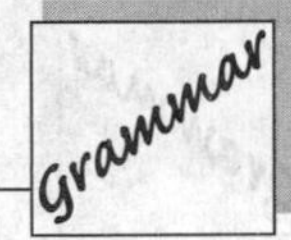

1	MASC./FEM. ADJECTIVE	ADVERB
	heureux/heureuse fortunate	**heureusement** fortunately
	franc/franche frank	**franchement** frankly
	extrême/extrême extreme	**extrêmement** extremely
2	MASC. ADJECTIVE	ADVERB
	désespéré desperate	**désespérément** desperately
	vrai true	**vraiment** truly
	résolu resolute	**résolument** resolutely
3	**gai** cheerful	**gaiement** OR **gaîment** cheerfully
4	**continu** continuous	**continûment** continuously
5	**constant** constant	**constamment** constantly
	courant fluent	**couramment** fluently
	évident obvious	**évidemment** obviously
	fréquent frequent	**fréquemment** frequently
6	**lent** slow	**lentement** slowly
	présent present	**présentement** presently

7 **Elle travaille bien**
She works well

8 **Il a expressément défendu qu'on parte**
He has expressly forbidden us to leave

9 **Un emploi mal payé**
A badly paid job

10 **J'ai été profondément ému**
I was deeply moved

11 **parler bas/haut**
to speak softly/loudly
coûter cher
to be expensive
voir clair
to see clearly
travailler dur
to work hard
chanter faux
to sing off key
sentir bon/mauvais
to smell nice/horrible

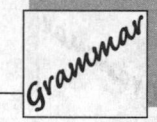

❒ Position of Adverbs

- When the adverb accompanies a verb in a simple tense, it generally follows the verb → [1]
- When the adverb accompanies a verb in a compound tense, it generally comes between the auxiliary verb and the past participle → [2]
  Some adverbs, however, follow the past participle → [3]
- When the adverb accompanies an adjective or another adverb it generally precedes the adjective/adverb → [4]

❒ Comparatives of Adverbs

These are formed using the following constructions:

plus … (que)	*more … (than)*	→ [5]
moins … (que)	*less … (than)*	→ [6]
aussi … que	*as … as*	→ [7]
si … que*	*as … as*	→ [8]

*used mainly after a negative

❒ Superlatives of Adverbs

These are formed using the following constructions:

le plus … (que)	*the most … (that)* → [9]
le moins … (que)	*the least … (that)* → [10]

Adverbs with irregular comparatives/superlatives

ADVERB	COMPARATIVE	SUPERLATIVE
beaucoup *a lot*	**plus** *more*	**le plus** *(the) most*
bien *well*	**mieux** *better*	**le mieux** *(the) best*
mal *badly*	**pis** OR **plus mal** *worse*	**le pis** OR **le plus mal** *(the) worst*
peu *little*	**moins** *less*	**le moins** *(the) least*

Examples

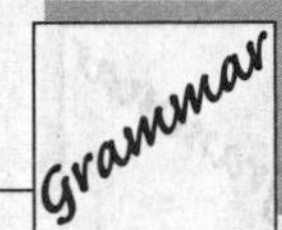

1 **Il dort encore**
He's still asleep

Je pense souvent à toi
I often think about you

2 **Ils sont déjà partis**
They've already gone

J'ai toujours cru que ...
I've always thought that ...

J'ai presque fini
I'm almost finished

Il a trop mangé
He's eaten too much

3 **On les a vus partout**
We saw them everywhere

Elle est revenue hier
She came back yesterday

4 **un très beau chemisier**
a very nice blouse

une femme bien habillée
a well-dressed woman

beaucoup plus vite
much faster

peu souvent
not very often

5 **plus vite**
more quickly

plus régulièrement
more regularly

Elle chante plus fort que moi
She sings louder than I do

6 **moins facilement**
less easily

moins souvent
less often

Nous nous voyons moins fréquemment qu'auparavant
We see each other less frequently than before

7 **Faites-le aussi vite que possible**
Do it as quickly as possible

Il en sait aussi long que nous
He knows as much about it as we do

8 **Ce n'est pas si loin que je pensais**
It's not as far as I thought

9 **Marianne court le plus vite**
Marianne runs fastest

Le plus tôt que je puisse venir c'est samedi
The earliest that I can come is Saturday

10 **C'est l'auteur que je connais le moins bien**
It's the writer I'm least familiar with

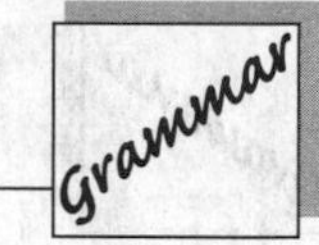

❒ Common adverbs and their usage

assez	*enough; quite*	→ 1 See also below
aussi	*also, too; as*	→ 2
autant	*as much*	→ 3 See also below
beaucoup	*a lot; much*	→ 4 See also below
bien	*well; very* *very much; 'indeed'*	→ 5 See also below
combien	*how much; how many*	→ 6 See also below
comme	*how; what*	→ 7
déjà	*already; before*	→ 8
encore	*still; yet* *more; even*	→ 9
moins	*less*	→ 10 See also below
peu	*little, not much; not very*	→ 11 See also below
plus	*more*	→ 12 See also below
si	*so; such*	→ 13
tant	*so much*	→ 14 See also below
toujours	*always; still*	→ 15
trop	*too much; too*	→ 16 See also below

◆ **assez, autant, beaucoup, combien** etc are used in the construction adverb + **de** + noun with the following meanings:

assez de	*enough*	→ 17
autant de	*as much; as many* *so much; so many*	
beaucoup de	*a lot of*	
combien de	*how much; how many*	
moins de	*less; fewer*	→ 17
peu de	*little, not much; few, not many*	
plus de	*more*	
tant de	*so much; so many*	
trop de	*too much; too many*	

◆ **bien** can be followed by a partitive article (see p 144) plus a noun to mean *a lot of; a good many* → 18

Examples

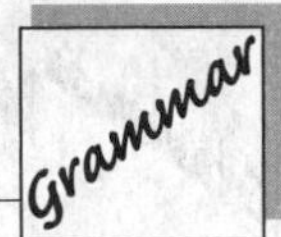

1	**Avez-vous assez chaud?** Are you warm enough?	**Il est assez tard** It's quite late
2	**Je préfère ça aussi** I prefer it too	**Elle est aussi grande que moi** She is as tall as I am
3	**Je voyage autant que lui**	I travel as much as him
4	**Tu lis beaucoup?** Do you read a lot?	**C'est beaucoup plus loin?** Is it much further?
5	**Bien joué!** Well played!	**Je suis bien content que ...** I'm very pleased that ...
	Il s'est bien amusé He enjoyed himself very much	**Je l'ai bien fait** I DID do it
6	**Combien coûte ce livre?** How much is this book?	**Vous êtes combien?** How many of you are there?
7	**Comme tu es jolie!** How pretty you look!	**Comme il fait beau!** What lovely weather!
8	**Je l'ai déjà fait** I've already done it	**Êtes-vous déjà allé en France?** Have you been to France before?
9	**J'en ai encore deux** I've still got two	**Elle n'est pas encore là** She isn't there yet
	Encore du café, Alain? More coffee, Alan?	**Encore mieux!** Even better!
10	**Travaillez moins** Work less	**Je suis moins étonné que toi** I'm less surprised than you are
11	**Elle mange peu** She doesn't eat very much	**C'est peu important** It's not very important
12	**Il se détend plus** He relaxes more	**Elle est plus timide que Sophie** She is shyer than Sophie
13	**Simon est si charmant** Simon is so charming	**une si belle vue** such a lovely view
14	**Elle l'aime tant**	She loves him so much
15	**Il dit toujours ça!** He always says that!	**Tu le vois toujours?** Do you still see him?
16	**J'ai trop mangé** I've eaten too much	**C'est trop cher** It's too expensive
17	**assez d'argent/de livres** enough money/books	**moins de temps/d'amis** less time/fewer friends
18	**bien du mal/des gens**	a lot of harm/a good many people

On the following pages you will find some of the most frequent uses of prepositions in French. Particular attention is paid to cases where usage differs markedly from English. It is often difficult to give an English equivalent for French prepositions, since usage *does* vary so much between the two languages.

In the list below, the broad meaning of the preposition is given on the left, with examples of usage following.

Prepositions are dealt with in alphabetical order, except **à, de** and **en** which are shown first.

à

at	**lancer qch à qn**	*to throw sth at sb*
	il habite à St. Pierre	*he lives at St. Pierre*
	à 2 euros (la) pièce	*(at) 2 euros each*
	à 100 km à l'heure	*at 100 km per hour*
in	**à la campagne**	*in the country*
	à Londres	*in London*
	au lit	*in bed* (also *to bed*)
	un livre à la main	*with a book in his/her hand*
on	**un tableau au mur**	*a picture on the wall*
to	**aller au cinéma**	*to go to the cinema*
	donner qch à qn	*to give sth to sb*
	le premier/dernier à faire	*the first/last to do*
	demander qch à qn	*to ask sb sth*
from	**arracher qch à qn**	*to snatch sth from sb*
	acheter qch à qn	*to buy sth from sb*
	cacher qch à qn	*to hide sth from sb*
	emprunter qch à qn	*to borrow sth from sb*
	prendre qch à qn	*to take sth from sb*
	voler qch à qn	*to steal sth from sb*

descriptive	**la femme au chapeau vert**	*the woman with the green hat*
	un garçon aux yeux bleus	*a boy with blue eyes*
manner, means	**à l'anglaise**	*in the English manner*
	fait à la main	*handmade*
	à bicyclette/cheval	*by bicycle/on horseback* (BUT note other forms of transport used with **en** and **par**)
	à pied	*on foot*
	chauffer au gaz	*to heat with/by gas*
	à pas lents	*with slow steps*
	cuisiner au beurre	*to cook with butter*
time, date: *at, in*	**à minuit**	*at midnight*
	à trois heures cinq	*at five past three*
	au 20ème siècle	*in the 20th century*
	à Noël/Pâques	*at Christmas/Easter*
distance	**à 6 km d'ici**	*(at a distance of) 6 km from here*
	à deux pas de chez moi	*just a step from my place*
destined for	**une tasse à thé**	*a teacup* (compare **une tasse de thé**)
	un service à café	*a coffee service*
after certain adjectives	**son écriture est difficile à lire**	*his writing is difficult to read* (compare the usage with **de**, p 206)
	prêt à tout	*ready for anything*
after certain verbs	see p 64	

de

from	**venir de Londres**	*to come from London*
	du matin au soir	*from morning till night*
	du 21 juin au 5 juillet	*from 21st June till 5th July*
	de 10 à 15	*from 10 to 15*
belonging to, *of*	**un ami de la famille**	*a family friend*
	les vents d'automne	*the autumn winds*
contents, composition, material	**une boîte d'allumettes**	*a box of matches*
	une tasse de thé	*a cup of tea* (compare **une tasse à thé**)
	une robe de soie	*a silk dress*
manner	**d'une façon irrégulière**	*in an irregular way*
	d'un coup de couteau	*with the blow of a knife*
quality	**la société de consommation**	*the consumer society*
	des objets de valeur	*valuable items*
comparative + a number	**il y avait plus/moins de cent personnes**	*there were more/fewer than a hundred people*
after superlatives: *in*	**la plus/moins belle ville du monde**	*the most/least beautiful city in the world*
after certain adjectives	**surpris de voir**	*surprised to see*
	il est difficile d'y accéder	*access is difficult* (compare the usage with **à**, p 205)
after certain verbs	see p 64	

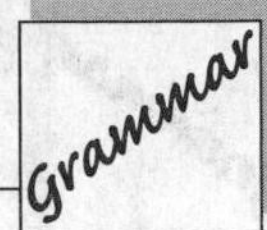

en

place: *to, in, on*	**en ville**	*in/to town*
	en pleine mer	*on the open sea*
	en France	*in/to France* (note that masculine countries use **à**)
dates, months: *in*	**en 1923**	*in 1923*
	en janvier	*in January*
transport	**en voiture**	*by car*
	en avion	*by plane* (but note usage of **à** and **par** in other expressions)
language	**en français**	*in French*
duration	**je le ferai en trois jours**	*I'll do it in three days* (i.e. *I'll take 3 days to do it:* compare **dans trois jours**)
material	**un bracelet en or**	*a bracelet made of gold* (note that the use of **en** stresses the material more than the use of **de**)
	consister en	*to consist of*
in the manner of, like a	**parler en vrai connaisseur**	*to speak like a real connoisseur*
	déguisé en cowboy	*dressed up as a cowboy*
+ present participle	**il l'a vu en passant devant la porte**	*he saw it as he came past the door*

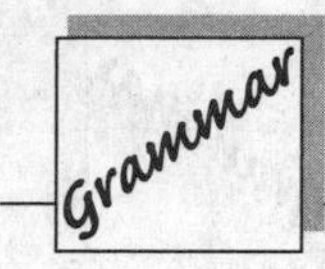

avant		
before	**il est arrivé avant toi**	*he arrived before you*
+ infinitive (add **de**)	**je vais finir ça avant de manger**	*I'm going to finish this before eating*
preference	**la santé avant tout**	*health above all things*
chez		
at the home of	**chez lui/moi** **être chez soi** **venez chez nous**	*at his/my house* *to be at home* *come round to our place*
at/to a shop	**chez le boucher**	*at/to the butcher's*
in a person, *among* a group of people or animals	**ce que je n'aime pas chez lui c'est son ...** **chez les fourmis**	*what I don't like in him is his ...* *among ants*
dans		
position	**dans une boîte**	*in(to) a box*
circumstance	**dans son enfance**	*in his childhood*
future time	**dans trois jours**	*in three days' time* (compare **en trois jours**, p 207)
depuis		
since: time	**depuis mardi**	*since Tuesday*
place	**il pleut depuis Paris**	*it's been raining since Paris*
for	**il habite cette maison depuis 3 ans**	*he's been living in this house for 3 years* (NOTE TENSE)

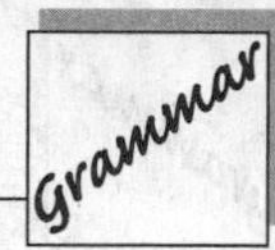

dès

past time	**dès mon enfance**	*since my childhood*
future time	**je le ferai dès mon retour**	*I'll do it as soon as I get back*

entre

between	**entre 8 et 10**	*between 8 and 10*
among	**Jean et Pierre, entre autres**	*Jean and Pierre, among others*
reciprocal	**s'aider entre eux**	*to help each other (out)*

d'entre

of, among	**trois d'entre eux**	*three of them*

par

agent of passive: *by*	**renversé par une voiture**	*knocked down by a car*
	tué par la foudre	*killed by lightning*
weather conditions	**par un beau jour d'été**	*on a lovely summer's day*
by (means of)	**par un couloir/sentier**	*by a corridor/path*
	par le train	*by train* (but see also **à** and **en**)
	par l'intermédiaire de M. Duval	*through Mr Duval*
distribution	**deux par deux**	*two by two*
	par groupes de dix	*in groups of ten*
	deux fois par jour	*twice a day*

pour		
for	**c'est pour vous**	*it's for you*
	c'est pour demain	*it's for tomorrow*
	une chambre pour 2 nuits	*a room for 2 nights*
	pour un enfant, il se débrouille bien	*for a child he manages very well*
	il part pour l'Espagne	*he's leaving for Spain*
	il l'a fait pour vous	*he did it for you*
	il lui a donné 5 euros pour ce livre	*he gave him 5 euros for this book*
	je ne suis pas pour cette idée	*I'm not for that idea*
	pour qui me prends-tu?	*who do you take me for?*
	il passe pour un idiot	*he's taken for a fool*
+ infinitive: *(in order) to*	**elle se pencha pour le ramasser**	*she bent down to pick it up*
	c'est trop fragile pour servir de siège	*it's too fragile to be used as a seat*
to(wards)	**être bon/gentil pour qn**	*to be kind to sb*
with prices, time	**pour 30 euros d'essence**	*30 euros' worth of petrol*
	j'en ai encore pour une heure	*I'll be another hour (at it) yet*
sans		
without	**sans eau**	*without water*
	sans ma femme	*without my wife*
+ infinitive	**sans compter les autres**	*without counting the others*

sauf

except (for)	**tous sauf lui**	*all except him*
	sauf quand il pleut	*except when it's raining*
barring	**sauf imprévu**	*barring the unexpected*
	sauf avis contraire	*unless you hear to the contrary*

sur

on	**sur le siège**	*on the seat*
	sur l'armoire	*on top of the wardrobe*
	sur le mur	*on (top of) the wall* (if the meaning is *hanging on the wall* use **à**, p 204)
	sur votre gauche	*on your left*
	être sur le point de faire	*to be on the point of doing*
on (to)	**mettez-le sur la table**	*put it on the table*
proportion: *out of, by*	**8 sur 10**	*8 out of 10*
	un automobiliste sur 5	*one motorist in 5*
	la pièce fait 2 mètres sur 3	*the room measures 2 metres by 3*

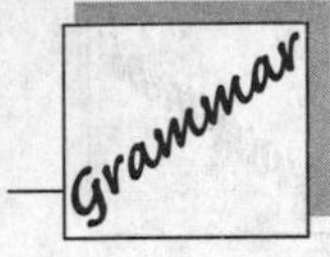

❐ Conjunctions

There are conjunctions which introduce a main clause, such as **et** *and*, **mais** *but*, **si** *if*, **ou** *or* etc, and those which introduce subordinate clauses like **parce que** *because*, **pendant que** *while*, **après que** *after* etc. They are all used in much the same way as in English, but the following points are of note:

- Some conjunctions in French require a following subjunctive, see p 58
- Some conjunctions are 'split' in French like *both … and, either … or* in English:

et … et	*both … and*	→ 1
ni … ni … ne	*neither … nor*	→ 2
ou (bien) … ou (bien)	*either … or (else)*	→ 3
soit … soit	*either … or*	→ 4

- **si + il(s) → s'il(s)** → 5
- **que**
  – meaning *that* → 6
  – replacing another conjunction → 7
  – replacing **si**, see p 62
  – in comparisons, meaning *as, than* → 8
  – followed by the subjunctive, see p 62
- **aussi** *so, therefore:* the subject and verb are inverted if the subject is a pronoun → 9

Examples

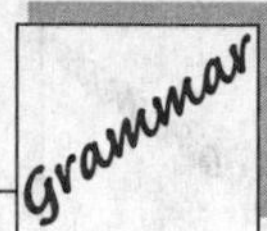

1 **Ces fleurs poussent et en été et en hiver**
These flowers grow in both summer and winter

2 **Ni lui ni elle ne sont venus**
Neither he nor she came
Ils n'ont ni argent ni nourriture
They have neither money nor food

3 **Elle doit être ou naïve ou stupide**
She must be either naïve or stupid
Ou bien il m'évite ou bien il ne me reconnaît pas
Either he's avoiding me or else he doesn't recognize me

4 **Il faut choisir soit l'un soit l'autre**
You have to choose either one or the other

5 **Je ne sais pas s'il vient/s'ils viennent**
I don't know if he's coming/if they're coming
Dis-moi s'il y a des erreurs
Tell me if there are any mistakes
Votre passeport, s'il vous plaît
Your passport, please

6 **Il dit qu'il t'a vu**
He says (that) he saw you
Est-ce qu'elle sait que vous êtes là?
Does she know that you're here?

7 **Quand tu seras plus grand et que tu auras une maison à toi, ...**
When you're older and you have a house of your own, ...
Comme il pleuvait et que je n'avais pas de parapluie, ...
As it was raining and I didn't have an umbrella, ...

8 **Ils n'y vont pas aussi souvent que nous**
They don't go there as often as we do
Il les aime plus que jamais
He likes them more than ever
L'argent est moins lourd que le plomb
Silver is lighter than lead

9 **Ceux-ci sont plus rares, aussi coûtent-ils cher**
These ones are rarer, so they're expensive

❒ Word Order

Word order in French is largely the same as in English, except for the following. Most of these have already been dealt with under the appropriate part of speech, but are summarized here along with other instances not covered elsewhere.

- Object pronouns nearly always come before the verb → [1]
  For details, see pp 166 to 170
- Certain adjectives come after the noun → [2]
  For details, see p 162
- Adverbs accompanying a verb in a simple tense usually follow the verb → [3]
  For details, see p 200
- After **aussi** *so, therefore*, **à peine** *hardly*, **peut-être** *perhaps*, the verb and subject are inverted → [4]
- After the relative pronoun **dont** *whose* → [5]
  For details, see p 182
- In exclamations, **que** and **comme** do not affect the normal word order → [6]
- Following direct speech:
  – the *verb* + *subject* order is inverted to become *subject* + *verb* → [7]
  – with a pronoun subject, the verb and pronoun are linked by a hyphen → [8]
  – when the verb ends in a vowel in the 3rd person singular, **-t-** is inserted between the pronoun and the verb → [9]

For word order in negative sentences, see p 216.
For word order in interrogative sentences, see pp 220 and 222.

Examples

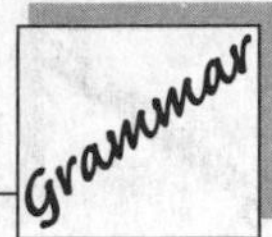

1 **Je les vois!**
I can see them!

Il me l'a donné
He gave it to me

2 **une ville française**
a French town

du vin rouge
some red wine

3 **Il pleut encore**
It's still raining

Elle m'aide quelquefois
She sometimes helps me

4 **Il vit tout seul, aussi fait-il ce qu'il veut**
He lives alone, so he does what he likes
À peine la pendule avait-elle sonné trois heures que ...
Hardly had the clock struck three when ...
Peut-être avez-vous raison
Perhaps you're right

5 Compare: **un homme dont je connais la fille**
a man whose daughter I know
and: **un homme dont la fille me connaît**
a man whose daughter knows me

If the person (or object) 'owned' is the *object* of the verb, the order is:
dont + verb + noun (1st sentence)
If the person (or object) 'owned' is the *subject* of the verb, the order is:
dont + noun + verb (2nd sentence)
Note also: **l'homme dont elle est la fille**
the man whose daughter she is

6 **Qu'il fait chaud!**
How warm it is!

Que je suis content de vous voir!
How pleased I am to see you!

Comme c'est cher
How expensive it is!

Que tes voisins sont gentils!
How kind your neighbours are!

7 **'Je pense que oui' a dit Luc**
' I think so', said Luke

'Ça ne fait rien' répondit Jean
'It doesn't matter', John replied

8 **'Quelle horreur!' me suis-je exclamé**
'How awful!' I exclaimed

9 **'Pourquoi pas?' a-t-elle demandé**
'Why not?' she asked
'Si c'est vrai', continua-t-il '...'
'If it's true', he went on '...'

❐ Negatives

ne ... pas	*not*
ne ... point (literary)	*not*
ne ... rien	*nothing*
ne ... personne	*nobody*
ne ... plus	*no longer, no more*
ne ... jamais	*never*
ne ... que	*only*
ne ... aucun(e)	*no*
ne ... nul(le)	*no*
ne ... nulle part	*nowhere*
ne ... ni	*neither ... nor*
ne ... ni ... ni	*neither ... nor*

◆ **Word order**

– In simple tenses and the imperative:
ne precedes the verb (and any object pronouns) and the second element follows the verb → 1

– In compound tenses:

i **ne ... pas, ne ... point, ne ... rien, ne ... plus, ne ... jamais, ne... guère** follow the pattern:
ne + auxiliary verb + **pas** + past participle → 2

ii **ne ... personne, ne ... que, ne ... aucun(e), ne ... nul(le), ne ... nulle part, ne ... ni (... ni)** follow the pattern:
ne + auxiliary verb + past participle + **personne** → 3

– With a verb in the infinitive:
ne ... pas, ne ... point (etc see i above) come together → 4

◆ For use of **rien**, **personne** and **aucun** as pronouns, see p 178.

Examples

1 **Je ne fume pas**
I don't smoke
Ne changez rien
Don't change anything
Je ne vois personne
I can't see anybody
Nous ne nous verrons plus
We won't see each other any more
Il n'arrive jamais à l'heure
He never arrives on time
Il n'avait qu'une valise
He only had one suitcase
Je n'ai reçu aucune réponse
I have received no reply
Il ne boit ni ne fume
He neither drinks nor smokes
Ni mon fils ni ma fille ne les connaissaient
Neither my son nor my daughter knew them

2 **Elle n'a pas fait ses devoirs**
She hasn't done her homework
Ne vous a-t-il rien dit?
Didn't he say anything to you?
Ils n'avaient jamais vu une si belle maison
They had never seen such a beautiful house
Tu n'as guère changé
You've hardly changed

3 **Je n'ai parlé à personne**
I haven't spoken to anybody
Il n'avait mangé que la moitié du repas
He had only eaten half the meal
Elle ne les a trouvés nulle part
She couldn't find them anywhere
Il ne l'avait ni vu ni entendu
He had neither seen nor heard him

4 **Il essayait de ne pas rire**
He was trying not to laugh

❐ Negatives (Continued)

◆ Combination of negatives. These are the most common combinations of negative particles:

ne ... plus jamais → [1]
ne ... plus personne → [2]
ne ... plus rien → [3]
ne ... plus ni ... ni ... → [4]
ne ... jamais personne → [5]
ne ... jamais rien → [6]
ne ... jamais que → [7]
ne ... jamais ni ... ni ... → [8]
(ne ... pas) non plus → [9]

non and **pas**

◆ **non** *no* is the usual negative response to a question → [10]
It is often translated as *not* → [11]

◆ **pas** is generally used when a distinction is being made, or for emphasis → [12]
It is often translated as *not* → [13]

Examples

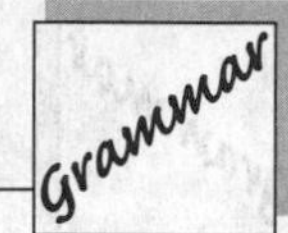

1 **Je ne le ferai plus jamais**
I'll never do it again

2 **Je ne connais plus personne à Rouen**
I don't know anybody in Rouen any more

3 **Ces marchandises ne valaient plus rien**
Those goods were no longer worth anything

4 **Ils n'ont plus ni chats ni chiens**
They no longer have either cats or dogs

5 **On n'y voit jamais personne**
You never see anybody there

6 **Ils ne font jamais rien d'intéressant**
They never do anything interesting

7 **Je n'ai jamais parlé qu'à sa femme**
I've only ever spoken to his wife

8 **Il ne m'a jamais ni écrit ni téléphoné**
He has never either written to me or phoned me

9 **Ils n'ont pas d'enfants et nous non plus**
They don't have any children and neither do we
Je ne les aime pas – Moi non plus
I don't like them – Neither do I; I don't either

10 **Vous voulez nous accompagner? – Non**
Do you want to come with us? – No (I don't)

11 **Tu viens ou non?**
Are you coming or not?
J'espère que non
I hope not

12 **Ma sœur aime le ski, moi pas**
My sister likes skiing, I don't

13 **Qui a fait ça? – Pas moi!**
Who did that? – Not me!
Est-il de retour? – Pas encore
Is he back? – Not yet
Tu as froid? – Pas du tout
Are you cold? – Not at all

❐ Question forms: direct

There are four ways of forming direct questions in French:

- by inverting the normal word order so that *pronoun subject* + *verb* → *verb* + *pronoun subject*. A hyphen links the verb and pronoun → [1]
  - When the subject is a noun, a pronoun is inserted after the verb and linked to it by a hyphen → [2]
  - When the verb ends in a vowel in the third person singular, **-t-** is inserted before the pronoun → [3]
- by maintaining the word order *subject* + *verb*, but by using a rising intonation at the end of the sentence → [4]
- by inserting **est-ce que** before the construction *subject* + *verb* → [5]
- by using an interrogative word at the beginning of the sentence, together with inversion *or* the **est-ce que** form above → [6]

Examples

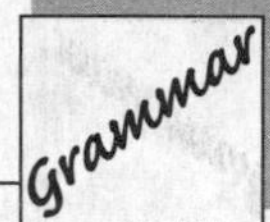

1 **Aimez-vous la France?**
Do you like France?
Est-ce possible?
Is it possible?
Part-on tout de suite?
Are we leaving right away?

Avez-vous fini?
Have you finished?
Est-elle restée?
Did she stay?

2 **Tes parents sont-ils en vacances?**
Are your parents on holiday?
Jean-Benoît est-il parti?
Has Jean-Benoît left?

3 **A-t-elle de l'argent?**
Has she any money?
La pièce dure-t-elle longtemps?
Does the play last long?
Mon père a-t-il téléphoné?
Has my father phoned?

4 **Il l'a fini**
He's finished it
Robert va venir
Robert's coming

Il l'a fini?
Has he finished it?
Robert va venir?
Is Robert coming?

5 **Est-ce que tu la connais?**
Do you know her?
Est-ce que tes parents sont revenus d'Italie?
Have your parents come back from Italy?

6 **Quel train** { **prends-tu?** / **est-ce que tu prends?** }
What train are you getting?

Lequel { **est-ce que ta sœur préfère?** / **ta sœur préfère-t-elle?** }
Which one does your sister prefer?

Quand { **êtes-vous arrivé?** / **est-ce que vous êtes arrivé?** }
When did you arrive?

Pourquoi { **ne sont-ils pas venus?** / **est-ce qu'ils ne sont pas venus?** }
Why haven't they come?

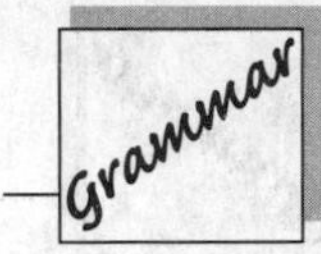

❒ Question forms: indirect

An indirect question is one that is 'reported', e.g. he asked me *what the time was*, tell me *which way to go*. Word order in indirect questions is as follows:

- *interrogative word* + subject + verb → [1]
- when the subject is a noun, and not a pronoun, the subject and verb are often inverted → [2]

❒ n'est-ce pas

This is used wherever English would use *isn't it?*, *don't they?*, *weren't we?*, *is it?* etc tagged on to the end of a sentence → [3]

❒ oui and si

Oui is the word for *yes* in answer to a question put in the affirmative → [4]

Si is the word for *yes* in answer to a question put in the negative or to contradict a negative statement → [5]

Examples

1 **Je me demande s'il viendra**
I wonder if he'll come
Je ne sais pas à quoi ça sert
I don't know what it's for
Dites-moi quel autobus va à la gare
Tell me which bus goes to the station
Il m'a demandé combien d'argent j'avais
He asked me how much money I had

2 **Elle ne sait pas à quelle heure commence le film**
She doesn't know what time the film starts
Je me demande où sont mes clés
I wonder where my keys are
Elle nous a demandé comment allait notre père
She asked us how our father was
Je ne sais pas ce que veulent dire ces mots
I don't know what these words mean

3 **Il fait chaud, n'est-ce pas?**
It's warm, isn't it?
Vous n'oublierez pas, n'est-ce pas?
You won't forget, will you?

4 **Tu l'as fait? – Oui**
Have you done it? – Yes (I have)

5 **Tu ne l'as pas fait? – Si**
Haven't you done it? – Yes (I have)

NUMBERS

Cardinal *(one, two etc)*		**Ordinal** *(first, second etc)*	
zéro	0		
un (une)	1	**premier (première)**	1er, 1ère
deux	2	**deuxième, second(e)**	2ème
trois	3	**troisième**	3ème
quatre	4	**quatrième**	4ème
cinq	5	**cinquième**	5ème
six	6	**sixième**	6ème
sept	7	**septième**	7ème
huit	8	**huitième**	8ème
neuf	9	**neuvième**	9ème
dix	10	**dixième**	10ème
onze	11	**onzième**	11ème
douze	12	**douzième**	12ème
treize	13	**treizième**	13ème
quatorze	14	**quatorzième**	14ème
quinze	15	**quinzième**	15ème
seize	16	**seizième**	16ème
dix-sept	17	**dix-septième**	17ème
dix-huit	18	**dix-huitième**	18ème
dix-neuf	19	**dix-neuvième**	19ème
vingt	20	**vingtième**	20ème
vingt et un (une)	21	**vingt et unième**	21ème
vingt-deux	22	**vingt-deuxième**	22ème
vingt-trois	23	**vingt-troisième**	23ème
trente	30	**trentième**	30ème
quarante	40	**quarantième**	40ème
cinquante	50	**cinquantième**	50ème
soixante	60	**soixantième**	60ème
soixante-dix	70	**soixante-dixième**	70ème
soixante et onze	71	**soixante-onzième**	71ème
soixante-douze	72	**soixante-douzième**	72ème
quatre-vingts	80	**quatre-vingtième**	80ème
quatre-vingt-un (une)	81	**quatre-vingt-unième**	81ème
quatre-vingt-dix	90	**quatre-vingt-dixième**	90ème
quatre-vingt-onze	91	**quatre-vingt-onzième**	91ème

NUMBERS

Cardinal		Ordinal	
cent	100	**centième**	100ème
cent un (une)	101	**cent unième**	101ème
cent deux	102	**cent deuxième**	102ème
cent dix	110	**cent dixième**	110ème
cent quarante-deux	142	**cent quarante-deuxième**	142ème
deux cents	200	**deux centième**	200ème
deux cent un (une)	201	**deux cent unième**	201ème
deux cent deux	202	**deux cent-deuxième**	202ème
trois cents	300	**trois centième**	300ème
quatre cents	400	**quatre centième**	400ème
cinq cents	500	**cinq centième**	500ème
six cents	600	**six centième**	600ème
sept cents	700	**sept centième**	700ème
huit cents	800	**huit centième**	800ème
neuf cents	900	**neuf centième**	900ème
mille	1000	**millième**	1000ème
mille un (une)	1001	**mille unième**	1001ème
mille deux	1002	**mille deuxième**	1002ème
deux mille	2000	**deux millième**	2000ème
cent mille	100.000	**cent millième**	100.000ème
un million	1.000.000	**millionième**	1.000.000ème
deux millions	2.000.000	**deux millionième**	2.000.000ème

Fractions		Others	
un demi, une demie	a half	**zéro virgule cinq (0,5)**	0.5
un tiers	a third	**un virgule trois (1,3)**	1.3
deux tiers	two thirds	**dix pour cent**	10%
un quart	a quarter	**deux plus deux**	2 + 2
trois quarts	three quarters	**deux moins deux**	2 - 2
un cinquième	one fifth	**deux fois deux**	2 x 2
cinq et trois quarts	five and three quarters	**deux divisé par deux**	2 ÷ 2

⚠ NOTE the use of points with large numbers and commas with fractions, i.e. the opposite of English usage.

❒ Other Uses

- **-aine** denoting approximate numbers:

une douzaine (de pommes)	about a dozen (apples)
une quinzaine (d'hommes)	about fifteen (men)
des centaines de personnes	hundreds of people
BUT: **un millier (de voitures)**	about a thousand (cars)

- measurements:

vingt mètres carrés	20 square metres
vingt mètres cubes	20 cubic metres
un pont long de quarante mètres	a bridge 40 metres long
avoir trois mètres de large/de haut	to be 3 metres wide/ high

- miscellaneous:

Il habite au dix	He lives at number 10
C'est au chapitre sept	It's in chapter 7
(C'est) à la page 17	(It's) on page 17
(Il habite) au septième étage	(He lives) on the 7th floor
Il est arrivé le septième	He came in 7th
échelle au vingt-cinq millième	scale 1:25,000

Telephone numbers

Je voudrais Édimbourg trois cent trente, vingt-deux, dix
I would like Edinburgh 330 22 10
Je voudrais le soixante-cinq, treize, vingt-deux, zéro deux
Could you get me 65 13 22 02
Poste trois cent trente-cinq
Extension number 335
Poste vingt-deux, trente-trois
Extension number 22 33

⚠ NOTE: In French, telephone numbers are broken down into groups of two or three numbers (never four), and are not spoken separately as in English. They are also written in groups of two or three numbers.

❒ Dates

Quelle est la date d'aujourd'hui? **Quel jour sommes-nous?**	What's the date today?
C'est ... **Nous sommes ...**	It's the ...
le premier février	1st of February
le deux février	2nd of February
le vingt-huit février	28th of February
Il vient le sept mars	He's coming on the 7th of March

⚠ NOTE: Use cardinal numbers except for the first of the month.

❒ Years

Je suis né en 1971
I was born in 1971

le douze février { **dix-neuf cent soixante et onze** / **mll neuf cent soixante et onze**

(on) 12th February 1971

⚠ NOTE: There are two ways of expressing the year (see last example). Note the spelling of **mil** *one thousand* in dates.

❒ Other expressions

dans les années cinquante	during the fifties
au vingtième siècle	in the twentieth century
en mai	in May
lundi (quinze)	on Monday (the 15th)
le lundi	on Mondays
dans dix jours	in 10 days' time
il y a dix jours	10 days ago

Quelle heure est-il? *What time is it?*
Il est … *It's …*

00.00 **minuit** *midnight, twelve o'clock*
00.10 **minuit dix, zéro heure dix**
00.15 **minuit et quart, zéro heure quinze**
00.30 **minuit et demi, zéro heure trente**
00.45 **une heure moins (le) quart, zéro heure quarante-cinq**

01.00 **une heure du matin** *one a.m., one o'clock in the morning*
01.10 **une heure dix (du matin)**
01.15 **une heure et quart, une heure quinze**
01.30 **une heure et demie, une heure trente**
01.45 **deux heures moins (le) quart, une heure quarante-cinq**
01.50 **deux heures moins dix, une heure cinquante**
01.59 **deux heures moins une, une heure cinquante-neuf**

12.00 **midi, douze heures** *noon, twelve o'clock*
12.30 **midi et demi, douze heures trente**

13.00 **une heure de l'après-midi, treize heures** *one p.m., one o'clock in the afternoon*
01.30 **une heure et demie (de l'après-midi), treize heures trente**

19.00 **sept heures du soir, dix-neuf heures** *seven p.m., seven o'clock in the evening*
19.30 **sept heures et demie (du soir), dix-neuf heures trente**

Examples

À quelle heure venez-vous? – À sept heures
What time are you coming? – At seven o'clock

Les bureaux sont fermés de midi à quatorze heures
The offices are closed from twelve until two

à deux heures du matin/de l'après-midi
at two o'clock in the morning/afternoon, at two a.m./p.m.

à sept heures du soir
at seven o'clock in the evening, at seven p.m.

à cinq heures précises *or* **pile**
at five o'clock sharp

vers neuf heures
about nine o'clock

peu avant/après midi
shortly before/after noon

entre huit et neuf heures
between eight and nine o'clock

Il est plus de trois heures et demie
It's after half past three

Il faut y être à dix heures au plus tard/au plus tôt
You have to be there by ten o'clock at the latest/earliest

Ne venez pas plus tard que onze heures moins le quart
Come no later than a quarter to eleven

Il en a pour une demi-heure
He'll be half an hour (at it)

Elle est restée sans connaissance pendant un quart d'heure
She was unconscious for a quarter of an hour

Je les attends depuis une heure
I've been waiting for them for an hour/since one o'clock

Ils sont partis il y a quelques minutes
They left a few minutes ago

Je l'ai fait en vingt minutes
I did it in twenty minutes

Le train arrive dans une heure
The train arrives in an hour('s time)

Combien de temps dure ce film?
How long does this film last?

Beware of translating word for word. While on occasion this is quite possible, quite often it is not. The need for caution is illustrated by the following:

- English phrasal verbs (i.e. verbs followed by a preposition) e.g. *to run away, to fall down* are often translated by one word in French → [1]
- English verbal constructions often contain a preposition where none exists in French, or vice versa → [2]
- Two or more prepositions in English may have a single rendering in French → [3]
- A word which is singular in English may be plural in French, or vice versa → [4]
- French has no equivalent of the possessive construction denoted by --*'s*/--s' → [5]

See also *at/in/to*, p 234.

Specific problems

-ing

This is translated in a variety of ways in French:

- *to be ...-ing is* translated by a simple verb → [6]
  EXCEPTION: when a physical position is denoted, a past participle is used → [7]
- in the construction *to see/hear sb ...-ing*, use an infinitive or **qui** + verb → [8]

-ing can also be translated by:
- an infinitive → [9]
  (see p 44)
- a perfect infinitive → [10]
  (see p 46)
- a present participle → [11]
  (see p 48)
- a noun → [12]

Examples

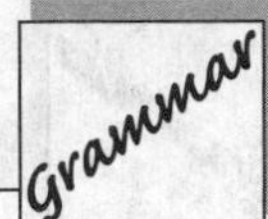

1 **s'enfuir** to run away — **tomber** to fall down — **céder** to give in

2 **payer** to pay for — **regarder** to look at — **écouter** to listen to
obéir à to obey — **nuire à** to harm — **manquer de** to lack

3 **s'étonner de** to be surprised at — **satisfait de** satisfied with
voler qch à to steal sth from — **apte à** capable of; fit for

4 **les bagages** the luggage — **ses cheveux** his/her hair
le bétail the cattle — **mon pantalon** my trousers

5 **la voiture de mon frère** my brother's car *(literally: … of my brother)* — **la chambre des enfants** the children's bedroom *(literally: … of the children)*

6 **Il part demain** He's leaving tomorrow — **Je lisais un roman** I was reading a novel

7 **Elle est assise là-bas** She's sitting over there — **Il était couché par terre** He was lying on the ground

8 **Je les vois** { **venir** / **qui viennent** } I can see them coming
Je l'ai entendue { **chanter** / **qui chantait** } I heard her singing

9 **J'aime aller au cinéma** I like going to the cinema — **Arrêtez de parler!** Stop talking!
Au lieu de répondre Instead of answering — **Avant de partir** Before leaving

10 **Après avoir ouvert la boîte, il …**
After opening the box, he …

11 **Étant plus timide que moi, elle …**
Being shyer than me, she …

12 **Le ski me maintient en forme**
Skiing keeps me fit

TRANSLATION PROBLEMS

to be

- Generally translated by **être** → [1]
  When physical location is implied, **se trouver** may be used → [2]
- In set expressions, describing physical and emotional conditions, **avoir** is used:

avoir chaud/froid	*to be warm/cold*
avoir faim/soif	*to be hungry/thirsty*
avoir peur/honte	*to be afraid/ashamed*
avoir tort/raison	*to be wrong/right*

- Describing the weather, e.g. *what's the weather like?*, *it's windy/sunny*, use **faire** → [3]
- For ages, e.g. *he is 6*, use **avoir** → [4]
- For state of health, e.g. *he's unwell, how are you?*, use **aller** → [5]

it is, it's

- Usually **il/elle est**, when referring to a noun → [6]
- For expressions of time, also use **il est** → [7]
- To describe the weather, e.g. *it's windy*, see above.
- In the construction: *it is difficult/easy to do sth*, use **il est** → [8]
- In all other constructions, use **c'est** → [9]

there is/there are

- Both are translated by **il y a** → [10]

can, be able

- Physical ability is expressed by **pouvoir** → [11]
- If the meaning is *to know how to*, use **savoir** → [12]
- *Can* + a 'verb of hearing or seeing etc' in English is not translated in French → [13]

Examples

1	**Il est tard** It's late	**C'est peu probable** It's not very likely
2	**Où se trouve la gare?** Where's the station?	
3	**Quel temps fait-il?** What's the weather like?	**Il fait beau/mauvais/du vent** It's lovely/miserable/windy
4	**Quel âge avez-vous?** How old are you?	**J'ai quinze ans** I'm fifteen
5	**Comment allez-vous?** How are you?	**Je vais très bien** I'm very well

6 **Où est mon parapluie? – Il est là, dans le coin**
Where's my umbrella? – It's there, in the corner
Descends la valise si elle n'est pas trop lourde
Bring down the case if it isn't too heavy

7 **Quelle heure est-il? – Il est sept heures et demie**
What's the time? – It's half past seven

8 **Il est difficile de répondre à cette question**
It's difficult to reply to this question

9 **C'est moi qui ne l'aime pas**
It's me who doesn't like him
C'est Charles/ma mère qui l'a dit
It's Charles/my mother who said so
C'est ici que je les ai achetés
It's here that I bought them
C'est parce que la poste est fermée que …
It's because the post office is closed that …

10 **Il y a quelqu'un à la porte**
There's somebody at the door
Il y a cinq livres sur la table
There are five books on the table

11 **Pouvez-vous atteindre cette étagère?**
Can you reach up to that shelf?

12 **Elle ne sait pas nager**
She can't swim

13	**Je ne vois rien** I can't see anything	**Il les entendait** He could hear them

TRANSLATION PROBLEMS

to (see also below)

- Generally translated by à → [1]
  (See p 204).
- In time expressions, e.g. *10 to 6*, use **moins** → [2]
- When the meaning is *in order to*, use **pour** → [3]
- Following a verb, as in *to try to do, to like to do,* see pp 44 and 64
- *easy/difficult/impossible* etc *to do:*
  The preposition used depends on whether a specific noun is referred to → [4] or not → [5]

at/in/to

- With feminine countries, use **en** → [6]
  With masculine countries, use **au** (**aux** with plural countries) → [7]
- With towns, use **à** → [8]
- *at/to the butcher's/grocer's* etc: use **à** + noun designating the shop, or **chez** + noun designating the shopkeeper → [9]
- *at/to the dentist's/doctor's* etc: use **chez** → [10]
- *at/to ...'s/...s' house:* use **chez** → [11]

Examples

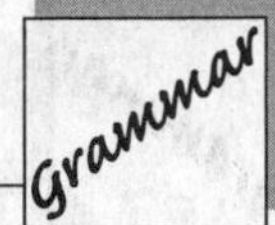

1 **Donne le livre à Patrick**
Give the book to Patrick

2 **dix heures moins cinq** — five to ten
à sept heures moins le quart — at a quarter to seven

3 **Je l'ai fait pour vous aider**
I did it to help you
Il se pencha pour nouer son lacet
He bent down to tie his shoelace

4 **Ce livre est difficile à lire**
This book is difficult to read

5 **Il est difficile de comprendre leurs raisons**
It's difficult to understand their reasons

6 **Il est allé en France/en Suisse**
He has gone to France/to Switzerland
un village en Norvège/en Belgique
a village in Norway/in Belgium

7 **Êtes-vous allé au Canada/au Danemark/aux États-Unis?**
Have you been to Canada/to Denmark/to the United States?
une ville au Japon/au Brésil
a town in Japan/in Brazil

8 **Il est allé à Vienne/à Bruxelles**
He has gone to Vienna/to Brussels
Il habite à Londres/à Genève
He lives in London/in Geneva
Ils logent dans un hôtel à St. Pierre
They're staying in a hotel at St. Pierre

9 **Je l'ai acheté** { **à l'épicérie** / **chez l'épicier** } I bought it at the grocer's
Elle est allée { **à la boulangerie** / **chez le boulanger** } She's gone to the baker's

10 **J'ai un rendez-vous chez le dentiste**
I've an appointment at the dentist's
Il est allé chez le médecin
He has gone to the doctor's

11 **chez Christian** — at/to Christian's house
chez les Pagot — at/to the Pagots' house

❒ General Points

- Activity of the lips

  The lips play a very important part in French. When a vowel is described as having 'rounded' lips, the lips are slightly drawn together and pursed, as when an English speaker expresses exaggerated surprise with the vowel 'ooh!' Equally, if the lips are said to be 'spread', the corners are pulled firmly back towards the cheeks, tending to reveal the front teeth.

  In English, lip position is not important, and vowel sounds tend to merge because of this. In French, the activity of the lips means that every vowel sound is clearly distinct from every other.

- No diphthongs

  A diphthong is a glide between two vowel sounds in the same syllable. In English, there are few 'pure' vowel sounds, but largely diphthongs instead. Although speakers of English may *think they* produce one vowel sound in the word 'day', in fact they use a diphthong, which in this instance is a glide between the vowels [e] and [ɪ]: [deɪ]. In French the tension maintained in the lips, tongue and the mouth in general prevents diphthongs occurring, as the vowel sound is kept constant throughout. Hence the French word corresponding to the above example, 'dé', is pronounced with no final [ɪ] sound, but is phonetically represented thus: [de].

- Consonants

  In English, consonants are often pronounced with a degree of laxness that can result in their practically disappearing altogether although not strictly 'silent'. In a relaxed pronunciation of a word such as 'hat', the 't' is often scarcely heard, or is replaced by a 'glottal stop' (a sort of jerk in the throat). This never occurs in French, where consonants are always given their full value.

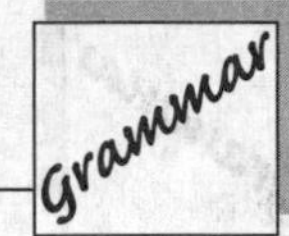

❒ Pronunciation of Consonants

Some consonants are pronounced almost exactly as in English: [b, p, f, v, g, k, m, w].

Most others are similar to English, but slight differences should be noted.

	EXAMPLES	HINTS ON PRONUNCIATION
[d]	**d**in**d**e	The tip of the tongue touches the upper front teeth and not the roof of the mouth as in English
[t]	**t**en**t**e	
[n]	**no**nn**e**	
[l]	**Lill**e	
[s]	tou**s** **ç**a	The tip of the tongue is down behind the bottom front teeth, lower than in English
[z]	**z**éro ro**s**e	
[ʃ]	**ch**ose ta**ch**e	Like the *sh* of English *shout*
[ʒ]	**j**e **g**ilet bei**g**e	Like the *s* of English *measure*
[j]	**y**eux pai**lle**	Like the *y* of English *yes*

Three consonants are not heard in English:

[R]	**r**a**r**e veni**r**	R is often silent in English, e.g. fa*r*m. In French the [R] is never silent, unless it follows an **e** at the end of a word e.g. cherch**er**. To pronounce it, try to make a short sound like gargling. Similar, too, to the Scottish pronunciation of *loch*
[ɲ]	vi**gn**e a**gn**eau	Similar to the *ni* of Spa*ni*ard
[ɥ]	h**u**ile l**u**eur	Like a very rapid [y] (see p 239) followed immediately by the next vowel of the word

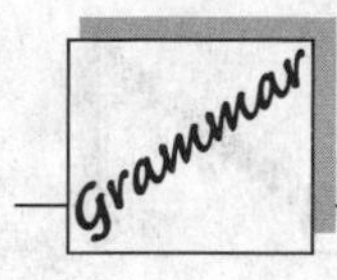

❐ Pronunciation of Vowels

	EXAMPLES	HINTS ON PRONUNCIATION
[a]	p**a**tte pl**at** **a**mour	Similar to the vowel in English *pat*
[ɑ]	b**as** p**â**te	Longer than the sound above, it resembles the English exclamation of surprise *ah!* Similar, too, to the English vowel in *car* without the final *r* sound
[ɛ]	l**ait** jou**et** m**er**ci	Similar to the English vowel in *pet*. Beware of using the English diphthong [eɪ] as in *pay*
[e]	**été** jou**er**	A pure vowel, again quite different from the diphthong in English *pay*
[ə]	l**e** pr**e**mier	Similar to the English sound in *butter* when the *r* is not pronounced
[i]	**ici** v**ie** l**y**cee	The lips are well spread towards the cheeks while uttering this sound. Shorter than the English vowel in *see*
[ɔ]	m**o**rt h**o**mme	The lips are well rounded while producing a sound similar to the *o* of English *cot*
[o]	m**ot** d**ô**me **eau**	A pure vowel with strongly rounded lips quite different from the diphthong in English *bone, low*

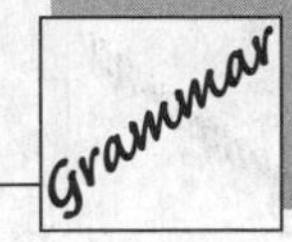

[u] gen**ou** r**oue** — A pure vowel with strongly rounded lips. Similar to the English *ooh!* of surprise

[y] r**ue** vêt**u** — Often the most difficult for English speakers to produce: round your lips and try to pronounce [i] (see above). There is no [j] sound (see p 237) as there is in English *pure*

[œ] s**œu**r b**eu**rre — Similar to the vowel in English *fir* or *murmur*, but without the *r* sound and with the lips more strongly rounded

[ø] p**eu** d**eux** — To pronounce this, try to say [e] (see above) with the lips strongly rounded

Nasal Vowels

These are spelt with a vowel followed by a 'nasal' consonant – **n** or **m**. The production of nasal vowels really requires the help of a teacher or a recording of the sound. However, to help you, the vowel is pronounced by allowing the air from the lungs to come partly down the nose and partly through the mouth, and the **n** or **m** is not pronounced at all.

[ɑ̃] l**ent** s**ang** d**ans**

[ɛ̃] mat**in** pl**ein**

[ɔ̃] n**on** p**ont**

[œ̃] br**un un** parf**um**

In each case, the vowel shown in the phonetic symbol is pronounced as described above, but air is allowed to come through the nose as well as the mouth

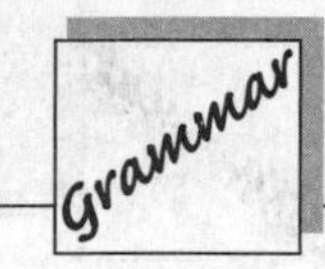

❒ From Spelling to Sounds

Although it may not seem so at first sight, there are some fairly precise 'rules' which can help you to know how to pronounce French words from their spelling.

Vowels

SPELLING	PRONOUNCED	EXAMPLES
a, à	[a]	ch**a**tte, t**a**ble
a, â	[ɑ]	p**â**te, p**a**s
e, é	[e]	**été**, march**er**
e, é, ê	[ɛ]	fen**ê**tre, f**e**rmer, ch**è**re
e	[ɔ]	doubl**e**, f**e**nêtr**e**
i, î, y	[i]	l**i**t, ab**î**mer, l**y**cée
o, ô	[o]	p**o**t, tr**o**p, d**ô**me
o	[ɔ]	s**o**tte, **o**range
u, û	[y]	batt**u**, f**û**t, p**u**r

Vowel Groups

There are several groups of vowels in French spelling which are regularly pronounced in the same way:

ai	[ɛ] or [e]	m**ai**son, march**ai**, f**ai**re
ail	[aj]	port**ail**
ain, aim, (c)in, im	[ɛ̃]	p**ain**, f**aim**, fr**ein**, **im**pair
au	[o]	**au**berge, land**au**
an, am, en, em	[ɑ̃]	pl**an**, **am**ple, **en**trer, t**em**ps
eau	[o]	bat**eau**, **eau**
eu	[œ] or [ø]	f**eu**, p**eu**r
euil(le), ueil	[œj]	f**euille**, rec**ueil**
oi, oy	[wa]	v**oi**re, v**oy**age
on, om	[ɔ̃]	t**on**, c**om**pter
ou	[u]	hib**ou**, **ou**til
œu	[œ]	s**œu**r, c**œu**r
ue	[y]	**rue**
un, um	[œ̃]	br**un**, parf**um**

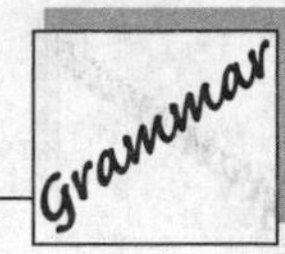

Added to these are the many groups of letters occurring at the end of words, where their pronunciation is predictable, bearing in mind the tendency (see p 242) of final consonants to remain silent:

TYPICAL WORDS	PRONUNCIATION OF FINAL SYLLABLE
pas, mât, chat	[ɑ] or [a]
marcher, marchez, marchais, marchait, baie, valet, mes, fumée	[e] or [ɛ]
nid	[i]
chaud, vaut, faux, sot, tôt, Pernod, dos, croc	[o]
bout, bijoux, sous, boue	[u]
fut, fût, crus, crûs	[y]
queue, heureux, bleus	[ø]
en, vend, vent, an, sang, grand, dans	[ɑ̃]
fin, feint, frein, vain	[ɛ̃]
on, pont, fond, avons	[ɔ̃]
brun, parfum	[œ̃]

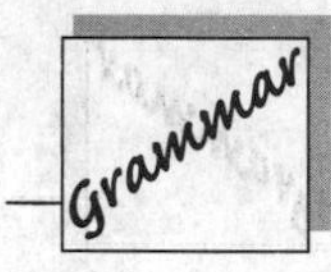

❒ From Spelling to Sounds (Continued)

Consonants

- Final consonants are usually silent → 1
- **n** or **m** at the end of a syllable or word are silent, but they have the effect of 'nasalizing' the preceding vowel(s) (see p 239 on Nasal Vowels)
- The letter **h** is either 'silent' ('mute') or 'aspirate' when it begins a word. When silent, the word behaves as though it started with a vowel and takes a liaison with the preceding word where appropriate.
When the **h** is aspirate, no liaison is made → 2
There is no way of predicting which words start with which sort of **h** – this simply has to be learnt with each word
- The following consonants in spelling have predictable pronunciations: b, d, f, k, l, p, r, t, v, w, x, y, z. Others vary:

SPELLING	PRONOUNCED	ENGLISH EXAMPLES	
c + a, o, u	[k]	**c**an, **c**ot, **c**ut	→ 3
+ **l, r**		**c**lass, **c**ram	
c + e, i, y	[s]	**c**eiling, i**c**e	→ 4
ç + a, o, u	[s]	**c**eiling, i**c**e	→ 5
ch	[ʃ]	**sh**op, la**sh**	→ 6
g + a, o, u	[g]	**g**ate, **g**ot, **g**un	→ 7
+ **l, r**		**g**lass, **g**ramme	
g + e, i, y	[ʒ]	lei**s**ure	→ 8
gn	[ɲ]	compa**ni**on, o**ni**on	→ 9
j	[ʒ]	mea**s**ure	→ 10
q, qu	[k]	**qu**ay, **k**it	→ 11
s between vowels:	[z]	ro**s**e	→ 12
elsewhere	[s]	**s**it	
th	[t]	**Th**omas	→ 13
t in **-tion**	[s]	**s**it	→ 14

Examples

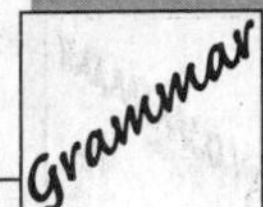

1	**éclat** [ekla]	**nez** [ne]	
	chaud [ʃo]	**aider** [ɛde]	
2	silent **h**: **des hôtels** [de zotɛl]	aspirate **h**: **des haricots** [de aʀiko]	
3	**café** [kafe]	**côte** [kot]	**culture** [kyltyʀ]
	classe [klas]	**croûte** [kʀut]	
4	**ceci** [səsi]	**cil** [sil]	**cycliste** [siklist]
5	**ça** [sa]	**garçon** [gaʀsɔ̃]	**déçu** [desy]
6	**chat** [ʃa]	**riche** [ʀiʃ]	
7	**gare** [gaʀ]	**gourde** [guʀd]	**aigu** [ɛgy]
	glaise [glɛz]	**gramme** [gʀam]	
8	**gemme** [ʒem]	**gilet** [ʒilɛ]	**gymnaste** [ʒimnast]
9	**vigne** [viɲ]	**oignon** [ɔɲɔ̃]	
10	**joli** [ʒɔli]	**Jules** [ʒyl]	
11	**quiche** [kiʃ]	**quitter** [kite]	
12	**sable** [sablə]	**maison** [mɛzɔ̃]	
13	**théâtre** [teɑtʀ]	**Thomas** [tɔma]	
14	**nation** [nasjɔ̃]	**action** [aksjɔ̃]	

❐ Feminine Forms and Pronunciation

- For adjectives and nouns ending in a vowel in the masculine, the addition of an **e** to form the feminine does not alter the pronunciation → [1]
- If the masculine ends with a silent consonant, generally **-d**, **-s**, **-r** or **-t**, the consonant is sounded in the feminine → [2]
  This also applies when the final consonant is doubled before the addition of the feminine **e** → [3]
- If the masculine ends in a nasal vowel and a silent **n**, e.g. **-an**, **-on**, **-in**, the vowel is no longer nasalized and the **-n** is pronounced in the feminine → [4]
  This also applies when the final **-n** is doubled before the addition of the feminine **e** → [5]
- Where the masculine and feminine forms have totally different endings (see pp 136 and 150), the pronunciation of course varies accordingly → [6]

❐ Plural Forms and Pronunciation

- The addition of **s** or **x** to form regular plurals generally does not affect pronunciation → [7]
- Where liaison has to be made, the final **-s** or **-x** of the plural form is pronounced → [8]
- Where the masculine singular and plural forms have totally different endings (see pp 138 and 148), the pronunciation of course varies accordingly → [9]
- Note the change in pronunciation in the following nouns:

SINGULAR		PLURAL		
bœuf	[bœf]	**bœufs**	[bø]	*ox/oxen*
œuf	[œf]	**œufs**	[ø]	*egg/eggs*
os	[ɔs]	**os**	[o]	*bone/bones*

245 Examples

	ADJECTIVES		NOUNS	
1	**joli**	→ **jolie**	**un ami**	→ **une amie**
	[ʒɔli]	[ʒɔli]	[ami]	[ami]
	déçu	→ **déçue**	**un employé**	→ **une employée**
	[desy]	[desy]	[ɑ̃plwaje]	[ɑ̃plwaje]
2	**chaud**	→ **chaude**	**un étudiant**	→ **une étudiante**
	[ʃo]	[ʃod]	[etydjɑ̃]	[etydjɑ̃t]
	français	→ **française**	**un Anglais**	→ **une Anglaise**
	[fʀɑ̃sɛ]	[fʀɑ̃sɛz]	[ɑ̃glɛ]	[ɑ̃glɛz]
	inquiet	→ **inquiète**	**un étranger**	→ **une étrangère**
	[ɛ̃kjɛ]	[ɛ̃kjɛt]	[etʀɑ̃ʒe]	[etʀɑ̃ʒɛʀ]
3	**violet**	→ **violette**	**le cadet**	→ **la cadette**
	[vjɔlɛ]	[vjɔlɛt]	[kadɛ]	[kadɛt]
	gras	→ **grasse**		
	[gʀɑ]	[gʀɑs]		
4	**plein**	→ **pleine**	**le souverain**	→ **la souveraine**
	[plɛ̃]	[plɛn]	[suvʀɛ̃]	[suvʀɛn]
	fin	→ **fine**	**Le Persan**	→ **la Persane**
	[fɛ̃]	[fin]	[pɛʀsɑ̃]	[pɛʀsan]
	brun	→ **brune**	**le voisin**	→ **la voisine**
	[bʀœ̃]	[bʀyn]	[vwazɛ̃]	[vwazin]
5	**canadien**	→ **canadienne**	**le paysan**	→ **la paysanne**
	[kanadjɛ̃]	[kanadjɛn]	[peizɑ̃]	[peizan]
	breton	→ **bretonne**	**le baron**	→ **la baronne**
	[bʀətɔ̃]	[bʀətɔn]	[baʀɔ̃]	[barɔn]
6	**vif**	→ **vive**	**le veuf**	→ **la veuve**
	[vif]	[viv]	[vœf]	[vœv]
	traître	→ **traîtresse**	**le maître**	→ **la maîtresse**
	[tʀɛtʀɛ]	[tʀɛtʀɛs]	[mɛtʀə]	[mɛtʀɛs]
7	**beau**	→ **beaux**	**la maison**	→ **les maisons**
	[bo]	[bo]	[mɛzɔ̃]	[mɛzɔ̃]
8	**des anciens élèves**		**de beaux arbres**	
	[de zɑ̃sjɛ̃ zelɛv]		[də bo zaʀbʀ(ə)]	
9	**amical**	→ **amicaux**	**un journal**	→ **des journaux**
	[amikal]	[amiko]	[ʒuʀnal]	[ʒuʀno]

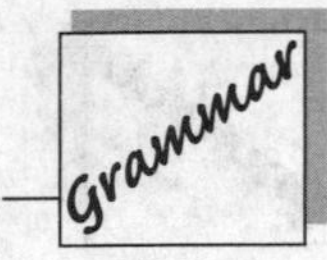

❒ The Alphabet

A, a	[ɑ]	**J, j**	[ʒi]	**S, s**	[ɛs]
B, b	[be]	**K, k**	[ka]	**T, t**	[te]
C, c	[se]	**L, l**	[ɛl]	**U, u**	[y]
D, d	[de]	**M, m**	[ɛm]	**V, v**	[ve]
E, e	[ə]	**N, n**	[ɛn]	**W,w**	[dubləve]
F, f	[ɛf]	**O, o**	[o]	**X, x**	[iks]
G, g	[ʒe]	**P, p**	[pe]	**Y, y**	[igʀɛk]
H, h	[aʃ]	**Q, q**	[ky]	**Z, z**	[zɛd]
I, i	[i]	**R, r**	[ɛr]		

Capital letters are used as in English except for the following:

- adjectives of nationality
  e.g. **une ville espagnole** **un auteur français**
  a Spanish town a French author

- languages
  e.g. **Parlez-vous anglais?** **Il parle français et allemand**
  Do you speak English? He speaks French and German

- days of the week:

lundi	Monday
mardi	Tuesday
mercredi	Wednesday
jeudi	Thursday
vendredi	Friday
samedi	Saturday
dimanche	Sunday

- months of the year:

janvier	January	**juillet**	July
février	February	**août**	August
mars	March	**septembre**	September
avril	April	**octobre**	October
mai	May	**novembre**	November
juin	June	**décembre**	December

INDEX

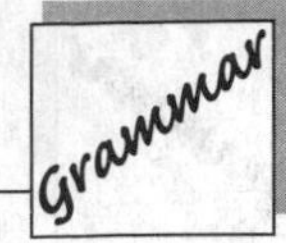

The following index lists comprehensively both grammatical terms and key words in French and English contained in this book.

a 146
à 204, 234
à governed by verbs 64
à with infinitives 44
à + le/les 140
à moins que 58
à peine 56, 214
ability 232
acheter 16
acquérir 76
address forms 164
adjectives 148
  position 162
  used as adverbs 198
adorer 44
adverbs 198
afin que 58
age 232
agent 209
agir s' 40
agreement:
  of adjectives 148, 154, 156, 158, 160
  of past participle 28, 32, 50
ago 227
aigu 152
aimer 44
aimer mieux 44
aller 28, 44, 232
  to express future 54
  conjugated 77
aller chercher 46
alphabet 246
among 180, 209
ancien 162
any 144
appeler 16
apposition, nouns in 142
après with perfect infinitive 46
arriver 28
articles 140
as 212
as ... as 154, 200
asseoir s' 32
conjugated 78
assez 202
at 204, 234
au 140, 234
aucun 178
auquel 180, 190
aussi 202, 212, 214
aussi ... que 154, 200
autant 202
autre 162
aux 140, 234
auxiliary verbs 22
auxquelles 180, 190
auxquels 180, 190
avant 208
avant que 58
avoir 42, 232
  auxiliary, 22, 46, 50
  conjugated 79
avoir peur (que) 60, 232
ayant 48
bad 154, 198
badly 198
barring 211
battre 80
be, to 232
beau 152, 162
beaucoup 200, 202
before 58, 208
bel 152
belle 152
belonging to 194, 206
best 60, 154, 200
better 154, 198, 200
between 180, 209
bien 198, 200, 202
bien que 58
bijou 138
blanc 152
blanche 152
bleu noun 138

bœuf(s) 244
boire 81
bon 154, 162, 198
bouillir 82
brave 162
bref 152, 198
brève 152
brièvement 198
by 209, 211
by (means of) 209
c'est 196, 232
c'était 196
ça 196
cage 133
caillou 138
calendar 227, 246
capitals, use of 246
cardinal numbers 224
ce demonstrative adjective 156
pronoun 184, 196
use of article following 146
ce que 184, 188
ce qui 184, 188
ce sont 196
ceci 196
céder 18
cela 196
celle 194
celles 194
celui 194
-cer verbs 14
certain pronouns 178
ces 156
cet 156
cette 156
ceux 194
chacun 178
chaque 162
cher 162
chez 208, 234
chou 138
-ci 156, 194
ciel, cieux 138
circumstance, expressing 208
colour adjectives 162
combien 202
commands, 20
comme 202, 214
comparative of adjectives 154, 212
comparative of adverbs 200, 212
compound tenses 22, 50
compter 44
conditional 6
conditional perfect 22, 24, 26
conjunctions 212
connaître 83
consonants: pronunciation 237
coucher se 32
coudre 84
countries 142, 234
courir 85
court 162
craindre 60, 86
crêpe 133
croire 60, 87
croître 88
cueillir 89
cuire 90
d'entre 209
dans 208
date 205, 207
days of the week 246
de preposition 206
governed by verbs 64
with infinitives 44
after superlative 154, 206
indefinite article 146
partitive 144
de + le/les 140
de crainte que 58
de façon que 58
de manière que 58
de peur que 58
de sorte que 58
défendre que 60
definite article 140
uses 142
déjà 202
demonstrative adjectives 156
demonstrative pronouns 194
depuis 208
use of tense

following 54, 56
dernier 60, 162
des 140
indefinite 146
partitive 144
dès 209
descendre 28, 44
désirer 44, 60
desquelles 180, 190
desquels 180, 190
détester 44
devenir 28
devoir 44, 52
conjugated 91
dire 92
direct object
pronouns 166
direct questions 220
direct speech 214
disjunctive
pronouns 172
distance 156, 205
distribution 209
donner 6
dont 182
word order
following 214
dormir 93
douter que 60
doux 152
du 140
partitive 144
duquel 180, 190
duration 207
each other 30
écrire 94
-eler verbs 16
elle 164, 172
elle-même 172
elles 164, 172
elles-mêmes 172
emotion, verbs of 60
emphasis 172, 196
en 207, 234
with present
participle 48
pronoun 170, 174
encore 202
énorme 198
énormément 198
entendre 44
entendre dire que 46
entendre parler de 46
entre 180, 209
entrer 28
envoyer 44, 95
envoyer chercher 46
épais 152
-er verbs 6
espérer 18, 44
essayer 16
essuyer 16
est-ce que 220
et 212
et ... et 212
étant 48
-eter verbs 16
être 232
auxiliary 22, 46
in passive 36
conjugated 96
être en train de 54
eux 172
eux-mêmes 172
except (for) 211
exclamatory
adjectives 158
faillir 44
faire 44
conjugated 97
to express the
weather 42, 232
faire entrer 46
faire venir 46
falloir 40, 44, 52
conjugated 98
faut, il 40, 58
faux 152
favori 152
fear 60
feminine:
formation 134, 148
nouns 132, 244
endings 133, 136, 150
pronunciation of 244
final 148
finir 6
first 60
first conjugation 6, 8
spelling irregu-

larities 14
fol 152
folle 152
for 210
in time
expressions 54, 56, 208
former, the 194
fou 152
fractions 225
fraîche 152
frais 152
franc(he) 152
from 204, 206
fuir 99
future perfect 22, 24, 26
use of 54
future tense 6
use of 54
future time, expressing 208
geler 16
gender 132
and meaning 133
generalizations 142
genou 138
-ger verbs 14
good 154, 198
grand 162
grec(que) 152
grêler 40
gros 152, 162
grosse 152
haïr 100
haleter 16
haut 162
he 164
hearing, verbs of 44, 230
her adjective 160
pronoun 166, 172
hers 192
herself 172
hibou 138
him 166, 172
himself 172
his adjective 160
pronoun 192
I 164
il 164
impersonal 40
il y a 42, 227, 232
ils 164
image 133
imperative 20
imperative
affirmative 30, 166, 168, 170
imperfect tense 6
use of 56
impersonal constructions 58
impersonal verbs 40
in 204, 205, 206, 207
in order to 210
indefinite article 146
indefinite pronouns 178
indirect object pronouns 168
indirect questions 222
infinitive 44, 230
infirmier/ière 132
interrogatives 220
interrogative adjectives 158
interrogative pronouns 186
intonation 220
intransitive verbs 28, 44
inversion 220
-ir verbs 6
irregular comparatives 154, 200
irregular superlatives 154, 200
irregular verbs 74
it 40, 164, 166, 172, 196
its 192
je, j' 164
jeter 16
jeune 162
joli 162
joujou 138
jusqu'à ce que 58
l' see **le, la**
l'un ... l'autre 30, 178
la article 140
pronoun 166
-là 156, 194
laisser 44

laisser tomber 46
lancer 14
languages 207, 246
laquelle 180, 190
last 60
latter, the 194
laver se 32, 34
le article 140
pronoun 166
le moins ... (que) 154
le plus ... (que) 154
least 154, 200
least, the 154
lequel 180, 190
les article 140
pronoun 166
lesquelles 180, 190
less 200, 202
less than 154, 200
leur possessive 160
pronoun 168
leur, le/la 192
leurs 160
leurs, les 192
lever 18
lever se 32
lire 101
livre 133
long(ue) 152, 162
lui 168, 172
lui-même 172
m' see **me**
ma 160
mal 198, 200
manche 133
manger 14
manner 205,206
manquer 42
masculine endings 133
masculine adjectives before vowel 152
masculine nouns 132
material 206, 207
mauvais 154, 162, 198
me 30, 166, 168
me 166, 172
means 205
meilleur 60, 150, 154, 198
même 162
mener 18
mes 160
mettre 102
mien, le 192
mienne, la 192
miennes, les 192
miens, les 192
mieux 198, 200
mine 192
modal auxiliary verbs 52
mode 133
moi 166, 168, 172
moi-même 172
moindre 154
moins 200, 202, 234
moins ... (que) 154, 200
mol 152
molle 152
mon 160
monter 28
months 207, 246
more 200, 202
more than 154, 200
most 200
most, the 154
mou 152
moudre 103
moule 133
mourir 28
conjugated 104
my 160
myself 172
nage 133
naître 28
conjugated 105
nasal vowels 239
nationality 162, 246
ne used with subjunctive 58, 60
ne ... aucun 216
ne ... guère 216
ne ... jamais 216
ne ... ni 216
ne ... nul 216
ne ... nulle part 216
ne ... pas 216
ne ... personne 216
ne ... plus 216

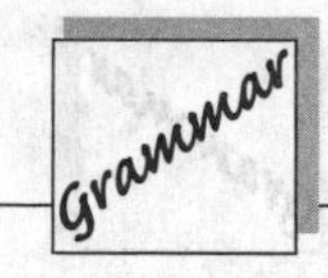

ne ... point 216
ne ... que 216
ne ... rien 216
n'est-ce pas 222
necessity 58
negative commands 20
negatives 216
combination of 218
form of article following 146
form of partitive following 144
neiger 40
neuter pronoun 166, 196
ni ... ni 212
nos 160
notre 160
nôtre, le/la 192
nôtres, les 192
noun endings 133
nouns 132, 244
nous 30, 164, 166, 168, 172
nous-mêmes 172
nouveau 152
nouvel 152
nouvelle 152
numbers 224
object pronouns 166, 168
œil 138
œuf(s) 244
of 206
on 36, 178
on 204, 207, 211
one's 160
oneself 172
only 60, 216
onto 211
opinion 60
order of object pronouns 170
orders 20, 60
ordinal numbers 224
ordonner 60
os 244
oser 44
ou ... ou 212
oui 222
our 160
ours 192
ourselves 172
out of 211
ouvrir 106
page 133
par 209
paraître 42
conjugated 107
parmi 180
partir 28
conjugated 108
partitive article 144
parts of the body 142
passer 28
passive 36, 209
past anterior 22, 24, 26
use of 56
past historic 6
use of 56
past participle:
formation 22
agreement 28, 32, 50
pauvre 162
payer 16
peler 16
penser que 60
perfect infinitive 46, 230
perfect tense 22, 24, 26
use of 56
permettre que 60
personal pronouns 164
personne 178
peser 18
petit 154, 162
peu 200, 202
peut-être 214
phrasal verbs 48, 230
physique 133
pire 154, 198
pis 198, 200
plage 133
plaire 109
pleut, il 40
pleuvoir 40, 110
pluperfect 22, 24, 26
plurals:
formation 138, 148
pronunciation 244

plus 202
plus ... (que) 154, 200
plusieurs 178
pneu 138
poêle 133
position:
of adjectives 162
of adverbs 200
of object pronouns 166
of indirect object pronouns 168
of **en** 174
of **y** 176
positive commands 20
possession 182, 230
possessive adjectives 160
possessive pronouns 192
possibility 58
pour 210
pour que 58
pourvu que 58
pouvoir 44, 52, 232
conjugated 111
préférer 44
premier 60
prendre 112
prepositions 204
present participle 48, 230
used with **en** 207
present tense 6
use of 54
prices 142, 210
professeur 132
pronoun objects:
position 20, 166, 168
pronouns 164
position 166,168
pronunciation 236
proportion 211
propre 162
proximity 156
public 152
publique 152
purpose 58
qu' see **que**
quality 206
que 186, 212, 214
pronoun 180
replacing **si** 62
to form an imperative 62
quel 158
quelle 158
quelles 158
quelque chose 178
quelques-uns 178
quelqu'un 178
quels 158
qu'est-ce que 186
qu'est-ce qui 186
question forms 220
qui 180, 186, 188, 230
qui est-ce que 186
qui est-ce qui 186
qui que 62
quoi 182, 184,186, 188
quoi que 62
quoique 58
rage 133
ras 150
-re verbs 6
recevoir 113
reflexive pronouns 30
position 30
reflexive verbs 30, 36
régler 18
regretter que 60
regular verbs 6
relative clauses 62
relative pronouns 180
rentrer 28
résoudre 114
ressembler se 32
rester 28, 42
result 58
retourner 28
revenir 28
rien 178
rire 115
rompre 116
s' see **se, si**
sa 160
sans 210
sauf 211
savoir 44, 52, 232
conjugated 117

se 30
sec 152
sèche 152
second conjugation 6, 10
seeing, verbs of 44, 230
sembler 42, 44
sentence structure 214
sentir 118
servir 119
ses 160
seul 60, 162
she 164
si 202, 212
si ... (que) 62, 154, 200
si *yes* 222
sien, le 192
sienne, la 192
siennes, les 192
siens, les 192
silence 133
simple 162
simple tenses 6
since 54, 56, 208
small 154
soi 172
soi-même 172
soit ... soit 212
some 144
somme 133
son 160
sortir 28, 120
sot(te) 152
souhaiter 44, 60
spelling 240
stem 6
stressed pronouns 172
subject pronouns 164
subjunctive:
present 6
imperfect 6
perfect 22, 24 , 26
pluperfect 22, 24, 26
use of 58
suffire 42, 121
suffixes 133
suivre 122
superlative of adjectives 154
superlative of adverbs 200
superlatives: use of subjunctive after 60
sur 211
t' see **te**
ta 160
taire se 123
tant 202
te 30, 166, 168
tel l62
telephone numbers 226
témoin 132
tenir 124
tenses: use of 54
tes 160
that adjective 156
relative pronoun 180
demonstrative pronoun 194, 196
conjunction 212
the 140
their 160
theirs 192
them 166, 172
themselves 172
there 176
there is/are 232
these adjective 156
pronoun 194
they 164
third conjugation 6, 12
this adjective 156
pronoun 194, 196
these adjective 156
pronoun 194
tien, le 192
tienne, la 192
tiennes, les 192
tiens, les 192
time 205, 210, 228
to 204, 207, 234
toi 30,166,168, 172
toi-même 172
tomber 28
ton 160
tonner 40
toujours 202
tour 133
tous 178

tout 178
tout ce que 184
tout ce qui 184
toutes 178
towards 210
transport 207
trop 202
trouver se 32, 232
tu 164
un article 146
uncertainty 60
une article 146
unique 60
us 166, 172
vaincre 125
valoir 126
valoir mieux 40, 44
vaut mieux, il 40
vendre 6
venir 28
  conjugated 127
venir de 54, 56
verb endings 6
verbs of motion 28, 44
verbs taking **être** 28
vêtir 128
vieil 152
vieille 152
vieux 152, 162
vivre 129
voile 133
voir 44, 130
vos 160
votre 160
vôtre, le/la 192
vôtres, les 192
vouloir 44, 52, 60
conjugated 131
vouloir dire 46
vous 30, 164, 166, 168,172
vous-même(s) 172
vowels:
  pronunciation 238
vrai 162
want 60
we 164
weather 42, 209, 232
well 198
what 184, 186
what a ... 146, 158
which 184
  pronoun 180, 190
  adjective 158
who 180,186
whom 180,186
whose 182
wishing, verbs of 60
without 210
word order 212, 214
  indirect questions 222
  negatives 216
worse 154, 198, 200
worst 154, 200
y 170, 176
years 227
-yer verbs 16
yeux 138
you 164, 166, 172
your 160
yours 192
yourself 172
yourselves 172